abbrev.	ABBREVIATION	*Eng*	England/English	*obs*	OBSOLETE
adj	adjective	*esp.*	especially	*pass.*	PASSIVE[2]
adv	adverb	*etc.*	and so on	*pl.*	plural
AmE	American English	*euph*	euphemistic	*pomp*	POMPOUS
&	and		(EUPHEMISM)	*prep*	PREPOSITION
apprec	APPRECIATIVE (2)	*fem.*	FEMININE (2)	*pron*	PRONOUN
bibl	biblical	*fig.*	FIGURATIVE	*S*	South
BrE	British English	*fml*	formal	*sbdy.*	somebody
cap.	CAPITAL[1] (3)	*humor*	humorous	*sing.*	singular
comb.	combining/combination	*infml*	informal	*sthg.*	something
comp.	COMPARATIVE[2]	*interj*	INTERJECTION (1)	*tdmk*	TRADEMARK
conj.	CONJUNCTION	*lit*	LITERARY	*tech*	TECHNICAL (2)
derog	DEROGATORY	*masc.*	MASCULINE (2)	*US*	United States
dial	DIALECT	*n*	noun	*usu.*	usually
E	East	*N*	North	*v*	verb
				W	West

tdmk Headwords that the editors have reason to believe constitute trademarks have been described as such. However, neither the presence nor absence of such description should be regarded as affecting the legal status of any trademark.

Grammar codes

[A] ATTRIBUTIVE; a word that is used before the noun that it is describing: *a main road*

[C] COUNTABLE; a noun that can be counted and has a plural form: *This is a dictionary. There are many dictionaries in the library.*

[F] PREDICATIVE; an adjective or adverb that is used only following the noun that it is describing, or following the verbs be and seem: *That car is three years old.* | *He was asleep.*

[I] INTRANSITIVE; a verb that has no OBJECT: *They all came yesterday.*

[P] plural; a noun that is used with a plural verb, and that has no singular noun form: *These pants are too tight.*

[S] singular; a noun that is used only in the singular, and that has no plural form: *There was a babble of voices.*

[T] TRANSITIVE; a verb that has a DIRECT OBJECT: *She rides a bicycle to school.*

[U] UNCOUNTABLE; a noun that cannot be counted, and that has no plural form: *We drink milk with our dinner.* | *There is not much milk left.* | *I found some information about the town.*

[no comp.] shows that an adjective or adverb does not have a COMPARATIVE[2] or a SUPERLATIVE[1] form with **-er** or **-est**, and that it cannot be used with **more** and **most**.

[+*that*] shows that a word can be followed by a CLAUSE beginning with that: *He read that oil prices were going down.*

[+(*that*)] shows that a word can be followed by a CLAUSE beginning with **that**. You don't have to use the word **that**: *He knew he would be late for work.*

[+*to-v*] shows that a word can be followed by an INFINITIVE verb with **to**: *I want to leave early today.*

[+*to-v*] shows that a verb can be followed by an INFINITIVE verb without **to**: *I saw him leave early today.*

[+*v-ing*] shows that a verb can be followed by another verb in the **-ing** form: *I enjoy playing football.*

[not *be*+*v-ing*] shows that a verb cannot be used in the **-ing** form after the verb **be**.

[after *n*] shows that an adjective, adverb, or noun can follow a noun: *a piece of wood three inches thick*

[*adv*+*adv/prep*] shows that an adverb can be followed by another adverb or by a PREPOSITION: *They live far away.* | *We could see far into the distance.*

LONGMAN

DICTIONARY
OF AMERICAN ENGLISH

LONGMAN

DICTIONARY
OF AMERICAN ENGLISH

A DICTIONARY FOR LEARNERS OF ENGLISH

Longman

LONGMAN DICTIONARY OF AMERICAN ENGLISH

Paper Edition
ISBN 0 582 79797 7

Case Edition
ISBN 0 582 90611 3

American College Edition
ISBN 0 582 79888 4

AUA Bangkok Edition
ISBN 0 582 79863 9

Asia Foundation Edition
ISBN 0 582 79889 2

ELS Edition
ISBN 0 582 79870 1

Delta Systems Edition
ISBN 0 8013 0616 7

Obunsha Edition
ISBN 0 8013 0493 8

Library of Congress Cataloging in Publication Data
Longman dictionary of American English.
1. English Language—United States—
   Dictionaries.
2. English Language—Text-books for foreign
   speakers.
I. Title.
PE2835.L6   1983   423   83-9388
ISBN 0-582-79797-7 (paper)
ISBN 0-582-90611-3 (case)

Cover: Piedad Palencia
Design: Paul Price-Smith
       SGS Education
Illustrations: Albert Lorenz

First printing 1983

Longman, 10 Bank Street, White Plains, N.Y. 10606

15 16 17 18 19-RN-96959493

Table of contents

General Consultants:
Virginia French Allen, Temple University, Emeritus
David E. Eskey, University of Southern California
Don L. F. Nilsen, Arizona State University
John W. Oller Jr., University of New Mexico
Richard C. Yorkey, St. Michael's College

Pronunciation Consultant:
William W. Crawford Jr., Georgetown University

Sponsoring Editors: Arley Gray
Della Summers

Coordinating Editor: Adrian Stenton

Editors: Leah Berkowitz, Julie Frank-McNeil, Henry Jorisch, Susan London, Jay Maurer, Jane Selden, Ellen Shaw

Senior Pronunciation Editor: Sharon Goldstein
Pronunciation Editor: Marjorie Fuchs

Administrative Assistants: Louis Morra, Marilyn Small

With Editorial Assistance from: John Ayto, Gillian Beaumont, Faye Carney, Steve Elsworth, Adam Gadsby, Andrew Gregg, Charlotte Grieg, Michael Rundell, Penelope Stock, Michael Upshall, Eve Watkins, Janet Whitcut

Preface

This *Dictionary* is for people who are learning English as a second or foreign language. If you are learning English you need a dictionary that gives you special kinds of information. This *Dictionary* has been written to help you as much as possible, both as a reference book and as an active learning tool.

How the *Dictionary* is helpful

The *Dictionary* is monolingual. Knowing the translation of a word gives you some information, but an English-English dictionary gives you complete definitions to help you understand words fully. This *Dictionary* gives clear definitions and many example sentences to explain the different meanings of a word. This will make it easier for you to understand and use English words.

The *Dictionary* is easy to understand. The definitions and examples are written using only 2,000 common English words. This means that you will be able to use the *Dictionary* even if you have been studying English for only a short time.

The *Dictionary* helps you use English. Of course, you must know the meanings of words, but you must also know how they are used in English grammar. This *Dictionary* gives clear, useful grammatical information. It also has ten full-page *Study Notes* that explain important but sometimes difficult points of grammar.

The *Dictionary* is easy to use, even if you have never used an English-English dictionary before. To help you get the information you need out of the *Dictionary*, there is a *Dictionary Skills Workbook* from page 12a to page 38a. The *Workbook* is your introduction and guide to the dictionary.

The *Dictionary* helps you build your vocabulary. There are cross-references to other words, such as synonyms (words with similar meanings) and antonyms (words with opposite meanings). In addition, there are 15 full-page illustrations of scenes from everyday life. Many objects in each picture are labeled. If you look at the illustration of an airport (page 17), for example, you will find many common words and phrases related to airports and travel.

How to get acquainted with your *Dictionary*

Turn to the *Table of Contents* and look at the parts of the *Dictionary* listed there. Look up a *Study Note* that interests you and see the kind of information it gives. Then look up an *Illustration* and see what you can learn from it. Notice the sections on *Word Building* and *Irregular Verbs* in the back of the *Dictionary*. Turn to these so you will know where to find them when you need them later.

Read a few entries. Look up several words. Try some you know and some you don't know. Read through the entries and note the kinds of information given.

Look at the inside covers. Important information on abbreviations, grammar, and pronunciation is given there.

Start doing the exercises in the *Dictionary Skills Workbook*. The information in these exercises is very important. If they seem too easy at first, keep going. Try to do a little work in the *Workbook* every time you use your *Dictionary*, or do it in class with your teacher. All of the answers to the exercises are printed at the end of the *Workbook*.

As you use your *Dictionary*, remember that it contains a lot of information not found in other dictionaries. By learning to use this *Dictionary* well, you will gain an important resource in your study of English.

Arley Gray, Sponsoring Editor

Spelling

Different spelling

judg·ment, judgement /ˈdʒʌdʒmənt/ *n* **1** an official decision given by a judge or a court of law: *The court passed judgment on the prisoner.*

Different spellings are shown here —see page 15a

American and British spelling

color¹ *AmE* ‖ **colour** *BrE* /ˈkʌlər/ *n* **1** [U] the quality which allows one to see the difference between (for example) a red flower and a blue flower when both are the same size and shape

British spellings are shown like this —see page 16a

Irregular plurals

po·ta·to /pəˈteɪtoʷ/ *n* **-toes** [C;U] a roundish root vegetable with a thin brown or yellowish skin, that is cooked and served in many different ways

Is the plural **-os** or **-oes**? We show the correct spelling here —see page 29a

Irregular verbs

hope¹ /hoʷp/ *v* **hoped, hoping** [I;T +*to-v*/ (*that*)/*for*] to wish and expect; desire in spite of doubts: *We're hoping to visit England this year.*

Does the spelling change? We show it here if it does —see page 31a

Sound/pronunciation

Sound

ap·ple /ˈæpəl/ *n* a hard round fruit with white juicy flesh, and a red, green, or yellow skin

The pronunciation of each word is shown like this —see page 16a

Stress

a·bil·i·ty /əˈbɪləṭiʸ/ *n* **-ties** [C;U] power and skill, esp. to do, think, make, etc.: *She has the ability to go to college, but she doesn't want to.*

Do you say **a**bility or a**bil**ity? —see page 19a

Meaning

Clear and simple explanations

egg /ɛg/ n **1** [C] a rounded object with a hard shell, which comes out of a female bird, snake, etc., and which contains a baby animal before it is born (HATCHed) **2** this when eaten as food: *I had a boiled egg for breakfast.*

Word meanings are simply explained and easy to understand. Words that you may not know are written in large letters like this. You can find all these words in the dictionary –see page 20a

More than one meaning

a·cute /əˈkyuʷt/ adj **1** (of the mind or the senses) able to notice small differences, esp. of meaning or sound; working very well; sharp: *Dogs have an acute sense of smell.* | *She has very acute hearing.* **2** severe; very great: *an acute lack of water* **3** (of a disease) coming quickly to a dangerous condition –compare CHRONIC **4** *tech* (of an angle) being less than 90 degrees –compare OBTUSE

Many words have more than one meaning. The first meaning is the most common one, but don't forget to check the others too –see page 22a

Examples of use

flinch /flɪntʃ/ v [I *from*] to move back a little when shocked by pain or fear: *Jane didn't flinch once when the doctor cleaned the cut in her arm.* | *He flinched when I raised my hand suddenly. He thought I was going to hit him.*

Many helpful examples show you how to use the word –see page 21a

Grammar

Parts of speech

age[1] /eʸdʒ/ n **1** the period of time a person has lived or a thing has existed: *He is ten years of age.*
age[2] v **aged**, **aging** or **ageing** [I;T] to (cause to) become old: *After his wife's death he aged quickly.*

These letters tell you if the word is a noun or a verb –see page 28a

Word families

a·brupt /əˈbrʌpt/ adj **1** sudden and unexpected: *The train came to an abrupt stop, making many passengers fall off their seats.* .... **–abruptly** adv: *The train stopped abruptly.* **–abruptness** n [U]

Words which are part of the same word family and which have different parts of speech are often shown like this –see page 27a

Grammar codes: countable and uncountable nouns

ac·tion /'ækʃən/ n **1** [U] movement using force or power for some purpose; doing things: *We have to take action* (=begin to act) *before it is too late.* **2** [C] something done; deed: *Actions are more important than words.*

These letters tell you if you can use the noun in the plural. [C] means you can. [U] means you cannot use this meaning in the plural –see page 29a

Transitive and intransitive verbs

ar·rive /ə'raɪv/ v **-rived**, **-riving** [I] **1** to reach a place, esp. at the end of a journey: *We arrived safely.*

ar·rest /ə'rɛst/ v [T] **1** to seize in the name of the law and usu. put in prison: *The policeman arrested the thief.*

These letters tell you if the word is followed by a direct object. [I] means you cannot use this verb with an object, [T] means you must use this verb with an object –see page 30a

Verbs followed by a preposition or adverb

ac·cuse /ə'kyuʷz/ v **-cused**, **-cusing** [T *of*] to charge (someone) with doing wrong or breaking the law; blame: *The police accused him of murder.*

This means that the verb is often followed by the preposition *of* –see page 31a

Verbs followed by another verb

en·joy /ɪn'dʒɔɪ/ v **-joyed**, **-joying** [T] **1** [+*v-ing*] to get happiness from; like: *I always enjoy going to the cinema.*

want¹ /wɑnt/ v **1** [T +*to-v*] to have a strong desire to or for; feel a strong desire to have: *I want to go to the movies tonight.*

These letters tell you that *enjoy* is often followed by a verb in the *-ing* form, and that *want* is often followed by a verb in the infinitive form –see page 32a

Phrasal verbs

account for sthg. v prep [T +*v-ing*] to give an explanation or reason for: *How do you account for all these mistakes?*

thrash sthg. ↔ **out** v adv [T] to reach agreement about (a problem) or produce (a decision) by much talk and consideration: *After a long discussion we were able to thrash out a plan.*

These letters tell you that the object always follows the preposition when you use *account for.* The arrow ↔ means that you can say *thrash the problem out* or *thrash out the problem* –see page 33a

Choosing the right word

Formal and informal

kid¹ /kɪd/ *n* **1** [C] *infml* a child: *There were three kids playing in the street.*

Would it be correct to use this word in a school essay? –see page 23a

American and British words

bulletin board /ˈ··· ˌ·/ *AmE* ‖ **notice board** *BrE*– a board on a wall on which notices and advertisements are placed

Shows the British word with the same meaning –see page 24a

Usage notes

a·lone /əˈloʷn/ *adv, adj* [F] **1** without others: *He lives alone.* | *The house stands alone on a hill. . . .*
USAGE **Alone** is neither good nor bad: *She reads a lot when she's* **alone. Solitary** and **lone,** when used of things, mean that there is only one: *a* **solitary/lone** *tree in the garden,* but when used of people they may show sadness, like **lonely** or **lonesome** (esp. *AmE*): *Come over and see me, I'm feeling a bit* **lonely.**

Usage Note explains the meaning and use of similar words –see page 26a

Synonyms

ab·surd /əbˈsɜrd, -ˈzɜrd/ *adj* against reason or common sense; clearly false or foolish; RIDICULOUS: *It's absurd not to wear a coat in such cold weather.*

fore·fin·ger /ˈfɔr,fɪŋgər, ˈfoʷr-/ also **index finger**– *n* the finger next to the thumb, with which one points

This shows another word you can use with the same meaning –see page 23a

Opposites

hap·py /ˈhæpiʸ/ *adj* **-pier, -piest 1** feeling, giving, or showing pleasure or contentment: *She is a happy child.* | *They have a happy marriage.*
–opposite **unhappy**

Shows a word with the opposite meaning –see page 25a

Related words

home·work /ˈhoʷmwɜrk/ *n* [U] schoolwork, such as essays, which is done outside the classroom, esp. at home, in a library, etc. –see also HOUSEWORK

Shows a word which is related or which might be confused –see page 24a

Dictionary Skills Workbook

This dictionary tells you a lot about English words and how to use them – in writing and speaking English, as well as in reading. Like any dictionary, it tells you the meaning of words and how to spell them, but it can also help you with grammar, pronunciation, word-building, and other important parts of the language.

   To use your dictionary well, you need to know how to find all the information in it. It is easy to do this once you understand how the dictionary works. These exercises will help you to learn how to use the dictionary and to understand the most important language points that you need to know. You can do them by yourself or with your teacher in class. The answers to the exercises are on pages 35a–38a.

Spelling

The words in this dictionary are listed in alphabetical order. Here is the alphabet:

a b c d e f g h i j k l m n o p q r s t u v w x y z
A B C D E F G H I J K L M N O P Q R S T U V W X Y Z

To put words in alphabetical order, look at the first letter of each word. The word whose first letter comes closest to the beginning of the alphabet is first in alphabetical order. The word whose first letter is next in the alphabet is second, and so on. For example, **able** comes before **be**, and **country** comes before **door**.

EXERCISE 1 Can you put these words in order? We have done the first two for you:

fight	_arm_
end	_bend_
arm	
car	
date	
bend	

EXERCISE 2 Now do the same with these words:

wind	_tell_
under	
zoo	
yellow	
Xmas	
visit	
tell	

When two words begin with the same letter, like **able** and **add**, you have to look at the second letter to find the word in the dictionary. So **able** comes before **add**, **man** comes before **meat**, and **wise** comes before **wood**.

EXERCISE 3 Can you put these words in order?

pen	_____
place	_____
pretend	_____
page	_____
poor	_____
piece	_____
pull	_____

If both the first and the second letters are the same, as in **grass** and **great**, then look at the third letter, and so on. So **grass** comes before **great**, and **through** comes before **throw**.

EXERCISE 4 Rewrite this list with all the words in the correct order:

illness	_____
month	_____
old	_____
money	_____
ill	_____
like	_____
kill	_____
jar	_____
name	_____
quick	_____
jam	_____
plate	_____

When you have done these exercises, turn to the answers on page 35a to see if you have listed them correctly.

Finding a word quickly

Because the words in this dictionary are listed in alphabetical order, this means that words beginning with **a** are listed at the front of the dictionary, words beginning with **z** are listed at the back, and words beginning with **m** are listed around the middle. So if you want to find the word **menu** you can turn straight to the middle of the dictionary. You don't have to start at the front and look through all the pages.

To help you to find words quickly, in the top corner of each page we print the first or the last word on that page. So you can work through the dictionary quickly just looking at these words until you find one which is spelled like the one you are looking for. You can then read down the page to find the word you want. For example, if you want to find the word **beetle**, turn the pages until you find **beet**. Then look down the page, and you will find **beetle**.

Two-word entries

Sometimes words are joined together with a hyphen, like **blue-collar**, and sometimes they are written as two words, like **ice cream** and **right angle**. Words like these are listed alphabetically as though they were just one word, so **ice cream** is listed after **icebox** and before **icicle**.

---

beet

---

beet /biʸt/ *n* **1** [C;U] *AmE*‖**beetroot** *BrE*- a plant with a large red round root, cooked and eaten as a vegetable **2** [C] also **sugar beet**- a plant which grows under the ground and from which beet sugar is obtained
beetle /ˈbiʸtl/ *n* an insect with hard wing coverings

---

icebox *n* **1** *AmE infml* for REFRIGERATOR **2** a box where food is kept cool with blocks of ice
ice cream *n* a sweet mixture which is frozen and eaten cold, usu. containing milk or other fat products: *chocolate ice cream*
ice hockey ‖ also **hockey** *esp. AmE*- a team game like FIELD HOCKEY played on ice
icicle *n* a pointed stick of ice formed when water freezes as it runs or DRIPs down: *icicles hanging from the roof*

EXERCISE 5   Put these two-word expressions in the right place in the lists below.

ice cream	absent-minded	all right	power station
ice	absent	allowable	power
ice age	absentee	allowance	powerful
iceberg	absently	alloy	powerless
ice cream			
icicle	absolute	allude to	pp.

Phrasal verbs

In English there are many two- or three-word verbs. These verbs (PHRASAL VERBS) have a different meaning from the main verb on its own, so they are listed separately, under the main verb, like this:

add *v* to put together with something else so as to increase the number, size, importance, etc.
add to *v prep* to increase: *The increase in electricity costs has added to our difficulties.*
addendum *n* something that is added or is to be added, as at the end of a speech or book

EXERCISE 6 Put these words in alphabetical order:

add up	*act*
act	_____
actual	_____
addition	_____
add	_____
act out	_____
act up	_____

Abbreviations

Abbreviations, like **CIA**, **a.m.**, and **e.g.** are listed in the dictionary in the usual way, so you will find **a.m.**, and **AM**, listed between **am** and **amalgamate**:

am *1st person sing. present tense of* BE
AM *abbrev. for* amplititude modulation; ...
a.m. *abbrev. for Latin* ante meridiem (= before midday)
amalgamate *v* (esp. of businesses, societies, groups, etc.) to join together

Different spelling

If you look up the word **judgment** in the dictionary, you will see that there are two different spellings for this word. Both of them are correct, but **judgment** is the more common one, so it is written first:

judgment, judgement *n* **1** an official decision given by a judge or a court of law: *The court passed judgment on the prisoner*, **2** an opinion: *to form a judgment* **3** the ability to judge correctly: *an* ERROR (=mistake) *of judgment*

EXERCISE 7 Find these words in the dictionary. Check (✓) the more common spellings:

judgment	___✓___	inquire	_____	enroll	_____
judgement	_____	enquire	_____	enrol	_____
generalise	_____	hankie	_____	yogurt	_____
generalize	_____	hanky	_____	yoghurt	_____

American and British spellings

If you look up the word **color**, you will see that there are two spellings for this word, and that **color** is used in American English (*AmE*), while **colour** is used in British English (*BrE*).

color *AmE* ‖ **colour** *BrE* *n* the quality which allows one to see the difference between (for example) a red flower and a blue flower when both are the same size and shape

In this dictionary American and British spelling differences are always shown with the sign ‖; the American spelling is on the left of this sign, with the label *AmE*, the British spelling is on the right, with the label *BrE*.

EXERCISE 8   Look up the following words in the dictionary. Which spelling would an American person use? Which spelling would a British person use? Write *AmE* for the American spelling, and *BrE* for the British.

center	*AmE*	defense	_____
centre	*BrE*	defence	_____
rumor	_____	cheque	_____
rumour	_____	check	_____

Sound/Pronunciation

As well as telling you how to spell words, the dictionary tells you how to pronounce them.

We use a special alphabet to show pronunciation, which is printed between sloping lines /...../, after the word, like this: **apple** /'æpəl/

apple /'æpəl/ *n* a hard round fruit with white juicy flesh, and a red, green, or yellow skin

Vowels and consonants

Look at the list of special (PHONETIC) letters on the inside back cover of this dictionary. You can see that this alphabet contains some letters that are the same as the English alphabet on page 12a, and some different ones.

In the list you will see common words next to the symbols. These words help you to learn to pronounce the sounds. For example:

VOWELS		CONSONANTS	
Symbol	Key Word	Symbol	Key Word
i^y	beat	p	**p**an
ɪ	bit	b	**b**an

This means that the phonetic letter /p/ is said like the **p** at the beginning of the word **pan**, and that the phonetic letter /b/ is said like the **b** at the beginning of the word **ban**. The phonetic letter /i^y/ is said like the **ea** in **beat**, and /ɪ/ is said like the **i** in **bit**. You don't have to learn all of the phonetic letters. Just remember to look at the list on the inside back cover when you're not sure how to say them.

EXERCISE 9 The words below contain one of these vowel sounds: /i^y/ as in **team**, /ɛ/ as in **bed**, /ɑ/ as in **pot**, and /u^w/ as in **do**. Look in the dictionary to see which sound each word uses, then write the word in one of the lists below, under the correct vowel:

> be̲d, bl̲u̲e̲, bo̲o̲t, bo̲x, br̲e̲ad, bu̲ry, d̲o̲, f̲ather, fi̲e̲ld, fr̲i̲end, gr̲o̲u̲p, ke̲y̲,
>
> m̲o̲ve, pe̲o̲ple, po̲t, sa̲i̲d, sc̲e̲ne, sh̲e̲ep, sh̲o̲e̲, te̲am, w̲atch

/i^y/	/ɛ/	/ɑ/	/u^w/
field	*bed*	*box*	*blue*

When you have made your lists, turn to the inside back cover to see how to say each sound.

Did you notice that the words **bed, bread, bury, friend,** and **said** all have the same /ɛ/ sound, even though they are spelled differently?

EXERCISE 10 The words in the list below contain one of these consonant sounds: /s/ as is **soon**, /f/ as in **few**, and /k/ as in **cool**. Look in the dictionary to see which sound each word uses for the underlined letters, then write the word in one of the lists below, under the correct consonant:

check, city, coffee, cool, cough, few, key, mice, photograph, psychology, queen, school, soon, science

/s/	/f/	/k/
city		

Now check the sounds on the inside back cover, and practice saying the words in the lists.

Did you notice that the words **coffee**, **cough**, **few**, and **photograph** all contain the same /f/ sound, even though they are spelled differently?

Spelling notes

Because many different letters can have the same sound in English, it is often difficult to know how to spell a word that you have not seen in writing. To help you to find these words, the dictionary contains a number of Spelling Notes, like the one shown here. This tells you that if you have heard a word that begins with the sound /f/, it may actually be spelt **ph-**, like **photograph**.

F, f

SPELLING NOTE
Words with the sound /f/ may be spelled **ph-**, like **photograph**

F, f the 6th letter of the English alphabet
fable *n* a short story, esp. about animals, that teaches a lesson (a MORAL) or truth

Words with the same spelling, but different sound

Look at the two entries for **row** here. You will see that they are both nouns, one meaning "a neat line (of people or things)," and one meaning "a noisy quarrel." If you look at the pronunciations of these two words you will see that they are said differently, even though they are spelled exactly the same. **Row** meaning "line" has a sound like **no**, and **row** meaning "quarrel" has a sound like **now**:

row /roʷ/ *n* a neat line (of people or things) side by side

row /raʊ/ *n* a noisy quarrel, sometimes with violent actions

EXERCISE 11   The words **lead** and **bow** can both be said in two different ways. Use your dictionary to decide how they should be pronounced in the sentences below. First find the correct meaning, then look at the pronunciation guide. Check (✓) the correct pronunciation.

Shall I **lead** the way? —————————————————	/liʸd/	✓
	/lɛd/	———
Lead is a dull gray soft metal. ————————————	/liʸd/	———
	/lɛd/	———
The ribbon in the girl's hair was tied in a **bow.** ———	/baʊ/	———
	/boʷ/	———
You must **bow** when the President enters the room. ———	/baʊ/	———
	/boʷ/	———

Stress

Most of the words in the exercises so far have been very short, and contain just one vowel sound. But many words, like **about**, **afraid**, and **alone** have two vowel sounds. They consist of two parts (or SYLLABLES).

about /əˈbaʊt/   **afraid** /əˈfreʸd/   **alone** /əˈloʷn/

If you look at the pronunciation guides for these words, you will see that they have an extra sign, a little bar /ˈ/ like the one in front of the /ˈb/ in **about**. This means that when we say these words we put more force (or STRESS) on the second part (or SYLLABLE) of the word:

ab<u>out</u>   **afr<u>aid</u>**   **al<u>one</u>**

Look at the pronunciation guides for **able**, **almost**, and **angry** below:

able /ˈeʸbəl/   **almost** /ˈɔlmoʷst/   **angry** /ˈæŋgriʸ/

Look for the sign /ˈ/. It's at the beginning of these words. This means that we put more force (STRESS) on the first SYLLABLE of these words:

<u>a</u>ble   **<u>al</u>most**   **<u>an</u>gry**

Practice saying the words **about**, **afraid**, and **alone**, and then say **able**, **almost**, and **angry**. Can you hear the difference? Remember to look for the sign /ˈ/.

EXERCISE 12   Look up the pronunciation guides for the words listed below. All of them have more than one SYLLABLE, so look for the sign /ˈ/. Underline the part of the word that has the stress put on it:

ab<u>il</u>ity	advantage	afternoon	afterwards

For more information on STRESS turn to page 792.

Nouns and verbs with different stress

Read through the following sentences:

> *I bought a new* **record** *today.*
> *The band went to the studio to* **record** *their new song.*

Did you say **record** the same or differently in the two sentences? They should be pronounced differently. Look in the dictionary and practice saying the sentences.

EXERCISE 13   Use your dictionary to check the pronunication of **increase** and **permit** in the sentences below. Underline the stressed syllable.

The school wants to **increase** the number of students next year.
There will be an **increase** in the number of students next year.

This card will **permit** you to enter the building.
You will need a **permit** to enter the building.

Syllables and hyphenation

It helps to learn the sound of a long word if you start by saying it one SYLLABLE at a time. Look at the entry for **ability** here:

a·bil·i·ty /ə'bɪləţiʸ/ *n* .....

The dots mean that the word **ability** has four SYLLABLEs, and you can learn to say it one SYLLABLE at a time:

a   bil   i   ty
/ə   'bɪl   ə   tiʸ/

Now say it quickly. Remember to put the stress on /'bɪl/: **abi̲lity**

The dots also show you where you can break a word at the end of a line of writing:

> *Jane shows a lot of* **abil-**
> **ity** *at school*

> *Jane shows a lot of* **abili-**
> **ty** *at school.*

But don't break a word after only one letter, and don't leave just one letter on the new line, after the hyphen.

Meaning

One of the main reasons that you need a dictionary is to find out the meaning of a word – its definition. In this dictionary, the definitions have been written using a limited defining vocabulary of only 2000 common words. This means that the definitions of even the most difficult words are easy to understand.

For example, look at the entry for **egg** shown here. Because there are no difficult words used in these definitions, you don't have to look up other words to understand what they mean.

egg *n* **1** a rounded object with a hard shell, which comes out of a female bird, snake, etc., and which contains a baby animal before it is born **2** this when eaten as food: *I had a boiled egg for breakfast.*

EXERCISE 14 Use your dictionary to answer these questions by looking up the words shown in **dark type** and reading their definitions. The first one has been done for you:

---

1. What would you write an **address** on?

Answer: *a letter,*
envelope or package

> **address** *n* the number of the building, name of the street and town, etc., where a person lives or works, esp. when written on a letter, envelope, or package

2. When you **abridge** something, do you make it longer or shorter?

Answer: _____

3. If two things are **adjacent**, are they close together or far apart?

Answer: _____

4. What can you describe as being **ajar**?

Answer: _____

5. What kinds of animals would you describe as **poultry**?

Answer: _____

6. Is an unmarried man a **spinster** or a **bachelor**?

Answer: _____

7. What might cause you to **flinch**?

Answer: _____

_____

_____

> **flinch** *v* to move back a little when shocked by pain or fear: *Jane didn't flinch once when the doctor cleaned the cut in her arm.* | *He flinched when I raised my hand suddenly. He thought I was going to hit him.*

The entry for **flinch** shown here has two examples after the definition, *printed like this.* These examples help you by giving you more information about what the word means and how to use it. So to answer question 7 you could have said "pain or fear," or you could have said "a doctor cleaning a wound," or "thinking that someone is going to hit you." Go on answering the questions, and remember: read the definitions and the examples.

8. What can be said to **act up**?

Answer: _____

9. What is often called "an **addition** to the family?"

Answer: _____

10. What two things might **adjoin** each other?

Answer: _____

More than one meaning

When you looked at the entry for **addition** to answer question 9, you probably noticed that it had two different meanings, numbered **1** and **2**. When an entry has more than one meaning like this, you should always read through all the meanings until you find the one that correctly explains the use of the word you are looking for.

> **addition** *n* **1** the act of adding, esp. of adding numbers together **2** something added: *A new baby is often called an addition to the family.*

EXERCISE 15   Look up these words in the dictionary. How many meanings does each one have?

able _2_   abroad ___   account ___   literally ___   poor ___   weak ___

EXERCISE 16   In the sentences below, the words in **dark type** all have more than one meaning. Look them up in the dictionary and decide which meaning correctly explains the use of the word in these sentences, and write the number in the blank:

1. She is a very **able** teacher.   _2_

2. I can't pay you. I have no money in my bank **account**.   ____

3. His essay was **poor**, so he got a low mark for it.   ____

4. John just won't listen to **reason** any more.   ____

5. I can't leave early. I'm up to my **neck** in work.   ____

When you look up the word **reason** to answer question 4, you will see that the example for definition **3** (the correct answer) includes the phrase **listen to reason**. This is in **dark type** to show that it is a very common expression.

up to one's neck is listed as a separate definition at **neck** because it is an IDIOM. You cannot guess the meaning of this special phrase, even if you know the meaning of all the words in it. So to help you find the meaning of idioms, we write them in **dark type** at the beginning of the definition, and we list them under the first important word, so **up to one's neck** is at **neck**, **pull someone's leg** is at **leg**, and **across the board** is at **board**.

The last few exercises have all helped you to find out what a word means. You should have no trouble finding the meaning of a word if you remember three things:

1. read both the definition and the example;
2. read all the definitions. If there are more than one, read until you come to the one that seems correct;
3. check to see if the word you are looking for is part of a special expression.

Using Your Dictionary to Choose the Right Word

In English you can sometimes use two different words to mean the same thing. For example, you can say:

Push the button with your **forefinger.** or:

Push the button with your **index finger**.

We show this in the dictionary by writing:

> **forefinger** also **index finger**– *n* the finger next to the thumb, with which one points

EXERCISE 17 Use your dictionary to find another word or phrase that means the same as the words in the list below:

aloud	*out loud*
anybody	_____
filing cabinet	_____
living room	_____
bathing suit	_____

Formal and informal

Most of the words in this dictionary can be used by all people in all parts of the world, and in any situation. But there are some words which are suitable in speech only on very formal occasions, and in writing by people in universities, government, and law. And there are some words which are suitable only for informal speech, or in a letter to a friend, for example. In the dictionary words which are suitable only for formal occasions are marked *fml*, and words which are suitable only for informal use are marked *infml*, like this:

> **destitute** *adj fml* without food, clothing, shelter, etc., or the money to buy them; very poor

> **kid** *n infml* a child: *How many kids do you have?*

EXERCISE 18 Some of the words in the list below would not be suitable for a letter or a school paper, because they are either too formal (*fml*), or too informal (*infml*). Check (✓) the words that you could use in your paper:

adorn	_____	lucky	_____
ad	_____	seek	_____
begin	✓	short	_____
commence	_____	succinct	_____
decorate	_____	TV	_____
erroneous	_____	television	_____
impart	_____	wrong	_____
look for	_____	zany	_____

If you look at the entry for **advertisement**, you'll see that it tells you that **ad** is another word for **advertisement**, but that it is only used in informal situations.

> **advertisement** *n* also **ad** *infml–* a notice of something for sale, job position to be filled, room to rent, etc., as in a newspaper, on television, or pasted on a wall

American and British words

We have already seen that words are sometimes spelled differently in American and British English, and there are some word differences too. For example, an American speaker would use **bulletin board** where a British speaker would use **notice board**. In the dictionary, words which are used only by American speakers are marked *AmE*, and words which are used only by British speakers are marked *BrE*, and they are separated by the sign ‖ like this:

> **bulletin board** *AmE* ‖ **notice board** *BrE– n* a board on a wall on which notices and advertisements are placed

> **notice board** *n BrE* for BULLETIN BOARD

This means that **notice board** is the British form of **bulletin board**, and that you turn to **bulletin board** for its meaning.

EXERCISE 19   Here is a list of British words. Write one of these words next to the American word in the list below which has the same meaning. Remember that you can look up either the British or the American word in the dictionary.

aeroplane   biscuit   lift   pavement

airplane   *aeroplane*

cookie   _____

elevator   _____

sidewalk   _____

See also/Compare

Look at the entries for **homework** and **housework** below:

> **homework** *n* schoolwork, such as essays, which is done outside the classroom, esp, at home, in a library, etc –compare HOUSEWORK

> **housework** *n* work done to keep the inside of a house clean and tidy –compare HOMEWORK

When you look up one of these words, the dictionary tells you to look at the other one so that you are sure that you have chosen the right word for the meaning you want.

EXERCISE 20   You can use the word **adapt** in one of the sentences below. Which word would you use in the other sentence?

They didn't have any children of their own, so they decided to
_____ one.

When they moved to a new country they had to _____
themselves to a different way of life.

Opposites

The dictionary also shows you words with the opposite meaning to the word you are looking up, like this:

> **happy** *adj* feeling, giving, or showing pleasure or contentment: *She is a happy child.* | *They have a happy marriage.* –opposite **unhappy**

This means that **unhappy** has the opposite meaning to **happy**.

> *Is she* **happy** *at school?* *No, she's very* **unhappy**.
> *She's not* **happy**; *she's* **unhappy**.

Opposites like **unhappy** are often formed by adding a small group of letters to the beginning of a word. So we have:

helpful opposite **unhelpful**
accurate opposite **inaccurate**
allow opposite **disallow**

EXERCISE 21   Look up the words below in the dictionary, and write down their opposites.

---

accurate   *inaccurate*

adaptable   _____

agree   _____

inflate   _____

logical   _____

mature   _____

Sometimes the opposite is a completely different word. For example the opposite of **heavy** is **light**, the opposite of **hard** is **soft** or **easy**. These opposites are shown in the same way:

> **hard** *adj* **1** firm and stiff; not easily broken or bent: *hard steel* | *hard skin* | *The snow has frozen hard* –opposite **soft** **2** difficult (to do or understand): *This question is too hard, I can't answer it.* –opposite **easy**

Usage notes

Look at the entry for **kill** here. After the definitions there is a Usage Note which tells you the different meanings and uses of a number of words which all mean "kill."

EXERCISE 22 Read through the Usage Note at **kill**, and use **kill**, **murder**, and **assassinate** to complete the sentences below. Some sentences should have more than one answer.

kill *v* **1** to cause to die: .....
USAGE **Kill** is a general word meaning to cause (anything) to die, but **murder** means to kill a person on purpose: *My uncle was* **killed** *in a plane crash.* | *The cold weather* **killed** *our tomato plants.* | *She was sent to prison for* **murdering** *her husband.* ..... To **assassinate** means to kill an important political figure: *an attempt to* **assassinate** *the governor*

He *murdered-killed* his friend because he was jealous.

There was an election after the President was _____.

The boy was _____ in a car accident.

Study notes

The Study Notes bring together a lot of words to tell you something about their meaning, use, or grammar. Turn to the Study Notes on **pairs of verbs** on page 481. This tells you the differences between **lend** and **borrow**, **bring** and **take**, and **say** and **tell**.

EXERCISE 23 Read the section on **lend** and **borrow**, and use one of the verbs **lend** and **borrow** in each of the sentences below:

Can I *borrow* your book? I left mine at home.

Will you _____ me your book? I left mine at home.

He _____ my book and he hasn't returned it yet.

I _____ him my book and he hasn't returned it yet.

Illustrations

The illustrations in this dictionary show you the different kinds of things you would find in, for example, a house or an office. They tell you what all the things are called, and show you how they are the same or different from other things. For example, if you turn to the illustration of a clothing store on page 123, you will see how a **pullover** is different from a **cardigan**, and what makes a **skirt** different from a **dress**.

EXERCISE 24 Turn to the illustration of a living room on page 399. What's the difference between a **couch** and an **armchair**?

Word families

Many words in English have several different forms, and these are often made by adding a group of letters to the end of a word. For example, we have the words:

abnormal, abnormally, abnormality
abrupt, abruptly, abruptness

These words have a different part of speech. Look at the entry for **abnormal**. **Abnormally** and **abnormality** are listed here because their meaning comes from **abnormal**, but they are used differently because they have different parts of speech. So we can say:

> **abnormal** *adj* not NORMAL; different (usu. in a bad sense) from what is ordinary or expected; unusual; peculiar: *Is the child abnormal in any way?* –**abnormally** *adv* –**abnormality** *n* -ties

Is the child **abnormal** *in any way?*   or

Does the child behave **abnormally** *at all?*   or

Does the child have any **abnormalities**?

EXERCISE 25   The sentences below all contain a word in **dark type** that is listed in the dictionary with one or more related words. Fill in the blanks with the correct related word.

It's an **abnormal** situation. In fact it's full of _abnormalities_

The train made an **abrupt** stop. It stopped very _____

I had to **adjust** the television. I made a small _____

She's a very **agile** girl. I admire her _____

Sometimes words that are related like this are listed separately in the dictionary. This is because their meanings are different, or because they are all very common words. Look at the entries here for **kind** and **kindly**, and note the three different meanings of **kindly**:

> **kind** *adj* helpful; (that shows one is) interested in the happiness or feelings of others: *It was very kind of you to visit me when I was ill.*
> **kindly** *adv* 1 in a kind manner: *She spoke kindly to the old man.* 2 please: *Would you kindly pass me that book?* 3 not take kindly to: not to accept easily or willingly: *He doesn't take kindly to being told how to behave.*

There is a list of all of these word endings at the back of the dictionary on pages 786–789. This list tells you what the endings mean, and gives you more examples.

Grammar

This dictionary tells you a lot about the grammar of words and how to use them in sentences.

Parts of speech

The first thing it tells you is whether a word is a noun, verb, adjective, etc. This information is shown like this:

n = noun	**action** *n* .....
v = verb	**add** *v* .....
adj = adjective	**afraid** *adj* .....
adv = adverb	**afterwards** *adv* .....
prep = PREPOSITION	**at** *prep* .....

EXERCISE 26 Choose the correct noun (*n*) from the list to complete these sentences:

active   activity   advice   advise

The market was very busy and there was a lot of ___*activity*___

My brother wanted to buy a car so he asked for my _____

EXERCISE 27 Choose the correct verb (*v*) to complete these sentences:

belief   believe   breath   breathe

Joan said that she found the ring, but I didn't _____ her.

I ran so fast that when I stopped I couldn't _____

EXERCISE 28 Now choose an adjective (*adj*) to complete these sentences:

height   high   heat   hot   afraid   fear

That huge building is over 200 feet _____

My little brother is _____ of dogs.

He burned his hand because he didn't know that the pan was _____.

Countable [C] and uncountable [U] nouns

If the word you look up is a noun, the dictionary shows you whether it has a plural or not. Nouns that don't have a plural are UNCOUNTABLE nouns, and are shown with a [U]; nouns that do have a plural are COUNTABLE nouns. We show these with a [C], or with no sign at all if they are only countable in all of their meanings (–see Study Notes on page 550). All of the meanings of the nouns shown here are COUNTABLE, so we don't need to use the sign [C].

bar *n* **1** a piece of wood, metal, etc. that is longer than it is wide: *an iron bar* | *a bar of soap/chocolate/gold* **2** a length of wood or metal across a door, gate, or window that keeps it shut or prevents movement through it: *There were metal bars across the windows of the prison.....*

child *n* **children** a young human being: *We have five children* (= sons and/or daughters) *but one's still a baby.....*

Irregular plurals

Most nouns form their plural by adding **-s** or **-es**, but if you look at the entry for **child** above, you will see that it has a special plural form, **children**. When a noun has a plural that changes its spelling, or where there is some doubt, we show it in the dictionary like this:

baby *n* **-bies** a very young child, esp. one who has not learned to speak

monkey *n* **-keys** a small tree-climbing animal with a long tail, and part of the class of animals most like man

potato *n* **-toes** a roundish root vegetable with a thin brown or yellowish skin, that is cooked and served in many different ways

radio *n* **-os** an apparatus made to receive sound broadcast through the air by means of electrical waves

foot *n* **feet** the movable part of the body at the end of the leg, below the ankle, on which a person or animal stands

sheep *n* **sheep** a grass-eating animal that is kept for its wool and its meat

EXERCISE 29   What is the plural of these nouns?

donkey	*donkeys*
tomato	_____
ox	_____
mouse	_____
car	_____
fish	_____

Nouns that are only singular [S] or only plural [P]

Look at the entries for **clatter** and **cattle** here:

clatter *n* [S] a number of rapid short knocking sounds as when a number of things fall to the ground: *There was a clatter of dishes in the kitchen.*

cattle [P] *n* large four-legged farm animals, esp. cows, kept for their meat or milk: *He has twenty* **head of cattle** *on his farm.*

The [S] means that **clatter** is usually used only in the singular, with a singular verb. It has no plural.

The [P] means that **cattle** is used only in the plural, with a plural verb. It has no singular form. Many of these [P] nouns are plural in form, like **scissors**, but some are not, like **cattle** and **police**.

Transitive [T] and intransitive [I] verbs

If the word you look up is a verb, the dictionary tells you a lot about how to use it in a sentence. First, it tells you whether the verb is TRANSITIVE or INTRANSITIVE (–see Study Notes on page 745). TRANSITIVE verbs are followed by a noun or noun phrase as a direct OBJECT, and are shown with a [T]; INTRANSITIVE verbs don't have a direct OBJECT, and are shown with an [I]:

kick *v* [T] to hit with the foot: *She kicked the ball.*

pause *v* [I] to stop for a short time before continuing: *She paused to light a cigarette, then continued reading.*

But many verbs can be both [T] and [I]. For example, **smell** can be [T], as in:

> *He stopped to* **smell** *the flower.*

or it can be [I], as in:

> *The flower* **smelled** *nice.*

smell *v* **1** [I] to have or use the sense of the nose: *The flower smelled nice.* **2** [T] to notice, examine, or recognize by this sense: *He stopped to smell the flower.*

EXERCISE 30 Some of these verbs need a noun or noun phrase to make a complete sentence. Use your dictionary to complete these sentences where necessary.

He **abandoned** _____

The storm **abated** _____

She was **adding** _____

The soldiers **advanced** _____

Verbs like *be* and *seem*

Some verbs, like **seem**, do not have an [I] or a [T] after them. These verbs are followed by another word which tells us something about the subject of the sentence. For example:

>*John* **seems** *happy today.*

>*This bag* **seems** *heavy; what's in it?*

You will find more information about these verbs in the Study Notes on page 745.

Irregular verbs

Most verbs add **-ed** for the past tense and PAST PARTICIPLE, and **-ing** for the PRESENT PARTICIPLE, like **help**:

>*Can you* **help** *me, please?*
>*I* **helped** *pass out the books yesterday.*
>*You've* **helped** *me a lot.*
>*I like* **helping** *people.*

But look at the sentences below, with the verbs **break** and **fly**:

>*Be careful or you'll* **break** *the glass.*   *Birds can* **fly**.
>*Who* **broke** *the window?*   *The aeroplane* **flew** *past.*
>*Somebody* **has broken** *the clock.*   *I've never* **flown** *in an airplane.*
>*You're always* **breaking** *things.*   *Do you like* **flying?**

There are a lot of irregular verbs, like **break** and **fly**, and to help you use them we list the different parts of the verb, like this:

break *v* **broke, broken, breaking** [I;T] to (cause to) come apart or separate into pieces, esp. suddenly or violently, but not by cutting or tearing

broken *v past participle of* BREAK

fly *v* **flew, flown, flying** [I] to move through the air on wings

flew *v past tense of* FLY

There is a list of irregular verbs with their different parts on pages 790–791.

Verbs followed by prepositions and adverbs [*of, from*]

Look at the sentences below:

The police accused John of stealing.
She accused me of breaking her watch.

You can see that both of these sentences use the verb **accuse**, and follow it with a direct object and then the PREPOSITION **of**. This is how we show this in the dictionary:

accuse *v* [*T of*] to charge (someone) with doing wrong or breaking the law; blame: *The police accused him (of murder).*

EXERCISE 31   Complete the sentences below by writing in the correct PREPOSITION:

He **absconded** ___*from*___ the bank with a lot of money.

I **abstained** _____ voting at the meeting.

We **adapted** _____ the cold weather very quickly.

This coat hook **adheres** _____ the wall.

I went to **apply** _____ the job, but it had already gone.

Verbs followed by another verb in the infinitive [+*to-v*]

Want and **decide** are examples of verbs that can be followed by the INFINITIVE form of another verb with **to**:

> *I **want to go** to the library.*
> *I **decided to rest** for a while.*

These verbs are shown in the dictionary like this. The examples tell you that you don't have to use a verb after **want**, but if you do it must be in the infinitive form with **to**.

> **want** *v* [T +*to-v*] to have a strong desire to or for; feel a strong desire to have: *I want a rest.* | *I want to rest.*

Verbs followed by another verb in the -*ing* form [+*v-ing*]

Enjoy and **approve of** are often followed by another verb in the **-ing** form:

> *I **enjoy riding** my bicycle.*
> *I don't **approve of** smoking.*

This is how this is shown in the dictionary. If you read the examples you can see that you can use either a noun or a verb after **enjoy**, but if you do use a verb it must be in the **-ing** form.

> **enjoy** *v* [T +*v-ing*] to get happiness from (things and experiences); like: *I enjoyed the movie.* | *I always enjoy going to the movies.*

EXERCISE 32 Complete the sentences below using the verbs in parentheses (....). Use your dictionary to see whether you should use the **to-** form or the **-ing** form:

I **enjoy** ___*playing*___ football.   (play)

I **want** _____ home.   (go)

I have **given up** _____   (smoke)

We **hope** _____ you again.   (see)

Verbs followed by a clause beginning with *that* [+*that*]

The sentences below all show verbs which are often followed by a clause beginning with the word **that**:

>*I* **think that** *he will be late.*
>*I* **believe that** *she is telling the truth.*

Think and **believe** are often used with **that**, so we show it in the dictionary:

> **think** *v* **2** [T +(*that*)] to believe; consider: *I think (that) he's wrong, don't you?*

Note that the word **that** is in parentheses (. . . . .) here because you can leave it out, as in: *I think he's wrong, don't you?*

Verbs not used in the *-ing* form [not *be* +*v-ing*]

With most verbs we can say:

>*I go to school every day.*

and

>*I am going to school tomorrow.*

But there are some verbs, like **know**, that we do not usually use in the **-ing** form. For example:

>*I* **know** *John quite well.*   NOT *I am knowing John quite well.*
>*I can* **see** *the book on the shelf.*   NOT *I am seeing the book on the shelf.*

Verbs like **know** and **see** are shown in the dictionary like this. Other verbs like this include **like**, **love**, **want**, **wish**, **believe**, **mean**, **understand**, **seem**, etc.

> **know** *v* [not *be* +*v-ing*] to have information (about) in the mind: *I know he's there because I saw him.*

Objects of phrasal verbs

The dictionary helps you to decide the correct position of the object when you are using a phrasal verb. Sometimes the object comes after the phrasal verb, and sometimes the object comes between the parts of the phrasal verb. Here are two examples:

> **look after** sbdy *v prep* [T]

> **push** sbdy **around** *v adv* [T]

I **looked after** *the sick man.*

The older boys were always **pushing** *the young boys* **around.**

You can see that the dictionary also tells you if the object is a person (sbdy.) or a thing (sthg.). The Study Note on phrasal verbs (page 501) tells you more about how the dictionary helps you to use and understand phrasal verbs correctly.

Adjectives

Most English adjectives can be used either before a noun or after a verb, like this:

It's a **long** *way into town.*   *The journey was quite* **long**.
He told us an **interesting** *story.*   *His story was very* **interesting**.

But some adjectives can be used in only one of these positions, and these adjectives are shown with the sign [A] or [F]. Turn to the Study Notes on page 9 for an explanation of these signs, and some examples.

More and most

When we want to express the idea of greater quantity or quality, we add **-er** and **-est** to short adjectives, and use **more** and **most** with long adjectives. For example:

She has **long** *hair. Yes, it's* **longer** *than it used to be.*
He told an **interesting** *story. Yes it was the* **most interesting** *story I've heard.*

A few adjectives have different **-er** and **-est** forms. For example:

good *adj* **better**, **best** having the right qualities	**big** *adj* **-gg-** of more than average size, weight, force, importance, etc.

This means that we say:

> *I had a* **good** *vacation this year, It was* **better** *than last year. In fact, it was the* **best** *vacation I've ever had.*

This means that we say:

> *The library is a* **big** *building, but the church is* **bigger**, *and the town hall is the* **biggest** *building in the town.*

Turn to page 135 for more examples of these COMPARATIVE and SUPERLATIVE adjectives.

Answers

EXERCISE 1
arm – bend – car – date – end – fight

EXERCISE 2
tell – under – visit – wind – Xmas – yellow – zoo

EXERCISE 3
page – pen – piece – place – poor – pretend – pull

EXERCISE 4
ill – illness – jam – jar – kill – like – money – month – name – old – plate – quick

EXERCISE 5
ice – ice age – iceberg – ice cream – icicle
absent – absentee – absently – absent-minded – absolute
power – powerful – powerless – power station – pp.

EXERCISE 6
act – act out – act up – actual – add – add up – addition

EXERCISE 7
judgment – generalize – inquire – hankie – enroll – yogurt

EXERCISE 8
AmE: center – rumor – defense – check
BrE: centre – defence – rumour – cheque

EXERCISE 9
With /iʸ/: field – key – people – scene – sheep – team
With /ɛ/: bed – bread – bury – friend – said
With /ɑ/: box – father – pot – watch
With /uʷ/: blue – boot – do – group – move – shoe

EXERCISE 10
With /s/: city – mice – psychology – soon – science
With /f/: coffee – cough – few – photograph
With /k/: check – cool – key – queen – school

EXERCISE 11
Shall I lead the way? /liʸd/
Lead is a dull gray metal. /lɛd/
The ribbon in the girl's hair was tied in a bow. /boʷ/
You must bow when the President enters the room. /baʊ/

EXERCISE 12
ability – advantage – afternoon – afterwards

EXERCISE 13
The school wants to increase the number of students next year.
There will be an increase in the number of students next year.
This card will permit you to enter the building.
You will need a permit to enter the building.

Exercise 14
1. a letter, envelope or package
2. shorter
3. close together
4. a door
5. farmyard birds, such as hens and ducks
6. a bachelor
7. pain or fear
8. a car
9. a new baby
10. rooms or houses

Exercise 15
able 2
abroad 2
account 10
literally 4
poor 3
weak 3

Exercise 16
1. able (2)
2. account (7)
3. poor (2)
4. reason (3)
5. neck (7)

Exercise 17
aloud *or* out loud
anybody *or* anyone
filing cabinet *or* file cabinet
living room *or* sitting room
bathing suit *or* swim suit

Exercise 18
Words that you could use in a school paper:
begin – decorate – look for – lucky – short – TV – television – wrong – zany

Exercise 19
airplane – aeroplane
cookie – biscuit
elevator – lift
sidewalk – pavement

Exercise 20
adopt – adapt. You **adopt** a child, but you **adapt** to a new way of life.

Exercise 21
inaccurate – unadaptable – disagree – deflate – illogical – immature

Exercise 22
murdered *or* killed
assassinated *or* killed
killed

Exercise 23
borrow – lend – borrowed – lent

Exercise 24
An armchair is a chair for one person only, but a couch is for two or more people.

Exercise 25
abnormalities – abruptly – adjustment – agility

Exercise 26
activity
advice

Exercise 27
believe
breathe

Exercise 28
high
afraid
hot

Exercise 29
donkeys – tomatoes – oxen – mice – cars – fish *or* fishes

Exercise 30
These sentences are complete: *The storm abated. The soldiers advanced.*
The others must have an object. There are many possible ways of completing the sentences; the dictionary gives you some examples.

Exercise 31
abscond from – abstain from – adapt to – adhere to – apply for

Exercise 32
enjoy playing
want to go
given up smoking
hope to see

Answers to illustration questions

Bedroom (page 55)
1. set, woke
2. make
3. asleep
4. go
5. overslept
6. late

KITCHEN (page 379)
1. snack
2. make
3. have/eat
4. garbage

OFFICE (page 467)
1. typewriter, word processor
2. copying machine
3. (coffee) break
4. get, go home

Answers to Study Notes questions

1. in, in, on
2. on, in
3. on
4. on, above/over
5. on
6. below
7. under
8. between
9. beside
10. in
11. on, on
12. at
13. in front of
14. between
15. behind
16. away from
17. into, out of

A, a

A, a /eʸ/ **A's, a's** or **As, as** the first letter of the English alphabet

A (in Western music) a musical note

a /ə; *strong* eʸ/ also (*before a vowel sound*) **an**– indefinite article, determiner **1** one: *a* THOU- SAND *pounds*|*a* DOZEN *eggs*|*I caught a fish yesterday.*|*He's a friend of mine.* (=one of my friends) **2** (before some words of quan- tity): *a few weeks*|*a little water*|*a lot of people* **3** (after *half, so, such, what, how, rather, too*): *What a nice girl (she is)!*|*I've never met such a nice girl.* **4** any; every; the thing called: *A bicycle has two wheels.* **5** a kind of: *Chablis is a very good wine.* **6** a container or UNIT (3) of: *I'd like a coffee, please.*|*A beer, please.* **7** (used before [S] nouns. Some of these words are actions): *Everyone needs a good cry now and then.* **8** each; every; PER: *six times a day*|*$2 a* DOZEN

AA /ˌeʸ 'eʸ/ *abbrev. for:* ASSOCIATE² (3) **of Arts**

AB /ˌeʸ 'biʸ/ → BA

ab·a·cus /'æbəkəs/ *n* **-cuses** a frame holding wires on which small balls can be moved, used for counting

a·ban·don /ə'bændən/ *v* [T] **1** to leave com- pletely and forever; desert: *The sailors aban- doned the burning ship.*|*He abandoned his wife and went away with all their money.* **2** to give up, esp. without finishing; stop: *The search was abandoned when night came.* **3** to give (oneself) up completely to a feeling or desire: *He abandoned himself to grief.*| *abandoned behavior* –**abandonment** *n* [U]

a·base /ə'beʸs/ *v* **-based, -basing** [T] *fml* to make (someone, esp. oneself) have less self-respect; make humble: *He won't abase himself by showing fear.* –**abasement** *n* [U]

a·bash /ə'bæʃ/ *v* [T *usu. pass.*] to cause to feel uncomfortable or ashamed in the presence of others: *He stood abashed.*

a·bate /ə'beʸt/ *v* **-bated, -bating** [I] *fml* (of storms, pain, sounds, etc.) to become less fierce; decrease: *The ship waited in the har- bor until the storm abated.* –see also UNA- BATED –**abatement** *n* [U]

ab·bess /'æbɪs/ *n* a woman who is the head of a religious establishment for women (CON- VENT) –compare ABBOT

ab·bey /'æbiʸ/ *n* (esp. formerly) a religious establishment in which Christian men (MONKs) or women (NUNs) live and work; MONASTERY or CONVENT

ab·bot /'æbət/ *n* [A;C] a man who is the head of a religious establishment for men (MONAS- TERY) –compare ABBESS

ab·bre·vi·ate /ə'briʸviʸˌeʸt/ *v* **-ated, -ating** [T] to make (a word, story, etc.) shorter

ab·bre·vi·a·tion /əˌbriʸviʸ'eʸʃən/ *n* a shor- tened form of a word, often one used in writing (such as *Mr.*)

ab·di·cate /'æbdɪˌkeʸt/ *v* **-cated, -cating** [I;T *from*] *fml* to give up (a position or right): *The King abdicated (from) the* THRONE (2).|*He*

abdicated all responsibility for the care of the child. –**abdication** /ˌæbdɪ'keʸʃən/ *n* [C;U]

ab·do·men /'æbdəmən, æb'doʷ-/ *n tech* a main part of the body, between the chest and legs –**abdominal** /æb'dɑmənəl/ *adj*

ab·duct /æb'dʌkt, əb-/ *v* [T] to take away (a person) unlawfully, often by force; KIDNAP: *The police think the woman has been ab- ducted.* –**abduction** /æb'dʌkʃən, əb-/ *n* [U]

a·bet /ə'bɛt/ *v* **-tt-** [T] **aid and abet** *law or humor* to help in a plan, esp. a crime

a·bey·ance /ə'beʸəns/ *n fml* the condition of not being in force or in use, at or for a certain time: *an old custom that has* **fallen into** abeyance|*Your plan is* **in abeyance.**

ab·hor /əb'hɔr, æb-/ *v* **-rr-** [T] to feel great hatred for; DETEST: *Most people abhor cruelty to children.*

ab·hor·rent /əb'hɔrənt, -'hɑr-, æb-/ *adj* [*to*] hateful; DETESTable: *The idea of killing ani- mals for food is abhorrent to many people.* –**abhorrence** *n* [U]

a·bide /ə'baɪd/ *v* **-bode** /'boʷd/ or **-bided, -biding 1** [T +*to-v/v-ing*] (usu. not in simple statements) to bear; TOLERATE: *I can't abide people who keep me waiting.* –see BEAR² (USAGE) **2** [I] *lit and old use* to stay; re- main; live (in or at a place)

    abide by sthg. *v prep* **-bided, -biding** [T *no pass.*] to obey (laws, agreements, etc.): *If you join the club you have to abide by its rules.*

a·bil·i·ty /ə'bɪlətiʸ/ *n* **-ties** [C;U] power and skill, esp. to do, think, make, etc.: *She has the ability to go to college, but she doesn't want to.*|*musical ability*|*a job more suited to his abilities* –see GENIUS (USAGE)

ab·ject /'æbdʒɛkt, æb'dʒɛkt/ *adj* **1** (of a con- dition) as low as possible; deserving great pity: *abject* POVERTY **2** not deserving respect; showing lack of self-respect: *an abject apol- ogy* –**abjectly** *adv*

a·blaze /ə'bleʸz/ *adj* [F] on fire: *The wooden house was quickly ablaze.* –see also BLAZE

a·ble /'eʸbəl/ *adj* **1** [F +*to-v*] having the power, skill, knowledge, time, etc., neces- sary to do something: *Will you be able to come?*|*I was able to reach the handle.* –op- posite **unable** –see Study Notes on page 434 **2** intelligent; skilled: *a very able student/ teacher*

a·bly /'eʸbliʸ/ *adv* in an able manner: *She controlled the meeting very ably.*

ab·nor·mal /æb'nɔrməl/ *adj* not NORMAL; dif- ferent (usu. in a bad sense) from what is ordinary or expected; unusual; peculiar: *Is the child abnormal in any way?* –**abnormally** *adv* –**abnormality** /ˌæbnɔr'mælətiʸ, -nər-/ *n* **-ties** [C;U]

a·board /ə'bɔrd, ə'boʷrd/ *adv,prep* [F] on or into (a ship, train, aircraft, bus, etc.): *The boat is ready to leave. All aboard!*|*They went aboard the ship.* –see also BOARD¹ (7)

a·bode /ə'boʷd/ *n lit, fml, or humor* place where one lives; home: (*law*) *a person of/with no fixed abode*

a·bol·ish /ə'balɪʃ/ *v* [T] to bring to an end by law; stop: *Slavery was abolished in the US in the 19th century.|There are many bad customs and laws that should be abolished.* –**abolition** /ˌæbə'lɪʃən/ *n* [U]: *the abolition of slavery* –**abolitionist** *n*

a·bom·i·na·ble /ə'bamənəbəl/ *adj* causing great dislike; hateful; DETESTABLE: *The judge said it was the most abominable crime he had ever heard of.|(infml) The food in this hotel is abominable.* –**abominably** *adv*

ab·o·rig·i·ne /ˌæbə'rɪdʒəniʸ/ *n* a member of a group, tribe, etc., that has lived in a place from the earliest times, esp. in Australia –**aboriginal** *adj,n*

a·bort /ə'bɔrt/ *v* **1** [T] to end (a PREGNANCY), or cause (a child) to be born too soon so that the child cannot live: *The doctor had to abort the baby/the pregnancy.* **2** [I;T] to give birth too early to (a dead child) –compare MISCARRY (1) **3** [I;T] to end or cause (a plan, job, etc.) to end before the expected time because of some trouble: *The space flight had to be aborted because of difficulties with the computer.*

a·bor·tion /ə'bɔrʃən/ *n* [C;U] (an example of) the act of giving birth or causing to give birth before the baby is properly developed so that the child cannot live, esp. when done intentionally –compare MISCARRIAGE, STILLBORN

a·bor·tive /ə'bɔrţɪv/ *adj* coming to nothing; not developing; unsuccessful: *an abortive attempt by the army to get rid of the government*

a·bound /ə'baʊnd/ *v* [I] to exist in large numbers or great quantity: *Wild animals abound here/in this park.*

  abound in/with sthg. *v prep* [T] to have in large numbers or great quantity: *The country abounds in valuable minerals.*

a·bout¹ /ə'baʊt/ *prep* **1** on the subject of: *a book about stars* **2** *BrE* for AROUND² (2a) **3** *fml* on the body of: *He had a gun hidden about his person.* (=in his clothes) **4 what/how about: a** what news or plans do you have concerning: *What about Jack? We can't just leave him here.* **b** (making a suggestion): *How about a drink?*

about² *adv* **1** a little more or less than: *about five miles|about ten years* **2** *BrE* for AROUND¹ (1,3) –see also BRING **about,** COME **about 3 be about to** to be just ready to; be going to: *We were about to leave when it started to rain.* **4 not about to** *AmE infml* very unwilling to: *I'm not about to lend you any more money.*

a·bove¹ /ə'bʌv/ *prep* **1** higher than; over: *We flew above the clouds.|(fig.) There's nothing in this store (for/at) above $10.* **2** more than: *The company values hard work above good ideas.* **3** higher in rank or power than: *The captain of a ship is above a seaman.* –opposite **below 4** too good, proud, or honest to: *He wouldn't steal; he's above that.|He's above stealing.* **5 above all** most important of all

above² *adv* **1** [F] in or to a higher place; higher: *The clouds above began to get thicker.|a cry from above* **2** more; higher: *20 and above|children of six and above* (=six or older)|*a military meeting for captains and above* (=of higher rank) **3** on an earlier page or higher on the same page: *the facts mentioned above* –compare BELOW¹ (3)

a·bove·board /ə'bʌvˌbɔrd, -ˌboʷrd/ *adj* [F] without any trick or attempt to deceive; honorable: *His part in the affair was (open and) aboveboard.*

a·bra·sive /ə'breʸsɪv, -zɪv/ *adj* **1** causing the wearing away of a surface **2** tending to annoy; rough: *She has an abrasive way of dealing with people.* –**abrasively** *adv*

a·breast /ə'brɛst/ *adv* [F] **1** side by side, on a level, and facing the same direction: *lines of soldiers marching five abreast* **2 keep/be abreast of** to know the most recent facts about (something): *She reads the papers to keep abreast of the times.*

a·bridge /ə'brɪdʒ/ *v* -**bridged,** -**bridging** [T] to make (something written or spoken) shorter –see also UNABRIDGED

a·bridg·ment, abridgement /ə'brɪdʒmənt/ *n* something, such as a story, book, or play, that has been made shorter: *an abridgment for television in five parts*

a·broad /ə'brɔd/ *adv* [F] **1** to or in another country: *He lived abroad for many years.* **2** *fml* over a wide area; everywhere: *The news of his death soon spread abroad.*

a·brupt /ə'brʌpt/ *adj* **1** sudden and unexpected: *The train came to an abrupt stop, making many passengers fall off their seats.* **2** (of behavior, character, etc.) rough, rather impolite –**abruptly** *adv* –**abruptness** *n* [U]

ab·scess /'æbsɛs/ *n* a swelling on or in the body where a thick yellowish poisonous liquid (PUS) has gathered

ab·scond /æb'skand, əb-/ *v* [I *from, with*] *fml* to go away suddenly and secretly because one has done something wrong: *He absconded with all the money.*

ab·sence /'æbsəns/ *n* **1** [U] the state of being away or of not being present: *Please look after my house during my absence.* –opposite **presence** [C] **2** an occasion or period of being away **3** [U] non-existence; lack: *The police were delayed by the absence of information about the crime.*

ab·sent¹ /'æbsənt/ *adj* **1** not present: *Four students are absent (from class) today.* **2** [A] showing lack of attention to what is happening: *an absent look on his face*

ab·sent² /æb'sɛnt, əb-/ *v* [T *from*] *fml* to keep (oneself) away: *He absented himself from the meeting.*

ab·sen·tee /ˌæbsən'tiʸ/ *n* a person who should be present but stays away: *There were many absentees from the meeting.*

ab·sen·tee·ism /ˌæbsən'tiʸˌɪzəm/ *n* [U] regular absence without good cause, esp. from work or duty

ab·sent·ly /'æbsəntliʸ/ *adv* in a manner showing lack of attention

absent-mind·ed /ˌ·· '···◄/ *adj* so concerned with one's thoughts as not to notice what is happening, what one is doing, etc. **–ab·sent-mindedly** adv **–absent-mindedness** n [U]

ab·so·lute /ˈæbsəˌluʷt, ˌæbsəˈluʷt/ adj **1** complete; perfect: a woman of absolute honesty|That's absolute nonsense! **2** having complete power; without limit: Absolute rulers can do just as they please. **3** not depending on or measured by comparison with other things: In absolute terms, wages have risen, but not in comparison with the cost of living. –compare RELATIVE² **–absoluteness** n [U]

ab·so·lute·ly /ˌæbsəˈluʷtliʸ, ˈæbsəˌluʷtliʸ/ adv **1** completely: It's difficult to cross the desert by car, but not absolutely impossible.|I'm absolutely BROKE. (=completely without money) –compare RELATIVELY; see Study Notes on page 363 **2** infml certainly: "Do you think so?" "Absolutely!"

USAGE The adverbs **absolutely** and **altogether** are pronounced /ˈ··, ·ˈ·/ when they come before the word they describe: I absolutely refuse.|altogether different. They are pronounced /ˌ··ˈ·/ when they come after the word they describe, or when they stand alone: different altogether|"Absolutely!"

ab·so·lu·tion /ˌæbsəˈluʷʃən/ n [U] (esp. in the Christian religion) forgiveness for a SIN

ab·solve /əbˈzɑlv, -ˈsɑlv/ v **-solved, -solving** [T from] to free (someone) from fulfilling a promise or a duty, or from having to be punished for a wrong

ab·sorb /əbˈsɔrb, -ˈzɔrb/ v [T] **1** to take or suck in (esp. liquids): Use the cloth to absorb the spilled ink.|The walls of the house absorb heat during the day.|(fig.) She's a good student and absorbs new ideas quickly. **2** [in, by] to take up all the attention of: I was absorbed in a book and didn't hear you call. **–absorption** /əbˈsɔrpʃən, -ˈzɔrp-/ n [U]

ab·sorb·ent /əbˈsɔrbənt, -ˈzɔr-/ adj able to ABSORB (1)

ab·sorb·ing /əbˈsɔrbɪŋ, -ˈzɔr-/ adj very interesting; ENGROSSING

ab·stain /əbˈsteʸn/ v [I from] to keep oneself from drinking, voting, etc.; REFRAIN (from something) **–abstainer** n

ab·sten·tion /əbˈstɛnʃən, -tʃən/ n [C;U] the act or an example of keeping oneself from doing something, esp. from voting: 50 votes for, 35 against, and 7 abstentions.

ab·sti·nence /ˈæbstənəns/ n [U] the act of keeping away from pleasant things, esp. from alcoholic drink **–abstinent** adj

ab·stract¹ /æbˈstrækt, əb-, ˈæbstrækt/ adj **1** thought of as a quality rather than as an object or fact; not real or solid: an abstract argument about justice|The word "honesty" is an **abstract noun**. –compare CONCRETE¹ –see Study Notes on page 550 **2** (in art) connected with or producing ABSTRACTS² (2)

ab·stract² /ˈæbstrækt/ n **1** a shortened form of a statement, speech, etc. **2** (in art) a painting, drawing, etc., that does not try to represent an object as it would be seen by a camera

ab·stract³ /æbˈstrækt, əb-/ v [T from] to remove by drawing out gently; separate: to

abstract the most important points from a long report

ab·stract·ed /æbˈstræktɪd, əb-/ adj not noticing what is happening; deep in thought **–abstractedly** adv

ab·strac·tion /æbˈstrækʃən, əb-/ n **1** [U] the state of not attending to what is going on; ABSENT-MINDEDNESS **2** [C] an idea of a quality as separate from any object: A good judge considers all the facts of a case as well as the abstraction "justice."

ab·struse /əbˈstruʷs, æb-/ adj fml difficult to understand **–abstrusely** adv **–abstruseness** n [U]

ab·surd /əbˈsɜrd, -ˈzɜrd/ adj against reason or common sense; clearly false or foolish; RIDICULOUS: It's absurd not to wear a coat in such cold weather. **–absurdly** adv **–absurdity** /əbˈsɜrdət̬iʸ, -ˈzɜr-/ n **-ties** [C;U]

a·bun·dance /əˈbʌndəns/ n [S;U] a great quantity; plenty: At the party there was food and drink **in abundance**.|The country has an abundance of skilled workers, but not enough jobs.

a·bun·dant /əˈbʌndənt/ adj more than enough: The country has abundant supplies of oil and gas. **–abundantly** adv

a·buse¹ /əˈbyuʷz/ v abused, abusing [T] **1** to do cruel things to (a person or animal): I won't allow you to abuse that dog. **2** to say cruel or rude things to or about (somebody or something) **3** to put to wrong use; use badly: to abuse one's power

a·buse² /əˈbyuʷs/ n **1** [U] harmful treatment (of a person or animal): child abuse|the prisoners were treated with abuse. **2** [U] unkind, cruel, or rude words: He greeted me with **a stream of abuse**. **3** [C;U] wrong use: the abuse of power|drug abuse

a·bu·sive /əˈbyuʷsɪv/ adj using or containing unkind, cruel, or rude language: an abusive letter/person **–abusively** adv

a·bys·mal /əˈbɪzməl/ adj very bad: The food was abysmal.

a·byss /əˈbɪs/ n a great hole which appears to have no bottom: (fig.) an abyss of sadness

AC abbrev. for alternating current; a flow of electricity that changes direction with regularity, and at a very rapid rate –compare DC

a·ca·cia /əˈkeʸʃə/ n acacias or acacia a tree, found mainly in hot countries, from which a GUM² (1) is obtained

ac·a·dem·ic¹ /ˌækəˈdɛmɪk/ adj **1** concerning teaching or studying, esp. in a college or university **2** concerning those subjects taught to provide skills for the mind rather than for the hand **3** derog not concerned with practical examples: The question of where we should go on our vacation is academic, since we don't have any money!

academic² n a college or university teacher

a·cad·e·my /əˈkædəmiʸ/ n **-mies 1** a society of people interested in the advancement of art, science, or literature **2** a school for training in a special art or skill: a military academy|an academy of music

ac·cede /ækˈsiʸd, ək-/ v **-ceded, -ceding** [I to] fml **1** to agree to a suggestion, plan, demand, etc., often after disagreeing: *to accede to a request* **2** to take a high post or position after someone has left it –see also ACCESSION

ac·cel·er·ate /ək'sɛləˌreʸt/ v **-ated, -ating** [I;T] to (cause to) move faster –opposite **decelerate**

ac·cel·er·a·tion /əkˌsɛlə'reʸʃən/ n [U] the act of increasing speed; rate at which speed is increased –opposite **deceleration**

ac·cel·er·a·tor /ək'sɛləˌreʸtər/ n the piece of apparatus in a car, etc., which is used to increase speed –see illustration on page 95

ac·cent¹ /'æksɛnt/ n **1** a particular way of speaking, usu. connected with a country, area, or class: *He speaks with a Southern accent.* **2** importance given to a word or part of a word (vowel or SYLLABLE) by saying it with more force: *The accent in the word "important" is on the second syllable.* **3** the mark used, esp. above a word or part of a word, in writing or printing to show what kind of sound is needed when it is spoken: *In French there are three possible accents on the vowel "e."*

ac·cent² /'æksɛnt, æk'sɛnt/ v [T] to pronounce (a word or a part of a word) with added force

ac·cen·tu·ate /ək'sɛntʃuʷˌeʸt, æk-/ v **-ated, -ating** [T] to give more importance to; direct attention to: *The dark frame accentuates the brightness of the picture.* –**accentuation** /əkˌsɛntʃuʷˈeʸʃən, æk-/ n [U]

ac·cept /ək'sɛpt/ v **1** [I;T] to take or receive (something offered or given), esp. willingly: *The police aren't allowed to accept rewards.|He asked her to marry him and she accepted (him).* –compare REJECT¹ (1) **2** [T +*that*] to believe; admit; agree to: *Did she accept your reasons for being late?|For a long time she could not accept that her husband was really dead.|accepted principles of behavior*

ac·cept·a·ble /ək'sɛptəbəl/ adj **1** good enough: *Your work is not acceptable; do it again.* **2** worth receiving; welcome: *The gift is very acceptable.* –opposite **unacceptable** –**acceptability** /əkˌsɛptə'bɪlətiʸ/ n [U] –**acceptably** /ək'sɛptəbliʸ/ adv

ac·cept·ance /ək'sɛptəns/ n **1** [C;U] the act of accepting or of being accepted **2** [U] favor; approval: *She won acceptance in her new job through a lot of hard work.*

ac·cess /'æksɛs/ n **1** [C] a means of entering; way in; entrance: *The only (means of) access to their house is along a narrow road.* **2** [U] means or right of using, reaching, or entering: *Students need easy access to books.*

ac·ces·si·ble /ək'sɛsəbəl/ adj that can be gotten or gotten to, into, or at: *The island is accessible only by boat.* –opposite **inaccessible** –**accessibility** /əkˌsɛsə'bɪlətiʸ/ n [U]

ac·ces·sion /ək'sɛʃən/ n fml the act of acceding (ACCEDE) or coming to a high position, office, etc.

ac·ces·so·ry /ək'sɛsəriʸ/ n **-ries 1** [usu. pl.] something which is not a necessary part of something larger but which makes it more useful, effective, etc.: *car accessories, including the roof rack and radio|a black dress*

with matching accessories (=hat, shoes, etc.) **2** also **accessary**– law a person who is not present at a crime but who helps another in doing something criminal

ac·ci·dent /'æksədənt, -ˌdɛnt/ n [C;U] something, esp. something unpleasant, undesirable, or damaging, that happens unexpectedly or by chance: *I had an accident in the kitchen and broke all the glasses.|We got back without accident.* **2 by accident** by chance

ac·ci·den·tal /ˌæksə'dɛntəl/ adj not happening by plan or intention; happening by chance –**accidentally** adv

accident-prone /'···ˌ·/ adj (of a person) more likely to have accidents than most people

ac·claim¹ /ə'kleʸm/ v [T as] to greet or publicly recognize: *The new drug has been acclaimed (as) the most important discovery for years.*

acclaim² n [U] strong expressions of approval and praise: *The book received considerable acclaim.*

ac·cla·ma·tion /ˌæklə'meʸʃən/ n [C;U] loud sounds of approval and praise; ACCLAIM

ac·cli·mate /'ækləˌmeʸt, ə'klaɪmɪt/AmE||also **acclimatize** /ə'klaɪməˌtaɪz/– v **-mated, -mating** [I;T to] to (cause to) become accustomed to the conditions of weather in a new part of the world: *We lived in Africa for five years, but we never really got acclimated (to the hot weather).|(fig.) He can't acclimate himself to working at night.* –**acclimation** /ˌæklə'meʸʃən/ n [U]

ac·co·lade /'ækəˌleʸd/ n strong praise and approval: *His new book received accolades from the papers.*

ac·com·mo·date /ə'kɑməˌdeʸt/ v **-dated, -dating** [T] **1** to provide with room in which to live or stay **2** to have enough space for **3** [to] fml to change (oneself, one's habits, etc.) to fit new conditions: *I can accommodate you/your wishes.* –**accommodation** /əˌkɑmə'deʸʃən/ n [C;U]: *I've already made my plans, but I can make an accommodation for you this time.*

ac·com·mo·dat·ing /ə'kɑməˌdeʸtɪŋ/ adj willing to help; ready to change to suit new conditions –**accommodatingly** adv

ac·com·mo·da·tions /əˌkɑmə'deʸʃənz/ n [P] AmE lodging, food, and services: *The high cost of accommodations makes traveling in the US expensive.*

ac·com·pa·ni·ment /ə'kʌmpəniʸmənt/ n **1** something which is usually or often found with something else **2** music played to support singing or another instrument

ac·com·pa·nist /ə'kʌmpənɪst/ n a person who plays a musical ACCOMPANIMENT (2)

ac·com·pa·ny /ə'kʌmpəniʸ/ v **-nied, -nying** [T] **1** to go with, as on a journey **2** to happen or exist at the same time as: *Lightning usually accompanies thunder.* **3** to make supporting music for –see also UNACCOMPANIED

ac·com·plice /ə'kɑmplɪs/ n a person who helps someone to do wrong –see also COMPLICITY

ac·com·plish /ə'kɑmplɪʃ/ v [T] to succeed in

doing; finish successfully: *We tried to settle the argument but accomplished nothing.*

ac·com·plished /ə'kʌmplɪʃt/ *adj* skilled; good at something, though not professional: *an accomplished singer*

ac·com·plish·ment /ə'kʌmplɪʃmənt/ *n* **1** [U] the act of ACCOMPLISHing or finishing work completely and successfully **2** [C] a skill; something in which one is ACCOMPLISHED: *Being able to play the piano well is just one of his accomplishments.*

ac·cord¹ /ə'kɔrd/ *v* [I *with*] *fml* to agree: *What you have just said does not accord with what you told us earlier.*

accord² *n* [U] *fml* **1** agreement: *The two governments are completely in accord on the question of preserving peace.* **2 of one's own accord** without being asked; willingly **3 with one accord** with everybody agreeing

ac·cord·ance /ə'kɔrdns/ *n* [U] *fml* agreement: *I sold the house,* **in accordance with** *your orders.*

ac·cord·ing·ly /ə'kɔrdɪŋli/ *adv* *fml* **1** in a suitable manner: *Please inform us if you are not satisfied with the car, and we will act accordingly.* (= by giving you another one) **2** therefore; so –see Study Notes on page 144

according to /·'··· ·/ *prep* **1** as said or shown by: *According to my watch it is 4 o'clock.|According to George, she's a really good teacher.* **2** in a way that agrees with: *We will be paid according to the amount of work we do.*

ac·cor·di·on /ə'kɔrdiᵛən/ *n* a musical instrument held in the hands and played by pressing the middle part together to force air through holes opened and closed by KEYS¹ (3) worked by the fingers –compare CONCERTINA

ac·cost /ə'kɔst, ə'kɑst/ *v* [T] to go up to and speak to (esp. a stranger), often in a threatening manner: *A strange man accosted him and asked for money.*

ac·count¹ /ə'kaʊnt/ *n* **1** [C] a written or spoken report; description; story: *Give us an account of what happened.| He is a great football player,* **by all accounts.** (= according to what everyone, the papers, etc., say) **2** [U] consideration; thought: *You must* **take into account** *the boy's long illness.* **3** [U] advantage; profit: *He* **put/turned** *his knowledge* **to good account.** **4** [C] a record or statement of money received and paid out, as by a bank or business: *The accounts show that business is beginning to improve.* **5** [C] an arrangement which allows one to buy goods and pay for them later: *I'll pay for the shirt now, but please put the shoes on my account.* **6** [C] a statement of money owed: *Please settle your account today.* (= pay what you owe) **7** [C] a sum of money kept in a bank which may be added to and taken from: *My account is empty, there is no money in it.* –see also CHECKING ACCOUNT, SAVINGS ACCOUNT **8 of great/no account** of great/no importance **9 on account of** because of –see Study Notes on page 144 **10 on no account** also **not on any account**– not for any reason: *On no account should you go there.|Don't go*

there on any account.

account² *v* →ACCOUNT FOR

ac·count·a·ble /ə'kaʊntəbəl/ *adj* [F *to, for*] responsible; having to give an explanation: *I am not accountable to you for my actions.*

ac·count·an·cy /ə'kaʊntənsiᵛ/ *n* [U] →ACCOUNTING

ac·count·ant /ə'kaʊntənt/ *n* a person whose job is to keep and examine the money accounts of businesses or people

account for sthg. *v prep* [T+*v-ing*] to give an explanation or reason for: *How do you account for the fact that you've been late every day this week?|She has to account to the director for all the money she spends.|Can you account for having spent so much money?* –see also UNACCOUNTABLE

ac·count·ing /ə'kaʊntɪŋ/ *AmE*‖ also **accountancy**– *n* [U] the work or job of an ACCOUNTANT

ac·cu·mu·late /ə'kyuʷmyə,leʸt/ *v* **-lated, -lating** [I;T] to make or become greater in quantity or size; collect or grow into a mass: *to accumulate a large fortune* –**accumulation** /ə,kyuʷmyə'leʸʃən/ *n* [C;U]: *an accumulation of work while I was on vacation*

ac·cu·ra·cy /'ækyərəsiᵛ/ *n* [U] the quality of being ACCURATE; exactness or correctness –opposite **inaccuracy**

ac·cu·rate /'ækyərɪt/ *adj* careful and exact; exactly correct: *Give me an accurate report of what happened.|Is that clock accurate?* –opposite **inaccurate** –**accurately** *adv*

ac·cu·sa·tion /,ækyə'zeʸʃən/ *n* [C;U] (a) charge of doing wrong: *The accusation was that he had murdered a man.*

ac·cuse /ə'kyuʷz/ *v* **-cused, -cusing** [T *of*] to charge (someone) with doing wrong or breaking the law; blame: *The police accused him (of stealing).|The angry man gave her an accusing look.|The judge asked the accused man to stand up.* –**accuser** *n* –**accusingly** *adv*

ac·cus·tom /ə'kʌstəm/ *v* [T *to*] to make used to: *He had to accustom himself to the cold weather of his new country.*

ac·cus·tomed /ə'kʌstəmd/ *adj* **1** [F *to*] more formal than used in the habit of: *I'm not accustomed to getting up so early.* **2** [A *no comp.*] *fml* regular; usual: *The director took her accustomed place at the end of the table.*

ace /eʸs/ *n* **1** a playing card that has a single mark or spot and usu. has the highest or the lowest value **2** *infml* a person of the highest class or skill in something: *She's an ace at cards/an ace card-player.*

ache¹ /eʸk/ *v* **ached, aching** [I] to have or suffer a continuous dull pain: *I ache all over.|My head aches.|(fig.) She was aching to go to the party, but her parents wouldn't let her.*

ache² *n* a continuous dull pain: *an ache in the arm|headache|*(fig.) *heartache*

a·chieve /ə'tʃiᵛv/ *v* **-chieved, -chieving** [T] **1** to finish successfully (esp. something, anything, nothing): *He will never achieve anything if he doesn't work.* **2** to gain (an aim, etc.) as the result of action: *As a result of advertising, we've achieved a big increase in sales this year.* –**achievable** *adj*

a·chieve·ment /ə'tʃiːvmənt/ n 1 [U] the successful finishing or gaining of something 2 [C] something successfully finished or gained esp. through skill and hard work

ac·id¹ /'æsɪd/ n 1 [C;U] a type of chemical substance containing HYDROGEN which may destroy things it touches: *The acid burned a hole in the carpet.* –compare ALKALI 2 [U] *infml* for LSD (1) 3 **acid test** a test or trial which will prove whether something is as valuable as it is supposed to be

acid² adj [A] 1 having a sour or bitter taste like that of unripe fruit or VINEGAR 2 hurtful in speech –compare SARCASTIC

a·cid·i·ty /ə'sɪdəti̯/ n [U] the quality of being acid; sourness

ac·knowl·edge /ək'nɑlɪdʒ/ v -edged, -edging [T] 1 [+v-ing/that] to accept or recognize (as); recognize the fact or existence (of): *When the election results were reported, the Senator acknowledged defeat/that she was defeated.|They acknowledged having been defeated.|She is acknowledged to be/as their best tennis player.* 2 to state that one has received (something): *We have to acknowledge his letter.* 3 to show that one recognizes (someone) as by smiling or waving: *He walked right past me without even acknowledging me.*

ac·knowl·edg·ment, -edgement /ək'nɑlɪdʒ mənt/ n 1 [U] the act of acknowledging (ACKNOWLEDGE): *He was given a gold watch in acknowledgment of his work for the business.* 2 [C] something given, done, or said as a way of thanking, showing that something has been received, etc.: *I wrote to them three weeks ago, and I haven't received an acknowledgment yet.*

ac·ne /'ækni̯/ n [U] a disease (common among young people) in which spots (PIMPLES (1)) appear on the face and neck

a·corn /'eɪkɔrn, 'eɪkərn/ n the nut of the OAK tree

a·cous·tics /ə'kuːstɪks/ n 1 [U] the scientific study of sound 2 [P] the qualities of a place, esp. a concert hall, theater, or large meeting room (AUDITORIUM), which make it good, bad, etc., for hearing music and speeches: *The acoustics of the theater are so good that you can hear everything even from the cheapest seats.*

ac·quaint /ə'kweɪnt/ v →ACQUAINT sbdy. WITH sthg.

ac·quaint·ance /ə'kweɪntns/ n 1 [C] a person whom one knows, esp. through work or business, but who may not be a friend 2 [S;U with] information or knowledge, as obtained through personal experience rather than careful study: *I have an/some acquaintance with the language.*

acquaint sbdy. **with** sthg. v prep [T] 1 *fml* to make (oneself or someone) familiar with: *I am already acquainted with the facts.* 2 **be acquainted (with)** to have met socially: *She and I are acquainted (with each other).*

ac·qui·esce /ˌækwiˈɛs/ v -esced, -escing [I in] *fml* to agree, often unwillingly but without raising an argument: *He acquiesced in the plans his parents had made for him.*

–**acquiescence** n [U] –**acquiescent** adj

ac·quire /ə'kwaɪər/ v -quired, -quiring [T] 1 to gain or come to possess by one's own work, skill, action, etc.: *He acquired a knowledge of computers by careful study.|The company has recently acquired a new office building in Chicago.* 2 **acquired taste** something that one must learn to like: *Coffee is an acquired taste and is not liked at first.*

ac·qui·si·tion /ˌækwəˈzɪʃən/ n 1 [U] the act of acquiring (ACQUIRE) 2 [C] something ACQUIRED: *This car is my latest acquisition.*

ac·quis·i·tive /ə'kwɪzətɪv/ adj often derog in the habit of acquiring (ACQUIRE) or collecting things: *He is very acquisitive and has filled his house with things he has bought.* –**acquisitiveness** n [U]

ac·quit /ə'kwɪt/ v -quitted, -quitting [T of] 1 to give a decision as in a court of law that (someone) is not guilty of a fault or crime: *They acquitted him of murder.* –opposite **convict** 2 *fml, usu. apprec* to cause (oneself) to act in the stated (usu. favorable) way: *She acquitted herself very well.*

ac·quit·tal /ə'kwɪtl/ n [C;U] the act of declaring or condition of being found not guilty, as in a court of law –opposite **conviction**

a·cre /'eɪkər/ n a measure of land; 4,840 square yards or about 4,047 square meters: *The total area of a soccer field is about two acres.*

a·cre·age /'eɪkərɪdʒ/ n [S;U] the area of a piece of land measured in ACRES

ac·rid /'ækrɪd/ adj (of taste or smell) bitter; causing a stinging sensation: *the acrid smell of burning plastic*|(fig.) *an acrid remark*

ac·ri·mo·ny /'ækrəˌmoʊni̯/ n [U] bitterness, as of manner or language –**acrimonious** /ˌækrəˈmoʊni̯əs/ adj –**acrimoniously** adv

ac·ro·bat /'ækrəˌbæt/ n a person skilled in walking on ropes or wires, balancing, walking on hands, etc., during a show, esp. at a CIRCUS (1) –**acrobatic** /ˌækrəˈbætɪk/ adj

ac·ro·bat·ics /ˌækrəˈbætɪks/ n [P;U] the art or tricks of an ACROBAT

a·cross /ə'krɔs/ prep,adv 1 from one side to the other (of): *The stream is six meters across.|a bridge across/over the river|Can you swim across?* 2 [F] on the opposite side (of): *They live across (the road) from us.* 3 so as to cross: *The two lines cut across each other.*

act¹ /ækt/ v [I] 1 [on, for, as] to take action: *The council must act before more people are killed on that dangerous road.|She acted on our suggestion.|In this case I'm acting for* (=in the interests of) *my friend Mr. Smith.|A trained dog can* **act as** (=fulfill the purpose of) *a guide to a blind person.* 2 to behave as stated: *The report said that the doctor had acted correctly.* 3 to represent or perform by action, esp. on the stage: *Olivier is acting tonight.*|(fig.) *I can't take her seriously because she always seems to be acting.* 4 [on, upon] to produce an effect; work: *Does the drug take long to act (on the pain)?*

act sthg.↔**out** v adv [T] to express (thoughts, unconscious fears, etc.) in actions and behavior rather than in words

act up v adv [I] infml to behave or perform badly: The car's acting up again.

act² n **1** a thing done; deed (of the stated type): a foolish act|an act of cruelty **2** (often cap.) a law: Congress has passed an Act forbidding the public sale of the drug. **3** (often cap.) one of the main divisions of a stage play: Hamlet kills the king in Act 5 Scene 2. **4** one of a number of short events in a theater or CIRCUS (1) performance: The next act will be a snake charmer. **5** derog infml an example of insincere behavior used for effect (often in the phrase **put on an act**): He doesn't really mean it; it's just an act. **6 get in on the/someone's act** infml to get a share of an/ someone's activity, and esp. any advantages that may come as a result

USAGE Compare **act** and **action**: When **action** is used as a [C] noun it means the same thing as **act**: a kind act/action. Certain fixed phrases use **act** and not **action**: an act of cruelty/of mercy|He was caught in the **act** of stealing. **Action**, unlike **act**, is also used as a [U] noun: the **action** of a runner/of a medicine (=the way or effect of doing something) or in other fixed phrases: to take (quick) **action** (=to act (quickly))

act·ing¹ /'æktɪŋ/ adj [A no comp.] appointed to carry out the duties of (an office or position) for a short time: Our director is in the hospital, but the acting director can see you.

acting² n [U] the art of representing a character, esp. in a play or movie

ac·tion /'ækʃən/ n **1** [U] movement using force or power for some purpose; doing things: We have to take action (=begin to act) before it is too late. –opposite **inaction 2** [C] something done; deed: Actions are more important than words. –see ACT² (USAGE) **3** [C usu. sing.] the way in which something moves or works: The horse had a fine action as it jumped the fence.|Today we'll study the action of the heart. **4** [C] effect: Photographs are made possible by the action of light on film. **5** [C usu. sing.] the main events in a play or book rather than the characters in it: The action takes place in a mountain village. **6** [C;U] a military fight or fighting: The action lasted five hours.|Many were killed **in action.** **7** [C;U] a charge or a matter for consideration by a court of law: If he doesn't pay us soon we will have to bring (an) action against him. **8 in/into action** in/into operation or a typical activity: He is a very good tennis player. You ought to see him in action. **9 out of action** out of operation; no longer able to do a typical activity: Can I borrow your car? Mine's out of action.

ac·ti·vate /'æktə‚veɪt/ v **-vated, -vating** [T] to cause to be active; bring into use: This button activates the heating system. –**activation** /‚æktə'veɪʃən/ n [U]

ac·tive /'æktɪv/ adj **1** doing things or always ready to do things; able or ready to take action: Although he is over 70, he is still active.|an active member of the club who goes to every meeting **2** able to produce the typical effects or act in the typical way: Be careful!

That dangerous chemical is still active! –opposite **inactive** (for **1,2**) **3** tech (of a verb or sentence) having as the subject the person or thing doing the action and as the object the person or thing receiving the action (as in The boy kicked the ball.) –compare PASSIVE¹ (2) –**actively** adv

active voice /‚·· '·/ also **active**– [the S] tech the ACTIVE¹ (3) part or form of a verb: "The boy kicked the ball" is in the active voice. –compare PASSIVE²

ac·tiv·ist /'æktəvɪst/ n a person taking an active part, esp. in a political movement

ac·tiv·i·ty /æk'tɪvəṭiⁱ/ n **-ties** [U] movement; action; the state of being active: a day full of activity|There's been a lot of activity on Main Street today. –opposite **inactivity 2** [C often pl.] something that is done or is being done: She has many activities that take up her time when she's not working.

ac·tor /'æktər/ n a person who acts in a play or movie

ac·tress /'æktrɪs/ n a woman who acts in a play or movie

ac·tu·al /'æktʃuʷəl, 'ækʃuʷəl/ adj [A no comp.] existing as a real fact: The actual cost of the repairs was a lot less than we had expected.

ac·tu·al·ly /'æktʃuʷəliⁱ, -tʃəliⁱ, 'ækʃuʷəliⁱ, -ʃəliⁱ/ adv **1** really: The people who actually have power are the owners of big industries.|Actually, you owe me more than this. **2** although it may seem strange: He not only invited me into his house but he actually offered me a drink.

a·cu·men /ə'kyuʷmən, 'ækyəmən/ n [U] fml ability to think and judge quickly and well: Her business acumen has made her very successful.

ac·u·punc·ture /'ækyə‚pʌŋktʃər/ n [U] the method of stopping pain and curing diseases by pricking certain parts of the body with needles, used esp. in China

a·cute /ə'kyuʷt/ adj **1** (of the mind or the senses) able to notice small differences, esp. of meaning or sound; working very well; sharp: Dogs have an acute sense of smell. **2** severe; very great: She was in acute pain.|an acute lack of food **3** (of a disease) coming quickly to a dangerous condition –compare CHRONIC (1) **4** tech (of an angle) being less than 90 degrees –compare OBTUSE (2) –**acutely** adv –**acuteness** n [U]

AD /‚eⁱ 'diⁱ/ abbrev. for: Latin Anno Domini; (in the year) since the birth of Christ: a battle in 1649 AD –compare BC

ad /æd/ n infml advertisement

ad·age /'ædɪdʒ/ n an old wise phrase; PROVERB

a·da·gio /ə'dɑdʒoʷ, -dʒiʸoʷ, -ʒiʸoʷ/ adv,adj,n (a piece of music) played slowly

ad·a·mant /'ædəmənt/ adj [+that] fml (esp. of a person or behavior) hard, immovable, and unyielding: I've tried to persuade him to change his mind, but he's adamant. –**adamantly** adv

Ad·am's ap·ple /'ædəmz ‚æpəl/ n that part at the front of the throat that is seen to move when a person, esp. a man, talks or swallows

a·dapt /ə'dæpt/ v [I;T to] to change so as to be or make suitable for new needs, different conditions, etc.: He adapted an old car motor to his boat.|When we moved to France, the children adapted (to the change) very well. –compare ADOPT

a·dapt·a·ble /ə'dæptəbəl/ adj often apprec able to change or be changed so as to be suitable for new needs, different conditions, etc. –opposite **unadaptable** –**adaptability** /ə,dæptə'bɪlətiʸ/ n [U]

ad·ap·ta·tion /,ædəp'teʸʃən, ,ædæp-/ n [C;U] the state of being ADAPTED or thing adapted: a new adaptation (of a book) for television

a·dapt·er, -or /ə'dæptər/ n something that ADAPTs, esp. an apparatus (PLUG¹ (2)) that makes it possible to use more than one piece of electrical machinery from a single supply point (SOCKET)

add /æd/ v **1** [T to] to put together with something else so as to increase the number, size, importance, etc.: Add a few more names to the list. **2** [T up] to join (numbers, amounts, etc.) so as to find the total: If you add 5 and/to 3 you get 8.|Add up these figures, please. –compare SUBTRACT **3** [T+that] to say also: I'd like to add that we are pleased with the result. **4 add insult to injury** to make matters even worse, esp. by causing annoyance as well as harm

add to sthg. v prep [T] to increase: The increase in electricity costs has added to our difficulties.

add up v adv [I] to make sense; seem likely: The facts in this case just don't add up.

ad·den·dum /ə'dendəm/ n **-da** /də/ tech something that is added or is to be added, as at the end of a speech or book

ad·der /'ædər/ n a small poisonous snake found in northern Europe and northern Asia

ad·dict /'ædɪkt/ n a person who is unable to free himself from a harmful habit, esp. of taking drugs

ad·dict·ed /ə'dɪktɪd/ adj [to] dependent on; unable to stop having, taking, etc.: addicted to HEROIN|(fig.) The children are addicted to television.

ad·dic·tion /ə'dɪkʃən/ n [C;U] (an example of) the state of being ADDICTED: Smoking can be a dangerous addiction.

ad·dic·tive /ə'dɪktɪv/ adj (of drugs, etc.) causing a person to become ADDICTED; habit-forming –opposite **non-addictive**

ad·di·tion /ə'dɪʃən/ n **1** [U] the act of adding, esp. of adding numbers together **2** [C] something added: A new baby is often called an addition to the family. **3 in addition (to)** as well (as): We play football in addition to soccer. –see Study Notes on page 144

ad·di·tion·al /ə'dɪʃənəl/ adj [no comp.] in addition; added: There is an additional charge for heavy bags. –**additionally** adv

ad·di·tive /'ædətɪv/ n a substance added in small quantities to something else, as to improve the quality, or add color, taste, etc.

ad·dress¹ /ə'dres/ v [T] **1** to write a name and ADDRESS² on (an envelope, package, etc.) **2** to direct speech to (a person or group):The mayor addressed the crowd.|Address your

remarks to me, please. **3** [to] fml to put (oneself) to work at: He addressed himself to the main difficulty.

ad·dress² /ə'dres, 'ædres/ n the number of the building, name of the street and town, etc., where a person lives or works, esp. when written on a letter, envelope, or package: I can't read the address on this letter.

ad·dress³ /ə'dres/ n a speech, esp. one that has been formally prepared

a·dept /ə'dept/ adj [at, in] highly skilled: Be careful when you play cards with him. He's very adept at cheating. –**adeptly** adv

ad·e·quate /'ædəkwɪt/ adj **1** [for] enough for the purpose, and no more: The city's water supply is no longer adequate. –compare AMPLE **2** [F to] having the necessary ability or qualities: I hope he will be adequate to the job. –opposite **inadequate** –**adequately** adv –**adequacy** /'ædəkwəsiʸ/ n [U for]

ad·here /əd'hɪər/ v **-hered, -hering** [I to] to stick firmly (to another or each other): The two surfaces adhered (to each other), and we couldn't get them apart.

adhere to sthg. v prep [T] often fml to favor strongly; be faithful to (an idea, opinion, belief, etc.): She adhered to her plan to leave early.

ad·her·ence /əd'hɪərəns/ n [U to] the act or condition of sticking to something firmly: (fig.) adherence to one's religious beliefs

ad·her·ent /əd'hɪərənt/ n a person who favors and remains with a particular idea, opinion, or political party

ad·he·sion /əd'hiʸʒən/ n [U] the state or action of sticking together

ad·he·sive /əd'hiʸsɪv, -zɪv/ n,adj (a substance, such as GLUE) that can stick or cause sticking

ad hoc /,æd 'hɑk, -'hoʷk/ adj Latin made, arranged, etc., for a particular purpose: an **ad hoc committee** specially established to deal with a particular subject

ad·ja·cent /ə'dʒeʸsənt/ adj [to] fml very close; touching or almost touching; next: The two families live on adjacent streets.

ad·jec·tive /'ædʒɪktɪv/ n a word which describes a noun (such as black in a black hat) –see Study Notes opposite –**adjectival** /,ædʒɪk'taɪvəl/ adj: an adjectival phrase

ad·join /ə'dʒɔɪn/ v [I;T] fml to be next to, very close to, or touching (one another): Our house adjoins theirs.|Our two houses adjoin.|the adjoining room

ad·journ /ə'dʒɜrn/ v [I;T for, till, until] (of a meeting, trial, etc.) to bring to or come to a stop for a particular period or until a later time: This trial has been adjourned.|The committee adjourned for an hour. –**adjournment** n [C;U]: The court met again after an adjournment of two weeks.

ad·ju·di·cate /ə'dʒuʷdɪˌkeʸt/ v **-cated, -cating** [I;T on] fml or tech to act as a judge: to adjudicate a singing competition –**adjudicator** n

ad·junct /'ædʒʌŋkt/ n **1** something that is added or joined to something else but is not a necessary part of it **2** a person in one of the

position of adjectives

Most English adjectives can come either before a noun or after a verb in a sentence. For example, we can say:

She lives in a **beautiful** *house.*
or
Her house is **beautiful.**

But some adjectives are different, and can be used in only one position.

For example:

main and **single** are used only before a noun. We can say:

The **main** *reason I came home was to see my parents.*
There was a **single** *house on the street.*

In the dictionary, adjectives like this are marked [A], to mean "only before a noun:"

> **main** *adj* [A] chief; most important: *a busy main road*

asleep and **unwell** are used only after a verb. We can say:

Is he **unwell***?*
No, he's **asleep***.*

In the dictionary, adjectives like this are marked [F], to mean "only after a verb:"

> **asleep** *adj* [F] sleeping: *He was* **sound/fast** *asleep.* (= completely asleep) – opposite **awake**

Some adjectives, esp. when used in expressions of measurement, are always used after a noun. We can say:

The hole is three meters **deep.**
The ladder is six feet **high** *and two feet* **wide.**

There are not many adjectives like this. In the dictionary they are marked [after *n*], to mean "only after a noun:"

> **thick** *adj* 2 [after *n*] measuring in depth or width: *ice five centimeters thick*

Some adjectives have an [A], [F], or [after *n*] for only one of their meanings, like **thick**.

When you find an adjective marked [A], [F], or [after *n*] in the dictionary, write it here to remind you how to use it. We have started the list for you:

[A]

medium

_____

_____

_____

_____

[F]

afraid

_____

_____

_____

_____

_____

[after *n*]

ago

_____

_____

_____

_____

_____

higher professions who is hired to work for an organization such as a university or a hospital for a short period of time and usu. for only a few hours per week: *an adjunct professor* |*I've been an adjunct there for years.*

ad·just /ə'dʒʌst/ v [I;T] to change slightly, esp. in order to set right or make suitable for a particular job or new conditions: *I have to adjust my watch. It's slow.*|*He adjusted (himself) very quickly to the heat of the country.* –**adjustable** adj –**adjustment** n [C;U]: *to make adjustments*

ad lib /ˌæd 'lɪb/ adv [F] Latin, infml spoken, played, performed, etc., without preparation: *He always performs ad lib.* –**ad-lib** /ˌ·'·◄/ adj: *The best joke in the play was ad-lib.*

ad-lib /ˌ·'·/ v -bb- [I;T] infml to invent and deliver (music, words, etc.) without preparation: *The actress forgot her lines but ad-libbed very well.*

ad·min·is·ter /əd'mɪnəstər/ v [T] fml 1 to direct or control (the affairs of a person or group): *Mr. Jones administers the company's accounts.*|*The courts administer the law.* 2 [to] to give: *She administered the medicine to the sick woman.*

ad·min·is·tra·tion /ədˌmɪnə'streɪʃən/ n 1 [U] the control or direction of affairs, as of a country or business: *You will need some experience in administration.* 2 [the C] esp. AmE (often cap.) the part of the national/state/city government under the control of the president/governor/mayor: *the Kennedy Administration*

ad·min·is·tra·tive /əd'mɪnə,streɪ ̯tɪv, -strə-/ adj [no comp.] of or concerning the control and direction of affairs, as of a country or business: *administrative responsibilities* –**administratively** adv

ad·min·is·tra·tor /əd'mɪnə,streɪ ̯tər/ n a person who controls or directs the affairs, as of a government office, school, or business

ad·mi·ra·ble /'ædmərəbəl/ adj worthy of admiration; very good: *an admirable meal*

ad·mi·ral /'ædmərəl/ n [A;C] (an officer who holds) a very high rank or the highest rank in a navy

ad·mi·ra·tion /ˌædmə'reɪ ̯ʃən/ n [U] a feeling of pleasure and respect: *I was filled with admiration for his courage.*

ad·mire /əd'maɪər/ v -mired, -miring [T for] to regard or look at with pleasure and respect; have a good opinion of: *We all admired her for the way she saved the children from the fire.*|*Stop looking in the mirror admiring yourself!* –see WONDER (USAGE) –**admirer** n: *He is one of her many admirers.*

ad·mis·si·ble /əd'mɪsəbəl/ adj able to be allowed or considered: *an admissible excuse*|*admissible* EVIDENCE –opposite **inadmissible** –**admissibility** /ədˌmɪsə'bɪləti ̯/ n [U]

ad·mis·sion /əd'mɪʃən/ n 1 [U] allowing or being allowed to enter or join a school, club, building, etc.: *Admission to the concert costs $5.* 2 [C] a statement saying or agreeing that something is true (usu. something bad); CON-

FESSION (1): *His admission of guilt surprised everyone.*|**By/On his own admission** (=as he himself admitted), *he is a bad driver.*

USAGE In the meaning "permission to go in" **admittance** is more formal than **admission**, which is the more ordinary word. The entrance price is **the admission**, not ***the admittance**. **Admittance** could not be used in an expression like *his* **admission** *of guilt.*

ad·mit /əd'mɪt/ v -tt- 1 [I;T +v-ing/(that)/to] to state or agree to the truth of (usu. something bad); CONFESS (1): *He never admits his mistakes/that he is wrong.*|*He admitted to the murder.*| *John has admitted (to) breaking the window* –compare DENY (1) 2 [T] to permit to enter; let in: *There were no windows to admit air.*|*He was admitted to the hospital suffering from burns.* 3 [T of] fml to allow: *The facts admit of no other explanation.*

ad·mit·tance /əd'mɪtns/ n [U] allowing or being allowed to enter; right of entrance: *Since the theater was full, I was unable to gain admittance.* –see ADMISSION (USAGE)

ad·mit·ted·ly /əd'mɪtɪdli ̯/ adv it must be admitted (that): *Admittedly, he works slowly, but the results are always excellent.*

ad·mon·ish /əd'manɪʃ/ v [T against, for] fml to scold or warn gently –**admonition** /ˌædmə'nɪʃən/ n [C;U]

a·do /ə'duʷ/ n 1 **without further/more ado** with no further delay or FUSS[1] (1): *Without further ado, I introduce our guest speaker.* 2 **with/without much ado** with a lot of/little delay or FUSS[1] (1): *With much ado, he introduced the guest.*|*He did the job quietly and without much ado.*

ad·o·les·cent /ˌædl'ɛsənt/ adj,n (of) a boy or girl in the period between being a child and being a grown person; young TEENAGER of about 13–16 –see CHILD (USAGE) –**adolescence** n [S;U]: *Adolescence is often a difficult time in one's life.*

a·dopt /ə'dapt/ v [T] 1 to take (someone else's child) into one's family and to take on the full responsibilities in law of a parent –compare FOSTER (2) 2 to take and use as one's own: *We adopted the new method of making wine.* 3 to approve formally; accept: *The committee adopted her suggestions.* –compare ADAPT

a·dop·tion /ə'dapʃən/ n [C,U] (an example of) the act of ADOPTING: *If you can't have children of your own, why not consider adoption?*

a·dop·tive /ə'daptɪv/ adj [no comp.] fml having ADOPTED (esp. a child): *her adoptive parents*

a·dor·a·ble /ə'dɔrəbəl, ə'doʷr-/ adj 1 worthy of being loved deeply 2 infml charming or attractive: *What adorable curtains!*

ad·o·ra·tion /ˌædə'reɪ ̯ʃən/ n [U] 1 religious worship 2 deep love and respect

a·dore /ə'dɔr, ə'doʷr/ v -dored, -doring [T not be +v-ing] 1 to worship; love deeply and respect highly: *an adoring look* |*He adores his elder brother.* 2 [+v-ing] infml to like very much: *She adores the movies/going to the movies.*

a·dorn /ə'dɔrn/ v [T with] fml to add beauty

or decoration to: (fig.) *He adorned his story with lies.* –see DECORATE (USAGE)

a·dorn·ment /ə'dɔrnmənt/ *n* [U] the act of ADORNing

a·dren·a·lin /ə'drɛnl-ɪn/ *n* [U] a chemical substance (HORMONE) made by the body during anger, fear, anxiety, etc., causing quick or violent action

a·drift /ə'drɪft/ *adv,adj* [F] (esp. of boats) not fastened, and driven by the sea or wind; loose

a·droit /ə'drɔɪt/ *adj* [*at, in*] having or showing ability to use the skills of mind or hand, esp. quickly –**adroitly** *adv* –**adroitness** *n* [U]

ad·u·la·tion /ˌædʒə'leʸʃən/ *n* [U] *fml* praise that is more than is necessary or deserved, esp. to win favor

a·dult /ə'dʌlt, 'ædʌlt/ *adj,n* (of) a fully grown person or animal, esp. a person over an age stated by law, usu. 18 or 21: *This movie is for adults, not children.*|*adult responsibilities*

adult ed·u·ca·tion /ˌ·, ··'··, ˌ·· ··'··/ *AmE*||**further education** *BrE*– *n* [U] education after leaving school, but not work towards a university degree –compare HIGHER EDUCATION

a·dul·ter·ate /ə'dʌltəˌreʸt/ *v* **-ated, -ating** [T *with*] to make impure or of poorer quality by the addition of something of lower quality: *wine adulterated with water* –see also UNADULTERATED –**adulteration** /əˌdʌltə'reʸʃən/ *n* [U]

a·dul·ter·y /ə'dʌltəriʸ/ *n* [U] sexual relations between a married person and someone outside the marriage –**adulterous** *adj* –**adulterer adulteress** /ə'dʌltərɪs/ *fem.–n*

ad·vance¹ /əd'væns/ *v* **-vanced, -vancing** [I;T *on, upon, against*] to (cause to) move forward: *Napoleon's army advanced on Moscow*|*advanced 30 kilometers in one day.*|*A month has passed and the work has not advanced.*|*(fml) The report advances* (=introduces) *the suggestion that safety standards should be improved.* –compare RETREAT¹ –**advancement** *n* [U]

advance² *n* **1** [C] forward movement: *You cannot stop the advance of old age.*|(fig.)*There have been great advances* (=developments) *in medicine in the last 50 years.* –compare RETREAT² **2** [C *of*] money that is paid before the proper time or lent: *I was given an advance of a month's pay.* **3** [A] going or coming before: *An advance party is a group (as of soldiers)that travels ahead of the main group.* **4 in advance** before in time: *We always pay the rent in advance.*

ad·vanced /əd'vænst/ *adj* far on in development: *advanced studies*|*the advanced industrial nations of the world*|*an advanced child*

ad·vanc·es /əd'vænsɪz/ *n* [P] efforts made to become friends with or to gain favorable attention from: *She refused his advances.*

ad·van·tage /əd'væntɪdʒ/ *n* **1** [C *over*] something that may help one to be successful or to gain a desired result: *He had the advantage (over other boys) of being born into a rich family.* **2** [U] profit; gain; BENEFIT¹ (1): *Is there any advantage in getting there early?*

–opposite **disadvantage** (for **1,2**) **3 Advantage X** (in tennis) (said when X has won the point after DEUCE): *Advantage Ms. Austin.* **4 take advantage of** to make use of, e.g. by deceiving someone

ad·van·ta·geous /ˌædvæn'teʸdʒəs, -vən-/ *adj* helpful; useful; bringing a good profit –opposite **disadvantageous** –**advantageously** *adv*

ad·vent /'ædvɛnt/ *n* **the advent of** the arrival or coming of (an important event, period, person, etc.): *Society has changed rapidly since the advent of the car.*

ad·ven·ture /əd'vɛntʃər/ *n* **1** [C] a journey, activity, experience, etc., that is strange, exciting, and often dangerous: *I told them of my adventures in the mountains.* **2** [U] excitement, as in a journey or activity; risk: *He lived for adventure.* –see VENTURE (USAGE)

ad·ven·tur·er /əd'vɛntʃərər/ **adventuress** /-rɪs/ *fem.–* *n* a person who has or looks for adventures

ad·ven·tur·ous /əd'vɛntʃərəs/ *adj* eager for or providing adventure: *an adventurous person/life* –opposite **unadventurous** –**adventurously** *adv*

ad·verb /'ædvɜrb/ *n* a word which describes or adds to the meaning of a verb, an adjective, another adverb, or a sentence, and which answers such questions as *how? when?* or *where?* (as in "He ran *slowly.*" "It was *very* beautiful." "Come *tomorrow.*" "Come *here.*") –**adverbial** /əd'vɜrbiʸəl, æd-/ *n,adj*

ad·ver·sar·y /'ædvərˌsɛriʸ/ *n* **-ies** *fml* an opponent or enemy

ad·verse /əd'vɜrs, æd-, 'ædvɜrs/ *adj fml* not in favor of; going against; opposing: *The judge gave us an adverse decision.*|*in adverse conditions* –compare AVERSE [adverse]

ad·ver·si·ty /əd'vɜrsətiʸ, æd-/ **-ties** *n* [C;U] (an example of) bad fortune; trouble: *A good friend will not desert you in time of adversity.*|*to meet with adversities*

ad·ver·tise /'ædvərˌtaɪz/ *v* **-tised, -tising 1** [I;T] to make (something for sale, services offered, room to rent, etc.) known to the public, as in a newspaper, or on television: *I advertised my house in the "Daily News."* **2** [I *for*] to ask (for someone or something) by placing an advertisement in a newspaper, store window, etc.: *We should advertise for someone to look after the house while we're away.* –**advertiser** *n*

ad·ver·tise·ment /ˌædvər'taɪzmənt, əd'vɜr tɪz-, əd'vɜrtɪs-/ *n* also **ad** *infml*– a notice of something for sale, job position to be filled, room to rent, etc., as in a newspaper, on television, or pasted on a wall –compare COMMERCIAL²

ad·ver·tis·ing /'ædvərˌtaɪzɪŋ/ *n* [U] the business of making known to people what is for sale and encouraging them to buy, esp. by means of advertisements

ad·vice /əd'vaɪs/ *n* [U] opinion given by one person to another on how that other should behave or act: *I asked the doctor for her advice.*|*On her advice I am staying in bed.*|*Let me give you a piece of advice.*

ad·vis·a·ble /əd'vaɪzəbəl/ *adj* [F] sensible; wise: *It is advisable to wear a safety belt when you're driving.* –opposite **inadvisable** **–advisability** /əd,vaɪzə'bɪlətiʸ/ *n* [U]

ad·vise /əd'vaɪz/ *v* **-vised, -vising 1** [I;T +*to-v/v-ing/(that)/on*] to tell (somebody) what one thinks should be done; give advice to (somebody): *I advise waiting till the right time.|I will do as you advise.|Can you advise me where to stay?|The doctor advised me to get more exercise.* **2** [T] *fml* to give notice to; inform: *We wish to advise you that you now owe the bank $500.* **3 well-advised/ill-advised** wise/unwise: *You would be well-advised to stay at home today.*

ad·vis·er ‖also **advisor** *AmE* /əd'vaɪzər/ *n* a person who gives advice, esp. to a government or business or to students in a high school or college: *the President's special adviser on foreign affairs|I have to see my adviser about changing my schedule.*

ad·vi·so·ry /əd'vaɪzəriʸ/ *adj* giving advice; having the power or duty to advise

ad·vo·cate¹ /'ædvə,keʸt/ *v* **-cated, -cating** [T +*v-ing*] to speak in favor of; support (esp. an idea or plan): *The opposition party advocates a reduction in taxes.*

ad·vo·cate² /'ædvəkɪt, -,keʸt/ *n* **1** a person who speaks for or supports an idea, way of life, etc.: *He is a strong advocate of the new method of teaching.* **2** *law* a person, esp. a lawyer, who speaks in defense of or in favor of another person

aer·i·al¹ /'ɛəriʸəl/ *n* →ANTENNA²

aerial² *adj* [A *no comp.*] of, from, or concerning the air; happening in the air: *an aerial battle*

aer·o·drome /'ɛərə,droʷm/ *n* *BrE* for AIRFIELD

aer·o·dy·nam·ics /,ɛəroʷdaɪ'næmɪks/ *n* **1** [U] the science that studies the forces that act on bodies moving through the air **2** [P] the qualities necessary for movement through the air **–aerodynamic** *adj* **–aerodynamically** *adv*

aer·o·plane /'ɛərə,pleʸn/ *n* *BrE* for AIRPLANE

aer·o·sol /'ɛərə,sɔl, -,sɑl/ *n* a small container from which liquid can be forced out in the form of a fine mist

aes·thet·ic ‖also **esthetic** *AmE* /ɛs'θɛtɪk, ɪs-/ *adj* of, concerning, or showing a sense of beauty: *The building is aesthetic, but not very practical.* **–aesthetically** *adv*

aes·thet·ics ‖also **esthetics** *AmE* /ɛs'θɛtɪks, ɪs-/ *n* [U] the study, science, or PHILOSOPHY (1) of beauty, esp. in art

a·far /ə'fɑr/ *adv* *lit* at a distance; far off

af·fa·ble /'æfəbəl/ *adj* easy to talk to; ready to be friendly; pleasant **–affability** /,æfə'bɪlətiʸ/ *n* [U] **–affably** /'æfəbliʸ/ *adv*

af·fair /ə'fɛər/ *n* **1** a happening; event; action: *The meeting was a noisy affair.* **2** [*often pl.*] something that has been done; something needing action or attention; business: *The President deals with important affairs of state.* **3** a sexual relationship between two people not married to each other, esp. one that lasts for some time

af·fect¹ /ə'fɛkt/ *v* [T] **1** to cause some result or

change in; influence: *Smoking affects health.* **2** to cause feelings of sorrow, anger, love, etc., in: *She was deeply affected by the news of his death.*

USAGE Compare **affect** and **effect**: *Will the department's policy be affected (=changed) by the appointment of a new chairwoman?|The new President hopes to effect (=produce) changes in the government's policy.*

affect² *v* [T +*to-v*] *fml, often derog* to pretend to feel, have, or do: *He affected illness to avoid going to work.|He affected not to hear her.* –see also UNAFFECTED (2)

af·fec·ta·tion /,æfɛk'teʸʃən/ *n* [C;U] *derog* an example of) behavior which is AFFECTED: *She is sincere and completely without affectation.*

af·fect·ed /ə'fɛktɪd/ *adj* *derog* not real or natural; pretended: *She showed an affected interest in his work.* –opposite **unaffected**

af·fec·tion /ə'fɛkʃən/ *n* [U] gentle, lasting love or fondness

af·fec·tion·ate /ə'fɛkʃənɪt/ *adj* showing gentle love **–affectionately** *adv*

af·fil·i·ate /ə'fɪliʸ,eʸt/ *v* **-ated, -ating** [I;T *with, to*] (esp. of a society or group) to join or connect: *Our club is affiliated with a national organization of similar clubs.* –opposite **disaffiliate** **–affiliation** /ə,fɪliʸ'eʸʃən/ *n* [C;U]

af·fin·i·ty /ə'fɪnətiʸ/ *n* **-ties 1** [C;U *between, with*] relationship, close likeness, or connection: *The French and Italian languages have many affinities (with each other).* **2** [C *for, to, between*] strong attraction: *He feels a strong affinity for/to her.|a strong affinity between them*

af·firm /ə'fɜrm/ *v* [T +*that*] *fml* to declare (usu. again, or in answer to a question): *The President affirmed the administration's intention to reduce taxes.* –compare DENY (1) **–affirmation** /,æfər'meʸʃən/ *n* [C;U]

af·firm·a·tive /ə'fɜrmətɪv/ *n,adj often fml* (a word) declaring "yes": *an affirmative answer|The answer was in the affirmative.* –opposite **negative** **–affirmatively** *adv*

af·fix¹ /ə'fɪks/ *v* [T *to*] *fml* to fix, fasten, or stick: *Please affix a stamp.*

af·fix² /'æfɪks/ *n* a group of letters added to the beginning of a word (in the case of a PREFIX) or the end of a word in the case of a SUFFIX) to change its meaning or its use (as in "un*tie*," "*mis*understood," "kind*ness*," "quick*ly*")

af·flict /ə'flɪkt/ *v* [T *usu. pass.*] to cause to suffer in the body or mind; trouble: *afflicted with blindness*

af·flic·tion /ə'flɪkʃən/ *n* [C;U] *fml* something causing suffering or grief

af·flu·ent /'æfluʷənt/ *adj* having plenty of money or other possessions; wealthy **–affluence** *n* [U]

af·ford /ə'fɔrd, ə'foʷrd/ *v* [T] **1** [+*to-v*] (*usu. with* can, could, able to) to be able to do, spend, buy, bear, etc., esp. without serious loss or damage: *Can you afford $100,000 for a house?|Since she lost her job, she can't afford (to have) a car.|I can't afford three weeks away from work.* **2** *fml & lit* to provide with; supply with; give: *The tree afforded us shelter from the rain.*

af·front /ə'frʌnt/ *n* an act, remark, etc., that is rude to someone or hurts his/her feelings, esp. when intentional or in public –compare EFFRONTERY

a·field /ə'fiʸld/ *adv* **far afield** far away, esp. from home: *Don't go too far afield or you might get lost.|We get a lot of tourists from Europe, and some from even further afield.*

a·flame /ə'fleʸm/ *adv,adj* [F] on fire: (fig.) *The forest was aflame with red and orange leaves.*

a·float /ə'floʷt/ *adv,adj* [F] floating; at sea: *Help me get my boat afloat.*

a·foot /ə'fʊt/ *adv,adj* [F] *often derog* being prepared, made ready, or in operation: *There is **a plan afoot** to tear down the old building.|There is some strange business afoot.*

a·fraid /ə'freʸd/ *adj* [F] **1** [+*to-v*/(*that*)/*of*] full of fear; FRIGHTENED: *Don't be afraid of the dog.|He was afraid that he would lose.|*(fig.) *Don't be afraid of asking for help.* **2** [+(*that*)] *polite* sorry for something that has happened or is likely to happen: *I am afraid I've broken your pen.|"Are we late?" "I'm afraid so."|"Are we on time?" "I'm afraid not."*

a·fresh /ə'frɛʃ/ *adv fml* once more; again: *I've ruined the painting and have to start afresh.*

Af·ri·can /'æfrɪkən/ *adj,n* of, from, or about Africa; a person from Africa

af·ter¹ /'æftər/ *prep* **1** following in time; later than: *We'll leave after breakfast.* (Compare *We'll leave in an hour.*) **2** following continuously: *Year after year went by.* **3** following in place or order; behind: *He entered the room after his father.|Your name comes after mine on the list.|Shut the door after you.* **4** because of: *After the way he treated me, I never want to see him again.* **5** in spite of: *After all my care in packing it, the clock arrived broken.* **6** in search of (esp. in order to punish); looking for: *The police are after me.* **7** with the name of: *The boy was named after his uncle.* **8 after all: a** in spite of everything: *So you see I was right after all!* **b** it must be remembered (that): *I know he hasn't finished the work, but after all, he is very busy.* –compare BEFORE²

after² *adv* [F or after *n*] later; afterwards: *John came last Tuesday, and I arrived the day after.* –compare BEFORE¹

after³ *conj* at a later time than (when): *I found your coat after you had left the house.* –compare BEFORE³

af·ter·ef·fect /'æftərɪˌfɛkt/ *n* [*often pl.*] an effect (usu. unpleasant) that follows some time after the cause or after the main effect: *the aftereffects of the storm.*

af·ter·life /'æftərˌlaɪf/ *n* **-lives** /ˌlaɪvz/ [*usu. sing.*] the life that is thought by some people to follow death

af·ter·math /'æftərˌmæθ/ *n* [*usu. sing.*] the result or period following a bad event such as an accident, storm, war, etc.: *Life was much harder in the aftermath of the war.*

af·ter·noon /ˌæftər'nuʷn◄/ *adj,n* (of) the period between midday and sunset: *I'll sleep in the afternoon.|I'll have an afternoon swim.*

af·ter·wards /'æftərwərdz/||also **afterward** *AmE*– *adv* later; after that: *She had her supper and went to bed soon afterwards.*

a·gain /ə'gɛn/ *adv* **1** once more; another time: *Please say that again.|Never do that again!|He told the story yet again.* **2** back to the place or condition as before: *She was ill but now she is well again.| He's home again now.* **3** besides; further: *That wasn't much; I could eat as much again.* **4** but; on the other hand: *He might go, but then again he might not.* **5 again and again** very often; repeatedly: *I've told you again and again not to play there.*

a·gainst /ə'gɛnst/ *prep* **1** in the direction of and meeting: *The rain beat against the windows.* **2** in opposition to: *We will fight against the enemy.|Stealing is against the law.* **3** in an opposite direction to: *We sailed against the wind.* **4** as a defense or protection from: *We are all taking medicine against the disease.* **5** having as a background: *The picture looks good against that light wall.* **6** touching, esp. for support: *I sat against the wall.*

age¹ /eʸdʒ/ *n* **1** [C;U] the period of time a person has lived or a thing has existed:*What is your age?|He is 10 years of age.|At your age you should know better.|What ages are your children?* **2** [U] one of the periods of life: *At the age of 40 a person has reached* **middle age**. **3** [U] the state of being old: *His back was bent with age.* **4** [U] the particular time of life at which a person becomes able or not able to do something: *People who are either* **under age** *or* **over age** *may not join.* **5** [C *usu. sing.*] (*usu. cap.*) a particular period of history: *The period in which man learned to make tools of iron is called the Iron Age.* **6** [C *often pl.*] *infml* a long time: *It's been ages|an age since we met.* **7 (be/come) of age** (to be or reach) the particular age when a person becomes responsible in law for his own actions, is allowed to vote, get married, etc.

age² *v* **aged, aging** *or* **ageing** [I;T] to (cause to) become old: *After his wife's death he aged quickly.* –**aging, ageing** /'eʸdʒɪŋ/ *n,adj* [U]: *an aging car that doesn't run well*

aged¹ /eʸdʒd/ *adj* [F] being of the stated number of years: *My son is aged 10 years.*

ag·ed² /'eʸdʒɪd/ *adj* very old: *an aged man|The sick and the aged need our help.*

age·less /'eʸdʒlɪs/ *adj* never growing old or never showing signs of growing old: *an ageless song*

a·gen·cy /'eʸdʒənsiʸ/ *n* **-cies 1** a business that makes its money esp. by arranging for people to meet others or the products of others: *I got this job through an employment agency.* **2** also **bureau**– a government department: *What agency is responsible for helping poor people?*

a·gen·da /ə'dʒɛndə/ *n* **-das** a list of the subjects to be considered at a meeting

a·gent /'eʸdʒənt/ *n* **1** a person who acts for another, esp. one who represents the business affairs of a firm: *Our agent in Rome* deals with all our Italian business.|a secret agent (=a political SPY) **2** a person or thing that works to produce a result: *Rain and sun are the agents which help plants to grow.|Soap is a cleaning agent.*

ag·gra·vate /'ægrə,veɪt/ v **-vated, -vating** [T] **1** to make more serious; make worse: *The lack of rain aggravated the already serious lack of food.* **2** to annoy: *If he aggravates me any more I'll hit him.|an aggravating delay* **–aggravation** /,ægrə'veɪʃən/ n [U]

USAGE Although **aggravate** is commonly used to mean "annoy," this is thought by some teachers to be incorrect. A *difficulty* is **aggravated;** a *person* is **irritated** or **annoyed.**

ag·gre·gate /'ægrəgɪt/ n [C;U] a total: *The football team had a low* GOAL *aggregate last season.* **–aggregate** *adj* [A]

ag·gres·sion /ə'greʃən/ n [U] the starting of a quarrel, fight, or war, esp. without just cause –see also NONAGGRESSION

ag·gres·sive /ə'gresɪv/ adj **1** *derog* always ready to quarrel or attack; threatening: *He's very aggressive; he's always arguing.* **2** *apprec* not afraid of opposition: *If you want to be a success in business, you must be aggressive.* **3** (of weapons) made for use in attack **–aggressively** *adv* **–aggressiveness** *n* [U]

ag·gres·sor /ə'gresər/ n *fml derog* a person or country that begins a quarrel, fight, war, etc., with another, esp. without just cause

ag·grieved /ə'griːvd/ adj *fml* suffering from a personal offense, showing hurt feelings, etc.

a·ghast /ə'gæst/ adj [F *at*] suddenly filled with surprise, fear, and shock: *aghast at the sight of blood on the floor*

ag·ile /'ædʒəl, 'ædʒaɪl/ adj able to move quickly and easily; active **–agility** /ə'dʒɪlətiː/ n [U]

ag·i·tate /'ædʒə,teɪt/ v **-tated, -tating 1** [T] to shake or move (a liquid) about **2** [T] to cause anxiety to; worry **3** [I *for*] to argue strongly in public for or against some political or social change

ag·i·ta·tion /,ædʒə'teɪʃən/ n [U] **1** painful excitement of the mind or feelings; anxiety **2** [*for, against*] public argument, action, unrest, etc., for or against political or social change

ag·i·ta·tor /'ædʒə,teɪtər/ n a person who excites and influences other people's feelings, esp. towards political or social change

a·glow /ə'gloʊ/ adj [F *with*] bright with color or excitement: *The sky was aglow with the setting sun.|Her face was aglow as she went to meet him.*

ag·nos·tic /æg'nɑstɪk, əg-/ n,adj (a person) who believes that nothing can be known about God or life after death –compare ATHEIST **–agnosticism** /æg'nɑstə,sɪzəm, əg-/ n [U]

a·go /ə'goʊ/ adv,adj [after n or adv] back in time from now; in the past: *He left 10 minutes ago.|He died long ago.|How long ago did he leave?*

USAGE 1 Ago is not used with verbs formed with *have.* Compare *I came here a year* **ago** and *I have been here* **for** *a year|since 1983.* **2 Before** shows the difference between a dis-

tant and a nearer point in the past: *My grandfather died five years* **ago;** *my grandmother had already died three years* **before.** (=eight years ago)

a·gog /ə'gɑg/ adj [F *with*] *infml* excited and expecting something to happen: *The children were all agog (with excitement) as the actor drew a gun from his pocket.*

a·go·nize ||also **-nise** *BrE* /'ægə,naɪz/ v **-nized, -nizing** [I *over*] *infml* to suffer great pain or anxiety: *to agonize over every decision|an agonized cry* (=expressing suffering)

a·go·niz·ing ||also **-nising** *BrE* /'ægə,naɪzɪŋ/ adj causing great pain or anxiety: *an agonizing decision|delay* **–agonizingly** *adv*

a·go·ny /'ægəniː/ n **-nies** [C;U] very great pain or suffering of mind or body: *He lay in agony until the doctor arrived.|in agonies of doubt*

a·grar·i·an /ə'greəriːən/ adj of land, esp. farmland or its ownership

a·gree /ə'griː/ v **-greed, -greeing 1** [I;T +*to-v/ (that)/on, upon, about, with*] to have or share the same opinion, feeling, or purpose: *She agreed with me.|We agreed to leave at once.|They agreed that they should ask him.|We agreed on a price for the car.|the price we agreed on|upon* –opposite **disagree;** see REFUSE (USAGE) **2** [I *to*] to say yes to an idea, opinion, etc., esp. after unwillingness or argument; accept; approve: *He agreed to my idea.|We met at the place we agreed on.*

agree with sbdy./sthg. *v prep* [T *no pass.*] **1** to be in accordance with: *Your story agrees with his in everything except small details.* **2** (usu. used in NEGATIVES[2]) *infml* to suit the health of: *The fruit did not agree with me. Now I've got a pain in my stomach.* –opposite **disagree with 3** (of nouns, adjectives, verbs, etc.) to have the same number, person, CASE[1] (6), etc., as (the subject)

a·gree·a·ble /ə'griːəbəl/ adj **1** to one's liking; pleasant: *agreeable weather* –opposite **disagreeable 2** [F *to*] ready to agree; willing: *Are you agreeable (to my suggestion)?*

a·gree·a·bly /ə'griːəbliː/ adv pleasantly: *I was agreeably surprised.* –opposite **disagreeably**

a·gree·ment /ə'griːmənt/ n **1** [U] the state of having the same opinion, feeling, or purpose: *We are in agreement with their decision.|The two sides were unable to reach agreement.* –opposite **disagreement 2** [C] an arrangement or promise of action, as made between people, groups, businesses, or countries: *You have broken our agreement by not doing the work you promised.*

ag·ri·cul·ture /'ægrɪ,kʌltʃər/ n [U] the art or practice of farming, esp. of growing crops **–agricultural** /,ægrɪ'kʌltʃərəl/ adv **–agricultur(al)ist** /,ægrɪ'kʌltʃər(əl)ɪst/ n

a·ground /ə'graʊnd/ adv,adj [F] (of a ship) on or onto the shore or bottom of a sea, lake, etc. (esp. in the phrase **run aground**)

ah /ɑ/ interj (a cry of surprise, pity, pain, joy, dislike, etc.): *Ah, there you are!*

a·ha /ɑ'hɑ/ interj (a cry of surprise, satisfaction, amused discovery, etc.:) *Aha, so it's you hiding there!*

a·head /ə'hɛd/ *adv,adj* [F] **1** in front; forward; in advance: *One man went ahead to see if the road was clear.|The road ahead was full of sheep.* **2** in or into the future: *to plan ahead* **3** in advance of; succeeding better: *Our team is ahead of the others in town.* **4 get ahead** to do well; succeed

a·hoy /ə'hɔɪ/ *interj* (a cry of greeting made by sailors, esp. from one ship to another)

aid¹ /eɪd/ *v* [T] to give support to; help

aid² *n* **1** [U] support; help: *He went to the aid of the hurt man.|What is the money in aid of?* **2** [C] a person or thing that supports or helps: *A dictionary is an important aid in learning a new language.* –see also VISUAL AID

aide /eɪd/ *n* a person who helps, esp. a person employed to help a government official

ail /eɪl/ *v* [I] *infml* to be ill and grow weak: (fig.) *the country's ailing* ECONOMY¹ (2)

ail·ment /'eɪlmənt/ *n* an illness, esp. one that is not serious: *He's always complaining of some ailment or another.*

aim¹ /eɪm/ *v* **1** [I;T *at, for*] to point or direct (a weapon, shot, remark, etc.) towards some object, esp. with the intention of hitting it: *He aimed the gun carefully.|He aimed it at the bottles.|My remarks were not aimed at you.* **2** [I +*to-v/at, for*] to direct one's efforts (towards doing or obtaining something); intend (to): *I aim to be a writer.|The factory must aim at increased production/at increasing production.*

aim² *n* **1** [U] the act of directing a weapon, remark, etc.: *The hunter took aim at the lion.|His aim was very good.* **2** [C] the desired result of one's efforts; purpose; intention: *What is your aim in working so hard?*

aim·less /'eɪmlɪs/ *adj* without any purpose; lacking intention: *his aimless life* –**aimlessly** *adv* –**aimlessness** *n* [U]

ain't /eɪnt/ *v nonstandard short form* for *am not, is not, are not, has not,* and *have not*: *It ain't right.|He ain't been there yet.*

air¹ /ɛər/ *n* **1** [U] the mixture of gases which surrounds the earth and which we breathe: *breathing in the fresh morning air |a hot airless room* **2** [U] the sky or the space above the ground: *He jumped into the air.|Mail goes quicker by air than by sea.* **3** [C] the general character of, or feeling caused by, a person or place: *There was an air of excitement at the meeting.|He had an air of sadness about him.* **4 into thin air** *infml* completely out of sight **5 on/off the air** broadcasting/not broadcasting –compare WIND¹ (1); see also AIRS

air² *v* **1** [I;T] to (cause to) dry in a place that is warm or has plenty of dry air: *If the sheets aren't aired properly, they won't dry.* **2** [T *out*] to cause to become fresh by letting in air: *We aired (out) the room by opening the windows.* **3** [T] to make known to others (one's opinions, ideas, complaints, etc.), often in an unwelcome way: *He's always airing his knowledge.* –**airing** *n* [C;U *usu. sing.*]: *to give the room/one's ideas a good airing*

air·borne /'ɛərbɔrn, -boʷrn/ *adj* **1** (esp. of

seeds) carried about by the air **2** (esp. of aircraft) in the air; in flight

air-con·di·tion·ing /'·· ·,···/ *n* [U] the system that uses one or more machines (**air-conditioners**) to keep air in a building or room cool –see illustration on page 55 –**air-conditioned** *adj*

air·craft /'ɛərkræft/ *n* **aircraft** a flying machine of any type, with or without an engine

aircraft car·ri·er /'·· ,···/ *n* a warship that carries aircraft and has a flat surface where they can take off and land

air·field /'ɛərfiʲld/ *n* a place where aircraft may land and take off but which need not have any large buildings –compare AIRPORT

air force /'· ·/ *n* the part of the military organization of a country that is concerned with attack and defense from the air

air host·ess /'· ,···/ also **hostess**– *n fem.* for FLIGHT ATTENDANT

air·i·ly /'ɛərəliʲ/ *adv* in a light manner; not seriously

air·lift /'ɛər,lɪft/ *n* the carrying of large numbers of people or amounts of supplies by aircraft, esp. to or from a place that is difficult to get to –**airlift** *v* [T]

air·line /'ɛərlaɪn/ *n* a business that runs a regular service for carrying passengers and goods by air

air·lin·er /'ɛər,laɪnər/ *n* a large passenger aircraft

air·lock /'ɛərlɑk/ *n* **1** a bubble in a tube or pipe that prevents the passage of a liquid **2** an enclosed space or room into which or from which air cannot accidentally pass, as in a spacecraft or apparatus for working under water

air·mail /'ɛərmeɪl/ *n* [U] **1** letters, packages, etc., sent by air –compare SURFACE³ **2** the system of sending things by air: *I sent it airmail/by airmail.*

air·man /'ɛərmən/ *n* **-men** /mən/ *AmE* a person in one of the lowest ranks in the air force

air·plane /'ɛərpleɪn/ *AmE* ‖**aeroplane** *BrE*– *n* an aircraft that is heavier than air, that has wings, and that has at least one engine –see illustration on page 17

air·port /'ɛərpɔrt, -poʷrt/ *n* a place where aircraft land and take off, which has several buildings, and which is regularly used by paying passengers –see illustration on page 17

air raid /'· ·/ *n* an attack by military aircraft

airs /ɛərz/ also **airs and graces** /,· · '··/– *n* [P] *derog* unnatural manners or actions intended to make people think one is more important than one really is (esp. in the phrases **give oneself airs, put on airs**)

air·ship /'ɛər,ʃɪp/ *n* (esp. formerly) an aircraft without wings, containing gas to make it lighter than air, with an engine to make it move

air·sick /'ɛər,sɪk/ *adj* sick because of the movement of an aircraft –**airsickness** *n* [U]

air·space /'ɛərspeʲs/ *n* [U] the air or sky above a country, regarded as the property of that country

air·strip /'ɛər,strɪp/ *n* a stretch of land used

by aircraft to take off and land, esp. in war or time of trouble

air·tight /ˌɛərˈtaɪt◂/ *adj* not allowing air to pass in or out: *airtight containers|*(fig.) *an airtight excuse* (an excuse that cannot be attacked)

air·wor·thy /ˈɛərˌwɜrðiʸ/ *adj* (of aircraft) in proper and safe working condition –**air-worthiness** *n* [U]

air·y /ˈɛəriʸ/ *adj* **-ier, -iest 1** of, in, or having plenty of air: *The large window makes the room seem airy.* **2** *derog* having little substance; empty: *Nothing results from his airy plans.* **3** *derog* of or having AIRS; AFFECTED **4** light-hearted; happy; careless

aisle /aɪl/ *n* a passage between rows of seats, as in a theater or a church

a·jar /əˈdʒɑr/ *adv,adj* [F] (of a door) not quite closed; slightly open

AK /əˈlæskə/ *written abbrev. said as:* Alaska (a state in the US)

a·kin /əˈkɪn/ *adj* [F *to*] having the same appearance, character, etc.; like: *Her beautiful writing is akin to drawing.*

AL /ˌæləˈbæmə/ *written abbrev. said as:* Alabama (a state in the US)

Ala. /ˌæləˈbæmə/ *written abbrev. said as:* Alabama (a state in the US)

à la carte /ˌɑ lə ˈkɑrt, ˌæ lə-, ˌɑ lɑ-/ *adj,adv* *French* (of food in a restaurant) according to a list (MENU) where each dish has its own separate price –compare TABLE D'HOTE

a·lac·ri·ty /əˈlækrətiʸ/ *n* [U] *fml* quick and willing readiness

a·larm¹ /əˈlɑrm/ *n* **1** [U] sudden fear and anxiety, as caused by the possibility of danger **2** [C] a warning of danger, as by ringing a bell or shouting: *I raised the alarm as soon as I saw the smoke.* **3** [C] any apparatus, such as a bell, noise, flag, by which a warning is given

alarm² *v* [T] to excite with sudden fear and anxiety

alarm clock /·ˈ· ˌ·/ also **alarm**– *n* a clock that can be set to make a noise at any particular time to wake up sleepers –see illustration on page 55

a·larm·ist /əˈlɑrmɪst/ *n derog* a person who always expects danger, often without cause, and says so to others

a·las /əˈlæs/ *interj lit* (a cry expressing grief, sorrow, or fear)

al·be·it /ɔlˈbiʸɪt, æl-/ *conj fml* even though; although: *It was a very important albeit small mistake.*

al·bi·no /ælˈbaɪnoʷ/ *n* **-nos** a person or animal with a pale milky skin, very light hair, and eyes that are pink because of a lack of coloring matter

al·bum /ˈælbəm/ *n* **1** a book used for collecting photographs, stamps, etc. **2** →LP

al·bu·men /ælˈbyuʷmən/ *n* [U] the white or colorless part of an egg

al·che·my /ˈælkəmiʸ/ *n* [U] (esp. in the MIDDLE AGES) the science concerned with finding a way to turn all metals into gold –**alchemist** /ˈælkəmɪst/ *n*

al·co·hol /ˈælkəˌhɔl, -ˌhɑl/ *n* [U] **1** the colorless liquid present in wine, beer, and SPIRITS¹

(7) that can make one drunk **2** the drinks containing this

al·co·hol·ic¹ /ˌælkəˈhɔlɪk, -ˈhɑ-/ *adj* of, caused by, or containing alcohol –opposite **non-alcoholic**

alcoholic² *n* a person who has the condition of ALCOHOLISM

al·co·hol·ism /ˈælkəhɔˌlɪzəm, -hɑ-/ *n* [U] the disease caused by the continued drinking of alcohol in great quantities

al·cove /ˈælkoʷv/ *n* a small partly enclosed space in a room or wall, for a seat, bed, etc. –compare RECESS (2)

al·der·man /ˈɔldərmən/ *n* **-men** /mən/ a local government officer having any of various duties

ale /eʸl/ *n* [U] any of various types of beer, esp. one that is pale in color

a·lert¹ /əˈlɜrt/ *adj* quick to see and act; watchful –**alertness** *n* [U]

alert² *n* **1** a warning to be ready for danger –compare ALL CLEAR **2 on the alert (for)** in a state of watchfulness for danger, as after a warning

alert³ *v* [T] **1** to put (esp. soldiers) on the ALERT² (2) **2** to warn: *The doctor alerted me to the danger of not getting enough sleep.*

al·fal·fa /ælˈfælfə/ *n* [U] *AmE* a plant used for feeding farm animals

alfalfa sprout /·ˈ·· ˌ·/ *n* young, undeveloped ALFALFA plants, used for food: *Alfalfa sprouts are good for you.*

al·gae /ˈældʒiʸ/ *n* [P] very simple, usu. very small plants that live in or near water

al·ge·bra /ˈældʒəbrə/ *n* [U] a branch of MATHEMATICS in which signs and letters are used to represent numbers and values –**algebraic(al)** /ˌældʒəˈbreʸɪk(əl)/ *adj* –**alge·braically** *adv*

al·go·rithm /ˈælgəˌrɪðəm/ *n* a list of instructions, esp. to a computer, which are carried out in a fixed order to find the answer to a question or esp. to calculate a number –**algorithmic** /ˌælgəˈrɪðmɪk/ *adj*

a·li·as¹ /ˈeʸliʸəs, ˈeʸlyəs/ *adv* (esp. of a criminal) also known as; also called: *The thief's real name was John Smith, alias Edward Ball.*

alias² *n* **-ases** a name other than the usual or officially recognized name, used esp. by a criminal; false name

al·i·bi /ˈæləˌbaɪ/ *n* **-bis** an argument or defense that a person who is charged with a crime was in another place when the crime was done and that he/she therefore could not have done it: *Jim's wife gave him an alibi by saying that he was at home with her on the night of the robbery.*

a·li·en¹ /ˈeʸliʸən, ˈeʸlyən/ *adj* **1** [*no comp.*] belonging to another country or race; foreign **2** [*to*] different in nature or character, esp. so different as to be opposed: *Their ideas are alien to our way of thinking.*

alien² *n* a person who has not become a citizen of the country where he/she is living –compare CITIZEN, NATIONAL²

a·li·en·ate /ˈeʸliʸəˌneʸt, ˈeʸlyə-/ *v* **-ated, -ating** [T] to cause to stop being or feeling friendly: *to alienate one's family/ someone's affections*

airplane

security check

departure lounge

baggage claim

GATE 2

NEWSSTAND

ARRIVALS   DEPARTURES

porter

check-in counter

ticket agent

garment bag   suitcase

baggage

backpack   baggage carousel

Pat arrived at the **airport** two hours ago to **catch** her **plane** to Tokyo. At the **check-in counter,** a **ticket agent** looked at her **ticket** and her **passport,** and her **baggage was checked in.** Pat's **suitcases** were very heavy, so she had to pay an **excess baggage charge** (amount of money for additional weight). Next she was given a **boarding pass** (a ticket that allows her to get on the plane). The boarding pass has a seat number written on it, and Pat was given a **window seat** in the **non-smoking section.** Her suitcases were labeled and sent off to be **loaded** into the **hold** of the **airplane.**

While waiting for her **flight** to be called, Pat went to the newsstand to buy a newspaper. Then she went through the **security check,** where her **carry-on luggage** (the bags she was keeping with her on the plane) was searched. Then Pat went into the **duty-free shop** where she had a chance to buy some things cheaply. The things she bought there were cheap because they were not taxed.

In the **departure lounge,** Pat joined the other passengers who were sitting and waiting until time for their flights to depart. After a few minutes Pat heard the announcement: "Flight 156 to Tokyo now **boarding** at **Gate Three,**" and she went to **board** (get on) her plane.

ticket   boarding pass   passport   baggage claim check

a·li·en·a·tion /ˌeʸliʸəˈneʸʃən, ˌeʸlyə-/ *n* [U *from*] a feeling of not belonging to or being part of one's surroundings: *The increasingly dull nature of industrial jobs has led to the alienation of workers.*

a·light[1] /əˈlaɪt/ **alighted** *or* **alit** /əˈlɪt/, **alighting** *v* [I *from*] *fml* to get off or down from something, esp. at the end of a journey

alight on/upon sthg. *v prep* [T] **1** to come down from the air onto **2** *fml becoming rare* to find unexpectedly; HAPPEN **on**

alight[2] *adj* [F] **1** lit up: *The room was alight with candles.* **2** on fire; in flames

a·lign ||also **aline-** *BrE* /əˈlaɪn/ *v* [I;T] to come, bring, form, or arrange into a line

align sbdy./ sthg. **with** *v prep* [T] **1** to cause to come into the same line as: *to align a picture with one directly opposite it* **2** to cause to come into agreement with: *They aligned themselves with the workers in the struggle for freedom.*

a·lign·ment ||also **aline-** *BrE* /əˈlaɪnmənt/ *n* [U] **1** the act of forming or arranging into a line: to *bring into/move out of alignment (with)* **2** (of people or countries with the same aims, ideas, etc.) the act of forming into groups, as in a war –opposite **nonalignment** (for **2**)

a·like /əˈlaɪk/ *adj,adv* [F] like one another; the same: *The two brothers are very much alike.|She treats all her children alike.*

al·i·men·ta·ry /ˌæləˈmɛntəriʸ/ *adj tech* concerning food and the way it is treated (DIGESTED[1] (1)) in the body

al·i·mo·ny /ˈæləˌmoʷniʸ/ *n* [S;U] money that a man or woman has been ordered to pay regularly to his/her former partner after they have been SEPARATED[1] (4) or DIVORCED[2] (1)

a·live /əˈlaɪv/ *adj* [F] **1** [*no comp.*] having life; not dead; living **2** full of life; active: *Although he's old, he's still very much alive.*|(fig.) *The argument was kept alive by the politicians.* **3 alive to** having full knowledge of: *He was alive to the dangers of the work.* **4 alive with** covered with or full of (living things): *The dead tree is alive with insects.*

al·ka·li /ˈælkəˌlaɪ/ *n* **-lis** *or* **-lies** [C;U] *tech* any of various substances that form chemical salts when combined with acids –compare ACID[1] (1) **–alkaline** /ˈælkəˌlaɪn, -lɪn/ *adj*

all[1] /ɔl/ *determiner,predeterminer* **1** the whole of: *He ate all his food.|He ate it all.|We walked all the way.|We worked hard all last year.* **2** every one (of): *We're all hungry.|All children like toys.|Please answer all the questions.|Answer them all.|We bought* **all kinds of** *things.* (=lots of different things) –see Study Notes on page 550 **3 all in** *infml* very tired **4 all out, all-out** *infml* using all possible strength and effort: *We* **went all out/made an all-out effort** *to climb the mountain.* –see also ALL RIGHT, ALL-AROUND

all[2] *adv* **1** [+*adj/adv/prep*] completely; wholly: *She sat all alone.|I got all dirty.|He got mud all over the seat.* **2** for each side: *The result of the game was three all; neither side won.* **3 all but** almost; nearly: *It's all but impossible.* **4 all over: a** everywhere (on an object or surface): *Paint it green all over!* **b** *esp. AmE* everywhere in a place: *We've been looking for her all over.* **c** right across; to every part of (a place): *to travel all over India* **d** finished: *Our hopes are all over.* **e** *infml* very like; thoroughly like: *He's always late; that's Billy all over.* **5 all the same** *infml* even so; in any case: *You say the bridge isn't safe. All the same I'm going to cross it.*

all[3] *pron* **1** everybody, everything, or everyone: *He gave all he had.|I brought all of them.* **2 (not) at all** (only used in NEGATIVES[2], questions, etc.) (not) in any way: *I do not agree with you at all.|Do you feel ill at all?|Do you feel at all ill?*

USAGE **All** is sing. with [U] nouns: **All** *the money is spent.* It is pl. with pl. nouns: **All** *the people have gone.*

Al·lah /ˈælə, ˈɑlə/ *n* (the Muslim name for) God

all-around /ˌ· ·ˈ·◂/ also **all-round**– *adj* [A] having ability in many things, esp. in various sports: *She's an all-around girl.*

al·lay /əˈleʸ/ *v* **-layed, -laying** [T] *fml* to make (fear, anger, doubt, etc.) less

all clear /ˌ· ˈ·/ *n* a signal (such as a whistle or loud cry) that danger is past –compare ALERT[2]

al·le·ga·tion /ˌæləˈgeʸʃən/ *n fml* a statement that charges someone with doing something bad or criminal but which is not supported by proof: *allegations of cruelty*

al·lege /əˈlɛdʒ/ *v* **-leged, -leging** [T +*that*] *fml* to state or declare without proof or before finding proof: *The police allege that the man was murdered but they have given no proof.* **–allegedly** /əˈlɛdʒɪdliʸ/ *adv*

al·le·giance /əˈliʸdʒəns/ *n* [C;U] loyalty, faith, and dutiful support to a leader, country, idea, etc.: *His allegiances are divided.*

al·le·go·ry /ˈæləˌgɔriʸ, -ˌgoʷriʸ/ *n* [C;U] (the style of) a story, poem, painting, etc., in which the characters and actions represent good and bad qualities **–allegorical** /ˌæləˈgɔrɪkəl, -ˈgɑr-/ *adj*

al·le·lu·ia /ˌæləˈluʷyə/ *n,interj* →HALLELUJAH

al·ler·gic /əˈlɜrdʒɪk/ *adj* [*to*] related to or suffering from an ALLERGY: *He is allergic to the fur of cats.|an allergic* REACTION *to cats*

al·ler·gy /ˈælərdʒiʸ/ *n* **-gies** a condition of being unusually sensitive to something eaten, breathed in, or touched, in a way that causes pain or suffering

al·le·vi·ate /əˈliʸviʸˌeʸt/ *v* **-ated, -ating** [T] to make (pain, suffering, anger, etc.) less **–alleviation** /əˌliʸviʸˈeʸʃən/ *n* [U]

al·ley /ˈæliʸ/ *n* **-leys 1** a narrow street or path between buildings in a town **2 up one's alley** *infml* suited to one's abilities or interests: *Cooking is (right) up his alley.* –see also BLIND ALLEY

al·li·ance /əˈlaɪəns/ *n* **1** [U] the act of allying or the state of being allied (ALLY[1]) (esp. in the phrase **in alliance (with)**) **2** [C] a close agreement or connection between countries, groups, families, etc.: *We are hoping for an alliance between government and industry.* **3** [C+*sing./pl.v*] a group or association, esp. of countries, formed to look after the interests of its members

al·lied /ə'laɪd, 'ælaɪd/ adj [to] related or connected, esp. by common qualities: painting and other allied arts

al·li·ga·tor /'ælə,geʸtər/ n -tors or -tor a large animal (REPTILE) like the CROCODILE

al·lit·er·a·tion /ə,lɪtə'reʸʃən/ n [U] the appearance of the same sound or sounds at the beginning of two or more words that are next to or close to each other (as in "Round the rocks runs the river") —**alliterative** /ə'lɪtə,reʸtɪv, -rətɪv/ adj

al·lo·cate /'ælə,keʸt/ also **allot–** v -cated, -cating [T] to set apart for somebody as a share or for some purpose: That space has already been allocated for building a new hospital.

al·lo·ca·tion /,ælə'keʸʃən/ n 1 [U] the giving of shares or places 2 [C] a share, as of money or space

al·lot /ə'lɑt/ v -tt- [T] →ALLOCATE

al·lot·ment /ə'lɑtmənt/ n 1 [C] a share, as of money or space 2 [U] the giving of shares or places

al·low /ə'laʊ/ v [T] 1 [+v-ing] to let (somebody) do something; let (something) be done; permit: They do not allow it/smoking/you to smoke.|You are allowed into the room. 2 to permit to be or to come: They won't allow dogs in the house. 3 [+that/of] to permit as possible; admit: The facts allow (of) no other explanation.|You must allow that people make mistakes. —opposite **disallow** (for **1,3**) 4 to provide (esp. money or time): You'll have to allow three days for that job.

allow for sbdy./sthg. v prep [T +v-ing] to take into consideration: Allowing for the train being late, we should be back by 10:30.

al·low·a·ble /ə'laʊəbəl/ adj that may be allowed or permitted

al·low·ance /ə'laʊəns/ n 1 [C] a something, esp. money, provided regularly: an allowance of $5,000 a year|a traveling allowance **b** AmE money given regularly (usu. weekly) to a child 2 [C;U] the taking into consideration of facts that may change something, esp. an opinion (esp. in the phrase **make allowance(s) for)**

al·loy /'ælɔɪ/ n a metal made by mixing together two or more different metals

all right /,· '·/ adv,adj [F no comp.] 1 safe, unharmed, or healthy: Was the driver all right after the accident? 2 infml satisfactory but not very good; acceptable; in a satisfactory or acceptable manner: His work is all right (but he could be faster). 3 (in answer to a suggestion, plan, etc.) I/we agree; yes: "Let's go now." "All right." —see ALRIGHT (USAGE)

all-round /,· '· ◂/ adj [A] →ALL-AROUND

al·lude to sbdy./sthg. /ə'luʷd/ v prep -luded, -luding [T +v-ing] fml to speak of but without going straight to the point: She did not say Mr. Smith's name, but it was clear she was alluding to him.

al·lure¹ /ə'lʊər/ v -lured, -luring [T] to attract by the offer of something pleasant; TEMPT (2): an alluring look

allure² n [S;U] attraction; charm

al·lu·sion /ə'luʷ·ʒən/ n [C;U to] fml the act of speaking of something in an indirect manner, or something spoken of without directness, esp. while speaking about something else: His allusions to my failures were unnecessary. —**allusive** /ə'luʷsɪv/ adj

al·lu·vi·al /ə'luʷviʸəl/ adj being, concerning, or made of soil put down by rivers, lakes, floods, etc.

al·ly¹ /ə'laɪ, 'ælaɪ/ v -lied, -lying [I;T with, to] to join or unite, as by political agreement or marriage: The small country allied itself with/to the stronger power.|They allied against the same enemy.

ally² /'ælaɪ, ə'laɪ/ n -lies a person or country that helps or supports one, esp. in war

al·ma ma·ter /,ælmə 'mɑtər, ,ɑl-/ n [usu. sing.] Latin fml & humor 1 the school, college, or university which one attended 2 AmE the song of a school, college, or university

al·ma·nac /'ɔlmə,næk/ n a book giving a list of the days of a year, together with the times of sunrise and sunset, changes in the moon, the rise and fall of the sea, etc.

al·might·y /ɔl'maɪtiʸ/ adj 1 (often cap.) having the power to do anything; OMNIPOTENT: God Almighty|(God,) the Almighty 2 infml very big, strong, great, etc.: an almighty crash

al·mond /'ɑmənd, 'æ-/ n 1 a fruit tree whose seeds are eaten as nuts 2 the nut of this tree

al·most /'ɔlmoʷst, ɔl'moʷst/ adv very nearly but not quite: I almost dropped the cake.|She said almost nothing.| almost the longest street|almost everybody

alms /ɑmz/ n [P] old use money, food, clothes, etc., given to poor people

a·loft /ə'lɔft/ adv [F] high up, as in the air or among the sails of a ship: The flag was flying aloft.

a·lone /ə'loʷn/ adv,adj [F] 1 without others: He lives/ works alone.|The house stands alone on the hill. 2 only: You alone can do it. (=you are the only person who can do it)|Time alone will show who was right. 3 **leave/let alone: a** to allow to be by oneself **b** to allow to remain untouched or unchanged: Leave that alone. It's mine. –see LET (4,5,12)

USAGE **Alone** is neither good nor bad: She lives on coffee and cake when she's **alone**. **Solitary** and **lone**, when used of things, mean that there is only one: a **solitary/lone** tree, but used of people they may show sadness, like **lonely** or (esp. AmE) **lonesome**: Come over and see me. I'm feeling a little lonely/lonesome.

a·long¹ /ə'lɔŋ/ prep 1 from one end of to the other: We walked along the road. 2 in a line next to the length of: Trees grew along the river bank. 3 at a point on the length of: His house is along this road.

along² adv 1 forward; on: She bicycled along, singing loudly. 2 with others or oneself: When we went to Paris, I took my sister along (with me). 3 [F] here or there; over; across: I'll be along soon.|Come along and visit us next week. 4 **all along** all the time: I knew the truth all along.

a·long·side /əˌlɔŋ'saɪd/ *prep,adv* close to and in line with the edge of (something); along the side: *We brought our boat alongside (their boat).*

a·loof /ə'luʷf/ *adj,adv* apart; distant in feeling or interest; RESERVED (1): *He held/kept himself aloof from the others.* –**aloofness** *n* [U]

a·loud /ə'laʊd/ also **out loud**– *adv* 1 in a voice that may be heard: *The teacher asked him to read the poem aloud.* 2 in a loud voice: *The pain caused him to cry aloud.*

al·pha /'ælfə/ *n* the first letter (α) in the Greek alphabet

al·pha·bet /'ælfəˌbɛt/ *n* the set of letters used in writing any language, esp. when arranged in order

al·pha·bet·i·cal /ˌælfə'bɛtɪkəl/ *adj* [no comp.] of, belonging to, or in the order of the alphabet: *In a dictionary the words are arranged in* **alphabetical order.** –**alphabetically** *adv*

al·pha·bet·ize ‖also **-ise** *BrE* /'ælfəbəˌtaɪz/ *v* **-ized, -izing** [T] to arrange in ALPHABETICAL order

al·pine /'ælpaɪn/ *adj* of or concerning **the Alps** or other high mountains

al·read·y /ɔl'rɛdiʸ/ *adv* 1 by or before a particular time; even before expected: *He had already gone (when I arrived).|She's here already; she's early.* 2 before: *I've been there already and don't want to go again.*

USAGE Note the difference between **already** and **all ready**: *We're* **all ready** means either that all of us are ready or that we are completely ready; **already** could not be used here. –see JUST² (USAGE)

al·right /ɔl'raɪt/ *adv* [no comp.] all right

USAGE **Alright** is often used instead of **all right,** but teachers prefer **all right.**

al·so /'ɔlsoʷ/ *adv* as well; besides; too: *The weather was* **not only** *cold,* **but also** *wet.* (=both cold and wet) –see Study Notes on page 144

al·tar /'ɔltər/ *n* a table or raised level surface used in a religious ceremony, as in the Christian Service of COMMUNION

al·ter /'ɔltər/ *v* [I;T] to (cause to) become different: *This shirt has to be altered. It's too large.|Do you think you will alter your travel plans?*

al·ter·a·tion /ˌɔltə'reʸʃən/ *n* 1 [U] the act of making or becoming different: *My coat needs alteration.* 2 [C] a change; something changed: *The alterations to your coat will take a long time.*

al·ter·ca·tion /ˌɔltər'keʸʃən/ *n fml* a noisy disagreement; quarrel

al·ter·nate¹ /'ɔltərnɪt/ *adj* 1 (of two things) happening by turns; first one and then the other: *a week of alternate rain and sunshine* 2 one of every two; every second: *He works on alternate days.* –see ALTERNATIVE¹ (USAGE) –**alternately** *adv*

al·ter·nate² /'ɔltərˌneʸt/ *v* **-nated, -nating** [I;T with, between] to (cause to) follow by turns: *We alternated periods of work and rest.|Work alternated with sleep.|My life alternated between work and sleep.* –**alternation** /ˌɔltər'neʸʃən/ *n* [C;U]

al·ter·na·tive¹ /ɔl'tɜrnətɪv/ *adj* [no comp.] (of two things) that may be used, had, done, etc., instead of another; other: *We returned by an alternative road.* –compare ALTERNATE¹

USAGE **Alternate** is sometimes used for **alternative:** *They had an* **alternate/alternative** *plan.* But **alternative** is thought to be better English. –**alternatively** *adv*

alternative² *n* [C;S *to*] something, esp. a course of action, that may be taken or had instead of one or more others: *The alternative to being taken prisoner was to die fighting.|We had to fight: there was no (other) alternative.|There are several alternatives to your plan.*

USAGE Sentences such as: *We have several* **alternatives** *to choose from.* are very common, but this is thought by teachers to be incorrect because there should be only *two* **alternatives.**

al·though /ɔl'ðoʷ/ *conj* in spite of the fact that; though: *They are generous although they are poor.|Although my car is very old, I don't want to buy a new one.* –see also THOUGH¹; see Study Notes on page 144

al·ti·tude /'æltəˌtuʷd, -ˌtyuʷd/ *n* 1 [usu. sing.] height, esp. of a mountain above sea level 2 [usu. pl.] a high place or area: *It is difficult to breathe at high altitudes.* –compare ELEVATION (2)

al·to /'æltoʷ/ *n* **-tos** (a person with) a singing voice between SOPRANO and TENOR

al·to·geth·er /ˌɔltə'gɛðər, 'ɔltəˌgɛðər/ *adv* 1 completely; thoroughly: *It is not altogether bad.|That's altogether different.* 2 considering all things; on the whole: *It was raining, but altogether it was a good trip.* –see ABSOLUTELY (USAGE)

al·tru·ism /'æltruʷˌɪzəm/ *n* [U] consideration of the happiness and good of others before one's own; unselfishness –compare EGOISM

al·tru·ist /'æltruʷɪst/ *n* a person who is habitually good to others –**altruistic** /ˌæltruʷ'ɪstɪk/ *adj*

a·lu·mi·num /ə'luʷmənəm/ *AmE*‖**aluminium** /ˌælyʊ'mɪniʸəm, ˌælə-/ *BrE*– *n* [U] a silver-white metal that is a simple substance (ELEMENT (1)) light in weight, and easily shaped

al·ways /'ɔlweʸz, -wiʸz, -wɪz/ *adv* 1 at all times; at each time: *The sun always rises in the east.|We've always lived here.* 2 forever: *I will love you always.* 3 (used with the *-ing* form of a verb) all the time and often in an annoying way: *He's always asking silly questions.* –see NEVER (USAGE)

am /m, əm; *strong* æm/ *1st person sing. present tense of* BE: *I am (living) here now.|Here I am!* –see AREN'T (USAGE)

AM /ˌeʸ 'ɛm◀/ amplitude modulation; a system of broadcasting in which the strength of the sound waves varies: *an AM radio* –compare FM

a.m. /ˌeʸ 'ɛm/ *Latin abbrev. for:* ante meridiem (=before midday) (used after numbers expressing time): *the 8 a.m. (train) from Chicago* –compare P.M.

a·mal·gam·ate /ə'mælgəˌmeʸt/ *v* **-ated, -ating** *v*

[I;T *with*] (esp. of businesses, societies, groups, etc.) to join; unite; combine –**amalgamation** /ə,mælgə'meɪʃən/ *n* [C;U]

a·mass /ə'mæs/ *v* [T] to gather or collect (money, goods, power, etc.) in great amounts

am·a·teur /'æmətʃər, -,tʃʊər, -,tɜr/ *n* **1** (of, by, or being) a person who performs plays, takes part in sports, takes photographs, etc., for enjoyment and without being paid for it: *an amateur photographer/football player| Only amateurs can compete in the Olympic Games.* –compare PROFESSIONAL² **2** (typical of) a person without experience or skill in a particular art, sport, etc.: *We did a pretty amateur job of painting the house.*

am·a·teur·ish /,æmə'tʃʊərɪʃ, -'tɜr-, -'tʃɜr-/ *adj derog* lacking skill; not good; poor –**amateurishly** *adv*

a·maze /ə'meɪz/ *v* -**mazed, -mazing** [T] to fill with great surprise; cause wonder in: *I was amazed by the news.|It amazed me to hear that you were leaving.* –**amazement** *n* [U]

a·maz·ing /ə'meɪzɪŋ/ *adj usu. apprec* causing great surprise or wonder because of quantity or quality: *The new plane goes at an amazing speed.|What an amazing performance!* –**amazingly** *adv* –see Study Notes on page 363

am·bas·sa·dor /æm'bæsədər, əm-/ *n* a person of high rank representing his/her country in the capital city of another country either for a special occasion or for a longer period in an EMBASSY –compare CONSUL –**ambassadorial** /æm,bæsədɔriʸəl, -'doʷr-, əm-/ *adj*

am·ber /'æmbər/ *n* [U] (the color of) a yellowish brown hard clear substance used for jewels, decorations, etc.

am·bi·dex·trous /,æmbɪ'dɛkstrəs/ *adj* able to use either hand with equal skill

am·bi·ence ‖also **ambiance** *AmE* /'æmbiʸəns, 'ambiʸans/ *n* [U] the character, quality, feeling, etc., of a place: *This little restaurant has a pleasant ambience.*

am·big·u·ous /æm'bɪgyuʷəs/ *adj* able to be understood in more than one way; of unclear meaning: *an ambiguous reply* –opposite **unambiguous**; compare AMBIVALENT –**ambiguously** *adv* –**ambiguity** /,æmbə'gyuʷətiʸ/ *n* -**ties** [C;U]: *Her reply was full of ambiguities.|You should try to avoid ambiguity in your writing.*

am·bi·tion /æm'bɪʃən/ *n* **1** [U] strong desire for success, power, riches, etc.: *That politician is full of ambition.* **2** [C] that which is desired in this way: *A big house in the country is my ambition.|One of her ambitions is to become a doctor.*

am·bi·tious /æm'bɪʃəs/ *adj* **1** having a strong desire for success, power, riches, etc.: *an ambitious man|She is ambitious to succeed in politics.* **2** demanding a strong desire for success, great effort, great skill, etc.: *an ambitious attempt to climb the dangerous mountain* –**ambitiously** *adv*

am·biv·a·lent /æm'bɪvələnt/ *adj* [*towards, about*] having opposing feelings towards, or opinions about, something or someone

–compare AMBIGUOUS –**ambivalence** *n* [U]

am·ble /'æmbəl/ *v* -**bled, -bling** [I *about, around*] to walk at an easy gentle rate –see WALK (USAGE) –**amble** *n* [S]

am·bu·lance /'æmbyələns/ *n* a motor vehicle for carrying sick or wounded people, esp. to a hospital –see illustration on page 673

am·bush¹ /'æmbʊʃ/ *v* [T] to attack from a place where one has hidden and waited

ambush² *n* [C; *in* U] a surprise attack from a place of hiding; the place where the attackers hide

a·me·lio·rate /ə'miʸlyə,reʸt/ *v* -**rated, -rating** [I;T] *fml* to make better or less bad; improve: *Hiring a new teacher will ameliorate the condition, but we still need more books and desks.* –**amelioration** /ə,miʸlyə're ʸʃən/ *n* [U]

a·men /,eʸ'mɛn, ,ɑ-/ *interj* (used at the end of a prayer or HYMN) may this be true; so be it

a·me·na·ble /ə'miʸnəbəl, ə'mɛ-/ *adj* [*to*] able to be guided or influenced (by): *She is amenable to reason.*

a·mend /ə'mɛnd/ *v* [T] to make changes in the words of (a rule or law)

a·mend·ment /ə'mɛndmənt/ *n* [C;U] (the act of making) a change, made in or suggested for a statement, etc.: *So many amendments were made to the law that its original meaning was completely changed.*

a·mends /ə'mɛndz/ *n* [P] **make amends** to repair or pay for some harm, unkindness, damage, etc.: *I'm sorry I broke your camera. How can I make amends (for what I did)?*

a·men·i·ty /ə'mɛnəti, ə'miʸ-/ *n* -**ties** [*often pl.*] a thing or condition in a town, hotel, place, etc., that one can enjoy and which makes life pleasant: *Parks and swimming pools are just some of the town's* **local amenities.**

A·mer·i·can /ə'mɛrɪkən/ *adj, n* (a person) belonging to North, Central, or South America, esp. the United States of America

A·mer·i·can·a /ə,mɛrɪ'kænə, -'kɑnə/ *n* [U] (a collection of) things concerning the United States, esp. its history

American foot·ball /·,··· '··/ *BrE*‖**football** *AmE*– *n* [U] →FOOTBALL

American In·di·an /·,··· '···/ *n* → INDIAN (1)

A·mer·i·can·ism /ə'mɛrɪkə,nɪzəm/ *n* a word, phrase, speech sound, etc., of English as spoken in America, esp. in the United States

A·mer·i·can·ize ‖also **-ise** *BrE* /ə'mɛrɪkə,naɪz/ *v* -**ized, -izing** [I;T] to (cause to) become American in character –**Americanization** /ə,mɛrɪkənə'zeʸʃən/ *n* [U]

Am·er·in·di·an /,æmə'rɪndiʸən/ *n* → INDIAN (1)

am·e·thyst /'æməθɪst/ *n* [C;U] (the color of) a purple stone, used in jewelery

a·mi·a·ble /'eʸmiʸəbəl/ *adj* of a pleasant nature; friendly –**amiability** /,eʸmiʸə'bɪlətiʸ/ *n* [U] –**amiably** /'eʸmiʸəbliʸ/ *adv*

am·i·ca·ble /'æmɪkəbəl/ *adj* suitable between friends; friendly: *We reached an amicable agreement.* –**amicably** *adv*

a·mid /ə'mɪd/ also **amidst** /ə'mɪdst/– *prep fml & lit* in the middle of; among: *He felt strange amid so many people.*

a·mi·no ac·id /ə,miʸnoʷ 'æsɪd, ,æmənoʷ-/ *n* a

substance coming from, found in, and necessary to living matter

a·miss /ə'mɪs/ adj,adv [F no comp.] fml **1** wrong(ly) or imperfect(ly): Is something amiss? **2 take something amiss** to be angry at something, esp. because of a misunderstanding

am·mo·nia /ə'mowⁿnyə/ n [U] a strong gas with a sharp smell, used in explosives, in chemicals (FERTILIZERs) to help plants grow, etc.

am·mu·ni·tion /,æmyə'nɪʃən/ n [U] bullets, bombs, explosives, etc., esp. things fired from a weapon: (fig.) The recent tax increases have provided the administration's opponents with plenty of ammunition.

am·ne·sia /æm'niʸʒə/ n [U] loss of memory, either in part or completely

am·nes·ty /'æmnəstiʸ/ n -ties [C;U] (a) general act of forgiveness, esp. as allowed by a state to political criminals

a·mok /ə'mʌk, ə'mɑk/ also **amuck**– adv **run amok** to run wild and out of control, esp. with a desire to kill people: (fig.) If public spending runs amok our taxes will increase.

a·mong /ə'mʌŋ/ also **a·mongst** /ə'mʌŋst/– prep **1** in the middle of; surrounded by: Their house is hidden among trees.|I was among the crowd. **2** in the group of; being one of: He is among the best of our students.|She's very good at sports: among other things, she plays tennis twice a week.|They talked about it among themselves. (=together) **3** (when things are shared by more than two people): Divide the money among the five of them. (Compare Divide the money between the two of them.) –see BETWEEN (USAGE)

a·mor·al /eʸ'mɒrəl, eʸ'mɑrəl, æ-/ adj having no understanding of right and wrong: Young children are amoral. –see also IMMORAL, MORAL –**amorality** /,eʸmə'rælətiʸ, ,æ-/ n [U]

am·o·rous /'æmərəs/ adj of love; easily moved to love, esp. sexual love: amorous looks|an amorous woman –**amorously** adv –**amorousness** n [U]

a·mor·phous /ə'mɔrfəs/ adj having no fixed form or shape: I can't understand his amorphous plans. –**amorphously** adv

a·mount /ə'maʊnt/ n a quantity or sum: Large amounts of money were spent on the bridge.|She could only pay half the amount she owed.

USAGE **Amount** is used with [U] nouns: the **amount** of money. With plurals it is better to use **number**: the **number** of mistakes.

amount to sth. v prep [not be + v-ing] to be equal to: Your words amount to a refusal.|His debts amount to over $1,000.

amp /æmp/ n **1** also **ampere** /'æmpɪər/ fml– tech the standard measure of the quantity of electricity that is flowing past a point –compare VOLT **2** infml for AMPLIFIER

am·phet·a·mine /æm'fɛtə,miʸn, -mɪn/ n [C;U] a drug used in medicine and by people wanting excitement

am·phib·i·an /æm'fɪbiʸən/ n an animal (such as a FROG) that is able to live both on land and in water –**amphibious** /æm'fɪbiʸəs/ adj: an amphibious animal|an amphibious vehicle

(=one which can travel both on land and in water)

am·phi·the·a·ter AmE‖**amphitheatre** BrE /'æmfə,θiʸətər/ n an open building with rows of seats all around a central area, used for competitions and plays, esp. in ancient Rome

am·ple /'æmpəl/ adj **1** (more than) enough: We have ample money for the journey. –compare ADEQUATE **2** large: The house has an ample yard. –**amply** adv

am·pli·fi·er /'æmplə,faɪər/ n an instrument, as used in radios and RECORD PLAYERs, that makes electrical current or power stronger, music louder, etc. –see illustration on page 399

am·pli·fy /'æmplə,faɪ/ v -fied, -fying **1** [I; on, upon] to make larger, esp. to explain in greater detail: He amplified (on) his remarks with drawings and figures. **2** [T] to increase the strength of (something, esp. sound from electrical instruments) –**amplification** /,æmpləfə'keʸʃən/ n [S;U]

am·pu·tate /'æmpyə,teʸt/ v -tated, -tating [I;T] to cut off (part of the body), esp. for medical reasons: Her leg was so badly damaged that the doctors had to amputate (it). –compare EXCISE² –**amputation** /,æmpyə'teʸʃən/ n [C;U]

a·muck /ə'mʌk/ adv → AMOK

a·muse /ə'myuʷz/ v -mused, -musing [T] **1** to cause laughter in; excite the sense of humor of: amused expression on one's face|an amusing story **2** to cause to spend time in a pleasant manner: The toys amused the child for hours.|The children amused themselves by playing games.

a·muse·ment /ə'myuʷzmənt/ n **1** [U] the state of being amused; enjoyment: To everybody's amusement the actor fell off the stage.|I listened in amusement. **2** [C] something that causes one's time to pass enjoyably: Big cities have theaters, movies, football games and many other amusements.

amusement park /·'·· ,·/ AmE‖**funfair** BrE– n a piece of ground out of doors where a noisy show is held, offering big machines to ride on, games of skill, and other amusements

an /ən; strong æn/ indefinite article, determiner (used when the following word begins with a vowel sound) a: an elephant, not a dog|an L.P.

USAGE When putting **a** or **an** before a set of letters like L.P. (an ABBREVIATION) one must know how they are said in speech. L.P. begins with the consonant "l", but the name of the consonant begins with the vowel sound /ɛ/; one says **an** L.P. but **a** C.P.A.

a·nach·ro·nism /ə'nækrə,nɪzəm/ n a person, thing, or idea that is or appears to be in the wrong period of time: It is an anachronism to say "Shakespeare traveled by plane."‖Sailing boats are an anachronism in this age of fast travel. –**anachronistic** /ə,nækrə'nɪstɪk/ adj –**anachronistically** adv

a·nae·mi·a /ə'niʸmiʸə/ n [U] esp. BrE for ANEMIA

an·aes·the·sia /,ænəs'θiʸʒə/ n [U] esp. BrE

for ANESTHESIA **–anaesthetic** /ˌænəsˈθetɪk/ n **–anaesthetist** /əˈnesθətɪst/ n **–anaesthetize, -tise** /əˈnesθəˌtaɪz/ v

an·a·gram /ˈænəˌgræm/ n a word or phrase made by changing the order of the letters in another word or phrase: *"Silent" is an anagram of "listen."*

a·nal /ˈeʸnl/ adj of, concerning, or near the ANUS

an·al·ge·sic /ˌænlˈdʒiʸzɪk, -sɪk/ n,adj [C;U] (a substance) which makes one unable to feel pain

a·nal·o·gous /əˈnæləgəs/ adj [F to] fml like or alike in some ways: *Your suggestion was analogous to one that was made earlier.*

a·nal·o·gy /əˈnælədʒiʸ/ n -gies **1** [C] a degree of likeness or sameness: *There is an analogy between the way water moves in waves and the way light travels.* **2** [U] the act of explaining by comparing something with another thing that is like it in some way

an·a·lyse /ˈænlˌaɪz/ v **-lysed, -lysing** [T] BrE for ANALYZE

a·nal·y·sis /əˈnæləsɪs/ n **-ses** /ˌsiʸz/ [C;U] **1** (an) examination of something together with thoughts and judgments about it: *His analysis of the accident showed what had happened.* **2** AmE for PSYCHOANALYSIS

an·a·lyst /ˈænl-ɪst/ n **1** a person who makes an ANALYSIS, esp. of chemicals **2** AmE for PSYCHOANALYST

an·a·lyt·ic /ˌænlˈɪtɪk/ also **analytical** /ˌænlˈɪtɪkəl/– adj of, concerning, or using ANALYSIS (1) **–analytically** adv

an·a·lyze AmE‖**analyse** BrE /ˈænlˌaɪz/ v **-lyzed, -lyzing** [T] to examine (something) carefully in order to find out about (it): *He analyzed the food and found it contained poison.*

an·ar·chism /ˈænərˌkɪzəm/ n [U] the political belief that society should have no government, laws, police, etc. **–anarchist** n

an·ar·chy /ˈænərkiʸ/ n [U] (lawlessness and disorder caused by) absence of government or control **–anarchic** /æˈnɑrkɪk/ adj

a·nath·e·ma /əˈnæθəmə/ n [S;U to] something hated: *Those terrible ideas are (an) anathema to me.*

a·nat·o·my /əˈnætəmiʸ/ n **-mies 1** [U] the scientific study of the bodies of living things, esp. by cutting up dead bodies **2** [C usu. sing.] the way a living thing works or is built: *to study the anatomy of insects/plants*|(fig.) *the anatomy of modern society* **–anatomical** /ˌænəˈtɑmɪkəl/ adj: *an anatomical description of the leg* **–anatomist** /əˈnætəmɪst/ n

an·ces·tor /ˈænˌsestər/ n a person, esp. one living a long time ago, from whom another is descended: *My ancestors came from Spain.* **–compare** DESCENDENT **–ancestral** /ænˈsestrəl/ adj [A]: *one's ancestral home*

an·ces·try /ˈænˌsestriʸ/ n **-tries** [C;U] a person's ANCESTORs considered as a group: *a person of noble ancestry*

an·chor¹ /ˈæŋkər/ n **1** a heavy piece of metal, usu. hooked, at the end of a chain or rope, for lowering into the water to keep a ship from moving **2** also **anchorman** /ˈæŋkərˌmæn/ **-men** /ˌmen/, **anchorwoman** /ˈæŋkərˌwʊmən/ **-women** /ˌwɪmɪn/– a broadcaster (usu. on TV) who is in charge of a news program and appears on it

anchor² v **1** [I] to stop sailing and lower the ANCHOR **2** [I;T] to (cause to) be fixed firmly

an·chor·age /ˈæŋkərɪdʒ/ n a place where ships may ANCHOR² (1)

an·cho·vy /ˈæn,tʃoʷviʸ, -tʃə-, ænˈtʃoʷviʸ/ n **-vies** or **-vy** a small strong-tasting fish

an·cient /ˈeʸnʃənt, ˈeʸntʃənt/ adj **1** in or of times long ago: *ancient Rome and Greece* **2** often humor very old **–see** OLD (USAGE)

an·cil·lar·y /ˈænsəˌleriʸ/ adj [to] fml or tech providing help, support, or additional service

and /ənd, ən; strong ænd/ conj **1** (joining two things, esp. words of the same type or sentences of the same importance) as well as; also: *a knife and fork*|*John and I*| *She was cold and hungry.*|*He started to shout and sing.* **–see** Study Notes on page 144 **2** then; afterwards: *I woke up and got out of bed.* **3** (used to express a reason or result): *Water the seeds and they will grow.*|*She was sick and took some medicine.* (=because she was sick) Compare *She took some medicine and was sick.* (=because she took the medicine) **4** (used instead of *to* after *come, go, try,* etc.): *Come and have a beer with me.*|*Try and get here before 4 o'clock.*

an·ec·dote /ˈænɪkˌdoʷt/ n a short interesting or amusing story about a particular person or event **–anecdotal** /ˌænɪkˈdoʷtl/ adj

a·ne·mi·a AmE‖also **anaemia** esp. BrE /əˈniʸmiʸə/ n [U] the unhealthy condition of not having enough red cells in the blood **–anemic** adj

a·nem·o·ne /əˈneməniʸ/ n **1** a plant with quite large red, white, or blue flowers **2** also **sea anemone**– a simple sea animal with a jelly-like body and brightly colored flower-like parts that can often sting

an·es·the·sia AmE‖also **anaesthesia** esp. BrE /ˌænəsˈθiʸʒə/ n [U] the state of being unable to feel pain, etc., as produced from ANESTHETIC

an·es·thet·ic AmE‖also **anaesthetic** esp. BrE /ˌænəsˈθetɪk/ n [C;U] a substance used in medical operations to produce an inability to feel pain, either in a limited area (**local anesthetic**) or in the whole body, together with unconsciousness (**general anesthetic**) **–anesthetist** /əˈnesθətɪst/ n: *The anesthetist gave the patient an* ANESTHETIC.

a·nes·the·tize AmE‖also **anaesthetize** esp. BrE /əˈnesθəˌtaɪz/ v [T] **-tized, -tizing** to make unable to feel pain, by giving an ANESTHETIC

a·new /əˈnuʷ, əˈnyuʷ/ adv lit in a new or different way; again

an·gel /ˈeʸndʒəl/ n **1** a messenger and servant of God, usu. represented as a person with wings and dressed in white **2** a person who is very kind, beautiful, etc. **–angelic** /ænˈdʒelɪk/ adj

an·ger¹ /ˈæŋgər/ n [U] a fierce feeling of displeasure, usu. leading to a desire to hurt or stop the person or thing causing it

anger² v [T] to make angry –see ANGRY (USAGE)

an·gle¹ /'æŋgəl/ n **1** the space between two lines or surfaces that meet or cross each other, measured in degrees that represent the amount of a circle that can fit into that space: *An angle of 90° is called a* **right angle.**|*The plant was growing* **at an angle.** (=not upright) **2** *infml* a point of view: *If you look at the accident from another angle you will see how funny it all was.*

angle² v **-gled, -gling** [T] **1** to turn or move at an angle **2** *often derog* to represent (something) from a particular point of view: *She angles her reports to suit the people she is speaking to.*

angle³ v [I] to fish with a hook and line –**angler** /'æŋglər/ n –**angling** n [U]

angle for sthg. v prep [T] *often derog* to try to get, esp. by tricks or questions which are not direct: *to angle for an invitation to a party*

An·gli·can /'æŋglɪkən/ n, adj (a member) of a branch (CHURCH OF ENGLAND) of the Christian religion –**Anglicanism** n [U]

an·gli·cize ‖also **-cise** *BrE* /'æŋglə‚saɪz/ v **-cized, -cizing** [I;T] to (cause to) become English in appearance, sound, character, etc.

An·glo-Sax·on /‚æŋgloʷ 'sæksən/ adj, n **1** [C] (of or concerning) a member of the people who lived in England in early times, from about 600 to 1066 AD **2** [U] (of or concerning) their language –see also SAXON

an·gry /'æŋgriʸ/ adj **1** filled with anger: *I was angry (with him) for keeping me waiting so long.* **2** (of the sky or clouds) stormy –**angrily** adv

USAGE **Bother** means "displease" or "trouble:" *Will it* **bother** *you if I turn the radio on?* Things, people, or events can **annoy** or **irritate** one without being bad enough to make one **angry** (=to **anger** one) or (*AmE infml*) **mad:** *He has an* **annoying/irritating** *habit of biting his nails.*|*I was* **angered** *by his refusal to help.*|*The teacher was* **angry** *because the children wouldn't stop talking.* To make someone **furious** (to **infuriate** someone) or drive someone into a **rage** are stronger expressions still. –see also AGGRA-VATE (USAGE)

an·guish /'æŋgwɪʃ/ n [U] very great pain and suffering, esp. of mind: *She was in anguish over her missing child.* –**anguished** adj: *anguished cries*

an·gu·lar /'æŋgyələr/ adj **1** having sharp corners **2** (of a person) with the bones able to be clearly seen; thin: *her sharp angular face* –**angularity** /‚æŋgyə'lærətiʸ/ n [U]

an·i·mal¹ /'ænəməl/ n **1** a living creature, having senses and able to move itself when it wants to: *Snakes, fish, and birds are all animals.*|*Of all the animals, man is the most intelligent.* **2** all this group except human beings: *Should animals be kept in cages?* **3** →MAMMAL

animal² adj **1** of, concerning, or made from animals **2** *usu. derog* concerning the body, not the mind or the spirit: *animal desires*

an·i·mate¹ /'ænəmɪt/ adj (of plants and ani-

mals) alive; living –opposite **inanimate**

an·i·mate² /'ænə‚meʸt/ v **-mated, -mating** [T] to give life or excitement to: *Laughter animated his face for a moment.*

an·i·mat·ed /'ænə‚meʸtɪd/ adj full of spirit, life, and excitement: *When the question was raised in Congress, there was an animated argument*/DEBATE¹.

an·i·ma·tion /‚ænə'meʸʃən/ n [U] **1** excitement; spirit; life: *They were full of animation as they talked of their vacation.* **2** the making of CARTOONS (2)

an·i·mos·i·ty /‚ænə'mɑsətiʸ/ n **-ties** [C;U against, towards, between] (an example of) powerful, often active, hatred

an·i·seed /'ænɪ‚siʸd/ n [U] the strong-tasting seeds of a plant (**anise**), used esp. in alcoholic drinks

an·kle /'æŋkəl/ n **1** the joint between the foot and the leg **2** the thin part of the leg just above the foot

an·nals /'ænlz/ n [P] *fml* a history or record of events, discoveries, etc., produced every year, esp. by societies for the advancement of learning or science: (fig.) *one of the most interesting periods in the annals* (=history) *of modern science*

an·nex¹ /ə'nɛks, 'ænɛks/ v [T to] to take control and possession of (land, a small country, etc.) esp. by force –**annexation** /‚ænɛk'seʸʃən, ‚ænɪk-/ n [C;U]

an·nex² ‖also **annexe** *esp. BrE* /'ænɛks, 'ænɪks/ n a building joined or added to a larger one: *a hospital annex*

an·ni·hi·late /ə'naɪə‚leʸt/ v **-lated, -lating** [T] to destroy completely: *We annihilated the enemy.* –**annihilation** /ə‚naɪə'leʸʃən/ n [U]

an·ni·ver·sa·ry /‚ænə'vɜrsəriʸ/ n **-ries** a day which is an exact year or number of years after something has happened: *Today is the anniversary of the day we met.*|*a wedding anniversary* –compare BIRTHDAY

An·no Dom·i·ni /‚ænoʷ 'dɑməniʸ, -‚naɪ/ *fml* for AD

an·no·tate /'ænə‚teʸt, 'ænoʷ-/ v **-tated, -tating** [T] *fml* to add notes to (a book) to explain certain parts –**annotation** /‚ænə'teʸʃən, ‚ænoʷ-/ n [C;U]

an·nounce /ə'naʊns/ v **-nounced, -nouncing** [T] **1** to state in a loud voice: *Everyone was silent as he announced the winner of the match.* **2** [+ *that*] to make known publicly: *The government announced that it would pay its debts.* –see also UNANNOUNCED –**announcement** n

an·nounc·er /ə'naʊnsər/ n a person who reads news or introduces people, acts, etc., esp. on radio or television

an·noy /ə'nɔɪ/ v **-noyed, -noying** [I;T] to cause (someone) trouble; make a little angry: *These flies are annoying me.* –see ANGRY (USAGE)

an·noy·ance /ə'nɔɪəns/ n **1** [C] something which annoys: *The noisy traffic is a continual annoyance.* **2** [U] the state of being annoyed

an·nu·al¹ /'ænyuʷəl/ adj (happening, appearing, etc.) every year or once a year; for one year: *an annual event* |*his annual wage* –**annually** adv

annual² *n* **1** a plant that lives for only one year or season –compare BIENNIAL **2** a book produced once each year having the same title but containing different stories, pictures, information, etc.

an·nu·i·ty /ə'nuʷətiʸ, ə'nyuʷ-/ *n* **-ties** a fixed sum of money paid each year to a person for a stated number of years or until death

an·nul /ə'nʌl/ *v* **-ll-** [T] *tech* to cause (a marriage, agreement, law, etc.) to cease to exist –**annulment** *n* [C;U]

an·ode /'ænoʷd/ also **positive pole**– *n tech* the part of an electrical instrument (such as a BATTERY (1)) which collects ELECTRONS, often a rod or wire shown as (+) –compare CATHODE

a·noint /ə'nɔɪnt/ *v* [T *with*] to put oil on (a person, head, or body), esp. in a religious ceremony –**anointment** *n* [C;U]

a·nom·a·ly /ə'naməliʸ/ *n* **-lies** *fml* a person or thing that is different from the usual type: *A cat with no tail is an anomaly.* –**anomalous** /ə'namələs/ *adj*: *in an anomalous position* –**anomalously** *adv*

a·non¹ /ə'nan/ *adv old use or lit* soon

anon.² *abbrev. for*: (esp. at the end of a poem, letter, etc.)

a·non·y·mous /ə'nanəməs/ *adj* with name unknown; without the writer's name: *It is unpleasant to receive anonymous letters.* –**anonymity** /,ænə'nɪmətiʸ/ *n* [U] –**anonymously** /ə'nanəməsliʸ/ *adv*

an·oth·er /ə'nʌðər/ *determiner, pron* **1** (being) one more of the same kind: *Have another drink and another piece of cake.* **2** a different one; some other: *He lost his book and borrowed one from another boy/from another one of the boys.* –see OTHER (USAGE)

an·swer¹ /'ænsər/ *n* **1** [C;U *to*] what is said or written when one is asked a question, sent a letter, etc.; reply: *I've had no answer to my letter yet.|I said good morning to him but he gave no answer.|My answer to his threat was to hit him.|In answer to my shouts people ran to help.* **2** [C] something which is discovered as a result esp. of thinking, using figures, etc.; SOLUTION (1): *The answer was 279.|* (fig.) *I'm getting too fat. The only answer is to stop eating sweets.*

answer² *v* [I;T] **1** [+ *that/with*] to give an answer (to); reply (to): *You didn't answer his question.|Why didn't you answer?|I answered (his words) with a smile.|I telephoned, but nobody answered (the telephone).* –see TELEPHONE (USAGE) **2** [*to*] to be as described in; equal; fit: *He answers (to) the description of the criminal.* **3** [*for*] to be satisfactory (for): *This tool will answer (for) our needs/ will answer (our needs) very well.*

USAGE **Answer** and **reply** are the usual verbs for answering questions; **respond** (*fml*) means the same thing but is much less common: *He answered/replied to the question/his mother.|"Are you coming?" "Yes," he answered/replied.|I spoke, but he didn't answer/reply/respond.|He answered/replied that he was coming.* **Retort** or (*rare*) **rejoin**

are angrier: *"Are you ready?" "Why should I be ready when you're not?" she* **retorted.**.

answer (sbdy.) **back** *v adv* [I;T *no pass.*] *infml* (esp. of children talking to grown-ups) to reply rudely (to): *Don't answer (me) back.|It's not polite.*

answer for sbdy./sthg. *v prep* [T *to*] **1** to be or become responsible for: *I will answer for his safety.* **2** to act, pay, or suffer as a result of: *You will have to answer for your violent behavior in court.*

an·swer·a·ble /'ænsərəbəl/ *adj* **1** able to be answered **2** [F *to, for*] responsible: *I'll be answerable for what he does.|I cannot do as I like; I am* **answerable to** *the government* **for** *any decision I make.*

ant /ænt/ *n* a small insect living on the ground and famous for hard work

an·tag·o·nism /æn'tægə,nɪzəm/ *n* [C;U] (an example of) active opposition or hatred between people or groups –**antagonist** /æn'tægənɪst/ *n* –**antagonistic** /æn,tæg ə'nɪstɪk/ *adj* –**antagonistically** *adv*

an·tag·o·nize /æn'tægə,naɪz/ *v* **-nized, -nizing** [T] to cause to become an enemy: *If you want to do well in this class, don't antagonize the teacher.*

ant·arc·tic /ænt'arktɪk, -'artɪk/ *adj,n* [*the* S] (*often cap.*) (of or concerning) the very cold most southern part of the world –compare ARCTIC

an·te /'æntiʸ/ → ANTE UP

an·te·ced·ent /,æntə'siʸdnt/ *n,adj* [*to*] *fml* (a thing, event, etc.) coming or being before

an·te·date /'ænti,deʸt, ,ænti'deʸt/ *v* **-dated, -dating** [T] to be earlier in history than: *This old carriage antedates the invention of the car.* –see also POSTDATE

an·te·lope /'æntəl,oʷp/ *n* **-lopes** *or* **-lope** a graceful animal like a deer, able to run very fast

an·te·na·tal /,æntiʸ'neʸtl/ *adj* [A] *BrE tech* for PRENATAL

an·ten·na¹ /æn'tɛnə/ also **feeler**– *n* **-nae** /niʸ/ a long thin sensitive hairlike organ, usu. in pairs, on the heads of some insects and animals that live in shells, and used to feel with

antenna² *AmE*||also **aerial**– *n* **-nas** a wire rod or framework put up, often on top of a house, to receive radio or television broadcasts

an·te·ri·or /æn'tiəriʸər/ *adj* [*to no comp.*] **1** *fml* earlier in time **2** *usu. tech* nearer the front –compare POSTERIOR

ante up (sthg.) *v adv* **-ted** *or* **-teed, -teing** [I;T *for*] *AmE infml* to pay (an amount of money), esp. in a game of chance; to provide (one's share of the money): *If you don't ante up for the trip by Friday, you can't go with us.*

an·them /'ænθəm/ *n* an esp. religious song of praise –see also NATIONAL ANTHEM

an·thol·o·gy /æn'θalədʒiʸ/ *n* **-gies** a collection of poems, or of other writings, often on the same subject, chosen from different books or writers –compare OMNIBUS (1)

an·thrax /'ænθræks/ *n* [U] a serious disease which attacks cattle, sheep, etc., and sometimes human beings

an·thro·poid /'ænθrə,pɔɪd/ *adj,n* (an animal)

like a human being

an·thro·pol·o·gy /ˌænθrə'pɑlədʒiʸ/ n [U] the scientific study of the human race, including its different bodily types and its beliefs, social habits, etc. –compare ETHNOLOGY, SOCIOLOGY –**anthropological** /ˌænθrəpə'lɑdʒɪkəl/ adj –**anthropologically** adv –**anthropologist** /ˌænθrə'pɑlədʒɪst/ n

an·ti·bi·ot·ic /ˌæntɪbaɪ'ɑtɪk, ˌæntaɪ-/ n,adj (a medical substance, such as PENICILLIN) produced by living things and able to stop the growth of, or destroy, harmful bacteria that have entered the body

an·ti·bod·y /'æntɪˌbɑdiʸ/ n -ies a substance produced in the body which fights disease

an·tic·i·pate /æn'tɪsəˌpeʸt/ v -pated, -pating [T] **1** [+v-ing/that] to expect: We are not anticipating (that there will be) trouble when the factory opens again.|We anticipate (meeting) opposition to our new plan. **2** to do something before (someone else): We anticipated our competitors by getting our book into the stores first. **3** [+that] to see (what will happen) and act as necessary, often to stop someone else doing something: We anticipated that the enemy would cross the river, and so we destroyed the bridge.|We're trying to anticipate what questions we'll be asked on the examination. –**anticipatory** /æn'tɪsəpəˌtɔri, -ˌtoʷriʸ/ adj

USAGE Although **anticipate** is commonly used to mean "expect," this is thought by teachers to be incorrect.

an·tic·i·pa·tion /ænˌtɪsə'peʸʃən/ n [U +that/ of] the act of anticipating (ANTICIPATE), esp. with hope: We waited at the station **in anticipation of** her arrival.

an·ti·cli·max /ˌæntɪ'klaɪmæks/ n something unexciting coming after something exciting: To be back in the office after climbing mountains for a week was an anticlimax for him. –see also CLIMAX¹ (1) –**anticlimactic** /ˌæntɪklaɪ'mæktɪk/ adj

an·ti·clock·wise /ˌæntɪ'klɑkwaɪz, ˌæntaɪ-/ adj,adv BrE for COUNTERCLOCKWISE

an·tics /'æntɪks/ n [P] strange or unusual behavior, esp. with odd, amusing, or foolish movements: Everyone laughed at his foolish antics.

an·ti·cy·clone /ˌæntɪ'saɪkloʷn/ n tech a mass of air that is heavy, causing settled weather, either hot or cold, in the area over which it moves –see also CYCLONE

an·ti·dote /'æntɪˌdoʷt/ n a substance to stop a poison working inside a person, or to prevent the effects of a disease: (fig.) We need an antidote to our present political troubles.

an·ti·freeze /'æntɪˌfriʸz/ n [U] a chemical substance put in water to stop it from freezing in very cold weather, used esp. in car engines

an·tip·a·thy /æn'tɪpəθiʸ/ n -thies [C;U to, towards, against, between] (an example of) a fixed dislike or hatred –**antipathetic** /ˌæntɪpə'θɛtɪk, ˌæntɪpə-/ adj

an·ti·quat·ed /'æntɪˌkweʸtɪd/ adj often derog old and not suited to present needs or conditions; not modern; old-fashioned –see OLD (USAGE)

an·tique /æn'tiʸk/ n,adj (a piece of furniture, jewelery, etc., that is) old and therefore becoming rare and valuable

an·tiq·ui·ty /æn'tɪkwətiʸ/ n -ties **1** [U] the state of being very old; great age: a building of great antiquity **2** [C;U] (a building, work of art, etc., remaining from) the ancient world, esp. of Rome or Greece

an·ti-Sem·i·tism /ˌæntiʸ 'sɛməˌtɪzəm, ˌæntaɪ-/ n [U] hatred of Jews –see also SEMITIC –**anti-Semitic** /ˌæntiʸ sə'mɪtɪk, ˌæntaɪ-/ adj

an·ti·sep·tic /ˌæntə'sɛptɪk/ n,adj (a chemical substance) able to prevent disease in a wound, etc., esp. by killing bacteria

an·ti·so·cial /ˌæntiʸ'soʷʃəl, ˌæntaɪ-/ adj **1** not social; causing damage to the way in which people live together peacefully: Playing music so loudly that it annoys everyone else in the street is antisocial. **2** not liking to mix with others: Jane's very friendly, but her husband's a little antisocial.

an·tith·e·sis /æn'tɪθəsɪs/ n -ses /ˌsiʸz/ [of, to] the direct opposite: The antithesis of death is life.

ant·ler /'æntlər/ n either of the pair of branched horns of a male deer (STAG) and other related animals

an·to·nym /'æntəˌnɪm/ n tech a word opposite in meaning to another word: "Pain" is the antonym of "pleasure." –compare SYNONYM

a·nus /'eʸnəs/ n tech the hole in the body through which solid food waste leaves the bowels –compare RECTUM

an·vil /'ænvɪl/ n a shaped iron block on which metals are hammered to the shape wanted

anx·i·e·ty /æŋ'zaɪətiʸ/ n -ties [C;U] **1** fear and worry, esp. as caused by uncertainty about something: They felt strong anxiety (for her safety/about her).|After hearing their advice he had no more anxieties. **2** [+to-v/that] a strong wish to do something; eagerness: anxiety to please

anx·ious /'æŋkʃəs, 'æŋʃəs/ adj **1** [for, about] feeling or causing anxiety; troubled: I was anxious about the children when they didn't come home from school.|an anxious wait for our examination results **2** [+to-v/that/for] having a strong wish to do something; eager: He was anxious to please his guests. –see NERVOUS (USAGE) –**anxiously** adv

an·y¹ /'ɛniʸ/ determiner,pron **1** every; no matter which (of more than two): They're all free. Take any you like.|Any child would know that. **2** (used only in NEGATIVES², questions, etc.): some; even the smallest number or amount: Do you have any money?|Are there any letters for me? I never seem to get any. (Compare There are **some** (letters for you.)|Come and see me if you have any time. –see EITHER¹ (USAGE) **3** as much as possible; all: He will need any help he can get. **4 in any case: a** also **at any rate**– whatever may happen: We may miss the next bus, but in any case we'll be there before midday. **b** besides; also: I don't want to go out tonight, and in any case we can't afford it.

an·y² adv (used only in NEGATIVES², questions,

etc.) in the least; at all: *I can't stay any longer.*|*Do you feel any better?*

an·y·bod·y /ˈɛniʸˌbɑdiʸ, -ˌbʌdiʸ, -bədiʸ/ also **anyone**– *pron* **1** all people; no matter who: *Anybody can cook–it's easy.*|*She's more intelligent than anybody else.* **2** (used only in NEGATIVEs[2], questions, etc.) any person: *Is anybody listening?*|*There isn't anybody listening.*|*If anybody is listening, I hope he/they will say so.*

an·y·how /ˈɛniʸˌhaʊ/ *adv infml* **1** carelessly; without any regular order: *His clothes were thrown down just anyhow.* **2** also **anyway**– in spite of that; in any case: *He told me not to buy it, but I bought it anyhow.* **3** also **anyway**– (used when going on with a story): "*Well, anyhow, I rang the bell...*"

an·y·one /ˈɛniʸˌwʌn, -wən/ *pron* anybody
USAGE Compare **anyone** and **any one**: *Don't let* **anyone** *in.*|*There are three possible answers*–**any one** *of them will be accepted.*

an·y·thing /ˈɛniʸˌθɪŋ/ *pron* **1** (used only in NEGATIVEs[2], questions, etc.) any one thing; something: *Is there anything in that box?*|*You can't believe anything she says.* **2** no matter what: *He will do anything for a quiet life.*|*Anything will do to keep the door open.* **3 anything but** not at all; far from: *That old bridge is anything but safe.* **4 anything like** at all like; at all: *It isn't anything like as cold as it was yesterday.* **5 as easy/fast/strong, etc., as anything** *infml* very easy/fast/strong, etc.: *Don't worry. The test is as easy as anything.* **6 like anything** *infml* (used to add force to a verb): *We ran like anything.* (=very fast/hard) **7 or anything** (suggests that there are other possibilities): *If you want to call me or anything, I'll be here all day.*

an·y·way /ˈɛniʸˌweʸ/ *adv infml* for ANYHOW (2,3)

an·y·where /ˈɛniʸˌhwɛər, -ˌwɛər/ *adv* **1** in, at, or to no matter what place: *Sit anywhere you like.* **2** (only in NEGATIVEs[2], questions, etc.) (in, at, or to) any place at all: *Did you go anywhere yesterday?* –see SOME (USAGE)

a·part /əˈpɑrt/ *adv* **1** [after *n*] separate by a distance: *The two buildings are three miles apart.*|*We planted the trees wide apart.*|*He and his wife are living apart.* **2** into parts: *He took the clock apart to repair it.* –see also COME **apart 3 apart from: a** without considering; except for: *good work, apart from a few slight faults* **b** as well as: *Apart from being too large, the hat doesn't suit me.* **4 tell/know apart** to be able to see the difference between: *I can't tell the two boys apart.*

a·part·heid /əˈpɑrtaɪt, -teʸt, -taɪd/ *n* [U] the separation of races in one country, esp. of blacks and whites in South Africa –compare SEGREGATION

a·part·ment /əˈpɑrtmənt/ *AmE*‖**flat** *esp. BrE*– *n* a set of rooms, including a kitchen and BATHROOM, usu. one of many such sets in a building: *an apartment on the fourth floor*|*a three-room apartment* –see HOUSE (USAGE)

apartment house /·'·· ˌ·/ also **apartment building** /·'·· ˌ·/– *n AmE* a building that is divided into separate APARTMENTs –see illustration on page 337

ap·a·thet·ic /ˌæpəˈθɛtɪk/ *adj* without feeling or interest; lacking desire to act –**apathetically** *adv*

ap·a·thy /ˈæpəθiʸ/ *n* [U] lack of feeling or interest in something or everything; lack of desire or ability to act in any way: *He was sunk in apathy after his failure.*

ape[1] /eʸp/ *n* a large monkey without a tail or with a very short tail (such as a GORILLA or CHIMPANZEE)

ape[2] *v* **aped, aping** [T] to copy (a person or a person's behavior, manners, speech, etc.); IMITATE

a·per·i·tif /əˌpɛrəˈtiʸf, ɑ-/ *n* a small alcoholic drink drunk before a meal

ap·er·ture /ˈæpərtʃər, -ˌtʃʊər/ *n* a hole, crack, or other narrow opening, esp. one that admits light into a camera

a·pex /ˈeʸpɛks/ *n* [*usu. sing.*] the top or highest part of anything: *the apex of a* TRIANGLE (1)|(fig.) *the apex of his popularity*

aph·o·rism /ˈæfəˌrɪzəm/ *n* a true or wise saying or principle expressed in a few words; MAXIM

aph·ro·dis·i·ac /ˌæfrəˈdɪziʸˌæk/ *n,adj* (a medicine, drug, etc.) causing sexual excitement

a·piece /əˈpiʸs/ *adv* to, for, or from each person or thing; each: *The apples cost fifty cents apiece.*

a·pol·o·get·ic /əˌpɑləˈdzɛtɪk/ *adj* expressing sorrow for some fault or wrong –**apologetically** *adv*

a·pol·o·gize‖also **-gise** *BrE* /əˈpɑləˌdʒaɪz/ *v* **-gized, -gizing** [I *to, for*] to say one is sorry, as for a fault or for causing pain: *I apologized (to her) (for stepping on her foot).*

a·pol·o·gy /əˈpɑlədʒiʸ/ *n* **-gies** a statement expressing sorrow for a fault, for causing trouble or pain, etc.: *I must offer her an apology for not going to her party.*|*I'll make an apology to her.*|*Please accept my apologies.*

ap·o·plex·y /ˈæpəˌplɛksiʸ/ *n* [U] the sudden loss of the ability to move, feel, think, etc.; STROKE[2] (3) –**apoplectic** /ˌæpəˈplɛktɪk/ *adj*

a·pos·tle /əˈpɑsəl/ *n* any of the 12 followers of Christ chosen by him to spread his message to the world

a·pos·tro·phe /əˈpɑstrəfiʸ/ *n* the sign (') used in writing **a** to show that one or more letters or figures have been left out of a word or figure (as in *don't* and *'47* for *do not* and *1947*) **b** before or after *s* to show possession (as in *John's hat, James' hat, lady's hat, ladies' hats, children's hats*) **c** before *s* to show the plural of letters and figures: *There are 2 f 's in off* and *Your 8's look like S's*

a·poth·e·car·y /əˈpɑθəˌkɛriʸ/ *n* **-ies** *old use* a person with a knowledge of chemistry who mixed and sold medicines; PHARMACIST

ap·pall *AmE*‖**appal** *BrE* /əˈpɔl/ *v* [T] to shock deeply; fill with fear, hatred, terror, etc.: *We were appalled when we heard she had been murdered.*

ap·pall·ing /əˈpɔlɪŋ/ *adj* **1** causing fear; shocking; terrible **2** *infml* very bad: *an appalling waste*|*an appalling play* –**appallingly** *adv*: *an appallingly bad driver*

ap·pa·rat·us /ˌæpəˈrætəs, -ˈreɪtəs/ n -uses or -us [C;U] a set of instruments, machines, tools, materials, etc., needed for a particular purpose: *The television workers set up their apparatus ready to film.*|*a piece of apparatus*

ap·par·el /əˈpærəl/ n [U] 1 *lit & old use* clothes, esp. of a fine or special sort: *priestly apparel* 2 *esp. AmE* (in comb.) clothes; clothing: *ladies' ready-to-wear apparel*

ap·par·ent /əˈpærənt, əˈpɛər-/ adj 1 [to] easily seen or understood; plain: *Her anxiety was apparent to everyone.* 2 not necessarily true or real; seeming: *Their apparent grief soon turned to laughter.*

ap·par·ent·ly /əˈpærəntliy, əˈpɛər-/ adv it seems (that); as it appears: *I wasn't there, but apparently she tried to drown him.*|*"Did she succeed?" "Apparently not."*

ap·pa·ri·tion /ˌæpəˈrɪʃən/ n the spirit of a dead person moving in bodily form; GHOST: *He saw the apparition of his dead wife.*

ap·peal¹ /əˈpiyl/ n 1 [C;U] (a) strong request for help, support, money, mercy, etc.: *His appeal for forgiveness went unanswered.*|*an appeal for money to build a new hall* 2 [U] power to move the feelings; attraction; interest: *Movies like that have lost their appeal for me.*|*sex appeal* 3 [C;U] a call to a higher court to change the decision of a lower court: *the right of appeal*|*a court of appeal*

appeal² v [I] 1 [+to-v/to, for] to make a strong request for help, support, money, mercy, etc.; beg: *The government is appealing to everyone to save water.* 2 [to] to please, attract, or interest: *Does the idea of working abroad appeal to you?*|*That music doesn't appeal (to people) any more.* 3 to call on a higher law court to change the decision of a lower court

appeal to sbdy./sthg. v prep [T for] to look for support in: *By appealing to his better nature, we persuaded the boy to tell the truth.*

ap·peal·ing /əˈpiylɪŋ/ adj 1 able to move the feelings: *the appealing eyes of a hungry dog* 2 attractive or interesting: *What an appealing little baby!* –opposite unappealing (for 2) –appealingly adv

ap·pear /əˈpɪər/ v [I] 1 to become able to be seen; come into sight: *In this disease, spots appear on the skin.*|*If I don't appear (=come) by 7 o'clock, I won't be coming at all.*|*Her new book will appear in the stores very soon.* –opposite disappear 2 [+to-v/(that)] to seem; look: *He appears to want to leave.*|*You appear well this morning.*|*It appears he's moving to another company.*|*So it appears.*|*It appears so.*|*It appears not.* 3 [I] to be present officially, as in a court of law: *He had to appear before the committee to explain his behavior.*

ap·pear·ance /əˈpɪərəns/ n 1 [C] the act of appearing, as to the eye, mind, or public: *My appearance at the party was not very welcome. He put in an appearance, but didn't stay long.* –opposite disappearance 2 [C;U] that which can be seen; outward qualities; look: *He had an unhealthy appearance.*|*They changed the whole appearance of the house just by painting it.*|*Don't judge by appearances.*

ap·pease /əˈpiyz/ v -peased, -peasing [T] to make calm or satisfy, esp. by yielding to demands or by giving or doing something: *The angry man was appeased when they said they were sorry.*|*to appease one's hunger/*CURIOSITY (1) –appeasement n

ap·pend /əˈpɛnd/ v [T to] *fml* to add (esp. something written onto the end of a letter or other piece of written material): *I append a list of those stores which sell our products.* –compare ENCLOSE (2)

ap·pend·age /əˈpɛndɪdʒ/ n something added, joined to, or hanging from something, esp. something larger

ap·pen·di·ci·tis /əˌpɛndəˈsaɪtɪs/ n [U] the diseased state of the APPENDIX (1)

ap·pen·dix /əˈpɛndɪks/ n -dixes or -dices /dəˌsiyz/ 1 a short wormlike organ leading off the bowel, and having little or no use 2 something added, esp. additional information at the end of a book

ap·per·tain to sthg. /ˌæpərˈteyn/ v prep [T no pass.] *fml* to belong to: *the responsibilities appertaining to the presidency*

ap·pe·tite /ˈæpəˌtaɪt/ n [C;U] a desire or wish, esp. for food: *Don't eat anything that will spoil your appetite for dinner.*|(fig.) *He had no appetite for hard work.*|*sexual appetites* –see DESIRE (USAGE)

ap·pe·tiz·er /ˈæpəˌtaɪzər/ n something small and attractive eaten at the beginning of a meal to increase the desire for food

ap·pe·tiz·ing /ˈæpəˌtaɪzɪŋ/ adj causing desire, esp. for food –opposite unappetizing –appetizingly adv: *food appetizingly cooked*

ap·plaud /əˈplɔd/ v [I;T] 1 to praise (a play, actor, performer, etc.), esp. by striking one's hands together (CLAPping) 2 to express strong approval of (a person, idea, etc.): *We all applauded the council's decision not to close the hospital.*

ap·plause /əˈplɔz/ n [U] loud praise for a performance or performer, esp. by striking the hands together (CLAPping)

ap·ple /ˈæpəl/ n 1 a hard round fruit with white juicy flesh and usu. a red, green, or yellow skin 2 apple of someone's eye *infml* the person or thing most liked

ap·pli·ance /əˈplaɪəns/ n an apparatus, instrument, or tool for a particular purpose, esp. a machine run by electricity and used in the house: *This house has several appliances such as a washing machine and clothes dryer.* –see MACHINE (USAGE)

ap·pli·ca·ble /ˈæplɪkəbəl, əˈplɪkəbəl/ adj 1 [to] able to have an effect on: *The new law is applicable beginning next Monday.*|*This rule is not applicable to foreigners.* 2 suitable for; correct –opposite inapplicable

ap·pli·cant /ˈæplɪkənt/ n a person who makes a request, esp. officially and in writing, for a job, etc.

ap·pli·ca·tion /ˌæplɪˈkeyʃən/ n 1 [C;U] (the act of making) a request, esp. in writing: *I made five applications for jobs but got nothing.* 2 [C;U of, to] the putting to use: *The application of new scientific discoveries* *to industrial production methods usually makes jobs easier to do.*|*the application of a medicine (onto the skin)* **3** [U] careful and continuous attention or effort: *He worked with great application to learn the new language.*

ap·plied /ə'plaɪd/ *adj* (esp. of a science) put to practical use: *applied* MATHEMATICS –compare PURE

ap·ply /ə'plaɪ/ *v* **-plied, -plying 1** [I *to, for*] to request something, esp. in writing: *I'll apply for the job today.* **2** [T *to*] to bring or put into use: *Apply as much force as is necessary.*|*to apply a new method* **3** [T *to*] to put on: *Apply some medicine to his wound.* **4** [I;T *to*] to (cause to) have an effect; be directly related: *This rule does not apply.* **5** [T *to*] to cause to work hard or carefully: *He applied himself to the job.*

ap·point /ə'pɔɪnt/ *v* [T] **1** to choose for a position, job, etc.: *We'll have to appoint a new teacher soon.*|*They appointed him (to be) chairman.* **2** *fml* to arrange; fix; decide: *Let's appoint a day to have dinner together.*|*She wasn't there at the appointed meeting place.*

ap·point·ment /ə'pɔɪntmənt/ *n* **1** [C] a meeting at an agreed time and place: *I have an appointment with the doctor.* **2** [U] the agreement of a time and place for meeting: *He will only see you by appointment.* **3** [C;U *of, as*] the choosing of someone for a position or job: *the appointment of John as director*/*to be director*/*a teaching appointment*

USAGE When you arrange to see someone at a fixed time you **make an appointment**. If you then actually see the person as arranged, you **keep your appointment**. If you cannot come, you write or telephone to **cancel the appointment**.

ap·por·tion /ə'pɔrʃən, ə'poʷr-/ *v* [T *between, among(st)*] *fml* to divide into and give as shares: *It was difficult to apportion the blame for the accident.*

ap·praise /ə'preʸz/ *v* **-praised, -praising** [T] *fml* to judge the worth, quality, or condition of; find out the value of: *They appraised the house carefully before they bought it.* –**appraisal** *n*

ap·pre·cia·ble /ə'priʸʃəbəl, -ʃiʸə-/ *adj* enough to be felt, noticed, or considered important: *an appreciable difference* –**appreciably** *adv*

ap·pre·ci·ate /ə'priʸʃiʸeʸt/ *v* **-ated, -ating 1** [T] to understand and enjoy the good qualities or value of: *to appreciate good wine*|*I appreciate your help.* **2** [I *in*] (of money, property, possessions, etc.) to increase in value: *Houses in this area have all appreciated (in value) since the new road was built.* –opposite **depreciate** (for 2) –**appreciation** /ə,priʸʃiʸeʸʃən/ *n* [C;U]

ap·pre·cia·tive /ə'priʸʃətɪv, -ʃiʸə-/ *adj* **1** grateful; thankful **2** feeling or showing understanding or admiration –opposite **unappreciative** –**appreciatively** *adv*

ap·pre·hend /,æprɪ'hɛnd/ *v* [T] *fml* to seize (a person who breaks the law): ARREST[1] (1)

ap·pre·hen·sion /,æprɪ'hɛnʃən, -tʃən/ *n* **1** [U] anxiety, esp. about the future; fear: *She felt apprehension for the safety of her son.* **2** [C;U] *fml* the act of seizing (a person who breaks the law); ARREST[2]

ap·pre·hen·sive /,æprɪ'hɛnsɪv/ *adj* [*for, about,* etc.] worried; anxious: *He looked apprehensive as he waited for the result to be broadcast.* –**apprehensively** *adv*

ap·pren·tice[1] /ə'prɛntɪs/ *n* a person who is under an agreement to serve, for a number of years and usu. for low wages, a person skilled in a trade, in order to learn that person's skill: *an apprentice electrician*|*He was apprentice to an electrician.*

apprentice[2] *v* **-ticed, -ticing** [T *to*] to make or send as an APPRENTICE: *He's apprenticed to an electrician.*

ap·pren·tice·ship /ə'prɛntɪ,ʃɪp, -tɪs,ʃɪp/ *n* [C;U] (the condition or period of) being an APPRENTICE

ap·proach[1] /ə'proʷtʃ/ *v* **1** [I;T] to come near or nearer (to): .*We approached the camp.*|*The time for us to leave is approaching.* **2** [T *about*] to speak to, esp. about something for the first time: *Did he approach you about lending him some money?* **3** [T] to begin to consider: *He approached the difficulty with great thought.*

approach[2] *n* **1** [U] the act of APPROACHing: *The approach of winter brings cold weather.* **2** [C] a means or way of entering: *All approaches to the town were blocked.* **3** [C] a manner or method of doing something: *a new approach to teaching English* **4** [C] speaking to someone for the first time: *I'm not very good at making approaches to strangers.*

ap·proach·a·ble /ə'proʷtʃəbəl/ *adj* **1** able to be reached **2** easy to speak to; friendly: *You'll find the director a very approachable person.* –opposite **unapproachable**

ap·pro·ba·tion /,æprə'beʸʃən/ *n* [U] *fml* praise; approval –opposite **disapprobation**

ap·pro·pri·ate[1] /ə'proʷpriʸɪt/ *adj* [*for, to*] correct or suitable: *His bright clothes were not appropriate for a funeral.* –opposite **inappropriate** –**appropriately** *adv* –**appropriateness** *n* [U]

ap·pro·pri·ate[2] /ə'proʷpriʸ,eʸt/ *v* **-ated, -ating** [T *for*] **1** *fml* to set aside for some purpose: *The government appropriated a large sum of money for building hospitals.* **2** *euph* to take for oneself; steal: *The mayor was found to have appropriated government money.* –**appropriation** /ə,proʷpriʸ'eʸʃən/ *n* [C;U]

ap·prov·al /ə'pruʷvəl/ *n* [U] **1** the act of approving –opposite **disapproval 2 on approval** *infml* (of goods taken or sent from a store) to be returned without payment if not found satisfactory

ap·prove /ə'pruʷv/ *v* **-proved, -proving** [T] to agree officially to: *The company president approved the building plans.* –**approvingly** *adv*

approve of sbdy./sthg. *v prep* [T +*v-ing*] to consider good, right, wise, etc.: *I don't approve of smoking in bed*/*people who smoke in bed.*

ap·prox. *written abbrev. said as:* APPROXIMATE(ly)[1]

ap·prox·i·mate[1] /ə'prɒksəmɪt/ *adj* [*no comp.*] almost correct but not exact: *The approximate number of students in the school is 300.* –**approximately** *adv: approximately 300*

ap·prox·i·mate[2] /ə'prɒksə,meʸt/ *v* **-mated, -mating** to come near to: *Your story only approximates the real facts.* –**approximation** /ə,prɒksə'meʸʃən/ *n* [C;U *of*]

ap·ri·cot /'æprɪ,kɒt, 'eʸ-/ *n* [C] a round soft orange or yellow fruit with a furry outside like a PEACH and a single large stone

A·pril /'eʸprəl/ also **Apr.** *written abbrev.* – *n* the 4th month of the year

April fool /ˌ·· '·/ *n* a person who has been deceived or made fun of by a trick played on April 1st (**April Fools' Day, All Fools' Day**)

a·pron /'eʸprən, 'eʸpərn/ *n* a simple garment worn over the front part of one's clothes to keep them clean, e.g. while cooking

apt /æpt/ *adj* **1** [F +*to-v*] having a tendency to do something; likely: *Please remind me about the party; I'm apt to forget the date.* **2** exactly suitable: *an apt remark* –**aptly** *adv* –**aptness** *n* [U]

ap·ti·tude /'æptə,tuʷd, -,tyuʷd/ *n* [C;U *for*] natural ability or skill, esp. in learning: *He showed great aptitude/an aptitude for learning languages./an aptitude test* –see GENIUS (USAGE)

a·quar·i·um /ə'kweəriʸəm/ *n* **-iums** *or* **-ia** /iʸə/ **1** a glass container for fish and other water animals **2** a building (esp. in a ZOO) containing many of these

A·quar·i·us /ə'kweəriʸəs/ *n* see ZODIAC

a·quat·ic /ə'kwætɪk, ə'kwɒtɪk/ *adj* living or happening in or on water: *aquatic plants/animals/Aquatic sports include swimming and rowing.*

aq·ue·duct /'ækwə,dʌkt/ *n* a bridge, pipe, or CANAL, that carries a water supply, esp. one that is built across a valley

aq·ui·line /'ækwə,laɪn, -lɪn/ *adj* of or like an EAGLE: *An aquiline nose is one that curves like an eagle's beak.*

AR *written abbrev. said as:* Arkansas /'ɑrkən,sɔ/ (a state in the US)

Ar·ab /'ærəb/ *n* a person who speaks ARABIC, esp. one from North Africa or the **Arabian peninsula**

A·ra·bi·an /ə'reʸbiʸən/ *adj* of Arabia, esp. the PENINSULA containing Saudi Arabia and several other countries: *the Arabian desert*

Ar·a·bic /'ærəbɪk/ *adj,n* [U] (of or concerning) the language or writing of the ARABs: *Arabic literature*

Arabic nu·mer·al /ˌ···'····/ *n* any of the signs most commonly used for numbers in the English and many other alphabets (such as 1, 2, 3, 4, etc.) –compare ROMAN NUMERAL

ar·a·ble /'ærəbəl/ *adj* (of land) suitable or used for growing crops

ar·bi·trar·y /'ɑrbə,treriʸ/ *adj often derog* **1** decided by or based on chance or personal opinion rather than reason: *I didn't know anything about any of the books so my choice was just arbitrary.* **2** of power that is

uncontrolled and used without considering the wishes of others: *The arbitrary decisions of the factory owners angered the workers.* –**arbitrarily** /ˌɑrbə'trerəliʸ/ *adv* –**arbitrariness** /'ɑrbə,treriʸnɪs/ *n* [U]

ar·bi·trate /'ɑrbə,treʸt/ *v* **-trated, -trating** [I;T *between*] to act as a judge in (an argument), esp. at the request of both sides: *Someone must arbitrate (between them).* –**arbitration** /ˌɑrbə'treʸʃən/ *n* [U]: *The workers agreed to* **go to arbitration** *to settle their pay claim.* –**arbitrator** /'ɑrbə,treʸtər/ *n*

arc /ɑrk/ *n* part of a circle or any curved line: *an arc of 110°*

ar·cade /ɑr'keʸd/ *n* a covered passage, esp. one with an arched roof, often with stores on one or both sides: *a shopping arcade*

arch[1] /ɑrtʃ/ *n* **1** the top curved part over a doorway, window, bridge, etc.: *The bridge had seven arches.* **2** something with this shape, esp. the middle of the bottom of the foot

arch[2] *v* [I;T] to form (into) an arch: *The cat arched its back in anger.|The trees arched over the path.*

ar·chae·ol·o·gy, archeology /ˌɑrkiʸ'ɒlədʒiʸ/ *n* [U] the study of the buried remains of ancient times, such as houses, pots, tools, and weapons –**archaeological** /ˌɑrkiʸə'lɒdʒɪkəl/ *adj* –**archaeologically** *adv* –**archaeologist** /ˌɑrkiʸ'ɒlədʒɪst/ *n*

ar·cha·ic /ɑr'keʸɪk/ *adj* belonging to the past; no longer used

arch·bish·op /ˌɑrtʃ'bɪʃəp◂/ *n* (in some branches of the Christian church) a priest of very high rank in charge of the churches and BISHOPs (1) in a large area

arch·er /'ɑrtʃər/ *n* a person who shoots arrows from a piece of bent wood (BOW[3] (1))

arch·er·y /'ɑrtʃəriʸ/ *n* [U] the art or sport of shooting arrows, esp. at a TARGET (1)

ar·chi·pel·a·go /ˌɑrkə'pelə,goʷ/ *n* **-goes** *or* **-gos** (an area of sea containing) a group of small islands

ar·chi·tect /'ɑrkə,tekt/ *n* a person who plans new buildings and sees that they are built properly: (fig.) *Julius Caesar was the architect of the Roman Empire.*

ar·chi·tec·ture /'ɑrkə,tektʃər/ *n* [U] **1** the art and science of building, including its planning, making, and decoration **2** the style or manner of building: *the architecture of ancient Greece/of the early 19th century* –**architectural** /ˌɑrkə'tektʃərəl/ *adj* –**architecturally** *adv*

ar·chives /'ɑrkaɪvz/ *n* [P] (a place for storing) old papers, such as records, reports, and letters of a particular group, country, etc., kept esp. for historical interest

arc·tic /'ɑrktɪk, 'ɑrtɪk/ *adj,n* [*the* S] (*often cap.*) (of or concerning) the very cold most northern part of the world –compare ANTARCTIC

ar·dent /'ɑrdnt/ *adj* strongly active; eager; fierce: *an ardent supporter of the government* –**ardently** *adv*

ar·dor *AmE*||**ardour** *BrE* /'ɑrdər/ *n* [C;U] *fml* strong excitement; burning eagerness: *His political ardor led to many arguments.*

ar·du·ous /'ɑrdʒuʷəs/ *adj* needing much effort; difficult: *an arduous climb|arduous work* –**arduously** *adv* –**arduousness** *n* [U]

are /ər; *strong* ɑr/ *v present tense pl. of* BE

ar·e·a /'ɛəriʸə/ *n* **1** [C;U] the size of a flat surface measured by multiplying the length by the width: *What's the area of your garden?* –compare VOLUME (2) **2** [C] a place; a part or division of the world; REGION: *There aren't any big stores in this area (of the town).* **3** [C] a particular space or surface: *There's a parking area behind the bank.* **4** [C] a subject, specialist field, or activity: *developments in the area of language teaching*

area code /'··· ,·/ *n AmE* (in the US and Canada) three numbers used before a telephone number when making a LONG-DISTANCE telephone call: *The area code for New York City is 212.*

a·re·na /ə'riʸnə/ *n* an enclosed area used for sports, public amusements, etc.: (fig.) *The small country became the arena of war between the two big powers.*

aren't /'ɑrənt/ *v short for:* **1** are not: *They aren't here.* **2** (in questions) am not: *I'm your friend, aren't I?*

USAGE There is no natural short form of "am *I* not?" Compare: 1 (*fml*) *I am your friend, am I not?* 2 (*infml*) *I'm your friend, aren't I?*

ar·gu·a·ble /'ɑrgyuʷəbəl/ *adj* **1** [*that*] able to be supported with reasons: *It is arguable that criminals are necessary members of society.* **2** doubtful in some degree: *an arguable decision* –**arguably** *adv*

ar·gue /'ɑrgyuʷ/ *v* -**gued**, -**guing** **1** [I *with, against, about*] to disagree in words; fight with words; quarrel: *Do what you are told and don't argue (with me).|They're always arguing about money.* **2** [I;T +*that*] to provide reasons for or against (something), esp. clearly and in proper order: *He argues well.|It could be argued that sending people to the moon is a waste of money.* **3** [I;T *about, against, over*] to reason strongly in defense of one's wishes or opinions, esp. in opposition to others: *He argued her into/out of going.|She is always ready to argue about politics.*

ar·gu·ment /'ɑrgyəmənt/ *n* **1** [C] a disagreement, esp. one that is noisy; quarrel **2** [C +*that*/*for, against*] a reason given to support or disprove something: *There are many arguments against smoking.* **3** [U] the use of reason to decide something: *We should try to settle this affair by argument, not by fighting.*

ar·gu·men·ta·tive /,ɑrgyə'mɛntət̬ɪv/ *adj derog* (of a person) liking to ARGUE (1)

a·ri·a /'ɑriʸə/ *n* a song that is sung by only one person in an OPERA

ar·id /'ærɪd/ *adj* (of land or a country) having so little rain as to be very dry and unproductive: (fig.) *arid studies that produce no new ideas*

Ar·ies /'ɛəriʸz/ *n* see ZODIAC

a·rise /ə'raɪz/ *v* **arose** /ə'rowˣz/, **arisen** /ə'rɪzən/, **arising** [I] **1** to come into being or to notice; happen; appear: *Difficulties will arise as we do the work.|A strong wind arose.*

2 *old use or lit* to get up –see RISE (USAGE)

ar·is·toc·ra·cy /,ærə'stɑkrəsiʸ/ *n* -**cies** the people of the highest social class, esp. people from noble families and with titles of rank: *They are considered the aristocracy in our town.* –compare UPPER CLASS

ar·is·to·crat /ə'rɪstə,kræt/ *n* a member of an ARISTOCRACY –**aristocratic** /ə,rɪstə'kræt̬ɪk/ *adj*

a·rith·me·tic¹ /ə'rɪθmə,tɪk/ *n* [U] the science of numbers; calculation by numbers –compare MATHEMATICS

ar·ith·met·ic² /,ærɪθ'mɛt̬ɪk/ *also* -**ical**– /ɪkəl/ *adj* of or concerning ARITHMETIC –**arithmetically** *adv*

Ariz. *written abbrev. said as:* Arizona /,ærə'zowˣnə/ (a state in the US)

Ark. *written abbrev. said as:* Arkansas /'ɑrkən,sɔ/ (a state in the US)

arm¹ /ɑrm/ *n* **1** either of the two upper limbs of a human being or other animal that stands on two legs: *She carried the box under her arm.|She welcomed them* **with open arms.** (=gladly)*|They walked down the street* **arm in arm.** (=with arms joined) **2** something that is shaped like or moves like an arm: *the arm of the chair* **3** the part of a garment, such as a coat, that covers the arm **4** **keep somebody at arm's length** to keep a safe distance away; avoid being friendly with somebody –**armless** *adj*

arm² *v* [I;T *with*] to supply with, fit with, or have, weapons or armor: *I warn you that I am armed.* (=have a gun)*|The country armed (itself) in preparation for war.|*(fig.) *He was armed with many facts and figures to prove his case.* –opposite **disarm**; see also UNARMED

ar·ma·da /ɑr'mɑdə, -'meʸ-/ *n lit* a collection (FLEET) of armed ships: *The Spanish Armada sailed to England in 1588.*

arm·band /'ɑrmbænd/ *n* a band of material worn around the arm to show official position, as a sign of MOURNING, etc.

arm·chair /'ɑrmtʃɛər/ *n* a chair with supports for the arms –see illustration on page 399

arm·ful /'ɑrmfʊl/ *n* all that a person can hold in one or both arms: *She brought an armful/several armfuls of fresh flowers.*

ar·mi·stice /'ɑrməstɪs/ *n* an agreement made during a war to stop fighting, usu. for a limited period of time

ar·mor *AmE||***armour** *BrE* /'ɑrmər/ *n* [U] **1** strong protective metal or leather covering as worn formerly in battle by fighting men and their horses **2** strong protective metal covering on fighting vehicles, ships, and aircraft

ar·mored *AmE||***armoured** *BrE* /'ɑrmərd/ *adj* (having fighting vehicles) covered with or protected by armor: **an armored car**|*an armored division*

ar·mor·y *AmE||***armoury** *BrE* /'ɑrməriʸ/ *n* -**ies** a place where weapons and other instruments of war are stored

arm·pit /'ɑrm,pɪt/ *n* the hollow place under the arm at the shoulder

arms /ɑrmz/ *n* [P] **1** weapons of war **2** →COAT OF ARMS **3** **up in arms** *infml* very angry and ready to argue, quarrel, or fight: *The women are up in arms over/about their low rate of pay.*

arms race /'· ·/ *n* a struggle between unfriendly countries in which each tries to produce more and better weapons of war than the other

ar·my /'ɑrmiʸ/ *n* **-mies 1** the military forces of a country, esp. those trained to fight on land **2** any large group, esp. one that is united for some purpose: *an army of workers/ants*

a·ro·ma /ə'roʷmə/ *n* a strong usu. pleasant smell: *the aroma of fresh coffee* –**aromatic** /ˌærə'mætɪk/ *adj: Aromatic plants are often used in cooking.*

a·rose /ə'roʷz/ *v past tense of* ARISE

a·round[1] /ə'raʊnd/ *adv* [no comp.] *esp. AmE* **1** also **about** *esp. BrE–* **a** here and there: *They travel around together.* **b** somewhere near: *Is there anybody around?* **2** also **about–** a little more or less than: *around five miles/around 30 years* **3** so as to face the other way: *He turned around when he heard a noise behind him.* **4** a moving in a circle; measured in a circle: *turning around and around|a tree nine feet around* **b** on all sides: *The children gathered around to hear the story.*

around[2] *prep* **1** on all sides of: *We sat around the table.|He put a frame around the picture.* **2 a** here and there in: *They walked around the streets.|books lying around the room* **b** near to: *He lives somewhere around Los Angeles.* **3** so as to get past: *Let's go around the town, not through it.*

a·rouse /ə'raʊz/ *v* **-roused, -rousing** [T] **1** to cause to wake; ROUSE (1): *We aroused him from his deep sleep.* **2** to cause to become active: *Her movements aroused him sexually.*

ar·raign /ə'reʸn/ *v* [T *for*] *tech* to call or bring before a court of law, esp. to face a serious charge –**arraignment** *n* [C;U]

ar·range /ə'reʸndʒ/ *v* **-ranged, -ranging** [T] **1** to set in a good or pleasing order: *to arrange flowers* –see also DISARRANGE **2** [+*to-v/-ing/that/about,for,with*] to plan in advance; prepare: *I have arranged a taxi (for us).|We arranged to meet them at 10 o'clock.|I arranged that we would meet them at the station.* **3** [*for*] to set out (a piece of music) in a certain way, as for different instruments: *a piece of music arranged for the piano*

ar·range·ment /ə'reʸndʒmənt/ *n* **1** [C;U +*to-v/about, for, with*] (the act of making) an agreement or plan; something arranged: *She's in charge of all the arrangements for the wedding.|I have an arrangement with my bank by which they let me have money before I have been paid.|We made an arrangement to meet at 10.* **2** [U] the act of putting into or of being put into order: *The arrangement of the flowers only took a few minutes.* **3** [C] something that has been put in order: *a beautiful flower arrangement* **4** [C;U] (an example of) the setting out of a piece of music in a certain way, as for different instruments

ar·ray[1] /ə'reʸ/ *v* **-rayed, -raying** [T] *fml or lit* **1** to set in order: *The soldiers were arrayed on*

the opposite hill. **2** to dress, esp. finely: *arrayed for her wedding*

array[2] *n* **-rays 1** a fine show, collection, or ordered group: *a beautiful array of dress materials|The crowd was met by an array of policemen.* –compare DISARRAY **2** *lit* clothes, esp. for a special occasion: *She put on her finest array.*

ar·rears /ə'rɪərz/ *n* [P] **1** money that is owed from the past and should have been paid: *He was in arrears with the rent.|The rent was two months in arrears.* **2** work that is still waiting to be done

ar·rest[1] /ə'rɛst/ *v* [T] **1** to seize in the name of the law and usu. put in prison: *The policeman arrested the thief.* **2** *fml* to bring to an end; stop: *The doctor arrested the growth of the disease.* **3** to catch and fix (esp. somebody's attention): *an arresting statement*

arrest[2] *n* [C;U] the act of ARRESTING[1] (1) or of being arrested: *The police made several arrests.|He was quickly* **put/placed under arrest.**

ar·riv·al /ə'raɪvəl/ *n* **1** [C;U] the act of arriving: *The arrival of the bus has been delayed.|On my arrival home I was greeted by my parents.* **2** [C] a person or thing that has arrived: *The new arrival was a healthy baby girl.*

ar·rive /ə'raɪv/ *v* **-rived, -riving** [I] **1** to reach a place, esp. the end of a trip: *We arrived home late.|What time does the plane arrive in New York?|*(fig.) *Now that her books were sold in every store she felt she had arrived.* (=won success) –compare DEPART **2** to happen; come: *At last our vacation arrived.|Her baby arrived* (=was born) *yesterday.*

arrive at sthg. *v prep* [T] to reach; come to: *After many hours of talk, the committee arrived at a decision.*

ar·ro·gant /'ærəgənt/ *adj* proud and self-important in a rude way that shows no respect for other people: *an arrogant official|arrogant manners* –**arrogantly** *adv* –**arrogance** *n* [U]: *His arrogance made him unpopular.*

ar·row /'æroʷ/ *n* **1** a thin straight stick with a point at one end and feathers at the other, which is shot in fighting or sport from a long piece of bent wood (BOW[3] (1)) **2** a sign like an arrow (→) used to show direction or the position of something

ar·se·nal /'ɑrsənəl/ *n* a usu. government building where weapons and explosives are made or stored: (fig.) *The police found an arsenal of knives and guns in the murderer's house.*

ar·se·nic /'ɑrsənɪk/ *n* [U] a very poisonous chemical substance used in medicine and for killing rats

ar·son /'ɑrsən/ *n* [U] the crime of setting fire to property in order to cause destruction –**arsonist** *n: The police are still looking for the arsonist who set fire to our house.*

art[1] /ɑrt/ **1** [U] the making or expression of what is beautiful or true, e.g. in a painting **2** [U] things produced in this way: *Japanese art|modern art|The painting was a* **work of**

art. **3** [C;U] fine skill in the making or doing of anything: *The art of painting well is not easily learned.|He is good at the art of making friends.|Driving a car in New York City is quite an art!* (=needs great skill)

art² *v* thou art *old use or bibl* (when talking to one person) you are

ar·ter·y /ˈɑrtəriʸ/ *n* -ies **1** a blood vessel that carries blood from the heart to the rest of the body –compare VEIN (1) **2** a main road, railroad, river, etc. –arterial /ɑrˈtɪəriʸəl/ *adj* [A]: **Arterial blood** *is bright red.|arterial roads leading into San Francisco*

art·ful /ˈɑrtfəl/ *adj* clever; skillful, often in a bad way; CUNNING: *He's very artful and usually succeeds in getting what he wants.* –see also ARTLESS –artfully *adv* –artfulness *n* [U]

ar·thri·tis /ɑrˈθraɪtɪs/ *n* [U] a disease causing pain and swelling in the joints of the body –arthritic /ɑrˈθrɪtɪk/ *adj,n*

ar·ti·choke /ˈɑrtəˌtʃoʷk/ *n* [C;U] a plant with a leafy kind of flower that may be eaten as a vegetable –see also JERUSALEM ARTICHOKE

ar·ti·cle /ˈɑrtɪkəl/ *n* **1** a particular or separate thing or object, esp. one of a group: *I need to buy several articles of clothing.* **2** a complete piece of writing in a newspaper, magazine, etc.: *an article on new industries* **3** *tech* the words "a" or "an" (**indefinite article**) and "the" (**definite article**)

ar·tic·u·late¹ /ɑrˈtɪkyəlɪt/ *adj* **1** *apprec* expressing or able to express thoughts and feelings clearly, esp. in words: *one of the most articulate supporters of the government* **2** (of speech) having clear separate sounds or words –opposite **inarticulate** –articulately *adv* –articulateness *n* [U]

ar·tic·u·late² /ɑrˈtɪkyəˌleʸt/ *v* -lated, -lating **1** [I;T] to speak, esp. clearly and effectively: *He articulated (each word) carefully.* **2** [T *usu. pass.*] to unite by joints that allow movements: *The bones of our fingers are articulated.|In an* **articulated vehicle/truck** *the driver's car is separate from the main part but joined to it to make turning corners easier.* –articulation /ɑrˌtɪkyəˈleʸʃən/ *n* [U]

ar·ti·fact, arte- /ˈɑrtəˌfækt/ *n* anything made by man, esp. something useful

ar·ti·fice /ˈɑrtəfɪs/ *n* **1** [C] a clever trick:*The use of mirrors in a room is an artifice to make the room look larger.* **2** [U] clever skill; CUNNING

ar·ti·fi·cial /ˌɑrtəˈfɪʃəl◄/ *adj* **1** made by man; not natural: *artificial flowers|artificial silk* –compare NATURAL, MAN-MADE **2** insincere; unreal: *She welcomed me with an artificial smile.* –artificially *adv* –artificiality /ˌɑrtəfɪʃiʸˈælətiʸ/ *n* [U]

artificial res·pi·ra·tion /ˌ···· ··ʹ··, ··,···· ··ʹ··/ *n* [C;U] the attempt to make a person who is nearly dead (esp. through drowning) breathe again, as by pressing the chest, moving the arms, and blowing air into the mouth

ar·til·ler·y /ɑrˈtɪləriʸ/ *n* [U] (the part of the army that uses) large guns

ar·ti·san /ˈɑrtəzən, -sən/ *n* a skilled worker, esp. in industry

art·ist /ˈɑrtɪst/ *n* **1** a person who practices or

works in one of the FINE ARTS, esp. painting **2** →ARTISTE

ar·tiste /ɑrˈtiʸst/ also **artist–** *n* a professional singer, actor, dancer, etc.

ar·tis·tic /ɑrˈtɪstɪk/ *adj* **1** [*no comp.*] of, concerning, or typical of art or artists **2** having or showing imagination and skill in art: *He's very artistic.|an artistic flower arrangement* –artistically *adv*

art·is·try /ˈɑrtəstriʸ/ *n* [U] *apprec* inventive imagination and ability; artistic skill

art·less /ˈɑrtlɪs/ *adj* not trying to deceive; simple, almost foolish; natural: *an artless village girl* –see also ARTFUL –artlessly *adv* –artlessness *n* [U]

arts /ɑrts/ *n* [P] those subjects or fields of study that are not considered to be part of science, esp. as taught at a university: *I'm studying the arts: history, literature, and French.* –compare the SCIENCES; see also BA, MA

art·y /ˈɑrtiʸ/ *adj* -ier, -iest *often derog* making a show of being interested in art –artiness *n* [U]

AS /ˌeʸ ˈɛs/ *abbrev. for:* ASSOCIATE² (3) **of science**

as¹ /əz; *strong* æz/ *adv,prep* **1** (used in comparisons) equally; like: *He's as old as me.|She's intelligent, but her brother is just as intelligent/not as intelligent/not so intelligent.* **2** in the condition of; when considered as being: *He works as a farmer.|As a writer, she's excellent, but as a teacher she's not very good.|This is regarded as* (=thought to be) *his best film.|She was dressed as a man.* **3 I thought as much!** *infml* I thought so!

as² *conj* **1** (used in comparisons): *He's as old as I am.|She doesn't run as/so fast as she used to.* **2** in the way or manner that: *Do as I say.* **3** while; when: *He saw her as she was getting off the bus.* **4** because: *As she has no car, she can't get there easily.* –see Study Notes on page 144 **5** though: *Tired as I was, I tried to help them.* **6 as it is** in reality; in fact: *I hoped things would get better, but as it is they are getting worse.* **7 as it were** so to speak; in a certain way: *He is my best friend, my brother, as it were.* –see also so as to, such as

USAGE **As** can be used in comparisons with or without "not": *He's as old/not as old as me.|He's as old/not as old as I am.* So can be used only with "not", but it is used less frequently than **as:** *He's not so old as me/not so old as I am.* –see also LIKE³ (USAGE)

as for /ˈ· ·/ *prep* (used when starting to talk about a new subject, connected with what came before) with regard to; concerning: *You can have a bed, but as for the children, they'll have to sleep on the floor.*

as if /ˈ· ˈ/ also **as though–** *conj* **1** as it would be if (something were true): *I couldn't move my legs. It was as if they were stuck to the floor.|Why doesn't she buy us a drink? It isn't as if she had no money!* (=she has plenty of money) **2** in a way that suggests that (something is true): *He shook his head as if to say no.|We've missed the bus. It looks as if we'll have to walk.*

as of /ˈ· ·/ *prep* starting from (the time

stated): *As of today you are in charge.*

as regards /· ·'·/ *prep* **1** (esp. in business letters) on the subject of; regarding: *As regards your recent inquiry…*|*As regards (doing) that, I haven't decided yet.* **2** according to: *correctly placed as regards size and color*

as to /'· ·/ *prep* **1** (used esp. when speaking of arguments and decisions) with regard to; concerning: *As to (doing) that, I haven't decided yet.*|*He's very uncertain as to whether it's the right job for him.* **2** according to; AS regards (2): *correctly placed as to size and color*

a.s.a.p. *written abbrev. said as:* as soon as possible

as·bes·tos /æs'bɛstəs, æz-, əs-, əz-/ *n* [U] a soft gray material that is made into clothes or solid sheets that protect against fire or heat

as·cend /ə'sɛnd/ *v* [I;T] *often fml* to climb; go, come, or move from a lower to a higher level: *The stairs ascended in a graceful curve.*|*He ascended the stairs.* –opposite **descend**

as·cend·an·cy, -ency /ə'sɛndənsiʸ/ *n* [U] governing or controlling influence; power: *He slowly gained ascendancy over/in the group.*

as·cent /ə'sɛnt/ *n* **1** [C;U] the act of going, moving, or climbing up; act of rising: *We made a successful ascent of the mountain.*|(fig.) *the ascent of man from his original state to modern civilization* **2** [U] a way up; upward slope, path, etc.: *a steep ascent* –opposite **descent**

as·cer·tain /ˌæsər'teʸn/ *v* [T +*that*] *fml* to discover (the facts of something); get to know: *to ascertain the truth*|*I ascertained that he was dead.*

as·cet·ic /ə'sɛtɪk/ *n,adj* (of) a person who does not allow himself/herself bodily pleasures, esp. for religious reasons –**asceticism** /ə'sɛtəˌsɪzəm/ *n* [U]

as·cot /'æskət, 'æskɑt/ *AmE*‖**cravat** *BrE*– *n* a piece of material worn loosely around the neck by men for decoration

as·cribe sthg. **to** sbdy./sthg. /ə'skraɪb/ *v prep* **-cribed, -cribing** [T] →ATTRIBUTE TO: *He ascribes his success to skill and hard work.*

ash¹ /æʃ/ *n* [U] the soft gray powder that remains after something has been burned: *cigarétte ash*|*The house burned to ashes.*

ash² *n* [C;U] (the hard wood of) a forest tree

a·shamed /ə'ʃeʸmd/ *adj* [F +*to-v/that/of*] feeling shame, guilt, sorrow, or unwillingness: *You should be ashamed (of yourself/your behavior)!* |*He was ashamed of asking/of having asked such a simple question.* –**ashamedly** /ə'ʃeʸmɪdliʸ/ *adv*

ash·en /'æʃən/ *adj* of (the color of) ashes; pale gray: *His ashen face showed how shocked he was.*

ash·es /'æʃɪz/ *n* [P] the remains of a dead body after it has been burned (CREMATED): *Her ashes were scattered over the sea.*

a·shore /ə'ʃɔr, ə'ʃoʷr/ *adv* [F] on, onto, or to the shore or land: *We came ashore from the boat.*

ash·tray /'æʃtreʸ/ *n* a small dish for cigarette

ash –see illustration on page 399

Ash Wednes·day /ˌ ·'··/ *n* the first day of LENT

A·sian /'eʸʒən, 'eʸʃən/ also **Asiatic** /ˌeʸʒiʸ'ætɪk, ˌeʸʃiʸ-, ˌeʸziʸ-/– *n,adj* (a person) of Asia

a·side¹ /ə'saɪd/ *adv* **1** to the side; out of the way: *She stepped aside to let them pass.*|*He put his work aside for a week.* **2** aside from →APART from

aside² *n* a remark in a low voice not intended to be heard by everyone present

ask /æsk/ *v* **1** [I;T +*to-v/that/for*] to call on (a person) for an answer (to); request: *Ask him who he is/where to go/if he'd like a drink.*|*If you need any help, just ask.*|*He asked (her) a question.*|*She asked him to wake her at 6 o'clock.*|*She asked (for) his advice.* **2** [T *for,of*] to demand; expect: *He is asking a lot of money (for his house).*|*The job asks a great deal (of me).* **3** [T *for,to*] to invite: *I have asked some friends (to come) (for/to dinner).*|*I asked her in/up/down/over for a drink.*

USAGE 1 Ask is the usual verb for questions: *He **asked** a question.*|*He **asked** (them) where they lived.*|*"Where do you live?" he **asked**.*|*If you don't know, you should **ask**.* **Inquire** (also **enquire**) is more formal but has the same meaning and could be used in the 3rd and 4th of these sentences, or in the 2nd without "them": *He **inquired** where they lived.* To **demand** means to ask for (something) very strongly: *I **demand** an explanation.*|*I **demand** to know the truth!* To **question** a person means to ask him/her many questions, and to **interrogate** suggests that the person being questioned is unwilling to answer, and force may be used: *The police **questioned/interrogated** the prisoner.* **2** Compare **ask** and **ask for** (*fml* **request**): *I saw the teacher and **asked for** (*fml* **requested**) a book.*|*I **asked** the teacher to give me a book.* –see ORDER (USAGE)

ask for sthg. *v prep* [T] *infml* to behave so as to cause (something bad): *If you climb mountains in misty weather, you're (really) **asking for it/trouble**!* –see also HEAD for

a·skew /ə'skyuʷ/ *adv* [F] not straight or in the proper manner: *He wore his hat askew.*

a·sleep /ə'sliʸp/ *adj* [F] **1** sleeping: *He was sound/fast* (=completely) *asleep.* –opposite **awake** **2** (of an arm or leg) that has been in one position too long) unable to feel; NUMB **3** **fall asleep** to go into a state of sleep

as·par·a·gus /ə'spærəgəs/ *n* **-gus** [C;U] a plant whose young green stems are eaten as a vegetable

as·pect /'æspɛkt/ *n* **1** a particular side of a many-sided state of affairs, idea, plan, etc.: *You have only considered one aspect of the problem, but there are many.* **2** the direction in which a window, room, front of a building, etc., faces: *The house has a southern aspect.* **3** *lit* appearance: *Her face had an angry aspect.*

as·per·sion /ə'spɜrʒən, -ʃən/ *n fml or humor* an unkind or harmful remark: *The newspaper **cast aspersions on** his ability to* *write good plays.*

as·phalt /'æsfɔlt/ *n* [U] a black sticky material that is firm when it hardens, used for the surface of roads: *an asphalt road (surface)*

as·phyx·i·ate /æ'sfɪksiʸˌeʸt, ə-/ *v* -ated, -ating [I;T] *fml* to (cause to) be unable to breathe; esp. to (cause to) die in this way; SUFFOCATE –**asphyxiation** /æˌsfɪksiʸ'eʸʃən, ə-/ *n* [U]

as·pi·rant /'æspərənt, ə'spaɪrənt/ *n* [*for*] *fml* a person who hopes for and tries to get something important: *There are many aspirants for the job.*

as·pi·ra·tion /ˌæspə'reʸʃən/ *n* [C;U] (a) strong desire, esp. to do something great or important: *She has aspirations to become a great writer.*

as·pire /ə'spaɪər/ *v* -pired, -piring [I +*to-v/to, after*] to direct one's hopes and efforts to some important aim: *He aspired after wealth/to the leadership of the party.*

as·pi·rin /'æspərɪn/ *n* -rin *or* -rins [C;U] (a TABLET (1) of) a medicine that lessens pain and fever

ass /æs/ *n* **1** an animal like a horse but smaller and with longer ears, e.g. a donkey **2** *infml* a stupid foolish person: *He's such an ass.* **3** *AmE infml* for BUTTOCKs: *I slipped and fell on my ass.*

as·sail /ə'seʸl/ *v* [T] *fml* to attack violently: *The army assailed the town.|to be assailed with rude words/doubts/worries*

as·sail·ant /ə'seʸlənt/ *n fml* an attacker

as·sas·sin /ə'sæsən/ *n* a person who murders (a ruler or politician) usu. for political reasons or reward

as·sas·si·nate /ə'sæsəˌneʸt/ *v* -nated, -nating [T] to murder (a ruler, politician, etc.) usu. for political reasons or reward –see KILL (USAGE) –**assasination** /əˌsæsə'neʸʃən/ *n* [C;U]

as·sault¹ /ə'sɔlt/ *n* [C;U] a sudden violent attack: *He led an assault against the castle.|(fig.) an assault on* (=attempt to climb) *Mount Everest|sent to prison for assault* (=an attack on another person)

assault² *v* [T] to attack suddenly and violently

as·sem·ble /ə'sɛmbəl/ *v* -bled, -bling **1** [I;T] to gather or collect together: *If we can assemble (everybody) quickly then we can leave.|The books are assembled on the shelves in alphabetical order.* **2** [T] to put together: *to assemble cars/machines*

as·sem·bly /ə'sɛmbliʸ/ *n* -blies **1** [C;U] (the meeting of) a group of people, esp. one gathered together for a special purpose: *School assembly will begin at nine o'clock.* **2** [C *usu. cap.*] a law-making body, esp. the lower of two such bodies: *the New York State Assembly*

as·sem·bly·man /ə'sɛmbliʸmən/ **assembly-woman** /-ˌwʊmən/ *fem.*– *n* -men /mən/ *AmE* a member of an ASSEMBLY of law-makers

as·sent /ə'sɛnt/ *v* [I +*to-v/to*] *fml* to agree to a suggestion, idea, etc.: *I won't assent to go/to her plan.* –opposite **dissent** –**assent** *n*

[U]: *We're waiting for the director to give his assent.*

as·sert /ə'sɜrt/ *v* [T] **1** [+*that*] to state or declare forcefully: *She asserted (her belief) that he was not guilty.* **2** to make a claim to; show, esp. forcefully, the existence of: *He asserted his* AUTHORITY (1) *by making them be quiet.|He asserted his rights.* **3** **assert oneself: a** to act in a way that shows one's power, control, etc. **b** to behave in a way that attracts notice

as·ser·tion /ə'sɜrʃən/ *n* [C;U +*that*] (the act of making) a forceful statement or claim: *He repeated his assertions that he was not guilty.*

as·ser·tive /ə'sɜrtɪv/ *adj* forceful; showing or expressing strong opinions or claims; CONFIDENT: *You couldn't fail to notice that assertive young man.* –**assertively** *adv* –**assertiveness** *n* [U]

as·sess /ə'sɛs/ *v* [T *at*] **1** to calculate or decide on the value of (property) or an amount for some special purpose: *They assessed the house (at $90,000).|to assess the amount of damage caused by a storm* **2** to judge the quality or worth of: *The teacher assessed his students' work.* –**assessment** *n* [C;U]

as·set /'æsɛt/ *n* something such as a building or furniture, that has value and that may be sold to pay a debt: *The company's assets were being sold.|(fig.) A sense of humor is a great asset.* –compare LIABILITY (3)

as·sid·u·ous /ə'sɪdʒuʷəs/ *adj* having or showing careful and continued attention –**assiduously** *adv*

as·sign /ə'saɪn/ *v* [T] **1** [*to*] to give as a share or for use: *They have assigned me (to)a small room.* **2** [*for, to*] to appoint; decide on: *I've been assigned to wash the dishes.|We assigned a day for our meeting.*

as·sign·ment /ə'saɪnmənt/ *n* **1** [C] a job which one is given or to which one is being sent: *an assignment in India* **2** [U] the act of ASSIGNING

as·sim·i·late /ə'sɪməˌleʸt/ -lated, -lating *v* **1** [I;T *to,into*] to (cause to) become part of: *America has assimilated many people from Europe.|They assimilated easily into their new jobs.* **2** [I;T] **a** to take (food) into the body after eating; DIGEST¹ (1) **b** (of food) to be taken into the body; be digested **3** [T] to understand or use properly: *You have to assimilate the facts, not just remember them.* –**assimilation** /əˌsɪmə'leʸʃən/ *n* [U]

as·sist /ə'sɪst/ *v* [I;T *in*] to help or support: *They assisted (him) in performing the operation.|Good glasses will assist you to read.* –see HELP (USAGE)

as·sist·ance /ə'sɪstəns/ *n* [U] help; support: *Can I be* **of any assistance**?*|She came to my assistance.*

as·sist·ant /ə'sɪstənt/ *n* a person who helps another, as in a job, and is under that person's direction: *When the store is busy, she employs an assistant.|He is an assistant cook.* –see OFFICER (USAGE)

assoc. *written abbrev. said as:* **1** ASSOCIATEd¹ (1) **2** association

as·so·ci·ate¹ /ə'soʷʃiʸˌeʸt, -siʸˌeʸt/ *v* -ated,

-ating 1 [I;T *with*] to (cause to) join as friends or business partners: *He associates with criminals.* **2** [T *with*] to connect in one's mind: *What do you associate with summer?* –see also DISSOCIATE

as·so·ci·ate² /ə'soʷʃiʸɪt, -siʸɪt/ *n* **1** a person connected with another, esp. in work: *He is not a friend; he's a business associate.* **2 associate degree** a degree given after two years' study, usu. at a COMMUNITY COLLEGE or a JUNIOR COLLEGE: *associate of arts|associate of science*

as·so·ci·a·tion /ə,soʷsiʸeʸʃən, -ʃiʸeʸ-/ *n* **1** [C+*to-v/of*] a society of people joined together for a particular purpose: *an association to help blind people* **2** [U *with*] joining or being joined with somebody or something: *I am working* **in association with** *another person.* **3** [U] the act of connecting things, esp. in the mind –opposite **dissociation** (for **2,3**)

as·sort·ment /ə'sɔrtmənt/ *n* a group of mixed things or of various examples of the same type of thing; mixture: *This box contains an assortment of candy.* –**assorted** *adj*: *a bag of assorted candy*

as·sume /ə'suʷm, ə'syuʷm/ *v* **-sumed, -suming** [T] **1** [+*(that)*] to take as a fact or as true without proof; suppose: *If he's not here in five minutes, we'll assume (that) he isn't coming.|Assuming it rains tomorrow, what will we do?* **2** to begin to use or perform (sometimes without the right): *The army assumed control of the government.* **3** to pretend to have or be: *He assumes a well-informed manner but in fact knows very little.* –**assumption** /ə'sʌmpʃən/ *n* [C;U]: *our wrong assumption that we would win|his assumption of power*

as·sur·ance /ə'ʃʊərəns/ *n* **1** [U] also **self-assurance**– strong belief in one's ability and powers: *The teacher lacked assurance in front of his class.* **2** [C +*that/of*] a firm statement; promise: *an assurance that he would come* **3** [U] *BrE* for insurance: *life assurance*

as·sure /ə'ʃʊər/ *v* **-sured, -suring** [T] **1** [+*that/of*] to try to cause (someone) to believe or trust in something; promise: *I assure you that this medicine cannot harm you.* **2** [+*that/of*] to make (oneself) sure or certain: *Before going to bed, he assured himself that the door was locked.* **3** *tech* to INSURE, esp. against death –see INSURE (USAGE)

as·sured /ə'ʃʊərd/ *adj* **1** also **self-assured**– having or showing certainty of one's own abilities: *an assured manner* **2** having or showing certainty: *There is an assured demand for such goods.* –**assuredly** /ə'ʃʊərɪdliʸ/ *adv*

as·ter·isk /'æstərɪsk/ also **star**– *n* a starlike mark (*) used to call attention to something written or printed

as·ter·oid /'æstə,rɔɪd/ *n* one of many small heavenly bodies (PLANETs) between MARS and JUPITER

asth·ma /'æzmə/ *n* [U] a diseased condition which makes breathing very difficult at times –**asthmatic** /æz'mætɪk/ *adj,n*: *He is (an) asthmatic.*

as·tig·ma·tism /ə'stɪgmə,tɪzəm/ *n* [U] the inability of the eye to see properly or clearly because of its shape

as·ton·ish /ə'stanɪʃ/ *v* [T] to produce great surprise or wonder in (someone): *We were astonished to hear that he had passed his driving test.|an astonished look|an astonishing price*

as·ton·ish·ment /ə'stanɪʃmənt/ *n* [U] great surprise or wonder: **To my astonishment** *he was early.*

as·tound /ə'staʊnd/ *v* [T] to surprise very much: *She was astounded when she heard she had won.*

a·stray /ə'streʸ/ *adj,adv* [F] off the right path or way: (fig.) *The attractions of the big city soon* **led** *the young man* **astray.** (=into bad ways)|*to go astray in a calculation*

a·stride /ə'straɪd/ *adv,prep* [F] with a leg on each side (of): *He rode astride.|astride a horse*

as·trin·gent /ə'strɪndʒənt/ *adj* **1** able to tighten up the skin or stop bleeding **2** severe; bitter: *an astringent remark*

as·trol·o·gy /ə'stralədʒiʸ/ *n* [U] the art of understanding the supposed influence on events and character of the stars and PLANETs –**astrological** /,æstrə'ladʒɪkəl/ *adj* –**astrologically** *adv* –**astrologer** /ə'stralədʒər/ *n*

as·tro·naut /'æstrə,nɔt/ *n* a person who travels in a spacecraft

as·tro·nom·i·cal /,æstrə'namɪkəl/ *adj* **1** of or concerning (the study of) the stars **2** *infml* very large: *Astronomical sums of money will be needed for this plan.* – **astronomically** *adv*

as·tron·o·my /ə'stranəmiʸ/ *n* [U] the scientific study of the sun, moon, stars, etc. –**astronomer** *n*

as·tute /ə'stuʷt, ə'styuʷt/ *adj* clever and able to see quickly something that is to one's advantage –**astutely** *adv* –**astuteness** *n* [U]

a·sy·lum /ə'saɪləm/ *n* [C;U] (a place which offers) protection and shelter, esp. as given by one country to people who have left another for political reasons

at /ət; *strong* æt/ *prep* **1** (shows a point in space): *at my house|at the bottom of a hole|He stood at the door.|We arrived at the airport.* (Compare *in Tokyo, in France, an island in the Atlantic*) **2** (shows a point in time): *at 10 o'clock|at midnight|at Christmas|at the moment* (Compare *on Tuesday, on July 1st, in the morning, in 1984*) **3** (shows an intended aim or object) in the direction of: *She shot at the bird, but she missed it.* (Compare *She shot the bird.* (=she did not miss it)|*He threw a stone at me.* (= to hurt me) (Compare *He threw the ball to me.* (= he wanted me to catch it)|*He shouted at the boy.* **4** (used when one acts or feels in answer to something): *I was surprised/ amused/ pleased at* (=by) *his behavior.|I laughed at his joke.* **5** (shows that somebody does something well, badly, etc.): *He's good/bad at arranging things.|He's good/bad at football.|She's a* GENIUS (1) *at chemistry.* **6** (shows what one is doing or the state one is in): *at work|at school|at war at peace* **7**

(used to measure a cost, rate, degree, level, age, speed, etc.): *bought at (a price or cost of) 10 cents each*|*the temperature at 40°*|*to stop working at (the age of) 60*|*to drive at 50 miles an hour* **8 at a/an** as a result of only one; in only one: *to reduce prices at a stroke*|*two at a time*

ate /eɪt/ v past tense of EAT

a·the·ism /'eɪθiɪy‚ɪzəm/ n [U] disbelief in the existence of God

a·the·ist /'eɪθiɪyɪst/ n a person who does not believe in the existence of God –compare AGNOSTIC –**atheistic(al)** /‚eɪθiɪy'ɪstɪk(əl)/ adj

ath·lete /'æθliɪyt/ n a person who practices bodily exercises and games that need strength and speed (ATHLETICS)

ath·let·ic /æθ'lɛtɪk/ adj **1** of or concerning ATHLETES or ATHLETICS **2** (of people) strong in body, with plenty of muscle

ath·let·ics /æθ'lɛtɪks/ n [U] the practice of bodily exercises and of sports demanding strength and speed, such as running and jumping

at·las /'ætləs/ n a book of maps

at·mos·phere /'ætməs‚fɪər/ n **1** the mixture of gases that surrounds any heavenly body, esp. the earth **2** the air, as in a room: *a smoky atmosphere*|(fig.) *There was an unfriendly atmosphere as I went in.*

at·mos·pher·ic /‚ætməs'fɪərɪk, -'fɛrɪk◄/ adj [A] of or concerning the earth's ATMOSPHERE (1)

at·om /'æṭəm/ n the smallest piece of a simple substance (ELEMENT (1)) that still has the same qualities and can combine with other substances (to form MOLECULES): (fig.) *There's not an atom of truth in that statement.*

atom bomb /‚·· '·/ also **atomic bomb** /·‚·· '·/– n a bomb whose very powerful explosion is caused by splitting an atom and setting free its force

a·tom·ic /ə'tɑmɪk/ adj **1** of or concerning an atom or atoms **2** working on or moving by ATOMIC ENERGY: *an atomic ship* –**atomically** adv

atomic en·er·gy /·‚·· '····/ also **nuclear energy**– n [U] the powerful force that is given out when an atom is split, used to make electricity, to drive large ships, in ATOM BOMBS, etc.

a·tone /ə'town/ v **-toned, -toning** [I for] to make repayment (for some crime, etc.): *He tried to atone for his crime by returning what he had taken.* –**atonement** n [U]

a·tro·cious /ə'trowʃəs/ adj **1** very cruel, shameful, shocking, etc.: *atrocious behavior* **2** infml very bad: *an atrocious meal* –**atrociously** adv

a·troc·i·ty /ə'trɑsəṭiy/ n **-ties** (an act of) great evil, esp. cruelty: *Many atrocities happened during the war.*

at·tach /ə'tætʃ/ v [T to] to fix; fasten; join: *The picture is attached to the wall by a nail.* –see also UNATTACHED

attach sbdy. to sbdy./sthg. v prep **1** [T] to cause (oneself) to join as a member of: *He attached himself to the group of leaders of the school.* **2 be attached to** to be fond of: *I am very attached to her.*

at·tach·ment /ə'tætʃmənt/ n **1** [U to] the act of attaching or of being attached (ATTACH **to**) **2** [C] something that is fixed to something else **3** [C for, to] fondness or friendship: *I felt an attachment for him.*

at·tack¹ /ə'tæk/ v **1** [I;T] to use violence (on), esp. with weapons: *The enemy attacked (us) at night.* **2** [T] to speak or write strongly against: *The Senator was attacked by the newspapers.* **3** [T] to harm, spoil, trouble, damage, etc., esp. by a continuing action: *The insects attacked the crops.* **4** [T] to begin with eagerness: *He attacked the problems at once.* –**attacker** n

attack² n **1** [C;U] (an act of) violence intended to harm: *The city came* **under attack** *during the night.* **2** [C on] writing or words intended to hurt or damage: *an attack on government action concerning unemployment* **3** [C of] a sudden or unexpected period of (serious) illness, esp. one which tends to return: *an attack of* MALARIA|*a* HEART ATTACK

at·tain /ə'teyn/ v [T] to succeed in arriving at, esp. after effort; reach: *She attained the position of director.* – **attainable** adj –**attainment** n [C;U]

at·tempt¹ /ə'tɛmpt/ v [T +to-v/v-ing] to make an effort at; try: *I attempted to speak/ speaking but was told to be quiet.*

attempt² n [C +to-v/at, on] an effort made to do something: *We failed in our attempt (to climb the mountain).*|*An attempt on her life* (=to kill her)|*I passed the test at the second attempt.* (=the second time I tried)

at·tend /ə'tɛnd/ v **1** [T] to be present at; go to: *I'll be attending the meeting.*|*to attend school* **2** [I to] fml to give one's attention; listen: *Are you attending (to what is being said)?* **3** [I;T] to look after; serve: *I have a good doctor attending me.* **4** [T] fml to go with: *Danger attended everything he did.*

USAGE People who **attend** a play or concert are the **audience;** people who **attend** a church service are the **congregation;** people who **attend** a game, such as football, are **spectators.** But an **attendant** is someone who is doing a job: *a swimming-pool* **attendant.**

attend to sbdy./sthg. v prep [T] to direct one's efforts and interest towards: *I have an urgent matter to attend to.*

at·tend·ance /ə'tɛndəns/ n **1** [U] the act of attending: *There is a doctor* **in attendance. 2** [C;U at] the act of being present, esp. regularly: *Attendance at school is demanded by law.* **3** [S at] the number of people present: *a large attendance at the meeting*

at·tend·ant /ə'tɛndənt/ n a person who looks after a place or person: –see ATTEND (USAGE)

at·ten·tion /ə'tɛnʃən, -tʃən/ n [U] **1** the act of fixing the mind on something, esp. by watching or listening; full thought and consideration: *You should* **pay attention to** *the teacher.* –opposite **inattention 2** particular care, notice, or action: *Old cars often need a lot of attention to keep them working.* **3** at/to attention in a military position in which a soldier stands straight and still

at·ten·tive /ə'tɛntɪv/ adj taking careful

notice: *The class was very attentive and quiet.|He was very attentive to the old lady and did everything for her.* –opposite **inattentive** –**attentively** *adv* –**attentiveness** *n* [U]

at·tic /ˈætɪk/ *n* the room in a building just below the roof

at·tire /əˈtaɪər/ [U] *fml* dress; clothes: *in formal attire*

at·ti·tude /ˈætəˌtuʷd, -ˌtyuʷd/ *n* **1** a way of feeling, thinking, or behaving: *She had an unfriendly attitude.|What is your attitude towards this idea?* **2** *fml* a position of the body

at·tor·ney /əˈtɜrniʸ/ *n* **-neys** *AmE* for LAWYER

at·tract /əˈtrækt/ *v* [T] to cause to like, admire, notice, or turn towards: *She/Her attention was attracted by his smile.|Flowers attract bees.|The moon attracts the earth's seas towards itself.*

at·trac·tion /əˈtrækʃən/ *n* **1** [U] the ability to attract; act of attracting: *The idea of traveling to the moon has little attraction for me.* **2** [C] something which attracts: *The city's bright lights, theaters, movies, etc., are great attractions.*

at·trac·tive /əˈtræktɪv/ *adj* **1** having the power to attract: *The idea is very attractive.* **2** pretty or HANDSOME: *an attractive girl/young man* –opposite **unattractive**; see BEAUTIFUL (USAGE) –**attractively** *adv* –**attractiveness** *n* [U]

at·tri·bute /ˈætrəˌbyuʷt/ *n* a quality forming part of the nature of a person or thing: *Kindness is just one of his attributes.*

attribute sth. **to** sbdy./sth. /əˈtrɪbyət, -byuʷt/ *v prep* **-uted, -uting** [T] to believe (something) to be the result or work of: *Susan attributes her success to hard work/to working hard.|This song is usually attributed to J. S. Bach.* –**attribution** /ˌætrəˈbyuʷʃən/ *n* [U]

at·trib·u·tive /əˈtrɪbyətɪv/ *adj* (of an adjective, noun, or phrase) describing and coming before a noun: *In "a green hat," green is an attributive adjective.* – compare PREDICATIVE –see Study Notes on page 9 –**attributively** *adv*

at·tune sbdy./sth; **to** sth. /əˈtuʷn, əˈtyuʷn/ *v prep* **-tuned, -tuning** [T *usu. pass.*] to cause to become used to or ready for: *I'm not really attuned to his way of thinking.*

au·burn /ˈɔbərn/ *adj,n* [U] (esp. of hair) reddish-brown

auc·tion¹ /ˈɔkʃən/ also **sale**– *n* a public meeting to sell goods to the person who offers the most money: *a furniture auction|I plan to sell my house by auction.*

auction² *v* [T *off*] to sell by AUCTION: *I'm going to auction off my house.*

auc·tion·eer /ˌɔkʃəˈnɪər/ *n* a person who is in charge of an AUCTION

au·da·cious /ɔˈdeʸʃəs/ *adj* **1** (foolishly) daring; brave **2** daringly impolite; CHEEKY –**audaciously** *adv*

au·dac·i·ty /ɔˈdæsətiʸ/ *n* [U] daring, boldness, or daring rudeness

au·di·ble /ˈɔdəbəl/ *adj* able to be heard –opposite **inaudible** –**audibility** /ˌɔdəˈbɪlətiʸ/ *n* –**audibly** /ˈɔdəbliʸ/ *adv*

au·di·ence /ˈɔdiʸəns/ *n* **1** the people listening to or watching a performance, speech, television show, etc.: *The audience was very excited by the show.* –see ATTEND (USAGE) **2** a formal meeting between somebody powerful and somebody less important: *an audience with the Pope*

au·di·o /ˈɔdiʸˌoʷ/ *adj* [A] connected with or used in the broadcasting or receiving of sound radio signals –compare VIDEO¹ (1)

audio-vis·u·al /ˌ··· ˈ···◄/ *adj* [no comp.] of, for, or concerning both sight and hearing: *The school's audio-visual department has lots of films and records.*

au·dit /ˈɔdɪt/ *v* [T] to make an official examination of (the accounts) of a business, etc., usu. done once each year. –**audit** *n*: *The yearly audit takes place each December.* –**auditor** *n*

au·di·tion¹ /ɔˈdɪʃən/ *n* a test performance requested of a singer, actor, etc., by the people from whom he/she hopes to get employment

audition² *v* [I;T] to give or cause (someone) to give an AUDITION

au·di·to·ri·um /ˌɔdəˈtɔriʸəm, -ˈtoʷr-/ *n* the space in a theater, hall, etc., where people sit when listening to or watching a performance

aug·ment /ɔgˈmɛnt/ *v* [I;T] *fml* to (cause to) become bigger, more valuable, better, etc.: *He augments his income by working in his free time.*

au·gur /ˈɔgər/ *v* **augur well/ill (for)** also **bode well/ill for**– *lit* to be a sign of good things/bad things in the future (for): *This rain augurs well for the farmers.*

au·gust /ɔˈgʌst/ *adj lit* causing feelings of great respect; noble and grand

Au·gust /ˈɔgəst/ also **Aug.** *written abbrev.*– *n* the eighth month of the year

aunt /ænt, ɑnt/ also (*infml*) **auntie, aunty** /ˈæntiʸ, ˈɑntiʸ/– *n* [A] the sister of one's father or mother or the wife of one's uncle: *Hello, Aunt Ruby!* –see illustration on page 247

au pair /ˌoʷ ˈpɛər/ *n French* a young foreigner, esp. a girl (an **au pair girl**), who lives with a family in return for doing light work in the house, usu. to learn the language

au·ra /ˈɔrə/ *n* an effect or feeling that seems to surround and come from a person or place: *an aura of decay in the empty village*

au·ral /ˈɔrəl/ *adj tech* of or received through hearing

aus·pic·es /ˈɔspəsɪz, -ˌsiʸz/ *n* [P] *fml* help, support, and favor: *This concert has been arranged* **under the auspices of** *the President.*

aus·pi·cious /ɔˈspɪʃəs/ *adj fml* giving, promising, or showing signs of future success –opposite **inauspicious** –**auspiciously** *adv*: *The year began auspiciously with good trade figures for January.*

aus·tere /ɔˈstɪər/ *adj* **1** lacking comfort; hard: *We led an austere life in the mountains.* **2** self-controlled; serious: *an austere person/manner|an austere style of painting* –**austerely** *adv* –**austerity** /ɔˈstɛrətiʸ/ *n* **-ties** [C;U]

au·then·tic /ɔˈθɛntɪk/ *adj* known to have been made, painted, written, etc., by the person who is claimed to have done it; GEN-

UINE (1) **–authentically** adv **–authenticity** /ˌɔːθenˈtɪsəti, ˌɒθən-/ n [U]

au·then·ti·cate /ɔːˈθentɪˌkeɪt/ v **-cated, -cating** [T] to prove (something) to be AUTHENTIC: To everyone's surprise, the painting was authenticated as a Rembrandt. **–authentication** /ɔˌθentɪˈkeɪʃən/ n [C;U]

au·thor /ˈɔːθər/ **authoress** /ˈɔːθərɪs/ fem. sometimes derog.– n the writer of a book, newspaper article, play, poem, etc.

au·thor·i·tar·i·an /ɔˌθɒrəˈteəriən, əˌθɒr-/ adj,n (a person) favoring or demanding obedience to rules and laws whether or not they are right: Don't be so authoritarian! You can't order people around like that!/ authoritarian government **–authoritarianism** n [U]

au·thor·i·ta·tive /əˈθɒrəˌteɪtɪv, əˈθɑr-/ adj **1** having or showing AUTHORITY; demanding respect or obedience: an authoritative voice **2** able to be trusted: We want a dictionary that will be an authoritative record of modern English. –compare DEFINITIVE **–authoritatively** adv

au·thor·i·ty /əˈθɒrəti, əˈθɑr-/ n **-ties 1** [C;U] (a person or group with) the ability, power, or right, to control and command: Who is in authority here?/What authority do you have for entering this house?/The government is the highest authority in the country./The authorities at city hall are slow to deal with complaints. **2** [U] power to influence: Although she has no official position in the party, she has a lot of authority. **3** [C] a person, book, etc., whose knowledge or information is dependable, good, and respected: He is an authority on plant diseases.

au·thor·ize‖also **-ise** BrE /ˈɔːθəˌraɪz/ v **-ized, -izing** [T] to give permission to or for: I authorized Mr. Jones to act for me while I was away./I authorized the payment of this bill. **–authorization** /ˌɔːθərəˈzeɪʃən/ n [C;U]

au·to·bi·o·graph·i·cal /ˌɔːtəˌbaɪəˈɡræfɪkəl/ also **autobiographic** /-ˈɡræfɪk/– adj of or concerning the facts of one's own life, esp. as written in a book **–autobiographically** adv

au·to·bi·og·ra·phy /ˌɔːtəbaɪˈɒɡrəfi/ n **-phies** a book written by oneself about one's own life –see also BIOGRAPHY

au·toc·ra·cy /ɔːˈtɒkrəsi/ n **-cies** [C;U] rule by one person with unlimited power

au·to·crat /ˈɔːtəˌkræt/ n **1** a ruler with unlimited power **2** a person who orders things to be done without considering the wishes of others **–autocratic** /ˌɔːtəˈkrætɪk/ adj **–autocratically** adv

au·to·graph¹ /ˈɔːtəˌɡræf/ n a person's name in his/her own writing (SIGNATURE), esp. the signature of someone famous: The little boys asked the football player for his autograph.

autograph² v [T] to sign (a letter, statement, book, etc.) with one's own name: I'll autograph this book for you./an autographed copy of a book

au·to·mate /ˈɔːtəˌmeɪt/ v **-mated, -mating** [I;T] to make (something) work by machinery and without the work of people

au·to·mat·ic /ˌɔːtəˈmætɪk◀/ adj **1** (esp. of a machine) able to work or move by itself without needing the operation of a person: The heating system here has an automatic temperature control. **2** done without thought, esp. as a habit: The movements needed to ride a bicycle soon become automatic. **3** certain to happen: You will get an automatic increase in pay every year. **–automatically** adv

au·to·ma·tion /ˌɔːtəˈmeɪʃən/ n [U] the use of machines that need little or no human control, esp. in place of workers

au·to·mo·bile /ˌɔːtəməˈbiːl, ˈɔːtəməˌbiːl/ n AmE fml for car: The automobile industry is doing well this year.

au·ton·o·mous /ɔːˈtɒnəməs/ adj governing itself: an autonomous country/REGION **–autonomously** adv

au·ton·o·my /ɔːˈtɒnəmi/ n [U] the condition of self-government, esp. of an area or group within a country

au·top·sy /ˈɔːˌtɒpsi/ n **-sies** →POSTMORTEM

au·tumn /ˈɔːtəm/ n [C;U] →FALL **–autumnal** /ɔːˈtʌmnəl/ adj

aux·il·ia·ry /ɔːɡˈzɪljəri, -ˈzɪləri/ adj offering or giving help; adding support: auxiliary workers/machinery **–auxiliary** n **-ries**

auxiliary verb /·,··· '·/ n tech a verb that goes with another verb to show person, tense, etc. (such as am, didn't, and have in "I am running," "I didn't climb," "they have heard")

av. written abbrev. said as: AVERAGE

a·vail /əˈveɪl/ n [U] lit profit; advantage; use: We tried and tried, but it was all of/to no avail; we failed.

a·vail·a·ble /əˈveɪləbəl/ adj able to be gotten, obtained, used, seen, etc.: I'm sorry, sir, those shoes are not available in your size./The doctor is (not) available now. –opposite **unavailable** **–availability** /əˌveɪləˈbɪləti/ n [U]

avail sbdy. **of** sthg. v prep [T] fml to give (oneself) the advantage of: You should avail yourself of every chance to improve your English.

av·a·lanche /ˈævəˌlæntʃ/ n a large mass of snow and ice crashing down the side of a mountain: (fig.) an avalanche of letters

a·vant-garde /ˌævɑnt ˈɡɑrd, ˌæ-◀/ adj French being, or produced by, one of the people who produce the newest ideas, esp. in the arts: avant-garde painters/painting

av·a·rice /ˈævərɪs/ n [U] fml too great eagerness and desire to get or keep wealth; GREED **–avaricious** /ˌævəˈrɪʃəs/ adj

a·venge /əˈvendʒ/ v **-venged, -venging** [T on,upon] esp. lit to get satisfaction for (a wrong) done to (someone) by punishing those who did it: They avenged his death by burning the village. –see REVENGE (USAGE) **–avenger** n

av·e·nue /ˈævəˌnyuː, -ˌnuː/ also **Ave.** written abbrev.– n (part of the name of) a wide street in a town: (fig.) They explored every avenue (=tried every possible way) but could not answer the question./5th Avenue

av·er·age¹ /ˈævərɪdʒ/ n **1** [C] the amount found by adding together several quantities and then dividing by the number of quantities: *The average of 3, 8, and 10 is 7.* **2** [C;U] a level or standard regarded as usual or ordinary: *He is* **above/below average** *in his lessons.*|*On the average we receive five letters each day.* –**average** *adj* [*no comp.*]: *What is the average rainfall for July?*|*There was nothing special about it. It was only average.* –see Study Notes on page 550

average² *v* **-aged, -aging** **1** to do, get, or come to an average: *My mail averages 20 letters a day.* **2** [T] to calculate the average of (figures)

average out *v adv* [I] *infml* to come to an average or ordinary level or standard, esp. after being higher or lower: *The good things and bad things in life average out in the end, don't they?*

a·verse /ə'vɜrs/ *adj* [F *to*] *fml or humor* opposed: *I am not averse to a good meal.* –compare ADVERSE

a·ver·sion /ə'vɜrʒən,-ʃən/ *n* [C;U *to*] (an object of) strong dislike; hatred: *She* **has an aversion** *to cats.*|*Cats are an aversion of hers.*

a·vert /ə'vɜrt/ *v* [T] **1** to prevent happening; avoid: *Accidents can be averted by careful driving.* **2** [*from*] *fml* to turn away (one's eyes, thoughts, etc.)

a·vi·ar·y /'eʸviʸˌeriʸ/ *n* **-ies** a large cage or enclosure for keeping birds in

a·vi·a·tion /ˌeʸviʸ'eʸʃən/ *n* [U] **1** the science or practice of the flight of aircraft **2** the aircraft industry

a·vi·a·tor /'eʸviʸˌeʸṭər/ *n old use* the pilot of an aircraft

av·id /'ævɪd/ *adj* [*for*] eager; keen: *an avid reader*|*He is avid for praise.* –**avidly** *adv*

av·o·ca·do /ˌævə'kɑdoʷ, ˌɑ-/ *n* **-dos** *or* **-does** a green tropical fruit with a large stone and smooth oily flesh

a·void /ə'vɔɪd/ *v* [T +*v-ing*] to miss or keep away from, esp. on purpose: *She avoided answering my questions.*|*To avoid the center of town, turn left here.* –**avoidable** *adj* –**avoidance** *n* [U]

av·oir·du·pois /ˌævərdə'pɔɪz/ *n,adj* [U] the system of weights in which the standard measures are the OUNCE (1), pound, and TON (1): *16 ounces avoirdupois* –compare METRIC

a·vow /ə'vaʊ/ *v* [T +*that*] *fml* to state openly; admit: *He avowed himself to be a supporter of the new group.* –**avowal** *n* [C;U]

a·vowed /ə'vaʊd/ *adj* [A] openly declared or admitted: *an avowed supporter of the government* –**avowedly** /ə'vaʊɪdliʸ/ *adv*

a·wait /ə'weʸt/ *v* [T] *fml* to wait for: *I am awaiting your reply.*|*A warm welcome awaits you.*

a·wake¹ /ə'weʸk/ *adj* [F] not asleep; having woken: *The children are still* **wide awake.** (=not at all sleepy)|(fig.) *He is* **awake to** (=conscious of) *the problem.*

awake² *also* **awaken** /ə'weʸkən/– *v* **awoke** /ə'woʷk/ *or* **awaked, awaked** *or* **awoken** /ə'woʷkən/, **awaking** [I;T +*to-v/to*] (to cause) to stop sleeping; wake: *The noise awoke me.*|(fig.) *Old memories awoke in her when she read the letter.*|(fig.) *Our people* **awake to/must be awakened to** *the danger.*

a·wak·en·ing /ə'weʸkənɪŋ/ *n* **1** the act of wak-

ing from sleep **2 rude awakening** a sudden consciousness of an unpleasant state of affairs: *We had all been enjoying ourselves, but the rude awakening came when our company started to lose money.*

a·ward¹ /ə'wɔrd/ *v* [T] to give, esp. as the result of an official decision: *He was awarded the prize for being the fastest runner.*|*The judge awarded a large sum of money to those hurt by the explosion.*

award² *n* something, esp. a prize or money, given as the result of an official decision: *an award of $5,000 to those hurt in the explosion*|*The award went to the youngest runner.*

a·ware /ə'wɛər/ *adj* [+*that/of*] having knowledge or understanding: *Are you aware of the difficulty/that there is a difficulty?*|*I'm aware (of) how you must feel.*|*She is politically/artistically aware.* –opposite **unaware** –**awareness** *n* [U]

a·wash /ə'wɑʃ, ə'wɔʃ/ *adj* [F] level with the water and washed over by the waves: *The river overflowed till the streets were awash.*

a·way¹ /ə'weʸ/ *adv* **1** [F] from here; from there; in another direction: *Go away!*|*He swam away from the ship.*|*They're away on vacation.*|*He lives far away.* **2** [after *n*] at a stated distance: *He lives three miles away.* **3** in a safe place: *He put the food away (in the cupboard).* **4** so as to be all gone or used up: *The sounds died away.*|*The water boiled away.*|*He gave all his money away.*|*He worked his life away.* **5** all the time; continuously: *They worked away all day.* **6 right away** *AmE*‖*also* **straight away** *BrE* without delay: *I'll do it right away.*

away² *adj* [A] (of a sporting event) played at the place, sports field, etc., of one's opponent: *an away game* –compare HOME³ (4)

awe /ɔ/ *n* [U] a feeling of respect mixed with fear and wonder: *He always stood in awe of his father.*

awe-in·spir·ing /'· ·ˌ··/ *adj* causing feelings of AWE

awe·some /'ɔsəm/ *adj* expressing or causing feelings of AWE (esp. when fear is present): *an awesome account of the terrors of war*

awe·struck /'ɔstrʌk/ *also* **awestricken** /'ɔˌstrɪkən/– *adj* filled with, made silent by, or showing AWE: *We sat in awestruck silence after hearing the truth at last.*

aw·ful /'ɔfəl/ *adj* **1** terrible; shocking: *The pain was awful.* **2** *infml* very bad; very great: *awful weather*|*an awful waste*

aw·ful·ly /'ɔfəliʸ/ *adv infml* very: *awfully cold*|*awfully nice* –see Study Notes on page 363

a·while /ə'hwaɪl, ə'waɪl/ *adv esp. lit* for a short time: *We rested awhile at the side of the road.*

awk·ward /'ɔkwərd/ *adj* **1** lacking skill in moving the body or parts of the body easily; CLUMSY (1): *The child was awkward with a knife and fork.* **2** not well made for use; causing difficulty: *an awkward tool to use* **3** difficult to deal with; inconvenient; EMBARRASSING: *Our visitors came at an awkward time.*|*a long awkward silence after their quarrel* –**awkwardly** *adv* –**awkwardness** *n* [U]

awn·ing /'ɔnɪŋ/ *n* a (CANVAS) covering, used

to protect shop windows, ships' DECKs, etc., from sun or rain

a·woke /əˈwoᵘk/ v past tense of AWAKE

a·wok·en /əˈwoᵘkən/ v past participle of AWAKE

ax¹ AmE‖also **axe** esp. BrE /æks/ n **axes** /ˈæksɪz/ a tool with a heavy metal blade on the end of a long handle, used to cut down trees, etc.

ax² AmE‖also **axe** esp. BrE v **axed, axing** [T] infml to remove suddenly and usu. without warning from a job, a list of plans for completion, etc.: We were going to build a new school, but the plan was axed by the government.

ax·i·om /ˈæksiᵞəm/ n a statement that is generally accepted as true —**axiomatic** /ˌæksiᵞəˈmætɪk/ adj

ax·is /ˈæksɪs/ n **axes** /ˈæksiᵞz/ the usu. imaginary line, around which a spinning body moves

ax·le /ˈæksəl/ n a bar with a wheel on either end, around which the wheels turn or which turns with the wheels, as on a car

aye /aɪ/ adv dial or lit (used esp. when voting or by sailors) yes: All in favor say "aye."‖(Aye, aye, sir.

AZ written abbrev. said as: Arizona /ˌærəˈzoᵘnə/ (a state in the US)

az·ure /ˈæʒər/ adj,n [U] bright blue, as of the sky

B, b

B, b /biᵞ/ **B's, b's** or **Bs, bs** the second letter of the English alphabet

b. written abbrev. said as: born: b. 1885

BA /biᵞ ˈeᵞ/ also **AB**— abbrev. for: Bachelor of Arts; (a title for someone who has) a first university degree in an ARTS subject: Susan Potter, BA‖He has a BA. –compare BS

baa /bɑ, bæ/ v **baaed, baaing** [I] to make the sound that a sheep or lamb makes –**baa** n

bab·ble /ˈbæbəl/ v **-bled, -bling** 1 [I;T] to talk quickly and foolishly or in a way that is hard to understand: During his fever he babbled without stopping.‖He babbled the secret (out) to his friends. 2 [I] to make continuous sounds like a stream: a babbling stream‖The baby babbled (away/on) for hours. –compare BURBLE –**babble** n [S;U]: a babble of voices‖the babble of running water

babe /beᵞb/ n 1 lit a baby 2 AmE infml a (usu. young) woman: "Hi, babe."

USAGE The use of **babe** or **baby** to speak about a woman is considered offensive by many people.

ba·boon /bæˈbuᵂn/ n a large doglike monkey of Africa or South Asia

ba·by /ˈbeᵞbiᵞ/ n **-bies** 1 [A;C] a very young child, esp. one who has not learned to speak –see CHILD (USAGE) 2 [A;C] a very young animal or bird: a baby monkey 3 [A;C] the youngest or smallest of a group: My brother John lives in Montreal. He's the baby of our family. 4 [C] AmE infml a person, esp. a girl or woman –see BABE (USAGE)

baby car·riage /ˈ·· ˌ·/ AmE‖also **pram** esp. BrE– n a four-wheeled carriage, pushed by hand, in which a baby can be taken around

ba·by·hood /ˈbeᵞbiᵞˌhud/ n [U] the period of time when one is a baby

ba·by·ish /ˈbeᵞbiᵞɪʃ/ derog like a baby: They told him it was babyish to cry

baby-sit /ˈ·· ˌ·/ v **-sat, -sitting** [I for] to take care of children while their parents are out –**baby-sitter** n

bach·e·lor /ˈbætʃələr/ n 1 an unmarried man –compare SPINSTER 2 a person who holds a first university degree, such as **Bachelor of**

Science (BS)/Arts (BA)

back¹ /bæk/ n 1 [C] the part of a person's or animal's body that is the side opposite the chest and goes from the neck to the bottom of the SPINE or the tail: The woman was carrying the baby on her back.‖You'll make your back ache if you carry those heavy buckets.‖If we really put our back into the job (=work very hard at it) we can finish it today.‖(fig.)He's always been kind to me. I can't just turn my back on (=desert) him now that he's ill and poor. 2 [the S] the part opposite the front: The back of the house looks out onto the river.‖You can't hear the speaker from the back of the hall.‖He feels safer sitting in the back of the car than in the front.‖There's a lot of useful information at the back of the dictionary. 3 [C] the part of a chair that one leans against when sitting 4 **be glad to see the back of someone** infml to be glad when someone or something goes away 5 **behind someone's back** unknown to the person concerned: This decision was made behind my back. 6 **have/with one's back to/against the wall** infml (to be) in the greatest possible difficulties, so that one must try very hard: At the end of the war, the country had its back to the wall, but now things are improving 7 **on/off someone's back** causing (or not causing) someone annoyance: The electricity company's on my back because I haven't paid my bill.‖I wish they'd get off my back! (=stop annoying me) 8 **put someone's back up** infml to annoy someone 9 **in back of** AmE at the back of: a room in back of the store 10 **back of beyond** a very distant place: They live on a farm somewhere in the back of beyond. –**backless** adj

back² adv 1 where someone or something was before: Put the book back on the shelf when you're finished with it.‖Back in Nigeria (where I come from) we used to play a lot of tennis.‖She came back to get the basket which she'd left behind. 2 towards or at the back; away from the front: She tied her hair back.|*Sit back so you can fasten your seat belt.* **3** away from the speaker: *Stand back! That dog bites.* **4** towards or in an earlier time: *We met him three years back/back in 1968.*|*to put the clock back* (=so that it shows an earlier time) **5** in return; in reply: *Call me back when you know the answer.*

back³ *adj* [A] **1** at the back: *the back door/back yard* **2** (of money) owed from an earlier time: *back pay/rent*

back⁴ *v* **1** [I;T] to (cause to) go backwards: *The car backed through the gate.*|*She backed the car through the gate.*|*The dog* **backed away** *as the man raised his whip.* **2** [T *up*] to support and encourage, often with money **3** [T] to put money on the success of in a race or competition; BET on: *The horse I backed came in last, so I lost my money.* **4** [T *with*] to put material on the inside of, as a LINING: *a dress backed with silk*

back down‖also **back off** *AmE*– *v adv* [I] to yield in argument, opinion, or claim; admit that one was wrong: *I saw that she was right, so I had to back down.*

back onto sthg. *v prep* [T] (of a place or building) to be near to at the back: *The house backs onto the river.*

back out *v adv* [I *from, of*] to fail to fulfill (a promise, contract, etc.): *I hope I can depend on you not to back out at the last moment.*

back sbdy./sthg. up *v adv* [T] to support: *The policeman wouldn't have believed me if you hadn't backed me up.* –see also BACKUP

back·bit·ing /ˈbækˌbaɪtɪŋ/ *n* [U] *derog* unkind talk about someone who is absent: *I didn't enjoy working there. There was too much backbiting.*

back·bone /ˈbækboʷn/ *n* **1** [C] →SPINE (1) **2** [S] the main support of a group, association, plan, etc.: *The small farmer is the backbone of this country!* **3** [U] firmness of mind; strength of character: *"No backbone," said the old man. "That's the trouble with young people today!"*

back·break·ing /ˈbækˌbreʸkɪŋ/ *adj* (of work) very hard to do: *a backbreaking job/load*

back·date /ˌbækˈdeʸt/ *v* **-dated, -dating** [T] to make effective from an earlier date: *The increase in pay agreed to in June will be backdated to January.* –see also POSTDATE

back·drop /ˈbækdrɑp/ *n* →BACKGROUND (2): *The events of the 1930's provided the backdrop for the movie.*

back·er /ˈbækər/ *n* someone who supports a plan, a political party, etc., with money

back·fire /ˈbækfaɪər/ *v* **-fired, -firing** [I] **1** (of a car, etc.) to make a loud noise as a result of an explosion in the engine which comes too soon **2** to have an effect opposite to the effect intended: *His plan to get rich backfired (on him), and he lost all his money.*

back·gam·mon /ˈbækˌgæmən/ *n* [U] a game for two players, using round wooden pieces and DICE on a special board

back·ground /ˈbækgraʊnd/ *n* **1** the scenery or ground behind the main object or event: *This is a picture of my house. In the background you can see the mountains.*|*She has a lot of power, but likes to remain in the*

background. –see also FOREGROUND **2** the conditions existing when something happens or happened: *The election took place against a background of widespread unemployment.*|*I'll need a little more background (information) before I can help you.* **3** a person's family, experience, and education: *a young man of excellent background*

back·hand /ˈbækhænd/ *n* (the ability to make) a stroke (as in tennis) with the back of the hand turned in the direction of movement: *He has an excellent backhand.* –see also FOREHAND

back·hand·ed /ˈbækˌhændɪd/ *adj, adv* **1** using or made with a BACKHAND **2** using, made, or done with the back of the hand: *He struck the man a backhanded blow.* **3 backhanded compliment** a remark that might cause either pleasure or displeasure: *He said my face was very unusual, which was a backhanded compliment.*

back·ing /ˈbækɪŋ/ *n* **1** [U] help or support, esp. from money: *The plan has plenty of backing and will probably succeed.* **2** [C;U] something that is used to make the back of an object: *(a) backing of cardboard* **3** [C] (esp. in popular music) the sound made by the instruments that support the main singer or instrumentalist

back is·sue /ˌ· ˈ··/ also **back number**– *n* a newspaper, magazine, etc., earlier than the most recent one

back·lash /ˈbæklæʃ/ *n* **1** a sudden violent backward movement **2** a strong but usu. delayed feeling by many people against a growing belief or practice, esp. against a political or social development

back·log /ˈbæklɔg, -lɑg/ *n* [C *usu. sing.*] a group of things to be done that were not done at the proper time: *After his vacation, he had a big backlog of work.*

back·pack /ˈbækpæk/ *n AmE* a kind of KNAPSACK carried on one's back, usu. supported by a light metal frame, used esp. by climbers and walkers

back·ped·al /ˈbækˌpɛdl/ *v* **-l-** *AmE*‖**-ll-** *BrE* **1** to PEDAL backwards, as on a bicycle **2** also **back track**– *infml* to take back a statement; undo something that has been done

back seat /ˌ· ˈ·◄/ *n* **1** [C] a seat at the back of a car **2** [S] a less important position: *She won't* **take a back seat** *to anyone.*

back·side /ˈbæksaɪd/ *n infml* the part of the body on which one sits

back street /ˌ· ˈ·◄/ *n* a street away from the main streets, esp. in a poor area of a town

back·stroke /ˈbækstroʷk/ *n* [S;U] a swimming stroke done on one's back

back talk /ˈ· ·/ *n* [U] *AmE infml* rude talk in reply to someone: *Listen to me carefully, and I don't want any back talk!*

back·track /ˈbæktræk/ *v* [I] **1** to go back over the same path **2** →BACKPEDAL (2): *The government is backtracking from its more expensive plans.*

back·up /ˈbækʌp/ *n* a thing or person ready to be used in place of or to help another

back·ward /ˈbækwərd/ *adj* **1** [*no comp.*] directed towards the back, the beginning, or the past: *a backward look* **2** late in development: *Some backward parts of the country do not have any electricity.|a backward child* –see also FORWARD[1] –**backwardly** *adv* –**backwardness** *n* [U]

back·wards /'bækwərdz/ also **backward** *AmE*– *adv* **1** towards the back, the beginning, or the past: *He looked backwards.|Can you say the alphabet backwards?* (=from Z to A) **2** with the back part in front: *to walk backwards|Your hat is on backwards.* **3** **backwards and forwards** first in one direction and then in the opposite direction **4** **know something backwards and forwards** to know something perfectly: *All the actors know the play backwards and forwards.* –see also FORWARD[2]

back·wa·ter /'bæk,wɔtər, -,wɑtər/ *n* **1** a part of a river where the water does not move **2** a place not influenced by outside events or new ideas: *There aren't any good stores in this town. It's just a backwater.*

back·woods /,bæk'wʊdz◀/ *n* [U +*sing./pl. v*] (esp. in North America) uncleared land far from towns

back·yard /,bæk'yɑrd◀/ *n AmE* a yard behind a house, usu. covered with grass: *The children are playing in the backyard.*

ba·con /'beykən/ *n* [U] salted or smoked meat from the back or sides of a pig

bac·te·ri·a /bæk'tɪəriə/ *n* [P] very small living things (related to plants), some of which cause disease. They exist in water, soil, air, plants, and the bodies of people and animals –compare GERM (1), VIRUS

bad /bæd/ *adj* **worse** /wɜrs/, **worst** /wɜrst/ **1** not good: *a very bad performance* (=not of acceptable quality)|*The recent rain has had a bad* (=unfavorable) *effect on the crops.|This fish has **gone bad**.* (=has become unfit to eat)|*He was sent to bed without any supper because of his bad behavior.|The game was stopped because of bad light.* (=because it was too dark)|*Smoking is bad for you|your health.|bad* (=incorrect) *grammar|I felt bad* (=ashamed or sorry) *about not being able to come last night.|I have some bad news for you, I'm afraid.|My leg's bad again.* (=is hurting)|*I'm **bad at** addition.* (=can't do it very well) **2** serious; severe: *a bad cold |a bad defeat* **3** **bad debt** a debt that is unlikely to be paid **4** **have/get a bad name** to lose or have lost people's respect: *That kind of car has a bad name among drivers.* **5** **in a bad way** very ill or in serious trouble **6** (**It's/That's**) **too bad** *infml* I'm sorry: *Too bad you couldn't come last night.* **7 not** (**so**) **bad** *infml* really rather good/well –**badness** *n* [U]

bade /bæd, beyd/ *v past tense and participle of* BID[1]

badge /bædʒ/ *n* a piece of metal or other material worn to show a person's employment, rank, membership of a group, etc.

badg·er[1] /'bædʒər/ *n* -**ger**, -**gers** an animal which has black and white fur, lives in holes in the ground, and is active at night

badger[2] *v* [T] to ask again and again; PESTER: *The children badgered me into taking them to the movies.*

bad·ly /'bædliy/ *adv* **1** in a bad manner: *badly made clothes|to play badly* –opposite **well 2** a great deal; very much: *They want help badly.|He is badly in need of a haircut.*

badly-off /,·· '·/ ‖also **bad-off** /,· '·/ *AmE*– *adj* **worse-off**, **worst-off** [F] poor –opposite **well-off** –see also OFF[1] (6)

bad·min·ton /'bæd,mɪntn/ *n* [U] a tennis-like game played by two or four people who hit a small feathered object (SHUTTLECOCK) over a high net

baf·fle /'bæfəl/ *v* -**fled**, -**fling** [T] to confuse so much that effective action is impossible: *The question baffled me completely and I couldn't answer it.* –**bafflement** *n* –**baffling** *adj* [U]: *a baffling question*

bag[1] /bæg/ *n* **1** a container made of cloth, paper, leather, etc., opening at the top: *a shopping bag* –see illustration on page 683 **2** also **bagful** /'bægful/– the amount held in a bag **3** **in the bag** *infml* certain to be won, gained, etc.: *We're sure to win. The game is in the bag.*

bag[2] *v* -**gg**- **1** [T] to put (material or objects in large quantities) into a bag or bags **2** *infml* to kill or catch (animals or birds): *We bagged a rabbit.*

bag·gage /'bægɪdʒ/ *AmE*‖also **luggage**– *n* [U] all the bags and other containers with which a person travels –see illustration on page 17

baggage room /'·· ,·/ *AmE*‖**left luggage office** *BrE*– *n* a place, esp. in a station, where bags can be left for a certain period, to be picked up later

bag·gy /'bægiy/ *adj* -**gier**, -**giest** *infml* hanging in loose folds; not tight: *His pants were baggy at the knees.*

bag·pipes /'bægpaɪps/ *n* [P] a musical instrument in which air stored in a bag is forced out through pipes to produce the sound: *to play the bagpipes|bagpipe music*

bah /bɑ, bæ/ *interj* (shows a low opinion of someone or something)

bail[1] /beyl/ *n v* [U] **1** money left with a court of law so that a prisoner may be set free until he/she is tried **2** **stand/go bail for someone** to pay money so that someone may be set free in this way BAIL OUT

bail·iff /'beylɪf/ *n AmE law* a court official who watches prisoners and keeps order in the courtroom

bail *v adv* **1** [T (**bail** sbdy.↔**out**)] to obtain (someone's) freedom by paying money (BAIL[1]) to ensure appearance in court: *Clark was charged with robbing the bank, and his family paid $500 to bail him out.* **2** [I;T (=**bail** sthg.↔**out**)] also **bale out** *BrE*– to remove water from (a boat) so as to prevent sinking: *When the storm rose on the lake, we had to bail out to reach the shore safely.* **3** [I of] *AmE*‖**bale out** *BrE*– to escape from an aircraft by PARACHUTE[1]

bait[1] /beyt/ *v* [T] **1** to put BAIT[2] on (a hook) to catch fish, or in (a trap) to catch animals **2** to make angry intentionally: *At school they baited the boy because of his strange clothes.*

bait[2] *n* [S;U] food or something like food used to attract and catch fish, animals, or birds:

(fig.) *Let's use free gifts as a bait to attract people to our new store.*

baize /beᵞz/ *n* [U] thick woolen cloth, usu. green, used esp. to cover tables on which certain games are played

bake /beᵞk/ *v* **baked, baking** [I;T] **1** to (cause to) cook using dry heat in an OVEN: *to bake bread|The bread is baking.* **2** to (cause to) become hard by heating: *In former times, bricks were baked in the sun.* –see COOK² (USAGE)

bak·er /'beᵞkər/ *n* a person who bakes bread and cakes, esp. professionally

bak·er·y /'beᵞkəriᵞ/ *n* **-ies** a place where bread and sometimes cakes are baked and/or sold

bal·ance¹ /'bæləns/ *n* **1** [S;U] a state in which all parts are of equal or proper weight; EQUILIBRIUM: *I found it hard to* **keep my balance** *on the icy path.|He* **lost his balance** *and fell over.|*(fig.) *We try to* **strike a** *proper* **balance** *between justice and mercy.* –opposite **imbalance 2** [C] a weight or influence on one side which equals a weight or influence on the other: *Mrs. Smith acts as a balance to Mr. Jones. Together, they are a good team.* **3** [C] an instrument for weighing things by seeing whether the amounts in two hanging pans are equal: (fig.) *The nation's future* **hangs in the balance.** (=is uncertain) **4** [C *usu. sing.*] something which is left over: *My bank balance isn't very large.* (=I don't have very much money in the bank)|*Can I take the balance of my vacation* (=the vacation I have not yet taken) *next month?* **5 on balance** (with) all things considered; taking everything into consideration

balance² *v* **-anced, -ancing 1** [I;T] to (cause to) be in a state of balance: *The dog balanced a ball on its nose.|Our accounts balance* (=show money spent to be equal to money received) *for the first time this year.* **2** [T] to consider or compare: *You have to balance the advantages of living in the country against the disadvantages.*

balance of pay·ments /,·· · '··/ also **balance of trade** /,·· · '·'–/ *n* [*the* S] the amount of money coming into a country or area in comparison with the amount going out

balance of pow·er /,·· · '··/ *n* [*the* S] a position in which power, esp. political or military power, is evenly balanced on all sides: *The growth of the new political party* **upset the balance of power.**

bal·co·ny /'bælkəniᵞ/ *n* **-nies 1** a place for people to stand or sit on, built out on the upstairs wall of a building: *You can see the sea from our balcony.* –compare PORCH (1); see illustration on page 337 **2** the seats upstairs in a theater

bald /bɔld/ *adj* **1** with little or no hair (on the head) **2** with little or no decoration; plain: *a bald statement* –**baldness** *n* [U]

bald·ing /'bɔldɪŋ/ *adj* becoming BALD (1): *a balding man/head*

bald·ly /'bɔldliᵞ/ *adv* spoken plainly, even cruelly: *The doctor told him baldly that if he didn't stop smoking he'd be dead in a year.*

bale /beᵞl/ *n* a large tightly tied mass of goods

or material ready to be taken away: *a bale of cotton/straw*

bale·ful /'beᵞlfəl/ *adj* (of appearance and behavior) full of hate and desire to do harm; evil: *a baleful look* –**balefully** *adv*

bale out *v adv BrE* for BAIL OUT

balk ‖also **baulk** *BrE* /bɔk/ *v* **1** [T] to stop or get in the way of on purpose **2** [I *at*] to be unwilling to face or agree to something difficult or unpleasant

ball¹ /bɔl/ *n* **1** a round object used in play; anything of like shape: *to throw a ball|The Earth is like a ball.|a ball of string|a snowball* **2** a rounded part of the body: *the ball of the foot|*EYEBALL **3 on the ball** *infml* showing up-to-date knowledge and skill and readiness to act: *That book/writer is really on the ball.* **4 play ball** *infml* for COOPERATE **5 start/keep the ball rolling** to begin/continue something

ball² *n* **1** a large formal occasion for social dancing **2** *infml* a very good time: *They all* **had a ball** *at the party.*

bal·lad /'bæləd/ *n* a simple song or a short story in the form of a poem

bal·last /'bæləst/ *n* [U] heavy material which is **a** carried on a ship to keep it steady **b** thrown from a BALLOON (1) to make it rise **c** put down under a road or railroad

ball bear·ing /,· '··/ *n* (one of the) metal balls moving in a ring around a bar in a machine so that the bar may turn more easily

ball·cock /'bɔlkɑk/ *n* an apparatus for opening and closing a hole through which water passes, worked by a hollow floating ball which rises and falls with the level of the water

bal·le·ri·na /,bælə'riᵞnə/ *n* a female BALLET dancer

bal·let /bæ'leᵞ, 'bæleᵞ/ *n* **1** [C] a kind of dance in which a story is told without speech or singing **2** [S;U] the art of doing such dances: *She has studied (the) ballet for six years.* **3** [C] a group of ballet dancers who work together: *the Bolshoi Ballet*

bal·lis·tics /bə'lɪstɪks/ *n* [U] the scientific study of the movement of objects that are thrown or forced through the air, such as bullets fired from a gun

bal·loon¹ /bə'luʷn/ *n* **1** a bag of strong light material filled with gas or heated air so that it can float in the air **2** a small rubber bag that can be blown up, used as a toy

balloon² *v* [I esp. *out*] to get rounder and rounder, like a BALLOON being blown up: *Her skirt ballooned out in the wind.*

bal·lot /'bælət/ *n* **1** a sheet of paper used to make a secret vote: *They are counting the ballots now.* **2** [*usu. sing.*] the action or system of secret voting: *The ballot is an important defense of political freedom.*

ball·point pen /,bɔlpɔɪnt 'pɛn/ also **ballpoint** /'bɔlpɔɪnt/– *n* a pen which has a ball at the end that rolls thick ink onto the paper

ball·room /'bɔlruʷm. -rʊm/ *n* a large room for a BALL² (1)

balm /bɑm/ *n* [C;U] (an) oily liquid with a strong but pleasant smell, often from trees, used as medicine or to lessen pain

balm·y /'bɑmiʸ/ *adj* **-ier, -iest** *apprec* (of air) soft and warm; MILD¹ (2)

bal·us·trade /'bæləˌstreʸd/ *n* a row of upright pieces of stone or wood with a bar along the top, guarding the outer edge of any place from which people might fall

bam·boo /ˌbæm'buʷ◂/ *n* **-boos** [C;U] a tall plant of the grass family, or its hard, hollow, jointed stems, used e.g. for making furniture

bam·boo·zle /bæm'buʷzəl/ *v* **-zled, -zling** [T *into/out of*] *infml* to deceive; trick; HOOD-WINK

ban¹ /bæn/ *v* **-nn-** [T] to forbid, esp. by law

ban² *n* [*on*] an order BANNing something: *There's a ban on smoking in theaters.*

ba·nal /bə'næl, bə'nɑl, 'beʸnl/ *adj derog* uninteresting because very common: *a banal remark* **–banality** /bə'næləṭiʸ/ *n* [C;U]

ba·nan·a /bə'nænə/ *n* a long finger-shaped tropical fruit, with a yellow skin and a soft, usu. sweet, inside

band¹ /bænd/ *n* **1** a thin flat narrow piece of material, **a** for fastening things together, or for putting around something to strengthen it **b** forming part of an article of clothing: *neckband|wristbands* **2** a line of a different color or pattern that stands out against the background on which it is painted or fixed: *There was an orange band on the snake's back.* **3** one of the parts into which a larger whole can be divided, such as a band of radio waves

band² *v* [T] to put a band or bands on
band together *v adv* [I] to unite, usu. with some special purpose

band³ *n* **1** a group of people formed for some common purpose and often with a leader: *a band of robbers* **2** a group of musicians with a leader, esp. a group that plays "popular" rather than "serious" music: *I heard a really great band last night.* –compare ORCHESTRA

ban·dage¹ /'bændɪdʒ/ *n* a piece of material, esp. cloth, for covering or binding around a wound or around a part of the body that has been hurt –see illustration on page 201

bandage² *v* **-daged, -daging** [T *up*] to tie up or bind around with a BANDAGE: *The doctor bandaged (up) his broken ankle.*

Band-Aid /'bænd eʸd/ *n tdmk AmE* (a thin band of) material that can be stuck to the skin to protect small wounds

ban·dit /'bændɪt/ *n* an armed robber, esp. one of an armed band

band·stand /'bændstænd/ *n* a raised place, open at the sides but with a roof, for a band when playing music outside

band·wag·on /'bændˌwægən/ *n* **jump on the bandwagon** to do or say something just because a lot of other people are doing or saying it

ban·dy¹ /'bændiʸ/ *v* **-died, -dying** [T] **bandy words (with)** to quarrel (with)
bandy sthg. **about** *v adv* [T] to spread (esp. unfavorable or untrue ideas) about by talking: *When the Websters' marriage failed, the news was quickly bandied about.*

bandy² *adj* **-dier, -diest 1** (of legs) curved outwards at the knees **2 bandy-legged** /'bændiʸ ˌlɛɡɪd, -ˌlɛɡd/ having such legs

bane /beʸn/ *n* **the bane of one's existence/life** a cause of bad things

bang¹ /bæŋ/ *v* **1** [T] to strike sharply; BUMP¹ (1): *He fell and banged his knee.* **2** [I;T] (to cause to) knock, beat, or push forcefully, often with a loud noise: *She banged the chair against the wall.* **3** [I] to make loud noise or noises: *There is someone banging around upstairs.*
bang sthg.↔**up** *v adv* [T] *AmE infml* to damage: *I banged up my leg in the accident.*

bang² *n* **1** a sharp blow **2** a sudden loud noise: *The door shut with a bang.*

bang³ *adv* [*adv* + *prep*] *infml* right; directly: *The lights went out bang* (=exactly) *in the middle of the performance.*

ban·gle /'bæŋgəl/ *n* a metal band worn around the arm or ankle as a decoration

ban·ish /'bænɪʃ/ *v* [T] to send away, usu. from one's own country, as a punishment: *She was banished by the government for political reasons.* –compare EXILE² **–banishment** *n* [U]

ban·is·ter /'bænəstər/ *n* a row of upright pieces of wood or metal with a bar along the top guarding the outer edge of stairs

ban·jo /'bændʒoʷ/ *n* **-jos** *or* **-joes** a stringed musical instrument with a long neck, and a body like a drum, used esp. to play popular music

bank¹ /bæŋk/ *n* **1** land along the side of a river, lake, etc. –see SHORE (USAGE) **2** earth which is heaped up in a field or garden, often making a border or division **3** a mass of snow, clouds, mud, etc.: *The banks of dark clouds promised rain.* **4** →SANDBANK

bank² *n* **1** a place in which money is kept and paid out on demand **2** a place where something is stored, esp. ORGANIC (1) products of human origin for medical use: *Hospital bloodbanks have saved many lives.*

bank³ *v* [T] to put or keep (money) in a bank
bank on sby./sthg. *v prep* [T *no pass.*] to depend on; trust in: *I'm banking on you to help me with the arrangements.*
bank up *v adv* [I;T (=**bank** sthg.↔**up**)] to form into a mass or heap: *The wind had banked the snow up against the wall.|At night we bank up the fire so that it's still burning in the morning.*

bank·er /'bæŋkər/ *n* a person who owns or controls or shares in the control of a BANK² (1): *Who are your bankers?* (=which bank do you use)

bank note /'· ·/ *n* a piece of paper money printed for the national bank of a country for public use

bank·rupt¹ /'bæŋkrʌpt, -rəpt/ *adj* unable to pay one's debts: *The company* **went bankrupt** *because it couldn't sell its products.*|(fig.) **morally bankrupt** (=completely without morals)

bankrupt² *v* to make BANKRUPT or very poor

bank·rupt·cy /'bæŋkˌrʌptsiʸ, -rəpsiʸ/ *n* **-cies** [C;U] (an example of) the quality or state of being BANKRUPT

ban·ner /'bænər/ *n* **1** *lit* a flag **2** a long piece of cloth on which a sign is painted, usu. carried between two poles: *The marchers' banners* said "We want work."

banns /bænz/ n [P] a public declaration, esp. in church, of an intended marriage

ban·quet /'bæŋkwɪt/ n a formal dinner for many people in honor of a special person or occasion, esp. one at which speeches are made

ban·tam /'bæntəm/ n a small variety of farm chicken

ban·ter /'bæntər/ v [I] to speak or act playfully or jokingly –**banter** n [U]: The actress exchanged banter with reporters.

bap·tism /'bæptɪzəm/ n [C;U] a Christian religious ceremony in which a person is touched or covered with water to make him/her pure and show that he/she has been accepted as a member of the Church –**baptismal** /bæp'tɪzməl/ adj

Bap·tist /'bæptɪst/ n a member of a branch of the Christian church which believes that BAPTISM should be only for people old enough to understand its meaning

bap·tize ‖also **-tise** BrE /bæp'taɪz, 'bæptaɪz/ v **-tized, -tizing** [T] to perform the ceremony of BAPTISM on

bar¹ /bɑr/ n **1** a piece of wood, metal, etc. that is longer than it is wide: an iron bar|a bar of soap/chocolate/gold –see illustration on page 51 **2** a length of wood or metal across a door, gate, or window that keeps it shut or prevents movement through it: There were metal bars across the windows of the prison.|(fig.) The fact that your English isn't very good may be a bar to (=may prevent) your getting that job. **3** a bank of sand or stones under the water, parallel to a shore, at the entrance to a harbor, etc. **4** a group of notes in music: She sang the first three bars of the song, and then stopped. **5** (a place with) a COUNTER¹ where alcoholic drinks are sold: a pleasant little bar –see illustration on page 581 **6 behind bars** in prison **7 prisoner at the bar** the person being tried in a court of law

bar² v **-rr-** [T] **1** to close firmly with a bar: to bar the door –opposite **unbar 2** to keep in or out by barring a door, gate, etc.: They barred themselves in. **3** to block (movement or action): to bar the way to the city/to success|(fig.) They have barred smoking at the dinner table.

bar³ prep except: The whole group was at the party, bar none.

Bar n [the S] AmE **1** (the members of) the profession of lawyer **2 be called to the bar** to become a lawyer

barb /bɑrb/ n the sharp point of a fish hook, arrow, etc., with a curved shape which prevents it from being easily pulled out –**barbed** adj: a barbed hook|(fig.) a barbed remark (=unkind; sharp)

bar·bar·i·an /bɑr'bɛəriyən/ n derog an uncivilized person, esp. one who is rude and wild in behavior: The barbarians conquered Rome.|Only a barbarian would not like the work of such a great writer. –**barbaric** /bɑr'bærɪk, -'bɛərɪk/ adj: barbaric people/customs|a barbaric punishment (=very cruel) –**barbarically** adv –**barbarism**

/'bɑrbə,rɪzəm/ n derog: Some words which used to be considered barbarisms are now acceptable. –**barbarous** /'bɑrbərəs/ adj –**barbarously** adv

bar·bar·i·ty /bɑr'bærəṭiy, -'bɛər-/ n **-ties** derog [C;U] (an example of) cruelty of the worst kind: The barbarities of the last war must not be repeated.

bar·be·cue¹ /'bɑrbɪ,kyuʷ/ n **1** a metal framework on which to cook meat over an open fire, usu. outdoors **2** a feast or party at which meat is prepared in this way and eaten: We had a barbecue on the beach.

barbecue² v **-cued, -cuing** [T] to cook (meat) **a** on a BARBECUE¹ (1) **b** in a very hot SAUCE

barbed wire /,· '·/ n [U] wire with short sharp points in it: They use barbed wire to keep the cattle in. –**barbed-wire** /,· '·◂/ adj: a barbed-wire fence

bar·ber /'bɑrbər/ n a person (usu. a man) who cuts men's hair and SHAVES them –compare HAIRDRESSER

bar·bi·tu·rate /bɑr'bɪtʃərɪt, -,reyt/ n [C;U] tech a drug that calms the nerves and puts people to sleep

bard /bɑrd/ n lit a poet

bare¹ /bɛər/ adj **1** uncovered; empty; without: bare skin|bare fields|a room bare of furniture **2** [A no comp.] not more than; only; I killed him with my bare hands. –**bareness** n [U]

bare² v **bared, baring** [T] to take off a covering; bring to view: The animal bared its teeth in anger.

bare·back /'bɛərbæk/ adj,adv [A] riding, esp. a horse, without a SADDLE (1): a bareback rider

bare·faced /'bɛərfeyst/ adj derog shameless: a barefaced lie

bare·foot /'bɛərfʊt/ adj,adv without shoes or other covering on the feet

bare·head·ed /'bɛər,hɛdɪd/ adj,adv without a hat

bare·ly /'bɛərliy/ adv **1** only just; hardly: We have barely enough money to last the weekend. –see HARDLY (USAGE) **2** in a bare way: The room was furnished barely. (=with very little furniture)

bar·gain¹ /'bɑrgɪn/ n **1** an agreement, esp. one to do something in return for something else: He made a bargain with his wife: "You do the shopping and I'll cook." **2** something that can be or has been bought cheaply: These shoes are a real bargain at such a low price. **3 drive a hard bargain** to get an agreement very much in one's own favor **4 into the bargain** in addition: She had to look after a house, her sick mother–and four children into the bargain.

bargain² v [I] to talk about the conditions of a sale, agreement, or contract: We bargained with her about the price.

bargain for sbdy./sthg. ‖ also **bargain on** sbdy./sthg. AmE– v prep [T] to take into account; consider: I had not bargained for such heavy rain, and I got very wet.

barge¹ /bɑrdʒ/ n a large low flat-bottomed boat used mainly for carrying heavy goods on a CANAL or river

barge² v **barged, barging** [I;T] to move in a heavy ungraceful way, often hitting against things: *He barged his way past us and got on the bus before everyone else.*

barge in v adv [I] to rush in rudely; interrupt: *The door burst open and the children barged in.*

bar·i·tone /'bærə¸town/ n (a man with) the male singing voice lower than TENOR and higher than BASS

bark¹ /bɑrk/ v **1** [I *at*] to make the sound that dogs make: *The dog always barks at the mailman.* **2** [T *out*] to say (something) in a sharp loud voice: *The officer barked (out) an order.* **3 bark up the wrong tree** *infml* to go to the wrong place or have a mistaken idea: *You're barking up the wrong tree if you ask her to help you, because she never helps anyone.*

bark² n **1** (a sound like) the sound made by a dog **2 His/Her bark is worse than his/her bite** *infml* He/She sounds worse than he/she is

bark³ n [U] the strong outer covering of a tree

bar·ley /'bɑrliy/ n [U] a grasslike grain plant grown for food and also used in the making of beer and SPIRITS¹ (7)

bar·man /'bɑrmən/ **barmaid** /'bɑrmeyd/ *fem.– n* **-men** /mən/ *esp. BrE* for BARTENDER

barn /bɑrn/ n a farm building for storing crops and food for animals, or for keeping the animals themselves in

bar·na·cle /'bɑrnəkəl/ n a small SHELLFISH which collects in large numbers on rocks and on the bottoms of ships, and which is hard to remove

barn·yard /'bɑrnyɑrd/ n a yard on a farm, usu. enclosed by a fence, with BARNs and perhaps other buildings round it

ba·rom·e·ter /bə'rɑmɪtər/ n an instrument for measuring the air pressure in order to help to judge probable changes in the weather or to calculate height above sea level –**barometric** /¸bærə'mɛtrɪk/ *adj* –**barometrically** *adv*

bar·on /'bærən/ n **1** [A;C] **baroness** /'bærənɪs/ *fem.–* (in Britain) (the title of) a nobleman with the lowest rank in the House of Lords **2** [C] a very powerful businessman: *an oil baron*

bar·on·et /¸bærə'nɛt, 'bærənɪt, -¸nɛt/ n (in Britain) (the rank of) a KNIGHT¹ (2) whose title passes on to his son when he dies

ba·ro·ni·al /bə'rowniyəl/ *adj* **1** of, like, or about a BARON (1) **2** large, rich, and noble: *a baronial hall*

bar·racks /'bærɪks/ n **barracks** a building or group of buildings that soldiers live in

bar·rage¹ /'bɑrɪdʒ/ n a manmade BAR¹ (3) built across a river usu. to provide water for farming

bar·rage² /bə'rɑʒ/ **1** the firing of a number of heavy guns at once **2** (of speech or writing) a large number of things put forward very quickly one after the other: *a barrage of questions*

bar·rel /'bærəl/ n **1** a round wooden container with curved sides and a flat top and bottom: *a beer barrel* **2** also **barrelful** /-¸fʊl/– the amount of liquid contained in a barrel **3** a part of something that serves as a container

and has the shape of a tube or CYLINDER (1): *a gun barrel*

bar·ren /'bærən/ *adj* **1** (of female animals) not able to REPRODUCE **2** (of trees or plants) bearing no fruit or seed **3** (of land) unable to produce a good crop **4** useless; empty; which produces no result: *It is useless to continue such a barren argument.* –compare FERTILE, FRUITFUL –**barrenness** n [U]

bar·ri·cade¹ /'bærə¸keyd, ¸bærə'keyd/ n a quickly-built wall of trees, earth, bricks, etc., put across a way or passage to block the advance of the enemy

barricade² v **-caded, -cading** [T] **1** to block off or close off with a BARRICADE **2** to put in a given place or condition by means of a BARRICADE: *to barricade oneself in one's room*

bar·ri·er /'æriyər/ n something placed in the way in order to prevent or control the movement of people or things: *The police put up barriers to control the crowd.*|*Deserts and high mountains have always been a barrier to the movement of people.*|(fig.) *The color of one's skin should be no barrier to success in life.*

bar·ring /'bɑrɪŋ/ *prep* except for: *The whole group was at the party, barring John.*|*We'll return at midnight, barring accidents.* (=if there are no accidents)

bar·ris·ter /'bærəstər/ n (esp. in England) a lawyer who has the right of speaking and arguing in the higher courts of law –compare SOLICITOR (2)

bar·row /'bærow/ n **1** a small cart, usu. with two wheels **2** →WHEELBARROW

bar·tend·er /'bɑr¸tɛndər/ *AmE* n a person who serves drinks in a bar (5): *Ask the bartender for two more beers, please.* –see illustration on page 581

bar·ter /'bɑrtər/ v [I;T *for, with*] to exchange goods for other goods: *They bartered farm products for machinery.*|*bartering for food* –**barter** n [U]

base¹ /beys/ n **bases** **1** the part of a thing on which the thing stands; the bottom: *the base of a pillar*|*We camped at the base of the mountain.*|*Draw a square with the line "xy" as its base.* **2** the part from which something originates or from which other things develop: *the base of the thumb* (=where it joins the hand)|*Several kinds of soup can be made using this vegetable base.*|*French is a Latin-based language.* **3** a center from which something is controlled, plans are made, etc.: *Our company's base is in Boston, but we have branches all around the world.*|*a New York-based firm* **4** a chemical substance which combines with an acid to form a salt **5** a military camp, esp. one intended to remain in use for some time **6** any (esp. the first three) of the four points which a BASEBALL player must touch in order to make a run **7 not get to first base (with)** *AmE infml* to not even begin to succeed (with): *He liked Susan very much, but he couldn't get to first base with her.*|*I tried to persuade them, but I didn't get to first base.*

base² *adj derog esp. lit* (of people, actions, etc.) low; dishonorable: *base conduct*

(=very bad behavior) –**basely** adv –**baseness** n [U]

base³ v →BASE sthg. ON sthg.

base·ball /'beⁱsbɔl/ n [U] a game played with a BAT and ball (**baseball**) between two teams of nine players each on a large field of which the center is four BASEs¹ (6): a baseball player/team

USAGE In **baseball** the **batter** tries to hit the ball thrown by the **pitcher**

base·ment /'beⁱsmənt/ n a room or rooms in a house which are below street level –compare CELLAR

base sthg. on/upon sthg. v prep **based, basing** [T] to do (something) using (something else) as the starting point or reason for it: You should always base your opinions on facts.

bash¹ /bæʃ/ v [T] infml to hit hard, so as to break or hurt in some way: He bashed his head (on the door).

bash² n usu. infml **1** a hard or fierce blow: He gave him a bash on the nose. **2** AmE infml an enjoyable party with a lot of noise, laughter, etc.

bash·ful /'bæʃfəl/ adj unsure of oneself; made unhappy by attention; SHY: The bashful child was nervous with strangers. –**bashfully** adv –**bashfulness** n [U]

ba·sic /'beⁱsɪk/ adj more necessary than anything else; on which everything else depends, or is built: the basic rules of good driving

ba·si·cal·ly /'beⁱsɪkliⁱ/ adv with regard to what is most important and BASIC, and in spite of surface behavior or details; in reality; FUNDAMENTALly: Basically, he's a nice person, but he doesn't always show it.|He's basically nice.

ba·sics /'beⁱsɪks/ n [the P] often infml of education are reading, writing, and simple calculations.

ba·sin /'beⁱsən/ n **1** a round hollow vessel for holding liquids or food; bowl **2** also **basinful**– the contents of a basin **3** a hollow place containing water, or where water collects: the basin of a FOUNTAIN **4** a circular or egg-shaped valley; all that area of country from which water runs down into a river: the Amazon Basin

ba·sis /'beⁱsɪs/ n **bases** /'beⁱsiⁱz/ that from which something is made, started, built, developed, or calculated: The basis of this drink is orange juice.|What is the basis of/for your opinion?

bask /bæsk/ v [in] to sit or lie in enjoyable heat and light: I was lying on the sand, basking in the sunshine.|(fig.) He wanted to bask in (=enjoy) his employer's approval.

bas·ket /'bæskɪt/ n **1** (the contents of) a usu. light container which is made of bent sticks or other such material: They were carrying several baskets of fruit.–see illustration on page 467 **2** an open net fixed to a metal ring high up off the ground, through which players try to throw the ball in the game of BASKETBALL

bas·ket·ball /'bæskɪt,bɔl/ n [C;U] (the ball used in) a usu. indoor game between two

teams of usu. five players each, in which each team tries to throw a large ball through the other team's BASKET (2). Do you play basketball?

bass¹ /bæs/ n **bass** or **basses** a fresh-water or salt-water fish that can be eaten

bass² /beⁱs/ adj (of a male singing voice or musical instrument) deep or low in sound: He has a fine bass voice.|a bass drum –compare TREBLE² (2)

bass³ /beⁱs/ n **1** (a man with) the lowest male singing voice –compare TENOR **2** the lowest part in written music **3** →DOUBLE BASS

bas·soon /bə'suʷn, bæ-/ n a wooden musical instrument, played by blowing through a double REED (2) that makes a deep sound

bas·tard /'bæstərd/ n **1** a child of unmarried parents **2** infml a person, esp. that one strongly dislikes: I'm going to get (=hurt, punish) you, you bastard!|The lucky bastard!

baste¹ /beⁱst/ v **basted, basting** [I;T] to join (pieces of cloth) together in long loose stitches; TACK² (3)

baste² v [I;T] to pour melted fat over (meat that is cooking)

bat¹ /bæt/ n **1** a specially shaped wooden stick used for hitting the ball in various games –see BASEBALL (USAGE) **2 at bat** (in BASEBALL) having a turn to hit the ball: Who's at bat? **3 off the bat** infml without delay: I asked her to help us, and (right) off the bat she said she would.

bat² v **-tt- 1** [T] to strike or hit with or as if with a BAT¹ (1): to bat a ball **2** [I] (in BASEBALL) to have a turn to bat: Who's batting now? –**batter** n

bat³ n **1** a flying mouselike animal that usu. eats insects or fruit and is active at night **2 as blind as a bat** infml not able to see well

bat⁴ v **not bat an eyelid** infml to show no sign of one's feelings or surprise: She heard the news without batting an eyelid.

batch /bætʃ/ n a quantity of material or number of things to be dealt with at one time: a batch of bread/ loaves|several batches of letters

bat·ed /'beⁱtɪd/ adj **with bated breath** hardly breathing at all (because of fear or other strong feeling): He waited for the news with bated breath.

bath¹ /bæθ/ n **baths** /bæðz, bæθs/ an act of washing one's whole body at one time: to take (AmE)/have (BrE) a bath|a nice hot bath –see also BATHS

bath² v BrE for BATHE¹ (1,2)

bathe¹ /beⁱð/ v **bathed, bathing 1** AmE‖**bath** BrE– to have a bath: No, you can't see you now; he's bathing. **2** [T] AmE‖**bath** BrE– to give a bath to: He's bathing the baby. **3** [T] to pour water or other liquid over; place in water or other liquid: Bathe your ankle twice a day. **4** [T] to spread over with (or as if with) light, water, etc.: The fields were bathed in sunlight. **5** [I] esp. BrE to go into a body of water or swimming pool for pleasure; to go swimming: I like to bathe in the sea. –**bather** n

bath·ing /'beⁱðɪŋ/ n [U] the act or practice of going into water to bathe or swim: Mixed bathing (=by men and women) is allowed in *this swimming pool.*

bathing suit /'·· ·/ also **swimsuit**– *n* the type of clothing worn for swimming

bath·robe /'bæθrowb/ *n* **1** a loose garment worn before and after bathing **2** *AmE* for DRESSING GOWN, esp. as worn by men

bath·room /'bæθruʷm, -rum/ *n* a room containing a BATHTUB and/or a TOILET –see illustration on page 51

baths /bæðz, bæθs/ *n* **baths** a public building with one or more rooms used for bathing or swimming: *the public baths*

bath·tub /'bæθtʌb/ *AmE* also **tub** *AmE*‖also **bath** esp. *BrE*– *n* a container in which one sits to wash the whole body –see illustration on page 51

ba·ton /bə'tɑn, bæ-/ *n* a short thin stick used esp. by a leader of music (CONDUCTOR) to show the beat of the music

bat·tal·ion /bə'tælyən/ *n* a group of 500 –1,000 soldiers made up of four or more companies (COMPANY (5)): *The second battalion is going abroad.*

bat·ten /'bætn/ *n* a long board used for fastening other pieces of wood

batten down sthg. *v adv* [T] (on ships) to fasten with boards of wood: *There's a storm coming, so let's* **batten down the hatches.** (=entrances to the lower parts of the ship)

bat·ter¹ /'bæṭər/ *v* **1** [I] to beat hard and repeatedly: *waves battering against the shore* **2** [T] to cause to lose shape, break, or be damaged: *The ship was battered to pieces by the storm.|a battered old hat*

batter² *n* [U] a mixture of flour, eggs, and milk, beaten together and used in cooking

bat·ter·ing ram /'··· ·/ also **ram**– *n* (in former times) a large heavy log with an iron end, used in war for breaking through the doors and walls of castles and towns

bat·ter·y /'bæṭəriʸ/ *n* **-ies 1** a piece of apparatus for producing electricity, consisting of a group of connected electric CELLs –see illustration on page 221 **2** a number of big guns together with the men and officers who serve them; set of guns positioned on a warship or fort **3** a group or set of things that are kept together: *They've got a battery of cooking pots in their kitchen.*

bat·tle¹ /'bæṭl/ *n* an esp. short fight between enemies or opposing groups; a struggle: *the Battle of Waterloo|a battle for power in the government|They died in battle.* –compare WAR

battle² *v* **-tled, -tling** [I] to fight or struggle: *The two fighters battled (with each other) for half an hour.*

bat·tle·field /'bæṭl,fiʸld/ also **battleground** /-,graund/ *n* a place at which a battle is or has been fought

bat·tle·ments /'bæṭlmənts/ *n* [*the* P] a low wall around the flat roof of a castle or fort, with spaces to shoot through

bat·tle·ship /'bæṭl,ʃɪp/ *n* the largest kind of warship, with the biggest guns and heaviest armor

bau·ble /'bɔbəl/ *n* a cheap jewel

baux·ite /'bɔksaɪt/ *n* [U] the clay (ORE) from which the metal ALUMINUM is made

bawd·y /'bɔdiʸ/ *adj* **-ier, -iest** funny about sex: *bawdy jokes* –**bawdily** *adv*

bawl /bɔl/ *v* [I;T] to shout or cry in a loud, rough, ugly voice: *He bawled at me/for his dinner.|The captain bawled (out) an order.*

bawl sbdy ↔ **out** *v adv* [T] *AmE infml* to scold: *He bawled me out for being late.*

bay¹ /beʸ/ *adj,n* (a horse whose color is) reddish-brown

bay² also **bay tree** /'· ·/– *n* a tree like the LAUREL, whose leaves may be used in cooking

bay³ *n* any one of the chief parts into which a building or hall is divided: *In the library, the books on history are all kept in one bay.* –see also SICKBAY

bay⁴ *n* **hold/keep at bay** to keep someone or something some distance away: *He kept me at bay with a knife.*

bay⁵ *n* a part of the sea or of a large lake enclosed in a curve of the land: *the Bay of Biscay|We swam in the bay.*

bay·o·net¹ /'beʸənɪt, -,nɛt, ,beʸə'nɛt/ *n* a long knife fixed to the end of a soldier's gun (RIFLE)

bayonet² *v* **-neted** *or* **-netted, -neting** *or* **-netting** [T] to drive a BAYONET into

bay·ou /'baɪuʷ, 'baɪoʷ/ *n* (esp. in the southeastern US) a body of water with a slow current and many water plants

ba·zaar /bə'zɑr/ *n* **1** (in Eastern countries) a marketplace or a group of shops **2** (in English-speaking countries) a sale to get money for some good purpose: *a church/hospital bazaar*

BC *adv abbrev. for:* (in the year) before the birth of Christ: *Rome was begun in 753 BC.* –compare AD

be¹ /bɪ; *strong* biʸ/ *v* [used as a helping verb with another verb]

present tense

singular	plural
I am, I'm	*We are, we're*
You are, you're	*You are, you're*
He/She/It is,	*They are, they're*
he's/she's/it's	

past tense

singular	plural
I was	*We were*
You were	*You were*
He/She/It was	*They were*

PAST PARTICIPLE	**been**
PRESENT PARTICIPLE	**being**
NEGATIVE *short forms*	**aren't, isn't, wasn't** *weren't*

For the pronunciation of these forms look them up in the dictionary at their own place. **1** [+*v-ing*] (forms the continuous tenses of verbs): *I'm working now.|She was reading.|We're leaving tomorrow.* (=it is arranged) **2** (used with the past participle to form the PASSIVE of verbs): *Smoking is not permitted.|The money was found.|The house is being painted.* **3** [+*to-v*] **a** (shows what must happen): *All prisoners are to be* (=must be) *in bed by 10 o'clock.*|*You are not to smoke here.* (=you must not smoke) **b** (shows arrangements for the future): *We are to be married next week.*|*We were to be married last week, but I was ill.*|*What am I to do?* (=what should I/can I do?) –see Study Notes on page 434 **c** (shows possible future happenings): *If I were to go home what would you say?* –see also BEEN

be² *v* [used as a connecting verb] **1** (shows that something or someone is the same as the subject): *January is the first month of the year.*|*The first person I met was my brother.* **2** (shows position or time): *The book is on the table.*|*The concert was last night.*|*Their party is* (=will take place) *on Saturday.* **3** to belong to a group or have a quality: *She's a doctor.*|*Horses are animals.*|*The leaves are green.*|*A knife is for cutting with.*|*You're right/wrong.* –see also BEEN

be³ *v* [I] to exist: *There is the possibility that he will arrive late.*|*Once upon a time there was a beautiful princess.* –see also BEEN

beach¹ /biːtʃ/ *n* a shore of an ocean, sea, or lake or the bank of a river covered by sand, smooth stones, or larger pieces of rock –see SHORE¹ (USAGE)

beach² *v* [T] to run or drive (a boat, etc.) onto the shore

beach ball /ˈ· ·/ *n* a large light ball, filled with air, for use at the BEACH

beach·comb·er /ˈbiːtʃˌkoʷmər/ *n* a person who lives on or near the BEACH, and sometimes earns money by selling things found there

bea·con /ˈbiːkən/ *n* **1** a signal fire on a hill, tower, or pole **2** a (flashing) light, to act as a guide or warning to sailors or airmen

bead /biːd/ *n* a small ball of glass or other material with a hole through it for a string or wire, worn with others on a thread, esp. round the neck, for decoration: *She was wearing a string of green beads.*|(fig.) *beads of* SWEAT¹ (1)

bead·y /ˈbiːdiʲ/ *adj* **-ier, -iest** (esp. of an eye) small, round, and shining, like a BEAD

bea·gle /ˈbiːgəl/ *n* a smooth-haired dog with short legs and large ears, used in hunting

beak /biːk/ *n* the hard horny mouth of a bird, a TURTLE, etc.

beak·er /ˈbiːkər/ *n* **1** a small glass cup shaped for pouring, as used in a chemical LABORATORY **2** a drinking cup with a wide mouth and usu. no handle

beam¹ /biːm/ *n* a large long heavy piece of wood, esp. one of the main ones used to support a building

beam² *n* **1** a line of light shining out from some bright object **2** radio waves sent out along a narrow path in one direction only, often to guide aircraft **3** a bright look or smile: *"How nice to see you!" she said, with a beam of welcome.*

beam³ *v* **1** [I] (of the sun or other shining objects) to send out light (and heat): *The sun beamed through the clouds.* **2** [I;T] to smile brightly and happily: *He beamed a cheerful welcome.* **3** [I;T] (of the radio) to send out in a certain direction: *The (radio) news was*

beamed *to East Africa.*

bean /biːn/ *n* **1** a seed of any of various upright climbing plants, esp. one that can be used as food **2** a plant bearing these seeds **3** a long container of these seeds (a POD), itself used as food when not yet fully grown **4** a seed of certain other plants, from which food or drink can be made: *coffee beans* **5 full of beans** *infml* full of active bodily strength and eagerness **6 spill the beans** *infml* to tell a secret, usu. unintentionally

bear¹ /bɛər/ *n* **bears** *or* **bear** a usu. large and heavy animal with thick rough fur that usu. eats fruit and insects as well as flesh

bear² *v* **bore** /bɔr, boʷr/, **borne** /bɔrn, boʷrn/, **bearing 1** [T] *fml* to carry from one place to another: *The bird seized the mouse and bore it off to its nest.*|(fig.)*He didn't do the job very well, but* **bear in mind** (=don't forget) *that he was ill at the time.* **2** [T] to support: *Will the ice on the lake bear your weight?*|(fig.) *All the costs of the repairs will be borne* (=paid) *by our company.* **3** [T] to have or show: *The letter bears her signature.*|*What he says* **bears no relation** *to the truth.* (=it is very different from the truth) **4** [T+*to-v*/*v-ing*] to suffer without complaining: *She bore the pain with great courage.*|(fig.) *I can't bear* (=greatly dislike) *the smell of tobacco smoke.*|*I couldn't bear to listen any longer, so I left the room.* –see USAGE **5** [T] to give birth to: *She bore/has borne three children.* –see BORN² (USAGE) **6** [I;T] to produce (a crop, fruit, or other product): *The tree is bearing a lot of apples this year.* **7** [I] to move in the stated direction: *Cross the field, bear left, and you'll soon reach the village.*

USAGE Compare **abide, bear, endure, stand, tolerate. 1 abide, bear, stand,** and **endure** are all used with "can" in questions and with NEGATIVE¹ (1) words to express great dislike; they have almost the same meaning, but **endure** is usu. only used about something really serious: *I can't* **abide/bear/stand** *strong coffee.*|*I can't* **endure** *talking to people who are* FASCISTs. **2 bear, endure,** and **stand** are also used for great bodily hardship; **endure** suggest pain that lasts a long time: *He* **bore/stood** *the pain as long as he could.*|*She had* **endured** *great pain for a number of years.* **3 tolerate** is used of people or behavior, but usu. not of suffering: *I find it hard to* **tolerate** *your behavior.*

bear down on/upon sbdy./sthg. *v adv prep* [T] to come near threateningly: *The ship bore down on the small boat.*

bear on/upon sthg. *v prep* [T] to show some connection with: *How does your news bear on this case?*

bear sthg.↔ **out** *v adv* [T] to support the truth of: *The prisoner's story was borne out by his wife.*

bear up *v adv* [I *under*] to show courage or strength by continuing (in spite of difficulties)

bear with sbdy./sthg. *v prep* [T] to show patience towards; PUT **up with**: *You must bear with his bad temper: he is very ill.*

bear·a·ble /ˈbɛərəbəl/ *adj* that can be borne

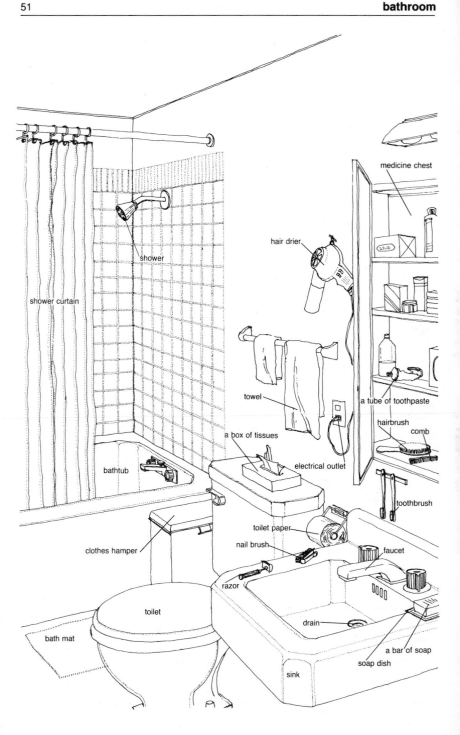

medicine chest

hair drier

shower

shower curtain

towel

a tube of toothpaste

hairbrush

comb

a box of tissues

electrical outlet

bathtub

toothbrush

toilet paper

clothes hamper

nail brush

faucet

razor

toilet

drain

bath mat

a bar of soap

soap dish

sink

or suffered without giving up one's courage: *The pain was just bearable.* –opposite **unbearable** –**bearably** *adv*

beard¹ /bɪərd/ *n* hair on the face below the mouth, often including the jaws, chin, and neck: *Not all men have beards.|John no longer wears a beard.* –compare MUSTACHE, WHISKERS –**bearded** *adj*: *a tall, bearded man|a gray-bearded old man*

beard² *v* [T] **beard the lion in his den** *lit* to face a person boldly on his own ground

bear·er /'bɛərər/ *n* **1** a person who bears or carries: *Please help the bearer of this letter.|the flagbearer* **2** also **pall bearer** *AmE*– a person who helps to carry the body at a funeral

bear·ing /'bɛərɪŋ/ *n* **1** [S;U] manner of holding one's body or way of behaving: *upright, proud bearing* **2** [S;U] connection with or influence on something: *What you have said has no bearing on the subject under consideration.* **3** [C] *tech* the part of a machine in which a turning rod is held, or which turns on a fixed rod –see also BALL BEARING **4** [C] *tech* a direction or angle as shown by a compass: *to take a (compass) bearing|*(fig.) *In all this mass of details I'm afraid I've* **lost my bearings.** (=become confused)

beast /biʸst/ *n* **1** a four-footed (farm) animal **2** *derog* a person (or sometimes a thing) that one doesn't like; BRUTE¹ (1): *a beast of a job|Her husband was a real beast.*

beast·ly /'biʸstliʸ/ *adj derog* that one does not like: *a beastly person/habit* –**beastliness** *n* [U] –**beastliness** *n* [U]

beat¹ /biʸt/ *v* **beat, beaten** /'biʸtn/ *or* **beat, beating** **1** [I;T] to hit repeatedly: *The rain was beating against the windows.|The police beat the door down in order to get into the house.|*(fig.) *The sun beat down all day.* **2** [T] to punish by hitting, esp. with heavy and repeated blows: *The child was taken away from her father because he beats her.* **3** [T] to mix with regular blows of a fork, spoon, etc.: *to beat two eggs* **4** [I;T] to move regularly: *You can hear its heart beating.|The bird beat its wings rapidly.* **5** [T] to defeat; do better than: *She beat her brother at tennis.|She's hoping to beat the world 1000 meter record.|*(fig.) **It beats me** *how he can have done it.* (=I can't understand it) –see WIN¹ (USAGE) **6 beat about the bush** *also* **beat around the bush** *AmE*– to delay talking about or considering the most important part of a subject **7 beat time** to make regular movements or noises by which the speed of music can be measured

beat sbdy.↔ down *v adv* [T] *infml* to persuade sbdy. to reduce a price: *He wanted $5 for the dress, but I beat him down to $4.50.*

beat sthg.↔ out *v adv* [T] to sound by beating: *The drummers beat out their music, and we all danced.*

beat sbdy.↔ up *adv infml* to wound severely by hitting: *The boys robbed the old man and then beat him up.*

beat² *n* **1** [C] a single stroke or blow, esp. as part of a group: *one beat of the drum every 60 seconds|*(fig.) *a heartbeat* **2** [S] a regular

sound produced by or as if by repeated beating: *the beat of the drum/of my heart* **3** [C; *the* S] time in music or poetry: *Every member of the band must follow the beat.* **4** [C] the usual path followed by someone on duty (esp. a police officer)

beat³ *adj* [F *no comp.*] *infml* very tired: *I'm (dead) beat after all that work!*

beat·en /'biʸtn/ *adj* [*no comp.*] **1** (of metal) made to take a certain shape by beating with a hammer: *a plate made of beaten gold* **2** given shape by the feet of those who pass along it: *We followed a well-beaten path through the forest.|Let's go somewhere* **off the beaten track/path** (=not well-known) *this summer.*

beat·er /'biʸtər/ *n* **1** a tool or instrument used for beating: *an egg beater* **2** a person who drives wild birds or animals towards the guns of those waiting to shoot them

be·a·tif·ic /ˌbiʸə'tɪfɪk/ *adj* giving or showing peaceful happiness: *a beatific smile on the holy man's face*

be·at·i·fy /biʸ'ætə,faɪ/ *v* -**fied, -fying** [T] (in the ROMAN CATHOLIC church) to declare (a dead person) officially blessed and holy –**beatification** /biʸ,ætəfɪ'keʸʃən/ [C;U]

beaut /byuʷt/ *AmE infml* for beauty (3): *That black eye is a real beaut!*

beau·ti·cian /byuʷ'tɪʃən/ *n* a person who gives beauty treatments (as to skin and hair)

beau·ti·ful /'byuʷtəfəl/ *adj* having beauty –**beautifully** *adv*

USAGE When used to describe a person's appearance, **beautiful** is a very strong word meaning "giving great pleasure to the senses." Its opposite is **ugly** or, even stronger, **hideous. Plain** is a less *derog* way of saying **ugly. Pretty, handsome, good-looking,** and **attractive** all mean "pleasant to look at;" but **pretty** is only used of women and children, and **handsome** (usually) only of men. **Good-looking, handsome,** and **plain** are normally only used of people, but the other words can also be used of things: *a* **pretty** *garden|a* **hideous** *dress.*

beau·ti·fy /'byuʷtə,faɪ/ *v* -**fied, -fying** [T] to make beautiful

beau·ty /'byuʷtiʸ/ *n* -**ties 1** [U] qualities that give pleasure to the senses or lift up the mind or spirit: *a woman/a poem of great beauty* **2** [C] someone (usu. female) or something beautiful: *She is a great beauty.|the beauties of the national parks* **3** [C] *infml* someone or something very good (or bad): *That apple is a real beauty.* **4 the beauty (of something)** the advantage (of something): *The beauty of my idea is that it would cost so little!*

beauty spot /'·· ˌ·/ *n* **1** a dark-coloured spot (natural or otherwise) on a woman's face, formerly considered attractive; PATCH¹ (7) **2** a place known for the beauty of its scenery

bea·ver /'biʸvər/ *n* -**ver** *or* -**vers** [C;U] (the valuable fur of) a type of water and land animal of the rat family, which builds DAMs across streams

be·bop /'biʸbap/ *n* [U] →BOP (2)

be·calmed /bɪ'kɑmd/ *adj* (of a sailing ship)

unable to move forward because of lack of wind

be·cause /bɪˈkɔz, -ˈkʌz/ conj for the reason that: *I was angry because he was late.*|*"Why can't I go?" "Because you're too young."* –see REASON (USAGE); see Study Notes on page 144

because of prep by reason of: *I came back because of the rain.*

beck /bɛk/ n **at someone's/one's beck and call** always ready to do everything someone/one asks

beck·on /ˈbɛkən/ v [I;T] to make a silent sign, as with the finger, to call (someone): *She's beckoning (to) me.*|*She beckoned me to follow her.*

be·come /bɪˈkʌm/ v **-came** /ˈkeɪm/, **-come**, **-coming** /ˈkʌmɪŋ/ **1** to come to be: *She became a lawyer.*|*The weather became warmer.* **2** [T] fml to be right or fitting for: *Those words do not become a person in your position.*

become of sbdy./sthg. v prep [T] to happen to (usu. a person or material thing), often in a bad way: *Whatever became of that little boy who ran away from home?*

USAGE Compare **become, come, go**: **Become** is the most formal, and can be used of people or things: *Mary* **became** *famous.*|*The sky* **became** *cloudy.*|*It* **became** *clear that he was lying.* People can **go** or **become** mad, blind, LAME, brown (=from the sun) or gray (=gray hair) but one cannot say **He went famous/angry.* One can use **go** to mean **become** about things: *The meat* **went** *bad.*|*Everything's* **going** *wrong.*|*The sky* **went** *cloudy.* Note also the use of **come** in the phrase: *Her dream* **came** *true.* –see GET[1] (USAGE)

be·com·ing /bɪˈkʌmɪŋ/ adj fml **1** apprec (of a hat, dress, color, etc.) looking very well on the wearer: *Blue always looks very becoming on her.* **2** proper; suitable; right: *His laughter was not very becoming on such a solemn occasion.* –opposite **unbecoming** –**becomingly** adv

bed[1] /bɛd/ n **1** [C;U] an article of furniture to sleep on: *a room with two beds*|*a comfortable bed for the night*|*It's time for bed*|*It's bedtime.*|*He helped me to* **make the bed.** (=put on the BEDCLOTHES or rearrange them after the bed has been slept in) –see illustration on page 55 **2** [C] a surface that forms the base or bottom of something: *The garage rests on a bed of cement.*|*I served the chicken on a bed of lettuce.*|*the bed of the river*|*the seabed* **3** [C] a piece of ground prepared for plants: *a flowerbed* **4** [C] a band of rock of a certain kind lying above or below others; STRATUM (1): *The building stands on a bed of rock.* **5 a bed of roses** infml a happy comfortable state **6 get up on the wrong side of the bed** infml to be in a bad temper

bed[2] v **-dd-** [T] **1** to fix on a base (or beneath the surface); EMBED: *The machine is bedded in cement.* **2** to plant in a bed or beds: *These young plants will soon be ready for bedding (out).*

bed down v adv **1** [T (=bed sbdy./ sthg.

down)] to make (a person or animal) comfortable for the night **2** [I] to make oneself comfortable for the night: *I'll bed down on these chairs.*

bed and board /ˌ· · ·ˈ·/ n [U] lodging and food

bed·clothes /ˈbɛdkloʊðz, -kloʊðz/ n [P] the sheets, covers, etc. put on a bed

bed·ding /ˈbɛdɪŋ/ n [U] **1** materials on which a person or animal can sleep: *This dried grass will make good bedding for the animals.* **2** →BEDCLOTHES

be·deck /bɪˈdɛk/ v [T with] fml to decorate: *The cars were all bedecked with flowers for the ceremony.*

be·dev·il /bɪˈdɛvəl/ v **-l-** AmE‖**-ll-** BrE [T] to trouble greatly: *The building of the bridge has been bedeviled by arguments over the plans.* –**bedevilment** n [U]

bed·lam /ˈbɛdləm/ n [S;U] infml a wild noisy place or activity

bed·pan /ˈbɛdpæn/ n a low wide vessel used by a sick person for emptying the bowels without getting out of bed –compare POT[1] (3)

be·drag·gled /bɪˈdrægəld/ adj with the clothes and hair in disorder: *a bedraggled appearance*

bed·rid·den /ˈbɛdˌrɪdn/ adj unable to get out of bed because of illness or old age

bed·room /ˈbɛdruʷm, -rʊm/ n a room for sleeping in –see illustration on page 55

bed·side /ˈbɛdsaɪd/ n the side of a bed: *He was called to the bedside of his sick father.*|*a bedside lamp*

bed·spread /ˈbɛdsprɛd/ n a decorative cloth spread over a bed –see illustration on page 55

bee /biʸ/ n **1** a stinging insect that makes HONEY and lives in groups **2 a bee in one's bonnet** infml a fixed idea: *He has a bee in his bonnet about health foods.*

beech /biʸtʃ/ n [C;U] also **beech tree** /ˈ· ·/– (the wood of) a tree with smooth grey trunk, spreading branches, and dark green or copper-colored leaves –sounds like **beach**

beef[1] /biʸf/ n [U] the meat of farm cattle –see MEAT (USAGE)

beef[2] v [I about] infml often derog to complain (about): *Stop beefing (about pay) and do some work!*

beef sthg.↔**up** v adv [T] AmE infml to strengthen: *We have to beef up the army with more soldiers.*

beef·y /ˈbiʸfiʸ/ adj **-ier, -iest** infml (of a person) big, strong, and perhaps fat

bee·hive /ˈbiʸhaɪv/ n →HIVE (1a)

bee·line /ˈbiʸlaɪn/ n **make a beeline for** infml to go quickly along a straight direct course for: *The hungry boy made a beeline for his dinner*

been /bɪn/ v **1** past participle of BE **2** (to have) gone and come back from: *Have you ever been to India?*

beer /bɪər/ n **1** [C;U] (a container of) a bitter alcoholic drink made from grain: *Do you like beer?*|*We had several beers.* **2** [U] (in comb) any of several kinds of drink, usu. non-alcoholic, made from roots or plants: *root beer* –**beery** adj: *unpleasant beery breath*

bees·wax /ˈbiʸzwæks/ n [U] wax made by

bees, used for making furniture polish, candles, etc.

beet /biˑt/ n 1 [C;U] AmE‖**beetroot** BrE– a plant with a large red round root, cooked and eaten as a vegetable 2 [C] also **sugar beet**– a plant which grows under the ground and from which beet sugar is obtained

bee·tle /ˈbiˑt̩l/ n an insect with hard wing coverings

beet·root /ˈbiˑt-ruˑt, -rʊt/ n **beetroot** or **beetroots** [C;U] BrE for BEET (1)

be·fall /bɪˈfɔl/ v -**fell** /ˈfɛl/, -**fallen** /ˈfɔlən/, -**falling** [I;T] fml (usu. of something bad) to happen (to), esp. as if by fate: Some misfortune must have befallen them.

be·fore¹ /bɪˈfɔr, -ˈfoʷr/ adv [no comp.] at an earlier time; earlier: Haven't I seen you before?|You should have told me this before. –see AGO (USAGE)

before² prep 1 earlier than: before 1937|the day before yesterday (=two days ago)|He got there before me. 2 in front of; ahead of: Your name comes before mine in the list.|You will have to swear before the judge. 3 in a more important position than: to put quality before quantity –compare AFTER¹

before³ conj 1 earlier than the time when: Say goodbye before you go. –compare AFTER³ 2 more willingly than; rather than: He will die before he will tell them what they want to know.

be·fore·hand /bɪˈfɔr,hænd, -ˈfoʷr-/ adv [no comp.] before something else happens: We knew they were coming, so we bought plenty of food beforehand.

be·friend /bɪˈfrɛnd/ v [T] fml to act as a friend to (someone younger, poorer, or weaker): He befriended me when I was young.

beg /bɛg/ v -**gg**- 1 [I;T +that/to-v/of, for] to ask humbly for (food, money, or other necessary things): He lives by begging (for money).|to beg a favor (of someone)|to beg that one (should/may) be allowed to go|He begged me to stay.|to beg (for) forgiveness 2 [T +to-v] fml to allow oneself: I beg to point out that your facts are incorrect.

beg·gar¹ /ˈbɛgər/ n 1 a person who lives by BEGging (1) 2 **Beggars can't be choosers** infml If you are asking for help, you must take what you are offered

beggar² v [T] fml to make very poor: They were beggared by trying to pay for their son's education.

beg·gar·ly /ˈbɛgərliˑ/ adj 1 of or like a BEGGAR 2 much too little for the purpose

be·gin /bɪˈgɪn/ v **began** /bɪˈgæn/, **begun** /bɪˈgʌn/, **beginning** [I;T +to-v/ v-ing] to start; take the first step: She began working here in 1962.|to begin by dancing/with a story/on a new book/at the beginning|It began to rain.|We can't go. To begin with, (=the first reason is) it's too cold. Besides, we don't have any money. –see START¹ (USAGE)

be·gin·ner /bɪˈgɪnər/ n a person who begins or has begun some activity, but who has very little experience –compare STARTER

be·gin·ning /bɪˈgɪnɪŋ/ n [C;U] the start; starting point; origin: She knows that subject from beginning to end.|at/in the beginning –compare ENDING

be·grudge /bɪˈgrʌdʒ/ v -**grudged**, -**grudging** [T +v-ing] →GRUDGE¹

be·guile /bɪˈgaɪl/ v -**guiled**, -**guiling** [T] fml 1 [into, out of] to deceive; cheat: He beguiled me into lending him my bicycle. 2 to charm: Her eyes and voice beguiled me. –**beguiling** adj

be·half /bɪˈhæf/ n **on behalf of someone/someone's behalf** also **in behalf of someone/someone's behalf** AmE– (acting, speaking, etc.) for someone; in the interests of someone: The President can't be here today, so I'm going to speak on his behalf.

be·have /bɪˈheʸv/ v -**haved**, -**having** [I] 1 to act; bear oneself: She behaved with great courage. 2 [I;T] to bear (oneself) in a socially-acceptable or polite way: Learn how to behave.|Behave (yourself)!|a well-behaved/badly-behaved child

be·hav·ior AmE‖**behaviour** BrE /bɪˈheʸvyər/ n [U] 1 way of behaving 2 **be on one's best behavior** to try to show one's best manners

be·head /bɪˈhɛd/ v [T] to cut off the head of, esp. as a punishment; DECAPITATE

be·hind¹ /bɪˈhaɪnd/ adv [no comp.] 1 towards or at the back: a house with a garage behind –compare FRONT¹ (1) 2 where something or someone was before: I can't unlock the car because I've left the keys behind.|They went for a walk but I stayed behind to look after the baby. 3 late; slow; BEHINDHAND: We're a month behind with the rent. (=we should have paid the rent a month ago)

behind² prep 1 towards or at the back of: We followed behind the advancing army.|She ran out from behind a tree. 2 less good than; below: We're three points behind the team in first place. 3 in support of; encouraging: We're all behind you (=we all agree with you) in this decision.

behind³ n euph infml the part of the body that a person sits on; BUTTOCKS: a kick in the behind

be·hind·hand /bɪˈhaɪnd,hænd/ adj, adv [with, in] fml late; slow: We're a month behindhand with the rent.

be·hold /bɪˈhoʷld/ v **beheld** /bɪˈhɛld/, **beholding** [T] lit & old use to have in sight; see –**beholder** n: Beauty is in the eye of the beholder.

beige /beʸʒ/ n, adj [U] a pale dull yellowish brown

be·ing /ˈbiʸɪŋ/ n 1 [U] existence; life: When did the club first come into being? 2 [C] a living thing, esp. a person: a human being

be·la·bor AmE‖**belabour** BrE /bɪˈleʸbər/ v [T] to work on or talk about to silly lengths: He kept belaboring the point until we were all tired.

be·lat·ed /bɪˈleʸt̩ɪd/ adj delayed; arriving too late –**belatedly** adv

belch /bɛltʃ/ v 1 [I] (of a person) to pass wind noisily from the stomach out through the throat 2 [T out] to throw out with force or in large quantities: Chimneys belch (out) smoke.

Bob usually **goes to bed** at about 11:00. He puts on his **pajamas** and **turns down the covers** of the bed. Before going to bed, he **sets his alarm** for 6:30. He usually **falls asleep** very quickly.

One night Bob forgot to set his alarm, and he **overslept.** He didn't **wake up** until 8:00, and was **late** for work.

When Bob's alarm **goes off** at 6:30, he **gets up.** He turns off the alarm, puts on his **bathrobe** and **slippers,** and then he's ready to **shower, get dressed,** and **have breakfast.** Before he goes to work, he **makes the bed.** On Saturdays, when Bob doesn't have to go to work, he likes to **sleep late.** Sometimes he doesn't get up until 9:00 on Saturdays.

Fill in the blanks.

1. When I went to bed, I _____ my alarm for 7:00, but I _____ up at 6:30.
2. Be sure to _____ your bed before leaving home.
3. I fell _____ while I was reading in bed.
4. I'd like to _____ to bed early tonight. I'm tired.
5. I'm sorry I'm late. I _____ this morning.
6. I'm tired. I'd like to sleep _____ tomorrow.

bel·fry /'bɛlfriʸ/ n -fries a tower for a bell (e.g. on a church)

be·lie /bɪ'laɪ/ v -lied, -lying [T] fml to give a false idea of: Her smile belied her real feelings of displeasure.

be·lief /bə'liʸf/ n 1 [S;U in] the feeling that something is true or that something really exists: (a) belief in God|my belief that he is right|His story is **beyond belief.** (=too strange to be believed) 2 [S;U in] trust; a feeling that someone or something is good or able: The failure of the operation has shaken my belief in doctors. 3 [C] something believed; an idea which is considered true, often one which is part of a system of ideas: my religious beliefs

be·liev·a·ble /bə'liʸvəbəl/ adj that can be believed –see also UNBELIEVABLE –**believably** adv

be·lieve /bə'liʸv/ v -lieved, -lieving [not be+v-ing] 1 to consider to be true or honest: to believe someone|to believe someone's reports –see also DISBELIEVE 2 [+(that)] to hold as an opinion; suppose: I believe (that) she is telling the truth.|I believe him to have done it.|I believe him (to be) honest.

   believe in sbdy./sthg. v prep [T] 1 to accept as true the existence of: Do you believe in fairies? 2 to have faith or trust in: Christians believe in Jesus. 3 to consider (something) to be of worth: Jim believes in going for a run every morning.

be·lit·tle /bɪ'lɪtl̩/ v -tled, -tling [T] fml to cause to seem little or unimportant: Don't belittle yourself/your efforts.

bell /bɛl/ n a round hollow metal vessel, which makes a ringing sound when struck

bell-bot·toms /'·· ,··ʸ/ n [P] pants with legs that become much wider at the bottom –see PAIR¹ (USAGE)

belle /bɛl/ n a popular and attractive girl or woman: the belle of the BALL (=the prettiest girl at the dance)

bel·li·cose /'bɛlɪˌkoʷs/ adj fml warlike; ready to quarrel or fight

bel·lig·er·ent /bə'lɪdʒərənt/ adj having or showing anger and readiness to fight: You said some very belligerent things. Were you trying to start a fight? –**belligerency** n [U]

bel·low /'bɛloʷ/ v 1 [I] to make the loud deep hollow sound typical of a BULL¹ (1) 2 [I;T] to shout (something) in a deep voice: to bellow (out) with excitement/pain|to bellow (out) orders|"Go away!" he bellowed. –**bellow** n

bel·lows /'bɛloʷz/ n bellows an instrument used for blowing air into a fire, ORGAN (3), etc. quickly –see PAIR¹ (USAGE)

bel·ly /'bɛliʸ/ n -lies 1 infml the part of the human body, between the chest and the legs, which contains the stomach and bowels 2 a surface or object curved or round like this part of the body: the belly of the plane/ship 3 –**bellied** having a BELLY of the stated type: a big-bellied man

bel·ly·ache /'bɛliʸˌeʸk/ v -ached, -aching [I about] infml often derog to complain, perhaps unjustly: Stop bellyaching and get on with the job!

belly but·ton /'·· ,··ʸ/ n infml for NAVEL

bel·ly·ful /'bɛliʸˌful/ n [S] infml too much: I've had a bellyful of your complaints.

be·long /bɪ'lɔŋ/ v [I] 1 to be in the right place: That chair belongs in the other room.|A man of his ability belongs in teaching.

   belong to sbdy./sthg. v prep [T no pass.] 1 to be the property of: That dictionary belongs to me. 2 to be a member of; be connected with: What party do you belong to?

be·long·ings /bɪ'lɔŋɪŋz/ n [P] those things which belong to one, which are one's property: She lost all her belongings in the fire.

be·loved /bɪ'lʌvd, bɪ'lʌvɪd/ adj,n [S] (a person who is) dearly loved: beloved by/of all her friends|His beloved (wife) had died.

be·low¹ /bɪ'loʷ/ adv [no comp.] 1 in a lower place; lower: He looked down from the mountain to the valley below.|officers of the rank of captain and below (=of lower rank)|children of seven and below (=younger) –opposite **above**; compare UNDER¹ 2 under the surface: miners working below (=under the earth)|The captain told the sailors to go below. (=to a lower DECK of the ship) 3 on a later page or lower on the same page: See page 85 below. –compare ABOVE² (3)

below² prep lower than; under: below the knee|a mile below the village|children below the age of seven (=younger than seven)|A captain is below a general. (=lower in rank)|below the surface of the water –opposite **above**; compare UNDER²

belt¹ /bɛlt/ n 1 a band worn around the waist: a leather belt –see illustration on page 123 2 a long circular piece of leather or other such material used for driving a machine or for carrying materials 3 an area that has some special quality: a green belt (=where grass and trees must not be replaced by buildings)|a cotton/corn belt (=where cotton/corn is the major crop) 4 **hit below the belt** infml to give an unfair blow (to) or attack unfairly 5 **tighten one's belt** infml to live more cheaply: In a period of mass unemployment a lot of people have to tighten their belts.

belt² v [T] 1 to fasten with a belt: She belted (up) her raincoat. –opposite **unbelt** 2 to hit with a belt: He really belted his son! 3 infml to hit very hard, esp. with the hand: I belted him in the eye.

be·moan /bɪ'moʷn/ v [T] fml to be very sorry because of: He bemoaned his fate.

be·mused /bɪ'myuʷzd/ adj having or showing inability to think properly: a bemused expression|He was bemused by/with all the questions.

bench /bɛntʃ/ n 1 [C] a long seat for two or more people: a park bench 2 [S] a judge or his seat in court: The bench declared....|to speak from the bench 3 [the U] judges as a group: What does the bench think about this? 4 [C] a long worktable

bend¹ /bɛnd/ v bent /bɛnt/, bending 1 [I;T] to (cause to) be forced into or out of a curve or angle: to bend the wire|(fig.) She is very firm about it: I can't bend her into changing her mind. **2** [I;T] to (cause to) slope or lean away from an upright position: *to bend over/down/forward/back|bent down with age* **3** [T] to direct (one's efforts): *He bent his mind to the job.* –see also BENT, BENT ON

bend² *n* **1** the act or action of bending or the state of being bent **2** something that is bent: *a bend in the road/river* **3 around the bend** *infml, often humor* mad: *He really drives me around the bend!*

be·neath¹ /bɪˈniʸθ/ *adv [no comp.] fml* below; underneath: *He looked down from the mountain to the valley beneath.* –compare BELOW¹, UNDER¹

beneath² *prep* **1** below; underneath: *a village beneath the hills|The ship sank beneath the waves.* **2** *fml* not worthy of: *Such behavior is beneath you.* –compare UNDER², BELOW²

ben·e·dic·tion /ˌbɛnəˈdɪkʃən/ *n* (the act of giving) a blessing

ben·e·fac·tion /ˌbɛnəˈfækʃən/ *n* [C;U] doing good or giving money for a good purpose; money so given

ben·e·fac·tor /ˈbɛnəˌfæktər/ **benefactress** /-trɪs/ *fem. n* a person who does good or who gives money for a good purpose

be·nef·i·cent /bəˈnɛfəsənt/ *adj fml apprec* doing good; kind **–beneficence** *n* [U]

ben·e·fi·cial /ˌbɛnəˈfɪʃəl/ *adj* (of non-living things) helpful; useful: *His vacation has had a beneficial effect.* **–beneficially** *adv*

ben·e·fi·ci·ar·y /ˌbɛnəˈfɪʃiʸˌɛriʸ, -ˈfɪʃəriʸ/ *n* **-ies** the receiver of a BENEFIT, esp. a person who receives money or property left by someone who has died

ben·e·fit¹ /ˈbɛnəfɪt/ *n* **1** [U] advantage; profit; good effect: *She had the benefit of a good education.|I've done it for his benefit.|It is of great benefit to everyone.* **2** [C] money provided by the government as a right, esp. in sickness or unemployment: *unemployment benefit|unemployment and sickness benefits* **3 benefit of the doubt** the right to favorable consideration in the absence of complete proof of wrongness or guilt: *We have to give him the benefit of the doubt until we are certain he's guilty.*

benefit² *v* **-fited, -fiting** [T] *fml* (of non-living things) to be useful, profitable, or helpful to: *Such foolish behavior will not benefit your case.*

benefit from/by sbdy./sthg. *v prep* [T] to gain by; receive BENEFIT¹ from: *Who would be most likely to benefit from the old man's death?*

be·nev·o·lent /bəˈnɛvələnt/ *adj* having or expressing a wish to do good –see also MALEVOLENT **–benevolently** *adv* **–benevolence** *n* [S;U]

be·nign /bɪˈnaɪn/ *adj* having or showing a kind or gentle nature: *A benign TUMOR will not cause you harm.* –compare MALIGNANT **–benignly** *adv*

bent¹ /bɛnt/ *n* [*for*] special natural skill or cleverness (in): *She has a natural bent for art.*

bent² *v past tense and participle of* BEND

bent on also **bent upon–** *adj* [F +*v-ing*] with one's mind set on; determined on: *She seems bent on becoming a musician.*

be·queath /bɪˈkwiʸð, bɪˈkwiʸθ/ *v* [T *to*] *fml* to give or pass on to others after death: *They bequeathed him a lot of money.* **–bequest** /bɪˈkwɛst/ *n: a bequest of $50,000 to his children*

be·reave /bəˈriʸv/ *v* **bereaved** *or* **bereft** /bəˈrɛft/, **bereaving** [T *of*] *fml* to take away, esp. by death: *He was bereaved (of his wife) last year|a bereaved mother* (=one whose child has died) **–bereavement** *n* [U]: *Bereavement is often a time of great grief.*

be·reft /bəˈrɛft/ *adj* [F *of*] completely without: *bereft of all hope*

be·ret /bəˈreʸ/ *n* a round usu. woolen cap with a tight headband and a soft full flat top

ber·ry /ˈbɛriʸ/ *n* **-ries** a small soft fruit

ber·serk /bərˈsɜrk, -ˈzɜrk/ *adj* [F] mad with violent anger: *On hearing the terrible news he went berserk.*

berth¹ /bɜrθ/ *n* **1** a place where a ship can stop and be tied up, as in a harbor **2** a sleeping place in a ship or train **3 give someone/something a wide berth** *infml* to stay at a safe distance from someone or something dangerous or unpleasant

berth² *v* [I;T] **a** (of a ship) to come into port to be tied up **b** to bring (a ship) into port to be tied up: *The captain berthed the ship at midday.*

be·seech /bɪˈsiʸtʃ/ *v* **besought** /bɪˈsɔt/ *or* **beseeched, beseeching** [T] *fml or lit* to ask eagerly and anxiously: *He besought a favor of the judge.*

be·set /bɪˈsɛt/ *v* **beset, besetting** [T *usu. pass.*] to trouble from all directions; attack without ceasing: *He was beset by doubts.|The plan was beset with difficulties.*

be·side /bɪˈsaɪd/ *prep* **1** by the side of; next to: *sitting beside the driver|a town beside the sea* **2** compared with: *The sales figures for this year don't look very good beside last year's results.* **3 beside oneself (with)** almost mad (with): *The children were beside themselves with excitement before the party.* **4 beside the point** having nothing to do with the main point or question: *I want to do it anyway: the cost is beside the point* –see BESIDES² (USAGE)

be·sides¹ /bɪˈsaɪdz/ *adv [no comp.]* in addition; also: *I don't want to go; (and) besides, I'm tired.|This car belongs to Mrs. Smith; she has two others besides.*

besides² *prep* as well as; in addition to: *There were three other people at the meeting besides Mr. Day.* –see Study Notes on page 144

USAGE **Besides** means "as well as" but **except** means "leaving out; but not." So *All of us spoke* **besides** *John* means that John spoke too, but *All of us spoke* **except** *John* means that John did not speak.

be·siege /bɪˈsiʸdʒ/ *v* **-sieged, -sieging** [T] to surround with armed forces: (fig.) *The crowd besieged the mayor with questions about their taxes.*

be·sot·ted /bɪˈsɑtɪd/ *adj* [F *with*] made dull or foolish: *besotted with drink/love/power*

be·sought /bɪˈsɔt/ *v past tense and participle of* BESEECH

best¹ /bɛst/ *adj* (SUPERLATIVE¹ *of* GOOD) **1** the

highest in quality; the most good: *the best tennis player in the world*|*She's my best friend.*|*What's the best thing to do?* –compare WORST[1] **2 the best part of** most of: *I haven't seen her for the best part of a week.*

best[2] *adv* (SUPERLATIVE[1] *of* WELL[3]) **1** in the best way; most well: *The one who does best will get the prize.* **2** to the best degree; most: *the best-loved singer*|*Tuesday will suit me best.* **3 as best one can** as well as one can **4 had best → had** BETTER[2] (3) –compare WORST[2]

best[3] *n* [S] **1** the most good thing or part; the greatest degree of good: *Only the best is good enough.* **2** one's best effort or state: *He did his best*|*tried his best to finish it.*|*to look one's best*|*I'm never* **at my best** *early in the morning.* **3 one's (Sunday) best** one's best clothes **4 All the best!** (*used when saying good-bye*) *I wish you success and happiness!* **5 at (the) best** if the best happens: *At best the company will take a big loss this year; at worst we may have to close down.* –compare WORST[3] **6 make the best of** to do as well as one can with (something not very good): *to make the best of a bad state of affairs*

bes·tial /ˈbestʃəl, ˈbiːs-/ *adj derog* **1** (of human beings and their behavior) of or like an animal in being nasty or shameful **2** very cruel; BRUTAL: *bestial cruelty* –COMPARE BEASTLY **–bestially** *adv* **–bestiality** /ˌbestʃiˈæləti, ˌbiːs-/ *n* [U]

best man /ˌ· '·/ *n* (at a marriage ceremony) the friend and attendant of the man who is to be married (BRIDEGROOM)

be·stow /bɪˈstoʊ/ *v* [T *on, upon*] to give: *Several gifts were bestowed on the President's visitors.* **–bestowal** *n*

best sel·ler /ˌ· '··/ *n* something (esp. a book) that sells in very large numbers

bet[1] /bet/ *n* **1** an agreement to risk money on the result of a future event: *I've made a bet that my party will win the next election.*|*to win/lose a bet* **2** a sum of money so risked: *a $5 bet*

bet[2] *v* **bet** *or* **betted, betting** [I;T +(*that*)/*on*] **1** to risk (money) on the result of a future event: *I bet (you) ($5) that they'll win the next election.*|*I bet on the wrong horse; it lost the race!* **2 I bet** *infml* I'm sure: *I bet it rains/will rain tomorrow!*

be·tide /bɪˈtaɪd/ *v lit* **Woe betide (you, him,** etc.) you, he, etc., will be in trouble: *Woe betide them if they're late!*

be·tray /bɪˈtreɪ/ *v* **-trayed, -traying 1** [*to*] to be disloyal or unfaithful to: *I thought he would be too loyal to betray his friends!* **2** [*to*] *fml* to give away or make known (esp. a secret): *He betrayed the secret to his friends.* **3** [+*that/to*] to show the real feelings or intentions of: *Her face betrayed her nervousness/betrayed (the fact) that she was nervous/betrayed what she was thinking.* **–betrayer** *n*

be·tray·al /bɪˈtreɪəl/ *n* [C;U] (an example of) the act of BETRAYing: *a betrayal of my principles*

be·troth /bɪˈtroʊð, bɪˈtrɔθ, bɪˈtroʊθ/ *v* [T *to*] *becoming rare* to promise to give (oneself) in marriage **–betrothal** /bɪˈtroʊðəl, bɪˈtrɔθəl, -ˈtroʊ-/ *n* [U]

bet·ter[1] /ˈbetər/ *adj* **1** (COMPARATIVE[2] *of* GOOD) higher in quality; more good: *Their house is better than ours.*|*much better weather than last week*|*I'm worse at chemistry than Jean, but I'm better at history.* **2** (COMPARATIVE[2] *of* WELL[5]) **a** improved in health: *I'm feeling a little better today.* **b** [*no comp.*] completely well again after an illness: *Now that he's better he can play football again.* **3 better than** *infml* more than: *Better than 100 people attended the meeting.* **4 one's better half** *infml humor* one's wife or husband **5 the better part of** more than half: *I haven't seen him for the better part of a month!* –compare WORSE[1]

better[2] *adv* (COMPARATIVE[2] *of* WELL[3]) **1** in a better way: *He swims better than he used to.* **2** to a greater degree: *She knows the story better than I do.* **3 had better** ought to; should: *You'd better go home now.*|*I'd better not tell him.* –compare WORSE[2]

better[3] *n* **1 a change for the better** a change with good results **2 get the better of** to defeat (someone) or deal successfully with (a difficulty): *to get the better of one's opponents* –compare WORSE[3]

better[4] *v* [I;T] to (cause to) improve (on): *They tried to better their living conditions.*|*Living conditions have bettered a great deal.*|*to better last year's results* –compare WORSEN

be·tween[1] /bɪˈtwiːn/ *prep* **1** (used to show that two things are separated): *She stood between John and Mary.*|*between five and six o'clock*|*You shouldn't eat between meals.*|*a color between blue and gray*|*There's a regular air service between New York and Washington.* **2** (used when things are shared by two): *Divide the money between the two of them.*|*Between us we can finish the job in an hour.* **3 between you and me** without anyone else knowing; privately: *Between you and me, (I think) he's dishonest.*

USAGE Compare **among** and **between**: In careful speech and writing, **between** should only be followed by two people, things, etc., and **among** by three or more. Some people use **between** in all cases, but teachers consider this incorrect. *Divide it between the two children/among all the children.* Note that we always use **between,** not **among,** when we speak of exact position in the middle of several things: *Ecuador lies between Colombia, Peru, and the Pacific Ocean.*

between[2] *adv* **1** in or into a space, or period of time, that is between: *I ate breakfast and dinner but nothing between.* **2 few and far between** *infml* rare and infrequent

bev·el /ˈbevəl/ *v* **-l-** *AmE*‖**-ll-** *BrE* [T] to make a sloping edge on (wood or glass) **–bevel** *n*

bev·er·age /ˈbevərɪdʒ/ *n fml* a liquid for drinking, esp. one that is not water, medicine, or alcohol: *We sell hot beverages.* (=tea, coffee, etc.)

be·wail /bɪˈweɪl/ *v* [T] *fml* to express deep sorrow for, esp. by or as if by weeping

be·ware /bɪˈwɛər/ *v* [I;T *of*] to be careful USAGE **Beware** is only used in giving or reporting warnings, and its form does not change: **Beware of** *the dog.*|*You must beware* of *accepting gifts from strangers.*

be·wil·der /bɪˈwɪldər/ *v* [T] to confuse: *Big city traffic bewilders me.*|*a bewildering mass of details*|*a bewildered look* **–bewilderment** *n* [U]: *Imagine my bewilderment when she said that!*

be·witch /bɪˈwɪtʃ/ *v* [T] **1** to have a magic effect, often harmful, on **2** to charm as if by magic: *a bewitching smile*

be·yond¹ /bɪˈyand/ *adv* on or to the further side; further: *I will go with you to the bridge, but not a step beyond.*|(fig.) *'to prepare for the changes of the 1980s and beyond'*

beyond² *prep* **1** on or to the further side of: *What lies beyond those mountains?* **2** past the limits of: *Don't stay there beyond midnight.*|*The fruit was beyond my reach.*|*It's beyond me* (=too hard for me to understand) *why she married him.* **3** besides; except for: *I own nothing beyond the clothes on my back.*|*I can't tell you anything beyond what you know already.*

bi·as¹ /ˈbaɪəs/ *n* **-ases** [C;U] **1** a tendency to be in favor of or against something or someone; PREJUDICE¹: *a bias towards/against the government* **2** a tendency of mind: *Her scientific bias showed itself in early childhood.*

bias² *v* **-s-** *or* **-ss-** [T] to cause to form settled favorable or unfavorable opinions without enough information to judge fairly; PREJUDICE² (1): *His background biases him against foreigners.*

bib /bɪb/ *n* a cloth or plastic shield tied under a child's chin to protect its clothes

bi·ble /ˈbaɪbəl/ *n* [C;*the* S] (*usu. cap.*) (a copy of) the holy book of the Christians and the Jews **–biblical** /ˈbɪblɪkəl/ *adj*

bib·li·og·ra·phy /ˌbɪbliˈagrəfiʸ/ *n* **-phies** a list of writings which share some quality, esp. a list of all writings used in the preparation of a book or article

bi·car·bon·ate /baɪˈkarbənɪt, -ˌneʸt/ *also* **bicarbonate of soda** /·ˌ···· · ˈ··/ *also* **bicarb** /baɪˈkarb/ *infml– n* [U] a chemical substance used esp. in baking and also taken with water to settle the stomach

bi·cen·ten·a·ry /ˌbaɪsɛnˈtɛnəriʸ, baɪˈsɛn tәˌnɛriʸ/ **-ries** *n* →BICENTENNIAL

bi·cen·ten·ni·al /ˌbaɪsɛnˈtɛniʸəl/ *n AmE* the day or year about 200 years after a particular event: *The US had its bicentennial in 1976.*

bi·ceps /ˈbaɪsɛps/ *n* **biceps** the large muscle on the front of the upper arm

bick·er /ˈbɪkər/ *v* [I *about, over*] to quarrel, esp. about small matters: *The two children were always bickering (with each other) (over/about their toys).*

bi·cy·cle¹ /ˈbaɪsɪkəl/ *also* **cycle, bike** *infml– n* a two-wheeled vehicle which one rides by pushing its PEDALs with the feet: *She goes to work on her bicycle/by bicycle.*|*He got on his bicycle and rode off.*

bicycle² *also* **cycle, bike** *infml– v* **-cled, -cling** [I] to travel by bicycle: *We bicycled/cycled to the beach.*

bid¹ /bɪd/ *v* **bid, bidding** [I;T] **1** to offer (a price) whether for payment or acceptance,

as at an AUCTION: *She bid $10 for the book.*|*What am I bid for this old book?* (=what will people bid for it?) **2** (in card games) to make a BID² (3): *I bid two SPADES².* **–bidder** *n*

bid² *n* **1** an offer to pay a certain price, esp. at an AUCTION: *a bid of $10 for that old book* **2** an offer to do some work at a certain price; TENDER³ (1): *Bids for building the bridge were invited from American and Japanese companies.* **3** (a chance or turn to make) a declaration of the number of games (TRICKs) a cardplayer says he intends to win: *a bid of two SPADES²* **4** an attempt to get or win: *The criminal made* **a bid for freedom** *by trying to run away.*

bid³ *v* **bade** /bæd, beʸd/ *or* **bid, bidden** /ˈbɪdn/ *or* **bid, bidding** *old use or lit* [T] **1** [*to*] to say (a greeting or goodbye to someone): *He bid me good morning as he passed.* **2** to order or tell (someone to do something): *She would never do as she was bidden.*|*She bade him come.*

bid·ding /ˈbɪdɪŋ/ *n* [U] **1** order; command (esp. in the phrases **at one's bidding, do someone's bidding**) **2** the act or action of making BIDs²

bide /baɪd/ *v* **bided** *or* **bode** /boʷd/, **biding**: **bide one's time** to wait, usu. for a long time, until the right moment: *He seems to be doing nothing, but really he's just biding his time.*

bi·det /bɪˈdeʸ/ *n* a kind of small low bath on which one sits to wash the lower parts of the body

bi·en·ni·al /baɪˈɛniʸəl/ *adj* **1** (of events) happening once every two years: *A biennial art show is held in the city: I saw it in 1970, 1972, and 1974.* **2** (of plants) living for two years and producing seeds in the second year **–compare** ANNUAL **–biennially** *adv*

bier /bɪər/ *n* a movable frame like a table, for supporting a dead body or COFFIN

bi·fo·cals /ˈbaɪˌfoʷkəlz, baɪˈfoʷkəlz/ *n* [P] eyeglasses having an upper part made for looking at distant objects, and a lower part made for reading **–see** PAIR¹ (USAGE) **–bifocal** *adj*

big /bɪg/ *adj* **-gg-** **1** of more than average size, weight, force, importance, etc.: *a big box*|*How big is it?*|*bigger than a house*|*a big mouse*|*That child is big for her age.*|*The big question is what to do next.*|(fig.) *big-hearted* (=generous; unselfish)|(fig.) *John is a big spender.* (=spends money freely)|*a big eater* **–compare** LITTLE¹, SMALL¹ **–see** Study Notes on page 550 **2** [F] *infml* very popular, successful, or important: *She's very big/a big name/in the big time in the music world.* **3** **too big for one's britches/boots** *infml* believing oneself to be more important than one really is **4** **that's big of (you, him, etc.)** *infml* that's generous of (you, him, etc.) **5** **big deal** *AmE infml* showing that one considers something unimportant: *"Be careful how you speak to him. He's the company president." "Big deal."* **6** **big mouth** *AmE infml* a person who talks too much: *You can't trust Peter with a secret. He's such a big mouth.* **7** **big shot** *AmE infml* an important and powerful person: *She thinks she's quite a big shot in the business world.* –**bigness** *n* [U]

big·a·my /ˈbɪɡəmiʸ/ *n* [U] the state of being married to two people at the same time: *Bigamy is considered a crime in many countries.* –see also MONOGAMY, POLYGAMY –**bigamist** /ˈbɪɡəmɪst/ *n* –**bigamous** /ˈbɪɡəməs/ *adj*

big broth·er /ˌ· ˈ···/ *n* (*usu. caps*) a political leader who has too much power, allows no freedom, and seems to be everywhere, watching

big·head /ˈbɪɡhɛd/ *n infml* a person who thinks too highly of his/her own importance

big·ot /ˈbɪɡət/ *n derog* a person who thinks unreasonably that his/her own strong opinion or belief is correct, esp. about matters of religion, race, or politics –**bigoted** *adj derog*: *bigoted people/opinions*

big·ot·ry /ˈbɪɡətriʸ/ *n* [U] *derog* acts or beliefs typical of a BIGOT

bike /baɪk/ *n, v* **biked, biking** [C;I] **1** *infml* for BICYCLE **2** *infml* for MOTORCYCLE

bi·ki·ni /bɪˈkiʸniʸ/ *n* a very small two-piece bathing suit for women

bi·lat·er·al /baɪˈlætərəl/ *adj* of, on, or with two sides; between or concerning two parties: *a bilateral agreement (between country A and country B)* –see also MULTILATERAL, UNILATERAL –**bilaterally** *adv*

bile /baɪl/ *n* [U] **1** a bitter green-brown liquid formed in the LIVER to help the body to DIGEST food **2** *fml* bad temper

bilge /bɪldʒ/ *n* **1** [C;U] (dirty water in) the bottom of a ship **2** [U] *infml* foolish talk: *Don't give me that bilge!*

bi·lin·gual /baɪˈlɪŋɡwəl/ *adj* **1** of, containing, or expressed in two languages: *a bilingual French-English dictionary* **2** able to speak two languages equally well

bil·ious /ˈbɪlyəs/ *adj* having sickness and pains in the head from too much BILE (1) in the body: *Fatty food makes some people bilious.* –**biliousness** *n* [U]

bill¹ /bɪl/ *n* **1** a list of things bought and their price: *She paid the bill (for the meal).* **2** a plan for a law, written down for the government to consider **3** *AmE‖note BrE–* a piece of paper money: *a five-dollar bill* **4** a printed notice: *Post No Bills* (a public warning on a wall, fence, etc.) **5 foot the bill (for)** *infml* to pay (for): *Who's going to foot the bill for the new library?*

bill² *n* the beak of a bird

bill³ *v* [T *for*] to send a bill to: *I can't pay now. Please bill me (for it) later.*

bill·board /ˈbɪlbɔrd, -boʷrd/ *n AmE* a high fence or board on which large advertisements are placed –see illustration on page 673

bil·let /ˈbɪlɪt/ *n, v* [C;T] (to provide) a house for lodging soldiers in, esp. for a short time: *The captain billeted his soldiers with Mrs. Smith.* (=in Mrs. Smith's house)

bill·fold /ˈbɪlfoʷld/ *n AmE* for WALLET

bil·liards /ˈbɪlyərdz/ *n* [U] a game played on a cloth-covered table (**billiard table**) with balls knocked with long sticks (CUEs) into pockets at the corners and sides

bil·lion /ˈbɪlyən/ *determiner, n, pron* billion or

billions (the number) 1,000,000,000 or 10⁹ –see Study Notes on page 550 –**billionth** *determiner, n, pron, adv*

bill of rights /ˌ· · ˈ·/ *n* **bills of rights** [*the* S] (*usu. caps*) a written list of the most important rights of the citizens of a country: *the Bill of Rights of the US* CONSTITUTION [*the* S]

bil·low¹ /ˈbɪloʷ/ *n* a wave, esp. a very large one: (*fig.*) *a great billow of smoke* –**billowy** *adj*

billow² *v* [I] to rise in waves; swell out: *billowing sails/skirts*

billy goat /ˈbɪliʸ ˌɡoʷt/ *n* (*used esp. by or to children*) a male goat –see also NANNY GOAT

bi·month·ly /baɪˈmʌnθliʸ/ *adv, adj* (appearing or happening) every two months: *a bimonthly magazine*

USAGE Expressions like **bi-weekly, -monthly** or **-annually** can mean either "twice in one week/month/year" or "once in two weeks/months/years," but in careful usage they have the latter meaning. **Semi-weekly, -monthly, -annually** mean twice in the stated period.

bin /bɪn/ *n* a large wide-mouthed container (esp. one with a lid) for bread, flour, coal, etc., or for waste

bi·na·ry /ˈbaɪnəriʸ/ *adj tech* **1** consisting of two things or parts; double: *A* **binary star** *is a double star, consisting of two stars turning around each other.* **2** using the two numbers, 0 and 1, as a base: *A binary system of numbers is used in many* COMPUTERs.

bind¹ /baɪnd/ *v* **bound** /baʊnd/, **binding 1** [T] to tie: *Bind the prisoner (to his chair) with rope.*|*Bind the prisoner's arms (together).*|(*fig.*) *He stood there, bound by the magic of the music.* **2** [T] BANDAGE²: *to bind (up) wounds* **3** [T] to strengthen or decorate with a cover or a band of material: *to bind a book* **4** [I;T] to (cause to) stick together: *This flour mixture isn't wet enough to bind properly.* **5** [T] to cause to obey, esp. by a law or a solemn promise: *I am bound by my promise.*|*a binding agreement*

bind² *n* [S] *infml* an annoying or difficult state of affairs, esp. in the phrase (**to be**) **in a bind**

bind·er /ˈbaɪndər/ *n* **1** a machine or person that binds, esp. books: *Your book is still at the binder's.* **2** a usu. removable cover, esp. for holding sheets of paper, magazines, etc.: *a three-ring binder for your school papers.*

bind·ing /ˈbaɪndɪŋ/ *n* **1** [C] a book cover: *The binding of this book is torn.* **2** [U] material sewn or stuck along the edge of something, such as a dress, for strength or decoration

bin·go /ˈbɪŋɡoʷ/ *n* [U] a game played for money or prizes by covering rows of numbered squares on a card

bin·oc·u·lars /bɪˈnɑkyələrz, baɪ-/ *n* [P] a pair of glasses like short TELESCOPEs¹ for both eyes, used for looking at distant objects: *I watched the horse-race through my binoculars.* –see PAIR¹ (USAGE)

bi·o·chem·is·try /ˌbaɪoʷˈkɛməstriʸ/ *n* [U] (the scientific study of) the chemistry of living things

bi·o·de·grad·a·ble /ˌbaɪoʷdɪˈɡreʸdəbəl/ *adj* able to decay or DISINTEGRATE naturally:

Plastic is not biodegradable.

bi·og·ra·phy /baɪ'ɑgrəfiʸ/ *n* **-phies** [C;U] (the branch of literature that deals with) a written account of a person's life –see also AUTOBIOGRAPHY –**biographer** *n* –**biographical** /ˌbaɪə'græfɪkəl/ *adj* –**biographically** *adv*

biological war·fare /ˌ····· '··/ also **germ warfare**– *n* [U] methods of fighting a war in which living things such as bacteria are used for harming the enemy

bi·ol·o·gy /baɪ'ɑlədʒiʸ/ *n* [U] the scientific study of living things –**biologist** *n* –**biological** /ˌbaɪə'lɑdʒɪkəl ◄/ *adj* –**biologically** *adv*

bi·on·ic /baɪ'ɑnɪk/ *adj infml* having powers (such as speed, strength, etc.) that are greater than those of ordinary human beings

bi·par·tite /baɪ'pɑrtaɪt/ *adj* being in two parts; shared by two parties: *a bipartite agreement*

bi·ped /'baɪpɛd/ *n tech* a two-footed creature –compare QUADRUPED

bi·plane /'baɪpleʸn/ *n* an aircraft with two sets of wings, one above the other –compare MONOPLANE

birch /bɜrtʃ/ *n* [C;U] (wood from) a tree, common in northern countries, with smooth wood and thin branches

bird /bɜrd/ *n* **1** a creature with wings and feathers, which can usu. fly in the air **2 early bird** *infml* a person who gets up or arrives early **3 kill two birds with one stone** *infml* to get two results (esp. good ones) with one action **4 (strictly) for the birds** *AmE infml* worthless; silly

bird of prey /ˌ·····'··/ *n* any bird that kills other birds and small animals for food

bird's-eye view /ˌ····'··/ *n* a view seen from high up: (fig.) *a bird's-eye view* (=general view) *of Roman history*

birth /bɜrθ/ *n* **1** [C;U] the act or time of being born, of coming into the world esp. out of the body of a female parent: *the birth of a child|Last year there were more births than deaths.|She weighed eight pounds at birth.|*(fig.)*the birth of a new political party|She* **gave birth to** *a fine healthy baby.* –compare DEATH **2** [U] family origin: *of noble birth|French by birth*

birth con·trol /'··,··/ *n* [U] various methods of limiting the number of children born

birth·day /'bɜrθdeʸ/ *n* **1** the date on which someone was born: *When is your birthday?* **2** the day in each year when this date falls: *Let me wish you a happy birthday!* –compare ANNIVERSARY

birth·day card /'··,·/ *n* a GREETING CARD sent to a person on his/her BIRTHDAY

birth·mark /'bɜrθmɑrk/ *n* an unusual mark on the body at birth

birth·rate /'bɜrθreʸt/ *n* the number of births for every 100 or every 1000 people during a given time: *a birthrate of 3 per 100*

bis·cuit /'bɪskɪt/ *n* **1** *AmE‖*scone *BrE*– a soft usu. round breadlike cake of a size for one person, made of flour, salt, milk, fat, and sometimes sugar, dried fruit, etc. and baked **2** *BrE* for COOKIE

bi·sect /'baɪsɛkt, baɪ'sɛkt/ *v* [T] *tech* to divide into two usu. equal parts –**bisection** /'baɪˌsɛkʃən, baɪ'sɛkʃən/ *n* [U]

bi·sex·u·al /baɪ'sɛkʃuʷəl/ *adj* **1** possessing qualities of both sexes: *a bisexual plant* **2** sexually attracted to people of both sexes: *bisexual love|a bisexual person* –see also HETEROSEXUAL, HOMOSEXUAL –**bisexuality** /ˌbaɪsɛkʃuʷæ'lətiʸ/ *n* [U]

bish·op /'bɪʃəp/ *n* **1** [A;C] (*often cap.*) (in some branches of the Christian church) a priest in charge of the churches and priests in a large area **2** [C] (in CHESS) a piece that can be moved only in a DIAGONAL direction

bish·op·ric /'bɪʃəprɪk/ *n* →DIOCESE

bi·son /'baɪsən, -zən/ *n* bison *or* bisons →BUFFALO

bis·tro /'biʸstroʷ, 'bɪ-/ *n* **-tros** (esp. in France) a small or simple BAR¹ (5), restaurant, or NIGHTCLUB

bit¹ /bɪt/ *n* **1** [C *of*] a small piece or quantity: *every bit of the food|He picked up all the bits of paper.|"I did a bit of Christmas shopping."* **2** [S] a short time: *I'm just going out for a bit.* **3** [S] some (in the phrases **a bit of luck/advice/news**) **4 a bit (of)** *infml* to some degree; rather: *a bit tired|That's a bit (too) much to pay.|"He's* **not a bit** *like that really."* (=he's not at all like that) –see USAGE **5 bits and pieces** *infml* small things of various kinds: *Let me get my bits and pieces together.* **6 bit by bit** also **a bit at a time**– *infml* a little at a time; gradually **7 every bit as** *infml* just as; quite as: *He's every bit as intelligent as you are.* **8 to bits** into small pieces: *The bridge was blown to bits by the explosion.*

USAGE Use **a bit** before adjectives: *I'm* **a** *(little)* **bit** *tired;* and **a bit of** before [U] nouns: **a bit of** *money|*a bit of *a problem*

bit² *n* **1** a metal bar, part of a BRIDLE, that is put in the mouth of a horse and used for controlling its movements **2** a part of a tool for cutting or making holes

bit³ *n* the standard measure of COMPUTER information

bitch¹ /bɪtʃ/ *n* **1** a female dog **2** *derog* a woman, esp. when unkind or bad-tempered: *You bitch!*

bitch² *v* [I *about*] *infml* to complain

bitch·y /'bɪtʃiʸ/ *adj* **-ier, -iest** having a tendency to make nasty jokes about other people and find fault with everything –**bitchily** *adv* –**bitchiness** *n* [U]

bite¹ /baɪt/ *v* **bit** /bɪt/, **bitten** /'bɪtn/, **biting** **1** [I;T] to cut, crush, or seize (something) with the teeth or to attack (someone or something) with the teeth: *Be careful, my dog bites.|The boy bit into the piece of cake.|He bit a large piece out of it.|The fierce dog bit me on the leg/bit a hole in my pants.|She bites her fingernails.|*(fig.) *a cold biting* (=painful) *wind* **2** [I;T] (of insects and snakes) to prick the skin (of) and draw blood: *He was bitten by a mosquito.* **3** [I] (of fish) to accept food on a fisherman's hook (and so get caught): (fig.) *I hoped she would be interested in my plan, but she didn't bite.* (=express any interest) **4** [I] to take hold of something firmly: *The ice on the road was so hard that the car tires would not bite.* **5** [I] to have or show an effect, unpleasant to some: *The government's new higher taxes are really beginning* *to bite.* **6 bite someone's head off** *infml* to speak to or answer someone rudely and angrily **7 bite the dust** *infml* to fall to the ground (esp. in a fight) **8 bite the bullet** to face up to a difficult state of affairs in spite of one's fear: *She bit the bullet and told the truth.*

bite sthg. ↔ **back** *v adv* [T] *infml* to control; prevent from being expressed: *Peter was about to tell the secret, but he bit his words back.*

bite² *n* **1** [C] (something removed or caused by) an act of biting: *A large bite had been taken out of the apple.|Her face was covered with insect bites.|He sat on the river bank for hours without (getting) a bite.* (=without catching a fish)|(fig.) *There's a real bite* (=sharpness) *in this cold wind.* **2** [S] *infml* something to eat: *He's hungry because he hasn't had a bite (to eat) all day.*

bit·ing /'baɪtɪŋ/ *adj* painful; cruel: *a cold and biting wind|He had some biting things to say about my homework.* –**bitingly** *adv: a bitingly cold wind*

bit·ter¹ /'bɪtər/ *adj* **1** having a sharp, biting taste, like beer or black coffee without sugar –compare SWEET¹ (1) **2** (of cold, wind, etc.) very sharp, keen, cutting, biting, etc.: *a bitter winter wind* **3** filled with or caused by hate, anger, sorrow, or other unpleasant feelings: *bitter enemies|bitter tears|It was a bitter disappointment to him when he failed his examination.* **4 to the bitter end** *infml* to the end in spite of all unpleasant difficulties –**bitterly** *adv* –**bitterness** *n* [U]

bitter² *n* [U] *BrE* a type of bitter beer: *A pint of bitter, please.*

bit·ter·sweet /ˌbɪtər'swiʸt◂/ *adj* **1** pleasant but mixed with sadness: *bittersweet memories of childhood* **2** *AmE* of, like, or related to a type of chocolate made with very little sugar

bi·tu·men /bɪ'tuʷmən, -'tyuʷ-, baɪ-/ *n* [U] a sticky substance (such as ASPHALT or TAR), esp. as used in road-making –**bituminous** /bɪ'tuʷmənəs, -'tyuʷ-, baɪ-/ *adj*

biv·ou·ac¹ /'bɪvuʷˌæk, 'bɪvwæk/ *n* a soldiers' camp without tents

bivouac² *v* **-ck-** [I] (esp. of soldiers) to spend the night in the open without tents: *They have/are bivouacked behind those trees.*

bi·week·ly /baɪ'wiʸkliʸ/ *adv,adj* appearing or happening every two weeks: *a biweekly magazine* –see BIMONTHLY (USAGE)

bi·zarre /bɪ'zɑr/ *adj* (esp. of appearance or happenings) strange; peculiar; odd –**bizarrely** *adv*

blab /blæb/ *v* **-bb-** [I] *infml* to tell a secret

black¹ /blæk/ *adj* **1** of the color of night; without light; having the color black: (fig.) *I like my coffee black.* (=without milk or cream) **2** (of feelings, behavior, news, etc.) very bad: *The bad news we've been getting means that things look very black for us.*|(fig.) *He gave me a black* (=very angry) *look.* **3** [no comp.] (of a person) of a black-skinned race –compare WHITE¹ (2) **4 black and blue** (darkly) discolored (BRUISED² (2)) as the result of a blow: *After the fight he*

was black and blue all over. **5 in black and white** in writing: *I want this agreement in black and white.* **6 black sheep** a worthless member of a respectable group: *He was the black sheep of the family after he had been to prison.* –**blackness** *n* [U]

black² *n* **1** [U] the darkest color: *After her husband died, she dressed in black for six months.* **2** [C] a person of a black-skinned race **3 in the black** having money in a bank account: *Our account is (nicely) in the black this month.* –opposite **in the red**

black³ *v* [T] to make black, as with a blow or by covering with a black substance: *to black someone's eye*

black out *v adv* **1** [I] to faint: *After the accident he blacked out and couldn't remember what had happened.* –see also BLACKOUT **2** [T (=**black** sthg.↔**out**)] to darken so that no light is seen: *During the war we had to black out all our windows.*

black·ber·ry /'blæk,bɛriʸ, -bəriʸ/ *n* **-ries** the fruit of a type of BRAMBLE, black or purple when ripe

black·bird /'blækbɜrd/ *n* a European and American bird of which the male is completely black

black·board /'blækbɔrd, -boʷrd/ also **chalkboard, board**– *n* a dark smooth surface (usu. black or green) used esp. in schools for writing or drawing on, usu. with chalk

black·en /'blækən/ *v* [T] to (cause to) become black or dark: *The smoke blackened his kitchen walls.*|(fig.)*Don't blacken my good name by spreading lies.*

black eye /ˌ· '·/ *n* the condition in which the skin around someone's eye is made black by a blow: *If he says that again, I'll give him a black eye.*

black·head /'blækhɛd/ *n* a kind of spot on the skin with a black center

black hole /ˌ· '·/ *n* an area in outer space into which everything near it, including light itself, is pulled

black·jack /'blækdʒæk/ *n* **1** also **twenty-one** *AmE*– a card game usu. played for money **2** [C] *AmE*‖**cosh** *BrE*– a short metal pipe or rubber tube usu. filled with heavy material such as metal or stone, and used as a weapon

black·list /'blæk,lɪst/ *v* [T] to put on a list of people, groups, countries, etc. who have done something wrong or who are to be punished: *blacklisted for non-payment of debts* –**blacklist** *n*

black mag·ic /ˌ· '··/ *n* [U] magic that is used for evil purposes

black·mail¹ /'blækmeʸl/ *n* [U] the obtaining of money or advantage by threatening, usu. to make known unpleasant facts about a person or group

blackmail² *v* [T *into*] to obtain money or advantage from (someone) by BLACKMAIL: *Don't think you can blackmail me (into doing that).* –**blackmailer** *n*

black mar·ket /ˌ· '··◂/ *n* [usu. sing.] the unlawful buying and selling of goods, foreign money, etc., when such trade is controlled: *They bought butter on the black market during the war.* –**black marketeer** /ˌ· ··'·/ *n*

blaze

Black Mus·lim /ˌ· ˈ··/ *n* a member of a group of black people that believes in the religion of Islam and wants the establishment of a separate black society

black·out /ˈblækaʊt/ *n* **1** a period of darkness enforced during wartime or caused by the failure of the electric power supply: *The streets were not lighted at night during the blackout.* **2** a loss of consciousness for a short time: *He had a blackout after the accident and could not remember what happened.* –see also BLACK³ **out**

black pow·er /ˌ· ˈ··/ *n* [S] (*usu. cap.*) the belief that in any country black people should have a share of political and ECONOMIC power which is in accordance with the number of black people in that country

black·smith /ˈblæk,smɪθ/ also **smith–** *n* a person who makes and repairs things made of iron, esp. horseshoes, usu. by hand

blad·der /ˈblædər/ *n* **1** a bag of skin inside the body of human beings or animals, in which waste liquid collects before it is passed out **2** a bag of skin, leather, or rubber which can be filled with air or liquid

blade /bleʸd/ *n* **1** the flat cutting part of a knife, sword, or other cutting tool or weapon such as a RAZOR **2** the flat wide part of an OAR, a PROPELLER, etc. **3** a long flat leaf of grass

blame¹ /bleʸm/ *v* **blamed, blaming** [T *for, on*] to consider (someone) responsible for (something bad): *They blamed the failure on George.|They blamed George (for the failure).|The children* **were (not) to blame for** (=(not) guilty of) *the accident.*

blame² *n* [U] responsibility for something bad: *The judge* **laid/put the blame** *for the accident on the driver of the car.|We were ready to* **take/bear the blame** *for what had happened.*

blame·less /ˈbleʸmlɪs/ *adj* free from blame; guiltless: *a blameless life* –**blamelessly** *adv*

blame·wor·thy /ˈbleʸm,wɜrðiʸ/ *adj fml* deserving blame

blanch /blæntʃ/ *v* **1** [T] to make (a plant or plant product) colorless, as by removing the skin or keeping out of the light: *blanched* ALMONDS **2** [T] to put (fruit, vegetables, etc.) into boiling water for a very short time **3** [I +*to-v/with, at*] to become pale with fear, cold, etc.: *Her face blanched with fear at the bad news.*

bland /blænd/ *adj* **1** (of food) not hurting the stomach and without much taste **2** (of people and behavior) not giving offense or being unusual in any way; not showing strong feelings –**blandly** *adv* –**blandness** *n* [U]

blank¹ /blæŋk/ *adj* **1** without writing, print, or other marks: *a blank page|Please write your name in the blank space at the top of the page.* **2** expressionless; without understanding; without interest: *I tried to explain, but he just gave me a blank look.* –**blankly** *adv* –**blankness** *n* [U]

blank² *n* **1** an empty space: *Write your name in the blank.|*(fig.) *When I tried to remember his name,* **my mind was a complete blank. 2** →BLANK CARTRIDGE **3 draw a blank** *infml* to be unsuccessful

blank³ *v AmE* to prevent an opponent from winning points in a game: *Our team blanked the other, 24-0.*

blank car·tridge /ˌ· ˈ··/ *n* a CARTRIDGE (1) that contains an explosive but no bullet

blank check *AmE*‖**cheque** *BrE* /ˌ· ˈ·/ *n* a check signed and given to someone to write in whatever amount he/she wishes to receive: (fig.) *He was given a blank check when he became director.* (=he can do whatever he wants as director)

blan·ket /ˈblæŋkɪt/ *n* **1** [C] a thick woolen covering used esp. on beds to protect from cold: (fig.) *The valley was covered with a blanket of snow.* **2** [A] including all cases, classes, or possible happenings; unlimited: *a blanket rule*

blank verse /ˌ· ˈ·/ *n* [U] poetry which does not RHYME: *Most of Shakespeare's plays are written in blank verse.*

blare /bleər/ *v* **blared, blaring** [I;T *out*] (of a horn or other loud sound-producing instrument) to sound or produce (sounds or words), sharply, loudly, and unpleasantly: *The radio blared out (the news).* –**blare** *n: the blare of a brass band|a blare of horns*

bla·sé /blɑˈzeʸ/ *adj* (typical of a person who is) tired of all forms of pleasure and not able to obtain further enjoyment: *You're being very blasé about it; aren't you glad you won the prize?*

blas·pheme /blæsˈfiʸm, ˈblæsfiʸm/ *v* **-phemed, -pheming** [I;T *against*] to speak without respect of or use bad language about (God or religious matters): *He can hardly speak without blaspheming (against) God.* –**blasphemer** *n* –**blasphemous** /ˈblæsfəməs/ *adj: blasphemous talk* –**blasphemously** *adv*

blas·phe·my /ˈblæsfəmiʸ/ *n* **-mies** [C;U] (an example of) disrespectful or bad language about God or holy things: *Their conversation was full of blasphemy/blasphemies.* –compare PROFANITY

blast¹ /blæst/ *n* **1** [C] a sudden strong movement of wind or air: *the icy blast(s) of the north wind* **2** [C;U] an explosion or the very powerful rush of air caused by an explosion **3** [C] a very loud usu. unpleasant sound of a brass wind instrument: *He blew several loud blasts on his horn.*

blast² *v* [I;T] to break up (esp. rock) by explosions: *The road is closed because of blasting.|They're trying to blast away the face of this rock.*

blast off *v adv* [I] (of a space vehicle) →TAKE **off** (2)

blast·ed /ˈblæstɪd/ *adj* [A] *euph* for DAMN² (1): *Make that blasted dog keep quiet!*

blast fur·nace /ˈ· ˌ··/ *n* a steel container where iron is separated from iron ORE by the action of heat and air blown through at great pressure

blast-off /ˈ· ·/ *n* (of a space vehicle) →TAKE OFF

bla·tant /ˈbleʸtnt/ *adj* shameless; offensively noticeable: *blatant disobedience* –**blatantly** *adv*

blaze¹ /bleʸz/ *n* [*usu. sing.*] **1** the sudden sharp shooting up of a flame; a very bright fire: *The fire burned slowly at first, but soon burst into a blaze.*|(fig.) *In a blaze of anger she shouted at them.*|(fig.) *The whole building was a blaze of light.* **2** a big dangerous fire: *The firemen were unable to control the blaze.* –see also ABLAZE

blaze² *v* **blazed, blazing** [I *with*] to (begin to) burn with a bright flame: *a blazing wood fire*|(fig.) *Lights blazed in every room.*|(fig.) *Her eyes were blazing with anger.* **–blazing** *adj*

blaze³ *v* **blaze a/the trail** to make marks along a path (TRAIL) for others to follow: (fig.) *Our company has blazed a trail in new methods of advertising.*

blaz·er /'bleɪʸzər/ *n* a JACKET (1) usu. light in weight, sometimes with the special sign of a school, club, etc., on it

bleach¹ /bliːʸtʃ/ *v* [I;T] to (cause to) become white or whiter: *There were only a few dry bones left, bleached by the sun.*

bleach² *n* [U] a substance used in BLEACHing: *My shirt was so dirty that I had to use bleach on it.*

bleak /bliːʸk/ *adj* cold, cheerless, and uninviting: *The weather in December was bleak and unpleasant.*|*a bleak hillside struck by the full force of the wind*|(fig.) *The future of this company will be very bleak if we keep losing money.* **–bleakly** *adv*

blear·y /'blɪəriʸ/ *adj* **-ier, -iest** (esp. of eyes) red and unable to see well because of tiredness, tears, etc.: *A bad cold has made him* **bleary-eyed.** **–blearily** *adv*

bleat /bliːʸt/ *v* **1** [I] to make the sound of a sheep, goat, or CALF¹ **2** [I;T] *infml* to speak or say (something) in a weak, shaking voice **–bleat** *n* [*usu. sing.*]

bleed /bliːʸd/ *v* **bled** /blɛd/, **bleeding 1** [I] to lose blood: *Your nose is bleeding.*|(fig.) *My heart bleeds for* (=I feel very sorry for) *those poor unhappy children.* **2** [T] to make (someone) pay too much money: *He bled them for every penny they had.*

bleep¹ /bliːʸp/ *n* a high, usu. repeated, sound sent out by a machine to attract someone's attention –compare BLIP

bleep² *v* **1** [I;T] to send out one or more BLEEPs¹: *The machine bleeped.*|*They're bleeping (for) you, doctor.* **2** *infml* to cut out a word or words from television or radio with BLEEPs: *The dirty words were bleeped.*

blem·ish¹ /'blɛmɪʃ/ *v* [T] to spoil the beauty or perfection of: *Her beautiful face was blemished by a big red spot on her nose.*

blemish² *n* a mark that spoils beauty or perfection: (fig.) *a blemish on his character*

blend¹ /blɛnd/ *v* **1** [I;T *together, with*] to (cause to) mix; produce by mixing: *Blend the sugar, flour, and eggs (together).*|*blended WHISKEY* **2** [I *with*] to go well together; HARMONIZE (2): *These houses seem to blend (in) well with the trees and the COUNTRYSIDE.*

blend² *n* a product of BLENDing¹: *We've been selling a great deal of this blend of coffee.*|*His manner was a blend of friendliness and respect.*

blend·er /'blɛndər/|| also **liquidizer** *BrE*– *n* a small electric machine used in the kitchen for

making solid foods into liquid-like forms, such as soups or juices –see illustration on page 379

bless /blɛs/ *v* **blessed** *or* **blest** /blɛst/, **blessing** [T] **1** to ask God's favor for: *The priest blessed the ship before it left port.* **2** to make or call holy: *The priest blessed the bread and wine.*|*Bless the name of the Lord!* **3 be blessed with** to be fortunate enough to have: *blessed with good health* –compare DAMN

bless·ed /'blɛsɪd/ *adj* holy; favored by God: *"Blessed are the peacemakers."* –compare DAMN² (1) **–blessedness** *n* [U]

bless·ing /'blɛsɪŋ/ *n* **1** [C] an act of asking or receiving God's favor, help, or protection: *The blessing of the Lord be upon you all.* **2** [U] approval; encouragement: *The government has given its blessing to the new plan.* **3 a blessing in disguise** something not very pleasant, which however is really a good thing after all: *The storm was a blessing in disguise because it kept us at home when you telephoned.*

blew /bluːʷ/ *v* past tense of BLOW¹

blight¹ /blaɪt/ **1** [U] a disease of plants **2** [C;U *usu. sing.*] something that spoils, or the condition of being spoiled: *The failure of his marriage* **cast a blight on** *his whole life.*

blight² *v* [T] to spoil with or as if with BLIGHT¹: *Her life was blighted by ill health.*

blind¹ /blaɪnd/ *adj* **1** unable to see: *blind from birth.*|*The blind do not always need our help.*|*blind in one eye*|(fig.) *The pilot made a blind landing in the mist.* (=using his instruments only and not looking outside) –compare SIGHTED **2** of poor judgment or understanding: *He is blind to the probable results of his behavior.*|*I have a blind spot where modern art is concerned.* (=I don't understand it) **3** uncontrolled: *blind haste/anger*|*the blind forces of nature* **4** at or in which one cannot see: *a dangerous blind corner* **5 turn a blind eye (to)** to pretend not to notice (something): *The teacher had turned a blind eye to their bad behavior for too long.* **–blindly** *adv* **–blindness** *n* [U]

blind² *v* [T] to make unable to see: *He was blinded by the smoke in the battle.*|*a blinding flash of light*|(fig.) *His desire to do it blinded him to all the problems.*

USAGE **blinded** and **deafened** are used only when referring to the event itself: **blinded** *by dust*|**blinded** *in the war*|*The music nearly* **deafened** *me.* For describing a state use the adjectives **blind** and **deaf:** *He became* **deaf/blind.**|*a* **blind/deaf** *child*

blind³ *n* **1** [*usu. sing.*] also **window shade** *AmE*– cloth or other material pulled down from a roller to cover a window **2** also **blinds, venetian blinds**– a window covering made of long thin flat bars of metal, plastic, or wood fixed to string so that the bars can be lowered, or turned to let in or shut out light and air –see illustration on page 399

blind al·ley /ˌ· '··/ *n* a narrow street that does not lead anywhere: *trapped in a blind alley*|(fig.) *We tried one idea after another, but they all seemed to be blind alleys.*

blind date /ˌ· '·/ *n infml* a social meeting

(DATE[1] (3)) between two people who have not met before

blind drunk /ˌ· '·/ adj [F] infml very drunk

blind·ers /'blaɪndərz/ AmE‖also **blinkers** esp. BrE– n [P] a pair of flat pieces of leather fixed beside a horse's eyes to prevent sight of objects at its sides: (fig.) David has blinders on when it comes to politics.

blind·fold[1] /'blaɪndfoʷld/ v [T] to cover (the eyes) with a piece of material

blindfold[2] n a piece of material that covers the eyes to prevent seeing

blink[1] /blɪŋk/ v [I,T] **1** to shut and open (the eyes) quickly, once or several times: She blinked (her eyes) as the bright light shone on her. **2** (of lights) to (seem to) go rapidly on and off: The driver is blinking his lights. –compare WINK

blink[2] n an act of BLINKing[1]

blink·ers /'blɪŋkərz/ n [P] → BLINDERS

blip /blɪp/ n a very short regular sound or image, produced by an electrical machine –compare BLEEP[1]

bliss /blɪs/ n [U] complete happiness –**blissfully** adv

blis·ter[1] /'blɪstər/ n **1** a thin watery swelling under the skin, caused by rubbing, burning, etc.: His new shoes gave him blisters. **2** a swelling on the surface of things such as painted wood or a rubber tire

blister[2] v [I;T] to (cause to) form BLISTERs[1] (on): His hands blister easily.|The heat had blistered the paint on the building.

blithe /blaɪð, blaɪθ/ adj (of behavior, language, spirits, etc.) happy; free from care –**blithely** adv: She continued on blithely in spite of all the problems.

blitz /blɪts/ n a sudden heavy attack, esp. from the air, or a period of such attacks: (fig.) an advertising blitz

bliz·zard /'blɪzərd/ n a long severe snowstorm –see WEATHER (USAGE)

bloat·ed /'bloʷtɪd/ adj unpleasantly swollen: the bloated body of a drowned animal

blob /blɑb/ n a drop or small round mass: a blob of paint on the floor

bloc /blɑk/ n **1** a group of people, political parties, or nations that act together: the COMMUNIST bloc **2 en bloc** /ˌɑn 'blɑk/ all together; all at once: Let's consider all the problems en bloc. –compare BLOCK[1]

block[1] /blɑk/ n **1** a solid usu. straight-sided mass or piece of wood, stone, etc.: The floor was made of wooden blocks.|a block of ice **2** (the distance along one of the sides of) a building or group of buildings built between two streets: The Empire State Building is four blocks from here.|We live on the same block. **3** a quantity of things considered as a single whole: a block of seats in a theater|a block of shares in a business **4** something that stops movement or activity: There's a block in the pipe somewhere, so the water isn't coming through.|He has a memory block. (=he can't remember anything) **5** a small usu. square piece of wood, etc. used as a child's toy: He made a house with his blocks. –compare BLOC

block[2] v [T] to prevent (the movement, ac-

tivity, or success of or through something): Something's blocking the pipe/the flow of water through the pipe.|Block the door so they can't get in.|My nose is all blocked up, and I can't breathe very well.|The government blocked our plan. –opposite unblock

block·ade[1] /blɑˈkeʸd/ n the shutting up of a place by warships or soldiers to prevent people or goods from coming or going –compare EMBARGO

blockade[2] v -aded, -ading [T] to put under a BLOCKADE[1]: The ships blockaded the enemy harbors.

block·age /'blɑkɪdʒ/ n something that causes a block: a blockage in the pipe

block·head /'blɑkhɛd/ n infml a stupid person

block let·ters /ˌ· '··/ n [P] the hand printing of words with each letter formed separately and written in its big (CAPITAL[2] (2)) form: Please print your name in block letters.

bloke /bloʷk/ n BrE infml a man; fellow

blond[1] /blɑnd/ adj (of hair) light-colored (usu. yellowish)

blond[2] /blɑnd/ n (fem. blonde) (blonde/same pronunciation/ (a person) with light-colored hair and skin –compare BRUNETTE

blood /blʌd/ n [U] **1** red liquid which flows through the body: His cruelty to his children really **makes my blood boil.** (=makes me very angry)|The sound of footsteps in the dark **made his blood run cold.** (=made him very afraid) **2** family relationship: a woman of noble blood|Farming **runs in their blood;** the people in their family have been farmers for 200 years. **3 fresh/new blood** a new person or new people (in a company, group, etc.): What we need here is some new blood with new ideas. **4 in cold blood** cruelly and on purpose: They killed the old man in cold blood! **5 -blooded: a** having a certain kind of blood: Fish are cold-blooded creatures. **b** showing a certain character: a hot-blooded young man (=showing strong feelings)

blood·bath /'blʌdbæθ/ n the killing at one time of many men, women, and children

blood·cur·dling /'blʌdˌkərdlɪŋ/ adj causing a feeling of fear to run through the whole body: bloodcurdling cries of pain

blood group /'· ·/ n → BLOOD TYPE

blood·hound /'blʌdhaʊnd/ n a large hunting dog with a very sharp sense of smell, used for tracking people or animals

blood·less /'blʌdlɪs/ adj without blood; without killing or violence: a bloodless victory –see also BLOODY[1] –**bloodlessly** adv

blood poi·son·ing /'· ˌ···/ also **septicemia** tech– n [U] a dangerous condition in which an infection spreads from a small area of the body through the BLOODSTREAM

blood pres·sure /'· ˌ··/ n [C;U] the measurable force with which blood travels through the BLOODSTREAM: Your blood pressure is a little high.

blood·shed /'blʌdʃɛd/ n [U] killing, usu. in fighting: There was a lot of bloodshed when the two countries went to war.

blood·shot /'blʌdʃɑt/ adj (of the eyes) having the white part colored red: His eyes were *bloodshot after too much drinking.* (=of alcohol)

blood·stain /'blʌdsteⁿn/ *n* a mark or spot of blood: *There were bloodstains on the floor where they had been fighting.* –**bloodstained** *adj*: (fig.) *This city has a bloodstained history.*

blood·stream /'blʌdstriʸm/ *n* [S] the blood as it flows through the blood vessels of the body: *Blood poisoning is a dangerous infection of the bloodstream.*

blood·thirst·y /'blʌd,θɜrstiʸ/ *adj* having or showing eagerness to kill or too much interest in violence –**bloodthirstily** *adv* –**bloodthirstiness** *n* [U]

blood type /'·· ·/ also **blood group**– *n* any of the four classes into which human blood can be separated: *What's your blood type?*

blood ves·sel /'· ,··/ *n* any of the tubes of various sizes through which blood flows in the body

blood·y¹ /'blʌdiʸ/ *adj* **-ier, -iest 1** covered with blood: *a bloody nose* **2** connected with wounding and killing: *a bloody battle* –see also BLOODLESS –**bloodily** /'blʌdl-iʸ/ *adv* –**bloodiness** *n* [U]

bloody² *adj,adv* [A] *BrE infml* not polite (used for giving force to a value judgment): *Don't be a bloody fool!|It's bloody wonderful!*

bloom¹ /bluʷm/ *n* **1** *apprec* a flower: *What beautiful blooms!|The roses are in full bloom.* **2 in the bloom of** at the best time of: *in the bloom of youth*

bloom² *v* [I] to produce flowers, come into flower, or be in flower: *The roses are blooming.|*(fig.) *Jane is blooming with health and beauty.* –compare BLOSSOM

bloom·ers /'bluʷmərz/ *n* [P] (esp. formerly) a woman's (outer or under) garment of short loose trousers gathered at the knee –see PAIR¹ (USAGE)

blos·som¹ /'blɑsəm/ *n* **1** [C] the flower of a tree or bush: *apple blossoms* **2** [U] the mass of such flowers on a single plant, tree, or bush: *a tree (covered) in blossom*

blossom² *v* [I] **1** (of a tree or bush) to produce or yield flowers; BLOOM²: *The apple trees are blossoming.* **2** [*out, into*] to develop: *a blossoming friendship|Sally is blossoming (out) (into a beautiful girl).* –compare BLOOM

blot¹ /blɑt/ *n* **1** a spot or mark that spoils or makes dirty, esp. as of ink dropped accidentally from a pen: *a blot of ink on the paper* **2** a fault or shameful act, esp. by someone usually of good character: *a blot on one's character*

blot² *v* **-tt-** [I;T] **1** to make one or more BLOTS¹ (on): (fig.) *He blotted his driving record by having an accident.* **2** to dry with BLOTTING PAPER

blot sthg. ↔ **out** *v adv* [T] to cover; hide: *The mist blotted out the sun.*

blotch /blɑtʃ/ *n* a large spot or mark on the skin, one's clothes, etc. –**blotchy** *adj*

blot·ter /'blɑtər/ *n* **1** a large piece of BLOTTING PAPER on which writing paper can be pressed face down to dry the ink –see illustration on page 467 **2** *AmE* a book where records are

first written, before the information is stored elsewhere: *the police blotter*

blotting pa·per /'·· ,··/ *n* [U] special thick soft paper which is used to dry wet ink on paper after writing

blouse /blaʊs, blaʊz/ *n* a usu. loose garment for women, reaching from the neck to about the waist –see illustration on page 123

blow¹ /bloʷ/ *v* **blew** /bluʷ/, **blown** /bloʷn/, **blowing 1** [I] to send out a strong current of air: *The wind's blowing hard tonight.|She blew on her food to make it cool.* **2** [I;T] to move by the force of a current of air: *The wind has blown my hat off.|My papers are blowing around the room. Close the window!|Several trees were blown down in the storm.* **3** [I;T] to (cause to) sound by blowing: *to blow a horn|The horn blew (loudly).* **4** [I] to take short quick breaths, usu. because of effort: *He was (PUFFing and) blowing as he climbed the stairs.* **5** [I;T] **a** (of an electrical FUSE¹) to suddenly stop working because a part has melted **b** to cause (a FUSE¹) to do this: *If you turn on the radio, the television, and the iron, it will blow the fuses.* **6** [T] *infml* to lose (money or a favorable chance) as the result of foolishness: *I blew $10 at cards the other night.|I've blown it!* **7 blow hot and cold (about)** *infml* to be favorable (to) at one moment and unfavorable (to) at the next **8 blow off steam** *infml* to give expression to anger or excitement **9 blow one's mind** *infml* to fill one with strong feelings of wonder or confusion **10 blow one's nose** to clean the nose by sending a strong breath through it into a handkerchief **11 blow one's own horn/trumpet** *infml* to say good things about oneself, usu. immodestly, so that others will know them **12 blow one's top/stack** *infml* to become violently angry **13 blow town** *AmE infml* to leave a town suddenly and quickly

blow out *v adv* **1** [I;T (=blow sthg.↔out)] to (cause to) stop burning by blowing: *Jane blew the candle out.* **2** [I] (esp. of a tire) to burst: *The tire blew out as I was driving to work.* **3** [I;T (=blow sthg.↔out)] to (cause to) be driven out by the force of air or other gas: *The explosion blew the windows out.* –compare BLOWOUT

blow over *v adv* [I] (of bad weather) to stop blowing; cease: *The storm has blown over.|*(fig.) *I hope your troubles will soon blow over.*

blow up *v adv* **1** [I;T (=blow sthg.↔ up)] to (cause to) explode or be destroyed by exploding: *to blow up the bridge|*(fig.) *My father blew up* (=was very angry) *when I arrived home late.* **2** [I;T (=blow sthg.↔ up)] to (cause to) become firm by filling with air: *Be sure to blow up the BALLOONs before the party.* **3** [T (=blow sthg.↔ up)] to enlarge (a photograph): (fig.) *This small matter has been blown up in order to cause trouble between us.*

blow² *n* act or example of blowing

blow³ *n* **1** a hard stroke with the open or closed hand, a weapon, etc.: *a blow on the head|The children came to blows with each other.* (=started fighting) **2** a shock or misfortune: *It was a great blow to her when her mother died.* **3 blow-by-blow account** an account which describes in detail all events in the order in which they happened

blow dry /'· ·/ v [T] to dry hair with a hand-held machine which blows hot air: *He blow dries his hair every morning after washing it.* **–blow drier** /'· ·/ n: *I bought a new blow drier on sale at the drug store.*

blow·fly /'bloʷflaɪ/ n **-flies** a fly that lays its eggs, esp. on meat or in wounds

blown /bloʷn/ v past participle of BLOW¹

blow·out /'bloʷaʊt/ n **1** the bursting of a container (esp. a tire): *He had a blowout on the road.* **2** *infml* a very gay noisy party with a lot of eating and drinking –see also BLOW up

blow·pipe /'bloʷpaɪp/ also **blowgun** /-gʌn/ n a tube used for blowing small stones or poisoned arrows (DARTS), used as a weapon

blow·torch /'bloʷtɔrtʃ/ also **blowlamp** /-læmp/– n a pipe from which a mixture of gas and air is blown out under pressure so as to give a small area of very hot flame

blow-up /'· ·/ n **1** a photographic ENLARGEment **2** a sudden moment of anger

blub·ber /'blʌbər/ n [U] the fat of sea creatures, esp. WHALES, from which oil is obtained

blue¹ /bluʷ/ adj **1** having the color blue: *The sky is deep blue.*|*He painted the door blue.*|*Your hands are* **blue with cold. 2** [F] *infml* sad and without hope: *I'm feeling kind of blue today.* **3 till one is blue in the face** unsuccessfully forever: *You can telephone her till you're blue in the face but, she'll never come.* **–blueness** n [U] **–bluish** adj

blue² n [C;U] **1** the color of the clear sky or of the deep sea on a fine day: *dressed in blue*|*(A) light blue would be a nice color for the door.* **2 out of the blue** unexpectedly: *John arrived out of the blue.*

blue·bell /'bluʷbɛl/ n a blue bell-shaped flower

blue·ber·ry /'bluʷˌbɛriʸ, -bəriʸ/ n **-ries** (the fruit of) a small bush which grows in North America

blue blood /'· ·/ n [U] the quality of being a nobleman or noblewoman by birth **–blue-blooded** /ˌ· '··◂/ adj

blue·bot·tle /'bluʷˌbatḷ/ n a large blue fly

blue-col·lar /ˌ· '··◂/ adj [A] of or relating to workers who do hard or dirty work with their hands: *blue-collar workers*|*He had lots of blue-collar jobs.* –compare WHITE-COLLAR

blue·fish /'bluʷˌfɪʃ/ n **bluefish** a sea fish with a bluish color caught for sport and food off the coast of North America

blue·grass /'bluʷgræs/ n [U] a kind of music from the Southern US, played on instruments with strings such as the GUITAR, VIOLIN, and BANJO, and usu. without electronic apparatus (an AMPLIFIER) to make it louder: *a bluegrass band*|*concert*

blue jay /'· ·/ n a common North American bird with a blue back and a showy growth of blue feathers on its head

blue jeans /'· ·/ n [P] *AmE* for JEANS

blue law /'· ·/ n *AmE infml* a law to control sexual morals, the drinking of alcohol, working on Sundays, etc.

blue mov·ie /ˌ· '··/ n a movie film about sex, esp. one that is shown at a private club

blue·print /'bluʷˌprɪnt/ n a copy of a plan for making a machine or building a house: *(fig.) The plans for the new educational system have only reached the blueprint stage so far.*

blues /bluʷz/ n [U +sing./pl. v] **1** a type of slow, sad music from the Southern US: *The blues was/were first performed by the black people of New Orleans.*|*a well-known blues singer* **2** *infml* the state of being sad: *a sudden attack of the blues*

bluff¹ /blʌf/ v **1** [I] to deceive by pretending to be stronger, cleverer, surer of the truth, etc., than one is: *He says he'll win the race, but he's only bluffing.* **2** [T through, out of] to find or make (one's way) by doing this: *He could bluff his way through any difficulty.* **bluff sbdy. into sthg.** v prep [T +v-ing] to persuade into (doing something) by BLUFFing¹ (1): *He bluffed me into thinking that his stick was a gun.*

bluff² n [U] **1** the action of BLUFFing¹ (1): *He threatened to dismiss me from my job, but it's all a bluff.* **2 call someone's bluff** to tell someone who is BLUFFing¹ (1) to do what he/she threatens to do, guessing that he/ she will not be able to

bluff³ adj (of a person or his/her manner) rough, plain, and cheerful: *Charles has a very kind heart in spite of his bluff way of speaking.* **–bluffly** adv **–bluffness** n [U]

blun·der¹ /'blʌndər/ n a stupid or unnecessary mistake

blunder² v [I] **1** to make a BLUNDER¹ **2** to move awkwardly or unsteadily, as if blind: *He blundered through the dark forest.* **–blunderer** n

blun·der·buss /'blʌndərˌbʌs/ n an old kind of gun with a wide mouth open to the barrel

blunt¹ /blʌnt/ adj **1** (of a knife, pencil, etc.) not sharp: *(fig.) Too much alcohol makes your senses blunt.* **2** (of a person or his speech) rough and plain, without trying to be polite or kind: *a blunt man*|*a few blunt words* **–bluntness** n [U]

blunt² v [T] to make BLUNT¹ (1)

blunt·ly /'blʌntliʸ/ adv roughly and plainly: *To speak bluntly, you are sure to fail.*

blur¹ /blɜr/ n [S] something whose shape is not clearly seen: *The houses appeared as a blur in the mist.*|*(fig.) My memory of the accident is only a blur.*

blur² v **-rr-** [T] to make difficult to see (through or with) clearly: *Tears blurred my eyes.*|*a very blurred photograph*

blurt sthg. ↔ out /blɜrt/ v adv [T] to say (something which should not be said) suddenly and without thinking: *Peter blurted out the news before he considered its effect.*

blush¹ /blʌʃ/ v [I at, with] to become red in the face, from shame or because people are looking at one: *He blushed with shame.*|*She blushed at their praises.* **–blushingly** adv

blush² n **1** [C] a case of BLUSHing¹: *His remark brought a blush (in)to my cheeks.* **2** [U] also **blush-on** /'· ·/, **blusher** /'blʌʃər/, **rouge–** a powder used to redden the face: *Mary* *looked pale, so I told her to put on some blush.*

blus·ter¹ /'blʌstər/ v [I] **1** to speak loudly and roughly, with noisy threats, often to hide lack of real power **2** (of wind) to blow roughly

bluster² n [U] **1** noisy threatening talk **2** the noise of rough wind or waves: *the bluster of the storm*

blus·ter·y /'blʌstəriʸ/ adj (of weather) rough, windy, and violent: *a blustery winter day*

B.O., bo /ˌbiʸ 'oʷ/ n [U] abbrev. for BODY ODOR

bo·a¹ /'boʷə/ also **boa constrictor** /ˌ·· ·'··/– n a large non-poisonous South American snake that kills creatures by crushing them

boa² also **feather boa**– n a long snake-shaped garment (STOLE) made of feathers, worn by women around the neck

boar /bɔr, boʷr/ n **boar** or **boars** a male pig on a farm that is kept for breeding (=is not CASTRATEd) –compare HOG¹ (1), SOW¹

board¹ /bɔrd, boʷrd/ n **1** [C] a long thin flat piece of cut wood; PLANK¹ (1) **2** [C] a flat piece of hard material used for a particular purpose: *She put the list on the* BULLETIN board.|*He wrote the date on the* BLACKBOARD.|*a nail sticking out of the* FLOOR-BOARD **3** [U] (the cost of) meals: *I pay $100 a week for room and board.* **4** [C often cap.] a committee or association, as of company directors, government officials, etc., with special responsibility: *He has joined/been elected to the board of a new company.*|*Mary is a workers' representative on the Board.*|*The Board is meeting the union today in the* **boardroom. 5 above board** (usu. of an action in business) completely open and honest **6 across the board** including all groups or members, as in an industry: *a wage increase of $20 a week across the board* **7 on board** in or on (a ship or public vehicle): *They got on board the train.*|*She enjoys life on board ship.* –compare ABOARD

board² v **1** [T *up, over*] to cover with BOARDs¹ (1): *Board the windows up.* **2** [T] to go on BOARD¹ (7) (a ship or public vehicle): *Passengers should board the train now.* **3** [I] (of an aircraft) to take on passengers: *Flight 387 for New York is now boarding at Gate 15.* **4** [I;T *at, with*] to get or supply with meals and usu. lodging for payment: *We're boarding some students from the university.*|*I'm boarding with a friend.*

board·er /'bɔrdər, 'boʷr-/ n a person who pays to live and to receive meals at another person's house; lodger: *Mrs. Brown takes in boarders for a living.*

board·ing·house /'bɔrdɪŋˌhaʊs, 'boʷr-/ n -houses /ˌhaʊzɪz/ a private lodging house (not a hotel) that supplies meals

boarding school /'·· ˌ·/ n [C;U] a school at which children live instead of going there daily from home

board·walk /'bɔrdwɔk, 'boʷrd-/ n AmE a footpath often made of boards, usu. beside the sea

boast¹ /boʷst/ n [C *that*] **1** usu. derog an expression of self-praise: *His boast that he*

was the strongest man in the village turned out to be untrue. **2** not derog a cause for pride: *It is one of their proudest boasts that nobody is sent to prison without trial.*

boast² v **1** [I;T *that/about, of*] usu. derog to say or talk (too) proudly: *She boasts that her car is faster than mine.*|*He boasted of/about the big fish he had caught.*|*Don't believe him; he's just boasting.* **2** [T] not derog (usu. not of people) to be lucky enough to own: *This little village boasts three parks.*

boast·ful /'boʷstfəl/ adj derog (of a person or his/her words) full of self-praise –**boastfully** adv –**boastfulness** n [U]

boat¹ /boʷt/ n **1** a small open vessel for travel-ing across water: *a small fishing boat/sailboat/rowboat*|*They crossed the river by boat/in a boat.* **2 in the same boat** in the same unpleasant conditions; facing the same dangers: *If you lose your job I'll lose mine, so we're both in the same boat.* **3 rock the boat** infml to make matters worse for a group by expressing differences of opinion

USAGE **Boats** are usually smaller than **ships**: *a fishing boat*|*Peter and Susan are spending the weekend on their boat.* However, the word may be used informally of a large passenger vessel: *We went to Australia by boat.* Large naval vessels are always called **ships**: *How many ships are there in the navy?*

boat·swain /'boʷsən/ n →BOSUN

boat train /'· ·/ n a train that takes people to or from ships in port

bob /bab/ v -bb- [I;T] to move (something) quickly and repeatedly up and down, as on water: *The small boat was bobbing up and down on the rough sea.*

bob·bin /'babɪn/ n a small roller on which thread is wound, as in a sewing machine –compare REEL¹

bob·by /'babiʸ/ n -bies BrE infml a policeman

bob·sled /'babsled/ also **bobsleigh** /-sleʸ/– v,n [C;I] (to ride in) a small vehicle that runs on metal blades and is used for sliding down snowy slopes (TOBOGGANing)

bode¹ /boʷd/ v boded, boding [I *well/ill*] lit →AUGUR

bode² v past tense of BIDE

bod·ice /'badɪs/ n the (usu. close-fitting) up-per part of a woman's dress or undergarment above the waist

bod·i·ly¹ /'badl-iʸ/ adj [A] of the human body: *He likes his bodily comforts.* –see also PHYSI-CAL (3)

bodily² adv (esp. of movement) in a body or as a whole; completely: *He picked the child up bodily and carried her to bed.*

bod·y /'badiʸ/ n -ies **1** [C] the whole of a person or animal as opposed to the mind or soul: *Her whole body was covered from head to toe with painful red spots.*|*He was there in body but not in spirit.* (=he wished he were somewhere else)|*Where did you bury the body?* (=of the dead person or animal) **2** [C] a body without the head or limbs: *He had a wound on his leg and two more on his body*|(fig.)*We sat in* **the body of** *the hall.* (=in the main part) **3** [C *of*] a (large) amount: *The oceans are large bodies of water.* **4** [C (some-*

times cap.)] a number of people who do something together in a planned way: *The United States Senate is an elected body.|The Governing Body of the College meets every Thursday.|They marched* **in a body** (=all together) *to the White House and demanded to see the President.* **5** [C] *tech* an object; piece of matter: *The sun, moon, and stars are* **heavenly bodies.|a foreign body** (=something that ought not to be there) *in one's eye* **6** [C] the main outside parts of a motor vehicle, as opposed to the motor, wheels, etc.: *repaint the body of the bus.* **7** [U] (of wine) full strong quality **8 bodied** having a certain kind of body: *a big-bodied man.*

USAGE One's **figure** is the shape of one's **body,** considered as to whether it is sexually attractive or to its relation to clothes: *She has a nice* **figure.** Body used here would be considered impolite. **Figure** is usually used of women; to talk about the shape and size of a man's body, the usual word is **physique**: *He has a powerful* **physique.** Build could be used of either a man or woman: *a man/woman of small* **build**

bod·y·guard /ˈbadiⁱˌgard/ *n* [+ *sing./pl. v*] a person or group of men whose duty is to guard an important person: *The President has always a bodyguard of several people.*

body lan·guage /ˈ·· ˌ··/ *n* [U] the movements of the body that express one's feelings: *She said she wasn't nervous, but her body language said she was.*

body o·dor /ˈ·· ˌ··/ also **B.O.**– *n* the unpleasant smell from a person's body, esp. as caused by SWEAT¹ (1)

bod·y·work /ˈbadiⁱˌwɜrk/ *n* **1** [U] the repair of a vehicle body: *This garage does good bodywork.* **2** [C] →BODY (6)

bog /bag, bɔg/ *n* [C;U] (a large area of) soft wet ground containing a great deal of decaying vegetable matter; SWAMP: *Don't walk across that field; it's a bog.* **–boggy** *adj*

bog down *v adv* **-gg-** [I;T (=**bog** sthg.↔ **down**) *usu.pass.*] to (cause to) sink (as if) into a BOG: *The car (got) bogged down in the mud.|*(fig.) *The talks with the workers (got) bogged down on the question of working hours.*

bo·gey , bogy, bogie /ˈbugiⁱ, ˈboʷgiⁱ/ *n* also **bogey man** /ˈ·· ˌ·/– (used by or to children) an imaginary evil spirit used for threatening children **2** an imaginary fear

bog·gle /ˈbagəl/ *v* **-gled, -gling** [I *at*] to make difficulties (about something) esp. owing to fear or surprise: **The/My mind boggles** *(at the idea)!* (=I can't imagine it)

bo·gus /ˈboʷgəs/ *adj derog* pretended; false

bo·he·mi·an /boʷˈhiʸmiʸən/ *adj,n becoming rare* (a person) that does not follow the usual rules of social life, though obeying the law: *Many writers, artists, and musicians are thought to be bohemians/to lead bohemian lives.*

boil¹ /bɔil/ *v* [I;T] **1 a** to cause (a liquid) to reach the temperature at which liquid changes into a gas: *Peter boiled the kettle.|I'm boiling the baby's milk.* **b** (of a liquid or the vessel containing it) to reach this tem-

perature: *Is the milk boiling yet?|The water is boiling away* (=is continuing to boil) *on the fire.|*(fig.) *boiling with anger|Injustice* **makes my blood boil.** (=makes me very angry) **2** to cook in water at 212°F, 100°C: *Boil the potatoes for 20 minutes.|I'll boil you an egg.|The potatoes have been boiling (away) for 20 minutes.* **3 boil dry: a** (of a liquid) to disappear by changing into a gas: *The water all boiled dry.* **b** to become dry because the liquid has disappeared in this way: *Don't let the pot/the vegetables boil dry.* –see also HARD-BOILED –see COOK² (USAGE)

boil away *v adv* [I] to be reduced to nothing (as if) by boiling: *The water had all boiled away and the pan was burned.*

boil down to sthg. *v adv prep* [T] *infml* to be or mean, leaving out the unnecessary parts: *The whole matter boils down to a power struggle between the trade union and the directors.*

boil over *v adv* [I] (of a liquid) to boil and flow over the sides of a container: *Turn off the gas; the milk is boiling over.|*(fig.) *The argument boiled over into open war.*

boil up *v adv* [I] (of troubles) to arise and reach a dangerous level: *Trouble is boiling up in downtown Chicago.*

boil² *n* [*the* S] →BOILING POINT: *Bring the soup to the boil.*

boil³ *n* a painful infected swelling under the skin, which bursts when ripe

boil·er /ˈbɔilər/ *n* a container for boiling, as in a steam engine, or to make hot water in a house

boiling point /ˈ·· ˌ·/ *n* **1** [C] the temperature at which a liquid boils: *Water has a boiling point of 212°F, 100°C.* **2** [S] the point at which high excitement, anger, etc., breaks into action

bois·ter·ous /ˈbɔistərəs/ *adj* (of a person or his/her behavior) noisily cheerful and rough **–boisterously** *adv* **–boisterousness** *n* [U]

bold /boʷld/ *adj* **1** (of a person or his/her behavior) daring; courageous; adventurous **2** *derog* (of a person) without respect or shame; rude: *She's a bold child/*as **bold as brass.** **3** (of the appearance of something) strongly marked; clearly formed: *a drawing done in a few bold lines* **–boldly** *adv* **–boldness** *n* [U]

bol·ster /ˈboʷlstər/ *n* a long round PILLOW

bolster sbdy./sthg. ↔ **up** *v adv* [T] to give necessary support and encouragement (to a person or his/her feelings or beliefs): *to bolster up someone's pride*

bolt¹ /boʷlt/ *n* **1** a screw with no point, which fastens onto a NUT (2) –compare NAIL¹ (1) to hold things together **2** a metal bar that slides across to fasten a door or window **3** →THUNDERBOLT

bolt² *v* **1** [I] (esp. of a horse) to run away suddenly, as in fear: *My horse bolted and threw me in the mud.|The thief bolted when he saw the policeman.* **2** [T] to swallow hastily: *She bolted (down) her breakfast.* **3** [I;T] to (cause to) fasten with a BOLT¹ (1,2): *I bolted the two parts together.|She bolted the door.|This door bolts on the inside.*

–opposite **unbolt** (for **3**)

bolt³ adv straight and stiffly: *He made the children sit bolt upright.*

bolt⁴ n [S] an act of running away: *The prisoner* **made a bolt for it.** (=tried to run away)

bomb¹ /bɑm/ n **1** [C] a hollow metal container filled with explosive: *They planted a bomb in the post office.* **2** [the S] the atomic bomb: *Has that country got the bomb now?* **3** (go) **like a bomb** *infml* (to go) very well: *My new car goes like a bomb.|The party went like a bomb.*

bomb² v [I;T] **1** to attack with bombs, esp. by dropping them from aircraft **2** [on, out] *AmE infml* to fail: "*How did he do on the last test?*" "*He bombed.*"

bom·bard /bɑm'bɑrd/ v [T] to keep attacking heavily (as if) with gunfire: *The warships bombarded the port.|The speaker was bombarded with questions.* –**bombardment** n

bombed /bɑmd/ adj *AmE infml* drunk: *He got really bombed at the party and passed out.*

bomb·er /'bɑmər/ n **1** an aircraft that carries and drops bombs –compare FIGHTER (2) **2** a person who puts bombs into buildings and other places

bomb·shell /'bɑmʃɛl/ n [usu. sing.] *infml* a great and often unpleasant surprise: *The news of the defeat was a bombshell to us.*

bo·na fide /'bownə ˌfaɪd, ˌbɑnə-, ˌbownə 'faɪdiʸ/ adj,adv *Latin law* real(ly); in good faith: *The hotel parking garage is only for bona fide guests.* (=only for people staying at the hotel)

bo·nan·za /bə'nænzə, bow-/ n something very profitable

bond¹ /bɑnd/ n **1** [C] an agreement, feeling, likeness, etc., that unites two or more people or groups: *two countries united in the bonds of friendship* **2** [C] a paper in which a government or an industrial firm promises to pay back with interest money that has been lent (INVESTED): *United States bond* **3** [S] a state of being stuck together: *This new paste makes a firmer bond.* **4** money paid as a promise: **Bail bond** *is money paid for* BAIL (1).

bond² v [I;T together,to] to (cause to) stick together as with paste: *These two substances won't bond (together).*

bond·age /'bɑndɪdʒ/ n [U] *lit* the condition of being a slave, or any state which seems like this

bonds /bɑndz/ n [P] *lit* chains, ropes, etc., used for tying up a prisoner: *to escape from one's bonds*

bone¹ /bown/ n [C;U] **1** (one of) the hard parts of the body, which protect the organs within and around which are the flesh and skin: *He broke a bone in his leg.* –see also SKELETON (1) **2 bone of contention** something that causes argument: *That island has been a bone of contention between our two countries for years.* **3 cut to the bone** to reduce (costs, services, etc.) as much as possible: *The bus service has been cut to the bone.* **4 feel in one's bones** to believe strongly though without proof: *I'm going to fail the examination! I can*

feel it in my bones. **5 have a bone to pick with someone** to have something to complain about to someone: *I've got a bone to pick with you. Why did you take my bicycle?* **6 make no bones about (doing) something** to feel no doubt or shame about (doing) something: *She made no bones about telling me the truth.* –**boneless** adj

bone² v **boned, boning** [T] to take the bones out of: *Will you bone this piece of fish for me?* –**boned** adj: *boned meat*

  bone up v adv [I;T for, on] *infml* to study hard, esp. for a special purpose: *You'd better bone up on the traffic laws if you expect to pass your driving test.|bone up for a test*

bone-dry /ˌ· '· ◄/ adj *infml* perfectly dry

bon·fire /'bɑnfaɪər/ n a large fire built in the open air, either to CELEBRATE something or to burn unwanted things

bon·go /'bɑŋgoʷ, 'bɔŋg-/ also **bongo drum** /'·· ˌ·-/ n **-gos** or **-goes** either of a pair of small drums played with the hands

bon·ho·mie /ˌbɑnə'miʸ/ n [U] cheerfulness; easy friendliness

bon·kers /'bɑŋkərz/ adj [F] *BrE infml humor* crazy: *You're completely bonkers.*

bon·net /'bɑnɪt/ n **1** a round head-covering tied under the chin, worn by babies and formerly by women –compare HAT (1) **2** *BrE* for HOOD (4)

bo·nus /'bownəs/ n **1** an additional payment beyond what is usual, necessary, or expected, e.g. to those who work for a business: *The workers got a Christmas bonus.* **2** *infml* anything pleasant in addition to what is expected: *We like our new house, and it's a real bonus that my mother lives so near.*

bon·y /'bowniʸ/ adj **-ier, -iest 1** very thin so that the bones can be seen: *her bony hand* **2** (of food) full of bones: *bony fish*

boo¹ /buʷ/ interj,n **boos** a shout of disapproval or strong disagreement

boo² v **booed, booing** [I;T] to express disapproval (of) or strong disagreement (with), esp. by shouting "BOO": *The crowd booed (the speaker).*

boob¹ /buʷb/ n *AmE infml* a foolish person

boob² n *derog* a woman's breast

boo-boo /'buʷbuʷ/ n **boo-boos** *AmE infml* a silly mistake

boo·by prize /'buʷbiʸ ˌpraɪz/ n a prize given (esp. as a joke) for the worst performance in a competition

booby trap /'·· ˌ·/ n **1** a hidden bomb which explodes when some harmless-looking object is touched **2** any harmless trap used for surprising someone

book¹ /bʊk/ n **1** a collection of sheets of paper fastened together as a thing to be read, or to be written in **2** [usu. pl.] written records of money, names, etc.: *How many names do you have on your books?* **3** any collection of things fastened together, esp. one with its own covers: *a book of stamps/tickets* **4** (bring (someone) to book** to punish or make (someone) pay **5 by the book** according to the rules **6 take a leaf out of someone's book** to behave as someone else does or has done:

Take a leaf out of her book. Start saving for your vacation now. **7 throw the book at (someone)** (esp. of the police or a judge) to make all possible charges against (someone) **8 the Good Book** also **the Book**– the BIBLE

book² *v* **1** [T] *infml* to enter charges against, esp. in police records: *He was booked on a charge of speeding.* **2** [I;T *up*] *esp. BrE* for RESERVE¹ (2)

book·case /'buk-ke^ys/ *n* a piece of furniture consisting of shelves to hold books –see illustration on page 399

book·end /'bukend/ *n* [*usu. pl.*] one of a pair of supports to hold a row of books

book·ing /'bukɪŋ/ *n* [C;U] *BrE* for RESERVATION (3)

book·keep·ing /'buk,ki^ypɪŋ/ *n* [U] the act of keeping the accounts of money of a business company, a public office, etc. –**bookkeeper** *n*

book·let /'buklɪt/ *n* a small book, usu. with a paper cover; PAMPHLET

book·mak·er /'buk,me^ykər/ also **bookie** /'buki^y/ *infml*– *n* a person who takes money (BETS¹ (2)) risked on the results of competitions, esp. horse races

book·mark /'bukmark/ also **bookmarker** /'buk,markər/– *n* something put between the pages of a book to keep a place in it

book·worm /'bukwɜrm/ *n often derog* a person who is very fond, perhaps too fond, of reading and study

boom¹ /bu^wm/ *v* [I] **1** to make a deep hollow sound; RESOUND (1): *The guns boomed.* **2** to grow rapidly, esp. in value: *Business is booming.*

boom out *v adv* [I;T (=**boom** sthg.↔ **out**)] to (cause to) come out with a deep hollow sound: *He boomed out his answer.|His answer boomed out.*

boom² *n* **1** a BOOMING¹ (1) sound or cry **2** a rapid growth or increase: *There has been a boom in* EXPORTS *this year.*

boom³ *n* **1** a long pole, esp. on a boat, to which a sail is fastened, or as part of an apparatus for loading and unloading **2** a heavy chain fixed across a river to stop things (esp. logs) floating down or prevent ships sailing up

boo·mer·ang /'bu^wmə,ræŋ/ *n* a curved stick which makes a circle and comes back when thrown, used by Australian ABORIGINES as a hunting weapon

boon /bu^wn/ *n* something favorable; a comfort; a help: *A car is a real boon when you live in the country.*

boor /buər/ *n derog* a rude ungraceful person –**boorish** *adj* –**boorishly** *adv* –**boorishness** *n* [U]

boost¹ /bu^wst/ *v* [T] **1** [*up*] to push up from below: *If you boost me up, I can just reach the window.* **2** to increase; raise: *to boost prices|plans to boost production by 30% next year|*(fig.) *We need a vacation to boost our spirits.*

boost² *n* **1** a push upwards **2** an increase in amount **3** an act that brings help or encouragement

boost·er /'bu^wstər/ *n* **1** a person or machine that BOOSTs¹ **2** a substance that increases the

effectiveness of a drug or medicine: *This medicine will last for a time, but after six months you'll need a booster.*

boot¹ /bu^wt/ *n* **1** [C *usu. pl.*] a covering of leather or rubber for the foot and ankle, usu. heavier and thicker than a shoe: *army boots/ hiking boots* **2** [C] *BrE* for TRUNK (5) **3** [*the S*] *infml* the act of sending someone away rudely, esp. from a job: *They gave him the boot for coming late.* –compare FIRE² (6) **4 lick someone's boots** *infml derog* to try to gain someone's favor by being too polite and too obedient **5 too big for one's boots** *infml* too proud

boot² *v infml* [T] to kick: *He booted the ball across the field.* [T] *infml* to send away rudely and sometimes

boot³ *n* **to boot** *fml or humor* (often of something unpleasant) besides; in addition: *He is dishonest, and a coward to boot.*

boot camp /'· ·/ *n* a camp where US navy, army, or MARINE RECRUITs are trained

boot·ee /'bu^wti^y/ *n* [*usu. pl.*] a baby's woolen boot

booth /bu^wθ/ *n* **booths** /bu^wðz, bu^wθs/ **1** (at a market or FAIR³) a tent or small building where goods are sold or games are played **2** an enclosed place big enough for one person at a time: *a telephone booth|a voting booth* **3** a partly enclosed place in a restaurant with a table between two long seats –see illustration on page 581

boot·leg /'bu^wtleg/ *v* **-gg-** [I;T] to make, carry, or sell (alcoholic drink) unlawfully –**bootlegger** *n*

boo·ty /'bu^wti^y/ *n* [U] goods stolen by thieves or taken by a victorious army

booze¹ /bu^wz/ **boozed, boozing** *v* [I] *infml* to drink alcohol, esp. too much alcohol: *He spends every night boozing with his friends.*

booze² *n* [U] *infml* alcoholic drink

booz·er /'bu^wzər/ *n infml* a person who BOOZEs, esp. habitually

bop /bap/ *n* **1** [C] *infml esp. AmE* a blow that strikes a person: *a bop on the head* **2** [U] also **bebop**– a type of JAZZ music

bor·der¹ /'bordər/ *n* **1** (land near) the dividing line between two countries: *soldiers guarding the border|over the border* **2** edge: *a border of flowers around the garden*

border² *v* [T] **1** to be a border to: *fields bordered by woods* **2** to have a common border with: *The United States borders Mexico along parts of the Rio Grande.*

border on/upon sthg. *v prep* [T] to be very much like: *His remarks bordered on rudeness.*

bor·der·line¹ /'bordər,laɪn/ *n* [C *usu. sing.*] (a line marking) a border: *the borderline between Connecticut and Massachusetts| between sleeping and waking*

borderline² *adj* [A *no comp.*] that may or may not belong to a certain type: *I'm not sure whether to pass him or fail him; he's* **a borderline case.**

bore¹ /bor, bo^wr/ *v* [I;T] to make a round hole or passage (in something): *This machine can bore through solid rock.|to bore a hole* –**borer** *n*

bore² *v past tense of* BEAR²

bore³ *n* **1** [C] *derog* a person who causes others to lose interest in him/her, as by continual dull talk **2** [S] *BrE infml* something one finds uninteresting: *Don't see that movie it's a real bore.|Studying all the time gets to be a bore.*

bore⁴ *v* [I;T] to make (someone) uninterested, e.g. by continual dull talk: *The lesson was boring.|The students were bored (by it).* **–boredom** /'bɔrdəm, 'boʷr-/ *n* [U]

bore⁵ *n* a measurement of the width of the hollow inside a gun barrel or pipe: *12-bore|small-bore|12-inch bore*

born¹ /bɔrn/ *adj* [*no comp.*] **1** [F] brought into existence by birth: *Shakespeare was born in 1564.|(fig.) The new political party was born at a small meeting/**born of** the disagreement between the two old political parties.* **2** [F] at birth; originally: *Tom was born American but grew up in Canada.* **3** [+*to-v*] having a stated quality from or as if from birth: *a born leader|born to succeed* **4 born and bred** having grown up from birth: *She was born and bred in Texas.|She was Texas born and bred.* **5 -born** born as stated: *new-born|first-born|still-born* (=born dead) –see also UNBORN

born² *v past participle of* BEAR²

USAGEThis is one of the two past participles of **bear** when it means "to give birth to". Compare: *He was **born** in 1950.|She has **borne** three children.*

borne /bɔrn, boʷrn/ *v* **1** *past participle of* BEAR² –see BORN² (USAGE) **2 -borne** carried as stated: *Some plants have windborne seeds.*

bor·ough /'bʌroʷ, 'bʌroʷ/ *n* a town, or a division of a large town, with powers of government: *the Borough of Brooklyn*

bor·row /'bʌroʷ, 'bɔroʷ/ *v* [I;T *from*] **1** to take or receive (something) for a certain time, intending to return it: *to borrow ($50) from a friend* –see Study Notes on page 481 **2** to take or copy (esp. ideas, words, etc.): *English has borrowed (words) from many languages.* **–borrower** *n*

bos·om /'buzəm, 'buʷ-/ *n often euph or lit* the front of the human chest, esp. the female breasts: *She held the child to her bosom.|a **bosom friend** (=a very close friend)*

boss¹ /bɔs/ *n infml* **1** a master; employer; person having control over others: *to ask the boss for more money|Good morning, boss.|Who's (the) boss?* (=who's in charge?) **2** *AmE usu. derog* a political party chief

boss² *v* [I;T *around*] *infml* to give orders (to); act in a BOSSY way: *Tom likes to boss younger children around.*

boss·y /'bɔsiʸ/ *adj* **-ier, -iest** *infml derog* having or showing too much liking for giving orders: *a bossy person| manner* **–bossiness** *n* [U] /boʷsən/ *n* a chief seaman on a ship: *Are we ready to sail, bosun?*

bo·sun, boatswain /'boʷsən/ *n* a chief seaman on a ship: *Are we ready to sail, bosun?*

bot·a·ny /'batn-iʸ/ *n* [U] the scientific study of plants **–botanical** /bə'tænɪkəl/ *adj* [A] **–botanist** /'batn-ɪst/ *n*

botch /batʃ/ *v infml* [T *up*] to do (something)

badly, esp. to repair (something) badly: *I tried to fix my watch myself, and I really botched it up.|a botched job* **–botch** also **botch-up** /'·· ·/– *n: I've **made a botch/ botch-up of** repairing the car.*

both /boʷθ/ *predeterminer,determiner,pron* **1** the two together; the one as well as the other: *Both children/Both of the children/Both the children won prizes.|She and her husband both like dancing.|"I don't know which to buy." "Why not buy both (of them)?"* –see EACH (USAGE) **2 both ... and ...** not only ... but also ... : *We visited both New York and London.|She both speaks and writes Swahili.|well known for both her kindness and her understanding*

both·er¹ /'baðər/ *v* **1** [T] to cause to be nervous; annoy or trouble, esp. in little ways: *I'm busy. Don't bother me.|That's what bothers me most.|(polite) I'm sorry to bother you, but can you tell me the time?* **2** [I +*to-v*/*with, about*] to cause inconvenience or trouble to oneself: *Don't bother with/about it.*

bother² *n* [C;U] trouble, inconvenience, or anxiety (usu. caused by small matters and lasting a short time): *We had a lot of bother finding our way here.|I don't want to be a bother to you, but could I stay here tonight?*

bot·tle¹ /'batl/ *n* **1** a container for liquids, usu. made of glass or plastic, with a narrow neck or mouth and usu. no handle –see illustration on page 683 **2** the quantity held by a bottle: *He drank a whole bottle/bottleful of wine!* **3 the bottle** alcoholic drink, esp. when drunk too much: *John's **on the bottle/hitting the bottle** again!*

bottle² *v* **-tled, -tling** [T] to put into bottles: *a machine for bottling wine/to bottle fruit to preserve it for the winter*

bottle sthg.↔ **up** *v adv* [T] to control in an unhealthy way: *Tell us what's worrying you. Don't bottle it up!*

bot·tle·neck /'batl,nɛk/ *n* a narrow space in a road which slows down traffic: *(fig.) We aren't making enough televisions because there's a bottleneck in production.*

bot·tom /'batəm/ *n* **1** [C] the base on which something stands; the lowest part, inside or outside: *at the bottom of the stairs|the bottom of his pant legs|The glasses all had wet bottoms.|some tea left at/in the bottom of your cup* **2** [*the* S *of*] the ground under the sea, a lake, or a river: *They sent the enemy ship to the bottom (of the sea).|the river-bottom* **3** [*the* S *of*] the least important or least worthy part of anything: *always at the bottom of the class* (=always getting low marks)|*He started life at the bottom/He started **at the bottom of the ladder** and worked his way up (to success).* **4** [*the* S *of*] the far end: *I'll walk with you to the bottom of the road.* –compare TOP¹ **5** [C] the part of the body on which one sits: *to fall on one's bottom* **6** [*the* S *of*] *often derog* the starting point; the cause; that on which everything else rests: *Who is **at the bottom of** all this trouble?|I intend to **get to the bottom of it.** (=find the cause) **7** [A] lowest; last: *in the bottom row* **8 bet one's**

bottom dollar *infml* to be completely sure: *You can bet your bottom dollar that she'll win.* **9 from the bottom of one's heart** truly; with real feeling: *I want to tell you from the bottom of my heart that I am truly sorry.*

bot·tom·less /'baṭəmlıs/ *adj* with no bottom or limit; very deep: (fig.) *The government's supply of money seemed bottomless, but now they have no more.*

bot·u·lism /'batʃə,lızəm/ *n* [U] a serious form of food poisoning caused by bacteria that are found in preserved meat and vegetables

bough /baʊ/ *n* a main branch of a tree

bought /bɔt/ *v* past tense and participle of BUY¹

boul·der /'boʷldər/ *n* a large stone or rock

bou·le·vard /'bʊlə,vard/ *n* (part of the name of) a broad street, often having trees on each side: *Sunset Boulevard*

bounce¹ /baʊns/ **bounced, bouncing** *v* **1** [I;T] **a** (of a ball) to spring back or up again from something solid **b** to cause (a ball) to do this: (fig.) *She bounced the baby (on her knee).* **2** [I] *infml* (of a check) to be returned by a bank as worthless

bounce² *n* [C;U] the act or action of bouncing (BOUNCE¹): |*The ball has plenty of bounce.*

bounc·ing /'baʊnsıŋ/ *adj* [A *no comp.*] *approc* (esp. of babies) healthy and active: *two bouncing babies*

bounc·y /'baʊnsiʸ/ *adj* **1** (showing that one is) full of life and eager for action: *a bouncy person/manner* **2** able to bounce: *a bouncy ball* **–bouncily** *adv* **–bounciness** *n* [U]

bound¹ /baʊnd/ *adj* intending to go (to); going (to): *bound for home/homeward-bound*

bound² *v* [T *usu. pass.*] to mark the edges of; keep within a certain space: *The US is bounded on the north by Canada and on the south by Mexico.* –see also UNBOUNDED

bound³ *adj* **1** [F *to*] fastened by or as if by a band; kept close to: *bound to one's job-|bound to a post|housebound* (=not often or ever leaving one's house)|*The airport was snowbound, so no aircraft could take off.* **2** [F+*to-v*] certain; sure: *It's bound to rain soon.|You're bound to succeed.* **3** [F+*to-v*] having to, by law or morally: *I felt bound to tell you.* **4** (of a book) fastened within covers: *a leather-bound book|a book bound in leather* **5 bound up in** busy with; very interested in: *She is bound up in her work.* **6 bound up with** dependent on; connected with: *His future is closely bound up with that of the company he works for.*

bound⁴ *n* a jump or LEAP²: *In a single bound, he was over the wall.*

bound⁵ *v* **1** to jump or LEAP¹: *He bounded away.* **2** to spring or BOUNCE¹ (1) back from a surface

bound·a·ry /'baʊndəriʸ/ *n* **-ries 1** the limiting or dividing line between surfaces, spaces, countries, etc.; border: *A river forms the boundary (line) between the two countries.* **2** the outer limit of something: *the boundaries of human knowledge* **3** (in sports) the line which marks the limit of the field of play: *A ball hit over the boundary*

bound·less /'baʊndlıs/ *adj* without limits: *boundless wealth/imagination* **–boundlessly** *adv* **–boundlessness** *n* [U]

bounds /baʊndz/ *n* [P] **1** the furthest limits or edges of something; the limits beyond which one may not go: *His foolishness was without bounds/went beyond the bounds of reason.* **2** *AmE* forbidden to be visited (by): *That movie is out of bounds (to you) because you're too young.*

boun·te·ous /'baʊntiʸəs/ also **bountiful** /'baʊntıfəl/– *adj fml or lit* given or willing to give freely: *bounteous gifts|a bounteous giver* **–bounteously** *adv* **–bounteousness** *n* [U]

boun·ty /'baʊntiʸ/ *n* [U] generosity: *a rich lady famous for her bounty to the poor*

bou·quet¹ /boʷ'keʸ, buʷ-/ *n* a bunch of flowers

bou·quet² /buʷ'keʸ/ *n* the smell of a wine: *a rich bouquet*

bour·bon /'bɜrbən/ *n* [U] a type of strong alcoholic drink (WHISKEY)

bour·geois /bʊər'ʒwa, 'bʊərʒwa/ *adj* **1** of, related to, or typical of the MIDDLE CLASS **2** *derog* too interested in material possessions and one's social position

bour·geoi·sie /,bʊərʒwa'ziʸ/ *n* [*the* U] the MIDDLE CLASS: *The bourgeoisie does no work with its hands.* –compare PROLETARIAT

bout¹ /baʊt/ *n* **1** a short period of fierce activity or illness: *a bout of drinking* (=drinking alcohol)|*several bouts of fever* **2** a BOXING match

bou·tique /buʷ'tiʸk/ *n* a small shop, or a department of a larger shop, that sells up-to-date clothes and other fashionable personal articles

bo·vine /'boʷvaɪn/ *adj* of or like a cow or ox

bow¹ /baʊ/ *v* **1** [I;T *down, to*] to bend forward the upper part of the body, or the head, to show respect, yielding, etc.: *Everyone bowed as the Queen walked into the room.|The guilty man bowed his head in shame.|He stood with bowed head at the funeral.* (fig.) *trees bowed down with snow* **2 bow and scrape** *usu. derog* to behave to someone with a politeness that is too great and may be false

bow out *v adv* [I *of*] to leave, or stop doing something: *The player bowed out of the game because he knew he wouldn't win it again.*

bow to sbdy./sthg. *v prep* [T] to yield to; obey: *I think you may be wrong, but I bow to your greater experience.*

bow² *n* **1** a bending forward of the upper part of the body, or the head, to show respect or yielding: *He moved aside for her with a polite bow.* –compare CURTSY **2 take a bow** to come on stage to receive praise (APPLAUSE) at the end of a performance

bow³ /boʷ/ *n* **1** a piece of wood held in a curve by a tight string and used for shooting arrows –see also CROSSBOW, LONGBOW **2** a long thin piece of wood with a tight string fastened along it, used for playing musical instruments that have strings **3** a knot formed by doubling a line, etc. into two or more round or curved pieces, and used for decoration in the hair, in tying shoes, etc.: *He tied the gift with a beautiful red bow.*

bow⁴ *v* [I] to bend or curve

bow⁵ /baʊ/ *n* the forward part of a ship –compare STERN²

bow·els /'baʊəlz/ *n* [P] **1** a system of tubes from the stomach which carries the waste matter out of the body; INTESTINES **2** the inner, lower part (of anything) (esp. in the phrase **the bowels of the earth**)

bow·er /'baʊər/ *n lit* (a summer house in) a pleasant shaded place under the trees

bowl¹ /boʊl/ *n* **1** a deep round container for holding liquids, etc.: *a soup bowl|a flower bowl|a sugar bowl* –see illustration on page 379 **2** the contents of a bowl: *a bowl/bowlful of sugar*

bowl² *v* **1** [I] to play the game of BOWLING: *He goes bowling every Saturday* **2** [I;T] to throw or roll (esp. a ball) as in some games –**bowler** *n: He's the best bowler on our team.*

   bowl sbdy.↔ **over** *v adv* [T] **1** to knock down: *Someone ran around the corner and nearly bowled me over.* **2** to give a great, esp. pleasant, surprise to: *Your news has really bowled me over.*

bow-legged /'boʊˌlɛgɪd, -lɛgd/ *adj* (esp. of people) having the legs curving outwards at the knee; BANDY² (2)

bowler /'boʊlər/ also **bowler hat** /ˌ·· '·/– *n BrE* for DERBY

bowl·ing /'boʊlɪŋ/ *n* [U] a game in which balls are rolled at an object or a group of objects: *Let's go bowling!*

bow tie /'boʊ taɪ/ *n* a NECKTIE fastened at the front with a knot in the shape of a BOW³ (3), worn esp. on formal occasions

box¹ /bɑks/ *n* **1** a container for solids, usu. with stiff sides and often with a lid: *a wooden box|a shoebox* –see illustration on page 683 **2** the contents of a box: *He ate a whole box/boxful of candy.* **3** a small room or enclosed space: *a box at the theater|the signal box on a railroad line*

box² *v* [T] to put in a box or boxes: *The oranges were boxed and sent off quickly.*

   box sbdy./sthg.↔**in/up** *v adv* [T] to enclose in a small space: *She feels boxed in living in that small apartment.*

   box sbdy./sthg.↔ **off** *v adv* [T] to separate by putting into an enclosed space: *We are each boxed off (from the others) in our own little offices.*

box³ *v* [I;T *with, against*] **1** to fight (someone) with closed hands (FISTs): *Have you seen Ali box?* –compare WRESTLE; see BOXING (USAGE) **2** to box someone's ears *infml* to hit someone on the ears with the hands –**boxer** *n*

box·er /'bɑksər/ *n* a large short-haired dog of German origin, usu. light brown in color

box·ing /'bɑksɪŋ/ *n* [U] the sport of fighting with tightly closed hands (FISTs)

USAGE One **boxes** in a **ring** wearing special **gloves** and wins on **points**, by winning more **rounds** than the other person, or by a **knockout**.

box num·ber /'· ˌ··/ *n* a number used as a mailing address, esp. in replying to newspaper advertisements

box of·fice /'· ˌ··/ *n* a place in a theater, concert hall, etc., where tickets are sold: *The play was a* **box-office success.** (= brought in a lot of money)

box spring /'· ˌ·/ *n* a base containing metal springs which is placed under a MATTRESS to make a bed

boy¹ /bɔɪ/ *n* **1** a young male: *Our new baby is a boy.|"Come here, boys!" shouted the old man.|a boy actor* **2** a son, esp. young **3** -**boy** a boy or man working at a certain job: *a cowboy|delivery boy|a messenger boy* **4** *infml esp. AmE* a male person of any age from a given place: *The people of our town are proud of the local boy who became governor.*

boy² *interj AmE infml* (expressing excitement): *Boy! What a game!*

boy·cott /'bɔɪkɑt/ *v* [T] to refuse to do business with, attend, or take part in: *They're boycotting the store because the people who work there aren't allowed to join a union.|to boycott a meeting* –**boycott** *n*

boy·friend /'bɔɪfrɛnd/ *n* a male companion, with whom one spends time and shares amusements a (woman's) favorite male companion –see also GIRLFRIEND

boy·hood /'bɔɪhʊd/ *n* [C;U *usu. sing.*] the time or condition of being a young boy: *a happy boyhood* –see also GIRLHOOD, CHILDHOOD

boy·ish /'bɔɪ-ɪʃ/ *adj often apprec* of or like a boy: *his boyish laughter|her boyish movements* –compare GIRLISH –**boyishly** *adv* –**boyishness** *n* [U]

boy scout /'· ·/ *fem.* **girl scout** *AmE*‖**girl guide** *BrE*– *n* (*often cap.*) a member of an association (the **Boy Scouts**) for training boys in character and self-help

Br. also **Brit.**– *written abbrev. said as:* British

bra /brɑ/ also **brassiere**– *n* a woman's undergarment worn to support the breasts –see illustration on page 123

brace¹ /breɪs/ *n* something used or worn for supporting, stiffening, or fastening

brace² braced, bracing *v* [T] **1** to make stronger: *We had to brace the walls when we put the new roof on.* **2** to provide or support with a brace: *His weak back was heavily braced.* **3** to prepare (oneself), usu. for something unpleasant or difficult: *Brace yourself for a shock!*

brace³ brace *n* (in hunting or shooting) two of a kind; a pair: *We brought back several brace of wild birds.* –compare PAIR¹, COUPLE¹

brace·let /'breɪslɪt/ *n* a band or ring, usu. of metal, worn round the wrist or arm as a decoration

brac·es /'breɪsɪz/ *n* [P] **1** wires worn inside the mouth, usu. by children, to straighten the irregular growth of teeth **2** *BrE* for SUSPENDERS

brac·ing /'breɪsɪŋ/ *adj apprec* (esp. of air) fresh and health-giving: *I love this bracing sea air!*

brack·en /'brækən/ *n* [U] a plant (FERN) which grows in forests, etc., and becomes rich red-brown in autumn

brack·et /'brækɪt/ *n* **1** a piece of metal or wood put in or on a wall to support something: *a lamp bracket* **2** [*usu. pl.*] either of a pair of signs with square corners used for enclosing a piece of information: *Information about the grammar of words in this dictionary is in brackets.* –compare **parenthesis 3** [+*sing./pl. v.*] a group of people who share some quality: *the upper income bracket/the 16–25 age bracket*

bracket² *v* [T] to enclose in BRACKETS¹ (2): *to bracket (off) some words*|(fig.) *to bracket two people (together) because they seem similar* –**brackishness** *n* [U]

brack·ish /'brækɪʃ/ *adj.* (of water) not pure; a little salty –**brackishness** *n* [U]

brag /bræg/ *v* **-gg-** [I;T +*that/about, of*] *derog* to speak in praise of oneself, often falsely; BOAST (1): *Don't brag!*|*He bragged about having won first prize/bragged that he had won first prize.*|*This work is* **nothing to brag about.**

Brah·man /'brɑmən/ also **Brahmin** /'brɑmən/– *n* a Hindu of the highest rank (CASTE)

braid¹ /breɪd/ *AmE*∥ also **plait** *esp. BrE*– *v* [T] to pass or twist three or more lengths of hair, dried stems of grass, etc. under and over each other to form one ropelike length: *The children braided each other's hair.*

braid² *AmE*∥also **plait** *esp. BrE*– *n* a length of something, esp. hair, made by BRAIDING¹

braille /breɪl/ *n* [U] (*sometimes cap.*) (a way of) printing with raised round marks which blind people can read by touching

brain¹ /breɪn/ *n* **1** [C] the organ of the body in the upper part of the head, which controls thought and feeling: *The brain is the center of higher nervous activity.*|*I've got that song on* **the brain.** (=I'm thinking about it continually) **2** [C] the mind; INTELLIGENCE (1): *a good brain*|*He's nice, but he doesn't have much of a brain.* **3** [C] *infml* a person with a good mind: *Some of the best brains in the country are here tonight.*

brain² *v* [T] *infml* to hit (someone) on the head very hard

brain·child /'breɪntʃaɪld/ *n infml* somebody's idea or invention, esp. if successful: *This brainchild of mine has saved us a lot of money.*

brain·less /'breɪnlɪs/ *adj derog* foolish; silly; stupid –see also BRAINY –**brainlessly** *adv*

brains /breɪnz/ *n* [U] **1** the material of which the brain consists **2** *infml* the ability to think: *She's got brains.* **3** **pick someone's brains** *infml* to find out someone's knowledge, e.g. by asking questions **4** **rack/beat one's brains** *infml* to think very hard so as to find an answer

brain·storm /'breɪnstɔrm/ *n infml* a sudden clever idea: *She had a brainstorm and got them all out of trouble.*

brain·wash /'breɪnwɑʃ, -wɔʃ/ *v* [T *into*] *infml derog* to cause (someone) to obey, change his/ her beliefs, etc., by very forceful persuasion: *Don't let all those television advertisements brainwash you into buying that soap.* – **brainwashing** *n* [U]

brain·wave /'breɪnweɪv/ *n* an electrical force produced by the brain: *That machine can measure brainwaves.*

brain·y /'breɪniy/ *adj* **-ier, -iest** *infml* with a good mind; intelligent –see also BRAINLESS –**braininess** *n* [U]

braise /breɪz/ **braised, braising** *v* [T] to cook (meat) slowly in liquid in a covered dish

brake¹ /breɪk/ *n* an apparatus for slowing or reducing movement and bringing a wheel, car, etc., to a stop: (fig.) *The government* **put the brakes on** *all our plans by giving us less money.* –see illustration on page 95

brake² *v* braked, braking [I;T] to (cause to) slow or stop by or as if by using a BRAKE: *I braked suddenly.*

bram·ble /'bræmbəl/ *n* a common wild prickly bush of the rose family, which bears blackberries (BLACKBERRY)

bran /bræn/ *n* [U] the crushed skin of wheat and other grain separated from the flour

branch¹ /bræntʃ/ *n* an armlike part or division of some material thing, esp. a tree: *a branch of a tree/a river/a branch road/railroad*|(fig.) *a branch of knowledge/ of a family/of the armed forces*|*Our company has branches in many cities.*

branch² *v* [I *off*] to become divided into or form branches: *Follow the main road until it branches, and then turn right.*|*Take the road that branches (off) to the right.*

  branch out *v adv* [I *into*] to add to the range of one's activities: *The bookstore has decided to branch out into selling music and records.*

brand¹ /brænd/ *n* **1** a class of goods which is the product of a particular firm or producer: *What is your favorite brand of soap?*|*The* **brand name** *of my favorite soap is "Flower."*|(fig.) *He has his own brand of humor.* **2** a mark made (as by burning) usu. to show ownership: *These cattle have my brand on them.* **3** *fml* a piece of burnt or burning wood

brand² *v* [T] to mark by or as if by burning, esp. to show ownership: *Our cattle are branded with the letter B.*|(fig.) *His unhappy childhood has branded him for life.*|*He is* **branded as** *a thief.*

bran·dish /'brændɪʃ/ *v* [T] to wave (something, esp. a weapon): *He brandished a gun threateningly.*

brand-new /ˌbræn 'nuw, -'nyuw, ˌbrænd-/ *adj apprec* new and completely unused: *a brand-new car*

bran·dy /'brændiy/ *n* **-dies** [C;U] (a type or single drink of) a strong alcoholic drink usu. made from wine

brash /bræʃ/ *adj* **1** *derog* rudely disrespectful and proud **2** hasty and too bold, esp. from lack of experience –**brashly** *adv* –**brashness** *n* [U]

brass /bræs/ *n* [U] **1** a very hard bright yellow metal, a mixture of COPPER¹ (1) and ZINC: *a brass ring*|*a brass band* (=a band consisting mostly of brass musical instruments) **2** (**get down to**) **brass tacks** *infml* (to come to) the really important facts or the real business

bras·siere /brə'zɪər/ *n fml* →BRA

brass knuck·les /ˌ· '···/ *n* [P] *AmE* a metal covering for the KNUCKLES, worn to make more damaging a blow with the closed hand (FIST)

brass·y /'bræsiʸ/ adj **-ier, -iest 1** like brass in color **2** like brass musical instruments in sound **3** (esp. of a woman) shameless and loud in manner

brat /bræt/ n derog a child, esp. a bad-mannered one **–bratty** adj

bra·va·do /brə'vɑdoʷ/ n [U] the (often unnecessary) showing of courage or boldness

brave¹ /breʸv/ adj apprec courageous, fearless, and ready to suffer danger or pain: brave soldiers/actions|Fortune favors the brave. **–bravely** adv **–bravery** /'breʸvəriʸ/ n [U]

brave² braved, braving v [T] to meet (danger, pain, or trouble) without showing fear: She braved her parents' displeasure by marrying him.|The teacher wants to see me about the examination results; I'd better go and **brave it out.**

brave³ n a young North American Indian WARRIOR (fighting man)

bra·vo /'brɑvoʷ, brɑ'voʷ/ interj,n **-vos** a shout of joy because someone (esp. a performer) has done well

brawl /brɔl/ n a noisy argument or fight, often in a public place, which usu. includes fighting **–brawl** v [I] **–brawler** n

brawn /brɔn/ n [U] muscle; MUSCULAR (1) strength **–brawny** adj: His brawny arms are very strong. **–brawniness** n [U]

bray /breʸ/ v,n [C;I] (to make) the sound that a donkey makes: (fig.) He brayed with laughter.

bra·zen /'breʸzən/ adj shameless; immodest: brazen disrespect **–brazenly** adv

brazen out v adv **brazen it out** to face trouble or blame with shameless daring, even when wrong

bra·zier /'breʸʒər/ n a container for burning coals

breach n /briʸtʃ/ **1** [C;U] an act of breaking, not obeying, or not fulfilling a law, promise, custom, etc.: Your action is a breach of our agreement.|You are **in breach of** your contract.|He was sent to prison for a **breach of the peace.** (=fighting in public) **2** [C] an opening, esp. one made in a wall by attackers **–breach** v [T]: The enemy breached the wall.

bread /brɛd/ n [U] **1** a common food made of baked flour: a loaf of bread|bread and butter (=bread spread with butter)|bread and cheese **2** food as a means of staying alive: our daily bread|Who is the **breadwinner** in your family? (=who works to supply the money, food, etc.?) **3** infml money **4 bread and butter** infml way of earning money: She doesn't just write for fun. Writing is her bread and butter. **5 know which side one's bread is buttered on** infml to know who or what will be of most gain to oneself

bread·crumb /'brɛdkrʌm/ n a very small bit of the inner part of a loaf of bread: breadcrumbs to feed the birds

breadth /brɛdθ, brɛtθ/ n [C;U] **1** fml (the) distance from side to side; width: What is the breadth of this river?|The breadth is 16 meters.|It's 16 meters in breadth.|a breadth of 16 feet –compare LENGTH (1) **2** a wide stretch:

His book showed the great breadth of his learning.|breadth of mind/opinions

break¹ /breʸk/ v **broke** /broʷk/, **broken** /'broʷkən/, **breaking 1** [I;T] to (cause to) come apart or separate into pieces, esp. suddenly or violently: to break a window/a leg|The rope broke when they were climbing.|The window broke into pieces.|to break a branch off a tree|A large piece of ice broke away from the main mass.|(fig.) You'll **break your neck** (=kill yourself) if you aren't more careful! **2** [I;T] to (cause to) become unusable by damage to one or more parts: He broke his wristwatch by dropping it.|This machine is broken and has to be repaired. **3** [I;T] to (cause to) become, suddenly or violently: The prisoner broke free/loose.|The box broke open when it fell.|They broke the door down. **4** [T] to disobey; not keep; not act in accordance with: to break the law/a promise **5** [I] to force a way (into, out of, or through): He broke into the store and stole $100. **6** [T] to bring under control: to break a person's spirit **7** [T] to do better than: to break a record (in sports, business, etc.) **8** [I;T] to (cause to) be destroyed: If he tries to take my customers, I'll break him!|He may break under continuous questioning. **9** [I;T] to interrupt (an activity): The bushes broke my fall.|Let's break for a meal and begin again afterwards. **10** [I;T] to (cause to) come to an end: to break the silence with a cry|The cold weather broke at the end of March.|The visit was **broken short** because there was talk of war. **11** [I;T] to (cause to) come esp. suddenly into being or notice: as day breaks|The storm broke.|The news broke.|Break the bad news gently. **12** [T] to discover the secret of: She broke their CODE¹ (1). (=secret writing) **13 break the back of** infml to finish the main or the worst part of: It took them all day to break the back of the job.

break away v adv [I] to escape (from someone): The criminal broke away from the policemen who were holding him.|(fig.) Modern music has broken away from the old rules. –see also BREAKAWAY

break cover of an animal to run out from a hiding place

break down v adv **1** [I;T (=break sthg. ↔ down)] to destroy; reduce or be reduced to pieces: They broke the door down.|The old cars were broken down for their metal and parts.|(fig.) I tried to break down his opposition to our plan.|His opposition broke down. **2** [I] (of machinery) to fail; stop working: The car broke down.|(fig.) The peace talks have broken down. **3** [I] (of a person) to lose control of one's feelings: Peter broke down and cried when his mother died. **4** [I;T (=break sbdy. down)] AmE for BREAK up (4) **5** [I;T (=break sthg. ↔ down) into] to (cause to) separate into different kinds or divide into types: The figures should be broken down into several lists.|Chemicals in the body break our food down into useful substances. –see also BREAKDOWN

break even v adv [I] to make neither a loss

nor a profit in doing business

break in *v adv* **1** [I] to enter a building by force: *He broke in and stole my money.* –see also BREAK-IN **2** [I] to interrupt: *She broke in with some ideas of her own.*|*She broke in on/upon my thoughts when she called me.* **3** [T] (**break** sthg.↔ **in**) to bring slowly into full use; make accustomed to something: *When horses are about six months old, they have to be broken in.*|*to break new shoes in* (=wear them to make them comfortable)|*to break in a new car*

break into sthg. *v prep* [T] **1** to enter by force: *to break into a house* **2** to interrupt: *to break into a conversation* **3** also **burst into** sthg.– to begin suddenly to sing, laugh, etc.: *to break into song/laughter* **4** to begin suddenly: *break into a run*

break sbdy. **of** sthg. *v prep* [T] to cure of (a bad habit): *Doctors keep trying to break him of smoking/of his dependence on the drug.*

break off *v adv* [I;T (=**break** sthg.↔ **off**)] **1** to (cause to) end; interrupt: *Those two countries have broken off relations (with each other).* **2** to (cause to) become separated from the main part with suddenness or violence, but not by cutting: *He broke off a branch.*|*A branch broke off (the tree).*

break out *v adv* [I] **1** to begin suddenly: *War/A fire broke out.* –see also OUTBREAK **2** [*in*] to show or give voice to, suddenly: *His face broke out* (=became covered) *in spots.*|*She broke out in curses.* **3** [*of*] to escape (from): *to break out of prison*

break through *v adv prep* [I;T (=**break through** sthg.)] **1** to force a way through: *Have our soldiers broken through (the enemy's defenses)?*|*The sun broke through (the clouds).* **2** to make a new discovery in (something), esp. after a long time: *The doctors broke through in their fight against heart disease.* –see also BREAKTHROUGH

break up *v adv* **1** [I;T (=**break** sthg.↔ **up**)] to (cause to) divide into smaller pieces: *The ice will break up when the warm weather comes.* **2** [I;T (=**break** sthg.↔ **up**)] to (cause to) come to an end: *The police broke up the fight.*|*The party broke up when the police arrived.*|*Their marriage broke up.* **3** [I] also **split up**– to separate: *What will happen to the children if Jim and Mary break up?*|*The crowd broke up.* **4** [I;T (=**break** sbdy. **up**)] to (cause to) suffer severe anxiety and pain: *He may break up under all this pressure.* **5** AmE [T =**break** sbdy. ↔ **up**] to amuse greatly: *Her funny story really broke me up.* –see also BREAK **down**, BREAKUP

break with sbdy./sthg. *v prep* [T] to cease one's connection with: *to break with one's former friends/with old ideas*

break² *n* **1** an opening made by breaking or being broken: *a break in the clouds* **2** a pause for rest; period of time between activities: *a break in the concert*|*a coffee break*|*We've worked eight hours without a break.* (=continuously) **3** a change from the usual pattern or custom: *a break from/with the past*|*a break in the weather* **4** the time of day before sunrise when daylight first appears: *the*

break of day|*at break of day*|*at daybreak* **5** *infml* a chance (esp. to make things better); piece of luck: *Give him a break and he'll succeed.* **6 a bad/lucky break** a bad/good piece of luck: *It was really a bad break when she lost her job.* **7 the breaks** fate (esp. in the phrase **those are the breaks**: *"It's to bad I wasn't born rich." "Those are the breaks."*

break·age *n* /'breᵞkɪdʒ/ [C;U] **1** (the action of causing) a broken place or part: *a breakage in the gas pipes* **2** the articles or (value of the) articles broken: *breakage of $50*

break·a·way *n* /'breᵞkə,weᵞ/ **1** [C] an act or example of BREAKing¹ **away** (as from a group or custom) **2** [A] wanting independence from an association of some kind: *A breakaway group within the old political party formed a new one.*

break·down /'breᵞkdaʊn/ *n* **1** a sudden failure in operation; a stop: *Our car had a breakdown.*|*a breakdown of talks between labor and employers*|*a **nervous breakdown*** (=being unable to continue one's usual life because of anxiety, etc.) **2** a division by types or into smaller groups; explanation in detail: *I'd like a breakdown of these figures, please.* –see also BREAK **down**, BREAKUP

break·fast /'brɛkfəst/ *n* [C;U] the first meal of the day: *He has breakfast at seven o'clock.*|*It happened at/during breakfast.*|*She likes eggs for breakfast.* –**breakfast** *v* [I on] : *We breakfasted early on orange juice and eggs.*

break-in /'··/ *n* the unlawful, forcible entering of a building: *$7,000 was stolen in the recent break-in* –see also BREAK **in**

break·neck /'breᵞknɛk/ *adj* [A] very fast or dangerous: **at breakneck speed**

break·through /'breᵞkθruᵂ/ *n* (the action of making) a discovery (often suddenly and after earlier failures) that will lead to other discoveries: *Scientists have made a breakthrough in their treatment of that disease.*|*an important scientific breakthrough* –see also BREAK **through**

break·up /'breᵞkʌp/ *n* **1** (esp. of a relationship or association) a coming to an end: *the breakup of a marriage* **2** a division into smaller parts: *the breakup of the large farms* –see also BREAK **up**, BREAKDOWN

break·wa·ter /'breᵞk,wɔtər, -,wɑtər/ *n* a thick wall built out into the sea to lessen the force of the waves near a harbor

breast /brɛst/ *n* **1** either of the two parts of a woman's body that produces milk, or the smaller part like this on a man's body: *a baby still at its mother's breast/at the breast* **2** *lit* the upper front part of the body between the neck and the stomach, esp. when considered as the part of the body where the feelings are supposed to be: *a troubled breast* –compare HEART (2), BOSOM **3 make a clean breast of** to tell the whole truth about (something, esp. something bad that one has done)

breast·stroke /'brɛst-stroᵂk/ *n* [S;U] a way of swimming with one's chest downwards, and one's arms pulling backwards HORIZONTALly from in front of one's head

breath /brɛθ/ n 1 [U] air taken into and breathed out of the lungs: *After all that running I have no breath left.* 2 [C] a single act of breathing air in and out once: *Take a deep breath.*|(fig.) *Let's go out for a breath of fresh air.*|*She claimed not to like the place, but* **in the next breath** *she said she was taking her vacation there.* 3 [S *of*] a sign or slight movement of (something): *There's a breath of spring in the air today.*|*There was hardly* **a breath of air.** (=there was very little wind) 4 **get one's breath (back) (again)**/ **catch one's breath** to return to one's usual rate of breathing: *I need time to catch my breath after running.* 5 **hold one's breath** to stop breathing for a time: (fig.) *The whole country held its breath* (=waited anxiously) *to see who would win the election.* 6 **out of breath** breathing very rapidly (as from tiring exercise); BREATHLESS (1) 7 **take one's breath away** to make one unable to speak (from surprise, pleasure, etc.): *She was so beautiful, it took my breath away.* 8 **under one's breath** in a low voice or a whisper 9 **save one's breath** to hold oneself back from talking: *Save your breath; he'll never believe you anyway.*

breathe /briːð/ v **breathed, breathing** 1 [I;T] to take (air, gas, etc.) into the lungs (and send it out again): *If you stop breathing you'll soon become unconscious.*|*The doctor told him to breathe in deeply* (=take air in) *and then breathe out.*|*He became ill after breathing coal dust for many years.*|(fig.) *breathing words of love into her ear* 2 [T *into*] to give or send out (a smell, a feeling, etc.): *The new general was able to breathe courage/new life into the army.*|(fig.) *He really* **breathes fire** *when he gets angry!* 3 **(be able to) breathe again** to stop feeling anxious: *He's gone; you can breathe (freely) again.* 4 **breathe down someone's neck** *infml* to keep too close a watch on what someone is doing

breath·er /briːðər/ n *infml* a short pause for a rest: *We've been working all day. Let's take a breather.*

breath·less /brɛθlɪs/ *adj* 1 breathing with difficulty; needing to breathe rapidly: *By the time I got to the top, I was completely breathless.* 2 not breathing; dead: *The murdered man lay breathless on the floor.* 3 causing one to stop breathing (because of excitement, fear, or other strong feeling) or to breathe with difficulty: *a breathless silence during the last scene of the movie*|*breathless haste/hurry/speed* –**breathlessly** *adv* –**breathlessness** *n* [U]

breath·tak·ing /brɛθˌteɪkɪŋ/ *adj* 1 very exciting: *a breathtaking horse race* 2 very unusual: *breathtaking beauty* –**breathtakingly** *adv* :*breathtakingly beautiful*

breech·es‖also **britches** *AmE* /brɪtʃɪz/– n [P] short trousers, esp. for men, fastened at or below the knee: *knee-breeches*|*riding breeches* –see PAIR[1] (USAGE)

breed[1] /briːd/ v **bred** /brɛd/, **breeding** 1 [I] (of animals) to produce young: *Some animals will not breed when kept in cages.*|(fig. derog) *Those people* **breed like rabbits.** 2 [T] to keep (usu. animals or fish) for the purpose of producing and developing young in controlled conditions: *He breeds cattle.*|*The winning horse was bred in Ireland.* 3 [T] to cause or be the beginning of: *Flies in food stores breed disease.*|*Dirt is the* **breeding-ground** *of disease.* (=the place where it can develop) –**breeding** n [U] *a person of fine breeding* (=trained in polite social behavior)

breed[2] n a kind or class of animal (or plant), usu. developed under the influence of people: *a breed of dog*|(fig.) *a fine breed of man*

breed·er /briːdər/ n a person who BREEDS[1] (2) animals, birds, or fish

breeze[1] /briːz/ n 1 a light gentle wind –see WEATHER 2 n *infml esp. AmE* something done easily: *Learning English is a breeze!* 3 **shoot the breeze** *AmE infml* to have a light conversation: *We were shooting the breeze while Fred poured the drinks.*

breeze[2] **breezing, breezed** v [I] *infml* to move swiftly and unceremoniously: *He just breezed in, smiled, and breezed out again.*

breeze through also **sail through** sthg.– v prep [T] *infml* to go through or pass easily: *She breezed through the examination with no trouble at all!*

breez·y /briːziː/ **-ier, -iest** *adj* 1 of or having fairly strong BREEZES[1] (1): *It's breezy today, so the clothes we washed will dry quickly.* 2 quick, cheerful, and bright in manner: *His breezy manner made him popular.* –**breezily** *adv* –**breeziness** *n* [U]

breth·ren /brɛðrən/ n [P] (used as a form of address to people, including women, attending a church service) brothers: *dearly beloved brethren*

brev·i·ty /brɛvətiː/ n [U] (of non-material things) shortness: *the brevity of his writing/his life*

brew /bruː/ v [I;T] 1 to make (beer) 2 [*up*] **a** to mix (tea or coffee) with hot water and prepare for drinking **b** (of tea or coffee) to become ready for drinking after being mixed with hot water: *The tea was brewing in the pot.*|(fig.) *Trouble/a storm was brewing.* –**brew** n: *a strong brew of tea/beer*

brew·er /bruːwər/ n a person who makes beer

brew·er·y /bruːwəriː/ **-ies** n a place where beer is made

bri·ar /braɪər/ n [C;U] →BRIER

bribe[1] /braɪb/ v **bribed, bribing** [T *with, into*] to influence unfairly (esp. someone in a position of trust) by favors or gifts: *He bribed the policeman (to let him go free/into letting him go free).*|(fig.) *The child was bribed with a piece of cake to go to bed quietly.*

bribe[2] n something offered or given in bribing (BRIBE[1]): *The official took bribes from people who wanted favors.*

brib·er·y /braɪbəriː/ n [U] giving or taking of a BRIBE

bric-a-brac /brɪk ə ˌbræk/ n [U] small decorations in a house

brick /brɪk/ n 1 [C;U] (a hard piece of) baked clay used for building: *They used yellow bricks to build the house.*|*The house is brick, not wood.* 2 [C] something in the shape of a brick: *a brick of gold* **3 beat/one's head against a brick wall** *infml* to waste one's efforts by trying to do something impossible **4 like a ton of bricks** *infml* with sudden crushing weight or force or in sudden anger: *He came down on me like a ton of bricks when I arrived late.* –see also BRICK UP

brick·lay·er /'brɪk,leɪ^yər/ *n* a worker who lays bricks (=puts bricks in place) –**bricklaying** *n* [U]

brick sthg. **up/in** *v adv* [T] to fill completely with bricks: *They've bricked up the space between the two rooms.*

bride /braɪd/ *n* a woman about to be married, or just married: *The bride wore a beautiful white dress.* –see also BRIDEGROOM –**bridal** *adj*

bride·groom /'braɪdgru^wm, -grʊm/ also **groom**– *n* a man about to be married, or just married –see also BRIDE

brides·maid /'braɪdzme^yd/ *n* an unmarried woman (usu. one of several) who attends the BRIDE on the day of the marriage ceremony –compare BEST MAN

bridge¹ /brɪdʒ/ *n* **1** something that carries a road or railway over a valley, river, etc. **2** the raised part of a ship on which the captain and other officers stand when controlling the ship **3** the bony upper part of the nose, between the eyes

bridge² *v* **bridged, bridging** [T] to build a bridge across: *to bridge a river*

bridge³ *n* [U] a card game for four players

bri·dle¹ /'braɪdl/ leather bands put on a horse's head for controlling its movements

bridle² *v* **bridled, bridling 1** to put a BRIDLE on: *to bridle a horse* **2** [I *at*] to show anger or displeasure, esp. by making a proud upward movement of the head and body: *He bridled (with anger) at my request.*

brief¹ /bri^yf/ *adj* short, esp. in time: *a brief look at the newspaper|a brief letter|It's a long letter, but* **in brief** (=in as few words as possible) *he says "No."* –**briefly** *adv:* *She spoke briefly.|Briefly, he said "No."*

brief² *n* a short spoken or written statement, esp. one giving facts or arguments about a law case

brief³ *v* [T] to give last instructions or necessary information to: *to brief the men before the attack|Before the meeting, let me brief you on what to expect.* –see also DEBRIEF –**briefing** *n* [C;U]: *Before the meeting, let me give you a briefing.*

brief·case /'bri^yfke^ys/ *n* a flat, usu. soft leather case for carrying papers or books, which opens at the top

briefs /bri^yfs/ *n* [P] very short close-fitting UNDERPANTS or women's PANTIES –see PAIR¹ (USAGE); see illustration on page 123

bri·er , briar /'braɪər/ *n* [C;U] (a) wild bush covered with prickles (THORNS), esp. the wild rose bush

bri·gade /brɪ'ge^yd/ *n* [+*sing./pl. v.*] **1** a part of an army, of about 5,000 soldiers **2** an organization formed to carry out certain duties, such as putting out fires: *the Fire Brigade*

brig·a·dier gen·er·al /,brɪgədɪər 'dʒɛnərəl/ *n*

an officer of high rank in the US army

bright /braɪt/ *adj* **1** full of light; shining; giving out or throwing back light very strongly: *The sun is brighter than the moon.|What a bright sunny day!|*(fig.) *One of the brightest moments in our country's history|a face bright with happiness|bright eyes* **2** (of a color) strong, clear, and easily seen: *bright red/yellow* **3** intelligent; quick at learning: *a bright child/idea* **4** showing hope or signs of future success: *You have a bright future ahead of you!* **5 look on/at the bright side (of things)** to be cheerful and hopeful in spite of difficulties –**brightly** *adv* –**brightness** *n* [U]

bright·en /'braɪtn/ *v* [I;T *up*] to (cause to) become bright: *The weather is brightening (up).|She brightened when she heard the good news.*

bril·liant /'brɪlyənt/ *adj* **1** very bright, splendid, or showy in appearance: *a brilliant sun/sea|an expensive and brilliant wedding|brilliant blue* **2** very intelligent; causing great admiration or satisfaction: *a brilliant speaker/scientist|a brilliant piece of music* –**brilliance, -cy** *n* [U] –**brilliantly** *adv*

brim¹ /brɪm/ *n* **1** the top edge of a cup, glass, bowl, etc., esp. with regard to how full it is: *The glass was full to the brim.* **2** the bottom part of a hat which turns outwards to give shade, or protection against rain –compare CROWN¹ (3) **3 -brimmed** (of hats) having a brim of the stated kind: *a wide-brimmed hat*

brim² *v* **-mm-** [I *over*] to be BRIMFUL: *His eyes brimmed (over) with tears.|a brimming cup of coffee*

brim over *v adv* [I *with*] to express a lot of (usu. a good feeling): *brimming over (with joy)*

brim·ful , -full /,brɪm'fʊl/ *adj* [F *of, with*] full to the top; overflowing: *to fill the bowl brimful with sugar|eyes brimful of tears|*(fig.) *She was brimful of suggestions.*

brine /braɪn/ *n* [U] water containing a lot of salt, used for preserving food –**briny** *adj*

bring /brɪŋ/ *v* **brought** /brɔt/, **bringing** [T] **1** [*to, for, over, across, etc.*] to come with, carry, or lead (to or towards): *Bring (me) the book.|Bring your friend to the party.|The prisoner was brought before the judge.|The beauty of the music brought tears to her eyes.* –see Study Notes on page 481 **2** to cause or lead to: *Spring rains bring summer flowers.|He could never bring himself to kill an animal or bird.* **3** to be sold for: *This old car will bring about $100.* **4** [*against*] *law* to make officially: *The policeman brought a charge against the drunk driver.* **5** to cause to come (to a certain place or state): *His cries brought the neighbors (running).|Bring them in/out/back/together.|That brings the total (up) to $300.|to* **bring something into being/to an end|**to **bring** *someone* **to his knees** (=to defeat)

bring sthg.↔ **about** *v adv* [T] to cause: *Science has brought about many changes in our lives.*

bring sbdy. **around/over** *v adv* [T] **1** to persuade into a change of opinion: *We must bring him around to our point of view.* **2**

bring sbdy./sthg.↔ **back** v adv [T to] **1** to cause to return: *If I go with you in your car, will you be able to bring me back?*|*Bring us back our books, please.*|*That old song certainly brings back memories!*|*They want to bring back hanging as a punishment.* (=hanging isn't used as a punishment now) **2** to obtain and return with: *When you go to the post office, would you please bring me back some stamps?*|*bring me some stamps back?*|*bring some stamps back for me?*

bring sthg./sthg.↔ **down** v adv [T] to cause to fall or come down: *The pilot brought the plane down gently.*|*He brought the deer down with one shot.*|(fig.) *to bring down prices*|*to bring someone down to your own level*|*to bring* **down** *trouble* **on** *the family*

bring sthg.↔ **forward** v adv [T] to introduce; suggest: *A new plan was brought forward to allow workers to share in the profits.*

bring sbdy./sthg.↔ **in** v adv [T] **1** to introduce: *to bring in a* BILL[1] (2) *(in Congress)*|*to bring in a new fashion*|*to bring in experienced people to help* **2** to produce as profit or earnings; earn: *The sale brought (us) in over $500.*|*She's bringing in $250 a week.* **3** to give a decision in court: *to bring in a* VERDICT *of guilty or not guilty* **4** to bring to a police station: *The policeman brought in two boys whom he had caught stealing.*

bring sthg. **into** sthg. v prep [T] to cause (an activity or condition) to start: *to bring a new system into being*|*into play*|*into force*

bring sthg.↔ **off** v adv [T] to succeed in doing (something difficult): *It was a very difficult job, but Anne was able to bring it off successfully.*

bring sthg.↔ **on**[1] v adv [T] to cause: *Going out in the rain brought on a fever.*

bring sthg. **on**[2]/**upon** sbdy. v prep [T] to cause (something, usu. unpleasant) to happen to (esp. oneself): *You brought this trouble on yourself.*

bring sbdy./sthg.↔ **out** v adv [T] **1** to produce: *to bring out a new kind of soap*|(fig.) *Sometimes a difficult state of affairs can bring out a person's best qualities.*|*to bring out the meaning*|*to bring out the best*|*the worst in someone* **2** also **draw** sbdy. ↔ **out**– to encourage, esp. to talk: *Bill is very quiet. Try to bring him out.* **3** to cause to advance, grow, or come earlier: *This warm weather should bring the roses out.*

bring sbdy. **to** also **bring** sbdy. **around** AmE‖**bring** sbdy. **round** BrE– v adv [T] to cause to regain consciousness: *They tried to bring the old man around after he fainted.*

bring sbdy. **through** sthg. also **carry** sbdy. **through** sthg.– v prep [T] to save (someone) from: *The doctor brought Mother through a serious illness.*|*The people's courage brought them through the war.*

bring sbdy./sthg.↔ **up** v adv **1** [T] to educate and care for in the family until grown-up: *to bring up children* –compare RAISE **2** [T] to raise or introduce (a subject): *to bring up the question of your vacation* –compare COME **up** (1) **3** **bring** sbdy. **up short** to cause to stop suddenly: *John was about to leave, when he*

was brought up short by a loud noise.

brink /brıŋk/ n [usu. sing.] an edge at the top of a cliff, at the side of water, etc.; VERGE: (fig.) **on the brink of** *disaster* (=a great misfortune)|*His failures brought him* **to the brink of** *ruin.*

brisk /brısk/ adj quick and active: *a brisk walker*|*walk*|(fig.) *a brisk wind* (=pleasantly cold and strong) –**briskly** adv –**briskness** n [U]

bris·tle[1] /ˈbrısəl/ n [C;U] (a) short stiff coarse hair: *His chin was covered with bristles.*

bristle[2] v **-tled**, **-tling** [I up, with] (esp. of hair, fur, etc.) to stand up stiffly: *The cat's fur bristled (up) with anger.*|(fig.) *The job* **bristled with** (=was full of) *problems.*

bris·tly /ˈbrısəliʲ/ adj **-tlier**, **-tliest** like or full of BRISTLES[1]: *a bristly face*

Brit. → BR

britch·es /ˈbrıtʃız/ n [P] **1** AmE for BREECHES **2 too big for one's britches** showing too high an opinion of oneself; full of CONCEIT: *He thinks he knows all the answers. He's getting too big for his britches.*

Brit·ish /ˈbrıtıʃ/ adj of Britain (or the British COMMONWEALTH)

brit·tle /ˈbrıtl/ adj hard but easily broken or damaged: *brittle glass*|(fig.) *a brittle friendship*|*a brittle nature*

broach /broʷtʃ/ v [T] to introduce as a subject of conversation: *At last he broached the subject of the new contract.*

broad /brɔd/ adj **1** large (or larger than usual) measured from side to side; wide: *broad shoulders*|*a broad river*|*the broad horizon* **2** [after n] (after a measurement) in width; across: *4 meters broad* **3** not limited; generous in thought: *a broad imagination*|*broadminded* **4** [A] general; not particular: *Give me a broad idea of your plans.* –compare NARROW[1] **5** [A] full and clear (esp. in the phrase **broad daylight**) **6** (of a way of speaking) typical; showing clearly where the speaker comes from: *She spoke with a broad Texas* ACCENT. –**broadly** adv: *Broadly (speaking), I agree with you.* –**broadness** n [U]

broad bean /ˈ· ·/ n a large flat kind of bean

broad·cast[1] /ˈbrɔdkæst/ n a single radio or television presentation: *Everyone paid careful attention to the radio broadcasts from the war area.*

broadcast[2] v **-cast**‖also **-casted** AmE, **-casting** **1** [I;T] to send out or give (radio or television presentations): *Channel 5 will broadcast the news at 10 o'clock.*|*The networks broadcast to all parts of the world.*|(fig.) *to broadcast* (=make widely known) *the news to all one's friends* **2** [I] to speak or perform on radio or television –**broadcaster** n –**broadcasting** n [U]

broad·en /ˈbrɔdn/ v [I;T out] to (cause to) become broad or broader: *Travel broadens the mind.*|*The river broadens (out) at this point.* –compare NARROW[2]

broad·mind·ed /ˌbrɔdˈmaındıd◄/ adj willing to respect the opinions (and actions) of others even if very different from one's own

–opposite **narrow-minded** –**broadminded-ness** n [U]

broad-side[1] /ˈbrɔdsaɪd/ n a forceful spoken or written attack: *She delivered a broadside (=made a strong attack) against the government.*

broadside[2] adv [on] sideways on: *The truck hit the car broadside.*

bro·cade[2] /browˈkeɪd/ n [U] decorative cloth usu. of silk, often with a raised pattern of gold or silver threads

broc·co·li /ˈbrɑkəliy/ n a vegetable similar to CAULIFLOWER whose young green flower heads are eaten

bro·chure /browˈʃʊər/ n a small thin book (BOOKLET; PAMPHLET), esp. one giving instructions or details of a service offered for money: *a travel brochure|an advertising brochure*

brogue[1] /browg/ n [usu. pl.] a strong thick shoe, esp. one with a pattern made in the leather –see PAIR [1] (USAGE)

brogue[2] n [usu. sing.] a way of speaking, esp. the way in which the Irish speak English

broil /brɔɪl/ v [I;T] AmE∥grill esp. BrE– to cook (something) over or under direct heat: (fig.) *It's really broiling (=it's very hot) today.* –see COOK [2] (USAGE)

broil·er /ˈbrɔɪlər/ n 1 AmE∥grill esp. BrE– an arrangement of a metal shelf under the gas flame or electric form of heat as part of a kitchen stove, used to cook food quickly –see illustration on page 379 2 a young small chicken bred esp. to be cooked by BROILing (or ROASTing[1]) 3 infml a very hot day: *Yesterday was a real broiler!*

broke[1] /browk/ adj [F no comp.] infml completely without money: *He/His company is* (**flat**) **broke.**|*His company has gone broke.*

broke[2] v past tense of BREAK[1]

bro·ken[1] /ˈbrowkən/ adj 1 violently separated into smaller pieces; damaged: *a window broken by a ball|a broken clock/leg|*(fig.) *broken dreams|a broken spirit|a broken man|a broken-down car (=a car in a state of disrepair)* 2 not kept to; destroyed: *a broken law/promise|a broken marriage/home* 3 imperfectly spoken or written: *broken English*

broken[2] v past participle of BREAK[1]

broken-heart·ed /ˌbrowkən ˈhɑrtɪd/ adj filled with grief: *He was broken-hearted when his wife died.* –**brokenheartedly** adv

bro·ker /ˈbrowkər/ n a person who does business for another, esp. in buying and selling shares in business or foreign money

bron·chi·tis /brɑŋˈkaɪtɪs/ n [U] an illness (INFLAMMATION) of the **bronchial tubes** (=the two branches connecting the WINDPIPE with the lungs), which causes coughing –**bronchitic** /brɑŋˈkaɪtɪk/ adj

bron·co /ˈbrɑŋkow/ -cos a wild or half-wild horse of the western US

bron·to·sau·rus /ˌbrɑntəˈsɔrəs/ -sauruses or -sauri /ˈsɔraɪ/ n a very large four-footed and probably plant-eating DINOSAUR

bronze[1] /brɑnz/ n [U] (the dark reddish-brown color of) a hard mixture (ALLOY) mainly of copper and tin

bronze[2] v bronzing, bronzed [T] to give the appearance or color of BRONZE to: *bronzed by the sun*

brooch /browtʃ, bruwtʃ/ n a decoration worn on women's clothes, fastened on by means of a pin

brood[1] /bruwd/ n a family of young creatures, esp. young birds: *The duck's brood was hungry.*

brood[2] v [I] 1 to sit on eggs as a hen does 2 [over, about] to continue to think esp. angrily or sadly (about something, often bad): *Don't just sit there brooding about your problems.* 3 [over] to hang closely over: *Dark clouds were brooding over the top of the mountain.* –**broody** adj –**broodily** adv –**broodiness** n [U]

brook /brʊk/ n a small stream

broom /bruwm, brʊm/ n a large sweeping brush, usu. with a long handle

broom·stick /ˈbruwm,stɪk, ˈbrʊm-/ n the long thin handle of a BROOM

broth /brɔθ/ n [C;U] soup in which meat, fish, rice, or vegetables have been cooked: *chicken broth*

broth·el /ˈbrɑθəl, -ðəl, ˈbrɔ-/ n a house of PROSTITUTEs[1], where sex can be had for money

broth·er /ˈbrʌðər/ n 1 a male relative with the same parents: *John and Peter are brothers.|John is Peter's brother* –see illustration on page 247 2 a male member of the same group: *a brother doctor [often cap.]* (a title for) a male member of a religious group, esp. a MONK: *a Christian Brother|Brother John will read the evening prayers.* –compare SISTER –**brotherly** adj: *brotherly love* –**brotherliness** n [U]

broth·er·hood /ˈbrʌðər,hʊd/ n 1 [U] the quality or state of being brothers 2 [C usu. sing.] the whole body of people in a business, profession, or association: *the medical brotherhood* –compare SISTERHOOD

brother-in-law /ˈ··· ·,·/ n **brothers-in-law** 1 the brother of one's husband or wife 2 the husband of one's sister 3 the husband of the sister of one's husband or wife –see also SISTER-IN-LAW; see illustration on page 247

brought /brɔt/ v past tense and participle of BRING

brow /braʊ/ n 1 [usu. pl.] →EYEBROW 2 →FOREHEAD 3 the upper part of a slope or a hill; the edge of a steep place

brow·beat /ˈbraʊbiyt/ v -beat, -beaten /ˌbiytn/, -beating [T into] to force to obey by using fierce looks or words: *to browbeat someone (into doing something)*

brown[1] /braʊn/ n,adj [C;U] (of) the color of earth: *brown shoes|He is very brown after his vacation.|dark brown|a dark brown*

brown[2] v [I;T] to (cause to) become brown or browner: *browned by the sun|First brown the meat in hot oil.*

brown·stone /ˈbraʊnstown/ 1 [U] a soft reddish-brown stone used in building 2 [C] a house with a front of this stone, common in New York City –see illustration on page 337

browse /braʊz/ v browsed, browsing [I] 1 to read parts of books, without any clear purpose, esp. for enjoyment: *to browse* *through/among someone's books|I had a good time browsing in the bookstore.* **2** to feed on young plants, grass, etc.: *cows browsing in the fields*

bruise¹ /bruᵂz/ *n* a discolored place where the skin of a human, animal, or fruit has been INJUREd by a blow but not broken

bruise² *v* **bruised, bruising** **1** [T] to cause one or more BRUISES on: *She fell and bruised her knee.|a bruised knee* **2** [I] to show one or more BRUISES: *The skin of a soft fruit bruises easily.*

brunch /brʌntʃ/ *n* [C;U] *infml* a late breakfast, an early LUNCH, or a combination of the two

bru·net /bruᵂˈnɛt/ *n* a man with dark hair –compare BLOND (2)

bru·nette /bruᵂˈnɛt/ *n* a woman with dark hair –compare BLONDE (2)

brunt /brʌnt/ *n* **bear the brunt of** to suffer the heaviest part of (an attack): *I had to bear the brunt of his anger alone since I was the only one in the office.*

brush¹ /brʌʃ/ *n* **1** an instrument for cleaning, smoothing, or painting, made of sticks, stiff hair, nylon, etc.: *a clothesbrush|a toothbrush|a hairbrush|a paintbrush* **2** an act of brushing: *I'll just give my coat/hair a quick brush.*

brush² *v* [I;T] **1** to clean or smooth with a brush: *to brush one's coat/the floor/one's teeth/one's hair|(fig.) The light wind gently brushed* (=passed lightly over or across) *his cheek.|She brushed* (=moved lightly or carelessly) *past me.* **2** to remove with or as if with a brush: *to brush away a fly (with one's hand)|to brush dirt off* **3** to put into the stated condition with or as if with a brush: *to brush one's coat clean|to brush a piece of paper off a table*

brush sbdy./sthg.↔**aside/away** *v adv* [T] to refuse to pay attention to: *to brush difficulties/opposition aside*

brush sbdy. **off** *v adv* [T] to refuse to listen to or have a relationship with –see also BRUSH-OFF

brush/polish sthg. **up** [T *on*] to improve one's knowledge of (something known but partly forgotten) by study: *I have to brush up (on) my French before I go to Paris.* –**brush-up** /'· ·/ *n*

brush³ *n* [U] **1** also **brushwood** /'brʌʃwʊd/– small branches broken off from trees or bushes **2** (land covered by) small rough trees and bushes

brush-off /'· ·/ *n* **brush-offs** *infml* a clear refusal to be friendly or to listen: *I wanted to speak to her/to ask her for more money, but she* **gave** *me* **the brush-off.** –see also BRUSH off

brusque /brʌsk/ *adj* quick and rather impolite: *a brusque person/manner/brusque behavior* –**brusquely** *adv* –**brusqueness** *n* [U]

brus·sels sprout /ˌbrʌsəlz ˈspraʊt, ˌbrʌsəl-/ also **sprout**– *n* [*usu. pl.*] a small tight bunch of leaves, used as a vegetable, which grows in groups on the sides of a high stem

bru·tal /'bruᵂtl/ *adj* having or showing no fine or tender human feeling; cruel: *a brutal lie/*

person|a brutal attack/attacker|(fig.) brutal weather/the brutal (=unpleasantly correct) *truth* –**brutally** /'bruᵂtl-i/ *adv* –**brutality** /bruᵂˈtæləti ʸ/ *n* [C;U]: *the brutality/ brutalities of war*

bru·tal·ize *AmE*||also **-ise** *BrE* /'bruᵂtl,aɪz/ *v* **-ized, -izing** [T] **1** to make BRUTAL or unfeeling **2** to treat in a BRUTAL manner: *He brutalized the children.* –**brutalization** /ˌbruᵂtlə 'zeʸʃ ən/

brute¹ /bruᵂt/ *n* **1** *often derog* an animal, esp. a large one: (fig.) *Her husband is an unfeeling brute.* **2** an unfortunate animal: *The horse broke its leg when it fell and the poor brute had to be destroyed.*

brute² *adj* [*no comp.*] like an animal in being unreasonable, cruel, or very strong: **brute force/strength**

brut·ish /'bruᵂtɪʃ/ *adj derog* suitable for or typical of animals rather than people: *The poor people lived in brutish conditions.|brutish behavior* –**brutishly** *adv,*

B.S. *AmE*|| also **B.Sc.** *esp. BrE*– *abbrev. for:* Bachelor of Science; (a title for someone who has) a degree from a university or four year college in a science subject: *He has a B.S. in Chemistry/Carmen Ortiz, B.S.* –compare B.A.

bub·ble¹ /'bʌbəl/ *n* a hollow ball of liquid containing air or gas: *bubbles on a boiling liquid|soap bubbles*

bubble² *v* **-bled, -bling** **1** [I] to form, produce, or rise as bubbles: *The gas bubbled to the surface of the water.|(fig.)She was* **bubbling over with** *joy.* (=showing great happiness) **2** to make the sound of bubbles rising in liquid: *We could hear the pot bubbling (away) quietly on the fire.*

bubble gum /'·· ·,·/ *n* [U] CHEWING GUM that can be blown into large bubbles

bub·bly /'bʌbliʸ/ *adj* **-blier, -bliest** **1** full of bubbles **2** showing good feelings freely: *bubbly people at a party*

buck¹ /bʌk/ *n* **1** **bucks** or **buck, doe** *fem.*– the male of certain animals, esp. the deer, the rat, and the rabbit **2** *infml* responsibility: *I don't know enough about it to decide, so I'll* **pass the buck** *(to you).* **4** *AmE infml* an American dollar

buck² *v* **1** [I] (esp. of a horse) to jump up with all four feet off the ground **2** [T] to throw off (a rider) by doing this: *The wild horse bucked its first rider off.* **3** *AmE infml* to oppose in a direct manner: *to buck the system* **buck up** *v adv infml* [I;T (=**buck** sbdy. **up**)] for CHEER up

buck·et /'bʌkɪt/ *n* **1** an open metal, plastic, or wooden container with a handle for carrying liquids; PAIL **2** its contents: *She poured a bucket/a bucketful of water over the floor.|(fig.) The rain came down* **in buckets.** (=it rained very hard) **3** **kick the bucket** /,· ·'··/ *humor infml* to die

buck·le¹ /'bʌkəl/ *n* a metal fastener used for joining the ends of a belt, or two leather bands (STRAPS), or for decoration

buckle² *v* **-led, -ling** [I;T *up, together*] **1** to (cause to) fasten or stay in a stated place with a BUCKLE: *He buckled (up) his belt* *tightly.* | *The belt buckled (up) easily.* | *The two ends buckle (together) at the back.* | *He buckled on his sword.* –opposite **unbuckle 2** to (cause to) become bent or wavy through heat, shock, pressure, etc.: *The accident buckled the wheel of my bicycle.* | *The wheel buckled.* | (fig.) *to buckle* (=yield) *under the attack and run away*

buckle down *v adv* [I *to*] *infml* to begin to work seriously (at): *to buckle down to work/working*

bud¹ /bʌd/ *n* [C;U] a young tightly rolled-up flower (or leaf) before it opens: *The plant will* **come into bud** *in spring.*

bud² *v* **-dd-** [I] to produce BUDs¹

Bud·dhism /'buwdizəm, 'bu-/ *n* [U] a religion of east and central Asia growing out of the teaching of Gautama Buddha that pureness of spirit is the answer to suffering –**Buddhist** *n*

bud·ding /'bʌdiŋ/ *adj* [A *no comp.*] beginning to develop: *a budding poet*

bud·dy /'bʌdiy/ *n* **-dies** *infml* **1** (esp. of a man) friend; partner: *We're good buddies.* **2** esp. *AmE* (used as a form of address, often in anger) fellow: *Get out of my way, buddy!*

budge /bʌdʒ/ *v* **budged, budging** [I;T] to (cause to) move a little: *I can't budge this rock.* | (fig.) *She won't budge from her opinions.*

budg·et¹ /'bʌdʒit/ *n* **1** a plan of how to arrange private or public income or spending: *a family/business/weekly budget* | *the government's efforts to* **balance the budget** (=make sure that no more money is being spent than is being earned) **2** the quantity of money stated in these plans: *a budget of $10,000,000.*

budget² *v* [I] to plan private or public spending within the limits of a certain amount of money: *careful budgeting.* | *She budgeted for* (=planned to save enough money for) *a vacation/buying a new car.* –**budgetary** /'bʌdʒə,tɛriy/ *adj* [*no comp.*]

buff¹ /bʌf/ *n,adj* [U] a faded yellow color: *buff yellow*

buff² *v* [T *up*] to polish (metal) with something soft

buff³ *n infml* a person who is very interested in and knowledgeable about the stated subject: *a film buff*

buf·fa·lo /'bʌfə,low/ *n* **-loes** *or* **-lo 1** a large wild cowlike animal formerly very common in North America and Europe with a very large head and shoulders covered with lots of hair; BISON **2** any of several kinds of very large black cattle with long flattish curved horns, found mainly in Asia and Africa

buff·er /'bʌfər/ *n* a person or thing that lessens the effect of a shock: (fig.) *A little money is a useful buffer in times of need.*

buf·fet¹ /'bʌfit/ *v* [T] to strike sharply or repeatedly: *We were buffeted by the wind and the rain.* | *We were buffeted about* (=thrown from side to side) *during the rough boat ride.*

buf·fet² /bə'fey, bu-/ *n* (a place, esp. a long table, where one can get) food, usu. cold, to be eaten standing up, or sitting down

somewhere else

buf·foon /bə'fuwn/ *n* a rough and noisy fool: *to play the buffoon at a party* –**buffoonery** /bə'fuwnəriy/ *n* [U]

bug¹ /bʌg/ *n* **1** *AmE* any small insect, creeping or flying –compare BEETLE **2** *infml* a small living thing causing disease; GERM: *I'm not feeling well: I must have picked up a bug somewhere.* **3** *infml* an apparatus for listening secretly to other people's conversations: *The police tested the room for bugs.* **4** [*the* S] *infml* an eager but sometimes foolish or not lasting interest in something: *bitten by the travel bug* | *the photography bug*

bug² *v* **-gg-** [T] *infml* **1** to fit with a secret listening apparatus: *The police have bugged my office.* **2** *AmE* to annoy (someone) continually: *Stop bugging me.*

bug·a·boo /'bʌgə,buw/ *n* **-boos** *n infml* esp. *AmE* an imaginary cause of fear: *childish bugaboos*

bu·gle /'byuwgəl/ *n* a brass musical instrument, played by blowing, like a TRUMPET¹ (1) but shorter, used esp. for army calls –**bugler** /'byuwglər/ *n*

build¹ /bild/ *v* **built** /bilt/, **building** [I;T *for, out of*] to make (one or more things) by putting pieces together: *That house is built (out) of brick(s). They're building (houses) in that area now.* | *He built me a model ship out of wood.* | (fig.) *Hard work builds character.* | *Reading builds* (=develops) *the mind* | *We are building for the future.* –**builder** *n*

build up *v adv* [I;T (=**build** sthg. ↔ **up**)] to (cause to) form steadily, become larger, or develop: *to build up one's strength* | *The clouds are building up.* | *She gradually built up a good business.* –see also BUILDUP

build² *n* [C;U] shape and size, esp. of the human body: *a powerful build* | *We are of the same build.* –see BODY (USAGE)

build·ing /'bildiŋ/ *n* **1** [C] something usu. with a roof and walls that is intended to stay in one place and not to be moved or taken down again: *Houses and churches are buildings.* **2** [U] the art or business of making buildings

build·up /'bildʌp/ *n* increase: *There's been a large buildup of traffic on the roads over the past year.* –see also BUILD **up**

built-up /ˌ· '·/ *adj* covered with buildings: *a built-up area*

bulb /bʌlb/ *n* **1** a round root of certain plants **2** any object of this shape, esp. the glass part of an electric lamp: *a light bulb*

bul·bous /'bʌlbəs/ *adj* *often derog* shaped like a BULB (1); fat and round: *a bulbous nose*

bulge¹ /bʌldʒ/ *n* a swelling of a surface caused by pressure from within or below –**bulgy** *adj* –**bulginess** *n* [U]

bulge² *v* **bulged, bulging** [I *with, out*] to swell out: *His stomach bulged (out).* | *His pockets were bulging with money.*

bulk /bʌlk/ *n* **1** [U] great size, shape, mass, or quantity **2** [C *usu. sing*] an unusually large, fat, or shapeless body: *The elephant lowered its great bulk.* **3** [*the* S *of*] the main or greater part (of): *The bulk of the work has already been done.* **4** **in bulk** in large quantities; not packed in separate packages: *to buy/ sell in bulk*

bulk·y /'bʌlkiʸ/ *adj* **-ier, -iest 1** having BULK (1), esp. if large of its kind or fat **2** having great size or mass in comparison with weight: *a bulky woolen garment* **–bulkiness** *n* [U]

bull /bʊl/ *n* **1** the male form of cattle, kept on farms to be the parent of young cattle **2** the male of certain other large land or sea animals: *a bull elephant* **3 a bull in a china shop** *infml* a rough, careless person in a place where skill and care are needed **4 take the bull by the horns** *infml* to face difficulties in spite of fear **–compare** COW¹

bull·dog /'bʊldɒg/ *n* a fierce dog of English origin, with a short neck and short thick legs

bull·doze /'bʊldoʷz/ *v* **-dozed, -dozing** [T] to force (objects, earth, etc. out of the way) with a special heavy machine (**bulldozer**) used when a level surface is needed: *to bulldoze the ground before building*|(fig.) *He bulldozed his plan through Congress.*|*They bulldozed her into agreeing.*

bul·let /'bʊlɪt/ *n* a type of shot fired from a gun, usu. long and with a rounded or pointed end: *A bulletproof car/garment stops bullets from passing through it.* **–compare** SHOT¹ (6), SHELL¹ (3)

bul·le·tin /'bʊlɪtn, 'bʊlətɪn/ *n* **1** a short public usu. official notice or news report intended to be made public without delay: *Here is the latest bulletin about the President's health.* **2** a PERIODICAL, esp. one produced by an association or group

bulletin board /'··· ,·/ *AmE*‖**notice board** *BrE–* *n* a board on a wall on which notices and advertisements are placed **–see illustration on page 467**

bull·fight /'bʊlfaɪt/ *n* a ceremonial fight between men and a BULL (1), esp. as practiced as a sport in Spain, Portugal, and Latin America **–bullfighter** *n* **–bullfighting** *n* [U]

bul·lion /'bʊlyən/ *n* [U] bars of gold or silver: *gold bullion*

bul·lock /'bʊlək/ *n* a young BULL (1) which cannot breed, often used for pulling vehicles **–compare** STEER¹

bull·ring /'bʊl,rɪŋ/ *n* a circular place (an ARENA) for BULLFIGHTs, surrounded by rows of seats

bull's-eye /'·· ·/ *n* the circular center of a TARGET that people try to hit when shooting: *That shot was a bull's eye.* (=it hit the center)|(fig.) *Your last remark really* **hit the bull's-eye**. *It was exactly right.*

bul·ly *v* **-lied, -lying** /'bʊliʸ/ [I;T *into*] to use one's strength to hurt (weaker people); make them afraid: *bullying smaller children (into doing things)* **–bully -lies** *n*

bul·rush /'bʊlrʌʃ/ *n* a tall grasslike waterside plant

bul·wark /'bʊlwərk, 'bʌl-/ *n* a strong wall built for defense or protection: (fig.) *Our people's support is a bulwark against the enemy.*

bum¹ /bʌm/ *n infml derog, esp. AmE* **1** a wandering beggar; TRAMP² (1) **2** a person who spends a lot of time on some game or

amusement: *a* BEACH *bum*

bum² *v* **-mm-** [T] *infml* to ask for (something) with no intention of returning it: *Can I bum a cigarette?*

bum around also **bum about** *BrE– v adv* [I] **1** to spend time lazily: *I didn't do anything last summer; I just bummed around.* **2** to spend time traveling for amusement: *I'd like to bum around (in) California for a few weeks.*

bum³ *adj infml* [A] **1** very bad: *He gave me some bum advice about buying a car.* **2** not working properly: *a bum knee*

bum·ble /'bʌmbəl/ *v* **-bled, -bling** [I *on, about*] *infml* to speak without making much sense, or so that the words are hard to hear clearly: *He kept bumbling on about something I couldn't understand.*

bum·ble·bee /'bʌmbəl,biʸ/ *n* a large bee which makes a loud noise when flying

bump¹ /bʌmp/ *v* **1** [I;T] to strike or knock with force or violence: *The car bumped (into) the tree.*|*The two cars bumped (together/each other).*|*I, bumped my knee (against/on the wall).*|*Something bumped against me.* **2** [I] to move (along) with much sudden shaking, as of a wheeled vehicle over uneven ground: *We bumped along/up and down.*

bump into sbdy. *v prep* [T] *infml* to meet by chance: *I bumped into an old college friend in a restaurant last night.*

bump sbdy.↔ **off** *v adv* [T] *infml* to kill; murder

bump² *n* **1** (the sound of) a sudden forceful blow or shock: *We heard a bump in the next room.* **2** a raised round swelling, often as caused by a blow: *a bump on his head* **–bumpy** *adj*: *a bumpy road/ride/skin* **–bumpiness** *n* [U]

bump·er¹ /'bʌmpər/ *n* a bar fixed on the front or back of a car to protect the car when it knocks against anything: *The traffic was* **bumper-to-bumper**. (=very close together) **–see illustration on page 95**

bumper² *adj* [A] very full or large: *a* **bumper crop**

bumper stick·er /'·· ,··/ *n* a printed message, usu. a short phrase or advertisement, fixed to the BUMPER¹ of a car

bun /bʌn/ *n* **1** a small bread ROLL¹ (2): *a* HAMBURGER *bun* **2** a small round sweet cake **3** hair fastened into a tight round shape, usu. at the back of the head: *She wears her hair in a bun.*

bunch¹ /bʌntʃ/ *n* [*of*] a number of things (usu. small and of the same kind) fastened, held, or growing together at one point: *a bunch of flowers/fruit/keys*|(*infml*) *This bunch of* (=group of) *girls enjoys swimming.*|*Susan is* **the best of the bunch**. (=the best person in a group)

bunch² *v* [I;T *up*] to (cause to) form into one or more bunches: *Bunch (up) together and you'll keep warm.*|*This cloth bunches up.* (=gathers into folds)

bun·dle¹ /'bʌndl/ *n* **1** [C *of*] a number of articles tied, fastened or held together, usu. across the middle **2** [S *of*] *infml* a mass (of):

I'm so anxious I'm just **a bundle of nerves.**|*She's* **a bundle of laughs**

bundle² *v* **-dled, -dling** [I;T] **1** to (cause to) move or hurry in a quick and rough manner: *The police bundled my friend into a car and drove away.*|*We all bundled into a car.*|*They bundled the children off (to school).* **2** [T] to put together or store in a disordered way: *Don't bundle all the clothes up like that/into that bag so carelessly.*

bundle up *v adv* to dress in a lot of warm clothing: *It's cold outside. You'd better bundle up/bundle the children up.*

bung /bʌŋ/ *n* a round piece of wood or other such material used to close the hole in a container

bun·ga·low /'bʌŋgə,lowʸ/ *n* a house which is all on one level –see HOUSE (USAGE)

bun·gle /'bʌŋgəl/ *v* **-gled, -gling** [I;T] to do (something) badly: *to bungle a job* –**bungler** *n* –**bungle** *n*

bun·ion /'bʌnyən/ *n* a painful swelling on the big toe

bunk /bʌŋk/ *n* a bed usu. fixed to the wall (as on a ship) and that is often one of two or more placed one above the other: **Bunk beds** *are useful in a small house/for children.*

bun·ker /'bʌŋkər/ *n* **1** a place to store coal, esp. on a ship or outside a house **2** a strongly-built shelter for soldiers, esp. one built underground

buoy¹ /'buʷiʸ, bɔi/ *n* a floating object fastened to the bed of the sea, e.g. to show ships where there are rocks

buoy² *v* [T *up usu. pass.*] to keep floating: *buoyed by the water*|(fig.) *Her spirits were buoyed up by hopes of success.*

buoy·an·cy /'bɔiənsiʸ, 'buʷyənsiʸ/ *n* [S;U] **1** the tendency of an object to float, or to rise when pushed down into a liquid: *the buoyancy of light wood*|(fig.) *a buoyancy of spirit that keeps her happy* **2** the power of a liquid to force upwards an object pushed down into it: *the buoyancy of water* –**buoyant** *adj* –**buoyantly** *adv*

bur·ble /'bɜrbəl/ *v* **-bled, -bling** [I] to make a sound like a stream flowing over stones –compare BABBLE

bur·den¹ /'bɜrdn/ *n fml* **1** a heavy load: (fig.) *the burden of duty/responsibility* **2 burden of proof** the responsibility of proving something: *The burden of proof lies with the person who makes the charge.*

burden² *v* [T] *fml* to load or trouble: *I will not burden you with a lengthy account of what happened*|*burdened with heavy taxation* –see also UNBURDEN

bu·reau /'byuərowʷ/ *n* **bureaus, bureaux** /'byuərowʷz/ **1** a government department **2** a business office, esp. one that collects and/or keeps facts: *an information bureau* **3** *AmE* chest of drawers for bedroom use

bu·reauc·ra·cy /byu'rɑkrəsiʸ/ *n* **-cies 1** [S] a group of government, business, or other officers who are appointed rather than elected **2** [C;U] *usu. derog* government by such officers, often supposed to be ineffective and full of unnecessary rules –**bureaucratic** /,byuərə'krætɪk/ *adj:* *too*

many bureaucratic rules

bu·reau·crat /'byuərə,kræt/ *n* a member of a BUREAUCRACY

bur·glar /'bɜrglər/ *n* a thief who breaks into houses, shops, etc., esp. during the night: *A burglar broke into my house and took my jewelry.* –see THIEF (USAGE)

bur·glar·ize /'bɜrglə,raiz/ *AmE*||also **burgle** /'bɜrgəl/ *esp. BrE*– *v* **-gled, -gling** [I;T] to break into a building and steal (from it or the people in it): *My apartment has been burglarized.*

bur·gla·ry /'bɜrgləriʸ/ *n* **-ries** [C;U] (an example of) the crime of entering a building (esp. a home) by force with the intention of stealing

bur·i·al /'bɛriʸəl/ *n* [C;U] the act, action, or ceremony of putting a dead body into a grave

bur·ly /'bɜrliʸ/ *adj* (of a person) strongly and heavily built –**burliness** *n* [U]

burn¹ /bɜrn/ *v* **burned** *or* **burnt** /bɜrnt/, **burning 1** [I] to be or become on fire: *The whole city's burning!*|*Coal of this quality doesn't burn very easily.*|(fig.) *He's burning with fever/desire.* –see USAGE **2** [I;T] to (cause to) suffer the effects of fire or heat: *I've burned my hand.*|*You should burn all those old papers.*|*The house was burned to the ground.*|*I've burned a hole in my shirt.*|*Turn the heat down on the stove or you'll burn the potatoes.*|*The potatoes have burned; we can't eat them.* **3** [T] to use for power, heating, or lighting: *lamps that burn oil*|*a coal-burning ship* **4** [I] *old use* to produce light; shine: *A light was burning in the window.* **5** [I] to produce or experience an unpleasant hot feeling: *the burning sands*|*My ears were burning after being out in the cold wind.* **6** [I +*to-v*] to be very eager: *She's burning to tell you the good news.* **7 burn one's boats/ bridges** *infml* to destroy all means of going back, so that one must go forward **8** [T *usu. pass.*] *AmE infml* to cause damage to; cheat or deceive: *She was burned in the business and lost a lot of money.*

USAGE In *AmE* **burned** is usually used as the past tense and participle of **burn**, but **burnt** may also be used, esp. as an adjective: **burnt sugar**. In *BrE*, the past tense and participle **burned** is used only when the verb is INTRANSITIVE: *The fire* **burned** *brightly.* Otherwise the *BrE* past tense and participle is **burnt**: *I've* **burnt** *the dinner.*

burn away *v adv* [I;T (=**burn** sthg. ↔ **away**)] to destroy or disappear by burning: *The pile of paper burned away to nothing.*

burn down *v adv* [I;T (=**burn** sthg. ↔ **down**)] to destroy (usu. a building) or be destroyed by fire: *The building (was) burned down and only ashes were left.* –see also BURN OUT

burn sthg. into sthg. *v prep* [T] to fix (as a mark) by burning, so that removal is impossible: *The owner's mark was burned into the animal's skin.*

burn sthg.↔ off *v adv* [T] to destroy by burning: *The farmers are burning off the* STUBBLE *from the fields.*

burn out v adv **1** [T usu. pass.] (**burn** sthg. **out**) to make hollow by fire: *The building was burned out and only the walls remained.* –see also BURN **down 2** [I,T (=**burn** sbdy./sthg. **out**)] to stop burning because there is nothing left to burn: *That small fire can be left to burn (itself) out.*|(fig.) *You'll burn yourself out if you work too hard.*|a **burned out** (=no longer active) *poet* **3** [I;T (=**burn** sthg. **out**)] to stop working through damage caused by heat: *The engine has/is burned out.*|a **burned out** (=worn out) *machine*

burn sbdy./sthg. **up** v adv **1** to destroy completely by fire: *All the wood has been burned up.* **2** *AmE infml* to cause to be very angry: *Her remarks really burned me up.*

burn² n [C;U] a mark, or the sensation produced by burning: *burns on her hand/her coat*

bur·ner /'bɜrnər/ n the part of a cooker, heater, etc. that produces flames –see illustration on page 379

burn·ing /'bɜrnɪŋ/ adj [A] **1** being on fire: *a burning house*|(fig.) *burning cheeks* (=cheeks that are hot and red)|*a burning* (=very strong) *interest in science* **2** producing (a sensation of) great heat or fire: *a burning fever*|*a burning sensation on the tongue* **3** having very great importance; urgent: *Unemployment is one of the burning questions of our time.*

bur·nish /'bɜrnɪʃ/ v [T] to polish (esp. metal), usu. with something hard and smooth

burnt /bɜrnt/ v past tense & participle of BURN¹

burp /bɜrp/ v *infml* **1** [T] to help (a baby) to get rid of stomach gas, esp. by rubbing or gently striking the back **2** [I] →BELCH¹ (1) –**burp** n

bur·ro /'bɜroʊ, 'bʊroʊ, 'bʌroʊ/ -ros *esp. AmE* a donkey, usu. small

bur·row¹ /'bɜroʊ, 'bʌroʊ/ n a hole in the ground made by an animal, esp. a rabbit, in which it lives or hides

burrow² v **1** [T] to make by or as if by digging: *to burrow a hole in the ground*|*to burrow a way through the sand* **2** [I] to move ahead by or as if by digging: *to burrow into/ through the sand* **3** [I;T] to (cause to) move as if looking for warmth, safety, or love: *She burrowed her head into my shoulder.*|*He burrowed against her back for warmth.*

bur·sar /'bɜrsər, -sɑr/ n a person in a college or school who is in charge of money, property, etc.

burst¹ /bɜrst/ v burst, bursting **1** [I;T + to-v] to (cause to) break suddenly, esp. by pressure from within: *The bottle/BALLOON burst.*|*She burst a blood vessel.*|*The storm burst and we all got wet.*|(fig.) *That bag is* **bursting with** (=filled very full with) *potatoes.*|(fig.) *My heart was* **bursting with** (=filled with) **grief/joy.**|*He is* **bursting to** (=very eager to) *tell you the news.* **2** to (cause to) come into the stated condition suddenly, often with force: *He burst free (from the chains).*|*She burst through the door*

into the room.|*The police burst open the door.*

burst in on/upon sbdy./sthg. v adv prep [T] to interrupt, usu. noisily: *They burst in on me while I was working.*

burst into sthg. v prep [T] **1** to enter hurriedly (usu. a room) **2** →BREAK **into** (3)

burst out v adv **1** [I +v-ing] to begin suddenly (to use the voice without speaking): *They burst out laughing/crying.* **2** [T] to say suddenly: *"I don't believe it!" burst out the angry man.* –see also OUTBURST

burst² n a sudden outbreak: *a burst of laughter/of speed/of gunfire*

bur·y /'beriy/ v -ied, -ying [T] **1** to put into the grave: *to bury a dead person*|(fig.) *to bury quarrels and forget the past* **2** to hide away esp. in the ground: *The dog buried a bone.*|(fig.) *They've buried themselves in the country.*|*The facts are buried in a few old books.*|*with one's head buried in a newspaper*|*He buried his head in his hands.* **3** **bury the hatchet** *infml* to become friends again after a quarrel

bus¹ /bʌs/ n a large passenger-carrying motor vehicle, esp. one which carries the public on payment of small amounts: *to travel* **by bus**|*I saw him on the bus.*|*to catch/miss the bus* –see illustration on page 673

bus² v -s-, -ss- [T] to carry students by bus to a school in a different area, esp. where students are of a different race: *The children are bused to a school in another town.* –**busing** n [U]: *Busing has been used in the US as a way to end* SEGREGATION.

bus·boy /'bʌsbɔɪ/ n a waiter's helper; one who removes dirty dishes and sets tables in a restaurant

bush /bʊʃ/ n **1** a small low tree: *a rose bush* **2** the bush uncleared wild country, esp. in Australia or Africa **3** *infml* to avoid coming to the main point: *Tell me the truth: don't beat around the bush.*

bush·el /'bʊʃəl/ n a dry measure equal to 2,150.42 CUBIC inches: *We bought a whole bushel of apples.*

bush·y /'bʊʃiy/ adj -ier, -iest (of hair) growing thickly: *a bushy beard/tail* –**bushiness** n [U]

busi·ness /'bɪznɪs/ n **1** [C;U] one's work or employment: *I'm in the insurance business.*|*I'm here on business, not for pleasure.* **2** [U] trade and the getting of money: "*How's business?*" "*Business is good.*"|*It's a pleasure to do business with you.* **3** [C] a particular money-earning activity or place, such as a shop: *to sell one's/the business* **4** [S] a duty: *It's a teacher's business to help children learn.* **5** [S] an affair; event; matter; thing: *I don't understand this business.*|*The business before the meeting tonight is…*|*a strange business* **6** **have no business doing something** also **have no business to do something**– to have no right to do something **7 Mind your own business** *infml* Don't ask about things that don't concern you **8 none of your business** *infml* nothing that concerns you

busi·ness·like /'bɪznɪs,laɪk/ adj having or showing the ability to succeed in business or to do things calmly and with common sense: *a businesslike person/ manner* –opposite **unbusinesslike**

busi·ness·man /ˈbɪznɪsˌmæn/ **businesswoman** /-ˌwʊmən/ *fem.*– *n* **-men** /-mɛn/ a person who works in business, e.g. the owner of a business firm

bus stop /ˈ· ·/ *n* a fixed place where buses stop for passengers: *I saw him waiting at the bus stop.* –see illustration on page 673

bust¹ /bʌst/ *v* [T] *infml* to break, esp. with force: *I busted my watch this morning.*

bust² *n* **1** the human head, shoulders, and chest, esp. as shown in a SCULPTURE¹ (2) **2** *euph* a woman's breasts; BOSOM **3** a measurement around a woman's breasts and back: *big around the bust*

bust³ *v* [T] *infml* **1** (of the police) to take to a police station; ARREST¹ (1): *He was busted for having* MARIJUANA. **2** (of the police) to enter without warning to look for something unlawful; visit on a RAID¹: *The police busted his house this morning and took some drugs away.* –**bust** *n: The bust was at three o'clock in the morning.*

bus·tle /ˈbʌsəl/ *v* **-tled, -tling** [I] to be busy, often with much noise: *He bustled around the house./The city bustles with* (=has lots of) *life.* –**bustle** *n* [S]: *the bustle of the big city/a bustle of activity*

bus·y¹ /ˈbɪziʸ/ *adj* **-ier, -iest 1** doing a lot of things, esp. working; not free: *She is busy now and cannot see you./He is busy writing./to be busy with some important work/a busy man* **2** full of work or activity: *a busy day/town* **3** *AmE* (of telephones) in use; ENGAGED (2): *I'm sorry, the line is busy.* **4 busy signal** *AmE* a sound made by a telephone when the line is in use: *I've called several times, and I always get a busy signal.* –**busily** *adv*

busy² *v* **busied, busying** [T *with*] to make or keep (esp. oneself) busy: *To forget his troubles, he busied himself with answering letters/in the kitchen.*

bus·y·bod·y /ˈbɪziʸˌbɑdiʸ/ *n* **-ies** *derog* a person who takes too much interest in the affairs of others

but¹ /bət; *strong* bʌt/ *conj* **1** yet at the same time; in spite of this: *He would like to go, but he can't./It's not cheap, but it's very good.* –see Study Notes on page 144 **2** except that: *We were coming to see you, but it rained (so we didn't.)/There's no doubt/no question but he's guilty.* **3** instead: *not one, but two!* **4** (shows disagreement): *"I'll give you $5." "But that's not enough!"*

but² *prep* (after **no, all, nobody, who, where,** etc.) other than; except: *There's no one here but me./Who but George would do such a thing?/everywhere but in New York/But for her, I would have drowned.*

USAGE Compare **but, except,** and **save.** In this sentence we can use all three: *We're all here but/except/* (*fml*) *save Mary.* But in this sentence **but** cannot be used: *The window is never opened except/save in summer.* Use **but** only after words like *none, all, nobody, anywhere, everything,* or after ques-

tion-words like *who, where, what.* It is usually followed by a noun or PRONOUN: *everywhere but in San Francisco/Who but John would say that?* –see ME (USAGE)

butch·er¹ /ˈbʊtʃər/ *n* a person who kills animals for food or one whose store sells meat: *I bought this chicken at the new butcher's/butcher./*(fig.) *That general/doctor is a real butcher!* (=causes death or hurt unnecessarily.)

butcher² *v* [T] to kill (animals) and prepare for sale as food: (fig.) *The soldiers butchered their enemies.* –see KILL (USAGE) –**butchery** *n* [U]

but·ler /ˈbʌtlər/ *n* the chief male servant of a house, in charge of the other servants

butt¹ /bʌt/ *v* [I;T] to strike or push against (someone or something) with the head or horns: *He butted (his head) against the wall.* –**butt** *n: The goat gave me a butt in the stomach!*

   butt in *v adv* [I *on,into*] *infml, often derog* to interrupt, usu. by speaking: *I wish you wouldn't keep butting in on our conversation!*

butt² *n* a person (or perhaps thing) that people make fun of: *Poor John was* **the butt of all their jokes.**

butt³ *n* a large, thick, or bottom end of something: *a cigarette butt* (=the last unsmoked end)

but·ter¹ /ˈbʌtər/ *n* [U] **1** yellow fat made from milk, spread on bread, used in cooking, etc. **2 Butter wouldn't melt in his/her mouth** *infml* He/She pretends to be kind and harmless but is not really so! –**buttery** *adj*

butter² *v* [T] **1** to spread with or as if with butter: *to butter bread* **2 know which side one's bread is buttered on** *infml* to know who or what will help one most, or bring one most gain

   butter sbdy. ↔ **up** *v adv* [T] *infml* to FLATTER (1) (someone): *She buttered him up by saying he was a good businessman.*

but·ter·cup /ˈbʌtərˌkʌp/ *n* a yellow wild flower

but·ter·fly /ˈbʌtərˌflaɪ/ *n* **-flies 1** any of several insects that fly by day and often have large beautifully-colored wings **2 have butterflies in one's stomach** *infml* to feel very nervous before doing something

but·ter·scotch /ˈbʌtərˌskɑtʃ/ *n* [U] a sweet food made from sugar and butter (and perhaps sweet SYRUP) boiled together

but·tock /ˈbʌtək/ *n* either of the two fleshy parts on which a person sits: *the left/right buttock*

but·ton¹ /ˈbʌtn/ *n* **1** a small usu. round or flat thing that is fixed to a garment or other object and usu. passed through an opening (BUTTONHOLE¹) to act as a fastener: *a row of buttons down the front of his shirt/a button nose* (=a small broad flattish nose) **2** a button-like part, object, or piece of apparatus, esp. one pressed to start a machine: *I pressed the button, and a bell rang.* **3** *AmE* a metal or plastic BADGE with a pattern or a short phrase expressing a usu. political or advertising message (SLOGAN): *wearing a button saying "Make Love Not War"/a* CAMPAIGN *button* **4**

on the button *infml esp. AmE* exactly right

button² *v* [I;T *up*] to (cause to) close or fasten with buttons: *to button (up) one's shirt|My shirt doesn't button (up) easily.*

but·ton·hole¹ /'bʌtn,hoʷl/ *n* a hole for a button to be put through to fasten a shirt, coat, etc.

buttonhole² *v* **-holed, -holing** [T] *infml* to stop and force to listen: *She buttonholed me outside the office, and told me about her plans for fighting unemployment.*

but·tress /'bʌtrɪs/ *n* a support for a wall –**buttress** *v:* (*fig.*) *Buttressed by its past profits, the company stayed in business through a difficult period.*

bux·om /'bʌksəm/ *adj apprec* (of a woman) attractively fat and healthy-looking; having a large BOSOM

buy¹ /baɪ/ *v* **bought** /bɔt/, **buying 1** [I;T *for,from,with*] to obtain (something) by giving money (or something else of value): *She bought me a book from them for $5.|He bought a new car.|When prices are low, I buy.* –compare SELL **2** [T] *infml* to accept; believe: *I don't buy that nonsense.* **3 buy time** *infml* to delay an action or decision that seems to be coming too soon: *He tried to buy time by doing a lot of talking.*

  buy sbdy.sthg.↔**off** *v adv* [T]→BRIBE¹

  buy sbdy./sthg.↔**out** *adv* [T] **1** to gain control of by buying the whole of: *to buy out a business* **2** to buy the business of: *We bought out the owners for $500,000.*

  buy sthg.↔**up** *v adv* [T] **1** to buy all the supplies of: *to buy up all the sugar on the market* **2** → BUY OUT

buy² *n infml* **1** an act of buying **2** something of value at a low price; BARGAIN¹ (2): *It's a good buy at that price!*

buy·er /'baɪər/ *n* a person who buys, esp. for a company or large store –compare SELLER

buzz /bʌz/ *v* **1** [I] to make a low noise (HUM), as bees do: (*fig.*) *The crowd/room buzzed with excitement.* **2** [I;T *for*] to call (someone) by using an electrical signaling apparatus (**buzzer**): *She buzzed (for) her secretary (to come).* –**buzz** *n* –**buzzer** *n: Come in when you hear the buzzer.*

  buzz off *v adv* [I] *infml* (in giving orders) to go away: *You're making me angry; buzz off!*

buz·zard /'bʌzərd/ *n* **1** (in America) a heavy slow-flying black bird that eats dead flesh; VULTURE **2** (in Britain) a heavy slow-flying bird that kills and eats other creatures; HAWK¹

buzz·word /'bʌzwɜrd/ *n* a word or phrase that sounds exact but lacks exact meaning, often used in politics and professions —see also CATCHWORD

by¹ /baɪ/ *prep* **1** near; beside: *standing by the window|Sit by me.* **2** past: *He walked/passed by me without noticing me.* **3** through the use of; through: *to enter by the door|to travel by train|to earn money by writing|to take the*

hammer by the handle|I did it by mistake.|What do you mean by that? **4** (shows the person or thing that does the action): *a play by Shakespeare|struck by lightning* **5** not later than: *Be here by four o'clock.|Will you finish it by tomorrow?* **6** in accordance with: *to play by the rules* **7** to the amount of: *They OVERCHARGEd me by $3.|It's better by far.* (=much better) **8** (in expressions of strong feeling and solemn promises): *By God he's done it!|to SWEAR (2) by heaven* **9** (in measurements and numbers): *a room 15 feet by 20 feet|to divide 10 by 5|to multiply 10 by 5* **10** (often with plurals or *the* +*singular*) (showing a measure or a rate): *paid by the hour|by result(s)|berries by the handful|to move along by inches* **11** (showing the size of groups that follow each other): *little by little|The animals went in two by two.* **12** during: *Cats sleep by day and hunt by night.* **13** with regard to: *a doctor by profession|French by birth* **14** (**all**) **by oneself** (completely) alone: *She was by herself.|He did it all by himself!* **15 by the way** *infml* (introducing a new subject or one that has not been mentioned earlier): *By the way, what happened to all the money I gave you?*

by² *adv* **1** past: *Please let me (get) by.|A lot of time has gone by since then.* **2** near: *some people standing by* **3** *AmE infml* at or to someone's home: *Stop/Come by for a drink after work.* **4 by and by** *infml* before long; a bit later: *I'll do it by and by.* **5 by and large** on the whole; in general: *By and large, your plan is a good one.* **6 lay/put/set (something) by** to keep or store (something, esp. money) for the future

bye /baɪ/ also **bye-bye** /,· '·, '· ·/, also **bye now** /'· ·/ *AmE interj infml* goodbye

by·gone /'baɪɡɔn, -ɡɑn/ *adj* [A *no comp.*] gone by; past: *in bygone days of long ago*

by·gones /'baɪɡɔnz, -ɡɑnz/ *n* **let bygones be bygones** *infml* to forget (and forgive) the bad things in the past

by·pass¹ /'baɪpæs/ *n* a road around something, esp. around a busy town: *a bypass avoiding the center of town*

bypass² *v* [T] to avoid: *If we bypass the town we'll miss all the traffic.*

by-prod·uct /'· ,··/ *n* **1** something additional formed when making or doing something: *Silver is often obtained as a by-product during the separation of lead from rock.* **2** an additional result, sometimes unexpected or unintended

by·stand·er /'baɪ,stændər/ *n* a person standing near, but not taking part in, what is happening; ONLOOKER: *The police asked some of the bystanders about the accident.*

by·way /'baɪ,weɪ/ also **byroad** /'baɪroʷd/– *n* a smaller road or path which is not well known

by·word /'baɪwɜrd/ *n* (the name of) a person, place, or thing that is taken as representing some quality: *The general's name had become a byword for cruelty in war.*

C, c

C, c /siʸ/ *C's, c's, cs-* **1** the third letter of the English alphabet **2** the ROMAN NUMERAL (number) for 100

c *written abbrev. said as:* **1** cent **2** CIRCA: *c 1834*

C *written abbrev. said as:* CENTIGRADE (=CELSIUS): *100°C*

CA *written abbrev. said as:* California /ˌkælə'fɔrnyə/ (state in the US)

cab /kæb/ *n* **1** a taxi: *Shall we walk or take a cab/go* **by cab**? –see illustration on page 95 **2** the part of a truck, train, etc., in which the driver sits or stands

cab·a·ret /ˌkæbə'reʸ/ *n* [C;U] (a) performance of popular music and dancing while guests in a restaurant have a meal, usu. at night

cab·bage /'kæbɪdʒ/ *n* [C;U] a large round vegetable with thick green leaves which are used (usu. cooked) as food –compare LETTUCE

cab driv·er /'· ˌ··/ also **cabby, cabbie** /'kæbiʸ/ *infml– esp. AmE* a person who drives a taxi

cab·in /'kæbɪn/ *n* **1** a small roughly built usu. wooden house: *They lived in a little log cabin in the mountains.* **2** the room at the front of an aircraft in which the pilot sits **3** a small room on a ship usu. for sleeping

cab·i·net /'kæbənɪt/ *n* **1** a piece of furniture, with shelves and doors, or drawers, used for showing or storing things: *a* FILING CABINET|*I put my collection of old glasses in the cabinet.* –see illustration on page 379 **2** (in various countries) the most important department heads of the government, who meet as a group to make decisions or to advise the head of the government: *The cabinet meets next week to consider this problem.*

ca·ble¹ /'keʸbəl/ *n* **1** [C;U] (a length of) thick heavy strong, esp. wire, rope used on board ships, to support bridges, etc. –compare WIRE **2** [C;U] a set of wires put underground or under the sea which carry electricity or telegraph and telephone messages: *Telegrams go from America to Europe by cable.* **3** [C] also **cablegram** /-ˌgræm/ *fml–* a telegram

cable² *v* **-bled, -bling** [I;T + *to-v/(that)*] to send (someone) (something) by telegraph: *I cabled (him) (some money).|She cabled him (to come).*

cable tel·e·vi·sion /ˌ·· '····/ also **cable TV** /ˌ·· ·'·/, **cable–** *n* [U] a system of broadcasting television by CABLE¹ (2), usu. paid for by the user: *I like cable television because the movies are better.|That broadcast is on cable.*

ca·cao /kə'kau, kə'kɑoʷ, kə'keʸoʷ/ *n* **-caos** (the South American tree which produces) a seed from which COCOA and chocolate are made

cack·le /'kækəl/ *v* **-led, -ling** [I] **1** to make the noise made by a hen **2** to laugh loudly and unpleasantly with a sound like this –**cackler** /'kæklər/ *n* –**cackle** *n*

cac·tus /'kæktəs/ *n* **-tuses** *or* **-ti** /taɪ/ a desert plant protected by sharp prickles, with thick fleshy stems and leaves

ca·dav·er /kə'dævər/ *n fml* a dead human body

ca·dence /'keʸdns/ *n* **1** a regular beat of sound **2** the rise and fall of the human voice esp. in reading poetry

ca·det /kə'det/ *n* a person studying to become an officer in one of the armed forces or the police

cadge /kædʒ/ *v* **cadged, cadging** [I;T] *infml derog* to get or try to get (something) by asking, often seeming to be taking advantage of someone: *He cadged 75 cents for cigarettes (from me) yesterday.* –**cadger** *n*

cae·sar·e·an, cesarean, caesarian, cesarian /sɪ'zɛəriʸən/ *n* an operation in which a woman's body is cut open to allow the baby to be taken out, when an ordinary birth may be difficult: *Our first baby was born by caesarean.*

ca·fe, café /kæ'feʸ, kə-/ *n* a small restaurant where light meals and drinks are served –compare RESTAURANT

caf·e·te·ri·a /ˌkæfə'tɪəriʸə/ *n* a restaurant where people serve themselves (get their own food and drink) often in a store, factory, college, etc. –compare CANTEEN (1)

caf·feine /kæ'fiʸn, 'kæfiʸn/ *n* [U] a chemical substance found in coffee and tea, often used in medicines as a STIMULANT (1)

cage¹ /keʸdʒ/ *n* an enclosure made of a framework of wires or bars, esp. for keeping animals or birds in

cage² *v* **caged, caging** [T] to put into a cage: *caged birds*|(fig.) *Mothers of young children often feel* **caged** *in staying at home all day.*

cag·ey /'keʸdʒiʸ/ *adj* **cagier, cagiest** *infml* careful; secretive; unwilling to talk or to be friendly: *She's very cagey about her past.* –**cagily** *adv* –**caginess** *n* [U]

ca·hoots /kə'huʷts/ *n* **in cahoots (with)** *infml esp. AmE* in partnership (with); **in** LEAGUE (3) **(with)**: *The bank robbers and the police were in cahoots.The bank robbers were in cahoots with the police.*

ca·jole /kə'dʒoʷl/ *v* **-joled, -joling** [T *into, out of*] to persuade by praise or deceit: *She's always cajoling people (into doing things for her).*

cake¹ /keʸk/ *n* **1** [C;U] (a piece of) a food made by baking a (usu. sweet) mixture of flour, eggs, etc.: *a birthday cake*|*Would you* like some cake? **2** [C] a round flat shaped piece of something: *a fish cake|a cake of soap* **3 (be) a piece of cake** *infml* (to be) very easy **4 (sell/go) like hot cakes** (to be sold) very quickly: *Those pictures are going like hot cakes; there will be none left soon.* **5 have one's cake and eat it (too)** *infml* to have the advantages of something without the disadvantages that go with it

cake² *v* **caked, caking** [T *with/on*] to (cause to) cover thickly; (cause to) become ENCRUSTED: *After walking through the field, my boots were caked with mud.*

Cal. *written abbrev. said as:* California /ˌkælə'fɔrnyə/ (a state in the US)

ca·lam·i·ty /kə'læmətiʸ/ *n* **-ties** a terrible or very bad event; serious misfortune: *50 people were killed in the calamity.* – **calamitous** *adj*

cal·ci·um /'kælsiʸəm/ *n* [U] a silver-white metal that is a simple substance (ELEMENT (1)) and is found in bones, teeth, and chalk

cal·cu·late /'kælkyə,leʸt/ *v* **-lated, -lating** [I;T +*(that)*] to work out or find out (something) by using numbers; COMPUTE: *Have you calculated the result?|I calculated (that) we would arrive at 6:00 p.m.|The scientists calculated when the spacecraft would reach the moon.* **2** [T +*(that)*] to plan; intend: *a calculated threat*

cal·cu·lat·ing /'kælkyə,leʸtɪŋ/ *adj usu. derog* coldly planning and thinking about future actions, esp. whether they will be good or bad for oneself –compare SHREWD

cal·cu·la·tion /ˌkælkyə'leʸʃən/ *n* [C;U] the act or result of calculating: *Her calculation was correct.|The calculations are based on these* STATISTICS.|*He lied with cold calculation.*

cal·cu·la·tor /'kælkyə,leʸtər/ *n* a small machine which can carry out number operations and which usu. has a MEMORY (5) –see illustration on page 221

cal·cu·lus /'kælkyələs/ *n* [U] (in MATHEMATICS) a way of making calculations about quantities which are continually changing, such as the speed of a falling stone or the slope of a curved line

cal·en·dar /'kæləndər/ *n* a list showing the days and months of the year: *I used the calendar to count how many days it was until my birthday.|From January 1st to February 1st is one* **calendar month.** –see illustration on page 467

calf¹ /kæf/ *n* **calves** /kævz/ the young of the cow or of some other large animals such as the elephant –see MEAT (USAGE)

calf² *n* **calves** the fleshy back part of the human leg between the knee and the ankle

cal·i·ber *AmE*‖**calibre** *esp. BrE* /'kæləbər/ *n* **1** [S;U] the quality of something or some-

---

one: *This work's of a very high caliber.* **2** [C] the size of a bullet: *a 32-caliber bullet*

cal·i·brate /'kælə,breʸt/ *v* **-brated, -brating** [T] to mark degrees and dividing points on (the scale of a measuring instrument) –**calibration** /ˌkælə'breʸʃən [C;U]

cal·i·co /'kælɪ,koʷ/ *n* [U] a type of heavy cotton cloth

Calif. *written abbrev. said as:* California /ˌkælə'fɔrnyə/ (a state in the US)

calipers *AmE*‖also **callipers** *esp. BrE* /'kæləparz/ *n* [P] an instrument with two legs used for measuring thickness, the distance between two surfaces, and inner width (DIAMETER) –PAIR (USAGE)

call¹ /kɔl/ *v* **1** [I;T *to, for, out*] to shout; speak or say in a loud clear voice: *He called for help.|"Hello!" she called.|I've been calling for five minutes; why doesn't she answer?|The fishermen called (out) to the people on the shore.* **2** [T] to name: *We'll call the baby Jean.* **3** [T] to (try to) cause to come by speaking loudly or officially or by sending an order or message: *Mother is calling me.|He called me over to his desk.|The President called his advisors to a meeting.|Call a doctor!* **4** [I] **a** to make a short visit to someone: *She called (on me) (on Tuesday).* **b** (of people esp. selling things) to make regular visits: *The milkman calls every day.* **5** [I;T] to (try to) telephone or radio (to): *I called him this morning but he was out.|The office called to find out where you were.* –see TELEPHONE¹ (USAGE) **6** [T] to cause to happen: *The President called a meeting.* **7** [T] to say or consider that (someone or something) is (something): *She called me a coward.|I don't call that a good painting.|How can you still call yourself my friend?|Did you hear what he called me?* **8** [I;T *to*] (of an animal) to make the usual cry to (another animal): *The birds are calling (each other).*

call back *v adv* **1** [T] (=**call** sbdy.↔ **back**) to cause to return: *Mrs. Jones was about to leave when her secretary called her back.* **2** [I;T] (=**call** sbdy. **back**)] to return a telephone call: *I'll call (you) back.* –see also CALL¹ (3); see TELEPHONE (USAGE)

call for sbdy./sthg. *v prep* [T] **1** to demand: *to call for the waiter|The opposition called for an inquiry.* **2** to need; deserve: *Your unkind remark was* **not called for.**|*It was* **uncalled-for. 3** to come and get: *I'll call for you at nine o'clock.*

call sbdy./sthg.↔ **in** *v adv* [T] **1** to ask to come to help: *Call the doctor in.* **2** to request the return of: *The company called in all the cars with dangerous faults.*

call sthg.↔ **off** *v adv* [T] **1** to cause not to take place: *The football game was called off because of the snow.* **2** to order to keep away: *Call off your dog; it tried to bite me!*

call on/upon sbdy. *v prep* [T] **1** to visit: *We can call on Mary tomorrow.* **2** *fml* to ask (someone) to do something: *The President called on everyone to work hard for their country.*

call sbdy.↔ **out** *v adv* [T] to order (some-

SPELLING NOTE

Words with the sound /k/, like **cut**, may be spelled **k-**, like **key**, or **qu-**, like **queen**. Words with the sound /s/, like **soon**, or **city**, may be spelled **s-**, like **soon**, or **ps-**, like **psychology**.

one) officially to come to one's help: *Call out the army.*

call up *v adv* **1** [I;T **call** sbdy.↔ **up**] to telephone: *I'll call you up this evening.* **2** [T **call** sbdy.↔ **up**] *infml* also **draft** *AmE infml*– conscript: *He was called up in 1917.* **3** [T **call** sthg.↔**up**] to bring back to memory; RECALL

call² *n* **1** a shout; cry: *They heard a call for help.*|*The call of this bird is very loud.* **2** [+ *to-v/to*] a command to meet, come, or do something; SUMMONS: *He felt a call (from God) to become a priest.* **3** an attempt to ring someone on the telephone; conversation over the telephone: *I have a call for you from Washington.*|*I gave my wife a call but she was out.*|*Ask him to return my call when he gets home, please.* **4** a short usu. formal visit: *The President is making/paying a call on the king.* **5 close call/shave/thing** something bad that nearly happened, but didn't: *That was a close call! We nearly hit the other car!* **6 no call for** no need for: *There's no call for worry.* **7 on call** not working but ready to work if needed: *The nurse is on call tonight.* **8 within call** near enough to hear a call

call box /'· ·/ *n BrE* for TELEPHONE BOOTH

call·er /'kɔlər/ *n* a person who makes a short visit: *John's a regular caller.*

call girl /'· ·/ *n* → PROSTITUTE

call·ing /'kɔlɪŋ/ *n* **1** [+*to-v, for*] a strong desire or feeling of duty to do a particular job; VOCATION (1, 3): *My son had a calling to become a priest.* **2** *fml* profession; trade: *"What was his calling?" "He was a teacher."*

cal·li·pers /'kæləpərz/ *n* [P] *esp. BrE* for CALIPERS

cal·lous /'kæləs/ *adj* unkind; without feelings for the sufferings of other people –compare CALLUS **–callously** *adv* **–callousness** *n* [U]

cal·low /'kæloʷ/ *adj derog* (of a person or behavior) young and without experience; IMMATURE

cal·lus /'kæləs/ *n* an area of thick hard skin: *calluses on his hands* –compare CALLOUS

calm¹ /kɑm/ *adj* **1** free from excitement; quiet; untroubled: *Even after the accident she was calm.* **2 a** (of weather) not windy: *After the storm it was calm.* **b** (of water) not rough; smooth; still: *The sea was calm.*

calm² *n* [S;U] **1** a time of peace and quiet; absence of excitement or worry **2** (of weather) an absence of wind or rough weather

calm³ *v* [T] to make calm: *She calmed her child by giving it some milk.*

calm down *v adv* [I;T] to become or make calm: *The excited girl quickly calmed down.*|*It was difficult to calm my brother down.*

cal·o·rie /'kæləriʸ/ *n* **1** a measure used when stating the amount of heat or ENERGY (3) that a food will produce: *One thin piece of bread has 90 calories.*|*I can eat only 1,500 calories a day on this DIET.* **2** a measure of heat

calves /kævz/ *n plural of* CALF

ca·lyp·so /kə'lɪpsoʷ/ *n* **-sos** or **-soes** a type of West Indian song

came /keʸm/ *v past tense of* COME

cam·el /'kæməl/ *n* a large long-necked animal with one or two large HUMPs on its back, used for riding or carrying goods in desert countries

ca·mel·lia /kə'miʸlyə/ *n* the large roselike sweet-smelling flower of an East Asian bush

cam·e·o /'kæmiʸoʷ/ *n* **-os** a piece of women's jewelery consisting of a raised shape or figure on a background

cam·er·a /'kæmərə/ *n* an apparatus for taking photographs or moving pictures

cam·ou·flage /'kæmə,flɑʒ, -,flɑdʒ/ *v* **-flaged, -flaging** [T] to make (esp. a military object) difficult to see or find esp. by the use of branches, paint, nets, etc. **–camouflage** *n* [C;U]

camp¹ /kæmp/ *n* a place where people live in tents or huts usu. for a short time: *a military camp*|*The climbers had a camp near the top of the mountain.*|*Let's go back to camp, it's getting dark*

camp² *v* [I] to set up (PITCH¹ (1)) or live in a camp: *The hunters camped near the top of the mountain.*|*We go camping every summer.*|*We camped out* (=outdoors) *last night.*

cam·paign¹ /kæm'peʸn/ *n* a connected set of military, political, or business actions intended to obtain a particular result: *The Spanish campaign and the campaign to seize Moscow were both failures.*|*The campaign succeeded and she won the election.*|*an advertising campaign*

campaign² *v* [I] to lead, take part in, or go on a CAMPAIGN: *Joan is campaigning for equal rights for women.* **–campaigner** *n*

cam·phor /'kæmfər/ *n* [U] a strong-smelling white substance, used esp. in medicine to prevent unconsciousness, and to keep insects away

cam·pus /'kæmpəs/ *n* **-puses** [C;U] the grounds of a university, college, or school

can¹ /kən; *strong* kæn/ *v* **could** /kəd; *strong* kʊd/, *3rd person sing. present tense* **can**, NEGATIVE *contraction* **can't** /kænt/ *or* **cannot** /'kænɑt, kæ'nɑt, kə-/ *past tense* NEGATIVE *contraction* **couldn't** /'kʊdnt/ [I +*to-v*] **1** to be able to; know how to: *She can speak French.*|*I can't remember where I put it.*|*Can you swim?*|*everything that money can buy*|*It can be* (=sometimes it is) *very cold in Canada.* **2** to be allowed to; have permission to; may: *You can't play football here.*|*Can we go home now, please?* (This use of **can** is now more common than **may**.) (used when asking someone to do something): *Can you help me please?* –see Study Notes on page 434

USAGE **Can** is often used with verbs which are marked [not *be* +*v-ing*], such as **see, hear,** and **believe:** *I'm looking at him and I can see him.*|*I'm listening hard but I can't hear it.*|*I can smell something burning.*|*I can believe that.*|*I can't imagine why.*|*Can you guess the answer?*|*Can you remember where they live?*

can² /kæn/ *n* **1** also **tin** *esp. BrE*– a small closed metal container in which foods or drinks are preserved without air: *He opened a can of beans/a can of beer.* –see illustration on page 379 **2** a usu. round metal container with an open top or removable lid and sometimes with handles, used for holding milk, coffee, oil, waste, ashes, etc. **3** the contents of such a container: *Add a can/canful of juice to the mixture and it will taste better.* **4** *infml esp. AmE* BUTTOCKS

can³ /kæn/ *v* **-nn-** [T] **1** to preserve (food) by putting in a closed metal container without air: *The fish is canned in this factory.|canned fruit* **2** *infml* for FIRE² (6)

ca·nal /kə'næl/ *n* a waterway dug in the ground, esp. to allow ships or boats to travel along it: *The Panama Canal joins two oceans.|Canals have been built to take water to the desert.|The goods are sent here by canal.*

ca·nar·y /kə'nɛəriʸ/ *n* **-ies** a small yellow bird usu. kept as a pet for its singing

can·cel /'kænsəl/ *v* **-l-**AmE**-ll-** BrE [T] **1** to give up or call off (a planned activity, idea, etc.): *She canceled her trip to New York because she felt ill.|She canceled her order for a new car.* **2** [out] to balance; equal: *The increase in the strength of their navy is canceled by that in our army.*

can·cel·la·tion /ˌkænsə'leʸʃən/ *n* [C;U] (an example of) the act of CANCELing (1): *The cancellation of the order for planes led to the closing of the factory.|Because there have been cancellations you can now have tickets.*

can·cer /'kænsər/ *n* [C;U] (a) diseased growth in the body, which may cause death: *He's got a cancer in his throat.|He's has cancer of the throat.|*(fig.) *Violence is the cancer of our society.* –compare CANKER –**cancerous** *adj*: *a cancerous growth*

Cancer *n* [S] see ZODIAC –see also TROPIC

can·did /'kændɪd/ *adj* directly truthful, even when telling the truth is uncomfortable or unwelcome –**candidly** *adv*

can·di·date /'kændəˌdeʸt, -dɪt/ *n* **1** a person who wants, or whom others want, to be chosen for a position, esp. in an election: *Jean was the best candidate for the job.|He was a candidate in the presidential election.* **2** a person taking an examination

can·dle /'kændl/ *n* a usu. round stick of wax containing a length of string (WICK (1)) which gives light when it burns

can·dle·stick /'kændl,stɪk/ *n* a holder for usu. one candle

can·dor *AmE*‖**candour** *BrE* /'kændər/ *n* [U] the state or quality of being sincerely honest and truthful (CANDID)

can·dy¹ /'kændiʸ/ *n* **-dies** [C;U] *esp. AmE* (a shaped piece of) various types of boiled sugar, or chocolate, or other sweets

candy² *v* **-died, -dying** [T] to preserve (food) by cooking in sugar: *candied fruit*

cane¹ /keʸn/ *n* **1** [C;U] (a length of) the hard smooth thin often hollow stem of certain plants (tall grasses such as BAMBOO): *cane*

SPELLING NOTE

Words with the sound /k/, like **cut**, may be spelled **k-**, like **key**, or **qu-**, like **queen**. Words with the sound /s/, like **city**, may be spelled **s-**, like **soon**, or **ps-**, like **psychology**.

---

furniture **2** [C] also **walking stick, stick**– thin rod of wood used for supporting the body when walking

cane² *v* **caned, caning** [T] to punish (someone) by striking with a CANE (1)

ca·nine /'keʸnaɪn/ *adj,n tech* (of, for, typical of) a dog or related animal

can·is·ter /'kænəstər/ *n* a usu. metal container used for holding a dry substance or a gas: *canisters for flour, sugar, and tea*

can·ker /'kæŋkər/ *n* [C;U] a sore or area of soreness caused by a disease which attacks the wood of trees and the flesh (esp. the mouth and ears) of animals and people: (fig.) *Violence is the canker in our society.* –compare CANCER –**cankerous** *adj*

can·na·bis /'kænəbɪs/ also **dope, pot, grass** *infml*– *n* [U] the drug produced from a particular type of HEMP plant (the **Indian hemp**), sometimes smoked in cigarettes to give a feeling of pleasure, leading to sleepiness: *Smoking cannabis is illegal in many countries.* –see also HASHISH, MARIJUANA

canned mu·sic /ˌkænd 'myuʷzɪk/ *n* [U] *derog* quiet recorded music played continuously in a public place, such as a restaurant or store

can·ni·bal /'kænəbəl/ *n* an animal or person that eats the flesh of its own kind –**cannibalism** *n* [U] –**cannibalistic** /ˌkænəbə'lɪstɪk/ *adj*

can·non¹ /'kænən/ *n* **cannons** *or* **cannon** a big gun, often fixed to the ground or onto a usu. two-wheeled carriage: *In this castle there are cannons from the 15th century.|Our fighter planes are all armed with cannon.* –compare CANON

cannon² *v* [I] to strike forcefully; knock: *He came running around the corner, cannoned into me, and knocked me over.*

can·not /'kænɑt, kæ'nɑt, kə-/ *v* can not: *Mr. Smith is sorry that he cannot accept your invitation to dinner.* –see also CAN'T

can·ny /'kæniʸ/ *adj* **-nier, -niest** clever; not easily deceived esp. in money matters: *The canny old lady knew that the book was too expensive.*

ca·noe¹ /kə'nuʷ/ *n* a long light narrow boat, pointed at both ends, and moved by a PADDLE¹ (1) held in the hands: *We crossed the lake by canoe/in a canoe.*

canoe² *v* **-noed, -noeing** [I] to travel by CANOE –**canoeist** *n*

can·on¹ /'kænən/ *n* **1** an established law of a Christian church **2** *fml* a generally accepted standard of behavior or thought: *His behavior offends the canons of good manners.* –compare CANNON –**canonical** /kə'nɑnɪkəl/ *adj*

canon² *n* [A;C] a Christian priest with special duties in a CATHEDRAL –compare CANNON

can·on·ize also **-ise** *BrE* /'kænəˌnaɪz/ *v* **-ized, -izing** [T] to declare (a dead person) a SAINT (2): *Joan of Arc was canonized in 1920.*

can o·pen·er /'·· ···/ *AmE*‖**tin opener** *BrE*– *n* an apparatus for opening cans –see illustration on page 379

can·o·py /'kænəpiʸ/ *n* **-pies** a cover usu. of cloth fixed above a bed or seat: (fig.) *a canopy of branches.*

canst /kənst; *strong* kænst/ **thou canst** *old use or bibl* (when talking to one person) you can

cant /kænt/ *n* [U] *derog* insincere talk about oneself, esp. about one's religious practices; HYPOCRISY

can't /kænt/ *v short for:* can not: *I can't come with you: I'm busy.|You can swim, can't you?* –see also CANNOT

can·ta·loupe||also **cantaloup** *AmE* /'kæntəl ,oᵂp/ *n* [C;U] a large round fruit (MELON) with a hard green or yellow skin and juicy reddish-yellow flesh

can·tan·ker·ous /kæn'tæŋkərəs/ *adj infml* bad-tempered; quarrelsome –**cantankerously** *adv*

can·teen /kæn'tiᵞn/ *n* **1** a place in a factory, military camp, etc., where people may buy and eat food, meals, drinks, etc. –compare CAFETERIA **2** a small usu. leather container in which water or other drink is carried

can·ter /'kæntər/ *n* [usu. sing.] (of a horse) a movement which is fast, but slower than a GALLOP –**canter** *v* [I;T]

can·vas /'kænvəs/ *n* [C;U] (a piece of) strong rough cloth used for tents, sails, bags, etc.: *We spent the night* **under canvas.** (=in a tent)|*The artist showed me his canvases.* (=pictures painted on pieces of canvas)

can·vass, -vas /'kænvəs/ *v* [I;T *for*] to go through (an area) or to (people) to ask for (esp. political support) or to find out (people's opinions): *We've canvassed the whole town, and we think our party will win the election.|I'm canvassing tonight.*

can·yon /'kænyən/ *n* a deep narrow steep-sided valley usu. with a river flowing through –see VALLEY (USAGE)

cap¹ /kæp/ *n* **1** a soft head-covering, esp. a flat closely fitting one, e.g. worn by nurses and soldiers: *a schoolboy's cap|an officer's cap* –compare HAT (1) **2** a protective covering for the top or end of an object: *Put the cap back on the bottle.* **3** also **diaphragm**– a small round object fitted inside a woman to allow her to have sex without having children –see also CONTRACEPTIVE

cap² *v* **-pp-** [T] **1** to put a cap on (someone or something); cover with a cap: (fig.) *Clouds capped the hills.* **2** to improve on (what someone has said or done): *He capped my story by telling a better one.* **3 to cap it all (off)** on top of everything else: *His wife left him, his car was stolen, then to cap it all (off) he lost his job!*

ca·pa·bil·i·ty /,keᵞpə'bɪləti̯ᵞ/ *n* **-ties** [C;U] the quality of being CAPABLE (1): *The child has great capabilities.|She has great capability as a singer and should be trained.|*NUCLEAR (1) *capability* (=the ability to fight a NUCLEAR (1) war)

ca·pa·ble /'keᵞpəbəl/ *adj* [*of*] **1** having the ability of doing or being, or the power to do or be: *A very capable doctor* (=a good doctor)|*She's capable of any crime.* **2** able to be; ready for; open to: *That remark is capable of being misunderstood.* –opposite **incapable** –**capably** *adv*

ca·pac·i·ty /kə'pæsəti̯ᵞ/ *n* **-ties 1** [S;U] the amount that something can hold or produce:

The seating capacity of this theater is 500.|working at full capacity (=producing the greatest amount possible)|*This factory has a production capacity of 200 cars a week.|The theater was* **filled to capacity.** (=completely full) **2** [C;U *for*] ability; power: *He has a capacity for enjoying himself.|Her capacity for remembering is very useful to her.|Understanding this book is beyond my capacity.* –see GENIUS (USAGE) **3** [C] character; position: *I'm speaking in* **my capacity as** *chairperson.*

cape¹ /keᵞp/ *n* a loose outer garment without SLEEVES, fastened at the neck and hanging from the shoulders: *a bicycle cape to keep off the rain* –compare CLOAK

cape² *n* (often in names) a piece of land joined to the coast and standing out into the sea: *the Cape of Good Hope*

ca·per¹ /'keᵞpər/ *v* [I] to jump about in a joyful manner: *The lambs were capering in the fields.*

caper² *n* **1** a gay jumping movement **2** *infml* an unlawful activity; crime

cap·il·lar·y /'kæpə,lɛri̯ᵞ/ *n* **-ies** a very fine hairlike tube, e.g. one of the smaller blood vessels in the body

cap·i·tal¹ /'kæpətl̩/ *n* **1** [C] a town or city where the center of government is: *Paris is the capital of France.* –compare CAPITOL **2** [S;U] wealth, esp. money used to produce more wealth or for starting a business; the machines, buildings, and goods used in a business: *This business was started with a capital of $10,000/with $10,000 capital.|*Capital gains *are profits made by selling possessions.* **3** [C] a CAPITAL² (2) letter, esp. one at the beginning of a word: *The word* DICTIONARY *is printed here in capitals.* –compare LOWER CASE

cap·i·tal² *adj* [A] **1** punishable by death: *Murder can be a capital offense.|*CAPITAL PUNISHMENT **2** (of a letter) written or printed in its large form (such as A, B, C) rather than in its small form (such as a, b, c)

cap·i·tal·ism /'kæpətl̩,ɪzəm/ *n* [U] the type of production and trade based on the private ownership of wealth –compare COMMUNISM

cap·i·tal·ist¹ /'kæpətl̩-ɪst/ *n* a person who owns or controls much wealth (CAPITAL¹ (2)) and esp. who lends it to businesses, banks, etc., at interest

capitalist² *adj* practicing or supporting CAPITALISM: *the capitalist countries of the West*

cap·i·tal·ize ||also **-ise** *BrE* /'kæpətl̩,aɪz/ *v* **-ized, -izing** [T] to write or print as a CAPITAL² (2) letter

capitalize on sthg. *v prep* [T] to use to one's advantage: *She capitalized on his mistake and won the game.*

capital pun·ish·ment /,··· '···/ *n* [U] punishment by death according to law; the death PENALTY (1)

Cap·i·tol /'kæpətl̩/ *n* [S] (in the US) the building in which the state or national law-making body meets: **The Capitol** *is the building in Washington, D.C. in which Congress meets.* –compare CAPITAL¹ (1)

ca·pit·u·late /kəˈpɪtʃəˌleʸt/ v **-lated, -lating** [I]
fml to yield to the enemy, usu. on agreed
conditions; SURRENDER **–capitulation**
/kəˌpɪtʃəˈleʸʃən/ n [C;U]

ca·price /kəˈpriʸs/ n [C;U] (a) sudden often
foolish change of mind or behavior usu.
without any real cause; sudden wish to have
or do something; WHIM

ca·pri·cious /kəˈprɪʃəs, -ˈpriʸ-/ adj often
changing; untrustworthy; caused by CAPRICE:
*We can't go camping while the weather is so
capricious.* **–capriciously** adv **–capricious-
ness** n [U]

Cap·ri·corn /ˈkæprɪˌkɔrn/ n see ZODIAC –see
also TROPIC

cap·size /ˈkæpsaɪz, kæpˈsaɪz/ v **-sized, -siz-
ing** [I;T] **a** (esp. of a boat) to turn over **b** to
turn (esp. a boat) over: *The boat capsized in
the storm, but luckily it didn't sink.*

cap·sule /ˈkæpsəl, -syuʷl/ n **1** a measured
amount of medicine inside an outer covering, the whole of which is swallowed **2** the
part of a spacecraft in which the pilots live
and work and from which the engine is
separated when the takeoff is completed

cap·tain¹ /ˈkæptən/ n **1** the leader of a team
or group **2** the person in command of a ship
or aircraft: *Are we ready to sail, Captain?* **3**
an officer of middle rank in the armed forces

captain² v [T] to be captain of; command;
lead: *to captain a team*

cap·tion /ˈkæpʃən/ n words written above or
below a picture, newspaper article, etc., to
explain what it is or give further information:
*I didn't understand the drawing until I read
the caption.*

cap·ti·vate /ˈkæptəˌveʸt/ v **-vated, -vating** [T]
to charm, excite, and attract (someone or
something): *the city's captivating beauty*

cap·tive¹ /ˈkæptɪv/ adj **1** taken prisoner, esp.
in war: *We were held captive for three
months.* **2** not allowed to move about freely;
imprisoned: *captive animals* **3** a captive audience one who cannot easily leave and must
therefore listen: *Lying in my hospital bed, I
was a captive audience to her uninteresting
stories.*

captive² n a person taken prisoner esp. in war

cap·tiv·i·ty /kæpˈtɪvətiʸ/ n [U] the state of
being CAPTIVE¹: *Many animals do not breed
when in captivity.*

cap·tor /ˈkæptər/ n usu. fml a person who has
CAPTURED¹ (1) someone or something: *I soon
escaped from my captors.*

cap·ture¹ /ˈkæptʃər/ v **-tured, -turing** [T] **1** to
take (a person or animal) prisoner: *He was
captured trying to escape from the country.* **2**
to take control of (something) by force from
an enemy; win; gain **3** to preserve on film, in
words, etc.: *In his book he tried to capture the
beauty of Venice.*

SPELLING NOTE
Words with the sound /k/, like **cut**, may
be spelled **k-**, like **key**, or **qu-**, like
queen. Words with the sound /s/, like
city, may be spelled **s-**, like **soon**, or
ps-, like **psychology**.

---

capture² n [U] the act of taking or being
taken by force

car /kɑr/ n **1** also **automobile** *AmE*‖also **motor
car** *BrE*– a vehicle with wheels, driven by a
motor, and used for carrying people: *She
goes to work by car.*–see illustration opposite **2** esp. *AmE* a carriage or vehicle for
use on railroads or CABLES¹ (1), esp. of a
stated kind: *This train has a sleeping car.*

car·a·mel /ˈkærəməl, -ˌmɛl, ˈkɑrməl/ n **1** [U]
burnt sugar used for giving food a special
taste and color **2** [C;U] (a piece of) sticky
boiled sugar containing this and eaten as
candy

car·at ‖also **karat** *AmE* /ˈkærət/ n a division
on the scale of measurement for expressing
the amount of gold in golden objects, or the
weight of a jewel: *a 24-carat gold ring*

car·a·van /ˈkærəˌvæn/ n **1** a group of people
with animals or vehicles traveling together
for protection through unfriendly esp. desert
areas **2** *BrE* for TRAILER (2) **3** *BrE* for WAGON
(1) –compare WAGON TRAIN

car·bo·hy·drate /ˌkɑrboʷˈhaɪdreʸt, -drɪt,
-bə-/ n [C;U] any of various types of substances, such as sugar, which consist of oxygen, HYDROGEN, and CARBON, which
provide the body with heat and power
(ENERGY) and if eaten in quantity make one
fat

car·bon /ˈkɑrbən/ n **1** [U] a simple substance
(ELEMENT (1)) found in a pure form as diamonds, etc., or in an impure form as coal,
gasoline, etc. **2** [C;U] also **carbon paper**– (a
sheet of) thin paper with a coat of colored
material on one side used between sheets of
typing paper for making one or more copies
3 [C] also **carbon copy** /ˌ··ˈ···/– a copy made
by using this paper; DUPLICATE¹: (fig.) *John is
a carbon copy of his father.*

car·bon·at·ed /ˈkɑrbəˌneʸtɪd/ adj containing
CARBON DIOXIDE: *Carbonated drinks have
small bubbles.*

carbon di·ox·ide /ˌkɑrbən daɪˈɑksaɪd/ n [U]
the gas produced when animals breathe out
or when CARBON (1) is burned in air

carbon mon·ox·ide /ˌkɑrbən məˈnɑksaɪd/ n
[U] a poisonous gas produced when CARBON
(1) (esp. gasoline) burns in a small amount of
air

car·bun·cle /ˈkɑrˌbʌŋkəl/ n a large ugly BOIL³

car·bu·re·tor *AmE*‖ **carburettor** *BrE* /ˈkɑrbə-
ˌreʸtər, -byə-/ n an apparatus, esp. used in
car engines, for mixing the necessary
amounts of air and gasoline to produce the
explosive gas which burns in the engine to
provide power

car·cass ‖also **carcase** *BrE* /ˈkɑrkəs/ n the
body of a dead animal, esp. one which is
ready to be cut up as meat

card /kɑrd/ n **1** also **playing card** *fml*– one of a
set (DECK) of 52 small sheets of plastic or stiff
paper marked to show class (SUIT¹ (1)) and
number and used for various games –see
CARDS (USAGE) **2** a small sheet of plastic or
stiff paper usu. with information printed on
it and having various uses: *a membership/a
calling card*‖*Let me give you my business
card.* **3** also **greeting card**– a piece of stiff

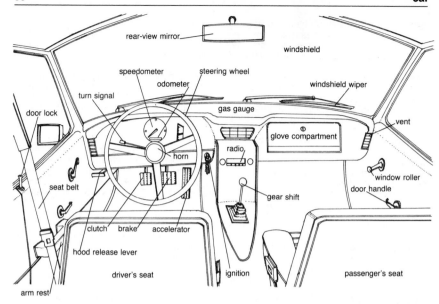

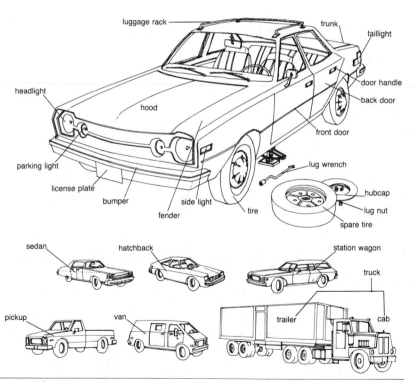

Useful Phrases
to fasten the seat belt
to turn left/right
to accelerate/speed up

to slow down
to park
to fill up the car (with gasoline)
to check the oil

paper, usu. with a picture on the front and a message inside, sent to a person by mail on special occasions (e.g. a birthday, Christmas, etc.): *I sent her a* **get-well card** *when she was in the hospital.*|*I bought a* **birthday card** *for Jack.* **4** →POSTCARD: *I received a card from my friend in Italy.* **5 have a card up one's sleeve** *infml* to have a secret, usu. effective, plan or intention

card·board /'kɑrdbɔrd, -boʷrd/ *n* [U] a thick stiff paperlike usu. brownish or grayish material used for making boxes, the backs of books, etc.

car·di·ac /'kɑrdiʸ,æk/ *adj* [A] *tech* connected with the heart or with heart disease

car·di·gan /'kɑrdəgən/ *n* a SWEATER or short KNITted coat with SLEEVEs (1), fastened at the front with buttons or a belt –see illustration on page 123

car·di·nal[1] /'kɑrdn-əl, 'kɑrd-nəl/ *n* **1** [A;C] a priest with one of the highest ranks of the ROMAN CATHOLIC church **2** [C] a North American bird (FINCH) the male of which is bright red in color

cardinal[2] *adj* [*no comp.*] *fml* most important; chief; main: *a cardinal idea*|*a cardinal sin*

cardinal num·ber /ˌ··· ˈ··/ *n* one of the numbers 1, 2, 3, etc. –compare ORDINAL number (first, second, third, etc.)

card in·dex /ˈ· ˌ··/ *n* (a case containing) a number of cards each carrying a particular piece of information and arranged in a special order

cards /kɑrdz/ *n* [P] **1** also **playing cards** *fml*–a set (DECK) of 52 CARDS[1] (1) **2** games played with such a set; card playing: *Let's play cards tonight.* **3 lay/put one's cards on the table** to be completely honest; say openly what one intends to do **4 in the cards** *infml* probable: *They say war's in the cards*

USAGE The **cards** used in card games come in two red **suits**, **hearts** and **diamonds**; and two black ones, **clubs** and **spades**. Each **suit** has an **ace**, a **king**, a **queen**, and a **jack**: *the* **king** *of* **hearts**|*the* **queen**, *and a* **jack**: *the* **king** *of* **hearts**|*the* **jack** *of* **clubs**.

care[1] /keər/ *n* **1** worry; anxiety; sorrow; grief; suffering of the mind: *free from care* **2** [C] an anxiety; worry; cause of sorrow, grief, etc. **3** [U] charge; keeping; protection; responsibility: *under the doctor's care*|*We left the baby in the care of our neighbor.* **4** [U] serious attention; effort: *Try to give more care to your work.* **5** [U] carefulness in avoiding harm, damage, etc.: *Glass; handle with care!*|*Cross the street with care.*|**Take care.** (=be careful) **6 care of** →c/o **7 take care of** to be responsible for: *Take care of the baby while I'm out.* –see CARE[2] (USAGE)

care[2] *v* **cared, caring 1** [I;T *about*] to be worried, anxious, or concerned (about); mind:

When her dog died, Alice didn't seem to care at all.|*After we lost the game, John said he didn't really care about it*|*didn't care whether we won or lost.* **2** [T +*to-v*] to like; want: *Would you care to go to dinner?*

care for sbdy./sthg. *v prep* [T] **1** to nurse or attend; look after: *He's very good at caring for sick animals.* **2** [*used only in questions and* NEGATIVES[2] (1); *no pass.*] to like: *I don't really care for tea; I like coffee better.* –see USAGE

USAGE Compare **care about, care for,** and **take care (of):** To **care about** something is to think it important, whether or not one likes it: *Does the government really care about the problems of old people?*|*I don't care about what people think.* To **care for** usually means "to have a liking for," or "to want," and is used only in questions and NEGATIVES[2] (1): *Would you care for some tea?* To **take care** is to be **careful: Take care** *not to drop it!* To **take care of** means "to look after": *Who takes care of the children while their parents are at work?*

ca·reer[1] /kə'rɪər/ *n* **1** a job or profession for which one is trained and which one intends to follow for the whole of one's life **2** (a part of) the general course of a person's working life: *She spent most of her career as a teacher.* –see JOB (USAGE)

career[2] *adj* [A] professional; intending to make a job one's CAREER[1] (1): *a career soldier*

career[3] *v* [I] to go at full speed; rush wildly: *The car careered uncontrollably down the hill.*

care·free /'keərfriʸ/ *adj apprec* free from anxiety; happy; without sorrow or fear: *On a fine spring day like this I feel carefree.* –see also CARELESS

care·ful /'keərfəl/ *adj* **1** [+*to-v*/*(that)*] taking care (with the intention of avoiding danger): *Be careful not to fall*|*that you don't fall off the ladder.*|*Be careful what you say.*|*You should have been more careful when you crossed the street.* **2** showing attention to details: *She's a careful worker.* **3** done with care; showing care: *The doctor made a careful examination.* –**carefully** *adv*: *Hold this glass carefully. I don't want it to break.* –see also CARELESS –**carefulness** *n* [U]

care·less /'keərlɪs/ *adj* **1** not taking care; inattentive: *He's a very careless driver; he never thinks about what he's doing.* **2** [A] not showing care: *This is careless work. Do it again!* –see also CAREFUL; compare: *After we finished our examinations we all felt happy and* **carefree**.|*He failed his examination because his work was* **careless** *and full of mistakes.* –**carelessly** *adv* –**carelessness** *n* [U]

ca·ress[1] /kə'rɛs/ *n* a light tender touch or kiss showing one's love for someone

caress[2] *v* [T] to give a CARESS to (someone): *She caressed his cheek lovingly.*

care·tak·er /'keər,teʸkər/ *n* **1** a person employed to look after a building **2** [C] *BrE* for JANITOR **3** [A;C] a government or person in charge for a usu. short time until another is elected: *a caretaker government*

car·fare /'kɑrfeər/ *n* [U] the money needed

(FARE¹ (1)) for a bus, taxi, etc., esp. for travel within a town or city

car·go /'kɑrgoʷ/ n -goes [C;U] (one load of) the goods (FREIGHT (2)) carried by a ship, plane, or vehicle: *We sailed with a cargo of coal.*

car·i·ca·ture /'kærəkə,tʃʊər, -tʃər/ n [C;U] (the art of making) a representation of a person, esp. in literature or art, made so that parts of his appearance or character seem more noticeable, odd, or amusing than they really are: *Newspapers often contain caricatures of well-known politicians.*|*Ted did a caricature of the teacher by talking in a deep voice.* –**caricature** v -tured, -turing [T] –**caricaturist** n

car·nage /'kɑrnɪdʒ/ n [U] fml the killing and wounding of many animals or esp. people: *The battlefield was a scene of great carnage.*

car·nal /'kɑrnl/ adj [A] usu. derog of the flesh, bodily, or esp. sexual: *carnal pleasures/desires*

car·na·tion /kɑr'neʸʃən/ n (a garden plant with) a sweet-smelling white, pink, or red flower

car·ni·val /'kɑrnəvəl/ n 1 [U] public rejoicing with feasting, dancing, drinking, and often processions and shows: *carnival time in Rio de Janeiro* 2 [C] a period when this takes place esp. in ROMAN CATHOLIC countries in the weeks before LENT 3 [C] a traveling amusement show

car·ni·vore /'kɑrnə,vɔr, -,voʷr/ n a flesh-eating animal: *Lions are carnivores; rabbits are not.* –**carnivorous** /kɑr'nɪvərəs/ adj: *Cows aren't carnivorous.*

car·ol /'kærəl/ n a religious song of joy and praise esp. sung at Christmas

ca·rouse /kə'raʊz/ v -roused, -rousing [I] lit to have fun, esp. by drinking large amounts of alcoholic drink

car·ou·sel, **carr-** /,kærə'sɛl/ n AmE for MERRY-GO-ROUND

carp¹ /kɑrp/ v [I] derog infml to find fault and complain continuously and unnecessarily: *Please stop carping about the way I dress.*

carp² n carp or carps a large FRESHWATER fish that lives in lakes, pools, and slow-moving rivers

car·pal /'kɑrpəl/ adj [A] tech of the wrist or the bones in the wrist

car park /'· ·/ n BrE 1 →PARKING LOT 2 →PARKING GARAGE

car·pen·ter /'kɑrpəntər/ n a person who is skilled at making and repairing wooden objects

car·pen·try /'kɑrpəntriʸ/ n [U] the art or work of a CARPENTER

car·pet¹ /'kɑrpɪt/ n 1 [U] heavy woven often woolen material for covering floors or stairs 2 [C] a shaped piece of this material, usu. fitted to the size of a particular room: (fig.) a *carpet of flowers*

carpet² v [T] to cover with or as if with a CARPET

car·riage /'kærɪdʒ/ n 1 [C] a wheeled vehicle, esp. a private horse-drawn vehicle 2 [C;U] the manner of holding one's head and body when standing or walking; DEPORTMENT 3 [U]

(the cost of) the act of moving goods from one place to another 4 [C] a wheeled support for moving a heavy object, esp. a gun 5 [C] a movable part of a machine: *A* TYPEWRITER *has a carriage which holds and moves the paper.* 6 BrE for CAR (2) 7 [C] AmE for BABY CARRIAGE

car·ri·er /'kæriʸər/ n 1 a person or thing that carries, esp. a business that carries goods or passengers from one place to another for payment 2 a person or thing that carries and passes diseases to others without himself or itself suffering from the disease

carrier bag /'··· ,·/ BrE for SHOPPING BAG

carrier pi·geon /'··· ,··/ also **homing pigeon**– n a PIGEON (a type of bird) that has been trained to carry messages from one place to another

car·rot /'kærət/ n 1 [C;U] (a plant with) a fairly long orange-red pointed root eaten as a vegetable: *Have some more carrots/carrot cake.* 2 [C] infml a promised reward or advantage for doing something: *Which shall it be? The carrot* (=reward) *or the stick* (=punishment)?

car·ry /'kæriʸ/ v -ried, -rying 1 [T] to move while supporting, containing, or taking: *She carried her child on her back.*|*Pipes carry oil across the desert.*|*In the US, the police usually carry* (=wear) *guns.*|(fig.) *Her ability carried her to the top of her profession.* 2 [T] to pass from one person to another; spread: *Many serious diseases are carried by insects.* 3 [T] to bear the weight of; support without moving: *This pillar carries the whole roof.*|(fig.) *His opinion* **carries** *a lot of* **weight** *with her.* (=influences her greatly) 4 [T] to contain: *The report carried a serious warning of future trouble.*|*All the newspapers carried articles about the President's plans.* 5 [T] to have as a usual or necessary result: *Such a crime carries a serious punishment.* 6 [I] to be able to reach a certain distance; cover space: *We couldn't hear her at the back of the hall because her voice doesn't carry (very well).* 7 [I;T usu. pass] a (esp. of a law or plan) to be approved b to cause (esp. a law or plan) to be approved: *The law was carried by 310 votes to 306.* 8 [T no pass.] to win the sympathy, support, or agreement of: *The President carried most of the states and won the election.* 9 [I;T] to put (a number) into the next upright row to the left as when doing addition: *What's 9+5? Write 4 and carry 1.* 10 **be carried away** to be excited: *She got carried away by the music at the concert and started to sing it herself.* 11 **carry the day** to win; be completely successful 12 **carry (something) too far** to do (something) for too long or to too great a degree

carry sthg.↔**forward/over** v adv [T] (when adding up accounts) to move a total from the bottom of one row of figures to the next row for further addition

carry sthg.↔**off** v adv [T] to perform or do (a part, action, duty, etc.) easily and successfully: *She carried off her part in the plan with no difficulty.*

carry on v adv 1 [I] infml to behave in a very

excited and anxious manner: *Stop carrying on!* **2** [I;T (=**carry** sthg. **on**) +*v-ing*] *esp. BrE* to continue, esp. in spite of an interruption or difficulties: *Carry on (doing) the good work!|We'll carry on (with) our conversation tomorrow.*

carry on with sbdy. *v adv prep* [T *no pass.*] *infml* to have a love affair with

carry sthg.↔ **out/through** [T] to fulfill; complete: *He carried out his threat to kill his enemy.|to carry out a plan, order, duty, etc.*

carry through¹ *v adv* **1** [T (**carry** sthg.↔ **through**)] CARRY out: *In spite of a long struggle we succeeded in carrying most of our plans through.* **2** [I] to continue to exist: *feelings that carry through to the present*

carry sbdy. **through**² *v adv; prep* [T] to help to continue in an effective way during (an illness, difficult period, etc.): *His courage carried him through (his illness).*

car·ry·all /'kæriʸˌɔl/ *n* a large bag or small case for carrying clothes and articles necessary for traveling

cart¹ /kɑrt/ *n* **1** a usu. two-wheeled wooden vehicle pulled by an animal, esp. a horse, or by hand, and used for farming or for carrying goods **2 put the cart before the horse** to put things in the wrong order

cart² *v* [T *off, away*] to carry in or as if in a cart: (fig.) *The police carted the prisoners off/away to prison.*

carte blanche /ˌkɑrt 'blɑnʃ, -'blɑntʃ, -'blɑʃ/ n **cartes blanches** /ˌkɑrts 'blɑnʃ, -'blɑntʃ, -'blɑʃ/ *n* [U +*to-v*] *French* full freedom, esp. in politics and in spending money: *She didn't say how I should use the money: she gave me carte blanche.*

car·ti·lage /'kɑrtl̩-ɪdʒ/ *n* [C;U] (a piece of) strong elastic substance found instead of bone in young animals and, esp. around the joints, in older animals: *There is a cartilage in the nose.* –compare GRISTLE

car·tog·ra·phy /kɑr'tɑgrəfiʸ/ *n* [U] the science or art of making maps

car·ton /'kɑrtn/ *n* a box made from stiff paper (CARDBOARD) used for holding goods –see illustration on page 683

car·toon /kɑr'tuʷn/ *n* **1** a humorous drawing, often dealing in an amusing (SATIRICAL) way with something of interest in the news **2** also **animated cartoon**– a MOTION PICTURE film made by photographing a set of drawings –see also COMIC STRIP –**cartoonist** *n*

car·tridge /'kɑrtrɪdʒ/ *n* **1** a usu. metal or paper tube containing an explosive and a bullet for a gun **2** (in a record player) a small case containing the needle (STYLUS) that picks up sound signals from a record **3** →CASSETTE

cart·wheel /'kɑrt-hwiʸl, -wiʸl/ *n* a circular movement in which a person turns over by

---

---

putting the hands on the ground and moving the legs sideways in the air: *to turn a cartwheel* –compare SOMERSAULT –**cartwheel** *v* [I]

carve /kɑrv/ *v* **carved, carving 1** [T] to cut (a special shape) out of (a piece of usu. wood or stone): *The artist carved an interesting decoration from/out of this piece of wood.|What did she carve (for) you?|*(fig.) *She carved (out) a good position for herself in the business.* –compare CHISEL² (1) **2** [I;T] to cut (cooked meat) into (pieces or SLICEs), esp. at a meal: *He carved me a nice piece of meat.*

carve up *v adv* [T] to divide, esp. in a way favorable to oneself

carv·ing /'kɑrvɪŋ/ *n* **1** [C] something made by carving (CARVE (1)) **2** [U] the work, art, or skill of a person who CARVEs

cas·cade¹ /kæˈskeʸd/ *n* **1** a steep high usu. small waterfall, esp. one part of a bigger waterfall **2** anything that seems to pour or flow downwards: *Her hair fell over her shoulders in a cascade of curls.*

cascade² *v* **-caded, -cading** [I;T] to (cause to) pour in quantity: *rainwater cascading down the window*

case¹ /keʸs/ *n* **1** [C] a single example: *It was a case of stupidity, not dishonesty.|Several cases of fever have been reported.* **2** [C] a particular occasion or state of affairs: *They might not offer me much money.* **In that case, I won't work for them.** **3** [C] a combination or set of events needing police or other inquiry or action: *a police case|a case study|a case of robbery with violence* **4** [C] a question to be decided in a court of law: *The case against Mr. Smith will be heard (=*judged) *today.* **5** [C *usu. sing.*] the facts and arguments supporting one side in a disagreement or in a question brought before a court of law: *The police have a clear case against the prisoner.* **6** [C;U] *(in grammar)* (changes in) the form of a word (esp. of a noun, adjective, or PRONOUN) showing its relationship with other words in a sentence: *"Me" is the* **objective case** *of "I."|"Mine" is the* **possessive case** *of "I."* **7 in any case** whatever happens: *In any case, you'll have to be at the station by nine.* **8 (just) in case** so as to be safe if (something happens): *Take your coat (just) in case it rains.|I'll cook plenty of potatoes just in case (they decide to stay for dinner).* **9 in case of** if or when something happens: *In case of fire, ring the bell.*

case² *n* **1** a large box in which goods can be stored or moved: *a case of wine* (=12 bottles) **2** the amount such a box holds: *a case/caseful of money* **3 lower case** (of letters of the alphabet) small: *The letter "e" is lower case.* **4 upper case** (of letters of the alphabet) large (CAPITAL² (2)): *The letter "E" is upper case.*

case³ *v* **cased, casing** [T] **1** to enclose or cover with a case **2** *infml* to examine, esp. with the intention of robbing: *the thief was* **casing the joint.** (=examining the place he intended to rob)

case·ment win·dow /ˌkeʸsmənt 'wɪndoʷ/ also **casement**– *n* a window that opens like a door –compare SASH WINDOW

case·work /'ke^yswɜrk/ n [U] SOCIAL WORK concerned with direct consideration of the difficulties of a particular person, family, etc. –**caseworker** n

cash¹ /kæʃ/ n [U] **1** money in coins and notes, rather than checks: *I don't have any cash on me. Can I pay by check?* **2** *infml* money in any form: *The business has a* **cash flow** *of $50,000 a month.* (=the flow of money payments to or from a firm or business) **3 cash on delivery** →C.O.D.

cash² v [T] to exchange (a check or other order to pay) for CASH¹ (1): *Can you cash this check/money order for me?|Where can I get this cashed?*

cash in v adv [I *on*] to take advantage or profit (from): *They cashed in on the chance to buy some land by the sea.*

cash crop /'· ·/ n a crop produced for sale rather than for use by the grower

cash·ew /'kæʃu^w, kæ'ʃu^w, kə-/ n (a tropical American tree with) a small curved nut

cash·ier /kæ'ʃɪər/ n a person in charge of money receipts and payments in a bank, hotel, restaurant, store, etc.

cash·mere /'kæʒmɪər, 'kæʃ-/ n [U] fine soft wool used esp. for KNITted clothes

cash reg·is·ter /'· ·,··/ n a business machine, esp. used in stores for calculating and recording the amount of each sale and the money received, and sometimes for giving change –see illustration on page 683

cas·ing /'ke^ysɪŋ/ n a protective covering: *This wire has a rubber casing.*

ca·si·no /kə'si^yno^w/ n **-nos** a building used for playing games for money

cask /kæsk/ n (the amount contained in) a barrel-shaped container for holding and storing liquids

cas·ket /'kæskɪt/ n **1** *AmE* for COFFIN **2** a small usu. decorative box for holding jewels, letters, and other small valuable things

cas·se·role /'kæsə,ro^wl/ [C;U] (the food cooked in) a deep usu. covered dish in which food, esp. a combination of foods may be cooked and served: *Would you like some more casserole?*

cas·sette /kə'set, kæ-/ n **1** a container holding MAGNETIC TAPE, which can be fitted into a **cassette player** (=a machine for playing a cassette) or VIDEO (2): *Put another cassette in the* **cassette player.** –compare CARTRIDGE (3); see illustration on page 399 **2** a container with photographic film already in it which can be fitted complete into a camera

cast¹ /kæst/ v **cast, casting** [T] **1** *often lit* to throw or drop: *The fishermen cast their nets into the sea.|*(fig.) *The evening sun casts long shadows.|*(fig.) *This misuse of public money has* **cast doubts on** *the actions of the whole government.* **2** [*off*] to throw off; remove: *He cast off his coat as he entered the room.* **3** to give an acting part to (a person) in (a play): *The director cast me as a mad scientist.* **4** to make (an object) by pouring (hot metal or plastic) into a specially shaped container (MOLD²): *to cast bronze* **5** to make (a vote, SPELL², etc.): *She cast her vote against the new tax.|In the story, the* WITCH *cast a spell on*

him, and made him ill.

cast sbdy./sthg.↔ **aside** v adv [T] to get rid of; DISCARD: *As soon as she became rich she cast aside all her old friends.*

cast sbdy.↔ **away** v adv [T *usu. pass.*] to leave somewhere as the result of a shipwreck: *We were cast away on an island without food or water.* –see also CASTAWAY

cast off v adv **1** [I;T (=**cast** sthg.↔ **off**)] **a** (of a boat or ship) to be set free on the water by a rope being untied **b** to set (a boat or ship) free by untying a rope **2** [T (**cast** sthg.↔ **off**)] to give or throw away (clothes no longer wanted) –see also CAST-OFF

cast sbdy.↔ **out** v adv [T *of*] *lit* to drive out or away; EXPEL: *to cast out the devil*

cast² n **1** [C] the actors in a play, film, etc.: *The cast is ready to start the play.* **2** [C] an act of throwing (esp. a fishing line) **3** [C] a hard stiff protective covering for holding a broken bone in place while it gets better –see illustration on page 201 **4** [S] general shape or quality: *an inquiring cast of mind*

cas·ta·nets /,kæstə'nets/ n [P] a musical instrument made from two shells of hard wood, plastic, etc., which are hit together repeatedly

cast·a·way /'kæstə,we^y/ n a person who escapes from a shipwreck and reaches the shore of a strange country or lonely island –see also CAST¹ **away**

caste /kæst/ n [C;U] (a group resulting from the) division of society based on class differences of wealth, rank, rights, profession, or job: *The caste system is still strong in India.*

cast·er, castor /'kæstər/ n a wheel fixed to the base of a piece of furniture so that it can be easily moved

cas·ti·gate /'kæstə,ge^yt/ v **-gated, -gating** [T] *fml* to punish or scold severely in order to correct

cast·ing /'kæstɪŋ/ n **1** [C] a usu. metal or plastic object made by having been CAST¹ (4) **2** [U] the act of CASTing¹ (3), esp. of actors for a play: *The play was a good one, but the casting was terrible.*

cast-i·ron /,· '··◄/ adj **1** made of CAST IRON **2** *infml* hard; strong; unyielding: *She has a cast-iron stomach; she can eat anything.|a cast-iron excuse*

cast iron /,· '··/ n [U] a hard but easily breakable type of iron

cas·tle /'kæsəl/ n **1** a large strongly-built building or set of buildings made in former times to be defended against attack **2** also **rook**– one of the powerful pieces in the game of CHESS

cast-off /'· ·/ n *infml* an unwanted article of clothing: *She gave her cast-offs to her younger sister.* –see also CAST¹ **off**

cas·tor /'kæstər/ n →CASTER

castor oil /,·· '·◄/ n [U] a yellowish medicinal oil used esp. as a LAXATIVE

cas·trate /'kæstre^yt/ v **-trated, -trating** [T] to remove all or part of the sex organs of (a male animal or person) –compare EMASCULATE –**castration** /kæ'stre^yʃən/ n [C;U]

cas·u·al /'kæʒu^wəl/ adj **1** resulting from

chance; not happening intentionally: *a casual meeting* **2** *informal: casual clothes|a casual host* **3** [A] not serious or thorough: *The casual newspaper reader wouldn't like articles on politics every day.|a casual* (=not close) *friendship* **4** [A] (of workers) employed for a short period of time –**casually** *adv* –**casualness** *n* [U]

cas·u·al·ty /'kæʒuʷəltiʸ, 'kæʒəltiʸ/ *n* **-ties 1** [C] a person hurt in an accident: *There were ten serious casualties in the train crash.|(fig.) The new school was never finished: it was a casualty of the recent spending cuts.* **2** [C] a military person lost through death, wounds, or illness

cat /kæt/ *n* **1** a small animal with soft fur, sharp teeth, and CLAWS (nails), often kept as a pet or in buildings to catch mice and rats: *A young cat is called a kitten.* **2** any of various animals related to this, such as the lion or tiger **3 let the cat out of the bag** *infml* to tell a secret (often unintentionally) **4 rain cats and dogs** *infml* to rain very heavily

cat·a·clysm /'kætə,klɪzəm/ *n fml* a violent and sudden change or event, esp. a serious flood or EARTHQUAKE –**cataclysmic** /,kætə'klɪzmɪk/ *adj*

cat·a·comb /'kætə,koʷm/ *n* [usu. pl.] an underground burial place made up of many passages and rooms

cat·a·log¹ *AmE*||also **-logue** *esp. BrE* /'kætl,ɔg, -,ɑg/ *n* a list of places, names, goods, etc. (often with information about them) put in a special order so that they can be found easily

catalog² *AmE*||also **-logue** *esp. BrE v* **-loged** *or* **-logued, -loging** *or* **-loguing** [T] **1** to make a CATALOG of goods, places, names, etc.): *Can you catalog the furniture you sell and send me a copy?* **2** to enter (a book, place, name, etc.) into a CATALOG

cat·a·lyst /'kætl-ɪst/ *n* [C;U] a substance which, without itself changing, causes chemical activity to quicken: (fig.) *The workers' demand for higher wages was a catalyst which led to important social changes.*

cat·a·pult¹ /'kætə,pʌlt, -,pʊlt/ *n* **1** a machine for throwing heavy stones, balls, etc., used as a weapon in former times **2** *BrE* for SLINGSHOT

catapult² *v* [I;T] to fire from a CATAPULT: *The attackers catapulted stones against the town hall.|(fig.) The car stopped suddenly and I was catapulted through the WINDSHIELD.*

cat·a·ract /'kætə,rækt/ *n* **1** a large waterfall **2** *tech* a diseased growth on the eye causing a slow loss of sight

ca·tas·tro·phe /kə'tæstrəfiʸ/ *n* a sudden, unexpected, and terrible event that causes great suffering, misfortune, or ruin; DISAS-

TER: *The flood was a terrible catastrophe in which many people died.* –**catastrophic** /,kætə'strɑfɪk/ *adj* –**catastrophically** *adv*

catch¹ /kætʃ/ *v* **caught** /kɔt/, **catching 1** [T] to get hold of (something moving in the air): *The dog caught the ball in its mouth.* **2** [T] to trap (esp. an animal) after chasing or hunting; take: *Cats like to catch mice.* **3** [T] to find unexpectedly; discover suddenly or by surprise: *The police caught him stealing a car.* **4** [T] to be in time for: *We had to drive very quickly in order to catch the train.* –opposite **miss 5** [T] to get (an illness); become infected with: *You'll catch (a) cold if you don't put a coat on.* **6** [I;T] to (cause to) become hooked, held, fastened, or stuck: *I caught my dress on a nail.|My skirt (got) caught in the door.* **7** [T] to attract (esp. interest or attention): *I'd like another drink; try to catch the waiter's eye.* (=look at him to attract his attention) **8** [T not *be+v-ing*] to get or notice for a moment: *I caught sight of my old friend in town today.|I thought I caught a smell of burning.* **9** [T not *be+v-ing*] to hear; understand: *I didn't catch what you said. Could you say it again please?* **10** [I;T] to start to burn: *The wood caught fire.*

catch on *v adv* [I] **1** to become popular: *The new song caught on really quickly.* **2** [to] to understand: *His teacher says he catches on quickly in math class.|At last we caught on to what she was doing.*

catch up *v adv* **1** [I;T *with*] to come up from behind; draw level (with): *Will we catch up with Japan in industrial production?|You go ahead and I'll catch up with you later.* (*BrE* also *catch you up later*) **2** [I *on*] to bring or come up to date: *I have to catch up on writing letters tonight so I can't go out.* **3 catch up in a:** very interested in: *caught up in conversation* **b** included in, often against one's wishes; INVOLVED (2) in: *The company seems to be caught up in difficulties.*

catch² *n* **1** [C] an act of seizing and holding a ball **2** [C] (the amount of) something caught: *The boat brought back a big catch of fish.* **3** [C] a hook or other apparatus for fastening something or holding it shut: *The catch on this chain is broken. I can't fasten it.* **4** [C] *infml* a hidden or awkward difficulty: *That house is very cheap; there must be a catch in it somewhere!* **5** [U] a simple game in which two or more people throw a ball to each other: *Let's play catch.*

catch·ing /'kætʃɪŋ/ *adj* [F] *infml* (of a disease) infectious

catch·word /'kætʃwɜrd/ *n* a word or phrase repeated so regularly that it becomes representative of a political party, newspaper, etc.; SLOGAN –see also BUZZWORD

catch·y /'kætʃiʸ/ *adj* **-ier, -iest** easy to remember: *a catchy song*

cat·e·chism /'kætə,kɪzəm/ *n* a set of questions and answers, often in the form of a small book, used for religious instruction in some branches of the Christian church

cat·e·gor·i·cal /,kætə'gɔrɪkəl, -'gɑr-/ *adj* unconditional; wholly fixed; made without any doubt in the mind of the speaker or

---

SPELLING NOTE

Words with the sound /k/, like **cut**, may be spelled **k-**, like **key**, or **qu-**, like **queen**. Words with the sound /s/, like **city**, may be spelled **s-**, like **soon**, or **ps-**, like **psychology**.

writer: *a categorical statement* –**categorically**
*adv: I asked her several times to come, but she
categorically refused.*

cat·e·go·rize ‖also **-rise** *BrE* /'kætəgə,raɪz/ *v*
-rized, -rizing [T *as*] to put in a CATEGORY

cat·e·go·ry /'kætə,gəriᵞ, -,goᵂriᵞ/ *n* **-ries** a
division or class in a system for dividing objects into groups according to their nature

ca·ter /'keᵞtər/ *v* [I;T] to provide and serve
food and drinks, usu. for payment, at a
public or private party rather than a
restaurant: *Who's catering (at) your
daughter's wedding?* –**caterer** *n*

  cater to sbdy./sthg. *AmE*‖**cater for**
sbdy./sthg. *BrE*– *v prep* [T] to take account
of and provide with what is necessary: *Our
newspapers and magazines try to cater to all
opinions.*

cat·er·pil·lar /'kætər,pɪlər, 'kætə,pɪlər/ *n* a
small long many-legged wormlike creature
(LARVA of the BUTTERFLY and other insects)
which feeds on the leaves of plants

cat·fish /'kæt,fɪʃ/ *n* **catfish** *or* **catfishes 1** [C] a
large fish with long fleshy hairlike growths
around the mouth **2** [U] this fish used as
food: *Do you like catfish?*

ca·the·dral /kə'θiᵞdrəl/ *n* the chief church of a
DIOCESE (an area with a BISHOP (1))

cath·ode /'kæθoᵂd/ also **negative pole**– *n* the
part of an electrical instrument (such as a
BATTERY (1)) from which ELECTRONS leave,
represented by the sign [-] –compare ANODE

cathode ray tube /'·· ,· ,·/ *n* →CRT

cath·o·lic /'kæθəlɪk/ *adj fml* (esp. of likings
and interests) general; widespread; broad:
catholic opinions

Catholic *adj,n* (a member) of the ROMAN
CATHOLIC church: *Catholic children/Cath-
olic schools/Is he (a) Catholic or (a) PROT-
ESTANT?* –**Catholicism** /kə'θalə,sɪzəm/ *n* [U]

cat·nap /'kætnæp/ *n infml* a very short light
sleep

cat's eye /'· ·/ *n* a small object fixed in the
middle of a road which shines when lit by car
lights in the dark

cat·sup /'kɛtʃəp, 'kæ-, 'kætsəp/ *n* [U]
→KETCHUP

cat·tle /'kætl/ *n* [P] large four-legged farm
animals, esp. cows, kept for their meat or
milk: *He has twenty* **head of cattle** *on his
farm.*

cat·ty /'kætiᵞ/ *adj* **-tier, -tiest** *derog infml* (esp.
of a woman or her behavior) marked by
hatred or anger that is not openly expressed
–compare SPITEFUL –**cattiness** *n* [U] –**cattily**
adv

caught /kɔt/ *v past tense & participle of* CATCH

cau·li·flow·er /'kɔli,flaᵘər, 'ka-/ *n* [C;U] (the
white part of) a garden vegetable with green
leaves around a large white head of
undeveloped flowers

cause¹ /kɔz/ *n* **1** [C] something which produces an effect; a person, thing, or event that
makes something happen –see REASON
(USAGE) **2** [U] reason: *Don't complain
without (good) cause.* **3** [C] a principle or
movement strongly defended or supported:
She fought for the cause all her life.

cause² *v* **caused, causing** [T] to lead to; be the

cause of: *What caused his illness?/His illness
caused him to miss the game./He often causes
trouble for people./This car has caused me a
lot of trouble.*

cause·way /'kɔzweᵞ/ *n* a raised road or path
esp. across wet ground or water

caus·tic¹ /'kɔstɪk/ *n* [C;U] (any of various
types of) chemical substance able to burn or
destroy (CORRODE) by chemical action

caustic² *adj* **1** able to burn or destroy by
chemical action; CORROSIVE **2** bitter; unpleasant; sour; nasty: *John's always making caus-
tic remarks about other people.*

cau·tion¹ /'kɔʃən/ *n* **1** [U] great care; the act
of paying attention to or of taking care **2** [C] a
spoken warning usu. given by a policeman,
judge, etc., when a person has broken the
law

caution² *v* [T *about*] to warn: *The policeman
said, "I must caution you that anything you
say may be used against you (at your trial)."*

cau·tion·ar·y /'kɔʃə,nɛriᵞ/ *adj [no comp.] fml*
giving advice or a warning

cau·tious /'kɔʃəs/ *adj* careful; paying attention; having or showing CAUTION¹ (1)
–**cautiously** *adv: I opened the door cautiously
so I wouldn't wake the baby.* –**cautiousness** *n*
[U]

cav·al·cade /'kævəl,keᵞd, ,kævəl'keᵞd/ *n*
[+*sing./pl. v*] a ceremonial procession of
riders, vehicles, etc.

cav·a·lier /,kævə'lɪər/ *adj* proud; thoughtless: *I'm annoyed at your cavalier treatment
of him.*

cav·al·ry /'kævəlriᵞ/ *n* [*the* U] (esp. in former
times) soldiers who fight on horseback
–compare INFANTRY

cave /keᵞv/ *n* a deep natural hollow place
either underground, or in the side of a cliff or
hill

cave in *v adv* [I] (of a roof or the covering
over a hollow place) to fall in or down: *The
roof of the old house caved in.*

cave·man /'keᵞvmæn/ *n* **-men** /mɛn/ a person
who lived in a cave in very ancient
(PREHISTORIC) times

cav·ern /'kævərn/ *n* a large deep cave –**cavernous** *adj: a cavernous hole*

cav·i·ar, -are /'kæviᵞ,ɑr, ,kæviᵞ'ɑr/ *n* [U] the
salted eggs (ROE) of various large fish, esp.
the STURGEON, highly regarded as food

cav·i·ty /'kævətiᵞ/ *n* **-ties** a hole or hollow
space in a solid mass: *a cavity in a tooth*

ca·vort /kə'vɔrt/ *v* [I] (esp. of a person) to
jump or dance about noisily –compare CAPER

caw /kɔ/ *n,v* [C;I] (to make) the loud rough
cry of various large birds (such as CROWS¹)

cay·enne pep·per /,kaɪen 'pɛpər, ,keᵞ-/ also
cayenne /,kaɪ'ɛn, ,keᵞ'ɛn◂/– *n* [C;U] (a
powder made from) a type of PEPPER¹ (2)
with long thin very hot-tasting red fruit

CB *abbrev. for:* CITIZEN'S BAND

cc *abbrev. for:* CUBIC CENTIMETER: *a 200 cc
engine*

CCTV *abbrev. for:* CLOSED CIRCUIT TELEVISION

cease /siᵞs/ *v* **ceased, ceasing**
[I;T +*to-v/v-ing*] *fml* to stop (esp. an ac-
tivity): *Cease fire!* (=Stop shooting!) *|At last
they ceased work(ing).* –see also CEASELESS

cease-fire /ˌ· '·, '· ·/ *n* an act of stopping fighting for a long or short period –compare TRUCE

cease·less /ˈsiʸslɪs/ *adj fml* unending; continuous; without ceasing: *ceaseless activity* –**ceaselessly** *adv: The baby cried ceaselessly.*

ce·dar /ˈsiʸdər/ *n* [C;U] (the reddish sweet-smelling wood of) a tall EVERGREEN tree

cede /siʸd/ *v* **ceded, ceding** [T *to*] *fml* to yield (usu. land or a right) to (another country or person), esp. after losing a war: *In 1871 France ceded Alsace–Lorraine to Germany.*

ceil·ing /ˈsiʸlɪŋ/ *n* **1** the inner surface of the top of a room –compare ROOF[1] (1) **2** a usu. official upper limit on wages, rents, etc.

cel·e·brate /ˈsɛləˌbreʸt/ *v* **-brated, -brating 1** [I;T] to mark (an event or special occasion) with public or private rejoicings: *We celebrated the New Year with a party.* **2** [T] to praise in writing, speech, etc. **3** [T] (of a priest) to perform (esp. the holiest part of the Christian religious service called the MASS) solemnly and officially

cel·e·brat·ed /ˈsɛləˌbreʸtɪd/ *adj* [*for*] well-known; famous: *Venice is celebrated for its beautiful buildings.*

cel·e·bra·tion /ˌsɛləˈbreʸʃən/ *n* **1** [U] the act of celebrating (CELEBRATE) **2** [C] an occasion of celebrating

ce·leb·ri·ty /səˈlɛbrətiʸ/ *n* **-ties** a famous person

cel·er·y /ˈsɛləriʸ/ *n* [U] (the greenish-white stems of) a small plant eaten as a vegetable: *He was eating a stick of celery.*

ce·les·tial /səˈlɛstʃəl/ *adj fml* of or belonging to the sky or heaven: *The sun, the stars, and the moon are celestial bodies.*

cel·i·bate /ˈsɛləbɪt/ *adj,n* (a person, esp. a PRIEST or NUN, who is) unmarried and without sexual activity or experience, esp. as the result of a religious promise –**celibacy** *n* [U] /ˈsɛləbəsiʸ/

cell /sɛl/ *n* **1** a small room **a** in a prison for one person or a small number of people **b** in a MONASTERY or CONVENT for one person **2** one small part of a larger whole **3** a very small division of living matter, with one center of activity (NUCLEUS (2)), able alone or with others to perform all the operations necessary for life **4** an apparatus for making a current of electricity by chemical action

cel·lar /ˈsɛlər/ *n* an underground room, usu. used for storing goods: *a wine cellar|Get some potatoes from the cellar, please.* –compare BASEMENT

cel·list /ˈtʃɛlɪst/ *n* a person who plays the CELLO

cel·lo /ˈtʃɛloʷ/ also **violoncello** *fml*– *n* **-los** a four-stringed musical instrument, like the VIOLIN but larger and producing a deeper

sound, that is held between the knees and played with a BOW[3] (2)

cel·lo·phane /ˈsɛləˌfeʸn/ *n* [U] *tdmk* thin transparent material used for wrapping goods

cel·lu·lar /ˈsɛlyələr/ *adj* consisting of CELLs (3)

cel·lu·loid /ˈsɛlyəˌlɔɪd/ *n* [U] *tdmk* a plastic substance made mainly from CELLULOSE, formerly used for making photographic film

cel·lu·lose /ˈsɛlyəˌloʷs/ *n* [U] the material from which the cell walls of plants are made, used in making paper, plastic, many man-made materials, etc.

Cel·si·us /ˈsɛlsiʸəs, -ʃəs/ *n,adj* [A or after *n*] CENTIGRADE: *10° Celsius*

Cel·tic /ˈsɛltɪk, ˈkɛl-/ *adj* of (the languages of) the Celts, a European people who include the Welsh and the Bretons

ce·ment[1] /sɪˈmɛnt/ *n* [U] **1** a gray powder, made from a burned mixture of lime and clay, which becomes hard like stone after having been mixed with water and allowed to dry **2** a thick sticky hard-drying chemical liquid (ADHESIVE) used for filling holes, as in the teeth, or for joining things together

cement[2] *v* [T] to join together or make firm with or as if with CEMENT: (fig.) *Our vacation together cemented our friendship.*

cem·e·ter·y /ˈsɛməˌtɛriʸ/ *n* **-ies** an area of ground, usu. not belonging to a church, set aside for the burial of dead people –compare CHURCHYARD, GRAVEYARD

cen·sor /ˈsɛnsər/ *n* an official who examines printed matter, films, or (sometimes in war) private letters with the power to remove anything offensive or (in war) helpful to the enemy –**censor** *v* [T] –**censorship** *n* [U]

cen·sure[1] /ˈsɛnʃər, -tʃər/ *n fml* [U] the act of blaming, unfavorably judging, or expressing strong disapproval: *a vote of censure on the official.*

censure[2] *v* **-sured, -suring** [T] *fml* to express strong disapproval of; judge severely and unfavorably

cen·sus /ˈsɛnsəs/ *n* **-suses** an official count of a country's total population, with other important information about the people

cent /sɛnt/ *n* 0.01 of certain money standards, such as the dollar

cen·ten·a·ry /sɛnˈtɛnəriʸ, ˈsɛntəˌnɛriʸ/ *n* **-ries** *esp. BrE* for CENTENNIAL

cen·ten·ni·al /sɛnˈtɛniʸəl/ *esp. AmE*‖**centenary** *esp. BrE*– *n* the day or year exactly 100 years after a particular event

cen·ter[1] *AmE*‖**centre** *BrE* /ˈsɛntər/ *n* **1** [C] a middle part or point; point equally distant from all sides; the exact middle, esp. the point around which a circle is drawn: *Although Washington, D.C. is the capital of the United States, it is not at the center of the country.* **2** [C] a point, area, person, or thing that is the most important to an interest, activity, or condition: *a shopping center|He likes to be the center of attention.* **3** [A; *the* S] a middle (MODERATE[1](2)) position, esp. in politics: *The political parties often move to the center just before an election.* –see MIDDLE[2] (USAGE)

SPELLING NOTE

Words with the sound /k/, like **cut**, may be spelled **k-**, like **key**, or **qu-**, like **queen**. Words with the sound /s/, like **city**, may be spelled **s-**, like **soon**, or **ps-**, like **psychology**.

center² *AmE*‖**centre** *BrE* *v* **1** [I;T *on, upon, around*] to (cause to) gather to a center; (cause to) have a center: *Our thoughts centered on the girl who had died.* **2** [T] to place in or at the center: *Center this picture on the wall please.*

center of grav·i·ty /,·· · '···/ *n* that point in any object on which it will balance

Cen·ti·grade /'sentə,greʸd/ also **Celsius**– *n* a scale of temperature in which water freezes at 0° and boils at 100° —compare FAHRENHEIT

cen·ti·me·ter *AmE*‖**centimetre** *BrE* /'sentə ,miʸtər/ *n* (a measure of length equal to) 0·01 meters or about 0·4 inches

cen·tral /'sentrəl/ *adj* **1** [A no comp.] being the center: *This is the central city of the whole area.* **2** at, in, or near the center: *The stores are in a central position in the city.* **3** [A no comp.] chief; main; of greatest importance: *The central aim of this government is social equality.*

central heat·ing /,·· '··/ *n* [U] a system of heating buildings in which heat is produced and controlled at a single point and carried by pipes to the various parts of the building in the form of hot air or water

cen·tral·ize ‖also **-ise** *BrE* /'sentrə,laiz/ *v* **-ized, -izing** [T] to gather (esp. of the controlling power of government) under central control: *Under the old political system power (was) centralized in the hands of one person.* –see also DECENTRALIZE –**centralization** /,sentrələ'zeʸʃən/ *n* [U]

cen·tre /'sentər/ *n,v* **-tred, -tring** *BrE* for CENTER

cen·trif·u·gal /sen'trɪfyəgəl, -fə-/ *adj* tending to move in a direction away from the center: *centrifugal force*

cen·tu·ri·on /sen'tuəriʸən, -'tyuər-/ *n* an army officer of ancient Rome, commanding a company of about 100 men

cen·tu·ry /'sentʃəriʸ/ *n* **-ries 1** a period of 100 years **2** (*sometimes cap.*) one of the 100-year periods counted forwards or backwards from the supposed year of CHRIST's birth: *the twentieth century*

ce·ram·ics /sə'ræmɪks/ *n* [P;U] (articles produced by) the art or practice of making bricks, pots, etc., by shaping pieces of clay and baking until hard –**ceramic** *adj* [A]

ce·re·al /'sɪəriʸəl/ *n* **1** [C] (a plant which is grown to produce) grain for food, such as wheat, rice, etc. **2** [C;U] (a) food made from grain, esp. eaten at breakfast

ce·re·bral /sə'riʸbrəl, 'serə-/ *adj tech* (often of illnesses) of or connected with the brain: (fig.) *a very cerebral person* (showing too much serious thinking)

cer·e·mo·ni·al /,serə'moʷniʸəl/ also **ceremonious**– *adj* marked by or done according to ceremony –**ceremonially** *adv*

cer·e·mo·ni·ous /,serə'moʷniʸəs/ *adj* **1** fond of ceremony and formal behavior; formally polite –see also UNCEREMONIOUS **2** →CEREMONIAL –**ceremoniously** *adv*

cer·e·mo·ny /'serə,moʷniʸ/ *n* **-nies 1** [C] a formal, solemn, and well-established action or set of actions used for marking an important esp. public, social, or religious event: *the wedding ceremony* **2** [U] the special order and formal behavior demanded by custom on particular occasions: *The wedding took place with the usual ceremony.*

cer·tain /'sɜrtn/ *adj* **1** sure; having no doubt: *I'm certain she saw me yesterday.*‖*There's no certain cure for this illness.* **2** [+to-v/(that)] sure to happen: *It's almost certain (that) the senator will lose the next election.* **3** [F +to-v/(that)] (of people) sure: *She's certain to do well on the examination.*‖*Are you certain (that) you'll get there in time?* **4 make certain** to do something in order to be sure: *Make certain (that) you know what time the train leaves.* –see also UNCERTAIN; see SURE¹ (USAGE)

certain² *determiner,pron* **1** (used like **some**, when something is not clearly known or described): *There are certain reasons why I have to say no.* (=I am not going to tell you what my reasons are)‖*Certain questions have never been answered.* **2** some but not a lot: *He makes a certain amount of profit from his business, but he'll never be rich.*

cer·tain·ly /'sɜrtnliʸ/ *adv* **1** without doubt; surely **2** (used as a polite or strong way of answering a question) yes; of course: *"Will you help me?" "Certainly."* **3 certainly not** (as a strong way of answering a question) no; of course not: *"Will you lend me $1000?" "Certainly not!"* –see SURE¹ (USAGE)

cer·tain·ty /'sɜrtntiʸ/ *n* **-ties 1** [U] the state of being certain; freedom from doubt: *I can't say with certainty what my plans are.* **2** [C] a clearly established fact: *Our victory is a certainty.* –see also UNCERTAINty

cer·tif·i·cate /sər'tɪfəkɪt/ *n* an official sheet of paper (DOCUMENT) on which is written or printed a statement made by an official person that a fact or facts are true: *a birth/marriage/death certificate*

certified pub·lic ac·count·ant /,··· ,·· ·'··/ also **CPA**– *n AmE* an ACCOUNTANT who has passed official examinations and received professional recognition

cer·ti·fy /'sɜrtə,fai/ *v* **-fied, -fying** [T] **1** to declare that (something) is correct or true: *The bank certified my accounts.*‖*A* **certified check** is a check given by a bank and which the bank promises is good. **2** [+that] to declare, esp. after some kind of test: *The doctor certified the prisoner healthy.* **3** to give a CERTIFICATE to (someone) declaring successful completion of a course of training for a particular profession: *a certified teacher* –**certification** /,sɜrtəfə'keʸʃən/ *n* [C;U] *He received his certification as a high school English teacher.*

cer·ti·tude /'sɜrtə,tuʷd, -,tyuʷd/ *n fml* [U +that] the state of being or feeling certain; freedom from doubt

cer·vix /'sɜrvɪks/ *n* **-vices** /-və,siʸz/ or **-vixes** *tech* a narrow necklike opening into an organ of the body, esp. into the WOMB –**cervical** /'sɜrvɪkəl/ *adj*

ce·sar·e·an, -ian /sɪ'zɛəriʸən/ *n* →CAESAREAN

ces·sa·tion /sɛ'seʸʃən/ *n fml* a short pause or

a stop; act of ceasing: *a cessation of fighting* (=with an enemy)

cess·pool /'sɛs-puʷl/ *n* an underground container or hole, in which a house's waste, esp. body waste (SEWAGE), is gathered

cf. *written abbrev. said as:* compare

chafe /tʃeʸf/ *v* **chafed, chafing 1** (to cause to) become sore, painful, or uncomfortable by rubbing: *Her skin chafes easily.*|*Her shoes chafed the skin on her feet.* **2** [I] to become or be impatient, or annoyed: *He chafed at the delay.*

chaff /tʃæf/ *n* [U] the outer seed covers (HUSKS), separated from the grain

chain¹ /tʃeʸn/ *n* **1** [C;U] (a length of) usu. metal rings, connected to or fitted into one another, used for fastening, supporting, decorating, etc.: *The bridge was supported by heavy iron chains hanging from two towers.*|*a lot of chain* **2** [C] a number of connected things, such as events, shops, restaurants, mountains, etc.: *a chain store* (=group of shops under one ownership)|*chain of events* **3 in chains** kept in prison or as a slave

chain² *v* [T *up*] to limit the freedom of with or as if with a chain: *The dogs were chained up for the night.*|*His job made him feel chained down.* –opposite **unchain**

chain re·ac·tion /'·· ·,··, ,· ·'··/ *n* a number of events or chemical changes in such a way related to each other that each causes the next

chain-smoke /'·· ·/ *v* **-smoked, -smoking** [I;T] to smoke (cigarettes) continually –**chain-smoker** *n*

chair¹ /tʃɛər/ *n* **1** [C] a piece of furniture on which one person may sit, which has typically a back, seat, usu. four legs, and sometimes arms –see also ARMCHAIR, WHEELCHAIR **2** [C] the office, position, or official seat of someone, such as a chairperson, in charge of a meeting *She holds the chair of chemistry in that university.* **3** [*the* S] *infml* for ELECTRIC CHAIR

chair² *v* [T] to be chairperson of a (meeting): *I wouldn't want to chair that committee. The members don't work well together.*

chair·man /'tʃɛərmən/ *also* **chairperson, chairwoman** (*fem.*)– *n* **-men** /mən/ a person **a** in charge of a meeting: *one of our most experienced chairmen* **b** who directs the work of a committee, department, etc.: *He was elected (the) chairman of the education committee.*

USAGE **Chairman** can be used for both men and women, but many people prefer to use **chairperson**, esp. when the sex of the person is not known.

chair·man·ship /'tʃɛərmən,ʃɪp/ *n* [*usu. sing.*] the rank, position, or period in office of chairman

chair·per·son /'tʃɛər,pɜrsən/ *n* **-persons** a

SPELLING NOTE
Words with the sound /ʃ/, like **chauffeur**, may be spelled **sh-**, like **shop**.

CHAIRMAN *or* CHAIRWOMAN –see CHAIRMAN (USAGE)

chair·wom·an /'tʃɛər,wumən/ *n* **-women** /,wimin/ a woman in charge of a meeting –see CHAIRMAN (USAGE)

cha·let /ʃæ'leʸ, 'ʃæleʸ/ *n* **1** a usu. wooden house with a steeply sloping roof, esp. common in Switzerland **2** a small house (BUNGALOW) or hut used esp. for vacationing –compare LODGE (2)

chal·ice /'tʃælɪs/ *n* a gold or silver decorative cup, used esp. to hold wine in Christian religious services

chalk¹ /tʃɔk/ *n* **1** [U] a type of soft white rock, used for making lime and various writing materials **2** [C;U] (a piece of) this material, white or colored, used for writing or drawing: *The teacher wrote on the (black)board with a piece of chalk/with chalk.* –**chalky** *adj* **-ier, -iest**

chalk² *v* [I;T] to write, mark, or draw with chalk

chalk sthg.↔ up *v adv* [T] *infml* to succeed in getting (esp. points in a game): *Our team has chalked up another victory.*

chal·lenge¹ /'tʃæləndʒ/ *v* **-lenged, -lenging** [T] **1** [*to*] to call (someone) to compete against one, esp. in a fight, game, etc.: *I challenged him to a game of tennis.*|(fig.) *a challenging* (=difficult) *problem* **2** to question the lawfulness or rightness of: *She challenged the justice of the new law.* –**challenger** *n*

challenge² *n* **1** [C +*to-v*] an invitation to compete in a fight, game, etc.: *He accepted his friend's challenge to swim across the river.* **2** [C;U] (something with) the quality of demanding competitive action, interest, or thought: *Building the bridge in a month was a real challenge.*

cham·ber /'tʃeʸmbər/ *n* **1** *old use* a room, esp. a bedroom **2** [*often pl.*] a room set aside for a special purpose: *Cases not heard (dealt with) in court are sometimes heard in the judge's chambers.* **3** an enclosed space, esp. in a body or machine: *The heart has four chambers.* **4** [*the* S] (the hall used for meetings of) a usu. elected law-making body: *In Britain the upper chamber of PARLIAMENT is the House of Lords, the lower the House of Commons.* **5 chamber of commerce** a group of businessmen and businesswomen, working together for the purpose of improving trade

cham·ber·maid /'tʃeʸmbər,meʸd/ *n* a female servant employed to clean bedrooms, esp. in a hotel

chamber mu·sic /'·· ,··/ *n* music written for a small group of instruments and suitable for performance in a private home or small hall

cha·me·leon /kə'miʸlyən, kə'miʸliʸən/ *n* a small four-legged animal with a long tail (LIZARD), which can change its color to match its surroundings

cham·pagne /ʃæm'peʸn/ *n* [C;U] a white wine containing a lot of bubbles, usu. drunk on special occasions: *True champagne comes only from an area of France, but wines with bubbles from other places are often called champagne, too.*

cham·pi·on¹ /'tʃæmpiʸən/ n **1** also **champ** /tʃæmp/ infml– a person or animal who has won competitions of courage, strength, or skill: a tennis champion **2** a person who fights for, supports strongly, or defends a principle, movement, person, etc.: a champion of women's rights/of the poor

champion² v [T] to fight for, support strongly, or defend (a principle, movement, person, etc.)

cham·pi·on·ship /'tʃæmpiʸən,ʃɪp/ n **1** a competition held to find the CHAMPION¹ (1) **2** the position, title, rank, or period of being CHAMPION¹ (1)

chance¹ /tʃæns/ n **1** [U] the force that seems to make things happen without cause or reason; luck; good or bad fortune: Chance plays an important part in many card games.|It happened by chance. **2** [C;U] (that)/of] (a) possibility; likelihood that something will happen: You'd have more chance of catching the train if you took a bus to the station instead of walking.|Is there any chance that our team will win?|(infml) **Chances are** (=it is likely) she has already heard the news. **3** [C+to-v] a favorable occasion; OPPORTUNITY: I never miss a chance to play football. **4** [C] a risk: The rope might break, but that's a chance I'll have to take! **5 on the (off) chance** in view of the (unlikely) possibility; in the hope: We went to the game on the (off) chance of seeing Paul there.

USAGE Compare **chance** and **opportunity**: You can have a **chance** or **opportunity** to do something, which means that it is luckily possible for you at a favorable moment: I had the **chance/opportunity** to visit Boston.|I had no **opportunity/chance** to see him. But we can also say There is a **chance** (=possibility) that I will see him, and **opportunity** could not be used here.

chance² v chanced, chancing [not be+v-ing] **1 chance it** infml to take a chance of success, though failure is possible: It was cloudy outside, but she chanced it without her raincoat. **2** [T+v-ing] to take a chance with; risk: You shouldn't chance all your money at once. **3** [I+to-v] fml to take place by chance; happen by accident: She chanced to be in the park when I was there.

chance on/upon sbdy./sthg. v prep [T] fml to meet by chance; find by chance

chance³ adj [A] accidental; unplanned: a chance meeting

chan·cel·lor /'tʃænsələr/ n **1** the head of some universities **2** (often cap.) a state or law official of high rank

chanc·y /'tʃænsiʸ/ adj -ier, -iest infml risky; uncertain as to the result: That was a chancy thing to do. You could have been killed.

chan·de·lier /ˌʃændə'lɪər/ n a usu. large decorative holder for electric lights or candles, usu. hanging from the CEILING

change¹ /tʃeⁱndʒ/ v changed, changing **1** [I;T] to make or become different: In fall the leaves change from green to brown.|Nothing will change him; he will always be the same.|The weather's changing. I think it's going to rain. **2** [T] to go from one to

another: He changed trains at Central Station.|Would you mind **changing places** (=exchanging positions) with me so that I can be nearer to the door? **3** [I;T into, out of] to put (different clothes) on oneself: She changed into her new dress.|She changed her dress.|I'm just going to change. **4** [T] to put (fresh clothes or coverings) on (a baby, child, bed, etc.): Did you change (the sheets on) your bed this week?|The baby needs changing. **5** [T] to give (money) in exchange for money of a different type: Where can I change my American money (for foreign money)?|Can you change a dollar (for me)? (=give me CHANGE² (5) for a dollar) **6** [T for] BrE for EXCHANGE² –compare EXCHANGE

change into v prep **1** [T (=**change into** sbdy./sthg.)] to become (something different): The next morning, the water had changed into ice. **2** [T (=**change** sbdy./sthg. **into** sbdy./sthg.)] to cause to become (something different): The scientist tried to change iron into gold.

change over v adv [I from, to] to make a complete change: The United States may change over to the metric system. –see also CHANGEOVER

change² n **1** [C;U] (an example of) the act or result of changing: If we are to avoid defeat we need a change of leadership.|The doctor said the woman had taken a **change for the worse** and was seriously ill.|a change in the weather **2** [C usu. sing.] something different done for variety, excitement, etc.: Let's go to a restaurant **for a change**.|She's on vacation; she needed a change (from work). **3** [C of] something new and fresh used in place of something else: He took a change of clothes with him, because he was going to stay until the next day.|Your car needs an oil change. **4** [U] the money returned when the amount given is more than the cost of the goods being bought: If it cost 25 cents and you gave her a dollar you should get 75 cents change. **5** [U] **a** coins of low value: How much do you have **in change**? **b** money in low-value coins or bills exchanged for a coin or bill of higher value: Can you give me change for/of a dollar? **6** [C;U] **change of life** → MENOPAUSE

change·a·ble /'tʃeⁱndʒəbəl/ adj (esp. of weather) likely to change; variable –**changeability** /ˌtʃeⁱndʒə'bɪlətiʸ/ n [U]

change·o·ver /'tʃeⁱn,dʒoʊvər/ n a change from one activity or system of working to another; an important change –see also CHANGE¹ over

chan·nel¹ /'tʃænl/ n **1** the deepest part of a river, harbor, or sea passage **2** a way, course, or passage for liquids. **3** a narrow sea passage connecting two seas or oceans: The English Channel separates England and France. **4** the shows, news, advertisements, etc., broadcast on a particular television station: Turn to the other channel. I don't like this show. **5** any course or way along which information travels: You should go through the official channels to get help.

channel² v **-l-** AmE‖**-ll-** BrE [T] **1** to direct: I decided to channel my abilities into some-

thing useful **2** to form a CHANNEL¹ (1,2) in

chant¹ /tʃænt/ *v* [I;T] **1** to sing (words) to a CHANT² (1) **2** to continuously repeat (words) in time: *The crowd chanted "Down with the government."*

chant² *n* [C;S] **1** an often-repeated tune, often with many words sung on one note, esp. used in religious services **2** words continuously repeated in time: *The crowd's chant was "More jobs! More money!"*

Cha·nu·kah /'hɑnəkə, 'xɑ-/ *n* [C;S] →HANUKKAH

cha·os /'keⁱɑs/ *n* [S;U] a state of complete and thorough disorder and confusion: *After the power failure, the city was in chaos.*

cha·ot·ic /keⁱ'ɑtɪk/ *adj* in a state of complete disorder and confusion; confused: *The traffic in the city was chaotic.* **–chaotically** *adv*

chap¹ /tʃæp/ *n infml esp. BrE* a man or boy; FELLOW¹ (1)

chap² *v* **-pp-** [I;T] to (cause to) become sore, rough, and cracked: *chapped hands*

chap·el /'tʃæpəl/ *n* **1** [C] a place, such as a small church, a room in a hospital, prison, etc., used for Christian worship –compare PARISH church **2** [U] the religious services held in such a place: *He goes to chapel every Sunday night.*

chap·er·on¹, **-one** /'ʃæpə,roʷn/ *n* (esp. formerly) an older person (usu. a woman) who goes with young people (or, in some countries, a young unmarried woman), in public, and is responsible for their behavior: *Her parents are going to be chaperons at the dance on Saturday.*

chaperon², **-one** *v* **-oned, -oning** [I;T] to act as a CHAPERON to (a person or people)

chap·lain /'tʃæplɪn/ *n* a priest or other religious minister responsible for the religious needs of a club, a college, a part of the armed forces, etc. –see PRIEST (USAGE)

chap·ter /'tʃæptər/ *n* **1** one of the main divisions of a book or long article, usu. having a number or title: (fig.) *The Civil War was a sad chapter in American history.* **2 chapter and verse** the exact details: *She told me chapter and verse where I could find the information.* **3** *esp. AmE* a local branch of an organization

char /tʃɑr/ *v* **-rr-** [I;T] to (cause to) become black by burning: *There was nothing left but a few charred remains.*

char·ac·ter /'kærɪktər/ *n* **1** [C;U] the qualities which make a person, thing, place, etc., different from another; nature: *a man of good character|When they tore down the old houses the whole character of the neighborhood was changed.* –compare CHARACTERISTIC², PERSONALITY (1), REPUTATION **2** [U] moral strength; honesty; INTEGRITY (1): *a woman of great character* **3** [C] a person in a book, play, etc.: *I find all the characters in his new play very amusing.* **4** [C]

SPELLING NOTE
Words with the sound /ʃ/, like **chauffeur**, may be spelled **sh-**, like **shop**.

infml a person as stated: *Some character just walked up and stole her bag.|He's a strange character.* **5** [C] *infml* an odd or humorous person: *She's a real character; she makes everyone laugh.* **6** [C] a letter, mark, or sign used in writing and printing: *The characters in Chinese writing look like small pictures.* **7 in/out of character** like/unlike one's usual nature

char·ac·ter·is·tic¹ /ˌkærɪktə'rɪstɪk/ *adj* typical; representing a person's or thing's usual character: *characteristic generosity* **–characteristically** *adv*

characteristic² *n* [*of*] a special and easily recognized quality of someone or something: *A characteristic of this animal is its ability to live for a long time without water.* –compare CHARACTER (1)

char·ac·ter·ize ‖also **-ise** *BrE* /'kærɪktə,raɪz/ *v* **-ized, -izing** [T] **1** to be typical of: *This kind of behavior characterizes the criminal mind.* **2** [*as*] to describe the character of: *She characterized him as lazy and selfish.* **–characterization** /ˌkærɪktərə'zeⁱʃən/ *n* [C;U]

cha·rade /ʃə'reⁱd/ *n* an act or position which is easily seen to be false or foolish

char·coal /'tʃɑrkoʷl/ *n* [U] the black substance made by burning wood in a closed container with little air, used as FUEL or for drawing with

charge¹ /tʃɑrdʒ/ *v* **charged, charging 1** [I;T] to ask in payment: *How much do you charge for your eggs?|The hotel charged me $30 for a room for the night.* –see COST (USAGE) **2** [T] to record (something) to someone's debt: *Don't forget to charge the money to my account.|I'll charge the ticket and pay later.* **3** [I;T *at, towards,* etc.] to rush in or as if in an attack: *Suddenly the wild animal charged at us.|The children charged out of school.* **4** [T *with*] to bring a CHARGE² (4) against; ACCUSE: *He was charged with stealing the jewels.|He was charged last night.* **5** [T+*to-v*] *fml* to command; give as a responsibility: *She charged me to look after her son.* **6** [I;T] to (cause to) take in the correct amount of electricity: *Does your car BATTERY (1) charge easily?*

charge² *n* **1** [C] the price asked or paid for goods or a service: *This store has a charge for delivery service.|What are the charges in this hotel?* **2** [U *of*] care; control; responsibility: *I'm in charge of this department.|She took charge of the family business when her father died.* **3** [C] *fml* a person or thing for which one is responsible: *I became my uncle's charge after my father's death.* **4** [C] a spoken or written statement blaming a person for breaking the law or for doing something morally wrong: *He was arrested on a charge of murder.|The police brought a charge of murder against him.|He faces a charge of murder.* **5** [C] a rushing forceful attack **6** [C] the amount of explosive to be fired at one time **7** [C;U] (a quantity of) electricity put into a BATTERY (1) or other electrical apparatus

charge ac·count /'· ·,·/ *n AmE*‖**credit**

account *BrE*– an account with a store which allows one to take goods home at once and pay for them later

charge card /ˈ· ·/ also **charge plate** /ˈ· ·/– *AmE* a small esp. plastic card usu. provided by one store which allows one to obtain goods the cost being charged to one's account and paid later –compare CREDIT CARD

char·i·ot /ˈtʃæriʸət/ *n* a two-wheeled horse-drawn vehicle with no seats, used in ancient times in battles and races –**charioteer** /ˌtʃæriʸəˈtɪər/ *n*

cha·ris·ma /kəˈrɪzmə/ *n* [U] the special charm or personal qualities which cause a person to win and keep the interest and love of other people: *a leader who has charisma* –**charismatic** /ˌkærɪzˈmætɪk/ *adj*

char·i·ty /ˈtʃærəṭiʸ/ *n* -**ties 1** [U] sympathy and kindness; the feeling of generosity, esp. towards poor people: *A feeling of charity made her give food to the old woman.*|*She did it out of* (=because of) **charity. 2** [C] a society or organization that gives help to the poor: *The Red Cross is an international charity.* –**charitable** /ˈtʃærəṭəbəl/ *adj*: *a charitable act/organization* –see also UNCHARITABLE

char·la·tan /ˈʃɑrlətən, -lətn/ *n derog* a person who deceives others by falsely claiming to have a special knowledge or skill: *He's not a doctor, he's a charlatan; he knows nothing about medicine.*

charm¹ /tʃɑrm/ *n* **1** [C;U] the power or ability to please, win over, or delight: *She has a lot of charm; she's very likeable.*|*This town has a charm you couldn't find in a big city.*|*He needed all his charm to persuade her he was right.* **2** [C] an object worn to keep away evil or bring good luck **3** [C] an act, expression, or phrase believed to have magical powers **4 work like a charm** to happen or take place with complete success

charm² *v* [T] **1** to please; win over; delight: *The child charms everyone.* **2** to control (something) as if by magic: *It seemed as if he had* **a charmed life;** *nothing bad ever happened to him.* –**charmer** *n*

charm·ing /ˈtʃɑrmɪŋ/ *adj* very pleasing; delightful: *What a charming young man!* –**charmingly** *adv*

chart¹ /tʃɑrt/ *n* **1** (a sheet of paper with) information written or drawn in the form of a picture, GRAPH, etc.: *a weather chart* **2** a map, esp. a detailed map of a sea area pular: *That record has been on the charts for weeks.*

chart² *v* [T] to make a map or CHART of; show or record on a chart: (fig.) *The book charts her rise to fame as an actress.*

char·ter¹ /ˈtʃɑrtər/ *n* **1** [C] a written or printed signed statement from a ruler, government, etc., giving rights, freedoms, etc., to the people, an organization, or a person: *The rights of the citizens are governed* **by charter. 2** [A;U] the practice of hiring or renting cars, buses, planes, etc., for special use: *This travel company specializes in charter flights.*

charter² *v* [T] **1** to give a CHARTER¹ (1) to (a country, firm, organization, etc.) **2** to hire or rent (a plane, train, bus, etc.) for a special use

charter mem·ber /ˌ·· ˈ···/ *n AmE* an original member of a society or organization: *She's a charter member of the club.*

char·y /ˈtʃɛəriʸ, ˈtʃæriʸ/ *adj* -**ier**, -**iest** [F *of*] *fml* careful; unwilling to take risks; CAUTIOUS: *The children are chary of crossing a busy main road.* –**charily** *adv*

chase¹ /tʃeʸs/ *v* **chased, chasing 1** [I;T] to follow rapidly in order to catch: *The cat chased the mouse but could not catch it.*|(fig.) *Why do people chase (after) material possessions?* **2** [T] to cause to leave or run away: *They chased the dog away.* **3** [I] to run; hurry: *The children are always* **chasing in and out/chasing around.**

chase² *n* **1** an act of chasing something: *There was a long chase before the criminal was caught.* **2 give chase** to chase someone: *The police saw the thief running up the street and gave chase in their car.*

chasm /ˈkæzəm/ *n* a very deep crack or opening in the surface of the earth or ice: (fig.) *There was a (deep) political chasm between the two countries which nearly led to war.*

chas·sis /ˈʃæsiʸ, ˈtʃæ-/ *n* **chassis** /ˈʃæsiʸz, ˈtʃæ-/ the framework on which the body and working parts of a vehicle, radio, etc. are fastened or built

chaste /tʃeʸst/ *adj* pure in word, thought, and deed, esp. without sexual activity –**chastely** *adv*

chas·ten /ˈtʃeʸsən/ *v* [T] *fml* to make (a person or behavior) pure; cause to improve: *He was chastened by the accident; he had nearly died.*

chas·tise /tʃæˈstaɪz, ˈtʃæstaɪz/ *v* -**tised, -tising** [T] *fml* to punish or blame severely, esp. by beating –**chastisement** *n* [C;U]

chas·ti·ty /ˈtʃæstəṭiʸ/ *n* [U] (esp. of young women) the state of being sexually pure: *Chastity before marriage is still demanded in some societies.* –compare VIRGINITY

chat¹ /tʃæt/ *v* -**tt-** [I *about,away*] to talk in a friendly familiar informal manner: *The two friends sat in a corner and chatted (away) about the weather.*

chat² *n* a friendly informal conversation

châ·teau , cha- /ʃæˈtoʷ/ *n* -**teaus** or -**teaux** /ʃæˈtoʷz, -ˈtoʷ/ *French* a castle or large country house in France

chat·tel /ˈtʃæṭl/ *n tech or fml* **1** an article of movable property **2** (esp. in former times) a slave

chat·ter¹ /ˈtʃæṭər/ *v* [I] **1** [*away, on, about*] (of people) to talk rapidly and at length, usu. about something unimportant: *The teacher told the children to stop chattering in class.*|*The monkeys were chattering away in the trees.* **2** (of the teeth or machines) to knock together, esp. through cold or fear: *I was so cold my teeth were chattering.* –**chatterer** *n*

chat·ter² *n* [U] **1** rapid informal unimportant conversation **2** a rapid knocking sound made by teeth, machines, etc.: *the chatter of the* MACHINE-GUN

chat·ter·box /ˈtʃæṭərˌbɑks/ *n infml* a person,

esp. a child, who talks a lot

chat·ty /'tʃætiʸ/ *adj* **-tier, -tiest** *infml* fond of talking: *a chatty letter|He's a friendly, chatty sort of person.*

chauf·feur /'ʃoʷfər, ʃoʷ'fɜr/ **chauffeuse** /ʃoʷ'fuz, ʃoʷ'fɜz/ *fem.–* ɪn *n* a person employed to drive someone's car –**chauffeur** *v* [I;T]

chau·vin·ism /'ʃoʷvə,nɪzəm/ *n* [U] **1** very great and often blind admiration of one's country; proud belief that one's country is politically, morally, and militarily better than all others **2** unreasoned belief that the sex to which one belongs is better than the other sex: *People who support equal rights for women fight against* **male chauvinism** *wherever it appears.*

chau·vin·ist /'ʃoʷvənɪst/ *n,adj* (a person or organization) favoring, feeling, or showing CHAUVINISM: *chauvinist government|Her husband's such a chauvinist that he tries to tell her how to vote.* –**chauvinistic** /,ʃoʷvə'nɪstɪk/ *adj* –**chauvinistically** *adv*

cheap¹ /tʃiʸp/ *adj* **1** low in price; costing little: *Fresh vegetables are very cheap in the summer.|Bread is cheap in this store because they bake it themselves.* **2** charging low prices: *This is the cheapest restaurant in town.* –compare DEAR¹ **3** of poor quality; SHODDY: *Her shoes looked cheap to me.* **4** needing little effort: *The army won a cheap victory over an enemy who had few guns and soldiers.* **5 feel cheap** *infml* to feel ashamed: *I felt cheap because I'd lied to my friend.* –**cheaply** *adv* –**cheapness** *n* [U]

cheap² *adv* **1** at a very low price: *I was very lucky to get it so cheap.* **2** *infml* in a way that lowers one's worth: *I wish she wouldn't act so cheap.*

cheap·en /'tʃiʸpən/ *v* [T] to make (esp. oneself) less popular or good: *By your dishonesty you've cheapened yourself in everyone's opinion.*

cheap·skate /'tʃiʸpskeʸt/ *n derog esp. AmE* a person who spends or gives unwillingly: *He's such a cheapskate he won't take his wife out to dinner on her birthday.*

cheat¹ /tʃiʸt/ *v* **1** [I *at*] to act dishonestly or deceitfully to win an advantage esp. in a game: *He always cheats at cards; I never play with him.|to cheat on an examination* **2** [T *out of*] to take from (someone) unfairly, dishonestly, or deceitfully: *He cheated the old woman (out of her money) by making her sign a paper she didn't understand.* **3** [T] *lit* to avoid or escape as if by deception: *The swimmers cheated death in spite of the storm.*

cheat² *n* a person who cheats; dishonest person

check¹ /tʃɛk/ *n* **1** [C *on*] an examination to make certain that something is correct: *a check on the quality of all goods leaving the factory* **2** [S] a stop; control; RESTRAINT:

SPELLING NOTE
Words with the sound /ʃ/, like **chauffeur**, may be spelled **sh-**, like **shop**.

We've kept the disease **in check** *for a year now.* **3** [C] *AmE|***tick** *BrE–* a mark (usu. ✓) put against something, such as an answer, name on a list, etc. to show that it is correct or the one of several chosen: *Check "yes" or "no" to answer the questions.* **4** [C] a receipt; ticket or object for claiming something: *I've lost the check for my coat.* **5** [C] *AmE* a bill at a restaurant –see illustration on page 581 **6** [C;U] a pattern of squares **7** [U] (in CHESS) the position of the king when under direct attack from an opponent's piece(s) **8** [C] *AmE|***cheque** *BrE* (a written order on) a small printed sheet of paper supplied by a bank used to pay someone a stated sum of money; *I always pay bills* **by check.***|My checkbook has two checks left.* **9 a blank check** *infml* full freedom to do something, esp. to spend money; CARTE BLANCHE: *I had/was given a blank check to buy books for the library.*

check² *v* **1** [I;T +*that*] to test, examine, or mark to see if something is correct; make sure; VERIFY: *Have you checked the examination papers yet, sir?|When I checked my shopping list, I found I'd forgotten to buy eggs.|"Is the baby asleep?" "I'll just go and check."* **2** [T] to find out and note: *He checked the temperature every morning before leaving home.* **3** [T] to stop; control; hold back; RESTRAIN: *A change of wind checked the fire.* –see also UNCHECKED **4** [T] (in CHESS) to move one's pieces so as to put (the opponent's king) under direct attack **5** [T *off*] *AmE|***tick** *BrE–* to show that something (an answer, name on a list, etc.) is correct by marking it with a CHECK¹ (3) **6** [T] to leave something (esp. a coat) somewhere to be kept safe: *They checked their coats before taking their seats in the theater.*

check in *v adv* [I *at, to*] to report one's arrival, as at a hotel desk, an airport, etc.: *Please check in at the airport an hour before your plane leaves.* –see also CHECK² **out** (1) –see illustration on page 17

check out *v adv* **1** [I *of*] to leave a hotel after paying the bill –see also CHECK² **in** **2** [I;T (=**check** sbdy./sthg. ↔ **out**)] *infml* **a** to find out whether something is true or correct by making inquiries: *to check out his story* **b** to be found to be true after inquiries have been made: *How does his story check out with the facts?* **3** [T *of*] *esp. AmE* to have the removal of (a thing) recorded: *She checked the books out of the library.*

check sthg.↔ **over** *v adv* [T] to examine: *Please check this piece of work over and tell me if you see any mistakes.*

check up on sbdy./sthg. *v adv prep* [T] *infml* to make thorough inquiries about: *The police were checking up on her so she left the country.*

checked /tʃɛkt/ *adj* having a pattern of squares (CHECKS¹ (6)): *Do you like these checked curtains?*

check·ered *AmE|***chequered** *BrE* /'tʃɛkərd/ *adj* marked by changes of good and bad luck; varying: *He's had a checkered past, but now he's determined to be successful.*

check·ers /'tʃɛkərz/ n AmE‖**draughts** BrE– [U] a game played by two people, each with 12 round pieces on a **checkerboard** of 64 squares.

checking ac·count /'·· ·ˌ·/ AmE‖**current account** BrE– n a bank account from which money can be taken out by check –compare SAVINGS ACCOUNT

check·list /'tʃɛkˌlɪst/ n a complete list of books, goods, voters, etc., so arranged as to provide an easy means of finding information about these things; CATALOG[1]

check·mate[1] /'tʃɛkmeɪt/ n [C;U] **1** (in CHESS) the position of a king when under direct attack from an opponent's pieces so that escape is impossible: *The game ended with a checkmate.* **2** (a) complete defeat

checkmate[2] v **-mated, -mating** [T] **1** (in CHESS) to win the game with a CHECKMATE **2** to stop; completely defeat

check·out coun·ter /'tʃɛk-aʊt ˌkaʊntər/ AmE‖**checkout** BrE– n the place in a supermarket where one shows the goods one has chosen and pays for them –see also CHECK OUT

check·point /'tʃɛkpɔɪnt/ n a place where a CHECK[1] (1) is made on people, traffic, goods, etc.: *There are a number of checkpoints on the border between East and West Berlin.*

check·room /'tʃɛk-ruːm, -rʊm/ n esp. AmE **also cloakroom**– a room, as in a theater, where hats, coats, bags, etc. may be left for a short time

check·up /'tʃɛk-ʌp/ n infml a general medical examination: *You don't look well. Why don't you go for a checkup?*

ched·dar /'tʃɛdər/ n [U] (*often cap.*) a firm smooth usu. yellowish cheese

cheek /tʃiːk/ n **1** [C] a fleshy part on either side of the face below the eye, esp. in human beings: *Her cheeks were red after she ran up the stairs.* **2** [U] infml bold disrespectful rude behavior **3** **-cheeked** having cheeks of the stated kind: *red-cheeked*

cheek·bone /'tʃiːkboʊn/ n the bone above the cheek, just below the eyes

cheek·y /'tʃiːkiː/ adj **-ier, -iest** infml disrespectful; rude **–cheekiness** n [U]

cheep /tʃiːp/ v,n [I;S] (to make) the weak high noise made by young birds

cheer[1] /tʃɪər/ n **1** [C] a shout of praise, encouragement, etc.: *I heard the cheers of the crowd, and I knew that our team was winning.* **2** [U] happiness of mind; good spirits; gaiety

cheer[2] v **1** [I] to shout in praise, approval, or support **2** [T on] to encourage by shouting approval or support: *The crowd cheered their team (on).* **3** [T] to give encouragement or hope to: *The President was cheered as he was driven through the streets.*

cheer up v adv [I;T (=**cheer** sbdy. **up**)] infml to (cause to) become happier or more cheerful: *Cheer up! The news isn't too bad.*

cheer·ful /'tʃɪərfəl/ adj happy; in good spirits: *a cheerful person/house* **–cheerfully** adv **–cheerfulness** n [U]

cheer·ing /'tʃɪərɪŋ/ adj encouraging; gladdening: *the cheering news that her opera-*

tion had been a success

cheer·i·o /ˌtʃɪəriˈoʊ/ interj BrE infml goodbye

cheer·lead·er /'tʃɪərˌliːdər/ n (esp. in the US) a person who calls for and directs cheering, as at a football game

cheer·less /'tʃɪərlɪs/ adj dull; without comfort; saddening: *a cheerless rainy day*

cheers /tʃɪərz/ interj infml, esp. BrE (when drinking with someone) good health

cheer·y /'tʃɪəriː/ adj **-ier, -iest** bright; cheerful: *He gave us a cheery greeting.* **–cheerily** adv **–cheeriness** n [U]

cheese /tʃiːz/ n [C;U] a soft or firm solid food made from pressed and sometimes ripened milk solids (CURDS): *cheese made from the milk of cows, sheep, or goats|a very good cheese*

cheese·burg·er /'tʃiːzˌbɜrgər/ n (esp. in the US) a HAMBURGER made with cheese on top

cheese·cake /'tʃiːzkeɪk/ n [C;U] a cake made from a mixture containing soft or unripe cheese

chee·tah /'tʃiːtə/ n a spotted African animal of the cat family, able to run very fast

chef /ʃɛf/ n a skilled cook, esp. the chief cook in a hotel or restaurant

chem·i·cal[1] /'kɛmɪkəl/ adj of, connected with, used in, or made by chemistry: *A chemical change takes place in paper when it burns.* **–chemically** adv

chemical[2] n any substance used in or produced by chemistry, esp. an ELEMENT (1) or COMPOUND[2]

chem·ist /'kɛmɪst/ n **1** a scientist who specializes in chemistry **2** esp. BrE for PHARMACIST

chem·is·try /'kɛməstriː/ n [U] the science which studies the substances (ELEMENTS (1)) which make up the earth, universe, and living things: *a chemistry student*

cheque /tʃɛk/ n BrE for CHECK[1] (8)

chequ·ered /'tʃɛkərd/ n BrE for CHECKERED

cher·ish /'tʃɛrɪʃ/ v [T not be +v-ing] fml to care for tenderly; love: *The old man cherished the girl as if she were his daughter.|(fig.)He cherished the memory of his dead wife.*

cher·ry[1] /'tʃɛriː/ n **-ries 1** [C] a small soft fleshy red, yellow, or black round fruit with a stonelike seed in the middle –compare GRAPE **2** [C;U] (the wood of) the tree on which this fruit grows

cherry[2] adj,n [U] (having) a varying but usu. middle red color

cher·ub /'tʃɛrəb/ n **-ubs** or **-ubim** /əbɪm, yə-bɪm/ **1** a beautiful and usu. winged child in paintings; ANGEL (1) **2** a beautiful child **–cherubic** /tʃəˈruːbɪk/ adj

chess /tʃɛs/ n [U] a game for two players, each of whom starts with 16 pieces (**chessmen**) which can be moved according to fixed rules across a **chessboard** in an attempt to trap (CHECKMATE) the opponent's king

chest /tʃɛst/ n **1** the upper front part of the body enclosing the heart and lungs **2** a large strong box in which valuable objects are kept, goods packed, etc.: *a chest of jewels|a* **chest of drawers** (=a piece of furniture with several drawers) *for her clothes* –see illustration on page 51 **3 get (something) off one's chest** to bring (a worry) out into the open by talking **4 -chested** having a chest of the stated kind: *flat-chested*

chest·nut¹ /'tʃɛsnʌt, -nət/ *n* **1** [C] a smooth reddish-brown nut that stays enclosed in a prickly case until ripe, eaten raw or cooked **2** [C;U] (the wood of) the tree on which this nut grows **3** [C] a reddish-brown horse

chestnut² *adj,n* [U] (having) a deep reddish-brown color

chest·y /'tʃɛstiʸ/ *adj* **-ier, -iest** *infml* sounding as if coming from the chest: *a deep, chesty voice* **–chestily** *adv*

chew /tʃuʷ/ *v* [I;T *up,on*] **1** to crush (food) with or as if with the teeth: *Chew your food well before you swallow it.* **2 bite off more than one can chew** *infml* to attempt more than one can deal with or succeed in finishing: *I bit off more than I could chew when I borrowed all that money from the bank.* **3 chew the fat** *infml* for CHAT¹

chew sbdy.↔out *v adv* [T] *infml esp. AmE* to scold: *He chewed out his secretary for being late to work every day.*

chew sthg.↔over *v adv* [T] *infml* to think about (a question, problem, etc.): *I'll chew it over for a few days and then let you have my answer.*

chewing gum /'·· ,·/ also **gum** – *n* [U] a substance usu. having a special, often sweet, taste, made to be CHEWed but not swallowed

chic /ʃiʸk/ *adj,n* [U] (showing) good style: *I think your hat is very chic.|She wears her clothes with chic.* **–chicly** *adv*

Chi·ca·no /tʃɪˈkɑnoʷ/ *n* **-nos** *AmE* a US citizen from Mexico or whose family came from Mexico: *Many Chicanos live in the Southwest of the US.*

chick /tʃɪk/ *n* **1** the young of any bird, esp. of a chicken **2** *infml* a young woman

chick·en¹ /'tʃɪkən/ *n* **1** [C;U] (the meat of) a common farmyard bird, esp. when young; FOWL: *He keeps chickens on his farm.|Would you like chicken for dinner?|A young chicken is called a **chick**, a female chicken is a **hen**, and a male chicken is a **rooster.** –see MEAT (USAGE)* **2** [C] *infml* a person who lacks courage; COWARD **3 count one's chickens before they're hatched** to make plans depending on something which has not yet happened

chicken² also **chicken-hearted** /,tʃɪkən 'hɑrtɪd ◄/ *adj* [F] *infml* lacking courage

chicken³ *v* →CHICKEN OUT

chick·en·feed /'tʃɪkən,fiʸd/ *n* [U] *infml* a small unimportant amount of money: *The bank offered to lend us $1000 but it's chicken-feed compared to what we need.*

chicken out *v adv* [I *of*] *derog infml* to decide not to do something because of being afraid: *I wanted to tell the director what I thought, but I chickened out at the last minute.*

SPELLING NOTE

Words with the sound /ʃ/, like **chauffeur**, may be spelled **sh-**, like **shop.**

---

chicken pox /'tʃɪkən ,pɑks/ *n* [U] a disease, caught esp. by children, that is marked by a slight fever and spots on the skin

chic·o·ry /'tʃɪkəriʸ/ *n* [U] **1** a plant whose leaves are eaten raw as a vegetable **2** a powder made from the dried crushed roots of this plant and added to coffee to give a special taste

chide /tʃaɪd/ *v* **chided** *or* **chid** /tʃɪd/, **chided** *or* **chid** *or* **chidden** /'tʃɪdn/, **chiding** [I;T *for, with*] *lit* to scold

chief¹ /tʃiʸf/ *n* [A;C] **1** a leader; ruler; person with highest rank; head of a party, organization, etc.: *The President is chief of the armed forces.|The chief of (the) police (department) demanded severe punishments for criminals.|an* INDIAN (1) *chief* **2 -in-chief** having the highest rank: *In World War Two Eisenhower was commander-in-chief of the armed forces.* **3 chief of staff** (in the US armed forces) the commander of the army or air force

chief² *adj* [A] **1** highest in rank; most important: *the chief clerk|chief priest|Rice is the chief crop in this area.* **2 Chief Executive** *AmE* President of the United States. **3 chief justice** the head judge of a court of justice, esp. the SUPREME COURT of the US.

chief·ly /'tʃiʸfliʸ/ *adv* **1** mainly; mostly but not wholly: *Bread is chiefly made of flour.|The accident happened chiefly because you were careless.* **2** above all; especially: *Chiefly, I ask you to remember to write to your mother.*

chief·tain /'tʃiʸftən/ *n* the leader of a tribe or other such group; chief

chif·fon /ʃɪˈfɑn, 'ʃɪfɑn/ *n* [U] a soft thin silky material used for SCARFs, dresses, etc.

child /tʃaɪld/ *n* **children** /'tʃɪldrən/ **1** a young human being: *We have five children* (=sons and/or daughters) *but one's still a baby.|Our first child died a month after he was born.|*(fig.) *Peter's a child* (=inexperienced) *in money matters.|*(fig.) *The atomic bomb is* **the child of** (=a product of) *20th-century science.* **2 child's play** something very easy to do: *Riding a bicycle is child's play when you've had some practice.* **3 be with child** *lit* to be PREGNANT

USAGE A very young **child** is a **baby** or (more formal) an **infant.** A child who has just learned to walk is a **toddler.** Children aged 13 to 19 are **teenagers** and younger **teenagers** may also be called **adolescents.** A **youth** [C] is an older, usually male, **teenager**, but this word often shows disapproval: *The police arrested several youths who were causing trouble at the football game.* **Youth** [U] means older teenagers and does not show disapproval: *Today's youth is the hope of the future.*

child·bear·ing /'tʃaɪld,bɛərɪŋ/ *n* [A;U] the act of giving birth to children: *a woman of childbearing age*

child·birth /'tʃaɪldbɜrθ/ *n* [U] the act of giving birth to a child

child·hood /'tʃaɪldhʊd/ *n* [C;U] **1** the time or condition of being a child: *He had a happy childhood in the country.|She could speak two languages from childhood.* **2 second**

childhood weakness of mind caused by old age; DOTAGE

child·ish /'tʃaɪldɪʃ/ adj **1** of, typical of, or for a child: *The little girl spoke in a high childish voice.* **2** derog having a manner unsuitable for a grown up; IMMATURE: *a childish remark* –compare CHILDLIKE –**childishly** adv –**childishness** n [U]

child·less /'tʃaɪldlɪs/ adj having no children: *a childless* COUPLE –**childlessness** n

child·like /'tʃaɪldlaɪk/ adj often apprec of or typical of a child, esp. having a natural lovable quality: *childlike trust* –compare CHILDISH (2)

chill[1] /tʃɪl/ v [I;T] to (cause to) become cold, esp. without freezing: *chilled beer*|*I want this wine to chill so I'll put it on ice for an hour.*|(fig.) *a chilling murder story* (=one which makes one afraid)

chill[2] n **1** an illness marked by coldness and shaking of the body: *I think I've* **caught a chill. 2** [usu. sing.] a certain coldness: *There was a chill in the air this morning.*|(fig.) *The bad news* **put a chill into** (=discouraged) *us all.*

chill[3] adj cold: *a chill wind*

chil·i AmE‖also **chile, chilli** /'tʃɪliʸ/ n **chilies, chiles, chillies 1** [C;U] (a powder made from) the seed case of the PEPPER (2) plant, used to give a hot taste to food **2** [U] a cooked dish of meat and sometimes beans given a special taste by the addition of this powder, and common in the southwestern and western US

chill·y /'tʃɪliʸ/ adj **-ier, -iest** rather cold; cold enough to be uncomfortable: *It grew chilly when the fire went out.*|*I feel chilly without a coat.*|(fig.) *The governor was given a chilly welcome when he arrived at the factory.* –**chilliness** n [S;U]

chime[1] /tʃaɪm/ n the sound made by or as if by a set of bells: *The chime of the clock woke him up.*

chime[2] v **chimed, chiming** [I;T] to make musical bell-like sounds; show (the time) in this way: *The clock chimed one o'clock.*

   chime in v adv [I;T +that/with] infml to interrupt or join in a conversation by expressing (an opinion): *He's always ready to chime in with his opinion.*

chim·ney /'tʃɪmniʸ/ n **-neys 1** a hollow passage often rising above the roof of a building, which allows smoke and gases to pass from a fire: *The factory chimneys poured smoke into the air.* –see illustration on page 337 **2** a glass tube often wide at the center and narrow at the top, put around a flame as in an oil lamp

chim·ney·pot /'tʃɪmniʸˌpat/ n a short EARTHENWARE or metal pipe fixed to the top of a chimney

chim·ney·sweep /'tʃɪmniʸˌswiʸp/ also **sweep** infml– n a person whose job is cleaning the insides of chimneys, esp. by pushing brushes up them

chim·pan·zee /ˌtʃɪmpænˈziʸ, tʃɪmˈpænziʸ/ also **chimp** /tʃɪmp/ infml– n a large dark-haired African monkey-like animal (APE) smaller than a GORILLA

chin /tʃɪn/ n **1** the front part of the face (esp. of a human being) where it stands out slightly below the mouth **2 (Keep your) chin up!** infml Don't stop trying to succeed or be cheerful!

chi·na /'tʃaɪnə/ n [U] **1** a hard white substance made by baking fine clay at high temperatures –compare PORCELAIN **2** plates, cups, etc., made from this or a substance like this; CROCKERY: *Please put the china away carefully.*

Chi·na·town /'tʃaɪnəˌtaʊn/ n an area in a city outside China where there are Chinese stores, restaurants, and clubs, and where many Chinese people live: *Let's go to Chinatown for dinner.*

chink /tʃɪŋk/ n a narrow crack or opening: *He watched the meeting secretly, through a chink in the wall.*|(fig.) *a chink of light in the darkness of the room*

chintz /tʃɪnts/ n [U] cotton cloth printed with brightly colored patterns, used for making curtains, furniture covers, etc.

chip[1] /tʃɪp/ n **1** a small piece of brick, wood, paint, etc., broken off something: *a chip of wood* **2** a crack or mark left when a small piece is broken off or knocked out of an object: *I was annoyed to find a chip in my new table.* **3** [usu. pl.] AmE for POTATO CHIP **4** [usu. pl.] BrE for FRENCH FRY: *fish and chips* **5** ‖also **counter** BrE– a flat plastic object used for representing money in certain games **6** →MICROCHIP **7 a chip off the old block** infml often apprec (usu. said by and about males) a person very like his father in character **8 have a chip on one's shoulder** infml to be quarrelsome, as a result of feeling badly treated: *She has a chip on her shoulder because she didn't go to college.*

chip[2] v **-pp-** [I;T] to (cause to) lose a small piece from the surface or edge: *This rock chips easily.*|*Someone chipped my best glass.*|*I'm so sorry. I've chipped your table.*

   chip away v adv **1** [T (**chip** sthg.↔ **away**)] to destroy (something) bit by bit, by breaking small pieces off: *At last he succeeded in chipping away the stone that held the door shut.* **2** [I at] to (try to) break small pieces off something: *He was chipping away at the rock with a hammer.*

   chip in v adv infml **1** [I;T +that/with] to enter a conversation suddenly with an opinion: *John chipped in that it was time to go home.* **2** [I;T (=**chip in** sthg.)] to add (one's share of money or activity): *I could only afford to chip in a few dollars.*|*Don't worry. I'm going to chip in.*

chip·munk /'tʃɪpmʌŋk/ n a small American SQUIRREL-like animal with a long bushy tail and bands of black and white color along its back

chi·rop·o·dist /kəˈrapədɪst, ʃə-/ n →PODIATRIST –**chiropody** n [U]

chirp /tʃɜrp/ also **chirrup** /'tʃɜrəp, 'tʃɪrəp/– v, n [C;I away, out] (to make) the short sharp sound(s) of small birds or some insects

chis·el[1] /'tʃɪzəl/ n a metal tool with a sharp cutting edge at the end of a blade, used for cutting into or shaping wood, stone, etc.

chisel² *v* **-l-** *AmE*‖**-ll-** *BrE* [I;T *away, into, out of*] **1** to cut or shape with a CHISEL¹: *She chiseled the rock into the figure of a lion.*|*He chiseled a hole in the door to fit a new lock.* –compare CARVE (1) **2** [T *out of*] *infml* to trick; deceive: *She chiseled me out of my money!*

chit /tʃɪt/ *n* a short letter, esp. a signed note showing a sum of money owed (for drinks, food, etc.)

chit·chat /'tʃɪt-tʃæt/ *n* [U] *infml* informal conversation

chiv·al·rous /'ʃɪvəlrəs/ *adj* (esp. of men) marked by politeness, honor, generosity, and good manners –opposite **unchivalrous** –**chivalrously** *adv*

chiv·al·ry /'ʃɪvəlriʸ/ *n* [U] **1** (in the MIDDLE AGES) the beliefs or practices of noble soldiers (KNIGHTs) as a group **2** (when speaking of a man) good manners, esp. towards women

chive /tʃaɪv/ *n* a plant related to the onion, with narrow grasslike leaves, used for giving a special taste to food

chlo·ri·nate /'klɔrə,neʸt, 'kloʷr-/ *v* **-nated, -nating** [T] to disinfect by putting CHLORINE into (a substance, esp. water): *Water is usually chlorinated in public swimming pools to keep it pure.*|*chlorinated water* –**chlorination** /,klɔrə'neʸʒən, ,kloʷr-/ *n* [U]

chlo·rine /'klɔriʸn, 'kloʷr-/ *n* [U] a gas that is a simple substance (ELEMENT (1)), greenish-yellow, strong-smelling, and used to DISINFECT

chlo·ro·form /'klɔrə,fɔrm, 'kloʷr-/ *n* [U] a colorless strong-smelling poisonous chemical liquid, used as an ANESTHETIC

chlo·ro·phyll /'klɔrə,fɪl, 'kloʷr-/ *n* [U] the green-colored substance in the stems and leaves of plants

chock /tʃak/ *n* a shaped piece of wood placed under something, such as a door, boat, barrel, or wheel to prevent it from moving –**chock** *v* [T]

chock-a-block /'tʃak ə ,blak, ,tʃak ə 'blak/ *adj,adv* [F *with*] *infml* very crowded; packed tightly: *The road was chock-a-block with cars again today.*

chock-full /,· '·◄/ *adj* [F *of*] *infml* completely full: *The cupboard is chock-full of food.*

choc·o·late /'tʃɔkəlɪt, 'tʃɑ-/ *n* **1** [U] a solid sweet usu. brown substance made from the crushed seeds of a tropical American tree (CACAO), eaten as candy: *Would you like a piece of chocolate?* **2** [C] a small candy made by covering a center, such as a nut, with this substance: *a box of chocolates* **3** [U] a sweet brown powder made by crushing this substance, used for giving a special taste to sweet foods and drinks **4** [C;U] (a cupful of) a drink made from hot milk (and water) mixed with this powder: *A hot chocolate, please.*

SPELLING NOTE
Words with the sound /ʃ/, like **chauffeur**, may be spelled **sh-**, like **shop**.

---

choice¹ /tʃɔɪs/ *n* **1** [C] the act or result of choosing: *What influenced you when you made your choice?*|*She is the people's choice for senator.* **2** [U] the power, right, or chance of choosing: *I have no choice but to do as he tells me.* **3** [C] a variety from which to choose: *There was a big choice of stores in the small town.*

choice² *adj* (esp. of food) worthy of being chosen; of high quality: *choice apples* –**choicely** *adv* –**choiceness** *n* [U]

choir /kwaɪər/ *n* a group of people who sing together esp. during religious services: *The church choir is singing tonight.*

choke /tʃoʷk/ *v* **choked, choking 1** [I;T] to (cause to) struggle to breathe or (cause to) stop breathing because of blocking of or damage to the breathing passages: *Water went down his throat and he started to choke.*|*I choked him to death.*| (fig.) *plants choked by long grass* **2** [T *up, with*] to fill (a space or passage) completely: *The roads were choked up with traffic.*|*The pipe was choked with leaves.*| (fig.) *I was choked up (with anger), and unable to speak.*

choke sthg.↔**back** *v adv* [T] to control (esp. violent or very sad feelings) as if by holding in the throat: *to try to choke back one's anger/one's tears*

choke² *n* **1** the act of choking (CHOKE¹ (1)) **2** an apparatus that controls the amount of air going into a car engine, esp. to help a cold engine start

chol·er·a /'kɑlərə/ *n* [U] an infectious disease of tropical countries which attacks esp. the stomach and bowels, and often leads to death

cho·les·ter·ol /kə'lɛstə,rɔl, -,roʷl/ *n* [U] a substance found in all cells of the body, which helps to carry fats

choose /tʃuʷz/ *v* **chose** /tʃoʷz/, **chosen** /'tʃoʷzən/, **choosing** [I;T] **1** [+*v-ing/ between, from*] to pick out from a greater number; show (what one wants) by taking: *Have you chosen a hat yet?*|*Will you help me choose a new coat?*|*He was chosen as President.*|*There are ten to choose from.*|*I had to choose between staying with my parents and going abroad.* **2** [+*to-v/that*] to decide: *He chose not to go home until later.*|*I choose that we leave later.* **3 There's little/not much to choose between them** They are very much alike

choos·y, choosey /'tʃuʷziʸ/ also **picky** *AmE*– *adj* **-ier, -iest** careful in choosing; hard to please: *Jean's very choosy about what she eats.*

chop¹ /tʃap/ *v* **-pp- 1** [I;T] to cut by repeatedly striking with a heavy sharp-ended tool, such as an axe: *She chopped the block of wood in half with a single blow.*|*We had to chop a path through the thick forest before we could get to the river.*|*to chop down a tree* **2** [T *up*] to cut into very small pieces: *Chop the onions up, please.*

chop² *n* **1** a quick short cutting blow as with an ax **2** a small piece of meat, esp. lamb or PORK, usu. containing a bone

chop·per /'tʃapər/ *n* **1** a heavy sharp-ended

tool for cutting wood or meat; ax **2** *infml* for HELICOPTER

chop·py /'tʃɑpiʸ/ *adj* **-pier, -piest** (of water) covered with many short rough waves: *The sea was choppy today because of the wind.* —**choppiness** *n* [U]

chop·stick /'tʃɑp,stɪk/ *n* [*usu. pl.*] either of a pair of narrow sticks held between the thumb and fingers and used in East Asian countries for lifting food to the mouth: *When we go to a Chinese restaurant we always use chopsticks instead of a knife and fork.*

cho·ral /'kɔrəl, 'koʷrəl/ *adj* [A *no comp.*] of, related to, or sung by a CHOIR or CHORUS¹ (1): *a choral group/society/choral music*

chord¹ /kɔrd/ *n* a combination of two or more musical notes sounded at the same time

chord² *n* a straight line joining two points on a curve

chore /tʃɔr, tʃoʷr/ *n* a small piece of regular work, quickly and easily done; necessary, but uninteresting job, esp. in a house or on a farm: *Every morning I get up and do the chores before I go out.|It's such a chore to do the shopping every day!*

cho·re·og·ra·phy /ˌkɔriʸ'ɑgrəfiʸ, ˌkoʷr-/ *n* [U] the art of dancing or of arranging dances for the stage —**choreographer** *n* : *The choreographer will direct her new dance next week.*

chor·tle /'tʃɔrtl/ *v,n* **-tled, -tling** [C;I] (to give) a laugh of pleasure or satisfaction; CHUCKLE

cho·rus¹ /'kɔrəs, 'koʷrəs/ *n* **1** [C] a group of people who sing together: *The chorus was very good today.* **2** [C] a piece of music played or sung after each group of lines (VERSE (2)) of a song **3** [S *of*] something said by a lot of people together: *The election results were greeted by a chorus of GROANS.*

chorus² *v* [I;T *that*] to sing or speak at the same time: *The papers all chorused praises for the President.*

chose /tʃoʷz/ *v past tense of* CHOOSE

cho·sen /'tʃoʷzən/ *v past participle of* CHOOSE

chow·der /'tʃaʊdər/ *n* [U] a thick soup prepared from pieces of fish and other sea animals (SHELLFISH), vegetables, meat, and often milk: CLAM *chowder*

Christ /kraɪst/ *n* also **Jesus Christ**– the man who started Christianity, considered by Christians to be the son of God and to be still alive in heaven

chris·ten /'krɪsən/ *v* [T] (in some Christian churches) to make (someone, esp. a child) a member of the church by BAPTISM and, usually the giving of a name: *The baby was christened by the priest.|We christened our baby John.|(fig.) The ship was christened the Queen Mary.*

Chris·ten·dom /'krɪsəndəm/ *n* [U] *old use* all Christian people in general

chris·ten·ing /'krɪsənɪŋ/ *n* [C;U] (in some Christian churches) the ceremony of BAPTISM or of naming a person, usu. a child

Chris·tian¹ /'krɪstʃən/ *n* a person who believes in the teachings of Jesus Christ

Christian² *adj* **1** believing in or belonging to any of the various branches of Christianity:

the Christian church|a Christian nation **2** of or related to CHRIST, Christianity, or Christians: *Christian ideas|He behaved in a Christian* (=kind and generous) *way to his enemies.* –opposite **unchristian** (for 2)

Chris·ti·an·i·ty /ˌkrɪstʃiʸ'ænəṭiʸ/ *n* [S] the religion based on the life and teachings of CHRIST: *to believe in Christianity*

Christian name /'·· ˌ·/ *n* → FIRST NAME

Christ·mas /'krɪsməs/ *n* [C;S] **1** also **Christmas Day** /ˌ·· '·/ a Christian holy day held on December 25th (or in some churches January 6th) in honor of the birth of Christ, usu. kept as a public holiday **2** the period just before and just after this: *Did you have a nice Christmas/a nice time at Christmas?*

Christmas Eve /ˌ·· '·/ *n* the day, and esp. the evening, before Christmas: *I always go to my parents' house on Christmas Eve.*

Christmas tree /'·· ˌ·/ *n* a real or man-made tree decorated with candles, lights, colored paper, etc., and set up in the home at Christmas

chrome /kroʷm/ *n* [U] a hard metal combination (ALLOY) of CHROMIUM with other metals, esp. used for covering objects with a thin shiny protective metal plate: *a lot of chrome on that car*

chro·mi·um /'kroʷmiʸəm/ *n* [U] a metal that is a simple substance (ELEMENT (1)) found only in combination with other chemicals, used for covering objects with a thin shiny protective plate: *chromium-plated*

chro·mo·some /'kroʷmə,soʷm/ *n* *tech* a threadlike body found in all living cells, which passes on and controls the nature, character, etc., of a young plant, animal, or cell

chron·ic /'krɑnɪk/ *adj* **1** (of a disease) continual; lasting a long time: *a chronic cough* –compare ACUTE (3) **2** [A] suffering from a disease or illness over a long period: *a chronic alcoholic/*INVALID –**chronically** *adv*

chron·i·cle¹ /'krɑnɪkəl/ *n* a record of historical events, arranged in order of time

chronicle² *v* **-cled, -cling** [T] to make a CHRONICLE of (events)

chron·o·log·i·cal /ˌkrɑnl'ɑdʒɪkəl/ *adj* [*no comp.*] arranged according to the order of time: *We'll make a list of the causes of the war in chronological order.* –**chronologically** *adv*

chro·nol·o·gy /krə'nɑlədʒiʸ/ *n* **-gies** *fml* **1** [U] the science which measures time and gives dates to events **2** [C] a list or table arranged according to the order of time: *a chronology of the events of last year*

chrys·a·lis /'krɪsəlɪs/ *n* (a hard case-like shell enclosing) a PUPA –compare COCOON

chry·san·the·mum /krɪ'sænθəməm/ *n* a garden plant with large brightly-colored flowers in autumn

chub·by /'tʃʌbiʸ/ *adj* **-bier, -biest** *infml* (of animals or people) having a full round usu. pleasing form; slightly fat –see THIN (USAGE) –**chubbiness** *n* [U]

chuck /tʃʌk/ *v* [T] *infml* to throw (something), esp. with a short movement of the arms: *Let's chuck all these old papers away! |(fig.) Don't be so noisy, or the driver will* *chuck us off (the bus).*|(fig.) *He's decided to chuck* (=leave) *his job.*

chuck sbdy./sthg.↔ **out** *v adv* [T] *infml* **1** to force (a person) to leave: *The waiter threatened to chuck us out (of the restaurant) if we made too much noise.* **2** to throw out; throw away: *I'm going to chuck out these old shoes.*

chuck·le¹ /'tʃʌkəl/ *v* **-led, -ling** [I] to laugh quietly: *I could hear him chuckling to himself as he read his book.*

chuckle² *n* a quiet laugh: *He gave a quiet chuckle and walked out of the room.*

chug /tʃʌg/ *v* **-gg-** [I] (of an engine) to make a repeated knocking sound while moving: *I heard the engine chugging away/along.* –**chug** *n* [S]: *the chug of the engine*

chum /tʃʌm/ *n infml* a good friend, esp. among boys

chum·my /'tʃʌmiʸ/ *adj* **-mier, -miest** *infml* friendly

chump /tʃʌmp/ *n infml* a fool: *He's a real chump.*

chunk /tʃʌŋk/ *n* a short thick piece or lump that is bigger than the pieces into which something is usually cut: (fig.) *That new car took a big chunk out of her wages.*

chunk·y /'tʃʌŋkiʸ/ *adj* **-ier, -iest** rather thick and solid; (of people) short and rather fat: *a chunky little man*

church /tʃɜrtʃ/ *n* **1** [C] a building made for public Christian worship: *I'm going to church today.* **2** [*the* S;U] the profession of the CLERGY (priests and people employed for religious reasons) of a religious body: *When he was 30 he joined the church and became a priest.*|*Do you agree with the separation of church* (=religious power) *and state?* **3** [*usu cap.*] the organization of Christian believers: *She was a loyal member of the Church.*|*the Church of England*|*the Catholic Church*

Church of Eng·land /ˌtʃɜrtʃ əv 'ɪŋglənd/ *n* [*the* S] the state church which is established by law in England and was separated from the ROMAN CATHOLIC church in the 16th century

church·yard /'tʃɜrtʃyard/ *n* an open space around and belonging to a church, often used for burials –compare CEMETERY, GRAVEYARD

churl·ish /'tʃɜrlɪʃ/ *adj lit derog* bad-tempered; rude –**churlishly** *adv* –**churlishness** *n* [U]

churn¹ /tʃɜrn/ *n* a container in which milk is beaten until it becomes butter

churn² *v* [I;T] **1** to make butter by beating (milk) **2** to (cause to) move about violently: *The ship churned the water up as it passed.*|(fig.) *My stomach started to churn when I thought about my exams.*

churn sthg. ↔ **out** also **crank out**– *v adv* [T] *infml* to produce a large quantity of, as if by

machinery: *She churns out about three new books every year.*

chute /ʃuʷt/ *n* a sloped passage along which something may be passed, dropped, or caused to slide: *a mail chute*

chut·ney /'tʃʌtniʸ/ *n* [U] a mixture of various fruits, hot-tasting seeds, and sugar, which is eaten with other dishes, such as meat or cheese

chutz·pah /'hʊtspə, 'xʊt-/ *n* [U] shamelessness: *You haven't returned the $500 I lent you, and now you want to borrow $1000! That takes chutzpah!*

CIA /ˌsiʸ aɪ 'eʸ/ *abbrev. for:* Central Intelligence Agency; the group of people in the US who gather information about other countries, esp. in secret: *a member of the CIA*

ci·der ‖also **cyder** *BrE* /'saɪdər/ *n* [C;U] **1** (a glass or bottle of) apple juice **2** also **hard cider** *esp. AmE–* (a glass or bottle of) an alcoholic drink made from apple juice

ci·gar /sɪ'gar/ *n* a tightly-packed tube-shaped roll of tobacco leaves for smoking –compare CIGARETTE

cig·a·rette ‖also **cigaret** *AmE–* /ˌsɪgə'rɛt, 'sɪgəˌrɛt/ *n* finely cut tobacco rolled in a narrow tube of thin paper for smoking –compare CIGAR

cinch /sɪntʃ/ *n* [S] *infml* **1** something done easily: *My examination was a cinch; I passed easily.* **2** something certain: *It's a cinch that our team will win.*

cin·der /'sɪndər/ *n* a small piece of partly burned wood, coal, etc., that is not yet ash and that can be burned further but without producing flames

cin·e·ma /'sɪnəmə/ *n* **1** [*the* S] also **movies** *AmE–* the art or industry of making moving pictures: *She's worked in the cinema all her life.* **2** [C] *esp. BrE* for MOVIE THEATER **3** [*the* S] *esp. BrE* for MOVIES

cin·na·mon /'sɪnəmən/ *n* [U] a sweet-smelling powder made from the tough outer covering (BARK) of a tropical Asian tree, used for giving a special taste to food

ci·pher ‖also **cypher** *BrE* /'saɪfər/ *n* **1** (a system of) secret writing; CODE¹ (1): *The government uses a secret cipher so that official messages are kept secret.* –see also DECIPHER **2** *lit* the number 0; zero **3** a person of no importance

cir·ca /'sɜrkə/ *prep fml* (used esp. with dates) about: *She was born circa 1060 and died in 1118.*

cir·cle¹ /'sɜrkəl/ *n* **1** (a flat round area enclosed by) a curved line that is everywhere equally distant from one fixed point **2** something having the general shape of this line; ring; group: *a circle of trees*|(fig.)*a large circle of friends*|(fig.)*In political circles there is talk of war.* **3** an upper floor in a theater, usu. with seats set in curved lines: *Shall we sit in the circle?* **4 come full circle** to go through a set of developments that lead back to the starting point: *It's January 1st again; the year has come full circle.*

circle² *v* **-cled, -cling** [I;T] to draw, form, or move in a circle: *The teacher circled the* *students' spelling mistakes in red ink.*|*The plane circled the airport before landing.*|*The birds were circling around in the air.*

cir·clet /'sɜrklɪt/ *n lit* a narrow round band of gold, silver, jewels, etc., worn (esp. by women) on the head, arms, or neck as decoration

cir·cuit /'sɜrkɪt/ *n* **1** a complete ring: *We made/did the circuit of the old city walls.* **2** (the establishments on) a regular journey from place to place: *The judge is* **on circuit** *for most of the year.* (=visits different courts)|*the tennis circuit* **3** the complete circular path of an electric current: *A break in the circuit had caused the lights to go out.*

cir·cu·i·tous /sər'kyuʷətəs/ *adj fml* going a long way round instead of in a straight line: *the river's circuitous course*|*a circuitous path* –**circuitously** *adv*

cir·cu·lar¹ /'sɜrkyələr/ *adj* **1** round; shaped like or nearly like a circle **2** forming or moving in a circle: (fig.) *a circular argument that doesn't lead anywhere*

circular² *n* a printed advertisement, paper, or notice intended to be given to a large number of people for them to read: *Did you see that circular from the new supermarket?*

cir·cu·late /'sɜrkyə‚leʸt/ *v* **-lated, -lating 1** [I;T] to (cause to) move or flow along a closed path: *Blood circulates around the body.*|*The heart circulates blood round the body.*|(fig.)*The news of the enemy's defeat quickly circulated around the town.*|(fig.)*A lot of false information has been circulated.* **2** [I] *infml* to move about freely: *He circulated at the party, talking to lots of people.* –**circulatory** /'sɜrkyələ‚tɔriʸ, -‚toʷriʸ/ *adj*

cir·cu·la·tion /‚sɜrkyə'leʸʃən/ *n* **1** [C;U] the flow of liquid around a closed system, esp. the movement of blood through the body: *Bad circulation can cause tiredness.* **2** [U] the movement of something such as news or money from place to place or from person to person: *The government has reduced the number of $50 bills* **in circulation.** –compare TRAFFIC (1) **3** [C] the average number of copies of a newspaper, magazine, book, etc., sold or read over a certain time: *This magazine has a circulation of 400,000.*

cir·cum·cise /'sɜrkəm‚saɪz/ *v* **-cised, -cising** [T] to cut off the skin (FORESKIN) at the end of the sex organ of (a man) or part of the sex organ (CLITORIS) of (a woman): *circumcised at birth* –**circumcision** /‚sɜrkəm'sɪʒən, 'sɜrkəm‚sɪʒən/ *n* [C;U]

cir·cum·fer·ence /sər'kʌmfərəns/ *n* the length around the outside of a circle; distance around a round object: *The earth's circumference is nearly 25,000 miles.*

cir·cum·spect /'sɜrkəm‚spɛkt/ *adj fml* (of a person or an action) done or acting after careful thought; CAUTIOUS –**circumspectly** *adv* –**circumspection** /‚sɜrkəm'spɛkʃən/ *n* [U]

cir·cum·stance /'sɜrkəm‚stæns/ *n* **1** [*usu. pl.*] a fact, condition, or event concerned with and influencing another event, person, or course of action: *We can't judge what he did until we know the circum-stances.*|*Circumstances forced me to accept a very low price when I sold the house.* **2** **in/under no circumstances** never; whatever happens **3** **in/under the circumstances** because of the conditions; because things are as they are: *I wanted to leave quickly, but under the circumstances (my uncle had just died) I decided to stay another night.*

cir·cum·vent /‚sɜrkəm'vɛnt, 'sɜrkəm‚vɛnt/ *v* [T] *fml* to avoid by or as if by passing around: *The company has opened an office abroad in order to circumvent our tax laws.* –**circumvention** /‚sɜrkəm'vɛnʃən, -tʃən/ *n* [U]

cir·cus /'sɜrkəs/ *n* **1** a public performance by a group of performers of various acts of skill and daring, often using animals and usu. traveling to different places **2** the tent-covered place where this performance happens, with seats round a ring in the middle

cis·tern /'sɪstərn/ *n* a container for storing water, esp. in a house for a TOILET

cit·a·del /'sɪtədl, -‚dɛl/ *n lit* a strong heavily-armed fort, usu. commanding a city, built to be a place of safety and defense in time of war: (fig.) *a citadel of freedom* –compare STRONGHOLD (1)

cite /saɪt/ *v* **cited, citing** [T] *fml* **1** to mention, esp. as an example in a statement, argument, etc.; QUOTE (2): *The mayor cited the latest crime figures as proof of the need for more police.* **2** to call (someone) to appear before a court of law; give a SUMMONS to: *He was cited in a DIVORCE case.*

cit·i·zen /'sɪtəzən/ *n* **1** a person who lives in a particular city or town, esp. one who has certain voting or other rights in that town **2 a** a person who is a member of a particular country by birth or by becoming NATURALIZEd (=being officially allowed to become a member) **b** a person who belongs to and gives his/her loyalty to a particular country and who expects protection from it: *She's an American citizen but lives in France.* –compare ALIEN², NATIONAL²

citizen's band /‚··· '·◂/ also **CB**– *n* [C;U] *AmE* certain radio frequencies (FREQUENCY (3)) set aside by the government in the US for use between private citizens: *A lot of truck drivers have citizen's band radios.*

cit·i·zen·ship /'sɪtəzən‚ʃɪp/ *n* [U] the state of being a citizen: *After eight years in the country he gained his citizenship.*

cit·rus ‖also **-rous** *BrE* /'sɪtrəs/ *adj* [*no comp.*] (of fruits) with thick skins and juicy flesh with a sour or sour-sweet taste: *I love citrus fruits, especially oranges.*

cit·y /'sɪtiʸ/ *n* **-ies** a usu. large and important group of houses, buildings, etc., esp. with a center where amusements can be found and business goes on. It is usu. larger and more important than a town. –compare TOWN, VILLAGE

city hall /‚·· '·/ *n* [C;U] *esp. AmE* (a public building used for) a city's local government.

civ·ic /'sɪvɪk/ *adj* of a city or its citizens: *The President's visit to the city was the most important civic event of the year.*|*civic duties*

civ·ics /'sɪvɪks/ *n* [U] a social science dealing

with the rights and duties of citizens, the way government works, etc.

civ·il /'sɪvəl/ *adj* **1** [*no comp.*] of, belonging to, or consisting of the general population; not military or religious: *We were married in a civil ceremony, not in church.* **2** [*no comp.*] (of law) dealing with the rights of private citizens; concerned with judging private quarrels between people rather than with criminal offenses: *Civil law is different from criminal law.* **3** polite enough to be acceptable, esp. if not friendly: *Try to be civil to him, even if you don't like him.*|**Keep a civil tongue in your head!** (=stop speaking rudely) –opposite **uncivil** (for 3); –see also CIVILLY

civil en·gi·neer·ing /ˌ·· ··'··/ *n* [U] the planning, building, and repair of public works, such as roads, bridges, large public buildings, etc. –**civil engineer** *n*

ci·vil·ian /sə'vɪlyən/ *n,adj* [*no comp.*] (a person) not of the armed forces: *civilian government*

ci·vil·i·ty /sə'vɪləṭiᵞ/ *n* -**ties** [C;U] (an act of) politeness; the quality of having good manners; helpfulness; COURTESY

civ·i·li·za·tion ‖also **-sation** *BrE* /ˌsɪvələ'zeᵞʃən/ *n* **1** [U] a stage of human social development, esp. one with a high level of art, religion, science, government, etc., and a written language **2** [C] the type of advanced society of a particular time or place: *to compare the civilizations of ancient China and Japan*

civ·i·lize ‖also **-lise** *BrE* /'sɪvəˌlaɪz/ *v* -**lized**, -**lizing** [T] **1** to (cause to) come from a lower stage of development to a more highly developed stage of social organization: *The Romans hoped to civilize all the tribes of Europe.* **2** *infml* to (cause to) improve in education and manners –see also UNCIVILIZED

civ·il·ly /'sɪvəliᵞ/ *adv* politely; in a CIVIL (3) manner

civil rights /ˌ·· '·/ *n* [P] **1** rights such as freedom, equality before the law, etc., which belong to all citizens without regard to their race, religion, color or sex **2 civil rights movement** a united effort in the US in support of civil rights for blacks and small racial or religious groups in the population

civil serv·ant /ˌ·· '··/ *n* a person employed in the CIVIL SERVICE –see OFFICER (USAGE)

civil serv·ice /ˌ·· '··/ *n* **1** [*the* S] all the various departments of the national government except the armed forces: *She works in/for the civil service.* **2** [U] all the people who are employed in this: *The civil service has too much power.*

civil war /ˌ·· '·/ *n* [C;U] (a) war between opposing groups of people from the same

country, fought within that country

clack /klæk/ *v* [I;T] to (cause to) make one or more quick sharp sounds –**clack** *n* [S]

clad /klæd/ *adj* [F *in; no comp.*] *lit* covered; clothed: *The old lady was clad in a fur coat.*|*The mountain was clad in mist.*|*an armor-clad ship*

claim¹ /kleᵞm/ *v* **1** [I;T *on, for*] to ask for, demand, or take (a title, property, money, etc.) as the rightful owner, or as one's right: *Did you claim on your insurance after your car accident?*|(fig.)*The flood claimed hundreds of lives.* **2** [T +*to-v*/(*that*)] to declare to be true; state esp. in the face of opposition; MAINTAIN (4): *He claims to be rich/claims that he is rich but I don't believe him.*

claim² *n* **1** [*for, on*] a demand for something as one's own by right: *The government would not even consider his claim for money.*|*They put in an insurance claim after their car accident.* **2** [*to, on*] a right to something: *He has a claim to the property; it was his mother's.*|*The town's only* **claim to fame** *is that it has the biggest parking lot in the country.* **3** [+*to-v*/*that*] a statement of something as fact: *His claim about the number of people killed in the war was clearly mistaken.* **4** something claimed, esp. an area of land or sum of money

clair·voy·ant /klɛər'vɔɪənt/ *adj,n* (of or related to the powers of) a person who can see what will happen in the future –**clairvoyance** *n* [U]

clam /klæm/ *n* a small soft-bodied sea animal with a double shell, that lives in sand or mud and is eaten

clam·ber /'klæmbər/ *v* [I *over*] to climb using both feet and hands, usu. with difficulty or effort: *Tell the children to stop clambering (around) over my new furniture.*

clam·my /'klæmiᵞ/ *adj* -**mier**, -**miest** unpleasantly sticky, slightly wet, and usu. cold: *clammy hands/weather* –**clammily** *adv* –**clamminess** *n* [U]

clam·or¹ *AmE*‖**clamour** *BrE* /'klæmər/ *n* a loud continuous usu. confused noise or shouting, esp. of people complaining: *a clamor of voices*|*public clamor for lower taxes* –**clamorous** *adj*: *clamorous demands for peace*

clamor² *AmE*‖ **clamour** *BrE* [I;T +*to-v*/*that*/*for*] to express (a demand) continually, loudly, and strongly: *The children were clamoring to be fed.*

clamp¹ /klæmp/ *n* an apparatus for fastening or holding things firmly together

clamp² *v* [T *together*] to fasten with a CLAMP¹: *Clamp these two pieces of wood together.*

clamp down *v adv* [I *on*] *infml* to become more firm; make limits: *The police are going to clamp down on criminal activity in this area.* –see also CLAMPDOWN

clamp·down /'klæmpdaʊn/ *n infml* a sudden usu. official limitation or prevention of doing or saying something: *The mayor has decided to put a clampdown on public spending.* –see also CLAMP² **down**

clam up *v adv* -**mm**- [I] *infml* to become

SPELLING NOTE

Words with the sound /k/, like **cut**, may be spelled **k-**, like **key**, or **qu-**, like **queen**. Words with the sound /s/, like **city**, may be spelled **s-**, like **soon**, or **ps-**, like **psychology**.

silent: *She clammed up when I mentioned the police.*

clan /klæn/ *n* **1** (esp. in Scotland) a group of families, all originally descended from one family; tribe **2** *humor* a large family

clan·des·tine /klæn'dɛstɪn/ *adj* done secretly or privately often for an unlawful reason: *a clandestine meeting* –**clandestinely** *adv*

clang /klæŋ/ *v* [I;T] to (cause to) make a loud ringing sound, such as when metal is struck: *The metal tool clanged when it hit the wall.|to clang a bell* –**clang** *n* [S]

clank /klæŋk/ *v* [I;T] to (cause to) make a short loud sound, like that of a heavy moving metal chain: *The prisoner's chains clanked as he walked.* –**clank** *n* [S]

clan·nish /'klænɪʃ/ *adj often derog* (of a group of people) tending keep together as a group, esp. supporting each other against those from outside –**clannishly** *adv*

clap¹ /klæp/ *v* -**pp**- **1** [I;T] to strike (one's hands) together with a quick movement and loud sound, esp. to show approval of a performance: *The teacher clapped her hands to attract the class's attention.|The people in the theater enjoyed the play and clapped loudly.* **2** [T *on*] to strike lightly with the open hand usu. in a friendly manner: *He clapped his son on the back.* **3** [T *in*] *infml* to put, place, or send usu. quickly and effectively: *The judge clapped her in prison before she had time to explain.*

clap² *n* **1** [C] a loud explosive sound: *a clap of thunder* **2** [S] an act of CLAPping¹ (1): *After he finished singing, there was a single clap from one person in the crowd.* –compare CLAP-PING, HAND¹ (5) **3** [S *on*] a light friendly hit, usu. on the back, with an open hand: *He gave me a clap on the back/shoulder and invited me for a drink.*

clap·per /'klæpər/ *n* the hammerlike object hung inside a bell which strikes the bell to make it ring

clap·ping /'klæpɪŋ/ *n* [U] the sound of hands being CLApped¹ (1); APPLAUSE: *The people enjoyed the performance so much that the clapping continued for a long time.|the sound of clapping* –compare CLAP² (2)

clap·trap /'klæptræp/ *n* [U] *infml* empty, insincere, and worthless speech or writing; nonsense

clar·i·fy /'klærə,faɪ/ *v* -**fied, -fying** [I;T] to (cause to) become clearer and more easily understood: *When will the administration clarify its position on equal pay for women?* –**clarification** /,klærəfə'keɪʃən/ *n* [C;U]: *He asked for (a) clarification of the government's position.*

clar·i·net /,klærə'nɛt/ *n* a long tubelike usu. wooden musical instrument, played by blowing

clar·i·ty /'klærəti/ *n* [U] clearness: *clarity of thinking/speech*

clash¹ /klæʃ/ *v* **1** [I *with*] to come into opposition: *The two armies clashed* (=fought) *near the border.|This shirt clashes with my pants.* (=the colors don't match)|*Her wedding clashed with* (=was at the same time as) *my examination, so I couldn't go.* **2** [I;T *together*] to (cause to) make a loud confused noise

clash² *n* **1** [S] a loud confused noise: *The soldiers were woken by the clash of weapons.* **2** [C] an example of opposition or disagreement: *a clash of interests|a border clash* (=fight at a border)

clasp¹ /klæsp/ *n* **1** a usu. metal fastener for holding two things or parts of one thing together: *the clasp on a belt* **2** [usu. *sing.*] a tight firm hold, esp. by the hand; GRIP –compare CLINCH

clasp² *v* [T] **1** to take or seize firmly; enclose and hold, esp. with the fingers or arms: *He clasped the money in his hands.* **2** [*together*] to fasten with a CLASP¹ (1) –opposite **unclasp**

class¹ /klæs/ *n* **1** [C] a social group whose members have the same political, social, and ECONOMIC (1) position and rank: *the ruling class|lower-class life|the upper classes* –see also MIDDLE CLASS, WORKING CLASS, UPPER CLASS **2** [U] the fact that there are different social groups with different social and political positions and points of view: *Class differences can divide a nation.|Is education class-based?*|**class consciousness** (having knowledge or feeling of belonging to a particular social class) **3** [C] a division of people or things according to rank, behavior, etc. **4** [C] a group of pupils or students taught together **5** [C;U] a period of time during which pupils or students are taught: *What time does the next class begin?* **6** [C] *esp. AmE* a number of students in a school or university finishing a course or degree in the same year: *We were both in the class of (19)80.* **7** [C] a level of quality of traveling conditions on a train, plane, boat, etc.: *A first-class ticket to Miami, please.* **8** [C] **class action** *AmE* a LAWSUIT set up by a group of people in the interests of themselves and all others with the same complaint: *The miners with lung diseases pressed a class-action suit against the company.*

class² *v* [T *as*] to put into a CLASS¹ (3); CLASSIFY

clas·sic¹ /'klæsɪk/ *adj* [A *no comp.*] **1** having the highest quality; of the first or highest class or rank **2** belonging to an established set of standards; well known, esp. as the best example: *a classic style of dress/building|a classic example/case* –compare CLASSICAL

classic² *n* a piece of literature or art of the first rank and of lasting importance: *That book is one of the classics of English literature.|*(fig.)*That joke's a classic; it really is funny.*

clas·si·cal /'klæsɪkəl/ *adj* **1** (*sometimes cap.*) in accordance with ancient Greek or Roman models in literature or art: *classical literature|a classical education* **2** [*no comp.*] (of music) put together and arranged (COMPOSED (2)) with serious artistic intentions: *Bach and Beethoven wrote classical music.* **3** of or related to a form or system established before modern times: *Classical scientific ideas about light were changed by Einstein.* –compare CLASSIC¹

clas·si·fi·ca·tion /ˌklæsəfə'keᵞʃən/ n 1 [U] the act or result of CLASSIFYing, esp. plants, animals, books, etc. 2 [C] a group, division, class, or CATEGORY into which something is placed

clas·si·fied /'klæsə,faɪd/ adj 1 divided or arranged in classes; placed according to class: a classified list of books in a library 2 (of government, esp. military, information) officially secret: This information is classified; only a few people can see it.

classified ad /ˌ··· '·/ also **want ad** AmE||also **small ad** BrE|| n a usu. small advertisement placed in a newspaper by a person wishing to sell or buy something, offer or get employment, etc.

clas·si·fy /'klæsə,faɪ/ v -fied, -fying [T] 1 to arrange or place (animals, plants, books, etc.) into classes or groups; divide according to class: People who work in libraries spend a lot of time classifying books. 2 esp. AmE to mark officially or declare (information) secret: The government has classified this information (as) secret.

class·room /'klæsruʷm, -rʊm/ n a room in a school, college, etc., in which a class meets for a lesson

class·y /'klæsiᵞ/ adj -ier, -iest infml stylish; fashionable; of high class or rank

clat·ter /'klætər/ n [S] a number of rapid short knocking sounds as when a number of things fall to the ground: There was a clatter of dishes in the kitchen. –**clatter** v [I;T]: The metal dish clattered down the stone steps

clause /klɔz/ n 1 (in grammar) a group of words containing a subject and a verb, usu. forming only part of a sentence. In "She came home when she was tired," She came home and when she was tired are two separate clauses –compare PHRASE, SENTENCE 2 a separate part or division of a written agreement or DOCUMENT with its own separate and complete meaning

claus·tro·pho·bi·a /ˌklɔstrə'foʷbiᵞə/ n [U] fear of being enclosed in a small closed space –**claustrophobic** /ˌklɔstrə'foʷbɪk/ adj

claw¹ /klɔ/ n 1 a sharp usu. curved nail on the toe of an animal or bird 2 a limb of certain insects and sea animals, such as CRABs, used for attacking and holding objects

claw² v [I;T] to tear, seize, pull, etc., with or as if with CLAWs: The cat clawed at the leg of the table.|It clawed a hole in my stocking.

clay /kleᵞ/ n [U] heavy firm earth, soft when wet, becoming hard when baked at a high temperature, and from which bricks, pots, EARTHENWARE, etc., are made –**clayey** /'kleᵞiᵞ/ adj

clean¹ /kliᵞn/ adj 1 free from dirt: Are your hands clean? 2 not yet used; fresh: clean

SPELLING NOTE

Words with the sound /k/, like **cut**, may be spelled **k-**, like **key**, or **qu-**, like **queen**. Words with the sound /s/, like **city**, may be spelled **s-**, like **soon**, or **ps-**, like **psychology**.

clothes|a clean piece of paper 3 morally or sexually pure: He led a clean life.| a clean joke (=not rude)|a clean fight (=a fair fight)|(infml) She is clean/has a clean record. (=is not a criminal) 4 having a smooth even edge or surface; regular: a clean cut|the car's clean lines 5 **come clean** infml to admit one's guilt; tell the unpleasant truth: Why don't you come clean and tell us your plans? –**cleanness** n [U]

clean² v [I;T] to (cause to) become clean: Please clean the windows. I can hardly see out.|Metal cleans easily. –**cleaning** n [S]: I have to give the windows a good cleaning.

clean sbdy./sthg.↔ **out** v adv [T] 1 to make (the inside of a room, box, drawer, etc.) clean and tidy 2 infml **a** to take all the money of (someone) by stealing or by winning: I got cleaned out playing cards. **b** to steal everything from (a place): The thieves cleaned out the store. –**cleanout** n [S]: I've just given my desk a good cleanout.

clean up v adv 1 [I;T (=**clean** sthg.↔ **up**)] to make clean or tidy: It's your turn to clean (the bedroom) up.|Clean up the pieces of broken bottle. 2 [I;T (=**clean up** sthg.)] infml to gain (money) as profit: He cleaned up (=made a lot of money) at the races today. –**cleanup** n [S]: I'm going to give the house a good cleanup.

clean³ adv infml [+ prep/adv; no comp.] completely: The bullet went clean through (his arm).|I'm clean out (of food) and the stores are closed.

clean·er /'kliᵞnər/ n 1 a person whose job is cleaning offices, houses, etc. 2 a machine, apparatus, or substance used in cleaning.

clean·er's /'kliᵞnərz/ n a place where clothes, material, etc., can be taken to be cleaned –see also DRY CLEAN

clean·li·ness /'klɛnliᵞnɪs/ n [U] habitual cleanness

clean·ly¹ /'klɛnliᵞ/ adj -lier, -liest careful to keep clean; always clean

clean·ly² /'kliᵞnliᵞ/ adv in a clean manner

cleanse /klɛnz/ v cleansed, cleansing [T] to make (usu. a cut, wound, etc.) clean or pure: The nurse cleansed the wound before stitching it.|(fig.) to cleanse someone of SIN

cleans·er /'klɛnzər/ n [C;U] a substance, such as a chemical liquid or powder, used for cleaning

clear¹ /klɪər/ adj 1 easy to see through: clear glass 2 free from anything that marks or darkens: a clear sky (=with no clouds) clear eyes|clear skin 3 (esp. of sounds, people, writing, etc.) easily heard, seen, read, or understood: a clear speaker|a clear article/ style of writing 4 (esp. of the mind or a person) thinking without difficulty; understanding clearly: a clear thinker 5 [F + (that)|about] (of a person) certain; feeling or showing CONFIDENCE (1): She seems quite clear about her plans/what to do. 6 open; empty; free from blocks, dangers; not OBSTRUCTED in any way: a clear road|a clear view|The road's clear of snow now. 7 [of] free from guilt or blame; untroubled: a clear conscience 8 plain; noticeable; OBVIOUS: a clear case of murder|*It's clear from his actions that he loves her.* **9 in the clear** *infml* free from danger, blame, guilt, etc.: *The police are gone, so we're in the clear.* –see also CLARITY –**clearness** *n* [U]

clear² *adv* **1** in a clear manner: *Speak loud and clear.* **2** [*no comp.*] out of the way; so as to be no longer inside or near: *She jumped clear (of the train).* **3** [*adv* +*prep*/*adv*; *no comp.*] completely; all the way: *You can see clear to the mountains today!* |*The prisoner got clear away.*

clear³ *v* **1** [I;T] to make or become clear: *After the storm was over, the sky cleared.*|*This soap should help clear your skin (of spots).* **2** [T *off, away, of, from*] to remove (something) from (an area); take away; get rid of: *I'll just clear off the plates; then we can use the table.*|*Whose job is it to clear snow from the road?*|*Please clear the table of all these papers.* **3** [T *of*] to show or declare to be free from blame: *The judge cleared the prisoner of any crime and set him free.* **4** [T] to give official permission to or for: *The plans for the new school have not yet been cleared by the council.* **5** [T] to pass by or over (something) without touching: *The horse easily cleared every fence.* **6** [T] to repay (a debt) in full **7 clear the air** to remove doubt and bad feeling by honest explanation, usu. by having an argument: *We had been annoyed with each other for weeks before we cleared the air by talking about it.*

clear sthg.↔ **away** *v adv* [T] to make an area tidy by removing (plates from a table, toys from a floor, etc.)

clear off *v adv* [I] *infml* to leave a place, often quickly: *When the two boys saw the policeman they cleared off as quickly as they could.*

clear out *v adv* **1** [I *of*] *infml* to leave esp. a building or enclosed space, often quickly: *When the police arrived, the thieves quickly cleared out of the house.* **2** [T (=**clear** sthg.↔ **out**)] to collect and throw away (unwanted objects): *I decided to clear out all the old clothes that we never wear.* **3** [T (=**clear** sthg. ↔ **out**)] to clean thoroughly: *I'm going to clear out my bedroom today.*

clear up *v adv* **1** [T (=**clear** sthg. ↔ **up**)] to find an answer to; explain: *to clear up the mystery* **2** [I;T (=**clear** sthg.↔ **up**)] to put in order; tidy up; finish: *I have lots of work to clear up by the weekend.*|*Would you clear up (this room) before our visitors arrive?* **3** [I] to become less bad or come to an end: *I hope the weather clears up before Sunday.*

clear·ance /'klɪərəns/ *n* [C;U] **1** the act or result of CLEARING³: *The ship sailed as soon as it got clearance from the port* AUTHORITY (1). **2** the distance between one object and another passing beneath or beside it: *There was a clearance of only ten centimeters between the bridge and the top of the bus.*

clear-cut /ˌ· '·◄/ *adj* **1** having a smooth regular neat shape (OUTLINE) **2** clear in meaning; DEFINITE: *The President provided Congress with clear-cut plans for future action.*

clear-head·ed /ˌ· '··◄/ *adj* having or showing a clear understanding; sensible –**clear-head-edly** *adv* –**clear-headedness** *n* [U]

clear·ing /'klɪərɪŋ/ *n* an area of land cleared of trees but surrounded by other trees

clear·ly /'klɪərliʸ/ *adv* **1** in a clear manner: *He spoke very clearly*; *I could hear every word.* **2** undoubtedly; OBVIOUSLY: *That's clearly a mistake.*|*Clearly, he's a very stupid person.*

clear-sight·ed /ˌ· '··◄/ *adj* able to see clearly and make good judgments –**clear-sightedly** *adv* –**clearsightedness** *n* [U]

cleav·age /'kliʸvɪdʒ/ *n* **1** [C] a division or break caused by splitting: *a sharp cleavage in society between rich and poor* **2** [U] the act of splitting **3** [C;U] *infml* the space between a woman's breasts, esp. that which can be seen when she is wearing a low-cut dress

cleave /kliʸv/ *v* **cleaved** *or* **cleft** /klɛft/ *or* **clove** /kloʷv/, **cleaved** *or* **cleft** *or* **cloven** /'kloʷvən/, **cleaving** [T] *becoming rare* to divide or make by a cutting blow: *The ax cleaved the piece of wood in two.*

cleav·er /'kliʸvər/ *n* an axlike tool, used esp. for cutting up large pieces of meat

clef /klɛf/ *n* a special sign put at the beginning of a line of written music to show how the notes should be played

cleft /klɛft/ *v past tense of* CLEAVE

clem·en·cy /'klɛmənsiʸ/ *n* [U] mercy, esp. when shown in making punishment less severe

clem·ent /'klɛmənt/ *adj* (esp. of the weather) not severe; MILD (2) –opposite **inclement** –**clemently** *adv*

clench /klɛntʃ/ *v* [T] to close or hold tightly: *She clenched her teeth*/FISTS.|*He clenched his money in his hand.*

cler·gy /'klɜrdʒiʸ/ *n* [P] the leaders of esp. the Christian religion who are allowed to perform religious services: *The clergy have a lot of power in some countries.*

cler·gy·man /'klɜrdʒiʸmən/ *n* **-men** /mən/ a Christian priest or MINISTER –see PRIEST (USAGE)

cler·i·cal /'klɛrɪkəl/ *adj* [*no comp.*] **1** of or concerning a clerk: *clerical work in an office* **2** of or concerning the CLERGY: *wearing a clerical collar* –**clerically** *adv*

clerk /klɜrk/ *n* **1** a person employed in an office, store, etc., to keep records, accounts, etc., and to do written work **2** an official in charge of the records of a court, town council, etc.: *town clerk* **3** *also* **salesclerk** *AmE*– a person who works in a store, esp. selling things

clev·er /'klɛvər/ *adj* **1** quick at learning and understanding; having a quick, skillful, and able mind or body: *a clever student*|*a clever worker*|*clever with his hands* **2** being the result of a quick able mind; showing ability and skill: *a clever idea* –**cleverly** *adv* –**cleverness** *n* [U]

cli·ché /kliʸˈʃeʸ/ *n derog* an idea or expression used so commonly that it has lost much of its meaning –compare PLATITUDE, TRUISM

click¹ /klɪk/ *n* a slight short sound, such as the noise of a key turning in a lock

click² *v* **1** [I;T] to (cause to) make a slight short sound: *The door clicked shut.* **2** [I *with*] *infml* to fall into place; be understood: *Her joke suddenly clicked (with us) and we all laughed.* **3** [I *with*] *infml* to be a success: *That movie's really clicked (with young people); it's very popular.*

cli·ent /'klaɪənt/ n **1** a person who pays a professional person, esp. a lawyer, for help and advice **2** →CUSTOMER –see CUSTOMER (USAGE)

cliff /klɪf/ n a high very steep face of rock, ice, earth, etc., esp. on a coast: *the white cliffs of Dover*|*She stood on the* **clifftop** *and looked out to sea.*

cliff·hang·er /'klɪf,hæŋər/ n *infml* a story or competition of which the result is in doubt until the very end: *The play was a real cliffhanger.*

cli·mac·tic /klaɪ'mæktɪk/ *adj* of or forming a CLIMAX –compare CLIMATIC

cli·mate /'klaɪmɪt/ n the average weather conditions at a particular place: *a tropical climate*|(fig.) *the present political climate* (=political opinions)

cli·mat·ic /klaɪ'mætɪk/ *adj* [*no comp.*] of or related to CLIMATE –compare CLIMACTIC –**climatically** *adv*

cli·max¹ /'klaɪmæks/ n **1** the most powerful or interesting part of a book, film, etc., usu. happening near the end of the story –see also ANTICLIMAX **2** → ORGASM

climax² v [I *in, with*] to reach a CLIMAX¹ (1): *His victory in the senatorial election climaxed a life of service.*

climb¹ /klaɪm/ v **climbed, climbing 1** [I;T] to move, esp. from a lower to a higher position, up, over, or through, esp. by using the hands and feet: *Do you think you can climb that tree?*|*to climb a ladder*|*The old lady climbs (up) the stairs with difficulty.*|*The child climbed into*/*out of the car.* **2** [I] to rise to a higher point; go higher: *It became hotter as the sun climbed in the sky.*|*The plane climbed quickly.*|*The road climbed steeply up the hill.*

climb down¹ (sthg.) v *adv; prep* [I;T] to go down, esp. by using the hands and feet: *We easily climbed down (the side of the cliff).*

climb down² v *adv* [I] *infml* to admit that one has been wrong, has made a mistake, etc., esp. in order to make a difficult state of affairs easier; BACK ⁴ **down**

climb² n [*usu. sing.*] **1** a journey upwards made by climbing; act of climbing: *After a climb of two hours, they reached the top of the mountain.*|*The governor's climb to power had taken 20 years.* **2** a place to be climbed; very steep slope: *There was a steep climb on the road out of town.*

climb·er /'klaɪmər/ n a person or thing that climbs: *a famous mountain climber*|(fig.)*He's always been a* **social climber.** (=tried to reach a higher social position)

SPELLING NOTE

Words with the sound /k/, like **cut,** may be spelled **k-,** like **key,** or **qu-,** like **queen.** Words with the sound /s/, like **city,** may be spelled **s-,** like **soon,** or **ps-,** like **psychology.**

---

clinch¹ /klɪntʃ/ v [T] *infml* to settle (a business matter or an agreement) firmly: *The two businessmen* **clinched the deal** *quickly.*|*The offer of more money clinched it for her. She accepted the job.*

clinch² n [S] the position of two people when holding each other tightly with the arms; EMBRACE: *The fighters*/*lovers were* **in a clinch.** –compare CLASP¹ (2)

cling /klɪŋ/ v **clung** /klʌŋ/, **clinging** [I *to*] to hold tightly; stick firmly; refuse to let go: *The wet shirt clung to his body.*|*The child was clinging to its mother.*|*She clung tightly to her few remaining possessions.*|(fig.) *She still clings to the belief that her son is alive.*

cling·ing /'klɪŋɪŋ/ *adj* **1** (esp. of clothes) tight-fitting; sticking tightly and closely to the body: *a clinging shirt* **2** too dependent upon the presence of another person: *a clinging child that will not leave its mother*

clin·ic /'klɪnɪk/ n a building or part of a hospital where usu. specialized medical treatment and advice is given: *The clinic is near the station.*|*an eye clinic*|*the ear, nose, and throat clinic*

clin·i·cal /'klɪnɪkəl/ *adj* **1** of or connected with a CLINIC or hospital **2** cold; not showing much personal feeling: *He seemed to have a rather clinical view of the breakup of his marriage.* –**clinically** *adv*

clink /klɪŋk/ v [I;T] to (cause to) make a slight knocking sound like that of pieces of glass or metal lightly hitting each other –**clink** n [S]

clip¹ /klɪp/ n a small variously-shaped plastic or usu. metal object for holding things tightly together or in place: *Fasten these sheets of paper together with a clip, please.*|*a paper clip*|*a hair clip*

clip² v **-pp-** [I;T *on, to, together*] to (cause to) fasten onto something with a CLIP¹: *Clip these sheets of paper together please.*|*Does your jewelry clip on?* –opposite **unclip**

clip³ v **-pp-** [T] to cut with scissors or another sharp instrument, esp. to cut small parts off something: *I'm going to clip this advertisement out of the paper.*|*We clipped 50 sheep today.* (=cut off the wool)|*The guard on the train clipped our tickets to show we'd used them.*

clip⁴ n **1** [C] the act or result of CLIPPING³ **2** [C] *infml* a short quick blow: *a clip around the ears* **3** [S] *infml* a fast speed: *He moved off at a good clip.*

clip·pers /'klɪpərz/ n [P] a usu. scissor-like tool used for CLIPPING³: *nail clippers* –see PAIR (USAGE)

clip·ping /'klɪpɪŋ/ n **1** a piece cut off or out of something: *nail clippings* **2** *AmE*‖**cutting** *BrE*– a piece cut out of a newspaper, magazine, etc., such as an article, advertisement, or photograph: *Did you save that newspaper clipping about my friend?*

clique /kliːk, klɪk/ n *derog* a small closely united group of people who do not allow others easily to join their group

clit·o·ris /'klɪtərɪs/ n a small front part of the female sex organ which becomes bigger when the female is sexually excited

cloak¹ /kloʊk/ n a loose outer garment, usu.

without arm-coverings (SLEEVEs), which is sometimes worn instead of a coat: (fig.) *His friendly behavior was a cloak for his evil intentions.*

cloak² /v/ [T] to hide, keep secret, or cover (ideas, thoughts, beliefs, etc.): *cloaked in secrecy*

cloak-and-dag·ger /ˌ· · '···/ adj [A] (esp. of plays, films, stories, etc.) dealing with adventure and mystery

cloak·room /'kloʷk-ruʷm, -rʊm/ n →CHECK-ROOM

clob·ber /'klɑbər/ v [T] *infml* to strike or attack severely and repeatedly: *I'll clobber you if you don't do what you're told.*|(fig.) *We were clobbered (severely defeated) at the last election.*

clock¹ /klɑk/ n **1** an instrument (not worn like a watch) for measuring and showing time: *According to the station clock, the train was an hour late.* **2 around the clock** all day and all night, usu. without stopping: *We worked around the clock to finish the job.* **3 put/set the clock back/ahead** (in countries which officially change the time at the beginning of winter and summer) to move the hands of a clock back/ahead one or two hours: *In Italy they put the clock back two hours every October.*|*In the United States they set the clock ahead an hour in the spring.* **4 turn/put the clock back** to set aside modern laws, ideas, plans, etc., and stay with or return to old-fashioned ones: *The administration has turned the clock back 20 years with its new plans for education.* **5 watch the clock** *derog infml* to think continually of how soon work will end: *A bad worker always watches the clock.*|*He's a clock-watcher.* **6 work against the clock** to work very quickly in order to finish a job before a certain time –see also O'CLOCK

USAGE If a **clock** or **watch** says 11:50 at 12 o'clock, then it is (*10 minutes*) **slow**; if it says 12:05, it is (*5 minutes*) **fast**. If it gets faster every day, it **gains** (time); if it gets slower every day, it **loses** (time). When one puts it to the right time one **sets** it: *I set my watch by the radio.* (=by listening to the radio time signal).

clock² v [T] →TIME² (2): *I clocked him while he ran a mile.*

  clock up sthg. v adv [T] *infml* to record (a distance traveled, points won, etc.): *We clocked up 1,000 miles coming here.*

clock·wise /'klɑk-waɪz/ adj,adv [no comp.] in the direction in which the hands of a clock move: *Turn the lid clockwise if you want to close it tightly.*|*a clockwise movement of the lid* –opposite **counterclockwise**

clock·work /'klɑk-wɜrk/ n [A;U] **1** machinery that can usu. be wound up with a key, and that is used esp. in clocks and toys: *clockwork toys* **2 like clockwork** *infml* smoothly; easily; regularly; without trouble

clod /klɑd/ n a lump or mass, esp. of clay or earth

clog¹ /klɑg/ n [*usu. pl.*] a kind of shoe **a** with a thick usu. wooden bottom **b** completely

made from one piece of wood –see PAIR (USAGE)

clog² v **-gg-** [I;T *up*] to (cause to) become blocked: *A machine won't work if it is clogged (up) with dirt.*|*a clogged sink*

clois·ter /'klɔɪstər/ n [*usu. pl.*] a covered passage which has open archways on one side facing into a garden or courtyard and which usu. forms part of a church, college, MONASTERY, or CONVENT

clois·tered /'klɔɪstərd/ adj shut away from the world in or as if in a CONVENT or MONASTERY: *a cloistered life*

clone /kloʷn/ n *tech* the descendant of a single plant or animal, produced by nonsexual reproduction of any one cell, and with exactly the same form as the parent

clop /klɑp/ v,n **-pp-** [I;S] (to make) a sound like horses' feet (HOOFs)

close¹ /kloʷz/ v **closed, closing 1** [I;T] to (cause to) shut: *Close the windows and keep out the cold air.*|*When does the store close?*|*The bank has decided to close (down) its Los Angeles branch.* **2** [T] to bring to an end: *She closed her speech with a funny joke.* –see OPEN (USAGE)

  close down v adv [I;T=**close** sthg.↔**down**] to (cause to) stop operation: *The company decided to close down the factory.*

  close in v adv [I] [*on, upon*] to surround gradually and usu. from all sides: *The people ran away when the enemy army began to close in.*|(fig.) *Night is closing in.*

  close up v adv **1** [T (=**close** sthg.↔ **up**)] to close completely; block: *The old road has now been closed up.* **2** [I] to come nearer each other: *The teacher told the children to close up to each other.*

close² /kloʷz/ n the end, esp. of an activity or of a period of time: *As the evening came/drew to a close the guests went home.*|*She brought the meeting to a close.*

close³ /kloʷs/ n **1** [C] an enclosed area or space, esp. the area around a large important church (CATHEDRAL); COURTYARD **2** [S *usu. cap.*] (part of the name of) a street in a town: *Spring Close*

close⁴ /kloʷs/ adj **1** near: *Our house is close to the park.* **2** [A] near in relationship: *He's one of my closest relatives/one of my closest friends.* –opposite **distant 3** tight; with little space: *When she sewed, she always used close stitches.* **4** thorough; careful: *We kept a close watch on the prisoners.*|*She made a close study of the subject.* **5** without fresh air, and perhaps too warm: *It's very close in here; open the window.* **6** decided by a very small difference: *a close result/game* –compare NARROW¹ (3) **7** [F] secretive: *She's always been very close about her past life.* **8 a close call/shave/thing** *infml* something bad that nearly happened but did not: *That was a close call! We nearly hit that car!* –see NEAR (USAGE) –**closely** adv –**closeness** n [U]

close⁵ /kloʷs/ adv [F] **1** near: *We live close to the church/close by the church.*|*to sit close together*|*to follow close behind*|*Don't come too close!* **2 close to** *infml* almost: *It happened close to 50 years ago.*

closed /kloʷzd/ adj **1** [to] (esp. of a store or public building) not open to the public: *The store is closed on Thursdays.*|*a club with a closed membership* **2 closed book** something of which one knows nothing: *Fishing is a closed book to me.*

closed cir·cuit tel·e·vi·sion /ˌ·ˌ·· '····/ n [U] a system which sends television signals by wire to a limited number of receivers: *That school uses closed circuit television to help teach some classes.*

closed sea·son /ˌ· '··/ also **close season** /ˈkloʷs ˌsiʸzən/ BrE– n the period of each year when certain animals, birds, or fish may not by law be killed for sport: *the closed season for fishing* –opposite **open season**

closed shop /ˌ· '·◄/ n a factory or other establishment in which the employer hires only members of a particular trade union

close-knit /ˌkloʷs 'nɪt◄/ also **closely-knit** /ˌ·· '·◄/ adj tightly bound together by social, political, religious, etc., beliefs and activities: *a close-knit* COMMUNITY

close-set /ˌkloʷs 'sɛt◄/ adj set close together: *close-set houses/eyes*

clos·et /ˈklɑzɪt/ n esp. AmE **1** a cupboard built into the wall of a room and going from floor to CEILING (1) –see illustration on page 55 **2 come out of the closet** infml to make public, and not to hide, esp. one's HOMOSEXUALity

close-up /ˈkloʷs ʌp/ n a usu. large-scale photograph taken from very near

clo·sure /ˈkloʷʒər/ n [C;U] (an example of) the act of closing: *Lack of money forced the closure of the company.* –compare OPENING[1]

clot[1] /klɑt/ n a thickened or half-solid mass or lump, usu. formed from a liquid, esp. blood: *a blood clot in his leg*

clot[2] v -tt- [I;T] to (cause to) form into CLOTs

cloth /klɔθ/ n **cloths** /klɔðz, klɔθs/ [C;U] (a piece of) material made from wool, hair, cotton, etc., by weaving, and used for making garments, coverings, etc.: *I need a lot of cloth if I'm going to make a long dress.*|*a tablecloth*|*Clean the windows with a cloth.* –see CLOTHES (USAGE)

clothe /kloʷð/ v **clothed** or **clad** /klæd/, **clothing** [T] to provide clothes for: *They have to work hard to feed and clothe their family.*|(fig.) *hills clothed in mist*

clothes /kloʷz, kloʷðz/ n [P] garments, such as pants, dresses, shirts, etc., worn on the body

USAGE Compare **clothes**, **cloth**, **clothing**, and **dress**: **Clothes** is the usual word for all the garments that one wears (such as shirts and dresses), and these are made from various kinds of **cloth** or **material** (such as wool and cotton): *He spends a lot of money on* **clothes.**|*She's got some lovely* **clothes.**|*How much* **cloth/material** *will I need to make a pair of pants?* **Clothing** is a more formal word for **clothes.** A **dress** is a kind of outer garment worn by women and girls, but in certain expressions **dress** [U] can mean a particular type of **clothing**: *What a pretty dress she's wearing today!!*|*My parents had to wear formal evening* **dress** *to go to the company dinner.*

clothes·horse /ˈkloʷzhɔrs, 'kloʷðz-/ n **1** a person who is concerned with clothing and fashion **2** a framework on which clothes are hung to dry, usu. indoors

cloth·ing /ˈkloʷðɪŋ/ n [U] often fml the garments, such as pants, dresses, shirts, etc., worn together on different parts of the body: *food, clothing, and shelter* –see CLOTHES (USAGE) –see illustration opposite

cloud[1] /klaʊd/ n **1** (a usu. white or gray mass of) very small drops of water floating high in the air: *When there are black clouds, you can tell it's going to rain.*| (fig.) *Clouds of smoke rose above the bombed city.*|(fig.) *a cloud of insects* **2** something that causes unhappiness or fear: *The clouds of war were gathering.* **3 under a cloud** out of favor; looked on with distrust: *He left his job under a cloud.* **4 on cloud nine** AmE infml very very happy

cloud[2] v [I;T over] to (cause to) become covered with or as if with clouds: *The sky clouded over: we could see it was going to rain.*|(fig.) *Age clouded his memory.*

cloud·burst /ˈklaʊdbɜrst/ n a sudden very heavy fall of rain

cloud·y /ˈklaʊdiʸ/ adj -ier, -iest **1** full of clouds; OVERCAST: *a cloudy day/sky* **2** not clear or transparent: *cloudy water*|*a cloudy mirror* –**cloudiness** n [U]

clout[1] /klaʊt/ n **1** [C] infml a blow or knock, esp. given with the hand **2** [U] esp. AmE infml influence: *Those senators have a lot of clout with the governor.*

clout[2] v [T] infml to strike, esp. with the hand

clove /kloʷv/ n the dried flower of a tropical Asian plant, used usu. whole for giving a special taste to food

clove[2] n any of the smallest pieces into which the root of the GARLIC plant can be divided: *a clove of garlic*

clove[3] v past tense of CLEAVE

clo·ven /ˈkloʷvən/ v past participle of CLEAVE: *Cows, sheep, and goats have* **cloven hoofs.** (=a foot divided into two parts)

clo·ver /ˈkloʷvər/ n [C;U] **1** a small usu. three-leafed plant with pink, purple, or white flowers, often grown as food for cattle **2 in clover** infml living in comfort

clown[1] /klaʊn/ n a performer, esp. in the CIRCUS (1), who dresses funnily and tries to make people laugh by his/her jokes, tricks, or actions

clown[2] v [I around, about] often derog to behave like a CLOWN[1]; act stupidly or foolishly

club[1] /klʌb/ n **1** (a building for) a society of people who join together for a certain purpose, esp. sport or amusement: *a health club*|*a tennis club*|*a social club* **2** a heavy stick, suitable for use as a weapon **3** a

---

SPELLING NOTE

Words with the sound /k/, like **cut**, may be spelled **k-**, like **key**, or **qu-**, like **queen**. Words with the sound /s/, like **city**, may be spelled **s-**, like **soon**, or **ps-**, like **psychology**.

Bill is looking for a new **jacket**. A **salesman** is helping him.

SALESMAN: I think this one is **your size**.
BILL: No, it's too **tight**. Do you have a larger one?
SALESMAN: **Try** this one **on**.
BILL: Yes, this **fits** (me) perfectly. Do you think it **goes with** these **pants**?
SALESMAN: Yes, I do. And it goes with your **tie**, too.

BILL: **What's it made of?**
SALESMAN: It's a **blend** of **wool** and **cotton**.
BILL: Hmm. **How much is it?**
SALESMAN: It's **on sale** this week. It's only $59.
BILL: Great. I'll take it.
SALESMAN: Fine. **Cash or charge?**
BILL: Charge, please.

specially shaped stick for striking a ball in certain sports, esp. GOLF: *a golf club* **4** a playing card with one or more three-leafed figures printed on it in black: *the three of clubs* –see CARDS (USAGE)

club² *v* **-bb-** [T] to beat or strike with a heavy stick (CLUB): *clubbed to death*

club sand·wich /ˌ·ˈ··/ *n AmE* three pieces of bread with some other usu. cold food between them, eaten with the hands

club so·da /ˌ·ˈ··/ [C;U] *AmE* for SODA WATER

cluck /klʌk/ *v,n* [C;I] (to make) the noise that a hen makes

clue /kluʷ/ *n* **1** something that helps to find an answer to a question, difficulty, etc.: *Have any clues been found that can help the police find the criminal?* **2 not have a clue** *infml* to be unable to understand; know nothing: *"Do you know what he's talking about?" "I don't have a clue."*

clump¹ /klʌmp/ *n* **1** [C] a group of trees, bushes, plants, etc., growing together **2** [C] a heavy solid lump or mass of dirt, soil, mud, etc. **3** [S] a heavy slow sound, such as made by slow footsteps

clump² *v* [I] to walk with slow heavy noisy footsteps

clum·sy /ˈklʌmziʸ/ *adj* **-sier, -siest** *derog* **1** awkward and ungraceful in movement or action; without skill or grace: *He's a terrible dancer; he's too clumsy and keeps hitting other people.* **2** difficult to handle or control: *You shouldn't wear such clumsy shoes.* –**clumsily** *adv* –**clumsiness** *n* [U]

clung /klʌŋ/ *v past tense and participle of* CLING

clus·ter¹ /ˈklʌstər/ *n* a number of things of the same kind growing or being close together in a group: *a cluster of stars*

cluster² *v* [I;T *around, together*] to (cause to) gather or grow in one or more CLUSTERS¹: *The boys clustered together around the fire and sang songs.*

clutch¹ /klʌtʃ/ *v* [T] to hold tightly: *The mother clutched her baby in her arms.|He clutched at* (=tried to hold) *the branch but could not reach it.*

clutch² *n* **1** [usu. sing.] the act of CLUTCHING¹; a tight hold: *His clutch was not tight enough, and he fell from the branch.* **2** an apparatus, esp. in a car, which allows working parts of an engine to be connected or disconnected: *You have to push in the clutch to change gears.* –see illustration on page 95 **3 in the clutches of** in the control, power, or possession of: *Once she was in the clutches of the enemy, she knew she'd never escape.*

clut·ter¹ /ˈklʌtər/ *v* [T *up*] to make untidy or confused: *Don't clutter up your room.|The room was cluttered with furniture.*

clutter² *n* [C;U] (a collection of) things scat-

tered about in a disorderly manner: *a room full of clutter*

cm *written abbrev. said as:* CENTIMETER(*s*)

c/o /ˌsiʸ ˈowˑ/ *written abbrev. also said as:* (in) care of; (esp. used when writing addresses) to be held or looked after by: *Send it to John Smith c/o Dorothy Smith.*

Co. /koʷ/ *written abbrev. also said as:* COMPANY (1): *James Smith & Co.*

CO *written abbrev. said as:* Colorado /ˌkɑləˈrædoʷ, -ˈrɑ-/, a state in the US

coach¹ /koʷtʃ/ *n* **1** a large enclosed four-wheeled horse-drawn carriage, used esp. in former times or in official ceremonies **2** also **car** *AmE*‖also **carriage** *BrE*– a railway passenger car **3** *BrE* for BUS¹ **4** a person who trains sportsmen and sportswomen for games, competitions, etc.: *a football coach* **5** also **coach class** *AmE*‖**economy** *BrE*–a cheap class for plane seats, etc.: *Is your ticket first class or coach?*

coach² *v* [I;T *in, at*] to train or teach (a person or a group of people); give instruction or advice to (a person or a group of people): *I coach people in singing.*

co·ag·u·late /koʷˈægyəˌleʸt/ *v* **-lated, -lating** [I;T] to (cause to) change from a liquid into a solid or nearly solid mass: *Blood coagulates when it meets air.|Air can coagulate blood.* –**coagulation** /koʷˌægyəˈleʸʃən/ *n* [U]

coal /koʷl/ *n* **1** [C;U] (a piece of) a black or dark brown mineral which is dug (MINEd) from the earth, which can be burned to give heat, and from which gas and many other products can be made: *A coal fell from the fire and burned the mat.* **2 drag/rake/haul over the coals** *infml* to scold someone for doing something wrong

co·a·lesce /ˌkoʷəˈlɛs/ *v* **-lesced, -lescing** [I] to grow together or unite so as to form one group, body, mass, etc. –**coalescence** *n* [U]

co·a·li·tion /ˌkoʷəˈlɪʃən/ *n* a union of political parties for a special purpose, usu. for a limited period of time: *Many different groups joined the coalition against government spending cuts.*

coal mine /ˈ· ·/ *n* a mine from which coal is obtained

coarse /kɔrs, koʷrs/ *adj* **1** not fine or smooth; lumpy; rough: *a coarse woolen garment|coarse grains of sand* **2** rough in manner; not delicate: *coarse behavior|a coarse joke* –**coarsely** *adv* –**coarseness** *n* [U]

coars·en /ˈkɔrsən, ˈkoʷr-/ *v* [I;T] to (cause to) become coarse: *The wrong kind of soap can coarsen the skin.*

coast¹ /koʷst/ *n* [usu. sing.] **1** the land next to the sea; seashore: *a trip to the coast* –see SHORE¹ (USAGE) **2 the coast is clear** *infml* all danger has gone: *When the coast was clear, the two thieves escaped.*

coast² *v* [I *along*] to keep moving, esp. down a hill, without any effort: *The children were enjoying coasting along (on their bicycles).*

coast·er /ˈkoʷstər/ *n* a small round mat placed under a bottle, glass, etc., to protect a table top or other surface –see illustration on page 399

coast guard /ˈ· ·/ *n* [U] (*often caps.*) a naval

or police organization intended to watch for ships in danger and prevent unlawful activity at sea

coast·line /'kowstlaın/ n the shape (OUTLINE) of a coast, esp. as seen from the sea

coat[1] /kowt/ n **1** an outer garment with long SLEEVEs, often fastened at the front with buttons, and usu. worn to keep warm or for protection **2** → JACKET (1): *a coat and skirt* **3** an animal's fur, wool, hair, etc. **4** also **coat·ing**– a covering spread over a surface: *a coat of paint*/*of dust*

coat[2] v [T *with*] to cover with a COAT[1] (4): *The table was coated with dust.*

coat of arms /ˌ· · '·/ n **coats of arms** a group of patterns or pictures, usu. painted on a shield, used by a noble family, town council, university, etc., as their special sign

coax /kowks/ v [T] **1** [*into, out of, to*] to persuade (someone) by gentle kindness or patience: *I coaxed him into going to school, even though I had to promise to go with him.* **2** to obtain (something) by gentle persuading: *I coaxed a kiss from her.* –**coaxingly** adv

cob /kab/ also **corncob** /'kɔrnkab/– n the long hard central part of an ear of corn

cob·bled /'kabəld/ adj (of a road) covered (PAVED) with COBBLESTONEs: *old cobbled streets*

cob·bler /'kablər/ n old use a person who repairs shoes

cob·ble·stone /'kabəlˌstown/ n [*often pl.*] a naturally rounded stone, used for covering the surface of roads in former times

co·bra /'kowbrə/ n an African or Asian poisonous snake

cob·web /'kabwɛb/ n a very fine network of sticky threads made by a SPIDER to catch insects

Co·ca-Co·la /ˌkowkə 'kowlə/ also **Coke** /kowk/– n [C;U] *tdmk* (a small bottle or glass of) a popular non-alcoholic dark-colored bubbly drink of American origin

co·caine /kow'keyn, 'kowkeyn/ also **coke** /kowk/ *infml*– n [U] a drug used for preventing pain, or taken (illegally) for pleasure

cock /kak/ n → ROOSTER

cock·a·too /'kakəˌtuw/ n **cockatoos** or **cockatoo** an Australian bird (PARROT) with a lot of large feathers (CREST) on the top of its head

cock-eyed /'kakaɪd/ adj infml turned or twisted to one side; CROOKED (1): *That picture's not hanging straight; it's cock-eyed.*|(fig.) *a cockeyed* (=foolish) *idea*

Cock·ney /'kakniy/ n a Londoner, esp. one from the poorer part near the sea ports (the **East End**)

cock·pit /'kakˌpɪt/ n the part of a plane or racing car in which the pilot or driver sits

cock·roach /'kak-rowtʃ/ n also **roach** AmE– a large black insect which lives in dark wet places and likes dirty houses

cock·tail /'kakteyl/ n **1** a mixed alcoholic drink **2** a small quantity of specially prepared SEAFOOD eaten at the start of a meal: *a shrimp cocktail*

cock·y /'kakiy/ also **cocksure** /ˌkak'ʃʊər◂/– adj **-ier, -iest** infml derog too sure of oneself:

I don't like him; he's too cocky. –**cockiness** n [U]

co·coa /'kowkow/ n **1** [U] a dark brown powder, used in making chocolate **2** [C;U] (a cupful of) a drink made from this powder

co·co·nut /'kowkəˌnʌt, -nət/ n [C;U] (the hard white flesh of) a very large nut with a hollow center filled with a milky juice

co·coon /kə'kuwn/ n a protective case of silky threads in which a CHRYSALIS is enclosed

cod /kad/ also **codfish** /'kad,fɪʃ/– n **cod** or **cods** [C;U] (the flesh of) a large North Atlantic sea fish

C.O.D. /ˌsiy ow 'diy/ abbrev. for: cash on delivery; with payment to be made when something is delivered

code[1] /kowd/ n **1** [C;U] a system of words, letters, numbers, etc., used instead of ordinary writing, esp. to keep messages secret: *a message written* in *code*/*a computer code* **2** [C;U] a system of signals used instead of letters and numbers in a message that is to be broadcast, telegraphed, etc.: *a telegraphic code* **3** [C] a system or collection of social customs or laws: *a code of behavior*

code[2] also **encode** fml– v **coded, coding** [T] to translate into a CODE[1] (1,2) –see also DECODE

co·ed /'kowɛd, ˌkow'ɛd/ n AmE infml a female student in a college or university open to both sexes

co·ed·u·ca·tion /ˌkowɛdʒə'keyʃən/ n [U] the system of educating boys and girls together –**coeducational** adj

co·erce /kow'ɜrs/ v **-erced, -ercing** [T] fml to make (an unwilling person or group of people) do something, by using force, threats of punishment, etc.: *The terrorists coerced the pilot into accepting their demands not to land.* –**coercion** /kow'ɜrʃən, -ʒən/ n [U]: *The terrorists got what they wanted by coercion.* –**coercive** /kow'ɜrsɪv/ adj

co·ex·ist /ˌkowɪg'zɪst/ v [I *with*] to exist together at the same time: *The war started because the two countries couldn't coexist peacefully.*

cof·fee /'kɔfiy/ n **1** [U] a brown powder made by crushing **coffee beans 2** [C;U] (a cupful of) a hot brown drink made from this powder: *Would you like a (cup of)/some coffee?*|*Two coffees, please!*

coffee table /'·· ˌ··/ a small long low table on which coffee may be served, magazines arranged, etc. –see illustration on page 399

cof·fer /'kɔfər, 'ka-/ n lit or humor a large strong chest for holding money, jewels, or other valuable objects

cof·fin /'kɔfɪn/ n the box in which a dead person is buried

cog /kag/ n any of the teeth around the edge of a wheel (**cogwheel**) that cause it to move or be moved by another wheel in a machine

co·gent /'kowdʒənt/ adj able to prove, or produce belief; forceful in argument; CONVINCING: *a cogent argument* –**cogently** adv –**cogency** n [U]

cog·i·tate /'kadʒəˌteyt/ v **-tated, -tating** [I *about, upon*] fml to think carefully and seriously about something –**cogitation** /ˌkadʒə'teyʃən/ n [U]

co·gnac /ˈkoʷnyæk, ˈkɑn-, ˈkɔn-/ n [C;U] (a glass of) a fine strong alcoholic drink (BRANDY) made in France

co·hab·it /ˌkoʷˈhæbɪt/ v [I with] fml (of two unmarried people) to live together as though married –**cohabitation** /koʷˌhæbəˈteʸʃən/ n [U]

co·here /koʷˈhɪər/ v **-hered, -hering** [I] fml **1** to stick together; be united **2** to be reasonably and naturally connected, esp. in thought

co·her·ent /koʷˈhɪərənt, -ˈhɛr-/ adj (esp. of speech, thought, ideas, etc.) naturally or reasonably connected; easily understood –opposite **incoherent** –compare CONSISTENT –**coherently** adv –**coherence** n [U]

co·he·sion /koʷˈhiʸʒən/ n [U] the act or state of sticking together tightly: We need more cohesion in the party if we're going to win the next election. –**cohesive** /koʷˈhiʸsɪv/ adj: cohesive forces in society

coif·fure /kwɑˈfyʊər, -ˈfyɜr/ n fml a style of arranging and combing a woman's hair –**coiffured** adj

coil¹ /kɔɪl/ v [I;T up] to (cause to) wind or twist into a ring or continuous circular shape (SPIRAL): Coil the rope up, please.|The snake coiled (itself) around the tree –opposite **uncoil**

coil² n **1** [C] (any of) a connected set of rings or twists into which a rope, wire, etc., can be wound: a coil of rope|a loose coil of hair **2** [C] tech an apparatus made by winding wire into a continuous circular shape, used for carrying an electric current **3** [C; the S] →I.U.D.

coin¹ /kɔɪn/ n [C;U] (a piece of usu. flat and round) metal made by a government for use as money: He paid me in coin.

coin² v [T] **1** to make (coins) from metal: The government has decided to coin more 50-cent pieces. **2** to invent (a word or phrase): Who coined the word "nuke?"

co·in·cide /ˌkoʷɪnˈsaɪd/ v **-cided, -ciding** [I with] **1** to happen at the same time or during the same period of time **2** (of ideas, opinions, etc.) to be in agreement: My religious beliefs don't coincide with yours.

co·in·ci·dence /koʷˈɪnsədəns, -ˌdɛns/ n [C;U] (a) combination of events, happening by chance, but in such a way that it seems planned or arranged: What a coincidence that I was in New York at the same time you were!

co·in·ci·den·tal /koʷˌɪnsəˈdɛntəl/ adj resulting from a COINCIDENCE: a coincidental meeting –**coincidentally** adv

coke¹ /koʷk/ n [U] the solid substance that remains after gas has been removed from coal by heating, burned as fuel

coke² n infml for **1** [C;U] tdmk for COCA-COLA **2** [U] → COCAINE

Col. written abbrev. said as: Colorado /ˌkɑləˈrædoʷ, -ˈrɑ-/, (a state in the US)

col·an·der /ˈkʌləndər, ˈkɑ-/ also **cullender** /ˈkʌl-/ n a bowl-shaped pan with many small holes in the bottom, used for separating liquid from food –see illustration on page 379

cold¹ /koʷld/ adj **1** having a low or lower than usual temperature; not warm: a cold night|a cold wind|It's a cold day for July, isn't it?|I'm (feeling) cold today. **2** (of people or their actions) showing a lack of (friendly) feelings; unkind **3** (of food) cooked but not eaten hot **4** (out) cold unconscious, esp. as the result of a severe blow to the head **5 know something cold** AmE to know something very well –**coldly** adv –**coldness** n [U]

cold² n **1** [the S] the absence of heat; low temperature; cold weather: Don't go out into the cold without a coat! **2** [C;U] an illness, esp. of the nose and/or throat, which is common in winter and may cause headaches, coughing, slight fever, and general discomfort (esp. in the phrases **catch/have (a) cold, the common cold) 3 (out) in the cold** infml not considered; seemingly unwanted: He was left out in the cold at school because he didn't like sports.

cold-blood·ed /ˌ·ˈ··◂/ adj **1** [no comp.] having a body temperature that changes according to the temperature of the surroundings: Snakes are cold-blooded. –compare WARM-BLOODED **2** derog showing complete lack of feeling; cruel: a cold-blooded murder –see also HOT-BLOODED

cold-heart·ed /ˌ·ˈ··◂/ adj lacking sympathy or feeling; unkind: a cold-hearted refusal –compare WARM-HEARTED –**cold-heartedly** adv –**cold-heartedness** n [U]

cold war /ˌ·ˈ·◂/ n (sometimes caps.) a severe political struggle, without actual fighting, between states with opposed political systems

col·ic /ˈkɑlɪk/ n [U] a severe pain in the stomach and bowels (esp. of babies)

col·lab·o·rate /kəˈlæbəˌreʸt/ v **-rated, -rating** [I with, on] **1** to work together or with someone else, esp. for a special purpose: The police and the army collaborated to catch the terrorists. **2** derog to help an enemy country which has taken control of one's own: Anyone who collaborated was shot. –**collaborator** n –**collaboration** /kəˌlæbəˈreʸʃən/ n [U]: The two companies are working in collaboration with each other.

col·lage /kəˈlɑʒ, koʷ-/ n a picture made by sticking various materials or objects onto a surface

col·lapse¹ /kəˈlæps/ v **-lapsed, -lapsing 1** [I;T] to (cause to) fall down or inwards suddenly: The bridge collapsed under the weight of the train.|(fig.) All opposition to the government collapsed because of the war. **2** [I] to fall helpless or unconscious: He collapsed at the end of the five-mile race. **3** [I;T] to fold into a shape that takes up less space: This table collapses, so I can store it easily when I'm not using it.

collapse² n **1** [S;U] (an example of) the act of

falling down or inwards: *The storm caused the collapse of the roof.*|(fig.) *The collapse of the peace talks caused more fighting.* **2** [C;U *usu. sing.*] (an example of) the act of suddenly and completely losing strength and/or will: *a state of near collapse*|*He suffered from a nervous collapse.*

col·laps·i·ble /kəˈlæpsəbəl/ *adj* that can be COLLAPSED[1] (3) for easy storing

col·lar[1] /ˈkɑlər/ *n* **1** the part of a shirt, dress, or coat that fits round the neck **2** a leather or metal band put round an animal's neck –see also BLUE-COLLAR, WHITE-COLLAR

collar[2] *v* [T] *infml* to catch and hold (someone): *The police collared him as he was getting on the boat.*

col·lar·bone /ˈkɑlərˌboʷn/ *n* either of a pair of bones joining the RIBs to the shoulders

col·late /kəˈleʸt, kɑ-, ˈkoʷleʸt, ˈkɑ-/ *v* [T] to arrange (the sheets of paper, book, etc.) in the proper order: *I've made the copies of your report, but I haven't collated them yet.*

col·lat·er·al /kəˈlæt̬ərəl/ *n* [S;U] *fml* property or something valuable promised to a lender of money in case repayment is not made: *He used his house as (a) collateral for the loan.* –compare SECURITY[3]

col·league /ˈkɑliʸg/ *n* a fellow worker, esp. in a profession

col·lect /kəˈlɛkt/ *v* **1** [I;T] to bring or gather together: *Collect the books and put them in a pile on my desk.*|*A crowd of people collected to see the new school.*|*I collect foreign coins.* (=as a HOBBY)|*The government could save money by improving the way it collects taxes.*|(fig.) *I tried to* **collect my thoughts** *but I was too excited.* **2** [T] to call for and take away: *The mailman collects the letters every morning.*

col·lect·ed /kəˈlɛktɪd/ *adj* having control of oneself, one's thoughts, senses, etc.; calm: *How can you stay so* **cool, calm, and collected** *after an argument?*

col·lec·tion /kəˈlɛkʃən/ *n* [C;U] the act of collecting, or set of things collected: *Janet has a very good collection of foreign stamps.*|*What does the church do with the money it gets from collections?*

col·lec·tive[1] /kəˈlɛktɪv/ *adj* [*no comp.*] of, by, or related to a number of people or groups of people considered or acting as one: *the collective opinion of the governments of Western Europe*|*collective ownership* –**collectively** *adv*

collective[2] *n* a business or firm owned and controlled by the people who work in it.: *The worker's collective doesn't like the new plan.*

collective bar·gain·ing /ˌ·ˌ·· ˈ···/ *n* [U] talks between unions and employers about working conditions, rules, wages, etc.

col·lec·tor /kəˈlɛktər/ *n* **1** a person employed to collect taxes, tickets, debts, etc. **2** a person who collects stamps, coins, etc., as a HOBBY: *a stamp collector*

col·lege /ˈkɑlɪdʒ/ *n* **1** [C;U] a school for higher and professional education, often connected to a university: *The college is next to the station.*|*He starts college in January.* **2** [C] *fml* a body of people with a common profession, purpose, duties, or rights

col·lide /kəˈlaɪd/ *v* **-lided, -liding** [I *with*] to meet and strike (together) violently: *Many people were hurt when the two buses collided.*

col·li·sion /kəˈlɪʒən/ *n* [C;U] (an example of) the act of colliding (COLLIDE): *Many people were hurt in the collision between the bus and the car.*

col·lo·qui·al /kəˈloʷkwiʸəl/ *adj* (of words, phrases, style, etc.) of or suitable for ordinary, informal, or familiar conversation –**colloquially** *adv* –**colloquialism** *n*

col·lu·sion /kəˈluʷʒən/ *n* [U] *fml* secret agreement between two or more people with the intention of cheating or deceiving others

Colo. *written abbrev. said as:* Colorado /ˌkɑləˈrædoʷ, -ˈrɑ-/ (a state in the US)

co·lon /ˈkoʷlən/ *n* a mark (:) used in writing and printing to introduce a statement, example, etc.

colo·nel /ˈkɜrnl/ *n* [A;C] an officer of middle rank in the army or air force

co·lo·ni·al /kəˈloʷniʸəl/ *adj* [A *no comp.*] of or related to colonies (COLONY (1)): *The African people have successfully fought against colonial rule.*

co·lo·ni·al·ism /kəˈloʷniʸəˌlɪzəm/ *n* [U] the having or keeping of colonies (COLONY(1)) abroad: *British colonialism led to the establishment of a large empire.* –compare IMPERIALISM –**colonialist** *adj,n*

col·o·nize ||also **-nise** *BrE* /ˈkɑləˌnaɪz/ *v* **-nized, -nizing** [I;T] to make (a country, area, etc.) into a COLONY (1): *The British first colonized North America in the 17th century.* –**colonization** /ˌkɑlənəˈzeʸʃən/ *n* [U] –**colonist** /ˈkɑlənɪst/ *n*

col·on·nade /ˌkɑləˈneʸd/ *n* a row of pillars with equal spaces between, usu. supporting a roof or row of arches

col·o·ny /ˈkɑləniʸ/ *n* **-nies 1** a country or area under the control of a distant country and often settled by people from that country **2** a group of people from the same country or with the same interests, living together: *the French colony in Tokyo* **3** a group of the same kind of animals or plants living or growing together: *a colony of plants*

col·or[1] *AmE*||**colour** *BrE* /ˈkʌlər/ *n* **1** [U] the quality which allows one to see the difference between (for example) a red flower and a blue flower when both are the same size and shape **2** [C] red, blue, green, black, brown, yellow, white, etc.: *"What color is this paint?" "It's red."*|*What color did you paint the door?* **3** [C;U] (a) paint; DYE: *The artist painted in* WATERCOLORS. **4** [U] the general appearance of the skin; COMPLEXION: *As she became more annoyed Jean's color changed.* **5** [U] details or behavior of a place, thing, or person, that interest the mind or eye and excite the imagination: *She loved the life, noise, and color of the market.*

USAGE When asking questions about color, say *What color is it?* (not *What* **color** *does it have?*) When answering, say *It's red.* (not *a red color*.)

color[2] *AmE*||**colour** *BrE* *v* **1** [T *in*] to cause (something) to have color, esp. with a

CRAYON or pencil rather than a brush: *The child is coloring the picture.* **2** [I] to take on or change color: *The leaves have already started to color; it will soon be winter.* **3** [T] to give a special effect or feeling to (a person, event, etc.): *Personal feelings colored his judgment.* **4** [I] to become red in the face; BLUSH: *He colored with anger at her suggestion.* –compare DISCOLOR

color bar /'·· ,·/ ‖also **color line** /'·· ,·/ *AmE–* *n* the set of customs or laws in some places which prevent people of different colors from mixing freely

color-blind /'·· ,·/ *adj* unable to see the difference between certain colors –**color blindness** /'·· ,·· / *n* [U]

col·ored[1] *AmE*‖**coloured** *BrE* /'kʌlərd/ *adj* **1** *old use* →BLACK[1] (3) **2** of the stated color: *She wore a cream-colored dress.*

colored[2] *AmE*‖**coloured** *BrE n often derog* any person belonging to a race that does not have a white skin

col·or·ful *AmE*‖**colourful** *BrE* /'kʌlərfəl/ *adj* **1** showily colored; full of color or colors; bright: *a bird with colorful wings* **2** likely to excite the senses or imagination; rich in expressive variety or detail: *a colorful period of history*

col·or·ing *AmE*‖**colouring** *BrE* /'kʌlərɪŋ/ *n* **1** [C;U] a substance used for giving a special color to another substance, esp. food; DYE: **2** [U] (healthy or ill appearance as expressed by) skin color: *People always think I'm ill because of my coloring.*

col·or·less *AmE*‖**colourless** *BrE* /'kʌlərlɪs/ *adj* **1** without color: *Water is a colorless liquid.* **2** dull; lacking variety, interest, excitement, etc.: *a colorless existence*

col·ors *AmE*‖**colours** *BrE* /'kʌlərz/ *n* [P] **1** the official flag of a country, ship, part of an army, etc. **2** a dress, cap, piece of material, etc., worn as a sign of one's club, school, team, etc. **3 with flying colors** with great success: *She passed her examination with flying colors.* **4 show one's true colors** to show one's real nature or character, esp. for the first time

co·los·sal /kə'lɑsəl/ *adj* very large: *a colossal building/debt* –see Study Notes on page 550

co·los·sus /kə'lɑsəs/ *n* -**suses** *or* -**si** /saɪ/ *a* person or thing of very great size, importance, or ability: *a colossus of a man*

colt /koʷlt/ *n* a young male horse –compare FILLY

col·umn /'kɑləm/ *n* **1** a pillar used in a building as a support or decoration or standing alone as a MONUMENT (1) **2** anything looking like a pillar in shape or use: *a column of smoke/to add up a column of figures/a column of soldiers marching down the road/This dictionary is arranged in two columns.* **3** an

SPELLING NOTE
Words with the sound /k/, like **cut**, may be spelled **k-**, like **key**, or **qu-**, like **queen**. Words with the sound /s/, like **city**, may be spelled **s-**, like **soon**, or **ps-**, like **psychology**.

article by a particular writer that regularly appears in a newspaper or magazine

col·um·nist /'kɑləmnɪst, 'kɑləmɪst/ *n* a person who writes a regular article for a newspaper or magazine

co·ma /'koʷmə/ *n* a state of long unnatural deep unconsciousness, from which it is difficult to wake up, caused by disease, poisoning, a severe blow, etc.: *After she drank the poison, she* **went into a coma.**

co·ma·tose /'koʷmə,toʷs, 'kɑ-/ *adj tech* in a COMA; deeply unconscious: (fig.) *feeling a bit comatose* (=very tired)

comb[1] /koʷm/ *n* a toothed piece of bone, metal, plastic, etc., used for tidying and straightening the hair –see illustration on page 51 –**combing** *n* [S]: *Your hair needs a good combing.*

comb[2] *v* [T] **1** to tidy, straighten, or arrange (esp. the hair) with a comb: *If you combed your hair more often you wouldn't look so untidy.* **2** to search (a place) thoroughly: *The police combed the woods for the missing boy.*

com·bat[1] /kəm'bæt, 'kɑmbæt/ *v* -**t-** *or* -**tt-** *AmE*‖-**tt-** *BrE* [I;T] *fml* to fight or struggle against: *to combat evil/The doctor spent his life combating disease.*

com·bat[2] /'kɑmbæt/ *n* [C;U] (a) struggle between two people, armies, ideas, etc.: *These soldiers have just been* **in combat.** (=fighting)

com·bat·ant /kəm'bætnt/ *n* a person playing a direct part in fighting: *In the last war as many noncombatants as combatants were killed.*

com·bi·na·tion /,kɑmbə'neʸʃən/ *n* **1** [U] the act of combining or state of being combined **2** [C] a number of people or things that are combined or united in a common purpose: *The club is supported by a combination of people from all social classes.* **3** [C] the list of special numbers or letters needed to open a special lock, SAFE[2], etc.

com·bine[1] /kəm'baɪn/ *v* -**bined**, -**bining** [I;T] to (cause to) come together, unite, or join together: *To make the cake, first combine the eggs, butter, and sugar.*

com·bine[2] /'kɑmbaɪn/ *n* a group of people, businesses, etc., joined or acting together

com·bus·ti·ble /kəm'bʌstəbəl/ *n,adj* (a substance) that can catch fire and burn easily: *Gasoline is highly combustible/a combustible, so don't smoke while you're handling it.*

com·bus·tion /kəm'bʌstʃən/ *n* [U] the act of catching fire and burning

come /kʌm/ *v* **came** /keʸm/, **come, coming** [I] **1** [+*v-ing*] to move towards the speaker or a particular place: *I recognized him as soon as he came towards me through the door.|The little girl came running to me for sympathy.|The train came slowly into the station.* **2** to arrive: *I've been waiting for hours, and he still hasn't come!|Darkness comes at six o'clock.|Christmas is coming soon.* **3** to reach: *The water came (up) to my neck.|Her hair comes (down) to her waist.* **4** to be in a particular place or position: *In this list the price comes next to the article.|A comes before B.|Monday comes after Sunday.|Your* family should always come before (=be more important than) *your job.* **5** [+*to-v*] to happen: *How did Jean come to be invited to this party?*|*No good will come of* (=happen as a result of) *all this.* **6** [+*to-v*] to begin: *In time you may come to enjoy school.* **7** to become: *The buttons on my coat came unfastened.*|*The door came open.* –compare COME **off**; see BECOME (USAGE) **8** to be offered, produced, etc.: *Shoes come in many shapes and sizes.*|*Milk comes from cows or other animals.* **9** come and go to pass or disappear quickly; change: *Fashions come and go, but this dress is always popular.* **10** come undone to meet with difficulties or failure: *The company's going to come undone if prices keep rising.* **11** how come? *infml* how did it happen (that): *How come you're so late?* **12** to come in the future: *the years/ days to come* –compare GO[1]

come about *v adv* [I +*that*] to happen: *How did this dangerous state of affairs come about?*|*How did it come about that you were an hour late on such a short trip?*

come across[1]/**upon** sbdy./sthg.– *v prep* [T *no pass.*] to meet or discover, esp. by chance: *I've just come across a beautiful poem in this book.*

come across[2] *v adv* [I] *infml* to be effective and well received: *Your speech came across very well; everyone liked it.*

come along *v adv* [I] **1** to advance; improve, esp. in health: *How's your work coming along?*|*Mother's coming along nicely, thank you.* **2** to happen; arrive by chance: *Take every chance that comes along.* **3** Come along! also Come on (now)!– *infml* Try harder! Hurry up!

come apart *v adv* [I] to break into pieces without the need of force: *I picked up the old book, and it just came apart in my hands.*

come around *v adv* [I] **1** also come to, come round– to regain consciousness **2** [*to*] to change sides or opinions: *He'll come around to our way of thinking sooner or later.* **3** to happen regularly: *Birthdays come around too quickly when one is older.* **4** to travel a longer way than usual: *We came around by the fields because we didn't want to go through the woods in the dark.* **5** →COME over[1] (2)

come at sbdy./sthg. *v prep* [T *no pass.*] to advance towards in a threatening manner: *She came at me with a knife.*

come back *v adv* [I] **1** to return: *When are you coming back?* **2** [*to*] to return to memory: *It's suddenly come back to me where I met you.* –see also COMEBACK **3** to become fashionable or popular again: *Do you think long dresses will ever come back?*

come between sbdy./sthg. *v prep* [T *no pass.*] to interrupt (two people or things); cause trouble between (two people or things): *John lets nothing come between himself and his work.*

come by sthg. *v prep* [T] to obtain or receive: *Jobs are hard to come by* (=difficult to find) *with so many people out of work.*

come down *v adv* [I] **1** to fall: *The roof came down during the night.*|(fig.) *I don't think gasoline will come down* (=fall in price) *this year, do you?*|(fig.) *Since Julia lost her job, she has really come down in the world.* (=fallen to a humbler standard of living) **2** to be passed on from one period of history to another: *This song comes down to us from the 10th century.* **3** come down in favor of/on the side of to decide to support: *The court came down on the side of the unions.* **4** come down to earth to return to reality –compare COMEDOWN

come down on sbdy./sthg. *v adv prep* [T *no pass.*] to punish: *The courts are going to come down heavily on young criminals.*

come down to sthg. *v adv prep* [T +*v-ing; no pass.*] to be able to be reduced to: *Our choices come down to going or staying.*

come down with sthg. *v adv prep* [T *no pass.*] *infml* to get; catch (an infectious illness): *I think I'm coming down with a cold.*

come forward *v adv* [I] to offer oneself to fill a position, give help to the police, etc.: *No one has come forward with information about the murder.*|*Only two people have come forward for election to the committee.*

come from sthg. *v prep* [T *no pass;* not *be* +*v-ing*] to have as a place of origin: *I come from Boston but have spent most of my life in Philadelphia.*|*Where do you come from?*

come in *v adv* [I] **1** to arrive as expected: *Has the train come in yet?* **2** to become fashionable, seasonal, etc.: *When did the short skirt first come in?* **3** come in handy to be useful: *This material will come in handy one day, so don't throw it away.*

come in on sthg. *v adv prep* [T *no pass.*] *infml* to join; take part in: *Let's ask Alice to come in on the plan.*

come into sthg. *v prep* [T] **1** to gain (a sum of money), esp. to INHERIT it after someone's death: *He came into a fortune when his mother died.* **2** (before nouns of type [U]) to begin to be in (a state or activity): *to come into fashion / existence / force / consideration*|*We were happy when the house came into sight because we had been walking for three hours.*

come of sthg. *v prep* [T *no pass.*] **1** to result from: *I don't know if any good will come of your actions.* **2** come of age to reach an age (usu. 18 or 21) when one is considered by law to be responsible for oneself and for obedience to the law

come off[1] *v adv* [I] **1** to become unfastened or disconnected: *A button came off my coat as I was climbing over the wall.* **2** to take place; happen, esp. successfully: *The wedding came off as planned.*

come off[2] *v prep* Come off it! (usu. in giving an order) to stop lying or pretending: *Come off it; tell the truth!*

come on *v adv* [I] *infml* to start: *I can feel a cold coming on.*|*The movie comes on at eight o'clock.*

come out *v adv* [I] **1** to appear: *The stars came out as soon as it was dark.*|*When will John's new book come out?* (=be offered for sale to the public) **2** to become known: *The news came out that the President was very sick.* **3** to be seen, as in a photograph: *Mary always comes out well in pictures.* **4** (of a photograph) to be DEVELOPED (3): *The pictures I took didn't come out; I'll have to take some more.* **5** (of color, a mark, etc.) to be removed; disappear: *I washed this shirt twice and the ink still didn't come out.* **6** to refuse to work: *Workers in all the factories are coming out in support of the dismissed men.* **7** to end in the stated way: *The answer to the problem came out wrong/right.*

come out against sthg. *v adv prep* [T +*v-ing;* no pass.] to declare one's opposition to: *The American government came out against the new British plane.*

come out with sthg. *v adv prep* [T no pass.] infml to say, esp. suddenly or unexpectedly: *John came out with a foolish remark which annoyed his old uncle.*

come over¹ *v adv* [I] **1** to make a short informal visit: *Come over and see us sometime.* **2** [*to*] to change sides or opinions; COME **around** (2) **3** →COME **across²**

come over² sbdy. *v prep* [T no pass.] (of a sudden strong feeling) to trouble or annoy (someone): *A feeling of faintness came over me, so I had to lie down.*

come through¹ *v adv* [I with] to do what is needed or expected: *I knew John would come through (with the money we need).*

come through² to continue to live after (something dangerous): *John was so ill he was lucky to come through (his operation).*

come to sbdy./sthg. *v prep* [T] **1** [no pass.] to reach; arrive at: *It has come to my notice* (=I have discovered) *that some money is missing.*|*to come to an end*|*The bill came to* (=amounted to) *$5.00.* **2** [+*v-ing;* no pass.] to concern: *When it comes to politics, I know nothing.* **3** [no pass.] to enter the mind suddenly: *Suddenly the words of the song came to me.* **4 come to pass** *fml* to happen **5 What is X coming to?** (asked when X is becoming worse) What is going to happen to X?: *What's the world coming to?*

come under sthg. *v prep* [T no pass.] **1** to be governed or controlled by: *This committee will come under the new Education Department.* **2** to receive: *We came under heavy enemy gunfire.* **3** to be able to be found below or after (a key word, heading, etc.): *What heading does this come under?*

come up *v adv* [I] **1** to come to attention or consideration: *Your question came up at the meeting.* **2** to happen: *I'll let you know if anything comes up.* **3** to come near: *He came up and said, "Pleased to see you."* **4 come up in the world** to reach a higher standard of living or social rank −opposite **come down in the world**

come up against sbdy./sthg. *v adv prep* [T no pass.] to meet (usu. a difficulty or opposition): *The workers came up against their employer's unwillingness to pay higher wages.*

come up to sthg. *v adv prep* [T] to equal: *Your recent work hasn't come up to your normal high standards.*

come up with sthg. *v adv prep* [T no pass.] infml to think of (a plan, answer, reply, etc.); produce: *He couldn't come up with an answer when I asked him why he was late.*

come·back /'kʌmbæk/ *n* a return to a former position of strength or importance: *We were losing, but we made a comeback in the second half of the game.* −see also COME **back** (2)

co·me·di·an /kə'miʸdiʸən/ *n* **1** an actor whose job is telling jokes or making people laugh **2** infml an amusing person: *Paul's a real comedian; he's always fun to be with.*

co·me·di·enne /kə,miʸdiʸ'ɛn/ *n* an actress whose job is telling jokes or making people laugh

come·down /'kʌmdaʊn/ *n* infml a fall in importance, rank, or respect: *It's a comedown to leave school and then not get a job.* −compare COME **down**

com·e·dy /'kʌmədiʸ/ *n* -**dies** [C;U] (a type of) funny play, film, or other work in which the story and characters are amusing and which ends happily −compare TRAGEDY

come-hith·er /,kʌm 'hɪðər/ *adj* [A] infml purposefully attractive in a sexual way: *She looked at me with come-hither eyes.*|*a come-hither look*

come·ly /'kʌmliʸ/ *adj* -**lier**, -**liest** *lit* attractive; having a pleasing appearance: *a comely young woman* −**comeliness** *n* [U]

com·et /'kʌmɪt/ *n* a heavenly body, with a very bright head and a long tail, that moves around the sun

com·fort¹ /'kʌmfərt/ *n* **1** [U] the state of being free from anxiety, pain, or suffering, and of having all one's bodily wants satisfied: *to live in comfort* **2** [C;U] (a person or thing that gives) strength, hope, or sympathy: *My husband was a great comfort to me when I was ill.*|*The priest spoke a few words of comfort to the dying man.* −see also DISCOMFORT

comfort² *v* [T] to give COMFORT¹ (2) to: *I tried to comfort Jean after her mother's death.* −**comforter** *n*

com·fort·a·ble /'kʌmftəbəl, 'kʌmfərtəbəl/ also **comfy** /'kʌmfiʸ/ -**fier**, -**fiest** infml− *adj* **1** having or providing comfort: *a comfortable chair*|*a comfortable income*|*a comfortable job* **2** [F] not experiencing (too much) pain, grief, anxiety, etc.: *The doctor said that Mother was comfortable after her operation.* −see also UNCOMFORTABLE −**comfortably** *adv*

com·ic¹ /'kʌmɪk/ *adj* **1** funny; causing laughter; humorous: *a comic performance* **2** [A] of COMEDY: *a comic actress*

comic² *n* **1** a person who is funny or amusing, esp. a professional COMEDIAN (1) **2** →COMIC BOOK

com·i·cal /'kʌmɪkəl/ *adj* slightly derog &

infml amusing in an odd way; strange: *That's a comical hat you're wearing, with all those flowers!*

comic book /'·· ,·/ *n AmE* also **comic**– a magazine for children containing COMIC STRIPS: *comic-book adventures*

com·ics /'kɑmɪks/ *n* [*the* P] *AmE* the part of a newspaper containing COMIC STRIPS

comic strip /'·· ,·/‖also **strip cartoon** /,· ·'·/ *BrE*– *n* a set of drawings telling a short story, often with words showing the speech of the characters in the pictures

com·ing[1] /'kʌmɪŋ/ *n* [S] **1** arrival: *With the coming of winter, days get shorter.* **2 comings and goings** *infml* acts of arriving and leaving: *We saw the comings and goings of the visitors from our bedroom window.*

coming[2] *adj* [A] that is coming or will come: *the coming winter*

com·ma /'kɑmə/ *n* the mark (,) used in writing and printing for showing a short pause

com·mand[1] /kə'mænd/ *v* **1** [I;T +*that*] to direct (a person or people), with the right to be obeyed; order: *She commanded us to come.|He commanded that the army attack at once.|The President commands the armed forces.* –see ORDER[2] (USAGE) **2** [T] to deserve and get: *This great man is able to* **command** *everyone's* **respect.**

command[2] *n* **1** [C] an order: *All his commands were quickly obeyed.* **2** [U *of*] control: *The army is under the President's direct command.|Who is* **in command of** *our navy?* **3** [S;U] the ability to control and use: *He has* **(a) good command** *of spoken French.*

com·man·deer /,kɑmən'dɪər/ *v* [T] to seize (private property) for public, esp. military use: *The soldiers commandeered the houses and used them for offices.*

com·mand·er /kə'mændər/ *n* [A;C] an officer of middle rank in a navy or air force

com·mand·ing /kə'mændɪŋ/ *adj* **1** [A] having command; being in charge: *Who's your commanding officer?* **2** deserving or expecting respect and obedience: *The teacher has such a commanding voice that everyone obeys her.*

com·mand·ment /kə'mændmənt/ *n* (often *cap.*) any of the ten laws (**Ten Commandments**) which according to the Bible were given by God to the Jews on Mount Sinai

com·man·do /kə'mændow/ *n* **-dos** *or* **-does** (a member of) a small fighting force specially trained for making quick attacks into enemy areas

com·mem·o·rate /kə'mɛmə,reyt/ *v* **-rated, -rating** [T] to be in memory of; give honor to the memory of: *This building commemorates those who died in the war.* –**commemoration** /kə,mɛmə'reyʃən/ *n* [U]: *A religious service will be held in commemoration of those who died in the war.* –**commemorative** /kə'mɛmərətɪv, -ə,reytɪv/ *adj*: *a commemorative stamp*

com·mence /kə'mɛns/ *v* **-menced, -mencing** [I;T +*to-v/ v-ing*] *fml* to begin; start: *Should we commence the attack?|After the election the new government commenced to build/building new houses.*

com·mence·ment /kə'mɛnsmənt/ *n* **1** [C;U]

fml the act of commencing (COMMENCE) **2** [C] *AmE* a ceremony at which students are given their degrees or DIPLOMAS

com·mend /kə'mɛnd/ *v* [T *to*] *fml* **1** to speak favorably of: *I can commend this man's work to you.|Our store has always been very highly commended.* **2** to put (esp. oneself) into the care or charge of someone else: *The dying man commended his soul/himself to God.*

com·mend·a·ble /kə'mɛndəbəl/ *adj* worthy of praise: *commendable efforts* –**commendably** *adv*

com·men·da·tion /,kɑmən'deyʃən/ *n* an official prize or honor given because of one's good qualities: *She was given a commendation for bravery after she saved the children from the fire.*

com·men·su·rate /kə'mɛnsərɪt, -ʃərɪt, -tʃərɪt/ *adj* [*with*] *fml* equal to; fitting; suitable: *He was given a job commensurate with his abilities.*

com·ment[1] /'kɑmɛnt/ *n* [C;U] (an) opinion, explanation, or judgment written or spoken about an event, person, state of affairs, etc.: *I asked her if she had any comments about the election.|No comment!* (=I have nothing to say)

comment[2] *v* [I;T +*that/on, upon*] to make a remark; give an opinion: *The teacher refused to comment on the examination results.|Jean commented that she thought it was time for a new car.*

com·men·tar·y /'kɑmən,tɛriy/ *n* **-ies 1** [C] a written collection of opinions, explanations, judgments, etc., on a book, event, person, etc. **2** [C;U] (a number of) opinions or descriptions spoken and usu. broadcast during an event, football game, etc.: *His commentary makes the game very interesting even on the radio.*

com·men·tate /'kɑmən,teyt/ *v* **-tated, -tating** [I *on*] to give a COMMENTARY (2) –**commentator** *n*: *a football commentator*

com·merce /'kɑmərs/ *n* [U] the buying and selling of goods, esp. between different countries; trade: *Our country has grown rich because of its commerce with other nations.*

com·mer·cial[1] /kə'mɔrʃəl/ *adj* **1** of, related to, or used in COMMERCE: *Our commercial laws are very old-fashioned.* **2** likely to produce profit: *Oil has been found in commercial quantities in Mexico.* –**commercially** *adv*

commercial[2] *n* an advertisement on television or radio

com·mer·cial·ize ‖also **-ise** *BrE* /kə'mɔrʃə-,laɪz/ *v* **-ized, -izing** [T] *often derog* to make (something) a matter of profit: *Do you agree that Christmas is too commercialized these days?* –**commercialism** /kə'mɔrʃə,lɪzəm/ *n* [U]

commercial ve·hi·cle /·,·· '···/ *n* a vehicle used for carrying goods from place to place

com·mie /'kɑmiy/ *n* *infml derog* for COMMUNIST

com·mis·er·ate with sbdy. /kə'mɪzə,reyt/ *v prep* **-ated, -ating** [T] to feel or express sympathy, sorrow, or pity for (a person): *I commiserated with my friend after he failed his exam.*

com·mis·er·a·tion /kə,mɪzə'reʸʃən/ *n* [C;U] (an expression of) sorrow, sympathy, or pity for the misfortune of another

com·mis·sion¹ /kə'mɪʃən/ *n* **1** [C;U] (an amount of) money, usu. related to the value of goods sold, paid to the salesman who sold them: *He gets 10% commission, so if he sells goods worth $100 his commission is $10.* **2** [U] the act of giving special powers or certain duties to a person or group of people **3** [C +*to-v*] the job, duty, or power given in such a way: *The commission for the new theater was given to a well-known* ARCHITECT. **4** [C] (*often cap.*) a group of people specially appointed to perform certain duties: *The minister established a commission to suggest improvements in the educational system.* | *The Commission meets twice a week.* –compare COMMITTEE **5** [C] (an official paper appointing someone to) any of several high ranks in the armed forces **6 out of commission** not ready for service; waiting for repair; out of ORDER¹ (3): *My car is out of commission; I have to take the bus.*

commission² *v* [T] to give a COMMISSION¹ (3,5) to (a person or group of people): *The artist was commissioned to paint a picture of the President.*

com·mis·sion·er /kə'mɪʃənər/ *n* (*often cap.*) **1** [A;C] (in some countries) an official in charge of a certain government department: *Commissioner Addo is responsible for education.* **2** [C] (*often cap.*) a member of a COMMISSION¹ (4)

com·mit /kə'mɪt/ *v* -**tt**- [T] **1** to do (something wrong, bad, or unlawful): *to commit a crime* | *commit* SUICIDE **2** [*to; usu. pass.*] to order (someone) to be placed under the control of another, esp. in a MENTAL (3) hospital: *He was committed to a* MENTAL *hospital at the age of thirty-two.* **3** [*to*] to promise (esp. oneself, one's property, etc.) to a certain cause, opinion, or course of action: *The government has committed itself to improving the Department of Education.* | *He won't* **commit himself on** (=give his opinion on) *women's rights.* **4 commit to memory** *fml* →MEMORIZE: *He committed the address to memory.*

com·mit·ment /kə'mɪtmənt/ *n* [C +*to-v*] a responsibility or promise to follow certain beliefs or a certain course of action: *We have to honor our commitments to other nations.* | *I don't want to get married because I don't want any commitments.* | *our government's* **commitment** *to* DEMOCRACY

com·mit·tal /kə'mɪtl/ *n* [C;U] (an example of) the act of sending a person to a MENTAL (3) hospital or a prison

com·mit·ted /kə'mɪtɪd/ *adj* [*to*] having given one's whole loyalty to a particular aim, job, or way of life: *Mary is a committed*

SPELLING NOTE

Words with the sound /k/, like **cut**, may be spelled **k-**, like **key**, or **qu-**, like **queen**. Words with the sound /s/, like **city**, may be spelled **s-**, like **soon**, or **ps-**, like **psychology**.

---

nurse/teacher. | *We are very committed to equal rights for women.*

com·mit·tee /kə'mɪtiʸ/ *n* a group of people chosen to do a particular job or for special duties: *He's on a lot of committees.* | *The committee believes that the hospital must be improved.* –compare COMMISSION¹ (4)

com·mod·i·ty /kə'madətiʸ/ *n* -**ties** an article of trade or COMMERCE, esp. a farm or mineral product: *Wine is one of the many commodities that France sells abroad.*

com·mo·dore /'kamə,dɔr, -,doʷr/ *n* [A;C] an officer of middle rank in the navy

com·mon¹ /'kamən/ *adj* **1** found or happening often and in many places; usual: *Wheat fields and corn fields are common in Nebraska.* **2** [*no comp.*] of no special quality; ordinary: *the common man/woman* | *the* **common cold 3** [*no comp.*] **a** belonging to or shared equally by two or more; united; JOINT²: *the common desire of the US and Canada* **b** of or belonging to society as a whole; public: **The common good** *would best be served by keeping prices from rising too quickly.* | *It is* **common knowledge** *among politicians that an election will soon be called.* | *When it comes to politics, my mother and I are* **on common ground.** (=we share the same beliefs) **4** *derog* coarse in manner; VULGAR: *The way you speak is very common.* | *I don't like him; he's* **as common as dirt.** (=very common) –**commonness** *n* [U]

common² *n* **1** (*often in names*) an area of grassland with no fences which all people are free to use: *Every Saturday Jean went riding on the village common.* **2 in common** in shared possession: *John and I have nothing in common.* (=no shared interests, qualities, etc.)

com·mon·er /'kamənər/ *n* a person who is not a member of a noble family; person without a title –compare NOBLE²

common law /,·· '·/ *n* [U] *tech* the unwritten law based on custom and court decisions rather than on laws passed by Congress, Parliament, etc. –**common-law** /,·· '·◄/ *adj* [A]: *She's his common-law wife because she's lived with him for three years without marrying him.*

com·mon·ly /'kamənliʸ/ *adv* usually; generally; ordinarily –compare UNCOMMONLY

Common Mar·ket /,·· '··◄/ [*the* S] *n* a society for trade made up of several European countries; the EUROPEAN ECONOMIC COMMUNITY

common noun /,·· '·/ *n* (in grammar) a noun that is not the name of a particular person, place, or thing: *"Book" and "sugar" are common nouns in English.* –see also PROPER NOUN

com·mon·place /'kamən,pleʸs/ *adj* common; ordinary: *Soon it will be commonplace for people to travel to the moon.*

common sense /,·· '·/ *n* [U] practical good sense and judgment gained from experience, rather than special knowledge from school or study: *Although he's not very intelligent, he's got lots of common sense.*

Com·mon·wealth /'kamən,wɛlθ/ *also* **Commonwealth of Nations** /,··· · '··/ *fml* – *n* [*the* S] an organization of independent states which were formerly parts of the British Empire, established to encourage trade and friendly relations among its members

com·mo·tion /kəˈmoʷʃən/ *n* [C;U] (an example of) great and noisy confusion or excitement: *"Why is there so much commotion coming from this room?" asked the angry teacher.|The imprisonment of the singer caused a commotion throughout the country.*

com·mu·nal /kəˈmyuʷnl, ˈkɑmyənl/ *adj* [*no comp.*] shared by or used by members of a group or a COMMUNITY: *communal land|communal tools*

com·mune¹ /kəˈmyuʷn/ *v* -muned, -muning [I *with, together*] *esp. lit* to exchange thoughts, ideas, or feelings: (fig.) *I often walk by the sea to commune with nature.*

commune² /ˈkɑmyuʷn, kəˈmyuʷn/ *n* **1** a group of people who live together, though not of the same family, and who share their lives and possessions **2** (esp. in COMMUNIST countries) a group of people who work as a team for the general good, esp. in raising crops and animals

com·mu·ni·ca·ble /kəˈmyuʷnɪkəbəl/ *adj fml* that can be (easily) COMMUNICATED (=passed from one person to another): *a communicable disease*

com·mu·ni·cate /kəˈmyuʷnəˌkeʸt/ *v* -cated, -cating *fml* **1** [T] to make (news, opinions, feelings, etc.) known: *I don't think the teacher communicates his ideas clearly.* **2** [I *with*] to share or exchange opinions, news, information, etc.: *Has the party leader communicated with the President yet?*

com·mu·ni·ca·tion /kəˌmyuʷnəˈkeʸʃən/ *n* **1** [U] the act of communicating (COMMUNICATE): *All communication stopped during the power failure.|Radio and television are important* **means of communication. 2** [C] something COMMUNICATEd; message: *This communication is secret; no one but you can see it.* –see also COMMUNICATIONS

com·mu·ni·ca·tions /kəˌmyuʷnəˈkeʸʃənz/ *n* [P] the various ways of traveling, moving goods and people, and sending information between places; roads, railways, radio, telephone, television, etc.: *Moscow has excellent communications with all parts of the Soviet Union.*

com·mu·ni·ca·tive /kəˈmyuʷnɪkətɪv, -ˌkeʸtɪv/ *adj* readily and eagerly willing to talk or give information; not secretive

com·mun·ion /kəˈmyuʷnyən/ *n* [U *with*] the sharing or exchange of beliefs, ideas, feelings, etc.

Communion also **Holy Communion**– *n* the religious service in Christian churches in which bread and wine are shared in a solemn ceremony; EUCHARIST –compare MASS

com·mu·ni·qué /kəˌmyuʷnəˈkeʸ, kəˈmyuʷnəˌkeʸ/ *n* an official report or declaration, usu. to the public or newspapers: *In its latest communiqué the government suggests that both sides will soon reach an agreement.*

com·mu·nism /ˈkɑmyəˌnɪzəm/ *n* [U] a classless social and political system in which the means of production are owned and con-

trolled by the state or the people as a whole –compare SOCIALISM, CAPITALISM

Communism *n* [U] the international political movement aimed at establishing COMMUNISM

com·mu·nist /ˈkɑmyənɪst/ *adj, n* (of or related to) a person who favors the principles of COMMUNISM

com·mu·ni·ty /kəˈmyuʷnəṭiʸ/ *n* -ties **1** [C] a group of people living together and/or united by shared interests, religion, nationality, etc.: *The Puerto Rican community in New York wants to keep its language and way of life alive.* **2** [*the* S] the public; people in general: *The job of a politician is to serve the community.*

com·mute¹ /kəˈmyuʷt/ *v* -muted, -muting **1** [I] to travel regularly a long distance between one's home and work, esp. by train: *She commutes from Scarsdale to New York|between Scarsdale and New York every day.* **2** [T] *fml* to make (a punishment) less severe: *His punishment was commuted from death to life imprisonment.*

commute² *n AmE infml* the trip made in commuting (COMMUTE¹ (1)): *It is a long commute from New York to Boston.*

com·mut·er /kəˈmyuʷṭər/ *n* a person who COMMUTEs¹ (1)

com·pact¹ /kəmˈpækt, kɑm-ˌˈkɑmpækt/ *adj* **1** firmly and closely packed together; solid: *The trees grew in a compact mass.* **2** arranged in or filling a small space: *a compact little apartment* –**compactly** *adv* –**compactness** *n* [U]

com·pact² /ˈkɑmpækt/ *n* **1** a small flat usu. round container for a woman's FACE POWDER and a mirror **2** also **compact car** /ˌ·· ˈ·/ *esp. AmE*– a small car

com·pact³ /ˈkɑmpækt/ *n fml* an agreement between two or more parties, countries, etc.

com·pact·ed /kəmˈpæktɪd/ *adj* pressed, joined together, or united firmly and closely: *a compacted mass*

com·pan·ion /kəmˈpænyən/ *n* **1** a person who spends time with another, because he/she is a friend or by chance, as when traveling: *He was my only companion during the war.|My fellow travelers made/were good companions.|*(fig.) *Ill health was his* **constant companion.** (=was with him all his life) **2** either of a pair or set of things; one thing that matches another: *I used to have a companion (piece) to that ornament, but I broke it.* **3** (usu. in titles) a book which gives one instructions on how to do something; guide; HANDBOOK: *the Traveler's Companion*

com·pan·ion·a·ble /kəmˈpænyənəbəl/ *adj* friendly; likely to be a good companion

com·pan·ion·ship /kəmˈpænyənˌʃɪp/ *n* [U] the relationship of companions; friendly company; fellowship: *He missed the companionship he'd enjoyed in the navy.*

com·pa·ny /ˈkʌmpəniʸ/ *n* -nies **1** [C] a group of people combined together for business, trade, artistic purposes, etc.: *a bus company|Which company do you work for?|The theater company makes a tour of the country every summer.* **2** [U] companionship; fellowship: *I was grateful for Jean's company when*

I traveled up to Boston.|*After two years of marriage they* **parted company**. (=ended their relationship) **3** [U] companions; the people with whom a person spends time: *John isn't very* **good company** (=a good person to be with) *when he's alone, but when Jean arrives he changes completely.* **4** [U] one or more guests: *No, you can't go out tonight; we're expecting company.* **5** [C] a body of (usu. about 120) soldiers, usu. part of a REGIMENT or BATTALION

com·pa·ra·ble /'kɒmpərəbəl/ *adj fml* that can be compared: *A comparable car would cost far more abroad.* –see also INCOMPARABLE –**comparably** *adv*

com·par·a·tive¹ /kəm'pærətɪv/ *adj* **1** making a comparison: *a comparative study of European languages* **2** measured or judged by comparison: *the comparative wealth of Kuwait* (=its wealth compared with the rest of the world) **3** of or related to the form of adjectives or adverbs expressing an increase in quality, quantity, or degree: *"Bigger" is the comparative form of "big."*|*"Worse" is the comparative form of "bad."* –see Study Notes opposite –**comparatively** *adv*

comparative² *n tech* the COMPARATIVE¹ (3) form of an adjective or adverb: *"Better" is the comparative of "good."*

com·par·a·tive·ly /kəm'pærətɪvliy/ *adv* **1** to a certain degree; rather: *Man is a comparatively new creature on the face of the earth.* **2** in a COMPARATIVE¹ (1) way: *These two languages must be studied comparatively.*

com·pare /kəm'pɛər/ *v* **-pared, -paring** [T *to, with*] **1** to examine or judge (one thing) against another in order to show the points of likeness or difference: *If you compare British football with American football, you'll find many differences.*|*If you compare both of our cars, you'll find they're very much alike.* **2** to show the likeness or relationship of (one thing and another): *It's impossible to compare the two cities; they're quite different.*

USAGE **Compare** can be followed by "to" or "with": *Los Angeles is large,* **compared** *to/with Boston.* **Compare to** usually means to say that one thing is similar to something else; **compare with** usually means to examine the ways in which one thing is similar to or different from another: *The writer of the poem* **compares** *his lover to a rose.* (=says she is like a rose)|*In today's lesson we will* **compare** *the Canadian system of government* **with** *the American.*

compare with sbdy./sthg. *v prep* [T +*v-ing*] to be worthy of comparison with: *Living in a city can't compare with living in the country.*

com·par·i·son /kəm'pærəsən/ *n* **1** [U] the act of comparing: *By/In comparison with Los Angeles, Boston is small.* **2** [C] the result of

comparing; a statement of the points of likeness and difference between two things **3** [U] likeness: *There is* **no comparison** *between frozen and fresh food.*

com·part·ment /kəm'pɑrtmənt/ *n* any of the parts into which an enclosed space is divided, such as **a** one of the small rooms in a railway carriage or **b** one of the small box-like containers inside the front of a car: *We sat in a compartment.*|*The driver kept his maps in the* **glove compartment** *in the front of his car.*

com·part·men·tal·ize ‖also **-ise** *BrE* /kəm,pɑrt'mentəl,aɪz, ,kɑmpɑrt-/ *v* **-ized, -izing** [T] to divide into separate COMPARTMENTS

com·pass /'kʌmpəs/ *n* **1** an instrument for showing direction, usu. consisting of a freely-moving MAGNETIC needle which always points to the north **2** [*often pl.*] a V-shaped instrument used for drawing circles, measuring distances on maps, etc. –see PAIR (USAGE) **3** [*usu. sing.*] *fml* an area; range; limit: *To help the old is well* **within the compass** *of the government's social responsibility.*

com·pas·sion /kəm'pæʃən/ *n* [U] pity or sympathy for the sufferings and misfortunes of others, causing a desire to give help or show mercy: *The world's main religions all teach us to have compassion for the poor and hungry.*

com·pas·sion·ate /kəm'pæʃənɪt/ *adj* feeling or showing COMPASSION –**compassionately** *adv*

com·pat·i·ble /kəm'pætəbəl/ *adj* [F *with*] that can exist or work in agreement together or with another: *Do you think that religion is compatible with science?*|*Their marriage ended because they were simply not compatible (with each other).* –opposite **incompatible** –**compatibly** *adv*

com·pa·tri·ot /kəm'peytriyət/ *n* a person who was born in or who is a citizen of the same country as another: *José and Reynaldo are compatriots because they both come from Mexico.*

com·pel /kəm'pɛl/ *v* **-ll-** [T] to make (a person or thing) do something by or as if by force; make necessary: *My father compelled us to stay indoors.*|(fig.) *Her intelligence and skill compel our admiration.* (=compel us to admire her) –**compelling** *adj* –**compellingly** *adv*

com·pen·di·um /kəm'pendiyəm/ *n* **-diums** or **-dia** /diyə/ *fml* a short but detailed and complete account of facts, information, a subject, etc.: *a compendium of useful information*

com·pen·sate /'kɑmpən,seyt/ *v* **-sated, -sating** [T +*v-ing*/*for*] to provide with a balancing effect for some loss or something lacking; make a suitable payment for some loss: *Many companies compensate their workers if they are hurt at work.*|*Nothing can compensate (me) for the loss of my wife*/*for losing my wife.* –**compensatory** /kəm'pensə,tɔriy, -,towriy/ *adj: compensatory payments*

com·pen·sa·tion /,kɑmpən'seyʃən/ *n* [S;U *for*] something given to COMPENSATE: *Did you get any compensation* (=any money)

STUDY NOTES comparatives: **more** and **most**, **-er** and **-est** ▐

The COMPARATIVE and SUPERLATIVE forms of adjectives and adverbs, which are used to show an increase in quality, quantity, or degree, are formed in three ways:

by adding **-er** and **-est** to the end of short words, like this:

Peter, David, and Stephen are all **tall**.
Peter is **taller than** *David.*
Stephen is **taller than** *both David and Peter.*
Stephen is **the tallest** *of the three.*

by adding **more** and **most** before longer words, like this:

All of these rings are **expensive**.
The gold ring is **more expensive than** *the silver ring.*
The diamond ring is **more expensive than** *both the silver ring and the gold ring.*
The diamond ring is **the most expensive**.

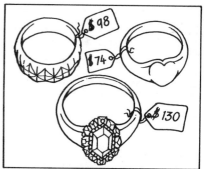

by using a different word, like this:

All of the girls' work is **good**.
Mary's work is **better than** *Anne's.*
Jane's work is **better than** *both Anne's and Mary's.*
Jane's work is **the best**.

Other words like this are **bad, far, well,** and **little** *adv.* Look these words up in the dictionary to see what their comparative and superlative forms are.

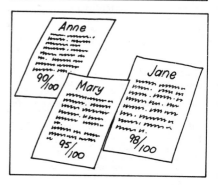

Note that some words, like **foreign** and **main**, have no comparative or superlative forms. These words cannot be used to show an increase in quality, quantity, or degree. They are marked in the dictionary like this [*no comp.*]:

main *adj* [*no comp.*] chief; most important: *a busy main road* *when you were dismissed from your job?*|*She received $10,000 in compensation for her husband's death.* –compare CONSOLATION, RECOMPENSE

com·pete /kəm'piʸt/ *v* **-peted, -peting** [I +*to-v*] to try to win something in competition with someone else: *John competed for a place at the school, but he didn't get in.*|*Although there were only four horses competing, it was an exciting race.*

com·pe·tence /'kampətəns/ *n* [U] ability to do what is needed; skill: *Janet drives with competence.* –opposite **incompetence** –see GENIUS (USAGE)

com·pe·tent /'kampətənt/ *adj* **1** having the ability or skill to do what is needed: *a competent swimmer/a competent teacher* –opposite **incompetent 2** satisfactory; ADEQUATE (1): *She did a competent job.* **–competently** *adv*

com·pe·ti·tion /,kampə'tɪʃən/ *n* **1** [U] the act of competing: *He was in competition with 10 others, so he did well to win the race.*|*There was great competition between the various teams fighting for first place.* **2** [C] a test of strength, skill, ability, etc.: *a dancing competition* **3** [U] the person or people competing: *There was a lot of competition for the job.*

com·pet·i·tive /kəm'pɛtətɪv/ *adj* of, related to, based on, or decided by competition: *the competitive nature of American university students* **–competitively** *adv* **–competitiveness** *n* [U]

com·pet·i·tor /kəm'pɛtətər/ *n* a person, team, firm, etc., competing with another or others; RIVAL: *There were seven competitors in the race.*

com·pi·la·tion /,kampə'leʸʃən/ *n* [C;U] (a report, book, etc. produced by) the act or action of compiling (COMPILE)

com·pile /kəm'paɪl/ *v* **-piled, -piling** [T] to make (a report, book, etc.) from facts and information found in various places: *It takes years of hard work to compile a good dictionary.* **–compiler** *n*

com·pla·cen·cy /kəm'pleʸsənsiʸ/ also **complacence** /-səns/– *n* [U] *usu. derog* a COMPLACENT feeling: *With the state of affairs in the world so dangerous, I see no reason for the administration's complacency.*

com·pla·cent /kəm'pleʸsənt/ *adj usu. derog* pleased or contented with oneself, perhaps unreasonably; self-satisfied: *After winning six times we became complacent; we thought we'd never lose.* **–complacently** *adv*

com·plain /kəm'pleʸn/ *v* [I;T +*that*] to express feelings of annoyance, pain, unhappiness, etc.; speak or say in an unhappy, annoyed, dissatisfied way: *Mary is always complaining (about something).*|*He complained that he couldn't find a job*

anywhere.|*Our neighbor said he'd complain about us to the police if we made any more noise.*|*My father is complaining of a pain in his chest.* **–complainingly** *adv*

com·plaint /kəm'pleʸnt/ *n* **1** [C] a cause or reason for complaining: *The workers made a list of their complaints.* **2** [C] a statement expressing annoyance, unhappiness, pain, dissatisfaction, grief, etc.: *The police received several complaints about the noise from our party.* **3** [U] the act of complaining: *If your neighbors are too noisy, then you have* **cause for complaint.**

com·plai·sant /kəm'pleʸsənt, -zənt/ *adj fml* ready and willing to please others; ready to agree **–complaisantly** *adv* **–complaisance** *n* [U]

com·ple·ment¹ /'kampləmənt/ *n* **1** something that completes or makes perfect: *A fine wine is a complement to a good meal.* **2** the quantity needed to make something complete: *The school's English department has its* **full complement** *of teachers.* (=has all the teachers it needs) –compare COMPLIMENT¹

com·ple·ment² /'kamplə,mɛnt/ *v* [T] to make (something) complete; be the COMPLEMENT¹ (1) of: *This wine complements the food perfectly.* –compare COMPLIMENT²

com·ple·men·ta·ry /,kamplə'mɛntəriʸ/ *adj* serving to complete; supplying what is needed for completion –compare COMPLIMENTARY

com·plete¹ /kəm'pliʸt/ *adj* **1** having all necessary, usual, or wanted parts; lacking nothing: *John's birthday did not seem complete without his father there.*|*We bought a house* **complete with** *furniture.* –opposite **incomplete 2** finished; ended: *When will work on the new school be complete?* **3** [A] thorough; full: *It was a complete surprise to see you on the bus yesterday.* **–completeness** *n* [U]

complete² *v* **-pleted, -pleting** [T] to finish; add what is missing or needed (to something) to form a finished whole: *I need one more stamp before my collection is completed.*|*When will work on the new school be completed?*

com·plete·ly /kəm'pliʸtliʸ/ *adv* altogether; totally: *The army made a completely successful attack on the enemy capital.* –see Study Notes on page 363

com·plex¹ /kəm'plɛks, kam-, 'kamplɛks/ *adj* **1** difficult to understand or explain: *Her political ideas were too complex to get support from ordinary people.* –compare SIMPLE **2** consisting of many closely connected parts: *There is a complex network of roads connecting the two cities.* **–complexity** /kəm'plɛks ətiʸ/ *n* **-ties** [C;U]

com·plex² /'kamplɛks/ *n* **1** a system consisting of a large number of closely connected parts: *The new sports complex has everything needed for many different activities.* **2** a group of unconscious wishes, fears, feelings, etc., which influence a person's behavior without him/her knowing it: *Andrew's complex about sex made his marriage a failure.*

com·plex·ion /kəm'plɛkʃən/ *n* **1** the natural

---

color and appearance of the skin, esp. of the face: *a good/dark/fair/pale complexion* **2** [*usu. sing.*] a general character or nature: *The new Congress has changed the whole complexion of the government.*

com·pli·ance /kəm'plaɪəns/ *n* [U *with*] *fml* obedience: *Compliance with the law is expected of all citizens.*

com·pli·ant /kəm'plaɪənt/ *adj* readily acting in accordance with a rule, order, the wishes of others, etc.: *I don't respect people who are too compliant.* –**compliantly** *adv*

com·pli·cate /'kɒmpləˌkeɪt/ *v* **-cated, -cating** [T] to make (something) difficult to understand or deal with: *It is a serious problem, complicated by the fact that we have no experience in this area.* –compare SIMPLIFY

com·pli·cat·ed /'kɒmpləˌkeɪtɪd/ *adj* difficult to understand or. deal with: *Don't ask me such complicated questions.|a complicated machine* –compare SIMPLE (2,3) –**complicatedly** *adv* –**complicatedness** *n* [U]

com·pli·ca·tion /ˌkɒmpləˈkeɪʃən/ *n* something that adds new difficulties: *The union's demand for higher wages was a complication that the company had not expected.*

com·plic·i·ty /kəmˈplɪsəti/ *n* [U] the act of taking part with another person in some wrongful action, esp. a crime –see also ACCOMPLICE

com·pli·ment¹ /'kɒmpləmənt/ *n* an expression of praise, admiration, or respect: *He received many compliments on his new suit.* –compare COMPLEMENT¹

com·pli·ment² /'kɒmpləˌment/ *v* [T *on*] to praise with a COMPLIMENT: *He complimented her, but she didn't want to listen.* –compare COMPLEMENT²

com·pli·men·ta·ry /ˌkɒmpləˈmentəriy/ *adj* **1** expressing admiration, praise, respect, etc. –opposite **uncomplimentary 2** given free: *complimentary tickets for the theater* –compare COMPLEMENTARY

com·pli·ments /'kɒmpləmənts/ *n* [P] good wishes: *That was an excellent dinner, Pierre: my compliments to the CHEF!*

com·ply /kəmˈplaɪ/ *v* **-plied, -plying** [I *with*] *fml* to act in accordance with a demand, order, rule, etc.: *People who refuse to comply with the law will be punished.*

com·po·nent /kəmˈpownənt/ *n* any of the parts that make up a whole (esp. a machine or system)

com·pose /kəmˈpowz/ *v* **-posed, -posing 1** [T] *more fml than* **make up** to make up (something); form (something): *Water is composed of* HYDROGEN *and* OXYGEN. –compare DECOMPOSE; –see COMPRISE (USAGE) **2** [I;T] to write (music, poetry, etc.) **3** [T] to make (esp. oneself) calm, quiet, etc.: *Adam was nervous at first but soon composed himself.*

com·pos·er /kəmˈpowzər/ *n* a person who writes music

com·pos·ite /kəmˈpɒzɪt, kɑm-/ *adj,n* (something) made up of a number of different parts or materials: *The police artist made a composite picture of the criminal.*

com·po·si·tion /ˌkɒmpəˈzɪʃən/ *n* **1** [C;U] (an example of) the act of composing (COMPOSE

(2)): *a piece of music of her own composition* **2** [C;U] the arrangement of the various parts of which something is made up: *Who decided (on) the composition of the committee?* **3** [C] a short piece of writing (ESSAY) done as an educational exercise **4** [C] a mixture of various substances: *a composition of different chemicals*

com·post /'kɒmpowst/ *n* [U] a mixture of decayed plant or animal matter, such as cut grass or leaves, used for making the soil richer

com·po·sure /kəmˈpowʒər/ *n* [U] complete control over one's feelings; calmness; steady manner or state of mind: *Keep calm: don't lose your composure.*

com·pound¹ /kəmˈpaʊnd, kɑm-/ *v* [T] **1** [*by*] to add to or increase (something bad): *Our difficulties were compounded by other people's mistakes.* **2** [*from, of*] to make (a substance or state) by combining various parts, qualities, etc.ꞌ

com·pound² /'kɒmpaʊnd/ *adj,n* (something) consisting of a combination of two or more parts –compare ELEMENT (1), MIXTURE

com·pound³ /'kɒmpaʊnd/ *n* a group of buildings enclosed by a wall, fence, etc.

com·pre·hend /ˌkɒmprɪˈhend/ *v* [I;T] *fml* to understand: *The judge said that it was difficult to comprehend the actions of the police in this matter.*

com·pre·hen·si·ble /ˌkɒmprɪˈhensəbəl/ *adj* able to be understood: *You often find a writer's books more comprehensible if you know about his life.* –opposite **incomprehensible** –**comprehensibility** /ˌkɒmprɪˌhensəˈbɪlətiy/ *n* [U]

com·pre·hen·sion /ˌkɒmprɪˈhenʃən, -tʃən/ *n* [U *of*] the act of understanding; ability to understand

com·pre·hen·sive /ˌkɒmprɪˈhensɪv/ *adj* thorough; broad; including much: *The government gave a very comprehensive explanation of its plans for industrial development.* –**comprehensively** *adv*

com·press /kəmˈpres/ *v* [T] **1** to force (a substance) into less space; press together: *compressed air* **2** to put (thoughts, ideas, etc.) into fewer words

com·pres·sion /kəmˈpreʃən/ *n* [U] **1** the act of COMPRESSING **2** the state of being COMPRESSED

com·prise /kəmˈpraɪz/ *v* **-prised, -prising** [not *be* + *v-ing*] to consist of; include; be made up of

USAGE Compare **comprise, compose, consist of, constitute,** and **include:** *The United States* **includes** *Alaska and Hawaii.* (=these are two of the states that make up the United States)|*North America* **consists of/is composed of/comprises** *The United States, Canada, and Mexico.* (=these are all the parts that make it up)|*The United States, Canada, and Mexico* **constitute/compose** (=make up) *North America.*

com·pro·mise¹ /'kɒmprəˌmaɪz/ *n* [C;U] (an example of) the act of settling an argument by each side taking a middle course acceptable to all sides: *The President and the Con-*

gress have been unable to reach **a compromise** on taxes.|to settle arguments by compromise, not with threats

compromise² v **-mised, -mising 1** [I] to settle an argument or differences of opinion by taking a middle course acceptable to all sides: *Jean didn't know whether to wear a formal dress or pants, so she compromised and wore a skirt.* **2** [T] to make (someone or something) open to dishonor, danger, etc.: *John felt he had compromised his beliefs by hiding the criminal.*

com·pul·sion /kəm'pʌlʃən/ n **1** [U] force or influence that makes a person do something: *The governor would use compulsion to make the people pay taxes.|I will pay nothing under compulsion.* **2** [C +to-v] a strong usu. unreasonable desire that is difficult to control: *Drinking is a compulsion with her.*

com·pul·sive /kəm'pʌlsɪv/ adj [A] resulting from a COMPULSION (2): *Compulsive eating is bad for one's health.* –**compulsively** adv

com·pul·so·ry /kəm'pʌlsəriʸ/ adj [no comp.] put into force by the law, orders, etc.: *Education is compulsory for all children in the US.* –compare VOLUNTARY (1) –**compulsorily** /kəm'pʌlsərəliʸ/ adv

com·punc·tion /kəm'pʌŋkʃən/ n [U] (*often in* NEGATIVE¹ (1) *sentences*) guilt; shame: *That woman didn't have the slightest compunction about telling me a lie.*

com·pute /kəm'pyuʷt/ v **-puted, -puting** [I;T] to calculate (a result, answer, sum, etc.)

com·put·er /kəm'pyuʷtər/ n an electric calculating machine that can store and recall information and make calculations at very high speeds

com·put·er·ize /kəm'pyuʷtə,raɪz/ v **-ized, -izing** [I;T] to use a computer to control (an operation, system, etc.): *The company has decided to computerize its sales department.*

com·rade /'kɑmræd/ n **1** [C] a close companion, esp. a person who shares difficult work or troubles **2** [A;C] (esp. used as a title in COMMUNIST countries) a citizen; fellow member of a union, political party, etc.: *We were met at the airport by three comrades from the local council.|Comrades, please be quiet.*

com·rade·ship /'kɑmræd,ʃɪp/ n [U] companionship; friendship

con¹ /kɑn/ n [C *usu. pl.*] see PRO¹

con² v **-nn-** [T *into, out of*] *infml* to trick (a trusting person) in order to make money: *They've conned me out of all my money!*

con·cave /,kɑn'keʸv◄/ adj *tech* curved inward, like the inside surface of a hollow ball: *a concave mirror* –opposite **convex**

con·ceal /kən'siʸl/ v [T] *more fml than* **hide**– to hide; keep from being seen or known: *He was very unhappy, but nobody knew,*

because he concealed his feelings. –**concealment** n [U]

con·cede /kən'siʸd/ v **-ceded, -ceding 1** [I;T +(that)] to admit as true, just, or proper, often unwillingly: *The government conceded defeat as soon as the election results were known.|I'm willing to concede (that) a larger car would have cost more, but I still think we should have bought one.* **2** [T] to give as a right; allow; yield: *After the First World War, Germany conceded her neighbors much valuable land.*

con·ceit /kən'siʸt/ also **conceitedness** /kən'siʸtɪdnɪs/– n [U] too high an opinion of one's own abilities, value, etc.: *That man's full of conceit.* –**conceited** adj

con·ceiv·a·ble /kən'siʸvəbəl/ adj that can be thought of or believed; imaginable: *It is conceivable that there will be a third world war, but I hope it won't happen.* –opposite **inconceivable** –**conceivably** adv

con·ceive /kən'siʸv/ v **-ceived, -ceiving 1** [T +(that)] to think of; imagine; consider: *Scientists first conceived the idea of the atomic bomb in the 1930's.* –see PERCEIVE (USAGE) **2** [I;T] *tech or bibl* to become PREGNANT with (a child): *The baby was conceived in March and born in December.*

conceive of sbdy./sthg. v prep [T +v-ing] to think of; imagine: *It's difficult to conceive of traveling to the moon.*

con·cen·trate¹ /'kɑnsən,treʸt/ v **-trated, -trating** [I;T] **1** [*on, upon*] to keep or direct (all one's thoughts, efforts, attention, etc.): *You should concentrate on the road while you're driving.|If you don't concentrate more on your work, you'll lose your job!* **2** to (cause to) come together in or around one place: *Industrial development is concentrated in the Northeast.|The crowds concentrated in the center of the town near the stores.*

concentrate² n [C;U] a CONCENTRATED (1) form of something: *orange juice concentrate*

con·cen·trat·ed /'kɑnsən,treʸtɪd/ adj **1** increased in strength by the removal of liquid or the addition of more of a substance **2** [A] very strong: *This student has made a concentrated effort to improve his work.*

con·cen·tra·tion /,kɑnsən'treʸʃən/ n **1** [U] close attention: *This book will need all your concentration.* **2** [C] a close gathering: *There is a concentration of industry in the north of the country.*

concentration camp /···'·· ,·/ n a large enclosed area where political prisoners are imprisoned

con·cen·tric /kən'sɛntrɪk/ adj *tech* having the same center: *concentric circles*

con·cept /'kɑnsɛpt/ n [C +that/of] a general idea, thought, or understanding: *I understand the concept of your plan, but I'm not sure about the details.*

con·cep·tion /kən'sɛpʃən/ n **1** [C;U +that/of] (a) general understanding; idea: *Different people have different conceptions of what he means.|Having studied history, I have some/a conception of what life was like in the past.* **2** [U] the act of forming an idea, plan, etc.: *The conception of the book took five* *minutes, but writing it took a year.* **3** [C;U] *tech* the starting of a new life by the union of a male and a female sex cell

con·cep·tu·al /kən'sɛptʃuʷəl/ *adj* of or based on (the formation of) CONCEPTS: *conceptual thinking* –**conceptually** *adv*

con·cern¹ /kən'sɜrn/ *v* [T] **1** [*no pass.*] to be about: *This story concerns a man who is wrongly imprisoned.* **2** to be of importance or interest to; have an effect on: *The results of a Presidential election concerns all the people who live in the country.* **3** [*about, with*] to worry (esp. oneself); interest (esp. oneself): *When she finished working, she concerned herself with looking after the old people in her area.*

concern² *n* **1** [C] a matter that is of interest or importance to someone: *The fact that you are unemployed isn't my concern.* **2** [U] worry; anxiety: *There is no* **cause for concern;** *the storm was not too serious.|a nurse's concern for a sick man* **3** [C] a business; firm: *Our concern makes shoes for children.|It was two years before the business was* **a going concern.** (=was making a profit)

con·cerned /kən'sɜrnd/ *adj* **1** [+*to-v/about*] anxious; worried: *I was very concerned about my mother's illness.* –see NERVOUS (USAGE) **2** [after *n*] interested; taking part: *All the people concerned very much enjoyed their afternoon visit to the theater.* **3** **as far as I'm concerned** (esp. with an expression of unfavorable feeling or opinion) in my opinion **4** **where X is/are concerned** in matters that have an effect on X: *Where work is concerned, I always try to do my best.* –see also UNCONCERNED

con·cern·ing /kən'sɜrnɪŋ/ *prep* more *fml* than **about** –about; with regard to: *Concerning your letter, I am pleased to inform you that your plans are quite acceptable to us.*

con·cert /'kansərt, -sɜrt/ *n* **1** a musical performance given by a number of singers or musicians or both –compare RECITAL (1) **2** **in concert** working together; in agreement: *The various governments decided to act in concert over this matter.*

con·cert·ed /kən'sɜrtɪd/ *adj* **1** planned or done together by agreement; combined: *a concerted effort by all governments to stop crime* **2** *infml* very strong: *This student has made* **a concerted effort** *to improve her work.* –**concertedly** *adv*

con·cer·ti·na /ˌkansər'tiʸnə/ *n* a small musical wind instrument of the ACCORDION family, held and played in the hands by pressing in from both ends

con·cer·to /kən'tʃɛrtoʷ/ *n* **-tos** or **-ti** /ṭiʸ/ a piece of music for one or more SOLO instruments playing with an ORCHESTRA

con·ces·sion /kən'sɛʃən/ *n* **1** [C;U] (a result of) the act of yielding, esp. after a disagreement: *The company's promise to increase our pay was a concession to union demands.* **2** [C +*to-v/from*] a right given or yielded by a government, owner of land, etc., to do something special: *oil concessions in the Gulf of Mexico|a food concession*

con·cil·i·ate /kən'sɪliʸˌeʸt/ *v* **-ated, -ating** [T]

to remove the anger or distrust of (someone); win the friendly feelings of

con·cil·i·a·tion /kənˌsɪliʸ'eʸʃən/ *n* [U] the act of conciliating (CONCILIATE): *Conciliation is the best way of regaining a person's trust after an argument.*

con·cil·i·a·to·ry /kən'sɪliʸəˌtɔriʸ, -ˌtoʷriʸ/ *adj* tending or intending to CONCILIATE: *He was very conciliatory but I still can't forgive him.*

con·cise /kən'saɪs/ *adj* short and clear; expressing much in few words: *a concise speech/book/speaker* –**concisely** *adv* –**conciseness** *n* [U]

con·clude /kən'kluʷd/ *v* **-cluded, -cluding 1** [I;T] *fml* to (cause to) come to an end: *We concluded the meeting at eight o'clock with a song.* **2** [T *with*] to arrange or settle (something): *We concluded an agreement with the enemy and soon made peace.* **3** [T +*that*] to come to believe after consideration of known facts: *The judge concluded that the prisoner was guilty.*

con·clu·sion /kən'kluʷʒən/ *n* **1** a judgment or decision: *What conclusions did you come to/draw/reach? |Be careful not to* **jump to conclusions.** (=to form a judgment too quickly) **2** *more fml than* **end**– the end; closing part: *The conclusion of her book was very exciting.* **3** an arrangement or agreement that introduces a changed state of affairs which is likely to last for some time: *The conclusion of peace is in the interests of both countries.* **4** **foregone conclusion** something decided in advance; something very likely to happen **5** **in conclusion** as the last thing: *In conclusion, I'd like to say how much I've enjoyed staying here.*

con·clu·sive /kən'kluʷsɪv/ *adj* putting an end to doubt or uncertainty: *conclusive proof that he was the murderer* –opposite **inconclusive** –**conclusively** *adv*

con·coct /kən'kakt, kan-/ *v* [T] to make (something) by mixing or combining parts: (fig.) *John concocted* (=made up) *an excuse for being late and the teacher believed him.* –**concoction** /kən'kakʃən, kan-/ *n*: *They gave me a very strange concoction to drink.*

con·com·i·tant /kən'kamətənt, kan-/ *adj,n fml* (something) existing or happening together with something else: *war with all its concomitant sufferings* –**concomitantly** *adv*

con·cord /'kaŋkɔrd/ *n* [U] *fml* friendly relationship; complete peace and agreement: *The two tribes had lived in concord for many centuries.* –compare DISCORD (1)

con·course /'kaŋkɔrs, -koʷrs/ *n fml* a large hall or open place where crowds of people can gather: *the airport concourse*

con·crete¹ *adj* /kan'kriʸt, 'kaŋkriʸt/ *adj* [*no comp.*] *fml* existing as something real or solid; actual: *Coal is a concrete object; heat is not.|*(fig.) *Do you have any concrete answers to this problem?* –compare ABSTRACT¹ (1) –**concretely** *adv*

con·crete² /'kaŋkriʸt, kan'kriʸt/ *v,n* **-creted, -creting** [T;U] (to cover with) a building material made by mixing sand, very small stones, cement, and water

con·cur /kən'kɜr/ *v* **-rr-** [I *on/with*] *fml* to

agree: *We concur on this matter.*

con·cur·rent /kən'kɜrənt, -'kʌrənt/ *adj fml* **1** (a case of) existing or happening at the same time **2** in agreement: *My opinions are concurrent with yours in this matter.* –**concurrently** *adv* –**concurrence** *n* [C;U]

con·cus·sion /kən'kʌʃən/ *n* [C;U] damaging of the brain caused by a heavy blow, shock, or violent shaking: *He suffered a concussion after falling off his bicycle.*

con·demn /kən'dem/ *v* [T] **1** to express strong disapproval of (someone or some action): *Most people are willing to condemn violence of any sort (as evil).* **2** [+to-v] to state the punishment for (a guilty person): *The prisoner was* **condemned to death.**|*The court condemned her to spend 30 years in prison.*|(fig.) *His bad leg condemned him to* (=forced him to remain in) *a wheelchair.* **3** to declare (something) officially unfit for use: *Although this house is condemned (as unfit), an old lady still lives here.* –**condemnation** /ˌkɑndem'neyʃən, -dəm-/ *n* [C;U]

con·den·sa·tion /ˌkɑnden'seyʃən, -dən-/ *n* **1** [U] drops of liquid formed when steam or hot air becomes cool: *There was condensation on the windows.* **2** [C;U] (the act or result of) condensing (CONDENSE)

con·dense /kən'dens/ *v* -**densed**, -**densing 1** [T] to put into a smaller or shortened form: *a condensed report* **2** [I;T] to (cause to) become liquid, or sometimes solid, esp. by cooling

con·de·scend /ˌkɑndɪ'send/ *v* [I +to-v] **1** to do something beneath one's social rank: *The general condescended to eat with the soldiers.* **2** *derog* to make oneself appear of a higher social rank than others: *I don't like Mrs. Smith: she's so condescending.* –**condescension** /ˌkɑndɪ'senʃən, -tʃən/ *n* [U]

con·di·ment /'kɑndəmənt/ *n* [*usu. pl.*] *fml* a powder or liquid used for giving a special taste to food: *Pepper and salt are condiments.*

con·di·tion¹ /kən'dɪʃən/ *n* **1** [C *of*] a state of being or existence: *The* ASTRONAUTS *soon got used to the condition of weightlessness.* **2** [U] the state of general health, fitness, or readiness for use: *Michael is* **out of condition** *because he never gets any exercise.*|*This car is in very good condition.*|*Her condition is improving.* (=she is getting well) **3** [C] something stated as necessary or desirable for something else: *She will join us* **on one condition:** *that we divide all the profits equally.*|*I'll come* **on condition that** (=if) *John is invited too.* –see also CONDITIONS

condition² *v* [T] **1** to settle; decide; control: *The amount of money I spend is conditioned by the amount I earn.* **2** *derog* to train: *Most people have been conditioned to accept what*

SPELLING NOTE

Words with the sound /k/, like **cut**, may be spelled **k-**, like **key**, or **qu-**, like **queen**. Words with the sound /s/, like **city**, may be spelled **s-**, like **soon**, or **ps-**, like **psychology**.

---

is advertised on television.

con·di·tion·al /kən'dɪʃənəl/ *adj* [*on,upon*] depending on a certain condition or conditions: *His agreement to buy our house was conditional on us leaving all the furniture in it.* –opposite **unconditional** –**conditionally** *adv*

con·di·tions /kən'dɪʃənz/ *n* [P] state of affairs; CIRCUMSTANCEs: *We were interested in working conditions in Africa.*|*What are housing conditions like in your country now?*|*Even under the best conditions, we couldn't get there in less than three days.* –compare CONDITION¹

con·do /'kɑndow/ *n* -**dos** *AmE infml* for CONDOMINIUM

con·do·lence /kən'dowləns/ *n* [C;U *often pl.*] (an expression of) sympathy for someone who has experienced great sorrow, misfortune, etc.: *Please accept my condolences on your mother's death.*

con·dom /'kɑndəm, 'kʌn-/ *n* a usu. rubber covering worn over the male sex organ during SEXUAL INTERCOURSE, used as a means of birth control and/or as a protection against disease

con·do·min·i·um /ˌkɑndə'mɪniyəm/ also **condo** *infml– n AmE* (an apartment in) an apartment building in which the people who live in the apartments own them –compare COOPERATIVE² (2)

con·done /kən'down/ *v* -**doned**, -**doning** [T] to forgive (wrong behavior); treat (a wrong action) as harmless: *I cannot condone the use of violence in politics.*

con·du·cive /kən'duwsɪv, -'dyuw-/ *adj* [F *to*] *fml* likely to produce: *Plenty of exercise is conducive to good health.*

con·duct¹ /kən'dʌkt/ *v* **1** [T] to direct or lead: *She conducts her business very successfully.*|*He conducted (us on) a tour of the city.* **2** [T] *fml* to behave (oneself): *Your children conduct themselves well.* **3** [I;T] to stand before and direct the playing of (musicians or a musical work) **4** [T] to act as the path for (electricity, heat, etc.): *Plastic and rubber won't conduct electricity, but copper will.*

con·duct² /'kɑndʌkt, -dəkt/ *n* [U] **1** *fml* behavior: *I'm glad to see your conduct at school has improved.* **2** direction of the course of (a business, activity, etc.)

con·duc·tor /kən'dʌktər/ *n* **1** a person who directs the playing of a group of musicians **2** a person employed to collect payments from passengers on a public vehicle: *a train conductor* **3** *AmE*||**guard** *BrE–* a railroad official in charge of a train **4** a substance that readily acts as a path for electricity, heat, etc.: *Wood is a poor conductor of heat.*

cone /kown/ *n* **1** a solid object with a round base and a point at the top **2** a hollow or solid object shaped like this: *an ice cream cone* **3** the fruit of a PINE² or FIR

con·fed·er·a·cy /kən'fedərəsiy/ *n* -**cies 1** *fml* an esp. political union of people, parties, or states **2** [*the* S] the Confederate States of America; union of southern states that fought against the northern states in the

American CIVIL WAR **–confederate** /kən-'fɛdərɪt/ *adj*

con·fed·er·ate[1] /kən'fɛdərɪt/ *n* **1** a member of a CONFEDERACY (1) **2** *derog* a person who shares in a crime

con·fed·er·ate[2] /kən'fɛdə,reʸt/ *v* **-ated, -ating** [I;T] to (cause to) combine in a CONFEDERACY (1) **–confederation** /kən,fɛdə'reʸʃən/ *n*

con·fer /kən'fɜr/ *v* **-rr-** [I *on,with*] *fml* to talk together; compare opinions: *The lawyers are still conferring on this matter.* **–conferment** *n* [C;U]

con·fer·ence /'kɑnfərəns/ *n* [C;U] a meeting held so that opinions and ideas on a subject, or a number of subjects, can be exchanged: *a conference of West European states|Ms. Chen cannot see you now: she is* **in conference.** **–see also** PRESS CONFERENCE

con·fess /kən'fɛs/ *v* [I;T *+v-ing/(that)*] **1** to admit (a fault, crime, something wrong): *The prisoner has confessed her crime.|She confessed (to) stealing the money.|Jean confessed (that) she'd broken the speed limit.|He confessed where he had hidden the money.* **2** *tech* to make (one's faults) known to a priest or God

con·fessed /kən'fɛst/ *adj* not secretive; open; by one's own admittance or declaration: *Mrs Jones is a (self-)confessed alcoholic.*

con·fes·sion /kən'fɛʃən/ *n* **1** [C;U] (an example of) the act of admitting one's crimes, serious faults, etc. **2** [U] *tech* a religious service at which a person tells his/her faults to a priest

con·fet·ti /kən'fɛtiʸ/ *n* [U] small pieces of colored paper thrown at weddings and other happy occasions

con·fi·dant /'kɑnfə,dænt, -,dɑnt, ,kɑnfə-'dænt, -'dɑnt/ **confidante** *fem.– n* a person to whom one tells one's secrets or with whom one talks about personal matters

con·fide /kən'faɪd/ *v* **-fided, -fiding** [T *+v-ing/that*] to tell (secrets, personal matters, etc.) secretly to a person one trusts: *Alice confided her dislike of her husband to Jean.|He confided to me that he had spent five years in prison.*

  confide in sbdy. *v prep* [T] to talk freely to, esp. about one's secrets: *John felt he could confide in his brother.*

con·fi·dence /'kɑnfədəns/ *n* **1** [U] full trust; belief in one's own or another's ability: *She has won his confidence; he trusts her.|Peter lacks confidence in himself.* **2** [C] a secret; some personal matter told secretly to a person **3 in confidence** privately; secretly: *I told you that in confidence, so why did you tell Nancy about it?*

con·fi·dent /'kɑnfədənt/ *adj* [F +*that/of*] feeling or showing CONFIDENCE (1): *a confident smile|The governor is confident of winning/that he will win the next election.* **–confidently** *adv*

con·fi·den·tial /,kɑnfə'dɛnʃəl, -tʃəl/ *adj* spoken or written in secret; to be kept secret: *confidential information* **–confidentially** *adv*

con·fid·ing /kən'faɪdɪŋ/ *adj* trustful: *her confiding nature* **–confidingly** *adv*

con·fine /kən'faɪn/ *v* **-fined, -fining** [T *to*] to enclose within limits; keep in a small space: *The animal was confined in a very small cage.|John was* **confined to bed** *for a week with his cold.* **–confinement** *n* [U]: *The prisoner was kept in* **solitary confinement.** (=kept completely alone)

con·fines /'kɑnfaɪnz/ *n* [P] limits; borders: *within the confines of one country|This is outside the confines of human knowledge.*

con·firm /kən'fɜrm/ *v* [T] **1** [+*(that)*] to support; make certain; give proof (of): *Please confirm your telephone message in writing.|The director confirmed that the meeting would be on June 20th.|His statement confirmed what we already believed.* **2** *tech* to admit (a person) to full membership of a church

con·fir·ma·tion /,kɑnfər'meʸʃən/ *n* [C;U] **1** [+*that*] something that CONFIRMs (1): *Your news was really confirmation for my beliefs.* **2** *tech* a religious service in which a person is made a full member of the church

con·firmed /kən'fɜrmd/ *adj* [A] firmly settled in a particular way of life: *He'll never get married: he's a confirmed* BACHELOR (1).

con·fis·cate /'kɑnfə,skeʸt/ *v* **-cated, -cating** [T] to seize (private property) officially and without payment, esp. as a punishment: *The teacher confiscated my radio because she heard me playing it in class.* **–confiscation** /,kɑnfə'skeʸʃən/ *n* [C;U]

con·fla·gra·tion /,kɑnflə,greʸʃən/ *n* *fml* a very large fire that destroys much property, esp. buildings or forests

con·flict[1] /'kɑn,flɪkt/ *n* [C;U] **1** (a) disagreement; argument; quarrel: *The two political parties have been* **in conflict** *since the election.* **2** (a) war; battle; struggle: *Armed conflict could start at any time.|There is a possibility of a serious conflict between the United States and Russia.*

con·flict[2] /kən'flɪkt/ *v* [I] to be in opposition (to another or each other); disagree: *Do our national laws conflict with any international laws?|My husband and I hold conflicting opinions on this matter.*

con·flu·ence /'kɑnfluʷəns/ *n* [C;U] *fml* the flowing together of two or more streams: *The city was established at the confluence of the Rhine and the Mosel.*

con·form /kən'fɔrm/ *v* [I *to*] *fml* to be obedient to, or act in accordance with established patterns, rules, etc.: *You must conform to the rules or leave the school.|Do you conform to your state's official religion?* **–conformity** /kən'fɔrmətiʸ/ *n* [U]

con·form·ist /kən'fɔrmɪst/ *adj, n* sometimes *derog* (of, concerning, or being) a person who acts and thinks in accordance and agreement with the established rules, values, and customs of society **–opposite noncon·formist**

con·found /kən'faʊnd, kɑn-/ *v* [T] to confuse and surprise (a person or group of people): *The election results confounded the ruling party.* **–confounded** *adj*

con·front /kən'frʌnt/ *v* [T] to face boldly or threateningly: *When I left the restaurant, I* *was confronted by two men who asked me for money.*

confront sbdy. **with** sthg. *v prep* [T] to bring face to face; cause to meet: *The police confronted her with the* EVIDENCE, *and she admitted that she had stolen the money.*

con·fron·ta·tion /ˌkɑnfrən'teɪʃən/ *n* [C;U] (an example of) the act of CONFRONTing: *The Arab-Israeli confrontation is causing serious difficulties to our company.|We cannot risk another confrontation with Russia.*

con·fuse /kən'fyuʷz/ *v* **-fused, -fusing** [T] **1** to mislead; cause to be mistaken: *I was confused by all the noise.|They confused the teacher by having the same names.* **2** [*with*] to mix up; fail to tell the difference between (two things): *I'm always confusing John and/with Paul. Which one is John?* –**confused** *adj* –**confusedly** /kən'fyuʷzɪdliʸ/ *adv* –**confusing** *adj* –**confusion** /kən'fyuʷʒən/ *n* [U]: *There was confusion as to whether we had won the battle or not.|To avoid confusion, the teams wore different colors.|*(fig.) *Your room is in complete confusion.* (=disorder)

con·geal /kən'dʒiʸl/ *v* [I;T] to (cause to) become thick or solid: *The liquid congealed.|congealed blood*

con·ge·nial /kən'dʒiʸnyəl/ *adj fml* pleasant; in agreement with one's nature: *congenial work|congenial company/companions* –opposite **uncongenial** –**congenially** *adv*

con·gen·i·tal /kən'dʒɛnəṭl/ *adj tech* (of diseases) existing at or from one's birth: (fig.) *a congenital liar* –**congenitally** *adv*

con·gest·ed /kən'dʒɛstɪd/ *adj* (of a street, city, narrow place, etc.) very full or blocked, esp. because of traffic: *Fifth Avenue is always very congested.|The baby couldn't breathe because its nose was congested.* (=blocked with MUCUS) –**congestion** /kən'dʒɛstʃən/ *n* [U]: *I don't like driving through New York because there's too much congestion.*

con·glom·er·ate /kən'glɑmərɪt/ *n* a large business firm producing goods of very different kinds

con·glom·er·a·tion /kənˌglɑmə'reɪʃən/ *n* a collection of many different things gathered together: *a strange conglomeration of objects in his pockets*

con·grat·u·late /kən'grætʃə,leɪt/ *v* **-lated, -lating** [T *on*] to speak to (a person) with praise and admiration for a happy event or something successfully done: *We congratulated her on having passed the examinations.| Let me congratulate you on the birth of your daughter.* –**congratulation** /kənˌgrætʃə-'leɪʃən/ *n* [U] –**congratulatory** /kən-'grætʃələ,tɔriʸ, -,toʷriʸ/ *adj*

con·grat·u·la·tions /kənˌgrætʃə'leɪʃəns/ also

SPELLING NOTE
Words with the sound /k/, like **cut**, may be spelled **k-**, like **key**, or **qu-**, like **queen**. Words with the sound /s/, like **city**, may be spelled **s-**, like **soon**, or **ps-**, like **psychology**.

congrats /kən'græts/ *infml– interj,n* [P *on*] an expression of joy for someone's success, good fortune, luck, etc.: *It's your birthday today? Congratulations!*

con·gre·gate /'kɑŋgrə,geɪt/ *v* **-gated, -gating** [I] to gather together: *The crowds congregated in the town square to hear the President.*

con·gre·ga·tion /ˌkɑŋgrə'geɪʃən/ *n* a group of people gathered together, esp. in a church for religious worship –see ATTEND (USAGE)

con·gress /'kɑŋgrɪs/ *n* **1** (*often cap.*) the elected law-making body of certain countries, esp. the US: *There will soon be elections to Congress.|Congress has approved the new education laws.* –compare SENATE **2** a formal meeting of representatives of societies, countries, etc., to exchange information and opinions: *The Congress of Vienna|a medical congress* –**congressional** /kən'grɛʃənəl/ *adj: congressional elections*

con·i·cal /'kɑnɪkəl/ also **conic** /'kɑnɪk/ *fml* – *adj* shaped like a CONE (1): *a conical hat|huts with conical roofs* –**conically** *adv*

con·i·fer /'kɑnəfər, 'koʷ-/ *n* a tree which bears CONES (3) and usu. keeps its leaves in winter –**coniferous** /koʷ'nɪfərəs, kə-/ *adj*

con·jec·ture /kən'dʒɛktʃər/ *n* [C;U] (the formation of) an idea, guess, etc., based on incomplete or uncertain information: *The senator didn't know the facts of the matter; what he said was pure conjecture.|I don't agree with his conjecture that prices will rise next year.* –**conjectural** /kən'dʒɛktʃərəl/ *adj*

con·ju·gal /'kɑndʒəgəl/ *adj* [A] *fml* concerning the relationship between husband and wife: *the conjugal bed|conjugal rights*

con·ju·gate /'kɑndʒə,geɪt/ *v* **-gated, -gating** [T] *tech* to give the various forms of (a verb) that show number, person, tense, etc.: *Can you conjugate "to have" in all its tenses?* –**conjugation** /ˌkɑndʒə'geɪʃən/ *n*

con·junc·tion /kən'dʒʌŋkʃən/ *n* **1** (in grammar) a word such as "but" or "and" that connects parts of sentences, phrases, etc. –see Study Notes on page 144 **2 in conjunction with** in combination with; together with; along with: *The army is acting in conjunction with the police in the hunt for terrorists.*

con·jure /'kɑndʒər/ *v* **-jured, -juring** [I;T] to cause to appear by or as if by magic: *The magician conjured a rabbit out of his hat.*

conjure sthg.↔ **up** *v adv* [T] **1** to imagine: *Try to conjure up a picture of life in ancient Egypt.* **2** to cause to be remembered: *to conjure up memories of the past* **3** to cause (spirits of the dead, etc.) to appear: (fig.) *Jean can conjure up a good meal in half an hour.*

con·jur·er, -juror /'kɑndʒərər/ *n* a person who practices magic, esp. to amuse others for payment

Conn. *written abbrev.* said as: Connecticut /kə'nɛṭɪkət/ (a state in the US)

con·nect /kə'nɛkt/ *v more fml than* **join**– **1** [T *up*] to join; unite; LINK: *They got two connecting rooms in the hotel.|The scientist connected the wires (up).* **2** [T *often pass.*] to think of as related: *She was connected with the crime.* **3** [T] to join by telephone: *I was* connected to the wrong person. **4** [T] to join to an electricity supply: *Make sure the machine's connected properly.* –opposite **disconnect** (for **3**, **4**) **5** [I *with*] (of one or more trains, buses, etc.) to be so planned that passengers can change from one to the other: *The next flight connects with a flight for Houston.*

con·nect·ed /kə'nɛktɪd/ *adj* **1** joined or related: *connected events* –opposite **unconnected 2** having social, professional, or business relationships of the stated kind: *You must be very **well-connected**: you seem to know all the right people.*

con·nec·tion ‖also **connexion** *BrE* /kə'nɛkʃən/– *n* **1** [U] the act of connecting: *the connection of the house pipes to the water supply* –opposite **disconnection 2** [C;U] (an example of) the state of being connected; relationship: *Do you know that there's a connection between smoking and heart disease?* **3** [C] a plane, train, bus, etc., planned to take passengers arriving by another one: *There are connections in New York for all European capitals.* **4** [C] anything that connects or is connected: *excellent road and railroad connections with the coast|a bad telephone connection|The machine won't work because of a faulty connection.* **5** [C usu. pl.] a person connected to others, e.g. by family or business: *We have connections with a company in Chicago.* **6 in connection with** with regard to: *In connection with your request of March 18, we are sorry to tell you that . . .*

con·nive /kə'naɪv/ *v* **-nived, -niving** [I +*to-v*/ *with*] *fml* to work together secretly, esp. for some wrong or unlawful purpose: *The student connived with her friend to cheat on the examination.* **–connivance** *n* [U *at, with*]: *The criminals could not have escaped without your connivance.*

con·nois·seur /ˌkanə'sɜr, -'suər/ *n apprec* a person with a good understanding of a subject for which knowledge and good judgment are needed: *a connoisseur of fine wines/art*

con·no·ta·tion /ˌkanə'teʸʃən/ *n* [*often pl.*] an idea suggested by a word in addition to the formal meaning of the word: *The word "good" sometimes has moral connotations.*

con·quer /'kaŋkər/ *v* **1** [I;T] to take (land) by force; win (land) by war: *The Normans conquered England in 1066.|a conquering army|a conquered city* **2** [I;T] to defeat (an enemy); be victorious over (an enemy) **3** [T] to gain control over (something unfriendly or difficult): *After many attempts to climb it, the mountain was conquered in 1982.* **–conqueror** *n*

con·quest /'kaŋkwɛst/ *n* **1** [U] the act of conquering: *The conquest of this rare disease has always been her aim.* **2** [C] something conquered, esp. land gained in war: *French conquests in Asia|(fig.) Peter is one of Jane's conquests; he's fallen in love with her already.*

Con·rail, ConRail /'kanreʸl/ *n* a system of railroads in the US set up under loose government control

con·science /'kanʃəns, -tʃəns/ *n* [C;U] an inner sense that knows the difference between right and wrong: *You should act according to your conscience.|to have a guilty conscience|a clear conscience*

con·sci·en·tious /ˌkanʃiʸ'ɛnʃəs, -tʃəs, -tʃiʸ-/ *adj* showing great care, attention, or seriousness of purpose: *a conscientious worker|a conscientious piece of work* –compare CONSCIOUS (3) **–conscientiously** *adv* **–conscientiousness** *n* [U]

con·scious /'kanʃəs, -tʃəs/ *adj* **1** [F] having one's mind and senses working; able to think, feel, etc.; awake: *He hurt his head in the accident, but he is still conscious.|Is he conscious enough to answer questions?* **2** [F +*(that)*/*of*] knowing; understanding: *Peter isn't conscious of his bad manners.|Jean's always been very conscious that she annoys people.* **3** [A] intentional: *a conscious decision to do something* –compare CONSCIENTIOUS **–consciously** *adv*

USAGE The opposite of **conscious** is **unconscious** in all the above meanings:|*He's not **yet** conscious/still unconscious after the accident.|I was conscious/unconscious of her presence.* But in PSYCHOLOGY, **conscious** is also compared with **subconscious**: *the conscious/subconscious/unconscious mind.*

con·scious·ness /'kanʃəsnɪs, -tʃəs-/ *n* **1** [U] the condition of being able to think, feel, understand what is happening, etc.: *Roger lost consciousness at four o'clock in the afternoon and died in the night.* **2** [U] all the ideas, opinions, etc., held by a person or a group of people: *the moral consciousness of a country|class consciousness* **3** [S;U +*that*/*of*] knowledge or a feeling, esp. of a not very clear kind; AWARENESS: *a consciousness that someone else was in the room*

con·script /kən'skrɪpt/ also **draft** *AmE*– *v* [T *into*] to make (someone) serve in one of the armed forces –**conscript** /'kan,skrɪpt/ *n*: *He's a conscript.* **–conscription** /kən'skrɪpʃən/ *n* [U]: *Some people feel that conscription is necessary for a country's defense.*

con·se·crate /'kansə,kreʸt/ *v* **-crated, -crating** [T] **1** to declare as holy in a special ceremony: *to consecrate a church* **2** to set apart solemnly for a particular purpose: *He consecrated his life to helping the poor.* **–consecration** /ˌkansə'kreʸʃən/ *n* [C;U]

con·sec·u·tive /kən'sɛkyətɪv/ *adj* following in regular or unbroken order: *The numbers 4, 5, 6 are consecutive.* **–consecutively** *adv*

con·sen·sus /kən'sɛnsəs/ *n* [*usu. sing.*] a general agreement; the opinion of a group: *What is the **consensus of opinion**?|Can we **reach a consensus** on this matter?*

con·sent¹ /kən'sɛnt/ *v* [I +*to-v*/*to*] to agree; give permission: *The father consented to his daughter's piano lessons.*

consent² *n* [U] **1** agreement; permission: *They did not give their consent to her marriage.* **2 age of consent** the age at which one may lawfully marry or have sex

con·se·quence /'kansə,kwɛns, -kwəns/ *n* **1** [C] something that follows from an action or

STUDY NOTES conjunctions

Words and phrases like **and, but, because**, and **so**, can be used to join two or more nouns, verbs, adjectives, or parts of a sentence.

ways of saying **and**

There are many words and phrases in English that can be used like **and** to join two or more ideas in a sentence. These ideas are often similar in meaning.

So instead of always saying:

When we went to town we visited the zoo **and** *the museum.*
Peter **and** *Paul came to the zoo.*

We can say:

We went to the zoo. We visited the museum, **as well**.
We went to the zoo. We went to the museum, **too**.
We went to the museum **as well as** *the zoo.*

We went to the zoo. We **also** *visited the museum.*
Not only *did we go to the zoo, we* **also** *went to the museum.*
Besides *going to the zoo, we went to the museum.*
In addition to *visiting the zoo, we went to the museum.*

Paul came to the zoo. Peter came **as well**.

Paul came to the zoo. Peter came, **too**.

Peter, **as well as** *Paul, came to the zoo with us.*
Paul came to the zoo. **So did** *Peter.*
Peter, and **also** *Paul, came with us to the zoo.*
Not only *Peter* **but also** *Paul came with us to the zoo.*
A lot of people came to the zoo **besides** *Peter and Paul.*
A number of people came to the zoo **in addition to** *Peter and Paul.*

If you look up these words in the dictionary, you will find more examples and definitions to help you to learn how to use them.

---

ways of saying **but**

There are many words and phrases like **but** that can be used to join two or more ideas in a sentence. These words can join verbs, nouns, adjectives, and whole sentences.

Look at these examples with **but**:

My room is small, **but** *it is comfortable.* (=because my room is small, you might not expect it to be comfortable, but it is)

She drove very fast to the airport, **but** *she missed the plane.* (=because she drove very fast, you might have expected her to get there on time, but she didn't)

We can express this meaning in a number of ways:

by using **yet** with two sentences, like this:
She drove very fast to the airport, **yet** *she missed the plane.*

by using **however** or **even so** with two sentences, like this:
My room is small; **however/even so**, *it's very comfortable.*

She drove very fast to the airport. **However/Even so**, *she missed the plane.*

by using **although** and **(even) though** with two subjects and verbs, like this:
Although/even though *my room is small, it is comfortable.*

My room is comfortable **although/even though** *it is small.*

by using **in spite of the fact that** or **despite the fact that** with two subjects and verbs:
My room is very comfortable **in spite of/despite the fact that** *it is small.*

Note that the part of a sentence beginning with **although, even though, in spite of the fact that,** or **despite the fact that** can come at the beginning or end of the sentence:
Even though *my room is small, it is very comfortable.*
My room is very comfortable **even though** *it is small.*

If you look up these ways of saying **but** in the dictionary, you will find more examples and definitions to help you use them. Other words that can be used to mean **but** are **nonetheless, nevertheless,** and **still**.

ways of saying **because**

There are many words and phrases like **because** that can be used to join two or more ideas in a sentence. These words and phrases all answer the question *Why?*

Some of these words and phrases that answer the question *why* show the *cause* of something:

She was late **because** *she missed the bus.*
She was late **because of** *missing the bus.*
Since/As *he has no money, he can't come.*
We had to stay inside **on account of** *the rain.*
His failure was **due to** *his lack of work.*
He failed **owing to** *his lack of work.*
We lost the game **through** *poor teamwork.*
The dog died **from** *eating poison.*

Some words and phrases that answer the question *why* show the *purpose* of something:

He only said it **to** *annoy me.*
He said it **in order to** *annoy me.*
I moved to California **in order that** *I might get a job.*
I had a big breakfast **so (that)** *I wouldn't be hungry later on.*
I had a big breakfast **so as** *not to be hungry later on.*

Note that the part of a sentence beginning with **because, in order that,** or **so (that)** can come at the beginning or end of the sentence:
She was late for school **because** *she missed the bus.*
Because *she missed the bus, she was late for school.*

---

ways of saying **so**

Words and phrases like **so** are used to show what happens as a result of something.
I was feeling ill, **so** *I went to bed.* (=Because I was feeling ill, I went to bed)
I was feeling ill. **That's why** *I went to bed.*

so and **that's why** are less formal ways of showing the result of something. More formal ways of expressing a similar meaning are:
Jane got a sore throat the night before the concert. **Therefore,** *she was unable to sing in it.*
The government does not wish to raise taxes. **Thus,** *it cannot give more money to the schools.*
I've never been to China. **Consequently/Hence,** *I know very little about it.*
Note that **thus, consequently, hence,** and **accordingly** are all marked *fml* in the dictionary.

Punctuation

and, but, yet, so, thus, hence

When these conjunctions join two sentences to make a single sentence, use a COMMA (**,**) before them:
I was very hungry, **but** *I didn't eat anything.*
I was very hungry, **so** *I ate dinner early.*

You may also begin a new sentence with **thus** and **hence,** but use a comma after the conjunction:
Very few people attended the meeting. **Thus,** *we couldn't make a decision.*
(You may also see sentences beginning with **and, but, so,** and **yet,** but some teachers do not like this usage.)

however, even so, therefore, consequently, nonetheless, nevertheless

When these conjunctions join two sentences to make a single sentence, use a SEMICOLON (**;**) before them and a comma after them:
Everyone attended the meeting; **however,** *we could not make a decision.*

These conjunctions may also begin a new sentence, but you must use a comma after them:
Everyone attended the meeting. **However,** *we could not make a decision.*

although, even though, though, in spite of the fact that, despite the fact that, because, since, as, in order that, so (that)

If one of these conjunctions introduces the first part of a sentence, use a comma between the two parts of the sentence:
Although *my room is small, it is very comfortable.*

But if the conjunction introduces the second part of a sentence, do not use a comma:
My room is very comfortable **although** *it is small.*

condition; result **2** [U] *fml* importance: *a matter of little/no consequence*

con·se·quent·ly /'kɑnsə,kwɛntliʸ, -kwənt-/ *adv* as a result; therefore: *The rain was heavy; consequently the road was flooded.* –see Study Notes on page 144

con·ser·va·tion /,kɑnsər'veʸʃən/ *n* [U] **1** the act of conserving (CONSERVE); preservation: *the conservation of wild life* **2** the controlled use of a limited supply of natural things, to prevent waste or loss: *Conservation of water is of great importance in desert areas.* –**conservationist** *n*: *The conservationists wanted the government to give more protection to wild animals.*

con·serv·a·tism /kən'sɜrvə,tɪzəm/ *n* [U] **1** dislike of change, esp. sudden change: *conservatism in matters of language* **2** the belief that the established order of society should be kept as it is for as long as possible and then changed only slowly: *political conservatism*

con·serv·a·tive /kən'sɜrvətɪv/ *adj* **1** favoring the established order of society; not liking change, esp. sudden change: *very conservative in matters of education* **2** not showy; modest: *She dresses in a rather conservative way.* **3** careful; kept within reasonable limits: *He made a conservative guess at the population of Hong Kong.* –**conservatively** *adv* –**conservative** *n*: *Aunt Mary's a real conservative. She doesn't like change at all.*

con·serv·a·to·ry /kən'sɜrvə,tɔriʸ, -,toʷriʸ/ *n* **-ries** **1** a glass enclosed room where plants are grown **2** a school where people are trained, esp. in music or acting

con·serve /kən'sɜrv/ *v* **-served, -serving** [T] to use (a supply) carefully; preserve: *We must conserve our forests if we are to make sure of a future supply of wood.*

con·sid·er /kən'sɪdər/ *v* **1** [I;T +*v-ing*] to think about; examine: *I considered changing my job, but in the end I decided not to.|We've decided to move and are considering where to go.* **2** [T not *be+v-ing*] to think of in a stated way: *I consider him (to be) a good musician.|I consider it a great honor to be here with you today.* **3** [T +*that*] to take into account; remember: *If you consider (the fact) that she's only been studying English a year, she speaks it very well.*

con·sid·er·a·ble /kən'sɪdərəbəl/ *adj* fairly large in amount, size, or degree: *a considerable length of time* –see also INCONSIDERABLE –**considerably** *adv*: *We have a considerably smaller house than theirs.*

con·sid·er·ate /kən'sɪdərɪt/ *adj apprec* thoughtful of the rights or feelings of others: *to be considerate towards old people* –opposite **inconsiderate** –**considerately** *adv* –**considerateness** *n* [U]

con·sid·er·a·tion /kən,sɪdə'reʸʃən/ *n* **1** [U *to*]

careful thought; attention: *We'll give your request for a pay raise (our) careful consideration.|I sent my poem to a magazine for (their) consideration.|consideration to detail* **2** [U *for*] thought for the wishes and feelings of others: *John never showed any/John had no consideration for anyone.* **3** [C] a fact to be considered when making a decision: *Cost is an important consideration for me when I buy new clothes.* **4 take into consideration** to remember about (something) when making a judgment: *Your teacher will take your recent illness into consideration when judging your examination.*

con·sid·ered /kən'sɪdərd/ *adj* [A] **1** reached after careful thought: *It is my* **considered opinion** *that you are wrong.* **2 all things considered** when one considers everything

con·sid·er·ing /kən'sɪdərɪŋ/ *prep,conj* if one remembers the rather surprising fact (of/that): *He did poorly in his examinations, considering how hard he had studied for them.*

con·sign /kən'saɪn/ *v* [T] **1** [*to*] to send (something) to a person or place for sale: *The goods were consigned to you by US mail and should have arrived by now.* **2** *fml* to put into the care of another; hand over: *Before her death my mother consigned me into my uncle's care.*

con·sign·ment /kən'saɪnmənt/ *n* **1** [U] the act of CONSIGNing (1) **2** [C] a number of goods CONSIGNed (1) together: *One consignment of bananas was bad.*

con·sist·en·cy /kən'sɪstənsiʸ/ also **consistence** /kən'sɪstəns/– *n* **-cies** **1** [U] the state of always keeping to the same principles or course of action: *Your actions lack consistency; you say one thing and do the other.* –opposite **inconsistency** **2** [C;U] the degree of firmness or thickness: *To make this cake, first you mix butter and sugar to the consistency of thick cream.*

con·sist·ent /kən'sɪstənt/ *adj* (of a person, behavior, beliefs, etc.) keeping to the same principles, line of reasoning, or course of action: *This statement is not consistent with what you said yesterday.* –opposite **inconsistent** –**consistently** *adv*

con·sist of sthg. /kən'sɪst/ *v prep* [T not *be+v-ing*, no pass.] to be made up of: *The city of New York consists of five boroughs.* –see COMPRISE (USAGE)

con·so·la·tion /,kɑnsə'leʸʃən/ *n* [C;U] (a person or thing that gives) comfort during a time of sadness or disappointment: *I got many letters of consolation when my mother died.|You were a consolation to me at such a sad time.*

con·sole¹ /kən'soʷl/ *v* **-soled, -soling** [T *with*] to give comfort or sympathy to (someone) in times of disappointment or sadness: *We tried to console her when her husband died, but it was very difficult.*

con·sole² /'kɑnsoʷl/ *n* a flat surface containing the controls for a machine, electrical apparatus, etc.

con·sol·i·date /kən'sɑlə,deʸt/ *v* **-dated, -dating** [I;T] **1** to make or become strong or firm:

SPELLING NOTE

Words with the sound /k/, like **cut**, may be spelled **k-**, like **key**, or **qu-**, like **queen**. Words with the sound /s/, like **city**, may be spelled **s-**, like **soon**, or **ps-**, like **psychology**.

Russia is trying to consolidate her position in eastern Europe. **2** to (cause to) combine into fewer or one: *Several small businesses consolidated to form a large powerful company.* —**consolidation** /kənˌsɑləˈdeɪʃən/ n [C;U]: *the consolidation of the three firms*

con·som·mé /ˌkɑnsəˈmeɪ/ n [C;U] (a) clear soup made from meat and/or vegetables

con·so·nant /ˈkɑnsənənt/ n (a letter representing) any of the speech sounds made by partly or completely stopping the flow of air as it goes through the mouth: *All the letters of the English alphabet except a,e,i,o, and u are consonants.* —compare VOWEL

con·sort /ˈkɑnsɔrt/ n the wife or husband esp. of a ruler

con·sor·ti·um /kənˈsɔrʃiʸəm, -ˈsɔrtiʸəm/ n **-tiums** or **-tia** /ʃiʸə, tiʸə/ [C +sing. pl. v] a combination of a number of companies, banks, etc., for a common purpose

consort with sbdy. /kənˈsɔrt/ v prep [T] *often derog* to spend time in the company of (esp. bad people): *She consorts with all kinds of strange people.*

con·spic·u·ous /kənˈspɪkyuʷəs/ adj noticeable; attracting attention: *She's always conspicuous because of her fashionable clothes.|He was conspicuous for his bad manners.* —opposite **inconspicuous** —**conspicuously** adv —**conspicuousness** n [U]

con·spir·a·cy /kənˈspɪrəsiʸ/ n **-cies** [C;U] (the act of making) a secret plan by two or more people to do something unlawful: *the generals' conspiracy to seize control of the government|They were guilty of conspiracy.*

con·spir·a·tor /kənˈspɪrətər/ n a person who takes part in a CONSPIRACY —**conspiratorial** /kənˌspɪrəˈtɔriʸəl, -ˈtoʷr-/ adj

con·spire /kənˈspaɪər/ v **-spired, -spiring** [I] **1** [+to-v] (of events) to combine: *Events conspired to produce great difficulties for the government.* **2** [+to-v/with, together] to plan together secretly (something unlawful or bad): *The criminals conspired to rob a bank.*

con·sta·ble /ˈkʌnstəbəl/ n [A;C] *BrE* a police officer of the lowest rank —compare POLICEMAN, POLICEWOMAN, PATROLMAN

con·stab·u·lar·y /kənˈstæbyəˌlɛriʸ/ n **-ies** the police force of a particular area or country

con·stan·cy /ˈkɑnstənsiʸ/ n [U] firmness of mind; freedom from change; faithfulness: *constancy of purpose|constancy between husband and wife* —opposite **inconstancy**

con·stant /ˈkɑnstənt/ adj **1** unchanging; fixed: *He drove at a constant speed.|(lit) a constant* (=loyal) *friend* —see also INCONSTANT **2** happening all the time: *I don't like these constant arguments.* —**constantly** adv

con·stel·la·tion /ˌkɑnstəˈleɪʃən/ n a group of fixed stars, often having a name, such as the Great Bear

con·ster·na·tion /ˌkɑnstərˈneɪʃən/ n [U] great shock and fear

con·sti·pa·tion /ˌkɑnstəˈpeɪʃən/ n [U] the (medical) condition of being unable to empty the bowels effectively —**constipated** /ˈkɑnstəˌpeɪtɪd/ adj

con·stit·u·en·cy /kənˈstɪtʃuʷənsiʸ/ n **-cies 1** an area of a country, represented in Con-

gress by one or more people **2** the voters living in such an area: *My constituency is opposed to the administration's plans, so I have to vote against it.*

con·stit·u·ent¹ /kənˈstɪtʃuʷənt/ n **1** a voter; member of a CONSTITUENCY (1) **2** any of the parts that make up a whole: *the constituents of an atom*

constituent² adj being one of the parts that makes a whole: *the constituent parts of an atom*

con·sti·tute /ˈkɑnstəˌtuʷt, -ˌtyuʷt/ v **-tuted, -tuting** *fml* [T not be +v-ing] to make up; form: *Seven days constitute a week.* —see COMPRISE (USAGE)

con·sti·tu·tion /ˌkɑnstəˈtuʷʃən, -ˈtyuʷ-/ n **1** [C] the laws and principles according to which a country is governed: *According to the American Constitution, Presidential elections are held every four years.* **2** [C] general 'condition of a person's body or mind: *an old man with a weak constitution* **3** [C] the way in which something is made up

con·sti·tu·tion·al /ˌkɑnstəˈtuʷʃənəl, -ˈtyuʷ-/ adj **1** limited or allowed by the CONSTITUTION (1): *There are severe constitutional limits on the President's power.* **2** of a person's CONSTITUTION (2): *a constitutional weakness of the mind* —**constitutionally** adv: *The government must always act constitutionally.*

con·strain /kənˈstreɪn/ v [T] *fml* to make (someone) do something by force or by strongly persuading: *I felt constrained to do what he told me.*

con·strained /kənˈstreɪnd/ adj awkward; unnatural: *a constrained manner* —opposite **unconstrained**

con·straint /kənˈstreɪnt/ n **1** [U] the condition of hiding one's natural feelings and behavior: *The children showed constraint in the presence of the new teacher.* **2** [C on] something that limits one's freedom of action: *lawful constraints on immoral behavior* **3** [U] the threat or use of force: *We acted under constraint.*

con·strict /kənˈstrɪkt/ v [T] to make narrower, smaller, or tighter: (fig.) *a constricted point of view* —**constrictive** adj —**constriction** /kənˈstrɪkʃən/ n [C;U]: *constriction of the blood vessels*

con·struct /kənˈstrʌkt/ v [T] *more fml than* **make**- to build; make by putting together or combining parts: *a difficult sentence to construct*

con·struc·tion /kənˈstrʌkʃən/ n **1** [U] the business or work of building: *I work in construction.|a construction company* **2** [U] the act or manner of CONSTRUCTING: *There are two new hotels near here* **under construction**. —see also DESTRUCTION **3** [C] something CONSTRUCTED, esp. a building: *a strangely shaped construction|A chair is a simple construction.*

con·struc·tive /kənˈstrʌktɪv/ adj helping to improve or develop something; helpful: *constructive suggestions/CRITICISM* —opposite **unconstructive** —**constructively** adv

con·strue /kənˈstruʷ/ v **-strued, -struing** [T] *fml* to place a certain meaning on (a statement etc.); understand; INTERPRET (2): *You can construe what she said in a number of different ways.* –see also MISCONSTRUE

con·sul /'kɑnsəl/ *n* a person appointed by a government to protect and help its citizens and its interests in trade in a foreign city –compare AMBASSADOR –**consular** /'kɑnsələr/ *adj*

con·sul·ate /'kɑnsəlɪt/ *n* **1** the official building in which a CONSUL lives or works **2** the rank of a CONSUL

con·sult /kən'sʌlt/ *v* [T] to go to (a person, book, etc.) for information, advice, etc.: *Have you consulted your doctor about your illness?* –**consultative** /kən'sʌltətɪv, 'kɑnsəl-ˌteʸtɪv/ *adj: a consultative committee*

  consult with sbdy. *v prep* [T] to exchange opinions, information, etc., with (a person or people): *Before we can accept the firm's offer we must consult with the workers.*

con·sult·ant /kən'sʌltənt/ *n* a person who gives specialist professional advice to others: *an industrial relations consultant|a firm of consultants*

con·sul·ta·tion /ˌkɑnsəl'teʸʃən/ *n* **1** [C] a meeting held to exchange opinions and ideas: *The doctors held a consultation concerning the new patient.* **2** [C;U] (an example of) the act of CONSULTing: *We made the decision in consultation with the others on the committee.*

con·sume /kən'suʷm/ *v* **-sumed, -suming** [T] **1** to eat or drink **2** to use up: *Arguing consumed many hours of the committee's time.* **3** (of a fire) to destroy: *The fire soon consumed the wooden buildings.|(fig.) She was consumed by hatred.*

con·sum·er /kən'suʷmər/ *n* a person who buys and uses goods and services: *The consumers complained about the increase in the price of meat.*

con·sum·mate¹ /kən'sʌmɪt, 'kɑnsə-/ *adj fml* perfect; complete: *consummate skill*

con·sum·mate² /'kɑnsə,meʸt/ *v* **-mated, -mating** [T] *fml* **1** to make perfect: *His happiness was consummated when she agreed to marry him.* **2** to make (a marriage) complete by having sex

con·sum·ma·tion /ˌkɑnsə'meʸʃən/ *n* **1** [C *usu. sing.*] the point at which something is made complete or perfect: *the consummation of ten years' work* **2** [U] the act of consummating (CONSUMMATE² (2)) a marriage

con·sump·tion /kən'sʌmpʃən/ *n* [U] **1** the act of consuming, or amount CONSUMEd: *The nation's consumption of oil increased last year.* **2** *old use* TUBERCULOSIS of the lungs: *She died of/from consumption.*

cont. *written abbrev. said as:* continued

con·tact¹ /'kɑntækt/ *n* **1** [U] the condition of meeting, touching, or receiving information

---

SPELLING NOTE

Words with the sound /k/, like **cut**, may be spelled **k-**, like **key**, or **qu-**, like **queen**. Words with the sound /s/, like **city**, may be spelled **s-**, like **soon**, or **ps-**, like **psychology**.

---

from: *Have you been in contact with your sister recently?|to make contact with the ship by radio|She has lost all contact with reality.* **2** [C] *infml* a social or business connection; person one knows who can help one: *I've got a contact in the tax office. She can help us.* **3** [C] an electrical part that can be moved to touch another part to complete an electrical CIRCUIT (3)

contact² *v* [T] to get in touch with (someone); reach (someone) by telephone, etc.

contact lens /'·· ˌ·/ also **contact–** *n* a very small LENS (1) specially shaped to fit closely over the eye to improve eyesight

con·ta·gious /kən'teʸdʒəs/ *adj* **1** (of a disease) that can be spread by touch or through the air: *(fig.) Her laughter is contagious.* **2** [F] (of a person) having a CONTAGIOUS disease –compare INFECTIOUS –**contagiously** *adv* –**contagiousness** *n* [U]

con·tain /kən'teʸn/ *v* [T] **1** to hold; have within itself: *This bottle contains two glasses of beer.|Beer contains alcohol.* **2** to hold back; keep under control: *Try to contain your anger/yourself!*

con·tain·er /kən'teʸnər/ *n* a box, bottle, etc., used for holding something

con·tam·i·nate /kən'tæmə,neʸt/ *v* **-nated, -nating** [T] to make impure or bad by mixing with dirty or poisonous matter: *Don't eat this food: it's been contaminated by flies.|The water was contaminated.* –**contamination** /kən,tæmə'neʸʃən/ *n* [U]

contd. *written abbrev. said as:* continued

con·tem·plate /'kɑntəm,pleʸt/ *v* **-plated, -plating** [I;T +*v-ing*] to consider or look at with continued attention; think about: *The doctor contemplated the difficult operation he had to perform.|I hope she isn't contemplating coming to stay with us!*

con·tem·pla·tion /ˌkɑntəm'pleʸʃən/ *n* [U *of*] deep thought: *She spent an hour in quiet contemplation.* –**contemplative** /kən'tɛmplətɪv, 'kɑntəm,pleʸtɪv/ *adj: a quiet, contemplative nature*

con·tem·po·ra·ne·ous /kən,tɛmpə'reʸniʸəs/ *adj* [with] *fml* existing or happening during the same period of time as another or each other –**contemporaneously** *adv*

con·tem·po·rar·y /kən'tɛmpə,rɛriʸ/ *adj* **1** modern; of the present: *contemporary history/art/morals|contemporary building* **2** [*no comp.*] of or belonging to the same (stated) time: *Contemporary reports of past events are often more interesting than the modern writer's view of them.* –see NEW (USAGE)

contemporary² *n* **-ies** a person living at the same time or of the same age as another: *Susan is my contemporary: we went to school together.*

con·tempt /kən'tɛmpt/ *n* [U] a lack of respect; the feeling that someone or something is of poor quality: *I feel nothing but contempt for such dishonest behavior.* –compare DISDAIN, SCORN

con·tempt·i·ble /kən'tɛmptəbəl/ *adj* deserving to be treated with CONTEMPT: *That was a contemptible trick to play on a friend!* –**contemptibly** *adv*

con·temp·tu·ous /kənˈtɛmptʃuᵂəs/ *adj* [*of*] feeling or expressing CONTEMPT: *She gave a contemptuous laugh.* **–contemptuously** *adv* –compare: *His speech was full of* **contemptuous** *remarks about his mother.*|*It was* **contemptible** (=very disrespectful) *of him to speak like that about her.*

con·tend /kənˈtɛnd/ *v* **1** [I *against, for, with*] to compete: *She contended for a gold medal at the Olympics.* **2** [T +*that*] to claim; say with strength: *The lawyer contended that there was no answer to the problem.*

con·tend·er /kənˈtɛndər/ *n* [*for*] (esp. in sports) a person who takes part in a competition

con·tent¹ /kənˈtɛnt/ *adj* [F +*to-v*/*with*] satisfied; happy: *Mary seems content to sit in front of the television all night.* –see also DISCONTENT

content² /kənˈtɛnt/ *v* [T *with*] to make happy or satisfied: *John contented himself with one glass of wine.*

con·tent³ /ˈkɑntɛnt/ *n* **1** [U] the subject matter, esp. the ideas, of a book, paper, etc.: *I like the style of this book, but I don't like the content.* –compare CONTENTS (2) **2** [S] the amount of a substance contained in something: *Oranges have a high water content.*

con·tent·ed /kənˈtɛntɪd/ *adj* [+*to-v*/*with*] satisfied; happy: *Jean seems contented just to sit and think.* –opposite **discontented** **–contentedly** *adv* **–contentment** *n* [U]: *the complete contentment of a well-fed baby*

con·ten·tion /kənˈtɛnʃən, -tʃən/ *n* **1** [U] the act of CONTENDING: *We're in trouble; this is no time for contention.* **2** [C +*that*] *fml* a claim; argument: *My contention is that the plan will never succeed.*

con·ten·tious /kənˈtɛnʃəs, -tʃəs/ *adj* **1** *fml* likely to cause argument: *Are lawyers contentious by nature?* **2** (of a person) tending to argue

con·tents /ˈkɑntɛnts/ *n* [P] **1** that which is contained in an object: *to drink the contents of the bottle* **2** (a table at the front of a book showing what a book contains: *Before buying a book, I look at the table of contents.* –compare CONTENT³ (1), INDEX

con·test¹ /ˈkɑntɛst/ *n* a struggle or fight; a competition: *a contest of skill*|*a beauty contest*

con·test² /kənˈtɛst, ˈkɑntɛst/ *v* [T] *fml* **1** to compete for; fight for: *How many people are contesting this seat on the council?* **2** to argue about the rightness of (something): *I intend to contest the judge's decision in another court.*

con·test·ant /kənˈtɛstənt/ *n* someone competing in a CONTEST¹: *There are 50 contestants in this competition.*

con·text /ˈkɑntɛkst/ *n* **1** the words around a word, phrase, etc., often used for helping to explain the meaning of the word, phrase, etc.: *You should be able to tell the meaning of this word from its context.* **2** the general conditions in which an event, action, etc., takes place **–contextual** /kənˈtɛkstʃuᵂəl/ *adj*

con·ti·nent /ˈkɑntən-ənt/ *n* any of the seven main large masses of land on the earth: *Africa is a continent.*

con·ti·nen·tal /ˌkɑntənˈɛntəl◄/ *adj* **1** related to or typical of a very large mass of land: *The weather in Siberia is typically continental.* **2** of, related to, or typical of Europe without the British Isles **3** *AmE* of, related to, or typical of North America: *The continental United States does not include Hawaii.*

con·tin·gen·cy /kənˈtɪndʒənsiʸ/ *n* **-cies** a possibility, esp. one that would cause problems if it happened: *We must be prepared for all contingencies.*|*contingency plans*

con·tin·gent¹ /kənˈtɪndʒənt/ *adj* [F *on, upon*] dependent on something uncertain: *Our arrival time is contingent on the weather.*

contingent² *n* **1** a group of soldiers, ships, etc., gathered together to help a larger force: *The army was strengthened by a large contingent of foreign soldiers.* **2** a group forming part of a large gathering: *Has the Scottish contingent arrived yet?*

con·tin·u·al /kənˈtɪnyuᵂəl/ *adj* repeated; frequent: *He has continual arguments with his father.* **–continually** *adv*

USAGE Compare **continual** and **continuous**. **Continual** means "happening again and again over a long period of time." and is often used of bad things; **continuous** means "continuing without interruption": **continual** *interruptions*|*six hours'* **continuous** *driving*|*The telephone has been ringing* **continually** *all morning.*|*The telephone rang* **continuously** *for five minutes.*

con·tin·u·a·tion /kənˌtɪnyuᵂˈeʸʃən/ *n* **1** [U] the act of continuing: *The Congress favors continuation of this tax system.* **2** [C] something which continues from something else: *The Baltic Sea is a continuation of the North Sea.*

con·tin·ue /kənˈtɪnyuᵂ/ *v* **-ued, -uing 1** [I;T +*to-v*/*v-ing*] to (cause to) go on happening: *The fighting continued for two days.* **2** [I;T +*to-v*/*v-ing*] to (cause to) start again after an interruption: *After a short break the play continued.*|*Will you continue reading after dinner?* **3** [I;T +*that*] to go on saying, esp. after an interruption: *"We must fight for racial equality,"* *continued the speaker.* –see also DISCONTINUE

continuing ed·u·ca·tion /ˌ·····   ··ˈ··/ *AmE*‖**further education** *BrE–* *n* [U] education after leaving school but not at a university –compare HIGHER EDUCATION

con·ti·nu·i·ty /ˌkɑntənˈuᵂəᵗiʸ, -ˈyuᵂ-/ *n* [U] uninterrupted connection or union: *There's no continuity between the parts of this book.*

con·tin·u·ous /kənˈtɪnyuᵂəs/ *adj* continuing without interruption; unbroken: *The brain needs a continuous supply of blood.* –opposite **discontinuous**; see CONTINUAL (USAGE) **–continuously** *adv*

con·tort /kənˈtɔrt/ *v* [I;T *with*] to (cause to) twist violently out of shape: *Her face was contorted with anger.*|*trees with contorted branches*|(fig.) *a contorted* (=difficult to understand) *line of reasoning* **–contortion** /kənˈtɔrʃən/ *n* [C;U]: *contortions of the body caused by poison*

con·tour /ˈkɑntuᵘər/ *n* **1** the shape of the edges

of an area: *the contour of the coast of Maine* **2** also **contour line** / '··· ,·/– a line drawn on a map to show the different heights of areas

con·tra·band /'kɑntrə,bænd/ *adj,n* [U] (of or concerning) goods which it is unlawful to bring into or send out of a country: *Contraband goods were found in his house.|contraband trade*

con·tra·cep·tion /,kɑntrə'sɛpʃən/ *n* [U] birth control; the methods of preventing sex from resulting in a woman becoming PREGNANT: *to practice contraception*

con·tra·cep·tive /,kɑntrə'sɛptɪv/ *adj,n* (of or concerning) a drug, object, or material used as a means of preventing an act of sex from resulting in a woman becoming PREGNANT: *Certain contraceptives make sex less enjoyable.* –see also DIAPHRAGM; CONDOM; IUD; PILL (2)

con·tract¹ /'kɑntrækt/ *n* **1** [+*to-v*] a formal agreement, having the force of law, between two or more people or groups: *Our shop has entered into/made a contract with a clothing firm to buy 100 coats a week.* **2** a signed paper on which the conditions of such an agreement are written: *We signed the contract!* –**contractual** /kən'træktʃuʷəl/ *adj: You have a contractual obligation to finish the building this month.* –**contractually** *adv*

con·tract² /kən'trækt/ *v* **1** [I;T] to (cause to) become smaller: *Metal contracts as it becomes cool.|In conversational English "is not" often contracts to "isn't."* –opposite **expand**, compare DILATE **2** [T] to get (an illness): *My son contracted a severe fever.*

con·tract³ /'kɑntrækt, kən'trækt/ *v* [I;T +*to-v*] to arrange by formal agreement: *They have contracted to build a bridge across the river.*

con·trac·tion /kən'trækʃən/ *n* **1** [U] the act of CONTRACTING² **2** [C] the shortened form of a word or words: *"Won't" is a contraction of "will not."*

con·trac·tor /'kɑn,træktər, kən'træk-/ *n* a person, business, or firm that provides building materials or labor

con·tra·dict /,kɑntrə'dɪkt/ *v* [I;T] to declare to be wrong or untruthful: *It's difficult to contradict someone politely.|Don't contradict!* **2** [T] (of a statement, action, fact, etc.) to be opposite in nature or character to: *His statements are contradicted by his actions.* –**contradictory** /'kɑntrə'dɪktəriʸ/ *adj* [*no comp.*]: *The prisoner's statement was contradictory to the one he'd made earlier.*

con·tra·dic·tion /,kɑntrə'dɪkʃən/ *n* **1** [U] the act of CONTRADICTing (1) **2** [C;U] a statement, action, or fact that CONTRADICTS (2) another or itself: *It is a contradiction to say you know him but he's a stranger.*

SPELLING NOTE

Words with the sound /k/, like **cut**, may be spelled **k-**, like **key**, or **qu-**, like **queen**. Words with the sound /s/, like **city**, may be spelled **s-**, like **soon**, or **ps-**, like **psychology**.

---

con·tral·to /kən'træltoʷ/ *n* **-tos** a female ALTO¹ (2)

con·trap·tion /kən'træpʃən/ *n infml* a strange-looking machine or apparatus: *I don't understand how this contraption works.*

con·trar·y¹ /'kɑn,trɛriʸ/ *adj* [*to*] **1** completely different; wholly opposed: *contrary suggestions* **2** **contrary to** in opposition to: *Contrary to all advice, he started to climb the mountain.*

con·trar·y² /'kɑn,trɛriʸ/ *n* **1** [*the* S] the opposite: *They say he is guilty, but I believe the contrary.* **2** **on the contrary** (*used for expressing strong opposition to what has just been said*) not at all; no: *"I hear you like your new job." "On the contrary, it's terribly uninteresting."* **3** **to the contrary** to the opposite effect; differently: *If you don't hear (anything) to the contrary I'll meet you at seven o'clock tonight.*

USAGE Compare **on the contrary, on the other hand, in contrast**: Use **on the contrary** to show complete disagreement with what has just been said: *"Does it rain a lot in the desert?" "On the contrary, it hardly ever rains."* Use **on the other hand** when adding a new and different fact to a statement: *It rarely rains in the desert, but on the other hand it rains a lot in the coastal areas.* Use **in contrast** to show the (surprising) difference between two very different facts: *It is hot in the desert in the day, but in contrast it is very cold at night.*

con·trar·y³ /'kɑn,trɛriʸ, kən'trɛəriʸ/ *adj* (of a person) difficult to handle or work with; unreasonable: *She is far too contrary to make friends easily.* –**contrarily** *adv* –**contrariness** *n* [U]

con·trast¹ /'kɑntræst/ *n* **1** [U] comparison of unlike objects, esp. to show differences: *In contrast with/ to your belief that we will fail, I know we will succeed.* –see CONTRARY (USAGE) **2** [C;U *between*] (a) difference or unlikeness: *such a contrast between brother and sister|This artist uses contrast (between light and dark) skillfully.*

con·trast² /kən'træst/ *v* [*with*] **1** [T] to compare (two things or people) so that differences are made clear: *In this book the writer contrasts Europe with/and America.* **2** [I] to show a difference when compared: *Your actions contrast unfavorably with your principles.*

con·tra·vene /,kɑntrə'viʸn/ *v* **-vened, -vening** [T] to act in opposition to; break (a law, rule, custom, etc.) *Your behavior contravened good manners.* –**contravention** /,kɑntrə'vɛnʃən, -tʃən/ *n* [C;U]

con·trib·ute /kən'trɪbyuʷt, -yət/ *v* **-uted, -uting** **1** [I;T *to, towards*] to join with others in giving (money, help, etc.): *Everybody contributed towards Jane's present when she left the office.* **2** [I *to*] to help in bringing about; have a share in: *Plenty of fresh air contributes to good health.* **3** [I;T *to*] to write and send (a written article) to a magazine, newspaper, etc.: *In general I write books, but sometimes I contribute to the newspaper.*

–**contribution** /ˌkɑntrəˈbyuʷʃən/ n [C;U]: *He gave a small contribution of $25.* –**contributor** /kənˈtrɪbyəṭər/ n: *a regular contributor to our magazine*

con·trib·u·to·ry /kənˈtrɪbyəˌtoriʸ, -ˌtoʷriʸ/ adj helping to bring about a result: *Your stupidity was a contributory cause of the fire.*

con·trite /kənˈtraɪt, ˈkɑntraɪt/ adj old use or lit feeling or showing guilt: *contrite tears* –**contritely** adv –**contrition** /kənˈtrɪʃən/ n [U]

con·trive /kənˈtraɪv/ v -**trived**, -**triving** [T +to-v] to succeed in (doing something), esp. in spite of difficulty: *After much difficulty I contrived to escape.*

con·trived /kənˈtraɪvd/ adj unnatural and forced: *the contrived cheerfulness of a worried doctor*

con·trol¹ /kənˈtroʷl/ v -**ll**- [T] to direct; fix the time, amount, degree, etc. of: *The pressure of steam in the engine is controlled by this button.*|*Control yourself/your temper; don't get angry.*|*The council controls the city.*

control² n **1** [U of, over] the power to control or direct: *Which political party has control of the city council? George took control of the business when his father died.*|*I lost control (of myself) and hit him.* **2** [U on, over] the act of controlling: *government control over industry/price controls* **3** [C often pl.] the place from which a machine, etc., is controlled: *He sat at the controls of the aircraft.*|*the control tower of an airport* **4 in control** in command; in charge **5 in the control of** controlled by **6 out of control** in(to) a state of not being controlled: *The car went out of control and crashed.* **7 under control** working properly; controlled in the correct way: *It took the teacher months to bring his class under control.*

con·tro·ver·sial /ˌkɑntrəˈvɜrʃəl/ adj causing much argument or disagreement: *a controversial speech/decision/person/book* –**controversially** adv

con·tro·ver·sy /ˈkɑntrəˌvɜrsiʸ/ n -**sies** [C;U] (a) fierce argument about something: *The new fashion has caused much controversy.*

con·va·lesce /ˌkɑnvəˈlɛs/ v -**lesced**, -**lescing** [I] to spend time getting well after an illness

con·va·les·cence /ˌkɑnvəˈlɛsəns/ n [S;U] the length of time a person spends getting well after an illness

con·va·les·cent /ˌkɑnvəˈlɛsənt/ adj,n (for, related to, or being) a person spending time getting well after an illness: *a convalescent nursing home*

con·vec·tion /kənˈvɛkʃən/ n [U] the movement in a gas or liquid caused by warm gas or liquid rising, and cold gas or liquid sinking: *a convection heater*|*Warm air rises by convection.*

con·vene /kənˈviʸn/ v -**vened**, -**vening** [I;T] **a** (of a group of people, committee, etc.) to meet or gather **b** to call (a group of people, committee, etc.) to meet or gather

con·ven·ience /kənˈviʸnyəns/ n **1** [U] fitness; suitableness: *We bought this house for its convenience. It's very near the stores.* –see also INCONVENIENCE **2** [C] an apparatus, service, etc., which gives comfort or advantage

to its user: *This house has all the modern conveniences.* **3** [U] personal comfort or advantage: *He thinks only of his own convenience.*|**Come at your** *earliest* **convenience.** (=as soon as is convenient for you)

con·ven·ient /kənˈviʸnyənt/ adj **1** suited to one's needs: *a convenient house/time/store* –opposite **inconvenient 2** [*to*] near; easy to reach: *Our house is very convenient to the stores.* –**conveniently** adv

con·vent /ˈkɑnvɛnt, -vənt/ n a religious establishment in which NUNs live and work –compare MONASTERY

con·ven·tion /kənˈvɛnʃən, -tʃən/ n **1** [C] a group of people gathered together with a shared purpose: *a teachers' convention*|*a national Democratic convention.* **2** [C;U] (an example of) generally accepted social behavior: *It is the convention for men to wear suits.* –see HABIT (USAGE) **3** [C] a formal agreement: *The countries all agreed to sign the convention.*

con·ven·tion·al /kənˈvɛnʃənəl, -tʃənəl/ adj often derog following accepted customs and standards, sometimes too closely: *conventional clothes/opinions/ideas* –opposite **unconventional 2** [*no comp.*] (of a weapon) not atomic –**conventionally** adv

con·verge /kənˈvɜrdʒ/ v -**verged**, -**verging** [I on] to come together towards a common point: *The roads converge just before the station.*|*converging lines* –compare DIVERGE –**convergent** adj [*no comp.*] –**convergence** n [C;U]

con·ver·sant /kənˈvɜrsənt/ adj [F *with*] fml familiar with: *I'm not conversant with chemistry because I've never studied it.*

con·ver·sa·tion /ˌkɑnvərˈseʸʃən/ n [C;U] (an) informal talk in which people exchange news, feelings, and thoughts: *Conversations with Tom are always interesting.* –**conversationally** adv

con·verse¹ /kənˈvɜrs/ v -**versed**, -**versing** [I on, about, with] more fml than **talk**– to talk informally: *I can converse with anyone about anything!*

con·verse² /kənˈvɜrs, ˈkɑnvɜrs/ adj fml opposite: *I hold the converse opinion.* –**conversely** adv

con·verse³ /ˈkɑnvɜrs/ n [*the* S] opposite: *I believe the converse of what you are saying.*

con·ver·sion /kənˈvɜrʒən, -ʃən/ n [C;U *of, from, into, to*] the act of CONVERTING¹; a change from one purpose, system, etc. to another: *The conversion of this building from a house to a school took place 100 years ago.*|*conversion from yards into meters* **2** [C *from, to*] a change in which a person accepts completely a new religion, belief, etc.: *His conversion from Hinduism to Buddhism happened in 1981.*

con·vert¹ /kənˈvɜrt/ v [I;T] **1** [*to, into*] to (cause to) change into another form, substance, or state, or from one purpose, system, etc. to another: *Coal can be converted to gas.*|*I want to convert some dollars into pounds.* **2** [*from, to*] (to persuade a person) to accept a particular religion, political belief, etc.: *John was converted to Bud-*

dhism.|*Anne has converted to Catholicism.*|*She converted him to her opinion.*

con·vert² /'kɑnvɜrt/ *n* a person who has been persuaded to accept a particular religion, political belief, etc.

con·vert·i·ble¹ /kən'vɜrtəbəl/ *adj* **1** that can be CONVERTED¹: *a convertible couch* (=a COUCH that can be unfolded to become a bed) **2** [*into*] (of a type of money) that can be freely exchanged for other types of money: *The dollar is convertible; the* RUBLE *is not.*

convertible² *n* a car with a roof that can be folded back

con·vex /,kɑn'vɛks◄, kən-/ *adj tech* curved outwards, like the outside edge of a circle: *a convex mirror* –opposite **concave**

con·vey /kən'veɪ/ *v* -veyed, -veying [T] **1** [*from, to*] to take or carry from one place to another: *to convey electricity from power stations to houses* **2** to make (feelings, ideas, thoughts, etc.) known: *I can't convey my feelings in words.*|*Words convey meaning.*

con·vict¹ /kən'vɪkt/ *v* [T *of*] to find (someone) guilty of a crime in a court of law: *The criminal was convicted of murder.* –opposite **acquit**

con·vict² /'kɑn,vɪkt/ *n* a person who has been found guilty of a crime and sent to prison, esp. for a long time: *an escaped convict*

con·vic·tion /kən'vɪkʃən/ *n* **1** [C] an occasion on which someone has been CONVICTED¹: *This was her third conviction for stealing.* –opposite **acquittal 2** [C;U] (a) very firm and sincere belief: *I speak with full conviction that our cause is just.*|*She was speaking from conviction.*

con·vince /kən'vɪns/ *v* -vinced, -vincing [T + *(that)*] to cause (someone) to believe; persuade (someone): *It took a long time to convince me of his guilt.*|*I was convinced* (=quite sure) *you were here.*|*It was hard to convince you (that) we couldn't afford a new car.*|*We convinced her to go to the movie.*

USAGE Compare **convince** and **persuade**: *The newspaper article has* **convinced** *me* (=made me believe) *that smoking is a dangerous habit.*|*The doctor* **persuaded** *me to stop smoking.*

con·vinc·ing /kən'vɪnsɪŋ/ *adj* able to CONVINCE: *a convincing speaker/speech* –opposite **unconvincing** –**convincingly** *adv*

con·viv·i·al /kən'vɪviʸəl/ *adj fml* friendly; with eating, drinking, and good company: *a very convivial party* –**conviviality** /kən,vɪv·iʸ'ælətiʸ/ *n* [U]

con·vo·lut·ed /'kɑnvə,luʷtɪd/ *adj fml* twisted; curved: (fig.) *a convoluted argument* –**convolution** /,kɑnvə'luʷʃən/ *n*

con·voy¹ /'kɑnvɔɪ/ *n* -voys (a group of ships or vehicles traveling with) a protecting force of armed ships, vehicles, etc.: *We decided to travel* **in convoy** *for safety.*|*The convoy was attacked at sea.*

convoy² *v* -voyed, -voying [T] (of an armed ship, vehicle, soldiers, etc.) to go with and protect (a group of ships, vehicles, etc.)

con·vulse /kən'vʌls/ *v* -vulsed, -vulsing [T *with*] to shake or upset (a person, society, etc.) violently

con·vul·sion /kən'vʌlʃən/ [*usu. pl.*] an unnaturally violent and sudden movement: *Her nervous illness often threw her into convulsions.* –**convulsive** /kən'vʌlsɪv/ *adj* –**convulsively** *adv*

coo /kuʷ/ *v* **1** [I] to make the low soft cry of a DOVE or PIGEON, or a sound like this **2** [I;T] to speak or say softly and lovingly: *to coo at a baby*

cook¹ /kʊk/ *n* a person who prepares and cooks food: *John's a cook in a hotel.*|*Peter's a better cook than Sarah, so he usually cooks for their family.* –compare CHEF

cook² *v* **1** [I;T] to prepare (food) for eating by using heat; make (a dish): *Do you want your vegetables cooked or raw?*|*I'm going to cook dinner tomorrow.* **2** [I] (of food) to be prepared in this way: *Make sure this meat cooks for at least an hour.*

USAGE A modern gas or electric **stove** (*BrE* **cooker**) usually has three parts: the **oven**, the **broiler** (*BrE* **grill**), and the **burners** on top. The **oven** is used for **baking** bread and cakes or **roasting** a large piece of meat. The **broiler** is an apparatus for cooking by direct heat, and can be used e.g. for **broiling** (*BrE* **grilling**) meat or **toasting bread** (=making it hard and brown). The **burners** can be used for **boiling** food in a pot with water; for **stewing** food (=cooking food slowly in liquid to make a stew); or for **frying** (=cooking food in hot fat or oil). **Simmering** is very gentle slow boiling.

cook sthg.↔ **up** *v adv* [T] to invent falsely: *I think she's cooked up that excuse. I don't believe it.*

cook·er /'kʊkər/ *adj BrE* for STOVE¹ –see COOK (USAGE)

cook·er·y /'kʊkəriʸ/ *n* [U] the science of preparation of food

cook·ie, cooky /'kʊkiʸ/ *n* -ies *AmE* **1** biscuit *BrE*– any of many types of sweetened and baked, flat, thin, dry cakes: *Have a chocolate cookie.* **2** *infml* a person: *a clever cookie.*

cook·out /'kʊk-aʊt/ *n esp. AmE infml* a meal cooked and eaten outdoors

cool¹ /kuʷl/ *adj* **1** neither warm nor cold; pleasantly cold: *a cool day* **2** calm; unexcited: *Even when you argue, you should try and keep cool.*|*John has* **a very cool head.** (=he never gets too excited) **3** [*towards*] (of a person, manner, behavior, etc.) not as friendly as usual: *Charles seemed very cool towards me today. I wonder if I've offended him.* **4** *infml apprec* living according to one's own standards; unconcerned about the opinion of other people –**coolly** /'kuʷl-liʸ, 'kuʷliʸ/ *adv* –**coolness** *n* [U]

cool² *v* [I;T *down*] to make or become cool: *Open the windows to cool the room.*|*Let your tea cool (down) a little before you drink it.*

–compare WARM[2]

cool down also **cool off**– v adv [I:T (= **cool** sbdy. **down**)] to (cause to) become calmer and less excited: *It took her a long time to cool down after the argument.|I tried to cool her down, but she was too angry.*

cool[3] n [*the* S] a temperature that is neither warm nor cold: *the cool of the evening*

cool·er kuᵂlər/ n a container that makes or keeps its contents cool –see illustration on page 581

coop /kuᵂp, kʊp/ n a cage for small creatures, esp. hens: *a chicken coop* –see COOP UP

co-op /'koᵂ ɑp/ n infml for COOPERATIVE[2]

co·op·er·ate, cooperate /koᵂ'ɑpə,reyt/ v **-ated, -ating** [I +*to-v/with, in*] to work or act together for a shared purpose: *The British cooperated with the French in building the new plane.|Let's all cooperate to get the work done quickly.*

co·op·er·a·tion, co-op- /koᵂ,ɑpə'reyʃən/ n [U] **1** the act of working together for a shared purpose **2** willingness to work together; help: *I need your cooperation in this matter.*

co·op·er·a·tive[1], **co-op-** /koᵂ'ɑpərəṭiv/ adj **1** helpful: *The teacher thanked her students for being so cooperative.* –opposite **uncooperative 2** [*no comp.*] made, done, or worked by people acting together: *a cooperative farm.* –**cooperatively** adv

cooperative[2], **co-op-** also **co-op** n **1** a COOPERATIVE[1] (2) firm, farm, etc.: *a farm cooperative* **2** esp. AmE (an apartment in) an apartment building that is owned by the people living in it –compare CONDOMINIUM

coop sbdy./sthg.↔ **up** /kuᵂp, kʊp/ v adv [T] to enclose; limit the freedom of (a person or animal): *cooped up in prison* –see COOP

co-opt /koᵂ'ɑpt/ v [T *into, onto*] (of an elected group) to choose (someone not elected) as a fellow member: *I wasn't elected to the committee: I was co-opted onto it.*

co·or·di·nate /koᵂ'ɔrdn,eyt/ v **-nated, -nating** [I;T] to (cause to) work together, esp. to increase effectiveness: *We need to coordinate our efforts.*

co·or·di·na·tion /koᵂ,ɔrdn'eyʃən/ n [U] **1** the act of coordinating (COORDINATE) **2** the way in which muscles work together when performing a movement: *Dancers need good coordination.*

coot /kuᵂt/ n a small gray water bird

cop[1] /kɑp/ n infml a policeman or policewoman

cop[2] v **-pp-** →COP OUT

cope /koᵂp/ v **coped, coping** [I *with*] to deal successfully with something: *I can't cope with (driving in) heavy traffic.*

co·pi·ous /'koᵂpiʸəs/ adj plentiful: *copious tears|She was a copious writer.* –**copiously** adv

cop out v adv **-pp-** [I *of, on*] infml often derog to fail to take the responsibility of making a difficult decision or to do what one thinks right: *You've got to do it: don't try to cop out (of it) by telling me you're too busy!* –**cop-out** /'·· ·/ n: *He used his illness as a cop-out for not passing the test.*

cop·per[1] /'kɑpər/ n **1** [U] a soft reddish metal

2 [C;U] a reddish-brown color –**coppery** /'kɑpəriʸ/ adj

copper[2] also **cop-** n infml a policeman

cop·ra /'kɑprə, 'koᵂ-/ n [U] the dried flesh of the coconut, from which oil is pressed for making soap

copse /kɑps/ n a small wood, usu. with small trees or bushes

cop·ter /'kɑptər/ n infml for HELICOPTER

Cop·tic Church /,kɑptɪk 'tʃɜrtʃ/ n a branch of the Christian Church based in Ethiopia and Egypt

cop·u·late /'kɑpyə,leyt/ v **-lated, -lating** [I *with*] fml to have sex –**copulation** /,kɑpyə'leyʃən/ n [U]

cop·y[1] /'kɑpiʸ/ n **-ies 1** a thing made to be exactly like another: *I asked my secretary to make me four copies of the letter.* **2** a single example of a magazine, book, newspaper, etc.: *Did you get your copy of "The News" today?*

copy[2] v **-ied, -ying 1** [T] to make a copy of (something) **2** [T] to follow (someone or something) as a standard or pattern: *Jean always copies the way I dress.* **3** [I;T *from, off*] to cheat by writing exactly the same thing as (someone else): *He never does his homework himself; he just copies his brother's.*

cop·y·cat /'kɑpiʸ,kæt/ n infml derog a person who without thought copies someone's manners, behavior, dress, etc.

cop·y·right /'kɑpiʸ,raɪt/ n [C;U] the right in law to be the only producer or seller of a book, play, movie, record, etc., for a fixed period of time: *Who has the copyright of/on/for your book?*

cor·al[1] /'kɔrəl, 'kɑrəl/ n [U] a white, pink, or reddish stonelike or hornlike substance formed from the bones of very small sea animals. *Coral is often used for making jewelry.*

coral[2] adj,n [U] (having) a pink or reddish orange color: *coral lips*

coral snake /'·· ,·/ also **coral** infml– n a brightly colored, poisonous snake found in America

cord /kɔrd/ n **1** [C;U] (a length of) thick string or thin rope **2** [C;U] (a piece of) wire with a protective covering, for joining electrical apparatus to a supply of electricity –see illustration on page 221 **3** [C] also **chord**– a part of the body, such as a nerve or number of bones joined together, that is like string: *the* VOCAL CORDS

cor·dial[1] /'kɔrdʒəl/ adj warmly friendly: *a cordial smile/welcome/invitation* –**cordiality** /,kɔrdʒiʸ'æləʒtiʸ, kɔr'dʒæ-/ n [U]

cordial[2] n [C;U] a strong alcoholic drink, usu. sweet and made from fruit

cor·dial·ly /'kɔrdʒəliʸ/ adv in a CORDIAL[1] manner: *You are cordially invited to the wedding.*

cor·don /'kɔrdn/ n a line or ring of police, military vehicles, etc., placed around an area to protect or enclose it

cordon sthg.↔ **off** v adv [T] to enclose (an area) with a line of police, soldiers, military vehicles, etc.

cords /kɔrdz/ also **corduroys** /'kɔrdə,rɔɪz,

,kɔrdə'rɔɪz/– n [P] *infml* pants made from CORDUROY –see PAIR (USAGE)

cor·du·roy /'kɔrdə,rɔɪ, ,kɔrdə'rɔɪ/ n [U] thick strong cotton cloth with thin raised lines on it, used esp. for making outer clothing

core¹ /kɔr, koʷr/ n **1** the hard central part containing the seeds of certain fruits, such as the apple: *An apple core is the part of an apple left after the flesh has been eaten.* **2** the most important or central part of anything **3 to the core** thoroughly; completely: *She's French to the core.*

core² v **cored, coring** [T] to remove the CORE¹ (1) from (a fruit)

cor·gi /'kɔrgiʸ/ n a small dog with short legs and a foxlike head

cork¹ /kɔrk/ n **1** [U] the outer covering (BARK) of the **cork oak** (=a tree from Southern Europe and North Africa) **2** [C] a round piece of this material fixed into the neck of a bottle to close it tightly: *I can't get the cork out of this wine bottle.*

cork² v [T *up*] to close (the neck of a bottle or other object) tightly with a CORK¹ (2) –opposite **uncork**

cork sthg.↔ up v adv [T] *infml* for BOTTLE **up**

cork·screw /'kɔrkskruʷ/ n **1** an apparatus of twisted metal with a handle, used for pulling CORKs¹ (2) out of bottles **2** →SPIRAL¹

cor·mo·rant /'kɔrmərənt/ n a large black fish-eating seabird with a long neck

corn¹ /kɔrn/ n [U] **1** *AmE*‖also **maize, sweet corn** *BrE*– (the seed of) a tall plant grown, esp. in America and Australia, for its ears of yellow seeds **2** *BrE* (the seed of) any of various types of grain plants, esp. wheat

corn² n a painful area of thick hard skin on the foot, usu. on or near a toe

corn bread /'·· ·/ n [U] (esp. in the US) coarse bread made from CORN¹ (1)

cor·ne·a /'kɔrniʸə/ n a strong transparent protective covering on the front outer surface of the eye –**corneal** *adj*

cor·ner¹ /'kɔrnər/ n **1** (the inside or outside of) the point at which two lines, surfaces, or edges meet: *the bottom corners of the page*|*the corner of the desk*|*the corner of a box* **2** the place where two roads, paths, or streets meet: *I'll meet you on/at the corner of Smith Street and Beach Road.* **3** [*often pl.*] a distant part of the world: *People came from all the corners of the world to hear her sing.* **4 cut corners** *infml* to do something in the easiest or quickest way, by paying no attention to rules, using simpler methods, etc. **5 in a tight corner** in a difficult or threatening position from which escape is difficult

corner² v **1** [T] to force (a person or animal) into a difficult position: *He fought like a cornered animal.* **2** [T] to gain control of (the

SPELLING NOTE

Words with the sound /k/, like **cut**, may be spelled **k-**, like **key**, or **qu-**, like **queen**. Words with the sound /s/, like **city**, may be spelled **s-**, like **soon**, or **ps-**, like **psychology**.

buying, selling, or production of goods): *By defeating their main competitor, this company will* **corner** *the (wheat) market.* **3** [I] (of a vehicle, driver, etc.) to turn a corner: *My car corners well even in wet weather.*

cor·ner·stone /'kɔrnər,stoʷn/ n **1** a stone set at one of the bottom corners of a building, often put in place at a special ceremony **2** something of first importance: *Free speech is the cornerstone of our way of life.*

cor·net /kɔr'nɛt/ n a small brass musical instrument like a TRUMPET

corn·flakes /'kɔrnfleʸks/ n [P] small FLAKES made from coarsely crushed corn, usu. eaten at breakfast, often with milk and sugar

cor·nice /'kɔrnɪs/ n a decorative border at the top edge of the front of a building or pillar or around the top inside edges of the walls in a room

cornstarch /'kɔrnstartʃ/ *AmE*‖**corn flour** /'· ·/ *BrE*– n [U] a fine white flour made from crushed corn, used in cooking to thicken liquids

corporal² n [A;C] a person of low rank in the armed forces

cor·po·rate /'kɔrpərɪt/ *adj* **1** of, belonging to, or shared by all the members of a group; COLLECTIVE: *corporate responsibility/effort* **2** of, belonging to, or related to a CORPORATION –**corporately** *adv*

cor·po·ra·tion /,kɔrpə'reʸʃən/ n a large business organization: *John works for a large chemical corporation.*

corps /kɔr, koʷr/ n **corps** /kɔrz, koʷrz/ **1** (*often cap.*) a trained army group with special duties: *the medical corps* **2** (*often cap.*) a branch of the army able to fight on its own **3** a group of people united in the same activity: *The President's PRESS corps is meeting tonight.*|*the DIPLOMATIC corps*

corpse /kɔrps/ n a dead body, esp. of a person

cor·pu·lent /'kɔrpyələnt/ *adj euph* very fat –**corpulence** n [U]

cor·pus /'kɔrpəs/ n **corpora** /'kɔrpərə/ or **corpuses** a collection of all the writings of a special kind: *the corpus of Shakespeare's works*

cor·pus·cle /'kɔrpəsəl, -,pʌsəl/ n any of the red or white cells in the blood

cor·ral /kə'ræl/ n,v (esp. in the West of the US) (to put in) an enclosed area where cattle, horses, etc., are kept: *After we corral the horses we'll have lunch.*

cor·rect¹ /kə'rɛkt/ *adj* **1** right; without mistakes: *a correct answer*|*correct spelling* **2** keeping to proper standards of manners, etc.: *correct behavior* –opposite **incorrect** –**correctly** *adv* –**correctness** n [U]

correct² v to make right or better; mark the mistakes in: *Correct my spelling if it's wrong.*

cor·rec·tion /kə'rɛkʃən/ n **1** [U] the act of CORRECTING² **2** [C] a change that corrects something: *Teachers usually make corrections in red ink.* **3** [U] *euph* punishment: *The prisoner was sent to a labor camp for correction.*

cor·rec·tive /kə'rɛktɪv/ *adj,n* (something) intended to correct: *corrective punishment*

–**correctively** *adv*

cor·re·la·tion /ˌkɔrəˈleⁱʃən, ˌkar-/ *n [between]* a shared relationship or causal connection: *a high correlation between unemployment and crime*

cor·re·spond /ˌkɔrəˈspand, ˌkar-/ *v* [I] **1** *[with, to]* to be in agreement; match: *These goods don't correspond with/ to the list of those I ordered.* **2** *[with]* to exchange letters regularly: *Janet and Bob corresponded (with each other) for many years.*

cor·re·spond·ence /ˌkɔrəˈspandəns, ˌkar-/ *n* [C;U] **1** agreement between particular things; likeness **2** the act of exchanging letters **3** the letters exchanged between people: *The library bought all the correspondence between President Kennedy and his mother.* |*to do/take a* **correspondence course** (=a course of lessons sent by mail)

cor·re·spond·ent /ˌkɔrəˈspandənt, ˌkar-/ *n* **1** a person with whom another person exchanges letters regularly **2** someone employed by a newspaper, television, etc., to report news from a distant area: *a war correspondent* |*our correspondent in Rome*

cor·re·spond·ing /ˌkɔrəˈspandɪŋ, ˌkar-/ *adj* matching; related: *All rights carry corresponding responsibilities with them.* –**correspondingly** *adv*

cor·ri·dor /ˈkɔrədər, -ˌdɔr, ˈkar-/ *n* **1** a passage, esp. between two rows of rooms: *Room 101 is at the end of the corridor.* **2** a narrow piece of land that passes through a foreign country: *the Polish Corridor (to the sea)*

cor·rob·o·rate /kəˈrabəˌreⁱt/ *v* **-rated, -rating** [T] to support (an opinion, belief, idea, etc.) by fresh information or proof: *A person who saw the accident corroborated the driver's statement.* |*This newspaper article corroborates my ideas on government spending.* –**corroborator** /kəˈrabəˌreⁱtər/ *n* –**corroborative** /kəˈrabərətɪv, -bəˌreⁱtɪv/ *adj* –**corroboration** /kəˌrabəˈreⁱʃən/ *n* [U]: *Is there any corroboration for that opinion?*

cor·rode /kəˈroʷd/ *v* **-roded, -roding** [I;T *away*] to (cause to) become worn or be destroyed slowly, esp. by chemical action: *Acid causes metal to corrode.* –**corrosive** /kəˈroʷsɪv/ *adj*

cor·ro·sion /kəˈroʷʒən/ *n* [U] **1** the act of corroding (CORRODE) **2** a substance, such as RUST[1] (1), produced by this act: *corrosion on the car's body*

cor·ru·gat·ed /ˈkɔrəˌgeⁱtɪd, ˈkar-/ *adj* having wavelike folds: *Sheets of corrugated iron are often used for roofs and fences.*

cor·rupt[1] /kəˈrʌpt/ *v* **1** [I;T] to make morally bad; cause to change from good to bad: *He could have been a great man, but he was corrupted by power.* **2** [T] to influence (esp. a public official) improperly; BRIBE[1]: *She was sent to prison for trying to corrupt a policeman (with money).* **3** [T] to change the original form of (a language, set of teachings, etc.) in a bad way: *Has the language been corrupted by the introduction of foreign words?* –**corruptible** *adj* –**corruptibility** /kəˌrʌptəˈbɪləti/ *n* [U]

corrupt[2] *adj* **1** immoral; wicked; bad: *a corrupt political system* **2** dishonest; able to be BRIBEd: *a corrupt judge* –see also INCORRUPTIBLE **3** containing mistakes; different from the original: *They spoke a corrupt form of French.* –**corruptly** *adv* –**corruptness** *n* [U]

cor·rup·tion /kəˈrʌpʃən/ *n* [U] **1** the act of CORRUPTing[1] **2** dishonesty; immoral behavior; the state of being CORRUPT[2] (2): *the corruption of the ancient Roman court* **3** decay; impurity: *the corruption of the body after death*

cor·set /ˈkɔrsɪt/ *n* a very tight-fitting undergarment worn, esp. by women, to give shape to the waist and HIPs –**corseted** *adj* **-tège**

cor·tege, -tège /kɔrˈtɛʒ, -ˈteⁱʒ/ *n fml* a procession of attendants, esp. at a funeral

cos·met·ic[1] /kazˈmɛtɪk/ *n [usu. pl.]* a face-cream, body-powder, etc., intended to make the skin or hair more beautiful: *"Do you use cosmetics?" "Yes, I use face-cream and wear LIPSTICK."*

cosmetic[2] *adj* **1** of, related to, or causing increased beauty of the skin or hair: *a cosmetic cream* **2** *derog* dealing with the outside appearance rather than the central part of a problem: *They made only cosmetic repairs on the house.*

cos·mic /ˈkazmɪk/ *adj* of or related to the whole universe –**cosmically** *adv*

cos·mo·naut /ˈkazməˌnɔt/ *n* a Soviet ASTRONAUT

cos·mo·pol·i·tan /ˌkazməˈpalətn/ *adj* **1** consisting of people from many different parts of the world: *New York is a very cosmopolitan city.* **2** (of a person, belief, opinion, etc.) not narrow-minded; showing wide experience of different people and places

cos·mos /ˈkazməs, -moʷs/ *n [the S]* the universe considered as an ordered system

cos·set /ˈkasɪt/ *v* **-tt-** [T] to pay a great deal of attention to making (a person) comfortable and contented

cost[1] /kɔst/ *n* **2** [C] the price of making or producing something: *Production costs can be very high.* **1** [S] the amount paid or asked for goods or services; price: *The cost of postage stamps is going up again next week.* |*He bought it at a cost of $300.* |(fig.) *She saved him from the fire, but at the cost of her own life.* |*We must avoid war,* **at all costs.** (=whatever might happen) **3** **cost of living** the cost of buying the necessary goods and services to provide a person with the average accepted things for living: *As the cost of living goes up my* **standard of living** *goes down.*

cost[2] *v* **cost, costing 1** [I;T *no pass.*] to have (an amount of money) as a price: *It will cost you $50 to fly to Paris.* |*The best goods usually cost most.* |(fig.) *That mistake cost him his life.* **2** [T *no pass.*] *infml* to be costly for (someone): *It will cost you to go by train. Why not go by bus?*

USAGE The **price** of a thing is what it **costs** you, or what the person who is selling it **charges** you for it: *What is the* **price** *of this watch?* |*What does it* **cost?** |*How much did he* charge you for repairing the car? The **value** of a thing is what it is worth: *He sold it at a* **price** *below its real value.* **Cost**, not **price**, is used **a** for services: *the* **cost** *of having the house painted* **b** for more general things: *the* **cost** *of living.* **Expense** is used like **cost**, esp. when this is thought of as too large: *the terrible* **expense** *of having the house painted.* A person **charges** a **charge**, a **price**, or (for professional services) a **fee**. A thing **costs** a sum of money: *This watch* **costs** *$10.*

cost³ *v* **costed, costing** [T] to calculate the price to be charged for (a job, someone's time, etc.): *The builder costed the job at about $150.*

co·star /ˈkoʷ star/ *n,v* **-starred, -starring** (to be) a famous actor or actress who appears together with another famous actor or actress in a movie or play: *Who's co-starring in this movie?*

cost·ly /ˈkɔstliʸ/ *adj* **-lier, -liest 1** costing a lot of money; EXPENSIVE **2** gained or won at a great loss: *the costliest war in our history* —**costliness** *n* [U]

cos·tume /ˈkɑstuʷm, -styuʷm/ *n* [C;U] the clothes typical of a certain period, country, or profession, esp. as worn in plays: *actors in strange costumes*

co·sy¹ /ˈkoʷziʸ/ *adj* **-sier, -siest** →COZY¹

cosy² *n* **-sies** →COZY²

cot /kɑt/ *n* **1** *AmE*‖**camp bed** *BrE–* a light narrow usu. single bed which folds flat and is easily carried **2** *BrE* for CRIB

cot·tage /ˈkɑtɪdʒ/ *n* a small house, esp. in the country –see HOUSE (USAGE)

cottage cheese /ˈ·· ˌ·, ˌ·· ˈ·/ *n* [U] soft lumpy white cheese made from sour milk

cot·ton¹ /ˈkɑtn/ *n* [U] **1** (a tall plant which produces) soft white hair used for making thread, cloth, etc. **2** thread or cloth made from this: *a cotton dress*‖a REEL *of white cotton thread*

cotton² *v* → COTTON ON; COTTON TO

cot·ton·mouth /ˈkɑtn̩ˌmaʊθ/ also **water moccasin–** *n* **-mouths** /ˌmaʊθs, ˌmaʊðz/ a poisonous snake found in low wet areas of the southern US

cotton on *v adv* [I *to*] *BrE infml* to understand: *It was a long time before I cottoned on (to what he meant).*

cotton to sbdy./sthg. *v prep* [T] *infml*, *esp. AmE* to like someone or something: *He's a friendly boy and will cotton (up) to anyone easily.*‖*I could never really cotton to his way of teaching.*

couch¹ /kaʊtʃ/ *n* a long piece of furniture, usu. with a back and arms, on which more than one person may sit or lie; SOFA –see illustration on page 399

couch² *v* [T *usu. pass.*] to express (words, a reply, etc.) in a certain way: *The President's*

SPELLING NOTE
Words with the sound /k/, like **cut**, may be spelled **k-**, like **key**, or **qu-**, like **queen**. Words with the sound /s/, like **city**, may be spelled **s-**, like **soon**, or **ps-**, like **psychology**.

refusal was couched in friendly language.

cou·chette /kuʷˈʃɛt/ *n* a narrow shelf-like bed on which a person can sleep on a train

cou·gar /ˈkuʷgər/ also **mountain lion, puma**‖also **panther** *AmE– n* **-gars** *or* **-gar** a large powerful brown wild cat from the mountainous areas of western North America and South America

cough¹ /kɔf/ *v* **1** [I] to push air out from the throat with a rough explosive noise, esp. because of discomfort in the lungs or throat during a cold or other infection **2** [T *up*] to clear (something) from the throat by doing this: *I knew she was seriously ill when she began to cough (up) blood.* **3** [I] to make a sound like a cough: *The engine coughed but would not start.*

cough up sthg. *v adv* [F] *infml* to produce (money or information) unwillingly

cough² *n* **1** [C] an act or sound of coughing: *She gave a nervous cough.* **2** [S] a (medical) condition marked by frequent coughing: *John had a bad cough all last week.*

could /kəd; *strong* kʊd/ *v negative contraction* **couldn't** /ˈkʊdnt/[I + *tə*v] **1** *past tense of* can: *I can't sing now, but I could when I was young.* **2** (used instead of *can* to describe what someone has said, asked, etc.): *He said we could smoke.* (=He said: "You can smoke.") **3** (used to show that something might be possible): *I could come tomorrow (if you would like me to).*‖*I could have bought it, but I didn't.* **4** (used when making a polite request): *Could you help me to lift it, please?* –see Study Notes on page 434

could·n't /ˈkʊdnt/ *v short for*: could not: *"Couldn't you see?" "No, I couldn't."*

coun·cil /ˈkaʊnsəl/ *n* a group of people appointed or elected to make laws or decisions, for a town, church, etc., or to give advice: *The housing council advised us to build apartments for old people.*

coun·cil·or *AmE*‖**-cillor** *BrE* /ˈkaʊnsələr/ *n* [A;C] a member of a council: *What do you think, Councilor Evans?*

coun·sel¹ /ˈkaʊnsəl/ *n* [U] **1** *law* the lawyer(s) speaking for someone in a court of law: *The judge asked (the) counsel for the* DEFENSE *to explain.* **2** *becoming rare* advice: *They refused to listen to the old man's counsel.* –sounds like **council**

counsel² *v* **-l-** *AmE*‖**-ll-** *BrE* [T + *v-ing*] *fml* to advise: *We were counseled against traveling/not to travel at night.*‖*the counseling service for new students*

coun·sel·or *AmE*‖**counsellor** *BrE* /ˈkaʊnsələr/ *n* **1** [C] an adviser: *a marriage guidance counselor* **2** [A;C] *esp. AmE* a lawyer **3** [C] one who takes care of a group of children, usu. in a summer camp: *My counselor's name is Susan.*

count¹ /kaʊnt/ *v* **1** [I;T *up, to*] to say or name the numbers in order, one by one or by groups: *He counted (up) to 100 and then came to find us.*‖*Count to 20, and then open your eyes.* **2** [T] to say or name (objects) one by one in order to find the whole number in a collection; total: *Count the apples in this box.*‖*Have the votes been counted yet?* **3** [T] to include: *There are six people in my family, counting my parents.* **4** [T] to consider; regard: *Pavlova was counted among the greatest dancers of the century.* **5** [I] to have value, force, or importance: *It is not how much you read but what you read that counts.*

count down *v adv* [I] to count backwards in seconds to zero, esp. before sending a spacecraft into space –see also COUNTDOWN

count sbdy. **in** *v adv* [T] *infml* to include: *If you're planning a trip to Florida, count me in.* –opposite **count out**

count on/upon sbdy./sthg. *v prep* **1** [T +*to-v*/*v-ing*] to depend on (someone, something, or something happening): *You can't count on the weather being good.*|*You can count on him to come.* **2** [T +*v-ing*] to expect; take into account: *I didn't count on John arriving so early.*

count sbdy./sthg.↔ **out** *v adv* [T] **1** to put down in turn while counting: *He counted out ten $5 bills.* **2** to declare (a BOXER[3] who fails to rise from the floor after ten seconds) to be loser of a fight **3** *infml* to leave out: *If you're playing football in this weather, you can count me out.* –opposite **count in**

count² *n* **1** an act of counting; total reached by counting **2 keep/lose count** to know/fail to know the exact number: *I lost count of how many times that actress has been married.* **3 be out for the count** (in BOXING) to be COUNTED[1] **out** (2); be unconscious

count³ *n* [A;C] (*often cap.*) (the title of) a European nobleman whose rank equals that of a British EARL

count·a·ble /ˈkaʊntəbəl/ *adj* that can be counted: *A* **countable noun** *is often marked* [C] *in this dictionary.* –opposite **uncountable** –see Study Notes on page 550

count·down /ˈkaʊntdaʊn/ *n* an act of counting backwards in seconds to zero: *a ten-second countdown before the spaceship takes off: ten, nine, eight, seven ...* –see also COUNT[1] **down**

coun·te·nance¹ /ˈkaʊntən-əns/ *n fml* the appearance or expression of the face: *a sad/fierce/angry countenance*

countenance² *v* **-nanced, -nancing** [T +*v-ing*] *fml* to give support or approval to; allow: *We will never countenance violence.*|*Your father won't countenance you/your marrying me.*

coun·ter¹ /ˈkaʊntər/ *n* **1** a narrow table or flat surface at which people in a shop, bank, restaurant, etc., are served –see illustration on page 683 **2 under the counter** privately, secretly, and often unlawfully: *During the war you could only get cigarettes under the counter, and at high prices.* **3 over the counter** (when buying drugs) without a PRESCRIPTION (a special note written by a doctor): *You can buy medicine for a headache over the counter in many stores.*

count·er² *n* **1** a person or machine that counts **2** a small flat object used in some table games instead of money

coun·ter³ *v* **1** [T] to oppose; move or act in opposition to (something): *My employer countered my request for more money by threatening to fire me.* **2** [I;T] to meet (an attack or blow) with another attack or blow; RETALIATE: *Try to counter with your left.* (=left hand)

counter⁴ *adv,adj* [F *to*] (in a manner or direction that is) opposed or opposite: *He acted counter to all advice.*

coun·ter·act /ˌkaʊntərˈækt/ *v* [T] to reduce or oppose the effect of (something) by opposite action: *This drug will counteract the snake's poison.* –**counteraction** /ˌkaʊntərˈækʃən/ *n* [C;U]

coun·ter·at·tack¹ /ˈkaʊntərəˌtæk/ *n* an attack made to stop, oppose, or return an enemy attack

coun·ter·at·tack² /ˌkaʊntərəˈtæk, ˈkaʊntər əˌtæk/ *v* [I;T] to make a COUNTERATTACK[1] (on)

coun·ter·bal·ance¹ /ˈkaʊntərˌbæləns/ also **counterpoise** /ˈkaʊntərˌpɔɪz/– *n* a weight or force that acts as a balance for another weight or force

coun·ter·bal·ance² /ˌkaʊntərˈbæləns, ˈkaʊn tərˌbæ-/ also **counterpoise**– *v* **-anced, -ancing** [T] to oppose or balance with an equal weight or force: *The man used his weight to counterbalance the load and prevent it from slipping.*

coun·ter·clock·wise /ˌkaʊntərˈklɑk-waɪz/ *AmE*||**anticlockwise** *BrE*– *adj,adv* in the opposite direction to the hands of a clock

coun·ter·feit¹ /ˈkaʊntərfɪt/ *v* [T] to copy (something) closely in order to deceive: *It is against the law to counterfeit money.* –**counterfeiter** *n*

counterfeit² *adj* made exactly like something real in order to deceive: *a counterfeit coin*

coun·ter·foil /ˈkaʊntərˌfɔɪl/ *n* a part of a check, money order, etc., kept by the sender as a record; STUB[1] (2)

coun·ter·mand /ˌkaʊntərˈmænd, ˈkaʊntər ˌmænd/ *v* [T] to declare (a command already given) ineffective, often by giving a different order

coun·ter·part /ˈkaʊntərˌpɑrt/ *n* a person or thing that serves the same purpose or has the same position as another: *A ruling queen is the female counterpart of a king.*

coun·ter·sign /ˈkaʊntərˌsaɪn/ *v* [T] to sign (a paper already signed by someone else): *He signed the agreement; it was then countersigned by his uncle.*

count·ess /ˈkaʊntɪs/ *n* [A;C] (*often cap.*) (the title of) a woman who holds the rank of EARL or COUNT for herself or because she is married to an EARL or COUNT

count·less /ˈkaʊntlɪs/ *adj* very many; too many to be counted

coun·try¹ /ˈkʌntriʸ/ *n* **-tries 1** [C] a nation or state with its land or population: *Some parts of this country are much warmer than others.* **2** [C] the people of a nation or state: *That country is opposed to war.* **3** [*the* S] the land outside cities or towns; land used for farming or left unused: *We're going to spend a day in the country tomorrow.* **4** [U] land with a special nature or character: *good farming country*

country² *adj* [A] of, in, from, or related to the

COUNTRY[1] (3): *country life|a country house*
country and west·ern /ˌ·· · '··/ also **country music** /ˌ·· '··/– *n* [U] popular music in the style of the southern and western US
coun·try·man /'kʌntriʸmən/ **countrywoman** /-ˌwʊmən/ *fem.*– *n* **-men** /mən/ a person from one's own country; COMPATRIOT
coun·try·side /'kʌntriʸˌsaɪd/ *n* [U] land outside the cities and towns, used for farming or left unused; country areas
coun·ty /'kaʊntiʸ/ *n* **-ties** a large area of land divided from others for purposes of local government
coup /kuʷ/ *n* **coups** /kuʷz/ **1** a clever move or action that obtains the desired result: *Getting the contract was quite a coup.* **2** →COUP D'ETAT
coup d'e·tat /ˌkuʷ deʸ'tɑ, -də-/ also **coup**– *n* **coups d'état** (*same pronunciation*) a sudden or violent seizure of power in a state by a small group that has not been elected
cou·pé /kuʷp, kuʷ'peʸ/ also **coupe** /kuʷp/– *n* an enclosed car with two doors and a sloping back
cou·ple[1] /'kʌpəl/ *n* **1** two things related in some way; two things of the same kind: *I found a couple of socks in the bedroom, but they don't make a pair.* **2** two people together, esp. when they are married, live together, or are on a DATE[1] (3): *Joanne and Jerry are a nice couple. Let's invite them to dinner.* **3** [*of*] *infml* a few; several; small number: *I'll just have a couple of drinks.*
USAGE Compare **pair** and **couple**: A **pair** means a set of two things which are not used separately from each other. These may be two things which are not joined together, such as *shoes,* or something made in two parts, such as *pants*: *a* **pair** *of socks/a* **pair** *of scissors/a* **pair** *of criminals who always work together.* Any two things of the same kind can be spoken of as a **couple:** *I saw a* **couple** *of cats in the yard.|Could you lend me a* **couple** *of dollars?* –see also PAIR (USAGE)
couple[2] *v* **-pled, -pling 1** [T *together*] to join together; connect: *They coupled the cars of the train together.* –opposite **uncouple 2** [I *with*] (of animals) to unite sexually; MATE
cou·pon /'kuʷpɑn, 'kyuʷ-/ *n* **1** a ticket that shows the right of the holder to receive some payment, service, etc.; VOUCHER: *I have a coupon for ten cents off this package of soap.* **2** a printed form e.g. in a newspaper, on which goods can be ordered, a competition entered, etc.
cour·age /'kɜrɪdʒ, 'kʌr-/ *n* [U] **1** the quality of mind that makes a person able to control fear in the face of danger, pain, misfortune, etc.; bravery: *a woman of courage |She showed great courage during the war.* **2 have the courage of one's (own) convictions** to be brave enough to do or say what one thinks is right

SPELLING NOTE
Words with the sound /k/, like **cut**, may be spelled **k-**, like **key**, or **qu-**, like **queen**. Words with the sound /s/, like **city**, may be spelled **s-**, like **soon**, or **ps-**, like **psychology**.

cou·ra·geous /kə'reʸdʒəs/ *adj* brave; fearless; marked by courage: *a courageous action/person* **–courageously** *adv* **–courageousness** *n* [U]
cou·ri·er /'kʊəriʸər, 'kɜr-, 'kʌr-/ *n* a messenger, esp. one on urgent or official business
course[1] /kɔrs, koʷrs/ *n* **1** movement from one point to another; continuous movement in space or time: *The enemy should be defeated* **in the course of** (=during) *the year.|During the course of the flight we'll be serving drinks.* **2** direction of movement taken by someone or something: *Our course is directly south.|the course of a stream|*(fig.) *Your best* **course of action** *is to complain to the director.|The ship is* **on/off course.** (=moving in the right/ wrong direction) **3** a set of lessons or studies: *a French course |an evening course |a four-year history course* **4** any of the several parts of a meal: *We had a three-course dinner.|The first course was soup.* **5** an area of land or water on which a race is held or certain types of sport played: *a* GOLF *course* **6 a matter of course** that which one expects to happen; something natural **7 in due course** without too much delay **8 of course** certainly; NATURALLY (4): *Of course I'll still love you when you're old.|"Were you glad to leave?" "Of course not!"*
course[2] *v* **coursed, coursing** [I] (of liquid) to flow or move rapidly: *Tears coursed down his cheeks.*
court[1] /kɔrt, koʷrt/ *n* **1** [C;U] a room or building in which law cases can be heard and judged: *The case was settled out of court.* (=without having to be heard by a judge) **2** [*the* S;U] people gathered together to hear and judge a law case: *The court stood when the judge entered.* **3** [C;U] (a part of) an area specially prepared and marked for various ball games, such as TENNIS: *Are the players on the court yet? |She knocked the ball right out of the court.* **4** [C] a short street enclosed by buildings on three sides: *They lived in Sniffin Court.* **5** [C;U] (people attending) the chief royal palace: *The British court is in London.* **6 take (someone) to court** to start an action in law against (someone)
court[2] *v* [T] **1** to pay attention to (an important or influential person) in order to gain favor, advantage, approval, etc. **2** to risk (something bad), often foolishly or without enough thought: *to court danger/defeat/ disaster* **3** *becoming rare* (of a man) to visit and pay attention to (a woman he hopes to marry): *Roger courted Ellen for years before she agreed to marry him.*
cour·te·ous /'kɜrṭiʸəs/ *adj* polite and kind; marked by good manners and respect for others –opposite **discourteous –courteously** *adv* **–courteousness** *n* [U]
cour·te·sy /'kɜrṭəsiʸ/ *n* **-sies** [C;U] (an example of) polite behavior or good manners –opposite **discourtesy**
court·house /'kɔrthaʊs, 'koʷrt-/ *n* **-houses** /ˌhaʊzɪz/ *AmE* a building containing courts

of law and government offices

cour·ti·er /ˈkɔrt̬iʸər, ˈkoʷr-/ n (in former times) a noble who attended at the court of a king or other ruler

court-mar·tial¹ /ˈ· ͵··/ n **courts-martial** or **court martials** [C;U] (a trial before) a military court of officers appointed to try people for offenses against military law

court-martial² v -**l-** AmE‖-**ll-** BrE [T] to try (someone) in a military court for an offense against military law

court·ship /ˈkɔrt-ʃɪp, ˈkoʷrt-/ n [C;U] (the length of time taken by) COURTING² (3)

court·yard /ˈkɔrtyɑrd, ˈkoʷrt-/ n a space enclosed by walls or buildings, next to or within a castle, large house, etc.

cous·in /ˈkʌzən/ n [A;C] the child of one's uncle or aunt –see illustration on page 247

cove /koʷv/ n a small sheltered opening in the coastline; small BAY

cov·en /ˈkʌvən, ˈkoʷ-/ n a gathering of WITCHES

cov·e·nant /ˈkʌvənənt/ n a formal solemn agreement between two or more people or groups

cov·er¹ /ˈkʌvər/ v **1** [T] to place or spread something upon, over, or in front of (something) in order to protect, hide, etc.: *The noise was so loud that she covered her ears with her hands.* –opposite **uncover 2** [T] to be or lie on the surface of (something); spread over (something): *furniture covered with dust* | *The town covers five square miles.* **3** [T] to include; consist of; take into account: *The doctor's talk covered the complete history of medicine.* **4** [T] to travel (a distance): *I want to cover 100 miles before it gets dark.* **5** [T] to report the details of (an event), e.g. for a newspaper: *Our best reporter covered the trial.* **6** [T] to be enough money for: *Will $40 cover the cost of a new skirt?* **7** [T] to protect as from loss; INSURE: *I'm covered against all accidents.* **8** [T] to keep a gun aimed at someone: *The policeman covered the criminal with a gun.* **9** [T] (in sports) **a** to guard the play of (an opponent) **b** to defend (an area or position) against attack by the other team **10** [I;T for] to act in place of (someone who is absent): *John's ill today, so will you cover for him?*

cover up ↔ sthg. v adv [T] to prevent (something) from being noticed: *She tried to cover up her nervousness.* –see also COVER-UP

cover up for sbdy. v adv prep [T] infml to hide something wrong or shameful in order to save (someone else) from punishment, blame, etc.: *He says he did it, but I think he's trying to cover up for a friend.*

cover² n **1** [C] anything that protects by covering, esp. a piece of material, lid, or top: *Put a cover on the chair before the cat sits on it.* | *a cushion cover* **2** [C] the outer front or back page of a magazine or PAPERBACK: *the photograph on the cover of the magazine* **3** [U] shelter or protection: *The flat land gave the soldiers no cover from enemy fire.* | *When it started raining we took cover under a tree.* **4** [U] insurance against loss, damage, etc.: *cover against fire* **5** [C usu. sing.] something

that hides or keeps something secret: *This business is a cover for unlawful activity.* **6** **break cover** to come out of hiding **7** **under separate cover** in a separate envelope: *"This is a receipt. The goods will be sent later under separate cover."*

cov·er·age /ˈkʌvərɪdʒ/ n [U] the amount of time and space given by television, a newspaper, etc., to report a particular event or piece of news.

cov·er·ing /ˈkʌvərɪŋ/ n something that covers or hides: *Put a covering over the hole.*

cover let·ter /ˈ·· ͵··/ n a letter or note containing an explanation or additional information, sent with a package, another letter, an application for a job, etc.

cov·ert /ˈkʌvərt, ˈkoʷ-, koʷˈvɜrt/ adj [no comp.] secret; hidden; not openly shown: *covert reasons* | *covert dislike* –opposite **overt** –**covertly** adv

cov·er-up /ˈ·· ͵·/ n an attempt to prevent something shameful or criminal from becoming publicly known –see COVER up

cov·et /ˈkʌvɪt/ v [I;T] bibl & derog to desire eagerly to possess (something, esp. something belonging to another person): *Never covet wealth and power.* –**covetous** adj –**covetousness** n [U]

cow¹ /kaʊ/ n **1** the fully-grown female form of cattle, kept on farms esp. to provide milk: *A young cow is called a calf.* **2** the female form of the elephant and certain other large sea and land animals: *a cow elephant* –compare BULL, CALF –see MEAT (USAGE)

cow² v [T] to conquer or bring under control by violence or threats: *The generals tried to cow the people by imprisoning some of their political leaders.*

cow·ard /ˈkaʊərd/ n a person unable to face danger, pain, etc. because he/she lacks courage; a person who shows fear in a shameful way: *You coward! Are you afraid of water?* –**cowardly** adj

cow·ard·ice /ˈkaʊərdɪs/ also **cowardliness** /ˈkaʊərdliʸnɪs/– n [U] lack of courage

cow·boy /ˈkaʊbɔɪ/ n a man employed to look after cattle, esp. in North America

cow·er /ˈkaʊər/ v [I] to bend low and draw back as from fear or shame; CRINGE: *The dog cowered when its master beat it.*

cow·girl /ˈkaʊgɜrl/ n a woman employed to look after cattle, esp. in North America

cowl /kaʊəl/ n a loose head covering (a HOOD), for the whole of the head except the face, worn esp. by MONKS

cow·man /ˈkaʊmən/ n -**men** /mən/ a man who owns cattle, usu. on a RANCH

cow·slip /ˈkaʊ͵slɪp/ n a wild plant with small yellow flowers

cox /kɑks/ also **coxswain** /ˈkɑksən, -sweʸn/ fml– n a person who guides and controls a rowing boat, esp. in races

coy /kɔɪ/ adj pretending to be modest or SHY¹ in the presence of others so as to attract attention –**coyly** adv –**coyness** n [U]

coy·ote /kaɪˈoʷt̬iʸ, ˈkaɪ-oʷt/ n **coyotes** or **coyote** a small WOLF¹ (1) that lives in western North America and Mexico

co·zy¹ AmE‖also **cosy** /ˈkoʷziʸ/ adj,n -**zier,**

-ziest *apprec* warm and comfortable: *a cozy little house* **–cozily** *adv* **–coziness** *n* [U]

cozy² *AmE*||also **cosy** *n* **-zies** a covering put over a boiled egg or teapot to keep the contents warm: *a tea cozy* |*an egg cozy*

CPA *abbrev. for:* CERTIFIED PUBLIC ACCOUNTANT

crab /kræb/ *n* **1** [C] a sea animal with a broad flat shell and five pairs of legs **2** [U] the flesh of this animal cooked as food

crab·by /'kræbiʸ/ *adj* **-bier, -biest** (of a person) bad-tempered

crack¹ /kræk/ *v* **1** [I;T *open*] to (cause to) break without dividing into separate parts; split: *Don't pour hot water into the glass or it will crack.*|*I don't like drinking from cracked cups.*|*I can't crack this nut.* **2** [I;T] to (cause to) make a sudden explosive sound: *The whip cracked threateningly.* **3** [I;T] to (cause to) strike with a sudden blow: *The boy fell and cracked his head against the wall.* **4** [I *up*] to fail or yield as a result of difficulties; lose control or effectiveness: *The pressures of work caused John to crack (up).* **5** [T] *infml* to tell (a joke) **6** [T] to discover the secret of (esp. a CODE¹) **7** [T] *infml* to open (a bottle) for drinking

crack down *v adv* [I *on*] to become more severe: *The military government decided to crack down on all political activity.* **–crackdown** /'krækdaʊn/ *n: a crackdown on drunken driving*

crack up *v adv infml* **1** [I;T(=**crack** sbdy. **up**)] to (cause to) laugh noisily: *That joke always cracks me up.*|*She cracked up when she heard the joke.* **2** [I] to lose control of one's feelings; to have a BREAKDOWN: *Paul cracked up after his wife died, and now he no longer leaves his house.*

crack² *n* **1** a line of division caused by splitting; thin mark or opening caused by breaking: *a crack in the window*|*a crack in the ice*|(fig.)*The door was opened just a crack.* **2** an explosive sound: *a crack of thunder*|*the crack of the guns* **3** a sudden sharp blow: *a crack on the head.* **4** *infml* an attempt: *This is her first* **crack** *at writing a book.* **5** a clever quick joke or remark: *He's always making cracks about my big feet.* **6 crack of dawn** the first light of day

crack³ *adj* [A *no comp.*] of high quality or good ability; skillful: *a crack shot* (=someone who is very good at shooting)

crack·er /'krækər/ *n* **1** a flat thin dry cake, round or square and unsweetened: *cheese and crackers* **2** → FIRECRACKER **3** *AmE infml usu. derog* a poor white person, esp. a man, usu. from the southeastern US

crack·le /'krækəl/ *v* **-led, -ling** [I;T] to (cause to) make small sharp sounds: *The fire crackled.* **–crackle** *n* [S]: *the crackle of burn-*

ing logs|a loud crackle

crack·ling /'kræklɪŋ/ *n* [U] **1** the hard easily broken brown skin of baked PORK **2** the sound of crackling (CRACKLE): *the crackling of the fire*

crack·pot /'krækpɑt/ *adj,n* [A;C] *infml & often humor* (of, belonging to, or being) a person with very strange, foolish, or mad ideas: *a crackpot scientist*

cra·dle¹ /'kreʸdl/ *n* **1** a small bed for a baby, esp. one that can be moved gently from side to side **2** the place where something begins; origin: *Greece was the cradle of Western civilization.* **3** a framework used for supporting something being built or repaired, or for doing certain jobs: *Ships are held in cradles while they're being built.*

cradle² *v* **-dled, -dling** [T] to hold gently as if in a CRADLE¹ (1): *John cradled the baby in his arms.*

craft¹ /kræft/ *n* a job or trade needing skill, esp. with one's hands: *the jeweler's craft*

craft² *n* **craft** a boat, esp. a small one; vessel: *The harbor was full of sailing craft.*

crafts·man /'kræftsmən/ *n* **-men** /mən/ a highly skilled worker: *furniture made by the finest craftsmen* **–craftsmanship** *n* [U]

craft·y /'kræftiʸ/ *adj* **-ier, -iest** cleverly deceitful: *The politician was very crafty.* **–craftily** *adv* **–craftiness** *n* [U]

crag /kræg/ *n* a high steep rough rock or mass of rocks

crag·gy /'krægiʸ/ *adj* **-gier, -giest** steep and rough; having many CRAGS:(fig.) *his craggy face*

cram /kræm/ *v* **-mm-** **1** [T] to force (a person or thing) into a small space: *to cram people into a railroad car* |*Have you seen the way he crams food down (his throat)?* **2** [T] to fill (something) too full: *Don't cram your bag too full of clothes.* **3** [I *for*] to prepare oneself for an examination by working very hard for a short time: *He sat up all night cramming (for his history exam).*

cramp¹ /kræmp/ *n* a severe pain from the sudden tightening of a muscle, which makes movement difficult: *The swimmer got a cramp in his leg and had to be lifted out of the water.*

cramp² *v* [T] **1** to keep within limits; prevent the natural growth or development of **2 cramp someone's style** *infml* to prevent someone from showing his/her abilities to the full

cramped /kræmpt/ *adj* limited in space: *a cramped little apartment*|*cramped writing* (=with letters written too closely together)

cran·ber·ry /'kræn‚bɛriʸ, -bəriʸ/ *n* **-ries** a small red sour-tasting berry

crane¹ /kreʸn/ *n* **1** a machine for lifting heavy objects by means of a very strong rope or wire fastened to a movable arm **2** a tall water bird with very long legs and neck

crane² *v* **craned, craning** [I;T] to stretch out (one's) neck esp. to get a better view: *Jane craned her neck to look for her friend in the crowd.*

cra·ni·um /'kreʸniʸəm/ *n* **-niums** or **-nia** /niʸə/ *tech* the bony framework of the animal or

---

SPELLING NOTE

Words with the sound /k/, like **cut**, may be spelled **k-**, like **key**, or **qu-**, like **queen**. Words with the sound /s/, like **city**, may be spelled **s-**, like **soon**, or **ps-**, like **psychology**.

human head; part of the SKULL that covers the brain –**cranial** /'kreⁱniⁱəl/ adj

crank /kræŋk/ n **1** an apparatus, such as a handle fixed at right angles to a rod, which changes movement in a straight line into circular movement. **2** infml, sometimes humor a person with very peculiar ideas

crank sthg.↔ **out** also **churn** sthg.↔ **out**– v adv [T] **1** to produce a large number of as if by machine: They crank out cars faster than they can sell them.

crank·y /'kræŋkiⁱ/ adj **-ier, -iest 1** esp. AmE bad tempered: a cranky, unfriendly old lady|a cranky baby **2** very strange; peculiar; odd

crap /kræp/ n [U] infml & derog **1** nonsense: His speech was **a lot of/a load of crap**.|"We'll never win against their team I'm sure of it." "Crap! We will win." **2** unwanted things: Get all this crap off the table.

craps /kræps/ n [U] **1** an American game played with two DICE for money **2 shoot craps** to play this game

crash¹ /kræʃ/ v **1** [I;T] to (cause to) have a violent and noisy accident: The car crashed on the bend, killing its driver and two passengers. **2** [I;T] to (cause to) fall or strike something noisily and violently: She crashed the plates angrily down on the table. **3** [I] to move violently and noisily: The angry elephant crashed through the forest. **4** [I] to make a sudden loud noise: The lightning flashed and the thunder crashed. **5** [I] (in the world of business and money matters) to fail suddenly; come to ruin: The New York STOCK EXCHANGE crashed in 1929.

crash² n **1** a violent vehicle accident: All the passengers were killed in the train/plane/car crash. **2** a sudden loud noise as made by a violent fall, break, etc.: a crash of thunder|the crash of breaking glass **3** a sudden severe business failure: the crash of the New York STOCK EXCHANGE

crash³ adj [A] marked by a very great effort to reach the desired results quickly: She wanted to lose weight, so she went on **a crash diet**.|a crash course in conversational French

crash hel·met /'· ‚··/ n a very strong protective head covering (HELMET) worn by racing car drivers, MOTORCYCLE riders, etc.

crash-land /‚· '·/ v [I;T] (to cause a plane) to crash in a controlled way so that as little damage as possible is done –**crash landing** /‚· '··/ n [C;U]

crass /kræs/ adj **1** stupid; unfeeling; coarse: crass behavior **2** (of stupidity, foolishness, etc.) complete; very great: crass stupidity/ignorance –**crassly** adv –**crassness** n [U]

crate /kreⁱt/ n a box or framework, esp. made of wood, for holding fruit, bottles, furniture, etc.: a milk crate |a crate of apples

cra·ter /'kreⁱtər/ n **1** the round bowl-shaped mouth of a VOLCANO **2** a rough round hole in the ground: a bomb crater|craters on the moon's surface

cra·vat /krə'væt/ n BrE for ASCOT

crave /kreⁱv/ v **craved, craving** [I;T] to have a very strong desire for (something): Some-

times I crave (for) a piece of chocolate.|(fml) to crave admiration/fame

cra·ven /'kreⁱvən/ adj derog completely lacking courage: a craven bully –**cravenness** n [U] –**cravenly** adv

crav·ing /'kreⁱvɪŋ/ n a very strong desire: a craving for sweets –see DESIRE (USAGE)

crawl¹ /krɔl/ v [I] **1** to move slowly with the body close to the ground or floor: The baby crawled across the room.|There's an insect crawling up your back!|(fig.) The traffic crawled along at ten miles an hour. **2** [with] to be completely covered by insects, etc.: The room was crawling with flies.|(fig.) The town was crawling with soldiers.

crawl² n [S] **1** a very slow movement **2** a rapid way of swimming on one's stomach, moving first one arm and then the other over one's head, and kicking the feet up and down: Do a/the crawl to the other side of the pool!

cray·fish /'kreⁱˌfɪʃ/ also **crawfish** /'krɔ-/– n **-fish** or **-fishes** [C;U] (the flesh of) a small LOBSTER-like animal that lives in rivers and streams

cray·on /'kreⁱɑn, -ən/ n a stick of colored wax or chalk used for writing or drawing, esp. on paper

craze¹ /kreⁱz/ n [for] a very popular fashion, usu. for a very short time: This new toy is the latest craze in Japan.

craze² v **crazed, crazing** [T usu.pass.] to make very excited, angry, or mad: a crazed expression|The climber was crazed by the freezing cold.

cra·zy /'kreⁱziⁱ/ adj **-zier, -ziest 1** ill in the mind; mad: The crazy man was considered too dangerous to be left alone. –compare INSANE **2** [+to-v] mad; foolish: He's crazy to go out in this weather!|a crazy idea **3** [F about] wildly excited; very fond (of) or interested (in): She's crazy about dancing. **4 like crazy** infml wildly and/or very actively: You'll have to work like crazy to get this finished. –**crazily** adv –**craziness** n [U]

creak¹ /kriⁱk/ v [I] to make the sound of a badly-oiled door when it opens: I'll have to oil this door to stop it from creaking.|(fig.) creaking with age

creak² n [C;S] the sound made by a badly-oiled door when it opens

creak·y /'kriⁱkiⁱ/ adj **-ier, -iest** that CREAKS¹: a creaky door –**creakily** adv –**creakiness** n [U]

cream¹ /kriⁱm/ n **1** [U] the thick fatty yellowish liquid that rises to the top of milk: Have some cream in your coffee.|a cream cake **2** [C;U] something similar to or containing this: ARTIFICIAL cream|a chocolate cream|cream of chicken soup **3** [C;U] a preparation made thick and soft like CREAM (1): face cream|Put some of this cream on that burn. **4** [the S] the best part of anything: the cream of society

cream² adj,n [U] (having) the color of CREAM; (having) a yellowish-white color: She wore a cream dress.

cream·y /'kriⁱmiⁱ/ adj **-ier, -iest** containing, or similar to, cream: creamy soap –**creaminess** n [U]

crease¹ /kriⁱs/ n a line made on cloth, paper,

etc., by folding or pressing: *There's a crease in your dress where you've been sitting.*

crease² *v* **creased, creasing** [I;T] to make or become pressed into CREASES¹: *He creased his trousers as he ironed them.|She creased the paper and put it in the envelope.*

cre·ate /kriˈeʸt/ *v* **-ated, -ating** [T] to cause (something new) to exist; produce (something new): *God created the world.|They created a new city where there was only desert before.|The new plans created (quite) a stir.* (=caused excitement)

cre·a·tion /kriˈeʸʃən/ *n* **1** [U] the act of creating (CREATE) **2** [C] something CREATEd; something produced by invention or imagination: *an artist's creation* **3** [U] the universe, world, and all living things: *Man is the lord of creation.*

cre·a·tive /kriˈeʸtɪv/ *adj* **1** producing new and original ideas and things: *creative thinking* **2** resulting from newness of thought or expression: *useful and creative work* **–creatively** *adv* **–creativity** /ˌkriʸeʸˈtɪvəṭiʸ/ also **creativeness** /kriʸˈeʸtɪvnɪs/– *n* [U]: *Someone with creativity is needed for this job.*

cre·a·tor /kriʸˈeʸtər/ *n* a person who CREATES **Creator** *n* [the S] God: *She gave thanks to the/her Creator.*

crea·ture /ˈkriʸtʃər/ *n* **1** an animal or being of some kind: *all God's creatures|creatures from outer space* **2** a person when considered in a particular way: *The poor creature had no family at all.*

crèche /krɛʃ, kreʸʃ/ *n* **1** a model of the scene of Christ's birth, often placed in churches and homes at Christmas time **2** *BrE* for DAY-CARE center

cre·dence /ˈkriʸdns/ *n* [U] *fml* acceptance as true; belief: *The newspapers are giving no credence to his latest statements.*

cre·den·tials /krəˈdɛnʃəlz, -tʃəlz/ *n* [P] a letter or other written proof of a person's position, trustworthiness, etc.

cred·i·bil·i·ty /ˌkrɛdəˈbɪləṭiʸ/ *n* [U] the state or quality of being CREDIBLE

cred·i·ble /ˈkrɛdəbəl/ *adj* deserving or worthy of belief; trustworthy: *a credible news report* –see also INCREDIBLE **–credibly** *adv*

cred·it¹ /ˈkrɛdɪt/ *n* **1** [U] a system of buying goods or services when they are wanted and paying for them later: *You can buy the furniture* **on credit.**|*six months' credit* –compare INSTALLMENT PLAN **2** [U] the quality of being likely to repay debts: *His credit is good. You can trust him.* **3** [U] (the amount of) money in a person's account, as at a bank: *on the credit side of the account* (=there is money in it) –compare DEBIT **4** [U] belief; trust; faith: *I place full credit in the government's abilities.|This story is gaining credit.* **5** [U] public attention; praise; favorable notice or

regard: *I got/was given no credit for my invention.* **6** [S;U] a cause of honor: *You're a credit to your team.|Our armed forces* **do us credit.** (=are a credit to us) **7** [C] (esp. in the US) a measure of work completed by a student, esp. at a university: *She doesn't have enough credits to receive her degree.* **8 to someone's credit: a** in someone's favor: *It is to his credit that he trained so hard for the race.* **b** as one's property; belonging to one: *She's only 30 years old, and already she has five books to her credit!* (=she's written five books)

credit² *v* [T] **1** [*with, to*] to place (an amount of money) in an account: *Please credit $200 to my account.|Credit my account with $200.* –compare DEBIT² **2** to believe: *Do you really credit the government's statement?* –see also DISCREDIT

credit sbdy. with sthg. *v prep* [T] to believe that a person has (something): *Please credit me with some sense!*

cred·it·a·ble /ˈkrɛdɪṭəbəl/ *adj* deserving praise, honor, approval, etc.: *a creditable effort to establish peace* –opposite **discreditable** **–creditably** *adv*

credit card /ˈ·· ˌ·/ *n* a small card which allows one to obtain goods and services, the cost being charged to one's account and paid later –compare CHARGE CARD

cred·i·tor /ˈkrɛdɪṭər/ *n* a person or firm to whom money is owed –compare DEBTOR

cred·u·lous /ˈkrɛdʒələs/ *adj* too willing to believe, esp. without real proof –see also INCREDULOUS **–credulously** *adv* **–credulousness** *n* [U] **–credulity** /krəˈduʷləṭiʸ, -ˈdyuʷ-/ *n* [U]

creed /kriʸd/ *n* a system of (esp. religious) beliefs or principles

creek /kriʸk, krɪk/ *n* **1** a small narrow stream or body of water **2 up the creek** *infml* in trouble: *I was up the creek when I lost the keys to my house.*

creep¹ /kriʸp/ *v* **crept** /krɛpt/, **creeping** [I] **1** to move slowly and quietly, esp. with the body close to the ground: *The cat crept silently towards the mouse.|The sea crept up the shore.* **2** to grow along the ground or a surface: *a creeping plant*

creep in *v adv* [I] to begin to happen: *Mistakes are creeping in which could have been avoided.*

creep into sthg. *v prep* [T *no pass.*] to begin to happen in: *You have to stop these mistakes from creeping into your work!*

creep² *n infml* an unpleasant person: *You ruined my party, you creep.*

creep·er /ˈkriʸpər/ *n* a plant which climbs up trees and walls or grows along the ground

creeps /kriʸps/ *n* [the P] *infml* an unpleasant sensation of fear: *The old empty house gives me the creeps.*

creep·y /ˈkriʸpiʸ/ *adj* **-ier, -iest** *infml* causing or feeling an unpleasant sensation of fear: *a creepy old house/man* **–creepily** *adv* **–creepiness** *n* [U]

cre·mate /ˈkriʸmeʸt, krɪˈmeʸt/ *v* **-mated, -mating** [T] to burn (a dead person) at a funeral ceremony –**cremation** /krɪ'meɪʃən/ n [C;U]

cre·ma·to·ri·um /ˌkriːməˈtɔːriːəm, -'toʷr-, ˌkrɛ-/ also **crematory** /'kriːmətɔːriʸ, -,toʷr-, 'krɛ-/– n **-riums** or **-ria** /riʸə/ a building in which dead people are CREMATED

cre·ole /'kriʸoʷl/ adj,n (often cap.) **1** [C;U] (of, being, related to) a language which is formed by the combination of a European language with one or more others and is the native language of its speakers –compare PIDGIN **2** [C] (of, being, or related to) a person of both European and African blood

cre·o·sote /'kriʸə,soʷt/ n [U] thick brown oily liquid used for preserving wood

crepe, crêpe /kreʸp/ n **1** [C] a very thin PANCAKE **2** [U] a light soft thin cloth with a slightly rough surface made from cotton, silk, wool, etc. **3** [U] also **crepe rubber** /ˌ· '··/– tightly pressed rubber used esp. for the bottoms of shoes

crept /krɛpt/ v past tense and past participle of CREEP

cre·scen·do /krə'ʃendoʷ/ n **-dos** a gradual increase of force or loudness, esp. of music: (fig.) The demands for an election rose to a crescendo.

cres·cent /'krɛsənt/ n **1** the curved shape of the moon during its first and last quarters, when it forms less than half a circle **2** something shaped like this, e.g. a curved row of houses or a curved street: The crescent is the sign of the Muslim faith.

cress /krɛs/ n [U] **1** → WATERCRESS **2** (esp. in the UK) a very small plant whose leaves are eaten raw

crest /krɛst/ n **1** the top of something, esp. of a mountain, hill, or wave **2** a special picture used as a personal mark on letters, envelopes, one's plates, etc. **3** a showy growth of feathers on top of a bird's head: (fig.) the crest on a soldier's HELMET

crest·fall·en /'krɛst,fɔːlən/ adj disappointed; low in spirits; sad

cre·tin /'kriʸtn/ n **1** infml a very stupid foolish person: You cretin! You've burned a hole in my best chair with your cigarette! **2** tech a person whose development of mind and body has stopped in early childhood

cre·vasse /krə'væs/ n a deep open crack, esp. in thick ice

crev·ice /'krɛvɪs/ n a narrow crack or opening, esp. in rock

crew /kruʷ/ n **1** all the people working on a ship, plane, etc., sometimes except for the officers: The crew is waiting for instructions from the ship's owner. **2** a group of people working together: the stage crew for the new play

crib¹ /krɪb/ n **1** AmE‖**cot** BrE– a small bed for a young child, usu. with movable sides so that the child cannot fall out **2** an open box or wooden framework holding food for animals; MANGER

crib² v **-bb-** [I;T from, off] infml to copy (something) dishonestly from someone else: I didn't know the answers so I cribbed them off John.

crick /krɪk/ n a painful stiffening of the

muscles, esp. in the back or the neck, making movement difficult

crick·et¹ /'krɪkɪt/ n an outdoor game played with a ball, BAT, and WICKETS, by two teams of 11 players each –**cricketer** n

cricket² n a small brown insect, the male of which makes loud noises by rubbing its wings together

cried /kraɪd/ v past tense and participle of CRY¹

cries /kraɪz/ v 3rd person sing. present tense of CRY¹

crime /kraɪm/ n **1** [C] an offense which is punishable by law: If you commit (=do) a crime you must expect to be punished.|(fig.) It's a crime (=a shame) that this food should be wasted. **2** [U] unlawful activity in general: It is the job of the police to prevent crime. –compare SIN

crim·i·nal¹ /'krɪmənəl/ n a person who is guilty of crime: The judge sent the criminal to prison.

criminal² adj **1** [A] of or related to crime or its punishment: a specialist in criminal law **2** of the nature of a crime: a criminal act|(fig.) It's criminal to waste money like that. –**criminally** adv

crim·son /'krɪmzən/ adj,n [U] (having) a deep slightly purplish red color

cringe /krɪndʒ/ v **cringed, cringing** [I] to bend and move back, esp. from fear: The dogs cringed when their master raised his whip.

crin·kle /'krɪŋkəl/ v **-kled, -kling** [I;T] to (cause to) become covered with fine lines: his crinkled face –**crinkle** n –**crinkly** /'krɪŋkliʸ/ adj **-klier, -kliest** –compare CREASE

crip·ple¹ /'krɪpəl/ n a person unable to use properly one or more of his/her limbs, esp. the legs: (fig.) He's a real cripple when it comes to social situations.

cripple² v **-pled, -pling** [T] to hurt or wound (a person) in such a way that use of one or more of the limbs is made difficult or impossible: (fig.) His business was crippled by the fire.

cri·sis /'kraɪsɪs/ n **-ses** /siʸz/ a turning point in the course of something; moment of great danger or difficulty: a governmental/political crisis|the crisis in Southern Africa|He's reached the crisis in his illness.

crisp¹ /krɪsp/ adj **1** hard; dry; easily broken: crisp pastry **2** firm; fresh: a crisp apple|crisp vegetables|a crisp $100 bill **3** (of style, manners, etc.) quick; showing no doubts or slowness; clear: a quick crisp reply **4** (of the air, weather, etc.) cold; dry; fresh: a crisp winter day|the crisp autumn wind –**crisply** adv –**crispness** n [U]

crisp² n BrE for POTATO CHIP

crisp·y /'krɪspiʸ/ adj **-ier, -iest** →CRISP¹ (1,2) –**crispiness** n [U]

criss·cross¹ /'krɪs-krɔs/ n [A;C] a pattern made by crossing a number of straight lines: a crisscross pattern

crisscross² v [I;T] to form a CRISSCROSS¹ pattern (on): Train tracks crisscross the country.

cri·te·ri·on /kraɪ'tɪəriʸən/ n **-ria** /riʸə/ or **-rions** an established standard or principle on which a judgment is based: What criteria do you use when judging a student's work?

crit·ic /'krɪtɪk/ n **1** a person skilled in forming

judgments about something, esp. art, music, etc. **2** a person who finds fault: *He's one of her strongest critics.*

crit·i·cal /ˈkrɪtɪkəl/ *adj* **1** [*of*] finding fault; judging severely: *Why are you so critical of the government?* –see also UNCRITICAL **2** very serious or dangerous: *a critical stage of the illness|His condition is reported as being critical.* **3** [A] of or related to the work of a CRITIC (1): *critical writings on art* –**critically** *adv*

crit·i·cism /ˈkrɪtəˌsɪzəm/ *n* [C;U] **1** the act of forming judgments about the good or bad qualities of anything, esp. artistic work; work of a CRITIC (1): *The students gave constructive* **criticism** (=helpful suggestions) *of the play.* **2** (an) unfavorable judgment; disapproval: *The government intends to stop unfavourable criticism by controlling the newspapers.|Your criticisms seem to have offended him.*

crit·i·cize ‖also **-cise** *BrE* /ˈkrɪtəˌsaɪz/ *v* **-cized, -cizing** [I;T *for*] **1** to find fault with; judge severely: *My father criticized my decision.* **2** to make judgments about the good and bad points of

cri·tique /krɪˈtiyk/ *n* an article, book, etc., criticizing(CRITICIZE (2)) the work of esp. a writer

croak[1] /krowk/ *v* **1** [I] to make a deep low noise such as a FROG makes **2** [I;T] to speak or say with a rough voice as if one has a sore throat **3** [I] *infml* to die

croak[2] *n* [C;S] a deep low noise such as a FROG makes

cro·chet[1] /krowˈʃey/ *n* [U] **1** a way of making clothes, decorations, etc., with a special hooked needle (**crochet-hook** /ˈ·· ˌ·/) **2** examples of work done in this way –compare KNITTING

crochet[2] *v* **-cheted** /ˈʃeyd/, **-cheting** /ˈʃeyɪŋ/ [I;T] to make by means of CROCHET[1]: *to crochet a dress for a baby*

crock·er·y /ˈkrɑkəriy/ *n* [U] cups, plates, pots, etc.

croc·o·dile /ˈkrɑkəˌdaɪl/ *n* **crocodiles** *or* **crocodile 1** [C] a large animal (REPTILE) with a long hard-skinned body and a long mouth with many teeth that lives on land and in lakes and rivers –compare ALLIGATOR **2** [U] the skin of this animal used as leather

cro·cus /ˈkrowkəs/ *n* **-cuses** a small plant with purple, yellow, or white flowers which open in early spring

crois·sant /kwaˈsɑnt, krwaˈsɑ̃/ *n French* a piece of buttery breadlike pastry, shaped like a CRESCENT (1)

cro·ny /ˈkrowniy/ *n* **-nies** *infml & sometimes derog* a friend or companion: *The mayor's always doing favors for his cronies.*

crook[1] /krʊk/ *n* **1** *infml* a thief **2** a bend or

SPELLING NOTE

Words with the sound /k/, like **cut**, may be spelled **k-**, like **key**, or **qu-**, like **queen**. Words with the sound /s/, like **city**, may be spelled **s-**, like **soon**, or **ps-**, like **psychology**.

---

curve: *She carried the package in the crook of her arm.*

crook[2] *v* [I;T] to bend: *She crooked her arm to carry the package.*

crook·ed /ˈkrʊkɪd/ *adj* **1** not straight; twisted; bent: *a crooked street* **2** *infml* dishonest –**crookedness** *n* [U]

croon /kruwn/ *v* [I;T] to sing gently in a low soft voice

crop[1] /krɑp/ *n* **1** a plant or plant product such as grain, fruit, or vegetables grown by a farmer: *Coffee is a widely grown crop in Brazil.* **2** the amount of such a product produced and gathered in a single season or place: *We've had the biggest wheat crop ever this year.|(fig.) à fine crop of hair|(fig.)a whole new crop of students*

crop[2] *v* **-pp-** [T] **1** (of an animal) to bite off and eat the tops of (grass, plants, etc.): *The sheep cropped the grass short.* **2** to cut (a person's hair or a horse's tail) short

crop up *v adv* [I] *infml* to happen or appear unexpectedly: *A problem has cropped up at work, so I'll be home late tonight.*

cro·quet /krowˈkey/ *n* [U] a game played on grass in which players knock balls through small metal arches (WICKETS) with a hammer (MALLET)

cross[1] /krɔs/ *n* **1** a mark, (x or +), often used **a** as a sign of where something is or should be **b** as a sign that something is incorrect **2** an upright post with a bar across it near the top on which people were bound or nailed and left to die as a punishment in ancient times: *Christ's death on* **the Cross 3** [*often cap.*] (an object of) this shape as the sign of the Christian faith or religion: *the sign of the Cross* **4** any of various representations of this, used for decoration, in art, JEWELS (2), etc.: *a gold cross* **5** an ornament of this shape worn as an honor (a MEDAL), esp. for military bravery: *He was given the Distinguished Service Cross.* **6** an example of sorrow or suffering as a test of one's patience or goodness: *Everyone* **has his own cross to bear** *in this life.* **7** a combination of two different things: *The drink tasted like a cross between coffee and hot chocolate.* –see also HYBRID

cross[2] *v* **1** [T] to go, pass, or reach across: *The soldiers took three days to cross the desert.|Be careful when you're crossing the street.* **2** [I;T] to place, lie, or pass across each other: *I'll meet you where the paths cross.|Jean crossed her legs.* –opposite **uncross 3** [T] to oppose (someone or his/her plans, wishes, etc.): *Anne hates to be crossed, so don't argue with her.* **4** [T] to make a movement of the hand forming a cross on (oneself) as a religious act: *She crossed herself as she left the church.* **5** [T] to cause (an animal or plant) to breed with one of another kind: *Is it possible to cross a tiger with/and a lion?*

cross sbdy./sthg. **off** (sthg.) *v adv; prep* [T] to remove (from) by drawing a line through: *If you don't want to come, cross your name off (the list).*

cross sthg.↔ **out** *v adv* [T] to draw a line through (writing): *I crossed out the mistakes* *in my sentence and wrote it again.*

cross³ *adj* angry; bad-tempered: *The old man was really cross when Jane broke his window.* **–crossly** *adv* **–crossness** *n* [U]

cross·bow /'krɔsbow/ *n* a powerful type of BOW³ (1), used in former times

cross·breed /'krɔsbriyd/ *n* an animal or plant which is a mixture of breeds **–crossbred** /ˌkrɔs'brɛd ◄/ *adj* : *a crossbred horse*

cross·check /ˌkrɔs'tʃɛk, 'krɔstʃɛk/ *v* [T] to find out the correctness of (a calculation, answer, etc.) by using a different method or information from different places

cross-coun·try /ˌ· '···◄/ *adj,adv* across the fields or open country: *a cross-country race|cross country skiing*

cross-ex·am·ine /ˌ· ·'··/ also **cross-question** /ˌ· '··/– *v* **-ined, -ining** [I;T] to question (esp. a witness) very closely, usu. in order to compare the answers with other answers given before **–cross-examination** /ˌ· ···'··/ *n* [C;U]

cross-eyed /'· ·/ *adj* having the eyes turned in towards the nose

cross·fire /'krɔsfaɪər/ *n* [U] one or more lines of gunfire firing across the direction of movement

cross·ing /'krɔsɪŋ/ *n* **1** a journey across the sea **2** a place where two lines, tracks, etc., cross **3** a place at which a road, river, etc., may be crossed

cross-leg·ged /ˌkrɔs 'lɛgɪd◄, -'lɛgd◄/ *adj,adv* having one leg placed over and across the other when sitting

cross·piece /'krɔs-piys/ *n* a piece of anything lying across something else

cross-pur·pos·es /ˌ· '···/ *n* **at cross-purposes** with different and opposing purposes in mind: *to talk at cross-purposes*

cross-re·fer /ˌ· ·'··/ *v* **-ferred, -ferring** [I;T *from,to*] to direct (the reader) from one place in a book to another place in the same book: *In this dictionary* CAPITAL *letters are used to cross-refer from one word to another.*

cross-ref·er·ence /ˌ· '···, ˌ· '··/ *n* a note directing the reader from one place to another in the same book: *In this dictionary cross-references are shown in* CAPITAL *letters.*

cross·roads /'krɔsrowdz/ *n* **crossroads 1** a place where two or more roads cross; INTERSECTION **2** a point at which an important decision must be taken

cross-sec·tion /'· ·,··/ *n* (a drawing of) a surface made by cutting across something, esp. at right angles to its length: *a cross-section of a worm/a plant stem|*(fig.) *a cross-section of society* (=a representative example of society)

cross·walk /'krɔswɔk/ *n AmE* a specially marked path where people on foot may cross a street –see illustration on page 673

cross·word puz·zle /'krɔswɔrd ˌpʌzəl/ also **crossword** – *n* a printed game in which words are fitted into a pattern of numbered squares in answer to numbered CLUES (=questions, information, etc. that help one to find the necessary word)

crotch /krɑtʃ/ *n* the place between the tops of the legs of the human body

crotch·et·y /'krɑtʃəṭiy/ *adj infml* (esp. of someone old) bad-tempered; liking to argue or complain

crouch /kraʊtʃ/ *v* [I *down*] to lower the body close to the ground by bending the knees and back: *The cat saw the bird and crouched down ready to jump.|The tall man had to crouch to get into the small car.*

crou·pi·er /'kruwpiy,eʸ, -ər/ *n* a person who collects the money lost and pays out the money won at a table where games such as ROULETTE are played for money

crow¹ /krow/ *n* **1** a large shiny black bird with a low loud cry **2 as the crow flies** in a straight line: *We're twenty miles from town as the crow flies, but nearly thirty by road.* **3 to eat crow** *infml* to be forced to admit humbly that one was wrong

crow² *v* [I] **1** to make the loud high cry of a ROOSTER (=a fully-grown male hen) **2** [*about,over*] *infml* to speak proudly: *I wish John would stop crowing about his examination results.*

crow³ *n* [S] the loud high cry of a ROOSTER (=a fully-grown male hen)

crow·bar /'krowbɑr/ *n* an iron bar used to raise heavy objects off the ground or to force open boxes, etc.

crowd¹ /kraʊd/ *n* **1** a large number of people gathered together: *a crowd waiting for a bus|There were crowds of people at the theater.* **2** a particular social group: *I don't like the college crowd.*

crowd² *v* [I] **1** (esp. of people) to come together in large numbers: *People crowded around the scene of the accident* **2** [T] (esp. of people) to fill: *Shoppers crowded the streets.*

crowd·ed /'kraʊdɪd/ *adj* completely full; filled with a crowd: *a crowded room|a crowded street*

crown¹ /kraʊn/ *n* **1** [C] a decoration for the head, usu. made of gold with jewels in it, worn by a king or queen as a sign of royal power:(fig.) *He won the crown* (=royal power) *by killing the old king.* **2** [C] a decoration of this shape used in art, HERALDRY, etc.: *a painted crown|a crown of flowers* **3** [C] the top or highest part of anything, e.g. of the head, a hat, a mountain, etc.: *the crown of a hill* **4** [*the* S] (*usu. cap.*) the governing power of a kingdom: *land belonging to the Crown* **5** [*the* S] a CHAMPIONSHIP title: *He won the boxing crown in 1981.*

crown² *v* [T] **1** to place a crown solemnly on the head of (a person) as a sign of royal power **2** to cover the top of (something): *Mist crowned the mountain.|Trees crowned the hill.* **3** to complete worthily: *Success in the peace talks has crowned this government's period in power.* **4 to crown it all** to complete good or bad fortune: *His house burned down, his car was stolen, and to crown it all he lost his job.*

crown jew·els /ˌ· '··/ *n* [P] the crowns, jewels, etc., worn by a king or queen on great state occasions

crown prince /ˌ· '·◄/ **crown princess** /ˌ· '··◄/ *fem.*– *n* [A;C] the man who has the lawful right to be king after the death of the present king or ruling queen

CRT /ˌsiy ɑr 'tiy/ *n* a glass instrument in which streams of ELECTRONs from the CATHODE (**cathode rays**) are directed onto a flat surface where they give out light, as in a television SCREEN¹ (6) –see illustration on page 221

cru·cial /'kruwʃəl/ *adj* [*to,for*] of the greatest importance: *at a crucial moment|Speed is crucial to our success.* –**crucially** *adv*

cru·ci·fix /'kruwsə,fɪks/ *n* a cross with a figure of Christ on it

cru·ci·fix·ion /ˌkruwsə'fɪkʃən/ *n* **1** [C;U] (an example of) the act of CRUCIFYing **2** [C] (usu. cap.) (a picture or other representation of) the death of Christ on the Cross

cru·ci·fy /'kruwsə,faɪ/ *v* -**fied, -fying** [T] to kill (someone) by nailing or binding to a CROSS¹ (2) and leaving to die: (fig.) *He was crucified by public opinion because his new book offended many people.*

crude /kruwd/ *adj* **1** in a raw or natural state; untreated: *crude oil|crude rubber* **2** lacking grace or sensitive feeling: *crude behavior|crude people* **3** not skillfully made or finished: *a crude shelter in the forest|crude ideas* –**crudely** *adv*

cru·di·ty /'kruwdətiy/ also **crudeness** /'kruwdnɪs/– *n* -**ties** [C;U] (an example of) the quality of being CRUDE

cru·el /'kruwəl/ *adj* -**ll**- **1** liking to cause pain or suffering; taking pleasure in the pain of another; merciless: *Anyone who likes watching people suffer is cruel.* **2** painful; causing suffering: *a cruel punishment/remark* |(fig.) *a cruel wind/disease* –**cruelly** *adv*

cru·el·ty /'kruwəltiy/ *n* -**ties 1** [U] also **cruelness** /'kruwəlnɪs/– the quality of being cruel: *cruelty to animals* **2** [C] a cruel act, remark, etc.

cru·et /'kruwɪt/ *n* a set of containers for pepper, salt, oil, MUSTARD, VINEGAR, etc., standing on a specially shaped holder of glass or metal, for use at meals

cruise¹ /kruwz/ *v* **cruised, cruising** [I] **1** to sail in an unhurried way **2** (of a car, plane, etc.) to move at a fairly high but steady speed, esp. on a long journey: *a cruising speed of 60 miles an hour*

cruise² *n* a sea voyage for pleasure

cruis·er /'kruwzər/ *n* **1** a fairly large pleasure boat, usu. covered and with places to sleep and prepare food **2** a large fast warship **3** *AmE* a police car

crumb /krʌm/ *n* a very small piece of dry food, esp. bread or cake: *Sweep up the crumbs from under the table.* |(fig.) *crumbs of knowledge/information*

crum·ble /'krʌmbəl/ *v* -**bled, -bling** [I;T] to break into very small pieces: *He crumbled the bread in his fingers.* |*As the years passed, the old church crumbled.* (=became a

ruin)|(fig.)*In the end, the Roman Empire crumbled.*

crum·bly /'krʌmbliy/ *adj* -**blier, -bliest** easily CRUMBLEd

crum·ple /'krʌmpəl/ *v* -**pled, -pling** [I;T *up*] to (cause to) become full of irregular folds by pressing, crushing, etc.: *I can't wear a crumpled dress.* |*The front of the car crumpled as he drove it into the wall.*

crunch¹ /krʌntʃ/ *v* **1** [I;T *on*] to crush (food) noisily with the teeth: *The dog was crunching (on) a bone.* **2** [I] to make a crushing noise: *Our feet crunched on the snow.* |*The stones crunched under the car tires.* –**crunchy** *adj* -**ier, -iest**

crunch² *n* [*the* S] **1** a sound as of CRUNCHing: *We could hear the crunch of their footsteps as they walked over the frozen snow.* **2** *infml* a difficult moment at which an important decision must be made (esp. in the phr. **when/if it comes to the crunch**)

cru·sade¹ /kruw'seyd/ *n* **1** (*usu. cap.*) any of the Christian wars to win back the Holy Land (Palestine) from the Muslims 800 years ago **2** a united effort for the defense or advancement of an idea, principle, etc.: *a crusade against crime|a crusade for women's rights*

crusade² *v* -**saded, -sading** [I *against, for*] to take part in a CRUSADE¹: *to crusade for women's rights* –**crusader** *n*

crush¹ /krʌʃ/ *v* **1** [T] to press with great force so as to destroy the natural shape or condition: *This machine crushes wheat grain to make flour.* |*The tree fell on top of the car and crushed it.*|(fig.) *The government has crushed all opposition.* **2** [I;T] to press tightly; CROWD²: *The people crushed through the gates.* **3** [I;T] →CRUMPLE

crush² *n* **1** [S] uncomfortable pressure caused by a great crowd of people: *There was such a crush on the train!* **2** [C *on*] *infml* a strong foolish and short-lived love for someone: *Ben has a crush on his music teacher.* **3** [U] a drink made by crushing fruit: *orange crush*

crust /krʌst/ *n* [C;U] **1** the hard usu. brown outer surface of baked bread **2** the baked pastry on a PIE **3** a hard outer covering (as of earth or snow): *the earth's crust* |*a thin crust of ice*

crus·ta·cean /krʌ'steyʃən/ *adj,n* (of, belonging to, or being) any of a group of animals with a hard outer shell: LOBSTERs, CRABs, *and* SHRIMP *are crustaceans.*

crust·y /'krʌstiy/ *adj* -**ier, -iest 1** having a hard well-baked CRUST: *a crusty loaf* **2** bad-tempered; bad-mannered: *a crusty old man*

crutch /krʌtʃ/ *n* a stick with a piece that fits under the arm, for supporting a person who has difficulty in walking: *When he broke his leg he had to walk on crutches.* –see illustration on page 201

crux /krʌks/ *n* [S] the central part of a problem: *The crux of the matter is …*

cry¹ /kraɪ/ *v* **cried, crying 1** [I;T] to produce (tears) from the eyes as a sign of sorrow, sadness, etc.: *She cried when she heard the news of her friend's death.* |*to cry oneself to*

SPELLING NOTE

Words with the sound /k/, like **cut**, may be spelled **k-**, like **key**, or **qu-**, like **queen**. Words with the sound /s/, like **city**, may be spelled **s-**, like **soon**, or **ps-**, like **psychology**.

sleep (=cry till one falls asleep) **2** [I *out*] to make a loud sound expressing fear, pain, or some other strong feeling: *The little boy cried out with pain when he burned his fingers.* **3** [I;T] to call loudly; shout: *The trapped woman cried out for help.|"Run, run!" he cried.* **4** [I] to make the natural sound of certain animals and birds: *Listen to the seabirds crying.* **5 cry one's eyes/heart out** to cry very bitterly: *When her dog died, my daughter cried her eyes out.*

cry out against sthg. *v adv prep* [T +*v-ing*] to express one's disapproval of

cry out for sthg. *v adv prep* [T] to be in great need of; demand: *The garden is crying out for rain.*

cry² *n* **cries 1** [C *of*] any loud sound expressing fear, pain, etc.: *a cry of anger/pain/fear* **2** [C] a loud call; shout: *a cry of "Stop, thief!"|a* **battle cry** (=a cry to show or encourage bravery in a battle)|(fig.) *a national cry for lower taxes* **3** [S] a period of crying: *You'll feel better after you've had a good cry.* **4** [C] the natural sound of certain animals or birds

cry·ba·by /ˈkraɪˌbeɪbiʸ/ *n* **-bies** a person, esp. a child, who cries or complains too readily or with little cause: (fig.) *Stop being such a crybaby. If you've lost your job, just go out and find another one.*

cry·ing /ˈkraɪ-ɪŋ/ *adj* [A] *infml* (esp. of something bad) that demands attention: *a crying need/shame*

crypt /krɪpt/ *n* an underground room, esp. under a church

cryp·tic /ˈkrɪptɪk/ *adj* hidden; secret; mysterious: *a cryptic message|a cryptic remark* (=with hidden meaning) **–cryptically** *adv*

crys·tal /ˈkrɪstəl/ *n* **1** [U] a transparent natural mineral that looks like ice **2** [U] colorless glass of very high quality: *a crystal wine glass* **3** [C] a small regular shape that becomes naturally by a substance when it becomes solid: *sugar and salt crystals* **4** [C] *AmE* the transparent cover over the face of a clock or watch

crys·tal·lize ‖also **-lise** *BrE* /ˈkrɪstəˌlaɪz/ *v* **-lized, -lizing** [I;T] **1** to (cause to) form CRYSTALS (3): *At what temperature does sugar crystallize?* **2** to (cause to) become clear or fixed in form: *She's trying to crystallize her ideas into a practical plan.* **–crystallization** /ˌkrɪstələˈzeɪʃən/ *n* [U]

CT *written abbrev. said as:* Connecticut /kəˈnɛtəkət/ (a state in the US)

cu. *written abbrev. said as:* CUBIC

cub /kʌb/ *n* the young of wild animals such as the lion, bear, etc.: *a lion and her cubs*

cube¹ /kyuʷb/ *n* **1** a solid object with six equal sides: *a sugar cube* **2** the number made by multiplying a number by itself twice: *The cube of 3 is 27.* $(3 \times 3 \times 3 = 27)$

cube² *v* **cubed, cubing** [T] **1** to cut (something) into CUBE-like shapes: *Cube the meat before putting it in the pan.* **2** to multiply a number by itself twice: *3 cubed* (written 3^3) *is 27.*

cu·bic /ˈkyuʷbɪk/ *adj* being a measurement of space when the length of something is

multiplied by the width and height of it: *a cubic inch/foot/meter*

cu·bi·cle /ˈkyuʷbɪkəl/ *n* a very small enclosed division of a larger room: *Do you have an office of your own, or do you work in a cubicle?*

cub scouts /ˈ· ·/ also **cubs** /kʌbz/– *n* [*the* P] a division of the BOY SCOUTS for younger boys: *My little brother's in the cub scouts/a cub scout.*

cuck·oo /ˈkuʷkuʷ, ˈkʊ-/ *n* **-oos** a gray European bird that has a call that sounds like its name

cu·cum·ber /ˈkyuʷkʌmbər/ *n* [C;U] a long, thin, round vegetable with a dark green skin and light green watery flesh

cud·dle¹ /ˈkʌdl/ *v* **-dled, -dling** [I;T *up*] to hold (someone, something, or each other) lovingly and closely in the arms: *The little girl picked up her dog and cuddled it.*

cuddle² *n* [S] an act of cuddling (CUDDLE¹)

cud·dly /ˈkʌdliʸ/ *adj* **-dlier, -dliest** lovable; suitable for cuddling (CUDDLE¹)

cudg·el /ˈkʌdʒəl/ *n* a short thick heavy object used as a weapon; short heavy CLUB¹ (2)

cue¹ /kyuʷ/ *n* (esp. in a play) a signal for the next person to speak or act: *The actor missed his cue and came onto the stage late.*

cue² *n* a long straight wooden rod used for pushing the ball in POOL² (2), BILLIARDS, etc. :*a pool cue*

cuff¹ /kʌf/ *n* **1** the end of a SLEEVE (=the arm of a garment) nearest the hand **2** *AmE*‖**turn up** *BrE*– a narrow band of cloth turned upwards at the bottom of a pant leg **3 off the cuff** without preparation: *I'm afraid I can't answer your question off the cuff.*

cuff² *n,v* [T] (to give) a light blow with the open hand: *Jane cuffed the dog when she found it on the chair.*

cui·sine /kwɪˈziʸn/ *n* [U] a style of cooking: *French cuisine*

cul-de-sac /ˌkʌl də ˈsæk, ˌkʊl-/ *n* **cul-de-sacs** *or* **culs-de-sac** a street with only one way in or out; BLIND ALLEY

cul·i·nar·y /ˈkʌləˌnɛriʸ, ˈkyuʷ-/ *adj* [no comp.] *fml* of, related to, or suitable for the kitchen or cooking

cull /kʌl/ *v* [T] to search through (a group of animals) and kill the weakest: *Every year some SEALS³ are culled because they eat too much fish.* **–cull** *n: a seal cull*

cul·len·der /ˈkʌləndər/ *n* →COLANDER

cul·mi·nate in sthg. /ˈkʌlməˌneɪt/ *v prep* **-nated, -nating** [T] *fml* to reach the highest point, degree, or development in: *The battle culminated in total victory.* **–culmination** /ˌkʌlməˈneɪʃən/ *n*

cul·pa·ble /ˈkʌlpəbəl/ *adj fml* deserving blame; guilty: *culpable behavior* **–culpability** /ˌkʌlpəˈbɪlətiʸ/ *n* [U] **–culpably** /ˈkʌlpəbliʸ/ *adv*

cul·prit /ˈkʌlprɪt/ *n* the person guilty of a crime or offense

cult /kʌlt/ *n* (the group of people believing in) a particular system of religious worship, principle, fashion, etc.: *When did he join the cult?|an ancient tribal cult|Her books have a* **cult following.** (=are read with great interest by a certain group)

cul·ti·vate /ˈkʌltə‚veʸt/ v **-vated, -vating** [T] **1** to prepare (land) for the growing of crops **2** to plant, grow, and raise (a crop) by preparing the soil, providing with water, etc.: (fig.) *to cultivate a love of art* **3** to encourage the growth of friendship with (a person): *John always tries to cultivate people who are useful to him.*

cul·ti·vat·ed /ˈkʌltə‚veʸtɪd/ adj having or showing good education, manners, etc. –opposite **uncultivated**

cul·ti·va·tion /‚kʌltəˈveʸʃən/ n [U] **1** the act of cultivating (CULTIVATE): *to bring new land under cultivation* **2** the state or quality of being CULTIVATED

cul·tur·al /ˈkʌltʃərəl/ adj of or related to CULTURE (1,2,3): *cultural independence|cultural activities* –**culturally** adv

cul·ture /ˈkʌltʃər/ n **1** [C;U] the particular system of art, thought, and customs of a society: *ancient Greek culture|a tribal culture* **2** [U] artistic and other activity of the mind and the works produced by this: *New York is a good city for anyone who is interested in culture.* **3** [U] a state of high development in art and thought: *a man of little culture* **4** [U] the practice of raising animals and growing plants: *bee culture*

cul·tured /ˈkʌltʃərd/ adj **1** having or showing good education, knowledge of the arts, good manners, sensitivity, etc.; CULTIVATED: *a cultured mind* –opposite **uncultured 2** grown or produced by man: *a cultured* PEARL

cum·ber·some /ˈkʌmbərsəm/ adj heavy and awkward to carry, wear, etc.: *a cumbersome package*

cu·mu·la·tive /ˈkyuʷmyələtɪv, -‚leʸ-/ adj increasing steadily in amount by one addition after another: *cumulative interest payable on a debt* –**cumulatively** adv: *At first, the drug does no harm, but cumulatively its effects are bad*

cun·ning /ˈkʌnɪŋ/ adj,n [U] (showing or having) cleverness in deceiving; clever: *as cunning as a fox|She showed her cunning in the way she avoided answering the question.* –compare GUILE –**cunningly** adv

cup¹ /kʌp/ n **1** a small round container, usu. with a handle, from which liquids are drunk: *to wash the coffee cups* –see illustration on page 379 **2** also **cupful** /ˈkʌpfʊl/– the amount held by one CUP¹ (1): *Add one cup of flour to half a cup of sugar.* **3** a specially shaped usu. silver vessel given as a prize in a competition: *Which team do you think will win the cup this year?* **4** a small circular object: *the cup of a flower*

cup² v **-pp-** [T] to form (esp. the hands) into the shape of a cup: *She cupped her cold hands around the bowl.*

SPELLING NOTE
Words with the sound /k/, like **cut**, may be spelled **k-**, like **key**, or **qu-**, like **queen**. Words with the sound /s/, like **city**, may be spelled **s-**, like **soon**, or **ps-**, like **psychology**.

cup·board /ˈkʌbərd/ n a set of shelves enclosed by doors, where clothes, plates, food, etc., may be stored –compare CLOSET¹

cu·pid·i·ty /kyuʷˈpɪdətiʸ/ n [U] fml & derog very great desire, esp. for money and property

cur /kɜr/ n a worthless bad-tempered dog, esp. of mixed breed –compare MONGREL

cu·rate /ˈkyuərɪt/ n an assistant appointed to help the priest of a PARISH

cu·ra·tor /kyuˈreʸtər, ˈkyuər‚eʸtər, -ətər/ n the person in charge of a MUSEUM, library, etc.

curb¹ /kɜrb/ n **1** *AmE‖***kerb** *BrE*– the edging of a SIDEWALK made of stones or cement –see illustration on page 673 **2** a controlling influence; CHECK¹ (1,2): *Keep a curb on your anger.*

curb² v [T] to control (one's feelings, temper, spending, etc.)

curd /kɜrd/ n [C;U] the thick soft substance that separates from milk when it becomes sour

cur·dle /ˈkɜrdl/ v **-dled, -dling** [I;T] to (cause to) form into CURDs; (cause to) thicken: (fig.) *a loud cry in the night which made his blood curdle* (=made him very afraid) –see also BLOODCURDLING

cure¹ /kyuər/ v **cured, curing** [T] **1** [*of*] to bring health to (a person) in place of disease or illness: *This medicine cured me of my cold.*|(fig.) *Parents try to cure their children of bad habits.* **2** to make (a disease, illness, etc.) go away, esp. by medical treatment: *The only way to cure backache is to rest.*|(fig.) *government action to cure unemployment* **3** to preserve (food, tobacco, etc.) by drying, hanging in smoke, covering with salt, etc.

cure² n **1** a medicine that cures an illness, disease, etc.: *There is still no cure for the common cold.*|(fig.) *Is there a cure for rising prices?* **2** a course of medical treatment: *He went for a cure at a famous hospital.* **3** a return to health after illness: *This drug should bring about a cure.*

cur·few /ˈkɜrfyuʷ/ n (a usu. military rule stating) a time during which all people should be indoors

cu·ri·o /ˈkyuəriʸ‚oʷ/ n **-os** a usu. small object, valuable because of its age, rarity, or beauty

cu·ri·os·i·ty /‚kyuəriʸˈasətiʸ/ n **-ties 1** [U] the desire to know or learn: *Curiosity is part of a child's nature.* **2** [C] a strange, interesting, or rare object, custom, etc.

cu·ri·ous /ˈkyuəriʸəs/ adj **1** [F +*to-v*] eager to know or learn: *A student should always be curious to learn.* –opposite **incurious 2** showing too much interest in other people's affairs: *He was so curious that he opened the letter even though it was addressed to his father.* **3** odd; strange; peculiar: *a curious state of affairs* –**curiously** adv: *Curiously (enough), I had met John's new friend before.*

curl¹ /kɜrl/ n **1** a small mass of twisted or waved hair –compare WAVE² (3) **2** something with the shape of the lines on a screw; SPIRAL: *a curl of smoke*

curl² *v* [I;T *up*] **1** (esp. of hair) to twist into or form a curl or curls: *I don't like my hair straight so I'm having it curled.*|*The leaves became brown, curled up, and died.*|(fig.) *She curled up in front of the fire with a book.*|*She curled herself/her feet up on the bed.* **2** to (cause to) wind: *The plant's stem curled around the branches of the tree.* —opposite **uncurl**

curl·y /'kɜrliʸ/ *adj* **-ier, -iest** having curls or tending to curl: *curly hair* —**curliness** *n* [U]

cur·rant /'kɜrənt, 'kʌr-/ *n* **1** a small dried seedless GRAPE, esp. used in baking cakes **2** the small black, red, or white juicy fruit that grows in bunches on certain bushes

cur·ren·cy /'kɜrənsiʸ, 'kʌr-/ *n* **-cies 1** [C;U] the particular type of money in use in a country: *The German currency is very strong now.* **2** [U] the state of being in general acceptance: *Reports about the president's illness are* **gaining currency** *among news reporters.*

cur·rent¹ /'kɜrənt, 'kʌr-/ *adj* **1** belonging to the present time; of the present day: *current fashions/events/prices* **2** commonly accepted; in general use: *That word is no longer in current use.* —see NEW (USAGE) —**currently** *adv*

current² *n* **1** [C] a continuously moving mass of liquid or gas: *The current is strongest in the middle of the river.*|*air currents*|(fig.) *the current of public opinion* **2** [C;U] the flow of electricity past a fixed point —see also A.C., D.C.

current ac·count /'·· ·,·/ *n BrE* for CHECKING ACCOUNT

cur·ric·u·lum /kə'rɪkyələm/ *n* **-la** /lə/ *or* **-lums** a course of study offered in a school, college, etc. —compare SCHEDULE

curriculum vi·tae /kə,rɪkyələm 'viʸtaɪ, 'vaɪtiʸ/ *n* [*usu. sing.*] *Latin fml* for RESUMÉ

cur·ry¹ /'kɜriʸ, 'kʌriʸ/ *n* **-ries** [C;U] **1** a CONDIMENT (=a powder or liquid that gives food a special taste) that is hot to the taste **2** an esp. Indian dish of meat, vegetables, etc., cooked in this CONDIMENT, usu. eaten with rice: *I like vegetable curry.*|*I'll have a chicken curry.*

curry² *v* **-ried, -rying** [T] to make (meat, vegetables, eggs, etc.) into CURRY¹ (2): *curried chicken*

curse¹ /kɜrs/ *n* **1** a word or sentence asking God, heaven, etc., to bring down evil or harm on someone or something **2** a cause of misfortune, evil, etc.: *Insects can be a curse to farmers.* **3** a word or words used in swearing; word or words expressing anger, hate, etc.

curse² *v* **cursed, cursing 1** [T] to call down evil or misfortune upon: *She cursed him/his name for ruining her life.* **2** [I;T] to swear (at): *The rider cursed his horse.*|*She cursed terribly.* **3** **cursed with** suffering misfortune or great harm because of

cur·so·ry /'kɜrsəriʸ/ *adj* (of work, reading, etc.) not thorough; done without attention to details —**cursorily** *adv*

curt /kɜrt/ *adj* (of a person, his/her manner, etc.) too short in speech to be polite: *a curt reply/answer/manner* —**curtly** *adv* —**curtness** *n* [U]

cur·tail /kər'teʸl/ *v* [T] *fml* to cut short; reduce; limit: *The government hopes to curtail public spending.* —**curtailment** *n* [C;U]

cur·tain /'kɜrtn/ *n* a piece of hanging cloth that can cover a window or door, divide a room in two, etc.: *Draw the curtains* (=pull them across the window); *it's getting dark.*|(fig.)*The burning house was hidden behind a curtain of smoke.* —compare DRAPES —see also IRON CURTAIN —see illustration on page 55

curt·sy¹, curtsey /'kɜrtsiʸ/ *n* **-sies** *or* **-seys** a woman's or young girl's act of respect to someone of higher rank, esp. nobility, made by bending the knees and lowering the head and shoulders —compare BOW² (1)

curtsy², curtsey *v* **-sied, -sying** [I] to make a CURTSY¹

cur·va·ture /'kɜrvətʃər, -,tʃʊər/ *n* [C;U] the degree to which something is curved; state of being curved: *the curvature of the earth's surface*

curve¹ /kɜrv/ *v* **curved, curving** [I;T] to (cause to) bend in the shape of a curve: *The road curved to the right.*

curve² *n* a line of which no part is straight and which contains no angles; rounded bend: *a curve in the road*

cush·ion¹ /'kʊʃən/ *n* **1** a bag filled with a soft substance on which a person can lie, sit, or rest comfortably: *He was lying on the floor with a cushion under his head.* **2** something like this in shape or purpose: *a cushion of air.*

cushion² *v* [T *against*] to lessen the force of: *Nothing can cushion (us against) the fear of death.*

cush·y /'kʊʃiʸ/ *adj* **-ier, -iest** *infml* (of a job, style of life, etc.) needing little effort; easy —**cushiness** *n* [U]

cus·tard /'kʌstərd/ *n* [U] a dessert made mainly with milk, eggs and sugar, and cooked

cus·to·di·an /kʌ'stoʷdiʸən/ *n* a person in charge of a public building; keeper of an apartment, office building, library, etc.

cus·to·dy /'kʌstədiʸ/ *n* [U] **1** the act or right of caring for someone, esp. when this right is given in a court of law: *After his divorce, the father was given custody of the children.* **2** the state of being guarded, esp. by the police: *The stolen car is now in police custody.*|*The criminal was taken into custody.*

cus·tom /'kʌstəm/ *n* **1** [C;U] (an) established socially accepted practice: *Social customs vary greatly from country to country.* **2** [C] the habitual practice of a person: *His custom was to get up early and take a cold bath.* **3** **custom-** (done or made) in accordance with the buyer's (CUSTOMER'S) wishes: *a custom-built car*|*custom-made clothes* —see HABIT (USAGE)

cus·tom·ar·y /'kʌstə,meriʸ/ *adj* established by custom; usual; habitual: *It is customary to give people gifts on their birthdays.* —**customarily** /,kʌstə'meərəliʸ/ *adv*

cus·tom·er /'kʌstəmər/ *n* a person who buys goods or services from a store, esp.

regularly: *The new store across the street has taken away most of my customers.*

USAGE When you go out to buy things, you are a **shopper**; when you buy goods from a particular store, you are that store's **customer**: *a busy street full of* **shoppers**|*Mrs. Stratton can't come to the telephone; she's with a* **customer**. If you are paying for professional services, e.g. from a lawyer, you are a **client**, but in the case of medical services you are a **patient**. If you are staying in a hotel, you are a **guest**.

cus·tom·ize /ˈkʌstəˌmaɪz/ *v* **-ized -izing** [T] *esp. AmE* to make or fix according to (someone's) specific likes, needs, etc.: *Bob had his car customized with special seats.*

cus·toms /ˈkʌstəmz/ *n* [P] **1** (*often cap.*) a place where travelers' belongings are searched when leaving or entering a country: *As soon as I got through customs, I felt at home.* **2** taxes paid on goods entering or leaving a country **3** (*often cap.*) the government organization established to collect these taxes

cut¹ /kʌt/ *v* **cut, cutting** **1** [I;T] to make a narrow opening in (something) with a sharp edge or instrument, accidentally or on purpose: *He cut his fingers on the broken glass.*|*This knife won't cut. It needs to be sharpened.*|(fig.) *His remark cut me deeply.* (=hurt my feelings) **2** [T *up*] to divide (something) or separate with a sharp edge or instrument: *The boys cut the cake in two and ate half each.* **3** [I] to be able to be divided or marked as with a sharp instrument: *A freshly baked cake doesn't cut easily.* **4** [I;T] to make (something) by using a sharp instrument: *They cut (their way) through the forest with their axes.*|*to cut a hole in a piece of paper* **5** [T *away,off,out*] to remove with a sharp instrument: *The snake's head was cut off with an axe.*|*Cut the dead wood away from the trees.* **6** [T] to shorten, take away, or lessen with or as if with a sharp instrument: *Your finger nails need to be cut.*|*Some violent scenes were cut from the film.* **7** [T *back*] to make smaller, less frequent, etc.: *They're cutting (back) train services and mail deliveries.* **8** [T] to grow (a tooth): *Our baby's cutting her first teeth, so she needs something to bite on.* **9** [T *off*] to interrupt (a supply of gas, electricity, etc.): *The water was cut off for two hours yesterday while the road was being repaired.* **10** [I;T] to divide (a pile of playing cards) in two before DEALing¹ (1) **11** [T] to cross: *The line AC is cut by line PQ.* **12** [T] to set free or loose by CUTting¹ (2) a rope, metal, etc.: *I cut myself free with my knife.* **13 cut corners** to do something in a less than perfect way in order to save time, money, etc. **14 cut it fine** to leave oneself

---

SPELLING NOTE

Words with the sound /k/, like **cut**, may be spelled **k-**, like **key**, or **qu-**, like **queen**. Words with the sound /s/, like **city**, may be spelled **s-**, like **soon**, or **ps-**, like **psychology**.

---

little time, money, etc., to do what is needed **15 cut one's losses** to stop taking part in a failing business, firm, etc., before one loses too much money

cut across sthg. *v prep* [T] **1** to take a shorter way across (a field, corner, etc.) **2** to go beyond or across the limits of: *a new group of members of Congress that cuts across party lines*

cut back *v adv* **1** [T] (**cut** sthg. ↔ **back**) to cut (a plant) close to the stem; PRUNE² **2** [I;T] (=**cut** sthg. ↔ **back**) *on* to reduce in size or amount: *We oppose any plans to cut back (on) production.* –see also CUTBACK

cut down *v adv* **1** [T] (**cut** sthg. ↔ **down**) to bring down by cutting; FELL²: *to cut down a tree* **2** [I;T] (=**cut down** sthg.) *on* to reduce in quantity or amount: *I have to cut down (on) smoking.* **3** [T] (**cut** sbdy. ↔ **down**) to knock down or kill (someone) esp. by striking with a sharp weapon

cut in *v adv* [I *on*] *infml* **1** →BUTT IN **2** to drive into a space between cars in a dangerous way: *You nearly caused a crash by cutting in (on me) like that!*

cut off *v adv* [T] **1** (**cut** sthg. ↔ **off**) to separate by cutting: *Cut off a piece of cheese for me, please.* **2** (**cut** sbdy./sthg. **off**) to disconnect: *We were cut off in the middle of our telephone conversation.*|*The water was cut off last week.* **3** (**cut** sbdy. **off**) to take away someone else's right to have one's property when one is dead; DISINHERIT: *If you marry that girl, I'll* **cut you off without a penny!** (=with no money) **4** (**cut** sbdy./sthg. **off**) [*from*] to block off or surround so that further movement out or in is impossible: (fig.) *Mary felt cut off from her friends when we moved.*

cut out *v adv* **1** [T *of*] (**cut** sthg. ↔ **out**) to remove by cutting: *She cut the advertisement out of the newspaper.* **2** [T] (**cut** sthg. ↔ **out**) to make by cutting: (fig.) *The rain and wind have cut out a deep valley.* **3** [T +*v-ing*] (**cut out** sthg.) *infml* to leave out; stop: *I must cut out smoking.* **4** [I] (of a motor) to stop suddenly: *Every time I got my car started the engine cut out.* **5 cut it/that out** *infml* to stop it: *Bob and Debbie were arguing, so their father told them to cut it out or go to bed.* **6 not cut out for something/to do something** not naturally well-suited for something: *I'm not cut out for this sort of work.*

cut up *v adv* **1** [T] (**cut** sthg. ↔ **up**) to cut into little pieces **2** [I] *infml* to behave in an amusing or annoying way: *I wish those children would stop cutting up.*|*He's always cutting up in class to make the other students laugh.*

cut² *n* **1** the result of cutting; an opening; wound: *a cut in the cloth*|*How did you get that cut on your hand?* **2** something obtained by cutting: *cuts* (=pieces) *of fresh lamb*|*a cut in* (=part taken out of) *a film* **3** [*in*] a reduction in size, amount, etc.: *cuts in government spending* **4** [*of,in*] *infml* a share: *The government plans to take a 50% cut of oil profits.* **5** the act of cutting (dividing) a pile of playing cards in two before DEALing¹ (1) **6 a cut above** *infml* better than; of higher quality or rank than: *This is a cut above all his other books.*

cut·and·dried /ˌ· · ˈ· ◄/ also **cut-and-dry** /ˌ· · ˈ· ◄/– *adj* already prepared and unlikely to be changed; fixed or settled in advance: *cut-and-dried opinions*

cut·back /ˈkʌtbæk/ *n* a planned decrease –see CUT[1] **back**

cute /kyuːt/ *adj esp. AmE* delightfully pretty and often small: *What a cute little baby!* –**cutely** *adv* –**cuteness** *n* [U]

cu·ti·cle /ˈkyuːtɪkəl/ *n* hard skin surrounding the lower edges of the nails on the toes and fingers

cut·lass /ˈkʌtləs/ *n* a short sword with a slightly curved blade, esp. as used formerly by a PIRATE

cut·ler·y /ˈkʌtləriː/ *n* [U] knives and other instruments used for eating

cut·let /ˈkʌtlɪt/ *n* a small piece of meat, usu. without bones: *a VEAL cutlet*

cut-rate /ˌ· ˈ· ◄/ *adj* [A] (of goods) cheap; sold at reduced prices: *cut-rate food/gas*

cut·ter /ˈkʌtər/ *n* **1** a small fast boat **2** an instrument for cutting: *a pair of wire-cutters*

cut·ting[1] /ˈkʌtɪŋ/ *n* **1** a stem, leaf, etc., cut from a plant, which can form roots and grow into a new plant **2** something produced by cutting, esp. a passage cut through higher land so that a road, railway, etc., can pass **3** *BrE* for CLIPPING (2)

cutting[2] *adj* **1** bitter; unkind: *The teacher was unpopular because he was always making cutting remarks.* **2** (esp. of the wind) uncomfortably strong and cold

cy·a·nide /ˈsaɪəˌnaɪd/ *n* [U] a very strong poison

cy·cla·men /ˈsaɪkləmən, ˈsɪ-/ *n* cyclamen a plant with white, purple, pink, or very red flowers

cy·cle[1] /ˈsaɪkəl/ *n* **1** a number of related events happening in a regularly repeated order: *the cycle of the seasons* **2** the period of time needed for this to be completed: *a 50-second cycle*

cycle[2] *v,n* **-cled, -cling** [I] →BICYCLE; MOTORCYCLE

cy·clic /ˈsaɪklɪk, ˈsɪ-/ also **cyclical** /ˈsaɪklɪkəl, ˈsɪ-/– *adj* happening in CYCLES[1] (1,2) –**cyclically** *adv*

cy·clist /ˈsaɪklɪst/ *n* a person who rides a bicycle

cy·clone /ˈsaɪkloʷn/ *n* a very violent wind moving rapidly in a circle around a calm central area; TORNADO –see also ANTICYCLONE

cyg·net /ˈsɪgnɪt/ *n* a young SWAN

cyl·in·der /ˈsɪləndər/ *n* **1** a hollow or solid body with a circular base and straight sides **2** the vessel within which a PISTON moves backwards and forwards as in an engine

cy·lin·dri·cal /səˈlɪndrɪkəl/ *adj* having the form of a CYLINDER (1) –**cylindrically** *adv*

cym·bal /ˈsɪmbəl/ *n* either of a pair of round thin metal plates struck together to make a loud ringing noise, used in music –**cymbalist** *n*

cyn·ic /ˈsɪnɪk/ *n sometimes derog* a person who thinks that people act only in their own interests, who sees little or no good in anything, and who shows this by making unkind remarks about people and things –**cynical** *adj: cynical remarks/behavior* –**cynically** *adv* –**cynicism** /ˈsɪnəˌsɪzəm/ *n* [U]

cy·press /ˈsaɪprəs/ *n* a tree with dark green leaves and hard wood, that does not lose its leaves in winter

cyst /sɪst/ *n* an enclosed hollow growth in or on the body, containing liquid matter

czar , tsar, tzar /zɑr/ *n* [A;C] (until 1917) the male ruler of Russia

cza·ri·na , tsarina, tzarina /zɑˈriːnə/ *n* [A;C] (until 1917) the female ruler of Russia and/or wife of the CZAR

D, d

D, d /diː/ **D's, d's** *or* **Ds, ds 1** the fourth letter of the English alphabet **2** the ROMAN NUMERAL (=number) for 500

d. *written abbrev. said as:* died: *d.1937*

-'d *short form of* **1** would: *I asked if he'd go.* (=if he would go) **2** had: *I asked if he'd gone.* (=if he had gone)

D.A. /ˌdiː ˈeɪ/ *AmE abbrev. for* →DISTRICT ATTORNEY

dab[1] /dæb/ *n* a slight or light touch: *He made a few dabs at the fence with the paintbrush but didn't really paint it.*

dab[2] *v* **-bb-** [I;T] to touch lightly or gently, usu. several times: *She dabbed (at) the wound with a wet cloth.*

dab·ble /ˈdæbəl/ *v* **-bled, -bling** [I *at, in*] *sometimes derog* to work at or study something without serious intentions: *to dabble in politics* –**dabbler** *n*

dachs·hund /ˈdɑkshʊnt, -hʊnd/ *n* a small dog with short legs and a long body

dad /dæd/ also **daddy** /ˈdædiː/– *n infml* (*used esp. by or to children*) father: *What are you doing, Dad?* –compare MOM

daf·fo·dil /ˈdæfəˌdɪl/ *n* a yellow flower of early spring

daf·fy /ˈdæfiː/ *adj* **-fier, -fiest** *AmE infml* silly; crazy: *a daffy idea*

daft /dæft/ *adj esp. BrE infml* silly; foolish: *a daft person/a daft thing to do* –**daftness** *n* [U]

dag·ger /ˈdægər/ *n* a short pointed knife used as a weapon, esp. formerly

dai·ly[1] /ˈdeɪliː/ *adj,adv* every day (or every day except Sunday and perhaps Saturday): *a daily journey/The mail is delivered twice daily./a daily newspaper/He gets paid daily.*

daily[2] *n* **-lies** a newspaper printed and sold every day except Sunday

dain·ty[1] /ˈdeɪntiː/ *adj* **-tier, -tiest** small, pretty, and delicate: *a dainty child/move-*

ment –**daintily** *adv* –**daintiness** *n* [U]

dain·ty² *lit n* -**ties** an especially nice piece of food; DELICACY (2)

dair·y /ˈdeəriⁱ/ *n* -**ies** 1 a place on a farm where milk is kept and butter and cheese are made 2 a shop where milk, butter, cheese, and eggs are sold

dairy cat·tle /ˈ·· ˌ··/ *n* [P] cattle kept for milk rather than for meat

da·is /ˈdeʸɪs, ˈdaɪ-ɪs/ *n* [*usu. sing.*] a raised part built at one end of a hall, for speakers to stand on

dai·sy /ˈdeʸziⁱ/ *n* -**sies** a very common small flower, white around a yellow centre

dale /deʸl/ *n lit* a valley

dal·ly /ˈdæleⁱ/ *v* -**lied, -lying** [I *over*] to be slow or waste time: *Don't dally or we'll be late.*

dal·ma·tian /dælˈmeʸʃən/ *n* (*usu. cap.*) a large dog, white with black spots

dam¹ /dæm/ *n* a wall or bank built to keep back water: *The Aswan Dam helps to control the River Nile in Egypt.*

dam² *v* -**mm-** [T *up*] 1 to build a dam across: *to dam (up) the river* 2 to keep back by means of a dam: *to dam (up) the water*|(fig.) *Damming up your anger leads to trouble.*

dam·age¹ /ˈdæmɪdʒ/ *n* [U] harm; loss: *The storm caused great damage.*|*This new law has done a lot of damage to the government's popularity.*

damage² *v* -**aged, -aging** [T] to cause damage to

dam·ag·es /ˈdæmɪdʒɪz/ *n* [P] *law* money that must be paid for causing damage: *The newspaper was ordered to pay damages to the movie star for printing an untrue story about him.*

dam·ask /ˈdæməsk/ *n,adj* [U] (a kind of cloth) decorated with a special pattern: *a beautiful damask cloth on the table*

dame /deʸm/ *n AmE infml* (esp. said by men) a woman:*What a dame!*

Dame *n* [A;C] (the title of) a woman who has been given a British rank of honor equal to that of KNIGHT¹ (2): *Dame Ellen Terry was a famous actress.*

damn¹ /dæm/ *v* [T] 1 (esp. of God) to send to punishment without end after death 2 (often used in curses): *(God) Damn it!*|*Damn you!* –compare BLESS 3 to declare to be bad: *The play was bad; the newspapers all damned it.* 4 to ruin: *He damned himself with one stupid remark.* 5 **I'll be damned if I will!** *infml* (a strong way of saying) I won't 6 **Well, I'll be damned!** *infml* (a strong way of saying) I'm very surprised

damn² also **damned–** *adj,adv* [A] *infml* 1 (used for giving force to an expression, good or bad): *a damn fool* |*damn foolish*|*He ran damn fast.* 2 **damn well** (used for giving force to a verb, usu. about something bad): *Don't lie to me: You knew damn well what was happening!*

damn³ also **damnation–** *interj infml* (an expression of anger or disappointment)

damn⁴ *n infml* (used in NEGATIVES², questions, etc.) even the smallest amount: *I don't* **give a damn** *what you do.*|*His promise isn't* **worth a damn.**

dam·na·tion /dæmˈneʸʃən/ *n* [U] the act of DAMNing¹ (1) or state of being damned

damn·ing /ˈdæmɪŋ/ *adj fml* very strongly against: *Some damning information against them was discovered.*

damp /dæmp/ *adj* rather wet: *damp air* |*a damp room* –**damply** *adv*

damp sthg. ↔ **down** also **dampen** sthg.↔ **down–** *v adv* [T] to make (a fire) burn more slowly: *Damp down the fire before you go to bed.*

damp·en /ˈdæmpən/ *v* 1 [I;T] to (cause to) become DAMP: *The rain hardly dampened the ground.* 2 [T] to make (feelings of happiness, eagerness, etc.) less strong: *Nothing can dampen my spirits on such a nice day!*

damp·ness /ˈdæmpnɪs/ also **damp–** *n* [U] wetness: *The dampness in the air makes me feel cold.*

dam·sel /ˈdæmzəl/ *n lit* a young unmarried woman of noble birth

dance¹ /dæns/ *v* **danced, dancing** [I;T *to*] to move to music: *She loves to dance to fast music.*|*She danced the* WALTZ *with me.*|(fig.) *The waves danced in the sunlight.* –**dancer** *n*

dance² *n* 1 an act of dancing: *Let's have one more dance before we go home.* 2 (the name of) a set of movements, esp. performed to music: *The* WALTZ *is a beautiful dance.* 3 a social meeting for dancing: *My parents are going to a dance tonight.*

dan·de·li·on /ˈdændəlˌaɪən/ *n* a small wild bright yellow flower

dan·druff /ˈdændrəf/ *n* [U] a common disease in which bits of dead skin form on the head and can be seen in the hair

dan·ger /ˈdeʸndʒər/ *n* 1 [U] the possibility of harm or loss: *The sign says "Danger! Falling rocks."*|*a danger signal*|*a place where children can play without danger*|*She has been very sick, but now she is* **out of danger.**|*He is* **in** (*great, real, etc.*) **danger of** *losing his job.* 2 [C] a case or cause of danger: *the dangers of smoking*

dan·ger·ous /ˈdeʸndʒərəs/ *adj* able to or likely to cause danger: *a dangerous criminal/ drug*|*It's dangerous to smoke.* –**dangerously** *adv: Don't drive so dangerously.*|*He is dangerously ill,*

dan·gle /ˈdæŋgəl/ *v* -**gled, -gling** 1 [I;T] to (cause to) hang or swing loosely: *keys dangling from a chain*|*He sat on the edge of the table dangling his legs.* 2 [T *in front of, before*] to offer as an attraction: *He dangled a trip to Paris in front of her to get her to work for him.*

dank /dæŋk/ *adj* unpleasantly wet and usu. cold: *an unhealthy house with dank stone walls*

dap·per /ˈdæpər/ *adj* (esp. of small men) (perhaps too) neat in appearance and quick in movements

dap·pled /ˈdæpəld/ *adj* marked with spots of color, or of sun and shadow: *a dappled horse*

dare¹ /deər/ *v* **dared, daring** 1 [I +*to-v*/*to-v*/not *be*+*v-ing*] to be brave or rude enough (to): *I dare not go.*|*I didn't dare (to) ask.*|*That's as much as I dare spend.*|*How dare you say that?* 2 [T] to (try to) persuade (someone) to do something dangerous: *I dared him to jump.*

dare² *n* a statement that someone else is not brave enough to do something; CHALLENGE: *I accepted his dare to climb the tree.*

dare·n't /'dɛərənt/ *v BrE short for* dare not: *I daren't ask him.*

dare·say /ˌdɛər'seɪ/ *v esp. BrE (only with "I")* [I;T +(*that*)] (I) suppose (that); perhaps: *I daresay you're right.|It will come, I daresay.*

dar·ing¹ /'dɛərɪŋ/ *adj* very brave (in a good or bad sense): *a daring attempt to save the children from the fire|a daring crime*

daring² *n* [U] bravery: *a person/an action of great daring*

dark¹ /dɑrk/ *adj* **1** partly or completely without light: *too dark to read|In winter it gets dark here early.* **2** tending towards black: *dark hair/green/clothes|a tall dark good-looking man|*(fig.) *Don't always look on the dark side of things.|*(fig.) *dark days ahead* **3** secret; hidden: *He kept his plans dark.* **4 dark horse** a person who may be successful although not much is known about him/her –**darkly** *adv* : *He spoke darkly of trouble to come.* –**darkness** *n* [U]

dark² *n* [*the* S;U] **1** the absence of light; darkness: *Can cats see in the dark?|Some children are afraid of the dark.|We don't go out* **after dark.**|*Get home* **before dark. 2 keep someone in the dark** to keep someone without knowledge: *They kept the public in the dark about their agreement.*

dark·en /'dɑrkən/ *v* [I;T] to make or become dark: *The sky quickly darkened after sunset.|His face darkened with anger when he heard the bad news.* –compare LIGHTEN

dar·ling¹ /'dɑrlɪŋ/ *n* (usu. used to address someone) a person who is very much liked or loved: *Darling, will you please hurry up!|My granddaughter is a little darling.*

darling² *adj* [A] dearly loved: *my darling husband/wife/child*

darn¹ /dɑrn/ *v* [I;T] to repair (a hole in cloth or a garment with a hole in it) by passing threads through and across: *to darn a sock/the hole in a sock* –**darn** *n*

darn² *n,adj,adv,interj euph* →DAMN²,³,⁴

dart¹ /dɑrt/ *n* **1** a small sharp-pointed object to be thrown, shot, etc., esp. one used as a weapon or in games: *a poisoned dart* **2** [S] a quick movement in a particular direction: *The prisoner* **made a dart for** *the door.* **3** a fold sewn into a garment, to make it fit better

dart² *v* **1** [I *across, out,* etc.] to move suddenly and quickly: *He darted out/towards the door.* **2** [T] to throw or send out suddenly and quickly: *The snake darted out its tongue.|She darted an angry look at her husband.*

darts /dɑrts/ *n* [U] a game in which DARTS¹(1) are thrown at a circular board (**dartboard**)

dash¹ /dæʃ/ *v* **1** [I] to run quickly and suddenly: *I have to dash (off) to catch my train.|He dashed across the street.* **2** [I;T] to (cause to) strike with great force: *The waves dashed the boat against the rocks.|The waves dashed against the rocks.* **3** [T] *esp. lit* to destroy (hopes, spirits, etc.): *The accident*

dashed John's hopes of playing on the football team. –see WALK (USAGE)

dash² *n* **1** [S] a sudden quick run: *The prisoners* **made a dash for** *freedom.* **2** [C] a small amount of something: *a dash of pepper/color* **3** [C] a mark (–) used in writing and printing: *The dash is longer than the* HYPHEN. **4** [U] a combination of bravery and style: *a person of great dash and spirit*

dash·board /'dæʃbɔrd, -bowrd/ *n* the instrument board in a car, where many of the controls are

dash·ing /'dæʃɪŋ/ *adj* having a lot of DASH² (4): *a dashing young officer* –**dashingly** *adv*

da·ta /'deɪtə, 'dætə, 'dɑtə/ *n* [P;U] facts; information: *The data is/are all ready for examination.|We keep the data in a* (**computer**) **data bank.**|

USAGE Although plural in its Latin form, **data** is now often used as a [U] noun: *This data is very interesting.*

date¹ /deɪt/ *n* **1** time shown by one or more of the following: the number of the day, the month, and the year (but not usu. by month alone): *The date on the coin is 1921.|What's the date today? It's the third of August.* **2** an arrangement to meet at a particular time and place: *They made a date to meet soon.* **3** *infml* a special social meeting between a man and woman, or boy and girl: *My mother tries to stop me from going out on dates.* **4** *AmE infml* a person with whom one has such a meeting: *Can I bring my date to your party?* **5 out of date: a:** not modern; old fashioned: *out-of-date methods* **b:** no longer able to be used: *This ticket is out of date.* **6 to date** until today: *To date he has done half the work.* **7 up to date** modern: *It was a modern factory–everything was really up to date.* –see also BLIND DATE

date² *v* **dated, dating 1** [T] to guess or show the date of: *I can't date the pot exactly, but it must be very old.|The shape of this pot dates it at about AD 400.* **2** [T] to write the date on: *Please date your letters to me in the future.* **3** [I;T] to (cause to) seem no longer in fashion: *This type of music is beginning to date.* **4** [I;T] *AmE infml* to go on or have a* DATE¹ (3) *with (another or each other): *They've been dating (each other) for months.*

date back to sthg. *v adv prep* [T *no pass.*] to have lasted since (the date of building or origin): *This church dates back to 1173.*

date from sthg. *v prep* [T *no pass.*] to have lasted since: *The custom dates from the time when men wore swords.*

date³ *n* a small brown sweet fruit with a long stone, from hot countries

dat·ed /'deɪtɪd/ *adj* out of DATE¹(5): *Those words all seem dated: I haven't heard them since about 1965!*

daub /dɔb/ *v* [T *with/ on*] to cover with something soft and sticky: *to daub the wall with paint|He daubed paint on the wall.*

daugh·ter /'dɔtər/ *n* someone's female child –compare SON (1) –see illustration on page 247 –**daughterly** *adj*

daughter-in-law /'··· ˌ·/ *n* **daughters-in-law**

the wife of someone's son –compare
SON-IN-LAW –SEE ILLUSTRATION ON PAGE 247

daunt /dɔnt, dɑnt/ v [T] to cause to lose
courage or the will to act: *He felt completely
daunted by the difficulties that faced
him.|The examination questions were
daunting.*

daunt·less /'dɔntlɪs, 'dɑnt-/ adj lit not
DAUNTed; fearless: *dauntless courage/
soldiers* –**dauntlessly** adv

daw·dle /'dɔdl/ v **dled, -dling** [I] infml to
waste time; be slow: *He dawdled all morn-
ing/all the way to school.* –**dawdler** n

dawn¹ /dɔn/ n [C;U] **1** the time of day when
light first appears; the first appearance of
light in the sky before the sun rises: *The
mailman has to get up before dawn every
day.|The dawns here in the mountains are
beautiful.|(fig.) the dawn of civilization* **2**
dawn is breaking light is just beginning to
appear –compare DUSK

dawn² v [I] (of the day, morning, etc.) to
begin to grow light just before the sun rises:
*The morning dawned fresh and clear after the
storm.*

dawn on/upon sbdy. v prep [T] to become
known by: *It suddenly/gradually dawned on
me that I had taken the wrong train.*

day /deɪ/ n **1** [C] a period of 24 hours: *There
are seven days in a week.|Christmas Day was
a Wednesday last year.* –see USAGE **2** [C;U]
the time between sunrise and sunset: *Call me
in the evening because I usually work during
the day.* –compare NIGHT (1) **3** [C] a period of
work within a 24-hour period: *She works an
eight-hour day.|They're demanding a
four-day week.* **4** [C] a period or point of
time: *People don't seem so polite these days.*
(=now, as opposed to in the past)|**In my day**
things were different.|**One day** (=at some
time in the future) *we'll get ourselves a new
car.|We've never heard the whole story* **to this
day.** (=up to and including now) **5** [S] a
period of success or fame: *He was a very fine
actor, but he has* **had his day** now. (=is no
longer good or popular) **6 call it a day** infml
to finish working for the day: *Let's call it a
day–I'm really tired.* **7 day after day/day in
day out** continuously **8 from day to day/day
by day** each day; as time goes on **9 make
someone's day** infml to make someone very
pleased or happy **10 the other day** in the
recent past: *I saw your friend the other day.*
USAGE If today is Wednesday, then Monday was **the day before yesterday** and Friday
will be **the day after tomorrow.** One cannot
leave out **the day** in these expressions.

day·break /'deɪbreɪk/ n [U] →DAWN¹ (1)

day·care /'deɪkeər/ n [U] the care of children
during the day while their parents are away
working –**daycare** adj [A]: *Large companies
sometimes have* **daycare centers.**

day·dream¹ /'deɪdriːm/ n a pleasant
dreamlike set of thoughts while one is
awake

daydream² v [I] to have DAYDREAMs: *She's
always daydreaming; she never listens to
what the teacher's saying.* –**daydreamer** n

day·light /'deɪlaɪt/ n [U] the light of day: *We*

use less electricity in summer because there's
more daylight.

daylight sav·ing time /ˌ·· '·· ˌ·/ AmE‖**summer time** BrE– n [U] the system of having the
time on the clocks usu. one hour later than
natural time according to the sun, so as to
make use of daylight hours in the summer

days¹ /deɪz/ n [P] life: *He began his days in a
small town.*

days² adv esp. AmE repeatedly by day; during any day: *they work days.*

day·time /'deɪtaɪm/ n [the S;U] →DAY (2): *I
can't sleep in the daytime.|daytime flights*
–opposite **nighttime**

day-to-day /ˌ· · '·◄/ adj [A] happening, etc.,
each day: *life's day-to-day difficulties* –compare EVERYDAY

daze¹ /deɪz/ v **dazed, dazing** [T] to make unable to think or feel clearly, esp. by a blow:
*After the accident John was dazed.|(fig.) The
news left him dazed.* –**dazedly** /'deɪzɪdliː/ adv

daze² n **in a daze** in a DAZEd condition

daz·zle /'dæzəl/ v **-zled, -zling** [T] to make
unable to see by throwing a strong light in
the eyes: *The lights of the car dazzled
me.|(fig.) She was dazzled by her success.*
–**dazzle** n [S]: *the dazzle of her smile*

DC abbrev. for: **1** direct current; a flow of
electricity that moves in one direction only
–compare AC **2** District of Columbia
/ˌdɪstrɪkt əv kəˈlʌmbiə/ (the area of the US
containing its capital): *Washington, DC*

DDT n [U] a chemical that kills insects: *The
farmer sprays DDT on his apples/sprays his
apples with DDT.*

dea·con /'diːkən/ **deaconess** /'diːkənɪs/ fem.–
n an officer of various Christian churches,
below a priest or minister

dead¹ /dɛd/ adj **1** no longer alive: *a dead man/
plant/leaf|Do the dead ever come back to
life?|(fig.) His love for you is now dead.|a
dead language/dead ideas* –compare INANI-
MATE –see USAGE **2** without the necessary
power: *a dead* BATTERY|*The telephone has
gone dead.* (=is not working) –compare
LIVE² (3) **3** [A] complete: *a dead stop/dead
silence* **4 dead center** the exact center **5 dead
heat** a race in which two or more people
finish at exactly the same time **6 dead wood**
useless people or things: *to cut out the dead
wood* (=to remove useless people or things)
USAGE Compare **dead** and **died**: Someone
(or something) that is no longer alive *is* dead
or has *died*: *My uncle died last week.|My
grandfather has been* **dead** *for years.|Our old
dog has just* **died.**|*These flowers are* **dead.**

dead² n **in the dead of** in the quietest or least
active period of: *in the dead of night/winter*

dead³ adv **1** suddenly and completely: *She
stopped dead.* **2** [adv + adj] infml completely: *dead certain/dead tired* **3**
[adv + adv] infml directly: *dead ahead*

dead·en /'dɛdn/ v [T] to cause to lose
(strength, feeling, brightness): *a medicine to
deaden the pain|Thick walls deaden noise.*

dead end n /ˌ·'·/ n **1** an end (as of a street)
with no way out **2** a position; state; or course
of action that leads to nothing further: *We've
come to a dead end in our efforts to reach an*

agreement.| *That's a real dead-end job.*

dead·line /'dɛdlaɪn/ *n* a date or time before which something must be done: *I hope we can finish this before the deadline!*

dead·lock /'dɛdlɒk/ *n* a disagreement which cannot be settled: *The talks about arms control have reached a complete deadlock.*

dead·ly¹ /'dɛdliʸ/ *adj* **-lier, -liest 1** dangerous; likely to cause death: *a deadly disease/weapon* **2** highly effective against something or someone: *a deadly remark* **3** [A] aiming to kill or destroy: *a deadly enemy/weapon* **4** *derog* very dull: *a deadly conversation* –**deadliness** *n* [U]

deadly² *adv* **1** very: *deadly serious|deadly dull* **2** like death: *deadly pale*

dead·pan /'dɛdpæn/ *adj infml* with no show of feeling, esp. when telling jokes: *deadpan humour|a deadpan expression*

dead weight /ˌ·'·/ *n* [S] the whole weight of something that does not move

deaf /dɛf/ *adj* **1** unable to hear at all or to hear well: *deaf people|a special school for the deaf* **2** [F *to*] unwilling to hear or listen: *deaf to all my prayers|She* **turned a deaf ear to** *his request.* –**deafness** *n* [U]

deaf·en /'dɛfən/ *v* [T] to make deaf: (fig.) *The music is deafening me!*

deal¹ /diʸl/ *v* **dealt** /dɛlt/, **dealing 1** [I;T *to, out*] to give out (playing cards) to players in a game **2** [T *to, out*] to divide among several; give each person his/her share: *Who's going to deal out the money?|I dealt (them) (out) three tickets each.* **3** [T] *fml* to strike (a blow): *She* **dealt** *him* **a blow** *on the side of his face.*

deal in sthg. *v prep* [T] to buy and sell; trade in: *This store deals in men's clothing.*

deal with sbdy./sthg. *v prep* [T] **1** to do business, esp. trade, with: *I've dealt with this store/person for 20 years.* **2** to treat; take action about: *Children are hard to deal with.|How do you deal with this problem?* **3** to be about: *This new book deals with the troubles in Ireland.*

deal² *n* **1** [C] an arrangement, esp. in business, to the advantage of both sides: *The car company has* **made a deal** *with a Japanese firm, which will supply engines in exchange for brakes.* **2** [S *of*] a quantity or degree, usu. large: *A great deal of money has been spent on the new hospital.|You will have to work a good deal faster.* **3** [the S;C] the act of giving out cards to players in a card game: *Who has the deal now?* **4 dirty/raw deal** *infml* bad treatment received

deal·er /'diʸlər/ *n* **1** a person in a stated type of business: *a used-car dealer* **2** a person who deals playing cards

deal·ing /'diʸlɪŋ/ *n* [U] method of business; manner of behaving: *I'm in favor of plain honest dealing.*

deal·ings /'diʸlɪŋz/ *n* [P] personal or business relations: *I've had dealings with him, but I don't know him very well.*

dean /diʸn/ *n* **1** (in some universities) an important officer **2** [A;C] (in several Christian churches) an officer in charge of several priests or church divisions

dear¹ /dɪər/ *adj* **1** much loved; precious: *a dear friend|Life is very dear to him.* **2** [A] *(usu. cap.)* (used at the beginning of a letter): *Dear Jane|Dear Sir* **3** *BrE* costly: *It's too dear. I can't afford it.* –compare CHEAP

dear² *n* a person who is loved or lovable: *Did you have a good day at work, dear?*

dear³ *interj* (used for expressing surprise, sorrow, slight anger): *Oh dear! I've lost my pen.|Dear! Dear! I'm sorry to hear that.*

dear·ly /'dɪərliʸ/ *adv* **1** with much feeling, usu. good feeling: *He loves his wife dearly.* **2** at a terrible cost in time, effort, pain, etc.: *He paid dearly for his mistake.*

dearth /dɛrθ/ *n* [S *of*] *fml* a lack (of); SHORTAGE (of): *There's a dearth of good restaurants in this city.*

death /dɛθ/ *n* **1** [C;U] the end of life; time or manner of dying: *He was happy till the day of his death.|His mother's death was a great shock to him.|Car accidents cause many deaths.|*(fig.) *Drinking will* **be the death of** *him.|If you go out without a coat, you'll* **catch your death of cold.** –compare BIRTH **2** [U] the state of being dead: *as still/cold as death* **3** [the S] the end or destruction (of something not alive): *a defeat that meant the death of all my hopes* **4 put to death** to kill, esp. with official permission: *The prisoners were all put to death.* **5 to death** beyond all acceptable limits: *I am sick to death of your complaints.*

death·blow /'dɛθbloʷ/ *n* [usu. sing.] an act, action, or event that destroys or ends someone or something: *His refusal to help us* **dealt a deathblow to** *our plans.*

death·ly /'dɛθliʸ/ *adj, adv* **-lier, -liest** like death: *a deathly cold body|a deathly silence*

death tax /'· ·/ *AmE*||**death duty** /'· ,·/ *BrE*— money that must be paid to a government on property left to a person when the original owner has died

death trap /'· ·/ *n* something or some state that may be very dangerous to life: *That old boat is a real death trap.*

death war·rant /'· ,··/ *n* a written official order to kill (EXECUTE (1)) someone

de·bar sbdy. **from** sthg. /diʸ'bɑr/ *v prep* **-rr-** [T] *fml* to prevent from

de·base /dɪ'beʸs/ *v* **-based, -basing** [T] to lower in quality, esp. in the opinion of others –**debasement** *n* [C;U]

de·bat·a·ble /dɪ'beʸtəbəl/ *adj* doubtful; perhaps not true: *They say their policies have not caused unemployment, but I think that's debatable.*

de·bate¹ /dɪ'beʸt/ *n* a usu. public meeting in which a question is talked about by at least two people or groups, each expressing a different point of view: *a long debate in the Senate*

debate² *v* **-bated, -bating** [I;T *about, upon, with*] to talk or argue about (something) with someone, usu. in an effort to persuade other people: *I debated the question with Mary.|They're debating whether to increase the price of gasoline.*

de·bauch /dɪ'bɔtʃ/ *v* [T] to lead away from socially approved forms of behavior, esp. in relation to sex and alcohol: *He had the look* of a debauched man.

de·bauch·er·y /dɪ'bɔtʃəriy/ n [U] derog behavior that goes beyond socially approved limits, esp. in relation to sex and alcohol

de·bil·i·tate /dɪ'bɪlə,teyt/ v -tated, -tating [T] to make weak: a debilitating disease

de·bil·i·ty /də'bɪlətiy/ n -ties [C;U] fml (a) weakness, esp. as the result of disease

deb·it[1] /'dɛbɪt/ n a record in a book of accounts of money spent or owed –compare CREDIT[1] (3)

debit[2] v [T] to charge with a DEBIT[1]: Debit Mr. Smith/Mr. Smith's account with $10. –compare CREDIT[1] (1)

deb·o·nair /,dɛbə'nɛər/ adj apprec becoming rare (usu. of men) cheerful and charming, but also polite and well-dressed: a debonair manner/young man

de·brief /diy'briyf/ v [T] to find out information from (someone on one's own side), by thorough questioning after an action: We debriefed our pilot after he had flown over the enemy's land. –see also BRIEF[3]

de·bris /də'briy, dey-/ n [U] the remains of something broken to pieces or destroyed; ruins: After the bombing there was a lot of debris.

debt /dɛt/ n 1 [C;U] something owed to someone else: a debt of $5/to pay one's debts |(fig.) a debt of GRATITUDE for your help 2 [U] the state of owing; the duty of repaying something: I'm heavily in debt at the moment, but hope to be out of debt when I get paid./in debt to him for his help 3 run into debt to begin to owe money

debt·or /'dɛtər/ n a person who owes money –compare CREDITOR

de·bunk /diy'bʌŋk, dɪ-/ v [T] infml to point out the truth about a wrong idea: A lot of people used to believe that, but now it's been completely debunked.

de·but /dey'byuw, dɪ-, 'deybyuw| n a first public appearance: The singer made his debut as Mozart's Don Giovanni.

deb·u·tante /'dɛbyu,tant/ also **deb** /dɛb/ infml– n a girl who is making, or has just made, her formal entrance into upper-class society

dec·ade /'dɛkeyd/ n a period of 10 years: Prices have risen steadily during the past decade.

dec·a·dent /'dɛkədənt/ adj marked by a fall from one level (esp. of morals) to a lower level: Many people believe that western society is becoming very decadent.|(fig.) How decadent to stay in bed all day! –decadence n

de·caf·fein·ate /diy'kæfə,neyt/ v -ated, -ating [T] to remove or reduce the CAFFEINE (esp. of coffee): decaffeinated coffee

de·cant /dɪ'kænt/ v [T] to pour (liquid, esp. wine) from one container into another

de·cant·er /dɪ'kæntər/ n a container (usu. of glass and decorated) for holding liquid (esp. wine)

de·cap·i·tate /dɪ'kæpə,teyt/ v -tated, -tating [T] fml to cut off the head of (esp. as a punishment); BEHEAD –decapitation /dɪ,kæpə'teyʃən/ n [C;U]

de·cay[1] /dɪ'key/ v 1 [I;T] (to cause) to go bad: Sugar can decay the teeth. 2 [I] to fall to a lower or worse state; lose health, power, etc.: It seems that all nations decay in time.

decay[2] n [U] the action, state, or result of decaying: The empty house has fallen into decay in the last twenty years.

de·ceased /dɪ'siyst/ n deceased fml & law the dead person: The deceased left a large sum of money to his wife. –deceased adj

de·ceit /dɪ'siyt/ n [U] derog the quality of being dishonest

de·ceit·ful /dɪ'siytfəl/ adj derog dishonest –deceitfully adv –deceitfulness n [U]

de·ceive /dɪ'siyv/ v -ceived, -ceiving [T in, into] to cause (someone) to accept as true or good what is false or bad: I trust him because I know he would never deceive me.|He deceived me. He lied about the money. –deceiver n

De·cem·ber /dɪ'sɛmbər/ also **Dec.** written abbrev.– n the 12th and last month of the year

de·cen·cy /'diysənsiy/ n [U] the quality of being DECENT

de·cent /'diysənt/ adj 1 socially acceptable; not causing shame or shock to others: Those tight pants of yours aren't decent!|decent behavior –opposite **indecent** 2 infml quite good: You can get a decent meal there without spending too much money. 3 infml nice; kind: That policeman was really very decent to us. –decently adv

de·cen·tral·ize also **-ise** BrE /diy'sɛntrə,laɪz/ v -ized, -izing [I;T] to (cause to) move from one big place to several smaller places –see also CENTRALIZE –decentralization /diy,sɛnt rələ'zeyʃən, ,diysɛn-/ n [U]

de·cep·tion /dɪ'sɛpʃən/ n [C;U] (an) act of deceiving

de·cep·tive /dɪ'sɛptɪv/ adj tending or having power to deceive; misleading –deceptively adv –deceptiveness n [U]

dec·i·bel /'dɛsə,bɛl, -bəl/ n tech a measure of the loudness of sound

de·cide /dɪ'saɪd/ v -cided, -ciding 1 [T +to-v/(that)] to arrive at an answer or an end to uncertainty about: to decide where to go/where they should go/She decided to go/I decided (that) it would cost too much to repair the car. 2 [I] to make a choice or judgment: I've been waiting all day for them to decide!/They decided in favor of him and against me. 3 [T] to bring to a clear or certain end: One blow decided the fight.

decide on sthg. v prep [T] to decide in favor of: I've decided on going to San Fransisco for my vacation.

de·cid·ed /dɪ'saɪdɪd/ adj fml 1 very clear and easily seen or understood: a decided change for the better 2 having or showing no doubt: a man of very decided opinions –decidedly adv –see also UNDECIDED

de·cid·u·ous /dɪ'sɪdʒuwəs/ adj tech having leaves that fall off in autumn: deciduous trees –compare EVERGREEN

dec·i·mal /'dɛsəməl/ adj based on the number 10

decimal[2] also **decimal fraction** /'··· ,··/ n a number like .5, .375, .06, etc.: You know 0.6 is a decimal because there's a **decimal point**

(also **decimal–**) *between the 0 and the 6.*

dec·i·mal·ize||also **-ise** *BrE* /'dɛsəməl,aɪz/ *v* **-ized, -izing** [I;T] to change to a DECIMAL¹ system of money, counting, etc. –**decimalization** /,dɛsəmələ'zeʸʃən/ *n* [U]

dec·i·mate /'dɛsə,meʸt/ *v* **-mated, -mating** [T] *fml* to destroy a large part of: *Disease decimated the population.* –**decimation** /,dɛsə'meʸʃən/ *n* [U]

de·ci·pher /dɪ'saɪfər/ *v* [T] to read (something difficult, esp. a CODE¹ (1)): *Your writing is difficult to decipher.* –see also CIPHER

de·ci·sion /dɪ'sɪʒən/ *n* **1** [C;U] (a) choice or judgment: *Who made the decision to go there?|Whose decision was it?|They expect to* **reach/come to a decision** *soon.* **2** [U] the quality of being able to make choices or judgments –opposite **indecision**

de·ci·sive /dɪ'saɪsɪv/ *adj* **1** showing determination or firmness: *A decisive person acts quickly.* **2** leading to a result: *It was a decisive battle; we won the war because of it.* **3** unquestionable: *a decisive victory* –opposite **indecisive** –**decisively** *adv* –**decisiveness** *n* [U]

deck¹ /dɛk/ *n* **1** the usu. wooden floor of a ship **2** a surface like this, such as the floor or level of a bus: *A double-deck bus has two levels.* **3** *AmE* a set of playing cards; PACK¹ (4) **4** *AmE* a built-out wooden entrance to a house, usu. the back or side, which is raised off the ground and is roofless: *Let's go out on the deck and get some sun.* –compare PATIO, PORCH **5** **-decker** having a certain number of DECKS (1,2) floors, or thicknesses: *A double-decker (bus) has two floors.|a triple-decker sandwich*

deck² *v* [T] *AmE infml* to knock someone to the floor

deck sbdy./sthg.↔**out** *v adv* [T *in*] to make more beautiful: *The street was decked out in flags.|Aren't you decked out tonight?* (You've dressed very well)

deck·chair /'dɛktʃɛər/ *n* a folding chair with a long seat of cloth (usu. CANVAS), used outdoors.

de·claim /dɪ'kleʸm/ *v* [T] *often derog* to say (something) loud and clear, with pauses and hand movements to increase the effect of the words –**declamation** /,dɛklə'meʸʃən/ *n* [C;U] –**declamatory** /dɪ'klæmə,tɔriʸ, -,toʷriʸ/ *adj*

dec·la·ra·tion /,dɛklə'reʸʃən/ *n* **1** the act of declaring: *a declaration of war* **2** a statement, giving information in an official manner: *Please make a written declaration of all the goods you bought abroad.*

de·clare /dɪ'klɛər/ *v* **-clared, -claring** [T] **1** to make known publicly or officially, according to rules, custom, etc.: *The U.S. declared war on England in 1812.|Jones was declared the winner.|I declare Mr. B. Schiff elected!* **2** [+(*that*)] to state (or show) with great force so that there is no doubt about the meaning: *He declared his position.|She declared (that) she knew nothing about the robbery.|He declared himself (to be) a member of their party.* **3** to make a full statement of (property for which tax may be owed to the government): *Do you have anything to declare?*

de·clared /dɪ'klɛərd/ *adj* openly admitted as:

a declared supporter of the government|It's their declared intention to increase taxes.

de·cline¹ /dɪ'klaɪn/ *v* **-clined, -clining 1** [I] to move from a better to a worse position, or from higher to lower: *Her power/health/ influence has begun to decline now that she is old.|The old man declined rapidly and soon died.* **2** [I;T +*to-v*] *fml* to refuse, usu. politely; be unwilling: *We asked them to come to our party, but they declined (the invitation).|The senator declined to make a statement.* –see REFUSE (USAGE)

decline² *n* [C *usu. sing.*;U] a period of declining (DECLINE¹ (1)), esp. as something or someone gets near the end: *There has been a sharp decline in interest in farming.|Interest in sports in our town is* **on the decline.**

de·code /diʸ'koʷd/ *v* **-coded, -coding** [T] to discover the meaning of (something written in a CODE¹ (1))

de·com·pose /,diʸkəm'poʷz/ *v* **-posed, -posing** [I;T] to (cause to) decay; break up into simple parts –**decomposition** /,diʸkɑmpə'zɪʃən/ *n* [U]

dé·cor, decor /deʸ'kɔr, 'deʸkɔr/ *n* [C;U] the decorative furnishing of a place, esp. a house or stage: *Who did the décor for your living room?*

dec·o·rate /'dɛkə,reʸt/ *v* **-rated, -rating 1** [T *with*] to serve as, or provide with, something added because it is beautiful, esp. for a special occasion: *The streets were decorated with flags.* **2** [I;T] to paint or put paper, etc., on the walls of a house: *How much will it cost to decorate the kitchen?* **3** [T *for*] to give (someone) an official mark of honor, such as a MEDAL

USAGE **Decorate, adorn, embellish,** and **garnish** are all verbs meaning "to add something to, so as to make more attractive." **Decorate,** as in (1) is normally used of places, and often of special occasions: *The children* **decorated** *the house for Christmas;* **adorn** is particularly used of things: *She* **adorned** *herself with jewels;* **embellish** is normally used of things: *The door of the church was* **embellished** *with* CARVINGS; and **garnish** is most often used of cooking: *a baked fish* **garnished** *with pieces of tomato.*

dec·o·ra·tion /,dɛkə'reʸʃən/ *n* **1** [U] the act or art of decorating; the state of being decorated **2** [C] an ornament; something that decorates: *decorations for a party* **3** [C] something given as a sign of honor, esp. military

dec·o·ra·tive /'dɛkərətɪv/ *adj* *apprec* attractive; used for decorating: *a decorative gold table* –**decoratively** *adv*

dec·o·ra·tor /'dɛkə,reʸtər/ *n* a person who chooses furniture, paint, curtains, etc. for a house, office, etc.

dec·o·rous /'dɛkərəs/ *adj fml* (of appearance or behavior) correct; properly serious in manner according to the customs of society –**decorously** *adv* –**decorum** /dɪ'kɔrəm, -'koʷr-/ *n* [U]: *I hope you will behave with decorum at the funeral.*

de·coy /'diʸkɔɪ, dɪ'kɔɪ/ *n* **-oys** something which is used for getting a person or bird into a trap –**decoy** /dɪˈkɔɪ, ˈdiːkɔɪ/ v [T *into*]

de·crease /dɪˈkriːs, ˈdiːkriːs/ v **-creased, -creasing** [I;T] to (cause to) become less in size, number, strength, or quality: *Our sales are decreasing.|The company decreased the number of workers.* –opposite **increase** –**decrease** /ˈdiːkriːs, dɪˈkriːs/ n [C;U *of, in*]

de·cree¹ /dɪˈkriː/ n an official command or decision

decree² v **-creed, -creeing** [I;T +(*that*)] to order officially, with the force of law: *They have decreed that all this fighting should end.*

de·crep·it /dɪˈkrɛpɪt/ adj derog weak or in bad condition from old age

de·cry /dɪˈkraɪ/ v **-cried, -crying** [T] fml to speak ill of; say bad things about

ded·i·cate /ˈdɛdəˌkeɪt/ v **-cated, -cating** [T *to*]
1 to give to, or declare for, a cause, purpose, or person: *The doctor dedicated his life/himself to finding a cure.|She dedicated her first book to her mother.*

ded·i·cat·ed /ˈdɛdəˌkeɪtɪd/ adj (esp. of people) very interested in or working very hard for an idea, purpose, etc.; COMMITTED: *She's very dedicated to her work.|a dedicated doctor.*

ded·i·ca·tion /ˌdɛdɪˈkeɪʃən/ n **1** [C;U] the act of dedicating (DEDICATE) **2** [C;U] the state of being DEDICATED: *She worked with great dedication to find a cure for the disease.* **3** [C] the words used in dedicating (DEDICATE (1))

de·duce /dɪˈduːs, dɪˈdjuːs/ v **-duced, -ducing** [T +(*that*)] to determine or decide (something) from general principles: *Because there were no clouds he deduced that it was going to be a cold night.* –see also DEDUCTION –**deducible** adj

de·duct /dɪˈdʌkt/ v [T *from*] to take away (an amount, a part) from a total –**deductible** adj

de·duc·tion /dɪˈdʌkʃən/ n **1** [C +(*that*)] that which is DEDUCEd: *Her deduction that he was now dead was correct.* **2** [C;U] the act or action of DEDUCTING **3** [C] that which is DEDUCTED: *She earned less money because of deductions from her wages.|income tax deductions.*

deed /diːd/ n **1** esp. lit something done on purpose: *good deeds* **2** law a written paper that is an official record of an agreement, esp. an agreement concerning ownership of land or a building: *You should keep the deeds to your house in a safe place.*

deem /diːm/ v [T +(*that*); not be +v-ing] fml to consider; have the opinion: *Do you deem this plan (to be) sensible?*

deep /diːp/ adj,adv **1** [adj, adv + prep/adv] going far down from the top: *The river is very deep here.|a mine two miles deep|knee-deep in work.|a deep breath* (=filling the lungs) **2** [adj, adv +prep/adv] going far in from the outside or the front edge: *a deep wound|a shelf 30 cm deep and 120 cm long|a house deep in the forest|*(fig.) *For some people, smoking is a* **deep-rooted** (=hard to stop) *habit.* **3** (of a color) strong and dark: *The sky was deep blue.* –compare LIGHT² (2), PALE¹ (2) **4** difficult to change; strong: *deep sleep|deep feeling* **5** seriously bad or damaging: *in deep trouble|deep in debt* **6** understanding

serious matters thoroughly: *a deep mind/thinker* **7** difficult to understand: *deep scientific principles* **8** **go off the deep end** infml **a** to go to an extreme (with something) **b** to lose one's mind **9** **in deep water** in serious trouble –see also DEPTH; compare SHALLOW –**deeply** adv –**deepness** n [U]

deep·en /ˈdiːpən/ v [I;T] to (cause to) become deeper: *We'll have to deepen the well if we want more water.|The color of the sky deepened as the sun went down.*

deep freeze /ˌ· ˈ·/ n →FREEZER (1)

deep-seat·ed /ˌ· ˈ··◂/ adj existing far below the surface: *a deep-seated sorrow*

deer /dɪər/ n **deer** a large fast four-footed animal, of which the males usu. have wide branching horns (ANTLERS) –sounds like **dear**

de·face /dɪˈfeɪs/ v **-faced, -facing** [T] to spoil the surface or appearance of, e.g. by writing or making marks on –**defacement** n [U]

de·fame /dɪˈfeɪm/ v **-famed, -faming** [T] fml to damage the good name of, usu. by unfair means –**defamatory** /dɪˈfæməˌtɔriː-, -ˌtoʊriː/ adj –**defamation** /ˌdɛfəˈmeɪʃən/ n [U]

de·fault /dɪˈfɔlt/ v [I *on*] to fail to fulfill a contract, agreement, or duty, esp. **a** to fail to pay a debt **b** to fail to take part in a competition –**default** n [U]: *She won* **by default**, *because her opponent refused to play.*

de·feat¹ /dɪˈfiːt/ v [T] **1** to win a victory over; beat: *Our team/army/political party has defeated our opponents!* **2** to cause to fail; FRUSTRATE (1): *It was lack of money that defeated their plan.*

defeat² n [C;U] **1** (an example of) the act of defeating: *the defeat of the losing army* **2** the act or state of being defeated: *their defeat by the winning army|After several defeats, the team is now doing well again.* –compare VICTORY

de·feat·ism /dɪˈfiːtɪzəm/ n [U] the practice of thinking or behaving in a way that shows an expectation of being defeated –**defeatist** n

def·e·cate /ˈdɛfəˌkeɪt/ v **-cated, -cating** [I] fml to pass waste matter from the bowels –**defecation** /ˌdɛfəˈkeɪʃən/ n [U]

de·fect¹ /ˈdiːfɛkt, dɪˈfɛkt/ n something lacking or imperfect; fault: *The machine is unsafe because of the defects in it.*

de·fect² /dɪˈfɛkt/ v [I *from,to*] to desert a country, political party, group, or movement, esp. in order to join an opposing one –**defection** /dɪˈfɛkʃən/ n [C;U]: *What caused his defection?* –**defector** n: *He's a defector.*

de·fec·tive /dɪˈfɛktɪv/ adj lacking something necessary; faulty: *defective machinery/ hearing* –**defectively** adv –**defectiveness** n [U]

de·fend /dɪˈfɛnd/ /dɪˈfɛnsəbəl/ v [T] **1** [*from, against*] to keep safe from harm; protect against attack: *The fort can't be defended against an air attack.|*(fig.) (in sport) *They defended their side of the field very well.* **2** to argue in favor of (something which is being attacked): *to defend one's beliefs* –compare ATTACK (1,2) **3** to act as a lawyer for (the person who has been charged) –compare PROSECUTE –**defensible** /dɪˈfɛnsəbəl/ adj

de·fend·ant /dɪˈfɛndənt/ n law a person

against whom a charge is brought –compare PLAINTIFF

de·fense *AmE*‖**defence** *BrE* /dɪ'fɛns/ *n* **1** [U] the act or action of defending: *the defense of one's country*|*He spoke* **in defense of** *justice.* **2** [C;U] means, methods, or things used in defending: *The government has increased its spending on defense.*|*Mountains are a defense against the wind.* **3** [C *usu. sing.*] arguments used in defending oneself: *The prisoner's defense was rather weak.* –compare PROSECUTION –**defenseless** *adj*

de·fen·sive /dɪ'fɛnsɪv/ *adj* able to defend: *defensive weapons*/*play*|*a defensive position* –see also OFFENSIVE –**defensively** *adv* –**defensiveness** *n* [U]

de·fer /dɪ'fɜr/ *v* -**rr**- [T] *fml* to delay until a later date; POSTPONE: *Let's defer action for a few weeks.*|*His military service was deferred until he finished college.* –**deferment** *n* [C;U]

defer to sbdy./sthg *v prep* [T] *fml* to yield to, esp. in opinion: *defer to your advice*

def·er·ence /'dɛfərəns/ *n* [U] *fml* regard for another's wishes, opinions, etc., because of the other's higher position or greater power –**deferential** /ˌdɛfə'rɛnʃəl, -tʃəl/ *adj*

de·fi·ant /dɪ'faɪənt/ *adj* showing no fear or respect; fearlessly refusing to obey –**defiance** *n* [U] –**defiantly** *adv*

de·fi·cien·cy /dɪ'fɪʃənsi/ *n* -**cies** [C;U] (a case of) the quality or state of being DEFICIENT; lack: *a vitamin deficiency*|*The deficiencies in this plan are very clear, and it can't possibly succeed.*

de·fi·cient /dɪ'fɪʃənt/ *adj* having none or not enough (of); lacking (in): *food deficient in iron*|*a deficient supply of water*|*deficient in skill* –**deficiently** *adv*

def·i·cit /'dɛfəsɪt/ *n* an amount by which something is less than what is needed, (esp.) the amount by which money that goes out is more than money that comes in: *The board of directors has reported a deficit of $2.5 million.* –opposite **surplus**

de·file /dɪ'faɪl/ *v* -**filed**, -**filing** [T] *fml* to destroy the pureness of: *The animals defiled the water.* –**defilement** *n* [U]

de·fine /dɪ'faɪn/ *v* -**fined**, -**fining 1** [I;T] to give the meaning(s) of (a word or idea); describe exactly: *Some words are hard to define.*|*This book defines the position of the national government in city affairs.* **2** [T] to show the limits or shape of: *I saw a clearly defined shape outside the window.* –see also INDEFINABLE

def·i·nite /'dɛfənɪt/ *adj* clear; without any uncertainty: *We demand a definite answer.*|*a definite success* –compare DEFINITIVE; see also INDEFINITE

def·i·nite·ly /'dɛfənɪtli/ *adv* without doubt; clearly: *That answer is definitely true.*|*That was definitely the best play I've seen all year.*|*He is definitely coming*/*definitely not coming.*|*Definitely not!*

def·i·ni·tion /ˌdɛfə'nɪʃən/ *n* **1** [C] an exact statement of the meaning, nature, or limits of something, esp. a word or phrase **2** [U] clearness of shape, color, or sound: *This photograph lacks definition.*

de·fin·i·tive /dɪ'fɪnətɪv/ *adj* **1** that provides a last decision that cannot be questioned: *a definitive answer* **2** that cannot be improved as a treatment of a particular subject: *She's written the definitive history of the Roman Empire.* –compare DEFINITE –**definitively** *adv*

de·flate /dɪ'fleɪt, diy-/ *v* -**flated**, -**flating** [I;T] **1** to (cause to) become smaller, esp. by losing air or gas: (fig.) *One sharp remark is enough to deflate him.* **2** to reduce the supply of money (of) or lower the level of prices (of) –opposite **inflate** –**deflation** /dɪ'fleyʃən, diy-/ *n* [C;U]

de·flect /dɪ'flɛkt/ *v* [I;T] to (cause to) turn from a straight course or fixed direction, esp. after hitting something: *Mary threw a rock at John, but it was deflected away from him when it hit a tree.* –**deflection** /dɪ'flɛkʃən/ *n* [C;U]

de·form /dɪ'fɔrm/ *v* [T] to spoil the form or appearance of: *a face deformed by disease*/*anger* –**deformation** /ˌdiyfɔr'meyʃən, ˌdɛfər-/ *n* [C;U]

de·form·i·ty /dɪ'fɔrməti/ *n* -**ties** [C;U] (an) imperfection of the body, esp. that can be seen: *He's very attractive in spite of his slight deformity.*

de·fraud /dɪ'frɔd/ *v* [T *of*] to deceive so as to get or keep something wrongly and usu. unlawfully

de·frost /dɪ'frɔst/ *v* [I;T] to remove ice from; unfreeze: *to defrost a REFRIGERATOR*|*Don't let the meat defrost too quickly.*

deft /dɛft/ *adj apprec* effortlessly skilfull: *a deft performance*/*catch* –**deftly** *adv* –**deftness** *n* [U]

de·funct /dɪ'fʌŋkt/ *adj fml or law* dead: (fig.) *defunct ideas*

de·fuse /diy'fyuwz/ *v* -**fused**, -**fusing** [T] to remove the FUSE³ (1) from (something explosive) so as to prevent an explosion: *to defuse a bomb*|(fig.) *to defuse a dangerous situation*

de·fy /dɪ'faɪ/ *v* -**fied**, -**fying** [T] **1** to show no fear of nor respect for: *These criminals are defying the law.*|(fig.)*This new invention seems to defy the laws of science.* **2** to ask (someone), very strongly, to do something considered impossible; dare; CHALLENGE: *I defy you to give me one good reason for believing you.*

de·gen·er·ate¹ /dɪ'dʒɛnərɪt/ *adj* having become worse in character, quality, etc., in comparison with a former state: *She was good before, but now she's just another degenerate artist.* –**degenerate** *n* –**degeneracy** /dɪ'dʒɛnərəsiy/ *n* [U]

de·gen·er·ate² /dɪ'dʒɛnəˌreyt/ *v* -**ated**, -**ating** [I *from,into*] **1** to pass from a higher to a lower type or condition: *The wide road degenerated into a little path.* **2** to sink into a low state of mind or morals: *a fine young man who has degenerated under the influence of bad company* –**degeneration** /dɪˌdʒɛnə'reyʃən/ *n* [U]

de·grade /dɪ'greyd/ *v* -**graded**, -**grading** [T] to bring down in the opinion of others, in self-respect, or in behavior: *Don't degrade yourself by arguing over money.*|*It was very degrading to be punished in front of the whole* *class.* **–degradation** /ˌdɛgrə'deɪʃən/ *n* [U]

de·gree /dɪ'griʸ/ *n* **1** [C] *tech* any of various measures: *Water freezes at 32 degrees* FAHRENHEIT *(32°F) or 0 degrees* CENTIGRADE *(0°C).|an angle of 90 degrees (90°)* **2** [C;U] a point on an imaginary line, which is used for measuring ability, progress, etc.: *The students have different degrees of ability.|To what degree can he be trusted?|He can be trusted to some/a certain degree.|He is getting better by degrees.* **3** [C] a title given by a university: *To do the job, you must have a degree in chemistry.*

de·hy·drate /diʸ'haɪdreʸt/ *v* **-drated, -drating** [T] to dry; remove all the water from: *to dehydrate milk to make milk powder* **–dehydrated** |diʸ'haɪdreʸtɪd| *adj* **–dehydration** /ˌdiʸhaɪ'dreʸʃən/ *n* [U]

de·i·fy /'diʸə,faɪ, 'deʸ-/ *v* **-fied, -fying** [T] *fml* to make a god of; take as an object of worship: *to deify trees and stones* **–deification** /ˌdiʸəfə'keʸʃən, ˌdeʸ-/ *n* [U]

deign /deʸn/ *v* [T +*to-v*] *derog* to lower oneself to do something or give something to people one considers unimportant: *Now that she is rich and famous, she doesn't deign to visit her former friends.* **–compare** CONDESCEND (1)

de·i·ty /'diʸətiʸ, 'deʸ-/ *n* **-ties** a god or goddess

dé·jà vu /ˌdeʸʒa 'vuʷ, -'vyuʷ/ *n* [U] *French* the feeling of remembering something that one is in fact experiencing for the first time

de·ject·ed /dɪ'dʒɛktɪd/ *adj* sad; having or showing low spirits: *a dejected look/person* **–dejectedly** *adv* **–dejection** /dɪ'dʒɛkʃən/ [U]

Del. *written abbrev. said as:* Delaware /'dɛləˌwɛər/ (a state in the US)

de·lay¹ /dɪ'leʸ/ *v* **-layed, -laying** **1** [T +*v-ing*] to do something later than planned; put off: *We decided to delay (going on) our vacation until next month.* **2** [I;T] to stop for a time, move slowly, or cause to be late: *What delayed you so long?*

delay² *n* **-lays** [C;U] the act of delaying or the state of being delayed: *Do it without (any) delay!|Delays of two hours or more were reported on the roads this morning.*

de·lec·ta·ble /dɪ'lɛktəbəl/ *adj apprec* very pleasing; delightful: *What a delectable meal!* **–delectably** *adv*

del·e·gate¹ /'dɛləgɪt, -ˌgeʸt/ *n* a person acting for one or more others, such as a representative to a meeting or an organization

del·e·gate² /'dɛləˌgeʸt/ *v* **-gated, -gating** [T *to*] to give (part or all of one's power, rights, etc.) for a certain time; appoint as one's DELEGATE¹: *I have delegated my command to Captain Roberts.|I have delegated her to serve in my place.*

del·e·ga·tion /ˌdɛlə'geʸʃən/ *n* **1** [U] the act of delegating (DELEGATE²) or the state of being delegated **2** [C] a group of DELEGATES¹

de·lete /dɪ'liʸt/ *v* **-leted, -leting** [T *from*] to take out or cut out (esp. words): *If you delete 50 words, we can put the whole story on one page.|Delete his name from the list.* **–deletion** /dɪ'liʸʃən/ *n* [C;U]

del·i /'dɛliʸ/ *n* **-is** *AmE* **1** [C] *infml* for DELICATESSEN **2** [U]*infml* the food sold in a

DELICATESSEN: *You can get very good deli in New York.*

de·lib·er·ate¹ /dɪ'lɪbərɪt/ *adj* **1** intentional; on purpose: *The car crash wasn't an accident; it was a deliberate attempt to kill him!* **2** (of speech, thought, or movement) slow; unhurried: *He stood up in a deliberate way and left the room.* **–deliberately** *adv* **–deliberateness** *n* [U]

de·lib·er·ate² /dɪ'lɪbəˌreʸt/ *v* **-ated, -ating** [I;T *upon, about*] *fml* to consider carefully, often in formal meetings with other people: *The judges are deliberating (the question).|They are deliberating (upon/about) what to do.* **–deliberation** /dɪˌlɪbə'reʸʃən/ *n* [C;U]

del·i·ca·cy /'dɛlɪkəsiʸ/ *n* **-cies** **1** [U] the quality of being DELICATE **2** [C] something pleasing to eat that is considered rare or costly: *That food is a great delicacy.*

del·i·cate /'dɛlɪkɪt/ *adj* **1** finely made; needing careful handling; easily broken, hurt, or made ill: *The body is a delicate machine.|Be careful with those plates. They're very delicate.* **2** needing careful treatment or TACT; likely to go wrong at any moment: *a delicate affair/position/subject.* **3** pleasing but not strong and not easy to recognize: *a delicate taste/smell/color* **4** sensitive: *That delicate instrument can record even very slight changes.* **–delicately** *adv*

del·i·ca·tes·sen /ˌdɛlɪkə'tɛsən/ *also* **deli** *infml n* a shop that sells foods ready to be served or delicacies (DELICACY (2))

de·li·cious /dɪ'lɪʃəs/ *adj* pleasing to one of the body's senses, esp. those of taste or smell: *Dinner was delicious!* **–deliciously** *adv*

de·light¹ /dɪ'laɪt/ *v* [I;T] to cause great satisfaction, enjoyment, or joy: *a book that is certain to delight|He delighted them with his performance.*

delight in *sthg. v prep* [T +*v-ing*] to take or receive great pleasure in: *She delights in (looking at) pictures.*

delight² *n* [C;U] (something that gives) great pleasure or satisfaction; joy: *I read your new book with real delight.|the delights of Houston's night life*

de·light·ful /dɪ'laɪtfəl/ *adj* highly pleasing: *a delightful little house* **–delightfully** *adv*

de·lin·quen·cy /dɪ'lɪŋkwənsiʸ/ *n* [U] (a tendency towards) behavior, esp. of young people, that is not in accordance with accepted social standards or with the law; the state of being DELINQUENT

de·lin·quent /dɪ'lɪŋkwənt/ *adj* having broken a law, esp. one which is not very important; having a tendency to break the law or to do socially unacceptable things: *delinquent behavior*

de·lir·i·ous /dɪ'lɪəriʸəs| *adj* in an excited dreamy state, esp. caused by illness: *He was so ill he became delirious.* **–deliriously** *adv*: *(fig.) deliriously happy* **–delirium**

de·liv·er /dɪ'lɪvər/ *v* [T] **1** [*to*] (in business) to take things to people's houses or places of work: *Letters are delivered every day.|Yes, we deliver newspapers.* **2** [*up, to*] to give; produce; hand over: *to deliver results* **3** to help in the birth of: *The doctor delivered her baby.* **4** to say; read aloud: *He delivered his speech effectively.* **5** [*from*] *fml* to set free

de·liv·er·ance /dɪˈlɪvərəns/ *n* [U *from*] *fml* the act of saving from danger or freeing from bad conditions or the state of being saved from danger

de·liv·er·y /dɪˈlɪvəriʸ/ *n* -**ies** **1** [C;U *to*] the act of taking something to somebody, or the things taken: *The next mail delivery is at 2 o'clock.|the delivery of letters to your house* **2** [C] the birth of a child: *The mother/The child had an easy delivery.* **3** [C;U] the act or style of speaking in public or throwing a ball in a game: *a good/slow delivery*

de·liv·er·y·man /dɪˈlɪvəriʸˌmæn, -mən/ -**men** /ˌmen, mən/ *esp. AmE* a man who delivers goods to people who have bought or ordered them, esp. locally

del·ta /ˈdeltə/ *n* **1** the fourth letter of the Greek alphabet(Δ, δ) **2** an area of low land shaped like a (Δ) where a river divides into branches towards the sea: *the Nile Delta in Egypt*

de·lude /dɪˈluʷd/ *v* -**luded**, -**luding** [T *with*, *into*] to mislead the mind or judgment of; deceive; trick: *Don't delude yourself with false hopes.*

del·uge¹ /ˈdelyuʷdʒ/ *n fml* **1** a great flood: (fig.) *a deluge of questions* **2** a very heavy rain

deluge² *v* -**uged**, -**uging** [T *with*] *fml* to pour out a great flood of things over: *The President was deluged with questions/cries/shouts.*

de·lu·sion /dɪˈluʷʒən/ *n* **1** [U] the act of deluding or the state of being DELUDED **2** [C] a false belief, esp. if strongly held: *He is* **under the delusion** *that he is Napoleon.|to* **suffer** **from** **delusions** –see ILLUSION (USAGE)

de·lu·sive /dɪˈluʷsɪv/ also **delusory** /dɪˈluʷsəriʸ/– *adj* **1** likely to DELUDE: *a delusive act/person* **2** that is a DELUSION; misleading: *a delusive belief* –**delusively** *adv*

de luxe /dɪ ˈlʌks, -ˈlʊks/ *adj* of especially good quality: *The de luxe model costs a lot more.*

delve /delv/ *v* **delved**, **delving** [I *into*, *among*] to search deeply: *He delved into lots of old books for the facts.*

dem·a·gogue /ˈdeməˌgag, -ˌgɔg/ *n derog* a leader who tries to gain, or has gained, power by exciting popular feelings rather than by reasoned argument –**demagogic** /ˌdeməˈgagɪk,-ˈgadʒɪk/ *adj*

de·mand¹ /dɪˈmænd/ *n* **1** [C *for*] an act of demanding; claim: *The workers' demand for higher wages seems reasonable.|*(fig.)* This work makes great demands on my time.* **2** [U *for*] the desire of people for particular goods or services: *Is there much demand/a great demand for teachers in this town? |Oil is* **in** **great demand** *these days.*

demand² *v* [T +*to-v/*(*that*)] to claim as if by right; ask for (something) very strongly: *I demand my rights/an answer.|I demanded to know the truth.|They demanded that they get more money.* – see ask (USAGE)

de·mand·ing /dɪˈmændɪŋ/ *adj* needing a lot

of effort or attention: *a very demanding child/job*

de·mar·ca·tion /ˌdiʸmarˈkeʸʃən/ *n* [U] limitation; separation: *a row of trees on the line of demarcation between the two farms*

de·mean /dɪˈmiʸn/ *v* [T] *fml* to lower in the opinion of oneself or others: *demeaning behavior/work*

de·mean·or *AmE*‖**demeanour** *BrE* /dɪˈmiʸn ər/ *n fml* behavior towards others: *His demeanor has always been that of a perfect gentleman.*

de·ment·ed /dɪˈmentɪd/ *adj* mad; of unbalanced mind –**dementedly** *adv*

de·mise /dɪˈmaɪz/ *n* [U] *law or euph* death: *Upon his demise his house passed to his son.* (fig.) *That friendship was his demise.*

dem·o /ˈdemoʷ/ *n* -**os** *AmE infml* an object used to DEMONSTRATE (1) esp. a car, radio, or record

de·mo·bi·lize‖also -**lise** *BrE* /diʸˈmoʷbə,laɪz, dɪ-/ -**lized**, -**lizing** *n* [T] *fml* to send (members of an army or other armed group) back to peacetime life –see also MOBILIZE –**demobilization** /dɪˌmoʷbələˈzeʸʃən, ˌdiʸmoʷ-/ *n* [U]

de·moc·ra·cy /dɪˈmakrəsiʸ/ *n* -**cies** **1** [U] government by elected representatives of the people: *representative democracy* **2** [C] a country governed by its people or their representatives

dem·o·crat /ˈdeməˌkræt/ *n* a person who believes in or works for DEMOCRACY

Democrat² *n* a member or supporter of the DEMOCRATIC party of the US –compare REPUBLICAN

dem·o·crat·ic¹ /ˌdeməˈkrætɪk/ *adj* **1** of, related to, or favoring DEMOCRACY **2** favoring and practicing social equality –**democratically** *adv*

Democratic² *adj* related to, or favoring one of the two largest political parties in the US (the **Democratic** **party**) –compare REPUBLICAN

de·mol·ish /dɪˈmalɪʃ/ *v* [T] to destroy; tear down: *They're going to demolish that old building.|*(fig.)*We've demolished all her arguments.*

dem·o·li·tion /ˌdeməˈlɪʃən, ˌdiʸ-/ *n* [C;U] (an example) of the action of DEMOLISHING

de·mon /ˈdiʸmən/ *n* an evil spirit: (fig.) *That child is a little demon.* –**demonic** /dɪˈmanɪk/ *adj*

de·mon·stra·ble /dɪˈmanstrəbəl/ *adj fml* that can be DEMONSTRATEd (1,2): *a demonstrable truth* –**demonstrably** *adv*

dem·on·strate /ˈdemənˌstreʸt/ *v* -**strated**, -**strating** **1** [T +(*that*)] to show clearly: *Please demonstrate how the machine works.* **2** [T +(*that*)] to prove or make clear, esp. by reasoning or giving many examples: *Galileo demonstrated that objects of different weight fall at the same speed.* **3** [I *about*, *against*] to take part in a public show of strong feeling or opinion, often with marching, big signs, etc.: *They demonstrated against the new law.* –**demonstrator** *n*

dem·on·stra·tion /ˌdemənˈstreʸʃən/ *n* **1** [C;U +(*that*)] the act of demonstrating (DEMONSTRATE): *the demonstration of a machine* **2**

de·mon·stra·tion [C] a public show of strong feeling or opinion, often with marching, big signs, etc.: *a demonstration against the war*

de·mon·stra·tive /dɪ'manstrətɪv/ *adj* showing feelings openly: *a demonstrative person/action* –compare RESERVED (1)

de·mor·al·ize also **-ise** *BrE* /dɪ'mɔrə,laɪz, -'mar-/ *v* **-ized,-izing** to lessen or destroy the courage and self-respect of: *The army was demoralized by defeat.* –**demoralization** /dɪ,mɔrələ'zeʸʃən, -,mar-/ *n* [U]

de·mote /dɪ'moʷt/ *v* **-moted, -moting** [T] to lower (someone) in rank or position –opposite **promote** –**demotion** /dɪ'moʷʃən/ *n* [C;U]

de·mur /dɪ'mɜr/ *v* **-rr-** [I *at*] *fml* to show signs of being against something: *They demurred at the idea of going to war.*

de·mure /dɪ'myʊər/ *adj* quiet and serious: *a demure young child* –**demurely** *adv*

den /dɛn/ *n* **1** the home of a usu. large fierce wild animal, esp. a lion: (fig.) *a den of thieves* **2** *AmE* a usu. informal room in a house for studying, resting, watching TV, etc: *The children like to play in the den.*

de·ni·al /dɪ'naɪəl/ *n* **1** [U] the act of DENYING **2** [C] an example or statement of this: *a denial of justice|a public denial of the story in the newspaper*

den·im /'dɛnəm/ *n* [U] a strong cotton cloth used esp. for JEANS

den·ims /'dɛnəmz/ *n* [P] pants made of DENIM; JEANS –see PAIR (USAGE)

de·nom·i·na·tion /dɪ,namə'neʸʃən/ *n* **1** a religious group; a division of a religious body: *There are many denominations among Christians.* **2** a standard, esp. of value: *coins of many denominations* **3** *fml* a name, esp. a general name for a class or type

de·note /dɪ'noʷt/ *v* **-noted, -noting** to be a name or mark of; mean: *The sign "=" denotes that two things are equal.|A smile often denotes pleasure.*

de·nounce /dɪ'naʊns/ *v* **-nounced, -nouncing** [T *to, as*] to speak or write against: *They denounced him to the police as a criminal.|The policeman's action was denounced in the newspapers.*

dense /dɛns/ *adj* **1** closely packed or crowded together: *a dense crowd|dense traffic* **2** difficult to see through: *a dense mist|*(fig.) *a dense book* **3** stupid; difficult to reach with ideas: *a dense mind|He's dense.* –**densely** *adv* –**denseness** *n* [U] –**density** /'dɛnsətiʸ/ *n* [U]

dent /dɛnt/ *n* a small hollow place in the surface of something man-made, which is the result of a blow or pressure: *a dent in a car|*(fig.) *a dent in one's pride* –**dent** *v* [I;T]: *I'm sorry, but I've dented your car.|That table dents easily.* –compare BUMP

den·tal /'dɛntəl/ *adj* of or related to the teeth: *dental decay*

den·tist /'dɛntɪst/ also **dental surgeon** /,·· '··/ *fml*– *n* a person professionally trained to treat the teeth –**dentistry** /'dɛntəstriʸ/ *n* [U]

den·tures /'dɛntʃərz/ *n* **-nuded, -nuding** [P] →FALSE TEETH

de·nude /dɪ'nuʷd, dɪ'nyuʷd/ *v* **-nuded, -nuding** [T *of*] *fml* to remove the covering from:

Rain denuded the mountainside of soil.|(fig.) *denuded of self-respect*

de·nun·ci·a·tion /dɪ,nʌnsiʸ'eʸʃən/ *n* [C;U] (an example of) the act of denouncing (DENOUNCE)

de·ny /dɪ'naɪ/ *v* **-nied, -nying** [T] **1** [+*v-ing/*(that)] to declare untrue; refuse to accept as a fact: *Can you deny the truth of his statement?|He denied telling me/that he had told me.* –compare AFFIRM, ADMIT **2** to refuse to give or allow: *I was denied the chance of going to college.* **3** *fml* to disclaim connection with or responsibility for: *He has denied his country and his principles!*

de·o·dor·ant /diʸ'oʷdərənt/ *n* [C;U] a substance that removes unpleasant smells, esp. those of the human body

de·o·dor·ize ||also **-ise** *BrE* /diʸ'oʷdə,raɪz/ **-ized, -izing** *v* [T] to remove or prevent the unpleasant smell of

de·part /dɪ'part/ *v* [I *from*] *fml* to leave esp. at the start of a trip; go away: *The train departed from the station at 12 o'clock.* –compare ARRIVE (1)

depart from sthg. *v prep* [T] *fml* to turn or move away from: *I'd like to depart from the main subject of my speech for a few moments.*

de·part·ed /dɪ'partɪd/ *adj* gone for ever: *to remember one's departed youth/fame*

de·part·ment /dɪ'partmənt/ *n* any of the important divisions or branches of a government, business, etc.: *the history department of a university|the toy department of a large store* –**departmental** /,diʸpart'mɛntəl, dɪ,part-/ *adj*

department store /·'·· ,·/ *n* a large store divided into departments, in each of which a different type of goods is sold

de·par·ture /dɪ'partʃər/ *n* [C;U] the action of DEPARTING; an act of DEPARTing: *What is the departure time of the flight?|The new system is a departure from our usual methods.*

de·pend /dɪ'pɛnd/ *v* **That (all) depends/It all depends** I have certain doubts about that/it

depend on/upon sbdy./sthg. *v prep* [T] **1** to trust (usu. a person): *We're depending on you to finish the job by Friday.|I depended on the map, but it was wrong.* **2** to be supported by: *His family depends on him.* **3** to vary according to: *Whether the game will be played depends on the weather.*

de·pend·a·ble /dɪ'pɛndəbəl/ *adj* that can be depended on or trusted –**dependably** *adv* –**dependability** /dɪ,pɛndə'bɪlətiʸ/ *n* [U]

de·pend·ence /dɪ'pɛndəns/ *n* [U *on, upon*] **1** the quality or state of being controlled or materially supported by another person **2** the need to have something, esp. certain drugs regularly

de·pend·ent[1] /dɪ'pɛndənt/ *adj* [*on*] that depends on: *a dependent child|The success of the show is dependent on the weather.*

dependent[2] , **-ant** *n* a person who depends on another for food, clothing, money, etc.: *Please state on the document whether you have any dependents.*

de·pict /dɪ'pɪkt/ *v* [T] *fml* to represent by a picture or describe: *This painting depicts the*

Battle of Waterloo. –**depiction** /dɪ'pɪkʃən/ *n* [C;U]

de·plete /dɪ'pliʸt/ *v* **-pleted, -pleting** [T] *fml* to lessen greatly: *The cost of this trip has depleted our money.* –**depletion** /dɪ'pliʸʃən/ *n* [U]

de·plore /dɪ'plɔr, dɪ'ploʷr/ *v* **-plored, -ploring** [T] to be very sorry about: *One must deplore such (bad) behavior.* –**deplorable** *adj: a deplorable* (=very bad) *performance* –**deplorably** *adv: She behaved deplorably.*

de·ploy /dɪ'plɔɪ/ *v* **-ployed, -ploying** [T] to arrange for esp. military action: *We must deploy our forces correctly in order to win the battle.* –**deployment** *n* [C;U]

de·port /dɪ'pɔrt, dɪ'poʷrt/ *v* [T] to send (an undesirable foreigner) out of the country –**deportation** /ˌdiʸpɔr'teʸʃən, -poʷr-/ *n* [C;U]

de·port·ment /dɪ'pɔrtmənt, -'poʷrt-/ *n* [U] *fml* the way a person behaves *(AmE)*/stands and walks *(BrE)*

de·pose /dɪ'poʷz/ *v* **-posed, -posing** [T] to remove from a high official position, esp. from that of ruler: *The head of state was deposed by the army.*

de·pos·it¹ /dɪ'pazɪt/ *v* [T] **1** to put down (usu. in a stated place): *Where can I deposit this load of sand?|A fine soil was deposited by winds carrying desert dust.* **2** to place in a bank or SAFE²: *He's deposited a lot of money recently.* –compare WITHDRAW (2)

deposit² *n* **1** [C;U] something DEPOSITED: *There are rich deposits of gold in those hills.* **2** [C *usu. sing.*] a part payment of money, which is made so that the seller will not sell the goods to anyone else: *You have to pay a deposit to the hotel if you want them to keep a room free for you.*

de·pot /'diʸpoʷ/ *n* **1** *AmE* a usu. small railroad or bus station **2** a storehouse for goods **3** a place where soldiers' stores are kept, and where new soldiers are trained

de·prave /dɪ'preʸv/ *v* **-praved, -praving** [T] to make bad in character: *The judge described the murderer as a depraved person.* –**depravity** /dɪ'prævətiʸ/ *n* **-ties** [C;U]

de·pre·ci·ate /dɪ'priʸʃiʸ,eʸt/ *v* **-ated, -ating** [I] (esp. of money, property, possessions, etc.) to fall in value –opposite **appreciate** –**depreciation** /dɪ,priʸʃiʸ'eʸʃən/ *n* [U]

de·press /dɪ'prɛs/ *v* [T] **1** to sadden; discourage: *The bad news depressed me.* **2** to make less active or strong: *The threat of war has depressed business activity.* **3** *fml* to press down: *Depress this button in case of fire.* –**depressing** *adj* –**depressingly** *adv*

de·pressed /dɪ'prɛst/ *adj* **1** low in spirits; sad **2** suffering from low levels of business activity: *depressed areas of the country*

de·pres·sion /dɪ'prɛʃən/ *n* **1** [C;U] a feeling of sadness and hopelessness: *He's suffering from depression.* **2** [C] a period of reduced business activity and high unemployment: *the great depression of the 1930's* **3** [C] a part of a surface lower than the other parts: *The rain collected in depressions on the ground.*

de·prive sbdy. **of** sthg. /dɪ'praɪv/ *v prep* **-prived, -priving** [T] to take away from; prevent from using: *They deprived the criminal*

of his rights. –**deprivation** /ˌdɛprə'veʸʃən/ *n* [C;U]

de·prived /dɪ'praɪvd/ *adj* (esp. of people) lacking food, money, etc.; poor: *deprived children*

dept. *n written abbrev. said as:* DEPARTMENT

depth /dɛpθ/ *n* [C;U] **1** the state of being deep; distance from the surface or front to the bottom or back: *What is the depth of this lake?|a depth of 30 feet|*(fig.)*the depth of her feeling* –compare HEIGHT **2 in depth** done with great thoroughness: *a study in depth of the problems of unemployment|an in-depth study* **3 out of one's depth: a** in water that is deeper than one's height **b** beyond one's ability to understand: *I'm out of my depth in this argument.*

dep·u·ta·tion /ˌdɛpyə'teʸʃən/ *n* a group of people DEPUTED to do something: *The government agreed to receive a deputation from the UN.*

dep·u·tize ‖also **-tise** *BrE* /'dɛpyə,taɪz/ *v* **-tized, -tizing** [I *for*] to act as DEPUTY

dep·u·ty /'dɛpyətiʸ/ *n* **-ties** a person who has the power to act for another: *Jean will be my deputy while I am away.*

de·rail /dɪ'reʸl, diʸ-/ *v* [I;T] to (cause to) run off the railroad track: *a derailed train* –**derailment** *n* [C;U]

de·range /dɪ'reʸndʒ/ *v* **-ranged, -ranging** [T] to put (esp. the mind) into a state of disorder: *The poor woman's mind has been deranged for many years.|She is deranged.* –**derangement** *n* [U]

der·by /'dɑrbiʸ/ *AmE*‖**bowler** *BrE–* *n* **-bies** a man's round hard hat, usu. black: *English businessmen often wear derbies.*

der·e·lict¹ /'dɛrə,lɪkt/ *adj* left to decay: *a derelict old house too dangerous to live in*

derelict² *n* a person, esp. an alcoholic, who has no home or any lawful means of support: *Many derelicts in the city live on the streets.*

de·ride /dɪ'raɪd/ *v* **-rided, -riding** [T +*v-ing*] *fml* to laugh at or make fun of as of no value

de·ri·sion /dɪ'rɪʒən/ *n* [U] the act of deriding or the state of being derided (DERIDE): *Everyone held the old man in derision.* –**derisive** /dɪ'raɪsɪv/ *adj: derisive laughter* –**derisively** *adv*

de·ri·so·ry /dɪ'raɪsəriʸ/ *adj* deserving to be DERIDEd because useless, ineffective, or not enough: *a derisory offer of $10 for something worth $100* –**derisorily** *adv*

de·riv·a·tive /dɪ'rɪvətɪv/ *n, adj* (something) coming from something else: *French is a derivative of Latin.|a rather derivative* (=not original or new) *piece of music*

de·rive from /dɪ'raɪv/ *v prep* **-rived, -riving** [T] **1** (**derive** sthg. **from** sbdy./ sthg.) to obtain from: *He derives a lot of pleasure from meeting new people.* **2** (**derive from** sthg.) to come from: *The word "*DERIVE*" derives from Latin.* –**derivation** /ˌdɛrə'veʸʃən/ *n* [C;U]

der·ma·ti·tis /ˌdɑrmə'taɪtɪs/ *n* [U] a disease of the skin, marked by redness, swelling, and pain

de·rog·a·to·ry /dɪ'rɑgətɔriʸ -ˌtoʷriʸ/ *adj fml* showing or causing lack of respect: *derogatory remarks about the government*

der·rick /ˈdɛrɪk/ n a CRANE¹ (1) for lifting and moving heavy weights, for example into or out of a ship

de·scend /dɪˈsɛnd/ v [I;T] fml to come, fall, or sink from a higher to a lower level; go down: The sun descended behind the hills.|She descended the stairs. —opposite **ascend**

  descend on/upon sbdy./sthg. v prep [T] sthg. **1** (of a group of people) to attack: Thieves descended on the traveler. **2** to arrive suddenly at: The whole family descended on us at Christmas.

  descend to sthg. v prep [T +v-ing] to lower oneself to: He descended to cheating.

de·scend·ant /dɪˈsɛndənt/ n a person or animal that has another as grandfather or grandmother, great-grandfather, etc.:He is a descendant of Queen Victoria. —compare ANCESTOR —**descended (from)** adj: descended from George Washington

de·scent /dɪˈsɛnt/ n **1** [C;U] the act or fact of going or coming down: The road makes a sharp descent just past the lake.|his descent into a life of crime —opposite **ascent 2** [U] family origins: She is of German descent.

de·scribe /dɪˈskraɪb/ v -scribed, -scribing [T] to say what something is like; give a picture (of) in words: to describe a man/a place/an event|Try to describe exactly what happened.

de·scrip·tion /dɪˈskrɪpʃən/ n [C;U] (the act of making) a statement or account that describes: I recognized the man from the description in the newspaper.|her powers of description —**descriptive** adj: descriptive writing —**descriptively** adv

des·e·crate /ˈdɛsəˌkreɪt/ v -crated, -crating [T] to use (something holy, such as a church) for purposes which are not holy —**desecration** /ˌdɛsəˈkreɪʃən/ n [C;U]

des·ert¹ /ˈdɛzərt/ n a large sandy piece of land where there is very little rain and not many plants: the Sahara Desert|a hot desert wind

de·sert² /dɪˈzɜrt/ v **1** [T] to leave empty or leave completely: the silent deserted streets of the city at night|All my friends have deserted me! **2** [I;T] to leave (military service) without permission n [C;U]

de·sert·er /dɪˈzɜrtər/ n a person who leaves military service without permission

de·serve /dɪˈzɜrv/ v -served, -serving [T +to-v; not be +v-ing] to be worthy of; be fit for: You've been working all morning. You deserve a rest.|She deserved to win.

de·serv·ed·ly /dɪˈzɜrvɪdliʸ/ adv rightly: Rembrandt is a deservedly famous artist.

des·ic·cate /ˈdɛsəˌkeɪt/ v -cated, -cating [I;T] fml to (cause to) dry up

de·sign¹ /dɪˈzaɪn/ v **1** [I;T] to make a drawing or pattern of; to draw the plans for: Who designed the Sante Fe Opera House? **2** [T] to develop for a certain purpose or use: a book designed mainly for use in colleges|This weekend party was designed to bring the two musicians together. —**designer** n: She's a dress designer/a book designer.

design² n **1** [C] a plan **2** [C] a drawing or pattern showing how something is to be made **3** [U] the art of making such drawings

or patterns: She attended a school of dress design. **4** [C] a decorative pattern

des·ig·nate /ˈdɛzɪgˌneɪt/ v -nated, -nating [T] fml **1** to point out or call by a special name: These x-marks on the drawing designate all the entrances to the building. **2** [for] to appoint (for special work): I am designating you to act for me while I am away. —**designation** /ˌdɛzɪgˈneɪʃən/ n [C;U]

  designate sbdy./ sthg. **as** sthg. v prep [T] fml to name officially as: The school has been designated as the meeting place for the evening art club.|She has been designated the Secretary of Education.

de·signs /dɪˈzaɪnz/ n [P on, against] evil plans: They have designs on your money/your life.

de·sir·a·ble /dɪˈzaɪərəbəl/ adj worth having, doing, or desiring: a desirable job/house —opposite **undesirable** —**desirability** /dɪˌzaɪərəˈbɪlətiʸ/ n [U] —**desirably** /dɪˈzaɪərəbliʸ/ adv

de·sire¹ /dɪˈzaɪər/ v -sired, -siring [T] **1** [+to-v/(that)] fml to wish or want very much: The judge desires to see you.|The President desires that you (should) come at once.|She desires you to come at once. **2** to wish to have sexual relations with

desire² n [C;U] **1** [+to-v/ that] a strong wish: filled with a/ the desire to see her family again **2** [for] a strong wish for sexual relations with: Antony's desire for Cleopatra

USAGE You can have a **desire** for anything: his **desire** for success|She has expressed a **desire** to attend our next meeting. You have an **appetite** only for things of the body: The baby has a good/ healthy **appetite** (=likes eating); and a **craving** is a strong desire, esp. for things that are thought to be bad: I can't cure my **craving** for cigarettes. **Lust** is a very strong and usu. derog word: **lust** for power/ sex.

de·sir·ous /dɪˈzaɪərəs/ adj [F +that, of] fml feeling or having a desire: The President is strongly desirous that you should attend the meeting.

de·sist /dɪˈzɪst, dɪˈsɪst/ v [I from] fml to cease doing: The judge told the man to desist from threatening his wife.

desk /dɛsk/ n **1** a table, often with drawers, at which one reads, writes, or does business —see illustration on page 467 **2** a place where a RECEPTIONIST sits: an information desk|the front desk at a hotel

des·o·late /ˈdɛsəlɪt/ adj sad and lonely: a desolate house|She was desolate after the death of her husband. —**desolately** adv —**desolation** /ˌdɛsəˈleɪʃən/ n [U]

de·spair¹ /dɪˈspɛər/ v [I of] to lose all hope (of): Don't despair: things will get better soon!|Sometimes I despair of ever passing my driving test!

despair² n [U] complete loss of hope: Defeat after defeat filled us with despair.

des·patch /dɪˈspætʃ/ n, v [C;T to] →DISPATCH

des·per·ate /ˈdɛspərɪt/ adj **1** (of a person) ready for any wild act because of loss of hope: a desperate criminal|He was desperate for work to provide food for his children. **2**

(of an action) wild or dangerous; done as a last attempt: *a last desperate effort to win* **3** (of a state of affairs) very difficult and dangerous: *The country is in a desperate state.* –**desperately** *adv*

des·per·a·tion /ˌdɛspəˈreʸʃən/ *n* [U] the state of being DESPERATE (1,2): *He kicked at the locked door in desperation.*

de·spic·a·ble /dɪˈspɪkəbəl, ˈdɛspɪ-/ *adj* that deserves to be DESPISED: *a despicable act* –**despicably** *adv*: *You behaved despicably!*

de·spise /dɪˈspaɪz/ *v* -**spised**, -**spising** [T] to regard as worthless, low, bad, etc.; dislike very strongly

de·spite /dɪˈspaɪt/ *prep fml* in spite of: *He came to the meeting despite his illness.* (=even though he was ill) –see Study Notes on page 144

de·spond·ent /dɪˈspɑndənt/ *adj* feeling a complete loss of hope and courage: *despondent about his poor health* –**despondently** *adv* –**despondency** *n* [U]

des·pot /ˈdɛspət, -pɑt/ *n derog* a person who uses great power unjustly or cruelly: *That mother rules her family like a real despot.* –**despotic** /dɛˈspɑtɪk, dɪ-/ *adj* –**despotism** /ˈdɛspəˌtɪzəm/ *n* [U]

des·sert /dɪˈzɜrt/ *n* [C;U] sweet food served at the end of a meal: *We had cake for dessert.*

des·ti·na·tion /ˌdɛstəˈneʸʃən/ *n* a place which is set for the end of a journey or to which something is sent: *The package was sent to the wrong destination.*

des·tined /ˈdɛstnd/ *adj* [+*to-v/for*] intended for some special purpose; intended by fate: *He was destined by his parents for life in the army.|His work was destined never to succeed.*

des·ti·ny /ˈdɛstəniʸ/ *n* -**nies** [C;U] fate; that which must or had to happen: *It was the great woman's destiny to lead her country.*

des·ti·tute /ˈdɛstəˌtuʷt, -ˌtyuʷt/ *adj* **1** without food, clothing, shelter, etc., or money to buy them **2** [F *of*] *fml* completely without: *She was destitute of human feeling.* –**destitution** /ˌdɛstəˈtuʷʃən, -ˈtyuʷ-/ *n* [U]

de·stroy /dɪˈstrɔɪ/ *v* -**stroyed**, -**stroying** [T] to ruin; put an end to the existence of (something): *The fire destroyed most of the building.*|(fig.)*All hopes of a peaceful settlement were destroyed by his violent speech.*

de·stroy·er /dɪˈstrɔɪər/ *n* **1** a person who destroys **2** a small fast warship

de·struc·tion /dɪˈstrʌkʃən/ *n* [U] the act of destroying or state of being destroyed: *the destruction of the forest by fire|The enemy bombs caused death and destruction.* –see also CONSTRUCTION

de·struc·tive /dɪˈstrʌktɪv/ *adj* **1** causing destruction: *a destructive storm* **2** wanting or tending to destroy –**destructively** *adv* –**destructiveness** *n* [U]

des·ul·to·ry /ˈdɛsəlˌtoriʸ, -ˌtoʷriʸ/ *adj fml* passing from one thing to another without purpose: *a desultory conversation, not serious at all*

de·tach /dɪˈtætʃ/ *v* [T *from*] to separate esp. from a larger mass and usu. without violence or damage –**detachable** *adj*

de·tached /dɪˈtætʃt/ *adj* **1** separate; not connected **2** (of a house) not connected with any other building –compare SEMIDETACHED **3** (of a person or an opinion) not influenced by personal feelings

de·tach·ment /dɪˈtætʃmənt/ *n* **1** [U] the act of DETACHING **2** [U] the state of being DETACHED (3) **3** [C] a group, esp. of soldiers, sent from the main group on special duty

de·tail /dɪˈteʸl, ˈdiʸteʸl/ *n* [C;U] a small point or fact: *Everything in her story is correct (down) to the smallest detail.|He has a good eye for detail. He notices everything.* –**detailed** *adj*: *a detailed account*

de·tain /dɪˈteʸn/ *v* [T] *fml* to keep (a person) somewhere for a certain time: *The police have detained two men for questioning at the police station.*

de·tect /dɪˈtɛkt/ *v* [T] to find out; notice: *Small quantities of poison were detected in the dead man's stomach.* –**detection** /dɪˈtɛkʃən/ *n* [U]: *His crime escaped detection* (=was not found out) *for many years.*

de·tec·tive /dɪˈtɛktɪv/ *n* a policeman, etc., whose special job is to find out information about criminals

dé·tente /deʸˈtɑnt/ *n* [C;U] *French* (a state of) calmer political relations between countries

de·ten·tion /dɪˈtɛnʃən, -tʃən/ *n* [C;U] (an example of) the act of preventing a person from going away for a period of time

de·ter /dɪˈtɜr/ *v* -**rr**- [T *from*] *fml* to prevent from acting, esp. by the threat of something unpleasant; DISSUADE: *The storm clouds deterred them from going out.* –**deterrent** /dɪˈtɜrənt, -ˈtʌr-/ *adj,n*: *a deterrent weapon|a* NUCLEAR *deterrent*

de·ter·gent /dɪˈtɜrdʒənt/ *n* [C;U] a chemical product used for cleaning esp. clothing and dishes –compare SOAP

de·te·ri·o·rate /dɪˈtɪəriʸəˌreʸt/ *v* -**rated**, -**rating** [I] to become worse: *his deteriorating health* –compare IMPROVE –**deterioration** /dɪˌtɪəriʸəˈreʸʃən/ *n* [U]

de·ter·mi·na·tion /dɪˌtɜrməˈneʸʃən/ *n* [U] **1** firmness of intention; strong will (to succeed, etc.): *The police chief announced his determination to catch the killers.|She showed great determination by continuing to play after hurting her foot.* **2** the act of determining (DETERMINE)

de·ter·mine /dɪˈtɜrmɪn/ *v* -**mined**, -**mining** [T] *fml* **1** to decide; find out: *to determine the rights and wrongs of the case|to determine the position of a star* **2** [+*to-v/(that)*] to (cause to) form a firm intention in the mind: *He determined to go at once/that he would go at once.*

de·ter·mined /dɪˈtɜrmɪnd/ *adj* firm; having a strong will: *a very determined woman|I am determined to go.*

de·ter·min·er /dɪˈtɜrmənər/ *n tech* a word that limits the meaning of a noun and comes before adjectives that describe the same noun: *In the phrase "his new car," the word "his" is a determiner.*

de·test /dɪˈtɛst/ *v* [T +*v-ing*] to hate with very strong feeling: *I detest people who deceive and tell lies.|They detest war.* –**detestable** *adj*

–**detestably** *adv*

det·o·nate /'dɛtn,eᵧt/ *v* **-nated, -nating** [I;T] to (cause to) explode suddenly: *They detonated the bomb and destroyed the bridge.* –**detonation** /,dɛtn'eᵧʃən/ *n*

de·tour /'diᵧtʊər/ *n* a way around something: *They* **made a detour** *to avoid the center of the town.*

de·tract from sthg. /dɪ'trækt/ *v prep n* [T] to take something away from; make less the value of: *All the decoration detracts from the beauty of the building's shape.*

det·ri·ment /'dɛtrəmənt/ *n* [U] *fml* harm; damage: *He did hard work* **without detriment to** *his health.|He smoked a lot,* **to the detriment of** *his health.* –**detrimental** /,dɛtrə'mɛntəl/ *adj*

deuce /duᵂs, dyuᵂs/ *n* **1** [C] a card or a DICE¹ of the value of 2 **2** [U] (in tennis) 40–40; 40 points to each player

de·val·u·a·tion /diᵧ,vælyuᵂ'eᵧʃən/ *n* [U] a reduction in the value of something, esp. the exchange value of money

de·val·ue /diᵧ'vælyuᵂ/ *v* **-ued, -uing 1** [I;T] to reduce the exchange value of (money): *That country had to devalue (its money) last year.* –see also REVALUE **2** [T] to cause or be responsible for a reduction in the value of (e.g. a person or a work of art): *Let's not devalue his work unjustly.*

dev·as·tate /'dɛvə,steᵧt/ *v* **-stated, -stating** [T] to destroy completely; make impossible to live in –**devastation** /,dɛvə'steᵧʃən/ *n* [U]

dev·as·tat·ing /'dɛvə,steᵧtɪŋ/ *adj* **1** completely destructive: *a devastating storm|* (fig.) *a devastating argument* **2** *infml* very good, attractive, etc.: *You look devastating in that new dress.* –**devastatingly** *adv*

de·vel·op /dɪ'vɛləp/ *v* **1** [I;T *from, into*] to (cause to) grow, increase, or become more complete: *to develop from a seed into a plant|to develop a business/one's mind/an idea* **2** [I;T] to (cause to) begin to be seen, become active, or show signs: *Trouble is developing among the sailors.|He seems to be developing a cold.* **3** [T] to put (something) through various stages of production: *developing the natural resources of a country|These photographs should be good when they're developed.*

de·vel·op·er /dɪ'vɛləpər/ *n* a person who hopes to make a profit from developing land or buildings

de·vel·op·ment /dɪ'vɛləpmənt/ *n* **1** [U] the act or action of developing or the state of being developed: *the development of a seed into a plant/of his shop into a big business* **2** [C] a result of developing: *This new rose is a development from a very old kind of rose.|there's a new* **housing development** *just outside of town.* **3** [C] a new event or piece of news: *the latest developments in the murder trial|The use of computers in business is an important new development.*

de·vi·ant /'diᵧviᵧənt/ also **deviate** /'diᵧviᵧɪt/ *AmE adj,n* (a person or thing) that is different from an accepted standard: *sexually deviant behavior|Deviant children need help.*

de·vi·ate /'diᵧviᵧ,eᵧt/ *v* **-ated, -ating** [I *from*]

to be different or move away from an accepted standard

de·vi·a·tion /,diᵧviᵧ'eᵧʃən/ *n* [C;U] (a) noticeable difference from what is expected, esp. from accepted standards of behavior: *sexual deviation*

de·vice /dɪ'vaɪs/ *n* **1** an instrument, esp. one that is cleverly thought out: *a device for sharpening pencils* **2** a plan, esp. for a purpose not wholly good **3 leave someone to his own devices** to leave (some one) alone, without help

dev·il /'dɛvəl/ *n* **1** [*the* S] (*usu.cap.*) the most powerful evil spirit; Satan **2** [C] an evil spirit **3** *infml* (in expressions of strong feeling) fellow; man; boy: *He failed his examination, (the) poor devil.|That devil took my car without asking me!*

dev·il·ish /'dɛvəlɪʃ/ *adj* evil; like the devil –**devilishness** *n* [U]

de·vi·ous /'diᵧviᵧəs/ *adj* **1** not going in the straightest or most direct way: *a devious path* **2** *derog* not direct and probably not completely honest: *Mary is a devious person, and I don't trust her.* –**deviously** *adv* –**deviousness** *n* [U]

de·vise /dɪ'vaɪz/ *v* **-vised, -vising** [T] to plan or invent (esp. cleverly): *He devised a plan for winning the game.*

de·void /dɪ'vɔɪd/ *adj* [F *of*] *fml* empty (of); lacking (in): *He is devoid of human feeling!*

dev·o·lu·tion /,dɛvə'luᵂʃən/ [U] the giving of governmental or personal power to another person or group

devolve on/upon sbdy. /dɪ'valv/ *prep* [T] (of power, work, etc.) to be passed to (another person or group): *While he's ill, most of his work will devolve on me.*

de·vote sthg. **to** sbdy./sthg. /dɪ'voᵂt/ *v prep* **-voted, -voting** [T] to set apart for; give wholly or completely to: *He has devoted his life to helping blind people.*

de·vot·ed /dɪ'voᵂtɪd/ *adj* [*to*] loyal; caring a great deal; fond of: *a devoted father/friend|He is very devoted to his wife.|devoted to football/helping others* –**devotedly** *adv*

dev·o·tee /,dɛvə'tiᵧ, -'teᵧ, -voᵂ-/ *n* [*of*] a person who admires someone or something: *a devotee of Bach* (=Bach's music)

de·vo·tion /dɪ'voᵂʃən/ *n* [U *to*] **1** the act of devoting or the condition of being DEVOTED to: *The devotion of too much time to sports leaves too little time for studying.* **2** great fondness **3** attention to religion; DEVOUTness

de·vour /dɪ'vaʊər/ *v* [T] to eat up quickly and hungrily: *The lion devoured the deer.|*(fig.) *She devoured the new book.*

de·vout /dɪ'vaʊt/ *adj* **1** (of people) seriously concerned with religion: *a devout Hindu* **2** [A] felt very deeply: *a devout hope* –**devoutly** *adv* –**devoutness** *n* [U]

dew /duᵂ, dyuᵂ/ *n* [U] the small drops of water which form on cold surfaces during the night –sounds like **due**; compare RAIN

dew·y /'duᵂiᵧ, 'dyuᵂiᵧ/ *adj* wet (as if) with DEW: *dewy-eyed*

dex·ter·i·ty /dɛk'stɛrətiᵧ/ *n* [U] *apprec* the quality of cleverness and skill, esp. in the use of the hands: *the dexterity with which she*

plays the piano **–dexterous** /'dɛkstərəs/ also
dextrous /'dɛkstrəs/ *adj*

di·a·be·tes /ˌdaɪə'biˠtɪs, -'biˠt̬iˠz/ *n* [U] a
disease in which there is too much sugar in
the blood

di·a·bet·ic /ˌdaɪə'bɛt̬ɪk/ *adj,n* (typical of or
suitable for) a person suffering from
DIABETES

di·a·bol·i·cal /ˌdaɪə'bɑlɪkəl/ *adj derog* **1** of or
like the devil **2** *infml* very unpleasant and
annoying: *What a diabolical plan!*
–diabolically *adv*

di·ag·nose /'daɪəgˌnoˠs, ˌdaɪəg'noˠs/ *v*
-nosed, -nosing [T *as*] to discover the nature
of (a disease): *The doctor diagnosed my illness (as a rare bone disease).*

di·ag·no·sis /ˌdaɪəg'noˠsɪs/ *n* **-ses** /siˠz/ [C;U
of] (a statement which is the result of) diag-
nosing (DIAGNOSE): *The two doctors
made/gave different diagnoses of my disease.*
–compare PROGNOSIS **–diagnostic** /ˌdaɪəg
ˌnɑstɪk/ *adj*

di·ag·o·nal /daɪ'ægənəl/ *n,adj* **1** a straight
line joining two opposite corners of a square,
or other four-sided figure: *The two diagonals
of a square cross in the center.* **2** (any straight
line) which runs in a sloping direction: *a
cloth with a diagonal pattern* **–diagonally** *adv*

di·a·gram /'daɪəˌgræm/ *n* a plan or figure
drawn to explain an idea; drawing which
shows how something works **–diagrammatic**
/ˌdaɪəgrə'mæt̬ɪk/ *adj* **–diagrammatically** *adv*

di·al¹ /'daɪəl/ *n* **1** the face of an instrument,
such as a clock, which shows measurements
by means of a pointer and figures **2** the wheel
on a telephone with numbered holes for the
fingers, which is moved when one makes a
telephone call

dial² *v* **-l-** *AmE*‖**-ll-** *BrE* [I;T] to make a
telephone call (to): *How do I dial
Detroit?|Put in the money before dialing.*
–see TELEPHONE (USAGE)

di·a·lect /'daɪəˌlɛkt/ *n* [C;U] a variety of a
language, spoken in one part of a country,
which is different from other forms of the
same language: *the Southern dialect; a poem
written in Scottish dialect* **–dialectal**
/ˌdaɪə'lɛktəl/ *adj*

di·a·lec·tic /ˌdaɪə'lɛktɪk/ also **dialectics**
/ˌdaɪə'lɛktɪks/ *n* [U] *tech* the art or method
of arguing according to certain rules of question and answer **–dialectical** *adj*

di·a·logue also **dialog** *AmE*– /'daɪəˌlɔg, -ˌlɑg/
n [C;U] **1** (a) written conversation in a book
or play: *a short dialogue between Hamlet and
his mother* **2** (a) conversation which examines differences of opinion, e.g. between
leaders: *At last there can be (a) reasonable
dialogue between our governments.* –see also
MONOLOGUE

di·am·e·ter /daɪ'æmət̬ər/ *n* (the length of) a
straight line going from one side of a circle to
the other side, passing through the center of
the circle –compare RADIUS (1)

di·a·met·ri·cal·ly /ˌdaɪə'mɛtrɪkliˠ/ *adv* completely; directly: *I am diametrically opposed
to* (=I completely disagree with) *his ideas.*

di·a·mond /'daɪəmənd/ *n* **1** [C;U] a very
hard, valuable, precious stone, usu. color-

less, which is used esp. in jewelry: *a diamond
ring|a diamond mine* **2** [C] a figure with four
straight sides of equal length that stands on
one of its points **3** [C] a playing card with one
or more of these figures printed on it in red:
the 4 of diamonds –see CARDS (USAGE)

di·a·per /'daɪəpər/ *AmE*‖**nappy** *BrE*– *n* a
piece of soft cloth or paper fastened and
worn between the legs and around the waist
of a baby

di·a·phragm /'daɪəˌfræm/ *n* **1** the muscle that
separates the lungs from the stomach **2** any
thin plate or piece of stretched material
which is moved, e.g. by sound: *The
diaphragm of a telephone is moved by the
sound of the voice.* **3** a small round object
fitted inside a woman to prevent her becoming PREGNANT

di·ar·rhe·a, -rhoea /ˌdaɪə'riˠə/ *n* [U] an illness
in which the bowels are emptied too often
and into liquid form

di·a·ry /'daɪəriˠ/ *n* **-ries** (a book containing) a
daily record of the events in a person's life:
Mary keeps (=writes) *a diary.*

dice¹ /daɪs/ *n* **-dice 1** a small six-sided block of
wood, plastic, etc., with a different number
of spots from 1-6 on the various sides, used in
games of chance: *to throw the dice|a pair of
dice* **2** **no dice** *infml, esp. AmE* no use

dice² *v* **-diced, -dicing 1** [T] to cut (food) into
small square pieces: *The meat should be
finely diced.* **2** [I *for,with*] to play with DICE¹

dic·ey /'daɪsiˠ/ *adj* **-ier, -iest** *infml* risky and
uncertain

di·chot·o·my /daɪ'kɑt̬əmiˠ/ *n* **-mies** [*between*]
fml a division into two (esp. opposite) parts
or groups: *the dichotomy between good and
evil*

dic·tate /'dɪkteˠt, dɪk'teˠt/ *v* **-tated, -tating**
[I;T *to*] **1** to say (words) for someone else to
write down or for a machine to record: *She
was dictating (a letter) to her secretary.* **2** to
state (demands, conditions, etc.) with the
power to enforce: *We're now in a position to
dictate (our own demands) to our employers.*

dic·ta·tion /dɪk'teˠʃən/ *n* **1** [U] the act of dictating or writing down what is DICTATEd(1): *a
secretary taking dictation* **2** [C] something
dictated to test one's ability to hear and write
a language correctly: *The teacher gave us two
French dictations today.*

dic·ta·tor /'dɪkteˠt̬ər, dɪk'teˠt̬ər/ *n derog* a
ruler who has complete power over a country, esp. if he/she has gained the power by
force **–dictatorial** /ˌdɪktə'tɔriˠəl, -'toˠr-/ *adj*

dic·ta·tor·ship /dɪk'teˠt̬ərˌʃɪp, 'dɪkteˠt̬ər-/ *n
derog* **1** [C;U] (the period of) government by
a dictator **2** [C] a country ruled by a dictator

dic·tion /'dɪkʃən/ *n* [U] the way in which a
person pronounces words: *Actors need training in diction.*

dic·tion·ar·y /'dɪkʃəˌnɛriˠ/ *n* **-ies** a book that
gives a list of words in alphabetical order,
with their meanings in the same or another
language: *a German-English dictionary|a
science dictionary* (=a dictionary of scientific
words)

did /dɪd, d;*strong* dɪd/ *v past tense of* DO

di·dac·tic /daɪ'dæktɪk/ *adj fml* (of speech or

writing) meant to teach, esp. to teach a moral lesson

did·n't /'dɪdnt/ *short for;* did not: *You saw him, I didn't.*

die¹ /daɪ/ *v* **died, dying** /'daɪ-ɪŋ/ [I] **1** (of creatures and plants) to stop living: *She's very ill and I'm afraid she's dying.|He died in his sleep.*(=while he was sleeping)|*He died of a fever/in an accident/by drowning/from a wound.*|(fig.) *My love for you will never die.*|(fig.) *His secret died with him.* (=was lost when he died) **2 be dying for/to** *infml* to have a great wish for/to: *I'm dying for a cigarette.|We're dying to hear what happened.* –see DEAD (USAGE)

die away *v adv* [I] (esp. of sound, wind, light) to fade and become less and less and cease

die down *v adv* [I] to become less strong or violent: *The fire is dying down.|The excitement died down.*

die off *v adv* [I] to die one by one: *As she got older, her relatives all died off.*|(fig.) *Local industry is gradually dying off as more and more people leave the area.*

die out *v adv* [I] (of families, races, practices, and ideas) to disappear completely: *Many old customs are dying out.*

die² *n* a metal block used for shaping metal, plastic, etc.

die·sel en·gine /'diːyzəl ˌendʒən, -səl-/ also **diesel–** *n* a type of oil-burning engine often used for trucks, buses and trains –compare GASOLINE ENGINE

di·et¹ /'daɪət/ *n* **1** [C;U] the sort of food and drink usually taken (by a person or group): *Proper diet and exercise are both important for health.|They lived on a diet of potatoes.* **2** [C] a limited list of food and drink that one is allowed: *The doctor ordered him to* **go on a diet** *to lose weight.|I can't eat chocolate. I'm* **on a diet.**

diet² *v* [I] to live on a DIET¹ (2): *No sugar in my coffee, please; I'm dieting.*

dif·fer /'dɪfər/ *v* [I] **1** [*from*] to be unlike: *Nylon and silk differ.|Nylon differs from silk in/as to its origin and cost.* **2** [*with*] to have an opposite opinion; disagree: *The two brothers often differ.|He differed with his brother about/on/over a political question.*

dif·fer·ence /'dɪfərəns/ *n* **1** [C *between*] a way of being unlike: *There are many differences between living in a city and living in the country.* **2** [S;U *between, in, of, to*] (an) amount or manner in which things are unlike: *The difference between 5 and 11 is 6.|Speaking the language makes no/a lot of difference when you travel to another country.|It doesn't make much/any/the least difference to me what you do.|When you're learning to drive, having a good teacher* **makes all the difference. 3** [C] a slight disagreement: *They've* **settled their differences** *and are friends again.*

dif·fer·ent /'dɪfərənt/ *adj* **1** [*from, than, to*] unlike; not of the same kind: *Mary and Jane are quite different.|Mary is different from/than/to Jane.|You look different with your hair cut.* **2** [A] various; several; not the same one or ones: *We make this dress in*

(three/a lot of) *different colors.|This is a different car from the one 1 drove yesterday.* –**differently** *adv*

USAGE **1** Although **different than** (*AmE*) and **different to** (*BrE*) are commonly used, teachers prefer **different from. 2** Compare **different** and **various:** Both mean "not the same" but **various** means "several not the same": *The judges gave* **various** *reasons* (=a number of different reasons) *for the court's decision.|The two judges gave* **different** *reasons for the court's decision.* (=they did not each give the same reason) Unlike **various, different** can also be used with a singular noun, and it then means that the noun is compared with something else that may or may not be mentioned: *You look* **different** (*from before*) *with your hair cut.|They each wanted to see a* **different** *film* (from *each other*).

dif·fer·en·tial /ˌdɪfə'rɛnʃəl, -tʃəl/ *n* the amount of difference between things, esp. difference in wages between workers at different levels in the same industry

dif·fer·en·ti·ate /ˌdɪfə'rɛnʃiyˌeyt, -tʃiy-/ *v* **-ated, -ating** [I;T *from, between*] to see, express, or make a difference (between): *I can't differentiate (between) these two sounds.|This company does not differentiate between men and women.* (=employs both equally) –**differentiation** /ˌdɪfəˌrɛnʃiyˈeyʃən, -tʃiy-/ *n* [C;U]

dif·fi·cult /'dɪfɪˌkʌlt, -kəlt/ *adj* **1** not easy; taking time or effort to do, make, or understand: *English is difficult/a difficult language to learn.* **2** (of people) unfriendly and always arguing; not easily pleased: *a difficult child*

dif·fi·cul·ty /'dɪfɪˌkʌltiy, -kəl-/ *n* **-ties 1** [U *in*] the quality of being difficult; trouble: *She had/found great difficulty in understanding him.|He did it without much/any difficulty.* **2** [C] something difficult; a trouble: *He's having* FINANCIAL (=money) *difficulties.|a small difficulty*

dif·fi·dent /'dɪfədənt/ *adj* [*about*] having or showing a lack of belief in one's own powers or ability: *He is diffident about expressing his opinions.* –compare CONFIDENT –**diffidently** *adv* –**diffidence** *n* [U]

dif·fuse¹ /dɪ'fyuʷs/ *adj fml* **1** widely spread; DIFFUSED²: *Direct light is better for reading than diffuse light.|a diffuse population scattered around the island* **2** *derog* using too many words and not keeping to the point: *a diffuse speech/writer* –**diffusely** *adv* –**diffuseness** *n* [U]

dif·fuse² /dɪ'fyuʷz/ *v* **-fused, -fusing** [I;T] *fml* to (cause to) spread out freely in all directions: *to diffuse knowledge* –**diffusion** /dɪ'fyuʷʒən/ *n* [U *of*]

dig¹ /dɪg/ *v* **dug** /dʌg/, **digging** [I;T] **1** to break up and move (earth): *to dig the ground|The dog has been digging in that corner for an hour.* **2** to make (a hole) by taking away earth: *We'll have to dig under the river/through the mountain/into the hill to lay this pipe.|The prisoners escaped by digging an underground passage.* **3** *infml* to like or understand: *I just don't dig this kind of music.*

dig sthg. **into** sbdy./sthg. *v prep* [T] to push into: *Dig a fork into the meat to see if it's cooked.*

dig sthg.↔**out** *v adv* [T of] **1** to find by searching: *I dug out this old dress to give to my daughter.* **2** to get out by digging; free from being buried: *He had to dig the car out of the snow.*

dig sthg.↔**up** *v adv* [T] **1** to make a hole in by taking away earth, etc.: *They're digging up the road outside our house.* **2** to find or take out of the ground, by digging: *Father dug up an old coin in the garden.*|(fig.) *The newspapers have dug up that unpleasant old story.*

dig² *n infml* **1** something said to make (playful) fun of or annoy (someone): *That remark was a dig at me.*|*He got in several digs at the director during his speech.* **2** a quick push: *John's falling asleep; just give him a dig!*

di·gest¹ /daɪˈdʒɛst, dɪ-/ *v* **1** [I;T] to (cause to) be changed into a form that the body can use: *Mary can't digest fat.*|*Cheese doesn't digest easily.* **2** [T] to think over and arrange in the mind: *to digest the contents of a book* –**digestible** *adj* –**digestive** *adj* [A]

di·gest² /ˈdaɪdʒɛst/ *n* a short account (of a piece of writing) which gives the most important facts: *a monthly digest*

di·ges·tion /daɪˈdʒɛstʃən, dɪ-/ *n* [C;U] (a) power of DIGESTING¹ (1) food: *Too much rich food is bad for your digestion.*|*Digestion is more difficult for old people.* –compare INDIGESTION

dig·it /ˈdɪdʒɪt/ *n* **1** any of the numbers from 0 to 9: *The number 2001 contains four digits.* **2** *fml* a finger or toe –**digital** /ˈdɪdʒətl/ *adj* [A]: *A* **digital** **watch** *shows the time by electronically lit up numbers, e.g. 12:14. It doesn't have any hands.*

dig·ni·fied /ˈdɪɡnəˌfaɪd/ *adj* having or showing DIGNITY: *a dignified manner*|*a dignified old man* –opposite **undignified**

dig·ni·tar·y /ˈdɪɡnəˌtɛriˠ/ *n* **-ies** *fml* a person holding a high position: *Many of the local dignitaries attended the mayor's funeral.*

dig·ni·ty /ˈdɪɡnətiˠ/ *n* [U] **1** true worth and nobleness of character: *She always acted with great dignity.* **2** calm and formal behavior: *The dignity of the occasion was lost when he fell down the steps.*

di·gress /daɪˈɡrɛs, dɪ-/ *v* [I from] *fml* (of a writer or speaker) to stop what one is saying and begin to talk about something else: *I'll tell you a funny story, if I may digress (from my subject) for a moment.* –**digression** /daɪˈɡrɛʃən, dɪ-/ *n* [C;U]

digs /dɪɡz/ *n* [P] *BrE infml* lodgings: *When his family left the city, Tom moved into digs.*

dike, dyke /daɪk/ *n* **1** a thick bank or wall built to control water and prevent flooding –compare DAM¹ **2** a narrow passage dug to carry water away; ditch

di·lap·i·dat·ed /dəˈlæpəˌdeˠtɪd/ *adj* (of things) broken and old; falling to pieces: *a dilapidated old car/house* –**dilapidation** /dəˌlæpəˈdeˠʃən/ *n* [U]

di·late /daɪˈleˠt, ˈdaɪleˠt/ *v* **-lated, -lating** [I;T] to make or become wider or further open by stretching: *Her eyes dilated with terror.* –compare CONTRACT² (1) –**dilation** /daɪˈleˠʃən/ *n* [U]

di·lem·ma /dəˈlɛmə/ *n* a difficult choice to be made between two courses of action: *She was* **in a dilemma** *as to whether to stay in school or get a job.*

dil·i·gent /ˈdɪlɪdʒənt/ *adj* (of people and behavior) hardworking; showing steady effort: *Though he's not quick, he's a diligent worker and should do well on the job.* –**diligently** *adv* –**diligence** *n* [U]

di·lute /daɪˈluˠt, dɪ-/ *v* **-luted, -luting** [T with] to make (a liquid) weaker or thinner by mixing another liquid with it: *He diluted the paint with water.*|(fig.) *The effect of the speech was diluted by the speaker's nervousness.* –compare CONCENTRATED (1) –**dilute** *adj*: *dilute acid* –**dilution** /daɪˈluˠʃən, dɪ-/ *n*

dim¹ /dɪm/ *adj* **-mm-** **1** not bright; not clear: *The light is too dim for me to read easily.*|*the dim shape of an animal in the mist* **2** *infml* (of people) stupid –**dimly** *adv* –**dimness** *n* [U]

dim² *v* **-mm-** [I;T] to (cause to) become DIM¹ (1): *The lights in the theater began to dim.*

dime /daɪm/ *n* **1** a coin of the US and Canada, worth 10 cents or 1/10 of a dollar **2 a dime a dozen** *AmE infml* very common; not at all unusual or valuable: *Used cars are a dime a dozen in this town.*

di·men·sion /dɪˈmɛnʃən, -tʃən, daɪ-/ *n* **1** a measurement in any one direction: *Length is one dimension, and width is another.*|*Time is sometimes called the fourth dimension.*|(fig.) *There is another dimension to this problem which you haven't mentioned.* **2 -dimensional** having the stated number of DIMENSIONS: *A three-dimensional object has length, depth, and height.*

di·men·sions /dɪˈmɛnʃənz, -tʃənz, daɪ-/ *n* [P] (measurements of) size: *What are the dimensions of this room?* (=its height, length, and width)|*a box of large dimensions*|*The dimensions of this difficulty have only recently been recognized.*

dime store /ˈ· ·/ *n AmE* →FIVE AND TEN

di·min·ish /dɪˈmɪnɪʃ/ *v* [I;T] *fml* to (cause to) become or seem smaller: *His illness diminished his strength.*|*the government's diminishing popularity* –**diminution** /ˌdɪməˈnuˠʃən, -ˈnyuˠ-/ *n* [C;U]

di·min·u·tive /dɪˈmɪnyətɪv/ *n, adj fml* **1** (a) word formed by adding an ending that means) very small: *Susie is a diminutive for* **Susan.** **2** very small: *This store has a lot of diminutive cameras.*

dim·ple /ˈdɪmpəl/ *n apprec* a little hollow place on the skin, esp. one formed in the cheek when a person smiles

din /dɪn/ *n derog* a loud, continuous, confused, and unpleasant noise

dine /daɪn/ *v* **dined, dining** [I] *fml* to eat dinner: *I'm going to dine with Peter/at Peter's tonight.*

dine out *v adv* [I] *fml* to eat dinner in a restaurant –compare EAT **out**

din·er /ˈdaɪnər/ *n* **1** *AmE* a small restaurant

beside the road **2** *AmE* a car on a train where food is served **3** a person who DINES, esp. in a restaurant

ding·dong /ˈdɪŋdɒŋ, -dɑŋ/ *adv,adj,n* [A;S] (like) the noise made by a bell: *The bells rang dingdong all morning.*

din·ghy /ˈdɪŋɡiʸ, ˈdɪŋiʸ/ *n* **-ghies** a small open boat

din·gy /ˈdɪndʒiʸ/ *adj* **-gier, -giest** (of things and places) dirty and faded: *a dingy little room* **–dingily** *adv* **–dinginess** *n* [U]

dining room /ˈ·· ˌ·/ *n* a room where meals are eaten in a house, hotel, etc.

din·ky /ˈdɪŋkiʸ/ **-kier, -kiest** *adj AmE derog* small and unimportant: *a dinky little room|hotel*

din·ner /ˈdɪnər/ *n* **1** [C;U] the main meal of the day, eaten either at midday or in the evening: *I'm busy cooking dinner.|It's dinner time/time for dinner.|We're having fish for (our) dinner.* **2** [C] a formal occasion in the evening when this meal is eaten: *The company is giving/holding/having an important dinner.*

USAGE If **dinner** is at midday, the evening meal is called **supper.** If **dinner** is in the evening, the midday meal is called **lunch.**

dinner jack·et /ˈ·· ˌ··/ →TUXEDO *n*

di·no·saur /ˈdaɪnəˌsɔr/ *n* a very large long-tailed creature (REPTILE) that lived in very ancient times and no longer exists

di·o·cese /ˈdaɪəsɪs, -ˌsiʸs, -ˌsiʸz/ *n* (in some churches of the Christian religion) the area under the government of a BISHOP **–compare** SEE

dip¹ /dɪp/ *v* **-pp- 1** [T *in, into*] to put (something) in/into a liquid for a moment: *to dip one's spoon into the coffee* **2** [I;T] to (cause to) drop slightly: *The sun dipped below the western sea.|The road dips just around the corner.*

  dip into sthg. *v prep* [T] **1** to read or study for a short time: *I haven't really read that book; I've only dipped into it.* **2** to put one's hand into (a place) and take something out: *He **dipped into his pocket** and bought drinks for his friends.* **3** to use part of: *He had to dip into his savings to buy the new car.*

dip² *n* **1** a slope down; slight drop in height: *a dip in the road* **2** *infml* a quick swim in the sea, a lake, etc.

diph·the·ri·a /dɪfˈθɪəriʸə, dɪp-/ *n* [U] a serious infectious disease of the throat which makes breathing difficult

diph·thong /ˈdɪfθɒŋ, -θɑŋ, ˈdɪp-/ *n tech* a compound vowel made by pronouncing two vowels quickly one after the other: *The vowel sound in "my" is a diphthong.*

di·plo·ma /dɪˈploʷmə/ *n* an official paper showing that a person has successfully finished a course of study: *She has a diploma in engineering.|a high school/college diploma*

di·plo·ma·cy /dɪˈploʷməsiʸ/ *n* [U] **1** the art and practice of establishing and continuing relations between nations **2** skill at dealing with people and getting them to agree: *He needed all his diplomacy to settle their quarrel.*

dip·lo·mat /ˈdɪpləˌmæt/ *n* a person employed in DIPLOMACY (1)

dip·lo·mat·ic /ˌdɪpləˈmætɪk◂/ *adj* **1** [A *no comp.*] of or related to DIPLOMACY (1): *Joan joined the diplomatic service.* **2** skilled in dealing with people; possessing TACT: *Try to be diplomatic when you refuse her invitation so you won't cause bad feelings.* **–opposite undiplomatic** (for 2) **–diplomatically** *adv*

dire /daɪər/ *adj* **1** very great; terrible: *in dire need of food* **2** [A] causing great fear for the future: *a dire warning*

di·rect¹ /dəˈrɛkt, daɪ-/ *v* [T] **1** [*to*] to tell (someone) the way to a place: *I'm lost. Can you direct me to the station?* **2** to control and be in charge of (the way something is done): *He directed the building of the new bridge.|Who directed that movie on television last night?* **3** [+*to-v/that*] *fml* to order: *The policeman directed the crowd to move back.* **4** [*to, at, towards*] to turn or aim (attention, remarks, movement, etc.) in the stated direction: *This warning is directed at you.* **–see** LEAD (USAGE)

direct² *adj* **1** straight; going from one point to another without turning aside: *What's the most direct way to get downtown?|a direct flight from New York to Los Angeles* **2** [*no comp.*] leading from one thing to another without anything coming between: *He was asked to leave school as a direct result of his behavior.* (=and for no other reason) **3** (of people and behavior) honest and easily understood: *He gave a direct answer to my question.* **–opposite indirect 4** [A] exact: *He's the direct opposite of his brother.* **–directness** *n* [U]

direct³ *adv* in a straight line; without stopping or turning aside: *The next flight doesn't go direct to Rome. It goes by way of Paris.*

di·rec·tion /dəˈrɛkʃən, daɪ-/ *n* **1** [U] the action of DIRECTING¹ (2); control: *The singing group is **under the direction** of Mr Blair.* **2** [C;U] the course on which a person or thing moves or is aimed: *He drove away **in the direction of** (=towards) Boston.|She has a good/bad sense of direction and never/always gets lost.* **3** [C] the point towards which a person or thing faces: *What direction does this house face?* **4** [C *usu. pl.*] a set of instructions on what to do or how to get somewhere: *He gave me directions to the station.|Follow the directions on the medicine bottle.*

di·rec·tive /dəˈrɛktɪv, daɪ-/ *n fml* an official order

di·rect·ly /dəˈrɛktliʸ, daɪ-/ *adv* **1** in a direct manner: *He lives directly opposite the church.|She answered me very directly and openly.* **–opposite indirectly 2** at once; very soon: (*infml*) *He should be here directly.*

di·rec·tor /dəˈrɛktər, daɪ-/ *n* **1** a person who directs an organization or company **2** a person who directs a movie or a play, instructing the actors, cameramen, etc. **–compare** PRODUCER

di·rec·to·ry /dəˈrɛktəriʸ, daɪ-/ *n* **-ries** a book or list of names, facts, etc., usu. arranged in alphabetical order: *The telephone directory* *gives people's names, addresses, and telephone numbers.* –see TELEPHONE (USAGE)

dirge /dɜrdʒ/ *n* a slow sad song sung over a dead person

dirt /dɜrt/ *n* [U] **1** unclean matter, esp. in the wrong place: *Wash the dirt off the floor/off your hands.|The floor is covered in/with dirt.* **2** soil; loose earth: *The children were outside playing happily in the dirt.* **3** impolite talk or writing about sex: *The newspaper was full of dirt about the senator.* **4 treat someone like dirt** to treat someone as though he/she were worthless

dirt farm·er /'· ,··/ *n AmE* a farmer who earns his living by farming his own land, esp. without hired help

dirt road /ˌ· '·/ *n AmE* a road of hard earth: *These dirt roads can be dangerous in the rain.*

dirt·y¹ /'dɜrtiʸ/ *adj* **-ier, -iest 1** not clean: *dirty hands|This dress is getting dirty. It needs to be washed.|Repairing cars is a dirty job.* **2** (of thoughts or words) concerned with sex in an impolite way: *They sat drinking and telling dirty stories.* **3 dirty trick** a mean trick **4** (**give someone**) **a dirty look** *infml* (to give someone) a look of great disapproval –**dirtily** *adv*

dirty² *v* **-ied, -ying** [I;T] to (cause to) become dirty: *Don't dirty the house.|White shoes dirty very quickly.*

dis·a·bil·i·ty /ˌdɪsəˈbɪlətiʸ/ *n* **-ties 1** [U] the state of being DISABLED **2** [C] something that DISABLES: *He gets money (a* **disability allowance***) from the government because of his disabilities.*

dis·a·ble /dɪsˈeʸbəl/ *v* **-bled, -bling** [T *from*] to make (a person) unable to do something, esp. to use his body properly: *He was disabled in the war; he lost his left arm.* –**disablement** *n* [C;U]: *to suffer from (a) disablement*

dis·a·bled /dɪsˈeʸbəld/ *n* [*the* P] DISABLED people: *The disabled will receive more money.*

dis·ad·van·tage /ˌdɪsədˈvæntɪdʒ/ *n* an unfavorable condition or position; anything which makes one less successful than other people: *His bad health is a great disadvantage to him.|If you don't speak good English, you'll be* **at a big disadvantage** *when you try to get a job.* –opposite **advantage** –**disadvantageous** /ˌdɪsædvænˈteʸdʒəs, -vən-, dɪsˌæd-/ *adj* [*to*]

dis·a·gree /ˌdɪsəˈgriʸ/ *v* **-greed, -greeing** [I *with*] to have or show different opinions: *I often disagree with him (about/over/as to what we ought to do).|These two reports of the accident disagree.* –opposite **agree**

disagree with sbdy. *v prep* [T *no pass.*] (of food or weather) to have a bad effect on; make ill: *Coffee always disagrees with me.* –opposite **agree with**

dis·a·gree·a·ble /ˌdɪsəˈgriʸəbəl/ *adj* unpleasant; not to one's liking: *a disagreeable job/person* –opposite **agreeable** –**disagreeably** *adv*

dis·a·gree·ment /ˌdɪsəˈgriʸmənt/ *n* [C;U] the fact or a case of DISAGREEing: *serious disagreement between the two political*

parties|The two parties are **in disagreement** *with each other on this question.|We have been having a few disagreements lately.*

dis·al·low /ˌdɪsəˈlaʊ/ *v* [T] *fml* to refuse officially to recognize or allow: *to disallow a claim* –opposite **allow**

dis·ap·pear /ˌdɪsəˈpɪər/ *v* [I] **1** to go out of sight: *The sun disappeared behind a cloud.* **2** to cease to exist; become lost: *These beautiful birds are fast disappearing.|My keys have disappeared off/from the table.* –opposite **appear** –**disappearance** /ˌdɪsəˈpɪərəns/ *n* [C;U]: *Her disappearance caused a lot of trouble.*

dis·ap·point /ˌdɪsəˈpɔɪnt/ *v* [T] to fail to fulfill the hopes of (a person): *I'm sorry to disappoint you, but I can't come after all.*

dis·ap·point·ed /ˌdɪsəˈpɔɪntɪd/ *adj* [*about, at, in, with*] unhappy at not seeing hopes come true: *Are you very disappointed about/at losing the race?|My parents will be disappointed in/with me if I fail the examination.* –**disappointedly** *adv*

dis·ap·point·ing /ˌdɪsəˈpɔɪntɪŋ/ *adj* causing one to be unhappy at not seeing hopes come true: *Her acting was disappointing; I hoped she would do better.|disappointing news* –**disappointingly** *adv*

dis·ap·point·ment /ˌdɪsəˈpɔɪntmənt/ *n* **1** [U] the state of being disappointed: **To his** *great* **disappointment,** *she wasn't on the train.* **2** [C] someone or something disappointing: *Our vacation has been a disappointment to us; it rained every day.*

dis·ap·prov·al /ˌdɪsəˈpruʷvəl/ *n* [U] the state of disapproving: *They showed their disapproval by not buying the product.|She shook her head* **in disapproval.** (=as a sign of disapproval) –opposite **approval**

dis·ap·prove /ˌdɪsəˈpruʷv/ *v* **-proved, -proving** [I *of*] to have a bad opinion (of): *We strongly disapprove of the* **company's new policy.** –opposite **approve** –**disapprovingly** *adv* –opposite **approvingly**

dis·arm /dɪsˈɑrm/ *v* **1** [T] to take the weapons away from: *The police disarmed the criminal.* **2** [I] (esp. of a country) to reduce the size and strength of armed forces –opposite **arm 3** [T] *apprec* to drive away anger from: *a disarming smile*

dis·ar·ma·ment /dɪsˈɑrməmənt/ *n* [U] the act or principle of DISARMing (2): *new plans for* **nuclear disarmament** –compare REARMAMENT

dis·ar·range /ˌdɪsəˈreʸndʒ/ *v* **-ranged, -ranging** [T] to upset the arrangement of –see also ARRANGE

dis·ar·ray /ˌdɪsəˈreʸ/ *n* [U] *fml* the state of disorder: *She rushed out of the burning house with her clothes* **in disarray.**

dis·as·so·ci·ate /ˌdɪsəˈsoʷʃiʸˌeʸt, -siʸ-/ *v* **-ated, -ating** [T *from*] →DISSOCIATE

dis·as·ter /dɪˈzæstər/ *n* [C;U] (a) sudden great misfortune: *The election results will bring political disaster.*

dis·as·trous /dɪˈzæstrəs/ *adj* very bad; causing a DISASTER: *a disastrous mistake|The results were disastrous.* –**disastrously** *adv*

dis·band /dɪsˈbænd/ *v* [I;T] to break up and

separate: *The club has disbanded.* –see also
BAND **together**

dis·be·lief /ˌdɪsbə'liʸf/ *n* [U] lack of belief: *He listened to my story with/in disbelief.*

dis·be·lieve /ˌdɪsbə'liʸv/ *v* **-lieved, -lieving** [T] to refuse to believe: *I was forced to disbelieve him.* –**disbeliever** *n*

USAGE **Disbelieve** is not often used in statements. People usually say: *I don't* **believe** *you.*/*I don't* **believe (in)** *that story.* **Disbelieve** is not used as the opposite of **believe** when it means **approve of.** People say: *I don't* **believe** *in letting children do whatever they like.*

disc /dɪsk/ *n* **1** →DISK **2** →RECORD² (4)

dis·card /dɪ'skɑrd/ *v* [T] to get rid of as useless: *to discard an old coat*/ *one's old friends*

dis·cern /dɪ'sɜrn, dɪ'zɜrn/ *v* [T +*that*; not *be* +*v-ing*] *fml* to see, notice, or understand, esp. with difficulty: *He was just able to discern the road in the dark.* –**discernible** *adj* –**discernibly** *adv*

dis·cern·ing /dɪ'sɜrnɪŋ, -'zɜr-/ *adj apprec* having or showing the power to decide and judge; having good taste: *a discerning man*/*mind* –**discernment** *n* [U]

dis·charge¹ /dɪs'tʃɑrdʒ, 'dɪstʃɑrdʒ/ *v* **-charged, -charging** *fml* **1** [T *from*] to allow or ask (a person) to go: *He was discharged from the army. The judge discharged the prisoner.*/*Although she was still ill, she discharged herself from hospital.* **2** [I;T] to send, pour, or let out (gas, liquid, etc.): *The chimney discharged smoke.* **3** [T] to perform (a duty or promise) **4** [T] to pay (a debt) in full **5** [I;T] to unload: *The ship discharged its cargo onto the dock.* **6** [T *at, into*] to fire or shoot (a gun, arrow, etc.)

dis·charge² /'dɪstʃɑrdʒ, dɪs'tʃɑrdʒ/ *n* [C;U] the action or result of discharging (DISCHARGE): *After my discharge from the army I went into business.*/*the discharge from the chimney*

dis·ci·ple /dɪ'saɪpəl/ *n* a follower of any great teacher (esp. religious), esp. one of the first followers of Christ

dis·ci·pli·nar·i·an /ˌdɪsəplə'nɛəriʸən/ *n* a person who can make people obey orders: *He's a good teacher, but he's not much of a disciplinarian.*

dis·ci·pline¹ /'dɪsəplɪn/ *n* [U] **1** training of the mind and body to produce obedience and self-control: *school/military discipline* **2** control gained as a result of this training: *The teacher can't keep discipline in her classroom.* **3** punishment: *That child needs discipline.* –**disciplinary** /'dɪsəplə,nɛriʸ/ *adj*

discipline² *v* **-plined, -plining** [T] **1** to provide DISCIPLINE¹ (1) for; train: *You must learn to discipline yourself.* **2** to punish: *She never disciplines her children and they are uncontrollable.*

disc jock·ey /'· ˌ··/ *n* →DISK JOCKEY

dis·claim /dɪs'kleʸm/ *v* [T +*v-ing*] to say that one does not own or does not claim; DENY: *He disclaimed all responsibility for the accident.*

dis·close /dɪs'kloʷz/ *v* **-closed, -closing** [T] **1** [+ *that*] to make known: *He disclosed that he had been in prison.* **2** to show by uncovering

dis·clo·sure /dɪs'kloʷʒər/ *n* [C;U] the act or result of disclosing (DISCLOSE (1)): *She made several surprising disclosures about her past life.*

dis·co /'dɪskoʷ/ *infml* **-cos** for DISCOTHEQUE

dis·col·or *AmE*‖**discolour** *BrE* /dɪs'kʌlər/ *v* [I;T] to (cause to) change color for the worse: *his discolored teeth* –**discoloration** /dɪsˌkʌlə'reʸʃən/ *n* [C;U]

dis·com·bob·u·late /ˌdɪskəm'bɑbyə,leʸt/ *v* **-lated, -lating** [T] *AmE infml* to confuse

dis·com·fort /dɪs'kʌmfərt/ *n* **1** [U] lack of comfort: *Your injury isn't serious, but it may cause some discomfort.*/*The presence of his former wife at the party caused him a lot of discomfort.* **2** [C] something that makes one uncomfortable: *the discomforts of travel*

dis·con·cert /ˌdɪskən'sɜrt/ *v* [T] to cause (someone) to feel doubt and anxiety: *She was disconcerted to see that she was being watched.*/*a disconcerting remark* –**disconcertingly** *adv*

dis·con·nect /ˌdɪskə'nɛkt/ *v* [T *from*] to undo the connection of: *They disconnected the telephone because I didn't pay the bill.* –**opposite connect** –**disconnection** /ˌdɪskə'nɛkʃən/ *n* [C;U]

dis·con·nect·ed /ˌdɪskə'nɛktɪd/ *adj* (of thoughts and ideas) badly connected; not well planned: *a few disconnected remarks*

dis·con·so·late /dɪs'kɑnsəlɪt/ *adj* [*about, at*] *fml* hopelessly sad, esp. at the loss of something: *The children were disconsolate about/at the death of their cat.* –**disconsolately** *adv*

dis·con·tent /ˌdɪskən'tɛnt/ also **discontentment** /-mənt/ *n* [U *with*] lack of contentment; dissatisfaction –**opposite content(ment)** –**discontented** *adj* –**discontentedly** *adv*

dis·con·tin·ue /ˌdɪskən'tɪnyuʷ/ *v* **-ued, -uing** [I;T +*v-ing*] *fml* to stop or end: *He will discontinue (teaching) his class after the summer.* –see also CONTINUE

dis·cord /'dɪskɔrd/ *n* [C;U] **1** *fml* (a case of) disagreement between people: *A good deal of discord has arisen over this question.* –see also CONCORD **2** (a) lack of agreement heard when sounds are made or notes played which do not sound good together –compare HARMONY –**discordant** /dɪs'kɔrdnt/ *adj: discordant opinions/music*

dis·co·theque /'dɪskəˌtɛk, ˌdɪskə'tɛk/ also **disco** *infml*– *n* a club where young people dance to recorded popular music

dis·count¹ /'dɪskaʊnt/ *n* a reduction made in the cost of buying goods in a shop: *a discount of 10 per cent* –compare REBATE

dis·count² /'dɪskaʊnt/ *v* [T] to reduce the price of goods

dis·count³ /dɪs'kaʊnt/ *v* [T] to pay little attention to; believe (a story or piece of news) to be not completely true: *Much of what he says must be discounted; he imagines things.*

dis·cour·age /dɪ'skɜrɪdʒ, -'skʌr-/ *v* **-aged, -aging** [T] **1** to take away courage and spirit from: *If you fail your driving test first time, don't let it discourage you/don't be discouraged.* **2** [+ *v-ing/from*] to try to prevent (an action, or someone from doing something) esp. by showing disfavor: *We discourage smoking in this school.*|*His mother discouraged him from joining the navy.* −opposite **encourage** −**discouragingly** *adv* −**discouragement** *n* [C;U]

dis·course /'dɪskɔrs, -koʷrs/ *n* [C;U *on, upon*] *fml* (a) serious conversation or speech

dis·cour·te·ous /dɪs'kɜrtiʲəs/ *adj fml* (of people or their behavior) not polite −opposite **courteous** −**discourteously** *adv* −**discourtesy** /dɪs'kɜrtəsiʲ/ −**sies** *n* [C;U]

dis·cov·er /dɪ'skʌvər/ *v* [T] **1** to find (something existing but not known before): *Columbus discovered America in 1492.* −compare INVENT **2** [+*to-v/that*] to find out (a fact, or the answer to a question): *Did you ever discover who sent you the flowers?*|*Scientists have discovered that this disease is carried by rats.* −**discoverer** *n*

dis·cov·er·y /dɪ'skʌvəriʲ/ *n* −**ies 1** [U] the event of discovering: *The discovery of oil on their land made the family rich.* **2** [C] something discovered: *to make an important scientific discovery.*

dis·cred·it /dɪs'krɛdɪt/ *v* [T] to cause people to lack faith in or respect for; stop people believing in: *The idea that the sun goes around the earth has long been discredited.*|*Much of his work has been discredited because we now know that he used false information.* −see also CREDIT² (2) −**discredit** *n* [U]

dis·cred·it·a·ble /dɪs'krɛdɪtəbəl/ *adj* (of behavior) shameful −opposite **creditable**

dis·creet /dɪ'skriʲt/ *adj* (of people, their behavior, or speech) careful and polite; showing good sense and judgment: *a discreet silence* −opposite **indiscreet** −**discreetly** *adv*

dis·crep·an·cy /dɪ'skrɛpənsiʲ/ *n* −**cies** [C;U between] difference; lack of agreement: *You said you paid $5 and the bill says $3. How do you explain the discrepancy?*

dis·cre·tion /dɪ'skrɛʃən/ *n* [U] **1** the quality of being DISCREET −opposite **indiscretion 2** the ability to decide what is most suitable to be done: *I won't tell you what time to leave. You're old enough to use your own discretion.*|*The hours of the meetings will be fixed at the chairman's discretion.* (=according to the chairman's decision)

dis·crim·i·nate /dɪ'skrɪmə,neʲt/ *v* −**nated, -nating** [I] **1** [*between*] to see or make a difference (between two or more things or people): *You must try to discriminate between facts and opinions.* **2** [*against/in favor of*] *usu. derog.* to treat (a person or group) as worse/better than others: *The government's policy discriminates against lower-paid workers.*

dis·crim·i·na·tion /dɪ,skrɪmə'neʲʃən/ *n* [U] **1** [*against*] *often derog* treating different things or people in different ways: *Pay us all the same thing! There should be no discrimination.* **2** *apprec* ability to choose the best by seeing small differences −**discriminating** /dɪ'skrɪmə,neʲtɪŋ/ *adj*

dis·cur·sive /dɪ'skɜrsɪv/ *adj fml* (of a person, words, or writing) passing from one subject

or idea to another in an informal way, without any clear plan: *to write in a discursive style* −**discursively** *adv*

dis·cus /'dɪskəs/ *n* **discuses** a heavy plate of wood, metal, or stone, which is thrown as far as possible, as a sport

dis·cuss /dɪ'skʌs/ *v* [T *with*] to talk about (with someone) from several points of view, esp. formally: *We discussed what to do and where we should go.*|*The committee discussed the plans for the new school.*

dis·cus·sion /dɪ'skʌʃən/ *n* [C;U] a case or the action of DISCUSSING: *to have/hold a discussion about/as to future plans*|*After much discussion the matter was settled.*|*Education is under discussion today.*

dis·dain¹ /dɪ'sdeʲn, dɪ'steʲn/ *n* [U] *fml* lack of respect; the feeling that someone or something is low and worthless −compare CONTEMPT, SCORN¹ −**disdainful** /dɪs'deʲnfəl, dɪ'steʲn-/ *adj* [*of, towards*] −**disdainfully** *adv*

disdain² *v* [T *not be* +*v-ing*] *fml* **1** to regard with DISDAIN: *Why do you disdain my offer of friendship?* −compare DESPISE **2** [+*to-v/v-ing; no pass.*] to refuse (to do an action) because of DISDAIN: *She disdained to answer/answering his rude remarks.*

dis·ease /dɪ'ziʲz/ *n* [C;U] (an) illness or disorder caused by infection or unnatural growth, not by an accident: *to catch/die of/suffer from/cure a disease*|*plant disease*|(fig.) *disease of the mind/of society* −**diseased** *adj*: *a diseased bone/plant*

USAGE 1 Though **illness** and **disease** are often used alike, **illness** is really a state, or length of time, of being unwell, which may be caused by a **disease**. **Diseases** can be caught and passed on if they are infectious or CONTAGIOUS, and **diseases** are the subjects of medical study: *Several children are away from school because of **illness**.*|*a rare heart disease.* **2** A person who has a **disease** is **ill** or (esp. *AmE*) **sick**. To be or feel **sick** also means to VOMIT or feel that one is going to vomit.

dis·em·bark /,dɪsɪm'bark/ *v* [I;T *from*] to (cause to) go on shore from a ship −opposite **embark** −**disembarkation** /,dɪsɛmbar'keʲʃən/ *n* [U]

dis·em·bod·ied /,dɪsɪm'badiʲd/ *adj* [A *no comp.*] existing as if without a body: *Disembodied voices could be heard in the darkness.*

dis·en·chant·ed /,dɪsɪn'tʃæntɪd/ *adj* (of a person) having lost one's belief (in the value of something): *disenchanted with my job* −**disenchantment** *n* [U]

dis·en·gage /,dɪsɪn'geʲdʒ/ *v* −**gaged, -gaging** [I;T *from*] *fml* **1 a** (esp. of parts of a machine) to come loose and separate **b** to loosen and separate (esp. parts of a machine): *Disengage the GEARS when you park the car.* **2** (of soldiers, ships, etc.) to stop fighting −opposite **engage**

dis·en·tan·gle /,dɪsɪn'tæŋgəl/ *v* −**gled, -gling** [I;T *from*] to make or become straight and free from knots: (fig.) *How can I disentangle the truth from all these lies?* −opposite **entangle** −**disentanglement** *n* [U]

dis·fa·vor *AmE*‖**disfavour** *BrE* /dɪs'feʲvər/ *n*

[U] *fml* **1** dislike; disapproval: *Mary seems to look upon/regard/*VIEW *John with disfavor.* **2** the state of being disliked: *John seems to be/have* **fallen into disfavor** *(with Judy).* –opposite **favor**

dis·fig·ure /dɪsˈfɪgyər/ *v* **-ured, -uring** [T] to spoil the beauty of: *The disease left his face disfigured.* –**disfigurement** *n* [C;U]

dis·grace[1] /dɪsˈgreɪs, dɪˈskreɪs/ *v* **-graced, -gracing** [T] **1** to be a DISGRACE[2] to: *He disgraced himself last night by drinking too much and starting a fight.* **2** to put (a public person) out of favor with DISGRACE[2]: *The dishonest congressman was publicly disgraced.*

disgrace[2] *n* [S;U *to*] (a cause of) shame or loss of honor and respect: *Being poor is no disgrace.|Harry is* **in disgrace** (=regarded with disapproval) *because of his behavior.|Doctors like that are a disgrace to our hospitals.* –**disgraceful** /dɪsˈgreɪsfəl, dɪˈskreɪs-/ –**disgracefully** *adv*

dis·grun·tled /dɪsˈgrʌntəld, dɪˈskrʌn-/ *adj* [*at,with*] annoyed and disappointed

dis·guise[1] /dɪsˈgaɪz, dɪˈskaɪz/ *v* **-guised, -guising** [T] **1** [*as*] to change the usual appearance, etc. of, so as to hide the truth: *She disguised herself as a man.* **2** to hide (the real state of things): *It is impossible to disguise the fact that business is bad.*

disguise[2] *n* **1** [C] something that is worn to hide who one really is: *Nobody saw through his disguise.*(=nobody recognized him) **2** [U] the state of being DISGUISED[1]: *He went to the party* **in disguise.**

dis·gust[1] /dɪsˈgʌst, dɪˈskʌst/ *n* [U *at*] strong feeling of dislike: *The food/The smell/His behavior filled her with disgust.*

disgust[2] *v* [T *at, with*] to cause a feeling of DISGUST[1] in: *We're all disgusted at the way his wife has treated him.|What a disgusting smell!* –compare REVOLT[1]

dish[1] /dɪʃ/ *n* **1** a large flat (often round or OVAL) vessel for holding or serving food: *A meat dish is a dish for meat; a wooden dish is a dish made of wood.* **2** (an amount of) cooked food of one kind: *Baked apples are his favorite dish.*

dish[2] *v* →DISH OUT; DISH UP

dis·heart·en /dɪsˈhɑrtn/ *n* [T] to cause to lose hope; discourage: *He's easily disheartened by difficulties.* –opposite **hearten**

dish·es /ˈdɪʃɪz/ *n* [P] all the dishes, plates, cups, knives, forks, etc., used for a meal: *Let's wash/do the dishes.*

di·shev·eled *AmE*‖**dishevelled** *BrE* /dɪˈʃɛvəld/ *adj* (of a person or his/her appearance) untidy

dis·hon·est /dɪsˈɑnɪst/ *adj* not honest; deceiving: *a dishonest politician|to get money by dishonest means* –**dishonestly** *adv* –**dishonesty** *n* [U]

dis·hon·or *AmE*‖**dishonour** *BrE* /dɪsˈɑnər/ *n* [S;U *to*] *fml* (something or someone that causes) loss of honor: *His desertion from the army brought dishonor to his family.* –**dishonor** *v* [T] –**dishonorable** *adj* –**dishonorably** *adv*

dish sthg.↔ **out** *v adv* [T] *infml* to serve out to

several people; HAND **out** (2): *to dish out the food/advice*

dish tow·el /ˈ·ˌ·/ *n* a cloth for drying cups, plates, etc. after they have been washed

dish (sthg.↔) **up** *v adv* [T] to put (the food for a meal) into dishes: *He dished up a big plate of beans.*

dish·washer *n* a person or machine that washes DISHES –see illustration on page 379

dis·il·lu·sion /ˌdɪsəˈluˠʒən/ *v* [T] to free from a wrong idea (ILLUSION): *I won't tell her her father is a thief; I don't want to disillusion her.* –**disillusionment** *n* [U]

dis·il·lu·sioned /ˌdɪsəˈluˠʒənd/ *adj* [*at, about, with*] feeling bitter and unhappy as a result of having been DISILLUSIONed: *He's very disillusioned about life.*

dis·in·clined /ˌdɪsɪnˈklaɪnd/ *adj* [F +*to-v*/*for*] unwilling: *I feel disinclined to exercise/go out in this weather.* –see also INCLINED –**disinclination** /ˌdɪsɪnkləˈneɪʃən, dɪsˌɪn-/

dis·in·fect /ˌdɪsɪnˈfɛkt/ *v* [T] to clean (things and places) with a chemical that can destroy bacteria –**disinfection** /ˌdɪsɪnˈfɛkʃən/ *n*

dis·in·fect·ant /ˌdɪsɪnˈfɛktənt/ *n* [C;U] a chemical used to DISINFECT

dis·in·her·it /ˌdɪsɪnˈhɛrɪt/ *v* [T] to take away from (usu. one's child) the lawful right to receive (INHERIT) one's goods after one's death

dis·in·te·grate /dɪsˈɪntəˌgreɪt/ *v* **-grated, -grating** [I;T] to (cause to) break up (as if) into small pieces: *The box was so old it just disintegrated when he picked it up.* –**disintegration** /dɪsˌɪntəˈgreɪʃən/ *n* [U]

dis·in·ter·est·ed /dɪsˈɪntrəstɪd, -ˈɪntəˌrɛstɪd, -ˈɪntərəstɪd/ *adj apprec* willing to judge or act fairly because not influenced by personal advantage: *She was chosen as a disinterested observer because she couldn't make money out of the affair.* –compare IMPARTIAL –**disinterestedly** *adv*

USAGE Compare **disinterested** and **uninterested**: *The argument can only be settled by someone who is* **disinterested**. (=who will not gain personally by deciding in favor of one side or another)|*Settle your own argument. I'm quite* **uninterested!** (=your argument doesn't interest me) Although **disinterested** is commonly used to mean "uninterested" this is thought by teachers to be incorrect.

dis·joint·ed /dɪsˈdʒɔɪntɪd/ *adj* (of words or ideas) not well connected; not following in reasonable order: *He gave a disjointed account of his vacation.* –**disjointedly** *adv* –**disjointedness** *n* [U]

disk, disc /dɪsk/ *n* **1** something round and flat: *the sun's disk|a computer disk* –see illustration on page 221 **2** a flat piece of strong bendable material (CARTILAGE) between the bones (VERTEBRAE) of one's back: *The pain was caused by a* **slipped disk.** **3** →RECORD[2] (4)

disk jock·ey /ˈ· ˌ··/ also **DJ** *infml*– a broadcaster who introduces records of popular music on a radio show

dis·like[1] /dɪsˈlaɪk/ *v* **-liked, -liking** [T +*v-ing*; not *be* +*v-ing*] to consider unpleasant; not to like: *I dislike being spoken to like that.*

dislike² n [C;U *of, for*] (a) feeling of disliking (DISLIKE): *to have a dislike of/for cats|She took a dislike to* him (=began to dislike him) *at once.*

dis·lo·cate /'dɪslow̩keʸt, dɪsˈlowkeʸt/ v -cated, -cating [T] to put (a bone) out of place: *He dislocated his shoulder.|a dislocated shoulder* –**dislocation** /ˌdɪslow̩'keʸʃən/ n [C;U]

dis·lodge /dɪsˈlɑdʒ/ v -lodged, -lodging [T *from*] to force or knock out of a position: *The government has been dislodged from power by the army.* –see also LODGE¹ (3)

dis·loy·al /dɪsˈlɔɪəl/ adj [*to*] not loyal –**disloyally** adv –**disloyalty** /dɪsˈlɔɪəltiʸ/ n -ties [C;U *to*]

dis·mal /'dɪzməl/ adj showing or causing sadness; lacking comfort: *a dismal song|dismal weather* –**dismally** adv

dis·man·tle /dɪsˈmæntəl/ v -tled, -tling [I;T] a to take (a machine or article) to pieces b (of a machine or article) to be able to be taken to pieces: *This engine dismantles easily.*

dis·may¹ /dɪsˈmeʸ/ v -mayed, -maying [T] to fill with DISMAY²

dismay² n [U *in, with*] strong feeling of fear and hopelessness: *They were* **filled with dismay** *by the news.|***To their dismay,** *the news was bad.*

dis·mem·ber /dɪsˈmɛmbər/ v [T] to cut or tear (a body) apart, limb from limb: *The young man's dismembered body was found by the police.*

dis·miss /dɪsˈmɪs/ v [T] **1** [*from*] *fml* to take away (the job of): *If you're late again you'll be dismissed (from you job).* **2** to send away: *The teacher dismissed the class early.|*(fig.) *He just laughed and dismissed the idea as impossible.* –**dismissal** n [C;U]

dis·mount /dɪsˈmaʊnt/ v [I] to get down (e.g. from a horse or bicycle) –opposite **mount**

dis·o·be·di·ent /ˌdɪsəˈbiʸdiʸənt/ adj [*to*] (of a person or his/her behavior) failing to obey: *a disobedient child|He was disobedient to his mother.* –opposite **obedient** –**disobediently** adv –**disobedience** n [U *to*]

dis·o·bey /ˌdɪsəˈbeʸ/ v -beyed, -beying [I;T] to fail to obey: *He disobeyed his mother and went to the party.*

dis·or·der /dɪsˈɔrdər/ n **1** [U] lack of order; confusion: *The house was in (a state of) disorder.* **2** [C;U] (a) violent public expression of political dissatisfaction: *public disorder because of the tax increases* **3** [C] a slight disease or illness: *suffering from a stomach disorder* –**disordered** adj: *a disordered mind*

dis·or·der·ly /dɪsˈɔrdərliʸ/ adj **1** untidy; confused: *a disorderly room* **2** violent in public: *disorderly conduct/youths;* –opposite orderly –see DRUNK¹ –**disorderliness** n [U]

dis·or·ga·nize ‖also **-nise** *BrE* /dɪsˈɔrgəˌnaɪz/ v -nized, -nizing [T] to throw (arrangements, a system, etc.) into disorder –see also ORGANIZE –**disorganization** /dɪsˌɔrgənəˈzeʸʃən/ n [U]

dis·o·ri·ent /dɪsˈɔriʸənt, -ˈoʷr-/ *AmE*‖also **disorientate** /dɪsˈɔriʸənˌteʸt, -ˈoʷr-/- v [T *usu. pass.*] to cause (someone) to lose the sense of time, direction, etc.; confuse: (fig.) *Father worked in the same job for 30 years, and he has been very disoriented since he stopped working.* –opposite **orient** –**disorientation** /dɪsˌɔriʸənteʸʃən, -ˌoʷr-/ n [U]

dis·own /dɪsˈoʷn/ v [T] to refuse to accept as one's own: *Peter's father disowned him when he was caught taking drugs.*

dis·par·age /dɪˈspærɪdʒ/ v [T] to make (someone or something) sound of little value or importance: *In spite of your disparaging remarks, I think she did well.* –**disparagingly** adv –**disparagement** n [C;U]

dis·par·i·ty /dɪˈspærətiʸ/ n -ties [C;U *between, in, of*] *fml* (an example of) difference or INEQUALITY: *There is (a) great disparity of/in age between him and his wife.* –see also PARITY

dis·pas·sion·ate /dɪsˈpæʃənɪt/ adj *apprec* (of a person or his behavior) calm and fair; not taking sides in an argument –**dispassionately** adv

dis·patch¹, **despatch** /dɪˈspætʃ/ v [T *to*] to send off: *The packages were dispatched yesterday.*

dispatch², **despatch** n **1** [U] a message carried by a government official, or sent to a newspaper by one of its writers: *to send/carry a dispatch from Chicago to St. Louis* **2** [U] *fml* speed and effectiveness: *He did the job with great dispatch.*

dis·pel /dɪˈspɛl/ v -ll- [T] to drive away (as if) by scattering: *His calm words dispelled our fears.*

dis·pen·sa·ble /dɪˈspɛnsəbəl/ adj not necessary; that can be DISPENSEd **with** –opposite **indispensable**

dis·pen·sa·ry /dɪˈspɛnsəriʸ/ n -ries a place where medicine is DISPENSEd (2), esp. in a hospital or school –see also PHARMACY (2)

dis·pen·sa·tion /ˌdɪspənˈseʸʃən, -pɛn-/ n [C;U] (a case of) permission to disobey a general rule or break a promise: *By a special dispensation from the Church, he was allowed to remarry.*

dis·pense /dɪˈspɛns/ v -pensed, -pensing [T] **1** [*to*] to deal out; give out (to a number of people): *A judge dispenses justice.|This machine dispenses coffee.* **2** to mix and give out (medicine) –**dispenser** n: *a coffee dispenser* –see illustration on page 467

dispense with sbdy./sthg. v prep [T] **1** to do without: *We'll have to dispense with a car; we can't afford it.* **2** to make unnecessary: *This new office machine dispenses with the need for a secretary.*

dis·perse /dɪˈspɜrs/ v -persed, -persing [I;T] to (cause to) scatter in different directions: *The wind dispersed the smoke.|The crowd dispersed when the police arrived.*

dis·pir·it·ed /dɪˈspɪrɪtɪd/ adj *lit* discouraged

dis·place /dɪsˈpleʸs/ v -placed, -placing [T] **1** to force out of the usual place: *He displaced a bone in his knee.|A displaced person is one who has been forced to leave his/her country.* **2** [*as*] to take the place of: *displaced by a younger person* –see REPLACE (USAGE) –**displacement** n [U]

dis·play /dɪˈspleʸ/ v -played, -playing [T]

more fml than **show**– to show: *to display goods in a store window|She displayed no emotion when she failed her exam.*

display² *n* [C;U] the act or result of DISPLAY-ing: *a display of skill|The goods were* **on display** *in the store window.*

dis·please /dɪs'pliyz/ *v* **-pleased, -pleasing** [T] *fml* to annoy, offend, or make angry: *The old lady was displeased with/by the children's noisy behavior.* –opposite **please** –**displeasure** /dɪs'plɛʒər/ *n*

dis·pos·a·ble /dɪ'spowzəbəl/ *adj* intended to be used once and then thrown away: *disposable paper plates*

dis·pos·al /dɪ'spowzəl/ *n* [U] **1** the act or action of getting rid of; removal: *garbage disposal* **2 at someone's disposal** available for someone to use: *During his visit I put my car at his disposal.*

dis·pose /dɪ'spowz/ *v* **-posed, -posing** [T *for*] *fml* to put (esp. armed forces) in place; set in readiness: *disposing soldiers for the battle* **dispose of** *sthg. v prep* [T] to get rid of; throw away; finish with: *Dispose of these old papers.|*(fig.) *I can dispose of your argument quite easily.*

dis·posed /dɪ'spowzd/ *adj* [F +*to-v*] *fml* willing: *I don't feel disposed to help you.* –compare INDISPOSED

dis·po·si·tion /,dɪspə'zɪʃən/ *n* [C;U +*to-v*] *fml* a general tendency of character, behavior, etc.; nature: *He has a happy disposition.*

dis·pos·sess /,dɪspə'zɛs/ *v* [T *of*] *fml* to take property away from

dis·pro·por·tion·ate /,dɪsprə'pɔrʃənɪt, -'powr-/ *adj* [*to*] unequal; too much or too little: *Her income is disproportionate to the amount of work she does.|We spend a disproportionate amount of our money on rent.* –opposite **proportionate** –**disproportionately** *adv*

dis·prove /dɪs'pruwv/ *v* **-proved, -proving** [T] to prove (something) to be false

dis·put·a·ble /dɪ'spyuwt̩əbəl, 'dɪspyə-/ *adj* not necessarily true; open to question –opposite **indisputable** –**disputably** *adv*

dis·pute /dɪ'spyuwt/ *v* **-puted, -puting 1** [I;T *about, over*] to argue, esp. angrily and for a long time: *They disputed for hours (about) whether to build a new school.* **2** [T] to call into question; doubt: *She disputed the truth of my statement.*

dispute² *n* an argument or quarrel: *The miners were* **in dispute** *with their employers about pay.*

dis·qual·i·fy /dɪs'kwɑlə,faɪ/ *v* **-fied, -fying** [T] to make or declare unfit, unsuitable, or unable to do something: *He won the game but was later disqualified because he cheated.* –**disqualification** /dɪs,kwɑləfə'keyʃən/ *n*

dis·qui·et /dɪs'kwaɪət/ *v* [T] *fml* to make anxious: *disquieted by his long silences|a disquieting remark* –**disquiet** *n* [U]

dis·re·gard /,dɪsrɪ'gɑrd/ *v* [T] to pay no attention to; IGNORE –**disregard** *n* [U *for, of*]: *his disregard of my instructions*

dis·re·pair /,dɪsrɪ'pɛər/ *n* [U] the state of being in need of repair: *The old houses had*

fallen into disrepair.

dis·rep·u·ta·ble /dɪs'rɛpyətəbəl/ *adj* having or showing a bad character; having a bad REPUTATION: *disreputable people/behavior* –opposite **reputable** –**disreputably** *adv*

dis·re·spect /,dɪsrɪ'spɛkt/ *n* [U] lack of respect or politeness –**disrespectful** /,dɪsrɪ'spɛktfəl/ *adj* –**disrespectfully** *adv*

dis·rupt /dɪs'rʌpt/ *v* [T] to bring or throw into disorder: *An accident has disrupted train service into and out of the city.* –**disruption** /dɪs'rʌpʃən/ *n* [C;U] –**disruptive** /dɪs'rʌptɪv/ *adj*: *He has a disruptive influence on the other children.*

dis·sat·is·fy /dɪ'sætɪs,faɪ, dɪs'sætɪs-/ *v* **-fied, -fying** [T] to fail to satisfy; displease –**dissatisfaction** /dɪ,sætɪs'fækʃən, dɪs,sætɪs-/ *n* [U *that*]: *dissatisfaction with her new job*

dis·sect /dɪ'sɛkt, daɪ-/ *v* [I;T] to cut up (esp. the body of a plant or animal) into parts, in such a way as to study the relationship of the parts: (fig.) *The witnesses' accounts were disected in order to find the truth.* –**dissection** /dɪ'sɛkʃən, daɪ-/ *n*

dis·sem·i·nate /dɪ'sɛmə,neyt/ *v* **-nated, -nating** [T] *fml* to spread (news, ideas, etc.) widely –**dissemination** /dɪ,sɛmə'neyʃən/ *n* [U]: *the dissemination of ideas*

dis·sen·sion /dɪ'sɛnʃən, -tʃən/ *n* [C;U] (a) disagreement, esp. leading to argument: *Her comments caused a great deal of dissension.*

dis·sent /dɪ'sɛnt/ *n* [U] disagreement; difference of opinion: *When I asked for agreement, there was no dissent* –opposite **assent** –**dissent** *v* [I *from*] –**dissenter** *n*

dis·serv·ice /dɪ'sɜrvɪs, dɪs'sɜr-/ *n* [S;U] harm or a harmful action: *You have done a serious disservice to your country by selling military secrets to our enemies.* –see also SERVICE¹ (3)

dis·si·dent /'dɪsədənt/ *adj,n* (a person) openly and often strongly disagreeing with an opinion or a group: *political dissidents* –**dissidence** *n* [U]

dis·sim·i·lar /dɪ'sɪmələr, dɪs'sɪ-/ *adj* unlike; not SIMILAR

dis·si·pate /'dɪsə,peyt/ *v* **-pated, -pating** *fml* **1** [I;T] (to cause to) disappear or scatter: *He tried to dissipate the smoke by opening a window.* **2** [T] to spend, waste, or use up foolishly: *He dissipated his large fortune in a few years.*

dis·si·pat·ed /'dɪsə,peytɪd/ *adj* (typical of a person) who wastes his/her life in search of foolish or dangerous pleasure

dis·so·ci·ate /dɪ'sowʃiy,eyt, -siy-/ *also* **disassociate**– *v* **-ated, -ating** [T *from*] to separate from association or union with something or someone else: *The politician dissociated himself from the decision to close the school.* –see also ASSOCIATE –**dissociation** /dɪ,sowsiy'eyʃən, -ʃiy-/ *n* [U]

dis·so·lute /'dɪsə,luwt/ *adj fml* (typical of a person) who leads a bad or immoral life: *a dissolute person/life* –**dissolutely** *adv* –**dissoluteness** *n* [U]

dis·so·lu·tion /,dɪsə'luwʃən/ *n* [U] *fml* the ending or breaking up of an association, group, marriage, etc.: *the dissolution of a friendship*

dis·solve /dɪˈzɑlv/ *v* **-solved, solving 1** [I;T] to make or become liquid by putting into a liquid: *Sugar dissolves in water.* **2** [I;T] **a** to cause (an association, group, etc.) to end or break up **b** (of an association, group, etc.) to end or break up **3** [I] to lose one's self-control under the influence of strong feeling: *to dissolve in/into tears/laughter*

dis·suade /dɪˈsweɪd/ *v* **-suaded, -suading** [T *from*] to advise (somebody) against doing something; persuade not to do: *I tried to dissuade her (from joining the club).* –compare PERSUADE –**dissuasion** /dɪˈsweɪʒən/ *n* [U]

dis·tance /ˈdɪstəns/ *n* **1** [C;U] (the amount of) separation in space or time: *What is the distance to Washington/between Washington and Miami/from Washington to Miami?|The school is some distance* (=quite far) *away.|within (easy) walking distance of home|The dog looked dangerous, so I decided to* **keep my distance** (=stay far away) *from it.|*(fig.) *There has been (a) great distance between us since our argument.* **2** [S *of*] a distant point or place: *One can see the ancient ruins from/at a distance of 20 miles/*in the distance.

dis·tant /ˈdɪstənt/ *adj* **1** separate in space or time; far off: *distant lands|the distant sound of a bell|the distant past* **2** [A] not very close: *a distant connection between two ideas|Those two girls are distant relatives.* **3** showing social distance or lack of friendliness: *a distant manner* –**distantly** *adv*: *Those two people/ideas are distantly related.*

dis·taste /dɪsˈteɪst/ *n* [S;U *for*] dislike; displeasure: *She looked at him with distaste.*

dis·taste·ful /dɪsˈteɪstfəl/ *adj* [*to*] causing DISTASTE: *The very idea of cheating him is distasteful to me.* –**distastefully** *adv* –**distastefulness** *n* [U]

dis·tend /dɪˈstɛnd/ *v* [I;T] *fml* to (cause to) swell: *His stomach was distended because of lack of food.* –**distension** /dɪˈstɛnʃən, -tʃən/ *n* [U]

dis·till *AmE*‖**distil** *BrE* /dɪˈstɪl/ *v* **-ll-** [T] to make (a liquid) into gas and then make the gas into liquid, as when separating alcohol from water: *Water can be made pure by distilling it.|distilled water* –**distillation** /ˌdɪstəˈleɪʃən/ *n* [C;U]

dis·till·er·y /dɪˈstɪləri/ *n* **-ies** a factory or business firm where WHISKEY is made

dis·tinct /dɪˈstɪŋkt/ *adj* **1** [*from*] different; separate: *Those two ideas are quite distinct (from each other).* **2** clearly seen, heard, understood, etc.; noticeable: *a distinct smell of burning* –opposite **indistinct** –**distinctly** *adv*: *He spoke very distinctly.* –**distinctness** *n* [U]

USAGE Anything clearly noticed is **distinct**: *There's a* **distinct** *smell of beer in this room.* A thing or quality that is clearly different from others of its kind is **distinctive**, or **distinct** *from*: *Beer has a very* **distinctive** *smell; it's quite* **distinct** *from the smell of wine.*

dis·tinc·tion /dɪˈstɪŋkʃən/ *n* **1** [C;U *between*] difference: *Can you* **make/draw a distinction** *between these two ideas?* **2** [S;U] the quality of being unusual, esp. of being unusually good; worth: *a writer of true distinction* **3** [C] a special mark of honor: *He had the distinction of being the first man to walk on the moon.*

dis·tinc·tive /dɪˈstɪŋktɪv/ *adj* clearly marking a person or thing as different from others: *She had a distinctive appearance.* –see DISTINCT (USAGE) –**distinctively** *adv* –**distinctiveness** *n* [U]

dis·tin·guish /dɪˈstɪŋgwɪʃ/ *v* **1** [T] to hear, see, or recognize: *He is easily distinguished by his uniform.|Can you distinguish objects at a distance?* **2** [I;T *from, between*] to make or recognize differences: *I can distinguish (between) those two objects/ideas.|to distinguish right from wrong* **3** [T] to set apart or mark as different: *Elephants are distinguished by their long noses* (TRUNKs). **4** [T] to behave (oneself) noticeably well: *He* **distinguished himself** *by his performance at the concert.*

dis·tin·guish·a·ble /dɪˈstɪŋgwɪʃəbəl/ *adj* [*from*] that can be clearly seen, heard, or recognized as different: *Those two objects/ideas are not easily distinguishable (from each other).* –opposite **indistinguishable**

dis·tin·guished /dɪˈstɪŋgwɪʃt/ *adj* marked by excellent quality or deserved fame: *a distinguished performance/politician/writer* –see FAMOUS (USAGE)

dis·tort /dɪˈstɔrt/ *v* [T] to twist out of a natural, usual, or original shape or condition: *a face distorted by/with anger|*(fig.) *He gave a distorted* (=untrue) *account of what had happened.* –**distortion** /dɪˈstɔrʃən/ *n* [C;U]

dis·tract /dɪˈstrækt/ *v* [T *from*] to take (a person, a person's mind) off what he/she is doing: *Don't distract me (from working).|She was distracted by the noise outside.*

dis·tract·ed /dɪˈstræktɪd/ *adj* [*by, with*] anxious or troubled about many things: *a distracted look* –**distractedly** *adv*

dis·trac·tion /dɪˈstrækʃən/ *n* **1** [C] something or someone that DISTRACTs; amusement: *There are too many distractions here for me to work.* **2** [U] an anxious confused state of mind: *The child's continual crying* **drove him to distraction.** **3** [U] the act of DISTRACTing or the state of being DISTRACTed

dis·traught /dɪˈstrɔt/ *adj* [*with*] very anxious and troubled: *distraught with grief/worry*

dis·tress¹ /dɪˈstrɛs/ *n* **1** [S;U] (a cause of) great suffering, pain, or discomfort: *The sick man showed signs of distress.|people in* **distress** *because of lack of money* **2** [U] a state of danger or great difficulty: *Send out a* **distress** *signal; the ship is sinking.*

distress² *v* [T] to cause DISTRESS¹ to

dis·tress·ing /dɪˈstrɛsɪŋ/ *adj* causing DISTRESS¹: *distressing news* –**distressingly** *adv*

dis·trib·ute /dɪˈstrɪbyət, -byuᵗ/ *v* **-uted, -uting** [T] **1** [*to, among*] to divide among several or many; give out: *to distribute the prizes to/among the winners* **2** [*over*] to spread out; scatter: *This new machine* *distributes seeds evenly and quickly (over the whole field).*

dis·tri·bu·tion /ˌdɪstrəˈbyuʷʃən/ *n* [C;U] an act of distributing or the state of being DISTRIBUTEd: *the distribution of prizes*

dis·trict /ˈdɪstrɪkt/ *n* an area of a country, city, etc., esp. made officially for particular purposes: *a postal district|District of Columbia|a poor district in a city*

district at·tor·ney /ˌ··· ·ˈ···/ also **D.A.**– *n (often caps) AmE* a government lawyer who acts for the State in bringing charges against criminals in a court of law

dis·trust[1] /dɪsˈtrʌst/ *v* [T] to lack trust in; mistrust: *He distrusts banks so he keeps his money at home.*

distrust[2] *n* [S;U] lack of trust; mistrust: *He regards banks with distrust.* –**distrustful** /dɪsˈtrʌstfəl/ *adj* –**distrustfully** *adv*

dis·turb /dɪˈstɜrb/ *v* [T] **1** to break in upon (esp. a person who is working); interrupt: *I'm sorry to disturb you but . . .* **2** to upset; worry: *disturbing news* **3** to change the usual or natural condition of: *A light wind disturbed the surface of the water.*

dis·turb·ance /dɪˈstɜrbəns/ *n* [C;U] **1** an act of DISTURBing or the state of being DISTURBED: *They were charged by the police with causing a disturbance.* **2** something that DISTURBS: *The noise of traffic is a continual disturbance.*

dis·turbed /dɪˈstɜrbd/ *adj* having or showing signs of an illness of the mind or the feelings: *emotionally disturbed*

dis·use /dɪsˈyuʷs/ *n* [U] the state of no longer being used: *That law has **fallen into disuse.***

ditch[1] /dɪtʃ/ *n* a not very deep V- or U-shaped passage cut into the ground, esp. for water to flow through: *The water flows into the ditch at the edge of the field.*

ditch[2] *v* [T] *infml* to get rid of; leave suddenly; ABANDON: *Her old car stopped working so she decided to ditch it.*

dith·er /ˈdɪðər/ *v* [I *about*] *infml* to act nervously or be unable to decide –**dither** *n* [S]

dit·to /ˈdɪtoʷ/ *n* **-tos** **1** a mark (″) meaning the same used in lists or tables to show that whatever is above is repeated: *a black pencil " blue " " red "* **2** *infml* the same: *"I'm hungry." "Ditto."* (=I am, too)

dit·ty /ˈdɪtiʸ/ *n* **-ties** a short simple song

di·van /ˈdaɪvæn, dɪˈvæn/ *n* a long soft seat or bed (**divan bed**) on a wooden base, usu. without back or arms

dive[1] /daɪv/ *v* **dived**‖also **dove** /doʷv/ *AmE*, **dived**, **diving** [I] **1** [*in, off, from, into*] to jump head first into the water: *The boy dived into the swimming pool from the **diving board.*** **2** [*down, for*] to go under the surface of the water; SUBMERGE: *They are diving for gold from the Spanish wreck.* **3** to move quickly, esp. downwards or out of sight: *The eagle dived down on the rabbit.|The rabbit dived into its hole.|He dived into the doorway so he wouldn't be seen.*

dive[2] *n* **1** an act of diving (DIVE): *a graceful dive into the pool|When the shots sounded, we made a dive for the nearest doorway.* **2** *infml* a not very respectable place, esp. for

meeting, eating, or amusement: *I'm not going to eat in a dive like that.*

div·er /ˈdaɪvər/ *n* a person who DIVEs, esp. one who swims to the bottom of the sea in special dress (a **diving suit** /ˈ·· ˌ·/) with a supply of air

di·verge /dəˈvɜrdʒ, daɪ-/ *v* **-verged, -verging** [I *from*] *fml* to separate and go on in different directions: *The road diverges ahead; you turn left.|I'm afraid our opinions diverge (from each other) on the subject of politics.* –see also CONVERGE –**divergence** *n* [C;U] –**divergent** *adj*

di·verse /dəˈvɜrs, daɪ-/ *adj fml* different; various: *many diverse interests* –**diversely** *adv*

di·ver·si·fy /dəˈvɜrsəˌfaɪ, daɪ-/ *v* **-fied, -fying** [I;T] to make different or various in form or quality; vary: *Our factory diversified several years ago.* (=started to make many different kinds of products)

di·ver·sion /dəˈvɜrʒən, daɪ-/ *n* **1** [C;U] a turning aside from a course, activity, or use: *the diversion of a river to supply water to the farms|The traffic had to follow a diversion because of an accident on the main road.* **2** [C] something that turns someone's attention away from something else that one does not wish to be noticed: *I think your last argument was a diversion to make us forget the main point.* **3** [C] something that DIVERTS or amuses: *Big cities have lots of movies, clubs, and other diversions.*

di·ver·si·ty /dəˈvɜrsətiʸ, daɪ-/ *n* [S;U *of*] the condition of being different or having differences; variety: *Mary has a great diversity of interests: she likes sports, travel, and photography.*

di·vert /dəˈvɜrt, daɪ-/ *v* [T] **1** [*from, to*] to cause to turn aside or from one use or direction to another: *They diverted the river to supply water to the town.|diverted traffic* **2** [*from*] to turn (a person or a person's attention) away from something, with good or bad result: *A loud noise diverted my attention.* **3** *fml* to amuse: *a game to divert the children*

di·vest sbdy. **of** sthg. /dəˈvɛst, daɪ-/ *v prep* [T] *fml* to take away (the position, rights, property, etc.) of: *They divested the king of all his power.*

di·vide /dəˈvaɪd/ *v* **-vided, -viding** **1** [T] to share: *Divide the cake (up) between|among you.|He divides his time between reading and writing.* **2** [I;T *into, from*] to (cause to) separate into parts: *This class is too large. We'll have to divide it.|The class divided into groups.|The new road will divide the farm.|(fig.) I hope this argument will not divide us.* **3** [I;T *by, into*] to find out how many times one number contains or is contained in another number: *15 divided by 3 is 5.|3 divides into 15 5 times.* –compare MULTIPLY

div·i·dend /ˈdɪvəˌdɛnd, -dənd/ *n* **1** that part of the money made by a business which is divided among those who own shares in the business: *The company declared a large dividend at the end of the year.* **2 pay dividends** to produce an advantage; be useful in the future: *I'm sure that new idea will pay dividends some day.*

di·vid·ers /dəˈvaɪdərz/ *n* [P] an instrument for measuring or marking off lines, angles, etc. –see PAIR (USAGE)

di·vine¹ /dəˈvaɪn/ *adj* **1** [*no comp.*] of, coming from, or being God or a god: *the divine right of kings* **2** *infml* very very good: *That play we saw last night was simply divine!* –**divinely** *adv*

divine² *v* **-vined, -vining** [I;T] **1** *fml* to discover or guess (the unknown, esp. the future) by or as if by magic **2** to be able to find (water or minerals) underground esp. by using a Y-shaped stick (a **divining rod** /·ˈ·· ˌ·/)

di·vin·i·ty /dəˈvɪnəṭiʸ/ *n* **-ties 1** [U] the quality or state of being DIVINE¹ (1) **2** [C] (*often cap.*) a god or goddess **3** [U] →THEOLOGY

di·vis·i·ble /dəˈvɪzəbəl/ *adj* that can be divided: *15 is divisible by 3.*

di·vi·sion /dəˈvɪʒən/ *n* **1** [U] separation or DISTRIBUTION: *the division of responsibility among the teachers* **2** [C] one of the parts into which a whole is divided: *He works in the foreign division of the company.* |*a naval division* (=a number of ships that fight together) **3** [C] something that divides or separates: *The river forms the division between the old and new parts of the city.* **4** [U] disagreement; lack of unity **5** [U] the act or action of finding out how many times one number or quantity is contained in another: *the division of 15 by 3*

di·vi·sive /dəˈvaɪsɪv, -ˈvɪ-/ *adj* tending to divide people; causing disunity or arguments: *He is a divisive influence at meetings.* –**divisively** *adv*

di·vorce¹ /dəˈvɔrs, dəˈvoʷrs/ *n* [C;U] (a case of) the ending of a marriage as declared by a court of law: *She got a divorce after years of unhappiness.* |*He is suing* (SUE) *for divorce.* (=trying to get a divorce) –compare SEPARATION (3)

divorce² *v* **-vorced, -vorcing 1** [I;T] to end a marriage between (a husband and wife) or to (a husband or a wife): *They divorced (each other).* |*the court divorced them.* **2** [T *from*] *fml* to separate: *It is hard to divorce love and duty* |*love from duty in one's mind.*

di·vor·cée /dəˌvɔrˈseʸ, -, voʷr-, dəˈvɔrseʸ, -ˈvoʷr-/ *n* a DIVORCED woman

di·vulge /dəˈvʌldʒ, daɪ-/ *v* **-vulged, -vulging** [T +*that*/ *to*] *fml* to tell (what has been secret): *Newsmen divulged that the President had been ill for some time before he died.*

Dix·ie /ˈdɪksiʸ/ *n* [S] *AmE infml* the Southern states of the US, especially the southeastern states where slaves were owned before the war between the States (the CIVIL WAR): *back home in Dixie*

diz·zy /ˈdɪziʸ/ *adj* **-zier, -ziest 1** having an unpleasant feeling of loss of balance, as if things are going round and round: *The room was so hot that she felt dizzy.* **2** causing this feeling: *a dizzy height* **3** *infml* foolish or stupid –**dizzily** *adv* –**dizziness** *n* [U]

DJ /ˈdiʸ dʒeʸ/ *n abbrev.* →DISK JOCKEY

DNA *abbrev. for: tech* deoxyribonucleic acid; the acid which carries GENETIC information in a cell

do¹ /də; *strong* duʷ/ *v*

present tense

singular	plural
I do	**We do**
You do	**You do**
He/She/It does	**They do**

past tense

singular	plural
I did	**We did**
You did	**You did**
He/She/It/ did	**They did**

PAST PARTICIPLE	**done**
PRESENT PARTICIPLE	**doing**
NEGATIVE *short forms*	**don't, doesn't didn't**

For the pronunciation of these forms look them up at their place in the dictionary.
1 [I] **a** (used as a helping verb with another verb): *Do you like it?* |*Don't stop.* |*He didn't answer.* |*Doesn't he look funny?* |*Why don't you come for the weekend?* (=please come!) **b** (used to make another verb stronger): *I really do like him!* |*"Why didn't you tell me?" "I did tell you!"* **2** [I] (used instead of another verb): *He likes it, and so do I.* |*He speaks English better now than he did before.* (=better than he used to speak it)| *"You stepped on my toe." "No, I didn't!"* **3** [T] (used instead of another verb): *"What are you doing?" "(I'm) cooking."*

do² /duʷ/ *v* **1** [T] (used of actions): *to do a sum* |*to do repairs* |*to do the cooking* |*to do the dishes* (=clean them)| *to do one's hair* (=arrange it) –see DO with (USAGE) **2** [T] (used in certain expressions): *I did my best (to help him).* |*I used to do business with him.* |*This medicine will do you good.* |*I have some work to do.* |*Do me a favor.* **3** [I] to be enough or be suitable: *Will $25 do?* |*This little bed will do for the baby.* |*You don't have to use milk. Water will do.* |*That will do! Stop!* **4** [I] to behave: *Do as you're told!* **5** [I] to advance: *They did well in the examination.* **6 do-it-yourself** *infml* the idea of doing repairs and building things oneself, instead of paying workmen: *She's very good at do-it-yourself repairs.* **7 How are you doing?** *infml esp. AmE* (an informal greeting) **8 How do you do?** *polite* (used when one is introduced to someone) **9 make do (with something)** also **make (something) do–** *infml* to use (something) even though it may not be perfect or enough: *We don't have any milk, so we'll have to make do with water.* **10 What do you do (for a living)?** What is your work? –see MAKE (USAGE); see also DOING

do away with sbdy./sthg. *v adv prep* [T] **1** to cause to end; ABOLISH: *The company did away with private offices.* **2** *infml* to kill or murder (someone or oneself)

do sbdy. **in** *v adv* [T] *infml* **1** to kill: *They did her in with an ax!* **2** to tire completely: *That* *long walk really did me in!*

do sbdy. **out of** sthg. *v adv prep* [T] *infml* to cause to lose, by cheating:*I've been done out of my rights.*

do sthg.↔**over** *v adv* [T] **1** to repaint (a room, wall, etc.): *Let's do the apartment over next month.* **2** *AmE* to do again: *This exercise has a lot of mistakes. You'd better do it over.*

do sbdy./sthg. **up** *v adv* [T] *infml* **1** to fasten: *Do up your buttons/my dress/this knot.* **2** to wrap: *to do up a package* **3** to make (oneself) more beautiful: *Mary did herself up for the party.*

do with sthg. *v prep* [T] **1** [+*v-ing; no pass.*] (*usu. after* could *or sometimes* can) to need or want: *I could do with a cup of coffee.|This room could do with (a) cleaning.* **2** to cause (oneself) to spend time doing: *The boys didn't know what to do with themselves when school ended.* **3** (*in questions with* "what") to do with regard to: *"What did you do with my pen?" "I put it away."* **4 have to do with** to have a connection with: *His job has to do with the government.* **5 have something/nothing/anything/a lot, etc.,to do with** to have some/no/any/a lot of, etc., connection with: *His job has nothing to do with the government.|Don't have anything to do with those silly people.|What he does at home has nothing to do with (=does not concern) his teacher.*

USAGE Compare **do to** and **do with**: *What did you* **do with** *my book?* means "Where is it?" *What did you* **do to** *my book?* suggests that you have damaged or changed it.

do without (sbdy./sthg.) *v adv; prep* [I;T] to continue to live without; DISPENSE **with**: *I don't have enough money to buy a car, so I'll just have to do without (one).*

do³ /duʷ/ *n* **do's** *or* **dos** /duʷz/ *infml* **1** a big party **2 do's and dont's** rules of behavior: *the do's and don'ts of working in an office*

doc·ile /'dɑsəl/ *adj* quiet and easily taught or led: *a docile child/animal* **–docility** /dɑ'sɪlətiʸ, doʷ-/ *n* [U]

dock¹ /dɑk/ *n* **1** a place where ships are loaded and unloaded, or repaired: *the docks of New York* **2** the place in a court of law where the prisoner stands

dock² *v* [I;T *at*] to (cause to) sail into, or remain at, a DOCK¹ (1)

dock³ *v* [T] to cut off the end of: *docking a horse's tail|*(fig.) *to dock a man's wages to pay for damage he had caused*

doc·tor¹ /'dɑktər/ *n* **1** [A;C] a person whose profession is to attend to and treat sick people (or animals): *an animal doctor|You should see a doctor.|Good morning, doctor.* –see illustration opposite **2** [A;C] a person holding one of the highest degrees given by a university (such as a Ph.D.)

USAGE In the US both medical doctors and dentists are addressed as **doctor.**

doctor² *v* [T] *infml* **1** to give medical treatment to **2** *derog* to change, esp. in a dishonest way: *They were charged with doctoring the election results.* **3** to change food by adding something, for example, alcohol: *He doctored the cake by adding rum.*

doc·tri·naire /ˌdɑktrə'nɛər/ *adj derog* typical of a person who tries to put into action some system of ideas (some DOCTRINE) without considering the practical difficulties: *doctrinaire beliefs*

doc·trine /'dɑktrɪn/ *n* **1** [C;U] a principle, or set of principles, that is taught: *religious doctrine* **2** [C] *esp. AmE* a statement of official government opinions and intentions, esp. in international relations: *the Monroe Doctrine* –see also INDOCTRINATE **–doctrinal** /'dɑktrənəl/ *adj*

doc·u·ment¹ /'dɑkyəmənt/ *n* a paper that gives information, proof, or support of something else: *Let me see all the official documents concerning the sale of this land.*

doc·u·ment² /'dɑkyə,mɛnt/ *v* [T] to prove or support with DOCUMENTs: *The history of this area is very well documented.* **–documentation** /ˌdɑkyəmɛn'teʸʃən, -mən-/ *n* [U]

doc·u·men·ta·ry¹ /ˌdɑkyə'mɛntəriʸ/ *adj* [A] of or related to DOCUMENTs¹: *documentary proof/evidence*

documentary² *n* **-ries** a film, or television or radio broadcast, that presents facts: *We saw a documentary about West Virginia coal miners.|a documentary film* –compare FEATURE¹ (4)

dod·der·ing /'dɑdərɪŋ/ also **doddery** /'dɑdəriʸ/ *adj infml* weak, shaky, and slow, usu. from age: *a doddering old man*

dodge /dɑdʒ/ *v* **dodged, dodging 1** [I;T] to avoid (something) by suddenly moving aside: *He dodged the falling rock and escaped unhurt.|He dodged past me.* **2** [T] *infml* to avoid by a trick or in some unlawful or dishonest way: *draft-dodging* (DRAFT¹ (3)) **–dodge** *n* **–dodger** *n*

do·do /'doʷdoʷ/ *n* **dodoes** *or* **dodos 1** a large bird that could not fly and that no longer exists **2** *infml* a fool: *He's a real dodo.*

doe /doʷ/ *n* **does** *or* **doe** the female of certain animals, esp. the deer, the rat, and the rabbit –compare BUCK

does /dəz, z, s; *strong* dʌz/ *v* 3rd person sing. present of DO¹,²

does·n't /'dʌzənt/ *short for:* does not: *She likes it, doesn't she?*

dog¹ /dɔg/ *n* **1** a common four-legged flesh-eating animal, esp. any of the many varieties used by man: *A young dog is called a* **puppy**. **2** the male of this animal and of certain animals like it, esp. the fox and the WOLF **3 lead a dog's life** *infml* to have an unhappy life with many troubles **4 Let sleeping dogs lie** Leave alone things which may cause trouble **5 not have a dog's chance** *infml* to have no chance at all **6 top dog** *infml* the person on top, who has power –compare UNDERDOG **7 treat someone like a dog** *infml* to treat someone very badly **8 You can't teach an old dog new tricks** people can't change their ways and habits easily

dog² *v* **-gg-** [T *by*] to follow closely (like a dog); PURSUE: *We were dogged by bad luck during the whole trip.*

dog-eared /'· ·/ *adj* (esp. of books and papers) having the corners of the pages bent down with use

examining room
stethoscope
nurse
thermometer
patient
doctor
examining table
crutch
sling
cast
bandage
receptionist's desk
receptionist
wheelchair
waiting room

Ms. Holtz is the **receptionist** for the **doctors** in this **clinic**. She answers the phone, keeps **medical records**, and welcomes people who come to the clinic. This morning, Suzanne Kelly's mother called.

MRS. KELLY: I'd like to **make an appointment** with Doctor Taylor, please. My daughter Suzanne is **ill.**

MS. HOLTZ: Doctor Taylor isn't **in** this morning, but she'll be **in** this afternoon. Will two o'clock be all right?

MRS. KELLY: That's fine.

MS. HOLTZ: What are Suzanne's **symptoms**?

MRS. KELLY: She **had a temperature** and a **sore throat** yesterday, and this morning she woke up with a **stomachache**.

MS. HOLTZ: Oh my. It sounds like she **has the flu**. There's a lot of it **going around**.

MRS. KELLY: Yes. At first I thought she just **had a cold**, but I think it's something worse.

MS. HOLTZ: Well, we'll see you at two o'clock.

MS. KELLY: Right. Thanks a lot.

dog·ged /'dɔgɪd/ adj having or showing a character which refuses to yield or give up in the face of difficulty or opposition: *She was not very intelligent, but by dogged effort she learned a good deal at school.* –**doggedly** adv –**doggedness** n [U]

dog·gie bag, doggy /'·· ˌ·/ n a small bag provided by a restaurant for taking home food remaining uneaten after a meal

dog·gy , doggie /'dɔgiʸ/ n -gies (*used esp. to or by children*) a dog

dog·house /'dɔghaus/ n **in the doghouse** *infml* in a state of disfavor or shame

do·gie /'dowʷgiʸ/ n AmE a motherless baby cow (CALF) in a group of cattle

dog·ma /'dɔgmə, 'dagmə/ n [C;U] an important belief or set of beliefs that people are expected to accept without reasoning: *church dogma|political dogma*

dog·mat·ic /dɔg'mæṭɪk, dag-/ adj **1** of or based on DOGMA **2** *usu. derog* (typical of a person) who puts forward beliefs expecting other people to accept them without question: *a dogmatic opinion/manner/person* –**dogmatically** adv

do·ing /'duwʷɪŋ/ n **1** [U] **a** something that one has done: *This must be your doing.* (=you did this) **b** hard work: *That job will take a lot of doing.* **2** [C *usu. pl.*] *infml* something that is done or that happens; social activity: *a lot of doings at Mr. Smith's house tonight*

dol·drums /'dowʷldrəmz, 'dal-/ n **in the doldrums** *infml* in a sad state of mind

dole¹ /dowʷl/ n **go/be on the dole** *infml* to (start to) receive money from the government because one is unemployed: *I've been on the dole for six months.*

dole² v → DOLE OUT

dole·ful /'dowʷlfəl/ adj causing or expressing unhappiness or low spirits: *a doleful look* –**dolefully** adv –**dolefulness** n [U]

dole sthg.↔ **out** v adv doled, doling [T *to*] to give (esp. money or food in small quantities) (to people in need)

doll¹ /dal/ n **1** a small figure of a person, esp. of a baby, for a child to play with **2** *infml* a pretty young woman **3** *AmE infml* a person that one likes: *You'll lend me $20? You're a doll.*

doll² v → DOLL UP

dol·lar /'dalər/ n **1** a standard of money, as used in the US, Canada, Australia,New Zealand, Hong Kong, etc. Its sign is $ and it is worth 100 cents **2** a piece of paper, a coin, etc. of this value **3** **dollars and cents** considered only with regard to the money value: *Our move to Houston was a dollars and cents decision.*

dol·lop /'daləp/ n [*of*] *infml* a shapeless mass, esp. of food: *a dollop of mashed potato*

doll sbdy.↔ **up** v adv [T] *infml* to dress (someone or oneself) prettily: *all dolled up to go to a party*

dol·ly /'daliʸ/ n -lies (*used esp. by and to children*) →DOLL (1)

dol·phin /'dalfɪn, 'dɔl-/ n a sea-animal two to three meters long, which swims about in groups

do·main /dowʷ'meyʷn, də-/ n **1** land(s) owned or controlled by one person, a government, etc. **2** a subject of activity, interest, or knowledge: *I can't answer your question about photography. It's not (in) my domain.*

dome /dowʷm/ n a rounded roof on a building or room

domed /dowʷmd/ adj covered with or shaped like a DOME

do·mes·tic¹ /də'mɛstɪk/ adj **1** of the house, home, or family: *domestic responsibilities/problems|not very domestic* (=not liking cooking, cleaning, etc.) **2** (of an animal) not wild: *The cat is a domestic animal in many countries.* **3** of one's own country or some particular country; not foreign: *the government's domestic policies.|domestic wine* –**domestically** adv

domestic² n a servant, usu. female, who works in a house

do·mes·ti·cate /də'mɛstəˌkeyʷt/ v -cated, -cating [T] **1** to make (an animal) able to live with people and serve them, esp. on a farm –compare TAME² **2** to cause to be interested in and enjoy home life and duties –**domestication** /dəˌmɛstə'keyʷʃən/ n [U]

do·mes·tic·i·ty /ˌdowʷmɛ'stɪsəṭiʸ/ n [U] (a liking for) home or family life

dom·i·cile /'damə,saɪl, -səl, 'dowʷ-/ n *fml* the place where one lives

dom·i·nance /'damənəns/ n [U] the fact or state of dominating (DOMINATE); importance, power, or controlling influence: *the director's dominance of the company* –compare DOMINATION

dom·i·nant /'damənənt/ adj dominating (DOMINATE): *My sister had a very dominant nature. We all did what she wanted.|The Town Hall was built in a dominant position on a hill where everyone could see it.*

dom·i·nate /'damə,neyʷt/ v -nated, -nating **1** [I;T] to have or exercise controlling power (over): *Her desire to dominate (other people) has caused trouble in her family.* **2** [I;T] to have the most important place or position (in): *Sports, and not learning, seem to dominate (in) that school.|That team has dominated football for years.* **3** [T] to rise or to be higher than; provide a view from a height above:*The church dominated the whole town.*

dom·i·na·tion /ˌdamə'neyʷʃən/ n [U] the act or fact of dominating or the state of being DOMINATEd: *His domination by his brother made him very angry.* –compare DOMINANCE

dom·i·neer·ing /ˌdamə'nɪərɪŋ/ adj *derog* showing a desire to control others, usu. without any consideration of their feelings or wishes: *a domineering person/manner*

do·min·ion /də'mɪnyən/ n **1** [U *over*] *lit* the power or right to rule: *Alexander the Great held dominion over a large area.* **2** [C] the land(s) held in complete control by one person, ruler, or government **3** [C] a self-governing nation of the British COMMONWEALTH: *the Dominion of Canada*

dom·i·no /'damə,nowʷ/ n -noes or -nos one of a set of flat pieces of wood, bone, etc., with a different number of spots on each, used for playing a game (**dominoes**)

do·nate /'downeyt, dow'neyt/ v **-nated, -nating** [I;T to] to make a gift of (something), esp. for a good purpose –see also DONOR

do·na·tion /dow'neyʃən/ n [C;U] the act of donating or something DONATED: *She made a donation of $1,000 to the Children's Hospital.*

done¹ /dʌn/ v past participle of DO¹,²

done² adj [F no comp.] **1** finished: *The job's nearly done.* **2** cooked enough to eat: *Are the potatoes done yet?* **3 Done!** I accept!: *"I'll give you $5 for it." "Done!"* **4 done for** to suffer an unavoidable misfortune: *If I make another mistake in this game I'm done for.* **5 done in** /,- '-/ very tired: *I feel completely done in!* **6 not done** not socially acceptable: *It isn't done to call your teachers by their first names in this school.*

don·key /'dɑŋkiy, 'dʌŋ-, 'dɔŋ-/ n **-keys** an animal like a horse, but smaller and with longer ears, used by man to carry loads; ASS

do·nor /'downər/ n **1** a person who gives, DONATES, or PRESENTS² (1) **2** a person who permits part of his/her body to be put into someone else for medical purposes: *a blood donor*

don't /downt/ short for: do not: *I don't know him very well.*

doo·dad /'duwdæd/ n AmE infml **1** → TRINKET **2** a small object whose name cannot be remembered or is not known: *Where's that doodad I need to fix my bicycle?*

doo·dle /'duwdl/ v **-dled, -dling** [I] to draw lines, figures, etc., aimlessly –**doodle** n

doom¹ /duwm/ n [C;U] a terrible fate; unavoidable destruction or death: *to meet one's doom*

doom² v [T usu. pass.] to cause to experience or suffer something unavoidable and unpleasant, such as death or destruction: *From the start, the plan was doomed (to failure/to fail).*

dooms·day /'duwmzdey/ n **till doomsday** infml for ever

door /dɔr, dowr/ n **1** a movable flat surface that opens and closes the entrance to a building, vehicle, room, or piece of furniture: *the kitchen/cupboard door|Most houses have a* **front door** *at the front and a* **back door** *at the back.|Will you* **answer** (=open) **the door?** *There's someone knocking (at it).|Mr. Brown is leaving now. Will you* **show him to** (=go with him to) **the door?**|(fig.) *This agreement opens the door to advances in every field.* –see illustration on page 95 **2** → DOORWAY: *to come through the door* **3** (in certain fixed phrases) a house; building: *My sister lives only two/a few doors away.|He sells books* **(from) door to door.** *|He is a* **door-to-door** *salesman.|My brother lives* **next door** *(to us).* **4 at death's door** lit near death **5 by the back door** secretly or by a trick **6 out of doors** →OUTDOORS

door·nail /'dɔrneyl, 'dowr-/ n (as) **dead as a doornail** infml dead: *That strange plan of yours is now as dead as a doornail. Nobody is interested in it any more.*

door·step /'dɔrstɛp, 'dowr-/ n a step outside an outer door

door·way /'dɔrwey, 'dowr-/ n an opening for an entrance door into a building or room: *She stood in the doorway, unable to decide whether or not to enter.*

dope¹ /dowp/ n infml **1** [U] a drug whose use is forbidden by law except on the orders of a doctor **2** [C] a stupid person

dope² v **doped, doping** [T up] infml to give DOPE¹ (1) to or put dope in: *to dope a person/a horse/oneself/a drink*

dop·ey, dopy /'dowpiy/ adj **-ier, -iest** infml **1** having or showing a dullness of the mind (as if) caused by alcohol or a drug; sleepy and unable to think clearly **2** stupid

dor·mant /'dɔrmənt/ adj inactive, esp. not actually growing or producing typical effects: *dormant animals asleep for the winter*|(fig.) *Many people disliked the plan, but opposition remained dormant because nobody could think of a better one.*

dor·mi·to·ry /'dɔrmə,tɔriy, -,towriy/ also **dorm** /dɔrm/ infml– n **-ries 1** AmE a building, esp. of a university, where students whose home is far away live, sleep, and study, usu. two to a room **2** a large room for sleeping, containing a number of beds: *a school dormitory*

dor·sal /'dɔrsəl/ adj tech [A] of, on, or near the back: *the dorsal* FIN *of a fish*

dos·age /'dowsɪdʒ/ n [usu. sing.] the amount of a DOSE¹

dose¹ /dows/ n a measured amount (esp. of liquid medicine) given or to be taken at a time: *Take one dose, three times a day.*|(fig.) *In the accident, the workers received a heavy dose of* RADIATION (3).|(fig.) *a dose of hard work*

dose² v **dosed, dosing** [T] to give a DOSE¹ to, esp. to give medicine to

dos·si·er /'dɑsiy,ey, 'dɔ-/ n a set of papers containing detailed information: *The police keep dossiers on all criminals.*

dot¹ /dɑt/ n **1** a small round mark: *a dot on the letter i*|(fig.) *He watched the train until it was only a dot in the distance.* **2 on the dot** infml at the exact point in time (or space): *The 3 o'clock train arrived on the dot.*

dot² v **-tt-** [T] **1** to mark with a dot: *to dot an i* **2** to cover (as if) with dots: *a lake dotted with boats*

dot·age /'dowtɪdʒ/ n [U] weakness of the mind caused by old age: *We have to look after Grandfather now that he's* **in his dotage.**

dote on/upon sbdy. /dowt/ v prep **doted, doting** [T] to have or show too much fondness for (esp. a person): *He dotes on his youngest son.*

dot·ing /'dowtɪŋ/ adj [A] having or showing (too) much fondness: *a doting husband* –**dotingly** adv

dot·ted line /,·· '·/ n **1** a line of dots on paper, on which something is to be written, esp. one's name **2 sign on the dotted line** infml to agree to something, usu. quickly and unconditionally

dot·ty /'dɑtiy/ adj **-tier, -tiest** infml weak-minded, foolish, or mad

dou·ble /'dʌbəl/ adj **1** in two parts; two together: *double doors|a double lock on the door|a cloth folded double* (=into two)|a *double meaning*|*a double* WHISKEY (=twice the usual amount) –compare SINGLE¹ (2) **2** made for two: *a double bed*|*a double (room) in a hotel* –**double** *adv*: *When you drink too much, you sometimes see double.*

double² *n* **1** [C;U] something that is twice another in size, quantity, value, etc.: *I paid only $2 for this old book and Mr. Smith offered me double* (=$4) *for it.*|*I'll have a double* (SCOTCH), *please.* **2** [C] a person who looks very much like another: *He is my double, though we are not related.* **3 on the double a** *infml* very quickly **b** (esp. of soldiers) at a rate between walking and running –see also DOUBLES

double³ *predeterminer* twice: *I bought double the amount of milk.*|*The cost of food is double what it was ten years ago.*

double⁴ *v* **-bled, -bling** [I;T] to make, be, or become twice as great or as many: *If you double five you get ten.*|*Prices doubled in five years.*|*Double the sheet* (=fold it once) *and you'll stay warmer.*

   double as sbdy./sthg. *v prep* [T] to have as a second use, job, etc.: *This chair doubles as a bed.*

   double back *v adv* [I] to return along the same path: *He started running towards the street but suddenly doubled back to the house.*

   double up *v adv* [I;T (=**double** sbdy.↔ **up**)] to (cause to) bend at the waist (usu. with pain or laughter): *They all doubled up (with laughter) when I told my joke.*|*He was doubled up (in pain) so we called the doctor.*

double-bar·reled *AmE*‖**-relled** *BrE* /ˌ··ˈ···◂/ *adj* (of a gun) having two barrels fixed side by side

double bass /ˌdʌbəl ˈbeʸs/ also **bass** – *n* the largest stringed musical instrument in the VIOLIN family, with a very deep sound

double-breast·ed /ˌ··ˈ···◂/ *adj* (of a coat or JACKET) made so that one side of the front is brought across the other side of the front and usu. having a double row of buttons

double-check /ˌ··ˈ·/ *v* [I;T] to examine (something) twice for exactness or quality

double chin /ˌ··ˈ·/ *n* a fold of loose skin between the face and neck

double-cross /ˌ··ˈ·/ *v* [T] *infml* to cheat by pretended friendship; BETRAY –**double cross** *n*

double date /ˌ··ˈ·/ *n infml* [I with] *esp. AmE* a DATE¹ (3) for two men and two women

double-date /ˌ··ˈ·/ *v* **-dated, -dating** [I with] *infml esp. AmE* to go on a DOUBLE DATE: *Let's double-date with Joanne and Jerry on Saturday night.*

double fea·ture /ˌ··ˈ··/ *n* a movie performance in which two main films are shown

double-glaze /ˌ··ˈ·/ *v* **-glazed, -glazing** [T] to provide (a window) with an additional sheet of glass –**double-glazing** *n* [U]

double-joint·ed /ˌ··ˈ···◂/ *adj* having joints that allow movement (esp. of the fingers) backwards as well as forwards: *He's double-jointed.*

double-park /ˌ··ˈ·/ *v* [I;T] to block a road by parking (a vehicle) beside a vehicle already

parked: *Because he double-parked, the policeman gave him a ticket.*

double-quick /ˌ··ˈ·◂/ *adj, adv infml* very quick(ly): *Get the doctor double-quick! Someone has fallen down the stairs.*

dou·bles /ˈdʌbəlz/ *n* **doubles** a match (esp. of tennis) played between two pairs of players: *Who'll win the men's/women's doubles at the US Open this year?* –compare SINGLES

double take /ˈ·· ˌ·/ *n infml esp. AmE* a quick but delayed movement of surprise usu. for humorous effect (esp. in the phrase **do a double take**)

double-talk /ˈ·· ˌ·/ *n* [U] *infml* language that appears to be serious and have meaning but in fact is a mixture of sense and nonsense –**double-talk** *v* [I;T] –**double-talker** *n*

dou·bly /ˈdʌbliʸ/ *adv* **1** to twice the degree: *Her life is doubly interesting because she became famous so young.* **2** in two ways: *That family is doubly troubled. They have no money and now their father is ill.*

doubt¹ /daut/ *v* [T +(*that*); not be +*v-ing*] **1** to be uncertain (about): *I doubt whether/if it's true.*|*I doubt his honesty.* **2** to consider unlikely: *I doubt that Tony will come.* –**doubter** *n*

USAGE In NEGATIVE¹ (2) statements, **doubt** may be followed by *that*, but not by *if* or *whether*: *I don't doubt that he's telling the truth.* In simple statements, *that, if,* and *whether* may be used: *I doubt that/if/whether he's coming.*

doubt² *n* **1** [C;U +*that*/*about*] (a feeling of) uncertainty of belief or opinion: *There is some doubt (as to/about) whether Peter will come on time.*|*There's no doubt that/* **Without doubt** *he'll come on time.*|*He says he can cure me, but I still have my doubts/am still in doubt (about him/it).* **2 in doubt** in a condition of uncertainty: *The whole matter is still in doubt.*

USAGE 1 **Doubt** is followed by *that* after *no* or *not*: *There is some* **doubt** (*as to*) *whether he is guilty.* |*There is no* **doubt** *that he is guilty.*2 **No doubt** and **doubtlessly** can be used as adverbs simply to mean "I think" or "I agree": **No doubt** *you'll be in the office tomorrow.* (=I expect you'll be there) But **without doubt** and **undoubtedly** express a stronger sense of knowing the real truth: *There will* **undoubtedly** (=certainly) *be trouble with the unions if she is fired.*

doubt·ful /ˈdautfəl/ *adj* **1** [*about*] full of doubt; uncertain: *I feel very doubtful about this/about whether to go.*|*The future is too doubtful for us to make plans.* **2** not probable; unlikely: *It is doubtful if we can get home before midnight.* –**doubtfully** *adv*

doubt·less·ly /ˈdautlisliʸ/ *AmE*‖also **doubtless**– *adv* **1** without doubt: *John will doubtlessly come early as he always does.* **2** probably: *It will doubtlessly rain on the day of the wedding.* –see DOUBT² (USAGE)

dough /doʷ/ *n* [U] **1** flour mixed with water ready for baking **2** *infml, esp. AmE* money

dough·nut /ˈdoʷnʌt, -nət/ *n* a small round, often ring-shaped, cake fried in fat and covered with sugar

dour /dauər, duər/ *adj* hard and cold in one's nature; unfriendly; unsmiling: *a dour look* –**dourly** *adv*

douse, dowse /daus/ *v* **doused, dousing** [T *with, in*] to put into water or throw water over

dove¹ /dʌv/ *n* a type of PIGEON; soft-voiced bird often used as a sign of peace: (fig) *That congressman is a dove.* (=against war)

dove² /dowv/ *v esp. AmE* a past tense of DIVE

dow·dy /'daudiʸ/ *adj* **-dier, -diest** *derog* (of clothes, esp. dresses) not attractive; old-fashioned; (of people) badly, dully dressed –**dowdily** *adv* –**dowdiness** *n* [U]

down¹ /daun/ *adv* [*no comp.*] **1** from above towards a lower place; to the floor, the ground, or the bottom: *The man bent down to kiss the child.|It gets cold quickly when the sun goes down.|She came down (the stairs) from her bedroom.|The telephone wires were blown down by the storm.* **2** in a low place: *down at the bottom of the sea* **3** from an upright or raised position: *You don't have to stand; please sit down.* **4** towards or in the south: *He's traveling down to Washington from New York.* –compare UP¹ (5) **5** along; away from the person speaking: *Will you walk down to the store with me?* **6** firmly; tightly; safely: *Did you press down the button?* **7** on paper; in writing: *"Did you write/copy/mark/put down the telephone number?" "I have it down somewhere."|to put one's name down on a list* **8** (showing a lower level or worse condition): *Production has gone down this year.* (=we have produced less)|*Let's mark down the prices.|The temperature's down ten degrees.* **9** (showing less noise, strength, activity, etc.): *Calm down.|Please turn the radio down* (=lower) *a bit.|They shouted the speaker down.* (=made him stop talking) **10** from the past: *These jewels have been passed down in our family from mother to daughter for 300 years.* **11 down under** *infml* in or to Australia or New Zealand **12 down with** ill with: *I'm coming down with a cold.* **13 Down with** I/We don't want: *Down with the taxes!* **14** *infml esp. AmE* finished; done: *eight down and two to go* (=eight have been finished, and there are two more to be done)

down² *adj* [F *no comp.*] **1** sad; in low spirits: *I feel really down today.* **2** *tech* (esp. of computers) not in operation: *The computer is down now but should be back up in an hour.*

down³ *prep* **1** to or in a lower place in; downwards by way of: *He ran down the hill.|The water poured down the pipe.|The bathroom is down those stairs.* **2** along; to or at the far end of: *He looked down the pipe.|They live just down the road.* **3** in the direction of the current of: *to go/be down the river*

down⁴ *v* [T] **1** to knock to the ground; defeat: *Our team easily downed theirs.* **2** to swallow quickly (esp. a liquid): *He downed his coffee and left.*

down⁵ *n* [U] fine soft feathers or hair – **downy** *adj* **-ier, -iest**

down-and-out /ˌ· · '·◂/ *adj* suffering from bad fortune, lack of money and work, etc.

down·cast /'daunkæst/ *adj* having or showing low spirits or sadness: *with downcast eyes*

down·fall /'daunfɔl/ *n* **1** (something that causes) a sudden fall (esp. from high rank); ruin: *Rising prices were the company's downfall.* **2** a sudden or heavy fall (esp. of rain); DOWNPOUR

down·grade /'daungreʸd/ *v* **-graded, -grading** [T] to lower in rank, position, or importance –opposite **upgrade**

down·heart·ed /ˌdaun'hartıd/ *adj* having or showing low spirits or sadness –**downheartedly** *adv*

down·hill¹ /ˌdaun'hıl/ *adv* **1** [after *n*] towards the bottom of a hill: *to run downhill|the road downhill* **2 go downhill** to move towards a lower or worse state or level: *His work has been going downhill recently. I hope it improves again soon:*

down·hill² /ˌdaun'hıl◂/ *adj* **1** [A] sloping or going towards the bottom of a hill **2** *infml* easy: *The hardest part of the work is over and the rest is downhill.*

down pay·ment /ˌ· '··/ *n* a part of the full price paid at the time of buying or delivery, with the rest to be paid later

down·pour /'daunpɔr, ˌ-powr/ *n* a heavy fall of rain

down·right /'daunrait/ *adv infml* (esp. with something bad) thoroughly; completely: *She was downright rude.* –**downright** *adj* [A]: *a downright cheat*

downs /daunz/ *n* [P] *BrE* low rounded grassy hills esp. as in the South of England: *the North/South Downs*

down·stairs /ˌdaun'steərz/ *adv* [F] on or to a lower floor and esp. the main or ground floor of a house: *to come downstairs|Is anyone downstairs yet?* –opposite **upstairs** –**downstairs** /ˌdaun'steərz◂/ *adj* [A]: *a downstairs bedroom*

down·stream /ˌdaun'strm◂/ *adv, adj* (moving) with the current, towards the mouth of a river, stream, etc.: *They traveled downstream.* –opposite **upstream**

down-to-earth /ˌ· · '·◂/ *adj* practical and honest; saying what one thinks: *a very down-to-earth person*

down·town¹ /ˌdaun'taun/ *adv* [*no comp.*] *esp. AmE* to, towards, or in the lower part or business center of a town or city: *to go/be down town*

down·town² /ˌdaun'taun◂/ *adj* [*no comp.*] *esp. AmE* of the lower part or business center of a town or city: *a downtown building*

down·trod·den /'daunˌtradn/ *adj esp. lit* treated badly by those in positions of power

down·ward¹ /'daunwərd/ *adj* [A] going down: *a downward movement of prices/of the head*

down·ward² *AmE*‖also **downwards** /'daunwərdz/– **1** going down: *The sun sank downward in the sky.* **2** with a particular side towards the ground: *He lay on the floor face downward.*

down·wind /ˌdaun'wınd◂/ *adj, adv* (going or being) in the direction that the wind is moving –opposite **upwind**

dow·ry /'dauəriʸ/ *n* **-ries** the property that a

woman brings to her husband in marriage

dowse /daʊs/ v dowsed, dowsing [T] →DOUSE

doze /dowz/ v dozed, dozing [I] to sleep lightly –**doze** n [S]: *He likes (to have) a doze after dinner.*

doze off also **drop off**, **nod off**– v adv [I] to fall asleep unintentionally: *I just dozed off (for a moment).*

doz·en /'dʌzən/ abbrev. **doz.**– determiner, n **dozen** or **dozens** a group of 12: *a dozen eggs| These eggs are 60 cents a half dozen.* (=60 cents for six) –see Study Notes on page 550

doz·y /'dowziy/ adj -ier, -iest sleepy: *a dozy feeling* –**dozily** adv –**doziness** n [U]

Dr. written abbrev. said as: Doctor

drab /dræb/ adj uninteresting; dull: *a drab color.|drab lives* –**drably** adv –**drabness** n [U]

drabs /dræbz/ n see DRIBS

draft¹ /dræft/ n 1 [C;U] the first rough written form of anything or a rough plan: *I've made a first draft of my speech for Friday.|a plan still only* **in draft** 2 [C;U] a written order for money to be paid by a bank, esp. from one bank to another: *paid by draft* –compare CHECK¹ (8) 3 [*the* S;U] *AmE*‖also **conscription**– the system of forcing people by law to serve in the armed forces 4 [C;U] *AmE*‖**draught** *BrE*– a current of air flowing through a room, a chimney, etc.: *You'll catch a cold if you sit in a draft.* 5 [C] *AmE*‖also **draught** esp. *BrE*– an act of swallowing liquid or an amount of liquid swallowed at one time

draft² v [T] 1 to make a DRAFT¹ (1) of 2 [*into*] *AmE*‖also **call up**, **conscript**– to order someone to join the armed forces

draft board /'· ·/ *AmE* a group of officials who select people to be DRAFTed (DRAFT² (2)) into the armed forces

draft·ee /dræf'tiy/ n a person who has been DRAFTed (DRAFT² (2)) into the armed forces: *He's a draftee.*

drafts·man *AmE*‖ **draughtsman** *BrE* /'dræftsmən/ n -**men** /mən/ 1 a person whose job is to make detailed drawings of all the parts of a new building, machine, etc. 2 *fml* a person who draws well

draft·y *AmE*‖**draughty** *BrE* /'dræftiy/ adj -ier, -iest with cold DRAFTs (4) blowing through: *a drafty room*

drag¹ /dræg/ n 1 [C;U] the action or an act of dragging 2 [C] something that is dragged along over a surface 3 [C *on, upon*] something or someone that makes it harder to advance towards a desired end: *He felt that his family was a drag on his career.* 4 [S] *infml* something dull and uninteresting: *The party was a drag, so we left early.* 5 [C] *infml* an act of breathing in cigarette smoke; PUFF² (1) 6 [U] *infml* woman's clothing worn by a man: *in drag*

drag² v -gg- 1 [T] to pull (a heavy thing) along: *dragging a branch along|*(fig.) *Why do you want to drag me out to a concert on this cold night!* 2 [I;T *along*] to (cause to) move along while touching the ground: *dragging his feet in the dust* 3 [I] to move along too slowly in space or time: *He dragged behind the others.*

drag on v adv [I] to last an unnecessarily long time: *The meeting seemed to drag on for hours.*

drag out v adv 1 [I;T (=**drag** sthg.↔**out**)] to (cause to) last an unnecessarily long time: *They dragged out the meeting with long speeches.* 2 [T *of*] (**drag** sthg.↔**out**) to force (something) to be told: *The police dragged the truth out of the prisoner.*

drag sthg.↔**up** v adv [T] *infml* to raise (a subject) unnecessarily: *The newspapers keep dragging up the politician's mistake.*

drag·on /'drægən/ n an imaginary fire-breathing animal in children's stories: (fig.) *That old woman's a real dragon!*

drag·on·fly /'drægən,flaɪ/ n -**flies** a large harmless brightly-colored insect

drain¹ /dreyn/ v [I;T] 1 [*away, off, out*] to (cause to) flow off gradually or completely: *to drain all the water out|The water drained (off/away).|Drain all the oil from/out of the engine.|*(fig.) *The old lady's strength is draining away.* 2 [*of*] to (cause to) become dry (as water or other liquid is removed): *Let the wet glasses drain (dry) before you put them away.|She was so afraid/angry that her face (was) drained of blood.|They want to drain the land to make crops grow better on it.|She drained her glass* (=drank all the contents) *and asked for more wine.|*(fig.) *His recent illness has really drained him.* (=made him weak)

drain² n 1 (the GRATING over) a pipe or ditch which carries esp. waste water away from buildings: *The drains are stopped up.* –see illustration on page 337 2 something that DRAINs, empties, or uses up: *All this spending is a drain on the money I have saved.* 3 **down the drain** *infml* used wastefully: (*The results of) years of work went down the drain in the fire.*

drain·age /'dreynɪdʒ/ n [U] a system or means for DRAINing: *soil with good drainage*

drain·board /'dreynbɔrd, -bowrd/ n a sloping board, usu. fixed to a SINK, on which dishes are placed after washing to allow them to dry

drake /dreyk/ n a male duck

dram /dræm/ n a small measure of weight

dra·ma /'dromə, 'dræmə/ n 1 [C] a serious work of literature that can be acted or read as a PLAY¹ (2) 2 [U] the art or study of PLAYs: *Which do you like better: music or drama?* 3 [U] a group of exciting events: *the drama of international politics|Their vacations are always full of drama.*

dra·mat·ic /drə'mætɪk/ adj 1 [*no comp.*] of or related to the DRAMA (2) 2 exciting; catching the imagination: *a dramatic moment when the movie star jumped from the window* –**dramatically** adv

dra·mat·ics /drə'mætɪks/ n [U] 1 the study or practice of theatrical arts such as acting 2 often derog DRAMATIC behavior or expression: *Your dramatics aren't going to change my mind.*

dram·a·tist /'dræmətɪst, 'dra-/ n a writer of plays, esp. serious ones; PLAYWRIGHT

dram·a·tize ‖also -**tise** *BrE* /'dræmə,taɪz, 'dra-/ v -**tized**, -**tizing** 1 [T] to change (a book, report, etc.) so that it can be acted or read as a play: *He's dramatizing the book about his life.* **2** [I;T] to present (something) in a DRAMATIC manner: *Don't dramatize so much—just give us the facts!* **–dramatization** /ˌdræmətəˈzeʸʃən, ˌdrɑ-/ *n* [C;U]

drank /dræŋk/ *v past tense of* DRINK¹

drape /dreʸp/ *v* **draped, draping** [T] **1** [*with, in, around, over*] to cover or decorate (something) with (folds of cloth): *We draped the picture of the war hero with/in the national flag.|Drape the flag around/over the picture.* **2** [*over, around*] to cause to hang or stretch out loosely or carelessly: *He draped his legs over the arm of the chair.*

drap·er·y /ˈdreʸpəriʸ/ *n* **-ies 1** [C;U] cloth or a garment arranged in folds: *walls covered with drapery|the drapery department of the store* **2** [U] *BrE for* DRY GOODS

drapes /dreʸps/ also **draperies–** *n* [P] *AmE* heavy curtains arranged in loose folds—compare CURTAIN

dras·tic /ˈdræstɪk/ *adj* strong, sudden, and often violent or severe: *Drastic changes are necessary to improve the government of the country.* **–drastically** *adv: She has changed drastically this year.*

draught ‖also **draft** *AmE* /dræft/ *n* [A;U] the drawing of a liquid from a large container such as a barrel: *Don't you have beer* **on draught** *here?* |*I want draught beer, not bottled beer!*

draughts /dræfts/ [U] *BrE for* CHECKERS

draw¹ /drɔ/ *v* **drew** /druʷ/, **drawn** /drɔn/, **drawing 1** [I;T] to make (pictures) with a pencil or pen: *Jane draws very well.|to draw a line/a map|He drew a house.* **2** [T] to cause to come, go, or move by pulling: *The horse drew the cart up the hill.|She* **drew me aside** *and whispered in my ear.|*(fig.) *Don't let yourself get drawn into the argument.|He drew the curtains.* (=opened or closed them) **3** [T] to take or pull out: *to draw water from the well.|He suddenly drew a knife and threatened me with it.|I drew $100 from my bank account today.|She drew the winning number in the lottery.|The insect bit him and* **drew blood** *from his arm.|*(fig.) *After three attempts he* **drew the conclusion** (=decided by reason) *that he would never pass the exam.* **4** [I] *rather lit* to move or go steadily or gradually: *Winter is drawing near.|The train drew into/ out of the station.* **5** [T] to attract: *The play is drawing large crowds/*AUDIENCES.*|Her shouts drew the attention of the police.* **6** [I;T] to end (a game, battle, etc.) without either side winning: *They drew (the match) 5 points to 5.* (=5 all)|*a drawn game* **–compare** TIE¹ (5) **7** to take (a breath) in: *She drew a deep breath and then continued.* **8** [I] to produce or allow a current of air, esp. to make a fire burn better: *The chimney/my pipe isn't drawing very well.* **9** **draw the line** to fix a limit of what one will not do or agree to: *to draw the line at stealing|I'm sorry but that's where I draw the line; I won't help him to cheat.* **10** [T] (of money, business shares, etc.) to earn: *money drawing interest in a bank*

draw away *v adv* **1** [I;T *from*] to move (something) away, usu. quickly: *He drew his hand away when she tried to shake it.* **2** [I *from*] to get further and further ahead (of): *The leader was gradually drawing away from the other runners.*

draw back *v adv* [I *from*] **1** to move oneself away from: *The crowd drew back in terror as the building crashed to the ground.* **2** to be unwilling to consider or fulfil (something): *The company drew back from (fulfilling) its agreement and wanted to talk about a new contract.* **–see** DRAWBACK

draw on/upon sthg. *v prep* [T] to make use of: *I'll have to draw on the money I've saved.|A writer has to draw on his imagination and experience.*

draw out *v adv* **1** [T] (**draw** sthg.↔ **out**) to cause to stretch in space or time: *a long-drawn-out speech* **2** [T] to have more hours of daylight: *The days are drawing out now that it's spring.*

draw up *v adv* **1** [T] (**draw** sthg.↔ **up**) to form and usu. write: *to draw up a plan/a contract/a check* **2** [I] (of a vehicle) to get to a certain point and stop: *The car drew up (at the gate) and three men got out.* **3** [T] (**draw** sbdy. **up**) to make (oneself) stand straight, often proudly: *to draw oneself up to one's full height*

draw² *n* **1** an act or example of DRAWING¹ (3), esp. in a LOTTERY: *He picked a winning number on the first draw.|He won and I lost: that's* **the luck of the draw.** **2** a result with neither side winning: *The game ended in/was a draw.* **3** a person or thing that attracts esp. a paying public: *That new singer is a big draw.*

draw·back /ˈdrɔbæk/ *n* a difficulty or disadvantage; something that can cause trouble: *The only drawback of the plan is that it costs too much.* **–see** DRAW¹ **back**

drawer /drɔr/ *n* a sliding boxlike container with an open top (as in a table or desk): *The paper is in my desk drawer.*

draw·ing /ˈdrɔ-ɪŋ/ *n* **1** [U] the art of drawing with lines made with a pen, pencil, etc.: *good at drawing* **2** [C] a picture made by drawing: *a drawing of a cat*

drawl /drɔl/ *v* [I;T] to speak or say slowly, with vowels greatly lengthened: *He spoke with a southern drawl.* **–drawl** *n :to speak in/with a drawl*

drawn¹ /drɔn/ *adj* (esp. of the face) changed as if by pulling or stretching: *a face drawn with sorrow*

drawn² *v past participle of* DRAW¹

dread¹ /dred/ *v* [T +*to-v/v-ing/that*] to fear greatly: *I dread her coming.|I* **dread to think** *what will happen if she comes.*

dread² *n* [S] a great fear, esp. of some harm to come: *He suffers from a great dread of heights.*

dread·ful /ˈdredfəl/ *adj* **1** causing great fear or anxiety; terrible: *the dreadful news of the accident|dreadful pain* **2** *infml* very unpleasant; unenjoyable; bad: *What a dreadful noise!|The play last night was just dreadful!*

dread·ful·ly /ˈdredfəliʸ/ *adv* **1** *infml polite* very: *I'm dreadfully sorry.* **2** in a DREADFUL manner: *dreadfully hurt*

dream¹ /driˠm/ *n* **1** a group of thoughts, images, or feelings experienced during sleep or when the mind is not completely under conscious control: *The child woke up in the middle of a bad dream.* **2** [*usu. sing.*] a state of mind in which one does not pay much attention to the real world: *John lives in a dream.* **3** something imagined and hopefully desired: *His dream was to live on a warm, sunny island.* **4** *infml* a thing or person notable for beauty, excellence, or enjoyable quality: *Their new house is a real dream.* –**dreamlike** *adj*

dream² *v* **dreamed** /driˠmd, drɛmt/ also **dreamt** /drɛmt/, *BrE* **dreaming** /'driˠmɪŋ/ [I;T +(*that*)/*of, about*] to have a dream (about something): *Do you dream at night?* |*I dreamed he would come.*|(fig.) *I never said that! You must have been dreaming.*|(fig.) *I* **wouldn't dream of** (=wouldn't consider) *hurting the child.*
USAGE For both the past tense and the past participle, **dreamed** and **dreamt** are both used in *BrE*, but **dreamed** is more often used in *AmE*.
dream sthg. ↔ **away** *v adv* [T] to spend (time) in dreaming or inactivity: *to dream away the hours*
dream sthg. ↔ **up** *v adv* [T] *infml often derog* to think of or imagine (something unusual or surprising): *They can always dream up some new excuse for the train arriving late.*

dream·er /'driˠmər/ *n* **1** a person who dreams **2** a person who has ideas or plans that are considered impractical

dream·y /'driˠmiˠ/ *adj* **-ier, -iest 1** (of a person) living more in the imagination than in the real world **2** *infml* wonderful; desirable; beautiful: *Isn't that dress dreamy!* –**dreamily** *adv* –**dreaminess** *n* [U]

drear·y /'drɪəriˠ/ *adj* **-ier, -iest** dull; sad; uninteresting: *a dreary day, cold and without sunshine*|*Addressing envelopes all the time is dreary work.* –**drearily** *adv* –**dreariness** *n* [U]

dredge /drɛdʒ/ *v* **dredged, dredging** [I;T *for*] to use a DREDGER (in, on, or for something): *Can we dredge the river to make it deeper?*

dredg·er /'drɛdʒər/ also **dredge–** *n* a machine or ship used for digging or sucking up mud and sand from the bottom of a river, canal, etc.

dregs /drɛgz/ *n* [P] bitter bits of matter in a liquid that sink to the bottom and are thrown away: (fig.) *Murderers and thieves are the dregs* (=worthless part) *of society.*

drench /drɛntʃ/ *v* [T] to make (usu. people, animals, or clothes) thoroughly wet: *I am drenched! I had no coat on when the rain started.*

dress¹ /drɛs/ *v* **1** [I;T] to put clothes on (oneself or someone else): *I'll be ready in a minute; I'm dressing.*|*Please dress the baby, George.* –see USAGE **2** [I;T] to provide (oneself or someone else) with clothes of the stated type: *She dresses well on very little money.*|*She's very well-dressed.*|*an old lady dressed in black* **3** [I] to put on formal clothes for the evening: *He said he would go to the*

party *if he didn't have to dress.* **4** [T] to clean and put medicine and a protective covering on (a wound) **5** [T] to treat (food) so as to make ready for cooking or eating: *a dressed chicken*|*He dressed the salad with oil and vinegar.*
USAGE Compare **dress, put on,** and **wear**: **Dress** can mean either "to put on clothes" or "to have on or wear clothes of the stated type," but **wear** cannot be used to mean "put on," or **put on** to mean "wear": *She got out of the bath and* **dressed**/*got* **dressed**/**put on** *her clothes.*|*Wait a minute–I'm just* **dressing** *the baby*/**putting** *the baby's clothes on.* Compare: *She always* **dresses** *in black*/**wears** *black.*|*He's not* **dressed** *in his uniform*/**wearing** *his uniform.*
dress sbdy. ↔ **down** *v adv* [T] to scold; TELL off (1) –**dressing-down** *n*: *He got a good dressing-down for being late so often.*
dress up *v adv* **1** [I] (usu. of children) to wear someone else's clothes for fun and pretense: *That little girl likes dressing up (in her mother's clothes).* **2** [I] to put on formal clothes or clothes which are not casual: *She wanted to go to dinner but didn't feel like dressing up.* **3** [T] (**dress** sbdy./sthg.↔ **up**) to make (something or someone) seem different or more attractive: *He dressed the facts up in amusing details.*

dress² *n* **1** [C] a woman's or girl's outer garment that covers the body from shoulder to knee or below –see illustration on page 123 **2** [U] clothing, esp. outer clothing: *Do we have to wear evening dress for this party?* –compare SKIRT; see CLOTHES (USAGE)

dress³ *adj* [A *no comp.*] **1** of or used for a dress: *dress material* **2** (of clothing) suitable for a formal occasion: *a dress shirt*/*coat*/*suit*

dress cir·cle /'· ,··/ *n* the first row of raised seats in a theater

dress·er /'drɛsər/ *n AmE* a chest of drawers, used esp. for clothing, often with a mirror on top –see illustration on page 55

dress·ing /'drɛsɪŋ/ *n* **1** [U] the act or action of a person who dresses: *Dressing is difficult for her since her accident.* **2** [C] material used to cover a wound: *a clean dressing* **3** [C;U] a usu. liquid mixture for adding to food, esp. a SALAD **4** [U] *AmE* for STUFFING (2)

dressing gown /'·· ,·/ *n* a garment rather like a long loose coat, worn after rising from bed and before putting on outer clothes

dressing ta·ble /'·· ,··/ *n* a low table with a mirror, usu. in a bedroom, at which one sits to arrange one's hair, etc.

dress·y /'drɛsiˠ/ *adj* **-ier, -iest** (of clothes) showy or ornamental, not for ordinary wear

drew /druˠ/ *v past tense of* DRAW¹

drib·ble /'drɪbəl/ *v* **-bled, -bling 1** [I;T] (of a liquid, esp. SALIVA) to flow or fall out in drops little by little: *The water dribbled from the tap.* **2** [I] to let a liquid, esp. SALIVA, fall or flow out slowly drop by drop: *The baby is dribbling. Wipe its mouth.* **3** [I;T] (in BASKETBALL) to move (a ball) by a number of short bounces –**dribble** *n*: *a dribble from the tap*

dribs /drɪbz/ *n* **dribs and drabs** *infml* small and unimportant amounts: *He's paying me* *back in dribs and drabs.*

dried /draɪd/ *v* past tense and participle of DRY²

dri·er /'draɪər/ *n* →DRYER

drift¹ /drɪft/ *n* **1** [C;U] the movement or course of something DRIFTING²: (fig.) *We have to stop this drift towards war.*|(fig.) *the drift of young people from the country to the city* **2** [C] a mass of matter (such as snow or sand) blown together by wind: *snow in great drifts*|*a snow drift* **3** [S] the general meaning: *I'm sorry; I can't* **catch/get the drift of** *what you're saying.*

drift² *v* **1** [I] to float or be driven along by wind, waves, or currents: *They drifted (out to sea).*|(fig.) *She just drifts from job to job.*|(fig.) *They had been married for a long time, but they gradually drifted apart until they separated.* **2** [I;T] to (cause to) pile up under the force of the wind or water: *The snow was drifting in great piles against the house.*

drift·er /'drɪftər/ *n* often derog a person who DRIFTS, esp. one who travels or moves about aimlessly

drill¹ /drɪl/ *v* [I;T] **1** to use a DRILL² (1) on (something); to make with a drill: *to drill a hole in the wall*|*The workmen have been drilling (the road) all day.* **2** to train and exercise (soldiers, students, etc.) by means of DRILLS² (2): *Let's drill them in English pronunciation.*

drill² *n* **1** [C] a tool or machine for making holes: *a road drill*|*a* DENTIST'S *drill* **2** [C;U] training and instruction in a subject, esp. by means of repeating and following exact orders **3** [C] practice in how to deal with a dangerous state of affairs: *a fire drill*

drill³ *n* **1** a machine used for planting seeds in rows **2** a row of seeds planted in this way

dri·ly /'draɪliʸ/ *adv* see DRY

drink¹ /drɪŋk/ *v* **drank** /dræŋk/, **drunk** /drʌŋk/, **drinking 1** [I;T *up*] to swallow (liquid): *Drink your coffee before it gets cold.*|(fig.) *drinking air into his lungs* **2** [I] to take in alcohol, esp. too much: *He doesn't smoke or drink.*|(fig.) *He drinks like a fish.*

drink sthg.↔ **in** *v adv* [T] to take in through the senses, esp. eagerly: *They drank in the sights and sounds of the city.*

drink to sbdy./sthg. *v prep* [T] to wish good health or success to; drink a TOAST¹ (2) to: *I drink to your health.*

drink² *n* [C;U] **1** a liquid suitable for swallowing **2** the habit or an act of drinking alcohol: *a drink of water*|*Their frequent arguments* **drove him to drink.**

drink·er /'drɪŋkər/ *n* a person who drinks alcohol, esp. too much: *a heavy drinker*

drip¹ /drɪp/ *v* **-pp-** [I;T] to fall or let fall in drops: *Water is dripping (down) from the roof.*|*The roof is dripping water.*|*The* TAP *is dripping.* (=water is dripping from the tap)

drip² *n* **1** [S] the action or sound of falling in drops: *All night I heard the drip drip drip of the water.* **2** [C] infml a dull and unattractive person

drip-dry /ˌ· '·◄/ *adj* (of clothing) that will dry smooth and needs no ironing when hung

while wet: *a drip-dry shirt*

drip·pings /'drɪpɪŋz/ *n* [P] fat and juices that have come from meat during cooking

drive¹ /draɪv/ *v* **drove** /drowᵛ/, **driven** /'drɪvən/, **driving** /'draɪvɪŋ/ **1** [I;T] to guide and control (a vehicle): *She drives well.*|*They drove to the station.*|*I never learned to drive a car.* –see LEAD (USAGE) **2** [T] to take (someone) in a vehicle: *Can you drive me to the station?* **3** [T] to force to go: *The farmer was driving his cattle along the road.*|*The bad weather has driven business away.* **4** [T] to provide the power for: *The engines drive the ship.* **5** [T] to force (someone) to work hard or to be or act as stated: *He drives his workers very hard.*|*It was her pride that drove her to do it.*|*driven mad with pain* **6** [T] to hit; push; move forward: *He drove the nail into the wood.*|*She drove the ball 150 yards.* **7** [I] (esp. of rain) to fall or move along with great force: *driving rain* **8** **drive something home (to)** to make something unmistakably clear (to)

drive at sthg. *v prep* [T *no pass.*] infml (in -ing form) to mean without actually saying; HINT: *What are you driving at?* (=What do you mean?)

drive sbdy./ sthg.↔ **off** *v adv* [T] to force away or back; REPEL: *He drove off his attackers.*

drive² *n* **1** [C] a journey in a vehicle **2** [C] a road, esp. one through a public park or to a private house **3** [C] an act of hitting a ball forcefully **4** [C] a strong well-planned effort by a group for a particular purpose: *The club is having a membership drive.* (=to get more members) **5** [C] an important natural need which must be fulfilled: *Hunger, thirst, and sex are among the strongest human drives.* **6** [U] a forceful quality of mind or spirit that gets things done: *He's intelligent but he won't succeed because he lacks drive.* **7** [C;U] the apparatus by which a machine is set or kept in movement: *This car has (a) front-wheel drive.* (=the engine turns the front wheels)

drive-in /'· ·/ *n,adj* [A;C] (a place) that people can use while remaining in their cars: *a drive-in (restaurant/movie theater/bank)*

driv·el /'drɪvəl/ *n,v* **1-** *AmE*‖**-ll-** *BrE* [I;U] (to talk) nonsense: *Don't talk drivel!*

driv·er /'draɪvər/ *n* a person who DRIVES: *Who was the driver of the car when the accident happened?*|*a cattle-driver*

driver's li·cense /'·· ˌ··/ *AmE*‖**driving licence** *BrE n* a LICENSE to drive a motor vehicle, obtained after success in a **driving test** /'·· ˌ·/

drive·way /'draɪvweʸ/ *n* a short private road leading from the street to a house or garage –see illustration on page 337

driz·zle¹ /'drɪzəl/ *v* **-zled, -zling** [it+I] to rain in very small drops or very lightly –see WEATHER (USAGE)

drizzle² *n* [S;U] a fine misty rain –**drizzly** *adj*: *drizzly rain*|*a drizzly day*

droll /drowl/ *adj* having a humorously odd or unusual quality: *a droll person/expression* –**drolly** /'drowl-liʸ, 'drowliʸ/ *adv*

drom·e·dar·y /'drɑməˌdɛriʸ/ *n* **-ies** a camel with one HUMP

drone¹ /drown/ v,n **droned, droning** [I;S] (to make) a continuous low dull sound like that of bees: *the drone of the enemy aircraft*|(fig.) *The politician droned on and on* (=spoke for a long time in an uninteresting manner) *about the President's new plans.*

drone² n a male bee

drool /druʷl/ v [I] *derog* to let liquid flow from the mouth: *At the sight of the food the dog started drooling.*|(fig.) *I don't like the way people drool* (=show pleasure in a foolish way) *over that singer.*

droop /druʷp/ v [I] to hang or bend downwards: *Her shoulders drooped with tiredness.*|*The flowers drooped and faded.*|(fig.) *Her spirits drooped.* (=she became sad) –**droop** n [S]

drop¹ /drɑp/ n **1** [C] a small round mass of liquid: *a drop of oil* |*a tear drop* |*Drops of rain fell on the window.*|(fig.) *"Would you like some more milk?" "Just a drop* (=a little) *please."* **2** [S] a distance or movement straight down: *a long drop to the bottom of the cliff* |*a drop in temperature/quantity/ quality*|*a drop of 10 feet* **3** [C] a small round candy: *fruit drops*|*chocolate drops* **4** (only) **a drop in the ocean** a small unimportant quantity

drop² v **-pp- 1** [I;T] to fall or let fall: *The fruit dropped* (*down*) *from the tree.*|*to drop one's voice* (*to a lower note*)|*Prices dropped* (=became lower) *in the first half of the year.*|*The wind has dropped.* (=has become less strong)|(fig.) *They worked until they dropped.* (=from tiredness) **2** [T] *infml* to allow (someone) to get out of a vehicle: *Drop me* (*off*) *at the corner.* **3** [T] to stop seeing, talking about, using, or practicing: *Let's drop the subject.* (=let's talk about something else)|*I'm going to drop history this year.* (=stop studying it)|*He's dropped all his old friends.* **4** [T] to leave out: *You drop the "o" when you combine "can" and "not" in "can't."*|*I've been dropped* (*from the team*) *for next Saturday's game.* **5** [I *in, by, around*] to visit unexpectedly or informally: *Drop in* (*and see us*) *next time you're in Atlanta.*|*Drop by* (=visit me) *one evening next week.* **6** [I *away, behind*] to get further away from a moving object by moving more slowly than it: *Our boat started the race well, but soon dropped away* (*from the others*)/*behind* (*the others*). **7** [T] *infml* to knock down; cause to fall: *dropped him with one blow* **8 drop dead** *infml* (often used in commands as an *INSULT*) to die suddenly **9 drop someone a line/note** to write a short letter to someone

drop in on sbdy. v adv prep [T no pass.] to visit without warning, informally

drop off v adv **1** [I] also **drop away**– to lessen; become fewer: *Interest in the game has dropped off.* **2** [T] (**drop** sbdy. **off**) *infml* to allow (sbdy.) to get out of a vehicle: *Just drop me off at the station.* **3** [T] (**drop** sthg. ↔ **off**) *infml* to deliver: *I want to drop off these books at Joanne's house on my way to school.* **4** [I] *infml* for *DOZE* **off**

drop out v adv [I] to stop attending or taking part: *He dropped out of college after only two weeks.*

drop·out /'drɑp-aʊt/ n a person who *DROPs* out of: **a** school or college without completing the course **b** ordinary society to practice another life style

drop·per /'drɑpər/ n a short glass tube with a rubber part (*BULB*) at one end used for measuring out liquids, esp. liquid medicine, in drops

drop·pings /'drɑpɪŋz/ n [P] waste matter from the bowels of animals and birds

drops /drɑps/ n [P] liquid medicine to be taken drop by drop: *eyedrops*

dross /drɔs, drɑs/ n [U] waste or impure matter

drought /draʊt/ n a long period of dry weather, when there is not enough water: *The crops died during the drought.*

drove¹ /droʷv/ n a large group of people or animals moving or acting together

drove² v past tense of *DRIVE*

drown /draʊn/ v **1** [I;T] to (cause to) die under water because unable to breathe **2** [T] to cover completely with water, esp. by a rise in the water level: *streets and houses drowned by the floods*|(fig.) *drowning the fruit with cream* **3** [T *out*] to cover up (a sound) by making a loud noise: *The band drowned out our conversation, so we sat and said nothing.* **4 drown one's sorrows** to drink alcohol in an attempt to forget one's troubles

drowse /draʊz/ v **drowsed, drowsing** [I *off*] to fall into a light sleep

drows·y /'draʊziʸ/ adj **-sier, -siest 1** ready to fall asleep **2** making one sleepy: *a drowsy summer afternoon* –**drowsily** adv –**drowsiness** n [U]

drudge¹ /drʌdʒ/ v **drudged, drudging** [I] to do hard, humble, or uninteresting work

drudge² n a person who *DRUDGEs*

drudg·er·y /'drʌdʒəriʸ/ n [U] hard dull humble uninteresting work

drug¹ /drʌg/ n **1** a medicine or material used for making medicines **2** a substance one takes, esp. as a habit, esp. for pleasure or excitement: *Tobacco and alcohol can be dangerous drugs.*|*Is he* **on drugs**? (=Does he takes drugs)|*Drug abuse is a serious problem among young people.*

drug² v **-gg-** [T] to add drugs or give drugs to, esp. so as to produce unconsciousness: *to drug a sick man in pain* |*The coffee was drugged.*

drug·gist /'drʌgɪst/ n *AmE* for *PHARMACIST*

drug·store /'drʌgstɔr, -stoʷr/ n esp. *AmE* a *PHARMACY*, esp. one which sells not only medicine, beauty products, film, etc., but also simple meals

drum¹ /drʌm/ n **1** a musical instrument consisting of a skin stretched tight over one or both sides of a hollow circular frame, and struck by hand or with a stick **2** something that looks like such an instrument, esp. a part of a machine or a large container for liquids: *an oil drum*

drum² v **-mm-** [I] **1** to beat or play a drum **2** to make drum-like noises, esp. by continuous beating or striking: *He drummed on the table* *with his fingers.*|*the sound of rain drumming against the window*

drum sthg. **into** sbdy. *v prep* [T] *infml* to put (an idea) firmly into (someone's mind) by steady effort or continuous repeating: *She drummed into the children that they should not cross the street alone.*

drum sthg.↔ **up** *v adv* [T] *infml* to obtain by continuous effort and esp. by advertising: *Let's try to drum up some more business.*

drum·mer /'drʌmər/ *n* a person who plays a drum

drum·stick /'drʌm,stɪk/ *n* **1** a stick for beating a drum **2** *infml* the lower meaty part of the leg of a bird, eaten as food

drunk¹ /drʌŋk/ *adj* [F] under the influence of alcohol: *The police charged him with being* **drunk and disorderly.**|*He got drunk on only two drinks.*|*He's* **dead/blind drunk.** (=very drunk)|(fig.) *drunk with power* –compare SOBER

drunk² also **drunkard** /'drʌŋkərd/– *n often derog* a person who is drunk, esp. often or continually

drunk³ *v past participle of* DRINK¹

drunk·en /'drʌŋkən/ *adj* [A] **1** drunk: *a drunken sailor* **2** resulting from or marked by too much drinking of alcohol: *a drunken sleep*|*a drunken driver* –**drunkenly** *adv* –**drunkenness** *n* [U]

dry¹ /draɪ/ *adj* **drier, driest 1** having no water or other liquid inside or on the surface; not wet: *Don't put your shirt on until it's dry.*|*The well has gone dry.*|*Be careful! The paint isn't dry yet.*|*dry skin* (=without natural liquids) **2** without rain or wetness: *dry weather* |*a dry month*|*dry heat* –compare HUMID **3** having or producing thirst: *I always feel dry in this hot weather.*|*It's dry work digging in the sun.* **4** (of alcoholic drinks, esp. wine) not sweet; not fruity in taste **5** amusing without appearing to be so; quietly IRONIC: *I like his dry humor.* **6** dull and uninteresting: *The book was* **as dry as dust.** (=very uninteresting) **7** not allowing the sale of alcoholic drink: *Are any parts of the US still dry?* **8 (as) dry as a bone** also **bone-dry**– *infml* very dry –**dryly, drily** *adv* –**dryness** *n* [U]

dry² *v* **dried, drying 1** [I;T *out, up*] to (cause to) become dry: *Dry your hands.*|*The wet clothes will soon dry (out) in the sun.*|*The hot summer sun dried up the lake.* **2** [T] to preserve (food) by removing liquid: *dried fruit/milk*

dry out *v adv* [I;T (=**dry** sbdy. **out**)] to (cause to) give up dependence on alcoholic drink

dry-clean /'· ·, ,· '·/ *v* [T] to clean (clothes, material, etc.), with chemicals instead of water, in a special store (**dry cleaner's**)

dry dock /'· ·/ *n* a place in which a ship is held in position while the water is pumped out, leaving the ship dry for repairs: *a ship* **in dry dock** *being painted*

dry·er, drier /'draɪər/ *n* a machine that dries – see illustration on page 51

dry goods /'· ·/ *AmE*‖**drapery** *BrE*– *n* [P] cloth, FABRICs, etc. as separate from food, HARDWARE, etc.

dry ice /ˌ· '·/ *n* [U] CARBON DIOXIDE in a solid state, used mainly to keep food and other things cold

dry rot /ˌ· '·/ *n* [U] diseased growth in wood (as in wooden floors) which turns wood into powder: *They didn't buy the house because it had dry rot.*

dry run /ˌ· '·/ *n* a practice exercise; REHEARSAL

du·al /'duwəl, 'dyuwəl/ *adj* [A] consisting of two parts or having two parts like each other; double: *He has a dual interest in the school. He teaches there, and his son is one of the students.*|*a dual-purpose instrument*

dub¹ /dʌb/ *v* **-bb-** [T] **1** *lit or old use* to make (someone) a KNIGHT by a ceremonial touch on the shoulder with a sword **2** *humor (or in newspapers)* to name humorously or descriptively: *They dubbed him Fatty because of his size.*

dub² *v* [T] **1** to give new or different sound effects to, or change the original spoken language of (a film, radio show, or television show): *Is the movie dubbed or does it have* SUBTITLES? **2** to record the sounds or images from one MAGNETIC TAPE to another, in order to make a copy: *I'd like to dub that* VIDEOTAPE *so I can watch it at home*

dub³ *n* a copy of a MAGNETIC TAPE made by DUBbing: *I can't give you the original tape, but I can make a dub for you.*

du·bi·ous /'duwbiyəs, 'dyuwˈ-/ *adj* **1** feeling doubt; undecided: *I'm still dubious about that plan.* **2** causing doubt; of uncertain value or meaning: *a dubious suggestion*|*a rather dubious character* (=a possibly dishonest person) –**dubiously** *adv* –**dubiousness** *n* [U]

duch·ess /'dʌtʃɪs/ *n* (*often cap.*) (the title of) **a** the wife of a DUKE **b** a woman who holds the rank of DUKE in her own right

duck¹ /dʌk/ **drake** *masc.*– *n* **ducks** *or* **duck 1** a common swimming bird with a wide beak, sometimes kept for meat, eggs, and soft feathers (**down**): *A young duck is called a* **duckling. 2 lame duck** *AmE* a political official whose term in office will soon end **3 like water off a duck's back** *infml* having no effect **4 (take to something) like a duck to water** *infml* (to learn or get used to something) naturally and very easily

duck² *v* **1** [I;T] to lower (one's head or body) quickly, esp. so as to avoid being hit or seen: *She had to duck to get through the low doorway.*|*He saw a policeman coming and ducked behind a car.* **2** [T] to push under water: *He ducked his head in the stream to get cool.* **3** [T] *infml* to try to avoid (a difficulty or unpleasant responsibility); DODGE: *Don't try to duck (out of) cleaning up the kitchen!* –**duck** *n*

duck out of sthg. *v adv prep* [T] *infml* to escape one's responsibility for: *Don't try to duck out of doing the dishes!*

duct /dʌkt/ *n* **1** a thin, narrow tube in the body or in plants which carries liquids, air, etc.: *tear ducts* **2** any kind of pipe or tube for carrying liquids, air, electric power lines, etc. –see AQUEDUCT, VIADUCT

dud /dʌd/ *n infml* a person or thing that is worthless or useless: *This new battery is a* *dud; it doesn't work!*

dude /duᵂd, dyuᵂd/ *n AmE infml* a city man, esp. an Easterner in the West

dude ranch /'·· ·/ *n* (in the US) a vacation place that offers activities (such as horseback riding) typical of western RANCHES (cattle farms)

due¹ /duᵂ, dyuᵂ/ *adj* **1** [F *to*] *fml* owed or owing as a debt or right: *A great deal of money is due to you.*|*Our grateful thanks are due to you.* –see DUE *to* (USAGE) **2** [A] *fml* proper; suitable; enough: *driving with due care and attention* **3** [F] payable: *a bill due today* **4** [F +*to-v*/ *for*] (showing arrangements made in advance) expected; supposed (to): *The next train to Los Angeles is due here at 4 o'clock.*|*I am due to leave very soon.*|*I am due for an increase in pay soon.* **5 in due course/ time** in or at the proper time –see also DULY

due to *prep* because of; caused by: *His illness was due to bad food.* –see Study Notes on page 144

USAGE Compare **due to** and **owing to**: As **due** is an adjective, **due to** should really be used only after nouns: *His absence was due to the storm.* Although it is now often used after verbs as well (in sentences like *He arrived late due to the storm.*), teachers prefer **owing to** or **because of** in these cases.

due² *n* something that rightfully belongs to someone, esp. something non-material: *I don't like him, but,* **to give him his due,** *he is a good singer.*

due³ *adv* (*before* north, south, east, *and* west) directly; exactly: *due north (of here)*

du·el¹ /'duᵂəl, 'dyuᵂəl/ *n* (esp. formerly) a fight with hand guns or swords between two people, to settle an argument: (fig.) *another duel between companies*

duel² *v* **-l-** *AmE*‖**-ll-** *BrE* [I *with*] to fight a DUEL **–dueler, duelist** *n*

due proc·ess /,· '··/ also **due process of law** /,· ·,··· '·/– *n* [*usu. sing.*] the fair operation of the law in US courts so that no citizen's rights are taken away: *He complained that he didn't get due process.*

dues /duᵂz, dyuᵂz/ *n* [P] official charges or payments: *harbor dues* |*union dues*|(fig.) *dues paying* (=actively involved) *member of a party, organization, etc.*

du·et /duᵂ'ɛt, dyuᵂ'ɛt/ *n* a piece of music for two performers –compare SOLO

duf·fel bag /'dʌfəl ,bæg/ *n* a loose bag made of a rough cloth, used for carrying clothes and other belongings on a trip

dug /dʌg/ *v* past tense and participle of DIG

dug·out /'dʌgaʊt/ *n* **1** a small light boat made by cutting out a deep hollow in a log: *a dugout CANOE* **2** [I] a (usu. military) shelter dug in the ground with an earth roof –compare TRENCH

duke /duᵂk, dyuᵂk/ *n* (*often cap.*) (the title of) a nobleman of the highest rank outside the Royal Family: *the Duke of Norfolk* |*He became a duke when his father died.* –see DUCHESS

dul·cet /'dʌlsɪt/ *adj lit* (esp. of sounds) sweet; pleasant; calming: *her dulcet tones* (=of her voice)

dull¹ /dʌl/ *adj* **1** not bright or shining: *a dress of some uninteresting dull color* |*It's a dull day; it'll probably rain.* **2** not clear or sharp: *a dull knocking sound somewhere in the house* | *a dull pain* **3** slow in thinking and understanding: *He couldn't teach such dull children.* **4** uninteresting; unexciting; lacking in imagination; boring (BORE⁴): *I slept through his dull speech.* **–dully** *adv*: *He spoke dully for what seemed like hours.* **–dullness** *n* [U]

dull² *v* [I;T] to (cause to) become dull: *eyes and ears dulled by age* |*Give me something to dull the pain.*

du·ly /'duᵂliʸ, 'dyuᵂliʸ/ *adv* [*no comp.*] *fml* in a DUE manner, time, or degree; properly: *The taxi that we had ordered duly arrived, and we drove off.*|*Your suggestion has been duly noted.*

dumb /dʌm/ *adj* **1** unable to speak: *dumb animals* |*The terrible news struck us all dumb.* **2** *infml* stupid: *That was a dumb thing to do!* **–dumbly** *adv* **–dumbness** *n* [U]

dumb·bell /'dʌmbɛl/ *n* **1** [*usu. pl.*] a weight consisting of two large metal balls connected by a short bar and usu. used in pairs for exercises **2** *infml esp. AmE* a stupid person

dumb·found, dumfound /dʌm'faʊnd, 'dʌm faʊnd/ *v* [T *usu. pass.*] to make unable to speak because of wonder, surprise, or lack of understanding: *He stood there, dumbfounded by the news.*

dum·my /'dʌmiʸ/ *n* **-mies 1** an object made to look like and take the place of a real thing: *a dummy gun made of wood* **2** something like a human figure made of wood or wax and used to make or show clothes: *a dressmaker's dummy* **3** *infml, esp. AmE* a stupid fool: *You dummy!*

dump¹ /dʌmp/ *v* [I;T] **1** to drop or unload (something) in a heap or carelessly: *Don't dump that sand in the middle of the path!* |*They dumped their bags on my floor and left!* |(fig.) *After she became rich and famous, she dumped all her old friends.* **2** *derog* to sell (goods) in a foreign country at a very low price

dump² *n* **1** a place for DUMPing something (such as waste material): *the town dump* **2** *derog infml* a dirty and untidy place: *This town's a real dump.*

dump·ling /'dʌmplɪŋ/ *n* **1** a lump of boiled DOUGH, often served with meat or having meat inside it **2** a sweet food made of pastry with fruit inside it: *apple dumplings*

dumps /dʌmps/ *n* **(down) in the dumps** *infml* sad; DEPRESSED

dump·y /'dʌmpiʸ/ *adj* **-ier, -iest** *infml* (esp. of a person) short and fat: *a dumpy little man*

dunce /dʌns/ *n* a slow learner; stupid person

dune /duᵂn, dyuᵂn/ also **sand dune**– *n* a sandhill (often long and low) piled up by the wind on the seashore or in a desert

dung /dʌŋ/ *n* [U] solid waste material passed from the bowels of animals (esp. cows and horses); animal MANURE

dun·ga·rees /,dʌŋgə'riʸz, 'dʌŋgə,riʸz/ *n* [P] pants made of heavy cotton cloth, usu. blue; JEANS –compare OVERALLS –see PAIR (USAGE)

dun·geon /'dʌndʒən/ *n* a dark underground

prison, esp. beneath a castle

dunk /dʌŋk/ v [T in] infml **1** to dip (esp. food) into liquid while eating: to dunk cookies in coffee **2** to put or cause (someone, oneself or something) to go under water, for a short period of time: She dunked her head in the water to cool off.

du·o /'duʷoʷ, 'dyuʷoʷ/ n **duos** two musicians who play or sing together

dupe¹ /duʷp, dyuʷp/ n a person who is tricked or deceived by someone else

dupe² v **duped, duping** [T into] to trick or deceive: The old lady was duped by the dishonest salesman.

du·plex /'duʷplɛks, 'dyuʷ-/ adj,n [A] AmE (a usu. costly apartment) having rooms on two floors of a building, with inside stairs connecting them –compare TRIPLEX

du·pli·cate¹ /'duʷpləkɪt, 'dyuʷ-/ adj,n [A;C] (something that is) exactly like another in appearance, pattern, or contents: If you've lost your key, I can give you a duplicate (key).|These two keys are duplicates (of each other).|copies in duplicate |duplicate copies

du·pli·cate² /'duʷplə,keʸt, 'dyuʷ-/ v [T] to copy exactly: Can you duplicate this key for me?|Can you duplicate these letters for me and send one to every student? –**duplication** /,duʷplə'keʸʃən, ,dyuʷ-/ n [U]

du·pli·ca·tor /'duʷplə,keʸtər, 'dyuʷ-/ n a machine that makes copies of written, printed, or drawn material

du·plic·i·ty /duʷ'plɪsəṭiʸ, dyuʷ-/ n [U] fml deceit; deception

dur·a·ble /'dʊərəbəl, 'dyʊər-/ adj long-lasting: durable clothing|We must make a durable peace. –**durability** /,dʊərə'bɪləṭiʸ, ,dyʊər-/ n [U]

du·ra·tion /dʊ'reʸʃən, dyʊ-/ n [U] the time during which something exists or lasts: He will be in the hospital for the duration of the school year.|an illness of short duration|We're in this together **for the duration.** (=for as long as it lasts)

du·ress /dʊ'rɛs, dyʊ-/ n [U] fml unlawful or unfair threats: You don't have to keep a promise made **under duress.**

dur·ing /'dʊərɪŋ, 'dyʊərɪŋ/ prep **1** all through (a length of time): He swims every day during the summer. (Compare He swam every day for three months.)|They lived abroad during the war. (=while the war was happening) **2** at some moment in (a length of time): He died during the night.

dusk /dʌsk/ n [U] the time when daylight is fading; darker part of TWILIGHT, esp. at night: The street lights go on at dusk. –compare DAWN¹ (2)

dusk·y /'dʌskiʸ/ adj **-ier, -iest** darkish in color; shadowy: the dusky light of the forest

dust¹ /dʌst/ n **1** [U] powder made up of very small pieces of waste or other matter: There was half an inch of dust on the books before I cleaned them.|gold dust/coal dust **2** [U] finely powdered earth: There is no grass here, and in the summer we have a great deal of dust.|The car left a cloud of dust as it went down the dirt road.

dust² v **1** [I;T] to clean the dust from; remove dust: Please dust all the books on the bottom shelf. **2** [T with] to cover with dust or fine powder: to dust the crops with a substance that will kill insects

dust·bin /'dʌst,bɪn/ n BrE for GARBAGE CAN

dust·er /'dʌstər/ n a cloth for dusting furniture

dust jack·et /'· ,··/ also **dust cover, jacket**– n a loose paper cover put as a protection around the hard cover of a book, often having writing or pictures describing the book

dust·pan /'dʌstpæn/ n a flat pan with a handle into which house dust can be brushed

dust·y /'dʌstiʸ/ adj **-ier, iest** dry and covered or filled with dust: In the summer the town becomes very dusty.

Dutch /dʌtʃ/ adj **1** of or related to the people, country, or language of the Netherlands (Holland) **2 go Dutch (with someone)**/**Dutch treat** to share expenses: Charles and Kate always go Dutch at the restaurant.

Dutch cour·age /,· '··/ n [U] infml the courage that comes from being drunk

du·ti·ful /'duʷtɪfəl, 'dyuʷ-/ adj (of people and their behavior) having or showing a sense of DUTY (1); with proper respect and obedience –**dutifully** adv

du·ty /'duʷtiʸ, 'dyuʷ-/ n **-ties** [C;U] **1** what one must do either because of one's job or because one thinks it right: His duties include taking the letters to the post office and arranging meetings.|to do one's duty |It's my duty to help you.|pay a duty visit (=because of conscience)|**duty bound** (=required by one's conscience) to visit an old aunt **2** a tax by the government, esp. on IMPORTED goods: CUSTOMS duties are paid on goods entering the country. **3 heavy duty** (as of a machine) able to do hard work: heavy duty tires **4 on/off duty** (esp. of policemen, soldiers, nurses, etc.) required/not required to work: When I'm off duty, I play tennis.

duty-free /,·· '· ◄/ adj,adv (of goods) allowed to come into the country without tax: You can bring in one bottle of wine duty-free.|the duty-free shop at the airport

dwarf¹ /dwɔrf/ n **dwarfs** or **dwarves** /dwɔrvz/ **1** a person, animal, or plant of much less than the usual size: a dwarf apple tree **2** a small imaginary manlike creature in fairy stories: Snow White and the Seven Dwarfs

dwarf² v [T] to cause to appear small by comparison: The new tall building dwarfs all the little stores.

dwell /dwɛl/ v **dwelt** /dwɛlt/ or **dwelled, dwelling 1** fml to live (in a place): They dwell in a forest/on an island. **2 -dweller** a person or animal that lives (in the stated place): cave-dwellers|city-dwellers

dwell on/upon sthg. v adv [T] to think, speak, or write a lot about: Don't dwell so much on your past.

dwell·ing /'dwɛlɪŋ/ n fml and humor a house, apartment, etc., where people live: Welcome to my humble dwelling!

dwin·dle /'dwɪndl/ v **-dled, -dling** [I away] to become gradually fewer or smaller: The number of people who live on the island is dwindling.

dye¹ /daɪ/ *n* [C;U] a vegetable or chemical substance, usu. liquid, used to color things esp. by dipping –compare PAINT² (1)

dye² *v* dyes, dyed, dyeing [I;T] to give or take (a stated) color by means of DYE: *She dyed the dress (red).|Will this dress dye?|*(fig.) *Sunset dyed the sky red.*

USAGE Compare **die** (verb): **dies, died, dying.**

dyed-in-the-wool /ˌ· · · '· ◄/ *adj often derog* impossible to change (as to the stated or known quality): *Emily is a dyed-in-the-wool Republican.*

dyke /daɪk/ *n, v* →DIKE

dy·nam·ic /daɪ'næmɪk/ *adj* **1** *often apprec* (of people, ideas, etc.) full of or producing power and activity: *a dynamic person|a dynamic period in history* **2** *tech* of or relating to force or power that causes movement –opposite **static** –**dynamically** *adv*

dy·nam·ics /daɪ'næmɪks/ *n* [U] **1** the science that deals with matter in movement **2** the forces that work in any system or matter: *the dynamics of international affairs*

dy·na·mism /'daɪnəˌmɪzəm/ *n* [U] (in a person) the quality of being DYNAMIC (1)

dy·na·mite¹ /'daɪnəˌmaɪt/ *n* [U] **1** a powerful explosive used in MINING **2** *infml* something or someone that will cause great shock, surprise, admiration, etc.: *That news story/That new singer is really dynamite!*

dynamite² *v* **-mited, -miting** [T] to blow up with DYNAMITE¹ (1)

dy·na·mo /'daɪnəˌmowˊ/ *n* **-mos** a machine (esp. small) which turns some other kind of power into electricity: *the dynamo on my bicycle* |(fig.) *Randolph is a real dynamo; he never stops working.* –compare GENERATOR

dy·nas·ty /'daɪnəstiˊ/ *n* **-ties** [C] a line of rulers all of the same family: *a dynasty of kings* –**dynastic** /daɪ'næstɪk/ *adj*

dys·en·ter·y /'dɪsənˌteriˊ/ *n* [U] a painful disease of the bowels that causes them to be emptied more often than usual and to produce blood and MUCUS

dys·lex·i·a /dɪs'leksiˊə/ also **word blindness**– *n* [U] *tech* inability to read, caused by difficulty in seeing letter shapes –**dyslexic** *adj*

dys·pep·sia /dɪs'pepʃə, -siˊə/ *n* [U] difficulty in DIGESTING food; INDIGESTION

dys·pep·tic /dɪs'peptɪk/ *adj* (typical of a person) suffering from DYSPEPSIA

E, e

E, e /iˊ/ **E's, e's** *or* **Es, es** the 5th letter of the English alphabet

E *written abbrev. said as:* east(ern)

each¹ /iˊtʃ/ *determiner,pron* every single one of two or more separately: *each foot|each of my feet|They each want to do something different.|She cut the cake into pieces and gave one to each of the children.*

USAGE Compare **each, every,** and **both: 1 Both** is used for two people or things taken together; **each** is used for any number of people or things taken separately; and **every** is used for a whole group: **Both** *my children* (=I have two children) *go to the same school.|***Each** *of my children* (=I have two or more children) *goes to a different school.|***Each** *child in the class gave a different answer.|***Every** *child in the class passed the examination.* **2 Both** always takes a plural verb; **every** always takes a singular verb: **Both** *our children go to the local school.|***Every** *child in the street goes to the local school.* **Each** usually takes a singular verb, except after a plural subject: **Each** *has his own room.|They* **each** *have their own rooms.* **3 Every** cannot be used in sentences like: **Both/Each** *of the boys...|The boys* **both/each**...

each² *adv* for or to every one: *The tickets are $5 each.*

each oth·er /ˌ· '··/ also **one another**– *pron* [*not used as the subject*] (means that each of two or more does something to the other(s)): *Susan and Robert kissed each other|one another* (=Susan kissed Robert and Robert kissed Susan)

USAGE Some teachers prefer **each other** to be used about two people or things, and **one another** about more than two: *After the tennis match, the two players shook hands with* **each other.**|*After the football match, the players all shook hands with* **one another.**

ea·ger /'iˊgər/ *adj* [+to-v/that/for, about] full of interest or desire; keen: *He listened to the story with eager attention.|He is eager for success/for you to meet his friends.* –**eagerly** *adv* –**eagerness** *n* [U]

ea·gle /'iˊgəl/ *n* a very large BIRD OF PREY with a hooked beak and very good eyesight

eagle-eyed /'·· ˌ·/ *adj* having very good eyesight: (fig.) *an eagle-eyed teacher, who sees the smallest mistake*

ear¹ /ɪər/ *n* **1** [C] either of the two organs of hearing, one on each side of the head: *Don't shout in my ear!* **2** [S for] good recognition of sounds, esp. in music and languages: *He doesn't like concerts; he has no ear for music.|Peter can play the most difficult piano music* **by ear.** (=without written musical notes) **3 out on one's ear** *infml* suddenly thrown out of a place because of bad behavior **4 play it by ear** *infml* to act as the situation changes rather than making plans in advance **5 up to one's ears in** *infml* deep in or very busy with: *I'm up to my ears in work/debt.* **6 -eared** having ears of a certain kind: *Rabbits are long-eared animals.*

ear² *n* the head of a grain-producing plant, used for food: *an ear of corn*

ear·drum /'ɪərdrʌm/ *n* a tight thin skin inside the ear, which allows one to hear sound

earl /ɜrl/ *n* (*often cap.*) (the title of) a British

nobleman of high rank: *the Earl of Warwick* –see also COUNTESS –**earldom** /'ɜrldəm/ *n*

ear·lobe /'ɪərlowᵇ/ *n* the fleshy bottom part of the EAR¹ (1)

ear·ly¹ /'ɜrliʸ/ *adj* **-lier, -liest 1** [after *n*] arriving, happening, etc., before the usual or expected time: *The train was ten minutes early.* **2** [A *no comp.*] happening towards the beginning of the day, a period of time, etc.: *She returned in the early morning.|I hope for an early answer to my letter.* –compare LATE¹ **3 at the earliest** and not sooner: *The letter will reach him on Monday at the very earliest.* –opposite **at the latest** –**earliness** *n* [U]

early² *adv* **-lier, -liest 1** before the usual, arranged, or expected time: *He always arrives early.* **2** towards the beginning of a period: *The bush was planted early (on) in the season.* –compare LATE²

ear·mark /'ɪərmɑrk/ *v* [T] to set aside (money, etc.) for a particular purpose: *Money earmarked for the schools*

earn /ɜrn/ *v* [T *by*] **1** to get (money) by working: *He earns $5,000 a year (by writing stories).* **2** to get (something that one deserves) because of one's qualities or actions: *She earned her place in the team by training hard.* –see WIN (USAGE)

ear·nest¹ /'ɜrnɪst/ *adj* determined and serious: *John is very earnest young man; he should relax more.* –**earnestly** *adv* –**earnestness** *n* [U]

earnest² *n* [U] seriousness: *It soon began to snow in earnest.* (=very hard)

earn·ings /'ɜrnɪŋz/ *n* [P] money which is earned by working

ear·phone /'ɪərfowⁿ/ *n* [*usu. pl.*] the part of a HEADPHONE that fits over the ear –see illustration on page 221

ear·ring /'ɪərɪŋ, 'ɪər,rɪŋ/ *n* a decoration worn on the ear –see PAIR (USAGE)

ear·shot /'ɪərʃɑt/ *n* **within/out of earshot** within/beyond the distance at which a sound can be heard

earth /ɜrθ/ *n* **1** [*the* S;U] the world on which we live: *They returned from the moon to the earth.|Earth is the third PLANET from the sun.|the most beautiful woman on earth* **2** [U] soil in which plants grow: *He planted the seeds in earth.* –see LAND (USAGE) **3** [C] the hole where certain wild animals live, esp. foxes: (fig.) *After searching everywhere, she finally* **ran him to earth** (=found him) *upstairs.* **4 down to earth** honest, direct, and practical; saying what one thinks **5 on earth** *infml* (used for giving force to a question with *what, who,* etc.): *What on earth are you doing?*

earth·en·ware /'ɜrθən,wɛər/ *n* [U] cups, dishes, pots, etc., made of baked clay: *an earthenware pot*

earth·ly /'ɜrθliʸ/ *adj* [A *no comp.*] **1** of this world as opposed to heaven; material: *earthly possessions* **2** [used only in questions, NEGATIVES², *etc.*] *infml* possible: *There's no earthly reason for me to go.|He hasn't an earthly* (*chance*) (=any hope) *of winning.* –compare EARTHY

earth·quake /'ɜrθkweʸk/ *n* a sudden usu.

violent shaking of the earth's surface: *The town was destroyed by the earthquake.*

earth·y /'ɜrθiʸ/ *adj* **-ier, -iest** concerned with things of the body, not of the mind: *Peter has an earthy sense of humor; he likes dirty jokes.* –compare EARTHLY –**earthiness** *n* [U]

ear·wig /'ɪər,wɪg/ *n* an insect with two curved parts on its tail

ease¹ /iʸz/ *n* [U] **1** the ability to do something without difficulty: *He jumped the wall* **with ease.** –compare EASILY (1) **2** the state of being comfortable and without worry or anxiety: *to lead a life of (the greatest) ease|Don't worry about meeting my father; I'm sure he'll* **put you at ease. 3 ill at ease** worried and nervous **4 (stand) at ease** (used as a military command) (to stand) with feet apart –compare **at** ATTENTION¹ (3)

ease² *v* **eased, easing 1** [I;T *off*] to make or become less severe: *I gave him some medicine to ease the pain.|The pain has eased (off).|I eased her mind by telling her that her children were safe.* **2** [I] to become less troublesome or difficult: *The relationship between the two countries has eased.* **3** [T] to cause (something) to move carefully, esp. slowly and gently: *The thief eased his body/himself through the window.*

ease up/off *v adv* [I *on*] *infml* to do (something) with less force: *It's time my father eased up (on his work) a little; he's getting old.*

ea·sel /'iʸzəl/ *n* a wooden frame to hold a BLACKBOARD, or to hold a picture while it is being painted

eas·i·ly /'iʸzəliʸ/ *adv* **1** without difficulty: *I can easily finish it today.* –compare EASE¹ (1), EASY¹ (1) **2** without doubt: *She is easily the most intelligent girl in the class.*

east¹ /iʸst/ *adv* (*often cap.*) towards the east: *The room faces East, so we get the morning sun.*

east² *n* [*the* S] (*often cap.*) **1** the direction in which the sun rises –compare EASTERN **2** one of the four main points of the compass, which is on the right of a person facing north **3** the eastern part a of the world, esp. Asia: *traveling in the Far East* –compare ORIENT **b** of a country: *the east of Canada*

Eas·ter /'iʸstər/ *n* **1** [C;S] the yearly feast-day when Christians remember Christ's death and his return to life **2** [A] happening at that time of the year: *Easter vacation*

east·er·ly /'iʸstərliʸ/ *adj* [*no comp.*] **1** towards the east: *in an easterly direction* **2** (of a wind) coming from the east

east·ern /'iʸstərn/ *adj* (*often cap.*) of or belonging to the east part of the world or of a country

east·ward /'iʸstwərd/ *adj* [*no comp.*] going towards the east: *an eastward journey* –**eastwards**‖also **eastward** *AmE*– *adv: to sail eastwards*

eas·y¹ /'iʸziʸ/ *adj* **-ier, -iest** [+*to-v*] **1** not difficult: *an easy book|John is easy to please.* (=it is not difficult to please him) –opposite **hard**; compare EASE¹ (1), EASILY (1) **2** comfortable and without worry or anxiety: *He isn't working now and leads a very easy* life.|with an easy mind |They completed the journey **in/by easy stages,** often stopping to rest. –compare EASE¹ (2) –**easiness** n [U]

easy² adv **-ier, -iest 1 easier said than done** harder to do than to talk about: *Passing exams is much easier said than done.* **2 easy does it** *infml* do something less quickly and more carefully **3 go easy on: a** to be kinder to (someone) **b** not to use too much of (something): *Go easy on the salt in the soup.* **4 take it/things easy** not to work too hard

easy chair /'·· ¡·/ n a big comfortable chair with arms

eas·y·go·ing /ˌiʸziʸ'goʷɪŋ◀/ adj taking life easily: *He's an easygoing person; he never gets angry.*

eat /iʸt/ v **ate** /eʸt/, **eaten** /'iʸtn/, **eating 1** [T up] to take (food) into the mouth and swallow it in order to feed the body: *Eat your dinner! |Tigers eat meat.*|(fig.) *A big house eats up money.* **2** [I] to have a meal: *What time do we eat?* **3** [I;T away, into] to damage or destroy (something), esp. by chemical action: *The acid ate away/ate a hole in/ ate into the metal.* **4 be eaten up with** to be completely and violently full of (jealousy, desire, etc.) **5 eat one's words** to admit to having said something wrong **6 eat out of someone's hand** *infml* to be very willing to obey or agree with someone

eat into sthg. v prep [T] to use part of: *Our trip has eaten into the money we saved.* –compare EAT (3)

eat out v adv [I] to eat a meal at a restaurant: *I don't feel like cooking. Let's eat out.*

eat·a·ble /'iʸţəbəl/ adj (of food) in a fit condition to be eaten

USAGE Compare **eatable** and **edible**: Something is **edible** if it can be used as food; food is **eatable** if it is fresh, nicely prepared, etc.: *Are these berries* **edible,** *or are they poisonous?*|*The food at my school is so bad it's* **uneatable/** *hardly* **eatable.**

eat·er /'iʸţər/ n a person who eats in a certain way: *He's a big eater.* (=he eats a lot)

eau de co·logne /ˌoʷ də kə'loʷn/ n [U] a sweet-smelling liquid made from alcohol and special oils, put on the wrists, behind the ears, etc., to make one feel fresh and smell pleasant

eaves /iʸvz/ n [P] the edges of a roof which come out beyond the walls: *birds nesting under the eaves*

eaves·drop /'iʸvzdrɑp/ v **-pp-** [I on] to listen secretly (to other people's conversation) –**eavesdropper** n

ebb¹ /ɛb/ n [U] **1** the flow of the sea away from the shore; the going out of the TIDE: *The tide is on the ebb.* –compare FLOW² (3) **2 at a low ebb** in a low state: *Fred is unhappy; he seems to be at a low ebb.*

ebb² v [I away] (of the sea) to flow away from the shore: (fig.) *His strength slowly ebbed away.* (=grew less)

eb·o·ny /'ɛbəniʸ/ n, adj [U] (having the color of) a hard black wood

e·bul·li·ence /ɪ'bʌlyəns, ɪ'bʊl-/ n [U] *fml* or *lit* the quality of being full of happiness and

excitement –**ebullient** adj: *He arrived at the party in a happy, ebullient mood.*

ec·cen·tric¹ /ɪk'sɛntrɪk/ adj (of a person or his behavior) peculiar; unusual; rather strange: *The old lady has some eccentric habits.* –**eccentrically** adv –**eccentricity** /ˌɛksɛn'trɪsəţiʸ, -sən-/ **-ties** [C;U] n

eccentric² n an ECCENTRIC person

ec·cle·si·as·tic /ɪˌkliʸziʸ'æstɪk/ n a (Christian) priest or MINISTER

ec·cle·si·as·ti·cal /ɪˌkliʸziʸ'æstɪkəl/ also **ecclesiastic–** adj connected with a Christian church: *ecclesiastical history/music*

ech·o¹ /'ɛkoʷ/ n **-oes** a sound sent back or repeated, e.g. from a wall or inside a cave

echo² v **-oed, -oing** [I;T with, to] to (cause to) come back as an ECHO¹: *Their voices echoed around the cave.*|*The room echoed with the sound of music.*|(fig.) *She echoes* (=repeats) *everything I say.*

é·clair /eʸ'klɛər, ɪ-, 'eʸklɛər/ n a finger-shaped pastry with a cream filling inside

e·clipse¹ /ɪ'klɪps/ n **1** [C] the disappearance, complete or in part, of the sun's light when the moon passes between it and the earth **2** [C;U] the loss of fame, power, success, etc.

eclipse² v **-clipsed, -clipsing** [T] **1** to cause an ECLIPSE¹ (1): *The moon is partly eclipsed.* **2** to do or be much better than; make (someone or something) lose fame: *She is eclipsed by her sister, who is very famous.*

e·col·o·gy /ɪ'kɑlədʒiʸ/ n [U] (the scientific study of) the pattern of the natural relations of plants, animals, and people to each other and to their surroundings –**ecologist** n –**ecological** /ˌɛkə'lɑdʒɪkəl, ˌiʸ-/ adj –**ecologically** adv

ec·o·nom·ic /ˌɛkə'nɑmɪk, ˌiʸ-/ adj [no comp.] **1** [A] connected with trade, industry, and wealth; of or concerning ECONOMICS: *The country is in a bad economic state.* **2** profitable: *She sold her house at an economic price.* –compare ECONOMICAL

ec·o·nom·i·cal /ˌɛkə'nɑmɪkəl, ˌiʸ-/ adj using money, time, goods, etc., without waste: *A small car is more economical than a large one, because it uses less gasoline.* –compare ECONOMIC

ec·o·nom·i·cal·ly /ˌɛkə'nɑmɪkliʸ, ˌiʸ-/ adv **1** not wastefully: *She cooks very economically.* –compare EXTRAVAGANTly **2** in a way which is connected with ECONOMICS

ec·o·nom·ics /ˌɛkə'nɑmɪks, ˌiʸ-/ n [P;U] the science or principles of the way in which industry and trade produce and use wealth: *The economics of national growth are of great importance to all governments.* –**economist** /ɪ'kɑnəmɪst/ n

e·con·o·mize ‖also **-mise** BrE /ɪ'kɑnəˌmaɪz/ v **-mized, -mizing** [I;T] to save (money, time, goods, etc.); to avoid waste: *to economize on gasoline* –compare ECONOMICAL

e·con·o·my¹ /ɪ'kɑnəmiʸ/ n **-mies 1** [C;U] (an example of) the careful use of money, time, etc.: *economy of effort* –compare ECONOMICAL **2** [C] the ECONOMIC (1) life or system of a country; operation of a country's money supply, industry, and trade: *The new Presi-*

dent promises to improve the state of the economy.

economy² *adj* [A] cheap; intended to save money: *Products sold in large economy sizes usually cost less.*

ec·sta·sy /ˈɛkstəsiˠ/ *n* **-sies** [C;U] a state of very strong feeling, esp. of happiness: *in an ecstasy of joy/delight*

ec·stat·ic /ɪkˈstætɪk, ɛk-/ *adj* causing or experiencing ECSTASY, esp. feeling very happy —**ecstatically** *adv*

ec·u·men·i·cal /ˌɛkyəˈmɛnɪkəl/ *adj* favoring, or tending towards, Christian unity all over the world

ec·ze·ma /ˈɛksəmə, ˈɛgzəmə, ɪgˈziˠmə/ *n* [U] a red swollen condition of the skin

ed·dy /ˈɛdiˠ/ *n* **-dies** a circular movement of water, dust, smoke, etc.

E·den /ˈiˠdn/ *n* (in the Bible) the garden where Adam and Eve lived before their disobedience to God

edge¹ /ɛdʒ/ *n* **1** the thin sharp cutting part of a blade, tool, etc. **2** the part along the outside of something: *the edge of a plate|Can you stand a coin up* **on its edge?***|the water's edge* **3 have the edge on** to be better than; have an advantage over: *He has the edge on the other students because he works harder.* **4 on edge** nervous; EDGY **5 -edged** having a certain kind or number of edges: *a two-edged knife*

edge² *v* **edged, edging 1** [T *with*] to place an edge or border on: *a white handkerchief edged with blue* **2** [I;T] to (cause to) move sideways little by little: *He edged (himself/his way) to the front of the crowd.*

edge·wise /ˈɛdʒwaɪz/ also **edgeways** /ˈɛdʒweˠz/– *adv* **1** in the direction of the edge; sideways **2 get a word in edgewise** (used only in NEGATIVES², questions, etc.) *infml* to get a chance to speak when someone else is speaking

edg·ing /ˈɛdʒɪŋ/ *n* [C;U] something that forms an edge or border: *a white handkerchief with (a) blue edging*

edg·y /ˈɛdʒiˠ/ *adj* **-ier, -iest** *infml* nervous: *She's been a little edgy lately because she's waiting for her examination results.*

ed·i·ble /ˈɛdəbəl/ *adj* fit to be eaten; eatable: *the difference between edible and poisonous berries* —opposite **inedible**; see EATABLE (USAGE)

e·dict /ˈiˠdɪkt/ *n fml* (in former times) an official public order; DECREE

ed·i·fice /ˈɛdəfɪs/ *n fml* a large fine building

ed·i·fy /ˈɛdə,faɪ/ *v* **-fied, -fying** [T] *fml* to improve (the character or mind of): *He read edifying books to improve his mind.* —**edification** /ˌɛdəfəˈkeˠʃən/ *n*

ed·it /ˈɛdɪt/ *v* [T] to prepare a book, newspaper, movie, etc., for printing or showing

e·di·tion /ɪˈdɪʃən/ *n* one printing, esp. of a book: *a first edition|a* **paperback** *edition* (=in paper covers)|*a* **hard-cover** *edition* (=in hard cardboard covers)

ed·i·tor /ˈɛdətər/ *n* a person who EDITs

ed·i·to·ri·al¹ /ˌɛdəˈtɔriˠəl, -ˈtoˠr-/ *adj* of an EDITOR: *an editorial office* —**editorially** *adv*

editorial² *n* a part of a newspaper giving an opinion on a problem or event

ed·u·cate /ˈɛdʒə,keˠt/ *v* **-cated, -cating** [T] to teach; train the character or mind of: *He was educated at a very good school.* —**educated** *adj*: *self-educated|educated tastes in art and literature*

ed·u·ca·tion /ˌɛdʒəˈkeˠʃən/ *n* [S;U] teaching or the training of mind and character: *She has had a good education.*

ed·u·ca·tion·al /ˌɛdʒəˈkeˠʃənəl/ *adj* of, about, or providing education: *an educational establishment/movie* —**educationally** *adv*

EEC /ˌiˠ iˠ ˈsiˠ/ *abbrev. for:* European Economic Community; COMMON MARKET: *to join the EEC*

eel /iˠl/ *n* a long snake-like fish

e'er /ɛər/ *adv lit short for:* EVER

ee·rie /ˈɪəriˠ/ *adj* causing fear because strange: *walking through the dark, eerie woods* —**eerily** *adv* —**eeriness** *n* [U]

ef·face /ɪˈfeˠs/ *v* **-faced, -facing** [T] *fml* to rub out; destroy the surface of: *Someone has effaced part of the address on this letter.* –see also SELF-EFFACING

ef·fect¹ /ɪˈfɛkt/ *n* [C;U] **1** a result: *the effects of an illness* |*One of the effects of bad weather is poor crops.* **2 in effect: a** in operation: *The rules will remain in effect until October.* **b** for all practical purposes: *Although she's his assistant, she has, in effect, full control.* **3 into effect** into operation: *The rule will come/be brought/be put/go into effect on Monday.* **4 take effect** to come into operation; start to have results: *The new tax system will take effect next May.|The medicine quickly took effect.*

effect² *v* [T] *fml* to cause, produce, or have as a result: *She effected several changes in the company.* –see AFFECT (USAGE)

ef·fec·tive /ɪˈfɛktɪv/ *adj* **1** producing the desired result: *His efforts to improve the school have been very effective.* –opposite **ineffective 2** [*no comp.*] actual; real: *Although there is a king, the army is in effective control of the country.* –compare EFFICACIOUS, EFFICIENT —**effectively** *adv* —**effectiveness** *n*

ef·fects /ɪˈfɛkts/ *n* [P] *fml or law* belongings; personal property: *He died poor and left no (personal) effects.*

ef·fec·tu·al /ɪˈfɛktʃuˠəl/ *adj fml* (of actions) producing the results intended: *effectual action against unemployment* –opposite **ineffectual** —**effectually** *adv*

ef·fem·i·nate /ɪˈfɛmənɪt/ *adj derog* (of a man or his behavior) having characteristics often thought to be usual in women; soft; weak —**effeminately** *adv* **effeminacy** /ɪˈfɛmənəsiˠ/ *n* [U]

ef·fer·vesce /ˌɛfərˈvɛs/ *v* **-vesced, -vescing** [I] *fml or tech* (of a liquid) to have bubbles forming inside; bubble —**effervescence** *n* [U] —**effervescent** *adj*

ef·fi·ca·cious /ˌɛfəˈkeˠʃəs/ *adj fml* (esp. of medicines) producing the desired effect —compare EFFECTIVE, EFFICIENT —**efficacy** /ˈɛfəkəsiˠ/ *n* [U]

ef·fi·cient /ɪˈfɪʃənt/ *adj* working well,

quickly, and without waste: *She is a quick, efficient worker.*|*This new machine is more efficient than the old one.* –Compare: *an efficient secretary* (=who does his/her job well) *an effective medicine* (=which produces the desired result: *opposite* **inefficient** –**efficiently** *adv* –**efficiency** /ɪˈfɪʃənsi/ *n* [U]: *attempts to improve efficiency*

ef·fi·gy /ˈɛfədʒiy/ *n* -**gies** *fml* a wooden, stone, etc., likeness of a person: *an effigy of Christ*

ef·flu·ent /ˈɛfluwənt/ *n* [C;U] *tech* (a type of) liquid waste that flows out from a factory, etc.: *Dangerous effluent is being poured into our rivers.*

ef·fort /ˈɛfərt/ *n* [C;U +to-v] (an example of) the use of strength; trying hard: *He lifted the heavy box **without effort**.*|*The prisoner **made an effort** to escape, but he failed.*

ef·fort·less /ˈɛfərtlɪs/ *adj* seeming to need or make no effort, yet very good: *He is a skillful and effortless player.* –**effortlessly** *adv* –**effortlessness** *n* [U]

ef·fron·ter·y /ɪˈfrʌntəriy/ *n* [U +to-v] bold rudeness without any sense of shame: *You wrecked my car and now you have the effrontery to ask me for my bicycle!* –compare AFFRONT

ef·fu·sive /ɪˈfyuwsɪv/ *adj* often *derog* showing too much feeling: *Her effusive welcome was not sincere.* –**effusively** *adv* –**effusiveness** *n* [U]

e.g. /ˌiy ˈdʒiy/ *abbrev. for:* Latin exempli gratia (=for example): *sweet foods, e.g. cake, chocolate, sugar, and ice cream*

e·gal·i·tar·i·an /ɪˌgæləˈtɛəriyən/ *adj* having the belief that all people are equal and should have equal rights –**egalitarianism** *n* [U]

egg /ɛg/ *n* **1** [C] a rounded object with a hard shell, which comes out of a female bird, snake, etc., and which contains a baby animal before it is born: *This hen lays beautiful brown eggs.* **2** [C;U] (the contents of) this when eaten as food: *The baby had egg all over his face* |*A dozen eggs, please.* **3** [C] the seed of life inside a female, which joins with the male seed (SPERM) to make a baby –see FERTILIZE **4 put all one's eggs in one basket** *infml* to depend completely on the success of one thing

egg·head /ˈɛghɛd/ *n usu. derog* a person who is (too) highly educated; HIGHBROW

egg sbdy. ↔ **on** *v adv* [T] to encourage strongly: *They egged me on to throw a stone through the window.*

egg·plant /ˈɛgplænt/ *n* [C;U] (a plant having) a large purple fruit that is eaten as a vegetable

e·go /ˈiygow/ *n* **egos** the way in which a person sees and feels about himself/herself: *Admiration by other people is good for one's ego.*

e·go·cen·tric /ˌiygowˈsɛntrɪk/ *adj derog* selfish; thinking only about (one)self

e·go·ism /ˈiygowˌɪzəm/ *n* [U] *derog* the quality of always thinking about oneself; selfishness –compare EGOTISM, ALTRUISM –**egoist** *n* –**egoistic** /ˌiygowˈɪstɪk/ *adj* –**egoistical** *adj*

eg·o·tism /ˈiygəˌtɪzəm/ *n* [U] *derog* the quality of talking too much about oneself –compare EGOISM –**egotist** *n* –**egotistic** /ˌiygəˈtɪstɪk/ *adj* –**egotistical** *adj*

ei·der·down /ˈaɪdərˌdaʊn/ *n* a thick warm bed covering filled with feathers (DOWN⁵)

eight /eyt/ *determiner,n,pron* (the number) 8 –**eighth** /eytθ, eyθ/ *determiner,n,pron,adv*

eight·een /ˌeyˈtiyn◄/ *determiner,n,pron* (the number) 18 –**eighteenth** *determiner, n,pron,adv*

eight·y /ˈeytiy/ *determiner,n,pron* -**ies** (the number) 80 –**eightieth** /ˈeytiyiθ/ *determiner, n,pron,adv*

ei·ther¹ /ˈiyðər, ˈaɪ-/ *determiner,pron* **1** one or the other of two: *There's coffee or tea; you can have either.*|*Is either of the boys coming?* –compare ANY¹; see also NEITHER **2** one and the other of two; each: *He sat in the car with a policeman on either side of him.* –compare BOTH¹

USAGE When **either, neither, none,** or **any** are used as PRONOUNS and followed by a plural, they usually take a singular verb in formal writing: **None/Neither** *of the boys has passed the examination.*|*Is* **any** *of these substances safe to eat.* In speech, however, a plural verb is often used, and this is quite acceptable: *Have* **any/either** *of you seen this movie before?*

either² *conj* (used to begin a list of possibilities separated by *or*): *The baby will be either a boy or a girl.*|*Either say you're sorry or (else) get out!*|*It's either red, blue, or green; I can't remember.*

USAGE In *fml* speech and writing, **either ... or** and **neither ... nor** are usually followed by a singular verb if the last noun is singular: *If either David or Janet come, they will want a drink*|*If my parents or my sister comes, please let them in.* If the last noun is plural, the verb is plural: *If my sister or my parents come, please let them in.* In *infml* usage, the verb is usually plural.

either³ *adv* (used with NEGATIVE² expressions) also; besides: *I haven't read this book, and my brother hasn't either.* (=both haven't read it)|*"I can't swim!" "I can't, either!"*|*"Neither can I."* (=I, too, am unable to swim)

e·jac·u·late /ɪˈdʒækyəˌleyt/ *v* -**lated, -lating** [I;T] **1** to throw out suddenly and with force from the body (esp. the male seed (SPERM)) **2** *fml* to cry out or say (something) suddenly –**ejaculation** /ɪˌdʒækyəˈleyʃən/ *n* [C;U]

e·ject /ɪˈdʒɛkt/ *v* [T *from*] *fml* to throw out with force: *The police came and ejected the noisy men from the restaurant.* –**ejection** /ɪˈdʒɛkʃən/ *n* [C;U]

eke sthg. ↔ **out** /iyk/ *v adv* **eked, eking** [T *with, by*] **1** to cause (a small supply) to last longer: *She eked out a small income by cleaning other people's houses.* **2 eke out a living** to make just enough money to live

e·lab·o·rate¹ /ɪˈlæbərɪt/ *adj* full of detail; carefully worked out and with a large number of parts: *an elaborate pattern* –**elaborately** *adv*

e·lab·o·rate² /ɪˈlæbəˌreyt/ *v* -**rated, -rating**

[I;T *on*] to add more detail to (something): *Just tell us the facts; don't elaborate (on them)*. **–elaboration** /ɪˌlæbəˈreʸʃən/ *n* [C;U]

e·lapse /ɪˈlæps/ *v* **-lapsed, -lapsing** [I] *fml* (of time) to pass away: *Three months have elapsed since he left home.*

e·las·tic¹ /ɪˈlæstɪk/ *adj* (of material such as rubber) able to spring back into shape after being stretched: *an elastic band* |(fig.) *The rules are elastic.* (=not fixed) **–elasticity** /ɪˌlæˈstɪsəṭiʸ, ˌiʸlæ-/ *n* [U]

elastic² *n* [U] (a piece of) ELASTIC¹ material

e·lat·ed /ɪˈleʸṭɪd/ *adj* [+*to-v/that/at*] filled with pride and joy: *The crowds were elated by the news.* **–elation** /ɪˈleʸʃən/ *n* [U]

el·bow¹ /ˈɛlboʷ/ *n* the joint where the arm bends, esp. the outer point of this

elbow² *v* [T] to push with the elbows: *He elbowed his way through the crowd.*

el·bow·room /ˈɛlboʷˌruʷm, -ˌrʊm/ *n* [U] space in which to move freely

el·der¹ /ˈɛldər/ *adj* [A] (of people, esp. in a family) older, esp. the older of two: *my elder brother* (=I have one brother, who is older than I am)| *My elder daughter is married.* (=I have two daughters)

USAGE Compare **elder** and **older**: **Older** is used of people or things, but **elder** is only used of people, and can never be used in comparisons: *Jane is Mary's* **elder** *sister.*|*Jane is* **older** *than* (not **elder than*) *Mary.*

elder² *n* **1** the older of two people: *Which is the elder (of the two sisters)?* |*Shouldn't we respect our elders?* (=older people) **2** a person holding a respected official position: *a Church elder* | *an elder* STATESMAN

elder³ *n* a small tree with white flowers and red or black berries

el·der·ly /ˈɛldərliʸ/ *adj* [*no comp.*] (of a person) getting near old age

el·dest /ˈɛldɪst/ *adj,n* (a person who is) oldest of three or more: *She has three children, and her eldest has just started school.*

e·lect¹ /ɪˈlɛkt/ *v* [T] **1** [*as,to*] to choose (someone) by voting: *They elected my brother (as) chairman.*|*to elect a new member to the committee* **2** [+*to-v*] *fml* to decide (to do something important): *She elected to return to work after her baby was born.*

elect² *adj* [after *n*] *fml* chosen, but not yet at work: *the president-elect*

e·lec·tion /ɪˈlɛkʃən/ *n* [C;U] (an example of) the choosing of representatives for a (political) position by vote: *to call a general election*|*the election results*|*Representatives are chosen by election.* **–elector** /ɪˈlɛktər/ *n* **–electoral** *adj* [A]: *the electoral system in this country*

e·lec·tive¹ /ɪˈlɛktɪv/ *adj fml* **1** (of a position) filled by election: *The office of President of the US is an elective one.* **2** having the power to elect: *an elective body* **3** *AmE* (of a course, esp. at a university) freely chosen; not RE-QUIRED; OPTIONAL

elective² *n AmE* an ELECTIVE¹ (3) course which is studied at school or college: *How many electives are you taking this year?*

e·lec·tor·ate /ɪˈlɛktərɪt/ *n* [C +*sing./pl.v*] all

the people in a country who have the right to vote: *The general electorate is voting today.*

e·lec·tric /ɪˈlɛktrɪk/ *adj* **1** [*usu.* A] producing or worked by electricity: *an electric clock*|*electric power* **2** very exciting: *His speech had an electric effect on the crowd; they stood and cheered him.* **–electrically** *adv*

USAGE Anything directly worked by or producing electricity is **electric**: *an* **electric** *clock/shock/light/*GENERATOR. Otherwise, the word is **electrical**, which is a more general expression, used of people and their work or of things: *an* **electrical** *engineer*|*an* **electrical** *apparatus*|*an* **electrical** *fault in the system.* –see also ELECTRONIC

e·lec·tri·cal /ɪˈlɛktrɪkəl/ *adj* [A] concerned with or using electricity: *an electrical* ENGINEER|*an electrical fault* –compare ELECTRIC **–electrically** *adv*

electric chair /·¹·· ˌ·/ also **chair** *infml– n* [*the* S] a punishment of death in some states of the US, in which electricity is passed through a person's body to kill him/her –see also ELECTROCUTE

e·lec·tri·cian /ɪˌlɛkˈtrɪʃən, ˌiʸlɛk-/ *n* a person whose job is to fit and repair electrical apparatus

e·lec·tric·i·ty /ɪˌlɛkˈtrɪsəṭiʸ, ˌiʸlɛk-/ *n* [U] the power which is produced by various means (e.g. by a BATTERY or GENERATOR) and which provides heat and light, drives machines, etc.

e·lec·tri·fy /ɪˈlɛktrəˌfaɪ/ *v* **-fied, -fying** [T] **1** to pass an electric current through (something) **2** to change (something) to a system using electric power: *The farm has not been electrified.* **3** to excite or surprise greatly: *The band gave an electrifying performance.* **–electrification** /ɪˌlɛktrəfəˈkeʸʃən/ *n* [U]

e·lec·tro·cute /ɪˈlɛktrəˌkyuʷt/ *v* **-cuted, -cuting** [T] to kill by passing electricity through the body **–electrocution** /ɪˌlɛktrəˈkyuʷʃən/ *n* [C;U]

e·lec·trode /ɪˈlɛktroʷd/ *n* either of the two points (the TERMINALs) at which the current enters and leaves a BATTERY, or other electrical apparatus

e·lec·tron /ɪˈlɛktrɑn/ *n* one of the parts of an atom; "bit" of NEGATIVE electricity –see also PROTON, NEUTRON

e·lec·tron·ics /ɪˌlɛkˈtrɑnɪks, ˌiʸlɛk-/ *n* [U] the branch of industry that makes products like radios, televisions, and recording apparatus **–electronic** *adj: an electronic watch*| *electronic music* –see illustration on page 221

el·e·gant /ˈɛləgənt/ *adj apprec* having the qualities of grace and beauty; stylish: *an elegant woman*|*elegant manners*|*an elegant piece of furniture* –opposite **inelegant** **–elegantly** *adv* **–elegance** *n* [S;U]

el·e·gy /ˈɛlədʒiʸ/ *n* **-gies** a poem or song written esp. to show grief

el·e·ment /ˈɛləmənt/ *n* **1** [C] any of certain simple substances that, alone or in combination, make up all substances: HYDROGEN *and* oxygen *are elements, but water, which is formed when they combine, is not.* **2** [S] a small amount: *There is an element of truth in what you say.* **3** [C] a part of a whole:

Honesty is an important element in anyone's character. **4** [C] the heating part of a piece of electrical apparatus **5 in/out of one's element** doing what one is most happy/unhappy doing

el·e·men·tal /ˌɛlə'mɛntəl/ *adj* of or like a great force of nature: *the elemental violence of the storm* –see also ELEMENTS

el·e·men·ta·ry /ˌɛlə'mɛntəriʸ/ *adj* **1** simple and easy **2** concerned with the beginnings, esp. of education and study: *some elementary exercises for the piano*

elementary school /····· ·/ also **primary school, grammar school, grade school**– *n AmE* a school in which basic subjects are taught for the first six or eight years of a child's education

el·e·ments /'ɛləmənts/ *n* [*the* P] **1** the beginnings; the first steps in a subject **2** *lit* the weather, esp. bad weather: *He walked on through the terrible storm, careless of the elements.* –see also ELEMENTAL

el·e·phant /'ɛləfənt/ *n* **-phants** *or* **-phant** a very large animal, with two long curved teeth (TUSKs) and a long nose called a TRUNK

el·e·vate /'ɛləˌveʸt/ *v* **-vated, -vating** [T] **1** to make (the mind, soul, etc.) better, higher, or more educated: *You should read an elevating book, not a love story.* **2** *fml* to raise: *He was elevated to the rank of captain.*

el·e·va·tion /ˌɛlə'veʸʃən/ *n* **1** [U] *fml* being ELEVATED: *elevation to the rank of a captain* **2** [S] height above sea-level: *Their house is at an elevation of 2,000 feet above sea level.* –compare ALTITUDE **3** [C] (a drawing of) a flat upright side of a building: *the front elevation of a house* –compare PLAN¹ (2), PERSPECTIVE, FACADE, SECTION

el·e·va·tor /'ɛləˌveʸtər/ *AmE*‖**lift** *BrE*– *n* an apparatus in a building for taking people and goods from one floor to another

el·ev·en /ɪ'lɛvən/ *determiner,n,pron* **1** (the number) 11: **2** a team of eleven players in football –**eleventh** *determiner,n,pron, adv*

elf /ɛlf/ *n* **elves** /ɛlvz/ a small fairy with pointed ears –**elfin** /'ɛlfɪn/ *adj*

el·ic·it /ɪ'lɪsɪt/ *v* [T *from*] *fml* to get, draw out (facts, information, etc.): *After much questioning, he elicited the truth.*

el·i·gi·ble /'ɛlədʒəbəl/ *adj* **1** [F +*to-v/as, for*] having the right (esp. by law) to do, receive, etc. (something): *He will become eligible to vote on his next birthday.* **2** suitable to be chosen: *I know an eligible young man who would be an excellent husband for Jane.* –opposite **ineligible** –**eligibility** /ˌɛlədʒə'bɪləṭiʸ/ *n* [U] –**eligibly** /'ɛlədʒəbliʸ/ *adv*

e·lim·i·nate /ɪ'lɪməˌneʸt/ *v* **-nated, -nating** [T *from*] to remove or get rid of: *to eliminate the mistakes from your writing* –**elimination** /ɪˌlɪmə'neʸʃən/ *n* [U]

e·lite /ɪ'liʸt, eʸ-/ *n often derog* the most powerful or most intelligent people in a group: *The power elite inside the government is controlling foreign policy.*

e·lit·ism /ɪ'liʸṭɪzəm, eʸ-/ *n* [U] (belief in) leadership or rule by an ELITE –**elitist** *adj,n*

e·lix·ir /ɪ'lɪksər/ *n* [C;U] *lit* an imaginary liquid having the power to change other metals into gold, or make life last forever

elk /ɛlk/ also **moose** *AmE*– *n* **elks** *or* **elk** a very large deer, with big flat ANTLERs (branching horns)

el·lip·ti·cal /ɪ'lɪptɪkəl/ also **elliptic**– *adj* having the curved shape of a circle when one looks at it sideways; OVAL: *The Earth's path around the sun is elliptical.* –**elliptically** *adv*

elm /ɛlm/ *n* [C;U] (the hard heavy wood of) a large tall broad-leaved tree

el·o·cu·tion /ˌɛlə'kyuʷʃən/ *n* [U] the art of good clear speaking in public

e·lon·gate /ɪ'lɔŋgeʸt, 'iʸlɔŋˌgeʸt/ *v* **-gated, -gating** [T] to make (a material thing) longer: *This painting doesn't look like her. The face is too elongated.* –**elongation** /ɪˌlɔŋ'geʸʃən, ˌiʸlɔŋ-/ *n* [C;U]

e·lope /ɪ'loʷp/ *v* **-loped, -loping** [I *with*] (of lovers) to run away secretly usu. with the intention of getting married: *She eloped with him.*|*They eloped last week.* –**elopement** *n* [C;U]

el·o·quent /'ɛləkwənt/ *adj fml* (of a person or speech) able to express ideas and opinions well, so that the hearers are influenced: *an eloquent speaker/speech* –**eloquently** *adv* –**eloquence** *n*

else /ɛls/ *adv* **1** (besides; also: *What else* (=what more) *can I say?* |*There's nothing else to eat.* **2** apart from that; otherwise: *Everybody else but me* (=all the other people) *has gone to the party.*|*She was wearing someone else's coat.* (=not her own coat)|*He must pay $1,000* **or else** *go to prison.*

else·where /'ɛls-hwɛər, -wɛər/ *adv* in or to another place; somewhere else: *This hotel is full. We will have to look for a room elsewhere.*

e·lu·ci·date /ɪ'luʷsəˌdeʸt/ *v* **-dated, -dating** [T] *fml* to explain or make clear (a difficulty or mystery): *Please elucidate the reasons for your decision.* –**elucidation** /ɪˌluʷsə'deʸʃən/ *n* [C;U]

e·lude /ɪ'luʷd/ *v* **-luded, -luding** [T] to escape from, esp. by means of a trick: *The fox eluded the hunters by turning back quickly.*|(fig.) *Her name eludes me for the moment.* (=I can't remember it)

e·lu·sive /ɪ'luʷsɪv/ *adj* difficult to catch, find, or remember: *I've been trying all day to reach him on the telephone, but he's very elusive.* –**elusively** *adv* –**elusiveness** *n* [U]

elves /ɛlvz/ *n pl. of* ELF

'em /əm/ *pron infml* →THEM

e·ma·ci·at·ed /ɪ'meʸʃiʸˌeʸṭɪd/ *adj* very thin, as a result of illness or lack of food –see THIN (USAGE) –**emaciation** /ɪˌmeʸʃiʸ'eʸʃən, -siʸ-/ *n* [U]

em·a·nate from sthg. /'ɛməˌneʸt/ *v prep* **-nated, -nating** [T *no pass.*] *fml* to come (out) from: *Light emanated from all the windows of the house.* –**emanation** /ˌɛmə'neʸʃən/ *n* [C;U]

e·man·ci·pate /ɪ'mænsəˌpeʸt/ *v* **-pated, -pating** [T *from*] to make free socially, politically, and in law –**emancipation** /ɪˌmænsə'peʸʃən/ *n*: *the emancipation of women*

em·balm /ɪm'bɑm/ *v* [T] to treat (a dead

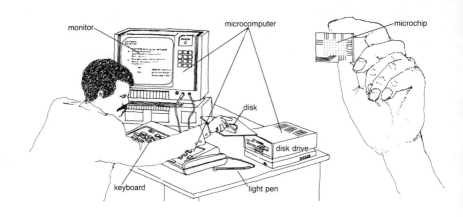

monitor
microcomputer
microchip
disk
disk drive
keyboard
light pen

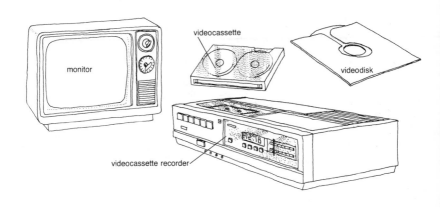

videocassette
videodisk
monitor
videocassette recorder

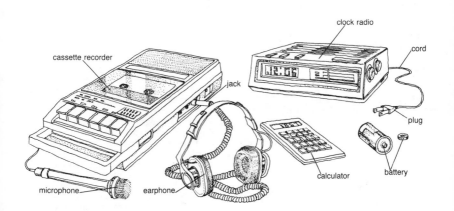

clock radio
cord
cassette recorder
jack
plug
microphone
earphone
calculator
battery

body) with chemicals, oils, etc., to prevent its decay **–embalmer** *n*

em·bank·ment /ɪm'bæŋkmənt/ *n* a wide wall, which is built to stop a river overflowing, or to carry a road or railroad over low ground

em·bar·go¹ /ɪm'bɑrgoʷ/ *n* **-goes** an official order forbidding trade: *to put/lay an oil embargo on an enemy country* –compare BLOCKADE

embargo² *v* **-goed, -going** [T] to put an EMBARGO on (something)

em·bark /ɪm'bɑrk/ *v* [I;T] to go, put, or take on a ship: *We embarked at Montreal, and disembarked in New York a week later.* **–embarkation** /ˌɛmbɑrˈkeʸʃən/ *n* [C;U]

embark on/upon sthg. *v prep* [T] to start (something new): *to embark on a new way of life*

em·bar·rass /ɪm'bærəs/ *v* [T] to cause to feel ashamed, uncomfortable, or anxious: *I don't like making speeches in public; it's so embarrassing.* **–embarrassment** *n* [C;U]: *a rude child, who was an embarrassment to his parents |He could not hide his embarrassment.*

em·bas·sy /'ɛmbəsiʸ/ *n* **-sies** (the official building of) a group of officials, usu. led by an AMBASSADOR, sent by a government to live in a foreign country and keep good relations with its government

em·bed /ɪm'bɛd/ *v* **-dd-** [T *in, with*] to fix (something) firmly and deeply: *a gold crown embedded with jewels |(fig.) That terrible day will be embedded in my memory.*

em·bel·lish /ɪm'bɛlɪʃ/ *v* [T *with*] to make more beautiful: *a white hat embellished with pink roses|(fig.) Tell the truth; do not embellish the story.* –see DECORATE (USAGE) **–embellishment** *n* [C;U]

em·ber /'ɛmbər/ *n* [*usu. pl.*] a red-hot piece of wood or coal, esp. in a fire that is no longer burning with flames

em·bez·zle /ɪm'bɛzəl/ *v* **-zled, -zling** [I;T] to steal (money that is placed in one's care): *The clerk embezzled $10,000 from the bank where he worked.* **–embezzlement** *n* [U] **–embezzler** *n*

em·bit·ter /ɪm'bɪtər/ *v* [T] to fill with painful or bitter feelings: *He was embittered by his many disappointments.*

em·bla·zon /ɪm'bleʸzən/ *v* [T *on, with;usu. pass.*] to decorate (a shield or flag) with a sign, usu. a COAT OF ARMS

em·blem /'ɛmbləm/ *n* [*of*] an object which is the sign of something: *The national emblem of America is an* EAGLE. –compare SYMBOL **–emblematic** /ˌɛmbləˈmætɪk/ *adj*

em·bod·y /ɪm'bɑdiʸ/ *v* **-ied, -ying** [T] **1** to express: *The letter embodied all his ideas.* **2** to contain or include: *The new car embodies many improvements.* **–embodiment** *n*: *The king was regarded by his enemies as the embodiment of evil.*

em·boss /ɪm'bɔs, ɪm'bɑs/ *v* [T *on, with*] to decorate (metal, paper, etc.) with a raised pattern: *The name and address of the company are embossed on its paper.*

em·brace¹ /ɪm'breʸs/ *v* **-braced, -bracing 1** [I;T] to take and hold (another or each other) in the arms as a sign of love: *She embraced her son tenderly.|The two sisters embraced.* **2** [T] *fml* to contain or include: *a course of study embracing several different subjects* **3** [T] *fml* to become a believer in: *He embraced the Muslim religion.*

embrace² *n* the act of embracing (EMBRACE¹ (1))

em·broi·der /ɪm'brɔɪdər/ *v* [I;T *with, in, on*] to do decorative needlework on (cloth): *to embroider a pattern|a dress embroidered with flowers in silk thread|(fig.) He always embroiders* (=adds untrue details to) *his stories to make them more exciting.*

em·broi·der·y /ɪm'brɔɪdəriʸ/ *n* [U] the act or result of EMBROIDERing: *a dress with a lot of embroidery on it*

em·broil /ɪm'brɔɪl/ *v* [T] to cause (oneself or another) to join in something troublesome: *to get embroiled in an argument*

em·bry·o /'ɛmbriʸ,oʷ/ *n* **-os** the young of any creature in its first state before it is born: *(fig.) His plans are still* **in embryo.** (=undeveloped) **–embryonic** /ˌɛmbriʸˈɑnɪk/ *adj*

em·cee /ˌɛmˈsiʸ/ *n AmE infml* a person who introduces the various acts in a stage or television show

em·er·ald /'ɛmərəld/ *adj,n* [C;U] (the color of) a bright green precious stone

e·merge /ɪ'mɜrdʒ/ *v* **-merged, -merging** [I] **1** [*from, out of*] to come or appear (from/out of somewhere): *The sun emerged from behind the clouds.* **2** [*from*] to become known as a result of inquiry: *It emerged that the driver of the car had been drunk.* **–emergence** *n* [U] *fml*

e·mer·gen·cy /ɪ'mɜrdʒənsiʸ/ *n* **-cies** an unexpected and dangerous happening which must be dealt with quickly: *Ring the bell in an emergency.|emergency* EXIT

emergency room /·'··· ,·/ *n AmE* a place in a hospital where people hurt in accidents or suffering from sudden illness are taken for treatment: *When Ann broke her arm, we took her to the emergency room.*

e·mer·gent /ɪ'mɜrdʒənt/ *adj* [A] beginning to be independent and noticeable: *the emergent countries of Africa*

e·met·ic /ɪ'mɛtɪk/ *n,adj* [C;U] *tech* (something, esp. medicine) eaten or drunk to cause a person to bring up food from the stomach: *If he drinks poison, give him an emetic at once.*

em·i·grate /'ɛmə,greʸt/ *v* **-grated, -grating** [I *from,to*] to leave one's own country in order to go and live in another **–emigrant** /'ɛməgrənt/ *n* **–emigration** /ˌɛməˈgreʸʃən/ *n* [C;U]

USAGE To **migrate** is to move from one country to another for a limited period; the word is esp. used of workers, called **migrants**, and birds, and the practice is called **migration**: *the spring* **migration** *of the wild ducks|migrants/migrant workers from Mexico.* To **emigrate** is to leave one country to go and become a citizen of another, and the practice is called **emigration**: *to* **emigrate** *to the US.* But from the point of view of the country which they enter, people who **emigr-ate** are **immigrants**, and the practice is called **immigration**. –compare IMMIGRATE

em·i·nent /'ɛmənənt/ *adj* (of people) famous and admired: *an eminent doctor* –Compare: *We are expecting the arrival of an eminent scientist.*|*The great man's arrival is imminent.* (=he will arrive very soon) –see FAMOUS (USAGE) –**eminence** *n* [U]

em·i·nent·ly /'ɛmənəntliʸ/ *apprec* (of qualities or abilities) very; unusually: *Your decision was eminently fair.*

e·mir /ə'mɪər/ *n* a Muslim ruler, esp. in Asia and parts of Africa

e·mir·ate /ə'mɪərɪt, -eʸt/ *n* the position, state, power, lands, etc., of an EMIR

em·is·sar·y /'ɛmə,sɛriʸ/ *n* -**ies** [*of*] *fml* a person who is sent with an official message or to do special work

e·mit /ɪ'mɪt/ *v* -**tt**- [T] *fml* to send out: *The chimney emitted smoke.*|(fig.) *John emitted a curse.* –**emission** /ɪ'mɪʃən/ *n* [C;U]

e·mol·u·ment /ɪ'mɑlyəmənt/ *n* [*usu. pl.*] *fml* money received for work; wage –compare SALARY; see PAY² (USAGE)

e·mo·tion /ɪ'mowʷʃən/ *n* **1** [C] any of the strong feelings of the human spirit: *Love, hatred, and grief are emotions.* **2** [U] strength of feeling; excited state of the feelings: *He described the accident in a voice shaking with emotion.* –**emotionless** *adj* –**emotionlessly** *adv*

e·mo·tion·al /ɪ'mowʷʃənəl/ *adj* **1** having feelings which are strong or easily moved: *He was very emotional; he cried when I left.* –opposite **unemotional 2** (of words, music, etc.) showing or causing strong feeling **3** concerning the EMOTIONS (1): *The child's bad behavior is a result of emotional problems.* –**emotionally** *adv*

e·mo·tive /ɪ'mowʷtɪv/ *adj* causing strong feeling: *"Home" is a much more emotive word than "house."*

em·pa·thy /'ɛmpəθiʸ/ *n* [S;U *with*] the power of imagining oneself to be another person, and so of sharing his/ her feelings

em·per·or /'ɛmpərər/ **empress** *fem.– n* the head of an empire

em·pha·sis /'ɛmfəsɪs/ *n* -**ses** /ˌsiʸz/ [C;U *on, upon*] special force given to something, to show that it is particularly important: *The dictionary places/lays/puts an emphasis on examples.* –**emphatic** /ɪm'fæṭɪk/ *adj*: *He answered the question with an emphatic "No."* –**emphatically** *adv*

em·pha·size ‖also -**sise** *BrE* /'ɛmfə,saɪz/ *v* -**sized**, -**sizing** [T] to place EMPHASIS on: *The band emphasized the last note.* (=played it loudly)| *I must emphasize the fact that they are only children.*

em·phy·se·ma /ˌɛmfə'siʸmə, -'ziʸ-/ *n* [U] *med* a diseased condition in which the lungs become swollen with air, causing difficulty in breathing and often preventing the proper action of the heart

em·pire /'ɛmpaɪər/ *n* (*often cap.*) a group of countries under one government, usu. ruled by an EMPEROR: *the Roman Empire*| (fig.) *the industrial empire of Standard Products*

em·pir·i·cal /ɪm'pɪrɪkəl, ɛm-/ *adj* (of people or methods) guided only by practical experience of the world than we see and feel, not by ideas out of books –**empirically** *adv* –**empiricism** /ɪm'pɪrə,sɪzəm, ɛm-/ *n* [U]

em·ploy /ɪm'plɔɪ/ *v* -**ployed**, -**ploying** [T] **1** [*as*] to use (a person) as a paid worker; appoint (a person) to a job: *We're employing three new secretaries on Monday.*|*We employ her as an adviser.* –see also UNEMPLOYED **2** [*as, in*] *fml* to use: *This bird employs its beak as a weapon.*

em·ploy·ee /ɪm'plɔɪ-iʸ, ˌɛmplɔɪ'iʸ, ɪm-/ *n* [*of*] a person who is employed: *a government employee*

em·ploy·er /ɪm'plɔɪər/ *n* a person or group that employs others: *The car industry is one of our biggest employers.*

em·ploy·ment /ɪm'plɔɪmənt/ *n* [U] **1** the state of being EMPLOYED (1) –opposite **unemployment 2** the act of EMPLOYING (2): *the employment of force*

employment a·gen·cy /·'·· ,···/ *n* a private business or (in the US) a government office which helps people to find work or workers

em·pow·er /ɪm'pauər/ *v* [T] *fml* to give (someone) a power or lawful right: *The new law empowered the police to search private houses.* –compare ENABLE, ENTITLE (2)

em·press /'ɛmprɪs/ *n* [*of*] **1** a female EMPEROR **2** the wife of an EMPEROR

emp·ti·ly /'ɛmptəliʸ/ *adv* in an EMPTY¹ (2) way

emp·ty¹ /'ɛmptiʸ/ *adj* **1** containing nothing: *an empty cup*|*There are three empty houses on our street.*|*He drove through streets empty of* (=without) *traffic.* –compare FULL¹ **2** [*of*] *derog* (of words, talk, etc.) without sense or purpose; meaningless; unreal: *empty promises* –**emptiness** *n* [U]

empty² *v* -**tied**, -**tying** [I;T] **1** to make or become EMPTY¹ (1): *They emptied the bottle.* (=drank all that was in it)|*The room emptied very quickly.* –compare FILL¹ **2** [*out, into, onto*] to put or move (the contents of a container) somewhere else: *He emptied out all his pockets onto the table.*

em·u·late /'ɛmyə,leʸt/ *v* -**lated**, -**lating** [T] *fml* to try to do as well as (another person): *You must work hard to emulate your sister's success.* –**emulation** /ˌɛmyə'leʸʃən/ *n* [U *of*]

e·mul·sion /ɪ'mʌlʃən/ *n* [C;U] a creamy mixture of liquids such as oil and water: *emulsion paint*

en·a·ble /ɪ'neʸbəl/ *v* -**bled**, -**bling** [T] to make able; give the power, means, or right: *The bird's large wings enable it to fly.*|*The new law enables a person to claim money from the state.*|*This dictionary enables you to understand English words.* –compare EMPOWER, ENTITLE (2)

en·act /ɪ'nækt/ *v* [T] **1** (of the government) to make or pass (a law) **2** to perform or represent (a part of a play) –**enactment** *n* [C;U]

en·am·el¹ /ɪ'næməl/ *n* [U] **1** a glassy substance which is melted, and put as decoration or protection onto objects made of metal, etc. **2** a kind of paint which produces a very shiny surface **3** the hard smooth outer surface of the teeth

enamel[2] v **-l-** AmE‖**-ll-** BrE [T] to cover or decorate with ENAMEL (1,2)

en·am·ored AmE‖**enamoured** BrE /ɪ'næmərd/ adj [F of, with] fml very fond of; charmed by: He's so (much) enamored of his own plan that he won't listen to me.

en·camp·ment /ɪn'kæmpmənt/ n a large esp. military camp

en·case /ɪn'keɪs/ v **-cased, -casing** [T in] to cover completely: His student card was encased in plastic.

en·chant /ɪn'tʃænt/ v [T] **1** to fill (someone) with delight: He was enchanted by/with the idea. **2** to use magic on: a palace in an enchanted forest **—enchanter, enchantress** /ɪn'tʃæntrɪs/ fem.– n **—enchantment** n [C;U]

en·chant·ing /ɪn'tʃæntɪŋ/ adj apprec delightful: an enchanting child **—enchantingly** adv

en·cir·cle /ɪn's3rkəl/ v **-cled, -cling** [T by, with, in] to surround; make a circle around: The army encircled the airport.

en·clave /'ɛnkleɪv, 'ɑŋ-/ n a part of a country or nation which is completely surrounded by another

en·close /ɪn'kloʊz/ v **-closed, -closing** [T by, in] **1** to surround with a fence or wall so as to shut in or close: a garden enclosed by a high wall **2** to put (esp. something sent with a letter) inside: I enclose a check for $50 (with this letter). **—compare** APPEND

en·clo·sure /ɪn'kloʊʒər/ n **1** a piece of land that is enclosed: There's a special enclosure where you can look at the horses before the race starts. **2** something that is put in with a letter

en·com·pass /ɪn'kʌmpəs/ v [T with] fml to surround on all sides: (fig.)My plan encompasses every possibility.

en·core /'ɑŋkɔr, 'ɑŋkoʊr, 'ɑn-/ n,interj (something which is performed again because of) a call (=Please do it again!) which is made by listeners who are pleased with a song or other performance

en·coun·ter /ɪn'kaʊntər/ v [T] fml to meet (something unexpected or dangerous): He encountered many problems.|He encountered a friend on the road. **—encounter** n [with]: an unpleasant encounter with a dangerous snake

en·cour·age /ɪn'k3rɪdʒ, -'kʌr-/ v **-aged, -aging** [T in] to give courage or hope to (someone); urge (someone) on: The new company has made an encouraging start.| Don't encourage her laziness by doing things for her. **—see also** DISCOURAGE **—encouragingly** adv **—encouragement** n [C;U]: He owed his success to his wife's encouragement.

en·croach /ɪn'kroʊtʃ/ v [I on, upon] to go beyond, or take more than, what is right or usual: His new farm buildings encroach on his neighbor's land. **—encroachment** n [C;U]

en·crust·ed /ɪn'krʌstɪd/ adj [with] covered in (gold, mud, jewels, etc.): a pipe encrusted with rust

en·cum·ber /ɪn'kʌmbər/ v [T with] to make free action or movement difficult: He is encumbered with debts. **—encumbrance** /ɪn'kʌmbrəns/ n

en·cy·clo·pe·di·a, -paedia /ɪn,saɪklə'piʸdiʸə/ n a book or set of books dealing with every branch of knowledge, or with one particular branch: an encyclopedia of modern science |A dictionary explains words, and an encyclopedia explains facts. **—encyclopedic** /ɪn,saɪklə'piʸdɪk/ adj

end[1] /ɛnd/ n **1** [of] the point where something stops: the ends of a rope/of a stick| Which end of the box has the opening?|He walked to the end of the road/the hall.| start work at the end of August.|The year is at an end/coming to an end. **2** a little piece that is left over: cigarette ends **—see also** ODDS AND ENDS **3** fml an aim or purpose: He wants to buy a house, and is saving money to/for this end.|to achieve one's ends **4** at loose ends AmE‖ at a loose end BrE – (restless and) having nothing to do **5** end to end with the points or the narrow sides touching each other: We can provide seats for ten people if we put these two tables end to end. **6** get (hold of) the wrong end of the stick to get a completely wrong idea **7** in the end at last: She tried many times to pass the examination, and in the end she succeeded. **8** make (both) ends meet to get just enough money for one's needs **9** no end of infml a very great deal of: That car has caused me no end of worry. **10** on end: a (of time) continuously: He sat there for hours on end. b upright: We had to stand the table on end to get it through the door. **11** put an end to to stop from happening any more

end[2] v [I;T] to (cause to) finish: The party ended at midnight.|The war ended in 1975.|He ended his letter (off) with good wishes to the family.

end in sthg. v prep [T] to result in: The battle ended in a victory/ in everyone dying.

end up v adv [I +v-ing] to finish in a particular place or way: She ended up (as) head of the company.

en·dan·ger /ɪn'deɪndʒər/ v [T] to cause danger to: You will endanger your health if you smoke.

en·dear sbdy. **to** sbdy. /ɪn'dɪər/ v prep [T] to cause (esp. oneself) to be loved: His kindness endeared him to everyone. **—endearing** adj: an endearing smile **—endearingly** adv

en·dear·ment /ɪn'dɪərmənt/ n [usu. pl] an expression of love: He was whispering endearments to her.

en·deav·or AmE ‖endeavour BrE /ɪn'dɛvər/ v [I+to-v] fml to try: You must endeavor to improve your work. **—endeavor** n [C;U]

en·dem·ic /ɛn'dɛmɪk, ɪn-/ adj [in,to] (esp. of diseases) found regularly in a particular place: an endemic disease of the chest among miners

end·ing /'ɛndɪŋ/ n the end, esp. of a story, movie, play, or word: a happy ending **—compare** BEGINNING

en·dive /'ɛndaɪv/ n [C;U] **1** also Belgian endive– leaves of CHICORY grown in a dark place to make them white, which are eaten raw or cooked **2** BrE for CHICORY (2)

end·less /'ɛndlɪs/ adj never finishing: The journey seemed endless. **—endlessly** adv

en·dorse, in- /ɪn'dɔrs/ v **-dorsed, -dorsing** [T]

1 to write, esp. one's name, on the back of (esp. a check) **2** *fml* to express approval or support of (opinions, actions, etc.) –**endorsement** *n* [C;U]

en·dow /ɪn'daʊ/ *v* [T] to give money to (a school, hospital, etc.) –**endowment** *n* [C;U] **endow** sbdy. **with** sthg. *v prep* [T *usu. pass.*] *apprec* to make rich in (a good quality or ability) from birth: *She is endowed with great musical ability.*

en·dur·ance /ɪn'dʊərəns, -'dyʊər-/ *n* [U] the state or power of enduring (ENDURE (1)): *When the pain was* **beyond/past endurance** (=impossible to bear), *she went to the doctor.*

en·dure /ɪn'dʊər, ɪn'dyʊər/ *v* **-dured, -during** **1** [T +*to-v/v-ing*] to bear (pain, suffering, etc.): *I can't endure that noise a moment longer.* –see BEAR² (USAGE) **2** [I] *fml* to last: *his fame as a great writer has endured.* –**endurable** *adj*

end·ways /'ɛndweʸz/ also **endwise** /'ɛnd waɪz/– *adv* with the end forward; not sideways: *The box is quite narrow when you look at it endways (on).*

en·e·my /'ɛnəmiʸ/ *n* **-mies 1** a person who hates or dislikes another person: *A politician often has many enemies.* (=many people dislike him)|*John and Paul are enemies.* (=of each other) **2** someone or something that wants to harm, or is against (someone or something): *Abraham Lincoln was the enemy of slavery.* –compare FRIEND (1) **3** the army with whom one is fighting: *The enemy is advancing.*

en·er·get·ic /,ɛnər'dʒɛtɪk/ *adj* full of ENERGY (1): *an energetic tennis player* –**energetically** *adv*

en·er·gy /'ɛnərdʒiʸ/ *n* [U] **1** (of people) the quality of being full of life and action; power and ability to be active, do a lot of work, etc.: *Young people usually have more energy than the old.*|*to* APPLY/DEVOTE *all one's energies to a job* **2** the power which does work and drives machines: *atomic/electrical energy*

en·force /ɪn'fɔrs, ɪn'foʷrs/ *v* **-forced, -forcing** [T] **1** to cause (a rule or law) to be carried out: *The new law about seat belts in cars will be difficult to enforce.* **2** to make (something) happen, esp. by threats or force: *the enforced silence of the newspapers under the military government* –**enforceable** *adj* –**enforcement** *n* [U]

en·fran·chise /ɪn'fræntʃaɪz/ *v* **-chised, -chising** [T] to give FRANCHISE (the right to vote at elections) to –opposite **disenfranchise** –**enfranchisement** /ɪn'fræntʃaɪzmənt, -tʃɪz-/ *n* [U]

en·gage /ɪn'geʸdʒ/ *v* **-gaged, -gaging 1** [T *as*] to arrange to employ (someone): *to engage a new secretary* **2** [T] to take up (time, thought, attention, etc.): *The new toy engaged the child's attention.* **3** [I;T *with*] to (cause to) fit into or lock together: *This wheel engages with that wheel and turns it.* **4** [T *in*] *fml* to attack: *They engaged the enemy (in battle).* –see also DISENGAGE

en·gaged /ɪn'geʸdʒd/ *adj* [F] **1** [*in, on*] (of people) busy; spending time on doing something: "*Can you come on Monday?*" "*No, I'm engaged.*" (=I've arranged to do something)|*engaged in politics/trade* **2** (of a telephone line) *BrE* for BUSY: *Sorry! The line/the number is engaged.* –see TELEPHONE (USAGE) **3** [+*to-v/to*] having agreed to marry: *My daughter is engaged (to a doctor).*|*They're engaged (to be married).*

en·gage·ment /ɪn'geʸdʒmənt/ *n* **1** an agreement to marry: *Have you heard that John has broken off his engagement to Mary?* (=said he no longer wishes to marry her) **2** an arrangement to meet someone or to do something, esp. at a particular time: *I can't come on Monday because I have an engagement.*

en·gag·ing /ɪn'geʸdʒɪŋ/ *adj apprec* charming: *an engaging smile* –**engagingly** *adv*

en·gine /'ɛndʒən/ *n* **1** a piece of machinery with moving parts which changes power from steam, electricity, oil, etc. into movement: *the engine of a car* –see MACHINE¹ (USAGE) **2** also **locomotive** *fml*–a machine which pulls a railroad train **3 -engined** having a certain number of engines or kind of engine: *a diesel-engined car* |*a four-engined aircraft*

en·gi·neer¹ /,ɛndʒə'nɪər/ *n* **1** a person who plans and understands the making of machines, roads, bridges, harbors, etc.: *an electrical/*CIVIL/MECHANICAL *engineer* **2** *AmE* a person who drives a railroad engine

engineer² *v* **1** to plan and make: *That mountain road is very well engineered.* [T] **2** to cause by secret planning: *He had powerful enemies who engineered* (=arranged) *his ruin.*

en·gi·neer·ing /,ɛndʒə'nɪərɪŋ/ *n* [U] the science or profession of an ENGINEER¹

Eng·lish /'ɪŋglɪʃ/ *adj* belonging to England, its people, etc.: *an English village*

English² *n* **1** [U] the language of the UK, the US, etc.: *Do you speak English?* |*She's Japanese, but her English is excellent.* **2** [the P] the people of England

en·grave /ɪn'greʸv/ *v* **-graved, -graving** [T *with, on*] to cut (words, pictures, etc.) on wood, stone, or metal: (fig.) *The terrible memory was engraved on his mind.* –**engraver** *n* –**engraving** *n* [C;U]

en·grossed /ɪn'groʷst/ *adj* [F *in*] having one's time and attention completely filled: *He was so engrossed in his work that he forgot to eat.*

en·gross·ing /ɪn'groʷsɪŋ/ *adj* very interesting; filling one's attention: *an engrossing book*

en·gulf /ɪn'gʌlf/ *v* [T] *lit* (of the earth, the sea, etc.) to destroy by swallowing up: *The stormy sea engulfed the small boat.*

en·hance /ɪn'hæns/ *v* **-hanced, -hancing** [T] to increase (good things such as value, power, or beauty): *Passing the examination should enhance your chances of getting a job.*

e·nig·ma /ɪ'nɪgmə/ *n* a mysterious person, thing, or event that is hard to understand: *I can't find out anything about her; she's an enigma.* –**enigmatic** /,ɛnɪg'mætɪk/ *adj* –**enigmatically** *adv*

en·joy /ɪn'dʒɔɪ/ *v* **-joyed, -joying** [T] **1**

[+*v-ing*] to get happiness from (things and experiences): *I enjoyed the movie.*|*I always enjoy going to the movies.* **2** *fml* to possess or use (something good): *to enjoy* (=have) *good health* **3 enjoy oneself** to be happy; experience pleasure: *Did you enjoy yourself at the party?* —**enjoyment** *n* [C;U]

en·joy·a·ble /ɪn'dʒɔɪəbəl/ *adj* (of things and experiences) pleasant: *an enjoyable vacation* —**enjoyably** *adv*

en·large /ɪn'lɑrdʒ/ *v* **-larged, -larging** [I;T] to (cause to) grow larger or wider: *We're enlarging the vegetable garden to grow more food.*|*This photograph probably won't enlarge well.* —**enlargement** *n* [C;U]: *I'm sending mother an enlargement of the baby's photograph.*

enlarge on sthg. *v prep* [T] to add more length and detail to

en·light·en /ɪn'laɪtn/ *v* [T] to cause to understand; free from false beliefs: *The child thought the world was flat until I enlightened him!* —**enlightened** *adj*: to hold enlightened opinions —**enlightenment** *n* [U]

en·list /ɪn'lɪst/ *v* **1** [I;T] to (cause to) enter the armed forces: *He enlisted when he was 18.* **2** [T *in*] to obtain (help, sympathy, etc.) —**enlistment** *n* [C;U]

en·liv·en /ɪn'laɪvən/ *v* [T] to make (people or events) more active, spirited, or cheerful

en·mi·ty /'ɛnməti/ *n* [U] the state or feeling of being an enemy or enemies

en·no·ble /ɪ'nowbəl/ *v* **-bled, -bling** [T] **1** to make better and more honorable: *His character has been ennobled by his sufferings.* **2** to make (someone) a nobleman/noblewoman

e·nor·mi·ty /ɪ'nɔrməti/ *n* **-ties 1** [C;U] (an act of) very great evil: *the enormity of his crime* **2** [U] the quality of being very large; ENORMOUSNESS: *the enormity of the job of feeding the whole school*

e·nor·mous /ɪ'nɔrməs/ *adj* very large indeed: *an enormous house/meal/amount of money* —see Study Notes on page 550 —**enormousness** *n* [U]

e·nor·mous·ly /ɪ'nɔrməsli/ *adv* very much indeed: *enormously rich*|*He's enormously popular.*

e·nough¹ /ɪ'nʌf/ *determiner, pron* [A or after *n*; +*to-v/for*] as much or as many as is necessary: *We have enough seats for everyone.*|*There's enough money/money enough to buy a car.*|*She doesn't have enough to do.*|*I've eaten more than enough.* (=too much)|*Is there food enough for everyone?*

USAGE **Enough** can come either before or after a plural or [U] noun, but the first position is more common: *Are there enough desks/desks enough for all the students?*|*Is there enough space/space enough for all the desks?*

enough² *adv* **1** [+*to-v*] to the necessary degree: *It's warm enough to swim.*|*He didn't run fast enough (to catch the train).* **2** not very, but in an acceptable way: *She runs well enough, but she would run very well if she tried harder.*|*He's lived in France for years, but strange enough* (=although this is rather

strange) *he can't speak French.*|*It's* **fair enough** (=reasonable) *to ask your own brother to help.* **3 sure enough** *infml* as expected: *He said he would come, and sure enough he did.*

en·quire /ɪn'kwaɪər/ *v* **-quired, -quiring** [I;T] →INQUIRE —see ASK (USAGE)

en·quir·y /ɪn'kwaɪəriʸ, 'ɪn,kwaɪ-, 'ɪnkwəriʸ/ *n* **-ies** →INQUIRY

en·rage /ɪn'reɪdʒ/ *v* **-raged, -raging** [T] to make very angry —**enraged** *adj* [+*to-v/that/at, by*]

en·rap·ture /ɪn'ræptʃər/ *v* **-tured, -turing** [T] to fill (someone) with great joy or delight (RAPTURE): *They were enraptured to meet the great singer.*

en·rich /ɪn'rɪtʃ/ *v* [T *by, with*] to make rich: *The discovery of oil will enrich the nation.*|(fig.) *Music can enrich your whole life.* —**enrichment** *n* [U]

en·roll, enrol /ɪn'rowl/ *v* **-ll-** [I;T *as, in*] to make (oneself or another person) officially a member of a group, school, etc. —**enrollment** *n* [C;U *as, in, of*]: *his enrollment as a member of the club*

en route /ɑn 'ruwt, ɛn-/ *adv* [F *for, from, to*] on the way: *I met her at the airport when I was en route to New York.*

en·sconce /ɪn'skɑns/ *v* **-sconced, -sconcing** [T] *fml or humor* to place or seat (oneself) comfortably in a safe place —**ensconced** *adj* [F *on, in*]

en·sem·ble /ɑn'sɑmbəl/ *n* **1** [C] a set of things that combine with or match each other to make a whole: *Your coat, hat, and shoes make an attractive ensemble.* **2** a small group of musicians who regularly play together —compare ORCHESTRA

en·sign /'ɛnsən, 'ɛnsaɪn/ *n* [C] a flag on a ship, esp. to show what nation the ship belongs to

en·sign 2 /'ɛnsən/ *n* [A;C] an officer of the lowest rank in the navy

en·slave /ɪn'sleɪv/ *v* **-slaved, -slaving** [T] to make into a slave —**enslavement** *n* [U]

en·sue /ɪn'suw/ *v* **-sued, -suing** [I *from*] *fml* to happen afterwards (often as a result): *A bomb exploded and I got lost in the ensuing confusion.*

en·sure /ɪn'ʃʊər/||also **insure** *AmE*– *v* **-sured, -suring** [T +*that*] to make (something) certain to happen: *If you want to ensure that you catch the plane, take a taxi.*

en·tail /ɪn'teɪl/ *v* [T] to make (an event or action) necessary: *Writing a history book entails a lot of work.*

en·tan·gle /ɪn'tæŋgəl/ *v* **-gled, -gling** [T *among, in, with*] to cause (something) to become twisted or mixed (with something else): *The bird entangled itself in the net/wire.*|(fig.) *He became entangled in dishonest business dealings.* —opposite **disentangle**; compare TANGLE, ENTWINE —**entanglement** *n* [C;U]

en·ter /'ɛntər/ *v* **1** [I;T] *more formal than* **go/come into** –to come or go into (a room, etc.): *to enter a room/a house*|*Please do not enter without knocking on the door.* **2** [T] to become a member of: *to enter the medical* *profession* **3** [T *in, up*] to write down (names, amounts of money, etc.) in a book

enter into sthg. *v prep* [T] **1** [*with*] to begin: *to enter into a contract with a company* **2** to take part in: *He entered into the spirit of the game with great excitement.*

en·ter·prise /'ɛntər,praɪz/ *n* **1** [C] a plan, esp. to do something new or difficult **2** [U] the courage that is needed to do something daring or difficult **3** [U] a way of organizing business: *Do you believe in* private *enterprise, or in government ownership of industry?* **4** [C] a business firm: *one of the largest enterprises of its kind*

en·ter·pris·ing /'ɛntər,praɪzɪŋ/ *adj apprec* having or showing ENTERPRISE (2) –opposite **unenterprising**

en·ter·tain /,ɛntər'teɪn/ *v* **1** [I;T] to amuse and interest: *A teacher should entertain as well as teach.* **2** [I;T] to give a party (for); to provide food and drink (for): *He does most of his entertaining in restaurants.* **3** [T] to be ready and willing to think about (an idea, doubt, etc.)

en·ter·tain·er /,ɛntər'teɪnər/ *n* a person who ENTERTAINS (1) professionally: *a popular television entertainer*

en·ter·tain·ing /,ɛntər'teɪnɪŋ/ *adj apprec* amusing and interesting: *an entertaining story* –**entertainingly** *adv*

en·ter·tain·ment /,ɛntər'teɪnmənt/ *n* **1** [U] the act of ENTERTAINING (2) people; the providing of food and drink **2** [C;U] (a) public amusement: *A movie theater is a place of entertainment.*

en·thrall, enthral /ɪn'θrɔl/ *v* [T] to hold the complete attention and interest of: *The boy was enthralled by his father's stories.* –**enthralling** *adj*

en·throne /ɪn'θroʷn/ *v* **-throned, -throning** [T] to place on a THRONE (official seat of a king or queen) –**enthronement** *n* [C;U]

en·thuse /ɪn'θuʷz/ *v* **-thused, -thusing** [I *about, over*] *infml* to show ENTHUSIASM: *He was enthusing about his new radio.*

en·thu·si·as·m /ɪn'θuʷziʸ,æzəm/ *n* [C;U *for, about*] a strong feeling of interest or admiration: *The new teacher is full of enthusiasm.* –**enthusiast** *n: a bicycling enthusiast* –**enthusiastic** /ɪn,θuʷziʸ'æstɪk/ *adj* –**enthusiastically** *adv*

en·tice /ɪn'taɪs/ *v* **-ticed, -ticing** [T *away, from, into*] to persuade (someone) to do something usu. wrong: *He enticed me away from working.* *n* [C;U]

en·tire /ɪn'taɪər/ *adj* [A] complete: *She spent the entire day in bed.* | *I am in entire agreement with you.* –**entirely** *adv* –see Study Notes on page 363

en·tire·ty /ɪn'taɪrətiʸ, ɪn'taɪrərtiʸ/ *n* [U] completeness; wholeness: *Consider the matter in its entirety.* (=as a whole)

en·ti·tle /ɪn'taɪtl/ *v* **-tled, -tling** [T] **1** to give a title to (a book, play, etc.) **2** [*to*] to give (someone) the right to do something: *This ticket entitles you to travel first class.* –compare ENABLE, EMPOWER –**entitlement** *n* [U]

en·ti·ty /'ɛntətiʸ/ *n* **-ties** something that has a single separate and independent existence:

Since the war Germany has been divided. It is no longer one political entity.

en·to·mol·o·gy /,ɛntə'mɑlədʒiʸ/ *n* [U] the scientific study of insects –compare ETYMOLOGY –**entomologist** *n*

en·tou·rage /,ɑntuʷ'rɑʒ/ *n* all the people who surround and follow an important person: *His entourage was traveling on the same plane.*

en·trails /'ɛntreʸlz/ *n* [P] *old use* the inside parts of an animal, esp. the bowels

en·trance¹ /'ɛntrəns/ *n* **1** [C] a gate, door, or other opening by which one enters: *Excuse me. Where is the entrance to the theater?* –compare ENTRY (3) **2** [C] the act of entering: *to make one's entrance* **3** [U] the right to enter: *the entrance* FEE (=money which must be paid) | *a school entrance examination*

USAGE Compare **entrance** and **entry**: Both words can be used to mean an act of entering: *to make one's* **entrance** *onto the stage* | *her late* **entry** *to the party;* or the right to enter: *a school* **entrance** *examination* | *an* **entry** *form*

en·trance² /ɪn'træns/ *v* **-tranced, -trancing** [T] *apprec* to fill (someone) with great wonder and delight

en·trant /'ɛntrənt/ *n* a person who enters into a profession, race, or competition

en·treat /ɪn'triʸt/ *v* [I;T +*that/for*] *fml* to beg humbly or very seriously: *She entreated her friend to forgive her.* –**entreaty** *n* **-ies** [C;U]

en·trenched /ɪn'trɛntʃt/ *adj often derog* (of rights, beliefs, etc.) firmly established: *his entrenched political ideas*

en·tre·pre·neur /,ɑntrəprə'nɜr, -'nʊər, -'nyʊər/ *n* a person who owns and runs a business

en·trust /ɪn'trʌst/ *v* [T *with, to*] to give (someone) (something) to take care of: *I entrusted the child to your care.*

en·try /'ɛntriʸ/ *n* **-tries 1** [C *into*] the act of coming or going in; ENTRANCE¹ (2): *Spain's entry into the war* **2** [U] the right to enter: *The sign on the door says "No Entry."* **3** [C] *esp. AmE* a door, gate, or passage by which one enters **4** [C;U] the act or result of writing something down on a list: *The next entry in this dictionary is the word "entwine."* **5** [C] a person or thing, entered in a race or competition: *This painting is Mrs. Smith's entry in the competition.* –see ENTRANCE¹ (USAGE)

en·twine /ɪn'twaɪn/ *v* **-twined, -twining** [T *in, around*] to twist together, around, or in: *They walked along with their fingers entwined.* –compare ENTANGLE

e·nu·mer·ate /ɪ'nuʷmə,reʸt, ɪ'nyuʷ-/ *v* **-rated, -rating** [T] *fml* to name (things on a list) one by one –**enumeration** /ɪ,nuʷmə'reʸʃən, ɪ,nyuʷ-/ *n* [C;U]

e·nun·ci·ate /ɪ'nʌnsiʸ,eʸt/ *v* **-ated, -ating** *fml* **1** [I;T] to pronounce (words): *An actor has to enunciate clearly.* **2** [T] to express (ideas, opinions, etc.) clearly and firmly –**enunciation** /ɪ,nʌnsiʸ'eʸʃən/ *n* [C;U]

en·vel·op /ɪn'vɛləp/ *v* [T *in*] to wrap up or cover completely: *The building was soon enveloped in flames.* –**envelopment** *n* [U]

en·ve·lope /'ɛnvə,loʷp, 'ɑn-/ *n* the paper

cover of a letter

en·vi·a·ble /'ɛnviʸəbəl/ *adj* causing ENVY; very desirable: *his enviable good luck|an enviable job* –opposite **unenviable** –**enviably** *adv*

en·vi·ous /'ɛnviʸəs/ *adj* feeling or showing ENVY: *She was envious of her sister's new job.* –see JEALOUS (USAGE) –**enviously** *adv*

en·vi·ron·ment /ɪn'vaɪrənmənt, -'vaɪərn-/ *n* [C; *the* S] the natural or social conditions in which people live: *We have to stop spoiling the environment.* (=the air, water, and land)|*Children need a happy home environment.|brougt up in a happy* **environment**. –**environmental** /ɪn,vaɪrən'mɛntəl, -,vaɪərn-/*adj: environmental* POLLUTION (=the making dirty of the *environment*)

USAGE Compare **environment** and **surroundings: Surroundings** are simply the physical things which surround a place or person: *a hotel set in pleasant* **surroundings.** Your **environment** means all the things around you, esp. as they influence your feelings and development. Compare *to grow up in beautiful* **surroundings**/*to grow up in a happy* **environment.**

en·vi·ron·men·tal·ist /ɪn,vaɪrən'mɛntəl-ɪst, -,vaɪərn-/ *n* a person who tries to prevent the ENVIRONMENT from being spoiled –**environmentalism** *n* [U]

en·vi·sion /ɪn'vɪʒən/ *AmE* –also **envisage** /ɪn'vɪzɪdʒ/ [T +*v-ing/that*] to see in the mind as a future possibility: *When do you envision being able to pay back the money?*

en·voy /'ɛnvɔɪ, 'an-/ *n* a messenger, esp. one sent by one government to do business with another

en·vy[1] /'ɛnviʸ/ *n* [U *at, of*] a feeling one has towards someone when one wishes that one had his/her qualities or possessions: *He feels envy towards his sister.|The boy's new toy was* **the envy of** *his friends.* (=it made them feel envy) –compare JEALOUSY

envy[2] *v* **-vied, -vying** [T] to feel ENVY[1] for or of: *I don't envy you your trip in this bad weather.*

en·zyme /'ɛnzaɪm/ *n* a chemical substance (CATALYST) produced by certain living cells, which can cause chemical change in plants or animals

ep·au·let, -lette /'ɛpə,lɛt, ,ɛpə'lɛt/ *n* a shoulder decoration, esp. on a military or naval uniform

e·phem·er·al /ɪ'fɛmərəl/ *adj* having a very short life: *Her success as a singer was ephemeral.*

ep·ic[1] /'ɛpɪk/ *adj usu. apprec* (of stories, events, etc.) full of brave action and excitement, like an EPIC[2]: *an epic journey to the South Pole*

epic[2] *n* a long poem about the deeds of gods and great men: *The Odyssey is an epic of ancient Greece.*

ep·i·cure /'ɛpɪ,kyuər/ *n* a person who takes great interest in the pleasures of food and drink; GOURMET –**epicurean** /,ɛpɪkyu'riʸən, -'kyuəriʸ-/ *adj,n*

ep·i·dem·ic /,ɛpə'dɛmɪk/ *n* a large number of cases of the same infectious disease at the same time: *an epidemic of* CHOLERA/*a* CHOLERA *epidemic* –**epidemic** *adj: (fig.) Violence is reaching epidemic levels in the city.*

ep·i·gram /'ɛpə,græm/ *n* a short clever amusing poem or saying –**epigrammatic** /,ɛpəgrə'mæʒtɪk/ *adj*

ep·i·lep·sy /'ɛpə,lɛpsiʸ/ *n* [U] a disease of the brain which causes sudden attacks of uncontrolled violent movement and loss of consciousness

ep·i·lep·tic /,ɛpə'lɛptɪk/ *adj,n* (being or concerning) a person who suffersfrom EPILEPSY: *an epileptic child/*FIT[3] (1)

e·pis·co·pal /ɪ'pɪskəpəl/ *adj* [A] **1** *fml* of or concerning BISHOPS **2** (*often cap.*) (of a church) governed by BISHOPS: **the Episcopal Church** (the CHURCH OF ENGLAND as established in the US)

ep·i·sode /'ɛpə,soʷd/ *n* (an account in a play or book of) one separate event: *There was an amusing episode at school yesterday.|The next episode of this television movie will be shown next week.*

e·pis·tle /ɪ'pɪsəl/ *n fml or humor* a (long and important) letter

Epistle *n* any of the letters written by the first followers (APOSTLEs) of Christ, in the Bible

ep·i·taph /'ɛpə,tæf/ *n* a short description of a dead person, often written on a stone above his/her grave

ep·i·thet /'ɛpə,θɛt/ *n* an adjective or descriptive phrase, esp. used of a person: *He cursed me, using a lot of rude epithets.*

e·pit·o·me /ɪ'pɪtəmiʸ/ *n* [*of*] a thing or person that shows, to a very great degree, a quality: *My cat is* **the epitome of** *laziness.* (=is very lazy)

e·pit·o·mize‖also **-mise** *BrE* /ɪ'pɪtə,maɪz/ **-mized, -mizing** [T] to be an EPITOME of; be very typical of: *He epitomizes the good qualities of his family.*

ep·och /'ɛpək/ *n* a period of historical time, during which certain events or developments happened –compare ERA

eq·ua·ble /'ɛkwəbəl, 'iʸ-/ *adj* (of temperature, or a person's character) without great changes; even and regular: *an equable climate|I like working with John because he's so calm and equable.* –**equably** *adv* –**equability** /,ɛkwə'bɪləʒtiʸ, iʸ-/ *n* [U]

e·qual[1] /'iʸkwəl/ *adj* **1** [*in, to; no comp.*] (of two or more) the same in size, number, value, rank, etc.: *Cut the cake into six equal pieces.|Women deserve equal pay* (=equal to men) *and to work* **on equal terms** (=as equals) *with men.* **2** [*to*] (of a person) having enough strength, ability, etc. (for): *Bill is equal to* (the job of) *running the office.* –opposite **unequal**

equal[2] *n* a person who is equal (to another or to oneself): *The teacher is popular because he treats the children as* (his) *equals.*

equal[3] *v* **-l-** *AmE* ‖ **-ll-** *BrE* [T not be +*v-ing*] **1** (of sizes or numbers) to be the same (as): *"x=y" means that x equals y.* **2** [*in, as*] to be as good, smart, etc. (as): *None of us can equal her, either in beauty or as a dancer.*

e·qual·i·ty /ɪ'kwɑləʒiʸ/ *n* [U] the state of being

equal: *the equality of man* (=of all people)|*racial equality* –*opposite* **inequality**

e·qual·ize||*also* **-ise** *BrE* /'iᵛkwə,laɪz/ *v* **-ized, -izing** [T] to make equal in size or numbers –**equalization** /,iᵛkwələ'zeᵛʃən/ *n* [U]

e·qual·ly /'iᵛkwəliᵛ/ *adv* **1** as (much); to an equal degree: *They can both run equally fast.* **2** in equal shares: *They shared the work equally between them.*

equal time /,·· '·/ *n* [U] the principle of providing the same amount of time for television or radio broadcasts to all CANDIDATEs in an election

e·qua·nim·i·ty /,iᵛkwə'nɪmətiᵛ, ,ɛ-/ *n* [U] *fml* calmness of mind: *He received the bad news with surprising equanimity.*

e·quate /ɪ'kweᵛt/ *v* **-quated, -quating** [T *with*] to consider or make (two or more things or people) equal: *You can't equate passing examinations with being educated.*

e·qua·tion /ɪ'kweᵛʒən/ *n tech* a statement that two quantities are equal: $x+2y=7$ *is an equation.*

e·qua·tor /ɪ'kweᵛtər/ *n* [*the* S] (*often cap.*) an imaginary line (of LATITUDE) drawn around the world halfway between its most northern and southern points (POLEs) –**equatorial** /,iᵛkwə'tɔriᵛəl, -'toᵛr-, ,ɛ-/ *adj*

e·ques·tri·an /ɪ'kwɛstriᵛən/ *adj* concerning horse-riding; of a rider on a horse: *an equestrian* STATUE (=stone figure)| *equestrian sports*

e·qui·lat·er·al /,iᵛkwə'læ'×ərəl/ *adj* (of a TRIANGLE) having all three sides equal

e·qui·lib·ri·um /,iᵛkwə'lɪbriᵛəm/ *n* [U] *fml* a state of balance: *He lost his equilibrium and fell into the lake.*

e·quine /'iᵛkwaɪn, -ɛ-/ *adj* of or like horses

e·qui·nox /'iᵛkwə,naks, 'ɛ-/ *n* [*the* C] one of the two times in the year when all places in the world have day and night of equal length –*compare* SOLSTICE

e·quip /ɪ'kwɪp/ *v* **-pp-** [T *with, for*] to provide (oneself or another) with what is necessary for doing something: *They can't afford to equip their army.*|*Your education will equip you to earn a good living.*

e·quip·ment /ɪ'kwɪpmənt/ *n* [U] the things needed for a particular activity: *office equipment*|*photographic equipment*

eq·ui·ty /'ɛkwətiᵛ/ *n* [U] the quality of being fair and just: *They shared the work of the house with perfect equity.* –*opposite* **inequity** –**equitable** /'ɛkwɪtəbəl/ *adj*: *an equitable division of the money* –*opposite* **inequitable** –**equitably** *adv*

e·quiv·a·lent[1] /ɪ'kwɪvələnt/ *adj* [*to*] (of time, amount, number, etc.) same; equal: *He changed his dollars for the equivalent amount in pounds*|*an equivalent amount of dollars.* –**equivalance** *n* [U]

equivalent[2] *n* something that is EQUIVALENT[1]: *Some American words have no British equivalents.*

e·quiv·o·cal /ɪ'kwɪvəkəl/ *adj* **1** (of words) having a double or doubtful meaning **2** (of behavior or events) questionable; mysterious –*opposite* **unequivocal** –**equivocally** *adv*

e·ra /'ɪərə, 'ɛrə/ *n* a set of years which is counted from a particular event or named after an important development: *The Christian era is counted from the birth of Christ.*|*the era of space travel* –*compare* EPOCH

e·rad·i·cate /ɪ'rædə,keᵛt/ *v* **-cated, -cating** [T] to end; destroy completely: *to eradicate crime/disease* –**eradication** /ɪ,rædə'keᵛʃən/ *n* [U]

e·rase /ɪ'reᵛs/ *v* **-rased, -rasing** [T] to rub out or remove (something, esp. pencil or chalk marks)

e·ras·er /ɪ'reᵛsər/ *n* **1** *AmE*||**rubber** *BrE*– something used for removing pencil marks **2** *also* **blackboard eraser**– *AmE* a piece of clothlike material with a stiff back which is used to ERASE a blackboard

e·rect[1] /ɪ'rɛkt/ *adj* upright; standing straight up on end: *Hold your head erect.* –**erectly** *adv* –**erectness** *n* [U]

erect[2] *v* [T] **1** *fml* to build: *This* MONUMENT *was erected in honor of Columbus.* **2** to fix or place in an upright position: *to erect a tent* –**erection** /ɪ'rɛkʃən/ *n* [C;U]

er·mine /'ɜrmɪn/ *n* **-mines** *or* **-mine** [C;U] (the white winter fur of) a small animal of the WEASEL family

e·rode /ɪ'roᵛd/ *v* **-roded, -roding 1** [T *away*] to eat into; wear or rub away: *The sea erodes the rocks.*|(fig.) *Jealousy is eroding our friendship.* **2** [I] to be or become worn away or rubbed away: *The coast is slowly eroding away.* –**erosion** /ɪ'roᵛʒən/ *n* [U]: *soil erosion by rain and wind*

e·rot·ic /ɪ'ratɪk/ *adj* of or concerning sexual love and desire: *erotic feelings* |*an erotic picture* –**erotically** *adv* –**eroticism** /ɪ'ratə,sɪzəm/ *n* [U]

USAGE Compare **erotic, sexual,** and **sexy: erotic** is used particularly for works of art: *an* **erotic** *film*|*some* **erotic** *Japanese pictures.* **sexual** just means connected with or in regard to sex: *the* **sexual** *organs*|*sexual* **habits.** and **sexy** means exciting in a **sexual** way: *You look very* **sexy** *in those tight pants!*

err /ɜr, ɛr/ *v* [I] *fml* to make a mistake; do something wrong: *To err is human.* (old saying)|*It is better to* **err on the side of** *mercy.* (=to be too merciful, rather than not merciful enough)

er·rand /'ɛrənd/ *n* a short journey made esp. to buy something: *I have no time to* **go on/run errands for** *you!*|*I've got a few errands to do* (things to go and get) in *town.*

er·rant /'ɛrənt/ *adj* [A] *old use or lit* mistaken; ERRING: *An errant husband is one who leaves his wife for other women.*

er·rat·ic /ɪ'rætɪk/ *adj* changeable without reason; not regular in movement or behavior: *an erratic tennis-player* (=sometimes good, sometimes bad) –**erratically** *adv*

er·ro·ne·ous /ɪ'roᵛniᵛəs/ *adj fml* (of a statement, a belief, etc.) incorrect: *the erroneous belief that the world is flat* –**erroneously** *adv*

er·ror /'ɛrər/ *n* **1** [C] a mistake; something done wrongly: *an error of judgment* **2** [U] the state of being wrong in behavior or beliefs: *The accident was caused by* **human error.**|*I did it* **in error.** (=by mistake)

USAGE An **error** is the same as a **mistake** except that a: **error** suggests a moral wrong, **mistake** a misjudgment: *It was a mistake buying that car.|the errors of his youth;* b: **error** is a more formal word: *Your work is full of spelling mistakes/(fml) errors;* c: in certain fixed phrases only one of them can be used: *an error of judgment|by mistake.* A small unintended mistake is a **slip** or an **oversight**: *I meant to write "son" not "sun." It was just a slip of the pen.|By an oversight, the letter was delivered to my neighbor instead of me.*

er·u·dite /ˈɛryə,daɪt, ˈɛrə-/ *adj fml* full of learning: *an erudite person/book* —**eruditely** *adv* —**erudition** /,ɛryəˈdɪʃən, ,ɛrə-/ *n* [U]

e·rupt /ɪˈrʌpt/ *v* [I] (of a VOLCANO) to explode and pour outfire: (fig.) *Violence erupted after the football game.* —**eruption** /ɪˈrʌpʃən/ *n* [C;U]: *a VOLCANO in a state of eruption*

es·ca·late /ˈɛskə,leʸt/ *v* -**lated, -lating 1** [T] to make (a war) more serious by stages —opposite **de-escalate 2** [I] (of prices and wages) to rise, one after the other: *The cost of living is escalating.* —**escalation** /,ɛskəˈleʸʃən/ *n* [U]

es·ca·la·tor /ˈɛskə,leʸtər/ *n* a set of moving stairs in a store, train station, airport, etc.

es·ca·pade /ˈɛskə,peʸd/ *n* a wild, exciting, and sometimes dangerous act, esp. one that disobeys rules or causes some trouble

es·cape¹ /ɪˈskeʸp/ *v* -**caped, -caping 1** [I;T *from*] to find a way out; get out: *They escaped from the burning house/ from prison.|Some gas is escaping from the pipe.* **2** [I;T +*v-ing*] (of a person) to avoid: *He narrowly (=only just) escaped being drowned.* **3** [T] (of an event, a fact, etc.) to be unnoticed or forgotten by: *I'm afraid your name escapes me.* (=I've forgotten it)|*Nothing escaped his attention.*

escape² *n* **1** [C;U *from, of, out of*] (an example or case of) the act of escaping or fact of having escaped: *an escape of gas|The thief jumped into a car and made his escape.* **2** [S;U] something that frees one from unpleasant or dull reality: *He reads adventure stories as an escape.* –see also ESCAPISM

es·cap·ism /ɪˈskeʸpɪzəm/ *n* [U] *derog* activity intended to provide escape from unpleasant or dull reality: *That story about three beautiful girls in a spacecraft is pure escapism!* —**escapist** *adj,n*

es·carp·ment /ɪˈskɑrpmənt/ *n* a long cliff on a mountain-side

es·cort¹ /ˈɛskɔrt/ *n* a person or people who go with another as aguard, or as a companion: *The prisoner traveled under police escort.* (=with some policemen)|*Mary's escort arrived to take her out for the evening.*

es·cort² /ɪˈskɔrt/ *v* [T] *fml* to go with (someone) as an ESCORT¹: *The senator was escorted by the workers as she toured the factory.*

e·soph·a·gus /ɪˈsɑfəgəs/ *n* -**gi** /,dʒaɪ, ,gaɪ/ the food tube leading from the back of the mouth down into the stomach

es·o·ter·ic /,ɛsəˈtɛrɪk/ *adj* limited to, or understood by, only a small number of people: *Some words are really too esoteric for this dictionary.* —**esoterically** *adv*

ESP /,iʸ ɛs ˈpiʸ/ *n* [U] *abbrev. for:* extrasensory perception; knowledge or feelings about outside, past, or future things, obtained without the use of the ordinary five senses

es·pe·cial /ɪˈspɛʃəl/ *adj* [A] *fml* for SPECIAL¹

es·pe·cial·ly /ɪˈspɛʃəliʸ/ *adv* **1** also **specially** *BrE*– to a particularly great degree: *"Do you like chocolate?" "Not especially."|I love Italy, especially in summer.* **2** also **specially** –for one particular purpose: *I made this cake especially for you.*

es·pi·o·nage /ˈɛspiʸə,naʒ, -nɪdʒ/ *n* [U] the action of SPYING; work of finding out (a country's) secret information and sending it to enemies

es·pla·nade /ˈɛsplə,nad, -,neʸd/ *n* a level open space for walking, often near the sea

Esq. /ˈɛskwaɪər, ɪˈskwaɪər/ *n* [after *n*] *esp. BrE written abbrev. said as:* esquire (used as a title of politeness usu. written after a man's full name): *The envelope is addressed to Peter Jones, Esq.*

es·say /ˈɛseʸ/ *n* a usu. short piece of writing on a subject esp. as part of a course of study: *We have to write an essay on the war with Napoleon.*

es·sence /ˈɛsəns/ *n* **1** [U *of*] the central or most important quality of a thing, which makes it what it is: *The essence of his religious teaching is love for all men.* **2** [C;U] the best part of a substance, taken out and reduced to a jelly, liquid, etc.: *essence of roses* **3 in essence** in its/one's nature; ESSENTIALLY

es·sen·tial /ɪˈsɛnʃəl, -tʃəl/ *adj* **1** [*to, for*] necessary: *We can live without clothes, but food and drink are essential to life.* **2** [A] central; most important or most notable: *What is the essential difference between these two political parties?* —**essential** *n*: *The room was furnished with the simplest essentials: a bed, a chair, and a table.*

es·sen·tial·ly /ɪˈsɛnʃəliʸ, -tʃə-/ *adv* in reality; BASICALLY: *She's essentially kind.*

es·tab·lish /ɪˈstæblɪʃ/ *v* [T] **1** to set up (esp. an organization): *This company/school was established in 1850.|The club has established a new rule allowing women to join.* **2** [*as, in*] to place (oneself or another) in a particular (esp. favorable) position: *He quickly established himself as a powerful member of the new company.* **3** [+*that*] to find out or make certain of (a fact, answer, etc.): *to establish the truth of a story* **4** to cause people to accept or recognize (a claim, fact, etc.): *His next film established his fame as an actor.* **5** to make (a religion) official for a nation: *The established religion of Egypt is Islam.*

es·tab·lish·ment /ɪˈstæblɪʃmənt/ *n* **1** [U] the act of ESTABLISHING: *the establishment of new industry by the government* **2** [C] *fml* a business organization: *The establishment you are looking for is on Fifth Avenue.*

Establishment *n* [*the* U] the powerful organizations and people who control public life and support the established order of society: *The Establishment is trying to hide the truth.*

es·tate /ɪ'steʸt/ n 1 [C] a (large piece of land in the country, usu. with one large house on it 2 [U] law the whole of a person's property, esp. after death 3 [C] BrE a piece of land on which buildings (of a stated type) have all been built together in a planned way: an industrial estate|a **housing estate**

es·teem[1] /ɪ'stiʸm/ n [U] fml respect; good opinion (of a person): All Ann's friends **held her in (high) esteem**. –compare ESTIMATION

esteem[2] v [T] fml 1 to respect and admire greatly: The old teacher was greatly loved and esteemed. 2 to believe to be (esp. something good): I did not esteem him to be worthy of trust.

es·thet·ics /es'θetɪks, iʸs-/ n [P;U] AmE for AESTHETICS

es·ti·ma·ble /'estəməbəl/ adj apprec (of a person or his behavior) worthy of ESTEEM[1] –see also INESTIMABLE

es·ti·mate /'estə,meʸt/ v -mated, -mating [I;T +that] to calculate (an amount, cost, etc.); form an opinion about (something): I estimate her age at about thirty-five.|I asked the building company to estimate the cost of the repairs to the roof. (=to tell me how much the repairs would cost) –see also INESTIMABLE UNDER/OVERESTIMATE; compare QUOTE (3) –**estimate** /'estəmɪt/ n [+that/of]: My estimate of her character was wrong.|We got three estimates before having the roof repaired, and accepted the lowest.

es·ti·ma·tion /,estə'meʸʃən/ n [U] judgment or opinion: He has lowered himself in my estimation. –compare ESTEEM[1]

es·trange /ɪ'streʸndʒ/ v -tranged, -tranging [T from] to make unfriendly: His behavior estranged him from his brother. –**estrangement** n [C;U from, with, between]

es·tu·ar·y /'estʃuʷ,eriʸ/ n -ies the wide lower part or mouth of a river, into which the sea enters at high TIDE

etc. /et 'setərə, -trə/ adv written abbrev. said as: et cetera; and the rest; and so on: They bought tea, coffee, sugar, etc.

etch /etʃ/ v [I;T on] to draw (a picture) by cutting lines on a metal plate with a needle and acid so that one can print from the plate: (fig.) The terrible event is etched forever in my memory. –**etching** n [C;U]: Mary is very good at etching.|a beautiful etching of a bird

e·ter·nal /ɪ'tɜrnl/ adj going on forever; without beginning or end: Rome has been called the Eternal City. –**eternally** adv

e·ter·ni·ty /ɪ'tɜrnəṭiʸ/ n -ties [S;U] time without end; state of time after death, which is said to last forever: (fig.) I was so anxious that every moment seemed an eternity.

e·ther /'iʸθər/ n [U] a light colorless liquid, easily changed into a gas, which is often used as an ANESTHETIC to put people to sleep before an operation

e·the·re·al /ɪ'θɪəriʸəl/ adj of unearthly lightness and delicacy; like a spirit –**ethereally** adv

eth·ic /'eθɪk/ n a system of moral behavior: the Christian ethic|a modern ethic

eth·i·cal /'eθɪkəl/ adj 1 of ETHICS (2): The use of animals in scientific tests raises some

difficult ethical questions. 2 [only used in NEGATIVES[2], questions, etc.] morally good: The judge said that the doctor's behavior had not been ethical. –opposite **unethical** (for 2) –**ethically** adv

eth·ics /'eθɪks/ n 1 [U] the science which deals with morals 2 [P] moral principles: What should I do? It's a matter of ethics.

eth·nic /'eθnɪk/ adj of or related to a racial, national, or tribal group

eth·nol·o·gy /eθ'nalədʒiʸ/ n [U] the science of the different human races –compare ANTHROPOLOGY

et·i·quette /'etɪkɪt, -,ket/ n [U] the formal rules of proper behavior

et·y·mol·o·gy /,etə'malədʒiʸ/ n [U] the scientific study of the origins, history, and changing meanings of words –compare ENTOMOLOGY

eu·ca·lyp·tus /,yuʷkə'lɪptəs/ n -tuses or -ti /taɪ/ [C;U] (the oil produced by) a tall tree, such as the Australian GUM[2] tree

Eu·cha·rist /'yuʷkərɪst/ n [the S] (the bread and wine taken at) the Christian ceremony based on Christ's last supper on Earth –see MASS, COMMUNION

eu·lo·gize‖ also **-gise** BrE /'yuʷlə,dʒaɪz/ v -gized, -gizing [T] fml to make a EULOGY about

eu·lo·gy /'yuʷlədʒiʸ/ n -gies [C;U on, of] fml (a speech or a piece of writing containing) high praise (usu. of a dead person or his/her qualities) –compare ELEGY

eu·nuch /'yuʷnək/ n a man who has been CASTRATEd (=had part of his sex organs removed)

eu·phe·mism /'yuʷfə,mɪzəm/ n [C;U] (an example of) the use of a pleasanter, less direct name for something thought to be unpleasant: "Pass away" is a euphemism for "die." –**euphemistic** /,yuʷfə'mɪstɪk/ adj

eu·pho·ri·a /yuʷ'foriʸə, -'foʷr-/ n [U] a feeling of happiness and cheerful excitement –**euphoric** /yu'forɪk, -'far-/ adj –**euphorically** adv

Eu·ro·pe·an /,yuərə'piʸən/ adj of or related to Europe

European Ec·o·nom·ic Com·mu·ni·ty /···,·· ··,·· ·'····/ n fml for COMMON MARKET

eu·tha·na·sia /,yuʷθə'neʸʒə/ n [U] the painless killing of incurably ill or old people

e·vac·u·ate /ɪ'vækyuʷ,eʸt/ v -ated, -ating [T] 1 to take all the people away from (a place): The village was evacuated because of the danger of a flood. 2 [from, to] to move (people) out of danger –**evacuation** /ɪ,væk yuʷ'eʸʃən/ n [C;U]

e·vac·u·ee /ɪ,vækyuʷ'iʸ/ n a person who has been EVACUATEd (2)

e·vade /ɪ'veʸd/ v -vaded, -vading [T] 1 [+ v-ing] derog to avoid, or avoid doing (something one should do): to evade (paying) your taxes|He evaded (=did not answer properly) the question. 2 to get out of the way of or escape from: After his escape he evaded the police|evaded CAPTURE (1) for several days.

e·val·u·ate /ɪ'vælyuʷ,eʸt/ v -ated, -ating [T] fml to calculate the value or degree of: The school has only been open for six months, so *it's too early to evaluate its success.* **–evaluation** /ɪˌvælyuʷˈeʸʃən/ *n* [C;U]

e·van·gel·i·cal /ˌiʸvænˈdʒelɪkəl, ˌɛvən-/ *adj,n* (*often cap.*) (a member) of certain PROTESTANT Christian churches which believe in the importance of faith and of studying the Bible, rather than in religious ceremonies

e·van·ge·list /ɪˈvændʒəlɪst/ *n* a person who travels from place to place and holds EVANGELICAL religious meetings **–evangelism** *n* [U]

e·vap·o·rate /ɪˈvæpəˌreʸt/ *v* **-rated, -rating** [I;T] to (cause to) change into steam and disappear: *The puddle evaporated in the sun.*|(fig.) *Hopes of reaching an agreement are beginning to evaporate.* (=to disappear) **–evaporation** /ɪˌvæpəˈreʸʃən/ *n* [U]

e·va·sion /ɪˈveʸʒən/ *n* **1** [C;U] *derog* an action, lack of action, or statement which EVADES (1): *George is in prison for tax evasion.*|*a speech full of evasions* (=which avoids the truth) **2** [U] the act of evading (EVADE (2)): *the fox's clever evasion of the dogs*

e·va·sive /ɪˈveʸsɪv/ *adj* which EVADES or tries to EVADE: *an evasive answer*|*If the enemy attacks,* **take evasive action.** **–evasively** *adv* **–evasiveness** *n* [U]

eve /iʸv/ *n* [S] **1** the night or day before a religious feast or holiday: *a party on New Year's Eve* **2** the time just before an important event: *on the eve of our examination*

e·ven¹ /ˈiʸən/ *adj* **1** level, smooth, regular; forming a straight line (with): *This table isn't very even; one of its legs is too short.*|*an even temperature* **2** [*with*] (of things that can be measured and compared) equal: *She won the first game and I won the second, so now we're even/now I'm even with her.*|*He cheated me, but I'll* **get even with** *him* (=harm him as he has harmed me) *one day!* **3** (of a number) that can be divided exactly by two: *2, 4, 6, 8, etc. are even numbers.* **–opposite odd –evenly** *adv* **–evenness** *n* [U]

even² *adv* **1** (used just before the surprising part of a statement, to make it stronger) which is more than might be expected: *Even wealthy people experienced hardship during the war.* (=so certainly everyone else did)|*He did not experience hardship even during the war.* (=so certainly not at any other time) **2** (used for making comparisons stronger): *It was cold yesterday, but it's even colder today.* **3 even if** no matter if; though: *Even if we could afford it, we wouldn't go abroad for our vacation.* (=because we don't want to) Compare *If we could afford it, we'd go abroad for our vacation.* (=but we can't) **4 even so** in spite of that; though that is true: *It's raining. Even so, we have to go out.* **–see** Study Notes on page 144

even³ *v* →EVEN OUT

eve·ning /ˈiʸvnɪŋ/ *n* [C;U] the end of the day and early part of the night: *Are you planning to go out this evening?*

evening dress /ˈ·· ˌ·/ *n* **1** [U] special clothes worn for formal occasions in the evening **2** [C] a usu. long dress worn by women for such an occasion

even out *v adv* [I;T (=**even** sthg.↔ **out**)] to (cause to) become level or equal: *Prices have been rising, but they should even out now.*

e·vent /ɪˈvɛnt/ *n* **1** a happening, usu. an important one: *the chief events of 1981*|*I'll probably see you tomorrow, but* **in any event** (=whatever may happen) *I'll call you.* **–see also** NONEVENT; **–compare** FACT (1) **2** any of the races, competitions, etc., arranged as part of a day's sports: *The next event will be the 100-yard race.* **3 in the event of (something)** if (something) happens: *In the event of rain, the party will be held indoors.*

e·vent·ful /ɪˈvɛntfəl/ *adj* full of important or interesting events: *an eventful life/meeting* **–opposite uneventful**

e·ven·tu·al /ɪˈvɛntʃuʷəl/ *adj* [A] (of an event) happening at last as a result: *the eventual success of his efforts* **–eventually** /ɪˈvɛntʃuʷəliʸ, -tʃəliʸ/ *adv: After failing four times, I eventually passed my driving test.*

e·ven·tu·al·i·ty /ɪˌvɛntʃuʷˈælətiʸ/ *n* **-ties** a possible, esp. unpleasant, event: *We should be prepared for all eventualities/for any eventuality.*

ev·er /ˈɛvər/ *adv* **1** (used mostly in questions, NEGATIVES², comparisons, and sentences with *if*) at any time: *Nothing ever makes him angry.*|*Have you ever been to San Francisco?*|*I hardly ever* (=almost never) *watch television.*|*If you ever come to Spain, we'll have to get together.*|*He ran faster than ever.*|*It was the best vacation we've ever had.* **2** (used for giving force to an expression): *He's been here ever since Monday.*|*Why ever not?* **–see** USAGE. **3** (in some expressions) always: *They lived happily* **ever after.** (at the end of a fairy story)|*Ever yours, John* (at the end of a letter)|*the ever-increasing population* **4 ever so/such** *infml* very: *It's ever so cold.*|*She's ever such a nice girl.* **–compare** NEVER

USAGE When **ever** is used after "how," "what," "when," etc. to show surprise or give force to a question, the two words should be written separately: Compare *What* **ever** *are you doing?* and *Do* **whatever** *she tells you.*

ev·er·green /ˈɛvərˌɡriʸn/ *adj,n* (a tree or bush) that does not lose its leaves in winter **–compare** DECIDUOUS

ev·er·last·ing /ˌɛvərˈlæstɪŋ◄/ *adj* **1** *fml* lasting forever; without an end: *He believes in everlasting life/in life everlasting.*|**2** [A] *derog* happening too often: *I'm tired of your everlasting complaints!*

ev·er·more /ˌɛvərˈmɔr, -ˈmoʷr/ *adv lit* always: *He swore to love her (for) evermore.*

ev·ery /ˈɛvriʸ/ *determiner* [A] **1** each or all (of more than two): *I believe every word he says.*|*I enjoyed every minute of the party.*|*She's* **every bit as** (=just as) *intelligent as her sister.* **–see** Study Notes on page 550 **2** (of things that can be counted) once (in) each: *He comes to see us every day/every three days.*|*Change the oil in the car every 5,000 miles.* **3** all possible; as much as possible: *She made every attempt to go.* **4 every other** (of things that can be counted)

the 1st, 3rd, 5th ... or the 2nd, 4th, 6th ... : *Take some medicine every other day.*
USAGE Compare **every one** and **everyone**: **Everyone** (or **everybody**) can only be used of people and is never followed by "of;" **every one** means each person or thing, and is often followed by "of": *Everyone in the class passed the exam.*|*There are 16 students and* **every one** *of them passed.* –see EACH (USAGE)

ev·ery·bod·y /'ɛvriˠ,badiˠ, -,bʌdiˠ, -bədiˠ/ also **everyone** /'ɛvriˠ,wʌn, -wən/ –pron every person: *Everybody else has gone home except me.*
USAGE Anybody, every, everybody, and **somebody** always take a singular verb, but they are often followed by a plural PRONOUN, except in formal speech and writing: *Has* **everybody** *finished their drinks/his or her drink.* (fml)?|*Anybody can use the library, can't they?*|*Somebody lost their coat/his coat* (fml).

ev·ery·day /'ɛvriˠ,deˠ/ adj [A no comp.] ordinary, common, and usual: *These are my everyday shoes, not my best ones.*

ev·ery·thing /'ɛvriˠ,θɪŋ/ pron [used with sing. verb] **1** each thing; all things: *Everything is ready now for the party.*|*I've forgotten everything I learned in school.* **2** all that matters: *Money isn't everything.* –compare NOTHING

ev·ery·where /'ɛvriˠ,hwɛər, -,wɛər/ ‖also **everyplace** /'ɛvriˠ,pleˠs/ AmE– adv in or to every place: *I can't find it, though I've looked everywhere.*|*She follows me everywhere I go.* –compare NOWHERE

e·vict /ɪ'vɪkt/ v [T from] to take (a person) away from a house or land by law: *If you don't pay your rent, you'll be evicted.* –**eviction** /ɪ'vɪkʃən/ n [C;U]

ev·i·dence /'ɛvədəns/ n [U +that/ of, for] **1** words or objects which prove a statement, support a belief, or make a matter more clear: *Can you show me any evidence for your statement?*|*The police have evidence that the killer was a woman.* **2 in evidence** able to be seen and noticed: *The police were very much in evidence* (=very noticeable) *whenever the President made a public appearance.*

ev·i·dent /'ɛvədənt, -,dɛnt/ adj plain, esp. to the senses; clear because of EVIDENCE: *It's evident that you've been drinking.*|*her evident unhappiness* –**evidently** /'ɛvədəntliˠ, -,dɛnt-, ,ɛvə'dɛntliˠ/ adv: *He is evidently not well.*

e·vil¹ /'iˠvəl/ adj **-l-** AmE‖ **-ll-** BrE fml very bad, esp. in thought or behavior; wicked; harmful: *evil thoughts* –see WICKED (USAGE) –**evilly** adv

evil² n [C;U] fml (a) great wickedness or misfortune: *"Deliver us from evil."* (prayer) –opposite **good**

e·vil·do·er /,iˠvəl'duˠər/ n fml a person who does evil

e·vince /ɪ'vɪns/ v -vinced, -vincing [T] fml (of a person or his/her behavior) to show clearly (a feeling, quality, etc.): *He evinced great sorrow for what he had done.*

e·voc·a·tive /ɪ'vakətɪv/ adj that produces memories and feelings: *The smell of those flowers is evocative of my childhood in India.*

e·voke /ɪ'voˠk/ v -voked, -voking [T] fml to produce or call up (a memory, a feeling, or its expression): *That old movie evoked memories of my childhood.* –**evocation** /,ɛvə'keˠʃən, ,iˠvoˠw-/ n [C;U]

ev·o·lu·tion /,ɛvə'luˠʃən/ n [U] (the scientific idea of) the development of the various types of plants, animals, etc., from fewer and simpler forms: *Some people do not believe in evolution.*|(fig.) *the evolution of modern aircraft* –**evolutionary** /,ɛvə'luˠʃə,nɛriˠ/ adj

e·volve /ɪ'valv/ v -volved, -volving [I;T] to (cause to) develop gradually: *The American political system has evolved over a long period of time.*

ewe /yuˠ/ n a fully-grown female sheep –compare RAM¹ (1)

ex·ac·er·bate /ɪg'zæsər,beˠt/ v -bated, -bating [T] fml to make worse (pain, diseases, problems, etc.): *The new law exacerbated relations between employers and workers.* –**exacerbation** /ɪg,zæsər'beˠʃən/ n [C;U]

ex·act¹ /ɪg'zækt/ adj **1** [A] correct and without mistakes; PRECISE: *an exact amount/weight*|*Your exact height is 5 feet 7 inches.* **2** marked by thorough consideration or careful measurement of small details of fact: *You have to be very exact in this job because a small mistake can make a big difference.* –opposite **inexact** –**exactness, exactitude** /ɪg'zæktə,tuˠd, -,tyuˠd/ n [U]

exact² v [T from] fml to demand and obtain by force, threats, etc.: *He exacted obedience from the children.*

ex·act·ing /ɪg'zæktɪŋ/ adj demanding much care, effort, and attention: *an exacting child/piece of work*

ex·act·ly /ɪg'zæktliˠ/ adv **1** (used with numbers and measures, and with *what, where, who,* etc.) with complete correctness: *Tell me exactly where she lives.*|*The train arrived at exactly 8 o'clock.* (=neither earlier nor later) **2** (used for adding force to an expression) just; really; quite: *Our new house is lovely. It's exactly what we've always wanted.* **3** (used as a reply to something that has been said) Right!: *"So you believe that we should spend more on education?" "Exactly!"*

ex·ag·ger·ate /ɪg'zædʒə,reˠt/ v -ated, -ating [I;T] to make (something) seem larger, better, worse, etc., than in reality: *That new machine is very useful, but he's exaggerating when he calls it the greatest invention ever made!* –**exaggerated** adj –**exaggeration** /ɪg,zædʒə'reˠʃən/ n

ex·alt /ɪg'zɔlt/ v [T] fml **1** to praise highly **2** to raise (a person) to a high rank –compare EXULT

ex·al·ta·tion /,ɛgzɔl'teˠʃən, ,ɛksɔl-/ n [U] fml or lit the joy of success

ex·alt·ed /ɪg'zɔltɪd/ adj (of a person or his/her position) of high rank

ex·am /ɪg'zæm/ n infml →EXAMINATION (1)

ex·am·i·na·tion /ɪg,zæmə'neˠʃən/ n **1** [C in, on] also **exam**– a spoken or written test of knowledge: *Did you pass your history exam?*|*When will we know the examination results?* **2** [C;U] (an act of) examining (EXAMINE): *Before we can offer you the job, you will have to have a medical examination.*|*The examination of all the witnesses took a week.*

ex·am·ine /ɪɡˈzæmɪn/ *v* **-ined, -ining** [T] **1** to look at (a person or thing) closely, in order to find out something: *My bags were examined when I entered the country.* **2** [*in, on*] to ask (a person) questions, in order to measure knowledge or find out something, as in a school or a court of law –compare CROSS-EXAMINE –**examiner** *n*

ex·am·ple /ɪɡˈzæmpəl/ *n* **1** something which shows a general rule: *Her rudeness was a typical example of her usual bad manners.*|*This house is a wonderful example of the* VICTORIAN *style of building.* **2** [*to*] *apprec* a person, or his behavior, that is worthy of being copied: *He arrived at the office early, to* set an example/a good example *to the others.* **3 for example** also **e.g.** *abbrev.* – here is one of the things or people just spoken of: *The government has reduced spending in several areas, for example education and health.* **4 make an example of someone** to punish someone so that others will be afraid to behave as he/she did

USAGE Compare set an example and give an example: When we ourselves are an example to be copied, then we set it: *Drink your milk and set a good example for the other children!* When we invent an example to explain what we mean– *large animals, for example, elephants*– we are giving an example

ex·as·per·ate /ɪɡˈzæspəˌreɪt/ *v* **-ated, -ating** [T] to annoy or make angry: *I was exasperated by/at all the noise.*|*an exasperating delay* –**exasperation** /ɪɡˌzæspəˈreɪʃən/ *n* [U]

ex·ca·vate /ˈɛkskəˌveɪt/ *v* [T] to make or uncover by digging: *They've excavated a hole in the road.*|*to excavate an ancient city* –**excavation** /ˌɛkskəˈveɪʃən/ *n* [C;U]

ex·ca·va·tor /ˈɛkskəˌveɪtər/ *n* a person or machine that EXCAVATEs

ex·ceed /ɪkˈsiːd/ *v* [T] *fml* **1** [not *be* +*v-ing*] to be greater than: *The cost will not exceed $100.* **2** to do more than (what is lawful, necessary, etc.): *Don't exceed* (=drive faster than) *the speed limit.*

ex·ceed·ing·ly /ɪkˈsiːdɪŋliː/ *adv* very; to an unusual degree: *Susan drove exceedingly fast.*

ex·cel /ɪkˈsɛl/ *v* **-ll-** [I;T *as, at, in*; not *be* +*v-ing*] *fml* to be very good; do or be better than: *She excels as a teacher of dancing.*

Ex·cel·len·cy /ˈɛksələnsiː/ *n* **-cies** (the word used when speaking to or of certain persons of high rank in the state or church): *The King will see you now, (your) Excellency.*|*His Excellency/their Excellencies will see you now.*|*His Excellency the Spanish* AMBASSADOR

ex·cel·lent /ˈɛksələnt/ *adj* very good; of very high quality: *excellent health*|*Your examination results are excellent.* –**excellently** *adv* –**excellence** *n* [U]: *the excellence of her cooking*

ex·cept¹ /ɪkˈsɛpt/ also **except for**– *prep,conj* leaving out; not including: *He answered all the questions except the last one.*|*I know nothing about it except what I read in the paper.*|*He can do everything except cook.*|*Except for one old lady, the bus was empty.* (=she was the only person in the bus) –see BESIDES (USAGE)

except² *v* [T] *fml* to leave out; not include: *You will all have to come on time; I can except no one.*

ex·cept·ed /ɪkˈsɛptɪd/ *adj* [after *n*] left out; apart from: *the whole family, John excepted* (=except John)

ex·cept·ing /ɪkˈsɛptɪŋ/ *prep* leaving out; except: *They were all saved excepting the captain.* (=he was not saved)|*They were all saved, not excepting the captain.* (=he was saved too)

ex·cep·tion /ɪkˈsɛpʃən/ *n* [C;U] **1** (a case of) EXCEPTing or being EXCEPTed: *You must answer all the questions without exception.*|*It's been very cold, but today's an exception; it's warm and sunny.*|*We don't usually accept checks, but we'll* make an exception *in your case.* **2 take exception (to)** to be made angry (by): *I took the greatest exception to his rude letters.* **3 with the exception of** except; apart from: *Everyone was tired with the exception of John.*

ex·cep·tion·al /ɪkˈsɛpʃənəl/ *adj* often *apprec* unusual, often in a good sense: *All her children are intelligent, but the youngest boy is really exceptional.* –**exceptionally** *adv*

ex·cerpt /ˈɛksɜːrpt/ *n* a piece taken from a book, speech, or musical work; EXTRACT

ex·cess¹ /ɪkˈsɛs, ˈɛksɛs/ *n* [S;U *of*] **1** the fact of EXCEEDing, or an amount by which something EXCEEDs (the stated amount): *This excess of losses over profits will ruin the business.*|*Never spend* in excess of (=more than) *your income.* **2** *derog* more than the reasonable degree or amount: *an excess of anger*|*to drink* to excess

ex·cess² /ˈɛksɛs, ɪkˈsɛs/ *adj* [A] additional; more than is usual, allowed, etc.: *pay excess charges for the additional bags*

ex·ces·sive /ɪkˈsɛsɪv/ *adj derog* too much; too great: *The food was bad and the bill was excessive.* –**excessively** *adv*

ex·change¹ /ɪksˈtʃeɪndʒ/ *n* **1** [C;U] (a case of) the act or action of exchanging: *an exchange of political prisoners between the two countries*|*He gave me an apple* in exchange for *a piece of cake.* **2** [C] also **telephone exchange**– (*often cap.*) a central place where telephone wires are connected so that people may speak to each other **3** [C] a place where people in business meet to buy and sell (goods): *They sell shares in companies at the* STOCK EXCHANGE.

exchange² *v* **-changed, -changing** [T *for, with*] to give and receive (something in return for something else): *The two armies exchanged prisoners.*|*John exchanged hats with Peter.* (=each gave the other his hat)|*Where can I exchange my dollars for lira?* –compare CHANGE¹ –**exchangeable** *adj*

exchange rate /·ˈ· ˌ·/ also **rate of exchange**– *n*

the value of the money of one country compared to that of another country

ex·cise¹ /'ɛksaɪz, 'ɛksaɪs/ *n* the government tax on certain goods produced and used inside a country –compare CUSTOMS (2)

ex·cise² /ɪk'saɪz/ *v* **-cised, -cising** [T] *fml* to remove (as if) by cutting out: *to excise a part of a book* –**excision** /ɪk'sɪʒən/ *n* [C;U]

ex·cit·a·ble /ɪk'saɪtəbəl/ *adj* easily excited –**excitability** /ɪkˌsaɪtə'bɪlətiʸ/ *n* [U]

ex·cite /ɪk'saɪt/ *v* **-cited, -citing** [T] **1** to cause (someone) to lose calmness and to have strong feelings, often pleasant: *The story excited the little boy very much.* **2** *fml* to cause (something to happen) by raising strong feelings: *The court case has excited a lot of public interest.*

ex·cit·ed /ɪk'saɪtɪd/ *adj* full of strong, pleasant feelings; not calm: *The excited children were opening their Christmas presents.* –**excitedly** *adv*

ex·cite·ment /ɪk'saɪtmənt/ *n* [C;U] (something which causes) the condition of being excited: *As the end of the game grew near, the crowd's excitement increased.*

ex·cit·ing /ɪk'saɪtɪŋ/ *adj* that excites one: *an exciting story/football game* –opposite **unexciting**

ex·claim /ɪk'skleʸm/ *v* [T +*that*] (*usu. used with the actual words of the speaker*) to say suddenly, because of strong feeling: *"Good heavens!" he exclaimed. "It's 6 o'clock."* compare EXPLAIN

ex·cla·ma·tion /ˌɛksklə'meʸʃən/ *n* the word(s) expressing a sudden strong feeling: *"Good heavens!" is an exclamation (of surprise).*

exclamation point /·····ˌ·/ *AmE*‖also **exclamation mark** *n* a mark (!) which is written after the actual words of an EXCLAMATION

ex·clude /ɪk'skluʷd/ *v* **-cluded, -cluding** [T] **1** [*from*] to keep or leave out: *They excluded people under 21 from (joining) the club.|You're all guilty; I can exclude no one from blame.* –opposite **include 2** to shut out from the mind (a reason or possibility): *We can't exclude the possibility that it will rain.* –**exclusion** /ɪk'skluʷʒən/ *n* [U *from*]

ex·clud·ing /ɪk'skluʷdɪŋ/ *prep* not counting; not including: *There were 30 people in the hotel, excluding the hotel workers.* –opposite **including**

ex·clu·sive¹ /ɪk'skluʷsɪv, -zɪv/ *adj* **1** that EX-CLUDEs socially unsuitable people and charges a lot of money: *one of New York's most exclusive night clubs* **2** [A] not shared with others: *This car is for the President's exclusive use.* **3 exclusive of** not taking into account; without; EXCLUDING: *The hotel charges $75 a day, exclusive of meals.* –opposite **inclusive of** –**exclusiveness** *n* [U]

exclusive² *n* a newspaper story at first given to or printed by only one newspaper –compare SCOOP

ex·clu·sive·ly /ɪk'skluʷsɪvliʸ, -zɪv-/ *adv* only; and nothing else/ no one else: *This room is exclusively for women.*

ex·com·mu·ni·cate /ˌɛkskə'myuʷnəˌkeʸt/ *v* **-cated, -cating** [T] to punish (someone) by

driving him/her out from active membership in the Christian church –**excommunication** /ˌɛkskəˌmyuʷnə'keʸʃən/ *n* [C;U]

ex·cre·ment /'ɛkskrəmənt/ *n* [U] *fml* the solid waste matter passed from the body through the bowels –compare EXCRETA

ex·cre·ta /ɪk'skriʸtə/ *n* [P] *fml* the solid and liquid waste matter (EXCREMENT, URINE, and SWEAT) passed from the body

ex·crete /ɪk'skriʸt/ *v* **-creted, -creting** [I;T] *fml* to pass out (EXCRETA) –see also SECRETE¹

ex·cre·tion /ɪk'skriʸʃən/ *n* [C;U] *fml* (the act of producing) EXCRETA

ex·cru·ci·at·ing /ɪk'skruʷʃiʸˌeʸtɪŋ/ *adj* (of pain) very bad: *an excruciating headache* –**excruciatingly** *adv*

ex·cur·sion /ɪk'skɜrʒən/ *n* a short journey made for pleasure, usu. by several people together: *to go on a day excursion* (=there and back in a day) *to Long Island.*

ex·cus·a·ble /ɪk'skyuʷzəbəl/ *adj* (of behavior) that can be forgiven –opposite **inexcusable** –**excusably** *adv*

ex·cuse¹ /ɪk'skyuʷz/ *v* **-cused, -cusing** [T] **1** [+*v-ing/for*] to forgive (someone) for a small fault: *Please excuse my bad handwriting/my opening your letter by mistake.* **2** (*mainly used in* NEGATIVES², *questions, etc.*) to make (bad behavior) seem less bad, or harmless: *Nothing can excuse his violent behavior.* **3** [*from*] to free (someone) from a duty: *Can I be excused (from) football practice today?* **4 Excuse me: a** (*a polite expression used when starting to speak to a stranger, when one wants to get past a person, or when one disagrees with something he/she has said*) Forgive me: *Excuse me, does this bus go to the airport?* **b** *AmE*‖also **sorry**– polite expression used when asking to be forgiven for wrong, usu. accidental behavior) *She said "Excuse me" when she stepped on my foot.* –see SORRY (USAGE)

ex·cuse² /ɪk'skyuʷs/ *n* [C;U *for*] the true or untrue reason given when asking to be forgiven for wrong behavior: *Do you have any excuse for coming so late?|Stop making excuses!*

USAGE Compare **reason, excuse,** and **pretext**: *His reason for leaving early was that his wife was sick.* (=she really was sick)|*His excuse for leaving early was that his wife was sick.* (=she may or may not have been sick)|*He left early on the pretext that his wife was sick.* (=she was not sick at all, and he had another reason for leaving early)

ex·e·cra·ble /'ɛksɪkrəbəl/ *adj fml* very bad: *What an execrable meal!* –**execrably** *adv*

ex·e·cute /'ɛksɪˌkyuʷt/ *v* **-cuted, -cuting** [T] **1** [*for*] to kill (someone) as a lawful punishment: *executed for murder* **2** to carry out (an order, plan, or piece of work): *He asked his brother to execute* (=carry out the orders in) *his* WILL² (4). **3** *fml* to perform (music, dance steps, etc.)

ex·e·cu·tion /ˌɛksɪ'kyuʷʃən/ *n* **1** [C;U] (a case of) legal killing as a punishment: *Executions used to be held in public.* **2** [U *of*] the carrying out (of an order, plan, or piece of work): *This good idea was never put into* execution.|*The execution of the court order may take a long time.*

ex·e·cu·tion·er /ˌɛksɪˈkyuᵂʃənər/ n the official who EXECUTEs (1) criminals

ex·ec·u·tive¹ /ɪgˈzɛkyətɪv/ adj [A] **1** concerned with making and carrying out decisions, esp. in business: *a woman of great executive ability* **2** having the power to carry out government decisions and laws: *the executive branch of government*

executive² n **1** a person in an EXECUTIVE¹ (1) position **2** the person or group in the EXECUTIVE¹ (2) position in agovernment: *The President of the US is the chief executive.*

ex·ec·u·tor /ɪgˈzɛkyətər/ **executrix** /ɪgˈzɛk yətrɪks/ *fem.*– n the person who carries out the orders in a WILL² (4)

ex·em·pla·ry /ɪgˈzɛmpləriʸ/ n [A] suitable as an example or as a warning: *exemplary behavior|an exemplary punishment*

ex·em·pli·fy /ɪgˈzɛmpləˌfaɪ/ v **-fied, -fying** [T] to be or give an example of: *The recent oil price increases exemplify the difficulties which the automobile industry is now facing.* –**exemplification** /ɪgˌzɛmpləfəˈkeʸʃən/ n [C;U]

ex·empt¹ /ɪgˈzɛmpt/ adj [F *from*] freed (from a duty, service, payment, etc.): *He is exempt from military service.*

exempt² v [T *from*] to make EXEMPT¹: *His bad health exempted him from military service.* –**exemption** /ɪgˈzɛmpʃən/ n [C;U *from*]

ex·er·cise¹ /ˈɛksərˌsaɪz/ n **1** [C;U] (a) use of any part of the body or mind so as to strengthen and improve it: *If you don't get more exercise, you'll get fat.|Here is a set of exercises which will strengthen your arm muscles.* **2** [C] a question or set of questions to be answered by a student for practice **3** [U] the use of a (stated) power or right: *the exercise of one's right to vote* **4** [C] a movement made by soldiers, naval ships, etc., in time of peace, to practise fighting: *naval exercises*

exercise² v **-cised, -cising 1** [I;T] to (cause to) get exercise: *You should exercise more.* **2** [T] *fml* to use (a power or right): *You should try to exercise patience.*

ex·ert /ɪgˈzɜrt/ v [T] to use (strength, skill, etc.): *My parents have been exerting a lot of pressure on me to change my job.|He never exerts himself* (=makes an effort) *to help anyone.*

ex·er·tion /ɪgˈzɜrʃən/ n [C;U] (a case of) EXERTing; (an) effort: *The doctor says he must avoid all exertion.*

ex·hale /eksˈheʸl, ɛkˈseʸl/ v **-haled, -haling** [I;T] to breathe out (air, gas, etc.) –opposite **inhale** –**exhalation** /ˌɛkshəˈleʸʃən, ˌɛksə-/ n [C;U]

ex·haust¹ /ɪgˈzɔst/ v [T] **1** to tire out: *What an exhausting day!* **2** to use up or deal with completely: *to exhaust the supply of oxygen|I think we've exhausted this subject: let's go on to the next one.*

exhaust² n [C] also **exhaust pipe** /·'·· ,·/ **1** the pipe which allows unwanted gas, steam, etc., to escape from an engine or machine **2** [U]

the gas or steam which escapes through this pipe

ex·haus·tion /ɪgˈzɔstʃən/ n [U] the state of being very tired: *to suffer from exhaustion*

ex·haus·tive /ɪgˈzɔstɪv/ adj thorough: *an exhaustive study* –compare: *The men made an* **exhaustive** *search of the forest, but couldn't find the missing children.|The men have spent an* **exhausting** (=very tiring) *day searching the forest.* –**exhaustively** adv

ex·hib·it¹ /ɪgˈzɪbɪt/ v [T] **1** to show in public, as for sale, or in a competition: *to exhibit paintings/flowers/new cars* **2** *fml* to show that one possesses (a feeling, quality, etc.): *to exhibit signs of fear/guilt*

exhibit² n **1** something that is EXHIBITed¹ (1), esp. in a MUSEUM **2** *AmE* a public show of objects: *an international trade exhibit.|The chilren's paintings are* **on exhibit** (being shown publicly) *at the school.*

ex·hi·bi·tion /ˌɛksəˈbɪʃən/ n **1** [of] an act of EXHIBITing¹ (2): *an exhibition of a bad temper* **2** →EXHIBIT²

ex·hi·bi·tion·ism /ˌɛksəˈbɪʃəˌnɪzəm/ n [U] often derog the behavior of a person who wants to be looked at and admired –**exhibitionist** n

ex·hib·i·tor /ɪgˈzɪbətər/ n a person, firm, etc., that EXHIBITs¹ (1)

ex·hil·a·rate /ɪgˈzɪləˌreʸt/ v **-rated, -rating** [T] to make cheerful and excited: *We felt very exhilarated after our day at the ocean.* –**exhilaration** /ɪgˌzɪləˈreʸʃən/ n [U] –**exhilarating** /ɪgˈzɪləˌreʸtɪŋ/ adj

ex·hort /ɪgˈzɔrt/ v [T +*to-v/to*] *fml* to urge or advise strongly: *The general exhorted his men to fight well/to courage.* –**exhortation** /ˌɛksɔrˈteʸʃən, ˌɛgzɔr-/ n [C;U]

ex·hume /ɪgˈzuᵂm, ɪgˈzyuᵂm, ɛksˈhyuᵂm/ v **-humed, -huming** [T] *fml* to take (a dead body) out of the grave –**exhumation** /ˌɛkshyuᵂˈmeʸʃən, ˌɛksyuᵂ-/ n [C;U]

ex·ile¹ /ˈɛgzaɪl, ˈɛksaɪl/ n **1** [S;U] unwanted absence from one's country, often for political reasons: *Napoleon was sent into exile.|to die in exile* **2** [C] a person who has been forced to leave his/her country, esp. for these reasons

exile² v **-iled, -iling** [T *to*] to send (someone) into EXILE¹ (1)

ex·ist /ɪgˈzɪst/ v [I] **1** to live or be real; to have being: *Does God exist?|The Roman Empire existed for several centuries.* **2** (of a person) to continue to live, esp. with difficulty: *She exists on bread and water.*

ex·ist·ence /ɪgˈzɪstəns/ n **1** [U] the state of existing: *a new country which* **came into existence** *in 1918* **2** [S] life; way of living: *Working as a writer can be a very lonely existence.*

ex·ist·ing /ɪgˈzɪstɪŋ/ adj [A] present: *Food will not get cheaper under existing conditions.*

ex·it¹ /ˈɛgzɪt, ˈɛksɪt/ n **1** (*often written over a door*) a way out, e.g. from a theater **2** an act of leaving, esp. of an actor leaving the stage: *Make your exit through the door at the back of the stage.*

exit² [I] (*used as a stage direction*) goes out;goes off stage: *Exit Hamlet, bearing the*

body of Polonius.
USAGE In stage directions, **exit** comes before its subject and has only one tense.
ex·o·dus /'ɛksədəs/ *n* [S *of, from*] a going out or leaving by a great number of people: *an exodus of cars from the city every evening*
ex·on·er·ate /ɪg'zɑnəˌreʸt/ *v* **-ated, -ating** [T *from*] *fml* to free (someone) from blame: *The report on the accident exonerates the company (from any responsibility).* **–exoneration** /ɪgˌzɑnə'reʸʃən/ *n* [U]
ex·or·bi·tant /ɪg'zɔrbəṭənt/ *adj* (of cost, demands, etc.) much greater than is reasonable: *That hotel charges exorbitant prices.* **–exorbitantly** *adv*
ex·or·cism /'ɛksɔrˌsɪzəm, -sər-/ *n* [C;U] an act or the art of exorcizing (EXORCIZE) **–exorcist** *n*
ex·or·cize ||also **-cise** *BrE* /'ɛksɔrˌsaɪz, -sər-/ *v* **-cized, -cizing** [T] to drive out (an evil spirit) from a person or place (as if) by solemn command
ex·ot·ic /ɪg'zɑṭɪk/ *adj usu. apprec* strange and unusual; (as if) from a distant country: *exotic flowers/food/smells* **–exotically** *adv*
ex·pand /ɪk'spænd/ *v* [I;T] to (cause to) grow larger: *Iron expands when it is heated.|The company has expanded its operations in Atlanta by building a new factory there.* –opposite **contract –expandable** *adj*
expand on sthg. *v prep* [T] to make (a story, argument, etc.) more detailed by addition: *There's no need to expand on your story; I understand it.*
ex·panse /ɪk'spæns/ *n* [*of*] a wide space: *an expanse of grass*
ex·pan·sion /ɪk'spænʃən, -tʃən/ *n* [U] the action of EXPANDing or state of being EXPANDed: *the expansion of metals when they are heated|The new school is large to allow room for expansion.*
ex·pan·sive /ɪk'spænsɪv/ *adj* **1** (of a person) friendly and willing to talk: *After she'd had a couple of drinks, Mary became very expansive.* **2** large and splendid –compare EXPENSIVE **–expansively** *adv*
ex·pa·tri·ate /ɛks'peʸtriʸɪt/ *n* a person living in a foreign country
ex·pect /ɪk'spɛkt/ *v* [T] **1** [+*to-v*/*(that)*] to think (that someone or something will come or that something will happen): *I expect (that) he'll pass the examination.|We expect to make a small profit this year.|We're expecting visitors.|I expect John home at 6 o'clock.|His weakness after the illness is* **to be expected.** (=usual) **2** to believe, hope, and think (that someone will do something): *The train leaves 8:30 so I'm expecting you all to be at the station on time.* **3** [+*(that)*; not *be* +*v-ing*] *infml esp. BrE* to think (that something is true): *"Who broke that cup?" "I expect it was the cat."* **4 be expecting (a baby)** (of a woman) to be PREGNANT (=carrying a child in her body)
ex·pect·an·cy /ɪk'spɛktənsiʸ/ *n* [U] hope; the state of expecting: *She waited for her lover in a state of happy expectancy.*
ex·pect·ant /ɪk'spɛktənt/ *adj* [*no comp.*] **1** hopeful: *The expectant crowds waited for the President to pass.* **2 expectant mother** a PREGNANT woman **–expectantly** *adv*
ex·pec·ta·tion /ˌɛkspɛk'teʸʃən/ *n* [C;U *of*] the condition of expecting; that which is expected: *We thought Mary would pass and John would fail, but* **contrary to expectation(s)** (=in spite of what was expected) *it was the other way around.|I usually enjoy his movies, but the latest one didn't* **come up to/live up to** *my* **expectations.** (=was not as good as I expected)
ex·pe·di·en·cy /ɪk'spiʸdiʸənsiʸ/ also **expedience** /ɪk'spiʸdiʸəns/– *n* [U] **1** the quality of being EXPEDIENT **2** *derog* regard only for one's own personal advantage: *All his actions are governed by expediency.*
ex·pe·di·ent[1] /ɪk'spiʸdiʸənt/ *adj* (of a course of action) useful or helpful for a purpose: *She thought it was expedient not to tell her mother where she had been.|It was an expedient plan.* –opposite **inexpedient –expediently** *adv*
expedient[2] *n* an EXPEDIENT plan, idea, or action
ex·pe·dite /'ɛkspəˌdaɪt/ *v* **-dited, -diting** [T] *fml* to make (a plan or arrangement) go faster: *The builders promised to expedite the repairs to the roof.*
ex·pe·di·tion /ˌɛkspə'dɪʃən/ *n* (the persons, vehicles, etc., going on) a (long) journey for a certain purpose: *an expedition to photograph wild animals in Africa* –see TRAVEL (USAGE)
ex·pe·di·tion·ar·y /ˌɛkspə'dɪʃəˌnɛriʸ/ *adj* [A] of or making up an EXPEDITION of war: *an* **expeditionary force**
ex·pel /ɪk'spɛl/ *v* **-ll-** [T *from*] **1** to dismiss officially (from a school, club, etc.): *He was expelled for cheating on an examination.* **2** *fml* to force out (from the body or a container): *to expel air from one's lungs*
ex·pend /ɪk'spɛnd/ *v* [T *in, upon*] to spend or use up (esp. time, care, etc.)
ex·pend·a·ble /ɪk'spɛndəbəl/ *adj* that may be used up for a purpose: *The officer regarded his soldiers as expendable and was willing to see them all killed in order to gain a victory.*
ex·pend·i·ture /ɪk'spɛndətʃər, -ˌtʃʊər/ *n* [S;U *of, on*] spending or using up: *the expenditure of time, effort, and money on a piece of work|efforts to reduce government expenditure*
ex·pense /ɪk'spɛns/ *n* [U] **1** cost of money, time, effort, etc.: *She* **spared no expense/went to great expense** (=spent a lot of money) *to make the party a success.|He finished the job* **at the expense of** (=causing the loss of) *his health.* –see COST (USAGE) **2 at someone's expense** with someone paying the cost: *He had his book printed at his own expense.|*(fig.) *He tried to be funny at my expense.* (=to make me seem silly)
ex·pens·es /ɪk'spɛnsɪz/ *n* [P] the money used or needed for a purpose: *traveling/vacation/monthly expenses*
ex·pen·sive /ɪk'spɛnsɪv/ *adj* costing a lot of money: *an expensive new coat|Buying that car was an expensive mistake.* –opposite **inexpensive –expensively** *adv*

ex·pe·ri·ence[1] /ɪk'spɪəriʸəns/ n **1** [U] (the gaining of) knowledge or skill which comes from practice rather than from books: *a teacher with five years' experience* **2** [C] something that happens to one and has an effect on the mind and feelings: *Getting caught in the flood was quite an experience.*

experience[2] v -enced, -encing [T] to feel, suffer, or know, as an experience: *to experience joy/difficulties/defeat*

ex·pe·ri·enced /ɪk'spɪəriʸənst/ adj [in] having knowledge, skill or experience: *an experienced doctor/traveler* —opposite **inexperienced**

ex·per·i·ment[1] /ɪk'spɛrəmənt/ n [C;U] (a) trial made in order to learn something or prove the truth of an idea: *to do/make/carry out/perform an experiment|It has been proven by experiment that the atom can be divided.*

ex·per·i·ment[2] /ɪk'spɛrə‚mɛnt, -mənt/ v [I on, upon, with] to make an EXPERIMENT[1]: *They experimented with new materials.|Many people disapprove of experimenting on animals.* —**experimentation** /ɪk‚spɛrəmən'teʸʃən, -mən-/ n [U]

ex·per·i·men·tal /ɪk‚spɛrə'mɛntəl/ adj used for or connected with EXPERIMENTS: *an experimental farm* —**experimentally** adv

ex·pert /'ɛkspɜrt/ adj,n [at, in, on] (a person) with special knowledge or training: *She's (an) expert on/in/at/teaching small chilren.* —**expertly** adv

ex·per·tise /‚ɛkspɜr'tiʸz/ n [U] skill in a particular field; KNOW-HOW: *Her expertise saved the business from failing.*

ex·pi·ra·tion /‚ɛkspə'reʸʃən/ n [U] the end of (something which lasts for) a period of time): *the expiration of a trade agreement between two countries|What is the **expiration date** on your driver's license?*

ex·pire /ɪk'spaɪər/ v -pired, -piring [I] **1** *more fml than* run out– (of something which lasts for a period of time) to come to an end: *Our trade agreement with China will expire next year.* **2** *lit* to die

ex·plain /ɪk'spleʸn/ v **1** [I;T +that/to] to give the meaning (of something); make (something) clear, by speaking or writing: *I don't understand this, but Paul will explain (it) (to us).|Explain what this word means.* **2** [T] to give or be the reason for; account for: *Can you explain your stupid behavior?|That explains why he's not here.*

ex·pla·na·tion /‚ɛksplə'neʸʃən/ n [C;U of, for] **1** (an act of) explaining: *She's giving an explanation of how the machine works.* **2** something that explains: *Can you think of any explanation for his bad behavior?*

ex·plan·a·to·ry /ɪk'splænə‚tɔriʸ,-,toʷriʸ/ adj (of a statement, a piece of writing, etc.) that explains –see also SELF-EXPLANATORY

ex·ple·tive /'ɛksplətɪv/ n an often meaningless word used to express violent feeling; OATH (2) or curse: *"DAMN" is an expletive.*

ex·pli·ca·ble /ɪk'splɪkəbəl, 'ɛksplɪ-/ adj [F] *fml* (of behavior or events) that can be explained –opposite **inexplicable** —**explicably** adv

ex·plic·it /ɪk'splɪsɪt/ adj (of statements, rules, etc.) clear and fully expressed: *to give explicit directions* –compare IMPLICIT –**explicitly** adv

ex·plode /ɪk'sploʷd/ v -ploded, -ploding [I;T] (esp. of a bomb or other explosive) to (cause to) blow up or burst: (fig.) *to explode with/in* (=violently show) *anger*

ex·ploit[1] /ɪk'splɔɪt/ v [T] **1** *derog* to use (esp. a person) unfairly for one's own profit: *to exploit women by making them work for less pay* **2** to use or develop (a thing) fully so as to get profit: *to exploit the oil under the sea* –**exploitation** /‚ɛksplɔɪ'teʸʃən/ n [U]

ex·ploit[2] /'ɛksplɔɪt/ n *apprec* a brave, bold, and successful deed

ex·plore /ɪk'splɔr, ɪk'sploʷr/ v -plored, -ploring [T] to travel into or through (a place) for the purpose of discovery: (fig.) *We must explore* (=examine carefully) *all the possibilities.* –**explorer** n –**exploration** /‚ɛksplə'reʸʃən/ n [C;U]: *an exploration to Antartica* –**exploratory** /ɪk'splɔrə‚tɔriʸ, ɪk'sploʷrə‚toʷriʸ/ adj

ex·plo·sion /ɪk'sploʷʒən/ n **1** (a loud noise caused by) an act of exploding: *When she lit the the gas stove there was a loud explosion.|*(fig.) *explosions of loud laughter* **2** a sudden increase: *population explosion*

ex·plo·sive[1] /ɪk'sploʷsɪv/ adj that can explode: *It's dangerous to smoke when handling explosive materials.|*(fig.) *The question of women's rights is an explosive one.* (=causes strong feelings) –**explosively** adv

explosive[2] n an explosive substance: *Gunpowder is an explosive.*

ex·po·nent /ɪk'spoʷnənt/ n [of] a person who expresses, supports, or is an example of (a stated belief or idea): *She's an exponent of the opinions of Freud.*

ex·port[1] /ɪk'spɔrt, ɪk'spoʷrt, 'ɛkspɔrt, 'ɛkspoʷrt/ v [I;T] to send (goods) out of a country for sale –compare IMPORT[1] –**exporter** n –**exportable** adj

ex·port[2] /'ɛkspɔrt, 'ɛkspoʷrt/ n **1** [U] also **exportation** /‚ɛkspɔr'teʸʃən, -spoʷr-/– (the business of) EXPORTING: *the export trade|The export/exportation of gold is forbidden.* **2** [C] something that is EXPORTED: *Wool is one of the chief exports of Australia.* –compare IMPORT[2]

ex·pose /ɪk'spoʷz/ v -posed, -posing [T] **1** [to] to uncover; leave unprotected: *to expose one's skin to the sun|*(fig.) *As a photographer in the war, she was exposed to many dangers.* **2** [to] to make known (a secretly guilty person or action): *I threatened to expose him (to the police).* **3** to uncover (film) to the light, when taking a photograph

ex·po·sé /‚ɛkspoʷ'zeʸ, -spə-/ n [of] a public statement of the (esp. shameful) facts (about something): *The movie is an exposé of his dishonest business methods.*

ex·po·si·tion /‚ɛkspə'zɪʃən/ n **1** [C;U] *fml* (an act of) explaining and making clear: *a full exposition of her political beliefs* **2** [C] an international show (EXHIBITION) of the products of industry

ex·po·sure /ɪk'spoʷʒər/ n **1** [C;U to] (a case

of) being EXPOSED (1): *We nearly died of exposure on the cold mountain.|much exposure to danger* **2** [C;U *of*] a case of exposing, or the experience of being EXPOSED (2): *I threatened him with public exposure.* **3** [C] the amount of film that must be EXPOSED (3) to take one photograph: *I have three exposures left on this roll of film.*

ex·pound /ɪk'spaʊnd/ *v* [T *to*] *fml* to give an EXPOSITION (1) of: *The priest expounded his religious ideas to us.*

ex·press¹ /ɪk'sprɛs/ *v* [T] to show (a feeling, opinion, or fact) in words or in some other way: *I can't express how grateful I am.|She expressed surprise when I told her you were coming.|The signs on the buses are expressed in both English and Spanish.|He expresses himself* (=speaks or writes) *in good clear English.*

express² *n* **1** [C] also **express train** /·'· ˌ·/– a fast train which stops at only a few stations **2** [U] a service or company for carrying things faster than usual: *Send the letter by express.*

express³ *adv* by EXPRESS² (2): *I sent the package express.*

express⁴ *adj* [A] **1** (of a command, wish, etc.) clearly stated or understood; EXPLICIT: *It was her express wish that you should have her jewels after her death.* **2** going or sent quickly: *an express letter/bus.* **3** (of a letter or package) sent faster and at a higher cost than usual: *express mail*

ex·pres·sion /ɪk'sprɛʃən/ *n* **1** [C;U] (an example of) the act of expressing: *A government should permit the free expression of political opinion.* **2** [U] the quality of showing or performing with feeling: *She doesn't sing with much expression.* **3** [C] a word or group of words: *"In the family way" is an old-fashioned expression meaning "PREGNANT."* **4** [C] a look on a person's face: *a wise/angry expression*

ex·pres·sion·less /ɪk'sprɛʃənlɪs/ *adj* (esp. of a voice or face) without EXPRESSION (2) –**expressionlessly** *adv*

ex·pres·sive /ɪk'sprɛsɪv/ *adj* [*of*] (esp. of words or a face) full of feeling and meaning: *A baby's cry may be expressive of hunger or pain.* –**expressively** *adv*

ex·press·ly /ɪk'sprɛsliʸ/ *adv* clearly; in an EXPRESS⁴ (1) way: *I told you expressly to lock the door.*

ex·press·way /ɪk'sprɛsˌweʸ/ *n* also **freeway, thruway** *AmE*‖**motorway** *BrE*– a very wide road built esp. for fast vehicles traveling long distances, and from which one may get off only at certain places (EXITs)

ex·pro·pri·ate /ɛks'proʷpriʸˌeʸt/ *v* -**ated**, -**ating** [T] *fml* to take away (something owned by another), often for public use: *The State expropriated all property owned by foreigners.* –**expropriation** /ɛksˌproʷpriʸ'eʸʃən/ *n* [C;U]

ex·pul·sion /ɪk'spʌlʃən/ *n* [C;U] (an act of) EXPELling or being EXPELled: *the expulsion of a child from school*

ex·pur·gate /'ɛkspərˌgeʸt/ *v* -**gated**, -**gating** [T] *fml* to make (a book, play, etc.) pure by taking out anything which is considered im-

proper –**expurgation** /ˌɛkspər'geʸʃən/ *n* [C;U]

ex·quis·ite /ɪk'skwɪzɪt, 'ɛkskwɪ-/ *adj apprec* very finely made or done; almost perfect: *exquisite manners/beauty|an exquisite piece of jewelery* –**exquisitely** *adv*

ex·tem·po·ra·ne·ous /ɪkˌstɛmpə'reʸniʸəs/ *adj* (spoken or done) in haste, without time for preparation: *an extemporaneous speech* –**extemporaneously** *adv*

ex·tend /ɪk'stɛnd/ *v* **1** [I] (of space, land, or time) to reach, stretch, or continue: *The hot weather extended into October.* **2** [T] to make longer or greater: *to extend the railroad to the next town* **3** [T] to stretch out (a part of one's body) to the limit: *a bird with its wings extended* **4** [T] *fml* to give or offer (help, friendship, etc.) to someone: *to extend a warm welcome to him|The bank will extend you* CREDIT. (=the right to borrow money)

ex·ten·sion /ɪk'stɛnʃən, -tʃən/ *n* **1** [U] the act of EXTENDING or condition of being EXTENDED (2,3,4): *the extension of our foreign trade* **2** [C] a part which is added to make something longer, wider, or greater: *to build an extension onto the house* **3** [C] any of many telephone lines which connect the SWITCHBOARD to various rooms or offices in a large building: *Could I have extension 45, please?*

ex·ten·sive /ɪk'stɛnsɪv/ *adj* large in amount or area: *an extensive library|extensive damage from the storm* –see also INTENSIVE –**extensively** *adv*

ex·tent /ɪk'stɛnt/ *n* **1** [U *of*] the length or area to which something EXTENDs (1): *The full extent of the desert is not known.|*(fig.) *I was surprised at the extent of her knowledge.* **2** [S;U] (a) (stated) degree: *I agree with what you say to some/a certain extent.* (=partly)

ex·ten·u·ate /ɪk'stɛnuʷˌeʸt/ *v* -**ated**, -**ating** [T] *fml* to lessen the seriousness of, by finding excuses for (bad behavior): *He stole the money, but there are* **extenuating circumstances.** (=facts to be considered) –**extenuation** /ɪkˌstɛnuʷ'eʸʃən/ *n* [C;U]

ex·te·ri·or¹ /ɪk'stɪəriʸər/ *adj* outer; on or from the outside (esp. of places): *the exterior walls of the building*– opposite **interior**; compare EXTERNAL

exterior² *n* the outside; the outer appearance or surface: *the exterior of the house* –opposite **interior**

ex·ter·mi·nate /ɪk'stɜrməˌneʸt/ *v* -**nated**, -**nating** [T] to kill (all the creatures or people in a place, or all those of a certain kind or race) –**extermination** /ɪkˌstɜrmə'neʸʃən/ *n* [U]

ex·ter·nal /ɪk'stɜrnl/ *adj* on, of, or for the outside: *This medicine is for external use, not to drink.|This newspaper doesn't pay much attention to external* (=foreign) *affairs.* –opposite **internal**; compare EXTERIOR –**externally** *adv*

ex·tinct /ɪk'stɪŋkt/ *adj* (esp. of a kind of animal) no longer existing: *The woolly elephant* (MAMMOTH) *has been extinct for a long time.|an extinct* (=no longer active) VOLCANO

ex·tinc·tion /ɪk'stɪŋkʃən/ *n* [U] **1** the state of

being or becoming EXTINCT: *Is the human race threatened with complete extinction?* **2** the act of EXTINGUISHing or making EXTINCT: *the extinction of his hopes*

ex·tin·guish /ɪkˈstɪŋgwɪʃ/ v [T] *fml* to put out (a light or fire): (fig.) *Nothing could extinguish his faith in human nature.*

ex·tin·guish·er /ɪkˈstɪŋgwɪʃər/ also **fire extinguisher**– n an instrument for putting out small fires by shooting liquid chemicals at them

ex·tol /ɪkˈstoʷl/ v **-ll-** [T] *fml* to praise very highly: *He keeps extolling the MERITS (=good qualities) of his new car.*

ex·tor·tion·ate /ɪkˈstɔrʃənɪt/ adj *derog* (of a demand, price, etc.) much too high; EXORBITANT **–extortionately** *adv*

ex·tort sthg. **from** sbdy. /ɪkˈstɔrt/ v prep [T] to obtain (esp. money) by force or threats: *He's been charged with extorting money from several small businesses.* **–extortion** /ɪkˈstɔrʃən/ n [U]: *a promise obtained by extortion*

ex·tra¹ /ˈɛkstrə/ adj,adv **1** [A] additional(ly); beyond what is usual or necessary: *an extra loaf of bread|to work extra hard* **2** [F] as well as the regular charge: *Dinner costs $10, and wine is extra.|They charge extra for wine.*

extra² n **1** something added, for which an EXTRA charge is made: *Breakfast is an extra at this hotel.* **2** a movie actor who has a very small part, e.g. in a crowd scene **3** a special EDITION (=one printing) of a newspaper

ex·tract¹ /ɪkˈstrækt/ v [T *from*] **1** to pull or take out, often with difficulty: *to extract a tooth|*(fig.) *He extracted a promise from me* (=made me promise) *that I'd come to the party.* **2** to take out with a machine or instrument, or by chemical means (a substance which is contained in another substance): *to extract gold from the rocks*

ex·tract² /ˈɛkstrækt/ n **1** [C;U *of*] (a) product obtained by EXTRACTING¹ (2): *meat extract* **–compare** ESSENCE (2) **2** [C *from*] a passage of written or spoken matter that has been taken from a book; EXCERPT: *She read me a few extracts from his letter.*

ex·trac·tion /ɪkˈstrækʃən/ n **1** [C;U *from*] the act or an example of EXTRACTING¹: *Her teeth are so bad that she needs five extractions.|the extraction of coal from a mine* **2** [U] (the stated) origin (of a person's family): *an American of Russian extraction* (=his family came from Russia)

ex·tra·cur·ric·u·lar /ˌɛkstrəkəˈrɪkyələr/ adj (esp. of activities such as sports, music, or acting) outside the regular course of work (CURRICULUM) in a school or college

ex·tra·dite /ˈɛkstrəˌdaɪt/ v **-dited, -diting** [T *from, to*] **1** to send (someone who may be guilty of a crime and who has escaped to another country) back for trial **2** to obtain (such a person) for trial in this way **–extradition** /ˌɛkstrəˈdɪʃən/ n [C;U]

ex·tra·ne·ous /ɪkˈstreʸniʸəs/ adj *fml* not belonging or directly connected: *His account of the war includes a lot of extraneous details.* **–extraneously** *adv*

ex·traor·di·nar·y /ɪkˈstrɔrdnˌɛriʸ/ adj **1** very

strange: *What an extraordinary idea!* **2** [A] more than what is ordinary: *a girl of extraordinary beauty|Owing to the danger of war, there will be an extraordinary* (=as opposed to regular) *meeting of Congress tonight.* **–extraordinarily** *adv*

ex·trap·o·late /ɪkˈstræpəˌleʸt/ v **-lated, -lating** [I;T] *fml* to guess (something in the future) from facts already known

ex·trav·a·gant /ɪkˈstrævəgənt/ adj *derog* **1** wasteful, esp. of money: *the government's extravagant policies* **2** (of ideas, behavior, and the expression of feeling) uncontrolled; beyond what is reasonable: *He makes the most extravagant claims for his new system.* **–extravagantly** *adv* **–extravagance** n [C;U]: *Try to shop carefully and avoid extravagance.|His latest extravagance is a hand-made silk shirt.*

ex·treme¹ /ɪkˈstriʸm/ adj **1** [A *no comp.*] the furthest possible; at the very beginning or very end: *extreme old age* **2** [A *no comp.*] the greatest possible: *extreme heat/ danger* **3** *often derog* (of opinions and those who hold them) going beyond the usual limits: *His political ideas are very extreme.|an extreme* RIGHT WING *party* **–compare** MODERATE¹ (2)

extreme² n **1** an EXTREME¹ (2) degree: *Sometimes he eats too much and sometimes he eats nothing. He goes from one extreme to the other.|She has been generous* **in the extreme.** (=very generous) **–compare** EXTREMITY **2** **go/be driven to extremes** to act too violently; to behave in an EXTREME¹ (3) way

ex·treme·ly /ɪkˈstriʸmliʸ/ adv very: *I'm extremely sorry.* **–see** Study Notes on page 363

ex·trem·ism /ɪkˈstriʸmɪzəm/ n [U] *derog* (esp. in politics) the quality or state of being EXTREME¹ (3) **–extremist** n,adj

ex·trem·i·ty /ɪkˈstrɛmətiʸ/ n **-ties 1** [S;U *of*] the highest degree (esp. of suffering and sorrow); (a case of) the greatest misfortune: *an extremity of pain/anger* **2** [C] the furthest point: *His extremities* (=hands and feet) *were frozen.*

ex·tri·cate /ˈɛkstrəˌkeʸt/ v **-cated, -cating** [T *from*] to set free from something that it is difficult to escape from: *I thought he was going to talk for hours, but I managed to extricate myself by saying I had to catch a train.* **–extricable** /ɪkˈstrɪkəbəl, ˈɛkstrɪ-/ adj **–extrication** /ˌɛkstrəˈkeʸʃən/ n [U]

ex·tro·vert , extravert /ˈɛkstrəˌvɜrt/ n a person who is cheerful and likes to be with and amuse other people rather than being quiet and alone **–see also** INTROVERT **–extroversion** /ˌɛkstrəˈvɜrʒən, ˈɛkstrəˌvɜrʒən/ n [U]

ex·u·ber·ant /ɪgˈzuʷbərənt/ adj overflowing with life and cheerful excitement: *an exuberant child|*(fig.) *the exuberant growth of a tropical rain forest* **–exuberantly** *adv* **–exuberance** n [U]

ex·ude /ɪgˈzuʷd, ɪkˈsuʷd/ v **-uded, -uding** [I;T] to (cause to) flow out slowly and spread in all directions: (fig.) *He's very popular with everyone; he exudes charm.*

ex·ult /ɪgˈzʌlt/ v [I *+to-v/at, in*] *fml or lit* to rejoice; to show delight: *The people exulted in/at the victory.* **–compare** EXALT **–exultant**

adj **–exultantly** *adv* **–exultation**
/ˌɛgzʌl'teʸʃən, ˌɛksʌl-/ [U *at, over*]: *The climber gave a cry of exultation when he reached the mountain top.*

exult over sbdy./sthg. *v prep* [T] to rejoice proudly over (esp. a defeated enemy)

eye¹ /aɪ/ *n* **1** the bodily organ with which one sees: *He lost an eye in an accident, and now he has a glass eye.│She has blue eyes.* **2** the power of seeing: *My eye fell upon* (=I noticed) *an interesting article in the newspaper.│She has* **a (good) eye for** (=the ability to see, judge, etc.) *fashion.* **3** the hole in a needle through which the thread passes **4** a small ring-shaped or U-shaped piece of metal into which a hook fits for fastening clothes: *Her dress was fastened with hooks and eyes.* **5 catch someone's eye** *infml* **a** to draw one's notice or attention to: *That painting caught my eye.│The student tried to catch the teacher's eye.* **6 in the eyes of** in the opinion of: *In her father's eyes, she can do nothing wrong.* **7 keep an eye on** *infml* to watch carefully: *Please keep an eye on the baby for me.* **8 keep an eye out for** to try to notice and remember; be on the LOOKOUT (1) for: *I want to move. Keep an eye out for an apartment, will you?* **9 keep one's eyes open** (also **peeled** *AmE*‖**skinned** *BrE*) to watch carefully (for): *The thieves kept their eyes peeled for the police.* **10 see eye to eye (with)** to agree completely (with): *He and his brother always see eye to eye.* **11 under/before one's very eyes** in front of one, so that one can see with no difficulty: *They stole the jewels under my very eyes.* **12 with one's eyes open** knowing what may possibly happen: *You married him with your eyes open, so don't complain now!* **13 look someone in the eye:** look straight into someone's face: *Can you look me in the eye and tell me a lie?* **14 more than meets the eye** *infml* more than actually appears or is seen: *The police said the death was an accident, but others are sure there is more than meets the eye.* **15 my eye!** *infml* (used for expressing strong disagreement or sometimes surprise): *A diamond, my eye! That's glass!* **16 a sight**

for sore eyes *AmE infml* something or someone that one is very glad to see **17 only have eyes for** to be interested only in looking at: *She only has eyes for her handsome husband.* **18 set/lay eyes on** *infml* see: *I knew he wasn't trustworthy the minute I laid eyes on him.* **19 -eyed** having eyes of the stated kind of number: *blue-eyed│one-eyed│bright-eyed* **–eyeless** *adj*

eye² *v* **eyed, eyeing** *or* **eying** [T] to look at closely, esp. with interest or distrust

eye·ball /'aɪbɔl/ *n* the whole of the eye, including the part hidden inside the head

eye·brow /'aɪbraʊ/ *n* **1** the line of hairs above each of the two human eyes **2 raise one's eyebrows (at)** to express surprise, doubt, or disapproval (at): *There were a lot of raised eyebrows/eyebrows raised at the news of the Secretary of State's dismissal.*

eye-catch·ing /'· ˌ··/ *adj* (of a thing) so unusual that one cannot help looking at it: *an eye-catching advertisement*

eye·lash /'aɪlæʃ/ *n* one of the small hairs which grow from the edge of each eyelid

eye·lid /'aɪˌlɪd/ *n* either of the pieces of covering skin which can move down to close each eye

eye·lin·er /'aɪˌlaɪnər/ *n* [U] solid paint used for giving more importance to the shape of the eyes

eye-o·pen·er /'· ˌ··/ *n* [S] something surprising, which makes a person see a truth he/she did not formerly believe: *I knew he was strong, but it was an eye-opener to me when I saw him lift that car.*

eye shad·ow /'· ˌ··/ *n* [U] colored paint used on the eyelids to give more attention to the eyes

eye·sight /'aɪsaɪt/ *n* [U] the power of seeing: *good/poor eyesight*

eye·sore /'aɪsɔr, -soʷr/ *n* something ugly to look at (esp. when many people can see it): *That new shopping center is a real eyesore.*

eye·strain /'aɪ-streʸn/ *n* [U] a painful and tired condition of the eyes, as caused by reading very small print

eye·wit·ness /'aɪˌwɪtnɪs/ *n* [*to, of*] a person who sees and is able to describe an event: *Were there any eyewitnesses to the crime?*

F, f

SPELLING NOTE

Words with the sound /f/ may be spelled **ph-**, like **photograph**.

F, f /ɛf/ **F's, f's** *or* **Fs, fs** the 6th letter of the English alphabet

F *written abbrev. said as:* FAHRENHEIT: *Water boils at 212°F.*

fa·ble /'feʸbəl/ *n* **1** [C] a short story, esp. about animals, that teaches a lesson (a MORAL) or truth **2** [C;U] a story or stories about great people who never actually

lived; LEGEND; MYTH

fab·ric /'fæbrɪk/ *n* **1** [C;U] cloth made of threads woven together **2** [U] the walls, roof, etc., of a building: (fig.) *The whole fabric* (=framework) *of society was changed by the war.*

fab·ri·cate /'fæbrəˌkeʸt/ *v* **-cated, -cating** [T] to make or invent (in order to deceive): *The story was fabricated and completely untrue.* **–fabrication** /ˌfæbrə'keʸʃən/ *n* [C;U]

fab·u·lous /'fæbyələs/ *adj* **1** nearly unbelievable: *a fabulous sum of money* **2** *infml* very good or pleasant; excellent: *We*

fabulously

had a fabulous vacation. **3** existing or told about in FABLES: *fabulous creatures*

fab·u·lous·ly /'fæbyələsliʸ/ *adv* very (rich, great, etc.)

fa·cade , façade /fə'sɑd/ *n* **1** the front of a building **2** a false appearance: *Her honesty was all a facade.*

face¹ /feʸs/ *n* **1** [C] the front part of the head from the chin to the hair: *a round face* **2** [C] an expression on the face: *their happy faces|She wore/pulled a long face.* (=looked sad) **3** [C] the front, top, or most important surface of something: *the face of a clock|We climbed the north face of the mountain.|They seem to have disappeared* **off the face of the earth. 4** [C] a rock surface, either above or below ground, from which coal, gold, diamonds, etc., are dug **5** [U] the condition of being respected: *He was afraid of risking failure because he didn't want to* **lose face.|Our team saved (their) face** *by getting 3 points in the last minute and drawing the match.* **6 face to face (with)** in the direct presence (of): *I've often talked to him on the telephone, but I've never met him face to face.|She came face to face with death.* **7 in the face of** in opposition to; in spite of: *She succeeded in the face of great difficulties.* **8 keep a straight face** to hide one's amusement (by not laughing or smiling): *It was hard to keep a straight face while I answered their questions.* **9 on the face of it** judging by what one can see; APPARENTLY **10 to someone's face** openly in someone's presence: *He wouldn't say rude things about her to her face.* **11 -faced** having a certain kind of face or expression: *red-faced|sad-faced*

face² *v* **faced, facing 1** [I;T] to have the face or front pointing (towards): *The house faces (towards the) north/faces the park.* **2** [T] to be in the presence of and oppose; CONFRONT: *She faced the danger bravely.|We're faced with a difficult decision.|I couldn't face another day at work, so I pretended to be sick.* **3** [T *with*] to cover esp. the front part of (something) with a different material: *The brick house was faced with stone.* **4 face the music** to meet and deal with the unpleasant results of one's actions

face up to sthg. *v adv prep* [T] to be brave enough to accept or deal with: *to face up to one's responsibilities*

face·cloth /'feʸs-klɔθ/ *n* →WASHCLOTH

face·less /'feʸslɪs/ *adj* without any clear character: *Crowds of faceless people pour into the city each day.*

face-lift /'· ·, ·/ *n* a medical operation to make the face look younger by tightening the skin: (fig.) *to give a room a face-lift* (=to improve its appearance)

face pow·der /'· ,··/ *n* [U] also **powder**– a powder spread on the face to change or improve the appearance

fac·et /'fæsɪt/ *n* any of the many flat sides of a

cut jewel or precious stone: (fig.) *The question had many facets.* (=parts to be considered)

fa·ce·tious /fə'siʸʃəs/ *adj derog* humorous; tending to use unsuitable jokes: *I became angry at his facetious remarks.* –**facetiously** *adv* –**facetiousness** *n* [U]

face val·ue /,· '··/ *n* [C;U] the value or cost as shown on the front of something, such as a postage stamp: (fig.) *If you take her remarks only* **at (their) face value** (=as they appear at first), *you won't understand her full meaning.*

fa·cial¹ /'feʸʃəl/ *adj* of or concerning the face: *facial hair* –**facially** *adv*

facial² *n* a beauty treatment for the face

fac·ile /'fæsəl/ *adj derog* **1** [A] easily done or obtained: *facile success* **2** too easy; not deep; meaningless: *facile remarks|a facile explanation*

fa·cil·i·tate /fə'sɪlə,teʸt/ *v* **-tated, -tating** [T] *fml* to make easy or easier; help: *The new machines will facilitate the job.*

fa·cil·i·ties /fə'sɪləti ʸz/ *n* [P] means to do things; that which can be used: *The college has excellent library facilities.*

fa·cil·i·ty /fə'sɪləti ʸ/ *n* **-ties 1** [C;U] *fml* (an) ability to do something easily: *His facility with/in languages is surprising.* **2** [C] an advantage; CONVENIENCE (2): *A free bus to the airport is a facility offered only by this hotel.* **3** [C] *AmE* something which is built (e.g. a hospital) or set up for a certain purpose: *a health facility|sports facility|psychiatric facility|The offender was sent to a correctional facility* (=a prison).

fac·ing /'feʸsɪŋ/ *n* [U] **1** an outer covering or surface, as of a wall, for protection, ornament, etc. **2** additional material sewn into the edges of a garment, to improve it, esp. in thickness

fac·sim·i·le /fæk'sɪməliʸ/ *n* an exact copy, esp. of a picture or piece of writing

fact /fækt/ *n* **1** [C] something that has actually happened or is happening; something known to be, or accepted as being, true: *Certain facts have become known about what the moon is made of.|It is a fact that Alexander Graham Bell invented the telephone.|She didn't answer my letter. The fact is she didn't even read it.* –compare EVENT (1) **2** [U] the truth: *Is this story fact or* FICTION? **3 as a matter of fact, in (actual) fact, in point of fact** really; actually: *She doesn't mind. In fact, she's very pleased.|He told us he'd seen it, but in point of fact he wasn't really there.* –compare INDEED

fac·tion /'fækʃən/ *n* [C;U] (disagreement in) a group or party within a larger group, esp. one that makes itself noticed

fac·tor /'fæktər/ *n* **1** any of the forces, conditions, influences, etc., that act with others to bring about a result: *His friendly manner is an important factor in his rapid success.* **2** (in MATHEMATICS) a whole number which, when multiplied by one or more whole numbers, produces a given number: *2, 3, 4, and 6 are all factors of 12.*

fac·to·ry /'fæktəriʸ/ *n* **-ries** a building or

SPELLING NOTE
Words with the sound /f/ may be spelled **ph-**, like **photograph**.

group of buildings where goods are made, esp. in great quantities by machines: *factory workers|a car factory*

facts of life /ˌ· · '·/ *n euph* the details of sex and how babies are born: *Have you told your child about the facts of life yet?*

fac·tu·al /'fæktʃuʷəl/ *adj* of, concerning, or based on facts: *a factual account of the war* –**factually** *adv*

fac·ul·ty /'fækəltiʸ/ *n* **-ties 1** a natural power or ability, esp. of the mind: *For a woman of 85, she still has all her faculties.|the faculty of hearing|He has the faculty to learn languages easily.* **2** a branch or division of learning, esp. in a university: *the law/science faculty* **3** all the teachers of a university or college

fad /fæd/ *n* a short-lived interest or practive: *Her interest in photography is only a passing fad.*

fade /feʸd/ *v* **faded, fading** [I;T] to (cause to) lose strength, color, freshness, etc.: *The sun has faded the material.|The sound of thunder faded (away) into the distance.|Hopes of a peace settlement are now fading.*

fade out *v adv* [I;T (=**fade** sth.↔ **out**)] (in film or sound mixing) to (cause to) disappear slowly by reducing the sound or strength: *to fade out the last scene*

fag /fæg/ *n* **1** *AmE infml derog* a male HOMOSEXUAL **2** *BrE* for CIGARETTE

fagged /fægd/ [F] *BrE infml* very tired: *I'm fagged (out) after that hard work.*

fag·got‖also **fagot** *AmE* /'fægət/ *n* **1** *AmE infml derog* a male HOMOSEXUAL **2** a bunch of small sticks for burning

Fahr·en·heit /'færən‚haɪt/ *n* a scale of temperature in which water freezesat 32° and boils at 212° –compare CENTIGRADE

fail¹ /feʸl/ *v* **1** [I;T] to be unsuccessful (in): *He failed (to pass) his driving test.* **2** [T] to decide that (somebody) has not passed an examination: *The teachers failed me on the written test.* –opposite **pass 3** [I;T +*to-v*] to not produce the desired result; not perform or do: *Last year the crops failed.|When money is in short supply many businesses fail.* (=are unable to continue)[*We waited half an hour, but the bus failed to arrive.* **4** [T] to disappoint: *I've got a lot of faith in the team; I'm sure they won't fail us.* **5** [I;T] to be not enough (for): *His courage failed him in the end.* **6** [I] to lose strength; become weak: *The sick woman is failing quickly.*

fail² *n* **1** an unsuccessful result in an examination –opposite **pass 2 without fail** certainly: *I'll bring you that book without fail.*

fail·ing¹ /'feʸlɪŋ/ *n* a fault or weakness: *This machine has one big failing.|human failings.*

failing² *prep* in the absence of; without: *Failing instructions, I did what I thought best.*

fail·ure /'feʸlyər/ *n* **1** [U] lack of success; failing: *Her plans ended in failure.* **2** [C] a person, attempt, or thing that fails: *As a writer, he was a failure.* **3** [C;U] the non-performance or production of something expected or desired: *crop failures|(a) heart failure|His failure to explain the noise worried us.*

faint¹ /feʸnt/ *adj* **1** [F] weak and about to lose consciousness: *We felt faint from lack of food.* **2** lacking clearness, brightness, strength, etc.: *a faint sound|The colors became more faint as the sun set.|faint-hearted* (=lacking in courage) **3** very small; slight: *a faint possibility|(infml) I don't have the faintest idea what you're talking about.* –**faintly** *adv* –**faintness** *n* [U]

faint² *v* [I] to lose consciousness –**faint** *n*

fair¹ /fɛər/ *adj* **1** free from dishonesty or injustice: *a fair decision|It is not fair to kick another player in football.|There must be* **fair play** (=just and honest treatment of all concerned) *in this competition.|They will win the election* **by fair means or foul.** (=in any way, honest or dishonest) –opposite **unfair 2** fairly good, but not excellent: *Her knowledge of the language is fair but not perfect.|a fair-sized garden* **3** (of weather) fine; clear **4** (having skin or hair that is) light in color; not dark **5** having a good clear clean appearance or quality: *I made you a fair copy of the report.* **6** (of women) *esp. old use* beautiful; attractive: **the fair sex** (=women as a group) –**fairness** *n* [U]

fair² *adv* **1** in a just or honest manner; fairly: *You must play fair.* **2 fair and square** honestly; justly: *It was a good game and they beat us fair and square.*

fair³ *n* **1** *AmE* a show of farm animals and produce, goods made by hand, etc. for judging, usu. held once a year: *a county/state fair* **2** a market, esp. one held at regular periods for selling farm produce **3** a very large show of goods, advertising, etc.: *a book fair*

fair·ground /'fɛərgraʊnd/ *n* an open space on which a FAIR³ (1,2) is held

fair·ly /'fɛərliʸ/ *adv* **1** in a manner that is free from dishonesty, injustice, etc.: *I felt that I hadn't been treated fairly.* –opposite **unfairly 2** for the most part; rather: *She speaks English fairly well.* –see RATHER (USAGE); see Study Notes on page 363

fair·y /'fɛəriʸ/ *n* **-ies** a small imaginary figure with magical powers and shaped like a human

fairy tale /'·· ‚·/ also **fairy story** /'·· ‚··/– *n* **1** a story about fairies and other small magical people **2** a story or account that is hard to believe

fait ac·com·pli /ˌfeʸt ækɒmˈpliʸ, ˌfɛt ɒkɒmˈpliʸ/ *n* **faits accomplis** /ˌfeʸt ækɒmˈpliʸz, ˌfɛz ɒkɒmˈpliʸ/ *French* something that has already happened or has been done and that cannot be changed

faith /feʸθ/ *n* **1** [U] strong belief; trust: *I'm sure she'll pass the test; I've got great faith in her.* **2** [U] (loyalty to one's) word of honor; promise: *I kept/broke faith with them.|The administration has acted* **in good/bad faith.** (=has kept/broken its promises) **3** [C;U] (a system of) religious belief; religion: *the Christian and Jewish faiths*

faith·ful /'feʸθfəl/ *adj* **1** full of or showing loyalty: *a faithful old dog* **2** true to the facts or to an original: *a faithful account/copy* **3** [*to*] loyal to one's (marriage) partner by having no sexual relationship with anyone else

–see also UNFAITHFUL; see FIDELITY –**faithful-ness** n [U]

faith·ful·ly /'feᵞθfəliᵞ/ adv **1** with faith: I promised you faithfully. **2** exactly: I copied the letter faithfully. **3 Yours faithfully** (used at the end of a business letter, before the signature) –compare SINCERELY, TRULY

faith·less /'feᵞθlɪs/ adj disloyal; false: a faithless friend –**faithlessly** adv –**faithlessness** n [U]

fake¹ /feᵞk/ v **faked, faking** [T] to make or copy (something, such as a work of art)in order to deceive: She got the money from the bank by faking her mother's handwriting.|(fig.) She faked illness so that she wouldn't have to go to school.

fake² n a person or thing that is not what he/she/it looks like: The painting looked old but was a recent fake.

fake³ adj [A] made and intended to deceive: fake money –compare GENUINE

fal·con /'fælkən, 'fɔl-/ n a bird that kills and eats other animals, and can be trained by man to hunt

fal·con·ry /'fælkənriᵞ, 'fɔl-/ n [U] the art of training FALCONS to hunt

fall¹ /fɔl/ v **fell** /fɛl/, **fallen** /'fɔlən/, **falling** [I] **1** to descend through the air: He fell off the ladder.|The rock fell 10 meters before reaching the bottom of the well. **2** to come down from a standing position,esp. suddenly: She slipped and fell (down/over).|Five trees fell over in the storm. **3** to become lower in level, degree, or quantity: The temperature fell 4°.|Their voices fell to a whisper. –opposite **rise 4** to hang loosely: Her hair falls over her shoulders. **5** (of the face) to take on a look of sadness, disappointment, etc.: Her face fell when I told her the bad news. **6** to be killed, esp. in battle: A prayer was said in memory of all who had fallen in the war. **7** to be defeated or conquered: The city fell (to the enemy).|The government has fallen. (=lost power) **8** to come or happen as if by descending: Night fell quickly.|A silence fell as he entered the room.|Christmas falls on a Friday this year. **9** to pass into a new condition; become: She fell ill.|He fell in love with her.|This old coat of mine is falling to pieces. **10 fall flat** to fail to produce the desired effect or result: His jokes fell flat: nobody laughed at them. **11 fall over backwards/oneself** to be very eager or too eager; do everything one can: I've fallen over backwards to please you: what more can I do? **12 fall on one's feet** infml to come out of a difficult state of affairs without harm **13 fall short** to fail to reach a desired result, standard, etc.: The government planned to build 700 new offices last year, but they fell short (of their aim).

fall back v adv [I] to move or turn back: The crowd fell back to let the doctor through.

fall back on sthg. v adv prep [T] to use when

there is failure or lack of other means: Acting is a very uncertain profession, so you need something to fall back on, such as a university degree.

fall behind also **get behind** – v adv [I with] to fail to produce something on time: to fall behind with the rent/ one's work

fall for sbdy./sthg. v prep [T] **1** to be cheated by: Don't fall for his tricks. **2** infml to fall in love with, esp. suddenly: She fell for him in a big way.

fall off v adv [I] to become less in quality, amount, etc.: Membership in the club has fallen off this year.

fall on sbdy./sthg. v prep [T] to attack eagerly: (fig.) The hungry children fell on the food.

fall out v adv [I with] to quarrel: Jean and Paul have fallen out with each other again.

fall through v adv [I] to fail to be completed: The plan fell through.

fall² n **1** [C] an act of falling: He had a bad fall and broke his wrist.|It's a fall of 200 feet to the bottom of the cliff.|(fig.) a fall from grace (=from favor) **2** [C; the S] AmE|also **autumn**– the season between summer and winter when leaves change color: We've had a beautiful fall this year.|We met in the fall of 1981. **3** [C] something that has fallen: A fall of rocks blocked the road.|a fall of snow **4** [C] a decrease in quantity, price, demand, degree, etc.: a sudden fall in temperature –opposite **rise 5** [S of] a defeat: the fall of France/of the government –see also FALLS

fal·la·cious /fə'leᵞʃəs/ adj fml **1** likely or intended to deceive **2** containing or based on false reasoning: a fallacious argument –**fallaciously** adv

fal·la·cy /'fæləsiᵞ/ n -**cies 1** [C] a false idea or belief: It is a popular fallacy that money always brings happiness. **2** [C;U] false reasoning, as in an argument

fall·en /'fɔlən/ v past participle of FALL

fall guy /'· ·/ n AmE infml a person who is easily cheated or tricked; SCAPEGOAT

fal·li·ble /'fæləbəl/ adj able or likely to make a mistake: Everybody is fallible. –opposite **infallible** –**fallibility** /,fælə'bɪləṭiᵞ/ n [U]

falling-out /,·· '·/ n **fallings-out** or **falling-outs** AmE a quarrel: They had a falling-out and haven't spoken to each other since then.

fall·out /'fɔlaʊt/ n [U] the dangerous dust, containing RADIOACTIVITY, that is left in the air after an atomic (or NUCLEAR) explosion

fal·low /'fæloʷ/ adj (of land) dug (or PLOWED) but left unplanted to improve its quality: We'll leave that field fallow for a year.

falls /fɔlz/ n [P] →WATERFALL: Niagara Falls

false /fɔls/ adj **1** not true or correct: false statements/ ideas|A **false start** in a race is when a runner leaves the starting line too soon. **2** not faithful or loyal: a false friend **3** not real: false teeth/diamonds **4** made or changed so as to deceive: false weights|The thieves got into the house **under false pretenses** by saying they had come to repair the telephone. **5 false alarm** a warning of something bad which does not happen: Someone shouted "Fire!" but it was a false alarm and

SPELLING NOTE

Words with the sound /f/ may be spelled **ph-**, like **photograph**.

there was no danger. –**falsely** *adv* –**falseness** *n* [U]

false·hood /'fɔlshʊd/ also **falsity** /'fɔlsətiʸ/– *n* [C;U] (the telling of) an untrue statement; lie

false teeth /ˌ· '·/ *n* [P] a set of teeth made of plastic and worn in the mouth of a person who has lost all or most of his/her natural teeth

fal·set·to /fɔl'sɛtoʷ/ *n* -**tos** [C;U] (a man with) an unnaturally high singing voice

fal·si·fy /'fɔlsəˌfaɪ/ *v* -**fied, -fying** [T] **1** to make false by changing something: *to falsify the records/facts* **2** to state or represent falsely: *Her speech before Congress was falsified by the newspapers.* –**falsification** /ˌfɔlsəfəˈkeʸʃən/ *n* [C;U]

fal·ter /'fɔltər/ *v* **1** [I;T *out*] to walk, move, or say (something) unsteadily, as through weakness or fear: *The sick man faltered a few steps then fell.|Her voice faltered, and then she lost consciousness.* **2** [I] to lose strength of purpose or action; HESITATE: *He faltered for a while and was unable to make a decision.* –**falteringly** *adv*

fame /feʸm/ *n* [U] the condition of being well known and talked about: *She hoped to find fame as a poet.* –**famed** *adj: The Rocky Mountains are famed for their beauty.*

fa·mil·iar /fə'mɪlyər/ *adj* **1** [*to*] generally known, seen, or experienced; common: *a familiar sight* **2** [F *with*] having a thorough knowledge (of): *Are you familiar with the rules of football?* –opposite **unfamiliar 3** *derog* too friendly for the occasion: *The man's familiar behavior angered the woman.*

fa·mil·iar·i·ty /fəˌmɪlˈyærətiʸ, -ˌmɪliʸˈær-/ *n* [U] **1** [*with*] thorough knowledge (of): *His familiarity with many foreign languages surprised us all.* **2** freedom of behavior usu. only expected in the most friendly relations: *They behaved towards each other with great familiarity.*

fa·mil·iar·ize *v* sbdy. **with** sthg.‖also -**ise** *BrE* /fə'mɪlyəˌraɪz/ *v prep* -**ized, -izing** [T] to make (oneself or someone else) informed about: *I spent the first few weeks familiarizing myself with the new job.*

fa·mil·iar·ly /fə'mɪlyərliʸ/ *adv* in an informal, easy, or friendly manner

fam·i·ly /'fæməliʸ/ *n* -**lies 1** [C] any group of people related by blood or marriage, esp. a group of two parents and their children: *My family is very large.|Everyone in my family is tall.|Our family has lived in this house for over a hundred years.|We are so close that we are like family. –see illustration on page 247* **2** [A] suitable for children as well as older people: *a family movie* **3** [S;U] children: *Do you have any family?* **4** [C] a group of things, esp. plants or animals, related by common characteristics: *The cat family includes lions and tigers.* **5 run in the family** (of a quality) to be shared by several members of a family: *She and her father both have a good sense of humour; it seems to run in the family.*

family man /'··· ˌ·/ *n* a man who is fond of home life with his family

family plan·ning /ˌ··· '··/ *n* [U] the control-

ling of the number of children born in a family by the use of any of various (CON-TRACEPTIVE) methods

family tree /ˌ··· '·/ *n* a plan of the relationship of the members of a family

fam·ine /'fæmɪn/ *n* [C;U] (a case of) very serious lack of food: *Many people die during famines every year.* –compare HUNGER

fam·ished /'fæmɪʃt/ *adj* [F] suffering from very great hunger

fa·mous /'feʸməs/ *adj* very well-known: *a famous actor|France is famous for its fine food and wine.*

USAGE Compare **famous, well-known, distinguished, eminent, notorious,** and **infamous: 1 Famous** is like **well-known,** but **famous** is a stronger word and means known over a wide area: *the doctor, the mailman, and other* **well-known** *people in the village|A* **famous** *movie star has come to live in our town.* **2 Distinguished** and **eminent** are used esp. of people who are famous for serious work in science, the arts, etc.: *a* **distinguished** *writer|an* **eminent** *scientist.* **3 Notorious** means famous for something bad; **infamous** also means very bad, but not necessarily famous: *Everyone was talking about the* **notorious** *murderer.|the* **infamous** *killing of an unarmed policeman.*

fa·mous·ly /'feʸməsliʸ/ *adv infml* very well: *She is doing famously in her new job.*

fan¹ /fæn/ *n* an instrument meant to make a flow of (cool) air, such as an arrangement of feathers or paper in a half circle waved by hand, or a series of broad blades turned by a motor

fan² *v* -**nn- 1** [T] to cause air to blow on (something) (as if) with a FAN¹: *She fanned her face with a newspaper.* **2** [I;T *out*] to spread like a FAN¹: *The soldiers fanned out across the hillside.*

fan³ *n* a very eager follower or supporter, esp. of a sport or famous person: *football fans|The famous singer employed two people to answer his* **fan mail**. (=letters sent to him by fans)

fa·nat·ic /fə'nætɪk/ also **fanatical** /fə'nætɪkəl/– *adj* showing very great and often unreasoning eagerness, esp. in religious or political matters –**fanatic** *n: a health food fanatic* –**fanatically** *adv* –**fanaticism** /fə'nætəˌsɪzəm/ *n* [C;U]

fan·ci·er /'fænsiʸər/ *n* a person who has a special interest, esp. in breeding or training certain types of birds, dogs, plants, etc.: *a dog-fancier*

fan·ci·ful /'fænsɪfəl/ *adj* **1** showing imagination rather than reason and experience: *a fanciful poet* **2** unreal; imaginary –**fancifully** *adv*

fan·cy¹ /'fænsiʸ/ *n* -**cies 1** [U] the power of creating imaginative ideas and expressions **2** [C] an image, opinion, or idea imagined: *I think he will come, but it's only a fancy of mine.* **3** [C] a liking formed without the help of reason: *I have* **taken a fancy to** *that silly hat.*

fancy² *v* -**cied, -cying** [T] **1** to form a picture of; imagine: *Fancy having a fool like that for* *a husband!*|*Fancy that!* **2** *esp. BrE* to have a liking for; wish for: *I fancy something sweet to eat.* **3** [+(*that*)] *fml esp. BrE* to think: *He fancied (that) he had met her before.* **4 fancy oneself** to have a very high (perhaps too high) opinion of oneself: *He fancies himself (as) the fastest swimmer.*

fancy³ *adj* **-cier, -ciest** ornamental or brightly colored; not ordinary: *fancy dresses*|*fancy cakes*|*They are too fancy for me.* **–fancily** *adv*

fancy-free /ˌ·· '·/ *adj* free to do anything or like anyone, esp. because not bound by love, esp. in the phrase **footloose and fancy-free**

fan·fare /'fænfɛər/ *n* a short loud piece of music played, esp. on the TRUMPET, to introduce a person or event

fang /fæŋ/ *n* a long sharp tooth, as of a dog or a poisonous snake

fan·tas·tic /fæn'tæstɪk/ *adj* **1** odd, strange, or wild in shape, meaning, etc.: *fantastic dream*|*story*|*fears* **2** (of an idea, plan, etc.) too unrelated to reality to be practical or reasonable **3** *infml* very good; wonderful: *a fantastic meal* **–fantastically** *adv*

fan·ta·sy /'fæntəsiʸ, -ziʸ/ *n* **-sies** [C;U] (a creation of) imagination: *The story is a fantasy.*|*He lives in a world of fantasy.* **–fantasize** /'fæntəˌsaɪz/ *v* [I;T *about*] **-sized, -sizing:** *He spends too much time fantasizing about things that will never happen.*

far¹ /fɑr/ *adj* **farther** /'fɑrðər/ *or* **further** /'fɜrðər/, **farthest** /'fɑrðɪst/ *or* **furthest** /'fɜrðɪst/ **1** distant; a long way off: *Shall we walk? It's not far.*|*a far country* **2** [A *no comp.*] (of one of two things) more distant: *Can we fish here, or must we cross to the far bank of the river?* **3 a far cry** a long way; very different: *This big house is a far cry from that little apartment they used to live in.* **–compare** NEAR

far² *adv* **farther** *or* **further, farthest** *or* **furthest** **1** [*adv* +*adv*/*prep*] a long way: *We walked far into the woods.*|*How far is it from here?* (=What is the distance?)|*It's not far beyond the church.*|*We worked far into the night.* (=very late)|*His rudeness went too far.* (=He was too rude) **2** very much: *far better*| *far too busy* **3 far as/so far as** to the degree that: *I will help you as far as I can.*|*So far as I know, they're coming.* **4 far from** rather than; instead of: *Far from being angry, he's delighted.* **5 how far** how much: *I don't know how far to believe him.* **6 so far: a** until now: *I've been here three weeks, and so far I've enjoyed it.* **b** up to a certain point: *You can trust him only so far and no further.* **7 far and wide** everywhere **8 so far, so good** things are satisfactory to this point, at least: *Our plan seems to be working. So far, so good.* –see also FAR-OFF, FAR-REACHING, FARSIGHTED –see FURTHER (USAGE)

USAGE **Far** is used in questions or NEGATIVES² about distance: *How far did you walk?*|*Did you walk far?*|*No, we didn't walk*

far. It is also used in simple statements after *too, as,* and *so: Yes, we walked as* **far** *as the river.*|*We walked much too* **far**! (compare *Yes, we walked a long way.* **Far** could not be used here.)

far·a·way /'fɑrəˌweʸ/ *adj* distant: *a faraway place*|*a faraway* (=dreamy) *look in her eyes*

farce /fɑrs/ *n* **1** [C;U] a (type of) light humorous play full of silly things happening **2** [C] an occasion or set of events that is a silly and empty show: *The talks were a farce since the President had already made the decision.* **–farcical** *adj* **–farcically** *adv*

fare¹ /fɛər/ *n* **1** [C] the price charged to carry a person, as by bus, train, or taxi **2** [C] a paying passenger, esp. in a taxi **3** [U] food, esp. as provided at a meal: *good*|*simple fare*

fare² *v* **fared, faring** *fml* to get along: *I think I fared pretty well on the examination.*

fare·well /ˌfɛər'wɛl/ *n,interj* →GOODBYE: *We'll have a farewell party before we leave.*

far·fetched /ˌfɑr'fɛtʃt◂/ *adj* improbable or difficult to believe: *a far-fetched excuse*

far-flung /ˌ· '·◂/ *adj* spread over a great distance: *Our far-flung trade connections cover the world.*

far-gone /ˌ· '·/ *adj infml* in an advanced state of something unpleasant such as debt, illness, etc.: *She always liked to drink, but now she's really far-gone.*

farm¹ /fɑrm/ *n* an area of land, with its buildings, concerned with the growing of crops or the raising of animals: *a chicken farm*|*We work on the farm.*

farm² *v* [I;T] to use (land) for growing crops, raising animals, etc.

   farm sthg.↔ **out** *v adv* [T] to send (work) for other people to do: *We have more work here than we can deal with, and so we have to farm some out.*

farm·er /'fɑrmər/ *n* a person who owns or plans the work on a farm

farm·house /'fɑrmhaus/ *n* the main house on a farm, where the farmer lives

farm·ing /'fɑrmɪŋ/ *n* [U] the practice or business of being in charge of or working on a farm

farm·yard /'fɑrmyɑrd/ *n* a yard surrounded by farm buildings

far-off /ˌ· '·◂/ *adj* distant in space or time

far-out /ˌ· '·◂/ *adj infml* very different or uncommon; strange: *far-out clothes*|*ideas*| *people*

far-reach·ing /ˌ· '··◂/ *adj* having a wide influence or effect: *They're demanding far-reaching political changes.*

far·sight·ed /ˌfɑr'saɪtɪd◂, 'fɑrˌsaɪtɪd/ *adj* **1** able to see the future effects of present actions –opposite **shortsighted 2** *AmE*|| **longsighted** *BrE*– able to see objects clearly or read things only when they are far from the eyes –opposite **nearsighted –farsightedness** *n* [U]

far·ther /'fɑrðər/ *also* **further–** *adv,adj* [*adv* +*adv*/*prep*] (COMPARATIVE² *of* FAR) more far: *We walked a mile farther*|*further down the road.*|*We can't go any farther*|*further ahead with this plan.* –see FURTHER (USAGE)

far·thest /'fɑrðɪst/ *also* **furthest–** *adv,adj* [*adv*

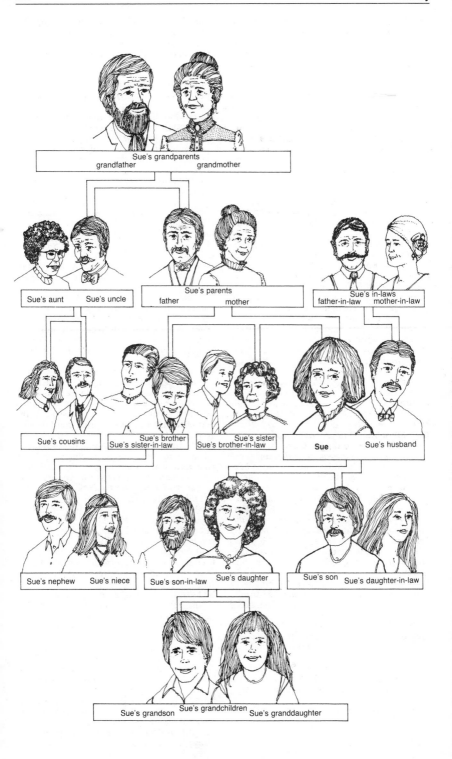

Sue's grandparents
grandfather   grandmother

Sue's aunt   Sue's uncle

Sue's parents
father   mother

Sue's in-laws
father-in-law   mother-in-law

Sue's cousins

Sue's brother
Sue's sister-in-law

Sue's sister
Sue's brother-in-law

Sue   Sue's husband

Sue's nephew   Sue's niece

Sue's son-in-law   Sue's daughter

Sue's son   Sue's daughter-in-law

Sue's grandson   Sue's grandchildren   Sue's granddaughter

+*adv/prep*] (SUPERLATIVE² of FAR) most far: *Who can swim farthest/furthest?*|*Our house is the farthest/furthest away from the center of town.* –see FURTHER (USAGE)

fas·ci·nate /'fæsə,neʸt/ *v* **-nated, -nating** [T *with/by*] to charm powerfully; be very interesting to: *I'm fascinated with/by Buddhist ceremonies.* –**fascinating** *adj*: *Your ideas are fascinating.* –**fascinatingly** *adv* –**fascination** /,fæsə'neʸʃən/ *n* [S;U]: *Old castles have a certain strange fascination for me.*

fas·cism /'fæʃizəm/ *n* [U] (*often cap.*) a political system in which all industrial activity is controlled by the state, no political opposition is allowed, nationalism is strongly encouraged, and SOCIALISM violently opposed

fas·cist /'fæʃist/ *n,adj* **1** (*often cap.*) (a supporter) of FASCISM: *fascist opinions*|*the Fascist party* **2** *derog* (a supporter) of very RIGHT WING ideas

fash·ion¹ /'fæʃən/ *n* **1** [C;U] the way of dressing or behaving that is considered the best at a certain time: *Long skirts are the latest fashion.*|*Fashions have changed since I was young.*|*Long hair is very much out of/in fashion* (=not) considered very modern) *now.* **2** [U] changing custom, esp. in women's clothing: *to study the history of fashion* **3** [S] *fml* a manner; way of making or doing something: *He behaves in a very strange fashion.* **4 after a fashion** not very well: *John speaks Russian after a fashion, but Jean speaks it much better.* **5 -fashion** in a certain way; like a certain person, animal, ect.: *She wore her hair schoolgirl-fashion.*

fashion² *v* [T] *fml* to shape or make, usually with one's hands: *He fashioned the clay into a pot.*

fash·ion·a·ble /'fæʃənəbəl/ *adj* (made, dressed, etc.) according to the latest fashion: *a fashionable hat/woman/restaurant* –opposite **unfashionable**; see also OLD-FASHIONED –**fashionably** *adv*: *fashionably dressed*|*to dress fashionably*

fast¹ /fæst/ *adj* **1** quick; moving quickly: *a fast car*|*fast music* **2** firm; firmly fixed: *The colors aren't fast, so be careful when you wash this shirt.*|*He made the rope fast* (=tied it firmly) *to the metal ring.* **3** [F; after *n*] (of a clock) showing a time that is later than the true time: *My watch is fast/is five minutes fast.* –compare SLOW

fast² *adv* **1** quickly: *You're learning very fast.*|*He ran faster and faster.* **2** firmly; tightly: *to stick fast in the mud* **3 fast asleep** sleeping deeply

fast³ *v* [I] to eat no food, esp. for religious reasons: *Muslims fast during Ramadan.*

fast⁴ *n* an act or period of FASTING³

fas·ten /'fæsən/ *v* [I;T *up, together, to*] to make or become firmly fixed or joined: *He fastened (up) his coat.*|*The bag doesn't fasten easily.*|*The door fastens with a hook.*|(fig.)

SPELLING NOTE
Words with the sound /f/ may be spelled **ph-**, like **photograph**.

She fastened her eyes on him. –opposite **unfasten**

fasten on/upon sthg. *v prep* [T] to seize on; take and use: *The President fastened on the idea at once.*

fas·ten·er /'fæsənər/ *n* something that fastens things together: *Please do up the fasteners on the back of my dress.* –compare ZIPPER

fas·ten·ing /'fæsənɪŋ/ *n* something that holds things shut, esp. doors and windows

fast food /ˌ· '·/ *n esp. AmE* [C;U] food that is prepared and served quickly, esp. HAMBURGERs and fried (FRY) chicken: *a fast-food restaurant/chain*

fas·tid·i·ous /fæˈstɪdiʸəs, fə-/ *adj* difficult to please; disliking anything at all dirty, unpleasant, or rough: *I knew he wouldn't enjoy going camping; he's too fastidious!* –**fastidiously** *adv*

fast·ness /'fæstnɪs/ *n* [U] the quality of being firm and fixed: *the fastness of a color*

USAGE There is no noun formed from **fast** when it means **quick**. Use instead **speed** or **quickness**: *The car went very fast/at great speed.*

fat¹ /fæt/ *adj* **-tt-** **1** (of creatures and their bodies) having (too) much fat: *fat cattle*|*You'll get even fatter if you eat all that cake.* **2** thick and well-filled; plentiful: *a fat bank account*|*fat profits* **3 a fat lot of** *infml* no; not any: *A fat lot of good that is!* –**fatness** *n* [U] –**fattish** *adj*

fat² *n* [U] **1** the material under the skins of animals and human beings which helps to keep them warm **2** this substance considered as food or used in cooking: *potatoes fried in deep fat* –compare LEAN² (2) **3 live on/off the fat of the land** to live in great comfort with plenty to eat –see CHEW (3) **the fat**

fa·tal /'feʸtl/ *adj* **1** [*to*] causing or resulting in death: *a fatal accident/illness* **2** very dangerous and unfortunate: *the fatal decision to return to the burning house* –compare FATEFUL –**fatally** *adv*: *fatally wounded*

fa·tal·ism /'feʸtl,ɪzəm/ *n* [U] the belief that events are decided by FATE (1) –**fatalist** *n* –**fatalistic** /,feʸtl'ɪstɪk/ *adj*

fa·tal·i·ty /feʸ'tælətiʸ, fə-/ *n* **-ties** [C;U] *fml* a violent accidental death: *It was a bad crash, but surprisingly there were no fatalities.*

fat cat /ˌ· '·/ *n AmE infml* a comfortable rich person, esp. one who gives money to a political party

fate /feʸt/ *n* **1** [S *often cap.*] the imaginary cause beyond human control that is believed to decide events: *He expected to spend his life in Italy, but fate had decided otherwise.* **2** [C] an end or result, esp. death: *They met with a terrible fate.* **3** [C] (a person's) future; what will happen to (one): *I wonder whether the examiners have decided our fate yet?*|*Now that oil is scarce, the fate of the automobile is uncertain.*

fat·ed /'feʸtɪd/ *adj* [F +*to-v/that*] caused or fixed by FATE (1): *It was fated that we should meet/We were fated to meet.*

fate·ful /'feʸtfəl/ *adj* important (esp. in a bad way) for the future: *the fateful night of the* *accident* –compare FATAL –**fatefully** *adv*

fa·ther[1] /ˈfɑðər/ *n* a male parent: *the fathers and mothers of the children*|(fig.) *He was the father* (=originator) *of modern scientific thought.* –see illustration on page 247 –**fatherless** *adj*

father[2] *v* [T] *old use or humor* (of a man) to cause the birth of (one's child):(fig.) *to father a plan*|*an invention*

Father [A] (a title of respect for) a priest, esp. in the ROMAN CATHOLIC Church: *Father O'Neal is our local priest.*

father fig·ure /ˈ·· ˌ·/ *n* an older man on whom one depends for advice and help

fa·ther·hood /ˈfɑðərˌhʊd/ *n* [U] the state of being a father: *the responsibilities of fatherhood*

father-in-law /ˈ··· · ˌ/ *n* **fathers-in-law** the father of one's wife or husband –see illustration on page 247

fa·ther·ly /ˈfɑðərliʸ/ *adj* like or typical of a father: *Let me give you some fatherly advice.* –**fatherliness** *n* [U]

Father's Day /ˈ·· ˌ·/ *n* a day on which respect and admiration are shown to fathers, usu. the third Sunday in June

fath·om[1] /ˈfæðəm/ *n* a measure (6 feet or 1·8 meters) of the depth of water: *The boat sank in 20 fathoms.*

fathom[2] *v* [T *out*] to get at the true meaning of; understand: *I can't fathom your meaning*|*fathom what you mean.*

fa·tigue[1] /fəˈtiʸg/ *n* [U] **1** great tiredness: *He was pale with fatigue after his sleepless night.* **2** *tech* the tendency of a metal to break as the result of repeated bending

fatigue[2] *v* **-tigued, -tiguing** [T] *fml* to make tired: *a very fatiguing job*

fa·tigues /fəˈtiʸgz/ also **fatigue uniform** /·ˈ· ˌ···/– *n* [P] *AmE* informal army clothes

fat·ten /ˈfætn/ *v* [T *up*] to make (a creature) fat: *Have some more cake! You need to fatten up.*

fat·ty /ˈfætiʸ/ *adj* **-tier, -tiest** (of food) containing a lot of fat –**fattiness** *n* [U]

fat·u·ous /ˈfætʃuʷəs/ *adj* very silly without seeming to know it: *What a fatuous remark!* –**fatuously** *adv* –**fatuity** /fəˈtuʷ-/ *n* [U]

fau·cet /ˈfɔsɪt/ *AmE*‖also **tap**– an apparatus for controlling the flow of liquid from a pipe, esp. in a kitchen or BATHROOM –compare HYDRANT; see illustration on page 379

fault[1] /fɔlt/ *n* **1** a mistake or imperfection: *a small electrical fault in the motor*|*Through no fault of her own* (=not because of any mistake she made) *she lost her job.*|*Which driver was at fault* (=in the wrong) *in the car crash?*|*She's always finding fault with* (=complaining about) *the way I do my hair.* **2** *tech* (in GEOLOGY) a crack in the earth's surface **3** be one's fault to be something for which one can rightly be blamed: *Whose fault is it (that) we're late? It's not my fault.*

fault[2] *v* [T] (used only in NEGATIVEs[2], questions, etc.) to find a FAULT[1] (1) in: *It was impossible to fault her performance.*

fault·less /ˈfɔltlɪs/ *adj* without a fault; perfect: *a faultless performance on the piano* –**faultlessly** *adv* –**faultlessness** *n* [U]

fault·y /ˈfɔltiʸ/ *adj* **-ier, -iest** having FAULTs[1] (1): *a faulty wire in the electrical system*|*faulty reasoning* –**faultily** *adv*

fau·na /ˈfɔnə/ *n* **-nas** or **-nae** /niʸ, naɪ/ [C;U] *tech* all the animals living in a particular place, or of a particular age in history: *the fauna of the forest* –compare FLORA

faux pas /ˌfoʷ ˈpɑ/ *n* **faux pas** /ˌfoʷ ˈpɑz/ a social mistake, in words or behaviour

fa·vor[1] *AmE*‖**favour** *BrE* /ˈfeʸvər/ *n* **1** [C] a kind act: *I want to ask a favor of you: will you lend me your car?*|*Do me a favor and turn off that radio!* **2** [U] active approval: *I'm afraid I'm out of favor with her* (=she is annoyed with me) *at the moment.*|*He worked hard to get back in the teacher's favor.*|*He did all he could to win her favor.* –see also DISFAVOR **3** [U] unfairly kind treatment to one person, to the disadvantage of others: *The teacher refused to have his daughter in his class for fear of showing favor to her.* **4 in favor** of approving or choosing: *Are you in favor of gun control?*|*He refused a job in the steel industry in favor of a university appointment.* **5 in one's favor** to one's advantage: *The bank has made an ERROR* (=mistake) *in your favor: we owe you $100.*

favor[2] *AmE*‖**favour** *BrE* *v* [T] **1** to be unfairly fond of; treat with FAVOR[1] (3): *A mother shouldn't favor one of her children more than the others.* **2** [T] to believe in (a plan or idea); regard with FAVOR[1] (2): *Did he favor your suggestion?*

favor sbdy. **with** sthg. *v prep* [T] *fml* to give (someone, something nice): *She favored him with a charming smile.*

fa·vor·able *AmE*‖**favourable** *BrE* /ˈfeʸvərəbəl/ *adj fml* **1** (of a message, answer, etc.) saying what one wants to hear: *I hear favorable accounts of your work.* **2** [*to*] (of conditions) advantageous: *The company will lend you money on very favorable terms.* –opposite **unfavorable**; compare FAVORITE[2] –**favorably** *adv*

USAGE Compare **favorable** and **favorite**: Your **favorite** (thing or person) is the one you like the best. Conditions are **favorable** when they are helpful, and words are **favorable** when they express agreement or approval: *What's your favorite television program?*|*John's a great favorite with me.*|*The game will be played on Saturday if the weather is favorable.*|*a favorable answer to my letter*

fa·vor·ite[1] *AmE*‖**favourite** *BrE* /ˈfeʸvərɪt/ *n* **1** something or someone that is loved above all others: *These books are my favorites.* **2** *derog* someone who receives too much FAVOR[1] (3): *A teacher shouldn't have/make favorites in the class.* **3** (in horseracing) the horse in each race that is expected to win: *The favorite came in second.* –compare OUTSIDER (2) –see FAVORABLE (USAGE)

favorite[2] *AmE*‖**favourite** *BrE* *adj* being a favorite: *What's your favorite television program?* –compare FAVORABLE; see FAVORABLE (USAGE)

fa·vor·it·ism *AmE*‖**favouritism** *BrE* /ˈfeʸvərə

ˌtızəm/ *n* [U] *derog* the practice of showing
FAVOR¹ (3)

favorite son /ˌ··· ᐧ·/ *n AmE* someone favored
by his state as a possible President of the US

fawn /fɔn/ *n* **1** [C] a young deer **2** [S;U] a light
yellowish-brown color

fawn on/upon sbdy. *v prep* [T] **1** (of dogs) to
jump on, rub against (someone), etc., as an
expression of love **2** to try to gain the favor of
(someone) by being (often insincerely) attentive: *They were fawning on their rich
uncle.*

FBI *n abbrev. for*: Federal Bureau of Investigation; the police department in the US
that is controlled by the central (FEDERAL)
government, and is particularly concerned
with matters of national SECURITY (=the protection of political secrets): *a member of the
FBI*

fear¹ /fɪər/ *n* [C;U +*that*] the feeling that one
has when danger is near; the feeling that
something (usu. unpleasant) is likely to happen: *I couldn't move for* (=because of)
*fear.|She has a great fear of fire.|The ad-
ministration's fear/fears that the unemployment figures would rise again was/were today
proved correct.|There's* **not much fear**
(=likelihood) *of snow at this time of
year.|We live in* **daily fear of** *an enemy attack.*

fear² *v* [not *be* +*v-ing*] *fml* **1** [T] to be afraid
of: *He has always feared mice.* **2** [I *for*] to be
afraid (for the safety of someone or something): *She feared for the lost child.* **3 I fear**
(*used when telling bad news*) I'm sorry that I
must say: *It's raining, I fear.|I fear we'll be
late.*

fear·ful /ˈfɪərfəl/ *adj* **1** [+*that/of*] *fml* afraid:
He was fearful of her anger. –opposite **fearless 2** causing fear: *a fearful storm* **3** very bad;
very great; FRIGHTFUL: *What a fearful waste
of time!* –**fearfully** *adv*: *a fearfully cold day*
–**fearfulness** *n* [U]

fear·less /ˈfɪərlɪs/ *adj* [*of*] without fear: *fearless of what might happen* –opposite **fearful**
–**fearlessly** *adv* –**fearlessness** *n* [U]

fear·some /ˈfɪərsəm/ *adj often humor* causing fear: *a fearsome sight*

fea·si·ble /ˈfiʸzəbəl/ *adj* able to be done;
possible: *Your plan sounds quite feasible.*
–**feasibility** /ˌfiʸzəˈbɪlətiʸ/ *n* [U] –**feasibly**
/ˈfiʸzəbliʸ/ *adv*

feast¹ /fiʸst/ *n* **1** a splendid esp. public meal:
The king gave/held a feast. **2** a day kept in
memory of a religious event: *Christmas is an
important feast for Christians.*

feast² *v* **1** [I *on, upon*] to eat and drink very
well **2** [T *on, upon*] *fml* to feed (someone)
especially well (on): (fig.) *He feasted his eyes
on the beautiful scene.*

feat /fiʸt/ *n* a clever action, showing strength,
skill, or courage: *It was quite a feat to move
that piano by yourself.*

feath·er /ˈfɛðər/ *n* **1** one of the many parts of
the covering which grows on a bird's body,

SPELLING NOTE
Words with the sound /f/ may be
spelled **ph-**, like **photograph**.

---

like a thin stick with soft hair-like material
on each side **2 a feather in one's cap** a
deserved honor that one is proud of: *They
want you to photograph the President?
That'll be quite a feather in your cap!* **3 birds
of a feather** people of the same (often bad)
kind

feather² *v* **feather one's nest** to make oneself
rich, esp. dishonestly, while in a trusted
position

feath·er·y /ˈfɛðəriʸ/ *adj* **1** covered with
feathers **2** soft and light: *feathery pastry*

fea·ture¹ /ˈfiʸtʃər/ *n* **1** a (typical or noticeable) part or quality: *Wet weather is a feature
of life in this country.* **2** any of the noticeable
parts of the face: *His nose is his best fea-
ture.|to have regular features* **3** a special long
newspaper article: *a front-page feature on
coal mining* **4** a full-length movie with an
invented story –compare DOCUMENTARY²

feature² *v* **-tured, -turing** **1** [T] to include as a
special FEATURE¹ (1): *a new movie featuring
Jack Nicholson* **2** [I] to be present as a FEA-
TURE¹ (1): *Work features largely in her life.*

Feb·ru·ar·y /ˈfɛbruʷˌɛriʸ, ˈfɛbyuʷˌɛriʸ/ also
Feb. *written abbrev.*– *n* the 2nd month of the
year

fe·ces *AmE*‖also **faeces** /ˈfiʸsiʸz/ *n* [P] *fml &
tech* the solid waste material passed from the
bowels

feck·less /ˈfɛklɪs/ *adj* (of a person or
behavior) worthless and without plans for
the future –**fecklessly** *adv* –**fecklessness** *n* [U]

fed¹ /fɛd/ *v past tense and participle of* FEED
–compare FED UP

fed² *n AmE infml* a FEDERAL officer who carries out the laws: *There have been several
inquiries into his business affairs by the feds.*

Fed *n* [*the* +S] *AmE infml* →FEDERAL RESERVE
BANK: *The Fed is going to raise interst rates.*

fed·er·al /ˈfɛdərəl/ *adj* **1** of or formed into a
political FEDERATION (1): *Switzerland is a
federal republic.* **2** (in the US) of or relating
to the central government of the FEDERATION
(1) as opposed to the states that form it: *to
pay both federal taxes and state taxes*

Federal Bu·reau of In·ves·ti·ga·tion
/ˌ··· ˌ··· ···ᐧ·/ *n* [*the* S] →FBI

fed·er·al·ism /ˈfɛdərəˌlɪzəm/ *n* [U] the belief
in political FEDERATION (1) –**federalist** *n,adj*

Federal Re·serve Bank ‖also **the Fed** *AmE
infml*– /ˌ··· ᐧ· ᐧ·/ *n* [*the* +S] (any of) 12 banks
set up in various parts of the US by the
central banking (**Federal Reserve**) system to
hold a supply (**reserve**) of money that can be
lent to other banks

fed·er·ate /ˈfɛdəˌreʸt/ *v* **-ated, -ating** [I;T] to
form or become a FEDERATION (1)

fed·er·a·tion /ˌfɛdəˈreʸʃən/ *n* **1** [C;U] (the
action of uniting) a group of states with one
government which decides foreign affairs,
defense, etc., but in which each state decides
its own affairs **2** [C] a group of societies,
organizations, etc., that have come together
in this way: *the American Federation of
Labor*

fed up /ˌ· ᐧ·/ *adj* [F +*that/about, with*] *infml*
unhappy, tired, and discontented: *I'm not
waiting any longer –I'm fed up!|I'm fed up*

with your complaints.

fee /fiʸ/ *n* a sum of money paid for professional services to a doctor, lawyer, private school, etc. –see PAY (USAGE)

fee·ble /'fiʸbəl/ *adj* weak; with little force: *Grandfather has been getting feebler lately.|a feeble joke* –**feebly** *adv* –**feebleness** *n* [U]

fee·ble·mind·ed /ˌfiʸbəl'maɪndɪd◄/ *adj euph* with less than the usual INTELLIGENCE (1)

feed¹ /fiʸd/ *v* **fed** /fɛd/, **feeding 1** [T *on, with*] to give food to: *to feed the dog|The baby will soon learn to feed himself.* |(fig.) *to feed the fire with logs* **2** [I] (esp. of animals or babies) to eat: *The horses were feeding quietly in the field.* **3** [T] to put, supply, or provide, esp. continually: *to feed the wire into/through the hole|The information is fed into the company's computer.*

feed on sthg. *v adv* [T] (of animals) to live on (a food): *Sheep feed mostly on grass.|(fig.)Her enemies fed on her misfortune.*

feed² *n* **1** [C] a meal taken by an animal **2** *infml humor* [S] a usu. large meal eaten by people: *That was a great feed we had last night.* **3** [U] food for animals: *a bag of chicken feed* –compare CHICKENFEED

feed·back /'fiʸdbæk/ *n* [U] information about the results of a set of actions, passed back to the person (or machine) in charge, so that changes can be made if necessary: *The company welcomes feedback from people who use the goods it produces.*

feed·bag /'fiʸdbæg/ *n AmE* **1** a bag hung around a horse's head to hold the food it eats **2** [U] **put on the feedbag** *infml humor* to eat: *I'm hungry. Let's put on the feedbag.*

feed·ing /'fiʸdɪŋ/ *n AmE* a meal taken by a baby: *When did the baby have her last feeding?*

feel¹ /fiʸl/ *v* **felt** /fɛlt/, **feeling 1** [T] to get knowledge of by touching with the fingers: *The doctor felt my arm to find out if it was broken.|I can't feel where the handle is.* **2** [T *for*] to search with the fingers rather than the eyes: *She felt in her bag for a pencil.* **3** [T] to experience the touch or movement of: *I felt an insect creep(ing) up my leg.* **4** [T] to suffer because of (a condition or event): *He feels the cold in winter.|She felt the death of her father very much.* **5** to have the experience of being, or seeming to oneself to be: *I feel ill.|She felt happy.|Please feel free to make suggestions.|I felt sure it was Marilyn.|I felt such a fool when I arrived three hours early.* **6** [I] to give a (sensation): *Your feet feel cold.|This sheet feels wet.|How does it feel to be famous?|I'm holding something that feels like a potato.* **7** [T+(*that*)] to have as an opinion; believe; but not as a result of reasoning: *I feel (that) you haven't been completely honest with me.|She felt unwanted.* **8** **feel as if/as though** to have or give the sensation that; seem to be: *I felt as if my leg had been broken.|My leg felt as though it was broken.* **9** **feel in one's bones that** to be certain that **10** **feel like** to have a wish for; want: *Do you feel like (having) a beer?|I don't feel like dancing now.* **11** **feel one's way: a** to

move carefully (as if) in the dark: *They felt their way down the dark passage.* **b** to act slowly and carefully: *He hasn't been on the job long and he's still feeling his way.*

feel for sbdy. *v prep* [T] to be sorry for; be unhappy about the suffering of

feel² *n* [S] **1** the sensation caused by feeling something: *Its skin has a rough feel.* **2** *infml* an act of feeling: *Let me have a feel in my pocket.* **3** **get the feel of** to become used to: *You'll soon get the feel of the new job/car.*

feel·er /'fiʸlər/ *n* **1** [*usu. pl.*] also **antenna**– the thread-like part on the front of an insect's head, with which it touches things **2** **put out feelers** to make a suggestion as a test of what others will think or do: *I'm putting out feelers to see if she'd like to come and work for us.*

feel·ing /'fiʸlɪŋ/ *n* **1** [S *of*] a consciousness of something felt: *a feeling of shame/danger/thirst/pleasure* **2** [S +(*that*)] a belief or opinion, not based on reason: *I have a feeling we're being followed.* **3** [U] the power to feel sensation: *He lost all feeling in his toes.* **4** [U] excitement of mind, esp. in a bad sense: *The new working hours caused a lot of* **bad/ill feeling** *at the factory.* **5** [U *for*] sympathy and understanding: *to play the piano with great feeling*

feel·ings /'fiʸlɪŋz/ *n* [P] sensations of joy, sorrow, hate, etc.; the part of a person's nature that feels, compared to the part that thinks: *She has very strong feelings on this subject.|You'll hurt his feelings* (=make him unhappy) *if you forget his birthday.*

feet /fiʸt/ *n pl. of* FOOT

feign /feʸn/ *v* [T +*that*] *fml* to pretend to have or be: *He feigned death.|a feigned illness*

feint /feʸnt/ *n* [*of*] *fml* a false attack or blow, made to draw the enemy's attention away from the real danger –sounds like **faint**

fe·line /'fiʸlaɪn/ *adj,n* (of or like) a member of the cat family: *Lions and tigers are felines.*

fell¹ /fɛl/ *v past tense of* FALL¹

fell² *v* [T] to cut or knock down: *a felled* OAK*|He felled the man at a* (=with one) *blow.*

fel·low¹ /'fɛloʷ/ *n* **1** *infml* a man: *See if those fellows want some beer.* **2** a GRADUATE¹ (3) student of a university to whom a certain amount of money is given for study **3** [*of*] a member (of a society connected with some branch of learning or of some university colleges)

fel·low² *adj* [A] another (of two or more things or people like oneself): *one's fellow creatures/prisoners/students|I have a lot of/a certain* **fellow feeling** (=sympathy) *for her because we were both born in the same country.*

fel·low·ship /'fɛloʷˌʃɪp, -lə-/ *n* **1** [C] a group or society: *Our son is a member of a youth fellowship.* **2** [C] the position or money given to a FELLOW¹ (2) **3** [U] the condition of being friends through sharing or doing something together; companionship

fel·o·ny /'fɛləniʸ/ *n* **-nies** *law* a serious crime: *Murder is a felony.* –compare MISDEMEANOR (2)

felt¹ /fɛlt/ *past tense and participle of* FEEL

felt² *n* [U] thick firm cloth made of wool, hair,

or fur, pressed flat: *a felt hat*

felt-tip pen /ˌ · · ' ·/ *n* a pen with a small piece of FELT at the end instead of a metal point

fem. *adj written abbrev. said as:* FEMININE –compare MASC.

fe·male¹ /'fiʸmeʸl/ *n* a female person or animal –compare MALE (2)

female² *adj* **1** (typical) of the sex that gives birth to young: *a female elephant|the female form* **2** (of plants or flowers) producing fruit

USAGE **Female** and **male** are used to show what sex a creature is. **Feminine** and **masculine** are used of the qualities that are supposed to be typical of the two human sexes: **feminine** INTUITION. Men can have **feminine** (but not **female**) qualities, and women can have **masculine** (but not **male**) ones: *her loud* **masculine** *voice.|He has a rather* **feminine** *walk.*

fem·i·nine /'fɛmənɪn/ *adj* **1** of or having the qualities suitable for a woman: *She has a very feminine appearance.|He has a very feminine voice.* –see FEMALE (USAGE) **2** *tech* (in grammar) of a certain class of words: *"Actress" is the feminine form of "actor."* –compare MASCULINE, NEUTER¹ (1)

fem·i·nin·i·ty /ˌfɛmə'nɪnətiʸ/ *n* [U] the quality of being FEMININE (1) –compare MASCULINITY

fem·i·nism /'fɛmə,nɪzəm/ *n* [U] the principle that women should have the same rights and chances as men –compare WOMEN'S LIBERATION –**feminist** *n,adj*

fe·mur /'fiʸmər/ *n* **femurs** *or* **femora** /'fɛmərə/ *tech* the long bone in the upper part of the leg

fence¹ /fɛns/ *n* **1** a wall made of wood or wire, dividing two areas of land: *a backyard fence.* –see illustration on page 337 **2** *infml* someone who buys and sells stolen goods **3 sit on the fence** *usu. derog* to avoid taking sides in an argument

fence² *v* **fenced, fencing** **1** [I] to fight with a long thin pointed sword (FOIL) as a sport **2** [I] to avoid giving an honest answer –compare HEDGE² (2) **3** [T *around, in*] to put a fence around: (fig.) *I felt fenced in because the room was so small.*

fence sthg.↔**off** *v adv* [T] to separate or shut out (an area) with a fence: *We fenced off the lake so the children wouldn't fall in.*

fenc·ing /'fɛnsɪŋ/ *n* [U] **1** the sport of fencing (FENCE) **2** (material for making) fences: *surrounded by wire fencing|by a wire fence*

fend /fɛnd/ *v* **fend for oneself** to take care of oneself: *I've had to fend for myself since I was 14.*

fend sbdy./sthg.↔**off** *v adv* [T] to push away; act to avoid: (fig.) *She fended off the difficult questions.*

fend·er /'fɛndər/ *n* **1** *AmE‖***wing** *BrE*– the guard over the wheel of a car –see illustration on page 95 **2** a low metal wall around an open fireplace, to stop the coal from falling out

fer·ment¹ /fər'mɛnt/ *v* [I;T] **1** to (cause to) be

in a state of FERMENTATION: *fermented apple juice|The wine is beginning to ferment.* **2 a** to be in a state of political trouble and excitement **b** to cause (this state): *His speeches fermented trouble among the workers.*

fer·ment² /'fɜrmɛnt/ *n* [U] (the condition of) political trouble and excitement: *The whole country was in a state of ferment.*

fer·men·ta·tion /ˌfɜrmən'teʸʃən, -mɛn-/ *n* [U] the period or event of chemical change caused by the action of certain living substances such as YEAST: *Leave the beer/wine on the shelf during fermentation.|Milk becomes cheese by fermentation.*

fern /fɜrn/ *n* **ferns** *or* **fern** a green plant with feathery shaped leaves and no flowers

fe·ro·cious /fə'roʷʃəs/ *adj* fierce, cruel, and violent: *a ferocious lion|ferocious punishments* –**ferociously** *adv* –**ferocity** /fə'rɑsətiʸ/, **ferociousness** *n* [U]

fer·ret /'fɛrɪt/ *v* [I *about, around*] to search: *I've been ferreting around among my papers for the missing letter.*

ferret sthg.↔**out** *v adv* [T] to discover (something) by searching: *to ferret out the truth*

Fer·ris wheel /'fɛrɪs ˌhwiʸl, -ˌwiʸl/ *n AmE* a large upright wheel with passenger cars that turns around, usu. found at AMUSEMENT PARKS: *Let's go for a ride on the Ferris wheel.*

fer·rous /'fɛrəs/ *adj tech* related to or containing iron: *ferrous metals* –opposite **nonferrous**

fer·ry¹ /'fɛriʸ/ *v* **-ried, -rying** [T] to carry on or as if on a FERRY² (1): *They ferried back and forth across the Mississippi River.|ferrying the children to and from school in my car*

ferry² *n* **-ries 1** also **ferryboat** /'fɛriʸˌboʷt/– a boat that carries people and things across a narrow stretch of water: *You can cross the river by ferry.* **2** a place from which a ferry leaves: *We had to wait three hours at the ferry.*

fer·tile /'fɜrtl/ *adj* able to produce or grow many young, fruits, or seeds; *Some fish are very fertile. They lay thousands of eggs.|Wheat grows well on fertile soil.|*(fig.) *a fertile* (=inventive) *imagination* –opposite **infertile**; compare STERILE –**fertility** /fər'tɪlətiʸ/ *n* [U]: *a man's/woman's fertility*

fer·til·ize ‖ also **-ise** *BrE* /'fɜrtl̩ˌaɪz/ *v* **-ized, -izing** [T] **1** to start the development of young in (a female creature or plant): *Bees fertilize the flowers.* **2** to put FERTILIZER on (land) –**fertilization** /ˌfɜrtl̩-ə'zeʸʃən/ *n* [U]

fer·til·iz·er /'fɜrtl̩ˌaɪzər/ *n* [C;U] (any type of) chemical or natural substance that is put on the land to make crops grow better –compare MANURE

fer·vent /'fɜrvənt/ *adj* feeling or showing strong and warm feelings: *a fervent desire to win|She's a fervent believer in free speech.* –**fervently** *adv*

fer·vor *AmE‖***fervour** *BrE* /'fɜrvər/ *n* [U] the quality of being FERVENT

fes·ter /'fɛstər/ *v* [I] (of a cut or wound) to become infected and diseased: (fig.)*Injustice was a growth festering in the society.*

fes·ti·val /'fɛstəvəl/ *n* **1** a time of public

SPELLING NOTE

Words with the sound /f/ may be spelled **ph-**, like **photograph**.

gaiety and celebration, esp. to mark a religious occasion: *Christmas is one of the festivals of the Christian religion.* **2** a group of artistic performances (musical, theatrical, etc.) held usu. regularly in a particular place: *the Cannes Film Festival*

fes·tive /ˈfɛstɪv/ *adj* of or suitable for a FESTIVAL (1): *Christmas is often called the festive season.*

fes·tiv·i·ty /fɛˈstɪvət̬iᵛ/ *n* **-ties** [*usu. pl.*] a FESTIVE event: *to stay in the city during the festivities*

fes·toon /fɛˈstuʷn/ *v* [T *with*] to ornament with chains of flowers, RIBBONs, etc.: *to festoon the room with flowers*

fe·tal , **foetal** /ˈfiᵛt̬l/ *adj* of, related to, or in the state or condition of a FETUS: *a fetal position*

fetch /fɛtʃ/ *v* [T] **1** to go and get and bring back: *Run and fetch the doctor!* **2** *infml* to be sold for: *The house'll fetch at least $30,000.*

fetch·ing /ˈfɛtʃɪŋ/ *adj becoming rare* attractive; pleasing: *You look very fetching in that hat.*

fete¹ /feᵛt/ *n* a day of public gaiety and amusement held usu. out of doors and often to collect money for a special purpose: *Our town is holding a fete to raise money for the building of the new school.*

fete² *v* **feted, feting** [T *usu. pass.*] to show honor to (someone) with public parties and ceremonies: *The ambassador was feted everywhere she went.*

fet·id /ˈfɛt̬ɪd, ˈfiᵛ-/ *adj* smelling bad: *fetid water*

fet·ish /ˈfɛt̬ɪʃ/ *n* **1** an object that is worshipped and thought to have magic power **2** something to which one pays an unreasonable amount of attention, or which one admires to a foolish degree: *Make sure you clean your room before he comes; he* **has a fetish about/makes a fetish of** *tidiness.*

fet·ter¹ /ˈfɛt̬ər/ *n* [*usu. pl.*] a chain for the foot of a prisoner: (fig.) *to escape from the fetters of an unhappy marriage*

fetter² *v* [T] *fml* to bind with or as if with FETTERs: *fettered by responsibility*

fet·tle /ˈfɛt̬l/ *n* [U] condition; state of body and mind (in the phrase **in fine/good fettle**)

fe·tus , **foetus** /ˈfiᵛt̬əs/ *n tech* a young creature inside the mother, esp. at a later state when all its parts have been developed for use at birth —compare EMBRYO

feud /fyuʷd/ *n* a state of strong dislike and/or violence which continues over some time as a result of a quarrel, usu. between two families: *the feud between Romeo's family and Juliet's*

feu·dal /ˈfyuʷdl/ *adj* [A] of or relating to the system by which people held land, and received protection, in return for giving work to the land owner, as practiced in Western Europe from about the 9th to the 15th century: *the feudal system/one's feudal lord* —**feudalism** *n* [U]

fe·ver /ˈfiᵛvər/ *n* [S;U] (a medical condition caused by) an illness in which the sufferer suddenly develops a very high temperature: *yellow fever/She is running/has a very high fever.*|(fig.) *in a fever of impatience*|(fig.)*Our*

excitement rose to **fever pitch** (a high degree of excitement) *as the great day came near.*

fe·ver·ish /ˈfiᵛvərɪʃ/ *adj* (as if) caused by fever: *in a feverish condition*|*a feverish dream* —**feverishly** *adv: working feverishly* (=very quickly and excitedly)*to finish the job*

few /fyuʷ/ *determiner,pron,n* **1** [U +*pl. v.*] (*used without a* **to** *show the smallness of a number*) not many; not enough: *She has very few friends.*|*So few (members) came that we were unable to hold the meeting.*|*There were* **no fewer than** (=there were at least) *a thousand cars.*|*Which of you has the fewest mistakes?* —compare PLENTY, LITTLE³ (1); see MORE (USAGE) **2** [*always sing. in form but takes a pl. v; no comp.*] (*used with a*) a small number, but at least some: *We need a few eggs and a little milk.*|*Let's stay a few days longer.*|*Why not invite a few of your friends?*|*There are only a few* (=there are not many) *left.* —compare LITTLE³ (2) —see Study Notes on page 550 **3 few and far between** not happening often: *Holidays are few and far between.* **4 quite a few** also **a good few**–a reasonable number:*Quite a few of us are getting worried.*|*You'll have to wait a good few weeks.*

USAGE *Only a* **few** and *only a* **little** are the commonest ways to express the idea of "not enough": *Only a* **few** *of the children can read.*|*I understood only a* **little** *of his speech.*

fez /fɛz/ *n* **fezzes** *or* **fezes** a round red hat with a flat top and no BRIM, worn by some Muslim men

fi·an·cé /ˌfiᵛɑnˈseᵛ, fiᵛˈɑnseᵛ/ **fiancée** (*same pronunciation*) *fem.*– *n* a man to whom a woman is ENGAGED (=whom she has promised to marry): *George is my fiancé.*| *Martha is my fiancée.*

fi·as·co /fiᵛˈæskoʷ/ *n* **-coes, -cos** [C;U] the complete failure of something planned: *The party was a total fiasco/ended in fiasco.*

fib¹ /fɪb/ *n infml* a small unimportant lie

fib² *v* **-bb-** [I] to tell FIBs¹ —**fibber** *n*

fi·ber *AmE*‖**fibre** *BrE* /ˈfaɪbər/ *n* **1** [C] one of the thin thread-like parts that form many animal and plant growths such as wool, wood, or muscle **2** [U] a mass of threads, used for making cloth, rope, etc.: *Cotton is a natural fiber; nylon is a man-made fiber.* **3** [U] strength of character: *He lacks moral fiber.* —**fibrous** /ˈfaɪbrəs/ *adj*

fi·ber·glass *AmE*‖**fibreglass** *BrE* /ˈfaɪbərˌglæs/ *n* [U] material made from glass FIBERs used for car bodies, furnishing materials, building light boats, etc.

fick·le /ˈfɪkəl/ *adj* not loyal in love or friendship; often changing: *He's changed his mind again; he's so fickle!* —**fickleness** *n* [U]

fic·tion /ˈfɪkʃən/ *n* **1** [U] stories or NOVELs about things that did not really happen, as compared to other sorts of literature like history or poetry: *a writer of popular fiction*|*Truth is sometimes stranger than fiction.* —see also NONFICTION **2** [S;U] an invention of the mind; an untrue story; invented information: *The newspaper's account of what happened was a complete fiction.* —compare FACT

fic·tion·al /'fɪkʃənəl/ *adj* belonging to FICTION (1); told as a story: *a fictional account of a journey to the moon* –compare FICTITIOUS

fic·ti·tious /fɪk'tɪʃəs/ *adj* [*no comp.*] untrue; invented; not real: *Hamlet was a fictitious character.* –Compare: *His account of the bank robbery was completely* **fictitious**. (=the robbery really happened, but his account of it was untrue)|*a* **fictional** *account of a bank robbery* (=a story of an imaginary event)

fid·dle¹ /'fɪdl/ *n infml* **1** a VIOLIN, or any musical instrument of that family: *Can you play the fiddle?*|*I'm tired of* **playing second fiddle to** (=taking a less important part than) *George. Why can't I run the business?* **2** a dishonest practice **3** (as) **fit as a fiddle** perfectly healthy

fiddle² *v* **-dled, -dling** *infml* **1** [I] to play the FIDDLE¹ (1) **2** [I *with, about, around*] to move or play (with something) aimlessly rather than acting with a purpose: *Stop fiddling (around) with that gun. It might go off!*|*Well, we'd better get started and stop fiddling around.* **3** [T *with*] to lie about (something) to gain money, etc.: *to fiddle with one's income tax* **-fiddler** /'fɪdlər/ *n*

fi·del·i·ty /fə'delətiʸ, faɪ-/ *n* [U] **1** [*to*] *fml* faithfulness; loyalty: *fidelity to one's leader*|*to one's wife or husband* –see also INFIDELITY; compare FAITHFUL (3) **2** (of something copied or reported) truthfulness; closeness in sound, facts, color, etc. to the original: *the fidelity of a translation*|*of a sound recording* –see also HI-FI

fidg·et /'fɪdʒɪt/ *v* [I] to move one's body around in a restless, impatient way: *children fidgeting in class* **-fidgety** *adj*

fidget² *n infml* someone, esp. a child, who FIDGETs: *He's such a fidget.*

field¹ /fiʸld/ *n* **1** [C] a stretch of land on a farm marked off in some way and used for animals or crops: *fields of corn* **2** [C] **a** any open area where **a** the stated game or other activity takes place: *a football field*|*a battlefield*|*An airfield is a place where aircraft can take off or land.* **b** the stated substance is MINED² (1): *a coalfield*|*an oilfield* **3** [C] a branch of knowledge or activity: *a lawyer famous in his own field*|*the field of politics*/*art*/*Greek history*|*That's outside my field.* (=not my special subject) **4** [*the* S] the place where real operations happen, as compared to places where they are studied: *He studies tribal languages in the field, not from books in the library.* –see also FIELDWORK **5** [C] the area in which the (stated) force is felt: *the moon's* GRAVITATIONAL *field*|*Our* **field of vision** (=the area within seeing distance) *is limited by that tall building.* **6** [*the* U] (in racing) all the horses, people, etc. in the race: *The rest of the field is far behind Big Red.* **7 have a field day** to enjoy oneself very much: *The newspapers had a field day when they found*

out about the movie star's marriage plans.

field² *v* [I;T] (IN BASEBALL) to catch or stop a ball: *He fielded the ball.*|*Our team is* BATTing *now and will be fielding later.*|(fig.)*The President fielded the reporters' questions.* (=answered the questions successfully) **-fielder** *n*

field day /'·· ·/ *n* **1** a day of army training, on whch soldiers give a public show of military skill **2** (*esp. AmE*) a sports day at school or college **3** a time of unusually pleasant or exciting action: *The newspapers will really have a field day with this story.*

field e·vent /'·· ·,·/ *n* a competitive sports event, such as weight-throwing or jumping

field glass·es /'· ,··/ *n* [P] → BINOCULARS –see PAIR (USAGE)

field hand /'· ·/ *n AmE* an outdoor farm worker

field hock·ey /'· ,··/ *esp. AmE*‖also **hockey**– an outdoor game played by two teams of 11 players each, with sticks and a ball –compare ICE HOCKEY

field·work /'fiʸldwɜrk/ *n* [U] scientific or social study done in the FIELD¹ (4), such as measuring and examining things or asking people questions: *doing fieldwork*

fiend /fiʸnd/ *n* **1** a devil or evil spirit **2** a person who is very interested in something stated: *a fresh air fiend*

fiend·ish /'fiʸndɪʃ/ *adj* **1** fierce and cruel: *a fiendish temper* **2** *infml* very clever; not plain or simple: *a fiendish plan* **-fiendishly** *adv*: *fiendishly cruel*|*a fiendishly difficult question* **-fiendishness** *n* [U]

fierce /fiʌrs/ *adj* **1** angry, violent, and cruel: *a fierce dog to guard the house*|*a fierce-looking man* **2** very great or strong: *the fierce heat of the sun*|*Because there is so much unemployment, the competition for jobs is very fierce.* **-fiercely** *adv* **-fierceness** *n* [U]

fi·er·y /'faɪəriʸ/ *adj* **-ier, -iest** flaming and violent; looking like fire: *fiery red hair*|(fig.) *a fiery temper*

fi·es·ta /fiʸ'estə/ *n* (esp. in ROMAN CATHOLIC countries) a religious holiday with public gaiety and celebration; FESTIVAL (1)

fif·teen /,fɪf'tiʸn◄/ *determiner,n,pron* (the number) 15 **-fifteenth** *determiner,n,pron, adv*

fifth /fɪfθ/ *determiner,n,pron,adv* 5th

fif·ty /'fɪftiʸ/ *determiner,n,pron* (the number) 50 **-fiftieth** /'fɪftiʸɪθ/ *determiner,n,pron,adv*

fifty-fifty /,·· '··◄/ *adj,adv* [A;F] (of shares or chances) equal(ly): *You have a fifty-fifty chance of winning.*|*We divided it up fifty-fifty*|*on a fifty-fifty* BASIS.|*Let's* **go fifty-fifty on** (=let's share equally) *the cost of the gas.*

fig /fɪg/ *n* (the tree that bears) a soft sweet fruit with many small seeds, growing chiefly in warm countries and often eaten dried

fig. *written abbrev. said as:* **1** FIGURE¹ (6) **2** FIGURATIVE: *In this dictionary, figurative uses of a word are marked* **fig.**

fight¹ /faɪt/ *v* **fought** /fɔt/, **fighting 1** [I;T] to use violence (against others): *Britain fought against*/*with the US in the* War *of Indepen-*

dence.|*Rome fought Carthage for/over* (=to gain) *control of the Mediterranean.*|*Did your father fight in the war?*|(fig.) *We must fight the government's education policy.*|(fig.) *to fight crime/a fire/for equal rights* **2** [I] to quarrel: *He and his wife are always fighting about who will take the car.* **3 fight one's way** to move along by fighting or pushing: *He had to fight his way through the crowd.* –**fighter** *n*
   fight back *v adv* [I] to defend oneself by fighting
   fight sthg.↔ **off** *v adv* [T] to keep (something) away with an effort: *to fight off a cold*
   fight on *v adv* [I] to continue fighting
   fight sthg.↔ **out** *v adv* [T] to settle (a disagreement) by fighting (esp. in the phrase **fight it out**)
fight² *n* **1** [C] a battle; an occasion of fighting: *to have a fight*|*The police were called to stop a fight outside the school.* **2** [U] also **fighting spirit** /ˌ··'··/– the power or desire to fight: *There's not much fight left in him now.* **3 put up a good/poor fight** to fight well/badly
fig·ment /'fɪgmənt/ *n* **a figment of one's imagination** something believed but not real
fig·u·ra·tive /'fɪgərətɪv/ *adj* (of words) used in some way to make a word picture or comparison: *"Sweet dreams" is a figurative expression, but "sweet coffee" is not.* –compare LITERAL (3) –**figuratively** *adv*
fig·ure¹ /'fɪgyər/ *n* **1** (the shape of) a whole human body, as shown in art or seen in reality: *a group of figures on the left of the picture* –see BODY (USAGE) **2** the human shape considered from the point of view of being attractive: *doing exercises to improve one's figure*|*What a* **fine figure of a man/woman**! (=a person with an attractive bodily shape) **3** an important person: *Mahatma Gandhi was both a political and a religious figure in Indian history.* **4** any of the number signs from 0 to 9: *Write the amount in words and in figures.*|*I'm no good at figures.* (=addition, subtraction, etc.)|*Her income is in five figures/She has a five-figure income.* (=$10,000 or more) **5** an amount, esp. of money **6** a numbered drawing, map, or DIAGRAM, used in a book to explain something: *Figure 10 shows the increase in average wages during this period.*
figure² *v* **-ured, -uring 1** [I *as, in*] to take part: *Roger figured as chief guest at the party.* **2** [I;T +(*that*)] *AmE* to consider; believe: *I figured (that) you'd want to go out.* **3 That figures!** That seems reasonable and what I expected, esp. when bad
   figure on sthg. *v prep* [T +*v-ing*] *esp. AmE* to plan on; include in one's plans: *I'm figuring on (getting) a pay increase.*
   figure sbdy./sthg.↔ **out** *v adv* [T] to understand by thinking: *I can't figure him out; he's a mystery!*|*We must figure out how to do it.*
figure eight /ˌ·· '·/ |**figure of eight** /ˌ·· · '·/ *BrE*– *n* anything of the shape of an 8, such as a knot, stitch, or pattern
fig·ure·head /'fɪgyər,hɛd/ *n* **1** the head or chief in name only: *The President is just a figurehead. It's the party leader who has the real power.* **2** an ornament on the front of a

ship, often in the shape of a person
figure of speech /ˌ·· '· ·/ *n* an example of the FIGURATIVE use of words: *I didn't really mean my partner is a rat; it was just a figure of speech.*
fil·a·ment /'fɪləmənt/ *n* a thin thread, such as that inside an electric light BULB: *spun glass/nylon filaments*
filch /fɪltʃ/ *v* [T] *infml* to steal secretly (something of small value)
file¹ /faɪl/ *n* a steel tool with a rough face, used for smoothing or cutting hard surfaces
file² *v* **filed, filing** [I;T] to use a FILE¹ on: *to file one's nails*|*to file through the bars*
file³ *n* **1** any of various arrangements of papers, shelves, boxes, or cases for storing papers in an office –see also FILING CABINET **2** [*on*] a collection of papers on one subject, stored in this way: *Here's our file on the Middle East.*|*I'll keep your report* **on file.** (=stored in a file)|*We* **keep/have a file on** each member of the party.
file⁴ *v* [T] **1** to put in a FILE³: *Please file this letter (away), Peter.* **2** *law* to send in or record officially: *to file an* APPLICATION
file⁵ *n* a line of people one behind the other (often in the phrase **in single file**) –compare RANK¹ (4)
file⁶ *v* [I] to walk in single FILE⁵: *They filed slowly past the grave of their leader.*
fil·et /fɪ'leɪ, 'fɪleɪ/ *n,v AmE* for FILLET
fil·i·al /'fɪliʸəl/ *adj fml* of or suitable to a son or daughter: *filial love*
fil·i·bus·ter /'fɪlə,bʌstər/ *v* [I] *esp. AmE* to try to delay or prevent action in a lawmaking body, such as the Senate by being very slow and making long speeches
fil·i·gree /'fɪlə,griʸ/ *n* [U] delicate ornamental wire work: *silver filigree jewellery*
filing cab·i·net /'·· ,···/ also **file cabinet**– *n* a piece of office furniture with drawers, for storing papers in –see illustration on page 467
fil·ings /'faɪlɪŋz/ *n* [P] very small sharp pieces that have been rubbed off a metal surface with a FILE¹: *iron filings*
fill¹ /fɪl/ *v* **1** [I;T *with*] to make or become full: *The house soon filled (with children).*|(fig.) *Laughter filled the room.*|*The thought fills me with pleasure.* **2** [T] to (cause to) enter (a position): *The office of chairperson remained unfilled.*|*Julie's the best person to fill this* VACANCY. **3** [T] to fulfil; meet the needs or demands of: *Can you fill this* PRESCRIPTION/*order, please?* –compare EMPTY²
   fill in *v adv* **1** [T] (**fill** sthg.↔ **in**) **a** to put in (whatever is needed to complete something): *You draw the trees and I'll fill in the sky.*|*Fill in your name on this check.* **b** also **fill** sthg.↔ **out** *esp. AmE*– to complete by putting in whatever is needed: *to fill in one's income tax* FORM¹ (3) **2** [T *on*] (**fill** sbdy. **in**) to supply the most recent information to: *Please fill me in on what happened at the meeting.* **3** [I *for*] to take someone's place: *Susan is ill. Can you fill in for her tonight?*
   fill out *v adv* **1** [I] to get fatter: *Her face is beginning to fill out.* **2** [T] (**fill** sthg.↔ **out**) →FILL IN (1b): *to fill out a form*

fill up v adv [I;T (=**fill** sthg. ↔ **up**)] to make or become completely full: *The room soon filled up with people.|fill up the gas tank*

fill² n a full supply; as much as is needed or wanted: *to drink one's fill|John annoys me; I've had my fill of him for one evening!*

fil·let¹ /ˈfɪleʸ, ˈfɪleʸ/ ‖also **filet** AmE– n a piece of fish or meat with the bones removed: *a fillet* STEAK*|fillets of* SOLE (3)

fillet² ‖also **filet** AmE– v **-leted** /ˈfɪleʸd, ˈfɪleʸd/, **-leting** /ˈfɪleʸɪŋ, ˈfɪleʸɪŋ/ [T] to remove the bones from (a piece of fish or meat); cut into FILLETS¹: *filleted* SOLE (3)

fill·ing /ˈfɪlɪŋ/ n **1** (the material put into) a hole in a tooth by a DENTIST to preserve it: *You've got a lot of fillings.* **2** a food mixture folded inside pastry, SANDWICHES, etc.

filling sta·tion /ˈ·· ,·ʳ/ n AmE →GAS STATION

fil·ly /ˈfɪliʸ/ n -lies a young female horse –compare COLT

film¹ /fɪlm/ n **1** [C;U] (a roll of) the substance on which one takes photographs or makes movies: *to buy a roll of film|some film for my camera* **2** [S;U] a thin skin of any material: *a sheet of plastic film|a film of dust* **3** [C] esp. BrE movie: *to* **shoot** (=make) **a film**|*Have you seen any good films lately?*

film² v [I;T] to make a movie (of): *We'll be filming all day tomorrow.|to film the President's arrival in Paris*

film star /ˈ· ·/ n esp. BrE for MOVIE STAR

film·strip /ˈfɪlm,strɪp/ n [C;U] (a length of) photographic film used to show (PROJECT² (3)) photographs, drawings, etc., one after the other as still pictures: *a filmstrip on the life of the ant*

film·y /ˈfɪlmiʸ/ adj **-ier, -iest** fine and thin, so that one can see through it: *a filmy silk dress* –**filminess** n [U]

fil·ter¹ /ˈfɪltər/ n **1** an apparatus through which substances can be passed so as to make them clean or to separate liquids from solids: *the oil filter in a car|a coffee filter* **2** a (colored) glass that changes light admitted into a camera

filter² v [I;T] to pass or send (as if) through a FILTER: *to filter the drinking water|Sunlight filtered through the curtains.|(fig.) The news slowly filtered through to everyone in the office.*

filter sthg.↔ **out** v adv [T] to remove by means of a FILTER: *to filter out the dirt|the blue light*

filth /fɪlθ/ n [U] **1** very nasty dirt: *Go and wash that filth off your hands.* **2** something rude or unpleasant or OBSCENE: *I don't know how you can read such filth.* –**filthy** adj **-ier, -iest** –**filthily** adv –**filthiness** n [U]

fin /fɪn/ n **1** a winglike part that a fish uses in swimming **2** a part shaped like this on a car, aircraft, or bomb

fi·nal¹ /ˈfaɪnl/ adj **1** [A] last; coming at the end: *Z is the final letter in the alphabet.|a final cup of coffee before we left* **2** (of a decision,

offer, etc.) that cannot be changed: *I won't go, and that's final!|Is that your final offer?*

final² n [often pl.] the last and most important test in **a** a set of matches: *the tennis finals* **b** a college course: *When do you take your finals?* (=final examinations)

fi·nal·e /fɪˈnæliʸ, -ˈnɑ-/ n the last division of a piece of music

fi·nal·ist /ˈfaɪnl-ɪst/ n one of the people or teams left in the FINAL² (**a**), after the others have been defeated

fi·nal·i·ty /faɪˈnæləṭiʸ, fɪ-/ n [U] the quality of being or seeming FINAL¹ (2): *"No!" she said with finality.*

fi·nal·ize ‖also **-ise** BrE /ˈfaɪnl,aɪz/ v **-ized, -izing** [T] to finish and make firm (plans, arrangements, etc.)

fi·nal·ly /ˈfaɪnl-iʸ/ adv **1** at last: *After several long delays, the plane finally left at 6 o'clock.* **2** so as not to allow further change: *It's not finally settled yet.*

fi·nance¹ /fəˈnæns, ˈfaɪnæns/ n [U] **1** the control of (esp. public) money **2** money, esp. provided by a bank or similar organization, to help run a business or buy something: *Unless we get more finance, we'll have to close the hotel.*

finance² v **-nanced, -nancing** [T] to provide money for: *The repairs to the school will be financed by the local council.*

fi·nanc·es /fəˈnænsɪz, ˈfaɪnænsɪz/ n [P] the amount of money owned by a person, organization, or government: *the present state of the country's finances*

fi·nan·cial /fəˈnænʃəl, -tʃəl, faɪ-/ adj connected with money: *New York is a great financial center.|Mr. Briggs is our financial adviser.* –**financially** adv

fin·an·cier /ˌfɪnənˈsɪər, fəˌnæn-, ˌfaɪnæn-/ n someone who controls or lends large sums of money

finch /fɪntʃ/ n a small singing bird

find¹ /faɪnd/ v **found** /faʊnd/, **finding** [T] **1** [not be +v-ing] to discover, esp. by searching: *I can't find my boots!|They found him a place to live|found a place for him to live.|Did you find what you were looking for?|They found the lost child (hiding) in the cave.|We've found oil in Alaska.* –compare LOSE **2** [+(that)/out] to learn or discover (something) by effort, chance, experience, etc.: *Please find (out) what time they're coming.|I find (that) I have plenty of time now.|When I woke up, I found myself* (=I found that I was) *in the hospital.|We went to her house but found that she was out.|I'm finding her (to be) a rather difficult person to work with.|This type of tree is found* (=exists) *only in Australia.* –compare FIND out (1) **3** fml (of things) to reach; arrive at: *The bullet found its mark.* **4** [not be +v- ing] to obtain by effort: *How ever do you find the time to make cakes?|At last she found the courage to tell him.* **5** [not be+v-ing] law to decide (someone) to be: *"How do you find the prisoner?" "We find him not guilty."|She was found guilty of stealing.*

find out v adv **1** [I;T (=**find** sthg.↔ **out**)] to learn or discover (a fact that was hidden):

Did you ever find out why he left his last job?
–compare FIND¹ (2) **2** [T] **(find** sbdy. **out)** to
discover in a dishonest act: *He was stealing
money from the company for years before
they found him out.*

find² *n* something (good) that is found: *This
little restaurant is quite a find/is a real find. I
didn't know it existed!*

find·ing /'faɪndɪŋ/ *n* **1** *law* a decision made by
a judge or JURY **2** something learned as the
result of an official inquiry: *the findings of
the committee on child care*

fine¹ /faɪn/ *n* an amount of money paid as a
punishment: *to pay a $5 fine*

fine² *v* **fined, fining** [T] to take money from as
a punishment: *They fined her heavily.|He
was fined $200.*

fine³ *adj* **1** [A] beautiful and of high quality;
better than most of its kind: *a fine
house/musician/wine/view|I've never seen a
finer animal.|We use only the finest materials
to make our furniture.* **2 a** very thin: *fine
hair/thread/silk|a pencil with a fine point*
–see THIN (USAGE) **b** in very small grains or
pieces: *fine sugar/dust* –opposite **coarse 3** (of
weather) bright and sunny; not wet: *The
weather turned out fine again.|a fine summer
morning* **4** [*no comp.*] (of a person or conditions) healthy and comfortable: *"How's
your wife?" "She's fine, thank you."|This
apartment's fine for two people, but not
more.* **5** [A] (of work) delicate and careful:
fine sewing/the finest workmanship|(fig.) *I
missed some of the finer points in the argu-
ment.|***Not to put too fine a point on it** (=to
express it plainly), *I think he's crazy.* **6** [A]
humor terrible: *That's a fine thing to
say!|This is a fine state of affairs.*

fine⁴ *adv* **1** also **finely**– so as to be very thin or
in very small pieces: *Cut up the vegetables
very fine.* **2** very well: *It suits me fine.|The
machine works fine if you oil it.*

fine arts /ˌ· '·/ *n* [*the* P] those arts such as
painting, music, and SCULPTURE, that are
chiefly concerned with producing beautiful
rather than useful things

fine·ly /'faɪnliʸ/ *adv* **1** closely and delicately:
These instruments are very finely set. **2** so as
to be in small grains or pieces: *finely cut
vegetables*

fin·er·y /'faɪnəriʸ/ *n* [U] gay, beautiful clothes
and ornaments: *the guests in their wedding
finery*

fi·nesse /fɪ'nɛs/ *n* [U] delicate skill: *She
handled the meeting with great finesse.*

fin·ger¹ /'fɪŋgər/ *n* **1** one of the movable parts
with joints, at the end of each human hand
(sometimes including the thumb) –compare
TOE¹ (1) **2 (have) a finger in every pie** *infml*
(to have) a part in everything that is going on
3 keep one's fingers crossed *infml* to hope for
the best: *I hope the weather stays fine for
tomorrow's game. We just have to keep our
fingers crossed.* **4 lift a finger** (*in* NEGATIVES²,
questions, *etc.*) to make any effort to help:
No one lifted a finger to save the prisoners. **5
put one's finger on** to find: *I can't quite put
my finger on what's wrong.* **6 get one's
fingers burned** to suffer because of a foolish

act or mistake: *George got his fingers burned
on that business deal.*

finger² *v* [T] **1** to feel or handle with one's
fingers: *She fingered the rich silk.* **2** *AmE
infml* to identify, esp. as a criminal: *The
witness fingered the criminal.*

fin·ger·nail /'fɪŋgər,neʸl/ also **nail**– *n* one of
the hard flat pieces that cover the ends of the
fronts of the fingers

fin·ger·print /'fɪŋgər,prɪnt/ *n* the mark of a
finger, esp. as used in the discovery of crime:
The police took the man's fingerprints.
(=made an image of them)

fin·ger·tip /'fɪŋgər,tɪp/ *n* the end of a finger:
(fig.) *You'd better ask David. He has all the
information **at his fingertips.*** (=has a ready
knowledge of it)

fin·ick·y /'fɪnɪkiʸ/ *adj* disliking many things;
FUSSY: *Eat your fish and don't be so finicky.*

fin·ish¹ /'fɪnɪʃ/ *v* **1** [I;T +*v-ing/up, off*] to
come or bring to an end; complete: *What
time does the concert finish?|When do you
finish college?|It's getting late. Let's finish up
and go home.|I haven't finished reading that
book yet.|The actress said she was finished
making movies.*(=wouldn't make any more
movies)*|I must finish this dress I'm making;
I'm just giving it the last **finishing touches.***
–compare START¹ **2** [T *up, off*] to eat or drink
the rest of: *The cat will finish (up) the
fish.|Let's finish (off) the wine.* **3** [T] *infml* to
take away all one's strength, hopes of success, etc.: *Climbing all those stairs has really
finished me.|The bad publicity finished his
career.*

finish with sbdy./sthg. *v prep* [T] to have no
more use for: *Could I use the scissors if
you're finished with them?|I'm finished with
Mary after the way she treated me.*

fin·ish² *n* **1** [S] the end or last part, esp. of a
race: *That was a close finish!* (=the competitors were almost tied) –compare START² **2**
[S;U] the appearance or condition of having
been properly finished, with paint, polish,
etc.: *the beautiful finish of old French
furniture*

fin·ished /'fɪnɪʃt/ *adj* **1** [F] ended; with no
hope of continuing: *If the bank refuses to
lend us the money, we're finished.* **2** [A] properly made and complete: *the finished pro-
duct/a beautifully finished old table*

fi·nite /'faɪnaɪt/ *adj* having an end or limit: *a
finite number of possibilities* –opposite
infinite

fi·ord /fyɔrd, fyoʷrd/ *n* →FJORD

fir /fɜr/ *n* a straight tree that keeps its its
sharp leaves (NEEDLES) in winter, and grows
esp. in cold countries. –sounds like **fur**

fire¹ /faɪər/ *n* **1** [U] burning with flames:
*Horses are afraid of fire.|insurance against
(destruction by) fire|The pile of papers
caught fire.* (=started to burn) *Someone
must have **set fire to** it/set it **on fire.***|(fig.) *Her
speech was full of fire.* (=strong feeling) **2**
[C] a mass of burning material, lit on purpose for cooking, heat, etc., or lit by accident: *The hunters lit a fire to keep warm at
night.|Put some more coal on the
fire.|Thousands of trees were lost in the forest*

fire. **3** [C] *BrE* a gas or electrical apparatus for warming a room, with the flames or red-hot wires able to be seen –compare STOVE **4** [U] shooting by guns: *We were under* **fire** (=being shot at) *from all sides.* **5 on fire** (of something not meant to burn) burning: *The house is on fire!* –compare FIERY

USAGE You **light** a **fire** or a candle (=make it burn), but you **fire** a gun (=shoot bullets from it), and you can also **fire** clay pots (=bake them in a KILN). If you **light** something that is not intended to burn, you **set fire to** it: *Someone* **set fire to** *the school bus.* When a thing begins to burn, it **catches fire:** *Her dress* **caught fire.**

fire² *v* **fired, firing 1** [I *at*] (of a person or a gun) to shoot off bullets: *He's firing at us!|The guns were firing all night.* **2** [T *at*] (of a person) to shoot bullets from (a gun): *He ran into the bank and fired his gun into the air.* **3** [T *at*] (of a person, gun, or BOW³ (1)) to shoot (bullets or arrows): *Hinckley fired five shots at the President.* **4** [T] to bake (clay pots, dishes, etc.) in a KILN **5** [T *with*] to produce (strong feelings) in (someone): *a speech that fired the crowd's imagination/fired them with anger against the government* **6** [T] *infml‖*also **sack** *BrE–* to dismiss from a job; *Get out! You're fired!*

fire a·larm /'· ·,·/ *n* a signal, such as a ringing bell, to warn people of fire

fire·arm /'faɪərɑrm/ *n* [*usu. pl*] a gun

fire·crack·er /'faɪər,krækər/ *AmE‖***cracker** *BrE–* *n* a small explosive charge used for making loud noises on special occasions: (fig.) *That child is a real firecracker.* (=very lively) –see also FIREWORK

fire de·part·ment /'· ·,··/ *AmE‖***fire brigade** /'· ·,·/ *BrE–* *n* [C +*sing./pl. v*] an organization for preventing and putting out fires: *The fire department is coming!*

fire en·gine /'· ,··/ *n* a special vehicle that carries firemen (FIREMAN) and special apparatus to put out fires –see illustration on page 673

fire es·cape /'· ·,·/ *n* a set of metal stairs leading down outside a building to the ground, by which people can escape in case of fire –see illustration on page 337

fire fight·er /'· ,··/ *n* → FIREMAN

fire·guard /'faɪərgɑrd/ *n* a protective metal framework put around a fireplace

fire hy·drant /'· ,··/ *n AmE* for HYDRANT (1)

fire·man /'faɪərmən/ also **firefighter–** *n* **-men** /mən/ a person whose job is putting out fires

fire·place /'faɪərpleɪs/ *n* the opening for a fire in the wall of a room, with a chimney above it and often a HEARTH and MANTELPIECE around it –see illustration on page 399

fire plug /'· ·/ *n AmE* for HYDRANT (1)

fire·side /'faɪərsaɪd/ *n* [*usu. sing.*] the area around the fireplace: *to sit by the fireside|a fireside chair*

fire sta·tion /'· ,··/ *n* a building for FIRE FIGHT-

> **SPELLING NOTE**
> Words with the sound /f/ may be spelled ph-, like **photograph.**

ERS and their fire-fighting apparatus

fire·wood /'faɪərwʊd/ *n* [U] wood cut to be used on fires

fire·work /'faɪərwɜrk/ *n* [*often pl.*] a small container filled with an explosive powder that is burned to produce a show of light, noise, and smoke –see also FIRE CRACKER

fir·ing squad /'faɪərɪŋ ,skwɑd/ *n* a group of soldiers with the duty of shooting an offender dead

firm¹ /fɜrm/ *adj* **1** strong; solid; hard: *Do you think the ice is firm enough to walk on?* **2** steady; strong and sure: *firm on one's feet|I don't think that chair's firm enough to stand on.|He kept a firm hold on my hand as he helped me over the fence.* **3** not changing or yielding: *a firm belief/believer in God|The price of gold stayed firm yesterday.|You'll have to be firm with him. He's a difficult child.* –**firmly** *adv* –**firmness** *n* [U]

firm² *n* a business company

fir·ma·ment /'fɜrməmənt/ *n* [*the* S] *lit* the sky

first¹ /fɜrst/ *n,pron* **1** [+*to-v*] the person or thing before all the others: *She was the first/one of the first to arrive.|Whoever is (the) first to finish will get a prize.* –compare LAST¹ **2 at first** at the beginning: *At first I didn't like him but now I do.* –compare LAST² (2) **3 from the (very) first** from the beginning

first² *determiner,adv* **1** before anything else; before the others: *"Let's go!" "I have to put on my shoes first."|George arrived first/was the first person to arrive.* **2** for the first time: *Is this your first visit to Los Angeles?|I remember when I first met him.* –compare LAST² **3** at the beginning: *When we first lived here there were no buses.* **4 first and foremost** most importantly; above all else: *She writes short stories, but first and foremost she's a poet.* **5 first of all** as the first thing: *First of all let me thank you for your present.* **6 first thing** at the earliest time in the morning: *We will leave first thing (in the morning).*

first aid /,· '·/ *n* [U] treatment to be given by an ordinary person to a person hurt in an accident or suddenly taken ill: *She pulled the drowning man from the water and gave him first aid.*

first base /,· '·/ *n* the first of the BASES¹ (6) which a BASEBALL player must reach in order to score a run

first class /,· '·◄/ *n* [U] the best and costliest method of travel or of sending mail: *Write "First Class" clearly on your letter, and it will get there quicker.|I like to travel in comfort, so I always go first class when I fly.* –see also SECOND CLASS

first-class *adj* of the highest or best quality: *Your work is first-class. I'm very pleased with it.*

first floor /,· '·◄/ *n* **1** also **ground floor–** (in the US) the floor of a building at ground level **2** (in Britain) the first floor of a building above ground level

first·hand /,fɜrst'hænd◄/ *adj,adv* (learned) directly from the point of origin: *I heard her news firsthand.* (=from her)*|firsthand information* –compare SECONDHAND¹ (2)

first la·dy /,· '··/ *n* [*the* S] (in the US) the wife

of the President: (fig.) *Ella Fitzgerald is often called the first lady of* JAZZ. (=one of the most important women in JAZZ)

first·ly /'fɜrstliʲ/ *adv* →FIRST² (1) –compare LASTLY

USAGE Teachers prefer **first** to **firstly** in sentences like this: *There are three reasons against it:* **first** . . .

first lieu·ten·ant /ˌ· ·'··/ *n* an officer of the second lowest rank in the US army, AIRFORCE, or MARINE CORPS

first name /'· ·/ also **given name**– *n* the name or names that stand before one's SURNAME (=family name); one's personal name: *Mr. Smith's first name is Peter.|His first names are Peter Alexander.|She's on a* **first-name basis** *with her teachers.* (=knows them well enough to call them by their first names)

USAGE In English-speaking countries, your **first name** is the one always used by your family and friends. People whose SURNAMEs come before their other names, as in Chinese, Hungarian, etc., may prefer to use **given name** rather than **first name.**

first per·son /ˌ· '··◄/ *n* [*the* S] **1** a form of verb or word standing for a noun (PRONOUN) used to show the speaker: *"I," "me," "we," and "us" are first person* PRONOUNS.*|"I am" is the first person present singular of "to be."* **2** a way of telling a story in which the teller uses himself/herself as the subject: *The story was written in the first person. It began "I was born in. . ."*

first-rate /ˌ· '·◄/ *adj* very good: *to use first-rate materials|This beer is first-rate!* –compare SECOND-RATE

fis·cal /'fɪskəl/ *adj fml* of or related to public money, taxes, debts, etc.

fish¹ /fɪʃ/ *n* **fish** *or* **fishes 1** [C] a creature which lives in water and uses its FINs and tail to swim: *We caught three little fishes/several fish.* **2** [U] its flesh when used as food: *We had fish/some fish/a piece of fish for dinner.*

fish² *v* **1** [I *for*] to try to catch fish; search (for something under water): *Let's go fishing.|to fish for* TROUT|(fig.) *Why are you* **fishing around** *in your pockets?*|(fig.) *I think he's just* **fishing for compliments.** **2** [T] to catch fish in (a piece of water): *This river has been fished too much.*

fish sthg.↔ out *v adv* [T] to bring out after searching: *to fish out a coin/a handkerchief from one's pocket*

fish·er·man /'fɪʃərmən/ *n* **-men** /mən/ a man who catches fish, for sport or as a job –compare ANGLER

fish·er·y /'fɪʃəriʲ/ *n* **-ies** a part of the sea where the industry of catching sea fish is practiced: *coastal fisheries*

fish·ing /'fɪʃɪŋ/ *n* [U] the sport or job of catching fish: *to do some fishing during vacation*

fish·mon·ger /'fɪʃˌmʌŋgər, -ˌmɑŋ-/ *n esp. BrE* (someone who works in) a shop that sells fish

fish·y /'fɪʃiʲ/ *adj* **-ier, -iest 1** tasting or smelling of fish **2** seeming false: *the fishiest story I've ever heard*

fis·sion /'fɪʃən/ *n* [U] *tech* the splitting into parts of certain cells or atoms

fis·sure /'fɪʃər/ *n fml* a deep crack in rock or earth: *grass growing in the fissures*

fist /fɪst/ *n* (the shape of) the hand with the fingers closed in tightly: *She shook her fist angrily.*

fit¹ /fɪt/ *v* **fitted** *or* **fit, fitting 1** [I;T] to be the right size or shape (for): *This dress doesn't fit (me).* **2** [T] to make suitable for: *Her special abilities fit her well for the job.* –see also FIT IN **3** [T] to provide and put correctly into place: *We're having new locks fitted on all the doors.* –see also FITTED (2) **4 fit the bill** to be just what one wants: *What do you want to drink? Will beer fit the bill?* **5 fit like a glove** to fit very well and closely

USAGE The usual past tense and past participle of **fit** is **fitted,** but in the first meaning **fit** is also used, esp. in *AmE: When he left the store, the suit* **fit** *him perfectly.*

fit in *v adv* **1** [I;T (=**fit** sthg.↔ **in**) *with*] to (cause to) be suitable (to): *to fit my arrangements in with yours|to fit in with his ideas|Wherever she went she fit in.* **2** [T] (**fit** sbdy./sthg.↔ **in**) to find a time to see (someone) or do (something): *Doctor Jones can fit you in on Thursday afternoon.*

fit sbdy./sthg.↔ **out** *v adv* [T] to supply with necessary things: *The ship has been newly fitted out.*

fit² *n* [S] the way in which something fits: *This coat's a beautiful fit.|I'll try to climb through, but it's a tight fit.*

fit³ *n* **1** a period of loss of consciousness, with strange uncontrolled movements of the body: (fig.) *Father will* **have a fit** (=be very angry) *when he hears what you have done.* **2** [*of*] a short attack (of a slight illness or violent feeling): *a fit of coughing|I hit her in a fit of anger.*|(fig.) *She kept them* **in fits (of laughter)** *with her jokes.* **3 by/in fits and starts** continually starting and stopping; not regularly

fit⁴ *adj* **-tt- 1** [+*to-v/for*] right and suitable: *She's not fit/not a fit person to be in charge of small children.|a meal fit for a king|The President has* **seen/thought fit** (=has decided) *to let the prisoner go free.* **2** in good health or bodily condition: *He runs three miles every morning; that's why he's so fit.* –opposite **unfit**

fit·ful /'fɪtfəl/ *adj* restless: *to spend a fitful night* –**fitfully** *adv*

fit·ness /'fɪtnɪs/ *n* [U] **1** the state of being fit in body: *doing exercises to improve their fitness* **2** [+*to-v/for*] the quality of being suitable: *his fitness to command the army*

fit·ted /'fɪtɪd/ *adj* **1** [F *with*] having (a part, piece of apparatus, etc.): *Is the car fitted with a radio?* **2** [A] fixed in place: *a fitted shelf*

fit·ter /'fɪtər/ *n* someone whose work is either **a** putting together machines or electrical parts or **b** cutting out and fitting clothes

fit·ting¹ /'fɪtɪŋ/ *adj fml* right; suitable: *It is fitting that we should remember him on his birthday.*

fitting² *n* an occasion of putting on clothes that are being made for one, to see if they fit:

I'm going for a fitting on Tuesday.

five /faɪv/ *determiner,n,pron* (the number) 5
five and ten /ˌ· · ˈ·/ also **dime store**– *n AmE* a store offering many items that cost little: *"Where can I buy some thread?" "There's a five and ten around the corner."*
fix¹ /fɪks/ *v* **1** [T] to fasten firmly: *He fixed the picture in position with a nail.*|(fig.) *Let me fix the address in my mind.*|(fig.) *The price was fixed at $50* **2** [I;T +*to-v*/*up*] to arrange: *If you want to meet them, I can fix it.*|*We haven't fixed (up) the date of her visit yet.* –compare FIX **on 3** [T] to arrange the result of unfairly: *The election/race was fixed.* **4** [T] to repair: *I have to get the radio fixed.* **5** [T] *esp. AmE* to prepare (esp. food or drink) for (someone): *Let me fix you a drink/Let me fix a drink for you.* **6** [T] *infml* to deal with; get even with (someone): *I'll fix him for calling me a liar!*
  fix on *v prep* [T] **1** (**fix** sthg. **on** sbdy./sthg.) to direct (one's eyes, attention, etc.) steadily at: *She fixed her eyes on the clock.* **2 fix the blame on** (**someone**) to decide that someone is guilty
  fix sbdy **up** *v adv* [T *with*] to provide with; make the arrangements for: *Let's fix him up with a job/with a room in the hotel.*
fix² *n infml* **1** an awkward or difficult position: *We're in a real fix. There's nobody to look after the baby.* **2** [*of*] (used by drug-takers) an INJECTION (of the stated drug)
fix·a·tion /fɪkˈseɪʃən/ *n* (in PSYCHOLOGY) a strong unhealthy feeling (about) or love (for): *He has a fixation about her/a mother fixation.*
fixed /fɪkst/ *adj* fastened; not movable or changeable: *The tables are firmly fixed to the floor.*|*The date is fixed now.*| (fig.) *He has very fixed ideas on this subject.*
fix·ed·ly /ˈfɪksɪdliʲ/ *adv* unchangingly; with great attention (in phrases like **to stare fixedly**)
fix·ture /ˈfɪkstʃər/ *n* **1** something that is fixed into a building and sold with it: *bathroom fixtures* –compare FITTING² **2** a match or sports competition taking place on an agreed date
fizz¹ /fɪz/ *v* [I] (of a liquid, usu. a drink) to produce bubbles, making the sound typical of this
fizz² *n* [S] the sound of FIZZing¹ –**fizzy** *adj* **-zier, -ziest**: *fizzy drinks*
fiz·zle out /ˈfɪzəl/ *v adv* **-zled, -zling** [I] to end in nothing after a good start: *The party fizzled out before midnight.*
fjord , fiord /fyɔrd, fyoʷrd/*|*/ *n* a narrow arm of the sea between cliffs or steep slopes, esp. in Norway
FL , also **Fla**– *written abbrev, said as:* Florida /ˈflɔrədə, ˈflɑr-/ (a state in the US)
flab·ber·gast·ed /ˈflæbər,gæstɪd/ *adj* [*at, by*] *infml* very surprised
flab·by /ˈflæbiʲ/ *adj* **-bier, -biest** having too

soft flesh; (of muscles) too soft: *I became a little flabby after I stopped playing football regularly.* –**flabbiness** *n* [U]
flac·cid /ˈflæksɪd, ˈflæsɪd/ *adj* not firm enough; weak and soft: *flaccid plant stems*
flag¹ /flæg/ *n* a square or OBLONG piece of cloth, usu. with a pattern or picture on it, fastened by one edge to a pole (**flagpole**) or rope: *to* FLY (=have on a pole) *the national flag of Mexico*|*flags hanging* **at half-mast** (=lower than the top of the pole) *as a sign of sorrow*
flag² *v* **-gg-** [I] to become weak and less alive or active: *After walking for three hours we began to flag.*|*his flagging interest in the subject* –see also UNFLAGGING
  flag sbdy./sthg.↔ **down** *v adv* [T] to cause (a vehicle) to stop by waving at the driver: *to flag down a taxi*
flag³ *n* →FLAGSTONE
flag·on /ˈflægən/ *n* a large container for liquids such as wine, usu. with a lid, a handle, and a lip or SPOUT for pouring
fla·grant /ˈfleɪʲgrənt/ *adj* (of a bad person or action) open and shameless: *flagrant cheating*|*a flagrant coward* –**flagrantly** *adv*
flag·ship /ˈflæg,ʃɪp/ *n* the chief ship, on which an ADMIRAL sails, among a group of warships
flag·stone /ˈflægstoʷn/ also **flag**– *n* a flat square of stone for a floor or path
flail /fleɪʲl/ *v* [I;T] to wave violently but aimlessly about: *Her legs flailed in the water.*
flair /fleər/ *n* [S;U *for*] the natural ability to do some special thing: *a flair for writing*|*He shows little flair for this subject.*
flake¹ /fleɪʲk/ *n* a light leaf-like little bit: *soap flakes*|*flakes of snow*|*of chocolate* –**flaky** *adj* **-ier, -iest**: *flaky pastry*
flake² *v* **flaked, flaking** [I *off*] to fall off in FLAKES: *The paint's beginning to flake (off).*
  flake out *v adv* [I] *infml* to faint or COL-LAPSE¹ (2)
flam·boy·ant /flæmˈbɔɪənt/ *adj* (of a thing or person) noticeable; showy, gay, and bold: *a flamboyant orange shirt* –**flamboyantly** *adv* –**flamboyance** *n* [U]
flame¹ /fleɪʲm/ *n* [C;U] **1** (a tongue of) red or yellow burning gas: *The dry sticks burst into flame(s).*|*The whole city was* **in flames. 2** *old* **flame** someone with whom one used to be in love: *Edward's an old flame of mine.*
flame² *v* **flamed, flaming** [I *out, up*] to become (red, bright, etc.) by or as if by burning: *The candles flamed brighter.*|*Her cheeks flamed red.*
fla·men·co /fləˈmeŋkoʷ/ *n* **-cos** *or* **-coes** a kind of Spanish dancing and music, very fast and exciting
flam·ing /ˈfleɪʲmɪŋ/ *adj* [A] burning brightly; bright; strong; (fig.) *I was* **in a flaming temper.**
fla·min·go /fləˈmɪŋgoʷ/ *n* **-gos** *or* **-goes** a tall tropical water bird with long thin legs and pink and red feathers
flam·ma·ble /ˈflæməbəl/ *adj AmE & tech* for INFLAMMABLE –opposite **non-flammable**
USAGE **Flammable** and **inflammable** are not opposites. They have the same meaning, but

flammable is used in the US and is also the *BrE tech* word.

flange /flændʒ/ *n* the flat edge that stands out from the main surface of an object such as a train wheel, to keep it in position

flank¹ /flæŋk/ *n* the side of an animal, person, or moving army: *The enemy attacked on the left flank.*

flank² *v* [T *with, by*] to be placed beside: *a road flanked with tall buildings*

flan·nel /ˈflænl/ *n* [U] a kind of smooth woolen cloth with a slightly furry surface: *a flannel shirt*

flan·nels /ˈflænlz/ *n* [P] men's FLANNEL pants

flap¹ /flæp/ *n* **1** [C] a wide flat part of anything that hangs down, esp. so as to cover an opening: *a cap with flaps to cover my ears |to creep under the flap of the tent|the flap on an en-velope* **2** [S] the sound of FLAPping² (1): *the slow flap of the sails* **3** [C] *infml* a state of excited anxiety: *Don't get in a flap; we'll find it.*

flap² *v* **-pp- 1** [I;T] to move (something large and soft) up and down or to and fro, making a noise: *The large bird flapped its wings.|The sails flapped in the wind.* **2** [I] *infml* to be in a FLAP¹ (3): *Quit flapping about it; we won't be late.*

flap·jack /ˈflæpdʒæk/ *n* a small PANCAKE

flare¹ /fleər/ *v* **flared, flaring** [I] to burn with a bright flame, but uncertainly or for a short time: *candles flaring in the wind*

   flare up *v adv* [I] to burn suddenly: (fig.) *Trouble may flare up in the big cities.*

flare² *n* **1** [S] a flaring (FLARE¹) light: *a sudden flare as she lit the gas* **2** [C] something that provides a bright light out of doors, often used as a signal: *As our ship began to sink, we sent out flares to attract attention.*

flared /fleərd/ *adj* (of pants or a skirt) shaped so as to get wider by degrees towards the bottom: *a very flared skirt*

flash¹ /flæʃ/ *v* **1** [I] (of a light) to appear or shine for a moment: *The lightning flashed.|the flashing lights of the cars|*(fig.) *flashing eyes* **2** [T *at*] to make a flash with; shine for a moment (at): *Why is that driver flashing his lights (at me)?|Stop flashing that light in my eyes.|*(fig.) *She flashed a sudden smile at him.|to flash a message on the movie* SCREEN **3** [T] to send (a telegraph or radio message): *They flashed the news back to Washington.* **4** [I] to move very fast: *A bright light flashed across the sky.|*(fig.) *The idea flashed into/across/through my mind.*

   flash back *v adv* [I *to*] to return suddenly (to an earlier time), as in a FLASHBACK: *My mind flashed back to last Christmas.* –see also FLASHBACK

flash² *n* **1** a sudden quick bright light: *flashes of lightning|*(fig.) *a sudden flash of merri-ment/of* INSPIRATION **2** a short news report, received by telegraph, radio, etc.: *A* **newsflash** *from Beirut says they've been shot.* **3** (in photography) the method or apparatus for taking photographs in the dark: *Did you use a flash?* **4 flash in the pan** a sudden success that will not be repeated: *This book was just a flash in the pan; he'll never write*

another one as good. **5 in a/like a flash** very quickly; at once

flash·back /ˈflæʃbæk/ *n* [C;U] part of a movie film that goes back in time to show what happened earlier in the story: *The events of his childhood are shown in (a) flashback.* –see also FLASH¹ **back**

flash·light /ˈflæʃlaɪt/ *n* **1** *esp. AmE* an electric hand-light (TORCH) **2** an apparatus for taking flash photographs: *Did you bring your flashlight/your flash?*

flash·y /ˈflæʃiʸ/ *adj* **-ier, -iest** over-orna-mented; unpleasantly big, bright, etc.: *a large flashy car|cheap flashy clothes* –**flashily** *adv: flashily dressed*

flask /flæsk/ *n* **1** a narrow-necked glass bot-tle, for containing liquids, esp. as used by scientists in the LABORATORY **2** a flat bottle for carrying alcohol or other drinks in the pocket, fastened to one's belt, etc. **3** also **thermos, thermos flask, vacuum flask**– a bot-tle which is specially made for keeping liquids either hot or cold

flat¹ /flæt/ *adj* **-tt- 1** smooth and level: *Find me something flat to write on.|He spread the map out flat on the floor.* **2** broad, smooth, and not very thick or high: *flat feet* (=without proper arches) **3** (of a tire) without enough air in it **4** (of beer and other gassy drinks) no longer fresh because the gas has been lost: *This beer's gone flat.|*(fig.) *Everything seems so flat* (=uninteresting) *since you left.* **5** (of a group of electric cells (BATTERY)) having no more electric current left inside **6** [after *n; no comp.*] (in music) lower than the true note: –compare SHARP¹ (9)**7** [A *no comp.*] com-plete; firm; with no more argument (in phrases like **flat refusal, flat denial**) –**flatness** *n* [U]

flat² *n* **1** [*usu. pl.*] a low level plain, esp. near water: *mud flats* **2** [*of*] the flat part or side (of): *I hit him with the flat of my hand/of my sword.* **3** (the sign for) a FLAT¹ (6) note in music –compare SHARP¹ (9)**4** *esp. AmE* a flat tire: *We had a flat on our way here.*

flat³ *adv* **1** completely: *He's flat BROKE.* –com-pare FLATLY (2) **2** (in music) lower than the true note: *You keep singing flat.* –compare SHARP¹ (9)**3** [after *n*] (after an expression of time, showing surprise at its shortness) ex-actly; and not more: *I got dressed in three minutes flat!* **4 flat out** at full speed: *working flat out|The car does 100 miles per hour flat out.*

flat⁴ *n esp. BrE* for APARTMENT

flat·car /ˈflætkɑr/ *n AmE* a railroad FREIGHT vehicle with no raised sides or ends and no roof

flat·ly /ˈflætliʸ/ *adv* **1** in a dull level way: *"It's hopeless," he said flatly.* **2** completely; firmly: *I flatly refuse to come.* –compare FLAT¹ (7)

flat rate /ˈ· ·/ *n* one charge including everything: *You can eat as much as you like for/at a flat rate of $6.*

flat·ten /ˈflætn/ *v* [I;T *out*] to make or become flat: *I flattened myself against the wall.|The hills flatten (out) here.*

flat·ter /ˈflætər/ *v* **1** [T *about, on*] to praise (someone) too much or insincerely in order to please: *We flattered her (on/about her cooking)*. **2** [I;T] (of experiences) to give pleasure to: *She was flattered at the invitation/to be invited/that they invited her.|a flattering invitation* **3** [I;T] (of a picture or photograph) to make (the person shown there) look too beautiful: *a flattering photograph of George|The picture certainly doesn't flatter you*. **4 flatter oneself (that)** to have the pleasant though perhaps mistaken opinion (that): *We flatter ourselves that we can do without their help*. **–flatterer** n

flat·ter·y /'flætəri/ n **-ies** [C;U] the action of FLATTERING, or a FLATTERING remark: *Flattery will get you nowhere!*

flat·u·lence /'flætʃələns/ n [U] fml too much gas in the stomach; WIND¹ (3)

flaunt /flɔnt, flɑnt/ v [T] derog to show for public admiration (something one is proud of): *to flaunt one's new fur coat* –compare: *She came into school flaunting her new red dress.|She flouted (=purposely broke) the school rules by not wearing the proper uniform*.

flau·tist /'flɔtɪst, 'flɑʊ-/ n esp. BrE for FLUTIST

fla·vor¹ AmE‖**flavour** BrE /'fleyvər/ n [C;U] **1** a substance that gives (a) taste; quality that only the tongue can experience: *a strong flavor of cheese|Choose from six popular flavors of ice cream!|This coffee has a nice flavor/has plenty of flavor.|*(fig.) *a story with an unpleasant flavor* **2 -flavored** having the stated flavor: *strawberry-flavored ice cream* **–flavorless** adj

flavor² AmE‖**flavour** BrE v [T with] to give FLAVOR¹ to: *I flavored the cake with chocolate*.

fla·vor·ing AmE‖**flavouring** BrE /'fleyvərɪŋ/ also **flavor** AmE– n [U] something added to food to give or improve the FLAVOR¹: *Add a spoonful of banana flavoring*.

flaw¹ /flɔ/ n a small sign of damage that makes an object not perfect: *a flaw in a plate|*(fig.) *the flaws in a contract*

flaw² v [T] to make a FLAW in: *The SCAR (=mark on the skin) flawed her skin*.

flaw·less /'flɔlɪs/ adj perfect; with no FLAW: *flawless beauty|*(fig.) *a flawless performance* **–flawlessly** adv

flax /flæks/ n [U] (the thread made from the stem of) a plant with blue flowers, used for making LINEN (1)

flax·en /'flæksən/ adj esp. lit (of hair) pale yellow: *flaxen curls/hair*

flea /fliy/ n a small jumping insect without wings, that bites human or animal flesh to live on blood

flea·bag /'fliybæg/ n AmE infml derog a cheap dirty hotel: *Let's find a better hotel. This one is a real fleabag!*

flea mar·ket /'· ,··/ n a market usu. in the street, where old or used goods are sold

fleck¹ /flɛk/ n a small mark or spot; a small piece (of something): *brown cloth with flecks of red|flecks of dust*

fleck² v [T usu. pass.] to mark or cover with FLECKS: *The grass under the trees was flecked with sunlight*.

flee /fliy/ v **fled** /flɛd/, **fleeing** [I;T] fml to escape (from) by hurrying away: *They all fled (from) the burning ship.|to flee the country* (=to go abroad for safety)

fleece¹ /fliys/ n a sheep's woolly coat

fleece² v **fleeced, fleecing** [T] infml to rob by a trick or by charging too much money: *They really fleeced us at that hotel!*

fleec·y /'fliysiy/ adj **-ier, -iest** woolly, like a FLEECE¹: *a coat with a warm fleecy LINING|little fleecy clouds*

fleet /fliyt/ n **1** a number of ships, such as warships in the navy: *The fleet is coming!* **2** a group of buses, aircraft, etc., under one control

fleet·ing /'fliytɪŋ/ adj (of time or periods) short; passing quickly: *a fleeting look* **–fleetingly** adv

flesh /flɛʃ/ n **1** [U] the soft substance including fat and muscle, that covers the bones and lies under the skin **2** [U] the soft part of a fruit or vegetable, which can be eaten **3** [the S] (the desires, esp. sexual, of) the human body as opposed to the mind or soul: *the pleasures of the flesh* **4 flesh and blood** relatives; family: *I have to help them because they're my own flesh and blood*. **5 in the flesh** in real life: *He's more handsome in the flesh than in his photographs*.

flesh·y /'flɛʃiy/ adj **-ier, -iest** of or like flesh; fat

flew /fluw/ v past tense of FLY

flex¹ /flɛks/ v [T] to bend and move (one of one's limbs, muscles, etc.) so as to stretch and loosen: *The runners flexed their muscles as they waited for the race to begin*.

flex² n [C;U] BrE for CORD

flex·i·ble /'flɛksəbəl/ adj **1** that can be bent easily **2** that can change or be changed to be suitable for new needs, changed conditions, etc.: *We can visit you on Saturday or Sunday; our plans are fairly flexible*. –opposite **inflexible**; compare RIGID **–flexibility** /ˌflɛksə'bɪlətiy/ n [U]

flex·time /'flɛks-taɪm/ also **flexitime** /'flɛksə,taɪm/– n [U] AmE a system of working hours in which workers can choose the times they start work and finish: *I'm on flextime, so I come to work at 10:30 and leave at 6:30*.

flick¹ /flɪk/ v **1** [I;T] to (cause to) move with a light quick blow: *to flick the SWITCH|The cow flicked the flies away with its tail*. **2** [T] to strike with a light quick blow from a whip, the finger, etc.: *The rider flicked the horse with her whip to make it go faster*.

flick² n a short light blow, stroke, or movement as with a whip, finger, etc.: *The horses ran faster with every flick of the whip*.

flick·er¹ /'flɪkər/ v [I] to burn or move unsteadily: *The wind blew the flickering candle out.|Shadows flickered on the wall.|*(fig.) *The hope that her husband might be alive still flickered within her*.

SPELLING NOTE

Words with the sound /f/ may be spelled **ph-**, like **photograph**.

flood

flicker² *n* [S] a FLICKERing¹ action: (fig.) *a flicker of hope*

fli·er, flyer /'flaɪər/ *n AmE* for HANDBILL

flight¹ /flaɪt/ *n* **1** [C;U] the act of flying: *a bird in flight|a bird's first flight from the nest|*(fig.) *a flight of the imagination* **2** [C] a trip by plane: *Did you have a good flight?|There are two flights to Tokyo* –see TRAVEL (USAGE) **3** a group of birds or aircraft flying together **4** [C] a set of stairs (between floors)

flight² *n* [C;U] (an example of) the act of running away or escaping (FLEEing): *When the police arrived, the thieves took (to) flight, leaving the jewels.*

flight at·tend·ant /'·· ·,··/ also **steward** (*masc.*), **stewardess, airhostess, hostess** (*fem.*)– *n* someone who looks after the comfort and safety of the passengers in an aircraft: *The flight attendant is demonstrating the use of the oxygen masks.*

flight·less /'flaɪtlɪs/ *adj* unable to fly: *The PENGUIN is a flightless bird.*

flight·y /'flaɪtiʸ/ *adj* **-ier, -iest** (esp. of one's behavior) unsteady; often changing –**flightiness** *n* [U]

flim·sy /'flɪmziʸ/ *adj* **-sier, -siest** not strong; light and thin: *flimsy cloth|*(fig.) *a flimsy argument* –**flimsiness** *n* [U]

flinch /flɪntʃ/ *v* [I *from*] to move back a little when shocked by pain or fear: *Jane didn't flinch once when the doctor cleaned the cut in her arm.| He flinched when I raised by hand suddenly. He thought I was going to hit him.*

fling¹ /flɪŋ/ *v* **flung** /flʌŋ/, **flinging** [T] to throw violently or with force: *Don't fling your clothes on the floor; hang them up.|Every morning he flings the windows open and breathes deeply.|She flung her shoe at the cat.|The military government flung its opponents into prison.*

fling² *n* **1** a short, often wild time of satisfying one's own desires, (esp. in the phrase **have one's/a fling**) **2** also **highland fling**– a spirited Scottish dance

flint /flɪnt/ *n* **1** [C;U] (a piece of) very hard gray stone that makes very small flashes of flame when struck with steel **2** [C] a small piece of metal used in cigarette lighters to light the liquid or gas

flip¹ /flɪp/ *v* **-pp- 1** [T] to send (something) spinning into the air with a light quick blow: *to flip a coin* **2** [I;T *over*] to turn over: *to flip an egg over in the pan* **3** [I *out*] *infml* also **flip one's lid** *AmE*– to become angry, excited, etc.: *My brother really flipped after his experiences in the war.|I knew you'd flip when you saw my new car.* **4** [I *for*] *AmE infml* to fall in love (with someone): *He really flipped (for her).* –compare FREAK OUT

flip through sthg. *v prep* [T] to read (a book, paper, etc.) rapidly and carelessly

flip² *n* [C] a quick light blow that sends something spinning into the air

flip·pant /'flɪpənt/ *adj* disrespectful about serious subjects, esp. when trying to be amusing: *flippant remarks* –**flippantly** *adv* –**flippancy** *n* [U]

flip·per /'flɪpər/ *n* **1** a limb of certain larger sea animals (esp. SEALs), with a flat edge used for swimming **2** a large flat shoe shaped like this, worn to aid swimming

flirt¹ /flɜrt/ *v* [I *with*] to behave with a member of the opposite sex in a way that attracts his/her attention: (fig.) *I've been flirting with* (=considering, but not very seriously) *the idea of changing my job.* –**flirtation** /flɜr'teɪʃən/ *n* [C;U] –**flirtatious** *adj*

flirt² *n* a person who generally FLIRTs¹ with members of the opposite sex

flit /flɪt/ *v* **-tt-** [I] to fly or move lightly or quickly: *The birds flitted from branch to branch.*

float¹ /floʷt/ *v* **1** [I;T] to (cause to) stay at the top of liquid or be held upin air without sinking: *Wood floats on water.|We are trying to float the sunken ship.|A feather floated down on the wind.* **2** [T] to establish (a business, company, etc.) by selling shares **3** [I;T] to allow the exchange value of (a country's money) to vary freely from day to day: *After the dollar was floated, its value went down.*

float² *n* **1** a piece of wood or other light object that floats, esp. as used on a fishing line or net **2** a large flat vehicle on which special shows, ornamental scenes, etc., are drawn in processions **3** a sum of money kept for use if an unexpected need arises –compare KITTY² (2)

float·ing /'floʷtɪŋ/ *adj* not fixed or settled: *The city has a large floating population.|People who do not always vote for the same political party are called **floating voters.***

flock¹ /flɑk/ *n* **1** a group of sheep, goats, or birds **2** *infml* a crowd; large number of people **3** the group of people who regularly attend a church: *The priest warned his flock against breaking God's law.*

flock² *v* [I *to, into*] to gather or move in large crowds: *People flocked to the theater to see the new movie.*

floe /floʷ/ *n* **floes** a large mass of ice floating on the surface of the sea

flog /flɑg, flɔg/ *v* **-gg-** [T] **1** to beat severely with a whip or stick, esp. as a punishment **2** **flog a dead horse** *infml* to waste one's time with useless efforts

flog·ging /'flɑgɪŋ, 'flɔ-/ *n* [C;U] a severe beating with a whip or stick, esp. as punishment

flood¹ /flʌd/ *n* **1** the covering with water of a place that is usu. dry; great overflow of water: *The town was destroyed by the floods after the storm.|The water rose to flood level.* **2** a large flow: *There was a flood of complaints about the bad language used in the show.*

flood² *v* [I;T] **1** to (cause to) be filled or covered with water: *Every spring the river floods (the valley).|Our street floods whenever we have rain.|After the rains we were* **flooded out.** (=forced to leave because of a flood) **2** to arrive (at) (a place) in large numbers: *After the show complaints flooded the television station's offices.|Requests for information flooded in after the advertisement.|Settlers flooded from Europe to*

America in the 19th century.

flood·gate /'flʌdgeɪt/ *n* a gate used for controlling the flow from a large body of water: (fig.) *The new law* **opened the floodgates** *of the people's bitterness and they marched down the streets demanding justice.*

flood·light¹ /'flʌdlaɪt/ *n* a large electric light used for lighting a stage, the outside of buildings, football grounds, etc., esp. at night –compare SEARCHLIGHT

floodlight² *v* **-lighted** *or* **-lit** /lɪt/, **lighting** [T] to light by using FLOODLIGHTS¹: *The White House is floodlit at night.*

floor¹ /flɔr, floʷr/ *n* **1** [C] the surface on which one stands indoors; surface nearest the ground: *A* **dance floor** *is a level area specially prepared for dancing.* **2** [C] a level of a building; STORY: *I live on the ground floor.* (=the floor level with the street)|*Our office is on the 6th floor.* **3** [*the* S] the part of a congress or council building where members sit and speak: *Senator Kennedy has the floor.*

floor² *v* [T] **1** to provide with a floor: *The room was floored with boards.* **2** *infml* to knock down: *The soldier floored his attacker with one heavy blow.*|(fig.) *The news completely floored me; I hadn't been expecting it.*

floor·board /'flɔrbɔrd, 'floʷrboʷrd/ *n* a board in a wooden floor

floor lamp /'· ·/ *n* a lamp on a tall base which stands on the floor –see illustration on page 399

flop /flɑp/ *v* **-pp-** [I] **1** to move or fall heavily or awkwardly: *He can't swim much; he just flops around in the water.* **2** *infml* (of a plan, a performance, etc.) to fail badly; be unsuccessful: *The new play flopped after only two weeks.* –**flop** *n* [C;S]: *He fell with a flop into the water.*|*The party was a complete flop; nobody enjoyed it.*

flop·house /'flɑphaʊs/ **-houses** /ˌhaʊzɪz/ *AmE infml* a cheap hotel, esp. one where homeless people stay: *Don't look for a hotel in that neighborhood. There's nothing but flophouses there.*

flop·py /'flɑpiʸ/ *adj* **-pier, -piest** soft and falling loosely: *a floppy hat*|*This material's too floppy for a coat.*|*a dog with floppy ears* –**floppily** *adv* –**floppiness** *n* [U]

flo·ra /'flɔrə, 'floʷrə/ *n* **-ras** *or* **rae** /riʸ, raɪ/ [C;U] *tech* all the plants growing wild in a particular place, or belonging to a particular age in history: *the flora of chalk areas*|*stone age flora* –compare FAUNA

flo·ral /'flɔrəl, 'floʷrəl/ *adj* [*no comp.*] of flowers: *floral patterns*

flor·id /'flɔrɪd, 'flɑrɪd/ *adj* **1** *often derog* having (too) much ornamentation: *florid language* **2** (of a person's face) having a red skin: *a florid* COMPLEXION –**floridly** *adv*

flo·rist /'flɔrɪst, 'floʷr-, 'flɑr-/ *n* (a person who keeps) a store for selling flowers

flo·til·la /floʷ'tɪlə/ *n* a group of small ships, esp. warships

---

SPELLING NOTE

Words with the sound /f/ may be spelled **ph-**, like **photograph**.

---

flounce /flaʊns/ *v* **flounced, flouncing** [I *out, off*] to move violently in anger: *She refused my advice and flounced out of the house.*

floun·der /'flaʊndər/ *v* [I] to move about with great difficulty, esp. making violent efforts not to sink: *The child floundered in the water until someone jumped in to save him.*|*The horse and its rider floundered through the deep snow.*|(fig.) *When one of his listeners laughed rudely, he floundered and forgot what he was saying.*

flour /flaʊər/ *n* [U] grain, esp. wheat, made into powder and used for making bread, pastry, cakes, etc. –sounds like **flower**

flour·ish¹ /'flɜrɪʃ, 'flʌrɪʃ/ *v* **1** [I] to grow healthily; be active or successful: *This plant will not flourish without water.*|*The company has really flourished since we moved our factory to Chicago.* **2** [T] to wave in the hand and so draw attention to (something): *"I've passed my examination!" shouted Jane, flourishing a letter.*

flourish² *n* a showy fancy movement or manner that draws people's attention to one: *He opened the door with a flourish.*

flout /flaʊt/ *v* [T] *fml* to treat without respect or consideration; go against: *She flouted all my offers of help and friendship.*|*You've flouted my orders.* (=disobeyed them)

flow¹ /floʷ/ *v* [I] (of liquid) to run or spread smoothly like a river; pour: *Blood was flowing from his wound.*|*Her tears flowed fast.*|(fig.) *The cars flowed in a steady stream along the main road.*|(fig.)*As they sat around the fire, the conversation began to flow freely.*|(fig.)*Her thick wavy hair flowed over her shoulders.*|(fig.)*The letter was written in graceful flowing handwriting.*

flow² *n* **1** [S *of*] a pouring out: *A flow of oil poured all over the floor.*|*a flow of meaningless words* **2** [*the* U *of*] (the rate of) a smooth steady movement: *the gentle flow of the river*|*the flow of gas*|*electricity to our homes* **3** [*the* S *of*] the rise (of the TIDE) –compare EBB¹ (L)

flow·er¹ /'flaʊər/ *n* **1** the part of a plant, often beautiful and colored, that produces seeds or fruit. **2** a plant that is grown for the beauty of this part: *We grow vegetables in the back of the house, and flowers in the front.*

flower² *v* [I] (of a plant) to produce flowers: *This bush flowers in the spring.*|*flowering plants*|(fig.) *Her genius as a painter flowered very early.*

flow·er·bed /'flaʊər,bɛd/ *n* a piece of ground, esp. in a garden, in which flowers are grown for ornament

flow·ered /'flaʊərd/ *adj* [A] ornamented with flower patterns: *flowered dress material*

flow·er·pot /'flaʊər,pɑt/ *n* a pot in which a plant can be grown in earth

flow·er·y /'flaʊəriʸ/ *adj* **-ier, -iest** **1** full of wild flowers **2** ornamented with flowers: *a flowery pattern*|(fig.) *flowery speech* (=full of fanciful words).

flown /floʷn/ *v* past participle of FLY

flu /fluʷ/ also **influenza** *fml or tech–* *n* [U] a disease which is like a bad cold but more serious

fluc·tu·ate /ˈflʌktʃuˌweʲt/ v -ated, -ating [I]
fml to rise and fall; change from one state to
another: *The price of vegetables fluctuates
according to the season.|fluctuating tem-
peratures|His feelings fluctuated between ex-
citement and fear.* —**fluctuation**
/ˌflʌktʃuˈweʲʃən/ n [C;U in]
flue /fluʷ/ n a metal pipe or tube up which
smoke or heat passes, usu. to a chimney
flu·en·cy /ˈfluʷənsiʲ/ n [U in] the quality or
condition of being FLUENT
flu·ent /ˈfluʷənt/ adj 1 [in] (of a person)
speaking or writing in an easy smooth manner: *He is fluent in five languages.* 2 (of
speech, writing, etc.) expressed readily and
without pause: *She speaks fluent though not
very correct English.* —**fluently** adv
fluff¹ /flʌf/ n [U] 1 soft light loose waste from
woolen or other materials: *The room hasn't
been properly cleaned; there's fluff and dust
under the furniture.* 2 very soft fur or hair on
a young animal or bird
fluff² v [T] 1 [out, up] to make (something
soft) appear larger by shaking or by brushing
or pushing upwards: *The bird fluffed out its
feathers in the sun. |She fluffed up her hair.* 2
infml to do (something) badly or unsuccessfully: *The actress fluffed her lines.*
(=forgot what she had to say)
fluff·y /ˈflʌfiʲ/ adj -ier, -iest like or covered
with FLUFF¹ (2) —**fluffiness** n [U]
flu·id¹ /ˈfluʷɪd/ adj having the quality of flowing, like liquids, air, gas, etc.; not solid:
(fig.) *Our ideas on the subject are still fluid.*
(=not fixed or settled) —**fluidity** /fluʷˈɪdətiʲ/
n [U]
fluid² n [C;U] a liquid
fluid ounce /ˌ·· ˈ·/ n (a measure of liquid
equal to) one 20th of a PINT or 0·0284 of a
liter
fluke /fluʷk/ n [S] *infml* a piece of accidental
good fortune: *He passed his examination by
a fluke; he knew very little about the sub-
ject.|She is not usually good at tennis; that
winning stroke was a fluke.*
flung /flʌŋ/ v past tense & participle of FLING
flunk /flʌŋk/ v AmE infml [I;T] to fail (someone) esp. in an examination or a course: *I
flunked the the final exam.|The teacher
flunked him in geography.*
  flunk out v adv AmE infml [I] to be
dismissed from a school or college for
failure: *She flunked out of college and went to
work as a waitress.*
flu·o·res·cent /fluəˈrɛsənt, flɔ-, floʷ-/ adj (of
a substance) having the quality of giving out
bright white light when electric or other
waves are passed through: *fluorescent lighting* —**fluorescence** n [U]
flur·ry¹ /ˈflɜriʲ, ˈflʌriʲ/ n -ries 1 [C] a sudden
sharp rush of wind or rain 2 [S of] a sudden
shared feeling: *A flurry of excitement went
around the crowd as the movie star arrived.*
flurry² v -ried, -rying [T] to confuse and make
(someone) have difficulty in thinking clearly
of what should be done; make nervous and
uncertain
flush¹ /flʌʃ/ n 1 [S of] (an act of cleaning with)
a sudden flow of liquid, esp. water): *The*

*pipe is blocked; give it a good flush.|(fig.) He
felt a flush of anger and hit her.* 2 [C;S] (a red
appearance of the face because of) a flow of
blood to the face:*The sick boy had an
unhealthy flush and breathed with difficulty.*
3 **in the first flush of** in the first part of
something pleasant: *In the first flush of suc-
cess he ordered drinks for everybody.|the first
flush of youth*
flush² v 1 [T out] to clean or drive out by a
sudden flow of water: *The pipe is blocked;
try flushing it (out) with hot water.|(fig.) The
police flushed the criminals out (of their hiding place).* 2 [I;T] to (cause to) become
empty of waste matter by means of a flow of
water: *The TOILET won't flush. I've tried
flushing it several times, but it won't work.* 3
[I;T] (of a person, the skin, or face) to (cause
to) become red: *She flushed when she
couldn't answer the question.|Her face was
flushed with fever.|(fig.) He was flushed with
(=excited by) excitement when he learned
that he'd won.*
flush³ adj 1 [with; no comp.] exactly on a
level (with); even in surface: *These cabinets
are flush with the wall.* (=they do not stick
out) 2 [F] *infml* having plenty of money: *I've
just been paid, so I'm feeling quite flush.*
flush⁴ adv [adv +adv/ prep] in a FLUSH³ (1)
way: *The door fits flush into its frame.*
flus·ter /ˈflʌstər/ v [T] to cause (someone) to
be hot, nervous, and confused: *The shouts of
the crowd flustered the speaker and he forgot
what he was going to say.* —**fluster** n [S]: *I got
in a fluster at some traffic lights, so I failed my
driving test.*
flute /fluʷt/ n a pipelike wooden or metal
musical instrument with finger holes, played
by blowing across a hole in the side
flut·ist /ˈfluʷtɪst/ n AmE‖ also **flautist** esp.
BrE– someone who plays the flute, esp. as a
profession
flut·ter¹ /ˈflʌtər/ v 1 [I;T] (of a bird, an insect
with large wings, etc.) to move (the wings)
quickly and lightly without flying: *I can hear
a bird fluttering in the chimney.* 2 [I] to fly by
doing this: *The BUTTERFLY fluttered into the
room.|(fig.) The dead leaves fluttered to the
ground.* 3 [I;T] to wave or move quickly up
and down or backwards and forwards: *The
flag fluttered in the wind.|to flutter one's
EYELASHes|(fig.) His heart fluttered with
excitement.*
flutter² n [S] a FLUTTERing¹ movement: *There
was a flutter of wings among the trees.|(fig.)
Everybody was **in a flutter** (of excitement) as
the President came in.|Her new book on sex
caused a flutter.*
flux /flʌks/ n [U] *fml* continual change; condition of not being settled: *Our future plans
are unsettled; everything is **in a state of flux**.*
fly¹ /flaɪ/ v flew /fluʷ/, flown /floʷn/, flying 1
[I] to move through the air on wings: *The
bird flew up into the tree.* 2 [I;T] **a** (of an
aircraft) to move through the air: *The plane
flew around the city several times.* **b** to cause
(an aircraft) to move through the air: *They
flew the plane around the world.* 3 [I] to
travel by aircraft: *He flew to Rome yesterday.*

4 [T] to move through the air over: *Powerful aircraft now fly the Atlantic in a few hours.* **5** to move rapidly or suddenly: *The train flew past.|She flew up the stairs.|The window flew open.|The day has simply flown (by).* (=has passed quickly)|(fig.) *He* **flew into a** (*terrible*) **temper.**|(fig.) *I'm late, I must fly.* (=leave quickly) **6** [I;T *from*] to escape (from); FLEE: *He's* **flown the coop** (=gone away or escaped) **7 fly off the handle** *infml* to become suddenly and unexpectedly angry **8 let fly (at)** to attack with words or blows

fly² *n* **flies 1** a small flying insect with two wings, esp. the **housefly 2** any of several other types of flying insect: *a* BUTTERFLY **3 fly in the ointment** a small unwanted thing that spoils the pleasure, perfection, etc. of an occasion **4 there are no flies on someone** someone is not a fool and cannot be tricked **5** the front opening of a pair of pants: *Your fly's open!*

fly·er /'flaɪr/ *n* →FLIER

fly·ing¹ /'flaɪ-ɪŋ/ *adj* [A *no comp.*] **1** (of a jump) made after running for a short distance: *He took a flying* LEAP *and jumped across the stream.* **2 get off to a flying start** to make a very good beginning **3 come off with/pass (a test, etc.) with flying colors** to succeed (on a test, etc.) particularly well **4 send flying** to knock (someone) over, backwards, or through the air, esp. with a violent blow

flying² *n* [U] the action of traveling by aircraft, as a means of getting from one place to another or as a sport: *I don't like flying; it makes me feel sick.|a flying club*

flying sau·cer /ˌ·· '··/ *n* a plate-shaped spaceship which is believed to come from another world

fly·o·ver /'flaɪˌoʷvər/ *n* BrE for OVERPASS

FM *abbrev. for:* **frequency modulation**; a system of broadcasting, usu. on VHF, in which the signal comes at a varying number of times per second: *an FM radio* –compare AM

foal /foʷl/ *n* a young horse

foam¹ /foʷm/ *n* [U] a whitish mass of bubbles on the surface of a liquid or on skin: *The breaking waves had edges of foam.|* **Foam rubber** *is soft rubber full of small air bubbles.* –**foamy** *adj* **-ier, -iest**

foam² *v* [I] to produce FOAM¹: *The dying animal was found* **foaming at the mouth.**

fob sbdy. **off** /fab/ *v adv* **-bb-** [T *with*] to take no notice of; wave (someone) aside (by means of): *I asked her for the money she owed me, but she just* **fobbed** *me* **off** (*with a stupid excuse*).

fo·cal point /'foʷkəl ˌpɔɪnt/ *n* [*the* U] →FOCUS¹ (2): *Television is now the focal point of family life in many American homes.*

fo·c'sle /'foʷksəl/ also **forecastle** *fml* – *n* the front part of a ship, where the sailors live

fo·cus¹ /'foʷkəs/ *n* **-cuses** *or* **-ci** /saɪ/ **1** [C] the

point at which beams of light or heat, or waves of sound meet after their direction has been changed **2** [*the* U *of*] the central point; place of greatest activity; center of interest: *Because of his strange clothes, he immediately became the focus of attention when he entered the room.* **3 in/out of focus** (not) giving a clear picture because the LENS is (not) correctly placed: *This picture of Carlos isn't in focus. I can't see his face clearly.* –**focal** /'foʷkəl/ *adj*

focus² *v* **-s-** *or* **-ss-** [I;T *on*] to bring or come into (a) FOCUS¹: *This photograph looks funny. I think you forgot to focus the camera.|The beams of light moved across the sky and focused on the plane.|*(fig.) *All eyes were focused on him.|*(fig.) *I've got to try to focus my mind on work.*

fod·der /'fadər/ *n* [U] food for horses and farm animals

foe /foʷ/ *n lit* an enemy

foe·tus /'fiʸtəs/ *n* →FETUS

fog¹ /fag, fɔg/ *n* [C;U] (a state or time of) very thick mist which makes it difficult to see

fog² *v* **-gg-** [I;T *up*] to (cause to) become difficult to see through because of a misty covering: *The steam has fogged my glasses.|My glasses have fogged up in this steamy room.*

fog·bound /'fagbaʊnd, 'fɔg-/ *adj* [*no comp.*] prevented by FOG¹ from traveling as usual: *We were fogbound at Kennedy Airport for 12 hours.|fogbound travelers*

fog·gy /'fagiʸ, 'fɔgiʸ/ *adj* **-gier, -giest 1** not clear because of FOG¹; very misty: *Foggy weather has made driving conditions very dangerous.* **2 not have the foggiest (idea)** *infml* not to know at all: *"What are you going to do this evening?" "I haven't (got) the foggiest."* –**foggily** *adv* –**fogginess** *n* [U]

foi·ble /'fɔɪbəl/ *n fml* a small rather foolish personal habit: *My grandfather always takes a cold bath in the morning. It's a foible of his.*

foil¹ /fɔɪl/ *v* [T *in*] *fml* to prevent (someone) from succeeding in (some plan): *The thief was foiled in his attempt to enter the house.|We foiled his attempt to escape.*

foil² *n* a light narrow sword with a covered point, used in FENCING

foil³ *n* **1** [U] (paper covered with) metal beaten or rolled into very thin paperlike sheets: *Chocolate is wrapped in foil to keep it fresh.* **2** [C *for, to*] a person or thing that makes more noticeable the better or different quality of another: *In the play, a wicked old uncle acts as a foil to the noble young prince.*

foist sbdy./sthg. **on** sbdy. /fɔɪst/ *v prep* [T] to cause (an unwanted person or thing) to be suffered for a time by (someone): *They didn't invite him to go out with them, but he foisted himself on them.|He's always trying to foist his political ideas on other people.*

fold¹ /foʷld/ *v* **1** [T *up*] to turn, bend, or press back one part of (something) and lay on the remaining part: *She folded the letter (up/in half).|She folded up the paper to make a toy plane.|He folded his arms.* (=crossed them over his chest) –opposite **unfold 2** [I] to be able to be bent back: *Does this table fold?*|*a folding bed* **3** [T] to wrap: *He folded the seeds in a piece of paper.* **4** [I *up*] (esp. of a business) to fail

fold² *n* a folded part or place: *The curtain hung in heavy folds.*|*the folds in a shirt that has been packed too tightly*

fold³ *n* a sheltered corner of a field where farm animals, esp. sheep, are kept for protection, surrounded by a fence or wall

-fold 1 by a certain number of times: *The price has increased fourfold.*|*a fourfold increase* **2** having a certain number of parts: *My ambition is twofold: to write books and become rich.*

fold·er /'fowldər/ *n* a folded piece of cardboard used for holding loose papers

fo·li·age /'fowliʸɪdʒ/ *n* [U] *fml* leaves

folk¹ /fowk/ also **folks** *AmE*– *n* [P] people (of one race or nation, or sharing a particular kind of life): *Some folk seem unable to spend money.*|*country folk*|*an old folks' home*

folk² *adj* [A *no comp.*] (esp. of music) of the ordinary people; often traditional: *folk music/songs/art*

folk·lore /'fowk-lɔr, -lowr/ *n* [U] (the study of) all the knowledge, beliefs, habits, etc., of a racial or national group, still preserved by memory, or in use from earlier and simpler times –see also LORE

folks /fowks/ *n* [P] *infml* **1** relations, esp. parents: *I'd like you to meet my folks.* **2** *AmE* for FOLK¹

fol·low /'fdlow/ *v* **1** [I;T] to come or go after: *You go first and I'll follow (you) later.*|*The child follows her mother around all day.* **2** [T] to go after in order to catch: *I think we're being followed!* **3** [I;T] to come next (after) in order: *The number 5 follows the number 4.*|*Disease often follows war.*|*The results were as follows.* (=as will now be listed)|*I'll have fish, with fruit to follow.* (=as the next dish) **4** [T] to go in the same direction as; continue along: *Follow the road until you come to the hotel.* **5** [T] to listen to carefully: *She followed the speaker with the greatest attention.* **6** [I;T] to understand clearly: *I didn't quite follow (you/what you said); could you explain it again?* **7** [T] to accept and act according to: *Did you follow the instructions on the packet?*|*These orders must be followed.*|*He followed his sister's example and went to college.*|*to follow one's conscience* **8** [I] to be a necessary effect or result: *Just because you are rich, it doesn't follow* (=you cannot reason from this) *that you are happy.* **9 follow in someone's footsteps** to follow an example set by someone in the past

follow sthg.↔ **through** *v adv* [T] to complete; carry out exactly to the end: *to follow through a line of inquiry*

follow sthg.↔ **up** *v adv* [T on] **1** to act further on (something): *That's an interesting suggestion, and I'll certainly follow it up.*|*The company tries to follow up on complaints.* **2** [*with*] to take further action after (something) (by means of something else): *He followed up his letter with a visit the next week.* –**follow-up** /'·· ,·/ *n* [A;C]: *She wrote a*

follow-up (=continuation) *to the story.*|*a* follow-up (=additional) *visit from the doctor*

fol·low·er /'fdlowər/ *n* an admirer or supporter of some person, belief, or cause: *He's a faithful follower of the Hindu faith.*|*St. Peter was one of Christ's first followers.*

fol·low·ing¹ /'fdlowɪŋ/ *adj* [*the* A] next (to be mentioned): *The child was sick in the evening, but on the following day he seemed well again.*|*Payment may be made in any of the following ways: by cash, by check, or by* CREDIT CARD.

following² *n* **following 1** [*the*] the one or ones about to be mentioned: *The following have been chosen to play in tomorrow's game: Roberto Lopez, Hugh Williams, Robin Sinclair . . .* **2** [*usu. sing.*] a group of supporters or admirers: *This senator has quite a large following in the South.*

following³ *prep* after: *Following the speech, there will be a few minutes for questions.*

fol·ly /'fdliʸ/ *n* **-lies** [C;U] *fml* (an act of) foolishness:*To reduce public spending on health would be an act of the greatest folly.*|*The old man smiled sadly as he remembered the follies of his youth.*

fond /fdnd/ *adj* **1** [*of*] loving in a kind, gentle, or tender way: *He signed the letter, "With fondest love, George."*|*She likes all her grandchildren, but she's especially fond of Peter.*|*I'm very fond of ice cream.* **2** [A] foolishly loving; yielding weakly to loving feelings: *A fond mother may spoil her child.* **3** [A] foolishly trusting or hopeful: *In spite of his failures, he has* **a fond belief** *in his own intelligence.* –**fondness** *n* [C;U *for*]

fon·dle /'fandl/ *v* **-dled, -dling** [T] to touch gently and lovingly; stroke softly: *The old lady fondled her cat as it sat beside her.*

fond·ly /'fandliʸ/ *adv* **1** in a loving way: *She greeted her old friend fondly.* **2** in a foolishly hopeful manner: *She fondly imagined that she could pass her examination without studying.*

font /fant/ *n* a large vessel in a church, usu. made of stone, that contains the water used for baptizing (BAPTIZE) people

food /fuwd/ *n* [C;U] **1** something that living creatures or plants take into their bodies to give them strength and help them to develop and to live: *Milk is the natural food for young babies.*|*a new kind of liquid plant food* **2** (an example of) something solid for eating: *They gave us plenty of food, but there wasn't enough to drink.*|*Too many rich foods will increase your weight.*|(fig.) *His father's advice gave the boy* **food for thought.** (=plenty to think about)

food stamps /'· ·/ *n* [usu. pl.] stamps given to poor people by the US government to buy food

fool¹ /fuwl/ *n derog* a silly person: *You fool! I asked for water, not wine.*|*I felt like such a fool when I realized I'd gotten on the wrong bus.*|*He's always afraid of* **making a fool of himself.** (=doing something silly)|*Are you trying to* **make a fool of me?** (=trick me)

fool² *v* **1** [T] to deceive; trick: *You can't fool him; he's much too intelligent for that.* **2** [I *around*] to behave in a silly way: *You'll never learn anything if you don't stop fooling around.|You shouldn't fool around with dangerous chemicals.* **3** [I] to speak without serious intention; joke: *I was only fooling.*

fool·er·y /ˈfuʷləriʸ/ *n* -ies [C;U] *usu.* derog (an example of) silly behavior

fool·har·dy /ˈfuʷlˌhardiʸ/ *adj* too bold; taking or needing useless or unwise risks: *a foolhardy attempt|You were very foolhardy to jump off the bus while it was still moving.* –**foolhardiness** *n* [U]

fool·ish /ˈfuʷliʃ/ *adj* derog without good sense; stupid; laughable: *It was very foolish of you to park the car in the middle of the road.|I couldn't answer the teacher's question, and this made me feel foolish.* –**foolishly** *adv* –**foolishness** *n* [U]

fool·proof /ˈfuʷlˈpruʷf/ *adj* [no comp.] **1** that cannot go wrong: *a foolproof plan|I've found a foolproof way of doing it.* **2** very simple to understand, use, work, etc.: *a foolproof machine*

fools·cap /ˈfuʷlzkæp/ *n* [U] a large size of paper, esp. writing paper

foot¹ /fʊt/ *n* compl **1** [C] the movable part of the body at the end of the leg, below the ankle, on which a person or animal stands: *I stepped on a piece of glass, and my foot's very sore.|It's nice to sit down after being on your feet* (=standing or walking) *all day.|He got to his feet* (=stood up) *when he heard the bell.|(fml) She said she wouldn't set foot in* (=enter) *the room until it was clean.* **2** [C] (pl. sometimes **foot**) (a measure of length equal to) 12 inches or about ·305 meters: *Three feet make one yard.|He's six feet/foot tall.* –see also **- footer 3** [U *of*] the bottom or lower part: *He stood at the foot of the stairs/bed.* –compare HEAD¹ (2) **4 get one's feet wet** to become used to new situations; settle in: *He's only been at the school for two weeks, and he hasn't really gotten his feet wet yet.* **5 get/have cold feet** to be too nervous to do something, esp. losing courage just before something: *They had cold feet at the last minute and refused to sell their house.* **6 have one foot in the grave** to be very old and near death **7 on foot** (by) walking: *My bicycle is broken, so I'll have to go on foot.* **8 put one's best foot forward** to make one's best effort: *Don't worry about the examination. Just put your best foot forward and do what you can.* **9 put one's feet up** infml to rest by lying down or sitting with one's feet supported on something: *It's nice to put your feet up after a long day's work.* **10 put one's foot down** infml to speak and act firmly on a particular matter: *The father didn't like his son staying out at night, so he put his foot down and ordered him not to do it again.* **11 put one's foot in it** infml to say the wrong thing or make an awkward mistake **12 be run off one's feet** infml to be very busy **13 -footed**

SPELLING NOTE

Words with the sound /f/ may be spelled **ph-**, like **photograph**.

---

having a certain number or kind of feet: *four-footed animals|Ducks are web-footed to help them move through the water.* **14 -footer** a person or thing a certain number of feet long, high, or tall: *My brother is a six-footer.*

foot² *v* [T] *infml* to pay (a bill): (fig.) *Who'll foot the bill for your stupid behavior?*

foot·ball /ˈfʊtbɔl/ *n* **1** [U] *AmE*‖**American football** *BrE*– a game played by two teams of 11 players each, in which a ball is passed from one player to another in an attempt to get GOALs (3) **2** [U] any of several games for two teams in which a ball is kicked and/or thrown around a field in an attempt to get GOALs: *They play football at school.|a football field* **3** [C] a large ball filled with air, usu. made of leather, used in these games: *a professional footballer*

foot·bridge /ˈfʊtˌbrɪdʒ/ *n* a narrow bridge to be used only by people walking

foot·hill /ˈfʊtˌhɪl/ *n* [of; usu. pl.] a low hill at the bottom of a mountain or chain of mountains: *the foothills of the Himalayas*

foot·hold /ˈfʊthoʷld/ *n* a space (as on a rock) where a foot can be placed to help one to continue to climb up or down: *The mountain climber couldn't find many footholds on the melting ice.|(fig.) It isn't easy to get a foothold as a movie actor.* –compare HOLD² (2)

foot·ing /ˈfʊtɪŋ/ *n* [S;U] a firm placing of the feet; room or a surface for the feet to stand on: *The roof of the house sloped steeply, so the man who was doing the repairs couldn't get much of a footing on it.|(fig.) Is this business on a firm footing?* (=well-planned, with enough money to support it)

foot·lights /ˈfʊtlaɪts/ *n* [P] a row of lights along the front edge of the floor of a stage at the theater, to show up the actors

foot·loose /ˈfʊtluʷs/ *adj* free to go wherever one pleases and do what one likes; having no family or business duties which control one's way of living (often in the phrase **footloose and fancy-free**)

foot·note /ˈfʊtnoʷt/ *n* a note at the bottom of a page in a book, to explain some word or sentence, add some special remark or information, etc.

foot·path /ˈfʊtpæθ/ *n* a narrow path or track for people to walk on: *a footpath across the fields* –compare SIDEWALK

foot·print /ˈfʊtˌprɪnt/ *n* a footshaped mark made by pressing a foot onto a surface: *Who left these muddy footprints on the kitchen floor?*

foot·sore /ˈfʊtsɔr, -soʷr/ *adj* having tender, painful, or swollen feet, esp. as a result of much walking: *After a long day seeing the sights of San Francisco, they came home tired and footsore.*

foot·step /ˈfʊtstɛp/ *n* a mark or sound of a person's step: *Her footsteps were clearly marked in the snow.|He heard soft footsteps coming up the stairs.*

foot·wear /ˈfʊtwɛər/ *n* [U] *tech* shoes and boots: *A store owner might say he sold footwear; we would say he sold shoes.*

foot·work /ˈfʊtwɜrk/ *n* [U] the use of the feet, esp. skilfully in dancing, sports, etc.

for¹ /fər; *strong* fɔr/ *prep* **1** meant to be given to, used by, or used in: *I made dinner for you.*|*We bought some new chairs for the office.*|*The doctor gave her some medicine for her cold.* **2** (shows purpose): *This knife is for cutting bread.*|*What's that handle for?* (=What is its purpose?) **3** instead of; so as to help: *Let me lift that heavy box for you.* **4** in favor, support, or defense of: *He plays baseball for the Yankees.* **5** towards; so as to reach: *The children left for school.*|*This train is for Boston.* **6** so as to have, catch, or get: *waiting for a bus*|*He went for a swim.*|*Run for your life!* (=so as to save your life)|*It's too early for dinner.* **7** as part of; as being: *She ate it for breakfast.*|*What do you want for a present?*|*I'm warning you for the last time.*|*For one thing, I don't like the color, and for another, the price is too high.* **8** meaning; as a sign of: *red for danger*|*What's the French word for "dog?"* **9** (shows payment, price, or amount): *You can get a room at the hotel for $20 a day.*|*She paid $3 for the book.*|*He was put in prison for speaking out against the government.*|*I wouldn't hurt him for anything.* (=whatever I was paid) **10** (shows length of time or distance): *We have been here for a week.* (Compare *We have been here* **since** *last Tuesday/We arrived a week* **ago**.)|*They ran for ten miles.*|*I haven't seen her for* (*AmE also in*) *years.* **11** at the time of: *We invited our friends for 6 o'clock.*|*She came home for Christmas.* **12** because of: *He was rewarded for his bravery.*|*She couldn't speak for laughing.* **13** in regard to; in connection with: *Eggs are good for you.*|*Italy is famous for its wine.*|*He has great respect for his father.* **14** considered as; considering: *She's tall for her age.* (=other girls the same age are not so tall)|*It's cold for April.* **15** (used in sentences like this): *There's no reason for you to worry.* (=no reason why you should worry)|*It's dangerous for him to run so fast.* (=that he should run so fast)|*Is there somewhere for me to sleep?* (=where I can sleep) **16 for all: a** in spite of: *For all his efforts, he didn't succeed.* **b** considering how little: *He may be dead, for all I know.* (=I don't know that he isn't dead) **17 if it weren't/ if it hadn't been for** if something were not true or had not happened: *If it hadn't been for your help* (=if you had not helped) *we would never have finished it.*

USAGE Verbs like **buy** or **make** can be used without **for**, in the first meaning, if something is bought or made **for** a person or animal: *She bought a present* **for** *her friend* or *She bought her friend a present.*|*He bought a new chair* **for** *the office,* but not *He bought the office a new chair.* –see also AS **for**; see AGO (USAGE)

for² *conj fml or lit* (*used after the main part of a sentence*) and the reason is that: *She doesn't go out now, for she is very old.*

for·age /ˈfɔrɪdʒ, ˈfɑr-/ *v* **-aged, -aging** [I] to wander around looking for food or other supplies: *The campers went foraging for wood to make a fire.*|(fig.) *He foraged around in his bag for 10 minutes, but couldn't*

find the ticket.

for·ay /ˈfɔreʸ, ˈfɑreʸ/ *n* a sudden rush into enemy country, usu. by a small number of soldiers, in order to damage or seize arms, food, etc.: (fig.) *his unsuccessful foray into politics*

for·bear /fɔrˈbɛər, fər-/ *v* **-bore** /ˈbɔr, ˈboʷr/, **borne** /ˈbɔrn, ˈboʷrn/, **-bearing** [I +to-v/ v-ing/from] *fml* to make no attempt to do something that one has the right to do (esp. in a generous and merciful way): *The judge said he would forbear (from) sending her to prison, on the condition that she promised not to steal again.*

for·bear·ance /fɔrˈbɛərəns, fər-/ *n* [U] *fml* control of one's feelings so as to show patient forgiveness: *The child doesn't understand that he's doing something wrong. You have to treat him with forbearance.*

for·bear·ing /fɔrˈbɛərɪŋ, fər-/ *adj apprec* long-suffering; gentle and merciful: *He has a forbearing nature; he accepts trouble with a smile.*

for·bid /fərˈbɪd, fɔr-/ *v* **-bade** /ˈbæd, ˈbeʸd/(*fml*) *or* **-bad** /ˈbæd/, **-bidden** /ˈbɪdn/ *or* **-bid** /ˈbɪd/, **-bidding** [T] to command not to do something: *I forbade my daughter to use my car.*|*Smoking is forbidden.*|*You are forbidden to smoke in class.* –compare ALLOW

for·bid·ding /fərˈbɪdɪŋ, fɔr-/ *adj* having a fierce, unfriendly, or dangerous look: *She has a forbidding manner and is slow in making friends.*|*a forbidding range of mountains* –**forbiddingly** *adv*

force¹ /fɔrs, foʷrs/ *n* **1** [U] natural or bodily power: *the force of the explosion*|*He had to use force to get the lid off the can.* **2** [U] violence: *The thief took the money from the old man by force.* **3** [C;U] someone or something that has a strong influence or great power: *Is religion a force for good in the world?*|*the forces of evil*|*I did it from* **force of habit. 4** [C;U] a power that changes or may produce change of movement in a body on which it acts: *The force of* GRAVITY *makes things fall to earth.* **5** [C] a group of people brought together and trained for special action, esp. fighting: *the* **police force**|*The navy is one of* **the armed forces. 6 in force** in large numbers: *The police were out in force to stop any trouble.* **7 in(to) force** (of a rule, order, law, etc.) in(to) effect

force² *v* **forced, forcing** [T] **1** to use bodily force or strong influence on: *I didn't want to give him the information; he forced me* (*to do it*).|*We had to force our way through the thick bushes.*|*She forced the window open.*|*The thieves forced the lock.* (=opened it by force)|*She was trying to force her foot into a shoe that was too small for it.* **2** to produce by unwilling effort, with difficulty, or unnaturally: *forced laughter*|*Don't try to force the high notes if you really can't sing them.* **3** to hasten the growth of (a plant) by the use of heat: (fig.) *forcing young minds with too much study* **4 force someone's hand** to make someone act as one wishes or before he or she is ready to

forced /fɔrst, foʷrst/ *adj* [A *no comp.*] done or made because of a sudden happening which makes it necessary to act without delay: *The plane had to make a forced landing because two of its engines were on fire.*

force·ful /'fɔrsfəl, 'foʷrs-/ *adj apprec* (of a person, words, ideas, etc.) strong; powerful: *a forceful speech|He isn't forceful enough to be a good leader.* –compare FORCIBLE **–forcefully** *adv* **–forcefulness** *n* [U]

for·ceps /'fɔrsəps, -sɛps/ *n* [P] a medical instrument used for holding objects firmly: *a pair of forceps* –see PAIR (USAGE)

forc·i·ble /'fɔrsəbəl, 'foʷr-/ *adj* [A] **1** using bodily force: *The police had to make a forcible ENTRY into the house where the thief was hiding.* **2** having power to influence the minds of others: *I haven't yet heard a really forcible argument in favor of the new plan.* –compare FORCEFUL

forc·i·bly /'fɔrsəbliʸ, 'foʷr-/ *adv* **1** by bodily force, esp. against one's will: *He complained that he was forcibly held by the police without good reason.* **2** in a strong manner that carries belief: *Her ideas are always forcibly expressed.* **3** strongly: *His manner of speaking reminded me forcibly of his father's.*

ford¹ /fɔrd, foʷrd/ *n* a place in a river where the water is not very deep, and where it can be crossed on foot, in a car, etc., without using a bridge **–fordable** *adj*

ford² *v* [T] to cross (a river, stream, etc.) by means of a FORD¹

fore /fɔr, foʷr/ *n* **come to the fore** to become well-known; come to have a leading position: *She was elected to Congress when she was 25, and soon came to the fore in national politics.*

fore·arm /'fɔrɑrm, 'foʷr-/ *n* the lower part of the arm between the hand and the elbow

fore·bod·ing /fɔr'boʷdɪŋ, foʷr-/ *n* [C;U +(*that*)] *fml* a feeling of coming evil: *I thought of a lonely future with foreboding.|She had a foreboding that she'd never see him again.*

fore·cast¹ /'fɔrkæst, 'foʷr-/ *v* **-cast** *or* **-casted**, **-casting** [T +*that*] to say, esp. with the help of some kind of knowledge (what is going to happen at some future time): *forecasting the future|The teacher forecast that 15 of his pupils would pass the examination.|Heavy rain has been forecast for tomorrow.* –compare PREDICT

forecast² *n* [+*that*] a statement of future events, based on some kind of knowledge or judgment: *Did you listen to the weather forecast on the radio?|The newspaper's forecast that the senator would be elected again was right.* –compare PREDICTION

fore·cas·tle /'foʷksəl, 'fɔr,kæsəl, 'for-/ *n fml* for →FO'C'SLE

fore·court /'fɔrkɔrt, 'foʷrkoʷrt/ *n* a courtyard in front of a large building

fore·fa·ther /'fɔr,fɑðər, 'foʷr-/ *n* [*usu. pl.*] a person from whom the stated person is descended; relative in the far past; (male) ANCESTOR: *One of his forefathers was an early settler in the United States.*

fore·fin·ger /'fɔr,fɪŋgər, 'foʷr-/ *also* **index finger–** *n* the finger next to the thumb, with which one points

fore·front /'fɔrfrʌnt, 'foʷr-/ *n* [*the* S] the most forward place; leading position: *The brave soldier was in the forefront of the fighting.*

fore·ground /'fɔrgraʊnd, 'foʷr-/ *n* [*the* S] the nearest part of a scene in a view, a picture, or a photograph: *This is a photograph of our new house, with my parents in the foreground.* –compare BACKGROUND (1)

fore·hand /'fɔrhænd, 'foʷr-/ *n,adj* [A;C] (in tennis) (a stroke) played with the inner part of the hand and arm facing forward –compare BACKHAND

fore·head /'fɔrɪd, 'fɑrɪd, 'fɔrhɛd, 'fɑr-/ *n* the part of the face above the eyes and below the hair

for·eign /'fɔrɪn, 'fɑrɪn/ *adj* [*no comp.*] **1** of a country or nation that is not one's own: *foreign travel|Do you speak any foreign languages?|an expert on* **foreign affairs** (=one who has special knowledge about the nation's relations with other countries) **2** [to] having no place (in): *He's a very good person; unkindness is foreign to his nature.|*(fig.) *The swelling on her finger was caused by a* **foreign body** *in it.* (=a small piece of some solid material that had entered it by accident) –compare STRANGE

for·eign·er /'fɔrənər, 'fɑr-/ *n* a person who comes from or was born in another country –compare STRANGER

fore·leg /'fɔrlɛg, 'foʷr-/ *n* either of the two front legs of a four-legged animal –compare HIND

fore·man /'fɔrmən, 'foʷr-/ *n* **-men** /mən/ **forewoman** /'fɔr,wʊmən, 'foʷr-/ *fem.–* **1** a skilled and experienced worker who is put in charge of other workers **2** *AmE* (in a court of law) the leader of the 12 people (JURY) appointed to decide whether a person on trial is guilty or not: *The foreman announced that the VERDICT was guilty.*

fore·most /'fɔrmoʷst, 'foʷr-/ *adj* [*the* A] *apprec* most important; leading: *Shakespeare is said to be the foremost writer in the English language.*

fore·name /'fɔrneʸm, 'foʷr-/ *n fml* for FIRST NAME (2)

fo·ren·sic /fə'rɛnsɪk, -zɪk/ *adj* [A] *tech* related to or used in the law and the tracking of criminals: *A specialist in* **forensic medicine** *was called as a witness in the murder trial.*

fore·run·ner /'fɔr,rʌnər, 'foʷr-/ *n* a person or thing that prepares the way for, or is a sign of the coming of, someone or something that follows: *Mrs. Pankhurst, who fought for the vote for women, was a forerunner of the modern women's movement.|Heavy clouds are the forerunners of a storm.*

fore·see /fɔr'siʸ, foʷr-/ *v* **-saw** /'sɔ/, **-seen** /'siʸn/, **-seeing** [T +(*that*)] to form an idea or judgment about (what is going to happen in the future); expect: *He couldn't foresee* *(that) his trip would be delayed by bad weather.|It's difficult to foresee whether she'll be well enough to go to work.*

fore·see·a·ble /fɔr'siʸəbəl, foʷr-/ *adj* [*no comp.*] that can be FORESEEN: *a foreseeable accident|The house needs a new roof, but we can't afford one* **in the foreseeable future.** (=as far ahead in time as we can see)

fore·shad·ow /fɔr'ʃædoʷ, foʷr-/ *v* [T] *esp. lit* to be a sign of (what is coming); represent or be like (something that is going to happen)

fore·sight /'fɔrsaɪt, 'foʷr-/ *n* [U] *usu. apprec* the ability to imagine what will probably happen, allowing one to act to help or prevent developments; care or wise planning for the future —compare HINDSIGHT

fore·skin /'fɔr,skɪn, 'foʷr-/ *n* a loose fold of skin covering the end of the male sex organ

for·est /'fɔrɪst, 'far-/ *n* [C;U] **1** (a large area of land thickly covered with) trees and bushes: *A large part of Africa is made up of thick forest.* –compare WOOD (2) **2 can't see the forest for the trees** missing what's clear by looking too closely

fore·stall /fɔr'stɔl, foʷr-/ *v* [T] *fml* to defeat (someone or someone's plan) by acting first: *I meant to meet my friend at the station, but she forestalled me by arriving on an earlier train and coming to the house.|She forestalled my plan to meet her.*

for·est·er /'fɔrəstər, 'far-/ also **forest ranger** /'·· ,··/ *AmE–* *n* a person who works in, or is in charge of, a forest

for·est·ry /'fɔrəstriʸ, 'far-/ *n* [U] the science of planting and caring for large areas of trees

fore·swear /fɔr'swɛər, foʷr-/ *v* [T] →FORSWEAR

fore·tell /fɔr'tɛl, foʷr-/ *v* **-told** /'toʷld/, **-telling** [T +(*that*)/*to*] to tell (what will happen in the future); PROPHESY: *Who can foretell what will happen to the world in 1000 years' time?*

fore·thought /'fɔrθɔt, 'foʷr-/ *n* [U] *often apprec* wise planning for future needs; consideration of what is to come: *If I'd had the forethought to bring my raincoat, I wouldn't have gotten wet in the storm.*

for·ev·er ‖also **for ever** *BrE* /fə'rɛvər, fɔ-/ *adv* **1** for all future time: *He wants to live forever (and ever).* **2** *(used with the -ing form of a verb)* all the time and in an annoying way; ALWAYS (3): *He's forever asking silly questions.*

fore·warn /fɔr'wɔrn, foʷr-/ *v* [T +*that*/*of*, *against*, *about*] to warn (someone) of coming danger, unpleasantness, etc.; advise (that something will happen or be done): *The electricity went off for several hours, but we had been forewarned about it, so we had plenty of candles.*

fore·word /'fɔrwɜrd, -wərd, 'foʷr-/ *n* a short introduction at the beginning of a book, esp. in which someone who knows the writer and his/her work says something about them —compare PREFACE

for·feit /'fɔrfɪt/ *v* [T] to have (something) taken away from one because some agreement or rule has been broken, or as a punishment, or as the result of some action: *If you don't return the radio to the store within a*

week, you forfeit your right to get your money back. **–forfeit** *n* [C; *the* U *of*]: *Some scientists who have studied dangerous substances have paid the forfeit of their lives in the cause of knowledge.*

for·gave /fər'geʸv/ *v* past tense of FORGIVE

forge¹ /fɔrdʒ, foʷrdʒ/ *v* **forged, forging** **1** [I;T] to make a copy of (something) in order to deceive: *He got the money by forging his brother's signature on a check.|a forged* PASSPORT **2** [T] to form by heating and hammering: *(fig.) forging a new unity in our political party*

forge² *n* **1** (a building or room containing) a large apparatus with a fire inside, used for heating and shaping metal objects: *Horseshoes are made in a forge.* **2** (a part of a factory containing) a large apparatus that produces great heat inside itself, used for melting metal, making iron, etc.

forge³ *v* **forged, forging** [I] to move with a sudden increase of speed and power: *He forged into the lead just before the end of the race.|(fig.) She didn't do very well at school, but she* **forged ahead** *in the last two years.*

forg·er /'fɔrdʒər, 'foʷr-/ *n* a person who FORGES¹ (1)

forg·er·y /'fɔrdʒəriʸ, 'foʷr-/ *n* **-ies** [C;U] (a result of) the act or an action of forging (FORGE¹ (1)): *He was sent to prison for forgery.|When he bought the picture he was told it was by Rubens, but he later found out that it was a forgery.*

for·get /fər'gɛt/ *v* **-got** /'gɑt/, **-gotten** /'gɑtn/, **-getting** [I:T] **1** [+*to-v/v-ing/*(*that*)] to fail to remember: *She asked me to visit her, but I forgot (about it)|I forgot to.|I've forgotten his name.|Don't forget the tickets.* (=remember to bring them)*|I forgot that you don't like coffee.|I'll never forget meeting you for the first time.|I forget who it was who said it.* **2** [*about*] to stop thinking (about); put out of one's mind: *Let's forget (about) our disagreements and be friends again.|"I'm sorry I broke your coffee cup." "Forget it."|"Did you lock the door?" "No, I forgot (all) about it."* **3 forget oneself** to lose one's temper or self-control, or act in a way that is unsuitable or makes one look silly: *The little cat annoyed him so much that he forgot himself and hit her.*

for·get·ful /fər'gɛtfəl/ *adj* [*of*] having the habit of forgetting: *One should not be forgetful of one's responsibilities.|My old aunt has become very forgetful.* **–forgetfully** *adv* **–forgetfulness** *n* [U]

forget-me-not /·'·· ,·/ *n* a small plant with blue flowers

for·give /fər'gɪv/ *v* **-gave** /'geʸv/, **-given** /'gɪvən/, **-giving** /'gɪvɪŋ/ [I;T *for*] to say or feel that one is no longer angry about and/or wishing to give punishment to (someone) for (something): *I'll never forgive you for what you said to me last night.|It's best to* **forgive and forget.**

for·give·ness /fər'gɪvnɪs/ *n* [U *of*] *fml* the act of forgiving or state of being forgiven: *He asked for forgiveness of his wrong-doings.*

for·giv·ing /fər'gɪvɪŋ/ *adj* *apprec* willing or

able to forgive: *She has a gentle forgiving nature.* –**forgivingly** *adv.*

for·go, fore- /fɔr'goʷ, foʷr-/ *v* **-went** /'wɛnt/, **-gone** /'gɔn, 'gɑn/, **-going** [T] to give up; (be willing) not to have (esp. something pleasant): *If we are going to finish this today, we'll have to forgo our lunch hour.*

fork¹ /fɔrk/ *n* **1** an instrument for holding food or carrying it to the mouth, having a handle at one end with two or more points at the other –see illustration on page 379 **2** a farm or gardening tool having a wooden handle with two or more metal points at the other end **3** a place where something long and narrow divides, or one of the divided parts: *We came to a fork in the road, and we couldn't decide whether to take the left fork or the right.*

fork² *v* [I] (of something long and narrow) to divide, esp. into two parts: *You'll see our house on the left, just before the road forks.*

fork sthg.↔ **out**‖also **fork** sthg. **up/over** *AmE*– *v adv* [I;T *for, on*] *infml* to pay (money) unwillingly: *I had to fork out over $1,000 to get the car repaired!*

forked /fɔrkt/ *adj* [*no comp.*] **1** having one end divided into two or more points: *Snakes have forked tongues.* **2** that divides into two or more parts at a point: *a forked road‖ forked lightning*

fork·lift /'fɔrk,lɪft/ *n* a small vehicle with a movable apparatus on the front, used for lifting and lowering heavy goods

for·lorn /fər'lɔrn, fɔr-/ *adj esp. lit or fml* **1** (typical of one who is) left alone and unhappy: *The little lost dog had a forlorn look on its face.*‖(fig.) *We saw a row of forlorn old buildings down by the harbor.* –see ALONE (USAGE) **2 forlorn hope** a plan or attempt that is very unlikely to succeed –**forlornly** *adv* –**forlornness** *n* [U]

form¹ /fɔrm/ *n* **1** [C;U] shape; appearance: *She has a tall graceful form.*‖*a bowl in the form of* (=shaped like) *a boat* **2** [C *of*] a kind; sort: *different forms of government‖This disease takes the form of* (=shows itself as) *high fever and sickness.*‖*I dislike any form of exercise.* **3** [C] an official printed paper with spaces in which to answer questions and give other information: *Please fill out this form, giving your name, age, and address.* **4** [U] condition of skill and fitness for taking part in sport, etc.: *He's been* **in bad form/out of form** *recently, and hasn't won a game for three months.* **5** [U] spirits: *Tom was* **in fine form**; *we all laughed at his stories.*

form² *v* [I;T] **1** to take or make into a shape: *A cloud of smoke formed over the burning city.*‖*She formed the clay into a bowl/formed a bowl from the clay.*‖(fig.) *School helps to form a child's character.* **2** to take the shape of: *She tied the two sticks together to form a cross.* **3** to (cause to) come into being: *A plan began to form in his mind.*‖*After the war a*

new government was formed. **4** to be: *Flour, eggs, fat, and sugar form the main contents of a cake.* **5** to (cause to) stand or move in (a certain order): *The men formed a chain to pass the goods from the trucks to the boats.*‖*The children formed a line.*

for·mal /'fɔrməl/ *adj* ceremonial; according to accepted rules or customs: *a formal dinner party‖Formal dress must be worn.*‖*Business letters are usually formal, but we write in a natural way to friends.*‖(fig.) *He's always very formal; he never joins in on a joke.* –**formally** *adv*

for·mal·i·ty /fɔr'mælətiʸ/ *n* **-ties 1** [C] **a** an act in accordance with law or custom: *There are a few formalities to settle before you become the lawful owner of the car.* **b** an act which has lost its real meaning: *The written part of the examination is just a formality; no one ever fails it.* **2** [U] careful attention to rules and accepted forms of behavior: *There's no time for formality in everyday life.*

for·mat /'fɔrmæt/ *n* **1** the size, shape, etc., in which something, esp. a book, is produced **2** the general plan or arrangement of something: *We're trying a new format for our television show this year.*

for·ma·tion /fɔr'meʸʃən/ *n* **1** [U] the shaping or developing of something: *School has a great influence on the formation of a child's character.* **2** [C;U] (an) arrangement of people, ships, aircraft, etc.; order: *The soldiers were drawn up in battle formation.* (=in correct position to begin a battle) **3** [C] a thing which is formed; way in which a thing is formed: *There are several kinds of cloud formations.*

form·a·tive /'fɔrmətɪv/ *adj* [A] having influence in forming or developing: *a child's formative years* (=the time when the character is formed)

for·mer¹ /'fɔrmər/ *adj* [A *no comp.*] *fml* of an earlier time: *a former President of the United States‖In former times we crossed the river by boat, but now we drive over the new bridge.*

former² *n* **former** *fml* the first of two people or things just mentioned: *Of Nigeria and Ghana, the former* (=Nigeria) *has the larger population.*‖*Did he walk or swim? The former* (=walking) *seems more likely.* –compare LATTER

for·mer·ly /'fɔrmərliʸ/ *adv* in earlier times: *This famous painting was formerly owned privately, but now it belongs to the nation.* –compare LATTERLY

for·mi·da·ble /'fɔrmədəbəl, fɔr'mɪdə-/ *adj fml* **1** causing fear, doubt, anxiety, etc.: *a formidable voice‖The teacher was a formidable old lady.* **2** difficult; hard to defeat: *They faced formidable difficulties in their attempt to reach the South Pole.*‖*The examination contained several formidable questions.* –**formidably** *adv*

form·less /'fɔrmlɪs/ *adj* without shape: *A strange formless creature came out of the sea.* –**formlessly** *adv* –**formlessness** *n* [U]

form let·ter /'· ˌ··/ *n AmE* a standardized letter sent to many people: *I expected a per-*

sonal response to my letter, and instead I got a form letter.

for·mu·la /'fɔrmyələ/ *n* **-las** *or* **-lae** /ˌliʸ, ˌlaɪ/ **1** [C *for*] *tech* a general law, rule, fact, etc., expressed shortly by means of a group of letters, signs, numbers, etc.: *The chemical formula for water is* H_2O. **2** [C *for*] a list of instructions for making something: *Someone has stolen the secret formula for the liquid that fires our new spacecraft.*|(fig.) *The two countries tried to make a peace formula.* **3** [C;U] *AmE* (a) liquid milklike food for babies

for·mu·late /'fɔrmyəˌleʸt/ *v* **-lated, -lating** [T] **1** to express in a short clear form **2** to invent and prepare (a plan, suggestion, etc.) **–formulation** /ˌfɔrmyə'leʸʃən/ *n* [U]

for·ni·cate /'fɔrnəˌkeʸt/ *v* **-cated, -cating** [I] *esp. law or bibl* to have sexual relations with someone outside marriage **–fornication** /ˌfɔrnə'keʸʃən/ *n* [U]

for·sake /fər'seʸk, fɔr-/ *v* **-sook** /'suk/, **-saken** /'seʸkən/, **-saking** [T] *fml* to desert; leave for ever; give up completely: *The little village had a forsaken look.* –see also GODFORSAKEN

for·swear , fore- /fɔr'swɛər/ *v* **-swore** /'swɔr, 'swor/, **-sworn** /'swɔrn, 'swoʷrn/ **-swearing** *fml* [T +*v-ing*] to make a solemn promise to give up or to stop doing (something): *The priests of some religions forswear wealth and marriage.*

fort /fɔrt, foʷrt/ *n* **1** [C] a strongly made building used for defense at some important place **2** [A;C] (*usu. cap. as part of name*) a (town containing a) fixed army camp: *In former times the American army kept lots of soldiers at Fort Apache.* **3 hold the fort** to look after everything while someone is away: *When our mother went into hospital, I had to hold the fort, as I was the oldest child.*

forte /fɔrt, foʷrt, 'fɔrteʸ/ *n* [*usu. sing.*] a strong point in a person's character or abilities: *Sports are his forte; he plays tennis and football excellently.*

forth /fɔrθ, foʷrθ/ *adv* **1** *esp. bibl or lit* (*after a verb*) out; forward: *He went forth into the desert to pray.*|*from this day forth* **2 and (so on and) so forth** etc.; and other like things: *She kept saying that she was sorry for what she'd done, she'd never do it again, it was just a mistake, and so forth.* **3 back and forth** first in one direction and then in the other

forth·com·ing /ˌfɔrθ'kʌmɪŋ◀, ˌfoʷrθ-/ *adj* **1** [*no comp.*] happening or appearing in the near future: *In the newspaper there was a list of forthcoming events in the city.* **2** [F *no comp.*] (*often with* NEGATIVE²) ready; supplied; offered when needed: *When she was asked why she was late, no answer was forthcoming.* **3** *infml* (*often with* NEGATIVE²) ready to be helpful and friendly: *I asked several villagers the way to the river, but none of them was very forthcoming.*

forth·right /'fɔrθraɪt, 'foʷrθ-/ *adj* direct in manner and speech; expressing one's thoughts and feelings plainly: *His forthright behavior shows that he's honest, but he seems rude to some people.* **–forthrightness** *n* [U]

forth·with /ˌfɔrθ'wɪθ, -'wɪð, ˌfoʷrθ-/ *adv* *esp.*

lit at once; without delay

for·ti·eth /'fɔrtiʸɪθ/ *determiner,n,pron,adv* 40th

for·ti·fi·ca·tion /ˌfɔrtəfə'keʸʃən/ *n* **1** [C *usu. pl.*] towers, walls, gun positions, etc., set up as a means of defense **2** [U] the act or science of FORTIFYing

for·ti·fy /'fɔrtəˌfaɪ/ *v* **-fied, -fying** [T] to build forts on; strengthen against possible attack: *a fortified city*|*We have to fortify the coastal areas against the enemy.*|(fig.) *A good breakfast will fortify you for the day's work.* **–fortifiable** *adj*

for·ti·tude /'fɔrtəˌtuʷd, -ˌtyuʷd/ *n* [U] *apprec* firm and lasting courage in bearing trouble, pain, etc., without complaining

fort·night /'fɔrtnaɪt, 'foʷrt-/ *n* [*usu. sing.*] *esp. BrE* two weeks **–fortnightly** *adj,adv*

for·tress /'fɔrtrɪs/ *n* a large fort; place strengthened for defense

for·tu·i·tous /fɔr'tuʷətəs/ *adj fml* happening by chance; accidental: *a fortuitous meeting* **–fortuitously** *adv*

for·tu·nate /'fɔrtʃənɪt/ *adj* more *fml than* **lucky–** having or bringing good fortune; lucky: *He's fortunate in having a good job.*|*She's fortunate enough to have very good health.*|*It was fortunate for her that she had enough money to repair the car.* **–opposite unfortunate**

for·tu·nate·ly /'fɔrtʃənɪtliʸ/ *adv* by good chance; luckily: *I was late in getting to the station, but fortunately for me, the train was late too.*|*Fortunately, he found the money that he'd lost.* **–opposite unfortunately**

for·tune /'fɔrtʃən/ *n* **1** [U] luck: *She had the good fortune to be free from illness all her life.* **2** [C] whatever happens to a person, good or bad: *Through all his changing fortunes, he never lost courage.* **3** [C] that which will happen to a person in the future: *He offered to* **tell** *my* **fortune.** (=to discover what he claims my future will be by using a special method, such as examining my hand) **4** [C] wealth; a large amount of money: *He* **made a fortune** *in* (=became rich by selling) *oil.*|*That new car must have cost you a fortune.*|*a* **small fortune.** (=a lot of money)

fortune-tell·er /'fɔrtʃənˌtɛlər/ *n* a person, usu. a woman, who claims to be able to tell FORTUNES (3)

for·ty /'fɔrtiʸ/ *determiner,n,pron* **-ties** (the number) 40

fo·rum /'fɔrəm, 'foʷrəm/ *n* **1** any place where public matters may be talked over and argued about: *The letters page of this newspaper is a forum for public argument.* **2** a meeting for such a purpose: *A group of schoolteachers are holding a forum on new ways of teaching history.*

for·ward¹ /'fɔrwərd/ *adj* **1** [A *no comp.*] towards the front, the end, or the future: *a forward movement*|*the forward part of the train* **2** [A *no comp.*] advanced in development: *a forward child*|*We aren't very far forward with our plans yet.* **3** too bold; too sure of oneself: *That little girl is very forward; she's always asking people for money.* **–compare** BACKWARD

forward² also **forwards** /ˈfɔrwərdz/– *adv* **1** towards the front, the end, or the future; ahead: *The soldiers crept forward under cover of darkness.|They never met again from that day forward.|Even though we have little money, our plans are going forward.* **2** towards an earlier time: *We'll bring the date of the meeting forward from the 20th to the 18th.* **3** into a noticeable position: *The lawyer brought forward some new reasons.* –compare BACKWARDS

forward³ *v* [T *to*] to send or pass on (letters, packages, etc.) to a new address: *When we moved, we asked the people who bought our old house to forward all our mail.|The man who left yesterday didn't leave* **forwarding instructions/a forwarding address,** *so I don't know where to send this letter.*

for·went , fore- /fɔrˈwɛnt, foʷr-/ *v past tense of* FORGO

fos·sil¹ /ˈfɑsəl/ *n* a hardened part or print of an animal or plant of long ago, that has been preserved in rock, ice, etc.

fossil² *adj* [A *no comp.*] **1** being or in the condition of a FOSSIL¹: *a fossil seashell* **2** being made of substances that were living things in the distant past: *Coal is a fossil* FUEL.

fos·sil·ize ‖also **-ise** *BrE* /ˈfɑsəˌlaɪz/ *v* **-ize, -izing** [I;T] to (cause to) become a FOSSIL¹: (fig.) *People's ideas sometimes become fossilized as they get older.*

fos·ter /ˈfɔstər, ˈfɑ-/ *v* [T] **1** *fml* to encourage (something) to grow or develop: *We hope these meetings will help foster friendly relations between our two countries.* **2** to care for (someone else's child) as one's own, usu. for a certain period and without taking on the full lawful responsibilities of the parent –compare ADOPT (1) **3 foster** giving or receiving parental care although not of the same family: *a foster parent|a foster home*

fought /fɔt/ *v past tense & participle of* FIGHT¹

foul¹ /faʊl/ *adj* **1** bad-smelling and impure: *foul air|*(fig.) **foul-mouthed** (=using foul language) **2** (of weather) rough; stormy: *It's a foul night tonight; it's pouring down rain.* **3** evil; wicked: *a foul murder* **4** *infml* very bad; unpleasant: *She has a foul temper.|I've had a foul morning; everything's gone wrong.* –**foully** *adv* –**foulness** *n* [U]

foul² *n* (in sport) an act that is against the rules: *The player committed a foul; he kicked his opponent intentionally.*

foul³ *v* [I;T] **1** to (cause to) become dirty, impure, or blocked with waste matter: *Industrial pollution has fouled the air.|*(fig.) *Don't* **foul up** *this chance!* (=spoil this chance) **2** (in sports, esp. BASKETBALL and SOCCER) to be guilty of a FOUL² (against): *The player ran into his opponent and fouled him just as he was kicking the ball.*

found¹ /faʊnd/ *v* [T] **1** [*on, upon*] to start building (something large); establish: *The*

castle is founded on solid rock.|The Romans founded a great city on the banks of this river.|This company was founded in 1724.|(fig.) *This story is founded on/upon fact.* **2** to start and support, esp. by supplying money: *The rich man founded a hospital and a school in the town where he was born.*

found² *v past tense & participle of* FIND¹

foun·da·tion /faʊnˈdeʸʃən/ *n* **1** [U] the act of starting the building or planning of something large, or starting some kind of organization: *The university has been famous for medical studies ever since its foundation.* **2** [C] the base on which something is supported or built: *The workers are laying the foundation of the new hospital.|She laid the foundation of her success by study and hard work.* **3** [C] (*often cap. as part of name*) an organization that gives out money for certain special purposes: *The Rockefeller Foundation gives money to help artists.* **4** [U] that on which a belief, custom, way of life, etc., is based; BASIS: *The foundation on which many ancient societies were built was the use of slaves.|The report was completely* **without foundation.** (=was untrue)

found·er¹ /ˈfaʊndər/ *n* a person who FOUNDs¹ something: *Mohammed was the founder of the Muslim religion.|a program in honor of the founders of the university*

foun·der² *v* [I] (of a ship) to fill with water and sink: *The ship foundered in the heavy seas.|*(fig.) *The plan was a good one, but it foundered for* (=because of) *lack of support.*

Founding Fa·thers /ˌ·· ˈ···/ *n* the American leaders who were members of the **American Constitutional Convention** of 1787

found·ry /ˈfaʊndriʸ/ *n* **-ries** a place where metals are melted down and poured into shapes to make separate articles or parts of machinery, such as bars, wheels, etc.: *an iron foundry|foundry workers*

foun·tain /ˈfaʊntn/ *n* (an ornamental apparatus producing) a stream of water that shoots straight up into the air: *The children played in the fountain in the park.|a drinking fountain*

four /fɔr, foʷr/ *determiner,n,pron* **1** (the number) 4 **2 on all fours** (of a person) on the hands and knees: *The baby was crawling around on all fours.*

four·teen /ˌfɔrˈtiʸn◄, ˌfoʷr-/ *determiner, n,pron* (the number) 14 –**fourteenth** *determiner,n,pron,adv*

fourth /fɔrθ, foʷrθ/ *determiner,n,pron,adv* **1** 4th **2** *AmE* for QUARTER: *27¾* (=said as twenty seven and three fourths)

Fourth of Ju·ly /ˌ·· ·ˈ·/ also **Independence Day** – *n* [*the* S] the national Independence Day of the US

fowl /faʊl/ *n* **fowl** or **fowls** *tech* a bird, esp. a hen –see also WILDFOWL

fox¹ /fɑks/ **vixen** /ˈvɪksən/ *fem.*– *n* **foxes** or **fox** a small doglike wild animal with reddish fur, which is often said to have a clever and deceiving nature

fox² *v* [T] *infml* to deceive cleverly; trick

fox·trot /ˈfɑks-trɑt/ *n* (a piece of music for) a dance with short quick steps

---

SPELLING NOTE

Words with the sound /f/ may be spelled **ph-**, like **photograph**.

fox·y /ˈfɑksiʸ/ adj -ier, -iest 1 derog like a fox, in appearance or nature; not to be trusted: a foxy character/smile 2 AmE infml (of a woman) attractive; sexy

foy·er /ˈfɔɪər/ n an entrance hall to a theater or hotel

fra·cas /ˈfreʸkəs, ˈfræ/ n a noisy quarrel in which a number of people take part, and which often ends in a fight

frac·tion /ˈfrækʃən/ n 1 (in MATHEMATICS) a division or part of a whole number: 1/3 and 5/8 are fractions. 2 a very small piece or amount: She's careful with her money, and spends only a fraction of her earnings. –**fractional** adj [no comp.]

frac·tion·al·ly /ˈfrækʃənəliʸ/ adv to a very small degree: If your calculations are even fractionally incorrect, the whole plan will fail.

frac·tious /ˈfrækʃəs/ adj fml (esp. of a child or an old or sick person) restless and complaining; bad-tempered about small things and ready to quarrel –**fractiously** adv –**fractiousness** n [U]

frac·ture¹ /ˈfræktʃər/ n [C;U of] tech (an example of) the act or result of breaking something, esp. a bone: Fracture of the leg can be very serious in old people.|A fracture in the gas pipe allowed a lot of gas to escape.

fracture² v -tured, -turing [I;T] tech to (cause to) break or crack: He fell and fractured his upper arm.|The ice on the lake fractured under the weight of the boys playing on it.

frag·ile /ˈfrædʒəl, -dʒaɪl/ adj 1 easily broken or damaged: This old glass dish is very fragile.|(fig.) a fragile relationship 2 slight in body or weak in health: a fragile old lady –**fragility** /frəˈdʒɪlətiʸ/ n [U]

frag·ment¹ /ˈfrægmənt/ n a small piece broken off; an incomplete part: She dropped the bowl on the floor, and it broke into fragments.|a fragment of a play

frag·ment² /ˈfrægmɛnt, fræɡˈmɛnt/ v [I] to break into FRAGMENTS¹: (fig.) He could remember only a fragmented account of the story. –**fragmentation** /ˌfrægmənˈteʸʃən, -mɛn-/ n [C;U]

frag·men·tar·y /ˈfrægmənˌtɛriʸ/ adj made up of pieces; not complete: His knowledge of the subject is no more than fragmentary.

fra·grance /ˈfreʸɡrəns/ n [C;U] apprec (the quality of having) a sweet or pleasant smell: This soap is made in several fragrances.

fra·grant /ˈfreʸɡrənt/ adj apprec having a sweet or pleasant smell (esp. of flowers): The air in the garden was warm and fragrant. –**fragrantly** adv

frail /freʸl/ adj weak in body or health: a frail old woman|She's still feeling a little frail.

frail·ty /ˈfreʸltiʸ/ n -ties [C;U] (an example of) the quality of being FRAIL: (fig.) One of the frailties (=weaknesses) of human nature is laziness.

frame¹ /freʸm/ v framed, framing [T] 1 to surround with a solid protecting edge; put a border around: I'm having this picture framed, so that I can hang it on the wall.|(fig.) A large hat framed the girl's face. 2 fml to form (words, sentences, ideas, etc.); express: A news reporter must frame his ques-

tions clearly. 3 infml to cause (someone) to seem guilty of a crime by means of intentionally false statements, proofs, etc.: He was framed by the real criminals and was sent to prison for a crime he hadn't done.

frame² n 1 the main supports over and around which something is stretched or built: In some parts of the world small boats are made of skins stretched over a wooden frame.|a bicycle frame|This old bed has an iron frame. 2 (the form or shape of) a human or animal body: a man with a powerful frame 3 a firm border or case into which something is fitted or set: I can't close the door; it doesn't fit into its frame.|a window frame|I haven't selected frames for my glasses yet. 4 **frame of mind** the state or condition of one's mind or feelings at a particular time: In her present frame of mind she shouldn't be left alone.

frame·work /ˈfreʸmwɜrk/ n a supporting frame; STRUCTURE: This building has a steel framework.|(fig.) the framework of modern government

franc /fræŋk/ n the standard coin of France, Switzerland, Belgium, and many countries that formerly belonged to France

fran·chise /ˈfræntʃaɪz/ n 1 [the U] fml the right to vote in a public election 2 [C] a special right given by a company to a person or group to sell that company's goods or services in a particular place

frank /fræŋk/ adj often apprec free and direct in speech; plain and honest; truthful: If you want my frank opinion, I don't think the plan will succeed.|Will you be frank with me about this matter? (=tell me the truth, without trying to hide anything) –**frankness** n [U]

frank·ly /ˈfræŋkliʸ/ adv speaking honestly and plainly: Frankly, I think your chances of getting the job aren't very good.

fran·tic /ˈfræntɪk/ adj very anxious, afraid, happy, etc.: There was a frantic rush to get everything ready for the President's visit. –**frantically** adv

fra·ter·nal /frəˈtɜrnl/ adj [A no comp.] of, belonging to, or like brothers –**fraternally** adv

fra·ter·ni·ty /frəˈtɜrnətiʸ/ n -ties 1 [C] any association of people having work, interests, etc., in common: He's a member of the medical fraternity. (=is a doctor)|The fraternity is meeting tomorrow to choose new members. 2 [U] fml the state of being brothers; brotherly feeling 3 [C] (at some American universities) a club of men students usu. living in the same house –compare SORORITY

frat·er·nize ‖also **-nise** BrE /ˈfrætər,naɪz/ v -nized, -nizing [I with] fml to meet and be friendly (with someone) as equals: Army officers may not fraternize with their men.

fraud /frɔd/ n 1 [C;U] (an act of) deceitful behavior for the purpose of gain, which may be punishable by law; dishonesty: She carried out a number of frauds on trusting people who lent her money.|The judge found the woman guilty of fraud. 2 [C] derog a person who pretends or claims to be what he/she is not: He said he was an insurance salesman, but later she realized he was a fraud.

fraud·u·lent /ˈfrɔdʒələnt/ adj fml deceitful; got or done by FRAUD (1): *She got the job of science teacher by fraudulent means; she pretended she'd studied at a university.* –**fraudulently** adv –**fraudulence** n [U]

fraught /frɔt/ adj fml [F with] full of (something unpleasant):*The long journey through the forest was fraught with danger.*

fray¹ /freɪ/ v **1** [T] to cause (rope, cloth, etc.) to become thin or worn by rubbing, so that loose threads develop: *This old shirt of mine is frayed at the collar.*|(fig.) *Her nerves were frayed by the noises in the street.* **2** [I] (of rope, cloth, etc.) to become thin or worn so that loose threads develop: *The electric wire is fraying and could be dangerous to handle.*|(fig.) *Tempers began to fray at the meeting.*

fray² n [the S] lit a fight, argument, quarrel, etc.: *Are you ready for the fray?*

freak v →FREAK OUT

freak¹ /friːk/ n **1** a living creature of unnatural form: *One of the new lambs is a freak; it was born with two tails.* **2** a peculiar happening: *By some strange freak, a little snow fell in Egypt a few years ago.* **3** infml a person who takes a special interest in the stated thing; FAN³: *a car freak*

freak² adj [A no comp.] unnatural in degree or type; very unusual: *The country's been having freak weather; it's been very hot during the winter.*|*a freak storm*

freak³ v →FREAK OUT

freak·ish /ˈfriːkɪʃ/ adj unusual; unreasonable; strange: *Her behavior's becoming so freakish that I'm worried about her.* –**freakishly** adv

freak out v adv [I;T (=**freak** sbdy.↔ **out**)] infml to (cause to) become greatly excited or anxious, esp. because of drugs

freck·le /ˈfrɛkəl/ n [often pl.] a small flat brown spot on the skin –**freckled** adj: *a freckled nose*

free¹ /friː/ adj **1** able to act as one wants; not in prison or under control: *She felt free when she left home and moved to the city.*|*The prisoner will be* **set free** *next week.*|*You are free to do as you wish.*|*This is a free country.* (=the state does not control everything) **2** not limited in any way, esp. by rule or custom: *The people won the right to* **free speech** *and a* **free press.** (=they could express ideas and judgments in public and in newspapers)|*a free translation* (=one in which the general meaning is translated without giving an exact translation of every single word) **3** [no comp.] without payment of any kind; costing nothing: *a free ticket for the concert*|*Anyone who joins this bank gets a free set of dishes.*|*"Are the drinks free?" "No, you have to pay for them."* **4** [no comp.] not busy; without work or duty: *He has very little free time.*|*a free moment*|*The doctor will be free in 10 minutes. Can you wait that*

SPELLING NOTE
Words with the sound /f/ may be spelled ph-, like **photograph**.

long?|*I'd like to talk to you when you're free.* **5** [no comp.] not being used; empty: *"Is this seat free?" "Yes; no one is using it."*|*She picked it up with her free hand.* **6** [F from, of] without (someone or something unwanted); untroubled by: *The old lady is never free from/of pain.*|*She was free from all blame for the accident.* **7** (esp. of bodily action) natural; graceful; not stiff or awkward: *free movement to music* **8** [F with] ready to give; generous: *She's very free with her money.*|*He's too free with his advice.* (=gives advice when it isn't wanted) **9 free and easy** lacking in too great seriousness and ceremony; cheerful and unworried: *She leads a free and easy life and never worries much about anything.* **10 -free** free from; without: *People with certain diseases have to eat salt-free foods.*|*a trouble-free journey*

free² adv **1** in a FREE¹ (1) manner: *Don't let the dog run free on the street.* **2** also **for free**– without payment: *Babies are allowed to travel free on buses.* **3** so as to become loose or disconnected: *Two of the screws in this old wooden door have worked themselves free.* (=loosened or fallen out as a result of use)

free³ v **freed** /friːd/, **freeing** [T from] **1** to set FREE¹ (1): *Free the prisoners!*|*She freed the bird from its cage.* **2** to move or loosen (someone or something that is stuck or trapped): *Can you free this window? It's stuck.* **3** [of] to take away something unpleasant from: *I need to go out; can you free me (from duty) for an hour?*|*She opened the window to free the room of smoke.*

free·bie , freebee /ˈfriːbiː/ n AmE infml something given or received without charge: *You don't have to pay for the ticket. It's a freebie.*

free·dom /ˈfriːdəm/ n **1** [U] the state of being free; state of not being under control: *The people there are fighting to gain freedom from foreign control.*|*During the summer vacation, the children enjoyed their freedom.*|*the freedom to choose what to do*|*freedom from fear* **2** [C;U +to-v/of] the power to do, say, think, or write as one pleases: *Two of the four freedoms spoken of by President Roosevelt in 1941 are freedom of speech and freedom of religion.* –compare LIBERTY

free-for-all /ˌ· · ·ˈ·/ n infml an argument, quarrel, etc., in which many people join and express their opinions, esp. in a noisy way: *The discussion about the new highway soon became a free-for-all.*

free·hand /ˈfriːhænd/ adj (of a drawing) done by hand, without the use of a ruler or other instrument –**freehand** adv

free·lance /ˈfriːlæns/ n,adj (done by) a writer or other trained worker who sells his/her work to a number of employers: *a freelance journalist/writer* –**freelancer** n

free·load /ˈfriːloʊd/ v [I off (of)] AmE infml to live on money and goods given by other people, without giving anything in return; SPONGE² (3): *He's been freeloading off (of) his friends for a year.* –**freeloader** n

free·ly /ˈfriːliː/ adv **1** willingly; readily: *I freely admit that what I said was wrong.*|*He* *gives his time freely to help the party.* **2** openly; plainly; without hiding anything: *You can speak quite freely in front of me; I won't tell anyone what you say.* **3** without any limitation on movement or action: *Oil the wheel; then it will turn more freely.*

free·think·er /ˌfriyˈθɪŋkər/ *n* a person who forms his/ her religious opinions on reason and not on the teaching of the Christian Church **–freethinking** /ˌ· ˈ··◂/ *adj*

free·way /ˈfriywey/ *n AmE* for EXPRESSWAY

free·wheel·ing /ˌfriyˈhwiylɪŋ◂, -ˈwiy-/ *adj* not greatly worrying about rules, formal behavior, responsibilities, or the results of actions

free will /ˌ· ˈ·/ *n* [U] the ability of a person to decide freely what he/she will do: *She did it of her own free will.* (=it was completely her decision)

freeze¹ /friyz/ *v* **froze** /frowz/, **frozen** /ˈfrowzən/, **freezing** **1** [I;T *up*] to (cause to) harden into or become covered with ice: *Water freezes at 32 degrees degrees* FAHRENHEIT *or 0 degrees* CENTIGRADE.│*The lake has frozen over/up.│The milk has frozen solid.│the hard frozen ground* –compare THAW, MELT **2** [I;T *up*] to (cause to) be unable to work properly as a result of ice or very low temperatures: *The engine has frozen up.│The cold has frozen the lock on the car door.* **3** [I] (of weather) to be at or below the temperature at which water becomes ice: *It's freezing tonight.* **4** [I;T] *infml* to (cause to) be, feel, or become very cold: *It's freezing in this room; can't you turn up the heat?│We nearly froze to death.* (=died of cold)│*I'm frozen stiff after sitting in that cold wind.* **5** [I;T] to preserve or be preserved by means of very low temperatures: *frozen dinners│Not all fruit freezes well.* **6** [I;T] to (cause to) stop suddenly or become quite still, esp. with fear: *The child froze at the sight of the snake.│A sudden terrible cry froze him to the spot.│A wild animal will sometimes freeze in its tracks when it smells an enemy.* **7** [T] to fix (prices or wages) officially at a given level for a certain length of time

freeze² *n* [S] **1** a period of very cold icy weather: *He slipped and broke his leg during the big freeze last winter.* **2** a fixing of prices or wages at a certain level: *a wage freeze*

freez·er /ˈfriyzər/ also **deep freeze–** *n* **1** a type of REFRIGERATOR in which supplies of food can be stored at a very low temperature for a long time –see illustration on page 379 **2** also **freezer compartment** /ˈ·· ·,··/– an enclosed part of a REFRIGERATOR in which there is a specially low temperature for making ice, storing frozen foods, etc.

freez·ing point /ˈfriyzɪŋ ˌpɔɪnt/ *n* **1** [U] also **freezing–** the temperature (32 degrees FAHRENHEIT or 0 degrees CENTIGRADE) at which water becomes ice: *It's very cold today; the temperature has dropped to the freezing point/below freezing.* **2** [C] the temperature at which any particular liquid freezes: *The freezing point of alcohol is much lower than that of water.*

freight /freyt/ *n* [U] **1** (money paid for) the

carrying of goods by some means of TRANS-PORT: *This aircraft company deals with freight only; it has no passenger service.│to send something by airfreight/freight train* **2** the goods carried in this way: *This freight must be carefully handled when loading.* **–freight** *v* [T]

freight·er /ˈfreytər/ *n* a ship for carrying goods

French¹ /frɛntʃ/ *adj* belonging to France, its people, etc.: *French wine*

French² *n* **1** [*the* P] the people of France **2** [U] the language of France: *We have a French lesson/French every Tuesday.*

French doors /ˌ· ˈ·/ *n* [P] a pair of light doors made up of squares of glass in a frame, usu. opening out onto the garden of, or separating two rooms of, a house

French fries /ˌ· ˈ·/ *AmE*║**chips** *BrE–* *n* [P] long thin pieces of potato cooked in deep fat

French·man /ˈfrɛntʃmən/ **Frenchwoman** /ˈfrɛntʃˌwumən/ *fem– n* **-men** /mən/ a French citizen born in France or of French parent(s)

fre·net·ic, phrenetic /frəˈnɛtɪk/ *adj* showing FRANTIC activity; overexcited **–frenetically** *adv*

fren·zied /ˈfrɛnziyd/ *adj* full of uncontrolled excitement and/or wild activity; FRANTIC: *The house was full of frenzied activity on the morning of the wedding.* **–frenziedly** *adv*

fren·zy /ˈfrɛnziy/ *n* [S;U] a state of great excitement or anxiety; sudden, but not lasting, attack of madness: *In a frenzy of hate he killed his enemy.│He worked himself up into a frenzy before his exams.*

fre·quen·cy /ˈfriykwənsiy/ *n* **-cies** **1** [U *of*] the repeated or frequent happening of something: *The frequency of accidents on that highway gives the doctors a lot of work.│Accidents are happening there with increasing frequency.* **2** [C] *tech* a rate at which something happens or is repeated: *This radio signal has a frequency of 200,000* CY-CLES¹ (2) *per second.* **3** [C] a particular number of radio waves per second at which a radio signal is broadcast: *This radio station broadcasts on three different frequencies.* –see also FM, VHF

fre·quent¹ /ˈfriykwənt/ *adj* common; found or happening often: *Sudden rainstorms are frequent on this coast.* –opposite **infrequent**; see NEVER (USAGE) **–frequently** *adv*

fre·quent² /friyˈkwɛnt, ˈfriykwənt/ *v* [T] *fml* to be often in (a place, someone's company, etc.): *She loves books and frequents the library.*

fresh /frɛʃ/ *adj* **1** (of food) not long gathered, caught, produced, etc., and therefore in good condition: *This fish isn't fresh; it smells!│fresh bread│fresh fruit* (=not canned or frozen) –compare STALE **2** [A *no comp.*] (of water) not salt; drinkable **3** (of air) pure and cool: *It's healthy to spend time in the fresh air.* (=outside) **4** [A *no comp.*] (an) other and different: *Let me make you a fresh pot of coffee.│It's time to take a fresh look at this subject.* **5** [*no comp.*] lately arrived, happened, supplied, or added: *There's been no* *fresh news of the fighting since yester-day.*|*The new teacher's fresh from university.* **6** (of skin) clear and healthy: *She has dark hair and a fresh* COMPLEXION. **7** [F] *infml* too bold (with someone of the opposite sex): *That girl's not behaving at all well; she's try-ing to* **get fresh with** *my brother.*|*He's not very polite; he's just a fresh kid.* –see also AFRESH –**freshness** *n* [U]

fresh·en /'frɛʃən/ *v* [I;T] to make or become fresher: (fig.) *The wind is freshening.* (=becoming stronger)
 freshen up *v adv* [I;T (**freshen** sbdy./sthg.↔ **up**)] to (cause to) feel more comfortable and attractive by washing: *Let me just go and freshen (myself) up.*|(fig.) *She's freshened up the house with a coat of paint.*

fresh·ly /'frɛʃliʸ/ *adv* (*before a past participle*) just lately; just now; recently: *"This coffee smells good." "Yes, it's freshly made."*|*His shirts have been freshly washed and ironed.*

fresh·man /'frɛʃmən/ also **fresher** /'frɛʃər/ *BrE*– *n* **freshmen** /-mən/ a student in his or her first year at a university or high school

fresh·wa·ter /'frɛʃ,wɒṭər, -,wɑṭər/ *adj* [A] of rivers or inland lakes; not belonging to the sea: *freshwater fish* –opposite **saltwater**

fret /frɛt/ *v* **-tt-** [I;T *about, over*] to be con-tinually worried and anxious, dissatisfied, or bad-tempered about small or unnecessary things: *Don't fret; everything will be all right.*|*Don't fret over small problems.*

fret·ful /'frɛtfəl/ *adj* complaining and anx-ious, esp. because of dissatisfaction or discomfort: *The child was tired and fretful.* –**fretfully** *adv* –**fretfulness** *n* [U]

fret·work /'frɛtwɜrk/ *n* [C;U] (the art of mak-ing) patterns cut in wood with a special tool (**fretsaw**)

Fri. *n written abbrev. said as:* Friday

fri·ar /'fraɪər/ *n* a man belonging to a Chris-tian religious group who, esp. in former times, was very poor and traveled around the country teaching the Christian religion –compare MONK

fri·ar·y /'fraɪəriʸ/ *n* **-ies** a building in which FRIARS live

fric·tion /'frɪkʃən/ *n* [U] **1** the natural force which tries to stop one surface sliding over another **2** the rubbing, often repeated, of two surfaces together: *The friction of the rope against the rock made the rope break and the climber fall.* **3** unfriendliness and disagreement caused by two different sets of opinions or natures: *Mary's neat and Jane's careless. If they have to share a room there'll probably be friction.*

Fri·day /'fraɪdiʸ, -deʸ/ *n infml* the 6th day of the week: *He'll arrive* (on) *Friday morn-ing.*|*Lots of people eat fish on Fridays.* (=ev-ery Friday) –see also GOOD FRIDAY

fridge /frɪdʒ/ *infml for* REFRIGERATOR

friend /frɛnd/ *n* **1** a person whom one knows well and likes, but who is not related:

Although Peter is **a close friend** *of mine, David is my* **best** (=closest) **friend.**|*Mary's* **an old friend**; *we've known each other/been friends for 16 years.* –compare ENEMY **2** [*of, to*] a helper; supporter; person showing kindness and understanding: *Vote for John-son –the people's friend!*|*He only got the job because he had* **friends in high places.** (=peo-ple in a position to influence others to help him) **3 a friend in need** a true friend, who is in trouble **4 make friends (with)** to form a friendship or friendships: *He has a pleasant manner, and makes friends very easily.*|*The little boys quarreled and then made friends.* (=forgave each other)|*Have you made friends with your new neighbors yet?* –see also BEFRIEND

friend·ly /'frɛndliʸ/ *adj* **-lier, -liest 1** [*to, with*] acting or ready to act as a friend: *A friendly dog came to meet us at the door.*|*He's not very friendly to newcomers.*|*a friendly nation* (=not an enemy)|*They quarreled once, but they're not friendly with each other now.* –op-posite **unfriendly 2** kind; generous; ready to help: *You're always sure of a friendly welcome at this hotel.* **3** not causing unpleas-ant feelings: *We've been having a friendly argument on politics.*|*Our two teams are playing* **a friendly game** *next Saturday. The game isn't part of a serious competition.* –**friendliness** *n* [U]

friend·ship /'frɛndʃɪp/ *n* [C;U] (an example of) the condition of sharing a friendly rela-tionship; feeling and behavior that exists be-tween friends: *True friendship is worth more than money.*|*His friendships never last very long.*

frieze /friʸz/ *n* an ornamental border along the top of a wall, either outside a building or inside a room –sounds like **freeze**

frig·ate /'frɪgɪt/ *n* a small fast-moving warship

fright /fraɪt/ *n* [C;U] (an experience that causes) the feeling of (usu. not very great) fear: *I was shaking with fright.*|*You* **gave me a fright** *by knocking so loudly on the door.*|*I got* **the fright of my life** (=the biggest fright I've ever had) *when the car burst into flames.*|*He* **took fright** *and ran away when he saw the policemen.*

fright·en /'fraɪtn/ *v* [T] **1** to fill with fear: *The child was frightened by the big dog.*|*a frightening dream* **2** to cause (someone) to do, go, etc., by frightening: *I frightened the bird away by moving suddenly.*|*He frightened off his attacker by shouting for help.*|*He frightened the old lady into/out of signing the paper.* –**frighteningly** *adv*

fright·ened /'fraɪtnd/ *adj* [+*to-v/(that)/at, of*] in a state of fear; afraid: *He was frightened at the thought of his coming examination.*|*I was frightened* (that) (=worried that) *you wouldn't come.*|*Some people are frightened of thunder, others of snakes.* –see also AFRAID (1)

fright·ful /'fraɪtfəl/ *adj* **1** causing a feeling of shock; very unpleasant: *The battlefield was a frightful scene.* **2** *infml, becoming rare* very bad; unpleasant: *We're having frightful weather this week.* –**frightfulness** *n* [U]

fright·ful·ly /'fraɪtfəliʸ/ adv infml, becoming rare very: I'm frightfully late.

frig·id /'frɪdʒɪd/ adj **1** tech very cold (fig.) a frigid (=rather unfriendly) welcome **2** (esp. of a woman) having an unnatural dislike of sexual activity –compare IMPOTENT **–frigidity** /frɪ'dʒɪdət̮iʸ/ n [U] **–frigidly** /'frɪdʒɪdliʸ/ adv

frill /frɪl/ n **1** an ornamental edge on a dress, curtain, etc., made of a band of cloth with a wavy edge **2** [usu. pl.] something ornamental or pleasant, but not necessary; EXTRA² (1): I just want an ordinary car without the frills.

frill·y /'frɪliʸ/ also **frilled** /frɪld/– adj **-ier, -iest** having many FRILLs (1): The little girl wore a frilly party dress. **–frilliness** n [U]

fringe¹ /frɪndʒ/ n **1** an ornamental edge of hanging threads on a curtain, tablecloth, garment, etc. **2** [of] the part farthest from the center; edge: It was easier to move about on the fringe of the crowd.|A **fringe group** separated from the main (political) party. **3 fringe benefit** [often pl.] added favors or services given with a job, besides wages: One of the fringe benefits of this job is free health insurance.

fringe² v **fringed, fringing** [T with] to act as a FRINGE¹ (1) to: A line of trees fringed the river.|a pool fringed with trees

frisk /frɪsk/ v **1** [I] (of an animal or child) to run and jump about playfully: The new lambs are frisking in the fields. **2** [T] infml to search (someone) for hidden weapons, goods, etc., by passing the hands over the body

frisk·y /'frɪskiʸ/ adj **-ier, -iest** overflowing with life and activity; joyfully alive: frisky lambs|The dog was very frisky when I took him out for a walk. **–friskily** adv **–friskiness** n [U]

frit·ter sthg. ↔ **a·way** /'frɪt̮ər/ v adv [T on] derog to waste (time, money, etc.): She fritters away all her money on cheap clothes.

fri·vol·i·ty /frɪ'vɑlət̮iʸ/ n **-ties** derog **1** [U] the condition of being FRIVOLOUS: Your frivolity makes you unsuitable for a responsible position. **2** [C] a FRIVOLOUS act or remark: A serious political speech should not be full of frivolities.

friv·o·lous /'frɪvələs/ adj derog not serious; silly: He failed his examination because he gave a frivolous answer to one of the questions.|He has a frivolous nature and won't take anything seriously. **–frivolously** adv **–frivolousness** n [U]

frizz /frɪz/ v [T up, out] infml to cause (hair) to go into short wiry curls

frizz·y /'frɪziʸ/ adj **-ier, -iest** infml (of hair) very curly: Some people have naturally frizzy hair.

fro /froʷ/ adv see TO-AND-FRO

frock /frɑk/ n becoming rare a woman's or girl's dress

frog /frɔg, frɑg/ n **1** a small hairless tailless jumping animal that lives in water and on land, and makes a deep rough sound (CROAK) –compare TOAD **2 a frog in one's/the throat** infml a difficulty in speaking because of roughness in the throat

frog·man /'frɔgmæn, -mən, 'frɑg-/ n **-men** /mɛn, mən/ a skilled underwater swimmer who wears a special apparatus for breathing, and large flat shoes (FLIPPERs) –compare SKIN DIVEr

frol·ic /'frɑlɪk/ v **-ck-** [I about] to play and jump about gaily: The young lambs were frolicking in the field. **–frolic** n: The children are having a frolic before bedtime.

from /frəm; strong frʌm, frɑm/ prep **1** starting at: the train from Boston|The shop is open from eight till five o'clock.|They stayed here from Monday to/till Friday.|Where do you come from? (=Where is your home?)|Can you translate this letter from Spanish into English? **2** sent or given by: a letter from John|She borrowed the money from her sister. **3** using; out of: Bread is made from flour.|She played the music from memory. **4** (shows separation, difference, or taking away): The village is five miles from the coast.|He needs a rest from work.|A tree gave us shelter from the rain.|She took the matches away from the baby.|Take 2 from 4.|He lives apart from his family.|I don't know one kind of car from another. **5** because of: suffering from heart disease|From his appearance, you wouldn't think he was old. –see Study Notes on page 144

frond /frɑnd/ n a leaf of a FERN or of a PALM

front¹ /frʌnt/ n **1** [the S of] the most forward position, part, or surface, farthest from or opposite to the back: The teacher called the boy up to the front of the class.|The front of the school faces south.|The front of the cupboard is made of glass.|The front of the postcard shows a picture of our hotel.|This dress closes in the front. **2** [S] the manner and appearance a person shows to others: She was nervous about meeting strangers, but she **put on a bold front** (=acted as if she wasn't afraid) and went to the party.|We must show a **united front** against the enemy. **3** [the S] a line along which fighting takes place in time of war: He lost his life at the front. **4** [C] (often cap.) a widespread and active political movement: The People's Front is gaining many supporters. **5** [C] tech a line of separation between two masses of air of different temperature: A cold front is the forward edge of a mass of moving cold air. **6** [A;C for] infml a person, group, or thing used for hiding the real nature of a secret or unlawful activity: A travel company was used as a front for bringing dangerous drugs into the country.|He is **the front man** for a criminal gang. **7 in front: a** ahead: The grandmother walked slowly, and the children ran in front. **b** in or at the part facing forwards: This dress closes in front. **c** in the most forward or important position: The driver sits in front, and the passengers sit behind. **8 in front of: a** towards or outside the front of: I can't read the notice because he's standing in front of it.|a car parked in front of the house –compare BEHIND¹ **b** in the presence of: Don't say that in front of the children! **9 in the front** in FRONT¹ (7b,c) **10 in the front of** in the most forward or important position: He's sitting in *the front of the car with the driver.*|*In the front of the picture is the figure of a man.*

front² *v* [I;T] (of a building) to have the front towards; face: *The hotel fronts (onto) the main road.*

front³ *adj* [A *no comp.*] being at the front: *Write your name on the front cover of the book.*|*his front teeth*|*front row seats*|*the front garden* –opposite **back**; see also REAR² (1)

front·age /ˈfrʌntɪdʒ/ *n* a part of a building or of land that stretches along a road, river, etc.: *The store has frontages on two busy streets.*

fron·tal /ˈfrʌntəl/ *adj* [A *no comp.*] **1** (of an attack) direct; (as if) from the front **2** of, at, or to the front –**frontally** *adv*

fron·tier /frʌnˈtiɪər/ *n* **1** a limit or border, esp. where the land of two countries meets: *They were shot trying to cross the frontier.*|*Sweden has frontiers with Norway and Finland.*|(fig.) *The frontiers of medical knowledge are being pushed further outwards every year.* **2** [*the* + C] the border between settled and wild areas of a country, esp. that in the US in the past

frost¹ /frɒst/ *n* **1** [U] a white powdery substance formed on outside surfaces from very small drops of water when the temperature of the air is below freezing point: *The car windows were covered with frost in the early morning.* –compare ICE **2** [C;U] (a period or state of) weather at a temperature below the freezing point of water: *Frost has killed several of our new young plants.*|*There was a hard frost last night.* (=a severe one)

frost² *v* **1** [I;T *over*] to (cause to) become covered with FROST¹ (1): *The cold has frosted the windows.*|*The fields have frosted over.* **2** [T *usu. pass.*] to make the surface of a sheet of (glass) rough so that it is not possible to see through: *a frosted glass door* **3** [T] to cover (a cake, COOKIE, etc.) with FROSTING

frost·bite /ˈfrɒstbaɪt/ *n* [U] swelling and discoloration of a person's limbs, caused by a great cold: *The mountain climbers were suffering from frostbite.* –**frostbitten** /ˈfrɒstˌbɪtn/ *adj*

frost·ing /ˈfrɒstɪŋ/ *n* [U] → ICING

frost·y /ˈfrɒstiʸ/ *adj* **-ier, -iest** very cold; cold with FROST¹ (2): *It was a cold frosty day.*|(fig.) *a frosty greeting* (=not friendly) –**frostily** *adv* –**frostiness** *n* [U]

froth¹ /frɒθ/ *n* [S;U] a white mass of bubbles formed on top of or in a liquid, or in the mouth; FOAM

froth² /frɒθ, frɒð/ *v* [I] to make or throw up FROTH¹: *The beer frothed as it was poured out.*|*The sick animal was frothing at the mouth.*

froth·y /ˈfrɒθiʸ, -ðiʸ/ *adj* **-ier, -iest** full of or covered with FROTH¹: *frothy beer* –**frothily** *adv* –**frothiness** *n* [U]

frown /fraʊn/ *v* [I] to draw the EYEBROWS together esp. in anger or effort, or to show disapproval, causing lines to appear on the

forehead: *The teacher frowned angrily at the noisy class.* –compare SMILE –**frown** *n*: *She looked at her examination paper with a frown.* –**frowningly** *adv*

frown on/upon sthg. *v prep* [T +*v-ing*] to disapprove of: *Mary wanted to go to France by herself, but her parents frowned on the idea.*

froze /frəʷz/ *v past tense of* FREEZE¹

fro·zen /ˈfrəʷzən/ *v past participle of* FREEZE¹

fru·gal /ˈfruʷgəl/ *adj* **1** careful in the use of money, food, etc.: *Although he's become rich, he's kept his frugal habits.* **2** small in quantity and cost: *a frugal supper of bread and cheese.* –**frugally** *adv* –**frugality** /fruʷˈgælətiʸ/ *n* [C;U]

fruit /fruʷt/ *n* [C;U] **1** (an example or type of) the part of a tree or bush that contains seeds, esp. considered as food: *Apples, oranges, and bananas are fruit.*|*The potato is a vegetable, not a fruit.*|*Would you like some more fruit?*|*a fruit store*|*This dish is made from a mixture of four different summer fruits.*|**the fruits of the earth** (=plants used for food) **2** a/the result: *The old man enjoyed the fruits of* (=rewards of) *his life's work.*|*Their plans haven't* **borne fruit.** (=had a successful result)

fruit·ful /ˈfruʷtfəl/ *adj* successful; useful; producing good results: *a fruitful meeting* –opposite **fruitless** –**fruitfully** *adv* –**fruitfulness** *n* [U]

fru·i·tion /fruʷˈɪʃən/ *n* [U] fulfilment (of plans, aims, desired results, etc.): *After much delay, the plan to build the new hospital came to/was brought to fruition.*

fruit·less /ˈfruʷtlɪs/ *adj* (of an effort) useless; unsuccessful; not bringing the desired result: *So far the search for the missing boy has been fruitless.* –opposite **fruitful** –**fruitlessly** *adv* –**fruitlessness** *n* [U]

fruit·y /ˈfruʷtiʸ/ *adj* **-ier, -iest 1** *usu. apprec* like fruit; tasting or smelling of fruit: *This red wine is soft and fruity.* **2** *infml* (of a person's voice) rich and deep: *a fruity laugh*

frus·trate /ˈfrʌstreʸt/ *v* **-trated, -trating** [T] **1** to prevent the fulfilment of; defeat (someone or someone's effort): *The bad weather frustrated all our hopes of going out.*|*In his attempts to escape, the prisoner was frustrated by a watchful guard.* **2** to cause (someone) to have feelings of annoyed disappointment or dissatisfaction: *I'm feeling frustrated in my present job.*|*After two hours' frustrating delay, our train finally arrived.* –**frustration** /frʌˈstreʸʃən/ *n* [C;U]: *Life is full of frustrations.*

fry¹ /fraɪ/ *v* **fried, frying** [I;T] to (cause to) be cooked in hot fat or oil: *Shall I fry the fish for dinner?*|*The eggs were frying in the pan.*|*fried rice* –see COOK (USAGE)

fry·ing pan /ˈ··ˌ·/ also **skillet** *AmE*– *n* a flat pan with a long handle, used for FRYING food

ft., ft *written abbrev. said as:* **1** feet: *4 ft long* **2** foot: *5 ft. long* –see FOOT¹ (2)

fuch·sia /ˈfyuʷʃə/ *n* a garden bush with hanging bell-like red, pink, or white flowers

fudge /fʌdʒ/ *n* [U] a soft creamy light brown

candy, made of chocolate, sugar, milk, butter, etc.

fu·el¹ /ˈfyuʷəl/ n [C;U] (a type of) material that is used for producing heat or power by burning: *Wood, coal, oil, and gas are different kinds of fuel.|Gasoline is no longer a cheap fuel.*

fuel² v **-l-** *AmE*‖ **-ll-** *BrE* [I;T] to take in or provide with FUEL¹: *Aircraft sometimes fuel while in the air.* –see also REFUEL

fu·gi·tive /ˈfyuʷdʒətɪv/ n a person escaping from danger, the police, etc.: *a fugitive from justice* –**fugitive** adj [A]

ful·crum /ˈfʊlkrəm, ˈfʌl-/ n **-crums** or **-cra** /krə/ the point on which a bar (LEVER) turns or is supported in lifting or moving something: *the fulcrum of a pair of SCALES*

ful·fill *AmE*‖also **fulfil** esp. *BrE* /fʊlˈfɪl/ v **-ll-** [T] **1** to perform or carry out (an order, duty, promise, etc.): *The doctor's instructions must be fulfilled exactly.|A chimney fulfills the FUNCTION of taking away smoke.|If you make a promise, you should fulfill it.* **2** to supply or satisfy (a need, demand or purpose): *The traveling library fulfills an important need for people who live far from the town.* **3** to make or prove to be true; cause to happen: *If he's lazy, he'll never fulfill his AMBITION to be a doctor.* **4** to develop fully the character and abilities of (oneself): *She fulfilled herself both as a mother and as a successful writer.*

ful·fill·ment *AmE*‖also **fulfilment** esp. *BrE* /fʊlˈfɪlmənt/ n [U] **1** the act of fulfilling or condition of being fulfilled: *After many years, his plans have come to fulfillment.* **2** satisfaction after successful effort: *a sense of fulfillment.*

full¹ /fʊl/ adj **1** [of] (of a container or space) filled completely; holding as much or as many as possible: *You can't put any more liquid into a full bottle.|The drawer was full of old clothes.|The train is full; there are no seats left at all.|a full train|The doctor had a very full day.* (=had work to do all the time)*|It's impolite to speak with your mouth full.* (=while you are eating)|(fig.) *a story full of sadness* **2** [of] (of a container) filled with liquid, powder, etc., as near to the top as convenient: *They brought us out a pot full of steaming coffee.|This bag of flour is only half full.* (=contains half the amount that it can hold)|*Don't fill my cup too full.* –compare EMPTY¹ (1) **3** [F of] containing or having plenty (of): *The field was full of sheep feeding on the new grass.|This work's full of mistakes.* **4** [up] infml well fed, often to the point of discomfort; satisfied: *I can't eat any more; I'm full (up).|a full stomach* **5** complete; whole: *Please write down your full name and address.|She rose to her full height.* (=stood up very straight and proudly)|*He has led a full life.* (=has had every kind of experience) **6** [A] the highest or greatest possible: *He drove the car at full speed through the town.* **7** [F of] having the mind and attention fixed only (on): *too full of my own troubles to care about the problems of others|She's always full of herself.* (=thinks she's very impor-

tant)|*He's full of his visit to America.* (=talks about it a lot) **8** (of a part of a garment) wide; flowing; fitting loosely: *a full skirt* **9** (of a shape or someone's body) often apprec round; rounded; fleshy: *a full moon|Her face was full when she was younger; now it's much thinner.* **10** [A] apprec (of color, smell, sound, or taste) deep, rich, and powerful: *wine with a full body* (=having strength and taste)

full² adv [adv+prep/adv] **1** straight; directly: *The sun shone full on her face.* **2** very; quite: *They knew full well that he wouldn't keep his promise.*

full³ n **1** in full completely: *The debt must be paid in full.* **2** to the full to the greatest degree; very greatly: *We enjoyed our trip to the full.*

full-blown /ˌ· ˈ·◂/ adj often lit (of a flower) completely open; (fig.) *We're afraid that the fighting on the border may develop into a full-blown* (=fully developed) *war.*

full-fledged /ˌfʊl ˈflɛdʒd◂/ *AmE*‖**fully-fledged** /ˌ·· ˈ·◂/ *BrE*– adj completely trained: *a full-fledged doctor*

full-grown /ˌ· ˈ·◂/ also **fully-grown** /ˌ·· ˈ·◂/ *BrE*– adj (esp. of an animal, plant, or (tech) person) completely developed: *A full-grown elephant can weigh over 6,000 kilograms.*

full-length /ˌ· ˈ·◂/ adj **1** (of a painting, mirror, etc.) showing a person from head to foot **2** (of a garment) reaching to the ground: *a full-length evening dress* **3** (of a play, book, etc.) not short; not shorter than is usual: *He has written several one-act plays, but only one full-length play.*

full moon /ˌ· ˈ·/ n [S;U] (the time of the month of) the moon when seen as a circle: *The/A full moon shone brightly.|There's a lot of light in the sky at full moon.*

full-scale /ˌ· ˈ·◂/ adj **1** (of a model, drawing, copy, etc.) of the same size as the object represented: *He made a full-scale model of an elephant, but he couldn't get it out of the room.* **2** [A] using all one's powers, forces, etc.: *a full-scale attack on an enemy position*

full stop /ˌ· ˈ·/ n **1** *BrE* for PERIOD (4) **2** come to a full stop to stop completely

full-time /ˌ· ˈ·◂/ adj,adv working for the normal number of hours or days in job, course of study, etc.: *a full-time student|full-time employment|He used to work full-time, but now he works only three days a week.* –compare PART-TIME

ful·ly /ˈfʊliʸ/ adv **1** completely; altogether; thoroughly: *I don't fully understand his reasons for leaving.|a fully trained nurse* **2** quite; at least: *It's fully an hour since he left.*

fum·ble /ˈfʌmbəl/ v **-bled, -bling 1** [I about, around] to move the fingers or hands awkwardly in search of something, or in an attempt to do something: *She fumbled around in her handbag for a pen.|*(fig.) *He's not a very good speaker; he often has to fumble for the right word.* **2** [I;T] to handle (something) without neatness or skill; mishandle: *The player fumbled and dropped the ball/fumbled his attempt to catch it.*

fume /fyuʷm/ v **fumed, fuming** [I] to show

signs of great anger and restlessness: *"Was he angry?" "Yes, he was really fuming."*

fumes /fyuᵂmz/ *n* [P] heavy strong-smelling air given off from smoke, gas, fresh paint, etc.: *The air in the railroad car was thick with tobacco fumes.|Gasoline fumes from car motors poison the air.*

fu·mi·gate /'fyuᵂmə,geʸt/ *v* **-gated, -gating** [T] to clear of disease, bacteria, or harmful insects by means of chemical smoke or gas: *The man was found to have an infectious disease, so all his clothes had to be fumigated.* –**fumigation** /,fyuᵂmə'geʸʃən/ *n* [U]

fun /fʌn/ *n* [U] **1** playfulness: *The little dog's full of fun.* **2** (a cause of) amusement; enjoyment; pleasure: *It's no fun spending the evening doing nothing.|Have fun!* (=enjoy yourself)*|He's learning French* **for fun/for the fun of it.** (=for pleasure)*|Swimming in the sea is* **great/good fun 3 in fun** as a joke; without serious or harmful intention: *I'm sorry I hid your car keys; I only did it in fun.* **4 make fun of/poke fun at** to (cause others to) laugh rather unkindly at: *People poke fun at her because she wears such strange hats.*

func·tion¹ /'fʌŋkʃən/ *n* **1** a usual purpose (of a thing) or special duty (of a person): *The function of an adjective is to describe or add to the meaning of a noun.|The function of a chairperson is to lead and control meetings.* **2** a large or important gathering of people for pleasure or on some special occasion: *This room may be rented for weddings and other functions.|The mayor has to attend all kinds of official functions.*

function² *v* [I] (esp. of a thing) to be in action; work: *The machine won't function well if you don't oil it.*

func·tion·al /'fʌŋkʃənəl/ *adj* made for or concerned with practical use without ornamentation: *functional furniture* –**functionally** *adv*

fund¹ /fʌnd/ *n* a supply or sum of money set apart for a special purpose: *government funds|the school sports fund|I'm a little* **short of funds.** (=without much money)*|*(fig.) *She has a fund of amusing jokes.*

fund² *v* [T] to provide money for (an activity, organization, etc.): *The search for a cure for this disease is being funded by the government.*

fun·da·men·tal¹ /,fʌndə'mentəl/ *adj* (of a non-material thing) of the greatest importance; deep; being at the base, from which all else develops: *The new government has promised to make fundamental changes.|Fresh air is fundamental* (=necessary) *to good health.* –**fundamentally** *adv* : *She is fundamentally unsuited to office work.*

fundamental² *n* [*of*] a rule, law, etc., on which a system is based: *If the boys are going camping for ten days, they'll need to know the fundamentals of cooking.*

fu·ner·al /'fyuᵂnərəl/ *n* [A;C] a ceremony, usu. religious, of burying or burning a dead person: *a funeral service|a funeral procession*

fu·ne·re·al /fyuᵂ'nɪəriʸəl/ *adj* heavy and sad; suitable to a funeral: *When news of the war was announced, we all sat in funereal silence.*

fun·gus /'fʌngəs/ *n* **fungi** /'fʌndʒaɪ, 'fʌŋgaɪ/ *or* **funguses 1** [C] a plant without flowers, leaves, or green coloring matter, with a fleshy stem supporting a broad rounded top (MUSHROOMS, TOADSTOOLS, etc.), or in a very small form, with a powderlike appearance (MILDEW, MOLD, etc.) **2** [U] these plants in general, esp. considered as a disease: *roses suffering from fungus*

fu·nic·u·lar /fyuᵂ'nɪkyələr, fə-/ also **funicular railway** / · ,··· '··/– *n* a small railway up a slope or a mountain, worked by a thick metal rope

funk·y /'fʌŋkiʸ/ *adj* **-ier, -iest** *apprec infml, esp. AmE* **1** (of JAZZ or similar music) having a simple coarse style and feeling, like the BLUES **2** fine; good: *a funky party*

fun·nel¹ /'fʌnl/ *n* **1** a tube-like vessel that is wide and round at the top and narrow at the bottom, used for pouring liquids or powders into a vessel with a narrow neck **2** a metal chimney for letting out smoke from a steam engine or steamship

funnel² *v* **-l-** *AmE*‖ **-ll-** *BrE* [I;T] to (cause to) pass through or as if through a FUNNEL¹ (1): *The large crowd funneled out of the gates after the football game.*

fun·ny¹ /'fʌniʸ/ *adj* **-nier, -niest 1** amusing; causing laughter: *I heard such a funny story this morning.|I don't think that's at all funny.* (=is a fit cause for laughter) **2** strange; unexpected; hard to explain; unusual: *What can that funny noise be?|It's a funny thing, but she put the book on the table five minutes ago, and now it can't be found.|When I saw them whispering to each other, I knew there was something funny* (=dishonest) *going on.* **3** [F no comp.] *infml* slightly ill: *She always feels a bit funny if she looks down from a height.* –**funniness** *n* [U]

funny² *AmE*‖**funnily** /'fʌnl-iʸ/ *BrE*– *adv* **1** in an unusual or amusing way: *She's been acting rather funny recently.* **2 funny enough** *AmE*‖**funnily enough** *BrE*– although this is strange: *There were black clouds and loud thunder, but funny enough it didn't rain.*

fur /fɜr/ *n* **1** [U] the soft thick fine hair that covers the body of some types of animal, such as bears, rabbits, cats, etc. **2** [A;C] a hair-covered skin of certain animals (such as foxes, rabbits, MINK, BEAVERS, etc.), used for clothing; a garment made of one or more of these: *Several valuable furs were stolen from the shop.|a fur coat* **3** [U] a hard covering on the inside of pots, hot-water pipes, etc. –see SCALE³ (2)

fu·ri·ous /'fyuəriʸəs/ *adj* **1** [+*to-v*] very angry in an uncontrolled way: *He'll be furious with us if we're late.|He'll be furious at being kept waiting.* –see ANGRY (USAGE) **2** wild; uncontrolled: *a furious temper|There was a furious knocking at the door.* –**furiousness** *n* [U] –**furiously** *adv*

furl /fɜrl/ *v* [T] to roll or fold up (a sail, flag, FAN, UMBRELLA, etc.) –see also UNFURL

---

fur·long /'fɜrlɔŋ/ n (a measure of length equal to) one-eighth of a mile, 220 yards or 201 meters, used mainly in horseracing

fur·nace /'fɜrnɪs/ n **1** an apparatus in a factory, in which metals and other substances are heated to very high temperatures in an enclosed space **2** a large enclosed fire used for producing hot water or steam: *The furnace broke down and our apartment has no heat.*|*This room's like a furnace.* (=it's much too hot)

fur·nish /'fɜrnɪʃ/ v [T] **1** to put furniture in (a room or building); supply with furniture: *The new hotel's finished, but it's not furnished yet.*|*They're renting a furnished house.* (=one with furniture already in it) **2** fml to supply (what is necessary for a special purpose): *This store furnishes everything you need for camping.*

fur·ni·ture /'fɜrnɪtʃər/ n [U] all large or quite large movable articles, such as beds, chairs, tables, etc., that are placed in a house, room, or other area: *This old French table is a very valuable piece of furniture.*|*garden furniture*

fu·ror /'fyʊərɔr/ *AmE*|| **furore** /'fyʊərɔr, -ɔʷr/ *BrE* n [S] a sudden burst of angry or excited interest among a large group of people: *There was a furor over the new taxes.*

fur·ri·er /'fɜriʷər, 'fʌr-/ n a person who prepares furs, makes fur garments, and/or sells them

fur·row[1] /'fɜroʷ, 'fʌroʷ/ n a long narrow track, esp. one cut by a PLOW in farming land: *The deep furrows made it difficult to walk across the field.*|(fig.) *Worry had caused deep furrows to appear on her forehead.*

furrow[2] v [T] to make FURROWS in: (fig.) *She looked at the examination paper with a furrowed* BROW. (=a forehead with lines in it)

fur·ry /'fɜriʸ/ adj **-rier, -riest** of, like, or covered with fur: *This furry material will make a warm coat for the winter.*|*a furry little rabbit*

fur·ther[1] /'fɜrðər/ adv,adj [adv+adv/prep] **1** (COMPARATIVE[2] of FAR) also **farther**– more far: *He can swim further/farther than I can.*|*She can't remember further back than 1970.* **2** more: *I have nothing further to say.*|*There will be a further performance* (=another performance) *of the play next week.*

USAGE **Farther** and **farthest** are only used when speaking of real places and distances: **farther/further** *down the road*|*What's the* **farthest/furthest** *place you've ever been to?* Otherwise, use **further** and **furthest**: *Nothing was* **further** *from my mind.*|*We'll have to wait a* **further** *two weeks to know the results.*

further[2] v [T] fml to help (something); advance; help to succeed: *the government's plans to further the cause of peace*

fur·ther·ance /'fɜrðərəns/ n [U of] fml helping forward; development; continuation: *He went to the university for the furtherance of his studies.*

further ed·u·ca·tion /ˌ··· ···'···/ n [U] *BrE* for CONTINUING EDUCATION

fur·ther·more /'fɜrðərˌmɔr, -ˌmoʷr/ adv fml besides what has been said: *The house is too small, and furthermore, it's too far from the city.*

fur·ther·most /'fɜrðər,moʷst/ adj [A] most distant; farthest away: *the furthermost station on the train line*

fur·thest /'fɜrðɪst/ also **farthest**– adv,adj [adv+adv/ prep] (SUPERLATIVE[2] of FAR) most far: *Who can swim furthest/farthest?*|*Our house is the furthest away.*|*Our house is the furthest/farthest from the stores.* –see FURTHER (USAGE)

fur·tive /'fɜrtɪv/ adj secret and/or not direct, as expressing guilty feelings; trying or hoping to escape notice: *The man's furtive manner made the policeman watch him to see what he would do.* **–furtively** adv **–furtiveness** n [U]

fu·ry /'fyʊəriʸ/ n **-ries 1** [S;U] (a state of) very great anger: *She was filled with fury/in a fury and could not speak.* **2** [U of] with force or activity: *At last the fury of the storm lessened.*

fuse[1] /fyuʷz/ n (a container with) a thin piece of wire, placed in an electric apparatus or system, which melts if too much electric power passes through it, and thus breaks the connection and prevents damage: *You'll* **blow a fuse** *if you put the electric heater and the TV and all the lights on at the same time. Then the whole place will be dark.*

fuse[2] v **fused, fusing 1** to (cause to) melt in great heat: *Lead will fuse at quite a low temperature.* **2** [together] to join or become joined by melting: *The aircraft came down in flames, and the heat fused most of the parts together into a solid mass.*|(fig.)*He was able to fuse his men together into a fighting force.*

fuse[3] n **1** a long string or a narrow pipe used for carrying fire to an explosive article and so causing it to blow up **2** an apparatus in a bomb, SHELL[1] (3), or other weapon, which causes it to explode when touched, thrown, etc.

fu·se·lage /'fyuʷsəˌlɑʒ, -ˌlɪdʒ, -zə-/ n the main body of an aircraft, in which travelers and goods are carried

fu·sion /'fyuʷʒən/ n [C;U of] (a) melting, mixing, uniting, or joining together: *This metal is formed by the fusion of two other types of metal.*|(fig.) *His work is a fusion of several different styles of music.*

fuss[1] /fʌs/ n [S;U] **1** unnecessary, useless, or unwelcome excitement, anger, impatience, etc.: *What a fuss about nothing!*|*Don't make so much fuss over losing a dollar.*|*There's sure to be a fuss when they find out that the window's broken.*|*Aunt Mary always* **makes a great fuss over** (=pays a lot of attention to) *her sister's daughter.* **2 kick up/make a fuss** to cause trouble, esp. by complaining loudly or angrily

fuss[2] v [I about] to act or behave in a nervous, restless, and anxious way over small matters: *Don't fuss; I'm sure we'll catch our train.*|*She fusses too much about her health; she's always going to the doctor.*

fuss·y /'fʌsiʸ/ adj **-ier, -iest** usu. derog **1** (of a person or a person's actions, character, etc.) nervous and excitable about small matters:

small *fussy movements of her hands* **2** (of a person) too much concerned about details: *He's fussy about his food; if it isn't cooked just right, he won't eat it.* –**fussily** *adv* –**fussiness** *n* [U]

fus·ty /ˈfʌstiʸ/ *adj* **-tier, -tiest** *derog* (of a room, box, clothes, etc.) having an unpleasant smell as a result of having been shut up for a long time, esp. when not quite dry –**fustiness** *n* [U]

fu·tile /ˈfyuʷtḷ, -taɪl/ *adj often derog* (of an action) having no effect; unsuccessful; useless: *All his attempts to unlock the door were futile, because he was using the wrong key.* | *Don't waste time by asking futile questions.* –**futility** /fyuʷˈtɪlətiʸ/ *n* [U]: *the futility of war*

fu·ture /ˈfyuʷtʃər/ *adj,n* **1** [A; *the* S] (in) time yet to come: *You should save some money. It's wise to provide for the future.* | *in future years* | *Keep this book for future use.* (=to use at a later time) | *In the future, we may all work fewer hours a day.* | *In the distant future* (=much later) *people may live on the moon.* | *We're hoping to move to Spain in the near future/in the not too distant future.* (=quite soon) –compare PAST[1] (1) **2** [A;C] (expected or planned for) a person's life in time yet to come; that which will happen to

someone or something: *I wish you a very happy future.* | *The company has had a difficult year, and its future is uncertain.* | *He has a bright future as a painter.* (=will be successful) | *my future husband/wife* (=the man/woman whom I am going to marry) | *We're leaving this country; our future home will be in Japan.* **3** [A; *the* S] *tech* (in grammar) (being) the tense of a verb that expresses what will happen at a later time: *The future (tense) of English verbs is formed with "will."* –compare PAST[1] (5) **4** [U] *infml* likelihood of success: *There's no future in trying to sell furs in a hot country.* **5 in future** (used in giving a warning) from now on: *In future, be more careful with your money.*

fu·tur·is·tic /ˌfyuʷtʃəˈrɪstɪk/ *adj infml* of strange modern appearance: *a futuristic building/design* –**futuristically** *adv*

fuzz[1] /fʌz/ *n* [U] *infml* a soft light substance such as rubs off a woolen article; FLUFF

fuzz[2] *n* [P] *infml* police: *Look out–the fuzz are coming!*

fuzz·y /ˈfʌziʸ/ *adj* **-ier, -iest** *infml* **1** (of hair) standing up in a light short mass **2** not clear in shape; misty: *The television picture is fuzzy tonight.* | (fig) *Her travel plans are still fuzzy.* **3** (of cloth, a garment, etc.) having a raised soft hairy surface –**fuzzily** *adv* –**fuzziness** *n* [U]

G, g

G, g /dʒiʸ/ **G's, g's** *or* **Gs, gs** the 7th letter of the English alphabet

G *abbrev. for: tech* **1** GRAVITY (2) **2** the amount of force caused by GRAVITY (2) on an object that is lying on the earth, used as a measure

Ga *written abbrev. said as:* Georgia /ˈdʒɔrdʒə/ (a state in the US)

gab[1] /gæb/ *n* [U] *infml* (**have**) **the gift of the gab** (have) the ability to speak well continuously

gab[2] *v infml* **-bb-** [I] to talk continuously: *We gabbed on the telephone for hours.*

gab·ble /ˈgæbəl/ *v* **-bled, -bling** [I;T] to say (words) so quickly that they cannot be heard clearly –**gabble** *n* [S;U]: *the gabble of excited children*

ga·ble /ˈgeʸbəl/ *n* the three-cornered upper end of a wall where it meets the roof

gad a·bout (sthg.) /gæd/ *v prep; adv* **-dd-** [I;T] *infml* to travel round (somewhere) to enjoy oneself: *She gads about (Europe) a lot.* –**gadabout** /ˈgædə,baʊt/ *n: He's a real gadabout.*

gadg·et /ˈgædʒɪt/ *n* a small machine or useful apparatus: *a nice little gadget for opening cans* –see MACHINE (USAGE)

gag[1] /gæg/ *n* **1** a piece of cloth, etc., put over or into the mouth to prevent the person from talking or shouting **2** *infml* a joke or funny story

gag[2] *v* **-gg-** [T] to prevent from speaking by putting a GAG[1] (1) into the mouth of: (fig.)

The newspapers have been gagged, so nobody knows what really happened.

gage /geʸdʒ/ *n,v* **gaged, gaging** *AmE* for GAUGE

gag·gle /ˈgægəl/ *n* a number of geese (GOOSE) together: (fig.) *a gaggle of noisy children*

gai·e·ty /ˈgeʸətiʸ/ *n* **-ties 1** [U] the state of being cheerful **2** [C *usu. pl.*;U] joyful events and activities, esp. at a time of public holiday

gai·ly /ˈgeʸliʸ/ *adv* in a cheerful manner

gain[1] /geʸn/ *v* **1** [T] to obtain (something useful, necessary, wanted, etc.): *I'm new on the job but I'm already gaining experience.* **2** [I;T] to make (a profit or increase in amount): *The car gained speed as it went down the hill.* | *My watch has gained ten minutes* (=by moving too fast) *since yesterday.* | *The People's Party is gaining ground* (=becoming stronger, more popular, etc.) *in the country.* –opposite **lose** (for 2); see WIN (USAGE)

gain on/upon sbdy./sthg.– *v prep* [T] to reduce the distance between oneself and (a competitor)

gain[2] *n* [C;U] (the act of making) an increase in wealth, amount, weight, etc.: *He put a lot of money into the firm with the hope of gain in the future.* | *The baby had a gain of half a pound (in weight) last week.* –opposite **loss**

gait /geʸt/ *n* a way or manner of walking: *He had a strange rolling gait, like a sailor on a ship.*

gal /gæl/ *n AmE infml* a girl or woman

ga·la /'geᵞlə, 'gælə, 'gɑlə/ *adj,n* (of) an occasion of feasting or public amusement: *a gala occasion*

gal·ax·y /'gæləksiᵞ/ *n* **-ies** any of the large groups of stars which make up the universe: (fig.) *a galaxy of film stars* **–galactic** /gə'læktɪk/ *adj*

gale /geᵞl/ *n* a strong wind: *The old tree was blown down in a gale.*|(fig.) *gales* (=sudden bursts) *of laughter* –see WEATHER (USAGE)

gall /gɔl/ *n* [U] **1** *old use* a bitter liquid formed by the LIVER **2 a** a feeling of bitterness or hatred **b** rudeness; bad manners: *They* **had the gall to** *call me fat!*

gal·lant¹ /'gælənt/ *adj* courageous: *a gallant deed/soldier* **–gallantly** *adv* **–gallantry** /'gæləntriᵞ/ *n* **-ries** [U;C]

gal·lant² /gə'lænt, gə'lɑnt, 'gælənt/ *adj lit* (of men) attentive and polite to women **–gallantly** *adv* **–gallantry** /'gæləntriᵞ/ *n* **-ries** [U;C]

gal·le·on /'gæliᵞən/ *n* a large sailing ship, formerly used esp. by the Spaniards

gal·ler·y /'gæləriᵞ/ *n* **-ies 1** a room, hall, or building where works of art are shown and sometimes offered for sale **2** an upper floor built out from an inner wall of a hall, from which activities in the hall may be watched **3** a long narrow room, such as one used for shooting practice **4** a level underground passage in a mine **5** the highest upper floor in a theater

gal·ley /'gæliᵞ/ *n* **-leys 1** a ship's kitchen **2** (in former times) a ship which was rowed by slaves, esp. an ancient Greek or Roman warship

gal·li·vant /'gælə,vænt, ,gælə'vænt/ *v* [I *about*] *infml & derog* to go around amusing oneself; GAD ABOUT: *to go gallivanting around town*

gal·lon /'gælən/ *n* (a measure for liquids equal to) 8 PINTS or 4 QUARTS (in America 3·78, in Britain 4·54 LITERs)

gal·lop¹ /'gæləp/ *n* **1** [S] the movement of a horse at its fastest speed: (fig.) *She went through the work at a gallop.* (=very quickly) **2** [C] a ride at this speed: *a long gallop*

gal·lop² *v* [I *off, away*] (of a horse, or a person riding a horse) to go at the fastest speed: *The horse galloped down the hill.*|*They galloped off (on their horses).*|(fig.) *to gallop through one's work*

gal·lows /'gæloʷz/ *n* **gallows** the wooden frame on which murderers used to be killed by hanging from a rope

Gal·lup poll /'gæləp ,poʷl/ *n tdmk* a special count of opinions in a country by questioning a number of people chosen by chance, esp. so as to guess the result of a coming election (=a POLL¹ (2))

ga·lore /gə'lɔr, gə'loʷr/ *adj* [after *n*] *apprec* (in) plenty: *money galore/friends galore*

ga·losh /gə'lɑʃ/ *n* [*usu. pl.*] a rubber shoe worn over an ordinary shoe when it rains or snows –see PAIR (USAGE)

gal·va·nize ||also **-nise** *BrE* /'gælvə,naɪz/ *v* **-nized, -nizing** [T] **1** to put a covering of metal, esp. ZINC, over (a sheet of another metal, esp. iron), by using electricity: *galvanized iron* **2** to shock (someone) into action: *The fear of losing his life galvanized him (into fighting back).*

gam·bit /'gæmbɪt/ *n* **1** an action made to produce a future effect, esp. an opening move in an argument or conversation –compare PLOY **2** (in CHESS) a set of opening moves in which a piece is risked so as to gain advantage later

gam·ble¹ /'gæmbəl/ *v* **-bled, -bling** [I] to risk one's money on horse races, in (card) games, business, etc.: *to spend the night gambling*|(fig.) *I escaped from the prison at night, gambling on the fact that* (=hoping that) *I wouldn't be seen because of the darkness.* **–gambler** /'gæmblər/ *n*

gamble sthg.↔ **away** *v adv* [T] to lose (money) by gambling (GAMBLE): *He gambled away all his money.*

gam·ble² *n* [S] a risky matter or act: *The operation may not succeed; it's a gamble whether he lives or dies.*

gam·bol /'gæmbəl/ *v* [I *about*] **-l-** *AmE*||**-ll-** *BrE* to jump about in play, as lambs or children do **–gambol** *n*

game¹ /geᵞm/ *n* **1** [C] a form of play or sport, or one example or type of this: *Football is a game which doesn't interest me.*|*Let's play a game of cards.* –see also GAMES; see RECREATION (USAGE) **2** [C] a single part of a set into which a match is divided, as in tennis, BRIDGE³, etc. **3** [U] wild animals, some birds, and some fish, which are hunted for food and as a sport: *a game bird/game laws* **4** [C] a trick or secret plan: *What's your game?*|*Try not to* **give the game away.** (=let it be known)

game² *adj* [+*to-v/for*] brave and ready (for action): *He fell and hurt himself, but he was game enough to get up and try again.*|*Who's game for a swim?* **–gamely** *adv*

game·keep·er /'geᵞm,kiᵞpər/ *n* a man employed to raise and protect GAME¹ (3), esp. birds, on private land

games /geᵞmz/ *n* **games 1** [*the* C +*sing./pl. v*] (in names) a particular set of games and sports competitions: *The* OLYMPIC GAMES *are held every four years.* **2** [U] *BrE* for PHYSICAL EDUCATION

gam·ut /'gæmət/ *n* [*the* S] **1** all the notes in music from the lowest to the highest **2** the whole range of a subject: *He's* **run the (whole) gamut of** (=experienced all of) *human experience.*

gan·der /'gændər/ *n* a male GOOSE

gang¹ /gæŋ/ *n* [C] **1** a group of people working together, esp. criminals, prisoners, or building workers: *The gang was planning a robbery.* **2** a group of friends: *Have you seen any of the gang lately?*

gang² *v* → GANG UP

gan·gling /'gæŋglɪŋ/ *adj* unusually tall and thin, so as to appear awkward in movement

gang·plank /'gæŋplæŋk/ *n* a board of wood which is used to make a bridge to get on or off a ship

gan·grene /'gæŋgriᵞn, gæŋ'griᵞn/ *n* [U] the decay of the flesh of part of the body because blood has stopped flowing there **–gangrenous** /'gæŋgrənəs/ *adj*

gang·ster /ˈgæŋstər/ n (esp. in modern times) a member of a group (GANG) of (armed) criminals

gang up v adv [I on, against] derog to work together as a close group (against someone):You've all ganged up on/against me!

gang·way /ˈgæŋweɪ/ n an opening in the side of a ship and the movable board (GANGPLANK) which is used to make a bridge from it to the land

gan·try /ˈgæntriɪ/ n -tries a metal frame which is used to support movable heavy machinery or railway signals

gap /gæp/ n an empty space between two objects or two parts of an object: The gate was locked but we went through a gap in the fence.|(fig.) There are wide gaps in my knowledge of history.|(fig.) I bridged a gap (=filled an empty moment) in the conversation by telling a joke.

gape /geɪp/ v gaped, gaping [I] 1 [at] to look hard in surprise, esp. with the mouth open: She gaped at the tall man, not believing that he was her younger brother. –compare GAWK 2 to be or come apart or open: a gaping hole/wound

ga·rage /gəˈrɑʒ, gəˈrɑdʒ/ n 1 a building in which motor vehicles can be kept –see illustration on page 337 2 a place where (gasoline can be bought and) cars can be repaired

garage² v -raged, -raging [T] to put in a garage

garage sale /ˈ·· ˌ·/ n a sale of used objects that takes place in a family's garage –compare RUMMAGE SALE

garb /gɑrb/ n [U] lit or humor clothing of a particular style: He went to the party in the garb of a Roman soldier.

gar·bage /ˈgɑrbɪdʒ/ n esp. AmE 1 waste material; RUBBISH: The street is covered with old cans and other forms of garbage. 2 derog stupid and worthless ideas, words, etc.

garbage can /ˈ·· ˌ·/ also **trash can** AmE‖**dustbin** BrE– n 1 a container (usu. found in the kitchen) having a lid and holding waste material (esp. food waste) until it can be taken away 2 this same container found outside the house –compare WASTEPAPER BASKET, see illustration on page 337

garbage col·lec·tor /ˈ·· ˌˌ·/ also **garbage man** /ˈ·· ˌ·/ AmE‖**dustman** /ˈdʌstmæn/ BrE– n a person employed (as by a town) to remove waste material from GARBAGE CANS

garbage truck /ˈ·· ˌ·/ AmE‖**dustcart** /ˈdʌstkɑrt/ BrE– n a specially made truck which goes from house to house or building to building to collect the contents of GARBAGE CANS

gar·bled /ˈgɑrbəld/ adj (of a statement) confused; giving a false idea of the facts: The newspaper gave a garbled account of the meeting.

gar·den¹ /ˈgɑrdn/ n 1 a piece of land, usu. near a house, on which flowers and vegetables may be grown 2 [often pl.] a public park with flowers, grass, paths, and seats 3 **lead (someone) up/down the garden path** to trick

(someone) into believing what is not true and acting on it

garden² v [I] to work in a garden, making plants grow –**gardener** n –**gardening** n [U]: My mother's very good at gardening.

gar·de·nia /gɑrˈdiɪnyə/ n a tropical bush or its large white or yellow sweet-smelling flowers

gar·gan·tu·an /gɑrˈgæntʃuʷən/ adj (usu. in connection with food) very big: a gargantuan meal/APPETITE

gar·gle /ˈgɑrgəl/ v -gled, -gling [I] to wash the throat with liquid by blowing through it at the back of the mouth –**gargle** n [S]

gar·goyle /ˈgɑrgɔɪl/ n a hollow figure of a person or animal esp. on the roof of a church, through whose mouth rainwater is carried away

gar·ish /ˈgɛərɪʃ, ˈgærɪʃ/ adj unpleasantly bright: garish colors/garish light –**garishly** adv –**garishness** n [U]

gar·land /ˈgɑrlənd/ n a circle of flowers, leaves, or both, esp. to be placed around the neck for ornament or as a sign of victory –compare WREATH –**garland** v [T]: garlanded with flowers

gar·lic /ˈgɑrlɪk/ n [U] a plant like an onion, which is used in cooking to give a strong taste

gar·ment /ˈgɑrmənt/ n fml (the name used, esp. by the makers, for) an article of clothing: This garment should be washed carefully.

gar·net /ˈgɑrnɪt/ n a type of red jewel

gar·nish¹ /ˈgɑrnɪʃ/ v [T] to add something to (esp. food) as a decoration –see DECORATE (USAGE)

garnish² n pieces of fruit, vegetable, or any of the things which are used to make food look better

gar·ret /ˈgærɪt/ n a usu. small room at the top of a house; ATTIC

gar·ri·son¹ /ˈgærəsən/ n a group of soldiers living in a town or fort and defending it: The garrison is preparing for another enemy attack.

garrison² v [T] (to send soldiers) to guard (something) in a GARRISON:The government will garrison the coastal towns.

gar·ru·lous /ˈgærələs, ˈgæryə-/ adj habitually talking too much, esp. about unimportant things –**garrulously** adv –**garrulity** /gəˈruʷləti̯/ also **garrulousness**– n [U]

gar·ter /ˈgɑrtər/ n a band of elastic material worn around the leg to keep a stocking up

gas¹ /gæs/ n gases 1 [C;U] (a type of) substance like air, which is not solid or liquid: There are several kinds of gas in the air. 2 [U] a substance of this type which is burned in the home for heating and cooking 3 [U] AmE infml GASOLINE 4 [C usu. sing.] infml esp. AmE a wildly funny or pleasant thing, or (sometimes) the opposite: I have to take 20 children to the movies. That'll be a real gas.

gas² v -ss- [T] to poison with gas

gas cham·ber /ˈ· ˌ··/ n a room which can be filled with gas so that animals or people may be put to death

gas·e·ous /ˈgæsiʷəs, ˈgæʃəs/ adj of or like gas

gash /gæʃ/ v [T] to make a deep cut in –**gash** n

gas·ket /'gæskɪt/ *n* a flat piece of soft material which is placed between two surfaces so that steam, oil, gas, etc., cannot escape

gas mask /'· ·/ *n* a breathing apparatus worn over the face to protect the wearer against poisonous gases

gas·o·hol /'gæsəˌhɔl, -ˌhɑl/ *n* [U] a mixture of alcohol and gasoline used esp. for producing power in the engines of cars

gas·o·line, -lene /ˌgæsə'liʸn, 'gæsəˌliʸn/ also **gas** *AmE infml*‖**petrol** *BrE–* *n* [U] a liquid obtained from PETROLEUM, used esp. for producing power in the engines of cars, aircraft, etc.: *We're almost out of gasoline.*

gasoline en·gine /'···ˌ··ˌ, '··· ˌ··/ *AmE*‖**petrol engine** *BrE–* a piece of machinery esp. in a car which changes power from GASOLINE into movement –compare DIESEL ENGINE

gasp /gæsp/ *v* [I] **1** to breathe quickly, esp. with difficulty, making a sudden noise: *I came out of the water and gasped for breath.* **2** to catch the breath suddenly, esp. because of surprise, shock, etc.: *I gasped with/in surprise at the unexpected news.* –**gasp** *n*: *He gave a gasp of surprise.*

gas sta·tion /'· ˌ··/ also **filling station, service station** *AmE*‖**petrol station** *BrE–* a place that sells gasoline and oil and repairs motor vehicles –see illustration on page 673

gas·sy /'gæsiʸ/ *adj* **-sier, -siest** full of (a) gas: *a gassy drink*

gas·tric /'gæstrɪk/ *adj* [A] *tech* of or belonging to the stomach: *the gastric juices* (=acids which break down food in the stomach)

gas·tro·en·ter·i·tis /ˌgæstrowˌɛntə'raɪtɪs/ *n* [U] an illness in which the food passages, including the stomach and INTESTINEs, are swollen

gas·tron·o·my /gæ'strɑnəmiʸ/ *n* [U] the art and science of cooking and eating good food –**gastronomic** /ˌgæstrə'nɑmɪk/ *adj* –**gastronomically** *adv*

gas·works /'gæswɜrks/ *n* **gasworks** a place where gas for use in the home is made from coal

gate /geʸt/ *n* **1** a movable frame, often with bars across it, which closes an opening in a fence, wall, etc.: *the garden gate*‖*park gates* –see illustration on page 337 **2** →GATEWAY **3** (the money paid by) the number of people who go in to see a sports event, esp. a football game

gate·crash·er /'geʸtˌkræʃər/ *n* a person who goes to a party without being invited: *There were so many gatecrashers that there wasn't enough food and the party was a failure.*

gate·post /'geʸtpowˢt/ *n* a post beside a gate, from which the gate is hung or to which it fastens

gate·way /'geʸt-weʸ/ *n* an opening in a fence, wall, etc., across which a gate may be put: (fig.) *Finishing college can be a gateway to* (=the way of finding) *success.*

gath·er /'gæðər/ *v* **1** [I;T *around*] to (cause to) come together: *Gather around, and I'll tell you a story.*‖*A crowd gathered to see what had happened.* **2** [T] to obtain (information or qualities) a little bit at a time: *As we came*

onto the open road we gathered speed. **3** [T *in, up*] to collect or pick (flowers, crops, etc.): *Gather your toys up.* **4** [T +(*that*)] to understand from something said or done: *I gather she's ill, and that's why she hasn't come.* **5** [T] to draw (material) into small folds by using a long thread: *a gathered skirt* (=at the waist)

gath·er·ing /'gæðərɪŋ/ *n* a meeting

gauche /gowʃ/ *adj* awkward (in social behavior); doing and saying the wrong things

gaud·y /'gɔdiʸ/ *adj* **-ier, -iest** too bright in color and/or with too much decoration –**gaudily** *adv* –**gaudiness** *n* [U]

gauge¹ ‖also **gage** *AmE* /geʸdʒ/ *n* **1** an instrument for measuring size, amount, etc., such as the width of wire, the amount of rain falling, etc. **2** a standard measure of weight, size, etc., to which objects can be compared

gauge² ‖also **gage** *AmE* *v* **gauged, gauging** [T] **1** to measure by means of a GAUGE **2** to judge the worth, meaning, etc. of (something or somebody's actions)

gaunt /gɔnt, gɑnt/ *adj* thin, as if ill or hungry –compare HAGGARD –**gauntness** *n* [U]

gaunt·let /'gɔntlɪt, 'gɑnt-/ *n* **1** a long GLOVE covering the wrist, which protects the hand (in certain sports, in industry, or formerly in battle) **2 run the gauntlet** to be open to or experience violent attack: (fig.) *He ran the gauntlet of newspaper attacks.* **3 throw down the gauntlet** to call someone to fight esp. when two people's beliefs are opposed: *Once he threw down the gauntlet, I had to fight.*

gauze /gɔz/ *n* [U] net-like material, sometimes used in medicine to cover wounds, or as a curtain: *cotton gauze*

gave /geʸv/ *v past tense of* GIVE

gav·el /'gævəl/ *n* a small hammer used by a judge in the US, a chairperson, or an AUCTIONEER, who strikes a table with it to get attention or to show that an object has been sold

gawk /gɔk/ *v* [I *at*] to look at something in a foolish way: *Don't stand there gawking (at it); do something.* –compare GAPE

gawk·y /'gɔkiʸ/ *adj* **-ier, -iest** (of a person) awkward in movement –**gawkiness** *n* [U]

gay /geʸ/ *adj* **1** cheerful; happy: *We were all gay at the thought of the coming holidays.* **2** bright or attractive: *We're painting the kitchen in gay colors.* **3** → HOMOSEXUAL

gaze¹ /geʸz/ *v* **gazed, gazing** [I *at*] to look steadily for a long or short period of time: *He sat gazing out of the window.*

gaze² *n* [S] a steady fixed look: *She turned her gaze from one person to the other.*

ga·zelle /gə'zɛl/ *n* **-zelles** *or* **zelle** a type of animal (ANTELOPE) like a small deer, which jumps in graceful movements

ga·zette /gə'zɛt/ *n* an official esp. one from the government newspaper, giving lists of people who have been employed by them, important notices, etc.

G.B., GB *abbrev. for:* Great Britain

gear¹ /gɪər/ *n* **1** [C;U] an arrangement, esp. of toothed wheels in a machine, which allows power to be passed from one part to another, esp. from the engine of a car to its wheels: *She changed gears to make the car go up the hill faster.*|*"The car isn't moving!" "That's because you're not in gear."* **2** [C] an apparatus or part of a machine which has a special use in controlling a vehicle: *the landing gear of an aircraft*|STEERing *gear* **3** [U] a set of things collected together, esp. for a particular purpose: *camping gear*

gear² *v →* GEAR TO

gear·box /'gɪərbɑks/ *n* a metal case containing the GEARS (1) of a vehicle; TRANSMISSION (3)

gear shift /'·· ·/ also **stick shift** *AmE*‖**gear lever** /'· ,··/, also **gear stick** /'·· ·/ *BrE*– *n* the apparatus which controls the GEARS (1) of a vehicle –see illustration on page 95

gear sthg. **to** sthg. *v prep* [T] to cause (one thing) to depend on or be fixed in relation to (another): *Education should be geared to the children's needs and abilities.*

geese /giˠs/ *n pl. of* GOOSE

gei·sha /'geˠʃə, 'giˠʃə/ also **geisha girl** /'·· ,·/– *n* a Japanese girl or woman who is trained to dance, sing, and perform various arts to amuse men

gel /dʒɛl/ *v* **-ll-** [I] →JELL (1,2)

gel·a·tin *AmE* /'dʒɛlətn/‖also **gelatine**– *n* [U] a clear substance from boiled animal bones, used for making food, medicines, and photographic film

ge·lat·i·nous /dʒə'lætn-əs/ *adj tech* like jelly; in a state between solid and liquid

gel·ig·nite /'dʒɛlɪg,naɪt/ *n* [U] a very powerful explosive

gem /dʒɛm/ *n* **1** a jewel; precious stone, esp. when cut into a regular shape **2** a thing or person of special value

Gem·i·ni /'dʒɛmə,naɪ, -,niˠ/ *n* see ZODIAC

gen·der /'dʒɛndər/ *n tech* **1** [U] (in grammar) the state of being MASCULINE, FEMININE, or NEUTER **2** [C] any of these states: *German has three genders.*

gene /dʒiˠn/ *n* a single part of the material at the center (NUCLEUS) of a cell, which controls the development of qualities in a living thing which have been passed on (INHERITED) from its parents

ge·ne·al·o·gy /,dʒiˠniˠ'ɑlədʒiˠ, -'ælə-, ,dʒɛ-/ *n* **-gies** [C;U] (the study of) the history of the members of a family, often shown in a drawing with lines and names spreading like the branches of a tree –**genealogist** *n* –**genealogical** /,dʒiˠniˠə'lɑdʒɪkəl, ,dʒɛ-/ *adj*

gen·er·al¹ /'dʒɛnərəl/ *adj* **1** [A] concerning or felt by everybody or most people: *the general public* (=the mass of ordinary people)|*The general feeling is* (=most people feel) *that it's wrong.*|*Worry about high food prices is now fairly general.*|*It's not in the general interest to close down railroads.* (=it's not good for most people) **2** not limited to one thing, place, etc.: *a general university degree* (=in several subjects)|*general education* (=in many subjects) **3** not detailed; describing the main things only: *Give me a general idea of the work.* **4** [after *n*] (as the second part of an official title) chief: *Postmaster-General*

general² *n* [A;C] **1** an officer of very high rank in an army or air force **2 in general: a** also **as a general rule** –usually; in most cases: *In general, people like her.* **b** (*after a pl. noun*) most: *People in general like her.* –compare GENERALLY

general e·lec·tion /,··· ·'··/ *n AmE* an election in which all the voters in the country choose members of local, state, and national governments

gen·er·al·i·ty /,dʒɛnə'rælətiˠ/ *n* **-ties 1** [U] the quality of being general **2** [C] a general statement; point for consideration which is not at all detailed: *The President's speech was full of generalities.*

gen·er·al·i·za·tion ‖also **-isation** *BrE* /,dʒɛnərələ'zeˠʃən/ *n* [C;U] (the act of making) a general statement, principle, or opinion resulting from the consideration of particular facts

gen·er·al·ize ‖also **-ise** *BrE* /'dʒɛnərə,laɪz/ *v* **-ized, -izing** [I] **1** to make a general statement (about): *Our history teacher is always generalizing. He never deals with anything in detail.* **2** to form a general principle, opinion, etc., after considering only a small number of the facts: *Is it fair to generalize from these two accidents and say that all young people are bad drivers?*

gen·er·al·ly /'dʒɛnərəliˠ/ *adv* **1** usually: *We generally go to the lake for our vacation.* **2** by most people: *The plan has been generally accepted.* **3** without considering details, but only the main points

general prac·ti·tion·er /,··· ·'··/ also **G.P.** *abbrev*– *n* a doctor who is trained in general medicine and whose work (**general practice** /,··· ·'·/) is to treat people in a certain local neighborhood

gen·er·ate /'dʒɛnə,reˠt/ *v* **-ated, -ating** [T] *tech* to produce (esp. heat or electricity): *Our electricity comes from a new generating station.*|(fig.) *The teacher's remark generated loud laughter.*

gen·er·a·tion /,dʒɛnə'reˠʃən/ *n* **1** [C] a single stage in the development of a family, or the average period of time (about 30 years) between each stage: *a family photograph showing three generations* (=myself, my parents, and my grandparents)|*It will take at least another generation to find an answer to the problem of hunger in the world.* **2** [C] all people of about the same age: *the younger generation* (=young people in general)|*Most people of my father's generation have experienced the hardships of war.* **3** [U] the act or action of generating (GENERATE): *Falling water may be used for the generation of electricity.*

gen·er·a·tor /'dʒɛnə,reˠtər/ *n* a machine which GENERATES, usu. electricity –compare DYNAMO

ge·ner·ic /dʒə'nɛrɪk/ *adj* **1** of or concerning a GENUS **2** shared by or typical of a whole class of things: ASPIRIN *is a generic drug.*

gen·er·ous /'dʒɛnərəs/ *adj* **1** showing readiness to give money, help, kindness, etc.: *It was very generous of you to lend me your car yesterday.* –compare MEAN¹ (4) **2** larger, kinder, etc., than usual: *a generous meal|a generous gift* –**generously** /'dʒɛnərəsliʸ/ *adv* –**generosity** /ˌdʒɛnə'rɑsətiʸ/ *n*

Gen·e·sis /'dʒɛnəsɪs/ *n* the first book of the Bible, in which the story of the beginning of the world is told

ge·net·ic /dʒə'nɛtɪk/ *adj* of or concerning GENES or GENETICS –**genetically** *adv*

ge·net·ics /dʒə'nɛtɪks/ *n* [U] the study of how living things develop according to the effects of those substances passed on in the cells from the parents –see GENE, HEREDITY

ge·nial /'dʒiʸnyəl, 'dʒiʸniʸəl/ *adj* **1** cheerful and kind; good-tempered **2** (of weather) gentle and good for the growth of plants –**genially** *adv* –**geniality** /ˌdʒiʸniʸ'ælətiʸ, dʒiʸn'yæ-/ *n* [U]

ge·nie /'dʒiʸniʸ/ *n* **-nies** a magical spirit in Arab fairy stories

gen·i·tals /'dʒɛnətlz/ also **genitalia** /ˌdʒɛnə'teʸlyə/ *fml n* [P] the outer sex organs –**genital** *adj* [A]

gen·i·tive /'dʒɛnətɪv/ *adj,n tech* (in grammar) (a form or a word) showing esp. possession or origin –compare POSSESSIVE¹ (2)

ge·nius /'dʒiʸnyəs/ *n* **1** [C;U] (a person of) very great ability: *Her latest book is a work of genius.* **2** [S *for*] a special ability: *She has a genius for MATHEMATICS.*

USAGE **Genius** is a very strong word, and is only used of a rare ability or the person who has it: *Einstein had genius/was a genius.* **Talent** also means a special ability (though not the person who has it), but it is not as strong a word as **genius**: *a young actress with a lot of talent|She has a talent for music.|He is a talented football player.* Both **talent** and **genius** are used of powers which a person is born with, but **skill**, which means the ability to do something well, is something that can be learned: *The senator answered his opponents' questions with great skill.|a skilled electrician.* You may be born with a **capacity** or **aptitude** for (doing) something, and this means that you will easily develop **skill** if you are taught: *The child shows a great capacity/aptitude for learning languages.* **Competence** is a satisfactory but not unusual degree of **skill**: *a test of one's competence as a driver/John's a competent teacher.*

gen·o·cide /'dʒɛnəˌsaɪd/ *n* [U] the act of killing a whole group of people, esp. a whole race

gen·teel /dʒɛn'tiʸl/ *adj* trying to show (unnaturally) polite manners –**genteelly** *adv* –**gentility** /dʒɛn'tɪlətiʸ/ *n* [U]

gen·tile /'dʒɛntaɪl/ *adj,n* [*sometimes cap.*] (a person who is) not Jewish

gen·tle /'dʒɛntəl/ *adj* not rough or violent in manner or movement; kind; soft: *Be gentle when you brush the baby's hair.|a gentle wind|a gentle slope* (=not steep) –**gentleness** *n* [U] –**gently** /'dʒɛntliʸ/ *adv*

gen·tle·man /'dʒɛntəlmən/ *n* **-men** /mən/ **1** a man who behaves well towards others and who can always be trusted to act honorably **2** *polite* a man

USAGE **Gentlemen** and **lady** are polite and rather old-fashioned words for **man** and **woman**. They are used esp. when speaking about someone in their presence, or when addressing a gathering of people: *Mr. Smith, there's a gentleman/lady here to see you. Shall I send him/her in?*|Ladies and gentlemen, *I'd like to introduce our speaker for tonight.* ... Otherwise, **man** and **woman** are the usual words: *Is the director a man or a woman?|the first woman prime minister.* **Man** is also used to mean human beings (men and women) in general: **Man** *is the only animal to make and use tools.* However, many people object to this use of **man** because of its SEXISM.

gen·try /'dʒɛntriʸ/ *n* [*the* P] people of high social class: *The landed gentry are those who own land from which they obtain their income.*

gen·u·ine /'dʒɛnyuʷɪn/ *adj* **1** (of an object) real; really what it seems to be: *a football made of genuine* (=not ARTIFICIAL) *leather* –compare FAKE³ **2** (of people or feelings) sincere; real, not pretended –**genuinely** *adv* –**genuineness** *n* [U]

ge·nus /'dʒiʸnəs/ *n* **genera** /'dʒɛnərə/ *tech* a division of a FAMILY (4) of living things, which usu. includes several closely related SPECIES (kinds of animal or plant) –see also GENERIC

ge·og·ra·pher /dʒiʸ'ɑgrəfər/ *n* a person who studies GEOGRAPHY (1)

ge·og·ra·phy /dʒiʸ'ɑgrəfiʸ/ *n* **1** [U] the study of the countries of the world and of the seas, rivers, towns, etc., on the earth's surface **2** [*the* S *of*] *infml* the arrangement or positions of the parts of (a particular place): *I can't show you the way, because I don't know the geography of the neighborhood.* –**geographical** /ˌdʒiʸə'græfɪkəl/ *adj* –**geographically** *adv*

ge·ol·o·gy /dʒiʸ'ɑlədʒiʸ/ *n* [U] the study of the materials (rocks, soil, etc.) which make up the earth, and their changes in the history of the world –**geological** /ˌdʒiʸə'lɑdʒɪkəl/ *adj* –**geologically** *adv* –**geologist** /dʒiʸ'ɑlədʒɪst/ *n*

ge·om·e·try /dʒiʸ'ɑmətriʸ/ *n* [U] the study in MATHEMATICS of the angles and shapes formed by the relationships of lines, surfaces, and solids in space –**geometric** /ˌdʒiʸə'mɛtrɪk/ *adj*: *geometric patterns* (=of straight lines and regular shapes)

Geor·gian /'dʒɔrdʒən/ **1** *adj* (in the style) of the period of rule of King George the First, Second, and Third, esp. from 1714 to 1811: *Georgian* ARCHITECTURE|*a beautiful Georgian house* **2** of or concerning the state of Georgia in the US

ge·ra·ni·um /dʒə'reʸniʸəm/ *n* a garden or pot plant with red or white flowers and rounded leaves

ger·i·at·rics /ˌdʒɛriʸ'ætrɪks, ˌdʒɪər-/ *n* [U] the medical treatment and care of old people –**geriatric** *adj* [A]: *a geriatric hospital*

germ /dʒɜrm/ *n* **1** a very small living thing which cannot be seen but may live on food or dirt or in the body, so causing disease –compare BACTERIA, MICROBE **2** a beginning point, esp. of an idea (esp. in the phrase **the germ of**)

Ger·man mea·sles /ˌdʒɜrmən 'miʸzəlz/ also

rubella *tech–* *n* [U] an infectious disease in which red spots appear on the body for a short time

ger·mi·nate /ˈdʒɜrməˌneʸt/ *v* **-nated, -nating** [I;T] **1** (of a seed) to start growing **2** to cause (a seed) to start growing **–germination** /ˌdʒɜrməˈneʸʃən/ *n* [U]

germ war·fare /ˌ· ˈ··/ *n* [U] →BIOLOGICAL WARFARE

ger·und /ˈdʒɛrənd/ *n* → VERBAL NOUN

ges·ta·tion /dʒɛˈsteʸʃən/ *n* [S;U] the carrying of a child or young animal inside the mother's body before birth

ges·tic·u·late /dʒɛˈstɪkyəˌleʸt/ *v* **-lated, -lating** [I] to make movements of the hands and arms to express something, esp. while speaking **–gesticulation** /dʒɛˌstɪkyəˈleʸʃən/ *n* [C;U]

ges·ture¹ /ˈdʒɛstʃər/ *n* **1** [C;U] movement, usu. of the hands, to express a certain meaning: *He made an angry gesture.|He always uses a lot of gestures when he's telling a joke.* **2** [C] an action which is done to show one's feelings: *We invited our new neighbors to dinner as a gesture of friendship.*

gesture² *v* **-tured, -turing** [I] to make a GESTURE¹ (1)

get /gɛt/ *v* **got** /gɑt/, **got** *or* **gotten** /ˈgɑtn/ *AmE* (see USAGE), **getting 1** [T] to receive or obtain: *I got a letter today.|He got three years in prison.|I'll get you* (=for you) *that book you wanted.|Can you get* (=hear) *Mexico on your radio?* **2** to become: *The food's getting cold.|She must have gotten lost.* **3** [I] to go or arrive: *We got home very late.|At last we're really getting somewhere.* (=arriving at success) **4** [T] to put into a place or state: *I'll get the car started.|We couldn't get the table through the door.* **5** [T] to cause to do: *I got him to help me when I moved the furniture.* **6** [T +to-v] to succeed in or be allowed: *He's very nice when you get to know him.|I never get to drive the car.* **7** [T] to prepare (a meal): *I'm just getting the dinner.* **8** [T] to catch (an illness): *He got a rare tropical disease.* **9** [T] *infml* to understand: *He didn't get the joke.|Do you get me/get what I mean?* **10** [T] *infml* to annoy: *His stupid remarks really get me.* **11** [T] *infml* to hit: *One of the stones got him in the eye.* **12 get something done: a** to cause something to be done: *I must get my shoes mended.* **b** to experience something that happens to one: *I got my hand caught in the door.* **13 have got** see HAVE² (1)

USAGE 1 In *AmE*, the past participle of **get** is **gotten** in every sense except (13), when **have got** means **have/possess.** In this case, the correct form is **got.** In *BrE*, the past participle is always **got.** 2 In formal writing it is better to avoid **get**, and to use **become, receive, obtain, move,** etc., according to the meaning.

get about *v adv* [I] → GET **around**

get across/over– *v adv* [I;T (=**get** sthg. **across**)] to (cause to) be understood (esp. by a large group): *Our teacher is intelligent, but not very good at getting his ideas across.* **–compare** GET **through¹** (2)

get ahead *v adv* [I *of*] to advance (beyond someone or something): *You have to get ahead of your competitors.|"How to Get Ahead* (=succeed) *in Business"* (title) **–compare** FALL **behind**

get along *v adv* [I] **1** (of people) to move away; leave: *I have to be getting along now.* **2** also **get on–** (of people and activities) to advance; go well:*How is your work getting along?* **3** to continue (often in spite of difficulties):*We can get along without your help.* **4** [*with*] also **get on–** (of people) to have a friendly relationship (with another or each other): *Do you get along well with your aunt?*

get around ‖also **get about** *esp. BrE–* **1** to be able to move again after an illness **2** *infml* to travel: *She gets around a lot because she works for an international company.* **3** ‖also **get round** *esp. BrE–* (of news, etc.) to spread

get around sbdy./sthg. *AmE*‖**get round** sbdy./sthg. *BrE– v prep* [T] **1** to avoid (something) or find a way to deal with (something) to one's advantage: *You can sometimes get around the tax laws.* **2** to persuade (someone) to accept one's own way of thinking: *You can get around him easily.*

get around to sthg. also **get round to** sthg.– *v adv prep* [T +*v-ing*] to find time, or have the time, for: *After a long delay, he got around to writing the letter.*

get at sbdy./ sthg. *v prep* [T] **1** [*pass. rare*] to reach: *Put the food where the cat can't get at it.|*(fig.) *to get at the truth* **2** [*no pass.*] (in tenses with the *-ing* form) to mean: *What are you getting at?*

get away *v adv* [I] to escape, e.g. from the scene of a crime: *The thieves got away (with all our money).|I'm sorry I'm late; I was in a meeting and couldn't get away.|*(fig.) *You* **can't get away from** (=you must admit) *the fact that...* **–see also** GETAWAY

get away with sthg. *v adv prep* [T +*v-ing*] to do (something bad) and escape punishment: *How did he get away with cheating?|You'll never get away with it.*

get back *v adv* [I] **1** to return to one's home, job, etc.: *I heard you were away. When did you get back?* **2** *infml* to speak or write to a person at a later time, usu. in order to give a decision or information that the person has asked for: *I can't answer your question now, but I'll get back to you tomorrow.* **3 get back at someone** *infml* to punish someone in return for a wrong done to oneself: *I'll get back at him one day!*

get behind *v adv* [I] →FALL¹ **behind**

get by *v adv* [I] **1** to continue one's way of life: *She can't get by on such a small income.* **2** to be good enough but not very good: *Your work will get by, but try to improve it.*

get down *v adv* [T] **1** (**get** sthg.↔ **down**) to swallow with difficulty: *Try to get the medicine down.* **2** (**get** sthg.↔ **down**) to record in writing: *Get down every word she says.* **3** (**get** sbdy. **down**) to make feel nervous, ill, or sad: *This continual wet weather is getting me down.*

get down to sthg. *v adv prep* [T +*v-ing*] to begin to give serious attention to: *to get down to work/business*

get in¹ *v adv* **1** [I] to arrive (inside a place):

The plane got in late. **2** [I] to be elected; come into power: *If Johnson gets in as mayor, I'll have to move out of this city.* **3** [T] (**get sbdy. in**) to call (someone) to one's help, esp. in the house: *Get the doctor in.* **4** [T] (**get sthg. in**) to say (something), esp. by interrupting a conversation: *Can I get a word in?* **5** [I *at, on*] to take part in (something): *to get in at the beginning*

get in[2] (**sthg.**) *v adv; prep* [I;T] to enter (a vehicle): *They got in and drove off.* –compare GET on[2], GET **out**

get into *v prep* [T] **1** (**get into sthg.**) →GET **in**[2]: *They got into the car and drove off.* **2** (**get sbdy.**) **into** sthg.) to put (oneself or someone else) into (a bad condition): *I've got (myself) into trouble/into the habit of smoking.|I'm sorry I got you into trouble with the teacher.* **3** [*no pass.*] (**get into** sthg.) to learn or become accustomed to: *I'll soon get into the work.* –compare GET **out of**

get off[1] sthg. *v adv; prep* [I;T] **1** to leave (work): *When do you get off (work)?* **2** to leave **a** a public vehicle: *Get off (the bus) at the hospital.* **b** a bicycle, horse, etc.; DISMOUNT (from) –compare GET **on**[2]

get off[2] *v adv* [I;T (=**get** sbdy. **off**) *with*] to (cause to) escape punishment: *The two boys got off with only a warning, but the judge sent the man to prison for a year.|A good lawyer might be able to get you off.*

get on[1] *v adv* [I] **1** →GET **along** (2,4) **2** (*in tenses with the* -ing *form*) to become later or older: *Time is getting on.* **3** [*with*] to continue, often after interruption: *Get on with your work!* **4** [*in*] to succeed: *All he ever thought about was getting on (in his job).*

get on[2] (sthg.) *v adv; prep* [I;T *to*] **1** to seat oneself on (a bicycle, horse, etc.) **2** to enter (a public vehicle): *They got on (the plane) at Cairo.* –compare GET **off**[1] (2), GET **in**[2]

get onto sbdy./sthg. *v prep* [T *no pass.*] **1** to find out about deceit by (someone): *He tricked people for years until the police got onto him.* **2** to begin to talk about or work at: *How did we get onto that subject?* **3** →GET **on**[2] –compare GET **in**[2]

get out *v adv* **1** [I *of*] to leave: *The meeting went on late, so I got out as soon as I could.|She got out of the car.* **2** [I;T (=**get** sbdy. **out**) *of*] to (cause to) escape: *Several men got out (of prison) yesterday.* **3** [T] (**get** sthg. ↔ **out**) to produce: *We hope to get the report out before the end of the month.* **4** [I] →LEAK[1] **out**: *How did the story get out?*

get out of *v adv prep* [T] **1** [+*v-ing*] (**get out of** sthg.) to escape responsibility for: *He tried to get out of helping me.* **2** [*no pass.*] (**get out of** sthg.) to be able to stop or leave: *to get out of a bad habit* –compare GET **into 3** (**get** sthg. **out of** sbdy.) to force from: *The police got the truth out of him.* **4** (**get** sthg. **out of** sthg.) to gain from: *I can't understand why people smoke. What do they get out of it?*

get over[1] *v adv* **1** [T *with*] (**get** sthg. **over**) to reach the end of (usu. something unpleasant): *You'll be glad to get your operation over (with).* **2** [I;T (=**get** sthg. **over**)] →GET **across**

get over[2] sbdy./sthg. *v prep* [T] **1** to return

to one's usual state of health, happiness, etc., after a bad experience of or with: *to get over an illness|She can't get over the death of her husband.* **2** *infml* to be very much surprised at (esp. in the phrase **can't get over**): *I can't get over how well I did on my examinations.*

get round sbdy./sthg. *v prep* [T] *BrE* for GET **around** sbdy./sthg.

get round to sthg. *v adv prep* [T +*v-ing*] *BrE* for GET **around to**

get through[1] *v adv* **1** [I *to*] to reach someone, esp. by telephone: *I tried to telephone you but I couldn't get through.* **2** [I;T (=**get** sthg. **through**) +*that/to*] to (cause to) be understood by (someone): *I can't get (it) through to him that he must rest.* –compare GET **across 3** [I *with*] to finish: *When you get through with your work, let's go out.*

get through[2] *v adv; prep* [I;T (=**get** (sbdy.) **through** (sthg.)] to (cause to) come successfully to the end of: *to get through/get someone through an examination/to get through the winter*

get together *v adv* [I *with*] to have a meeting or party: *When can we get together?* –see also GET-TOGETHER

get up *v adv* **1** [I;T (=**get** sbdy. **up**)] to (cause to) rise from bed: *What time do you normally get up?* **2** [T] (**get up** sthg.) to increase the amount of: *get up steam/speed* –see also GETUP

get up to sthg. *v adv prep* [T] **1** to reach: *What page did you get up to?*

get·a·way /ˈgɛtəˌweɪ/ *n* [A;S] *infml* an escape: *The thieves made a quick getaway.|a getaway car* –see also GET **away**

get-to·geth·er /ˈ·· ·ˌ··/ *n* a friendly informal meeting for enjoyment: *the old school get-together that you both went to* –see also GET **together**

get·up /ˈgɛtʌp/ *n infml* a set of clothes, esp. unusual clothes –see also GET **up**

gey·ser /ˈgaɪzər/ *n v adv prep* a natural spring of hot water which from time to time rises suddenly into the air from the earth

ghast·ly /ˈgæstliː/ *adj* **-lier, -liest 1** causing great fear or shock: *Hearing of their death was the most ghastly news.* **2** *infml* very bad: *We had a ghastly time at the party.* **3** (of a person) very pale and ill-looking

gher·kin /ˈgɜrkɪn/ *n* a small green CUCUMBER, usu. eaten as a PICKLE

ghet·to /ˈgɛtoʊ/ *n* **-tos** a part of a city in which a group of people live who are poor and/or are not accepted as full citizens

ghost /goʊst/ *n* **1** (the spirit of) a dead person who appears again: *Do you believe in ghosts?* (=that they exist) **2 to give up the ghost** to die **3 a ghost of a** the slightest: *You haven't got a ghost of a chance of getting the job.*

ghost·ly /ˈgoʊstliː/ *adj* like a GHOST, esp. having a faint or uncertain color and shape: *I saw a ghostly light ahead of me in the darkness.* **–ghostliness** *n* [U]

ghost town /ˈ· ·/ *n* an empty town, esp. one that was once busy because people came to find gold, and left when it was finished

ghoul /guːl/ *n* **1** a spirit which (in the stories

told in Eastern countries) takes bodies from graves to eat them **2** a person who delights in (thoughts of) dead bodies and other nasty things –**ghoulish** *adj*

GI /ˌdʒiʸ ˈaɪ/ *n* **GI's** *or* **GIs** a soldier in the US army, esp. during World War Two

gi·ant /ˈdʒaɪənt/ *n* **1** [C] a man who is much bigger than is usual: (fig.) *Shakespeare is a giant among writers.* **2** [A] very large: *The giant (size) package gives you more for less money!* **3** [C] (in fairy stories) a very big strong man, often unfriendly and very cruel –compare DWARF[1] (2)

gib·ber·ish /ˈdʒɪbərɪʃ, ˈgɪ-/ *n* [U] meaningless sounds or talk

gib·bon /ˈgɪbən/ *n* an animal like a monkey (APE) with no tail and long arms

gibe, jibe /dʒaɪb/ *n* a remark which makes someone look foolish

gib·lets /ˈdʒɪblɪts/ *n* [P] the parts of a bird, such as the heart and LIVER, which are taken out before it is cooked

gid·dy /ˈgɪdiʸ/ *adj* **-dier, -diest 1** (of a person) feeling unsteady, as though everything is moving around oneself: *The children enjoyed going around and around, but I felt giddy just watching them.* **2** causing a feeling of unsteady movement and/or falling:*We looked down from a giddy height.* **3** (of a person) acting silly: *He was giddy after just one drink.* –**giddily** *adv* –**giddiness** *n* [U]

gift /gɪft/ *n* **1** something which is given freely; present **2** a natural ability to do something: *He has a gift for music.*

gift·ed /ˈgɪftɪd/ *adj* having one or more special abilities (TALENTs): *a gifted painter*|*Their daughter is very gifted.* (=unusually intelligent)

gig /gɪg/ *n infml* a musician's job or performance: *They're doing a gig in Los Angeles next month.*

gi·gan·tic /dʒaɪˈgæntɪk/ *adj* unusually large in amount or size –see Study Notes on page 550 –**gigantically** *adv*

gig·gle /ˈgɪgəl/ *v* **-gled, -gling** [I] to laugh in a silly, uncontrolled manner –**giggle** *n*

gild /gɪld/ *v* **gilded** *or* **gilt** /gɪlt/, **gilding** [T] to cover with a thin coat of gold (paint): (fig.) *Sunshine gilded the rooftops.*

gill[1] /gɪl/ *n* one of the organs through which a fish breathes

gill[2] /dʒɪl/ *n* a measure equal to ¹/₄ PINT or 0.142 LITERS

gilt /gɪlt/ *n* [U] shiny material, esp. gold, used as a thin covering: *The plates have a gilt edge.*

gim·mick /ˈgɪmɪk/ *n infml* a trick or object which is used to draw attention: *The pretty girl on the cover of the book is just a sales gimmick.* (=to encourage people to buy the book) –**gimmicky** *adj*

gin /dʒɪn/ *n* [U] a colorless alcoholic drink made from grain and certain berries

gin·ger[1] /ˈdʒɪndʒər/ *n* [U] a plant with a root which can be used in cooking to give a hot strong taste

ginger[2] *adj,n* [U] (of) an orange-brown color

ginger ale /ˈ·· ˌ·, ˌ·· ˈ·/ *n* [U] a gassy non-alcoholic drink made with GINGER[1]

gin·ger·ly /ˈdʒɪndʒərliʸ/ *adv* carefully and

with controlled movements so as not to cause harm: *I reached out gingerly to touch the snake.*

ging·ham /ˈgɪŋəm/ *n* [U] a type of cotton woven with a pattern of squares (CHECKs[1] (6))

gip·sy /ˈdʒɪpsiʸ/ *n* **-sies** *esp. BrE* for GYPSY

gi·raffe /dʒəˈræf/ *n* **-raffes** *or* **-raffe** an African animal with a very long neck and legs and orange skin with dark spots

gird·er /ˈgɜrdər/ *n* a strong beam, usu. of iron or steel, which supports a floor or roof or part of a bridge

gir·dle /ˈgɜrdl/ *n* an undergarment for women meant to hold the flesh firm; light CORSET

girl /gɜrl/ *n* **1** a young female person: *There are more girls than boys in this school.*|*My little girl* (=my daughter) *is ill.* **2** a woman: *The men have invited the girls to play football against them.*|*office girls* **3** →GIRLFRIEND: *John's girl* –**girlish** *adj: his girlish movements* –compare BOYISH –**girlishly** *adv* –**girlishness** *n* [U]

girl·friend /ˈgɜrlfrɛnd/ *n* **1** a female companion with whom one spends time and shares amusements: *She is always talking on the telephone to her girlfriends.* **2** a male's favorite female companion: *He seems to have a new girlfriend every week.* –see also BOYFRIEND

girl·hood /ˈgɜrlhʊd/ *n* [S;U] the time or condition of being a young girl –see also BOYHOOD, CHILDHOOD

girl scout /ˈ· ·/ *AmE*‖ **girl guide** /ˌ· ˈ·/ *BrE n* a member of an association (the **Girl Scouts**) for training girls in character and self-help –compare BOY SCOUT

girth /gɜrθ/ *n* [C;U] *fml* the measure of thickness around something: *the girth of a tree*

gist /dʒɪst/ *n* [the S] the main points (as of an argument): *I don't have time to read this report. Can you give me the gist of it?*

give[1] /gɪv/ *v* **gave** /geʸv/, **given** /ˈgɪvən/, **giving 1** [I;T] to cause (someone) to have or own (something): *She gave him a book for his birthday.*|*Give me the baby while you find your keys.*|*He gives freely to the poor.* **2** [T] to allow to have: *Give him enough time to get home before you telephone.*|*Give me a chance to try the job.* **3** [T] to produce (an effect) on (someone); cause to experience: *The cold wind gave me a pain in the ears.*|*I hope my son hasn't given you a lot of trouble.*|*The news gave us a shock.* **4** [T] to produce; supply with: *Cows give milk.*|*Can you give me more information?*|*Does that clock give the right time?* **5** [T *to*] to set aside (time, thought, strength, etc.) for a purpose: *She gives all her time to her family.*|*Many have given their lives in the cause of truth.* **6** [T *for*] to pay in exchange: *How much did you give to have the roof fixed?* **7** [T] to do (an action) (to): *She gave a sudden shout of surprise.*|*Give me a kiss.*|*to give an order*|*to give permission*|*He gave the door a push.* **8** [T] to admit the truth of: *It's not cheap, I give you that, but it's a really good hotel.* **9** [T *often pass.*] to cause to believe because of information one has received: *I was given to* *understand that he was ill.* **10** [I] to bend or stretch under pressure: *The branch he was sitting on began to give.* **11 give or take** (a certain amount) or (a certain amount) more or less: *It will take an hour, give or take a few minutes (either way).* **12 give way (to): a** to yield, as in traffic or in an argument: *The truck refused to give way to the car, and so they caused an accident.|He refused to give way and admit he was wrong.* **b** to break: *The floor gave way under the weight.* **c** to become less useful or important than: *Steam trains gave way to electric trains.* **d** to allow oneself to show (esp. a feeling) **13 What gives?** *infml* What's going on? **14 give one's word** to promise: *I give you my word that I'll never smoke cigarettes again.* **15 give it to someone** *infml* to scold someone, esp. in an angry or direct way: *Mr. Sutton gave it to Linda when she broke his window.* **–giver** *n*

give sbdy./sthg. ↔ **away** *v adv* [T] **1** to make someone a present or prize of (something): *She gave away all her money to the poor.|(fig.) Our team just gave the game away by playing so badly.* **2** to deliver or formally hand over (a woman) to the husband at the wedding: *Mary was given away by her father.* **3** to make known (a secret) intentionally or unintentionally: *He tried to pretend that he wasn't worried, but his shaking hands gave him away/gave the game away.* (=showed his real feelings) –see also GIVEAWAY

give sbdy. **back** sthg. *v adv* [T] to return (something) to the owner or original possessor: *Give me back my pen.|Give me my pen back.* –see Study Notes on page 481

give in *v adv* [I] to yield: *The boys fought until one gave in.|Don't give in to him.*

give off sthg. *v adv* [T] to send out (esp. a liquid, gas, or smell): *to give off steam*

give out *v adv* **1** [T] (**give** sthg. ↔ **out**) to give to each of several people: *Give out the examination papers.|Give the money out to the children.* **2** [I] *esp. BrE* for RUN *out*

give up *v adv* **1** [T +*v-ing*] (**give up** sthg.) to stop having or doing: *The doctor told him to give up smoking.|I've given up the idea.|She gave up (seeing) her lover to save her marriage.* **2** [I;T (=**give** sthg. ↔ **up**)] to stop working at or trying to do (something): *to give up one's studies|He tried to run twelve miles, but had to give up halfway.* **3** [T] (**give** sbdy. **up**) to stop believing that (someone) can be saved, esp. from death: *The boy was* **given up for lost/for dead**. **4** [T *to*] (**give** sbdy. **up**) to offer (someone or oneself) as a prisoner: *He gave himself up (to the police).* **5** [T *to*] (**give** sthg.↔ **up**) to deliver or allow to pass (to someone else): *Give your seat up to the old lady.*

give² *n* [U] the quality of moving (esp. bending, stretching, or loosening) under pressure: *Shoes get slightly larger after you've worn them because of the give in the leather.*

give-and-take /ˌ· · ·ˈ·/ *n* [U] willingness of each person to yield to (some of) the other's wishes: *We can only settle this argument if* there is a little give-and-take on both sides.

give·a·way /ˈgɪvəˌweɪ/ *n* [S] something unintentional that makes a secret known: *She tried to hide her feelings, but the tears in her eyes were* **a dead giveaway**. –see also GIVE away

giv·en¹ /ˈgɪvən/ *adj* **1** fixed for a purpose and stated as such: *The work must be done within the given time.* **2** if allowed or provided with: *Given the chance, I'd come and see you in California*

given² *prep* if one takes into account: *Given their inexperience/Given that they're inexperienced, they've done a good job.*

given name /ˈ·· ˌ·/ *n AmE* for FIRST NAME

giz·zard /ˈgɪzərd/ *n* the second stomach of a bird, where food is broken into powder

gla·cial /ˈgleɪʃəl/ *adj* of or concerning ice or GLACIERS

gla·cier /ˈgleɪʃər/ *n* a mass of ice which moves very slowly down a mountain valley

glad /glæd/ *adj* **-dd-** **1** [F +*to-v/(that)/about, of*] (of people) pleased and happy: *I'm glad he got the job/about his new job.|Thanks for the help; I was very glad about it.|I'll be glad to help you repair the car.* **2** [A] causing happiness: *glad news of victory* –compare SAD **–gladness** *n* [U]

glad·den /ˈglædn/ *v* [T] to make glad or happy: *The sight of the child running and playing after his long illness gladdened his father's heart.* –compare SADDEN

glade /gleɪd/ *n lit* an open space without trees in a wood or forest

glad·i·a·tor /ˈglædiˌeɪtər/ *n* (in ancient times in Rome) an armed man who fought against men or wild animals in a public place (ARENA)

glad·ly /ˈglædli/ *adv polite* very willingly; eagerly: *I'll gladly come and help you.*

glam·or *AmE* ‖ also **glamour** esp. *BrE* /ˈglæmər/ *n* [U] a special quality of charm and beauty; attractiveness: *the glamor of foreign countries.|She added a touch of glamor by wearing a beautiful dress.*

glam·or·ize ‖ also **-ise** *BrE* /ˈglæməˌraɪz/ *v* **-ized, -izing** [T] to make (something) appear better, more attractive, etc., than in reality

glamorous, -ourous /ˈglæmərəs/ *adj* having GLAMOR: *a glamorous job/girl* **–glamorously** *adv*

glance¹ /glæns/ *v* **glanced, glancing** [I] to give a rapid look: *He glanced at his watch.|I glanced around the room before I left.|She glanced down the list of names.*

glance off (sthg.) *v adv; prep* [I;T] to hit and BOUNCE off at once: *The rock fell down and glanced off the car.*

glance² *n* **1** a rapid look or movement of the eyes: *One glance at his face told me he was ill.|He gave it an admiring glance.* **2 at a glance** with one look; at once: *She saw at a glance that he'd been crying.*

USAGE Compare **glance** and **glimpse**: *As I waited for John to arrive, I* **glanced at**/*took a* **glance at the clock** (=had a quick look at it) *and saw that he was late.|I caught a* **glimpse** *of the Town Hall clock* (=saw it just for a moment) *as we drove quickly past.* The verb to

glimpse has the same meaning as the noun but is not common.

glanc·ing /ˈglænsɪŋ/ adj [A] (of a blow) which slips to one side: a glancing blow on the chin

gland /glænd/ n an organ of the body which treats materials from the bloodstream to produce various liquid substances: a SWEAT gland –**glandular** /ˈglændʒələr/ adj: glandular fever

glare¹ /gleər/ v glared, glaring [I] 1 [at] to look in an angry way: They didn't fight, but stood there glaring at one another. 2 to shine with a strong light esp. in a way that hurts the eyes: The sun glared out of the blue sky.

glare² n [S] 1 an angry look or STARE: I started to offer help, but the fierce glare on his face stopped me. 2 a hard, unpleasant effect given by a strong light: There was a red glare over the burning city.

glar·ing /ˈgleərɪŋ/ adj 1 too bright: This glaring light hurts my eyes.|a glaring red 2 (of mistakes) very noticeable: The report is full of glaring errors. –**glaringly** adv

glass /glæs/ n 1 a hard transparent solid material made from melted sand: a glass bottle/window|I cut my hand on some broken glass. 2 [U] a collection of objects made of this: glass and CHINA 3 [C] a a drinking vessel –see illustration on page 379 b also **glassful** /ˈglæsfʊl/– the amount which this holds –see also GLASSES

glass·es /ˈglæsɪz/ n [P] two pieces of specially-cut glass usu. in a frame and worn in front of the eyes to help a person to see: I have to wear glasses for reading.|some new glasses (=a new pair of glasses) –see also SUNGLASSES; see PAIR (USAGE)

glass·ware /ˈglæsweər/ n [U] glass objects generally, esp. dishes, drinking glasses, etc.

glass·y /ˈglæsiʸ/ adj -ier, iest 1 like glass, esp. (of water) smooth and shining 2 (of eyes) of a fixed expression, as if without sight or life: After he hit his head, his eyes went glassy and we knew he was seriously hurt.

glaze¹ /gleyz/ v glazed, glazing 1 [T] to cover (esp. window frames) with glass 2 [T] to put a shiny surface on (pots and bricks) 3 [I over] (of eyes) to become dull and lifeless: His eyes glazed (over), and he fell unconscious.

glaze² n a shiny surface, esp. one fixed on pots

gla·zier /ˈgleyʒər/ n a worker who fits glass into window frames

glaz·ing /ˈgleyzɪŋ/ n [C;U] the piece of glass used to fill a window –see also DOUBLE GLAZE

gleam¹ /gliʸm/ n 1 a shining light, esp. one making objects bright: The red gleam of the firelight 2 a sudden showing of a feeling or quality for a short time: A gleam of interest came into her eye.|a gleam of hope –compare GLIMMER

gleam² v [I] to give out a bright light: The furniture gleamed after being polished.

glean /gliʸn/ v [T] fml to gather (esp. information) in small amounts and often with difficulty

glee /gliʸ/ n [U] a feeling of joyful satisfaction at something which pleases one: The child danced with glee when she heard the good news. –**gleeful** /ˈgliʸfəl/ adj –**gleefully** adv

glen /glen/ n a narrow mountain valley, esp. in Scotland

glib /glɪb/ adj -bb- 1 able to speak well and easily, whether speaking the truth or not: a glib talker 2 spoken too easily to be true: a glib excuse|His answer was just too glib. –**glibly** adv –**glibness** n [U]

glide¹ /glaɪd/ v glided, gliding [I] 1 to move (noiselessly) in a smooth, continuous manner,which seems easy and without effort: The boat glided over the river.|The dancers glided across the floor. 2 to fly in a plane which has no engine (GLIDER) but follows movements of the air currents

glide² n a gliding movement (GLIDE¹)

glid·er /ˈglaɪdər/ n a plane without an engine

glid·ing /ˈglaɪdɪŋ/ n [U] the sport of flying GLIDERS

glim·mer /ˈglɪmər/ v,n [I] (to give) a very faint, unsteady light: A faint light glimmered at the end of the hall.|(fig.) a glimmer of hope –compare GLEAM

glimpse¹ /glɪmps/ v glimpsed, glimpsing [T] to have a quick view of: I glimpsed her among the crowd just before she disappeared from sight.

glimpse² n [at, of] a quick look at or incomplete view of: I only **caught a glimpse** of the thief, so I can't really describe him. –see GLANCE (USAGE)

glint¹ /glɪnt/ v [I] to give out small flashes of light: The gold was glinting in the sunlight.|(fig.) His eyes glinted when he saw the money.

glint² n a flash of light, as from a shiny metal surface: (fig.) I knew he was angry by the glint in his eye.

glis·ten /ˈglɪsən/ v [I with] to shine from or as if from a wet surface: eyes glistening with tears|I polished it till it glistened.

glit·ter /ˈglɪtər/ v [I] to shine brightly with flashing points of light: The diamond ring glittered on her finger. –**glitter** n [S;U]: the glitter of broken glass

glit·ter·ing /ˈglɪtərɪŋ/ adj [A] splendid; excellent: one of the glittering stars of the modern theater|a glittering performance

gloat /glowt/ v [I over] to look at something or think about it with satisfaction, often in an unpleasant way: He gloated over his brother's failure to win the prize.|a gloating look –**gloatingly** adv

glob·al /ˈglowbəl/ adj 1 of or concerning the whole earth: global travel|global changes 2 taking account of all possible considerations: The report takes a global view of the company's problems. –**globally** adv

globe /glowb/ n 1 the earth: She has traveled all over the globe. 2 an object in the shape of a round ball, esp. one on which a map of the earth is painted 3 a round glass bowl, esp. used as a cover for a lamp (LAMPSHADE)

globe·trot·ter /ˈglowb,tratər/ n a person who habitually travels around the world

glob·u·lar /ˈglabyələr/ adj 1 in the form of a GLOBULE 2 in the form of a GLOBE

glob·ule /ˈglabyuʷl/ n a small drop of a liquid

or melted solid: *Globules of wax fell from the candle.*

gloom /gluʷm/ *n* **1** [U] darkness: *He couldn't see the house in the gloom.* **2** [C;U] a feeling of deep sadness:*The news of defeat filled them with gloom.*

gloom·y /'gluʷmiʸ/ *adj* **-ier, -iest 1** almost dark: *a gloomy day* **2** having or giving little hope or cheerfulness: *Our future seems gloomy.|gloomy news* **–gloomily** *adv*

glo·ri·fy /'glɔrə̩faɪ, 'gloʷr-/ *v* **-fied, -fying** [T] **1** to give glory, praise, or fame to **2** to cause to appear more important than in reality: *She calls it a country house, but I call it a glorified hut.* **–glorification** /ˌglɔrəfə'keʸʃən, ˌgloʷr-/ *n* [U]

glo·ri·ous /'glɔriʸəs, 'gloʷr-/ *adj* **1** having, or worthy of, great fame and honor: *a glorious victory* **2** beautiful; splendid: *glorious colors|a glorious day* **–gloriously** *adv*

glo·ry /'glɔriʸ, 'gloʷriʸ/ *n* **-ries 1** [U] great fame or success; praise and honor: *He was* **bathed in glory** *on the day he became President.|Glory be to God.* **2** [U] beauty; splendid appearance: *The bright moonlight showed the Taj Mahal* **in all its glory.** **3** [C *usu. pl.*] special beauty or cause for pride: *That building is one of the glories of the city.*

glory in sthg. *v prep* **-ried, -rying** [T] to enjoy, often in a selfish way: *He gloried in his victory after the election.*

gloss /glɔs, glɑs/ *n* **1** [S;U] shiny brightness on a surface: *high gloss paint|the gloss on her hair|*(fig.) *They hide their hatred of each other under a gloss of good manners.* **2** [C] an explanation of a piece of writing, esp. in the form of a note at the end of a page or book: *I wouldn't have been able to understand this page without the gloss.*

glos·sa·ry /'glɑsəriʸ, 'glɔ-/ *n* **-ries** a list of esp. unusual words, with an explanation of their meanings, at the end of a book

gloss o·ver sthg. *v adv* [T] to speak kindly of (something bad); hide (faults): *to gloss over his failure*

gloss·y /'glɔsiʸ, 'glɑ-/ *adj* **-ier, -iest** shiny and smooth: *Our cat has glossy black fur.|A* **glossy magazine** *has lots of color pictures in it and is printed on good quality paper.*

glove /glʌv/ *n* **1** a garment which covers the hand, with separate parts for the thumb and each finger –compare MITTEN; see PAIR (USAGE); see illustration on page 123 **2 fit like a glove** to fit perfectly **3 handle with kid gloves** to treat very gently and carefully

glow¹ /gloʷ/ *v* [I *with*] **1** to give out heat and/or light without flames or smoke: *The iron bar was heated till it glowed.|The fire was glowing.|The cat's eyes glowed in the darkness.* **2** to show redness and heat in the face, esp. after hard work or because of strong feelings: *glowing cheeks|glowing with health and happiness*

glow² *n* [S] **1** a light from something burning without flames or smoke: *the red glow in the sky above the town|The oil-lamp gives a soft glow.* **2** brightness of color: *the glow of copper in the kitchen* **3** the feeling and/or signs of heat and color in the body and face, as after

exercise or because of good health: *the glow of health|a glow of happiness*

glow·er /'glaʊər/ *v* [I *at*] to look with an angry expression: *Instead of answering, he just glowered (at me).|a glowering look* **–gloweringly** *adv*

glow·ing /'gloʷɪŋ/ *adj* showing a favorable picture: *She gave a glowing description of the movie.* **–glowingly** *adv*

glow-worm /'· ·/ *n* a type of insect with a tail that shines in the dark

glu·cose /'gluʷkoʷs/ *n* [U] a natural form of sugar found in fruit

glue¹ /gluʷ/ *n* [U] a sticky substance used for joining things together **–gluey** *adj* **-ier, -iest**

glue² *v* **glued, gluing** *or* **glueing** [T] to join with GLUE¹: *She glued the two pieces of wood together.|*(fig.) *The children are always glued to* (=always watching) *the television.*

glum /glʌm/ *adj* sad; in low spirits, esp. because of disappointment: *Why do you look so glum?* **–glumly** *adv* **–glumness** *n* [U]

glut¹ /glʌt/ *v* **-tt-** [T] **1** to supply with too much; overfill: *They glutted the stores with cheap fruit from abroad.* **2 glut oneself** to fill oneself (esp. by eating): *He glutted himself on chocolate.*

glut² *n* [*usu. sing.*] a larger supply than is necessary: *a glut of eggs (on the market)|a glut of old movies on television*

glu·ti·nous /'gluʷtn-əs/ *adj fml* sticky: *a bowl of glutinous rice*

glut·ton /'glʌtn/ *n* **1** a person who eats too much **2** [*for*] *infml* a person who is always ready to do more of something hard or unpleasant: *She kept coming to work even when she was ill; she's a real* **glutton for punishment.**

glut·ton·ous /'glʌtn-əs/ *adj* GREEDY, esp. for food

glut·ton·y /'glʌtn-iʸ/ *n* [U] the habit of eating (and drinking) too much

glyc·er·in, -ine /'glɪsərɪn/ *n* [U] a sweet sticky colorless liquid used in making soap, medicines, and explosives

gm. *n written abbrev. said as:* GRAM

GMT *abbrev. for:* GREENWICH MEAN TIME

gnarled /nɑrld/ *adj* rough and twisted, with hard lumps, esp. as a result of age or hard work: *a gnarled tree trunk|the old man's gnarled hands*

gnash /næʃ/ *v* [T] **gnash one's teeth** to make a noise with (one's teeth) by biting hard in anger or worry

gnat /næt/ *n* a small flying insect that bites

gnaw /nɔ/ *v* [I;T *away, at*] to keep biting steadily on (a bone etc.), esp. until one makes (a hole, etc.): *Our dog likes to gnaw bones.|Rats have gnawed their way through the wall/gnawed a hole in the wall.|*(fig.) *Something's gnawing at* (=worrying) *my mind.*

gnaw·ing /'nɔ-ɪŋ/ *adj* [A *no comp.*] painful or worrying in a small but continuous way: *gnawing hunger/anxiety*

gnome /noʷm/ *n* (in fairy stories) a little (old) man who lives under the ground and guards piles of gold

GNP *abbrev. for:* Gross National Product;

(the total worth of all the goods and services produced in a country, usu. in a single year) **go¹** /gəʊ/ *v* **went** /wɛnt/, **gone** /gɔn, gɑn/, **going 1** [I] to leave the place where the speaker is (so as to reach another): *It's late; I must go/be going.*|(fig.) *The summer is going fast.* –compare COME (1) **2** [I] to move or travel: *We went by bus.*|*The car's going too fast.*|*We went to Mexico for our vacation.*|*His hand went to his gun.* **3** [I +*v-ing*] to travel somewhere to do (an activity): *to go walking/shopping/swimming* **4** [I] to reach (as far as stated): *Which street goes to the station?*|*The valley goes from east to west.*|*The roots of the plant go deep.* **5** [I] to be placed, esp. usually placed: *"Where do the knives go?" "In this drawer."* **6** to become: *Her hair's going gray.*|*She went red in the face and rushed out angrily.*|*to go mad/blind* **7** to remain (in a certain state): *Should a criminal go free?* |*When the crops fail, the people go hungry.* **8** [I] (of machines) to work (properly): *The car won't go.* **9** [I *for*] to be sold: *The car was going cheap.*|*It went for $500.* **10** [I] to become weakened or worn out: *My voice is going because of my cold.*|*These old shoes are going.* **11** [T] to have the stated words or make the stated sound: *How do the words to this song go?* |*Ducks go "quack."* **12** [I] to match or fit: *It won't go in the box.*|*Blue and green don't go (together).*|*The belt won't go around (my waist).* –compare GO **with**, GO **together 13** [I] to be allowable, esp. in the phrase **anything goes**: *In this school, anything goes.* **14 be going to (do or happen)** (shows the future, esp. for events and actions which are intended, planned, or probable): *He's going to buy her some shoes.* (compare *He will buy her some shoes if she asks him to.*)|*Is it going to rain?*|*I'm going to be sick!* |*She's going to have a baby.* –see GONNA (USAGE) **15 go and: a** to go in order to: *I'll go and get my book.*|*I went and bought* (=I went and I bought) *another one.* **b** *infml* (expresses surprise): *She's gone and bought a new car!* **16 to go: a** left before something happens: *Only three days to go before/to Christmas!* **b** *AmE* (of food) to be taken away from a restaurant and eaten elsewhere: *Two hamburgers to go, please.* **17 -goer** a person who goes regularly to a certain place or activity: *churchgoers/moviegoers* –see also GOING¹

USAGE The usual past participle of **go** is **gone,** but if it means "visited" or "arrived (and left)" it is **been.** Compare: *George has* **gone** *to Paris.* (=he's there now, not here)|*George has* **been** *to Paris.* (=he has visited Paris in the past)|*The doctor hasn't* **gone** *yet.* (=he is still here)|*The doctor hasn't* **been** *here yet.* (=he has not yet arrived) –see BECOME (USAGE)

go about¹ *v adv* →GO¹ **around** (1,2)

go about² sthg. *v prep* [T] **1** to perform or do: *to go about one's business*|*They went about it wrong.* **2** [+*v-ing*] also **set about**– to begin working at: *How do you go about repairing this clock?*

go after/for sbdy./sthg. *v prep* [T *pass. rare*] to try to obtain or win; chase: *to go after a job/a girl/a prize*

go against sbdy./sthg. *v prep* [T *no pass.*] **1** to act or be in opposition to: *She went against her mother/her mother's wishes.*|*It goes against his principles to borrow money.* –compare GO **along** (2) **2** to be unfavorable to: *Opinion is going against us.*|*The case may go against you.*

go ahead *v adv* [I *with*] to begin or continue: *The council gave us permission to go ahead with our building plans.*|*Work is going ahead on the new bridge.* –see also GO-AHEAD

go along *v adv* [I] **1** to continue: *I like to add up my bank account as I go along.* **2** [*with*] to agree with; support: *We'll go along with you/your suggestion.* –compare GO **against** (1)

go around/round *v adv* [I] **1** (*usu. in tenses with the -ing form*) (of an illness) to spread: *There are a lot of colds going around.* **2** [*with*] to spend time in public (with someone): *Why do you go around with such strange people?* **3** to be enough for everyone: *If there are not enough chairs to go around, some people will have to stand.*

go at/for sbdy./sthg. *v prep* [T *no pass.*] to attack: *Our dog went at the mailman.*|(fig.) *He went at his breakfast as if he hadn't eaten for a week.*

go back *v adv* [I] **1** to return: *Let's go back to what the chairman said earlier.* **2** [*to*] to reach backwards in time: *My family goes back to the 18th century.*

go back on sthg. *v adv prep* [T *pass. rare*] to break or not keep (a promise, agreement, etc.): *to go back on a promise*

go by¹ *v adv* [I] to pass (in place or time): *A car went by.*|*Two years went by.*|*He let the chance go by.*

go by² sthg. *v prep* [T *no pass.*] **1** to act according to; be guided by; judge by: *to go by the rules/the book*|*You can't go by what he says.*|*Going by her clothes, she must be very rich.* **2 go by the name of** to be called, esp. in addition to one's real name

go down *v adv* [I] **1** to become lower: *The floods are going down.*|*The standard of work has gone down.*|*Eggs are going down (in price).* –compare GO **up** (1) **2** to sink: *Three ships went down in the storm.*|*before the sun goes down* **3** to become less swollen: *The swelling on my ankle has gone down, so I should be able to walk soon.*|*This tire is going down; I'll pump it up.* **4** [*with*] to be accepted: *He/His speech went down well (with the crowd).* **5** [*in*] to be recorded: *This day will go down in history.*

go far *v adv* [I] **1** to be successful; succeed: *She is smart and will go far (in her job).* **2** to satisfy many needs: *This food won't go far when there are ten people to feed.*

go for sbdy./sthg. *v prep* [T *no pass.*] **1** →GO **at 2** →GO **after: 2** *to go for a job/a prize* **3** to like or be attracted by: *I don't go for men of his type.* **4** to concern or be true for (someone or something) in the same manner as for others: *I find this report badly done, and that goes for all the other work done in this office.*

5 to be sold for (esp. in the phrase **go for a song**) **6 go for nothing/naught** to be wasted; have no result: *All my hard work went for nothing/naught.*

go in for sthg. *v adv prep* [T +*v-ing*] to make a habit of (doing), esp. for enjoyment: *I don't go in for sports.*

go into sthg. *v prep* [T] **1** [*no pass.*] to enter (a place, a profession, etc.): *to go into town/politics* **2** to examine or concern oneself with: *The police are going into the murder case.|Let's not go into details.*

go off¹ *v adv* [I] **1 a** to explode **b** to ring or sound loudly: *The* ALARM *went off when the thieves got in.* **2** to succeed or fail: *The party went off very well/badly.* (=was a success/failure) **3** to fall asleep or lose consciousness: *Has the baby gone off yet?* –compare DROP **off** (2) **4** to cease operation: *The heating goes off at night.* –compare GO **on** (4) **5 go off with** to take away without permission: *He's gone off with my car!*

go off² sbdy./sthg. *v prep* [T] to lose interest in or liking for: *I've gone off coffee; give me some tea.*

go on¹ *v adv* [I] **1** to take place or happen: *What's going on here?* **2** [+*to-v/v-ing/with*] to continue (to behave in a certain way): *He went on talking even though no one was listening.|Go on with your work.|If he goes on like this, he'll lose his job.* **3** (of time) to pass: *As the day went on, it became hotter.* **4** to be put into operation: *The lights went on at 6 o'clock.* –compare GO **off** (4) **5** [*at*] to keep complaining or scolding: *He's always going on at his wife.* **6** to keep talking: *She can really go on!* **7 go on (with you)!** I don't believe you!

go on² sthg. *v prep* [T *no pass.*] to use as a reason, proof, or base for further action: *A bloody handkerchief and the name "Margaret" were all the police had to go on to catch the killer.*

go out *v adv* [I] **1** to leave the house, esp. for amusement: *She went out for a walk.|We go out three times a week.|He's not old enough to go out to work.* **2** [*together, with*] (usu. in the *-ing form*) to spend time regularly (usu. with someone of the other sex):*They've been going out together for two years.* **3** [*to*] to travel (to a distant place): *My friends went out to Africa.* **4** (of a fire, light, etc.) to stop burning or shining: *Without more coal, the fire will soon go out.|*(fig.) *He went out like a light.*(=to sleep, or into unconsciousness) **5** (of the sea or TIDE) to go back to its low level –compare COME **in** 6 **6** to cease to be fashionable or customary: *Short skirts went out a few years ago, but they've come back again.* **7** [*to*] (of feelings) to be in sympathy (with): *Our thoughts go out to our friends abroad.*

go over¹ sthg. *v prep* [T] **1** to look at or examine: *We went over the list of names and chose two.* **2** to repeat: *I'll go over the explanation of how it works.*

go over² *v adv* [I *from* and/or *to*] to change (one's political party, religion, etc.): *She went over to the Republicans after their election victory.*

go round *v adv* [I] →GO **around**

go through¹ *v adv* [I] to be approved officially: *Their business arrangements went through.*

go through² sthg. *v prep* [T] **1** to suffer or experience: *The country has gone/been through too many wars.* **2** →GET **through²** (2) **3** to pass through or be accepted by: *The new law has gone through Congress.* **4** →GO **over¹** (2)

go through with sthg. *v adv prep* [T] to complete (something which has been agreed or planned), often with difficulty: *He promised to sign the contract, but now he doesn't want to go through with it.*

go to sthg. *v prep* [T *no pass.*] **1** to cause oneself to experience: *She went to a lot of trouble for me.|They went to great expense to educate me.* **2** to enter or start experiencing (a state) (in phrases like **go to sleep, go to war**)

go together *v adv* [I] (of two things) to GO **with** (1) each other; match

go under *v adv* [I] (of a ship or floating object) to sink: (fig.) *After he got into debt, his business went under.* (=failed) –compare GO **down** (2)

go up *v adv* [I] **1** to rise: *Prices have gone up again.* –compare GO **down** (1) **2** to be built: *How many houses have gone up this year?* **3** to BLOW **up** (1) or be destroyed in fire: *The whole house went up in flames.*

go with sthg. *v prep* [T *no pass.*] **1** to match or suit: *Mary's blue dress goes with her eyes.* **2** [+*v-ing*] to be often found with; ACCOMPANY: *Happiness doesn't necessarily go with (having) money.*

go without (sthg.) *v prep; adv* [I;T +*v-ing*] **1** →DO **without**: *I'm afraid there's no coffee, so we'll just have to go without (it).* **2 it goes without saying** it's clear without needing to be stated

go² *n* **goes** *infml* **1** [U] the quality of being full of activity: *The children are full of go.* **2** [C] an attempt to do something: *He had several goes at the examination before he passed.* **3** [C *usu. sing.*] one's turn (esp. in a game): *It's my go now.* **4 on the go** working all the time –see also GO **ahead**

goad /gowd/ *n* something which urges a person to action

goad sbdy. **into** sthg. *v prep* [T] to cause (someone) to (do something) by strong or continued annoyance: *They goaded him into doing it by saying he was a coward.*

go-a·head /'· ·,·/ *n* [*the* S] permission to act: *We're all ready to start the new building, as soon as we get the go-ahead from the council.* –see also GO **ahead**

goal /gowl/ *n* **1** one's aim or purpose; something one wishes to obtain or reach: *His goal is a job at the university.|The company has* ACHIEVE*d all its goals this year.* (=done everything it planned to do) **2** (in games like football) the place, usu. between two posts (**goalposts**), sometimes with a net between them, where the ball must go for a point to be gained: *She keeps goal* (=defends the goal) *for the school team.* **3** the point(s) gained (SCORE*d*) when the ball is caused to do this: *We won by three goals to one.*

goal·keep·er /ˈgoʷl̩ˌkiʸpər/ also **goalie** /ˈgoʷliʸ/ *infml–* *n* (in games like soccer, hockey, etc.) the player who is responsible for preventing the ball from getting into his/her team's GOAL (2)

goat /goʷt/ *n* a four-legged animal related to the sheep, which has horns and gives milk and a rough sort of wool –see also BILLY GOAT, NANNY GOAT, KID¹ (1)

gob·ble¹ /ˈgɑbəl/ *v* **-bled, -bling** [I;T *up*] to eat very quickly, and sometimes noisily: *The children gobbled up their food and rushed out to play.*

gobble² *v,n* (to make) the sound a TURKEY makes

go-be·tween /ˈ·· ·ˌ·/ *n* a person who takes messages from one person or side to another, because they themselves cannot meet: *The business was arranged by a trustworthy go-between.*

gob·let /ˈgɑblɪt/ *n* a drinking vessel, usu. of glass or metal, with a base and stem but no handles, and used esp. for wine

gob·lin /ˈgɑblɪn/ *n* a usu. unkind or evil spirit which plays tricks on people

god /gɑd/ *n* **goddess** /ˈgɑdɪs/ *fem.–* a being (one of many) which is worshipped, as one who made or rules over (a part of) the life of the world

God *n* **1** the being who in the Christian, Jewish, and Muslim religions is worshipped as maker and ruler of the world **2 God forbid that** may it not happen that **3 God (alone) knows** *infml* it's impossible to say: *God knows where he went!* **4 God willing** if all goes well **5 Oh God/My God/Good God** (expressions of surprise, fear, etc.) **6 Thank God** (an expression of gladness that trouble has passed): *Thank God you're safe!*

god·child /ˈgɑdtʃaɪld/ *n* the child (**godson** or **goddaughter**) for whom one takes responsibility by making promises at a religious ceremony –see also GODPARENT

god-fear·ing /ˈ· ·ˌ··/ *adj fml* good and well-behaved according to the rules of religion; GODLY

god·for·sak·en /ˈgɑdfərˌseʸkən, ˌgɑdfərˈseʸ-/ *adj* (of a place) empty, containing nothing useful or interesting, etc.

god·less /ˈgɑdlɪs/ *adj fml* wicked; not showing respect to or belief in God

god·like /ˈgɑdlaɪk/ *adj* like or suitable to God or a god: *godlike beauty/calm*

god·ly /ˈgɑdliʸ/ *adj* **-lier, -liest** *fml* showing obedience to God by leading a good life; GOD-FEARING

god·par·ent /ˈgɑdˌpɛərənt, -ˌpær-/ *n* the person (**godfather** or **godmother**) who makes promises to see that a child is raised with the religious teachings of its parents –see also GODCHILD

god·send /ˈgɑdsɛnd/ *n* an unexpected lucky chance or thing: *It was a godsend to have him there just when we needed someone.*

go·fer /ˈgoʷfər/ *n AmE infml* a person who gets things or carries messages for another

gog·gle /ˈgɑgəl/ *v* **-gled, -gling** [I *at*] to look hard with the eyes wide open, as in surprise:

They all goggled at my funny clothes. –compare STARE

gog·gles /ˈgɑgəlz/ *n* [P] (a pair of) large round glasses with an edge which fits against the skin so that dust, water, etc., cannot get near the eyes: *motorcycle goggles* –see PAIR (USAGE)

go·ing¹ /ˈgoʷɪŋ/ *n* [U] **1** the act of leaving: *Her going will be a great loss to the company.* **2** the act or speed of travel or work: *We climbed the mountain in three hours, which was good going.* **3** the condition or possibility of travel: *The mud made it rough/hard/heavy going for the car.*|(fig.) *This book is very heavy going.* (=very difficult to read)|(fig.) *Let's leave* **while the going's good.** (=while we can) **4 -going** going regularly to a certain place or activity: *theater going/churchgoing* –see also **-goer** (GO¹ (17))

going² *adj* [A] **1** as charged at present: *The* **going rate** *for the job is $10 per hour.* **2** in operation: *a going* CONCERN (=an active profitable business) **3 going for someone** *infml* working in one's favor: *She has a lot going for her: brains, beauty, and wealth.*

going-o·ver /ˌ·· ˈ··/ *n* **goings-over** *infml* a (thorough) examination and/or treatment: *The car needs a good going-over before we use it again.*

goings-on /ˌ·· ˈ·/ *n* [P] activities, usu. of an undesirable kind: *There was shouting, and loud music, and all sorts of goings-on I can't describe!*

going to /ˈ·· ·, ˈgɔnə, gɔnə/ →GO¹ (14) –see GONNA (USAGE)

go-kart /ˈgoʷ kɑrt/ *n* a very small low racing car made of an open framework with little or no BODY (6)

gold /goʷld/ *n* [U] **1** a valuable soft yellow metal (an ELEMENT (1)) used for making coins, jewelry, etc.: *He wore a gold watch.*|*Gold is found in rock and streams.* **2** the color of this metal: *gold paint* **3 as good as gold** (esp. of children) very well behaved

gold·en /ˈgoʷldən/ *adj* of or like gold: *a golden crown*|*golden hair*|(fig.) *a golden* (=very fortunate) OPPORTUNITY

gold·fish /ˈgoʷldˌfɪʃ/ *n* **goldfish** *or* **goldfishes** a small fish which is kept as a pet in glass bowls or in ornamental pools

gold·mine /ˈgoʷldmaɪn/ *n* **1** a place where gold is taken (MINEd) from the rock **2** a successful business or activity which makes large profits: *With this new invention, we're* **sitting on a goldmine.** (=we possess something very valuable)

golf¹ /gɑlf, gɔlf/ *n* [U] a game in which people hit small hard balls into holes, using any of a special set of sticks (**golf clubs**), trying to do so with as few strokes as possible, on a piece of land called a **golf course**

golf² *v* [I] (*esp. in the* -ing *form*) to play GOLF¹: *to go golfing* –**golfer** *n*

golf club /ˈ· ·/ *n* **1** a club for GOLFers² with the buildings and land it uses **2** a long-handled wooden or metal stick used for hitting the ball in GOLF¹

gon·do·la /ˈgɑndələ/ *n* a long narrow

flat-bottomed boat with high points at each end, used only on the waterways (CANALs) which run between the houses in Venice in Italy

gon·do·lier /ˌgɑndə'lɪər/ n a man who guides and rows a GONDOLA

gone /gɔn, gɑn/ v past participle of GO –see GO (USAGE)

gong /gɔŋ, gɑŋ/ n a round piece of metal hanging from a frame, which when struck with a stick makes a deep ringing sound

gon·na /'gɔnə, gənə/ going to
USAGE When **going to** is used before another verb, to show the future, it is sometimes pronounced in this way. It may be written **gonna** in stories, to show an informal way of speaking: *You gonna tell him?* (=are you going to tell him?) But **going to** in *I'm going to Montreal* is not pronounced in this way.

gon·or·rhe·a, -rhoea /ˌgɑnə'riʸə/ n [U] a disease of the sex organs, passed on during sexual activity –compare SYPHILIS

good¹ /gʊd/ adj better /'bɛtər/, best /bɛst/ 1 having the right qualities; satisfactory; enjoyable: *a good play|good weather|Have a good time!* 2 suitable; favorable: *It's a good day for a swim.|a good chance of getting a job* 3 suitable for its purpose: *a good idea|good advice* 4 [for] useful to the health or character: *Milk is good for you.|It isn't good (for you) to have everything you want.* 5 morally right: *to do a good deed|to lead a good life* 6 [of, to] (of people) kind; helpful: *She's always been very good to me.|It's good of you to help.* 7 (esp. of children) well-behaved: *Be good when we visit your aunt.* 8 [at] skillful; having the ability to do something: *a good cook|She's good at languages.* –opposite **bad** 9 [A no comp.] complete; thorough: *Have a good look.|Their team gave us a good beating.* 10 [A no comp.] large in size, amount, etc.: *We waited a good while.* 11 [A no comp.] at least or more than: *It's a good five miles away.* 12 **a good deal** quite a lot: *We're expecting a good deal of support for our new movement.* 13 **as good as** almost (the same thing as): *He as good as refused.|We're as good as ruined.* 14 **Good!** I agree or I'm glad 15 **in good time** early

good² n [U] 1 that which is right and useful in accordance with religious beliefs or moral standards: *You must learn the difference between good and evil.* 2 that which causes gain or improvement: *I don't want to punish you, but it's **for your own good**.|Milk does you good.* (=is good for your health)|**It's no good** (=it's useless) *crying now!|Is this new paint any good?* (=is it good paint?)|**What's the good of/What good is** *having a car if you can't drive.* –compare HARM¹ (1) 3 **for good** for ever: *We thought they'd come just for a visit, but it seems they're staying for good.* 4 **up to no good** doing or intending to do something wrong or bad

good af·ter·noon /· ˌ··'·/ interj,n (an expression used when meeting someone in the afternoon)

good·bye /gʊd'baɪ/ interj,n (an expression

used when leaving, or being left by, someone): *"Goodbye, Mrs. Smith."|They said their goodbyes and left.* –compare HELLO

good eve·ning /· '··/ interj,n (an expression used when meeting someone in the evening) –compare GOOD NIGHT

good-for-noth·ing /ˌ··'··, '··ˌ··/ adj,n [A;C] (a person who) is worthless, who does no work, etc.: *Get out of bed, you good-for-nothing (fool)!*

Good Fri·day /ˌ· '··/ n the Friday before EASTER

good-hu·mored *AmE*‖**-humoured** *BrE* /ˌ· '··◄/ n having or showing a cheerful, friendly state of mind: *He was very good-humored about repairing the clock I broke.* –**good-humoredly** adv

good·ish /'gʊdɪʃ/ adj [A no comp.] 1 pretty good, but not very good 2 rather large, long, far, etc.: *Their house was a **goodish distance** from the bus-stop.*

good-look·ing /ˌ· '··◄/ adj attractive: *a good-looking man* –see BEAUTIFUL (USAGE)

good morn·ing /· '··/ interj,n (an expression used when meeting someone in the morning)

good-na·tured /ˌ· '··◄/ adj naturally kind; ready to help, to forgive, not to be angry, etc. –**good-naturedly** adv

good·ness /'gʊdnɪs/ n [U] 1 the quality of being good 2 the best part, esp. (of food) the part which is good for the health: *All the goodness has been boiled out of the vegetables.* 3 (used in expressions of surprise and annoyance): *My goodness!|Goodness me!|**For goodness' sake**, stop making so much noise!*

good night /· '·/ interj,n (an expression used when leaving, or being left by, someone at night, esp. before going to bed or to sleep) –compare GOOD EVENING

goods /gʊdz/ n [P] 1 movable articles (e.g. clothes, food, kitchen materials, etc.) which can be owned, bought, or sold: *This store sells a variety of goods.* 2 *BrE* for FREIGHT

good·will, good will /ˌgʊd'wɪl/ n [U] 1 kind feelings towards or between people: *There is goodwill between the former enemies.* 2 the popularity of a business, usu. included as part of its selling price: *We paid $20,000 for the store, and $5,000 for its goodwill.*

good·y¹ /'gʊdiʸ/ n -ies [usu. pl.] infml something particularly attractive, pleasant, or desirable, esp. something nice to eat

goody² interj (an expression of pleasure used esp. by children)

goody-good·y /ˌ··'··/ n **goody-goodies** often derog a person who likes to appear faultless in behavior so as to please others, not because he or she is really good

goo·ey /'guʷiʸ/ adj -ier, -iest 1 sticky and (usu.) sweet: *gooey cakes* 2 over-sweet; SENTIMENTAL (2): *a gooey story*

goof /guʷf/ v,n [C;I] infml esp. *AmE* (to make) a silly mistake

goof off v adv [I] *AmE* infml to waste time: *You can't goof off on this job.*

goof off /'· ·/ n *AmE* infml a person who GOOFS off: *He's a real goof off.*

goof·y /ˈguʷfiʸ/ adj **-ier, -iest** silly; slightly mad

goon /guʷn/ n **1** infml a silly, foolish person **2** AmE infml a hired criminal

goose /guʷs/ **gander** masc.– n **geese** /giʸs/ a large white bird which looks like a duck and makes a HISSING noise

goose·ber·ry /ˈguʷs,bɛriʸ, -bəriʸ, ˈguʷz-/ n **-ries** the small, round, green fruit of a bush grown in gardens: a gooseberry bush

goose·flesh /ˈguʷsflɛʃ/ n [U] a condition in which the skin is raised up in small points, as when a person is cold or frightened

goose pim·ples /ˈ· ,··/ n [P] →GOOSEFLESH

go·pher /ˈgoʷfər/ n a ratlike animal of North and Central America which makes and lives in holes in the ground

gore /gɔr, goʷr/ v **gored, goring** [T] (of an animal) to wound with the horns or TUSKs

gorge /gɔrdʒ/ n a narrow valley with steep sides usu. made by a stream running through it –see VALLEY (USAGE)

gorge sbdy. **on** sthg. also **gorge** sbdy. **with** sthg.– v prep **gorged, gorging** [T] to fill (oneself) with (food)

gor·geous /ˈgɔrdʒəs/ adj infml delightful; very beautiful: gorgeous colors|a gorgeous day (=warm and bright) –**gorgeously** adv

go·ril·la /gəˈrɪlə/ n the largest of the manlike monkeys

gor·y /ˈgɔri, ˈgoʷriʸ/ adj **-ier, -iest** full of violence; bloody: a gory movie|all the gory details of the murder

gosh /gɑʃ/ interj (an expression of surprise)

gos·ling /ˈgɑzlɪŋ/ n a young GOOSE

gos·pel /ˈgɑspəl/ also **gospel truth** /,·· ·ˈ–/ [U] infml something which is completely true: What I'm telling you is gospel/the gospel truth.

Gospel n any of the four accounts in the Bible of Christ's life

gos·sa·mer /ˈgɑsəmər/ n [U] **1** light, silky thread which SPIDERs leave on grass, bushes, etc. **2** a very light thin material

gos·sip¹ /ˈgɑsəp/ n **1** [C;U] (an example of) talk or writing, often untruthful, about other people's actions and private lives: I don't approve of gossip.|two neighbors having a gossip in the street|I read about it in the **gossip column**. (=writing in a newspaper about the private lives of well-known people) –compare RUMOR **2** [C] a person who likes talking about other people's private lives

gossip² v [I with, about] to talk or write GOSSIP¹ (1)

got /gɑt/ v past tense and past participle of GET –see GOTTEN (USAGE)

Goth·ic /ˈgɑθɪk/ adj **1** of a style of building common in Western Europe between the 12th and 16th centuries, with pointed arches, arched (VAULTed¹ (1)) roofs, and tall thin pillars (PIERs) **2** of a style of writing in the 18th century which produced stories (NOVELs) set in lonely fearful places: Gothic novels

got·ta /ˈgɑtə/ got to

USAGE **got to** is sometimes pronounced in this way. It may be written **gotta** in stories to show an informal way of speaking: I've gotta

go. (=I have got to go, I must go) Sometimes **have** is left out, but not **has**: You('ve) gotta do it|She's gotta do it.

got·ten /ˈgɑtn/ v AmE past participle of GET

USAGE In AmE, **gotten** is much more common than **got** as the past participle of **get**, except when it means a "possess": compare I've got a new car. (=I possess one) and I've gotten a new car. (=I've bought one); or **b** "must": compare I've got to go. (=I must go)|I've gotten to go. (=I've succeeded in going). But Americans often say I have a new car.|I have to go instead of having/has got (to). **Gotten** is not used in BrE.

gouge sthg.↔ **out** /gaʊdʒ/ v adv **gouged, gouging** [T] to press or dig out with force: to gouge out someone's eyes

goug·er /ˈgaʊdʒər/ n **price gouger** a person who cheats (someone) by charging too much money (for something): I never shop in that store; the owner is a real price gouger.

gou·lash /ˈguʷlɑʃ, -læʃ/ n [C;U] meat and vegetables cooked together with PAPRIKA, which gives a hot taste

gourd /gɔrd, goʷrd, gʊərd/ n a large fruit with a hard shell which is often used as a drinking vessel or dish

gour·met /gʊərˈmeʸ, ˈgʊərmeʸ/ n a person who knows a lot about and enjoys good food and drink

gout /gaʊt/ n [U] a disease which makes esp. the toes, knees, and fingers swell and give pain

gov·ern /ˈgʌvərn/ **1** [I;T] to rule (a country, city, etc., and its people): The President governs the country. **2** [T] to control or determine: The need for money governs all his plans.|The price of coffee is governed by the quantity which has been produced.

gov·ern·ess /ˈgʌvərnɪs/ n (esp. in former times) a female teacher who lives with a family and educates their children at home

gov·ern·ment /ˈgʌvərmənt, ˈgʌvərnmənt/ n **1** [U] the action, form, or method of ruling: The country has always had fair government. **2** [C] (often cap.) the people who rule: The Government is planning new tax increases. –compare ADMINISTRATION (2) –**governmental** /,gʌvərˈmɛntəl, -vərˈmɛn-/ adj

gov·er·nor /ˈgʌvənər, -vər-/ n a person who controls any of certain types of organization or place; (in the US) who leads the administration of a state: the governor of California –**governorship** n [U]

gown /gaʊn/ n **1** old use or AmE a long dress, esp. one worn on formal occasions: an evening gown **2** a (long) loose usu. black outer garment worn for special ceremonies by judges, teachers, lawyers, etc.

G.P. n abbrev. for: GENERAL PRACTITIONER: Do you know a good G.P.?

grab¹ /græb/ v **-bb-** [I;T at] to seize with a sudden, rough movement, esp. for a selfish reason: He grabbed the money and ran off.|(fig.) When she was offered work in India, she eagerly grabbed (at) the chance to travel.

grab² n **1** a sudden attempt to seize something: The thief **made a grab at** my bag but I *pushed him away.* **2 up for grabs** *infml* able to be taken by anyone: *All this old clothing is up for grabs. Do you want any of it?*

grace[1] /greɪs/ *n* **1** [U] the quality of being fine, effortless, and attractive in movement, form, or behavior: *to dance with grace* **2** [U] kindness; willingness to do what is right: *She had the grace to say that he was right.|He agreed that he was wrong with good/bad grace.* (=willingly/unwillingly) **3** [U] favor; mercy: *By the grace of God the ship came safely home through the storm.|She fell from grace with the king.* (=displeased him) **4** [U] a delay allowed as a favor for payment, work, etc.: *The bill should be paid by Friday, but they're giving us a week's grace.* **5** [C;U] a prayer before or after meals, giving thanks to God: *Who'll say grace today?* **6** [C *usu. cap.*] a way of speaking to or of a DUKE, DUCHESS, or ARCHBISHOP: *Your/His/Her Grace|Their Graces*

grace[2] *v* **graced, gracing** [T] *fml or humor* to decorate; add a fine quality to by one's presence; HONOR: *We were graced with the presence of our chairman.*

grace·ful /'greɪsfəl/ *adj* **1** (of shape or movement) attractive to see: *a graceful dancer/runner* **2** (of speech and feeling) suitably and pleasantly expressed –see GRACIOUS (USAGE) –**gracefully** *adv*

grace·less /'greɪsləs/ *adj* **1** awkward in movement or form **2** lacking in good manners –**gracelessly** *adv* –**gracelessness** *n* [U]

gra·cious /'greɪʃəs/ *adj fml* **1** polite, kind, and pleasant: *She was gracious enough to show us around her home.* –opposite **ungracious 2** [A] having those qualities which are made possible by wealth, such as comfort, beauty, and freedom from hard work: *gracious living* **3** [A] used in speaking of royal persons: *Her Gracious* MAJESTY *Queen Elizabeth* –**graciously** *adv* –**graciousness** *n* [U]

USAGE Compare **gracious** and **graceful**. **Graceful** means attractive or pleasant, and is used esp. to describe bodily movements or form, though it can also used of people's manners: *a graceful dancer|a deer running gracefully through the forest|He admitted gracefully that he was wrong.* **Gracious** is normally used of people's manners and suggests a very grand person being polite to someone less important: *The Senator thanked them graciously.*

gra·da·tion /greɪˈdeɪʃən/ *n* a stage in a set of changes or degrees of development: *A good actor can express every gradation of feeling from joy to grief.*

grade[1] /greɪd/ *n* **1 a** a degree of rank or quality **b** the members of the group at this level: *This grade of wool can be sold at a lower price.* **2** *AmE* a class for the work of a particular year of a school course: *She's in the second/eighth grade.* **3** *esp. AmE* a mark for the standard of a piece of schoolwork **4** *AmE* for GRADIENT **5 make the grade** to succeed; reach the necessary standard

grade[2] *v* **graded, grading** [T] to separate into levels: *These potatoes have been graded ac-*

cording to size and quality.

grade school /'· ·/ *n AmE* for ELEMENTARY SCHOOL

gra·di·ent /'greɪdiyənt/ *n* the degree of slope, as on a road: *A gradient of 1 in 4 is a rise or fall of one meter for every four meters forward.*

grad·u·al /'grædʒuwəl/ *adj* happening slowly and by degrees; not sudden: *There has been a gradual increase in the number of people owning cars.|a gradual rise in the path* –**gradually** *adv*

grad·u·ate[1] /'grædʒuwɪt/ *adj,n* [A;C] **1** *AmE* a person who has completed a course at a university, college, school, etc.: *He's a high school/college graduate.* **3** *esp. AmE||* **postgraduate** *esp. BrE*– (a person doing studies that are) done at a university after one has received one's first degree: *graduate school|a graduate student*

grad·u·ate[2] /'grædʒuw,eɪt/ *v* **-ated, -ating 1** [I *from*] to obtain a degree at a university, esp. a first degree **2** [I *from*] *AmE* to complete an educational course **3** [T] to arrange in order of degree, amount, or quality (GRADE): *The salary scale is graduated so that you get more money each year.* **4** [T] *tech* to make marks showing degrees of measurement (on): *a graduated ruler*

graduate school /'··· ,·/ *n AmE* a place of education where students can obtain a higher degree (as an M.A., M.S., or PH.D.) after they have received a first degree

grad·u·a·tion /,grædʒuw'eɪʃən/ *n* [C;U] the act of graduating with, or ceremony at which one receives, a university degree or American high school DIPLOMA

graf·fi·ti /grəˈfiytiy/ *n* [U] drawings or writing on a wall, esp. of a rude or political nature

graft[1] /græft/ *n* **1** [C] a piece cut from one plant and bound inside a cut in another, so that it grows there **2** [C] a piece of healthy living skin or bone taken from a person's body, and placed on or in another part of the body which has been damaged: *a skin graft on the burned leg* **3** [U] *esp. AmE* the practice of gaining money or advantage by the dishonest use of political influence

graft[2] *v* [T *on, onto*] to put (a piece) as a GRAFT[1] on a tree or body

grain /greɪn/ *n* **1** [C] a seed of rice, wheat, or other such food plants **2** [U] crops from plants which produce such seeds, esp. from wheat **3** [C] a piece of a substance which is made up of many small hard pieces: *a grain of sand/salt|*(fig.) *There is not a grain of truth* (=there is no truth at all) *in your statement.* **4** [*the* U] the natural arrangement of the threads or FIBERS in wood, flesh, rock, and cloth, or the pattern of lines one sees as a result of this: *It is easiest to cut wood in the direction of the grain.|*(fig.) **It goes against the grain** *for me to borrow money.* (=I don't like doing it) **5** [C] the smallest measure of weight, as used for medicines (1/7000 of a pound or .0648 gram)

gram /græm/ *n* (a measure of weight equal to) 1/1000 of a kilogram

gram·mar /'græmər/ *n* **1** [U] (the study and

use of) the rules by which words change their forms and are combined into sentences: *I find German grammar very difficult.|You must try to improve your grammar.* **2** [C] a book which teaches these rules: *This is the best Italian grammar I've seen.*

grammar school /'··· ,·/ *n* **1** *AmE becoming rare* for ELEMENTARY SCHOOL **2** (in Britain, esp. formerly) a school for children over the age of 11, who are specially chosen to study for examinations which may lead to higher education

gram·mat·i·cal /grə'mætɪkəl/ *adj* **1** [A] concerning grammar **2** correct according to the rules of grammar: *That is not a grammatical sentence.* **–grammatically** *adv*

gra·na·ry /ˌgreᵞnəriᵞ, 'græ–/ *n* **-ries** a storehouse for grain, esp. wheat: (fig.) *The Mid-West is the granary of the US.*

grand¹ /grænd/ *adj* **1** splendid in appearance; IMPRESSIVE: *There's a grand view of the mountains from this hotel.* **2** (of people) important, or (esp.) thinking oneself so **3** *infml* very pleasant; delightful: *That was a grand party.* **4** [A] complete (esp. in the phrase **the grand total**) **–grandly** *adv* **–grandness** *n* [U]

grand² *n* grand *infml* 1,000 dollars, pounds, etc.: *He paid fifteen grand for that car.*

grand·dad /'grændæd/ *n infml* grandfather

grand·child /'græntʃaɪld/ *n* **grandchildren** /'græn,tʃɪldrən/ the child (**grandson** or **granddaughter**) of someone's son or daughter –see illustration on page 247

grand·daugh·ter /'græn,dɔtər/ *n* the daughter of someone's son or daughter –see also GRANDSON; see illustration on page 247

gran·deur /'grændʒər, -dʒuər/ *n* [U] *fml* great beauty or power, often combined with great size: *the grandeur of nature|He has delusions of grandeur.* (=he thinks he is more important than he really is)

grand·fa·ther /'græn,faðər, 'grænd–/ *n* father of someone's father or mother –see also GRANDMOTHER; see illustration on page 247

grandfather clock /'··· ,·/ *n* a tall clock which stands on the floor, with a wooden outer case and the face at the top

gran·di·ose /'grændiᵞˌoʷs, ˌgrændiᵞ'oʷs/ *adj often derog* intended to have the effect of seeming important, splendid, etc.: *She's always producing grandiose plans that never work.*

grand·ma /'grænmɑ, 'græmɑ, 'grændmɑ/ *n infml* grandmother –see also GRANDPA

grand·moth·er /'græn,mʌðər, 'grænd–/ *n* the mother of someone's father or mother –see also GRANDFATHER; see illustration on page 247

grand·pa /'grænpɑ, 'græmpɑ, 'grændpɑ/ *n infml* grandfather –see also GRANDMA

grand·par·ent /'græn,peərənt, -,pær-, 'grænd–/ *n* the parent (**grandfather** or **grandmother**) of someone's father or mother –see illustration on page 247

grand pi·an·o /ˌ· ·'··/ *n* a large expensive piano, usu. played at concerts

grand·son /'grænsʌn, 'grænd–/ *n* the son of someone's son or daughter –see also GRAND-

DAUGHTER; see illustration on page 247

grand·stand /'grænstænd, 'grænd–/ *n* the seats, arranged in rows and sometimes covered by a roof, from which people watch sports events, races, etc.

gran·ite /'grænɪt/ *n* [U] a hard gray rock, used for building and making roads

gran·ny, grannie /'græniᵞ/ *n* **-nies** *infml* grandmother

gra·no·la /grə'noʷlə/ *n* [U] a dry breakfast food consisting of grains, nuts, fruit, etc.

grant¹ /grænt/ *n* money given esp. by the state for a particular purpose, e.g. to a university or to support a student during his/her studies: *She finds it difficult to live on her student grant.*

grant² *v* [T] **1** *fml* to give, esp. what is wanted or requested: *The boys were granted an extra day's vacation.* **2** [+*that*] to admit to (the truth of (something)): *I grant you that the senator isn't very popular at the moment, but I think he will win the next election.* **3 granted** yes (but): *"We've been very successful this year." "Granted. But can we do it again next year?"* **4 take something/someone for granted: a** to accept a fact, action, etc., without question: *I took it for granted that you would want to see the play, so I bought you a ticket.* **b** to treat something or someone with no attention or thought; not realize the true value of: *He's so busy with his job that he takes his family for granted.*

gran·u·lat·ed /'grænyəˌleᵞtɪd/ *adj* consisting of small bits (GRAINS (3) or GRANULEs): *granulated sugar* (=sugar that can be poured out, not large lumps)

gran·ule /'grænyuʷl/ *n* a small bit like a fine grain: *a granule of salt* **–granular** /'grænyələr/ *adj*

grape /greᵞp/ *n* **1** a small round juicy fruit usu. green (called "white") or dark purple (called "black"), which grows on a VINE and is often used for making wine: *a bunch of grapes* **2 sour grapes** the act of pretending to dislike what one really desires, because it is unobtainable: *Since losing the election, John says he never really wanted to become a politician anyway, but I think it's just sour grapes.*

grape·fruit /'greᵞpfruʷt/ *n* **grapefruit** or **grapefruits** a large round yellow fruit with a thick skin, like an orange but with a more acid taste

grape·vine /'greᵞpvaɪn/ *n* **1** [C] the climbing plant that bears GRAPEs **2** [*the* S] a secret way of spreading news or RUMOR: *I heard about your new job on/through the (office) grapevine.*

graph /græf/ *n* a drawing showing the relationship between two changing quantities; for example a line which shows the monthly profits of a business

graph·ic /'græfɪk/ *adj* [A] **1** concerned with written signs, usu. letters or drawings: *the graphic arts* **2** which gives a clear and detailed description or lifelike picture, esp. in words: *a graphic description of the accident*

graph·i·cal·ly /'græfɪkliᵞ/ *adv* **1** in a GRAPHIC

(2) manner: *She described the events so graphically that I could almost see them.* **2** *fml* by means of a GRAPH

grap·ple with sbdy./sthg. /'græpəl/ *v prep* **-pled, -pling** [T] to seize and struggle with: *He grappled with the bank robber, but was thrown to the ground.*|(fig.) *to grapple with a difficult problem*

grasp¹ /græsp/ *v* [T] **1** to take or keep a firm hold of, esp. with the hands: (fig.) *to grasp an* OPPORTUNITY **2** to succeed in understanding: *I grasped the main points of the speech.*
  grasp at sthg. *v prep* [T] reach for: *He grasped at anything that might help him.*

grasp² *n* [S] **1** a firm hold: *I kept her hand in my grasp.* **2** →REACH² (1): *Success is within her grasp.* **3** understanding: *This work is beyond my grasp.*|*She has a good grasp of the English language.*

grasp·ing /'græspɪŋ/ *adj derog* eager for more, esp. money: *Don't let those grasping taxi drivers charge you too much.*

grass /græs/ *n* **1** [U] a common low-growing green plant growing in fields and on hills: *She was lying on the grass.*|*We played football on the grass.* **2** [C] a green plant with tall, straight stems and flat blades: *Cows eat all kinds of grasses.* **3** [U] *infml* for MARIJUANA

grass·hop·per /'græs,hɑpər/ *n* an insect which can jump high and make a sharp noise by rubbing parts of its body together

grass·land /'græslænd/ *n* [U] a stretch of land covered mainly with grass, esp. land used for cattle to feed on

grass roots /,· '·/ *n* [P] the ordinary people in a country, political party, etc., not the ones with power: *grass roots opinion*|*a grass roots movement*

gras·sy /'græsiʸ/ *adj* **-sier, -siest** covered with growing grass

grate¹ /greʸt/ *n* the bars and frame which hold the coal, wood, etc., in a fireplace –sounds like **great**

grate² *v* **grated, grating 1** [T] to rub (usu. food) on a hard, rough surface so as to break into small pieces: *grated cheese* **2** [I *on*] to make a sharp sound, unpleasant to the hearer: *The nails in his boots grated on the stones.*|*His whistling grated on her nerves.*

grate·ful /'greʸtfəl/ *adj* [*to, for*] feeling or showing thanks to another person: *I was grateful to John for bringing the books*|*for his kindness.* –opposite **ungrateful**; see also GRATITUDE –**gratefully** *adv* –**gratefulness** *n* [U]

grat·i·fy /'grætə,faɪ/ *v* **-fied, -fying** [T] *fml* to give pleasure and satisfaction to: *It gratified me to know that soon he would be well again.* –**gratification** /,grætəfə'keʸʃən/ *n* [U] –**gratifying** /'grætə,faɪ-ɪŋ/ *adj* [+*to-v*]: *It was gratifying to know of the success of our efforts.*

grat·ing¹ /'greʸtɪŋ/ *n* a frame or network of bars, usu. metal, to protect a hole or window: *The coin fell through a grating at the side of the street.*

grating² *adj* (of a noise or sound) sharp, hard, and unpleasant –**gratingly** *adv*

gra·tis /'grætɪs, 'greʸ-, 'grɑ-/ *adv,adj* [F] *fml* free; (given) without payment

grat·i·tude /'grætə,tuʷd, -,tyuʷd/ *n* [U *to, for*] the state or feeling of being grateful; kind feelings towards someone who has been kind: *She showed me her gratitude by inviting me to dinner.* –opposite **ingratitude**

gra·tu·i·tous /grə'tuʷətəs, -'tyuʷ-/ *adj* **1** done freely, without reward or payment being expected **2** *derog* not deserved or necessary: *a gratuitous, rude remark*|*His movies are full of gratuitous violence.* –**gratuitously** *adv*

gra·tu·i·ty /grə'tuʷətiʸ, -'tyuʷ-/ *n* **-ties** a gift of money for a service done; TIP³

grave¹ /greʸv/ *n* **1** the place in the ground where a dead person is buried: (fig.) *Is there life beyond the grave?* (=after death) **2 make someone turn in his/her grave** to do something which would anger a person now dead: *That use of English would make Shakespeare turn in his grave.*

grave² *adj* serious or solemn: *His face was grave as he told them about the accident.*|*The sick man's condition is grave.* (=he is seriously ill) –**gravely** *adv*

grav·el¹ /'grævəl/ *n* [U] a mixture of small stones with sand, used on the surface of roads or paths

gravel² *v* **-l-** *AmE*||**-ll-** *BrE* [T] to cover (a road) with GRAVEL¹: *a graveled path*

grave·stone /'greʸvstoʷn/ *n* a stone put up over a grave bearing the name, dates of birth and death, etc., of the dead person –see also HEADSTONE

grave·yard /'greʸvyɑrd/ *n* a piece of ground, sometimes near a church, where people are buried –compare CEMETERY, CHURCHYARD

grav·i·tate to·ward sthg. /'grævə,teʸt/ also **gravitate to** sthg.– *v prep* **-tated, -tating** [T] to be drawn toward and move to: *In the 19th century, industry gravitated toward the north of England.*|(fig.) *He gravitates toward the arts.*

grav·i·ta·tion /,grævə'teʸʃən/ *n* [U] **1** the act of gravitating (GRAVITATE TOWARD) **2** →GRAVITY (2) –**gravitational** *adj*

grav·i·ty /'grævətiʸ/ *n* [U] **1** seriousness (as of manner, of a situation, etc.): *He doesn't understand the gravity of his illness.* –see GRAVE² **2** the natural force by which objects are attracted to each other, esp. that by which a large mass pulls a smaller one to it: *Anything that is dropped falls to the ground, pulled by the force of gravity.*

gra·vy /'greʸviʸ/ *n* [U] **1** the juice which comes out of meat as it cooks **2** the thickened liquid made from this (with flour, etc., added) to serve with meat and vegetables

gray¹ *AmE*||**grey** *esp. BrE* /greʸ/ *adj* **grayer, grayest 1** of the color like black mixed with white; of the color of lead, ashes, rain clouds, etc.: *Her hair is going gray with worry.*|*a gray coat*|(fig.) *His life in prison was gray* (=dull) *and lonely.* **2** having gray hair: *She became gray within a few weeks.* **3** (of the skin of the face) of a pale color because of sudden fear or illness: *His face turned gray as he heard the bad news.* –**grayness** *n* [U]

gray² *AmE*||**grey** *esp. BrE n* [C;U] (a) gray color: *She was dressed in gray*|*dull grays and browns*

gray³ *AmE*‖**grey** *esp. BrE v* [I] (of hair) to become gray: *graying hair*

graze¹ /greʸz/ *v* **grazed, grazing 1** [I] (of animals) to feed on grass: *The cattle are grazing in the field.* **2** [T] to cause (animals) to feed on grass: *We're grazing the sheep in the next field.*

graze² *v* [T] **1** to break the surface of (esp. the skin) by rubbing against something: *She fell down and grazed her knee.* **2** to touch (something) lightly while passing: *The car just grazed the gate as it drove through.*

graze³ *n* [*usu. sing.*] a surface wound

grease¹ /griʸs/ *n* [U] **1** animal fat when soft after being melted: *It was difficult to get the* BACON *grease off the plates.* **2** a thick oily substance: *He puts grease on his hair to make it shiny.*

grease² /griʸs, griʸz/ *v* **greased, greasing** [T] to put GREASE¹ on: *If you grease the lock it will turn more easily.*‖*Grease the pan with butter before baking the cake.*

greas·y /ˈgriʸsiʸ, -ziʸ/ *adj* **-ier, -iest** covered with or containing GREASE; slippery: *greasy food/skin/hair* –**greasily** *adv* –**greasiness** *n* [U]

great /greʸt/ *adj* **1** of excellent quality or ability: *the great women of the past*‖*a great king, artist, etc.* **2** [A] important: *a great occasion* **3** large in amount or degree: *Take great care.*‖*It was a great loss to us all.*‖*a great deal*‖*a great many* **4** [A] (of people) unusually active in the stated way: *He's a great talker.*‖*We're great (=very close) friends.* **5** [A] (*usu. before another adj. of size*) big: *a great (big) tree* **6** *infml* unusually good; very enjoyable: *What a great idea!*‖*This new singer is really great!* **7 great-:** **a** being the parent of a person's grandparent: *great-grandfather* **b** being the child of a person's grandchild: *great-granddaughter* **c** being the brother or sister of a person's grandparent: *great-aunt* **d** being the child of a person's nephew or niece: *great-nephew* –see illustration on page 247 –**greatness** *n* [U]

great·ly /ˈgreʸtliʸ/ *adv* (*with verb forms, esp. the past participle*) to a large degree; very: *greatly moved by his kindness*‖*greatly to be feared*

greed /griʸd/ *n* [U *for*] *usu. derog* strong desire to obtain a lot or more than what is fair, esp. of food, money, or power: *He eats because of greed, not hunger.*‖*greed for gold*

greed·y /ˈgriʸdiʸ/ *adj* **-ier, -iest** *usu. derog* full of GREED, esp. for food: *The greedy little boy ate all the food at the party.*‖*greedy for power* –**greedily** *adv* –**greediness** *n* [U]

green¹ /griʸn/ *adj* **1** of a color between yellow and blue; of the color of leaves and grass: *a green* SALAD‖*The fields and woods are very green* (=covered in fresh leaves and grass) *in the spring.* **2** unhealthily pale in the face, as though from sickness **3** [F] also **green with envy**– very jealous **4** *infml* young and/or inexperienced and therefore easily deceived and ready to believe anything **5 have a green thumb**‖*AmE* **green fingers** *BrE* to have natural skill in making plants grow well **6 the green light** the sign, or permission, to begin

an action: *We're ready to rebuild our house. We're just waiting for the green light from the town council.* –**greenness** *n* [U]

green² *n* **1** [U] the color which is green: *She was dressed in green.* **2** [C] a smooth stretch of grass, for a special purpose, as for playing a game or for the general use of the people of a town: *They are dancing on the village green.*‖*In his first game of* GOLF *he hit his ball onto the green in one stroke!*

green belt /ˈ· ·/ *n* [C;U] a stretch of land around a town, where building is not allowed, so that fields, woods, etc., remain

green·er·y /ˈgriʸnəriʸ/ *n* [U] green leaves and plants (FOLIAGE), esp. when used for decoration

green·gage /ˈgriʸngeʸdʒ/ *n* a soft juicy greenish-yellow fruit; kind of PLUM

green·gro·cer /ˈgriʸnˌgroʷsər/ *n esp. BrE* (a person who has) a store selling vegetables and fruit: *I bought some oranges at the greengrocer's.*

green·horn /ˈgriʸnhɔrn/ *n* **1** a young, inexperienced person who is easily cheated **2** *esp. AmE* a recently arrived IMMIGRANT, esp. male **3** a beginner, esp. male, at some kind of work or skill

green·house /ˈgriʸnhaʊs/ *n* **-houses** /ˌhaʊzɪz/ a building made of glass, used for growing plants which need heat, light, and protection from winds

greens /griʸnz/ *n* [P] green leafy vegetables that are cooked and eaten

Green·wich Mean Time /ˌgrɪnɪdʒ ˈmiʸn ˌtaɪm, -nɪtʃ, ˌgrɛ-/ (*abbrev.* **GMT**) *n* the time at a place near London (Greenwich) which is on an imaginary line dividing east from west: *Times in the rest of the world are fixed in relation to Greenwich Mean Time.*‖*European time is usually one hour later than Greenwich Mean Time.*

greet /griʸt/ *v* [T] **1** to welcome on meeting: *She greeted us by shouting a friendly* "HELLO!"‖*He greeted her with a loving kiss.*‖(fig.) *As we entered the room, we were greeted by complete disorder.* **2** to receive with an expression of feeling: *The speech was greeted by loud cheers.*

greet·ing /ˈgriʸtɪŋ/ *n* **1** a form of words or an action used on meeting someone:*"Good morning," I said, but she didn't return the greeting.* **2** [*usu. pl.*] a good wish: *We sent a card with birthday/Christmas greetings.*

greeting card *AmE*‖**greetings card** *BrE* /ˈ·· ˌ·/ *n* →CARD (3)

gre·gar·i·ous /grɪˈgɛəriʸəs/ *adj* living in groups; enjoying the companionship of others –**gregariously** *adv* –**gregariousness** *n* [U]

gre·nade /grəˈneʸd/ *n* a small bomb which can be thrown by hand or fired from a gun

grew /gruʷ/ *v* past tense of GROW

grey /greʸ/ *esp. BrE* for GRAY

grey·hound /ˈgreʸhaʊnd/ *n* a thin dog with long legs, which can run swiftly in hunting and racing

grid /grɪd/ *n* **1** a set of bars set across each other in a frame; GRATING¹: *a grid over a drain* **2** a network of electricity supply wires connecting the power stations: *the national grid* **3** a system of numbered squares printed on a map so that the exact position of any place on it may be stated or found

grid·dle /'grɪdl/ *n* an iron plate or pan, usu. round, which can be used for cooking over a fire

grid·lock /'grɪdlɒk/ *n* [U] *AmE* continuous lines of traffic which block street corners and INTERSECTIONS (2) and prevent traffic from moving in any direction

grief /griːf/ *n* [U] **1** great sorrow or feelings of suffering, esp. at the death of a loved person: *She went nearly mad with grief after the child died.|His wild behavior was a cause of grief to his parents.* **2 come/be brought to grief** to fail, causing harm to oneself: *My plan came to grief, and I was left penniless.* **3 good grief!** (an expression of surprise and some dislike)

griev·ance /'griːvəns/ *n* a report of or cause for complaint, esp. of unjust treatment: *a committee to deal with workers' grievances*

grieve /griːv/ *v* **grieved, grieving 1** [I *for*] to suffer from grief and sadness, esp. over a loss: *She is still grieving (for her dead husband).* **2** [T] to cause grief to; make very unhappy: *It grieves me to see him in such bad health.*

griev·ous /'griːvəs/ *adj* [A] *fml* very seriously harmful; severe: *a grievous mistake|grievous wounds* **–grievously** *adv*

grill¹ /grɪl/ *v* **1** [I;T] to cook (something) on a GRIDDLE or a GRILL² (1): *a grilled cheese sandwich* –compare BROIL; see COOK (USAGE) **2** [I;T] *esp. BrE* for BROIL¹ **3** [T] *infml* (esp. of the police) to question severely and continuously: *He was grilled for two hours before the police let him go.*

grill² *n* **1** a set of bars which can be put over a hot open fire, so that food can be cooked quickly: *Put the hamburgers on the grill.* **2** *esp. BrE* for BROILER (1) **3** meat cooked this way (esp. in the phrase **a mixed grill** =several types together)

grille /grɪl/ *n* a framework of usu. upright metal bars filling a space in a door or window, esp. in a bank or other place where money is handled and must be protected

grim /grɪm/ *adj* **-mm- 1** cruel, hard, or causing fear: *Her expression was grim when she told them they had lost their jobs.|the grim news of his death* **2** determined, esp. in spite of fear: *a grim smile* **3** *infml* unpleasant; not cheerful: *What grim weather!* **–grimly** *adv* **–grimness** *n* [U]

grim·ace /'grɪməs, grɪ'meɪs/ *v* **-aced, -acing** [I *at, with*] to make an expression of pain, annoyance, etc., which makes the face look unnaturally twisted: *The teacher grimaced as he looked at my work.|He grimaced with pain.* **–grimace** *n*: *a grimace of pain*

grime /graɪm/ *n* [U] a surface of thick black dirt: *His face and hands were covered with grime from the coal dust.*

grim·y /'graɪmiː/ *adj* **-ier, -iest** covered with dark dirt or GRIME **–griminess** *n* [U]

grin¹ /grɪn/ *v* **-nn-** [I *with, at*] **1** to make a GRIN: *They grinned with pleasure when I gave them the candy.* **2 grin and bear it** *infml* to suffer

what is unpleasant without complaint

grin² *n* a smile, esp. a very wide smile: *I knew she was joking because she had a big grin on her face.*

grind¹ /graɪnd/ *v* **ground** /graʊnd/, **grinding** [T] **1** to crush into small pieces or a powder by pressing between hard surfaces: *Grind up the wheat to make flour.|freshly-ground coffee* **2** to make smooth or sharp by rubbing on a hard surface: *A man came to grind the knives and scissors.* **3** to press upon, or press together, with a strong, twisting movement: *The dirt was deeply ground into the floor.|Some people grind their teeth during their sleep.* **4 grind to a halt** to come slowly and/or noisily to a stop

grind sbdy.↔ **down** *v adv* [T] →OPPRESS: *The people were ground down by lack of food and money.*

grind sthg.↔ **out** *v adv* [T] *derog* to produce (esp. writing or music of poor quality) continuously, like a machine

grind² *n* **1** [S] hard uninteresting work: *He finds any kind of study a real grind.|daily grind of the housework* **2** [C] *AmE infml* a student who is always working

grind·er /'graɪndər/ *n* a person or machine that GRINDS¹ (1): *a coffee grinder*

grind·stone /'graɪndstəʊn/ *n* **1** a round stone which is turned to sharpen tools, knives, etc. **2 one's nose to the grindstone** *infml* in a state of hard dull work: *He's got to keep his nose to the grindstone to feed his five children.*

grip¹ /grɪp/ *v* **-pp-** [I;T] to take a very tight hold (of): *Grip harder.|He gripped my hand in fear.|(fig.) The pictures gripped my imagination.*

grip² *n* **1** [C *usu. sing.*] a very tight forceful hold: *The policeman would not loosen his grip on the thief.|(fig.) He keeps a firm grip on his children.* (=controls them a great deal) **2** [S] the power of understanding or doing: *I played badly; I seem to be **losing my grip**.* **3** [C] *AmE or old use* a bag or case for a traveler's personal belongings **4** [C] (a part of) an apparatus which GRIPS **5 come/get to grips with** to deal seriously with (something difficult): *The speaker talked a lot but never really came to grips with the subject.*

gripe¹ /graɪp/ *v* **griped, griping** [I *at, about*] *infml* to complain continually: *He's griping about his income tax again.*

gripe² *n infml* a complaint: *My main gripe is, there's no hot water.*

grip·ping /'grɪpɪŋ/ *adj* that holds the attention: *a gripping movie* **–grippingly** *adv*

gris·ly /'grɪzliː/ *adj* **-lier, -liest** unpleasant because of destruction, decay, or death which is shown or described: *the grisly remains of the bodies|a grisly story about people who ate human flesh* –compare GRUESOME

gris·tle /'grɪsəl/ *n* [U] the material in meat which is too tough to eat, found near the bones –compare CARTILAGE **–gristly** *adj* **-ier, -iest**

grit¹ /grɪt/ *n* [U] **1** small pieces of a hard material, usu. sand or stone: *His hands were covered with grit after working in the garden.* **2** *infml* determination; lasting courage;

grit² v -tt- **grit one's teeth** to become determined when in a position of difficulty: *The snow was blowing in her face, but she gritted her teeth and went on.*

griz·zly bear /ˈgrɪzliʸ bɛər/ also **grizzly**– n a large brownish-gray bear of the Rocky Mountains of North America

groan¹ /groʷn/ v [I] to make a GROAN²: *The old man who had been in the accident lay groaning beside the road.*|(fig.) *The table groaned with food.* (=there was lots of food on it)|(fig.) *The people groaned under the load of taxes.*

groan² n a rather loud sound of suffering, worry, or disapproval, made in a deep voice: *There were loud groans when he asked them for money.*|(fig.) *The old chair gave a groan when the fat man sat down on it.*

gro·cer /ˈgroʷsər/ n a storekeeper who sells food and other things for the home, such as matches and soap

gro·cer·ies /ˈgroʷsəriʸz/ n [P] the goods sold by a GROCER: *He brought the bag of groceries in from the car.*

gro·cer·y /ˈgroʷsəriʸ/ also **grocery store** /ˈ··· ˌ·/– n -ies a store where groceries are sold

grog·gy /ˈgrɑgiʸ/ adj -gier, -giest [F] infml weak because of illness, shock, etc., esp. when not able to walk steadily: *When I left my bed after my long illness, I felt too groggy to stand.* –**groggily** adv

groin /grɔɪn/ n the place where the tops of the legs meet the front of the body

groom¹ /gruʷm, grʊm/ n **1** a person who is in charge of horses **2** →BRIDEGROOM

groom² v [T] **1** to take care of the appearance of (oneself), by dressing neatly, keeping the hair tidy, etc.: *a well-groomed look* **2** [for] to prepare (someone) for a special position or occasion: *grooming her for stardom* (=to play big parts in plays or films) **3** to take care of (horses), esp. by rubbing, brushing, and cleaning

groove /gruʷv/ n a long narrow path or track made in a surface, esp. to guide the movement of something: *The needle moves along the groove on a record.*|*The cupboard door slides open along a groove.*

grope /groʷp/ v **groped, groping** [I;T for] to search about with the hands in or as if in the dark; feel: *He groped in his pocket for his ticket.*|*I groped my way to a seat in the dark movie theater.*|(fig.) *We are groping after the truth.*

gross¹ /groʷs/ adj **1** unpleasantly fat **2** (of people's speech and habits) rough, impolite, and offensive: *She was shocked by his gross behavior at the party.* **3** inexcusable; FLAGRANT: *gross negligence* (=carelessness) **4** [no comp.] total: *The gross weight of the box of chocolates is more than the weight of the chocolates alone.* –compare NET³ (1,3) –**grossly** adv –**grossness** n [U]

gross² v [T] to gain as total profit or earn as a total amount: *The company grossed $2,000,000 last year.* –compare NET³

gross³ determiner,n **gross** or **grosses** a group of 144; 12 DOZEN

gro·tesque /groʷˈtɛsk/ adj strange and unnatural so as to cause fear or be laughable:*The fat old man looked grotesque in tight pants.* –**grotesquely** adv –**grotesqueness** n [U]

grot·to /ˈgrɑtoʷ/ n -toes or -tos a natural cave, esp. of limestone, or a man-made one in a garden

grouch¹ /graʊtʃ/ n infml **1** a person who keeps complaining **2** a bad-tempered complaint

grouch² v [I] infml to complain; GRUMBLE¹ (1)

ground¹ /graʊnd/ n **1** [the S;U] the surface of the earth: *The branch broke and fell to the ground.* –compare FLOOR¹ (1)|*They built a bomb shelter below ground/ underground.*|(fig.) *The book says nothing new; it just goes over the same old ground/doesn't break new ground.*|*You're on dangerous ground if you mention modern music to him. He hates it!* **2** [U] soil; earth: *The ground is too dry for planting seeds.* –see LAND (USAGE) **3** [C] a piece of land used for a particular purpose: *a playground* **4** [U] an argument or position which one will defend: *He refused to give ground in the argument.* (=would not admit the point) **5** [C] →BACKGROUND (1): *The curtains have white flowers on a blue ground.* **6** [C usu. sing.] AmE‖**earth** BrE– (an additional safety wire which makes) a connection between an electrical apparatus and the ground **7** gain ground to have more success or become more popular: *The opposition party seems to be gaining ground.* **8** get off the ground to make a successful start –see also GROUNDS

ground² v **1** [I] (of a boat) to strike against the bottom or the ground **2** [T] to cause (a pilot or plane) to come to or stay on the ground, instead of flying **3** [T on, in] to base: *an argument grounded on personal experience* **4** [T] AmE‖**earth** BrE– to make (an electrical apparatus) safer by connecting it to the ground with a wire

ground³ v past tense and participle of GRIND

ground floor /ˌ· ˈ·◀/ also **first floor** AmE– n **1** the part of a building, often the lowest, at ground level: *I live on the ground floor.* –see also FIRST FLOOR **2** get/be in on the ground floor infml to be part of an activity from the time it starts

ground·ing /ˈgraʊndɪŋ/ n [S] a complete training in the main points which will enable thorough study or work on some subject: *a good grounding in English grammar*

ground·less /ˈgraʊndlɪs/ adj (of feelings, ideas, etc.) without base or good reason: *groundless fears/worries* –**groundlessly** adv

ground·nut /ˈgraʊndnʌt/ n BrE for PEANUT

ground rule /ˈ· ˌ·/ n [often pl.] esp. AmE **1** a rule used as a base for deciding how to deal with something **2** a rule for an informal sporting event

grounds /graʊndz/ n [P] **1** land surrounding a large building, such as a country house or hospital, usu. made into gardens and enclosed by a wall or fence: *a walk through*

cheerful effort made during difficulty –**gritty** adj -tier, -tiest *the grounds* **2** a reason: *We have good grounds for thinking that she stole the money.*|*He left* **on (the) grounds of** *poor health.* **3** small bits of solid matter which sink to the bottom of a liquid, esp. coffee

ground·work /'graʊndwɜrk/ *n* [U] the work which forms the base for some kind of study or skill

group¹ /gruʷp/ *n* **1** a number of people, things, or organizations placed together or connected in a particular way: *a photograph of a family group*|*a group of tall trees*|*Schoolchildren are taught according to age groups.*|*French and Spanish are in the same language group.* **2** a usu. small number of players of popular music: *My favorite group is playing here tonight.*

group² *v* [I;T] to form into one or more groups: *We can group animals into several types.*

group·ie /'gruʷpiʸ/ *n infml* a person, esp. a young girl, who follows POP⁴ group players to the concerts they give

group·ing /'gruʷpɪŋ/ *n* [*usu. sing.*] a (way of) arrangement into a group: *The new grouping of classes means that there are larger numbers in each class.*

group ther·a·py /ˌ· '·—·/ *n* [U] a way of treating disorders of the mind by bringing sufferers together to talk about their difficulties, usu. with a doctor or specially trained leader

grouse¹ /graʊs/ *n* **grouse** a smallish fat bird which is shot for food and sport

grouse² *v,n* **groused, grousing** [C;I] *infml* (to make) a complaint; GRUMBLE¹,²

grove /groʷv/ *n lit* a small group of trees

grov·el /'grʌvəl, 'grʌ-/ *v* -l- *AmE*‖-ll- *BrE* [I to] *derog* to lie or move flat on the ground, esp. in fear of or obedience to someone powerful: *The dog groveled at his feet when he shouted at it.*|(fig.) *I had to grovel in front of my employer before she would agree to increase my pay.* –**groveller** *n*

grow /groʷ/ *v* **grew** /gruʷ/, **grown** /groʷn/, **growing** **1** [I] (of (parts of) living things) to increase in size by natural development: *Grass grows after rain.*|*He's grown six inches (taller).*|*A lamb grows into a sheep.*|*She's letting her hair grow.*|*a growing boy*|*The children have grown.*|*The population is growing* (=increasing in numbers) *too quickly.* **2** [I] (of plants) to exist and be able to develop, esp. after planting: *Cotton grows very well in Texas.*|*Oranges grow wild here.* **3** [T] to cause to or allow to grow (esp. plants and crops): *Mary grows vegetables.*|*Plants grow roots.*|*He grew a beard.*|*She's grown her hair long.* **4** [+*to-v*] to become (gradually): *She's growing fat.*|*The noise grew louder.*|*It's growing dark; we must go home soon.*|*I think you'll grow to like him when you know him better.*

grow away from sbdy. *v adv prep* [T *no pass.*] to have a less close relationship with (esp. one's parents, husband, or wife): *Since she went to college, she's grown away from the family.*

grow into sbdy./sthg. *v prep* **1** to become:

She's grown into a fine young woman. **2** [T *no pass.*] to become big enough for (clothes): *The coat is too long, but she'll grow into it.* –compare GROW **out of** (1)

grow on sbdy. *v prep* [T] to become gradually more pleasing or more of a habit to: *Modern music is difficult to listen to, but it starts to grow on you.*

grow out of sthg. *v adv prep* [T +*v-ing*] **1** to become too big or too old for (esp. clothes, shoes, etc.): *My daughter has grown out of all her old clothes* –compare GROW **into** (2) **2** [*no pass.*] to develop as a result of: *Her political beliefs grew out of her hatred of injustice.*

grow up *v adv* [I] **1** (of people) to develop from child to man or woman **2** to arise; develop into something lasting: *The custom grew up of dividing the father's land between the sons.*

grow·er /'groʷər/ *n* a person who grows plants, fruit, etc., for sale

growl /graʊl/ *v,n* [C;I] (to make) a deep rough sound in the throat, or a sound like this: *Our dog always growls at visitors.*|*the growl of distant thunder*

grown /groʷn/ *adj* [A] of full size or development; ADULT: *A grown man like you shouldn't act like that.*

grown-up /ˌ· '·◄/ *adj* fully developed; ADULT: *She has a grown-up daughter who lives abroad.* –**grown-up** /'· ·/ *n infml: Go to bed now and let the grown-ups have a little time to themselves.*

growth /groʷθ/ *n* **1** [U] the act or rate of growing and developing: *the rapid growth of* POVERTY **2** [S;U] increase in numbers or amount: *the growth of large companies*|*a sudden growth in the membership of the club* **3** [C] something which has grown: *Nails are growths at the ends of the fingers.* **4** [C] a lump produced by an unnatural and unhealthy increase in the number of cells in a part of the body –compare TUMOR

grub¹ /grʌb/ *n* **1** [C] an insect in the wormlike form it has when just out of the egg **2** [U] *infml* food

grub² *v* -bb- [I] to turn over the soil; dig: *The dog was grubbing (around) under the bush, looking for a bone.*

grub·by /'grʌbiʸ/ *adj* -**bier**, -**biest** dirty

grudge¹ /grʌdʒ/ also **begrudge**– *v* **grudged, grudging** [T +*v-ing*] to give or allow (something) unwillingly: *He grudged paying so much for such bad food.*

grudge² *n* [*against*] **1** a cause for dislike, real or imagined, esp. of another person: *I feel he has a grudge against me, although I don't know why.* **2** **bear a grudge/grudges** to continue to have feelings of anger about someone's past actions: *He bears a grudge against me because I took his place on the team.*

grudg·ing /'grʌdʒɪŋ/ *adj* ungenerous; unwilling (to give): *She was very grudging in her thanks.* –**grudgingly** *adv*

gru·el /'gruʷəl/ *n* [U] a thin liquid food, esp. for sick people

gru·el·ing *AmE*‖**gruelling** *BrE* /'gruʷəlɪŋ/ *adj* very hard and tiring

grue·some /ˈgruʷsəm/ *adj* (esp. of something connected with death or decay) terrible to the senses; shocking and sickening –compare GRISLY –**gruesomely** *adv* –**gruesomeness** *n* [U]

gruff /grʌf/ *adj* (of a person's voice or way of speaking) rough and unfriendly: *Although he has a gruff manner, he is really very kind.* –**gruffly** *adv* –**gruffness** *n* [U]

grum·ble¹ /ˈgrʌmbəl/ *v* **-bled, -bling** [I] **1** [*about*] to express discontent or dissatisfaction; complain, not loudly, but angrily: *He has everything he needs. He has nothing to grumble about.* **2** (of thunder and certain noises) RUMBLE –**grumbler** /ˈgrʌmblər/ *n*

grumble² *n* a complaint or expression of dissatisfaction

grump·y /ˈgrʌmpiʸ/ *adj* **-ier, -iest** bad-tempered, esp. because of low spirits: *You're very grumpy today. What's the matter?* –**grumpily** *adv* –**grumpiness** *n* [U]

grun·gy /ˈgrʌndʒiʸ/ *adj AmE infml* **-gier, -giest** dirty: *What a grungy old coat!*

grunt /grʌnt/ *v,n* [C;I] (to make) a short deep rough sound in the throat, as if the nose were closed: *a grunting pig|He didn't say anything. He just gave a grunt of agreement.*

guar·an·tee¹ /ˌgærənˈtiʸ/ *n* [+*to-v/that/of*] **1** a formal declaration that something will be done, esp. a written agreement by the maker of an article, to repair or replace it if it is found imperfect within a period of time: *The radio has a two-year guarantee.|The television is less than a year old, so it is still under guarantee.*|(fig.) *Clear skies are no guarantee that the weather will stay fine.* **2** an agreement to be responsible for the fulfillment of someone else's promise, esp. for paying a debt **3** something of value given to someone to keep until the owner has fulfilled a promise, esp. to pay: *He gave them the papers which proved his ownership of the land, as a guarantee that he would repay the money.* –compare SECURITY (3)

guarantee² *v* **-teed, -teeing** [T] **1** to give a promise of quality, payment, or fulfillment (a GUARANTEE¹) about: *The watch is guaranteed for three years.|They have guaranteed delivery within a month.* **2** [+*to-v/that*] to promise (that something will certainly be so): *I guarantee that you'll enjoy yourself.*

guar·an·tor /ˈgærən͵tɔr, -tər/ *n law* a person who gives a GUARANTEE¹ (2)

guar·an·ty /ˈgærəntiʸ/ *n* **-ties** *law* a GUARANTEE, esp. of payment

guard¹ /gɑrd/ *n* **1** [U] a state of watchful readiness to protect or defend: *There are soldiers* **on guard** *at the gate, to prevent anyone getting in or out.|They are keeping/standing guard over the house.* **2** [U] a position for defense, esp. in a fight: *He hit him* **when his guard was down.** (=when he was not ready to defend himself) **3** [C] a person, esp. a soldier, policeman, or prison officer, who guards someone or something: *The camp guards are changed every night.* **4** [C] a group of people, esp. soldiers, whose duty is to guard someone or something: *The prisoner was brought in* **under** *armed*

guard.|*The guard is changed every hour.* **5** [C] an apparatus which covers and protects: *A fireguard prevents children getting near the fire.|a mudguard over the chain of a bicycle* **6** **on/off one's guard** ready/not ready to deal with a sudden trick or attack: *Be on your guard against thieves.*

guard² *v* [T] **1** [*against, from*] to defend; keep safe, esp. by watching for danger: *The dog guarded the house (against strangers).|The soldiers were guarding the bridge.* **2** to watch (a prisoner) in order to prevent escape: (fig.) *Guard the secret with your life; don't tell it to anyone.*

guard against sthg. *v prep* [T +*v-ing*] to (try to) prevent by special care: *You should wash your hands before preparing food to guard against spreading infection.*

guard·ed /ˈgɑrdɪd/ *adj* (of speech) careful; not saying too much –**guardedly** *adv*

guard·i·an /ˈgɑrdiʸən/ *n* **1** a person or place that guards or protects: *That bank is the guardian of their wealth.|A* **guardian angel** *is believed to be a good spirit which protects a person or a place.* **2** *law* a person who has the responsibility of looking after a child not his/her own, esp. after the parents' death –see also WARD (3)

gua·va /ˈgwɑvə/ *n* (a small tropical tree bearing) a round fruit with pink or white flesh and seeds in the center

gu·ber·na·to·ri·al /ˌguʷbərnəˈtɔriʸəl, -ˈtoʷr-, ͵gyuʷ-/ *adj fml* of or concerning a governor: *a gubernatorial election in Florida*

guer·ril·la, guerilla /gəˈrɪlə/ *n* a member of an unofficial fighting group which attacks the enemy in small groups unexpectedly: *guerrilla warfare*

guess¹ /gɛs/ *v* **1** [I;T +*(that)/at*] to form (a judgment) or risk giving (an opinion) without knowing or considering all the facts: *Can you guess (at) the price?|Guess how much/what it cost.* **2** [T] to get to know by guessing: *She guessed my thoughts.* **3** [T +*(that)*] *infml esp. AmE* to suppose; consider likely: *I guess you don't have time to go out now that you have young children.* **4** **keep someone guessing** to keep someone uninformed and uncertain about what will happen next

guess² *n* **1** an attempt to guess: *I took a guess at the answer.* **2** an opinion formed by guessing: *My guess is that he didn't come because he was angry with us.* **3** **at a guess** by guessing, without being certain or exact: *At a guess, I'd say she was 35.*

guess·ti·mate /ˈgɛstəmɪt/ *n infml* an ESTIMATE based on GUESSWORK rather than facts: *My guesstimate is that it will cost $200 to fly to Miami.* –**guesstimate** /ˈgɛstə͵meʸt/ *v* **-mated, -mating** [I;T]

guess·work /ˈgɛswɜrk/ *n* [U] the act of guessing, or the judgment which results

guest /gɛst/ *n* **1** a person who is in someone's home by invitation, for a short time (as for a meal), or to stay (one or more nights): *I can't go out now; we have guests.* –compare VISITOR **2** a person who is invited out and paid for at a theater, restaurant, etc.: *They are com-*

ing to the concert as my guests. |a **guest artist** (=actor or singer who is invited to perform) **3** a person who is lodging in a hotel, or in someone's home: *While Tom was a guest in my house, he stayed in the* **guest room.** |*She takes in* **paying guests. 4 be my guest!** *infml* I would not mind if you did so; please feel free to do so: *"May I borrow your pen?" "Be my guest!"* –see CUSTOMER (USAGE)

guest·house /'gɛsthaʊs/ *n* **-houses** /ˌhaʊzɪz/ **1** a separate house for guests **2** a private house where visitors may stay and have meals for payment

guf·faw /gə'fɔ/ *v,n* [C;I] (to make) a loud and perhaps rude laugh

guid·ance /'gaɪdns/ *n* [U] help; advice

guide¹ /gaɪd/ *n* **1** something or somebody that shows the way, esp. someone whose job is to show a place to tourists: *You need a guide to show you the city.* **2** something which influences or controls a person's actions or behavior: *It may not be a good thing to take your friend's experience as a guide.* **3** [*to*] also **guide book** /'· ·/– a book which gives a description of a place, for the use of visitors, or which teaches something

guide² *v* **guided, guiding** [T] to act as a guide to: *She guides people around the city.* |*The light guided them back to harbor.* |(fig.) *The government will guide the country through the difficulties ahead.* –see LEAD (USAGE)

guide·lines /'gaɪdlaɪnz/ *n* [P] the main points about something which is to be dealt with (esp. something official)

guild /gɪld/ *n* an association of people who share the same interests or (esp. in former times) the same skills or profession: *the tailors' guild*

guile /gaɪl/ *n* [U] deceit, esp. of a clever, indirect kind –compare CUNNING –**guileful** /'gaɪlfəl/ *adj*

guile·less /'gaɪl-lɪs/ *adj* (appearing to be) lacking in any deceit: *Even though she had a guileless manner, he knew he couldn't really trust her.*

guil·lo·tine¹ /'gɪlə͵tiʸn, 'gɪʸə-, ͵gɪlə'tiʸn, ͵gɪʸə-/ *n* **1** [C; *the* S] a machine used in France for cutting off the heads of criminals, which works by means of a heavy blade sliding down between two posts **2** [C] a machine for cutting paper

guillotine² *v* **-tined, -tining** [T] to use a GUILLOTINE¹ (1) as punishment on: *Many members of noble families were guillotined in France in the late 18th century.*

guilt /gɪlt/ *n* [U] **1** the fact of having broken a law: *There can be no doubt about the guilt of a man who is found with stolen money in his pockets.* –opposite **innocence 2** responsibility for something wrong; blame: *The children behave badly, but the guilt lies with the parents, who don't care about their behavior.* **3** the knowledge or belief that one has done wrong; shame: *His face showed guilt, although he said he had done nothing wrong.* –**guiltless** *adj* –**guiltlessness** *n* [U]

guilt·y /'gɪltiʸ/ *adj* **-ier, -iest 1** [*of*] having broken a law or disobeyed a moral or social rule: *guilty of murder* |*He was found*

(=declared) *guilty.* –compare INNOCENT **2** [A] having or showing a feeling of guilt: *I have a* **guilty conscience** *about forgetting to mail your letter.* –**guiltily** *adv* –**guiltiness** *n* [U]

guin·ea pig /'gɪniʸ ͵pɪg/ *n* **1** a small roundish furry animal rather like a rat without a tail, which is often kept by children as a pet, and is sometimes used in scientific tests **2** a person who is the subject of some kind of test: *I have to try my cooking out on someone. Will you be my guinea pig?*

guise /gaɪz/ *n* [*usu. sing.*] *fml* an outer appearance, often one which is intended to deceive: *The thieves came into the house* **in/under the guise** *of television repair men.*

gui·tar /gɪ'tɑr/ *n* a musical instrument with six or more strings, a long neck, and a wooden body like a VIOLIN but larger, played by PICK-ing¹ (6) the strings with the fingers

gulch /gʌltʃ/ *n esp. AmE* (esp. in the western US) a narrow stony valley with steep sides formed by a rushing stream

gulf /gʌlf/ *n* **1** a large deep stretch of sea partly enclosed by land: *the Gulf of Mexico* **2** a deep hollow place in the earth's surface: *The ground trembled, and suddenly a great gulf opened before us.* **3** a great area of division or difference, esp. between opinions: *a huge gulf between them*

gull /gʌl/ also **seagull**– *n* a largish flying seabird with a loud cry

gul·let /'gʌlɪt/ *n infml* the (inner) throat; foodpipe from mouth to stomach

gul·li·ble /'gʌləbəl/ *adj* easily tricked, esp. into a false belief: *He's so gullible you could sell him anything.* –**gullibility** /ˌgʌlə'bɪlətiʸ/ *n* [U] –**gullibly** /'gʌləbliʸ/ *adv*

gul·ly /'gʌliʸ/ *n* **-lies 1** a small narrow valley cut esp. into a hillside by heavy rain **2** a man-made deep ditch or other small waterway

gulp /gʌlp/ *v* **1** [T *down*] to swallow hastily: *Don't gulp your food.* **2** [I] to make a sudden swallowing movement as if surprised or nervous –**gulp** *n*

gulp sthg.↔ **back** *v adv* [T] to prevent the expression of feeling by or as if by swallowing: *She gulped back her tears.*

gum¹ /gʌm/ *n* [*usu. pl.*] either of the two areas of firm pink flesh in which the teeth are fixed, at the top and bottom of the mouth

gum² *n* **1** [U] sticky substance obtained esp. from the stems of some trees and bushes, used for sticking things together **2** [U] →CHEWING GUM

gum³ *v* **-mm-** [T] to stick (something somewhere) with GUM² (1): *He gummed the labels on the boxes.*

gum sthg.↔ **up** *v adv* [T] *infml* to make unworkable: *Her illness gummed up our plans for a party.*

gum·bo /'gʌmboʷ/ *n* **-bos 1** [C]→ OKRA **2** [U] a type of American soup made with meat or fish, vegetables, and OKRA to thicken it

gum·drop /'gʌmdrɑp/ *AmE*||**gum** *BrE*– *n* a small jelly-like candy

gump·tion /'gʌmpʃən/ *n* [U] *infml* common sense

gun¹ /gʌn/ n **1** a weapon from which bullets or larger metal objects (SHELLS¹ (3)) are fired through a metal tube (BARREL) –compare CANNON **2 jump the gun** infml to start before getting permission **3 stick to one's guns** to continue to fight, argue, or keep one's point of view in spite of attacks, esp. on one's beliefs

gun² also **rev up**– v **-nn-** infml [T] to feed GASOLINE to and cause an engine to move quickly: She gunned the engine and sped away.

gun sbdy.↔**down** v adv to shoot, causing to fall to the ground dead or wounded

gun for sbdy. v prep to look for someone in order to start an argument

gun·boat /'gʌnbowt/ n a small but heavily armed naval warship

gun·fire /'gʌnfaɪər/ n [U] the sound or act of firing one or more guns

gung ho /ˌgʌŋ 'howⁱ/ adj AmE infml having a strong feeling of interest; enthusiastic (ENTHUSIASM)

gunk /gʌŋk/ n [U] infml esp. AmE any unpleasant, dirty, and/or sticky substance

gun·man /'gʌnmən/ n **-men** /mən/ a criminal armed with a gun

gun·ner /'gʌnər/ n [A;C] a soldier in a part (REGIMENT) of the army, navy, or air force which uses heavy guns (ARTILLERY)

gun·point /'gʌnpɔɪnt/ n **at gunpoint** under a threat of death by shooting: We were robbed at gunpoint.

gun·pow·der /'gʌnˌpaʊdər/ n [U] an explosive material made of various substances, in the form of a powder

gun·run·ner /'gʌnˌrʌnər/ n a person who unlawfully and secretly brings guns into a country, esp. for the use of those who wish to fight against their own government –**gunrunning** n [U]

gun·shot /'gʌnʃɑt/ n **1** [C] the act or sound of firing a gun: a gunshot wound **2** [U] the distance reached by a shot from a gun: We were careful not to come **within gunshot** of the enemy.

gur·gle /'gɜrgəl/ v,n **-gled, -gling** [C;I] (to make) a sound like water flowing unevenly, as out of an opening: The baby lay gurgling in her bed.|The water gurgled out of the bottle.

gu·ru /'guʷruʷ, 'guəruʷ, gʊ'ruʷ/ n **-rus** [A;C] an Indian priest or teacher of religious practices that produce peace of mind: (fig.) Mr. Brown is the President's guru on all matters concerning defense.

gush¹ /gʌʃ/ v [I] **1** (of liquids) to flow or pour out in large quantities, as from a hole or wound: Oil gushed out from the broken pipe.|Blood gushed from his wound. **2** [over] to express too much admiration, pleasure, etc., in a great flow of words, foolishly or without true feeling –**gushing** adj: a gushing spring|gushing praise –**gushingly** adv

gush² n [S] a (sudden) flow (of liquid): There was a gush of blood as the wound reopened.|(fig.) a gush of interest/ ENTHUSIASM

gust /gʌst/ n [of] a sudden strong rush of air,

rain, smoke, etc., carried by wind: A gust of wind blew the door shut. –compare PUFF² (2) –**gusty** adj **-ier, -iest**: gusty weather

gus·to /'gʌstoʷ/ n [U] eager enjoyment (in doing or having something): He started painting **with great gusto.**

gut¹ /gʌt/ n **1** [C;U] the food pipe which passes through the body **2** [U] strong thread made from this part of animals:The fishing line is made of gut.

gut² v **-tt-** [T] **1** to take out the inner organs (esp. GUTS) of (a dead animal) **2** to destroy completely the inside of (a building), esp. by fire: The huge factory was gutted in minutes.

gut³ adj [A] infml arising from or concerning one's strongest feelings and needs, not from thought: a gut feeling that something terrible would happen|a **gut reaction** against the new government

guts /gʌts/ n [P] infml **1** the bowels or IN-TESTINES **2** bravery; determination: She has a lot of guts; she went on arguing even though no one agreed with her.

gut·ter /'gʌtər/ n **1** [C] a small hollow or ditch beside a street, or an open pipe fixed to a roof, to collect and carry away rainwater **2** [the S] the lowest poorest social conditions, as in a dirty part of a city: After losing all his money, he ended up in the gutter.

gut·tur·al /'gʌtərəl/ adj of or in the throat: Unable to speak, she made a few guttural sounds in reply.

guy /gaɪ/ n infml esp. AmE a man; fellow: a nice guy

guz·zle /'gʌzəl/ v **-zled, -zling** [I;T] to eat or drink eagerly and greedily (GREED): Pigs guzzle their food.|He's been guzzling beer all evening. –**guzzler** n

gym /dʒɪm/ n infml **1** [C] →GYMNASIUM **2** [U] →PHYSICAL EDUCATION: a gym class|I have gym at 11:00.

gym·na·si·um /dʒɪm'neʸziʸəm/ n a hall with wall bars, ropes, and other such things, for climbing, jumping, etc.

gym·nast /'dʒɪmnæst/ n a person who trains and is skilled in certain bodily exercises

gym·nas·tics /dʒɪm'næstɪks/ n [U] the art of training the body by means of certain exercises, often done in competition with others –**gymnastic** adj [A]

gy·ne·col·o·gy AmE‖**gynaecology** BrE /ˌgaɪnə'kɑlədʒiʸ, ˌdʒaɪ-/ n [U] the study in medicine of the workings of the female sex organs and the study and treatment of their diseases –**gynecological** /ˌgaɪnəkə'lɑdʒɪkəl, ˌdʒaɪ-/ adj –**gynecologist** /ˌgaɪnə'kɑlədʒɪst, ˌdʒaɪ-/ n

gyp /dʒɪp/ v **-pp-** AmE infml derog. [T] to cheat: He gypped me out of $10.

gyp·sy esp. AmE‖**gipsy** esp. BrE /'dʒɪpsiʸ/ n **-sies 1** (sometimes cap.) a member of a dark-haired race which may be Indian in origin and travels around in covered carts (CARAVANS), earning money as horse dealers, musicians, FORTUNE-TELLERS, etc. **2** infml & sometimes derog a person who habitually wanders and who has the habits of someone who does not stay for long in one place

gy·rate /ˈdʒaɪreʸt, dʒaɪˈreʸt/ v **-rated, -rating** [I] to swing round and round a fixed point, in one direction or with changes of direction: *The dancers gyrated quickly to the strong beat of the music.* –**gyration** /dʒaɪˈreʸʃən/ n [C;U]

gy·ro·scope /ˈdʒaɪrəˌskoʷp/ also **gyro** /ˈdʒaɪroʷ/ *infml*– n a heavy wheel which spins inside a frame, used for keeping ships and aircraft steady, and as a children's toy –**gyroscopic** /ˌdʒaɪrəˈskɑpɪk/ adj

H, h

H, h /eʸtʃ/ **H's, h's** *or* **Hs, hs** the 8th letter of the English alphabet

ha /hɑ/ *interj* a shout of surprise, interest, etc.

hab·er·dash·er /ˈhæbərˌdæʃər/ n **1** *AmE* a storekeeper who sells men's clothing, esp. hats, GLOVEs, etc. **2** *BrE* a storekeeper who sells pins, sewing thread, and other small things used in dressmaking

hab·er·dash·er·y /ˈhæbərˌdæʃəriʸ/ n **-ies** [C;U] (the goods sold in) a HABERDASHER's shop or department in a department store

hab·it /ˈhæbɪt/ n **1** [C;U] (an example of) customary behavior: *It was her habit to go for a walk before lunch.|I smoke* **out of habit**, *not for pleasure.* **2** [C] a special set of clothes, esp. that worn by MONKs and NUNs in religious ORDERs[1] (10)

USAGE A **habit** usually means something done regularly by a single person, and a **custom** usually means something that has been done for a long time by a whole society: *He has an annoying* **habit** *of biting his nails.|the* **custom** *of giving presents at Christmas.* **Practice** is like **custom** but is often *derog: the* **practice** *of eating one's enemies.* The **conventions** of a society are its generally accepted standards of behavior: *As a matter of* **convention**, *people attending funerals wear dark clothes.*

hab·it·a·ble /ˈhæbətəbəl/ adj which can be lived in (INHABITed) –opposite **uninhabitable**

hab·i·tat /ˈhæbəˌtæt/ n the natural home of a plant or animal: *plants in their natural habitat*

hab·i·ta·tion /ˌhæbəˈteʸʃən/ n *fml* [U] the act of living in (INHABITing): *a house unfit for human habitation*

ha·bit·u·al /həˈbɪtʃuʷəl/ adj [A no comp.] **1** usual; customary: *She gave her habitual greeting.* **2** (done) by habit: *He's a habitual smoker; he always has a cigarette after dinner.* –**habitually** adv: *habitually late*

hack[1] /hæk/ v [I;T *at, away*] to cut (up), esp. roughly and in uneven pieces: *He hacked away (at the trees) all night.|They hacked their way through the forest.*

hack[2] n **1** an old tired horse **2** a light horse for riding **3** a writer who does a lot of poor quality work **4** *AmE infml* a taxi

hacking cough /ˌ·· ˈ·/ n a cough with a rough unpleasant sound

hack·neyed /ˈhækniʸd/ adj (of a saying) meaningless because used and repeated too often

hack·saw /ˈhæksɔ/ n a tool (SAW) that has a fine-toothed blade and is used for cutting metal

had /d, əd, həd; *strong* hæd/ v **1** *past tense and* *past participle of* HAVE **2 be had** *infml* to be tricked or made a fool of: *I've been had! The camera I bought doesn't work.*

had·dock /ˈhædək/ n **haddock** *or* **haddocks** [C;U] a common fish found in northern seas, used as food

had·n't /ˈhædnt/ v *short for:* had not: *They hadn't arrived when I got there.*

hag /hæg/ n an ugly or unpleasant woman, esp. one who is old and is thought to be evil

hag·gard /ˈhægərd/ adj having lines on the face and hollow places around the eyes and in the cheeks, as if through tiredness: *a haggard look* –compare GAUNT

hag·gle /ˈhægəl/ v **-gled, -gling** [I *over/about* and/or *with*] to argue over something, esp. over fixing a price: *He haggled for hours over the price of the horse.*

ha-ha /ˌ· ˈ·/ *interj* (a shout of laughter)

hail[1] /heʸl/ n [U] frozen rain drops which fall as little hard balls: (fig.) *a hail of bullets* –see WEATHER (USAGE)

hail[2] v [*it* I] (of HAIL) to fall: *It's hailing.*

hail[3] v [T] to call out to (someone) in greeting or to gain attention: *Because I missed the last bus I hailed a taxi.*

   hail sbdy./sthg. **as** sthg. v prep [T] to recognize as (something good): *They hailed it as a work of art.*

   hail from sthg. v prep [T no pass.] to come from; have as one's home: *She hails from New Orleans.*

hail·stone /ˈheʸlstoʷn/ n a ball of HAIL[1]

hail·storm /ˈheʸlstɔrm/ n a storm when HAIL[1] falls heavily

hair /hɛər/ n **1** [C] a fine threadlike growth from the skin of a person or animal: *The cat has left her loose hairs all over my clothes.* **2** [U] a mass of such growths, such as that on the head of human beings: *My hair has grown very long.* –compare FUR (1) **3 get in someone's hair** *infml* to annoy someone **4 let one's hair down** *infml* to do as one likes; behave wildly, esp. after one has had to be controlled in behavior, as after a formal occasion **5 make someone's hair stand on end** to make someone very afraid; TERRIFY **6 split hairs** *derog* to be too concerned with unimportant differences, esp. in arguments –see also HAIR-SPLITTING **7 -haired** having a certain kind of hair: *long-haired|fair-haired*

hair·brush /ˈhɛərbrʌʃ/ n a brush used for the hair to get out dirt and to make the hair smooth –see illustration on page 51

hair·cut /ˈhɛərkʌt/ n **1** an occasion of having the hair cut **2** the style the hair is cut in

hair·do /ˈhɛərduʷ/ n **-dos** *infml* **1** an occasion

of a woman's having her hair shaped into a style **2** the style a woman's hair is shaped into: *Do you like my new hairdo?*

hair·dress·er /'hɛərˌdrɛsər/ *also* **hair stylist** /'· ˌ··/– *n* a person who shapes the hair into a style by cutting, SETTING[1] (14), etc., or who changes its color –compare BARBER –**hairdressing** *n* [U]

hair·line /'hɛərlaɪn/ *n* **1** the place on the forehead where the hair starts growing **2** a very thin line: *a* **hairline crack** *in the cup*

hair·net /'hɛərnɛt/ *n* a net (worn esp. by women) which stretches over the hair to keep it in place

hair·piece /'hɛərpiʸs/ *n* a piece of false hair used to make one's own hair seem thicker

hair·pin /'hɛərˌpɪn/ *n* a pin made of wire bent into a U-shape to hold the hair in position on the head

hairpin curve /ˌ·· '·/ **hairpin turn** *AmE*‖**hairpin bend** *esp. BrE*– *n* a narrow U-shaped curve where a road turns back, as when going up a steep hill

hair-rais·ing /'· ˌ··/ *adj* that makes one very afraid: *a hair-raising experience*

hairsbreadth /'hɛərzbrɛdθ, -brɛtθ/ *also* **hairbreadth** /'hɛərbrɛdθ, -brɛtθ/– *n* a very short distance: *We missed the other car by a hairsbreadth and narrowly avoided an accident.*

hair-split·ting /'· ˌ··/ *n* [U] too much interest in unimportant differences and points of detail, esp. in argument

hair spray /'· ·/ *n* [C;U] (an AEROSOL containing) liquid which is sprayed onto the hair in a fine mist to hold it in place: *She uses too much hair spray.*|*There's a new hair spray I'd like to try.*

hair·y /'hɛəriʸ/ *adj* **-ier, -iest 1** (when used of people, not usu. describing the hair on the head) having a lot of hair: *hairy legs*|*a hairy chest* **2** *infml* exciting in a way that causes fear, or dangerous: *It was very hairy driving down that narrow road in the darkness.* –**hairiness** *n* [U]

hal·cy·on /'hælsiʸən/ *adj* [A *no comp.*] *lit* calm or peaceful (esp. in the phrase **halcyon days**)

hale /heʸl/ *adj* **hale and hearty** /ˌ· · '··/ very healthy

half[1] /hæf/ *n,pron* **halves** /hævz/ **1** either of two equal parts of something; ½; 50%: *the bottom half of the class*|*the first half of the football game*|*Half of it was broken.*|*Half of them are already here.*|*a pound and a half* (=1½ pounds) *of rice*|*Cut it* **in half.** (=into two halves) –compare WHOLE[2] (1,2) **2** the number ½: *3 halves make 1½.* **3 go halves (in/on something) (with someone)** *infml* to share (the cost of something) (with someone)

half[2] *predeterminer,adj* ½ in amount: *Half the car was damaged.*|*Half the boys are already here.*|*half a minute*|*half a mile*|*a half mile*|*a half smile* (=not quite complete)

half[3] *adv* **1** partly; not completely: *half cooked*|*She's half French and half English.* **2 half and half** /ˌ· · '·/ half of one and half of the other; two equal parts of two things: *"Is it made with milk or water?" "Half and half."* –see also HALF AND HALF **3 not half** not at all: *The food's not half bad.* (=quite good)

half a doz·en /ˌ· · '··/ *also* **(a) half dozen** /ˌ· '··/– *determiner,n* **half dozens** six; a set of six: *half a dozen eggs*|*I'll have two half dozens.* (=two groups of half a dozen) –see also DOZEN

half and half /ˌ· · '·/ *n* [U] a liquid that is half cream and half milk: *Do you like half and half in your coffee?*

half·back /'hæfbæk/ *n* (in games like football) a player or position between the center players and the back players

half-baked /ˌ· '·◂/ *adj* (of ideas) stupid; not sensible

half-broth·er /'· ˌ··/ *n* a brother related through one parent only

half-cocked /ˌ· '·/ *adj* **go off half-cocked** to begin without enough preparation

half-heart·ed /ˌ· '··◂/ *adj* showing little effort and no real interest: *a half-hearted attempt to fix the window* –see also WHOLE-HEARTED –**half-heartedly** *adv* –**half-heartedness** *n* [U]

half-mast /ˌ· '·/ *n* a point near the middle of a flagpole where the flag flies as a sign of sorrow: *All the flags were* **at half-mast** *when President Kennedy died.*

half-sis·ter /'· ˌ··/ *n* a sister related through one parent only

half time /'· ·/ *n* [U] the period of time between two parts of a game, such as a football game

half truth /'· ·/ *n* a statement that is only partly true

half·way /ˌhæf'weʸ◂/ *adj,adv* **1** at the midpoint between two things: *the halfway point between Detroit and Chicago* **2** by a small or incomplete amount: *You can't go halfway when you're painting the walls. Once you've started you have to finish the job.* **3 meet someone halfway** to make an agreement with someone which partly satisfies the demands of both sides: *You want to pay $10 but I want $20. Meet me halfway and make it $15.*

half-wit /'· ·/ *n usu. derog* a person of weak mind –**half-witted** /ˌ· '··◂/ *adj*

hal·i·but /'hæləbət, 'haˌ-/ *n* -**but** *or* -**buts** [C;U] a very large fish used as food

hall /hɔl/ *n* **1** a large room in which meetings, dances, etc., can be held **2** the passage just inside the entrance of a house, from which the rooms open **3** (in a college or university) the room where the members live or eat together: *I live in a* **residence hall.**

hal·le·lu·ja /ˌhælə'luʷyə/ *also* **alleluia**– *interj,n* (a song, cry, etc., that is an expression of) praise, joy, and thanks to God

hall·mark[1] /'hɔlmɑrk/ *n* the mark made on objects of precious metal to prove that they are silver or gold: (fig.) *Clear expression is the hallmark of a good writer.* (=the sign which shows that the writer is good)

hallmark[2] *v* [T] to make a HALLMARK[1] on (something)

hal·lo /hə'loʷ, hɛ-, hæ-/ *interj, n* -**los** *BrE for* HELLO

hal·low /'hæloʷ/ *v* [T *usu. pass.*] to make

holy: (fig.) *the hallowed memories of great people*

Hal·low·een, -e'en /ˌhælə'wiᵛn, ˌhɑ-/ *n* the night of October 31, when children play tricks and dress up in strange clothes

hal·lu·ci·nate /hə'luᵂsə͵neᵛt/ *v* **-nated, -nating** [I] to see things which are not there: *Some drugs cause people to hallucinate.*

hal·lu·ci·na·tion /hə͵luᵂsə'neᵛʃən/ *n* [C;U] (the experience of seeing) something that is imagined although it is not really there, often as the result of a drug or mental illness

hall·way /'hɔlweᵛ/ *n esp. AmE* for HALL (2)

ha·lo /'heᵛloᵂ/ *n* **-loes** *or* **-los** a golden circle representing light around the heads of holy people in religious paintings

halt¹ /hɔlt/ *v* [I;T] *fml* to (cause to) stop: *The train was halted by work on the line ahead.*

halt² *n* [S] a stop or pause: *The car came to a halt just in time to prevent an accident.*

hal·ter /'hɔltər/ *n* **1** a rope or leather band fastened around a horse's head, esp. to lead it **2** *also* **halter top** /'·· ͵·/, **halter neck–** a garment that leaves the wearer's back uncovered and is held in place by a narrow band of material passed around the neck

halt·ing /'hɔltɪŋ/ *adj* stopping and starting as if uncertain: *a halting voice* **–haltingly** *adv*

halve /hæv/ *v* **halved, halving** [T] **1** to divide into halves: *Let's halve the work between the two of us.* **2** to reduce to half

halves /hævz/ *n pl. of* HALF

ham /hæm/ *n* **1** [C;U] preserved meat from the upper part of a pig's leg **2** [C] *infml* an actor, performer, speaker, etc., whose performance is unnatural **3** a person who receives and/or sends radio messages using his/her own apparatus

ham·burg·er /'hæm͵bɜrgər/ *n* a flat circular cake of very small pieces of meat, esp. eaten in a ROLL¹ (2) of bread

ham·let /'hæmlɪt/ *n* a small village

ham·mer¹ /'hæmər/ **1** a tool with a heavy head used esp. for driving nails into wood **2** something made to hit something else, as in a piano, or part of a gun **3 be/go at it hammer and tongs** (of two people) to fight or argue violently

hammer² *v* **1** [I;T] to strike (something) with a hammer: *Hammer the nails in.*|(fig.) *The police hammered* (=knocked hard) *at the door.* **2** [T] *infml* to conquer (someone) by fighting, or in a game: *We hammered the other team.*

hammer sthg.↔ **out** *v adv* [T] to talk about in detail and come to a decision about: *The government tried to hammer out an agreement with the workers.*

ham·mock /'hæmək/ *n* a long piece of sailcloth (CANVAS) or net which can be hung up by the ends to form a bed

ham·per¹ /'hæmpər/ *v* [T] to cause difficulty in movement or activity: *The snow hampered my movements.*

hamper² *n* **1** a large basket with a lid, often used for carrying food **2** *AmE* a large basket with a lid, in which dirty clothing, sheets, TOWELs, etc., are put ready for washing –see illustration on page 51

ham·ster /'hæmstər/ *n* a small animal with pockets (POUCHES) in its cheeks for storing food, kept as a pet

ham·string¹ /'hæm͵strɪŋ/ *n* a cordlike TENDON at the back of the leg, joining a muscle to a bone

hamstring² *v* **-strung** /strʌŋ/, **-stringing** [T] to cut the HAMSTRING of, destroying the ability to walk: (fig.) *Congress is trying to hamstring the President in this matter by refusing to approve the money he needs.*

hand¹ /hænd/ *n* **1** [C;U] the movable parts at the end of the human arm, including the fingers: *She had a book in her hand.*|*I can't carry that bag; my hands are full.* (=I'm holding things in both hands)|*I can't come today; I've* **got my hands full.** (=I'm very busy)|*It was written* **by hand.** (=not printed) **2** [C] a pointer or needle on a clock or machine: *The minute hand is bigger than the hour hand.* **3** [C] a set of playing cards held by one person in a game **4** [C] a worker who uses his/her hands, esp. a sailor: *All hands on* DECK! (=a call for all sailors to come up to deal with some trouble)|*a factory hand*|*She's* **a good hand at** *making bread.*|(fig.) *I'm* **an old hand** (=an experienced person) *at this game; you can't trick me.* **5** [S] encouragement or approval given to a performer by striking the hands together; APPLAUSE: *They gave the singer* **a big hand.** –compare CLAP² (2) **6** [S] help: *Could you* **give/lend** *me* **a hand** *to move this box, please?* **7** [U] control: *The meeting is* **getting out of hand.** *Can we have just one speaker at a time.*|*Don't worry; I have the matter* **well in hand.** (=I'm dealing with it) **8 at hand a** *fml* near in time or place: *Election day is at hand.* **b** within reach: *I don't have my telephone book at hand so I'll have to check later.* **9 at second/third/fourth hand** as information passed on through one, two, or three people –see also FIRSTHAND, SECOND- HAND **10 change hands** to go from the possession of one person to that of another: *The car had changed hands five times* (=had six owners) *before I bought it.* **11 first hand** by direct experience of oneself or another person: *I found out about it first hand from my neighbor.* (=he saw it happen) **12 get/keep one's hand in** to become/stay used to an activity by practicing **13 get the upper hand (of)** to get control or power (over something/somebody difficult) **14 give somebody a free hand** to allow somebody to do things in his/her own way **15 hand in hand: a** holding each other's hand: *They walked down the street hand in hand.* **b** always happening together: *Dirt and disease go hand in hand.* **16 have a hand in** to share (an activity); be partly responsible for: *I had a hand in arranging the party.* **17 on hand** ready for use or to take part **18 on the one/other hand** (used for comparing different things or ideas) as one point in the argument/as an opposite point: *On the one hand this job doesn't pay very much, but on the other (hand) I can't get another one.* **19 play into (someone's) hands** to do something which gives (one's opponent) an advantage

20 turn one's hand to to begin to practice (a skill) **21 wait on (somebody) hand and foot** to do everything for somebody, as if they were unable to look after themselves **22 -handed** having or using a certain kind of hand or hands: *right-handed|heavy-handed|a one-handed throw* –see also HANDS

hand² *v* [T] **1** to give from one's own hand into that of (someone else): *Hand me that book, please.|She handed the book back to him.|Please hand the sweets round.* (=offer them to everyone) **2 (have to) hand it to (someone)** to (have to) admit the high quality or success of (someone): *You have to hand it to her, she's a good talker.*

hand sthg.↔ **down/on** also **pass** sthg.↔ **down/on** *v adv* [T] **1** to give or leave to people who are younger or come later: *This ring has been handed down from my grandmother.* **2** *AmE* to make a public statement about: *The directors will hand down their decision tomorrow.*

hand sthg.↔ **in** *v adv* [T] to deliver; give by hand: *Please hand in your books to me at the end of the lesson.*

hand sthg.↔ **on** *v adv* [T] to give from one person to another (esp. something which can be used by many people one after the other): *Please read this notice and hand it on.*

hand sthg.↔ **out** *v adv* [T *to*] to give, esp. one of (a set of things) to each member of a group of people: *Hand out the pencils.* –see also HANDOUT

hand sbdy./sthg.↔ **over** *v adv* [T *to*] to give into someone else's care, control, etc.: *The thief was handed over to the police.|Hand over your money, or I'll shoot.*

hand·bag /'hændbæg, 'hæn-/ ‖also **purse, pocketbook** *AmE*– *n* a small bag for a person, usu. a woman, to carry money and personal things in

hand·bill /'hænd,bɪl, 'hæn-/ ‖also **flier, flyer** *AmE*– *n* a small printed notice or advertisement to be given out by hand

hand·book /'hændbʊk, 'hæn-/ *n* a short book giving all the most important information about a subject –compare MANUAL

hand·cuff /'hændkʌf, 'hæn-/ *v* [T] to put HANDCUFFS on

hand·cuffs /'hændkʌfs, 'hæn-/ *n* [P] metal rings joined together, for fastening the wrists of a criminal –see PAIR (USAGE)

hand·ful /'hændfʊl, 'hæn-/ *n* **1** an amount which is as much as can be held in the hand: *I picked up a handful of letters and began to open them.* **2** a small number (of people): *We invited thirty people, but only a handful of them came.* **3** a living thing which is so active that it is difficult to control: *That child is quite a handful.*

hand·gun /'hændgʌn, 'hæn-/ *n esp. AmE* a small gun held in one hand while firing, not raised against the shoulder; PISTOL

hand·i·cap¹ /'hændiʸkæp/ *n* **1** a disability or disadvantage: *Blindness is a great handicap.|Being small is a handicap in a crowd like this.* **2** (in a race or other sport) a disadvantage given to the stronger competitors, such

as carrying more weight or running further than others

handicap² *v* **-pp-** [T] **1** to cause (someone) to have a disadvantage: *Lack of money handicapped him badly.* **2** [*usu. pass.*] (of a disability of mind or body) to prevent (someone) from acting or living normally: *He is handicapped by bad eyesight.|physically handicapped*

hand·i·craft /'hændiʸkræft/ *n* [*usu. pl.*] a skill needing careful use of the hands, such as sewing, weaving, etc.

hand·i·work /'hændiʸwɜrk/ *n* [U] **1** work demanding the skillful use of the hands **2** action, usu. showing some sign of the person who has done it: *Nature is God's handiwork.*

hand·ker·chief /'hæŋkərtʃɪf, -,tʃiʸf/ *n* **-chiefs** a piece of cloth for drying the nose, eyes, etc.

han·dle¹ /'hændl/ *n* **1** a part of an object which is specially made for holding it or for opening it –see illustration on page 95 **2 fly off the handle** *infml* to lose one's temper

handle² *v* **-dled, -dling** [T] **1 a** to feel in the hands **b** to move by hand: *Glass–handle with care.* **2** to deal with; control: *He handled a difficult argument skillfully.|Ms. Brown handles the company's accounts.|A good teacher must know how to handle children.* **3** to use (goods) in business; DEAL **in**: *We don't handle that sort of book.* **–handleable** *adj*

han·dle·bars /'hændl,bɑrz/ *n* [P] the bar above the front wheel of a bicycle or motorcycle, which controls the direction it goes in

han·dler /'hændlər/ *n* a person who controls an animal

hand lug·gage /'· ,··/ *n* [U] a traveler's light or small bags, cases, etc., which can be carried by hand

hand·made /,hænd'meʸd◀, ,hæn-/ *adj* made by hand, not by machine

hand-me-down /'·· ,·/ *n AmE infml* a garment used by one person after belonging to another: *wearing my brother's hand-me-downs*

hand·out /'hændaʊt/ *n* **1** something given free, such as food, clothes, etc., esp. to someone poor **2** information given out, esp. a printed sheet: *Please read the handout carefully.* –see also HAND² **out**

hand·picked /,hænd'pɪkt, ,hæn-/ *adj* chosen with great care

hands /hændz/ *n* [P] possession: *A valuable book has come into my hands.|I know the child's in good hands* (=being well cared for) *when she's with her aunt.|I've been trying to lay my hands on* (=get possession of) *a good cheap bicycle.|Now the children are off my hands* (=I am no longer responsible for them) *I have a lot of free time.* –see also HAND

hand·shake /'hændʃeʸk, 'hæn-/ *n* an act of taking each other's right hand when two people meet or leave each other

hand·some /'hænsəm/ *adj* **1** (esp. of men) good-looking; of attractive appearance –see BEAUTIFUL (USAGE) **2** generous; plentiful: *a handsome reward* **–handsomely** *adv*

hand·stand /'hændstænd, 'hæn-/ *n* a movement in which the legs are kicked into the air so that the body is upside down and supported on the hands

hand-to-mouth /ˌ··ˈ·◂/ *adj,adv* (of a way of life) spending one's money as soon as it comes in

hand·writ·ing /ˈhændˌraɪtɪŋ/ *n* [U] (a particular person's style of) writing done by hand: *She has very clear handwriting.*

hand·y /ˈhændiʸ/ *adj* **-ier, -iest 1** useful and simple to use: *This is a handy little tool.|A few more traveler's checks may* **come in handy** (=may be useful) *on our vacation.* **2** clever in using the hands: *handy with a needle* **3** *infml* near; **at** HAND (9): *The stores are quite handy.* –**handily** *adv*

hand·y·man /ˈhændiʸˌmæn/ *n* **-men** /ˌmɛn/ a person who does repairs and practical jobs well, esp. in the house

hang¹ /hæŋ/ *v* **hung** /hʌŋ/, **hanging 1** [I;T] to fix or be fixed at the top so that the lower part is free: *to hang curtains |Hang your coat (up) in the closet.|The curtains hang well.* **2** [T] to fix (wallpaper) on a wall: *Her paintings were hung in the living room.*

  hang around *v adv;prep infml* **1** [I;T (=**hang around** sthg.)] esp. *AmE*||**hang about** *BrE*– to wait or stay near (a place) without purpose or activity: *I hung around (the station) for an hour but he didn't come.* **2** [I] *AmE*||**hang about** *BrE*– to delay or move slowly; DAWDLE: *Don't hang around. We have a train to catch!*

  hang back *v adv* [I] to be unwilling to act or move: *The bridge looked so unsafe that we all hung back in fear.*

  hang on *v adv* [I] *infml* **1** [*to*] to keep hold of; keep possession of: *Hang on (to the* STRAP). *The bus is starting.* **2** to wait: *Hang on a minute: I'm coming.|I'm afraid the line (=telephone line) is busy, would you like to hang on?* –compare HANG **up** (1) **3** to keep doing something: *You must be tired, but try to hang on till all the work's finished.*

  hang onto sthg. also **hold onto** sthg.– *v prep* [T] to try to keep: *We should hang onto the house until prices are higher.*

  hang out *v adv* [I *with*] to live or spend much time in a place or with someone: *He hangs out in the local bar/with his friends from school.* –see also HANGOUT

  hang up *v adv* [I] **1** to finish a telephone conversation by putting the RECEIVER back: *I was so angry I hung up on her.* (=while she was talking) –compare HANG **on** (2); see TELEPHONE (USAGE) **2 be hung up on/about** *infml* to be anxious or have a fixed idea about –see also HANGUP

hang² *v* **hanged** /hæŋd/, **hanging** [I;T] to (cause to) die, esp. in punishment for a crime, by dropping with a rope around the neck: *He was hanged for murder.*

hang³ *n* **get/have the hang of something** *infml* to develop the skill of doing something, or an understanding of how something works: *Press this button when the light goes on. You'll soon get the hang of it.*

hang·ar /ˈhæŋər, ˈhæŋgər/ *n* a big building where planes are kept

hang·er /ˈhæŋər/ also **coat hanger, clothes hanger** – *n* a hook and crosspiece to fit inside

the shoulders of a dress, coat, etc., to keep the shape of the garment when it is hung up

hanger-on /ˌ··ˈ·/ *n* **hangers-on** *usu. derog* a person who tries to be friendly with another person or group, esp. for his/her own advantage

hang glid·ing /ˈ· ˌ··/ *n* [U] the sport of GLIDING using a large KITE (2) instead of a plane

hang·ing /ˈhæŋɪŋ/ *n* [C;U] death by hanging (HANG²): *Are you in favor of hanging?*

hang·man /ˈhæŋmən/ *n* **-men** /mən/ the person whose work is hanging criminals

hang·out /ˈhæŋaʊt/ *n infml* a place where one lives or is often to be seen: *Their hangout is the bar around the corner.* –see also HANG **out**

hang·o·ver /ˈhæŋˌoʷvər/ *n* **1** the feeling of headache, sickness, etc., the day after drinking too much alcohol **2** a condition or effect resulting from an earlier event or state: *His cough is a hangover from a bad illness he had.*

hang-up /ˈhæŋʌp/ *n infml* something which a person gets unusually worried about, finds very difficult, etc.: *One of his hangups is that he's afraid to fly alone.* –see also HANG **up** (2)

han·ker for sthg. /ˈhæŋkər/ also **hanker after** sthg.– *v prep* [T] *infml* to have a strong wish for (usu. something one cannot have); LONG for: *He's lonely and hankers after friendship.* –**hankering** *n* [*for*]: *a hankering for something sweet to eat*

han·kie, -ky /ˈhæŋkiʸ/ *n* **-kies** *infml* a handkerchief

han·ky-pan·ky /ˌhæŋkiʸ ˈpæŋkiʸ/ *n* [U] *infml* deceit or improper behavior of a not very serious kind

Ha·nuk·kah, Chanukkah /ˈhɑnəkə, ˈxɑ-/ *n* an eight-day Jewish holiday marking an ancient victory in Israel

hap·haz·ard /ˌhæpˈhæzərd/ *adj* happening in an unplanned disorderly manner: *It's a very haphazard system. It doesn't always work properly.* –**haphazardly** *adv*

hap·pen /ˈhæpən/ *v* **1** [I *to*] to take place: *A funny thing happened yesterday.|Did you hear what happened to Peter last night?* **2** [I +*to-v*; not *be*+*v-ing*] to have the good or bad luck (to): *I happened to see him yesterday.* **3** [*it*+I+*that*; not *be*+*v-ing*] to be true by or as if by chance (note the phrases as **it happens/happened**): *It (so) happened that I saw him yesterday.* (=I saw him yesterday, as it happens)

USAGE People or things **become** something, in the meaning of passing from one state to another: *Douglas* **became** *an engineer* (not *became engineer).|The horse* **became/got** *thirsty.|This idea is* **becoming/getting** *fashionable.* Events **happen** (usually by accident) or **take place** (usually by arrangement): *When did the explosion* **happen**?| *When will the wedding* **take place**?

  happen on/upon sbdy./sthg. also **chance (up)on** sbdy./sthg.– *v prep* [T *no pass.*] to find or meet by chance: *I happened on an old country hotel and stopped to have a meal.*

hap·pen·ing /ˈhæpənɪŋ/ *n* something which happens; event

hap·pi·ly /ˈhæpəliʸ/ *adv* **1** in a happy manner:

laughing happily **2** fortunately: *Happily, the accident was prevented.*

hap·pi·ness /'hæpiʸnɪs/ *n* [U] the state of being happy

hap·py /'hæpiʸ/ *adj* **-pier, -piest 1** feeling/giving pleasure and contentment: *a happy child/marriage* –opposite **unhappy 2** (of behavior, thoughts, etc.) suitable: *That was not a very happy remark.* **3** [F+*to-v*/*that;. no comp.*] *polite* pleased; not finding it difficult (to): *I'll be happy to meet him when I have time.* **4** [A] (of wishes) joyful: **Happy New Year|Happy Birthday**

happy-go-luck·y /ˌ··· '··◄/ *adj usu.* not *derog* (of people or their acts) showing a lack of careful thought or planning; CAREFREE

ha·rangue /həˈræŋ/ *v,n* **-rangued, -ranguing** [C;T] (to attack or try to persuade with) a long often loud and scolding speech

ha·rass /həˈræs, ˈhærəs/ *v* [T] to make (somebody) worried by causing trouble, esp. on repeated occasions: *I felt harassed by all the work at the office.* –**harassment** *n* [U]

har·bor¹ *AmE*‖**harbour** *BrE* /ˈhɑrbər/ *n* [C;U] an area of water which is sheltered from rough waters, esp. the sea, so that ships are safe inside it

harbor² *AmE*‖**harbour** *BrE* *v* [T] to give protection and shelter, usu. to something/someone bad: *Harboring criminals is an offense under the law.*|(fig.) *He harbors* (=keeps in his mind) *a secret wish to be a singer.*

hard¹ /hɑrd/ *adj* **1** firm and stiff; not easily broken or bent: *hard rock|hard skin|The snow has frozen hard.* –opposite **soft 2** [+*to-v*] difficult (to do or understand): *This question is too hard; I can't answer it.*|*It's hard to know what he's really thinking.* –opposite **easy 3** needing or using force of body or mind: *Give it a hard push, then it will move.*|*She doesn't mind hard work; she's a hard worker.*|*We must take a long hard look at this plan.* (=examine it very carefully) **4** full of difficulty and trouble; not pleasant: *a hard life|It's been a hard winter.* (=very cold and snowy)|*The police gave him a hard time.* (=hurt him physically and/or mentally) **5** [*on*] showing no kindness; severe: *Don't be too hard on him; he didn't mean to do it.*|*He takes a hard line on the question of punishing young criminals.* –see also HARDLINE **6** (of water) containing lime, that prevents soap from mixing properly with the water **7** [A *no comp.*] (of a drug) being one on which a user can become dependent (ADDICTED) in such a way that he/she is ill without it **8** [*no comp.*] (in English pronunciation): **a** (of the letter *c*) pronounced as /k/ rather than /s/ **b** (of the letter *g*) pronounced as /g/ rather than /dʒ/: *The letter "g" is hard in "get" and soft in "gentle."* –opposite **soft** (for 1,6,7,8); see also HARD UP; see HARDEN (USAGE) –**hardness** *n* [U]

hard² *adv* **1** with great effort: *Push hard!|She's working hard.|I had to think long and hard before I could find the answer.* **2** in large amounts; heavily: *It's raining harder than ever.* **3 be hard hit (by)** to suffer loss because of (some event): *The farmers were hard hit by the bad weather.* **4 be hard put (to it) to (do something)** to have great difficulty (in doing something) **5 hard at it** *infml* working with great effort: *She's hard at it preparing for her examinations.* **6 take (it) hard** to suffer deeply: *She failed her examination, and she's taking it very hard.*

hard-and-fast /ˌ· · · '··◄/ *adj* [A] (of rules) fixed and unchangeable

hard·back /ˈhɑrdbæk/ *n* also **hardcover** /ˈ· ˌ··/– a book with a strong stiff cover (BINDING): *a hardback/a hardback book* –compare PAPERBACK

hard-boiled /ˌ· '·◄/ *adj* **1** (of eggs) boiled until the yellow part is hard –see also SOFT-BOILED **2** (of people) not showing feeling, esp. when made bitter through bad experience

hard cash /ˌ· '·/ *n* [U] coins and bills, not a check: *We wanted to give him a check, but he demanded hard cash.*

hard-core /ˌ· '·◄/ *adj* [A *no comp.*] often *derog* refusing to change, yield, or improve: *hard-core opposition to the government's plans*

hard core /ˌ· '·/ *n* [U] often *derog* the people most concerned at the center of an activity, esp. when opposed to some other group: *There is a hard core in the party which makes all the decisions.*

hard drink /ˌ· '·/ *n* [C;U] (a) drink which contains alcohol: *They served hard drinks at the party.*|*He likes hard drink.*

hard·en /ˈhɑrdn/ *v* [I;T] to (cause to) become hard or firm: *The snow hardened until ice was formed.*|*My hands hardened when I was working on the farm.*|(fig.) *Don't harden your heart against* (=don't be hard and unkind toward) *him.*|(fig.) *He became hardened to pain.* –compare SOFTEN

USAGE **Harden** means "to make or become hard," but should only be used when hard means "firm and stiff" or "unkind and severe." Otherwise, use **get harder.** Compare: *Leave the jelly in a cool place to* **harden.** (=become firm)|*to* **harden** *one's heart* (=show unkindness), and *The exercises in this book gradually* **get harder.** (=become more difficult)|*Life seems to be* **getting harder** (=becoming more troublesome) *for everyone.*

harden sbdy. **to** sthg. *v prep* [T +*v-ing; usu. pass.*] to make (someone) less sensitive to (something or doing something): *I'm quite hardened to the cold weather here now.*

hard·head·ed /ˌhɑrdˈhɛdɪd◄/ *adj* tough and practical: *a hardheaded businesswoman*

hard-heart·ed /ˌ· '··◄/ *adj* having no kind feelings; HARD¹ (5) –opposite **soft-hearted** –**hard-heartedly** *adv* –**hard-heartedness** *n* [U]

hard·line /ˌhɑrdˈlaɪn◄/ *adj infml* unwilling to move from a fixed, usu. strict, position; UNCOMPROMISING: *hardline supporters of the government's policies* –see also HARD (5) –**hardliner** *n*

hard luck /ˌ· '·/ also **tough luck**‖also **hard lines** *BrE*– *interj,n* [U] *infml* (sorry about your) bad luck: *You failed your examination? Hard luck!*

hard·ly /'hɑrdliʸ/ *adv* **1** almost not: *I could hardly wait to hear the news.*|*I was so angry that I could hardly speak.*|**I hardly ever** (=almost never) *go out these days.* **2** only just: *I hardly know the people I work with.*|*Hardly had we started our journey* (=we had only just started) *when the car got a flat tire.*|*We'd hardly arrived before we had to go back.* **3** not at all; not reasonably: *I can hardly ask him directly for more money.*|*This is hardly the time for buying new clothes–I've only got just enough money for food.*

USAGE Compare **hardly, scarcely, barely,** and **no sooner: 1** Hardly, scarcely, and barely are followed by *when*, but **no sooner** is followed by *than*, in sentences like these: *The game had* **hardly/scarcely/barely** *begun when it started raining.*|*The game had* **no sooner** *begun than it started raining.* **2** The word order in all these sentences can be changed like this: **Hardly/barely/scarcely** *had the game begun when it started raining.*| **No sooner** *had the game begun than it started raining.* **3 Hardly, scarcely,** and (less commonly) **barely** can be followed by *any, ever,* and *at all,* to mean "almost no," "almost never," and "almost not:" *We've* **hardly/scarcely/barely** *any money left.*|*He's* **hardly/scarcely** *ever late for work.*

hard of hear·ing /,· · '··/ *adj* [F] *euph* unable to hear properly; (rather) DEAF

hard·ship /'hɑrd,ʃɪp/ *n* [C;U] (an example of) difficult conditions of life, such as lack of money, food, etc.

hard up /,· '·◄/ *adj* [F *for*] in need (of); not having enough esp. money: *We were very hard up when I lost my job.*|*The company is hard up for new ideas.*

hard·ware /'hɑrdwɛər/ *n* [U] **1** goods for the home and garden, such as pans, tools, etc.: *a hardware store* **2** machinery which makes up a computer –compare SOFTWARE

hard·wood /'hɑrdwʊd/ *n* [U] strong heavy wood from trees like the OAK, used to make good furniture –opposite **softwood**

har·dy /'hɑrdiʸ/ *adj* **-dier, -diest 1** (of people or animals) strong; able to bear cold, hard work, etc. **2** *tech* (of plants) able to live through the winter above ground –**hardiness** *n* [U]

hare /hɛər/ *n* **hares** *or* **hare** an animal rather like a rabbit, but usu. larger, with long ears, a short tail, and long back legs which make it able to run fast –sounds like **hair**

hare·brained /'hɛərbreʸnd/ *adj* (of people or plans) very impractical; quite foolish

hare·lip /'hɛər,lɪp/ *n* the top lip divided into two parts, because of its not developing properly before birth –**harelipped** /'hɛər,lɪpt/ *adj*

har·em /'hɛərəm, 'hærəm/ *n* **1** the place in a Muslim house where the women live **2** the women who live in this place

hark back /hɑrk/ *v adv* [I *to*] *infml* to mention things which happened in the past: *You're always harking back to how things were when you were young.*

har·lot /'hɑrlət/ *n old use* for PROSTITUTE

harm¹ /hɑrm/ *n* [U] **1** damage; wrong: *He means no harm* (=doesn't intend to do anything hurtful) *by saying what he thinks.*|*It wouldn't do him any harm* (=it would be good for him) *to work a little harder.*|*The ship was caught in a bad storm, but it* **came to no harm.** (=it wasn't harmed)|*She spilled wine on the carpet, but there was no harm done.* (=nothing was spoiled) –compare GOOD² (2) **2 out of harm's way** out of danger; safe from danger –**harmful** /'hɑrmfəl/ *adj* –**harmfully** *adv* –**harmfulness** *n* [U]

harm² *v* [T] to hurt; spoil; damage: *There was a fire in our street, but our house wasn't harmed at all.*|*She wouldn't harm a fly.* (=She's very gentle by nature)

harm·less /'hɑrmlɪs/ *adj* that cannot cause harm: *The dog seems fierce, but he's harmless.*|*a harmless question* –**harmlessly** *adv* –**harmlessness** *n* [U]

har·mon·i·ca /hɑr'mɑnɪkə/ *also* **mouth organ–** *n* a type of small musical instrument played by being held in the mouth, passed backward and forward across the lips, and blown into or sucked through

har·mo·nize ‖*also* **-nise** *BrE* /'hɑrmə,naɪz/ *v* **-nized, -nizing** [I;T] **1** to sing or play (a piece of music) in HARMONY (1) **2** [*with*] (to cause to) be in agreement, esp. in style, color, etc., with each other or something else

har·mo·ny /'hɑrməniʸ/ *n* **-nies 1** [C;U] notes of music combined together in a pleasant sounding way **2** [U] a state of agreement (in feelings, ideas, etc.); peacefulness: *My cat and dog never fight–they live together* **in perfect harmony.** –compare DISCORD –**harmonious** /hɑr'mowniʸəs/ *adj* –**harmoniously** *adv*

har·ness¹ /'hɑrnɪs/ *n* [C *usu. sing.*; U] the bands which are used to control a horse or fasten it to a cart, or to support a baby

harness² *v* [T] **1** [*to*] to put a HARNESS¹ on (esp. a horse) and/or fasten to a vehicle such as a cart **2** to use a natural force to produce useful power: *River water is harnessed to produce electricity.*

harp /hɑrp/ *n* a large musical instrument with strings running from top to bottom of an open three-cornered frame, played by stroking (STROKE) or PICKing¹ (6) the strings with the hands –**harpist** *n*

harp on sthg. *also* **harp on about** sthg.– *v prep;adv derog* [T] to talk a lot about (one's misfortunes): *My grandfather still harps on (about) the death of his youngest son.*

har·poon /hɑr'puʷn/ *n,v* [T] (to strike with) a spear with a long rope, which is used for hunting large sea animals, esp. WHALEs

harp·si·chord /'hɑrpsɪ,kɔrd/ *n* a musical instrument used, esp. formerly, like a piano except that the strings are PICKed¹ (6) rather than struck

har·row·ing /'hæroʷɪŋ/ *adj* which causes feelings of pain and worry: *To see someone killed is a very harrowing experience.*

harsh /hɑrʃ/ *adj* **1** unpleasant in causing pain to the senses: *a harsh light* (=too strong for the eyes)|*harsh colors*|*a harsh voice* –opposite SOFT **2** (of people, punishments, etc.) showing cruelty or lack of kindness –**harshly** *adv* –**harshness** *n* [U]

har·vest¹ /'harvɪst/ *n* **1** the act of gathering the crops: *We all helped with the harvest.* **2** the time of year when crops are picked **3** the (amount of) crops gathered: *a good harvest|a large harvest*

harvest² *v* [T] to gather (a crop) –compare REAP

has /s, z, əz, həz; *strong* hæz/ *v 3rd pers. sing. present tense of* HAVE

has-been /'· ·/ *n infml* a person or thing no longer important, useful, etc.

hash /hæʃ/ *n* **1** [C;U] a meal containing meat cut up in small pieces, esp. when re-cooked **2** [S] a mixed-up affair; MESS or MUDDLE (esp. in the phrase **make a hash of it**) **3** [U] *infml* for HASHISH

hash·ish /'hæʃiːʃ, hæ'ʃiːʃ/ also **hash** *infml*– *n* [U] a drug made from the hardened juice of the CANNABIS plant

has·n't /'hæzənt/ *v short for* has not: *Hasn't he finished yet?*

hasp /hæsp/ *n* a metal fastener for a box, door, etc., which usu. fits over a hook and is kept in place by a PADLOCK

has·sle¹ /'hæsəl/ *n infml esp. AmE* **1** a difficult argument **2** a struggle of mind or body: *It's a real hassle to get this child to eat.*

hassle² *v* **-sled, -sling** [I;T] *infml esp. AmE* to cause trouble or difficulties (for)

haste /heɪst/ *n* [U] (too) quick movement or action: *In his haste, he forgot to put on his coat.*

has·ten /'heɪsən/ *v* **1** [I;T] to (cause to) move or happen faster: *She hastened home.* **2** [I +to-v] to be quick (to say), because the hearer may imagine something else has happened: *He told her about the accident, but hastened to add that her son was not seriously hurt.*

hast·y /'heɪstiː/ *adj* **-ier, -iest** done in a hurry: *a hasty meal* (=made/eaten in a hurry) **2** too quick in acting or deciding, esp. with a bad result: *His hasty decision was a bad mistake.* –**hastily** *adv* –**hastiness** *n* [U]

hat /hæt/ *n* **1** a covering placed on top of the head –compare CAP, BONNET **2** **at the drop of a hat** suddenly **3** **old hat** /,·'·/ old-fashioned **4** **pass the hat around** to collect money, esp. to give to someone who deserves it **5** **take one's hat off to (someone)** to show that one admires (someone) for an action: *I take my hat off to him for the way he arranged the party.* **6** **talking through one's hat** *infml* saying something stupid **7** **hat in hand** humbly **8** **I'll eat my hat** (an expression of disbelief): *If they win tomorrow, I'll eat my hat.* **9** **keep (something) under one's hat** to keep (something) secret

hatch¹ /hætʃ/ *v* **1** [I;T *out*] **a** (of an egg) to break, letting the young bird out: *Three eggs have already hatched.* **b** to cause (an egg) to break in this way: *We hatch the eggs by keeping them in a warm place.* **2** [I *out*] (of a young bird) to break through an egg: *Three chickens have hatched (out).* **3** [T] to make (a plan or idea): *They hatched a plan to murder the king.*

hatch² *n* (the cover used to close) an opening on a ship or aircraft through which people and things can pass

hatch·back /'hætʃbæk/ *n* a car having a door at the back which opens upwards –see illustration on page 95

hatch·et /'hætʃɪt/ *n* a small ax with a short handle

hate¹ /heɪt/ *n* [U] a strong feeling of dislike: *She looked at me with hate in her eyes.* –opposite **love**

hate² *v* **hated, hating** [T +*to-v/v-ing*] **1** to have a great dislike of: *I hate violence.|The two enemies hated each other.* –opposite **love** **2** *infml* to dislike: *He hates people asking him for money.|I hate (having) to tell you, but I've damaged your car.*

hate·ful /'heɪtfəl/ *adj* very unpleasant to experience: *Ironing shirts is a hateful job.* –**hatefully** *adv*

ha·tred /'heɪtrɪd/ *n* [S;U *of, for*] the state or feeling of hating; hate: *She is full of hatred for the driver who killed her dog.* –opposite **love**

hat·ter /'hætər/ *n* a maker and/or seller of hats (esp. in the phrase **as mad as a hatter** (=completely mad))

haugh·ty /'hɔtiː/ *adj* **-tier, -tiest** *fml derog* (of people or their acts) appearing proud; showing that one thinks other people less important than oneself –**haughtily** *adv* –**haughtiness** *n* [U]

haul¹ /hɔl/ *v* **1** [I;T *away, on, up*] to pull hard: *to haul the logs along the ground|to haul up the fishing nets|They hauled away on the ropes.* **2** [T *up*] to force to appear: *The police have hauled Jane (up) before the court for drunk driving.*

haul² *n* **1** [S] the act of hauling or the distance HAULed: (fig.) *It was a long haul home, carrying our bags up the hill.* **2** [C] **a** the amount of fish caught when fishing with a net **b** *infml* the amount of something gained, esp. stolen goods

haul·age /'hɔlɪdʒ/ *n* [U] (the charge for) the business of carrying goods by road

haunch /hɔntʃ, hɑntʃ/ *n* [usu. pl.] the fleshy part of the body between the waist and knee

haunt¹ /hɔnt, hɑnt/ *v* [T] **1** (esp. of a dead person) to visit, usu. appearing in a strange form: *A headless man haunts the castle.* **2** [not *be +v-ing*] to visit (a place) regularly **3** [not *be +v-ing; usu. pass.*] to be always in the thoughts of (someone): *I was haunted by his last words to me.*

haunt² *n* a place where someone goes regularly: *This bar is one of my favorite haunts.*

haunt·ing /'hɔntɪŋ, 'hɑn-/ *adj* remaining in the thoughts: *a haunting memory* –**hauntingly** *adv*

have¹ /v, əv, həv; *strong* hæv/ *v*

present tense

singular	plural
I **have**, I**'ve**	We **have**, we**'ve**
You **have**, you**'ve**	You **have**, you**'ve**
He/She/It **has**, he**'s**/she**'s**/it**'s**	They **have**, they**'ve**

past tense
singular   plural

I **had**, I'**d**   We **had**, we'**d**
You **had**, you'**d**   You **had**, you'**d**
He/She/It **had**   They **had**, they'**d**
he'**d**/she'**d**/it'**d**

PAST PARTICIPLE   **had**

PRESENT PARTICIPLE   **having**

NEGATIVE short forms   **haven't, hasn't
                                  hadn't**

For the pronunciation of these forms look them up in the dictionary at their own place. [I] (used as a helping verb with another verb) **1** (used with the past participle to form the perfect tenses of verbs): *I've/I have written a letter.|He's/He has gone to Detroit.|Have you finished?|She said she'd been/had been there before.* **2** [+*to-v*] also **have got to**– to be forced to; must: *Do you have to go now?| I'll have to telephone later.* –see GOTTA (USAGE) –see Study Notes on page 434 **3 have had it** *infml* to have experienced, worked, or suffered all one can: *I'm afraid this car's finally had it.|The friendship is over; I've had it with her behavior.|She's had it–let her rest.*

USAGE 1 Compare *I* **have** *seen that film before.* (=at some time in the past)|*I saw that film on Saturday /last night/ in 1980.* (=at a particular time in the past) 2 When **have** is used in this sense, its pronunciation is usually /hæf/: *I have to* /'hæftə/ *eat.*

have² /hæv/ *v* **had, having** [T *no pass.*] **1** also **have got**– to possess; own: *She has blue eyes.|Have you got a pencil? Do you have a pencil?* (*AmE*)|*This coat has no pockets.| He's got a bad cold.|I've no idea what to do.* –see GOTTEN (USAGE) **2** to receive or obtain: *Have some coffee!* **3** to experience or enjoy: *to have breakfast|to have a bath/a fight|Have a look* (=look) *at this.|We're having a party/a meeting.|I had my watch stolen.* **4** [*over*] to ask (somebody) to one's home: *We're having some people (over) for drinks tonight.* **5** to allow; permit: *I can't have (you) running up and down the stairs all day.* **6** to cause (something) to be done or to happen: *I had my hair cut.|We'll soon have your car out of the ditch.* **7** to give birth to; become the mother of: *She had her baby in hospital.* **8 have done with** to finish; put an end to **9 have it in for (someone)** *infml* to be as unkind as possible to (someone) on purpose: *One of the teachers really has it in for that child. She shouts at him all the time.* **10 have to do with** to have a connection with: *Her job has (something) to do with looking after old people.|Does the government's unpopularity have anything to do with the recent tax increases?* **11 have nothing on** *infml* be not nearly as good as: *Sam may have money, but for brains he has nothing on Janet.*

have on *v adv* [*no pass.*] [T] **1** [not *be* +*v-ing*] (**have** sthg. ↔ **on**) also **have got on**– to be wearing (something): *He had nothing on except a hat.* **2** [not *be* +*v-ing*] (**have** sthg. **on**) also **have got on**– to have arranged to do: *I*

don't have anything on tonight/I have nothing on (for) tonight.

have sthg. **out** *v adv* [T *no pass.*] **1** to get something taken out, usu. a tooth or organ of the body: *to have a tooth out/have one's* AP-PENDIX *out* **2** [*with*] to settle a difficulty by talking freely or angrily: *This disagreement has gone on for too long: it's time we had it/ the whole thing out!*

ha·ven /'heɪvən/ *n lit* a place of calm and safety: (fig.) *safe in the haven of his books*

have·n't /'hævənt/ *v short for* have not: *You haven't been here before, have you?*

hav·oc /'hævək/ *n* [U] widespread damage or confusion: *His arrival that night* **played havoc with** (=caused confused changes in) *my plans.|The rain will* **wreak havoc on** (=damage) *plans to drive to Boston.*

hawk¹ /hɔk/ *n* **1** a usu. large bird which catches other birds and small animals for food **2** a person, esp. a politician, who believes in using force or in increasing violence in war –opposite **dove**

hawk² *v* [T] to sell (goods) on the street or at the doors of houses, esp. while traveling from place to place: (fig.) *to hawk one's ideas around* –**hawker** *n*

haw·thorn /'hɔθɔrn/ *n* a tree which has white or red flowers, and red berries in autumn

hay /heɪ/ *n* **1** [U] grass which has been cut and dried, esp. for cattle food **2 make hay** to make use of chances: *Make hay while you are in Chicago and look for a job there.* –**haymaking** /'heɪˌmeɪkɪŋ/ *n* [U]

hay fe·ver /'· ˌ··/ *n* [U] an illness rather like a bad cold, but caused by breathing in POLLEN dust from plants

hay·stack /'heɪstæk/ *n* a large pile of HAY built for storing **2 (like looking for) a needle in a haystack** (like looking for) something impossible to find among so many other things

hay·wire /'heɪwaɪər/ *adj* **go haywire** (of plans, arrangements, etc.) to become confused and DISORGANIZED

haz·ard¹ /'hæzərd/ *n* a danger: *a hazard to health/a health hazard* –**hazardous** /'hæzərdəs/ *adj* –**hazardously** *adv* –**hazardousness** *n* [U]

hazard² *v* [T] *fml* to risk; put in danger: *He hazarded all his money in the attempt to save the business.|I'll hazard a guess.* (=I'll make a guess but I may be wrong)

haze¹ /heɪz/ *n* [C;U] a light mist or smoke: *a haze of cigarette smoke*

haze² *v* **hazed, hazing** *AmE* [T] **1** to worry and trouble by forcing to do unpleasant work or by saying rude things; HARASS **2** to play tricks on (a young college student) as part of the ceremony of admittance to a club

ha·zel¹ /'heɪzəl/ *n* a tree which bears nuts that can be eaten

hazel² *n,adj* [U] (of) a light or greenish brown color: *She has hazel eyes.*

haz·y /'heɪzi/ *adj* **-ier, -iest** misty; rather cloudy: *The mountains were hazy in the distance.*|(fig.) *I'm rather hazy* (=uncertain) *about the details of the arrangement.* –**hazily** *adv* –**haziness** *n* [U]

H-bomb /'eɪtʃ bɑm/ n →HYDROGEN BOMB

he¹ /iʸ; *strong* hiʸ/ *pron* (used as the subject of a sentence) **1** that male person or animal already mentioned: *"Where's John?" "He went to the movies."|Be careful of that dog–he sometimes bites.* **2** that person: *Everyone should do what he thinks best.* –see ME (USAGE)

he² /hiʸ/ n a male person or animal: *Is your dog a he or a she?|a he-goat*

head¹ /hɛd/ n **1** [C] the part of the body which contains the eyes, ears, nose and mouth, and the brain **2** [*the* S] the end where this part rests: *at the head of the bed|the grave* –compare FOOT¹ (3) **3** [C] the mind or brain: *Can't you get these facts into your head?|Try not to let your heart* (=feelings) *rule your head.|It never entered his head to help me.* (=he never even thought of helping)*|He suddenly took it into his head* (=decided) *to learn Russian.|I don't have much of a head for figures.* (=I'm not very good at adding, subtracting, etc.)*|We must put our heads together* (=talk together) *and decide what to do.* **4** [C] a ruler or leader: *the head of a company|the family|heads of state| government* **5** [C; *the* S] the part at the top or front; the most important part: *the head of the nail|Put your address at the head of the letter.|He sat at the head of the table.|Move to the head of the line of people.* **6** [*usu. pl.*] the front side of a coin which often bears a picture of the ruler's head: *"Let's* TOSS *for it." –"Heads." –"Heads it is,"* (=the front fell so as to be seen) *so you win."* –opposite **tails 7** [S] **a** a person (only in the phrase **a/per head**): *It cost $25 a head to eat there.* **b** (used in counting farm animals) an animal: *three head of cattle* **8** [C] the pressure or force produced by a quantity of steam or water **9 above/over someone's head** beyond someone's understanding; too difficult **10 a: bring something to a head** to cause (an event) to reach a point where something must be done or decided **b: come to a head** to reach this point **11 go to someone's head: a** to over-excite or INTOXICATE someone **b** to make someone too proud, or CONCEITED **12 have one's head in the clouds** to be impractical; not act according to the realities of life **13 head over heels: a** a turning over in the air head first **b** very much; completely: *head over heels in love* **14 keep one's head** to remain calm **15 lose one's head** to act wildly or without reason because afraid, angry, confused, etc. **16 not be able to make heads or tails of** *infml* to be unable to understand **17 bury one's head in the sand** to avoid facing some difficulty **18 have a swollen head** *also* **have a swelled head** *AmE*– to be too proud of oneself or something one has done **19 have something hanging over one's head** to feel the threat of something bad about to happen **20 (do something) standing on one's head** (to do something) easily or without any trouble **21 -headed** having a certain type of head or hair: *curly-headed|red-headed| two-headed|empty-headed*

head² v **1** [T] to lead; be at the front of: *The car headed the procession.* **2** [T] to be in

charge of: *Who heads the government?* **3** [I;T] to (cause to) move in a certain direction: *We headed him towards the house.|We're heading home.*

head for sthg. *v prep* [T] to move towards; go to: *Where are you heading/headed for?|(fig.) You're heading for an accident if you drive after drinking.*

head off *v adv* [T] to cause to move in a different direction by getting in front of: *They were running towards the door, but we headed them off from outside.*

head·ache /'hɛdeʸk/ n a pain in the head: *(fig.) The problem of unemployment is a big headache for the government.*

head·band /'hɛdbænd/ n a band worn on the forehead, usu. to keep the hair back from the face

head·dress /'hɛd-drɛs/ n an ornamental covering for the head

head·first /ˌhɛd'fɜrst/ *also* **headlong**– *adj,adv* (moving or entering) with the rest of the body following the head

head·gear /'hɛdgɪər/ n [C;U] (a) covering for the head

head·hunt·er /'hɛdˌhʌntər/ n **1** a person who cuts off his enemies' heads and keeps them **2** a person who tries to attract especially able people to other jobs by offering them better pay and more responsibility

head·ing /'hɛdɪŋ/ n the words written as a title at the top of (each part of) a piece of writing

head·land /'hɛdlənd, -lænd/ n a narrow piece of land running out into the sea

head·light /'hɛdlaɪt/ ‖*also* **headlamp** /'hɛdlæmp/ *BrE*– n a powerful light fixed at the front of a vehicle, usu. one of a pair

head·line /'hɛdlaɪn/ n **1** the heading printed in large letters above a story in a newspaper **2** [*usu. pl.*] a main point of the news, as read on radio or television

head·long /'hɛdlɔŋ, ˌhɛd'lɔŋ◄/ *adv,adj* **1** →HEADFIRST **2** (done) with great haste, often without thought: *He rushed headlong into buying the car, and then saw it was a mistake.*

head·mas·ter /'hɛdˌmæstər, hɛd'mæ-/ **head·mistress** /'hɛdˌmɪstrɪs, ˌhɛd'mɪ-/ *fem.*– n the teacher in charge of a private school

head-on /ˌ·'·◄/ *adv,adj* with the head or front parts meeting, usu. violently: *a head-on collision*

head·phones /'hɛdfoʷnz/ n [P] an apparatus made of two parts of metal, plastic, etc., which fits over the ears and is used to receive radio messages, listen to records, etc.

head·quar·ter /'hɛdˌkwɔrtər/ *v AmE* [T; *usu. pass.*] to have HEADQUARTERS in/at: *The F.B.I is headquartered in Washington.|The army was headquartered at Valley Forge.*

head·quar·ters /'hɛdˌkwɔrtərz/ *also* **HQ**– n **-ters** [+*sing./pl. v*] the office or place where the people work who control a large organization, such as the police or army: *F.B.I. headquarters is/are in Washington D.C.*

head·room /'hɛd-ruʷm, -rʊm/ n [U] space above a vehicle passing under a bridge, through a TUNNEL, etc.

head·set /'hɛdsɛt/ n esp. AmE (a set of) HEADPHONES

head·shrink·er /'hɛd‚ʃrɪŋkər/ n humor for PSYCHIATRIST

head start /‚· '·/ n [S over, on] an advantage, esp. in a race: (fig.) He has a head start over his friends who are learning French because he has already lived in France for a year.

head·stone /'hɛdstoʷn/ n a stone which marks the top end of a grave, usu. having the buried person's name on it; GRAVESTONE

head·strong /'hɛdstrɒŋ/ adj (of people) determined to do what one wants against all other advice

head·way /'hɛdweʸ/ n make headway to advance in dealing with a difficulty

head·wind /'hɛd‚wɪnd/ n a wind blowing directly against one

head·y /'hɛdiʸ/ adj -ier, -iest 1 (of alcohol and its effects) tending to make people drunk, GIDDY, etc. (to INTOXICATE) 2 with a feeling of lightness and excitement: heady with success

heal /hiʸl/ v [I;T over, up] to (cause to) become healthy, esp. to grow new skin: His wounds are healing (over/up).|(fig.) Their disagreements healed (over) with time and they became close friends. –healer n

health /hɛlθ/ n [U] 1 the state of being well, without disease: Health is more important to me than money. –compare SICKNESS 2 the condition of the body: in poor/good health

health·y /'hɛlθiʸ/ adj -ier, -iest 1 strong, not often ill; usually in good health 2 likely to produce or showing good health: healthy country air|a clear healthy skin|(fig.) The children have a healthy (=natural) dislike of school. –opposite unhealthy –healthily adv –healthiness n [U]

heap¹ /hiʸp/ n a pile or mass of things one on top of the other: The books lay in a heap on the floor.|(fig.) She was so tired that she fell in a heap on her bed.

heap² v [T on, with, up] to pile up in large amounts: He heaped the plate with food.|He heaped food on the plate.

hear /hɪər/ v heard /hɜrd/, hearing 1 [I;T not be +v-ing] to receive and understand (sounds) by using the ears: I can't hear very well.|I heard him say so.|I can hear someone knocking. 2 [T +(that); not be+v-ing] to be told or informed: I heard (that) he was ill. 3 [T] to listen with attention (esp. to a case in court): The judge heard the case.|She heard what he had to say. 4 won't/wouldn't hear of refuse(s) to allow: You are my guest; I won't hear of you paying for dinner. 5 Hear! Hear! (a shout of agreement)

USAGE Compare hear and listen: To hear is to experience with the ears; to listen is to hear with attention: I was asleep when the telephone rang, so I didn't hear it.|We always listen to the 6 o'clock news on the radio.|If you listen hard, you can hear what the neighbors are saying.

hear about sbdy./sthg. v prep [T +v-ing] to get to know (about): Have you heard about Jim coming to Houston?|We've been hearing a lot about that young tennis player lately.

hear from sbdy. v prep [T not be +v-ing] to receive news from (someone), usu. by letter: I heard from her last week.|I haven't heard from him since he telephoned.

hear of sbdy./sthg. v prep [T +v-ing; be+v-ing] (usu. in questions, NEGATIVES², etc.) to know of (a fact/the existence of something or somebody): Who's he?–I've never heard of him.|We've never heard of anyone doing a thing like that.

hear sbdy. **out** v adv [T] to listen to (someone who is speaking) until he/she has finished: Don't interrupt, just hear me out before you start talking.

hear·ing /'hɪərɪŋ/ n 1 [U] the sense by which one hears sound: Her hearing is getting worse. She needs a hearing aid. (=a small electric machine which makes sounds louder) 2 [U] the distance at which one can hear; EARSHOT: Don't talk about it in his hearing. (=so that he can hear)|Are you within hearing distance of his voice? 3 [C] law a trial of a case before a judge

hear·say /'hɪərseʸ/ n [U] things which are said rather than proved: I don't know if he's really leaving his job; it may only be hearsay.

hearse /hɜrs/ n a car which is used to carry a body in its COFFIN to the funeral

heart /hɑrt/ n 1 [C] the organ inside the chest which controls the flow of blood by pushing it around the body 2 [S;U] this organ when thought of as the center of the feelings, esp. kind feelings: He seems rather mean, but he has a kind heart/he is kind at heart/his heart is in the right place.|Have a heart! (=Don't be unkind to me)|I pity them with all my heart/from the bottom of my heart. (=with deep feeling) 3 [C] the center: the heart of a cabbage/of the city/a problem|Let's get to the heart of the matter. 4 [U] courage; firmness of purpose: Take heart and go on trying.|I used to work in the garden every week, but I lost heart when all the plants died.|I didn't have the heart to tell him the bad news. 5 [C] a playing card with one or more heart-shaped figures printed on it in red: the Queen of Hearts –see CARDS (USAGE) 6 after one's own heart of the type like oneself or which one likes: He's a man after my own heart. 7 break someone's heart to make someone very unhappy 8 by heart by memory: to know/learn by heart 9 set one's heart on (doing) something to want very much to have or do something 10 take (something) to heart to feel the effect of something deeply (and take suitable action) 11 eat one's heart out to be very troubled; be worrying a lot 12 wear one's heart on one's sleeve to show one's feelings (esp. to show that one is in love with a certain person) instead of hiding these feelings 13 -hearted /'hɑːtɪd/ adj having a certain type of HEART (2,4): kind-hearted-|cold-hearted|lion-hearted (=very brave)

heart·ache /'hɑrteʸk/ n [U] deep feelings of sorrow and pain

heart at·tack /'· ·‚·/ n a very dangerous medical condition in which the heart suddenly stops working properly: He died of a heart attack.

heart·beat /'hɑrtbiʸt/ *n* [C;U] (the) movement of the heart as it pushes the blood: *The doctor listened to the rapid heartbeat of the sick child.*

heart·break /'hɑrtbreʸk/ *n* [C;U] deep sorrow

heart·break·ing /'hɑrt₁breʸkɪŋ/ *adj* causing great sorrow –**heartbreakingly** *adv*

heart·bro·ken /'hɑrt₁broʷkən/ also **broken-hearted**– *adj* (of a person) deeply hurt

heart·burn /'hɑrtbɜrn/ *n* [U] a condition in which one feels an unpleasant burning in the chest, caused by INDIGESTION

heart·en /'hɑrtn/ *T* *fml* to encourage: *He was heartened by her kindness.|heartening news.* –opposite **dishearten**

heart·felt /'hɑrtfɛlt/ *adj* deeply felt; sincere; true: *She gave him her heartfelt thanks for all his help.*

hearth /hɑrθ/ *n* the area around the fire in one's home, esp. the floor of the fireplace

heart·i·ly /'hɑrt̬l-iʸ/ *adv* **1** (done) with strength, force, APPETITE, etc.: *They ate heartily.* **2** very: *I'm heartily tired/sick of your questions.*

heart·less /'hɑrtlɪs/ *adj* cruel; unkind; pitiless –**heartlessly** *adv* –**heartlessness** *n* [U]

heart·rend·ing /'hɑrt₁rɛndɪŋ/ *adj* which causes a feeling of deep sorrow or pity: *the heartrending cries of the wounded* –**heartrendingly** *adv*

heart·strings /'hɑrt₁strɪŋz/ *n* [P] someone's deep feelings of love and pity

heart-to-heart /₁· · '· ◄/ *adj,n* (a talk) done freely, mentioning personal details, without hiding anything

heart·warm·ing /'hɑrt₁wɔrmɪŋ/ *adj* giving a feeling of pleasure, esp. because of a kindness done: *We don't need your help, but it was a heartwarming offer.*

heart·y /'hɑrt̬iʸ/ *adj* **-ier, -iest** **1** warm and friendly: *a hearty greeting* **2** strong and healthy (esp. in the phrase **hale and hearty**) **3** (of meals) large: *a hearty breakfast* –**heartiness** *n* [U]

heat¹ /hiʸt/ *n* [U] **1** the quality or quantity of being warm or cold **2** [S;U] hotness; WARMTH: *The heat from the fire dried their clothes.|I can't walk around in this heat.* (=hot weather)|(fig.) *In the* **heat of the moment/argument** *I lost my self-control.* **3** (**be**) **in heat** *AmE*‖**on heat** *BrE*– (of certain female animals, e.g. dogs) (to be) in a state in which CONCEPTION (3) can occur **4** [C] a part of a race or competition whose winners compete against other winners until there is a small enough number to decide the end result

heat² *v* [I;T *up*] to (cause to) become warm or hot: *We'll heat (up) some soup for lunch.*

heat·ed /'hiʸt̬ɪd/ *adj* angry or excited: *a heated argument* –**heatedly** *adv*

heat·er /'hiʸt̬ər/ *n* a machine for heating air or water, such as those which burn gas, oil, or electricity to produce heat

hea·then /'hiʸðən/ *n,adj* old use or humor (of) a person who does not belong to one of the large established religions: *heathen gods* –compare PAGAN

heath·er /'hɛðər/ *n* [U] a plant which grows on open windy land (MOORS) and has small usu. pink or purple flowers

heat·ing /'hiʸt̬ɪŋ/ *n* [U] a system for keeping rooms and buildings warm –see also CENTRAL HEATING

heat·stroke /'hiʸtstroʷk/ *n* [U] →SUNSTROKE

heat wave /'· ·/ *n* a period of unusually hot weather

heave¹ /hiʸv/ *v* **heaved, heaving** **1** [T] to pull and lift with effort, esp. towards oneself: *We heaved him to his feet.|They all heaved on the rope, and at last the rock moved.* **2** [I] to rise and fall regularly: *Her chest heaved as she breathed deeply after the race.* **3** [T] *infml* to throw: *The children have just heaved a brick through my window.* **4** [I] →RETCH **5 heave a sigh** to let out a deep breath with a sound expressing sadness

heave² *v* **hove** /hoʷv/, **heaving** [I] (esp. of a ship) to move in the stated direction or manner: *As we came into harbor another ship hove into view.*

heave to *v adv* [I] *tech* (of a ship) to stop moving; come to rest: *When the ship received the signal, she hove to.*

heave³ *n* **1** a pull or throw: *Just one more heave, and the stone will be in the right place.* **2** an act of RETCHing: *The sight of the dead body gave me the* **dry heaves.** (=retching without result)

heav·en /'hɛvən/ *n* **1** [U] the place where God or the gods are supposed to live; place of complete happiness where the souls of good people go after death –compare HELL (1) **2** [C *usu. pl.*] the sky: *Just as the game started,* **the heavens opened** *and it* **poured with rain.**

heav·en·ly /'hɛvənliʸ/ *adj* [*no comp.*] **1** [A] of, from, or like heaven; in or belonging to the sky: *The sun, moon, and stars are* **heavenly bodies.** **2** *infml* wonderful: *What heavenly weather!* –compare HELLISH

heav·en·wards /'hɛvənwərdz/ also **heavenward** /'hɛvənwərd/ *AmE*– *adv* towards the sky or heaven

heav·y /'hɛviʸ/ *adj* **-ier, -iest** **1** of a certain weight, esp. of a weight that makes carrying, moving, or lifting difficult: *The bag is too heavy for me to carry.* **2** of unusual force or amount: *heavy rain|a heavy blow|a heavy punishment|heavy traffic|A* **heavy smoker/drinker** *is one who smokes/drinks a lot or too much.|I'm such a* **heavy sleeper** *that the explosion didn't wake me.* **3** serious, esp. if uninteresting: *This book is heavy reading.* **4 a** feeling or showing difficulty or slowness in moving: *My head is heavy.|heavy movements* **b** difficult and causing tiredness: *I've had a heavy day at the office.|Moving that piano was heavy work.* **5** (of food) rather solid and bad for the stomach **6** (of weather) **a** still, without wind, dark, etc. **b** (at sea) stormy, with big waves **7** unhappy: *a heavy heart* –opposite **light** –**heavily** *adv*: *moving/breathing/drinking heavily* –**heaviness** *n* [U]

heavy-du·ty /₁·· '··◄/ *adj* (of clothes, tires, machines, oil, etc.) made to be used a lot, or strong enough for rough treatment

heavy-hand·ed /ˌ·· '··◄/ *adj* unkind or unfair in one's treatment of others; not careful in speech and action **–heavy-handedly** *adv* **–heavy-handedness** *n* [U]

heav·y·heart·ed /ˌhɛviʸ'hɑrtɪd◄/ *adj* sad **–opposite light-hearted**

heavy in·dus·try /ˌ·· '···/ *n* [U] organizations that produce goods (such as coal, steel, or chemicals) which are used in the production of other goods **–compare** LIGHT INDUSTRY

heav·y·weight /'hɛviʸ,weʸt/ *n,adj* (a BOXER (2)) of the heaviest class: (fig.) *He is a real heavyweight around the office.* (=a person of importance)

He·brew /'hiʸbruʷ/ *adj,n* (of) the language used by the Jews, in ancient times and at present the language of Israel

heck·le /'hɛkəl/ *v* **-led, -ling** [I;T] to interrupt (a speaker, performer, or performance) with confusing or unfriendly remarks **–heckler** *n*

hec·tare /'hɛktɛər/ *n* (a measure for the area of land which equals) 10,000 square meters

hec·tic /'hɛktɪk/ *adj* full of excitement and hurried movement: *a hectic day* **–hectically** *adv*

he'd /iʸd; *strong* hiʸd/ *v short for* **1** he would: *He'd go there now if he could afford it.* **2** he had: *He'd gone.|He'd already seen the movie.*

hedge[1] /hɛdʒ/ *n* **1** a row of bushes or small trees dividing one yard or field from another **–see** illustration on page 337 **2** [*against*] a protection: *Buying a house is the best* **hedge against inflation**. (=protection against one's money losing its value)

hedge[2] *v* **hedged, hedging 1** [I;T] to make a HEDGE around (a field) **2** [I] to refuse to answer directly: *You're hedging again–have you or haven't you got the money?* **3 hedge one's bets** to protect oneself against loss by favoring or supporting more than one side in a competition or struggle

hedge·hog /'hɛdʒhɔg, -hɑg/ *n* a small insect-eating animal which has SPINEs (sharp needle-like hairs) standing out from its back **–compare** PORCUPINE

hedge·row /'hɛdʒroʷ/ *n* a row of bushes, esp. along country roads, or separating fields

he·do·nism /'hiʸdn,ɪzəm/ *n* [U] the idea that pleasure is the most important thing in life **–hedonist** *n* **–hedonistic** /ˌhiʸdn'ɪstɪk/ *adj*

heed[1] /hiʸd/ *v* [T] *fml* to give attention to: *She didn't heed my warning.*

heed[2] *n* [U] *fml* attention; notice: **Take heed of/pay heed to** *what I say, if you want to succeed.* **–heedful** /'hiʸdfəl/ *adj* **–heedless** *adj* [*of*]

heel[1] /hiʸl/ *n* **1** the back part of the foot **2** the part of a shoe, sock, etc., which covers this, esp. the raised part of a shoe underneath the foot: *There's a hole in the heel of my stocking.|to wear high heels* (=shoes with high heels) **–compare** SOLE[1] (2) **3** *AmE infml* an unpleasant person (usu. a man) who treats others badly **4 at/on one's heels** very closely behind: *He followed (hot) on my heels.* **5 down at heel** (of a person) untidy and uncared for in appearance **6 cool one's heels**

to be made to wait for some time unwillingly **7 kick up one's heels: a** to jump and make kicking movements in play **b** to be free and enjoy oneself

heel[2] *v* [T] to put a heel on (a shoe) **–compare** SOLE[2]

heft·y /'hɛftiʸ/ *adj* **-ier, -iest** big and/or strong: *a hefty man/meal/blow to the jaw*

heif·er /'hɛfər/ *n* a cow which has not yet given birth to a CALF (=a young cow)

height /haɪt/ *n* **1** [C;U] the quality or degree of being tall or high: *His height makes him stand out in the crowd.* **2** [C] (a point at) a fixed or measured distance above another given point: *a window at a height of ten feet above the ground|During the floods the river water rose to the height of the main road beside it.* **–compare** DEPTH **3** [C] a high position or place: *We looked down from a great height to the town below.* **4** [*the* S] the main point; highest degree: *It's the height of stupidity to go sailing when you can't swim.|at the height of the storm*

height·en /'haɪtn/ *v* [I;T] to (cause to) become greater in degree: *As she waited, her excitement heightened.|The performance heightened my admiration for the actor.*

heir /ɛər/ **heiress** /'ɛərɪs/ *fem.–n* [*to*] the person who has the lawful right to receive the property or title of an older member of the family who dies: *The king's eldest son is the heir to the* THRONE. (=kingdom)

heir·loom /'ɛərluʷm/ *n* a valuable object given by older members of a family to younger ones over many years or even several centuries

heist /haɪst/ *n AmE infml for* BURGLARY; ROBBERY (1)

held /hɛld/ *v* past tense and past participle of HOLD

hel·i·cop·ter /'hɛlɪ,kɑptər/ also **chopper, copter** *infml– n* an aircraft which is made to fly by a set of large fast-turning metal blades fixed on top of it

hel·i·port /'hɛlə,pɔrt, -,poʷrt/ *n* a HELICOPTER airport

he·li·um /'hiʸliʸəm/ *n* [U] a gas that is a simple substance (ELEMENT) that is lighter than air, will not burn, and is used e.g. in BALLOONs[1] (1)

hell[1] /hɛl/ *n* [U] **1** (esp. in the Christian and Muslim religions) a place where the souls of the wicked are said to be punished after death: (fig.) *Driving a car in a snowstorm is real hell!* **–compare** HEAVEN (1) **2** *infml* (a swear word, used in anger or to strengthen an expression): *What the hell's that thing on your head?|That's* **a hell of** *a good car.|Stop telling me what to do–(you can)* **go to hell!**|*I had to run* **like hell** *to catch the bus.* **3 for the hell of it** *infml* for fun: *Then we decided to go swimming at midnight just for the hell of it.* **4 give someone hell** *infml* to treat or scold (someone) very roughly in anger: *My father wasn't there when I came in late, but he gave me hell in the morning.*

hell[2] *interj infml not polite* (an expression of strong anger or disappointment): *Oh, hell! I've missed the last train.*

he'll /ɪl, iʸl, hɪl; *strong* hiʸl/ *short for* **1** he will **2** he shall

hell·ish /'hɛlɪʃ/ *adj infml* terrible; very unpleasant: *The weather's been hellish recently.* –compare HEAVENLY

hel·lo /hə'loʷ, hɛ'loʷ, 'hɛloʷ/ also **hallo, hullo** *BrE– interj,n* **-los 1** (the usual word of greeting): *Hello, John! How are you?* **2** (the word used for starting a telephone conversation): *Hello, who's speaking, please?* –compare GOODBYE **3** *BrE* (an expression of surprise): *Hello! Somebody's left their hat behind.* **4** (a call for attention to a distant person): *Hello! Is anybody there?*

helm /hɛlm/ *n* the TILLER which guides a ship: (fig.) *How long has she been* **at the helm of** (=in control of) *the company?*

hel·met /'hɛlmɪt/ *n* a covering to protect the head, as worn by soldiers, motorcyclists, policemen, miners, etc.

helms·man /'hɛlmzmən/ *n* **-men** /mən/ a person who guides and controls, esp. when STEERING at the HELM of a boat

help¹ /hɛlp/ *v* **1** [I;T *out*] to do something for (someone who needs something done for them); AID; ASSIST: *Please help me; I can't do it alone.|My father helped me (out) with money when I needed it.|Could you help me (to) lift this box?|The money you lent me will help a lot.|Trade helps the development of industry.* **2** [I;T] to make better: *Crying won't help (you).|It won't help (you) to cry.|Have you got anything to help a cold?* **3** [T +*v-ing*] to avoid; prevent; change; (only in the phrase **can/can't/couldn't help):** *I couldn't help crying.|She can't help herself. She doesn't mean to be so rude.|He never does any more work than he can help.|***I can't help it.** (=it's not my fault)|*You've broken it now,* **it can't be helped.** (=we must accept it) **4** [T *to*] to take for (oneself), esp. dishonestly: *The money was on the table and no one was there, so he helped himself (to it).|"Can I have a drink?" "Help yourself!"|***Help yourself to** *a drink.* **5 so help me** on my solemn promise: *I'll pay you back, so help me (I will)!*

USAGE **Assist** is like **help** but **a** it is more formal, and **b** it suggests that the person being assisted is also doing part of the work: *I can't push the car on my own–will somebody* **help**/(*fml*) **assist** *me? If someone is in difficulties, you* **help** (not **assist**) them: *His job consists of* **helping** *old people who live alone.|I'm afraid I'm lost–can somebody* **help** *me?*

help² *n* **1** the act of helping; ASSISTANCE; AID: *You're not (of) much help to me just sitting there.|If you want any help, just ask me.* **2** [C *to*] something or somebody that helps: *This machine is a great help in making car parts more quickly.* **3 Help!** Please bring help, I'm in danger **4** [U] *esp. AmE* workers, esp. HOUSEKEEPERS: *Good help is hard to find.*

help·ful /'hɛlpfəl/ *adj* [*to, in*] willing to help; useful –opposite **unhelpful** –**helpfully** *adv* –**helpfulness** *n* [U]

help·ing /'hɛlpɪŋ/ *n* a serving of food; PORTION (3)

help·less /'hɛlplɪs/ *adj* unable to look after oneself or to act without help: *a helpless child* –**helplessly** *adv* –**helplessness** *n* [U]

hel·ter-skel·ter /ˌhɛltər 'skɛltər/ *adv,adj* (done) in a great hurry; disordered/ disorderly: *She worked helter-skelter.*

hem¹ /hɛm/ *n* the edge of a piece of cloth when turned under and sewn down, esp. the lower edge of a skirt or dress: *This dress is too long; I have to take the hem up.* (=make it shorter)

hem² *v* **-mm-** [T] to put a HEM¹ on

hem sbdy./sthg. ↔ **in** *v adv* [T] to surround tightly; enclose: *The whole army was hemmed in by the enemy, and there was no hope of escape.*

hem·i·sphere /'hɛməˌsfɪər/ *n* **1** half a SPHERE (an object which is round like a ball) **2** a half of the earth, esp. the northern or southern half above or below the EQUATOR, or the eastern or western half

hem·line /'hɛmlaɪn/ *n* the position of the HEM; length of a dress, skirt, etc.

hem·lock /'hɛmlɑk/ *n* [C;U] (a plant which produces) a poisonous drug

he·mo·glo·bin /'hiʸməˌgloʷbɪn/ *n* [U] red coloring matter in the blood which carries oxygen

he·mo·phil·i·a /ˌhiʸmə'fɪliʸə, -'fiʸlyə/ *n* [U] a disease which shows its effects only in males and which makes the sufferer bleed for a long time after a cut –**hemophiliac** /ˌhiʸmə'fɪliʸˌæk, -'fiʸ-/ *n, adj*

hem·or·rhage /'hɛmərɪdʒ/ *n* [C;U] a flow of blood, esp. a long or large and unexpected one

hem·or·rhoid /'hɛməˌrɔɪd/ *n* [*usu. pl.*] *tech or fml* a swollen blood vessel at the opening (ANUS) at the lower end of the bowel –see also PILES

hemp /hɛmp/ *n* [U] any of a family of plants which are used for making strong rope and a rough cloth, and one of which (**Indian hemp**) produces the drug CANNABIS

hen /hɛn/ *n* **1** the female bird often kept for its eggs on farms; female chicken **2** a female bird of which the male is the ROOSTER: *a hen* PHEASANT

hence /hɛns/ *adv* **1** for this reason: *The town was built on the side of a hill: hence the name Hillside.* –see Study Notes on page 144 **2** *fml* from here or from now: *three days hence* –compare THENCE

hence·forth /'hɛnsfɔrθ, -foʷrθ, ˌhɛns'fɔrθ, -'foʷrθ-/ also **henceforward** /ˌhɛns'fɔrwərd, -'foʷr-/– *adv fml* from now on: *I promise to behave better henceforth.*

hench·man /'hɛntʃmən/ *n* **-men** /mən/ *usu. derog* a faithful supporter, esp. of a political leader, who obeys without question and may use violent or dishonest methods

hen·na /'hɛnə/ *n* [U] a reddish-brown DYE made from a type of bush and used to color the hair, fingernails, etc.

hep·a·ti·tis /ˌhɛpə'taɪtɪs/ *n* [U] a disease (INFLAMMATION) of the LIVER

her¹ /ər, hər; *strong* hɜr/ *determiner* (POSSESSIVE *form of* SHE) **1** of that female person or animal already mentioned: *Mary sat down in* her chair. **2** (used of things, esp. vehicles or countries, that are thought of as female): *the ship with all her passengers*

her² *pron (object form of* SHE): *Where is Mary? Can you see her?|I saw her running across the road.|God bless this ship and all who sail on her!* –see ME (USAGE)

her·ald¹ /'hɛrəld/ *n* (in former times) a person who carried messages from a ruler and gave important news to the people: (fig.) *Early flowers are heralds* (=signs) *of spring.*

herald² *v* [T *in*] to be a sign of something coming: *The singing of the birds heralded (in) the day.*

her·ald·ry /'hɛrəldriʸ/ *n* [U] the study and use of COATS OF ARMS –**heraldic** /hə'rældɪk/ *adj*

herb /ɜrb, hɜrb/ *n* any of several kinds of plant which are used to make medicine or to improve the taste of food –compare SPICE –**herbal** *adj: a herbal medicine*

her·ba·ceous /hɜr'beʸʃəs, ɜr-/ *adj* (of a plant) soft-stemmed, not woody: *We have a* **herbaceous border** (=border of herbaceous plants) *around our garden.*

herb·al·ist /'ɜrbəlɪst, 'hɜr-/ *n* a person who treats disease with HERBS

her·biv·o·rous /hɜr'bɪvərəs, ɜr-/ *adj* (of animals) which eat grass and plants –see also CARNIVORE

herd¹ /hɜrd/ *n* **1** a group of animals of one kind which live and feed together: *a herd of elephants* **2** (*in comb.*) someone who looks after a group of animals; HERDSMAN: SHEPHERD|*goatherd* **3** *derog* people generally, thought of as acting or thinking all alike: *to follow the herd*

herd² *v* [I;T *into*] to (cause to) group together (as if) in a herd: *We all herded into the corner.|The farmer herded the cows into the field.*

herds·man /'hɜrdzmən/ *n* -**men** /mən/ a man who looks after a HERD of animals

here /hɪər/ *adv* **1** at, in, or to this place: *I live here.|Come over here.|It's two miles from here.|My friend here will help you.* **2** at this point: *Here we agree.* **3** (used for drawing attention to someone or something): *Here comes Mary.* (=I can see Mary coming)|*Here is the news...* –compare THERE (1,2,3) **4 here and there** scattered about **5 Here goes!** *infml* Now I'm going to try something: *I've never been on a horse before–well, here goes!* **6 Here's to** (said when drinking a TOAST¹ (2)): *Here's to John in his new job!* **7 Here you are** Here's what you want **8 neither here nor there** not important; IRRELEVANT: *I know you want a bigger car, but that's neither here nor there; we can't afford it.*

here·a·bout *AmE* /'hɪərə,baʊt, ,hɪərə'baʊt/ also **hereabouts** /'hɪərə,baʊts, ,hɪərə'baʊts/ *esp. BrE– adv* near here

here·af·ter¹ /,hɪər'æftər/ *adv fml or law* after this time; in the future

hereafter² *n* [*the* S] the life after death

here·by /,hɪər'baɪ, 'hɪərbaɪ/ *adv fml or law* now; by doing or saying this: *I hereby declare her elected.*

he·red·i·tar·y /hə'rɛdə,tɛriʸ/ *adj* [*no comp.*] which can be or is passed down from parent

to child: *a hereditary disease|a hereditary ability|a hereditary* PEERAGE (2)

he·red·i·ty /hə'rɛdətiʸ/ *n* [U] the passing on of qualities from parent to child in the cells of the body: *Some diseases develop because of the conditions one lives in; others are present by heredity.*

here·in /,hɪər'ɪn/ *adv fml or law* in this piece of writing

her·e·sy /'hɛrəsiʸ/ *n* -**sies** [C;U] (the fact of holding) a (religious) belief against what is accepted

her·e·tic /'hɛrətɪk/ *n* a person who favors HERESY or is guilty of a heresy –**heretical** /hə'rɛtɪkel/ *adj*

here·with /,hɪər'wɪθ, -'wɪð/ *adv fml or law* with this piece of writing: *I send you herewith two copies of the contract.*

her·it·age /'hɛrətɪdʒ/ *n* [*usu. sing.*] something which is passed down over many years within a family or nation: *Much of our country's artistic heritage* (=pictures and beautiful buildings) *was destroyed during the war.*

her·met·ic /hɜr'mɛtɪk/ *adj* very tightly closed; AIRTIGHT: *A* **hermetic seal** *is used at the top of this glass bottle.* –**hermetically** *adv*

her·mit /'hɜrmɪt/ *n* (esp. in former times) a person who lives alone, thinking and praying –compare RECLUSE

her·mit·age /'hɜrmətɪdʒ/ *n* a place where a HERMIT lives or has lived

her·ni·a /'hɜrniʸə/ also **rupture**– *n* [C;U] the medical condition in which an organ pushes through its covering wall, usu. when the bowel is pushed through the stomach wall

he·ro /'hɪəroʷ/ **heroine** /'hɛroʷɪn/ *fem.– n* -**roes 1** a person remembered or admired for (an act of) bravery, strength, or goodness **2** the most important character in a play, poem, story, etc.

he·ro·ic /hɪ'roʷɪk/ *adj* **1** showing the qualities of a HERO (1): *a heroic effort* **2** *tech* concerned with heroes: *heroic poems* –**heroically** *adv*

he·ro·ics /hɪ'roʷɪks/ *n* [P] speech or actions which are meant to appear great, though they mean nothing

her·o·in /'hɛroʷɪn/ *n* a drug from MORPHINE, which is used for lessening pain, and which one can become dependent on (ADDICTED to)

her·o·ism /'hɛroʷ,ɪzəm/ *n* [U] great courage: *It was an act of heroism to go back into the burning building.*

her·on /'hɛrən/ *n* -**ons** *or* -**on** a long-legged bird which lives near water

hero sand·wich /,·· '··, '·· ,··/ *AmE* a usu. large sandwich consisting of a small loaf of bread (roll) for one person, cut through and filled with meat, cheese, onions, etc.

her·ring /'hɛrɪŋ/ *n* -**ring** *or* -**rings 1** a fish which swims in large groups (SHOALS) in the sea, and is used for food **2 red herring** a fact or point of argument which draws attention away from the main point

hers /hɜrz/ *pron* (POSSESSIVE *form of* SHE) of that female person or animal already mentioned: *I cleaned my shoes, and Mary cleaned hers.|That's my coat and hers is over there.*

her·self /ər'sɛlf; *strong* hər'sɛlf/ *pron* **1** (used as the object of a verb, or after a PREPOSI-TION, when the same female person or animal does the action and is the object of the action): *She cut herself.*|*She's proud of herself.*|*Sarah looked at herself in the mirror.* **2** (used to make *she,* or the name of a female person or animal, stronger): *She herself said so.*|*She went there herself.*|*She'd like to speak to the doctor herself.*

he's /iᵧz; *strong* hiᵧz/ *v short for* **1** he is: *He's a writer.*|*He's coming.* **2** (*in compound tenses*) he has: *He's seen the movie.*|*He's had a cold*

hes·i·tant /'hɛzətənt/ *adj* showing uncertainty or slowness about deciding to act; tending to HESITATE: *She's hesitant about making new friends.* –**hesitantly** *adv* –**hesitancy** /'hɛzətənsiᵧ/ *also* **hesitance**– *n* [U]

hes·i·tate /'hɛzə,teᵧt/ *v* **-tated, -tating** [I +*to*-*v*] **1** to pause in or before an action: *She hesitated before crossing the road.*|*He hesitated over the choice between the two suits.* **2** (*polite*) to be unwilling; find it unpleasant: *I hesitate to ask you, but will you lend me some money?* –**hesitating** *adj* –**hesitatingly** *adv* –**hesitation** /,hɛzə'teᵧʃən/ *n* [C;U]: *Without a moment's hesitation, she jumped into the river.*|*I have no hestitation in saying . . .*

het·er·o·ge·ne·ous /,hɛtərə'dʒiᵧniᵧəs, -'dʒiᵧnyəs/ *adj* of (many) different kinds: *a heterogeneous group of people* –compare HOMOGENEOUS

het·er·o·sex·u·al /,hɛtərə'sɛkʃuᵂəl/ *adj,n* (of or being) a person attracted to people of the other sex –compare BISEXUAL, HOMOSEXUAL –**heterosexually** *adv* –**heterosexuality** /,hɛtərə,sɛkʃuᵂ'ælətiᵧ/ *n* [U]

het up /,hɛt 'ʌp/ *adj* [F *about*] *infml* (of people) excited; anxious: *He's all het up about tomorrow's examination.*

hew /hyuᵂ/ *v* **hewed, hewed** *or* **hewn** /hyuᵂn/, **hewing** [I;T] *fml or lit* to cut by striking blows with an axe or other tool; HACK: *to hew down a tree*|*Miners hew coal (out of the rock).*

hex·a·gon /'hɛksə,gɑn/ *n* a figure with six sides –**hexagonal** /hɛk'sægənəl/ *adj*

hey /heᵧ/ *interj* (a shout used to call attention or to express surprise, interest, etc.): *Hey! Where are you going?*

hey·day /'heᵧdeᵧ/ *n* [S] the best period (of some desirable state): *In the heyday of their empire, the Romans controlled most of the western world.*|*In his heyday, he was one of the best football players in the world.*

hi /haᵧ/ *interj infml* HELLO

HI *written abbrev. said as:* Hawaii /hə'waɪ-iᵧ, -'wɑ-/ (a state in the US)

hi·a·tus /haɪ'eᵧţəs/ *n* **-tuses,** *or* **-tus** [*usu. sing.*] *fml* a space or GAP where something is missing

hi·ber·nate /'haɪbər,neᵧt/ *v* **-nated, -nating** [I] (of animals) to be or go into a sleep-like state during the winter –**hibernation** /,haɪbər 'neᵧʃən/ *n* [U]

hic·cup, hiccough /'hɪkəp/ *n* (a sudden sharp sound caused by) a movement in the chest which stops the breath: *In the middle of the prayer there was a loud hiccup from my son.* –**hiccup, hiccough** *v* [I]

hick /hɪk/ *n AmE infml* a person from the

country who is inexperienced in the way of life in the city.

hick·o·ry /'hɪkəriᵧ/ **-ries** *n* [C;U] (the wood of) a type of tree of North America which provides hard wood and bears nuts

hide¹ /haɪd/ *v* **hid** /hɪd/, **hidden** /'hɪdn/ *or* **hid, hiding** /'haɪdɪŋ/ **1** [T] to put or keep out of sight; make or keep secret: *I hid the broken plate in the drawer.*|*You're hiding some important facts. Don't hide your feelings; say what you think.* **2** [I] to place oneself or be placed so as to be unseen: *I'll hide behind the door.*|*Where's that book hiding?*

hide² *n* an animals's skin, esp. when removed to be used for leather: *I'll tan your hide.* (=give you a beating)

hide·bound /'haɪdbaʊnd/ *adj* (of people) having fixed, unchangeable opinions; NARROW-MINDED

hid·e·ous /'hɪdiᵧəs/ *adj* having a terrible effect on the senses, esp. shocking to the eyes: *a hideous face/noise/wound* –see BEAUTIFUL (USAGE) –**hideously** *adv* –**hideousness** *n* [U]

hid·ing¹ /'haɪdɪŋ/ *n infml* a beating: *I'll give you a (good) hiding when we get home!*

hiding² *n* [U] **go into hiding/be in hiding** to hide oneself/be hidden: *The escaped prisoner had been in hiding for two weeks when the police found him.*

hi·er·ar·chy /'haɪə,rɑrkiᵧ/ *n* **-chies** [C;U] (an) organization of a system into higher and lower, esp. official ranks: *The party hierarchy* (=its most powerful members) *will never accept him as leader.*|(fig.) *a hierarchy of moral values* –**hierarchical** /,haɪə'rɑrkɪkəl/ *adj* –**hierarchically** *adv*

hi·er·o·glyph·ics /,haɪərə'glɪfɪks/ *n* [P] the system of writing which uses picture-like signs (=**hieroglyphs** /'haɪərə,glɪfs/) to represent words, esp. as used in ancient Egypt

hi-fi /,haɪ 'faɪ/ *n,adj* **hi-fis** [C;U] HIGH FIDELITY (=very sensitive) apparatus for reproducing recorded sound; STEREO *When you listen to my hi-fi (set), it's like sitting in the concert hall!*

hig·gle·dy-pig·gle·dy /,hɪgəldiᵧ 'pɪgəldiᵧ/ *adj,adv infml* in disorder; mixed together without system

high¹ /haɪ/ *adj* **1** (not usu. of living things) having a top that is some distance, esp. a large distance above ground: *How high is it?*|*It's a very high building.*|*a high mountain*|*twelve feet high* **2** at a point well above the ground or above what is usual: *That shelf is too high for me; I can't reach it.*|(fig.) *the high* (=great) *cost of food*|*traveling at high* (=great) *speed*|*a high musical note*|*Their vacation is the* **high spot** (=something remembered with pleasure) *of the year.* **3** showing goodness; worthy of admiration: *high principles* **4** [A *no comp.*] of or concerning people of great wealth or rank: *high society/the high life* **5** [A *no comp.*] (of time) at the most important or mid-point of: *high summer*|*high noon*|*It's high time we went.* (=we have to go now; it's getting late) **6** [F] *infml* **a** drunk **b** under the effects of drugs

–opposite **low** (for 1,2,3,4)
USAGE People, and things that are narrow as well as high, are **tall** rather than **high**. Compare: *A* **high** *wall surrounds the prison.|a room with a* **high** *ceiling and a* **tall** *tree|a* **tall** *man*

high² *adv* [*adv* +*prep*/*adv*] **1** to or at a high level in position, movements, or sound: *They climbed high.|The plane flew high above.|The bird sang high and clearly.|*(fig.): *He's risen high in the world.* –opposite **low 2 high and dry** *infml* without help; deserted: *He took all the money and left me high and dry.* **3 high and low** everywhere: *I looked/searched high and low for it.* **4 high on the hog** *AmE infml* well and richly: *they've been living high on the hog since they found oil on their land.*

high³ *n* **1** [C] a high point; the highest level: *The price of food reached a new high this week.* –opposite **low 2** [C] *infml* a state of great excitement and happiness produced (as if) by a drug **3** a high place, esp. heaven (only in the phrase **on high**)

high·boy /ˈhaɪbɔɪ/ *AmE*||**tallboy** *BrE*–*n* a tall piece of wooden furniture containing several drawers

high·brow /ˈhaɪbraʊ/ *n,adj* sometimes derog (typical of) a person thought to show more than average knowledge of art and INTELLECTUAL interests –compare LOWBROW

high chair /ˈ· ·/ *n* a chair with long legs at which a baby or small child can sit, esp. when eating

high-class /ˌ· ˈ·◂/ *adj* **1** of good quality **2** of high social position

high com·mis·sion·er /ˌ· ·ˈ··/ *n* (*often caps.*) a person (like an AMBASSADOR) who represents one COMMONWEALTH country in another

high court /ˌ· ˈ·◂/ *n* the court which is above all the rest and which can be asked to change the decision of a lower court

high·er ed·u·ca·tion /ˌ··· ··ˈ··/ *n* [U] education at a university or college –compare CONTINUING EDUCATION

high fi·del·i·ty /ˌ· ·ˈ····/ also **hi-fi**– *adj* (of TAPE RECORDERS, RECORD PLAYERS, etc.) able to give out sound which represents very closely the details of the original sound before recording

high-flown /ˌ· ˈ·◂/ *adj* (of language) grand-sounding, though lacking in meaning

high-grade /ˌ· ˈ·◂/ *adj* [no comp.] of high quality: *high-grade cloth for suits*

high-hand·ed /ˌ· ˈ··◂/ *adj derog* using one's power too forcefully: *It was rather high-handed to punish the child for the accident.* –**high-handedly** *adv* –**high-handedness** *n* [U]

high jinks /ˈ· ·/ *n* [P;U] wild fun of a harmless type

high jump /ˈ· ·/ *n* a sport in which people jump over a bar which is raised higher and higher –compare LONG JUMP

high·land /ˈhaɪlənd/ *adj,n* (of) a mountainous area: *highland cattle|the Scottish Highlands* –compare LOWLAND

high-lev·el /ˌ· ˈ··◂/ *adj* [A] (involving people) of high importance: *high-level peace talks*

high·light¹ /ˈhaɪlaɪt/ *n* an important detail which stands out from the rest:*a film of the highlights of the competition*

highlight² *v* [T] to pick out (something) as an important part; throw attention onto

high·ly /ˈhaɪliʸ/ *adv* **1** (*esp. before adjectives made from verbs*) to a high degree; very: *highly skilled|highly enjoyable* **2** (very) well: *highly paid* |*He speaks very highly of you.*

high-strung /ˌ· ˈ·◂/ also **highly-strung** /ˌ·· ˈ·◂/ – *adj* nervous; excitable

high-mind·ed /ˌ· ˈ··◂/ *adj* (of people) having high principles –**high-mindedness** *n* [U]

High·ness /ˈhaɪnɪs/ *n* (a title used of or to certain royal persons): *His/Her/Your Highness|His Highness Prince Leopold*

high-pow·ered /ˌ· ˈ··◂/ *adj* showing great force (in an activity): *high-powered selling methods|a high-powered car*

high-pres·sure /ˌ· ˈ··◂/ *adj* **1** (of a machine or substance) which uses or is at high pressure **2** (of an action, job, or person) carried out or working with great speed and force: *A high-pressure salesman may make you buy something you don't want.*

high-rise /ˈ· ·/ *adj,n* [A;C] (a building, esp. a block of apartments) with many floors (STORYS): *She lives in a high-rise (apartment).*

high school /ˈ· ·/ *n* [C;U] *esp. AmE* (*caps. in names*) a SECONDARY school esp. for children over age 14

high-spir·it·ed /ˌ· ˈ···◂/ *adj* full of fun; adventure-loving

high tide /ˌ· ˈ·/ *n* [C;U] the moment when the water is highest up the seashore because the TIDE has come in –see also LOW TIDE

high·way /ˈhaɪweʸ/ *n esp. AmE* a broad main road used esp. by traffic going from one town to another

high·way·man /ˈhaɪweʸmən/ *n* -**men** /mən/ (in former times) a man who used to stop travellers on the roads and rob them of their money

hi·jack /ˈhaɪdʒæk/ *v* [T] to take control of (a vehicle or aircraft) by force of arms, often for political aims –**hijacker** *n* –**hijacking, hijack** *n* [C;U]

hike¹ /haɪk/ *n* a long walk in the country

hike² *v* **hiked, hiking** [I] **1** to go on a HIKE¹ **2** [T] *infml esp. AmE* (of prices) to raise suddenly or with one movement: *to hike rents* –**hiker** *n* –**hiking** *n* [U]

hi·lar·i·ous /hɪˈlɛəriʸəs, -ˈlær-/ *adj* full of or causing laughter: *a hilarious film* –**hilariously** *adv*

hi·lar·i·ty /hɪˈlærətiʸ, -ˈlɛər-/ *n* [U] cheerfulness, expressed in laughter

hill /hɪl/ *n* **1** a raised part of the earth's surface, not as high as a mountain, and not usu. as bare, rocky, etc. **2** the slope of a road or path –**hilly** *adj* -**ier, -iest**

hill·bil·ly /ˈhɪlˌbɪliʸ/ *n,adj* -**lies** *AmE often derog* (for, concerning) a person, from a small country place, usu. the mountainous area of the southeastern US: *hillbilly music*

hill·ock /ˈhɪlək/ *n* a little hill

hill·side /ˈhɪlsaɪd/ *n* the slope of a hill, as

opposed to the top (**hilltop**)

hilt /hɪlt/ *n* the handle of a sword, or of a knife which is used as a weapon: (fig.) *She's in trouble (**up**) to the hilt.* (=completely)

him /ɪm; *strong* hɪm/ *pron* (*object form of* HE): *That dog never comes when I call him.|Which is your brother? Is that him?|I heard him singing outside.* –see ME (USAGE)

him·self /ɪm'sɛlf; *strong* hɪm'sɛlf/ *pron* **1** (used as the object of a verb, or after a PREPOSITION, when the same male person or animal does the action and is the object of the action): *He hurt himself.|Did he enjoy himself?|Tom's old enough to look after himself.|*(with general meaning) *A man should be able to defend himself.* **2** (used to make *he*, or the name of a male person or animal, stronger): *He himself told me.|He ate it himself.|I want the director himself, not his secretary.*

hind /haɪnd/ *adj* [A *no comp.*] (usu. of animals' legs) belonging to the back part –compare FORELEG

hin·der /'hɪndər/ *v* [T] to prevent (someone from doing something or something from being done): *You're hindering (me in) my work by talking all the time.*

hind·quar·ters /'haɪnd,kwɔrtərz/ *n* [P] the back part of an animal including the legs –compare HAUNCHES

hin·drance /'hɪndrəns/ *n* [*to*] something or somebody that HINDERs: *He said he'd help me do the job, but he was more of a hindrance than a help.*

hind·sight /'haɪndsaɪt/ *n* [U] the ability to see how and why something happened, esp. to know that it could have been prevented: *I now know with hindsight that it was a mistake to buy that car.* –compare FORESIGHT (1)

Hin·du /'hɪnduʷ/ *adj,n* (of) a person whose religion is Hinduism

Hin·du·ism /'hɪnduʷ,ɪzəm/ *n* [U] the chief religion of India, notable esp. for its social ranks (CASTE system) and the belief that one returns after death in another form (REINCARNATION)

hinge¹ /hɪndʒ/ *n* a metal part which joins two objects together and allows the first to swing freely, such as one joining a door to a frame, or a lid to a box: *Oil the hinges; the door is* CREAK*ing.* (=making an unpleasant noise)

hinge² *v* **hinged, hinging** [T] to fix (something) on HINGEs

hinge on/upon sthg.– *v prep* [T +*v-ing*] depend on: *Everything hinges on what we do next.*

hint¹ /hɪnt/ *n* **1** a small or indirect suggestion: *I kept looking at my watch, but he just continued talking: he can't* **take** (=understand) **a hint. 2** a small sign: *There's a hint of summer in the air, although it's only April.* **3** useful advice: *helpful hints*

hint² *v* [I;T +*that*] to suggest indirectly: *I hinted (to him) that I was dissatisfied with his work.*

hint at sthg. *v prep* [T] to speak about in an indirect way: *She hinted at leaving early.*

hin·ter·land /'hɪntər,lænd/ *n* the inner part of a country, beyond the coast or the banks of an important river: *They got away from the excitement of New York by taking a trip to the hinterlands.*

hip /hɪp/ *n* the fleshy part of either side of the human body above the legs: *Swimming is good for the hips.*

hip·pie , hippy /'hɪpiʸ/ *n* -**pies** *becoming rare* (esp. in the 1960's) a person who is (thought to be) against the standards of ordinary society, showing this esp. by having long hair, dressing in a colorful way, and (sometimes) taking drugs for pleasure

hip·po·pot·a·mus /,hɪpə'pɑtəməs/ *also* **hip·po** /'hɪpoʷ/ *infml* –*n* -**muses** *or* -**mi** /,maɪ/ a large African animal with a thick body and thick hairless skin, which lives near water

hire¹ /haɪər/ *v* **hired, hiring** [T] **1** to employ (someone) for a time for payment: *The fruit is picked by hired laborers.* **2** *BrE* for RENT² (3) –see RENT (USAGE)

hire sbdy. ↔ **out** *v adv* [T *to*] to give (one's) services for payment: *Farm laborers used to hire themselves out for the summer.*

hire² *n* [U] (payment for) the act of hiring or state of being hired: *To work for hire*

his /ɪz; *strong* hɪz/ *determiner,pron* (POSSESSIVE *form of* HE) **1** of that male person or animal already mentioned: *Peter sat down in his chair.|I cleaned my shoes, and John cleaned his.|That's my coat, and his is over there.* **2** of that person: *I hope Steve does his best in the race.*

hiss /hɪs/ *v* [I;T *at*] to make a sound like a continuous "s," esp. to show anger, disapproval, etc.: *The cat hissed as the dog came near it.|Gas escaped with a hissing noise from the broken pipe.|The crowd hissed (at) the speaker when he said taxes should be increased.* –**hiss** *n: The snake gave an angry hiss.*

his·to·ri·an /hɪ'stɔriʸən, -'stoʷr-/ *n* a person who studies and/or writes about history

his·tor·ic /hɪ'stɔrɪk, -'stɑr-/ *adj* important in history –see HISTORY (USAGE)

his·tor·i·cal /hɪ'stɔrɪkəl, -'stɑr-/ *adj* **1** connected with history as a study: *He gave all his historical papers to the library.* **2** which represents a fact/facts of history: *a historical play/*NOVEL*|Is it a historical fact (=is it true) that Washington slept in this house?* –see HISTORY (USAGE) –**historically** *adv*

his·to·ry /'hɪstəriʸ/ *n* -**ries 1** [U] (the study of) events in the past, esp. events concerning the rulers and government of a country, social and trade conditions, etc.: *History is my favorite subject at school.|For the first time in our country's history, we have a President who is divorced.* **2** [C] a (written) account of history: *a short history of the last war* **3** [C] a set of events relating to a place or person: *Mr. Jones has a long history of heart trouble.* **4 make history** to do something important which will be recorded and remembered

USAGE A **story** is an account of a number of connected events which may or may not have really happened. **History** is concerned with real events of the past, and **historical** characters or events are those that have really existed or happened. A place is **historic** if it has a long **history,** and an event is **historic** if it will be remembered in **history.** Compare: *a* **historic** *meeting between two great leaders|a meeting of the local* **historical** *society* (=a society concerned with history)

his·tri·on·ic /ˌhɪstriˈɑnɪk/ *adj* **1** concerning the theater or acting **2** *derog* done or performed in a theatrical way; showing pretended feelings, not real ones **–histrionically** *adv*

his·tri·on·ics /ˌhɪstriʸˈɑnɪks/ *n* [P] *derog* behavior which is like a theatrical performance, with no real feelings behind it

hit¹ /hɪt/ *v* **hit, hitting** [T] **1** to give a blow to; strike: *He hit the other man.|He hit the ball (with the* BAT*).* **2** to (cause to) come against (something) with force: *The ball hit the window.|She hit her head on the table.* **3** *infml* to reach: *We hit the main road after traveling two miles on a side road.|Price increases hit* (=have a bad effect on) *everyone's pocket.* (=money) **4 hit it off (with)** *infml* to have a good relationship (with): *I'm glad to see the two girls hitting it off so well.* **5 hit the roof** also **hit the ceiling** *AmE– infml* to show or express great anger **6 hit the nail on the head** to be exactly right (in saying something) **7 hit someone where it hurts (most)** to attack someone through his/her weaknesses **8 hit the bottle** *infml* to (start to) drink too much alcohol **9 hit the hay/sack** *infml* to go to bed **10 hit the road** *esp. AmE* to leave **11 hit the brakes** *AmE* to step on or use the BRAKE¹*s* suddenly (to stop a car, bicycle, etc.)

hit on/upon sthg. *v prep* [T] to find by lucky chance or have a good idea about: *Peter hit on an idea that will get us out of our difficulty.*

hit² *n* **1** a blow; stroke: *He aimed a wild hit at his attacker.|That was a good hit. It almost saved the game.* **2** the act of successfully striking something aimed at: *I* SCORE*d a direct hit with my first shot.* –compare MISS² **3** something, esp. a recorded song or other performance, that is very successful: *The song was a hit at once.|*(fig.) *You've* **made a hit with** *him; he likes you.*

hit-and-run /ˌ· · '· ◄/ *adj* [A] **1** (of a road accident) of a type in which the guilty driver does not stop to help **2** (of a driver) who behaves in this way

hitch¹ /hɪtʃ/ *v* **1** [T] to fasten by hooking a rope or metal part over another object: *He hitched the horse's rope over the pole.|Another train car has been hitched on.* **2** [I;T] *infml* to travel by getting rides in other people's cars: *He hitched across Canada.|Let's hitch a ride.*

hitch sthg. ↔ **up** *v adv* [T] **1** to pull upwards into place: *John hitched up his pants.* **2** to fasten (to something) by HITCHING¹: *I hitched up the horses (to the cart).*

hitch² *n* a difficulty which delays something for a while: *a slight hitch|A* **technical hitch** *prevented the lights from working.*

hitch·hike /ˈhɪtʃhaɪk/ *v* **-hiked, -hiking** [I] to go on a journey by getting rides in other people's cars **–hitchhiker** *n*

hith·er /ˈhɪðər/ *adv* **1** *old use* to this place:

Come hither! **2 hither and thither** in all directions

hith·er·to /ˌhɪðərˈtuʷ, ˈhɪðərˌtuʷ/ *adv fml* up until now: *Hitherto we have always paid the rent on Mondays.*

hit-or-miss /ˌ· · '·/ *adj* which depends on chance; not planned carefully

hive /haɪv/ also **beehive–** *n* a place where bees live, like a small hut or box: (fig.) *What a* **hive of industry!** (=a crowded busy place)

h'm /hm, hmh/ *interj* → HUMPH

HMS *abbrev. for:* His/Her MAJESTY's Ship (a title for a ship in the British Royal Navy): *HMS Belfast*

hoard¹ /hɔrd, hoʷrd/ *v* [T] to store secretly in large amounts **–hoarder** *n*

hoard² *n* a (secret) store, esp. of something valuable to the owner

hoar·frost /ˈhɔrfrɒst, ˈhoʷr-/ *n* [U] white frozen drops of water, as seen on grass and plants after a cold night

hoarse /hɔrs, hoʷrs/ *adj* (of a person or voice) HARSH-sounding, as during a cold –compare HUSKY **–hoarsely** *adv* **–hoarseness** *n* [U]

hoar·y /ˈhɔriʸ, ˈhoʷriʸ/ *adj* **-ier, -iest** (of hair) gray or white with age

hoax /hoʷks/ *n* a trick, esp. one which makes someone believe something which is not true, and take action upon that belief: *We all left the building after a telephone caller said there was a bomb, but it was just a hoax.* **–hoax** *v* [T]

hob·ble /ˈhɑbəl/ *v* **-bled, -bling** [I] to walk in an awkward way, with difficulty: *I hurt my foot and had to hobble home.*

hob·by /ˈhɑbiʸ/ *n* **-bies** an activity which one enjoys doing in one's free time –see RECREATION (USAGE)

hob·by·horse /ˈhɑbiʸˌhɔrs/ *n* **1** a child's toy like a horse's head on a stick **2** a fixed idea to which a person keeps returning in conversation

hob·nob /ˈhɑbnɑb/ *v* **-bb-** [I *with*] *sometimes derog* to have a (pleasant) social relationship, often with someone in a higher position: *I've been hobnobbing with the directors at the office party.*

ho·bo /ˈhoʷboʷ/ *n* **-boes** or **-bos** *AmE infml* a wanderer who has no regular work; TRAMP² (1)

hock¹ /hɑk/ *n* a cut of meat from an animal's leg, above the foot

hock² *v infml* [T] → PAWN¹

hock³ *n infml* **in hock** being held by a PAWNBROKER

hock·ey /ˈhɑkiʸ/ *n* **1** *AmE* for FIELD HOCKEY **2** *esp. AmE* for ICE HOCKEY

hodge·podge /ˈhɑdʒpɑdʒ/ *n* [usu. sing.] a number of things mixed up without any sensible order of arrangement

hoe¹ /hoʷ/ *n* a long-handled garden tool used esp. for removing wild plants (WEED*s*)

hoe² *v* **hoed, hoeing** [I;T] to use a HOE (on)

hog¹ /hɑg, hag/ *n* **hogs** or **hog 1** *esp. AmE* a pig, esp. a fat one for eating –compare BOAR, sow **2** a dirty, selfish person who eats too much **3 go whole hog** *infml* to do something thoroughly

hog² v **-gg-** [T] *infml* to take and keep (all of something) for oneself: *Drivers who* **hog the road** *leave no room for other cars.*

hoist¹ /hɔɪst/ v [T *up*] to raise up by force, esp. when using ropes on board a ship: *He hoisted it over his shoulder.|The sailors hoisted the flag.*

hoist² n **1** an upward push **2** an apparatus for lifting heavy goods

hold¹ /howᵘld/ v **held** /held/, **holding 1** [T] to keep or support with a part of the body, esp. with the hands: *This cup is too hot for me to hold.|The dog held the newspaper in its mouth.* **2** [T] to put or keep (a part of the body) in the stated position: *She held her arm still while the doctor looked at it.* **3** [T] to keep in position; support: *She held her hair back with a pin.|a roof held up by strong supports* **4** [T] to keep back or control: *The police held the angry crowd back.* **5** [T] to be able to contain: *How much water does the pan hold?|(fig.) Life holds many surprises.* **6** [T] to have or keep in one's possession: *He holds a half share in the business.|She holds the office of chairwoman.|(fig.) His speech held their attention* **7** [T] to make (something) happen: *We held a meeting on Tuesday.* **8** [T] to keep in the stated position or condition: (fig.) *We held ourselves in readiness for bad news.* **9** [T +*that*] *infml* to express one's belief (that); consider: *I hold (the view) that he's a fool.* **10** [I] to be or remain in a certain state; continue: *What he said still holds/holds good.* (=is true)|*Can the good weather hold?|The bridge failed to hold and crashed into the river below.* **11 Hold it!** Stay like that; don't move! **12 hold one's breath** to stop breathing, e.g. through fear or expectation **13 be left holding the bag** (*AmE*)|**baby** (*BrE*) to find oneself responsible for doing something which someone else has started and left unfinished **14 hold one's own** to keep one's (strong) position even when attacked **15 hold the line** to wait on the telephone –compare HOLD **on**(1)

hold sthg. **against** sbdy. v prep [T] to allow (something bad that someone has done) to have an effect on one's feelings about (this person): *We shouldn't hold it against him that he spent some time in prison.|We shouldn't hold his past mistakes against him.*

hold back v adv **1** [T] (**hold** sbdy./sthg.↔ **back**) also **keep back**– to cause to stay in place; control: *We built banks of earth to hold back the rising flood waters.|Police held the crowds back.|(fig.) Jim was unable to hold back his anger any longer.* **2** [T] (**hold** sbdy.↔ **back**) to prevent the development of: *You could become a good musician, but your lack of practice is holding you back.* **3** [I;T] (=**hold** sthg.↔ **back**) to keep (something) secret: *We must have the whole story: don't hold (anything) back.*

hold sthg.↔ **down** v adv [T] **1** to keep (esp. a job): *Jim seems unable to hold down a job for more than a few weeks.* **2** to keep at a low level: *to hold prices down* –see also KEEP **down** (1)

hold forth v adv [I *on*] *often derog* to speak at length

hold off v adv [I;T (=**hold** sbdy./sthg.↔ **off**)] **1** also **keep off**– to (cause to) remain at a distance: *We must hold off the enemy's attack.|Will the rain hold off until after the game?* **2** also **put off**– to delay: *The leaders will hold off making a decision until Monday.*

hold on v adv [I] **1** to wait (often on the telephone); HANG **on**: *Could you hold on? I'll just see if he's in.* **2** to continue (in spite of difficulties); HANG **on¹** (3); HOLD **out** (2)

hold onto sthg. v prep [T] →HANG **onto**

hold out v adv **1** (**hold out** sthg.) to offer: *I don't hold out much hope that the weather will improve.|She held out her hand in friendship.* **2** also **hang on, hold on**– to last (in spite of difficulties); ENDURE: *The town was surrounded, but the people held out until help came.|I think the car will hold out until we reach Chicago.* **3** [I;T *on*] to refuse or to be slow to act on or agree to something: *Everyone has agreed on the plan but Peter. He's still holding out.*

hold out for sthg. v adv prep [T] to demand firmly and wait in order to get: *The men are still holding out for more pay.*

hold sthg. **over** v adv [T] to move to a later date: *The concert was held over until the following week because of the singer's illness.*

hold (sbdy.) **to** sthg. v prep [T] *fml* to (cause to) follow exactly or keep to: *We tried to change his mind, but he held to his decision.*

hold/keep sthg.↔ **together** v adv [T] to cause to remain united: *I used a pin to hold the belt together|A child often holds a marriage together.*

hold sbdy./ sthg.↔ **up** v adv [T] **1** to delay: *The building of the new road has been held up by bad weather.* **2** to stop in order to rob: *The criminals held up the train and took all the money.* **3** to show as an example: *Grandfather always held up his youngest son as a model of hard work.* –see also HOLDUP

hold with sthg. v prep [T] to approve of; agree with: *I don't hold with some of the strange ideas you believe in.*

hold² n **1** [C;U] the act of holding; GRIP² (1): *Take/get/catch hold of the rope, and we'll pull you up.|Keep hold of/Don't lose hold of my hand.|(fig.) He's got a good hold of his subject.|I have to get hold of* (=find) *John/some more writing paper.* **2** [C] something which can be held, esp. in climbing: *Can you find a hold for your hands so that you can pull yourself up?* –compare FOOTHOLD **3 have a hold over** to know something which gives one an influence over **4 no holds barred** all methods are permitted

hold³ n the part of a ship (below DECK) where goods are stored

hold·er /ˈhowᵘldər/ n **1** a person who has control of or possesses a place, a position, or money: *The holder of this office is responsible for arranging meetings.* –compare HOLD¹ (6) **2 -holder: a** a person who holds property; TENANT: *a* LEASE-*holder/house-holder* **b** something which holds or contains: *a cigarette holder*

hold·ing /ˈhoʷldɪŋ/ n something which one possesses, esp. land or SHARES¹ (2)

hold·out /ˈhoʷldaʊt/ n infml esp. AmE a person who will not or is slow to act on or agree to something

hold·o·ver /ˈhoʷld,oʷvər/ n [from] esp. AmE something that has continued to exist longer than expected: His long hair is a holdover from the 60's.

hold·up /ˈhoʷldʌp/ n **1** a delay, as of traffic **2** also **stickup** infml –an attempt at robbery by threatening people with a gun –see also HOLD up (2)

hole¹ /hoʷl/ n **1** an empty space within something solid: The men have dug a hole in the road.|There's a hole in my sock. **2** the home of a small animal: a rabbit hole **3** (in GOLF) a hollow place into which the ball must be hit **4** infml a small unpleasant place: His apartment is a hole. **5 poke/pick holes in something** to say what is wrong with something, esp.when it is not really faulty

hole² v **holed, holing** [I;T] to put (a ball) in a hole in GOLF: to hole in one (=one stroke)

hole up v adv [I] infml esp. AmE to hide as a means of escape: After the bank robbery, the criminals holed up in an old factory.

hol·i·day /ˈhalə,deʸ/ n **1** a time of rest from work, a day (often originally of religious or historical importance) or longer **2** BrE for VACATION –see VACATION (USAGE) –**holiday** v [I]

ho·li·ness /ˈhoʷliʸnɪs/ n **1** [U] the state or quality of being holy **2** (usu. cap.) (a title of the POPE): Your Holiness|His Holiness Pope John Paul

hol·ler /ˈhalər/ v [I;T to,at] infml esp. AmE to shout out: "Let go," she hollered. –**holler** n: He let out a holler as soon as he saw me.

hol·low¹ /ˈhaloʷ/ adj **1** having an empty space inside: The pillars look solid, but in fact they're hollow. (fig.) the hollow (=insincere) promises of politicians|hollow cheeks (=with the skin sinking inwards) **2** having a ringing sound like the note when an empty container is struck: the hollow sound of a large bell –**hollowly** adv –**hollowness** n [U]

hollow² n a space sunk into something, esp. into the ground

hollow out v adv [T] **1** to make a hollow place in sthg.: to hollow out a log **2** [of] to make by doing this: to hollow a CANOE out of a log

hol·ly /ˈhaliʸ/ n [U] a small tree with dark green shiny prickly leaves and red berries

Hol·ly·wood /ˈhaliʸˌwʊd/ n an area in Los Angeles, California, famous because many popular movies have been made there: a Hollywood movie

hol·o·caust /ˈhalə,kɔst, ˈhoʷ-/ n the loss of many lives, esp. by burning

hol·ster /ˈhoʷlstər/ n a leather holder for a PISTOL (=small hand gun), esp. one that hangs on a belt around the waist

ho·ly /ˈhoʷliʸ/ adj -**lier, -liest 1** connected with God and religion: the Holy Bible|the holy city of Mecca/Benares **2** (of a person or life) in the service of God and religion; pure and blameless

hom·age /ˈhamɪdʒ, ˈa-/ n [U] signs of great respect: They **paid homage to** the king.

home¹ /hoʷm/ n **1** the place where one usually lives, esp. with one's family: "Where do you live?" "Well, Nigeria is my home, but I'm living in New York just now."|The White House is the home of the President and his family.|He's not **at home** (=in the house) now; he should be back at seven. –see USAGE **2** a place where a thing lives, exists, etc.: India is the home of elephants and tigers.|America is the home of BASEBALL. **3** a place for the care of a group of people or animals of the same type,who do not live with a family: a children's home **4** be/feel **at home** to be comfortable; not feel worried, esp. because one has the right skills or experience: He's completely at home working with children. **5 make oneself at home** to behave freely, sit where one likes, etc., as if at home –**homeless** adj –**homelessness** n [U]

USAGE We use the simple tenses of live (not *stay) when talking about **home**. –see HOUSE (USAGE)

home² adv **1** to or at one's home: Is she home yet?|I have to be getting home. **2** to the right place: He struck the nail home. **3 bring home to/come home to someone** to (cause to) be fully understood by someone: At last it's come home to me how much I owe to my parents.

home³ adj [A] **1** of, related to, or being a home, place of origin, or base of operations: the home office of an international firm|Boston is my **home town**. **2** not foreign; DOMESTIC¹ (3): the home country|home affairs|the islanders are demanding **home rule.** (=self-government) **3** prepared, made, or done in a home: home cooking|**homemade** clothes/jam|These **homegrown** apples (=grown at home) taste better than the ones from abroad. **4** working, playing, or happening in a home area: the home team|home games –compare AWAY²

home·com·ing /ˈhoʷm,kʌmɪŋ/ n an arrival home, esp. after long absence

home in on sthg. v adv prep [T] to aim exactly towards

home·land /ˈhoʷmlænd/ n one's native country

home·ly /ˈhoʷmliʸ/ adj -**lier, -liest 1** simple, not grand: a homely meal of bread and cheese **2** AmE (of a person) not good-looking –**homeliness** n [U]

home·mak·er /ˈhoʷm,meʸkər/ n a person who takes care of a home

ho·me·op·a·thy esp. AmE‖**homoeo-** BrE /,hoʷmiʸˈapəθiʸ/ n [U] the practice of treating a disease by giving small amounts of a drug which, in larger amounts, would produce an illness like the disease –**homeopath** /ˈhoʷmiʸə,pæθ/ n –**homeopathic** ,hoʷmiʸə'pæθɪk/ adj –**homeopathically** adv

home run /,· '·/ also **homer** /ˈhoʷmər/ infml– n in BASEBALL, a long hit which allows a player to go around all the bases and score a point

home·sick /ˈhoʷm,sɪk/ adj feeling a great wish to be at home, when away from it –**homesickness** n [U]

home·stead /'howmstɛd/ n **1** a house and land; a farm with its buildings **2** *esp. AmE* a piece of land given by the state (esp. in former times) on condition that the owner farm it for a certain length of time

home truth /ˌ·'·/ n a fact about someone which is unpleasant for him/her to know, but true

home·ward /'howmwərd/ adj going towards home: *the homeward journey* –opposite **outward** –**homeward** *AmE*‖ also **homewards**– adv: *hurrying homeward*

home·work /'howmwɜrk/ n [U] schoolwork, such as essays, which is done outside the classroom, esp. at home, in a library, etc. –compare HOUSEWORK

hom·ey, homy /'howmiy/ **-ier, -iest** adj AmE infml pleasant, like home

hom·i·ci·dal /ˌhɑmə'saɪdl◂/ adj likely to murder

hom·i·cide /'hɑmə,saɪd/ n fml or law **1** [C;U] (an act of) murder **2** [C] a murderer

hom·i·ly /'hɑməliy/ n **-lies** fml **1** →SERMON **2** usu. derog a long talk giving one advice on how to behave

hom·ing /'howmɪŋ/ adj [A] having the ability **a** (esp. of PIGEONS) to find one's way home **b** (esp.of modern weapons of war) to guide themselves onto the place they are aimed at: *a* MISSILE *with a homing device*

ho·mo·ge·ne·ous /ˌhowmə'dʒiyniyəs, -'dʒiy nyəs, ˌhɑ-/ adj formed of parts of the same kind –compare HETEROGENEOUS –**homogeneity** /ˌhowmədʒə'niyətiy, -'ney-, ˌhɑ-/ [U] –**homogeneously** /ˌhowmə'dʒiyniy əsliy, -'dʒiy nyəs-, ˌhɑ-/ adv

ho·mog·e·nize‖also **-nise** BrE /hə'mɑdʒə ˌnaɪz/ v **-nized, -nizing** [T] to make (the parts of a whole) become evenly spread: *homogenized milk* (=with no cream, because the fat is broken up all through the liquid)

hom·o·nym /'hɑmə,nɪm, 'how-/ n a word which has the same sound and usu. the same spelling as another, though different in meaning or origin: *The noun "bear" and the verb "bear" are homonyms (of each other).*

hom·o·phone /ˌhɑmə,fown, 'how-/ n a word which sounds the same as another but is different in meaning, origin, or spelling: *"knew" and "new" are homophones (of each other).*

ho·mo·sex·u·al /ˌhowmə'sɛkʃuwəl/ adj,n (of or being) a person sexually attracted to people of the same sex –compare BISEXUAL, HETEROSEXUAL, LESBIAN

hone /hown/ v **honed, honing** [T] to sharpen (knives, swords, etc.)

hon·est /'ɑnɪst/ adj **1** (of people) trustworthy; not likely to lie or to cheat **2** (of actions, appearance, etc.) showing such qualities: *an honest face/opinion* –opposite **dishonest**

hon·est·ly /'ɑnɪstliy/ adv **1** in an honest way –opposite **dishonestly 2 a** really; speaking truthfully: *I didn't tell anyone; honestly I didn't.* **b** (used for expressing strong feeling usu. mixed with disapproval): *Honestly! What a stupid thing to do!*

hon·es·ty /'ɑnəstiy/ n [U] the quality of being honest –opposite **dishonesty**

hon·ey /'hʌniy/ n **-eys 1** [U] the sweet sticky soft material produced by bees, which is eaten on bread **2** [C] esp. AmE →DARLING

hon·ey·comb /'hʌniy,kowm/ n a container made by bees of beeswax and consisting of six-sided cells in which honey is stored

hon·ey·moon /'hʌniy,muwn/ n the holiday taken by a man and woman who have just gotten married v [I]: *We honeymooned in Paris.* –**honeymooner** n

hon·ey·suck·le /'hʌniy,sʌkəl/ n [C;U] a climbing plant with sweet-smelling yellow flowers

honk /hɑŋk, hɔŋk/ v,n [I;T] (to make) the sound (like that) of a GOOSE or a car horn: *honking geese* (GOOSE)‖*As she drove past, she honked the horn/gave the horn a honk.*

hon·or¹ AmE‖**honour** BrE /'ɑnər/ **1** [U] great respect, often publicly expressed: *a party* **in honor of** (=to show respect to) *the visiting president* –opposite **dishonor 2** [U] high standards of character that cause one to be respected by others: *a man of honor*‖*to fight for/to save the honor of one's country* **3** [S] something that brings pride or pleasure: *It's a great honor to have the President visiting our town.* **4** [C] (a title of respect for a judge): *Your/His Honor* **5 on one's honor** in a position which would bring shame on oneself if one did not do what one has promised to: *He was (put) on his honor not to tell the secret.*

hon·or² AmE‖**honour** BrE [T] **1** to show respect to: *Today the President is honoring us with his presence.*‖*I'm honored that you should remember me.* **2** to keep (an agreement), often by making a payment:*You must have enough money to honor your checks before writing them.*

hon·or·a·ble AmE‖**honourable** BrE /'ɑnər əbəl/ adj showing or deserving honor –opposite **dishonorable**; –compare HONORARY –**honorably** adv

Honorable AmE‖**Honourable** BrE **Hon.** adj [A] (a title given to judges and various official people, including Members of Parliament): *Will the Honorable member please answer the question?*‖*As my Honorable friend has said, . . .*

hon·or·a·ry /'ɑnə,reriy/ adj **1** (of a rank, university degree, etc.) given as a sign of HONOR, not according to the usual rules **2** (of an office or position held) without payment for one's services: *He's the honorary chairman.* –compare HONORABLE

honor roll /'·· ˌ·/ n AmE a list of the names of people who have earned praise, as by passing an examination, a course, or showing bravery in battle etc.

hon·ors AmE‖**honours** BrE /'ɑnərz/ n [A;P] **1** a specialized university UNDERGRADUATE degree: *She graduated with honors.*‖*an honors degree* **2 (full) military honors** ceremonies at which soldiers attend esp. to bury a great person **3 do the honors** infml to act as the host or hostess, as by offering drink

hood /hʊd/ n **1** a covering for the whole of the

head and neck (except the face), often fastened to a coat **2** *AmE*‖**bonnet** *BrE*– a metal lid over the front of a car –see illustration on page 95

hood·wink /'hʊd,wiŋk/ v [T] to trick or deceive

hoof /hʊf, huʷf/ n **hoofs** or **hooves** /hʊvz, huʷvz/ the hard foot of certain animals, as of the horse

hook¹ /hʊk/ n **1 a** a curved piece of metal, plastic, etc., for catching something on or hanging things on: *a fish hook*|*Hang your coat on the hook.* **b** a small one used with an EYE¹ (4) to fasten clothing **2** (*usu. in comb.*) a tool for cutting grass, branches, etc. **3** (in BOXING) a blow given with the elbow bent **4 be/get off the hook** to be/get out of a difficult situation **4 by hook or by crook** by any means possible **6 hook, line, and sinker** (with expressions of belief) completely: *I swallowed the unlikely story hook, line, and sinker*

hook² v [T] **1** to catch (as if) with a HOOK¹ (1): *to hook a fish* **2** to hang on or fasten (as if) with a HOOK¹(1): *Hook my dress up.*|*Hook the rope over that nail.*

hook *sthg.*↔ **up** v adv [I] to connect to a power supply or central system: *Is the television hooked up?*

hooked /hʊkt/ adj **1** shaped like a hook: *a hooked nose* **2** [F *on*] *infml* **a** dependent (on drugs) **b** having a great liking for and very frequently using, doing, eating, etc.: *She's hooked on old movies.* –compare ADDICTED (to)

hook·y, hookey /'hʊkiʸ/ n [U] *AmE infml* →TRUANT (only in the phrase **play hooky**)

hoo·li·gan /'huʷlɪgən/ n a noisy, rough person who causes trouble by fighting, breaking things, etc. –**hooliganism** n [U]

hoop /huʷp, hʊp/ n a circular band of wood or metal, esp. around barrel or used as a child's toy

hoo·ray /hʊ'reʸ, hə'reʸ/ interj,n →HURRAY

hoot¹ /huʷt/ v [I;T *at, with*] to (cause to) make a HOOT²: *When he began to sing, we all hooted at him.*

hoot² n **1** the sound made by an OWL, a ship's horn, or (*BrE*) a car horn **2** a shout of dislike, unpleasant laughter, etc.: *His speech was greeted with loud hoots.* **3 not give/care a hoot/two hoots** *infml* not to care at all: *He doesn't give a hoot whether he passes his examination or not.*

hooves /hʊvz, huʷz/ n pl. of HOOF

hop¹ /hɑp/ v **-pp-** [I] **1 a** (of people) to jump on one leg **b** (of small creatures) to jump: *The bird hopped onto my finger.* **2** [*on, in*] *infml* to get quickly onto or into: *She hopped on her bicycle*|*in(to) her car and rushed off.* **3 hopping mad** very angry

hop² n **1** an act of HOPping; jump **2** *infml* a distance traveled by a plane before landing: *It's a short hop from Washington to New York.*

hop³ n a tall climbing plant with flowers whose seed-cases (**hops**) are dried and used in making beer

hope¹ /hoʷp/ v **hoped, hoping** [I;T +*to-v*/(*that*)/*for*] to wish and expect; desire

in spite of doubts: *I hope he'll come tomorrow.*|*We're hoping to visit France this year.*|*After this dry weather, everyone hopes for rain.*

USAGE Compare **hope** and **wish**: You can **wish** for impossible things, but you can **hope** only when the thing you want is possible: *I* **wish** *I were 20 years younger.*|*I* **hope** *you'll be better soon.* –see also WAIT (USAGE)

hope² n [C;U +(*that*)/ *of*] **1** the expectation of something happening as one wishes: *There's not much hope that he'll come/of him coming.* **2** a person or thing that seems likely to bring success: *Please help me; you're my only hope/last hope.* **3 hold out hope** to give reason to expect: *He can hold out no hope of succeeding.* **4 raise someone's hopes** to make someone hope for success, esp. when it is unlikely

hope·ful /'hoʷpfəl/ adj [+*that*] feeling or giving cause for hope: *I'm hopeful that he'll arrive early.*|*There are hopeful signs that an agreement will be reached.* –**hopefulness** n [U]

hope·ful·ly /'hoʷpfəliʸ/ adv **1** in a hopeful way **2** if our hopes succeed: *Hopefully we'll be there by dinnertime.*

USAGE This second meaning of **hopefully** is now very common, esp. in speech, but it is thought by some teachers to be incorrect.

hope·less /'hoʷp-lɪs/ adj **1** showing or giving no hope: *hopeless tears* |*The doctor said Ann's condition was hopeless.* (=incurable) **2** *infml* useless: *Your work is hopeless, and so are you.* –**hopelessly** adv –**hopelessness** n [U]

hop·scotch /'hɑpskɑtʃ/ n [U] a children's game in which a stone is thrown onto numbered squares and each child HOPs from one to another

horde /hɔrd, hoʷrd/ n a large number or crowd: *A horde/Hordes of children ran through the building.* –sounds like **hoard**

ho·ri·zon /hə'raɪzən/ n the limit of one's view across the surface of the earth, where the sky seems to meet the earth or sea

hor·i·zon·tal /,hɔrə'zɑntəl, ,hɑr-/ adj in a flat position, along or parallel to the ground: *Stand the table on its legs, so that the top is horizontal.* –compare VERTICAL –**horizontally** adv

hor·mone /'hɔrmoʷn/ n any of several substances directed from organs of the body into the bloodstream so as to influence growth, development, etc.

horn /hɔrn/ n **1** [C] a hard pointed growth found in a pair on the top of the heads of cattle, sheep, and goats **2** [U] the material that these growths are made of: *The knife has a horn handle.* **3** [C] an apparatus, as in a car, which gives a warning sound: *The driver blew/sounded his horn when the child stepped in front of his/her car.* –see illustration on page 95 **4** [C] any of a number of musical instruments consisting of a long metal tube, usu. bent several times and played by blowing: *the French horn*|*a hunting horn*

hor·net /'hɔrnɪt/ n a large insect which can sting, related to the WASP

horn·pipe /'hɔrnpaɪp/ *n* (the music for) a dance, esp. performed by sailors

horn·y /'hɔrniʸ/ *adj* **-ier, -iest** hard and rough: *The old gardener had horny hands.*

hor·o·scope /'hɔrə,skoʷp, 'har-/ *n* a set of ideas about someone's character, life, and future, which are gained by knowing the positions of the stars or PLANETs at the time of his birth

hor·ren·dous /hə'rendəs, hɔ-, ha-/ *adj* really terrible; causing great fear **–horrendously** *adv*

hor·ri·ble /'hɔrəbəl, 'har-/ *adj* **1** causing HORROR: *a horrible accident* **2** *infml* very unkind, unpleasant, or ugly: *What a horrible dress!* **–horribly** *adv*

hor·rid /'hɔrɪd, 'harɪd/ *adj esp. BrE* [*to*] very unpleasant or unkind; HORRIBLE (2): *I've had a horrid day.|Don't be so horrid (to Aunt Jane)!* **–horridly** *adv* **–horridness** *n* [U]

hor·rif·ic /hɔ'rɪfɪk, ha-, hə-/ *adj* able to or meant to HORRIFY, shock, etc.: *The film showed the most horrific murder scenes.* **–horrifically** *adv*

hor·ri·fy /'hɔrə,faɪ, 'har-/ *v* **-fied, -fying** [T] to shock; fill with HORROR: *I was horrified at/by the news.|a horrifying story* **–horrifyingly** *adv*

hor·ror /'hɔrər, 'harər/ *n* **1** [U] a feeling of great shock, fear, and dislike: *We were filled with horror at the bad news.|I cried out* **in horror** *as I saw the cars crash.* **2** [C] an unpleasant person: *The little horror never stops playing tricks on his parents.* **3 horror movie** a movie in which strange and fearful things happen, such as dead people coming to life, people turning into animals, etc.

hors d'oeu·vre /ɔr 'dɜrv/ *n* **-d'oeuvres** /'dɜrvz/ *or* **-d'oeuvre** *French* any of several types of food served in small amounts at the beginning of a meal

horse /hɔrs/ *n* **1** a large four-legged animal with hard feet (hooves(HOOF)), which people ride on and use for pulling heavy things **2** also **vaulting horse**– a wooden apparatus which people can VAULT² over for exercise **3 dark horse** a person whose abilities are hidden or unknown **4 (straight) from the horse's mouth** *infml* told one directly, from the person concerned: *"Who told you she was leaving?" "I heard it straight from the horse's mouth."* (=she herself told me) **5 put the cart before the horse** to do or put things in the wrong order **8 eat/work like a horse** eat/work a lot **9 hold your horses!** don't rush hastily into an activity or decision

horse·back /'hɔrsbæk/ *n* **1** [A] *esp. AmE* or on the back of a horse: *Do you like horseback riding?* **2 on horseback** (riding) on a horse

horse chest·nut /'· ,··/ *n* (a nut from) a large tree with white or pink flowers **–compare** CHESTNUT¹ (1,2)

horse·man /'hɔrsmən/ **horsewoman** /'hɔrs-,wʊmən/ *fem.*– *n* **-men** /mən/ a person who rides a horse, esp. one who rides well

horse·play /'hɔrs-pleʸ/ *n* [U] rough noisy behavior

horse·pow·er /'hɔrs,paʊər/ *abbrev.* **HP–** *n*

horsepower a measure of the power of an engine

horse·rac·ing /'hɔrs,reʸsɪŋ/ *n* [U] the sport of racing horses ridden by JOCKEYs, for money

horse·rad·ish /'hɔrs,rædɪʃ/ *n* a plant whose root is used to make a strong-tasting SAUCE (**horseradish sauce**) to be eaten with meat

horse·shoe /'hɔrʃ-ʃuʷ, 'hɔrs-/ also **shoe–** *n* **1** a curved piece of iron nailed on under a horse's foot **2** something made in this shape, believed to bring good luck

hors·y /'hɔrsiʸ/ *adj* **-ier, -iest 1** *often derog* (too) interested in horses, fond of riding, etc. **2** looking like a horse **–horsiness** *n* [U]

hor·ti·cul·ture /'hɔrtə,kʌltʃər/ *n* [U] the science of growing fruit, flowers, and vegetables **–horticultural** /,hɔrtə'kʌltʃərəl/ *adj* **–horticulturist** *n*

hose¹ /hoʷz/ *n* [C;U] (a piece of) rubber or plastic tube used to direct water onto fires, a garden, etc.

hose² *v* **hosed, hosing** [T *down*] to use a HOSE¹ on: *hosing the car down|to hose the garden*

hose³ *n* [P] (used esp. in shops) stockings or socks

ho·sier·y /'hoʷʒəriʸ/ *n* [U] socks, stockings, underclothes, etc.

hos·pi·ta·ble /'haspɪtəbəl, ha'spɪ-/ *adj* (of people or their acts) showing attention to the needs of others, esp. by asking them into one's home, feeding them, etc. **–opposite inhospitable –hospitably** *adv* **–hospitality** /,haspə'tæləti·ʸ/ *n* [U]: *Mrs. Brown is known for her hospitality.*

hos·pi·tal /'haspɪtl/ *n* [C;U] a place where ill people stay and have treatment: *After her accident, Jane was taken to the hospital.*

hos·pi·tal·ize also **-ise** *BrE* /'haspɪtl,aɪz/ *v* **-ized, -izing** [T] to put (a person) into a hospital: *He broke a leg and was hospitalized for a month.* **–hospitalization** /,haspɪtl-ə'zeʸʃən/ *n* [C;U]

host¹ /hoʷst/ *n* **1** a man who receives guests: *He acted as host to his father's friends.*|(fig.) **the host country** *for the Olympic Games* **2** a person who introduces other performers, such as those on a TV show: *Here is your host, Michael Parkinson.*

host² *v* [T] to act as host at (a party, friendly meeting, etc.)

host³ *n* [C] a large number: *A whole host of difficulties have arisen.*

hos·tage /'hastɪdʒ/ *n* a person kept by an enemy so that the other side will do what the enemy wants: *The man with the gun* **took/held** *the child* **hostage**.

hos·tel /'hastl/ *n* a building in which certain types of persons can live and eat, as for students, young people working away from home, etc.: *a youth hostel*

hos·tel·ry /'hastl-riʸ/ *n* **-ries** *old use or humor* a hotel

host·ess /'hoʷstɪs/ *n* **1** a female host **2** →FLIGHT ATTENDANT

hos·tile /'hastl, 'hastaɪl/ *adj* **1** [*to*] unfriendly; showing dislike **2** belonging to an enemy

hos·til·i·ties /ha'stɪlətiʸz/ *n* [P] acts of fighting in war: *Hostilities have broken out be* *tween the two countries.*

hos·til·i·ty /hɑ'stɪlətiy/ *n* [U] the state of being unfriendly

hot /hɑt/ *adj* **-tt- 1** having a certain degree of heat, esp. a high degree: *How hot is the water?* | *The water isn't hot yet.* | *Now the water is so hot I burned my finger in it.* | (fig.) *hot* (=very recent) *news* | *a hot temper* | *hot feelings* | *A* **hot- blooded** *person is one who easily shows strong feelings.* | (*infml*) *She's very* **hot on** (=well-informed on and interested in) *history.* **2** causing a burning taste in the mouth: *Pepper makes food hot.* **3 hot air** meaningless talk or ideas **4 hot and bothered** worried by a feeling that things are going wrong **5 hot on someone's trail/track** chasing and ready to catch someone **6 hot on the heels (of)** following or happening just after **7 hot under the collar** angry or excited and ready to argue **8 not so hot** *infml* not very good; not as good as expected **9 the hot seat** *infml* a position of difficulty from which one must make important decisions **10** *infml* (of stolen goods) difficult to pass on because still known to the police, esp. soon after the crime has taken place

hot·bed /'hɑtbɛd/ *n* a place or condition where something undesirable can exist and develop: *The city is a hotbed of crime.*

hot-blood·ed /ˌ·'··◄/ *adj* showing strong feelings; showing PASSION –see also COLD-BLOODED (2)

hot dog /'· ·/ *n* a special sort of long red SAUSAGE in a bread ROLL¹ (2)

ho·tel /howʷtɛl/ *n* a building where people can stay in return for payment

hot·foot /'hɑtfʊt/ *v* **hotfoot it** *infml* to move fast: *We hotfooted it down the street.* **–hotfoot** *adv* : *We ran hotfoot to find out the news.*

hot·head /'hɑthɛd/ *n* a person who does things in haste, without thinking –**hot headed** /ˌhɑt'hɛdɪd ◄/ *adj* –**hotheadedly** /ˌhɑt'hɛdɪdliy/ *adv*

hot·house /'hɑthaʊs/ *n* **-houses** /ˌhaʊzɪz/ a warm building where flowers and delicate plants can grow; GREENHOUSE

hot·ly /'hɑtliy/ *adv* **1** in anger and with force **2** closely and eagerly: *He was* **hotly pursued** *by his dog.*

hot·plate /'hɑtpleyt/ *n* a metal surface, usu. on a cooking STOVE, which is heated and on which food can be cooked in a pan –see COOK (USAGE)

hot-wa·ter bot·tle /ˌ·'···ˌ··/ *n* a rubber container which is filled with hot water and is placed inside a bed to warm it

hound¹ /haʊnd/ *n* a hunting dog, esp. a foxhound

hound² *v* [T] to chase or worry continually: *I've got to finish the work so I don't have him hounding me all the time.*

hour /aʊər/ *n* **1** [C] any of the 24 equal periods of time into which a whole day is divided: *There are 60 minutes in an hour.* | *It's only an hour away.* (=it takes only an hour to travel there) **2** a time of day when a new such period starts: *He arrived* **on the hour.** (=exactly at 1 o'clock, 2 o'clock, etc.) **3** [C] a fixed point or period of time: *No one helped*

me **in my hour of need.** (=when I needed help) | **Visiting hours** (=the time when one is allowed to visit) *at the hospital are 3:00 to 5:00.* **4** [C] a certain period of time: *The hours I spent with you were the happiest of my life.* | *I've been waiting here* **for hours.** (=for a long time) **5 after hours** /ˌ·· '·/ later than the usual times of work or business **6 at all hours** (at any time) during the whole day and night **7 (at) the eleventh hour** (at) the last moment; very late **8 the wee hours** the hours soon after midnight (1, 2, 3 o'clock)

hour·ly /'aʊərliy/ *adj,adv* (happening, appearing, etc.) every hour or once an hour

house¹ /haʊs/ *n* **houses** /'haʊzɪz/ **1** a building for people to live or work in **b** the people in such a building: *The whole house was awakened.* —see, illustration on page 337 **2** a building for the stated purpose: *a hen house* | *a storehouse* | *the* **House of Representatives** (=the building and people partly responsible for making US laws; its members are elected by the people) **3** (*cap. in names*) an important family, esp. noble or royal: *The House of Windsor is the British royal family.* **4** [*usu. sing.*] a theater, or the people in it: *a full house* | *His jokes* **brought the house down.** (=brought loud laughter, admiration, etc. from everyone in the theater) **5 like a house on fire** very quickly: *That new fashion caught on like a house on fire.* **6 on the house** (usu. of drinks) paid for by the owner of a bar, restaurant, etc. **7 keep house** to do cleaning, cooking, and other things usu. done to keep a house in order

USAGE A **house** is a building for people to live in, and is usually built on more than one level (STORY). A **cottage** is a small, old house, esp. in the country, and a **bungalow** is a house built on only one level. A set of rooms (including a kitchen and bathroom) within a larger building is an **apartment** (**flat** *esp. BrE*), and a small one-room apartment is called a **studio.** A very large house is called a **mansion,** or (if it belongs to a king or queen) a **palace.** The place where you live is your **home,** whatever type of house it is: *After the party, we went* **home** *to our apartment.*

house² /haʊz/ *v* **housed, housing** [T] to provide with a place to live

house ar·rest /'· ·ˌ·/ *n* **under house arrest** forbidden by the government to leave one's house

house·boat /'haʊsbowt/ *n* a boat fitted with everything necessary for living there

house·bound /'haʊsbaʊnd/ *adj* not able to move out of the house, esp. because of illness

house·break·er /'haʊsˌbreykər/ *n* a thief who enters a house by force

house·bro·ken /'haʊsˌbrowkən/ *AmE* ‖ **house-trained** /'· ·/ *BrE adj* (of house pets) trained to go out of the house to empty the bowels or BLADDER

house·hold /'haʊshowld, 'haʊsowld/ *n* all the people living together in a house: *The whole household was up early.*

house·hold·er /'haʊsˌhowldər, 'haʊˌsowl·/ *n* a person who owns or is in charge of a house

household word /ˌ·· '·/ also **household name**– n a thing or person known and spoken of by almost everybody

house·keep·er /ˈhaʊsˌkiʸpər/ n a person who has charge of the running of a house

house·keep·ing /ˈhaʊsˌkiʸpɪŋ/ n [U] work done in looking after a house and the people who live in it

house·warm·ing /ˈhaʊsˌwɔrmɪŋ/ n a party given for friends when one has moved into a new house

house·wife /ˈhaʊswaɪf/ n -wives /waɪvz/ a woman who works at home for her family, cleaning, cooking, etc., esp. one who does not work outside the home

house·work /ˈhaʊswɜrk/ n [U] work done to keep the inside of a house clean and tidy –compare HOMEWORK

hous·ing /ˈhaʊzɪŋ/ n 1 (the action of providing) places to live: More money should be spent on the housing of old people.|Too many people are living in bad housing. 2 [C] protective covering, as for machinery: the engine housing

housing de·vel·op·ment /'·· ·,···/ n esp. AmE a group of houses and/or apartments built in one place by one owner and rented or sold

housing proj·ect /'·· ,··/ n esp. AmE a HOUSING DEVELOPMENT, esp. a public one, usu. built with government money for low-income families

hove /hoʷv/ v past tense and past participle of HEAVE[1]

hov·el /ˈhʌvəl, ˈhɑ-/ n a small dirty place to live in

hov·er /ˈhʌvər, ˈhɑ-/ v [I over, around] 1 (of birds, certain aircraft, etc.) to stay in the air in one place 2 (of people) to wait around one place: I was trying to read a book, but the children kept hovering around me.|(fig.) He's hovering between life and death.

hov·er·craft /ˈhʌvərˌkræft, ˈhɑ/ n a boat which moves over land or water with a strong force of air underneath lifting it above the ground, sea, etc.: We crossed the lake on a hovercraft/by hovercraft. –compare HYDROFOIL

how[1] /haʊ/ adv 1 (used in questions) a in what way: How do you spell it? b in what state of health: How is your mother? c (in questions about amount or number): How old are you? 2 (used in expressions of feeling): How they cried!|How nice of you to come!|How difficult it is! (compare What a difficult book it is!) 3 How come? infml Why is it?: How come we weren't invited to the party? 4 How do you do? polite, esp. BrE (used when one is first introduced to someone): "This is my wife." "How do you do?" 5 and how! infml esp. AmE Very much so: "So they enjoyed themselves?" "And how!" 6 How can you, he, etc. you, he shouldn't: How can you say such an unkind thing? 7 How are you? a (a question about someone's health) b (a phrase used when meeting again a person already known). The reply is often "Fine (thanks). (And) how are you?

how[2] conj the way in which; the fact that: I

remember how they laughed.

how·ev·er[1] /haʊˈɛvər/ conj in whatever way: However I cook eggs, she still refuses to eat them.

however[2] adv 1 in spite of this: It's raining hard. However, I think we should go out.|He may, however, come later. –see Study Notes on page 144 2 to whatever degree: She always goes swimming, however cold it is. 3 also how ever– (showing surprise) in what way: How ever did you get here?

howl[1] /haʊl/ v [I;T] to make HOWLs[2]: The dogs howled all night.|The wind howled in the trees.|We howled with laughter.|(fig.) The baby's howling. (=weeping loudly)

howl sbdy.↔ **down** adv [T] to make a loud disapproving noise so as to prevent (someone) from being heard

howl[2] n a long loud cry, esp that made by wolves (WOLF) and dogs

HP abbrev. for: HORSEPOWER

HQ abbrev. for: HEADQUARTERS: See you back at HQ.

hr., hrs. written abbrev. said as: hour, hours

hub /hʌb/ n 1 the central part of a wheel, around which it turns and to which the outside edge (RIM) is connected by SPOKEs 2 the center of activity or importance

hub·bub /ˈhʌbʌb/ n [S] a mixture of loud noises

hub·cap /ˈhʌbkæp/ n a metal covering over the center of the wheel of a motor vehicle –see illustration on page 95

huck·le·ber·ry /ˈhʌkəlˌbɛriʸ,-bəriʸ/ -ries n a dark blue fruit which grows in North America

huck·ster /ˈhʌkstər/ n often derog a person who sells small things in the street or at the doors of houses

hud·dle[1] /ˈhʌdl/ v -dled, -dling [I;T] to (cause to) crowd together, in a group or in a pile: The boys huddled together under the rock to keep out of the wind.

huddle[2] n a number of people or things close together and not in any ordered arrangement: The football players went into a huddle.

hue /hyuʷ/ n fml a color: The diamond shone with every hue under the sun.

hue and cry /ˌ· · '·/ n the expression of worry, anger, etc., by noisy behavior: They raised a (great) hue and cry against the new rule.

huff /hʌf/ n (in/into) a huff (in/into) a state of bad temper when offended: She's in a huff because my brother didn't remember her name.

hug[1] /hʌg/ v -gg- [T] 1 to hold tightly in the arms, esp. as a sign of love 2 to go along while staying near: The boat hugged the coast.

hug[2] n the act of hugging (HUG[1]): She gave her little boy a hug before he went to bed.

huge /hyuʷdʒ/ adj very big: a huge house|The movie was a huge success. –see Study Notes on page 550 –hugeness n [U]

huge·ly /hyuʷdʒliʸ/ adv infml very much: hugely successful

huh /hʌ/ interj (used for asking a question or

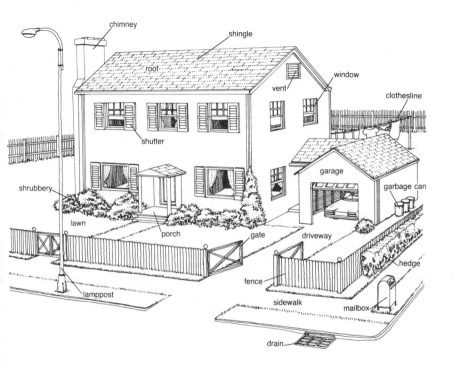

chimney
shingle
roof
vent
window
clothesline
shutter
garage
garbage can
shrubbery
lawn
porch
gate
driveway
fence
hedge
lamppost
sidewalk
mailbox
drain

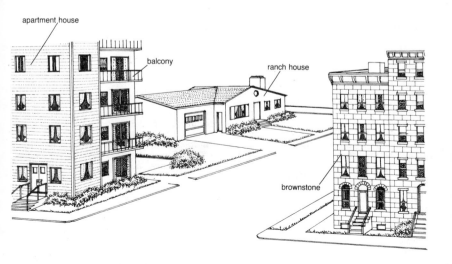

apartment house
balcony
ranch house
brownstone

for expressing surprise or disapproval)

hulk /hʌlk/ n the body of an old ship, no longer used at sea and left in disrepair: (fig.) *a great hulk of a man* (=heavy and awkward)

hulk·ing /ˈhʌlkɪŋ/ adj [A] big, heavy, and awkward: *We can't move this hulking table on our own.*

hull¹ /hʌl/ n the main body of a ship

hull² v [T] to take the outer covering off (certain grains and seeds, esp. PEAS and beans): *Rice is gathered, cleaned, and hulled before being sold.* –compare SHELL

hul·la·ba·loo /ˈhʌləbəˌluʷ, ˌhʌləbəˈluʷ/ n -loos [usu. sing.] a lot of noise, esp. of voices

hul·lo /həˈloʷ, hʌ-/ interj,n -los esp. BrE for HELLO

hum /hʌm/ v -mm- 1 [I] (esp. of bees) to make a continuous BUZZ 2 [I;T] (of people) to make a sound like a continuous **m**, esp. as a way of singing music with closed lips: *to hum a song* 3 [I with] (of work being carried out) to be active; to move fast: *Things are starting to hum (with activity).* n [S]

hu·man¹ /ˈhyuʷmən/ adj 1 of or concerning people: *the human voice|a newspaper story with lots of* **human interest** (=concerning someone's personal life and problems, not affairs of state, etc.) 2 showing the feelings, esp. those of kindness, which people are supposed to have: *He seems quite human when you know him.* –see also INHUMAN –compare HUMANE

human² also **human being**– |ˌ·· ˈ··/ n a man, woman, or child, not an animal

hu·mane /hyuʷˈmeʸn/ adj showing human kindness and the qualities of a civilized person –opposite inhumane; compare HUMAN –humaneness n [U]

hu·man·ism /ˈhyuʷməˌnɪzəm/ n [U] a system of beliefs concerned with the interests and values of man, and not with religious principles –humanist n

hu·man·i·tar·i·an /hyuʷˌmænəˈtɛəriʸən/ n,adj (a person) concerned with trying to improve people's lives, by giving them better conditions to live in, fighting injustice, etc.

hu·man·i·ties /hyuʷˈmænəṭiʸz/ n [the P] studies such as literature, languages, history, etc.; the ARTS –compare the SCIENCES

hu·man·i·ty /hyuʷˈmænəṭiʸ/ n [U] 1 the quality of being HUMANE or human: *a politician of great humanity* 2 human beings generally: *This new drug will help all humanity.* also -ise BrE

hu·man·ize also -ise BrE /ˈhyuʷməˌnaɪz/ v -ized, -izing [T] to make human or HUMANE

hu·man·ly /ˈhyuʷmənliʸ/ adv (only used in questions, NEGATIVES², etc.) within human powers: *It's not humanly possible to complete all the work in such a short time.*

hum·ble¹ /ˈhʌmbəl/ adj 1 having a low opinion of oneself and a high opinion of others: *a humble man* –see also HUMILITY; compare PROUD 2 low in rank or position; unimportant: *a humble job* –humbly adv

humble² v -bled, -bling [T] to make (someone or oneself) humble or lower in position: *to humble one's enemy*

hum·bug /ˈhʌmbʌg/ n [U] becoming rare nonsense

hum·drum /ˈhʌmdrʌm/ adj too ordinary; without variety or change: *to lead a humdrum life*

hu·mer·us /ˈhyuʷmərəs/ n the bone in the top half of the arm –sounds like **humorous**

hu·mid /ˈhyuʷmɪd/ adj (of air and weather) containing a lot of water VAPOR; DAMP: *The weather was so hot and humid that we all felt uncomfortable.*

hu·mid·i·fy /hyuʷˈmɪdəˌfaɪ/ v -fied, -fying [T] to make HUMID

hu·mid·i·ty /hyuʷˈmɪdəṭiʸ/ n [U] the (amount of) water VAPOR contained in the air: *It's difficult to work because of the humidity.*

hu·mil·i·ate /hyuʷˈmɪliʸˌeʸt/ v -ated, -ating [T] to cause to feel humble or to lose the respect of others: *The teacher told the whole class that my family was poor. I've never felt so humiliated.* –humiliation /hyuʷˌmɪliʸˈeʸʃən/ n [C;U]

hu·mil·i·ty /hyuʷˈmɪləṭiʸ/ n [U] the quality of being humble

hu·mor¹ AmE‖**humour** BrE /ˈhyuʷmər, ˈyuʷ-/ n [U] 1 the ability to be amused: *a sense of humor* 2 the quality of causing amusement: *a play with no humor in it* 3 -humored AmE‖-humoured BrE of the stated condition of mind: *She's always good-humored.|He's ill-humored today.*

humor² AmE‖**humour** BrE v [T] to keep (someone) happy or calm by acceptance of (esp.) foolish wishes, behavior, etc.: *Don't argue; just humor him, and he'll stop.*

hu·mor·ist /ˈhyuʷmərɪst, ˈyuʷ-/ n a person who makes jokes, esp. in writing

hu·mor·ous /ˈhyuʷmərəs, ˈyuʷ-/ adj funny; making people laugh: *a humorous film/remark/character in a play* –humorously adv

hump /hʌmp/ n a lump or round part which stands out noticeably, esp, on the back, e.g. on a camel

humph, h'm /hmh, hm, hʌmf/ interj a sound made with the lips closed to express doubt, disagreement, or dissatisfaction with something said or done.

USAGE This sound is usually spelled **humph** in writing. Some people pronounce it /hʌmf/ when they are reading aloud.

hu·mus /ˈhyuʷməs/ n [U] rich soil made of decayed plants, leaves, etc.

hunch¹ /hʌntʃ/ n [+ (that)] an idea based on feeling rather than on reason: *I have a hunch (that) he didn't really want to go.*

hunch² v [T up] to pull ((part of) the body) into a rounded shape: *She hunched her shoulders over her book.|She sat with her shoulders hunched up.*

hunch·back /ˈhʌntʃbæk/ n (a person with) a back misshaped by a round lump (HUMP) –hunchbacked adj

hun·dred /ˈhʌndrɪd/ determiner,n,pron -dred or -dreds (the number) 100 –see Study Notes on page 550 –**hundredth** /ˈhʌndrɪdθ, -drɪtθ/ determiner,n,pron,adv

USAGE 1 We say numbers like this: *326 = three* **hundred and** *twenty six. 92,804,326 =*

ninety two **million,** *eight* **hundred and** *four* **thousand,** *three* **hundred and** *twenty six.* We only say **and** after **hundred.** 2 Words like **hundred** and **thousand** can also be used in the plural when there is no number before them: **Hundreds** *of people attended the concert*|**Millions** *of dollars have been spent on the new hospital.*

hun·dred·weight /ˈhʌndrɪdˌweʸt/ (*written abbrev.* **cwt**)– *n* -**weight** (a measure of weight equal to) (in America) 100 pounds, (in Britain) 112 pounds

hung /hʌŋ/ *v past tense and past participle of* HANG¹

hun·ger /ˈhʌŋgər/ *n* [U] **1** the wish or need for food: (fig.) *his hunger for excitement* **2** lack of food: *There is hunger in all the places where the crop was spoiled.* –compare FAMINE

hunger for sthg. also **hunger after** sthg.– *v prep* [T] to want very much

hunger strike /ˈ··· ˌ·/ *n* a refusal to eat as a sign of strong dissatisfaction: *The prisoners* **went on (a) hunger strike** *because of the conditions in the prison.* –**hunger striker** *n*

hun·gry /ˈhʌŋgriʸ/ *adj* -**grier,** -**griest 1** feeling or showing hunger **2** causing hunger: *hungry work* **3 go hungry** to remain without food: *If you won't cook your own dinner, then you'll have to go hungry.* –**hungrily** *adv*

hunk /hʌŋk/ *n* a thick piece, esp. of food, broken or cut off

hunt¹ /hʌnt/ *v* **1** to chase in order to catch and kill (animals and birds) either for food or for sport **2** to search (for): *He went through the whole house hunting for his books*

hunt sbdy./sthg.↔ **down** *v adv* [T] to succeed in finding after much effort: to *hunt down a criminal*

hunt² *n* an act of hunting: *It was an exciting hunt, but the fox escaped.*|*an elephant hunt*|*Our hunt* (=search) *for a house is at last at an end.*

hunt·er /ˈhʌntər/ *n* a person or animal that hunts, usu. wild animals. (fig.) *a fortune hunter* (=someone eagerly searching for a lot of money)

hur·dle¹ /ˈhɜrdl/ *n* **1** a frame for jumping over in a race **2** a difficulty which is to be conquered

hurdle² *v* -**dled,** -**dling** [I] to run a HURDLE¹ race –**hurdler** *n*

hurl /hɜrl/ *v* [T] to throw with force: *He hurled a brick through the window.*|(fig.) *The drunk hurled curses at the policeman.*

hur·ly-bur·ly /ˌhɜrliʸ ˈbɜrliʸ/ *n* [S;U] noisy activity: the *hurly-burly of city life*

hur·ray, hooray /həˈreʸ, hʊˈreʸ/ also **hurrah** /həˈrɑ, həˈrɔ, hʊ-/ *becoming rare– interj,n* a shout of joy or approval: *Three cheers for the losing team:* **Hip, hip, hurray!**|*We've done it!* *Hurray!*

hur·ri·cane /ˈhɜrəˌkeʸn, ˈhʌr-/ *n* a storm with a very strong fast wind; CYCLONE or TYPHOON –see WEATHER (USAGE)

hurricane lamp /ˈ··· ˌ·/ *n* a lamp which has a strong cover to protect the flame inside from wind

hur·ried /ˈhɜriʸd, ˈhʌr-|* *adj* done in haste:

hurried work – **hurriedly** *adv*

hur·ry¹ /ˈhɜriʸ, ˈhʌriʸ/ *v* -**ried,** -**rying 1** to (cause to) be quick in action, sometimes too quick: *Don't hurry; we're not late.*|*He hurried across the road in front of a car.* **2** [T] to send or bring quickly: *Doctors and nurses were hurried to the accident.*

hurry up *v adv* [I;T (=**hurry** sbdy./sthg.↔ **up**) to (cause to) move faster; *I tried to hurry him up, but he wouldn't walk any faster.*|*We'll have to hurry up (the work) in order to finish on Friday.*

hurry² *n* [U] **1** haste; quick activity **2** need for haste: *Don't drive so fast; there's no hurry.* **3 in a hurry: a** hastily: *You make mistakes if you do things in a hurry.* **b** eager: *I'm not in a/any hurry to change my job.* **c** *infml* (usu. with a NEGATIVE ²) quickly; easily: *I won't forget her kindness in a hurry.*

hurt /hɜrt/ *v* **hurt, hurting 1** [T] to cause pain and/or damage (INJURY) to (esp. a part of the body): *He hurt his leg when he fell.*|(fig.) *My feelings were hurt when he didn't ask me to the party.* **2** [I;T] to cause (a person or other living creature) to feel pain: *My leg hurts.*|*Is that tight shoe hurting (you/your foot)*|(fig.) *It* **won't hurt you** (=it won't be bad for you) *to miss breakfast for once.* – **hurt** *n* [U]

USAGE When **hurt** is used in the sense of bodily damage, you may be *slightly/ badly/seriously* **hurt** but do not use these adverbs when speaking of unhappiness caused by someone's behavior. Compare: *She was badly/ slightly* **hurt**, *when she fell from the ladder,* and *She was very* **hurt** *by his unkind words.* –see WOUND (USAGE)

hurt·ful /ˈhɜrtfəl/ *adj* harmful; painful to the feelings: *There's no need to make such hurtful remarks.* –**hurtfully** *adj* –**hurtfulness** *n* [U]

hur·tle /ˈhɜrtl/ *v* -**tled,** -**tling** [I] to move or rush with great speed: *Rocks hurtled down the cliffs/through the air.*

hus·band /ˈhʌzbənd/ *n* the man to whom a woman is married –see illustration on page 247

hus·band·ry /ˈhʌzbəndriʸ/ *n* [U] *fml* farming: *animal husbandry*

hush¹ /hʌʃ/ *v* [I;T *often in commands*] to (cause to) be silent and/or calm –compare SHUSH

hush sthg.↔ **up** *v adv* [T] to keep from being public knowledge: *The President tried to hush up the fact that his adviser had lied.*

hush² *n* [S;U] (a) silence, esp. a peaceful one: *A hush fell over the room.*

hush-hush /ˌ· ˈ·◂/ *adj infml* (of plans, arrangements, etc.) hidden, or to be hidden, from other people's knowledge; secret

husk /hʌsk/ *n* the dry outer covering of some fruits and seeds: *Brown bread contains the husk of wheat.*

husk·y¹ /ˈhʌskiʸ/ *adj* -**ier,** -**iest 1** (of a person or voice) difficult to hear and breathy, as if the throat were dry –compare HOARSE **2** (of a person) big and strong –compare HEFTY –**huskily** *adv* –**huskiness** *n* [U]

hus·ky² *n* -**kies** a working dog with thick hair, used to pull SLEDGEs over the snow

hus·sy /'hʌsiʸ, 'hʌziʸ/ *n* **-sies** *old use or humor* a girl or woman who behaves in a sexually improper manner (note the phrases **brazen/shameless hussy**)

hus·tings /'hʌstɪŋz/ *n* [*the* P] the speeches, attempts to win votes, etc., which go on before an election

hus·tle¹ /'hʌsəl/ *v* **-tled, -tling** [I;T] **1** to (cause to) move fast: *I hustled the children off to school.* **2** [I;T *into*] *esp. AmE* to persuade someone by forceful, esp. deceitful activity: *He hustled me into buying the car, even though I didn't really want it.* **3** [I] *AmE infml* to work as a PROSTITUTE

hustle² *n* [U] hurried activity (esp. in the phrase **hustle and bustle**)

hus·tler /'hʌslər/ *n esp. AmE* **1** a person who HUSTLES¹ (2) **2** *AmE infml* for PROSTITUTE

hut /hʌt/ *n* a small building, often made of wood, esp. one used for living in or for shelter –compare SHED¹

hutch /hʌtʃ/ *n* a small box or cage with one side made of wire netting, esp. one for keeping rabbits in

hy·a·cinth /'haɪəsɪnθ/ *n* a plant with bell-shaped flowers, which grows from a BULB in spring

hy·ae·na /haɪ'iʸnə/ *n* →HYENA

hy·brid /'haɪbrɪd/ *n* something, esp. an animal or plant, that is produced from parents of different breeds; CROSS¹ (7): *The hybrid from a donkey and a horse is called a MULE.*

hy·drant /'haɪdrənt/ *n* **1**‖also **fire hydrant, fire plug** *AmE*– a water pipe in the street from which one may draw water for putting out a fire **2** a water pipe outside a house or building from which one may draw water for plants, cleaning, etc. —compare FAUCET

hy·drau·lic /haɪ'drɔlɪk/ *adj* concerning or moved by the pressure of water or other liquids: *hydraulic power│a hydraulic engineer* –**hydraulically** *adv*

hy·drau·lics /haɪ'drɔlɪks/ *n* [U] the science which studies the use of water to produce power

hy·dro·e·lec·tric /,haɪdrowɪ'lɛktrɪk/ *adj* concerning or producing electricity by the power of falling water: *a hydroelectric power station* –**hydroelectrically** *adv*

hy·dro·foil /'haɪdrəˌfɔɪl/ *n* a large motorboat with legs which raise it out of the water as it moves: *to travel* **by hydrofoil** –compare HOVERCRAFT

hy·dro·gen /'haɪdrədʒən/ *n* [U] a gas that is a simple substance (ELEMENT), without color or smell, that is lighter than air and that burns very easily

hydrogen bomb /'··· ,·/ also **H-bomb, fusion bomb** – *n* a very powerful type of ATOM BOMB

hy·dro·pho·bi·a /,haɪdrə'fowbiʸə/ *n* [U] → RABIES

hy·dro·plane /'haɪdrəˌpleʸn/ *n* a flat-bottomed motor-boat which can move very fast over the surface of water

hy·e·na, hyaena /haɪ'iʸnə/ *n* a wild dog-like animal of Africa and Asia, which eats meat and has a cry like a laugh

hy·giene /'haɪdʒiʸn/ *n* [U] **1** the study and practice of how to keep good health, esp. by paying attention to cleanliness **2** cleanliness generally

hy·gi·en·ic /,haɪdʒiʸ'ɛnɪk, -'dʒɛnɪk/ *adj* **1** causing or keeping good health **2** clean –opposite **unhygienic** –**hygienically** *adv*

hymn /hɪm/ *n* a song of praise, esp. to God, usu. one of the religious songs of the Christian church which all the people sing together during a service

hy·per·bo·le /haɪ'pɜrbəliʸ/ *n* [C;U] (the use of) a form of words which makes something sound bigger, smaller, louder, etc. than it really is

hy·phen /'haɪfən/ *n* a short written or printed line (-) which can join words or SYLLABLES –compare DASH² (3)

hy·phen·ate /'haɪfəˌneʸt/ *v* **-ated, -ating** [T] to join with a HYPHEN –**hyphenation** /,haɪfə'neʸʃən/ *n* [U]

hyp·no·sis /hɪp'nowˢsɪs/ *n* [U] (the production of) a sleep-like state in which a person's mind and actions can be controlled by another person –**hypnotic** /hɪp'nɑtɪk/ *adj* –**hypnotically** *adv*

hyp·no·tism /'hɪpnəˌtɪzəm/ *n* [U] the practice of hypnotizing ⟨HYPNOTIZE⟩ someone –**hypnotist** *n*

hypnotize‖also **-tise** *BrE* /'hɪpnəˌtaɪz/ *v* **-tized, -tizing** [T] to produce HYPNOSIS in (someone)

hy·po·chon·dri·ac /,haɪpə'kɑndriʸ,æk/ *n* a person suffering from a state of anxiety and (unnecessary) worry about his/her health (**hypochondria** /,haɪpə'kɑndriʸə/)

hy·poc·ri·sy /hɪ'pɑkrəsiʸ/ *n* [U] the act or practice of pretending to believe, feel, or be something very different from, and usu. better than, what one actually believes, feels, or is

hyp·o·crite /'hɪpəˌkrɪt/ *n* a person who says one thing and does another, usu. something worse; one who practises HYPOCRISY: *You say you care about the poor, but you walk past them in the street; you hypocrite!* –**hypocritical** /,hɪpə'krɪtɪkəl/ *adj* –**hypocritically** *adv*

hy·po·der·mic /,haɪpə'dɜrmɪk/ *adj,n* (of) an instrument or means of putting drugs into the body which is made to enter or INJECTed beneath the skin: *A hypodermic needle/ SYRINGE is sometimes just called a hypodermic.* –**hypodermically** *adv*

hy·po·ther·mi·a /,haɪpə'θɜrmiʸə/ *n* [U] a medical condition in which the body temperature falls below the usual level, esp. as happens with old people who do not keep warm at home: *Every winter some old people die from hypothermia.*

hy·poth·e·sis /haɪ'pɑθəsɪs/ *n* **-ses** /,siʸz/ an idea which is not necessarily true, but which is thought suitable to explain the facts about something: *According to the government's hypothesis, the high cost of living is caused by increased wages.* –compare THEORY

hy·po·thet·i·cal /,haɪpə'θɛtɪkəl/ *adj* supposed to be so; not yet proved to be true or known to have happened –**hypothetically** *adv*

hys·ter·ec·to·my /,hɪstə'rɛktəmiʸ/ *n* **-mies** [C;U] the medical operation for removing the WOMB –compare VASECTOMY

hys·ter·i·a /hɪˈstɛriʸə, -ˈstɪər-/ n [U] **1** a condition of nervous excitement in which the sufferer laughs and cries uncontrollably and/or shows strange changes in behavior or bodily state **2** wild excitement, as of a crowd of people

hys·ter·i·cal /hɪˈstɛrɪkəl/ adv **1** (of people) in a state of HYSTERIA: *The doctor slapped the hysterical child to make him calmer.* **2** (of feelings) expressed wildly, in an uncontrolled manner: *hysterical laughter* **3** AmE infml wildly funny: *The movie was hysterical. I couldn't stop laughing.* – **hysterically**

I, i

SPELLING NOTE
Words with the sound /aɪ/ may be spelled e-, like **eye**, or ai-, like **aisle**.

I, i /aɪ/ **I's, i's** or **Is, is 1** the 9th letter of the English alphabet **2** the ROMAN NUMERAL (number) for 1

I /aɪ/ pron (used as the subject of a sentence) the person who is speaking: *I'm your mother, aren't I?|My husband and I are glad to be here.* –see ME (USAGE)

IA written abbrev. said as: Iowa /ˈaɪəwə/ (a state in the US)

ice¹ /aɪs/ n **1** [U] water which has frozen to a solid: *There is ice on the lake in winter.|Her hands were like ice/were as cold as ice/were ice-cold.* **2** [C] a type or a serving of a cold sweet food like ice cream, but made with fruit juice instead of cream **3 break the ice** to begin to be friendly with people one did not know before: *A few drinks will help to break the ice at the party.* **4 cut no ice (with someone)** to have little effect on someone **5 (skating) on thin ice** (being) in a dangerous or difficult position **6 keep (something) on ice** to keep for later use: *It's an interesting suggestion, and we'll keep it on ice.*

ice² v **iced, icing** [T] **1** to make very cold by using ice: *iced drinks* **2** to cover (a cake) with ICING

   ice over also **ice up**– v adv to become covered with ice: *The lake iced over during the night.*

ice age /ˈ· ·/ n any of several periods when ice covered many northern countries

ice bag /ˈ· ·/ also **ice pack**– n AmE a bag containing ice, used to make parts of the body cool

ice·berg /ˈaɪsbɜrg/ n a very large piece of ice floating in the sea, most of which is below the surface

ice·box /ˈaɪsbɑks/ n **1** AmE infml for REFRIGERATOR **2** a box where food is kept cool with blocks of ice

ice cream /ˈ· ·/ n [C;U] a sweet mixture which is frozen and eaten cold, usu. containing milk or other fat products: *chocolate ice cream*

ice hock·ey /ˈ· ˌ··/ ‖also **hockey** esp. AmE– n [U] a team game like FIELD HOCKEY played on ice

ice-skate /ˈaɪskeʸt/ v **-skated, -skating** [I] to SKATE on ice **–ice-skater** n **–ice- skating** n [U]:

Ice-skating is my favorite winter sport.

ice skate /ˈ· ·/ n either of a pair of metal blades fitted to the bottom of shoes for moving swiftly on ice

i·ci·cle /ˈaɪsɪkəl/ n a pointed stick of ice formed when water freezes as it runs or DRIPs down: *icicles hanging from the roof*

ic·ing /ˈaɪsɪŋ/ also **frosting**– n [U] a mixture of fine powdery sugar and liquid, used to decorate cakes

i·con, ikon /ˈaɪkɑn/ n an image of a holy person, used in the worship of the Eastern branches of Christianity

ic·y /ˈaɪsiʸ/ adj **-ier, -iest 1** very cold: *My hands are icy.|(fig.) She gave me an icy look.* **2** covered with ice: *Icy roads are dangerous.* **–icily** adv **–iciness** n [U]

I'd /aɪd/ short for: **1** I had: *I'd gone* **2** I would: *I'd go*

ID written abbrev. said as: Idaho /ˈaɪdəˌhoʷ/ (a state in the US)

ID /ˌaɪ ˈdiʸ/ n abbrev. for: IDENTIFICATION (2): *Before we accept your check, we need to see two forms of ID.|an ID card.*

i·de·a /aɪˈdiʸə/ n **1** [C;U] a picture in the mind: *I've got a good idea of what he wants.|Do you have any idea of what I'm trying to explain?|You have no idea (=you can't imagine) how worried I was.* **2** [C] an opinion; thought: *He'll have his own ideas about that.|I have an idea (=I think) that he's on vacation this week.* **3** [C] a plan; suggestion: *I have an idea for a new book.|What a good idea! Let's do it.|She's full of good ideas.*

i·de·al¹ /aɪˈdiʸəl/ adj [no comp.] perfect: *an ideal marriage*

ideal² n **1** a perfect example: *That's my ideal of what a house should be like.* **2** [usu. pl.] (a belief in) high or perfect standards: *a woman with high ideals*

i·de·al·ism /aɪˈdiʸəˌlɪzəm/ n [U] the belief that one should live according to one's IDEALs² (2): *youthful idealism* **idealist** n **–idealistic** /ˌaɪdiʸəˈlɪstɪk, aɪˌdiʸə-/ adj **–idealistically** adv

i·de·al·ize ‖also **-ise** BrE /aɪˈdiʸəˌlaɪz/ v **-ized, -izing** [I;T] to imagine or represent as perfect or as better than in reality: *He tends to idealize his life in the army.* **–idealization** /aɪˌdiʸələˈzeʸʃən/ n [C;U]

i·de·al·ly /aɪˈdiʸəliʸ/ adv **1** in an IDEAL¹ way: *ideally beautiful* **2** in an IDEAL¹ state of affairs: *Ideally, I would like to be a teacher,* *but there are so few jobs now.*

i·den·ti·cal /aɪˈdɛntɪkəl, ɪ-/ *adj* [*no comp.*] **1** [*with, to*] exactly alike: *You and your brother have almost identical voices.|Your voice is identical to hers.|***Identical twins** *look exactly alike.* **2** the same: *This is the identical hotel that we stayed in last year.* **–identically** *adv*

i·den·ti·fi·ca·tion /aɪˌdɛntəfəˈkeʸʃən, ɪ-/ *n* [U] **1** the act of IDENTIFYing or state of being identified: *identification of the dead body by the brother* **2** something (such as an official paper) which proves who one is: *His only* **means of identification** *was his passport.*

i·den·ti·fy /aɪˈdɛntəˌfaɪ, ɪ-/ *v* **-fied, -fying** [T] to prove or show the IDENTITY of: *I identified the coat at once; it was my brother's.|I identified the criminal.*

identify with *v prep* [T] **1** (**identify** sbdy. **with** sthg.) to cause or consider (someone) to be connected with: *That politician is too closely identified with the senator to become a member of our committee.* **2** [T] (**identify with** sbdy./sthg.) to feel sympathy for (someone), or feel that one shares (something): *Reading this book, we can identify with the main character's struggle.*

i·den·ti·ty /aɪˈdɛntətiʸ, ɪ-/ *n* **-ties 1** [C;U] who or what a particular person or thing is: *He had lost his* **identity card** (=a document which shows one's identity) *and was being questioned by the police.|What's the identity of this piece of metal?* (=what type of metal is it?) **2** [U] sameness; exact likeness

i·de·ol·o·gy /ˌaɪdiʸˈaləʤiʸ, ˌɪdiʸ-/ *n* **-gies** [C;U] a set of ideas, esp. if typical of a social or political group **–ideological** /ˌaɪdiʸˈlaʤɪkəl, ˌɪdiʸ-/ *adj* **–ideologically** *adv*: *Ideologically, they have many differences.* **–ideologist** /ˌaɪdiʸˈaləʤɪst, ˌɪdiʸ-/ *n*

id·i·o·cy /ˈɪdiʸəsiʸ/ *n* **-cies** [C;U] (an act of) stupidity

id·i·om /ˈɪdiʸəm/ *n* **1** a phrase which means something different from the meanings of the separate words: *To be "hard up" is an English idiom meaning to lack money.* **2** the way of expression typical of a person or a people in their use of language: *the idiom of the young* **–idiomatic** /ˌɪdiʸəˈmætɪk/ *adj a Frenchman who speaks idiomatic English |"To call it a day" is an idiomatic expression.* **–idiomatically** *adv*

id·i·o·syn·cra·sy /ˌɪdiʸəˈsɪŋkrəsiʸ/ *n* **-sies** a peculiarity of one person: *One of his idiosyncrasies is keeping pet snakes.*

id·i·ot /ˈɪdiʸət/ *n* **1** a foolish person: *Idiot! You've dropped my watch!* **2** old use or tech a person of very weak mind usu. from birth **–idiotic** /ˌɪdiʸˈɑtɪk/ *adj* **–idiotically** *adv*

i·dle¹ /ˈaɪdl/ *adj* **1** not working: *Men are left idle when machines break down.* **2** of no use; having no result: *idle gossip/talk|His words were just* **idle threats**; *he can't harm us.* **3** lazy: *That boy is really idle; he just sits*

SPELLING NOTE
Words with the sound /aɪ/ may be spelled **e-**, like **eye**, or **ai-**, like **aisle**.

---

around the house all day. **–idleness** *n* [U] **–idly** *adv*

idle² *v* **-dled, -dling 1** to waste time doing nothing: *idling in the park* **2** (of an engine) to run slowly **–idler** *n*

idle sthg. **away** *v adv* to waste (time) doing nothing: *We idled away a few hours by talking.*

i·dol /ˈaɪdl/ *n* an image worshipped as a god: (fig.) *The football player was the idol of many young people.*

i·dol·a·try /aɪˈdalətriʸ/ *n* [U] the worship of IDOLs **–idolatrous** *adj*

i·dol·ize ‖ also **-ise** *BrE* /ˈaɪdlˌaɪz/ *v* **-ized, -izing** [T] to treat as an IDOL: *He idolizes his father.*

i·dyll, idyl /ˈaɪdl/ *n* (a description of) a simple, happy scene, esp. in the country **–idyllic** /aɪˈdɪlɪk/ *adj: an idyllic scene* **–idyllically** *adv*

i.e. /ˌaɪ ˈiʸ/ *abbrev. for:* Latin id est (=that is to SAY¹ (5)): *females, i.e. girls and women*

if /ɪf/ *conj* **1** supposing that; on condition that: *If you pour oil on water, it floats.|We'll go if it doesn't rain/unless it rains.|If John were/was here, he would know what to do.|If he told you that, he was lying.* **2** even if; although: *a pleasant if noisy child* **3** (used after verbs like ask, know, wonder) whether: *Do you know if/whether she's coming?* **4** (used after words expressing feelings): *I'm sorry if she's annoyed.|Do you mind if I smoke?* (=May I smoke?) **5 if I were you** (used when giving advice): *If I were you, I'd go home.* (=you ought to go home) **6 ifs, ands, or buts** reasons given for delay: *I don't want any ifs, ands, or buts; do it at once!*

USAGE **If** is only followed by *will/won't*, when they mean "be willing"/"be unwilling": **If** *you won't come* (=if you refuse), *I'll go alone.* Compare: **If** *it rains tomorrow, I'll go alone.* –see also **as if**, **even if**, **if only**

if·fy /ˈɪfiʸ/ *adj infml* uncertain, doubtful: *She was very iffy about whether she would take the job.*

ig·loo /ˈɪgluʷ/ *n* **-loos** a house made of hard icy blocks of snow

ig·ne·ous /ˈɪgniʸəs/ *adj tech* (of rocks) formed from LAVA

ig·nite /ɪgˈnaɪt/ *v* **-nited, -niting** [I;T] *fml* to (cause to) start to burn: *The liquid ignited when somebody dropped a match in it.*

ig·ni·tion /ɪgˈnɪʃən/ *n* **1** [C] the electrical CIRCUIT which starts an engine –see illustration on page 95 **2** [U] *fml* the act or action of igniting (IGNITE)

ig·no·ble /ɪgˈnoʷbəl/ *adj lit* not noble; dishonorable; which one should be ashamed of: *ignoble acts/deeds*

ig·no·min·y /ˈɪgnəˌmɪniʸ/ *n* **-ies** *fml* [C;U] (an act of) shame or dishonor **–ignominious** /ˌɪgnəˈmɪniʸəs/ *adj: ignominious behavior |an ignominious defeat* **–ignominiously** *adv*

ig·no·ra·mus /ˌɪgnəˈreʸməs, -ˈræ-/ *n* **-muses** *derog* an IGNORANT person

ig·no·rance /ˈɪgnərəns/ *n* [U *of*] lack of knowledge: *Ignorance of the law is no excuse.*

ig·no·rant /ˈɪgnərənt/ *adj* [*of*] **1** lacking knowledge: *ignorant of even the simplest* *facts* –see IGNORE (USAGE) **2** *infml* rude, impolite, esp. because of lack of social training

ig·nore /ɪgˈnɔr, ɪgˈnoʷr/ *v* **-nored, -noring** [T] to refuse to notice; take no notice of: *Ignore the child if he misbehaves, and he'll soon stop.*

USAGE Compare **ignore** and **be ignorant**: *He was driving very fast because he was* **ignorant** *of the fact that* (=he didn't know that) *there was a speed limit.|He* **ignored** *the speed limit* (=he knew about it, but paid no attention to it) *and drove very fast.*

i·kon /ˈaɪkɑn/ *n* → ICON

IL *written abbrev. said as:* Illinois /ˌɪləˈnɔɪ/ (a state in the US)

ill¹ /ɪl/ *adj* worse /wɜrs/, worst /wɜrst/ **1** [F] not well in health: *She's* **seriously ill** (=very ill) *in the hospital.* **2** [A] bad; harmful: *ill luck|He suffers from* **ill health.***|I feel no* **ill will** (=dislike) *towards her in spite of her unkindness.* –see DISEASE (USAGE)

ill² *adv* [*no comp.*] **1** badly; unpleasantly: *to speak ill of one's neighbors.|She seems* **ill-suited** *to this job.|The child has been* **ill-treated.***|He was* **ill-advised** (=unwise) *to buy that old house.|an* **ill-fated** (=unlucky) *attempt* **2** hardly; not easily: *I can ill afford the time.* **3 ill at ease** uncomfortable: *He felt ill at ease at the party.*

ill³ *n* [*often pl.*] a bad thing: *the ills of life*

I'll /aɪl/ *v short for:* **1** I will **2** I shall

il·le·gal /ɪˈliʸgəl/ *adj* [*no comp.*] not LEGAL; against the law: *It's illegal to park your car here.* –**illegally** *adv*

il·le·gal·i·ty /ˌɪliʸˈgæləṭiʸ/ *n* **-ties 1** [U] the state of being ILLEGAL **2** [C] an act against the law

il·leg·i·ble /ɪˈlɛdʒəbəl/ *adj* not LEGIBLE; which cannot be read: *illegible handwriting* –**illegibly** *adv* –**illegibility** /ɪˌlɛdʒəˈbɪləṭiʸ/ *n* [U]

il·le·git·i·mate /ˌɪlɪˈdʒɪṭəmɪt/ *adj* **1** [*no comp.*] born to parents who are not married: *an illegitimate child* **2** not allowed by the rules: *an illegitimate action* –opposite **legitimate**; compare ILLEGAL –**illegitimately** *adv* –**illegitimacy** /ˌɪlɪˈdʒɪṭəməsiʸ/ *n* [U]

il·lic·it /ɪˈlɪsɪt/ *adj* [*no comp.*] (done) against a law or a rule: *an illicit act|illicit trade in drugs* –**illicitly** *adv*

il·lit·er·ate /ɪˈlɪṭərɪt/ *adj,n* [*no comp.*] (a person who is) not LITERATE; unable to read and write: *About half the population is still illiterate.|He's an illiterate.* –**illiteracy** /ɪˈlɪṭərəsiʸ/ *n* [U]

ill·ness /ˈɪlnɪs/ *n* [C;U] (a) disease; unhealthy state of the body: *A serious illness has prevented her from working for a year.* –see DISEASE (USAGE)

il·log·i·cal /ɪˈlɑdʒɪkəl/ *adj* **1** (of people or ideas) going against LOGIC **2** *infml* not sensible –opposite **logical** –**illogically** *adv*

il·lu·mi·nate /ɪˈluʷməˌneʸt/ *v* **-nated, -nating 1** to give light to: *The room was illuminated by candles.* **2** to decorate (buildings, streets, etc.) with lights for a special occasion

il·lu·mi·nat·ing /ɪˈluʷməˌneʸt̬ɪŋ/ *adj* helping to explain: *an illuminating remark, that showed her real character*

il·lu·mi·na·tion /ɪˌluʷməˈneʸʃən/ *n* [U] the act of illuminating or state of being ILLUMINATEd

il·lu·sion /ɪˈluʷʒən/ *n* something seen wrongly, not as it really is; a false belief or idea: *The lake in the desert was just an* **optical illusion.***|She is* **under the illusion** *that she's passed the exam, but I know she failed.|I* **have no illusions** *about him; I know he's a liar.*

USAGE Compare **illusion** and **delusion**: An **illusion** is usu. something that seems true to the senses, but is known to be false; a **delusion** is something which, though false, is believed to be true: *the* **illusion** *that the sun goes around the earth* (=it seems to, but we know it does not)*|man's earlier* **delusion** *that the sun went around the earth* (=people believed this really happened).

il·lus·trate /ˈɪləˌstreʸt/ *v* **-trated, -trating** [T] **1** to add pictures to (something written): *This book is a beautifully illustrated history of science.* **2** to show the meaning of (something) by giving related examples: *The story he told about her illustrates her true generosity very clearly.*

il·lus·tra·tion /ˌɪləˈstreʸʃən/ *n* **1** a picture, esp. in a book: *It's not a very good book, but I like the illustrations.* **2** an example which explains the meaning of something: *That's a typical illustration of his meanness.* **3 by way of illustration** as an example

il·lus·tra·tive /ɪˈlʌstrəṭɪv/ *adj* used for explaining the meaning of something: *an illustrative example* –compare ILLUSTRATE (2) –**illustratively** *adv*

il·lus·tra·tor /ˈɪləˌstreʸṭər/ *n* a person who draws pictures, esp. for a book

il·lus·tri·ous /ɪˈlʌstriʸəs/ *adj apprec* famous; known for one's great works: *the illustrious name of Shakespeare* –**illustriously** *adv*

I'm /aɪm/ *short for:* I am

im·age /ˈɪmɪdʒ/ *n* **1** a picture, esp. in the mind: *An image of a country garden came into my mind.* **2** the opinion which others have of one: *The President will have to improve his image if he wants to win the next election.* **3** a copy: *He's the (very) image of his father.* **4** an object made to represent a god or person to be worshipped –compare IDOL **5** a METAPHOR or SIMILE; phrase suggesting something by means of a poetical form

im·age·ry /ˈɪmɪdʒriʸ/ *n* [U] the use of IMAGES (5) in literature

i·mag·i·na·ble /ɪˈmædʒənəbəl/ *adj* that can be imagined: *every imaginable possibility*

i·mag·i·nar·y /ɪˈmædʒəˌnɛriʸ/ *adj* not real, but imagined: *All the characters in this book are imaginary.|My little daughter has an imaginary friend.* –compare IMAGINATIVE

i·mag·i·na·tion /ɪˌmædʒəˈneʸʃən/ *n* **1** [C;U] the act of imagining or the ability to imagine: *The little boy's story shows plenty of imagination.|a vivid imagination* **2** [C] the mind: *The difficulties are all in your imagination.*

i·mag·i·na·tive /ɪˈmædʒənəṭɪv/ *adj* using or having imagination: *imaginative writing |She is an imaginative child.* –compare: *an imaginative story |All the events described in this story are* **imaginary.** (=they didn't really happen) –opposite **unimaginative**

–**imaginatively** adv

i·**mag·ine** /ɪ'mædʒɪn/ v -**ined**, -**ining** [not be + v-ing] **1** [T + v-ing] to form (a picture or idea) in the mind: Can you imagine George cooking dinner for twenty people? **2** [T +(that)] to suppose or have an idea about, esp. mistakenly or without proof: She imagines that people don't like her.

i·**mam** /ɪ'mɑm/ n a Muslim priest and/or prince, or someone who studies Muslim law

im·**bal·ance** /ɪm'bæləns/ n a lack of balance or proper relationship, esp. between two qualities or between two examples of one thing: When more males are born than females, there is a population imbalance.

im·**be·cile** /'ɪmbəsəl, -,sɪl/ n a person of weak mind –compare IDIOT –**imbecility** /,ɪmbə'sɪlətiʸ/ -**ties** n [C;U]

im·**bibe** /ɪm'baɪb/ v -**bibed**, -**bibing** [I;T] fml to drink or take in (esp. alcohol)

im·**bue** sbdy. **with** sthg. /ɪm'byuʷ/ v prep -**bued**, -**buing** [T usu. pass.] fml to fill with a strong feeling or opinion): A President should be imbued with a sense of responsibility for the nation.

im·**i·tate** /'ɪmə,teʸt/ v -**tated**, -**tating** [T] to copy the behavior, appearance, speech, etc., typical of (a person): James can imitate his father's speech perfectly.|You should imitate her way of doing things. –see also INIMITABLE –compare IMPERSONATE –**imitative** /'ɪmə,teʸtɪv/ adj –**imitator** /'ɪmə,teʸtər/ n

im·**i·ta·tion** /,ɪmə'teʸʃən/ n [C;U] the act or result of imitating (IMITATE): His imitation of that singer is perfect.|imitation jewelry (=a copy of the real thing)

im·**mac·u·late** /ɪ'mækyəlɪt/ adj very clean and unspoiled: immaculate white shoes –**immaculately** adv: immaculately dressed

im·**ma·te·ri·al** /,ɪmə'tɪəriəl/ adj unimportant: When it happened is immaterial; I want to know why it happened.

im·**ma·ture** /,ɪmə'tʃʊər, -'tʊər, -'tyʊər/ adj (typical of someone who is) not MATURE; not fully formed or developed: His foolish behavior is very immature for a man of 30. –**immaturely** adv –**immaturity** /,ɪmə'tʃʊərətiʸ, -'tʊər-, -'tyʊər-/ n [U]

im·**meas·ur·a·ble** /ɪ'mɛʒərəbəl/ adj [no comp.] too large to be measured: immeasurable depths/stupidity

im·**me·di·a·cy** /ɪ'miʸdiʸəsiʸ/ also **immediateness** /ɪ'miʸdiʸɪtnɪs/ – n [U] the nearness or urgent presence of something: He did not realize the immediacy of the problem.

im·**me·di·ate** /ɪ'miʸdiʸɪt/ adj [no comp.] **1** done or needed at once: I want an immediate reply. **2** nearest; next: in the immediate future |My immediate family consists of my son and my wife.

im·**me·di·ate·ly** /ɪ'miʸdiʸɪtliʸ/ adv [adv + prep/adv] at once: I left immediately after I heard the news.|Stop that, immediately!

im·**me·mo·ri·al** /,ɪmə'mɔriʸəl, -'moʷr-/ adj

SPELLING NOTE
Words with the sound /aɪ/ may be spelled e-, like **eye**, or ai-, like **aisle**.

---

going back to ancient times: People have fought wars **from/since time immemorial**.

im·**mense** /ɪ'mɛns/ adj usu. apprec very large: an immense room/improvement –see Study Notes on page 550 –**immensity** n [U]: the immensity of space

im·**mense·ly** /ɪ'mɛnsliʸ/ adv apprec very much: I enjoyed it immensely.

im·**merse** /ɪ'mɜrs/ v -**mersed**, -**mersing** [T in] to put deep under water: He lay immersed in a hot bath.|(fig.) She was so immersed in her work that she didn't notice me. –**immersion** /ɪ'mɜrʒən, -ʃən/ n [U]

im·**mer·sion heat·er** /·'··· ,··/ n an electric water heater placed in a tank which provides all the hot water for use in the home

im·**mi·grant** /'ɪməgrənt/ n a person coming into a country from abroad to make his home there

im·**mi·grate** /'ɪmə,greʸt/ v -**grated**, -**grating** [I] to come into a country to make one's life and home there –see EMIGRATE (USAGE) –**immigration** /,ɪmə'greʸʃən/ n [U]: the immigration office at the airport

im·**mi·nence** /'ɪmənəns/ n [U] the nearness of something which is going to happen: The imminence of their exams made them work harder.

im·**mi·nent** /'ɪmənənt/ adj [no comp.] which is going to happen very soon: There's a storm imminent. –compare EMINENT, IMPENDING –**imminently** adv

im·**mo·bile** /ɪ'moʷbəl, -,biʸl/ adj not MOBILE; not able to move; unmoving –**immobility** /,ɪmoʷ'bɪlətiʸ/ n [U]

im·**mo·bi·lize** ‖also -**lise** BrE /ɪ'moʷbə,laɪz/ v -**lized**, -**lizing** [T] to make unable to move: When she broke her leg, Alice was immobilized for weeks.

im·**mod·er·ate** /ɪ'madərɪt/ adj not MODERATE; not (done) within sensible limits: immoderate eating –**immoderately** adv

im·**mod·est** /ɪ'madɪst/ adj derog **1** not modest; telling the good things about oneself instead of hiding them **2** likely to shock because improper or impure: an immodest dress |immodest behavior –compare INDECENT –**immodestly** adv –**immodesty** n [U]

im·**mor·al** /ɪ'mɔrəl, ɪ'mɑr-/ adj not moral; not considered good or right, esp. in sexual matters: Using other people for one's own profit is immoral.|A PROSTITUTE lives off **immoral earnings**.|an immoral book –compare AMORAL –**immorally** adv –**immorality** /,ɪmə'rælətiʸ, ,ɪmɔ-/ -**ties** [C;U]

im·**mor·tal** /ɪ'mɔrtl̩/ adj [no comp.] not MORTAL; that will not die; that continues for ever: Nobody is immortal |(fig.) immortal fame –**immortality** /,ɪmɔr'tælətiʸ/ n [U]

im·**mor·tal·ize** ‖also -**ise** BrE /ɪ'mɔrtl̩,aɪz/ v -**ized**, -**izing** [T in] to give endless life or fame to (someone): Charlie Chaplin was immortalized in his early silent movies.

im·**mov·a·ble** /ɪ'muʷvəbəl/ adj which cannot be moved: (fig.) The government is immovable on the new drinking laws. –**immovably** adv

im·**mune** /ɪ'myuʷn/ adj **1** [to] unable to be harmed because of special powers in oneself:

immune to disease |*immune to unpleasant- ness* **2** [*from*] protected (from): *The criminal was told he would be immune from punish- ment if he said what he knew about the murder.* –**immunity** *n* [U]

im·mu·nize ||also **-nise** *BrE* /'ɪmyəˌnaɪz/ *v* [T] to make (someone) safe against disease by putting certain substances into the body, usu. by means of a HYPODERMIC needle –see also INOCULATE, VACCINATE –**immunization** /ˌɪmyənə'zeʸʃən/ *n* [C;U]

im·mu·ta·ble /ɪ'myuʷtəbəl/ *adj fml* unchangeable: *immutable laws of nature*

imp /ɪmp/ *n* a little devil: (fig.) *That child is a real imp.* –see also IMPISH

im·pact /'ɪmpækt/ *n* the force of one object hitting another: *The cup hit the wall and broke on impact.* |(fig.) *Her new idea made a great impact in the office.*

im·pair /ɪm'pɛər/ *v* [T] to spoil or weaken: *His hearing was impaired after the explosion.* –**impairment** *n* [U]

im·pale /ɪm'peʸl/ *v* **-paled, -paling** [T *on*] to run a sharp stick or weapon through (some- one's body): *He fell out of the window and was impaled on the fence.*

im·part /ɪm'pɑrt/ *v* [T *to*] *fml* to give (qualities, knowledge, etc.): *She imparted the secret to a friend.*

im·par·tial /ɪm'pɑrʃəl/ *adj* [*no comp.*] fair; giving equal attention to all concerned: *an impartial judge* –see also DISINTERESTED –**im- partially** *adv* –**impartiality** /ɪmˌpɑrʃiʸ'ælət̬iʸ/ *n* [U]

im·pass·a·ble /ɪm'pæsəbəl/ *adj* which cannot be traveled over: *The snow has made the road impassable.* –compare IMPOSSIBLE

im·passe /'ɪmpæs, ɪm'pæs/ *n* [*usu. sing.*] a point where further movement is blocked: *to reach an impasse in discussions* (=where neither side will agree)

im·pas·sioned /ɪm'pæʃənd/ *adj* (usu. of speech) moved by deep feelings: *an impas- sioned demand for the prisoners to be freed*

im·pas·sive /ɪm'pæsɪv/ *adj sometimes derog* (of people) showing or having no feelings; unusually calm –**impassively** *adv*: *He watched impassively as his house burned down.* –**impassivity** /ˌɪmpæ'sɪvət̬iʸ/ *n* [U]

im·pa·tient /ɪm'peʸʃənt/ *adj* **1** not patient; unable to wait calmly or bear the weaknesses of others: *too impatient with slow learners* **2** [F +*to-v*/*for*] eager: *impatient for his dinner* –**impatience** *n* [U + *to-v*/*for*]: *Try to control your impatience.* –**impatiently** *adv*: *He waited impatiently for the train to arrive.*

im·peach /ɪm'piʸtʃ/ *v* [T] *law* to charge (esp. a public official) with a serious crime, esp. against the state –**impeachment** *n* [C;U]

im·pec·ca·ble /ɪm'pɛkəbəl/ *adj* faultless: *im- peccable manners*/*behavior* –**impeccably** *adv*

im·pe·cu·ni·ous /ˌɪmpɪ'kyuʷniʸəs/ *adj fml, sometimes humor* having little or no money, esp. continued

im·pede /ɪm'piʸd/ *v* **-peded, -peding** [T] *fml* to get in the way of; make (something) difficult to do: *The attempt to rescue the climbers was impeded by bad weather.*

im·ped·i·ment /ɪm'pɛdəmənt/ *n* a fact or

event which makes action difficult or impos- sible: *It's difficult to understand him because he has a speech impediment.*

im·pel /ɪm'pɛl/ *v* **-ll-** [T *in, into*] *fml* (esp. of an idea, feeling, etc.) to push (someone) for- ward: *Hunger impelled me to finish my work quickly.*

im·pend·ing /ɪm'pɛndɪŋ/ *adj* (usu. of some- thing unpleasant) about to happen: *the im- pending examinations* –compare IMMINENT

im·pen·e·tra·ble /ɪm'pɛnətrəbəl/ *adj* **1** which cannot be gone into or through: *the im- penetrable forest* |(fig.) *impenetrable dark- ness* (=in which nothing can be seen) **2** not able to be understood or helped: *an im- penetrable mystery* –see also PENETRATE

im·per·a·tive¹ /ɪm'pɛrət̬ɪv/ *adj* [+*that*] *fml* urgent; which must be done: *It's imperative that he go now.* –**imperatively** *adv*

imperative² *n tech* (an example of) the form which shows the use of the verb to express a command: *In "Come here!" the verb "come" is in the imperative.*

im·per·cep·ti·ble /ˌɪmpər'sɛptəbəl/ *adj* not PERCEPTIBLE; unable to be noticed because of smallness or slightness: *an almost impercep- tible movement in the dark* –**imperceptibly** *adv* –**imperceptibility** /ˌɪmpərˌsɛptə'bɪlət̬iʸ/ *n* [U]

im·per·fect¹ /ɪm'pɔrfɪkt/ *adj* not perfect; faulty: *an imperfect knowledge of French* –**imperfectly** *adv* –**imperfection** /ˌɪmpər- 'fɛkʃən/ *n* [C;U]

imperfect² *n tech* (an example of) the tense of the verb which shows incomplete action in the past: *In "we were walking down the road" the verb "were walking" is in the imperfect.* –see also PERFECT¹ (5)

im·pe·ri·al /ɪm'pɪəriʸəl/ *adj* (often cap.) con- cerning an empire or its ruler –compare IM- PERIOUS –**imperially** *adv*

im·pe·ri·al·ism /ɪm'pɪəriʸəˌlɪzəm/ *n* [U] **1** (belief in) the making of empires **2** *derog* the gaining of political and trade advantages over poorer nations by a powerful country which rules them or helps them with money –compare COLONIALISM –**imperialist** *adj,n*

im·per·il /ɪm'pɛrəl/ *v* **-l-** *AmE* ||**-ll-** *BrE* [T] to put in danger

im·pe·ri·ous /ɪm'pɪəriʸəs/ *adj fml* (too) com- manding; expecting obedience from others: *an imperious voice* –compare IMPERIAL –**im- periously** *adv* –**imperiousness** *n* [U]

im·per·son·al /ɪm'pɔrsənəl/ *adj* not showing personal feelings: *an impersonal letter* |*a large, impersonal organization* –**imper- sonally** *adv*

im·per·so·nate /ɪm'pɔrsəˌneʸt/ *v* **-nated, -nating** [T] to pretend to be (another person) by copying his/her appearance, behavior, etc.: *He impersonates all the well-known politicians.* –compare IMITATE –**impersona- tion** /ɪmˌpɔrsə'neʸʃən/ *n* [C;U] –**impersona- tor** /ɪm'pɔrsəˌneʸtər/ *n*

im·per·ti·nent /ɪm'pɔrtn-ənt/ *adj* rude or not respectful, esp. to an older or more impor- tant person –**impertinence** *n* [U] –**imperti- nently** *adv*

im·per·turb·a·ble /ˌɪmpər'tɔrbəbəl/ *adj* that

cannot be worried; that remains calm and steady in spite of difficulties or confusion –**imperturbably** *adv* –**imperturbability** /ˌɪmpərˌtɜrbəˈbɪlətiʸ/ *n* [U]

im·per·vi·ous /ɪmˈpɜrviʸəs/ *adj* [*to; no comp.*] **1** not allowing anything to pass through: *This material is impervious to gases and liquids.* **2** too certain in one's opinions to be changed or influenced (by): *impervious to reason/threats/criticism*

im·pet·u·ous /ɪmˈpɛtʃuʷəs/ *adj* showing swift action but lack of thought: *an impetuous driver/decision* –**impetuously** *adv* –**impetuosity** /ɪmˌpɛtʃuʷˈɑsətiʸ/ *n* [U]

im·pe·tus /ˈɪmpətəs/ *n* **1** [U] the force of something moving; MOMENTUM: *The car ran down the hill under its own impetus.* **2** [C;U] (an) encouragement: *The President's plan gave fresh impetus to industry.*

im·pi·e·ty /ɪmˈpaɪətiʸ/ *n* -ties [C;U] (an act showing) lack of PIETY; lack of respect, esp. for religion

im·pinge on/upon sthg. /ɪmˈpɪndʒ/ *v prep* -pinged, -pinging [T] to have an effect on: *The need to see that justice is done impinges on every decision made in the courts.*

im·pi·ous /ˈɪmpiʸəs, ɪmˈpaɪəs/ *adj* lacking PIETY; showing IMPIETY –opposite pious –**impiously** *adv*

imp·ish /ˈɪmpɪʃ/ *adj* like a little devil (IMP): *an impish smile* –**impishly** *adv* –**impishness** *n* [U]

im·plac·a·ble /ɪmˈplækəbəl, -ˈpleyʸ-/ *adj* impossible to satisfy or PLACATE: *an implacable enemy* |*implacable dislike*

im·plant /ɪmˈplænt/ *v* [T *in, into*] to fix in deeply, usu. into the body or mind

im·ple·ment¹ /ˈɪmpləmənt/ *n* a tool or instrument: *farming/cooking implements*

im·ple·ment² /ˈɪmpləˌmɛnt/ *v* [T] to carry out or put into practice: *The committee's suggestions will be implemented immediately.*

im·pli·cate /ˈɪmplɪˌkeyʸt/ *v* -cated, -cating [T *in*] *fml* to show that (someone else) is also to blame: *The police found a letter which implicated him in the robbery.* –compare INVOLVE

im·pli·ca·tion /ˌɪmplɪˈkeyʸʃən/ *n* **1** [U] the act of IMPLYING: *She said very little directly, but a great deal* **by implication.** **2** [C] a suggestion not expressed but understood: *He smiled, but the implication was that he didn't believe me.* –compare INSINUATION **3** [U] *fml* the act of implicating (IMPLICATE)

im·plic·it /ɪmˈplɪsɪt/ *adj* **1** [*in*] (of a statement, rule, etc.) meant though not plainly expressed; suggested: *an implicit threat* |*The threat was implicit in the way he looked.* –compare EXPLICIT **2** [A] unquestioning and complete: *She has implicit trust in her doctor.* –**implicitly** *adv*: *She trusted the doctor implicitly.*

im·plore /ɪmˈplɔr, ɪmˈploʷr/ *v* -plored, -ploring [T] to ask (someone) in a begging man-

ner (for something or to do something): *an imploring look* |*I implore you to go now.*

im·ply /ɪmˈplaɪ/ *v* -plied, -plying [T +*that*] to express indirectly; suggest: *His manner implies that he would like to come with us.* |*The fact that nobody answered the telephone implies that they're not at home.* |*Refusal to answer implies guilt.* –see INFER (USAGE)

im·po·lite /ˌɪmpəˈlaɪt/ *adj* not polite –**impolitely** *adv* –**impoliteness** *n* [C;U]

im·pol·i·tic /ɪmˈpɑləˌtɪk/ *adj* (of an action) not POLITIC; not well-judged for one's purpose; not wise

im·pon·der·a·ble /ɪmˈpɑndərəbəl/ *adj* of which the importance cannot be calculated or measured exactly –**imponderable** *n* [*usu. pl.*]: *Many imponderables influence the result of an election.*

im·port¹ /ˈɪmˌpɔrt, ɪmˈpoʷrt, ˈɪmpɔrt, ˈɪmpoʷrt/ *v* [T *from*] to bring in (something), esp. from abroad: *imported silk* –compare EXPORT¹ –**importer** *n*

im·port² /ˈɪmpɔrt, ˈɪmpoʷrt/ *n* **1** [C *often pl.*] something brought into a country from abroad: *Imports rose last month.* (=we imported more goods than in the month before) **2** [U] the act of IMPORTING: *the import of food from abroad* –compare EXPORT² **3** [S] *fml* the meaning: *The import of the speech was difficult to understand.* **4** [U] *fml* IMPORTANCE: *a matter of no/great import*

im·por·tance /ɪmˈpɔrtns/ *n* [U] **1** the quality or state of being important –opposite **unimportance 2** the reason why something or someone is important: *The importance of washing one's hands is that it prevents infection.*

im·por·tant /ɪmˈpɔrtnt/ *adj* having great effect, value, etc.: *It's important to learn to read.* |*a very important meeting* |*She's one of the most important people in the company.* –opposite **unimportant** –**importantly** *adv*

im·por·ta·tion /ˌɪmpɔrˈteyʸʃən, -poʷr-/ *n* [C;U] the act or result of IMPORTING

im·por·tu·nate /ɪmˈpɔrtʃənɪt/ *adj fml* always demanding things –**importunately** *adv*

im·por·tune /ˌɪmpɔrˈtuʷn, -ˈtyuʷn, ɪmˈpɔrtʃən/ *v* -tuned, -tuning [T] *fml* to beg (someone) repeatedly for things or to do things

im·pose /ɪmˈpoʷz/ *v* -posed, -posing [*on, upon*] **1** [T] to establish (an additional payment) officially: *A new tax has been imposed on wine.* **2** [I] to take unfair advantage, in a way that causes additional work and trouble: *Thanks for your offer of help, but I don't want to impose on you.* **3** [T] to force the acceptance of; establish: *She imposed herself as their leader.* –**imposition** /ˌɪmpəˈzɪʃən/ *n* [C;U *of, on, upon*]: *It's an imposition to ask us to stay at work until seven o'clock at night.*

im·pos·ing /ɪmˈpoʷzɪŋ/ *adj* powerful in appearance; strong or large in size: *an imposing view across the valley* |*an imposing building* –**imposingly** *adv*

im·pos·si·ble /ɪmˈpɑsəbəl/ *adj* **1** [*no comp.*] not possible: *It's impossible to do all that work before tomorrow!* **2** hard to bear; very unpleasant: *His bad temper makes life im-*

possible for his whole family.|an impossible child –compare IMPASSABLE –**impossibility** /ɪmˌpɑsəˈbɪləṭiʸ/ n [U] –**impossibly** /ɪmˈpɑsəbliʸ/ adv: (not used with verbs): impossibly difficult

im·pos·tor ‖also **-ter** AmE /ɪmˈpɑstər/ n someone who deceives by pretending to be someone else: You're not my brother, you impostor!

im·po·tent /ˈɪmpəṭənt/ adj **1** [+to-v] lacking power to do things: The city government seems impotent in dealing with the rising crime rate. **2** (of a man) unable to perform the sex act –see also POTENT –**impotence** n [U] –**impotently** adv

im·pound /ɪmˈpaʊnd/ v [T] fml or law to take and shut up officially until claimed (esp. something lost or not taken care of): If you leave your car there, the police will impound it.

im·pov·er·ish /ɪmˈpɑvərɪʃ/ v [T] to make poor: (fig.) The world was impoverished by the death of that great artist.

im·prac·ti·ca·ble /ɪmˈpræktɪkəbəl/ adj not PRACTICABLE; that cannot be used in practice: Those new building plans are impracticable. –**impracticably** adv –**impracticability** /ɪmˌpræktɪkəˈbɪləṭiʸ/ n [U]

im·prac·ti·cal /ɪmˈpræktɪkəl/ adj not practical; not sensible or reasonable: It's impractical not to be able to even boil an egg.|an impractical suggestion –**impractically** adv –**impracticality** /ɪmˌpræktɪˈkæləṭiʸ/ n [U]

im·preg·na·ble /ɪmˈprɛgnəbəl/ adj which cannot be entered or conquered by attack: an impregnable castle

im·preg·nate /ɪmˈprɛgneʸt/ v **-nated, -nating** [T] **1** [with] to cause (a substance) to enter and spread completely through (another substance): a new kind of furniture-cleaning cloth that's impregnated with polish **2** fml to make PREGNANT (1)

im·pre·sa·ri·o /ˌɪmprəˈsɑriʸˌoʷ, -ˈsɛɑr-/ n **-os** a person who arranges performances in theaters, concert halls, etc.

im·press /ɪmˈprɛs/ v [T] **1** to fill (someone) with admiration: I was very impressed by/with their new house. **2** [on, with] to make the importance of (something) clear to (someone); EMPHASIZE: My father impressed on me the value of hard work.

im·pres·sion /ɪmˈprɛʃən/ n **1** the image or feeling a person or thing gives to someone's mind, esp. as regards its strength or quality: a strong impression|I made a bad impression on the teacher by arriving late on my first day.|First impressions are often wrong.|What's your impression of him as a worker? |I **got the impression** (that) they'd just had an argument.|I was **under the impression** that he was the head of the company, but he wasn't **2** a mark left by pressure: I saw the impression of a foot in the mud. **3** an attempt to copy a person's appearance or behavior, esp. when done as a theatrical performance: He did/gave an impression of the teacher which made us all laugh.

im·pres·sion·a·ble /ɪmˈprɛʃənəbəl/ adj easy to influence: The child is at an impression-

able age.

im·pres·sion·ism /ɪmˈprɛʃəˌnɪzəm/ n [U] (often cap.) a style of painting (esp. in France, 1870–1900) which produces effects by light and color rather than by details of form –**impressionist** n

im·pres·sion·is·tic /ɪmˌprɛʃəˈnɪstɪk/ adj based on IMPRESSIONs (1) rather than on knowledge, fact, or detailed study: an impressionistic account of what happened –**impressionistically** adv

im·pres·sive /ɪmˈprɛsɪv/ adj causing admiration by giving one a feeling of size, importance, quality, etc.: an impressive speech/speaker –opposite **unimpressive** –**impressively** adv –**impressiveness** n [U]

im·print /ɪmˈprɪnt/ v [T on] to print or press (a mark) on something: (fig.) Every detail is imprinted on my mind. –**imprint** /ˈɪmˌprɪnt/ n

im·pris·on /ɪmˈprɪzən/ v [T] to put in prison or keep in a place or state from which one cannot get out as one wishes –**imprisonment** n [U]

im·prob·a·ble /ɪmˈprɑbəbəl/ adj not probable; not likely to happen or to be true: an improbable idea –**improbably** adv –**improbability** /ɪmˌprɑbəˈbɪləṭiʸ, ˌɪmprɑ-/ **-ties** n [C;U]

im·promp·tu /ɪmˈprɑmptuʷ, -tyuʷ/ adj, adv (said or done) at once without preparation: an impromptu speech –compare IMPROVISE

im·prop·er /ɪmˈprɑpər/ adj **1** not suitable: His casual style of dress was improper for a formal dinner. **2** showing thoughts which are socially undesirable, esp. about sex: an improper suggestion/remark –see also PROPER –**improperly** adv

im·pro·pri·e·ty /ˌɪmprəˈpraɪəṭiʸ/ n **-ties** fml **1** [U] the quality or state of being IMPROPER **2** [C] a socially undesirable act –see also PROPRIETY

im·prove /ɪmˈpruʷv/ v **-proved, -proving** [I;T] to (cause to) become better: I want to improve my English.|I think your English is improving.|Our new improved dish soap gets all your dishes really clean.

improve on/upon sthg. v prep [T] to produce or be something better than; BETTER⁴: Tom has improved on his first attempt (at drawing).

im·prove·ment /ɪmˈpruʷvmənt/ n [C;U] (a sign of) the act of improving or the state of being improved: There's been a great improvement in his work this term.|His health is showing signs of improvement.

USAGE An **improvement** in something means that it has gotten better, but one can speak of an **improvement** on something only when two things are compared: There has been an **improvement** in the weather.|Today's weather is an **improvement** on yesterday's.

im·prov·i·dent /ɪmˈprɑvədənt/ adj fml (esp. of someone who wastes money) not PROVIDENT; not preparing for the future –**improvidence** n [U] –**improvidently** adv

im·pro·vise /ˈɪmprəˌvaɪz/ v **-vised, -vising** [I;T] to do or make (something one has not prepared for) because a sudden need has arisen: *I forgot the words of my speech, so I had to improvise.* **–improvisation** /ɪmˌprɑvə'zeᵉʃən, ˌɪmprəvə-/ *n* [C;U] *–compare* IMPROMPTU

im·pru·dent /ɪm'pruʷdnt/ *adj* not PRUDENT; unwise and thoughtless (in one's actions) **–imprudence** *n* [U] **–imprudently** *adv*

im·pu·dent /'ɪmpyədənt/ *adj* shamelessly bold, esp. to an older or more important person: *an impudent child/remark* **–impudence** *n* [U] **–impudently** *adv*

im·pulse /'ɪmpʌls/ *n* **1** [C;U] a sudden wish to do something: *She had a sudden impulse to go on vacation.|He bought the car* **on impulse. 2** [C] *tech* a single push, or a force acting for a short time in one direction along a wire, nerve, etc.: *an electrical impulse*

im·pul·sive /ɪm'pʌlsɪv/ *adj* having or showing a tendency to act suddenly without thinking about the suitability, results, etc., of one's acts **–impulsively** *adv* **–impulsiveness** *n* [U]

im·pu·ni·ty /ɪm'pyuʷnəṭiʸ/ *n* [U] certainty of not being punished: *He behaved badly* **with impunity** *since he knew the teacher was weak.*

im·pure /ɪm'pyuər/ *adj* **1** not pure; morally bad; of bad sexual habits: *impure thoughts* **2** not pure, but mixed with something else: *impure drugs*

im·pu·ri·ty /ɪm'pyuərəṭiʸ/ *n* **-ties 1** [C] something mixed with something else so that it is not pure **2** [C;U] the state of not being pure, or an act showing this *–see also* PURITY

im·pute sthg. to sbdy./sthg. /ɪm'pyuʷt/ *v prep* **-puted, -puting** [T] *fml* to blame (something) on: *The police impute the rise in crime to high unemployment* **–imputation** /ˌɪmpyə'teᵉʃən/ *n* [C;U]

in¹ /ɪn/ *prep* **1** (shows a position surrounded by something else) contained by; so as to be contained by; not beyond: *living in a house |money in a box|to sit in a car* (but *on a bicycle*)*|to swim in the sea* (compare *to sail on the sea*)*|cows in a field|She jumped in/into the water.|We arrived in Boston.* (compare *we arrived at the airport.*)*|in France |an island in the Atlantic |in the hospital |in prison|in church* **2** (when speaking of time) *a* during: *in January |in the spring|in 1984|in the night* (compare *at night, at 10 o'clock, on July 1st, on Saturday*)*|in the past* **b** after not more than: *It's two o'clock. I'll come in an hour.* (=at three o'clock) **3** shown or described as the subject of: *a character in a story |the people in this photograph* **4** (shows employment): *She's in politics.|a job in insurance* **5** wearing: *a girl in red/in uniform* **6** towards (a direction): *in the wrong direction|The sun was in my eyes.* (=shining directly towards them) **7** using; with: *Write it in pencil/in French.* **8** (shows the way something happens): *in public* (=publicly)*|in secret* (=secretly)*|ten feet in length* (=as to

length)*|in danger|in a hurry |in reply* (=as a reply) **9** so as to be divided or arranged: *in rows |in a circle |They arrived in large numbers.* (=large numbers of them arrived) **10** (shows the larger one in a relation) per: *a slope of 1 in 3 |1 in (every) 5 women*

in² *adv* **1** so as to be contained or surrounded; away from the outside: *Open the bag and put the money in.|Come in!* (said when someone knocks at a door) **2** present; at home, indoors, etc.: *I'm afraid Mr. Jones is out, but he'll be in soon.|The train isn't in yet.* **3** from a number of people, or from all directions to a central point: *Letters have been coming/pouring in from everybody who heard the news on the radio.|Papers/marks must be in by Monday.* **4 a** of one side: (fig.) *The Republican party is in.* (=elected) **b** (of the ball in a game such as tennis) inside the line **5** fashionable: *Long skirts came in* (=became fashionable) *last year.* **6** (of the TIDE) close to the coast; high: *The TIDE is coming in now.* *–opposite* **out** (for 2,4,5,6) **7 day in, day out; year in, year out** etc. day after day, year after year, etc., without change **8 in for** to be about to have (esp. something bad): *I'm afraid we're in for some trouble.* **9 in on** having a share in: *people who were in on* (=knew) *the secret* **10 in and out (of)** sometimes inside and sometimes outside: *He's been in and out of prison for years.* **11 in with** friendly with **12 the ins and outs (of something):** the various parts and difficulties to be seen when something is looked at in detail: *the ins and outs of politics*

in³ *adj* [A] **1** directed towards; used for sending or going in: *I took the letters from my in box.* *–opposite* **out 2** [A] *infml* fashionable: *the in place to go |an in joke*

IN *written abbrev. said as:* Indiana /ˌɪndiʸ'ænə/ (a state in the US)

in·a·bil·i·ty /ˌɪnə'bɪləṭiʸ/ *n* [S;U +*to-v*] lack of ability; lack of power or skill: *(an) inability to work alone*

in·ac·ces·si·ble /ˌɪnək'sɛsəbəl/ *adj* [*to*] not ACCESSIBLE; which cannot be reached: *Heavy snow made the town inaccessible (to traffic).* **–inaccessibly** *adv* **–inaccessibility** /ˌɪnəkˌsɛsə'bɪləṭiʸ/ *n* [U]

in·ac·cu·rate /ɪn'ækyərɪt/ *adj* not ACCURATE; not correct **–inaccurately** *adv* **–inaccuracy** /ɪn'ækyərəsiʸ/ *n n* [C;U]

in·ac·tion /ɪn'ækʃən/ *n* [U] lack of action or activity; quality or state of doing nothing

in·ac·tive /ɪn'æktɪv/ *adj* not active **–inactivity** /ˌɪnæk'tɪvəṭiʸ/ *n* [U]

in·ad·e·qua·cy /ɪn'ædəkwəsiʸ/ *n* **-cies** [C;U] (an example of) the quality or state of being INADEQUATE

in·ad·e·quate /ɪn'ædəkwɪt/ *adj* [*to, for*] not ADEQUATE; not good enough in quality, ability, size, etc. (for some act): *I felt inadequate in my new job, so I left.|The food was inadequate for 14 people.* **–inadequately** *adv*

in·ad·vert·ent /ˌɪnəd'vɜrtnt/ *adj* (done) without paying attention or by accident **–inadvertently** *adv*: *He inadvertently knocked over his cup of coffee.*

in·al·ien·a·ble /ɪn'eᵉlyənəbəl/ *adj* [*no comp.*]

which cannot be taken away: *Freedom of speech should be an* **inalienable right.**

in·ane /ɪ'neɪn/ *adj* empty of meaning; really stupid: *an inane remark* **–inanely** *adv* **–inanity** /ɪ'nænəti/ *n* **-ties**

in·an·i·mate /ɪn'ænəmɪt/ *adj* not ANIMATE¹; not living: *Stone is inanimate.* –compare DEAD **–inanimately** *adv* **–inanimateness** *n* [U]

in·ap·pli·ca·ble /ɪn'æplɪkəbəl/ *adj* not APPLICABLE; which cannot be used or is unrelated to the subject **–inapplicability** /ɪn,æplɪkə'bɪləti/ *n* [U] **–inapplicably** /ɪn'æplɪkəbli/ *adv*

in·ap·pro·pri·ate /,ɪnə'proʷpriɪt/ *adj* [for, to] not APPROPRIATE; not suitable: *Your short dress is inappropriate for a formal party.* **–inappropriately** *adv* **–inappropriateness** *n* [U]

in·ar·tic·u·late /,ɪnɑr'tɪkyəlɪt/ *adj* **1** (of speech) not ARTICULATE, not well-formed; not clearly expressed **2** (of a person) speaking unclearly, so that the intended meaning is not expressed or is hard to understand **–inarticulately** *adv* **–inarticulateness** *n* [U]

in·as·much as /,ɪnəz'mtʃ əz/ *conj fml* owing to the fact that; because: *Their father is also guilty, inasmuch as he knew what they were going to do.*

in·at·ten·tion /,ɪnə'tɛnʃən, -tʃən/ *n* [U *to*] lack of attention

in·at·ten·tive /,ɪnə'tɛntɪv/ *adj* [to] not giving attention: *Julia is an inattentive pupil.* **–inattentively** *adv* **–inattentiveness** *n* [U]

in·au·di·ble /ɪn'ɔdəbəl/ *adj* not AUDIBLE; too quiet to be heard **–inaudibly** *adv* **–inaudibility** /ɪn,ɔdə'bɪləti/ *n* [U]

in·au·gu·rate /ɪ'nɔgyə,reʸt, -gə-/ *v* **-rated, -rating** [T] **1** [*usu. pass.*] to introduce (someone important) into a new place or job by holding a special ceremony **2** to open (a new building) or start (a public affair) with a ceremony: *The new school was inaugurated last week.* **–inaugural** /ɪ'nɔgyərəl, -gə-/ *adj* [A]: *an inaugural ceremony to open the new hospital* **–inauguration** /ɪ,nɔgyə'reʸʃən, -gə-/ *n* [C;U]

in·aus·pi·cious /,ɪnɔ'spɪʃəs/ *adj* not AUSPICIOUS; seeming to show bad luck to come; not giving good hopes for the future: *an inauspicious start to the term* **–inauspiciously** *adv* **–inauspiciousness** *n* [U]

in·born /,ɪn'bɔrn◄/ *adj* present from birth; part of one's nature: *Birds have an inborn ability to fly.*

in·bred /,ɪn'brɛd◄/ *adj* **1** having become part of one's nature as a result of early training **2** (resulting from being) bred from closely related members of a family

in·breed·ing /'ɪn,briʸdɪŋ/ *n* [U] breeding from (closely) related members of a family

Inc. /ɪŋk, ɪn'kɔrpə,reʸtɪd/ *abbrev. for*: (in the US) INCORPORATED: *General Motors, Inc.* –compare LTD

in·cal·cu·la·ble /ɪn'kælkyələbəl/ *adj* which cannot be counted or measured, esp. if very great: *an incalculable risk* **–incalculably** *adv*

in·can·des·cent /,ɪnkən'dɛsənt, -kæn-/ *adj* giving a bright light when heated **–incandescence** *n* [U] **–incandescently** *adv*

in·can·ta·tion /,ɪnkæn'teʸʃən/ *n* [C;U] (the saying of) words used in magic

in·ca·pa·ble /ɪn'keʸpəbəl/ *adj* [*of*] not CAPABLE; not able to do something: *I'm incapable of deceiving you.* **–incapably** *adv* **–incapability** /ɪn,keʸpə'bɪləti/ *n* [U]

in·ca·pac·i·tate /,ɪnkə'pæsə,teʸt/ *v* **-tated, -tating** [T *for*] to make (someone) not able to do something: *He was incapacitated after the accident.*

in·ca·pac·i·ty /,ɪnkə'pæsəti/ *n* **-ties** [S;U +to-v/for] lack of ability or power (to do something): *an incapacity to lie*

in·car·cer·ate /ɪn'kɑrsə,reʸt/ *v* **-ated, -ating** [T] *fml* to imprison **–incarceration** /ɪn,kɑrsə'reʸʃən/ *n* [U]

in·car·nate /ɪn'kɑrnɪt, -neʸt/ *adj* [after *n*] in the form of a body (not a spirit or idea): *the devil incarnate*|*She was happiness incarnate.*

in·car·na·tion /,ɪnkɑr'neʸʃən/ *n* **1** [U] the act of putting an idea, spirit, etc. into bodily form; state of being INCARNATE **2** [C] a person or thing that is the perfect example of a quality: *She's the incarnation of all goodness.*

in·cen·di·ar·y /ɪn'sɛndiʸ,eriʸ/ *adj* [A] which causes fires: *an incendiary bomb*

in·cense¹ /'ɪnsɛns/ *n* [U] a substance that gives off a sweet smell when burned, often used in religious services

in·cense² /ɪn'sɛns/ *v* **-censed, -censing** [T *at*] to make (someone) very angry: *I was incensed at his rudeness.*

in·cen·tive /ɪn'sɛntɪv/ *n* [C;U +to-v] an encouragement to greater activity: *His interest gave me (an) incentive, and I worked twice as hard.*|*He's got no/little incentive to work.*

in·cep·tion /ɪn'sɛpʃən/ *n fml* the beginning: *He's worked for that company from its inception.*

in·ces·sant /ɪn'sɛsənt/ *adj* never stopping: *incessant noise* **–incessantly** *adv*

in·cest /'ɪnsɛst/ *n* [U] a sexual relationship between close relatives in a family, as between brother and sister **–incestuous** /ɪn'sɛstʃuʷəs/ *adj* **–incestuously** *adv*

inch¹ /ɪntʃ/ *n* **1** a measure of length; 1/12 of a foot (about 0·025 meters) **2 inch by inch** by a small amount at a time

inch² *v* [I;T] to (cause to) move slowly and with difficulty in the way stated: *I inched (my way) through the narrow space between the cars.*

in·ci·dence /'ɪnsədəns/ *n* [S] the rate of happening: *There's a high incidence of disease there.*

in·ci·dent /'ɪnsədənt/ *n* an event, esp. one in a story: *In a recent incident two bombs exploded.*

in·ci·den·tal /,ɪnsə'dɛntəl◄/ *adj,n* [to] **1** (something) happening or appearing irregularly or as a less important part of something important **2** (something, esp. a fact or detail which is) unimportant: *an incidental remark*

in·ci·den·tal·ly /,ɪnsə'dɛntliʸ/ *adv* (used for adding something to what was said before, either on the same or another subject) by the way¹ (8): *I have to go now. Incidentally, if you want that book, I'll bring it next time.*

in·cin·er·ate /ɪn'sɪnə,reʸt/ *v* **-ated, -ating** [T]

fml to destroy (unwanted things) by burning
–**incineration** /ɪnˌsɪnəˈreɪʃən/ *n* [C;U]
in·cin·er·a·tor /ɪnˈsɪnəˌreɪtər/ *n* a machine for burning unwanted things
in·cip·i·ent /ɪnˈsɪpiʲənt/ *adj* [*no comp.*] *fml* at an early stage: *incipient disease*
in·ci·sion /ɪnˈsɪʒən/ *n* [C;U] *fml* the act of cutting or a cut into something, done with a special tool for a special reason: *An incision was made into the diseased organ.*
in·ci·sive /ɪnˈsaɪsɪv/ *adj apprec* going directly to the center or main point of the matter that is being considered: *incisive statements* –**incisively** *adv*
in·ci·sor /ɪnˈsaɪzər/ *n* any of the teeth at the front of the mouth, which have one cutting edge
in·cite /ɪnˈsaɪt/ *v* **-cited, -citing** [T] **1** to (try to) cause or encourage (someone) to a strong feeling or action: *a violent speech inciting the army to attack the government* **2** to (try to) cause or lead to (a strong feeling or action): *He was charged with inciting a* RIOT. –**incitement** *n* [C;U]
in·clem·ent /ɪnˈklɛmənt/ *adj fml* (of weather) not CLEMENT; bad, esp. cold or stormy
in·cli·na·tion /ˌɪnkləˈneɪʃən/ *n* **1** [C;U +*to-v*/*to*, *towards*] that which one likes; liking: *You always follow your own inclinations instead of thinking of our feelings.*|*I have no inclination to be a doctor.* **2** [C] a movement from a higher to a lower place: *He gave an inclination of the head/the hand.* **3** [S] *fml or tech* a slope; sloping position
in·cline[1] /ɪnˈklaɪn/ *v* **-clined, -clining 1** [I;T +*to-v*/*to*, *towards*] to encourage or cause (someone) to feel, think, etc.: *I am inclined to think she is telling the truth.* –compare INCLINED (1) **2** [T] *fml* to cause to move downward: *She inclined her head (in greeting).*
in·cline[2] /ˈɪnklaɪn/ *n* a slope: *a steep incline*
in·clined /ɪnˈklaɪnd/ *adj* [F +*to-v*] **1** encouraged; feeling a wish (to): *The news makes me inclined to change my mind.* –see also DISINCLINED **2** likely; tending (to): *I'm inclined to get tired easily.*
in·clude /ɪnˈkluʷd/ *v* **-cluded, -cluding** [T +*v-ing*] **1** to have as a part; contain in addition to other parts: *The price includes postage charges.* –opposite **exclude**; see COMPRISE (USAGE) **2** to put in with something else: *I included eggs on the list of things to buy.*
in·clud·ed /ɪnˈkluʷdɪd/ *adj* [after *n*] INCLUDING: *Take all of us, me included.*
in·clud·ing /ɪnˈkluʷdɪŋ/ *prep* having as a part; which includes: *There are six people, including three women.*|*Take all of us, including me.* –opposite **excluding**
in·clu·sion /ɪnˈkluʷʒən/ *n* **1** [U] the act of including or state of being included –opposite **exclusion 2** [C] something that is included

in·clu·sive /ɪnˈkluʷsɪv/ *adj* **1** containing or including everything (or many things): *an inclusive charge*|*an* **all-inclusive** *price* **2** [after *n*] (of a price or charge) including other costs that are often paid separately: *The rent is $10 inclusive of heating.*|*The rent is $10 inclusive (of everything).* **3** [after *n*] including all the numbers or dates: *Read pages 25 to 50 inclusive.* –see also EXCLUSIVE –**inclusively** *adv*
USAGE With expressions of time, **through** instead of **inclusive** is often used in *AmE*: *Monday* **through** *Friday*
in·cog·ni·to /ˌɪnkagˈniʲtoʷ, ɪnˈkagnəˌtoʷ/ *adj,adv* [F] hiding one's IDENTITY, esp. by taking another name when one's own is well-known: *traveling incognito*
in·co·her·ent /ˌɪnkoʷˈhɪərənt/ *adj* not COHERENT; showing lack of suitable connections between ideas or words: *He became quite incoherent as the disease got worse.* –**incoherence** *n* [U] –**incoherently** *adv*
in·come /ˈɪnkʌm, ˈɪŋ-/ *n* [C;U] money which one receives regularly, usu. payment for one's work, or interest from INVESTMENTS: *(a) very small/low income* |*Low-income families need government help.* –see PAY (USAGE)
in·com·ing /ˈɪnˌkʌmɪŋ/ *adj* [A] coming towards one; about to enter or start (to be): *the incoming* TIDE|*incoming traffic* –compare OUTGOING (1)
in·com·mu·ni·ca·do /ˌɪnkəˌmyuʷnɪˈkadoʷ/ *adv,adj* [F] (of people) kept away from people outside, and not able to give or receive messages
in·com·pa·ra·ble /ɪnˈkampərəbəl/ *adj* [*no comp.*] too great in degree to be compared with other examples of the same type; very great: *incomparable wealth* –see also COMPARABLE –**incomparability** /ɪnˌkampərəˈbɪ ləṭiʲ/ *n* [U] –**incomparably** /ɪnˈkampərəbliʲ/ *adv*: *incomparably beautiful*
in·com·pat·i·ble /ˌɪnkəmˈpæṭəbəl/ *adj* [*with*] not COMPATIBLE; not suitable to be together with (another thing or person/each other): *Their natures are incompatible.*|*His plan is incompatible with my intentions.* –**incompatibly** *adv* –**incompatibility** /ˌɪnkəmˌpæṭ əˈbɪləṭiʲ/ *n* **-ties** [C;U]
in·com·pe·tence /ɪnˈkampəṭəns/ *n* [U] lack of COMPETENCE; lack of ability and skill resulting in useless work
in·com·pe·tent /ɪnˈkampəṭənt/ *adj,n* [+*to-v*] (a person who is) not COMPETENT; completely unskillful (in something): *an incompetent teacher* |*He is a total incompetent.* –**incompetently** *adv*
in·com·plete /ˌɪnkəmˈpliʲt/ *adj* not complete; not perfect –**incompletely** *adv* –**incompleteness** *n* [U]
in·com·pre·hen·si·ble /ˌɪnkamprɪˈhɛnsəbəl, ɪnˌkam-/ *adj* [*to*] not COMPREHENSIBLE; which cannot be understood and/or accepted: *This new law is incomprehensible.* –**incomprehensibly** *adv* –**incomprehensibility** /ˌɪnkamprɪˌhɛnsəˈbɪləṭiʲ, ɪnˌkam-/ *n* [U]
in·con·ceiv·a·ble /ˌɪnkənˈsiʲvəbəl/ *adj* [*to*] **1** which is too strange to be thought real: *It once seemed inconceivable (to everyone) that*

men would travel to the moon. **2** infml impossible; which can't happen: He can't go on vacation alone: it's inconceivable. **–inconceivably** adv

in·con·clu·sive /ˌɪnkən'kluʷsɪv/ adj not CONCLUSIVE; which has not led to a decision or result: an inconclusive discussion **–inconclusively** adv **–inconclusiveness** n [U]

in·con·gru·ous /ɪn'kɑŋgruʷəs/ adj [with] comparing strangely with what surrounds it: The modern church looks incongruous in that old-fashioned village. **–incongruously** adv **–incongruousness** n [U] **–incongruity** /ˌɪnkɑŋ'gruʷətiʸ, -kən-/ n n [C;U]

in·con·se·quen·tial /ˌɪnkɑnsə'kwɛnʃəl, -tʃəl, ɪnˌkɑn-/ adj unimportant: an inconsequential idea **–inconsequentially** adv

in·con·sid·er·a·ble /ˌɪnkən'sɪdərəbəl/ adj of small size or worth: $10 is an inconsiderable amount of money to a rich man. | **a not inconsiderable** (=large) sum of money –see also CONSIDERABLE

in·con·sid·er·ate /ˌɪnkən'sɪdərɪt/ adj derog not CONSIDERATE; not thinking of other people's feelings: He's inconsiderate to his family because he never tells them he's working late. **–inconsiderately** adv **–inconsiderateness** n [U]

in·con·sist·ent /ˌɪnkən'sɪstənt/ adj **1** [with] (of ideas, etc.) not CONSISTENT; not agreeing with something else/one another: Those remarks are inconsistent with what you said yesterday. | The two remarks are inconsistent. **2** likely to change: English weather is very inconsistent; one moment it's raining and the next it's sunny. **–inconsistently** adv **–inconsistency** n **-cies** [C;U]

in·con·sol·a·ble /ˌɪnkən'soʷləbəl/ adj unable to be comforted because of great sorrow, or too great to be removed by comforting: She is inconsolable over the loss of her dog. | inconsolable grief **–inconsolably** adv: inconsolably sad

in·con·spic·u·ous /ˌɪnkən'spɪkyuʷəs/ adj not CONSPICUOUS; not easily seen; not attracting attention **–inconspicuously** adv **–inconspicuousness** n [U]

in·con·ti·nent /ɪn'kɑntən-ənt/ adj unable to control the water in the BLADDER, so that it is passed from the body when one does not wish to pass it **–incontinence** n [U]

in·con·tro·vert·i·ble /ˌɪnkɑntrə'vɜrtəbəl, ɪnˌkɑn-/ adj which cannot be disproved; INDISPUTABLE **–incontrovertibly** adv

in·con·ven·ience¹ /ˌɪnkən'viʸnyəns/ n [C;U] (an example of) a state of difficulty when things do not suit one: It causes a lot of inconvenience when buses don't come. | All that travel will be a great inconvenience to me. –see also CONVENIENCE

inconvenience² v **-ienced, -iencing** [T] to make things difficult for (someone): I hope it won't inconvenience you to drive me to the station.

in·con·ven·ient /ˌɪnkən'viʸnyənt/ adj not CONVENIENT; causing difficulty; not what suits one: The meeting is at an inconvenient time for me; I can't come. **–inconveniently** adv

in·cor·po·rate /ɪn'kɔrpə,reʸt/ v **-rated, -rating** [T in, into, with] to make (something) a part of a group; include: They incorporated his new ideas into their plans. | The new plan incorporates the old one. **–incorporation** /ɪnˌkɔrpə'reʸʃən/ n [U]

in·cor·po·rat·ed /ɪn'kɔrpə,reʸtɪd/ also **Inc** abbrev.– adj [after n] fml esp. AmE formed into a CORPORATION according to law –compare LIMITED (2)

in·cor·rect /ˌɪnkə'rɛkt/ adj not correct **–incorrectly** adv **–incorrectness** n [U] –compare WRONG¹ (1)

in·cor·ri·gi·ble /ɪn'kɔrədʒəbəl, -'kɑr-/ adj (of people or behavior) very bad and unable to be changed for the better: She's an incorrigible liar. **–incorrigibly** adv **–incorrigibility** /ɪnˌkɔrədʒə'bɪlətiʸ, -ˌkɑr-/ n [U]

in·cor·rupt·i·ble /ˌɪnkə'rʌptəbəl/ adj too honest to be improperly influenced or BRIBED –see also CORRUPT

in·crease¹ /ɪn'kriʸs/ v **-creased, -creasing** [I;T] to make or become larger in amount or number: The population of this town has increased. | They have increased the price of oil again. –opposite **decrease**

in·crease² /'ɪnkriʸs, 'ɪŋ-/ n [C;U] a rise in amount, numbers, etc.: Crime is **on the increase.** (=increasing) –opposite **decrease**

in·creas·ing·ly /ɪn'kriʸsɪŋliʸ/ adv more and more all the time: I'm finding it increasingly difficult to pay my bills.

in·cred·i·ble /ɪn'krɛdəbəl/ adj **1** too strange to be believed; unbelievable: an incredible idea/story/excuse –see also CREDIBLE **2** infml wonderful; unbelievably good: She has an incredible house. **–incredibly** adv **–incredibility** /ɪnˌkrɛdəbɪlətiʸ/ n [U]

in·cred·u·lous /ɪn'krɛdʒələs/ adj showing disbelief: an incredulous look –see also CREDULOUS **–incredulously** adv **–incredulity** /ˌɪnkrə'duʷlətiʸ, -'dyuʷ-/ n [U]

in·cre·ment /'ɪnkrəmənt, 'ɪŋ-/ n [C;U] (an) increase in money or value: She receives a salary increment every year. **–incremental** /ˌɪnkrə'mɛntəl, -ˌɪŋ-/ adj

in·crim·i·nate /ɪn'krɪmə,neʸt/ v **-nated, -nating** [T] to cause (someone) to seem guilty of a crime or fault: incriminating EVIDENCE **–incrimination** /ɪnˌkrɪməneʸʃən/ n [U]

in·cu·bate /'ɪŋkyə,beʸt, 'ɪn-/ v **-bated, -bating** [I;T] **1** to sit on and keep (eggs) warm until the young birds come out **2** (of eggs) to be kept warm until HATCHed **–incubation** /ˌɪŋkyə'beʸʃən, ˌɪn-/ n [U]

in·cu·ba·tor /'ɪŋkyə,beʸtər, 'ɪn-/ n a machine for **a** keeping eggs warm until they HATCH **b** keeping alive PREMATURE babies

in·cul·cate /ɪn'kʌlkeʸt, 'ɪnkʌlˌkeʸt/ v **-cated, -cating** [T with/into] fml to fix (ideas, principles, etc.) in the mind of (someone): He inculcated his opinions into his children.

in·cum·bent /ɪn'kʌmbənt/ adj **1** [F on, upon] fml being the moral duty of (someone): It's incumbent on you to advise your son before he leaves home. **2** [A] holding the stated office: the incumbent president

in·cur /ɪn'kɜr/ v **-rr-** [T] to receive (some unpleasant thing) as a result of certain actions: *I incurred his dislike from that day on.|to incur a debt*

in·cur·a·ble /ɪn'kyʊərəbəl/ *adj* that cannot be cured: *an incurable disease* **–incurably** *adv* **–incurability** /ɪn,kyʊərə'bɪləti/ *n* [U]

in·cur·sion /ɪn'kɜrʒən/ *n fml* a sudden attack on or entrance into a place which belongs to other people

in·debt·ed /ɪn'dɛtɪd/ *adj* [*to*] very grateful to (someone) for help given: *I'm indebted to all the people who worked so hard to make the party a success.* **–indebtedness** *n* [U]

in·de·cent /ɪn'diʸsənt/ *adj* not DECENT (1); offensive to general standards of behavior: *an indecent remark/joke* **–compare** IM-MODEST (2) **–indecently** *adv: indecently dressed* **–indecency** *n* **-cies** [C;U]

in·de·ci·sion /,ɪndɪ'sɪʒən/ *n* [U] lack of DECISION; uncertainty before deciding to do something, choose something, etc.: *His indecision caused him to lose the chance of a new job.*

in·de·ci·sive /,ɪndɪ'saɪsɪv/ *adj* **1** (of people) not DECISIVE; unable to make decisions **2** giving an uncertain result: *an indecisive answer/victory* **–indecisively** *adv* **–indecisiveness** *n* [U]

in·deed /ɪn'diʸd/ *adv* **1** (said in answers) yes, certainly: *"Did you hear the explosion?" "Indeed I did."* **2** (used after *very* to make the meaning stronger): *very cold indeed* **3** (shows surprise and often disbelief): *"I earn $1,000 a day." "Indeed!"*

in·de·fen·si·ble /,ɪndɪ'fɛnsəbəl/ *adj* which cannot be excused or defended: *indefensible behavior*

in·de·fin·a·ble /,ɪndɪ'faɪnəbəl/ *adj* which cannot be DEFINEd or described: *There's an indefinable air of tension in this town.* **–indefinably** *adv*

in·def·i·nite /ɪn'dɛfənɪt/ *adj* not definite; not clear; not fixed, esp. as to time: *indefinite opinions |He's away for an indefinite period (of time).* **–indefiniteness** *n* [U]

in·def·i·nite·ly /ɪn'dɛfənɪtliʸ/ *adv* for a period of time without a fixed end: *You can borrow the book indefinitely.*

in·del·i·ble /ɪn'dɛləbəl/ *adj* which cannot be erased: *indelible ink|an indelible pencil* **–indelibly** *adv: an experience indelibly printed on my memory*

in·del·i·cate /ɪn'dɛlɪkɪt/ *adj* not delicate; not polite or modest; rough in manners: *Her indelicate remark hurt his feelings.* **–indelicately** *adv* **–indelicacy** /ɪn'dɛlɪkəsiʸ/ *n* **-cies** [C;U]

in·dem·ni·fy /ɪn'dɛmnə,faɪ/ *v* **-fied, -fying** [T *against, for*] to (promise to) pay (someone) in case of loss, hurt, or damage **–indemnification** /ɪn,dɛmnəfə'keʸʃən/ *n* [C;U]

in·dem·ni·ty /ɪn'dɛmnətiʸ/ *n* **-ties 1** [U] protection against loss, esp. in the form of a promise to pay **2** [C] payment for loss of money, goods, etc.: *When a country has been* defeated in war, it sometimes has to pay an indemnity to the winners.

in·dent /ɪn'dɛnt/ *v* [I;T] to start (a line of writing) further into the page than the others: *You should indent the first line of a new paragraph.*

in·de·pend·ence /,ɪndɪ'pɛndəns/ *n* [U *from*] the quality or state of being independent; freedom: *This money gives me independence from my family.|The United States gained independence from Britain in 1776.*

Independence Day /··'·· ,·/ *n* the public holiday on the day when a country declared or gained its independence from another: *In the US, Independence Day is celebrated on July 4.*

in·de·pend·ent /,ɪndɪ'pɛndənt◄/ *adj* **1** not governed by another country: *Zimbabwe became independent in 1980.* **2** [*of*] not needing other things or people: *She's very independent and lives all alone.|This is an independent decision; I wasn't influenced by anyone else.* **–see also** DEPENDENT **–independently** *adv*

in·de·scrib·a·ble /,ɪndɪ'skraɪbəbəl/ *adj* which cannot be described, e.g. because beautiful beyond belief **–indescribably** *adv*

in·de·struct·i·ble /,ɪndɪ'strʌktəbəl/ *adj* being too strong to be destroyed **–indestructibility** /,ɪndɪ,strʌktə'bɪləti/ *n* [U] **–indestructibly** /,ɪndɪ'strʌktəbliʸ/ *adv*

in·de·ter·mi·nate /,ɪndɪ'tɜrmənɪt/ *adj* not clearly seen as, or not fixed as, one thing or another: *Our vacation plans are still at an indeterminate stage.*

in·dex¹ /'ɪndɛks/ *n* **-dexes** or **-dices** /də,siʸz/ **1** an alphabetical list at the back of a book, of names, subjects, etc., mentioned in it and the pages where they can be found **–compare** CONTENTS **2** the system of numbers by which prices, costs, etc., can be compared to a former level: *the cost of living index*

index² *v* [T] to provide with or include in an INDEX

index fin·ger /'·· ,··/ *n* → FOREFINGER

In·di·an /'ɪndiʸən/ *n,adj* **1** also **American Indian, Native American, Amerindian–** (a person) belonging to or connected with any of the original peoples of America except the Eskimos **2** (a person) belonging to or connected with India

Indian corn /,·· '·/ also **maize–** *n* [U] *AmE* a type of CORN¹ (1) of various colors

in·di·cate /'ɪndə,keʸt/ *v* **-cated, -cating 1** [T] to point at; draw attention to: *I asked him where my sister was, and he indicated the store across the street.* **2** [T +(*that*)] to show by a sign; make clear: *I indicated that his help was not welcome.* **3** [I;T +(*that*)] to show (the direction in which one is turning in a vehicle) by hand signals, lights, etc.: *He's indicating left.|Don't forget to indicate.* **–indication** /,ɪndə'keʸʃən/ *n* [C;U +*that/of*]: *There is every indication* (=a strong likelihood) *of a change in the weather.*

in·dic·a·tive /ɪn'dɪkətɪv/ *adj* [F +*that/of*] showing; suggesting: *His presence is indicative of his wish to help/that he wishes to help.* **–indicatively** *adv*

---

in·di·ca·tor /ˈɪndəˌketytər/ n **1** a needle or pointer on a machine showing the measure of some quality **2** any of the lights on a car which flash to show which way it is turning

in·di·ces /ˈɪndəˌsiᵛz/ n plural of INDEX

in·dict /ɪnˈdaɪt/ v [T for] fml to charge (someone) formally with an offense in law –**indictment** n [C;U] –**indictable** adj: an indictable offense

in·dif·fer·ent /ɪnˈdɪfərənt/ adj **1** [to] not interested in; not caring about or noticing: I was so excited to see snow that I was indifferent to the cold. **2** not very good: good, bad, or indifferent?|I'm an indifferent cook. –see DIFFERENT (USAGE) –**indifferently** adv –**indifference** n [U to, towards]: He treats me with indifference.

in·dig·e·nous /ɪnˈdɪdʒənəs/ adj [to] fml or tech native; belonging (to a place) –**indigenously** adv: These plants were not found here indigenously, but were introduced many years ago.

in·di·gest·i·ble /ˌɪndɪˈdʒestəbəl, -daɪ-/ adj (of food) not easily broken down in the stomach into substances to be used by the body –see also DIGEST¹ –**indigestibility** /ˌɪndɪˌdʒestəˈbɪlətiᵛ, -daɪ-/ n [U]

in·di·ges·tion /ˌɪndəˈdʒestʃən, -daɪ-/ n [U] illness or pain caused by the stomach being unable to deal with the food which has been eaten –see also DIGESTION

in·dig·nant /ɪnˈdɪgnənt/ adj [at, over, about] expressing or feeling surprised anger (at something which should not be so) –**indignantly** adv

in·dig·na·tion /ˌɪndɪgˈneᵛʃən/ n [U at, over, about] feelings of anger (against something wrong): I expressed my indignation at being unfairly dismissed.

in·dig·ni·ty /ɪnˈdɪgnətiᵛ/ n -ties [C;U] (an example of) a state which makes one feel less respected (less DIGNIFIED) or that one is on public show: I suffered the indignity of having to say I was sorry in front of all those people.

in·di·rect /ˌɪndəˈrɛkt◄, -daɪ-/ adj not straight; not directly connected (to or with): The taxi driver took an indirect ROUTE to avoid the center of town.|The accident was an indirect result of her lack of care.|(fig.) an indirect answer –opposite direct –**indirectly** adv –**indirectness** n [U]

in·dis·ci·pline /ɪnˈdɪsəplɪn/ n [U] lack of DISCIPLINE¹ (2); state of disorder because of lack of control

in·dis·creet /ˌɪndɪˈskriᵛt/ adj not DISCREET; not acting carefully and politely, esp. in the choice of what one says and does not say –**indiscreetly** adv

in·dis·cre·tion /ˌɪndɪˈskreʃən/ n [C;U] (an example of) the state or quality of being INDISCREET; lack of DISCRETION (1)

in·dis·crim·i·nate /ˌɪndɪˈskrɪmənɪt/ adj [no comp.] not choosing or chosen carefully: the terrorists' indiscriminate murder of ordinary people –**indiscriminately** adv

in·dis·pen·sa·ble /ˌɪndɪˈspɛnsəbəl/ adj [to] that is too important to live or be without: She's become quite indispensable to the company. –compare DISPENSABLE –**indispensably** adv –**indispensability** /ˌɪndɪˌspɛnsəˈbɪlətiᵛ/ n [U]

in·dis·posed /ˌɪndɪˈspoᵛzd/ adj fml [F] not very well (in health): His wife says he's indisposed, but I know he's drunk. –compare DISPOSED

in·dis·pu·ta·ble /ˌɪndɪˈspyuᵛtəbəl/ adj being too certain to be questioned –opposite disputable –**indisputably** adv

in·dis·tinct /ˌɪndɪˈstɪŋkt/ adj not DISTINCT (2); not clear to the eye or mind or ear: I have only an indistinct memory of my father.|There is a large indistinct area in the photograph. –**indistinctly** adv –**indistinctness** n [U]

in·dis·tin·guish·a·ble /ˌɪndɪˈstɪŋgwɪʃəbəl/ adj [from] not DISTINGUISHABLE; which cannot be seen or recognized to be different from something else or each other: The material is indistinguishable from real silk but much cheaper. –**indistinguishably** adv

in·di·vid·u·al¹ /ˌɪndəˈvɪdʒuᵛəl/ adj (often with each) single; particular; separate: Each individual leaf on the tree is different.|Individual attention must be given to every fault in the material.|She wears very individual clothes. (=different from other people's)

individual² n **1** a single being or member of a group, treated separately: The rights of the individual are the most important in a free society. **2** infml a person: What a bad-tempered individual you are!

in·di·vid·u·al·i·ty /ˌɪndəˌvɪdʒuᵛˈælətiᵛ/ n -ties [S;U] the character and qualities which make someone or something different from all others: Her work shows great individuality.

in·di·vid·u·al·ly /ˌɪndəˈvɪdʒuᵛəliᵛ/ adv one by one; separately: Individually, the children are quite nice, but in a group they're very badly-behaved.

in·di·vis·i·ble /ˌɪndəˈvɪzəbəl/ adj which cannot be divided or separated into parts –**indivisibly** adv –**indivisibility** /ˌɪndəˌvɪzəˈbɪlətiᵛ/ n [U]

in·doc·tri·nate /ɪnˈdaktrəˌneᵛt/ v -nated, -nating [T with] usu. derog to put ideas into (someone's) mind: They have those political opinions because they've been indoctrinated all their lives. –**indoctrination** /ɪnˌdaktrəˈneᵛʃən/ n [U]

in·do·lent /ˈɪndələnt/ adj fml lazy; not liking to be active: an indolent worker –**indolently** adv –**indolence** n [U]

in·dom·i·ta·ble /ɪnˈdamətəbəl/ adj fml too strong to be discouraged: a man of indomitable spirit –**indomitably** adv

in·door /ˈɪndor, ˈɪndoᵛr/ adj [A] which is (happening, done, used, etc.) inside a building: indoor sports|indoor clothes –opposite outdoor

in·doors /ˌɪnˈdorz, ˌɪnˈdoᵛrz/ adv to(wards), in, or into the inside of a building: We went indoors.|We stayed indoors. –opposite outdoors

in·du·bi·ta·ble /ɪnˈduᵛbətəbəl, -ˈdyuᵛ-/ adj fml which cannot be doubted to be so; unquestionable **–indubitably** *adv*

in·duce /ɪn'duːs, ɪn'dyuːs/ *v* **-duced, -ducing**
[T] *fml* **1** to lead (someone) (into an act)
often by persuading: *I was induced to come
against my will.* **2** to cause or produce: *Too
much food induces sleepiness.*

in·duce·ment /ɪn'duːsmənt, -'dyuːs-/ *n*
[C;U +*to-v*] (something which provides) encouragement to do something: *I gave him
money as an inducement to leave.*

in·duc·tion /ɪn'dʌkʃən/ *n* [U] the act or
ceremony of introducing a person to a new
job, organization, etc: *his induction into the
army*

in·dulge /ɪn'dʌldʒ/ *v* **-dulged, -dulging** [I;T] **1**
to allow (someone) to do or have what they
want: *He indulges his children.* **2** [*in*] *infml* to
let (oneself) have what one wants, esp. too
much: *He's not really a drinker, but he in-
dulges at parties.|I sometimes* **indulge in** *a
cigarette.*

in·dul·gence /ɪn'dʌldʒəns/ *n* **1** [U] the habit
of allowing someone to do or have what they
want: *His indulgence to his children was bad
for them.* **2** [C] something in which someone
INDULGES (2): *Candy is my only indulgence.*
-indulgent *adj*: *indulgent parents* **–in-
dulgently** *adv*

in·dus·tri·al /ɪn'dʌstriʸəl/ *adj* **1** of industry
and the people who work in it: *industrial
unrest* **2** having highly developed industries
–compare: *Japan is an* **industrial** *nation.|The
Japanese are an* **industrious**
(=hard-working) *nation.* **–industrially** *adv*

in·dus·tri·al·ist /ɪn'dʌstriʸəlɪst/ *n* a person
who is closely concerned in the system of
earning profits in industry, esp. a factory
owner

in·dus·tri·al·ize ‖also **-ise** *BrE* /ɪn'dʌstriʸə
ˌlaɪz/ *v* **-ized, -izing** [I;T] to (cause to)
become industrially developed **–industrial-
ization** /ɪnˌdʌstriʸələ'zeʸʃən/ *n* [U]

in·dus·tri·ous /ɪn'dʌstriʸəs/ *adj* hard-work-
ing –compare INDUSTRIAL **–industriously** *adv*
–industriousness *n* [U]

in·dus·try /'ɪndəstriʸ/ *n* **-tries 1** [U] (the work
of) factories and large organizations
generally: *The country is supported by industry.* **2** [C] a particular sort of work, usu.
employing lots of people and using
machinery to produce goods: *the clothing
industry* **3** [U] continual hard work

in·e·bri·at·ed /ɪ'niʸbriʸˌeʸtɪd/ *adj fml or pomp*
drunk **–inebriation** /ɪˌniʸbriʸ'eʸʃən/ *n* [U]

in·ed·i·ble /ɪn'ɛdəbəl/ *adj* not EDIBLE; not
suitable for eating

in·ef·fa·ble /ɪn'ɛfəbəl/ *adj fml* too wonderful
to be described in words: *ineffable joy* **–in-
effably** *adv*

in·ef·fec·tive /ˌɪnə'fɛktɪv/ also **ineffectual**
/ˌɪnə'fɛktʃuʷəl/– *adj* not EFFECTIVE; which
does not produce any result or who cannot
do anything well: *An ineffective person
should not be our leader.|an ineffectual per-

---

son/plan* –compare EFFECTUAL **–ineffectively**
adv **–ineffectiveness** *n* [U]

in·ef·fi·cient /ˌɪnə'fɪʃənt/ *adj* not EFFICIENT;
that does not work well so as to produce
good results quickly: *an inefficient ma-
chine|an inefficient secretary* **–inefficiently**
adv **–inefficiency** *n* [U]

in·el·e·gant /ɪn'ɛləgənt/ *adj* not ELEGANT;
lacking grace; awkward **–inelegantly** *adv* **–in-
elegance** *n* [U]

in·el·i·gi·ble /ɪn'ɛlədʒəbəl/ *adj* [+*to-v/for*]
not ELIGIBLE: *He was ineligible to vote,
because he didn't belong to the club.* **–in-
eligibility** /ɪnˌɛlədʒə'bɪlətiʸ/ *n* [U]

in·ept /ɪ'nɛpt/ *adj* **1** foolishly unsuitable: *an
inept remark* **2** totally unable to do things:
He's inept at tennis. **–ineptly** *adv* **–ineptitude**
/ɪ'nɛptəˌtuʷd, -ˌtyuʷd/ also **ineptness**– *n* [U]

in·e·qual·i·ty /ˌɪniʸ'kwɑlətiʸ/ *n* **-ties** [C;U] (an
example of) lack of equality: *social ine-
quality |There are many inequalities in the
law.*

in·ert /ɪ'nɜrt/ *adj* [*no comp.*] **1** lacking the
power or will to move: *inert matter |He stood
inert as the car came towards him.* **2** tech not
acting chemically with other substances: *inert gases* **–inertly** *adv*

in·er·tia /ɪ'nɜrʃə/ *n* [U] the force which makes
a person or thing stay in the state or position
which they are in: (fig.) *I get a feeling of
inertia on a hot summer day.*

in·es·cap·a·ble /ˌɪnə'skeʸpəbəl/ *adj* which
cannot be escaped from or avoided

in·es·sen·tial /ˌɪnə'sɛnʃəl, -tʃəl/ *adj,n* [*to*]
(something which is) not ESSENTIAL; not at
all necessary

in·es·ti·ma·ble /ɪn'ɛstəməbəl/ *adj* too great
to be calculated; very important: *a jewel of
inestimable value* –see also ESTIMATE **–in-
estimably** *adv*

in·ev·i·ta·ble /ɪ'nɛvətəbəl/ *adj* **1** which cannot be prevented from happening: *An argument was inevitable because they disliked
each other so much.* **2** [A] *infml* which always
happens, or is present with someone or
something else: *Aunt Sue was wearing her
inevitable large hat.* **–inevitably** *adv* **–in-
evitability** /ɪˌnɛvətə'bɪlətiʸ/ *n* [U]

in·ex·act /ˌɪnɪg'zækt/ *adj* not exact **–inexacti-
tude** /ˌɪnɪg'zæktəˌtuʷd, -ˌtyuʷd/ also **inexact-
ness**– *n* [U]

in·ex·cus·a·ble /ˌɪnɪk'skyuʷzəbəl/ *adj* which
is too bad to be excused: *inexcusable
behavior/lateness* –opposite **excusable** **–inex-
cusably** *adv*

in·ex·haust·i·ble /ˌɪnɪg'zɔstəbəl/ *adj* which is
in such large quantities that it can never be
finished **–inexhaustibly** *adv*

in·ex·o·ra·ble /ɪn'ɛksərəbəl/ *adj fml* whose
actions or effects cannot be changed or prevented by one's efforts **–inexorably** *adv* **–in-
exorability** /ɪnˌɛksərə'bɪlətiʸ/ *n* [U]

in·ex·pe·di·ent /ˌɪnɪk'spiʸdiʸənt/ *adj* (of acts)
not EXPEDIENT; not suitable or advisable: *It
would be inexpedient to go out without a coat.*
–inexpediency also **inexpedience**– *n* [U]

in·ex·pen·sive /ˌɪnɪk'spɛnsɪv/ *adj fml* not EX-
PENSIVE; cheap; low in price **–inexpensively**
adv

SPELLING NOTE
Words with the sound /aɪ/ may be
spelled **e-**, like **eye**, or **ai-**, like **aisle**.

in·ex·pe·ri·ence /ˌɪnɪk'spɪəriʸəns/ n [U] lack of experience

in·ex·pe·ri·enced /ˌɪnɪk'spɪəriʸənst/ adj (of people) not experienced; lacking the knowledge which one gains by experiencing some activity or life generally: *an inexperienced driver*

in·ex·plic·a·ble /ˌɪnɪk'splɪkəbəl, ɪn'ɛksplɪkə-/ adj not EXPLICABLE; which is too strange to be explained or understood: *The inexplicable disappearance of the woman worried everyone.* –**inexplicably** adv

in·ex·press·i·ble /ˌɪnɪk'sprɛsəbəl/ adj (of feelings) too great or too strong to be expressed in words –**inexpressibly** adv

in·ex·tri·ca·ble /ɪn'ɛkstrɪkəbəl, ˌɪnɪk'strɪ-/ adj fml which cannot be escaped from –**inextricably** adv: *Our fates are inextricably joined.*

in·fal·li·ble /ɪn'fæləbəl/ adj 1 (of people) not FALLIBLE; never making mistakes or doing anything bad 2 (of things) always having the right effect: *an infallible cure* –**infallibility** /ɪnˌfælə'bɪlətiʸ/ n [U]

in·fa·mous /'ɪnfəməs/ adj well known for wicked behavior: *an infamous criminal* –see FAMOUS (USAGE)

in·fa·my /'ɪnfəmiʸ/ n -**mies** [C;U] (an example of) the quality of being INFAMOUS

in·fan·cy /'ɪnfənsiʸ/ n [S;U] early childhood: *a happy infancy* |(fig.) *Our new plan is still only in its infancy.*

in·fant /'ɪnfənt/ n [A;C] a very young child: *a high rate of infant MORTALITY* –see CHILD (USAGE)

in·fan·tile /'ɪnfən,taɪl, -tɪl/ adj like, concerning, or happening to small children: *infantile illnesses* |*His behavior is infantile* (=very foolish) *for a man of 35.*

in·fan·try /'ɪnfəntriʸ/ n [U] soldiers who fight on foot: *The infantry was fighting bravely.* –compare CAVALRY

in·fat·u·at·ed /ɪn'fætʃuʷ,eʸtɪd/ adj [with] (of people) filled with a strong unreasonable feeling of love for (someone) –**infatuation** /ɪnˌfætʃuʷ'eʸʃən/ n [C;U with]

in·fect /ɪn'fɛkt/ v [T with] to put disease into the body of (someone): *The disease infected her eyes, and she became blind.*|(fig.) *Violence is infecting our society.*

in·fec·tion /ɪn'fɛkʃən/ n [C;U] (an example of) the state or result of being infected, or the action of infecting: *infection from impure water/by flies*|*She is suffering from a lung infection.*

in·fec·tious /ɪn'fɛkʃəs/ adj (of a disease) which can be spread by infection, esp. in the air: *Colds are infectious.*|(fig.) *infectious laughter* –compare CONTAGIOUS –**infectiously** adv –**infectiousness** n [U]

in·fer /ɪn'fɜr/ v -**rr-** [T +(that)/from] to reach an opinion after thinking about (something): *I infer from your letter that you do not wish to see us.* –compare IMPLY –**inference** /'ɪnfərəns/ n [C;U]

USAGE Compare **imply** and **infer**. The speaker or writer **implies** something, and the listener or reader **infers** it: *His remarks implied* (=suggested indirectly) *that he hadn't*

enjoyed his trip.|*I* **inferred** from his *remarks that he hadn't enjoyed his trip.* (=this was the meaning I drew). Although **infer** is often used to mean **imply**, this is not correct.

in·fe·ri·or¹ /ɪn'fɪəriʸər/ adj [to] (of people and things) not good or less good in quality or value: *His work is inferior to mine.*|*He's so clever he makes me feel inferior.* –opposite **superior**; see MAJOR (USAGE) –**inferiority** /ɪnˌfɪəriʸ'ɔrətiʸ, -'ɑr-/ n [U]

in·fe·ri·or² n often derog a person of lower rank, esp. in a job: *You shouldn't be afraid of making your inferiors work harder.* –compare SUPERIOR² (1), SUBORDINATE

in·fer·nal /ɪn'fɜrnl/ adj 1 infml very bad; very annoying: *Stop that infernal noise!* 2 of HELL⁴ (1): *the infernal powers* –**infernally** adv

in·fer·no /ɪn'fɜrnoʷ/ n -**nos** a place or state that is like HELL⁴ (1): *The burning building became an inferno.*

in·fer·tile /ɪn'fɜrtl/ adj not FERTILE; not able to produce young; (of land) not able to grow plants –compare STERILE –**infertility** /ˌɪnfɜr'tɪlətiʸ/ n [U]

in·fest /ɪn'fɛst/ v [T with] to cause trouble to or in, by being present in large numbers: –**infestation** /ˌɪnfɛ'steʸʃən/ n [C;U]

in·fi·del /'ɪnfədl, -ˌdɛl/ n old use (used esp. in former times by Christians and Muslims of each other) an unbeliever

in·fi·del·i·ty /ˌɪnfə'dɛlətiʸ/ n -**ties** [C;U] (an example or act of) disloyalty; UNFAITHFULness, esp. to one's marriage partner –see also FIDELITY

in·fight·ing /'ɪn,faɪtɪŋ/ n [U] competition and disagreement, often bitter, between close members of a group

in·fil·trate /ɪn'fɪl,treʸt, 'ɪnfɪl-/ v -**trated**, -**trating** [T in, into] to (cause to) go into and among (the parts or members of something), esp. quietly and with an unfriendly purpose: *to infiltrate a political party* –**infiltrator** n –**infiltration** /ˌɪnfɪl'treʸʃən/ n [U]

in·fi·nite /'ɪnfənɪt/ adj [no comp.] not FINITE; without limits or end: *infinite kindness* –**infinitely** adv: *That was infinitely* (=much) *better than his last film.*

in·fin·i·tes·i·mal /ˌɪnfɪnə'tɛsəməl/ adj [no comp.] very, very small –**infinitesimally** adv

in·fin·i·tive /ɪn'fɪnətɪv/ n,adj tech (of) the form of the verb that can be used after other verbs and with to before it (such as *go* in *I can go, I want to go,* and *It is important to go*)

in·fin·i·ty /ɪn'fɪnətiʸ/ n [S;U] limitless time or space: *the infinity of the universe*|(fig.) *I seemed to wait for an infinity.*

in·firm /ɪn'fɜrm/ adj fml weak in body or mind, esp. from age: *old and infirm*

in·fir·ma·ry /ɪn'fɜrməriʸ/ n -**ries** a hospital or other place where the sick are given care and treatment: *the school infirmary*

in·fir·mi·ty /ɪn'fɜrmətiʸ/ n -**ties** fml [C;U] (an example of) weakness of body or mind: *The old woman was suffering from age and infirmity.*

in·flame /ɪn'fleʸm/ v -**flamed**, -**flaming** [T with] to fill (someone) with strong feelings: *inflamed with desire/anger*

in·flamed /ɪn'fleʸmd/ adj (of a part of the

body) red and swollen because hurt or diseased: *an inflamed eye*

in·flam·ma·ble /ɪnˈflæməbəl/ ‖also **flamma-ble** *esp. AmE*– *adj* which can be set on fire: *Oil is highly inflammable.* –opposite **nonflammable** –compare INFLAMMATORY; see FLAMMABLE (USAGE)

in·flam·ma·tion /ˌɪnfləˈmeɪʃən/ *n* [C;U] swelling and soreness, which is often red and hot to the touch

in·flam·ma·to·ry /ɪnˈflæmə‚tɔriʲ, -‚toʷriʲ/ *adj* likely to cause strong feelings to rise, or violence to happen: *an inflammatory speech* –see also INFLAME; compare INFLAMMABLE

in·flat·a·ble /ɪnˈfleʲtəbəl/ *adj* which can be INFLATED for use

in·flate /ɪnˈfleʲt/ *v* **-flated, -flating** [I;T] *fml* **1** to (cause to) fill until swelled with air, gas, etc.; BLOW **up** (2) **2** to increase the supply of money (of) or raise the level of prices of –opposite **deflate**

in·flat·ed /ɪnˈfleʲtɪd/ *adj* **1** blown up (as with air): *an inflated tire* **2** *fml* filled with pride: *He has an inflated opinion of his own importance.*

in·fla·tion /ɪnˈfleʲʃən/ *n* [U] the condition in which prices keep rising, esp. to an undesirable degree: *The rate of inflation was 10%* (=prices rose by 10%) *last year.* –opposite **deflation** –**inflationary** /ɪnˈfleʲʃə‚neriʲ/ *adj*: *the government's inflationary policies*

in·flect /ɪnˈflɛkt/ *v* [I;T] *tech* **1** (of a word) to change in form at its end according to use: *The word "child" inflects differently in the plural from the word "boy."*‖*an inflected verb* **2** to cause (a word) to change in form according to use **3** to cause (the voice) to change, esp. in level, according to the needs of expression –**inflection** /ɪnˈflɛkʃən/ *n* [C;U]: *In "longest," -EST is the inflection meaning "most."*‖*He had an angry inflection in his voice.*

in·flex·i·ble /ɪnˈflɛksəbəl/ *adj* not FLEXIBLE; which cannot be bent; (of people) not easily turned away from their purpose: *You'll never get her to change her mind; she's so inflexible.* –**inflexibly** *adv* –**inflexibility** /ɪnˌflɛksəˈbɪlətiʲ/ *n* [U] –compare FLEX¹

in·flict sth. **on/upon** sbdy. /ɪnˈflɪkt/ *v prep* [T] to force (something unwanted or unpleasant) on: *Don't inflict your ideas on me.*‖(fig.) *Mary inflicted the children on her mother for the weekend.*

in·flu·ence¹ /ˈɪnfluʷəns/ *n* **1** [C;U *over, with, on, upon*] **a** (the action of) power to gain an effect on the mind of or get results from, without asking or doing anything: *He has a strange influence over the girl.*‖*Her influence made me a better person.*‖*He used his influence* (=power) *to get his friend a job.* **b** a person with this power: *He's an influence for good in the club.*‖*He is a good/bad influence on my daughter.* **2 under the influence of** in the power of; experiencing the effects of

(people, things): *driving under the influence of alcohol*

influence² *v* **-enced, -encing** [T] to have an effect on; AFFECT¹: *Don't let me influence your decision.*‖*What influenced you to do it?*

in·flu·en·tial /ˌɪnfluʷˈɛnʃəl, -tʃəl/ *adj* having great influence: *an influential decision/man* –**influentially** *adv*

in·flu·en·za /ˌɪnfluʷˈɛnzə/ *n* [U] *fml* or *tech* for FLU

in·flux /ˈɪnflʌks/ *n* [*usu. sing.*] the arrival, or movement inwards, of large numbers/quantities: *There was a sudden influx of goods onto the market.*

in·form /ɪnˈfɔrm/ *v* [T + *that/of, about*] *fml* to tell; to give information to: *I informed him (about) where to go.* –see SAY (USAGE)

inform against/on/upon sbdy. *v prep* [T] to tell the police, or someone in charge, about (someone who has done something wrong)

in·for·mal /ɪnˈfɔrməl/ *adj* not formal; without ceremony: *an informal meeting/informal clothes/language* –**informality** /ˌɪnfɔrˈmælətiʲ/ *n* [U] –**informally** /ɪnˈfɔrməliʲ/ *adv*

in·form·ant /ɪnˈfɔrmənt/ *n* a person who gives information –compare INFORMER

in·for·ma·tion /ˌɪnfərˈmeʲʃən/ *n* [U] (something which gives) knowledge in the form of facts: *The police don't have enough information to catch the criminal.*

in·form·a·tive /ɪnˈfɔrmətɪv/ *adj* that tells one some useful things: *an informative television program* –opposite **uninformative** –**informatively** *adv*

in·formed /ɪnˈfɔrmd/ *adj* knowing things; having all the information: *well-informed*‖*badly informed*‖*I read the newspapers to keep myself informed about what is happening.* –opposite **uninformed**

in·form·er /ɪnˈfɔrmər/ *n* a person who IN-FORMS against another, esp. to the police –compare INFORMANT

in·fra·red /ˌɪnfrəˈrɛd◂/ *adj* of the heat-giving RAYS of light of longer wave-length than the red light which can be seen –compare ULTRAVIOLET

in·fra·struc·ture /ˈɪnfrə‚strʌktʃər/ *n* the system which supports the operation of an organization: *the country's transport infrastructure* (=its roads, railways, etc.)

in·fre·quent /ɪnˈfriʲkwənt/ *adj* not frequent; not (happening) often: *infrequent visits* –**infrequently** *adv* –**infrequency** *n* [U]

in·fringe /ɪnˈfrɪndʒ/ *v* **-fringed, -fringing** [T] to go against or take over (the right of another): *to infringe on/upon a nation's fishing rights at sea* –**infringement** *n* [C;U]: *Stealing is an infringement of the law.*

in·fu·ri·ate /ɪnˈfyʊəriʲ‚eʲt/ *v* **-ated, -ating** [T] to make (someone) very angry

in·fuse /ɪnˈfyuʷz/ *v* **-fused, -fusing 1** [*with*] to fill (someone) with a quality **2** [T] to put (a substance such as tea) in hot water so as to make a liquid of a certain taste –**infusion** /ɪnˈfyuʷʒən/ *n* [C;U]: *an infusion of new ideas*

in·ge·nious /ɪnˈdʒiʲnyəs/ *adj* having or showing cleverness at making or inventing things: *an ingenious person/idea/toy* –compare: *He*

SPELLING NOTE

Words with the sound /aɪ/ may be spelled **e-**, like **eye**, or **ai-**, like **aisle**.

invented an **ingenious** *excuse for being late.|Only the most* **ingenious** *person would believe such a weak excuse!* –**ingeniously** adv

in·ge·nu·i·ty /ˌɪndʒəˈnuːətiʸ,-ˈnyuːʷ-/ n [U] skill and cleverness in making or arranging things

in·gen·u·ous /ɪnˈdʒɛnyuʷəs/ adj (of people and their acts) simple, direct, and inexperienced: *He is too ingenuous in believing what people say.* –compare INGENIOUS –**ingenuously** adv –**ingenuousness** n [U]

in·got /ˈɪŋgət/ n a lump of metal in a regular shape, often brick-shaped; bar (of gold or silver)

in·grained /ɪnˈgreʸnd, ˈɪngreʸnd/ adj fixed deep (inside) so that it is difficult to get out or destroy: *ingrained dirt|ingrained habits*

in·gra·ti·ate /ɪnˈgreʸʃiʸ,eʸt/ v -ated, -ating [T with] to make (oneself) very pleasant to someone in order to gain favor: *He ingratiated himself with his employer.* –**ingratiating** adj: *an ingratiating smile* –**ingratiatingly** adv

in·grat·i·tude /ɪnˈgrætə,tuʷd, -,tyuʷd/ n [U] lack of GRATITUDE; ungratefulness

in·gre·di·ent /ɪnˈgriʸdiʸənt/ n one of a mixture of things from which something is made: *There's a list of the ingredients on the side of the box.|(fig.) Imagination and hard work are the ingredients of success.*

in·hab·it /ɪnˈhæbɪt/ v [T not be +v-ing] to live in –see also UNINHABITABLE –**inhabitable** adj: *an inhabitable area*

in·hab·it·ant /ɪnˈhæbətənt/ n a person who lives in a particular place: *inhabitants of large cities*

in·hale /ɪnˈheʸl/ v -haled, -haling [I;T] to breathe in (air, gas, etc.): *He inhaled deeply.|He inhaled (smoke) deeply from his cigarette.* –opposite **exhale**

in·her·ent /ɪnˈhɪərənt, -ˈhɛr-/ adj [in] forming a natural part (of a set of qualities, a character, etc.): *The desire for freedom is inherent in us all.*

in·her·ent·ly /ɪnˈhɪərəntliʸ, -ˈhɛr-/ adv in itself or oneself; by its or one's nature; as such; INTRINSICALLY

in·her·it /ɪnˈhɛrɪt/ v [I;T from] to receive (property, a title, etc.) left by someone who has died: *(fig.) She inherited all her mother's beauty.* –see also DISINHERIT –**inheritance** n [C;U]

in·hib·it /ɪnˈhɪbɪt/ v [T from] to hold back (from something); to make INHIBITED: *His presence inhibits me.*

in·hib·it·ed /ɪnˈhɪbɪtɪd/ adj (of people and character) unable to express what one really feels or do what one really wants: *She is too inhibited to laugh freely/to talk about sex.* –compare UNINHIBITED –**inhibitedly** adv

in·hi·bi·tion /ˌɪnhɪˈbɪʃən, ˌɪnə-/ n [C;U] the state of, or a feeling of, being INHIBITED: *She soon loses her inhibitions when she's had two or three glasses of wine.*

in·hos·pit·a·ble /ˌɪnhɑˈspɪtəbəl, ɪnˈhɑspɪ-/ adj not HOSPITABLE; not showing kindness, esp. not giving food and shelter in one's own home –**inhospitably** adv

in·hu·man /ɪnˈhyuʷmən/ adj too cruel, lacking in feelings, etc., to be worthy of human

behavior –compare INHUMANE; see also HUMAN

in·hu·mane /ˌɪnhyuʷˈmeʸn/ adj (of people and their acts) not HUMANE; not showing human kindness: *inhumane treatment of animals* –compare INHUMAN –**inhumanely** adv

in·hu·man·i·ty /ˌɪnhyuʷˈmænətiʸ/ n -ties [C;U] (an example of) lack of HUMANITY (1); the quality or state of being cruel and harming other human beings: *the inhumanities of war*

in·im·i·ta·ble /ɪˈnɪmətəbəl/ adj too good for anyone else to copy with the same high quality –see also IMITATE –**inimitably** adv

in·iq·ui·tous /ɪˈnɪkwətəs/ adj fml very unjust or wicked –**iniquitously** adv –**iniquity** n -ties [C;U]

i·ni·tial¹ /ɪˈnɪʃəl/ adj [A no comp.] which is (at) the beginning of a set: *The initial talks were the base of the later agreement.* –**initially** adv: *Initially, she opposed the plan, but later she changed her mind.*

initial² n a large letter at the beginning of a name: *Steven Lane's initials are S.L.*

initial³ v -l- AmE||-ll- BrE [I;T] to sign one's name on (a piece of writing) by writing one's INITIALS, usu. to show approval or agreement: *Please initial here.*

i·ni·ti·ate /ɪˈnɪʃiʸ,eʸt/ v -ated, -ating 1 [T] to start (something) working: *The company will now initiate the new agreement on vacation time and sick days.* 2 [into] to introduce (someone) into a club, group, etc., esp. with a special ceremony –**initiation** /ɪ,nɪʃiʸˈeʸʃən/ n [C;U]: *initiation into a secret society*

i·ni·tia·tive /ɪˈnɪʃətɪv, -ʃiʸə-/ n 1 [C] the first movement or act which starts something happening: *He **took the initiative** in organizing a party after his brother's wedding.* 2 [U] the ability to make decisions and take action without the help of others 3 **on one's own initiative** (done) according to one's own plan and without help

in·ject /ɪnˈdʒɛkt/ v [T with/into] to put (liquid) into (someone) with a special needle (SYRINGE): *They are injecting him with new drugs.|(fig.) We hope to inject new life/interest into our work.*

in·jec·tion /ɪnˈdʒɛkʃən/ n [C;U] the act of INJECTING, or the amount injected: *The nurse gave him an injection for/against typhoid.*

in·ju·di·cious /ˌɪndʒuʷˈdɪʃəs/ adj fml (of acts) not JUDICIOUS; not wise or sensible to do; showing poor judgment –**injudiciously** adv –**injudiciousness** n [U]

in·junc·tion /ɪnˈdʒʌŋkʃən/ n [+to-v/ +that/against] fml or law a command or official order to do or not to do something

in·jure /ˈɪndʒər/ v -jured, -juring [T] to hurt (a living thing): *She was injured badly in the accident.|The injured (people) were taken to the hospital.* –**injurious** /ɪnˈdʒuəriʸəs/ adj: *Smoking is injurious to health.* –see WOUND¹ (USAGE)

in·ju·ry /ˈɪndʒəriʸ/ n -ries 1 [C;U] (an example of) harm; damage to a living thing: *insurance against injury at work|He suffered serious injuries to the arms and legs.|(fig.) injury to one's pride* 2 **add insult to injury** to do or say something more against someone when one has already harmed them enough

in·jus·tice /ɪn'dʒʌstɪs/ *n* [C;U] **1** (an act of) not being just; unfairness –see also JUSTICE **1 do someone an injustice** to judge someone in an unfair way and/or believe something bad about them which is untrue

ink /ɪŋk/ *n* [U] colored liquid used esp. for writing

ink·ling /'ɪŋklɪŋ/ *n* [S;U *of, as to*] a possible idea or a suggestion: *He* **had no/some inkling** *of the difficulties.*

in·laid /'ɪnleʸd, ɪn'leʸd/ *adj* [*with*] having another substance set in: *wood inlaid with gold|inlaid wood*

in·land¹ /'ɪnlənd/ *adj* [A] done or placed inside a country, not near the coast or other countries: *the inland forests|inland trade*

in·land² /'ɪnlænd, 'ɪnlənd/ *adv* [F] towards or in the heart of the country: *We walked inland.|There are mountains inland.*

in-laws /'··/ *n* [P] the father and mother of the person someone has married, and also (sometimes) other relatives by marriage

in·lay /'ɪnleʸ/ *n* a pattern, surface, or substance set into another: *wood with an inlay of gold*

in·let /'ɪnlɛt, 'ɪnlɪt/ *n* **1** a narrow stretch of water reaching from a sea, lake, etc., into the land or between islands **2** a way in (for water, liquid, etc.) –compare OUTLET

in·mate /'ɪnmeʸt/ *n* a person living in the same room or building as others, esp. unwillingly as in a hospital or prison

in me·mo·ri·am /ɪn mə'mɔriʸəm, -'moʷr-/ *prep Latin* (used before the name marked on a stone above a grave) in memory of: *In Memoriam John Jones, 1871–1956.*

inn /ɪn/ *n* a small hotel or place esp. in the country where one can stay and/or drink alcohol, eat meals, etc.: *On our trip to New England, we stayed in a beautiful old inn.*

in·nate /ˌɪ'neʸt◄/ *adj* (of qualities) which someone was born with: *innate kindness* –**innately** *adv*

in·ner /'ɪnər/ *adj* [A *no comp.*] **1** (placed) inside: *the inner ear|an inner room|*(fig.) *Her words have an inner* (=secret) *meaning.* **2** closest to the center (and in control) of what is happening: *the inner circle of power* –compare OUTER

in·ner·most /'ɪnər,moʷst/ *adj* farthest inside: *the innermost depths of the cave|one's innermost desires* –opposite **outermost**

in·ning /'ɪnɪŋ/ *n* the period of time in a baseball game during which each team bats BATS

inn·keep·er /'ɪn,kiʸpər/ *n old use* a person who (owns and) runs an inn

in·no·cent /'ɪnəsənt/ *adj* **1** [*of*] (of people) guiltless: *He was innocent of the crime.* –opposite **guilty 2** (of things) harmless: *innocent pleasures* **3** (of people) simple; not able to recognize evil: *a trusting innocent young child* –**innocently** *adv* –**innocence** *n* [U]

SPELLING NOTE
Words with the sound /aɪ/ may be spelled **e-**, like **eye**, or **ai-**, like **aisle**.

in·noc·u·ous /ɪ'nɑkyuʷəs/ *adj* (esp. of actions, statements, etc.) harmless; not intended to offend –**innocuously** *adv* –**innocuousness** *n* [U]

in·no·va·tion /ˌɪnə'veʸʃən/ *n* [C;U] (an example of) the introduction of something new: *The innovation of air travel during this century has made the world seem smaller.|There have been many recent innovations in printing methods.* –**innovative** /'ɪnə,veʸtɪv/ *adj* –**innovator** *n*

in·nu·en·do /ˌɪnyuʷ'ɛndoʷ/ *n* **-does** *or* **-dos** [C;U] (an example of) the act of suggesting something unpleasant in words without saying it directly: *He made innuendoes about her coming home at four o'clock in the morning.*

in·nu·mer·a·ble /ɪ'nuʷmərəbəl, ɪ'nyuʷ-/ *adj* [*no comp.*] too many to be counted

in·oc·u·late /ɪ'nɑkyə,leʸt/ *v* **-lated, -lating** [I;T *with/ against*] to introduce a weak form of a disease into (a living body) as a protection against the disease –compare VACCINATE, INJECT, IMMUNIZE –**inoculation** /ɪ,nɑkyə'leʸʃən/ *n* [C;U]

in·of·fen·sive /ˌɪnə'fɛnsɪv/ *adj* (of people and their acts) not OFFENSIVE (1); not causing any harm; not causing dislike in other people: *He has an inoffensive manner.|Anne is a quiet inoffensive sort of woman.* –**inoffensively** *adv* –**inoffensiveness** *n* [U]

in·op·por·tune /ɪn,ɑpər'tuʷn, -'tyuʷn, ˌɪnɑ-/ *adj fml* not opportune; unsuitable (for the time): *an inopportune visit/remark|He called at an inopportune moment, when we were busy.* –**inopportunely** *adv* –**inopportuneness** *n* [U]

in·or·di·nate /ɪn'ɔrdn-ɪt/ *adj fml* beyond reasonable limits: *an inordinate amount of work* –**inordinately** *adv: inordinately great demands*

in·or·gan·ic /ˌɪnɔr'gænɪk◄/ *adj* not ORGANIC; not of living material –**inorganically** *adv*

in·put /'ɪnpʊt/ *n* [S;U] something put in for use, esp. by a machine, such as electrical current or information for a computer –see also PUT **in** –compare OUTPUT

in·quest /'ɪnkwɛst/ *n* an official inquiry usu. to find out the cause of a sudden and unexpected death, esp. when there is a possibility of crime

in·quire, en- /ɪn'kwaɪər/ *v* **-quired, -quiring 1** [T] to ask: *I inquired* ((*fml*) *of him*) *what he wanted/whether he would come.* **2** [I] to ask for information: *I'll* **inquire about** *the trains.|She* **inquired after** (=asked about) *my mother's health.|We* **inquired into** (=searched for information about) *his story and found it was true.*

in·quir·ing, en- /ɪn'kwaɪərɪŋ/ *adj* showing an interest in learning about things: *a child with an inquiring mind*

in·quir·y, en- /ɪn'kwaɪəriʸ, 'ɪn,kwaɪ-, 'ɪnkwəriʸ/ *n* **-ies** [C;U] (an example of) the act of inquiring (INQUIRE): *My inquiry about his health was never answered.|The police are making inquiries about the crime.*

USAGE **Enquiry** and **inquiry** are almost the same, but **enquiry** is more often used for a simple request for information, and **inquiry** for a long serious study: *Thank you for your* **enquiry**/*your* **enquiries** *about my health.*/*a government* **inquiry** *into the dangers of smoking*

in·qui·si·tion /ˌɪnkwəˈzɪʃən/ *n usu. derog* an inquiry, esp. one that is carried out with little regard for the rights of the people being questioned

in·quis·i·tive /ɪnˈkwɪzətɪv/ *adj* (of people and their acts) trying to find out (too many) details about things and people: *Don't be so inquisitive: I'm not telling you what I did last night.* –**inquisitively** *adv* –**inquisitiveness** *n* [U]

in·roads /ˈɪnrowdz/ **make inroads into/on** to take away or use up: *Studying* **makes inroads into/on** *my free time.*

in·sane /ɪnˈseyn/ *adj* (of people and their acts) not SANE; mad –**insanely** *adv*: *insanely jealous*

in·san·i·tar·y /ɪnˈsænəˌteriy/ *adj* → UNSANITARY

in·san·i·ty /ɪnˈsænətiy/ *n* [U] madness: (fig.) *We pointed out the insanity of going out in the rain.* –opposite **sanity**

in·sa·tia·ble /ɪnˈseyʃəbəl, -ʃiyə-/ *adj* that cannot be satisfied: *I can't believe you're still hungry; you're insatiable!* –**insatiably** *adv*

in·scribe /ɪnˈskraɪb/ *v* **-scribed, -scribing** [T *in, into, on/with*] *fml* to write (something) by marking into (a surface); mark (a surface) with (something written, esp. a name): *She inscribed his name on the book.*/(fig.) *The pages of history were inscribed with their names.* –**inscription** /ɪnˈskrɪpʃən/ *n*

in·scru·ta·ble /ɪnˈskruwtəbəl/ *adj* (of people and their acts) whose meaning is hidden or hard to find out; mysterious: *an inscrutable smile* –**inscrutably** *adv* –**inscrutability** /ɪnˌskruwtəˈbɪlətiy/ *n* [U]

in·sect /ˈɪnsɛkt/ *n* a small creature with no bones and a hard outer covering, six legs, and a body divided into three parts, such as an ant or fly

in·sec·ti·cide /ɪnˈsɛktəˌsaɪd/ *n* [C;U] (a) chemical substance made to kill insects

in·se·cure /ˌɪnsɪˈkyuər/ *adj* **1** (of people) (feeling) not SECURE; afraid or unsure of oneself **2 a** not safe; which cannot support people, things, etc.: *an insecure wall* **b** unsafe; not supported: *I feel insecure on this high ladder.* –**insecurity** /ˌɪnsɪˈkyuərətiy/ *n* [U] –**insecurely** /ˌɪnsɪˈkyuərliy/ *adv*

in·sen·si·ble /ɪnˈsɛnsəbəl/ *adj fml* **1** not conscious –compare SENSELESS (1) **2** lacking knowledge of: *insensible of his danger*
USAGE **Insensible** is *not* the opposite of **sensible**.

in·sen·si·tive /ɪnˈsɛnsətɪv/ *adj* [*to*] **1** (of people and their acts) not SENSITIVE; not kind to others because one does not understand how they feel; TACTless: *an insensitive remark* **2** not having the feeling which is usual when one meets a (certain) experience: *insensitive to pain* –**insensitively** *adv* –**insensitivity** /ɪnˌsɛnsəˈtɪvətiy/ *n* [S;U]

in·sep·a·ra·ble /ɪnˈsɛpərəbəl/ *adj* [*from*] not SEPARABLE; that cannot be separated (from

something else or from one another): *The two girls are inseparable friends.* –**inseparably** *adv* –**inseparability** /ɪnˌsɛpərəˈbɪlətiy/ *n* [U]

in·sert¹ /ɪnˈsɜrt/ *v* [T *in, to*] to put something inside (something else): *He inserted the key in the lock and opened the door.*

insert² /ˈɪnsɜrt/ *n* a thing INSERTed: *An insert in the newspaper advertised the opening of the new restaurant.*

in·ser·tion /ɪnˈsɜrʃən/ *n* [C;U] the act or action of INSERTING, or the thing inserted

in·shore /ˌɪnˈʃɔr◂, -ˈʃowr◂/ *adv* [F] near, towards, or to the shore –see also OFFSHORE, ONSHORE –**inshore** *adj* [A]

in·side¹ /ɪnˈsaɪd, ˈɪnsaɪd/ *n* **1** the area within (something else); the part that is nearest to the center, or that faces away from other people or from the open air: *paint the inside of the house* –opposite **outside 2** [*often pl.*] *infml* the stomach: *a pain in one's insides*

inside² *prep,adj* **1** within or into something: *inside the car*/*the house*/*my mouth*/*He opened the box and looked inside.*/*the inside pages of a book* **2** to or on the edge of a road: *the inside* LANE (2) (=where cars drive slowly) **3** *infml* in less time than: *He'll be here* **inside** *of an hour.* **4** of or from the secret center of something: *inside information* (=from someone who knows the secret truth) **5** with the usual inside parts on the outside: *He put his socks on* **inside out.** –opposite **outside** (for **1,2**)
USAGE Compare **within** and **inside**: 1 Both words can express the idea of being surrounded, but **inside** is more usual in this sense; **within** is formal and only used of large areas: **inside** *the box*/**within** *the prison* (fml). 2 Both words can mean "not beyond." but **within** is more usual, and **inside** is informal: *Your shoes will be ready* **within**/**inside** (infml) *a week.*

in·sid·er /ɪnˈsaɪdər/ *n* someone who is in a group whose membership gives him special information and/or power –compare OUTSIDER

in·sid·i·ous /ɪnˈsɪdiyəs/ *adj* unnoticed in action but causing something very bad in the end; secretly harmful: *the insidious growth of decay* –**insidiously** *adv* –**insidiousness** *n* [U]

in·sight /ˈɪnsaɪt/ *n* [C;U *into*] (an example of) the power of using one's mind to understand something deeply, esp. without help from outside information: *Visiting Los Angeles gave me insight into the lives of the people who live there.*

in·sig·ni·a /ɪnˈsɪgniyə/ *n* **-as** *or* **-a** [P] a BADGE or object which represents the power of an official or important person, such as the STRIPEs of an officer

in·sig·nif·i·cant /ˌɪnsɪgˈnɪfəkənt/ *adj* not SIGNIFICANT; not of value and/or importance –**insignificance** *n* [U] –**insignificantly** *adv*

in·sin·cere /ˌɪnsɪnˈsɪər/ *adj* not sincere –**insincerity** /ˌɪnsɪnˈsɛrətiy/ *n* [U]

in·sin·u·ate /ɪnˈsɪnyuwˌeyt/ *v* **-ated, -ating** [T +(*that*)/*to*] to suggest (something unpleasant) by one's behavior or questions: *Are* *you insinuating that I'm not telling the truth?* |*an insinuating remark*

in·sin·u·a·tion /ɪnˌsɪnyuʷˈeⁱʃən/ *n* [C;U] (an example of) the act or action of insinuating (INSINUATE): *She blamed him, not directly but by insinuation.* |*They made unpleasant insinuations that he might not be honest.* –compare IMPLICATION (2)

in·sip·id /ɪnˈsɪpɪd/ *adj* lacking a strong effect, esp. a taste: *insipid food* |*an insipid character* –**insipidly** *adv* –**insipidness** *n* [U]

in·sist /ɪnˈsɪst/ *v* [I;T] **1** [+(*that*)/*on, upon*] to declare firmly (when opposed): *I insisted (to everyone) that he was wrong.* |*I insisted on my correctness.* **2** [+(*that*)/*to*] to order (something to happen): *I insisted on him going.* |*I insisted that he leave.* |*You've got to come with us: I insist.*

in·sist·ence /ɪnˈsɪstəns/ *n* [U] **1** the act of INSISTING: *I did it, but only at your insistence.* **2** the quality or state of being INSISTENT (1)

in·sist·ent /ɪnˈsɪstənt/ *adj* **1** [+(*that*)/*on, upon*] (of people) repeatedly INSISTING or making demands: *He's very insistent that he'll finish in time.* |*an insistent refusal* **2** (of acts) needing to be done, answered, etc.; urgent: *the insistent ringing of the telephone* –**insistently** *adv*

in si·tu /ˌɪn ˈsaɪtuʷ, -tyuʷ, -ˈsɪ-/ *adv* [F] *Latin* in its original place

in so far as /ˌ· · ˈ· ·/ also **insofar as** /ˌɪnsəˈfɑr əz, -soʷ-/, **in as far as**– *conj* to the degree that: *I'll help you in so far as I can.*

in·so·lent /ˈɪnsələnt/ *adj* (of people and their acts) showing disrespectful rudeness; IN-SULTING –**insolently** *adv* –**insolence** *n* [U]

in·sol·u·ble /ɪnˈsɑlyəbəl/ ‖also **insolvable** /ɪnˈsɑlvəbəl/ *AmE*– *adj* **1** which cannot be made right, brought to a good result, or SOLVED **2** which cannot be DISSOLVED (esp. 1,2): *insoluble in water* –opposite **soluble**

in·sol·vent /ɪnˈsɑlvənt/ *adj* not SOLVENT; not having money to pay what one owes –**insolvency** *n* [U]

in·som·ni·a /ɪnˈsɑmniʸə/ *n* [U] habitual inability to sleep –**insomniac** /ɪnˈsɑmniʸˌæk/ *n,adj*: *She's an insomniac; she only sleeps for two or three hours a night.*

in·spect /ɪnˈspɛkt/ *v* [T] **1** to examine (the details of something) **2** to make an official visit to judge the quality of (an organization, machine, etc.)

in·spec·tion /ɪnˈspɛkʃən/ *n* [C;U] (an example of) the act of INSPECTING or the state of being inspected: *a tour of inspection* |*I gave the radio a thorough inspection before I bought it.*

in·spec·tor /ɪnˈspɛktər/ *n* **1** [C] an official who INSPECTS: *a health inspector* **2** [A;C] in some police departments, a police officer of middle rank

in·spi·ra·tion /ˌɪnspəˈreⁱʃən/ *n* **1** [C;U] (something or someone which causes) an urge to produce good and beautiful things,

esp. works of art: *Dante was the inspiration for my book on Italy.* |*Her hard work and imagination are an inspiration to everyone in the company.* **2** [C] a good idea: *I've had an inspiration; let's go to the country.* –**inspirational** *adj*

in·spire /ɪnˈspaɪər/ *v* -**spired, -spiring** [T] **1** [+*to-v*/*to*] to encourage in (someone) the ability to act, esp. with a good result: *You inspire me to greater efforts.* |*I was inspired to work harder.* |*an inspiring speech* **2** to be the force which produces (usu. a good result): *His best music was inspired by the memory of his mother.* **3** [*with*/*in*] to put (a feeling towards the subject) into (someone): *You inspire me with admiration.* |*He inspires hate/dislike in me.*

in·spired /ɪnˈspaɪərd/ *adj* so excellent as to seem to show INSPIRATION (2), esp. from God: *an inspired guess* |*She sang as if inspired.* –opposite **uninspired**

in·sta·bil·i·ty /ˌɪnstəˈbɪlətiʸ/ *n* [U] lack of STABILITY; unsteadiness, esp. of character

in·stall /ɪnˈstɔl/ *v* [T *in*] **1** to set (an apparatus) up, ready for use: *We're installing a new heating system.* **2** to settle (someone) in an official position, esp. with ceremony: *The new head of the university will be installed today.* |(fig.) *I installed myself in front of the fire.* –**installation** /ˌɪnstəˈleⁱʃən/ *n* [C;U]

in·stall·ment *AmE*‖also **instalment** /ɪnˈstɔlmənt/ *n* **1** a single payment of a set which, in time, will complete full payment: *I'll soon pay the last installment of my debt.* **2** a single part of a book, play, or television show which appears in regular parts until the story is completed

installment plan /·ˈ·· ˌ·/ *AmE n* [C; *the* S] a system of payment for goods by which one pays small sums of money regularly after receiving the goods (usu. paying more than the original price): *buying by the installment plan* –compare CREDIT¹ (1)

in·stance /ˈɪnstəns/ *n* **1** [*of*] a single fact, event, etc., expressing a general idea; example; case: *an instance of bad behavior* **2** **for instance** for example: *You can't depend on her: for instance, she arrived late for an important meeting yesterday.* **3** **in the first instance** first of all; as a beginning

in·stant¹ /ˈɪnstənt/ *n* a moment or point of time: *Not for an instant did I believe he had lied.* |(*At*) *The instant I saw him I knew he was angry.*

instant² *adj* [*no comp.*] **1** happening at once: *instant change* **2** [A] (of food etc.) which can be very quickly prepared for use: *instant coffee/potatoes*

in·stan·ta·ne·ous /ˌɪnstənˈteⁱniʸəs/ *adj* [*no comp.*] happening at once –**instantaneously** *adv* –**instantaneousness** *n* [U]

in·stant·ly /ˈɪnstəntliʸ/ *adv* [*no comp.*] at once: *The police came to my help instantly.*

in·stead /ɪnˈstɛd/ *adv* **1** in place of that: *It's too wet to walk, so we'll go swimming instead.* |*She never studies. Instead, she plays tennis all day.* **2** **instead of** in place of: *I should be at school instead of lying here in bed.* |*Will you go to the party instead of me?*

in·step /'ɪnstɛp/ *n* the upper surface of the foot between the toes and the ankle

in·sti·gate /'ɪnstə,geʸt/ *v* **-gated, -gating** [T] *fml* to start (something happening, often something bad) by one's action: *He instigated the ending of free school milk.* **–instigator** *n* **–instigation** /,ɪnstə'geʸʃən/ *n* [U]: *We have come* **at your instigation.** (=at your suggestion)

in·still *AmE*‖**instil** *esp. BrE-* /ɪn'stɪl/ *v* **-ll-** [T *in, into*] *fml* to put (ideas, feelings, etc.) into someone's mind by a continuing effort: *I instilled the need for good manners into all my children.* **–instillation** /,ɪnstə'leʸʃən/ *n* [U]

in·stinct /'ɪnstɪŋkt/ *n* [C;U +*to-v*] the natural force in people and animals which causes certain behavior patterns, such as nest-building, which are not based on learning or thinking: *Some animals hunt by instinct.*‖(fig.) *Trust your instincts and do what you think is right.* **–instinctive** /ɪn'stɪŋktɪv/ *adj: instinctive fear of snakes* **–instinctively** *adv: Instinctively, I knew she was ill.*

in·sti·tute¹ /'ɪnstə,tuʷt, -,tyuʷt/ *n* a society formed for a special purpose: *a scientific institute*

institute² *v* **-tuted, -tuting** [T] to set up for the first time (a society, rules, actions in law, etc.)

in·sti·tu·tion /,ɪnstə'tuʷʃən, -'tyuʷ-/ *n* **1** [C] (a large building for) an organization which provides people with help, work, medical treatment, or protection, such as a school or hospital **2** [C] a habit, custom, etc., which has been in existence for a long time: *Marriage is an institution in most societies.* **3** [C;U] the act or action of instituting (IN-STITUTE²): *the institution of a new law* **–institutional** *adj* **–institutionalize** /,ɪnstə'tuʷʃənəl,aɪz, -'tyuʷ-/ *v* [T]

in·struct /ɪn'strʌkt/ *v* [T +*that/to-v*] **1** to give knowledge or information to: *They instructed me in the best ways of doing the job.* **2** to give orders to: *I've been instructed to wait here until the teacher arrives.* **–**see ORDER² (USAGE)

in·struc·tion /ɪn'strʌkʃən/ *n* **1** [U] the act or action of instructing; teaching: *He's not yet trained; he's still receiving instruction.* **2** [C often *pl.*] an order (to a person or machine), or advice on how to do something: *an instruction book*‖*a book of instructions* **–instructional** *adj*

in·struc·tive /ɪn'strʌktɪv/ *adj* giving useful information **–instructively** *adv*

in·struc·tor /ɪn'strʌktər/ *n* a person who teaches an activity: *a driving instructor*

in·stru·ment /'ɪnstrəmənt/ *n* **1** an object used to help in work: *medical instruments* **2** also **musical instrument** /,··· '···/ – an object which is played to give musical sounds (such as a piano, a horn, etc.)

in·stru·men·tal /,ɪnstrə'mɛntəl/ *adj* **1** [*in*] helpful (in); (part of) the cause of: *I was instrumental in catching the criminal.* **2** (of music) for instruments, not voices: *an instrumental work*

in·sub·or·di·nate /,ɪnsə'bɔrdn-ɪt, -'bɔrdnɪt/ *adj* (of a person of lower rank, or his/her behavior) disobedient; not showing willingness to take orders **–insubordination** /,ɪnsə'bɔrdn'eʸʃən/ *n* [C;U]

in·sub·stan·tial /,ɪnsəb'stænʃəl, -tʃəl/ *adj* lacking firmness or solidity; weak or unsatisfying: *an insubstantial meal* **–**see also SUBSTANTIAL

in·suf·fer·a·ble /ɪn'sʌfərəbəl/ *adj* unbearable (in behavior); too proud in manner: *insufferable rudeness*‖*He's insufferable.* **–insufferably** *adv*

in·suf·fi·cient /,ɪnsə'fɪʃənt/ *adj* [*for*] not SUFFICIENT; not enough: *They gave insufficient help.*‖*The food was insufficient for our needs.* **–insufficiently** *adv* **–insufficiency** *n* [S;U *of*]: *(an) insufficiency of money*

in·su·lar /'ɪnsələr, 'ɪnsʸə-/ *adj* narrow (in mind); interested only or mainly in a small group, country, etc. **–insularity** /,ɪnsə'lærəti̯ʸ, ,ɪnsʸə-/ *n* [U]

in·su·late /'ɪnsə,leʸt, 'ɪnsʸə-/ *v* **-lated, -lating** [T *from, against*] **1** to cover (something) so as to prevent the passing of unseen forces such as electricity, heat, or sound: *Many houses could be warmer if they were insulated so that the heat is not lost.* **2** to protect (a person) from ordinary experiences: *Very wealthy people are insulated from many of the difficulties faced by ordinary people.*

in·su·la·tion /,ɪnsə'leʸʃən, ,ɪnsʸə-/ *n* [U] **1** the action of insulating or the state of being INSULATED **2** material which INSULATES

in·sult¹ /ɪn'sʌlt/ *v* [T *by*] to offend, by speech or act: *You have insulted me by saying that.*‖*an insulting remark*

in·sult² /'ɪnsʌlt/ *n* [C;U] (an example of) speech or action which INSULTS¹: *He shouted insults at the boy who had kicked him.*

in·su·per·a·ble /ɪn'suʷpərəbəl/ *adj fml* (of something in one's way) too difficult to be conquered or passed: *insuperable difficulties/BARRIERS* **–**compare INSURMOUNTABLE **–insuperably** *adv*

in·sur·ance /ɪn'ʃʊərəns/ *n* **1** [U] (the business of making an) agreement by contract to pay money, esp. in case of a misfortune (such as illness, death, or accident): *life insurance*‖*car insurance*‖*an* **insurance policy** (=a written contract of insurance)‖*He worked in insurance.* **2** [U] money paid (by an **insurance company**) as a result of such a contract, or (to an **insurance company**) in order to make or keep such a contract **3** [S;U *against*] protection (against something): *I bought another lock as additional insurance against thieves.*

in·sure /ɪn'ʃʊər/ *v* **-sured, -suring** **1** [T *against*] to protect (oneself or another), esp. against loss of (money, life, goods, etc.) by INSURANCE (1): *My house is insured against fire.*‖*I am insured.* **2** [T +(*that*)] *esp. AmE* for ENSURE

USAGE Compare **insure, ensure,** and **assure:** 1 **Insure** and **assure** are both words for gaining protection through **insurance,** but **assure** is normally only used for insurance against death: *life* **assurance**‖*fire* **insurance** 2 **Assure** is also used more generally to mean "to make certain" and is similar to **ensure**: *I went back to the car to* **assure** *myself that I had locked it properly.*|*I put in a new lock to* **ensure** *that the car would not be stolen.*|*My car is* **insured** *against being stolen* (=if it is stolen, I will get money from the* **insurance company**). 3 **Reassure** means "to comfort someone who is anxious" (not "to **assure** again") 4 The social quality of **assurance** means that one is sure of oneself and not afraid of people: *She seems very* **self-assured.**

in·sur·gent /ɪnˈsɜrdʒənt/ *adj,n* [A;C] (a person who is) ready to take power by or as if by force, after rising against the people who have power

in·sur·mount·a·ble /ˌɪnsərˈmaʊntəbəl/ *adj* too large, difficult, etc., to be dealt with –compare INSUPERABLE

in·sur·rec·tion /ˌɪnsəˈrekʃən/ *n* [C;U] the act or occasion of rising against the people who have power, such as the government –**insurrectionist** *n*

in·tact /ɪnˈtækt/ *adj* [F] whole because no part has been touched or spoiled: *The delicate package arrived intact.* –**intactness** *n* [U]

in·take /ˈɪnteɪk/ *n* [S] the amount or number allowed to enter, or taken in: *a large intake of food*|*the yearly intake of students*

in·tan·gi·ble /ɪnˈtændʒəbəl/ *adj* which by its nature cannot be known by the senses, though it can be felt: *an intangible quality*|*We felt an intangible presence in the room.* –see also TANGIBLE –**intangibly** *adv* –**intangibility** /ɪnˌtændʒəˈbɪlətiy/ *n* [U]

in·te·gral /ˈɪntəgrəl/ *adj* [A no comp.] necessary (to complete something): *an integral part of the argument*

in·te·grate /ˈɪntəˌɡreɪt/ *v* **-grated, -grating** [I;T *into, with*] 1 to (cause to) join to something else so as to form a whole: *I integrated your suggestion into my plan.* 2 (of members of social groups) to join in and mix with society as a whole; to cause (members of social groups) to do this: *They've lived in this country for 10 years but have never really integrated/become integrated.* –compare SEGREGATE –**integration** /ˌɪntəˈgreyʃən/ *n* [U]

in·te·grat·ed /ˈɪntəˌgreytɪd/ *adj* showing a usu. pleasing mixture of qualities, groups, etc.: *This is an integrated school with children of different races and social classes.*

in·teg·ri·ty /ɪnˈtegrətiy/ *n* [U] 1 strength and firmness of character or principle; honesty that can be trusted: *a man of complete integrity* 2 *fml* state of wholeness; completeness: *Our integrity as a nation is threatened.*

in·tel·lect /ˈɪntəlˌekt/ *n* [C;U] the ability to reason (rather than to feel or act) –see INTELLIGENT (USAGE)

in·tel·lec·tu·al¹ /ˌɪntəlˈektʃuwəl/ *adj* 1 concerning the INTELLECT: *intellectual subjects* –compare SPIRITUAL¹ (1) 2 able to use the INTELLECT well; showing unusual reasoning powers: *an intellectual argument/family* –see

INTELLIGENT (USAGE); –**intellectually** *adv*

intellectual² *n* a person who works and lives by using his mind, and who is interested in activities which include thinking and understanding rather than feeling and doing

in·tel·li·gence /ɪnˈtelədʒəns/ *n* [U] 1 (good) ability to learn and understand: *an intelligence test*|*Use your intelligence.* 2 information gathered esp. about an enemy country, or the group of people who gather it: *the Central Intelligence* AGENCY *of the US*

in·tel·li·gent /ɪnˈtelədʒənt/ *adj* having or showing powers of reasoning or understanding: *All human beings are much more intelligent than animals.*|*an intelligent suggestion* –opposite **unintelligent** –**telligently** *adv*

USAGE Compare **intelligent** and **intellectual**. Anyone with a quick and clever mind is **intelligent**, but an **intellectual** (person) is someone who is well-educated and interested in subjects that exercise the mind. A small child, or even a dog, can be **intelligent** but cannot be called an **intellectual**.

in·tel·li·gi·ble /ɪnˈtelədʒəbəl/ *adj* [*to*] (esp. of speech or writing) which can be understood –opposite **unintelligible**; compare ARTICULATE¹ (1,2) –**intelligibly** *adv* –**intelligibility** /ɪnˌtelədʒəˈbɪlətiy/ *n* [U]

in·tend /ɪnˈtend/ *v* [T +*to-v/that*] 1 to plan; to mean (to do): *I intended to catch the early train, but I didn't get up in time.*|*I intend to report you to the police.* 2 to mean to be: *The flowers were intended for you, but my mother thought they were for her.*|*It was intended as a joke.*|*It was intended to be cooked slowly.*

in·tense /ɪnˈtens/ *adj* strong (in quality or feeling): *intense cold*|*intense sorrow*|*She is a very intense person who cares deeply about everything.* –**intensely** *adv*

in·ten·si·fi·er /ɪnˈtensəfaɪər/ *n* a word which makes an adjective stronger in feeling –see Study Notes opposite

in·ten·si·fy /ɪnˈtensəˌfaɪ/ *v* **-fied, -fying** [I;T] to (cause to) become more INTENSE: *Police have intensified their search for the criminal.* –**intensification** /ɪnˌtensəfəˈkeyʃən/ *n* [U]

in·ten·si·ty /ɪnˈtensətiy/ *n* [U] the quality of being INTENSE: *The poem shows great intensity of feeling.*

in·ten·sive /ɪnˈtensɪv/ *adj* which gives a lot of attention or action to a small amount of something/in a small amount of time: *Intensive care in hospitals is given to the seriously ill.* –see also EXTENSIVE –**intensively** *adv*

in·tent¹ /ɪnˈtent/ *n* [U] 1 purpose; INTENTION: *with good intent*|*He entered the building with intent to steal.* 2 **to all intents (and purposes)** in almost every way; very nearly

intent² *adj* [*on*] showing fixed attention (in doing or wishing to do): *an intent look*|*He's intent on his studies/on going to France.* –**intently** *adv* –**intentness** *n* [U]

in·ten·tion /ɪnˈtenʃən, -tʃən/ *n* [C;U] (an example of) a determination to act in a certain way: *I've got no intention of changing my mind.*|*It wasn't my intention to make you miss your train.*|*He is full of* **good intentions** *but can do nothing to help.*

SPELLING NOTE

Words with the sound /aɪ/ may be spelled e-, like **eye**, or ai-, like **aisle**.

STUDY NOTES intensifiers ▰▰▰▰▰▰▰▰▰

Some adverbs, like **very, quite, rather,** etc., can be used to change the meaning of a word, phrase, or sentence. They can be used to make the meaning stronger:

It's **very** *hot today.* (=more than just hot)

Or they can be used to make the meaning less strong:

It's **fairly** *hot today.* (=less than just hot, but definitely not cold)

In the diagram below, the meaning of the groups of words get stronger as you move down the page:

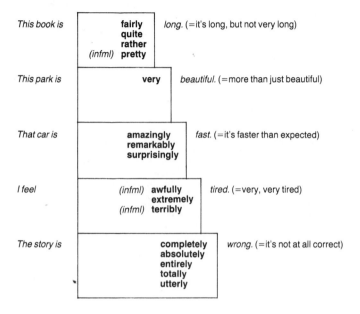

This book is	**fairly** *long.* (=it's long, but not very long)
	quite
	rather
(infml)	**pretty**
This park is	**very** *beautiful.* (=more than just beautiful)
That car is	**amazingly** *fast.* (=it's faster than expected)
	remarkably
	surprisingly
I feel	*(infml)* **awfully** *tired.* (=very, very tired)
	extremely
	(infml) **terribly**
The story is	**completely** *wrong.* (=it's not at all correct)
	absolutely
	entirely
	totally
	utterly

Look up these words in your dictionary to find more examples of their different meanings and uses.

---

in·ten·tion·al /ɪnˈtɛnʃənəl, -tʃənəl/ *adj* (done) on purpose –opposite **unintentional** –**intentionally** *adv*

in·ter /ɪnˈtɜr/ *v* -**rr**- [T] *fml* to bury (a dead person) –opposite **disinter**

in·ter·act /ˌɪntəˈrækt/ *v* [I *with, against*] to have an effect on each other or something else –**interaction** /ˌɪntəˈrækʃən/ *n*

in·ter·cede /ˌɪntərˈsiʸd/ *v* -**ceded, -ceding** [I *with, for*] to speak in favor of another, esp. in order to save him/her from punishment: *He intel·ceded with the governor for me, and I was saved.* –**intercession** /ˌɪntərˈsɛʃən/ *n* [C;U]

in·ter·cept /ˌɪntərˈsɛpt/ *v* [T] to stop and usu. seize (a person or thing moving from one place to another): *The drugs were intercepted by the police before they were delivered.* –**interception** /ˌɪntərˈsɛpʃən/ *n* [C;U]

in·ter·change /ˈɪntərˌtʃeʸndʒ/ *n* **1** [C;U] (an example of) the act or action of exchanging: *a useful interchange of ideas* **2** [C] *esp. AmE* a point where one drives onto a road without crossing any of the roads which join there

in·ter·change·a·ble /ˌɪntərˈtʃeʸndʒəbəl/ *adj* [*with*] which can be used in place of each other/something else –**interchangeably** *adv: The two words are used interchangeably.*

in·ter·com /ˈɪntərˌkɑm/ *n* a system by which one can talk through a machine to people in a near place, as used e.g. in an office by someone to speak to a secretary in an outer room

in·ter·con·ti·nen·tal /ˌɪntərˌkɑntənˈɛntəl/ *adj* (used, done, connected with, etc.) different land masses (CONTINENTs): *intercontinental trade*

in·ter·est¹ /ˈɪntrɪst, ˈɪntərɪst/ *n* **1** [C;U *in*] a readiness to give attention: *I have no interest in politics.* | *He's showing an interest in music.*

2 [U] a quality of causing attention to be given: *That's of no interest to me.* **3** [C] an activity, subject, etc., to which one gives time and attention: *Eating seems to be his only interest in life.* **4** [C;U *often pl.*] advantage, advancement, or favor: *It's* **in your interest** *to put your point of view first.*|*Come into my office and you will hear something* **to your interest. 5** [U] money paid for the use of money: *He lent me the money at 6% interest.*

interest² *v* [T *in*] **1** to make (someone) feel interest: *Football doesn't interest me at all.* **2** to make (someone) want to buy, take, do something, etc.: *Can I interest you in a cup of coffee?*

in·ter·est·ed /ˈɪntrəstɪd, ˈɪntəˌrɛstɪd, ˈɪntərəstɪd/ *adj* **1** [+ *to* -v/*in*] concerned; having or showing interest: *I was interested in your remark/to hear your remark.*|*an interested look on his face* –opposite **uninterested 2** [A] personally concerned; on whom there will be an effect; who cannot make a fair judgment from the outside: *the interested* PARTY (=*tech* person) –see DISINTERESTED (USAGE) –**interestedly** *adv*

in·ter·est·ing /ˈɪntrəstɪŋ, ˈɪntəˌrɛstɪŋ, ˈɪntərəstɪŋ/ *adj* which takes (and keeps) one's interest: *an interesting idea* –opposite **uninteresting** –**interestingly** adv

in·ter·fere /ˌɪntərˈfɪər/ *v* -**fered**, -**fering** [I *with, in, between*] **1** to get in the way of another; block the action of another **2** *derog* to push oneself into a matter which does not concern one: *I don't like interfering old busybodies* (BUSYBODY).

USAGE Compare **interfere** *in* and **interfere** *with:* *Stop* **interfering** *in my work!* (=taking part when you are not wanted)|*This noise is* **interfering** *with my work.* (=preventing me from doing it properly)

in·ter·fer·ence /ˌɪntərˈfɪərəns/ *n* [U] **1** [*with*] the act or action of interfering (INTERFERE) **2** the noises and shapes which spoil the working of electrical apparatus, esp. when a radio station is difficult to listen to because of the effect of another one near its WAVELENGTH

in·ter·im¹ /ˈɪntərəm/ *n* **1** the time between two events **2 in the interim** → MEANWHILE (1)

interim² *adj* good enough for a limited time, but not meant to last: *The full report isn't ready yet, but you can see the interim report.*

in·te·ri·or /ɪnˈtɪəriər/ *adj,n* (the part which is) inside, indoors, or farthest from the edge or outside: *He went into the interior (of the country).* (=the part farthest from the coast)|*An* **interior decorator** *is a person who plans the colors and furnishings for the inside of a house.* –opposite **exterior**

in·ter·ject /ˌɪntərˈdʒɛkt/ *v* [I;T] *fml* to make (a sudden remark) between others: *"Don't do it like that!" he interjected while explaining how to fasten the wires.*

in·ter·jec·tion /ˌɪntərˈdʒɛkʃən/ *n fml* **1** [C] a phrase, word, or set of sounds used as a sudden remark usu. expressing surprise, anger, etc.; EXCLAMATION: *interjections such as "oh!" or "Well done!"* **2** [U] the act of INTERJECTING

in·ter·lock /ˌɪntərˈlɑk/ *v* [I;T] to fasten or be fastened together, esp. so that movement of one part causes movement in others: *to interlock the fingers of two hands*

in·ter·lop·er /ˈɪntərˌloʷpər/ *n fml* a person found in a place, esp. among others, who has no right to be there –compare INTRUDER

in·ter·lude /ˈɪntərˌluʷd/ *n* **1** a free period of time between activities **2** (something, esp. music, used for filling) the time (INTERVAL) between parts of a play, film, concert, etc.

in·ter·mar·ry /ˌɪntərˈmæriʸ/ *v* -**ried**, -**rying** [I *with*] (of different groups of people) to marry each other: *The two families have been intermarrying for 100 years.* –**intermarriage** /ˌɪntərˈmærɪdʒ/ *n* [U]

in·ter·me·di·ar·y /ˌɪntərˈmiʸdiʸˌɛriʸ/ *n* -**ies** a person who comes between two other groups, people, etc., often so as to bring them into agreement

in·ter·me·di·ate /ˌɪntərˈmiʸdiʸɪt/ *adj* (done or happening) between two others; halfway: *an intermediate level English class* (=between the highest and lowest levels)

in·ter·ment /ɪnˈtɜrmənt/ *n* [C;U] *fml* burial –see also INTER; –compare INTERN

in·ter·mi·na·ble /ɪnˈtɜrmənəbəl/ *adj* (seeming) endless: *I had interminable problems with my last car: it never worked well.* –**interminably** *adv*

in·ter·mis·sion /ˌɪntərˈmɪʃən/ *n esp. AmE*‖**interval** *BrE*– a period of time between parts of a play, concert, etc.: *During the intermission, let's go out for some fresh air.*

in·ter·mit·tent /ˌɪntərˈmɪtnt/ *adj* happening with pauses in between; not continuous: *an intermittent fault/noise* –**intermittently** *adv*

in·tern¹ /ɪnˈtɜrn/ *v* [T] to put in prison or limit the freedom of movement of (someone considered dangerous), esp. in wartime or for political reasons –**internment** *n* [U] –compare INTERMENT

intern², **-terne** /ˈɪntɜrn/ *n AmE* a JUNIOR (2) doctor completing hospital training

in·ter·nal /ɪnˈtɜrnl/ *adj* **1** of or in the inside, esp. of the body: *internal damage* **2** inside a country; not foreign: *internal trade* –opposite **external** –**internally** *adv*

internal-com·bus·tion en·gine /·ˌ··· ·ˈ·· ˌ··/ *n* an engine (such as a car engine) which produces power by the burning of a substance (such as gasoline) inside itself

in·ter·na·tion·al /ˌɪntərˈnæʃənəl/ *adj* between nations; concerning more than one nation –**internationally** *adv*

in·ter·plan·e·tar·y /ˌɪntərˈplænəˌtɛriʸ/ *adj* (happening or done) between the PLANETs: *interplanetary travel/space*

in·ter·play /ˈɪntərˌpleʸ/ *n* [U] the action or effect of (two) things on each other: *the interplay of light and sound*

in·ter·pose /ˌɪntərˈpoʷz/ *v* -**posed**, -**posing** [I;T *between, among, in*] *fml* to put, come, or say between: *She interposed a few questions into the senator's speech.*

SPELLING NOTE
Words with the sound /aɪ/ may be spelled e-, like **eye**, or ai-, like **aisle**.

in·ter·pret /ɪn'tɜrprɪt/ v **1** [T] to put (a language) into the words of another language usu. by talking –compare TRANSLATE **2** [T as] to understand or show the meaning of (something): *I interpret his answer as a refusal.* | *The actor interprets Shakespeare in a new way.* –see also MISINTERPRET

in·ter·pre·ta·tion /ɪn,tɜrprə'teʸʃən/ n [U] the act or the result of INTERPRETing; explanation

in·ter·pret·er /ɪn'tɜrprətər/ n a person who INTERPRETS (1)

in·ter·ro·gate /ɪn'tɛrə,geʸt/ v -gated, -gating [T] to question formally for a special purpose –see ASK (USAGE) –interrogation /ɪn,tɛrə'geʸʃən/ n [C;U] –interrogator /ɪn'tɛrə,geʸtər/ n

in·ter·rog·a·tive /,ɪntə'ragətɪv/ adj,n (a sentence, phrase, or word) which asks a question –interrogatively adv

in·ter·rupt /,ɪntə'rʌpt/ v [I;T] **1** to break the flow of speech of (someone) by saying something: *Stop interrupting me; I'm trying to talk to your mother!* **2** to break the flow of (something continuous) –interruption /,ɪntə'rʌpʃən/ n [C;U]

in·ter·sect /,ɪntər'sɛkt/ v [I;T] (of lines, roads, etc.) to be in such a position as to cut across (each other or something else)

in·ter·sec·tion /,ɪntər'sɛkʃən, 'ɪntər,sɛk-/ n **1** [U] the act or action of INTERSECTing **2** [C] a place where two or more highways or streets cross

in·ter·sperse /,ɪntər'spɜrs/ v -spersed, -spersing [T with] to set here and there: *a field full of grass, interspersed with a few flowers*

in·ter·val /'ɪntərvəl/ n **1** a period of time between events: *There was a long interval before he replied.* **2** BrE for INTERMISSION **3** at intervals (of) happening regularly after equal periods of time or appearing at equal distances (of): *The bell rang at 20-minute intervals.*

in·ter·vene /,ɪntər'viʸn/ v -vened, -vening [I] **1** [in] (of people) to interrupt something, esp. to prevent a bad result: *They were starting to fight when their father intervened.* **2** to happen between events: *in the intervening years* –intervention /,ɪntər'vɛnʃən, -tʃən/ n [C;U]

in·ter·view¹ /'ɪntər,vyuʷ/ n a meeting where a person is asked questions **a** to decide whether he/she can take up a job or **b** to find out about his/her actions, opinions, etc., sometimes broadcast on radio or television

interview² v [T] to ask questions of (somebody) in an INTERVIEW¹ –interviewer n

in·ter·weave /,ɪntər'wiʸv/ v -wove /'woʷv/, -woven /'woʷvən/, -weaving [T with] to weave together: *curtains made of red cloth interwoven with gold* | (fig.) *Our lives are interwoven.*

in·tes·tate /ɪn'tɛsteʸt, -stɪt/ adj law not having made a WILL² (6) which leaves one's property to named people: *He died intestate.*

in·tes·tine /ɪn'tɛstɪn/ n the tube carrying food from the stomach; bowels –compare BOWELS (1) –intestinal adj

in·ti·ma·cy /'ɪntəməsiʸ/ n [U with] **1** the state of being INTIMATE¹ **2** close friendship

in·ti·mate¹ /'ɪntəmɪt/ adj **1** [with] close in (a sexual) relationship: *intimate friends* | *They had been intimate* / **on intimate terms** *for some time.* **2** personal; private: *one's intimate beliefs* **3** detailed; resulting from close study: *an intimate knowledge of the city* –intimately adv

in·ti·mate² /'ɪntə,meʸt/ v -mated, -mating [T +(that)] fml to make known indirectly; suggest: *He intimated that he wanted to go.* –intimation /,ɪntə'meʸʃən/ n [C;U]

in·tim·i·date /ɪn'tɪmə,deʸt/ v -dated, -dating [T] to make (someone) fearful, esp. by threatening violence, because one wants them to do something –intimidation /ɪn,tɪmə'deʸʃən/ n [U]

in·to /'ɪntə, -tʊ; strong 'ɪntuʷ/ prep **1** so as to be in or inside: *It was raining, so they went into the house.* | *She jumped into the water.* | *He went into* (=got a job in) *business.* | *They worked far into the night.* | *You'll get into trouble.* **2** so as to be: *to translate it into French* | *She developed into a beautiful woman.* **3** (used when dividing one number by another): *Three into six goes twice.* **4** against; so as to hit: *to run into a wall* **5** infml keen on; interested in: *He's given up photography now, and he's into religion and modern music.*

in·tol·er·a·ble /ɪn'talərəbəl/ adj not TOLERABLE; too difficult, painful, etc., to be borne; unbearable –intolerably adv

in·tol·er·ant /ɪn'talərənt/ adj not TOLERANT; not able to accept ways of thinking and behaving which are different from one's own: *They're intolerant of any opposition.* –intolerantly adv –intolerance n [U]

in·to·na·tion /,ɪntə'neʸʃən, -toʷ-/ n [U] rise and fall in the level (PITCH²) of the voice

in·tox·i·cate /ɪn'taksə,keʸt/ v -cated, -cating [I;T] to make drunk: *driving while intoxicated* | (fig.) *Success intoxicated him.* –intoxication /ɪn,taksə'keʸʃən/ n [U]

in·trac·ta·ble /ɪn'træktəbəl/ adj (of people and their acts) difficult to control –intractability /ɪn,træktə'bɪlətiʸ/ n [U]

in·tran·si·gent /ɪn'trænsədʒənt, -zə-/ adj fml (of people and their acts) showing strong ideas which cannot be changed by others' wishes –compare STUBBORN –intransigence n [U]

in·tran·si·tive /ɪn'trænsətɪv, -zə-/ n,adj (a verb) which has a subject but not an object: *In this dictionary the mark* [I] *shows an intransitive verb.* –see Study Notes on page 745

in·tra·ve·nous /,ɪntrə'viʸnəs/ adj (done) within a VEIN (=blood vessel taking blood back to the heart): *an intravenous* INJECTION –intravenously adv

in·trep·id /ɪn'trɛpɪd/ adj (of people and their acts) showing no fear –intrepidly adv –intrepidity /,ɪntrə'pɪdətiʸ/ n [U]

in·tri·ca·cy /'ɪntrɪkəsiʸ/ n -cies **1** [U] the quality of being INTRICATE **2** [C] something INTRICATE: *the intricacies of political behavior*

in·tri·cate /'ɪntrɪkɪt/ adj containing many detailed parts and thus difficult to understand: *an intricate pattern/story* –**intricately** *adv*

in·trigue¹ /ɪn'triᵞg/ *v* **-trigued, -triguing 1** [T] to interest greatly: *Your story intrigues me.|an intriguing idea* **2** [I] to make a secret plan

in·trigue² /'ɪntriᵞg, ɪn'triᵞg/ *n* [C;U] (the act or practice of making) a secret plan: *intrigues between political groups*

in·trin·sic /ɪn'trɪnsɪk, -zɪk/ *adj* [*to, in*] being part of the nature of the stated thing: *The intrinsic value of a coin is the value of the metal it is made of.* –**intrinsically** *adv*

in·tro·duce /ˌɪntrə'duᵂs, -'dyuᵂs/ *v* **-duced, -ducing** [T] **1** to make known by name for the first time to each other or someone else: *I introduced John to Mary last year.|Let me introduce myself: my name is Steve Orlando.* **2** to bring in for the first time: *Potatoes were introduced into Europe from South America.* **3** to produce the first part of (something), esp. to suggest or explain the main part: *This song introduces the most important part of the play.*

in·tro·duc·tion /ˌɪntrə'dʌkʃən/ *n* **1** [U *of, to, into*] the act of introducing or the state of being introduced: *the introduction of a new product* **2** [C] an occasion of telling people each others' names: *Mary made the introductions and we all shook hands.* **3** [C *to*] **a** a written or spoken explanation at the beginning of a book or speech **b** a book which gives one a knowledge of the most important things before going on to advanced studies: *"An Introduction To Chemistry"*

in·tro·duc·to·ry /ˌɪntrə'dʌktəriᵞ/ *adj* which INTRODUCES (3): *a few introductory remarks before the main points*

in·tro·spec·tion /ˌɪntrə'spɛkʃən/ *n* [U] the habit of looking into one's own thoughts and feelings –**introspective** *adj*

in·tro·vert /'ɪntrəˌvɜrt/ *n* an INTROVERTED person –see also EXTROVERT

in·tro·vert·ed /'ɪntrəˌvɜrtɪd/ *adj* concerning oneself with one's own thoughts, acts, personal life, etc., rather than spending time with others –**introversion** /ˌɪntrə'vɜrʒən, -ʃən, 'ɪntrəˌvɜr-/ *n* [U]

in·trude /ɪn'truᵂd/ *v* **-truded, -truding** [I;T *into, on, upon*] to bring or come in when not wanted: *I don't want to intrude on them if they're busy.|I hope I'm not intruding.*

in·trud·er /ɪn'truᵂdər/ *n* a person who has come in unasked and perhaps secretly

in·tru·sion /ɪn'truᵂʒən/ *n* [C;U *on*] the act or an example of intruding (INTRUDE): *The police action was an intrusion on my private life.* –**intrusive** /ɪn'truᵂsɪv/ *adj*

in·tu·i·tion /ˌɪntuᵂ'ɪʃən, -tyuᵂ-/ *n* **1** [U] the power of understanding something without reasoning **2** [C +*that*] an example of this, or a piece of knowledge that results: *She had an intuition that her friend was ill.* –**intuitive** /n'tuᵂətɪv, -'tyuᵂ-/ *adj* –**intuitively** *adv*

SPELLING NOTE
Words with the sound /aɪ/ may be spelled **e-**, like **eye**, or **ai-**, like **aisle**.

---

in·un·date /'ɪnənˌdeʸt/ *v* **-dated, -dating** [T *with*] to flood over, esp. in very large quantities or numbers: (fig.) *I was inundated with requests for money.* –**inundation** /ˌɪnən 'deʸʃən/ *n*

in·vade /ɪn'veʸd/ *v* **-vaded, -vading 1** [I;T] to attack and spread into so as to take control of (a country, city, etc.) **2** [I;T] to enter in large numbers: *Tourists invaded the seaside town during the summer.* **3** [T] to enter into and spoil: *to invade someone's* PRIVACY –**invader** *n*

in·va·lid¹ /'ɪnvəlɪd/ *n* a person made weak by illness: *my invalid mother*

in·val·id² /ɪn'vælɪd/ *adj* not VALID; not correct or correctly expressed, esp. in law: *an invalid claim/ticket*

in·val·i·date /ɪn'væləˌdeʸt/ *v* **-dated, -dating** [T] to make (something) INVALID²; show that (something) is not correct –opposite **validate** –**invalidation** /ɪnˌvælə'deʸʃən/ *n* [U]

in·val·u·a·ble /ɪn'vælyəbəl, -yuᵂəbəl/ *adj* (of qualities) too valuable for the worth to be measured: *your invaluable help* –see WORTHLESS (USAGE)

in·var·i·a·ble /ɪn'vɛəriᵞəbəl/ *adj* which cannot vary or change –opposite **variable** –**invariably** *adv*: *It invariably* (=always) *rains when I go on vacation.*

in·va·sion /ɪn'veʸʒən/ *n* **1** an act of invading (INVADE) **2** the incoming or spread of something usu. harmful

in·vec·tive /ɪn'vɛktɪv/ *n* [C;U] *fml* forceful, attacking speech, used for blaming someone for something and often including swearing

in·vent /ɪn'vɛnt/ *v* [T] **1** to make up, think of, or produce for the first time: *Alexander Graham Bell invented the telephone in 1876.* **2** to make up (something unreal or untrue): *The whole story was invented.*

USAGE One **discovers** something that existed before but was not known, such as a place or a fact. One **invents** something that did not exist before, such as a machine or a method.: *Who* **discovered** *America?|Who* **invented** *the computer?*

in·ven·tion /ɪn'vɛnʃən, -tʃən/ *n* **1** [U] the act of inventing: *the invention of the telephone* **2** [C] something invented: *The telephone is a wonderful invention.*

in·ven·tive /ɪn'vɛntɪv/ *adj apprec* able to invent: *an inventive person/mind* –**inventively** *adv* –**inventiveness** *n* [U]

in·ven·tor /ɪn'vɛntər/ *n* a person who invents something new

in·ven·to·ry /'ɪnvənˌtɔriᵞ, -ˌtoʷriᵞ/ *n* **-ries** a list, esp. one of all the goods in a place

in·verse /ɪn'vɜrs, 'ɪnvɜrs/ *adj,n* [A;C] (something is) opposite in order or position: *The inverse of ¼ is 4* (=4/1). –**inversely** *adv*

in·vert /ɪn'vɜrt/ *v* [T] to put in the opposite position or order, esp. upside down: *She caught the insect by inverting her cup over it.* –**inversion** /ɪn'vɜrʒən, -ʃən/ *n* [C;U]

in·ver·te·brate /ɪn'vɜrtəbrɪt, -ˌbreʸt/ *adj,n tech* (a living creature) which has no SPINE (1) –see also VERTEBRATE

inverted com·ma /·ˌ·· '··/ *n BrE* for QUOTATION MARK

in·vest /ɪnˈvɛst/ v [I;T *in*] to use (money) to make more money out of something that will increase in value: *She invested in a house/a painting.*|(fig.) *I've invested a lot of time and effort in this plan.*

in·ves·ti·gate /ɪnˈvɛstəˌgeʸt/ v **-gated, -gating** [I;T] to examine carefully, or inquire about the reasons for (something), the character of (someone), etc.: *to investigate the crime* **–investigator** /ɪnˈvɛstəˌgeʸtər/ n **–investigation** /ɪnˌvɛstəˈgeʸʃən/ n [C;U]

in·ves·ti·ture /ɪnˈvɛstətʃər, -ˌtʃʊər/ n a ceremony giving someone a high rank

in·vest·ment /ɪnˈvɛstmənt/ n **1** [U] the act or action of INVESTING **2** [C] an amount of money INVESTED: *an investment of $1,000 in a growing business*

in·vet·er·ate /ɪnˈvɛtərɪt/ adj [A] settled in a (bad) habit: *an inveterate LIAR*|*inveterate hatred*

in·vid·i·ous /ɪnˈvɪdiʸəs/ adj [A] which will make people unjustly offended or jealous: *They all sing equally well, so I don't want to make invidious distinctions between them.* **–invidiously** adv

in·vig·o·rate /ɪnˈvɪgəˌreʸt/ v **-rated, -rating** [T] to give a feeling of strength and/or power to: *an invigorating swim in the lake*

in·vin·ci·ble /ɪnˈvɪnsəbəl/ adj too strong to be conquered **–invincibly** adv **–invincibility** /ɪnˌvɪnsəˈbɪləti ʸ/ n [U]

in·vis·i·ble /ɪnˈvɪzəbəl/ adj **1** not VISIBLE; that cannot be seen; hidden from sight **2** not recorded, esp. in statements of profit and loss: *invisible earnings/EXPORTS* **–invisibly** adv **–invisibility** /ɪnˌvɪzəˈbɪləti ʸ/ n [U]

in·vi·ta·tion /ˌɪnvəˈteʸʃən/ n **1** [C +*to-v*] an often written request to go somewhere or do something: **2** [U] the act of inviting: *entrance by written invitation only*

in·vite /ɪnˈvaɪt/ v **-vited, -viting** [T] **1** [*to*] to ask (somebody) to a social occasion: *She invited me to her party.*|*Why don't you invite me in (to the house)?* **2** to ask for; encourage: *I invited her to go for a walk.*|(fig.) *Some stores invite crime by making it easy to take goods.*

USAGE This word is not used when one is actually **inviting** someone. We may say "*Would you like to come to the party?*" and then later remark "*I* **invited** *them to the party.*"

in·vit·ing /ɪnˈvaɪtɪŋ/ adj attractive: *the food on the table looks inviting* **–opposite uninviting –invitingly** adv

in·voice /ˈɪnvɔɪs/ v,n **-voiced, -voicing** [T] (to make or send) a bill for goods received

in·voke /ɪnˈvoʷk/ v **-voked, -voking** [T] **1** to call out to (a power, esp. God) for help **2** to request or beg for: *I invoked their help/their forgiveness.*

in·vol·un·tar·y /ɪnˈvɑlənˌtɛriʸ/ adj not (done) from choice or intention; unwilled: *He gave an involuntary smile/gasp.* **–see also** VOLUNTARY **–involuntarily** /ɪnˌvɑlənˈtɛərəliʸ/ adv

in·volve /ɪnˈvɑlv/ v **-volved, -volving** [T] **1** [*in, with*] to cause (someone) to become connected or concerned: *Don't involve other*

people in your mistakes. **2** [+*v-ing*] to have as a part or result: *Taking the job involves living abroad.* **–involvement** n [U]

in·volved /ɪnˈvɑlvd/ adj **1** difficult to understand; COMPLICATED **2** [*with*] (of a person) closely connected in relationships and activities with others, esp. in a personal or sexual way: *They are deeply involved with each other.*

in·ward¹ /ˈɪnwərd/ adj **1** on or towards the inside **2** of the mind or spirit: *inward peace* **–opposite outward –inwardly** adv: *inwardly happy*

inward² ‖also **inwards** esp. BrE– adv towards the inside **–opposite outward**

i·o·dine, -din /ˈaɪəˌdaɪn, -dɪn/ n [U] a simple substance (ELEMENT (1)) that is used in photography, and on wounds to prevent infection

i·on /ˈaɪən, ˈaɪɑn/ n an atom which has been given (+) POSITIVE¹ or (-) NEGATIVE¹ force by the taking away or addition of an ELECTRON

i·o·ta /aɪˈoʷtə/ n [S] (only used in NEGATIVEs², questions, etc.) a very small amount: *There's not an iota of truth in that.*

IOU /ˌaɪ oʷ ˈyuʷ/ abbrev. for: "I owe you"; a piece of paper saying that one owes a certain amount of money to someone else, with one's signature at the bottom: *I can't give you the money now; can I give you an IOU for $25?*

IPA /ˌaɪ piʸ ˈeʸ/ abbrev. for: International PHONETIC Alphabet; a system of signs used for representing speech sounds

IQ /ˌaɪ ˈkyuʷ/ abbrev. for: intelligence quotient; a measure of INTELLIGENCE (1), with 100 as the average: *a very high IQ*

i·ras·ci·ble /ɪˈræsəbəl, aɪ-/ adj (of a person) tending to get angry **–irascibly** adv **–irascibility** /ɪˌræsəˈbɪləti ʸ, aɪ-/ n [U]

i·rate /ˌaɪˈreʸt◂/ adj fml angry: *an irate letter* **–irately** adv

ir·i·des·cent /ˌɪrəˈdɛsənt/ adj lit showing changing colors as light falls on it: *iridescent soap bubbles* **–iridescence** n [U]

i·ris /ˈaɪrɪs/ n **1** the round, colored part of the eye **2** a tall yellow or purple flower with large leaves

irk /ɜrk/ v [T] to annoy; trouble: *It irks him to have to clean his house.*

irk·some /ˈɜrksəm/ adj troublesome; annoying

i·ron¹ /ˈaɪərn/ n **1** [U] a very common and useful metal that is a simple substance (ELEMENT (1)), is used in the making of steel, and is found in very small quantities in certain foods and in the blood **2** [C] a heavy flat-bottomed object with a handle on top, which is heated and used for making clothing and cloth smooth **3** [A] of great strength (of character); unyielding: *an iron will*

iron² v [T] to make (clothes) smooth with an IRON¹ (2): *I've been (doing the) ironing all day.*|*Would you like to iron my shirt for you?*

iron sthg. ↔ out adv [T] infml to remove or find an answer to: *to iron out the difficulties*

Iron Cur·tain /ˌ·· ˈ··/ n sometimes derog for: the western border between the USSR (and other COMMUNIST countries) and the rest of the world, which cannot be easily crossed for purposes of trade, the exchange of information, travel, etc. (note the phrase **behind the Iron Curtain**)

i·ron·ic /aɪˈrɒnɪk/ also **ironical**– /aɪˈrɒnɪkəl/ adj expressing IRONY –**ironically** adv: He smiled ironically.

ironing board /ˈ··· ,·/ n a long narrow table on which clothes are spread to be made smooth (IRONED)

iron lung /, ·· ˈ·/ n a machine fitted over the body which helps a person to breathe

i·rons /ˈaɪərnz/ n [P] chains to keep a prisoner from moving

i·ro·ny /ˈaɪrəniʸ, ˈaɪərniʸ/ n -nies **1** [U] (amusing) use of words which are clearly opposite to one's meaning (as by saying "This is beautiful weather" when the weather is bad) **2** [C;U] a course of events or a condition which has the opposite result from what is expected, usu. a bad result: life's little ironies

ir·ra·tion·al /ɪˈræʃənəl/ adj **1** (of people and their acts) not (done by) using reason; against reasonable behavior **2** (of living things) not RATIONAL; without power to reason –**irrationally** adv

ir·rec·on·cil·a·ble /ɪˌrekənˈsaɪləbəl, ɪˈrekən ˌsaɪ-/ adj (of people and their acts) which cannot be brought into agreement –**irreconcilably** adv

ir·re·fut·a·ble /ɪˈrefyətəbəl, ˌɪrɪˈfyuʷtə-/ adj too strong to be disproved: an irrefutable argument –see also REFUTABLE –**irrefutably** adv

ir·reg·u·lar /ɪˈregyələr/ adj **1** (of shape) not regularly; having different-sized parts; uneven; not level **2** (of time) at unevenly separated points; not equal **3** not according to the usual rules, habits, etc. **4** (in grammar) not following the usual pattern: an irregular verb –**irregularly** adv –**irregularity** /ɪˌregyə ˈlærətiʸ/ n -ties [C;U]

ir·rel·e·vance /ɪˈreləvəns/ also **irrelevancy**– /ɪˈreləvənsiʸ/ n -cies **1** [U] the state of being IRRELEVANT **2** [C] a remark or fact which is IRRELEVANT

ir·rel·e·vant /ɪˈreləvənt/ adj not RELEVANT; not having any real connection with or relation to something else: If he can do the job well, his age is irrelevant. (=does not matter) –**irrelevantly** adv

ir·rep·a·ra·ble /ɪˈrepərəbəl/ adj which is too bad to be repaired or put right: The flood did irreparable damage to the house. –**irreparably** adv

ir·re·place·a·ble /ˌɪrɪˈpleʸsəbəl/ adj too special or unusual to be REPLACEd (2)

ir·re·press·i·ble /ˌɪrɪˈpresəbəl/ adj too strong or forceful to be held back: irrepressible high spirits –**irrepressibly** adv

ir·re·proach·a·ble /ˌɪrɪˈproʷtʃəbəl/ adj (of people and their acts) without blame; faultless –**irreproachably** adv

ir·re·sist·i·ble /ˌɪrɪˈzɪstəbəl/ adj too strong, powerful, pleasant, etc., to be RESISTed: an irresistible argument/force –**irresistibly** adv

ir·re·spec·tive of /ˌɪrɪˈspektɪv əv/ prep without regard to: They send information every week, irrespective of whether it's useful or not.

ir·re·spon·si·ble /ˌɪrɪˈspɒnsəbəl/ adj (of people and their acts) not RESPONSIBLE; showing lack of ability to behave carefully, think of the effect of actions on others, etc. His behavior was very irresponsible; he might have hurt somebody. –**irresponsibly** adv –**irresponsibility** /ˌɪrɪˌspɒnsəˈbɪlətiʸ/ n [U]

ir·rev·er·ent /ɪˈrevərənt/ adj (of people and their acts) showing lack of respect, esp. for religion –**irreverence** n [U] –**irreverently** adv

ir·rev·o·ca·ble /ɪˈrevəkəbəl/ adj that cannot be changed: an irrevocable decision –**irrevocably** adv

ir·ri·gate /ˈɪrəˌgeʸt/ v -gated, -gating [T] to supply water to (dry land) esp. by providing it with man-made streams (CANALs) –**irrigation** /ˌɪrəˈgeʸʃən/ n [U]

ir·ri·ta·ble /ˈɪrətəbəl/ adj easily made angry by small things –**irritably** adv –**irritability** /ˌɪrətəˈbɪlətiʸ/ n [U]

ir·ri·tant /ˈɪrətənt/ n,adj [A;C] (a substance) which IRRITATEs (2)

ir·ri·tate /ˈɪrəˌteʸt/ v -tated, -tating [T] **1** to make angry or excite in an unpleasant way –see ANGRY (USAGE) **2** to make painful and sore: Wool irritates my skin. –**irritation** /ˌɪrəˈteʸʃən/ n

is /s, z, əz; strong ɪz/ v third person sing. present of BE

Is·lam /ɪsˈlɑm, ˈɪslɑm, -ləm, ˈɪz-/ n (the people and countries that practice) the Muslim religion, started by Mohammed –**Islamic** /ɪsˈlɑmɪk, -ˈlæ-, ɪz-/ adj

is·land /ˈaɪlənd/ n **1** a piece of land surrounded by water: Manhattan is an island|(fig.) an island of pleasure among the sorrows of life **2** also **traffic island**||also **safety island** AmE– a raised place in the middle of the road where people crossing can wait for traffic to pass

isle /aɪl/ n lit an island

is·n't /ˈɪzənt/ v short for: is not: Today isn't Monday. It's Tuesday.

i·so·late /ˈaɪsəˌleʸt/ v -lated, -lating [T] to keep apart or separate from others: Several towns have been isolated by the floods. –**isolation** /ˌaɪsəˈleʸʃən/ n [U]: Living in complete isolation in the country

i·so·lat·ed /ˈaɪsəˌleʸtɪd/ adj standing alone; the only one of its type: On one isolated occasion I saw him laugh.|an isolated farmhouse

is·sue¹ /ˈɪʃuʷ/ n **1** [U] the act of coming out or bringing out something: I bought the book the day after its issue. **2** [C] something, esp. something printed, brought or given out: There's a new issue of Christmas stamps every year. **3** [C] an important matter: The real issue is . . . **4** [U +sing./pl. v] old use and law children: He died without issue. **5 at issue** of importance; under consideration

is·sue² v -sued, -suing [T] **1** to bring out (esp.

SPELLING NOTE

Words with the sound /aɪ/ may be spelled **e-**, like **eye**, or **ai-**, like **aisle**.

something printed and/or official) for the notice of the public **2** [*to*] to supply or provide officially: *They issued guns to the soldiers.*

issue from sthg. *v prep* [T] to come or result from: *His difficulties issue from his lack of knowledge.*

isth·mus /'ısməs/ *n* a narrow area of land which joins two larger land masses

it /ıt/ *pron* (*used as subject or object*) **1 a** that thing, group, idea, etc., already mentioned: *"Whose coat is this?" "It's mine."|"Where's my dinner?" "The cat ate it."|The government has become very unpopular since it was elected.|They were all shouting. It* (=the shouting) *was terrible!* **b** (used of a person or animal whose sex is unknown or not thought to be important): *What a beautiful baby; is it a boy or a girl?* **2** that person: *"Who's that?" "It's me!"/"It's Harry!"/"It's the mailman!"* **3** (used in statements, esp. about weather time, or distance, as a meaningless subject or object: *It's raining.|It's Thursday.|It's a four hour drive from New York to Boston.|It's my turn.|If it weren't for the snow,* (=if there were no snow) *we could climb the mountain.* **4** (used in sentences where the real subject comes later): *It's fun being a singer.* (=Being a singer is fun.)*|It's no use worrying.|It's a pity that you forgot.|It seems that she lost her way.* **5** (used with the verb *be*, to make part of a sentence more important): *It was John who told me.* (=John told me, not Peter)*|It was yesterday that he told me.* (=not today) **6 that's it: a** there's nothing more to come: *You can have a boiled egg and that's it.* **b** that's right: *Hold the ladder for me; that's it!*

i·tal·ics /ı'tælıks, aı-/ *n* [P;U] (the style of) printing with small sloping letters: *This sentence is printed in italics.* –**italic** *adj*

itch¹ /ıtʃ/ *v* **1** [I] to feel or cause soreness which makes one want to SCRATCH: *The wound itches all the time.|I itch all over.* **2** [T] *infml* to have a desire to do something soon:

I'm itching to go.|He seems to be itching for a fight.

itch² *n* **1** a sore feeling which makes one want to rub or SCRATCH the skin **2** a strong desire –**itchy** *adj* **-ier, -iest** –**itchiness** *n* [U]

it'd /'ıtəd/ *short for:* **1** it would: *It'd be all right if I had enough money.* **2** it had: *It'd been raining earlier that morning.*

i·tem /'aıtəm/ *n* **1** a single thing among a set or on a list **2** also **news item**– a piece of news in a newspaper

i·tem·ize ‖also **-ise** *BrE* /'aıtə,maız/ *n* **-ized, -izing** [T] to set out all the details of (each ITEM): *an itemized bill*

i·tin·er·ant /aı'tınərənt/ *adj* [A] traveling from place to place: *an itinerant judge*

i·tin·er·ar·y /aı'tınə,reriy/ *n* **-ies** a plan of a journey

it'll /'ıtḷ/ *short for:* **1** it will: *It'll rain.* **2** it shall

its /ıts/ *determiner* (*possessive form of* IT) of that thing, animal, etc., already mentioned: *The cat drank its milk and washed its ears.*

it's /ıts/ *short for:* **1** it is: *It's raining.* **2** it has: *It's rained.*

it·self /ıt'sɛlf/ *pron* **1** (used as the object of a verb, or after a PREPOSITION, when the same thing or creature does the action and is the object of the action): *The cat's washing itself.|The city government has made itself unpopular.* **2** (used to make *it*, or the name of a thing or creature, stronger): *We won't buy new tires when the car itself is so old.* **3 in itself** without considering the rest; as such

IUD /,aı yuwʷ 'diʸ/ *abbrev. for:* intrauterine device; an object placed in the childbearing organ of a woman to prevent her from having children

I've /aıv/ *short for:* I have: *I've been here before.|I've got lots of time.|(BrE) I've lots of time.*

i·vo·ry /'aıvəriʸ/ *n* [U] (the color of) a hard white substance, of which elephants' TUSKs are made

i·vy /'aıviʸ/ *n* [U] a climbing plant with shiny three- or five-pointed leaves

J, j

SPELLING NOTE
Words with the sound /dʒ/ may be spelled **g-**, like **general**

J, j /dʒeʸ/ **J's, j's** *or* **Js, js** the 10th letter of the English alphabet

jab¹ /dʒæb/ *v* **-bb-** [I;T *away, at*] to push (something pointed); strike quick blows: *He jabbed his stick into the ground.|The fighters jabbed (away) at each other for a long time.*

jab² *n* **1** a sudden forceful push or blow **2** *infml* for INJECTION

jab·ber /'dʒæbər/ *v* [I;T] to talk or say (something) quickly and not clearly: *I can't understand you if you keep jabbering (away) like that.* –**jabber** *n* [S;U]

jack¹ /dʒæk/ *n* **1** an apparatus for lifting a heavy weight, such as a car, off the ground **2** also **knave** –a playing card with a picture of a man on it –see CARDS (USAGE)

jack² *v* → JACK UP

jack·al /'dʒækəl/ *n* **-als** *or* **-al** a wild animal of the dog family

jack·daw /'dʒækdɔ/ *n* a bird of the CROW family, believed to steal small bright objects

jack·et /'dʒækıt/ *n* **1** a short coat with SLEEVES (1) –see illustration on page 123 **2** the skin of a potato: *potatoes cooked in their jackets* **3** an outer cover for certain machines or engines that get very hot **4** → DUST JACKET **5** *AmE* for SLEEVE (2)

jack-in-the-box /'· · · ,·/ *n* a children's toy which is a box from which an amusing figure jumps when the top is opened

jack knife /'· ·/ *n* **jack knives** a usu. large folding pocket knife

jack-knife *v* **-knifed, -knifing** [I] (esp. of an ARTICULATEd vehicle) to bend suddenly in the middle as in an accident

jack-of-all-trades /,· ·' ·, ·, , ' ·' ·/ *n* **jacks-of-all-trades** (*sometimes cap.*) a person who can do many different kinds of work

jack·pot /'dʒækpɒt/ *n* **1** the biggest amount of money to be won in a game of cards or chance **2 hit the jackpot** *infml* to win the JACKPOT, or have a big success

jack sthg.↔ **up** *v adv* [T] to lift with a JACK (1): *Jack up the car.*

jade /dʒeʸd/ *n* [U] (the color of) a precious usu. green stone from which ornaments and jewelery are made

jad·ed /'dʒeʸdɪd/ *adj* tired because of having had too much of something

jag·ged /'dʒægɪd/ *adj* having a rough uneven edge –**jaggedly** *adv*

jag·uar /'dʒægwɑr, 'dʒægyuʷˌɑr/ *n* a large spotted wild cat of Central and South America

jail¹ ‖also **gaol** *BrE* /dʒeʸl/ *n* [C;U] a prison or place where criminals are kept as part of their punishment

jail² ‖also **gaol** *BrE* *v* [T] to put in JAIL¹

jail·er , jailor ‖also **gaoler** *BrE* /'dʒeʸlər/ *n* a person who is in charge of a prison or prisoners

ja·lop·y /dʒə'lɑpiʸ/ *n* **-ies** *humor* a worn-out old car

jam¹ /dʒæm/ *n* [U] fruit boiled and preserved in sugar and used esp. for spreading on bread –compare JELLY (1b)

jam² *v* **-mm- 1** [T *together*] to pack or crush tightly: *I can't jam another thing into this bag.|The crowds jammed the streets, and no cars could pass.* **2** [T] to push forcefully and suddenly: *She jammed the top of the box down on my finger.|I jammed on the brakes/jammed the brakes on.* **3** [I *up*] (of parts of machines) to get stuck **4** [T] to block (radio messages) by broadcasting noise

jam³ *n* **1** a mass of people or things JAMMED so close together that movement is difficult or impossible: *a traffic jam* **2 get into/be in a jam** *infml* in trouble

jamb /dʒæm/ *n* a side post of a door or window

jam·bo·ree /,dʒæmbə'riʸ/ *n* a happy party or gathering, esp. of BOY SCOUTS

jam-packed /,· '· ◀/ *adj* [*with*] *infml* with many people or things very close together; very CROWDED

jan·gle /'dʒæŋgəl/ *v* **-gled, -gling** [I;T] to (cause to) make a sharp unpleasant sound, as of metal striking against metal: *The bell jangled.*

jan·i·tor /'dʒænətər/ *n* *AmE*‖**caretaker** *BrE*– a person who is employed to take care of a building

---

SPELLING NOTE

Words with the sound /dʒ/ may be spelled **g-**, like **general**

Jan·u·ar·y /'dʒænyuʷˌɛriʸ/ *n* **-ies** also **Jan.** *written abbrev.* the first month of the year

jar¹ /dʒɑr/ *n* (the contents of) a short-necked wide-mouthed pot made of glass, stone, clay, etc.: *a jar of juice* –see illustration on page 683

jar² *v* **-rr- 1** [I *on*] to make an unpleasant sound **2** [T] to give an unpleasant shock to: *The fall jarred every bone in my body.* **3** [I *with*] to go badly together: *jarring opinions/colors*

jar³ *n* (something that causes) an unpleasant shock

jar·gon /'dʒɑrgən/ *n* [C;U] *often derog* language that is hard to understand, esp. because it is full of words known only to the members of a certain group

jaun·dice /'dʒɔndɪs, 'dʒɑn-/ *n* [U] a disease that causes a yellowness of the skin, the white part of the eyes, etc.

jaun·diced /'dʒɔndɪst, 'dʒɑn-/ *adj* **1** suffering from JAUNDICE **2** mistrustful; tending to judge others unfavorably: *He has rather jaundiced opinions about all these modern ideas.*

jaunt /dʒɔnt, dʒɑnt/ *n,v* [I;C *about, around*] (to go on) a short journey, usu. for pleasure

jaun·ty /'dʒɔntiʸ, 'dʒɑn-/ *adj* **-tier, -tiest** (showing that one feels) satisfied with oneself and pleased with life: *a jaunty wave of the hand* –**jauntily** *adv* –**jauntiness** *n* [U]

jav·e·lin /'dʒævəlɪn/ *n* a light spear for throwing, esp. in sport

jaw /dʒɔ/ *n* one of the two bony parts of the face in which the teeth are set: *the upper/lower jaw*

jay /dʒeʸ/ *n* a noisy brightly-colored bird of the CROW family

jay·walk /'dʒeʸwɔk/ *v* [I] to cross streets in a careless and dangerous way –**jaywalker** *n*

jazz /dʒæz/ *n* [U] music originated by black Americans, usu. with some free playing by each musician in the band

jazz sthg.↔ **up** *v adv* [T] *infml* to make more active, bright, or enjoyable: *to jazz up the room with some bright red curtains*

jazz·y /'dʒæziʸ/ *adj* **-ier, -iest** *infml* **1** like JAZZ music **2** attracting attention, as with bright loud colors: *a very jazzy dress* –**jazzily** *adv*

jeal·ous /'dʒɛləs/ *adj* [*of*] *often derog* **1** wanting to keep what one has; POSSESSIVE: *He is jealous of his possessions/of his wife's love.* **2** wanting to get what someone else has; ENVIOUS: *He is jealous of their success.* –**jealously** *adv* : *The dog jealously guarded its bone.*

USAGE **Jealousy** is a stronger and more unpleasant feeling than **envy**. Compare: *Peter's new job sounds very nice –I'm envious/full of envy/I envy him* (=I wish I had a job like his). *Jane is full of jealousy/is jealous of Peter* (=feels a strong dislike for him) *because she thinks she should have gotten the job instead of him.*

jeal·ous·y /'dʒɛləsiʸ/ *n* **-ies** [C;U] (a) JEALOUS feeling

jeans /dʒiʸnz/ *n* [P] pants made of a strong, usu. blue, cotton cloth, worn informally –see PAIR¹ (USAGE)

jeep /dʒiˑyp/ n a small car suitable for travelling over rough ground: *to cross the desert by jeep*

jeer /dʒɪər/ v [I;T] to laugh rudely (at): *The crowd jeered (at) the prisoners.* –**jeer** n

jell /dʒel/ v [I] **1** also **gel** –to become firmer, like JELLY **2** to take a clear shape

jel·ly /'dʒeliˑy/ n -**lies 1** [C;U] a soft food made **a** with GELATIN: *an orange jelly* **b** out of fruit juice boiled with sugar, so as to become clear, and used for spreading on bread: *apple jelly* –compare JAM¹ **2** [S;U] any material that is between a liquid and a solid state

jel·ly·fish /'dʒeliˑy,fɪʃ/ n -**fish** or -**fishes** a sea creature with a body like jelly

jem·my /'dʒemiˑy/ n -**mies** *BrE* for JIMMY

jeop·ard·ize ‖also -**ise** *BrE* /'dʒepər,daɪz/ v -**ized, -izing** [T] *fml* to put in danger: *If you are rude to the boss, it may jeopardize your chances of success.*

jeop·ard·y /'dʒepərdiˑy/ n [U] *fml* danger: *His foolish behavior may put his whole future in jeopardy.*

jerk¹ /dʒɜrk/ v **1** [T] to pull suddenly: *She jerked out the knife that was stuck in the wood.* **2** [I] to move with a JERK² or jerks: *The old bus jerked to a stop.*

jerk² n **1** a short quick pull or movement: *The knife was stuck, but she pulled it out with a jerk.* **2** *AmE derog infml* a foolish and ungraceful person: *You jerk! That was a terrible thing to say to me.* –**jerky** *adj* -**ier, -iest** –**jerkily** *adv*

jer·kin /'dʒɜrkɪn/ n a short coat, usu. SLEEVELESS

jer·ry-built /'dʒeriˑy ,bɪlt/ *adj derog* (esp. of houses) built quickly, cheaply, and not well

jer·sey /'dʒɜrziˑy/ n -**seys** a tight KNITted woolen garment for the upper part of the body

Je·ru·sa·lem ar·ti·choke /dʒə,ruˑwsələm 'ɑrtə ,tʃoʷk/ also **sunchoke** *AmE*– a plant with a potato-like root that may be eaten as a vegetable –see also ARTICHOKE

jest /dʒest/ v [I] *fml* to speak without serious intention; joke: *She always jests about her feelings towards him.* –**jest** n: *He said it in jest.* (=as a joke) –**jesting** *adj: a jesting person/remark*

jest·er /'dʒestər/ n a man kept in former times by a ruler to amuse him, tell jokes, etc.

jet¹ /dʒet/ n **1** a narrow stream of liquid, gas, etc., coming forcefully out of a small hole: *The firemen directed jets of water at the burning house.* **2** a narrow opening from which this is forced out: *Put a match to the gas jet to light the gas.* **3** an aircraft with a JET ENGINE: *traveling by jet*

jet² v -**tt-** [I;T *out*] to come or send out in a JET¹ (1): *The water jetted out.*

jet³ n [U] a hard black material, used, when polished, for making ornaments

jet-black /,· '· ◄/ *adj* of the color of JET³; very dark shiny black

jet en·gine /,· '··/ n an engine that pushes out a stream of hot air and gases behind it, and is used for making aircraft fly

jet-pro·pelled /,· ·'·◄/ *adj* (of a plane) pushed through the air by a JET ENGINE –**jet**

propulsion /,· ·'··/ n [U]

jet set /'· ·/ n [U] rich, successful, and fashionable people

jet·ti·son /'dʒetəsən, -zən/ v [T] to get rid of by throwing out

jet·ty /'dʒetiˑy/ n -**ties** a wall built out into water, used either for getting on and off ships or as a protection against the force of the waves

Jew /dʒuʷ/ n a member of a people, whose religion is JUDAISM, who lived in ancient times in the land of Israel, some of whom now live in the modern state of Israel and others in various countries throughout the world –**Jewish** *adj: the Jewish religion*

jew·el /'dʒuʷəl/ n **1** a precious stone **2** a decoration that contains one or more of these and is worn in clothes or on the body

jew·eled *AmE*‖**jewelled** *BrE* /'dʒuʷəld/ *adj* decorated with, or having, jewels

jew·el·er *AmE*‖**jeweller** *BrE* /'dʒuʷələr/ n a person who buys and sells jewels, watches, etc. containing jewels

jew·el·ry /'dʒuʷəlriˑy/ n [U] JEWELs (2)

jib /dʒɪb/ n a small sail

jibe¹ /dʒaɪb/ n → GIBE

jibe² v **jibed, jibing** [I] *infml* to agree with: *Your story doesn't jibe with the facts.*

jif·fy /'dʒɪfiˑy/ n [S] *infml* a moment: *I'll be ready in a jiffy.*

jig¹ /dʒɪg/ n (music for) a quick merry dance

jig² v -**gg- 1** [I] to dance a JIG¹ **2** [I;T] to (cause to) move with quick short movements up and down: *jigging the baby on his knee*

jig·ger /'dʒɪgər/ n **1** a measure used in mixing alcoholic drinks, usu. 1½ ounces **2** *infml esp. AmE* any small piece of apparatus: *Have you seen that jigger I fix the radio with?*

jig·gle /'dʒɪgəl/ v -**gled, -gling** [I;T] *infml* to (cause to) move from side to side with short quick light JERKs²: *Carry the cup carefully and don't jiggle it, or you'll spill the coffee.* –**jiggly** *adj* –**jiggle** n

jig·saw puz·zle /'dʒɪgsɔ ,pʌzəl/ also **jigsaw**– n a picture stuck onto wood and cut up into many small irregular pieces to be fitted together for amusement

jilt /dʒɪlt/ v [T] to refuse to see (a lover) anymore; unexpectedly refuse to marry (someone) after having promised to do so

jim crow /,dʒɪm 'kroʷ/ n [A] *AmE (often caps)* **1** the system of unfair treatment of black Americans: *Jim Crow laws* **2** for black Americans only, and usu. of poor quality: *Jim Crow schools/businesses*

jim·my *AmE*‖**jemmy** *BrE* /'dʒɪmiˑy/ n -**mies** an iron bar used esp. by thieves to break open doors, windows, etc.

jin·gle¹ /'dʒɪŋgəl/ v -**gled, -gling** [I;T] to (cause to) sound with a JINGLE² (1): *He jingled the money in his pocket.*

jingle² n **1** a repeated sound as of small bells ringing or light metal objects striking against each other **2** a simple poem with a very regular beat, usu. of poor quality, esp. as a radio or TV advertisement

jinx¹ /dʒɪŋks/ n something that brings bad luck; a curse: *There seems to be a jinx on our team, because we always lose.*

jinx² *v* [T] *infml* to bring bad luck to

jit·ters /'dʒɪtərz/ *n* [*the* P] *infml* anxiety before an event: *I've got the jitters about that examination.* –**jittery** /'dʒɪtəriʸ/ *adj*

jive /dʒaɪv/ *n* [U] **1** (dancing performed to) a type of popular music with a strong regular beat **2** *AmE infml* deceiving or foolish talk

job /dʒɑb/ *n* **1** regular paid employment: *She has a good job in a bank.|She's been out of a job* (=unemployed) *for months.* **2** a piece of work: *I've got a job for you: wash these dishes.* **3** something hard to do; difficulty: *It was a (real) job to see the teacher.* **4** a dishonest or harmful piece of work, esp. robbery: *He's in prison for pulling a job at the bank.* **5 on the job** (of people or, sometimes, machines) at work, working, busy

USAGE What you do to earn your living is your **job**, your **work**, or (more formal) your **occupation**: *Do you like your job?|Please state your name, age, and occupation on the form.* **Post** and **position** are more formal (words for a particular job): *Please send me details of the post/position which is advertised in today's paper.* A skilled job in which you use your hands is a **trade**: *She's an electrician by trade.* And a job for which you need special training and a high level of education (such as being a doctor or lawyer) is a **profession**. Some professions, such as teaching, nursing, and the Church, are also called **vocations**, which suggests that people do them in order to help others. A **career** is a job or profession that you follow for your whole life. *Her political career began when she was elected to the Senate 20 years ago.* –see WORK¹ (USAGE)

job lot /'· ·/ *n* a group of things of different kinds, bought or sold together

jock /dʒɑk/ *n infml* **1** an athlete **2** → JOCKSTRAP

jock·ey¹ /'dʒɑkiʸ/ *n* **-eys** a person who rides in horse races, esp. professionally

jockey² *v* **-eyed, -eying** to get (someone to do something or into a certain position) by skillful tricks: *Mary jockeyed for a good position in her company.*

jock·strap /'dʒɑkstræp/ also **jock–** *n* a tight fitting undergarment for supporting the sex organs, worn by men taking part in sports

joc·u·lar /'dʒɑkyələr/ *adj fml* meaning to cause laughter: *a jocular reply/person* –**jocularly** *adv* –**jocularity** /ˌdʒɑkyə'lærətiʸ/ *n* **-ties** [C;U]

joc·und /'dʒɑkənd, 'dʒoʷ-/ *adj lit* merry; cheerful –**jocundity** /dʒoʷ'kʌndətiʸ/ *n* [U]

jog¹ /dʒɑg/ *v* **-gg- 1** [T] to give a slight push or knock with the arm, hand, etc.: *You jogged my elbow and spoiled what I was drawing.* **2** [I] to move slowly and unsteadily: *The carriage jogged along on the rough road.* **3** [I] to run slowly and steadily: *I go jogging in the park before breakfast.* –see WALK (USAGE)

SPELLING NOTE

Words with the sound /dʒ/ may be spelled **g-**, like **general**

---

4 jog someone's memory to make someone remember

jog² *n* **1** a slight shake, push, or knock **2** a slow steady run

john /dʒɑn/ *n AmE infml* for BATHROOM

joie de vi·vre /ˌʒwɑ də 'viʸv, -'viʸvrə/ *n* [U] the joy of life

join /dʒɔɪn/ *v* **1** [I;T *to, together, up*] to come or bring together; connect (with); unite: *Join this pipe to the other one.|Join the two ends of the rope together.|Where do the two roads join (up)?|to join two people in marriage* **2** [I;T *in*] to take part together (with): *Will you join me in a drink?* (=have a drink with me)|*Sarah never joins in; she always plays on her own.* **3** [T] to become a member of: *to join the army/the Democratic party* **4 join forces (with)** to come together or unite for a common purpose

join up *v adv* [I] to enter military service; esp. by one's own choice

joint¹ /dʒɔɪnt/ *n* **1** a place where things (esp. bones) join **2** *BrE* for ROAST² (1) **3** *infml derog & humor* a public place, esp. one where people go for amusement **4** *infml* a cigarette containing the drug CANNABIS **5 put someone's nose out of joint** *infml* to annoy someone by saying or doing something that offends them **6 out of joint** (of a joint of the body) out of the proper position

joint² *adj* [A] shared by two or more people: *to take joint action |joint owners* –**jointly** *adv*

joist /dʒɔɪst/ *n* one of the beams onto which a floor is fixed

joke¹ /dʒoʷk/ *n* **1** anything said or done to cause laughter or amusement: *I was laughing because she just told me a very funny joke.|Your bad behavior has gone beyond a joke.* (=has become too serious to laugh at) **2 no joke** *infml* a serious or difficult matter: *It was no joke carrying those heavy bags.* **3 play a joke on someone** to do something to make other people laugh at someone –see also PRACTICAL JOKE

joke² *v* **joked, joking** [I *with, about*] to tell jokes: *Don't joke with him about religion.|joking remarks* –**jokingly** *adv*: *I'm sure his remarks were meant jokingly.*

jok·er /'dʒoʷkər/ *n* **1** a person who likes to make jokes **2** an additional playing card, which in some games may have any value

jol·ly¹ /'dʒɑliʸ/ *adj* **-lier, -liest** merry; happy; pleasant: *a jolly person/laugh* –**jollity** /'dʒɑlətiʸ/ *n* [U]

jolly² *v* **-lied, -lying** [T] *infml* to make (someone) willing or eager (to do something); urge gently: *They jollied her into going with them.*

Jolly Rog·er /ˌdʒɑliʸ 'rɑdʒər/ *n* the flag of a PIRATE of former times, showing a SKULL and bones crossed under it

jolt /dʒoʷlt/ *v* [I;T] to (cause to) shake or be shocked: *The cart jolted (along) over the rough road.|Her angry words jolted him out of the belief that she loved him.* –**jolt** *n*

jon·quil /'dʒɑŋkwɪl/ *n* a type of sweet-smelling spring flower of the NARCISSUS family

josh /dʒɑʃ/ *v* [I] *AmE infml* **1** to joke **2** [T] to make fun of, without wanting to hurt: *His* *friends joshed him about his wish to become mayor.*

jos·tle /'dʒɑsəl/ v **-tled, -tling** [I;T] (of a person) to knock or push against (someone): *Don't jostle (against) me.*

jot¹ /dʒɑt/ n [S] a very small amount; a bit: *not a jot of truth in it*

jot² v **-tt-** [T *down*] to write quickly, esp. without preparation

jour·nal /'dʒɜrnl/ n **1** a DIARY **2** a magazine, esp. of a particular group, association, etc.: *She's reading the Canadian Medical Journal.*

jour·nal·ism /'dʒɜrnl,ɪzəm/ n [U] the profession of producing, esp. writing for, newspapers or magazines **–journalistic** /,dʒɜrnl'ɪstɪk/ adj

jour·nal·ist /'dʒɜrnl-ɪst/ n a person whose profession is JOURNALISM

jour·ney¹ /'dʒɜrniʸ/ n **-neys** a trip of some distance, usu. by land: *He's going on/making a long journey.|They broke (=interrupted) their journey by spending the night in a hotel.* –see TRAVEL² (USAGE)

journey² v **-neyed, -neying** [I] *lit* to travel: *She's journeyed all over the world.*

joust /dʒaʊst/ v [I *with*] (in former times) to fight on horseback with LANCEs as sport

jo·vi·al /'dʒoʷviʸəl/ adj full of good humor; friendly: *a jovial old man/voice* **–jovially** adv **–joviality** /,dʒoʷviʸ'æləti̯ʸ/ n [U]

jowl /dʒaʊl/ n the lower part of the side of the face, esp. loose skin and flesh near the lower jaw

joy /dʒɔɪ/ n **1** [C;U] great happiness: *He was filled with joy.|To her parents' joy, she won first prize.|My children are a great joy to me.* **2 for joy** because of (feeling) joy: *He jumped for joy when he opened his present.*

joy·ful /'dʒɔɪfəl/ adj full of joy: *a joyful person/event* **–joyfully** adv **–joyfulness** n [U]

joy·less /'dʒɔɪlɪs/ adj without joy; unhappy **–joylessness** n [U]

joy·ous /'dʒɔɪəs/ adj lit full of or causing joy: *a joyous heart/event* **–joyously** adv **–joyousness** n [U]

joy·ride /'dʒɔɪraɪd/ n infml a ride for pleasure in a (stolen) vehicle, often with careless driving

joy·stick /'dʒɔɪ,stɪk/ n a stick whose movement directs the movement of an aircraft

J.P. n abbrev. for: Justice of the Peace; a person who gives judgments in a less important court of law

ju·bi·lant /'dʒuʷbələnt/ adj filled with or expressing great joy: *a jubilant person/shout* **–jubilantly** adv **–jubilation** /,dʒuʷbə'leɪʃən/ n [U]

ju·bi·lee /'dʒuʷbə,liʸ, ,dʒuʷbə'liʸ/ n a period of great rejoicing, esp. to mark or remember some event

Ju·da·ism /'dʒuʷdiʸ,ɪzəm, -deʸ-, -də-/ n [U] the religion and civilization of the Jews

judge¹ /dʒʌdʒ/ v **judged, judging** [I;T] **1** to act as a judge (in): *Who will judge the next case?|to judge horses* **2** [+*that*] to form or give an opinion about (someone or something): *Judge whether he's right or wrong.* –see also MISJUDGE

judge² n **1** [A;C] a public official who has the power to decide questions brought before a court of law: *a Judge of the Supreme Court* **2** [C] a person who has the right to make a decision, esp. in a competition **3** [C *of*] a person who has the knowledge and experience to give valuable opinions: *She's a good judge of wine.*

judg·ment, judgement /'dʒʌdʒmənt/ n **1** [C] an official decision given by a judge or a court of law: *The court passed (=gave)* **judgment on** *the prisoner.* **2** [C] an opinion: *to form a judgment* **3** [U] the ability to judge correctly: *an ERROR (=mistake) of judgment*

judgment day /'·· ,·/ also **last judgment, day of judgment–** n (*often cap.*) the day when God will judge everybody

ju·di·cial /dʒuʷ'dɪʃəl/ adj of a court of law, a judge, or his/her judgment –compare: *a* **judicial** *decision|a* **judicious** *(=wise) decision* **–judicially** adv

ju·di·ci·ar·y /dʒuʷ'dɪʃiʸ,eriʸ, -ʃəriʸ/ n **-ies** fml the judges (in law) considered as one group

ju·di·cious /dʒuʷ'dɪʃəs/ adj having or showing good judgment –opposite **injudicious**; compare JUDICIAL **–judiciously** adv **–judiciousness** n [U]

ju·do /'dʒuʷdoʷ/ n [U] a type of fighting from Asia based on holding and throwing the opponent

jug /dʒʌg/ n **1** also **pitcher** AmE– a pot for liquids with a handle and a lip for pouring **2** AmE a large deep container with a narrow opening, roughly made and often containing cheap WHISKEY, wine or CIDER (1) **3 jug wine** AmE cheap wine in a large jug

jug·ger·naut /'dʒʌgər,nɔt/ n a great force or object that destroys everything it meets

jug·gle /'dʒʌgəl/ v **-gled, -gling** [I;T *with*] **1** to keep (several objects) in the air at the same time by throwing them up quickly and catching them again **2** to play tricks (with): *He went to prison for juggling his firm's accounts.* **–juggler** n

juice /dʒuʷs/ n [C;U] **1** the liquid part of fruit, vegetables, and meat: *orange juice* **2** the liquid in certain parts of the body, esp. the stomach, that helps people and animals to use (DIGEST) food **3** infml anything that produces power, such as electricity, gasoline, etc.: *Turn on the juice and let's see if this radio works now.*

juic·y /'dʒuʷsiʸ/ adj **-ier, -iest** **1** having a lot of juice: *a juicy orange* **2** interesting, esp. because providing information about bad or improper behavior: *I want all the juicy details.* **–juiciness** n [U]

juke·box /'dʒuʷkbɑks/ n a machine which plays music (or records) when a coin is put into it

Ju·ly /dʒʊ'laɪ, dʒə-/ also **Jul.** written abbrev.– n **-lies** the seventh month of the year

jum·ble /'dʒʌmbəl/ v **-bled, -bling** [I;T] to mix in disorder: *Her books/thoughts (were) all jumbled (up/ together).* **–jumble** n [S *of*]

jum·bo /'dʒʌmboʷ/ also **jumbo-sized** /'·· ,·/– adj [A] larger than others of the same kind: *a jumbo* JET¹ (3)

jump[1] /dʒʌmp/ *v* **1** [I] to push oneself into the air by the force of one's legs; spring: *The horse jumped over the fence.|She jumped out of the window.|(fig.) He keeps jumping from one subject of conversation to another.* **2** [T] to spring over: *The dog jumped the stream.* **3** [I] to make a quick sudden anxious movement: *The noise of the gun made him jump.* **4** [I] (esp. of prices and quantities) to rise suddenly and sharply: *The price of oil jumped sharply in 1973.* **5 jump the gun** to start something (like a race) too soon **6 jump down someone's throat** *infml* to begin to disagree with someone before they have finished talking

jump at sthg. *v prep* [T] to be eager to accept: *She jumped at the chance to go abroad.*

jump[2] *n* **1** an act of jumping **2 be/stay one jump ahead** *infml* having an advantage over others by being in advance of them

jump·er /ˈdʒʌmpər/ *n AmE* a dress without SLEEVES, usu. worn over a BLOUSE

jump·y /ˈdʒʌmpiʸ/ *adj* **-ier, -iest** nervous: *I knew that something was going to happen, and I was very jumpy.* **–jumpily** *adv* **–jumpiness** *n* [U]

junc·tion /ˈdʒʌŋkʃən/ *n* an example or, usu., a place of joining, meeting, or uniting: *a railroad junction where lines from all over the country meet.*

junc·ture /ˈdʒʌŋktʃər/ *n fml* a state of affairs or point in time: **At this juncture** *in our nation's affairs, we need firm leadership.*

June /dʒuʷn/ also **Jun.** *written abbrev.– n* the sixth month of the year

jun·gle /ˈdʒʌŋgəl/ *n* [C;U] a tropical forest too thick to walk through easily: *jungle animals/birds|(fig.) the jungle of business/of the big city*

jun·ior /ˈdʒuʷnyər/ *n,adj* **1** [*to*] younger: *She is junior to me.|You are my junior.* **2** of lower rank or position: *a junior officer/minister* –compare SENIOR[1,2]; see MAJOR (USAGE) **3** *AmE* (of) a student in the third year of a high school or university course

Junior *n AmE* [after *n*] the younger: *John Smith Junior is the son of John Smith.*

junior col·lege /ˌ·· ˈ··/ *n* (in the US) a two-year school of higher education at which one can complete the first two years of a university education: *I went to the junior college for my first two years and then transferred to the University of California* –see also COMMUNITY COLLEGE

junk[1] /dʒʌŋk/ *n* [U] *infml* old useless things: *What will you pay me for all this old junk?*

junk[2] *n* a flat-bottomed Chinese sailing ship

jun·ket /ˈdʒʌŋkɪt/ *n,v AmE infml* (to go on) a trip or journey, esp. one made by a government official and paid for with government money: *That senator is always junketing/taking junkets to Europe.*

junk food /ˈ· ·/ *n infml* [U] food with little value to one's health

junk·ie, junky /ˈdʒʌŋkiʸ/ *n infml* a person who takes drugs, esp. HEROIN, as a habit

junk mail /ˈ· ·/ [U] *AmE derog* mail, usu. for advertising, that is sent to people even if they have not asked to receive it

jun·ta /ˈhʊntə, ˈdʒʌntə/ *n often derog* a (military) government that has come to power by force

Ju·pi·ter /ˈdʒuʷpətər/ *n* the largest PLANET of the group that includes the Earth, fifth in order from the sun

ju·ris·dic·tion /ˌdʒʊərəsˈdɪkʃən/ *n* [U] the right to use the power held by an official body, esp. a court of law: *The court can/cannot deal with this matter, as it is* **within/outside its jurisdiction.**

ju·ris·pru·dence /ˌdʒʊərəsˈpruʷdns/ *n* [U] *fml* the science or knowledge of law

ju·rist /ˈdʒʊərɪst/ *n fml* a person with a thorough knowledge of law

ju·ror /ˈdʒʊərər/ also **juryman** /ˈdʒʊəriʸmən/, **jurywoman** /-ˌwʊmən/ *fem. – n* a member of a JURY

ju·ry /ˈdʒʊəriʸ/ *n* **-ries 1** a group of usu. 12 people chosen to decide questions of fact in a court of law: *The jury has decided that the prisoner is guilty.* **2** a group of people chosen to judge a competition: *the jury of the Miss World competition*

just[1] /dʒʌst/ *adj* fair; in accordance with what is right and true: *a very just man|You have received a just reward/punishment.* **–opposite unjust –justly** *adv* **–justness** *n* [U]

just[2] /dʒəst; *strong* dʒʌst/ *adv* **1** exactly at that time or place; exactly: *He was just sitting here.|He came just as I was leaving.|That's just what I wanted.* (–compare *That's not quite what I wanted.*) **2** only a little bit; almost not; hardly: *The skirt comes just below my knees.|I can just lift it.* (=it is almost too heavy for me to lift) **3** only: *I don't want any dinner, just coffee.|Answer me; don't just stand there laughing.|Just listen to this!* (=used to make a command stronger) **4 just now: a** at this moment: *We're having dinner just now; come back later.* **b** a moment ago: *Paul telephoned just now; he wants some money.*

USAGE **Already, yet,** and **just** were formerly not used with the simple past tense when speaking of time. Expressions like: *I already saw him.|The bell just rang.|Did you eat yet?* are often used, but some teachers do not like them.

just about *adv* almost; very nearly: *They had just about won the game when they had to stop playing.*

jus·tice /ˈdʒʌstɪs/ *n* **1** [U] the quality of being just; rightness; fairness: *The justice of these remarks was clear to everyone.* **–opposite injustice 2** [U] the action or power of the law: *to bring a criminal to justice|a court of justice* **3** [C] *AmE* a judge (of a law court) **4 do justice to someone/do someone justice** to treat someone in a fair way

Justice of the Peace /ˌ·· ·· · ˈ·/ *n fml* → J.P.

jus·ti·fi·a·ble /ˈdʒʌstəˌfaɪəbəl, ˌdʒʌstəˈfaɪ-/ *adj* that can be justified (JUSTIFY) **–opposite**

unjustifiable **–justifiably** *adv*
jus·ti·fy /'dʒʌstə,faɪ/ *v* **-fied, -fying** [T +*v-ing/to*] to be or give a good reason for: *How can you justify your rude behavior?* **–justification** /,dʒʌstəfə'keʸʃən/ *n* [U] **–justified** /'dʒʌstə,faɪd/ *adj*: *Is he justified in his behavior?*
jute /dʒuʷt/ *n* [U] a substance from a plant used for making rope and rough cloth
jut out /dʒʌt/ *v adv* **-tt-** [I] to be in a position

further forward than its surroundings: *The wall juts out here to allow room for the chimney.*
ju·ve·nile¹ /'dʒuʷvə,naɪl, -nl/ *adj* of, like, by, or for young people: *juvenile books|a juvenile court*
juvenile² *n fml or tech* a young person
jux·ta·pose /'dʒʌkstə,poʷz, ,dʒʌkstə'poʷz/ *v* **-posed, -posing** [T] *fml* to place side by side or close together **–juxtaposition** /,dʒʌkstəpə'zɪʃən/ *n* [U]

K, k

K, k /keʸ/ **K's, k's** *or* **Ks, ks** the 11th letter of the English alphabet
ka·bob /kə'bɑb/ *n* → KEBAB
ka·lei·do·scope /kə'laɪdə,skoʷp/ *n* a tube fitted at one end with mirrors and pieces of colored glass which shows many colored patterns when turned: (fig.) *At sunset the sky became a kaleidoscope of colors.* **–kaleidoscopic** /kə,laɪdə'skɑpɪk/ *adj* **–kaleidoscopically** *adv*
kan·ga·roo /,kæŋgə'ruʷ/ *n* **-roos** an Australian animal which jumps along on its large back legs and which carries its young in a special pocket of flesh
ka·o·lin /'keʸəlɪn/ *n* [U] a fine white clay used for making cups, plates, etc., and also in medicine
kar·at /'kærət/ *n* → CARAT
ka·ra·te /kə'rɑṭiʸ/ *n* [U] an Asian style of fighting using blows with the hands and feet
kay·ak /'kaɪæk/ *n* a narrow covered boat, esp. as used by Eskimos
ke·bab, kabob, kebob /kə'bɑb/ *n* a dish of small pieces of meat cooked on a stick, sometimes with vegetables
keel /kiʸl/ *n* **1** a bar along the bottom of a boat from which the whole frame of the boat is built up **2 on an even keel** without any sudden changes; steady; steadily
keel o·ver *v adv* [I] to fall over sideways: *The ship keeled over in the storm.*
keen /kiʸn/ *adj* **1** (of the mind, the feelings, the five senses, etc.) good, strong, quick at understanding, deeply felt, etc.: *a keen mind|a keen desire|keen sight* **2** [+*to-v*] having a strong, active interest; eager: *a keen student of politics|keen competition for the job|(esp. BrE) She's keen on* (=very interested in) *football/passing the examination.* **3** sharp; with a fine cutting edge: *Careful with that knife: it's got a keen edge!* **–keenly** *adv* **–keenness** *n* [U]
keep¹ /kiʸp/ *v* **kept** /kɛpt/, **keeping 1** [T] to have without the need of returning: *You can keep it; I don't need it.|I gave him $5 for the*

food and told him to keep the change. **2** [T] to have for some time or for more time: *Please keep this for me until I come back for it.|These old clothes aren't worth keeping.* **3** [I;T +*v-ing*] to (cause to) stay, remain, or continue: *It's hard to keep warm in this cold weather.|Her sickness kept her in the hospital for six weeks.|He keeps (on) interrupting.* (=interrupts continually)|*Keep off the grass!* (=don't walk on it)|*Try to keep out of trouble.|The work is hard, but I'll keep at it until it's finished.* **4** [T] to know (a secret) without telling: *She kept his secret for 15 years.* **5** [T] to make regular written records of or in: *Keep an account of what you spend.|I've always kept a* DIARY. **6** [T] to take care of and provide with food, money, etc.: *She kept her brother's children when he died.* **7** [T *from*] *fml* to guard; protect: *May God keep you (from harm)!* **8** [T] to own (and make money from): *She keeps chickens.* **9** [I] (of food) to remain fresh and fit to eat: (fig.) *"I've got something to tell you." "Won't it keep until later?"* **10** [I;T *from*] to hold back; delay or prevent: *You're late; what kept you?|I know you're busy; I won't keep you.|Can't you keep your dog from coming into my yard?* **11** [T] to fulfil: *She kept her promise/appointment.* **12 keep one's head** to remain calm **13 keep someone company** to remain with someone: *I don't want to be alone; will you keep me company?*

keep sthg.↔ **back** *v adv* [T] not to tell or give; WITHHOLD: *She told us most of the story but kept back the part about her uncle.*

keep sbdy./sthg.↔ **down** *v adv* [T] **1** to control; prevent from increasing: *Chemicals are used for keeping insects down.* **2** to keep in a state like slavery; OPPRESS (1)

keep on *v adv* [I;T] (=**keep on** sthg.) +*v-ing*) to continue (doing something): *Prices keep on increasing.*

keep out *v adv* [I;T] (=**keep** sbdy./sthg.↔ **out**) *of*] to (cause to) remain outside: *Warm clothing will keep out the cold.*

keep to *v prep* [T] **1** (**keep to** sthg.) to move, or stay in (a certain position): *Traffic in Britain keeps to the left.|He kept to his room.* **2** (**keep to** sthg.) to limit oneself to: *keep to the subject* **3** to keep (**keep** sthg. **to** sbdy.) private to (oneself): *He kept the news to him-*

self.|*She doesn't go out much; she likes to* **keep to herself.**

keep up *v adv* **1** [T] (**keep** sthg. ↔ **up**) to cause to remain high: *a belt to keep my pants up*|(fig.) *She kept up her spirits by singing.* **2** [T] (**keep** sthg.↔ **up**) to keep in good condition: *How do you keep up this large house?* **3** [I;T] (=**keep up** sthg.) to continue: *Keep up the good work.*|*Will the warm weather keep up?* **4** [I;T] (=**keep** sbdy. **up**) to (cause to) remain out of bed: *I hope I'm not keeping you up.* **5** [I *with*] to remain level: *I had to run to keep up (with the girls).* **6 keep up with the Joneses** *derog* to stay level with social changes; compete with one's neighbors socially

keep² *n* **1** [U] (the cost of providing) necessary goods and services, esp. food and lodgings: *He doesn't do enough to* **earn his keep. 2** [C] a great tower of a castle

keep·er /'kiʸpər/ *n* a person who guards, protects, or looks after: *The keeper is feeding the animals.*|*shopkeeper*|*doorkeeper*

keep·ing /'kiʸpɪŋ/ *n* [U] **1** care or charge: *Don't worry; your jewels are* **in safe keeping.** (=being guarded carefully) **2 out of/in keeping (with** something**)** not in/in agreement (with something): *Her words and her actions are out of keeping (with each other).*

keep·sake /'kiʸpseʸk/ *n* something, usu. small, given to be kept in memory of the giver

keg /kɛg/ *n* a small barrel

ken·nel¹ /'kɛnl/ *n AmE* a place where small animals, esp. dogs, are looked after while their owners are away

kennel² *v* **-l-** *AmE*‖**-ll-** *BrE* [T] to keep or put in a KENNEL¹

kept /kɛpt/ *v past tense and past participle of* KEEP

kerb /kɜrb/ *BrE for* CURB

ker·chief /'kɜrtʃɪf/ *n old use* a square piece of cloth worn (usu. by women) to cover the head, neck, etc.

ker·nel /'kɜrnl/ *n* **1** the part, usu. eatable, of a nut, fruit stone, or seed inside its hard covering or shell **2** the important or main part of something, often surrounded by unimportant or untrue matter

ker·o·sene, -sine /'kɛrəˌsiʸn, ˌkɛrə'siʸn/ *AmE*‖ **paraffin** *BrE*– *n* [U] an oil made from PETROLEUM, coal, etc., burned for heat and in lamps for light

ketch·up ‖also **catsup** *AmE* /'kɛtʃəp, 'kæ-/ *n* [U] a thick red sour liquid made from TOMATOes, used for giving a special taste to food

ket·tle /'kɛtl/ *n* a metal pot with a lid, a handle, and a SPOUT (=a narrow curved mouth for pouring), used mainly for boiling water –see illustration on page 379

ket·tle·drum /'kɛtlˌdrʌm/ *n* a musical instrument consisting of a large metal drum with a round curved-up bottom

SPELLING NOTE
Words with the sound /k/ may be spelled c-, like **cool**, or qu-, like **queen**.

key¹ /kiʸ/ *n* **keys 1** an instrument, usu. made of metal, that one puts into a hole and turns, to lock or unlock a door, start or stop a car engine, etc. **2** [*to*] something that explains, answers, or helps you to understand: *a key to the grammar exercises*|(fig.) *Her unhappy childhood is the key to her character.* **3** any of the parts in a writing or printing machine or musical instrument that are pressed down to make it work: *the keys of a piano*|a TYPEWRITER **4** a set of musical notes based on a particular note: *a song in the key of C*

key² *v* **keyed, keying** [T *to*] to make (more) suitable: *The rate of production must be keyed to the level of public buying of our product.*

key³ *adj* [A] very important; necessary for success: *She has a key position in the company.*

key·board /'kiʸbɔrd, -boʷrd/ *n* a row of KEYS¹ (3) on a musical instrument or machine: *the keyboard of a piano*|a TYPEWRITER –see illustration on page 212

keyed up /ˌkiʸd 'ʌp/ *adj* [about] excited or nervous: *We're all very keyed up about the examination.*

key·hole /'kiʸhoʷl/ *n* a hole for the key in a lock, a clock, etc.

key·note /'kiʸnoʷt/ *n* **1** [C] the particular note on which a musical KEY¹ (4) is based **2** [A;C] (containing) a central or the most important idea: *The keynote of her speech was that we need higher wages.*

key·punch /'kiʸpʌntʃ/ *AmE*‖**card punch**– *BrE n* a machine that puts information onto cards in such a way that computers can read and understand it

key ring /'· ·/ *n* a ring or ring-shaped thing on which keys are kept

kg. *written abbrev. said as:* KILOGRAM(s)

kha·ki /'kækiʸ, 'kɑ-/ *adj,n* [U] **1** a yellow-brown color **2** cloth of this color, esp. as worn by soldiers

kib·butz /kɪ'buts/ *n* **-butzim** /ˌbut'siʸm/ *or* **-butzes** a farm or settlement in Israel where many people live and work together

kick¹ /kɪk/ *v* **1** [T] to hit with the foot: *She kicked the ball against the wall.* **2** [T] to make or* SCORE² (1) by doing this: *He kicked a hole in the door.*|*He kicked a field* GOAL (3). **3** [I] to move the foot or feet as if to strike a blow: *Babies kick to exercise their legs.* **4** [I] (of a gun) to move backwards forcefully when fired

kick sbdy. **around** *v adv* [T] *inf* to treat someone roughly with speech or actions

kick off *v adv* [I] to start a game of football –see also KICKOFF

kick sbdy.↔ **out** *v adv* [T *of*] to remove or dismiss, esp. violently

kick up sthg. *v adv* [T] *infml* to cause or make (a FUSS or a ROW³): *I know he didn't want to go, but he shouldn't have* **kicked up a fuss** *about it.*

kick² *n* **1** [C] an act of kicking: *Give the door a kick to open it.* **2** [C] *infml* a strong feeling of excitement, pleasure, etc.: *She drives fast (just) for kicks.* **3** [U] *infml* power to produce an effect: *This wine has a lot of kick to it.*

kick·back /'kɪkbæk/ n infml money for services (often illegal) that have helped one make money: a kickback of $1,000

kick·off /'kɪk-ɔf/ n the kick which begins a game of football: The kickoff is at three o'clock today. –see also KICK¹ off

kid¹ /kɪd/ n **1** [C] infml a child: How many kids do you have? **2** [C] infml esp. AmE a young person: college kids **3** [C;U] (leather made from the skin of) a young goat: a goat and two young kids(fig.) Don't treat those criminals with kid gloves. (=gently)

kid² adj [A] AmE infml (of a brother or sister) younger: his kid sister

kid³ v -dd- infml [I;T on] to pretend, esp. in a playful manner; deceive: He's not really hurt; he's only kidding.|Don't kid me; I know you're not telling the truth.

kid·nap /'kɪdnæp/ v -p- or -pp- AmE -pp-BrE [T] to take (someone) away unlawfully in order to demand money or something else for his/her safe return –**kid·napper** n

kid·ney /'kɪdniʸ/ n -neys **1** one of the pair of human or animal organs in the lower back area, which separate waste liquid from the blood **2** one of these animal organs cooked and eaten

kidney bean /'·· ˌ·/ n a type of bean that is OVAL shaped, dark red, and eaten as a vegetable

kidney ma·chine /'·· ·ˌ·/ n a machine that can do the work of diseased human KIDNEYS

kill¹ /kɪl/ v **1** [I;T] to cause to die: to kill insects/one's enemies|(fig.) My feet are killing me! (=hurting very much)|(fig.) She killed our chances of winning.|(fig) He killed the bottle of wine. (=drank all of it) **2** kill time to make free time pass by finding something to do: While waiting for the train he killed time by going for a walk. **3** kill two birds with one stone to get two good results from one action

USAGE **Kill** is a general word meaning to cause (anything) to die, but **murder** means to kill a person on purpose: My uncle was **killed** in a plane crash.|The cold weather **killed** our tomato plants.|She was sent to prison for **murdering** her husband. **Slaughter** and **butcher** mean to kill animals for food, but both words are also used to describe cruel or unnecessary killing of humans: Our army was **butchered** by the enemy's much larger forces.|Thousands of people are needlessly **slaughtered** in car accidents. To **assassinate** means to kill an important political figure: an attempt to assassinate the Governor; and to **massacre** means to kill large numbers of (esp. defenseless) people: After their victory, the army entered the city and **massacred** the women and children.

kill sbdy./sthg.↔ **off** v adv [T] to kill (living things) one at a time: The trees were killed off by the severe winter.

kill² n **1** [S] the bird or animal killed in hunting: The lion didn't leave his kill until he had satisfied his hunger. **2** [the S] the act of killing, esp. hunted birds or animals

kill·er /'kɪlər/ n infml [A;C] a person, animal, or thing that kills: killer SHARKS|This disease is a killer.

kill·ing¹ /'kɪlɪŋ/ n **make a killing** to make a large amount of money suddenly, esp. in business

killing² adj that kills or makes very tired: This work is really killing. –**killingly** adv

kill·joy /'kɪldʒɔɪ/ n a person who spoils the pleasure of other people

kiln /kɪln, kɪl/ n a box-shaped heating apparatus for baking or drying: a brick kiln

kil·o·gram ‖also **-gramme** BrE /'kɪləˌgræm/ also **kilo** /'kiʸloʷ/ infml– n 1,000 grams

kil·o·me·ter AmE‖**-tre** BrE /kɪ'lɑmətər, 'kɪləˌmiʸṭər/ n 1,000 meters

kil·o·watt /'kɪləˌwɑt/ n 1,000 WATTS

kilt /kɪlt/ n a short skirt with many pressed folds, worn traditionally by Scotsmen

ki·mo·no /kə'moʷnə, -noʷ/ n -nos a long coatlike garment worn in Japan

kin /kɪn/ n [P] old use & fml members of one's family: His **next of kin** (=closest relative(s)) were told of his death. –see also KITH AND KIN

kind¹ /kaɪnd/ n [C of] a group, the members of which share certain qualities; type; sort: We sell hats of all kinds/all kinds of hats.|Haven't you got any other kind?|that kind of book **2** [U] nature or type: They are different in size but not in kind. **3 in kind: a** (of payment) using goods or natural products rather than money **b** with the same treatment: I paid him back in kind for hitting me. **4 kind of** infml esp. AmE rather; in a certain way: I'm feeling kind of tired.|She kind of hoped to be invited. **5 of a kind: a** old use of the same sort: They're all of a kind. **b** of a not very good sort: She gave us coffee of a kind, but we couldn't drink it.

USAGE Sentences like: Those **kind**/**sort** of parties always make me nervous are common in speech, but are thought by teachers to be incorrect. In writing it is better to use this form: That **kind**/**sort** of parties always make me nervous.

kind² adj helpful; (that shows one is) interested in the happiness or feelings of others: a kind person/action/thought|She's very kind to animals.|It was very kind of you to visit me when I was ill. –opposite **unkind**

kin·der·gar·ten /'kɪndərˌgɑrtn, -ˌgɑrdn/ n a school or class for children aged four to six which they attend, usu. for one year before entering grade school— compare NURSERY SCHOOL

kind-heart·ed /ˌ· '·· ◂/ adj having or showing a kind nature: a kind-hearted person/action –**kind-heartedly** adv

kin·dle /'kɪndl/ v -dled, -dling [I;T] to (cause to) start to burn: The wood was wet and wouldn't kindle easily.|(fig.) The police action kindled the crowd's anger.

kin·dling /'kɪndlɪŋ/ n [U] materials for lighting a fire, esp. dry wood, leaves, grass, etc.

kind·ly¹ /'kaɪndliʸ/ adj -lier, -liest pleasant; friendly: a kindly smile|She's the kindliest/the most kindly person I have ever met. –**kindliness** n [U]

kind·ly² adv **1** in a kind manner: She spoke kindly to him. –opposite **unkindly 2** please:

Will you kindly pass me that book? **3 not take kindly to** not to accept easily or willingly: *He didn't take kindly to being told how to behave.*

kind·ness /'kaɪndnɪs/ *n* **1** [U] the quality of being kind **2** [C] a kind action: *Please have the kindness to answer this letter quickly.*

kin·dred¹ /'kɪndrɪd/ *n old use & lit* **1** [U] family relationship **2** [P] one's relatives or family: *Only a few of his kindred were present at his funeral.* –compare KIN

kindred² *adj* [A] belonging to the same group; having almost the same habits, interests, etc.: *She and I are* **kindred spirits:** *we both enjoy music and dancing.*

ki·net·ic /kɪ'nɛtɪk/ *adj fml and tech* of or about movement –**kinetically** *adv*

ki·net·ics /kɪ'nɛtɪks/ *n* [U] the science that studies the action of force in producing or changing movement

kin·folk /'kɪnfoʷk/ also **kinfolks**– *n* [P] *old use* members of one's family

king /kɪŋ/ *n* **1** [A;C *of*] (*sometimes cap.*) (the title of) the male ruler of a country, usu. the son of a former ruler: *the King of Spain|King Edward* –compare QUEEN **2** [C *of*] the most important member of a group: *The lion is the king of the* JUNGLE. **3** [C] **a** (in CHESS) the most important piece **b** playing card with a picture of a king –see CARDS USAGE

king·dom /'kɪŋdəm/ *n* **1** a country governed by a king (or queen) **2** any of the three great divisions of natural objects: *the animal/vegetable/mineral kingdom*

USAGE A **kingdom** may be ruled over by a **queen.**

king·fish·er /'kɪŋ,fɪʃər/ *n* a small brightly-colored bird that feeds on fish in rivers, lakes, etc.

king·ly /'kɪŋliʸ/ *adj* that belongs or is suitable to a king: *a kingly way of doing things*

king·pin /'kɪŋ,pɪn/ *n* the most important person in a group, upon whom the success of the group depends

kink /kɪŋk/ *n* **1** a backward turn or twist in hair, a rope, chain, pipe, etc. **2** a peculiarity of the mind or character –**kinky** *adj* **-ier, -iest**

kins·man /'kɪnzmən/ **kinswoman** /-,wʊmən/ *fem.*– *n* **-men** /mən/ *old use* a relative

ki·osk /'kiʸask, kiʸ'ask/ *n* **1** a small open building, such as one used for selling newspapers on the street **2** *BrE fml* a public telephone box

kip·per /'kɪpər/ *n* a salted fish (HERRING) that is cut open and preserved by being treated with smoke

kiss¹ /kɪs/ *v* [I;T] to touch with the lips as a sign of love or as a greeting: *They kissed (each other) when they met.|(fig.) The wind kissed* (=gently touched) *her hair.*

kiss² *n* **1** an act of kissing: *She gave him a kiss.* **2 kiss of death** something that makes failure certain

kit /kɪt/ *n* **1** (a box for) a set of articles, esp.

SPELLING NOTE
Words with the sound /k/ may be spelled **c-**, like **cool**, or **qu-**, like **queen.**

---

tools, needed for a particular purpose: *This toy ship is made from a kit.*(=a set of small separate pieces)/*a shaving kit*/*a first aid kit* **2** the clothes and other articles needed by a soldier, sailor, etc., or carried by a traveler

kitch·en /'kɪtʃən/ *n* a room used for cooking –see illustration opposite

kitch·en·ette /,kɪtʃə'nɛt/ *n* a very small (part of a room used as a) kitchen

kitchen gar·den /,·· '···/ *n* a garden where fruit and vegetables are grown

kite /kaɪt/ *n* **1** a wooden or metal frame covered with paper or cloth for flying in the air, often as a plaything, at the end of a long string **2** a large bird (HAWK) that eats small birds and animals

kith and kin /,kɪθ ən 'kɪn/ *n* **1** [P] (friends, esp. from one's own country, and) relatives: *We may not agree with their politics, but we should remember that they are our kith and kin.* **2** [S] one of these: *Don't quarrel with him; he's your own kith and kin.*

kit·ten /'kɪtn/ *n* a young cat

kit·ten·ish /'kɪtn-ɪʃ/ *adj* of or like a KITTEN; playful

kit·ty¹ /'kɪtiʸ/ *n* **-ties** a cat or KITTEN: *"Here, kitty kitty," called the little girl.*

kitty² *n* **1** (in some card games) a sum of money put in the center of the table by all the players at the beginning, and taken by the winner **2** *infml* a sum of money collected by a group of people, and used for an agreed purpose

ki·wi /'kiʸwiʸ/ *n* [C] **-wis 1** a New Zealand bird with very short wings that cannot fly **2** [C;U] a fruit with a brown skin and green flesh

Klee·nex /'kliʸnɛks/ also **tissue** *n* – [C;U *usu. sing.*] *tdmk* (a sheet of) thin soft paper, used instead of a handkerchief

klep·to·ma·ni·a /,klɛptə'meʸniʸə/ *n* [U] a disease of the mind causing an uncontrollable desire to steal –**kleptomaniac** /,klɛptə'meʸniʸ,æk/ *n*

km. *written abbrev. said as:* kilometer(s)

knack /næk/ *n* [*of*] *infml* a special skill or ability, usu. the result of practice: *He has a/the knack of making friends wherever he goes.*

knap·sack /'næpsæk/ also **rucksack**– *n* a bag fastened to the shoulders and carried on the back in which climbers, walkers, etc., carry their belongings

knave /neʸv/ *n* **1** *old use* a dishonest man **2** → JACK (2) –**knavery** /'neʸvəriʸ/ *n* [U]

knead /niʸd/ *v* [I;T] **1** to mix together and make a paste of (something, such as flour and water for making bread) by pressing with the hands **2** to press or make other movements on (a muscle or other part of the body) to cure pain, stiffness, etc.

knee¹ /niʸ/ *n* **1** the middle joint of the leg **2** the part of a garment that covers the knee: *big holes in the knees of his old trousers* **3 go/fall on one's knees** to admit defeat and ask for mercy

knee² *v* **kneed, kneeing** [T *in*] to hit with the knee

knee·cap /'niʸkæp/ *n* the bone in front of the knee

cabinet

whisk

mug

colander

coffee pot

electrical outlet

dish drainer

faucet

sink

freezer

teapot

blender

cord

spatula

mixer

mixing bowl

dishwasher

skillet

saucepan

kettle

burner

refrigerator

stove

garbage can

oven

stool

broiler

can

cutting board

can opener

glass

kitchen knife

napkin

fork

cup

saucer

kitchen knife

plate

knife

spoon

toaster

tablecloth

place mat

Useful Phrases

to make breakfast/lunch/dinner
to boil an egg
to fry some fish/meat
to broil a steak
to bake some bread/some cookies
to roast a chicken
to slice an onion/a carrot
to chop some celery/an onion
to peel an orange/some potatoes
to make a pot of coffee/some tea/a sandwich
to have/eat breakfast/lunch/dinner
to have a snack

to wash the dishes
to dry the dishes
to run the dishwasher
to put away the dishes
to take out the garbage

Fill in the Blanks

1. I like to have a _____ when I come home
   from school.
2. Let's _____ a pot of tea.
3. We like to _____ dinner at 7:30.
4. Don't forget to take out the _____ .

knee-deep /ˌ· '·◄/ adj [F in] deep enough to reach the knees: *The water is knee-deep.*|(fig.) *knee-deep in debt*

kneel /niʸl/ v **knelt** /nɛlt/ or **kneeled, kneeling** [I *down, on*] to go down or remain on the knee(s): *She knelt (down) to pray.*

knell /nɛl/ n the sound of a bell rung esp. for a death or funeral

knew /nuʷ, nyuʷ/ v past tense of KNOW¹

knick·ers /'nɪkərz/ n [P] esp. AmE short loose pants made to fit tightly around the legs just above the knee

knickknack, nicknack /'nɪknæk/ n infml a small ornament of any type, esp. for the house

knife¹ /naɪf/ n **knives** /naɪvz/ **1** a blade fixed in a handle used for cutting as a tool or weapon –see Study Notes on page 379 **2 stick a knife in someone's back** infml to do harm on purpose to somebody who trusts you
USAGE Note the word order in this fixed phrase: **knife and fork**

knife² v **knifed, knifing** [T *in*] to strike with a knife used as a weapon: *During the fight he was knifed in the stomach.*

knight¹ /naɪt/ n **1** (in former times) a noble soldier on horseback **2** a man who has been given a title which has a rank below that of LORD¹ (2): *Sir George (Smith) was made a knight by the Queen for his service to his country.* **3** (in CHESS) a piece, usu. with a horse's head, that moves two squares forward in a straight line and one to the side

knight² v [T] to make (someone) a KNIGHT¹ (1): *Sir George (Smith) was knighted by the Queen in 1981.*

knight·hood /'naɪthʊd/ n [C;U] the rank, title, or state of a KNIGHT¹ (1)

knit /nɪt/ v **knit** or **knitted, knitting** [I;T] **1** [*for*] to make (things to wear) by uniting threads into a close network by means of long needles: *I'm knitting (you) a pair of socks.* **2** [*together*] to unite or join closely: *I hope the two edges of that broken bone will knit (together) smoothly.* **3 knit one's brows** to show displeasure, worry, or deep thought by FROWNING

knit·ting /'nɪtɪŋ/ n [U] something which is being KNITted (1): *She keeps her knitting in a bag.*

knives /naɪvz/ n pl. of KNIFE¹

knob /nɑb/ n **1** a round lump, esp. on the surface or at the end of something: *a stick with a knob on the end* **2** a round handle or control button

knob·by /'nɑbiʸ/ AmE‖**knobbly** /'nɑbliʸ/ BrE adj **-bier, -biest** having round KNOBlike lumps: *He has very thin legs and knobby knees.*

knock¹ /nɑk/ v **1** [I] to strike a blow; hit, usu. making a noise when doing so: *Please knock (on/at the door) before entering.* **2** [T] to hit; strike: *She knocked the cup off the table.*|*He knocked the fish on the head to kill it quickly.*

3 [T] infml to express unfavorable opinions (about someone): *Stop knocking him; he's a good singer really.*

knock around¹ sthg. v prep [T] infml to lie unnoticed in (a place): *That old thing has been knocking around the house for years.*

knock around² v adv infml **1** [I] to be present or active: *"Who's that man? I haven't seen him before." "Oh, he's been knocking around here for years."* **2** [I *with*] to have a relationship or be seen (with someone): *Sally's been knocking around with Jim for years.* **3** (**knock** sbdy. **around**) to treat roughly: *They say he knocks children around.*

knock sbdy./sthg.↔ **down** v adv [T] **1** to destroy (a building, bridge, etc.) by means of blows: *Our house is being knocked down to make way for a new road.* **2** also **knock over**– to strike (a person) to the ground: *Alex was knocked down by a crowd of people* **3** [*to*] to (cause to) reduce (a price): *The price was knocked down to $3.*|*I knocked him down to $3.*

knock off v adv **1** [I;T (**knock off** sthg.)+v-ing] infml to stop: *Let's knock off (work) early today.* **2** [T] (**knock** sthg.↔ **off**) to take from a total payment: *I'll knock $2 off.* **3** [T] (**knock** sthg.↔ **off**) to steal from: *They knocked off the bank and got away with $4000.*

knock sbdy.↔ **out** v adv [T] **1** (of a drug) to cause sleep **2** (in BOXING) to make (one's opponent) lose consciousness or be unable to rise before a count of 10 seconds **3** to cause to be dismissed from a competition: *Our team was knocked out in the first part of the competition.* –see also KNOCKOUT

knock sbdy.↔ **up** v adv [T]AmE derog infml to cause (a woman) to become PREGNANT

knock² n **1** (the sound of) a blow: *a knock at the door* **2** a piece of bad luck or trouble: *He's taken/had quite a few knocks recently.*

knock·er /'nɑkər/ also **doorknocker**– n a metal instrument fixed to a door and used by visitors for knocking at the door

knock-kneed /'·'·/ adj having knees that turn inwards and knock together, or at least touch, when walking (**knock-knees**)

knock·out /'nɑk-aʊt/ n **1** also **KO** infml– a KNOCKing out of one fighter (BOXER³) by another: *He won the fight by a knockout.* **2** infml someone (or something) causing great admiration (or surprise): *You are really a knockout in your new dress.* –see also KNOCK¹ out

knoll /noʷl/ n a small round hill

knot¹ /nɑt/ n **1** a fastening formed by tying together the ends of pieces of string, rope, wire, etc.: *She tied her belt with a knot.* **2** a hard mass in wood where a branch joins a tree **3** a small group of people close together: *a knot of people whispering in the corner* **4** a measure of the speed of a ship, about 1,853 meters (about 6,080 feet) per hour –compare NAUTICAL MILE

knot² v **-tt-** [I;T] to make a knot in or join together with a knot: *Knot the ends of the*

SPELLING NOTE

Words with the sound /k/ may be spelled **c-**, like **cool**, or **qu-**, like **queen**.

rope together.|*This wire is too stiff to knot easily.*

knot·ty /ˈnɑtiʸ/ *adj* **-tier, -tiest** containing one or more KNOTS¹ (2)

know¹ /noʷ/ *v* **knew** /nuʷ, nyuʷ/, **known** /noʷn/, **knowing 1** [I;T +(*that*); not *be + v-ing*] to have information (about) in the mind: *I know he's there because I saw him. I know that is true.*|*He doesn't know how to do it.*|*I know what happened.*|*"He's very ill." "Yes, I know."* **2** [T] to have met and spoken to (someone) several times: *I've known Martin for years.* **3** [T] (used only in past tenses) to have seen, heard, etc.: *I've known her (to) drink twelve glasses of beer in an evening.* **4** [T *by*] to be able to recognize: *You'll know her by the color of her hair.* **5** [T] *lit* to have experienced: *He has known much unhappiness.* **6 know a thing or two/the ropes** *infml* to have practical useful information gained from experience **7 know something backwards** to understand something perfectly **8 know one's own mind** to know what one wants **9 you know** (used for adding force to a statement): *You'll have to try harder, you know, if you want to succeed.* –see also UNKNOWN

USAGE Compare **know** and **learn**: To **know** is to be conscious of (a fact), to have skill in (a subject), or to have met (a person) before: *I knew I had passed the test.*|*She knows all about computers.*|*Do you know how to drive?* (not *Do you know to drive?*)|*"Do you know my brother?" "No, we've never met."* To **learn** is to get to know (a fact or subject, not a person): *I learned that I had passed the test.*|*She's learning all about computers.*|*I'm learning (how) to drive.* Compare *I know how to drive* (not *I am knowing*)

know better *v adv* [I *than*] to be wise or well-trained enough (not to): *She should know better than to spend all her money on books.*

know sbdy./sthg. from sbdy./sthg. *v prep* [T] to be able to tell the difference between: *He doesn't know his left hand from his right.*

know of sbdy./sthg. *v prep* [T] **1** to have heard of or about: *Although I know of her, I don't really know her.*|*Do you know of a good restaurant near here?* **2 Not that I know of** Not so far as I know

know² *n* **in the know** well-informed; having more information (about something) than most people

know-how /ˈ· ·/ *n* [U] *infml* practical ability or skill; "knowing how" to do something

know·ing¹ /ˈnoʷɪŋ/ *adj* **1** (showing that one is) well-informed or possessing secret understanding: *a knowing person/smile/look* **2** because I know: *Knowing John, he'll be late.* (=he's always late)

knowing² *n* **there's no knowing** it's impossible to know: *There's no knowing what the weather will be like.*

know·ing·ly /ˈnoʷɪŋliʸ/ *adv* **1** in a KNOWING¹ manner **2** intentionally; with knowledge of the probable effect: *She would never*

knowingly hurt anyone. –opposite **unknowingly**

know-it-all /ˈ· · ˌ·/ also **know-all** /ˈ· ·/ *esp. BrE*– *n derog* a person who behaves as if he/she knows everything

knowl·edge /ˈnɑlɪdʒ/ *n* [S;U] **1** understanding: *a knowledge of/not much knowledge of the truth* **2** learning; that which is known: *a knowledge of/not much knowledge of French* **3** familiarity with; information about: *She has a good knowledge of politics.*

knowl·edge·a·ble /ˈnɑlɪdʒəbəl/ *adj* (of a person) having a good deal of knowledge; well-informed: *He's very knowledgeable about football.* –**knowledgeably** *adv*: *He speaks very knowledgeably about football.*

known¹ /noʷn/ *adj* **1** [A] also **well-known**– generally recognized (as being something): *He's a known criminal.* **2 known as: a** generally recognized as: *She's known as a great singer.* **b** also publicly called; named: *Samuel Clemens, known as Mark Twain, was a famous American writer.* **3 make it known that . . .** *fml* to declare or cause to know that . . .: *He made it known to his friends that he did not want to enter politics.*

known² *v past participle of* KNOW¹

knuck·le /ˈnʌkəl/ *n* a finger joint

knuckle down *v adv* **-led, -ling** [I *to*] *infml* to start working hard: *You'll really have to knuckle down (to your work) if you want to pass the examination.*

knuckle-dust·er /ˈ·· ˌ·/ *BrE for* BRASS KNUCKLES

knuckle un·der *v adv* [I *to*] to admit defeat; yield

K O /ˌkeʸ ˈoʷ/ *n infml* → KNOCKOUT (1)

ko·a·la /koʷˈɑlə/ also **koala bear** /·ˈ·· ˌ·/ – *n* an Australian tree-climbing animal like a small furry bear

Ko·ran /kɔˈræn, -ˈrɑn, koʷ-, kə-/ *n* [the S] the holy book of the Muslims

ko·sher /ˈkoʷʃər/ *adj* of or about food, esp. meat, which is lawful for Jews to eat: *kosher meat*|*a kosher restaurant*

kow·tow /ˌkaʊˈtaʊ, ˈkaʊtaʊ/ *v* [I *to*] *infml* to obey without question; be too humble (towards): *Be polite, but don't kowtow (to him).*

Krem·lin /ˈkremlɪn/ *n* [the U] (the group of buildings in Moscow which are the center of) the government of the Soviet Union: *How is the Kremlin going to answer the latest message from Washington?*

KS *written abbrev. said as:* Kansas /ˈkænzəs/ (a state in the US)

ku·dos /ˈkuʷdɑs, -doʷs, ˈkyuʷ-/ *n* [U] honor, praise, glory, and thanks (for something done): *She got a lot of kudos for her work at the university.*

kung fu /ˌkʌŋ ˈfuʷ, ˌkʊŋ-/ *n* [U] a Chinese style of fighting using blows with the hands and feet, related to KARATE

kw *written abbrev. said as:* KILOWATT(s)

KY *written abbrev. said as:* Kentucky /kənˈtʌkiʸ/ (a state in the US)

L, l

L, l /ɛl/ **L's, l's** *or* **Ls, ls 1** the 12th letter of the English alphabet **2** the ROMAN NUMERAL (=number) for 50

LA *written abbrev. said as:* Louisiana /luʷˌiʸziʸˈænə/ (a state in the US)

lab /læb/ *n infml* for LABORATORY

la·bel[1] /ˈleʸbəl/ *n* a piece of paper, cloth, etc. fixed to something, on which is written what it is, who owns it, etc.

label[2] *v* **-l-** *AmE*‖**-ll-** *BrE* [T] **1** to fix or tie a LABEL[1] on: *The doctor labeled the bottle (poison/poisonous).* **2** to put into a kind or class; describe as: *His enemies labeled him a thief.*

la·bor[1] *AmE*‖**labour** *BrE* /ˈleʸbər/ *n* **1** [C;U] work, esp. tiring physical work, or effort **2** [U] workers, esp. those who use their hands: *skilled/unskilled labor* **3** [S;U] the act of giving birth: *She was in labor for three hours.* **4** **labor of love** work done gladly and without thought of gain

labor[2] *AmE*‖**labour** *BrE* *v* **1** [I] to work, esp. hard **2** [I] to move or act with difficulty; struggle: *She labored up the hill with her bags.*|*The engine was laboring.* **3** [T] to work something out in too great detail or at unnecessary length (often in the phrase **labor the point**)

labor under sthg. *v prep* [T] to suffer from; be troubled by: *He labored under a misunderstanding/misapprehension.*

lab·o·ra·to·ry /ˈlæbrəˌtɔriʸ, -ˌtoʷriʸ/ *n* **-ries** a building or room which contains scientific apparatus and in which a scientist works

Labor Day *AmE*‖**Labour Day** *BrE* /ˈ·· ˌ·/ *n* a holiday held on the first Monday of September in the US and Canada to honor workers

la·bor·er *AmE*‖**labourer** *BrE* /ˈleʸbəˌrər/ *n* a worker whose job needs strength rather than skill

la·bo·ri·ous /ləˈbɔriʸəs, -ˈboʷr-/ *adj* needing great effort: *a laborious* TASK **–laboriously** *adv* **–laboriousness** *n* [U]

labor un·ion /ˈ·· ˌ·/ *AmE*‖also **trade union** *esp. BrE n* an organization of workers to represent their interests and deal as a group with employers

Lab·ra·dor re·triev·er /ˌlæbrədɔr rɪˈtriʸvər/ also **Labrador** /ˈlæbrəˌdɔr/, **Lab** *infml– n* a large black or yellow dog

lab·y·rinth /ˈlæbəˌrɪnθ/ *n* a network of narrow twisting passages or paths, through which it is difficult to find one's way: (fig.) *the labyrinth of his mind* **–compare** MAZE **–labyrinthine** /ˌlæbəˈrɪnθɪn, -θaɪn, -θiʸn/ *adj* [A]

lace[1] /leʸs/ *n* **1** [C] a string or cord used for fastening something, esp. shoes **2** [U] a netlike ornamental cloth made of fine thread: *lace curtains*

lace[2] *v* **laced, lacing** [T] **1** [T *up*] to draw together or fasten with a LACE[1] (1) **–opposite**

unlace 2 [T *with*] to add a small amount ofstrong alcoholic drink to (weaker drink)

lac·er·ate /ˈlæsəˌreʸt/ *v* **-ated, -ating** [T] *fml* to tear (the flesh, an arm, etc.) roughly; cut: *Her face was badly lacerated by the broken glass.* **–laceration** /ˌlæsəˈreʸʃən/ *n* [C;U]

lack[1] /læk/ *v* [T] to be without; not have enough of: *We lacked food.*

lack[2] *n* [S;U] absence or need: *The plants died through/for lack of water.*

lack·ey /ˈlækiʸ/ *n* **-eys** *derog* a person who behaves like a servant by obeying others without question

lack·ing /ˈlækɪŋ/ *adj* [F] *fml* **1** not present; missing: *Help was lacking during the storm.* **2** **be lacking in** to have little of; need: *Is she lacking in courage?*

la·con·ic /ləˈkɑnɪk/ *adj* using few words **–laconically** *adv*

lac·quer /ˈlækər/ *v,n* [C;T;U] (to cover with) a transparent substance which forms a hard shiny surface, or makes hair stay in place; *hair lacquer*|*She lacquered the old table.* **–compare** VARNISH[1,2]

la·crosse /ləˈkrɔs/ *n* [U] a game played on a field by two teams, each player having a long stick with a net at the end to throw, catch, and carry the ball

lac·tic /ˈlæktɪk/ *adj tech* concerning or obtained from milk

lac·y /ˈleʸsiʸ/ *adj* **-ier, -iest** of or like LACE[1] (2)

lad /læd/ *n infml* a boy; youth: *He's just a lad.*

lad·der /ˈlædər/ *n* **1** a frame with steps (RUNGS), used for climbing, as up a building or the side of a ship: (fig.) *climbing the ladder of success* **2** *BrE* for RUN[2] (9): *a ladder in a stocking*

lad·en /ˈleʸdn/ *adj* [*with*] heavily loaded: *The bushes were laden with fruit.*|(fig.) *laden with sorrow*

La·dies' room /ˈleʸdiʸz ˌruʷm, -ˌrʊm/ *AmE*‖also **Ladies, -dies'** *esp. BrE– n* **Ladies, -dies'** a women's public LAVATORY

la·dle[1] /ˈleʸdl/ *n* a large spoon with a long handle: *a soup ladle*

ladle[2] *v* **-dled, -dling** [T *into, out, out of*] to serve (food, soup, etc.) with a LADLE[1]

la·dy /ˈleʸdiʸ/ *n* **-dies 1** [C] *polite* a woman, esp. one of good social position –see GENTLEMAN (USAGE) **2** [A] also **woman**– female: *a woman doctor*

Lady *n* **-dies** [A;C] a title put before the name of a woman of noble rank

la·dy·bug /ˈleʸdiʸˌbʌg/ *AmE*‖also **ladybird** /ˈleʸdiʸˌbɜrd/– *n* a small round flying BEETLE, usu. red with black dots

lady-in-wait·ing /ˌ·· ··· ˈ··/ *n* **ladies-in-waiting** a lady who is the servant of a queen or princess

lag /læg/ *v* **-gg-** [I *behind*] to move or develop more slowly (than others): *The children always lag behind when we go for a walk.*

la·ger /'lɑgər/ n [C;U] (a drink, glass, or bottle of) a light kind of beer

la·goon /lə'guːn/ n a lake of sea water, partly or completely separated from the sea

laid /leʸd/ v past tense and participle of LAY¹

lain /leʸn/ v past participle of LIE¹

lair /lɛər/ n the place where a wild animal hides, rests, and sleeps: *a wolf in its lair*|(fig.) *The thieves hid in their lair.*

lake /leʸk/ n a large mass of water surrounded by land: *We took a boat across the lake.* –compare POND

la·ma /'lɑmə/ n a Buddhist priest of Tibet, Mongolia, etc.

lamb¹ /læm/ n **1** [C] a young sheep **2** [U] the meat of a young sheep –see MEAT (USAGE)

lamb² v [I] (of sheep) to give birth to lambs

lame¹ /leʸm/ adj **1** not able to walk properly as a result of some weakness in a leg or foot **2** not easily believed; weak: *He gave a lame excuse for being absent.* –**lamely** adv –**lameness** n [U]

lame² v **lamed, laming** [T] to make LAME¹ (1)

lame duck /ˌ· '·/ n **1** AmE a political official whose period in office will soon end **2** a person or business that is helpless or ineffective

la·ment¹ /lə'mɛnt/ v fml [I;T +v-ing] to feel or express grief or sorrow (for or at)

lament² n **1** [for] a strong expression of grief or deep sorrow **2** a song or piece of music expressing sorrow, esp. for the death of somebody

lam·en·ta·ble /lə'mɛntəbəl/ adj causing one to be very dissatisfied or to wish that something had not happened –**lamentably** adv

lam·i·nate¹ /'læməˌneʸt/ v **-nated, -nating** [T] to make (a strong material) by firmly joining many thin sheets of material on top of each other

lam·i·nate² /'læmənɪt, -ˌneʸt/ n [C;U] material made by laminating (LAMINATE¹) sheets, e.g. of plastic

lamp /læmp/ n an apparatus for giving light, as from oil, gas, or electricity –see illustration on page 399

lam·poon¹ /læm'puːn/ n a piece of writing attacking a person, government, etc., by making them look foolish

lampoon² v [T] to attack by means of a LAMPOON¹

lamp·post /'læmp-poʷst, 'læmpoʷst/ n a tall thin pillar supporting a lamp which lights a street or other public area –see illustration on page 337

lamp·shade /'læmpʃeʸd/ n a cover, usu. decorative, for a lamp

lance /læns/ n a long spearlike weapon used by soldiers on horseback in former times

land¹ /lænd/ n **1** [U] the solid dry part of the earth's surface: *She traveled over land and sea.* **2** [C] a part of the earth's surface forming a political whole; country; nation **3** [U] a part of the earth's surface all of the same natural type: *the forest lands of Norway* **4** [U] earth; soil: *He works (on) the land.* **5** [U] ground owned as property: *You are on my land.*|*Land prices have risen.*

USAGE The earth's surface when compared with the sea is the **land**, but when compared with the sky it is the **earth**: *After a week at sea, the sailors saw* **land**.|*After a week in space, the spacecraft returned to* **earth**. An area considered as property is a piece of **land**: *the high price of* **land** *in California.* The substance in which plants grow is the **ground, earth** or **soil. Ground** also means the surface we walk on, but when this is indoors it is the **floor**: *The horse fell to the* **ground**.‖*The plate fell on the* **floor.**

land² v **1** to come to, bring to, or put on land: *The ship landed the goods at Baltimore.* **2** [I] (of something moving through the air) to settle, come to rest, or fall: *The bird landed on the branch.*|*The plane landed safely.*|*The ball landed in the water.* **3** [T] infml to put or arrive in a condition, place, or position: *That will land him in prison.* **4 land on one's feet: a** to have good luck **b** to come successfully out of difficulty

land·ed /'lændɪd/ adj [A] owning large amounts of land: *a landed family*|*the landed gentry*

land·ing /'lændɪŋ/ n **1** the act of arriving or bringing to land: *The plane's landing was delayed because of fog.* –compare TAKEOFF **2** a place where people and goods are landed, esp. from a ship **3** the level space or passage at the top of a set of stairs in a building: *I'll meet you on the landing, not in my room.*

land·la·dy /'lændˌleʸdiʸ, 'lænleʸdiʸ/ n **-dies** a female LANDLORD

land·locked /'lændlɑkt, 'lænlɑkt/ adj enclosed or almost enclosed by land: *a land locked country, that has no port*

land·lord /'lændlɔrd, 'lænlɔrd/ n **1** a person, esp. a man, from whom someone rents all or part of a building, land, etc.

land·mark /'lændmɑrk, 'lænmɑrk/ n **1** an easily recognizable object, such as a tall tree or building, by which one can tell one's position **2** something that marks an important point or change, e.g. in a person's life: *The discovery of electricity was a landmark in history.*

land·scape¹ /'lændskeʸp, 'lænskeʸp/ n **1** a wide view of country scenery **2** a picture of such a scene

landscape² v **-scaped, -scaping** [T] to make (the land around new houses, factories, etc.) more beautiful, esp. by adding trees and plants

land·slide /'lændslaɪd, 'lænslaɪd/ n **1** a sudden fall of earth or rocks down a slope, hill, etc.: *The road was blocked by a landslide.* **2** a very large success for a person, political party, etc., in an election: *He won by a landslide.*

lane /leʸn/ n **1 a** a narrow, often winding, road, esp. in the country **b** (part of the name of) a street in a town **2** a division of a wide road, usu. marked by white lines so that fast and slow cars can stay apart **3** a fixed path across the sea or through the air used regularly by ships or aircraft

lan·guage /'læŋgwɪdʒ/ n **1** [U] the system of human expression by means of words in speech or writing **2** [C] a particular system of words, as used by a people or nation: *He speaks two foreign languages.|the language of science* (=the particular words used by scientists) **3** [C;U] any system of signs, movements, etc., used to express meanings or feelings: *the language of music/mathematics|a computer language*

language lab·o·ra·to·ry /'··· ,···/ *n* a room in which people can learn languages by means of special machines, esp. TAPE RECORDERS

lan·guid /'læŋgwɪd/ *adj* lacking strength or will; slow and weak –**languidly** *adv*

lan·guish /'læŋgwɪʃ/ *v* [I] *fml or lit* **1** to be or become lacking in strength or will **2** [*in*] to experience long suffering: *to languish in prison*

lan·guor /'læŋgər/ *n* [U] *lit* **1** tiredness of mind or body; lack of strength or will **2** pleasant or heavy stillness: *The languor of a summer afternoon.* –**languorous** *adj* –**languorously** *adv*

lank /læŋk/ *adj* (of hair) straight and lifeless –**lankly** *adv* –**lankness** *n* [U]

lank·y /'læŋkiʸ/ *adj* **-ier, -iest** (esp. of a person) very thin and ungracefully tall –**lankily** *adv* –**lankiness** *n* [U]

lan·tern /'læntərn/ *n* a container, usu. of glass and metal, that encloses the flame of a light: *a* KEROSENE *lantern*

lap¹ /læp/ *n* the front part of a seated person between the waist and the knees: *Come and sit on my lap.*

lap² *v* **-pp-** [T] (in racing) to pass (another competitor) so as to be at least one LAP³ ahead of him/her

lap³ *n* (in racing) a single journey around a track or across the length of a swimming pool

lap⁴ *v* **-pp- 1** [T *up*] to drink by taking up with quick movements of the tongue: *The cat lapped up the milk.* **2** [I *against*] to move or hit with little waves and soft sounds: *The sea lapped against the rocks.*

lap sthg.↔ **up** *v adv* **-pp-** [T] to listen eagerly to; accept without thought: *The silly boy lapped up all their praise.*

lap⁵ *n* the act or sound of LAPping⁴: *the lap of the waves*

la·pel /lə'pɛl/ *n* the part of the front of a coat (or JACKET) that is joined to the collar and folded back on each side towards the shoulders

lapse¹ /læps/ *n* **1** a small fault, mistake, or failure in behavior, esp. one that is quickly put right: *a lapse of memory* **2** a gradual passing away, esp. of time: *After a lapse of several years he came back to see us.*

lapse² *v* **lapsed, lapsing** [I] **1** [*into*] to sink, pass, or fall by degrees: *to lapse into silence* **2** [*from*] to fail with regard to behavior, belief, etc.: *a lapsed Catholic* (=who no longer practices his/her religion) **3** (of business agreements, titles, etc.) to come to an end, esp.because of lack of use or failure to claim

lar·ce·ny /'lɑrsəniʸ/ *n* **-nies** [C;U] *law* (an act of) stealing –compare THEFT

larch /lɑrtʃ/ *n* [C;U] (the wood of) a tall tree with bright green needle-like leaves and hard-skinned fruit (CONES)

lard /lɑrd/ *n* [U] pig fat used in cooking

lar·der /'lɑrdər/ *n* a cupboard or small room in a house where food is stored –see also PANTRY

large /lɑrdʒ/ *adj* **1** more than usual in size, number, or amount; big –opposite **small** –see Study Notes on page 550 **2 at large: a** (esp. of dangerous people or animals) free; uncontrolled **b** as a whole; altogether: *The country at large is hoping for great changes.* **3 larger than life** not able to be mistaken; real –see also BY² (5) –**largeness** *n* [U]

large·ly /'lɑrdʒliʸ/ *adv* to a great degree; chiefly: *This country is largely desert.|He left his job largely because he was bored.*

lar·gesse ‖also **largess** *AmE* /lɑr'dʒɛs, lɑr'ʒɛs/– *n* [U] generosity to those in need

lar·i·at /'læriʸət/ *n AmE* for LASSO¹

lark¹ /lɑrk/ *n infml* something done for a joke or amusement; *He did it for a lark, he didn't mean any harm.*

lark² *n* a small light brown singing bird with long pointed wings, e.g. the SKYLARK

lar·va /'lɑrvə/ *n* **-vae** /viʸ/ the wormlike young of an insect –**larval** *adj*

lar·yn·gi·tis /,lærən'dʒaɪtɪs/ *n* [U] a painful swollen condition of the LARYNX, which makes speech difficult

lar·ynx /'lærɪŋks/ also **voice box** *infml*– **larynxes** or **larynges** /lə'rɪndʒiʸz/ the hollow boxlike part in the throat, in which the sounds of the voice are produced by the VOCAL CORDS

las·civ·i·ous /lə'sɪviʸəs/ *adj* feeling or showing uncontrolled sexual desire –**lasciviously** *adv* –**lasciviousness** *n* [U]

la·ser /'leʸzər/ *n* an apparatus for producing a very powerful narrow beam of light

lash¹ /læʃ/ *v* **1** [T] to strike with or as if with a whip: (fig.) *a tongue lashing* (=a scolding) **2** [I;T *about*] to strike or move violently or suddenly: *The cat's tail lashed angrily.* **3** [T] to tie firmly, esp. with rope: *During the storm all the boxes had to be lashed down.*

lash out *v adv* [I *at, against*] **1** to strike or attack violently with a weapon, hand, foot, etc. **2** to attack with violent speech

lash² *n* **1** (a stroke given with) the thin striking part of a whip **2** a sudden or violent movement: *the lash of the waves on the rocks*

las·so¹ /'læsoʷ, læ'suʷ/ also **lariat** *AmE*– *n* **-sos** or **-soes** a rope with one end that can be tightened in a circle (NOOSE), used(esp. in the US) for catching horses and cattle

lasso² *v* [T] to catch with a LASSO

last¹ /læst, lɑst/ *n,pron* **1** [+*to-v*] the person or thing after all the others: *He was the very last to arrive.* –compare FIRST¹ (1) **2 at (long) last** in the end; after a long time: *At long last we found out what had really happened.* **3 to the last** until the end

last² *determiner,adv* [*no comp.*] **1** after everything else; after the others: *George arrived last/was the last person to arrive.|This is my last $1.* (=the only remaining one) –compare FIRST² **2** on the occasion nearest in the past; most recent: *When did you last see him?|They've lived here for the last three years.* (=the three years up to this year)|*This week's class was shorter than last week's.* (not the last week's) –compare NEXT² (2) **3 last but not least** important, although coming at the end

last³ v **1** to measure in length of time; go on; continue: *The hot weather lasted until September.* **2** [I] to remain in use, in good condition, or unweakened: *This cheap watch won't last (for) very long.*

last·ing /'læstɪŋ,'lɑ-/ adj [A] continuing for a long time; unending: *a lasting sorrow*

last·ly /'læstli,'lɑstli/ adv after everything else; in the end: *. . . Lastly, let me mention the help I had from my parents.* –compare FIRSTLY

latch¹ /lætʃ/ n **1** a fastening for a door, gate, window, etc., worked by dropping a bar into a U-shaped space **2** a spring lock for a house door that can be opened from the outside with a key

latch² v [I;T] to fasten or be able to be fastened with a LATCH¹ –opposite **unlatch**
latch on v adv [I to] infml to understand
latch onto sbdy./sthg. v prep [T] infml **1** to understand **2** to refuse to allow (someone) to go; CLING TO

late¹ /leʸt/ adj **1** arriving, happening, etc., after the usual, arranged, or expected time: *The train was 10 minutes late.* **2** happening towards the end of the day, life, a period, etc.: *She returned in the late afternoon.* –compare EARLY¹ **3** [A] happening only a short time ago: *Some late news has just come in.* **4** [A] who has died recently: *her late husband* –**lateness** n [U]

late² adv **1** after the usual, arranged, or expected time: *The bus arrived five minutes late.* **2** towards the end of a period: *The bush was planted late in the season.* –compare EARLY² **3 of late** recently

late·ly /'leʸtli/ adv in the recent past

la·tent /'leʸtnt/ adj existing but not yet noticeable or fully developed: *latent ability/talent* –**latency** n [U]

lat·er·al /'lætˌərəl/ adj [A] tech of, at, from, or towards the side: *a lateral* SHOOT *on a plant*|(fig.) *a lateral idea* –**laterally** adv

lat·est /'leʸtəst/ n [U] infml the most recent news, fashion, or example: *Have you heard the latest about the war?*

la·tex /'leʸteks/ n [U] a thick whitish liquid produced esp. by the rubber tree

lathe /leʸð/ n a machine that turns a piece of wood or metal round against a sharp tool that gives it shape

lath·er¹ /'læðər||'lɑðər/ n [S;U] a **a** white mass produced by shaking a mixture of soap and water: *He put some lather on his chin, and then began to* SHAVE. **b** any mass like this, (e.g. of SWEAT)

lather² v **1** [I] (esp. of soap) to produce a LATHER¹ **2** [T] to cover with LATHER¹

Lat·in /'lætn/ n,adj **1** [U] (of) the language of the ancient Romans **2** [C] (a member) of any nation that speaks a language that comes from LATIN(1), such as Spanish, Portuguese, Italian, or French

Latin A·mer·i·ca /ˌ·· ·'···/ n the Spanish- or Portuguese-speaking countries of South and Central America –**Latin American** /ˌ··

·'··· ◄/ adj: *Latin American politics/history*

lat·i·tude /'lætə,tuʷd, -,tyuʷd/ n [S;U] **1** the distance north or south of the EQUATOR measured in degrees: *The latitude of the ship is 20 degrees south.* –compare LONGITUDE **2** freedom in action, opinion, expression, etc.: *That school allows its students a great deal of latitude in deciding which subjects to study..*

lat·i·tudes /'lætə,tuʷdz, -,tyuʷdz/ n [P] an area at a certain LATITUDE: **High latitudes** are those areas a long way north or south of the EQUATOR.

la·trine /lə'triʸn/ n (esp. in camps) a hole in the ground used as a TOILET

lat·ter /'lætər/ adj fml **1** [A] (after the, this, or these) nearer to the end; later: *the latter years of her life* **2** [A] the second (of two people or things just mentioned): *Of the pig and the cow, the latter (animal) is more valuable.*|*Of pigs and cows, the latter (=cows) are more valuable.*|*Did he walk or swim? The latter seems unlikely.* –compare FORMER²

lat·ter·ly /'lætərliʸ/ adv recently; lately –compare FORMERLY

lat·tice /'lætɪs/ n a wooden or metal framework used as a fence, a support for climbing flowers, etc.

laud·a·ble /'lɔdəbəl/ adj fml (esp. of behavior, actions, etc.) deserving praise –**laudability** /ˌlɔdə'bɪlətiʸ/ n [U] –**laudably** /'lɔdəbliʸ/ adv

laugh¹ /læf/ v **1** [I at] to express amusement, happiness, careless disrespect, etc., by making explosive sounds with the voice, usu. while smiling: *It was so funny, I couldn't stop laughing.* **2** [T] to bring, put, drive, etc., with laughing: *They laughed her out of the house.*|*He laughed himself sick.* **3 laugh in somebody's face** to show clear disrespect or disobedience towards somebody **4 no laughing matter** serious
laugh sthg.↔ **off/away** v adv [T] to cause, by laughing, to seem less or unimportant: *She bravely laughed off her pain.*

laugh² n **1** an act or sound of laughing **2 have the last laugh** to win after earlier defeats

laugh·a·ble /'læfəbəl/ adj causing laughter; funny; foolish –**laughably** adv

laugh·ter /'læftər/ n [U] the act or sound of laughing

launch¹ /lɔntʃ, lɑntʃ/ v [T] **1** to set a (newly-built) boat into the water **2** to send (esp. a ROCKET) into the sky **3** to cause (an activity, plan, way of life, etc.) to begin: *to launch an attack/a new product* **4** [at] to throw with great force

launch² n [S] the act of LAUNCHing¹

launch³ n a large motor boat used for carrying people on rivers, lakes, etc.

laun·der /'lɔndər, 'lɑn-/ v [T] to wash (or wash and iron) (clothes, sheets, etc.)

laun·dro·mat /'lɔndrə,mæt, 'lɑn-/ AmE‖also **launderette** /ˌlɔndə'rɛt, ˌlɑn-/ esp. BrE– n a place where people pay to wash their clothes in machines

laun·dry /'lɔndriʸ, 'lɑn-/ n -**dries 1** [C] a place or business where clothes, etc., are washed and ironed **2** [U] clothes, sheets, etc., needing washing or that have just been washed **3**

[C] →LAUNDROMAT

lau·rel /ˈlɔrəl, ˈlɑrəl/ n a small tree with smooth shiny leaves that do not fall in winter

la·va /ˈlɑvə, ˈlævə/ n [U] 1 rock in a very hot liquid state flowing from an exploding mountain (VOLCANO) 2 this material when it has become cool and turned into a gray solid

lav·a·to·ry /ˈlævəˌtɔriʸ, -ˌtoʷriʸ/ n -ries AmE 1 a WASHBOWL in a BATHROOM 2 BATHROOM

lav·en·der /ˈlævəndər/ n [U] a plant with small strongly-smelling pale purple flowers

lav·ish /ˈlævɪʃ/ adj 1 generous or wasteful in giving or using: a lavish spender|lavish with help 2 given, spent, or produced in great quantity: lavish praise |a lavish feast –lavishly adv –lavishness n [U]

lavish on v prep [T] to give or spend freely, generously, or wastefully: He lavished money/kindness on his friends.

law /lɔ/ n 1 [C] a rule that is supported by the power of government and that governs the behavior of members of a society: a law against drinking and driving 2 [the S] the whole body of such rules in a country: The law forbids stealing.|Murder is against the law.|Law and order is necessary for a peaceful society. 3 [U] such rules, either in total or in part, and the way in which they work: She's studying law at the university.|business law 4 [C] a rule of action in a sport, art, business, etc.: the laws of tennis 5 [C] a statement expressing what has been seen always to happen in certain conditions: Boyle's law is a scientific principle.|the laws of physics 6 [the U] infml the police or a policeman: The law was there in large numbers.

law·a·bid·ing /ˈ· ·,···/ adj obeying the law

law·ful /ˈlɔfəl/ adj fml 1 allowed by law: their lawful king 2 obeying the law: lawful citizens –opposite unlawful –see LEGAL (USAGE) –lawfully adv –lawfulness n [U]

law·less /ˈlɔlɪs/ adj fml 1 uncontrolled; wild 2 (of a country or place) not governed by laws –lawlessly adv –lawlessness n [U]

lawn /lɔn/ n a stretch of usu. flat ground covered with closely cut grass –see illustration on page 337

law·suit /ˈlɔsuʷt/ also suit– n a noncriminal case in a court of law

law·yer /ˈlɔyər, ˈlɔɪər/ also attorney AmE– n a person whose business it is to advise people about laws and to represent them in court

lax /læks/ adj 1 not giving attention to details or to what is correct or necessary 2 careless or lazy 3 lacking in control –laxly adv –laxity /ˈlæksəṭiʸ/ also laxness– n [C;U]

lax·a·tive /ˈlæksəṭɪv/ n,adj (a medicine) that causes the bowels to empty easily

lay¹ /leʸ/ v laid /leʸd/, laying 1 [T down] to put down so as to lie flat: Lay your coat on the bed.|We're going to lay a new carpet. 2 [T] to set in proper order or position: This workman is able to lay bricks very quickly. 3 [T] to cause to lie flat, settle, disappear, or cease to be active: Her fears were soon laid (to rest). 4 [I;T] (of birds, insects, etc.) to produce (an egg or eggs): The hens aren't laying. 5 [T] to make (a statement, claim, charge, etc.) in an official way: The police have laid a serious

charge against you. 6 [T on] to risk (esp. money) on the result of some happening, such as a race; BET²

USAGE Do not confuse lay [T] (laid, laid) with lie [I] (lay, lain). A person can lay his coat on the bed; when he has done this his coat is lying on the bed. A third verb lie [I] (lied, lied) means "to tell a lie."

lay down sthg. v adv [T] 1 to put down (tools, arms, etc.) as a sign that one will not use them 2 to state firmly: to lay down the law

lay into sbdy. v prep [T] to attack with words or blows

lay sbdy. **low** v adv [T] 1 to knock down 2 to make ill: I was laid low by a fever.

lay sbdy.↔ **off** v adv [T] to stop employing (a worker) for a period in which there is little work: They laid us off for three months. –compare TAKE on; see also LAY-OFF

lay sbdy./ sthg.↔ **out** v adv [T] 1 to spread out or arrange 2 to plan (a building, town, garden, etc.) 3 to knock or strike (a person) down –see also LAYOUT

lay over also **stop over**– v adv [I] AmE to make a short stay (usu. at an airport) before continuing a journey

lay sbdy./ sthg.↔ **up** v adv [T] 1 [usu. pass.] to cause to be kept indoors or in bed with an illness: I was laid up with a cold. 2 to put (a boat) out of service, esp. for repairs

lay sthg. **waste** v adv [T] to make (a place) bare, esp. by violence; destroy, as in war

lay² adj [A] 1 of, to, or performed by people who are not in official positions within a religion 2 not having knowledge of a particular branch of learning, such as law or medicine

lay³ v past tense of LIE¹

lay·er¹ /ˈleʸər/ n 1 a thickness of some material (often one of many) laid over a surface: These seeds must be covered with a layer of earth. 2 a person or thing that lays something: a bricklayer

layer² v [T] to make a LAYER¹ (1) of; put down in LAYERS¹ (1)

lay·man /ˈleʸmən/ n -men /mən/ 1 a person who is not a priest in a religion 2 a LAY² (2) person

lay-off /ˈ· ·/ n the stopping by a business of a worker's employment at a time when there is little work –see also LAY¹ off

lay·out /ˈleʸaʊt/ n 1 the planned arrangement of a town, garden, etc. 2 a drawing or plan of a building. –see also LAY¹ out

laze¹ /leʸz/ v lazed, lazing [I;T away, around, about] to rest lazily; to waste (time) enjoyably: I spent the morning just lazing (around).|I lazed away the morning.

laze² n [S] a short period of restful and lazy inactivity

la·zy /ˈleʸziʸ/ adj -zier, -ziest 1 disliking and avoiding activity or work: He won't work: he's just too lazy! –compare IDLE¹ 2 (esp. of periods of time) encouraging inactivity: a lazy afternoon 3 moving slowly: a lazy river –lazily adv –laziness n [U]

lb written abbrev. said as: pound (weight)

lead¹ /liʸd/ v led /lɛd/, leading 1 [I;T] to bring

or show the way to (a person or animal) by going in front: *She led the blind man down the stairs.|The horses were led into the yard.|You lead and we'll follow.* **2** [I;T] to be the means of reaching a place, going through an area, etc.: *This road will lead you to the center of town.|The path leads through the woods.* **3** [T] to persuade or influence (someone) to do something: *What led you to believe I was sick?* **4** [I;T] to direct, control, or govern (an army, a movement, a meeting, etc.) **5** [I;T] to be ahead in sports or games: *Boston was leading Chicago 15–0 at half time.* **6** [T] to (cause to) experience (a kind of life): *He led a hard life.*

USAGE To **lead** is to show the way by going first, to **guide** is to show the way and explain things, and to **direct** is to explain to someone how to get to a place: *He led them down the mountain.|She guided the tourists round the castle.|Could you direct me to the station, please?* To **drive** is either to control a moving vehicle, or to make animals move forward by going behind them: *Driving the cattle to market.* To **steer** is to control the direction of a moving vehicle or boat.

lead sbdy. **on** *v adv infml* [T] to cause to believe something that is not true: *I don't believe you; you're just leading me on!*

lead to sthg. *v prep* [T +*v-ing*] to have as a result; cause: *Smoking cigarettes leads to lung disease.*

lead up to sthg. *v adv prep* [T] to be an introduction to: *He was leading up to a request for money with his kind words.*

lead² *n* **1** [*the* S] the chief or front position: *Los Angeles was* **in the lead** (=winning the game) *at half time.|He's* **playing the lead** (=the chief acting part) *in the new play.|Japan has* **taken the lead** *in car production.* (=is now producing more than anyone else) **2** [S *of, over*] the distance, number of points, etc., by which a person or thing is in advance of another: *Our product still has a good lead over that of our competitor.* **3** [C] a piece of information that may lead to a discovery or something being settled; CLUE: *The police have several useful leads.* **4** [C] a guiding suggestion or example: *I'll follow your lead.* **5** [C] an electric wire for taking the power from the supply point to an instrument or apparatus

lead³ /lɛd/ *n* **1** [U] a soft heavy easily melted grayish-blue metal, used for pipes, to cover roofs, etc. **2** [C;U] a thin stick of a black substance (a kind of CARBON (1)) used in pencils: *I need a soft lead pencil.*

lead·en /ˈlɛdn/ *adj* **1** of the color of lead; dull gray: *a leaden sky* **2** dull; heavy; sad: *a leaden heart*

lead·er /ˈliʸdər/ *n* **1** a person or thing that leads or is in advance of others: *The leader (of the race) is just coming into view.* –compare WINNER **2** a person who guides or directs a group, movement, etc.: *the leader of a political party|a* SCOUT² (2) *leader*

lead·er·ship /ˈliʸdərˌʃɪp/ *n* [U] **1** the position of LEADER (2): *the battle for the leadership of the Republican Party* **2** the qualities neces-

sary in a LEADER (2)

lead·ing /ˈliʸdɪŋ/ *adj* [A] **1** most important; chief; main: *She is a* **leading light** (=an important and influential person) *in the modern theater.* **2** guiding, directing, or controlling: *A* **leading question** *is one formed in such a way that it suggests the desired answer.*

leaf /liʸf/ *n* **leaves** /liʸvz/ **1** [C] one of the usu. flat and green parts of a plant that are joined to its stem or branch **2** [C] a thin sheet of paper, esp. a page in a book **3** [U] metal, esp. gold or silver, in a very thin sheet: *gold leaf* **4** [C] part of a tabletop, usu. with HINGEs, that may be folded up or down to make the table bigger or smaller **5 turn over a new leaf** to begin a new course of improved behavior, habits, etc.

leaf·let /ˈliʸflɪt/ *n* a small sheet of printed matter, usu. given free to the public

leaf through (sthg.) *v prep; adv* [I;T] to turn the pages of (a book, magazine, etc.) quickly without reading much

leaf·y /ˈliʸfiʸ/ *adj* **-ier, -iest** covered with leaves (LEAF (1))

league /liʸg/ *n* **1** a group of people, countries, etc., who have joined together to work for some aim **2** a group of sports clubs or players that play games among themselves in competition **3 in league (with)** working together, often secretly or for a bad purpose **4 in the same league (with)** equal (to)

leak¹ /liʸk/ *n* **1** a small accidental hole or crack, esp. in a container, pipe, etc., through which something flows in or out **2** the liquid, gas, etc., that escapes through such a hole: *I can smell a gas leak.* **3** an accidental or intentional spreading of news, facts, etc., that ought to be secret

leak² *v* **1** [I;T] to let (a liquid, gas, etc.) in or out of a LEAK¹ (1): *The bottle leaks.* **2** [I] (of a liquid, gas, etc.) to pass through a LEAK¹ (1) **3** [T *out, to*] to make known (news, facts, etc., that ought to be secret): *The politician leaked the news to the newspapers.*

leak out *v adv* [I] (of news, facts, etc., that ought to be secret) to become known

leak·age /ˈliʸkɪdʒ/ *n* [U] the act or result of LEAKing² (2)

leak·y /ˈliʸkiʸ/ *adj* **-ier, -iest** letting liquid LEAK² (2) in or out: *a leaky bucket*

lean¹ /liʸn/ *v* **leaned** *or* **leant** /lɛnt/ *esp. BrE,* **leaning 1** [I] to be in a position that is not upright; slope: *That wall leans so much it might fall over.* **2** [I] to bend (from the waist): *He leaned forward/over to hear what she was saying.* **3** [I;T] to rest (oneself or something) on or against something: *She leaned against the door.*

lean on/upon sbdy. *v prep* [T] also **lean upon** sbdy.– to depend on: *to lean on my friends for help*

lean toward *AmE*‖also **lean towards** *BrE– v prep* [T] to favor (an opinion, idea, etc.)

lean² *adj* **1** (of people and animals) very thin **2** (of meat) without much fat **3** producing or having little value: *This has been a lean year for business.* –**leanness** *n* [U]

lean·ing /ˈliʸnɪŋ/ *n* [*towards*] a feeling or opinion (in favor of): *Most young people have a* *leaning towards rock music.*

leap¹ /liˠp/ *v* **leaped** *or* **leapt** /lɛpt/ *esp. BrE,* **leaping** /'liˠpɪŋ/ **1** [I] to jump through the air, often landing in a different place: *He leaped into the air.|They leaped over the stream.* **2** [T] to jump over: *He leaped the wall and ran away.*

leap at sthg. *v prep* [T] to accept (a chance, offer, etc.) eagerly

leap² *n* **1** a sudden jump, spring, or movement **2** the distance crossed by LEAPING¹: *a leap of three feet* **3** a sudden increase: *a leap in the number of births.*

leap year /'· ·/ *n* [C;U] a year, every fourth year, in which February has 29 days instead of 28 days

learn /lɜrn/ *v* **learned** /lɜrnd, lɜrnt/ ‖also *BrE* **learnt** /lɜrnt/ **learning 1** [I;T +*to-v*] to gain knowledge (of) or skill (in): *The child is learning quickly.|I'm trying to learn French.|He is learning to be a dancer.|She is learning how to play the drums.* –compare TEACH **2** [T] to fix in the memory; MEMORIZE: *Learn this list of words.* **3** [I;T (*of, about*)] to become informed (of): *His mother learned of her son's success in the newspapers.* **4 learn one's lesson** to suffer so much from doing something that one will not do it again

USAGE For the past tense and past participle, **learned** is the usual *AmE* form but **learned** and **learnt** are equally common in *BrE.* –see KNOW (USAGE)

learn·ed /'lɜrnɪd/ *adj* having or showing much knowledge: *a learned woman/book* **–learnedly** *adv*

learn·er /'lɜrnər/ *n* a person who is learning: *She's a rather slow learner.* (=is slow at learning)

learn·ing /'lɜrnɪŋ/ *n* [U] deep and wide knowledge gained through study –compare KNOWLEDGE

lease¹ /liˠs/ *n* **1** a written agreement by which a building, piece of land, etc., is given (RENTed² (2)) to somebody for a certain time in return for rent: *His lease is for five years.* **2 a new lease on life** *AmE* new strength or desire to be happy, successful, etc.

lease² *v* **leased, leasing** [T *out*] to give or take the use of (land or buildings) on a LEASE¹

leash /liˠʃ/ *n AmE* a length of rope, leather, chain, etc., tied to a dog to control it: *Dogs must be kept on a leash.*

least¹ /liˠst/ *adv* (*superlative of* LITTLE) **1** in the smallest degree: *It happened just when we least expected it.|No one listened, least of all* (=especially not) *the children!* –compare MOST¹ **2 least of all** especially not: *I don't want to see anyone today, least of all him!*

least² *determiner,pron* (*superlative of* LITTLE) **1** the smallest number or amount: *Buy the one that costs the least.|He's **not in the least*** (=not at all) *worried.* **2 at least: a** not less than; if not more: *They cost at least $5/$5 at least.* **b** if nothing else; anyway: *The food wasn't good, but at least it was cheap.*

leath·er /'lɛðər/ *n* [U] treated animal skin used for making shoes, bags, etc.: *a leather coat*

leath·er·y /'lɛðəriˠ/ *adj* like leather; hard and

stiff: *leathery meat*

leave¹ /liˠv/ *v* **left** /lɛft/, **leaving 1** [I;T] to go away (from): *I hope they'll leave soon. I want to go to bed.|I hear (that) his brother has left home.|The ship is leaving for* (=to go to) *New York soon.* **2** [T] to allow to remain, esp. after going away: *The mailman left a letter for us.|Someone has left the window open.|Is there any coffee left or did you drink it all?|You've left your food* (=not eaten it); *don't you like it?|I can't deal with it now. I'll leave it until tomorrow.|Let's just leave it at that.* (=not talk or argue about it any longer) **3** [T *behind*] to fail to take or bring, esp. by accident: *Don't leave your coat (behind)!* **4** [T] to give after one's death: *I'm leaving you $5,000 in my* WILL² (4). **5** [T +*v-ing/with, to*] to give into the care or charge of someone: *He left his cat with us.|I'll leave (it to) you to buy the tickets.|I'll leave buying the tickets to you.* **6** [T] to cause to remain after doing a sum: *2 from 8 leaves 6.* **7 leave one cold** to fail to excite or interest one

leave sbdy./sthg.↔**out** *v adv* [T *of*] to fail to put in or include: *I left out the important point.|They left me out of the team.*

leave sbdy./sthg. **behind** *v adv* [T] to fail to take or bring esp. by accident

leave off *v adv* [I] to stop: *I left off in the middle of page 10.*

leave² *n* **1** [C;U] (a period of) time away from work or duty, esp. in the armed forces: *The soldiers are on leave.|I'm spending my next leave in Greece.* –see VACATION (USAGE) **2** [U +*to-v*] *fml* permission: *Have you been given leave to swim here?* **3 take leave (of)** to say goodbye (to); go away (from)

leaves /liˠvz/ *n pl. of* LEAF

lech·er·ous /'lɛtʃərəs/ *adj derog* (usu. of a man) having a desire for continual sexual pleasure **–lecherously** *adv* **–lecherousness** *n* [U]: *His lecherousness is famous.* **–lecher** *n* [C]: *He's a real lecher.*

lech·er·y /'lɛtʃəriˠ/ *n* [U] *derog* continual searching for sexual pleasure

lec·tern /'lɛktərn/ *n* a sloping table for holding a book

lec·ture /'lɛktʃər/ *n,v* **-tured, -turing** [C;I;T *on, about*] **1** (to give) a speech to a group of people, esp. as a method of teaching at universities: *She lectures on English history.|a history lecture* **2** (to give) a long solemn scolding or warning

lec·tur·er /'lɛktʃərər/ *n* a person who teaches or gives LECTUREs usu. at a university or college, usu. in a **lecture hall –lectureship** /'lɛktʃər,ʃɪp/ *n: She's got a lectureship at Yale.*

led /lɛd/ *v past tense and past participle* LEAD¹

ledge /lɛdʒ/ *n* **1** a narrow flat shelf, esp. one on the edge of an upright object: *He keeps some books on the window ledge, and some on a shelf on the wall.* **2** a flat shelf of rock

ledg·er /'lɛdʒər/ *n* an account book recording money going in and out of a business, bank, etc.

leech /liˠtʃ/ *n* a small wormlike creature that lives by drinking the blood of living animals

leek /liˠk/ *n* a vegetable like the onion but

with a long white fleshy stem and large long leaves

leer¹ /lɪər/ n an unpleasant smile or sideways look expressing cruel enjoyment or thoughts of sex

leer² v [I at] to look with a LEER¹: *He leered at the young girl.* –**leeringly** adv

leer·y /'lɪəriʸ/ adj [no comp. (of)] infml watchful and not trusting

lee·way /'liʸweʸ/ n [C;U] additional time, space, money, etc., that allows a chance to succeed in doing something: *Ten minutes should be (a big) enough leeway to allow for delays.*

left¹ /lɛft/ adj [A] **1** on or belonging to the side of the body that usu. contains the heart: *one's left arm/eye* **2** on, by, or in the direction of one's left side: *the left bank of the stream* –opposite **right**

left² n **1** [the+U] the left side or direction: *Keep to the left.* **2** [C] the left hand **3** [U] political parties or groups that generally support LIBERAL political views: *The left is going to win the election.* –compare RIGHT²

left³ adv towards the left –opposite **right**

left⁴ v past tense and past participle of LEAVE¹

left-hand /ˌ· '·◄/ adj [A] **1** on, to, or going to the left: *the left-hand page|a left-hand turn* **2** of, for, with, or done by the left hand: *a left-hand stroke*

left-hand·ed /ˌ· '··◄/ adj **1** using the left hand for most actions **2** made for use by a left-handed person: *left-handed scissors* –opposite **right-handed** –**left-handedly** adv –**left-handedness** n [U]

left lug·gage of·fice /ˌ· '·· ˌ··/ n BrE for BAGGAGE ROOM

left·o·vers /'lɛft,oʷvərz/ n [P] food remaining uneaten after a meal

left·ward /'lɛftwərd/ AmE∥also **leftwards** /'lɛftwərdz/ esp. BrE– adv on or towards the left –opposite **rightward** –**leftward** adj

left wing /ˌ· '·◄/ adj,n [U] (the members) of a political party or of a group that favor greater political changes: LEFT² (3): *left-wing ideas|The left wing hasn't voted yet.* –opposite **right wing** –**left-winger** /ˌ· '·· / n

leg /lɛg/ n **1** one of the limbs on which an animal walks and which support its body **2** that part of this limb above the foot **3** the part of a garment that covers the leg: *There's a hole in your pants leg.* **4** one of the long thin supports on which a piece of furniture stands **5** one part or stage, esp. of a journey or competition: *The last leg of the journey always seems the longest.* **6** on one's/its last legs: **a** very tired **b** nearly worn out or failed **c** close to death **7** pull someone's leg to make fun of a person in a playful way, as by making him/her believe something that is not true **8** stretch one's legs to take a short walk, esp. when feeling stiff after sitting for a long time **9** -legged having legs of the stated number or kind: *four-legged|sitting cross-legged*

leg·a·cy /'lɛgəsiʸ/ n -cies **1** money, etc., that passes to someone on the death of the owner according to his/her official written wish (WILL² (4)) **2** something passed on or left behind by someone else: (fig.) *Disease and famine are often legacies of war.*

le·gal /'liʸgəl/ adj **1** allowed or made by law; lawful: *a legal claim* –opposite **illegal 2** [A] of, concerning, or using the law: *He took legal action to stop his neighbors making so much noise.* –**legally** adv –**legality** /lɪ'gæləṭiʸ/ n [U]

USAGE **Legal** and **lawful** both mean "allowed by the law." *Children can't buy alcohol: it's not* **legal/lawful. Legal** also means "connected with the law;" *the* **legal** *profession|Do you know your* **legal** *rights?* **Legitimate** is a similar word meaning "lawful and correct," but it can also mean "reasonable and acceptable": *You should only stay away from school if you have a* **legitimate** *reason, such as illness.*

legal aid /ˌ·· '·/ n [U] the services of a lawyer in a court case provided free to people who cannot pay for them

le·gal·ize ∥also -ise BrE /'liʸgə,laɪz/ v - ized, -izing [T] to make legal: *Will the government legalize* ABORTION? –**legalization** /ˌliʸgələ'zeʸʃən/ n [U]

le·ga·tion /lɪ'geʸʃən/ n [C sing./pl. v] a group of government employees who represent their government in a foreign country

leg·end /'lɛdʒənd/ n **1** [C] an old story about ancient times which is probably not true **2** [U] such stories collectively: *a character in legend* **3** [C] a famous person or act, esp. in a particular area of activity: *He is a legend in his own lifetime for his scientific discoveries.*

leg·end·ar·y /'lɛdʒən,deriʸ/ adj **1** of, like, or told in a LEGEND (1) **2** famous

leg·gings /'lɛgɪnz/ n [P] an outer covering worn to protect the legs, esp. from foot to knee –see PAIR¹ (USAGE)

leg·gy /'lɛgiʸ/ adj -gier, -giest (esp. of children and women, and young animals) having long legs –**legginess** n [U]

leg·i·ble /'lɛdʒəbəl/ adj (of handwriting or print) that can be read, esp. easily –opposite **illegible** –**legibility** /ˌlɛdʒə'bɪləṭiʸ/ n [U] –**legibly** /'lɛdʒəbliʸ/ adv: *Please write legibly.*

le·gion /'liʸdʒən/ n [C +sing./pl. v] **1** a group of soldiers or other armed men **2** a large group of people: *a legion of admirers*

leg·is·late /'lɛdʒə,sleʸt/ v -lated, -lating [I for, against] to make laws

leg·is·la·tion /ˌlɛdʒə'sleʸʃən/ n [U] **1** the act of making laws **2** a body of laws

leg·is·la·tive /'lɛdʒə,sleʸṭɪv/ adj [A] **1** of or concerning the making of laws **2** having the power and duty to make laws –**legislatively** adv

leg·is·la·ture /'lɛdʒə,sleʸtʃər/ n the body of people who have the power to make and change laws

le·git·i·mate /lə'dʒɪṭəmɪt/ adj **1** according to law; lawful or correct **2** born of parents who are lawfully married to each other –opposite **illegitimate 3** reasonable; sensible: *They had a legitimate reason for being late.* see LEGAL (USAGE) –**legitimately** adv –**legitimacy** /lə'dʒɪṭəməsiʸ/– n [U]

lei·sure /'liʸʒər, 'lɛ-/ n **1** [U] time when one is free from employment; free time: *Tennis and swimming are her leisure activities.* **2** at

leisure: a not working or busy; free **b** without hurry

lei·sured /ˈliːʒərd, ˈlɛ-/ adj having plenty of free time

lei·sure·ly /ˈliːʒərliʸ, ˈlɛ-/ adj (done) without haste: a leisurely walk

lem·on /ˈlɛmən/ n [C;U] (a tree bearing) a fruit with a thick yellow skin and sour juice: a lemon drink

lem·on·ade /ˌlɛməˈneʸd/ n [U] **1** AmE a drink made from fresh LEMONS with sugar and water added **2** BrE a transparent drink tasting of LEMONS, containing small bubbles, to which water is not added before drinking

lend /lɛnd/ v lent /lɛnt/, lending [T to] **1** to give (someone) the possession or use of (something) for a limited time: Can you lend me $10? I'll return it next week.|I lent her some bread; she'll bring me some more tomorrow. –see Study Notes on page 481 **2** fml to add or give: The flags lent color to the streets. –compare BORROW, LOAN

length /lɛŋkθ, lɛŋθ/ n **1** [C;U] the measurement or distance from one end to the other or of the longest side of something: The length of the room is 10 meters; it is 10 meters in length.|We walked the length of the street. (=from one end to the other)|The students complained about the length of the exam. (=said there were too many questions) –compare BREADTH **2** [C of] a piece of something, esp. of a certain length or for a particular purpose: a length of string **3** at length: **a** after a long time; at last **b** in detail; using many words **4** go to any/great/considerable lengths to be prepared to do anything, however dangerous, unpleasant, or wicked: He would go to any lengths to keep his government in power.

length·en /ˈlɛŋkθən, ˈlɛŋθən/ v [I;T] to make or become longer –opposite **shorten**

length·wise /ˈlɛŋkθwaɪz, ˈlɛŋθ-/ also **lengthways** /ˈlɛŋkθweʸz, ˈlɛŋθ-/– adv in the direction of the length: Measure/fold it lengthways.

length·y /ˈlɛŋkθiʸ, ˈlɛŋθiʸ/ adj -ier, -iest very long; too long –**lengthiness** n [U]

le·ni·ent /ˈliʸniʸənt, ˈliʸnyənt/ adj merciful in judgment; gentle: a lenient punishment –compare STRICT –**lenience** also **leniency** n [U]

lens /lɛnz/ n **1** a special piece of glass, curved on one or both sides, used to make glasses for the eyes, cameras, microscopes, etc. **2** a part of the eye, behind the PUPIL² **3** →CONTACT LENS

lent /lɛnt/ v past tense and past participle of LEND

Lent n the 40 days before EASTER, during which many Christians FAST³

len·til /ˈlɛntəl/ n the small round seed of a beanlike plant, dried and used for food

Le·o /ˈliʸoʷ/ n see ZODIAC

leop·ard /ˈlɛpərd/ **leopardess** /ˈlɛpərdɪs/ fem. – n a large fierce catlike animal, yellowish with black spots, found in Africa and Southern Asia

le·o·tard /ˈliʸəˌtɑrd/ n a single close-fitting garment that covers the body, worn esp. by dancers

lep·er /ˈlɛpər/ n a person who has LEPROSY: a leper hospital

lep·ro·sy /ˈlɛprəsiʸ/ n [U] a disease in which the skin becomes rough and thick, and fingers, toes, etc., drop off –**leprous** /ˈlɛprəs/ adj

les·bi·an /ˈlɛzbiʸən/ adj,n (of or concerning) a woman who is sexually attracted to other women –compare HOMOSEXUAL –**lesbianism** n [U]

le·sion /ˈliʸʒən/ n tech a wound

less¹ /lɛs/ adv (comparative of LITTLE) [than] **1** (with adjectives and adverbs) not so; to a smaller degree (than): The next train will be less crowded than this one. **2** (with verbs) not so much: Try to shout less.|He works less than he used to. –compare MORE¹ (1)

less² determiner,pron (comparative of LITTLE) [of, than] **1** a smaller amount: They buy less beer and fewer cigarettes now.|Can we have less noise/less of that noise?(=Be quiet!)|She gives them less to eat in summer.|It's less than a mile to the ocean. –see MORE (USAGE) **2** less and less (an amount) that continues to become smaller: less and less work|less and less able to work **3** no less (than) (expressing surprise at a large number or amount): No less than 1000 people came. **4** none the less but all the same; in spite of everything; NEVERTHELESS: I can't really afford it, but I want to buy it none the less. **5** the less (used to show that two things get smaller, or change, together): The less he eats, the thinner he gets.

less³ prep not counting; subtracting: You will be paid $100 less tax, so you should take home about $75.

less·en /ˈlɛsən/ v [I;T] to make or become less in size, importance, appearance, etc.

less·er /ˈlɛsər/ adj,adv [A no comp.] fml (not used with than) not so great or so much: the lesser of two evils |one of the lesser-known African writers

les·son /ˈlɛsən/ n **1** something taught to or learned by a pupil, esp. in school; the period of time a pupil or class studies a subject: Each history lesson lasts 40 minutes. **2** something, e.g. an experience, from which one should learn: His car accident was a lesson to him/taught him a lesson; he won't drive so fast again.

lest /lɛst/ conj fml for fear that; in case: I wrote down the date of his birthday lest I should forget it.

let /lɛt/ v let, letting [T] **1** to allow to do or happen: She lets her children play in the street.|I don't smoke because my father won't let me (smoke).|He's letting his beard grow.|He let a week go by before answering the letter.|They let the prisoners go. (=set them free) **2** must; is to: Let each man decide for himself.|Let there be no mistake about it.|Let the line AB be equal to the line XY. **3** [to, out] BrE for RENT **4** let alone not to mention; even less: The baby can't even walk, let alone run. **5** let/leave someone/something alone/be to stop worrying someone/something; not to touch, scold, etc.: *Let him be; he's not hurting anybody.*|*Leave those books alone; they're not yours!* **6 let go (of)** to stop holding: *Don't let go (of) the handle.*|*Let go! You're hurting my arm.* **7 let oneself go: a** to behave more freely and naturally than usual: *She really lets herself go at parties.* **b** to take less care of one's appearance than usual: *Since his wife died he's just let himself go.* **8 let someone know** to tell someone; inform: *Will you let me know if you can't come to dinner?* **9 let us: a** allow us to: *Please let us buy you a drink!* **b** also **let's–** (used when suggesting a plan that includes the person spoken to) we must/should: *Let's have a party.*|*Let's hurry!*|*Let's not go yet.* **10 let it go at that** to agree or decide not to say/do any more **11 let (it) slip** to allow a fact to be known accidentally **12 let well enough alone** *AmE* to allow existing conditions to remain as they are, for fear of making things worse

let sbdy./sthg.↔ **down** *v adv* [T] **1** to cause to be disappointed; fail to keep a promise to (someone) –see also LETDOWN **2** to make (clothes) longer –opposite **take up** (for 2)

let sbdy./sthg.↔ **in** *v adv* [T] to admit; allow to enter (a house, room, etc.): *There's someone at the door; let them in, will you?*

let sbdy. **in for** sthg. *v adv prep* [T] to cause (esp. oneself) to have (something unwanted): *He let himself in for a lot of work when he agreed to fix that car.*

let sbdy. **in on** sthg. *v adv prep* [T] to allow (someone) to share (a secret)

let sbdy. **off**[1] (sthg.) *v adv; prep* [T] to excuse from (punishment, duty, etc.): *She let him off (doing) his homework because he was ill.*|*The police let him off, but warned him not to do it again.*

let sbdy./sthg.↔ **off**[2] *v adv* [T] to allow to leave a vehicle; DROP **off** (2)

let on sthg.↔ *v adv* [I;T +*that/about*] *infml* to tell (a secret): *He asked me where John was, but I didn't let on.*

let sthg.↔ **out**[1] *v adv* [T] **1** to express; UTTER (2): *He let out a cry of pain.* **2** to make (clothes) bigger –opposite **take in** (for 2)

let out[2] *v adv* [I] *AmE* to end: *The movie lets out at 10:00.*

let sbdy./sthg.↔ **through** *v adv* [T] to allow to pass

let up *v adv* [I] to lessen; gradually cease; stop: *When will this rain let up?* –see also LETUP

let·down /'lɛtdaʊn/ *n infml* a disappointment: *We were going out today, but now it's raining so we can't. What a let down!* –see also LET **down**

le·thal /'liɣθəl/ *adj* able to kill: *a lethal DOSE*[1] *of a poison*

leth·ar·gy /'lɛθərdʒiɣ/ *n* [U] state of being sleepy or unnaturally tired; lazy state of mind –**lethargic** /ləˈθɑrdʒɪk/ *adj*

let·ter /'lɛtər/ *n* **1** [C] a written or printed message sent usu. in an envelope: **2** [C] one of the signs in writing or printing that represents a speech sound **3** [S] the words of an agreement, law, etc., rather than its real or

intended meaning: *be bound by the letter of the law* –compare SPIRIT[1] (6)

let·ter·box /'lɛtər,bɑks/ *BrE* for MAILBOX

let·ter·head /'lɛtər,hɛd/ *n* the name and address of a person or business printed at the top of the owner's writing paper

let·ter·ing /'lɛtərɪŋ/ *n* [U] letters or words written or drawn, esp. with regard to their style

letter-per·fect /,·· '···◄/ *n* having or showing correctness in every detail: *Her speech was letter-perfect.*

let·tuce /'lɛtɪs/ *n* [C;U] a common garden plant with large pale green leaves, used in SALADS

let·up /'lɛtʌp/ *n* [C;U] (a) stopping or lessening of activity –see also LET **up**

leu·ke·mia ‖also **-kae-** *BrE* /luwˈkiɣmiɣə/ *n* [U] a serious disease of the blood during which a person becomes very weak and often dies

lev·el[1] /'lɛvəl/ *n* **1** [C;U] a position of height: *The top of this mountain is two miles above sea level.*|*The garden is arranged on two levels.* (=it has two separate pieces of ground, one higher than the other)|(fig.) *The level* (=quality) *of your work is not satisfactory.*|(fig.) *The matter is being considered at government level.* (=by politicians) **2** [C] a smooth flat surface, esp. a wide area of flat ground: *You should build on the level, not on the slope.* **3** [C *of*] amount, size, or number: *The workmen have been told to increase their production level.* **4 on the level** *infml* honest(ly); truthful(ly)

level[2] *v* **-l-** *AmE*‖**-ll-** *BrE* **1** [I;T *out, off*] to make or become flat and even, so that no one part is raised above the rest: *Level the ground off before you plant the seeds.*|*Prices have begun to level off.* (=stay the same after rising or falling) **2** [T] to knock or pull down to the ground: *They leveled all the old trees to make way for the road.*

level sthg. **at** sbdy. *v prep* [T] **1** to aim (a weapon) at **2** also **level** sthg. **against** sbdy. –to bring (a charge) against: *A serious charge was leveled at the judge.*

level with sbdy. *v prep* [T] to speak freely and truthfully to; not hide facts from: *I'm going to level with you. I'm the one who broke your watch.*

level[3] *adj* **1** having no part higher than the rest; even: *If the table top isn't level, things will roll off.*|*A football field must be level.* **2** [*no comp.*] equal in position or standard: *The child's head is level with his father's knee.*|*The quality of their work is about equal.* **3** steady and unvarying: *He gave me a level look.* **4** also **level-headed** /,·· '···◄/ – calm and sensible in judgment: *She has a level head/is level-headed about money.* **5 one's level best** *infml* one's best effort; all that one can

level[4] *adv* so as to be level

level cross·ing /,·· '··/ *BrE* for GRADE CROSSING

lev·er[1] /'lɛvər, 'liɣ-/ *n* **1** a bar used for moving something heavy or stiff. One end is placed under or against the object, the middle rests on something, and the other end is pushed down **2** any part of a machine working in the same way: *Push the lever, and the machine will start.* **3** something which may be used for influencing someone

lever² *v* [T] to move (something) with a LEVER¹: *They levered it into position.|He had to lever open the window.|(fig.) They're trying to lever him out of his job.*

lev·er·age /'lɛvərɪdʒ, 'liːv-/ *n* [U] **1** the action, use, or power of a LEVER¹ **2** power, influence, or other means of obtaining a result: *He has some leverage over the politician.*

lev·i·tate /'lɛvə,teɪt/ *v* **-tated, -tating** [I;T] to (cause to) rise and float in the air as if by magic –**levitation** /,lɛvə'teɪʃən/ *n* [U]

lev·i·ty /'lɛvəṭiː/ *n* [U] *fml or pomp* lack of seriousness

lev·y¹ /'lɛviː/ *n* **-ies 1** an official demand for, or collection of, a tax or people to become soldiers **2** the money, soldiers, etc., collected

levy² *v* **-ied, -ying** [T *on, upon*] to demand and collect officially: *to levy a tax on tobacco*

lewd /luːᵂd/ *adj* **1** wanting or thinking about sex, esp. in a manner that is not socially acceptable **2** impure; rude; OBSCENE: *lewd songs* –**lewdly** *adv* –**lewdness** *n* [U]

lex·i·cal /'lɛksɪkəl/ *adj tech* of or concerning words –**lexically** *adv*

lex·i·con /'lɛksɪ,kɑn, -kən/ *n* a dictionary, esp. of an ancient language or of words from a single subject: *a lexicon of words related to space flight*

li·a·bil·i·ty /,laɪə'bɪləṭiː/ *n* **-ties 1** [U] the condition of being LIABLE **2** [C] something for which one is responsible, esp. by law **3** [C] the amount of debt that must be paid –compare ASSET

li·a·ble /'laɪəbəl/ *adj* [F] **1** [+ *v-ing/for*] responsible, esp. in law, for paying for something: *He said that he was not liable for his son's debts.* **2** likely to, esp. from habit or tendency: *He's liable to shout when angry.*

li·aise /liː'eɪz/ *v* **-aised, -aising** [I *with*] to work together so that all the people working are informed about what is being done: *We should liaise closely with the government about this.*

li·ai·son /'liːə,zɑn, liː'eɪzɑn/ *n* [*with, between*] **1** a working association or connection **2** a sexual relationship between two people not married to each other

li·ar /'laɪər/ *n* a person who tells lies

lib /lɪb/ *n* [U] *infml* →LIBERATION (esp. in the phrases **women's lib, gay lib** (see GAY (3))

li·bel¹ /'laɪbəl/ *n* [C;U] *law* (the making of) a written statement, picture, etc., that unfairly damages the good opinion held about a person by others: *My reputation was ruined by that libel.* –compare SLANDER

libel² *v* **-l-** *AmE*‖**-ll-** *BrE* [T] to print a LIBEL¹ against

li·bel·ous *AmE*‖**libellous** *BrE* /'laɪbələs/ *adj* **1** being or containing a LIBEL¹: *a libelous article in a newspaper* **2** in the habit of writing LIBELS –**libellously** *adv*

lib·er·al¹ /'lɪbərəl/ *adj* **1** willing to respect the ideas and feelings of others: *a liberal mind/thinker* **2** favoring some change, as in political or religious affairs: *The church has*

become more liberal in this century. –compare REACTIONARY, RADICAL **3** favoring a wide general knowledge and wide possibilities for self-expression: *a liberal education* **4** giving or given freely and generously: *a liberal supporter of the hospital* –**liberalism** *n* [U]

liberal² *n* a person with wide understanding, who is in favor of change –compare REACTIONARY

lib·e·ral·i·ty /,lɪbə'ræləṭiː/ *n* [U] also **liberalness** /'lɪbərəlnɪs/- **1** generosity **2** broadness of mind

lib·er·al·ly /'lɪbərəliː/ *adv* generously; freely; in great amount; in large quantities

lib·er·ate /'lɪbə,reɪt/ *v* **-ated, -ating** [T *from*] *fml* to set free (from control, prison, etc.): *The prisoners were liberated by the army.* –**liberator** *n*

lib·er·at·ed /'lɪbə,reɪṭɪd/ *adj* having freedom of action in social and sexual matters: *a liberated young person*

lib·e·ra·tion /,lɪbə'reɪʃən/ *n* [U] the act of setting free or state of being LIBERATED

lib·er·ty /'lɪbərtiː/ *n* **-ties 1** [U] personal or political freedom from outside control: *People often have to fight for their liberty.* **2** [U] the chance or permission to do or use something **3 at liberty: a** free from prison, control, etc. **b** not busy; free **c** having permission or the right (to do something) **4 take liberties (with): a** to act in a rude, too friendly way (towards) **b** to make changes (in): *They took several liberties with the original story when they turned it into a film.* –compare FREEDOM

li·bi·do /lɪ'biːdoʊᵂ/ *n* **-dos** *tech* the sexual urge

Li·bra /'liːbrə, 'laɪ-/ *n* [S] see ZODIAC

li·brar·i·an /laɪ'brɛəriːən/ *n* a person who is in charge of or helps to run a library –**librarianship** *n* [U]

li·brar·y /'laɪ,brɛriː, -brəriː, -briː/ *n* **-ries 1** a building or room which contains usu. books that may be looked at or borrowed by the public (**public library**) or by members of a special group: *a record/toy library* (=containing records/toys) **2** a collection of books

lice /laɪs/ *n pl. of* LOUSE

li·cense¹ *AmE*‖also **licence** *esp. BrE* /'laɪsəns/- *n* **1** [C] an official paper, card, etc., showing that permission has been given to do something, usu. for a payment: *a driver's license|a license to sell alcohol* **2** [U] (too much) freedom of action, speech, thought, etc. –see also POETIC LICENSE

license² **-cence** *v* **-censed, -censing** [T] to give official permission to or for

license plate *AmE*‖**numberplate** *BrE*– /'·· ,·/ *n* either of the signs (usu. at the front and back ends) of a vehicle showing its official number –see illustration on page 55

li·cen·tious /laɪ'sɛnʃəs, -tʃəs/ *fml* behaving in a sexually uncontrolled manner –**licentiously** *adv* –**licentiousness** *n* [U]

li·chen /'laɪkən/ *n* [U] a flat spreading plant that covers the surfaces of stones and trees

lick¹ /lɪk/ *v* [T] **1** to move the tongue across (a surface) in order to taste, clean, make wet, etc.: *to lick a postage stamp|The dog licked the dish clean.|(fig.) The flames licked against the building.* **2** [*up, out, off*] to take into the mouth with the tongue: *The cat licked up the milk.* **3** *infml* to defeat in a game, race, fight, etc.

lick² *n* **1** the act of LICKing¹ **2** [*of*] a small amount (of cleaning, paint, etc.): *This door needs a lick of paint.*|*He hasn't done a lick of work all week.* **3 a lick and a promise** quick performance of a piece of work

lic·o·rice, liquorice /'lɪkərɪs, -rɪʃ/ *n* [U] a sweet black substance used in medicine and sweets

lid /lɪd/ *n* **1** the piece that covers the open top of a pot, box, or other container and that lifts up or can be removed **2** →EYELID

lie¹ /laɪ/ *v* **lay** /leɪ/, **lain** /leɪⁿn/, **lying,** /'laɪ-ɪŋ/ [I] **1** to be in a flat position on a surface: *The book is lying on the table.*|*He lay on the floor, reading a book.*|*Father is lying down* (=resting on a bed) *for a while.* **2** [*down*; not *be+v-ing*] to put the body into such a position: *I'm tired. I have to lie down.* **3** to be in the stated position; be placed: *The town lies to the east of us.*|(fig.) *The truth lies somewhere between the statements of the two men.*|(fig.)*The decision lies with you.* (=you must make it) **4** to remain or be kept in the stated condition or position: *The machines have lain* IDLE (=unused) *for weeks now.*|*The man lay in prison for seven years.*|*Don't leave your money lying in the bank; spend it.* **5 lie low** to be in hiding or avoid being noticed

　lie around *v adv* [I] to be lazy; do nothing
　lie behind sthg. *v prep* [T] to be the reason for: *I wonder what lies behind his decision to leave.*

lie² *v* **lied, lying** [I] to tell a lie

lie³ *n* an untrue statement purposely made to deceive: *to tell lies*

lieu /luːʷ/ *n* **in lieu (of)** instead (of): *I'll take your watch in lieu of payment.*

lieu·ten·ant /luːʷ'tɛnənt/ *n* an officer of low rank in the armed forces

life /laɪf/ *n* **lives** /laɪvz/ **1** [U] the active force that enables (animals and plants) to continue existing: *Stones do not have life.*|*Is there life after death?* **2** [U] living things: *There is no life on the moon.*|*plant life* **3** [U] human existence: *Life isn't all fun.*|*You won't see life* (=all the different experiences of human existence) *if you stay at home for ever.* **4** [C] the period during which one is alive: *She led a long and happy life.*|*They have very busy lives.*|*I have lived in Chicago all my life, but I will spend the rest of my life in Florida.*|*He had only a short married life.* (=he was married for only a short time)|*Her working life was full of accidents.* **5** [C] a person: *Several lives were lost* (=people died) *in the accident.* **6** [U] activity; movement: *There were* **signs of life** *in the forest as the sun rose.*|*The children are* **full of life** *this morning.* **7** [S] a person or thing that is the cause of enjoyment or activity in a group: *He was* **the life and soul of** *the party.* **8** [U] also **life imprisonment** /ˌ··'···/ – the punishment of being put in prison for as long as one lives: *She got* **life (imprisonment)** *for killing the policeman.* **9** [C] also **life story** /ˌ· '··/ –a written, filmed, or other account of a person's existence; BIOGRAPHY **10 not on your life!** certainly not! **11 take one's (own)/someone's life** to kill oneself/someone **12 the life of** (sthg.) the most active part of: *He's so amusing that he's the life of any party.* –compare DEATH

life belt /'· ·/ *n* a LIFE PRESERVER worn as a belt

life·blood /'laɪfblʌd/ *n* [U] something that gives continuing strength and force: *Trade is the lifeblood of most modern states.*

life·boat /'laɪfboʷt/ *n* a boat used for saving people in danger at sea

life·guard /'laɪfgɑrd/ *n* a swimmer employed to help swimmers in danger

life jack·et /'· ˌ··/ *n* an air-filled garment that is worn around the chest to support a person in water

life·less /'laɪflɪs/ *adj* **1** having no life; dead: *a lifeless corpse* **2** lacking strength, interest, or activity: *This town is lifeless; nothing ever happens.*|*I feel lifeless today.* –compare LISTLESS **–lifelessly** *adv* **–lifelessness** *n* [U]

life·like /'laɪflaɪk/ *adj* very much like real life or a real person: *a lifelike photograph*

life·line /'laɪflaɪn/ *n* a rope used for saving life, esp. at sea: (fig.) *The telephone is my lifeline to the world.*

life·long /'laɪflɒŋ/ *adj* [A] lasting all one's life: *my lifelong friend*

life pre·serv·er /'· ·ˌ··/ *n AmE* a life-saving apparatus for use in the water (such as a LIFE BELT or LIFE JACKET)

life-size /ˌ· '·◄/ also **life-sized** /ˌ· '·◄/ – *adj* (of a work of art) of the same size as that which it represents

life·time /'laɪftaɪm/ *n* the time during which a person is alive

lift¹ /lɪft/ *v* **1** [T *up*] to bring from a lower to a higher level: *These bags are too heavy; I can't lift them.*|*Stop looking at the ground; lift your head up.* **2** [I] (esp. of clouds, mist, etc.) to move upwards and often disappear **3** [T] to bring to an end; remove: *The unpopular tax was soon lifted.* **4** [T] *infml* to steal (esp. small articles) –see also SHOPLIFT **5** [T] *infml* to take and use (other people's ideas, writings, etc.) as one's own without stating that one has done so

　lift off *v adv* [I] (of an aircraft or space craft) to take off –see also LIFT-OFF

lift² *n* **1** [C] the act of lifting, rising, or raising **2** [C;U] a lifting force, such as an upward pressure of air on the wings of an aircraft **3** [C] a free ride in a vehicle, esp. one given to a traveler: *Can you give me a lift into town?* **4** *BrE* for ELEVATOR **5** [S] *infml* a feeling of increased strength, higher spirits, etc.: *I was given a lift when I heard that I passed my exams.*

lift-off /'· ·/ also **blast-off**– *n* the start of the flight of a space vehicle –see also LIFT¹ **off**

lig·a·ment /'lɪgəmənt/ *n* one of the strong bands that join bones or hold some part of the body in position: *He tore a ligament playing football.*

light¹ /laɪt/ *n* **1** [U] the natural force that is produced by or redirected (REFLECTED (1)) from objects, so that we see them: *sunlight*|*firelight*|*This light is too poor to read by.*|*I* *can't read in this bad light.|She worked by the light of a candle.* **2** [U] the light of the sun or the time it lasts: *I want to finish this painting while the light lasts|before the light goes.* **3** [C] something that produces light and causes other things to be seen, such as a lamp or TORCH: *Turn off the lights when you go to bed.* **4** [C] something, such as a match or cigarette LIGHTER, that will set something else, esp. a cigarette, burning: *Can you give me a light, please?* **5** [S;U] brightness, as in the eyes, showing happiness or excitement **6** [U] the condition of being known: *Some new information has* **come to light** *about the accident.* **7** [C] the way in which something or someone appears or is regarded: *The workers and the employers look at the difficulties in quite a different light.|He tried to put my actions* **in a good/bad light.** (=favorably/unfavorably) **8 in (the) light of** taking into account; considering **9 see the light: a** to be made public **b** to understand or accept an idea or the truth of something **c** to understand or accept a religious belief; have a SPIRITUAL (2) experience which changes one's beliefs **10 throw/shed light on** to make clear; explain

light² *adj* **1** easy to see in; bright: *a light room* **2** not deep or dark in color; pale: *light green*

light³ *v* lit /lɪt/ *or* lighted, lighting **1** [I;T *up*] to (cause to) start to burn: *He lit (up) a cigarette.|The fire won't light.* **2** [T] to give light to: *The room is lit by several large lamps.* **3** [I;T *up*] to (cause to) become bright with pleasure or excitement: *Suddenly a smile lit (up) her face.|Her eyes lit up when she saw me.*

USAGE Use **lit** as the past participle of **light**, except when it stands as an adjective before the noun: *He's* **lit** *a match.|The match is* **lit.** |*a* **lighted** *match.*

light up *v adv* **1** [I;T (=light sthg.↔ up)] to give light to; make or become bright with light or color: *The candles lit up the room.* **2** [I] *infml* to begin to smoke a cigarette or pipe

light⁴ *adj* **1** of little weight; not heavy: *as light as air|It's very light, a child could lift it.* **2** not using or needing great effort; not powerful, severe, or serious: *A light touch is needed in playing quiet music.|a light wind|light reading/music|a light meal* (=small in amount) **3** (of sleep) from which one wakes easily; not deep: *A light sleeper is a person whose sleep is easily ended, for example by a soft noise.* **4 make light of** to treat as of little importance

light⁵ *adv* without many possessions (LUGGAGE): *I always travel light.*

light bulb /'· ·/ *n* →BULB (2)

light·en¹ /'laɪtn/ *v* [I;T] to make or become brighter or less dark –compare DARKEN

lighten² *v* [I;T] **1** to make or become less heavy, forceful, etc. **2** to make or become more cheerful or less troubled

light·er /'laɪtər/ *n* **1** that which lights or sets on fire **2** also **cigarette lighter**– an instrument that produces a small flame for lighting cigarettes, pipes, or CIGARS

light-fin·gered /ˌ· '··◄/ *adj infml* having the habit of stealing small things

light-head·ed /ˌ· '··◄/ *adj* **1** unable to think clearly, as during fever or after drinking alcohol; GIDDY (1): *I feel a bit light-headed. I think I'll sit down.* **2** not sensible or serious; foolish –**light-headedly** *adv* –**light-headedness** *n* [U]

light-heart·ed /ˌ· '··◄/ *adj* cheerful; happy

light·house /'laɪthaʊs/ *n* -**houses** /ˌhaʊzɪz/ a building with a powerful flashing light that guides ships or warns them of dangerous rocks

light in·dus·try /ˌ· '···/ *n* [U] organizations that produce light and usu. small goods, e.g. radios, clothes, books, etc. –compare HEAVY INDUSTRY

light·ing /'laɪtɪŋ/ *n* [U] **1** the act of making something give light or start burning **2** the system or apparatus that lights a room, building, etc., or the quality of the light produced: *soft* (=not very bright) *lighting in a restaurant*

light·ly /'laɪtliʸ/ *adv* **1** with little weight or force; gently: *He pressed lightly on the handle.* **2** to a slight or little degree: *lightly cooked|lightly armed* **3** without careful thought or reasoning: *I didn't start this court action lightly, you know!* **4** without proper respect

light·ning /'laɪtnɪŋ/ *n* **1** [U] a powerful flash of light in the sky, usu. followed by thunder **2** [A] very quick, short, or sudden: *a lightning visit|a lightning* STRIKE² (1)

lightning bug /'··ˌ·/ *n* →FIREFLY

light pen /'· ˌ·/ *n* an apparatus shaped like a pen, which can cause letters or shapes to appear or change when it is pointed at a MONITOR (2) –see illustration on page 221

light·weight /'laɪt-weʸt/ *n,adj* **1** (a person or thing) of less than average weight: (fig.) *a lightweight thinker* **2** (a BOXER) weighing between 126 and 135 pounds –see also HEAVYWEIGHT

light year /'· ·/ *n* (a measure of length equal to) the distance that light travels in one year(about 6,000,000,000,000 miles)

lik·a·ble, likeable /'laɪkəbəl/ *adj* (of a person) pleasant; attractive

like¹ /laɪk/ *v* **liked, liking** [T not *be*+*v*-*ing*] **1** to be fond of; find pleasant: *Do you like bananas?|I've never liked her brother.|I like sailing.|How do you like my new bicycle?* –opposite **dislike 2** [+*to-v*] to wish or choose: *I'd like* (=I want) *to see you.|I'd like you to come and see me.|I don't like to ask my parents for money.|Which one would you like, the red or the blue?|Do you like milk in your coffee?* **3 I like that!** What an annoying thing! *So you're not going to give me my money? Well, I like that!* **4 if you like** if you do not want something else: *We can go out if you like.|"Shall we go?" "(Yes.) If you like."*

USAGE When **like** means "to be fond of or enjoy," it is used alone; when it means "to want," it is used with *would.* (Compare: I **like** *beer.* (=I'm fond of it) and *I'd* **like** (=want) *a glass of beer.|Do you* **like** *going to the movies?|Would you* **like** *to go to the movies tonight?* The verb **love** is used in the same way: I **love** *swimming.*|*I'd love to go swimming.*

like² *adj* **1** the same in many ways; of the same kind: *running, swimming, and like sports*|*like ideas* –see also UNLIKE **2 -like: a** the same as in many ways: *lifelike* **b** typical of: *ladylike*|*childlike*

like³ *prep* **1** in the same way as; of the same kind as: *Do it like this.*|*He was like a son to me.*|*When the car is painted it will look like new.* **2** typical of; showing the usual manner of: *It was (just) like her.* **3** for example: *I asked lots of people, like Mrs. Jones and Dr. Simpson.*

USAGE Note the difference between these uses of **like** and **as**: *He has been playing tennis* **as** *a professional for two years* (=he is a professional tennis player).|*He plays tennis* **like** *a professional* (=he is not a professional tennis player, but he plays as well as someone who is).

like⁴ *n* [S] something which is the same or as good: *running, swimming, and the like* –see also LIKES

like⁵ *conj infml* **1** in the same way as: *Do it like I tell you.* **2** as if: *He acted like he owned the shop.*

like·li·hood /'laɪkliʸ,hʊd/ *n* [U*of*] the fact or degree of being likely

like·ly¹ /'laɪkliʸ/ *adj* **-lier, -liest 1** [+*to-v*] probable; expected: *Are we likely to arrive in time?*|*It seems likely that she'll pass her exams.*|*The likeliest result of the game is a tie.* –opposite **unlikely 2** suitable to give results: *a likely plan*|*He's the most likely*/*the likeliest of the people to ask for the job.*

likely² *adv* **1** (esp. after *most, very*) probably: *They'll very likely come by car.* **2 as likely as not** probably **3 not likely!** *infml* certainly not!

like·ness /'laɪknɪs/ *n* [C;U] sameness in form: *a family likeness*

lik·en sbdy./sthg. **to** sbdy./sthg. /'laɪkən/ *v prep* [T] *fml* to compare with: *Our little company can be likened to a big family.*

likes /laɪks/ *n* [P] things that one likes (usu. in the phrase **likes and dislikes**)

like·wise /'laɪk-waɪz/ *adv* [*no comp.*] **1** in the same way; the same: *John took off his shoes, and Peter did likewise.* (=they both took off their shoes) **2** also; too: *For this job you need a lot of patience; likewise you need a sense of humor.*

lik·ing /'laɪkɪŋ/ *n* [S *for*] fondness: *to have a liking for sweets*

li·lac /'laɪlək, -lɑk, -læk/ *n* **1** [C] a tree with pinkish, purple, or white flowers giving a sweet smell **2** [U] a purple color

lilt /lɪlt/ *v,n* [I;S] (to have) a regular pattern of pleasant sound: *a lilting voice*/*tune*|*She speaks with a Southern lilt.*

lil·y /'lɪliʸ/ *n* **-ies** a plant usu. with large clear white flowers

lily-liv·ered /,·· '·· ◄/ *adj* cowardly

li·ma bean /'laɪmə ,biʸn/ *n* a type of bean with flat seeds that can be eaten

limb /lɪm/ *n* **1** a leg, arm, or wing of an animal **2** a (large) branch of a tree **3 out on a limb** alone without support, esp. in opinions or argument **4 -limbed** having limbs of the

stated kind: *strong-limbed*

lim·ber up /'lɪmbər ʌp/ *v adv* [I] to prepare for a race, etc. by stretching one's muscles through exercise

lim·bo /'lɪmboʷ/ *n* **-bos** [C;U] a state of uncertainty: *I'm in limbo, waiting to know if I've got the job or not.*

lime¹ /laɪm/ *n* [U] a white substance obtained by burning a special type of stone (**limestone**), used in making cement

lime² *n* **1** also **lime tree** /'· ·/, **linden** – a tree with yellow sweet-smelling flowers **2** (a tree which bears) a small green fruit which is juicy and tastes sour

lime·light /'laɪmlaɪt/ *n* [*the* S] a lot of attention from the public: *That politician has been* **in the limelight** *recently because of his strong opinions.*

lim·er·ick /'lɪmərɪk/ *n* a short poem with five lines, usu. humorous

lim·it¹ /'lɪmɪt/ *n* **1** [*of*] the farthest point or edge (of something): *the limit of one's patience*|*I can't walk 10 miles; I know my own limits.* –compare EDGE¹ **2 off limits** (to) *AmE* where one is not allowed **3 within limits** up to a reasonable point (in amount, time, etc.)

limit² *v* [T *to*] to keep below or at a certain point or amount: *We must limit our spending.*|*We must limit ourselves to an hour*/*to one drink each.*

lim·i·ta·tion /,lɪmə'teʸʃən/ *n* **1** [U] the fact or conditions of limiting or being limited **2** [C usu. pl.] a weakness of body or character which limits one's actions: *I know my limitations*; *I won't even try to build my own house.*

lim·it·ed /'lɪmɪtɪd/ *adj* **1** small in amount, power, etc., and not able to increase: *His ability to improve his work is very limited.* –opposite **unlimited 2** [A or after *n*] also **Ltd.** – (of a company) having a reduced duty to pay back debts: *Dixon and Son Limited*

lim·it·ing /'lɪmɪtɪŋ/ *adj* which prevents improvement, increase, etc.: *A limiting* FACTOR *in the improvement of health is the lack of doctors.*

lim·ou·sine /'lɪmə,ziʸn, ,lɪmə'ziʸn/ also **limo** /'lɪmoʷ/ *infml*– *n* an expensive car with the driver's seat separated from the back by a sheet of glass, usu. driven by a paid driver (CHAUFFEUR)

limp¹ /lɪmp/ *n,v* [I;S] (to walk with) an uneven step, one foot or leg moving less well than the other: *He has*/*walks with a limp.*

limp² *adj* lacking strength or stiffness: *She went limp and fell to the ground.*|*This card got wet and went limp.* –**limply** *adv* –**limpness** *n* [U]

lim·pet /'lɪmpɪt/ *n* a very small sea animal with a shell, which holds on tightly to the rock where it lives

lim·pid /'lɪmpɪd/ *adj lit* (esp. of liquid) clear; transparent: *eyes like limpid pools* –**limpidly** *adv*

lin·den /'lɪndən/ *n* →LIME² (1)

line¹ /laɪn/ *v* **lined, lining** [T (*with*)] **1** to cover the inside of something with material (e.g. a coat with light cloth or a box with paper or something soft) **2** to be an inner covering for: *the soft slippery substance that lines the* *stomach* **3 line one's pocket(s)/purse** to make money for oneself

line² *n* **1** a thin mark with length but no width, which can be drawn on a surface: *Can you draw a straight line?|a line drawing|*(fig.) *The old man's face is covered with lines.* (=of folded skin) **2** a long mark that acts as a limit or border: *Which of the runners was the first to cross the (finish) line?* (=to win the race)|*The ship crossed the line* (=the EQUATOR) *at midday.|There's a very fine line between punishment and cruelty.* **3** a row: *a line of people walking into a theater|75 lines of printed words on a page.* **4** a piece of string, wire, or cord: *a clothes line|a fishing line* **5** a telephone connection or wire: *The lines have crossed.* (=there's a wrong connection)|*The lines went down in the storm.* **6** a railway track: *Passengers are not allowed to cross the lines.|the main line from Washington D.C. to Baltimore* **7** (*usu. in combination*) a (company that provides a) system for traveling or moving goods, esp. by sea or air: *an airline|a shipping line* **8** a direction; course: *You're standing right in the line of fire.* (=the direction in which the guns are shooting)|(fig.) *Let's try a different line of approach to the problem.* **9** a business, profession, trade, etc.: *My line is selling.|She's in the selling line.|*(fig.) *Fishing isn't really my line.* (=does not interest me) **10** a type of goods: *a new line in hats* **11** a set of people following one another in time, esp. a family: *He comes from a long line of actors.* **12** an official point of view; POLICY (esp. in phrase **take a strong line**): *the party line* **13 draw the line (at)** to state a limit to what one is prepared to do: *I said I'd help you to make some money, but I draw the line at stealing.* **14 in line for** being considered for and likely to get: *in line for the job* **15 in line with** in accordance with: *That isn't in line with my ideas at all.* **16 read between the lines** to find a meaning which is not actually stated: *In her letter she says she's having a good time, but reading between the lines I don't think she's very happy.*

line³ *v* **lined, lining** [T] **1** to draw or mark lines on: *lined paper|Worry lined his face.* **2** to form rows along: *The crowds lined the streets.*

line up *v adv* **1** [I;T (=**line** sbdy./sthg.↔**up**)] to (cause to) move into a row: *He lined up behind the others to wait his turn.|Line up the glasses and I'll fill them.* **2** [T] (**line** sbdy./sthg.↔**up**)to arrange (a show, event, etc.): *I've lined up a famous singer for the school concert.* –compare LINEUP

lin·e·ar /'lɪniʸər/ *adj* **1** of or in lines: *a linear DIAGRAM* –compare LINE² (1) **2** of length: *linear measurements*

line·man /'laɪnmən/ *also* **linesman**– *n* **-men** /mən/ – **1** a man whose job is to take care of railroad lines or telephone wires **2** *AmE* a football player in the attacking forward line –compare LINESMAN

lin·en /'lɪnən/ *n* [U] **1** cloth made from FLAX **2** sheets and bedclothes, tablecloths, etc.: *to buy bed linen*

lin·er /'laɪnər/ *n* **1** a large passenger ship **2** a

piece of material used inside another to protect it: *a fur liner*

lines /laɪnz/ *n* [P] the words learned by an actor to be said in a play

lines·man /'laɪnzmən/ *n* **-men** /mən/ **1** (in sports) an official who stays near the side of the playing area and decides which team has gone outside the limits, done something wrong, etc. –compare REFEREE¹ **2** →LINEMAN (2)

line·up /'laɪnʌp/ *n* [*usu. sing.*] **1** an arrangement of people or things, esp. in a line **2** a set of events, following one after the other –see also LINE³ **up**

lin·ger /'lɪŋgər/ *v* [I *on,over*] **1** to wait for a time instead of going; delay going: *She lingered over her meal till it was too late to go out.|He lingered outside the school after everybody else had gone home.* **2** to be slow to disappear: *The pain lingered on for weeks.|a lingering fear, after an accident* –**lingerer** *n*

lin·ge·rie /ˌlɑnʒəˈreʸ, ˈlænʒəˌriʸ, -dʒə-/ *n* [U] *fml & tech* underclothes for women

lin·guist /'lɪŋgwɪst/ *n* **1** a person who studies the science of language (LINGUISTICS) **2** a person who studies and is good at foreign languages

lin·guis·tic /lɪŋˈgwɪstɪk/ *adj* [A] **1** concerning one or more languages: *great linguistic knowledge* **2** concerning LINGUISTICS –**linguistically** *adv*

lin·guis·tics /lɪŋˈgwɪstɪks/ *n* [U] the study of language in general and of particular languages

lin·i·ment /'lɪnəmənt/ *n* [C;U] an oily liquid to be rubbed on the skin, esp. to help soreness and stiffness of the joints

lin·ing /'laɪnɪŋ/ *n* a piece of material covering the inner surface of a garment, box, etc.

link¹ /lɪŋk/ *n* **1** something which connects two other parts: *Is there a link between smoking and lung diseases?|There's a new rail link between the two towns.*(=a train runs between them) **2** one ring of a chain

link² *v* [I;T *together, up*] to join or connect: *The road links all the new towns.|They walked with linked arms.|She was able to link up all the different pieces of information.*

link·age /'lɪŋkɪdʒ/ *n* **1** a set of LINKS **2** [S;U] the fact or way of being connected

links /lɪŋks/ *n* **links** [C] a piece of ground on which GOLF is played: *He played the links in the country.*

link-up /'lɪŋk-ʌp/ *n* a point of joining or connection: *a road linkup|a television linkup*

li·no·le·um /lɪˈnoʷliʸəm/ *n* [U] a floor-covering made up of strong cloth and other substances

lin·seed oil /'lɪnsiʸd ˌɔɪl/ *n* [U] an oil made from FLAX, used in some paints, inks, etc.

lint /lɪnt/ *n* [U] tiny pieces of thread or fiber

lin·tel /'lɪntəl/ *n* a piece of stone or wood across the top of a window or door, forming part of the frame

li·on /'laɪən/ **lioness** /'laɪənɪs/ *fem.*– *n* **lions** *or* **lion 1** a large yellow four-footed animal of the cat family which lives mainly in Africa **2** a famous and important person **3 the lion's**

share (of) the greatest part (of); most (of)

lip /lɪp/ *n* **1 a** one of the two edges of the mouth where the skin is delicate and rather red: *He kissed her on the lips.* **b** the ordinary skin below the nose **2** the edge (of a hollow vessel or opening): *the lip of the cup* **3 stiff upper lip** a lack of expression of feeling **4 pay lip service to** to support in words, but not in fact **5 -lipped** having lips of a certain color, shape, etc.: *red-lipped|thin-lipped with anger*

lip-read /'lɪp riʸd/ *v* [I] (usu. of people who cannot hear) to watch people's lip movements so as to understand what they are saying **–lipreading** *n* [U]

lip·stick /'lɪp,stɪk/ *n* [C;U] (a stick-shaped mass of) material for brightening the color of the lips: *I'm putting on some lipstick.*

liq·ue·fy /'lɪkwə,faɪ/ *v* **-fied, -fying** [I;T] to (cause to) become liquid: *Butter liquefies in heat.* **–liquefaction** /,lɪkwə'fækʃən/ *n* [C]

li·queur /lɪ'kɜr, lɪ'kʊər/ *n* a very strong alcoholic drink which has a special, rather sweet taste

liq·uid¹ /'lɪkwɪd/ *n* [C;U] (a type of) substance not solid or gas, which flows and has no fixed shape: *Water is a liquid.*

liquid² *adj* **1** (esp. of something which is usu. solid or gas) in the form of a liquid: *liquid gold|liquid oxygen* **2** (esp. of food) soft and watery **3** (of sounds) clear and flowing, with pure notes

liq·ui·date /'lɪkwə,deʸt/ *v* **-dated, -dating** [T] **1** to get rid of; destroy **2** to arrange the end of business for (a company), esp. when it is unable to pay its debts (=is BANKRUPT) **–liquidation** /,lɪkwə'deʸʃən/ [U]: *The company has gone into liquidation.* (=is BANKRUPT)

liq·uid·ize /'lɪkwə,daɪz/ *v* **-ized, -izing** [T] to crush (esp. fruit or vegetables) into a liquid-like form

liq·uid·iz·er /'lɪkwə,daɪzər/ *n BrE* for BLENDER

liq·uor /'lɪkər/ *n* [U] **1** *AmE* strong alcoholic drink, such as WHISKEY **2** *BrE fml or tech* alcoholic drink

liq·uo·rice /'lɪkərɪs, -rɪʃ/ *n* [U] → LICORICE

lisp¹ /lɪsp/ *v* [I;T] to speak or say with /s/ sounds which are not clear, making the /s/ seem like /θ/ **–lispingly** *adv*

lisp² *n* [S] the fault in speech of LISPING¹: *She speaks with a lisp.*

lis·som, lissome /'lɪsəm/ *adj* (of a person or the body) graceful in shape and movement **–lissomly** *adv* **–lissomness** *n* [U]

list¹ /lɪst/ *n* a set of names of things written one after the other, so as to remember them or keep them in order: *a list of things to do.|a shopping list|He made a list of their names.*

list² *v* [T] to write in a list: *He listed all the things he had to do.*

list³ *v* [I] (esp. of a ship) to lean or slope to one side **–list** *n* [S]

lis·ten¹ /'lɪsən/ *v* [I *to*] to give attention in hearing: *She's listening to the radio.|Listen to the music.* –see HEAR (USAGE)

listen for *v prep* [T] to pay attention so as to be sure of hearing: *Listen for the moment when the music changes.*

listen in *v adv* [I] **1** [*to*] to listen to (a broadcast on) the radio: *to listen in to the news* –see also TUNE² **in 2** [*on, to*] to listen to (the conversation of) other people, esp. when one should not –compare EAVESDROP

listen² *n* [S] *infml* an act of listening: *Have a listen.*

list·ing /'lɪstɪŋ/ *n AmE* a list, esp. for the telephone, TV and radio: *Check your TV listing for the time and station of the program.*

list·less /'lɪstlɪs/ *adj* (of a person who is) lacking power of movement, activity, etc.: *Heat makes some people listless.* –compare LIFELESS **–listlessly** *adv* **–listlessness** *n* [U]

lit /lɪt/ *v* past tense and past participle of LIGHT

lit·a·ny /'lɪtn-iʸ/ *n* **-nies** a form of prayer in the Christian church

li·ter /'liʸtər/ *n AmE*‖**litre** *BrE* a measure of liquid equal to about 1¾ PINTS

lit·er·a·cy /'lɪtərəsiʸ/ *n* [U] the state of being able to read and/or write (=being LITERATE (3)): *an adult literacy campaign* (=a movement to teach people to read) –opposite **illiteracy**

lit·er·al /'lɪtərəl/ *adj* **1** exact: *a literal account of a conversation* **2** giving one word for each word (as in a foreign language): *a literal translation* **3** following the usual meaning of the words, without any additional meanings: *The literal meaning of the word "pig" is an animal, not a person who eats too much.* –compare FIGURATIVE **4** not showing much imagination: *a literal APPROACH² (3) to a subject* **–literalness** *n* [U]

lit·er·al·ly /'lɪtərəliʸ/ *adv* **1** exactly: *to do literally nothing at all* **2** (used for giving force to an adjective): *literally blue with cold* –see USAGE **3** word by word: *to translate literally* **4** according to the words and not the intention: *I took what he said literally, but afterwards it became clear that he really meant something else.*

USAGE **Literally** should really be used to mean "exactly as stated," It is often used more loosely to give force to an expression, but this is thought by teachers to be incorrect. Compare: *Their house is* **literally** *10 yards from the sea* (=this is a true statement).|*He* **literally** *exploded with anger* (=he did not in fact explode).

lit·er·ar·y /'lɪtə,reriʸ/ *adj* of, concerning, or producing literature: *a literary woman| magazine*

lit·er·ate /'lɪtərɪt/ *adj* **1** able to read and write **2** well-educated –opposite **illiterate** **–literately** *adv* **–literateness** *n* [U]

lit·er·a·ture /'lɪtərətʃər, -,tʃʊər, 'lɪtrə-/ *n* **1** [U] written works which are of artistic value: *English literature|modern literature* **2** *infml* printed material, esp. giving information: *Have you any literature on the new car?*

lithe /laɪð/ *adj* (of a person or the body) able to bend and move easily **–lithely** *adv*

lit·i·gate /'lɪtə,geʸt/ *v* **-gated, -gating** [I;T] *tech* to bring or defend (a case) in a court of law **–litigation** /,lɪtə'geʸʃən/ *n*

lit·mus /'lɪtməs/ *n* [U] a coloring material which turns red when touched by an acid

substance and blue when touched by an
ALKALI: *litmus paper*
li·tre /ˈliːtər/ *BrE* for LITER
lit·ter¹ /ˈlɪtər/ *n* **1** [U] things (to be) thrown
away, esp. paper scattered untidily: *a litter
bin/basket* –see illustration on page 673 **2** [C]
a group of young animals born at the same
time to one mother, as of KITTENS: *The litter
has all lived.*
litter² *v* [T] to scatter; spread; cover untidily:
*to litter the room with papers/papers littering
the room*
lit·ter·bug /ˈlɪtərˌbʌg/ *AmE*‖**litterlout** /ˈlɪt
ərˌlaʊt/ *BrE*– *n* a person who leaves on
public ground things which should be thrown
away at home or in a special place
lit·tle¹ /ˈlɪtl/ *adj* **1** [A] small: *two little insects* **2**
[A] short: *a little time* –see Study Notes on
page 550 **3** young: *my little girl* (=daughter)
|*She's too little to ride a bicycle.*|*my little
brother/sister* (=my younger brother/sister)
4 not important: *the little things of life* –compare BIG
little² *adv* **less** /lɛs/, **least** /liːst/ **1** not much: *a
little known fact*|*She goes out very little.* **2** not
at all: *Little did they know that the truth
would be discovered.*
little³ *determiner, pron* **less**, **least 1** [U] (used
without *a*, to show the smallness of the
amount) not much; not enough: *I have very
little (money) left.*|*I understood little of his
speech.*|*It's no less than a mile* (=it's at least a
mile) *to the station.*|*Buy the one that costs the
least (money).* **2** [S *no comp.*] **a** a small
amount, but at least some: *a few eggs and a
little milk*|*May I have a little of that cake?*|**b** a
short time: *You'd better stay in bed for a little
while.* –see Study Notes on page 550 **3 a little**
rather: *I was a little annoyed.* **4 little by little**
gradually: *We collected enough money little
by little.* **5 make little of** to treat as unimportant see FEW (USAGE)
little fin·ger /ˌ·· ˈ·/ *n* The smallest finger on
the hand
lit·ur·gy /ˈlɪtərdʒi/ *n* **-gies** a form of worship
in the Christian church, using prayers,
songs, etc., according to fixed patterns
–**liturgical** /lɪˈtɜːrdʒɪkəl/ *adj*
liv·a·ble, liveable /ˈlɪvəbəl/ *adj* **1** suitable to
live in: *make the house livable* **2** worth living;
acceptable to experience: *My life's not livable right now.*
live¹ /lɪv/ *v* **lived, living 1** [I] to be alive; have
life: *She lived a long time.* **2** to continue to be
alive: *His illness is so serious, he is unlikely to
live.*|*He managed to live through two world
wars.* **3** to have one's home; DWELL: *Where
do you live?*|*I live in an apartment in Detroit.*
4 to afford what one needs: *to earn enough to
live* **5** (of characters in books, plays, etc.) to
seem real **6 live and let live** to accept others'
behavior; TOLERATE other people
live by sthg. *v prep* [T] **1** [+*v-ing*] to make
an income from: *He lives by stealing.* **2** to
behave according to the rules of: *He lives by
the book.* (=does nothing wrong)
live sthg.↔**down** *v adv* [T] to cause (a bad
action) to be forgotten, esp. by future good
behavior: *He was drunk at school; he'll*

never live it down.
live in *v adv* [I] to sleep and eat in a house
where one is employed
live off sbdy./sthg. *v prep* [T] **1** to produce
one's food or income from: *I live off the
money from my first book.* **2** *usu. derog* to
get money for one's needs from: *to live off
one's parents*
live on sthg. *v prep* [T] to have as one's only
food or income: *to live on fruit*|*to live on the
rent from one's property*
live out sthg. *v adv* [T] to live till the end of:
Will the old man live out the month?
live up to sthg. *v adv prep* [T] to keep to the
high standards of: *Did the film live up to your
expectations?* (=was it as good as you
expected?)
live with sbdy./sthg. *v prep* [T] **1** *euph* to
live in the same house as lovers **2** to accept
(an unpleasant thing): *I don't enjoy the pain,
but I can live with it.*
live² /laɪv/ *adj* [*no comp.*] **1** [A] alive; living:
The cat was playing with a live mouse. –opposite **dead 2** in a state in which it could
explode: *a live bomb* **3** carrying free
electricity which can shock anyone who
touches it: *a live wire* **4** (of broadcasting)
seen and/or heard as it happens: *It wasn't a
recorded show; it was live.*
live·li·hood /ˈlaɪvliˌhʊd/ *n* the way by which
one earns one's money: *I like playing in the
band, but I don't do it just for fun. It's my
livelihood.*
live·ly /ˈlaɪvli/ *adj* **-lier, -liest 1** full of quick
movement, thought, etc.: *a lively mind/song*
2 lifelike; as if real; VIVID (2): *a lively description* –**liveliness** *n* [U]
liv·en up /ˈlaɪvən/ *v adv* [I;T] to make or
become LIVELY (1)
liv·er /ˈlɪvər/ *n* **1** [C] a large organ in the body
which produces BILE and cleans the blood **2**
[U] this organ from animals used as food:
Chicken livers with rice
lives /laɪvz/ *n pl. of* LIFE
live·stock /ˈlaɪvstɑk/ *n* [U] animals kept on a
farm: *The livestock is locked up for the night.*
liv·id /ˈlɪvɪd/ *adj* **1** blue-gray, as of marks on
the skin (BRUISES) after being hit **2** *infml* very
angry –**lividly** *adv*
liv·ing¹ /ˈlɪvɪŋ/ *adj* **1** alive now: *She has no
living relatives.*|*The living are more impor-
tant to us than the dead.* **2** existing in use: *a
living language*
living² *n* **1** [C] earnings with which one buys
what is necessary to life: *to make a living in
industry* **2** [U] a standard one reaches in
food, drink, etc.: *The cost of living increased
by 10% last year.*
living room /ˈ·· ˌ·/‖also **sitting room** *esp.
BrE*– *n* the main room in a house where
people can do things together, (usu.) apart
from eating –see illustration opposite
liz·ard /ˈlɪzərd/ *n* a (usu.) small REPTILE, with
a rough skin, four legs, and a long tail
ll *written abbrev. said as:* lines: *see ll 104-201*
-'ll /əl, l/ *v* short for will; shall: *He'll soon be
here.*
lla·ma /ˈlɑmə/ *n* **-mas or -ma** an animal of
South America with thick woolly hair, some-

blinds

lamp

bookcase

turntable
amplifier
tuner

table lamp

floor lamp

couch

armchair

vase

mantel

fireplace

cassette

record

end table

speaker

fireplace screen

coffee table

television

ashtray

coaster

rug

times used for carrying goods

load¹ /lowd/ n **1** an amount being carried, or to be carried, esp. heavy: *a load of furniture*|(fig.) *Her grief is a heavy load to bear.* **2** the amount which a certain vehicle can carry: *a car load of people* **3** the work done by an engine, etc. **4** the power of an electricity supply **5 loads of** also **a load of**– *infml* a large amount of; a lot of: *She's got loads of money.*|*That book is a load of nonsense.*

load² v **1** [I;T *up, with*] to put a load on or in (something): *Load the car (with the packages)*/*the parcels into the car.*|*Have you finished loading up?*|(fig.) *They loaded me with gifts.* **2** [T] to put a CHARGE² (6) or roll of film into (a gun or camera)

load sbdy./sthg.↔ **down** v adv [T *with*] to load with a great weight: *I was loaded down with books.*

load·ed /'lowdɪd/ adj **1** giving an unfair advantage: *The argument was loaded in his favor.* **2** containing a hidden trap: *a loaded question* **3** [F] *infml* having lots of money: *Why pay him? He's loaded.* **4** [F] *AmE infml* to be drunk: *He's so loaded he can't stand up.*

loaf¹ /lowf/ n **loaves** /lowvz/ bread shaped and baked in one piece, usu. fairly large –compare ROLL¹ (2) –see illustration on page 683

loaf² v [I *about*] *infml* to waste time, esp. by not working when one should –**loafer** n

loam /lowm/ n [C;U] good soil –**loamy** adj **-ier, -iest**

loan¹ /lown/ n **1** something which is lent: *The book is a loan, not a gift.*|*a $1,000 loan* **2** the act of lending: *the loan of a book*

loan² v [T *to*] **1** *AmE* to give (someone) the use of; lend –see Study Notes on page 481 **2** to lend formally for a long period: *She loaned her pictures to the MUSEUM.*

loath, loth /lowθ, lowð/ adj [F +*to-v*] unwilling: *loath to lend money*

loathe /lowð/ v **loathed, loathing** [T +*v-ing*] to feel hatred or great dislike for –**loathing** n [C;U]

loath·some /'lowðsəm, 'lowθ-/ adj which causes great dislike; very unpleasant: *the loathsome smell of burning flesh* –**loathsomely** adv –**loathsomeness** n [U]

loaves /lowvz/ n pl. of LOAF¹

lob¹ /lɑb/ v **-bb-** [T] to send (a ball) in a LOB²

lob² n (in tennis) a ball thrown or hit in a high gentle curve

lob·by¹ /'lɑbiʸ/ n **-bies 1** [C] a hall or passage, not a room, which leads from the entrance to the rooms inside a building: *the hotel lobby* **2** [C] a group of people who unite for or against an action, so that those in power will change their minds: *The clean air lobby is against the plans for the new chemical factory.*

lobby² v **-bied, -bying 1** [I;T] to meet (a member of a law-making body) in order to persuade (him/her) to support one's actions and needs **2** [I] to be active in making actions, plans, etc., public, so as to bring about a change of some kind

lobe /lowb/ n **1** also **earlobe**– the round fleshy piece at the bottom of the ear **2** *tech* any

rounded division of an organ, esp. the brain and lungs

lob·ster /'lɑbstər/ n [C;U] an eight-legged sea animal with a shell, the flesh of which may be eaten

lo·cal¹ /'lowkəl/ adj **1** of or in a certain place, esp. the place one lives in: *the/our local doctor*|*local news*|*a local bar* –see TOPICAL (USAGE) **2** *tech* concerning a particular part, esp. of the body: *a local infection*

local² n **1** *infml* a person who lives in the place he is in: *I don't know of a cheap restaurant. Ask one of the locals.* **2** a bus, a train, etc., making all stops

lo·cal·i·ty /low'kæləṭiʸ/ n **-ties** a place or area, esp. in which something happens or has happened

lo·cal·ize ‖ also **-ise** *BrE* /'lowkə,laɪz/ v **-ized, -izing** [T] to keep within a small area: *to localize the pain* –**localization** /,lowkələ'zeʸʃən/ n [U]

lo·cal·ly /'lowkəliʸ/ adv [*no comp.*] **1** in a local area **2** →NEARBY: *Do you work locally?*

lo·cate /'lowkeʸt, low'keʸt/ v **-cated, -cating 1** [T] to learn the position of: *We located the library, schools, and stores as soon as we moved into the town.* **2** [T] to fix or set in a certain place: *to locate one's home in the country*|*The house is located next to the river.* **3** [I *in*] *AmE* to settle down in a place: *Her company located in Chicago.*

lo·ca·tion /low'keʸʃən/ n **1** a place or position: *a suitable location for a camp* **2 on location** in a town, country, etc., to make a movie

lock¹ /lɑk/ n **1** an apparatus for closing and fastening something by means of a key: *He put new locks on the doors.* –see illustration on page 95 **2** a stretch of water closed off by gates, esp. on a CANAL, so that the level can be raised or lowered to move boats up or down a slope **3 lock, stock and barrel** completely **4 under lock and key: a** safely hidden and fastened in **b** imprisoned

lock² v **1** [I;T] to fasten with a lock: *Lock the door.*|*The door won't lock.* **2** [T] to put in a place and lock the entrance: *to lock one's jewels in the closet* **3** [I] to become fixed or blocked: *I can't move the car; the wheels have locked.* –**lockable** adj

lock sthg.↔ **away** v adv [T] to keep safe or secret, (as) by putting in a locked place

lock sbdy.↔ **in** v adv [T] to put (esp. a person or animal) inside a place and lock the doors

lock sbdy.↔ **out** v adv [T *of*] to keep out of a place by locking the entrance –see also LOCKOUT

lock up v adv **1** [I;T (=lock sthg.↔ up)] to make (a building) safe by locking the doors, esp. for the night **2** [T] (lock sbdy./sthg. ↔ up) to put in a place of safety and lock the entrance: *to lock up one's possessions*|*People like that should be locked up!* (=in prison)

lock³ n a small piece of hair: *a curly lock*

lock·er /'lɑkər/ n a small usu. metal closet for keeping things in, esp. at a school where there is one for each pupil or in a sports building where clothes may be kept after changing

lock·et /ˈlɑkɪt/ n a small decoration for the neck, a metal case on a chain in which small pictures can be kept

lock·out /ˈlɑk-aʊt/ n the employers' action of not allowing workers to go back to work, esp. in a factory, until they accept an agreement –see also LOCK² out

lo·co·mo·tive¹ /ˌloʷkəˈmoʷṭɪv/ adj tech concerning or causing movement: *locomotive powers* –**locomotion** /ˌloʷkəˈmoʷʃən/ n [U]

locomotive² n fml a railway engine

lo·cust /ˈloʷkəst/ n an insect of Asia and Africa which flies in large groups, often destroying crops

lodge¹ /lɑdʒ/ v **lodged, lodging 1** [I] to stay, usu. for a short time and paying rent:*to lodge at a friend's house*/*with friends* **2** [I] to live in lodgings **3** [I;T] to settle or fix firmly in a position: *A chicken bone lodged in his throat.*|*He lodged the stick in the hole.* –see also DISLODGE **4** [T] to make (a statement) officially: *to lodge a complaint*

lodge² n **1** a small house on the land of a larger house **2** a small house for hunters, SKIers, etc., to stay in while crossing wild country –compare CHALET (2)

lodg·er /ˈlɑdʒər/ n a person who pays rent to stay in somebody's house

lodg·ing /ˈlɑdʒɪŋ/ n [S;U] a place to stay for payment: *a lodging for the night*|*to find lodging*

lodg·ings /ˈlɑdʒɪŋz/ n [P] a house where rooms are rented out: *to stay in lodgings*

loft /lɔft/ n a room under the roof of a building; ATTIC

loft·y /ˈlɔftiʸ/ adj -ier, -iest **1 a** of unusually high quality of thinking, feeling, etc.: *lofty aims* **b** showing belief of being better than other people: *a lofty smile* **2** lit high: *the lofty walls of the city* –**loftily** adv –**loftiness** n [U]

log¹ /lɔg, lɑg/ n **1** a thick piece of wood from a tree: **2** an official written record of a journey, as in a ship, plane, etc.: *The captain described the accident in the ship's log.* **3 sleep like a log** to sleep deeply without moving

log² v **-gg-** [T] to record in a LOG¹ (2)

lo·gan·ber·ry /ˈloʷgənˌbɛriʸ, -bəriʸ/ n **-ries** a red fruit grown from a plant which is half BLACKBERRY and half RASPBERRY

log·a·rithm /ˈlɔgəˌrɪðəm, ˈlɑ-/ also **log** infml– n a number which represents a value of another number, and which can be added to another logarithm instead of multiplying the original number –**logarithmic** /ˌlɔgəˈrɪðmɪk, ˌlɑ-/ adj

log·ger·heads /ˈlɔgərˌhɛdz, ˈlɑ-/ n **at loggerheads (with)** always disagreeing (with)

log·ic /ˈlɑdʒɪk/ n [U] **1** the science of reasoning by formal methods **2** a way of reasoning **3** infml reasonable thinking: *There's no logic in spending money on useless things.* –compare LOGISTICS

log·i·cal /ˈlɑdʒɪkəl/ adj **1** in accordance with the rules and science of LOGIC: *a logical argument* **2** having or showing good reasoning; sensible –opposite **illogical**; –compare

REASONABLE (1) –**logically** adv

lo·gis·tics /loʷˈdʒɪstɪks, lə-/ n [P;U] organization of work, materials, moving, etc.: *The logistics of the operation are very difficult because there are 90,000 soldiers involved.* –compare LOGIC –**logistic** adj –**logistically** adv

loin·cloth /ˈlɔɪnklɔθ/ n **-cloths** /klɔðz, klɔɪs/ a loose covering for the LOINS, worn in hot countries

loins /lɔɪnz/ n [P] the lower part of the body below the waist and above the legs

loi·ter /ˈlɔɪtər/ v **1** AmE to stand around doing nothing usu. in a public place: *the sign said, "No loitering."* **2** [I] to walk about slowly with frequent stops: *The policeman watched the two men, who were loitering near the door to the bank.* –**loiterer** n

loll /lɑl/ v **1** [I about, around] to be lying in a lazy loose position: *She was lolling in a chair with her arms hanging over the sides.* **2** [I;T out] to (allow to) hang down loosely: *The dog's tongue lolled out*

lol·li·pop /ˈlaliʸˌpɑp/ also **lolly** /ˈlaliʸ/ BrE– n **1** a hard sweet made of boiled sugar set around a stick **2** anything like this, esp. frozen juice on a stick

lone /loʷn/ adj [A no comp.] without (other) people: *a lone rider* –see ALONE (USAGE)

lone·ly /ˈloʷnliʸ/ adj **-lier, -liest** alone and unhappy; away from other people: *When his wife died, he was very lonely.*|*a lonely house in the country* –see ALONE (USAGE) –**loneliness** n [U]

lon·er /ˈloʷnər/ n a person who spends a lot of time alone, esp. by choice

lone·some /ˈloʷnsəm/ adj AmE infml lonely: *Why don't you come over? I'm feeling lonesome.* –see ALONE (USAGE)

long¹ /lɔŋ/ adj **longer** /ˈlɔŋgər/, **longest** /ˈlɔŋgɪst/ **1** measuring a large amount in length, distance, or time: *long hair*|*a long journey*|*He took a long time to get here.* –opposite **short 2** covering a certain distance or time: *How long was her speech?*|*It was an hour long.*|*The room is 20 feet long and 15 feet wide.* **3** (of a vowel) longer lasting than a short vowel in the same position **4 not by a long shot** AmE‖**chalk** BrE infml not at all; not nearly: "*Is he ready yet?*" "*No, not by a long shot.*" **5 in the long run** in the end: *The company is in difficulties at the moment, but we expect it to do well in the long run.*

long² adv **1** (for) a long time: *I can't wait much longer.*|*Will you be long?* (=will it take you a long time?)|*He hasn't been back long.* (=he has only just returned) **2 as/so long as** if; on condition that: *You can go out, as long as you promise to be back before 11 o'clock.* **3 long ago** at a distant time in the past **4 no longer/(not) any longer** (used only in NEGATIVES², questions, etc.) (not) any more; not now: *He no longer lives here*/*He doesn't live here any longer.* **5 so long** infml goodbye

long³ n **1** a long time: *I'll be back before long.* (=soon)|*Were you there for long?*|*It won't take long to fix the car.* **2 the long and the short of it** the general result

long⁴ v [I;T +to-v/for] to want very much:

I'm longing to go.|I'm longing for him to come home.

long·bow /'lɒŋbowʲ/ n a large powerful BOW³ (1) made of a single curved piece of wood, for use with arrows

long-dis·tance /ˌ· '·◄/ adj,adv [A no comp.] from one point to a far point: *a long-distance runner|a long-distance (telephone) call|to call long-distance*

lon·gev·i·ty /lɒn'dʒɛvətiʲ, lɔn-/ n [U] fml long life

long·hand /'lɒŋhænd/ n [U] ordinary writing by hand, not in any shortened or machine-produced form —compare SHORTHAND

long·ing /'lɒŋɪŋ/ n,adj [C;U for] (showing) a strong feeling of wanting something: *a longing for fame|secret longings|longing looks* **–longingly** adv

lon·gi·tude /'lɒndʒəˌtuʷd, -ˌtyuʷd/ n [C;U] the distance east or west of a MERIDIAN, measured in degrees –compare LATITUDE (1) **–longitudinal** /ˌlɒndʒə'tuʷdn-əl, -'tyuʷd-/ adj

long jump /'· ·/ n [C; the S] a sport in which people jump as far as possible along the ground –compare HIGH JUMP

long·last·ing /ˌlɒŋ'læstɪŋ◄/ adj AmE something that can be used for along time without wearing out even when used a lot

long-play·ing rec·ord /ˌ· ·· '··/ also **album–** n → LP

long-range /ˌ· '·◄/ adj [A] covering a long distance or time: *long-range weapons/ long-range planning*

long·shore·man /ˌlɒŋ'ʃɔrmən, -'ʃoʷr-, 'lɒŋˌʃɔrmən, -ˌʃoʷr-/ **-men** /mən/ AmE for STEVEDORE

long·sight·ed /ˌlɒŋ'saɪtɪd/ adj BrE for FARSIGHTED

long·stand·ing /ˌlɒŋ'stændɪŋ◄/ adj which has existed for a long time: *a long standing trade agreement between two countries*

long-term /ˌ· '·◄/ adj for or in the distant future: *a long-term plan|No one knows what the long-term effects of new drugs will be.* –see also SHORT-TERM

long wave /ˌ· '·◄/ n [U] radio broadcasting on waves of 1,000 meters or more

long·ways /'lɒŋweʲz/ adv →LENGTHWISE

long·wind·ed /ˌlɒŋ'wɪndɪd◄/ adj saying too much in a dull way: *a longwinded speech*

look¹ /lʊk/ v **1** [I at, out of, away, etc.] to turn the eyes so as to see, examine, or find something: *You are looking at this dictionary.|"I can't find it." "You could see it if you'd only look."|I looked away as the doctor put the needle in my arm.|He looked out of the window.* **2** to have the appearance of being (ill, well, etc.): *You look tired.|He looks like my brother.* **3** [T] to see and notice carefully: *Look what I've done!|Look where you're going!* **4** [I] (of a thing) to face in the stated direction: *Our house looks east/looks out on the river.* **5** **look as if/look like** to seem probable that: *It looks as if we're going to miss the plane.|It looks like they'll win the election.* **6** **look someone in the eye/face** to look directly and boldly at someone **7** **not much to look**

at not attractive

look after sbdy./sthg. *v prep* [T] to take care of: *Who will look after the baby?|I can look after myself.*

look ahead *v adv* [I] to plan for the future

look around also **look round** *BrE– v adv* **1** [I for] to search **2** [I] to examine the surroundings: *He went into the old building just to look around.* **3** [I;T = **look around** sthg.] to look at everything, esp. before buying: *Would you like to look around?|looking around the stores.*

look at sbdy./sthg. *v prep* [T] **1** to watch: *looking at the traffic going past the window|Look at him jumping!* –see SEE¹ (USAGE) **2** to regard; judge: *He looks at work in a different way now that he's in charge.* **3** to consider; examine: *I wouldn't look at such a small offer.|to look carefully at a problem* **4** to remember and learn from: *Look at Mrs. Jones; she died of a heart attack when she was still young.*

look back *v adv* [I] **1** [to, on] to remember **2** **never look back** to have complete success: *After he won the first game, he never looked back.*

look down on sbdy. *v adv prep* [T] to have a low opinion of (esp. someone thought less socially important) –compare LOOK **up to**

look for sbdy./sthg. *v prep* [T] to try to find

look forward to sthg. *v adv prep* [T +v-ing] to expect to enjoy (something that is going to happen): *I'm looking forward to seeing you.*

look into sthg. *v prep* [T] to examine the meaning or causes of: *We're looking into the reasons for the fire in your house.*

look on¹ *v adv* [I] to watch while others take part –see also ONLOOKER

look on²/upon sbdy./sthg. [T as, with] to consider; regard: *I look on him as a friend.*

look out *v adv* [I for] to take care; watch (for): *Look out! You'll hit that car!* –see also LOOKOUT

look sthg. ↔ **over** *v adv* [T] to examine quickly –compare OVERLOOK

look through sthg. *v prep* [T] to examine, esp. for points to be noted

look up *v adv* **1** [I] to get better; improve: *Things are looking up!* **2** [T] (**look** sthg.↔ **up**) to find (information) in a book: *Look up the word in the dictionary.* **3** [T] (**look** sbdy. ↔ **up**) to visit when in the same area: *Look me up, next time you're in town.*

look up to sbdy. *v adv prep* [T] to respect –compare LOOK **down on**

look² n **1** an act of looking: *Have/Take a look at that!|She gave me an angry look.* (=looked angrily at me) **2** an expression on the face: *I knew she didn't like it by the look on her face.* **3** an appearance: *He has the look of a winner.|By the look(s) of it,* (=probably) *we shan't have much rain this month.|This year's fashion introduces a new look in skirts.|I don't like the look of that hole in the roof.* (=it suggests something bad to me) –see also LOOKS ·

look³ also **look here** /ˌ· '·/– interj (an expression, often angry, used to draw a person's attention): *Look (here), I don't mind your* *borrowing my car, but you should ask me first.*

look-a·like /'· ·,·/ *n AmE* something of the same appearance as something else; DOU-BLE² (2): *Those two girls could be sisters. They're look-alikes.*

look·out /'lʊk-aʊt/ *n* **1** [S] the act of watching or searching for: *She's* **on the lookout for** *a job.* **2** [C] **a** a place to watch from **b** a person whose duty is to watch **3 one's own lookout** *infml* one's own affair: *If the teacher finds out you've been cheating, it's your own lookout.* –see LOOK¹ **out**

looks /lʊks/ *n* [P] an attractive appearance: *He kept his (good) looks even in old age.*

loom¹ /luːm/ *n* a frame or machine for weaving cloth

loom² *v* [I *up*] to come into sight in a way that seems large and unfriendly: *A figure loomed (up) out of the mist.*|(fig.) *The fear of failure* **loomed large** *in his mind.*

loon·y /'luːniː/ *n,adj infml* **-ier, -iest** (a person who is) mad or foolish; LUNATIC

loop¹ /luːp/ *n* the circular shape made by a piece of string, wire, rope, etc., when curved back on itself: *The loop of string makes a handle for the package.*|(fig.) *The plane made a loop in the sky.*

loop² *v* [I;T] **1** to make or form a LOOP¹ **2** to fasten with a LOOP¹: *Loop the rope around the gate.*

loop·hole /'luːphoʊl/ *n* a way of avoiding something, esp. one provided by faults in a rule or agreement: *a loophole in the tax laws*

loose¹ /luːs/ *adj* **1** [F *no comp.*] not fastened, tied up, shut up, etc.; free from control: *The animals broke loose and ran away.*|*I have one hand loose but the other is tied.* **2** [*no comp.*] not bound together: *The store won't sell the candy loose. You have to buy a box.* **3** not firmly fixed; not tight: *This pole is coming loose and will soon fall over.*|*a loose button* **4** (of clothes) not fitting tightly **5** not exact: *a loose translation* **6** without morals: *loose living* **7 at loose ends** having nothing to do **8 let loose** to free: *The children were let loose from school.* –**loosely** *adv* –**looseness** *n* [U]

loose² *v* **loosed, loosing** [T] *fml or lit* to free from control; untie –compare LOOSEN

loose³ *adv* in a loose manner; loosely

loose⁴ *n* **on the loose** free from control, esp. of law: *A dangerous criminal is on the loose.*

loos·en /'luːsən/ *v* [I;T] to make or become less firm, fixed, or tight; set free; unfasten: *He loosened his collar.* –compare LOOSE², TIGHTEN

    loosen up *v adv* [I] to exercise the muscles ready for action: *The runners are just loosening up before the race.*

loot¹ /luːt/ *n* [U] goods stolen by thieves, soldiers, etc., in time of war or social unrest

loot² *v* [I;T] to take LOOT¹ (from): *Following the explosions in the center of town, crowds of people looted the stores.* –**looter** *n*

lop /lɒp/ *v* **-pp-** [T *away, off*] to cut off; remove: *to lop off branches from a tree*

lope /loʊp/ *v* **loped, loping** [I] (esp. of animals) to move easily and quite fast with springing steps –**lope** *n* [S]

lop-sid·ed /'· ·,··/ *adj infml* having one side not balanced with the other

lo·qua·cious /loʊ'kweɪʃəs/ *adj fml* talking a great deal –**loquacity** /loʊ'kwæsətiː/ *n* [U]

lord¹ /lɔːd/ *n* **1** a ruler or master **2** a nobleman

lord² *v* **lord it (over someone)** *esp. derog* to behave like a lord (to someone)

Lord¹ *n* **1** [*the* S] God **2** [A;C] (a title of certain official people), esp. in Britain: *the Lord MAYOR of London* **3 Lord (only) knows** no one knows

Lord² *interj* a term of surprise or worry: *Good Lord!*|*Oh Lord, I forgot!*

lord·ly /'lɔːdliː/ *adj* **-lier, -liest** like a lord; grand

lord·ship /'lɔːdʃɪp/ *n* (the title used for) a judge, a BISHOP, or certain noblemen (esp. in Britain): *Good morning, your lordship(s).*

lore /lɔː, loʊr/ *n* [U] knowledge or old beliefs not written down: *old sea lore* –see also FOLKLORE

lor·gnette /lɔːn'jet/ *n* a pair of glasses held in front of the eyes by a long handle

lor·ry /'lɒriː, 'lɑriː/ *n* **-ries** *BrE* for TRUCK (1)

lose /luːz/ *v* **lost** /lɒst/, **losing 1** [T] to come to be without, e.g. through carelessness; fail to find: *I lost my book.*|*She lost her way in the darkness.* **2** [T] to (cause to) have taken away; (cause to) have no longer, as a result of time, death, or destruction: *I've lost all interest in football.*|*His foolish behavior lost him his job.*|*She lost her parents when she was very young.* (=they died)|*He lost an eye in the accident.* **3** [I;T] to fail to win, gain, or obtain: *He lost the argument.*|*Argentina lost to* (=was beaten by) *Spain.* **4** [I;T] to (cause to) have less (money) than when one started: *We lost $200 on that job.*|*We lost on that job.*|*That job lost us $200.* **5** [T] to have less of: *He's lost a lot of weight.* **6** [T] to fail to use; waste: *The doctor lost no time in getting the sick man to hospital.* **7** [T] to (cause to) fail to hear, see, or understand: *I'm sorry, I've lost you/you've lost me; could you explain it again?* **8** [I;T] (of a watch or clock) to work too slowly by (an amount of time): *This watch loses (5 minutes a day).* –opposite **gain**

    lose out *v adv* [I *on*] *infml* to make a loss; have no success: *The firm lost out on the deal.*

los·er /'luːzər/ *n* a person who has been defeated: *He always gets annoyed when I beat him at cards: he's a bad loser.*|*I'm a* **born loser.** (=I'm always defeated) –compare WINNER

loss /lɒs/ *n* **1** [U] the act or fact of losing possession (of something): *Did you report the loss of your car to the police?* **2** [C] a person, thing, or amount that is lost or taken away: *His death was a great loss to his friends.* **3** [C] a failure to make a profit: *The company had a big loss/big losses this year.* **4 at a loss** confused; uncertain what to do or say **5 be a dead loss** *infml* to have no worth or use

lost¹ /lɒst/ *past tense and participle of* LOSE

lost² *adj* **1** that cannot be found: *lost keys* **2** no longer possessed: *lost youth*|*a lost chance* **3** [F] unable to find the way: *I got lost in the* snow. **4** [F] destroyed, killed etc.: *men lost at sea*

lot¹ /lɑt/ *n* **1** [C] a great quantity, number, or amount: *He has a lot of friends.|She has lots (and lots) of money.|There was lots to drink at the party.|That's a lot!* –see Study Notes on page 363 **2** *esp. BrE* [*the* U +*sing./ pl. v*] the whole quantity, number, or amount: *Give me the lot.|The whole lot of you are wrong!* **3** [C] a group or amount of people or things of the same type: *The last lot of apples wasn't very good.*

lot² *n* **1** [C] *esp. AmE* an area of land used for building or parking cars on: *a parking lot|a house on a big lot* **2** [C;U] (the use of) objects of different sizes or with different marks to make a choice or decision by chance: *We* **drew/ cast lots** *to decide who should go.* **3** [S] *lit* one's way of life; fate **4** [C] an article or articles sold together in an AUCTION sale: *Lot 49, a set of silver spoons* **5 a bad lot** *infml* a bad person

lo·tion /ˈloʷʃən/ *n* [C;U] a liquid mixture, used to make skin or hair clean and healthy

lot·ter·y /ˈlɑtəriʸ/ *n* -**ies** a system in which a few out of many numbered tickets sold to people are picked by chance, and prizes given to those who bought them –compare RAFFLE

lo·tus /ˈloʷṭəs/ *n* a white or pink flower that grows, esp. in Asia, on the surface of lakes

loud¹ /laʊd/ *adj* **1** having or producing great strength of sound; not quiet; noisy: *loud music|a loud radio* **2** unpleasantly noisy or colorful: *loud behavior|loud wallpaper* –**loudly** *adv* –**loudness** *n* [U]

loud² *adv* loudly; in a loud way: *Try to sing louder.*

loud·speak·er /ˈlaʊdˌspiʸkər/ also **speaker**– *n* the part of a radio or record player that produces the sound

lounge¹ /laʊndʒ/ *n* a comfortable room for sitting in, as in a house or hotel

lounge² *v* **lounged, lounging** [I *about, around*] to stand or sit in a lazy manner; pass time doing nothing

lour /ˈlaʊər/ *v* [I] → LOWER³

louse /laʊs/ *n* **lice** /laɪs/ **1** a small insect that lives on the skin and in the hair of people and animals **2** *infml* a worthless person

louse sthg.↔ **up** *v adv* **loused, lousing** [T] *AmE infml* to deal unsuccessfully with; MESS sthg. UP

lous·y /ˈlaʊziʸ/ *adj* -**ier**, -**iest 1** *infml* very bad, useless, etc.: *What lousy weather!* **2** [F] covered with lice (LOUSE)

lout /laʊt/ *n* a rough young man with bad manners –**loutish** *adj*

love¹ /lʌv/ *n* **1** [U] a strong feeling of fondness for a person: *a mother's love for her child|a man and a woman* **in love** (*with each other*) –opposites **hate, hatred 2** [U *of, for*] warm interest and enjoyment (in): *love of art/sports* **3** [C *of*] the object of attraction or liking: *Music was the love of his life.* **4** [C] a person who is loved: *Yes, my love.* **5** [U] (in tennis) no points; NIL: *McEnroe leads 15-love.* **6 give/send somebody one's love** to send friendly greetings to **7 not for love nor money** not by any means

love² *v* **loved, loving 1** [I;T not *be+v-ing*] to feel love, desire, or strong friendship (for): *I love my husband.* **2** [T +*to-v/ v-ing*] to like very much; take pleasure in: *He loves singing.|I'd love a drink.|I'd love you to come.|She loves old Humphrey Bogart films.* –opposite **hate**; see LIKE¹ (USAGE)

love af·fair /ˈˈ· ·ˌ·/ *n* an experience of (sexual) love between two people

love·ly /ˈlʌvliʸ/ *adj* -**lier**, -**liest 1** beautiful; that one loves or likes: *a lovely view of the mountains* **2** very pleasant: *a lovely meal* –**loveliness** *n* [U]

lov·er /ˈlʌvər/ *n* **1** a person who loves and/or has sex with another person outside marriage: *He is her lover.* **2** a person who loves something: *an art lover*

love·sick /ˈlʌvˌsɪk/ *adj* sad or ill because of unreturned love

lov·ing /ˈlʌvɪŋ/ *adj* showing or feeling love: *a loving look* –**lovingly** *adv*

low¹ /loʷ/ *adj* **1** being or reaching not far above the ground, floor, base, or bottom; not high: *a low wall/bridge/roof/shelf*|(fig.) *That comes low on the list of jobs to be done.* **2** small in size, degree, amount, worth, etc.: *a low figure|The temperature was very low yesterday.|a low price|a low opinion|Our supply of sugar is getting low.* (=is nearly finished) **3** [F] lacking in strength or spirit; weak or unhappy: *She's still feeling a little low after her operation.* **4** [A] having only a small amount of a particular substance, quality, etc. : *low-fat milk* **5** not loud; soft **6** (of a musical note) deep **7** near the bottom in position or rank: *a man of low birth* **8** for a slow or the slowest speed: *Use a low* GEAR *to drive up the hill.* –opposite **high** (for **1, 2, 4, 5, 6, 7, 8**) **9** not worthy, respectable, good, etc.: *a low* (=dishonest) TRICK (3) –**lowness** *n* [U]

low² *adv* **1** in or to a low position, point, degree, manner, etc.: *Shoot low.* **2** near the ground, floor, base, etc.; not high **3** (in music) in or with deep notes –opposite **high 4** quietly; softly

low³ *n* a point, price, degree, etc., that is low: *Profits have reached a new low this month.* –opposite **high**

low·brow /ˈloʷbraʊ/ *n,adj usu. derog* (typical of) a person who has no interest in literature, the arts, etc. –compare HIGHBROW

low·down /ˈloʷdaʊn/ *n* [*the* S *on*] *infml* the plain facts or truth, esp. when not generally known

low-down /ˈ· ·/ *adj* [A] worthless; dishonorable: *a low-down trick*

low·er¹ /ˈloʷər/ *adj* [A] in or being the bottom part (of something): *The bottle is on the lower shelf.* –opposite **upper**

lower² /ˈloʷər/ *v* **1** [I;T] to make or become smaller in amount or degree: *Lower the price/your voice.* **2** [I;T] to move or let down: *Lower the flags.|to lower one's eyes* –opposite **raise** (for **1,2**) **3** [T] (*usu. only in* NEGATIVES², *questions, etc.*) to bring (oneself) down in worth: *I wouldn't lower myself to speak to him.*

low·er³, lour /'lauər/ v [I at] lit to look in a bad-tempered, threatening manner; FROWN: (fig.) a lowering sky before the storm

lower case /ˌ·· '·◄/ n,adj [U] (a type of letter) printed in its small form (a, b, c) rather than in its large (CAPITAL² (2)) form (A, B, C)

lower class /ˌ·· '·◄/ n [C; the U] often derog the WORKING CLASS as regarded by those outside it: The lower class has serious social problems.|lower-class habits –see WORKING CLASS (USAGE)

low-key /ˌ· '·◄/ also **low-keyed**– adj controlled in style or quality; not loud or bright

low·land /'loᵂlənd/ n,adj [U] (an area of land) lower than the land surrounding it: lowland areas|the Lowlands of Scotland –compare HIGHLAND

low·ly /'loᵂliʸ/ adv,adj 1 in a low position, manner, or degree: lowly paid workers 2 not proud; simple; humble –**lowliness** n [U]

low·ly·ing /ˌ· '··◄/ adj (of land) not much above the level of the sea; not high

low tide /ˌ· '·/ n [C;U] the moment when the water is lowest down the seashore because the TIDE has gone out –see also HIGH TIDE

loy·al /'lɔɪəl/ adj true to one's friends, group, country, etc.; faithful: a loyal supporter|He has remained loyal to the team even though they lose every game. –opposite **disloyal** –**loyally** adv –**loyalty** n -ties [C;U]

loy·al·ist /'lɔɪəlɪst/ n a person who remains faithful to an existing ruler or government when opposed by those who want change

loz·enge /'lazəndʒ/ n a small flat substance made of sugar and usu. medicine: a cough lozenge

LP /ˌɛl 'piʸ/ also **long-playing record, album**– n a record, with recorded music, speech, etc., which plays for about 20 minutes each side –compare SINGLE² (1)

LSD /ˌɛl ɛs 'diʸ/ also **acid** infml– n [U] a strong drug that causes one to see things in a strange and different way

Ltd. esp. BrE written abbrev. said as: LIMITED (2): Dixon and Son, Ltd., –compare INC.

lu·bri·cant /'luᵂbrəkənt/n [C;U] a substance, esp. oil, which helps parts (e.g. in a machine) to move easily

lu·bri·cate /'luᵂbrə‚keʸt/‖also **lube** /luᵂb/ AmE infml– v -cated, -cating [T] to make smooth and able to move easily by adding a LUBRICANT: to lubricate the engine –**lubrication** /ˌluᵂbrə'keʸʃən/ n [U]

lu·cid /'luᵂsɪd/ adj 1 easy to understand; clear: a lucid explanation 2 able to express one's thoughts clearly; not confused: The old man's usually mad but he does have lucid moments. –**lucidly** adv –**lucidity** /luᵂ'sɪdəṭiʸ/ n [U]

Lu·cite /'luᵂsaɪt/ n [U] tdmk a strong transparent plastic material: a Lucite table

luck /lʌk/ n [U] 1 that which happens, either good or bad, to a person by, or as if by, chance; fortune: Luck was with us and we won easily.|I've had bad luck all week. 2 good fortune: I wish you luck.|Give me one more kiss for luck. 3 be down on one's luck to have bad luck; be without money 4 be in/out of luck to have/not have good fortune

luck out v adv [I] AmE infml to be lucky: You really lucked out that time.

luck·y /'lʌkiʸ/ adj -ier, -iest having, resulting from, or bringing good luck: a lucky man/discovery/charm –opposite **unlucky** –**luckily** adv: Luckily, she was in when I called. –**luckiness** n [U]

lu·cra·tive /'luᵂkrəṭɪv/ adj fml producing a lot of money; profitable: a lucrative business deal –**lucratively** adv

lu·di·crous /'luᵂdɪkrəs/ adj causing laughter; very foolish; RIDICULOUS: a ludicrous suggestion

lug¹ /lʌg/ v -gg- [T] infml to pull or carry with great effort and difficulty

lug² n a little piece that sticks out of something, such as the handle on a cooking pot –see illustration on page 95

lug·gage /'lʌgɪdʒ/ n [U] the cases, bags, boxes, etc., of a traveler; BAGGAGE: I put my luggage on the train.

lu·gu·bri·ous /lə'guᵂbriʸəs, -'gyuᵂ-/ adj fml unhappy; too sorrowful or dull: a lugubrious face/song –**lugubriously** adv

luke·warm /ˌluᵂk'wɔrm◄/ adj 1 (of liquid) not very hot 2 showing hardly any interest

lull¹ /lʌl/ v [T] to cause to sleep, rest, or become less active: The motion of the train soon lulled me to sleep.

lull² n [S in] a period in which activity is less: a lull in the fighting

lul·la·by /'lʌlə‚baɪ/ n -bies a pleasant song used for causing a child to sleep

lum·ba·go /lʌm'beʸgoᵂ/ n [U] pain in the lower back

lum·ber¹ /'lʌmbər/ v [I] to move in a heavy awkward manner

lumber² n [U] esp. AmE TIMBER (1) which has been cut into boards

lum·ber·jack /'lʌmbər‚dʒæk/ n (esp. in the US and Canada) a person whose job is to cut down trees for wood

lu·mi·nar·y /'luᵂmə‚nɛriʸ/ n -ies fml a person whose mind, learning, or actions are famous and respected

lu·mi·nous /'luᵂmənəs/ adj shining in the dark: luminous paint –**luminously** adv

lump¹ /lʌmp/ n 1 a mass of something solid with no special size or shape: a lump of lead/clay 2 a hard swelling on the body: She found a lump in her left breast. 3 a small square-sided block (of sugar): I take one lump of sugar in my tea. 4 **a lump in the throat** a tight sensation in the throat caused by feeling pity, sorrow, etc.

lump² adj **lump sum** /ˌ· '·◄/ a single undivided amount of money: You can pay for the television either in a lump sum, or in monthly INSTALLMENTS.

lump³ v **lump it** infml to accept bad conditions without complaint: I can't afford a better car, so you'll have to **like it or lump it.**

lump sth·g.↔ together v adv [T] to put (two or more things) together: The cost of these two trips can be lumped together.

lump·y /'lʌmpiʸ/ adj -ier, -iest having lumps: a lumpy bed

lu·na·cy /'luᵂnəsiʸ/ n [U] 1 madness 2 foolish or wild behavior

lu·nar /'luʷnər/ *adj* of, for, or to the moon: *a lunar voyage* –compare SOLAR

lunar month /ˌ·· '·/ *n* a period of 28 days (the time the moon takes to circle the earth)

lu·na·tic /'luʷnə.tɪk/ *n,adj* (a person who is) mad, foolish, or wild

lunch[1] /lʌntʃ/ also **luncheon** /'lʌntʃən/ *fml– n* [C;U] **1** a meal eaten in the middle of the day: *I'm hungry. Let's have lunch.* **2 out to lunch** *infml* silly or foolish

lunch[2] *v* [I] to eat LUNCH[1]: *We're lunching with John today.*

lunch·eon·ette /ˌlʌntʃə'nɛt/ *n AmE* a place where light LUNCHes are sold

lunch·time /'lʌntʃ-taɪm/ *n* [U] the time at or during which LUNCH is eaten

lung /lʌŋ/ *n* either of the two breathing organs in the chest of man or certain animals

lunge /lʌndʒ/ *v,n* lunged, lunging [I *at,out*] (to make) a sudden forceful forward movement, esp. with the arm: *He lunged at me with a knife.*

lurch[1] /lɜrtʃ/ *n* **leave someone in the lurch** *infml* to leave someone alone and without help when he/she is in difficulty

lurch[2] *n* a sudden, uncontrolled movement: *The boat gave a lurch sideways towards the rocks.*

lurch[3] *v* [I] to move with irregular sudden steps: *The drunken man lurched across the street.*

lure[1] /lʊər/ *n* [C;S *of*] **1** something that attracts: *the lure of money* **2** something used to attract animals so that they can be caught

lure[2] *v* lured, luring [T] to attract; TEMPT (2): *She's been lured to the Middle East by the promise of high wages.*

lu·rid /'lʊərɪd/ *adj* **1** shocking; unpleasant: *The papers gave the lurid details of the murder.* **2** unnaturally bright; strongly colored: *a lurid picture of a sunset* –**luridly** *adv*

lurk /lɜrk/ *v* [I] to wait in hiding, esp. for an evil purpose: *The murderer lurked behind the trees.*

lus·cious /'lʌʃəs/ *adj* having a very pleasant, sweet taste, smell, or appearance: *luscious fruit/wine* –**lusciously** *adv* –**lusciousness** *n* [U]

lush[1] /lʌʃ/ *adj* **1** (of plants, esp. grass) growing very well; thick and healthy **2** *infml* rich; comfortable

lush[2] *n AmE infml* a person who is frequently drunk

lust /lʌst/ *n* [C;U *for*] strong (esp. sexual) desire; eagerness to possess: *lust for power* –**lust** *v* [I *after/for*]: *lusting for power* –see DESIRE[2] (USAGE)

lus·ter *AmE*‖**lustre** *BrE* /'lʌstər/ *n* [S;U] brightness of a polished, shiny surface –**lustrous** /'lʌstrəs/ *adj*: *lustrous black hair* –**lustrously** *adv*

lust·ful /'lʌstfəl/ *adj* full of strong (sexual) desire –**lustfully** *adv*

lust·y /'lʌsti/ *adj* -ier, -iest **1** full of strength, health, etc.: *lusty singing* **2** full of sexual desire –**lustiness** *n* [U]

lute /luʷt/ *n* a type of old musical instrument with strings, a long neck, and a body shaped like a PEAR

lux·u·ri·ant /lʌg'ʒʊəriʸənt, lʌk'ʃʊər-/ *adj* growing well, esp. in health and number: *Luxuriant forests covered the hills.* –compare LUXURIOUS –**luxuriantly** *adv* –**luxuriance** *n* [U]

lux·u·ri·ate in sthg. /lʌg'ʒʊəriʸeʸt, lʌk'ʃʊər-/ *v prep* -ated, -ating [T] to enjoy oneself lazily in (doing something)

lux·u·ri·ous /lʌg'ʒʊəriʸəs, lʌk'ʃʊər-/ *adj* very fine and costly; very comfortable: *a luxurious hotel* –compare LUXURIANT –**luxuriously** *adv*

lux·u·ry /'lʌkʃəriʸ, 'lʌgʒəriʸ/ *n* -ries **1** [U] great comfort, as provided by wealth: *a life of luxury.|a luxury apartment* **2** [C] a pleasant thing that is not necessary or often had: *Champagne is a luxury.|We can't afford to spend money on luxuries.*

ly·chee /'liʸtʃiʸ, 'laɪtʃiʸ/ *n* an Asian fruit with a hard shell and sweet white flesh

ly·ing /'laɪ-ɪŋ/ *v* present participle of LIE[1] and LIE

lynch /lɪntʃ/ *v* [T] (esp. of a crowd of people) to attack and kill (someone thought to be guilty of a crime), without a lawful trial

lynx /lɪŋks/ *n* lynxes *or* lynx a wild animal of the cat family with a short tail

lyre /laɪər/ *n* an ancient Greek musical instrument with strings stretched on a U-shaped frame

lyr·ic /'lɪrɪk/ *n,adj* (a short poem) like a song or expressing strong personal feelings: *lyric poetry*

lyr·i·cal /'lɪrɪkəl/ *adj* full of pleasure, strong feelings, etc.: *She became quite lyrical about his gift.* –**lyrically** *adv*

lyr·i·cist /'lɪrəsɪst/ *n* a writer of LYRICS; songwriter

lyr·ics /'lɪrɪks/ *n* [P] the words of a song

M, m

M, m /ɛm/ **M's, m's** *or* **Ms, ms** **1** the 13th letter of the English alphabet **2** the ROMAN NUMERAL (number) for 1,000

m *written abbrev. said as:* METER

-'m /m/ *short for:* am: *I'm ready.*

ma /mɑ, mɔ/ *n infml* (a name for mother): *Ma, can I have some more milk?*

MA *written abbrev. said as:* Massachusetts /ˌmæsə'tʃuʷsɪts, -zɪts/ (a state in the US)

M.A. /ˌɛm 'eʸ/ *abbrev. for:* Master of Arts; (a title for someone who has) a higher university degree: *Mary Jones, M.A.|an M.A.*

ma'am /mæm/ *n* **1** (a short form of MADAM) **2** *AmE* (a polite way of addressing a woman): *Yes, ma'am.|Excuse me, ma'am.*

ma·ca·bre /mə'kɑbrə, mə'kɑb, mə'kɑbər/ *adj*

mac·a·ro·ni /ˌmækəˈrowniʸ/ n [U] a food made from flour paste (PASTA) in the form of short thin pipes which are boiled in water before eating –compare SPAGHETTI

ma·caw /məˈkɔ/ n a large brightly-colored bird (PARROT) with a long tail

mace /meʸs/ n 1 [C] an ornamental rod which is carried by an official in certain ceremonies as a sign of power 2 [U] (usu. caps) tdmk a chemical sprayed in the face that causes tears, pain in the eyes and an ill feeling: Do you think people should be allowed to carry Mace if they're afraid of being robbed?

Mach /mak/ n [S] the speed of an aircraft in relation to the speed of sound: If a plane is flying at Mach 2, it is flying at twice the speed of sound.

ma·che·te /məˈʃɛtiʸ, -ˈtʃɛ-/ n a knife with a broad heavy blade, which is used as a cutting tool and weapon

ma·chine¹ /məˈʃiʸn/ n a man-made instrument or apparatus which uses power (such as electricity) to perform work: a sewing machine

USAGE Machines, appliances, tools, and **gadgets** are all instruments for doing work. A **machine** performs work by using power, which is provided by an **engine** or **motor**: A lot of work on farms is now done by **machines**. Electrical **machines** used in the home (such as washing machines and REFRIGERATORS) are often called **appliances**. A **tool** is a simpler form of **machine**, usually worked by hand, and a **gadget** is a small, useful **tool** for doing a particular job: a store selling spades and other garden **tools**|a clever little **gadget** for opening wine bottles

machine² v -chined, -chining [T] to make or produce by machine –**machinist** n

ma·chine-gun /·ˈ· ˌ·/ n a quick-firing gun which fires continuously when the TRIGGER is pressed

ma·chin·er·y /məˈʃiʸnəriʸ/ n [U] 1 machines in general: Nowadays, most farm work is done by machinery. 2 the working parts of an apparatus 3 the operation of a system or organization: The machinery of the law works slowly.

mack·er·el /ˈmækərəl/ n **mackerels** or **mackerel** [C;U] a strong-tasting sea fish which can be eaten

mack·in·tosh /ˈmækɪn.tɑʃ/ also **mack, mac** /mæk/ infml– n esp. BrE a coat made to keep out the rain

mac·ro·bi·ot·ic /ˌmækrowbaɪˈɑtɪk/ adj concerning a type of food (esp. vegetable products grown without chemicals etc.) which is thought to produce good health

mad /mæd/ adj 1 also **crazy**– ill in the mind: She went mad after the death of her son. 2 [F at,with] infml angry: I got mad at him for being late.|She was **hopping mad**. (=very angry) 3 [F about, for] filled with strong feeling, interest, etc.: He's mad about football. 4 very foolish and careless of danger: You're mad to drive so fast! 5 **drive someone mad** to annoy someone very much 6 **like mad** infml

very hard, fast, loud, etc.: to work like mad

mad·am /ˈmædəm/ also **ma'am** AmE– n (a polite way of addressing a woman, e.g. a customer in a store): Can I help you, madam? –compare SIR

Madam n **Mesdames** /meʸˈdɑm/ (a formal word of address used e.g. when addressing women in certain official positions or in a business letter to a woman): Madam President, may I ask you . . .|Dear Madam . . . –compare SIR (2), MISTER

mad·den /ˈmædn/ v [T] to make angry; annoy

mad·den·ing /ˈmædn-ɪŋ, ˈmædnɪŋ/ adj infml very annoying –**maddeningly** adv

made¹ /meʸd/ v past tense and participle of MAKE¹

made² adj [F] 1 [of] formed: Clouds are made (up) of water. 2 [for] completely suited: a night made for love 3 sure of success: When you find gold you're made.

mad·ly /ˈmædliʸ/ adv 1 as if mad: She rushed madly out of the room. 2 infml very (much): madly in love

mad·man /ˈmædmæn, -mən/ **madwoman** /ˈmæd.wʊmən/ fem.– n **-men** /mɛn, mən/ a person who is mad: He drives like a madman.

mad·ness /ˈmædnɪs/ n [U] 1 the state of being mad 2 behavior that appears mad: It would be madness to increase taxes just before the election.

Ma·don·na /məˈdɑnə/ n [C; the S] (a picture or figure of) Mary, the mother of Christ in the Christian religion

mad·ri·gal /ˈmædrɪgəl/ n a song for singers without instruments

mael·strom /ˈmeʸlstrəm/ n esp. lit 1 a violent WHIRLPOOL 2 [usu. sing.] the violent, destructive force of events

mae·stro /ˈmaɪstrowʸ/ n **-stros** a great or famous musician

Ma·fi·a /ˈmɑfiʸə/ n [the S] an organization of (originally Sicilian) criminals who control many activities by unlawful or violent means: The Mafia is powerful in the US.

mag·a·zine /ˌmægəˈziʸn, ˈmægə.ziʸn/ n 1 also **mag** /mæg/ infml– a sort of book with a paper cover, which contains writing, photographs, and advertisements, usu. on a special subject or for a certain group of people, and which is printed every week or month: a fashion magazine 2 a storehouse or room for arms, bullets, etc. 3 the part of a gun in which bullets (CARTRIDGES) are placed before firing

ma·gen·ta /məˈdʒɛntə/ n,adj [U] (of) a dark purplish red color

mag·got /ˈmægət/ n a wormlike creature, the young of flies or other insects, often found on meat

mag·ic /ˈmædʒɪk/ n [U] 1 the system of trying to control events by calling on spirits, secret forces, etc. 2 the art of a theatrical performer (CONJURER) who produces unexpected objects and results by tricks 3 a charming quality or influence –**magic** adj [A]: the magic touch

mag·i·cal /ˈmædʒɪkəl/ adj of strange power, mystery, or charm: a magical evening beneath the stars –**magically** adv

ma·gi·cian /məˈdʒɪʃən/ n a person who practices magic; CONJURER

ma·gis·te·ri·al /ˌmædʒəˈstɪəriᵊl/ adj 1 fml having or showing the power of a master or ruler 2 [A] of or done by a MAGISTRATE

ma·gis·trate /ˈmædʒɪˌstreʸt, -strɪt/ n an official who judges cases in the lowest law courts; J.P.

mag·nan·i·mous /mægˈnænəməs/ adj unusually generous towards others –**magnanimity** /ˌmægnəˈnɪməṭiʸ/ adv

mag·nate /ˈmægneʸt, -nɪt/ n a person of wealth and power in business or industry

mag·ne·sia /mægˈniʸʒə, -ʃə/ n [U] a light white powder used as a stomach medicine

mag·ne·si·um /mægˈniʸziʸəm, -ʒiʸəm/ n [U] a silver-white metal that burns with a bright white light and is used in making FIREWORKS

mag·net /ˈmægnɪt/ n any object, esp. a piece of iron, which can draw other (metal) objects towards it, either naturally or because of an electric current being passed through it –**magnetic** /mægˈnɛtɪk/ adj: The iron has lost its magnetic force.|(fig.) a magnetic person –**magnetically** adv

mag·net·ic field /·,·· ˈ·/ n the space in which the force of a MAGNET is effective

magnetic pole /·,·· ˈ·/ n either of two points near the NORTH POLE and the SOUTH POLE of the earth towards which the compass needle points

magnetic tape /·,·· ˈ·/ n [C;U] (a length of) narrow plastic material covered with a MAGNETIC substance on which sound or other information can be recorded

mag·net·ism /ˈmægnəˌtɪzəm/ n [U] 1 (the science dealing with) the qualities of MAGNETs 2 strong personal charm

mag·net·ize ‖also **-ise** BrE /ˈmægnəˌtaɪz/ v [T] to make into a MAGNET: Iron can be magnetized by passing an electric current around it.

mag·nif·i·cent /mægˈnɪfəsənt/ adj great, grand, etc.: The royal wedding was a magnificent occasion. –**magnificence** n [U] –**magnificently** adv

mag·ni·fy /ˈmægnəˌfaɪ/ v **-fied, -fying** [T] to make (something) appear larger than it is –**magnification** /ˌmægnəfəˈkeʸʃən/ n [C;U]: This MICROSCOPE has a magnification of ten. (=It makes things look eight times larger)

magnifying glass /ˈ···· ,·/ n a curved piece of glass (LENS) which makes objects seen through it look bigger

mag·ni·tude /ˈmægnəˌtuʷd, -ˌtyuʷd/ n [U] fml greatness of size or importance: I hadn't realized the magnitude of the problem.

mag·no·lia /mægˈnoʷlyə/ n a tree with large sweet-smelling flowers

mag·pie /ˈmægpaɪ/ n a noisy black and white bird which likes to pick up and steal bright objects

ma·ha·ra·ja, -jah /ˌmɑhəˈrɑdʒə, -ˈrɑʒə/ n (often cap.) (the title of) an Indian prince

ma·hog·a·ny /məˈhɑgəniʸ/ n [U] (the color of) a dark reddish wood, used for making good furniture

maid /meʸd/ n a female servant: a housemaid

maid·en¹ /ˈmeʸdn/ also **maid–** n lit a girl who is not married

maiden² adj [A] 1 first; not done before: The ship made its maiden voyage last year. 2 (of a woman, esp. an older woman) unmarried: a maiden aunt |a maiden lady

maid·en·ly /ˈmeʸdnliʸ/ adj esp. lit like a MAIDEN¹; sweet, modest, etc.

maiden name /ˌ·· ˈ·/ n the family name a woman has or had before marriage

mail¹ /meʸl/ n [U] 1 the postal system: Airmail is quicker than sea mail.|(AmE) It came in the mail. 2 letters and anything else sent by the postal system: Is there any mail today?

mail² esp. AmE‖**post** BrE– v [T to] to take a letter, package, etc. to a post office or put into a collection box for sending: I mailed the letter two days ago. It should arrive soon.

mail·bag /ˈmeʸlbæg/ n a bag for carrying letters and packages

mail·box /ˈmeʸlbɑks/ n 1 AmE‖**postbox** BrE– a place for collecting mail. There's a mailbox just down the street. 2 AmE‖**letterbox** BrE– a place where one's mail is left, either near one's house or at a post office –see illustration on page 337

mail·man /ˈmeʸlmæn, -mən/ AmE‖also **postman**– n **-men** /mɛn, mən/ a person employed to collect and deliver letters, packages, etc.

maim /meʸm/ v [T] to harm (someone) so that part of the body can no longer be used: After the car accident she was maimed for life, and could not walk.

main¹ /meʸn/ adj [A no comp.] chief; most important: a busy main road|the main meal of the day|Here are the main events in today's news again. –**mainly** adv: His money comes mainly from business interests.

main² n 1 [usu. pl.] a chief pipe or wire supplying water, gas, or electricity 2 **in the main** usually; mostly

main·land /ˈmeʸnlænd, -lənd/ n [the S] a land mass, considered without its islands

main·spring /ˈmeʸnˌsprɪŋ/ n [usu. sing.] the chief reason behind an action: His belief in freedom was the mainspring of his fight against slavery.

main·stay /ˈmeʸnsteʸ/ n [usu. sing. of] someone or something which provides the chief support: Farming is still the mainstay of this country.

main·stream /ˈmeʸnstriʸm/ n [the S] the main or usual way of thinking or acting in a subject

main·tain /meʸnˈteʸn/ v [T] 1 to continue to have, do, etc., as before: He maintained his interest in football all his life. 2 to support with money: to maintain a family 3 to keep in good condition; take care of: the high cost of maintaining an old house 4 [+ (that)/to be] to (continue to) argue for (an opinion): Some people still maintain that the earth is flat.|He maintained his right to enter the building.

main·te·nance /ˈmeʸntənəns/ n [U] the act of MAINTAINING: car maintenance

maize /meʸz/ n [U] 1 AmE for INDIAN CORN 2 BrE for CORN¹ (1)

maj·es·ty /ˈmædʒəstiʸ/ n [U] greatness; a show of power, as of a king or queen –**majestic** /məˈdʒɛstɪk/ adj –**majestically** adv

Majesty n **-ties** (a title for speaking to or of a

king or queen: *Her Majesty the Queen/Their Majesties the King and Queen opened the new hospital yesterday.|Thank you, your Majesty.*

ma·jor¹ /ˈmeʸdʒər/ *adj* [A] greater when compared with others, in size, number, or importance: *The car needs major repairs.|a major operation* –opposite **minor**

USAGE Although it means "of greater importance than others," **major** is not used in comparisons with *than: a* **major** *new book about American politics* (not **This book is* **major** *than that one*). **Minor** is used in the same way. **Superior, inferior, senior,** and **junior** can be used in comparisons, but they are followed by *to,* not *than: This restaurant is* **superior** *to* (not **than*) *the one we went to last week.|She is* **senior** *to everyone else in the company.*

major² *n* **1** [A;C] (*often cap.*) an officer of middle rank in an army or airforce **2** [C] *AmE* the chief subject(s) which one studies at a college or university: *She entered college as a history major.|History is her major.*

major in *sthg. v prep* [T] *AmE* to study as the chief subject(s) when completing one's degree: *She majored in history.*

ma·jor·i·ty¹ /məˈdʒɔrəṭiˀ, -ˈdʒɑr-/ *n* **-ties 1** [U] the greater number or amount (esp. of people): *The majority of voters voted for the President.|At the meeting, young people were* **in the majority.** –see also PLURALITY **2** [C *usu. sing.*] the difference in number between a large and smaller group: *She won by a large majority/a majority of 900 votes.* **3** [C *usu. sing.*] *law* the age when one becomes fully responsible in law for one's actions: *She left home when she reached her majority.*

majority² *adj* [A] reached by agreement of most members of a group: *a majority decision*

make¹ /meʸk/ *v* **made** /meʸd/, **making 1** [T] to produce by work or action: *I'm making a cake.|Will you make me a cup of coffee?|The children are making a lot of noise.|I'm going to make a skirt out of this material.|Congress makes laws.|He's made his decision.* (=has decided)*|I'll make you an offer of* (=offer you) *$5 for it.|*(fig.) *She made an important discovery.* (=discovered something important) **2** [T] to put into the stated condition, position, etc.; cause to be: *Overeating made him ill.|I'm going to make this material into a skirt.|I want to make you my wife.* (=marry you)*|He made himself heard across the room.* **3** [T] to force or cause (someone to do something/something to happen): *The pain made him cry out.|How do you make this machine work?|She was made to wait for over an hour.|If you won't do it willingly, I'll make you (do it).* **4** [T] to tidy (a bed that has been slept in) by straightening the sheets, pulling over the cover, etc. **5** [T] to earn (money): *He makes a lot (of money) on his job.* **6** [T] to calculate (and get as a result): *What time do you make it?* **7** to add up to: *Two and two make four.* **8** to be counted as (first, second, etc.): *This makes our third party this month.|That makes four who want*

to go. **9** [I;T] to have the qualities of (esp. something good): *This coat will make a good present for my mother.|This story makes good reading.|The hall would make a good theater.* **10** [T] to arrive at or on: *We just made the train.* (=almost missed it)*|Can you make* (=attend) *the party?* **11** [T] *infml* to give the particular qualities of; complete: *The bright paint really makes the room.|The good news made my day.* **12 make believe** to pretend: *The children are making believe that they're princes and princesses.* –see MAKE-BELIEVE **13 make do (with something)** also **make (something) do** to use (something) even though it may not be very good or enough: *We don't have any wine, so we'll have to make do with water.* **14 make it** *infml* **a** to arrive in time **b** to succeed **15 make one's way** to go: *I made my way home/ up the stairs.* **16 make or break** which will cause success or complete failure: *a make or break decision* **17 make love (to)** to have sex (with): *They made love.|He made love to her.* **18 make room** to clear a space for something or someone

USAGE **1** Compare **do** and **make**: **Do** and **make** are used in many fixed expressions like do *a favor,* make *war,* and there is no rule about these. Usually, however, you **do** an action, and **make** something that was not there before: *to* **make** *a noise/a fire/to* **do** *the shopping/one's exercises/"What are you* **doing**?" "Cooking."*|"What are you* **making**?" "A cake."* **2** Compare **made from** and **made of**: We use **from** when the original substance has been completely changed, and **of** when something simpler has been done and we are naming the materials used: *Paper is* **made of** *wood.|Bread is* **made from** *wheat|a bag made of leather.* **3** When **make** means to force or cause (*meaning 3*), do not use *to* before a following verb, unless the sentence is passive: *It* **made** *me cry.|He was* **made** *to walk home.*

make away/off with *sthg. v adv prep* [T] *infml* to steal

make for *sthg. v prep* [T *no pass.*] **1** to move (quickly) in the direction of: *It started raining, so she made for the house.* **2** to result in: *The large print makes for easy reading.*

make *sthg.* **of** *sthg. v prep* [T *no pass.*] to understand by: *I don't know what to make of his behavior.* (=I can't understand it)

make off *v adv* [I] to escape in a hurry

make out *v adv* **1** [T] (**make** *sbdy./sthg.*↔ **out**) to see or understand with difficulty: *I can just make out the writing.|Can you make out what he's trying to say?* **2** [T] (**make** *sthg.* ↔ **out**) to write in complete form: *to make out a bill/a list|Make the check out to me.* **3** [I] *infml* to succeed, in business, personal relationships, or life generally: *How did he make out while his wife was away?|They seem to be making out very well together.* **4** [T +(*that*)] (**make out** *sthg.*) *infml* to claim or pretend, usu. falsely: *He makes out that he's younger than me.* **5** [T] (**make** *sbdy./sthg.* **out** to be *sthg.*) to claim or pretend that someone, esp. oneself, is something: *He makes himself out* to be very important.|He's not as bad as they make him out to be.

make sthg.↔ **over** v adv [T] **1** [into] to change: The basement has been made over into a playroom. **2** [to] to pass over, esp. in law: His wealth was made over to his children.

make up v adv **1** [T] (**make** sthg.↔ **up**) to invent (a story, excuse, etc.), esp. in order to deceive: I don't believe your story; you're making it up. **2** [I;T] (=**make** sbdy. **up**)] to put special paint and powder on the face of (someone or oneself) so as to change or improve the appearance: She makes herself up/makes up her face in the morning. –see also MAKE-UP **3** [T] (**make** sthg.↔ **up**) to put together into a form ready for use: Bring the sheets and make up the bed.|I'll make up a bed on the floor. **4** [T] (**make** sthg.↔ **up**) to make (an amount or number) complete: They made up a four at tennis.|You must make up the money (to the right amount). **5** [T] (**make** sthg.↔ **up**) to repay or give (an amount) in return: You must make up what you owe before the end of the month. **6** [I] to become friends again after (a quarrel): Let's kiss and make up.|At last they've made up after their quarrel. **7 make up one's mind** to decide

make up for sthg. v adv prep [T +v-ing] to repay with something good; COMPENSATE for: This beautiful fall makes up for/is making up for the wet summer.|Work fast, to **make up for lost time.**

make up to sbdy. v adv prep [T] **1** to try to gain the favor of **2 make it up to someone** to repay someone with good things in return for something: You've been so kind. I'll make it all up to you one day.

make² n **1** a type of product, esp. as produced by a particular maker: "What make is your car?" "It's a Ford." **2 on the make** infml & derog **a** searching for personal profit or gain **b** trying to obtain a sexual experience with someone

make-be·lieve /ˌ· ·'· ◂/ n [U] a state of pretending or the things which are pretended: She lives in a world of make-believe. –see also MAKE¹ (12)

mak·er /'meʸkər/ n a person or firm that makes something: makers of fine furniture|a dressmaker

make·shift /'meʸkˌʃɪft/ adj [A] used for a time because there is nothing better: They made a makeshift table from boxes.

make·up /'meʸk-ʌp/ n **1** [C;U] powder, paint, etc., worn on the face: Too much makeup looks unnatural. **2** [C] the combination of qualities (in a person's character) –see also MAKE **up**

mak·ing /'meʸkɪŋ/ n **1** [U] the act or business of making something, esp. with the hands: dressmaking|shoemaking **2** [the S of] the cause of improvement: Hard work will be the making of him. **3 in the making** ready to be produced: There's a fortune in the making for anyone willing to work hard.

mak·ings /'meʸkɪŋz/ n [the P of] the possibility of developing (into): She has the

makings of a good doctor.

mal·ad·just·ed /ˌmælə'dʒʌstɪd◂/ adj (of a person) having mental or behavior problems which prevent a happy normal life –opposite **well-adjusted**

mal·a·dy /'mælədiʸ/ n -**dies** fml & lit a disease; sick state

mal·aise /mæ'leʸz/ n [C;U] a feeling of mental or physical discomfort, esp. with no obvious cause: A social malaise in the country

ma·lar·i·a /mə'lɛəriʸə/ n [U] a disease caused by the bite of a certain type of mosquito, in hot countries –**malarial** adj [A]

mal·con·tent /ˌmælkən'tɛnt, 'mælkən,tɛnt/ n a person dissatisfied with a (political) state of affairs

male /meʸl/ adj,n **1** (of) the sex that does not give birth to young: In most birds, the male is more brightly-colored than the female.|a male monkey **2** (suitable to or typical of) this sex, rather than the female sex: a male voice –see FEMALE (USAGE)

ma·lev·o·lent /mə'lɛvələnt/ adj lit having or expressing a wish to do evil to others –compare BENEVOLENT –**malevolence** n [U] –**malevolently** adv

mal·for·ma·tion /ˌmælfor'meʸʃən/ n [C;U] tech (the condition of having) a wrongly-shaped part, e.g. of the body –**malformed** /ˌmæl'formd◂/ adj

mal·ice /'mælɪs/ n [U] **1** the wish to hurt other people **2 bear malice** to feel continuing dislike for someone –**malicious** /mə'lɪʃəs/ adj –**maliciously** adv

ma·lign /mə'laɪn/ v [T] to express evil of, esp. wrongly: This politician has been maligned by the newspapers.

ma·lig·nant /mə'lɪgnənt/ adj **1** full of hate and a strong wish to hurt: a malignant nature **2** tech (of a disease or condition) serious enough to cause death if not prevented: a malignant growth (TUMOR) on the body –compare BENIGN –**malignantly** adv –**malignancy** n [U]

ma·lin·ger /mə'lɪŋgər/ v [I] to avoid work by pretending to be ill –**malingerer** n

mall /mɔl/ n AmE **1** an area of streets where one can walk to and around stores **2** →SHOPPING CENTER

mal·lard /'mælərd/ n mallards or mallard a wild duck

mal·le·a·ble /'mæliʸəbəl/ adj **1** (of metals) that can be made into a new shape **2** (of people) easily changed or influenced –**malleability** /ˌmæliʸə'bɪlətiʸ/ n [U]

mal·let /'mælɪt/ n a wooden hammer

mal·nu·tri·tion /ˌmælnuʷ'trɪʃən, -nyuʷ-/ n [U] (bad health resulting from) lack of food, or the wrong kind of food –see also NUTRITION

mal·prac·tice /ˌmæl'præktɪs/ n [C;U] (an example of) unlawful activity for personal advantage, or bad treatment given by a person in a position of responsibility, e.g. a doctor or lawyer

malt /mɔlt/ n [U] grain, usu. BARLEY, which has been specially treated and is used for making drinks, esp. beer

mal·treat /mæl'triʸt/ v [T] fml to treat cruelly

–**maltreatment** n [U]

mam·mal /'mæməl/ n an animal of the type which is fed when young on its mother's milk

mam·moth /'mæməθ/ n **1** [C] a large hairy kind of elephant which lived on earth in early times **2** [A] very large: *Building the new railroad will be a mammoth job.*

man[1] /mæn/ n **men** /mɛn/ **1** [C] a fully-grown human male: *men, women, and children|The army will make a man of you.* (=a strong courageous person) –see also WOMAN (1) **2** [C] a human being, male or female: *All men must die.* **3** [S] human beings in general; the human race: *Man cannot live by bread alone.* **4** [C] a fully-grown male in employment or of low rank in the armed forces: *officers and men* **5** [C] any of the objects moved by each player in a board game: CHESS men **6 as one man** with the agreement of everyone **7 man about town** a (rich) man who does not work but spends time at social gatherings, in clubs, theaters, etc. **8 man and wife** husband and wife **9 the man in the street** (the idea of) the average person, who represents general opinion **10 man of the world** a man with a lot of experience of life **11 to a man** every person: *They agreed to a man.* **12 man to man** to speak honestly: *They had a man to man talk.* **13 -man** /mən/ **-woman** /ˌwʊmən/ *fem*: – **a** a person who lives in a certain place: *a Frenchman|a caveman* **b** a person who has a certain kind of job, skill, position, etc.: *a businessman|a postman* –see GENTLEMAN (USAGE)

man[2] v **-nn-** [T] to provide with men for operation: *Man the guns.*

man[3] *interj AmE infml* (used for expressing strong feelings, e.g. excitement, surprise, etc.)

man·a·cle /'mænəkəl/ n,v **-cled, -cling** [C;T] (to put on) a chain for fastening the hands or feet of a prisoner

man·age /'mænɪdʒ/ v **-aged, -aging 1** [T] to control or guide (esp. a business): *to manage a hotel/a house|She manages the money very well.* **2** [I;T +to-v] to succeed in dealing with (a problem): *The box is heavy, but I can manage (to carry) it.|We don't have much money, but we manage.|Do you think we'll manage to finish the work by Friday?*

man·age·a·ble /'mænɪdʒəbəl/ *adj* possible to control or deal with –opposite **unmanageable**

man·age·ment /'mænɪdʒmənt/ n **1** [U] the art or practice of managing (MANAGE) something, e.g. a business or money **2** [C] the people in charge of a firm, industry, etc.: *The management is having talks with the workers.*

man·ag·er /'mænɪdʒər/ n a person who directs the affairs of a business, a sports team, a singer, etc.: *the manager of a football team/a* POP[4] *group|My bank manager, Mrs. Perez, said I could have the money.|That was a terrible meal. I'm going to complain to the manager.*

man·a·ge·ri·al /ˌmænə'dʒɪriᵊl/ *adj* [A] of or concerning a MANAGER or MANAGEMENT: *a managerial position*

man·date /'mændeᵊt/ n **1** the right and power given to a body of people to act according to the wishes of those who voted for it: *The government has a mandate from the people to increase taxes.* **2** a formal command given by a higher to a lower official

man·da·to·ry /'mændəˌtɔriʸ, -ˌtoʷriʸ/ *adj fml* containing a command which must be obeyed

man·di·ble /'mændəbəl/ n *tech* a jaw which moves, usu. the lower jaw of an animal or fish

man·do·lin /ˌmændəl'ɪn, 'mændəl-ɪn/ n a musical instrument with eight metal strings, which is rather like a LUTE

mane /meᵊn/ n the long hair on the back of a horse's neck, or around the face and neck of a lion

ma·neu·ver[1] *AmE*||**manoeuvre** *BrE* /mə'nuʷvər, -'nyuʷ-/ n **1** (a set of) planned moves of an army or of warships, e.g. for training purposes: *Army maneuvers on land* **2** a skillful move or clever trick

ma·neu·ver[2] *AmE*||**manoeuvre** *BrE* v [I;T] **1** to (cause to) perform one or more MANEUVERS **2** to move (skillfully) to a position: *It was difficult to maneuver the furniture through the door.*

ma·neu·ver·a·ble *AmE*||**manoeuvrable** *BrE* /mə'nuʷvərəbəl, -'nyuʷ-/ *adj* that can be moved or directed easily: *a very maneuverable car* –**maneuverability** /məˌnuʷvərə'bɪlətiʸ, -ˌnyuʷ-/ n [U]

man·ga·nese /'mæŋgəˌniʸz, -ˌniʸs/ n [U] a grayish white metal used in making glass, steel, etc.

mange /meᵊndʒ/ n [U] a skin disease of animals, esp. dogs and cats, leading to the loss of hair or fur –**mangy** *adj* **-gier, -giest**

man·ger /'meᵊndʒər/ n **1** a long open container used for feeding horses and cattle **2 dog in the manger** a person who does not wish others to enjoy what he/she cannot use for his/her own enjoyment

man·gle[1] /'mæŋgəl/ v **-gled, -gling** [T] to tear or cut to pieces; crush: *After the accident the bodies were too badly mangled to be recognized.*

mangle[2] n a machine with rollers turned by a handle, between which water is pressed from clothes, sheets, etc., being passed through

man·go /'mæŋgoʷ/ n **-goes** or **-gos** (a tropical tree which bears) a fruit with sweet yellow-colored flesh

man·grove /'mæŋgroʷv/ n a tree of tropical countries which grows on muddy land (a SWAMP) and near water

man·han·dle /'mænˌhændl/ v **-dled, -dling** [T] to move, esp. roughly, using force: *She complained that she had been manhandled by the police.*

man·hole /'mænhoʷl/ n a covered opening in a road, through which a person can go down to repair underground pipes and wires

man·hood /'mænhʊd/ n [U] the condition or qualities of being a man: *Members of certain tribes perform special ceremonies when they reach manhood.*

ma·ni·a /'meᵊniᵊə/ n **1** [U] *tech* a dangerous

disorder of the mind **2** [C;U *for*] (a) very strong desire or interest: *a mania for (driving) fast cars|car mania*

ma·ni·ac /'me^yni^yˌæk/ *n* **1** a person who suffers from MANIA (1): *a dangerous sex maniac* **2** a wild thoughtless person: *He drives like a maniac.*

man·ic /'mænɪk/ *adj* of or suffering from MANIA

man·i·cure /'mænɪˌkyʊər/ *n* [C;U] (a) treatment for the hands and fingernails, including cleaning, cutting, etc. –**manicure** *v* **-cured, -curing** [T] –**manicurist** *n*

man·i·fest¹ /'mænəˌfɛst/ *adj fml* plain and clear to see: *Fear was manifest on his face.* –**manifestly** *adv*

manifest² *v* [T] *fml* to show plainly: *The disease manifests itself in yellowness of the skin and eyes.*

man·i·fes·ta·tion /ˌmænəfɛ'ste^yʃən,-fə-/ *n* [C;U] *fml* (an) act of showing or making clear

man·i·fes·to /ˌmænə'fɛsto^w/ *n* **-tos** or **-toes** a (written) statement making public the intentions, opinions, etc., of a political party or group

man·i·fold¹ /'mænəˌfo^wld/ *adj fml* many in number and/or kind: *The problems facing the government are manifold.*

manifold² *n tech* a pipe with holes, to allow gases to enter or escape from an engine, e.g. in a car

ma·nil·a, -nilla /mə'nɪlə/ *n* [A] strong brown paper

ma·nip·u·late /mə'nɪpyəˌle^yt/ *v* **-lated, -lating** [T] **1** to handle or control skillfully: *to manipulate the controls of the machine* **2** to control and influence (someone) for one's own purpose –**manipulative** /mə'nɪpyə lətɪv,-ˌle^ytɪv/ *adj* –**manipulation** /məˌnɪpyə 'le^yʃən/ *n* [C;U]

man·kind /ˌmæn'kaɪnd/ *n* [U +*sing.*/ *pl. v*] the human race, both men and women: *the worst war in the history of mankind*

man·ly /'mænli^y/ *adj* **-lier, -liest** having or showing the qualities suitable to a man; strong, brave, etc.: *a manly act of courage* –**manliness** *n* [U]

man-made /ˌ· '· ◄/ *adj* **1** produced by people; not found in nature: *a man-made lake* **2** (of materials) made from chemical, not natural, substances; SYNTHETIC: *Nylon is a man-made* FIBER. –compare NATURAL¹ (1)

manned /mænd/ *adj* (of machines) having people on board: *a manned spacecraft* –opposite **unmanned**

man·ner /'mænər/ *n* **1** [C of usu. sing.] the way or style of doing something: *The sheets are usually folded in this manner.|a painting in the French 19th century manner* **2** [S] a personal way of acting or behaving: *I don't like his manner; it's very rude.|a pleasant manner* **3 all manner of** every sort of **4 not by any manner of means** not at all

man·ner·ism /'mænəˌrɪzəm/ *n* a typical habit of behaviour, speech, etc.

man·ners /'mænərz/ *n* [P] **1** (polite) social practices or habits: *Children should be taught (good) manners.* **2** –**mannered** having

a certain type of manners: *good/ well-mannered|bad/ill-mannered*

ma·noeu·vra·ble *adj BrE* for MANEUVERABLE –**manoeuvrability** /məˌnuːwvərə'bɪləti^y, -ˌnyuw-/ *n* [U]

ma·noeu·vre /mə'nuːwvər, -'nyuw-/ **-vred, -vring** *n;v BrE* for MANEUVER

man·or /'mænər/ *n* **1** a large house with land: *a manor house* **2** the land belonging to a nobleman (the **lord of the manor**) under the FEUDAL system

man·pow·er /'mænˌpaʊər/ *n* [U] the number of people needed for a certain type of work: *The new machines will cause a reduction in manpower.*

man·sion /'mænʃən, -tʃən/ *n* a large house, usu. belonging to a wealthy person –see HOUSE (USAGE)

man·slaugh·ter /'mænˌslɔtər/ *n* [U] *law* the crime of killing a person, unlawfully but not intentionally –compare MURDER

man·tel /'mæntəl/ also **mantelshelf** /-ˌʃelf/ *old use* – *n* the shelf above a fireplace –see illustration on page 399

man·tle /'mæntəl/ *n lit or old use* a loose outer garment; CLOAK: (fig.) *a mantle of snow on the trees*

man·u·al¹ /'mænyu^wəl/ *adj* of or using the hands: *Manual work is tiring.* –**manually** *adv*

manual² *n* a (small) book of information about how to do something, or use esp. a machine –compare HANDBOOK

man·u·fac·ture¹ /ˌmænyə'fæktʃər/ *v* **-tured, -turing** [T] to make or produce by machinery, esp. in large quantities: *manufactured goods|manufacturing industry.* –**manufacturer** *n*

manufacture² *n* [U] the act of manufacturing (MANUFACTURE)

ma·nure /mə'nʊər, mə'nyʊər/ *n* [U] waste matter from animals which is put on the land to make it produce better crops –compare FERTILIZER

man·u·script /'mænyəˌskrɪpt/ *n* **1** the first copy of a book or piece of writing, esp. written by hand before being printed **2** a handwritten book, of the time before printing was invented: *a collection of valuable old manuscripts*

man·y /'mɛni^y/ *determiner,pron* more /mɔr, mo^wr/ most /mo^wst/ **1** (used without *a* to show the large size of a number): *How many letters are there in the alphabet?|There are (far) too many people here.|Not many of the children* (=Only a few of the children) *can read.|He bought four tickets, which was one too many.* (=he only needed three)|*Many people learn French at school.* –see Study Notes on page 550 **2 a good/ great many** a large number of **3 many a man, time, etc.** many men, times, etc.: *Many a man would have run away, but he didn't.* **4 many is the time** there have been many times: *Many's the time I've wondered what he meant.*

map¹ /mæp/ *n* a representation or plan showing the shape and position of countries, towns, rivers, etc.: *a map of Europe/central San Juan*

map² *v* **-pp-** [T] to make a map of

map sthg. ↔ **out** *v adv* [T] to plan (an event) in the future: *We spent weeks mapping out our holiday.*

ma·ple /'meɪᵖəl/ *n* a tree with many-pointed leaves, which yields a sugary liquid

mar /mɑr/ *v* **-rr-** [T] *esp. lit* to spoil: *The big new road mars the beauty of the countryside.*

mar·a·thon /'mærəˌθɑn/ *n* **1** [C] **a** 26-mile running race **b** any activity that tests one's power over a long time **2** [A] very long: *a marathon speech of six hours*

ma·raud·ing /mə'rɔdɪŋ/ *adj* [A] searching for something to steal, burn, or destroy: *They were attacked by marauding soldiers.* –**marauder** *n*

mar·ble /'mɑrbəl/ *n* **1** [A;U] a hard sort of stone used for building, SCULPTURE, etc., and usu. showing an irregular pattern of colors: *a white marble gravestone* **2** [C *usu. pl.*] a small hard ball of colored glass used by children to play a game in which they roll the balls along the ground: *Let's have a game of marbles.*

march¹ /mɑrtʃ/ *v* **1** [I] to walk with a regular, esp. forceful, step like a soldier: *The soldiers marched along the road.|She was very angry and marched out (of the house).|*(fig.) *Time marches on.* –see WALK (USAGE) **2** [T] to force to walk (away): *The police marched him off to prison.* **3 Quick march!** (a command to soldiers to start marching)

march² *n* **1** [*the* U] the act of marching: *The soldiers went past at the march/on the march.|*(fig.) *the march of time* **2** [C] the distance covered while marching in a certain period of time: *It was a short/a day's march from the city to the camp.* **3** [C] a piece of music for marching to **4** [C] marching by a large number of people from one place to another to show their opinions or dissatisfactions: DEMONSTRATION (2): *a hunger march*

March also **Mar.** *written abbrev.– n* the third month of the year

mare /mɛər/ *n* a female horse or donkey –compare STALLION

mar·ga·rine /'mɑrdʒərɪn/ *n* [U] a food made from animal or vegetable fats, used instead of butter on bread or in baking

mar·gin /'mɑrdʒɪn/ *n* **1** a space near the edge of a page: *to make notes in the margin of a book* **2** an amount above what is necessary: *He left home early and caught the train by a good margin.* (=of time) **3** (in business) the amount of profit: *high profit margins*

mar·gin·al /'mɑrdʒənl/ *adj* of small importance or small amount: *The new law will cause a marginal increase in the cost of living.* –**marginally** *adv*

mar·i·gold /'mærəˌgoʷld/ *n* a flower with a yellow head

mar·i·jua·na, -huana /ˌmærə'wɑnə, -'hwɑnə/ *n* [U] the common form of the drug CANNABIS, usu. smoked in cigarettes for pleasure

ma·ri·na /mə'riʸnə/ *n* a small harbor for pleasure boats

mar·i·nate /'mærəˌneʸt/ also **marinade** /ˌmærə'neʸd, 'mærəˌneʸd/– *v* **-nated, -nating** [T] to leave (meat or fish) in a mixture of wine, oil, SPICEs, etc. before cooking –**marinade** *n* [C;U]

ma·rine¹ /mə'riʸn/ *adj* [A] **1** of, near, or living in the sea: *Marine plants grow on the sea bed.* **2** of ships and sea trade: *marine insurance*

marine² *n* [A;C] a soldier who serves on a naval ship

Marine Corps /·ˈ· ˌ·/ also **Marines** /mə'riʸnz/– *n* [*the* U] (in the US) a small army-like force connected to the navy

mar·i·ner /'mærənər/ *n lit* a sailor or seaman

mar·i·o·nette /ˌmæriʸə'nɛt/ *n* a small figure of a person, animal, etc., moved by strings or wires; sort of PUPPET

mar·i·tal /'mærətl/ *adj* of or concerning marriage –**maritally** *adv*

mar·i·time /'mærəˌtaɪm/ *adj* [A] **1** concerning ships or the sea: *maritime law|a great maritime power* (=with a strong navy) **2** living or existing near the sea

mar·jo·ram /'mɑrdʒərəm/ *n* [U] a plant (HERB) with sweet-smelling leaves used in cooking

mark¹ /mɑrk/ *n* **1** a spot, line, or cut that spoils the natural color or appearance of something: *His feet left (dirty) marks all over the floor.|*(fig.) *His years in prison have left their mark on him.* **2** an object or sign serving as a guide, giving information, or showing a quality: *We followed the marks that the car had left in the grass.|They stood as a mark of respect when he came in.|a question mark|*(fig.) *He certainly* **made his mark** (**on the place**) *while he was here.* (=had a great influence on it) **3** a figure, letter, or sign which represents a judgment of quality in someone's work, behavior, or performance: *The highest mark in the test was nine out of ten.* **4** a particular type of a machine: *The Mark 4 car is more powerful than the old Mark 3.* **5 not (quite) up to the mark** not of good enough quality **6 On your marks, get set, go!** (used for starting a running race)

mark² *v* **1** [I;T] to make a mark on, or to receive a mark, in a way that spoils the appearance: *The hot cups have marked the table.|Don't put hot cups on the table. It marks easily.|The disease marked her face for life.* **2** [T] to be a sign of: *The pile of stones marks his grave.|Today's ceremony marks 100 years of trade between our countries.|She has the qualities that mark a good doctor.* **3** [T] to give marks (MARK¹ (3)) to: *I've got a pile of examination papers to mark.|The teacher marked my test 10 out of 10.* **4 Mark my words!** Take note of and remember what I say **5 mark time** to spend time on work, business, etc., without advancing

mark sthg. ↔ **down/up** *v adv* [T] to lower/raise (goods) in price: *These winter coats have been marked down from $100 to $65.* –see also MARKUP

mark stgh. ↔ **off** *v adv* [T] to draw lines around (an area): *they marked off the tennis court with white paint.*

mark sbdy./stgh. ↔ **out** *v adv* [T *for*] to show as suitable (for): *Her powerful speeches marked her out for political success.*

mark³ *n* a German coin

marked /mɑrkt/ *adj* **1** noticeable: *He showed a marked lack of interest.* **2** [F *by*] (typically) having: *This writer's plays are marked by a gentle humor.* **3 marked man** a man who is in danger from an enemy **–markedly** /'mɑrkɪdliʸ/ *adv*

mark·er /'mɑrkər/ *n* **1** a tool for making marks **2** an object which marks a place

mar·ket¹ /'mɑrkɪt/ *n* **1** a building or open place where people meet to buy and sell goods: *a cattle market|the market square* **2** a gathering of people to buy and sell on certain days at such a place: *Monday is market day.* **3** an area or country where there is a demand for goods: *They sell to foreign markets|the home market.* **4** demand for goods: *There's not much of a market for woolen clothes in a tropical country.* **5 a buyer's/seller's market** a situation favoring the buyer/seller: *Not many people can afford new cars right now, so it's a buyer's market.* **6 on the market** (of goods) for sale **7 in the market (for)** ready to buy

market² *v* [T] to offer for sale: *The company markets many types of goods.* **–marketable** *adj*

mar·ket·ing /'mɑrkɪtɪŋ/ *n* [U] **1** the various activities by which goods are advertised and sold **2** *AmE* for shopping, esp. for food: *to do the marketing.*

marks·man /'mɑrksmən/ **markswoman** /-,wʊmən/ *fem.– n* **-men** /mən/ a person who can shoot well with a gun

mark·up /'mɑrk-ʌp/ *n* the amount by which a price is raised: *a markup of 20 cents* –see also MARK² **down/up**

mar·ma·lade /'mɑrmə,leʸd/ *n* [U] a sweet food (JAM) which is spread on bread, made from fruits, esp. oranges

ma·roon¹ /mə'ruʷn/ *v* [T] to leave (someone) alone, esp. in a place where no one lives, with no means of getting away: *The boat sank and we were marooned on a little island.*

maroon² *n,adj* [U] (of) a very dark red-brown color

mar·quee /mɑr'kiʸ/ *n* **1** *AmE* a cover usu. of glass and metal over the entrance of a building, esp. of a theater. **2** a large tent used for outdoor public events

mar·quis /'mɑrkwɪs, mɑr'kiʸ/ also **marquess** /'mɑrkwɪs/- **-quises** /kwɪsɪz/ *or* **-quis** /'kiʸz/ (*fem.* **marchioness** /'mɑrʃənɪs, ,mɑrʃə'nɛs/) (the title of) a nobleman of high rank

mar·riage /'mærɪdʒ/ *n* [C;U] **1** the union of a man and woman by a ceremony in law: *The marriage took place in church.* **2** the state of being so united: *Her first marriage was not very happy.* (=her life with her first husband)

mar·riage·a·ble /'mærɪdʒəbəl/ *adj fml* suitable to be married

mar·ried /'mæriʸd/ *adj* **1** having (as) a husband or wife: *a married man|*(fig.) *He's married to his work.* (=gives it all his attention) –compare SINGLE **2** [A] of the state of marriage: *married life*

mar·row /'mæroʷ/ *n* [U] the soft fatty substance in the hollow center of bones

mar·ry /'mæriʸ/ *v* **-ried, -rying 1** [I;T] to take (a person) in marriage: *He got married late in life/never married.* |(fig.) *She married (into)*

money. (=a rich man) **2** [T] (of a priest or official) to perform the ceremony of marriage for (two people): *An old friend married them.* **3** [T *to*] to cause to take in marriage: *She wants to marry her son to a rich woman.*

Mars /mɑrz/ *n* the PLANET fourth in order from the sun, and next to the Earth

marsh /mɑrʃ/ *n* [C;U] (an area of) low land that is soft and wet **–marshy** *adj* **-ier, -iest**

mar·shal¹ /'mɑrʃəl/ *n* **1** [A;C] an officer of the highest rank in certain armies and air forces **2** [C] an official who arranges a public ceremony or event **3** [A;C] (in the US) **a** an official who carries out the judgments given in a court of law **b** a chief officer of a police or fire-fighting force

marshal² *v* **-l-** *AmE*‖**-ll-** *BrE* [T] **1** to arrange in good order: *He gave a good speech, in which he marshaled the facts very clearly.* **2** to lead or show the way to the correct place

marsh·mal·low /'mɑrʃ,meloʷ, -,mæloʷ/ *n* a type of soft round sweet substance, eaten as candy

mar·su·pi·al /mɑr'suʷpiʸəl/ *adj,n tech* (one) of the type of animal which carries its young in a pocket of skin (POUCH) on the mother's body

mar·tial /'mɑrʃəl/ *adj* [A] of or concerning war, soldiers, etc.: *martial music*

martial law /,·· '·/ *n* [U] government by the army under special laws

Mar·tian /'mɑrʃən/ *adj,n* (a being) of the PLANET MARS, usu. in imaginary stories

mar·tyr¹ /'mɑrtər/ *n* **1** a person who dies or suffers for his/ her beliefs **2 make a martyr of oneself** to give up one's own wishes to help others, or in the hope of being praised

martyr² *v* [T] to kill or cause to suffer for a belief

mar·tyr·dom /'mɑrtərdəm/ *n* [U] the death or suffering of a martyr

mar·vel¹ /'mɑrvəl/ *n* a wonder; wonderful thing or example: *The operation was a marvel of medical skill.*

marvel² *v* **-l-** *AmE*‖**-ll-** *BrE* [I;T +(*that*), *at*] to wonder; be surprised at: *We marveled at their skill.*

mar·vel·ous *AmE*‖**marvellous** *BrE* /'mɑr vələs/ *adj* wonderful; surprisingly good: *What marvelous weather!* **–marvelously** *adv*

Marx·ism /'mɑrksɪzəm/ *n* [U] the teaching of Karl Marx on which COMMUNISM is based, which explains the changes in history according to the struggle between social classes **–Marxist** *n,adj*

mar·zi·pan /'mɑrzə,pæn, 'mɑrtsə,pɑn/ *n* [U] a very sweet paste, of nuts, sugar, and egg, used for making some sweet foods

masc. *adj. written abbrev. said as:* MASCULINE –compare FEM.

mas·car·a /mæ'skærə/ *n* [U] a dark substance for coloring the EYELASHES

mas·cot /'mæskət/ *n* an object, animal, or person thought to bring good luck

mas·cu·line /'mæskyəlɪn/ *adj* **1** of or having the qualities suitable for a man –compare FEMININE; see FEMALE (USAGE) **2** *tech* (in grammar) of a certain class of words: *"Drake" is the masculine form of "duck."*

match –compare FEMININE

mas·cu·lin·i·ty /ˌmæskyəˈlɪnətiᵞ/ *n* [U] the quality of being MASCULINE (1) –compare FEMININITY

mash¹ /mæʃ/ *v* [T] to crush into a soft substance: *Mash the potatoes with a fork.*

mash² *n* [C;U] **1** a mixture of grain and water used as food for animals **2** [U] a mixture of MALT with hot water, used in making beer or whiskey

mask¹ /mæsk/ *n* a covering for the face to hide or protect it: *Everyone who enters the chemical factory must wear a mask.*|(fig.) *He hid his hatred under a mask of loyalty.* –see also GAS MASK **–masked** /mæskt/ *adj*

mask² *v* [T] to cover with a MASK; hide: (fig.) *She masked her feelings.* –see also UNMASK

mas·och·ism /ˈmæsəˌkɪzəm/ *n* [U] the wish to be hurt so as to gain (esp. sexual) pleasure –compare SADISM **–masochist** *n* **–masochistic** /ˌmæsəˈkɪstɪk/ *adj*

ma·son /ˈmeᵞsən/ *n* →STONEMASON

ma·son·ry /ˈmeᵞsənriᵞ/ *n* [U] a stone part of a building: *She was hit by a piece of falling masonry.*

mas·quer·ade¹ /ˌmæskəˈreᵞd/ *n* **1** a dance or party where people wear MASKs **2** something pretended; hiding of the truth

masquerade² *v* **-aded, -ading** [I *as*] to pretend (to be): *He got a free ticket to the play by masquerading as a friend of the actors.*

mass¹ /mæs/ *n* **1** [C *of*] a solid lump, quantity, or heap, or large number: *a solid mass of rock*|*(infml) masses of people* **2** [U] (in science) the amount of matter in a body

mass² *v* [I;T] *lit* to gather together in large numbers: *Dark clouds massed, and we expected rain.*

mass³ *adj* [A] of or for a great number of people: *a mass murderer*|*a mass meeting*

Mass *n* [C;U] (esp. in the ROMAN CATHOLIC church) the main religious service, based on Christ's last supper

Mass. *written abbrev. said as:* Massachusetts /ˌmæsəˈtʃuᵂsɪts, -zɪts/ (a state in the US)

mas·sa·cre¹ /ˈmæsəkər/ *n* a killing of large numbers of people who cannot defend themselves

massacre² *v* **-cred, -cring** [T] to kill a large number of people: (fig.) *Their team was much better than ours, and we were massacred.* –see also KILL (USAGE)

mas·sage /məˈsɑʒ, məˈsɑdʒ/ *n* [C;U] (an example of) treatment of the body by pressing and rubbing one's hands on it to take away pain or stiffness **–massage** *v* **-saged, -saging** [T]

mass·es /ˈmæsɪz/ *n* [*the* P] the lower, poorer classes in society; the WORKING CLASS

mas·seur /məˈsɜr, mæ-/ **masseuse** /məˈsuᵂs, -ˈsuᵂz, -ˈsɜz, mæ-/ *fem.– n* a person who gives MASSAGEs

mas·sive /ˈmæsɪv/ *adj* very big; strong and powerful: *the massive walls surrounding the city*|*a massive increase in the cost of living* **–massively** *adv*

mass me·di·a /ˌ· ˈ···/ *n* [*the* U +*sing./ pl. v*] the means of giving news and opinions to large numbers of people, esp. radio,

television, and the newspapers: *The mass media is/are sympathetic towards the government.* –see also MEDIUM

mass pro·duc·tion /ˌ· ·ˈ··/ *n* [U] the making of large numbers of the same article by a fixed method **–mass-produce** /ˌ· ·ˈ·/ *v* **-duced, -ducing** [T]: *cheap mass-produced furniture*

mast /mæst/ *n* **1** a long upright pole for carrying sails on a ship **2** a flagpole –see also HALF-MAST

mas·ter¹ /ˈmæstər/ *n* **1** [*of*] **mistress** *fem.–* a man in control of people, animals, or things: *He's the master of the house.*|*the dog's master* **2 mistress** *fem.– fml esp. BrE* a male teacher **3** a man of great skill in art or work with the hands: *a master builder*|CRAFTSMAN|*The painting is the work of a master.* –see also OLD MASTER

master² *adj* [A] chief; most important: *the master bedroom*

master³ *v* [T] to gain control over or learn throughly: *to master a horse*|*It takes years to master a new language.*

mas·ter·ful /ˈmæstərfəl/ *adj* having an ability to control others –compare MASTERLY **–masterfully** *adv*

master key /ˌ·· ˈ·/ *n* a key that will open several different locks

mas·ter·ly /ˈmæstərliᵞ/ *adj* showing great skill: *a masterly speech* –compare MASTERFUL **–masterliness** *n* [U]

mas·ter·mind¹ /ˈmæstərˌmaɪnd/ *n* a very intelligent person, esp. one who is responsible for a plan: *The police never found the mastermind behind the jewel robbery.*

mastermind² *v* [T] *infml* to plan (a course of action) cleverly: *to mastermind a crime*

mas·ter·piece /ˈmæstərˌpiᵞs/ *n* a piece of work, esp. art, which is the best of its type or the best a person has done

mas·ter's /ˈmæstərz/ *n* **master's** *infml esp. AmE (often cap.)* an M.A. or M.S. degree: *She has her master's in physics.*

mas·ter·y /ˈmæstəriᵞ/ *n* [U *over, of*] control (over) or skill (in): *The enemy had complete mastery of the seas, and no ships could get through.*

mas·ti·cate /ˈmæstəˌkeᵞt/ *v* **-cated, -cating** [I;T] *fml* to bite on and through (food); CHEW **–mastication** /ˌmæstəˈkeᵞʃən/ *n* [U]

mas·tiff /ˈmæstɪf/ *n* a large powerful guard dog

mas·tur·bate /ˈmæstərˌbeᵞt/ *v* **-bated, -bating** [I;T] to excite the sex organs (of), by handling, rubbing, etc. **–masturbation** /ˌmæstərˈbeᵞʃən/ *n* [U]

mat¹ /mæt/ *n* **1** a piece of rough strong material or small RUG used for covering part of a floor **2** a small piece of material used for putting under objects on a table: *Put the hot dish down on the mat, so you don't burn the table.* –see illustration on page 379

mat² →MATT

mat·a·dor /ˈmætəˌdɔr/ *n* the person who kills the BULL in a BULLFIGHT

match¹ /mætʃ/ *n* **1** [C] a game or sports event in which teams or people compete: *a tennis match* **2** [S *for*] a person who is equal or better in strength, ability, etc., (to another):

I'm no match for her when it comes to painting. (=she's much better than me)|*He was very good at tennis, but* **he met his match** (=met someone who could beat him) *when he played McEnroe.* **3** [S *for*] a thing or set of things that is like or suitable to another or each other: *The hat and shoes are a perfect match.*

match² *v* **1** [I;T] to be like or suitable for use with (another or each other) (): *The curtains don't match the paint.|The curtains and paint don't match.* **2** [T *in, for*] to be or find an equal to: *This hotel can't be matched for good service and food.* **3** [T *up*] to find something like or suitable for use with: *I'm trying to match this yellow wool; do you have anything like it?* **4 well-/ill-matched** suitable/not suitable to be with, or to compete with, each other: *John and his wife are well-matched.|The two fighters aren't very well-matched.* (=one is much better than the other)

match³ *n* a short thin stick, usu. of wood, with a substance at the end which burns when struck against a rough surface: *a box of matches*

match·box /'mætʃbɑks/ *n* a small box in which matches are sold, with rough material along one or both sides on which to strike them

match·ing /'mætʃɪŋ/ *adj* [A] (esp. of colors) which are the same or suited

match·less /'mætʃlɪs/ *adj fml* which has no equal in quality

match·mak·er /'mætʃ,meʸkər/ *n* a person who encourages people (who he/she thinks suitable) to marry each other

mate¹ /meʸt/ *n* **1** [C] a fellow workman or friend: *They are my mates/roommates/teammates/classmates.* **2** [C] *AmE* a husband or wife. **3** *BrE infml* (a way of addressing a man): *"What time is it, mate?"* **4** the rank below a ship's captain: *first mate/second mate* **5** one of a male and female pair of animals

mate² *v* **mated, mating** [I;T *with*] to become or make into a couple, esp. of animals, for the production of young: *Birds mate in the spring.|the* **mating season**|*They mated a horse with a donkey.*

ma·te·ri·al¹ /mə'tɪəriʸəl/ *adj* **1** of or concerning matter or substance, not spirit: *The storm did a great deal of material damage.* (=to buildings, property, etc.) **2** of the body, rather than the mind or soul: *Our material needs are food and clothing.* —compare SPIRITUAL —**materially** *adv*

material² *n* **1** [C;U] anything from which something is or may be made: *Rubber is a widely used material.|Building materials are costly.* **2** [C;U] cloth: *dress material|a light material* —see CLOTHES (USAGE) **3** [U *for*] knowledge of facts from which a (written) work may be produced: *She's collecting material for a book.*

ma·te·ri·al·ism /mə'tɪəriʸə,lɪzəm/ *n* [U] **1** *esp. derog* (too) great interest in the pleasures of the world, money, etc. **2** the belief that only matter exists, and that there

is no world of the spirit —**materialistic** /mə,tɪəriʸə'lɪstɪk/ *adj* —**materialistically** *adv* —**materialist** /mə'tɪəriʸəlɪst/ *adj,n*

ma·te·ri·al·ize /mə'tɪəriʸə,laɪz/||also **-ise** *BrE*– *v* **-ized, -izing** [I] to take on bodily form; become real: *The shape of a man materialized out of the shadows.|His hopes never materialized.*

ma·ter·nal /mə'tɜrnl/ *adj* **1** of, like, or natural to a mother **2** [A] related through the mother's part of the family: *my maternal grandfather* —see also PATERNAL —**maternally** *adv*

ma·ter·ni·ty /mə'tɜrnəṭiʸ/ *adj,n* [A;U] (of) motherhood or the bodily condition of becoming a mother; for PREGNANCY and giving birth: *a maternity dress|a maternity hospital/WARD*

math·e·ma·ti·cian /,mæθəmə'tɪʃən/ *n* a person who studies MATHEMATICS

math·e·mat·ics /,mæθə'mætɪks/ also **math** /mæθ/ *infml*– *n* [U] the study or science of numbers —compare ARITHMETIC —**mathematical** *adj* —**mathematically** *adv*

mat·i·née /,mætn'eʸ/ *n* a performance of a play or movie given in the afternoon

ma·tri·arch /'meʸtriʸ,ɑrk/ *n* a woman who rules a family or a group of people –see also PATRIARCH —**matriarchal** /,meʸtriʸ'ɑrkəl/ *adj*

ma·tri·ar·chy /'meʸtriʸ,ɑrkiʸ/ *n* **-chies** [C;U] (an example of) a social system in which women, not men, have power over the family and possessions –see also PATRIARCHY

mat·ri·cide /'mætrə,saɪd/ *n* [C;U] the crime of killing one's mother –see also PATRICIDE

ma·tric·u·late /mə'trɪkyə,leʸt/ *v* **-lated, -lating** [I;T] to (allow to) become a member of a university, esp. after an examination or test —**matriculation** /mə,trɪkyə'leʸʃən/ *n* [C;U]

mat·ri·mo·ny /'mætrə,moʷniʸ/ *n* [U] *fml* the state of marriage —**matrimonial** /,mætrə'moʷniʸəl/ *adj*

ma·trix /'meʸtrɪks/ *n* **matrices** /'meʸtrə,siʸz, 'mæ-/ *or* **matrixes** *tech* **1** a hollow container (MOLD²) into which melted metal is poured to form a shape **2** the rock or stone in which hard stones or jewels have been formed **3** (in MATHEMATICS, science, etc.) an arrangement of numbers, figures, or signs

ma·tron /'meʸtrən/ *n* **1** (the title of) a woman **a** in a hospital who has control over the the nurses **b** in a school, prison, etc. who is in charge of housekeeping **2** *lit* an older married woman

ma·tron·ly /'meʸtrənliʸ/ *adj* **1** *euph* (of a woman) rather fat –see THIN (USAGE) **2** (of a woman) having or showing DIGNITY like a MATRON (2)

matt, mat||also **matte** *AmE* /mæt/ *adj* of a dull, not shiny, surface: *matt paint*

mat·ted /'mæṭɪd/ *adj* twisted in a thick mass: *matted hair*

mat·ter¹ /'mæṭər/ *n* **1** [U] the material which makes up the world and everything in space which can be seen or touched **2** [C] a subject to which one gives attention; an affair: *There are several important matters I wish to talk to you about.|I've decided to* **let the matter drop.** (=take no further action to deal with the affair)|*Looking after 15 noisy children is* **no laughing matter.** (=is difficult) **3** [*the* S] a trouble or cause of pain, illness, etc.: **What's the matter;** *why are you crying?*|There's **nothing the matter/Nothing's the matter with** *me.* (=nothing's wrong)|**What's the matter with** *the radio; why isn't it working?* **4** [U] written material: *I must take some* **reading matter** (=books, magazines, etc.) *for the journey.* **5 a matter of: a** a little more or less than; about: *We only had to wait a matter of (ten) minutes.* **b** having as a part or result; needing: *Answering this question is just a matter of using your intelligence.* **6 a matter of course** a normal or usual event: *When I go out of the house I lock the door* **as a matter of course. 7 a matter of life or death** something so serious that failure to do it may result in death **8 a matter of opinion** a subject on which different persons may think differently **9 as a matter of fact** really; in fact: *"I thought you wouldn't mind." "Well, as a matter of fact I don't; but you should have asked me first."* –see also MATTER- OF-FACT **10 for that matter** (used when mentioning another possibility) as concerns the thing mentioned: *Your mother would never allow it, and for that matter, neither would I.* **11 mind over matter** a strong will conquering bodily weakness **12 no matter** (**how, where, etc.**) it makes no difference: *We'll have to finish the job, no matter how long it takes.*

matter² *v* [I *to*] to be important: *It doesn't matter if I miss my train, because there's another one later.*|*I don't think anybody matters to her apart from herself.*

matter-of-fact /ˌ·· ·ˈ·◂/ *adj* concerned with facts, not imagination or feelings; practical –see also MATTER¹ (9)

mat·ting /ˈmætɪŋ/ *n* [U] rough material for mats and for packing goods

mat·tress /ˈmætrɪs/ *n* a large bag of solid but yielding material for sleeping on

ma·ture¹ /məˈtʃʊər, məˈtʊər, məˈtjʊər/ *adj* **1 a** fully grown and developed **b** typical of an older person; sensible: *You're not a child; you must behave in a more mature way.* –opposite **immature 2** (of cheese, wine, etc.) ready to be eaten or drunk; ripe –**maturely** *adv* –**maturity** /məˈtʃʊərətiʸ, -ˈtʊər-, -ˈtjʊər-/ *n* [U]

mature² *v* **-tured, -turing** [I;T] to (cause to) become MATURE: *In six years the wine will have matured.*

maud·lin /ˈmɔdlɪn/ *adj fml* showing foolish sadness in a pitiful way: *He always becomes maudlin after he's had a few drinks.*

maul /mɔl/ *v* [T *about*] **1** (esp. of animals) to hurt by tearing the flesh: *The hunter was mauled by a lion.* **2** to handle roughly or in an unwelcome way: *Stop mauling me!*

mau·so·le·um /ˌmɔsəˈliʸəm, -zə-/ *n* a fine stone building (TOMB) raised over a grave

mauve /moʷv/ *adj,n* [U] (of) a pale purple color

mav·er·ick /ˈmævərɪk/ *n* **1** a person, esp. a politician, who acts differently from the rest of the group **2** *AmE* a young cow without its owner's mark

max·im /ˈmæksɪm/ *n* a rule for good and sensible behavior, often expressed in a short saying

max·i·mize ‖also **-mise** *BrE* /ˈmæksəˌmaɪz/ *v* **-mized, -mizing** [T] to increase to the greatest possible size –compare MINIMIZE

max·i·mum /ˈmæksəməm/ *n* **-ma** /mə/ *or* **-mums 1** [C] the most, or the largest possible, quantity, number or degree: *He smokes a maximum of 15 cigarettes a day.*|*This lamp will give you the maximum of light.*|*The sound has reached its maximum.* (=is at its loudest) **2** [A] largest, or largest possible (in amount, degree, etc.): *Today's maximum temperature will be 65 degrees.*|*maximum speed* –see also MINIMUM

may /meyʸ/ *v* negative contraction **mayn't** /ˈmeyʸənt/ *esp. BrE*[I + *to*-v] **1** (shows a possibility): *He may come or he may not.*|*"Why hasn't he come?" "He may have missed the train."* (=perhaps he has missed it)|I may have thought that once, but I don't now. **2** to have permission to; be allowed to: *You may come in now.*|*May we go home, please?* (This is now less common than **can**) –see Study Notes on page 434 **3** (used when expressing a wish): *May there never be another world war!* **4 may/might as well** to have no strong reason not to: *There's nothing to do, so I might as well go to bed.* –see CAN, MIGHT (USAGE)

May *n* the 5th month of the year

may·be /ˈmeyʸbiʸ/ *adv* perhaps: *"Will they come?" "Maybe."*

may·day /ˈmeyʸdeyʸ/ *n* a radio signal used as a call for help from a ship or plane

May Day /ˈ· ·/ *n* 1st May, when dances, games, etc. are held to welcome spring, and when political parties of the LEFT² (3) hold public events

may·n't /ˈmeyʸənt/ *v esp. BrE* short for **may not**: *They mayn't have arrived yet, if the traffic's been bad.*

USAGE **May** and **not** are usu. not contracted in *AmE*: *They may not be here yet.* |(fml) You may not swim here unless you are a member of this club.

may·on·naise /ˌmeyʸəˈneyʸz, ˈmeyʸəˌneyʸz/ *n* [U] a thick yellowish SAUCE made from eggs, oil, VINEGAR, etc., often used on SALADs

may·or /ˈmeyʸər, mɛər/ *n* a person elected to be head of a city or town –**mayoral** *adj*

may·pole /ˈmeyʸpoʷl/ *n* a tall pole which can be ornamented with flowers and around which people dance on **May Day** (May 1st), esp. formerly in villages

maze /meyʸz/ *n* an arrangement of paths, often bordered with tall HEDGES¹ (1), which twist and turn, and are sometimes blocked, within an enclosed area. *In a maze, you try to find the center and then the way out again.| We were lost in the maze for several hours.*|(fig.) *a maze of narrow winding streets* –compare LABYRINTH

MD, Md. *written abbrev. said as:* Maryland /ˈmɛrələnd/ (a state in the US)

M.D. *abbrev. for:* Doctor of Medicine: *Joan Snow, M.D.*

me /miyʸ/ *pron* (*object form of* I): *Can you see*

me?|He bought me a drink.|He bought a drink for me.|That's me on the left of the photograph.
USAGE **Him, her, me, us,** and **them** are used in speech after *as, than,* and *be,* but in formal writing **he, she, I, we,** and **they** are sometimes used instead: *I'm a better player than* **him**/ *than* **he** *(fml).|I'm not as pretty as* **her**/*as* **she** *(fml).|It's* **me**!/*It is* **I** *(fml)*
ME, Me. *written abbrev. said as:* Maine /meⁱn/ (a state in the US)
mead·ow /ˈmɛdoʷ/ *n* [C;U] (a field of) grassland on which cattle, sheep, etc., may feed
mea·ger AmE‖**meagre** BrE /ˈmiʸgər/ *adj* not enough in quantity, quality, strength, etc.: *He cannot exist on his meager income.* **–meagerly** *adv* **–meagerness** *n* [U]
meal[1] /miʸl/ *n* **1** an amount of food eaten at one time: *She cooks a hot meal in the evenings.|The dog has one meal a day.* **2** also **mealtime** /ˈmiʸltɑɪm/– the occasion or time of eating a meal: *The whole family meets at meals.*
meal[2] *n* [U] grain which has been crushed into a powder, esp. for flour **–mealy** *adj* **-ier, -iest**
meal·y-mouthed /ˌ··ˈ·◂/ *adj* expressing things indirectly, not plainly, esp. when something unpleasant must be said: *mealy-mouthed politicians/ statements*
mean[1] /miʸn/ *adj* **1** unkind; nasty: *It was very mean of you not to let the children play in the snow.* **2** *esp. AmE* bad-tempered; liking to hurt: *That's a mean dog. Be careful –it may bite you.* **3** *lit* (typical of a person) of low social position; humble: *a man of mean birth|They live in a mean little house.* **4** ungenerous; unwilling to share or help: *He's very mean with his money.* **5 no mean (something)** a very good (something): *He's no mean cook.|Running 10 miles is no mean* ACHIEVEMENT. **–meanly** *adv* **–meanness** *n* [U]
mean[2] *v* **meant** /mɛnt/, **meaning** /ˈmiʸnɪŋ/ [T] **1** [+(that); not be +v-ing] to represent (a meaning): *What does this French word mean?|The red light means "Stop".|The sign means that cars cannot enter.* **2** [+to-v/ (that)] to have in mind or for a purpose; intend: *She said Tuesday, but she meant Thursday.|I meant to go yesterday.|Those flowers were meant for you; I meant you to have them.|I said I would rescue him and I meant it.* (=I am determined to do so)|*When I asked you to do it I didn't mean (that) you should take all day.|I've been meaning to ask you–how's your mother?* **3** [+v-ing/ (that); not be +v-ing] to be a sign of: *The dark clouds mean rain.|That expression on his face means (that) he's angry.|Missing the train means waiting for an hour.* (=we will have to wait) **4** [to; not be +v-ing] to be of importance by (a stated amount): *Her work means a lot/means everything to her.* **5 be meant to** *esp. BrE* to have to; be supposed to: *You're meant to take your shoes off when you enter a Hindu temple.* **6 mean business** *infml* to act with serious intentions **7 mean well** to do or say what is intended to help, but often doesn't
mean[3] *n* **1** an average amount, figure, or

value: *The mean of 7, 9, and 14 is found by adding them together and dividing by 3.* **2** a state, way of behavior, etc., which is not too strong or weak, great or small, etc., but in between
mean[4] *adj* [A no comp.] (of measurements) average: *The mean yearly rainfall is 20 inches.*
me·an·der /miʸˈændər/ *v* [I] **1** (of rivers and streams) to flow slowly, with many turns **2** (of people or talk) to speak or move on in a slow aimless way **–meanderingly** *adv* **–meanderings** *n* [P]
mean·ing[1] /ˈmiʸnɪŋ/ *n* [C;U] **1** the idea which is intended to be understood: *One word can have several meanings.|What's the meaning of this?* (often said to demand an explanation of something that has angered one) **2** importance or value: *He says his life has lost its meaning (for him) since his wife died.*
meaning[2] *adj* [A] which gives an effect of important (hidden) meaning or thought: *a meaning smile*
mean·ing·ful /ˈmiʸnɪŋfəl/ *adj* of important meaning; containing information: *That statement is not very meaningful.|He gave her a meaningful look.* **–meaningfully** *adv* **–meaningfulness** *n* [U]
mean·ing·less /ˈmiʸnɪŋlɪs/ *adj* without meaning or purpose: *a meaningless remark/action* **–meaninglessly** *adv* **–meaninglessness** *n* [U]
means /miʸnz/ *n* **means 1** [C of] a method or way (of doing): *The quickest means of travel is by plane.|Use whatever means you can to . . .* **2** [P] money, income, or wealth, esp. large enough for comfort: *Have you the means to support a family?|a man of means* (=a rich man) **3 by all means** certainly; please do **4 by means of** by using: *She could not speak, but made her wishes known by means of signs.* **5 by no means** *fml* not at all: *I am by no means pleased with this behavior.*
meant /mɛnt/ *v past tense and participle of* MEAN[2]
mean·time /ˈmiʸntɑɪm/ *n* **in the meantime** in the time between two events: *We can't go out yet because it's raining, so let's play a game in the meantime.*
mean·while /ˈmiʸnhwɑɪl, -wɑɪl/ also **meantime** *infml*– *adv* during this time; in the same period of time: *They'll be here in ten minutes. Meanwhile, we'll have some coffee.*
mea·sles /ˈmiʸzəlz/ *n* [the U] an infectious disease in which the sufferer has a fever and small red spots on the face and body
mea·sly /ˈmiʸzliʸ/ *adj* **-slier, -sliest** *infml* of small value, size, etc.: *a measly little piece of cheese* **–measliness** *n* [U]
meas·ur·a·ble /ˈmɛʒərəbəl/ *adj* large enough or not too large to be reasonably measured **–see also** IMMEASURABLE **–measurably** *adv*: *Your work has improved measurably* (=a lot) *this year.*
meas·ure[1] /ˈmɛʒər/ *n* **1** [U] a system for calculating amount, size, weight,etc.: *An* OUNCE *in liquid measure is different from an* OUNCE *in dry measure.* **2** [C] an amount in such a system: *An hour is a measure of time.*

3 [C] an instrument used for calculating amount, length, weight, etc.: *The glass is a pint measure.* –see also TAPE MEASURE **4** [S;U of] *fml* an amount or quality: *He has not become rich, but he has had* **a certain measure of** *success/***some measure of** *success.* **5** [C *usu. pl.*] an action taken to gain a certain end: *The administration has promised to* **take measures** *to help the unemployed.* **6 for good measure** in addition; as something extra: *After I'd weighed the apples, I put in another one for good measure.*

measure² *v* **-ured, -uring 1** [I;T] to find the size, length, amount, degree, etc., (of) in standard measurements: *He measured (the height of) the desk.* **2** [T] to show or record amount, size, length, etc.: *A clock measures time.* **3** [not *be*+*v*-ing] to be of a certain size: *The picture measures 10 by 14 inches.*

measure sthg.↔ **out** *v adv* [T] to take a measured quantity of (something taken from a larger amount): *To make the cake, measure out 2 cups of flour and half a cup of butter.*

measure up *v adv* [I *to*] to show good enough qualities (for): *He didn't measure up to the job.*

meas·ure·ment /'mɛʒərmənt/ *n* **2** [U] the act of measuring **1** [C *usu. pl.*] a length, height, etc., found by measuring: *Which measurement should I take first–the width or the length of the room?*

meat /miːt/ *n* [U] **1** the flesh of animals (sometimes including birds, but not including fish) which is eaten: *There's not much meat on that bone/chicken.|His religion forbids the eating of meat.* **2** valuable matter, ideas, etc.: *It was an interesting speech, but there was no real meat in it.* –**meaty** *adj* **-ier, -iest**: *a meaty soup|*(fig.) *a meaty story*

USAGE The meat from some animals has a different name from the animal itself. For example, the meat from a **cow** is called **beef**, the meat from a **pig** is **pork** or **ham**, and the meat from a **calf** (a young cow) is **veal**. But the meat from a **lamb** is **lamb**, and for birds and fish the same word is used for both the meat and the creature: *They keep* **chickens** *and* **ducks** *in their yard.|Should we have* **chicken** *or* **duck** *for dinner?*

meat·ball /'miːtbɔl/ *n* a small round ball made out of finely cut-up meat, several of which may be eaten together at a meal

me·chan·ic /mɪ'kænɪk/ *n* a person who is skilled in using, repairing, etc., machinery: *a car mechanic*

me·chan·i·cal /mɪ'kænɪkəl/ *adj* [*no comp.*] of, connected with, moved, worked, or produced by machinery: *a mechanical toy|*(fig.) *He was asked the same question so many times that the answer became mechanical.* (=as if made by a machine) –**mechanically** *adv*

me·chan·ics /mɪ'kænɪks/ *n* [U] **1** the science of the action of forces on objects **2** the science of making machines **3 the mechanics of** the ways in which something works, produces results, etc.: *She has natural ability, but hasn't yet learned the mechanics of the job.*

mech·a·nism /'mɛkə,nɪzəm/ *n* the different parts of something, esp. of a small machine, arranged together, and the action they have: *The clock doesn't work. There's something wrong with the mechanism.|the mechanism of the brain|the mechanism of local government*

mech·a·nize ‖also **-nise** *BrE* /'mɛkə,naɪz/ *v* **-nized, -nizing** [T] to use machines for, instead of using the effort of human beings or animals: *If we can mechanize farming we can produce more crops with fewer people.* –**mechanization** /,mɛkənə'zeɪʃən/ *n* [U]

med·al /'mɛdl/ *n* a round flat piece of metal, or a cross, with a picture and/or words marked on it, which is usu. given to a person as an honor for an act of bravery or strength: *She won a gold medal at the Olympic Games.*

med·al·ist *AmE*‖ **medallist** *BrE* /'mɛdl-ɪst/ *n* a person who has won a MEDAL, esp. in sports

me·dal·lion /mə'dælyən/ *n* a round MEDAL like a large coin, used for ornament

med·dle /'mɛdl/ *v* **-dled, -dling** [I *in, with*] to interest oneself or take action (in something which it is not one's concern); INTERFERE (2) –**meddler** *n* –**meddlesome** *adj*: *a meddlesome old man, always giving unwanted advice*

me·di·a /'miːdiyə/ *n* [U +*sing./pl. v*] the newspapers, television, and radio; MASS MEDIA: *The media controls/control the news* –see also MEDIUM

me·di·ae·val /,miːdiy'iːvəl, mɛ-, ,mɪ-/ *adj* →MEDIEVAL

me·di·ate /'miːdiy,eɪt/ *v* **-ated, -ating** [I;T *between*] *fml* to act or produce as a peacemaker: *The government mediated between the workers and the employers.|The army leaders have mediated a* CEASE-FIRE/*a settlement.* –**mediation** /,miːdiy'eɪʃən/ *n* [U] –**mediator** /'miːdiy,eɪtər/ *n*

med·i·cal¹ /'mɛdɪkəl/ *adj* [*no comp.*] **1** of or concerning medicine and treating the sick: *a medical student|a medical examination* (=of the body by a doctor) **2** of the treatment of disease by medicine rather than by operation –compare MEDICINAL –**medically** *adv*

medical² *n infml* a medical examination (of the body)

med·i·care /'mɛdɪ,kɛər/ *n* [U] (*often cap.*) (in the US) a system of government medical care, esp. for old people

med·i·cat·ed /'mɛdɪ,ketɪd/ *adj* including or mixed with a medical substance: *medicated* SHAMPOO

med·i·ca·tion /,mɛdɪ'keɪʃən/ *n* [C;U] *esp. AmE* a medical substance, esp. a drug: *It is better to sleep naturally, without taking medication.*

me·dic·i·nal /mə'dɪsənəl/ *adj* [*no comp.*] **1** used for medicine: *medicinal alcohol* (=not for drinking) **2** having the effect of curing, like medicine: *medicinal* HERBS –compare MEDICAL¹ –**medicinally** *adv*

med·i·cine /'mɛdəsən/ *n* **1** [C;U] a substance used for treating disease, usu. taken by mouth: *a bottle of medicine|Keep all medicines away from children.* **2** [U] the science of treating and understanding disease **3 give someone a taste/dose of his own**

medicine *infml* to treat someone as (badly as) he has treated others as a punishment

me·di·e·val, mediaeval /ˌmɪ^ydiˑ'ï^yvəl, ˌme-, ˌmɪ-/ *adj* of the period in history between about 1100 and 1500 (the MIDDLE AGES)

me·di·o·cre /ˌmɪ^ydi^y'o^wkər/ *adj* of not very good or bad quality or ability: *a mediocre essay* **—mediocrity** /ˌmɪ^ydi^y'akrəṭi^y/ *n* [U]

med·i·tate /'mɛdəˌte^yt/ *v* **-tated, -tating** [I] **1** to fix and keep the attention on one matter, having cleared the mind of thoughts, esp. for religious reasons and/or to gain peace of mind **2** to think seriously or deeply: *He meditated for two days before giving his answer.*

med·i·ta·tion /ˌmɛdə'te^yʃən/ *n* [C;U] the act or result of meditating (MEDITATE)

med·i·ta·tive /'mɛdəˌte^yṭɪv/ *adj* thoughtful; showing deep thought **—meditatively** *adv*

me·di·um¹ /'mɪ^ydi^yəm/ *n* **-dia** /di^yə/ *or* **-diums** **1** a method for giving information; form of art: *He writes stories, but the theater is his favorite medium.|Television can be a medium for giving information, for amusing people, and for teaching them.* **–see also** MASS MEDIA, MEDIA **2** a substance in which objects or living things exist, or through which a force travels; surroundings: *A fish in water is in its natural medium.|Sound travels through the medium of air.* **3** a middle position: *There's a happy medium between eating all the time and not eating at all.*

medium² *n* **-diums** a person who claims to have power to receive messages from the spirits of the dead

medium³ *adj* [A] of middle size, amount, quality, value, etc.: *a medium-sized cabbage* –see Study Notes on page 550

med·ley /'mɛdli^y/ *n* **-leys 1** a piece of music made up of parts of other musical works **2** a mass or crowd (of different types) mixed together: *a medley of different ideas*

meek /mi^yk/ *adj* gentle in nature; yielding to others' actions and opinions **—meekly** *adv* **—meekness** *n* [U]

meet¹ /mi^yt/ *v* **met** /mɛt/, **meeting 1** [I;T] to come together (with), by chance or arrangement: *Let's meet for dinner.|I met him on the street.|The whole school met to hear the speech.|I'll drive to the station and meet her at the train.|The two cars met* HEAD-ON. (=had an accident) **2** [I;T] to get to know or be introduced (to) for the first time: *Come to the party and meet some interesting people.|Haven't I met you somewhere before?* **3** [I;T] to touch, (as if) naturally: *Their lips met (in a kiss).* **4** [I] to join: *The two roads meet just north of Boston.* **5** [T] to find or experience; MEET with (1): *She met her death in a plane crash.* **6** [T *with*] to answer, esp. in opposition: *His speech was met with cries of anger.* **7** [T] to satisfy: *Does the hotel meet your expectations?|This new truck meets our needs.* **8** [T] to pay: *Can you meet your debts?* **9 more** (in/to something) **than meets the eye** hidden facts, difficulties, or reasons (in or for something): *We thought the job would be easy, but there's more to it than meets the eye.* **10 make ends meet** to use one's (small amount of) money carefully so as to afford

what one needs

meet up *v adv* [I *with*] *infml* to meet, by arrangement: *Let's meet up after the play.* **a** to join (someone): *"You go ahead; I'll meet up with you at the restaurant."* **b** to catch (someone): *When I meet up with him, he'll have to pay.*

meet with sbdy./sthg. *v prep* [T] **1** to experience or find by chance: *I met with some difficulties when I tried to enter the country.|They met with an accident on their way back.* **2** *esp AmE* to have a meeting with: *Our representatives met with several heads of state.*

meet² *n* a gathering of people, esp. (*BrE*) on horses with hunting dogs (HOUNDS) to hunt foxes or (*AmE*) for sports events: *a swimming meet*

meet·ing /'mi^yṭɪŋ/ *n* **1** a gathering of people, esp. for a purpose: *I was late for the meeting so they started without me.* **2** the coming together of two or more people, by chance or arrangement: *Our meeting at the station was quite by chance.*

meg·a·lo·ma·ni·a /ˌmɛgəlo^w'me^yni^yə/ *n* [U] (the condition in which one holds) the belief that one is more important, powerful, etc., than one really is **—megalomaniac** /ˌmɛgəlo^w'me^yni^yˌæk/ *n*

meg·a·phone /'mɛgəˌfo^wn/ *n* an instrument shaped like a horn which makes the voice louder when spoken through it, so that it can be heard over a distance

meg·a·ton /'mɛgəˌtʌn/ *n* a measure of force of an explosion equal to that of a million tons of explosive: *a 5-megaton atomic bomb*

mel·an·chol·y¹ /'mɛlənˌkɑli^y/ *n* [U] sadness, esp. over a period of time and not for any particular reason **—melancholic** /ˌmɛlən'kɑlɪk/ *adj*

melancholy² *adj* sad: *alone and feeling melancholy|melancholy news*

me·lee /'me^yle^y, me^y'le^y/ *n* [*usu. sing.*] a struggling or disorderly crowd

mel·lif·lu·ous /mə'lɪflu^wəs/ *adj* (of words, music, or a voice) with a sweet smooth flowing sound

mel·low¹ /'mɛlo^w/ *adj* **1** (of fruit and wine) sweet and ripe or MATURE, esp. after being kept for a long time **2** (of colors and surfaces) soft, warm, and smooth **3** (of people) wise and gentle through age or experience **—mellowly** *adv* **—mellowness** *n* [U]

mellow² *v* [I;T] to (cause to) become (more) MELLOW with the passing of time: *The colors mellowed as the sun went down.|The years have mellowed him.*

me·lod·ic /mə'lɑdɪk/ *adj* **1** [*no comp.*] of or having a MELODY **2** →MELODIOUS

me·lo·di·ous /mə'lo^wdi^yəs/ *adj* sweet-sounding; tuneful **—melodiously** *adv*

mel·o·dra·ma /'mɛləˌdrɑmə, -ˌdræmə/ *n* [C;U] a (type of) exciting play, full of sudden events and strong feelings: (fig.) *There was quite a melodrama when the child lost his mother in the street.*

mel·o·dra·mat·ic /ˌmɛlədrə'mæṭɪk/ *adj* showing, or intended to produce, strong and excited feelings; (too) EMOTIONAL (1): *He* *says he's going to kill himself, but he's just being melodramatic.*

mel·o·dy /'mɛlədiᵞ/ n -dies 1 a song or tune 2 the part which forms a clearly recognizable tune in a larger arrangement of notes

mel·on /'mɛlən/ n [C;U] a large round fruit, with a firm skin and juicy flesh which can be eaten

melt /mɛlt/ v 1 [T] to cause (a solid) to become liquid: *The sun melted the snow.* 2 [I] (of a solid) to become liquid: *The ice is melting in the sun.* |(fig.) *His anger quickly melted.* (=disappeared) –compare FREEZE
USAGE The adjective **molten** means **melted**, but is used only of things that melt at a very high temperature: **molten** *rock/metal* |**melted** *chocolate/ice.*

melt away v adv [I] to disappear easily: *The opposition melted away when they realized they had no support.*

melt sthg.↔ **down** v adv [T] to make (a metal object) liquid by heating, esp. so as to use the metal again –compare MELTDOWN

melt·down /'mɛltdaʊn/ n an accident in which the central part of a NUCLEAR REACTOR could melt –see also MELT **down**

melting pot /'·· ,·/ n 1 a place where there is a mixture of people of different races and nations: *America has been a melting pot since its beginnings.* 2 a container in which metals can be melted

mem·ber /'mɛmbər/ n [of] a person belonging to a club, group, etc.: *a member of the family* |*a Member of Congress* |*a member of a political party* –opposite **non-member**

mem·ber·ship /'mɛmbər,ʃɪp/ n 1 [U] the state of being a member of a club, society, etc.: *My membership is due for renewal.* 2 [*the* S] all the members of a club, society, etc.

mem·brane /'mɛmbreᵞn/ n [C;U] soft thin skin in the body, covering or connecting parts of it

me·men·to /mə'mɛntoʷ/ n -tos a small object which reminds one, esp. of a vacation, a friend, etc.

mem·o /'mɛmoʷ/ n -os a note from one person or office to another within an organization: MEMORANDUM

mem·oirs /'mɛmwɑrz/ n [P] the story of a person's own life, esp. that of an important public figure: *The old general has started to write his memoirs.*

mem·o·ra·bil·i·a /,mɛmərə'bɪliᵞə, -'bɪlyə, -'biᵞl-/ n [P] things that are very interesting and worth remembering, esp. in connection with a famous person or event: *Kennedy memorabilia*

mem·o·ra·ble /'mɛmərəbəl/ adj worth remembering; special in some way: *The film was memorable for* (=remembered because of) *the fine acting of the two main characters.* |*a memorable trip abroad* –**memorably** adv

mem·o·ran·dum /,mɛmə'rændəm/ n -da /də/ or -dums fml for MEMO

me·mo·ri·al /mə'mɔriᵞəl, -'moʷr-/ n 1 an object, such as a stone MONUMENT, in a public place in memory of a person, event, etc.: *a war memorial* 2 a custom which serves the

same purpose: *The church service is a memorial to those killed in the war.*

Memorial Day /·'··· ,·/ n (in the US) a holiday at the end of May when soldiers killed in war and other dead people are remembered

mem·o·rize ||also -rise BrE /'mɛmə,raɪz/ v -rized, -rizing [T] to learn and remember, on purpose: *He memorized the list of dates.*

mem·o·ry /'mɛməriᵞ/ n -ries 1 [C;U] (an) ability to remember events and experience: *She's got a good memory for dates/faces.* |*He played the tune* **from memory.** (=without written music) 2 [C *of*] an example of remembering: *one of my earliest memories* 3 [S] the time during which things happened which can be remembered: *There have been two wars within the memory of my grandfather/* **within living memory.** (=which can be remembered by people now alive) 4 [C] the opinion held of someone after his death: *to praise his memory* 5 the part of a computer or CALCULATOR in which information (DATA) can be stored until it is wanted

men /mɛn/ n pl. of MAN

men·ace¹ /'mɛnɪs/ n 1 [C;U *to*] something which suggests a threat or brings danger: *He spoke with menace in his voice.* |*The busy street outside the school is a menace to the children's safety.* 2 [C] *infml* a troublesome person or thing: *That child is a menace.*

menace² v -aced, -acing [T] *esp. fml* to threaten: *The people are being menaced by the threat of war.*

men·ac·ing /'mɛnəsɪŋ/ adj threatening: *a menacing look* |*Those dark clouds look menacing.* (=there may be a storm) –**menacingly** adv

me·nag·er·ie /mə'nædʒəriᵞ, -ʒə-/ n a collection of wild animals kept privately or for the public to see; ZOO

mend¹ /mɛnd/ v 1 [I;T] to repair (a hole, break, fault, etc.) in (something): *I'll mend that shirt.* 2 [I] to regain one's health: *He's mending nicely after his accident.* 3 **mend one's ways** to improve one's behavior –**mender** n

mend² n 1 a part mended after breaking or wearing; part PATCHED or DARNED 2 **on the mend** getting better after illness

me·ni·al /'miᵞniᵞəl, 'miᵞnyəl/ adj (of a job) humble and not interesting or important: *menial work* –**menially** adv

men·o·pause /'mɛnə,pɔz/ also **change of life**– n [U] the time when a woman's PERIODS¹ (5) stop, usu. in middle age

men's room /'· ·/ *AmE* ||gents *BrE*– n a public RESTROOM for men

men·stru·al /'mɛnstruᵞəl, -strəl/ adj concerning a woman's PERIOD¹ (5)

men·stru·ate /'mɛnstruᵞw,eᵞt/ v -ated, -ating [I] to have a PERIOD¹ (5) –**menstruation** /,mɛnstruᵞw'eᵞʃən/ n [C;U]

men·tal /'mɛntəl/ adj [no comp.] 1 of the mind: *mental powers* |*mental illness* –compare PHYSICAL 2 [A] done only in or with the mind, esp. without the help of writing: *mental* ARITHMETIC 3 [A] concerning disorders or illness of the mind: *a mental hospital* |*mental treatment* |*a mental patient* –**mentally** adv

men·tal·i·ty /mɛn'tælətiʸ/ n **-ties 1** [U] the abilities and powers of the mind: *of weak mentality* **2** [C] character; habits of thought: *I can't understand the mentality of anyone who would do a terrible thing like that!*

men·thol /'mɛnθɒl, -θɑl, -θoʷl/ n [U] a white substance with a MINTY¹ taste **–mentholated** /'mɛnθə,leʸtɪd/ adj

men·tion¹ /'mɛnʃən, -tʃən/ v [T] **1** [+*that*] to tell about in a few words, spoken or written: *He mentioned their interest in sport/that they were interested in sport.* **2** to say the name of: *He mentioned a useful book.* **3 Don't mention it** polite There's no need for thanks; I'm glad to help: *"Thanks very much." "Don't mention it."* **4 not to mention (something/the fact that)** and in addition there's . . .: *They have three dogs to look after, not to mention the cat and the bird.* –see also UNMENTIONABLE

mention² n [U] **1** the act of mentioning: *There was no mention of our team's success in the newspaper.* **2** formal recognition as a reward: *He did not win, but he did get honorable mention.*

men·tor /'mɛntɔr, -tər/ n a person who habitually advises another

men·u /'mɛnyuʷ/ n **-us** a list of dishes in a meal or to be ordered as separate meals, esp. in a restaurant –see illustration on page 581

me·ow AmE‖**miaow** BrE /miʸ'aʊ/ n, v [C;I] (to make) the crying sound a cat makes

mer·ce·nar·y¹ /'mɜrsə,nɛriʸ/ n **-ies** a soldier who fights for any country or group that pays him, not for his own country

mercenary² adj derog influenced by the wish to gain money or other reward

mer·chan·dise /'mɜrtʃən,daɪz, -,daɪs/ n [U] things for sale; goods for trade

mer·chant /'mɜrtʃənt/ n a person who buys and sells goods, esp. in large amounts: *a jewelry merchant*

merchant ma·rine /,·· ·¹·/ n [C; the S] (the people who work on) those ships of a nation which are used in trade, not in war

mer·ci·ful /'mɜrsɪfəl/ adj showing mercy; willing to forgive instead of punishing: *The merciful king saved him from death.|a merciful death* (=it was fortunate to die, rather than suffer) **–mercifully** adv

mer·ci·less /'mɜrsɪlɪs/ adj [to] showing no mercy; willing to punish rather than forgive: *a merciless judge* **–mercilessly** adv **–mercilessness** n [U]

mer·cu·ri·al /mər'kyʊəriʸəl/ adj [no comp.] quick to change: *a mercurial temper* **–mercurially** adv

mer·cu·ry /'mɜrkyəriʸ/ also **quicksilver–** n [U] a heavy silver-white metal that is liquid at ordinary temperatures and is used in THERMOMETERS, BAROMETERS, etc.

mer·cy /'mɜrsiʸ/ n **1** [U] willingness to forgive, not to punish: *The general showed no mercy, and his prisoners were all killed.* **2** [S] a fortunate event: **It's a mercy** *the accident happened so close to the hospital.* **3 at the mercy of** powerless against: *They were lost at sea, at the mercy of wind and weather.*

mercy kill·ing /'·· ,·¹·/ n [U] → EUTHANASIA

mere /mɪər/ adj **1** [A no comp.] nothing more than (a): *She lost the election by a mere 20 votes.* **2 the merest** as small or unimportant as possible: *The merest little thing makes him nervous.*

mere·ly /'mɪərliʸ/ adv only . . . and nothing else: *He merely wants to know the truth.*

merge /mɜrdʒ/ v **merged, merging 1** [I *into*] to become lost in or part of something else/each other: *One color merged into the other.|My friends merged into the crowd and I lost sight of them.* **2** [I;T *with*] to join together so as to become one: *The roads merge a mile ahead.|The two companies merged to become stronger.*

merg·er /'mɜrdʒər/ n a joining together of two or more companies or firms

me·rid·i·an /mə'rɪdiʸən/ n an imaginary line drawn from the top point of the earth (NORTH POLE) to the bottom (SOUTH POLE) over the surface of the earth, one of several used on maps to show position

me·ringue /mə'ræŋ/ n [C;U] (a light round cake made of) a mixture of sugar and the white part of eggs, beaten together

mer·it¹ /'mɛrɪt/ n **1** [U] the quality of deserving praise, reward, etc.; personal worth:*There's little merit in passing the examination if you cheated.* **2 on its/his, etc., (own) merits** by or for its/his, etc., own qualities, good or bad, not by one's own opinions: *We must judge this plan on its own merits.*

merit² v [T +*v-ing*] fml to deserve; have a right to: *He merited all the praise they gave him.*

mer·i·toc·ra·cy /,mɛrə'tɑkrəsiʸ/ n **-cies** a social system which gives the highest positions to those with the most ability

mer·i·to·ri·ous /,mɛrə'tɔriʸəs, -'toʷr-/ adj fml deserving reward or praise: *a meritorious performance*

mer·maid /'mɜrmeʸd/ n (in stories) a young woman with the bottom half of her body like a fish's tail

mer·ri·ment /'mɛrɪmənt/ n [U] laughter and sounds of enjoyment

mer·ry /'mɛriʸ/ adj **-rier, -riest 1** cheerful; fond of laughter, fun, etc.: *a merry person|a merry smile* **2 Merry Christmas!** Have a happy time at Christmas **–merrily** adv **–merriness** n [U]

merry-go-round ‖/'·· ·,·/ also **carousel** AmE‖also **roundabout** BrE– n a machine in an amusement park on which people can ride around and around sitting on wooden animals

mer·ry·mak·ing /'mɛriʸ,meʸkɪŋ/ n [U] infml lit fun and enjoyment, esp. eating, drinking, and games: *There was a lot of merrymaking in the office at Christmas.*

Mes·dames /meʸ'dɑm/ n pl. of MADAM

mesh¹ /mɛʃ/ n **1** [C;U] (a piece of) material woven in a fine network with small holes between the threads: *We put some/a fine wire mesh over the chimney so that the birds wouldn't fall in.* **2** [C usu. pl.] the threads in such a network: *The fish were caught in the meshes of the net.*

mesh² v [I with] to connect; be held (together): The teeth on the GEARs mesh as they turn round.

mes·mer·ize ‖also **-ise** BrE /'mɛzmə,raɪz/ v **-ized, -izing** [T] to surprise very much, esp. so as to make speechless and unable to move: We stood by the lake, mesmerized by the flashing colors of the fish.

mess /mɛs/ n **1** [S;U] a state of disorder or untidiness; dirty material: This room's (in) a mess.|You dropped the food so you can clean up the mess.|The company's affairs are in a terrible mess. **2** [C usu. sing.] infml a person whose appearance, behavior, or thinking is in a disordered state: You look a mess–you can't go to the office like that. **3** [C] a place to eat and relax for members of the armed forces: the officers' mess **4** [S] infml trouble: You're really in a mess now that you've been caught cheating. **5 make a mess of** infml to disorder, spoil, ruin, etc.: This illness has made a mess of my vacation plans.

mess a·round ‖also **mess about** BrE– v adv [I] **1** to be lazy: He spent all day Sunday just messing around. **2** to act or speak stupidly: Stop messing around and tell me clearly what happened!

mes·sage /'mɛsɪdʒ/ n **1** [C +to-v/that] a spoken or written piece of information passed from one person to another: There's a message for you from your brother.|Let's leave her a message to meet us at the station. **2** [the S] the important or central idea: the message of this book **3 get the message** infml to understand what is wanted or meant

mes·sen·ger /'mɛsəndʒər/ n a person who brings one or more messages

mes·si·ah /mə'saɪə/ n [usu. sing.] (often cap.) **1** the expected deliverer and ruler of the Jewish people **2** Christ, the leader in the Christian religion

Messrs. /'mɛsərz/ abbrev. (used chiefly in writing as the pl. of MR., esp.in the names of firms): Messrs. Ford and Dobson, piano repairers

mess sthg.↔ **up** v adv [T] infml to disorder, spoil, etc.: Her late arrival messes up our plans. –**mess-up** /'· · ·/ n

mess with sthg. v prep [T usu. neg. imper.] infml to cause trouble to: Don't mess with me, or you'll be sorry!

mess·y /'mɛsiʸ/ adj **-ier, -iest 1** untidy **2** (causing the body to become) dirty: It's a messy business having a tooth taken out. –**messily** adv –**messiness** n [U]

met /mɛt/ v past tense and participle of MEET

me·tab·o·lism /mə'tæbə,lɪzəm/ n the chemical activities in a living thing by which it gains power (ENERGY),esp. from food

met·al /'mɛtl/ n [C;U] any usu. solid shiny mineral substance which can be shaped by pressure and used for passing an electric current: Copper and silver are both metals.|a metal box

me·tal·lic /mə'tælɪk/ adj of or like metal: metallic colors|a metallic sound

met·al·lur·gy /'mɛtl,ɜrdʒiʸ/ n [U] the study and practice of removing metals from rocks,

melting them, and using them –**metallurgist** n

met·a·mor·pho·sis /,mɛtə'mɔrfəsɪs/ n **-ses** /,siʸz/ [C;U] (a) complete change from one form to another: A BUTTERFLY is produced by metamorphosis from a CATERPILLAR.

met·a·phor /'mɛtə,fɔr/ n [C;U] (the use of) a phrase which describes one thing by stating another thing with which it can be compared (as in the roses in her cheeks or The rain came down in buckets) without using the words "as" or "like" –compare SIMILE –**metaphorical** /,mɛtə'fɔrɪkəl, -'far-/ adj –**metaphorically** adv

met·a·phys·ics /,mɛtə'fɪzɪks/ n [U] a branch of the study of thought (PHILOSOPHY) concerned with the science of being and knowing –**metaphysical** adj –**metaphysically** adv

me·te·or /'miʸtiʸər/ n a small piece of matter floating in space that forms a line of light if it falls into the earth's air (ATMOSPHERE)

me·te·or·ic /,miʸtiʸ'ɔrɪk, -'ɑr-/ adj like a METEOR, esp. in being very fast or in being bright and short-lived: a meteoric rise to fame –**meteorically** adv

me·te·or·ite /'miʸtiʸə,raɪt/ n a small METEOR that has landed on the earth without being totally burned up

me·te·or·ol·o·gy /,miʸtiʸə'ralədʒiʸ/ n [U] the study of weather conditions –**meteorological** /,miʸtiʸərə'lɑdʒɪkəl/ adj –**meteorologist** /,miʸtiʸə'ralədʒɪst/ n

me·ter¹ /'miʸtər/ n a machine which measures the amount of something used: a gas meter|a PARKING METER

meter² AmE‖**metre** BrE (a measure of length equal to) 39.37 inches

meter³ AmE‖**metre** BrE n [C;U] (any type of) arrangement of notes or esp. words (as in poetry) into strong and weak beats –see also RHYTHM –**metrical** /'mɛtrɪkəl/ also **metric**- adj –**metrically** adv

meth·od /'mɛθəd/ n **1** [C] a way or manner (of doing): We use new methods so that we can do the job quickly and cheaply.|old-fashioned teaching methods **2** [C;U] (the use of) an orderly system or arrangement: There's not much method in the way they do their accounts. **3 method in one's madness** a hidden system behind disordered actions –see also METHODOLOGY

me·thod·i·cal /mə'θɑdɪkəl/ adj careful; using an ordered system: a methodical person|She has a methodical way of doing things. –**methodically** adv

Meth·od·ism /'mɛθə,dɪzəm/ n [U] the beliefs of a Christian group which follows the teachings of John Wesley –**Methodist** adj, n

meth·od·ol·o·gy /,mɛθə'dalədʒiʸ/ n **-gies** [C;U] tech the set of methods used for study or action in a particular subject, as in science or education: a new methodology of teaching –see also METHOD –**methodological** /,mɛθədl'adʒɪkəl/ adj –**methodologically** adv

me·tic·u·lous /mə'tɪkyələs/ adj very careful, with attention to detail: meticulous drawings|a meticulous worker –**meticulously** adv –**meticulousness** n [U]

me·tre /'miʸtər/ n BrE for METER²,³

met·ric /ˈmɛtrɪk/ *adj* concerning the system of measurement (**metric system**) based on the metre and kilogram

met·ri·ca·tion /ˌmɛtrɪˈkeʸʃən/ *n* [U] the change from standards of measurement that had been used before (as, the foot and the pound) to meters, grams, etc.

met·ro /ˈmɛtroʷ/ *n* **-ros** [C; *the* S] (*often cap.*) an underground railway system in cities in France or various other countries: *the Washington/Montreal Metro|Can you get there by metro?* –compare SUBWAY

met·ro·nome /ˈmɛtrəˌnoʷm/ *n* an instrument with an arm that moves from side to side to give the speed at which a piece of music should be played

me·trop·o·lis /məˈtrɑpəlɪs/ *n* [C; *the* S] *fml* a chief city or the capital city of a country –**metropolitan** /ˌmɛtrəˈpɑlətn/ *adj*: *The New York metropolitan area includes parts of New Jersey, Connecticut, and Long Island.*

met·tle /ˈmɛtl/ *n* [U] *fml often apprec* courage; the will to continue: *The runner fell, but he showed his mettle by continuing in the race.*

mew /myuʷ/ *n*, *v* [C;I] → MEOW

mews /myuʷz/ *n* **mews** a street, in a city, where horses were once kept, now partly rebuilt for people to live in

mez·za·nine /ˈmɛzəˌniʸn/ *n* a floor that comes between two other floors of a building

mg *written abbrev. said as:* MILLIGRAM

MI *written abbrev. said as:* Michigan /ˈmɪʃɪgən/ (a state in the US)

mi·aow /miʸˈaʊ/ *n*, *v* [C;I] *BrE* for MEOW

mice /maɪs/ *n pl. of* MOUSE

Mich. *written abbrev. said as:* Michigan /ˈmɪʃɪgən/ (a state in the US)

mi·crobe /ˈmaɪkroʷb/ *n* a living creature that is so small that it cannot be seen without a microscope, and that may cause disease

mi·cro·chip /ˈmaɪkroʷˌtʃɪp/ also **chip** *infml*– *n* a tiny set of connected electrical parts produced as a single unit on a slice of material such as SILICON –see illustration on page 221

mi·cro·cosm /ˈmaɪkrəˌkazəm/ *n* [*of*] a little self-contained world that represents all the qualities, activities, etc., of something larger

mi·cro·fiche /ˈmaɪkrəˌfiʃ/ *n* **-fiche** *or* **-fiches** [C;U] a sheet or piece of MICROFILM

mi·cro·film¹ /ˈmaɪkrəˌfɪlm/ *n* [C;U] (a length of) film for photographing a page, a letter, etc., in a very small size so that it can be easily stored and made larger by means of a machine when one wants to read it

microfilm² *v* [T] to photograph (something) using MICROFILM

mi·cro·or·ga·nism /ˌmɪkroʷˈɔrgəˌnɪzəm/ *n* a living creature too small to be seen without a microscope

mi·cro·phone /ˈmaɪkrəˌfoʷn/ also **mike** *infml*– *n* an instrument for receiving sound waves and changing them into electrical waves, used in broadcasting or recording sound (as in radio, telephones, TAPE RECORDERS, etc.) or in making sounds louder: *Speak into the microphone, or the people at the back won't be able to hear you.* –see illustration on page 221

mi·cro·proc·es·sor /ˌmaɪkroʷˈprasɛsər/ *n* *tech* a very small computer, or part of this, which contains one or more MICROCHIPs –see illustration on page 221

mi·cro·scope /ˈmaɪkrəˌskoʷp/ *n* an instrument that makes objects which are too small to be seen by the eye look larger, and so can be used for examining them –compare TELESCOPE¹

mi·cro·scop·ic /ˌmaɪkrəˈskɑpɪk/ *adj* **1** by or as if by means of a microscope **2** *infml* very small: *It's impossible to read his microscopic handwriting.* –see Study Notes on page 550 –**microscopically** *adv*

mi·cro·wave /ˈmaɪkrəˌweʸv/ *n* an electric wave of very short length, used in sending messages by radio, in RADAR, and esp. in cooking food: *a microwave oven*

mid·day /ˈmid-deʸ/ *n* [U] the middle of the day; 12 o'clock NOON: *We have lunch at midday.* –compare MIDNIGHT

mid·dle¹ /ˈmɪdl/ *adj* [A] in or nearly in the center: *Ours is the middle house in that row of five.*

middle² *n* [*the* S] **1** the central part, point, or position: *He planted rose trees in the middle of the garden.|This bill must be paid not later than the middle of the month.* **2** *infml* the waist or the part below the waist: *He's getting fatter around the middle.* **3 in the middle of something/doing something** in the course of or busy with something/doing something

USAGE **Center** is similar to **middle**, but it suggests an exact point: *Their house is in the* **middle** *of a field.|At the beginning of the game, the football is placed in the* **center** *of the field.*

middle age /ˌ·· ˈ·◂/ *n* [U] the years between youth and old age –**middle-aged** /ˌ·· ˈ·◂/ *adj*: *He's nearly 60, but he still considers himself to be middle-aged.*

Middle Ag·es /ˌ·· ˈ··/ *n* [*the* P] the period in European history between about AD 1100 and 1500

middle class /ˌ·· ˈ·◂/ *adj,n* [U] (of) the social class to which people belong who are neither very wealthy nor workers with their hands –see WORKING CLASS (USAGE)

Middle East /ˌ·· ˈ·◂/ also **Mid East** /ˌmɪd ˈiʸst ◂/ *AmE*– *n* [*the* S] the countries in Asia west of India, such as Iran, Iraq, Syria, etc., –**Middle Eastern** *adj*

mid·dle·man /ˈmɪdlˌmæn/ *n* **-men** /ˌmɛn/ anyone coming between two people, groups, esp. a person who buys goods from a producer, and sells (at a gain) to a storekeeper or directly to a user

middle-of-the-road /ˌ·· ··· ˈ·◂/ *adj* favoring ideas, esp. political ideas, that most people would agree with; not EXTREME¹ (3)

mid·dling /ˈmɪdlɪŋ/ *adj infml* between large and small, neither good nor bad, etc.; average

midge /mɪdʒ/ *n* a very small flying insect, like a mosquito, that bites

midg·et /ˈmɪdʒɪt/ *n* **1** [C] a very, or unusually, small person **2** [A] very small, compared with others of the same kind: *midget cars|midget cameras*

mid·land /'mɪdlənd/ adj [A no comp.] of the middle or central part of a country

mid·night /'mɪdnaɪt/ n [U] 12 o'clock at night: *The party finished at/continued until midnight.|We went for a midnight swim.* (=in the middle of the night) –compare MIDDAY

mid·riff /'mɪdrɪf/ n the part of the human body between the chest and the waist

mid·ship·man /'mɪd,ʃɪpmən, ,mɪd'ʃɪp-/ n -men /mən/ [A;C] a boy or young man who is being trained to become a naval officer

midst /mɪdst/ n [U] *lit or old use* the middle part or position: *The soldier was always in the midst of the fight.|the enemy* **in our midst** (=among us)

mid·way /ˌmɪd'weɪ◄/ adj, adv halfway or in a middle position: *There's a small village midway between these two towns.*

mid·week /'mɪdwiːk, ˌmɪd'wiːk◄/ n, adj [U] (happening during) the middle days of the week; Tuesday, Thursday, and esp. Wednesday

mid·wife /'mɪdwaɪf/ n -wives /waɪvz/ someone who has received special training to help women when they are giving birth to children

mien /miːn/ n *lit* a person's appearance, manner, or expression: *a thoughtful and solemn mien*

miffed /mɪft/ adj *infml* slightly angry

might¹ /maɪt/ v *negative contraction* **mightn't** /'maɪnt/ *BrE* [I + *to*-v] **1** (shows a possibility): *He might come, but it's very unlikely.|He might have missed the train.* (=perhaps he missed it)|*I might have thought that once, but I don't believe it now.* –see USAGE **2** (used as the past of *may*): *I thought it might rain.* (=I thought *"It may rain!"*)|*They asked if they might go home.* (=They asked *"May we go home?"*) **3** *BrE* (used instead of *may*, for asking permission politely): *"Might I come in?" "Yes, you may."* **4** (used like *ought*): *You might at least say "thank you" when someone helps you.|You might have offered to help!* (=I wish you had, but you didn't)|*I might have known she'd refuse!* (=it was typical of her to refuse) –see Study Notes on page 434 **5 might well** to be likely to: *We lost the football game, but we might well have won if one of our players hadn't been hurt.* **6 might as well** MAY as well (MAY (4)): *No one will eat this food; it might just as well be thrown away.*

USAGE When it is showing a possibility, **might** sometimes suggests a smaller possibility than **may**, but often these words are used to mean the same thing: *I may/might go to the movies on Friday; I just don't know yet.*

might² n [U] power; strength; force: *He tried with all his might to move the heavy rock from the road.*

mightn't /'maɪnt/ v *BrE short for* might not: *They mightn't come.*

might·y /'maɪtiː/ adj -ier, -iest **1** *esp. lit* having great power or strength; very great: *He gave the rock a mighty blow.|Even the mightiest of empires comes to an end.* **2 high and mighty**

derog showing too much pride and a feeling of one's own importance –**mightily** adv

mi·graine /'maɪgreɪn/ n [C;U] a severe and repeated headache, usu. with disorder of the eyesight

mi·grant /'maɪgrənt/ n a person or animal or esp. bird that MIGRATES or is migrating: *Migrant workers move from country to country in search of work.*

mi·grate /maɪ'greɪt/ v -grated, -grating [I from, to] **1** (of birds and fish) to travel regularly from one part of the world to another, according to the seasons of the year –see EMIGRATE (USAGE) **2** to move from one place to another; change one's place of living, esp. for a limited period: *Some tribes migrate with their cattle in search of fresh grass.* –**migratory** /'maɪgrəˌtɔːriː, -ˌtoʊriː/ adj

mi·gra·tion /maɪ'greɪʃən/ n [C;U] (an example of) the act of migrating (MIGRATE): *Scientists have studied the migration of fish over long distances.|Wars always cause great migrations of people.*

mike /maɪk/ n *infml* → MICROPHONE

mild /maɪld/ adj **1** usu. *apprec* (of a person) gentle: *He has too mild a nature to get angry, even if he has good cause.* **2** not hard or causing much discomfort or suffering; slight: *The thief was given a milder punishment than he deserved.|It's been a mild winter this year.* (=not a cold winter) –compare SEVERE (2) **3** (of food, drink, etc.) not strong or bitter in taste: *mild cheese* –**mildness** n [U]

mil·dew¹ /'mɪlduː, -djuː/ n [U] a soft usu. whitish growth that forms on food, leather, plants, etc., that have been kept for a long time in warm and slightly wet conditions –**mildewy** adj

mildew² v [I;T] to (cause to) become covered with MILDEW: *mildewed plants*

mild·ly /'maɪldliː/ adv **1** in a MILD (1) manner: *She complained loudly to the owner of the store, who answered her mildly.* **2** slightly: *I was only mildly interested in the story I read in the newspaper.* **3 to put it mildly** describing something as gently as possible: *The government's policy has not been a great success, to put it mildly.*

mile /maɪl/ n (a measure of length equal to) 1,609 meters or 1,760 yards: *He has a 10-mile drive each day to and from his work.|They walked for miles* (=a very long way) *without seeing another person.|*(fig.) *He was* **miles off** *in his calculations.* (=they were completely wrong)

mile·age /'maɪlɪdʒ/ n **1** [C usu. sing.; U] the distance that is traveled, measured in miles: *What mileage does your car get?|What mileage does your car get per gallon?* **2** [U] *infml* an amount of use: *The newspapers are getting a lot of mileage out of the accident. There's a new story about it every day.*

mile·stone /'maɪlstoʊn/ n **1** a stone at the side of a road, on which is marked the number of miles to the next town **2** an important event in a person's life or in history: *The invention of the wheel was a milestone in the history of the world.*

mi·lieu /miːl'juː, -'jɜː, miːˈjuː-/ n -lieus *or* -lieux (same pronunciation) [*usu. sing.*] surroundings, esp. a person's social surroundings

mil·i·tant¹ /'mɪlətənt/ *adj* having or expressing a readiness to fight or use force: *A few militant members of the crowd started throwing stones at the police.|a militant speech* –compare MILITARY **–militancy** /'mɪlətənsiʸ/ *n* [U] **militantly** *adv*

militant² *n* a MILITANT person: *They say these student disorders have been caused by a few militants.*

mil·i·tar·y¹ /'mɪlə,teriʸ/ *adj* [A] of, for, by, or connected with soldiers, armies, or war fought by armies: *In some countries all the young men do a year's military service.|combined naval and military operations|a military hospital* –compare MILITANT

military² *n* [*the* P] soldiers; the army: *Since the police were no longer able to keep order in the city, they called in the military.*

mil·i·tate a·gainst sthg. /'mɪlə,teʸt/ *v prep* **-tated, -tating** [T +*v-ing*] to act as a reason against: *The fact that he'd been in prison militated against his chances of getting a job in a bank.*

mi·li·tia /mə'lɪʃə/ *n* [C +*sing./pl. v*] a body of men not belonging to a regular army, but trained as soldiers to serve only in their home country: *The militia is sometimes used for dealing with* RIOTS.

milk¹ /mɪlk/ *n* [U] **1** a white liquid produced by human or animal females for the feeding of their young, and (in the case of cows' and goats' milk) often drunk by human beings or made into butter and cheese: *a bottle of milk* **2** a whitish liquid or juice obtained from certain plants and trees: COCONUT milk **3 cry over spilt milk** to waste time being sorry about something bad that cannot be repaired or changed for the better

milk² *v* **1** [I;T] **a** to take milk from (a cow, goat, or other animal): *The farmer milks (the cows) twice a day.* **b** (of a cow, goat, etc.) to give milk: *There's something wrong with this cow; she isn't milking very well.* **2** [T] *infml* to get money, knowledge of a secret, etc., from (someone or something) by clever or dishonest means: *The politician was too experienced to be milked by newspaper men.* (=he refused to give them any news)

milk·man /'mɪlkmæn/ *n* **-men** /mɛn/ a man who sells milk, esp. one who goes from house to house each day to deliver it

milk shake /'· ·/ *n* a drink of milk and usu. ice cream shaken up together and given the taste of fruit, chocolate, etc.

milk·y /'mɪlkiʸ/ *adj* **-ier, -iest 1** made of, containing, or like milk **2** (of water or other liquids) not clear; cloudy; having a milklike appearance **–milkiness** *n* [U]

mill¹ /mɪl/ *n* **1** (a building containing) a large machine for crushing corn or grain into flour –see also WINDMILL **2** a factory or WORKSHOP (1): *Cotton cloth is made in a cotton mill.|Paper is made in a paper mill.* **3** a small machine, used esp. in a kitchen, in which a stated material can be crushed into powder: *a coffee mill|a pepper mill*

mill² *v* [T] **1** to crush (grain) in a mill **2** to

produce (flour) by this means

mill about/around– *v adv* [I] *infml* to move without purpose in large numbers: *There were a lot of people milling about in the streets.*

mil·len·ni·um /mə'lɛniʸəm/ *n* **-niums** or **-nia** /niʸə/ **1** a period of 1,000 years **2 the millennium** a future age in which all people will be happy and contented

mil·le·pede /'mɪlə,piʸd/ *n* → MILLIPEDE

mill·er /'mɪlər/ *n* a man who owns or works a mill that produces flour

mil·let /'mɪlɪt/ *n* [U] the small seeds of certain grasslike plants used as food: *millet cakes|a bag of millet*

mil·li·gram‖also **-gramme** *BrE* /'mɪlə,græm/ *n* (a measure of weight equal to) 1,000th of a gram

mil·li·me·ter *AmE*‖ **-tre** *BrE* /'mɪlə,miʸtər/ *n* (a measure of length equal to) 1,000th of a meter

mil·li·ner /'mɪlənər/ *n* a person who makes and/or sells women's hats

mil·li·ner·y /'mɪlə,nɛriʸ/ *n* [U] the articles made or sold by a MILLINER: *the millinery department in a large store*

mil·lion /'mɪlyən/ *determiner, n, pron* **million** or **millions** (the number) 1,000,000; 10^6 –see HUNDRED (USAGE); see Study Notes on page 550 **–millionth** *determiner, n, pron, adv*

mil·lion·aire /,mɪlyə'nɛər/ **millionairess** /,mɪlyə'nɛrɪs/ *fem.– n* a person who has 1,000,000 pounds or dollars; very wealthy person

mil·li·pede, millepede /'mɪlə,piʸd/ *n* a small creature rather like a worm, with a lot of legs

mill·stone /'mɪlstoʷn/ *n* a person or thing that gives someone great trouble, anxiety, etc.: *His lazy son is* **a millstone around his neck.**

mime¹ /maɪm, miʸm/ *n* **1** [C;U] an act or the practice of using actions without language to show meaning: *I couldn't speak Chinese, but I showed in mime that I wanted a drink.|the art of mime* **2** [C] an actor who performs without using words –compare MIMIC¹

mime² *v* **mimed, miming** [I;T] to act (something) in MIME¹: *The actor was miming the movements of a bird.* –compare MIMIC²

mim·e·o·graph¹ /'mɪmiʸə,græf/ *AmE*‖**duplicating machine** *BrE– n* a machine that copies exactly by using a STENCIL

mimeograph² *AmE*‖**duplicate** *BrE– v* to copy exactly by using a MIMEOGRAPH¹: *a mimeographed copy*

mim·ic¹ /'mɪmɪk/ *n* a person who is good at copying another's manners, speech, etc., esp. in a way that causes laughter –compare MIME¹

mimic² *v* **-ck-** [T] to copy the action of: *She made us all laugh by mimicking the teacher/the teacher's way of speaking.* –compare MIME² **–mimicry** /'mɪmɪkriʸ/ *n* [U]

min·a·ret /,mɪnə'rɛt, 'mɪnə,rɛt/ *n* a tall thin tower on a mosque, from which Muslims are called to prayer

mince¹ /mɪns/ *v* **minced, mincing 1** [T] to cut (esp. meat) into very small pieces **2** *derog* to walk in an unnatural way, taking little short steps **3 not to mince matters/one's words** to speak of something bad or unpleasant using plain direct language

mince² *n* [U] **1** *AmE* for MINCEMEAT **2** *BrE* for MINCEd meat

mince·meat /ˈmɪnsmiˑt/ *n* [U] **1** a mixture of CURRANTS, dried fruit, dried orange skin, etc. (not meat) used as a sweet filling to put inside pastry **2 make mincemeat of** *infml* to defeat or destroy (a person, belief, etc.) completely

mind¹ /maɪnd/ *n* **1** [C;U] a person's way of thinking or feeling; thoughts: *Her mind is filled with dreams of becoming a great actress.|She has a very quick mind.|A number of possibilities* **come to mind.** (=I can think of a number) **2** [U] memory: *I couldn't quite* **call** *his name* **to mind.** (=remember it)|*I'm afraid it* **went** *right* **out of my mind.** (=I forgot about it).|*I'll* **bear/keep** *your* suggestion **in mind.** (=continue to consider it)|*You* **put** *me* **in mind of** (=remind me of) *my brother.* **3** [C] attention: **Keep your mind on** *your work.|You can do it if you* **put your mind to it.** (=give all your attention to it)|*She found that hard work was the best way to* **take her mind off** *her problems.|Let us now* **turn our minds to** (=begin to consider) *tomorrow's meeting.* **4** [C] intention: *Nothing was further from my mind.* (=that was not at all what I intended)|*Those boys have been stealing my apples again; I* **have a good mind/half a mind to** (=I think I may) *report them to the police.|If he's* **set his mind on** *doing it* (=decided firmly to do it), *nothing will stop him.* **5** [C] opinion: *We are* **of one/of the same mind** *on this matter.* (=we both or all think the same about it)|**To my mind** (=in my opinion) *you're quite wrong.* **6** [C] a person considered for his/her ability to think well: *She's among the best minds* (=most intelligent people) *in the country.* **7 change one's mind** to change one's intentions or opinion: *I was going to leave tomorrow, but I've changed my mind.|I used to think he was stupid, but I'm beginning to change my mind about him.* **8 in one's right mind** (*used only in* NEGATIVES², questions, etc.) altogether sensible or SANE: *No one in their right mind would have paid $3000 for that old car.* **9 make up one's mind** to reach a decision or firm opinion (about) **10 on one's mind** troubling one's thoughts: *She's had a lot on her mind recently.* **11 out of one's mind** not sensible or SANE; CRAZY **12 -minded** /ˈmaɪndɪd/ having the stated kind of mind: *strong-minded/open-minded*

mind² *v* **1** [T] to take care or charge of; look after: *Our neighbor is minding our dog while we're away.* **2** [I;T +*v-ing/that*; not *be/v-ing*] (*often used with* would, *in requests, or in* NEGATIVE¹ *sentences*) to have a reason against or be opposed to (a particular thing); be troubled by or dislike: *"Would you mind if I went home early?" "Yes, I'd mind very much."|Would you mind making* (=please make) *a little less noise?|I wouldn't mind a drink.* (=I'd like one)|*Do you mind the window (being) open?* (=that it is open) **3** [I;T

+(*that/out*] (*usu. in commands*) *esp. BrE* to be careful (of); pay close attention (to): *Mind that step; it's loose!|Mind you don't drop it!|Just get on with your work; don't mind me.* (=don't pay any attention to my presence) **4** [I;T] (*said esp. to children*) to obey: *The boy was told to mind his grandmother while his mother went out shopping.|"If you don't mind, you won't get any cake," said the children's mother.* **5 mind one's own business** (*usu. in commands*) to pay attention to one's own affairs, and not to other people's **6 mind you** take this fact into account: *Grandfather spends a lot of time in bed now; mind you, he is 93!* **7 never mind** it doesn't matter; don't worry: *"We've missed the train!" "Never mind; there will be another one in ten minutes."|Never mind that now; we can deal with it later.*

mind·less /ˈmaɪndlɪs/ *adj derog* not having, needing, or using the power of thinking; stupid: *mindless cruelty* **–mindlessly** *adv* **–mindlessness** *n* [U]

mine¹ /maɪn/ *pron* (POSSESSIVE¹ (3) form of *I*) of the person who is speaking: *That bag's* **mine.***|That's your coat, and mine is over here.*

mine² *n* **1** a deep hole or network of holes under the ground from which coal, gold, tin, and other mineral substances are dug: *a tin mine* |*Many men were buried underground when there was an accident at the mine.* |(fig.) *The old man was* **a mine of information** *about the village where he had lived for 50 years.* –compare QUARRY **2** a kind of bomb that is placed just below the ground or in the sea and is exploded electrically from far away or when touched, passed over, etc.

mine³ *v* **mined, mining 1** [I;T *for*] to dig or work a MINE² (1) in (the earth): *mining for coal* **2** [T] to obtain by digging from a MINE² (1): *Coal is mined in Pennsylvania.* **3** [T] to put MINES² (2) in or under: *All the roads leading to the city had been mined.*

mine·field /ˈmaɪnfiˑld/ *n* a stretch of land or water in which MINES² (2) have been placed

min·er /ˈmaɪnər/ *n* a worker in a MINE² (1) –compare MINOR²

min·er·al /ˈmɪnərəl/ *n* any of various esp. solid substances that are formed naturally in the earth (such as stone, coal, salt, etc.), esp. as obtained from the ground for man's use

mineral wa·ter /ˈ··· ˌ··/ *n* [C;U] water that comes from a natural spring and contains minerals, often drunk for health reasons

min·gle /ˈmɪŋɡəl/ *v* **-gled, -gling** [I;T *with, together*] *esp. lit* to mix (with another thing or with people) so as to be an undivided whole: *The king often left his palace at night, and mingled with the people in the streets.*

mini /ˈmɪniˑ/ *infml* very small compared with others of its kind: *She's wearing a mini (skirt).*

min·i·a·ture /ˈmɪniˑətʃər, ˈmɪnətʃər, -ˌtʃuər/ *n* **1** [C] a very small copy or representation of anything **2** [A] (esp. of something copied or represented) very small: *The child was playing with his miniature trains.* **3** [C] a very small painting of a person

min·i·bus /'mɪniᵛˌbʌs/ *n* a small bus with seats for between six and twelve people: *The children go to school in a minibus/by minibus.*

min·i·mal /'mɪnəməl/ *adj* of the smallest possible amount, degree, or size: *Fortunately, the storm only did minimal damage to the crops.* –**minimally** *adv*

min·i·mize ‖**also -mize** *BrE* /'mɪnəˌmaɪz/ *v* **-mized, -mizing** [T] to lessen to the smallest possible amount or degree: *You can minimize the dangers of driving by taking care to obey all the rules of the road.|He'd made a bad mistake, but tried to minimize its seriousness.* (=treat it as if it were not serious) – compare MAXIMIZE

min·i·mum /'mɪnəməm/ *n* **-ma** /mə/ *or* **-mums 1** [C] the least, or the smallest possible, quantity, number, or degree: *This price is his minimum; he refuses to lower it any further.|We will try to keep the cost of repairs down to a minimum.* **2** [A] smallest, or smallest possible (in amount, degree, etc.): *The minimum pass mark in this examination is 70 out of 100. |He couldn't join the police, because he was below the minimum height allowed by the rules.|The minimum wage is now $3.25 per hour.* –opposite **maximum**

min·ing /'maɪnɪŋ/ *n* [U] the action or industry of getting minerals out of the earth by digging: *coalmining|a mining company*

min·is·ter¹ /'mɪnəstər/ *n* **1** the religious leader in some Christian churches –see PRIEST (USAGE) **2** (not in the US) a politician who is a member of the government and is in charge of a particular government department: *the Minister of Transport*

minister² *v* → MINISTER TO

min·is·te·ri·al /ˌmɪnə'stɪəriᵛəl/ *adj* of a MINISTER (2): *As part of her ministerial duties, she often had to travel abroad.*

minister to sbdy. *v prep* [T] *esp. lit* to serve; perform duties to help: *ministering to the sick*

min·is·try /'mɪnəstriᵛ/ *n* **-tries** (*often cap.*) **1** [*the* S] the profession of a church MINISTER (1): *Our son wants to enter the ministry* **2** [C] a government department led by a MINISTER (2): *The army, navy, and air force are all controlled by the Ministry of Defense.* **3** [C] the office or position of a MINISTER (2)

mink /mɪŋk/ *n* **minks** *or* **mink** [C;U] (the valuable brown fur of) a type of small WEASEL-like animal: *a mink coat*

Minn. *written abbrev. said as:* Minnesota /ˌmɪnə'soᵂtə/ (a state in the US)

mi·nor¹ /'maɪnər/ *adj* [*no comp.*] lesser or smaller in degree, size, etc.; of little importance: *He left most of his money to his sons; his daughter received only a minor share of his wealth.|The young actress was given a minor part in the new play.|a very minor illness* see –MAJOR (USAGE)

minor² *n law* a person below the age (usu. 18 or 21 in the US) at which he/she is fully responsible in law for his/her actions –compare MINER

mi·nor·i·ty /mə'nɔrətiᵛ/ *n* **-ties** the smaller number or part; a number or part that is less

than half: *The nation wants peace; only a minority wants the war to continue.* **2** [C] a small part of a population which is different from the rest in race, religion, etc.: *a law to protect religious minorities* **3** [A] of or supported by a small, or the smaller, number of people: *I agree with the minority opinion.* –compare MAJORITY

min·strel /'mɪnstrəl/ *n* (in the MIDDLE AGES) a musician who traveled around the country singing songs and poems

mint¹ /mɪnt/ *n* **1** [U] a small plant whose leaves have a particular fresh smell and taste and are used in preparing drinks, making CHEWING GUM, etc. **2** [C] *infml→* PEPPERMINT (2): *Have one of these mints!*

mint² *n* **1** [C] a place in which coins and banknotes are officially made by the government **2** [S] *infml* a large amount (of money) **3 in mint condition** (of objects which people collect, such as books, postage stamps, coins, etc.) in perfect condition, as if unused

mint³ *v* [T] to make (a coin)

min·u·et /ˌmɪnyuᵂ'et/ *n* (a piece of music for) a type of slow graceful dance

mi·nus¹ /'maɪnəs/ *prep* **1** made less by (the stated figure or quantity): *17 minus 5 leaves 12* **2** being the stated number of degrees below the freezing point of water: *The temperature was minus 10 degrees.* –compare PLUS¹

minus² also **minus sign** /'·· ˌ·/ *n* a sign (–) used for showing that the second number is to be taken away from the first, or that a number is less than zero –compare PLUS²

minus³ *adj* [A] (of a number or quantity) less than zero –compare PLUS³

min·us·cule /'mɪnəˌskyuᵂl/ *adj* very, very small

min·ute¹ /'mɪnɪt/ *n* **1** [C] (a unit of time equal to) a 60th of an hour: *The train arrived at exactly four minutes past eight.|It's only a few minutes' walk from here to the station.* (=a walk taking a very short time) **2** [S] *infml* a very short space of time: *I'll be ready in a minute.* (=very soon)*|"Are you ready yet?" "No, but I won't be a minute."* (=I'll be ready very soon) **3** [C] (a unit of measurement equal to) a 60th of a degree: *The exact measurement of this angle is 80 degrees 30 minutes (80° 30″)* **4 the minute (that)** as soon as: *Although we hadn't met for 25 years, I recognized him the minute (that) I saw him.* –see also MINUTES

mi·nute² /maɪ'nuᵂt, -'nyuᵂt, mɪ-/ *adj* **1** very small: *His writing's so minute that it's difficult to read.* –see Study Notes on page 550 **2** giving attention to the smallest points; very careful and exact: *minute details* –**minuteness** *n* [U] –**minutely** *adv*

min·utes /'mɪnɪts/ *n* [P] a written record of business done, suggestions made, decisions taken, etc., at a meeting: *Before the committee started its work, the minutes of the last meeting were read.|to take* (=write) *minutes*

mir·a·cle /'mɪrəkəl/ *n* an act or happening (usu. having a good result), that cannot be explained by the laws of nature, esp. one done by a holy person: *According to the*

Bible, Christ worked many miracles such as turning water into wine.|Doctors do their best to treat the sick, but they can't perform miracles.|(fig.) *The teacher told me that it'd be a miracle if I passed the examination.* **–miraculous** /mɪˈrækyələs/ *adj: The army won a miraculous victory over a much stronger enemy.* **–miraculously** *adv: It was a terrible explosion but, miraculously, no one was killed.*

mi·rage /mɪˈrɑːʒ/ *n* a strange effect of hot air conditions in a desert, in which objects appear which are not really there

mir·ror[1] /ˈmɪrər/ *n* a piece of glass, or other shiny or polished surface that throws back (REFLECTS) images that fall on it: *The driver saw in his mirror that a police car was following him.* –see illustration on page 55

mirror[2] *v* [T] to show, as in a mirror: (fig.) *The election results mirror public opinion quite well.* (=give a true representation of it)

mirth /mɜːθ/ *n* [U] *esp. lit* merriness and laughter **–mirthless** *adj*

mis·ad·ven·ture /ˌmɪsədˈventʃər/ *n* [C;U] *esp. law or lit* an accident; (event caused by) bad luck: **death by misadventure** (=accidental death)

mis·an·throp·ic /ˌmɪsənˈθrɑpɪk/ *adj* (of a person) who hates everybody, trusts no one, and avoids being in the company of others

mis·ap·ply /ˌmɪsəˈplaɪ/ *v* **-plied, -plying** [T] *fml* to put to a wrong use; use wrongly or for a wrong purpose **–misapplication** /ˌmɪsæpləˈkeɪʃən/ *n* [C;U *of*]

mis·ap·pre·hend /ˌmɪsæprɪˈhend/ *v* [T] *fml* to understand (something) in a mistaken way: *The accident was caused by one driver completely misapprehending the intentions of the other.* **–misapprehension** /ˌmɪsæprɪˈhenʃən, -tʃən/ *n* [C;U +*that*]

mis·ap·pro·pri·ate /ˌmɪsəˈprowpriˌeɪt/ *v* **-ated, -ating** [T] *fml or law* to take dishonestly and put to a wrong use: *The lawyer was sent to prison for misappropriating money placed in his care.* **–misappropriation** /ˌmɪsəˌprowpriˈeɪʃən/ *n* [C;U *of*]

mis·be·have /ˌmɪsbɪˈheɪv/ *v* **-haved, -having** [I;T] to behave (oneself) badly or improperly: *The pupil was punished, not for bad work, but for misbehaving (himself) in class.*

mis·be·hav·ior *AmE*‖**misbehaviour** *BrE* /ˌmɪsbɪˈheɪvyər/ *n* [U] bad improper behavior

mis·cal·cu·late /ˌmɪsˈkælkyəˌleɪt/ *v* **-lated, -lating** [I;T] to calculate (figures, time, etc.) wrongly; form a wrong judgment of (something): *I missed the train. I'd miscalculated the time it would take me to reach the station.* **–miscalculation** /ˌmɪskælkyəˈleɪʃən/ *n* [C;U]

mis·car·riage /ˌmɪsˈkærɪdʒ, ˈmɪsˌkærɪdʒ/ *n* **1** an act or case of producing lifeless young, esp. early in their development, before the proper time of birth –compare ABORTION, STILLBORN **2 miscarriage of justice** (a) failure by the law courts to do justice, esp. as when a person who is not guilty is sent to prison

mis·car·ry /ˌmɪsˈkæriy/ *v* **-ried, -rying** [I] **1** (of a woman) to have a MISCARRIAGE **2** (of an intention, plan, etc.) to be unsuccessful; fail to have the intended or desired result

mis·cel·la·ne·ous /ˌmɪsəˈleyniyəs/ *adj* several kinds or different kinds; having a variety of sorts, qualities, etc. **–miscellaneously** *adv*

mis·chance /ˌmɪsˈtʃæns/ *n* [C;U] *fml* (an example of) bad luck: *Only a serious mischance will prevent him from arriving tomorrow.*

mis·chief /ˈmɪstʃɪf/ *n* [U] **1** bad, but not seriously bad, behavior (esp. of children) probably causing trouble, and possibly damage: *If his parents leave him alone for five minutes, the little boy gets into mischief.|She knew the children were* **up to** some **mischief** (=doing or planning something wrong), *and she found them in the garden digging up the flowers.* **2** *fml* damage or harm; wrong-doing: *The storm did a lot of mischief to the crops.* – see WICKED (USAGE) **–mischievous** /ˈmɪstʃəvəs/ *adj:* *One expects healthy children to be mischievous at times.* **–mischievously** *adv* **–mischievousness** *n* [U]

mis·con·ceive /ˌmɪskənˈsiyv/ *v* **-ceived, -ceiving** [T] to think (something) out badly and without proper consideration for what is suitable: *The government's plan for the railroads is completely misconceived.*

mis·con·cep·tion /ˌmɪskənˈsɛpʃən/ *n* [C;U] (an example of) understanding wrongly; state of being mistaken in one's understanding

mis·con·duct /ˌmɪsˈkɑndʌkt/ *n* [U] *fml* bad behavior sexual behaviour

mis·con·struc·tion /ˌmɪskənˈstrʌkʃən/ *n* [C;U] *fml* (an example of) mistaken understanding: *A law must be stated in the clearest language, so that it is not* **open to misconstruction.** (=so that there is no possibility that it will be wrongly understood)

mis·con·strue /ˌmɪskənˈstruw/ *v* **-strued, -struing** [T] *fml* to place a wrong meaning on (something said or done) –see also CONSTRUE

mis·deed /ˌmɪsˈdiyd/ *n fml or lit* a wrong or wicked act: *He deserved long imprisonment for his many misdeeds.*

mis·de·mean·or *AmE*‖**misdemeanour** *BrE* /ˌmɪsdɪˈmiynər/ *n* **1** a bad or improper act that is not very serious **2** *law* a crime that is less serious than, for example, stealing or murder –compare FELONY

mis·di·rect /ˌmɪsdəˈrekt, -daɪ-/ *v* [T] to direct wrongly: *I asked a boy the way to the station, but he misdirected me.*

mi·ser /ˈmaɪzər/ *n derog* a person who hates spending money, and who becomes wealthy by storing it **–miserly** *adj* **–miserliness** *n* [U]

mis·er·a·ble /ˈmɪzərəbəl/ *adj* **1** very unhappy: *The child is cold, hungry, and tired, so of course he's feeling miserable.* **2** very poor (in quality or amount): *a miserable failure|What miserable weather!* **–miserably** *adv: a miserably cold day|She failed miserably.*

mis·er·y /'mɪzəriʸ/ n [U] great unhappiness or great pain and suffering (of body or of mind): *Her baby died and, to add to her misery, her husband deserted her.*

mis·fire /ˌmɪs'faɪər/ v **-fired, -firing** [I] **1** (of a gun) to fail to send out the bullet when fired **2** (of a plan, joke, etc.) to fail to have the desired or intended result

mis·fit /'mɪs,fɪt/ n a person who does not fit well and happily into his/her social surroundings, or who is not suitable for the position he/she holds

mis·for·tune /mɪs'fɔrtʃən/ n [C;U] (an example of) bad luck, often of a serious nature: *His failure in business was due not to misfortune, but to his own mistakes.*

mis·giv·ing /mɪs'gɪvɪŋ/ n [C;U] (feeling of) doubt, fear of the future, and/or distrust: *He looked with misgiving at the strange food on his plate.|I could see he had some misgivings about lending me his car.*

mis·gov·ern /ˌmɪs'gʌvərn/ v [T] to govern (a country) badly or unjustly **–misgovernment** /ˌmɪs'gʌvərnmənt, -vərmənt/ n [U]

mis·guid·ed /mɪs'gaɪdɪd/ adj (of behavior, an action, etc.) directed to wrong or foolish results; badly judged **–misguidedly** adv

mis·han·dle /ˌmɪs'hændl/ v **-dled, -dling** [T] to handle or treat roughly, without skill, or insensitively: *Our company lost an important order because the whole affair was mishandled by the directors.*

mis·hap /'mɪshæp/ n an unfortunate, often slight, accident; unfortunate happening: *He hurt his knee during the football game, but this mishap didn't stop him from playing.*

mis·in·form /ˌmɪsɪn'fɔrm/ v [T about] to tell (someone) something that is incorrect or untrue, either on purpose or by accident: *He charged the government with misinforming the nation about the cost of its plans.*

mis·in·ter·pret /ˌmɪsɪn'tɜrprɪt/ v [T] to put a wrong meaning on (something said, done, etc.); explain wrongly: *The driver misinterpreted the policeman's signal and made a wrong turn.* –see also INTERPRET **–misinterpretation** /ˌmɪsɪn,tɜrprə'teʸʃən/ n [C;U]

mis·judge /ˌmɪs'dʒʌdʒ/ v **-judged, -judging** [T] to judge (a person, action, time, distance, etc.) wrongly; form a wrong opinion of: *He's honest, and you misjudge him if you think he isn't.* **–misjudgment, -judgement** n [C;U of]

mis·lay /mɪs'leʸ/ v **-laid** /'leʸd/, **-laying** [T] to put (something) in a place and forget where; lose (something) in this way, often only for a short time

mis·lead /mɪs'liʸd/ v **-led** /'lɛd/, **-leading** [T] to cause (someone) to form a mistaken idea or to act wrongly or mistakenly: *I was misled by the car's appearance–it looked much newer than it really was.|Don't let his friendly manner mislead you into trusting him.|a misleading description* **–misleadingly** adv

mis·man·age /ˌmɪs'mænɪdʒ/ v **-aged, -aging** [T] to control or deal with (private, public, or business affairs) badly, unskilfully, etc.: *It's not surprising the company's in debt–it's been completely mismanaged.* **–mismanagement** n [U of]

mis·no·mer /ˌmɪs'noʷmər/ n a wrong or unsuitable name: *To call it a school is a misnomer–it was more like a prison!*

mi·sog·y·nist /mɪ'sɑdʒənɪst/ n a person who hates women

mis·place /ˌmɪs'pleʸs/ v **-placed, -placing** [T] **1** to have (good feelings) for an undeserving person or thing: *Your trust in that man is misplaced.* **2** →MISLAY: *I've misplaced my glasses again.* **–misplacement** n [U of]

mis·print /'mɪs,prɪnt/ n a mistake in printing

mis·pro·nounce /ˌmɪs-prə'naʊns/ v **-nounced, -nouncing** [T] to pronounce (a word, letter,etc.) incorrectly **–mispronunciation** /ˌmɪs-prə,nʌnsiʸ'eʸʃən/ n [C;U]

mis·quote /ˌmɪs'kwoʷt/ v **-quoted, -quoting** [T] to make a mistake in reporting (words) spoken or written by (a person): *The politician complained that the newspapers had misquoted him.* **–misquotation** /ˌmɪs-kwoʷ'teʸʃən/ n [C;U]

mis·read /ˌmɪs'riʸd/ v **-read** /'rɛd/, **-reading** /'riʸdɪŋ/ [T] to read or understand (something) wrongly: *He misread the date on the letter; it was October 15th, not 16th.|The general misread the enemy's intentions and didn't expect an attack.*

mis·rep·re·sent /ˌmɪsrɛprɪ'zɛnt/ v [T] to give an untrue explanation or description of (someone, or someone's words or actions), in such a way that unfavorable ideas may be spread: *Our decision to reduce taxes has been misrepresented as an attempt to gain popularity.* **–misrepresentation** /ˌmɪsrɛprɪzɛn'teʸʃən/ n [C;U]

miss¹ /mɪs/ v **1** [I;T +v-ing] to fail to hit, catch, find, meet, see, hear, add, etc.: *The falling rock just missed my head.|He arrived too late and missed the train.|He shot at me but missed.|I don't want to miss seeing that play on television tonight.|You missed an important fact in your account of the accident.* **2** [T +v-ing] to feel sorry or unhappy at the absence or loss of: *Her children have gone to California and she misses them very much.|I miss living in the country.|Give the beggar a coin; you won't miss it.* **3** [T] to discover the absence or loss of: *I didn't miss the key until I got home and found it wasn't in my bag.* **4 miss the boat** infml to lose a good chance, esp. by being too slow–see also HIT-OR-MISS, MISSING

miss out v adv [I on] to lose a chance to gain advantage or enjoyment: *You really missed out by not coming to the party.*

miss² n a failure to hit, catch, hold, etc., that which is aimed at: *The car almost hit the bus; it was a near miss.*

miss³ n (sometimes cap.) (a form of address used to) waitress, woman/girl working in a store, female stranger in the street, etc.: *Miss, could you tell me where the post office is, please?*

Miss n [A] (a title placed before the name of) an unmarried woman or a girl: *Miss Brown*|*The Miss Browns*|*The Misses Brown are sisters.* –compare MRS., MS.

Miss. *written abbrev. said as:* Mississipi /ˌmɪsəˈsɪpiʸ/ (a state in the US)

mis·shap·en /ˌmɪsˈʃeʸpən, ˌmɪˈʃeʸ-/ *adj* badly or wrongly shaped or formed

mis·sile /ˈmɪsəl/ n **1** an explosive weapon which can fly under its own power (ROCKET), and which can be aimed at a distant object **2** *fml* an object or a weapon thrown by hand or shot from a gun: *The angry crowd at the football game threw bottles and other missiles at the players.*

miss·ing /ˈmɪsɪŋ/ *adj* not to be found; not in the proper or expected place; lost: *One of the duties of the police is to try to find missing persons.*|*I noticed that he had a finger missing from his left hand.*

mis·sion /ˈmɪʃən/ n **1** a group of people who are sent abroad for a special reason: *A Canadian trade mission to China* **2** the duty or purpose for which these people are sent: *The soldiers' mission was to blow up the enemy's radio station.* **3** a place where a particular form of religion is taught, medical services are given, etc.: *They come to the mission from many miles around to see a doctor or a priest.* **4** the particular work for which one believes oneself to have been sent into the world: *Her mission in life seems to be helping lonely old people.*

mis·sion·ar·y /ˈmɪʃəˌneriʸ/ n **-ies** a person who is sent usu. to a foreign country, to teach and spread religion there

mis·spell /ˌmɪsˈspɛl/ v **-spelled** *or* **-spelt** /ˈspɛlt/, **-spelling** [T] to spell wrongly –**misspelling** n [C;U]

mis·spend /ˌmɪsˈspɛnd/ v **-spent** /ˈspɛnt◂/, **-spending** [T] to spend (time, money, etc.) wrongly or unwisely; waste

mist¹ /mɪst/ n [C;U] (an area of) clouds of very small drops of water floating in the air, near or reaching to the ground; thin FOG: *The mountain top was covered in mist.*

mist² v [I;T *over, up*] to (cause to) be covered with MIST¹: *The train became so hot that the air misted (up) the windows.*|*The windows misted up.*

mis·take¹ /mɪˈsteʸk/ v **mistook** /mɪˈstʊk/, **mistaken** /mɪˈsteʸkən/, **mistaking** [T] to have a wrong idea about; understand wrongly: *She doesn't speak very clearly so I mistook what she said.*|*He'd mistaken the address and gone to the wrong house.* –see also UNMISTAKABLE

mistake sbdy./sthg. **for** sbdy./sthg. v prep [T] to think wrongly that (a person or thing) is (someone or something else): *They mistook him for his brother.*

mistake² n a wrong thought, act, etc.; something done, said, believed, etc., as a result of wrong understanding, lack of knowledge or skill, etc.: *There were several spelling mistakes in your written work.*|*There must be some mistake in this bill; please add up the figures again.*|*She put salt into her tea* **by mistake.** –see ERROR (USAGE)

mis·tak·en /mɪˈsteʸkən/ *adj* wrong; incorrect: *If you thought she intended to be rude, you were mistaken.*|*I had the mistaken idea that it would be quicker to take the train.* –**mistakenly** *adv*

Mister /ˈmɪstər/ n [A] → MR.

mis·time /ˌmɪsˈtaɪm/ v **-timed, -timing** [T] to do or say (something) at a wrong or unsuitable time: *The general mistimed his attack; it should have been made an hour earlier.*

mis·tle·toe /ˈmɪsəlˌtoʷ/ n [U] a plant with small white berries that is often hung in rooms at Christmas time

mis·treat /ˌmɪsˈtriʸt/ *AmE*‖**maltreat** *esp. BrE*– v [T] to treat cruelly: *He mistreats his dogs.*

mis·tress /ˈmɪstrɪs/ n **1** a woman who is in control (of a family, school, etc.): *She felt she was no longer mistress in her own house when her husband's mother came to stay.*|*All the girls like their new* **headmistress.** (=leader of a private girls' school) –compare MASTER¹ **2** a woman with whom a man has a sexual relationship, usu. not a socially acceptable one: *His wife left him when she discovered he had a mistress.*

mis·trust /mɪsˈtrʌst/ v [T] not to trust –**mistrust** n [S;U *of*]: *He keeps his money at home because he has a great mistrust of banks.* –**mistrustful** /ˌmɪsˈtrʌstfəl/ *adj* [*of*]

mist·y /ˈmɪstiʸ/ *adj* **-ier, -iest** full of or covered with MIST: *a misty morning*| (fig.) *eyes misty with tears*

mis·un·der·stand /ˌmɪsʌndərˈstænd/ v **-stood** /ˈstʊd/, **-standing** [not *be* +*v*-ing] **1** [I;T] to understand wrongly; put a wrong meaning on: *I think you misunderstood me*/*misunderstood what I said.* **2** [T] to fail to see or understand the true character or qualities of (someone): *He complains that his wife misunderstands him.*

mis·un·der·stand·ing /ˌmɪsʌndərˈstændɪŋ/ n **1** [C;U] (an example of) the act of putting a wrong meaning (on something); confusion: *I think there's been some/a misunderstanding: I meant that we should meet at nine in the morning, not nine at night.* **2** [C] *often euph* a disagreement less serious than an argument

mis·use¹ /ˌmɪsˈyuʷz/ v **-used, -using** [T] to use (something) in a wrong way or for a wrong purpose

mis·use² /ˌmɪsˈyuʷs/ n [C;U *of*] (an example of) bad, wrong, or unsuitable use: *an unforgivable misuse of his power*

mite /maɪt/ n **1** a type of very small insect-like creature **2** a small child, esp. for whom one feels sorry

mi·ter *AmE*‖also **mitre** *esp. BrE* /ˈmaɪtər/ n a tall pointed hat worn by priests of high rank (BISHOPS and ARCHBISHOPS)

mit·i·gate /ˈmɪtəˌgeʸt/ v **-gated, -gating** [T] *fml* to lessen the seriousness of (wrong or harmful action): *The judge said that nothing could mitigate the cruelty with which the mother had treated her child.*|*Are there any* **mitigating circumstances** *in this case?* (=conditions that lessen the seriousness of a crime) –see also UNMITIGATED –**mitigation** /ˌmɪtəˈgeʸʃən/ n [U]

mitt /mɪt/ n **1** an especially strong hand covering (GLOVE) worn by a BASEBALL player **2** → MITTEN **3** infml a hand: Those are my cigarettes; get your mitts off them.

mit·ten /ˈmɪtn/ n a garment for the hand (GLOVE) in which all four fingers are covered by one large baglike part –see PAIR (USAGE)

mix¹ /mɪks/ v [I;T up/with] to (cause to) be combined so as to form a whole, of which the parts cannot (easily) be separated one from another: You can't mix oil and water.| Oil and water don't mix.|Oil doesn't mix with water.|Put the flour, eggs, and milk into a bowl and mix them together.|You can mix blue and yellow to produce green. **2** [I with] (of a person) to be, or enjoy being in the company of others: He's such a friendly person that he mixes well in any company.

mix sbdy./sthg.↔ **up** v adv [T] **1** [with] to confuse or mistake: It's easy to mix him up with his brother; they're very much alike. **2** to put into disorder: If you mix up those papers, we won't find the one we need quickly. –see also MIX-UP

mix² n **1** [C;U] a combination of different substances, prepared to be ready, or nearly ready, for (the stated) use: cake mix **2** [S of] a group of different things, people, etc.; mixture: There was a strange mix of people at the party.

mixed /mɪkst/ adj **1** of different kinds: I have mixed feelings about the book.(=I like it in some ways, but not in others) **2** of or for both sexes: a mixed school|mixed swimming

mixed up /ˌ· ˈ·◄/ adj **1** [F in/with] connected (with someone or something bad): I'm afraid he's mixed up in some dishonest business. **2** confused: I've heard so many different points of view about it that I'm a little mixed up.

mix·er /ˈmɪksər/ n **1** a machine by or in which substances are mixed: a food mixer –see illustration on page 379 **2** a person who MIXES¹ (2) well or badly with other people: To do this job well, you need to be a good mixer.

mix·ture /ˈmɪkstʃər/ n **1** [C;U] a set of substances mixed together: This tobacco is a mixture of three different sorts.|You need some cough mixture. (=medicine for preventing coughing) **2** [S] a combination (of things or people of different types or qualities): I listened to his excuse with a mixture of amusement and disbelief. **3** [U] fml the action of mixing or state of being mixed

mix-up /ˈ· ·/ n infml a state of disorder, as caused by bad planning, faulty arrangements, etc.: There was a mix-up at the station and some of our group got on the wrong train. –see also MIX **up**

MN written abbrev. said as: Minnesota /ˌmɪnəˈsoʷtə/ (a state in the US)

mm written abbrev. said as: MILLIMETERS

MO, Mo. written abbrev. said as: Missouri /mɪˈzʊəriʸ, mɪˈzʊərə/ (a state in the US)

moan¹ /moʷn/ n a low sound of pain, grief, or suffering: From time to time there was a moan (of pain) from the sick man.

moan² v [I] **1** to make the sound of a MOAN¹:

The sick child moaned a little, and then fell asleep. **2** derog to complain; speak in a complaining voice: Stop moaning; you really have nothing to complain about. –**moaner** n

moat /moʷt/ n a long deep hole that in former times was dug for defense around a castle, fort, etc., and was usually filled with water

mob¹ /mɑb/ n **1** [A] often derog a large noisy crowd, esp. one which is violent: An angry mob gathered outside the palace. **2** [A] derog of, by, or for the common people: The government feared mob rule. **3** [the S] often cap. a group of criminals (MOBSTERs)

mob² v **-bb-** [T] (of a group of people) to crowd around (someone) esp. because of interest or admiration: When he left the hall after his speech, the party leader was mobbed by his supporters.

mo·bile¹ /ˈmoʷbəl/ adj movable; able to move, or be moved, quickly and easily; not fixed in one position: She's much more mobile (=able to move from place to place) now that she's bought a car.|Out here in the country, we buy all our food from the mobile shop. (=a shop in a vehicle which is driven from place to place) –see also IMMOBILE –**mobility** /moʷˈbɪlətiʸ/ n [U]

mo·bile² /ˈmoʷbiʸl/ n an ornament or work of art made of small models, cards, etc., tied to wires or string and hung up so that they are moved by currents of air

mobile home /ˌ·· ˈ·/ also **trailer house**– a vehicle which can be pulled by a car or TRUCK and which has several rooms including a kitchen and bathroom: They bought a mobile home with three bedrooms.

mo·bi·lize ‖also **-lise** BrE /ˈmoʷbəˌlaɪz/ v **-lized, -lizing** [I;T] to (cause to) gather together for a particular service or use, esp. for war: Our country's in great danger; we must mobilize (the army).|He's trying to mobilize all the support/supporters he can get for his new political party. –see also DEMOBILIZE –**mobilization, -sation** /ˌmoʷbələˈzeʸʃən/ n [C;U]

mob·ster /ˈmɑbstər/ n a member of the MOB¹ (3); GANGSTER

moc·ca·sin /ˈmɑkəsən/ n a shoe made of soft leather –see PAIR (USAGE)

mock¹ /mɑk/ v [I;T] to laugh (at) or make fun (of), esp. unkindly or unfairly: The student did his best, and the teacher was wrong to mock (his efforts). **2** [T] to make fun of by copying: He made all the other boys laugh by mocking the way the teacher spoke and walked. –**mockingly** adv

mock² adj [A no comp.] not real or true; like (in appearance, taste, etc.) something real: The army training exercises ended with a mock battle.|He spoke to her in a mock-serious manner.

mock·er·y /ˈmɑkəriʸ/ n **-ies 1** [U] the act or action of MOCKing **2** [S] something that is not what it is supposed to be: The medical examination was a mockery; the doctor hardly looked at the child. **3** **make a mockery of** to cause to appear worthless, stupid, etc.: His failure made a mockery of all the teacher's efforts to help him.

mo·dal verb /ˌmoʷdəl ˈvɜrb/ *n* –see Study Notes on pages 434 and 435

mode /moʷd/ *n fml* a way of acting, behaving, speaking, writing, living, etc.: *He suddenly became wealthy, which changed his whole mode of life.*

mod·el¹ /ˈmɑdl/ *n* **1** [A;C] a small representation or copy of something: *a model of the Eiffel Tower made out of matchsticks|model plane* **2** [C] a person, esp. a young woman, employed to wear clothes and show them to possible buyers (as in a store, by being photographed, etc.) **3** [C] a person employed to be painted, drawn, photographed, etc. by an artist **4** [A;C] a person or thing that can serve as a perfect example or pattern, worthy to be followed or copied: *This student's written work is a model of care and neatness.* **5** [C] a particular type of vehicle, weapon, machine, instrument, or garment, as made by a particular maker: *Chrysler has produced two new models this year.*

model² *v* **-l-** *AmE*‖**-ll-** *BrE* **1** [T] to make a model of: *He modeled a ship out of bits of wood.* **2** [T] to shape (a soft substance, such as clay) into an article **3** [I] to work as a MODEL¹ (2,3) **4** [T] to wear and show (a garment) as a MODEL¹ (2): *Angela is modeling an attractive blue silk dress.*

   model sbdy. **on/upon/after** sbdy. *v prep* [T] to form the character, qualities, etc., of (oneself) as a copy of (another person): *She modeled herself on her mother.*

mod·er·ate¹ /ˈmɑdərɪt/ *adj* **1** of middle degree; neither large nor small, high nor low, fast nor slow, etc.: *At the time of the accident, the train was traveling at a moderate speed.|a child of only moderate ability* (=not especially intelligent)|*moderate wage demands* **2** not favoring political or social ideas that are very different from those of most people; not EXTREME¹ (3): *moderate political opinions* –see also IMMODERATE

mod·er·ate² /ˈmɑdəˌreʸt/ *v* **-ated, -ating** [I;T] to make or become less in force, degree, rate, etc.; reduce: *He should moderate his language when children are present.* (=shouldn't use words not fit for them to hear)

mod·er·ate³ /ˈmɑdərɪt/ *n* a person whose opinions are MODERATE¹ (2)

mod·er·ate·ly /ˈmɑdərɪtliʸ/ *adv* [*no comp.*] to a MODERATE¹ (1) degree; not very: *a moderately successful film*

mod·er·a·tion /ˌmɑdəˈreʸʃən/ *n* [U] **1** the ability or quality of keeping one's desires within reasonable limits; self-control: *He showed great moderation in answering so calmly the attacks made on his character.* **2 in moderation** within sensible limits: *Some people say that smoking in moderation isn't harmful to one's health.*

mod·ern /ˈmɑdərn/ *adj* of the present time, or of the not far distant past; not ancient: *The modern history of Italy begins in 1860, when the country became united.|In this part of the city, you can see ancient and modern buildings next to each other.|modern languages* (=as opposed to Latin, Greek, etc.)|*a very modern train station built of* CONCRETE² *and glass* –see NEW (USAGE) –**modernity** /mɑˈdɜrnətiʸ, mə-/ *n* [U]

mod·ern·ize ‖also **-ise** *BrE* /ˈmɑdərˌnaɪz/ *v* **-ized, -izing** [T] to make (something) suitable for modern use, or for the needs of the present time: *The house needs to be modernized: it has no bathroom or electricity.* –**modernization** /ˌmɑdərnəˈzeʸʃən/ *n* [C;U]

mod·est /ˈmɑdɪst/ *adj* **1** *apprec* having or expressing a lower opinion than is probably deserved, of one's own abilities: *She's very modest about her success and says it's just the result of good luck.* **2** not large in quantity, size, value, etc.: *There has been a modest rise in house prices this year.* **3** *apprec* (esp. of a woman or her clothes) avoiding or not showing anything that is improper –see also IMMODEST –**modestly** *adv*

mod·es·ty /ˈmɑdəstiʸ/ *n* [U] *often apprec* the quality, state, or fact of being MODEST: *His natural modesty saved him from being spoiled by fame and success.*

mod·i·cum /ˈmɑdɪkəm/ *n* [S *of*] a small amount (of anything): *If he had a modicum of sense, he wouldn't do such a foolish thing.*

mod·i·fi·ca·tion /ˌmɑdəfəˈkeʸʃən/ *n* **1** [U] the act of MODIFYing or state of being modified **2** [C] a change made in something: *A few simple modifications to this plan would greatly improve it.*

mod·i·fy /ˈmɑdəˌfaɪ/ *v* **-fied, -fying** [T] to change (a plan, an opinion, a condition, or the form or quality of something), esp. slightly: *The car has been modified so that it can be used in the desert.*

mod·ish /ˈmoʷdɪʃ/ *adj* fashionable

mod·u·late /ˈmɑdʒəˌleʸt/ *v* **-lated, -lating** [T] *fml or tech* to vary the strength, nature, etc., of (a sound)

mod·ule /ˈmɑdʒuʷl/ *n* **1** a part having a standard shape and size, used in building, making furniture, etc. **2** a part of a space vehicle that can be used independently from the other parts –**modular** /ˈmɑdʒələr/ *adj: modular furniture*

mo·hair /ˈmoʷhɛər/ *n* [U] (cloth made from) the long fine silky hair of a kind of goat (=**Angora goat**)

Mo·ham·med·an /moʷˈhæmədən/ also **Muhammadan**– *adj,n* → MUSLIM

Mo·ham·med·an·ism /moʷˈhæmədənˌɪzəm/ *n* [U] → ISLAM

moist /mɔɪst/ *adj* slightly wet; DAMP: *The thick steam in the room had made the walls moist.|eyes moist with tears* –**moistly** *adv* –**moistness** *n* [U]

moist·en /ˈmɔɪsən/ *v* [I;T] to make or become slightly wet

mois·ture /ˈmɔɪstʃər/ *n* [U] water, or other liquids, in small quantities or in the form of steam or mist: *The desert air's so dry that it contains hardly any moisture.*

mo·lar /ˈmoʷlər/ *n* any of the large teeth at the back of the mouth used for breaking up food

mo·las·ses /məˈlæsɪz/ *n* [U] **1** a thick dark sweet liquid produced from newly cut sugar plants **2** a very thick sticky dark liquid pro-

STUDY NOTES modal verbs ▰▰▰▰▰▰

The verbs below are all modal verbs. They are used as helping verbs with another verb to change its meaning in some way. This list tells you what the modal verbs mean and how to use them.

expressing ability	She **can** speak French. I **could** swim when I was five. I **was able to** lift the box.	
asking and giving permission	**Can** I go home now? **Could** I turn the radio down? You **may** come in now.	**can** is now the most common word. **could** and **may** are more polite ways of asking permission.
making requests and suggestions	**Can** you close the door, please? **Could** you help me, please? **Shall** we go to the movies tonight?	**could** is more polite than **can**. **shall** is used only with I and we.
expressing necessity	I **have to/have got to** leave now. I **had to** leave early last night. You children **must** go to bed now. I **must** hurry or I'll be late.	**must** is most often used in fml usage or when one person has power over another, as when parents speak to children, or in the first PERSON to show strong necessity.
expressing lack of necessity	You **don't have to** arrive until 10:30. I **didn't have to** put on my heavy coat.	
giving advice	You **should/ought to** be ashamed of yourself. I **shouldn't have/oughtn't to have** said that.	**should/ought to** are used for actions which are thought to be good or right. **must/have to** are used for necessary actions. **shouldn't/oughtn't to** are used for actions which are thought to be bad or wrong. **don't have to** is used for unnecessary actions.
giving commands	You **must not** tell anyone. You **must** keep it secret. You **are not to** go. You **are to** stay here.	
expressing near certainty and impossibility	You've worked all day. You **must** be tired. You haven't worked at all. You **can't** be tired. They're not here. They **must have** gone home. Their car is still here. They **can't have** gone home.	**must** and **must have** are the opposites of **can't** and **can't have** in this meaning.
talking about the future	It **will** rain tomorrow. I **shall** write to you again when we have made a decision.	**will** is more common than **shall**. **shall** is fml and is used only with I and we.
expressing possibility	It **may/might** snow tonight.	**might** makes something sound less likely than **may**.
talking about the past	We **used to** work in the same office. We **would** often go to the movies together.	

Here are some ways of using these modal verbs in different types of sentences:

	with not and n't	in a question	describing what someone said
can	*She* **can't/cannot** *speak French.*	**Can** *she speak French?*	*She said she* **could** *speak French.*
could	*I* **couldn't/could not** *swim when I was five.*	**Could** *you swim when you were five?*	*He said he* **could** *swim when he was five.*
may	*You* **may not** *go to the party.*	**May** *I go to the party?*	*I said you* **may** *go.*
might	*He* **might not** *be in his office.*	*Where* **might** *he be?*[1]	*He said he* **might** *leave early.*
shall	*We* **shall not** *go to the movies.*	**Shall** *we go to the movies?*	*They said we* **should** *go to the movies.*
must	*You* **must not** *go.*	**Must** *you go now?*	*They said they* **must** *go.*
have to	*You* **don't/do not have to** *go.*	**Do** *you* **have to** *go?*	*They said they* **had to** *go.*
are to	*You* **aren't/are not to** *stay.*	**Are** *you* **to** *stay there?*	*They said they* **were to** *stay.*
should	*He* **shouldn't/should not** *go.*	**Should** *he go?*	*They said he* **should** *go.*
ought to	*You* **oughtn't/ought not to** *go there.*	**Ought** *you* **to** *go there?*	*They said you* **ought to** *go.*
will	*It* **won't/will not** *rain.*	**Will** *it rain?*	*They said it* **would** *rain.*
used to	*I* **didn't use to** *work there.*	**Did** *you* **use to** *work there?*	*They said they* **used to** *work there.*
would	*I* **wouldn't/would not** *go.*	**Would** *you go there?*	*They said they* **would** *often go there.*

[1]Questions with **might** are rare. **Could** is more often used: *Where* **could** *he be?*

duced when sugar is being REFINED (=made pure)

mold¹ *AmE*‖**mould** *BrE* /moʷld/ *n* [U] a soft greenish growth on bread, cheese, etc. that has been kept too long or on objects that have been left for a long time in warm wet air

mold² *AmE*‖**mould** *BrE* *n* a hollow vessel having a particular shape, into which some soft substance is poured, so that when the substance becomes cool and hard, it takes this shape: *a jelly mold shaped like a rabbit*

mold³ *AmE*‖**mould** *BrE* *v* [T] to shape or form (something solid) esp. using a MOLD²: *The car body is molded in the factory.*|*a figure of a man molded out of/in clay.*|(fig.) *His character has been molded more by his experiences than by his education.*

mold·ing *AmE*‖**moulding** *BrE* /ˈmoʷldɪŋ/ *n* **1** [U] the act, work, or way of giving shape to something, esp. to a soft substance **2** [C] an ornamental edge or band of stone, wood, etc. around a window, at the top of a wall, etc.

mold·y *AmE*‖**mouldy** *BrE* /ˈmoʷldiʸ/ *adj* **-ier, -iest** of or covered with MOLD¹ (1): *moldy cheese*|*The old house smells moldy.* –**moldiness** *n* [U]

mole¹ /moʷl/ *n* a small dark brown mark on the skin

mole² *n* a small furry almost blind animal that digs passages underground to live in

mol·e·cule /ˈmɑlə,kyuʷl/ *n* the smallest part of any substance that can exist without losing its own chemical nature, consisting of one or more atoms –**molecular** /məˈlɛkyələr/ *adj*

mole·hill /ˈmoʷl,hɪl/ *n* **1** a small heap of earth made by a MOLE² digging underground **2 make a mountain out of a molehill** to make an unimportant matter seem more important than it is

mo·lest /məˈlɛst/ *v* [T] **1** to annoy or attack: *A dog that molests sheep has to be killed.* **2** *euph* to attack (esp. a woman or a child) sexually –**molestation** /,moʷlɛsˈteʸʃən, ,mɑ-/ *n* [U]

mol·li·fy /ˈmɑlə,faɪ/ *v* **-fied, -fying** [T] to make calmer: *He bought his angry wife a gift, but she refused to be mollified.* –**mollification** /,mɑləfəˈkeʸʃən/ *n* [U]

mol·lusk *AmE*‖also **mollusc** /ˈmɑləsk/ *n* any of a class of animals with soft bodies and no backbone or limbs and usu. covered with a shell: SNAILs *and* OCTOPUSES *are mollusks.*

molt *AmE* **moult** *esp. BrE* /moʷlt/ *v* [I;T] (of a bird or animal) to lose or throw off (feathers, hair, or fur)

mol·ten /ˈmoʷltn/ *adj* (of metal or rock) turned to liquid by very great heat; melted –see MELT (USAGE)

mom /mɑm/ *AmE*‖**mum** *BrE* *n* (used esp. by or to children) mother: *Could I borrow your car, mom?*

mo·ment /ˈmoʷmənt/ *n* **1** [C] a very short period of time: *It will only take a moment.*|*I'll be back in a moment/in a few moments.* (=very soon)|*Just a moment* (=wait); *I want to speak to you.* **2** [S] a particular point in time: *Just at that moment, the door opened and the teacher walked in.* **3** [C +to-v/for;

usu. sing.] the right time for doing something: *Now is the moment to attack, while the enemy is at its weakest.* **4** [U] *fml* importance: *a matter of (the greatest) moment* **5 at any moment** at an unknown time only a little after the present: *He might come back at any moment.* **6 at the moment** at the present time; now **7 the moment (that)** just as soon as; at exactly the time when: *I recognized him the moment (that) I saw him.*

mo·men·ta·ry /ˈmoʷmən,tɛriʸ/ *adj* lasting for a very short time: *Her feeling of fear was only momentary; it soon passed.* –compare MOMENTOUS –**momentarily** /,moʷmənˈtɛrəliʸ/ *adv: He was so surprised that he was momentarily unable to speak.*

mo·men·tous /moʷˈmɛntəs, mə-/ *adj* of very great importance or seriousness: *We listened on the radio to the momentous news that war had begun.* –compare MOMENTARY

mo·men·tum /moʷˈmɛntəm, mə-/ *n* [U] esp. *tech* the quantity of movement in a body: *As the rock rolled down the mountainside, it gathered momentum.* (=moved faster and faster)|(fig.) *The struggle for independence is gaining momentum* (=growing stronger) *every day.*

mom·my /ˈmɑmiʸ/ *AmE*‖**mummy** *BrE*– *n* **-mies** (used esp. by or to children) (a word for) mother: *I want my mommy!*

Mon. written *abbrev. for:* Monday

mon·arch /ˈmɑnərk, ˈmɑnɑrk/ *n* a ruler of a state (such as a king, queen, etc.) who has the right to rule by birth –**monarchic** /məˈnɑrkɪk/ also **monarchical**– *adj*

mon·arch·ist /ˈmɑnərkɪst/ *n* a person in favor of the idea that kings, queens, etc., should rule, rather than elected leaders

mon·ar·chy /ˈmɑnərkiʸ/ *n* **-chies 1** [U] rule by a king or queen **2** [C] a state ruled by a king or queen –compare REPUBLIC

mon·as·ter·y /ˈmɑnəs,tɛriʸ/ *n* **-ies** a religious establishment in which MONKs live and work –compare CONVENT

mo·nas·tic /məˈnæstɪk/ *adj* of monasteries (MONASTERY) or MONKs

mo·nas·ti·cism /məˈnæstə,sɪzəm/ *n* [U] the life, or way of life, of MONKs in a MONASTERY

Mon·day /ˈmʌndiʸ, -deʸ/ *n* the second day of any week; the day after Sunday: *He'll arrive on Monday evening.* (=during the evening of next Monday).|*Many people do their week's washing on Mondays.*|*He arrived on the Monday and left on the Wednesday.* (=arrived on the second day of the week being spoken of)|*He arrived on a Monday* (=not a Sunday, Tuesday, etc.).|(esp. *AmE*) *She works Mondays.*

mon·e·tar·y /ˈmɑnə,tɛriʸ/ *adj* of or connected with money: *The monetary system of certain countries used to be based on gold.*

mon·ey /ˈmʌniʸ/ *n* [U] **1** coins or paper notes with their value printed on them, given and taken in buying and selling: *He doesn't usually carry much money on him.* (=in his pockets)|*The repairs will cost a lot of money.* **2** wealth: *Money doesn't always bring happiness.*|*If this old picture really is by a famous artist, we're in the money.* (=we will be wealthy) **3 one's money's worth** full value for the money one has spent: *We enjoyed the film so much that we felt we'd got our money's worth.* –see also POCKET MONEY

money or·der /'·· ‚·'/ *AmE*‖**postal order** *BrE*– *n* an official paper of a stated value which can be bought from a post office, bank, etc. and sent in place of money

mon·gol /'maŋgəl, -goʷl/ *n* a person born with a weakness of the mind and a broad flattened head and face and sloping eyes

mon·grel /'maŋgrəl, 'mʌŋ-/ *n* an animal, esp. a dog, whose parents were of mixed breeds or different breeds –compare PEDIGREE

mon·i·tor¹ /'manətər/ *n* **1** a pupil chosen to help the teacher in various ways **2** the part of an electrical apparatus, such as a television or a computer, that has a SCREEN on which pictures or information appear –see illustration on page 221

monitor² *v* [T] to watch, listen to, or examine (esp. the working of a machine, or radio and television broadcasts): *We have been monitoring the enemy's radio broadcasts to try to find out their plans.*

monk /mʌŋk/ *n* a member of an all-male religious group that lives together in a MONASTERY –compare FRIAR, NUN –**monkish** *adj*

mon·key /'mʌŋkiʸ/ *n* -**keys 1** a long-tailed active tree-climbing animal, belonging to that class of animals most like man **2** *infml* a child who is full of annoying playfulness and tricks

monkey a·round *v adv* [I] *infml* to play in a foolish way: *The boys were monkeying around in the playground and one got hurt.*

monkey with sbdy./sthg. *v prep* [T] *infml* to touch, use, or examine (esp. something that is not one's concern) without skill and so possibly causing damage: *You'll break the T.V. if you don't stop monkeying with it.*

monkey wrench /'·· ‚·/ *n* a tool that can be ADJUSTED for holding or turning things of different widths

mon·o¹ /'manoʷ/ *adj* **1** using a system of sound recording, broadcasting, or receiving in which the sound appears to come from one direction only when played back: *a mono record/record player* –compare STEREO **2 mono-** one; single

mono² *n* [U] *AmE infml* for MONONUCLEOSIS

mon·o·chrome /'manə‚kroʷm/ *adj* having, using, or showing one color only: *a monochrome television set* (=one showing black and white pictures, not colored ones)

mon·o·cle /'manəkəl/ *n* an apparatus like glasses, but for one eye only

mo·nog·a·my /mə'nagəmiʸ/ *n* [U] the custom or practice of having only one wife or husband at one time –compare BIGAMY, POLYGAMY –**monogamous** *adj*

mon·o·gram /'manə‚græm/ *n* a figure made of two or more letters, esp. the first letters of a person's names, often printed on writing paper, etc. –**monogrammed** *adj*

mon·o·lith /'manl‚ɪθ/ *n* a large pillar made from one piece or mass of stone and standing by itself

mon·o·lith·ic /‚manl'ɪθɪk/ *adj* **1** of or like a MONOLITH: *a monolithic building* **2** *often derog* forming a large unchangeable whole: *a monolithic system of government* –**monolithically** *adv*

mon·o·logue ‖also **monolog** *AmE* /'manl‚ɔg, -‚ɑg/ *n* **1** a long speech, part in a play or film, etc., spoken by one person only **2** *infml often derog* a rather long speech by one person, which prevents others from taking part in the conversation –compare DIALOGUE

mon·o·nu·cle·o·sis /‚manoʷ‚nuʷkliʸ'oʷsɪs, -‚nyuʷ-/ also **mono** *AmE infml*–‖ **glandular fever** *BrE*– *n* [U] an infectious disease which causes one's GLANDS to swell and which causes a fever and tiredness

mon·o·plane /'manə‚pleʸn/ *n* an aircraft having a single wing on each side of it –compare BIPLANE

mo·nop·o·lize ‖also **-lise** *BrE* /mə'napə‚laɪz/ *v* -**lized, -lizing** [T] to have or obtain a MONOPOLY of; have or get complete unshared control of: *These two company's are so big that they monopolize the cigarette industry.*‖(fig.) *The naughty child monopolized the teacher's attention.* –**monopolization** /mə‚napələ'zeʸʃən/ *n* [U *of*]

mo·nop·o·ly /mə'napəliʸ/ *n* -**lies 1** [C] (a person, company, etc. that has) the right or power, shared with no one else, to provide a service, trade in anything, produce something, etc.: *The postal services are a government monopoly.* **2** [S] possession of, or control over, something, which is not shared by another or others: *He seems to think he has a monopoly on brains.* (=that he alone is intelligent)‖*A university education shouldn't be the monopoly of those whose parents are rich.*

mon·o·rail /'manə‚reʸl/ *n* (a train traveling on) a railroad with a single rail

mon·o·syl·lab·ic /‚manəsɪ'læbɪk/ *adj* **1** (of a word) having one SYLLABLE **2** (of speech, a remark, etc.) formed of words with one SYLLABLE; short and rather rude: *He would give only monosyllabic replies, such as "yes" and "no."*

mon·o·syl·la·ble /'manə‚sɪləbəl/ *n* a word of one SYLLABLE: *"Can, hot, neck" are monosyllables.*

mon·o·tone /'manə‚toʷn/ *n* [S] a manner of speaking or singing in which the voice continues on the same note: *to speak in a monotone*

mo·not·o·nous /mə'natn-əs/ *adj* having a tiring uninteresting sameness or lack of variety: *My job at the car factory is very monotonous.* –**monotonously** *adv* –**monotony** *n* [U]

mon·soon /man'suʷn/ *n* [C; *the* S] **1** the (period or season of) heavy rains which fall in India and neighboring countries **2** the wind that brings these rains –see WEATHER (USAGE)

mon·ster /'manstər/ *n* **1** [C] a creature, imaginary or real, that is unnatural in shape, size, or qualities, and usu. causes fear: *a sea monster*‖*Children love to hear stories about terrible monsters.* **2** [C *of*] a very evil person:

The judge told the murderer that he was a monster/a monster of cruelty. **3** [A;C] an animal, plant, or thing of unusually great size or strange form: *That dog's a real monster; I've never seen such a big one.|a monster potato*

mon·stros·i·ty /mɑnˈstrɑsəṭiʸ/ n **-ties** something made or built in such a way that it is, or is considered, very ugly: *Have you seen that new office building in the center of town? It's a monstrosity!*

mon·strous /ˈmɑnstrəs/ adj **1** of unnaturally large size, strange shape, etc. **2** shocking: *monstrous cruelty|Your behavior in class is monstrous!* –**monstrously** adv

Mont. written abbrev. said as: Montana /mɑnˈtænə/ (a state in the US)

month /mʌnθ/ n **1** any of the 12 named divisions of the year **2** a period of about four weeks: *The baby was born on September 23, so he'll be exactly six months old tomorrow (March 23).* –see also LUNAR MONTH

month·ly /ˈmʌnθliʸ/ adj, adv (happening, appearing, etc.) every month or once a month: *a monthly meeting*

mon·u·ment /ˈmɑnyəmənt/ n **1** a building, pillar, STATUE, etc., that preserves the memory of a person or event: *This pillar is a monument to all those who died in the war.|(fig.) That big empty office building is a monument to bad planning.* **2** an old building, etc., or what remains of it, considered worthy of preservation for its historic interest or beauty: *an ancient monument*

mon·u·men·tal /ˌmɑnyəˈmɛntl◂/ adj **1** of, intended for, or having the nature of a MONU-MENT (1) **2** very large, and of great and lasting worth: *The artist spent years on his monumental painting, which covered the whole roof of the church.* **3** very great in degree: *monumental stupidity*

moo /muʷ/ n,v [I] (to make) the noise that a cow makes

mood /muʷd/ n **1** [C] a state of the feelings at a particular time: *The beautiful sunny morning put him in a happy mood.|His moods change very quickly.|The teacher's in a bad mood* (=in a bad temper) *today.* **2** [C] a state of feeling in which one is bad-tempered: *Don't ask him to lend you money when he's in one of his moods.* **3** [the S +to-v/for] the right state of mind (for a particular activity, thing, etc.): *She was very tired, and in no mood for dancing.*

mood·y /ˈmuʷdiʸ/ adj **-ier, -iest** usu. derog **1** having MOODs (1) that change often and quickly **2** bad-tempered, angry, displeased, or unhappy, etc. –**moodily** adv –**moodiness** n [U]

moon /muʷn/ n **1** [the S] the body which moves round the earth once every 28 days, and can be seen shining in the sky at night **2** [S] this body as it appears at a particular time: *Last night there was a full moon.* (=appearing as a full circle) **3** [C] a body that turns round a PLANET other than the earth: *Saturn has several moons.* **4** once in a blue moon once in a very long time –**moonless** adj

moon around also **moon about**– v adv [I]

infml to wander around or behave in an aimless unhappy way

moon·beam /ˈmuʷnbiʸm/ n a beam of light from the moon

moon·light /ˈmuʷnlaɪt/ n [U] the light of the moon: *The moonlight on the calm sea added to the beauty of the scene.*

moon·lit /ˈmuʷnˌlɪt/ adj [A] given light by the moon: *a beautiful moonlit night*

moor¹ /mʊər/ n [often pl.] esp. BrE a wide, open area of land, covered with rough grass or low bushes and not farmed because of its bad soil

moor² v [I;T to] to fasten (a ship, boat, etc.) to land, the bed of the sea, etc. by means of ropes, chains, an ANCHOR, etc.

moor·ings /ˈmʊərɪŋz/ n [P] a place where a ship or boat is MOORED: *Several ships broke away from their moorings in the storm.*

moose /muʷs/ n moose a type of large deer that lives in north America (and in northern Europe, where it is called an ELK)

moot point /ˌmuʷt ˈpɔɪnt/ n an undecided point; point on which there is disagreement or doubt

mop¹ /mɑp/ n **1** a tool for washing floors or dishes, made of a stick with either a number of threads of thick string, or a piece of SPONGE¹ (2), fastened to one end **2** infml a thick usu. untidy mass (of hair)

mop² v **-pp-** [T] **1** to clean with, or as if with, a MOP¹ (1): *I usually mop the kitchen floor twice a week.* **2** to make dry by rubbing with something dry: *to mop one's BROW* (2) *with a handkerchief*

mop sthg.↔ **up** v adv [T] to remove (unwanted liquid, dirt, etc.) with, or as if with, a MOP¹ (1): *It was you who spilled the milk; you'll have to mop it up.*

mope /moʷp/ v **moped, moping** [I] to be in low spirits, often without trying to become more cheerful

mo·ped /ˈmoʷpɛd/ n a bicycle which has a small engine, to help the rider esp. when going uphill

mor·al¹ /ˈmɔrəl, ˈmɑrəl/ adj **1** [A no comp.] concerning or based on the difference between right and wrong or good and evil: *a man of high moral standards|She refused to join the army on moral grounds, because she thought it was wrong to kill people.|I don't think you have any right to make moral judgments about me.* **2** keeping exactly to what is (considered by society to be) good or acceptable in behavior, esp. in matters of sex: *My grandfather was a very moral man; he never told a lie in his life.* –see also AMORAL, IM-MORAL **3 moral support** support given without material help; encouragement **4 moral victory** the result of a contest or argument in which the losing side feels it has proved itself to be right or just

moral² n a good lesson in behavior, the right way of leading one's life, etc. that can be learned from a story or event: *The moral of this story is that crime does not pay.*

mo·rale /məˈræl/ n [U] the state of mind (of a person, team, army, etc.) esp. with regard to pride, determination not to yield, etc.:

Despite their defeat over the weekend, the team's morale is still high.

mor·al·ist /'mɔrəlɪst, 'mɑr-/ *n usu. derog* a person who concerns himself/ herself with trying to control the MORALS of other people –**moralistic** /ˌmɔrə'lɪstɪk, ˌmɑr-/ *adj*

mo·ral·i·ty /mə'ræləti^y/ *n* [U] rightness or pureness of behavior, of an action, etc.: *One sometimes wonders if there's any morality in politics.* –opposite **immorality**

mor·al·ize ‖also **-ise** *BrE* /'mɔrəˌlaɪz, 'mɑr-/ *v* **-ized, -izing** [I *about, on, upon*] *usu. derog* to express one's thoughts on the rightness or wrongness of behavior, actions, etc. –**moralizer** *n*

mor·al·ly /'mɔrəli^y, 'mɑr-/ *adv* **1** *apprec* in a MORAL¹ (3) manner –opposite **immorally 2** with regard to right or good behavior: *What you did wasn't actually against the law, but it was morally wrong.*

mor·als /'mɔrəlz, 'mɑr-/ *n* [P] standards of behavior, esp. in matters of sex: *a person of loose morals* (=bad sexual behavior)|*In his business affairs he has no morals.* (=he acts dishonestly, etc.)

mo·rass /mə'ræs/ *n* a stretch of soft, wet, low ground that is dangerous for walking: (fig.) *The report took a long time to read because of the morass of details.*

mor·a·to·ri·um /ˌmɔrə'tɔri^yəm, -'to^wr-, ˌmɑr-/ *n* **-ria** /ri^yə/ *or* **-riums 1** a declaration that a particular activity will be stopped or delayed for a time: *a moratorium on the building of new houses by the town council* **2** the length of such a delay

mor·bid /'mɔrbɪd/ *adj derog* having or showing an unhealthy unnatural interest in or liking for unpleasant subjects, esp. concerning death –**morbidly** *adv* –**morbidity** /mɔr'bɪdəti^y/ *n* [U]

more¹ /mɔr, mo^wr/ *adv* (COMPARATIVE² of *many, much*) [*than*] **1** to a greater degree: *This book is more interesting than that one.*|*I sleep more in the winter.* –compare LESS¹ –see Study Notes on page 550 **2** (with *once, no*) again: *I'll repeat the question once more.*|*The ship sank below the waves and was seen no more.* (=never again)

more² *determiner, pron* (COMPARATIVE² of *many, much*) [*of, than*] **1** a greater number or amount: *There are more rooms in this house than in mine.*|*As he grows older, he spends more (of his) time in bed.*|*It's no more than a mile to the ocean.* –see (USAGE) **2** an additional number or amount: *Have some more coffee!*|*Could I have a little more of that cake?*|*I have to write two more letters this morning.* (=besides those already written) –see Study Notes on page 135 **3 any more** any longer; now: *They don't live here any more.* **4 more and more** increasingly; (an amount) that continues to increase: *more and more difficult*|*I seem to spend more and more money on food every week!* **5 more or less** about; not exactly: *The repairs will cost $75, more or less.* **6 the more** (used to show that two things get larger, or change, together): *The more he eats, the fatter he gets.* –compare LESS²

USAGE **More** is the opposite of both **less** (for amounts) and **fewer** (for numbers). Compare: *a few/three/many* **more** (opposite **fewer**) *friends*|*a bit/rather/much* **more** (opposite **less**) *money*

more·o·ver /mɔr'o^wvər, mo^wr-/ *adv fml* besides what has been said: *The price is too high, and, moreover, the house isn't in a suitable position.*

morgue /mɔrg/ *n* a building in which dead bodies of unknown people are kept until it is discovered who they were –compare MORTUARY

Mor·mon /'mɔrmən/ *n* a member of a religious body originally formed in the US, and calling itself **The Church of Jesus Christ of Latter-Day Saints**

morn /mɔrn/ *n* a morning

morn·ing /'mɔrnɪŋ/ *n* **1** [C;U] the first part of the day, usu. until the time when the midday meal is eaten: *I must go shopping sometime this morning.*|*I don't want to telephone him tonight; can't it wait until morning?*|*I'll see you in the morning.* (=tomorrow morning)|*I met him in town this morning.*|*He didn't get home until two o'clock in the morning.* **2** [A] of, in, or taking place in this part of the day: *an early morning cup of coffee*|*the morning newspapers*

morn·ings /'mɔrnɪŋz/ *adv esp. AmE* in or during early morning, or most mornings: *Mornings I usually go for a run.*

mo·ron /'mɔran, 'mo^wran/ *n usu. derog* a very foolish person –**moronic** /mə'ranɪk/ *adj* –**moronically** *adv*

mo·rose /mə'ro^ws/ *adj* bad-tempered; not cheerful –**morosely** *adv* –**moroseness** *n* [U]

mor·phine /'mɔrfi^yn/ *n* [U] a powerful drug used for stopping pain

mor·row /'mɔro^w, 'mɑro^w/ *n* [*the* S] *lit* the day following today: *Let's hope that the morrow will bring better news.*

mor·sel /'mɔrsəl/ *n* a very small piece (of food): (fig.) *He hasn't a morsel of sense.*

mor·tal¹ /'mɔrtl/ *adj* **1** that must die; not living for ever –opposite **immortal 2** causing death: *a mortal wound* **3** [A] very great (in degree): *in mortal danger*

mortal² *n esp. lit* a human being (as compared with a god, a spirit, etc.): *We're all mortals, with our human faults and weaknesses.*

mor·tal·i·ty /mɔr'tæləti^y/ *n* **1** [S;U] (the rate of) the number of deaths from a certain cause, among a certain type of people, etc.: *If this disease spreads, the doctors fear that there'll be a high mortality.*|*Infant mortality* (=the rate at which deaths of babies take place) *is still very high in some countries.* **2** [U] the condition of being MORTAL¹ (1) –opposite **immortality** (for 2)

mor·tal·ly /'mɔrtl-i^y/ *adv* in a manner that causes death: *He fell to the ground, mortally wounded.*|(fig.) *She was mortally* (=greatly) *offended by your remarks.*

mor·tar¹ /'mɔrtər/ *n* **1** a heavy gun with a short barrel, firing an explosive that falls from a great height **2** a bowl made from a hard material, in which substances are crushed with a PESTLE into very small pieces or powder

mortar² *n* [U] a mixture of lime, sand, and water, used in building

mort·gage¹ /'mɔrgɪdʒ/ *n* **1** an agreement to have money lent, esp. so as to buy a house, by which the house or land belongs to the lender until the money is repaid **2** the amount lent on a mortgage

mortgage² *v* **-gaged, -gaging** [T] to give the right or the claim to the ownership of (a house, land, etc.) in return for money lent for a certain period

mor·ti·fy /'mɔrtə,faɪ/ *v* **-fied, -fying** [T] to hurt (a person's) feelings, causing shame, anger, etc.: *The teacher was mortified by his own inability to answer such a simple question.* –**mortification** /,mɔrtəfə'keʸʃən/ *n* [U]

mor·tu·ar·y /'mɔrtʃuʷ,eriʸ/ *n* **-ies** a place esp. in a hospital where a dead body is kept until the time of the funeral –compare MORGUE

mo·sa·ic /moʷ'zeʸɪk/ *n* [C;U] (a piece of ornamental work produced by) the fitting together of small pieces of colored stone, glass, etc., so as to form a pattern or picture

mo·sey /'moʷziʸ/ *v* **-seyed, -seying** I] *AmE infml* to walk in an unhurried manner; SAUNTER: *It's getting late. We'd better mosey along.*

Mos·lem /'mɑzləm, 'mɑs-/ *n, adj* →MUSLIM

mosque /mɑsk/ *n* a building in which Muslims worship

mos·qui·to /mə'skiʸtoʷ/ *n* **-toes** a small flying insect that pricks the skin and then drinks blood, and can in this way cause the disease of MALARIA

moss /mɔs/ *n* [U] a small flat green or yellow flowerless plant that grows in a thick furry mass on wet soil, or on a wet surface –**mossy** *adj*

most¹ /moʷst/ *adv* (SUPERLATIVE *of much*) **1** to the greatest degree: *the most comfortable hotel in this town|What annoyed me most was the way he laughed at my mistake.* –compare LEAST¹ –see Study Notes on page 135 **2** *fml* very: *a most enjoyable party|I'll most certainly attend the meeting.*

most² *determiner, pron* (SUPERLATIVE of *many, much*) [*of*] **1** the greatest number or amount: *Most people take their vacations in the summer.|He spends most of his time traveling.|She bought the one that cost the most.* –see Study Notes on page 135 **2 at most** not more than; if not less: *She's at most 25 years old.* –compare LEAST² **3 for the most part** mainly: *Summers in the south of France are for the most part dry and sunny.* **4 make the most of** to get the best advantage from: *We've only got one day in San Francisco, so let's make the most of it and see everything.*

most·ly /'moʷstliʸ/ *adv* mainly; in most cases or most of the time: *She uses her car mostly for going to work.*

mo·tel /moʷ'tɛl/ *n* a hotel especially built for traveling motorists

moth /mɔθ/ *n* **moths** /mɔðz, mɔjs/ a quite large winged insect, related to the BUT-TERFLY, which flies mainly at night. The young of some types of moth (the **clothes-moth**) eat and make holes in clothes

moth·ball /'mɔθbɔl/ *n* [*usu. pl.*] a small ball made of a strong-smelling substance, used for keeping MOTHs away from clothes

moth-eat·en /'·· ,··/ *adj* (of a garment) destroyed, or partly destroyed, by MOTHs: *(fig.) a moth-eaten* (=very worn out) *old chair*

moth·er¹ /'mʌðər/ *n* **1** a female parent: *His mother and father are both doctors.|a mother hen and her young CHICKS|Would you like a cup of coffee, Mother?* –see illustration on page 247 **2 the/one's mother country** the country of one's birth **3 the/one's mother tongue** one's native language –**motherless** *adj*

mother² *v* [T] **1** (esp. of a woman) to care for (someone) like a mother **2** *derog* to treat (someone) with too great protectiveness and care

moth·er·hood /'mʌðər,hʊd/ *n* [U] the state of being a mother: *Motherhood doesn't suit her; she shouldn't have had children.*

mother-in-law /'·· · ,·/ *n* **mothers-in-law** the mother of a person's husband or wife –see illustration on page 247

moth·er·ly /'mʌðərliʸ/ *adj apprec* having or showing the love, kindness, etc., of amother –**motherliness** *n* [U]

mother-of-pearl /,·· · '·/ *n* [U] a hard smooth variously colored substance on the inside of certain shells, used for making ornamental articles

Mother's Day /'·· ,·/ *n* a day on which respect and admiration are shown to mothers, in the US on the second Sunday in May

mother su·pe·ri·or /,·· ·'··/ *n* (*usu. caps.*) the female head of a CONVENT

mo·tif /moʷ'tiʸf/ *n* a subject, pattern, idea, etc., forming the base on which something, esp. a work of art, is made

mo·tion¹ /'moʷʃən/ *n* **1** [U] the act, manner, or state of moving: *The gentle rocking motion of the ship made me feel sleepy.|The train was already in motion when he jumped on.|Parts of the movie were shown again in slow motion.* (=making the movements appear slower than in real life)|*Press this button to put/set the machine in motion.* (=start it working) **2** [C] a single or particular movement or way of moving: *He made a motion with his hand, as if to tell me to keep back.* **3** [C +*to-v/that*] a suggestion formally put before a meeting: *The motion to increase the club's membership charges was defeated by 15 votes to 10.*

motion² *v* [I;T] to direct (someone) by means of a movement, usu. with the hand: *She motioned (to) me to come into the room.*

mo·tion·less /'moʷʃənlɪs/ *adj* without any movment; quite still: *The cat remained motionless, waiting for the mouse to come out of its hole.* –**motionlessly** *adv* –**motionlessness** *n* [U]

motion pic·ture /,·· '··/ also **movie** *AmE*||**film** *esp. BrE*– *n* a story or events put on film and shown to people

mo·ti·vate /'moʷtə,veʸt/ *v* **-vated, -vating** [T] to provide (someone) with a reason or cause for doing something: *His attempt to get* *elected was motivated only by a desire for power.*

mo·ti·va·tion /ˌmoʷtə'veʸʃən/ n [C;U] the act or state of being MOTIVATEd; need or purpose: *The stronger the motivation, the more quickly a person will learn a foreign language.*

mo·tive /'moʷtɪv/ n a cause of or reason for action; that which urges a person to act in a certain way: *In a case of murder, the police question everyone who might have a motive.|What do you think his motives were in buying the director a drink?* –**motiveless** *adj*

mot·ley /'mɑtliʸ/ *adj derog or humor* of many different kinds, classes, etc.: *a motley crowd of people*

mo·tor¹ /'moʷtər/ n a machine that changes power, esp. electrical power, into movement: *This machine is driven by a small electric motor.* –see MACHINE (USAGE)

motor² *adj* [A] **1** driven by an engine: *a motor-boat|a motor SCOOTER* **2** *BrE* of, for, or concerning vehicles driven by an engine, esp. those used on roads: *the motor industry|trade|motor racing*

motor³ *v* [I] *BrE* for DRIVE¹ (1)

mo·tor·bike /'moʷtər,baɪk/ n **1** *AmE* a small light MOTORCYCLE **2** *BrE infml* for MOTORCYCLE

mo·tor·cade /'moʷtər,keʸd/ n *AmE* a line of motor vehicles moving forward in an orderly way, as in a PARADE: *The President's motorcade will pass by in about 20 minutes.*

mo·tor·car /'moʷtər,kɑr/ n *BrE fml* a car

mo·tor·cy·cle¹ /'moʷtər,saɪkəl/ also **motorbike**– n a large heavy bicycle driven by an engine: *to go to work by motorcycle* –**motorcyclist** n

motorcycle also **cycle**– **-cled, -cling** *v* [I] to ride on a motorcycle: *They motorcycled all the way from Boston*

mo·tor·ist /'moʷtərɪst/ n *fml* a person who drives a car –compare PEDESTRIAN

mo·tor·ize ‖also **-ise** *BrE* /'moʷtə,raɪz/ *v* **-ized, -izing** [T] to provide (soldiers, an army, etc.) with motor vehicles

mo·tor·way /'moʷtər,weʸ/ n *BrE* for EXPRESSWAY

mot·tled /'mɑtld/ *adj* marked irregularly with variously colored spots or parts: *The underside of this snake is all yellow, but its back is mottled.*

mot·to /'mɑtoʷ/ n **-tos** or **-toes** a short sentence or few words taken as the guiding principle of a person, a school, etc.: *The school motto is "Never lose hope."* –compare SLOGAN

mould /moʷld/ n [U] *BrE* for MOLD

moult /moʷlt/ *v* [I;T] *BrE* for MOLT

mound /maʊnd/ n [of] a heap (of earth, stones, etc.); small hill: (fig.) *There's a mound of papers on my desk.*

mount¹ /maʊnt/ n [A;C] *old use or (cap.)* as part of a name a mountain: *Mount Everest*

mount² *v* **1** [I;T] to get on (a horse, a bicycle, etc.): *He mounted (his horse) and rode away.* –opposite **dismount** **2** [I;T] *fml* to go up; climb: *The old lady can mount the stairs only with difficulty.* **3** [I *up*] to rise in level or

increase in amount: *His debts continued to mount up.* **4** [T] to fix on a support or in a frame: *She mounted the photograph on stiff paper.* **5** [T] to prepare or begin (an attack): *The unions are getting ready to mount a powerful attack on the administration.*

mount³ n an animal on which one rides: *This old donkey is a good quiet mount for a child.*

moun·tain /'maʊntn/ n a very high hill, usu. of bare or snow-covered rock: *He looked down from the top of the mountain in the valley far below.|mountain goats|*(fig.) *She has a mountain of work to do.*

moun·tain·eer /ˌmaʊntn'ɪər/ n a person who climbs mountains as a sport or profession –**mountaineering** n [U]

moun·tain·ous /'maʊntn-əs/ *adj* full of or containing mountains: *mountainous country*

mourn /mɔrn, moʷrn/ *v* [I;T *for, over*] to feel and/or show grief, esp. for the death of someone: *The old woman still mourns for her son, 30 years after his death.|The whole nation mourned her death.*

mourn·er /'mɔrnər, 'moʷr-/ n a person who attends a funeral, esp. a relative or friend of the one who is dead

mourn·ful /'mɔrnfəl, 'moʷrn-/ *adj sometimes derog* sad; causing, feeling, or expressing sorrow –**mournfully** *adv* –**mournfulness** n [U]

mourn·ing /'mɔrnɪŋ, 'moʷr-/ n [U] (the expression of) grief, esp. for a death: *All the theaters were closed, as a sign of mourning for the dead President.*

mouse /maʊs/ n **mice** /maɪs/ a small furry animal with a long tail that lives in houses and in fields: *a field mouse|I think we've got mice in the kitchen.*

mousse /muʷs/ n [C;U] (a sweet dish made from) cream, eggs, and other substances mixed together and then frozen: *chocolate mousse*

mous·tache /'mʌstæʃ, mə'stæʃ/ n *esp. BrE* for MUSTACHE

mous·y /'maʊsiʸ, -ziʸ/ *adj* **-ier, -iest** **1** *often derog* (of hair) having a dull brownish-gray color **2** *derog* (of a person) unattractively plain and quiet; DRAB

mouth¹ /maʊθ/ n **mouths** /maʊðz/ **1** the opening on the face through which a person or animal may take food into the body and speak or make sounds **2** an opening, entrance, or way out: *the mouth of a cave|the mouth of a river* (=where it joins the sea) **3** **by word of mouth** by speaking and not by writing **4** **down in the mouth** not cheerful; in low spirits **5** **put words into someone's mouth: a** to tell someone what to say **b** *derog* to suggest or claim, falsely, that someone has said a particular thing **6** **take the words out of someone's mouth** to say something that someone else was going to say, before he/she has had time or a chance to speak **7** **-mouthed** /maʊðd, maʊθt/ *usu. derog.* having the stated way of speaking: *loud-mouthed*

mouth² /maʊð/ *v* [I;T] **1** to speak or say (something), esp. repeatedly without understanding or sincerity, or in a displeasing way:

He walked out of the room, mouthing curses. **2** to move the lips as if speaking but without making any sound

mouth·ful /'maʊθʊl/ *n* **1** [C] as much (food or drink) as fills the mouth: *I'm so full I couldn't eat another mouthful.* **2** [S] *infml, usu. humor* a big long word that one finds difficulty in saying or pronouncing: *Her name is quite a mouthful!*

mouth·or·gan /'maʊθ,ɔrgən/ *n* → HARMONICA

mouth·piece /'maʊθpiʸs/ *n* **1** the part of anything (such as a musical instrument, a telephone, etc.) that is held in or near the mouth **2** [*of*] *often derog* a person, newspaper, etc. that expresses the opinions of others: *This newspaper is the mouthpiece of the government.*

mouth·wash /'maʊθwɑʃ, -wɔʃ/ *n* [C;U] a liquid used in the mouth, for making it feel fresh, helping to cure infected parts, etc.

mouth·wa·ter·ing /'·ˌ····/ *adj* (of food) that makes one want to eat

mov·a·ble , moveable /'muʷvəbəl/ *adj* that can be moved; not fixed in one place or position: *toy soldiers with movable arms and legs* –see also IMMOVABLE

move¹ /muʷv/ *v* **moved, moving** **1** [I;T] to (cause to) change place or bodily position: *Please move your car. It's blocking the road.|Can you sit still without moving for 10 minutes?|He was trapped in the crashed car and could not move his legs.|The talks have been moved from London to Paris.|That student should be moved up to a higher class.* **2** [I] to be in movement; go, walk, run, etc., esp. in a particular way: *Don't get off the train while it's still moving.|The dancer moves very gracefully.|That car is really moving!* (=traveling very fast) **3** [I] (of work, events, etc.) to advance; get nearer to an end: *Work on the new building is moving along more quickly than was expected.* **4** [I] to change one's place of living: *Their present house is too small, so they've decided to move.* **5** [I] to lead one's life or pass one's time (esp. with or among people of a certain kind): *She lives in Paris and moves with a lot of writers and artists.* **6** [T +to-v/to] to cause (to act from) feelings of pity, sadness, anger, admiration, etc.: *The child's suffering moved his father to tears.|I was very moved by her story.* –see also MOVING, UNMOVED **7** [I;T +that/for] to put forward, at a meeting (a suggestion on which arguments for and against are heard, and a decision taken, esp. by voting): *I move that we support the introduction of this law.|We moved for an ADJOURNMENT of half an hour.*

move along *v adv* **1** [I] to move further towards the front or back: *The people standing in the bus moved along, to make room for others.* **2** [I;T (=move sbdy. along)] →MOVE on (2)

move around *v adv* [I; T = move sthg./sbdy. around] to (cause to) move continually; fail to keep still: *I can hear somebody moving around upstairs.|I can hear the neighbors moving their furniture around again.*

move away *v adv* [I] to go to a new home in a different area: *"Do the Rossi's still live here?" "No, they've moved away."*

move in *v adv* [I] to take possession of a new home: *We've bought the house, but we can't move in until next month.*

move off *v adv* [I] to leave; DEPART: *The guard blew his whistle, and the train moved off.*

move on *v adv* **1** [I to] to change (to something new): *I think we've talked enough about that subject; let's move on.* **2** [I;T (=move sbdy. on)] to (order to) go away to another place or position: *The man was annoying people, so the policeman moved him on.*

move over *v adv* [I] to change position in order to make room for someone or something else: *Move over and let your grandmother sit down.*

move² *n* **1** [S] an act of moving; movement: *If you make a move, I'll shoot.* **2** [C] an act of going to a new home, office, etc. **3** [C] (in games such as CHESS) an act of taking a piece from one square and putting it on another **4** [C] a (step in a) course of action towards a particular result: *New moves to settle the disagreement between the workers and employers have ended in failure.* **5 get a move on** *infml* (*often in commands*) to hurry up

move·ment /'muʷvmənt/ *n* **1** [C;U] (an act of) moving or of being moved;(example of) activity: *Movement can be painful when you've hurt your back.|the movement of goods by road|I noticed a sudden movement behind the curtain.|The police are watching this man's movements* (=all his activities) *very carefully.* **2** [C] a group of people who make united efforts for a particular purpose: *The anti-war movement was against the war in Vietnam.* **3** [C] a general feeling, way of thinking, acting, etc. towards something new, not directed by any particular person or group: *The movement towards greater freedom for women still has a long way to go.* **4** [C] a main division of a musical work, esp. of a SYMPHONY **5** [C] the moving parts of a piece of machinery, esp. a clock or watch

mov·ie /'muʷviʸ/ *n esp. AmE* a film; MOTION PICTURE

mov·ies /'muʷviʸz/ *esp. AmE‖***pictures** *BrE–* *n* [*the* P] **1** a showing of a MOTION PICTURE: *Let's go to the movies tonight.* **2** the MOTION PICTURE industry: *He's worked in the movies all his life.* **3** the art of making MOTION PICTURES: *Are movies replacing theater as an art form?* – see also CINEMA

movie star /'·· ˌ·/ *AmE‖*also **film star** *BrE– n* a well-known movie actor or actress: *a famous movie star of the 30's*

movie the·a·ter /'·· ˌ···/ also **theater** *AmE‖***cinema** *BrE– n* a theater in which movies are shown

mov·ing /'muʷvɪŋ/ *adj* **1** causing strong feelings, esp. of pity: *The book was so moving that she almost wept.* –see also MOVE¹ (6) **2** [A no comp.] that moves; not fixed: *Oil the moving parts of this machine regularly.* **–movingly** *adv*

moving van /'·· ,·/ *AmE*‖**removal van** *BrE*– *n* a large covered vehicle (VAN) used for moving furniture

mow /mow/ *v* **mowed, mown** /mown/ *or* **mowed, mowing** [I;T] to cut (grass, corn, etc.) with a MOWER or a SCYTHE
mow sbdy.↔**down** *v adv* [T] to kill, destroy, or knock down, esp. in great numbers: *The soldiers were mown down by fire from the enemy's guns.*

mow·er /'mowər/ *n* a machine for MOWING, esp. (a **lawnmower**) one for cutting grass

mpg *written abbrev. said as:* miles per GALLON (esp. of gasoline): *a car that gets 35 mpg*

mph *written abbrev. said as:* miles per hour: *driving along at 60 mph*

Mr. /'mɪstər/ *n* [A] **1** a title for a man who has no other title: *Mr. Smith* |*Mr. John Smith* –compare MESSRS. **2** a title used when addressing certain men in official positions: *Mr. Chairman* |(in the US) *Mr. President*

Mrs. /'mɪsɪz/ *n* [A] a title for a married woman: *Mrs. Jones* |*Mrs. Sarah Jones* –compare MISS, Ms.

Ms. /mɪz/ *n* [A] a title for a woman who does not wish to call herself either "Mrs." or "Miss"

MS[1] *pl* **MSS** *written abbrev. said as:* MANUSCRIPT

MS[2] *written abbrev. said as:* Mississippi /ˌmɪsəˈsɪpiy/ (a state in the US)

M.S. *AmE*‖**M.Sc.**– *abbrev. for:* Master of Science; (a title for someone who has) a university degree which can be taken one or two years after a B.S.: *Jill Smith, M.S.*|*an M.S.*

Mt. *written abbrev. said as:* MOUNT[1]: *Mt. Everest*

MT *written abbrev. said as:* Montana /man'tænə/ (a state in the US)

much[1] /mʌtʃ/ *adv* **more** /mɔr, mowr/, **most** /mowst/ **1** by a great degree: *much fatter than I am*|*much too busy*|*I'd much rather not.*|*Thank you very much.* **2** nearly; in most ways: *much the same as usual*
USAGE Use **much** with adjectives made from the PASSIVE[1] (2) form of verbs, in the same way as **very** is used with ordinary adjectives: *This picture is* **much** *admired/is* **very** *beautiful.*

much[2] *determiner, pron, n* **more, most** [U] (*used in questions and* NEGATIVES[2] *and after* so *and* too, *but not usu. in simple statements*) a great amount: *not very much time*|*far too much work*|*How much does it cost?*|*The movie has just started–we haven't missed very much.*|(*fml*) *I have much pleasure in giving you this prize.* –see Study Notes on page 363 **2 as much again** twice as much **3 I thought as much** I expected that (esp. something bad): *So they found out he's been cheating. I thought as much.* **4 make much of** to treat as important **5 much as** although: *Much as I want to, I can't come.* **6 not much of a** not a very good: *It's not much of a day for a walk.* **7 not up to much** *infml* not busy: *She's not up to much since she retired.* **8 so much for** that is the end of: *It's raining–so much for my idea of taking a walk.* **9 this/that much** the parti-

cular amount or words: *I'll say this much, he's a good worker (although I don't like him personally).* **10 too much for** too hard for: *Climbing the stairs is too much for her now.*

muck /mʌk/ *n* [U] *infml* **1** dirt **2** waste matter dropped from animals' bodies, esp. as used for spreading on the land; MANURE –**mucky** *adj* **-ier, -iest**

mu·cus /'myuwkəs/ *n* [U] a slippery liquid produced in certain parts of the body, esp. the nose

mud /mʌd/ *n* [U] **1** very wet earth in a sticky mass **2 one's name is mud** one is spoken badly of after causing trouble

mud·dle[1] /'mʌdl/ *n* [*usu. sing*] a state of confusion and disorder: *I was in such a muddle that I didn't know what day it was.*

muddle[2] *v* **-dled, -dling** [T *up*] **1** to put into disorder: *You're muddling up the papers.* **2** to confuse: *She gave me so many different instructions that I got muddled (up).*
muddle along *v adv* [I] to continue in a confused manner, without a plan
muddle through *v adv* [I] to have successful results without the best methods of reaching them: *The government is in trouble, but I expect the country will muddle through.*

mud·dy[1] /'mʌdiy/ *adj* **-dier, -diest** covered with or containing mud: *the muddy waters of the river*|*Take off those muddy boots.*

muddy[2] *v* **-died, -dying** [T] to make dirty with mud: *Your dog's muddying the kitchen floor.*

mud·guard /'mʌdgɑrd/ *n AmE* a piece of rubber or other heavy material hanging behind the wheels of vehicles, esp. TRUCKs, to keep the mud from flying up –compare FENDER

mud·sling·er /'mʌdˌslɪŋər/ *n* a person who says damaging things about another

muf·fin /'mʌfɪn/ *n AmE* a type of small ROLL[1] (2) (which may be eaten with butter)

muf·fle /'mʌfəl/ *v* **-fled, -fling** [T *usu. pass.*] to make (a sound) less easily heard, esp. with a material: *muffled voices coming from the next room*

muf·fler /'mʌflər/ *n* **1** a SCARF worn to keep one's neck warm **2** *AmE*‖**silencer** *BrE*– an apparatus for reducing the noise of a gasoline engine which fits into the pipe where burned gases come out

mug[1] /mʌg/ *n* **1** (the contents of) a kind of cup with a flat bottom, straight sides, and handle, but without a SAUCER: *a mug of coffee* –see illustration on page 379 **2** *derog. infml* the face of a person: *Where have I seen that mug before?*

mug[2] *v* **-gg-** [T] to rob with violence, esp. on a dark street –**mugger** *n* –**mugging** *n* [C;U]

mug·gy /'mʌgiy/ *adj* **-gier, -giest** (of weather) unpleasantly warm and not dry (HUMID) –**mugginess** *n* [U]

Mu·ham·mad·an /muˈhæmədən, mow-/ *adj,n* →MUSLIM

mu·lat·to /məˈlætow, -ˈlɑ-, myuw-/ *n* **-tos, -toes** a person with one parent of the black race and one of the white race

mul·ber·ry /'mʌlˌbɛriy, -bəriy/ *n* **-ries** (a tree with) a dark purple fruit which can be eaten

mulch /mʌltʃ/ *n* [S;U] a covering of material,

often made from decaying plants, which is put over the soil and over the roots of plants to protect and improve them

mule /myuʷl/ n the animal which is the young of a donkey and a horse

mull /mʌl/ v [T] to heat (wine or beer) with sugar, SPICES, and other things: *mulled wine* –compare

mull sthg.↔ **over** v adv; prep [T] to think over; consider for a time: *I haven't decided what to do; I'm mulling it over.*

mul·lah /'mʌlə, 'mʊlə/ n a Muslim teacher of law and religion

mul·ti·far·i·ous /ˌmʌltə'fɛəriʲəs/ adj [no comp.] of many different types: *multifarious interests* –**multifariously** adv

mul·ti·lat·er·al /ˌmʌltɪ'lætərəl/ adj concerning or including more than two (usu. political) groups of people: *a multilateral agreement on world oil prices* –compare BILATERAL, UNILATERAL –**multilaterally** adv

mul·ti·ple¹ /'mʌltəpəl/ adj [no comp.] including many different parts, types, etc.: *The driver of the crashed car received multiple injuries.* (INJURY)

multiple² n [of] a number which contains a smaller number an exact number of times: *3×4=12; so 12 is a multiple of 3.*

mul·ti·pli·ca·tion /ˌmʌltəplə'keʲʃən/ n [U] the method of combining two numbers by adding one of them to itself as many times as the other states: *2×4=8 is an example of multiplication.*

mul·ti·plic·i·ty /ˌmʌltə'plɪsəṭiʲ/ n [S] a large number or great variety: *a multiplicity of ideas*

mul·ti·ply /'mʌltəˌplaɪ/ v -**plied, -plying** [I;T] **1** [by] to combine by MULTIPLICATION: *to multiply 2 by 3|2 multiplied by 3 (2×3)=2+2+2.|You added when you should have multiplied.* –compare DIVIDE (3) **2** to increase: *to multiply one's chances of success|When animals have more food, they generally multiply* (=breed) *faster.*

mul·ti·ra·cial /ˌmʌltɪ'reʲʃəl◂/ adj consisting of or involving several races of people

mul·ti·sto·ry /ˌmʌltɪ'stɔriʲ◂, -'stoʷriʲ◂/ adj [A] (of a building) having several levels or floors: *a multistory office building*

mul·ti·tude /'mʌltəˌtuʷd, -ˌtyuʷd/ n **1** fml a large number: *A multitude of thoughts filled her mind.* **2** old use & bibl a large crowd

mum¹ /mʌm/ n BrE for MOM

mum² n AmE infml for CHRYSANTHEMUM

mum·ble /'mʌmbəl/ v -**bled, -bling** [I;T +that] to speak (words) unclearly: *The old woman mumbled a prayer.|I wish you wouldn't mumble–I can't hear what you're saying.*

mum·mi·fy /'mʌməˌfaɪ/ v -**fied, -fying** [T] to preserve (a dead body) as a MUMMY²

mum·my¹ /'mʌmiʲ/ n -**mies** BrE for MOMMY

mummy² n a dead body preserved from decay by treatment with special substances

mumps /mʌmps/ n [the U] an infectious illness in which the GLANDS (=organs which send substances into the bloodstream) swell, particularly those around the neck and mouth

munch /mʌntʃ/ v [I;T] to eat (something)

with a strong movement of the jaw, esp. making a noise: *munching an apple*

mun·dane /mʌn'deʲn/ adj usu. derog ordinary, with nothing exciting or unusual in it; uninteresting: *a mundane life*

mu·nic·i·pal /myuʷ'nɪsəpəl/ adj concerning (the parts of) a town, city, etc., under its own government: *municipal buildings|the municipal council* –**municipally** adv

mu·nic·i·pal·i·ty /myuʷˌnɪsə'pæləṭiʲ/ n -**ties** a town, city, or other small area having its own government for local affairs

mu·nif·i·cence /myuʷ'nɪfəsəns/ n [U] fml generosity –**munificent** adj

mu·ni·tions /myuʷ'nɪʃənz/ n [P] large arms for war, such as bombs, guns, etc.

mu·ral /'myuʊrəl/ n a painting which is painted on a wall

mur·der¹ /'mɜrdər/ n **1** [C;U] the crime of killing a human being unlawfully: *She was found guilty of murder.|Police are still looking for the murder weapon.* –compare MANSLAUGHTER **2** [U] infml a very difficult or tiring experience: *At last I repaired the clock, but it was murder getting the pieces back in.*

murder² v [T] **1** to kill unlawfully, and on purpose: *a murdered man* –see KILL (USAGE) **2** to ruin (language, music, etc.) by using or performing it badly –**murderer** n

mur·der·ous /'mɜrdərəs/ adj of, like, or suggesting murder: *murderous intentions|a murderous expression on his face* –**murderously** adv

murk·y /'mɜrkiʲ/ adj -**ier, -iest** dark and unpleasant: *a murky night|*(fig.) *a criminal with a murky past*

mur·mur¹ /'mɜrmər/ n **1** a soft low sound: *the murmur of the stream* **2** without a murmur without complaint: *The children went to bed without a murmur.*

murmur² v [I;T +that] to make a soft sound, esp. to speak or say in a quiet voice: *a child murmuring in her sleep|As she delivered her speech, the crowd murmured its approval.*

mus·cle /'mʌsəl/ n **1** [C;U] (one of) the pieces of elastic material in the body which can tighten to produce movement, esp. bending of the joints: *to develop one's arm muscles by playing tennis* **2** [U] strength: *the military muscle of the big world powers* **3** not move a muscle to stay quite still

muscle in v adv -**cled, -cling** [I on] infml to force one's way into (esp.) a group activity, usu. so as to gain a share in what is produced

mus·cu·lar /'mʌskyələr/ adj **1** of, concerning, or done by muscles: *a muscular disease* **2** having big muscles; strong-looking: *a muscular body|He's big and muscular.*

muse /myuʷz/ v **mused, musing** [I over, (up)on] to think deeply, forgetting about the world around one: *She sat musing for hours.*

mu·se·um /myuʷ'ziʲəm/ n a building where objects are kept and usu. shown to the public because of their scientific, historical, or artistic interest: *the Museum of Modern Art*

mush /mʌʃ/ n [U] **1** a soft mass of half-liquid, half-solid material, esp. food **2** AmE boiled corn meal –**mushy** adj -**ier, -iest**: *mushy potatoes|mushy PEAS*

mush·room¹ /'mʌʃruʷm, -rʊm/ *n* any of several types of plant (FUNGUS), some of which can be eaten, which grow and develop very quickly

mushroom² *v* [I] to grow and develop fast: *Since the opening of the first store new branches have mushroomed all over the country.*

mu·sic /'myuʷzɪk/ *n* [U] **1** the arrangement of sounds in pleasant patterns and tunes: *That's a beautiful piece of music.|What's your favorite kind of music?* **2** the art of doing this: *to study music|a music student* **3** a written or printed set of notes: *a sheet of music|I've lost my music.* **4 face the music** to admit to blame, responsibility, etc., and accept the results, esp. punishment or difficulty

mu·si·cal¹ /'myuʷzɪkəl/ *adj* **1** [A] of, like, or producing music: *musical instruments|a rather musical way of speaking* **2** skilled in and/or fond of music: *a very musical child*

musical² *n* a play or film with songs and often dances

mu·si·cian /myuʷ'zɪʃən/ *n* a person who performs on a musical instrument, or who writes music

musk /mʌsk/ *n* [U] a strong-smelling substance used in making PERFUMEs **−musky** *adj* **-ier, -iest** : *a musky smell*

mus·ket /'mʌskɪt/ *n* an early type of gun

mus·ket·eer /,mʌskə'tɪər/ *n* a soldier who was armed with a MUSKET

Mus·lim /'mʌzləm, 'mʊz-, 'mʊs-/ also **Moslem, Mohammedan, Muhammadan** *n,adj* (a person) of the religion started by Mohammed −see also ISLAM

mus·lin /'mʌzlɪn/ *n* [U] a very fine thin cotton material, used (esp.formerly) for light dresses

muss /mʌs/ *v* [T *up*] *infml esp. AmE* to disorder or make a MESS of (esp. the hair)

mus·sel /'mʌsəl/ *n* a small sea animal (a MOLLUSK) living inside a black shell, whose soft body can be eaten as food

must¹ /məst; strong mʌst/ *v negative contraction* **mustn't** /'mʌsənt/ [I + *to*-v] **1** (past usu. **had to**) (used to show what it is necessary for one to do, what one ought to do, or what one is forced to do): *I must leave at six today.* (but *I had to leave at six yesterday.*) |*You mustn't tell anybody about this–it's a secret.|You must go and see that new movie; you'll really enjoy it.|"Dogs must be kept on a* LEASH" (notice) **2** (past **must have**) to be likely or certain to: *You must feel tired after your long walk.|There's nobody here – they must have all gone home.|You must be* (=I suppose that you are) *the new English teacher.* −see Study Notes on page 434

USAGE 1 **Must** is used in two ways, expressing (1) what is necessary, and (2) what is certain or probable. For sense (1) the past is usually **had to**: *I had to get up early yesterday;* and the NEGATIVE² is either **must not** (=it is forbidden) or **don't have to**: *You must not smoke in this part of the train.|You don't have to arrive at the airport until 10:30.* For sense (2) the past is **must have,** and the NEGA-

TIVE² is **can't** (present) and **can't have** (past): *They must have gotten lost.* (=I'm sure they have).|*They can't have gotten lost* (=I'm sure they haven't) **2 Ought to** and **should** can be used as less strong forms of **must** in both these senses. Compare: *The doctor told me I must stop smoking.|My friends told me I ought to/should stop smoking.|The game must have finished by now.* (=I'm sure it has).|*The game ought to/should have finished by now.* (=I expect it probably has). **3** Using **must** to express "what is necessary" is considered very strong in *AmE.* It can be used when the speaker has power over the person spoken to, as a parent or teacher to a child, or a doctor to a patient. It is also used on official papers and signs. In most other cases, it is more polite to use **should, ought to,** or **have to.**

must² /mʌst/ *n* [S] something which it is necessary or very important to have or experience: *Warm clothes are a must in the mountains.*

mus·tache *AmE*‖also **moustache** *esp. BrE* /'mʌstæʃ, mə'stæʃ/ *n* hair growing on the upper lip

mus·tang /'mʌstæŋ/ *n* a small American horse which lives wild on the plains

mus·tard /'mʌstərd/ *n* [U] (a yellow-flowered plant whose seeds produce) a hot-tasting powder which is mixed with water and eaten in small quantities with meat and other food

mus·ter /'mʌstər/ *v* [I;T] to gather or collect: *to muster one's courage|The* TROOPS *mustered on the hill.*

must·n't /'mʌsənt/ *v* short for must not: *You mustn't talk in class.*

must·y /'mʌstiʸ/ *adj* **-ier, -iest** with an unpleasant smell as if old: *musty old books* **−mustiness** *n* [U]

mu·ta·tion /myuʷ'teʸʃən/ *n* [C;U] (an example of) the action of change in the cells of a living thing producing a new quality in the material or parts of the body

mute¹ /myuʷt/ *adj* silent; without speech **−mutely** *adv*

mute² *n* a person who cannot speak

mut·ed /'myuʷtɪd/ *adj* (of a sound or a color) made softer than is usual

mu·ti·late /'myuʷtl,eʸt/ *v* **-lated, -lating** [T] to damage by removing a part of: *She was mutilated in the accident and now has only one leg.|The police found a badly mutilated body.* **−mutilation** /,myuʷtl'eʸʃən/ *n* [C;U]

mu·ti·neer /,myuʷtn'ɪər/ *n* a person who takes part in a MUTINY

mu·ti·nous /'myuʷtn-əs/ *adj* taking part in a MUTINY: (fig.) *The mutinous children refused to obey their teacher.* **−mutinously** *adv*

mu·ti·ny¹ /'myuʷtn-iʸ/ *n* **-nies** [C;U] (an example of) the act of taking power from the person in charge, esp. from a captain on a ship

mutiny² *v* **-nied, -nying** [I] to take part in a MUTINY

mutt /mʌt/ *n AmE infml* a dog of no particular breed whose parents were of mixed or different breeds

mut·ter /'mʌtər/ v [I;T +*that*] to speak (usu. angry or complaining words) in a low voice, not easily heard: *He muttered a threat.|She's muttering to herself.* –**mutter** n [S]: *to speak in a mutter*

mut·ton /'mʌtn/ n [U] the meat from a sheep –see MEAT (USAGE)

mu·tu·al /'myuᵂtʃuᵂəl/ adj [*no comp.*] **1** equally so, one towards the other: *Stalin and Trotsky were mutual enemies.|their mutual dislike* (=she dislikes him and he dislikes her) **2** equally shared by each one: *mutual interests|our mutual friend* –**mutually** adv

mutual fund /,··· '·/ *AmE*‖**unit trust** *BrE*– n a company formed to control INVESTMENTs of many different types

muz·zle¹ /'mʌzəl/ n **1** the front part of an animal's face, with the nose and mouth **2** the front end of a gun barrel **3** a covering around an animal's mouth, to prevent it from biting

muzzle² v **-zled, -zling** [T] to put a MUZZLE¹ (3) on: (fig.) *Those who know the truth have been muzzled* (=kept silent) *by those in power.*

my /maɪ/ determiner (POSSESSIVE *form of* I) **1** of the person who is speaking: *my car|my mother* **2** (used as a cry of surprise or pleasure): *My, my! What a clever boy you are!*

my·op·ic /maɪ'ɑpɪk, -'oᵂ-/ adj unable to see clearly objects which are not close; NEARSIGHTED

myr·i·ad /'mɪriᵞəd/ adj,n lit (of) a great and varied number

my·self /maɪ'sɛlf/ pron **1** (used as the object of a verb, or after a PREPOSITION, when the person who is speaking does the action and is the object of the action): *I hurt myself.|I'm feeling pleased with myself.|I can take care of myself.*

mys·te·ri·ous /mɪ'stɪəriᵞəs/ adj not easily understood; full of mystery: *the mysterious disappearance of my brother|They're being very mysterious* (=not telling anyone) *about their vacation plans.* –**mysteriously** adv –**mysteriousness** n [U]

mys·ter·y /'mɪstəriᵞ/ n **-ies 1** [C] something which cannot be explained or understood: *Her death is a mystery.* **2** [U] a strange secret nature or quality: *stories full of mystery*

mys·tic /'mɪstɪk/ n a person who practices MYSTICISM

mys·ti·cal /'mɪstɪkəl/ also **mystic** adj **1** concerning MYSTICISM **2** of hidden religious power and importance –**mystically** adv

mys·ti·cism /'mɪstə,sɪzəm/ n [U] the attempt to gain, or practice of gaining, a knowledge of real truth and union with God by prayer and MEDITATION

mys·ti·fy /'mɪstə,faɪ/ v **-fied, -fying** [T] to make (someone) wonder; completely BEWILDER: *I'm completely mystified about what happened.* –**mystification** /,mɪstəfə'keᵞʃən/ n [C;U]

mys·tique /mɪ'stiᵞk/ n [*usu. sing.*] a feeling of mystery or separateness which surrounds certain activities, professions, etc.: *the mystique of the film industry*

myth /mɪθ/ n **1** [C] an ancient story, usu. containing religious or magical ideas, which may explain natural or historical events **2** [U] such stories generally: *an idea common in myth* **3** [C +*that*] a false story or idea, which may be widely believed: *the myth that men are better drivers than women*

myth·i·cal /'mɪθɪkəl/ adj [*no comp.*] **1** of or in a MYTH (1) **2** not real; imagined or invented

my·thol·o·gy /mɪ'θɑlədʒiᵞ/ n **-gies** [C;U] (a system of beliefs contained in) MYTHs (1) –**mythological** /,mɪθə'lɑdʒɪkəl/ adj

N, n

N, n /ɛn/ **N's, n's** *or* **Ns, ns** the 14th letter of the English alphabet

n written abbrev. for: **1** noun **2** note

N written abbrev. for: North(ern)

nab /næb/ v **-bb-** [T] infml to seize (esp. as a thief): *He was nabbed before he could escape with the money.*

nag¹ /næg/ v **-gg-** [I;T +*to-v/at*] **1** to find fault with; try to persuade (someone) by continuous complaining: *I wish you'd stop nagging. I'm doing my best.|He's been nagging (at) me all week to mend his shirt.* **2** to worry or annoy continuously: *a nagging headache*

nag sbdy. **into** sthg. v prep [T +*v-ing*] to cause to do (something) by NAGging: *The*

children have nagged me into taking them to the movies.

nag² n **1** derog a person who NAGS¹: *I don't like working with him because he such a nag.* **2** a horse that is old or in bad condition

nail¹ /neᵞl/ n **1** a thin pointed piece of metal for hammering into pieces of wood, usu. to fasten them together –compare BOLT¹ (1), SCREW¹ (1) **2** a→ FINGERNAIL **b** rare→ TOENAIL **3** hard as nails infml without any tender feelings **4** hit the nail on the head infml to do or say something exactly right

nail² v [T, on] to fasten (as) with a nail or nails: *She nailed a sign to/on the door.*

nail sthg.↔**down** v adv [T] **1** to fasten down, with a nail or nails: *Would you nail down that loose board in the floor?* **2** [*to*] to force (someone) to tell plans or wishes clearly: *Before they repair the car, nail them down to a price.* (=make them tell you how much it will cost)|*I can never nail her down (to anything).*

nail·brush /ˈneɪlbrʌʃ/ n a small stiff brush for cleaning hands, and esp. FINGERNAILS –see illustration on page 51

nail file /ˈ· ·/ n a small instrument with a rough surface for shaping FINGERNAILS

nail pol·ish /ˈ· ˌ··/ AmE‖**nail varnish** BrE /ˈ·ˌ··/– n [U] colored or transparent liquid which dries to give a hard shiny surface, used esp. by women on their FINGERNAILS

na·ive, naïve /nɑˈiˠv/ adj having or showing no experience (as of social rules or behavior), esp. because one is young: The youngest boy was laughed at for his naive remarks.|It's naive (of you) to believe he'll do what he says. –**naively, naïvely** adv –**naiveté, naïveté** /ˌnaiˠvˈteˠ, naˈiˠvte/ n [U] –**naivety, naïvety** /naˈiˠvtiˠ,naˈiˠvətiˠ/ n [U]

na·ked /ˈneɪkɪd/ adj 1 (of (a part of) a person's body) not covered by clothes: He was naked to the waist. (=wore nothing above his waist)|(fig.) a naked window (=with no curtain or other covering over it) 2 **with the naked eye** without any instrument to help one see: Bacteria are too small to see with the naked eye. –**nakedly** adv –**nakedness** n [U]

name¹ /neɪm/ n 1 [C] the word(s) that someone or something is called or known by: Her name is Mary Wilson. Her first name is Mary.|What's the name of the river that flows through Boston?|Do you know a boy **by the name of** (=called) David?|I like to buy **name-brand** (=well-known) foods. 2 [S] fame; the opinion others have of one: Its slow service gave the restaurant a bad name.|She **made a name for herself/made her name** (=became famous) as a painter. 3 to **one's name** infml (esp. of money) as one's property: He hasn't got a penny to his name.

name² v named, naming [T] 1 to give a name to: They named their baby son John. (=gave him the name John)|She was named after/for (=given the same name as) her mother. 2 to say what the name of (someone or something) is: Can you name this plant? 3 to choose or appoint: The President named him (as) Secretary of State.|"How much will you sell me this for?" "Name your own price."

name·drop /ˈneɪmdrɑp/ v **-pp-** [I] derog & infml to mention famous people's names to make it seem that one knows them or their work well: He doesn't really know any famous scientists. He's just namedropping. –**namedropper** n –**namedropping** n [U]

name·less /ˈneɪmlɪs/ adj 1 not known by name; ANONYMOUS: the work of a nameless 13th century poet|a certain person who must/shall be nameless (=whose name I will not tell) 2 too terrible to describe or name: guilty of nameless crimes

name·ly /ˈneɪmliˠ/ adv (and) that is (to say): Only one person can do the job, namely you.

name·sake /ˈneɪmseˠk/ n one of two or more people with the same name: I often get letters that are addressed to my namesake John Smith down the street.

nan·ny /ˈnæniˠ/ n **-nies** esp. BrE (esp. in rich families) a woman employed to take care of children

nanny goat /ˈ·· ˌ·/ n (used esp. by or to children) a female goat –compare BILLY GOAT

nap¹ /næp/ n a short sleep, esp. during the day: Father always takes/has a nap in the afternoon.

nap² v **catch someone napping** infml to find, or take advantage of, someone off guard or not doing his/her duty

na·palm /ˈneˠpɑm/ n [U] a jelly made from gasoline, which burns fiercely and is used in bombs

nape /neˠp/ n [S] the back (of the neck): the nape of the neck

nap·kin /ˈnæpkɪn/ n 1 a piece of cloth or paper used for protecting one's clothes and for cleaning one's hands and lips during a meal –see illustration on page 581 2 BrE fml for NAPPY

nap·py /ˈnæpiˠ/ n **-pies** BrE for DIAPER

nar·cis·sus /nɑrˈsɪsəs/ n **-sus** or **-suses** or **-si** /ˌsaɪ/ a white or yellow spring flower, such as the DAFFODIL

nar·cot·ic /nɑrˈkɑtɪk/ n [often pl.] a drug which in small amounts causes sleep or takes away pain, and in large amounts is harmful and habit-forming: He was sent to prison on a narcotics charge. (=an offense concerning selling or using these drugs) –**narcotic** adj

nar·rate /ˈnæreˠt, næˈreˠt/ v **-rated, -rating** [T] fml to tell (a story); describe (an event or events) in order: Shall I narrate a strange experience of mine? –**narration** /næˈreˠʃən/ n [C;U] –**narrator** /ˈnæˌreˠtər, næˈreˠ-, ˈnærətər/ n

nar·ra·tive /ˈnærətɪv/ n [C;U] (the act or practice of telling) a story: a narrative of last week's events –**narrative** adj [no comp.]: a narrative poem

nar·row /ˈnæroˠ/ adj 1 small from one side to the other, esp. in comparison with length or with what is usual: They live in a narrow little street just off the main road.|The gate is too narrow for a car; we'll have to walk through. –compare BROAD, WIDE 2 limited; RESTRICTED (3): The secret is known only to a narrow group of people.|She has very narrow ideas about religion. 3 only just successful: to win by a narrow MAJORITY (2)|a narrow escape –compare CLOSE⁴ (6); see THIN (USAGE) –**narrowness** n [U]

narrow² v [I;T] to (cause to) decrease in width: The river narrows at this point. –compare BROADEN, WIDEN

nar·row·ly /ˈnæroˠliˠ/ adv hardly; only just: One car went too fast and narrowly missed hitting another car.

narrow-mind·ed /ˌ·· ˈ··◂/ adj derog unwilling to respect the opinions (or actions) of others when different from one's own; PREJUDICED: The narrow-minded articles in this newspaper make me angry. –opposite **broad-minded** –**narrowmindedness** n [U]

na·sal /ˈneˠzəl/ adj of or related to the nose: to breathe through the nasal passage|His nasal (=making sounds through the nose) voice is hard to listen to. –**nasally** adv

nas·ty /ˈnæstiˠ/ adj **-tier, -tiest** 1 unpleasant in manner; angry or threatening: Who's that nasty old woman?|He turned **nasty**

(=started to threaten me) *when I said I couldn't pay him.* **2** very ugly or unpleasant to see, taste, smell, etc.: *cheap and nasty furniture* **3** painful; severe; dangerous: *a nasty accident with one person killed* |*a nasty cut on the head* **4** morally bad or improper; OBSCENE: *You've got a nasty mind.* **–nastily** *adv* **–nastiness** *n* [U]

na·tion /'neʸʃən/ *n* **1** a large group of people living in one area and usu. having an independent government: *The President spoke on radio to the nation.* –compare COUNTRY¹ (1) **2** a large group of people with the same race and language: *the American Indian nations in the western United States* –see RACE³ (USAGE)

na·tion·al¹ /'næʃənəl/ *adj* of, concerning, or belonging to a nation: *a national newspaper* (=one read everywhere in the country)| *a national holiday* (=a holiday everywhere in the country)|*The national news comes after the international news.*|*The National Theater is supported by the government.* **–nationally** *adv*

national² *n* a person, esp. someone abroad, who belongs to another, usu. stated, country: *American nationals in England* –compare CITIZEN, ALIEN²

national an·them /ˌ··· '··/ *n* the official song of a nation, to be sung or played on certain formal occasions

na·tion·al·ism /'næʃənəlˌɪzəm/ *n* [U] **1** love of and pride in a country shown by its people **2** desire by a racial group (nation) to form an independent country

na·tion·al·ist /'næʃənəlɪst/ *adj,n* (a person) believing in NATIONALISM (2): *a Basque nationalist*|*the nationalist party in Quebec*

na·tion·al·is·tic /ˌnæʃənəl'ɪstɪk/ *adj* often *derog* of or showing (too) great love of one's country: *a nationalistic election speech* **–nationalistically** *adv*

na·tion·al·i·ty /ˌnæʃə'næləṭiʸ/ *n* **-ties** [C;U] membership in a particular nation by a person: *She lives in France but has British nationality.*|*people of many different nationalities*

na·tion·al·ize ‖also **-ise** *BrE* /'næʃənəlˌaɪz/ *v* **-ized, -izing** [T] (of a central government) to buy or take control of (a business, industry, etc.) for the state: *Some people think that the government should nationalize the medical industry.* **–nationalization** /ˌnæʃənələ'zeʸʃən/ *n* [U]

national park /ˌ··· '·/ *n* an area of land, usu. large, which is kept in its natural state by the government for people to visit

national serv·ice /ˌ··· '··/ *n BrE* for DRAFT¹ (3)

na·tion·wide /ˌneʸʃən'waɪd◂/ *adj* (used esp. in newspapers, on the radio, etc.) happening, existing, etc., over a whole country; NATIONAL¹: *a nationwide broadcast* (=heard

---

SPELLING NOTE
Words with the sound /n/ may be spelled **kn-**, like **know**, or **pn-**, like **pneumonia**.

---

everywhere in the country)

na·tive¹ /'neʸtɪv/ *adj* **1** [A] belonging to or being the place of one's birth: *her native language*|*a native New Yorker* **2** [A] (of a person) belonging to a country from birth: *native speakers of English* (=those who learn English as their first language) **3** [*to*] growing, living, produced, found, etc., in a place: *a plant native to the eastern US* **4** belonging to someone from birth; not learned; INNATE: *native ability/intelligence*

native² *n* **1** someone who was born (in a place): *a native of California* **2** *often derog and becoming rare* (esp. used by Europeans of non-Europeans) one of the original people living in a place: *The government of the island treated the natives badly.*|*a native village*

Native A·mer·i·can /ˌ·· ·'···/ *n* → INDIAN (1)

Na·tiv·i·ty /nə'tɪvəṭiʸ/ *n* the birth of Christ

NATO /'neʸtoʷ/ *n abbrev. for:* North Atlantic Treaty Organization; a group of countries (including the US and Britain) which give military help to each other

nat·ty /'næṭiʸ/ *adj* **-tier, -tiest** *infml* neat in appearance: *a very natty dresser* (=a person who dresses in a neat, fashionable style) **–nattily** *adv*

nat·u·ral¹ /'nætʃərəl/ *adj* **1** of, concerning, or being what exists or happens ordinarily in the world, esp. not caused, made, or controlled by people: *the natural mineral wealth of a country*|*death from natural causes*| *natural foods* –compare MAN-MADE, ARTIFICIAL **2** usual; ordinary: *It's natural to feel nervous when you go to a new school.* **3** not looking or sounding different from usual; UNAFFECTED: *Try to look natural for your photograph.* **4** [A *to*] belonging to someone from birth; not learned: *natural charm*|*a natural musician* (=with natural musical ability) –see also UNNATURAL, SUPERNATURAL **–naturalness** *n* [U]

natural² *n* [*usu. sing.*] *infml* someone or something well suited (to a job, part in a play, etc.) or certain to succeed: *As an actor, he's a natural.*

natural gas /ˌ··· '·/ *n* [U] gas which is taken from under the earth or sea and mainly burned for cooking and heating

natural his·to·ry /ˌ··· '···/ *n* [U] the study of plants, animals, and rocks

nat·u·ral·ist /'nætʃərəlɪst/ *n* a person who studies plants or animals

nat·u·ral·ize ‖also **-ise** *BrE* /'nætʃərəˌlaɪz/ *v* **-ized, -izing** [T] to make (a person born elsewhere) a citizen of a country: *He was naturalized after living in the US for five years.* **–naturalization** /ˌnætʃərələ'zeʸʃən/ *n* [U]

nat·u·ral·ly /'nætʃərəliʸ/ *adv* **1** according to the nature of someone or something: *Her cheeks are naturally red.* **2** without trying to look or sound different from usual: *Speak naturally when talking on the telephone.* **3** of course; as one could have expected: *"Did you win the game?" "Naturally."*|*Naturally you will be tired after your long walk.* **4** **come naturally to** also **come natural to** *infml* –to be easy or be easily learned by (someone): *She's a good player; the game comes naturally to her.*

natural re·sourc·es /ˌ··· ˈ···/ *n* [P] the land, forests, mineral wealth, etc., that a country possesses

natural sci·ence /ˌ··· ˈ··/ *n* [C;U] BIOLOGY, chemistry, and PHYSICS –compare SOCIAL SCIENCE

natural se·lec·tion /ˌ··· ·ˈ··/ *n* [U] *tech* the course of events by which only the plants and animals best suited to the conditions around them continue to live

na·ture /ˈneʸtʃər/ *n* **1** [U] everything that exists in the world independently of human beings, such as earth and rocks, the weather, and plants and animals: *They stopped to admire the beauties of nature.* (=scenery)|*Trying to grow crops on this bad land is a struggle against nature.* **2** [C;U] the qualities which make someone different from others; character:*She has a generous nature/is generous* **by nature.***|It's (in) her nature to be generous.* **3** [S] a type; sort: *ceremonies of a solemn nature* **4 second nature** a firm habit that has become part of one's character: *He's been teaching for so long that it's second nature to him now.* **5 back to nature** returning to the living conditions that existed before the spread of civilization: *Many people are getting back to nature by eating only natural foods.*

naught /nɔt/ *n* [U] *old use & lit* nothing: *All his hopes* **came to naught** *when he failed the exam.*

naugh·ty /ˈnɔtiʸ/ *adj* **-tier, -tiest 1** (esp. of children) bad in behavior; not obeying a parent, teacher, set of rules, etc.: *You naughty boy! I told you not to play in the street.* –see WICKED (USAGE) **2** *euph* morally, esp. sexually, improper: *an amusing and naughty book* –**naughtily** *adv* –**naughtiness** *n* [U]

nau·se·a /ˈnɔziʸə, ˈnɔʒə, ˈnɔsiʸə, ˈnɔʃə/ *n* [U] a feeling of sickness and desire to VOMIT (to throw up the contents of the stomach through the mouth)

nau·se·ate /ˈnɔziʸˌeʸt, -ʒiʸ-, -siʸ-, -ʃiʸ-/ *v* **-ated, -ating** [T] to cause to feel NAUSEA: *a nauseating smell*|(fig.) *Violence in movies is often nauseating.* (=very unpleasant) –**nauseous** /ˈnɔʃəs, ˈnɔziʸəs/ *adj: a nauseous feeling*

nau·ti·cal /ˈnɔt̪ɪkəl/ *adj* of or concerning sailors, ships, or sailing –**nautically** *adv*

nautical mile /ˌ··· ˈ·/ *n* a measure of distance, used at sea, equal to 1,852 meters –compare KNOT[1] (4)

na·val /ˈneʸvəl/ *adj* of a navy or ships of war: *naval officer/battles*

nave /neʸv/ *n* the long central part of a church usu. between two AISLES

na·vel /ˈneʸvəl/ *n* a small sunken place in the middle of the stomach, left when the connection to the mother (the UMBILICAL CORD) is cut at birth

nav·i·ga·ble /ˈnævəgəbəl/ *adj* (of a body of water) deep and wide enough to allow ships to travel: *The St. Lawrence River is navig-*

able from the Great Lakes to the sea.

nav·i·gate /ˈnævəˌgeʸt/ *v* **-gated, -gating** [I;T] to direct the course of (a ship, plane, etc.): (fig.) *I'll drive if you hold the map and navigate.*

nav·i·ga·tion /ˌnævəˈgeʸʃən/ *n* [U] the act, practice, or science of navigating (NAVIGATE): *Navigation is difficult on this river because of the rocks.*

nav·i·ga·tor /ˈnævəˌgeʸtər/ *n* the officer on a ship or aircraft who controls its course

na·vy /ˈneʸviʸ/ *n* **-vies 1** the organization, including ships, people, buildings, etc., which makes up the power of a country for war at sea: *He joined the navy nearly 30 years ago.* **2** the ships of war belonging to a country: *a small navy of ten ships|one of the smallest navies in the world*

navy blue /ˌ··· ·ˈ◄/ also **navy–** *adj,n* [U] very dark blue (color)

nay /neʸ/ *adv lit* (used for adding something stronger to what has been said) no

NB *abbrev. for:* (used esp. in writing) Latin nota bene (=note well)

NC, N.C. *written abbrev. said as:* North Carolina /ˌnɔrθ ˌkærəˈlaɪnə/ (a state in the US)

NCO /ˌɛn siʸ ˈoʷ/ *n abbrev. for:* NONCOMMISSIONED OFFICER: *He became an NCO at 18.*

ND, N.D., N.Dak. *written abbrev.said as:* North Dakota /ˌnɔrθ dəˈkoʷtə/ (a state in the US)

NE *written abbrev. said as:* northeast(ern) **1** also **Neb.** –Nebraska /nəˈbræskə/ (a state in the US) **2** northeast(ern)

near[1] /nɪər/ *adj* [*to*] not far; not at much distance: *the near future|Go and pick an apple from the nearest tree.|We live in the center of town,, so my office is quite near.|He's one of my nearest relatives.* (=is closely related to me) –**nearness** *n* [U *to*]

USAGE **Near** and **close** are almost the same in meaning, but there are certain phrases in which one must be used and not the other. Notice *the* **near** *future/the* **near** *distance* (not **close**); *a* **close** *friend/***close** *behind* (not **near**). **Close** cannot be used as a PREPOSITION, but **close** to can: *I live close to/near the station.*

near[2] *adv,prep* [*to*] not far (from): *We live near (to) the church.|Don't go too near (to) the edge of the cliff.|The bus is nowhere near as fast as/not nearly as fast as* (=much slower than) *the train.*

near[3] *v* [I;T] to come closer in distance or time (to); APPROACH[1] (1): *He got more and more nervous as the day neared.*

near[4] *almost: a near-perfect performance|a near-impossible decision*

near·by /ˌnɪərˈbaɪ◄/ *adv,adj* [no *comp.*] near; close by: *a nearby mailbox|a football game being played nearby*

near·ly /ˈnɪərliʸ/ *adv* [no *comp.*] almost; not far from, but not quite: *He nearly died.|The train was nearly full.|not nearly enough money* (=far too little money)

near miss /ˌ· ·ˈ·/ *n* **1** a bomb, shot, etc., which does not hit exactly the right spot but comes close to it **2** *infml* something which fails but almost succeeds, or which fails to be completely successful: *Her idea was a near miss; it won second prize.*

near·sight·ed /ˌnɪərˈsaɪtɪd◂, ˈnɪərˌsaɪtɪd/ *AmE*‖**shortsighted** *BrE*– *adj* unable to see objects clearly or read things in writing if they are not close to the eyes –**nearsightedness** *n* [U]

neat /niːt/ *adj* **1** in good order; showing care in appearance; tidy: *neat handwriting*|*He keeps his office neat and tidy.* **2** clever and effective: *a neat trick*/*description* **3** also **straight** *esp. AmE*– (of alcoholic drinks) without ice or water or other liquid:*I like my* WHISKEY *neat.* **4** *AmE infml* very good; very pleasant; fine: *It was a really neat party; I enjoyed myself.* –**neatly** *adv* –**neatness** *n* [U]

neb·u·lous /ˈnɛbyələs/ *adj* not clear; not DIS-TINCT (2); VAGUE (1): *nebulous political ideas*

nec·es·sar·i·ly /ˌnɛsəˈsɛrəliˈ/ *adv* in a way that must be so; unavoidably: *Food that looks good doesn't necessarily taste good.* (=it might taste bad)

nec·es·sar·y /ˈnɛsəˌsɛriˈ/ *adj* [*to, for*] that must be; that must be had or obtained; needed: *Food is necessary for life.*|*Is it really necessary for me to attend the meeting?*|*to make the necessary arrangements* –see also UNNECESSARY

ne·ces·si·tate /nəˈsɛsəˌteɪt/ *v* -**tated, -tating** [T *+v-ing*] *fml* to cause a need for; make necessary: *Your mistakes will necessitate doing the work again.*

ne·ces·si·ty /nəˈsɛsətiˈ/ *n* -**ties 1** [S;U *+to-v*/ *of,for*] the condition of being necessary, needed, or unavoidable; need: *Is there any necessity for another election?*|*We're faced with the necessity of buying* (=we have to buy) *a new car.*|*He was forced* **by necessity** *to steal a loaf of bread because he was so hungry.* **2** [C] something that is necessary: *Food and clothing are necessities of life.*

neck¹ /nɛk/ *n* **1** the part of the body by which the head is joined to the shoulders **2** the part of a garment that goes around this part of the human body: *the neck of a shirt* **3** a narrow part that sticks out from a broader part: *the neck of a bottle* **4 neck and neck** *infml* (of two horses, people, etc., in competition) equal so far; with an equal chance of winning **5 stick one's neck out** *infml* to take a risk; say or do something which may fail, be wrong, or hurt one **6 neck of the woods** *infml esp. AmE* area or part of the country: *People don't do that in my neck of the woods.* **7 up to one's neck (in)** also **up to one's ears (in)**– *infml* busy (with), deeply concerned (with or by): *I'm up to my neck in debt.* (=I owe a lot of money) **8 -necked** (of a piece of clothing) having a certain shape or style of neck: *a V-necked dress* |*an open-necked shirt* (= unbuttoned at the neck)

neck² *v* [I] *infml* to kiss, CARESS, etc., but without having full sexual relations: *a boy*

SPELLING NOTE
Words with the sound /n/ may be spelled **kn-**, like **know**, or **pn-**, like **pneumonia**.

and girl necking in the back of a car

neck·lace /ˈnɛk-lɪs/ *n* a string of jewels, BEADS, PEARLS, etc., or a chain of gold, silver, etc., worn around the neck for decoration

neck·line /ˈnɛk-laɪn/ *n* the line made by the neck opening of a piece of women's clothing: *a low neckline*

neck·tie /ˈnɛktaɪ/ *AmE*‖also **tie**– *n* a band of cloth worn around the neck, usu. inside a shirt collar and tied in a knot at the front –compare BOW TIE –see illustration on page 123

nec·tar /ˈnɛktər/ *n* [U] **1** (in ancient Greek and Roman literature) the drink of the gods: (fig.) *A cold beer is like nectar when you're thirsty.* **2** the sweet liquid collected by bees from flowers

née /neɪ/ *adv* (*used after a married woman's name and before her original family name*) formerly named: *Mrs. Carol Cook née Williams*

need¹ /niːd/ *n* **1** [S;U *of, for*] the condition of lacking or wanting something necessary or very useful: *There is a growing need for new housing in this area.*|*The doctor told me I was* **in need of** *a good rest.*|*Take money from the bank* **as the need arises.** (=whenever it is necessary) **2** [S;U *+to-v*/*for*] a necessary duty; what must be done: *There's no need for you to come too.*|(fig.) *There's no need to be* (=you shouldn't be) *so rude.* **3** [C *usu. pl.*] *fml* something necessary to have: *The hotel* STAFF¹ (=workers) *will attend to all your needs*/*your every need.* **4** [U] *fml & euph* the state of not having enough food or money: *We are collecting money for children in need.* **5 if need be** if it is necessary **6 a friend in need** *infml* a true friend, who comes to help one in trouble

need² *v* [T *+to-v*/*v-ing;* not *be*+*v-ing*] to have a need for; want for some useful purpose; lack: *Children need milk.*|*This soup needs salt.*|*My hair needs cutting*/*needs to be cut.*|*I need my hair cut.*|*If I need you to come and help I'll call.*|*You don't need to come if you don't want to.*

need³ *v negative contraction* **needn't** /ˈniːdnt/ [I *+to-v;* not *be*+*v-ing*] *esp. BrE* (used as a helping verb and another verb in questions and NEGATIVES² (1), not in simple statements) to have to: *"Need you go so soon?" "No, we needn't."*/*Yes, we must."*|*You needn't talk so loud; I can hear you very well.*

nee·dle¹ /ˈniːdl/ *n* **1** a long pointed metal pin with a hole in one end for the thread, used in sewing **2** a thin pointed object that looks like this: *a* PINE² *needle* (=a thin leaf of this tree) **3** a thin pointed rod used in working with long threadlike pieces of wool: KNITting *needles* **4** (in a RECORD PLAYER) the very small pointed jewel or piece of metal which picks up the sound recorded on a record; STYLUS **5** a very thin hollow pointed tube, at the end of a HYPODERMIC SYRINGE, which is pushed into someone's skin to put a liquid (esp. medicine) into the body **6** a long thin pointer: *The needle of the compass shows that we're facing north.*

needle² *v* -**dled, -dling** [T *about*] *infml* to

annoy (someone) by repeated unkind remarks, stupid jokes, etc.; TEASE (1): *The boys always needled Jim about being fat.*

need·less /'niʸd-lɪs/ *adj* **1** not needed; unnecessary: *needless trouble preparing for guests who didn't come* **2** **needless to say** of course; as was to be expected: *Needless to say, it rained when I left my window open.* **–needlessly** *adv*

nee·dle·work /'niʸdl‚wɜrk/ *n* [U] sewing and EMBROIDERY: *tired eyes from doing fine needlework*

need·n't /'niʸdnt/ *v esp. BrE short for:* NEED³ not: *You needn't go if you don't want to.|I needn't have put on this thick coat.* (=but I did)

need·y /'niʸdiʸ/ *adj* **-ier, -iest** poor; without food, clothing, etc.: *a needy family|money to help the needy*

ne'er /nɛər/ *adv lit* never: *Will he ne'er come home again?*

ne'er-do-well /'nɛər duʷ ‚wɛl/ *n* **-wells** *derog* a useless or lazy person

ne·far·i·ous /nɪ'fɛəriʸəs/ *adj fml* against laws or moral principles; wicked: *His nefarious activities include selling drugs and stolen goods.* **–nefariously** *adv*

neg·a·tive¹ /'nɛgəṭɪv/ *adj* **1** saying or meaning "no": *a negative answer to my request|negative expressions like "not at all"* –opposite **affirmative** **2** without any active qualities or results: *negative advice that only tells you what not to do|The test for bacteria was negative.* (=none were found) **3** (of electricity) of the type that is based on ELECTRONS **4** in MATHEMATICS (of a number or quantity) less than zero: *a negative profit* (=a loss)*|If x is* POSITIVE¹ (5) *then −x is negative.* –opposite **positive** (for 2, 3, 4) **–negatively** *adv*

negative² *n* **1** a word, expression, or statement saying or meaning "no": *The answer to my request was* **in the negative.**|*"Never" and "not at all" are negatives.* –opposite **affirmative 2** a photograph or film showing dark areas in nature as light and light areas as dark –compare POSITIVE²

ne·glect¹ /nɪ'glɛkt/ *v* [T] **1** [+*v-ing*] to give too little attention or care to: *neglected children|You've been neglecting your work.* **2** [+*to-v*] to fail (to do something), esp. because of carelessness or forgetfulness: *Don't neglect to lock the door when you leave.*

neglect² *n* [U] **1** the action of NEGLECTing: *the owner's neglect of repairs to his house* **2** the condition or fact of being NEGLECTed: *The building is in a state of neglect.*

ne·glect·ful /nɪ'glɛktfəl/ *adj* in the habit of NEGLECTing things: *a mother who is neglectful of her children* **–neglectfully** *adv* **–neglectfulness** *n* [U]

neg·li·gee /‚nɛglɪ'ʒeʸ, 'nɛglɪ‚ʒeʸ/ *n* a woman's light and usu. fancy NIGHTGOWN

neg·li·gent /'nɛglɪdʒənt/ *adj* not taking enough care; in the habit of NEGLECTing things: *He was negligent in not locking the doors as he was told to do.* **–negligently** *adv* **–negligence** *n* [U]: *The driver's negligence*

was the cause of the accident.

neg·li·gi·ble /'nɛglɪdʒəbəl/ *adj* too slight or unimportant to be worth any attention: *The damage to my car is negligible.* **–negligibly** *adv*

ne·go·ti·a·ble /nɪ'goʷʃiʸəbəl, -ʃəbəl/ *adj* **1** that can be settled or changed by being NEGOTIATEd: *a negotiable contract|He says his claim is not negotiable.* **2** (of a check or order to pay money) than can be exchanged for money **3** *infml* that can be passed through, along, etc.: *The road is only negotiable in the summer time.*

ne·go·ti·ate /nɪ'goʷʃiʸ‚eʸt/ *v* **-ated, -ating 1** [I +*to-v/ with*] to talk with another person or group in order to try to come to an agreement: *The two governments were negotiating to bring an end to the fighting.* **2** [T *with*] to produce (an agreement) or settle (a piece of business) in this way: *The union negotiated a new contract with the City.* **3** [T] *infml* to go safely over, through, along, etc.: *Will this small car negotiate that steep hill?* **–negotiator** *n*

ne·go·ti·a·tion /nɪ‚goʷʃiʸ'eʸʃən/ *n* [C;U] an act or the action of negotiating (NEGOTIATE (1,2)): *The agreement was the result of long negotiation(s).|the negotiation of new wages|The contract is* **under negotiation.** (=now being settled)

Ne·gro /'niʸgroʷ/ **Negress** /'niʸgrɪs/ *fem.–* **-groes** a person belonging to a dark-skinned race; BLACK¹ (3) person

USAGE In the US the word **black** is preferred to **Negro.**

neigh /neʸ/ *v,n* [I] (to make) the loud and long cry of a horse

neigh·bor *AmE*||**-bour** *BrE* /'neʸbər/ *n* one of two or more people who live near one another: *my next-door neighbor* (=the person living in the next house)*|We're neighbors now.*

neigh·bor·hood *AmE*||**-bourhood** *BrE* /'neʸbər‚hʊd/ *n* **1** [C] (the people living in) a small area within a larger place such as a town: *a quiet neighborhood with good stores|a neighborhood school* **2** [S] the area around a point or place: *You'll find it somewhere* **in the neighborhood (of** *the station).*

neigh·bor·ing *AmE*||**-bouring** *BrE* /'neʸbərɪŋ/ *adj* [A *no comp.*] (esp. of places) near or close by: *bus service between here and the neighboring cities*

neigh·bor·ly *AmE*||**-bourly** *BrE* /'neʸbərliʸ/ *adj* friendly; like (that of) a good neighbor –opposite **unneighborly –neighborliness** *n* [U]

nei·ther¹ /'niʸðər, 'naɪ-/ *determiner,pron* not one and not the other of two: *Neither road|Neither of the streets is very good.* (=they are both bad)*|Neither of them wanted to go.|"Will you have tea or coffee?" "Neither!"* –see also EITHER¹

neither² *conj* **1** not either: *He neither ate, drank, nor smoked.|Neither my father nor I were there.* –see EITHER (USAGE) **2** (*used with* NEGATIVE¹ (1) *expressions*) also not: *I haven't read this book, and neither has my* *brother.* (=both haven't read it)|*"I can't swim!" "Neither can I!"* (=both of us are unable to swim)

USAGE Notice the word order of **Neither/Nor** *can I*, which is the same as that of a question.

nem·e·sis /'nɛməsɪs/ *n* -ses /ˌsiʸz/ **1** [U] *lit* (*sometimes cap.*) just and esp. unavoidable punishment **2 a** a person who carries out such punishment **b** a powerful enemy or opponent

ne·o·lith·ic /ˌniʸə'lɪθɪk/ *adj* (*often cap.*) of the period in time when people began to settle in villages, grow crops, and keep animals –compare PALEOLITHIC

ne·on /'niʸɑn/ *n* [U] a chemically inactive gas that is a simple substance (ELEMENT) and is present in small amounts in the air

neon light /ˌ·· '·/ *n* a glass tube filled with NEON which lights when an electric current goes through it, often shaped to form a sign advertising something

neph·ew /'nɛfyuʷ/ *n* the son of one's (wife's or husband's) brother or sister –compare NIECE –see illustration on page 247

nep·o·tism /'nɛpəˌtɪzəm/ *n* [U] the practice of favoring one's relatives when one has power, esp. by giving them good jobs

Nep·tune /'nɛptuʷn, -tyuʷn/ *n* the PLANET 8th in order from the sun

nerd /nɜrd/ *n AmE infml derog* a dull or unattractive person

nerve¹ /nɜrv/ *n* **1** [C] any of the threadlike parts of the body which form a system to carry feelings and messages to and from the brain **2** [U] strength or control of mind; courage: *a man of nerve*|*a test of nerve*|*I wanted to write an angry letter but I lost my nerve when I sat down to do it.* **3** [S;U] *derog* boldness; EFFRONTERY: *She must be forty pounds overweight, and She has the nerve to tell me to lose weight.*|*What nerve!*

nerve² *v* **nerved, nerving** [T] *fml* to give courage to (someone, esp. oneself) –see also UNNERVE

nerve-rack·ing /'·ˌ··/ *adj infml* difficult to do or bear calmly, esp. because dangerous: *a nerve-racking drive through the high mountains*

nerves /nɜrvz/ *n* [P] *infml* **1** a condition of great nervousness: *She gets nerves before every examination.* **2** **get on someone's nerves** to make someone annoyed or bad-tempered: *That loud music is getting on my nerves.*

nerv·ous /'nɜrvəs/ *adj* **1** afraid; worried: *I always get nervous before a plane trip.*|*a nervous smile* **2** of or related to the NERVOUS SYSTEM of the body, or to the feelings: *a nervous disease* –**nervously** *adv* –**nervousness** *n* [U]

USAGE Compare **nervous, concerned**, and **anxious**: You can be **nervous** (=rather

afraid) while something is happening, and **concerned** (=worried) about something that is happening, but **anxious** means worried about what might happen: *I didn't play well because I was too nervous.*|*We're rather concerned about father's health.*|*Your mother will be anxious until she hears that you're safe.*

nervous break·down /ˌ··· '··/ *n* a serious medical condition of deep worrying, anxiety, weeping, and tiredness

nervous sys·tem /'··· ˌ··/ *n* (in people and animals) the system (=the brain, SPINE, and NERVES) which receives and passes on feelings, messages, etc. from inside and outside the body

nerv·y /'nɜrviʸ/ *adj* -ier, -iest *infml* **1** *AmE* having NERVE¹ (3); BRASH (2) **2** *BrE* nervous and anxious

nest¹ /nɛst/ *n* **1** a hollow place built or found by a bird for a home and a place to keep its eggs **2** the home of certain other animals or insects: *an ants' nest* **3** a group of like objects which fit closely into or inside one another: *a nest of tables/boxes*

nest² *v* [I] to build or use a nest: *Most birds nest in trees.*

nest egg /'· ·/ *n* an amount of money saved for future use

nes·tle /'nɛsəl/ *v* -tled, -tling [T *down*] to settle or lie warmly, closely, or comfortably: *villages nestling among the hills*|*She nestled her head on/against his shoulder.*

net¹ /nɛt/ *n* **1** [C;U] a material of strings, wires, threads, etc. twisted, tied, or woven together with regular spaces between them **2** [C] any of various objects made from this, such as **a** a large piece spread out under water to catch fish **b** a trap: *a BUTTERFLY net* **c** a length dividing the two sides of the court in tennis, BADMINTON, etc. **d** an enclosure at the back of the GOAL (2) in SOCCER, HOCKEY, etc.

net² *v* -tt- [T] to catch (as if) in a net: *We netted three fish.*

net³ ‖also **nett** *BrE*– *adj* [A or after *n*] (of an amount) when nothing further is to be subtracted: *net profit* (=after tax, rent, etc. are paid)|*net weight* (=of an object without its package)|*This jar of coffee weighs 7 ounces net.* –compare GROSS¹ (4)

net⁴ *v* -tt- [T *for*] to gain as a profit: *The sale netted a fat profit for the company.* –compare GROSS²

neth·er /'nɛðər/ *adj* [A] *lit or humor* lower; under: *the nether regions* (=lower parts) *of the body*

net·ting /'nɛtɪŋ/ *n* [U] string, wire, etc., made into a net: *a fence of wire netting*

net·tle¹ /'nɛtl/ *n* a wild plant having leaves which may sting and make red marks on the skin

nettle² *v* -tled, -tling [T] to make (someone) angry or impatient: *I was nettled by his impolite behavior.*

net·work /'nɛt-wɜrk/ *n* **1** a large system of lines, tubes, wires, etc., that cross or meet one another: *the country's railroad network*|*the network of blood vessels in the body*|(fig.) *a network of friends in different*

SPELLING NOTE

Words with the sound /n/ may be spelled **kn-**, like **know**, or **pn-**, like **pneumonia**.

parts of the country **2** a group of radio or television stations in different places using many of the same broadcasts

neu·ro·sis /nʊˈrowsɪs, nyʊ-/ *n* **-ses** /siᵞz/ [C;U] *tech* a disorder of the mind marked by strong unreasonable fears and ideas about the outside world

neu·rot·ic /nʊˈraṭɪk, nyʊ-/ *adj* related to or suffering from NEUROSIS: *(infml) Stop worrying about it! You're really getting neurotic.* —**neurotic** *n*

neu·ter¹ /ˈnuʷṭər, ˈnyuʷ-/ *adj* **1** (in grammar) in or related to a class (GENDER) of words which are neither MASCULINE (2) nor FEMININE (2): *a neuter noun/ending* **2** (of plants or animals) with no or undeveloped sexual organs: *Worker bees are neuter.*

neuter² *n* (the class of) a NEUTER word or word form: *How do you put this adjective into the neuter?*

neuter³ *v* [T *usu. pass.*] to remove part of the sex organs of (an animal) by an operation —compare CASTRATE

neu·tral¹ /ˈnuʷtrəl, ˈnyuʷ-/ *adj* **1** without any feelings on either side of a question: *I'm neutral in this argument; I don't care who wins.* **2** being or belonging to a country which is not fighting or helping either side in a war: *a neutral country* **3** having no qualities of the stated kind, as of something **a** very weak or colorless: *trousers of a neutral colour* **b** (in chemistry) neither an acid nor a BASE¹ (4) **c** with no electrical charge —**neutrally** *adv*

neutral² *n* **1** [U] the position of the GEARS in a car or other machine, in which no power is carried from the engine to the wheels: *When you start the engine, be sure the car is in neutral.* **2** [C] a NEUTRAL¹ (2) person or country

neu·tral·i·ty /nuʷˈtrælət̬iᵞ/ *n* [U] the condition or quality of being NEUTRAL¹, esp. in a war

neu·tral·ize ‖also **-ise** *BrE* /ˈnuʷtrəˌlaɪz, ˈnyuʷ-/ *v* **-ized, -izing** [T] to cause to have no effect; destroy the qualities, force, or activity of: *to neutralize an acid with a* BASE¹ (4)|*High taxes will neutralize increased wages.* —**neutralization** /ˌnuʷtrələˈzeᵞʃən, ˌnyuʷ-/ *n* [U]

neu·tron /ˈnuʷtran, ˈnyuʷ-/ *n* a very small piece of matter that helps to form the central part of an atom and carries no electricity —see also ELECTRON, PROTON

nev·er /ˈnevər/ *adv* not ever; not at any time: *I've never been to Paris.|He never goes anywhere without his dog.|Never forget to lock the door at night.|Never have I met such a strange person.*

USAGE Compare **never, sometimes, often,** etc.: School starts at 9 o'clock, and in January Peter arrived at school before 9 o'clock every day. Mary was late for school just twice in the month. Jane was late on 4 days, and Jim was late on 10 days. So we can say: *Peter never arrives late/always comes on time.|Mary is **rarely/hardly ever**/(fml) **seldom** late; she's **usually/nearly always** on time.|Jane is **occasionally/sometimes** late, and Jim is **often/frequently** late*

nev·er·more /ˌnevərˈmɔr, -ˈmoʷr/ *adv lit* never again

nev·er·the·less /ˌnevərðəˈles◂/ also **none-theless**– *adv* in spite of that: *What you said was true but nevertheless unkind.|I can't go. Nevertheless, thank you for inviting me.* –see Study Notes on page 144

new /nuʷ, nyuʷ/ *adj* **1** recently begun, made, built, etc.: *a new President|new fashions|We sell new and used furniture.|Have you seen her new car?* **2** [A] **a** only recently found or known: *the discovery of a new star* **b** having been in the stated position only a short time: *a new member of the club* **3** [A *no comp.*] different; (an)other: *to learn a new language* **4** [A *no comp.*] just beginning to be used, etc.; fresh: *They've gone to Mexico to start a new life.* **5** **new to** just beginning to know about or do; still unfamiliar with: *a young clerk new to the job* **6 new-** newly; recently: *a newborn baby|a new-found friend* –**newness** *n* [U]

USAGE **New** is a general word for something that exists now but has only been in existence for a short time: *a new building/law/book.* **Recent** describes something that happened or came into existence a short time ago, and is used esp. of events: *our recent vacation|We elected a new senator in the recent election.* **Modern** covers a greater period of time than **new**, and means "belonging to the present time or not too distant past": *an examination in modern history, from 1550 to 1982|Modern medical science has conquered many diseases.* **Contemporary** means "belonging to the present or the recent past," and **current** describes something that exists now, but may or may not be **new**: *contemporary art/politics|the government's current ideas on defense|The firm's current director has been in the job for 25 years.* –compare OLD (USAGE)

new·com·er /ˈnuʷˌkʌmər, ˈnyuʷ-/ *n* [to] one who has recently come; or has begun coming: *a newcomer to the city* (=visiting or living there for the first time)|*The team is a newcomer to the competition.* (=hasn't been in it before)

new·fan·gled /ˌnuʷˈfæŋgəld◂, ˌnyuʷ-/ *adj* [A] *derog or humor* (of ideas, inventions, etc.) new and unnecessary or of no value: *We need better teachers, not newfangled ideas on education!*

new·ly /ˈnuʷliᵞ, ˈnyuʷliᵞ/ *adv* (used before a past participle) recently; freshly: *a newly built house*

new·ly·wed /ˈnuʷliᵞˌwed, ˈnyuʷ-/ *n* [usu. pl.] a man or woman recently married: *Mr. and Mrs. Smith are newlyweds/are a newlywed* COUPLE.

news /nuʷz, nyuʷz/ *n* [U] what is reported (esp. in newspapers and on radio and television) about a recent event or events; new information: *news of the election results|I heard it on the seven o'clock news.|Have you heard the news about Mary? She's going to have a baby.*

news·cast·er /ˈnuʷzˌkæstər, ˈnyuʷz-/ ‖also **newsreader** /ˈnuʷzˌriᵞdər, ˈnyuʷz-/ *BrE*– *n* a person who broadcasts news on radio or television

news con·fer·ence /'· ,···/ n →PRESS CONFERENCE

news·deal·er /'nuᵂz‚diᵞlər, 'nyuᵂz-/ AmE‖ **newsagent** /'nuᵂz‚eᵞdʒənt, 'nyuᵂz-/ BrE n a person in charge of a store selling newspapers and magazines: You can get that paper at your local newsdealer's.

news·let·ter /'nuᵂz‚lɛtər,'nyuᵂz-/ n a small sheet of news sent weekly or monthly to a particular group of people: the company newsletter

news·pa·per /'nuᵂz‚peᵞpər, 'nyuᵂz-/ also **paper-** n **1** [C] a paper printed and sold usu. daily or weekly, with news, notices, advertisements, etc.: an evening newspaper|the Sunday papers **2** [U] paper on which these have been printed: Wrap it up in newspaper.

news·print /'nuᵂz‚prɪnt, 'nyuᵂz-/ n [U] tech a cheap paper used mostly for newspapers

news·reel /'nuᵂzriᵞəl, 'nyuᵂz-/ n a short movie film of news

news·stand /'nuᵂzstænd, 'nyuᵂz-/ n a small store, often inside a shelter outdoors, from which newspapers, magazines, etc. are sold

news·wor·thy /'nuᵂz‚wɜrðiᵞ, 'nyuᵂz-/ adj important and interesting enough to be reported as news

newt /nuᵂt, nyuᵂt/ n a small four-legged animal living both on land and in water

New Tes·ta·ment /‚· '···◄/ n the part of the Bible containing writings about the life of Christ –compare OLD TESTAMENT

New World /‚· '·/ n [the S] North, Central, and South America; the Western HEMISPHERE

new year /‚· '·◄/ n (often caps.) the year which has just begun or will soon begin: We are hoping for better business in the new year than in this past year.|Happy New Year! (=a greeting spoken at the beginning of the year)

New Year's Day /‚· · '·/ n (in Western countries) January 1st

New Year's Eve /‚· · '·/ n (in Western countries) December 31st

next¹ /nɛkst/ adj **1** nearest; without anything coming between: They live in the next house to ours.|We'll have to stop at the next gasoline station.|The best way is by air; the **next best** (=the second best) is by train. **2** the nearest after: If I miss this train I'll catch the next|the next one.|Are you coming to our next meeting?|I'll be on vacation next week. (not the next week)

next² adv **1** just afterwards: What will you do next? **2** the first time after this or that: I'll tell you the answer when we next meet. –compare LAST² (2) **3 next to: a** close beside: sitting next to Mary **b** almost: He earns next to nothing. (=very little money)

next-door /‚· '·◄/ adj [A] in or being the next building, esp. in a row: next-door neighbors

---

SPELLING NOTE

Words with the sound /n/ may be spelled **kn-**, like **know**, or **pn-**, like **pneumonia.**

---

next door /‚· '·/ adv [F to] in or being the next building: We live next door to a movie theater.

next of kin /‚· · '·/ n **next of kin** law the person most closely related to someone: Her next of kin was/were informed about the accident.

nib /nɪb/ n the pointed piece on the end of a pen, usu. metal, out of which the ink flows

nib·ble /'nɪbəl/ v **-bled, -bling** [I;T away, at, on] to take small bites (out of something): Aren't you hungry? You're only nibbling (at) your food.|The mice have nibbled away part of the cheese. **–nibble** n

nice /naɪs/ adj **1** infml good; pleasant; pleasing: How nice of you to do that!|a nice piece of work|a nice day (=with good weather)|That's a nice dress.|How nice to see you! (=a greeting) **2** fml showing or needing careful understanding; fine; delicate: a nice difference between two meanings **3** derog & infml bad; unpleasant: Don't be so rude; that's a nice way to behave to your aunt! **–niceness** n [U]

USAGE Nice is very commonly used in speech, but in formal writing it is better to avoid it and use **amusing, beautiful, interesting,** etc., according to the meaning.

nice·ly /'naɪsliᵞ/ adv well; in a good, pleasant, kind, or skillful way: to smile nicely|The man is doing nicely (=his condition is quite good) in the hospital after his accident. **2** in an exact, fine, or delicate way

ni·ce·ty /'naɪsətiᵞ/ n **-ties** a fine or delicate point; detail: Let's answer the question in general: we don't have time to consider all the niceties.

niche /nɪtʃ/ n **1** a hollow place in a wall, usu. made to hold a piece of art (like a BUST² (1) or STATUE) **2 find a niche for oneself** to find a suitable place, job, position, etc.

nick¹ /nɪk/ n **1** a small (accidental) cut in a surface or edge: not badly hurt, only nicks and cuts **2 in the nick of time** just in time: I caught the baby in the nick of time before he fell down the stairs.

nick² v [T] to make or cut a NICK¹ in: A bullet nicked the soldier's leg.

nick·el /'nɪkəl/ n **1** [U] a hard silver-white metal that is a simple substance (ELEMENT) and is used in the production of other metals **2** [C] the coin of the US and Canada worth five cents: Can you give me a DIME for two nickels?

nick·name¹ /'nɪkneᵞm/ n a name used informally instead of (some)one's own name, usu. given because of one's character or appearance or as a short form of the actual name: His real name is Mr. MacDonald, but his nickname is "Mac."

nickname² v **-named, -naming** [T] to give (someone) a NICKNAME: They nicknamed him "Fats" because of his weight.

nic·o·tine /'nɪkə‚tiᵞn/ n [U] a poisonous chemical contained in tobacco

niece /niᵞs/ n the daughter of one's (wife's or husband's) brother or sister –compare NEPHEW –see illustration on page 247

nif·ty /'nɪftiᵞ/ adj **-tier, -tiest** infml very good, attractive, or effective: a nifty little car

nig·gard·ly /'nɪgərdliʸ/ *adj derog* **1** (of a person) not willing to spend money, time, etc.; STINGY **2** small or limited; MEAN¹ (4): *a niggardly offer for such a good bicycle* –**niggardliness** *n* [U]

nig·ger /'nɪgər/ *n taboo infml* a BLACK¹ (3) person; NEGRO

nig·gle /'nɪgəl/ *v* **-gled, -gling** [I] **1** to pay too much attention to small details: *She niggled over every detail of the bill, to avoid paying too much for the meal.* **2** to annoy or worry continually *adj* [A]: *a niggling doubt*

nigh /naɪ/ *adv,prep* **1** *lit & old use* near **2 well nigh** also **nigh on**– *dial or old use* almost: *He worked at his job well nigh 50 years.*

night /naɪt/ *n* **1** [C;U] the dark part of each day, when the sun cannot be seen: *The nights are longer in winter.*|*I slept well last night.*|*Cats can see well at/by night.*|*She lay awake* **all night (long)**. (=from the time she went to bed until morning)|*The baby woke up twice* **in the night**.|*tomorrow night* –compare DAY (2) **2** [C] an evening, considered as an occasion: *We saw the show on its first night.* (=at its first performance, in the evening) **3 night after night** *infml* regularly every night: *He goes out drinking night after night.* **4 night and day** also **day and night**– *infml* all the time

night·cap /'naɪtkæp/ *n* **1** a usu. alcoholic drink taken before going to bed **2** a soft cloth cap worn in bed in former times

night·club /'naɪtklʌb/ *n* a club open late at night where people may eat, drink, dance, and often see a show

night·dress /'naɪtdres/ *n* →NIGHTGOWN

night·fall /'naɪtfɔl/ *n* [U] the beginning of night; DUSK

night·gown /'naɪtgaʊn/ *AmE*‖also **nightdress, nightie** /'naɪti/ *infml* – *n* a piece of women's clothing like a loose dress, made to be worn in bed

night·in·gale /'naɪtnˌgeʸl, 'naɪtɪŋ-/ *n* any of several European birds (THRUSHES) known for their beautiful song

night·life /'naɪtlaɪf/ *n* [U] the activity of people who go out to enjoy themselves at night in BARS¹ (5), NIGHTCLUBS,etc.

night·ly /'naɪtliʸ/ *adj,adv* (happening, done, used, etc.) every night: *a play performed nightly*|*a nightly news broadcast*

night·mare /'naɪtmeər/ *n* a terrible dream: (fig.) *Driving through that snowstorm was a nightmare.* –**nightmarish** *adj* –**nightmarishly** *adv*

night school /'· ·/ *n* a school or set of classes meeting in the evening, esp. for people who have jobs during the day: *You can learn French in night school.*

night shift /'· ·/ *n* (a period of) work done during the night, as in a factory: *He worked (on) the night shift.*|*a night-shift worker*

night·stick /'naɪtˌstɪk/ *AmE*‖**baton, truncheon** *BrE*– *n* a short thick stick often carried by policemen

night·time /'naɪt-taɪm/ *n* [U] the time each day when it is dark –opposite **daytime**

night watch·man /ˌ· '··/ *n* a man with the job of guarding a building at night

nil /nɪl/ *n* nothing; zero: *The new machine reduced labor costs to almost nil.*

nim·ble /'nɪmbəl/ *adj apprec* quick, light, and neat in movement; AGILE: *a nimble climber* –**nimbleness** *n* [U] –**nimbly** *adv*

nin·com·poop /'nɪnkəmˌpuʷp, 'nɪŋ-/ *n infml* a stupid person; fool

nine /naɪn/ *determiner, n, pron* **1** (the number) 9 **2 nine times out of ten** *infml* almost always: *Even before I open my mouth, my wife knows what I am going to say nine times out of ten.*

nine·teen /ˌnaɪn'tiʸn◄/ *determiner,n,pron* (the number) 19 –**nineteenth** *determiner,n, adv,pron*

nine·ty /'naɪntiʸ-/ *determiner,n,pron* **-ties** (the number) 90 –**ninetieth** /'naɪntɪʸɪθ/ *determiner,n,adv,pron*

nin·ny /'nɪniʸ/ *n* **-nies** *infml & derog* a silly foolish person

ninth /naɪnθ/ *determiner,n,adv,pron* 9th

nip¹ /nɪp/ *v* **-pp-** **1** [I;T] to catch in a tight sharp hold between two points or surfaces, such as between the finger and thumb: *The dog nipped* (=has bitten) *the mailman on the leg.* **2 nip in the bud** to do harm to (something) at an early stage of its development, so as to keep from succeeding: *Her plans to go out were nipped in the bud when her mother arrived for the evening.*

nip² /nɪp/ *n* [S] **1** a coldness: *There's a nip in the air today: winter's coming.* **2** the act or result of NIPPING¹: *I gave my fingers a bad nip by catching them in the door.*

nip³ /nɪp/ *n infml* a small amount of an alcoholic drink, not beer or wine: *a nip of* WHISKEY

nip·ple /'nɪpəl/ *n* **1** one of the areas of darker skin which stands out from the breasts and through which a baby may suck milk from a woman –compare TEAT **2** *AmE* the piece of rubber shaped like this on the end of a baby's bottle **3** a small opening shaped like this on a machine, for oil or GREASE (2)

nip·py /'nɪpiʸ/ *adj* **-pier, -piest** having a NIP² (1): *a nippy winter morning* –**nippiness** *n* [U]

nit /nɪt/ *n* an egg of an insect (usu. a LOUSE) that is sometimes found in people's hair

nit·pick·ing /'nɪtˌpɪkɪŋ/ *adj,n* [U] *derog infml* paying too much attention to small and unimportant points: *He can't understand a general argument; he always asks nitpicking little questions.*

ni·trate /'naɪtreʸt/ *n* [C;U] any of several chemicals used mainly (as FERTILIZER) in improving soil for growing crops: SODIUM nitrate

ni·tric ac·id /ˌnaɪtrɪk 'æsɪd/ *n* [U] a powerful acid (HNO_3) which eats away (CORRODES) other materials and is used in explosives and other chemical products

ni·tro·gen /'naɪtrədʒən/ *n* [U] a gas that is a simple substance (ELEMENT), without color or smell, that forms most of the earth's air

ni·tro·glyc·er·in, -ine /ˌnaɪtrə'glɪsərɪn, -troʷ-/ *n* [U] a powerful liquid explosive used in DYNAMITE

nit·wit /'nɪtˌwɪt/ *n infml* a silly foolish person

no¹ /noʷ/ *determiner,adv* **1** (used in an answer expressing refusal or disagreement): *"Is it* *raining?" "No, it's snowing."|"Will you mail this letter for me?" "No, I don't want to go out."* –opposite **yes 2** not any; not at all: *There's no sugar in the bowl.|I've no time to talk to you just now.|I'm feeling no better.* (=feeling the same or worse)|(used in warnings and road signs) *No parking* (=do not park here)|*It's no distance to the station.* (=not far at all) –see Study Notes on page 144

USAGE Compare **no** and **not**. Use **no** before nouns (**no** *money*), before noun-like verbs (**no** *smoking*), before adjectives followed by a noun (**no** *black shoes*), or before adverbs of comparison (**no** *better*). Use **not: a** before verbs, to change them to the opposite of their meaning: *I'm* **not** *coming.* **b** before **a, all, both, every, half, the,** etc. (DETERMINERS): **not** *a chance*|**not** *all of us*|**not** *enough* **c** before names (**not** *George*), adverbs (**not** *often*), PREPOSITIONS (**not** *on Sunday*), and most adjectives where no noun follows (*they're* **not** *stupid!*).

no² *n* [S] an answer or decision of no: *a clear no to my request for money* –opposite **yes**

no. nos. *written abbrev. said as:* NUMBER¹ (2)

no·bil·i·ty /noʷˈbɪləti̯/ *n* **1** [*the* U] (in certain countries) the group of people of the highest social class: *The British nobility no longer has much political power.* **2** [U] the quality or condition of being NOBLE¹: *a man of great nobility*

no·ble¹ /ˈnoʷbəl/ *adj* **1** of high (moral) quality; deserving praise; worthy: *noble and generous feelings* –opposite **ignoble 2** of or belonging to a high social titled rank: *a woman of noble birth*

noble² *n* (esp. in FEUDAL times) a person of the highest and most powerful social class –compare COMMONER

no·ble·man /ˈnoʷbəlmən/ **noblewoman** /ˌwʊmən/ *fem.– n* **-men** /mən/ a member of the NOBILITY (1); PEER¹ (2,3)

no·bly /ˈnoʷbli̯/ *adv* in a noble way, esp. in a way deserving of praise: *She nobly did my work as well as hers while I was ill.*

no·bod·y¹ /ˈnoʷˌbadi̯, -bədi̯, -ˌbadi̯/ also **no one–** *pron* no person; not anybody: *There's nobody* (or *there isn't anybody*) *in the room.|Can you help me? Nobody else* (=no other person) *can.*

nobody² *n* **-ies** a person of no importance: *I want to be famous! I'm tired of being a nobody.*

noc·tur·nal /nakˈtɜrnl/ *adj fml or tech* of, happening, or active at night: *a nocturnal visit/bird* –**nocturnally** *adv*

nod /nad/ *v* **-dd- 1** [I;T] to bend (one's head) forward and down, esp. to show agreement or give a greeting or sign: *She nodded (her head) when she passed me in the street.|I asked her if she was ready to go and she nodded.*|(fig.) *flowers nodding in the wind* **2**

[T] to show in this way: *They nodded their agreement.* **3** [I *off*] to let one's head drop in falling asleep: *I nodded off in the meeting and didn't hear what was said.* –**nod** *n: He greeted us with a nod (of the head).*|(fig.) *We waited for Charles to* **give the nod to** (=approve of) *our plan.*

nod·ule /ˈnadʒuʷl/ *n* a small round mass or lump esp. on a plant or a person's body –**nodular** /ˈnadʒələr/ *adj*

No·el /noʷˈɛl/ *n lit* (the season of) Christmas

noise /nɔɪz/ *n* [C;U] (an) unwanted, unpleasant, or confused sound: *I heard a strange noise last night.|There's so much noise in this restaurant I can hardly hear you talking.* –**noiseless** *adj* –**noiselessly** *adv* –**noiselessness** *n* [U]

USAGE A **sound** is anything that you hear: *the sound of voices/of music/of breaking plates.* A **voice** is the sound of a person speaking or singing: *to have a loud voice.* A **noise** is usually a loud unpleasant sound: *Stop making so much noise!*

nois·y /ˈnɔɪzi̯/ *adj* **-ier, -iest** making a lot of noise: *a noisy car|It's very noisy in this office.|This is a very noisy office.* –**noisily** *adv* –**noisiness** *n* [U]

no·mad /ˈnoʷmæd/ *n* a member of a tribe which travels around, esp. to find grass for its animals: *the nomads of the desert* –**nomadic** /noʷˈmædɪk/ *adj: nomadic tribes|a nomadic life* –**nomadically** *adv*

no-man's-land /ˈ·· ˌ·/ *n* [S] the area of land between two opposing armies, belonging to neither

nom de plume /ˌnam də ˈpluʷm/ *n* **noms de plume** (*same pronunciation*) → PEN NAME

no·men·cla·ture /ˈnoʷmənˌkleʸtʃər/ *n* [C;U] *fml* a system of naming things, esp. in a branch of science: *the nomenclature of chemical compounds* –compare TERMINOLOGY

nom·i·nal /ˈnamənl/ *adj* **1** in name or form but usu. not in reality: *The old man is only the nominal head of the business; his daughter makes all the decisions.* **2** (of an amount of money) very small; NEGLIGIBLE: *sold at a nominal price* (=a very low price) –**nominally** *adv: The company is nominally his, but he has nothing to do with it now.*

nom·i·nate /ˈnaməˌneʸt/ *v* **-nated, -nating** [T] **1** [*for*] to suggest or name (someone) officially for election to a position, office, honor, etc.: *I wish to nominate Jane Morrison for president of the club.* **2** [*as*] to appoint (someone) to such a position, office, etc.: *The president nominated me (as/to be) his representative at the meeting.*

nom·i·na·tion /ˌnaməˈneʸʃən/ *n* [C;U] (an example of) the act or result of nominating or being nominated (NOMINATE): *The club agreed to all the committee's nominations.|Who will get the nomination for president?*

nom·i·na·tive¹ /ˈnamənətɪv/ *adj* showing that a word is the subject of a verb: *nominative endings|"We" is nominative, but "us" is accusative.*

nominative² *n* the CASE¹ (6) (set of forms)

SPELLING NOTE

Words with the sound /n/ may be spelled **kn-**, like **know**, or **pn-**, like **pneumonia**.

showing that a word is the subject of a verb: *Put this noun in(to) the nominative.*

nom·i·nee /ˌnɑmə'niy/ *n* a person who has been NOMINATED

non·ag·gres·sion /ˌnɑnə'grɛʃən/ *n* [A] not attacking: *a nonaggression agreement* (=each side promising not to attack the other) –see also AGGRESSION

non·a·ligned /ˌnɑnə'laɪnd/ *adj* (of a country) not supporting the actions of any particular powerful country or group of countries –see also ALIGN –**nonalignment** *n* [U]

non·cha·lant /ˌnɑnʃə'lɑnt, -tʃə-/ *adj* showing calmness, and often lack of interest; COOL (2): *He appeared nonchalant in court even when the judge ordered him to pay $10,000.* –**nonchalance** *n* [S;U]: *She showed a surprising nonchalance the first time she flew a plane.* –**nonchalantly** *adv*

non·com·bat·ant /ˌnɑnkəm'bætnt, -'kɑm bətənt/ *n* a person, esp. in the armed forces (such as a CHAPLAIN), who does not take part in actual fighting: *military duty as a noncombatant|noncombatant duty*

non·com·mis·sioned of·fi·cer /ˌnɑnkə ˌmɪʃənd 'ɔfəsər, 'ɑfə-/ *n* an officer of low rank in the armed forces –see also COMMISSION²

non·com·mit·tal /ˌnɑnkə'mɪtl/ *adj* not expressing a clear opinion or intention: *I asked him if he approved of our plan, but he was noncommittal.* –see also COMMIT (3) –**noncommittally** *adv*

non·con·form·ist /ˌnɑnkən'fɔrmɪst/ *adj,n* (of, concerning, or being) a person who does not follow some customary way(s) of living, acting, thinking, etc.: *a political nonconformist|nonconformist habits* –opposite conformist –**nonconformity, nonconformism** *n* [U]

non·con·trib·u·to·ry /ˌnɑnkən'trɪbyə,tɔriy, -,towriy/ *adj* [A] not having to make payments: *a noncontributory* PENSION *plan*

non·de·script /ˌnɑndɪ'skrɪpt◀/ *adj* without any strong or interesting qualities; dull: *Her clothes were so nondescript that I can't remember what she was wearing.*

none¹ /nʌn/ *pron* **1** not any: *None of the money is mine.|None of my friends ever comes/come to see me.* (=I have more than two friends, but they don't come to see me. Use *neither of my friends* when there are only two)|*Even an old car is better than none at all.* –see EITHER¹ (USAGE); see Study Notes on page 144 **2 none but** *fml* only **3 none other** (*shows surprise*) no one else: *It was none other than Tom! We thought he was in Africa!*

none² *adv* **1 none the** not at all; no: *My car is none the worse for* (=is no worse because of) *the accident.* **2 none too** not very: *The food is none too good here.*

non·en·ti·ty /nɑn'ɛntətiy/ *n* **-ties** a person without much ability, character, or importance: *a weak government, full of politicians who are nonentities*

none·the·less /ˌnʌnðə'lɛs◀/ *adv* in spite of that; NEVERTHELESS –see Study Notes on page 144

non·e·vent /ˌnɑnɪ'vɛnt/ *n infml* a happening that is much less important, interesting, etc., than expected: *The election was a real non-event; only a few people voted.*

non·ex·ist·ent /ˌnɑnɪg'zɪstənt◀/ *adj* not existing: *This year's profits were very small; in fact, they are almost nonexistent.*

non·fic·tion /ˌnɑn'fɪkʃən/ *n* [U] literature other than poetry, plays, stories, and NOVELs –see also FICTION

non·flam·ma·ble /ˌnɑn'flæməbəl/ *adj* difficult or impossible to burn –opposite **inflammable, flammable**

non·in·ter·ven·tion /ˌnɑnɪntər'vɛnʃən, -tʃən/ also **noninterference** /ˌnɑnɪntər'fɪərəns/– *n* [U] the practice by a government of taking no part in the affairs or disputes of another country –see also INTERVENE

non·pay·ment /ˌnɑn'peymənt/ *n* [U *of*] failure to pay (bills, tax, etc.): *This letter is about nonpayment of your income tax.*

non·plussed /ˌnɑn'plʌst/ *adj* surprised; not knowing what to think or do: *The speaker was completely nonplussed by the angry remarks from his listeners.*

non·prof·it /ˌnɑn'prɑfɪt/ *AmE*‖**nonprofit-making** /ˌnɑn'prɑfɪt,meykɪŋ/ *adj* not run in order to make a profit: *This is a nonprofit organization.*

non·pro·lif·er·a·tion /ˌnɑnprə,lɪfə'reyʃən/ *n* [U] the result of keeping atomic weapons in only the same amounts and in the same countries as at the (present) time: *a nonproliferation agreement* –see also PROLIFERATE

non·sense /'nɑnsɛns, -səns/ *n* [U] speech, writing, thinking, behavior, etc., that is stupid: *A lot of the government's new ideas are nonsense.|I've never heard such nonsense!|Stop that nonsense, children! Behave yourselves.* –see also SENSE¹ (3)

non·sen·si·cal /nɑn'sɛnsɪkəl/ *adj* full of NONSENSE; foolish or ABSURD: *nonsensical opinions* –**nonsensically** *adv*

non se·qui·tur /ˌnɑn 'sɛkwɪtər/ *n* **non sequiturs** *fml & Latin* a statement which does not follow from the facts or arguments which are given

non·stand·ard /ˌnɑn'stændərd◀/ *adj* (of words, expressions, pronunciations, etc.) not usually used by educated native speakers of a language –compare SUBSTANDARD, STANDARD² (2)

non·stick /ˌnɑn'stɪk◀/ *adj* [A] (of a cooking pan) having a specially treated smooth inside surface that food will not stick to

non·stop /ˌnɑn'stɑp◀/ *adj,adv* without a pause or interruption; without stopping: *a nonstop flight to New York|You can now fly nonstop from London to Singapore.*

non·vi·o·lence /ˌnɑn'vaɪələns/ *n* [U] opposition without using force or violence, shown esp. by not obeying laws or orders *adj: nonviolent* PROTEST¹ –**nonviolently** *adv*

noo·dle /'nuwdl/ *n* [*usu. pl.*] a usu. long thin piece of paste made from flour, water, and eggs, boiled until soft and eaten in soups, with meat, etc.

nook /nʊk/ *n lit or humor* a sheltered and private place: *a shady nook in the garden*

noon /nuʷn/ *n* 12 o'clock in the daytime; MIDDAY: *We left home at noon.|Noon is the earliest time I can come.*

noon·day /'nuʷndeʸ/ *n lit for* MIDDAY: *the noonday sun*

no one /'·· ·/ *pron* → NOBODY[1]

noose /nuʷs/ *n* a ring formed by the end of a cord, rope, etc., which closes more tightly as it is pulled (esp. as used to hang a person)

nope /nowp/ *adv infml for* NO[1] (1)

no-place /'nowpleʸs/ *adv* → NOWHERE

nor /nər; *strong* nɔr/ *conj* **1** (used in a list of NEGATIVE possibilities, often after *neither*): *It can't be done by you nor me nor anyone.|Neither my father nor I was there.* –see EITHER[2] (USAGE) **2** (used with NEGATIVE[1] (1) expressions) also not; neither: *"I can't swim." "Nor can I!"* (=both of us are unable to swim) –see NEITHER (USAGE)

norm /nɔrm/ *n* **1** a standard of proper behavior or principle of right and wrong; rule: *social norms* **2** a usual or expected number, amount, pattern of action or behavior, etc.; average: *The norm in this examination is 70 out of 100.*

nor·mal /'nɔrməl/ *adj* according to what is expected, usual, or average: *normal working hours from nine to five|Rainfall has been above/below normal this July.|She is a normal child in every way.* –see also ABNORMAL

nor·mal·i·ty /nɔr'mælətiʸ/ also **normalcy** /'nɔrməlsiʸ/ *AmE– n* [U] the quality or fact of being NORMAL

nor·mal·ize ‖also **-ise** *BrE* /'nɔrmə,laɪz/ *v* **-ized, -izing** [I;T] (esp. in relations between countries) to (cause to) come back to a good or friendly state: *The two countries tried to normalize relations after the war.* –**normalization** /,nɔrmələ'zeʸʃən/ *n* [U]

nor·mal·ly /'nɔrməliʸ/ *adv* **1** in a NORMAL way or to a NORMAL degree: *He was behaving normally in spite of his anxiety.* **2** in the usual conditions; ordinarily: *I normally go to bed early, but I stayed up late last night.*

north[1] /nɔrθ/ *n* [*the* S] (*often cap.*) **1** (the direction of) one of the four main points of the compass, which is on the left of a person facing the rising sun: *I'm lost. Which direction is north?* |*a window facing the north|the north wall of a building* **2** [A] (of a wind) coming from this direction: *a cold north wind* **3** the North (in the US) the northern part of the US: *The problem of unemployment is much worse in the North than in the South.*

north[2] *adv* (*often cap.*) towards the NORTH[1] (1): *to travel (further) north|The room faces north, so it's always cold.|San Francisco is (a long way) north of Los Angeles.*

north·bound /'nɔrθbaʊnd/ *adj* traveling towards the north: *northbound traffic*

north·east[1] /,nɔrθ'iʸst◂/ *n* **1** [*the* S] (the direction of) the point of the compass which is half-way between north and east **2** (of a

wind) coming from this direction: *a northeast wind* –**northeasterly** /,nɔrθ'iʸstərliʸ/ *adj*

northeast[2] *adv* towards the NORTHEAST[1] (1): *to sail northeast*

north·er·ly /'nɔrðərliʸ/ *adj* **1** towards or in the north: *a northerly direction* **2** (of a wind) coming from the north: *a cold northerly wind*

north·ern /'nɔrðərn/ *adj* (*often cap.*) of or belonging to the north part of anything, esp. of the world or of a country: *The northern half of the Earth is called the Northern HEMISPHERE.*

north·ern·most /'nɔrðərn,mowst/ *adj* furthest north: *the northernmost parts of Canada*

North Pole /,· '·/ *n* [*the* S] (the lands around) the most northern point on the surface of the earth –see also SOUTH POLE

north·ward /'nɔrθwərd/ *adj* going towards the north: *a northward journey* –**northward** *AmE*‖also **northwards**– *adv: to sail northward*

north·west[1] /,nɔrθ'wɛst◂/ *n* **1** [*the* S] (the direction of) the point of the compass which is half-way between north and west **2** (of a wind) coming from this direction: *a northwest wind* –**northwesterly** /,nɔrθ'wɛstərliʸ/ *adj*

northwest[2] *adv* towards the NORTHWEST[1] (1): *Chicago is northwest of New York.*

nose[1] /nowz/ *n* **1** [C] the part of the face above the mouth, which is the organ of smell and through which air is breathed **2** [C] *infml* this organ regarded as representing too great interest in things which do not concern one: *Keep your nose out of/Stop poking your nose into my affairs!* **3** [S] the sense of smell: *This dog has a good nose.*|(fig.) *A newspaper reporter must have a nose for a good story.* (=have a special ability to find one) **4** [C] the front end of something, such as a car, plane, tool, or gun **5 cut off one's nose to spite one's face** to do something to one's own disadvantage because one is angry **6 look down one's nose at** *infml* to have or show a low opinion of (someone thought to be less socially important) **7 on the nose** *infml* exactly correct: *You guessed the winning number on the nose.* **8 pay through the nose** *infml* to pay far too much **9 put someone's nose out of joint** *infml* to make someone jealous by taking his/her place as the centre of attention **10 under someone's (very) nose** *infml* right in front of someone; quite openly: *They stole the jewels from under the (very) nose(s) of the police.* **11 turn up one's nose (at)** *infml* to consider (something) not good enough to eat, take part in, etc.: *I wish my children wouldn't turn up their noses at eating vegetables.* **12 -nosed** having a certain shape or kind of nose: *red-nosed|broken-nosed*

nose[2] *v* **nosed, nosing 1** [I;T] to move or push ahead slowly or carefully: *I nosed the car/The car nosed (out) into the traffic.* **2** [I] *infml* to attempt to find out esp. things that do not concern one; search: *I found her nosing around among my private papers.|Stop nosing into my affairs!*

nose·bag /'nowzbæg/ also **feedbag** *AmE– n* a

bag hung around a horse's head to hold its
food

nose·bleed /'noᵂzbliʸd/ n a case of bleeding
from the nose: *I had a nosebleed today.*

nose·dive./'noᵂzdaɪv/ v **-dived, -diving** [I] (of
an aircraft) to drop suddenly with the nose
pointing straight down: (fig.) *Profits have
nosedived* (=gone down very sharply) *in the
last year.* **–nosedive** n

nosh /nɑʃ/ n infml for SNACK *I don't need a
whole meal, I just want a nosh.* **–nosh** v [I on]:
He's noshing on an apple.

nos·tal·gia /nɑ'stæld3ə, nə-/ n [U] fondness
for something in the past: *I was filled with
nostalgia from hearing my favorite old song.*
–nostalgic adj **–nostalgically** adv

nos·tril /'nɑstrəl/ n either of the two openings
at the end of the nose, through which one
breathes

nos·y, nosey /'noᵂziʸ/ adj derog interested in
things that do not concern one; PRYING¹: *Our
nosy neighbors are always looking into our
windows.* **–nosiness** n [U]

not /nɑt/ adv shortened to **n't** /ənt/ after helping verbs **1** (used for changing a word or
expression to one with the opposite mean-
ing): *not thirsty|not on Sunday|We're not/We
aren't coming.|It's a cat, not a dog.|Not
everyone likes this book.* (=some people
don't like it) **2** (used in place of a whole
expression): *"Will it rain?" "I hope not."* (=I
hope it won't rain)|*I'll try to be there by nine,
but if not, start the meeting without me.* **3 not
a** not even one: *"How much did this cost?"
"Not a cent!"* (=nothing) **4 not at all** (an
answer to polite praise or thanks): *"Thanks
for helping me." "Not at all. I enjoyed it."* **5
not that** although it is not true that: *Where
were you last night? Not that I care, of course.*
–see NO (USAGE)

no·ta·ble¹ /'noᵂtəbəl/ adj [for] worthy of
notice; REMARKABLE; OUTSTANDING: *notable
events|a notable lawyer* **–notability** /ˌnoᵂ
tə'bɪlətiʸ/ n [U]

notable² n [usu. pl.] a famous or important
person

no·ta·bly /'noᵂtəbliʸ/ adv **1** especially; particularly: *Many members were absent, notably
the vice-chairman.* **2** noticeably: *notably
higher sales*

no·ta·ry /'noᵂtəriʸ/ **-ries** also **notary public**
/ˌ··· ˈ···/– n a person with the power in law to
witness the signing of written statements and
make them official **–notarize** /'noᵂtəˌraɪz/
-rized, -rizing v [T]

no·ta·tion /noᵂ'teʸʃən/ n [C;U] (writing that
uses) a set of written signs to describe the
stated kinds of things: *a page covered with
musical notation*

notch¹ /nɑtʃ/ n **1** a V-shaped cut in a surface
or edge: *He cut a notch in the stick with a
sharp knife.* **2** infml a degree: *He's a notch
above the rest of the workers.* **3** AmE a narrow passage between mountains

notch² v [T] **1** to make a notch in **2** [up] infml
to win or record (a victory or gain): *The team
notched (up) their third victory in a row.*

note¹ /noᵂt/ v **noted, noting** [T] **1** to pay attention to and remember: *Please note that this*

bill must be paid within ten days. **2** to write
down as a record or reminder: *He noted
down my new address.*

note² n **1** also **tone** AmE– (a written sign
representing) a single musical sound of a
particular degree of highness or lowness: *I
can't sing the high notes.* **2** a quality (of
voice): *There was a note of anger in what he
said.* **3** a record or reminder in writing: *Make
a note of how much money you spend.|She
takes* (=writes down) *good notes of
everything that's said in class.* **4** a remark
added to a piece of writing and placed outside the main part of the writing (as at the
bottom of a page), esp. to give additional
information **5** a short letter, usu. informal **6**
also **bill** AmE– a piece of paper money: *a $5
note* **7 compare notes** infml **a** (with) to tell
one's experiences and opinions of something
(to) **b** (of 2 people) to tell these. to one
another: *Mary and I have been comparing
notes about our trips to Mexico.* **8 of note** fml
of fame or importance: *She's a musician of
(some/great) note.* **9 take note of** to pay
attention to: *Take (careful) note of what I
say, and please don't forget it.*

note·book /'noᵂtbʊk/ n a book in which
NOTES² (3) may be written

not·ed /'noᵂtɪd/ adj [for] well-known;
famous: *a noted performer|a town noted for
its beauty*

note·pa·per /'noᵂtˌpeʸpər/ n [U] paper for
writing letters and NOTES² (5) –see also WRIT-
ING PAPER

note·wor·thy /'noᵂtˌwɜrðiʸ/ adj (esp. of
things and events) worthy of attention;
NOTABLE¹

noth·ing /'nʌθɪŋ/ pron **1** not any thing; no
thing: *There's nothing in this box; it's
empty.|I've got nothing to do.|There's
nothing he likes more than playing football.* **2**
something of no importance: *She means
nothing to me.|They* **think nothing of** *walking
20 miles.* **3 for nothing: a** for no money; free:
He gave me this bicycle for nothing. **b** with no
good result: *All her efforts were for nothing.*
4 nothing but only: *He's nothing but a criminal.* **5 nothing doing** infml I won't! No!:
*"Come to the movies with me." "Nothing
doing. I have to stay home and work."* **b** no
result, interest, action, permission, etc.: *We
went to a party last night, but there was
nothing doing so we left early.* **6 nothing like:
a** nothing better than: *There's nothing like a
cup of tea when you're thirsty.* **b** not nearly:
It's nothing like it was yesterday. **7 nothing to
do with** no connection with **8 to say nothing
of** as well as; including: *Three people were
badly hurt, to say nothing of the damage to
the building.* **9 nothing much** infml not much;
very little: *"Is anything interesting happening?" "No, nothing much."* –compare SOME-
THING¹, EVERYTHING

nothing² n [usu. sing.] a thing or person with
no value or importance: *She's an interesting
person but her husband is a real nothing.*

noth·ing·ness /'nʌθɪŋnɪs/ n [U] the state of
being nothing; not being: *Is there only
nothingness after death?*

no·tice¹ /'noʷtɪs/ n **1** [U] warning or information about something that will happen: *These rules may be changed without notice.|The factory is closed* **until further notice.** (=until you are informed of its reopening)|*Can you be ready in ten minutes' notice/***at short notice**? (=if I tell you only ten minutes/a short time before)|*I gave notice at work today.* (=officially informed my employers that I intend to leave)|*The owners of my apartment have given us six weeks' notice to leave.* (=told us we have to leave in six weeks) **2** [U] attention: **Don't take any/Take no notice of** (=pay no attention to) *what they say.|His writings brought him public notice.* **3** [C] a usu. short written statement of information or directions to the public: *The notice on the wall says "No smoking."* **4** [C] a statement of opinion, esp. in a newspaper, about a new book, play, etc.; REVIEW¹ (2): *The new play got favorable notices in the newspapers.*

notice² v **-ticed, -ticing** [I;T +(*that*)] to be aware of, esp. by seeing: *She was wearing a new dress, but he didn't even notice (it).|I noticed (that) he wasn't wearing any socks.|Did you notice where I put it?|I noticed her leave/leaving.*

no·tice·a·ble /'noʷtɪsəbəl/ adj that can be noticed; worth noticing: *a noticeable drop in the amount of crime* **–noticeably** adv: *There was noticeably less rain this year.*

notice board /'·· ‚·/ n BrE for BULLETIN BOARD

no·ti·fy /'noʷtə‚faɪ/ v **-fied, -fying** [T *of*] to tell (someone), esp. formally: *to notify the police of a crime|I'll notify my lawyer to write out the agreement.* **–notification** /‚noʷtəfə'keʸʃən/ n [C;U]

no·tion /'noʷʃən/ n [+*that/of*] an idea, belief, or opinion; CONCEPTION (1): *I haven't the faintest notion (of) what you're talking about.|He is full of silly notions.*

no·to·ri·e·ty /‚noʷtə'raɪətiʸ/ n [U] the state of being NOTORIOUS

no·to·ri·ous /noʷ'tɔriʸəs, -'toʷr-/ adj derog famous for something bad; widely and unfavorably known: *a notorious thief/ prison|an area notorious for crime* –see FAMOUS (USAGE) **–notoriously** adv

not·with·stand·ing /‚nɑtwɪθ'stændɪŋ, -wɪð-/ prep,adv fml in spite of (this): *Notwithstanding any other agreements, we will make a new contract with the firm.|He tried to prevent the marriage but it took place notwithstanding.*

nought /nɔt/ n **1** esp. BrE (the figure) 0; zero: *0.6 is usually read "nought point* SIX*."* **2** esp. old use & lit nothing; NAUGHT

noun /naʊn/ n a word that is the name of a person, place, thing, quality, action, etc., and can be used as the subject or object of a verb. *Nouns are marked "n" in this dictionary.* –compare PRONOUN

SPELLING NOTE
Words with the sound /n/ may be spelled **kn-**, like **know**, or **pn-**, like **pneumonia**.

---

nour·ish /'nɜrɪʃ, 'nʌrɪʃ/ v [T] to cause to stay alive or grow by giving food, water, etc.: *nourishing food|a well-nourished baby* –see also UNDERNOURISH

nour·ish·ment /'nɜrɪʃmənt, 'nʌr-/ n [U] something that NOURISHES; food: *The child took no nourishment all day.*

nov·el¹ /'nɑvəl/ n a long written story dealing with invented people and events: *"War and Peace," the great novel by Leo Tolstoy*

novel² adj new; not like anything known before: *a novel suggestion, something we hadn't tried before*

nov·el·ist /'nɑvəlɪst/ n a writer of NOVELs

nov·el·ty /'nɑvəltiʸ/ n **-ties** **1** [U] the state or quality of being NOVEL² **2** [S] something new and unusual: *I go out so rarely that it was a novelty for me to go to the movies last night.* **3** [C] an unusual cheap, usu. not very useful, small object: *stores full of Christmas novelties*

No·vem·ber /noʷ'vɛmbər, nə-/ also **Nov.** written abbrev.– n the 11th month of the year

nov·ice /'nɑvɪs/ n **1** a person with no experience in a skill or subject; BEGINNER: *a novice swimmer/a novice at swimming* **2** a person who has recently joined a religious group to become a MONK or NUN

now¹ /naʊ/ adv **1 a** at this time; at present: *We used to live in Washington but now we live in New York.|We've had dinner; now let's have some coffee.|Goodbye for now.|From now on* (=starting now) *I will try to do better.* **b** at the time mentioned in a story: *He opened the door. Now the noise was very loud.* **2** (used for starting a new subject, or to warn someone or tell them what to do): *Now, let's move on to the next question.|Now then, what's happened? |Be careful, now!|Now, now, stop crying!* **4 just now: a** at this moment: *I'm busy just now; come back later.* **b** a moment ago: *He telephoned just now.*

now² also **now that**– conj because something has happened: *Now (that) John's arrived, we can begin.*

now·a·days /'naʊə‚deʸz/ adv at the present time: *Gasoline costs a lot nowadays.*

no·where /'noʷhwɛər, 'noʷwɛər/ adv **1** not anywhere; in or to no place: *The book was nowhere to be found.|The poor old man has nowhere to live.|(fml) Nowhere have I seen so many beautiful houses.* **2** also **noplace**– AmE infml no purpose or result: *That kind of talk will* **get** (you) **nowhere** (=will not do you any good).|*Five dollars goes nowhere now.* (=will hardly buy anything) –compare SOMEWHERE, EVERYWHERE

nox·ious /'nɑkʃəs/ adj fml harmful: *noxious chemicals in the river water*

noz·zle /'nɑzəl/ n a short tube fitted to the end of a HOSE, pipe, BELLOWS, etc., to direct and control the stream of liquid or gas coming out

n't /ənt/ short for not: *hadn't|didn't| wouldn't|isn't*

nu·ance /'nuwɑns, 'nyuʷ-, nuʷ'ɑns, nyuʷ-/ n a slight difference in color, meaning, etc.: *nuances of taste which are hard to describe*

nu·bile /'nuʷbəl, -baɪl, 'nyuʷ-/ *adj fml or humor* (of a girl) young and sexually attractive

nu·cle·ar /'nuʷkliʸər, 'nyuʷ-/ *adj* **1** of, concerning, or using the NUCLEUS of an atom, ATOMIC ENERGY, or the ATOM BOMB: *a nuclear power station|nuclear war|nuclear PHYSICS* **2** of, concerning, or being a NUCLEUS (1): *A father, mother, and children make up a* **nuclear family**.

nuclear dis·ar·ma·ment /ˌ··· ·'···/ *n* [U] the giving up of atomic weapons by agreement between nations

nuclear en·er·gy /ˌ··· '···/ also **atomic energy**– *n* [U] the powerful force that is given out when the middle part (NUCLEUS) of an atom is split or joined to another atom, used to make electricity, drive large ships, in ATOM BOMBS, etc.

nuclear re·ac·tor /ˌ··· ·'··/ also **reactor, atomic pile**– *n* a large machine that produces NUCLEAR ENERGY

nu·cle·us /'nuʷkliʸəs, 'nyuʷ-/ *n* **1** an original or central point, part, or group inside a larger thing, group, organization, etc.: *100 books as the nucleus of a new school library* **2** the central part of an atom, made up of NEUTRONS and PROTONS

nude¹ /nuʷd, nyuʷd/ *adj* not covered by clothes; NAKED

nude² *n* **1** [C] (a piece of art showing) a person without clothes **2** [U] the state of being NUDE: *They went swimming* **in the nude.**

nudge /nʌdʒ/ *v* **nudged, nudging** [T] to touch or push gently, esp. with one's elbow: *He nudged his friend to let him know it was time to leave.* –**nudge** *n: He felt a sharp nudge in his side.*

nud·ism /'nuʷdɪzəm, 'nyuʷ-/ *n* [U] the practice of living without clothes, esp. in a group –**nudist** *adj,n: a nudist camp* (=a place where nudists go for vacations)

nu·di·ty /'nuʷdəʈiʸ, 'nyuʷ-/ *n* [U] the quality or state of being NUDE: *There has been a lot of nudity in recent movies.*

nug·get /'nʌgɪt/ *n* a small rough lump of a precious metal, found in the earth: *a gold nugget*

nui·sance /'nuʷsəns, 'nyuʷ-/ *n* a person, animal, or action that annoys or causes trouble: *Sit down and stop being a nuisance|making a nuisance of yourself.|What a nuisance! I forgot my ticket.*

nuke /nuʷk, nyuʷk/ *n,v* **nuked, nuking** [C;T] *infml* (to attack with) a NUCLEAR weapon

null and void /ˌnʌl ən 'vɔɪd/ *adj fml & law* without force or effect in law: *The court ruled that the claim was null and void.*

nul·li·fy /'nʌlə,faɪ/ *v* **-fied, -fying** [T] *fml* to cause or declare to have no effect (in law): *a claim nullified by the court* –**nullification** /ˌnʌləfə'keʸʃən/ *n* [U]

numb¹ /nʌm/ *adj* [*with*] (of the body) unable to feel anything: *My hands are numb after an hour outside on such a cold day.* (fig.) *numb with shock* –**numbly** /'nʌmliʸ/ *adv* **numbness** *n* [U]

numb² *v* [T] to cause to feel nothing or no pain; make NUMB¹: *fingers numbed with cold|the numbing effect of the drug* –**numbingly** *adv*

num·ber¹ /'nʌmbər/ *n* **1** [C] (a written sign representing) a member of a system used in counting: *1, 2, and 3 are numbers.|Choose any number between one and ten.|What is your telephone number?* **2** [A] (usu. written No., no.) having the stated size, place in order, etc.: *We live at No. 57, Church Street.* (=our house has the number 57) **3** [C;U] (a) quantity or amount: *The number of chairs in the room is 10.|Members are few in number.|***A number of** (=several) *visitors came to the meeting.|I've told you* **any number of** (=very many) *times not to do that.|Our army was beaten by* **sheer weight of numbers.** (=by the large amount of enemy soldiers) **4** [C] a (copy of a) magazine printed at a particular time; ISSUE¹ (2): *The latest number of "Vogue" magazine* **5** [C] a piece of (popular) music **6 have someone's number** *infml* to have knowledge useful in annoying or defeating someone: *Our team couldn't do anything right; the opposing team had their number.*

USAGE Plural nouns after a number usually take a plural verb, but if you are giving an opinion about the size of the number itself, use a singular verb. Compare: *25 bottles of wine* **were** *drunk at the office party.|25 bottles of wine* **is** *too much for the office party.* –see AMOUNT (USAGE)

number² *v* **1** [T] to give a number to: *Number the questions (from) 1 to 10.* **2** to reach as a total; be in number: *The people at the meeting numbered several THOUSANDS.* **3** [*among, as, with*] to be included: *He is numbered among the best of modern writers.* **4 someone's days are numbered** *infml* someone cannot continue or live much longer

num·ber plate /'nʌmbər,pleʸt/ *n BrE* for LICENSE PLATE

nu·mer·al /'nuʷmərəl, 'nyuʷ-/ *adj,n* (any of the systems of signs) used for representing a number or numbers; (of) NUMBER¹ (1) –compare ROMAN NUMERAL, ARABIC NUMERAL

nu·mer·i·cal /nuʷ'merɪkəl, nyuʷ-/ *adj* of, concerning, showing, or shown by a number or numbers: *numerical ability* (=skill with numbers)*|numerical order* –**numerically** *adv: numerically greater* (=greater in number(s))

num·er·ous /'nuʷmərəs, 'nyuʷ-/ *adj* many: *one of my numerous relatives|for numerous reasons* –**numerously** *adv*

nun /nʌn/ *n* a member of an all-female religious group that lives together in a CONVENT –compare MONK

nun·ner·y /'nʌnəriʸ/ *n* **-ies** a building in which NUNS live; CONVENT –compare MONASTERY

nup·tial /'nʌpʃəl, -tʃəl/ *adj* [A] *pomp or tech* of or concerning marriage or the marriage ceremony: *the nuptial day* –**nuptials** *n* [P]: *The nuptials were performed by the local priest.*

nurse¹ /nɜrs/ *n* **1** [A;C;S] a person who is trained to take care of sick, hurt, or old people, esp. as directed by a doctor in a hospital: *a student nurse* (=a person learning to be a nurse)|*a private nurse taking care of him at home* –see illustration on page 201 **2** a woman employed to take care of a young child

nurse² *v* **nursed, nursing 1** [T] to take care of as or like a nurse: *He nursed her back to health.*|*She spends her time nursing her old father.* **2** [I;T] to give (a baby) milk from the breast: *a nursing mother* **3** [T] to hold (esp. a bad feeling) in the mind: *She still nursed a grudge* (=kept an angry feeling) *against her old enemy.*

nurse·maid /'nɜrsmeʸd/ *n* → NURSE¹ (2)

nurs·er·y /'nɜrsəriʸ/ *n* **-ies 1** a place where small children are taken care of while their parents are at work, shopping, etc. **2** an area where young plants and trees are grown **3** *esp. old use* a small child's bedroom or playroom in a house

nurs·er·y·man /'nɜrsəriʸmən/ *n* **-men** /mən/ a person who grows plants in a NURSERY (2)

nursery rhyme /'··· ˌ·/ also **Mother Goose rhyme** *AmE*– *n* a short usu. old and well-known song or poem for small children

nursery school /'··· ˌ·/ *n* a school for young children of three to five years of age: *children at nursery school* –compare KINDERGARTEN

nurs·ing /'nɜrsɪŋ/ *n* [U] the job of a NURSE¹ (1): *If you like helping sick people, why not go into nursing?* (=become a nurse)

nursing home /'··· ˌ·/ *n* a usu. private establishment where old or sick people are cared for by nurses

nur·ture /'nɜrtʃər/ *v* **-tured, -turing** [T] *lit* to give care and food to: *nurtured by loving parents*

nut /nʌt/ *n* **1 a** a dry fruit with a seed (KERNEL) surrounded by a hard shell **b** this seed, which is eaten **2** a small piece of metal for screwing onto a BOLT¹ (1) **3** *infml* a person who is or seems to be unbalanced in the mind; a crazy (1) person **4** *infml* one's head: *You must be off your nut!* (=mad) **5** *infml* a person with a very strong interest of the stated kind;

FREAK¹ (3): *She's a health food nut; she only eats fruits and vegetables.* **6 a hard/tough nut to crack** *infml* a difficult question, person, etc.,to deal with

nut·crack·er /'nʌtˌkrækər/ *n* a tool for cracking the shell of a nut: *Do we have a nut cracker/a pair of nutcrackers in the house?* –see PAIR (USAGE)

nut·meg /'nʌtmɛg/ *n* [C;U] a seed or powder used (as a SPICE) to give a particular taste to food

nu·tri·ent /'nuʷtriʸənt, 'nyuʷ-/ *adj,n tech* (a chemical or food) providing for life and growth

nu·tri·tion /nuʷ'trɪʃən, nyuʷ-/ *n* [U] the action of providing or state of being provided with food; NOURISHMENT: *Good nutrition is important for good health.* –see also MALNUTRITION

nu·tri·tious /nuʷ'trɪʃəs, nyuʷ-/ *adj* valuable to the body as food; NOURISHING: *Eat lots of good nutritious food.*

nuts /nʌts/ *adj* [F] *infml* mad; CRAZY (1): *I'll go nuts if I have to wait much longer.*

nut·ty /'nʌtiʸ/ *adj* **-tier, -tiest 1 a** tasting like nuts: *wine with a nutty taste* **b** filled with nuts: *a nutty cake* **2** *infml* mad; CRAZY –**nuttiness** *n* [U]

nuz·zle /'nʌzəl/ *v* **-zled, -zling** [I;T *up, against*] (esp. of an animal) to rub, touch, or push with the nose: *The dog nuzzled the sleeping child.*

NW *written abbrev. said as:* northwest(ern)

ny·lon /'naɪlən/ *n* [U] a strong man-made material made into clothes, string, and plastics: *nylon thread/thread made of nylon*|*a nylon shirt*

ny·lons /'naɪlənz/ *n* [P] *becoming rare* women's nylon stockings: *a pair of nylons* –see PAIR (USAGE)

nymph /nɪmf/ *n* (in Greek and Roman literature) any of the less important goddesses of nature, represented as young girls

nym·pho·ma·ni·ac /ˌnɪmfə'meʸniˌæk/ *n,adj* (of or being) a woman who has unusually strong sexual desires

O, o

O, o /oʷ/ **O's, o's** *or* **Os, os 1** the 15th letter of the English alphabet **2** (in speech) zero

oaf /oʷf/ *n* a stupid ungraceful person (esp. male): *You* CLUMSY *oaf!* –**oafish** *adj* –**oafishly** *adv* –**oafishness** *n* [U]

oak /oʷk/ *n* [C;U] (the hard wood of) a large tree which grows ACORNs

oar /ɔr, oʷr/ *n* a long pole with a wide flat blade, used for rowing a boat: *He pulled hard on the oars.* –compare PADDLE¹

o·a·sis /oʷ'eʸsɪs/ *n* **-ses** /siʸz/ a place with trees and water in a desert

oath /oʷθ/ *n* **oaths** /oʷðz, oʷθs/ **1** a solemn promise: *to swear/take an oath* –compare VOW¹ **2** an expression of strong feeling using religious or sexual words improperly: *oaths*

and CURSES (3) **3 be on/under oath** *law* to have made a solemn promise to tell the truth

oat·meal /'oʷtmiʸl/ *n* [U] crushed OATS used for making cakes and breakfast food

oats /oʷts/ *n* [P] **1** a grain that provides food for people and animals **2** → OATMEAL **3 feel one's oats** *infml* to feel full of life and ready for action **4 sow one's wild oats** to chase pleasure foolishly while still young

ob·du·rate /'abdərɪt, -dyər-, -dʒər-/ *adj fml* unchangeable in beliefs or feelings; STUBBORN –**obdurately** *adv* –**obduracy** *n* [U]

o·be·di·ent /ə'biʸdiʸənt, oʷ-/ *adj* doing what one is ordered to do; willing to obey: *an obedient child/dog* –opposite **disobedient** –**obediently** *adv* –**obedience** *n* [U]

ob·e·lisk /'abəlɪsk/ n a tall pointed stone pillar built usu. in honor of a person or event

o·bese /owˈbiˑys/ adj fml very fat –see THIN (USAGE) –**obesity** n [U]

o·bey /owˈbeˑy, ə-/ v **-beyed, -beying** [I;T] to do (what one is asked or ordered to do) by (someone): *Obey (the law/orders/your teachers) or you will be punished.* –opposite **disobey**

o·bit·u·ar·y /əˈbɪt∫uˑwˌeriˑy, owˈ-/ n **-ies** a formal report, esp. in a newspaper, that someone has died, esp. with an account of the dead person's life

ob·ject¹ /'abdʒɪkt, 'abdʒɛkt/ n **1** a thing that can be seen or touched **2** [of] something that produces interest or other effect: *an object of admiration/of fear* **3** purpose; aim: *The object of his visit was to open the new hospital.* **4** *tech* a term used in grammar to describe words in a certain situation. In the sentences *John gave Mary a book; John gave a book to Mary, "(to) Mary"* is the **indirect object** of the verb, and *"book"* is the **direct object** –compare SUBJECT¹ (6) –see Study Notes on page 745 **5 no object** to a difficulty: *I will pay anything; money is no object.*

ob·ject² /əbˈdʒɛkt/ v **1** [I to] to be against; feel dislike: *Do you object to smoking?* **2** [T +(that)] to give as an OBJECTION: *I wanted to climb the hill, but Bill objected that he was too tired.* –**objector** n

ob·jec·tion /əbˈdʒɛk∫ən/ n [to] **1** a statement or feeling of dislike, disapproval, or opposition: *to raise/voice an objection* **2** a reason or argument against

ob·jec·tion·a·ble /əbˈdʒɛk∫ənəbəl/ adj unpleasant; offensive: *objectionable people/ behavior* –**objectionably** adv

ob·jec·tive¹ /əbˈdʒɛktɪv/ adj **1** not influenced by personal feelings; fair: *an objective decision* **2** existing outside the mind; real –compare SUBJECTIVE –**objectively** adv: *Objectively (speaking), he can't possibly succeed.* –**objectivity** /ˌabdʒɛkˈtɪvətiˑy/ n [U]

objective² n an object to be won; purpose of a plan

ob·jet d'art /ˌɔbʒeˑy ˈdɑr, ˌab-/ n **objets d'art** (*same pronunciation*) French an object, usu. small, having some artistic value

ob·li·gate /'abləˌgeˑyt/ v **-gated, -gating** [T usu. pass.] fml to make (someone) feel it necessary (to do something); OBLIGE (1): *He felt obligated to visit his parents.*

ob·li·ga·tion /ˌabləˈgeˑy∫ən/ n a duty; necessity: *Have a look around the store; you're under no obligation to buy anything.*

o·blig·a·to·ry /əˈblɪgəˌtɔriˑy, -ˌtowriˑy/ adj necessary; which must be done by law, rule, etc. –compare OPTIONAL

o·blige /əˈblaɪdʒ/ v **-bliged, -bliging** [T] **1** [usu. pass.] to force (someone to do something): *He felt obliged to leave after such an unpleasant argument.* **2** polite to do (someone) a favor: *Could you oblige me by opening the window?* **3 (I'm) much obliged (to you)** polite (I'm) very grateful (to you)

o·blig·ing /əˈblaɪdʒɪŋ/ adj kind and eager to help –**obligingly** adv

o·blique /owˈbliˑyk, ə-/ adj **1** indirect: *an oblique remark* **2** in a sideways direction; sloping: *an oblique line* **3** tech (of an angle) more or less than 90°

ob·lit·er·ate /əˈblɪtəˌreˑyt/ v **-ated, -ating** [T] to remove all signs of; destroy –**obliteration** /əˌblɪtəˈreˑy∫ən/ n [U]

ob·liv·i·on /əˈblɪviˑyən/ n [U] **1** the state of having forgotten; unconsciousness; OBLIVIOUSNESS **2** the state of being forgotten

ob·liv·i·ous /əˈblɪviˑyəs/ adj [to, of] not noticing: *He was quite oblivious to the danger he was in.* –**obliviously** adv –**obliviousness** n [U]

ob·long /'ablɔŋ/ adj,n (a figure) with four straight sides, forming four right angles, which is longer than it is wide; RECTANGLE –compare SQUARE¹ (1)

ob·nox·ious /əbˈnak∫əs/ adj fml unpleasant; nasty: *an obnoxious smell/person* –**obnoxiously** adv

o·boe /'owˑbow/ n a musical WIND INSTRUMENT made of wood

ob·scene /əbˈsiˑyn, ab-/ adj (esp. of ideas, books, etc., usu. about sex) nasty; offensive –**obscenely** adv –**obscenity**; /əbˈsɛnətiˑy/ n **-ties** [C;U]

ob·scure¹ /əbˈskyʊər/ adj **1** hard to understand; not clear: *a speech full of obscure political jokes* **2** not well known: *an obscure poet* –**obscurely** adv –**obscurity** n **-ties** [C;U]

obscure² v **-scured, -scuring** [T] to hide; make difficult to see: *My view was obscured by the trees.*

ob·se·qui·ous /əbˈsiˑykwiˑyəs/ adj fml too eager to obey or serve; too humble: *He has an obsequious manner.*

ob·serv·ance /əbˈzɜrvəns/ n [U] fml behavior in accordance with a law, ceremony, or custom: *the observance of the speed limit/of Christmas*

ob·serv·ant /əbˈzɜrvənt/ adj **1** quick at noticing things –opposite **unobservant 2** acting in accordance with law or custom (esp. religious)

ob·ser·va·tion /ˌabzərˈveˑy∫ən, -sər-/ n **1** [C;U] action of noticing **2** [U] ability to notice things: *His powers of observation are poor.* (=he doesn't notice things) **3** [C] a remark: *He made the observation that …* **4 under observation** being carefully watched during some period of time: *She is in the hospital under observation.* (=to see if she is ill)

ob·serv·a·to·ry /əbˈzɜrvəˌtɔriˑy, -ˌtowriˑy/ n **-ries** a place from which scientists watch the moon, stars, etc.

ob·serve /əbˈzɜrv/ v **-served, -serving** [T] **1** [(that)] to see and notice; watch carefully: *to observe the stars | They were observed entering the bank.* **2** to act in accordance with (law or custom (esp. religious)) **3** [(that)] to make a remark; say

ob·serv·er /əbˈzɜrvər/ n **1** one who OBSERVES (1,2) **2** one who attends meetings, classes, etc., to OBSERVE (1) only, not to take part

ob·sess /əbˈsɛs/ v [T] to fill (someone's) mind continuously: *He's obsessed with football and talks about nothing else.*

ob·ses·sion /əbˈsɛ∫ən/ n [about, with] a fixed

idea from which the mind cannot be freed *adj*

ob·ses·sive /əb'sɛsɪv/ *adj* of or like an OBSESSION: *his obsessive interest in sex*

ob·so·les·cent /ˌɑbsə'lesənt/ *adj* becoming OBSOLETE —**obsolescence** *n* [U]

ob·so·lete /ˌɑbsə'liᵛt, 'ɑbsəˌliᵛt/ *adj* no longer used; out of date: *obsolete machinery* |(fig.) *obsolete ideas* –see OLD (USAGE)

ob·sta·cle /'ɑbstɪkəl/ *n* [*to*] something which stands in the way and prevents action or success: *She felt that her family was an obstacle to her work.*

ob·stet·rics /əb'stɛktrɪks/ *n* [U] the branch of medicine concerned with the birth of children –**obstetric(al)** *adj*

ob·sti·nate /'ɑbstənɪt/ *adj* not willing to change one's opinion, obey, etc.: *Don't be so obstinate! Do as you're told.* –**obstinately** *adv* –**obstinacy** *n* [U]

ob·struct /əb'strʌkt/ *v* [T] **1** to block up: *to obstruct a road* **2** to put difficulties in the way of: *to obstruct a plan* –**obstruction** /əb'strʌkʃən/ *n* [C;U]: *an obstruction in the road* –**obstructive** /əb'strʌktɪv/ *adj* –**obstructively** *adv* –**obstructiveness** *n* [U]

ob·tain /əb'teᵛn/ *v* [T] *more fml than* **get**– to get: *By this method, you obtain good results.* –**obtainable** *adj: I'm sorry, but the record that you asked for is no longer obtainable.*

ob·tru·sive /əb'truᵂsɪv/ *adj* displeasingly noticeable or active –see also UNOBTRUSIVE –**obtrusively** *adv* –**obtrusiveness** *n* [U]

ob·tuse /əb'tuᵂs, əb'tyuᵂs, ɑb-/ *adj* **1** *fml* stupid **2** *tech* (of an angle) between 90° and 180° –compare ACUTE (4) –**obtusely** *adv* –**obtuseness** *n* [U]

ob·vi·ous /'ɑbviᵛəs/ *adj* easy to understand; clear; which must be recognized: *It's very obvious that he's lying.* –**obviousness** *n* [U]

ob·vi·ous·ly /'ɑbviᵛəsliᵛ/ *adv* it can be easily seen (that); plainly: *Obviously, you didn't read it.*

oc·ca·sion /ə'keᵛʒən/ *n* **1** a time when something happens: *On that occasion I was not at home.* **2** a special event or ceremony: *The opening of a new school is always a great occasion.* **3 on occasion** from time to time; occasionally

oc·ca·sion·al /ə'keᵛʒənəl/ *adj* [A] happening from time to time; not regular: *We get an occasional visitor here.* –see NEVER (USAGE) –**occasionally** *adv*

oc·cult /ə'kʌlt, ɑ-/ *adj* secret; magical and mysterious; hidden from ordinary people

oc·cu·pant /'ɑkyəpənt/ *n* [*of*] *fml* a person who lives in a certain place: *Are you the occupant of this house?* –**occupancy** /'ɑkyəpənsiᵛ/ *n* [U]: *Occupancy of this apartment by more than four people is against the law.*

oc·cu·pa·tion /ˌɑkyə'peᵛʃən/ *n* **1** [C] a job; employment –see JOB (USAGE) **2** [U *of*] taking possession of: *The workers' occupation of the factory lasted three weeks.*

oc·cu·pa·tion·al /ˌɑkyə'peᵛʃənəl/ *adj* of or about an OCCUPATION (1): *For professional football players, broken bones are an occupational hazard.* (=a risk connected with their

work) –**occupationally** *adv*

oc·cu·pi·er /'ɑkyəˌpaɪər/ *n* an OCCUPANT, esp. of a house

oc·cu·py /'ɑkyəˌpaɪ/ *v* **-pied, -pying** [T] **1** to be in (a place): *to occupy a house/a bed/a hotel room* **2** to fill (a certain position, space, or time): *His books occupy a lot of space.* |*Voluntary work occupies a lot of his spare time.* **3** to cause to spend time (doing something): *He occupied himself in/with collecting stamps.* |*For most of the day I was occupied in writing letters.* **4** to move into and hold possession of (an enemy's country, town, etc.)

oc·cur /ə'kɜr/ *v* **-rr-** [I] **1** *more fml than* **happen**– (esp. of unplanned events) to happen; take place: *Many accidents occur in the home.* **2** (esp. of something not alive) to exist: *That sound doesn't occur in his language.*

occur to sbdy. *v prep* [T] (of an idea) to come to (someone's) mind: *Just as I was leaving the house, it occurred to me that I had forgotten my keys.*

oc·cur·rence /ə'kɜrəns, ə'kʌr-/ *n* an event; happening

o·cean /'oᵂʃən/ *n* **1** (*the* U) the great mass of salt water that covers most of the earth **2** [C] (*often cap. as part of a name*) any of the great seas into which this mass is divided: *the Pacific Ocean* –**oceanic** /ˌoᵂʃiᵛ'ænɪk/ *adj*

o'clock /ə'klɑk/ *adv* (used with the numbers from 1 to 12 in telling time) exactly the hour stated according to the clock: *"What time is it?" "It's 9 o'clock."*

oc·ta·gon /'ɑktəˌgɑn/ *n tech* a flat figure with eight sides and eight angles –**octagonal** /ɑk'tægənəl/ *adj*

oc·tave /'ɑktɪv/ *n* a space of eight degrees between musical notes

Oc·to·ber /ɑk'toᵂbər/ *also* **Oct.** *written abbrev. n* the 10th month of the year

oc·to·pus /'ɑktəpəs/ *n* **-puses** *or* **-pi** /ˌpaɪ/ a deep-sea creature with eight arms (TENTACLES)

oc·u·list /'ɑkyəlɪst/ *n fml* an eye-doctor

odd /ɑd/ *adj* **1** strange; unusual: *odd behavior*|*an odd person* **2** [A] separated from a pair or set to which it belongs: *an odd shoe* **3** (of a number) that cannot be divided exactly by 2: *1, 3, 5, 7, etc., are odd.* –opposite **even 4** [A] not regular; OCCASIONAL: *He does an odd job for me from time to time.*|*I only get a chance to read at odd moments.* **5** [after *n*] *infml* (after numbers) with rather more: *20-odd years*

odd·i·ty /'ɑdəṭiᵛ/ *n* **-ties** a strange person, thing, etc.

odd·ly /'ɑdliᵛ/ *adv* strangely: *He spoke oddly.*|*Oddly enough, he didn't seem to remember his own birthday.*

odd·ment /'ɑdmənt/ *n* [*often pl.*] something left over or remaining

odds /ɑdz/ *n* [P] **1** the probability that something will or will not happen: *The odds are 10 to 1 that her horse will not win the race.*|*The odds are that he will fail his exam.* **2 at odds (with)** in disagreement (with)

odds and ends /ˌ· · '·/ *n* [P] small articles

without much value: (fig.) *There are a few odds and ends of business I'd like to talk to you about.*

odds-on /ˌ·'·◄/ *adj* very likely (to win): *The odds-on favorite* (=horse) *came in last, to everyone's surprise.*

ode /oʷd/ *n* a usu. long poem

o·di·ous /'oʷdiʸəs/ *adj fml* hateful; very unpleasant **–odiously** *adv*

o·dom·e·ter /oʷ'dɑmətər/ *n* an instrument fitted in a vehicle to record the distance it travels –see illustration on page 95

o·dor *AmE*‖**odour** *BrE* /'oʷdər/ *n* a smell, esp. an unpleasant one **–odorless** *adj*

o'er /ɔr, oʷr/ *adv, prep lit* over

of /əv, ə; *strong* ʌv, ɑv/ *prep* 1 belonging to (something not alive): *the leg of the table* (but note *John's leg*|*the dog's leg*)|*the color of her hair*|*the size of the room* 2 made from: *a dress of silk*|*a crown of gold* 3 containing: *a bag of potatoes* 4 (shows a part or amount): *two pounds of sugar*|*several miles of bad road·*|*much of the night*|*the members of the team*|*a blade of grass*|*both of us* 5a that is/are; being: *the City of New York*|*the art of painting*|*at the age of eight*|*two friends of mine·*|*some fool of a boy* (=some foolish boy) b happening in or on: *the University of California*|*the Battle of Waterloo*|*my letter of the 19th* 6 (of works of art or literature) a by: *the plays of Shakespeare* b about: *stories of adventure*|*a picture of John* 7 in relation to; in connection with: *the king of England*|*a teacher of English*|*the time of arrival*|*a lover of music*|*to die of hunger*|*to cure someone of a disease*|*fond of swimming*|*within a mile of here* (=not more than a mile from here) 8 with; having: *an area of hills*|*a matter of no importance* 9 (shows what someone or something is or does): *the laughter of the children*|*How kind of John to buy the tickets.* 10 a (used in dates): *the 27th of February* b *AmE* (used in telling time) before: *It's five (minutes) of two.* (=1:55) c during: *They always like to go there of an evening.*

off¹ /ɔf/ *adv, adj* [F] 1 from or no longer in a place or position; away: *They got into the car and drove off.*|*The door handle fell off.*|*She stood a few yards off.*|*Catch this bus and get off* (=out of the bus) *at the station.*|*He took his shoes off.* (=from his feet)|*Christmas is only a week off!*|*They're off!* (=the race has started)|*(fml) Be off with you!* (=go away)|*I'm taking Monday off.* (=away from work) 2 not lit or working: *Turn the light/TAP off.*|*The T.V. is off.* –opposite **on** 3 so as to be completely finished or no longer there: *Finish the work off before you go home.*|*Kill the animals off.* 4 not quite right; not as good as usual: *Her work has been off lately.* 5 [F] not going to happen after all: *I'm afraid the party's off.* –compare ON² (6) 6 having little or a lot of something, esp. money: *They're not very well off.* (=they're poor)|*They're better off than we are.* 7 to be supported by, usu. with money: *He lives off his father; he's never worked a day in his life.* 8 **off and on** also **on and off**– from time to time; sometimes

off² *prep* 1 not on; away from: *Keep off the grass.*|*He jumped off the bus.*|*She cut a piece off the loaf.*|*We're getting off the subject.* 2 (esp. of a road) turning away from (a larger one): *a narrow street off Third Avenue* 3 in the sea near: *an island off the coast of France* 4 no longer wanting or having something: *He's off cigarettes.*|*The doctor took him off drugs.* –opposite **on**

off³ *adj* [A] 1 (of a time) a not as good as usual: *This is one of his off days; he usually plays better.* b quiet and dull: *Tickets are cheaper during the off season.* 2 **on the off chance** *infml* just in case; with the unlikely chance

of·fend /ə'fɛnd/ *v* 1 [T] to hurt the feelings of: *I was very offended that you forgot my birthday.* 2 [T] to cause displeasure to: *Cruelty offends many people.* 3 [I *against*] to do wrong

of·fend·er /ə'fɛndər/ *n euph* a criminal

of·fense *AmE*‖**offence** *BrE* /ə'fɛns/ *n* 1 [C *against*] a wrong; crime: *Driving while drunk is a serious offense.* 2 [C;U] cause for hurt feelings: *to give/cause offense to someone*|*to take offense at something*

of·fen·sive¹ /ə'fɛnsɪv/ *adj* 1 causing offense; unpleasant: *offensive behavior*|*an offensive person* –opposite **inoffensive** 2 of or about attacking: *charged with carrying an offensive weapon* –see also DEFENSIVE **–offensively** *adv* **–offensiveness** *n* [U]

offensive² *n* 1 a continued attack 2 **on the offensive** making a continued attack

of·fer¹ /'ɔfər, 'ɑfər/ *v* 1 [T *to, for*] to hold out (to a person) for acceptance or refusal: *Offer the guests some coffee.*|*They've offered us $75,000 for the house. Should we take it?* 2 [I;T +*to-v*] to express willingness (to do something): *She offered to help.* 3 [T *up, to*] to give (to God): *He offered (up) a prayer.*

offer² *n* 1 [+*to-v/of*] a statement offering (to do) something: *Thanks for your offer of help.* 2 [*of*] something which is offered: *He made me an offer of $10.*

of·fer·ing /'ɔfərɪŋ, 'ɑ-/ *n* something offered, esp. to God

off·hand /ˌɔf'hænd◄/ *adv, adj* 1 careless; disrespectful: *an offhand manner* 2 at once; without time to think **–offhandedly** *adv* **–offhandedness** *n* [U]

of·fice /'ɔfɪs, 'ɑ-/ *n* 1 [C] a place where business is done: *I work in an office.*|*a ticket office* –see illustration on page 467 2 [C] (*usu. caps.*) a government department: *the Passport Office* 3 [C;U] a position of responsibility or power, esp. in government: *to hold/enter/leave office*|*Our party has been in/out of office for three years.*

of·fi·cer /'ɔfəsər, 'ɑ-/ *n* 1 a person in a position of command in the armed forces 2 a policeman 3 a person who holds a position of some importance, esp. in government, a business, or a group: *a local government officer*

USAGE **Civil servants** are people who work for the government, and an **official** is someone who works for a government or other large organization in a position of responsibility: *a meeting between* **civil servants** *from the Department of Transportation and important railroad* **officials.** An **officer** is usually a member of the armed forces in a position of command, or a member of the police force, but the word is sometimes used like **official.** A **clerk** is an office worker of fairly low rank. This word is also used in *AmE* for someone who works in a store (a **sales clerk**), but the *BrE* word is **shop assistant.**

of·fi·cial¹ /ə'fɪʃəl/ *n* a person who holds an OFFICE (3): *a union official* –see OFFICER (USAGE)

official² *adj* of, about, or from a position of trust, power, and responsibility: *an official position|an official occasion* –Compare: *an* **official** *letter concerning my income tax|an* **officious** *letter from my neighbor complaining about the noise from my radio* –opposite **unofficial**

of·fi·cial·ly /ə'fɪʃəliʸ/ *adv* **1** in an official manner **2** as (believed to have been) stated by officials: *Gold is officially worth $400 an* OUNCE, *but I can buy it at a cheaper price.* –opposite **unofficially**

of·fi·ci·ate /ə'fɪʃiʸ,eʸt/ *v* **-ated, -ating** [I *at*] to perform official duties: *Who's going to officiate at your wedding?*

of·fi·cious /ə'fɪʃəs/ *adj derog* too eager to give orders or to offer advice –compare OFFICIAL² **–officiously** *adv* **–officiousness** *n* [U]

off·ing /'ɔfɪŋ/ *n* **in the offing** about to happen

off-peak /,· '·◄/ *adj* [A] **1** less busy: *Telephone rates are lower during off-peak hours.* **2** existing during less busy periods: *off-peak electricity* –compare PEAK¹ (2)

off·set /'ɔfsɛt, ,ɔf'sɛt/ *v* **-set, -setting** [T] to make up for; balance: *The cost of getting there was offset by the fact that I found a very cheap place to live.*

off·shoot /'ɔfʃuʷt/ *n* a new stem or branch: (fig.) *an offshoot of a large organization*

off·shore /,ɔf'ʃɔr◄, -'ʃoʷr◄/ *adv,adj* in the water, at a distance from the shore: *America's offshore oil|two miles offshore* –compare ONSHORE, INSHORE

off·side /,ɔf'saɪd◄/ *adj,adv* (in certain sports) in a position in which play is not allowed –opposite **onside**

off·spring /'ɔf,sprɪŋ/ *n* [U] *fml or humor* a child or children; the young of an animal: *Their offspring all became musicians.*

off-white /,· '·◄/ *n,adj* [U] a color that is not a pure white

oft /ɔft/ *adv lit often*: *oft-repeated advice*

of·ten /'ɔfən/ *adv* **1** many times: *"How often do you go there?" "Once a month, but I wish I could go more often."* **2** in many cases: *It's often very difficult to understand what he's saying.* **3 as often as not** quite often; at least half the time: *As often as not, he forgets his homework.* **4 every so often** sometimes; OCCASIONALLY **5 more often than not** more than half of the time; usually: *More often than not, she's late for school.* –see NEVER (USAGE)

o·gle /'oʷgəl/ *v* **-gled, -gling** [I;T *at*] to look (at) with great interest, esp. sexual interest

o·gre /'oʷgər/ **ogress** /'oʷgrɪs/ *fem.– n* **1** (in fairy stories) a fierce creature like a very large man, who is thought to eat children **2** a person who makes others afraid

oh /oʷ/ *interj* (expressing surprise, fear, etc.)

ohm /oʷm/ *n* a measure of electrical RESISTANCE (4)

oil¹ /ɔɪl/ *n* [U] a fatty liquid (from animals, plants, or under the ground) used for burning, for making machines run easily, for cooking, etc.: *corn oil |OLIVE oil |motor oil*

oil² *v* [T] to put oil onto or rub oil on or into

oil paint·ing /'·,··/ *n* **1** [U] the art of painting in OILS **2** [C] a picture painted in OILS

oil·rig /'ɔɪl,rɪg/ *n* an apparatus for getting oil from underground, esp. from land that is under the sea

oils /ɔɪlz/ *n* [P] paints (esp. for pictures) containing oil –compare WATERCOLOR

oil·skin /'ɔɪl,skɪn/ *n* [C;U] (a garment made of) cloth treated with oil so that water will not pass through it

oil slick /'· ·/ *n* a thin sheet of oil floating on water, esp. as a result of an accident to an oil-carrying ship

oil·y /'ɔɪliʸ/ *adj* **-ier, -iest** **1** of, about, or like oil: *an oily liquid* **2** covered with or containing oil: *dirty oily clothes|oily food* **3** *derog* too polite: *I don't like his oily manner.*

oink /ɔɪŋk/ *v,n* [C;I] *infml* (to make) the sound that a pig makes

oint·ment /'ɔɪntmənt/ *n* [C;U] a substance (often medicinal) to be rubbed on the skin

o·kay¹, OK /oʷ'keʸ/ *adj,adv infml* [F] **1** all right: *That car runs okay now.|She's OK now.* **2** (asking for or expressing agreement, or giving permission) all right; agreed; yes: *Let's go there, okay?| "Should we go there?" "Okay."|"Can I use your car?" "Okay."*

okay², OK *v* **okayed, okaying** [T] *infml* to approve: *Has the bank okayed your request for a loan?*

okay³, OK *n* **okays, OK's** *infml* approval; permission: *I got the OK to leave early.*

o·kra /'oʷkrə/ *n* [U] a type of green vegetable from southern countries

old /oʷld/ *adj* **1** advanced in age; of age: *"How old is the baby?" "She's eight months old."|My mother is not as old as you.* **2** having lived or existed for a long time: *an old man|old and young people|old and new books|The old* (=old people) *do not always understand young people.* **3** having been in use for a long time: *old shoes|an old car* **4** [A] having continued in the stated relationship for a long time: *We are old friends.* **5** [A] known for a long time: *Don't tell me the same old story again!|Good old John!* **6** [A] former: *He got his old job back.* **7 of old: a** long ago; in the past: *days of old* **b** since a long time ago: *I know him of old.*

USAGE **1** Note that **old,** not **young** or **new,** is used when measuring age: *a* **young** *baby|a* **new** *car,* but *How* **old** *is the baby?|How* **old** *is your car?|a* **three week old** *baby,* etc. **2 Old** is a general word for great age, and **elderly** is a polite way of saying old when speaking of people: *an* **old** *church|an* **old/elderly** *lady.* **Venerable** is used of someone who is old and

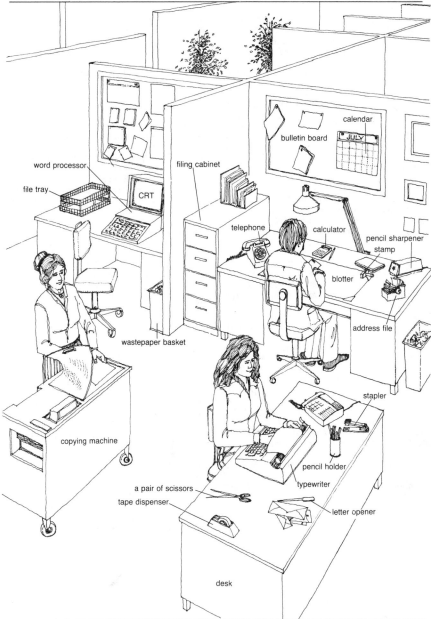

word processor
file tray
CRT
filing cabinet
bulletin board
calendar
JULY
telephone
calculator
pencil sharpener
stamp
blotter
address file
wastepaper basket
stapler
copying machine
pencil holder
typewriter
a pair of scissors
tape dispenser
letter opener
desk

These people work in a large office. They **get to work** at 9:00 in the morning and **go home** at 5:00 in the afternoon. Sometimes they have to work **overtime**.

They usually take a **coffee break** in the morning and another break in the afternoon.

Their job is to **answer the phone** and **take messages**. They also **type** letters and reports, using either a **typewriter** or the **word processor**. They can **make copies** of their work on the **copying machine**. They **file** papers carefully so that they will be able to find them again.

Everyone in this office works hard, but the modern **office equipment** helps them do their work quickly.

Fill in the blanks.
1. You can use a _____ or a _____ to type letters.
2. You can make copies on a _____ .
3. If you're feeling tired, you should take a _____ .
4. What time do you _____ to work in the morning?
   What time do you _____ in the afternoon?

respected: *a* **venerable** *white-haired priest.*
Ancient is the word used for civilizations of
the distant past or their products: *ancient
Egypt|an* **ancient** *Greek bowl.* **Antique** is
used of things that are rare and valuable as
well as old: *an* **antique** *French writing desk.*
Things or ideas that are no longer suitable or
useful are **antiquated**, and when something
new takes their place they become **obsolete:**
antiquated *beliefs/methods|The new com-
puter has made this old machine* **obsolete.**
Old-fashioned is like **antiquated**, but it is less
derog and can also be used of people. –see
also ELDER (USAGE), NEW (USAGE)

old age pen·sion /ˌ· '··/ *n* [U; *the* S] money
paid regularly by the State to old people –**old
age pensioner** *n*

old·en /'owldən/ *adj* [A] *lit & old use* past;
long ago: **in olden days|in olden times**

old-fash·ioned /ˌ· '···◄/ *adj* (of a type that is)
no longer common: *old-fashioned ideas|an
old-fashioned house* –see OLD (USAGE)

old mas·ter /ˌ· '··/ *n* (a picture by) an important painter of an earlier period

Old Tes·ta·ment /ˌ· '···◄/ *n* [*the* S] the first
half of the Bible, containing ancient Hebrew
writings about the Jews –compare NEW
TESTAMENT

old-tim·er /ˌ· '··/ *n* **1** a person who has been
somewhere or done something for a long
time **2** *AmE* an old man

ol·i·gar·chy /'alə,garkiʸ/ *n* **-chies 1** [C;U] (a
state which has) government or rule by a few
people, (often) for their own interests **2** [C]
the group who govern such a state

ol·ive /'alɪv/ *n* **1** [C] (the small egg-shaped
fruit of) a tree grown in Mediterranean
countries **2** [U] also **olive green** /ˌ· '·◄/–
light green

olive branch /'·· ,·/ *n* [*the* S] a sign of peace

O·lym·pic Games /ə,lɪmpɪk 'geʸmz, oʷ-/ also
Olympics /ə'lɪmpɪks, oʷ-/ *n* [*the* P] an international sports event held once every four
years in different countries –**Olympic** *adj* [A]

o·me·ga /oʷ'meʸgə, -'mɛ-, -'miʸ-/ *n* the last
letter of the Greek alphabet (Ω ω)

om·e·let, -lette /'aməlɪt/ *n* eggs beaten
together and cooked in hot fat (by FRYing): *a
cheese omelet*

o·men /'oʷmən/ *n* [*of*] a sign that something is
going to happen in the future: *a good/bad
omen*

om·i·nous /'amənəs/ *adj* being an OMEN, esp.
of something bad: *ominous black clouds*
–**ominously** *adv*

o·mis·sion /oʷ'mɪʃən, ə-/ *n* **1** [U] the act of
OMITTing or state of being omitted: *He's an-
noyed about his omission from the team.* **2**
[C] something (or someone) OMITTed

o·mit /oʷ'mɪt, ə-/ *v* **-tt-** [T] **1** to leave out; not
include, by mistake or on purpose **2**
[+*to-v/v-ing*] to leave undone; not do: *He
omitted to tell me when he was leaving.*

om·nip·o·tent /am'nɪpətənt/ *adj* all-powerful
–**omnipotence** *n* [U]

om·ni·scient /am'nɪʃənt/ *adj* all-knowing;
knowing everything –**omniscience** *n* [U]

on¹ /ɑn, ɔn/ *prep* **1** also **upon** *fml*– **a** touching,
supported by, hanging from, or connected

with: *a lamp on the table/ the wall|a ring on
my finger|a ball on a string|the wheels on my
car|He cut his foot on* (=against) *a piece of
glass.* **b** towards; in the direction of: *on my
right|to march on the capital|an attack on the
enemy* **c** at the edge of; along: *a town right on
the river|trees on both sides of the street* **d**
directly after and because of: *acting on your
advice|On thinking about it, I decided not to
go.* **e** about (a subject): *a book on India* **f** in
(a large vehicle): *on the train* **g** (before words
about traveling): *on a journey|on my way to
school* **h** directed towards: *a tax on in-
come|They spent their money on beer.* **i**
following continuously; AFTER¹ (2): *to suffer
defeat on defeat* **2 a** (used with days, dates,
and times): *on Tuesday|on July 1st|on time*
(=not late or early)|*on the hour* (=exactly at
two, three, etc.)|*on a hot day* (compare *in the
morning, in 1984, at 6 o'clock*) **b** using; by
means of: *on foot|on a bicycle|to live on
potatoes|A car runs on gasoline.|I can't
afford to live on my pay.|I heard it on the
radio.|talking on the telephone* **c** in a state of:
on fire|on sale|on vacation|on purpose (but
by accident) **d** working for; belonging to: *to
serve on a committee|a job on a newspaper
|Which side was she on in the game?* **e** *infml*
paid for by: *Drinks are on me!*

on² *adv,adj* [F] **1** continuously, instead of
stopping: *He worked on (and on) all night.* **2**
further; forward: *If you walk on, you'll come
to the church.|If any letters come, can I send
them on to you?* (=to your new address)|*I'll
do it later on.* (=afterwards) **3** so as to be
fastened or in place: *with his coat on|He had
nothing* (=no clothes) *on.|The bus stopped,
and we got on.* (=into the bus) **4** with the
stated part in front: *The two cars crashed
head on.* **5** lit; working: *Turn the light/the* TAP
on. –opposite **off 6** happening or going to
happen: *There's a new movie on at the thea-
ter.|I've got nothing on tonight, so let's go
out.* –compare OFF¹ (5) **7 go on about** *infml* to
keep talking (about something/to someone)
in a dull or complaining way: *What's he going
on about now?* **8 on and on** without stopping
9 on and off also **off and on**– from time to
time; sometimes **10 be on** arranged: *Our
trip's on; let's start packing.*

once¹ /wʌns/ *adv* **1** one time and no more:
*We've met only once.|They go to the movies
once a week.|I'll help you just this once.* **2**
some time ago; formerly: *He once knew her,
but they are no longer friends.* **3 all at once**
suddenly **4 at once: a** now; without delay: *Do
it at once!* **b** at the same time; together: *Don't
all speak at once!* **5 (just) for once** for this one
time only: *For once he was telling the truth.* **6
once and for all** for the last time: *Once and
for all, I won't go!* **7 once in a while** now and
then; sometimes **8 once more: a** one more
time **b** also **once again**– now again as before:
John's back home once more. **9 once or twice**
(only) a few times: *I've been there once or
twice.* **10 once upon a time** (beginning a story
for children) at some time in the past: *Once
upon a time there lived a king ...*

once² *conj* from the moment that; when:

Once he arrives, we can start.

once-o·ver /'· ˌ·ˈ·/ *n* [*usu. sing.*] *infml* a quick look or examination: *He gave the car the once-over and decided not to buy it.*

on·com·ing /'ɒnˌkʌmɪŋ, 'ɔn-/ *adj* [A] coming towards one: *oncoming cars*

one¹ /wʌn/ *determiner,n* **1** the number 1: *Only one person came.*|TWENTY-one|*one o'clock*|*page one*|*one dollar and 50 cents*| *one*|*a liter of wine*|*one of your friends* (=a friend of yours)|*She's the one person* (=the only person) *who can do it.*|*I for one* (=this is my personal opinion) *think it's pretty good.* –see Study Notes on page 550 **2** a certain; some: *I saw her one day in June.*|*Come and see us one evening.* **3** the same: *They all ran in one direction.*|*She's president and secretary all in one.* (=she's both) **4** (used with *another*, *the other*, etc.) a particular example or type (of): *He can't tell one tree from another.*|*One (of them) went North, the other went South.* **5 be one up (on someone)** to have the advantage (over someone) –see also ONE-UPMANSHIP **6 one after another/after the other** singly; one by one

one² *pron* **1** (*pl.* ones) a single thing or person mentioned: *Do you have any books on farming? I want to borrow one.* (=a book on farming) (compare *I want to borrow some* = some books on farming)|*There are only hard chocolates left; we've eaten all the soft ones.* **2** (*no pl.*) *fml* anybody at all; YOU (2): *One should do one's duty*|(*AmE*) *his duty.* **3** (*pl.* ones) a person or a thing: *I want to be with my loved ones.*

one an·oth·er /ˌ· ·ˈ·ˈ·/ *pron* →EACH OTHER: *They hit one another.*|*We often stay in one another's houses.* –see EACH OTHER (USAGE)

one-armed ban·dit /ˌ· · ˈ·ˈ·/ *n infml* for SLOT MACHINE

on·er·ous /'ɒnərəs, 'oʷ-/ *adj fml* difficult; heavy; troublesome: *an onerous duty* –**onerously** *adv* –**onerousness** *n* [U]

one·self /wʌn'sɛlf/ *pron* **1** (used as the object of a verb, or after a PREPOSITION, when the subject is *one*): *One can't enjoy oneself if one*|*if he* (*AmE*) *is too tired.* **2** (used to make *one* stronger): *To do something oneself is often easier than getting someone else to do it.* **3 be oneself** to be in one's usual state of mind or body: *She was very ill yesterday, but she's more like herself today.*|*I'll forgive you; I know you weren't yourself when you said that.* **4 by oneself** alone; without help: *The baby can walk by himself now.*|*Do they live all by themselves in that big house?* **5 to oneself** for one's own private use; not to be shared: *I want a bedroom to myself.*

one-sid·ed /ˌ· ˈ·ˈ·◀/ *adj* **1** seeing only one side (of a question); unfair: *a one-sided view of the problem* **2** with one side much stronger than the other: *a one-sided football game* –**one-sidedly** *adv* –**one-sidedness** *n* [U]

one-time /'wʌntaɪm/ *adj* [A] former

one-up·man·ship /ˌwʌn'ʌpmən،ʃɪp/ *n* [U] the art of getting an advantage over others

one-way /ˌ· ˈ·◀/ *adj* [A] **1** moving or allowing movement in only one direction: *one-way*

traffic|*a one-way street* **2** *esp. AmE*||**single** *BrE*– (of a ticket or its cost) for a trip from one place to another but not back again –compare ROUND-TRIP

on·go·ing /'ɒnˌgoʷɪŋ, 'ɔn-/ *adj* continuing; that go(es) on

on·ion /'ʌnyən/ *n* [C;U] a strong-smelling round white vegetable used in cooking

on·look·er /'ɒnˌlʊkər, 'ɔn-/ *n* a person who sees something happening without taking part in it –see also LOOK on

on·ly¹ /'oʷnliʸ/ *adj* [A] with no others in the same group: *the only person who wants the job*|*an only child* (=with no brothers or sisters)

only² *adv* **1** nothing more than; and nobody or nothing else: *only five minutes more*|*Ladies only!*|*not only he but the whole family*|*I saw him only yesterday.* (=and no longer ago)|*Only a doctor can do that.*|*Don't eat it; it will only make you ill.* (=that is the only possible result) **2 if only** (expressing a wish): *If only she would come!* **3 only too** very; completely: *It's only too true.*

USAGE In writing, put **only** just before the part of the sentence that it is about: *Only John saw the lion.* (=no one else saw it)|*John only saw the lion.* (=he didn't shoot it)|*John saw only the lion.* (=he didn't see the tiger)

only³ *conj* except that; but: *He wants to go, only he can't.*

on·rush /'ɒnrʌʃ, 'ɔn-/ *n* a strong movement forward –**onrushing** *adj* [A]

on·set /'ɒnsɛt, 'ɔn-/ *n* [the S] the first attack or beginning (of something bad): *the onset of a nasty cold*

on·shore /ˌɒn'ʃɔr◀, -'ʃoʷr◀, ˌɔn-/ *adv,adj* on (to) or on the shore: *the search for onshore oil* –compare OFFSHORE

on·side /ˌɒn'saɪd◀, ˌɔn-/ *adj,adv* not OFFSIDE

on·slaught /'ɒnslɔt, 'ɔn-/ *n* [on] a fierce attack (on): *The politician made a strong onslaught* (=attacking speech) *on taxes.*

on·to /'ɒntə, -tuʷ, 'ɔn-/ *prep* to a position or point on: *He jumped onto*|*on the horse.*

o·nus /'oʷnəs/ *n* [the S *of*] duty; responsibility: *The onus of proof lies with you.*

on·ward /'ɒnwərd, 'ɔn-/ *adj* [A] forward in space or time: *the onward march of events* –**onwards**||also **onward** *AmE*– *adv: from breakfast onwards*

on·yx /'ɒnɪks/ *n* [C;U] a precious stone having bands of various colors in it

oops /ʊps, uʷps/ *interj infml* (said when someone has made an ungraceful mistake): *Oops! I nearly dropped my cup of tea!*

ooze¹ /uʷz/ *n* [U] mud or thick liquid, as at the bottom of a river –**oozy** *adj* **-ier, -iest**

ooze² *v* **oozed, oozing 1** [I] (of liquid) to pass or flow slowly: (fig.) *Their courage oozed away.* **2** [T] to allow (liquid) to pass slowly out: *The meat just oozed blood.*|(fig.) *He oozes charm.*

o·pal /'oʷpəl/ *n* [C;U] a precious stone which looks like milky water with colors in it

o·paque /oʷ'peʸk/ *adj* **1** not allowing light to pass through **2** hard to understand –compare TRANSPARENT –**opaquely** *adv* –**opaqueness**, **opacity** /oʷ'pæsəṭiʸ/ *n* [U]

OPEC /'oʷpɛk/ *abbrev. for:* Organization of Petroleum Exporting Countries; a group of countries who produce oil (=PETROLEUM), and plan together how to sell it

o·pen¹ /'oʷpən/ *adj* **1** not shut: *an open door* |*with open eyes*|(fig.) *an open mind* (=not closed to new ideas) **2** [A] not enclosed: *the open country*|*open fields* **3** [A] not covered: *an open boat*|*the open air* **4** not fastened: *an open shirt* **5** not finally decided: *an open question*|*The job is still open.* **6** not hiding anything; honest: *Let's be open with each other.*|*open hatred* **7** ready for business: *The bank isn't open yet.* **8** that anyone can enter: *an open competition* **9 open to**: a not safe from: *This book is open to misunderstanding.* **b** willing to receive **c** not closed to –compare CLOSED

open² *v* **1** [I;T] to (cause to) become open: *Open your eyes.* **2** [I;T *up, out*] to (cause to) spread out or unfold: *to open a book* **3** [I;T] to (cause to) start: *The story opens with a snowstorm.*|*The store opens at nine o'clock.* **4** [T] to make usable (a passage) by removing the things that are blocking it **5 open fire (at/on)** to start shooting (at) –compare CLOSE¹

USAGE One **opens** or **shuts** doors, windows, or boxes. One **turns** water or gas TAPs **on** or **off**. One **turns** or **switches** electrical things **on** or **off**.

open up *v adv* **1** [T *to*] (**open** sthg.↔ **up**) to make possible the development of; start: *They opened the country up (to trade).* **2** [I *often in commands*] *infml* to open a door **3** [I] *AmE* to speak more freely: *He finally opened up about his problems.*

open³ *n* [*the* U] **1** the outdoors: *life in the open* **2 in(to) the open** (of opinions, secrets, etc.) in(to) general knowledge

open-air /ˌ·· '·◄/ *adj* [A] of or in the outdoors: *an open-air theater* –opposite **indoor**

open-and-shut /ˌ·· · '·◄/ *adj* easy to settle: *It is an open-and-shut case of murder.*

open-end·ed /ˌ·· '··◄/ *adj* without any definite end, aim, or time limit set in advance: *an open-ended discussion*

o·pen·er /'oʷpənər/ *n* a person or thing that opens something: *a bottle opener*

open-hand·ed /ˌ·· '··◄/ *adj* generous –**open-handedly** *adv* –**open-handedness** *n* [U]

o·pen·ing¹ /'oʷpənɪŋ/ *n* **1** [C;U] the act of becoming or causing to become open: *the opening of a new university* –compare CLOSURE **2** [C *in*] a hole or clear space; GAP: *an opening in the fence* **3** [C *for*] a favorable set of conditions (for): *good openings for business*

opening² *adj* [A] first; beginning: *her opening words* –opposite **closing**

o·pen·ly /'oʷpənliʸ/ *adv* not secretly: *They talked openly about their plans.* –**openness** *n* [U]

open-mind·ed /ˌ·· '··◄/ *adj* willing to consider new arguments, ideas, opinions, etc.: *Even though my parents are old, they're very open-minded.* –compare BROADMINDED, SMALL-MINDED –**open-mindedly** *adv*

op·er·a /'ɑpərə/ *n* [C;U] (the art of making) a musical play in which many or all of the words are sung –**operatic** /ˌɑpə'rætɪk/ *adj* –**operatically** *adv*

op·er·ate /'ɑpəˌreʸt/ *v* **-ated, -ating 1** [I;T] to (cause to) work: *to operate a machine*|*a factory*|*The new law doesn't operate in our favor.* **2** [I] to be in action: *That business operates in several countries.* **3** [I *on*] to cut the body in order to set right or remove a diseased part, usu. in a special room (**operating room**) in a hospital

op·er·a·tion /ˌɑpə'reʸʃən/ *n* **1** [U] (a state of) working; the way a thing works: *The operation of a new machine can be hard to learn.*|*When does the new law* **come into operation?** **2** [C] a thing (to be) done; an activity: *to begin operations*|*a difficult operation* **3** [C *on*] the cutting of the body in order to set right or remove a diseased part: *She will perform an operation on the patient at 4 o'clock.* **4** [C] an (esp. military) action; movement: *the army's operations in the Middle East*

op·er·a·tion·al /ˌɑpə'reʸʃənəl/ *adj* **1** [F] (of things) in operation; ready for use: *The new machines are not yet operational.* **2** [A] of or about operations: *operational costs* –compare OPERATIVE –**operationally** *adv*

op·er·a·tive /'ɑpərətɪv, 'ɑpəˌreʸ-/ *adj* [F] (of plans, laws, etc.) in operation; producing effects –compare OPERATIONAL

op·er·a·tor /'ɑpəˌreʸtər/ *n* a person who works a machine, apparatus, telephone SWITCHBOARD, etc. –see TELEPHONE (USAGE)

oph·thal·mol·o·gy /ˌɑfθæl'mɑlədʒiʸ, -θəl-, -θə'mɑ-, ˌɑp-/ *n* [U] *tech* the study of the eyes and their diseases —**ophthalmologist** *n*

o·pin·ion /ə'pɪnyən/ *n* **1** [C;U] what a person thinks about something: *His opinions are always interesting.*|**In my opinion** *you're wrong.*|**Public opinion** *is against him.* **2** [C] professional judgment or advice: *I asked for a second opinion from another doctor.* **3 have a good/bad/high/low opinion of** to think well/badly of

o·pin·ion·at·ed /ə'pɪnyəˌneʸtɪd/ *adj derog* very sure of the rightness of one's opinions

o·pi·um /'oʷpiʸəm/ *n* [U] a sleep-producing drug made from the seeds of the white POPPY

o·pos·sum /ə'pɑsəm, 'pɑsəm/ *also* **possum** *AmE infml* – *n* **-sums** *or* **-sum** a small American tree-climbing animal that pretends to be dead when it is caught

op·po·nent /ə'poʷnənt/ *n* a person who takes the opposite side, esp. in playing or fighting –see also PROPONENT

op·por·tune /ˌɑpər'tuʷn, -'tyuʷn/ *adj* **1** (of times) right for a purpose: *an opportune moment* **2** coming at the right time: *an opportune remark* –opposite **inopportune** –**opportunely** *adv*

op·por·tun·ism /ˌɑpər'tuʷˌnɪzəm, -'tyuʷ-/ *n* [U] *derog* the taking advantage of every chance for success, sometimes at other people's cost –**opportunist** *n*

op·por·tu·ni·ty /ˌɑpər'tuʷnətiʸ, -'tyuʷ-/ *n* **-ties** [C;U *+to-v/for, of*] a favorable (OPPORTUNE) moment or occasion (for doing something):

a wonderful opportunity to go shopping/I took the opportunity *to visit my brother.* –see CHANCE (USAGE)

op·pose /ə'po^wz/ *v* **-posed, -posing** [T] **1** to be or act against: *We opposed the building of a new road through the park.* **2 as opposed to** as completely different from; in CONTRAST or opposition to **3 be opposed to** to oppose: *I am opposed to that plan.*

op·po·site¹ /'apəzit, -sit/ *n* a person or thing that is as different as possible (from another): *Black and white are opposites.*/*You are nice; he is just the opposite.*

opposite² *adj* [*to*] **1** as different as possible from: *the opposite direction* |(fig.) *the opposite sex* **2** [F] facing: *the houses opposite*/*He sits opposite.* **3 opposite number** a person in the same job elsewhere: *She's my opposite number in the company's Texas office.*

opposite³ also **opposite to** /'··· ·/ – *prep* facing: *the houses opposite (to) ours*

op·po·si·tion /,apə'zɪʃən/ *n* **1** [U *to*] the act or state of being opposed to or fighting against: *There will be a lot of opposition to that new road.* **2** [C] a political party that is opposed to the person holding political office: *The opposition will vote against the President's new tax laws.*

op·press /ə'prɛs/ *v* [T] **1** to rule in a hard and cruel way **2** [*usu. pass.*] to cause to feel ill or sad: *I feel oppressed by/ with worry.*

op·pres·sion /ə'prɛʃən/ *n* [U] the condition of oppressing or being OPPRESSED (esp. 1)

op·pres·sive /ə'prɛsɪv/ *adj* **1** cruel; unjust: *an oppressive government* **2** causing feelings of illness or sadness: *oppressive heat* **–oppressively** *adv* **–oppressiveness** *n* [U]

op·pres·sor /ə'prɛsər/ *n* a person (or group) that OPPRESSES (1)

opt /apt/ *v* →OPT FOR, OPT OUT

opt for sthg. *v prep* [T] to choose (a particular thing) rather than any others –see also OPT OUT

op·tic /'aptɪk/ *adj* [A] of or belonging to the eyes: *the optic nerve*

op·ti·cal /'aptɪkəl/ *adj* [A] of or about the sense of sight: *optical instruments* **–optically** *adv*

op·ti·cian /ap'tɪʃən/ *n* a person who makes and sells glasses for the eyes

op·tics /'aptɪks/ *n* [U] the scientific study of light

op·ti·mism /'aptə,mɪzəm/ *n* [U] the belief that whatever happens will be good, and that things will end well –compare PESSIMISM **–optimist** *n* **–optimistic** /,aptə'mɪstɪk/ *adj* **–optimistically** *adv*

op·ti·mum /'aptəməm/ *adj* [A] best or most favorable: *optimum conditions for growing rice*

op·tion /'apʃən/ *n* **1** [U] the freedom to choose: *You have to do it; you have no option.* **2** [C] something chosen or offered for choice: *The government has two options: either to reduce spending or to increase taxes.*

op·tion·al /'apʃənəl/ *adj* which may be freely chosen or not chosen: *optional subjects at school* –compare OBLIGATORY **–optionally** *adv*

opt out *v adv* [I *of*] *infml* to choose not to take part (in something) –see also OPT FOR

op·u·lence /'apyələns/ *n* [U] (a state of) very great and showy wealth **–opulent** *adj* **–opulently** *adv*

or /ər; *strong* ɔr/ *conj* **1** (used in a list of possibilities): *What would you like, coffee or tea?*/*Either say you're sorry or get out!* |*She wants to live in London or Paris or Rome*/*London, Paris, or Rome.* **2** (*after a* NEGATIVE² (1)) and not: *He never smokes or drinks.* **3** if not; otherwise: *Wear your coat or (else) you'll be cold.*/*He can't be ill, or he wouldn't have come.* **4 or so** about; or more: *a minute/three minutes or so* |*five dollars or so*

or·a·cle /'ɔrəkəl, 'ɑr-/ *n* **1** a person who is thought to be very wise and able to give the best advice **2** (in ancient Greece) a place where a god was believed to answer people's questions, often in words hard to understand

o·ral /'ɔrəl, 'o^wrəl/ *adj* **1** spoken, not written: *an oral examination* **2** of, about, or using the mouth **–orally** *adv*

or·ange¹ /'ɔrɪndʒ, 'ɑr-/ *n* a very common reddish-yellow round fruit with a bitter-sweet taste and a thick skin

orange² *adj,n* [U] (of) the color of an orange

o·rang·u·tang /ə'ræŋə,tæŋ/ also **-tan** /,tæn/ *n* a large red-haired monkey with no tail

o·ra·tion /ɔ're^yʃən, o^w-, ə-/ *n fml* a formal and solemn public speech

or·a·tor /'ɔrətər, 'ɑr-/ *n* **1** a person who delivers (makes) an ORATION **2** a good public speaker **–oratory** /'ɔrə,tɔriy, -,to^wri^y, 'ɑr-/ *n* [U]

orb /ɔrb/ *n* a ball-like object, esp. one carried by a king or queen on formal occasions

or·bit¹ /'ɔrbɪt/ *n* the path of something moving around a heavenly body, e.g. the moon or a spacecraft moving around the earth **–orbital** /'ɔrbɪtl/ *adj*

orbit² *v* [I;T] to move in an ORBIT¹ around (something)

or·chard /'ɔrtʃərd/ *n* a field where fruit trees grow

or·ches·tra /'ɔrkɪstrə, 'ɔr,kɛstrə/ *n* **1** [*the* S] a large group of people who play music together on stringed and other instruments: *The orchestra is playing well tonight.* **2** [*the* S] *AmE*||**stalls** *BrE*– the seats on the main level of a theater: *Let's sit in the orchestra. I don't like the balcony.* **–orchestral** /ɔr'kɛstrəl/ *adj* [A]

or·chid /'ɔrkɪd/ *n* a plant with very showy flowers

or·dain /ɔr'de^yn/ *v* [T] **1** to make (someone) a priest or religious leader: *She was ordained (as) the first woman priest of her church.* **2** [+*that*] *fml* (of God, the law, etc.) to order

or·deal /ɔr'di^yəl/ *n* a difficult or painful experience

or·der¹ /'ɔrdər/ *n* **1** [U] the special way in which things are arranged in connection with each other: *The words in a dictionary are shown in alphabetical order.* **2** [U] the state in which things are carefully and neatly arranged in their proper place: *Your room is very untidy; go put it in order.* –opposite

disorder 3 [U] fitness for use or operation: *The telephone's* **out of order.** (=does not work) **4** [U] the condition in which laws and rules are obeyed: *That young teacher can't keep order in his classroom.* –opposite **disorder;** see also LAW (2) **5** [C;U +*to-v*/ *that*] a command; direction: *You must obey my orders.*|*I have orders to search your room.* (=I have been commanded to do so)|*I'm here* **by order** *of the general.* (=he commanded me to come)|*The ship left* **under orders** *to sail to the Pacific.* (=having been commanded to do so) **6** [C] a request to supply goods: *an order for three bottles of milk to be sent to us each day* **7** [C] the goods supplied in accordance with such a request: *I'm going to collect my order from the store.* **8** [C] a written or printed paper which allows the holder to do something, e.g. to be paid money –see also MONEY ORDER **9** [C] *tech* (in BIOLOGY) a division, used in putting animals, plants, etc., in groups according to relationship **10** [C] a society of people who lead a holy life of service according to a particular set of religious rules, esp. a group of MONKs or NUNs **11** [*the C of*] (*often cap. as part of a name*) a group of people who have all received special honor given for service, bravery, etc. **12** [C] a quantity of food asked for in a restaurant: *an order of potatoes.* **13 in order to** also **in order that** (*fml*)– with the purpose of: *We used the computer in order to save time*|(*fml*) *in order that we might save time.* –see Study Notes on page 144 **14 made to order** made to fit a particular person's body or according to the exact needs, description, or plan of a particular person. **15 on order** asked for from the maker or supplier but not yet supplied **16 out of order a** not working: *This elevator is out of order.* **b** not following or not in accordance with the rules of a formal meeting –see also ORDER (3)
order² *v* **1** [T +*that*] to give an order (to or for); command: *The general has ordered an advance*|*ordered that the army (should) advance.*|*The doctor ordered (him) a complete rest.* **2** [I;T] to ask for (something) to be brought, made, etc., in return for payment: *Don't forget to order more pencils.*|*I've ordered you a beer.*|*"Have you ordered yet, madam?" asked the waiter.* **3** [T] to arrange; direct: *We must order our affairs better.*
USAGE People whose position gives them the right to be obeyed can **order** or give **orders,** but **command** is normally only used in a military sense: *The doctor* **ordered** *me to rest for a week.*|*The general* **ordered/commanded** *his men to advance.* **Instruct, tell,** and **ask** are similar to **order,** but not as strong.

order sbdy. **around/about–** *v adv* [T] to annoy by giving many orders, esp. unpleasantly

or·dered /ˈɔrdərd/ *adj* arranged; tidy; regular: *an ordered life*
or·der·ly¹ /ˈɔrdərliʸ/ *adj* **1** well-arranged **2** of a tidy nature and habits **3** peace-loving and well-behaved: *The crowd at the football game was very orderly.* –opposite **disorderly**

–**orderliness** *n* [U]
orderly² *n* **-lies 1** a soldier who attends an officer **2** an attendant in a hospital
or·ders /ˈɔrdərz/ *n* [P] *tech* the state of being a priest or other person permitted to perform Christian services and duties (esp. in the phrase **holy orders**)
or·di·nal num·ber /ˌɔrdn-əl ˈnʌmbər,ˌɔrd-nəl/– *n* a number showing position or order in a set: *1st, 2nd, and 3rd are all ordinal numbers.* –compare CARDINAL NUMBER
or·di·nar·i·ly /ˌɔrdn'erəliʸ/ *adv* **1** in an ordinary way **2** usually: *Ordinarily, he's back by five o'clock.*
or·di·nar·y /ˈɔrdn,eriʸ, ˈɔrd,neriʸ/ *adj* **1** not unusual; common **2 out of the ordinary** unusual; uncommon –see also EXTRAORDINARY –**ordinariness** *n* [U]
or·di·na·tion /ˌɔrdn'eʸʃən/ *n* [C;U] the act or ceremony of ORDAINing a priest
ore /ɔr, oʷr/ *n* [C;U] rock, earth, etc., from which metal can be obtained
o·reg·a·no /əˈrɛgə,noʷ/ *n* [U] a plant used in cooking.
or·gan /ˈɔrgən/ *n* **1** a part of an animal or plant that has a special purpose: *The* LIVER *is an organ and so is the heart.*|*the sexual organs* **2** an organization, usu. official, that has a special purpose: *the organs of the government* **3** a musical instrument that uses air to produce sounds, played like a piano and often found in churches
or·gan·ic /ɔr'gænɪk/ *adj* **1** [A] of living things: *organic life*/*chemistry*/*diseases* –opposite **inorganic** [A] made of parts with specialized purposes: *an organic whole*/ *system* **3** (of food) grown without the help of chemical FERTILIZERs –opposite **nonorganic** –**organically** *adv*
or·gan·ism /ˈɔrgə,nɪzəm/ *n* **1** a living being **2** a whole made of specialized parts
or·gan·ist /ˈɔrgənɪst/ *n* a musician who plays an ORGAN (3)
or·ga·ni·za·tion ‖also **-sation** *BrE* /ˌɔrgənə'zeʸʃən/ *n* **1** [C] a group of people with a special purpose, such as a club or business **2** [U] the arrangement or planning of parts so as to form an effective whole –**organizational** *adj* –**organizationally** *adv*
or·ga·nize ‖also **-nised** *BrE* /ˈɔrgə,naɪz/ *v* **-nized, -nizing 1** [T *into*] to arrange into a good working system; make necessary arrangements for (something) –see also DISORGANIZE **2** [I;T] *esp. AmE* for UNIONIZE –**organizer** *n*
or·ga·nized ‖also **-nised** *BrE* /ˈɔrgə,naɪzd/ *adj* arranged into a system that works well –opposite **disorganized**
or·gasm /ˈɔrgæzəm/ *n* [C;U] the highest point of sexual pleasure –**orgasmic** /ɔr'gæzmɪk/ *adj*
or·gy /ˈɔrdʒiʸ/ *n* **-gies** a wild party, usu. with alcohol, often with sex
O·ri·ent /ˈɔriʸənt, -,ɛnt, ˈoʷr-/ *n* [*the* S] *fml or lit* Asia; the (Far) East –**Oriental** /ˌɔriʸ'ɛntəl◂, ˌoʷr-/ *n,adj: Do you like Oriental art?*
o·ri·ent /ˈɔriʸ,ɛnt, -ənt, ˈoʷr-/ *AmE* ‖**orientate** /ˈɔriʸən,teʸt, ˈoʷr-/ *esp. BrE* – *v* [T] to give

direction or guidance to: *I need some time to get oriented whenever I go to a new place.* – see also DISORIENT

o·ri·en·ta·tion /ˌɔriᵞən'teᵞʃən, ˌoʷr-/ *n* [C;U] **1** becoming familiar with some place or something: *Orientation for new students is held during the first week of school.* **2** a position or direction: (fig.) *a new orientation in life*

or·i·fice /'ɔrəfɪs, 'ɑr-/ *n fml* an opening or hole

or·i·gin /'ɔrədʒɪn, 'ɑr-/ *n* **1** [C;U] a starting point: *the origin of a river*/*of a belief* |*a word of unknown origin* **2** [U] parents and conditions of early life: *a woman of humble origin(s)* (=from a low social class)

o·rig·i·nal¹ /ə'rɪdʒənəl/ *adj* **1** [A *no comp.*] first; earliest: *The original owner of the house was Thomas Jefferson.* **2** *often apprec* new; different; unlike others: *an original idea/invention/thinker/painting* –opposite **unoriginal** (for 2)

original² *n* **1** [C] (usu. of paintings) the one from which copies can be made **2** [*the* S] the language in which something was originally written: *Have you read Homer in the original?*

o·rig·i·nal·i·ty /əˌrɪdʒə'nælətiᵞ/ *n* [U] *often apprec* the quality of being ORIGINAL¹ (2): *Her book shows great originality.*

o·rig·i·nal·ly /ə'rɪdʒənəliᵞ/ *adv* **1** in the beginning; formerly: *The family originally came from France.* **2** in a new or different way

o·rig·i·nate /ə'rɪdʒəˌneᵞt/ *v* **-nated, -nating** [I;T] to (cause to) begin: *Her book originated in/from a short story.* –**orginator** *n*

or·na·ment¹ /'ɔrnəmənt/ *n* **1** [C] an object possessed because it is (thought to be) beautiful rather than because it is useful: *Their house is full of little ornaments.* **2** [U] something which is added to make something else more beautiful

or·na·ment² /'ɔrnəˌmɛnt/ *v* [T *with*] to add ORNAMENT to

or·na·men·tal /ˌɔrnə'mɛntəl◀/ *adj* **1** providing or serving as ORNAMENT **2** *often derog* perhaps beautiful, but not really necessary –**ornamentally** *adv*

or·nate /ɔr'neᵞt/ *adj sometimes derog* having a great deal of decoration; not simple: *an ornate style* –**ornately** *adv* –**ornateness** *n* [U]

or·ni·thol·o·gy /ˌɔrnəˈθɑlədʒiᵞ/ *n* [U] the scientific study of birds –**ornithologist** *n* –**ornithological** /ˌɔrnəθə'lɑdʒɪkəl/ *adj*

or·phan /'ɔrfən/ *v,n* (to cause to be) a person (esp. a child) lacking one or both parents: *She was orphaned when her parents died in a plane crash.*

or·phan·age /'ɔrfənɪdʒ/ *n* a place where ORPHAN children live

or·tho·dox /'ɔrθəˌdɑks/ *adj* **1** generally or officially accepted: *orthodox ideas* **2** holding accepted opinions, esp. in religion: *an orthodox Muslim* –see also UNORTHODOX –**orthodoxy** *n* [U]

Orthodox Church /ˌ··· '·/ *n* [*the* S] any of several Christian churches esp. in eastern Europe

or·tho·pe·dic, -paedic /ˌɔrθə'piᵞdɪk◀/ *adj*

[A] of the branch of medicine that deals with (the putting straight of) bones: *After hurting his leg in the accident, he spent three months in an orthopedic hospital.*

Os·car /'ɑskər/ *n* an American movie prize

os·cil·late /'ɑsəˌleᵞt/ *v* **-lated, -lating** [I] *tech* to keep on moving from side to side, between two limits, or between two choices; VACILLATE –**oscillation** /ˌɑsə'leᵞʃən/ *n* [C;U]

os·prey /'ɑspriᵞ, 'ɑspreᵞ/ *n* **-preys** a large fish-eating bird

os·ten·si·ble /ɑ'stɛnsəbəl/ *adj* [A] seeming or pretended, but perhaps not really true –**ostensibly** *adv: He did it ostensibly for love, but really for money.*

os·ten·ta·tion /ˌɑstən'teᵞʃən, -tɛn-/ *n* [U] *derog* unnecessary show of wealth, knowledge, etc. –**ostentatious** *adj* –**ostentatiously** *adv*

os·tra·cize ‖also **-cise** *BrE* /'ɑstrəˌsaɪz/ *v* **-cized, -cizing** [T] (of a group of people) to refuse to have social dealings with (another person or group of people) –**ostracism** /'ɑstrəˌsɪzəm/ *n* [U]

os·trich /'ɔstrɪtʃ, 'ɑ-/ *n* **-triches** *or* **-trich** a very large African bird which runs very quickly but cannot fly

oth·er /'ʌðər/ *determiner,pron* **1** the second of two; the remaining (one or ones): *holding the wheel with one hand and waving with the other (one)*|*They live on the other side of the street.*|*a voice at the other end of the telephone*|*Mary's here. Where are the others?* **2** more of the same kind: *John and two other boys* (Compare *John and two girls*)|*These are red, and the others are brown.* **3** not the same; not this, not oneself, not one's own, etc.: *He enjoys spending other people's money.* (=not his own)| *Others may laugh at her, but I like her.* **4 other than** except: *There's nobody here other than me.*|*You can't get there other than by car.* **5 the other day/afternoon/evening/night** on a recent day/afternoon/evening/night –see also EACH OTHER

USAGE **Other** is not used after **an.** The word is then **another:** *Would you like* **another**/*some* **others?**

oth·er·wise /'ʌðərˌwaɪz/ *adv* **1** in a different way; differently: *I hate him, and I won't pretend otherwise.* (=pretend I don't)|*We'll get there somehow, by train or otherwise.* **2** in every other way; apart from that: *The soup was too salty, but otherwise the meal was excellent.* **3** if not: *Do it now. Otherwise, it will be too late.*

ot·ter /'ɑtər/ *n* **-ters** *or* **-ter** a swimming fish-eating animal with brown fur

ouch /aʊtʃ/ *interj* (an expression of sudden pain)

ought /ɔt/ *v present tense negative contraction* **oughtn't** /'ɔtnt/ [I +*to-v*] (used as a helping verb with another verb) **1** (to show a moral duty): *She ought to/she should look after her children better.*|*You ought to be ashamed of yourself.*|*He ought to be punished.* (=someone should punish him)|*He oughtn't to have said that (but he did).*|*This old coat ought to be thrown away.* (=it would be sensible to throw it away) –see Study Notes on page 434 **2** (to show that something can be naturally expected): *Prices ought to come down soon.|You ought to be hungry by now.*

ounce /aʊns/ *written abbrev.* **oz**– *n* **1** [C] (a measure of weight equal to) 1/16 of a pound; approx 28 grams **2** [S *of*] (even) a small amount: *Haven't you got an ounce of sense?*

our /aʊər, ɑr/ *determiner* (POSSESSIVE[1] (2) *form of* WE) of the people who are speaking: *our daughter|our modern world*

ours /aʊərz, ɑrz/ *pron* (POSSESSIVE[1] (2) *form of* WE) of the people who are speaking: *This is your room, and ours* (=our room) *is down the hall.|Ours is/are on the table.|"a friend of ours"*

our·selves /aʊər'sɛlvz, ɑr-/ *pron* **1** (used as the object of a verb, or after a PREPOSITION, when the people who are speaking do the action and are the objects of the action): *We saw ourselves on television.|John and I have bought ourselves* (=for ourselves) *a new car.* **2** (used to make WE stronger): *We built the house ourselves.*

oust /aʊst/ *v* [T *from*] to force out; cause to leave: *The government has been ousted by the army.*

out¹ /aʊt/ *adv,adj* [F] **1** in or to the open air or the outside: *Open the bag and take the money out.|Shut the door to keep the wind out.|He put his tongue out.|She opened the cage and let the bird out.* (=let it go free) **2** absent; away from a place: *I'm afraid Mr. Jones is out/has gone out; he'll be in soon.|They went out to Africa.|We've given out all the tickets.* (=to everyone)*|You can wash out the dirty spots.* (=so that they won't be there) **3** so as to be clearly seen, shown, understood, etc.: *The sun came out.|I tore my coat on a nail that was sticking out from the wall.* **4 a** (of a baseball player) no longer batting (BAT² (2)) **b** (of the ball in a game such as tennis) outside the line **5** so as to be no longer fashionable: *Long skirts are out this year.* **6** (of a fire or light) no longer burning: *The fire's out.|Please put your cigarette out.* **7** completely: *to clean out the room|I'm tired out.* **8** in a loud voice; aloud: *Read/Call out the names.* **9** impossible: *Visiting Jim is out; he left for Europe yesterday.* **10** (of a flower) fully open and ripe **11** (of the TIDE) away from the coast; low: *The TIDE is going out now.* **12 out for** trying to get: *Don't trust him; he's only out for your money.* **13 out to** trying to: *Be careful: he's out to get* (=harm) *you.|They're out to win.* –compare IN¹ **14 Out with it!** *imper.* say it

out of *prep* **1** from inside; away from: *to jump out of bed |to walk out of a room|to wake up out of a deep sleep|She'll soon be out of danger.* (=safe) **2** from among: *Three out of four people choose this soap!* **3** not having; lacking: *We're nearly out of gasoline.* **4** because of: *I came out of real interest, not just to have a good time!* **5** (shows what something is made from): *made out of wood* **6 out of it** lonely and unhappy because one is not included in something: *I felt a little out of it when we all went to the lake, be-*

cause I can't swim.

out² *adj* [A] **1** directed outwards; used for sending or going out: *Put the letter in the out* TRAY. –opposite **in 2 out and out** complete; total: *an out-and-out lie*

out³ *n* [S] *infml* **1** an excuse for leaving an activity or avoiding blame: *He had an out. He said his father was ill.* **2** *infml* **be on the outs with** to be separated from someone's friendship

out·age /'aʊtɪdʒ/ *n* a period during which there is no (usu. electrical) power: *The power outage lasted three hours.*

out·bid /aʊt'bɪd/ *v* **-bid, -bidding** [T] to offer more than (someone else)

out·board mo·tor /ˌaʊtbɔrd 'moʊtər, -boʊrd-/ *n* a motor fixed to the back end of a small boat

out·break /'aʊtbreɪk/ *n* [*of*] a sudden appearance or beginning of something bad: *an outbreak of disease/of insects/of fighting* –compare BREAK¹ **out**

out·burst /'aʊtbɜrst/ *n* [*of*] a sudden powerful expression of feeling or activity: *outbursts of weeping/laughter/gunfire*

out·cast /'aʊtkæst/ *n,adj* (a person) forced from his home or deserted by his/her friends

out·class /aʊt'klæs/ *v* [T] to be very much better than

out·come /'aʊtkʌm/ *n* [*of*] an effect or result: *What was the outcome of the election?*

out·crop /'aʊtkrɑp/ *n* a rock which stands up out of the ground

out·cry /'aʊtkraɪ/ *n* **-cries** a public show of anger: *If they try to close the library, there'll be a great outcry.*

out·dat·ed /ˌaʊt'deɪtɪd◄/ also **out-of-date**– *adj* no longer in general use

out·dis·tance /aʊt'dɪstəns/ *v* **-tanced, -tanc·ing** [T] to go further or faster than

out·do /aʊt'duw/ *v* **-did** /'dɪd/, **-done** /'dʌn/, **-doing**, **-does** *3rd pers. sing. pres. t.* /'dʌz/ [T] to do or be better than: *She outdid him in running and swimming.*

out·door /'aʊtdɔr, -doʷr/ *adj* [A] which is (happening, done, or used) in the open air: *outdoor shoes|outdoor life* –opposite **indoor**

out·doors /ˌaʊt'dɔrz, -'doʷrz/ also **out of doors** /ˌ· · '·/ – *adv,n* [*the* S] (in) the open air –opposite **indoors**

out·er /'aʊtər/ *adj* [A *no comp.*] on the outside; at a greater distance from the middle: *the outer walls|outer islands* –compare INNER

out·er·most /'aʊtərˌmoʷst/ *adj* [A] furthest outside or furthest from the middle: *the outermost stars* –compare INNERMOST

outer space /ˌ· · '·/ *n* [U] the area where the stars and other heavenly bodies are

out·fit /'aʊtˌfɪt/ *n* **1** all the things, esp. clothes, needed for a particular purpose **2** *infml* a group of people, esp. if working together

out·flank /aʊt'flæŋk/ *v* [T] to go around the side of (an enemy) and attack from behind

out·go·ing /'aʊtˌgoʷɪŋ/ *adj* **1** [A *no comp.*] who is finishing a period in office, esp. in political office: *the outgoing president* –compare INCOMING **2** having or showing eagerness to mix socially with others; friendly: *She's very outgoing.*

out·go·ings /'aʊt,goʷɪŋz/ n [P] amounts of money that are spent

out·ing /'aʊtɪŋ/ n a short pleasure trip

out·land·ish /aʊt'lændɪʃ/ adj strange and unpleasing: *What an outlandish hat!* –**outlandishly** adv –**outlandishness** n [U]

out·last /aʊt'læst/ v [T] to last longer than

out·law¹ /'aʊtlɔ/ n (esp. in former times) a criminal who has not been caught by the police

outlaw² v [T] **1** to declare (someone) a criminal **2** to declare (something) unlawful

out·lay /'aʊtleʸ/ n [on, for] money spent for a purpose

out·let /'aʊtlɛt, -lɪt/ n [for] a way out (usu. for a liquid or a gas): (fig.) *an outlet for his feelings* –compare INLET

out·line¹ /'aʊtlaɪn/ n [of] **1** the shape (of something): *the outline of her face in the light of the candle* **2** the main ideas or facts (of something): *an outline of history/of the main points of the talk*

outline² v **-lined, -lining** [T] to make an OUTLINE¹ of: *The director outlined his plans for the company's future.*

out·live /aʊt'lɪv/ v **-lived, -living** [T] to live longer than

out·look /'aʊtlʊk/ n **1** a view on which one looks out **2** future probabilities **3** [on] one's general point of view –see VIEW (USAGE)

out·ly·ing /'aʊt,laɪ-ɪŋ/ adj [A] far from the center: *an outlying area of the country*

out·ma·neu·ver AmE‖**outmanoeuvre** BrE /,aʊtmə'nuʷvər/ v [T] to make more effective movements than (an opponent); put in a position of disadvantage

out·mod·ed /aʊt'moʷdɪd/ adj no longer in fashion

out·num·ber /aʊt'nʌmbər/ v [T] to be larger in numbers than: *We were heavily outnumbered by the enemy.*

out-of-date /,· · ' · ◄/ adj →OUTDATED

out-of-the-way /,· · · ' · ◄/ adj **1** distant; far away from people and places **2** not known by ordinary people

out·pa·tient /'aʊt,peʸʃənt/ n a sick person who goes to a hospital for treatment while continuing to live at home

out·post /'aʊtpoʷst/ n [of] a group of people or settlement at some distance from the main group or settlement

out·put /'aʊtpʊt/ n [U] something produced for use, such as goods or information from a computer: *an output of 10,000 cars a year* –compare INPUT

out·rage¹ /'aʊt-reʸdʒ/ n [C;U] (anger caused by) a very wrong or cruel act

outrage² v **-raged, -raging** [T] to offend greatly: *The closing of the hospital has outraged public opinion.*

out·ra·geous /aʊt'reʸdʒəs/ adj very offensive –**outrageously** adv

out·right¹ /aʊt'raɪt, 'aʊt-raɪt/ adv **1** completely: *He's been paying for that house for years; now he owns it outright.* **2** openly: *I told him outright what I thought.*

outright² /'aʊt-raɪt/ adj [A] complete: *an outright loss*

out·set /'aʊtsɛt/ n [the S] the beginning: *At/from the outset there was trouble.*

out·shine /aʊt'ʃaɪn/ v **-shone** /'ʃoʷn/, **-shining** [T] to shine more brightly than: (fig.) *She outshines* (=is much better than) *all the other competitors.*

out·side¹ /,aʊt'saɪd◄, 'aʊtsaɪd/ n [the S] the outer part of a solid object; the part that is furthest from the center, or that faces away: *to paint the outside of the house|This coat is cloth on the inside and fur on the outside.* –opposite **inside 2 at the (very) outside** at the most: *$100 at the outside*

outside² adv,adj,prep [no comp.] **1** out of or beyond something; towards or in the open air: *outside the door/the town/my experience|an outside covering|children playing outside in the street* **2** of or from elsewhere: *We can't do it ourselves; we need outside help.* **3** greater; more than: *an outside figure of $100|anything outside $100* **4** (of a chance or possibility) slight; unlikely; distant **5** away from the edge of a road: *If you want to drive fast, use the outside* LANE –compare INSIDE²

outside of /,·'· ·/ prep AmE infml **1** except for: *Outside of John, there's no one for the job.* **2** outside: *People were marching outside of the building.*

out·sid·er /aʊt'saɪdər/ n **1** a person who is not accepted as a member of a particular social group –compare INSIDER **2** a person or animal not considered to have a good chance to win –compare FAVORITE¹ (3)

out·size /'aʊtsaɪz/ also **outsized** /'aʊtsaɪzd/– adj [A] (esp. of clothing) larger than the standard sizes

out·skirts /'aʊtskərts/ n [P of] (esp. of a town) the outer areas: *They live on the outskirts of Paris.*

out·smart /aʊt'smart/ v [T] infml to defeat by acting more cleverly than; OUTWIT

out·spo·ken /aʊt'spoʷkən/ adj expressing openly what is thought or felt –**outspokenly** adv –**outspokenness** n [U]

out·spread /,aʊt'sprɛd◄/ adj spread out flat or to full width: *with arms outspread*

out·stand·ing /aʊt'stændɪŋ/ adj **1** better than others; very good **2** not yet done or paid: *some work still outstanding|outstanding debts* –**outstandingly** adv

out·stretched /,aʊt'strɛtʃt◄/ adj stretched out to full length

out·strip /aʊt'strɪp/ v **-pp-** [T] to do better than

out·ward¹ /'aʊt-wərd/ adj [A] **1** away: *the outward voyage* –opposite **homeward 2** on the outside: *outward cheerfulness* –see also INWARD

outward² AmE‖also **outwards** /-wərdz/– adv towards the outside –opposite **inward**

out·ward·ly /'aʊt-wərdli/ adv seeming to be, but in reality probably not being: *He was outwardly calm, but ...*

out·weigh /aʊt'weʸ/ v [T] to be more important than: *My love for her outweighs everything else.*

out·wit /aʊt'wɪt/ v **-tt-** [T] to defeat by being more intelligent than

out·worn /,aʊt'wɔrn◄, -'woʷrn◄/ adj (of an idea, custom, etc.) no longer useful or used

–compare WORN-OUT

o·val /'oʷvəl/ *n,adj* (anything which is) egg-shaped

o·va·ry /'oʷvəriʸ/ *n* **-ries** the part of a female that produces eggs

o·va·tion /oʷ'veʸʃən/ *n* a joyful expression of public approval: *a standing ovation* (=when people stand and APPLAUD)

ov·en /'ʌvən/ *n* a box used for cooking, baking clay, etc. –see COOK (USAGE); see illustration on page 379

o·ver¹ /'oʷvər/ *adv* **1** downwards from an upright position: *He pushed me and I fell over.* **2** across an edge, a distance, or an open space: *The milk's boiling over!*|*We flew over to Europe.* (=across the Atlantic)|*Come and sit over here.* (=on this side of the room) **3** from one person or group to another: *He signed the money over to his son.* **4** above; more: *The plane flew over at 3 o'clock.*|*children of seven and over* (=older) –opposite **under 5** so that another side is shown: *Turn the page over.*|*dogs rolling over (and over) on the grass* **6** so as to be covered and not seen: *Let's paint it over in green.*|*Cover her over with a sheet.* **7** completely through; from beginning to end: *You'd better think/talk it over carefully.* **8** (showing that something is repeated): *I've told him several times over/told him over and over not to do it.* **9** *esp. AmE* during or beyond a certain period: *Don't leave now. Why don't you stay over till Monday?* **10** so as to be in each other's positions: *Let's change these two pictures over and hang this one up there.* **11** too much; too: *Don't be over anxious about it.* **12** *AmE* again: *I failed my driving test, so I'm going to take it over (again) next week.*

over² *prep* **1** directly above; higher than, but not touching: *The lamp hung over/above the table.*|*The doctor leaned over the sick child.* **2** so as to cover: *He put the newspaper over his face.* **3** from side to side of, esp. by going up and then down again: *to jump over the wall/the ditch* (Compare *across the ditch*, but not *across the wall)|*If we can't go over the mountain, we have to go around it.*|*The car ran over* (not *across) *a dog and killed it.*|*to fall over* (=across the edge of) *a cliff* **4** on the far side of: *They live (just) over/across the street.* **5** in many parts of; everywhere in: *They traveled (all) over Europe.* **6** commanding; in control of: *He ruled over a large kingdom.*|*I don't want anyone over me, telling me what to do.* **7** more than; above: *over 30 books*|*children over seven* (=older than seven) **8** during: *to hold a meeting over dinner*|*Will you be at home over Christmas?* **9** by means of; using: *I don't want to say it over the telephone.*|*I heard it over the radio.* **10** on the subject of; about: *difficulties over his income tax*|*"taking a long time over it"* (=in doing it) **11 over and above** as well as; besides –compare UNDER²

over³ *adj* [F *with*] finished; ended: *I'm sorry, the program is over; it's finished.*|*At last the exams are over and done with.* (=completely finished)

o·ver·all /,oʷvər'ɔl◄/ *adj,adv* [A; after *n*] **1** including everything: *the overall measurements of the room*|*The fish measured 5 feet 3 inches overall.* **2** on the whole; generally: *Overall, prices are still rising.*

o·ver·alls /'oʷvər,ɔlz/ *n* [P] loose trousers often fastened over the shoulders and worn by workers over other clothes –compare DUNGAREES

o·ver·arm /'oʷvər,arm/ *adj,adv* OVERHAND

o·ver·awe /,oʷvər'ɔ/ *v* **-awed, -awing** [T] to fill with respect and fear

o·ver·bal·ance /,oʷvər'bæləns/ *v* **-anced, -ancing** [I;T] to (cause to) become unbalanced and fall over

o·ver·bear·ing /,oʷvər'bɛərɪŋ◄/ *adj* trying to make other people obey without regard for their ideas or feelings –**overbearingly** *adv*

o·ver·board /'oʷvər,bɔrd, -,boʷrd/ *adv* **1** over the side of a ship or boat into the water **2 go overboard for/about** *infml* to become very attracted to

o·ver·bur·den /,oʷvər'bɜrdn/ *v* [T *with*] to make (someone or something) carry or do too much

o·ver·cast /,oʷvər'kæst◄/ *adj* dark with clouds: *an overcast sky/day*|(fig.) *Her face was overcast with sadness.*

o·ver·charge /,oʷvər'tʃardʒ/ *v* **-charged, -charging** [I;T] to charge (someone) too much: *They overcharged me (by) $5 for the food.* –see also UNDERCHARGE

o·ver·coat /'oʷvər,koʷt/ *n* a long warm coat worn over other clothes in cold weather

o·ver·come /,oʷvər'kʌm/ *v* **-came** /'keʸm/, **-come, -coming 1** [I;T] to fight successfully against; defeat: *to overcome the enemy/a bad habit* **2** [T] (usu. of feelings) to take control and influence the behavior of (someone): *I was overcome by tiredness/grief.*

o·ver·com·pen·sate /,oʷvər'kampən,seʸt/ *v* **-sated, -sating** [I *for*] to try to correct some weaknesses by taking too strong an action in the opposite direction –**overcompensation** /,oʷvər,kampən'seʸʃən/ *n* [U]

o·ver·crowd /,oʷvər'kraʊd/ *v* [T *with*] to put or allow too many people or things in (one place): *an overcrowded classroom*

o·ver·do /,oʷvər'duʷ/ *v* **-did** /'dɪd/, **-done** /'dʌn/, **-doing** [T] **1** to do, decorate, perform, etc., too much: *The love scenes in the play were a little overdone.*|*I've been overdoing it.* (=working too much) **2** to use too much: *Don't overdo the salt.*

o·ver·done /,oʷvər'dʌn◄/ *adj* cooked too much –see also UNDERDONE

o·ver·dose /'oʷvər,doʷs/ *n* too much of a drug: *He died by taking an overdose.*

o·ver·draft /'oʷvər,dræft/ *n* permission from a bank to OVERDRAW; the sum by which one has OVERDRAWN

o·ver·draw /,oʷvər'drɔ/ *v* **-drew** /'druʷ/, **-drawn** /'drɔn/, **-drawing** [I;T] to get a bank to pay one more money than one has in (one's account): *My account is $300 overdrawn/overdrawn by $300.*

o·ver·due /,oʷvər'duʷ◄, -'dyuʷ◄/ *adj* [after *n*] **1** left unpaid too long **2** later than expected: *The train is 15 minutes overdue.*

o·ver·es·ti·mate /ˌoʷvərˈɛstəˌmeʸt/ v **-mated, -mating** [I;T] **1** to give too high a value for (an amount): *We overestimated the cost, so we still have some money left.* **2** to have too high an opinion of: *I think you're overestimating his abilities.*

o·ver·flow¹ /ˌoʷvərˈfloʷ/ v [I;T] **1** to flow over the edges (of): *The river overflowed (its banks).* **2** [into] to go beyond the limits (of): *The crowd overflowed the theater into the street.*|(fig.) *His heart is overflowing with sadness.*

o·ver·flow² /ˈoʷvərˌfloʷ/ n **1** an act of OVERFLOWING **2** something that OVERFLOWS: *Bring a pot to catch the overflow from this pipe.* **3** a pipe or CHANNEL (2) for carrying away water that is more than is needed

o·ver·grown /ˌoʷvərˈgroʷn◂/ adj [with] covered with plants growing uncontrolled

o·ver·hand /ˈoʷvərˌhænd/ also **overarm**— adj,adv (in sports) with the arm moving above the shoulder: *He threw the ball overhand.*|*an overhand throw* —opposite UNDERARM

o·ver·hang /ˌoʷvərˈhæŋ/ v **-hung** /ˈhʌŋ/, **-hanging** [I;T] to hang over (something): *overhanging cliffs* —**overhang** /ˈoʷvərˌhæŋ/ n

o·ver·haul /ˌoʷvərˈhɔl, ˈoʷvərˌhɔl/ v [T] to examine thoroughly and perhaps repair if necessary: *to overhaul a car* —**overhaul** /ˈoʷvərˌhɔl/ n

o·ver·head¹ /ˌoʷvərˈhɛd◂, ˈoʷvərˌhɛd/ adv, adj above one's head: *electricity carried by overhead wires* (=not underground)

o·ver·head² /ˈoʷvərˌhɛd/ n [U] money spent regularly to keep a business running: *Their office is in midtown Manhattan, so their overhead is very high.*

o·ver·hear /ˌoʷvərˈhɪər/ v **-heard** /ˈhɜrd/, **-hearing** [T] to hear (what others are saying) without their knowledge: *I overheard them talking about me.*

o·ver·joyed /ˌoʷvərˈdʒɔɪd/ adj [F +to-v/that] very pleased; full of joy

o·ver·land /ˈoʷvərˌlænd/ adv,adj across or by land and not by sea or air

o·ver·lap¹ /ˌoʷvərˈlæp/ v **-pp-** [I;T] to cover (something) partly: *Some roofs are made with overlapping* SLATES¹.|(fig.) *History and politics overlap and should be studied together.*

o·ver·lap² /ˈoʷvərˌlæp/ n [C;U] the amount by which two or more things OVERLAP¹ each other

o·ver·load /ˌoʷvərˈloʷd/ [T] **1** to load too heavily **2** to cause (a machine) to work too hard, and so use too much electricity: *Don't overload the electrical system by using too many machines.*

o·ver·look /ˌoʷvərˈlʊk/ v [T] **1** to have or give a view of from above: *Our room overlooked the sea.* **2** to look at but not see; not notice; miss **3** to pretend not to see; forgive: *I'll overlook your lateness this time, but don't be late again.* —see also LOOK over

o·ver·ly /ˈoʷvərliʸ/ adv [no comp.] too much; very: *I'm not overly interested in music.*

o·ver·much /ˌoʷvərˈmʌtʃ◂/ adv, determiner, pron [usu. with NEGATIVES²] too much; very

much: *He doesn't like me overmuch.*

o·ver·night /ˌoʷvərˈnaɪt◂/ adv,adj **1** for or during the night: *an overnight trip*|*an overnight bag* **2** suddenly: *After flying across the Atlantic, Charles Lindbergh became famous overnight.*

o·ver·pass /ˈoʷvərˌpæs/ AmE‖**flyover** BrE— n a place where roads, etc. cross each other and where one passes high over the other by way of a kind of bridge

o·ver·pop·u·lat·ed /ˌoʷvərˈpɑpyəˌleʸtɪd/ adj having too many people —**overpopulation** /ˌoʷvərˌpɑpyəˈleʸʃən/ n [U]

o·ver·pow·er /ˌoʷvərˈpaʊər/ v [T] **1** to conquer (someone) by greater power **2** →OVERCOME

o·ver·rate /ˌoʷvərˈreʸt/ v **-rated, -rating** [T] to put too great or high a value on: *I think that movie has been overrated; it isn't really very good.* —see also UNDERRATE

o·ver·re·act /ˌoʷvər-riʸˈækt/ v [I;T to] to react in a way stronger than necessary: *Whenever we discuss politics, he always overreacts.*

o·ver·ride /ˌoʷvərˈraɪd/ v **-rode** /ˈroʷd/, **-ridden** /ˈrɪdn/, **-riding** [T] to take no notice of (another person's orders, claims, etc.)

o·ver·rule /ˌoʷvərˈruʷl/ v **-ruled, -ruling** [T] to decide against (someone in a lower position, or something): *The judge overruled us/our claim.*

o·ver·run /ˌoʷvərˈrʌn/ v **-ran** /ˈræn/, **-run** /ˈrʌn/, **-running 1** [T] to spread over, usu. causing harm: *The enemy overran the conquered country.* **2** [I;T] to continue beyond (a time limit or an appointed stopping place)

o·ver·seas /ˌoʷvərˈsiʸz◂/ adv,adj across the sea: *They've gone to live overseas.*|*overseas students*

o·ver·see /ˌoʷvərˈsiʸ/ v **-saw** /ˈsɔ/, **-seen** /ˈsiʸn/, **-seeing** [T] to watch to see that work is properly done: *to oversee the work/the workers* —**overseer** /ˈoʷvərˌsiʸər, -ˌsɪər/ n

o·ver·shad·ow /ˌoʷvərˈʃædoʷ/ v [T] **1** to throw a shadow over **2** to make appear less important: *Her new book will overshadow all her earlier ones.*

o·ver·shoot /ˌoʷvərˈʃuʷt/ v **-shot** /ˈʃɑt/, **-shooting** [I;T] to go too far or beyond at a fast speed, and miss: *The train overshot the station.*

o·ver·sight /ˈoʷvərˌsaɪt/ n [C;U] (an) unintended failure to notice or do something: *The mistake was the result of (an) oversight.* —see ERROR (USAGE)

o·ver·sim·pli·fy /ˌoʷvərˈsɪmpləˌfaɪ/ v **-fied, -fying** [I;T] to express (something) so simply that its true meaning is changed or lost —**oversimplification** /ˌoʷvərˌsɪmpləfəˈkeʸʃən/ n [C;U]

o·ver·sleep /ˌoʷvərˈsliʸp/ v **-slept** /ˈslɛpt/, **-sleeping** [I] to sleep too long or too late

o·ver·state /ˌoʷvərˈsteʸt/ v **-stated, -stating** [T] to cause (something) to seem to appear better, worse, or more important than it really is: *She overstated her case, so we didn't believe her.* —see also UNDERSTATE

o·vert /oʷˈvɜrt, ˈoʷvɜrt/ adj fml public; not secret —opposite **covert** —**overtly** adv

o·ver·take /ˌoʷvərˈteʸk/ v **-took** /ˈtʊk/, **taken**

/'teʸkən/, **-taking** [I;C] to come up level with and pass: *A car overtook me, although I was going very fast.*

o·ver·throw /ˌoʷvər'θroʷ/ *v* **-threw** /'θruʷ/, **-thrown** /'θroʷn/, **-throwing** [T] to defeat; remove from official power: *to overthrow the government* –**overthrow** /'oʷvərˌθroʷ/ *n* [*the* S]

o·ver·time /'oʷvərˌtaɪm/ *n,adv* [U] (time) beyond the usual time, esp. working time: *They're working overtime to finish the job quickly.*

o·ver·ture /'oʷvərtʃər, -ˌtʃʊər/ *n* a musical introduction to a large musical piece, esp. an OPERA: *the overture to Mozart's "Don Giovanni"*

o·ver·tures /'oʷvərtʃərz, -ˌtʃʊərz/ *n* [P] an offer to begin to deal with someone in the hope of reaching an agreement: *to make peace overtures to the enemy*

o·ver·turn /ˌoʷvər'tɜrn/ *v* [I;T] to (cause to) turn over: *The boat/The lamp overturned.*

o·ver·weight /ˌoʷvər'weʸt◄/ *adj* [after *n*] weighing too much: *This package/person is overweight by two pounds/is two pounds overweight.|an overweight person* –compare UNDERWEIGHT; see THIN (USAGE)

o·ver·whelm /ˌoʷvər'hwɛlm, -'wɛlm/ *v* [T] 1 to defeat or make powerless (usu. a group of people) by much greater force of numbers 2 (of feelings) to OVERCOME (2) completely and usu. suddenly

o·ver·whelm·ing /ˌoʷvər'hwɛlmɪŋ, -'wɛl-/ *adj* very large or great; too large or great to oppose –**overwhelmingly** *adv*

o·ver·work¹ /ˌoʷvər'wɜrk/ *v* [I;T] to (cause to) work too much

overwork² /'oʷvərˌwɜrk/ *n* [U] too much work; working too hard

o·ver·wrought /ˌoʷvər'rɔt◄/ *adj* too nervous and excited

ow /aʊ/ *interj* (an expression of sudden pain)

owe /oʷ/ *v* **owed, owing** [T] 1 [*to, for*] to have to pay: *He owes (me) $20 (for my work).* –see Study Notes on page 481 2 [*to*] to feel

grateful (to) (for): *We owe our parents a lot.*

ow·ing /'oʷɪŋ/ *adj* [F or after *n*] still to be paid: *How much is owing to you?|There is still $5 owing.*

owing to /'··ˌ·/ *prep* because of: *We were late, owing to the snow.* –see Study Notes on page 144

owl /aʊl/ *n* a night bird, supposed to be very wise –**owlish** *adj*

own¹ /oʷn/ *determiner, pron* 1 belonging to oneself and to nobody else: *I only borrowed the book; it's not my own.|The country has its own oil and doesn't need to buy any from abroad.|She would rather have a room of her (very) own than sleep with her sisters.* 2 **have/get one's own back (on someone)** to succeed in doing harm (to someone) in return for harm done to oneself 3 **on one's own** by oneself; without help: *I can't carry it on my own; it's too heavy.*

own² *v* [T] 1 to possess (something), esp. by lawful right: *Who owns this house/this dog?* 2 [+(*that*)] *fml* to admit –**own up** *v adv* [*I to*] *to admit a fault or crime:* *She took the money, but she wouldn't own up to taking it.*

own·er /'oʷnər/ *n* a person who owns something, esp. by lawful right –**ownership** *n* [U]

ox /ɑks/ *n* **oxen** /'ɑksən/ a large animal of the cattle type, wild or used by man

ox·ide /'ɑksaɪd/ *n* [C;U] a chemical substance in which something is combined with oxygen: *iron oxide*

ox·i·dize ‖also **-dise** *BrE* /'ɑksəˌdaɪz/ *v* **-dized, -dizing** [I;T] to (cause to) combine with oxygen, esp. in such a way as to make or become RUSTY –**oxidation** /ˌɑksə'deʸʃən/ *n* [U]

ox·y·gen /'ɑksɪdʒən/ *n* [U] a gas present in the air, without color, taste, or smell, but necessary for all forms of life on earth

oys·ter /'ɔɪstər/ *n* a flat shellfish which can produce a jewel called a PEARL

oz. *written abbrev. said as:* OUNCE *or* OUNCES

o·zone /'oʷzoʷn/ *n* [U] 1 *tech* a type of oxygen 2 *infml* air that is pleasant to breathe, esp. near the sea

P, p

P, p /piʸ/ **P's, p's** *or* **Ps, ps** the 16th letter of the English alphabet

p¹ *abbrev. for:* (*BrE infml*) (new) penny/ pence: *This newspaper costs 8p.* –see PENNY (USAGE)

p² *written abbrev. said as:* page –see also PP

PA, Pa. *written abbrev. said as:* Pennsylvania /ˌpɛnsəl'veʸnyə, -'veʸniʸə/ (a state in the US)

PA /ˌpiʸ 'eʸ/ *n abbrev. for:* public-address system; an electrically controlled apparatus used for making a speaker clearly heard by large groups of people, esp. out of doors, usu. by using LOUDSPEAKERS: *I can hear you loud and clear over the PA.*

pace¹ /peʸs/ *n* 1 [S;U] rate or speed in walk-

ing, running, etc.: *a slow pace|The fastest runner* **set the pace** *and the others followed.|She works very fast: I can't* **keep pace with** (=work at the same speed as) *her.* 2 [C] (the distance moved in) a single step in running or walking: *The fence is ten paces from the house.* 3 **put someone through his/her paces** to make someone do something as a test or proof of his/her abilities

pace² *v* **paced, pacing** 1 [I;T] to walk (across) with slow, regular, steady steps, esp. backwards and forwards:*The people outside the theater paced up and down, trying to keep warm.|The lion paced the floor of its cage.* 2 [T *off, out*] to measure by taking steps of an equal and known length: *to pace out a room*

3 [T] to set the speed or rate of movement for: *She knew how fast she was running, because her trainer was pacing her on a bicycle.*

pace·mak·er /ˈpeɪsˌmeɪkər/ *n* **1** also **pacesetter** *AmE*– **a** a person who sets a speed that others in a race try to equal **b** a person who sets an example for others **2** a machine used to make weak or irregular heartbeats regular

pace·set·ter /ˈpeɪsˌsɛtər/ *n esp. AmE* for PACEMAKER (1)

pac·i·fi·er /ˈpæsəˌfaɪər/ *n* a rubber thing for sucking, put in a baby's mouth to keep it quiet

pac·i·fism /ˈpæsəˌfɪzəm/ *n* [U] the belief that all wars are wrong

pac·i·fist /ˈpæsəfɪst/ *n* an active believer in PACIFISM; person who refuses to fight in a war because of such a belief

pac·i·fy /ˈpæsəˌfaɪ/ *v* **-fied, -fying** [T] to make calm, quiet, and satisfied: *to pacify a crying baby* –**pacification** /ˌpæsəfəˈkeɪʃən/ *n* [U]

pack¹ /pæk/ *n* **1** a number of things wrapped or tied together, or put in a case, esp. for carrying on the back:*The climber carried some food in a pack on his back.*|*They used* **packhorses** *to carry their food and tents across the mountains.* **2** a group of wild animals (esp. the WOLF) that hunt together, or a group of dogs trained together for hunting **3** *derog* a collection, group, etc. (esp. in the phrases **pack of thieves, pack of lies**) **4** a complete set of cards used in playing a game **5** *AmE*‖also **packet**– a small package; a number of small things tied or put together into a small box, case, or bag: *a pack of cigarettes/envelopes*

pack² *v* **1** [I;T] to put (things, esp. one's belongings) into (a case, boxes, etc.) for traveling or storing: *She packed her bags and left.*|*I'm leaving in an hour, and I haven't packed yet!*|*He packed some bread and cheese for his dinner.*|*a packed meal* –see also UNPACK **2** [T] to cover, fill, or surround closely with a protective material: *Pack some paper around the dishes in the box so that they will not break.* **3** [I;T *in, down*] to fit, crush, or push into a space: *If you pack those things down, we can get some more clothes into the box.* **4** *AmE infml* to carry regularly (esp. in the phrase **to pack a gun**)

pack sbdy./sthg.↔ *in v adv* [T] *infml* **1** to attract in large numbers: *That movie is really packing them in.* (=attracting large crowds) **2 pack it in** *infml* **a** to cease an activity: *We've been working at this long enough; it's time to pack it in and go home.* **b** to eat large amounts

pack sbdy.↔ **off** *v adv* [T *to*] *infml*→BUNDLE off: *He packed his children off to school and then went out.*

pack up *v adv* [I] *infml* to finish work

pack·age¹ /ˈpækɪdʒ/ *n* a thing or things wrapped in paper and tied or fastened for easy carrying, mailing, etc.: *He carried a large package of books under his arm.*|*I'm taking this package to the post office.* –see illustration on page 683

package² *v* **-aged, -aging** [T *up*] to place in or

tie up as a PACKAGE¹: *Books are packaged in the shipping department.*|*packaged food-*|*Too much packaging increases the cost of the food we buy.*

package deal /ˈ·· ˌ·/ also **package**– *n infml* an agreement that includes a number of things all of which must be accepted together

package tour /ˈ·· ˌ·/ *n* a completely planned vacation arranged by a company at a fixed price

packed /pækt/ *adj* (of a room, building, etc.) full of people; CROWDED

pack·er /ˈpækər/ *n* a person who PACKS² (1,2) esp. **a** food for preserving **b** the furniture, clothing, etc., of people moving from one house to another

pack·et /ˈpækɪt/ *n* →PACK¹ (5): *a packet of envelopes/cigarettes*

pack·ing /ˈpækɪŋ/ *n* [U] material used in PACKING² (2)

packing case /ˈ·· ˌ·/ *n* a strong wooden box in which things are packed to be stored or sent elsewhere

pact /pækt/ *n* a solemn agreement: *a pact of peace between the two nations*

pad¹ /pæd/ *n* **1** anything made or filled with a soft material used to protect something, make it more comfortable, etc.: *American football players wear shoulder pads for protection.*|*Put a clean pad of cotton over the wound.* **2** a number of sheets of paper fastened together, used for writing letters, drawing pictures, etc.: *a writing pad* **3** the thick-skinned underpart of the foot of some four-footed animals

pad² *v* **-dd-** [T] to fill with soft material in order to protect, shape, or make more comfortable: *a coat with padded shoulders*|(fig.) *I made my speech longer by padding it with a few jokes.*

pad³ *v* **-dd-** to walk steadily and usu. softly: *John rode his bicycle slowly, and his dog padded along beside him.*

pad·ding /ˈpædɪŋ/ *n* [U] material used to PAD² something

pad·dle¹ /ˈpædl/ *n* **1** a short pole with a wide flat blade at one or both ends, used for pushing and guiding a small boat (esp. a CANOE¹). Unlike an OAR, it is not fastened in position on the side of the boat **2** a specially shaped wooden stick used for hitting the ball in TABLE TENNIS –compare RACKET¹

paddle² *v* **-dled, -dling** [I;T] to move (a small light boat, esp. a CANOE¹) through water, using one or more PADDLES¹; row gently

paddle steam·er /ˈ·· ˌ··/ *n* a steamship which is pushed forward by PADDLE WHEELS

paddle wheel /ˈ·· ˌ·/ *n* a large wheel fixed to the side or back of a ship, and turned by a steam-engine to make the ship move forward through the water

pad·dock /ˈpædək/ *n* a small field where horses are kept and exercised, or where horses are brought together before a race so that people may see them

pad·dy /ˈpædi/ also **rice paddy, paddy field** /ˈ·· ˌ·/– *n* **-dies** a field where rice is grown in water

pad·lock /ˈpædlɑk/ *n* a movable lock with a

U-shaped metal bar, which can be used to lock gates, bicycles, cupboards, etc. **–padlock** v [T]: *Did you remember to padlock the gate?*

pa·dre /'pɑdreʸ, -driʸ/ n *infml* a priest, esp. one in the Armed Forces; CHAPLAIN –see PRIEST (USAGE)

pa·gan /'peʸgən/ n a person who is not a believer in any of the chief religions of the world **–pagan** *adj*: *a pagan ceremony*

page¹ /peʸdʒ/ n one or both sides of a sheet of paper in a book, newspaper, etc.:*There is a picture of a ship on page 44.|Someone has torn a page out of this book.*

page² n **1** a (usu. young) person who carries messages, usu. uniformed: *It is an honor to work as a page in Congress.* **2** a boy servant in a hotel, club, etc., usu. uniformed **3** (at a wedding) a boy attendant on the BRIDE (=the woman getting married)

page³ v **paged, paging** [T] (in a hotel, hospital, etc.) to call aloud for (someone who is wanted for some reason), esp. through a LOUDSPEAKER

pag·eant /'pædʒənt/ n a public show or ceremony, usu. out of doors, esp. **a** one in which there is a procession of people in rich dress **b** one in which historical scenes are acted

pag·eant·ry /'pædʒəntriʸ/ n [U] splendid show of ceremonial grandness with people in fine dress: *the pageantry of a royal wedding*

pa·go·da /pə'goʷdə/ n a temple (esp. Buddhist or Hindu) built on several floors with an ornamental roof at each level

paid /peʸd/ v *past tense and participle of* PAY¹

paid-up /,· '·◀/ *adj* having paid in full (esp. so as to continue being a member) –compare PAY¹ **up**

pail /peʸl/ n a bucket used for carrying liquids: *a milk pail*

pain¹ /peʸn/ n **1** [U] suffering; great discomfort of the body or mind:*She was in pain/crying with pain after she broke her arm.|His behavior caused his parents a great deal of pain.* **2** [C] a feeling of suffering or discomfort in a particular part of the body –compare ACHE² **3** [S] also **pain in the neck** /,· ··'·/– *infml* a person, thing, or happening that causes annoyance or displeasure; NUISANCE: *He's a real pain.* –see also PAINS

pain² v [T] to cause to feel pain in the mind; hurt

pained /peʸnd/ *adj* showing that one is displeased or hurt in one's feelings: *After they had quarreled, there was a pained silence between them.*

pain·ful /'peʸnfəl/ *adj* causing pain: *a painful cut on my thumb* **–painfully** *adv* **–painfulness** n [U]

pain·kill·er /'peʸn,kɪlər/ n a medicine which lessens or removes pain

pain·less /'peʸnlɪs/ *adj* causing no pain: (fig.) *The examination was quite painless.* **–painlessly** *adv*

pains /peʸnz/ n [P] trouble; effort: *He tried very hard, so we gave him something for his pains.|The teacher* **was at/took (great) pains** (=took great trouble) *to make sure that we all understood.*

pains·tak·ing /'peʸnz,teʸkɪŋ, 'peʸn,steʸ-/ *adj* careful and thorough: *painstaking care* **–painstakingly** *adv*

paint¹ /peʸnt/ n [U] liquid coloring matter which can be put or spread on a surface to make it a certain color: *a can of green paint|* **Wet Paint** (a warning sign placed near a freshly-painted surface) –compare DYE¹

paint² v [I;T] **1** to put paint on (a surface): *She painted the door blue/a bright color.* **2** to make (a picture of) (somebody or something) using paint:*Who painted this picture?|I wish I could paint as well as you.|*(fig.) *Her letters paint a wonderful picture of her life in Burma.* **3 paint the town red** *infml* to go out and have a good time, usu. when celebrating (CELEBRATE) something

paint·er /'peʸntər/ n **1** a person whose job is painting houses, rooms, etc. **2** a person who paints pictures; artist: *a PORTRAIT painter*

paint·ing /'peʸntɪŋ/ n **1** [U] the art or practice of painting pictures **2** [C] a picture made in this way

paints /peʸnts/ n [P] a set of small tubes or cakes of paint of different colors, usu. in a box (**paint box**), as used by an artist: *a set of oil paints*

pair¹ /pɛər/ n **pairs** *or* **pair 1** something made up of two parts that are alike and are joined and used together: *a pair of pants|a pair of scissors* **2** two things that are alike or of the same kind, and are usu. used together: *a pair of shoes|a beautiful pair of legs|a pair of kings* (=two playing cards of the same value) **3** two people closely connected, esp. a COUPLE¹ (2): *The happy pair are going to Spain after their wedding.* –see COUPLE (USAGE)

USAGE Some words for two things joined together, like **pants** and **scissors**, are used like plural nouns, but they are not thought of as having a number. So one can say *These* **pants**/*My other* **pants** *are dirty,* or *two more* **pairs** *of* **pants,** but not *two* **pants,** *both* **pants. Pair** is also used for things like **shoes,** which are not joined together, so that one can say *one* **shoe,** *both* **shoes,** as well as *a* **pair** *of* **shoes.** Any word in this dictionary which is followed by the note "see PAIR (USAGE)" can be used in the expression *a* **pair** *of* **X.**

pair² v [I;T] **1** [off, up] to (cause to) form into one or more PAIRs¹ (2,3): *Birds often pair in the spring.|We have been trying for years to pair Jane and David off.* **2** to make, or join with somebody to make, a PAIR¹ (3)

pair up v *adv* [I;T] (=**pair** sbdy.↔ **up**) *with*] to (cause to) join in pairs, esp. for purposes of work or sport

pa·ja·mas *AmE*‖**pyjamas** *BrE* /pə'dʒɑməz, -'dʒæ-/ n [P] a soft loose-fitting pair of pants and short coat made to be worn in bed –see illustration on page 55

pal /pæl/ n *infml* a close friend: *an old pal of mine*

pal·ace /'pælɪs/ n a large and splendid house, esp. where a king or queen officially lives: (fig.) *Her house is a palace compared to ours!* –see HOUSE (USAGE)

pal·at·a·ble /'pælətəbəl/ *adj* **1** pleasant to

STUDY NOTES pairs of verbs ▮▮▮▮▮▮▮

lend and borrow

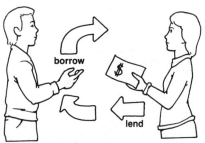

The boy wants to **borrow** a dollar **from** the girl. The girl **lends** a dollar **to** the boy.

If she **lends** (also **loans** *AmE*) the money to him, it is a **loan**. He will have to **pay back** (or **repay**) the money to her.

If he has **borrowed** the money and has not **paid** it **back**, he **owes** her the money.

"I don't have enough money for my bus fare. Can I borrow a dollar? / Can you lend me a dollar?"

"O.K. I'll lend you a dollar, but you have to pay me back / pay it back / give it back on Monday."

bring and take

*I asked the waiter to **bring** me a cup of coffee, and to **take away** the dirty dishes.*

bring means "to cause to come with one to the place where the speaker is or will be"

*They came to my party and **brought** me a lovely present.*

take means "to cause to go with one to another place"

*We went to her party and **took** her a present.*

say and tell

say and **tell** are very similar in meaning, but we use them differently in sentences. We usually **say** something, but **tell** somebody something. Compare:

*I **said**, "Be quiet!"*

*She **said** a few words and then sat down.*

*He **said**, "I'm very tired."*
*He **said** (that) he was very tired.*

*He **said** ⟨(to me)⟩ that he was tired.*

*I **told** ⟨you⟩ to be quiet!*

*She **told** ⟨us⟩ a very funny story.*

*He **told** ⟨me⟩ (that) he was very tired.*

Note the use of **tell** in the phrases **tell a lie**, **tell the truth**, **tell a story**, **tell the time**.

taste **2** agreeable to the mind; pleasant –opposite **unpalatable**

pal·ate /'pælɪt/ n **1** the top part (ROOF¹ (4)) of the inside of the mouth **2** [usu. sing.] the ability to judge food or wine

pa·la·tial /pə'leʸʃəl/ adj (usu. of buildings) like a palace; large and splendid: a palatial hotel

pale¹ /peʸl/ adj **1** (of a person's face) having less than the usual amount of color; rather white **2** (esp. of colors) not bright; weak: pale blue|the pale light of the moon –**paleness** n [U]

pale² v **paled, paling** [I] to become pale: (fig.) All our other worries paled (=began to seem unimportant) beside the possibility that the country would go to war.

pa·le·o·lith·ic /ˌpeʸliʸə'lɪθɪk, ˌpæ-/ adj (often cap.) of the earliest known period of human existence (**Old Stone Age**), when people made weapons and tools of stone: a paleolithic ax –compare NEOLITHIC

pal·ette /'pælɪt/ n a board with a curved edge and a hole for the thumb, on which an artist mixes colors

paling /'peʸlɪŋ/ n a fence made out of pointed pieces of wood

pall¹ /pɔl/ n **1** a covering of dark cloth spread over a COFFIN (a box in which a dead body is carried): (fig.) a pall of smoke hiding the city **2** AmE a COFFIN with a body inside

pall² v [I on] to become uninteresting or dull, esp. through being done, heard, etc., too often or for too long: His interest in his new job began to pall after a while.

pall·bear·er /'pɔl,bɛərər/ n a person who walks beside or helps to carry a COFFIN at a funeral

pal·lid /'pælɪd/ adj (esp. of the face, skin, etc.) unusually or unhealthily pale; WAN: She had a pallid look, as if she had been indoors too long. –**pallor** /'pælər/ n [S;U]

palm¹ /pɑm/ also **palm tree** /'· ·/– n a tall tropical tree with a branchless stem and a mass of large leaves at its top: a DATE palm –see COCONUT

palm² n the inner surface of the hand between the base of the fingers and the wrist

palm³ v → PALM sthg. ↔ OFF

palm·ist /'pɑmɪst/ n a person who claims to be able to tell someone's future by examining the lines on his or her PALM² –**palmistry** n [U]

palm sthg.↔ off v adv [T on, as] infml to sell (or gain profit from) something by wrongly describing it; deceitfully gain acceptance for: She tried to palm the painting off as a real Renoir.|The fruit seller palmed off some bad oranges on the old man.

pal·pa·ble /'pælpəbəl/ adj fml easily and clearly known by the senses or the mind; OBVIOUS: a palpable lie –**palpably** adv: What you say is palpably false.

pal·pi·ta·tion /ˌpælpə'teʸʃən/ n [C;U often pl.] an irregular or too rapid beating of the heart, caused by illness, too much effort, etc.

pal·try /'pɔltriʸ/ adj -**trier, -triest** unimportant; worthlessly small: He sold his paintings for a paltry sum of money.

pam·pas /'pæmpəz, -pəs/ n [the P;S] the large wide treeless plains in parts of South America

pam·per /'pæmpər/ v [T] to show too much attention to making (somebody) comfortable; treat too kindly: a pampered cat

pam·phlet /'pæmflɪt/ n a small book with paper covers which deals usu. with some matter of public interest: a political pamphlet on education

pan¹ /pæn/ n any of various kinds of metal container used in cooking, usu. with one long handle and sometimes with a lid –see also BEDPAN, DUSTPAN, FRYING PAN, SAUCEPAN

pan² v -**nn**- **1** [I;T for] to wash (soil or GRAVEL) in a type of SIEVE, looking for a precious metal: panning for gold **2** [T] infml to pass severe judgment on; CRITICIZE very severely

pan³ v -**nn**- [I;T over, around, to] to move (a camera while filming), from side to side, up and down, back, etc.

pan·a·ce·a /ˌpænə'siʸə/ n often derog something that is said to cure any illness, put right all troubles, etc.

pa·nache /pə'næʃ, pə'nɑʃ/ n [U] a manner of doing things that is showy and splendid, and without any seeming difficulty

pan·cake /'pænkeʸk/ n a thin soft flat cake made of flour, milk, eggs, etc. (BATTER²), cooked in a flat pan and eaten hot

pan·da /'pændə/ also **giant panda**– n **pandas** or **panda** a large bearlike animal with black and white fur, originally from China

pan·de·mo·ni·um /ˌpændə'moʷniʸəm/ n [U] a state of wild and noisy disorder

pan·der to sbdy./sthg. /'pændər/ v prep [T] derog to provide something that satisfies (the low or undesirable wishes of): a newspaper that panders to people's interest in sex

pane /peʸn/ n a single sheet of glass for use in a frame, esp. of a window

pan·el¹ /'pænl/ n **1** a separate usu. four-sided division of the surface of a door, wall, etc., which is different in some way from the surface around it **2** a board on which controls or instruments of various kinds are fastened **3** a group of speakers who answer questions to inform or amuse the public, usu. on a radio or television show: a panel game|What does the panel think? –see also PANELIST **4** a piece of cloth of a different color or material, set in a dress **5** AmE a group of people who decide something: A panel discussion|a panel of judges to pick the best singer.

panel² v -**l**- AmE‖-**ll**- BrE [T] to divide into or decorate with PANELS¹ (1,4): a room paneled with/in polished wood

pan·el·ing AmE‖**panelling** BrE /'pænl-ɪŋ/ n [U] PANELS¹ (1)

pan·el·ist AmE‖**panellist** BrE /'pænl-ɪst/ n a member of a PANEL¹ (3)

pang /pæŋ/ n a sudden sharp feeling of pain: pangs of hunger|a pang of sadness

pan·han·dle¹ /'pæn,hændl/ n esp. AmE a thin stretch of land joined to a larger area like the handle of a pan: the Oklahoma panhandle.

panhandle² -**dled, -dling** v [I] AmE infml to

beg, esp. in the streets –**panhandler** n: *There are a lot of panhandlers on the streets of New York.*

pan·ic¹ /'pænɪk/ n [C;U] (a state of) sudden uncontrollable fear or terror: *There was (a) panic when the fire started.*

panic² v **-ck-** [I;T *at*] to (cause to) feel PANIC¹: *The crowd panicked at the sound of the guns.* | *The thunder panicked the horses.*

panic-strick·en /'·· ,··/ adj filled with wild terror

pan·nier /'pænyər, 'pæniyər/ n a basket, esp. one of a pair, carried by a horse or donkey, on a bicycle, etc.

pan·o·ram·a /,pænə'ræmə, -'rɑ-/ n a complete view over a wide area: –**panoramic** /,pænə'ræmɪk/ adj : *a panoramic view of the city from the tenth floor of the building*

pan·sy /'pænziy/ n **-sies** a small plant with wide flat flowers

pant¹ /pænt/ v [I;T] to take quick short breaths, or say (something) in this way, esp. after great effort or in great heat: *The dog panted in the heat.*

pant² n a short quick breath

pan·the·ism /'pænθiy,ɪzəm/ n [U] the religious idea that God and the universe are the same thing –**pantheist** n

pan·ther /'pænθər/ n **panthers** or **panther 1** a LEOPARD, esp. a black one **2** *AmE* for COUGAR

pant·ies /'pæntiyz/ also **pants** esp. *BrE*– n [P] a short close-fitting undergarment worn below the waist by women and girls –see also UNDERPANTS; see PAIR¹ (USAGE) –see illustration on page 123

pan·to·mime /'pæntə,maɪm/ also **mime** *infml*– n [C;U] (an example of) a kind of play where movements of the face and body, rather than spoken words, tell the story

pan·try /'pæntriy/ n **-tries** a small room with shelves in a house, where dishes, food etc. are kept –compare LARDER

pants /pænts/ n [P] **1** an outer garment worn by men and women covering the body from the waist down, with two parts, each fitting a leg –compare TROUSERS –see illustration on page 123 **2** →UNDERPANTS or PANTIES –see PAIR (USAGE)

pa·pa /'pɑpə/ n *AmE infml* (a name for father)

pa·pa·cy /'peypəsiy/ n [*the* S] the power and office of the POPE

pa·pal /'peypəl/ adj [A] of the POPE or of the PAPACY

pa·pa·ya /pə'paɪə/ n [C;U] (the large yellow-green fruit of) a tall tree grown in tropical countries

pa·per¹ /'peypər/ n **1** [U] material made in the form of sheets from very thin threads of wood or cloth, used for writing on, covering packages or walls, etc.: *a sheet of paper* | *paper bag/handkerchief* **2** [C] *infml* a newspaper: *Have you seen today's paper?* **3** [C] →TERM PAPER **4** [C] a piece of writing for specialists, often read aloud **5 on paper** as written down or printed, but not yet tested by experience: *These plans seem good on paper, but we cannot be sure they will work.*

paper² v [T] to cover (a wall or walls) with WALLPAPER: *She papered the room green/in green/with green paper.*

pa·per·back /'peypər,bæk/ n [A;C] a book with a thin cardboard cover: *This bookstore only sells paperbacks.* | *a paperback* NOVEL²/*a* NOVEL² **in paperback** –compare HARDBACK

paper clip /'·· ,·, ,·· '·/ n a small piece of curved wire used for holding sheets of paper together

pa·pers /'peypərz/ n [P] pieces of paper with writing on them, esp. as used for official purposes

pa·per·weight /'peypər,weyt/ n a heavy object placed on top of loose papers to keep them from being scattered

pa·per·work /'peypər,wɜrk/ n [U] regular work of writing reports, letters, keeping records, etc., esp. as part of a job

pa·pier-mâ·ché /,peypər mə'ʃey/ n [U] paper mixed with GLUE to form a soft mass, and used for making boxes, trays, etc.

pa·pri·ka /pæ'priykə, 'pæprikə/ n [U] a red powder (PEPPER) used in cooking to give a hot taste to food

pa·py·rus /pə'paɪrəs/ n **-ri** /raɪ/, or **-ruses** [U] paper made in ancient Egypt from a grasslike plant

par /pɑr/ n [S] **1** a level which is equal or almost the same; PARITY: *These two things are* **on a par** *(with each other).* **2** (in the game of GOLF) the number of strokes the average player should take to hit the ball into a hole **3 below par** *infml* not in the usual or average condition (of health, activity, etc.)

par·a·ble /'pærəbəl/ n a short simple story which teaches a moral or religious lesson

pa·rab·o·la /pə'ræbələ/ n a curve like the line made by a ball when it is thrown forward in the air and falls to the ground

par·a·chute¹ /'pærə,ʃuʷt/ n an apparatus made of cloth, fastened to persons or objects dropped from aircraft in order to make them fall slowly: *a parachute jump*

parachute² v **-chuted, -chuting** [I;T] to (cause to) drop from an aircraft by means of a PARACHUTE¹

pa·rade¹ /pə'reyd/ n **1** [C;U] (an example of) a gathering together for the purpose of being officially looked at, or for a march or ceremony: *The soldiers are* **on parade**.| *The Olympic Games begin with a parade of all the competing nations.* **2** [C] a wide public path or street, often beside the seashore

parade² v **-raded, -rading 1** [I;T] (esp. of soldiers) to gather together in ceremonial order, for the purpose of being officially looked at, or for a march **2** [T] *often derog* to show in order to gain admiration: *He is always parading his knowledge/his wealth.*

par·a·dise /'pærə,daɪs, -,daɪz/ n **1** [S] (*usu. cap.*) Heaven **2** [S] (*usu. cap.*) (in the Bible) the Garden of Eden, home of Adam and Eve **3** a place of perfect happiness: (fig.) *This hotel is a sportsman's paradise.* (=has everything a sportsman needs) **4 fool's paradise** a state of great contentment for which there is no real reason and which is unlikely to last

par·a·dox /'pærə,dɑks/ n **1** a statement which

seems to be impossible, because it says two opposite things, but which has some truth in it: *"More haste, less speed" is a paradox.* **2** an improbable combination of opposing qualities, ideas, etc.: *It is a paradox that in such a rich country there should be so many poor people.* **–paradoxical** /ˌpærə'dɑksɪkəl/ *adj* **–paradoxically** *adv*

par·af·fin /'pærəfɪn/ *n* [U] *BrE* for KEROSENE

par·a·gon /'pærəˌgɑn, -gən/ *n* [*of*] a person or thing that is a perfect model to copy (often in the phrase **a paragon of virtue**)

par·a·graph /'pærəˌgræf/ *n* a division of a piece of writing made up of one or more sentences, of which the first word starts a new line: *Look at the third paragraph on page 23.*

par·a·keet /'pærəˌkiʸt/ *n* a kind of small PARROT

par·al·lel¹ /'pærəˌlɛl, -ləl/ *adj* [*no comp.*] **1** (of lines or rows) running side by side but never getting nearer to or further away from each other: *parallel lines|The railroad track runs parallel with/to the road.* **2** comparable (to): *My experience in this matter is parallel to yours.*

parallel² *n* **1** a parallel line, row, or surface **2** a comparable person or thing: *an actor without (a) parallel in modern movies|There are few parallels* (=points of likeness) *between American football and soccer.* **3** also **parallel of latitude** /ˌ··· · '···/– any of a number of lines on a map drawn parallel to the EQUATOR

parallel³ *v* **-l-** [T] to equal; match: *No one has paralleled her success in business.* –see also UNPARALLELED

par·al·lel·o·gram /ˌpærə'lɛləˌgræm/ *n tech* a flat four-sided figure with opposite sides equal and parallel

pa·ral·y·sis /pə'ræləsɪs/ *n* **-ses** /ˌsiʸz/ [C;U] (a) loss of feeling in and control of the body muscles: *paralysis of the arm*

par·a·lyt·ic /ˌpærə'lɪtɪk/ *n,adj* **1** (a person) suffering from PARALYSIS **2** causing PARALYSIS: *a paralytic STROKE² (3)* **–paralytically** *adv*

par·a·lyze *AmE*‖**-lyse** *BrE* /'pærəˌlaɪz/ *v* **-lyzed, -lyzing** [T] to make (the body muscles) unable to move: *paralyzed with fear|(fig) The electricity failure paralyzed the train service.*

par·a·med·ic /ˌpærə'mɛdɪk/ *n AmE* a person who helps a doctor of medicine or a nurse in caring for the sick

par·a·mil·i·tar·y /ˌpærə'mɪləˌtɛriʸ/ *adj* like or used as a regular military force: *In some countries the police have paramilitary duties.*

par·a·mount /'pærəˌmaʊnt/ *adj* great above all others; highest in power or importance: *of paramount importance*

par·a·noi·a /ˌpærə'nɔɪə/ *n* [U] a disease of the mind in which the sufferer believes that others hate him/her and are purposely mistreating him/her, or that he/she is a person of high importance **–paranoiac** /ˌpærə'nɔɪæk, -'nɔɪ-ɪk/ *adj,n*

par·a·noid /'pærəˌnɔɪd/ *adj* (as if) suffering from PARANOIA: *My father locks every door in*

the house because he is paranoid about being robbed.

par·a·pet /'pærəpɪt, -ˌpɛt/ *n* a low wall at the edge of a roof, bridge, etc.

par·a·pher·na·lia /ˌpærəfər'neʸlyə, -fə'neʸl-/ *n* [U] a number of small articles of various kinds, esp. personal belongings or those needed for some skill or work: *I keep all my photographic paraphernalia in that room.*

par·a·phrase /'pærəˌfreʸz/ *v* **-phrased, -phrasing** [T] (to make) a re-expression of (something written or said) in words that are easier to understand

par·a·ple·gic /ˌpærə'pliʸdʒɪk/ *adj,n* (of or being) a person suffering from PARALYSIS of the lower part of the body –see also QUADRIPLEGIC

par·a·site /'pærəˌsaɪt/ *n* **1** a plant or animal that lives on or in another and gets food from it **2** a useless person who is supported by the wealth or efforts of other people **–parasitic** /ˌpærə'sɪtɪk/ *adj: a parasitic plant* **– parasitically** *adv*

par·a·sol /'pærəˌsɔl, -ˌsɑl/ *n* a light umbrella used for protection from the sun

par·a·troop·er /'pærəˌtruʷpər/ *n* a soldier trained to drop from an plane using a PARACHUTE

par·a·troops /'pærəˌtruʷps/ *n* [P] a group of PARATROOPERS

par·boil /'pɑrbɔɪl/ *v* [T] to boil until partly cooked

par·cel /'pɑrsəl/ *n* **1** a package **2 part and parcel of** a most important part that cannot be separated from the whole of

parcel sthg. **↔ out** *v adv* **-l-***AmE*‖**-ll-** *BrE* [T] to divide into parts or shares

parch /pɑrtʃ/ *v* [T] (of the sun) to make hot and dry: *Give me a drink; I'm parched!* (=very thirsty)

parch·ment /'pɑrtʃmənt/ *n* [U] **1** a writing material used esp. in ancient times, made from the skin of a sheep or goat **2** a paper of good quality that looks like this material

par·don¹ /'pɑrdn/ *n* **1** [C;U] (an act or example of) forgiveness **2** [C] *law* an action of a court or ruler forgiving a person for an unlawful act, and giving freedom from punishment **3 I beg your pardon** also **pardon me**– *polite* **a** "Please excuse me for having accidentally touched/pushed you." **b** also **pardon** *infml*– "I did not hear/understand what you said and would like you to repeat it."

pardon² *v* [T *for*] **1** to forgive; excuse: *We must pardon him his little faults.* **2** to give an official PARDON¹ (2) to or for

par·don·a·ble /'pɑrdənəbəl/ *adj* that can be pardoned: *a pardonable mistake* **–opposite unpardonable**

pare /pɛər/ *v* **pared, paring** [T] to cut away the thin outer covering, edge, or skin of: *to pare an apple*

pare sthg. **↔ down** *v adv* [T] to reduce (esp. a cost)

par·ent /'pɛərənt, 'pær-/ *n* [*often pl.*] the father or mother of a person or animal: *John and Mary have become parents.* (=They have become the father and mother of a child) –see illustration on page 247 –**parental** /pəˈrɛntəl/ adj [A]

par·ent·age /ˈpɛərəntɪdʒ, ˈpær-/ n [U] origin; birth: *a child of unknown parentage*

pa·ren·the·sis /pəˈrɛnθəsɪs/ n -ses /ˌsiʸz/ **1** [*usu. pl.*] – either of a pair of small curved lines ( ), used in writing to enclose added information **2** an added explanation or thought enclosed in this way –**parenthetic** /ˌpærənˈθɛtɪk/ also **parenthetical** – adj: *Parenthetic remarks should be short.* –**parenthetically** adv

par·ent·hood /ˈpɛərəntˌhʊd, ˈpær-/ n [U] the state or condition of being a parent

par ex·cel·lence /ˌpar ˌɛksəˈlans/ adj [*after n*] *French* without equal, as the best and/or most typical of its kind

pa·ri·ah /pəˈraɪə/ n a person not accepted by society

par·ish /ˈpærɪʃ/ n an area in the care of a single priest and served by one main church: *a parish church/priest*

pa·rish·ion·er /pəˈrɪʃənər/ n a person living in a particular PARISH, esp. one who regularly attends the PARISH church

par·i·ty /ˈpærəṭiʸ/ n [U] the state or quality of being equal: *parity between men's and women's pay* –see also DISPARITY

park¹ /park/ n a large usu. grassy enclosed piece of land in a town, used by the public for pleasure and rest

park² v [I;T] to put (a car or other vehicle) somewhere for a time: *Don't park (the car) in this street.|I'm parked over there.* (=My car is parked over there)|(fig.) *Don't park your books on my desk!* –see PARKING (USAGE)

par·ka /ˈparkə/ n a short coat which has a protective cover (HOOD) for the head, and which keeps out wind and rain

park·ing /ˈparkɪŋ/ n [U] the leaving (parking) of a car or other vehicle in a particular place for a time

USAGE You can **park** (your car) in a **parking lot** or **(parking) garage**, where there is space for many cars. A space for one car, usu. on a street and marked with painted lines, is a **parking place/space**. The sign **Parking** means "Permission to **park**." It is *not* the name of a place, so you cannot ask *Where is the* **parking**?

parking ga·rage /ˈ·· ·ˌ·/ AmE‖**car park** BrE– n an enclosed PARKING LOT often having several stories

parking lot /ˈ·· ˌ·/ AmE‖**car park** BrE– n an open place where cars and other vehicles can be parked, sometimes for payment

parking me·ter /ˈ·· ˌ·/ n an apparatus at the side of a street, into which one puts a coin to pay for parking a car beside it for a certain time –see illustration on page 673

par·lance /ˈparləns/ n [U] fml a particular manner of speech or use of words: *In naval parlance, the left side of a ship is the* PORT² *side.*

par·lia·ment /ˈparləmənt/ n (*usu. cap.*) **1** a body of people wholly or partly elected by the people of a country to make laws **2** (in the United Kingdom) the main law-making body, made up of the King or Queen, the Lords, and the elected representatives of the people: *Parliament sits* (=meets regularly) *at Westminster.* –**parliamentary** /ˌparləˈmɛnt əriʸ/ adj

par·lia·men·tar·i·an /ˌparləmɛnˈtɛəriʸən, -mən-/ n a person whose duty is to make sure that the business of a meeting is done according to established rules

par·lor AmE‖**parlour** BrE /ˈparlər/ n **1** esp. AmE (*in comb.*) a store for some kind of personal service or for selling a particular type of article: *an ice cream parlor|a* PIZZA *parlor* **2** now rare a room in a private house used for receiving guests, reading, etc.

pa·ro·chi·al /pəˈroʷkiʸəl/ adj **1** (of the mind, one's interests, opinions, etc.) limited; narrow **2** of a PARISH –**parochially** adv –**parochialism** n [U]

par·o·dy¹ /ˈpærədiʸ/ n -dies **1** [C *of*] a weak and unsuccessful copy: *The trial was a parody of justice.* **2** [C;U *of, on*] (a piece of) writing or music intended to amuse by copying the style of a known writer or musician

parody² v -died, -dying [T] to make a PARODY¹ (2) of

pa·role¹ /pəˈroʷl/ n [U] the letting out of a person from prison, conditional upon good behavior, before the end of the official period of imprisonment: *She was a good prisoner, so she was let out* **on parole.**

parole² -roled, -roling [T] to set free on PAROLE¹

par·ox·ysm /ˈpærəkˌsɪzəm/ n a sudden uncontrollable explosive expression: *paroxysms of anger/laughter*

par·quet /parˈkeʸ/ n [A;U] small flat blocks of wood fitted together in a pattern onto the floor of a room: *a parquet floor*

par·rot /ˈpærət/ n any of a large group of tropical birds, having a curved beak and usu. brightly colored feathers, that can be taught to copy human speech

par·ry¹ /ˈpæriʸ/ v -ried, -rying [T] to turn aside or keep away (an attacking blow or a weapon): (fig.) *She parried the unwelcome question skillfully.*

parry² n -ries an act of PARRYing¹, esp. in fencing (FENCE² (1))

par·si·mo·ni·ous /ˌparsəˈmoʷniʸəs/ adj fml too careful with money; unwilling to spend –**parsimoniously** adv –**parsimony** /ˈparsəˌmoʷniʸ/ n [U]

pars·ley /ˈparsliʸ/ n [U] a small garden plant (HERB) used in cooking or on uncooked foods

pars·nip /ˈparsnɪp/ n a garden plant with a thick white or yellow root that is used as a vegetable

par·son /ˈparsən/ n a Christian religious leader in charge of a PROTESTANT church

par·son·age /ˈparsənɪdʒ/ n the house where a PARSON lives

part¹ /part/ n **1** [C;U *of*] a piece which is less than the whole: *Which part of the town do you live in?|Part of the house was/Parts of the house were damaged by the fire.|She lived there for the greater part of* (=most of) *her life.* **2** [C] any of the pieces into which something is divided: *Cut the cake into eight equal parts.*|*I didn't like the first part of the book.*|*You can see Part Two of this story next week.* **3** [C] a necessary or important piece of a machine or other apparatus: *Do you sell parts for Ford cars?* **4** [S;U] a share or duty in some activity: *Did you* **take part in/have any part in** *the meeting?*|*Luck* **played a part in** (=helped to cause) *his success.* **5** [C] (the words spoken by) a character acted by an actor in a play: *In our next production, I will take the part of a policeman.*|*Have you learned your part yet?* **6** [U] a side or position in an argument: *He always takes his sister's part.* (=supports her) **7** [C] a line on the head made when hair is separated by combing **8 for my part** as far as I am concerned; speaking for myself **9 for the most part** *fml* mostly; most of the time: *She is for the most part a well-behaved child.* **10 in part** in some degree; partly **11 on the part of someone** by someone; of someone: *It was a mistake on your part to sign the agreement before reading it.*

part² *v* **1** [I;T] to (cause to) become separate or no longer together: *She tried to part the two fighting dogs.*|*If we must part, I hope we can part (as) friends.*|*The clouds parted, and the sun shone down.* **2** [T] to separate (hair on the head) along a line with a comb **3 part company (with): a** to end a relationship (with) **b** no longer to be together (with) **c** to disagree (with)

part with sthg. *v prep* [T] to give up, esp. unwillingly: *It's not easy to part with one's favorite possessions.*

part³ *adv* →PARTLY (esp. in the phrase **part ⋯, part ⋯**): *The English exam is part written, part spoken.*

part⁴ *adj* [A] not complete; PARTIAL (1): *I will give you $150 in part payment.*

par·take /par'teʸk/ *v* **-took** /'tʊk/, **taken** /'teʸkən/, **-taking** [I *of*] old use or humor to eat or drink, esp. something offered: *Will you partake of a drink with us?*

par·tial /'parʃəl/ *adj* **1** [no comp.] not complete: *The play was only a partial success.* **2** favoring one person, side, etc., more than another, esp. in a way that is unfair –opposite **impartial 3** [F *to*] having a strong liking for: *I'm very partial to sweet foods.*

par·ti·al·i·ty /ˌparʃiʸ'æləṭiʸ, -'ʃælə-/ *n* **1** [U] the quality or fact of being PARTIAL (2); BIAS¹ (1) –opposite **impartiality 2** [S *for*] a special liking

par·tial·ly /'parʃəliʸ/ *adv* **1** not completely; PARTLY: *I am partially to blame for the accident.* **2** in a PARTIAL (2) way

par·tic·i·pant /par'tɪsəpənt, pər-/ *n* [in] a person who takes part or has a share in an activity or event

par·tic·i·pate /par'tɪsə,peʸt, pər-/ *v* **-pated, -pating** [I *in*] to take part or have a share in an activity or event –**participation** /par,tɪsə'peʸʃən, pər-/ *n* [U]

par·ti·ci·ple /'parṭə,sɪpəl, -səpəl/ *n* (in English grammar) either of two forms of a verb (PAST PARTICIPLE and PRESENT PARTICIPLE) which may be used in compound forms

of the verb or as adjectives –**participial** /ˌparṭə'sɪpiʸəl/ *adj*

par·ti·cle /'parṭɪkəl/ *n* **1** a very small piece of matter: *dust particles floating in the sunlight*|(fig.) *There wasn't a particle of truth in what he said.* **2** (in grammar) any of several usu. short words in a sentence apart from the subject, verb, etc.: *"But, and, out, up" are used as particles in some sentences.*

par·tic·u·lar /pər'tɪkyələr/ *adj* **1** [A no comp.] worthy of notice; special; unusual: *There was nothing in the letter of particular importance.* **2** [A no comp.] single and different from others; of a certain sort: *I don't like this particular hat, but the others are quite nice.* **3** showing (too) much care or interest in small matters; hard to please: *He is very particular about his food.* **4 in particular** especially: *I noticed his eyes in particular, because they were very large.*

par·tic·u·lar·ly /pər'tɪkyələrliʸ/ *adv* especially; in a way that is special and different from others: *He isn't particularly intelligent.*

par·tic·u·lars /pər'tɪkyələrz/ *n* [P *of*] the facts or details (esp. about an event)

part·ing¹ /'parṭɪŋ/ *n* **1** [C;U] (an example of) the action of PARTING² (1) **2 the parting of the ways** the point at which two people must separate, or a choice must be made

parting² *adj* [A] done or given at the time of PARTING² (1): *a parting kiss*

par·ti·san, -zan /'parṭəzən, -sən/ *n* **1** a strong supporter of a party, group, plan, etc.: *a partisan speech* **2** a member of an armed group that fights in secret against an enemy that has conquered their country

par·ti·tion¹ /par'tɪʃən, pər-/ *n* **1** [U] division into two or more parts (esp. of a country) **2** [C] something that divides, esp. a thin wall inside a house

partition² *v* [T] to divide into two or more parts

partition sthg.↔ **off** *v adv* [T] to make (esp. a part of a room) separate by means of a PARTITION¹ (2)

part·ly /'partliʸ/ *adv* in some degree but not completely: *I have partly finished it.*|*What you say is partly true.*

part·ner /'partnər/ *n* **1** a person who shares in the same activity, esp. either of two people dancing together or playing together in games such as tennis or BRIDGE³ **2** any of the owners of a business, who share the profits and losses

part·ner·ship /'partnər,ʃɪp/ *n* **1** [U] the state of being a partner, esp. in business: *We've been in partnership for five years.* **2** [C] a business owned by two or more partners

part of speech /ˌ· · '·/ *n* (in grammar) any of the classes into which words are divided according to their use: *"Noun," "verb," and "adjective" are parts of speech.*

par·took /par'tʊk/ *v* past tense of PARTAKE

par·tridge /'partrɪdʒ/ *n* **-tridges** *or* **-tridge** [S;U] (the meat of) a middle-size bird shot for sport and food

part-time /ˌ· '·◄/ *adj,adv* (working or giving work) during only a part of the regular working time: *a part-time job*|*She works* *part-time.* –see also FULL-TIME

par·ty /ˈpɑːtiʸ/ *n* **-ties 1** [C] a gathering of people, usu. by invitation, for food and amusement: *to give* (=have) *a party│Did you enjoy Susie's party?│a party dress* **2** a group of people doing something together: *The table is for a party of four.│a* **search party,** *looking for the lost child* **3** an association of people having the same political aims, esp. as formed to try to win elections: *What is* **the party line** (=the official opinion of the party) *on nuclear weapons?* **4** [A] the system of government based on political parties: *the party system│party politics* **5** [C] *law* one of the people or sides in an agreement or argument –see also THIRD PARTY

pass¹ /pæs/ *v* **1** [I;T] to reach and move beyond (a person or place): *I passed the restaurant on my way to the library.* **2** [I] to go forward; advance: *The road was so crowded that the car could not pass (through).│A cloud passed across the sun.* **3** [I;T] to go through or across: *No one is allowed to pass the gates of the camp.│*(fig.) *I'll let that remark pass.* (=I will not say anything about that remark)│(fig.) *Angry words passed between them.* **4** [T] to put; cause to go: *She passed the rope around the tree and knotted it.* **5** [T] to give (esp. by hand): *Please pass me the salt!* **6** [I;T] (in various sports) to kick, throw, hit, etc. (esp. a ball) to a member of one's own side **7** [I;T] **a** (of time) to go by **b** to cause (time) to go by, esp. in a way that does not seem too long or dull: *She passed the time by reading a book.* **8** [I] to change: *When you melt ice, it passes from a solid to a liquid state.* **9** [I] to go from one person's control or possession to another's: *When she dies, her money will pass to her son.* **10** [I;T] to give official acceptance to (a suggested law or other formal suggestion) **11** [I;T] to succeed in (an examination): *She passed her driving test on her first try.* –opposite **fail 12** [T] to accept after examination: *I can't pass you; your work wasn't good enough.* –opposite **fail 13** [T *on, upon*] to give (a judgment, opinion, etc.) –see SENTENCE¹ (2) **14** [T] to say (a remark or comment): *He's always passing rude remarks about me.* **15** [I] to come to an end: *Summer passed quickly.│Your headache will soon pass if you lie down.* **16 pass the time of day (with)** to give a greeting (to), and/or have a short conversation (with) **17 pass water** *euph* →URINATE –see PAST¹ (USAGE)

pass away/on *v adv* [I] *euph* (esp. of a person) to die: *She passed away in her sleep.*

pass sthg.↔ **along** *v adv* [T] *AmE* →HAND² **down** (1)

pass by *v adv* **1** [I] to go past **2** [T] (**pass** sbdy.↔ **by**)also **pass over**– to pay no attention to; disregard: *The voters passed him by.│Life has passed me by.*

pass sthg.↔ **down** *v adv* [T] →HAND² **down** (1)

pass for *v prep* to be (mistakenly) accepted as: *She could pass for a much younger woman.*

pass sbdy./sthg. **off** *v adv* [T *as*] to present

falsely: *She passed herself off as an experienced doctor.*

pass on *v adv* **1** [I] →PASS **away 2** [T] (**pass** sthg. ↔ **on**) →HAND² **on** (1)

pass out *v adv* **1** [I] to faint **2** [T] (**pass** sthg. ↔**out**) *AmE* for HAND² **out**; DISTRIBUTE (1)

pass sbdy.↔ **over¹** *v,adv* [T] →PASS **by** (2)

pass over² sthg. *v prep* [T] to try not to notice or mention: *Let us pass over his rude remarks in silence.*

pass sthg.↔**up** *v adv* [T] to let go; miss: *Don't pass up a chance like that!*

pass² *n* a way by which one may go through, esp. over a range of mountains

pass³ *n* **1** an act of moving past: *The plane made a few passes over the enemy camp, but didn't drop any bombs.* **2** a piece of printed paper which shows that one is permitted to do a certain thing, such as travel on a train without paying, enter a building, etc. **3** a successful result in an examination –opposite **fail 4** an act of PASSING¹ (6) a ball **5** *infml* an attempt to make somebody sexually interested in one, by words or by touching, stroking, etc.: *He* **made a pass at** *her, and she hit him.*

pass. *written abbrev. said as:* PASSIVE¹ (2)

pass·a·ble /ˈpæsəbəl/ *adj* **1** (just) good enough to be accepted; not bad **2** (of a road or river) fit to be used, crossed, etc. –opposite **impassable** (for 2)

pas·sage /ˈpæsɪdʒ/ *n* **1** [C] a usu. narrow way through; opening: *He forced a passage through the thick forest.* **2** [U *of*] the action of going across, by, over, through, etc., in space: *The bridge is not strong enough to allow the passage of heavy vehicles.* **3** [C] also **passageway**– a narrow connecting way, esp. inside a building; CORRIDOR **4** [U *of*] (of time) the course; onward flow **5** [S] (the cost of) a long journey by ship: *She paid for his passage to Bermuda.* **6** [C] a usu. short part of a speech or a piece of writing or music

pas·sage·way /ˈpæsɪdʒˌweʸ/ →PASSAGE (3)

pas·sé /pæˈseʸ/ *adj* [F] *derog* no longer considered modern; old-fashioned

pas·sen·ger /ˈpæsəndʒər/ *n* a person, not the driver, traveling in a public or private vehicle

pass·er·by /ˌpæsərˈbaɪ/ *n* **passersby** /-sərz-/ a person who happens (by chance) to pass by a place

pass·ing¹ /ˈpæsɪŋ/ *adj* [A *no comp.*] **1** moving or going by: *She watched the passing cars.* **2** not lasting very long: *She did not give the matter even a passing thought.*

passing² *n* in passing in the course of a statement (esp. one about a different matter): *He was talking about Spain, and he mentioned in passing that you went there last year.*

pas·sion /ˈpæʃən/ *n* [C;U] (a) strong, deep, often uncontrollable feeling, esp. of love, hatred, or anger: *The poet expressed his burning passion for the woman he loved.│*(fig.) *He has a passion for ice cream.*

pas·sion·ate /ˈpæʃənɪt/ *adj* showing or filled with PASSION: *a passionate speech/woman/interest in politics* –**passionately** *adv*

pas·sive /ˈpæsɪv/ *adj* **1** *sometimes derog* not

active; influenced by outside forces but not doing anything; suffering without opposition **2** (of a verb or sentence) expressing an action which is done to the subject of a sentence: *"Was thrown" is a passive verb in "The boy was thrown from his horse."* –compare AC-TIVE (3) –**passively** *adv*

passive voice /,·· '·/ also **passive**– *n* [*the* S] *tech* (in grammar) the PASSIVE¹ (2) part or forms of a verb –compare ACTIVE VOICE

pas·siv·i·ty /pæ'sɪvətiʸ/ also **passiveness** /'pæsɪvnɪs/– *n* [U] the state or quality of being PASSIVE (1)

Pass·o·ver /'pæs,oʷvər/ *n* [C;S] (in the Jewish religion) a holiday in memory of the freeing of the Jews from Egypt

pass·port /'pæspɔrt, -poʷrt/ *n* a small official book that proves the nationality of a person, and is used esp. when entering a foreign country: (fig.) *Do you think that money is a passport to happiness?* –see illustration on page 17

pass·word /'pæswɜrd/ *n* a secret word or phrase which one has to know in order to be allowed to enter a building, camp, etc.

past¹ /pæst/ *adj* **1** [A; after *n*] (of time) much earlier than the present: *In past years/years past they never would have done that.* –compare FUTURE¹ **2** [A; after *n*] (*with the* PERFECT¹ (5) *tenses*) (of time) a little earlier than the present; up until the time of speaking: *I haven't been feeling very well for the past few days.* **3** finished; ended: *Winter is past and spring has come.* **4** [A] former; not any longer: *She's a past president of the club.* **5** [A] (of a verb form) expressing an action or event that happened before the present moment: *the past tense*

USAGE The past participle of **pass** is **passed**, but it is not used as an adjective. Instead, use **past**, which has the same pronunciation. Compare: *This week has* **passed** *quickly.*|*the* **past** *week*

past² *prep* **1 a** farther than: *The hospital is about a mile past the school.* **b** up to and then beyond: *We drove past the house.* **2** beyond in time or age: *It's half past three.*|*She's past* (=older than) *eighty.* **3 past caring** in a state of no longer caring what happens: *He's been without a job so long that he's past caring.* –**past** *adv*: *The children came running past/by.*|*A whole year went past/by before we saw them again.*

past³ *n* [S] **1** (what happened in) time before the present: *In the past I have had many jobs.*|*Our country has a glorious past.* (=history) **2** the past tense

pas·ta /'pɑstə/ *n* [U] food made, in various different shapes, from flour paste, and often covered with SAUCE and/or cheese

paste¹ /peʸst/ *n* [C;U] **1** a thin soft mixture used for sticking paper together, or onto other surfaces **2** any soft wet mixture of powder and liquid that is easily shaped or spread: *toothpaste*|*Make a paste of flour, fat, and water.* **3** a food made by crushing solid foods into a smooth soft mass, used for spreading on bread: *meat paste/fish paste* –compare PÂTÉ

paste² *v* **pasted, pasting** [T] to stick or fasten (paper) with paste: *a notice pasted to/on the door*

pas·tel /pæ'stɛl/ *n* (a picture drawn with) a stick of chalklike coloring matter

pas·teur·ize ‖also **-ise** *BrE* /'pæstʃə,raɪz, -stə-/ *v* **-ized, -izing** [T] to heat (a liquid, esp. milk) in a certain way in order to destroy bacteria –**pasteurization** /,pæstʃərə'zeʸʃən, -stə-/ *n* [U]

pas·tille /pæ'stiʸl/ *n* a small round hard candy, esp. one containing a medicine for the throat

pas·time /'pæs-taɪm/ *n* something done to pass one's time in a pleasant way

past mas·ter /,· '···/ *n* [*at, in, of*] a person who is very skilled (in a particular subject or action)

pas·tor /'pæstər/ *n* a Christian religious leader in charge of a church and its members (esp. of a PROTESTANT Church)

pas·to·ral /'pæstərəl/ *adj* **1** of or concerning the members of a religious group, or its leader's duties towards them: *The priest/RABBI makes pastoral visits every Tuesday.*|*pastoral care* (=spiritual help, and advice) **2** *lit* concerning simple peaceful country life: *a pastoral scene of cows drinking from a stream/pastoral poetry.*

past par·ti·ci·ple /,· '····/ *n* (in grammar) a form of a verb which may be used (in compound forms of the verb) to express actions done or happening in the past, or sometimes as an adjective: *"Done" and "walked" are the past participles of "do" and "walk."* –see LIST OF IRREGULAR VERBS

past per·fect /,· '···/ *n* also **pluperfect**– *adj* (a tense) that expresses an action completed before a particular time in the past (stated or understood), and is formed in English with *had* and a past participle –see also PRESENT PERFECT

pas·try /'peʸstriʸ/ *n* **-tries 1** [C] a small sweet cake made from flour, fat, milk or water and usu. sugar, sometimes containing cream or fruit, eaten when baked **2** [U] a mixture of flour, fat, and milk or water, eaten when baked, used esp. to enclose other foods

pas·ture¹ /'pɑstʃər/ *n* [C;U] (a piece of) grassy land where cattle feed

pasture² *v* **-tured, -turing** [T] to put (farm animals) in a PASTURE¹

past·y /'peʸstiʸ/ *adj* **-ier, -iest** (of the face) white and unhealthy-looking

pat¹ /pæt/ *n* **1** a light friendly touch with the flat hand: *She gave the dog a pat as she walked past.* **2** a small shaped mass of butter **3 pat on the back** *infml* an expression of praise or satisfaction for something done

pat² *v* **-tt-** [T] to touch gently and repeatedly, esp. with the flat hand (often to show kindness, pity, etc.): *He looked at himself in the mirror and patted his hair.*

patch¹ /pætʃ/ *n* **1** a (usu. small) piece of material used to cover a hole or a damaged place **2** an area on a surface that is different (being wet, rough, etc.) from the surface around it: *wet patches on the wall*|*There will be a few patches of mist near the coast.* **3** a (usu. small) piece of ground, esp. as used for growing vegetables: *a potato patch*

patch² *v* [T] to put a PATCH¹ (1) on a hole, worn place, etc. in (esp. a garment): *patched pants*

patch sthg.↔ up *v adv* [T] **1** to mend with PATCHES¹ (1): *to patch up an old coat*|(fig.) *The doctors patched up the soldier and sent him home.* **2** →MAKE¹ **up** (1): *to patch up a quarrel*

patch·work /'pætʃwɜrk/ *n* [A;C;U] sewn work made by joining together a number of pieces of cloth of different colors, patterns, and shapes: *a patchwork bedcover*|(fig.) *From the plane we could see a patchwork of fields of different shapes and colors.*|*a patchwork* QUILT

patch·y /'pætʃiʸ/ *adj* **-ier, -iest 1** made up of, or appearing in, PATCHES¹ (2): *patchy mist* **2** *usu. derog* incomplete; uneven: *My knowledge of science is patchy.*|*patchy fog* –**patchily** *adv* –**patchiness** *n* [U]

pâ·té /pɑ'teʸ, pæ-/ *n* [U] a food made by crushing solid foods (esp. LIVER) into a smooth soft mass –compare PASTE¹ (3)

pa·tent¹ /'peʸtnt, 'pætnt/ *adj* (esp. of things that are not material) easy and plain to see; OBVIOUS

pat·ent² /'pætnt/ also **patented** /'pætntɪd/ *adj* protected, by a PATENT³, from being copied or sold by those who do not have a right to do so: *a patent lock*

pat·ent³ /'pætnt/ *n* a piece of writing from a government office (**Patent Office**) giving someone the right to make or sell a new invention for a certain number of years

pat·ent⁴ /'pætnt/ *v* [T] to obtain a PATENT³ for

pat·ent leath·er /ˌpætnt 'leðər◄, ˌpætn-/ *n* [U] fine very shiny black leather: *patent leather shoes*

pa·tent·ly /'peʸtntliʸ, 'pæt-/ *adv derog* clearly and plainly: *a patently false statement*

pa·ter·nal /pə'tɜrnl/ *adj* **1** of, like, or received from a father: *paternal love* **2** *derog* protecting people like a father but allowing them no freedom **3** related to a person through the father's side of the family: *my paternal grandmother* (=my father's mother) –compare MATERNAL –**paternally** *adv*

pa·ter·nal·ism /pə'tɜrnlˌɪzəm/ *n* [U] *derog* the PATERNAL (2) way of ruling a country, controlling a company, etc. –**paternalist** *n* –**paternalistic** /pəˌtɜrnl'ɪstɪk/ *adj*

pa·ter·ni·ty /pə'tɜrnəṭiʸ/ *n* [U] *law* origin from the male parent

path /pæθ/ *n* **1** also **pathway**– a track or way made by people walking over the ground: *a path through the woods* **2** an open space made to allow forward movement: *The police cleared a path through the crowd.* **3** a line along which something moves: *the path of an arrow*

pa·thet·ic /pə'θeṭɪk/ *adj* **1** causing a feeling of pity or sorrow: *the child's pathetic cries of pain* **2** *derog* worthless; hopelessly unsuccessful: *He's a really pathetic actor!* –**pathetically** *adv*

path·o·log·i·cal /ˌpæθə'lɑdʒɪkəl/ *adj* **1** [A] *tech* of or concerning PATHOLOGY **2** *tech*

caused by disease, esp. of the mind **3** *infml* unreasonable; caused by the imagination only: *a pathological fear of the dark* –**pathologically** *adv*: *pathologically jealous*

pa·thol·o·gist /pə'θɑlədʒɪst, pæ-/ *n* a specialist in PATHOLOGY (esp. a doctor who examines a dead body to find out how the person has died)

pa·thol·o·gy /pə'θɑlədʒiʸ, pæ-/ *n* [U] *tech* the study of disease

pa·thos /'peʸθɑs, -θɔs/ *n* [U] *lit* the quality in speech, writing, etc., that causes a feeling of pity and sorrow

path·way /'pæθweʸ/ *n* →PATH (1)

pa·tience /'peʸʃəns/ *n* [U] **1** the quality of being patient: *You need a lot of patience if you want to get served in this restaurant.*|*She showed great patience with her stupid husband.* –opposite **impatience 2** *BrE* for SOLITAIRE

pa·tient¹ /'peʸʃənt/ *adj* having or showing the ability to bear long waiting, or anything unpleasant, calmly and without complaining –opposite **impatient** –**patiently** *adv*

patient² *n* a person receiving medical treatment from a doctor and/or in a hospital –see CUSTOMER (USAGE) –see illustration on page 201

pat·i·o /'pæṭiʸˌoʷ/ *n* **-os** an open space between a house and garden, with a stone floor, used for sitting on in good weather –compare DECK¹ (3)

pa·tri·arch /'peʸtriʸˌɑrk/ *n* **1** an old and much-respected man **2** (*usu. cap.*) one of the chief BISHOPs of the eastern churches

pa·tri·arch·y /'peʸtriʸˌɑrkiʸ/ *n* **-ies** [C;U] a social system ruled or controlled only by men –**patriarchal** /ˌpeʸtriʸ'ɑrkəl/ *adj*: *a patriarchal society*

pat·ri·cide /'pætrəˌsaɪd/ *n* [C;U] the crime of killing one's father

pat·ri·mo·ny /'pætrəˌmoʷniʸ/ *n* **-nies** [S;U] property INHERITed (=received by right of birth) from one's father, grandfather, etc. –**patrimonial** /ˌpætrə'moʷniʸəl/ *adj*

pa·tri·ot /'peʸtriʸət, -ˌɑt/ *n apprec* a person who loves his/her country

pa·tri·ot·ism /'peʸtriʸəˌtɪzəm/ *n* [U] love for and loyalty to one's country –**patriotic** /ˌpeʸtriʸ'ɑṭɪk/ *adj* –**patriotically** *adv*

pa·trol¹ /pə'troʷl/ *n* **1** [U] the act of PATROLling²: *We're on patrol.* **2** (in military use) a small group of people sent to search for the enemy, or to protect a place from the enemy

patrol² *v* **-ll-** [I;T] to go at regular times around (an area, building, etc.) to see that there is no trouble, that no one is trying to get in or out unlawfully, etc.

patrol car /·'·, ˌ·'·/ *n esp. BrE* for SQUAD CAR

pa·trol·man /pə'troʷlmən/ *n* **-men** /mən/ *AmE* a policeman who regularly PATROLs² a particular area

pa·tron /'peʸtrən/ *n* **1** a person who uses a particular store, hotel, etc., esp. regularly: *a special offer for our regular patrons* **2** [*of*] a person who supports and regularly gives money to a worthy purpose, or to another person or group of people: *a patron of the arts*

pa·tron·age /ˈpeʸtrənɪdʒ, ˈpæ-/ n [U] **1** the support given by a PATRON **2** *sometimes derog* the right to appoint people to important positions

pa·tron·ize ‖also **-ise** BrE /ˈpeʸtrə,naɪz, ˈpæ-/ v **-ized, -izing** [T] **1** to act towards as if better or more important than: *He cannot speak to women without patronizing them.* |*a patronizing smile* **2** to be a PATRON (2) of

patron saint /ˌ·· ˈ·/ n a Christian holy man or woman of former times (SAINT), regarded as giving special protection to a particular place, activity, etc.: SAINT *Christopher is the patron saint of travelers.*

pat·ter[1] /ˈpætər/ n,v [I;S] (to make) the sound of something striking a hard surface lightly, quickly, and repeatedly: *the patter of rain on the window* |*The dog pattered down the stairs.*

patter[2] n [U] very fast continuous amusing talk, esp. as used by a person telling jokes or doing tricks

pat·tern[1] /ˈpætərn/ n **1** a regularly repeated arrangement (esp. of lines, shapes, etc., on a surface or of sounds, words, etc.): *The cloth has a pattern of red and white squares.* **2** the way in which something happens or develops: *The illness is not following its usual pattern.* **3** a shape used as a guide for making something, esp. a piece of paper used to show the shape of a part of a garment: *a dress pattern*

pattern[2] v [T] **1** to make a decorative PATTERN[1] (1) on: *a patterned carpet* **2** to make as if according to a PATTERN[1] (3); copy exactly

paunch /pɔntʃ, pantʃ/ n derog or humor a fat stomach, esp. a man's **–paunchy** adj **-ier, -iest**

pau·per /ˈpɔpər/ n a person who is very poor

pause[1] /pɔz/ n a short but noticeable break in activity or speech: *a pause in the conversation*

pause[2] v **paused, pausing** [I] to stop for a short time before continuing: *She paused to light a cigarette, then continued reading.*

pave /peʸv/ v **paved, paving** [T] to cover (a path, area, etc.) with a surface of flat stones: *a paved courtyard* |(fig.) *This agreement will* **pave the way for** (=make possible) *a lasting peace.*

pave·ment /ˈpeʸvmənt/ n **1** [U] AmE the hard surface of a street **2** [C] BrE for SIDEWALK

pa·vil·ion /pəˈvɪlyən/ n **1** a large usu. decorative building used for public amusements or EXHIBITs (1), esp. one intended to be used only for a short time **2** a large tent

pav·ing /ˈpeʸvɪŋ/ n [U] material used to PAVE a surface: *a paving stone*

paw[1] /pɔ/ n an animal's foot that has nails or CLAWs

paw[2] v [I;T] **1** [at] (of an animal) to touch or try to touch with a PAW[1]: *The dog pawed (at) the bone.* **2** [at] infml (of a person) to feel or touch with the hands, esp.in a rough or sexually improper manner: *She wanted to watch the movie, but he kept pawing her/pawing at her.*

pawn[1] /pɔn/ v [T] to leave (something of value) with a PAWNBROKER as a promise that

one will repay the money one has borrowed

pawn[2] n **1** (in CHESS) one of the eight smallest and least valuable of a player's pieces **2** an unimportant person used by somebody else for his/her own advantage

pawn·bro·ker /ˈpɔn,broʷkər/ n a person to whom people bring valuable articles so that they may borrow money for a time

pay[1] /peʸ/ v **paid** /peʸd/, **paying 1** [I;T +to-v/for] to give (money) to (someone) in return for goods bought, work done, etc.: *I paid $5 for that book/to have my radio repaired.* |*I'll pay you $3 to clean my car.* |*Did you pay for that, sir?* |*I've already paid.* **2** [T] to settle (a bill, debt, etc.): *Have you paid the electricity bill yet?* **3** [T in, into] to put (money, a check, etc.,) into a bank account to be kept safe **4** [I;T] to be profitable to or worth the effort of (someone): *If we can't make our farm pay, we'll sell it.* |*a well-paying job* (=job that pays a lot of money) |*It won't pay you* (=be to your advantage) *to argue with him.* |*Crime doesn't pay.* **5** [I for] to suffer for some bad action: *I'll make him pay for being so rude to me.* **6** [T] to make or say (esp. in the phrases **pay a visit, pay a call, pay a compliment, pay one's respects**): *I'll pay you a visit next week.* **7** [T to] to give (one's attention): **Pay attention** *to what I'm saying.* **8 pay one's way** to pay money for things as one buys them, so as not to go into debt

pay sbdy./sthg.↔ **back** v adv [T] **1** to return what is owed: *Have I paid (you) back the $10 you lent me?* –see Study Notes on page 481 **2** to return bad treatment, rudeness, etc. to (someone who has done something wrong to oneself): *I'll pay you back for what you did to me!*

pay off v adv **1** [T] to pay the whole of (a debt) **2** [T] (**pay** sbdy.↔ **off**) →BRIBE[1] **3** [I] to be successful: *Our plan certainly paid off; it was a great idea.* –see also PAYOFF

pay sthg.↔ **out** v adv [T] **1** to lift and slowly give out (a rope) **2** to give (money) in return for goods or services: *I paid out a lot of money for that car.*

pay up v adv [I] to pay a debt in full, often unwillingly –compare PAID-UP

pay[2] n [U] **1** [I;T] money received for work: *He gets his pay each Thursday.* **2 in the pay of** derog employed by: *This man is in the pay of the enemy.*

USAGE **Pay** is a general word for the money you receive from work, but **income** means any money you receive, whether from work or from money INVESTED, rents, etc.: *Have you any* **income** *apart from your pay?* **Remuneration** is like **pay**, but much more formal. **Wages** and **salary** are both **pay** received at regular times, but a **salary** is usually paid monthly or every two weeks, and **wages** are usually paid weekly and are calculated by the hour, day, or week. Money paid for certain professional services (e.g. to a lawyer) is a **fee**.

pay·a·ble /ˈpeʸəbəl/ adj [F] that may or must be paid: *This bill is payable within seven days.* |*Your check should be made payable to "The Union Gas Company."* (=this name should be written on the check)

pay·day /'peʸdeʸ/ n [C;S] the day on which wages are (to be) paid

pay·ee /peʸ'iʸ/ n tech a person to whom money is or should be paid

pay·ment /'peʸmənt/ n **1** [U] the act of PAYing[1] (1,2): Here is a check in payment of my account. –see also NONPAYMENT **2** [C] an amount of money (to be) paid: monthly payments for rent

pay·off /'peʸɔf/ n [the S] infml **1** the act or time of paying wages, debts, etc. **2** punishment; RETRIBUTION –see also PAY[1] **off**

pay phone /'· ·/ also **pay telephone** /'· ·,···/– n a public telephone which one can use only after putting a coin into a special machine

pay·roll /'peʸrowl/ n **1** [C] a list of workers employed by a company and the amount of wages each person is to be paid **2** [S] the total amount of wages paid in a particular company

PE /piʸ 'iʸ/ n abbrev for: PHYSICAL EDUCATION: a PE class

pea /piʸ/ n a round green seed, used for food

peace /piʸs/ n **1** [S;U] a condition or period in which there is no war **2** [the S] a state of freedom from disorder within a country, with the citizens living according to the law: We should all **keep the peace. 3** [U] calmness; quietness; freedom from anxiety: Let me do my work in peace.|All I want is some **peace and quiet.**|peace of mind

peace·a·ble /'piʸsəbəl/ adj disliking argument or quarreling –**peaceably** adv

peace·ful /'piʸsfəl/ adj **1** quiet; untroubled: to spend a peaceful day in the garden **2** liking peace: peaceful nations –**peacefully** adv –**peacefulness** n [U]

peace·time /'piʸs-taɪm/ n [U] a time when a nation is not at war –opposite **wartime**

peach /piʸtʃ/ n **1** [C] a round fruit with soft yellowish-red skin and sweet juicy flesh, and a large seed in its center **2** [U] the color of the skin of this fruit; yellowish-red

pea·cock /'piʸkak/ n -**cocks** or -**cock** a large male bird famous for its long beautiful tail feathers

peak[1] /piʸk/ n **1** a sharply pointed mountain top: The (mountain) peaks are covered with snow all the year. **2** the highest point or level of a varying amount, rate, etc.: Sales have reached a new peak.|The roads are full of traffic at peak hours. –compare OFF-PEAK **3** the flat curved part of a cap which sticks out in front above the eyes

peak[2] v [I] to reach a PEAK[1] (2): Sales have now peaked, and we expect them to decrease soon.

peaked /piʸkt/ adj [A] having a PEAK[1] (3)

peal[1] /piʸl/ n **1** the sound of the loud ringing of bells **2** a loud long sound or number of sounds one after the other: a peal of thunder

peal[2] v [I;T out] to (cause to) ring out or sound loudly

pea·nut /'piʸnʌt/ n a nut which grows in a shell under the ground, and can be eaten

pea·nuts /'piʸnʌts/ n infml esp. AmE a sum of money so small that it is not worth considering: This job pays peanuts.

peanut but·ter /'·· ,··/ n [U] a soft substance made of crushed PEANUTs, usu. eaten on bread

pear /pɛər/ n a sweet juicy fruit, narrow at the stem and wide at the other

pearl /pɜrl/ n **1** [C] a small hard round white mass formed inside the shell of OYSTERS, very valuable as a jewel **2** [U] the color of this; silvery-white **3** [A;U] →MOTHER-OF-PEARL

pearl·y /'pɜrliʸ/ adj -**ier, -iest** like or decorated with PEARLS (1): pearly teeth|a pale pearly gray

peas·ant /'pɛzənt/ n **1** (now used usu. of developing countries or former times) a person who works on the land, esp. one who owns and lives on a small piece of land **2** derog a person without education or manners

peas·ant·ry /'pɛzəntriʸ/ n [the U] all the PEASANTs (1) of a particular country: The peasantry is tired of the government's promises.

peat /piʸt/ n [U] partly decayed vegetable matter which takes the place of ordinary soil in certain areas, and is used for burning instead of coal –**peaty** adj -**ier, -iest**

peb·ble /'pɛbəl/ n a small roundish smooth stone found esp. on the seashore or on a riverbed

peck[1] /pɛk/ v [I;T at] (of birds) to strike (at something) with the beak: That bird tried to peck me.|(fig.)You're only pecking at your food: what's wrong? **2** [T] infml to kiss in a hurry or without much feeling

peck[2] n **1** a stroke or mark made by PECKing[1] (1) **2** infml a hurried kiss

pe·cu·liar /pɪ'kyuʷlyər/ adj **1** strange; unusual (esp. in a troubling or displeasing way): This food has a peculiar taste; do you think it's all right? **2** [F to] belonging only to (a particular person, place, etc.): This style of cooking is peculiar to the Southwest.

pe·cu·li·ar·i·ty /pɪ,kyuʷliʸ'ærətiʸ/ n -**ties 1** [U] the quality of being PECULIAR **2** [C] something which is PECULIAR: One of the peculiarities of her behavior is that she shouts instead of talking.

pe·cu·liar·ly /pɪ'kyuʷlyərliʸ/ adv **1** especially; more than usually: This question is peculiarly difficult. **2** strangely

pe·cu·ni·a·ry /pɪ'kyuʷniʸ,ɛriʸ/ adj fml & pomp connected with or consisting of money

ped·a·go·gy /'pɛdə,gowdʒiʸ, -,ga-/ n [U] fml the study of ways of teaching –**pedagogic** /,pɛdə'gadʒɪk, -'gow-/ adj

ped·al[1] /'pɛdl/ n a kind of bar which is part of a machine and can be pressed with the foot in order to control the working of the machine: One of the pedals has come off my bicycle.

pedal[2] v -**l-** AmE‖-**ll-** BrE [I;T] to move (esp. a bicycle) along by using PEDALS[1]: She pedaled the bicycle up the hill.|I was just pedaling along.

ped·ant /'pɛdnt/ n derog a person whose attention to detail is too great –**pedantic** /pə'dæntɪk/ adj: Our English teacher is very pedantic about correct grammar.

ped·dle /'pɛdl/ v -**dled, -dling** [I;T] to try to sell (small goods) by going from place to place

ped·dler, pedlar /'pɛdlər/ n **1** a person who PEDDLES **2** →PUSHER

ped·es·tal /'pɛdəstl/ n **1** the base on which a pillar or STATUE stands **2** put/set somebody on a pedestal to consider somebody better, nobler, etc., than oneself or others

pe·des·tri·an[1] /pə'dɛstriʸən/ n a person walking (esp. in a street used by cars) –compare MOTORIST

pedestrian[2] adj not interesting or unusual; lacking in imagination: He was rather a pedestrian student.

pedestrian cross·ing /·,··· '··/ n a special place for PEDESTRIANS to cross the road

pe·di·a·tri·cian /ˌpiʸdiʸə'trɪʃən/ n a doctor who specializes in PEDIATRICS

pe·di·at·rics /ˌpiʸdiʸ'ætrɪks/ n [U] the branch of medicine concerned with children and their diseases

ped·i·gree /'pɛdə,griʸ/ n **1** [A] (of animals, esp. dogs) descended from a recorded (and usu. specially chosen) family, and therefore of high quality **2** [C;U] (a set of) people (or animals) from whom a person (or animal) is descended; ANCESTRY: a dog of unknown pedigree –compare MONGREL

ped·lar /'pɛdlər/ →PEDDLER (1)

pee[1] /piʸ/ v [I] infml for URINATE

pee[2] n [S;U] infml an act or result of urinating (URINATE)

peek[1] /piʸk/ v [I at] infml to look (at something) quickly, esp. when one should not: He just had time to peek into the room before the door closed. –compare PEEP[1], PEER[2]

peek[2] n [S] infml an act of PEEKing

peel[1] /piʸl/ v **1** [T] to remove the outer covering from (a fruit, vegetable, etc.): a machine that peels potatoes **2** [T off] to remove (the outer covering) from something: Peel the skin off (the banana).|They peeled off their clothes and jumped into the water. **3** [I] (of an outer covering or surface) to come off, esp. in small pieces: My skin always peels when I've been in the sun.|The paint was peeling (off the walls).

peel[2] n [U] the outer covering, esp. of those fruits and vegetables which one usu. PEELs[1] (1) before eating: orange/apple peel –compare RIND

peel·ings /'piʸlɪŋz/ n [P] parts PEELed[1] (1) off (esp. from potatoes)

peep[1] /piʸp/ v [I at] to look quickly and secretly: His hands were covering his face, but I could see him peeping through his fingers. –compare PEEK[1], PEER[2]

peep[2] n [S at] a short, incomplete, and perhaps secret look: He took a peep at the back of the book to find the answers.

peep[3] n [S] a short high sound as made by a young bird or a mouse: (fig.) I don't want to hear a peep (even the smallest sound) out of you until dinnertime.

peer[1] /pɪər/ n **1** an equal in rank, age, quality, etc.: The opinion of his peers/his peer group is more important to him than his parents' ideas. –see also PEERLESS **2** (in Britain) a member of any of five noble ranks (BARON, VISCOUNT, EARL, MARQUIS, and DUKE) **3** (in Britain) a person who has a TITLE (4)

peer[2] v [I at] to look very carefully or hard, esp. as if not able to see well:She peered through the mist, trying to find the right path.|He peered at me over the top of his glasses. –compare PEEK[1], PEEP[1]

peer·age /'pɪərɪdʒ/ n [C;U] **1** the whole body of PEERs[1] (2,3) **2** the rank of a PEER[1] (2,3)

peer·less /'pɪərlɪs/ adj fml without an equal; better than any other –see also PEER[1] (1)

peeve[1] /piʸv/ v peeved, peeving [T usu. pass.] infml to annoy

peeve[2] n something that annoys or displeases

peev·ish /'piʸvɪʃ/ adj bad-tempered; easily annoyed by unimportant things –peevishly adv –peevishness n [U]

peg[1] /pɛg/ n **1** a short piece of wood, metal, etc., used for fastening things, hanging things on, etc.: Hang your coat on the peg in the hall.|First hammer the tent pegs into the grond, and then tie the ropes onto them. **2** square peg in a round hole a person who is not suited to the position or group in which he/she is placed **3** take somebody down a peg (or two) infml to show somebody that he/she is not as important as he/she thought he was

peg[2] v -gg- [T] **1** to fasten with a PEG[1] (1): She pegged the tent so it wouldn't blow in the wind. **2** to fix or hold (prices, wages, etc.) at a certain level

peg away v adv [I at] infml to work hard and steadily at

pe·jor·a·tive /pɪ'dʒɔrətɪv, -'dʒɑr-/ n,adj fml (a word, phrase, etc.) that suggests that somebody or something is bad or worthless: "Mean" is a more pejorative word than "economical."

Pe·king·ese, Pekinese /ˌpiʸkə'niʸz, -'niʸs/ n a small dog with long silky hair

pel·i·can /'pɛlɪkən/ n a large water bird which catches fish and stores them in a long baglike part under its beak

pel·let /'pɛlɪt/ n **1** a small ball of any soft material made by or as if by rolling between the fingers **2** a small ball of metal made to be fired from a gun

pelt[1] /pɛlt/ n the skin of a dead animal, esp. with the fur still on it

pelt[2] v **1** [T with] to attack by throwing things at: He pelted us with stones. **2** [I down] (of rain) to fall heavily and continuously: I'm not going out there; it's really pelting (down)!

pel·vis /'pɛlvɪs/ n the bowl-shaped frame of bones at the base of the backbone (SPINE (1)) –pelvic adj

pen[1] /pɛn/ n an instrument for writing or drawing with ink, such as a BALLPOINT PEN or FELT-TIP PEN

pen[2] n a small piece of land enclosed by a fence, used esp. for keeping animals in

pen[3] v -nn- [T] pomp to write: to pen a few lines of poetry

pen[4] v -nn- [T up, in] to shut (animals) in a PEN[2]: (fig.) I'm tired of being penned (up) in the office all day.

pe·nal /'piʸnl/ adj [no comp.] **1** of punishment (by law): penal laws |penal servitude (=imprisonment in which one also has to do hard work) **2** for which one may be punished by law: a penal offense

pe·nal·ize ‖also **-ise** *BrE* /'piːnl̩ˌaɪz, 'pɛn-/ *v* **-ized, -izing** [T *for*] **1** to punish, esp. unfairly **2** (in sports) to punish (a player's action) by giving an advantage to the other team: *Their team was penalized for intentionally wasting time.*

pen·al·ty /'pɛnltiː/ *n* **-ties 1** the punishment for breaking a law, rule, or agreement in law: *She has* **paid the penalty** *for her crimes.*|(fig.) *One of the penalties of fame is that people point at you in the street.* **2** something (such as a number of years in prison or an amount of money to be paid) that is ordered as a punishment: *Fishing in this river is forbidden, and the penalty is $25.* **3** (in sports) a disadvantage suffered by a player or team for breaking a rule: *Our player was put in the* **penalty box** *after he kicked an opponent.*

pen·ance /'pɛnəns/ *n* [U] self-punishment suffered, esp. for religions reasons, to show that one is sorry for having done wrong

pence /pɛns/ *BrE pl. of* PENNY –see also SIX-PENCE; see PENNY (USAGE)

pen·chant /'pɛntʃənt/ *n* [*for*] *French* a strong liking: *a penchant for Indian food*

pen·cil¹ /'pɛnsəl/ *n* a narrow pointed instrument, usu. wooden, containing a thin stick of a black substance or colored material, used for writing, drawing, or (an **eyebrow pencil**) for darkening the EYEBROWS

pencil² *v* **-l-** *AmE*‖**-ll-** *BrE* [T] to draw, write, or mark with a PENCIL¹

pend·ant, -ent /'pɛndənt/ *n* a hanging piece of jewelry, esp. a chain worn round the neck with a small decorative object hanging from it

pend·ing¹ /'pɛndɪŋ/ *prep* until: *This matter must wait pending her return from Europe.*

pending² *adj* [F *no comp.*] waiting to be decided or settled

pen·du·lous /'pɛndʒələs, -dyə-/ *adj fml* hanging down loosely so as to swing freely

pen·du·lum /'pɛndʒələm, -dyə-/ *n* a weight hanging from a fixed point so as to swing freely, esp. as used to control the working of a clock

pen·e·trate /'pɛnəˌtreɪt/ *v* **-trated, -trating 1** [I;T *through, into*] to enter, cut, or force a way (into or through something):*The knife penetrated his stomach.*|*Rain has penetrated right through this coat.*|*The car lights penetrated the darkness.* **2** [T] to understand: *to penetrate the mystery of the atom* –see also SO IMPENETRABLE –**penetrable** /'pɛnətrəbəl/ *adj* –**penetrability** /ˌpɛnətrə'bɪlətiː/ *n* [U]

pen·e·trat·ing /'pɛnəˌtreɪtɪŋ/ *adj* **1** (of the eye, questions, etc.) sharp and searching **2** (of a person, the mind, etc.) able to understand clearly and deeply **3** (of sounds) sharp and loud: *a penetrating voice* –**penetratingly** *adv*

pen·e·tra·tion /ˌpɛnə'treɪʃən/ *n* [U] **1** the act or action of penetrating (PENETRATE) **2** the ability to understand quickly and clearly

pen·guin /'pɛŋgwɪn, 'pɛn-/ *n* a large black-and-white flightless seabird of esp. the ANT-ARCTIC

pen·i·cil·lin /ˌpɛnə'sɪlɪn/ *n* [U] a substance used as a medicine to destroy certain bacteria in people and animals

pe·nin·su·la /pə'nɪnsələ, -syə-/ *n* a piece of land almost completely surrounded by water: *Italy is a peninsula.* –**peninsular** /pə'nɪnsələr, -syə-/ *adj*

pe·nis /'piːnɪs/ *n* **-nises** or **-nes** /niːz/ the outer sex organ of males

pen·i·tent /'pɛnətənt/ *adj fml* feeling or showing sorrow for having done wrong, with the intention not to do so again –opposite **impenitent** –**penitently** *adv* –**penitence** *n* [U]

pen·i·ten·tia·ry /ˌpɛnə'tɛnʃəriː, -tʃəriː/ *n* **-ries** a prison, esp. in the US

pen·knife /'pɛn-naɪf/ *n* **-knives** /naɪvz/ a small knife with usu. two folding blades, usu. carried in the pocket –compare JACK KNIFE

pen name /'· ·/ *n* a name used by a writer instead of his/her real name –see also PSEUDONYM

pen·nant /'pɛnənt/ *n* a long narrow pointed flag, esp. as used by schools, sports teams, etc., or on ships for signaling

pen·ni·less /'pɛnɪlɪs/ *adj* having no money

pen·ny /'pɛniː/ *n* **pennies** or **p** *BrE infml* **1** [C] (in the US and Canada) (a coin worth) a cent **2** [C] also **copper, p** *BrE infml*– (in Great Britain after 1971) a small copper and tin (BRONZE) coin, 100 of which make a pound **3** [C] also **copper** *BrE infml*– (in Great Britain before 1971) a BRONZE coin, 12 of which made a shilling **4** [S] (*used in* NEGATIVE¹ (1) *sentences*) a small amount of money: *The trip won't cost you a penny if you come in my car.* **5 a pretty penny** *infml* a rather large amount of money

USAGE In the US, Canada, and Britain, the plural **pennies** is used when speaking of the coins themselves, not as an amount of money. In Britain the plural **pence** or **p** is used when speaking of an amount of money: *She had several coins in her pocket, but no pennies.*|It only cost a few **pence**/30 **pence**/five **p.**

pen pal /'· ·/ *n AmE*‖**pen friend** *BrE*– a person, esp. in a foreign country, whom one has come to know by the friendly exchange of letters, but whom one has never met

pen·sion /'pɛnʃən, -tʃən/ *n* an amount of money paid regularly (esp. by a government or a company) to someone who no longer works, esp. because of old age or illness –see also OLD AGE PENSION, SOCIAL SECURITY

pen·sion·a·ble /'pɛnʃənəbəl, -tʃənə-/ *adj* giving one the right to receive a PENSION: *When will you reach pensionable age?*

pen·sion·er /'pɛnʃənər, -tʃənər/ *n* a person who is receiving a PENSION

pension sbdy.↔ **off** *v adv* [T] to dismiss from work but continue to pay a PENSION to

pen·sive /'pɛnsɪv/ *adj* deeply, perhaps sadly, thoughtful: *The woman in this painting has a pensive smile.* –**pensively** *adv* –**pensiveness** *n* [U]

pen·ta·gon /'pɛntəˌgɑn/ *n* a flat shape with five sides and five angles –**pentagonal** /pɛn'tægənl/ *adj*

Pentagon *n* [*the* S] (the chief officers working in) the building in Washington from which the armed forces of the US are directed

pen·ta·gram /ˈpɛntəˌgræm/ n a five-pointed star, used as a magic sign

pen·tath·lon /pɛnˈtæθlɑn, -lən/ n a sports event in which those taking part have to compete in five different sports (running, swimming, riding, shooting, and FENCING)

pent·house /ˈpɛnthaʊs/ n -houses /ˌhaʊzɪz/ a desirable small house or set of rooms built on top of a tall building

pent up /ˌpɛnt ˈʌp◂/ adj [A;F] shut up within narrow limits: I don't like being pent up in the house all the time.|(fig.) **pent-up feelings**

pe·nul·ti·mate /pɪˈnʌltəmɪt/ adj [A] next to the last: November is the penultimate month of the year.

pen·u·ry /ˈpɛnyəriy/ n [U] fml the state of being very poor; POVERTY

peo·ple¹ /ˈpiypəl/ n **1** [P] persons in general; persons other than oneself: Were there many people at the meeting? |If you do that, people will start to talk (about your behavior).|People who live in the South speak in a different way from people who live in the North. **2** [the P] all the persons in a society, esp. those who do not have special rank or position: a politician who belonged to the (common) people **3** [C] a race; nation: The Chinese are a hard-working people.|the peoples of Africa **4** [P] the persons from whom one is descended and to whom one is related: His people have lived in this valley for over 200 years. –see PERSON (USAGE)

people² v **-pled, -pling** [T] fml to fill with PEOPLE¹ (1): a desert peopled only by wandering tribes

pep /pɛp/ n [U] infml quick activity and forcefulness; VIGOR

pep·per¹ /ˈpɛpər/ n **1** [U] a hot-tasting powder made from the crushed seeds of certain plants, used for making food taste better **2** [C] a large round, or long and narrow, red or green fruit, sometimes with a hot taste, used as a vegetable **–peppery** adj

pepper² v [T] **1** to add or give the taste of PEPPER¹ (1) to (food) **2** [with] to hit repeatedly (esp. with shots or with small but annoying things)

pep·per·mint /ˈpɛpərˌmɪnt/ n **1** [U] a MINT¹ (1) plant with a special strong taste, used esp. in making candy and medicine **2** [C] also **mint**– a candy with this taste

pep pill /ˈ· ·/ n infml a small ball of solid medicine (PILL) taken to make one happier, or quicker in thought and action, for a short time

pep talk /ˈ· ·/ n infml a talk intended to fill the listener(s) with an urge to do something well, to win, etc.

per /pər; strong pɜr/ prep for each: apples costing 30 cents per pound|Our charge for the work will be $6 per hour|an hour.|My rent is $5000 **per annum**. (=per year)

per·am·bu·la·tor /pəˈræmbyəˌleytər/ n BrE fml for BABY CARRIAGE

per·ceive /pərˈsiyv/ v **-ceived, -ceiving** [T +(that)] fml to have or come to have knowledge of (something) through one of the senses (esp. sight) or through the mind; see: I told the judge that I couldn't perceive any difference between the two coins.|We perceived that we were unwelcome and left. **–perceivable** adj

USAGE Compare **perceive** and **conceive**: You **perceive** (=become conscious of) something that already exists. You **conceive** (=form in the mind) a completely new idea: We **perceived** that the teacher was angry with us.|She **conceived** a bold plan of escape.

percent, per cent /pərˈsɛnt/ adv,n (one part) in or for each 100; %: The restaurant has a service charge of ten percent (10%).|(fig.) I am 100 percent in agreement with you. (=totally in agreement)

per·cent·age /pərˈsɛntɪdʒ/ n [usu. sing.] an amount stated as if it is part of a whole which is 100; PROPORTION (3): What percentage of people die of this disease every year?

per·cep·ti·ble /pərˈsɛptəbəl/ adj fml able to be PERCEIVEd; noticeable –opposite **imperceptible –perceptibly** adv

per·cep·tion /pərˈsɛpʃən/ n **1** [U] also **perceptiveness**– the ability to PERCEIVE; clear natural understanding: a woman of great perception **2** a result of perceiving (PERCEIVE); something noticed and understood: my sudden perception of the difficulty

per·cep·tive /pərˈsɛptɪv/ adj quick to notice and understand **–perceptively** adv **–perceptiveness** n [U]

perch¹ /pɜrʃ/ n **1** a branch, rod, etc., where a bird rests **2** a high position in which a person or building is placed: From our perch up there on top of the cliff, we can see the whole town.

perch² v **1** [I] (of a bird) to come to rest from flying: The birds perched on the telephone wires. **2** [I;T] to (cause to) go into or be in the stated position (esp. unsafely, or on something narrow or high): She perched (herself) on a tall chair.|a house perched on the edge of the cliffs

perch³ n perch or perches a lake and river fish with prickly FINs, used as food

per·co·late /ˈpɜrkəˌleyt/ v **-lated, -lating 1** [I through] (of liquid) to pass slowly (through a material having small holes or GAPs in it): (fig.) Opposition to the President began to percolate through the Senate **2** [T] also **perk** infml– to make (coffee) in a special pot by the slow and repeated passing of hot water through crushed coffee beans **–percolation** /ˌpɜrkəˈleyʃən/ n [C;U]

per·co·la·tor /ˈpɜrkəˌleytər/ n a pot in which coffee is PERCOLATEd (2)

per·cus·sion /pərˈkʌʃən/ n [U] **1** the forceful striking together of two (usu. hard) objects **2** musical instruments that are played by being struck, esp. as a division of a band (**percussion section**): The drum is a percussion instrument.|The percussion is too loud.

per·cus·sion·ist /pərˈkʌʃənɪst/ n a person who plays PERCUSSION (2) instruments

pe·remp·to·ry /pəˈrɛmptəriy/ adj fml (of a person, his/her manner, etc.) showing an expectation of being obeyed at once and without question; impolitely quick and unfriendly **–peremptorily** adv

pe·ren·ni·al¹ /pəˈrɛniʸəl/ adj 1 lasting forever or for a long time; CONSTANT: *Politics provides a perennial subject of argument.* 2 (of a plant) living for more than two years –**perennially** adv

perennial² n a PERENNIAL¹ (2) plant

per·fect¹ /ˈpɜrfɪkt/ adj 1 of the very best possible kind, degree, or standard: *The weather during our vacation in California was perfect.*|(fig.) *a perfect crime* (=one in which the criminal is never discovered) 2 complete, with nothing missing, spoiled, etc.: *She's 75, but she still has a perfect set of teeth.* 3 suitable and satisfying in every way: *This big house is perfect for our large family.* 4 [A] *often infml* complete; thorough; UTTER: *a perfect stranger* 5 [A] *tech* (of verb forms, tenses, etc.) concerning a period of time up to and including the present (**present perfect**), past (**past perfect**), or future (**future perfect**) (as in "She has gone," "She had gone," "She will have gone"): *the perfect tense* –see also IMPERFECT²

per·fect² /pərˈfɛkt/ v [T] to make perfect: *She went to Italy to perfect her singing voice.*

per·fec·tion /pərˈfɛkʃən/ n [U] 1 the state or quality of being perfect: *The meat was cooked to perfection.* –opposite **imperfection** 2 the act of developing completely or making perfect: *The perfection of this new medical treatment may take several years.* 3 the perfect example: *As an actress, she is perfection itself.*

per·fec·tion·ist /pərˈfɛkʃənɪst/ n *sometimes derog* a person who is not satisfied with anything other than PERFECTION (1): *It takes him hours to cook a simple meal because he's such a perfectionist.*

per·fect·ly /ˈpɜrfɪktliʸ/ adv 1 in a perfect way: *She speaks French perfectly.* –opposite **imperfectly** 2 very; completely: *The walls must be perfectly clean before you paint them.*

per·fid·i·ous /pərˈfɪdiʸəs/ adj *fml & lit* disloyal; TREACHEROUS (1) –**perfidiously** adv

per·fi·dy /ˈpɜrfədiʸ/ n -dies [C;U] *fml & lit* (an example of) disloyalty; TREACHERY

per·fo·rate /ˈpɜrfəˌreʸt/ v -rated, -rating [T] to make a hole or holes through (something): *This machine perforates the sheets of stamps so that they can be easily torn off.*

per·fo·ra·tion /ˌpɜrfəˈreʸʃən/ n 1 [U] the action of perforating (PERFORATE) 2 [C *often pl.*] a small hole or line of holes made by perforating something

per·form /pərˈfɔrm/ v 1 [T] to do; carry out (a piece of work, an order, etc.): *The doctor performed the operation.*|*Who will perform the marriage ceremony for them?* 2 [I;T] to give, act or show (a play, a part in a play, a piece of music, etc.) esp. before the public: *What play will be performed tonight?*|*She will be performing at the piano.*|*a performing bear* 3 [I] to work or carry out an activity (in the stated way): *This car performs well/badly on hills.*

per·form·ance /pərˈfɔrməns/ n 1 [C;U] the action of PERFORMing (1,2), or an action PERFORMed (1,2): *Our football team's performance has been excellent this year.*|*His*

performance of/as Othello was terrible.*|*The band will give two more performances before leaving Boston.* 2 [U] (of people or machines) the ability to do something, esp. needing skill: *The car's performance on corners needs to be improved.*

per·form·er /pərˈfɔrmər/ n a person (or thing) that PERFORMs (2), esp. an actor, musician, etc. –compare SPECTATOR

per·fume¹ /ˈpɜrfyuʷm, pərˈfyuʷm/‖ also **scent** *BrE*– n [C;U] 1 a sweet or pleasant smell, as of flowers 2 sweet-smelling liquid, often made from flowers, for use esp. on a woman's face, wrists, and body

per·fume² /pərˈfyuʷm, ˈpɜrfyuʷm/ v -fumed, -fuming [T] 1 *fml or lit* to fill with PERFUME¹ (1): *roses perfuming the air* 2 to put PERFUME¹ (2) on: *a perfumed handkerchief*

per·func·to·ry /pərˈfʌŋktəriʸ/ adj *fml* done hastily and without thought, interest, or care –**perfunctorily** adv –**perfunctoriness** n [U]

per·haps /pərˈhæps/ adv 1 it may be; possibly: *Perhaps it'll rain.*|"Will he come?" "Perhaps not." 2 (used when asking for something politely): *Perhaps you could help me ...?* (=please help me)

per·il /ˈpɛrəl/ n *fml* 1 [U] danger, esp. of being harmed or killed 2 [C] something that causes danger 3 **at one's peril** (used when advising someone not to do something) with the near certainty of meeting great danger

per·il·ous /ˈpɛrələs/ adj *fml* dangerous; risky –**perilously** adv

pe·rim·e·ter /pəˈrɪmətər/ n the border around any closed flat figure or special area of ground, esp. a camp or airfield: *The perimeter of the airfield is protected by guard-dogs.*|*a perimeter fence*

pe·ri·od /ˈpɪəriʸəd/ n 1 a stretch of time with a beginning and an end, but not always of measured length: *There were long periods when we had no news of him.*|*Tomorrow's weather will be dry with sunny periods.* 2 a particular stretch of time in the development of a person, a civilization, the earth, an illness, etc.: *the Victorian period of English history*|*a play about the French Revolution, with all the actors wearing period clothes* (=clothes of that period) 3 a division of a school day; lesson: *a history period* 4 *AmE*‖**full stop** *BrE*– a point (.) marking the end of a sentence or a shortened form of a word 5 also **menstrual period** *fml*– a monthly flow of blood from the body of a woman –see also MENSTRUATE

pe·ri·od·ic /ˌpɪəriʸˈɑdɪk/ also **periodical**– adj happening occasionally, usu. at regular times: *periodic attacks of fever* –**periodically** adv

pe·ri·od·i·cal /ˌpɪəriʸˈɑdɪkəl/ n a magazine which appears at regular times (e.g. every month)

per·i·pa·tet·ic /ˌpɛrəpəˈtɛtɪk/ adj *fml or tech* traveling about; going from place to place

pe·riph·er·al /pəˈrɪfərəl/ adj 1 of slight importance by comparison; not central: *matters of peripheral interest* 2 of or connected with a PERIPHERY –**peripherally** adv

pe·riph·er·y /pəˈrɪfəriʸ/ n -ies *fml* [usu. sing.]

a line or area enclosing something; outside edge: *the periphery of the town*

per·i·scope /'perəˌskoʷp/ *n* a long tube with mirrors fitted in it so that people who are lower down (esp. in SUBMARINES) can see what is above them

per·ish /'perɪʃ/ *v* [I] (in writing, and esp. in newspapers) to die, esp. in a terrible or sudden way; be completely destroyed: *Almost a hundred people perished in the hotel fire last night.*

per·ish·a·ble /'perɪʃəbəl/ *adj* (of food) that quickly decays –opposite **nonperishable** –**perishables** *n* [P]

per·jure /'pɜrdʒər/ *v* **-jured, -juring: perjure oneself** to tell a lie on purpose after promising solemnly to tell the truth (esp. in a court of law)

per·jur·er /'pɜrdʒərər/ *n* a person who PERJUREs him/herself

per·ju·ry /'pɜrdʒəriʸ/ *n* [U] the act of perjuring oneself (PERJURE)

perk¹ /pɜrk/ also **perquisite** *fml*– *n* [usu. pl.] *infml* money and goods (or non-material advantage) that one gets regularly from one's work apart from pay: *The perks include a company car.*|*One of the perks of this job is that you don't have to work on Tuesdays.*

perk² *v* [I;T] *infml* for PERCOLATE (2)

perk up *v adv* [I;T (=perk sbdy.↔ up)] *infml* to (cause to) become more cheerful, show interest, etc.

perk·y /'pɜrkiʸ/ *adj* **-ier, -iest** boldly cheerful; full of life and interest –**perkily** *adv* –**perkiness** *n* [U]

perm¹ /pɜrm/ *n BrE* for PERMANENT²

perm² *v* [T] *infml* to give a PERMANENT² to

per·ma·nence /'pɜrmənəns/ *n* [U] the state of being PERMANENT –opposite **impermanence**

per·ma·nent¹ /'pɜrmənənt/ *adj* lasting or intended to last for a long time or forever: *a permanent job/address* –compare TEMPORARY –**permanently** *adv*

permanent² *AmE*‖**perm** *BrE infml*, also **permanent wave** /ˌ··· '·/ *fml*– *n* waves or curls put into hair by chemical treatment so that they will last for several months

per·me·ate /'pɜrmiʸˌeʸt/ *v* **-ated, -ating** [I;T *through*] *more fml than* **pass through**– to pass through or into every part of (something): *Water permeated through the cracks in the wall.*|*A strong desire for political change permeated the country.* –**permeation** /ˌpɜrmiʸ'eʸʃən/ *n* [U]

per·mis·si·ble /pər'mɪsəbəl/ *adj* allowed; permitted

per·mis·sion /pər'mɪʃən/ *n* [U +to-v] an act of PERMITting¹; agreement; CONSENT: *We asked his permission to use the car.*|*Did she give you permission to take that?*

per·mis·sive /pər'mɪsɪv/ *adj often derog* allowing a great deal of, or too much, freedom, esp. in sexual matters (often in the phrase **the permissive society**) –**permissively** *adv* –**permissiveness** *n* [U]

per·mit¹ /pər'mɪt/ *v* **-tt-** *more fml than* **allow**– **1** [T +to-v/v-ing] to allow: *I cannot permit this to happen.*|*The rules of the club do not*

permit smoking. **2** [I] to make it possible (for a stated thing to happen): *I will come in June if my health permits.*|*weather permitting* (=if the weather is good enough to allow it) **3** [T] also **permit of** *fml*– to allow as possible; admit: *The facts permit (of) no other explanation.*

per·mit² /'pɜrmɪt, pər'mɪt/ *n* an official written statement giving one the right to do something: *You can't enter the building without a permit.*

per·mu·ta·tion /ˌpɜrmyʊ'teʸʃən/ *n* [C;U] (esp. in MATHEMATICS) (the act of) changing the order of a set of things arranged in a group: *The six possible permutations of ABC are ABC, ACB, BCA, BAC, CAB, and CBA.*

per·ni·cious /pər'nɪʃəs/ *adj fml* very harmful; having an evil effect –**perniciously** *adv* –**perniciousness** *n* [U]

per·ox·ide /pə'rɑksaɪd/ also **hydrogen peroxide** *fml*– *n* [U] *infml* a chemical liquid used to take the color out of dark hair and to kill bacteria

per·pen·dic·u·lar /ˌpɜrpən'dɪkyələr/ *adj* **1** exactly upright; not leaning to one side or the other **2** [*to*] (of a line or surface) at an angle of 90 degrees to a line or surface –**perpendicularly** *adv*

per·pe·trate /'pɜrpəˌtreʸt/ *v* **-trated, -trating** [T] *fml or humor* to be guilty of; do; COMMIT (1) (something wrong or criminal) –**perpetration** /ˌpɜrpə'treʸʃən/ *n* [U] –**perpetrator** /'pɜrpəˌtreʸtər/ *n*

per·pet·u·al /pər'petʃuʷəl/ *adj* **1** lasting forever or for a long time: *the perpetual snow on the mountains* **2** *often derog* happening often or uninterruptedly: *I'm tired of your perpetual complaints.* –**perpetually** *adv*

per·pet·u·ate /pər'petʃuʷˌeʸt/ *v* **-ated, -ating** [T] to preserve; cause to be continued or remembered –**perpetuation** /pərˌpetʃuʷ'eʸʃən/ *n* [U]

per·pe·tu·i·ty /ˌpɜrpə'tuʷətiʸ, -'tyuʷ-/ *n* [U] *fml* **in perpetuity** for a time without end: *The land was given to them in perpetuity.*

per·plex /pər'pleks/ *v* [T] to cause to feel confused and troubled by being difficult to understand or answer –**perplexed** /pər'plekst/ *adj*: *They looked perplexed when I told them that their parents had gone.* –**perplexedly** /pər'pleksɪdliʸ/ *adv*

per·plex·i·ty /pər'pleksətiʸ/ *n* [U] the state of being PERPLEXed

per·qui·site /'pɜrkwəzɪt/ *n fml* for PERK¹

per se /ˌpɜr 'seʸ/ *adv Latin fml* considered alone and not in connection with other things

per·se·cute /'pɜrsɪˌkyuʷt/ *v* **-cuted, -cuting** [T] to treat cruelly; cause to suffer (esp. for religious or political beliefs) –**persecution** /ˌpɜrsɪ'kyuʷʃən/ *n* [C;U] –**persecutor** /'pɜrsɪˌkyuʷtər/ *n*

per·se·ver·ance /ˌpɜrsə'vɪərəns/ *n* [U] continual steady effort made to fulfill some aim

per·se·vere /ˌpɜrsə'vɪər/ *v* **-vered, -vering** [I *at, in, with*] to continue firmly in spite of difficulties –**persevering** *adj*

per·sist /pər'sɪst, -'zɪst/ *v* [I] **1** [*with, in*] to continue firmly (and perhaps unreasonably) in spite of opposition or warning: *If you persist in breaking the law, you will go to prison.* **2** to continue to exist: *The cold weather will persist for the rest of the week.*

per·sist·ent /pərˈsɪstənt, -ˈzɪs-/ *adj often derog* **1** continuing in a habit or course of action, esp. in spite of opposition or warning: *a persistent thief|your persistent attempts to annoy me* **2** continuing to exist, happen, or appear for a long time, esp. for longer than is usual or desirable: *a persistent cough* –**persistence** *n* [U]: *He showed such persistence that they finally had to give him a job.* –**persistently** *adv*

per·snick·e·ty /pərˈsnɪkətiʸ/ *adj infml & often derog* worrying (too much) about small things; FUSSY (2)

per·son /ˈpɜrsən/ *n* **1** [C] a human being: *You're just the person I wanted to see.* **2** [C] *sometimes derog* a human being, esp. somebody unknown or not named –see USAGE **3** [C;U] (in grammar) any of the three special forms of verbs or PRONOUNs that show the speaker (**first person**), the one spoken to (**second person**),or the human being or thing spoken about (**third person**) **4 in person** *personally*: *I can't attend the meeting in person, but I'm sending someone to speak for me.*

USAGE The usual plural of **person** is **people**: *Only one* **person**/*A lot of* **people** *replied to our advertisement.* **Persons** is formal, and often used in official writings, notices, etc.: *He was murdered by a* **person** *or* **persons** *unknown.*|**Persons** *wishing to enter this building must have permission.*

per·so·na /pərˈsoʷnə/ *n* (in PSYCHOLOGY) the outward character a person takes on in order to persuade other people (and him/herself) that he/she is a particular type of person

per·son·a·ble /ˈpɜrsənəbəl/ *adj* attractive in appearance or character: *a personable young man*

per·son·age /ˈpɜrsənɪdʒ/ *n fml or pomp* a famous or important person: *the mayor and other local personages*

per·son·al /ˈpɜrsənəl/ *adj* **1** concerning, belonging to, or for the use of a particular person; private: *father's personal chair|a letter marked "Personal"|Here are Jane's* **personal effects** (=belongings) **2** done or made directly by a particular person, not by a representative: *The mayor made a personal visit to the scene of the fighting.* **3** of the body or appearance: *Personal cleanliness is important for health.* **4** (of remarks) directed against (the appearance or character of) a particular person: *I told them not to make personal remarks about her.* **5** (in grammar) showing the PERSON (3) –see also IMPERSONAL, PERSONAL PRONOUN

personal col·umn /ˈ··· ˌ··/ *n* a part of a newspaper that gives or asks for messages, news, etc., about particular persons

per·son·al·i·ty /ˌpɜrsəˈnælətiʸ/ *n* **-ties 1** [C;U] the whole nature or character of a particular person: *He has a weak personality.* **2** [U] unusual, strong, exciting character: *She became an actress because she has so much*

personality. **3** [C] a person who is well known to the public or to people connected with some particular activity: *a television personality*

per·son·al·ize *AmE*‖also **-ise** *BrE* /ˈpɜrsənəˌlaɪz/ *v* **-ized, -izing 1** [I;T] *often derog* to change so as to be concerned with personal matters or relationships rather than with facts: *Let's not personalize (this argument).* **2** [T] to make PERSONAL (1), esp. by adding one's address or one's name: *personalized handkerchiefs*

per·son·al·ly /ˈpɜrsənəliʸ/ *adv* **1** directly and not through somebody acting for one: *He is personally in charge of all the arrangements.* **2** speaking for oneself only; as far as oneself is concerned: *She said she didn't like it, but personally I thought it was very good.* **3** as a person; not considered for any qualities that are not PERSONAL (1): *Personally she may be very charming, but is she a good doctor?* **4** as directed against oneself in a PERSONAL (4) way: *You must not take my remarks about your plan personally.*

personal pro·noun /ˌ··· ˈ··/ *n* a word standing for a noun (PRONOUN) and used for showing the speaker, the one spoken to, or the one spoken of: *"I," "you," and "they" are personal pronouns.*

per·son·i·fy /pərˈsɑnəˌfaɪ/ *v* **-fied, -fying** [T] to be a (perfect) example of; be the living form of (some quality) –**personification** /pərˌsɑnəfəˈkeʸʃən/ *n* [C;U]: *Although she is poor, she is* **the personification of** (=a perfect example of) *generosity.*

per·son·nel /ˌpɜrsəˈnɛl/ *n* [P] all the people employed by a company, in the armed forces, etc.: *army personnel* |*New personnel are needed for our operations in the Middle East.*

per·spec·tive /pərˈspɛktɪv/ *n* **1** [U] (the rules governing) the art of drawing solid objects on a flat surface so that they give a natural effect of depth, distance, and solidity (esp. in the phrases **in perspective, out of perspective**): *The picture looks strange because it has no perspective.*|*The objects in the background are out of perspective.* **2** [C;U] the way in which a matter is judged, so that background, future or possible problems, etc., are taken into consideration: *We have to look at the problem* **in perspective/in its proper perspective**. **3** [C *of*] a view, esp. one stretching far into the distance: (fig.) *a perspective of our country's history*

per·spi·ca·cious /ˌpɜrspɪˈkeʸʃəs/ *adj fml or humor* having or showing keen judgment and understanding –**perspicacity** /ˌpɜrspɪˈkæsətiʸ/ *n* [U]

per·spi·ra·tion /ˌpɜrspəˈreʸʃən/ *n* [U] →SWEAT[1] (1)

per·spire /pərˈspaɪər/ *v* **-spired, -spiring** [I] →SWEAT[2] (1)

per·suade /pərˈsweʸd/ *v* **-suaded, -suading 1** [*into, out of*] to cause to do something by reasoning, arguing, begging, etc.:*Try to persuade him to come with us.*|*They persuaded us into/out of going* (=to go/not to go) *to the party.* **2** to cause to feel certain; CONVINCE:

She was not persuaded of the truth of his statement. –see also DISSUADE –see CONVINCE (USAGE)

per·sua·sion /pər'swe^yʒən/ *n* **1** [U] the act of persuading (PERSUADE) **2** [U] the ability to influence others **3** [C] a group holding a particular belief: *People of many different political persuasions attended the meeting.*

per·sua·sive /pər'swe^ysɪv/ *adj* having the power to influence others into believing or doing what one wishes –**persuasively** *adv* –**persuasiveness** *n* [U]

pert /pɜrt/ *adj* slightly disrespectful in a bold and rather amusing way –**pertly** *adv* –**pertness** *n* [U]

per·tain to sthg. /pər'te^yn/ *v prep* [T] *fml* to belong to or have a connection with

per·ti·na·cious /ˌpɜrtn'e^yʃəs/ *adj fml* determined; STUBBORN –**pertinacity** /ˌpɜrtn'æsəti^y/ *n* [U]

per·ti·nent /'pɜrtn-ənt/ *adj* [*to*] *fml* connected directly (with something that is being considered); RELEVANT: *several pertinent questions* –opposite **irrelevant** –**pertinently** *adv*

per·turb /pər'tɜrb/ *v* [T] *fml* to cause to worry; put into a state of disorder

pe·ruse /pə'ru^wz/ *v* -**rused**, -**rusing** [T] *fml or humor* to read through carefully –**perusal** /pə'ru^wzəl/ *n* [C;U]

per·vade /pər've^yd/ *v* -**vaded**, -**vading** [T] *fml or lit* (of smells and of ideas, feelings, etc.) to spread through every part of: *The smell of cooking pervaded the room.*

per·va·sive /pər've^ysɪv/ *adj sometimes derog* of a kind that will probably or easily PERVADE; widespread: *the pervasive influence of television* –**pervasively** *adv* –**pervasiveness** *n* [U]

per·verse /pər'vɜrs/ *adj* (of people, actions, etc.) purposely continuing in what is wrong, unreasonable, or against the wishes of others: *We all wanted to go tomorrow, but he had to be perverse, and chose to go today.* –**perversely** *adv* –**perversity** /pər'vɜrsəti^y/ *also* **perverseness**– *n* -**ties** [C;U]

per·ver·sion /pər'vɜrʒən, -ʃən/ *n* **1** [U] the action of PERVERTing[1] **2** [C] a PERVERTed[1] form (of what is true, reasonable, considered to be natural, etc.): *His interest in dead bodies is one of his many perversions.*

per·vert[1] /pər'vɜrt/ *v* [T] **1** to turn (someone) away from what is right and natural, esp. to influence in the direction of (what are considered) unnatural sexual habits **2** to use for a bad purpose: *Scientific knowledge is often perverted to help cause destruction and war.*|*To pervert the course of justice is to prevent justice being done.*

per·vert[2] /'pɜrvɜrt/ *n derog* a person whose sexual behavior is different from (what is considered) natural

pe·se·ta /pə'se^ytə/ *n* a Spanish coin, on which the Spanish money system is based

pes·ky /'pɛski^y/ *adj* -**kier**, -**kiest** *AmE infml* annoying and causing trouble: *What a pesky child!*

pes·si·mism /'pɛsəˌmɪzəm/ *n* [U] the habit of thinking that whatever happens will be bad –see also OPTIMISM –**pessimist** *n*: *A few*

pessimists think we will lose the election, but most of us are sure we will win. –**pessimistic** /ˌpɛsə'mɪstɪk/ *adj* –**pessimistically** *adv*

pest /pɛst/ *n* **1** a usu. small animal or insect that harms or destroys food supplies **2** *infml* an annoying person or thing

pes·ter /'pɛstər/ *v* [I;T *for, with*] to annoy (somebody) continually, esp. with demands: *The children pestered the travelers for money.*|*My son has been pestering me to take him with me.*

pes·ti·cide /'pɛstəˌsaɪd/ *n* [C;U] a chemical substance used to kill PESTS (1)

pes·ti·lence /'pɛstələns/ *n* [C;U] *esp. old use* a disease that causes death and spreads quickly to large numbers of people

pes·tle /'pɛsəl, 'pɛstl/ *n* an instrument with a heavy rounded end, used for crushing substances in a special bowl (MORTAR)

pet[1] /pɛt/ *n* [A;C] **1** an animal kept in the home as a companion: *a pet dog* |*She keeps a monkey as a pet.* **2** a person (esp. a child) or thing specially favored above others: *She is the teacher's pet.* **3 pet peeve** special dislike: *Her pet peeve is people talking during a movie.*

pet[2] *v* -**tt**- **1** [T] to touch kindly with the hands, showing love **2** [I;T] *infml* to kiss and touch (another or each other) in sexual play

pet·al /'pɛtl/ *n* any of the (usu. colored) leaflike divisions of a flower

pe·ter out /'pi^ytər/ *v adv* [I] to come gradually to an end

pe·tite /pə'ti^yt/ *adj apprec* (esp. of a woman, her appearance, etc.) small

pe·ti·tion[1] /pə'tɪʃən/ *n* (a paper containing) a request or demand made to a government or other body, usu. signed by many people: *a petition against the closing of the library*

petition[2] *v* [I;T +*to-v*/*for*] to make a PETITION[1] or request: *The people petitioned (the government) to be allowed to return to their island.*

pet·ri·fy /'pɛtrəˌfaɪ/ *v* -**fied**, -**fying** **1** [T] *infml* to put into a state of great shock or fear: *I was so petrified by the face in the window that I couldn't move.* **2** [I;T] to turn into stone: *the Petrified Forest in Arizona*

pet·ro·chem·i·cal /ˌpɛtro^w'kɛmɪkəl/ *n* a chemical substance obtained from PETROLEUM or natural gas: *the petrochemical industry*

pet·rol /'pɛtrəl/ *n* [U] *BrE* for GASOLINE

pe·tro·le·um /pə'tro^wli^yəm/ *n* [U] a mineral oil obtained from below the surface of the earth, and used to produce gasoline, KEROSENE, and various chemical substances

petroleum jel·ly /·ˌ··· '··/ *n* [U] a solid substance made from PETROLEUM, used esp. as a medicine for the skin

petrol sta·tion /'·· ˌ··/ *n BrE* for GAS STATION

pet·ti·coat /'pɛti^yˌko^wt/ *n* → SLIP[2] (3)

pet·ty /'pɛti^y/ *adj* -**tier**, -**tiest 1** (by comparison) unimportant: *Our difficulties seem petty when compared to those of people who never get enough to eat.* **2** *derog* having or showing a mind that is narrow and ungenerous: *petty acts of unkindness* –**pettily** *adv* –**pettiness** *n* [C;U]

petty cash /ˌ·· ˈ·/ n [U] an amount of money kept ready in an office for making small payments

petty of·fi·cer /ˌ·· ˈ···◂/ n [A;C] a NONCOM-MISSIONED OFFICER in the navy

pet·u·lant /ˈpɛtʃələnt/ adj showing childish bad temper over unimportant things, or for no reason at all **–petulantly** adv **–petulance** n [U]

pew /pyuʷ/ n a long seat (BENCH (1)) for people to sit on in church

pew·ter /ˈpyuʷtər/ n [U] (dishes and vessels made from) a grayish metal made by mixing lead and tin

pha·lanx /ˈfeʸlæŋks/ n **-lanxes** or **-langes** /fəˈlændʒiʸz/ **1** (in ancient Greece) a group of soldiers packed closely together for better protection **2** any group of people packed closely together for attack or defense

phal·lus /ˈfæləs/ n an image of the male sex organ (PENIS), esp. as used as a sign of sexual power **–phallic** /ˈfælɪk/ adj

phan·tom /ˈfæntəm/ n a shadowy likeness of a dead person; GHOST

phar·aoh /ˈfɛərowʷ, ˈfeʸrowʷ/ n [A;C] (often cap.) (the title of) the ruler of ancient Egypt

phar·ma·ceu·ti·cal /ˌfɑrməˈsuʷtɪkəl/ adj [A] connected with (the making of) medicine: a pharmaceutical company

phar·ma·cist /ˈfɑrməsɪst/ also **druggist** AmE‖**chemist** BrE– n fml a person who prepares and sells medicine

phar·ma·col·o·gy /ˌfɑrməˈkɑlədʒiʸ/ n [U] the scientific study of medicines and drugs **–pharmacologist** n

phar·ma·cy /ˈfɑrməsiʸ/ n **-cies 1** [U] the making and/or giving out of medicine **2** [C] also **drug store** AmE‖**chemist's (shop)** BrE– a store where medicines are sold **–compare** DISPENSARY

phase¹ /feʸz/ n **1** a stage of development: a new and dangerous phase in the relations between the two nations|Most children **go through a phase** of opposing all their parents' wishes. **2** any of a number of changes in the appearance of the moon or a PLANET as seen from the earth at different times: the phases of the moon

phase² v **phased, phasing** [T] to plan or arrange in separate PHASES¹ (1): The introduction of the plan is being carefully phased. (=done in stages)
   phase sthg.↔ **in/out** v adv [T] to introduce/remove in stages or gradually

Ph.D. /ˌpiʸ eʸtʃ ˈdiʸ/ n abbrev. for: (a person who has gained) an advanced university degree: She's working for/towards/on her Ph.D.

pheas·ant /ˈfɛzənt/ n **pheasant** or **pheasants** [C;U] (the meat of) a large long-tailed bird hunted for food

phe·nom·e·nal /fɪˈnɑmənl/ adj very unusual; scarcely believable: phenomenal strength **–phenomenally** adv

phe·nom·e·non¹ /fɪˈnɑmə,nɑn, -nən/ n **-na** /nə/ a fact or event in nature (or society), esp. one that is unusual and/or of scientific interest: the phenomena of nature|Snow in Egypt is an almost unknown phenomenon.

phenomenon² n **-nons** a very unusual person, thing, event, etc.

phew, whew /fyuʷ, hwyuʷ/ interj (the sound of) a quick short whistling breath, either in or out, expressing gladness, tiredness, or shock

phi·al /ˈfaɪəl/ n a small bottle, esp. one of liquid medicine

phi·lan·der /fɪˈlændər/ n [I] lit to amuse oneself by making love to another, with no serious intentions **–philanderer** n

phi·lan·thro·pist /fɪˈlænθrəpɪst/ n a person who is kind and helpful to those who are poor or in trouble, esp. by making generous gifts of money

phi·lan·thro·py /fɪˈlænθrəpiʸ/ n [U] a feeling of kindness and love for all people, esp. as shown in an active way by giving help **–philanthropic** /ˌfɪlənˈθrɑpɪk/ adj

phi·lat·e·ly /fɪˈlætl-iʸ/ n [U] tech stamp-collecting **–philatelist** n

phil·is·tine /ˈfɪlə,stiʸn/ n derog a person who has no understanding of, or interest in, art, music, beautiful things, etc.

phi·lol·o·gy /fɪˈlɑlədʒiʸ/ n [U] tech the science of the nature and development of words, language, or a particular language **–philologist** n

phi·los·o·pher /fɪˈlɑsəfər/ n **1** a person who studies (and sometimes teaches) PHILOSOPHY (1) **2** a person who has formed a PHILOSOPHY (2)

phil·o·soph·i·cal /ˌfɪləˈsɑfɪkəl/ also **philo·sophic** /ˌfɪləˈsɑfɪk/– adj **1** accepting (esp. difficulty or unhappiness) with calmness and quiet courage **2** of or concerning PHILOSOPHY (1): the philosophical writings of Sartre **–philosophically** adv

phi·los·o·phize AmE‖also **-phise** BrE /fɪˈlɑsə,faɪz/ v **-phized, -phizing** [I about] to think, talk, or write like a PHILOSOPHER

phi·los·o·phy /fɪˈlɑsəfiʸ/ n **-phies 1** [U] the study of the nature and meaning of existence, reality, knowledge, goodness, etc. **2** [C] any of various systems of thought having this as its base: the philosophy of Aristotle|(fig.) Eat, drink, and be merry; that's my philosophy! (=my rule for living)

phlegm /flɛm/ n [U] the thick jelly-like substance produced in the nose and throat (esp. when one has a cold); yellow or green MUCUS

phleg·mat·ic /fleɡˈmætɪk/ adj fml calm and unexcitable **–phlegmatically** adv

pho·bi·a /ˈfowʷbiʸə/ n a strong and usu. unreasonable fear and dislike: He has a phobia about water and won't learn to swim.

phoe·nix /ˈfiʸnɪks/ n an imaginary bird of ancient times, believed to burn itself at the end of its life and be born again from the ashes

phone¹ /fowʷn/ n a telephone: Elaine does most of her business over the phone.|Tom is always on the phone.

phone² v **phoned, phoning** [I;T +to-v/up] to telephone: Phone me (up) when you arrive at the station.|He phoned (me) to say he couldn't come. **–see** TELEPHONE (USAGE)

pho·net·ic /fəˈnɛtɪk/ adj **1** of or concerning the sounds of human speech **2** using signs to represent the actual sounds of speech: *This dictionary uses a phonetic alphabet as a guide to pronunciation.* –**phonetically** *adv*

pho·net·ics /fə'nɛṭɪks/ *n* [U] *tech* the study and science of speech sounds

pho·ny , phoney /'foʷniʸ/ *adj* **-nier, -niest** *infml derog* pretended; false –**phony, phoney** *n* **-ies, -eys:** *He's a phony!*

pho·no·graph /'foʷnə,græf/ *n AmE* for RECORD PLAYER

phos·pho·res·cence /,fɑsfə'rɛsəns/ *n* [U] the giving out of light with little or no heat –**phosphorescent** *adj*

phos·pho·rus /'fɑsfərəs/ *n* [U] a poisonous yellowish waxlike simple substance (ELEMENT (1)) that shines faintly in the dark and starts to burn when brought out into the air

pho·to /'foʷtoʷ/ *n* **-tos** *infml* a photograph

pho·to·cop·i·er /'foʷtə,kɑpiʸər, 'foʷtoʷ-/ *n* a machine that makes photocopies (PHOTOCOPY)

pho·to·cop·y /'foʷtə,kɑpiʸ, 'foʷtoʷ-/ *v,n* **-ied, -ying; -ies** [C;T] (to make) a photographic copy of a letter, drawing, etc. –compare XEROX

pho·to·e·lec·tric cell /,foʷtoʷɪ,lɛktrɪk 'sɛl/ *n* an instrument by which light is made to start an electrical apparatus working

photo fin·ish /,·· '··/ *n* the end of a race in which the leaders finish so close together that a photograph has to be taken to show which is the winner

pho·to·gen·ic /,foʷtə'dʒɛnɪk/ *adj* (esp. of people) having an appearance that looks pleasing or effective when photographed

pho·to·graph¹ /'foʷtə,græf/ also **photo, picture** *infml*– *n* a picture obtained by using a camera and film sensitive to light: *Have you seen John's photograph in the newspaper?* (=a photograph of John)|*Visitors to the museum are not allowed to* **take photographs.**

photograph² *v* [T] to take a photograph of

pho·tog·ra·pher /fə'tɑgrəfər/ *n* a person who takes photographs, esp. as a business or an art

pho·to·graph·ic /,foʷtə'græfɪk/ *adj* [A] concerning, got by, or used in producing photographs –**photographically** *adv*

pho·tog·ra·phy /fə'tɑgrəfiʸ/ *n* [U] the art or business of producing photographs

pho·to·stat /'foʷtə,stæt/ *n,v* **-tt-** [T] *tdmk sometimes cap.* →PHOTOCOPY

phras·al verb /,freʸzəl 'vɜrb/ *n* a small group of words that acts like a verb and consists usu. of a verb with an adverb and/or a PREPOSITION: *"Run out" and "use up" are phrasal verbs.* –see Study Notes opposite

phrase¹ /freʸz/ *n* **1** (in grammar) a small group of words forming part of a sentence: *"Walking along the road"* and *"a packet of cigarettes"* are phrases. –compare SENTENCE, CLAUSE **2** a short expression, esp. one that is clever and very suited to what is meant

phrase² *v* **phrased, phrasing** [T] to express in (particular) words: *a politely-phrased refusal*

phrase book /'· ·/ *n* a book giving and explaining phrases of a particular (foreign)

language, for people to use when they go abroad

phra·se·ol·o·gy /,freʸziʸ'ɑlədʒiʸ/ *n* [U] *fml* the way in which words are chosen, arranged, and/or used: *I don't understand all this scientific phraseology.*

phys·i·cal /'fɪzɪkəl/ *adj* **1** of or concerning material things (as opposed to things of the mind, spirit, etc.): *the physical world* –compare MENTAL **2** of or according to the laws of nature: *Is there a physical explanation for these strange happenings?* **3** of or concerning the body: *physical exercise* –compare BODILY¹ **4** [A] concerning the natural formation of the earth's surface: *physical* GEOGRAPHY **5** [A] (of certain sciences) of the branch that is connected with PHYSICS: *physical chemistry*

physical ed·u·ca·tion /,··· ··'··/ also **PE** *infml AmE*‖**physical training** /,··· '··/ *BrE*– *n* [U] development of the body by games, exercises, etc., esp. in schools

phys·i·cal·ly /'fɪzɪkliʸ/ *adv* **1** according to the laws of nature: *It's* **physically impossible** *to travel faster than the speed of light.* **2** with regard to the body: *The old man is still physically fit, but mentally* (=with regard to the mind) *rather confused.*

physical ther·a·py /,··· '··/ *n* [U] → PHYSIOTHERAPY

phy·si·cian /fɪ'zɪʃən/ *n* a doctor, esp. one who treats diseases with medicines (as opposed to a SURGEON, who performs operations)

phys·i·cist /'fɪzəsɪst/ *n* a person who studies PHYSICS

phys·ics /'fɪzɪks/ *n* [U] a science concerned with the study of matter and natural forces (such as light, heat, movement, etc.)

phys·i·ol·o·gy /,fɪziʸ'ɑlədʒiʸ/ *n* [U] a science concerned with the study of how the bodies of living things, and their various parts, work –**physiologist** *n* –**physiological** /,fɪziʸə'lɑdʒɪkəl/ *adj*

phys·i·o·ther·a·py /,fɪziʸoʷ'θɛrəpiʸ/ also **physical therapy**– *n* [U] the use of exercises, rubbing, heat, etc., in the treatment of disease, broken limbs, etc. –**physiotherapist** *n*

phy·sique /fɪ'ziʸk/ *n* the form and character of a human body –see BODY (USAGE)

pi /paɪ/ *n* (in GEOMETRY) a Greek letter (π) used for representing the fixed RATIO of the CIRCUMFERENCE of a circle to its DIAMETER: *Pi equals about 22/7 or 3.14159.*

pi·an·ist /piʸ'ænɪst, 'piʸənɪst/ *n* a person who plays the piano

pi·an·o /piʸ'ænoʷ/ *n* **-os** a large musical instrument, played by pressing narrow black or white bars (KEYS¹ (3)) which cause small hammers to hit wire strings

pic·co·lo /'pɪkə,loʷ/ *n* **-los** a small musical instrument that looks like a FLUTE but plays higher notes

pick¹ /pɪk/ *v* [T] **1** to choose: *He picked the biggest cake he could find.* **2** to pull or break off (part of a plant) by the stem from a tree or plant; gather: *He picked her a rose.*|*They've gone fruit-picking today.* **3** to take up or

STUDY NOTES phrasal verbs

Verbs like **give up**, **look after**, and **put up with** are very common in English. This dictionary makes it very easy for you to understand what they mean and how to use them.

give up, **look after**, and **put up with** do not mean the same as **give**, **look**, and **put**. For example, to **give** something **up** means "to stop having or doing something."

The dictionary lists them under the main verb so that they can be easily found. For example, **give up** is listed under **give**, after the meanings of the main verb:

> **give** *v* [T] to cause (someone) to have or own (something): *She gave him a book for his birthday.* | *Give me the baby while you find the keys* . . .
> **give up** *v adv* to stop having or doing: *The doctor told me to give up smoking.* | *I've given up the idea.*

The entry for **give up** tells you that it means "to stop having or doing." This means that instead of saying:

I **stopped** *playing tennis after I left school.*

you could say:

I **gave up** *playing tennis after I left school.*

These PHRASAL VERBs, just like main verbs, can be INTRANSITIVE or TRANSITIVE (see Study Notes on page 745). If they are intransitive, they are shown like this:

> **get by** *v adv* [I] to continue one's way of life: *She can't get by on such a small income*

When they are transitive, this means that they must be followed by a noun or noun phrase (direct OBJECT). Transitive phrasal verbs are shown like this:

> **bring off** *v adv* [T] to succeed in doing (something difficult): *It was a very difficult job, but Anne was able to bring it off successfully.*

Phrasal verbs are made up of a verb and a PREPOSITION, or a verb and an adverb, or both. This means that direct objects can sometimes follow the verb, and sometimes follow the preposition or adverb.

To help you to use phrasal verbs correctly, this dictionary actually shows you where the object goes, using the words:

sbdy. (=somebody)
sthg. (=something)

> **look after** sbdy. *v prep* [T] to take care of

this means that the object is a person, and that it can only follow the preposition:

Can you **look after** *the baby while I go out?*

> **push** sbdy. **around** *v adv* [T] to treat roughly and unfairly

this means that the object is a person, and that it can only follow the verb:

That big boy **pushes** *all the smaller boys* **around**. *Don't* **push** *me* **around**!

> **make** sthg. ↔ **up** *v adv* [T] to invent (a story, excuse etc.)

this means that the object is a thing, in this case a story, excuse, etc., and the ↔ means that it can follow either the verb or the adverb:

He **made up** *a story for the children.*
He **made** *a story* **up** *for the children.*

But note that PRONOUNs *always* follow the verb.

He **made** *it* **up.**

> **acquaint** sbdy. **with** sthg. *v prep* [T] to make (oneself or someone) familiar with

this means that the phrasal verb has two objects. The first object is a person, and follows the verb, the second object is a thing, and follows the preposition:

I **acquainted** *the doctor* **with** *the facts.*

> **put** sthg. **down to** sbdy./sthg. *v adv prep* [T] to state that (something) is caused by

this means that the phrasal verb has two objects; a thing that follows the verb, and a person or a thing that follows **to** (not the adverb **down**):

I **put** *his mistake* **down to** *his bad memory.*
I **put** *all the trouble* **down to** *Anne.*

remove, usu. with the fingers or a pointed instrument, esp. separately or bit by bit: *picking the meat from a bone* **4** to remove unwanted pieces from, esp. with a finger or a pointed instrument: *Don't pick your nose!* **5** to make with or as with a pointed instrument (usu. in the phrase **pick a hole/holes in**) **6** *AmE*‖also **pluck**– to play a stringed musical instrument by quickly pulling (the strings): *How fast can you pick the* BANJO? **7** to bring about intentionally (usu. in the phrase **pick a fight/quarrel with someone**) **8** to steal or take from, esp. in small amounts: *It's easy to have your pocket picked in a big crowd.|He's good at picking people's brains.* (=getting people to say what their ideas are, esp. so that he can use them for himself) **9** to unlock (a lock) with any instrument other than a key, esp. secretly and for a bad purpose: *They picked the lock and entered the house.* **10 pick and choose** to choose very carefully, considering each choice for a long time **11 pick holes in** usu. *derog* to find fault with; find the weak points in: *She picked holes in my argument.*

  pick at sthg. *v prep* [T] to eat (a meal) with little effort or interest: *to pick at her food*

  pick sbdy./sthg.↔**off** *v adv* [T] to shoot (people or animals) one by one, by taking careful aim

  pick on sbdy. *v prep* [T] *infml* to choose, esp. for punishment or blame: *Why pick on me?*

  pick sbdy./sthg.↔**out** *v adv* [T] **1** to choose **2** to see clearly among others: *Can you pick out your sister in this crowd?*

  pick sbdy./sthg.↔**over** *v adv* [T] to examine (too) carefully in order to choose the best or remove the unwanted: *You should pick over the beans before you cook them.*

  pick up *v adv* **1** [T] (**pick** sbdy./sthg.↔**up**) to take hold of and lift up: *Pick up the box by the handles.* **2** [T] (**pick** sthg.↔**up**) to gather together; collect: *Please pick up all your toys when you've finished playing.* **3** [I] to improve: *Trade is picking up again.|Mary has been ill, but she's picking up now.* **4** [T] (**pick** sthg.↔**up**) to gain; get: *Where did you pick up that book/your excellent English?* **5** [I;T (=**pick** sthg.↔**up**)] to (cause to) start again: *to pick up (the conversation) where we left off* **6** [T] (**pick** sbdy./sthg.↔**up**) to collect; arrange to go and get: *Pick me up at the hotel.|I'm going to pick up my coat from the cleaner's.* **7** [T] (**pick** sbdy./sthg.↔**up**) to collect in a vehicle **8** [T] (**pick** sbdy.↔**up**) *infml* to become friendly with during a short meeting, usu. with sexual intentions: *I didn't like him; he was just trying to pick me up.* **9** [T] (**pick** sbdy.↔**up**) to catch (a criminal): *The bank robbers have been picked up at the airport.* **10** [T] (**pick** sthg.↔**up**) to be able to hear or receive (on a radio): *We picked up signals for help from the burning plane.* **11** [T] (**pick** sthg. **up**) to raise (oneself) after a fall or failure: *Pick yourself up!* –see also PICK-UP

  pick up on sthg. *v adv prep* [T] *infml* to understand: *He didn't pick up on my argument until I had talked for 15 minutes.*

pick² *n* [U] **1** choice: *Which one do you want* –**take your pick!** **2** the best (of many) (esp. in the phrase **the pick of**)

pick³ *n* **1** a sharp pointed, usu. small instrument: *an ice pick| a* TOOTHPICK|*a hair pick* **2** *infml* for PICKAX

pick⁴ also **plectrum**– *n* a small thin piece of wood, plastic, etc. used for playing string instruments such as the GUITAR

pick·ax *AmE*‖**pickaxe** *BrE* /'pɪk-æks/ *n* a large tool with a wooden handle fitted into a curved iron bar with two sharp points, used for breaking up roads, rock, etc.

pick·er /'pɪkər/ *n* a person or instrument that gathers: *The fruit pickers in California have formed a union.*

pick·et¹ /'pɪkɪt/ *n* **1** a person placed at the entrance to a factory, store, etc., to prevent anyone (esp. other workers) from going in during a STRIKE² **2** *infml* for PICKET LINE **3** a strong pointed stick fixed into the ground, esp. used with others to make a fence (**picket fence**) **4** a soldier or group of soldiers with the special job of guarding a camp

picket² *v* [I;T] to surround or guard with or as PICKETS¹ (1): *No coal could be delivered to the factory, because the workers were picketing the gates.*

picket line /'·· ‚·/ *n* a group or line of PICKETS¹ (1)

pick·le¹ /'pɪkəl/ *n* **1** [U] a liquid (esp. VINEGAR or salt water) used to preserve meat or esp. vegetables **2** [C;U] a (piece or pieces of) vegetable, esp. CUCUMBER, preserved in this **3 in a pickle** *infml* in a difficult position or condition

pickle² *v* **-led**, **-ling** [T] to preserve (food) in PICKLE¹ (1)

pick·led /'pɪkəld/ *adj* **1** (of food) which has been PICKLED²: *pickled onions* **2** [F] *infml* drunk

pick-me-up /'·· ‚·/ *n infml* something, esp. a drink or a medicine, that makes one feel stronger and more cheerful

pick·pock·et /'pɪk‚pɑkɪt/ *n* a person who steals things from people's pockets, esp. in a crowd –see THIEF (USAGE)

pick-up /'· ·/ *n* **1** an act of PICKING **up 2** the part of a record-player which receives and plays the sound from a record **3** a light truck having an open body with low sides –see illustration on page 95

pick·y /'pɪkiʸ/ *adj* **-ier**, **-iest** *esp. AmE derog* careful in choosing; hard to please: *She's a very picky eater.|Don't be so picky.*

pic·nic¹ /'pɪknɪk/ *n* **1** a pleasure trip in which (cold) food is taken to be eaten somewhere outdoors: *They went on/for a picnic in the country.* **2** *infml* (usu. in NEGATIVEs) something especially easy or pleasant to do: *It's no picnic riding the train to work every day.*

picnic² *v* **-ck-** [I] to go on or have a PICNIC¹

pic·to·ri·al /pɪk'tɔriʸəl, -'toʷr-/ *adj* having, or expressed in, PICTURES¹ (1) –**pictorially** *adv*

pic·ture¹ /'pɪktʃər/ *n* **1** [C] a painting or drawing: *Draw a picture of that tree.* **2** [C] a photograph: *May I take your picture?* (=a picture of you) **3** [S] a person or thing that is beautiful to look at: *This garden is a picture in the* summer. **4** [S] the perfect example: *That baby is* **the picture of** *health.* **5** [C *usu. sing.*] what is seen on a television set or at the movies: *You can't get a clear picture on this set.* **6** [C] a movie: *There's a good picture being shown this week.* –see PICTURES **7** [C *usu. sing.*] an image in the mind, esp. an exact one produced by a skillful description: *This book gives a good picture of life in England 200 years ago.* **8 get the picture** *infml* to understand **9 in/out of the picture** *infml* in/not in the position of knowing all the facts: *I've been away for two months, so I'm not really in the picture.*

picture² *-tured, -turing* [T] **1** to imagine: *I can't quite picture myself as a mother.* **2** to paint or draw so as to give an idea of: *The artist has pictured him as a young man.*

pic·tures /ˈpɪktʃərz/ *n* [*the* P] *infml esp. BrE* for MOVIES

pic·tur·esque /ˌpɪktʃəˈrɛsk/ *adj* **1** charming or interesting enough to be made into a picture **2** (of language) unusually clear, strong, and descriptive

pid·dling /ˈpɪdlɪŋ/ *adj derog* small and unimportant

pidg·in /ˈpɪdʒən/ *n* [C;U] a language which is a mixture of two or more other languages, esp. as used between people who do not speak each other's languages

pie /paɪ/ *n* [C;U] **1** a pastry case filled with meat or fruit, baked usu. in a deep dish (**pie dish**): *an apple pie* |*a meat pie* |*Have some more pie.* **2** (**as**) **easy as pie** *infml* very easy **3 have a finger in every pie** to concern oneself with or be connected with different matters **4 pie in the sky** *infml* a hopeful plan or suggestion that has not been, or has little chance of being, put into effect

pie·bald /ˈpaɪbɔld/ *adj,n* (a horse) colored with large black and white shapes (PATCHES (2))

piece /piːs/ *n* **1** a bit, such as: **a** a part (of anything solid) which is separated, broken, or marked off from a larger or whole body: *a piece of land* |*He tore off a small piece of paper.* |(fig.) *Let me give off a small piece of paper.* (fig.) *Let me give you a piece of advice.* **b** a single object that is an example of a kind or class, or that forms part of a set: *a piece of paper* (=a whole sheet) |*a piece of furniture* **2 a** any of many parts made to be fitted together: *I bought this table in pieces, but one piece is missing.* **b** an object or person forming part of a set: *an 80-piece band* (=one with 80 players or instruments) **3** one of a set of small objects or figures used in playing certain board games, esp. CHESS **4** an example of something made or done, esp. of a stated quality: *This watch is a fine piece of work.* |*a quiet piece of music* |*Did you see the piece in the newspaper about Mrs. Smith's accident?* **5** a coin: *a 50-cent piece* **6 a piece of cake** *infml* something very easy to do **7 give somebody a piece of one's mind** to tell somebody angrily what one thinks of him/her; scold somebody severely **8 in one piece** *infml* **a** (of a thing) undamaged; still whole **b** (of a person) unharmed, esp. after

an accident **9 piece by piece** one by one; one part at a time

piece sthg.↔**together** *v adv* **pieced, piecing** [T] **1** to make (esp. a story) complete by adding part to part: *The policeman tried to piece together the facts.* **2** to put together (the separate parts of)

pi·èce de ré·sis·tance /piˈ(y)ɛs də rɪˌzi(y)ˈstɑns, -re(y)-, ˌpyɛs də ˌre(y)ziˈ(y)ˈstɑs/ *n* **pièces de résistance** (*same pronunciation*) *French* the best or most important thing or event, among a number of things or events

piece·meal /ˈpiˈ(y)smiˈ(y)l/ *adj,adv* (done, made, etc.) only one part at a time: *We used to do the work piecemeal, but now we do everything in one operation.*

piec·es /ˈpiˈ(y)sɪz/ *n* **1 go** (**all**) **to pieces** to lose the ability to think or act clearly because of fear, sorrow, etc. **2 in pieces** broken; destroyed **3 pull to pieces** to show to be ineffective: *She pulled their argument to pieces.* **4 take to pieces** to (cause to) separate into parts: *Take this engine to pieces and see what's wrong with it.* **5 to pieces** into (small) bits: *It fell to pieces in my hand.* |(fig.) *Sam went to pieces when he heard the bad news.*

piece·work /ˈpiˈ(y)swɜrk/ *n* [U] work paid for by the amount done rather than by the hours worked

pied /paɪd/ *adj* [A] (esp. of certain types of bird) irregularly colored with two or more colors

pier /pɪər/ *n* **1** a bridgelike framework built out into the sea at which boats can stop to take in or land their passengers or goods **2** a framework like this at places where people go for vacations, with small buildings on it where people can eat and amuse themselves **3** a pillar used to support a bridge or the roof of a high building

pierce /pɪərs/ *v* **pierced, piercing** [I;T] **1** to make a hole in or through (something) with a point: *The needle pierced her finger.* |*He pierced the rubber ball with a knife.* **2** to force or make (a way) into or through (something): *We pierced our way through the thick forest.* |(fig.) *A sudden cry pierced the silence.*

pierc·ing /ˈpɪərsɪŋ/ *adj* **1** very sharp, esp. in an unpleasant way: *a piercing cry* |*a piercing wind* **2** going to the center or the main point; searching: *a piercing look* –**piercingly** *adv*

pi·e·ty /ˈpaɪətiˈ(y)/ *n* [U] deep respect for God and religion –opposite **impiety**

pig /pɪg/ *n* **1** a fat, usu. pink, short-legged animal kept on farms for food –see MEAT (USAGE) **2** *derog* an ill-mannered person who eats too much: *John really* **made a pig of himself** *at the party.*

pi·geon /ˈpɪdʒən/ *n* **pigeons** or **pigeon** (the meat of) a quite large light-gray short-legged bird

pi·geon·hole¹ /ˈpɪdʒənˌhoʷl/ *n* one of a set of boxlike divisions in a frame (e.g. on a wall or on top of a desk) for putting esp. papers in: *There's a letter in your pigeonhole.*

pigeonhole² *v* **-holed, -holing** [T] *infml* to separate (someone or something) in one's mind as belonging to a particular group or class

pigeon-toed /'·· ,·/ *adj* (of a person) having the feet pointing inwards

pig·gy·back /'pɪgyˌbæk/ *adj,adv,n* (a ride given to a child who is) carried in a sitting position on one's back

pig·gy bank /'·· ,·/ *n* a small container, usu. in the shape of a pig, used by children for saving coins

pig·head·ed /'pɪgˌhɛdɪd/ *adj derog* determinedly holding to an opinion or course of action in spite of argument, reason, etc.; STUBBORN –**pigheadedly** *adv* –**pigheadedness** *n* [U]

pig·let /'pɪglɪt/ *n* a young pig

pig·ment /'pɪgmənt/ *n* **1** [C;U] (a) coloring matter that is mixed with oil, water, etc., to make paint **2** [U] natural coloring matter of plants and animals, as in leaves, hair, skin, etc.

pig·men·ta·tion /ˌpɪgmən'teyʃən/ *n* [U] the coloring of living things

pig·my /'pɪgmiy/ *n* →PYGMY

pig·sty /'pɪgstaɪ/ also **pigpen** /'pɪgpɛn/ *AmE– n* -**sties 1** also **sty–** an enclosure with a small building in it, where pigs are kept **2** *infml* a very dirty room or house

pig·tail /'pɪgteyl/ *n* (worn esp. by young girls) a length of hair that has been twisted together (BRAIDED) and hangs down the back of the neck and shoulders –compare PONYTAIL

pike¹ /paɪk/ *n* **pike** *or* **pikes** a large fish-eating fish that lives in rivers and lakes

pike² *n AmE infml for* TURNPIKE

pike³ *n* a long-handled spear formerly used by soldiers fighting on foot

pil·chard /'pɪltʃərd/ *n* a small sea fish like the HERRING, often preserved in cans as food

pile¹ /paɪl/ *n* **1** a heap, esp. as made of a number of things of the same kind placed on top of each other: *We put the newspapers in piles on the floor.* **2** [*usu. pl.*] *infml* a lot: *I've got piles of work to do today.* **3** [*usu. sing.*] *infml* a very large amount of money; fortune: *She made a pile from her books, so she doesn't need to work now.*

pile² *v* **piled, piling 1** [T] to make a PILE¹ (1) of: *He piled the boxes one on top of the other.* **2** [T] to load, fill, or cover: *The cart was piled high with fruit.* **3** [I *in(to)*, *out* (*of*)] *infml* (of people) to come or go in a (disorderly) crowd: *We opened the doors, and they all piled in.*

    pile up *v adv* [I;T (**pile** sthg.↔**up**)] to (cause to) form into a mass or large quantity: *We piled up the boxes outside the house.|My work is piling up.* –see also PILEUP

pile³ *n* a heavy wooden, metal, or stonelike (CONCRETE (2)) post hammered upright into the ground as a support for a building, a bridge, etc.

pile⁴ *n* [C;U] the soft surface of short threads on floor coverings (CARPETS) and some cloths (esp. VELVET)

pile driv·er /'·· ,··/ *n* a machine for hammering PILES³ into the ground

piles /paɪlz/ *n* [P] *infml for* HEMORRHOIDS

pile-up /'paɪlʌp/ *n infml* a traffic accident in which a number of vehicles crash into each other –see also PILE **up**

pil·fer /'pɪlfər/ *v* [I;T] to steal (something small or a lot of small things): *a boy found pilfering from other children's desks* –**pilferer** *n*

pil·grim /'pɪlgrəm/ *n* a person who travels (esp. a long way) to a holy place as an act of religious love and respect

pil·grim·age /'pɪlgrəmɪdʒ/ *n* [C;U] (a) journey made by a PILGRIM: *Aziz is planning to* **go on/make a pilgrimage** *to Mecca.* –see TRAVEL (USAGE)

pill /pɪl/ *n* **1** [C] a small ball of solid medicine, made to be swallowed whole **2** [*the* S] (*often cap.*) a PILL (1) taken regularly by women as a means of birth control: *The doctor asked her if she was* **on the pill.** (=taking it regularly)

pil·lage¹ /'pɪlɪdʒ/ *n* [U] *old use* the act of pillaging (PILLAGE²); PLUNDER

pillage² *v* **-laged, -laging** [T] *old use* to steal things violently from (a place taken in war); PLUNDER

pil·lar /'pɪlər/ *n* **1** a tall upright usu. round post made of stone used as a support or ornament **2** [*of*] something in the shape of this: *a pillar of smoke* **3** an important member and active supporter: *She has been a pillar of the church all her life.*

pillar-box /'·· ,·/ also **postbox–** *n BrE* a round pillar-shaped box in the street, into which letters are mailed –see also LETTERBOX; MAILBOX

pil·lion /'pɪlyən/ *n* a seat for a second person on a motorcycle, placed behind the driver: *a pillion passenger*

pil·low /'pɪlow/ *n* a cloth bag longer than it is wide, filled with soft material, used for supporting the head in bed –see illustration on page 55

pil·low·case /'pɪlowˌkeys/ also **pillow slip** /'·· ,·/– *n* a washable cloth covering for a PILLOW

pi·lot¹ /'paɪlət/ *n* **1** a person who flies an aircraft **2** a person with a special knowledge of a particular stretch of water, who is employed to go on board and guide ships that use it

pilot² *v* [T] **1** to act as PILOT¹ of (an aircraft or ship) **2** to help and guide: *She piloted the old man through the crowd to his seat.*

pilot³ *adj* [A] serving as a trial for something: *We're doing a pilot study to see if this product will sell well, and if it does we will go into full production.*

pilot light /'·· ,·/ *n* a small gas flame kept burning all the time, used for lighting larger gas burners when the gas in them is turned on

pimp /pɪmp/ *n* a man who provides a woman (PROSTITUTE) for the satisfying of someone's sexual desires

pim·ple /'pɪmpəl/ *n* a small raised diseased spot on the skin –**pimply** *adj: pimply skin*

pin¹ /pɪn/ *n* **1** a short thin piece of metal that looks like a small nail, used for fastening together pieces of cloth, paper, etc. **2** a thin piece of metal, pointed at one end and with an ornament at the other, used esp. as a form of jewelry **3** a short piece of wood or metal used as a support, for fastening things together, etc.; PEG

pin² v -nn- [T] **1** to fasten or join with a pin or pins –opposite **unpin 2** to keep in one position: *In the accident, he was pinned under the car.*

  pin sbdy./sthg.↔**down** v adv [T] **1** to fasten down; prevent from moving **2** to make (someone) give clear details, make a firm decision, etc.; NAIL down: *I won't pin you down to a particular time: come any day next week.*

  pin sthg. **on** sbdy./sthg. v prep [T] to fix (guilt, etc.) on: *Don't try to pin the blame on me!*

pin·a·fore /'pɪnə,fɔr, -,foʷr/ n a loose garment that does not cover the arms or back, worn over a dress to keep it clean

pin·cers /'pɪnsərz, -tʃərz/ n [P] **1** a tool made of two crossed pieces of metal and used for holding tightly and pulling small things, such as a nail from wood –compare PLIERS; see PAIR¹ (USAGE) **2** the horny CLAWS of certain shellfish, used for seizing food

pinch¹ /pɪntʃ/ v **1** [I;T] to press (esp. a person's flesh) tightly between two hard surfaces, or between the thumb and a finger, accidentally or on purpose: *He pinched her arm.* **2** [I] to give pain by being too tight: *Don't buy the shoes if they pinch.* **3** [T] *infml* to take without permission; steal: *Somebody's pinched my bicycle!*

pinch² n **1** an act of PINCHING¹ (1) **2** an amount that can be picked up between the thumb and a finger: *a pinch of salt* **3** **in a pinch** *AmE*‖**at a pinch** *BrE*– if necessary **4** feel the **pinch** to be in difficulties because of lack of money

pinched /pɪntʃt/ adj [F *with*] (of the face) thin or tired-looking: *pinched with cold/ anxiety/poverty*

pin·cush·ion /'pɪn,kuʃən/ n a filled bag like a small CUSHION into which PINS¹ (1) are stuck until they are needed

pine¹ /paɪn/ v **pined, pining** [I] **1** [*away*] to become thin and lose strength and health slowly, through disease or esp. grief **2** [+*to-v/for*] to have a strong but esp. unfulfillable desire

pine² n **1** [C] also **pinetree** /'·· ·/– a tall tree with thin sharp leaves (**pine needles**) that do not drop off in winter and woody fruits (**pine cones**), found esp. in colder parts of the world **2** [U] the white or yellowish soft wood of this tree

pine·ap·ple /'paɪn,æpəl/ n [C;U] (the sweet yellow flesh of) a large dark yellow tropical fruit with a mass of stiff leaves on top: *canned pineapple*

ping /pɪŋ/ v,n [I;S] (to make) a short sharp ringing sound, e.g. by hitting a glass with something hard

ping-pong /'pɪŋpɑŋ, -pɔŋ/ n [U] *infml* for TABLE TENNIS

pin·ion /'pɪnyən/ v [T] *fml* to prevent the movement of (a person or animal) by holding or tying up the limbs: *Two of them pinioned me to the wall, while a third searched my pockets.*

pink /pɪŋk/ n,adj [U] **1** pale red **2** → ROSE **3 in the pink (of condition/health)** *usu. humor* in perfect health; very well

pink·ie, -y /'pɪŋkiʸ/ n -ies *AmE infml* the last and smallest finger of the human hand

pink·ish /'pɪŋkɪʃ/ adj slightly PINK

pin mon·ey /'·· ,··/ n *infml* [U] a small amount of money that is earned, esp. by doing small jobs

pin·na·cle /'pɪnəkəl/ n **1** a pointed stone decoration built on a roof, esp. in old churches and castles **2** a thin tall pointed rock or rocky mountain top **3** the highest point or degree: *the pinnacle of one's success*

pin·point /'pɪnpɔɪnt/ v [T] **1** to find or describe the exact nature or cause of **2** to show the exact position of

pin·prick /'pɪn,prɪk/ n a small mark made (as if) by a pin

pins and nee·dles /,· · '··/ n [P] *infml* **1** slight continuous pricking feelings in a part of the body (esp. a limb) to which the supply of blood is returning **2 on pins and needles** nervous

pin·stripe /'pɪnstraɪp/ n any of a number of thin (usu. white) lines repeated at regular spaces along (usu. dark) cloth to form a pattern: *Some businessmen wear pinstripe suits.* –**pinstriped** adj

pint /paɪnt/ n **1** a measure for liquids, equal to about 0.57 of a liter; half a QUART **2** *BrE infml* a drink of beer of this amount

pin-up /'pɪnʌp/ n a picture of an attractive person, such as a popular singer, a person wearing no clothes, etc., esp. as stuck up on a wall

pi·o·neer¹ /,paɪə'nɪər/ n **1** one of the first settlers in a new or unknown land **2** a person who does something first and so prepares the way for others: *a pioneer of operations on the human heart*

pioneer² v [T] to begin or help in the early development of

pi·ous /'paɪəs/ adj showing and feeling deep respect for God and religion –opposite **impious** –**piously** adv

pip /pɪp/ n a small fruit seed, esp. of an apple, orange, etc.

pipe¹ /paɪp/ n **1** a tube used for carrying liquids and gas: *a gas pipe*‖*a hot-water pipe* **2** a small tube with a bowl-like container at one end, used for smoking tobacco: *He lit his pipe.* **3 a** a simple tubelike musical instrument, played by blowing **b** any of the tubelike metal parts through which air is forced in an ORGAN (3)

pipe² v **piped, piping 1** [T *into, to*] to carry (esp. liquid or gas) through PIPES¹ (1) **2** [I;T] to play (music) on a PIPE¹ (3a) or on BAGPIPES

  pipe down v adv [I] *infml* to stop talking; be quiet

  pipe up v adv [I] *infml* to begin to speak or sing, esp. in a high voice

pipe dream /'· ·/ n an impossible hope, plan, idea, etc.

pipe·line /'paɪp-laɪn/ n **1** a long line of PIPES¹ (1), often underground, for carrying liquids or gas **2 in the pipeline** on the way

pip·er /'paɪpər/ n a musician who plays on a

PIPE[1] (3a), or esp. on BAGPIPES

pipes /paɪps/ *n* [P] *infml* for BAGPIPES

pip·ing[1] /ˈpaɪpɪŋ/ *n* [U] **1** a number or system of PIPES[1] (1); pipes in general: *The piping outside the house needs painting.* **2** the act or art of playing on a PIPE[1] (3a) or BAGPIPES

piping[2] *adv* **piping hot** (esp. of liquids or food) very hot: *piping hot soup*

pi·quant /ˈpiːᵏkənt, ˈpiːᵏkɑnt, piːᵏˈkɑnt/ *adj fml* **1** having a pleasant sharp taste **2** pleasantly interesting and exciting to the mind –**piquancy** /ˈpiːᵏkənsiᵞ/ *n* [U] –**piquantly** /ˈpiːᵏkɑntliᵞ, -kɑnt-, piːᵞˈkɑnt-/ *adv*

pique[1] /piːᵏk/ *n* [U] a feeling of displeasure, esp. caused by the hurting of one's pride: *He left* **in a fit of pique.**

pique[2] *v* **piqued, piquing** [T *usu. pass.*] to make angry by hurting the pride

pi·ra·cy /ˈpaɪrəsiᵞ/ *n* [U] **1** robbery by PIRATES[1] (1) **2** the action of pirating (PIRATE)

pi·ra·nha /pɪˈrɑnyə, -ˈræn-, -ˈrɑnə/ *n* a fierce South American meat-eating river fish

pi·rate[1] /ˈpaɪrɪt/ *n* **1** (esp. formerly) a person who sails the seas stopping and robbing ships **2** a person who uses the work of other people without official permission, e.g. one who prints and sells a book without the writer's permission to do so –**piratical** /paɪˈrætɪkəl/ *adj*

pirate[2] *v* **-rated, -rating** [T] to make and sell (a book, newly invented article, etc.) without permission, when the right to do so belongs to someone else

pir·ou·ette[1] /ˌpɪruːˈɛt/ *n* a very fast turn made on the front part of one foot, esp. as done by a BALLET dancer

pirouette[2] *v* **-etted, -etting** [I] to dance one or more PIROUETTES[1]

Pis·ces /ˈpaɪsiᵞz/ *n* -ces see ZODIAC

piss[1] /pɪs/ *v* [I] *taboo* for URINATE

piss[2] *n* [U] *taboo* for URINE

pis·ta·chi·o /pɪˈstæʃiᵞˌoᵂ, -ˈstɑ-/ *n* **-os** a small green nut, used as food

pis·tol /ˈpɪstl/ *n* a small gun held and fired in one hand

pis·ton /ˈpɪstən/ *n* (in pumps and engines) a solid pipe-shaped piece of metal that fits tightly into a tube (CYLINDER (2)) in which it moves up and down by pressure or explosion, and so gives movement to other parts of the machine

pit[1] /pɪt/ *n* **1** a large natural or man-made hole in the ground: *The children were playing in the sandpit.* **2** a deep hole dug in the ground to get materials, esp. coal, out: *He worked all his life down in the pit.* **3** [*usu. pl.*] (in motor racing) a place beside a track where cars can come during a race to be quickly examined and repaired **4** a natural hollow in the surface of a living thing (esp. in the phrase **pit of the stomach** =the hollow place just below the bones of the chest, esp. thought of as being the place where fear is felt) –see also ARMPIT **5** [*usu. pl.*] a small hollow mark or place in the surface of something, esp. as left on the face after certain diseases, esp. SMALLPOX **6** [*usu. sing.*] (the people sitting in) the seats at the back of the ground floor of a theater, behind the

ORCHESTRA (2) **7** also **orchestra pit**– the space below and in front of a theater stage where musicians sit and play during a (musical) play

pit[2] *v* **-tt-** [T] to mark with PITS[1] (5): *a pitted face*

pit[3] *AmE*‖also **stone** esp. *BrE*– *n* the hard central part of certain types of fruit

pit[4] *AmE*‖also **stone** esp. *BrE*– *v* **-tt-** [T] to take the seeds or PITS out of (fruit): *Please pit these peaches for me.*

pit sbdy./sthg. **a·gainst** sbdy./sthg. *v prep* [T] to match or set against, in a fight, competition, struggle, etc.: *He's pitting his strength against that of a man twice his size.*

pitch[1] /pɪtʃ/ *v* **1** [I;T] to set up (a tent, camp, etc.) in position on open ground, esp. for a certain time only –opposite **strike 2** [I;T] (in the game of BASEBALL) **a** to aim and throw (a ball): (fig.) *We pitched those noisy people out (of the club).* **b** to be a PITCHER[2] **3** [T] to set the degree of highness or lowness of (a sound, music, etc.) **4** [T] to give a particular feeling or expression to (something said or written): *He pitched his speech at a very simple level so that even the children could understand.* **5** [I;T] to (cause to) fall heavily or suddenly forwards or outwards: *His foot caught in a rock, and he pitched forwards.* **6** [I] (of a ship or aircraft) to move along with the back and front going up and down independently –compare ROLL (6)

pitch in *v adv* [I] *infml* to start to work or eat eagerly

pitch[2] *n* **1** [C] the degree of highness or lowness of a musical note or speaking voice **2** [S] a degree; level: *The children were at a high pitch of excitement before the holiday.* **3** [C;S;U] (esp. in building) amount or degree of slope: *the pitch of the roof* **4** [S] (of a ship or aircraft) a backward and forward movement; the action of PITCHING[1] (6) –compare ROLL[1] (4) **5** [C] (in BASEBALL) the way or act of PITCHING[1] (2a) a ball **6** [C] *infml* a salesman's special way of talking about the goods he is trying to sell: *He has a very good* **sales pitch.**

pitch[3] *n* [U] a black substance that is melted into a sticky material used for making hard protective coverings, or for putting between cracks (esp. in a ship) to stop water coming through

pitch-black /ˌ· ˈ· ◄/ also **pitch-dark**– *adj* very dark; difficult to see in –**pitch-blackness** *n* [U]

pitch·er[1] /ˈpɪtʃər/ *n* a large container for holding liquids with a handle and a lip for pouring

pitcher[2] *n* (in BASEBALL) a player who throws the ball towards the person who is BATTING

pitch·fork /ˈpɪtʃfɔrk/ *n* a long-handled farm tool with two or three curved metal points at one end, used esp. in lifting dried cut grass (HAY)

pit·e·ous /ˈpɪtiᵞəs/ *adj* causing or intended to cause pity: *The hungry dog gave a piteous cry.* –**piteously** *adv*

pit·fall /ˈpɪtfɔl/ *n* an unexpected danger or difficulty; mistake that may easily be made:

There are many pitfalls in English spelling for foreign students.

pith /pɪθ/ *n* [U] **1** a soft white substance that fills the stems of certain plants and trees **2** a white material just under the skin of oranges and other fruit of the same type

pith·y /ˈpɪθiʸ/ *adj* **-ier, -iest 1** of, like, or having much PITH (1,2) **2** (of something said or written) strongly stated without wasting any words **–pithily** *adv* **–pithiness** *n* [U]

pit·i·a·ble /ˈpɪtiʸəbəl/ *adj* worthy of pity **–pitiably** *adv*

pit·i·ful /ˈpɪtɪfəl/ *adj* **1** causing or deserving pity: *The poor old man was a pitiful sight.* **2** *derog* not worthy or deserving respect; worthless: *my pitiful attempts to play the piano* **–pitifully** *adv*

pit·i·less /ˈpɪtɪlɪs/ *adj* showing no pity; merciless; severe: *a pitiless ruler who made all his people suffer*|(fig.) *a cold and pitiless wind blowing from the north* **–pitilessly** *adv* **–pitilessness** *n* [U]

pit·tance /ˈpɪtns/ *n* [*usu. sing.*] a very small ungenerous amount of pay

pit·ter-pat·ter /ˈpɪtər ˌpætər, ˌpɪtər ˈpætər/ *adv,adj,n* [*the* S] (making or having) the sound or movement of a number of quick light beats or steps: *the pitter-patter of little feet*|*My heart went pitter-patter with fear.*

pit·y[1] /ˈpɪtiʸ/ *n* **1** [U] sensitiveness to and sorrow for the suffering or unhappiness of others: *Don't help me* **out of pity**, *but only if you think I deserve it.* **2** [S] a sad or inconvenient state of affairs: *What a pity you won't be back before I leave!* **3 have/take pity on (someone)** to help (someone) as a result of feeling PITY[1] (1)

pity[2] *v* **-ied, -ying** [T] **1** to feel PITY[1] (1) for **2** *derog* to consider to be PITIFUL (2): *I pity you if you can't answer such a simple question!*

piv·ot[1] /ˈpɪvət/ *n* a fixed central point or pin on which something turns **–pivotal** *adj*

pivot[2] *v* [I *on*] to turn around on or as if on a PIVOT[1]: (fig.) *The whole war pivoted on* (=depended on) *a single battle.*

pix·ie, pixy /ˈpɪksiʸ/ *n* **-ies** a small fairy believed to like playing tricks on people

piz·za /ˈpiʸtsə/ *n* [C;U] a flat usu. round piece of bread DOUGH or pastry baked with a mixture of cheese, TOMATOES, etc., on top

pl. *written abbrev. said as:* plural

plac·ard /ˈplækɑrd, -kərd/ *n* a large printed or written notice or advertisement

pla·cate /ˈpleʸkeʸt, ˈplæ-/ *v* **-cated, -cating** [T] to cause to stop feeling angry **–placatory** /ˈpleʸkəˌtɔriʸ, -ˌtoʷriʸ, ˈplæ-/ *adj*: *His placatory words had little effect on the angry travelers.* –see also IMPLACABLE

place[1] /pleʸs/ *n* **1** [C] a particular part of space or position in space: *This is the place where the accident happened.*|*I think this is the best place to put the clock.*|(fig.) *Sports never had a place in his life.* (=was not important to him) **2** [C] a particular spot or area on a surface: *I've got a sore place in the middle of my back.* **3** [C] a particular part of the earth's surface, town, etc.: *Moscow is a very cold place in winter.* **4** [C] a proper or usual position or occasion: *Put it back in its*

place.|*A business meeting isn't the place in which to talk about private affairs.*|*Electric trains have* **taken the place of** (=are used instead of) *steam trains.* **5** [C] a building, room, or piece of land used for a stated purpose: *parks and other places of amusement*|*a marketplace* **6** [C] a position in relation to a set of other things: *She finished in second place in the race.* (=was the second to finish)|*Please* **keep my place** *in the line* (=line of waiting people) *until I come back.*|*I've lost my place in my book.* (=I can't find the page that I was reading) **7** [C] the position of a figure in a row of figures, to the right of a decimal point: *1.222 is written to three decimal places.* **8** [*the* S] a numbered point in an argument, explanation, etc.: **In the first place** *I don't want to go, and* **in the second place** *I can't afford to.* **9** a seat: *There were a lot of empty places in church today.* **10** [C *usu. sing.*] a position of employment, in a team, etc.: *a place on the football team* **11** [C] social position; rank: *The Senator said that there was* CORRUPTION *in high places.* (=among people of high rank and influence)|*That remark really* **put** *him* **in his place.** (=reminded him that he is not as important as he would like to be) **12** [S] duty; what one should or must do: *It's not your place to tell me what to do.* **13** [C] *infml* a house; home: *Come over to my place tomorrow.* **14 all over the place** *infml* **a** everywhere **b** in disorder: *She left her books spread all over the place.* **15 go places** *infml* to be increasingly successful: *He's really going places in his new job.* **16 in/out of place: a** in/not in the proper position **b** suitable/unsuitable **17 in place of** instead of **18 take place** to happen: *When did this conversation take place?* –see HAPPEN (USAGE)

USAGE **Room** [U] and **place** [C] both mean free space that can be used for a purpose; but **place** is used for a single particular piece of space, while **room** means space in general: *"Is there any* **room** *for me to sit down in here?" "Yes, there's a* **place** *in the corner."*|*This is the* **place** *where we keep the food.*|*There's no* **room** *for any more coal in here.*

place[2] *v* **placed, placing** [T] **1** to put in a certain position: *He placed the book on the shelf.*|(fig.) *You place me in a very difficult position.*|(fig.) *I place a great deal of importance on correct grammar.* (=consider it to be very important)|(fig.) *I would place her among the best singers in the country.* **2** to pass to a person, company, etc., who can do the needed action: *I* **placed an order** *with them for 500 pairs of shoes.* **3** [*usu. pass.*] to declare officially that (a runner) has finished a race in the stated position: *My horse was placed second.* **4** to remember fully the name of, or where one last saw or heard, someone or something: *I can remember your face, but I can't place where we met.*

pla·ce·bo /pləˈsiʸboʷ/ *n* **-bos** *or* **-boes** a substance given instead of real medicine, as to a person who only imagines that he/she is ill

place·ment of·fice /ˈpleʸsmənt ˌɔfɪs, -ˌɑfɪs/ *n*

an office in a college or university that helps its students find jobs, esp. students who have GRADUATEd

placement test /'·· ,·/ *n* a test usu. taken at the beginning of a course used to divide a large number of students into different classes: *Have you taken the English placement test yet?*

plac·id /'plæsɪd/ *adj* **1** (of people or animals) quiet; not easily angered or excited **2** (of things) calm; peaceful: *the placid surface of the lake* –**placidly** *adv*

pla·gia·rism /'pleʸdʒə‚rɪzəm/ *n* **1** [U] the action of plagiarizing (PLAGIARIZE) **2** an idea, story, etc., that is PLAGIARIZED –**plagiarist** *n*

pla·gia·rize *AmE*‖also **-rise** *BrE* /'pleʸdʒə‚raɪz/ *v* **-rized, -rizing** [I;T] to take (words, ideas, etc.) from someone else's work and use as one's own without admitting one has done so

plague¹ /pleʸg/ *n* **1** [C; *the* S;U] a quick-spreading quick-killing disease, esp. a particular one that produces high fever and swellings on the body **2** [C] a widespread, uncontrollable, and harmful mass or number of something: *a plague of rats*

plague² *v* **plagued, plaguing** [T] to annoy by doing some repeated action: *You've been plaguing me with silly questions all day!*

plaid /plæd/ *n* [C;U] (a long piece of) woolen cloth, often with a special colored pattern (TARTAN) as worn over the shoulder by Scottish people

plain¹ /pleʸn/ *n* a large stretch of flat land: *the Great Plains of the US*

plain² *adj* **1** clear; easy to see, hear, or understand: *It's quite plain that you don't agree.|Explain it in plain language.* **2** simple; without decoration or pattern: *plain food|plain paper* (=without lines) **3** *euph* not pretty or good-looking; rather ugly –see BEAUTIFUL (USAGE) **4** (of a person or what he/she says) direct and honest; expressing exactly what is meant; FRANK¹ –**plainness** *n* [U]

plain³ *n* [U] *tech* a simple stitch in KNITTING

plain-clothes /‚· '··◄/ *adj* (of a policeman) wearing ordinary clothes while on duty, rather than a uniform

plain·ly /'pleʸnliʸ/ *adv* in a PLAIN² (1,2,4) manner; as is plain: *The door's locked, so plainly they must be out.*

plain sail·ing /‚· '··/ *n* [U] a course of action that is simple and free from trouble

plain·spo·ken /‚pleʸn'spoʷkən◄/ *adj* direct in the use of words, often in a rude way

plain·tiff /'pleʸntɪf/ *n law* a person who brings a charge against somebody (DEFENDANT) in court

plain·tive /'pleʸntɪv/ *adj* **1** expressing suffering and a desire for pity: *the plaintive cries of the child locked in the room* **2** expressing gentle sadness: *a plaintive old song* –**plaintively** *adv* –**plaintiveness** *n* [U]

plait /pleʸt, plæt/ *n,v BrE* for BRAID

plan¹ /plæn/ *n* **1** a (carefully considered) arrangement for carrying out some future activity: *Have you made any plans for tomorrow night?* **2** a line drawing (often one

of a set) showing something (such as a building, room, or piece of machinery) as it might be seen from above: *a street-plan of Chicago|Have you seen the plans for the new library|*SUBMARINE¹ (1)? –compare ELEVATION (3), SECTION¹ (2) **3 go according to plan** to happen as planned, without any difficulties

plan² *v* **-nn-** **1** [I;T +*to-v/for,on,ahead*] to make a plan for (something): *We've been planning this visit for months.|She never plans (ahead); she doesn't like too much organization.|I'd planned on doing/I'd planned to do some work this afternoon.|Where do you plan to spend your vacation?* **2** [T] to make drawings, models, or other representations of (something to be built or made)

plane¹ /pleʸn/ *n* a tool with a blade that takes very thin pieces off wooden surfaces to make them smooth

plane² *v* **planed, planing** [I;T] to use a PLANE¹ on (something)

plane³ *n* **1** (in GEOMETRY) a flat or level surface **2** a level; standard: *Let's keep the conversation on a friendly plane.* **3** *infml* for AIRPLANE

plan·et /'plænɪt/ *n* a large body in space that moves around a star, esp. around the sun: *The Earth is a planet.* –**planetary** /'plænə‚teriʸ/ *adj* [A]: *planetary movements*

plan·e·tar·i·um /‚plænə'tɛəriʸəm/ *n* **-iums** or **-ia** /iʸə/ a building containing an apparatus that throws spots of light onto the inside of a curved roof to show an image of the movements of planets and stars

plane tree /'· ·/ also **plane**– *n* a broad-leaved wide-spreading tree that commonly grows in towns

plank¹ /plæŋk/ *n* **1** a long, usu. heavy, flat narrow piece of wood: *a plank bridge across a stream* **2** a main principle of a political party's stated group of aims: *One of the planks of the party's election* CAMPAIGN *is fighting unemployment.*

plank² *v* [T *with*] to cover with PLANKs¹ (1)

plank·ton /'plæŋktən/ *n* [U] the very small forms of plant and animal life that live in water (esp. the sea) and form the food of many fish

plan·ner /'plænər/ *n* a person who plans, esp. who plans the way in which towns are to develop: *a city planner*

plant¹ /plænt/ *v* **1** [I;T] to put (plants or seeds) in the ground to grow: *April is the time to plant.|*(fig.) *His evil talk planted the seeds of hatred in their hearts.* **2** [T *with*] to supply (a place) with seeds or growing plants: *We're planting a small garden.|The hillside was planted with trees.* **3** [T] to fix or place firmly or with force: *He planted himself in a chair by the fire.* **4** [T *on*] *infml* to hide (esp. stolen goods) on a person so that he/she will seem guilty: *Those drugs aren't mine; the police planted them on me!*

plant² *n* **1** [C] a living thing that has leaves and roots, and grows usu. in earth, esp. the kind smaller than trees: *All plants need water and light.|the plant life of the area |a potato plant* **2** [C] **a** a machine; apparatus: *We have our own small power plant for electricity.* **b** a factory: *They've just built a new chemical plant.*

plan·ta·tion /plæn'teɪʃən/ *n* **1** a large piece of land, esp. in hot countries, on which crops such as tea, sugar, and rubber are grown: *a rubber plantation* **2** a large group of growing trees planted esp. to produce wood

plant·er /'plæntər/ *n* a person who owns or is in charge of a PLANTATION (1): *a cotton planter*

plaque /plæk/ *n* **1** [C] a flat metal or stone plate with writing on it, fixed to a wall in memory of a person or event, or as an ornament **2** [U] *tech* a substance that forms on teeth in the mouth, and in which bacteria live and breed –compare TARTAR (1)

plas·ma /'plæzmə/ *n* [U] the liquid part of blood

plas·ter¹ /'plæstər/ *n* [U] **1** a pastelike mixture of lime, water, sand, etc., which hardens when dry and is used, esp. on walls, to give a smooth surface **2 in plaster** in a PLASTER CAST (2)

plaster² *v* [T] **1** [*over*] to put wet PLASTER¹ (1) on; cover with plaster: *These rough places on the wall could be plastered over.* **2** [*with/on*] to spread (something), perhaps too thickly, on: *They plastered the wall with signs.|They plastered signs on the wall.*

plaster cast /ˌ· '·/ *n* **1** a copy of a stone or metal figure (STATUE) made from PLASTER OF PARIS **2** also **cast–** a case made from PLASTER OF PARIS, placed around a part of the body to protect or support a broken bone

plas·tered /'plæstərd/ *adj* [F] *humor* drunk

plas·ter·er /'plæstərər/ *n* a person whose job is to PLASTER² (1) esp. walls

plaster of Par·is /ˌplæstər əv 'pærɪs/ *n* [U] a quick-drying whitish paste made of a chalklike powder mixed with water, used for PLASTER CASTs, in decorative building work, etc.

plas·tic¹ /'plæstɪk/ *n* [C;U] a light man-made material produced chemically from oil or coal, which can be made into different shapes when soft and keeps its shape when hard: *a plastic spoon|The spoon is plastic.|Plastics are used in many modern articles instead of wood and metal.*

plastic² *adj* **1** (of a substance) easily formed into various shapes by pressing **2** [A] *fml* connected with the art of shaping forms in clay, stone, wood, etc. (esp. in the phrase **the plastic arts**)

plas·tic·i·ty /plæs'tɪsəṭiʸ/ *n* [U] the state or quality of being PLASTIC² (1)

plas·tics /'plæstɪks/ *n* [U] the science of producing PLASTIC¹ materials: *Plastics is an important branch of chemistry.*

plastic sur·ger·y /ˌ·· '···/ *n* [U] the repairing or improving of damaged or badly shaped parts of the body

plate¹ /pleɪt/ *n* **1** [C] **a** a flat, usu. round dish with a slightly raised edge from which food is eaten or served: *a dinner plate|a paper plate* **b** also **plateful** /'pleɪtfʊl/– the amount of food that this will hold: *two plates of meat* –see illustration on page 379 **2** [U] metal articles, usu. made of gold or silver, as used at meals or in services at church: *All the church plate*

has been locked up. **3** [U] common metal with a thin covering of gold or silver: *gold plate|It's only plate, so it's not very valuable.* **4** [*the* S] **a** a round metal or wooden dish used to collect money in a church **b** a collection of money taken in church: *The plate was more than $10.* **5** [C] (*often in comb.*) a flat, thin, usu. large piece of metal, glass, etc., for use in building, in parts of machinery, as a protection, etc. **6** [C *usu. sing.*] **a** also **dental plate–** a thin piece of pink plastic shaped to fit inside a person's mouth, into which false teeth are fixed **b** also **denture** *fml–* a set of false teeth fixed into this **7** [C] a picture in a book, printed on different paper from the written part and often colored **8** [C] a small sheet of metal, usu. brass, fixed to the entrance to an office, bearing the name of the person who works there, or of a company **9 hand/give somebody something on a plate** *infml* to hand/give somebody something desirable, too willingly and easily

plate² *v* **plated, plating** [T *with*] to cover (a metal article) thinly with another metal, esp. gold, silver, or tin: *The ring wasn't solid gold; it was only plated.|a silver-plated spoon*

pla·teau /plæ'toʷ/ *n* **-teaus** *or* **-teaux** /'toʷz/ **1** a large stretch of level land much higher than the land around it **2** a state in which an activity ceases developing: *Business has now reached a plateau, but we hope it will begin to increase again soon.*

plate glass /ˌ· '·◄/ *n* [U] fine clear glass made in large, quite thick sheets for use esp. in store windows **–plate-glass** *adj* [A]

plat·form /'plætfɔrm/ *n* **1** a raised floor of boards for speakers, performers, etc. **2** a raised flat surface built along the side of the track at a railroad station for travelers getting on or off a train: *The Boston train is now on Platform One.* **3** [*usu. sing.*] the main ideas and aims of a political party, esp. as stated before an election: *The party is fighting the election from a platform which supports the end of the war.*

plat·ing /'pleɪṭɪŋ/ *n* [U] a thin covering of metal put on by plating (PLATE²)

plat·i·num /'plætn-əm, 'plɑtnəm/ *n* [U] an expensive grayish-white metal that is a simple substance (ELEMENT (1)) and is used esp. in very valuable jewelry: *a platinum ring|This ring is (of) platinum.*

plat·i·tude /'plætəˌtuʷd, -ˌtyuʷd/ *n derog* a statement that is true but not new, interesting, or clever: *He seems to have no original ideas; his speech was full of platitudes.* –compare CLICHÉ, TRUISM **–platitudinous** /ˌplætə'tuʷdn-əs, -'tyuʷd-/ *adj*

pla·ton·ic /plə'tɑnɪk/ *adj* (of love or friendship between two people) only of the mind and spirit; not sexual **–platonically** *adv*

pla·toon /plə'tuʷn/ *n* a small body of soldiers which is part of a COMPANY (5) and is commanded by a LIEUTENANT

plat·ter /'plæṭər/ *n esp. AmE* a large flat dish used for serving food

plat·y·pus /'plæṭəpəs/ also **duck-billed platypus–** *n* a small furry Australian animal that lays eggs and has a beak like a duck's, but gives milk to its young

plau·dit /'plɔdɪt/ *n fml* [*usu. pl.*] a show of pleased approval: *She smiled and waved when she heard the plaudits of the crowd.*

plau·si·ble /'plɔzəbəl/ *adj* **1** (of a statement, argument, etc.) seeming to be true or reasonable: *Your explanation sounds plausible; I think I believe it.* –opposite **implausible 2** (of a person) skilled in producing (seemingly) reasonable statements which may not be true: *a plausible liar* –**plausibly** *adv* –**plausibility** /ˌplɔzə'bɪlətiy/ *n* [U]

play¹ /pley/ *n* **1** [U] activity for amusement only, esp. among the young: *We watched the children at play.* **2** [C] (a performance of) a piece of writing to be acted in a theater or on TV: *I saw two plays last month.*|*I've just read a wonderful new play; they're going to put it on* (=perform it) *next year.* **3** [C;U] (an) action in a sport: *There was some exciting play in the baseball game.* **4** [U] the condition of being allowed by the rules to be kicked, hit, etc., in a game: *He tried to keep the ball in play.*|*The ball went out of play.* **5** [U] freedom of movement given by slight looseness: *Give the rope some play.*|(fig.) *He gave free play to his feelings and shouted angrily.* **6** [U] action; effect; use: *She had to bring all her experience into play to do the job.* **7** [U] quick, not lasting movement: *the play of sunshine and shadow among the trees* **8** [U] *esp. AmE* a calculated move towards a result (esp. in the phrase **make a play for**): *make a play for the job*

play² *v* **1** [I] (esp. of the young) to do things that pass the time pleasantly, esp. including running and jumping and using toys: *He was playing with his toy bear.* **2** I;T] to take part in (a sport or game) (against): *Shall we play cards?*|*If you were fitter, you'd play better.*|*Detroit and Dallas are playing football tomorrow.* **3** [I;T] to place (one of one's playing cards) face upwards on the table **4** [T] to strike and send (a ball), esp. in the stated way: *She played the ball just over the net.* **5** [T] to plan and carry out for one's own amusement or gain: *They played a cruel joke on her.*|(fig.) *I thought my eyes must be playing tricks on me.* (=deceiving me) **6** [I;T] to produce esp. musical sounds (from or of): *The radio was playing very loudly.*|*She plays the piano well.*|*Tonight I will play you some Mozart.* **7** [T] (of an actor) to perform: *The part of Hamlet was played by Derek Jacobi.* **8** to pretend to be: *He likes to play the great man.*|*He played dead.* **9** [I] to move lightly and irregularly: *A smile played across her lips.* **10** [I;T] to direct or be directed, esp. continuously: *The fireman played water onto the burning house.* **11 play for time** to cause delay, in order to gain time for thinking, avoid defeat, etc. **12 play hard to get** to pretend one is not sexually interested in someone, in the hope that they will become even more interested in oneself **13 play into someone's hands** to act in a way that gives someone an advantage over one **14 play it by ear** *infml* to act as things develop, rather than making plans in advance, esp. in a

difficulty **15 play (it) safe** to act in such a way that one has the best chance of avoiding a misfortune **16 play one's cards right** to use well the chances, conditions, facts, etc., that one has **17 play the fool** to act foolishly **18 play the game** to be fair, honest, and honorable **19 play with fire** to take great risks

play at sthg. *v prep* [T +*v-ing*] →PLAY² (8)

play sthg.↔ **back** *v adv* [T] to go through and listen to (something that has just been recorded on a machine)

play sthg.↔ **down** *v adv* [T] to cause to seem less important

play sbdy./sthg.↔ **off** *v adv* [T *against*] to set in opposition, esp. for one's own advantage: *She played one friend off against the other.* –compare PLAY-OFF

play on/upon sthg. *v prep* [T] to try to increase or strengthen (esp. the feelings of others) for one's own advantage: *I played on his generosity and in the end he agreed to lend me his car.*

play sthg.↔ **up** *v adv* [T] *infml* to cause something to seem more important than it really is: *He played up his accident to get more time off from work.*

play-act /'· ·/ *v* [I] to pretend; behave with an unreal show of feeling –**play-acting** *n* [U]

play·boy /'pleybɔɪ/ *n* a man who lives mainly for pleasure

play·er /'pleyər/ *n* **1** a person taking part in a game or sport **2** *esp. old use* an actor

play·ful /'pleyfəl/ *adj* **1** gaily active; full of fun: *a playful little dog* **2** not intended seriously: *a playful kiss on the cheek* –**playfully** *adv* –**playfulness** *n* [U]

play·ground /'pleygraʊnd/ *n* a piece of ground kept for children to play on, esp. at a school

play·house /'pleyhaʊs/ *n* -**houses** /ˌhaʊzɪz/ (*usu. cap. as part of a name*) a theater: *the Provincetown Playhouse*

playing card /'·· ˌ·/ *n fml* for CARD³ (1)

play·mate /'pleymeyt/ *n fml* a companion who shares in children's games and play

play-off /'· ·/ *n* a second match played to decide a winner, when the first has not done so –compare PLAY **off**

play on words /ˌ· · '·/ *n* **plays on words** →PUN

play·pen /'pleypɛn/ *n* a frame enclosed by bars or a net for a small child to play safely in

play·room /'pleyruʷm, -rʊm/ *n* a room set aside for children's play

play·thing /'pleyˌθɪŋ/ *n* **1** a toy **2** a person who is treated lightly and without consideration by another

play·time /'pleytaɪm/ *n* a (short) period of time, esp. at a school, when children can go out to play

play·wright /'pleyraɪt/ *n* a writer of plays

pla·za /'plazə, 'plæzə/ *n* a public square or marketplace: *a shopping plaza*

plea /pliy/ *n* **1** [C *for*] *fml* an eager or serious request: *his plea for forgiveness* **2** [*the* S] *fml* an excuse: *He refused the invitation to dinner on the plea of being too busy.* **3** [C *of*] *law* a statement by a person in a court of law, saying whether or not he is guilty of a charge:

a plea of guilty/not guilty

plead /pliːd/ *v* **pleaded** *or* **plead** /plɛd/ *also* **pled** /plɛd/ *AmE*, **pleading 1** [I *with*] to make continual and deeply felt requests: *He pleaded (with her) until she agreed to do as he wished.* **2** [T] to give as an excuse for an action: *I'm sorry I didn't answer your letter; I can only plead forgetfulness.* **3** [I] *law* to answer a charge in court: *The girl charged with murder was said to be* INSANE *and unfit to plead.* **4** [I;T] *law* to declare in official language that one is (in a state of): *She pleaded guilty/not guilty.|They made him plead* INSANITY.

pleas·ant /ˈplɛzənt/ *adj* **1** pleasing to the senses, feelings, or mind; enjoyable: *What a pleasant surprise!|a flower with a pleasant smell.|It's* (=the weather is) *usually pleasant here in August.* **2** (esp. of people) likeable; friendly: *She seems a pleasant woman.|Make an effort to be pleasant at the party.* –opposite **unpleasant** –**pleasantly** *adv:He smiled pleasantly when we arrived.*

pleas·ant·ry /ˈplɛzəntriː/ *n* **-ries** a light amusing remark; pleasant joke

please¹ /pliːz/ *v* **pleased, pleasing 1** [I;T] to make (someone) happy; give pleasure (to): *You can't please everybody.|Do it to please me.|The woman in the library is always eager to please (everybody).* –opposite **displease 2** [I] (*not as the main verb of a sentence*) to choose; like: *Come and stay as long as you please.* **3 if you please** *fml* (used to give force after a request) PLEASE²: *Come this way, if you please.* **4 please yourself** *infml* do as you wish, it doesn't matter to me

please² *interj* (used when asking politely for something): *A cup of tea, please.|Please be quiet.|Would you go now, please?|"More coffee?" "Please."* (=yes, please)

pleased /pliːzd/ *adj* feeling or showing satisfaction or happiness: *I'm very pleased you've decided to come.|She had a pleased look on her face.|I'm pleased with your work.|He was looking very* **pleased with himself,** *so I knew he had passed his driving test.* –opposite **displeased**

pleas·ing /ˈpliːzɪŋ/ *adj* giving pleasure or satisfaction: *a pleasing result to our talks* –**pleasingly** *adv*

pleas·ur·a·ble /ˈplɛʒərəbəl/ *adj fml* enjoyable; pleasant –**pleasurably** *adv*

pleas·ure /ˈplɛʒər/ *n* **1** [U] the feeling of happiness or satisfaction resulting from an experience that one likes: *He listened with pleasure to the beautiful music.|It gives me no pleasure to have to tell you this.|He* **took great pleasure in** (=greatly enjoyed) *telling me that my team had lost.* –opposite **displeasure 2** [C] a cause of happiness, enjoyment, or satisfaction: *It's been a pleasure to talk to you.|Some old people have very few pleasures in life.* **3** [U] enjoyment; RECREATION: *Are you here on business or just for pleasure?* **4** [S] *polite* something that is not inconvenient and that one is pleased to do (esp. in the phrase **a/my/our pleasure**): *"Thank you for helping me." "My pleasure./It was a pleasure."*

pleat¹ /pliːt/ *v* to make PLEATS² in: *a pleated skirt*

pleat² *n* a specially pressed narrow fold in cloth

ple·be·ian /plɪˈbiːən/ *n,adj derog* (a member) of the lower social classes: *plebeian habits*

pleb·i·scite /ˈplɛbəˌsaɪt/ *n* a direct vote by all the people of a nation on a matter of national importance: *to hold a plebiscite|It was decided* **by plebiscite.** –compare REFERENDUM

plec·trum /ˈplɛktrəm/ *n* **-tra** /trə/ *or* **-trums** →PICK⁴

pled /plɛd/ *v AmE past tense and participle of* PLEAD

pledge¹ /plɛdʒ/ *n* **1** [C] something given or received as a sign of faithful love or friendship: *Take this ring as a pledge of our friendship.* **2** [C] something valuable left with someone else as proof that one will fulfill an agreement **3** [C;U] a solemn promise or agreement: *It was told me under pledge of secrecy.*

pledge² *v* **pledged, pledging** *fml* **1** [T+*to-v/that*] to make a solemn promise or agreement: *They have pledged that they will always remain faithful.* **2** [T *to*] to bind (someone) with a solemn promise: *She was pledged to secrecy.*

ple·na·ry /ˈpliːnəriː, ˈplɛ-/ *adj fml* **1** (of power of government) complete; without limit **2** (of a meeting) attended by all who have the lawful right to attend

plen·i·po·ten·tia·ry /ˌplɛnəpəˈtɛnʃəriː, -tʃə-, -ʃiˌeriː, -tʃiː-/ *n,adj* **-ries** (a person) having full power to act in all matters, as a representative of one's government, esp. in a foreign country

plen·te·ous /ˈplɛntiːəs/ *adj lit* for PLENTIFUL

plen·ti·ful /ˈplɛntɪfəl/ *adj* existing in quantities or numbers that are (more than) enough: *The camp has a plentiful supply of food.* –**plentifully** *adv*

plen·ty /ˈplɛntiː/ *n* [U +*sing./pl. v*] as much or as many as one needs; enough: *plenty of money|$100 is plenty.|There are plenty more chairs in here.|He gave them plenty to eat.|The farms have water in plenty.* (=lots of water)*|Don't get any more sugar; we've got plenty.* –compare LOT¹

pleth·o·ra /ˈplɛθərə/ *n* [S *of*] *fml* an amount or supply much greater than is needed

pli·a·ble /ˈplaɪəbəl/ *also* **pliant** /ˈplaɪənt/– *adj* **1** easily bent without breaking **2** easily influenced; yielding to the wishes and commands of others –**pliability** /ˌplaɪəˈbɪlətiː/ *also* **pliancy** /ˈplaɪənsiː/– *n* [U]

pli·ers /ˈplaɪərz/ *n* [P] a small tool made of two crossed pieces of metal with long flat jaws at one end, used to hold small things or to bend or cut wire –compare PINCERS and see PAIR¹ (USAGE)

plight /plaɪt/ *n* [*usu. sing.*] a (bad, serious, or sorrowful) condition or state: *The poor girl was in a terrible plight.|the plight of these poor homeless children*

plod /plɒd/ *v* **-dd- 1** [I] to walk slowly, esp. with difficulty and great effort: *The old man plods along, hardly able to lift each foot.* **2**

[*esp. away (at)*] to work steadily, esp. at something uninteresting: *The boy plodded away (at the work) all night but couldn't finish it.*

plod·der /ˈplɑdər/ n a slow, not very clever, but steady worker who often succeeds in the end

plop /plɑp/ v,n,adv **-pp-** [*adv +prep/adv; S*] *infml* (to fall with) a sound as of something dropping smoothly into liquid: *The stone plopped into the stream.*|*There was a loud plop as the bag fell to the floor and burst.*|*The soap fell plop into the bath.*

plot¹ /plɑt/ n **1** a small marked or measured piece of ground for building or growing things: *a building plot*|*I grow potatoes on my little plot of land.* **2** the set of connected events on which a story, play, movie, etc., is based **3** a secret plan to do something usu. against a person, needing combined action by several people: *They've discovered a plot to kill the Queen.*

plot² v **-tt- 1** [T] to mark (the position of a moving aircraft or ship) on a map **2** [T] to express or represent by means of pictures or a map **3** [T] to make (a line or curve showing certain stated facts) by marking on paper marked with small squares: *to plot (a line showing) the increase in sales this year* **4** [I;T+*to-v*] to plan together secretly: *They're plotting against him.*|*They're plotting to kill him/plotting his murder/plotting how to murder him.* –**plotter** n [*usu. pl.*]

plow¹ *AmE*‖also **plough** /plaʊ/ n **1** a farming tool with a heavy cutting blade drawn by a motor vehicle or animal(s) and used to break up and turn over the earth, esp. before seeds are planted **2** any tool or machine that works like this one –see also SNOWPLOW

plow² *AmE*‖also **plough** v **1** [I;T] to break up or turn over (land) with a PLOW¹ (1): *Farmers plow (their fields) in fall or spring.* **2** [I] to force a way or make a track: *The great ship plowed across the ocean.*|(fig.) *He plowed through the book to the end.* (=the book was very dull or difficult)

plow sthg.↔ **back** v adv [T] to put (money earned) back into a business so as to build up the business

ploy /plɔɪ/ n *infml* a way of behaving in order to gain some advantage: *His usual ploy is to pretend to be ill so that people will take pity on him.*

pluck¹ /plʌk/ v **1** [T] to pull the feathers off (a dead chicken, duck, etc., being prepared for cooking) **2** [T *out, from, off*] to pull sharply; pick: *She tried to pluck out some of her gray hairs.*|(*lit*) *He plucked a rose/an apple.* **3** [I;T *at*] →PICK¹ (6)

pluck up v adv **pluck up (one's) courage** to show bravery in spite of (one's) fears: *He could not pluck up enough courage to ask her to marry him.*

pluck² n [U] courage and will: *Mountain climbers need a lot of pluck.*

pluck·y /ˈplʌkiʸ/ adj **-ier, -iest** brave and determined –**pluckily** adv

plug¹ /plʌg/ n **1** a small piece of rubber, wood, metal, etc., used for blocking a hole,

esp. in a pipe: *She pulled the plug out of the bath and the water ran out.* **2** a small plastic object with two or three metal pins which are pushed into an electric power point (SOCKET) to obtain power for an electrical apparatus –see illustration on page 221 **3** *infml* a favorable opinion, esp. given on radio or television, about a record, book, etc., meant to make people want to buy the thing spoken of

plug² v **-gg-** [T] **1** to block, close, or fill up with a PLUG¹ (1): *Use this to plug the hole in your boat.* –opposite **unplug 2** *infml* to advertise (something) by repeatedly mentioning: *He's been plugging his new book on the radio.*

plug away at sthg. v adv prep [T] *infml* to work with the will to complete (a difficult job)

plug sthg.↔ **in** v adv [T] to connect to a supply of electricity

plum /plʌm/ n **1** [C] a sweet smooth-skinned fleshy fruit, usu. dark red, with a single hard seed (PIT³) **2** [U] a dark reddish-blue color **3** [A;C] *infml* something very desirable: *That job's a real plum.*

plum·age /ˈpluʷmɪdʒ/ n [U] a bird's covering of feathers

plumb¹ /plʌm/ n a mass of lead tied to the end of a string (**plumb line**), used to find out the depth of water or whether a wall is built exactly upright

plumb² v [T] **1** to (try to) find out the meaning of: *plumbing the deep mysteries of man's mind* **2 plumb the depths (of)** to reach the lowest point (of): *to plumb the depths of unhappiness*

plumb·er /ˈplʌmər/ n a person whose job is to fit and repair water pipes, etc., in a building

plumber's help·er /ˌ·· ˈ··/ n *AmE infml* for PLUNGER (1)

plumb·ing /ˈplʌmɪŋ/ n [U] **1** all the pipes, containers for storing water, etc., in a building: *an old house with noisy plumbing* **2** the work of a PLUMBER

plume /pluʷm/ n a feather, esp. a large or showy one: (fig.) *a plume of smoke*

plum·met /ˈplʌmɪt/ v [I *down*] to fall steeply or suddenly: *The damaged aircraft plummeted (down) to earth.*|*Prices have plummeted.* –compare ROCKET²

plump¹ /plʌmp/ adj usu. apprec (of people, animals, or parts of the body) pleasantly fat; nicely rounded: *a baby with plump little arms and legs* –see THIN (USAGE) –**plumpness** n [U]

plump² v →PLUMP UP, PLUMP FOR

plump for sthg. v prep [T+*v-ing*] *infml* to support (an idea, plan, etc.): *We're plumping for buying a new car.*

plump sthg.↔ **up** v adv [T] to make (esp. bed coverings) rounded and soft by shaking

plun·der¹ /ˈplʌndər/ v [I;T] to seize (goods) unlawfully or by force from (people or a place), esp. in time of war: *They plundered the helpless town/plundered all the valuable things they could find.*

plunder² n [U] goods seized by PLUNDERing¹

plunge¹ /plʌndʒ/ v **plunged, plunging 1** [I;T]

to (cause to) move or be thrown suddenly forwards and/or downwards: *The car stopped suddenly and he plunged forward.*|(fig.) *Prices have plunged.* (=become suddenly lower) **2** [I] (of the neck of a woman's garment) to have a low curve or V-shape that shows a quite large area of the chest: *a plunging* NECKLINE

plunge into *v prep* [T] **1** (**plunge** (sthg.) **into** sbdy./sthg.) to push or rush suddenly or violently into the depths or thickness of: *He plunged into the water.*|*She plunged the knife into his back.* **2** (**plunge** sbdy./sthg. **into** sthg.) to cause to feel or be in a state of: *The room was plunged into darkness.*

plunge² *n* [S] **1** an act of plunging (PLUNGE¹), esp. head first into water **2 take the plunge** to decide upon and perform an act determinedly, after having delayed through anxiety or uncertainty

plung·er /'plʌndʒər/ *n* a rubber cup on the end of a handle, used for unblocking pipes by means of SUCTION

plunk¹ /plʌŋk/ *n,adv* [*adv* +*prep/adv*; S] *infml* (with) a hollow sound as of something dropping or falling onto a metal object: *I heard a plunk, and saw that the box had fallen off the table.*|*The box fell plunk on the floor.*

plunk² *v* [T] *infml* to put down heavily or with force: *She plunked herself in the chair and refused to move.*

plu·per·fect /ˌpluːwˈpɜrfɪkt/ *adj,n* → PAST PERFECT

plu·ral /'plʊərəl/ *adj,n* (a word or form) that represents more than one: *"Dogs" is a plural noun.*|*"Dogs" is the plural of "dog."* –compare SINGULAR

plu·ral·i·ty /plʊəˈrælətiy/ *n* **1** [U] (in grammar) the state of being plural **2** [C] *tech, esp. AmE* the largest number of votes in an election, esp. when less than a MAJORITY (2)

plus¹ /plʌs/ *prep* with the addition of (the stated figure or quantity): *3 plus 6 is 9 (3+6=9).*|*It costs a dollar, plus ten cents for postage.* (=the total spent is $1.10) –compare MINUS¹

plus² also **plus sign** /'·· ·/– *n* a sign (+) showing that two or more numbers are to be added together, or that a number is greater than zero –compare MINUS² (1)

plus³ *adj* **1** [A] (of a number or quantity) greater than zero: *a plus quantity* –compare MINUS³ **2** [after *n*] and above (a stated number): *All the children here are 12 plus.* (=are 12 years old or older)

plush /plʌʃ/ *adj* [A] *infml* splendid and costly: *the plush new hotel*

Plu·to /'pluːwtow/ *n* the PLANET 9th in order from the sun, the most distant of the group that includes the Earth

plu·to·crat /'pluːwtəˌkræt/ *n* a person who has power because of his/her wealth –**plutocratic** /ˌpluːwtəˈkrætɪk/ *adj*

plu·to·ni·um /pluːˈtowniʸəm/ *n* [U] a man-made simple substance (ELEMENT (1)) that is used esp. in the production of atomic power

ply¹ /plaɪ/ *v* **plied, plying 1** [I;T *between*] (of taxis, buses, and esp. boats) to travel regularly (in or on): *This ship plies between London and Australia.* **2** [T] *lit* to work (regularly) at (a trade): *The newspaper-seller* **plies his trade** *in the streets.*

ply sbdy. **with** sthg. *v prep* [T] to keep supplying with (esp. food, drink, or questions)

ply² *n* [U] a measure of the thickness of woolen thread, rope, PLYWOOD, etc., according to the number of single threads or sheets of material it is made from: *What ply is this wool?*|*This is four-ply wool.*|*three-ply wood*

ply·wood /'plaɪwʊd/ *n* [U] strong board made of several thin sheets of wood stuck together

p.m. /ˌpiʸ ˈɛm/ *abbrev. for:* Latin post meridiem (=after midday) (used after numbers expressing time): *He caught the 5 p.m. (train) from Washington D.C.* –compare A.M.

PM *abbrev. for:* (*infml esp. BrE*) PRIME MINISTER

pneu·mat·ic /nʊˈmætɪk, nyʊ-/ *adj* **1** worked by air pressure: *a pneumatic* DRILL² (1) **2** containing air: *a pneumatic tire* –**pneumatically** *adv*

pneu·mo·nia /nʊˈmownyə, nyʊ-/ *n* [U] a serious disease of the lungs with INFLAMMATION and difficulty in breathing

P.O. *written abbrev. said as:* POST OFFICE

poach¹ /powtʃ/ *v* [T] to cook (esp. eggs or fish) in gently boiling water or other liquid: *poached eggs*

poach² *v* [I;T *for, on*] **1** to catch or shoot (animals, birds, or fish) without permission on private land: *poaching (for) rabbits*|*Don't let me catch you poaching (on my land) again.* **2** to take or use unfairly (a position or idea belonging to someone else) –**poacher** *n*

P.O. Box /ˌpiʸ ˈow ˌbaks/ *n* →POST OFFICE BOX

pock·et¹ /'pakɪt/ *n* **1** [C] a small flat cloth bag sewn into or onto a garment, for keeping small articles in: *The policeman wanted to know what was in my pockets.* **2** [C] a container made by fitting a piece of cloth, net, etc., into the inside of a case or a car door, onto the back of an aircraft seat, etc. **3** [C *of*] a small area or group that exists separated from others like it: *pockets of mist*|*There are pockets of unemployment in the industrial areas.* **4** [A] small enough to be carried in the pocket: *a pocket camera* **5 have someone in one's pocket** to have complete influence over someone **6 out of pocket** having spent money without any good result: *I bought a new cigarette lighter and it broke. Now I'm $10 out of pocket.*

pocket² *v* [T] **1** to put into one's POCKET¹ (1) **2** to take (money or something small) for one's own use, esp. dishonestly: *He spent some of the money as we asked, but he pocketed most of it.*

pock·et·book /'pakɪtˌbʊk/ *n AmE* for HANDBAG

pock·et·ful /'pakɪtˌfʊl/ *n* [*of*] the amount that a POCKET¹ (1) will hold

pocket mon·ey /'·· ˌ··/ *n* [U] **1** *AmE* a small amount of money carried in the event one may need it **2** *BrE* for ALLOWANCE (1b)

pock·mark /'pakmark/ *n* a hollow mark left

on the skin where a raised spot has been –**pockmarked** *adj*

pod[1] /pɑd/ *n* a long narrow seed vessel of various plants, esp. beans and PEAs: *a PEA pod*

pod[2] *v* -**dd**- [T] to take (beans, PEAs, etc.) from the POD[1] before cooking

po·di·a·trist /pəˈdaɪətrɪst/ *n* a doctor who cares for and treats the human foot –**podiatry** *n* [U]: *He decided to study podiatry after he became a doctor.*

po·di·um /ˈpoʷdiʸəm/ *n* -**diums** *or* -**dia** /diʸə/ a raised part of a floor, or a large movable block, for a performer, speaker, musical CONDUCTOR, etc., to stand on

po·em /ˈpoʷəm/ *n* a piece of writing, arranged in patterns of lines and of sounds, expressing in IMAGINATIVE language some deep thought, feeling, or human experience

po·et /ˈpoʷɪt/ *n* a person who writes poems

po·et·ic /poʷˈɛtɪk/ also **poetical** /poʷˈɛtɪkəl/– *adj* of, like, or connected with poets or poetry: *poetic language|Some plays are written in poetic form.* –**poetically** *adv*

poetic jus·tice /ˌ·· '··/ *n* [U] perfect justice, by which wrong-doers are justly punished

poetic li·cense /ˌ·· '··/ *n* [U] the freedom allowed by custom in the writing of poetry to change facts, not to obey the usual rules of grammar, etc.

po·et·ry /ˈpoʷətriʸ/ *n* [U] **1** the art of a poet **2** poems in general: *a book of poetry* –compare PROSE **3** *apprec* a quality of beauty, grace, and deep feeling: *This dancer has poetry in her movements.*

poign·ant /ˈpɔɪnyənt/ *adj* producing a sharp feeling of sadness or pity: *poignant memories of my childhood* –**poignantly** *adv* –**poignancy** *n* [U]

point[1] /pɔɪnt/ *n* **1** [C *of*] a sharp end: *She pricked herself with/on the point of a needle.* **2** [C] a position in space or time; a particular place, moment, or state: *The bus stops at four or five points along this road.|It was* **at that point** (=moment) *that I saw him leave.|I've* **come to the point** *where I can't stand her arguing any longer.* **3** [C] a scoring (SCORE) system used in deciding who is the winner in various sports and games: *We won the game by 12 points to 3.* **4** [C] also **decimal point**– a sign (.) used for separating a whole number from any following decimals: *When we read out 4.23, we say "four point two three".* **5** [C;U] a degree of temperature: *Heat the water till it reaches its* **boiling point. 6** [C] a single particular idea, fact, or part of an argument or statement: *There are two or three points in your speech that I didn't understand.|You've got a* **point** *there.* (=what you have said may well be right) **7** [*the* S;U] the idea contained in something said or done, which gives meaning to the whole: *I didn't* **see the point** *of his last remark.|I* **missed the point**. *What did he mean?|I* **take your point.** (=I understand your suggestion)|**That's not the point.** (=not really important to or connected with the main thing being talked about)|*I'm in a hurry, so* **come/get to the point.** (=speak about

the most important or urgent matter)|*The fact that he's your brother is* **beside the point.** (=has nothing to do with the main matter) **8** [C] (*often cap. as part of name*) a piece of land with a sharp end that stretches out to the sea **9** [C] (in GEOMETRY) an imaginary spot or place that has position but no size **10** [C] also **compass point, point of the compass**– any of the 32 marks on a compass **11** [U] the dangerous end of a weapon, considered as a means of having power or influence over someone: *He forced his prisoner* **at gun point/at the point of** *a gun to stand against the wall.* **12** [C] a noticeable quality or ability of someone or something: *Work isn't her strong point; she's pretty lazy.* **13** [U] purpose; use: *There's not much point in washing it if you're going to make it dirty again five minutes later.* **14** **at the point of** just before: *at the point of death* **15** **beside the point** not related to the subject under consideration **16** **in point** which proves or is an example of the subject under consideration: *What happened to us on our trip is* **a case in point. 17** **on the point of** just starting to; just about to **18** **point of no return** a point in doing something at which one has to decide whether to stop or go on, because if one continues, one will not be able to stop **19** **point of order** a matter connected with the proper running of an official meeting **20** **point of view** a way of considering or judging a thing, person, event, etc.: *We need someone with a fresh point of view to improve this scheme.|Look at it from my point of view.* (=see how it affects me) **21** **to the point of** so as to be almost: *Her manner of speaking is direct to the point of rudeness.* **22** **when it comes/came to the point** when the moment for action or decision comes/came

point[2] *v* **1** [I *at, to*] to hold out a finger, a stick, etc., in order to show direction or position or to cause someone to look: *She pointed at him and said, "He's the thief!"|He pointed to the house on the corner and said, "That's where I live."* **2** [T *at, towards*] to aim, direct, or turn: *He pointed his gun at the floor and fired.* **3** [T] to fill in and make smooth the spaces between the bricks of (a wall, house, etc.) with MORTAR[2] or cement **4** **point the finger at** *infml* to hold (someone) up to public blame; ACCUSE

point sbdy./sthg.↔ **out** *v adv* [T +*that/to*] to draw attention to: *He pointed her out to me.|May I point out that if we don't leave now we'll miss the bus?*

point towards sthg. *v prep* [T] to suggest the strong possibility of; be a sign of

point-blank /ˌ·'·◄/ *adj,adv* **1** (fired) from a very close position: *a point-blank shot at his head|He fired at the animal point-blank.* **2** (in a way that is) forceful and direct: *a point-blank refusal|He refused point-blank.*

point·ed /ˈpɔɪntɪd/ *adj* **1** shaped to a point at one end: *long pointed fingernails* **2** (of something said or done) directed, in a noticeable and often unfriendly way, at a particular person or group: *She looked in a pointed manner at the clock, and I understood that it was time to leave.* –**pointedly** *adv*

point·er /ˈpɔɪntər/ n **1** a stick used by someone to point at things on a large map, board, etc. **2** a small needlelike piece of metal that points to the numbers on a measuring apparatus **3** a type of hunting dog **4** a useful suggestion or piece of advice

point·less /ˈpɔɪntlɪs/ adj **1** often derog meaningless **2** useless; unnecessary –**pointlessly** adv –**pointlessness** n [U]

poise¹ /pɔɪz/ v **poised, poising** [T] to hold or place lightly in a position in which it is difficult to remain steady: He poised the glass on the edge of the shelf.

poise² n [U] **1** good judgment, self-control, and a quiet belief in one's abilities **2** the way of holding one's head or body: We admired the graceful poise of the dancer.

poised /pɔɪzd/ adj **1** [F] in a state of balance: The sick man is poised between life and death. **2** [F +to-v/for] in a state of readiness to act or move: The army was poised for action. **3** apprec having POISE² (1)

poi·son¹ /ˈpɔɪzən/ n [C;U] (a) substance that harms or kills if a living animal or plant takes it in: He tried to kill himself by taking poison.

poison² v [T] **1** to give poison to; harm or kill with poison: We decided to kill the rats by poisoning them. **2** to put poison into or onto (something): Someone tried to poison the water supply.|a poisoned arrow **3** to influence (someone's behavior, mind, etc.) in a harmful or evil way: She tried to poison her husband's mind against his sister. –**poisoner** n

poi·son·ous /ˈpɔɪzənəs/ adj containing, or having the effects of, poison: poisonous snakes/berries|This medicine is poisonous if taken in large quantities.|(fig.) poisonous (=evil, nasty) ideas –opposite **nonpoisonous** –**poisonously** adv

poke¹ /poʷk/ v **poked, poking** [I;T] **1** to push sharply out of or through an opening: His elbow was poking through his torn shirt SLEEVE.|She poked her head around the corner. **2** to push (a pointed thing) into (someone or something): You nearly poked me (in the eye) with your pencil.|Stop poking (me)! **3 poke fun at** to make jokes against **4 poke one's nose into something** infml to inquire into something that does not concern one
  poke around v adv [I] infml **1** to search: She poked around in her bag for her ticket. **2** also **poke along** n → DAWDLE: If you keep poking around like that, we'll be late.

poke² n an act of poking (POKE¹ (2)) with something pointed

pok·er¹ /ˈpoʷkər/ n a thin metal rod used to move the wood or coal in a fire in order to make it burn better

poker² n [U] a card game usu. played for money

poker face /ˈ·· ˌ·/ n a face that shows nothing of what a person is thinking or feeling –**poker-faced** /ˈ·· ˌ·/ adj

pok·y /ˈpoʷkiʸ/ adj **-ier, -iest** infml (of a place) uncomfortably small: a poky little house

po·lar /ˈpoʷlər/ adj [A] of, near, like, or coming from lands near the North or South POLES² (1)

polar bear /ˈ·· ˌ·/ n bears or bear a large white bear that lives near the North POLE

po·lar·i·ty /poʷˈlærətiʸ, pə-/ n **-ties** [C;U] the state of having or developing two opposite qualities: a growing polarity between the opinions of the company and those of the labor union

po·lar·ize AmE‖also **-ise** BrE /ˈpoʷlə.raɪz/ v **-ized, -izing** [I;T] to (cause to) gather around two opposite points: The government's policy seems to have polarized society into two classes.|Society has polarized into two classes. –**polarization,** /ˌpoʷlərə'zeʸʃən/ n [C;U]

Po·lar·oid /ˈpoʷlə.rɔɪd/ n tdmk **1** [U] a material used in the glass in SUNGLASSES, car windows, etc., to make light shine less brightly through it **2** [C] a camera that produces a finished photograph only seconds after the picture has been taken

pole¹ /poʷl/ n a long usu. thin round stick or post: a flagpole|a beanpole (=for supporting climbing bean plants)|telephone poles beside the railroad line

pole² n **1** either end of an imaginary straight line (AXIS) around which a solid round mass turns, esp. **a** (the lands around) the most northern and southern points on the surface of the earth **b** the two points in the sky to the north and south around which stars seem to turn –see also MAGNETIC POLE, NORTH POLE, SOUTH POLE **2** either of the points at the ends of a MAGNET **3** either of the two points at which wires may be fixed onto an electricity-storing apparatus (BATTERY) –the **negative pole** and the **positive pole 4 poles apart** widely separated; having no shared quality, idea, etc.

pole·cat /ˈpoʷlkæt/ n AmE infml for SKUNK

pole star /ˈ· ·/ also **North Star** /ˌ· ˈ·/– n [S] (often cap.) the rather bright star that is nearest to the center of the heavens in the northern part of the world

pole vault /ˈ· ·/ n (the sport of making) a jump over a high raised bar, using a long pole –**pole-vault** v [I]

po·lice¹ /pəˈliʸs/ n [the P] an official body of men and women whose duty is to protect people and property, to make everyone obey the law, to catch criminals, etc.: The police have caught the murderer.|the police force|a police car

police² v **-liced, -licing** [T] to keep order in (a place) by or as if using police: Dangerous areas have to be carefully policed at night.

po·lice·man /pəˈliʸsmən/ n **-men** /mən/ a male police officer –see illustration on page 673

police officer /·ˈ·· ˌ···/ n a member of a police force

police state /·ˈ· ˌ·/ n derog a country in which most activities of the citizens are controlled by (secret) political police

police sta·tion /·ˈ· ˌ··/ n the local office of the police in a town, part of a city, etc.

po·lice·wom·an /pəˈliʸs.wumən/ n **-women** /ˌwɪmɪn/ [A;C] a female police officer

pol·i·cy¹ /ˈpɑləsiʸ/ n **-cies** [C;U] a plan or course of action in directing affairs, esp. as chosen by a political party, government, business company, etc.: *One of the party's policies is to control public spending.*|*It's against government policy to sell weapons to that country.*

policy² *n* a written statement of the details of an agreement with an insurance company

po·li·o /'po^wli^yˌo^w/ *also* **poliomyelitis** /ˌpo^wli^yo^wˌmaɪə'laɪtɪs/ *n* [U] a serious infectious disease of the nerves in the backbone (SPINE), often resulting in a lasting loss of the power to move certain muscles (PARALYSIS)

pol·ish¹ /'palɪʃ/ *v* **1** [I;T *up*] to make or become smooth and shiny by continual rubbing: *Polish your shoes with a brush.*|*Silver polishes easily with this special cloth.* **2** [T] to make (a speech, piece of writing, performance, etc.) as perfect as possible: *The musicians gave a very polished performance.*

polish sthg.↔ **off** *v adv* [T] *infml* to finish (food, work, etc.)

polish² *n* **1** [C;U] a liquid, powder, paste, etc., used in polishing a surface: *a can of shoe polish*|*I keep my polishes in this cupboard.* **2** [S] a smooth shiny surface produced by rubbing: *That hot plate will spoil the polish on this table.* **3** [U] *apprec* fine quality or perfection (of manners, education, writing, etc.)

po·lite /pə'laɪt/ *adj* having or showing good manners, consideration for others, and/or correct social behavior: *What polite well-behaved children!* —opposite **impolite** —**politely** *adv* —**politeness** *n* [U]

pol·i·tic /'paləˌtɪk/ *adj fml* **1** (of behavior or actions) well-judged with regard to one's own advantage: *He felt it was politic to be on time his first day on the new job.* —opposite **impolitic** **2** (of a person) skillful in acting to obtain a desired result

po·lit·i·cal /pə'lɪtɪkəl/ *adj* **1** of or concerning politics and/or government: *a political party*|*the loss of political freedoms*|*They are political prisoners, in prison because of their political beliefs.* —opposite **nonpolitical** **2** very interested in or active in politics: *The students in this university are very political.* —opposite **apolitical** —**politically** *adv*

pol·i·ti·cian /ˌpalə'tɪʃən/ *n* a person whose business is politics

pol·i·tics /'paləˌtɪks/ *n* **1** [U] the art, science, or business of government: *Tom is studying politics at university.*|*She takes an active part in local politics.*|*Politics has/have never interested me.* **2** [P] political opinions: *What are your politics? I support the* DEMOCRATIC *Party.*

pol·ka /'po^wlkə, 'po^wkə/ *n* (a piece of music for) a quick simple dance for people in pairs

poll¹ /po^wl/ *n* **1** [C] the giving of votes at an election: *The result of the poll won't be known until midnight.* **2** [C] *also* **opinion poll**– a questioning of a number of people chosen by chance, to find out the general opinion about something or someone **3** [S] the number of votes recorded at an election: *a heavy poll* (=with a large number of people voting)

poll² *v* [T] to receive (a stated number of votes) at an election: *She polled 10,542 votes.*

pol·len /'palən/ *n* [U] fine yellow dust on the male part of a flower that causes other flowers to produce seeds when it is carried to them

pollen count /'·· ˌ·/ *n* a measure of the amount of POLLEN floating in the air

pol·li·nate /'palə,ne^yt/ *v* **-nated, -nating** [T] to cause (a flower or plant) to be able to produce seeds by bringing POLLEN —**pollination** /ˌpalə'ne^yʃən/ *n* [U]

poll·ing /'po^wlɪŋ/ *n* [U] the giving of votes at an election; voting: *Polling was quite heavy.* (=lots of people voted)

polling booth /'·· ˌ·/ *n esp. BrE* for VOTING BOOTH

pol·lut·ant /pə'lu^wtnt/ *n* [C;U] a substance or thing that POLLUTEs

pol·lute /pə'lu^wt/ *v* **-luted, -luting** [T] to make (air, water, soil, etc.) dangerously impure or unfit for use: *The river has been polluted by factory waste.*|(fig.) *His teachings polluted the students' minds.*

pol·lu·tion /pə'lu^wʃən/ *n* [U] **1** the action of polluting (POLLUTE) **2** a substance or other thing that POLLUTEs: *There's so much pollution in the air here that it's becoming an unhealthy place to live.*

po·lo /'po^wlo^w/ *n* [U] a ball game played between two teams of players on horseback with long-handled wooden hammers

polo neck /'·· ˌ·/ *n BrE* for TURTLENECK

pol·ter·geist /'po^wltərˌgaɪst/ *n* a spirit that is said to make noises, throw objects around a room, etc.

pol·y·an·dry /'pali^yˌændri^y, ˌpali^y'æn-/ *n* [U] the custom or practice of having more than one husband at the same time

pol·y·es·ter /ˌpali^y'ɛstər, 'pali^yˌɛstər/ *n* [U] a man-made material used esp. to make cloth for garments: *a shirt made of polyester and cotton*

pol·y·eth·yl·ene /ˌpali^y'ɛθəˌli^yn/ *AmE*||**polythene** *BrE*– *n* [U] a type of plastic not easily damaged by water or certain chemicals, used esp. as a protective covering, for making household articles, etc.: *a polyethylene bag*

po·lyg·a·my /pə'lɪgəmi^y/ *n* [U] the custom or practice of having more than one wife at the same time —compare MONOGAMY, BIGAMY —**polygamist** *n* —**polygamous** /pə'lɪgəməs/ *adj*: *a polygamous society*

pol·y·gon /'pali^yˌgan/ *n* (in GEOMETRY) a figure on a flat surface having five or more straight sides

pol·y·sty·rene /ˌpali^y'staɪri^yn/ *n* [U] a light plastic, used esp. for making containers

pol·y·tech·nic /ˌpali^y'tɛknɪk/ *adj* of or concerning a place of higher education providing training in many arts and esp. trades connected with skills and machines: *the New York Polytechnic Institute*

pol·y·thene /'paləˌθi^yn/ *n* [U] *BrE* for POLYETHYLENE

pom·e·gran·ate /'paməˌgrænɪt, 'pʌmə-/ *n* a round fruit containing a mass of small seeds in a red juicy flesh

pom·mel /'pʌməl/ *v* **-l-** *AmE*||**-ll-** *BrE AmE* for PUMMEL

pomp /pamp/ *n* [U] grand solemn ceremonial

show, esp. on some public or official occasion

pom·pom /ˈpɑmpɑm/ n a small ball made of bits of wool worn as a decoration on garments: *a hat with a pompom*

pomp·ous /ˈpɑmpəs/ adj derog foolishly solemn and self-important: *pompous language*|*a pompous official* –**pomposity** /pɑmˈpɑsət̬iʸ/ also **pompousness** /ˈpɑm pəsnɪs/– n [U] –**pompously** adv

pon·cho /ˈpɑntʃoʷ/ n -**chos** a garment consisting of a single long wide piece of usu. thick woolen cloth with a hole in the middle for the head

pond /pɑnd/ n an area of still water smaller than a lake: *a duck pond in the park*

pon·der /ˈpɑndər/ v [I;T *on, over*] fml to spend time in considering (a fact, difficulty, etc.): *When I asked her advice, she pondered (the matter) and then told me not to go.*|*The prisoner pondered (on) how to escape.*

pon·der·ous /ˈpɑndərəs/ adj fml slow and awkward because of size and weight: (fig.) *a ponderous style of writing* –**ponderously** adv –**ponderousness** n [U]

pon·tiff /ˈpɑntɪf/ n [the S usu.cap.] (in various religions) a chief priest, esp. the POPE

pon·tif·i·cate /pɑnˈtɪfəˌkeʸt/ v -**cated, -cating** [I *about, on*] usu. derog to speak or write as if one's own judgment is the only correct one

pon·toon /pɑnˈtuʷn/ n any of a number of flat-bottomed boats fastened together side by side to support a floating bridge (**pontoon bridge**) across a river

po·ny /ˈpoʷniʸ/ n -**nies** a small horse

po·ny·tail /ˈpoʷniʸˌteʸl/ n a bunch of hair tied high at the back of the head –see also PIGTAIL

poo·dle /ˈpuʷdl/ n a type of dog with thick curling hair, usu. cut in special shapes

pooh /puʷ/ interj **1** (said when smelling something unpleasant) **2** derog (said to show disbelief or disapproval at a suggestion, idea, etc.)

pooh-pooh /ˌ·ˈ·/ v [T] infml to treat as not worthy of consideration: *They pooh-poohed the idea.*

pool¹ /puʷl/ n **1** a small area of still water in a hollow place, usu. naturally formed: *After the rain, there were little pools of water in the street.* **2** [*of*] a small amount of any liquid on a surface: *She was lying in a pool of blood.* **3** →SWIMMING POOL

pool² n **1** [C] a common supply of money, goods, workers, etc., which may be used by a number of people: *Our company has a car pool, so if I need a car there's always one there.*|*A* **typing pool** *is a group of* TYPISTS *in one large office, who do all the typing (*TYPE²*) for the company.* **2** [U] a type of American BILLIARDS: *to shoot pool (=*to play pool)

pool³ v [T] to combine; share: *If we pool our ideas, we may be able to produce a really good plan.*

pool⁴ n infml an arrangement by which people risk small amounts of money on the results of certain events

poop /puʷp/ n tech the back end of a ship

pooped /puʷpt/ also **pooped out** /ˌ·ˈ·/– adj

AmE infml very tired: *I'm really pooped tonight.*

poor /puʊər/ adj **1** having very little money: *He was too poor to buy shoes for his family.*|*"The government's plan will hurt the poor, the ill, and the unemployed."* –compare RICH (1) **2** below the usual standard; low in quality: *in poor health*|*a poor crop of beans* **3** [*no comp.*] deserving or causing pity: *The poor old man had lost both his sons in the war.*

poor·ly¹ /ˈpuʊərliʸ/ adv badly; not well: *poorly dressed/paid*

poorly² adj [F] esp. BrE ill: *I'm feeling rather poorly today.*

poor·ness /ˈpuʊrnɪs/ n [U *of*] a low standard; lack of a desired quality: *the poorness of the quality of the materials* –compare POVERTY

pop¹ /pɑp/ v -**pp- 1** [I;T] to (cause to) make a short sharp explosive sound: *The bottle stopper (*CORK*) popped when he pulled it out.* **2** [I] infml to spring: *The child's eyes almost popped out of her head with excitement.* **3** [I;T] infml to go, come, or put suddenly, quickly, etc.: *I've just popped in to return your book.*|*I'm afraid she's just popped out for a few minutes.*|*He popped his head around the door.* **4 pop the question (to)** infml to make an offer of marriage (to); PROPOSE (3) (to)

pop² n **1** [C] a sound like that of a slight explosion: *When he opened the bottle, it went pop.* **2** [U] infml for SODA (2)

pop³ n AmE infml father: *Can I borrow the car, Pop?*

pop⁴ n [U] modern popular music, esp. as favored by younger people: *Which do you like better,* CLASSICAL (2) *music or pop (music)?*|*a pop group (=*a group of people who sing and play pop music)|*a pop concert*

pop⁵ written abbrev. said as: **1** population **2** popularly

pop·corn /ˈpɑpkɔrn/ n [U] grains of corn that have been swollen and burst by heat, usu. eaten with salt and butter

pope /poʷp/ n [A;C] (often cap.) the head of the ROMAN CATHOLIC Church: *the election of a new pope*|*Pope John Paul*

pop·lar /ˈpɑplər/ n [C;U] (the wood of) a very tall straight thin tree

pop·py /ˈpɑpiʸ/ n -**pies** a plant with showy esp. red flowers

pop·u·lace /ˈpɑpyələs/ n [U] fml all the common people of a country: *The populace no longer supports this policy.*

pop·u·lar /ˈpɑpyələr/ adj **1** favored by many people; well liked: *a popular song*|*She's very popular with her pupils.* –opposite **unpopular 2** [A] sometimes derog suited to the understanding, liking, or needs of the general public: *The popular newspapers take a great interest in the President's family.* **3** [A *no comp.*] fml of or for the general public: *popular opinion*|*the popular vote*

pop·u·lar·i·ty /ˌpɑpyəˈlærət̬iʸ/ [U] the quality or state of being well liked, favored, or admired –opposite **unpopularity**

pop·u·lar·ize *AmE*‖also -**ise** *BrE* /ˈpɑp yələˌraɪz/ v -**ized, -izing** [T] **1** to make (something difficult) easily understandable to ordinary people by a simple explanation **2** to make (something new) generally known and used –**popularization** /ˌpɑpyələrə'zeyʃən/ *n* [C;U]

pop·u·lar·ly /'pɑpyələrliy/ *adv* generally; by most people: *It's popularly believed that smoking is bad for one's health.*

pop·u·late /'pɑpyə,leyt/ *v* **-lated, -lating** [T *often pass.*] (of a group) to settle or live in (a particular area): *a thickly-populated area| North America was mainly populated by new settlers from abroad.*

pop·u·la·tion /ˌpɑpyə'leyʃən/ *n* **1** [C;U *of*] the number of people (or animals) living in a particular area, country, etc.: *What was the population of Europe in 1900?* **2** [U] the people living in an area: *The population in these villages has to get its water from wells.*

pop·u·lous /'pɑpyələs/ *adj* (of a place) having a large population, esp. when compared with size

por·ce·lain /'pɔrsəlɪn, 'powr-/ *n* [U] (cups, dishes, etc., made of) thin shiny material of very fine quality, which is produced by baking a clay mixture

porch /pɔrtʃ, powrtʃ/ *n* **1** *AmE*‖also **veranda** *esp. BrE*– an addition to a house, built out from any of the walls, having a floor and a roof (usu. supported by pillars) but no outside walls –compare DECK, BALCONY –see illustration on page 337 **2** a built-out roofed entrance to a house or church

por·cu·pine /'pɔrkyə,paɪn/ *n* a short-legged animal that has very long stiff prickles (QUILLs) all over its back and and sides

pore /pɔr, powr/ *n* a very small opening (esp. in the skin) through which liquids (esp. SWEAT¹ (1)) may pass

pore o·ver sthg. *v prep* **pored, poring** [T] to study or give close attention to (usu. something written or printed)

pork /pɔrk, powrk/ *n* [U] meat from pigs –compare BACON, HAM; see MEAT (USAGE)

por·nog·ra·phy /pɔr'nɑgrɑfiy/ also **porn** /pɔrn/ *infml*– *n* [U] **1** the treatment of sexual subjects in pictures or writing in a way that is meant to cause sexual excitement **2** books, photographs, films, etc., containing this –**pornographer** *n* –**pornographic** /ˌpɔrnə'græfɪk/ *adj*

po·rous /'pɔrəs, 'powrəs/ *adj* allowing liquid to pass slowly through: *porous soil|This clay pot is porous.* –opposite **nonporous**

por·poise /'pɔrpəs/ *n* a large fishlike sea animal like a DOLPHIN that swims about in groups

por·ridge /'pɔrɪdʒ, 'pɑr-/ *n* [U] →OATMEAL (2)

port¹ /pɔrt, powrt/ *n* **1** (a) harbor: *There is only one port along this rocky coast.|We have to reach port by evening.* **2** a town with a harbor: *The ship will call at several ports.|Port of New Orleans|Our next port of call* (=the next place at which the ship will stop) *is Lisbon.* –see AIRPORT

port² *n* [S] the left side of a ship or aircraft as one faces forward: *The damaged ship was leaning over to port.|on the port side* –compare STARBOARD

port³ *n* [U] strong usu. sweet Portuguese wine usu. drunk after a meal –compare SHERRY

port·a·ble /'pɔrtəbəl, 'powr-/ *adj* that can be (easily) carried or moved; quite small and light: *a portable television*

por·tal /'pɔrtl, 'powrtl/ *n fml or lit* a (very grand) door or entrance to a building

port·cul·lis /pɔrt'kʌlɪs, powrt-/ *n* (in old castles, forts, etc.) a strong gatelike framework hung above an entrance and lowered as a protection against attack

por·tend /pɔr'tɛnd, powr-/ *v* [T] *fml* to be a sign or warning of (a future undesirable event): *Those black clouds portend a storm.*

por·tent /'pɔrtɛnt, 'powr-/ *n fml or lit* a (wonderful or terrible) sign or warning, esp. of something strange or undesirable: *portents of war*

por·ten·tous /pɔr'tɛntəs, powr-/ *adj fml or lit* that warns or FORETELLS (of evil happenings); threatening –compare OMINOUS

por·ter /'pɔrtər, 'powr-/ *n* a person employed to carry travelers' bags, esp. at railroad stations, airports, etc. –see illustration on page 17

port·fo·li·o /pɔrt'fowliy,ow, powr-/ *n* **-os 1** a large flat case like a very large book cover, for carrying drawings, business papers, etc. **2** a collection of drawings or other papers (such as would be contained in this) **3** the office and duties of an official of state: *the portfolio of foreign affairs*

port·hole /'pɔrthowl, 'powrt-/ *n* a small usu. circular window along the side of a ship or aircraft

por·ti·co /'pɔrtɪ,kow, 'powr-/ *n* **-coes** or **-cos** a grand entrance to a building, consisting of a roof supported by pillars

por·tion /'pɔrʃən, 'powr-/ *n* [*of*] **1** a part separated or cut off: *passengers traveling in the front portion of the train* **2** a share: *A portion of the blame for the accident must be borne by the driver.* **3** a quantity of food for one person as served in a restaurant

portion sthg.↔ **out** *v adv* [T *along, between*] to share

port·ly /'pɔrtliy, 'powr-/ *adj* **-lier, -liest** *euph or humor* (of a grown-up person, often rather old) round and fat: *the portly old general* –**portliness** *n* [U]

port·man·teau /pɔrt'mæntow, powrt-, ˌpɔrt mæn'tow, ˌpowrt-/ *n* **-teaus** or **-teaux** /tow z, 'towz/ a large traveling case for clothes, esp. one that opens out in the middle into two equal parts

por·trait /'pɔrtrɪt, -treyt, 'powr-/ *n* [*of*] **1** a painting, drawing, or photograph of a real person: *She's just painted a portrait of the Royal Family.* **2** a lifelike written description

por·trai·ture /'pɔrtrɪtʃər, 'powr-/ *n* [U] the art of making PORTRAITs (esp. 1)

por·tray /pɔr'trey, powr-/ *v* **-trayed, -traying** [T] **1** to represent (someone or something) in painting, in a book, etc., esp. according to one's own ideas or so as to produce a certain effect: *Her book portrays her father as a cruel man.* **2** to act the part of (a particular character) in a play –**portrayal** *n* [C;U]

pose¹ /powz/ *v* **posed, posing 1** [I;T *for*] to

(cause to) sit or stand in a particular effective position, esp. for a photograph, painting, etc.: *After the wedding we all posed for a photograph.* **2** [T] to set; offer for consideration: *You've posed us an awkward question.|This new law poses several problems for the farmers.*

  pose as sbdy. *v prep* [I] to pretend to be: *The prisoner posed as a prison officer in order to escape.*

pose² *n* **1** a position of the body, esp. as taken up to produce an effect in art: *She asked me to stand in various poses so that I could be photographed.* **2** *derog* an unnatural way of behaving which is intended to produce an effect

posh /pɑʃ/ *adj infml derog or apprec* for, or typical of, people of high social rank: *a posh hotel|She has a rather posh way of speaking.*

po·si·tion¹ /pəˈzɪʃən/ *n* **1** [C;U] the place where someone or something is or should be: *We can find our position by looking at this map.|One of the chairs is out of position.|Put it back in position.* **2** [C;U *in*] a particular place or rank in a group: *She's in top position in the class.* **3** [C *usu. sing.*] a condition or state: *By telling her that, you've put me in a very difficult position.|In the company's present position, they cannot afford to offer higher wages.|I'd like to help you, but I'm afraid I'm not in a position to do so.* (=I can't) **4** [C] the way or manner in which someone or something is placed or moves, stands, sits, etc.: *He had to work in a most uncomfortable position under the car.* **5** [C] a job; employment: *She has a good position in an oil company.* –see JOB (USAGE)

position² *v* [T] to put in the stated or proper POSITION¹ (1): *He positioned himself on the corner of the street to watch for the car.*

pos·i·tive¹ /ˈpɑzətɪv/ *adj* **1** allowing no room for doubt; DEFINITE: *We still don't have a positive answer as to how he died.|a positive refusal* **2** [F +(that)/of] (of a person) having no doubt about something; sure: *Are you positive he's the man you saw yesterday?* **3** effective; actually helpful: *It's no use just telling me to do it; give me positive advice as to how to do it.|positive thinking* **4** [no comp.] (in grammar) of or being the simple form of an adjective or adverb, which expresses no COMPARISON –compare COMPARATIVE, SUPERLATIVE **5** [no comp.] (in MATHEMATICS) (of a number or quantity) greater than zero **6** [no comp.] (of a photograph) having light and dark areas as they are in nature, not the other way around **7** [no comp.] (of a medical test) showing signs of disease –opposite **negative** (for 3, 5, 6, 7) **8** [A no comp.] *infml* (used for giving force to a noun) complete; real: *It was a positive delight to hear her sing so beautifully.*

positive² *n* **1** (in grammar) the POSITIVE¹ (4) degree or form of an adjective or adverb: *The positive of "prettiest" is "pretty."* **2** (in MATHEMATICS) a quantity greater than zero **3** a POSITIVE¹ (6) photograph –compare NEGATIVE

pos·i·tive·ly /ˈpɑzətɪvliʸ, ˌpɑzəˈtɪvliʸ◄/ *adv* **1**

(as if) with certainty: *He said quite positively that he would come, so we were all surprised when he didn't.* **2** *infml* (used for adding force to an expression) really; indeed: *This food is positively wonderful!* –compare POSITIVE¹ (8)

pos·sess /pəˈzɛs/ *v* [T not *be* +*v-ing*] **1** *fml* to own; have: *They asked me if I possessed a gun.* **2** (of a feeling or idea) to influence (someone) so completely as to control or direct actions: *What possessed you to act so strangely?* (=caused you ...)

pos·sessed /pəˈzɛst/ *adj fml or lit* wildly mad, (as if) controlled by an evil spirit: *She must have been possessed, to attack her own mother.*

pos·ses·sion /pəˈzɛʃən/ *n* **1** [U *of*] ownership: *Does the possession of wealth bring happiness?|She was found in possession of dangerous drugs.|The soldiers took possession of* (=captured) *the enemy's fort.* **2** [C often *pl.*] a piece of personal property: *The child's favorite possession was a little wooden dog.*

pos·ses·sive¹ /pəˈzɛsɪv/ *adj* **1** *derog* unwilling to share (something one owns, someone's attention, etc.) with other people **2** (in grammar) of or being a word that shows ownership or connection: *"My" and "its" are possessive adjectives.* –compare GENITIVE –**possessively** *adv* –**possessiveness** *n* [U]

possessive² *n* a POSSESSIVE¹ (2) word or form: *"Hers" is the possessive of "she."*

pos·ses·sor /pəˈzɛsər/ *n fml* an owner: *He is the fortunate possessor of a fine singing voice.*

pos·si·bil·i·ty /ˌpɑsəˈbɪlətiʸ/ *n* -ties **1** [S;U +*that/of*] the state or fact of being possible; a (degree of) likelihood: *Police are considering the possibility that the fire was started intentionally.|Is there any possibility that you'll be able to come tomorrow?* **2** [C] something that is possible: *The general would not accept that defeat was a possibility.|Your product has possibilities; with our help it could be a great success.* –see also IMPOSSIBLE

pos·si·ble /ˈpɑsəbəl/ *adj* **1** that can exist, happen, or be done: *It's no longer possible to find a cheap apartment in New York City.|I'll help you if possible.* (=if it is possible) *Try to finish the job as soon as possible.* –opposite **impossible** **2** that may or may not be, happen, or be expected: *It is possible but not probable that I'll go there next week.* **3** acceptable; suitable: *one of many possible answers*

pos·si·bly /ˈpɑsəbliʸ/ *adv* **1** in accordance with what is POSSIBLE (1): *I'll do all I possibly can.|You can't possibly walk 20 miles in an hour.* **2** perhaps: *"Will you come with us tomorrow?" "Possibly."*

pos·sum /ˈpɑsəm/ *n* **1** *infml* for OPOSSUM **2** **play possum** to pretend to be asleep or dead

post¹ /poʷst/ *n* **1** [C] a strong upright pole or bar made of wood, metal, etc., usu. fixed into the ground: *The fence was made of posts joined together with wire.|a gate post|a signpost* **2** [*the* S] the starting or finishing place in a race, esp. a horse race: *My uncle's* *horse was* **first past the post.**|*the* **finishing post**

post² *v* [T] **1** to make public or show by fixing to a wall, board, post, etc.: *The names of the members of the team will be posted today.* **2** [T *usu. pass.*] to make known (as being) by putting up a notice: *The ship was posted missing.*

post³ *n BrE* for MAIL¹

post⁴ *v* [T] **1** *BrE* for MAIL²: *Did you post that letter I gave you yesterday?* **2 keep someone posted** to continue to give someone all the latest news about something

post⁵ *n* **1** a job: *The post was advertised in today's newspaper.* –see JOB (USAGE) **2** a special place of duty, esp. on guard or on watch: *The soldiers must be at their posts by 8:30.* **3** a small distant fort, camp, etc., at which a body of soldiers is kept

post⁶ *v* [T] to place (soldiers, etc.) on duty in a special place: *Post a guard outside the camp.*

post·age /ˈpoʷstɪdʒ/ *n* [U] the charge for carrying a letter, package, etc., by post

postage stamp /ˈ·· ˌ·/ *n fml* for STAMP² (1)

post·al /ˈpoʷstl/ *adj* [A] connected with the public letter service: *Postal charges have risen again.*

postal or·der /ˈ·· ˌ··/ *n BrE* for MONEY ORDER

post·box /ˈpoʷstbɑks/ also **letterbox**– *n BrE* for MAILBOX

post·card /ˈpoʷstkɑrd/ also **card**– *n* a card on which a message may be sent by post, sometimes having a picture or photograph on one side (a **picture postcard**)

post·date /ˌpoʷstˈdeʸt/ *v* **-dated, -dating** [T] **1** to write on (a letter, check, etc.) a date later than the date of writing: *I'll give you a post-dated check; you can take it to the bank in two weeks.* **2** to be later in history than –see also PREDATE, BACKDATE

post·er /ˈpoʷstər/ *n* a large printed notice or (colored) drawing put up in a public place

pos·te·ri·or /pɑˈstɪəriʸər, poʷ-/ *n humor* the part of the body a person sits on; BUTTOCKs

pos·ter·i·ty /pɑˈsterəṭiʸ/ *n* [U] *fml* people who will be born and live after one's own time

post·grad·u·ate /ˌpoʷstˈgrædʒuʷɪt/ *n,adj* →GRADUATE¹ (3)

post·haste /ˌpoʷstˈheʸst/ *adv lit* at very great speed; in a great hurry

post·hu·mous /ˈpɑstʃəməs/ *adj* coming after one's death: *posthumous fame* –**posthumously** *adv*: *His last book was published posthumously.*

post·man /ˈpoʷstmən/ *n* **-men** /mən/ →MAILMAN

post·mark /ˈpoʷstmɑrk/ *n* an official mark made on letters, packages, etc., usu. over the stamp, showing when and from where they are sent –**postmark** *v* [T *usu. pass.*]: *The package was postmarked Los Angeles.*

post·mas·ter /ˈpoʷstˌmæstər/ **postmistress** /-ˌmɪstrɪs/ *fem.*– *n* a person officially in charge of a post office

post·mor·tem /ˌpoʷstˈmɔrtəm/ *n Latin* an examination of a dead body to discover the cause of death; AUTOPSY: (fig.) *There will have to be a postmortem on the company's poor sales results.*

post of·fice /ˈ· ˌ··/ *n* a building or office which deals with the mail

post of·fice box /ˈ· ·· ˌ·/ also **P.O. box** *infml*– *n* a numbered box in a post office, to which a person's mail can be sent: *For further details, write to post office box 301.*

post·pone /poʷstˈpoʷn, poʷsˈpoʷn/ *v* **-poned, -poning** [T +*v-ing/until, to*] to delay; move to some later time: *We're postponing our vacation until August.* –**postponement** *n* [C;U]

post·script /ˈpoʷstˌskrɪpt, ˈpoʷsˌskrɪpt/ also **P.S.** *infml*– *n* a short addition to a letter, below the place where one has signed one's name

pos·tu·late /ˈpɑstʃəˌleʸt/ *v* **-lated, -lating** [T +*that*] *fml* to accept (something that has not been proved) as true, as a base for reasoning

pos·ture¹ /ˈpɑstʃər/ *n* **1** [U] the general way of holding the body: *Upright posture is natural only to humans.* **2** [C] a fixed bodily position: *She photographed me in various postures: sitting, standing, etc.*

posture² *v* **-tured, -turing** [I] *often derog* to place oneself in a fixed bodily position, esp. in order to make other people admire one

post·war /ˌpoʷstˈwɔr◄/ *adj* [A] belonging to the time after a war

po·sy /ˈpoʷziʸ/ *n* **-sies** a small bunch of flowers

pot¹ /pɑt/ *n* **1** [C] a round vessel of baked clay, metal, glass, etc., used for containing liquids or solids and esp. for cooking: *a pot of soup*|*a teapot* **2** [C *of*] also **potful** /ˈpɑtfʊl/– the amount that a POT (1) will hold: *a pot of tea for two, please.* **3** [*the* S] *esp. AmE* all the money risked on one card game (esp. POKER) and taken by the winner **4** [*the* S] *AmE* all the money put together by a number of people for some common purpose (such as their weekly food supply) **5** [U] *infml* for MARIJUANA **6 go to pot** *infml* to become ruined or worthless, esp. from lack of care

pot² *v* **-tt-** [T] **1** to shoot and kill, esp. for food or sport **2** to put (a young plant) in a pot filled with earth

po·tas·si·um /pəˈtæsiʸəm/ *n* [U] a silver-white soft easily melted metal that is a simple substance (ELEMENT (1))

po·ta·to /pəˈteʸtoʷ, -ṭə-/ *n* **-toes** [C;U] a roundish root vegetable with a thin brown or yellowish skin, that is cooked and served in many different ways: *baked potatoes* –see also SWEET POTATO

potato chip /·ˈ·· ˌ·/ also **chip** *AmE*‖**crisp** *BrE*– *n* a thin piece of potato cooked in very hot fat, dried, salted, and usu. sold in bags

pot·bel·ly /ˈpɑtˌbeliʸ/ *n* **-lies** *often derog or humor* a large rounded noticeable stomach –**potbellied** /ˈpɑtˌbeliʸd/ *adj*

po·tent /ˈpoʷtnt/ *adj fml* (of medicines, drugs, drinks, etc.) having a strong and/or rapid effect on the body or mind: (fig.) *a potent* (=effective) *argument* –see also IMPOTENT

po·ten·tate /ˈpoʷtnˌteʸt/ *n* (esp. in former times) a ruler with direct power over his/her people, not limited by a law-making body

po·ten·tial¹ /pəˈtenʃəl, -tʃəl/ adj [no comp.] existing in possibility; not at present active or developed, but able to become so: *Every seed is a potential plant.*|*She is seen as a potential leader of the party.* –**potentially** adv

potential² n [U] (the degree of) possibility for developing or being developed: *a new invention with a big sales potential*

pot·hole /ˈpɑthoʷl/ n **1** a deep round hole in the surface of rock by which water enters and flows underground, often through a cave **2** a hole in the surface of a road caused by traffic or bad weather

po·tion /ˈpoʷʃən/ n lit a single drink of a liquid mixture, intended as medicine, poison, or a magic charm: *a sleeping/love potion*

pot·luck /ˌpɑtˈlʌk◄/ n **take potluck: a** to choose without enough information: *There are so many to chose from; I think I'd better take potluck and have–it doesn't matter, really–this one.* **b** (esp. of an unexpected guest) to have the same meal as everyone else: *Come home with us and have supper, if you don't mind taking potluck.*|*a potluck dinner*

pot·shot /ˈpɑt-ʃɑt/ n infml a carelessly aimed shot: *I took a potshot at the rabbit, but I missed.*|*She took potshots at my ideas.*

pot·ted /ˈpɑtɪd/ adj [A] (of meat, fish, or chicken) made into a paste and preserved in a pot, for eating when spread on bread

pot·ter /ˈpɑtər/ n a person who makes pots, dishes, etc., out of baked clay, esp. by hand

potter a·bout v adv [I] infml esp. BrE for PUTTER AROUND

pot·ter·y /ˈpɑtəriʸ/ n [U] **1** the work of a POTTER **2** (objects made out of) baked clay: *Modern pottery is usually decorated.*|*a pottery dish*

pot·ty /ˈpɑtiʸ/ n -ties a round vessel for liquid and solid body waste, used by children, now usu. made of plastic

pouch /paʊtʃ/ n **1** a small leather bag, esp. to hold tobacco or (formerly) gunpowder **2** a pocket of skin, esp. one in the lower half of the body, in which certain animals (MARSUPIALS) carry their young

poul·tice /ˈpoʷltɪs/ n a soft heated wet mass of any of various substances, spread on a thin cloth and laid against the skin to lessen pain, swelling, etc.

poul·try /ˈpoʷltriʸ/ n **1** [P] farmyard birds, such as hens, ducks, etc., kept for supplying eggs and meat: *Our poultry are kept at the rear of the garden.* **2** [U] hens, ducks, etc., considered as meat: *Poultry is cheap this week.*

pounce /paʊns/ v **pounced, pouncing** [I at, on, upon] to fly down or spring suddenly in order to seize something: *The cat pounced on the bird.*|(fig.) *Policemen were hiding in the bank, ready to pounce on the thieves.*

pound¹ /paʊnd/ n **1** [C] a standard measure of weight equal to 16 OUNCES (.454 kilograms): *Sugar is sold by the pound.*|*Two pounds of apples, please.*|*I lost several pounds last month.* (=became lighter by that amount) **2** [C; the S] also **pound sterling** fml– the British standard of money, divided into 100 pence:

Five pounds is usually written "£5."|*a five-pound note*|*Recently, the pound has* **grown stronger against** (=has increased in value in relation to) *the dollar.* **3** [C] the standard of money in several countries: *the Egyptian pound* **4** **-pounder** something weighing a certain number of pounds: *I went fishing and caught a five-pounder.*

pound² v **1** [T up] to crush into a soft mass or powder by striking repeatedly with a heavy object: *This machine pounds the stones into a powder.* **2** [I;T away, against, at, on] to strike or beat repeatedly, heavily, and noisily: *The stormy waves pounded against the rocks.*|*My heart pounded with excitement.*

pound³ n a place where lost dogs and cats, or cars that have been unlawfully parked, are kept by the police until claimed

pour /pɔr, poʷr/ v **1** [I;T away, in, out] (cause to) flow steadily and rapidly: *Blood poured from the wound.*|*Shall I pour you another cup of coffee?*|*At four o'clock the children poured out of school.*|(fig.) *The government has been pouring money into the steel industry recently.* **2** [it I down] to rain hard and steadily: *It's pouring (down).*|*in the pouring rain* –see WEATHER (USAGE)

pour sthg.↔ out v adv [T] to tell (a story, news, one's troubles, etc.) freely and with feeling

pout /paʊt/ v [I;T] to show childish bad temper and displeasure by pushing (the lips) forward –**pout** n

pov·er·ty /ˈpɑvərtiʸ/ n [U] the state of being very poor: *Poverty prevented the boy from continuing his education.*

poverty-strick·en /ˈ··· ˌ··/ adj very poor indeed

POW, P.O.W. /ˌpiʸ oʷ ˈdʌbəlyuʷ/ abbrev. for: PRISONER OF WAR: *a POW camp*

pow·der¹ /ˈpaʊdər/ n [C;U] (a kind of) substance in the form of very fine dry grains: *He stepped on the piece of chalk and crushed it to powder.*|*a packet of soap powder*|*face powder* (=a type of COSMETIC¹)

powder² v [T] to put POWDER¹ (esp. face powder, TALCUM POWDER) on: *John powdered the baby after its bath.*

pow·dered /ˈpaʊdərd/ adj produced or dried in the form of powder: *powdered milk*

powder room /ˈ··· ˌ·/ n euph a women's public BATHROOM in a theater, hotel, restaurant, big store, etc.

pow·der·y /ˈpaʊdəriʸ/ adj like or easily broken into powder: *powdery snow*

pow·er¹ /ˈpaʊər/ n **1** [C;U +to-v/of] what one can do; ability: *Man is the only animal that has the power of speech.*|*She claims to have the power to see into the future.*|*He did everything in his power* (=all he could) *to help her.*|*When she wrote this book, she was at the height of her powers as a writer.* **2** [U] force; strength: *You can really feel the power of the sun here.*|*a nation's sea power* (=the strength of its navy) **3** [U] force that may be used for doing work, driving a machine, or producing electricity: *Mills used to depend on wind power or water power.*|*The damaged ship was able to reach port* **under her own**

power. –see HORSEPOWER, MANPOWER **4** [C +*to-v*] right to act, given by law or official position: *The police have been given special powers to deal with this state of affairs.*|*She has the* **power of attorney** (=a signed, official paper giving the right) *to act for her brother.* **6** [C] a person, group, nation, etc., that has influence or control: *There must be a meeting of world powers* (=the strongest nations in the world) *to try to avoid war.*|(fig.) *No power on earth can make me do what I don't want to.* **7** [C] (in MATHEMATICS) the number of times that an amount is to be multiplied by itself: *The amount 2 to the power of 3 is written* 2^3, *and means* $2 \times 2 \times 2$. **8** [U] a measure of the degree to which a microscope, TELESCOPE, etc., is able to make things seen through it look larger **4** [U] control over others: *The power of the Church in national affairs has lessened.*|*Which political party is* **in power** *now?* (=which one is the government party?) **9** [S *of*] *infml* a large amount; great deal: *Your visit did me a power of good.* **10 the powers that be** *often humor* the people in high official positions who make decisions that have an effect on one's life **11 -powered** using or producing a certain type or amount of POWER (3): *a low-powered engine*|*a gas-powered heating system*

power² *v* **1** [T *usu. pass*] to supply power to (esp. a moving machine): *This train is powered by electricity.* **2** *infml* to move or travel powerfully and at speed

pow·er·ful /'pauǝrfǝl/ *adj* **1** having great power; very strong; full of force: *a powerful swimmer*|*a meeting of the world's most powerful nations*|*The ship is driven by two powerful motors.* **2** having a strong effect: *The mayor made a powerful speech.*|*a powerful drug* **–powerfully** *adv: He's very powerfully built.* (=has a big strong body)

pow·er·less /'pauǝrlis/ *adj* [+*to-v*] lacking power or strength; weak; unable: *The car went out of control, and the driver was powerless to stop it.* **–powerlessly** *adv* **–powerlessness** *n* [U]

power sta·tion /'·· ,··/ also **power plant** /'·· ,·/ *AmE*– a large building in which electricity is made

pp *written abbrev. said as:* pages: *see pp 15-37* –see also P²

P.R., PR *abbrev. for:* **1** PUBLIC RELATIONS **2** Puerto Rico /ˌpwertǝ 'riʸkoʷ, 'pɔr-, ˌpoʷr-/

prac·ti·ca·ble /'præktɪkǝbǝl/ *adj* that can be successfully used or acted upon (though not yet tried): *Is it practicable to try to grow crops in deserts?* –opposite **impracticable** –**practicably** *adv* –**practicability** /ˌpræktɪkǝ'bɪlǝtiʸ/ *n* [U]

USAGE Do not confuse **practicable** and **practical**. Although they can sometimes mean the same thing (a **practicable/practical** plan or suggestion is one that will work), **practicable** is never used of people and only rarely of objects.

prac·ti·cal¹ /'præktɪkǝl/ *adj* **1** concerned with action, practice, or actual conditions and results, rather than with ideas: *She has studied medicine but has not had much prac-*

tical experience with hospital work. **2** effective or convenient in actual use; suited to actual conditions: *a very practical little table that folds up out of the way when not needed* **3** *often apprec* sensible; clever at doing things and dealing with difficulties: *We've got to be practical and buy only what we can afford.* –opposite **impractical** (for 2, 3) –see PRACTICABLE (USAGE) –**practicality** /ˌpræktɪ'kæl ǝtiʸ/ *n* **-ties** [C;U]: *I'm not sure about the practicality of that suggestion.*

practical² *n infml* a PRACTICAL¹ (1) lesson, test, or examination, as in science: *a chemistry practical*

practical joke /ˌ··· '·/ *n* a trick played upon one person to give amusement to others

prac·ti·cal·ly /'præktɪkliʸ/ *adv* **1** usefully; suitably **2** very nearly; almost: *The holidays are practically over; there's only one day left.*

prac·tice¹, -tise /'præktɪs/ *n* **1** [C;U] (a) (regularly) repeated performance or exercise in order to gain skill in an activity: *It takes a lot of practice to be really good at this sport.*|*a football practice*|*teaching practice*|*I'm* **out of practice** *at playing the piano.* (=unable to play well because of lack of practice) **2** [U] the actual doing of something: *It sounded like a good idea, but* **in practice** *it didn't work.*|*We've made our plans, and now we must put them into practice.* –compare THEORY (2) **3** [C;U] *fml* something that is regularly or habitually done: *It is not the usual practice for offices to stay open after six o'clock.* –see HABIT (USAGE) **4** [C *usu. pl.*] *often derog* an act that is often repeated, esp. secretly, in a fixed manner or with ceremony: *the tribe's religious practices* **5** [C] the business of a doctor or lawyer

practice² *AmE*‖also **-tise** *v* **-ticed, -ticing** **1** [I;T+*v-ing*] to do (an action) or perform on (a musical instrument) regularly or repeatedly in order to gain skill: *She's been practicing the piano for nearly an hour.*|*You'll never learn to ride a bicycle if you don't practice.* **2** [T] to act in accordance with, esp. habitually: *They were prevented from practicing their religion.*|*a practicing Jew*|(*fml*) *We have to learn to practice* ECONOMY. (=avoid spending money) **3** [I;T] to do the work of a doctor or lawyer: *She practices medicine*|*practices as a doctor.*|*She's a practicing doctor.* **4 practice what one preaches** to do oneself what one is always telling others to do

prac·ticed *AmE*‖also **-tised** /'præktɪst/ *adj* skilled through practice: *a practiced cheat*|*thoroughly practiced in the art of dancing*

prac·ti·tion·er /præk'tɪʃǝnǝr/ *n* a person who works in a profession, esp. a doctor or lawyer: *medical practitioners* –see GENERAL PRACTITIONER

prag·mat·ic /præg'mætɪk/ *adj* dealing with matters in the way that seems best under the actual conditions, rather than following a rule; practical **–pragmatically** *adv*

prag·ma·tism /'prægmǝˌtɪzǝm/ *n* [U] PRAGMATIC thinking or way of considering things

prai·rie /'prɛǝriʸ/ *n* (esp. in North America) a wide treeless grassy plain

praise¹ /preʸz/ v **praised, praising** [T *for*] **1** to speak favorably and with admiration of **2** *fml or lit* to offer thanks and honor to (God), esp. in song in a church service

praise² n [U] **1** expression of admiration: *The new film has received a lot of praise.*|*a book in praise of country life* **2** *fml or lit* glory; worship: *Let us give praise to God.* **3** **sing the praises of** to praise (too) eagerly: *He's always singing his own praises.* (=praising himself)

praise·wor·thy /'preʸz₁wɜrðiʸ/ adj apprec deserving praise –**praiseworthiness** n [U]

pram /præm/ also **perambulator** fml– n BrE for BABY CARRIAGE

prance /præns/ v **pranced, prancing** [I] (of a horse) to jump high or move quickly by raising the front legs and springing forwards on the back legs: (fig.) *Jane pranced into the room wearing her new clothes.*

prank /præŋk/ n a playful but foolish trick, not intended to harm: *a schoolboy prank*

prat·tle¹ /'prætl/ v **-tled, -tling** [I *on, about*] usu. derog. to talk meaninglessly or lightly and continually in a childish way: *He prattled on about his job.*

prattle² n [U] infml often derog childish or unimportant talk

prawn /prɔn/ n a small ten-legged sea animal, used for food –compare SHRIMP

pray /preʸ/ v **prayed, praying** [I;T + to-v/ that/for, to] to speak, often silently, to God (or gods), showing love, giving thanks, or asking for (something): *They went to the mosque to pray.*|*I will pray to God for your safety.*|(infml) *The baseball game is on Saturday, so we're praying for* (=strongly hoping for) *a nice day.*

prayer /prɛər/ n **1** [U] the act of praying to God or gods: *They believe that prayer can bring peace to the world.* **2** [C] a solemn request made to God or gods: *Her prayer was answered and her parents came home safely.* **3** [C usu. pl.] a daily religious service among a group of people, mainly concerned with praying: *school prayers*

prayer book /'·· ·/ n a book containing prayers

preach /priʸtʃ/ v **1** [I;T +that/to] to give (a religious talk (SERMON)) esp. as part of a service in church: *Christ preached to large crowds.*|*The priest preached (about) the importance of caring for the old and sick.* **2** [T] to advise or urge others to accept (something that one believes in): *She's always preaching the value of fresh air.* **3** [I *at*] derog to offer (unwanted) advice on matters of right and wrong: *My sister has been preaching at me again about my lack of neatness.* –**preacher** n

pre·am·ble /'priʸˌæmbəl, priʸ'æmbəl/ n fml or derog a statement at the beginning of a speech or piece of writing, giving its reason and purpose

pre·ar·range /ˌpriʸə'reʸndʒ/ v **-ranged, -ranging** [T] to arrange in advance: *at a prearranged signal*

pre·car·i·ous /prɪ'kɛəriʸəs/ adj unsafe; not firm or steady: *The climber had only a precarious hold on the slippery rock.*|*The com-*

pany has started making a profit again, but its position is still precarious. –**precariously** adv –**precariousness** n [U]

pre·cau·tion /prɪ'kɔʃən/ n an action done in order to avoid possible known danger, discomfort, etc.: *We will* **take** *all the* **precautions** *we can against the painting being stolen.* –**precautionary** /prɪ'kɔʃəˌnɛriʸ/ adj

pre·cede /prɪ'siʸd/ v **-ceded, -ceding** [I;T] fml to come or go (just) in front (of): *The senator's statement preceded* (=came before) *the President's speech.* –compare SUCCEED (2) –**preceding** adj [A]: *I remember the war but not much of the preceding years.*

prec·e·dence /'prɛsədəns, prɪ'siʸdns/ n [U] (the right to) a particular place before others, esp. because of importance: *Studying* **has/takes precedence over** *playing football.*|*Let us deal with the questions* **in order of precedence.** (=the most important one being answered first)

prec·e·dent /'prɛsədənt/ n [C;U] (the use of) a former action or case that acts as an example or rule for present action: *When he decided the case, the judge had to follow the precedent which had been established in 1920.*|*If you let the children stay up late tonight, you will* **set a precedent**, *and they'll expect to stay up late every night.*

pre·cept /'priʸsɛpt/ n a guiding rule on which behavior, a way of thought or action, etc., is based

pre·cinct /'priʸsɪŋkt/ n **1** AmE a division of a town or city for election or police purposes: *These policemen are from the twelfth precinct.* **2** [of usu. pl.] the space, often enclosed by walls, that surrounds an important building or group of buildings: *It's quiet within the precincts of the old college.*

pre·cincts /'priʸsɪŋkts/ n [P of] fml neighborhood; area around (a town or other place): *The precincts of the port are full of seamen when the ships are in.*

pre·cious¹ /'prɛʃəs/ adj of great value: *a precious jewel*|*That old toy bear is John's most precious* (=most dearly loved) *possession.*

precious² adv infml very (esp. in the phrases **precious little/few**)

precious met·al /ˌ·· '··/ n [C;U] a rare and valuable metal, such as gold or silver

precious stone /ˌ·· '·/ also **stone–** n a rare and valuable jewel, such as a diamond, EMERALD, etc. –compare SEMIPRECIOUS

prec·i·pice /'prɛsəpɪs/ n a steep or almost upright side of a high rock, mountain, or cliff

pre·cip·i·tate¹ /prɪ'sɪpəˌteʸt/ v **-tated, -tating** **1** [T] fml to hasten the coming of (an unwanted event): *The sudden increase in the cost of oil precipitated the failure of his company.* **2** [I;T] (in chemistry) to (cause to) separate from a liquid because of chemical action

pre·cip·i·tate² /prɪ'sɪpətɪt, -ˌteʸt/ n [C;U] (in chemistry) a solid substance that has been separated from a liquid by chemical action –compare PRECIPITATION (3)

precipitate³ /prɪ'sɪpətɪt/ adj fml wildly hasty; acting or done without care or thought –compare PRECIPITOUS –**precipitately** adv

pre·cip·i·ta·tion /prɪˌsɪpə'teᵞʃən/ *n* [U] **1** *fml* unwise haste **2** *tech* (amount of) rain, snow, etc. **3** (in chemistry) the act of precipitating (PRECIPITATE¹ (2))

pre·cip·i·tous /prɪ'sɪpətəs/ *adj* dangerously steep –compare PRECIPITATE³

pré·cis /preᵞ'siᵞ, 'preᵞsiᵞ/ *n* **précis** /preᵞ'siᵞz, 'preᵞsiᵞz/ a shortened form of a speech or piece of writing, giving only the main points

pre·cise /prɪ'saɪs/ *adj* **1** exact (in form, detail, measurements, time, etc.): *very precise calculations*|*Our train leaves at about half past ten, or*–**to be precise**–*10:33.* **2** careful and correct in regard to the smallest details: *A scientist must be precise in making tests.* –opposite **imprecise** –**preciseness** *n* [U]

pre·cise·ly /prɪ'saɪsliᵞ/ *adv* **1** exactly: *The train leaves precisely at 10 o'clock.* **2** yes, that is correct; you are right: *"So you think we ought to wait until next fall?" "Precisely."*

pre·ci·sion /prɪ'sɪʒən/ *n* **1** [U] also **preciseness**– exactness: *She doesn't express her thoughts with precision, so people often misunderstand her.* –opposite **imprecision 2** [A] used for producing very exact results: *precision instruments*

pre·clude /prɪ'kluʷd/ *v* **-cluded, -cluding** [T +*v-ing*/*from*] *fml* to prevent: *Let us be exact in what we say so as to preclude any possibility of misunderstanding.* –**preclusion** /prɪ'kluʷʒən/ *n* [U]

pre·co·cious /prɪ'koʷʃəs/ *adj sometimes derog* (of a young person or his/her abilities) showing unusually early development of mind or body –**precociously** *adv* –**precociousness** *n* [U] –**precocity** /prɪ'kɑsətiᵞ/ *n* [U]

pre·con·ceived /ˌpriᵞkən'siᵞvd/ *adj* (of an idea, opinion, etc.) formed in advance, without (enough) knowledge or experience –**preconception** /ˌpriᵞkən'sɛpʃən/ *n*: *Most of my preconceptions about New York were proved wrong when I actually went to live there.*

pre·cur·sor /prɪ'kɜrsər, 'priᵞˌkɜrsər/ *n* [*of*] *fml* a person or thing that comes before and is a sign or earlier type of one that is to follow: *The precursor of the modern car was a horseless carriage with a gasoline engine.*

pre·date /ˌpriᵞ'deᵞt/ *v* **-dated, -dating** [T] to write on (a letter, check, etc.) a date earlier than the date of writing –see also POSTDATE

pred·a·tor /'prɛdətər, -ˌtɔr/ *n* a PREDATORY (1) animal

pred·a·to·ry /'prɛdəˌtɔriᵞ, -ˌtoʷriᵞ/ *adj* **1** (esp. of a wild animal) living by killing and eating other animals **2** concerned with or living (as if) by robbery and seizing the property of others: *predatory tribes*|(fig.) *This city is full of predatory hotel keepers!*

pred·e·ces·sor /'prɛdəˌsɛsər/ *n* **1** a person who held an (official) position before someone else: *Our new doctor is much younger than his predecessor.* **2** something formerly used, but which has now been changed for something else: *This latest plan to save the company seems to me no better than any of its predecessors.*

pre·des·ti·na·tion /ˌpriᵞdɛstə'neᵞʃən, priᵞˌdes-/ *n* [U] the belief that God or fate has decided everything that will happen, and that no human effort can change things –compare FREE WILL

pre·des·tine /priᵞ'dɛstɪn/ *v* **-tined, -tining** [T] *fml* to fix, as if by God or fate, the future of: *He felt that he was predestined to lead his country to freedom.*

pre·de·ter·mine /ˌpriᵞdɪ'tɜrmɪn/ *v* **-mined, -mining** [T *usu. pass.*] to fix unchangeably from the beginning: *The color of a person's eyes is usually predetermined by that of his parents.*

pre·dic·a·ment /prɪ'dɪkəmənt/ *n* a difficult or unpleasant state of affairs in which one must make a difficult choice: *I'm in a predicament. Should I take this new job, or stay home with my baby?*

pred·i·cate /'prɛdɪkɪt/ *n* the part of a sentence which makes a statement about the subject: *In "Birds fly" and "She is an artist," "fly" and "is an artist" are predicates.*

pred·i·ca·tive /'prɛdɪˌkeᵞtɪv, -kəṭɪv/ *adj* (of an adjective, noun, or phrase) coming after the noun being described or after the verb of which the noun is the subject: *In "He is alive," "alive" is a predicative adjective.* –compare ATTRIBUTIVE –see Study Notes on page 9

pre·dict /prɪ'dɪkt/ *v* [T +(*that*)] to see or describe (a future happening) in advance as a result of knowledge, experience, reason, etc.: *She predicted that he would marry a doctor.*|*Can you predict when the work will be finished?*

pre·dict·a·ble /prɪ'dɪktəbəl/ *adj* that can be PREDICTED –opposite **unpredictable** –**predictably** *adv*

pre·dic·tion /prɪ'dɪkʃən/ *n* **1** [C +*that*] something that is PREDICTED **2** [U] the act of PREDICTING

pred·i·lec·tion /ˌprɛdl'ɛkʃən, ˌpriᵞd-/ *n* [*for*] a special liking that has become a habit: *Charles has always had a predilection for red-haired women.*

pre·dis·pose /ˌpriᵞdɪ'spoʷz/ *v* **-posed, -posing** [T *to*] *fml* to influence (someone) in the stated way: *I have heard nothing that predisposes me to dislike her.*|*His weak chest predisposes him to* (=makes him likely to get) *winter colds.*

pre·dis·po·si·tion /ˌpriᵞdɪspə'zɪʃən/ *n fml* [*to*] a state of body or mind that is favorable (to something, often something bad)

pre·dom·i·nant /prɪ'dɑmənənt/ *adj* [*over*] most powerful, noticeable, or important: *Bright red was the predominant color in the room.* –**predominance** *n* [S;U]

pre·dom·i·nant·ly /prɪ'dɑmənəntliᵞ/ *adv* mostly; mainly: *The votes were predominantly in favor of the new law.*

pre·dom·i·nate /prɪ'dɑməˌneᵞt/ *v* **-nated, -nating** [I *over*] to be greater or greatest in numbers, force, influence, etc.

pre·em·i·nent /priᵞ'ɛmənənt/ *adj usu. apprec* above all others in the possession of some (usu. good) quality, ability, or main activity –**preeminence** *n* [U] –**preeminently** *adv*

pre·empt /priᵞ'ɛmpt/ *v* [T] to cause to have no influence or force by means of taking action in advance: *The council found that their plans had been preempted by a government decision.* –**preemptive** *adj: a preemptive strike by the army*

preen /priʸn/ *v* **1** [T] (of a bird) to clean or smooth (itself or its feathers) with the beak **2** [I;T] (of a person) to make (oneself) neat; to show self-satisfaction: *John stood preening (himself) in front of the mirror.*

pre·fab /priʸˈfæb, ˈpriʸfæb/ *n infml* a small prefabricated house

pre·fab·ri·cate /priʸˈfæbrə,keʸt/ *v* **-cated, -cating** [T] to make (the parts of a building, ship, etc.) in a factory ready for fitting together in any place chosen for building –**prefabricated** *adj* –**prefabrication** /,priʸfæbrəˈkeʸʃən/ *n* [U]

pref·ace¹ /ˈprɛfɪs/ *n* [*to*] an introduction to a book or speech, usu. written by the writer –compare FOREWORD

preface² *v* **-aced, -acing** [T *with, by*] to provide with a PREFACE¹: *He prefaced his speech with an amusing story.*

pre·fect /ˈpriʸfɛkt/ *n* (*sometimes cap.*) (in certain countries today) a public officer or judge with duties in government, the police, or the army: *the Prefect of Police of Paris*

pre·fer /prɪˈfɜr/ *v* **-rr-** [T] **1** [+*to-v/v-ing/to*] to choose (one thing or action) rather than another; like better: *I prefer dogs to cats.|"Would you like meat or fish?" "I prefer meat, please."|Would you prefer that I come on Monday instead of Tuesday?* **2** [*against*] *law* to put forward for official consideration or action according to law (esp. in the phrases **prefer charges/a charge**)

pref·er·a·ble /ˈprɛfərəbəl/ *adj* [*to no comp.*] better (esp. because more suitable); to be PREFERred: *Anything is preferable to having them with us for the whole week!* –**preferably** *adv*

pref·er·ence /ˈprɛfərəns/ *n* **1** [C;U *for, to*] (a) desire or liking (for one thing rather than another): *They've always had a preference for taking their vacations abroad.* (=rather than in their own country)*|I'd choose the small car in preference to the larger one.* (=rather than the larger one) **2** [U] special favor or consideration shown to a person, group, etc.: *In considering people for jobs in our company, we give preference to those with some experience.*

pref·er·en·tial /,prɛfəˈrɛnʃəl, -tʃəl/ *adj* [A] of, giving, receiving, or showing PREFERENCE (2): *The President admitted that he gave preferential treatment to people from his own party.*

pre·fix /ˈpriʸˌfɪks/ *n* (in grammar) an AFFIX that is placed at the beginning of a word or base: *"Re-" (meaning "again") is a prefix in "refill."* –compare SUFFIX

preg·nan·cy /ˈprɛgnənsiʸ/ *n* **-cies** [C;U] (an example of) the condition of being PREGNANT (1): *Is it unwise to smoke during pregnancy?*

preg·nant /ˈprɛgnənt/ *adj* **1** [after *n*] (of a woman or female animal) having a developing child or young in the body: *How long has she been pregnant?|She is five months pregnant.* **2** [A] full of important but unexpected

meaning: *His words were followed by a pregnant pause.*

pre·hen·sile /prɪˈhɛnsəl, -saɪl/ *adj tech* (of a part of the body) able to curl around, seize, and hold things: *a monkey hanging from the tree by its prehensile tail*

pre·his·tor·ic /,priʸhɪˈstɔrɪk, -ˈstɑr-/ *adj* of or belonging to a time before recorded history: *prehistoric man|prehistoric burial grounds* –**prehistory** /priʸˈhɪstəriʸ/ *n* [U]

pre·judge /,priʸˈdʒʌdʒ/ *v* **-judged, -judging** [T] to form an (unfavorable) opinion about (someone or something) before knowing or examining all the facts –**prejudgment, -judgement** *n* [C;U]

prej·u·dice¹ /ˈprɛdʒədɪs/ *n* [C;U] (an example of) unfair and often unfavorable feeling or opinion not based on reason or enough knowledge: *A judge must be free from prejudice.|a new law to discourage **racial prejudice** (=prejudice against members of other races)|He has a prejudice against women drivers.*

prejudice² *v* **-diced, -dicing** [T] **1** [*against, in favor of*] to cause (someone or someone's mind) to have a PREJUDICE¹; influence: *He is prejudiced against French wine because he is Italian.* **2** to weaken; harm (someone's case, expectations, etc.): *Your bad spelling may prejudice your chances of getting this job.*

prej·u·diced /ˈprɛdʒədɪst/ *adj usu. derog* feeling or showing PREJUDICE¹; unfair –opposite **unprejudiced**

prej·u·di·cial /,prɛdʒəˈdɪʃəl/ *adj* [F *to*] *fml* harmful: *His lawyer told him that the new information would be prejudicial to his case.*

prel·ate /ˈprɛlɪt/ *n* a priest of high rank, esp. a BISHOP or someone with a higher rank

pre·lim·i·nar·y¹ /prɪˈlɪmə,nɛriʸ/ *n* **-ies** [*usu. pl.*] a preparation; PRELIMINARY² act or arrangement: *There are a lot of preliminaries to be gone through before you can visit that country.*

preliminary² *adj* [A] coming before and introducing or preparing for something more important: *The students take a preliminary test in March, and the main examination in July.*

prel·ude /ˈprɛlyuʷd, ˈpreʸluʷd, ˈpriʸluʷd/ *n* [*to usu. sing.*] **1** something that comes before and acts as an introduction to something more important: *The widespread fighting in the streets may be a prelude to more serious trouble.* **2** a short piece of music that introduces a large musical work

pre·mar·i·tal /,priʸˈmærətḷ/ *adj* happening or existing before marriage: *premarital sex* –**premaritally** *adv*

pre·ma·ture /,priʸməˈtʃʊər, -ˈtʊər, -ˈtyʊər/ *adj* developing, happening, or coming before the natural or proper time: *His premature death at the age of 32 is a great loss.|The baby had to be kept in the hospital because it was two months premature.* (=born two months earlier than expected)*|I think your attack on the new law is a little premature since we don't know all the details yet.* –**prematurely** *adv*

pre·med·i·tat·ed /priˠ'mɛdə,teˠtɪd/ adj intentional; done on purpose; planned: *premeditated murder*

pre·mier¹ /prɪ'mɪər, -'myɪər, 'priˠmɪər/ adj [A] *fml* first (in position or importance): *America's premier medical school*

premier² n [A;C] (*often cap.*) the head of the government (PRIME MINISTER) in certain countries: *a meeting between the Irish Premier and the President of the US* –**premiership** n

pre·miere, **-mière** /prɪ'mɪər, -'myɪər, -'myɛər/ n the first public performance of a play or a movie

prem·ise /'prɛmɪs/ n [C +*that*] *fml* a statement or idea on which reasoning is based: *The lawyer based his argument on the premise that people are innocent until they are proven guilty.*

prem·is·es /'prɛmɪsɪz/ n [P] a building with any surrounding land, considered as a particular piece of property: *I have warned you before to keep off my premises!|Food bought in this store may not be eaten* **on the premises.** (=must be taken away before being eaten)

pre·mi·um /'priˠmiˠəm/ n **1** a sum of money paid (regularly) to an insurance company to protect oneself against some risk of loss or damage **2 at a premium** rare or difficult to obtain, and therefore worth more than usual: *During the vacation months of July and August, hotel rooms are at a premium.*

pre·mo·ni·tion /,priˠmənɪʃən, ,prɛ-/ n [C +*that/of*] a feeling that something (esp. something unpleasant) is going to happen; forewarning: *The day before her accident, she had a premonition of danger.*

pre·mon·i·to·ry /prɪ'manə,tɔriˠ, -,towˠriˠ/ adj *fml* giving a warning

pre·na·tal /,priˠ'neˠt̬l/ adj *tech esp. AmE* existing or happening before birth: *Women who are going to have a baby should go to a doctor regularly for* **prenatal examinations.**

pre·oc·cu·pa·tion /priˠ,akyə'peˠʃən, ,priˠak-/ n **1** [U] the state of being PREOCCUPIED: *his preoccupation with his health* **2** [C] a matter which takes up all one's attention

pre·oc·cu·pied /priˠ'akyə,paɪd/ adj with the mind fixed on something else (esp. something worrying); inattentive to present matters: *You were too preoccupied to recognize me in the street yesterday.*

pre·oc·cu·py /priˠ'akyə,paɪ/ v **-pied, -pying** [T] to fill the thoughts of (someone) almost completely, esp. so that not enough attention is given to other (present) matters

prep·a·ra·tion /,prɛpə'reˠʃən/ n **1** [U] the act of preparing: *He didn't do enough preparation for his examination.|Plans for the new school are now* **in preparation.** (=being prepared) **2** [C *for, usu. pl.*] an arrangement (for a future event): *Preparations for the party are almost complete.* **3** [C] something that is made ready for use by mixing a number of (chemical) substances: *a new preparation for cleaning metal*

pre·par·a·to·ry /prɪ'pærə,tɔriˠ, -,towˠriˠ, -'pɛər-, 'prɛpərə-/ adj [A] **1** done in order to

get ready for something **2 preparatory to** *prep fml* before: as a preparation for: *I have a few letters to write preparatory to beginning the day's work.*

preparatory school /·'····· ,·/ also **prep school** *infml–* n (in the US) a private high school where students are made ready to attend college

pre·pare /prɪ'pɛər/ v **-pared, -paring 1** [I;T +*to-v/for*] to get ready; make ready: *First prepare the rice by washing it, then cook it in boiling water.|They are busy preparing to go on vacation.|Will you help me prepare for* (=get everything ready for) *the party?* **2** [T *for*] to accustom (someone or someone's mind) to some (new) idea, event, or condition: *He prepared himself for defeat.*

pre·pared /prɪ'pɛərd/ adj [*no comp.*] **1** gotten ready in advance: *The chairman read out a prepared statement.* –opposite **unprepared 2** [F +*to-v*] willing: *I'm not prepared to listen to your weak excuses.*

pre·pay /,priˠ'peˠ/ v **-paid** /'peˠd/, **-paying** [T] to pay for (something) in advance

pre·pon·der·ance /prɪ'pandərəns/ n [S;U *of*] *fml* the quality or state of being greater in amount, number, etc.: *There is now a preponderance of women on the company's senior staff.* –**preponderant** adj –**preponderantly** adv

prep·o·si·tion /,prɛpə'zɪʃən/ n a word used with a noun or PRONOUN to show its connection with another word: *In "He walked into the house" and "She succeeded by working hard," "into" and "by" are prepositions.* –see Study Notes on page 528 –**prepositional** adj: *"In a soft bed" and "on top" are prepositional phrases.*

pre·pos·sess·ing /,priˠpə'zɛsɪŋ/ adj *fml* (of a person or a quality of his/her character) very pleasing; charming –opposite **unprepossessing**

pre·pos·ter·ous /prɪ'pastərəs/ adj completely unreasonable or improbable; ABSURD: *That's the most preposterous idea I've ever heard!* –**preposterously** adv

prep school /'prɛp skuwl/ n [C;U] *infml* for PREPARATORY SCHOOL

pre·req·ui·site /priˠ'rɛkwəzɪt/ n,adj *fml* [*to, for*] (something) that is necessary before something else can happen or be done: *Every student must take certain prerequisite classes before beginning study in their field of interest.*

pre·rog·a·tive /prɪ'ragətɪv/ n *fml* [*usu. sing.*] a special right belonging to someone by rank, position, or nature: *A judge may use his prerogative of mercy towards a criminal.*

pres·age /'prɛsɪdʒ, prɪ'seˠdʒ/ v **-aged, -aging** [T not *be* +*v-ing*] *lit* to be a warning of; FORETELL

Pres·by·te·ri·an /,prɛzbə'tɪriˠən, ,prɛs-/ n,adj (a member) of a PROTESTANT Church governed by a body of official people all of equal rank

pres·by·ter·y /'prɛzbə,tɛriˠ, 'prɛs-/ n **-ies 1** (in the PRESBYTERIAN Church) a local court or ruling body **2** (in the ROMAN CATHOLIC Church) the house in which a priest lives

pre·scribe /prɪ'skraɪb/ v **-scribed, -scribing** [I;T for] **1** to order the use of (something, esp. a medicine or treatment): *The doctor prescribed a medicine for the child's stomach pains.* **2** fml (of a person or body that has the right to do so) to state (what must be done in certain conditions): *What punishment does the law prescribe for this crime?*

pre·scrip·tion /prɪ'skrɪpʃən/ n **1** [U] the act of prescribing (PRESCRIBE) **2** [C] something that is PRESCRIBED: (fig.) *What's your prescription for a happy marriage?* **3** [C] (a written order describing) a particular medicine or treatment ordered by a doctor: *Take this prescription to your local* PHARMACY.

pres·ence /'prɛzəns/ n [U] **1** (the fact or state of) being present: *She was so quiet that her presence was hardly noticed.|Your presence is requested at the meeting on Thursday.* –opposite **absence 2** [U] personal appearance and manner, as having a strong effect on others **3** in the presence of someone also in someone's presence– close enough to be seen or heard by someone **4** presence of mind the ability to act calmly, quickly, and wisely in conditions of sudden danger or surprise: *When the fire started in the kitchen, John had the presence of mind to turn off the gas.*

pres·ent¹ /'prɛzənt/ n a gift: *They unwrapped their Christmas presents.*

pre·sent² /prɪ'zɛnt/ v [T] more fml than **give– 1** to give (something) away, esp. at a ceremonial occasion: *He presented a silver cup to the winner/presented the winner with a silver cup.* **2** (of non-material things) to be the cause of; give: *The question should present no difficulty to you.* **3** to offer (esp. in the phrases **present one's apologies/compliments/respects**, etc.) **4** to offer for consideration or bring to someone's attention: *The committee is presenting its report next week.* **5** to provide for the public to see in a theater, movie theater, etc.: *The theater company is presenting "Hamlet" next week.* **6** fml to introduce (someone) esp. to someone of higher rank: *May I present Mr. Johnson (to you)?* **7** to introduce and take part in (a television or radio show)

pres·ent³ /'prɛzənt/ adj **1** [F] in the place talked of or understood: *How many people were present at the meeting?* –opposite **absent 2** [A] existing or being considered now: *What is your present address?|It's usually best to wait, but in the present case* (=in this case) *I'd do it now.* **3** [A] (of a tense or a form of a verb) expressing an existing state or action: *In "he wants" and "they are coming," the verbs are in the present tense.*

pres·ent⁴ /'prɛzənt/ n **1** [the S] the PRESENT³ (2) time: *We learn from the past, experience the present, and hope for success in the future.* **2** [C] the PRESENT³ (3) tense **3** at present at this time; now **4** for the present now but not necessarily in the future

pre·sent·a·ble /prɪ'zɛntəbəl/ adj fit to be shown, heard, etc., in public; fit to be seen and judged **–presentably** adv

pres·en·ta·tion /ˌprɛzən'teɪʃən, ˌpriʸ-/ n **1** [C;U of] the act or action of PRESENTing² something: *The presentation of prizes will begin at three p.m.* **2** [U of] the way in which something is said, offered, shown, explained, etc., to others

pres·ent-day /ˌprɛzənt 'deɪ◄/ adj [A] modern; existing now: *present-day prices*

pre·sen·ti·ment /prɪ'zɛntəmənt/ n [C +that/of] fml an unexplained uncomfortable feeling that something (esp. something bad) is going to happen; PREMONITION

pres·ent·ly /'prɛzəntliʸ/ adv **1** soon: *The doctor will be here presently.* **2** esp. AmE at present; now: *The doctor is presently writing a book.*

present par·ti·ci·ple /ˌ·· '····/ n (in grammar) a form of a verb which ends in -ing and may be used in compound forms of the verb to express actions done or happening in the past, present, or future, or sometimes as an adjective: *In the sentence "I'm going," "going" is a present participle.*

present per·fect /ˌ·· '··/ also **perfect, perfect tense–** n tech (of a verb) the tense of a verb that shows a period of time up to and including the present, and in English is formed with *has* or *have* and a PAST PARTICIPLE –see PERFECT¹ (5), PAST PERFECT

pres·er·va·tion /ˌprɛzər'veɪʸʃən/ n [U] **1** [of] the act or action of preserving (PRESERVE): *The police are responsible for the preservation of law and order.* **2** the state of being or remaining in (a stated) condition after a long time: *The old building is in a good state of preservation except for the wooden floors.*

pre·serv·a·tive /prɪ'zɜrvətɪv/ n,adj [C;U] a usu. chemical substance) that can be used to PRESERVE¹ (3) foods

pre·serve¹ /prɪ'zɜrv/ v **-served, -serving** [T] **1** to keep (someone or something) alive, safe from destruction, etc.: *The Town Council has spent a lot of money to preserve this remarkable old building.* **2** to cause (a condition) to last; keep unchanged: *It is the duty of the police to preserve public order.* **3** to keep (something, esp. food) in good condition for a long time by some special treatment: *preserved fruit|The Ancient Egyptians knew how to preserve dead bodies from decay.* –compare CONSERVE

preserve² n **1** [C usu. pl.; U] a substance made from fruit boiled in sugar, used esp.for spreading on bread; JAM **2** [C] a stretch of land or water kept for private hunting or fishing **3** [C] something considered to belong to or be for the use of only a certain person or limited number of people: *She considers the arranging of flowers in the church to be her own preserve.*

pre·side /prɪ'zaɪd/ v **-sided, -siding** [I at] to be in charge; lead: *the presiding officer at the election*

preside over sthg. v prep [T] **1** to direct (a committee or other formal group of people): *The meeting was presided over by the chairman.*

pres·i·den·cy /'prɛzədənsiʸ/ n **-cies 1** [of] the office of president: *Roosevelt was elected four times to the presidency of the US.* **2** the

STUDY NOTES prepositions

The radio is **on** the refrigerator.
The milk is **in** the refrigerator.
Fill in the blanks with _in_ or _on_.
1. "Is there any orange juice?"
   "Yes, it's _____ a bottle _____ the refrigerator.
   It's _____ the top shelf."
2. "Is there any bread?"
   "Yes, it's _____ the refrigerator. It's _____ a
   plastic bag."

There's a cover **over** the cake.
There's a cake **on** the table.
There's a light **over/above** the table.
Fill in the blanks with _on_, _over_, or _above_.
3. "Where's the teapot?"
   "It's _____ the stove."
4. "I can't find the sugar."
   "It's _____ the shelf _____ the stove."

A boy is fishing **on** the bridge.
His friend is fishing **below** the bridge.
There's a boat **under** the bridge.

Fill in the blanks with _on_, _under_, or _below_.
5. The car is _____ the bridge.
6. The town is _____ the bridge.
7. The river is flowing _____ the bridge.

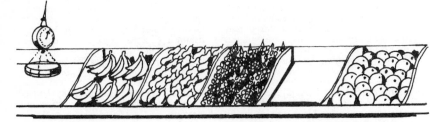

The bananas are **beside** the pears.
The pears are **between** the bananas and the
grapes.

Fill in the blanks with _beside_ or _between_.
8. "Where should I put these apples?"
   "Put them _____ the grapes and the oranges."
9. "Where do these lemons go?"
   "_____ the bananas."

Mr. and Mrs. Brown live **in** this house.
They live **on** 14th Street.
They live **on** the corner of 14th and Stonewall.
They live **at** 803 East 14th Street.
They live **in** a small town.

Fill in the blanks with *in, on,* or *at*.

10. "Where do you live?"
    "I live _____ a small town in New Jersey."
11. "Where's your school?"
    "It's _____ Main Street. It's _____ the corner
    of Main and Spring Streets."
12. "Please deliver this package to my sister.
    She lives _____ 3225 North Thomas Avenue."

The truck is **in front of** the large car.
The small car is **between** the truck and the
motorcycle.
The small car is **behind** the motorcycle.

**Fill in the blanks with *in front of, behind,* or
between.**

13. The motorcycle is _____ the small car.
14. The truck is _____ the large car and the
    small car.
15. The large car is _____ the truck.

A woman is going **into** the bank.
The man is coming **out of** the drug store.
The little girl is walking **towards** the candy store,
and the little boy is walking **away from** it.

**Fill in the blanks with *towards, away from,
into,* or *out of*.**

16. The policeman is walking _____ the phone
    booth.
17. The old man is waiting to go _____ the
    phone booth. A woman is coming _____ it.
    She's just made a call.

length of time a person is president

pres·i·dent /'prɛzədənt/ n 1 [C;A] (often cap.) the head of government in many modern states that do not have a king or queen: the President of France|President Reagan 2 [C] (sometimes cap.) the head of a club or society, some universities or colleges, some government departments, etc.: the President of the Board of Trade|of Corpus Christi College 3 [C] AmE (sometimes cap.) the head of a business company, firm, bank, etc. –**presidential** /ˌprɛzə'dɛnʃəl, -tʃəl/ adj [A]

press¹ /prɛs/ v 1 [I;T] to push firmly and steadily: Press this button to start the engine. 2 [T] to direct weight or force on (something) in order to crush, flatten, pack tightly, or get juice out: To make wine, first you press the GRAPES.|pressed flowers 3 [T] to give (clothes) a smooth surface and a sharp fold by using a hot iron 4 [T] to hold firmly as a sign of friendship, love, pity, etc.: He pressed my hand warmly when we met. 5 [I;T] to continue to force (an attack, hurried action, etc.) on (someone): We must hurry, time is pressing. (=we don't have much time) 6 [T] to continue to demand or ask for: She pressed her guest to stay a little longer.|The company is pressing (me) for a decision.

press on/forward fml– v adv [I with] to continue; advance with courage or without delay: Let's press on with our work.

press² n 1 [S] an act of pushing steadily against something 2 [the U] (writers and reporters for) newspapers and magazines in general (often including the news-gathering services of radio and television): the power of the press|a press photographer|The press has been invited to a meeting to hear the President's speech. 3 [S] treatment given by newspapers in general when reporting about a person or event: The play received a good press. (=the newspapers said it was good) 4 [C] →PRINTING PRESS 5 [C] (usu. cap.) a business for printing (and sometimes also for selling) books, magazines, etc.: the University Press 6 [C] an act of smoothing a garment with a hot iron 7 [C] a machine used for pressing 8 **go to press** (of a newspaper for any particular day) to start being printed

press a·gent /'· ˌ··/ n a person in charge of keeping a politician, actor, theater, etc., in favorable public notice by supplying photographs, interesting facts, details of coming performances, etc., to newspapers

press con·fer·ence /'· ˌ···/ also **news conference**– n a meeting arranged by an important person to which news reporters are invited to listen to a statement or to ask questions

press cut·ting /'· ˌ··/ n a short notice, picture, etc., cut out of a newspaper or magazine

pressed /prɛst/ adj [F for] having hardly enough (of): I'm pressed for time this morning so I'll see you in the afternoon.

press·ing /'prɛsɪŋ/ adj demanding or needing attention, action, etc., now: Pressing

business matters prevented her from taking a vacation.

press re·lease /'· ·ˌ·/ n a prepared statement given out to news services and newspapers

pres·sure¹ /'prɛʃər/ n 1 [U of] the action of pressing with force or weight: The pressure of the water turns this wheel, and this is used to make electric power. 2 [C;U] the strength of this force: These air containers will burst at high pressures. 3 [C;U] the (force of the) weight of the air: Low pressure often brings rain. 4 [U] forcible influence: We must put **pressure on** the government to change this law.|He didn't want to leave the country; he only agreed to go **under pressure**. (=after being forcibly persuaded to do so) 5 [U of] the conditions of work, a style of living, etc., which cause anxiety and difficulty: The pressure of work became too much for him, and his doctor suggested a vacation. –see BLOOD PRESSURE

pressure² esp. AmE‖**pressurize** BrE– v -sured, -suring [T into] to (try to) make (someone) do something by means of forceful demands or influence: They pressured him into freeing the prisoners.

pressure cook·er /'·· ˌ··/ n a tightly covered metal cooking pot in which food can be cooked very quickly by the pressure of hot steam

pressure group /'·· ˌ·/ n a group of people that actively tries to influence public opinion and government action, usu. for its own advantage

pres·sur·ize‖also **-ise** BrE /'prɛʃəˌraɪz/ v -ized, -izing [T] 1 to control the air pressure inside (an aircraft) so that the pressure does not become much lower than that on earth: a pressurized CABIN 1 BrE for PRESSURE²

pres·tige /prɛ'stiʒ, -'stiʸdʒ/ n [U] general respect or admiration felt for someone or something by reason of rank, proved high quality, etc.: The universities of Harvard and Yale have a lot of prestige.

pres·tig·ious /prɛ'stɪdʒəs, -'stiʸ-/ adj usu. apprec having or bringing PRESTIGE

pre·sum·a·bly /prɪ'zuːʷməbliʸ/ adv probably; it may reasonably be supposed that: Presumably there's a good reason for her absence because she doesn't usually stay home from work.

pre·sume /prɪ'zuːʷm/ v -sumed, -suming 1 [I;T +(that)] to take (something) as true without direct proof; suppose: From the way they talked I presumed they were/them to be married. 2 [I +to-v] fml to dare to do something which one has no right to do: Are you presuming to tell me how the work should be done?

presume upon/on sthg.– v prep [T] fml to make a wrong use of (someone's kindness) by asking for help, etc.

pre·sump·tion /prɪ'zʌmpʃən/ n 1 [C +that] an act of supposing: Your presumption that I would agree with your plan is false. 2 [U] improper boldness that shows too high an opinion of oneself

pre·sump·tu·ous /prɪ'zʌmptʃuʷəs/ adj derog showing too much boldness towards others as a result of having too high an opinion of oneself –**presumptuously** *adv*

pre·sup·pose /ˌpriʸsə'poʷz/ *v* -**posed, -posing** [T +*that*] to suppose or take to be true; ASSUME –**presupposition** /ˌpriʸsʌpə'zɪʃən/ *n* [C;U +*that*]: *Your judgment of the case is based on the presupposition that the witness is telling the truth.*

pre·tend /prɪ'tɛnd/ *v* [I;T +*to-v*/(*that*)] **1** to give an appearance of (something that is not true), with the intention of deceiving: *She pretended she didn't know me when I passed her in the street.|He pretended to be reading.|She wasn't really crying; she was only pretending.* **2** (usu. of a child) to imagine as a game: *Let's pretend we're on the moon!*

pre·tend·er /prɪ'tɛndər/ *n* [*to*] a person who makes a (doubtful or unproved) claim to some high position, such as to be the rightful king

pre·tense *AmE*‖also **-tence** /'priʸtɛns, prɪ'tɛns/ *n* [S;U] **1** a false appearance, reason, or show intended to deceive or as a game: *She isn't really ill; it's only pretense.|He didn't like the food, but he **made a pretense of** eating some of it since he was a guest.* **2** false pretenses *law* acts intended to deceive (esp. in the phrase **by/under false pretenses**)

pre·ten·sion /prɪ'tɛnʃən, -tʃən/ *n* **1** [C *often pl.*] a claim to possess skill, qualities, etc.: *I make no pretensions to skill as an artist, but I enjoy painting.* **2** [U] *fml* the quality of being PRETENTIOUS

pre·ten·tious /prɪ'tɛnʃəs, -tʃəs/ *adj* claiming (in an unpleasing way) importance that one does not possess: *a pretentious style of writing* –opposite **unpretentious** –**pretentiously** *adv* –**pretentiousness** *n* [U]

pre·text /'priʸtɛkst/ *n* a reason given for an action in order to hide the real intention; excuse: *He came to the house **under/on the pretext** of seeing Mr. Smith, but he really wanted to see me.* –see EXCUSE (USAGE)

pret·ty¹ /'prɪtiʸ/ *adj* -**tier, -tiest 1** (esp. of a woman, a child, or a small fine thing) pleasing or nice to look at, listen to, etc.; charming but not beautiful or grand: *She looks much prettier with long hair than with short hair.|What a pretty picture!* –see BEAUTIFUL (USAGE) **2 sitting pretty** *infml* (of a person) in a favorable position or condition –**prettily** *adv* –**prettiness** *n* [U]

pretty² *adv* **1** rather; quite but not completely: *pretty comfortable|pretty cold* –see Study Notes on page 363 **2 pretty much** also **pretty well** almost: *pretty much the same|pretty well impossible*

pre·vail /prɪ'veʸl/ *v* [I] *fml* **1** [*against, over*] to gain control or victory; win a fight: *Justice has prevailed; the guilty man has been punished.* **2** [*among, in*] to (continue to) exist or be widespread: *A belief in magic still prevails among some tribes.*

   prevail upon/on sbdy. *v prep* [T] *fml* to persuade: *Can I prevail upon you to stay a little longer?*

pre·vail·ing /prɪ'veʸlɪŋ/ *adj* [A *no comp.*] **1** (of a wind) that blows over an area most of the time **2** most common or general (in some place or at some time): *He wore his hair in the prevailing fashion.*

prev·a·lent /'prɛvələnt/ *adj* [*among, in*] *fml* existing commonly, generally, or widely (in some place or at sometime): *Eye diseases are prevalent in some tropical countries.* –**prevalence** *n* [U *of*]

pre·var·i·cate /prɪ'værə,keʸt/ *v* -**cated, -cating** [I] *fml* to try to hide the truth by not answering questions clearly or completely truthfully: *Tell me where you've been, and don't prevaricate!* –**prevarication** /prɪ,værə'keʸʃən/ *n* [C;U]

pre·vent /prɪ'vɛnt/ *v* [T *from*] more *fml* than **stop**– to keep (something) from happening or stop (someone) from doing something: *What can we do to prevent this disease (from) spreading?* –**preventable** *adj*

pre·ven·tion /prɪ'vɛnʃən, -tʃən/ [U *of*] the act or action of PREVENTing: *the prevention of crime*

pre·ven·tive /prɪ'vɛntɪv/ also **preventative** /prɪ'vɛntətɪv/– *n,adj* (something that is) intended to prevent something, esp. illness: *preventive medicine*

pre·view /'priʸvyuʷ/ *n* [*of*] a private showing of paintings, a movie, etc., before they are shown to the general public

pre·vi·ous /'priʸviʸəs/ *adj* [A *no comp.*] **1** happening, coming, or being earlier in time or order: *Have you had any previous experience, or is this kind of work new to you?* **2 previous to** *fml* before; PRIOR to –**previously** *adv*: *I hadn't seen him previously.*

pre·war /ˌpriʸ'wɔr◂/ *adj* [A] belonging to the time before a war

prey /preʸ/ *n* [U] **1** an animal that is hunted and eaten by another animal **2** a way of life based on killing and eating other animals (in the phrases **beast/bird of prey**): *A tiger is a beast of prey.*

prey on/upon sbdy./sthg. *v prep* [T] **1** (of an animal) to hunt and eat as PREY: *Cats prey on birds and mice.* **2** (of sorrow, troubles, etc.) to trouble greatly: *This problem has been preying on my mind* (=troubling me) *all day.*

price¹ /praɪs/ *n* **1** an amount of money that must be paid to buy something: *What is the price of this suit?|House prices are getting higher/rising/going up.|*(fig.) *Isn't loss of your health too high a price to pay for the pleasure of smoking* **2 at a price** for a lot of money: *You can buy excellent wine here–at a price.* **3 not at any price** not in any condition, even if favorable –see COST (USAGE)

price² *v* **priced, pricing** [T] **1** to fix the price of: *highly priced goods* **2** to mark (goods in a shop) with a price **3 price oneself out of the market** to make one's prices so high that people are unwilling to buy one's goods or services: *The photographer priced himself out of the market by charging such high prices.*

price·less /'praɪslɪs/ *adj* **1** of very great value; of worth too great to be described or calculated: *a priceless collection of paintings* –see WORTHLESS (USAGE) **2** *infml* very funny or laughably foolish: *You look price-*

less in those pants! They're much too tight.

prick¹ /prɪk/ n **1** a small sharp pain: *She felt a sharp prick when the needle went into her finger.* **2** a small mark or hole made by pricking

prick² v **1** [T *with, on, in*] to make a very small hole or holes in the skin or surface of (something or oneself) with a sharp-pointed object: *She pricked herself with a needle.* **2** [I;T] to (cause to) feel a sensation of light sharp pain on the skin: *The leaves of this plant prick if you touch them.*|(fig.) *Her conscience pricked her.*

prick up v adv **prick up its ears** (esp. of an animal) to raise the ears so as to listen attentively: *He pricked up his ears* (=began to listen) *when they started to talk about him.*

prick·le¹ /'prɪkəl/ n a small sharp-pointed growth on the skin of some plants or animals: *A* PORCUPINE *is covered with prickles.*

prickle² v **-led, -ling** [I;T] to give or feel a pricking sensation: *Woolen clothes often prickle when they touch one's skin.*

prick·ly /'prɪkliʸ/ adj **-lier, -liest 1** covered with prickles: *prickly bushes* **2** that gives a pricking sensation

pride /praɪd/ n **1** [U] (a feeling of) satisfaction and pleasure in what one can do or has done, or in someone or something connected with oneself: *They* **take great pride in** *their daughter, who is now a famous scientist.* **2** [U] self-respect: *I think you hurt his pride by laughing at the way he speaks English.* **3** [U] derog too high an opinion of oneself because of one's rank, wealth, abilities, etc.: *their wicked pride* **4** [the S] the most valuable person or thing: *This fine picture is* **the pride of** *my collection.*|*It is my* **pride and joy.** (=something that is greatly valued)

pride sbdy. **on/upon** sthg. v prep **prided, priding** [T] to be pleased and satisfied with (oneself) about: *She prides herself on her ability to speak eight languages.*

priest /priʸst/ n **1** (in the Christian Church, esp. in the ROMAN CATHOLIC Church) a specially trained person, usu. a man, who performs various religious duties and ceremonies for a group of worshippers **2 priestess** fem.– a specially-trained person with related duties and responsibilities in certain non-Christian religions

USAGE **Clergyman** is a general word for someone who is in charge of the religious worship of a group of Christian people, but the word **priest** is used in the ROMAN CATHOLIC Church, the ORTHODOX Church, and in the EPISCOPAL Church. In other PROTESTANT Churches the usual word is **minister** or **pastor**. A **clergyman** who is responsible for the religious needs of a large organization (such as a university or hospital) or in the armed forces is a **chaplain**.

priest·hood /'priʸsthʊd/ n [the U] the office, position, or rank of a priest: *He entered the priesthood.* (=became a priest)

prig /prɪg/ n derog a person who believes himself/herself morally better than others **–priggish** adj **–priggishness** n [U]

prim /prɪm/ adj **-mm-** usu. derog having a stiff

self-controlled manner; easily shocked by anything improper or rude: *She's much too* **prim and proper** *to enjoy such a dirty joke.* **–primly** adv **–primness** n [U]

pri·ma·cy /'praɪməsiʸ/ n [U of] fml the state or quality of being first in rank, importance, position, etc.

pri·ma don·na /ˌpriʸmə 'dɑnə, ˌprɪmə-/ n **1** the leading woman singer in (an) OPERA **2** derog an excitable self-important person who expects everyone to do as he/she wishes

pri·mae·val /praɪ'miʸvəl/ adj →PRIMEVAL

pri·mar·i·ly /praɪ'mɛərəliʸ/ adv mainly; chiefly: *We do sell paintings here, but this is primarily a furniture store.*

pri·mar·y¹ /'praɪˌmɛriʸ, -məriʸ/ adj **1** chief; main: *The primary cause of Tom's failure was his laziness.* **2** [A] (of education or a school) for children between five and 11 years old –compare SECONDARY (1), ELEMENTARY (2)

primary² n **-ies** (esp. in the US) an election at which the members of a political party vote for the person that they would like to see as their party's choice (CANDIDATE) for a political office

primary col·or /ˌ··· '··/ n any of three colors (red, yellow, and blue) from which all other colors can be made by mixing

pri·mate¹ /'praɪmeʸt/ n a member of the most highly developed group of breast-feeding animals (MAMMALS), which includes men, monkeys, and related animals

pri·mate² /'praɪmɪt, -meʸt/ n (often cap.) a priest of the highest rank; ARCHBISHOP

prime¹ /praɪm/ n [S] the state or time of (someone's or something's) greatest perfection, strength, or activity: *Many young soldiers were cut off* **in their prime.** (=killed in battle while still young)

prime² adj [A no comp.] **1** first in time, rank, or importance; chief: *a matter of prime importance* **2** of the very best quality or kind: *a prime cut of* BEEF|*The show was on television during* **prime time,** *when everyone was watching.*

prime³ v **primed, priming** [T] to prepare **a** (a machine) for working by filling with water, oil, etc. **b** (a surface) for painting by covering with a layer of paint, oil, etc.: (fig.) *It was a difficult case, but the man on trial had been carefully primed* (=instructed in advance) *by his lawyer.*

prime min·is·ter /ˌ· '···/ also **P.M.** infml– n (often caps.) the chief minister and leader of the government in Britain and many other countries with a Parliament

prime num·ber /ˌ· '··/ n tech a number that can be divided exactly only by itself and the number one: *23 is a prime number.*

prim·er /'praɪmər/ n [C;U] a paint or other substance spread over the bare surface of wood before the main painting

pri·me·val, -mae- /praɪ'miʸvəl/ adj [no comp.] of the earliest period of the earth's existence; very ancient: *primeval forests*

prim·i·tive /'prɪmətɪv/ adj **1** [A] of or belonging to the earliest stage of development, esp. of life or of man: *Primitive man made primi-*

tive tools from sharp stones and animal bones. | *primitive art on the walls of caves* **2** simple; roughly made or done; not greatly developed or improved: *Small seashells have sometimes been used as a primitive kind of money.* –**primitively** *adv* –**primitiveness** *n* [U]

prince /prɪns/ *n* [A;C] *(often cap.)* **1** a son or other near male relation of a king or queen: *Prince Edward is the Queen's youngest son.* **2** a ruler of a usu. small country or state: *Prince Rainier of Monaco* | *In former times parts of India were ruled by princes.*

prince·ly /'prɪnsliʸ/ *adj* **1** of or belonging to a PRINCE **2** fine; splendid; generous: *a princely gift*

prin·cess /'prɪnsɪs, -sɛs/ *n* [A;C] *(often cap.)* **1** a daughter or other near female relation of a king or queen **2** the wife of a PRINCE

prin·ci·pal¹ /'prɪnsəpəl/ *adj* [A *no comp.*] chief; main; most important; of highest rank: *The principal character in the story is a young artist.* –compare PRINCIPLE

principal² *n* **1** [C] *(often cap.)* the head of some universities, colleges, and schools **2** [S] a sum of money lent, on which interest is paid **3** [C *often pl.*] a leading performer in a play, group of musicians, etc. –compare PRINCIPLE

prin·ci·pal·i·ty /ˌprɪnsə'pælətiʸ/ *n* **-ties** a country that a PRINCE (2) rules

prin·ci·pal·ly /'prɪnsəpliʸ/ *adv* chiefly; mostly: *Although he's a lawyer, he's principally employed in controlling a large business.*

prin·ci·ple /'prɪnsəpəl/ *n* [C +*that/of*] **1** a general truth or belief that is used as a base for reasoning or action: *One of the principles of this dictionary is that explanations should be in simple language.* | *They agreed to the plan* **in principle**, (=regarding the main idea) *but there were several details they didn't like.* **2** a law of nature, esp. as governing the making or working of a machine, apparatus, etc.: *A bicycle and a motorcycle are built on the same principle, though the force that moves them is different.* **3** **on principle** because of settled fixed beliefs: *I refuse to go there, on principle.* –compare PRINCIPAL

prin·ci·ples /'prɪnsəplz/ *n* [P] **1** the general rules on which a skill, science, etc., is based: *This course teaches the principles of cooking.* **2** high personal standards of what is right and wrong, used as a guide to behavior: *He has no principles; he'll do anything for money.*

print¹ /prɪnt/ *n* **1** [C] a mark made on a surface showing the shape, pattern, etc., of the thing pressed into it: *a* FOOTPRINT | (fig.) *Sorrow had left its print on her face.* **2** [U] letters, words, or language in printed form: *I can't read small print without my glasses.* | *I wouldn't have believed it if I hadn't seen it* **in print.** (=in a book, newspaper, etc.) **3** [C] a photograph printed on paper **4** [C] a picture printed from a small sheet of metal **5** **in/out of print** (of a book) that can still/no longer be obtained from the printer **6 small print** a part of an agreement in law that is printed in very small letters and which, as people often do

not take the trouble to read it, may have disadvantageous details included in it

print² *v* **1** [I;T] to press (letters or pictures) onto (esp. paper) by using shapes covered with ink or paint: *The last line on this page hasn't been properly printed.* | *This machine can print 60 pages a minute.* **2** [I;T] to make (a book, magazine, etc.) by pressing letters or pictures onto paper: *This company prints a lot of educational books.* **3** [T] to cause to be included in or produced as a book, newspaper, etc.: *All today's newspapers have printed the President's speech in full.* **4** [T] to make or copy (a photograph) on paper sensitive to light, from a specially treated sheet of photographic film **5** [I;T] to write without joining the letters: *Please print the address clearly in capital letters.*

print·er /'prɪntər/ *n* **1** a person who owns or works in a printing business **2** the part of a computer that prints letters, PRINTOUTs, etc. stored in the computer's memory

print·ing /'prɪntɪŋ/ *n* [U] the act or art of PRINTing (esp. 2): *The invention of printing was an important event in the history of education.*

printing press /'·· ˌ·/ also **press**– *n* a machine that prints books, newspapers, etc.

print·out /'prɪntˌaʊt/ *n* [C;U] a printed record produced by a computer

pri·or¹ /'praɪər/ *adj* [A *no comp.*] **1** earlier; coming or planned before: *I was unable to attend the wedding because of* **a prior engagement.** **2** more important; coming first in importance: *I stopped playing football because my work had a prior claim on my time and attention.* **3** **prior to** *fml* before: *The contract will be signed prior to the ceremony.*

prior² **prioress** /'praɪərɪs/ *fem.*– *n* [A;C] the head of a PRIORY

pri·or·i·ty /praɪ'ɔrətiʸ/ *n* **-ties 1** [U] the state or right of being first in position or earlier in time: *The badly wounded* **have/take priority** **for** *medical attention* **over** *those only slightly hurt.* **2** [C] something that needs attention, consideration, service, etc., before others: *The government should try to* **get** *its* **priorities right/straight.** (=deal with what is most important first)

pri·o·ry /'praɪəriʸ/ *n* **-ries** *(often cap.)* a Christian religious house or group of men (MONKs) or women (NUNs) living together, which is smaller and less important than an ABBEY

prism /'prɪzəm/ *n* **1** (in GEOMETRY) a solid figure with a flat base and parallel upright edges **2** a transparent three-sided block, usu. made of glass, that breaks up white light into different colors

pris·on /'prɪzən/ *n* **1** a large (government) building where criminals are kept locked up as a punishment: *The thief was sent to prison for a year.* **2** a place or condition in which one is shut up or feels a loss of freedom: *Tom hates school; it's a prison to him.*

pris·on·er /'prɪzənər/ *n* **1** a person kept in a prison for some crime or while waiting to be tried: *The prisoners were trying to escape.* | *He was* **taken prisoner** *by enemy soldiers.* | *They* **kept/held** *him* **prisoner** *for three months.* **2** a person or animal (seized and) held with limited freedom of movement

pris·on·er of war /,··· · '·/ also **POW** *infml–* n a member of the armed forces caught by the enemy during a war and kept as a prisoner

pri·va·cy /'praɪvəsiʸ/ n [U] the state of being away from the presence, notice, or activities of others: *There's not much privacy in these apartments: the walls are so thin you can hear everything your neighbor is saying.*

pri·vate¹ /'praɪvɪt/ adj **1** intended only for oneself or a chosen group; not shared with everyone in general: *You shouldn't read people's private letters.|Don't repeat what I told you to anyone; it's private.* –opposite PUBLIC **2** not connected with or paid for by the government, public service, etc.: *a private hospital* **3** not connected with one's business, work, rank, etc.; unofficial: *The President is on a private visit to Mexico.* **4** quiet; without lots of people: *Is there a private corner where we can sit and talk by ourselves?* **5 in private** without other people listening or watching –**privately** adv: *May I speak to you privately?*

private² n [A;C] (often cap.) a soldier of the lowest rank

private en·ter·prise /,·· '···/ n [U] →CAPITALISM

private school /,·· '·/ n a school, not supported by government money, where education must be paid for –compare PUBLIC SCHOOL

pri·va·tion /praɪ'veʸʃən/ n [C;U] fml (a) lack of the necessary things or the main comforts of life: *Everyone suffered privations during the war, when there wasn't enough food in the country.*

priv·i·lege /'prɪvəlɪdʒ/ n **1** [C;U] (a) special right or advantage limited to one person or a few (fortunate) people of a particular kind: *In countries where there are still not many schools, education is a privilege.* **2** [S] a special favor; advantage that gives one great pleasure: *He's a fine musician; it's a privilege to hear him play.* –**privileged** /'prɪvəlɪdʒd/ adj: *We are privileged tonight to have as our main speaker the Foreign Minister of France.*

priv·y /'prɪviʸ/ adj [F to] fml sharing secret knowledge (of)

prize¹ /praɪz/ n something of value given to someone who is successful in a game, race, competition, etc., or given for some deed that is admired: *Her beautiful roses won first prize at the flower show.*

prize² adj [A] **1** that has gained a PRIZE¹: *prize cattle|a prize rose* **2** infml & humor worthy of a PRIZE¹ for quality, size, etc.: *That hen has produced a prize egg, bigger than any I've ever seen.* **3** given as a PRIZE¹: *prize money*

prize³ v prized, prizing [T] to value highly: *The boy's bicycle was his most prized possession.*

prize⁴ v prized, prizing [T] →PRY²: *We prized the top off the box with an iron bar.*

prize·fight /'praɪzfaɪt/ n a public BOXING match for a money prize

pro¹ /proʷ/ n pros [usu. pl.] an argument or reason in favor (of something): *We should hear all the **pros and cons** of the matter before*

we make a decision.

pro² n pros infml for PROFESSIONAL: *a football pro|a pro football player*

prob·a·bil·i·ty /,prɑbə'bɪlətiʸ/ n -ties **1** [U] the state or quality of being probable **2** [U +that/of] likelihood: *There's little probability of reaching San Francisco tonight.|In all probability* (=almost certainly) *we will be late.* **3** [C +that/of] a probable event or result: *War is a real probability in the present state of affairs* –opposite **improbability 4** [C +that/of] (in MATHEMATICS) the chance of an event happening, expressed as a calculation based on known numbers

prob·a·ble /'prɑbəbəl/ adj that has a good chance of being true or correct; likely: *It's possible that it will rain, but with such a blue sky it doesn't seem probable.|a probable result* –opposite **improbable** –**probably** adv: *John probably told his father all about what happened; he usually tells him everything.*

pro·ba·tion /proʷ'beʸʃən/ n [U] **1** (the time of) the testing of a person's character, behavior, abilities, etc., esp. for a job, to be a member of some society, etc. (esp. in the phrase **on probation**) **2** law the system of allowing a law-breaker to go free and unpunished if he/she will promise to behave well (esp. in the phrase **on probation**) –**probationary** /proʷ'beʸʃə,nɛriʸ/ adj

pro·ba·tion·er /proʷ'beʸʃənər/ n a person who is on PROBATION (1,2)

probation of·fi·cer /·'··· ,···/ n a person whose job is to watch, advise, and help law-breakers who are put on PROBATION (2)

probe¹ /proʷb/ n **1** a long thin metal instrument, usu. with a rounded end, esp. one used to search the inside of a wound, a hole in a tooth, etc. **2** also **space probe**– an apparatus sent into the sky to examine conditions in outer space **3** (esp. in newspapers) a careful and thorough inquiry or examination

probe² v probed, probing [I;T into] to search with a PROBE¹ (1):(fig.) *She tried to probe* (=search into) *my mind and discover what I was thinking.*

pro·bi·ty /'proʷbətiʸ/ n [U] fml perfect honesty

prob·lem /'prɑbləm/ n **1** a (serious) difficulty that needs attention and thought: *The unemployment problem in this area is getting worse.* **2** a question (esp. connected with numbers, facts, etc.) for consideration or for which an answer is needed: *The little boy can already do simple problems in addition and subtraction.*

prob·lem·at·ic /,prɑblə'mætɪk/ also **problematical** /-kəl/– adj doubtful; not settled: *The future of our business is problematic.* –**problematically** adv

pro·bos·cis /prə'bɑsɪs/ n -boscises or -boscides /'bɑsə,diʸz/ tech **1** the long movable nose of certain animals, esp. the elephant **2** a long tubelike part of the mouth of some insects

pro·ce·dure /prə'siʸdʒər/ n [C;U] a set of actions necessary for doing something properly: *Writing a check is a simple pro-*

cedure.|PARLIAMENTARY *procedure* –compare PROCESS[1] –**procedural** *adj*

pro·ceed /prəˈsiʸd, proʷ-/ *v* [I] **1** [+*to-v*/*with*] to begin and continue (some course of action): *Tell us your name and then proceed with your story.*|*As soon as he came in he proceeded to tell us all his troubles.* **2** [*with*] *fml* to continue (after stopping): *Don't let me stop you; proceed with your work.* **3** *fml* to advance; move along a course: *Do not proceed across a main street without first looking to the right and the left.*

pro·ceed·ings /prəˈsiʸdɪŋz, proʷ-/ *n* [P] **1** an action taken in law (esp. in the phrases **start/take (legal) proceedings**) **2** (undesirable or unlawful) happenings

pro·ceeds /ˈproʷsiʸdz/ *n* [P] money gained from the sale of something, or as the result of some activity for getting money

proc·ess[1] /ˈprɑsɛs, ˈproʷ-/ *n* **1** [C] any continued set of natural actions over which man has little control: *the process of breathing*|*Coal was formed out of dead forests by chemical processes.* **2** [C] a continued set of actions performed intentionally in order to reach some result: *the process of learning to read* **3** [U] course; time during which something is still being done: *The firm is now* **in the process of** *moving the machines to a new factory.* **4** [C] a particular system or treatment of materials used esp. in producing goods –compare PROCEDURE

process[2] *v* [T] **1** to treat by a particular PROCESS[1] (4): *processed cheese*|*One has to process a photographic film to print pictures from it.* **2** to put (facts, numbers, etc.) into a computer for examination

pro·ces·sion /prəˈsɛʃən/ *n* **1** [C] a line of people, vehicles, etc., moving forward in an orderly, often ceremonial, way **2** [U] a continuous onward movement of people or things: *The workers marched* **in procession** *to the government office.*

pro·ces·sion·al /prəˈsɛʃənəl/ *adj* [A] connected with or used in a solemn religious procession: *a processional march*

pro·claim /proʷˈkleʸm, prə-/ *v* [T +*that*] **1** *fml* to make known publicly; declare officially: *The ringing bells proclaimed the news of the end of the war.*|*A national holiday was proclaimed.* **2** *lit* to show clearly: *His pronunciation proclaimed that he was an American.*

proc·la·ma·tion /ˌprɑkləˈmeʸʃən/ *n* **1** [C] an official public statement: *a proclamation by the city's mayor* **2** [U] the action of PROCLAIMing

pro·cras·ti·nate /proʷˈkræstəˌneʸt, prə-/ *v* -nated, -nating [I] *fml* to delay repeatedly and without good reason in doing some necessary act –**procrastination** /proʷˌkræstəˈneʸʃən, prə-/ *n* [U]

pro·cre·ate /ˈproʷkriʸˌeʸt/ *v* -ated, -ating [I;T] *fml or tech* to produce or give life to (young): *All animals have to procreate (their* SPECIES*).* –**procreation** /ˌproʷkriʸˈeʸʃən/ *n* [U]

pro·cure /proʷˈkyʊər, prə-/ *v* -cured, -curing **1** [T *for*] *fml* to obtain, esp. by effort or careful attention **2** [I;T *for*] to provide (a woman) for someone else's sexual satisfaction

prod /prɑd/ *v* -dd- [I;T *at, with*] to push or press (something or someone) with a pointed object; POKE (2): (fig.) *John is lazy; he won't do any work if he's not prodded into it.* (=urged to do it) –**prod** *n: He gave the snake a prod with his toe.*

prod·i·gal /ˈprɑdɪɡəl/ *adj fml* carelessly wasteful, esp. of money –**prodigality** /ˌprɑdɪˈɡælətiʸ/ *n* [U] *adv*

pro·di·gious /prəˈdɪdʒəs/ *adj* wonderful, esp. because of size, amount, or quality; very great: *He never forgets anything; his memory is prodigious.* –**prodigiously** *adv*

prod·i·gy /ˈprɑdədʒiʸ/ *n* -gies something unusual and wonderful, esp. a person who has unusual and very noticeable abilities: *He's only six years old, yet he plays the piano beautifully. He's a* **child prodigy.**

pro·duce[1] /prəˈduʷs, -ˈdyuʷs/ *v* -duced, -ducing **1** [T] to show, bring out, or offer for examination or consideration: *Can you produce any proof that you weren't near the bank at the time of the robbery?* **2** [T] to grow or supply: *Canada produces good wheat.* **3** [T] to give birth to (esp. young animals):(fig.) *the finest writer our country has ever produced* **4** [I;T] to make (something, esp. goods) from materials: *Gas can be produced from coal.*|*The factory hasn't begun to produce yet.* **5** [T] to cause; have as a result or effect: *Her jokes produced a great deal of laughter.* **6** [T] to prepare in all details and bring before the public:*The book/play was badly produced.* –see PRODUCTION (USAGE)

prod·uce[2] /ˈprɑduʷs, -dyuʷs, ˈproʷ-/ *n* [U] something that has been produced by growing or farming:*The wine bottle was marked "Produce of Spain."* –see PRODUCTION (USAGE)

pro·duc·er /prəˈduʷsər, -ˈdyuʷ-/ *n* **1** a person or company that produces goods, foods, or materials **2** a person who has general control esp. of the money for a play, movie, or broadcast, but who does not direct the actors –compare DIRECTOR, IMPRESARIO

prod·uct /ˈprɑdʌkt, -dəkt/ *n* **1** something useful produced by growth or from the ground, or made in a factory: *Fruit and wine are important products of California.* **2** something that is produced as a result of thought, will, planning, conditions, etc.: *Criminals are sometimes the product of bad homes.* **3** (in MATHEMATICS) the number gotten by multiplying two or more numbers: *The product of 3 multiplied by 2 multiplied by 6 is 36.*

pro·duc·tion /prəˈdʌkʃən/ *n* **1** [U *of*] the act of producing (PRODUCE[1] (1,2,4,6)): *Entrance is permitted only on production of a ticket.*|*the production of cloth by hand* **2** [U] the amount produced: *Production of iron has increased in the last few weeks.* **3** [C;U] (the act of producing) a play, movie, or broadcast: *This new theater is becoming known for its good productions.* –see also MASS PRODUCTION

USAGE Compare **produce** (*n*), **product**, and **production**: Things **produced** on a farm are

produce; things **produced** by industry are **products**; and plays, movies, etc., **produced** for the theater, television, etc., are **productions**: *The market sells a variety of fresh produce.|The company's products include washing machines and radios.|a new production of "Hamlet"*

pro·duc·tive /prə'dʌktɪv/ *adj* **1** that produces well or much: *a very productive writer/meeting* **2** [F *of*] causing or producing (a result): *It was a very long meeting, but it wasn't productive (of any important decisions).* –opposite **unproductive** –**productively** *adv*

pro·duc·tiv·i·ty /,proʷdʌk'tɪvəṭiʸ, ,prɑdək-/ *n* [U] the (measured) ability to grow things or the (calculated) rate of making goods

Prof. *written abbrev. said as:* PROFESSOR:

pro·fane¹ /proʷ'feʸn, prə-/ *adj fml* having or showing disrespect for God or for holy things: *To smoke in a church or mosque would be a profane act.* –compare SACRED –**profanity** *adv*

profane² *v* **-faned, -faning** [T] *fml* to treat (esp. something holy) disrespectfully

pro·fan·i·ty /proʷ'fænəṭiʸ, prə-/ *n* **-ties** [C;U] *fml* (an example of) PROFANENESS: *The men were rough and their conversation was full of profanities.* –compare BLASPHEMY

pro·fess /prə'fɛs, proʷ-/ *v* [T] **1** *fml* to declare plainly (some personal feeling, belief, etc.): *She professed a belief in spirits.* **2** to claim (often falsely): *I don't profess to know anything about poetry.* –**professed** /prə'fɛst, proʷ-/ *adj* [A]: *a professed Muslim*

pro·fes·sion /prə'fɛʃən/ *n* **1** [C] a form of employment, esp. one that is respected in society and is possible only after training (such as law, medicine, and the Church): *He is a lawyer* **by profession**. –see JOB (USAGE) **2** [U] the whole body of people in a particular profession: *The teaching profession claims to be badly paid.* **3** [C *of*] *fml* a declaration (of one's belief, opinion, or feeling)

pro·fes·sion·al¹ /prə'fɛʃənəl/ *adj* **1** [A *no comp*] working in one of the professions: *A doctor is a professional man.* **2** *usu. apprec* showing or using the qualities of training of a member of a profession: *The magician performed his tricks with professional skill.|professional standards* –see also UNPROFESSIONAL **3** [*no comp.*] doing for money what others do for enjoyment: *a professional painter* –compare AMATEUR (2) **4** [*no comp.*] done by people who are paid: *professional football* –compare AMATEUR (1) –**professionally** *adv*

professional² *n* **1** a person who earns money by practicing a particular skill or sport: *He has just* **turned** (=become a) **professional. 2** *apprec* a person who has great experience and high professional standards: *She's a real professional.* –compare AMATEUR (2)

pro·fes·sion·al·ism /prə'fɛʃənəl,ɪzəm/ *n* [U] **1** the behavior, skill, or qualities shown by a PROFESSIONAL¹ (1) person **2** *apprec* the quality of being a PROFESSIONAL² (2)

pro·fes·sor /prə'fɛsər/ *n* [A;C;U] (the title of) a teacher of the highest rank in a univer-

sity department: *My new history professor is Professor Ward.|He is Professor of History at the university.* –**professorial** /,proʷfə'sɔriʸəl, -'soʷr-, ,prɑ-/ *adj*

prof·fer /'prɑfər/ *v* [T *to*] *fml* to offer: *He refused the proffered drink.*

pro·fi·cient /prə'fɪʃənt/ *adj* [*at, in*] thoroughly skilled: *She is proficient at/in swimming.* –**proficiently** *adv* –**proficiency** *n* [U *at, in*]

pro·file /'proʷfaɪl/ *n* **1** [C;U] a side view, esp. of someone's head: *He drew her* **in profile. 2** [C] a short description, esp. of a person's life and character, as given on television or in a newspaper **3** **keep a low profile** to avoid drawing attention to oneself or one's actions

prof·it¹ /'prɑfɪt/ *n* **1** [C;U] money gain; money gained by business: *He sold his house* **at a profit** (=sold it for more than it had cost him)|*He* **made a profit** *of $5,000 on the sale.* –opposite **loss 2** [U] *fml* advantage gained from some action: *reading for profit and pleasure*

profit² *v* [T] *fml or old use* (of a thing) to be of use or advantage to (someone or something): *It will profit you nothing* (=will not help you) *to do that.*

profit by/from sthg.– *v prep* [T +*v-ing*] to learn or gain advantage from: *You can profit by my mistakes and avoid them yourself.*

prof·it·a·ble /'prɑfɪṭəbəl/ *adj* useful; resulting in gain (of money): *The company has had a profitable year.* –opposite **unprofitable** –**profitably** *adv*

prof·it·eer /,prɑfə'tɪər/ *v* [I] *derog* to make unfairly large profits –**profiteer** *n*

profit mar·gin /'·· ,··/ *n* the difference between the cost of production and the selling price

prof·li·gate /'prɑfləgɪt, -,geʸt/ *adj fml* **1** [*of*] (of a person or spending of money) carelessly and boldly wasteful **2** wicked; shamelessly immoral –**profligacy** /'prɑfləgəsiʸ/ *n* [U] *fml* –**profligate** *n*

pro·found /prə'faʊnd/ *adj more fml than* **deep– 1** [A] deep; complete: *There was a profound silence in the empty church.|the profound depths of the ocean* **2** *often apprec* having, showing, or using thorough knowledge and deep understanding: *He is a profound thinker.|He has a profound mind.* –**profoundly** *adv*: *I am profoundly* (=very) *grateful.*

pro·fun·di·ty /prə'fʌndəṭiʸ/ *n* **-ties** [C;U] *more fml than* **depth** – depth or thoroughness, esp. of mind or feeling

pro·fuse /prə'fyuʷs/ *adj* [F *in, of*] (too) freely produced or poured out: *Her head was covered with a profuse mass of curls.|profuse tears|She was profuse in her thanks.* –**profusely** *adv* –**profusion** /prə'fyuʷʒən/ *n* [S;U]: *There is a profusion of flowers in the garden in summer; flowers grow there* **in profusion**.

prog·e·ny /'prɑdʒəniʸ/ *n* [U +*sing./pl.v*] *tech or lit, sometimes humor* children (of a person) or the young (of an animal): *Her* NUMEROUS *progeny was/were all asleep.*

prog·no·sis /prɑg'noʷsɪs/ *n* **-noses** /'noʷsiʸz/

tech a doctor's opinion, based on medical experience, of what course a disease will probably take –compare DIAGNOSIS

pro·gram[1] /'prowgræm, -grəm/ *AmE*‖**programme** *BrE*– *n* **1** a list of performers or things to be performed at a concert, a theater, a sports competition, etc. **2** a complete show or performance: *What is your favorite television program?* **3** a fixed plan of what one is going to do: *a new political program intended to win votes.* **4** a plan of the operations to be performed by a computer when dealing with a set of facts

program[2] *v* **-mm-** *or* **-m-** [T] **1** to plan or arrange: *The central heating system is programmed to start working at six o'clock each morning.* **2** to supply (a computer) with a plan of the operations to be performed: *Please program the computer to give me more information.*

pro·gram·mer, programer /'prowgræmər, -grəmər/ *n* a person who prepares a PROGRAM[1] for a computer

prog·ress[1] /'pragrɛs, -grəs/ *n* [U] **1** advance; journey onward: *The ship made slow progress through the rough sea.*|*Please do not enter while a lesson is* **in progress.** (=continuing) **2** continual improvement or development: *Jane is still sick in the hospital, but she's* **making progress.** (=is getting better)

pro·gress[2] /prə'grɛs/ *v* [I] **1** to advance: *The year is progressing. It will soon be autumn.* **2** to improve; develop (favorably): *Mary is progressing in the art of cooking; her meals are becoming quite good.* –compare REGRESS

pro·gres·sion /prə'grɛʃən/ *n* [S;U] (the action of) PROGRESSING[2], esp. by stages

pro·gres·sive /prə'grɛsɪv/ *adj* **1** [*no comp.*] moving forward continuously or by stages **2** that favors or uses new ideas: *This is a very progressive firm; it uses the most modern systems* –**progressively** *adv: It got progressively worse/better.*

pro·hib·it /prow'hɪbɪt, prə-/ *v* [T +*v-ing/from*] *fml* **1** to forbid by law or rule: *Smoking in this theater is prohibited.* **2** to prevent; make impossible: *His lack of height prohibits his becoming a policeman.*

pro·hi·bi·tion /,prowə'bɪʃən/ *n* **1** [U *of*] the act of PROHIBITING (1) **2** [C *against*] *fml* an order forbidding something **3** [U] (*usu. cap.*) (in the US) the time (from 1920 to 1933) during which a national law forbade the making or sale of alcoholic drinks

pro·hib·i·tive /prow'hɪbətɪv, prə-/ *adj* preventing the use or misuse of something: *The government has put a prohibitive tax* (=higher than anyone can pay) *on foreign goods.* –**prohibitively** *adv: prohibitively* EXPENSIVE

proj·ect[1] /'pradʒɛkt, -dʒɪkt/ *n* (a plan for) work or activity of any kind: *This student is doing a special project; he's building a small machine for his science class.*

pro·ject[2] /prə'dʒɛkt/ *v* **1** [I;T] to (cause to) stand out beyond an edge or surface: *His ears project noticeably.*|*He has projecting ears.* **2** [T] to (aim and) throw through the air with force **3** [T *into, onto*] to cause (heat,

sound, light, or shadow) to be directed into space or onto a surface: *A singer must learn to project his voice so as to be heard in a large hall.* **4** [T] to consider as a possible thing to do; plan: *our projected visit to Australia*

pro·jec·tile /prə'dʒɛktəl, -,taɪl/ *n* an object or weapon that shoots or is shot forward, esp. from a gun

pro·jec·tion /prə'dʒɛkʃən/ *n* **1** [U *of*] the act of PROJECTING[2] **2** [C *of*] something that has been PROJECTED[2] (3) or PROJECTS[2] (1)

pro·jec·tion·ist /prə'dʒɛkʃənɪst/ *n* a person who works a PROJECTOR, esp. in a movie theater

pro·jec·tor /prə'dʒɛktər/ *n* an apparatus for PROJECTING[2] (3) films or pictures onto a surface

pro·le·tar·i·an /,prowlə'tɛriyən/ *n,adj often derog* (a member) of the PROLETARIAT

pro·le·tar·i·at /,prowlə'tɛriyət/ *n* [U] the class of (esp. unskilled) workers who have to work for wages: *The proletariat has strong opinions on this matter.* –compare BOURGEOISIE

pro·lif·er·ate /prə'lɪfə,reyt, prow-/ *v* **-ated, -ating** [I] to increase rapidly in numbers –see also NONPROLIFERATION –**proliferation** /prə,lɪfə'reyʃən, prow-/ *n* [S;U *of*]

pro·lif·ic /prə'lɪfɪk, prow-/ *adj fml* producing many or much: *a prolific writer* –**prolifically** *adv*

pro·log *AmE*‖also **prologue** /'prowlɔg, -lɑg/ *n* [*to*] (*sometimes cap.*) an introduction to a play, long poem, etc.

pro·long /prə'lɔŋ/ *v* [T] to make longer; LENGTHEN: *They're prolonging their visit; they've decided to stay another week.* –**prolongation** /,prowlɔŋ'geyʃən/ *n* [C;U *of*]

pro·longed /prə'lɔŋd/ *adj* continuing for a long time: *a prolonged absence*

prom /pram/ *n AmE* a formal dance party given for students by a HIGH SCHOOL or college class

prom·e·nade[1] /,pramə'neyd, -'nad/ *n* **1** a wide path beside a road along the coast in a town **2** *fml* an unhurried walk, ride, or drive for pleasure or exercise

promenade[2] *v* **-naded, -nading** [I;T] *fml* to walk slowly and to and fro along (a place, street, etc.)

prom·i·nent /'pramənənt/ *adj* **1** standing out (beyond a surface): *her prominent teeth* **2** [*in*] of great ability, fame, etc.: *a politician who is prominent in matters concerning trade* **3** noticeable or easily seen –**prominently** *adv* –**prominence** *n* [C;U]: *He is* **coming into prominence** *as an artist.*

pro·mis·cu·ous /prə'mɪskyuwəs/ *adj derog* not limited to one sexual partner: *a promiscuous life* –**promiscuously** *adv* –**promiscuity** /,pramɪ'skyuwətiy, ,prow-/ *also* **promiscuousness**– /prə'mɪskyuwəsnɪs/ *n* [U]

prom·ise[1] /,pramɪs/ *n* **1** [C +*to-v/that/of*] a statement, which someone else has a right to believe and depend on, that one will or will not do something, give something, etc.: *If you* **make a promise** *you should keep it; you should not* **break a promise.** **2** [S;U *of*] (signs or reasons for) expectation or hope (of something good): *The boy is* **showing** *great* **promise** *as a student.*

promise² *v* **-ised, -ising** [I;T] **1** [+*to-v/(that)*] to make a promise to do or give (something) or that (something) will be done: *I promise to return your bicycle in good condition.*|*"She's not coming tonight." "But she promised!"*| *I can't give you the book; I* **promised** *it to Susan.* **2** [+*to-v*] to cause one to expect or hope for (something); to give PROMISE¹ (2): *It promises to be a fine day.*

prom·is·ing /'promɪsɪŋ/ *adj apprec* full of PROMISE¹ (2); showing signs of advance towards success –opposite **unpromising** –**promisingly** *adv*

prom·on·to·ry /'promən,tɔriʸ, -,toʷriʸ/ *n* **-ries** a high point of land stretching out into the sea

pro·mote /prə'moʷt/ *v* **-moted, -moting** [T] **1** [*to*] to advance (someone) in position or rank: *The young army officer was promoted to captain/promoted to the rank of captain.* –opposite **demote 2** to help actively in forming, arranging, or encouraging (a business, concert, play, etc.): *Who is promoting this* BOXING *match?*|*How can we promote the sales of this product?*

pro·mot·er /prə'moʷtər/ *n* a person who PROMOTES (2) activities or people

pro·mo·tion /prə'moʷʃən/ *n* [C;U *of*] **1** (an) advancement in rank or position: *There are good chances of promotion in this firm.* –opposite **demotion 2** (an) action to help something develop or succeed (esp. publicly): *This year's sales promotions haven't been very successful.*

prompt¹ /prompt/ *v* **1** [T] to cause or urge: *Hunger prompted him to steal.* **2** [I;T] to remind (an actor) of the next words in a speech

prompt² *adj* [F] done, given, or acting quickly, at once, or at the right time: *Prompt payment of bills helps keep our accounts in order.*|*This worker is always prompt in his duties.* –**promptly** *adv: When he called me a thief I promptly hit him.*|*The performance will start promptly at seven o'clock.* –**promptness** *n* [U]

prompt·er /'promptər/ *n* a person who PROMPTS¹ (2) actors who forget their words

prone /proʷn/ *adj* **1** [F +*to-v/to*] likely to suffer (usu. something unpleasant or unwanted): *He's very prone to colds in winter.*|*Mary's always falling over; she's* **accident-prone. 2** (of a person or position) stretched out flat with the face and front of the body downwards –compare SUPINE

prong /prɔŋ/ *n* **1** a thin sharp-pointed piece or part esp. of a fork **2** **-pronged: a** having a certain number of prongs: *a four-pronged fork* **b** (of an attack) coming from a certain number of directions at the same time: *a two-pronged attack*

pro·noun /'proʷnaʊn/ *n* (in grammar) a word that is used in place of a noun or a noun phrase: *Instead of saying "the man came" you can use a pronoun and say "he came."*

pro·nounce /prə'naʊns/ *v* **-nounced, -nouncing 1** [I;T] to make the sound of (a letter, a word, etc.): *In the word "knew," the "k" is not pronounced; the word is pronounced without the "k."* **2** [T +*that*] *fml* to declare (officially): *Everyone pronounced the dinner to be very good.*|*At the end of the marriage ceremony, the priest said: "I now pronounce you man and wife."*

pro·nounced /prə'naʊnst/ *adj* very strong or noticeable: *You won't easily make him change his opinion; he has very pronounced ideas on everything.*|*a pronounced* LIMP

pro·nounce·ment /prə'naʊnsmənt/ *n* [+*that/on, upon*] a (solemn or official) declaration or statement

pron·to /'prontoʷ/ *adv* [no comp.] *infml* at once; very quickly

pro·nun·ci·a·tion /prə,nʌnsiʸ'eʸʃən/ *n* **1** [U] the way in which something is pronounced **2** [S;U] a particular person's way of pronouncing

proof¹ /pruʷf/ *n* **1** [C;U +*that/of*] (a) way of showing that something is true: *I wouldn't demand proof of honesty from a friend.* **2** [C] a test or trial: *A soldier's courage is* **put to the proof** *in battle.* **3** [C;U] a test copy made of something printed, so that mistakes can be put right before the proper printing is done **4** [U after *n*] the standard of strength of some kinds of alcoholic drink: *This* GIN *is 15 per cent proof.* –see PROVE

proof² *adj* **1** [F *against*] giving or having protection against something harmful or unwanted:|*a waterproof coat*|*a soundproof room*|(fig.) *His courage is proof against* (=not influenced by) *the greatest pain.* **2** [after *n*] (of certain types of alcoholic drink) of the stated alcoholic strength in comparison with some standard: *In the US,* WHISKEY *of 90 proof is 45% alcohol.*

prop¹ /prop/ *n* a support placed to hold up something heavy: (fig) *Her daughter was a prop to* (=supported) *her during her illness.*

prop² *v* **-pp-** [T *up*] to support or keep in position: *Prop the gate open with a brick.*|*He propped his bicycle (up) against the fence.*

prop³ also **property** *fml– n* [*usu. pl.*] any small article that is used on the stage in the acting of a play

prop·a·gan·da /,propə'gændə/ *n* [U] *often derog* ideas, false or true information, etc. spread about officially, esp. by a government: *The propaganda of a political party is planned to gain votes, and isn't always the exact truth.*

prop·a·gate /'propə,geʸt/ *v* **-gated, -gating 1** [I] (of living things) to increase in number by producing young: *Most plants propagate by seed.* **2** [T] to cause to have descendants: *Insects propagate themselves by means of eggs.* **3** [T] to cause to spread to a great number of people: *The political party started the newspaper to propagate its ideas.* –**propagator** /'propə,geʸtər/ *n* –**propagation** /,propə'geʸʃən/ *n* [U *of*]

pro·pel /prə'pɛl/ *v* **-ll-** [T] to move, drive, or push forward: *One has to depend on the wind to propel a sailing boat.*

pro·pel·ler /prə'pɛlər/ *n* two or more blades fixed to a central bar that is turned at high speed by an engine, used for driving a ship or aircraft

pro·pen·si·ty /prə'pɛnsətiʸ/ n **-ties** [+to-v/for, to, towards] fml a natural tendency towards a particular (usu. undesirable) kind of behavior: a propensity for complaining|a propensity to sudden anger

prop·er /'prɑpər/ adj **1** [A no comp.] right; suitable; correct: The child is too ill to be nursed at home; she needs proper medical attention at a hospital.|These pages aren't in their proper order; page 22 comes after page 26. **2** sometimes derog paying great attention to what is considered correct in society: I don't think a that short dress is proper for going to church in. −see also IMPROPER **3** [A] infml real; actual: The little boy wanted a proper dog as a pet, not a toy dog. **4** [after n, no comp.] itself; in its actual, most limited meaning: Many people call themselves New Yorkers though they live outside, not in the city proper.

prop·er·ly /'prɑpərliʸ/ adv **1** suitably; correctly: I'm learning German, but I still can't speak it properly. **2** really; actually; exactly: I'm not, properly speaking, a nurse, since I haven't been trained, but I've had a lot of experience looking after sick people.

proper noun /ˌ·· '·/ also **proper name**− n (in grammar) a name used for a single particular thing or person, and spelled with a CAPITAL letter: "James," "London," and "China" are proper nouns. −see also COMMON NOUN

prop·er·ty /'prɑpərtiʸ/ n **-ties 1** [U] something which is owned; possession(s): The police found some stolen property hidden in the thief's house. **2** [U] land, buildings, or both together: The city is growing and property in the center of town is becoming more valuable. **3** [C] a building, piece of land, or both together: Several properties in this street are for rent. **4** [C of] a quality, power, or effect that belongs naturally to something: Many plants have medicinal properties. **5** [C usu. pl.] fml for PROP³

proph·e·cy /'prɑfəsiʸ/ n **-cies 1** [U] the foreseeing and foretelling of future events **2** [C+that] a statement telling something that is to happen in the future: The teacher's prophecy that the boy would become famous was later fulfilled.

proph·e·sy /'prɑfəˌsaɪ/ v **-sied, -sying** [I;T +that] to give (a warning, statement about some future event, etc.): I wouldn't like to prophesy who will win the election.

proph·et /'prɑfɪt/ n **1** (in the Christian, Jewish, and Muslim religions) a man who believes that he is directed by God to make known and explain God's will and/or to lead or teach a religion **2** prophetess fem.− an important thinker, poet, etc., who introduces and teaches some new idea **3 prophet of doom** derog a person who is always foretelling ruin, destruction, misfortune, etc.

pro·phet·ic /prə'fɛtɪk/ also **prophetical** /-kəl/ adj **1** [of] correctly telling of things that will happen in the future **2** of or like a PROPHET (2) −**prophetically** adv

pro·pi·ti·ate /prə'pɪʃiʸˌeʸt, proʷ-/ v **-ated, -ating** [T] fml to win the favor of (someone who is angry or unfriendly) by some pleasing act −**propitiation** /prəˌpɪʃiʸ'eʸʃən, proʷ-/ n [U for, of]

pro·pi·tious /prə'pɪʃəs/ adj [for, to] fml advantageous; favorable: Some people believe that finding a penny is a propitious sign. −**propitiously** adv

pro·po·nent /prə'poʷnənt/ n [of] a person who argues in favor of something −see also OPPONENT

pro·por·tion /prə'pɔrʃən, -'poʷr-/ n **1** [U] the correct relationship between the size, position, and shape of the different parts of a whole: This drawing isn't **in proportion**; the car is larger than the house. −opposite **disproportion 2** [C;U of] the compared relationship between two things in regard to size, importance, etc.: The proportion of men to women in the population has changed so that there are now fewer women and more men.|Are you paid **in proportion to** (=according to) the number of hours you work? −compare RATIO **3** [C of] a part or share (as measured in amount and compared with the whole): "What proportion of your wages do you spend on rent?" "About a quarter." **4 in/out of proportion** (not) according to real importance; (not) sensibly: When one is angry one often does not see things **in proportion**. **5 sense of proportion** ability to judge what matters, without being influenced by personal feelings

pro·por·tion·al /prə'pɔrʃənəl, -'poʷr-/ adj **1** concerning PROPORTION (2) **2** [to] in (correct) PROPORTION (2): His pay is proportional to the amount of work he does. −opposite **disproportional** (for 2) −**proportionally** adv

pro·por·tion·ate /prə'pɔrʃənɪt, -'poʷr-/ adj [to] in right PROPORTION (1,2) −compare DISPROPORTIONATE −**proportionately** adv

pro·pos·al /prə'poʷzəl/ n **1** [+to-v/at/for, often pl.] a plan or suggestion: peace proposals **2** [of] an offer of marriage −compare PROPOSITION¹ (3) **3** [+to-v/that/of] the act of proposing (PROPOSE): the proposal that we should rest for a while

pro·pose /prə'poʷz/ v **-posed, -posing 1** [T +to-v/(that)/as, for] to suggest; put forward for consideration: I propose resting for half an hour.|I propose that we take a rest.|(fml) I wish to propose Charles Robson for membership of the club. **2** [T +to-v] to intend: I propose to go to Washington on Tuesday. **3** [I;T to] to make an offer of (marriage) (to someone)

prop·o·si·tion¹ /ˌprɑpə'zɪʃən/ n **1** [+that] a statement in which an opinion or judgment is expressed **2** a suggested business offer or arrangement: He **made me a proposition** concerning the sale of my car. **3** euph an offer to have sex with someone (esp. in the phrase **make someone a proposition**) −compare PROPOSAL

proposition² v [T] infml to make (someone) a PROPOSITION¹ (3)

pro·pound /prə'paʊnd/ v [T] fml to put forward as a question or matter for consideration

pro·pri·e·tar·y /prə'praɪə,tɛriʸ/ *adj* [A] privately owned or controlled

pro·pri·e·ties /prə'praɪəṭiʸz/ *n* [*the* P] *fml* the rules of proper social behavior

pro·pri·e·tor /prə'praɪəṭər/ **proprietress** /prə'praɪətrɪs/ *fem.– n esp. fml* an owner (esp. of a business, etc.): *I wasn't satisfied with our hotel, so I will complain to the proprietor.*

pro·pri·e·ty /prə'praɪəṭiʸ/ *n* [U] *fml* **1** rightness of social or moral behavior: *You can trust John to behave with perfect propriety.* **2** fitness; rightness: *I doubt the propriety of making a public statement on prison conditions before we have studied the official reports.* –see also IMPROPRIETY

pro·pul·sion /prə'pʌlʃən/ *n* [U] *tech* force that drives (PROPELS) something, esp. a vehicle, forward: *This aircraft works by* JET *propulsion.* (=it has JET engines)

pro·sa·ic /prowʷ'zeʸɪk/ *adj* dull; uninteresting: *a prosaic job/article* –**prosaically** *adv*

pro·scribe /prowʷ'skraɪb/ *v* **-scribed, -scribing** [T] *fml* to forbid (esp. something dangerous or harmful), esp. by law –**proscription** /prowʷ'skrɪpʃən/ *n* [C;U]

prose /prowʷz/ *n* [C;U] written language in its usual form (as different from poetry): *Newspaper articles are written in prose.* –compare POETRY

pros·e·cute /'prasə,kyuwʷt/ *v* **-cuted, -cuting** [I;T *for*] to bring a criminal charge against (someone) in a court of law: *He was prosecuted for stealing.*

pros·e·cu·tion /,prasə'kyuwʷʃən/ *n* **1** [C;U] (an example of) prosecuting or being PROSECUTED by law **2** [*the* U] the group of people who bring a criminal charge against someone in court: *The prosecution is coming into court.|A famous lawyer has been asked to appear* **for the prosecution.** –compare DEFENSE

pros·e·cu·tor /'prasə,kyuwʷtər/ *n* the person (often a lawyer) who PROSECUTES another –see DISTRICT ATTORNEY

pros·pect¹ /'praspɛkt/ *n* **1** [C;U *of*] (a) reasonable hope or chance (of something happening): *There's not much prospect of my being able to see you soon.|a job with excellent prospects* (=chances of future success) **2** [S;U *of*] something which is probable: *She doesn't like the prospect of having to live alone.* **3** [C *usu. sing.*] *fml* a wide or distant view: *From the top of the hill there's a beautiful prospect over the valley.* –see VIEW (USAGE)

prospect² *v* [I;T *for*] to examine (land, an area, etc.) in order to find gold, silver, oil, etc. –**prospector** /'praspɛktər/ *n*

pro·spec·tive /prə'spɛktɪv/ *adj* expected; probable; intended: *a prospective buyer for the house*

pro·spec·tus /prə'spɛktəs/ *n* a printed statement giving details of a university, a new business, etc.

pros·per /'praspər/ *v* [I] to become successful

pros·per·i·ty /pra'spɛrəṭiʸ/ *n* [U] good fortune and success, esp. in money matters

pros·per·ous /'praspərəs/ *adj* successful; rich –**prosperously** *adv*

pros·ti·tute¹ /'prastə,tuwʷt, -,tyuwʷt/ **male prostitute** *masc.– n* a person, esp. a woman, who earns money by having sex with a person who will pay for it –**prostitution** /,prastə'tuwʷʃən, -'tyuwʷ-/ *n* [U *of*]

prostitute² *v* **-tuted, -tuting** [T] *fml* **1** to hire (oneself) as a PROSTITUTE¹ **2** to put to a dishonorable use, for money: *He prostituted his abilities by acting in bad movies.*

pros·trate¹ /'prastreʸt/ *adj* **1** lying flat, with the face to the ground –compare PRONE (2) **2** having lost all strength, courage, and ability to act, as a result of some experience: *She was prostrate with grief.* –**prostration** /pra'streʸʃən/ *n* [C;U]

prostrate² *v* **-trated, -trating** [T] **1** to put in a PROSTRATE¹ (1) position **2** [*usu. pass.*] to cause to be PROSTRATE¹ (2): *a prostrating illness*

pro·tag·o·nist /prowʷ'tægənɪst/ *n* **1** [*of*] a supporter or leader of some (new) idea or purpose: *Ms. Jerome was one of the chief protagonists of women's rights.* **2** the chief character in a play or story

pro·tect /prə'tɛkt/ *v* [T *against, from*] to keep safe, by guarding or covering: *He raised his arm to protect his face from the blow.* –**protector** /prə'tɛktər/ *n: knee protectors*

pro·tec·tion /prə'tɛkʃən/ *n* **1** [U *against, for*] the act of protecting or state of being protected: *A thin coat gives little protection against the cold.* **2** [S] a person or thing that protects: *Shoes are a protection for the feet.*

pro·tec·tive /prə'tɛktɪv/ *adj* **1** [A] that gives protection **2** [*towards*] wishing to protect: *protective clothing|protective parents* –**protectively** *adv* –**protectiveness** *n* [U]

pro·tec·tor·ate /prə'tɛktərɪt/ *n* a country controlled and protected by a more powerful nation

pro·té·gé /'prowʷṭə,ʒeʸ, ,prowʷṭə'ʒeʸ/ **protégée** *fem. (same pronunciation)– n* a person who is guided and helped by someone of influence or power: *This young politician is the Senator's protégé.*

pro·tein /'prowʷtiʸn/ *n* [C;U] any of many substances (present in such foods as meat and eggs) that help to build up the body and keep it healthy

pro·test¹ /'prowʷtɛst/ *n* [C;U] **1** (a) complaint or strong spoken expression of dissatisfaction, disagreement, opposition, etc. (often in the phrases **enter/lodge a protest (against something)**): *They refused to buy meat,* **in protest. 2 under protest** unwillingly

pro·test² /prə'tɛst, prowʷ-, 'prowʷtɛst/ *v* **1** [I *about, against, at*] to express one's disagreement, feeling of unfairness, annoyance, etc.: *They protested about the bad food at the hotel.|They protested to the owner.* **2** [T+*that*] to declare, esp. in complaint or opposition: *We urged her to come to the party with us, but she protested that she was too tired.* –**protester** *n*

Prot·es·tant /'praṭɪstənt/ *n,adj* (a member) of a part of the Christian church that separated from the ROMAN CATHOLIC Church in the 16th century –**Protestantism** n [U]

prot·es·ta·tion /ˌprɑtɪˈsteʸʃən, ˌproʷ-/ n [+*that/of*] *fml* a (solemn) declaration, esp. against opposition: *The meeting ended with protestations of friendship from everyone.*

pro·to·col /ˈproʷtəˌkɔl, -ˌkɑl/ n [U] the system of fixed rules and accepted behavior used esp. by representatives of governments on official occasions

pro·ton /ˈproʷtɑn/ n a very small piece of matter that helps to form the central part of an atom –see also ELECTRON, NEUTRON

pro·to·type /ˈproʷtəˌtaɪp/ n [*of*] the first form of anything, from which all later (improved) forms develop: *the prototype of a new car*

pro·tract·ed /proʷˈtræktɪd, prə-/ adj lasting a long time, esp. longer than expected: *a protracted argument|a protracted stay in hospital*

pro·trac·tor /proʷˈtræktər, prə-/ n an instrument usu. in the form of a half-circle, used for measuring and drawing angles

pro·trude /proʷˈtruʷd/ v **-truded, -truding** [I;T] *fml* to (cause to) stick out: *The policeman saw a gun protruding from the man's pocket.|protruding teeth* –**protrusion** /proʷˈtruʷʒən/ n [C;U *of*]

pro·tu·ber·ance /proʷˈtuʷbərəns, -ˈtyuʷ-/ n *fml* a swelling: *protuberances on a stem*

proud /praʊd/ adj **1** *apprec* having and showing self-respect –compare HUMBLE[1] (1) **2** *derog* having too high an opinion of oneself: *He's too proud to be seen in public with his poorly-dressed mother.* **3** [+*to-v/that/of*] having or expressing personal satisfaction and pleasure in something: *Tom is very proud of his new car.|Our football team feels proud that it has won every game this year.* **4** [A] splendid; noble; grand; glorious: *This proud and great university has produced many famous people.* **5 do (someone) proud a** to treat someone, esp. a guest, splendidly **b** to give (someone) cause for pride or satisfaction –see PRIDE –**proudly** adv

prove /pruʷv/ v **proved, proved** or **proven** /ˈpruʷvən/ *esp. AmE,* **proving 1** [T +*that/to*] to give proof of; show to be true: *He has proved his courage in battle.|The marks of the prisoner's fingers on the gun proved that he had held it; they proved him to be the guilty man.* –see also DISPROVE **2** [I;T] to show in the course of time or experience, etc.,to be of the quality stated: *At his new job he proved himself to be a good worker.|As it happened, my advice proved to be wrong.* –*see also* PROOF[1]

prov·en /ˈpruʷvən/ also **proved**– adj [A] *apprec* that has been tested and shown to be true: *a man of proven ability* –opposite **unproven**

prov·erb /ˈprɑvɜrb/ n a short well-known saying usu. in popular language: *"Don't put all your eggs in one basket" is a proverb.*

pro·ver·bi·al /prəˈvɜrbiʸəl/ adj **1** of, concerning, or like a PROVERB: *the proverbial eggs in the basket* **2** very widely known and spoken of; undoubted: *His generosity is proverbial.* –**proverbially** adv

pro·vide /prəˈvaɪd/ v **-vided, -viding** [T] **1** [*for/with*] to supply (something needed or useful): *That hotel provides good meals.* **2** [+*that*] (of a law, rule, agreement, etc.) to state a special arrangement that must be fulfilled: *The law provides that valuable ancient buildings must be preserved by the government.*

provide for sbdy. v prep [T] to support; supply with the necessary things of life: *He has a wife and five children to provide for.*

pro·vid·ed /prəˈvaɪdɪd/ also **provided that, providing, providing that** /·ˈ··· ·/– conj if and only if; on condition that: *I will go, (always) provided (that) you go too.*

prov·i·dence /ˈprɑvədəns/ n [S;U] a special event showing God's care or the kindness of fate (often in the phrase **divine providence**): *It seemed like providence that the doctor happened to be passing just at the time of the accident.*

prov·i·dent /ˈprɑvədənt/ adj (careful in) providing for future needs, esp. by saving or storing –opposite **improvident** –**providently** adv

prov·i·den·tial /ˌprɑvəˈdɛnʃəl, -tʃəl/ adj *fml* happening just when needed; lucky –**providentially** adv

prov·ince /ˈprɑvɪns/ n **1** [C] one of the main divisions of some countries (and formerly of some empires) that forms a separate whole for purposes of government control **2** [U] a branch of thought, knowledge, or study: *I know nothing about Persian art; that's outside my province. My province is European art.*

prov·inc·es /ˈprɑvɪnsɪz/ n [P] the parts of a country that are distant from the main city: *I saw the new movie in London; it's not yet being shown in the provinces.*

pro·vin·cial[1] /prəˈvɪnʃəl, -tʃəl/ n a PROVINCIAL[2] (esp. 2) person

provincial[2] adj **1** [A] of a PROVINCE (1), or the PROVINCES **2** *often derog* having or showing the old-fashioned manners, opinions, customs, etc., regarded (esp. in former times) as typical of people of the PROVINCES –**provincially** adv

pro·vi·sion[1] /prəˈvɪʒən/ n **1** [U *of*] the act of providing: *The provision of a new library has been of great advantage to the students.* **2** [*against, for*] preparation (for future needs): *They spend all their money and* **make no provision for** *the future.* **3** [C +*that*] a condition in an agreement or law; PROVISO: *According to the provisions of the agreement the money must be paid back quickly.*

provision[2] v [T *for*] to provide with food and other supplies in large quantities

pro·vi·sion·al /prəˈvɪʒənəl/ adj for the present time only, with the probability of being changed –compare TEMPORARY –**provisionally** adv

pro·vi·sions /prəˈvɪʒənz/ n [P] food supplies

pro·vi·so /prəˈvaɪzoʷ/ n **-sos** [C +*that*] something added that limits the conditions in which an agreement will be accepted, esp. in business matters: *I agreed to do the work, with the proviso that I'm paid before I do it.*

prov·o·ca·tion /ˌprɑvəˈkeʸʃən/ n **1** [U] the act

of provoking or state of being PROVOKED **2** [C] something that PROVOKEs: *the provocations of teaching a class of badly-behaved children*

pro·voc·a·tive /prə'vɒkətɪv/ *adj* causing argument, anger, or (sexual) interest: *He made a provocative speech that caused a great deal of argument.|to wear a provocative dress* –**provocatively** *adv*

pro·voke /prə'voʷk/ *v* **-voked, -voking** [T] **1** to make angry or bad-tempered: *That dog is very dangerous when provoked.* **2** to cause (a feeling or action): *Her rudeness provoked me to strike her.|Don't throw one bone to two dogs; you'll only provoke a fight.*

pro·vok·ing /prə'voʷkɪŋ/ *adj usu. fml* annoying –**provokingly** *adv*

prow /praʊ/ *n esp. lit* the pointed front part of a ship or boat; BOW⁵

prow·ess /'praʊɪs/ *n* [U *as, at, in*] *fml or lit* unusual ability or skill: *His prowess as a football player makes it certain that he'll be chosen for the team.*

prowl¹ /praʊl/ *v* [I] (esp. of an animal looking for food, or of a thief) to move about quietly trying not to be seen or heard: *I woke up in the middle of the night and heard someone prowling around* (=a **prowler**) *my yard.*

prowl² *n* [S] *infml* an act of PROWLing¹: *a lion on the prowl, looking for food*

prox·im·i·ty /prɒk'sɪmətiʸ/ *n* [U *to*] *fml* **1** nearness **2** in the proximity of *fml* near

prox·y /'prɒksiʸ/ *n* **-ies** (a person having) the right to act for or represent another person, esp. as a voter at an election: *to vote* **by proxy**

prude /pruʷd/ *n derog* a person who makes a show of being easily shocked and does not do or say anything supposed to be impure –**prudish** /'pruʷdɪʃ/ *adj* –**prudishly** *adv* –**prudishness** *n* [U]

pru·dent /'pruʷdnt/ *adj* sensible and wise; careful: *It's prudent to wear a heavy coat when the weather is cold.* –opposite **imprudent** –**prudently** *adj* –**prudence** *n* [U]: *Prudence prevented John from disobeying his father, who had a fierce temper.*

prud·er·y /'pruʷdəriʸ/ *n* [U] *derog* the behavior of a PRUDE

prune¹ /pruʷn/ *n* a dried PLUM

prune² *v* **pruned, pruning** [T] [*back*] to cut off or shorten some of the branches of (a tree or bush) in order to improve the shape and growth

pry¹ /praɪ/ *v* **pried, prying** [I *into*] to try to find out about someone else's private affairs: *Stop prying: you shouldn't read my letters!|prying newspaper reporters*

pry² also **prize–** *v* [T] to move, lift, or break with a tool or metal bar: *I couldn't pry the cover off this wooden box without breaking it.*

P.S. /ˌpiʸ 'ɛs/ *n infml abbrev. for:* POSTSCRIPT: *Yours sincerely, J. Smith. P.S. I won't be able to come before Thursday.*

psalm /sɑm/ *n* a song or poem in praise of God, esp. one of the collection of Psalms in the Bible

pseu·do·nym /'suʷdn,ɪm/ *n* an invented name used, esp. by a writer of books, in

place of the real name: *Eric Blair wrote* **under the pseudonym of** *George Orwell.* –compare PEN NAME

psych /saɪk/ *v →* PSYCH OUT, PYSCH UP

psy·che /'saɪkiʸ/ *n* [*usu. sing.*] *tech or fml* the human mind, soul, or spirit

psy·che·del·ic /ˌsaɪkə'dɛlɪk/ *adj* **1** (of a mind-influencing drug) having the effect of making the senses seem keener than in reality **2** (of a form of art) producing an effect on the brain by means of strong patterns of noise, color, lines, moving lights, etc.

psy·chi·a·trist /saɪ'kaɪətrɪst, sɪ-/ *n* a doctor trained in PSYCHIATRY

psy·chi·a·try /saɪ'kaɪətriʸ, sɪ-/ *n* [U] the study and treatment of diseases of the mind –**psychiatric** /ˌsaɪkiʸ'ætrɪk/ *adj: psychiatric help|a psychiatric hospital*

psy·chic /'saɪkɪk/ also **psychical** /'saɪkɪkəl/– *adj* **1** concerning the mind or soul: *psychic disorders* **2** concerning the truth of strange happenings not explained by scientists, such as the power to see into the future –**psychically** *adv*

psy·cho·a·nal·y·sis /ˌsaɪkoʷə'næləsɪs/ *n* [U] a way of treating certain disorders of the mind by examination of the sufferer's past life, dreams, etc., in an effort to find past experiences that may be causing the illness

psy·cho·an·a·lyst /ˌsaɪkoʷ'ænl-ɪst/ also **analyst** *AmE–* *n* a person who is trained in PSYCHOANALYSIS

psy·cho·an·a·lyze *AmE‖* also **-lyse** /ˌsaɪkoʷ 'ænl,aɪz/ *v* **-lyzed, -lyzing** [T] to treat by PSYCHOANALYSIS

psy·cho·log·i·cal /ˌsaɪkə'lɑdʒɪkəl/ *adj* **1** of or connected with the way that the mind works: *There must be some psychological explanation for his bad temper.* **2** [A] using PSYCHOLOGY: *Psychological tests may be used to find out a person's character.* –**psychologically** *adv*

psy·chol·o·gist /saɪ'kɑlədʒɪst/ *n* a person who is trained in PSYCHOLOGY

psy·chol·o·gy /saɪ'kɑlədʒiʸ/ *n* **-gies 1** [U] the study or science of the mind and the way it works **2** [C;U] *infml* the mind and character of a particular person or group: *I can't understand that man's psychology.*

psy·cho·path /'saɪkə,pæθ/ *n tech* a person who has a serious disorder of character that may cause violent or criminal behavior –**psychopathic** /ˌsaɪkə'pæθɪk/ *adj*

psy·cho·sis /saɪ'koʷsɪs/ *n* **-choses** /'koʷsiʸz/ [C;U] *tech* a serious disorder of the mind that may produce character changes

psy·cho·so·mat·ic /ˌsaɪkoʷsə'mætɪk/ *n tech* (of an illness) caused by fear or anxiety rather than by a bodily disorder –**psychosomatically** *adv*

psy·cho·ther·a·py /ˌsaɪkoʷ'θɛrəpiʸ/ *n* [U] *tech* treatment of disorders of the mind using PSYCHOLOGY rather than drugs, etc. –**psychotherapist** *n*

psy·chot·ic /saɪ'kɑtɪk/ *n,adj tech* (of or being) a person suffering from a PSYCHOSIS: *psychotic behavior*

psych sbdy./sthg. ↔ **out** *v adv* [T] *infml* **1** to

pugnacious

figure out the intentions of sbdy. or the solution of sthg. by using PSYCHOLOGY **2** to make sbdy. frightened or uneasy by means of PSYCHOLOGY: *We psyched out the other team by telling them how big our players were.*

psych sbdy. ↔ **up** *v adv* [T] *infml* to make one's feelings ready for sbdy. or sthg.: *We psyched ourselves up for the big game.*

P T A /ˌpiy tiy 'ey/ *abbrev. for:* Parent-Teacher Association

pub /pʌb/ also **public house** /'·· ,·/ *BrE fml– n* (esp. in Britain) a building (not a club or hotel) where alcohol may be bought and drunk during fixed hours –compare BAR¹ (5)

pu·ber·ty /'pyuwbərtiy/ *n* the stage of change in the human body from childhood to the grown-up state in which it is possible to produce children

pu·bic /'pyuwbɪk/ *adj* [A] of or near the sexual organs: *pubic hair*

pub·lic¹ /'pʌblɪk/ *adj* **1** of, for, or concerning people in general; not private: *The town has its own public library and public school.*|**Public opinion** (=what most people think or believe) *was against the old political system.*|*This place is too public for talk about our personal affairs; anyone might hear what we're saying.* **2** known to all or to many: *The news of the ruler's death was not* **made public** *for several days.* **3 in the public eye** often seen in public or on television, or mentioned in newspapers –**publicly** *adv*

public² *n* [*the* U] **1** people in general: *The American public is interested in sports.* **2** a group in society considered for its interest in a particular person, activity, etc.: *a famous singer who tries to please his public by singing its/their favorite songs* **3 in public** in the presence of other people –opposite **in private**

pub·li·can /'pʌblɪkən/ *n BrE* a person who runs a PUB

pub·li·ca·tion /ˌpʌbləˈkeyʃən/ *n* **1** [U *of*] the act of making something known to the public: *the publication of the results of the election* **2** [U] the offering for sale to the public of something printed: *The book is ready for publication.* **3** [C] something PUBLISHED (1), such as a book or magazine

pub·li·cist /'pʌbləsɪst/ *n* a person whose business is to bring something to the attention of the public; PRESS AGENT

pub·lic·i·ty /pʌˈblɪsətiy/ *n* [U] **1** public notice or attention: *The actress's marriage got a lot of publicity.* **2** the business of bringing someone or something to (favorable) public notice, esp. for purposes of gain

pub·li·cize /'pʌbləˌsaɪz/ *v* **-cized, -cizing** [T] to bring to public notice or attention

public pros·e·cu·tor /ˌ·· '··· ·/ *n* (*often caps.*) →DISTRICT ATTORNEY

public re·la·tions /ˌ·· ·'··/ *n* [P] the relations between an organization and the general public, which must be kept friendly: *If we plant flowers in front of the factory it will be good (for) public relations.*

public school /'·· ,·/ *n* **1** (in the US) a free local PRIMARY school for children who study there but live at home –compare PRIVATE SCHOOL **2** (in the UK) a private SECONDARY school for children who usu. live as well as study there

public spir·it·ed /ˌ·· '···◄/ *adj apprec* showing willingness and the desire to serve people and do what is helpful for all

pub·lish /'pʌblɪʃ/ *v* **1** [I;T] (of a business firm) to choose, arrange, have printed, and offer for sale to the public (a book, magazine, newspaper, etc.) **2** [T] to make known generally: *The death of the ruler was kept secret; the news wasn't published for several days.*

pub·lish·er /'pʌblɪʃər/ *n* a person or company whose business is to PUBLISH (1) books, newspapers, etc., or (sometimes) to make and sell records

pub·lish·ing /'pʌblɪʃɪŋ/ *n* [U] the business or profession of preparing and offering books, newspapers, etc., for sale

puce /pyuws/ *n,adj* [U] (of) a dark brownish purple color

puck /pʌk/ *n* a hard flat circular piece of rubber used instead of a ball in the game of ICE HOCKEY

puck·er /'pʌkər/ *v* [I;T *up*] to tighten into (unwanted) folds: *to pucker (up) one's lips* –**pucker** *n*

pud·ding /'pʊdɪŋ/ *n* [C;U] **1** a sweet dish that is soft and creamy, and served for DESSERT: *We're having chocolate pudding tonight.* **2** a usu. solid dish based on pastry, rice, eggs, etc., usu. served hot: *an apple pudding/a rice pudding*

pud·dle /'pʌdl/ *n* a small amount of rainwater lying in a hollow place in the ground: *The children played in the puddles after the rain.*

pudg·y /'pʌdʒiy/ *adj* **-ier, -iest** *infml* (of a person or part of the body) short and fat

pu·er·ile /'pyuərəl, -raɪl/ *adj fml* fit only for children; silly –**puerility** /ˌpyuə'rɪlətiy/ *n* **-ties** [C;U]

puff¹ /pʌf/ *v* **1** [I;T *away, at, on*] to (cause to) blow out repeatedly, esp. in small amounts: *Don't puff cigarette smoke in my face.*|*She was puffing away (at a cigarette) nervously.* **2** [I] to breathe rapidly and with effort, usu. during or after hurried movement: *He puffed up the steep slope.* **3** [I] to move while sending out little clouds of smoke: *The railroad train puffed into the station.*

puff out *v adv* [I;T (=**puff** sthg.↔**out**) *with*] to (cause to) enlarge, esp. with air: *The bird puffed out its feathers.*

puff up *v adv* [I;T (=**puff** sthg.↔**up**) *with, usu. pass.*] to (cause to) swell

puff² *n* **1** an act of PUFFING¹ (1,2): *He took a puff at his cigarette.* **2** a sudden short rush of air, smoke, etc.: *a puff of wind* –compare GUST **3** a hollow piece of light pastry (**puff pastry**) that is filled with a soft (usu. sweet) mixture: *a cream puff*

puf·fin /'pʌfɪn/ *n* a North Atlantic seabird that has a very large brightly colored beak

puff·y /'pʌfiy/ *adj* **-ier, -iest** rather swollen –**puffiness** *n* [U]

pug /pʌg/ *n* a small short-haired dog with a wide flat face and a turned-up nose

pug·na·cious /pʌgˈneyʃəs/ *adj fml* fond of quarreling and fighting: *pugnacious people/*

behavior –**pugnaciously** *adv* –**pugnacity** /pʌɡˈnæsətiʸ/ *n* [U] *fml*

puke /pyuʷk/ *v* **puked, puking** [I;T] *infml* to be sick; VOMIT –**puke** *n* [U]

pull¹ /pʊl/ *v* **1** [I;T] to move (something) along behind one while moving: *The train is pulled by a powerful engine.*|*Help me move this piano; you pull and I'll push.* **2** [I;T *up, on, at, out*] to move (someone or something) towards oneself, sometimes with force: *He pulled his chair up to the table.*|*The cupboard door is stuck and I can't pull it open.*|*The child pulled (at) its mother's coat.* **3** [T] to draw or press towards one in order to cause an apparatus to work: *To fire the gun, pull the* TRIGGER. **4** [T *in*] to attract: *The football game pulled in great crowds.*|*He's not popular enough to pull in many votes in the election.* **5** [I] (of an apparatus) to move when drawn or pressed towards one: *The handle pulls so easily that a child could open the door.* **6** [T] to bring out (a small weapon) ready for use: *He pulled a gun on me.* (=took out a gun and aimed it at me) **7 pull a face** to make an expression with the face to show rude amusement, disagreement, dislike, etc. **8 pull a fast one (on)** *infml* to get the advantage (over) by a trick **9 pull one's weight** to do one's full share of work **10 pull to pieces** to say or show that (something or someone) is bad or worthless by pointing out the weak points or faults –compare PUSH¹

pull away *v adv* [I *from*] (esp. of a road vehicle) to start to move off: *He jumped onto the bus just as it was pulling away.*

pull sthg.↔**down** *v adv* [T] → TEAR **down**

pull in *v adv* **1** [I] (of a train) to arrive at a station **2** [I] also **pull over**– (of a vehicle or boat) to move to one side (and stop) **3** [T] (**pull** sthg.↔**in**) *infml* to earn (a lot of money): *He's pulling in quite a bit in his new job.*

pull off *v adv* **1** [T] (**pull** sthg.↔**off**) *infml* to succeed in (a difficult attempt): *The trick looked impossible, but she pulled it off.* **2** [I] to drive a vehicle onto the side of the road –compare PULL **in** (2), PULL **over**

pull out *v adv* **1** [I] (of a train) to leave a station **2** [I;T (=pull sbdy.↔out)** *of*] to (cause to) leave a place or time of trouble: *Jim saw that the company was going to be ruined, so he pulled out.*

pull over *v adv* [I;T (=pull** sthg.↔**over)]** to direct or move (one's vehicle) over to one side of the road –compare PULL **in** (2), PULL **off** (2)

pull through *v adv* [I;T (=pull** sbdy. **through)] 1** to (cause to) live in spite of illness or wounds **2** to (help to) succeed in spite of difficulties: *Margaret had difficulty with her work for the examinations, but her teacher pulled her through.*

pull together *v adv* **1** [I] (of a group of people) to work so as to help a common effort **2** [T *no pass.*] (**pull** sbdy. **together**) to control the feelings of (oneself): *Stop acting like a baby!* **Pull yourself together!**

pull up *v adv* [I;T (=pull** sthg. **up)** to (cause to) come to a stop: *The car pulled up*

outside the station.

pull² *n* **1** [C;U] (an act of) pulling: *Give the rope a pull.* (=pull it)|*the moon's pull on the sea* **2** [U] *infml* special influence; (unfair) personal advantage **3** [C] a rope, handle, etc., used for pulling something or causing something to act by pulling: *a bellpull* –compare PUSH²

pul·let /ˈpʊlɪt/ *n* a young hen during its first year of laying eggs

pul·ley /ˈpʊliʸ/ *n* **-leys** an apparatus consisting of a wheel over which a rope or chain can be moved, used for lifting heavy things

pull·o·ver /ˈpʊlˌoʷvər/ *n* a woolen or cotton garment for the top half of the body, that has no fastenings and is pulled on over the head –compare SWEATER –see illustration on page 123

pul·mo·nar·y /ˈpʊlməˌnɛriʸ, ˈpʌl-/ *adj* [A] *tech* of, concerning, or having an effect on the lungs

pulp¹ /pʌlp/ *n* **1** [S;U] a soft almost liquid mass, such as the soft inside part of many fruits or vegetables: *A banana is mainly pulp, except for its skin.*|*You've boiled these vegetables too long; you've boiled them to a pulp.* **2** [U] wood or other vegetable materials softened and used for making paper

pulp² *v* [I;T] to (cause to) become PULP¹

pul·pit /ˈpʊlpɪt, ˈpʌl-/ *n* a small raised enclosure of wood or stone in a church, from which the priest addresses the worshippers

pul·sate /ˈpʌlseʸt/ *v* **-sated, -sating** [I *with*] **1** to shake very regularly **2** →PULSE² –**pulsation** /pʌlˌseʸʃən/ *n* [C;U]

pulse¹ /pʌls/ *n* [*usu.sing.*] the regular beating of blood in the main blood vessels carrying blood from the heart, esp. as felt by a doctor at the wrist: *His pulse raced.* (=his heart beat very quickly)|*The doctor felt/took the woman's pulse.* (=counted the number of beats per minute)

pulse² also **pulsate**– *v* **pulsed, pulsing** [I *through, with*] to beat steadily as the heart does: *He could feel the blood pulsing through his body as he waited for the next explosion.*|*pulsing with excitement*

pulse³ *n* [C;U] (the seeds of) beans, PEAS, LENTILS, etc., used as food

pul·ver·ize ‖also **-ise** *BrE* /ˈpʌlvəˌraɪz/ *v* **-ized, -izing 1** [I;T] to (cause to) become a fine powder or dust by crushing **2** [T] *infml* to defeat thoroughly

pu·ma /ˈpyuʷmə, ˈpuʷmə/ *n* **pumas** *or* **puma** →COUGAR

pum·ice /ˈpʌmɪs/ also **pumice stone** /ˈ·· ˌ·/– *n* [U] a very light, silver-gray rock, used for cleaning and for rubbing surfaces smooth

pum·mel /ˈpʌməl/‖also **pommel** *AmE*– *v* **-l-** *AmE*‖ **-ll-** *BrE* [T] to hit repeatedly, esp. with the closed hand

pump¹ /pʌmp/ *n* **1** [C] a machine for forcing liquids, air, or gas into or out of something: *The heart is a kind of natural pump that moves the blood around the body.*|*a water pump*|*a gasoline pump*|*a bicycle pump* **2** [S] an act of PUMPing²

pump² *v* **1** [I;T] to (cause to) empty or fill

with a liquid or gas by means of a PUMP¹ (1): *He pumped up his car tires.|They had pumped the well dry and could get no more water.|His heart was pumping fast.* **2** [T] *infml* to ask (someone) questions in the hope of finding out something that one wants to know

pum·per·nick·el /ˈpʌmpər,nɪkəl/ *n* [U] a type of heavy dark brown bread

pump·kin /ˈpʌmpkɪn, ˈpʌŋkɪn/ *n* [C;U] (a plant with) a very large dark yellow roundish fruit that grows on the ground

pun¹ /pʌn/ also **play on words**– *n* an amusing use of a word or phrase that has two meanings, or of words having the same sound but different meanings: *He made the following pun: "Seven days without water make one weak."* (=week)

pun² *v* -nn- [I *on, upon*] to make PUNs¹: *He punned on the likeness of "weak" and "week."*

punch¹ /pʌntʃ/ *v* **1** [I;T] to strike (someone or something) hard with the closed hand (FIST): *He punched the man in the chest/in the nose.* **2** [T *in*] to make (a hole) in (something) using a PUNCH³: *Did he punch (a hole in) your ticket?*

punch² *n* **1** [C *in, on*] a quick strong blow made with the closed hand (FIST): *I'd like to give that man a punch in the nose.* **2** [U] *apprec* forcefulness; effective power: *That statement lacks punch; it sounds weak.*

punch³ *n* a steel tool for cutting holes: *a ticket punch*

punch⁴ *n* [U] a drink made from fruit juice, wine, sugar, water, etc.

punch line /ˈ· ·/ *n* [usu. *sing.*] the last few words of a joke or story, that give meaning to it and cause amusement or surprise

punc·til·i·ous /pʌŋkˈtɪliˑəs/ *adj fml, usu. approc* very exact and particular about details, esp. of behavior –**punctiliously** *adv* –**punctiliousness** *n* [U]

punc·tu·al /ˈpʌŋktʃuˑəl/ *adj* not late; happening, doing something, etc., at the exact time: *She's never punctual in answering letters; she's always late.* –opposite **unpunctual** –**punctuality** /,pʌŋktʃuˑˈæləti/ *n* [U] –**punctually** *adv*

punc·tu·ate /ˈpʌŋktʃuˑeɪt/ *v* -ated, -ating [T] **1** to divide (written matter) into sentences, phrases, etc., by means of PUNCTUATION MARKS **2** [usu. *pass.*] to interrupt repeatedly: *The football game was punctuated by the cheers of supporters.*

punc·tu·a·tion /,pʌŋktʃuˑeɪʃən/ *n* [U] (the marks used in) punctuating (PUNCTUATE (1)) a piece of writing

punctuation mark /·· ·· ,·/ *n* any sign used in punctuating (PUNCTUATE (1)), such as a COMMA (,), a PERIOD (.), a QUESTION MARK (?), etc.

punc·ture¹ /ˈpʌŋktʃər/ *n* a small hole made with a sharp point through a soft surface, esp. a tire: *I'm sorry I'm late: I had a puncture in my tire, so I had to change it.*

puncture² *v* -tured, -turing [I;T] to make or get a PUNCTURE¹: *A nail on the road punctured the tire.|He is in the hospital,* *suffering from a punctured lung.*

pun·dit /ˈpʌndɪt/ *n often humor* a person of knowledge (in a particular subject): *political pundits*

pun·gent /ˈpʌndʒənt/ *adj* having a strong, sharp, stinging taste or smell: (fig.) *pungent* (=sharp) *remarks* –**pungently** *adv* –**pungency** /ˈpʌndʒənsi/ *n* [U]

pun·ish /ˈpʌnɪʃ/ *v* [T] **1** [*for*] to cause (someone) to suffer for (a fault or crime): *People should be punished severely for dangerous driving.|Dangerous driving should be severely punished.* **2** to deal roughly with (an opponent), esp. by taking advantage of a weakness

pun·ish·a·ble /ˈpʌnɪʃəbəl/ *adj* [by, *for*] that may be punished by law: *Murder is punishable by death in some countries.*

pun·ish·ing /ˈpʌnɪʃɪŋ/ *adj infml* that makes one thoroughly tired and weak: *a long and punishing climb* –**punishingly** *adv*

pun·ish·ment /ˈpʌnɪʃmənt/ *n* **1** [U] the act of punishing or condition of being punished: *The boy accepted his punishment without complaining.* **2** [C] a way in which a person is punished: *A just judge will try to make the punishment fit the crime.*

pu·ni·tive /ˈpyuʷnəṭɪv/ *adj* **1** intended as punishment **2** very severe: *punitive taxes* –compare PUTATIVE –**punitively** *adv*

punk¹ /pʌŋk/ *n AmE derog infml* **1** [C; *you* +N] a rough and unpleasant young man or boy, esp. one in the habit of fighting and breaking the law (often in the phrase **young punk**) **2** [C] an inexperienced young man or boy

punk² *adj* [A] (in the US and esp. in Britain since the 1970s) of a movement among certain young people who are opposed to the values of money-based society and who express this esp. in loud, often violent music (**punk rock**), strange clothing, and hair of unusual colors

punt /pʌnt/ *n,v* [C;I] (to go for a journey by) a long narrow flat-bottomed river boat, moved by someone pushing a long pole against the bottom of the river

pu·ny /ˈpyuʷniˑ/ *adj* -nier, -niest *derog* small and weak; poorly developed: *puny little arms and legs*

pup /pʌp/ *n* **1** a young SEAL³ or OTTER **2** →PUPPY

pu·pa /ˈpyuʷpə/ *n* -pas *or* -pae /piˑ/ an insect in the middle stage of its development, contained in and protected by a covering

pu·pil¹ /ˈpyuʷpəl/ *n* a person, esp. a child, who is being taught

pupil² *n* the small black round opening in the middle of the colored part of the eye, through which light passes

pup·pet /ˈpʌpɪt/ *n* **1** [C] a toylike jointed wooden or cloth figure of a person or animal, that is made to move by someone pulling wires or strings that are fixed to it –see MARIONETTE **2** [C] a toylike cloth figure of a person or animal, moved by putting the hand inside it **3** [A] *often derog* not independent, but controlled by someone else: *a puppet government*

pup·pet·eer /ˌpʌpɪˈtɪər/ n a person who performs with PUPPETs (1,2)

pup·py /ˈpʌpiʸ/ also **pup–** n **-pies** a young dog

pur·chase¹ /ˈpɜrtʃəs/ v **-chased, -chasing** [T for] fml or tech to buy: to purchase a new house in the country

purchase² n **1** [U] buying: He gave his son some money for the purchase of his school books. **2** [C often pl.] **a** an act of buying: She made several purchases in the department store. **b** an article that has just been bought

pur·chas·er /ˈpɜrtʃəsər/ n tech a person who buys goods from another

pure /pyʊər/ adj **1** not mixed with any other substance, esp. dirt or other harmful matter: pure silver|The air by the sea is pure and healthy. **2** free from evil; without sexual thoughts or experience: a pure young girl –see also IMPURE **3** clear; not mixed: a cloudless sky of the purest blue|The voices of the young boys were high and pure. **4** [A] infml complete; thorough; only: By pure chance he found the rare book he needed in a little store. **5** [A] (of an art or branch of study) considered only for its own nature as a skill or exercise of the mind, separate from any use that might be made of it: pure science –compare APPLIED

pu·ree /pyʊˈreʸ, ˈpyʊəreʸ/ n,v **-reed, -reeing** [C;U;T] (to prepare) food boiled to a soft half-liquid mass and rubbed through a fine wire frame: an apple puree

pure·ly /ˈpyʊərliʸ/ adv completely; wholly; only: I helped him purely (and simply) out of friendship.

pur·ga·tive /ˈpɜrgətɪv/ n,adj (a medicine) that causes the bowels to empty: This fruit often has a purgative effect.

pur·ga·to·ry /ˈpɜrgəˌtoriʸ, -ˌtoʷriʸ/ n **-ries 1** [U] (often cap.) (esp. according to the ROMAN CATHOLIC religion) a state or place in which the soul of a dead person must be made pure by suffering for wrong-doing on earth, until it is fit to enter Heaven **2** [C;U] often humor a place, state, or time of suffering

purge¹ /pɜrdʒ/ v **purged, purging** [T from, of] **1** to make clean and free from (something evil or impure): Try to purge your spirit (of hatred).|The people wished to purge their SINs. **2** to get rid of (an unwanted person) in (a state, political party, group, etc.) by unjust or forceful means **3** to clear (waste matter) from (the bowels) by means of medicine

purge² n an act or set of actions intended to get rid of unwanted members of a (political) group, suddenly, often unjustly, and often by force: The new President carried out a purge of disloyal army officers.

pu·ri·fy /ˈpyʊərəˌfaɪ/ v **-fied, -fying** [T of] to make PURE (esp. 1,3): This salt has been specially purified for use in medicine. –**purification** /ˌpyʊərəfəˈkeʸʃən/ n [U of]

pur·ist /ˈpyʊərɪst/ n a person who is always (too) careful to practice the correct way of doing something, esp. in matters of grammar, use of words, etc.

pu·ri·tan /ˈpyʊərətn/ adj,n usu. derog (of,

like, or being) a person who has rather hard fixed standards of behavior and self-control, and thinks pleasure is unnecessary or wrong –**puritanical** /ˌpyʊərəˈtænɪkəl/ adj: a puritanical father who wouldn't allow his children to watch television. –**puritanically** adv

pu·ri·ty /ˈpyʊərətiʸ/ n [U] the quality or state of being pure –see also IMPURITY

purl /pɜrl/ n,v [I;T;U] tech (to make) a simple stitch in KNITTING –**purl** v

pur·loin /pərˈlɔɪn, ˈpɜrlɔɪn/ v [T] fml to steal (esp. something of small value)

pur·ple /ˈpɜrpəl/ adj,n (of) a dark color made of a mixture of red and blue –compare VIOLET

pur·port¹ /pərˈport, -ˈpoʷrt/ v [T+to-v] to have an (intended) appearance of being: His plans are not what they purport to be.

pur·port² /ˈpɜrport, -poʷrt/ n [U of] fml the general meaning or intention (of someone's words or actions): The purport of the message seemed to be this.

pur·pose /ˈpɜrpəs/ n **1** [C] an intention or plan; reason for an action: Did you come to Texas **for the purpose of** seeing your family or for business purposes?|It wasn't an accident; you did it **on purpose**. (=intentionally) **2** [C] use; effect; result: Don't waste your money; put it to some good purpose.|I don't have a pen, but a pencil will **answer/serve the same purpose**. (=will do what is needed) **3** [U] steady determined following of an aim; willpower

pur·pose·ful /ˈpɜrpəsfəl/ adj directed towards a special purpose –**purposefully** adv

pur·pose·less /ˈpɜrpəslɪs/ adj aimless; meaningless –**purposelessly** adv

pur·pose·ly /ˈpɜrpəsliʸ/ adv intentionally: I purposely didn't come yesterday because I knew you'd be out.

purr /pɜr/ v,n [C;I] (to make) a low continuous sound produced in the throat by a pleased cat: (fig.) The big car purred along the road.

purse¹ /pɜrs/ n **1** a small flattish leather or plastic bag used, esp. by women, for carrying money –compare WALLET **2** AmE for HANDBAG **3** an amount of money collected for some good purpose or offered as a gift or as a prize to a winner: a purse of $10,000.

purse² v **pursed, pursing** [T] to draw (esp. the lips) together into little folds: She pursed her lips to show her dislike.

purs·er /ˈpɜrsər/ n an officer on a ship who keeps the ship's accounts and is also in charge of the travelers' rooms, comfort, etc.

pur·sue /pərˈsuʷ/ v **-sued, -suing** [T] **1** more fml than **chase–** to follow, esp. in order to catch, kill, or defeat: The police are pursuing an escaped prisoner.|Wherever the travelers went in the city, they were pursued by beggars. **2** to continue (steadily) with; be busy with: He is pursuing his studies at the university.

pur·su·er /pərˈsuʷər/ n a person or animal that PURSUEs (1): The deer ran faster than its pursuers.

pur·suit /pərˈsuʷt/ n **1** [U] the act of pursuing (PURSUE) someone or something: The police *car raced through the streets* **in pursuit of** *another car.* **2** [C] any activity to which one gives one's time, whether as work or for pleasure: *One of the boy's favorite pursuits is stamp collecting.*

pur·vey /pər'veʸ/ *v* **-veyed, -veying** [T *to*] *fml or tech* to supply (food or other needed goods) as a trade –**purveyor** /pər've ̓ʸər/ *n* [*of, to*]

pus /pʌs/ *n* [U] a thick yellowish liquid produced in an infected wound or poisoned part of the body

push¹ /pʊʃ/ *v* **1** [I;T] to use sudden or steady pressure in order to move (someone or something) forward, away from oneself, or to a different position: *He pushed me suddenly, and I fell into the water.*|*Don't push; there's enough room for everyone.* **2** [I;T] to make (one's way) by doing this: *She pushed past me.*|*He pushed his way to the front of the crowd.* **3** [T] to try to force (someone) to do something by continual urging: *If you push a worker too hard, he may make mistakes.*|*My friends are all pushing me to enter politics.* **4** [I;T] *infml* to force (someone or something) on the notice of others, as a means of success: *The company is pushing its new product.* (=advertising it widely) **5** [T] *infml* to sell (unlawful drugs) **6 push one's luck** to take an increasing risk –compare PULL¹

  push sbdy. around *v adv* [T] *infml* to treat roughly and unfairly; ORDER² **around**

  push off *v adv* [I] *infml* to go away

  push sbdy./sthg. through (sthg.) *v adv, prep* [T] to force to be successful (in): *push the student through (the examination)*

push² *n* **1** [C] an act of pushing: *They gave the car a push* (=pushed it) *to start it.* **2** [C] a planned attack and advance of great strength by an army **3** [U] *infml* active will to succeed, esp. by forcing oneself and one's wishes on others –compare PULL²

push·er /'pʊʃər/ *n infml* a person who sells unlawful drugs

push·o·ver /'pʌʃ ̩oʷvər/ *n* [C;S] *infml* something that is very easy to do or win: *The examination was a pushover: I knew the answers to most of the questions.*

push-up /'· ·/ *n AmE* a form of exercise in which a person lies face down on the ground and pushes his body up with his or her arms

push·y /'pʊʃiʸ/ also **pushing** /'pʊʃɪŋ/– *adj* **-ier, -iest** *usu. derog* too active and forceful in getting things done, esp. for one's own advantage

puss·y /'pʊsiʸ/ also **puss** /pʊs/, **pussycat** /'pʊsiʸ ̩kæt/– *n* **-ies** *infml* (a word used for calling) a cat

pus·tule /'pʌstʃuʷl/ *n tech* a small raised spot on the skin containing poisonous matter

put¹ /pʊt/ *v* **put, putting** [T] **1** to move, place, lay, or fix in, on, or to a stated place: *Put the chair near the fire.*|*You put too much salt in this food.*|*She picked it up, then quickly put it down.*|*He put the children to bed.* (fig.) *Let's* **put an end to** *this nonsense.* (=stop it)| *Everyone* **puts the blame on** *me.* (=blames me)|*The murderer was* **put to death.** (=killed) **2** to cause to be: *He put his books*

in order. **3** to make, place, set, or fix (something or someone), in connection with something else as an act of will or the mind: *It's time to put an end to the meeting* (=end it).|*The prisoner was put to death* (=was killed). **4** to give expression to; say: *She is–how should I put it?–not exactly fat, but a little heavy.* **5** to write down: *Put your name at the top of the page.* **6** to throw (a heavy metal ball (SHOT)) as a form of sporting competition **7** to calculate, or form an opinion of (something): *I put your monthly costs at $1,000.*

  put sthg. ↔across/over– *v adv* [T] to cause to be understood; explain: *I'm not putting my meaning across very well.*

  put sthg. ↔aside *v adv* [T] to save (money, etc.), usu. for a special purpose: *He has a little money put aside for a trip to Europe.*|*Put the rest of the cake aside for tomorrow.* –compare PUT **away** (2), PUT **by**

  put sthg. ↔away *v adv* [T] **1** to remove to a place where it is usually stored: *Put the books away neatly on the shelf.* **2** to save (esp. money) for later use –compare PUT **aside 3** *infml* to eat (usu. large quantities of food) **4** *infml* to place (someone) in prison or in a hospital for INSANE people

  put sthg. ↔back *v adv* [T] **1** to cause to show an earlier time: *put the clocks back* –compare PUT **forward** (2) **2** to delay: *The fire in the factory has put back production.*

  put sthg. ↔by *v adv* [T] →PUT **away** (2)

  put sbdy./sthg. ↔down *v adv* [T] **1** to control; defeat: *put down the opposition* **2** *infml* to make feel humble: *She really put him down when she called him lazy.* **3** to pay (an amount) as part of the cost of something with a promise to pay the rest over a period of time –see also DOWN PAYMENT

  put sbdy. down for sthg. *v adv prep* [T] to put (someone's name) on a waiting list for a race, a school, etc.

  put sthg. down to sthg. *v adv prep* [T] to state that (something) is caused by: *I put his bad temper down to his recent illness/to having had an unhappy childhood.*

  put sbdy./sthg. forward *v adv* [T] **1** to offer: *May I put your name forward as a possible chairman of the committee?* **2** to cause to show a later time: *put the clocks forward* –compare PUT **back**

  put sthg. ↔in *v adv* [T] **1** to make or send (a request or claim): *If the goods were damaged in the mail, you can put in a claim to the post office.* **2** to do or spend, esp. for a purpose: *put in three years' work*|*put in an hour at one's studies* –see INPUT

  put in for sthg. *v adv prep* [T] to make a formal request for; APPLY (1) for: *They've put in for more money.*

  put into *v prep* [T] **1** (**put** sthg. **into** sthg.) to add to: *Put more effort into your work!* **2** (**put into** sthg.) (of a ship) to enter (a port): *The boat has to put into Sydney for supplies.*

  put sbdy./sthg. ↔off *v adv* [T] **1** [+*v-ing/till, until*] to move to a later date; delay: *I feel ill; I'll have to put off my visit*|*put off going till next month.*|*We've invited them to dinner,* *but we will have to put them off because the baby's sick.* **2** to make excuses to (someone) in order to avoid a duty: *I put him off with a promise to pay him next week.* **3 a** to discourage: *The speaker was trying to make a serious point, but people kept putting him off by shouting.* **b** to cause to feel dislike: *His bad manners put her (right) off.*

put sbdy. **off** sthg. *v prep* to discourage from: *Don't talk, it puts him off his game.|The smell put me off eating for a week!*

put on *v adv* [I] *infml* to give the appearance of feeling sthg.: *He's not really crying. He's just putting on.* –see also PUT-ON

put sbdy./sthg.↔**on 1** to cover (part of) the body with (esp. clothing): *She put her hat and coat on.|He put on his glasses to read the letter.* –opposite **take off** –see DRESS (USAGE) **2** to increase: *She put on weight.* **3** to perform (a play, show, etc.) on a stage. **4** to provide: *So many people wanted to go to the game that another train had to be put on.* **5** *AmE infml* to play a trick on; deceive **6** →TURN **on** (1): *Put on the light/the radio.*

put sthg. **on** sthg. *v prep* [T] to risk (money) on; BET[2]

put out *v adv* [T] **1** (**put** sthg.↔**out**) to make stop burning: *She put the light/the fire out.* **2** (**put** sbdy. **out**) to trouble or annoy: *She was so put out by the man's rudeness that she didn't know what to say.|Will it put you out if I bring another guest?* **3** (**put** sthg.↔**out**) to broadcast or print: *The government will put out a new statement next week.* **4 put oneself out** to take trouble: *No one likes her; she never puts herself out to help people.*

put sthg.↔**over** *v adv* [T] →PUT **across**: *He wasn't elected because he didn't put his ideas over clearly enough.*

put through *v adv* [T] **1** (**put** sbdy. **through**) [*to*] to connect (a telephone caller) by telephone: *Can you put me through to this number?* **2** (**put** sthg.↔**through**) to complete (a piece of business) successfully

put sbdy. **through** sthg. *v prep* [T] to cause to experience: *You've put him through a lot of pain.*

put to *v prep* [T] **1** (**put** sbdy./sthg. **to** sbdy.) to ask (a question) of or make (an offer) to **2** (**put** sbdy./sthg. **to** sthg.) to test by using the stated means: *Let's put the matter to a vote.* **3** (**put** sbdy. **to** sthg.) to cause to be in (a certain place or condition): *She put the child to bed.* **4 be hard put to (do something)** to find it difficult to (do something): *You'd be hard put to find water in a desert.*

put together *v adv* [T] **1** (**put** sthg.↔**together**) to form; make a group of: *He wanted to put a team together.* **2** [*usu. pass.*] to combine: *His share was more than all the others' put together.|They* **put their heads together** (=combined ideas) *to answer the question.*

put up *v adv* [T] **1** (**put** sthg.↔**up**) to raise: *to put up a tent* **2** (**put** sthg.↔**up**) to put in a public place: *put up a notice* –opposite **take down 3** (**put** sthg.↔**up**) to increase (a price) **4** (**put** sbdy.↔**up**) to provide food and lodging for: *I'm afraid I can't put you up; you'll have to go to a hotel.* **5** (**put up** sthg.) to offer,

show, make, or give, esp. in a struggle: *What a coward; he didn't even put up a fight!* **6** (**put** sthg. **up**) to offer for sale: *She's putting her house up (for sale).*

put sbdy. **up to** sthg. *v adv prep* [T] to give the idea of (doing esp. something bad): *Who put you up to this trick?*

put up with sbdy./sthg. *v adv prep* [T] to suffer without complaining: *I can't put up with your rudeness any more; leave the room.|That woman has a lot to put up with.* (=has many troubles to bear)

put[2] *adj* **stay put** *infml* to remain where placed: *The lid won't stay put; it keeps falling off.*

pu·ta·tive /ˈpyuʷtətɪv/ *adj* [A] *fml* generally accepted or supposed to be: *his putative parents* –compare PUNITIVE

put-on /ˈ·· ·/ *n AmE infml* **1** a person who pretends to have a feeling, opinion, etc.: *Don't believe her when she says she's angry. She's a real put-on.* **2** something not intended seriously –**put-on** *adj* [A]

pu·tre·fy /ˈpyuʷtrəˌfaɪ/ *v* **-fied, -fying** [I;T] *more fml than* **rot**– to decay; (cause to) become PUTRID –**putrifaction** /ˌpyuʷtrə ˈfækʃən/ *n* [U] *fml or tech*

pu·trid /ˈpyuʷtrɪd/ *adj* (esp. of an animal or plant substance) very decayed and bad-smelling

putt /pʌt/ *v* [I;T] (in the game of GOLF) to strike (the ball) gently along the ground towards or into the hole –**putt** *n*

put·ter a·round /ˈpʌtər/ *AmE‖***potter about** esp. *BrE*– *v adv* [I] to spend time in activities that demand little effort: *I spent the afternoon puttering around in the garden.*

put·ty /ˈpʌtiʸ/ *n* [U] a soft oily paste, used esp. in fixing glass to window frames

put up·on /ˈ·· ·,·/ *adj* [F] (of a person) used for someone else's advantage: *The way his neighbor always borrows things from him makes him feel put upon.*

puz·zle[1] /ˈpʌzəl/ *v* **-zled, -zling 1** [T *often pass.*] to cause (someone) difficulty in the effort to explain or understand: *The woman's illness puzzled the doctor; he couldn't find the cause.* **2** [I *about,over,as to*] to make a great effort of the mind in order to understand or find the answer to a difficult question: *He was puzzling over the map, trying to find the easiest way to cross the mountains.* –**puzzled** *adj*: *a puzzled expression on his face|I'm puzzled about what to do next.*

puzzle[2] *n* **1** [*usu. sing.*] something that one cannot understand or explain **2** a game, toy, or apparatus in which parts must be fitted together correctly, intended to amuse or exercise the mind: *a* CROSSWORD *puzzle|a book of puzzles|a* JIGSAW PUZZLE

pyg·my, pigmy /ˈpɪgmiʸ/ *n* **-mies 1** a member of a race of very small people **2** any person or animal of much less than usual height

py·ja·mas /pəˈdʒɑməz, -ˈdʒæ-/ *n* [P] *esp. BrE* for PAJAMAS

py·lon /ˈpaɪlən/ *n* a tall framework of steel bars used for supporting wires that carry electricity over land

pyr·a·mid /'pɪrəmɪd/ n **1** (in GEOMETRY) a solid figure with a flat usu. square base and straight flat three-angled sides that slope upwards to meet at a point **2** (often cap.) a very large ancient stone building in the shape of this, used formerly, esp. in Egypt, as the burial place of a king

pyre /paɪər/ n a high mass of wood for the ceremonial burning of a dead body

py·thon /'paɪθən, -θən/ n a large non-poisonous tropical snake that kills animals for food by winding around them and crushing them

Q, q

Q, q /kyuʷ/ **Q's, q's** or **Qs, qs** the 17th letter of the English alphabet

quack¹ /kwæk/ v,n [C;I] (to make) the sound that ducks make

quack² n a person dishonestly claiming to have medical knowledge or skills: a quack doctor

quad¹ /kwɑd/ also **quadrangle** /'kwɑdræŋgəl/ fml– n a square open area with buildings around it, esp. in a college or a university

quad² n infml for QUADRUPLET

quad·rant /'kwɑdrənt/ n **1** a quarter of a circle **2** an instrument for measuring angles

quad·ri·lat·er·al /ˌkwɑdrə'lætərəl/ adj,n (a figure) with four sides

quad·ri·ple·gic /ˌkwɑdrə'pliʸdʒɪk/ adj,n (of or being) a person suffering from PARALYSIS of both arms and both legs –see also PARAPLEGIC

quad·ru·ped /'kwɑdrə,pɛd/ n an animal (MAMMAL) with four legs –compare BIPED

quad·ru·ple¹ /kwɑ'druʷpəl, 'kwɑdrʊpəl/ v **-pled, -pling 1** [T] to multiply (a number or amount) by four **2** [I] to become four times as great: Our profits quadrupled this year.

quadruple² predeterminer,n,adv [U] fml (an amount which is) four times as big as something mentioned or usual: quadruple the amount of profit

quad·ru·plet /kwɑ'drʌplɪt, -'druʷ-, 'kwɑdrʊplɪt/ also **quad** infml– n [usu. pl.] one of four children born of the same mother at the same time

quag·mire /'kwæɡmaɪər, 'kwɑɡ-/ n a large area of soft wet ground; BOG

quail¹ /kweʸl/ n **quail** or **quails** [C;U] (meat of) a type of small bird, highly regarded as food

quail² v [I with, at] to be afraid; tremble: He quailed (with fear) at the thought of telling her the bad news.

quaint /kweʸnt/ adj unusual and attractive, esp. because old: a quaint old village –**quaintly** adv –**quaintness** n [U]

quake¹ /kweʸk/ v **quaked, quaking** [I with, at] to shake; tremble: to quake with fear

quake² n infml for EARTHQUAKE

Quak·er /'kweʸkər/ n,adj (a member) of a Christian religious group which opposes violence

qual·i·fi·ca·tion /ˌkwɑləfə'keʸʃən/ n **1** [C +to-v/for] ability, experience, or training enabling one to do something: She has the right qualifications for the job/to do the job **2** [C] something which limits the meaning of something said: We support their policy, but with certain qualifications. **3** [U] the act of QUALIFYing

qual·i·fied /'kwɑlə,faɪd/ adj **1** [+to-v/for] having suitable knowledge, ability, or experience, esp. for a job: He's not qualified to teach young children. **2** limited: She gave qualified agreement.

qual·i·fy /'kwɑlə,faɪ/ v **-fied, -fying 1** [I;T +to-v] to (cause to) gain a certain level of knowledge, ability, or performance: This course will qualify you to teach swimming.|Will our team qualify for the final competition? **2** [T] to limit (esp. the meaning of something stated): I'd like to qualify my last remark.

qual·i·ta·tive /'kwɑlə,teʸtɪv/ adj of or about quality: a qualitative judgment –compare QUANTITATIVE –**qualitatively** adv

qual·i·ty /'kwɑlətiʸ/ n **-ties 1** [C;U] a (high) degree of goodness: material of low/poor quality|an actor of real quality (=a very good actor) **2** [C] something typical of a person or material: Kindness is his best quality.|She shows qualities of leadership.

qualm /kwɑm, kwɔm/ n [about] a feeling of nervousness or uncertainty: He **had no qualms about** working in a foreign country.

quan·da·ry /'kwɑndəriʸ/ n **-ries** [about, over] a feeling of not knowing what to do: I was **in a quandary** about whether to go.

quan·ti·fy /'kwɑntə,faɪ/ v **-fied, -fying** [T] fml to measure (an amount or quantity): It is difficult to quantify the value of a good education. –**quantifiable** adj –**quantification** /ˌkwɑntəfə'keʸʃən/ n [U]

quan·ti·ta·tive /'kwɑntə,teʸtɪv/ adj of or about quantity –compare QUALITATIVE –**quantitatively** adv

quan·ti·ty /'kwɑntətiʸ/ n **-ties 1** [U] a measurable property of something: The quantity of food was enough (=there was plenty of it), but the quality was not very good. **2** [C] an amount or number: Police found a large quantity of illegal drugs. –see Study Notes on page 550 **3 an unknown quantity** something or someone whose true nature or value is not yet known: Their new player is an unknown quantity.

quar·an·tine¹ /'kwɔrən,tiʸn, 'kwɑr-/ n [S;U] a period of time when a person or animal that may be carrying disease is kept separate from others so that the disease cannot spread: Because of the disease, the house was put under quarantine (=no one was allowed

countable nouns

apple and **chair** are both COUNTABLE nouns because they are separate things that we can count:

an apple   *three apples*   *a chair*   *two chairs*

These nouns can be used in the plural and can be used with **a** or **an** when they are singular.

uncountable nouns

sand and **water** are UNCOUNTABLE nouns, because they are substances which cannot be counted:

water   *sand*

These nouns are not usually used in the plural, and they cannot be used with **a** or **an**.

There are some nouns, like **love** and **beauty** (ABSTRACT nouns) which cannot be counted because they are not physical things like apples and chairs. These are uncountable nouns too.

In the dictionary, [C] means countable, and [U] means uncountable. If a noun does not have a [C] or a [U] printed by it, this means that it is always countable.

---

more and less

The lists below show you which words to use with [C] and [U] nouns to show quantity. They answer questions like *How many?* and *How much?*

How many?
(use with [C] nouns)

Every *student/***All** *the students came to the meeting.*

Most *of my friends came to the party.*

There are **a lot of** *people here.*
There aren't **many** *people here.*
Many *people walk to school every day.*

Some *of these apples taste sour.*
Several *people were waiting for the bus.*

There are **not many/only a few** *tickets left.*
There are **few** *children in this part of town.*

He couldn't answer **any** *of the exam questions.*
There are **no** *eggs left;* **none** *at all.*

all

How much?
(use with [U] nouns)

He ate **all** *the bread.*

He spends **most** *of his time reading.*

There's **a lot of** *milk left.*
There isn't **much** *milk left.*
Much *time was wasted discussing impossible solutions to our problem.*

There's **some** *bread on the table.*

There's **only a little/not much** *room left.*

Hurry up! There's **little** *time left.*

She didn't give me **any** *help.*

There is **no** *gasoline in the car;* **none** *at all.*

a lot of and many/much

Use **a lot of**, not **many** or **much**, after an AFFIRMATIVE verb:
We have **a lot of** *eggs/milk.*

Use **many** or **much** after a NEGATIVE verb:
There aren't **many** *eggs left.* | *There isn't* **much** *milk left.*
Note that **a lot of** can also be used here, but this usage is less common.

Use either **a lot of** or **many/much** with the subject of a sentence:
Many/A lot of *books were stolen from the library last year.* | **Much** *of what you say is true.*
Note that **many** and **much** are more *fml* than **a lot of** in this use.

some and any

any is usually used instead of **some** in questions and sentences with *not*:
Do you have **any** *eggs/milk?* | *No, I don't have* **any** *eggs/milk.*

It is also possible to use **some** in questions, especially when you expect the answer to be *yes*:
Would you like **some** *cookies?* | *Would you like* **some** *more coffee?*

nouns that are both countable and uncountable

Some nouns, like **light** and **coffee**, can be [C] (countable) in one meaning and [U] (uncountable) in another. When they are [C] they can become plural; when they are [U] they cannot. For example:

[U] *the **light** of the sun*

[C] *turn on the lights*

[U] *a jar of **coffee***

[C] *Three **coffees** please.*
   (=three cups of coffee)

plural and singular nouns

Some nouns, like **scissors**, are used only in the plural, i.e. they take a plural verb. These nouns are often plural in form, like **scissors**, but sometimes not. For example, **police** is a plural noun. Plural nouns are marked [P] in the dictionary:

> **scissors** *n* [P] two sharp blades with handles at one end with holes for the fingers, fastened at the center so that they can cut when they close: *I cut his hair with scissors.* | *Do you have a pair of scissors?*

Some nouns, like **yen** are usually used only in the singular. These nouns are used with **a** or **an**, and are marked [S] in the dictionary:

> **yen** *n* [S] a strong desire: *He has a yen to travel.*

---

number and size

The lists below show you how to use these words to show quantity in numbers and in size. Quantity in numbers answers the question *How many?*, and quantity in size answers the question *How big?*

How many?	very many, very big	**How big?**

How many?

*There are **billions** of stars in the sky.*
*The world's population is more than four **billion** people.*

Millions *of people watched the football game on television.*
*There are about five **million** people in this city.*

*Their new car cost **thousands** of dollars.*
*It cost 15 **thousand** dollars.*

*There were **hundreds** of people on the beach.*
*They bought two **hundred** new books for the library.*

*There were **dozens** of people waiting in the line.*
*We need two **dozen** eggs.*

*Only **one or two** of my friends noticed that I'd had my hair cut.*

very few, very small

How big?

*China is a **vast/huge/enormous** country.*
*There is a **gigantic/colossal/immense** new building in the center of the city.*

*There was a **big/large/great big** box on the floor.*

*She is about **average** height.*
*The room is **medium** sized.*

*He was a **little** man–thin and not very tall.*
*She carried a **small** bag in her hand.*

*There was a **tiny** insect on the flower.*

*I can't read his **minute/microscopic** writing.*

to leave or enter) *for two weeks.*

quarantine² *v* **-tined, -tining** [T] to put in/under QUARANTINE¹

quar·rel¹ /'kwɔrəl, kwarəl/ *n* **1** [*with*] an angry argument **2** [only used in NEGATIVES², questions, etc.] a cause for disagreement: *I have no quarrel with what the governor says.*

quarrel² *v* **-l-** *AmE*‖**-ll-** *BrE* [I *about, over, with*] to have an angry argument: *She quarreled (about politics) with George.*

quar·rel·some /'kwɔrəlsəm, 'kwar-/ *adj* (of a person) likely to argue; often arguing

quar·ry¹ /'kwɔriʸ, 'kwariʸ/ *n* **-ries** a place on the surface of the earth from which stone, sand, etc. are dug out –compare MINE² (1)

quarry² *v* **-ried, -rying** [I;T] to dig out (stone, sand, etc.) from a QUARRY¹

quarry³ *n* [S] the person or animal that one is hunting

quart /kwɔrt/ *n* a measure for liquids which is 1/4 of a GALLON; two PINTS

quar·ter¹ /'kwɔrtər/ *n* **1** a 4th part of a whole: *a quarter of a mile*|*a quarter of a pound of cookies* **2** 15 minutes before or after the hour: *It's (a) quarter past 10.* (=10:15)|*(a) quarter to 10/of 10 (AmE)* (=9:45)|*in three quarters of an hour* (=45 minutes) **3** a period of three months of the year, used esp. for making payments: *I have to make a payment on my bank loan each quarter.* **4** (in the US and Canada) a coin worth 25 cents (=¹/₄ of a dollar) **5** a place or person(s), often from which something comes: *Help is arriving from all quarters.* **6** a part of a town, often typical of certain people: *the student quarter* **7 at close quarters** near together –see also QUARTERS

quarter² *v* [T] **1** to cut or divide into four parts **2** to provide lodgings for (esp. soldiers)

quar·ter·back /'kwɔrtər,bæk/ *n AmE* the member of a football team who calls the signals to direct offensive play

quar·ter·fi·nal /ˌkwɔrtər'faɪnl/ *n* any of four matches in a competition of which the winners will play in the two SEMIFINAL matches

quar·ter·ly /'kwɔrtərliʸ/ *adj,adv* (happening, appearing, etc.) every three months: *to pay the phone bill quarterly*|*a quarterly magazine*

quar·ter·mas·ter /'kwɔrtər,mæstər/ *n* a military officer in charge of provisions

quarter note /'·· ,·/ *n AmE tech* a musical note

quar·ters /'kwɔrtərz/ *n* [P] lodgings: **Married quarters** *are houses where soldiers live with their families.*

quar·tet /kwɔr'tɛt/ *n* (a piece of music written for) four people playing instruments or singing together

quartz /kwɔrts/ *n* [U] a hard mineral substance, now used in making very exact watches and clocks

quash /kwaʃ/ *v* [T] **1** to officially refuse to accept: *The high court judge quashed the decision of the lower court.* **2** → SUPPRESS

qua·ver /'kweyvər/ *v* [I] (of a voice) to shake –**quaver** *n* –**quavery** *adj*

quay /kiʸ/ *n* a fixed place, usu. built of stone, where ships can land

quea·sy /'kwiʸziʸ/ *adj* **-sier, -siest** feeling sickness: *I felt a little queasy on the ship.* –**queasily** *adv* –**queasiness** *n* [U]

queen /kwiʸn/ *n* **1** [A;C] (the title of) **a** a female ruler of a country: *Queen Elizabeth the Second of England* **b** the wife of a king **2** [C] the winning female in a competition: *a beauty queen* **3** [C] the large leading female insect of a group: *the queen ant/bee* **4** [C] **a** (in CHESS) the most powerful piece **b** a playing card with a picture of a queen –see CARDS (USAGE)

queen·ly /'kwiʸnliʸ/ *adj* **-lier, -liest** like, or suitable for, a queen

queer¹ /kwɪər/ *adj* **1** strange; ODD: *What a queer story!* **2** *infml* not well: *I'm feeling a little queer; I think I'll go home.* **3** *infml derog* for HOMOSEXUAL –**queerly** *adv* –**queerness** *n* [U]

queer² *n infml derog* a male HOMOSEXUAL

quell /kwɛl/ *v* [T] to stop; SUPPRESS: *The police were called in to quell the violence.*

quench /kwɛntʃ/ *v* [T *with,in*] to take away the force of (flames, desire, etc.) esp. with water: *to quench one's thirst with a glass of water*

quer·u·lous /'kwɛrələs, 'kwɛryə,-/ *adj fml derog* complaining –**querulously** *adv* –**querulousness** *n* [U]

que·ry¹ /'kwɪəriʸ/ *n* **-ries** a question or doubt: *to* **raise** *a few* **queries**

query² *v* **-ried, -rying** [T] to express a doubt about: *Nobody would query her ability.*|*to query a point*

quest /kwɛst/ *n* [*of, for*] *esp. lit* a search; an attempt to find: *the long quest for a cure for the disease*|*They traveled* **in quest of** *gold.*

ques·tion¹ /'kwɛstʃən/ *n* **1** [C] a sentence or phrase which asks for information: *I asked you a question and you didn't answer.*|*The question is: how was he killed?* **2** [C] a difficulty or matter to be settled; PROBLEM (1): *It's a question of finding enough time.* **3** [C;U] (a) doubt: *There was some question as to his honesty.* **4 call (something) into question** to raise doubts about (something): *His honesty was called into question.* **5 in question** under consideration; being talked about: *That is not the point in question.* **6 out of the question** impossible: *You can't go to the wedding in that old shirt; it's out of the question.* **7 there's no question about/that** there's no doubt about that **8 there's no question of** there's no possibility of

question² *v* [T] **1** [*about*] to ask (someone) a question/questions **2** to raise doubts about: *I would never question her honesty.* –see ASK (USAGE)

ques·tion·a·ble /'kwɛstʃənəbəl/ *adj* that may be QUESTIONED² (2); perhaps not true or right: *a questionable idea*|*questionable behavior in money matters* –**questionably** *adv*

ques·tion·ing /'kwɛstʃənɪŋ/ *adj* appearing to question: *She gave him a questioning look.* –**questioningly** *adv*

question mark /'·· ,·/ *n* the mark (?)

ques·tion·naire /ˌkwɛstʃə'nɛər/ *n* a piece of paper, usu. given to several people, showing a set of questions to be answered in order to provide information

queue[1] /kyu^w/ *n BrE* a line of people, cars, etc., waiting to move, to get on a vehicle, or to enter a building; set of people waiting for something: *a long queue outside the theater*

queue[2] *v* **queued, queuing** [I *up, for*] *BrE* to form or join a line while waiting: *We queued (up) for the bus.|We queued for hours.*

quib·ble /ˈkwɪbəl/ *v* **-bled, -bling** [I *about, over, with*] to argue about small points: *Don't quibble over the money; pay her what she asks.* **–quibble** *n* **–quibbling** *adj*

quick[1] /kwɪk/ *adj* **1** [+*to-v*/*about, at, with*] swift; soon finished: *a quick drink|a quick answer|She's quick to learn/quick at learning.* **2** easily showing anger (in the phrases **a quick temper, quick tempered**) **–quickly** *adv* **–quickness** *n* [U]

quick[2] *n* [*the* U] the flesh to which the fingernails and toenails are joined: (fig.) *He* **cut me to the quick** (=hurt me deeply) *with that unkind remark.*

quick[3] *adv* **1** quickly: *Come quick; something terrible has happened!* **2** (in comb.): *a quick-acting medicine*

quick·en /ˈkwɪkən/ *v* [I;T] to (cause to) become quick: *The music quickened, and the dancing got faster.*

quick·sand /ˈkwɪksænd/ *n* [C;U] wet sand which sucks in anyone or anything that tries to cross it

quick·sil·ver /ˈkwɪkˌsɪlvər/ *n* [U] → MERCURY

quick-wit·ted /ˌˈ ˈ···◀/ *adj* quick to understand and act

qui·es·cent /kwaɪˈɛsənt, kwiʸ-/ *adj fml* still; at rest **–quiescence** *n* **–quiescently** *adv*

qui·et[1] /ˈkwaɪət/ *adj* **1** with little noise: *quiet music|a quiet voice* –compare LOUD[1] (1) **2** without unwanted activity; at rest; calm: *a quiet life* **3** not making oneself noticed by activity: *The children are unusually quiet today.* **–quietly** *adv* **–quietness** *n* [U]

quiet[2] *n* [U] **1** state of being quiet; quietness: *an evening of* **peace and quiet 2 on the quiet** *infml* without telling anyone; secretly

quiet[3] *AmE*‖**quieten** /ˈkwaɪətn/ *esp. BrE*– *v* [I;T *down*] to (cause to) become QUIET[1]: *The children quickly quieted down.|quiet his fears*

quill /kwɪl/ *n* **1** (a pen made from) a bird's long stiff feather **2** a sharp prickle on some animals, such as the PORCUPINE

quilt /kwɪlt/ *n,v* [I;T] (to make, esp. the outer part of) a cloth cover for a bed filled with soft warm material –see also PATCHWORK

quilt·ed /ˈkwɪltɪd/ *adj* made with cloth containing soft material and with stitching across it

quince /kwɪns/ *n* a hard fruit related to the apple, used esp. in jelly

qui·nine /ˈkwaɪnaɪn/ *n* [U] a drug used for treating fevers, esp. MALARIA

quint·es·sence /kwɪnˈtɛsəns/ *n fml* the perfect type or example: *John is* **the quintessence** *of good manners.* **–quintessential** /ˌkwɪntəˈsɛnʃəl, -tʃəl/ *adj* **–quintessentially** *adv*

quin·tet /kwɪnˈtɛt/ *n* (a piece of music written for) five people playing instruments or singing together

quin·tu·plet /kwɪnˈtʌplɪt, -ˈtuʷ-, -ˈtyuʷ-,

'kwɪntʊplɪt/ *n* [*usu. pl.*] one of five children born of the same mother at the same time

quip /kwɪp/ *v,n* **-pp-** [C;I] (to make) a clever-sounding remark

quirk /kwɜrk/ *n* **1** a strange happening or accident: *By some quirk of fate the two of us were on the same train.* **2** (a tendency to) a strange type of behavior: *He has some unusual quirks in his character.*

quis·ling /ˈkwɪzlɪŋ/ *n* someone who helps another country that has taken over his/her own

quit /kwɪt/ *v* **quit** *AmE*‖**quitted** or **quit** *BrE*, **quitting** [I;T +*v-ing*] to stop (doing something) and leave: *I've quit my job.|I've quit working.|I'd had enough, so I quit.* **–quitter** *n: Elaine is a quitter; she never finishes anything that she begins.*

quite /kwaɪt/ *predeterminer, adv* **1** [*adv* +*adv*/*adj*/*prep*] completely; perfectly: *quite different|Are you quite sure?|not quite ready* **2** to some degree; rather: *quite small|quite a lot of people|It was quite good, but not perfect.* –see Study Notes on page 363 **3 quite something** *infml* unusual, esp. unusually good: *It's quite something to be made a judge at the age of 29.*

quits /kwɪts/ *adj* [F *with*] *infml* back on an even level with someone after an argument, after repaying money which is owed, etc.: *Give him $5 and* **call it quits.** (=agree that the argument is settled)

quiv·er[1] /ˈkwɪvər/ *v* [I *with, at*] to tremble a little: *I quivered (with fear) at the sound.|a quivering movement* **–quiver** *n: a quiver of excitement*

quiver[2] *n* a container for arrows which is carried on the back

quix·ot·ic /kwɪkˈsɑtɪk/ *adj* trying to do the impossible, often for others, while oneself running into danger **–quixotically** *adv*

quiz[1] /kwɪz/ *n* **-zz-** a competition or game where questions are put

quiz[2] *v* **-zz-** [T *about*] to ask questions of (someone): *He quizzed me about where I'd been last night.*

quiz·zi·cal /ˈkwɪzɪkəl/ *adj* suggesting the idea **a** that one knows something and/or is laughing at the other person **b** that one is asking a question without saying anything: *a quizzical smile/*GLANCE[2] (1) **–quizzically** *adv*

Quon·set hut /ˈkwɑnsɪt ˌhʌt/ *n AmE tdmk* a large shelter with a cement floor and a round roof made of iron sheets

quo·rum /ˈkwɔrəm, ˈkwoʷrəm/ *n fml* a stated number of people, without whom a meeting cannot be held: *We couldn't vote because we didn't have a quorum.*

quo·ta /ˈkwoʷtə/ *n* a stated number or amount, or a limit on numbers: *The quota of students the university is allowed to accept has been reduced.*

quot·a·ble /ˈkwoʷtəbəl/ *adj* worthy of being QUOTEd

quo·ta·tion /kwoʷˈteʸʃən/ *n* **1** [U] the act of quoting (QUOTE[1]) **2** [C] also **quote** *infml*– a sentence drawn from literature **3** [C] the calculated cost of a piece of work: *He gave me a quotation for fixing the roof.* (=he told me how much it would cost)

quotation mark /ˈ··· ˌ·/ *n* either of a pair of marks (" ") (' ') showing the beginning and end of words QUOTED (often in the phrase **in quotation marks**)

quote /kwoʷt/ *v* **quoted, quoting 1** [I;T *from*] to repeat in speech or writing the words of (a book or writer): *He quotes (from) the Bible to support his beliefs.* **2** [T] to mention (an

example) to give force to one's arguments: *She quoted me several cases to support what she was saying.* **3** [T *to*] to give a price: *I can quote you a price lower than anyone else's!*

quo·tient /ˈkwoʷʃənt/ *n* a number which is the result when one number is divided by another: *If you divide 10 by 2, the quotient is 5.*

R, r

SPELLING NOTE
Words with the sound /r/ may be spelled **wr-**, like **wrong**.

R, r /ɑr/ **R's, r's** *or* **Rs, rs 1** the 18th letter of the English alphabet **2 the three R's** reading, writing, and ARITHMETIC, thought to form the beginning of a child's education

rab·bi /ˈræbaɪ/ *n* **-bis** (the title of) a Jewish religious leader and teacher of Jewish law

rab·bit¹ /ˈræbɪt/ *n* [C;U] (the fur or meat of) a common small long-eared animal of the HARE family that lives in a hole (BURROW) in the ground

rab·ble /ˈræbəl/ *n* a disordered crowd of noisy people

rabble-rous·ing /ˈ·· ˌ··/ *adj* [A] (of a speaker or speech) exciting the mass of the people to hatred and violence: *a rabble-rousing speech*

rab·id /ˈræbɪd/ *adj* **1** suffering from RABIES: *a rabid dog* **2** [A] *derog* (of a person or his/her opinions) unreasonably violent: *a rabid opponent of the government*

ra·bies /ˈreʸbiʸz/ *also* **hydrophobia** *fml*– *n* [U] a disease of certain animals, including humans, passed on by the bite of an infected animal, esp. a dog, and causing death

rac·coon /ræˈkuʷn/ ‖*also* **coon** *AmE*– *n* [C;U] (the thick fur of) a small meat-eating North American animal with a long tail

race¹ /reʸs/ *n* [*against, between, with*] a competition in speed: *to have/run/lose/win a race*|*a boat race*|*a race against time*

race² *v* **raced, racing 1** [I;T] to compete in a race (against): *She's a very good swimmer and often races.*|*I'll race you to the end of the road.* **2** [I;T] to (cause to) go very fast: *We raced the sick woman to hospital.*|(fig.) *The vacation raced by.* **3** [T] to cause (an animal or vehicle) to run a race: *My horse has hurt his foot so I can't race him.* –see WALK (USAGE) **4** [I] (of an engine) to work too fast

race³ *n* **1** [C] one of the divisions of human beings, each with a different type of body: *the black/white/brown races* **2** [C] a group of people with the same history, language, customs, etc.: *the German race* **3** [C] a (stated) type of creature: *the human race* (=people in general) **4** [A] of or between races (RACE³ (1)): *race relations*

USAGE **Race, nation, state,** and **tribe** are all words for large groups into which human beings may be divided. The largest of these groups is a **race**, and this word is used of people of the same color and/or physical type. A **nation** is a group of people (smaller than a **race**) who have a common history and language, and usually live in the same place. Unlike **race** and **nation**, a **state** is a political division and can mean either an independent country or one of the partly-independent divisions in a country like the US: *The German* **nation** *is divided into two* **states,** *East Germany and West Germany.*|*the Indian* **nations** *of North America*|*the modern* **states** *of Africa*|*the* **State** *of Texas.* A **tribe** is a social group, smaller than a **nation,** which has the same customs and beliefs, and often the same language: *a* **tribe** *of hunters living in the Amazon forest*|*Which* **tribe** *does the President of Uganda belong to?*

race·course /ˈreʸs-kɔrs, -koʷrs/ *n* a track around which horses race

rac·es /ˈreʸsɪz/ *n* [*the* P] an occasion when horse races are held at a RACECOURSE: *a day at the races*

race·track /ˈreʸs-træk/ *n* a course around which runners, cars, etc., race

ra·cial /ˈreʸʃəl/ *adj* connected with (one's own) RACE³ (1): *racial pride/customs/origin/type*

ra·cial·ly /ˈreʸʃəliʸ/ *adv* from the point of view of RACE³ (1): *Racially, there is no difference between the two nations.*

rac·ing /ˈreʸsɪŋ/ *n* [A] used for racing in competitions: *a racing car*|*a racing horse*

rac·ism /ˈreʸsɪzəm/ *also* **racialism** /ˈreʸʃəˌlɪzəm/– *n* [U] *derog* political and social practices based on the belief that one's own race is the best –**racist, racialist** *adj,n*

rack¹ /ræk/ *n* **1** [C] a framework with bars, hooks, etc., for holding things: *He put the bottles of wine in a rack.*|*a* LUGGAGE *rack on a train* **2** [*the* S] an instrument of TORTURE consisting of a frame on which people used to be stretched by turning its wheels

rack² *v* [T] to cause great pain: *a racking headache*|*He was racked with pain/by doubts.*

rack³, wrack *n* [U] **rack and ruin** the ruined state caused by lack of care: *The house went to/is in rack and ruin.*

rack·et¹, racquet /ˈrækɪt/ *n* a light instrument consisting of a network usu. of nylon stretched in a frame with a handle, used for hitting the ball in games such as tennis

racket² /ˈ/ n infml 1 [S] a loud noise: *Stop making such a racket! I can't sleep.* 2 a dishonest way of getting money, e.g. by threatening or cheating people

rack·et·eer /ˌrækəˈtɪər/ n derog someone who works a RACKET² (2)

rac·on·teur /ˌrækɒnˈtɜr/ n French someone good at telling stories

rac·y /ˈreɪsiʸ/ adj -ier, -iest (of speech or writing) amusing, full of life, and perhaps sex: *Paul shocked the priest with his racy stories.* –**racily** adv –**raciness** n

ra·dar /ˈreɪdɑr/ n [U] a method of finding the position of solid objects by receiving radio waves seen on a glass plate (SCREEN¹ (6))

ra·di·ance /ˈreɪdiʸəns/ n [U] the quality of being RADIANT (1,2)

ra·di·ant /ˈreɪdiʸənt/ adj 1 [A] sending out light or heat in all directions; shining: *the radiant sun* 2 [with] (of a person or his/her appearance) showing love and happiness: *her radiant face* 3 [A] tech sent out by RADIATION: *radiant heat* –**radiantly** adv

ra·di·ate /ˈreɪdiʸˌeʸt/ v -ated, -ating [T] to send out (light or heat): (fig.) *She radiated happiness.*

   radiate from sthg. v prep [T no pass.] to come out or spread in all directions from: *a system of roads radiating from the center of town*

ra·di·a·tion /ˌreɪdiʸˈeʸʃən/ n 1 [U] the radiating (RADIATE) of heat, light, etc. 2 [C] something which is radiated: *This apparatus produces harmful radiations.* 3 [U] → RADIOACTIVITY: *the effects of atomic radiation*

ra·di·a·tor /ˈreɪdiʸˌeʸtər/ n 1 an apparatus, esp. one consisting of pipes with steam or hot water passing through them, used for heating buildings –see illustration on page 55 2 an apparatus which keeps the engine of a motor vehicle cool

rad·i·cal¹ /ˈrædɪkəl/ adj 1 (of changes) thorough and complete: *The government made radical improvements to the tax system.* 2 (of a person or his opinions) in favor of thorough and complete political change –compare REACTIONARY –**radically** adv

radical² n a person who wishes to make rapid and thorough social and political changes –**radicalism** n [U]

ra·di·i /ˈreʸdiʸˌaɪ/ n pl. of RADIUS

ra·di·o¹ /ˈreʸdiʸˌoʷ/ n -os 1 [U] the sending or receiving of sounds through the air by electrical waves: *The police talked to each other by radio.* 2 [C] an apparatus made to receive sounds broadcast through the air by means of electrical waves: *a transistor radio* –see illustration on page 95 3 [U] the radio broadcasting industry: *Her first job was in radio.* 4 **on the radio: a** (of a sound) broadcast: *I heard it on the radio.* **b** (of a person) broadcasting

radio² v -oed, -oing [I;T] to send (a message) by radio: *The ship radioed for help.*

ra·di·o·ac·tiv·i·ty /ˌreʸdiʸoʷækˈtɪvətiʸ/ n [U] the quality, harmful to living things, that some simple substances (ELEMENTS (1)) have

of giving out force (ENERGY (2)) by the breaking up of atoms –**radioactive** /ˌreʸdiʸoʷˈæktɪv/ adj: *The train was carrying dangerous radioactive waste.*

ra·di·og·ra·phy /ˌreʸdiʸˈɑgrəfiʸ/ n [U] the taking of photographs made with short waves (X-RAYS), usu. for medical reasons –**radiographer** n

ra·di·o·ther·a·py /ˌreʸdiʸoʷˈθɛrəpiʸ/ n [U] the treatment of diseases by RADIOACTIVITY or X-RAYS

rad·ish /ˈrædɪʃ/ n a small vegetable or its red or white hot-tasting root which is eaten raw, esp. in SALADS

ra·di·um /ˈreʸdiʸəm/ n [U] a rare shining white metal that is a simple substance (ELEMENT), has a high level of RADIOACTIVITY, and is used in the treatment of certain diseases, esp. CANCER

ra·di·us /ˈreʸdiʸəs/ n -dii /diʸˌaɪ/ 1 (the line marking) the distance from the center of a circle or SPHERE (1) to its edge or surface –compare DIAMETER 2 a circular area measured from its center point: *He lives somewhere within a two-mile radius of the town.*

raf·fi·a /ˈræfiʸə/ n [U] the soft string-like substance from the leaf stems of a PALM tree, used for making hats, baskets, etc.

raf·fle¹ /ˈræfəl/ n a sale of an article by selling numbered tickets of which one is chosen by chance to be the winner: *He won a car in the raffle.* –compare LOTTERY

raffle² v -fled, -fling [T off] to sell in a RAFFLE

raft /ræft/ n 1 a flat boat or floating surface made of large pieces of wood fixed together 2 also **life raft**– a flat rubber boat that can be filled with air and carried by planes and ships to save life 3 **a raft of** AmE infml a large number or amount of: *A whole raft of people came for drinks.*

raf·ter /ˈræftər/ n one of the large sloping, esp. wooden beams that hold up a roof

rag¹ /ræg/ n 1 [C;U] (a small piece of) old cloth: *He cleaned the machine with an oily rag/a piece of oily rag.* 2 [C] an old worn-out garment: *The beggar was dressed in rags.* 3 [C] infml derog a badly-written newspaper: *Why are you reading that rag?* 4 **glad rags** infml best clothes

rag² v -gg- [T] to play rough tricks on or make fun of; TEASE: *They ragged him about his big ears.*

rag·a·muf·fin /ˈrægəˌmʌfɪn/ n lit a dirty young child in torn clothes

rag·bag /ˈrægbæg/ n often derog a confused mixture: *His argument is a ragbag of disconnected facts.*

rage¹ /reʸdʒ/ n 1 [C;U] (a state of) wild uncontrollable anger: *The child wept with rage.|My father is in one of his rages.|He **flies into a rage** every time I mention money.|(fig.) the rage of the storm.* –see ANGRY (USAGE) 2 [C] infml a fashion: *Short hair is (all) the rage* (=very fashionable) *now.*

rage² v raged, raging [I] 1 [against, at] to be in a RAGE¹ (1) 2 to be full of violent force: *The battle raged.|a raging headache|The disease raged through the city.*

rag·ged /'rægɪd/ *adj* **1** old and torn: *a ragged shirt*|(fig.) *ragged clouds in the sky* **2** dressed in old torn clothes: *a ragged little boy* **3** (of work) unfinished and imperfect: *The musicians gave a ragged performance.* –**raggedly** *adv* –**raggedness** *n* [U]

rag·time /'rægtaɪm/ *n* [U] a type of music of black US origin, popular in the 1920's: *a ragtime band*

raid¹ /reɪd/ *n* [*on*] **1** a quick attack on an enemy position: *to make a raid on the enemy coast*|an **air raid** (=an attack by aircraft)|(fig.) *The children made a raid on the kitchen and took all the cookies.* **2** an unexpected visit by the police, in search of criminals or illegal goods: *During their raid on the house, the police found a lot of drugs.*

raid² *v* [I;T] to visit or attack (a place) on a RAID: *raid a house* –**raider** *n*

rail¹ /reɪl/ *n* **1** [C] a fixed bar, esp. one to hang things on or for protection: *Keep your hand on the rail as you climb the steps.* **2** [C] one of the pair of metal bars fixed to the ground, along which a train runs: (fig.) *Jane has gone slightly off the rails* (=become disordered in mind) *since the accident.* **3** [A] connected with railroads: *rail travel*|*send it by rail* (=by train)

rail² *v* [I *against, at*] *fml* to complain noisily: *railing against the latest tax increases*

rail·ing /'reɪlɪŋ/ *n* [C;U] one of a series of RAILS¹ (1) making up a fence: *The dog got its head stuck between the railings.*

rail·road¹ /'reɪlroʷd/ *AmE*‖**railway** /'reɪlweʸ/ *esp. BrE*– *n* (a system, including engines, stations, etc. of) track for trains: *I work for the railroad.*

railroad² *v* [T] **1** to hurry (someone) unfairly: *The workers were railroaded into signing the agreement.* **2** to pass (a law) or carry out (a plan) quickly in spite of opposition: *The chairman railroaded the plan through the committee.*

rai·ment /'reɪmənt/ *n* [U] *lit* clothes

rain¹ /reɪn/ *n* **1** [U] water falling in separate drops from the clouds: *The rain fell continuously.*|*She went out in the rain without a coat.*|*Don't go out because it looks like rain* (=as if it will rain). –compare DEW **2** [S] a thick fall of anything: *a rain of bombs*|*of questions* **3 as right as rain** *infml* in perfect health: *Jane's been ill, but she's as right as rain now.* –see WEATHER (USAGE)

rain² *v* **1** [*it* +I] (of rain) to fall: *It's raining.*|*It began to rain hard.* **2** [I;T *down*] to (cause to) fall like rain: *Tears rained down her cheeks.*|*Their rich uncle rained gifts upon the children.* **3 rain cats and dogs** to rain very heavily

rain sthg.↔ **out** *v adv* [T] *infml esp. AmE* to cause to stop because of rain: *The game was rained out.*

rain·bow /'reɪnboʷ/ *n* an arch of different colors that sometimes appears in the sky immediately after rain

rain check /'· ·/ *n AmE infml* an agreement that one may claim later something that is being offered now: *I don't want a drink now, but I'll take a rain check on it.*

rain·coat /'reɪnkoʷt/ *n* a light coat worn to keep dry when it rains

rain·drop /'reɪndrɑp/ *n* a single drop of rain

rain·fall /'reɪnfɔl/ *n* [C;U] the amount of rain that falls in an area in a certain time –compare PRECIPITATION (2)

rain for·est /'· ,··/ *n* a wet tropical forest with tall trees growing thickly together

rains /reɪnz/ *n* [*the* P] →MONSOON (1): *The rains have started early this year.*

rain·y /'reɪniʸ/ *adj* **-ier, -iest** having a lot of rain: *a very rainy day*|*place*|*Save your money* **for a rainy day.** (=for a time when you need it)

raise¹ /reɪz/ *v* **raised, raising** [T] **1** to lift, push, or move upwards: *to raise the lid of a box*|*raise one's hat*|*She raised her finger to her lips as a sign for silence.*|*The car raised a cloud of dust as it rushed past.*|*He raised the fallen child to his feet.* (=helped him to stand) **2** to make higher in amount, degree, size, etc.: *to raise the rent*|*the temperature*|*someone's pay* –opposite **lower** (for 1,2) **3** to collect together: *to raise an army*|*We couldn't raise enough money to buy the house.* **4** to produce, cause to grow or increase, and look after (living things); BRING **up** (1) (children): *raise a family*|*raise horses* **5** to mention (a subject): *There's an important point I want to raise.* **6 a** to make (a noise): *The men raised a cheer.* **b** to cause people to make (a noise) or have (feelings): *Her joke raised a laugh.*|*His long absence raised doubts*|*fears about his safety.* **7 raise hell/the roof** *infml* to become very angry: *Mother will raise hell if you don't clean up your room.* –see RISE (USAGE)

raise² *AmE*‖**rise** *BrE*– *n* an increase in wages: *I got a $50-a-week raise last month.*

rai·sin /'reʸzən/ *n* a sweet dried fruit (GRAPE) used in cakes, etc.

ra·jah , raja /'rɑdʒə/ *n* [C;S] (the title of) an Indian ruler

rake¹ /reʸk/ *n* a tool consisting of a row of teeth at the end of a long handle, used for making the soil level, gathering up dead leaves, etc.

rake² *v* **raked, raking 1** [I;T] to make (a place) level with a RAKE¹: *Rake the garden paths (smooth).* **2** [T *together, up*] to collect with a RAKE¹: *Rake up the dead leaves.* **3** [I *around*] to search carefully by turning over a mass: *She raked around among her papers to see if she could find it.*

rake sthg.↔ **in** *v adv* [T] *infml* to earn or gain (a lot of money): *He must be raking in $1500 a week!*

rake sthg.↔ **up** *v adv* [T] *infml* **1** to remember and talk about (something that should be forgotten): *Please don't rake up that old quarrel again.* **2** to collect together, esp. with difficulty: *to rake up enough money for the rent*

rake³ *n old use* a man who has led a wild life

SPELLING NOTE
Words with the sound /r/ may be spelled **wr-**, like **wrong**.

with regard to drink and women

rake-off /'· ·/ n a (usu. dishonest) share of profits: *The taxi driver gets a rake-off from the hotel if he takes travelers there.*

rak·ish /'reʸkɪʃ/ adj bold and wild like (that of) a RAKE³: *lead a rakish life|She wore her hat at a rakish angle.* (=sideways on her head) –**rakishly** adv –**rakishness** n [U]

ral·ly¹ /'ræliʸ/ v -lied, -lying 1 [I;T] to come or bring together (again) for a purpose: *The whole nation rallied to the government.|The leader rallied his tired soldiers, and they drove the enemy back.* 2 [I] to recover from illness or unhappiness: *He soon rallied from the shock of his father's death.*

rally around v adv [I] infml (esp. of a group) to come to someone's help: *Her friends all rallied around when she was ill.*

rally² n -lies 1 a large (esp. political) public meeting 2 a car race over public roads 3 (in tennis) a long struggle to gain a point, with each player hitting the ball again and again

ram¹ /ræm/ n 1 a fully-grown male sheep –compare EWE 2 → BATTERING RAM 3 any machine that repeatedly drops or pushes a weight onto or into something

ram² v -mm- [T] 1 to run into (something) very hard: *His car rammed the wall.* 2 [down] to force into place with heavy pressure: *He rammed his clothing into the drawer.|*(fig.) *I don't like math, but my teacher keeps ramming it down my throat.* (=forcing it on me)

Ram·a·dan /ˌræməˈdɑn/ n the 9th month of the Muslim year, during which no food or drink may be taken between sunrise and sunset

ram·ble¹ /'ræmbəl/ v -bled, -bling [I] 1 [around] to go on a RAMBLE²: *They rambled through the woods.* 2 [about] to talk or write in a disordered way: *The old man rambled on (about the days of his youth).* –**rambling** n [U]

ramble² n a (long) walk for enjoyment, often in the country: *go for/on a ramble through the woods*

ram·bler /'ræmblər/ n a person who goes on RAMBLES²

ram·bling /'ræmblɪŋ/ adj 1 (of speech or writing) disordered and wandering: *a long and very rambling letter* 2 (of houses, streets, etc.) of irregular shape; twisting and winding: *The old building was full of rambling passages.* 3 (of a plant) growing loosely in all directions: *a rambling rose*

ram·i·fi·ca·tion /ˌræməfəˈkeʸʃən/ n fml something that follows from an action or decision; CONSEQUENCE: *What are the ramifications of our decision to join the union?*

ram·i·fy /'ræməˌfaɪ/ n -fied, -fying [I;T] to (cause to) branch out in all directions; form a network

ramp /ræmp/ n 1 a man-made slope that connects two levels: *Drive the car up the ramp.* 2 AmE a road for driving onto or off of a highway, esp. an EXPRESSWAY

ram·page /'ræmpeʸdʒ, ræm'peʸdʒ/ v -paged, -paging [I] to rush about wildly or angrily: *The elephants rampaged through the forest.*

–**rampage** /'ræmpeʸdʒ/ n [the S]: *football crowds* on the rampage

ramp·ant /'ræmpənt/ adj (of crime, disease, beliefs, etc.) widespread and impossible to control: *Sickness was rampant in the country.* –**rampantly** adv

ram·part /'ræmpɑrt/ n [usu. pl.] a wide bank of earth built to protect a fort or city

ram·rod /'ræmrɑd/ n a stick for pushing the gunpowder into or cleaning a gun

ram·shack·le /'ræmˌʃækəl/ adj (of a building or vehicle) badly made or needing repair; falling to pieces: *a ramshackle old house*

ran /ræn/ v past tense of RUN

ranch /ræntʃ/ n (in the western US and Canada) a very large farm, esp. one where sheep, cattle, or horses are produced

ranch·er /'ræntʃər/ n a person who owns or works on a RANCH

ranch house /'·· ·/ n AmE 1 a house built on one level, usu. with a roof that does not slope much –see illustration on page 337 2 a house on a RANCH in which the RANCHER and his/her family live

ran·cid /'rænsɪd/ adj (of oily food or its taste or smell) not fresh: *rancid butter*

ran·cor AmE‖ **rancour** BrE /'ræŋkər/ n [U] fml a feeling of bitter, unforgiving spite and hatred –**rancorous** /'ræŋkərəs/ adj –**rancorously** adv

ran·dom¹ /'rændəm/ adj [A] made or done aimlessly, without any plan: *a random choice|a random sample of people* (=people chosen in such a way that anyone is equally likely to be chosen) –**randomly** adv –**randomness** n [U]

random² n at random aimlessly; without any plan: *She asked questions at random.*

rand·y /'rændiʸ/ adj -ier, -iest infml (of a person or his/ her feelings) full of sexual desire –**randiness** n [U]

rang /ræŋ/ v past tense of RING

range¹ /reʸndʒ/ n 1 [C] a connected line of mountains, hills, etc.: *a mountain range* 2 [C] an area where shooting is practiced, or where MISSILEs are tested: *a firing range* 3 [C] (in North America) a wide stretch of grassy land where cattle feed 4 [U] the distance at which one can see or hear: *Shout as soon as she comes within range.* 5 [S;U] the distance that a gun can fire: *He shot the rabbit at short/close/long range.|What's the range of this gun?* 6 [S] the measurable limits between which something varies: *a country with a wide range of temperature|people in the $15,000-$20,000 income range* 7 a set of different objects of the same kind: *a complete range of gardening tools* 8 →STOVE

range² v ranged, ranging 1 [I not be+v-ing] to vary between limits; reach from one limit to another: *The children's ages range from 5 to 10/ between 5 and 10.* 2 [I;T through,over; no pass.] lit to wander freely (through, over): *We ranged (over) the hills and valleys.* 3 [T] to put in position; arrange: *She ranged the goods neatly in the store window.*

range over sthg. v prep [T] (of thoughts or speech) to be concerned with; include, one after the other: *Our conversation ranged* *over many subjects.*

rang·er /ˈreʸndʒər/ *n* (in North America) **a** a forest guard **b** a policeman on horseback in a country area

rank¹ /ræŋk/ *n* **1** [C;U] (a) degree of value, ability, importance, etc., in a group: *the rank of general|He's above me in rank.* **2** [C;U] (high) social position: *people of all ranks* **3** a line of people, esp. soldiers or things: *Taxis stand in a (taxi) rank waiting to be hired.*|(fig.) *the ranks* (=the large group) *of the unemployed* **4 rank and file** the ordinary people in an organization as opposed to the leaders

rank² *v* **1** [I;T *as, among*] to be or put in (a certain class): *This town ranks (high) among New England beauty spots.*

rank³ *adj* **1** (of a plant) too thick and widespread: *rank grass* **2** (of smell or taste) very strong and unpleasant: *rank tobacco* **3** [A] (esp. of bad things) complete; UTTER: *He's a rank beginner at the job, but he'll learn.* **–rankly** *adv* **–rankness** *n* [U]

rank·ing /ˈræŋkɪŋ/ *adj* [A] *AmE* (of an officer) of highest rank present: *Who's the ranking officer here?*

ran·kle /ˈræŋkəl/ *v* **-kled, -kling** [I] to continue to be remembered with bitterness and anger: *His rudeness to me still rankles.*

ran·sack /ˈrænsæk/ *v* [T] to search through and rob: *Enemy soldiers ransacked the town.*|(fig.) *She ransacked her pockets for the keys.*

ran·som /ˈrænsəm/ *n* (a sum of money paid for) the freeing of a prisoner: *They took away* (KIDNAPped) *the boy and* **held him for ransom.** (=kept him prisoner so as to demand payment) **–ransom** *v* [T]

rant /rænt/ *v* [I *on*] to talk in a loud excited way: *The priest ranted on about the devil and all his works.*

rap¹ /ræp/ *n* **1** (the sound of) a quick light blow: *to hear a rap on the door* **2** *infml* a conversation **3 beat the rap** *AmE infml* to escape punishment **4 take the rap (for)** *infml* to receive the punishment (for someone else's crime)

rap² *v* **-pp-** [I;T *at, on*] to strike quickly and lightly: *someone rapping loudly at the door/ on the table*
  rap sthg.↔**out** *v adv* [T] to say sharply and suddenly: *The officer rapped out an order.*

rap³ *v* **-pp-** [I] *AmE infml* to talk freely and easily: *We rapped for a while before the meeting.*

ra·pa·cious /rəˈpeʸʃəs/ *adj fml* taking everything one can, esp. by force: *a rapacious band of robbers* **–rapaciously** *adv* **–rapaciousness** *n* [U] **–rapacity** /rəˈpæsətiʸ/ *n* [U]

rape¹ /reʸp/ *v* **raped, raping** [T] to have sex with a person against his or her will

rape² *n* [C;U] **1** (a case of) the act and crime of raping (RAPE¹): *He was sent to prison for*

SPELLING NOTE
Words with the sound /r/ may be spelled **wr-**, like **wrong.**

rape. **2** *fml* spoiling: *the rape of our beautiful forests*

rap·id¹ /ˈræpɪd/ *adj* quick-moving; fast: *The improvement was rapid.|to ask questions in rapid* SUCCESSION|*The school promised rapid results in the learning of languages.* **–rapidity** /rəˈpɪdtiʸ/ *n* [U] **–rapidly** /ˈræpɪdliʸ/ *adv*

rapid² *n* [*usu. pl.*] a part of a river where the water moves very fast over rocks

ra·pi·er /ˈreʸpiʸ-ər/ *n* a long sharp thin sword

rap·ist /ˈreʸpɪst/ *n* a man guilty of RAPE² (1)

rap·port /ræˈpɔr, ræˈpoʷr, rə-/ *n* [U *between, with*] close agreement and understanding: *to have/feel/develop rapport with someone*

rap·proche·ment /ˌræproʷˈmã/ *n fml* a coming together again in friendship of former enemies: *At last there are signs of a rapprochement between our two countries.*

rapt /ræpt/ *adj* giving one's whole mind (to): *We listened with rapt attention.* **–raptly** *adv* **–raptness** *n* [U]

rap·ture /ˈræptʃər/ *n* [P;U] *fml* great joy and delight: *She* **went into raptures** (= became full of joy) *at/about the news.* **–rapturous** /ˈræptʃərəs/ *adj: a rapturous welcome* **–rapturously** *adv*

rare¹ /rɛr/ *adj* **1** unusual; not common: *a rare event|It's very rare for him to be late.* **2** (esp. of air) thin; light: *the rare air of the mountains* **–rareness** [U]

USAGE Uncommon and perhaps valuable things are **rare**: *a* **rare** *bird/coin.* Common useful things that we do not have enough of are **scarce**: *Potatoes were* **scarce** *last winter.* We can use **rare**, but not **scarce**, about time: *one of my* **rare** (=not happening often) *visits to Paris.*

rare² *adj* (of meat, esp. STEAK) lightly cooked **–compare** WELL-DONE

rar·e·fied /ˈrɛrəˌfaɪd/ *adj* **1** (of air in high places) light; thin **2** *humor* very high and pure; grand: *He moves in very rarefied circles; his friends are all extremely wealthy.*

rare·ly /ˈrɛrliʸ/ *adv* not often: *I have rarely seen such a beautiful sunset.* **–compare** SCARCELY; see NEVER (USAGE)

rar·ing /ˈrɛrɪŋ/ *adj* [F +*to-v*] *infml* very eager: *The children were* **raring to go.** (=eager to start)

rar·i·ty /ˈrɛrətiʸ/ **-ties 1** [U] the quality of being RARE¹ (1) **2** [C] something uncommon: *This type of flower is becoming a rarity.*

ras·cal /ˈræskəl/ *n* **1** a dishonest person **2** *humor* a person, esp. a child, who misbehaves: *You little rascal! Where have you hidden my shoes?*

rash¹ /ræʃ/ *adj* foolishly bold; not thinking enough of the results: *a rash decision|a rash young soldier|I promised* **in a rash moment** *to take the children swimming.* **–rashly** *adv* **–rashness** *n* [U]

rash² *n* [S] a set of red spots on the face and/or body, caused by illness: *She* **broke out in** (=become covered with) **a rash** *today.*|(fig.) *a rash of complaints* (=large number)

rash·er /ˈræʃər/ *n* a thin piece of BACON: *a few rashers (of BACON) for breakfast*

rasp /ræsp/ *v* [T] **1** to rub, producing a sensation of roughness: *The cat's tongue rasped my hand.*|(fig.) *His loud voice rasped (on)* (=had an annoying effect on) *my nerves.* **2** to say in a rough voice

rasp·ber·ry /ˈræzˌbɛriˠ, -bəriˠ/ *n* **-ries 1** a soft sweet red berry (or its bush): *raspberries and cream* **2** *infml* a rude sound made by putting one's tongue out and blowing

rat¹ /ræt/ *n* **1** a long-tailed animal (RODENT) related to but larger than the mouse **2** *infml* a low worthless disloyal person: *But you promised to help us, you rat!* **3 smell a rat** *infml* to guess that something wrong is happening

rat² *v* **-tt-** [I *on*] *infml* to act in a disloyal way by breaking a promise, informing the police, etc.: *They said they'd help, but they've ratted (on us).*

ratch·et /ˈrætʃɪt/ *n* a toothed wheel or bar provided with a piece of metal that fits between its teeth so as to allow movement in one direction but not the other

rate¹ /reɪt/ *n* **1** [C *of*] a value, cost, speed, etc. measured by its relation to some other amount: *to travel at the rate of 100 miles an hour*|*The* **birth rate** *is the number of births compared to the number of the people.*|*to drive at a steady rate* **2** [C] a charge or payment fixed according to a standard scale: *They're demanding higher rates of pay.* **3** [A] of the (numbered) quality: *a* **first-rate** (=very good) *performer* **4 at any rate** in any case; whatever happens **5 at this/that rate** if events continue in the same way as now/ then: *At this rate we won't be able to afford a vacation.* **6 rate of exchange** the relationship between the money of two countries: *What's the rate of exchange today between the Yen and the dollar?*

rate² *v* **rated, rating** [T] to consider; set a value on: *I rate her highly as a poet.*

rath·er¹ /ˈræðər/ *predeterminer,adv* **1** to some degree; QUITE (2): *a rather cold day*|*rather a cold day*|*rather cold weather*|*driving rather fast*|*These shoes are rather big.*|*It rather surprised me.* –see Study Notes on page 363 **2** more willingly: *I'd rather play tennis than swim.*|*"Have a drink?" "No thanks, I would rather/sooner not."* **3** more truly: *He ran rather than walked.*|*She came home very late last night, or rather very early this morning.*

USAGE **Fairly** *cold weather* or *driving* **fairly** *fast* mean "cold enough," "fast enough," but **rather** *cold*, **rather** *fast* may mean "too cold," "too fast."

rath·er² /ræˈðɜr/ *interj esp. BrE infml* (used as an answer) Yes, certainly!: *"Would you like a swim?" "Rather!"*

rat·i·fy /ˈrætəˌfaɪ/ *v* **-fied, -fying** [T] *fml* to make official by signing (a written agreement): *The heads of the two governments met to ratify the* TREATY. –**ratification** /ˌrætəfəˈkeɪʃən/ *n* [U]

rat·ing /ˈreɪtɪŋ/ *n* the place given to a person or thing in respect to rank, position, quality, popularity, etc.: *This television* PROGRAM *has been getting high ratings.*|*She has a good* CREDIT¹ (2) *rating so she can borrow a lot of money.*

ra·ti·o /ˈreɪʃiˠˌoʷ, ˈreɪʃoʷ/ *n* **-os** a figure showing the number of times one quantity contains another: *The ratio of 10 to 5 is 2 to 1.*|*We divided it in the ratio 2:1.* –compare PROPORTION

ra·tion¹ /ˈræʃən, ˈreɪˠ-/ *n* a share (of food, gasoline, etc.) allowed to one person for a period, esp. during a war, a time of short supply, etc.

ration² *v* [T] **1** [*to*] to limit (someone) to a fixed RATION¹: *She rationed them to two eggs a week.* **2** to limit and control (supplies): *They had to ration gasoline during the war.*

ration sth.↔**out** *v adv* [T] to give out (supplies) in RATIONS¹: *He rationed out the water to the sailors.*

ra·tion·al /ˈræʃənəl/ *adj* **1** (of people) able to reason **2** (of ideas and behavior) sensible; according to reason: *a rational suggestion/explanation* –opposite **irrational** –**rationally** *adv* –**rationality** /ˌræʃəˈnæləti/ *n* [U]

ra·tion·ale /ˌræʃəˈnæl/ *n* [C;U] *fml* the reason(s) on which a system or practice is based

ra·tion·al·ize *also* **-ise** *BrE* /ˈræʃənəlˌaɪz/ *v* **-ized, -izing** [I;T] to find reasons for (one's own unreasonable behavior or opinions): *She tried to rationalize getting into the argument by saying that her husband started it.* **2** [T] to improve (a method or system) and make it less wasteful by reasonable thinking, using a set of principles: *to rationalize the spelling system of English* –**rationalization** /ˌræʃənələˈzeɪʃən/ *n* [C;U]

rat race /ˈ· ·/ *n* [*the* S] *infml* the endless competition for success in business or life: *Susan got so tired of the rat race that she went to work on a farm.*

rat·tle¹ /ˈrætl/ *v* **-tled, -tling 1** [I;T] to (cause to) make a lot of quick little noises: *The beggar rattled the coins in his cup.*|*The cart rattled along the stony road.* **2** [T] *infml* to make nervous or anxious: *Keep calm; don't get rattled.*

rattle/reel sth.↔**off** *v adv* [T] to repeat quickly and easily from memory: *She rattled off the poem.*

rattle on/away *v adv* [I] to talk quickly and continuously: *He kept rattling on about his problems.*

rattle through sth. *v prep* [T] to perform quickly: *to rattle through his speech/her work*

rattle² *n* [C;S] (a toy or instrument that makes) a rattling noise (RATTLE¹ (1)): *The baby was playing with the rattle.*|*the rattle of milk bottles*

rat·tle·snake /ˈrætlˌsneɪk/ ‖*also* **rattler** /ˈrætlər/ *AmE infml* – *n* a poisonous American snake that makes a rattling noise (RATTLE¹ (1)) with its tail

rat·ty /ˈrætiˠ/ *adj* **-tier, -tiest 1** →SHABBY **2** of or like a rat

rau·cous /ˈrɔkəs/ *adj* (of voices) rough and unpleasant: *raucous shouts* –**raucously** *adv* –**raucousness** *n* [U]

raun·chy /ˈrɔntʃiˠ, ˈrɑn-/ *adj* **-chier, -chiest** *AmE infml* dirty; nasty: *a raunchy movie* –**raunchiness** *n* [U]

rav·age /'rævɪdʒ/ v **-aged, -aging** [T] **1** to ruin: *crops ravaged by storms* **2** to rob (an area) with violence: *The conquering army ravaged the country.*

rav·ag·es /'rævɪdʒɪz/ n [P *of*] the destroying effects: *the ravages of fire/war*

rave /reɪv/ v **raved, raving** [I *about, against, at*] to talk wildly as if mad: *He raved all night about his boss.*

  rave about sbdy./sthg. v prep [T] *infml* to speak about with (too) great admiration: *Everybody raved about the new singer.*

rav·el /'rævəl/ v **-l-** *AmE*‖**-ll-** *BrE* [I;T] to UNRAVEL

ra·ven /'reɪvən/ n [A;C] (the color of) a large shiny black bird with a deep unmusical voice (CROAK)

rav·en·ous /'rævənəs/ adj very hungry **–ravenously** adv

ra·vine /rə'viːn/ n a deep narrow valley with steep sides –see VALLEY(USAGE)

rav·ing /'reɪvɪŋ/ adj,adv *infml* talking wildly: *a raving madman*‖*He's raving (mad).* **–ravings** n [P]: *the ravings of a madman/of the sick woman*

rav·i·o·li /ˌrævi'oʊliʲ/ n [U] small cases of flour paste (PASTA) filled with meat, cheese, etc. and boiled –compare SPAGHETTI, MACARONI

rav·ish /'rævɪʃ/ v [T] *lit* **1** to RAPE **2** [*by, with; usu. pass.*] to fill with delight: *ravished by her personality*

rav·ish·ing /'rævɪʃɪŋ/ adj very beautiful; causing great delight: *a ravishing sight* **–ravishingly** adv

raw /rɔː/ adj **1** (of food) not cooked: *raw vegetables* **2** in the natural state: *raw silk/cotton*‖**Raw materials** are the natural substances from which industrial products are made. **3** (of a person) not yet trained; not experienced: *a raw RECRUIT who has just joined the army* **4** (of a part of the body) painful; sore: *a raw wound/hands raw with cold* **5** (of weather) cold and wet: *a raw winter day* **6 raw deal** *infml* unfair or cruel treatment: *to have/get (rather) a raw deal* **–rawly** adv **–rawness** n [U]

ray /reɪ/ n [*of*] a narrow beam (of heat, light, etc.): *the sun's rays*‖an X-RAY *photograph*‖(fig.) *a ray* (=a small bit) *of hope*

ray·on /'reɪɑn/ n [U] a smooth silk-like material made from wool or cotton (CELLULOSE)

raze /reɪz/ v **razed, razing** [T] *fml* to flatten (buildings, towns, etc.): *a bomb attack that razed the city* **to the ground**

ra·zor /'reɪzər/ n a sharp sometimes electric instrument for removing hair from the skin –see SAFETY RAZOR –see illustration on page 51

R.C. n abbrev. for: ROMAN CATHOLIC

Rd written abbrev. said as: road

re /riʲ, reɪ/ prep [U] (esp. in business letters) on the subject of; with regard to: *re your*

letter of October 19th

're /ər/ short for: are: *We're ready, but they're not.*

reach¹ /riʲtʃ/ v **1** [T] to arrive at; get to: *They reached New Orleans on Thursday.*‖*to reach the end of the book*‖*The news only reached me yesterday.*‖*to reach the age of 50*‖*My income reached five figures* (= at least $10,000) *last year.*‖(fig.) *He doesn't allow the problems of other people to reach* (=affect) *him.* **2** [I] to stretch out a hand or arm for some purpose: *I reached up and put the package on the top shelf.* **3** [I;T] to be able to touch (something) by stretching out a hand or arm: *"Can you reach that apple on the tree?" "I'm not tall enough to reach (it)."* **4** [I;T] (of things or places) to be big enough to touch; stretch out as far as: *The ladder won't quite reach (as far as) the window.*‖(fig.) *His influence hasn't reached the capital yet.* **5** [T] to get or give by stretching out a hand or arm: *Reach (me) down the box from the shelf.* **6** [T] to get a message to; CONTACT²: *She can always be reached at her office during the day.*

  reach out v adv [I;T(=**reach out** sthg.)(*no pass.*)] to stretch out a hand or arm: *She reached out (a hand) and took the book.*

reach² n **1** [U *of*] the distance that one can touch or travel: *The bottle was within (his) reach.* (=he could touch it)‖*The medicine was beyond/out of (her) reach.* (=she couldn't touch it)‖*to live within easy reach of the stores* **2** [S] the length of one's arm: *He has a longer reach than I have, so he can climb better.* **3** [C] a straight stretch of water between two bends in a river: *the upper reaches of the river*

re·act /riʲ'ækt/ v [I] **1** [*to, against*] to act in reply; to behave differently as a result: *The company reacted to the workers' complaints by dismissing the director.*‖*How did she react to your suggestion?*‖*He reacted against his father's influence by running away.* **2** [*with, on*] *tech* (of a substance) to change when mixed with or brought into contact with another: *An acid can react with a BASE to form a salt.*

re·ac·tion /riʲ'ækʃən/ n **1** [C *to*] a case of REACTING (1): *What was your reaction to the news?* **2** [U] *fml derog* the quality of being REACTIONARY: *The REVOLUTION was defeated by the forces of reaction.* **3** [C;U] *tech* (a) change caused in a chemical substance by the action of another

re·ac·tion·ar·y /riʲ'ækʃəˌnɛriʲ/ adj,n **-ies** *derog* (a person) strongly opposed to social or political change –compare RADICAL¹

re·ac·ti·vate /riʲ'æktəˌveɪt/ v **-ated, -ating** [T] to cause (esp. machinery) to become active again

re·ac·tor /riʲ'æktər/ n → NUCLEAR REACTOR

read /riʲd/ v **read** /rɛd/, **reading** /'riʲdɪŋ/ **1** [I;T] to understand (something printed or written): *The child is learning to read.*‖*She reads well for a six-year-old.*‖*I often read a book at night.*‖*to read music*‖*to read a map*‖*I can read French, but I can't speak it.*‖(fig.) *I can read your thoughts (from your face).* **2**

[I;T +*that*] to get (the stated information) from print or writing: *I read about the murder/read the account of the murder in the paper.*|*I read that the new director was a woman.* **3** [I not *be*+*v-ing*] (of something written) to be or mean (in the stated way): *Her letters always read well/always read as if she copied them from books.*|*The name reads "Benson" not "Fenton".*|*His letter reads as follows . . .* **4** [I;T] to say (printed or written words) to others: *He read the children a story.*|*The teacher read (the poem) aloud to the class.*|*She read out the football results.* **5** [T] (of measuring instruments) to show: *The* THERMOMETER *reads 33 degrees.* **6** [T] *esp. BrE* to study (a subject) at a university: *Helen's reading history/law at Harvard.* **7** **read between the lines** to find a meaning that is not expressed: *If you read between the lines, this letter is really a request for money.* **8** **take something as read** to accept something to be true or satisfactory, without any need to consider it further: *We can take his ability as read, but will he be interested in doing the job?* **9** -**read: a** (of a person) having a certain amount of knowledge gained from books: *a well-read woman* **b** (of a book, newspaper, etc.) read by a certain number of people: *a little-read* NOVEL

read sthg. **into** sthg. *v prep* [T] to believe (something) to be meant though not expressed by (something else): *Don't read more into her letter than she intended.*

read up on sthg. *v adv* [T] *infml* to study a subject thoroughly: *to read up on the tax laws*

read·a·ble /'riˢdəbəl/ *adj* **1** interesting or easy to read **2** → LEGIBLE –**readability** /ˌriˢdə'bɪlətiˢ/ *n* [U]

re·ad·dress /ˌriˢə'drɛs/ *also* **redirect**– *v* [T *to*] to write a different address on (a letter): *Readdress my letters (to the new house).*

read·er /'riˢdər/ *n* a person who reads (a stated thing or in a stated way): *Are you a fast reader?*|*We have received many letters on this subject from our readers.* (in a newspaper)

read·er·ship /'riˢdərˌʃɪp/ *n* [S] the number or type of READERs (1) of a newspaper: *The paper has a readership of 500,000/a very well-educated readership.*

read·i·ly /'rɛdl-iˢ/ *adv* **1** willingly: *He readily promised to help.* **2** with no difficulty: *Vegetables can readily be bought anywhere in the city.*

read·i·ness /'rɛdiˢnɪs/ *n* **1** [S;U +*to-v*] (a) willingness: *to show (a) great readiness to learn* **2** [*in* U] the state of being ready: *to have everything* **in readiness for** *the party*

read·ing /'riˢdɪŋ/ *n* **1** [U] the act or practice of reading: *Children learn reading and writing at school.* **2** [C *of*] an opinion about the meaning of something: *My reading of the law is that we don't have to pay.* **3** [C] a figure shown by a measuring instrument: *What are the temperature readings for this machine?* **4** [U] something to be read: *suitable reading for children* **5** [A] for reading: *the reading room at the library*|*a reading lamp*

re·ad·just /ˌriˢə'dʒʌst/ *v* [I;T *to*] to get or put

back into the proper position: *to readjust (oneself) to school life after summer vacation* –**readjustment** *n* [C;U]: *a period of readjustment*

read·out /'riˢd-aʊt/ *n* [U] the (work of removing) information from a computer and of showing it in an understandable form

read·y¹ /'rɛdiˢ/ *adj* -**ier**, -**iest 1** [F +*to-v/for*] prepared and fit (for use): *Is breakfast ready?*|*The letters are ready to be mailed/ready to be signed.*|*They* **made ready** (=prepared) *for the attack.* **2** [F +*to-v*] willing: *She's always ready to help.* **3** [A] (of mental abilities) quick: *a ready understanding of difficult problems*

ready² *interj* **Ready, set, go!** *also* **on your mark(s), get set, go!**– (used when telling people to begin a race)

ready³ *adv* (used before a past participle) in advance: *a ready-cooked dinner*

ready⁴ *v* -**ied**, -**ying** [T] *esp. AmE* to prepare (oneself or something): *They readied themselves for the race by training every day for a month.*

ready-made /ˌ·· '·◄/ *adj* (esp. of clothes) not made specially for the buyer; able to be used at once: *a ready-made suit* |(fig.) *He doesn't think about politics; he just gets ready-made ideas from the newspapers.* –see also TAILOR-MADE –compare **made to** ORDER¹ (14)

re·al¹ /riˢəl/ *adj* actually existing; true not false: *Is your ring real gold?*|*a story of real life* –**realness** *n* [U]

real² *n infml esp. AmE* **for real: a** seriously: *They were fighting for real.* **b** serious: *He couldn't believe their threats were for real.*

real³ *adv infml esp. AmE* very: *I'm real sorry.*

real es·tate /'· ·ˌ·/ *n* [U] **1** *fml and law* property in land and houses **2** *esp. AmE* houses and land to be bought: *sell real estate*

real estate a·gent /'· ·· ˌ··/ *also* **realtor** *tdmk*, **real estate broker** *AmE*‖**estate agent** *BrE* – *n* a person whose business is to buy and sell houses, property, land, etc. for people

re·al·ism /'riˢəˌlɪzəm/ *n* [U] **1** determination to face facts and deal with them practically, without being influenced by feelings **2** (in art and literature) the showing of things as they really are –**realist** *n*

re·al·is·tic /ˌriˢə'lɪstɪk/ *adj* **1** showing REALISM (1): *Our income has gotten smaller, so we must be realistic and give up our car.* –opposite **unrealistic 2** (of art or literature) life-like: *a realistic drawing of a horse* –**realistically** *adv*

re·al·i·ty /riˢ'ælətiˢ/ *n* -**ties 1** [U] the quality or state of being real; real existence: *She believes in the reality of God.*|*Everyone trusted the stranger, but* **in reality** (=in actual fact) *he was a criminal.* **2** [C;U] something or everything that is real: *His dream of marrying Annie became a reality.*|*to escape from reality by going to the movies*

re·al·i·za·tion, -sation /ˌriˢələ'zeˢʃən/ *n* **1** [S; the U +*that/of*] (an experience of) understanding and believing: *the full realization that she was guilty* **2** [*the* U *of*] the becoming real (of a hope or plan): *the realization of my hopes*

re·al·ize||also **-ise** *BrE* /'riʸə‚laɪz/ *v* **-lized, -liz-ing** [T] **1** [+*(that)*] to understand and believe (a fact): *He didn't realize he was wrong.*|*I didn't realize how late it was.* **2** to make real (a hope or purpose); CARRY out: *She realized her intention of becoming an actress.* **3** *fml* to get (money) by selling property: *The house* (=the selling of it) *realized a profit.*

real·ly /'riʸəliʸ/ *adv* **1** in fact; truly: *Did she really say that?*|*I really don't*/ *I don't really want any more.*|*It's really a nice picture.*|*You really should have asked me first.* **2** thoroughly: *It's really cold today.*|*a really cold day*|*I really hate him.* **3** (shows interest or slight displeasure): *"I collect rare coins." "Really?"*|*Well, really! What a terrible thing to do!*

re·al·tor /'riʸəltər/ *n AmE tdmk* for REAL ESTATE AGENT

realm /rɛlm/ *n* **1** (*often cap.*) *lit & law* a kingdom: *the defense of the Realm* **2** a world; area of activity: *the realm of science*|*within the realms of possibility*

ream /riʸm/ *n* **1** a measure for sheets of paper **a** (in the US) 500 sheets **b** (in Britain) 480 sheets **2** *infml* a lot (of writing): *She wrote reams of notes.*

reap /riʸp/ *v* [I;T] to cut and gather (a crop of grain): (fig.) *to reap a reward*/*a profit* –compare SOW, HARVEST

reap·er /'riʸpər/ *n* a person or machine that REAPS

re·ap·pear /‚riʸə'pɪər/ *v* [I] to appear again after an absence –**reappearance** /‚riʸə'pɪərəns/ *n* [U]

re·ap·prais·al /‚riʸə'preʸzəl/ *n fml* [C;U] (a new judgment formed by) examining something again to see whether one should change one's opinion of it: *Our relations with the other government needed (a) reappraisal.*

rear¹ /rɪər/ *v* **1** [T] to care for until fully grown: *to rear a large family* –compare RAISE¹ (esp. 4) **2** [I] (of a four-legged animal) to rise upright on the back legs: *The horse reared and threw me off.* **3** [T] to lift up (one's head, etc.): *The lion suddenly reared its head.*|(fig.) *A problem has just* **reared its ugly head.** (=just appeared)

rear² *n* **1** [U] the back: *a garage at the rear of the house*|*a rear window* –compare FRONT **2** [C] *euph* the part of the body on which one sits; BUTTOCKS **3** **bring up the rear** to come last (as in a procession)

re·arm /riʸ'ɑrm/ *v* [I;T *with*] to provide (oneself or others) with weapons again, or with new weapons: *to rearm the country with modern MISSILES* –compare DISARM (1) –**rearmament** /riʸ'ɑrməmənt/ *n* [U]

re·ar·range /‚riʸə'reʸndʒ/ *v* **-ranged, -ranging** [T] to put into a different order: *Let's rearrange (the furniture in) the room.* –**rearrangement** *n* [C;U]

rear·ward /'rɪərwərd/ *adj* [A] *fml* at or towards the back: *in a rearward direction*

–**rearward** *AmE*|| also **rearwards**– *adv* : to look rearwards

rea·son¹ /'riʸzən/ *n* **1** [C;U +*to-v*/*that*] the cause of an event; the explanation or excuse for an action: *The reason for the flood was all that heavy rain.*|*The reason that*/*why he died was lack of medical care.*|*There is*/*We have reason to believe that she was murdered.*|*What is your reason for wanting to enter the country?*|*She thinks,* **with reason** (=rightly) *that I don't like her.* **2** [U] the power to think, understand, and form opinions: *People are different from animals because they possess the power of reason.* **3** [U] good sense: *Why won't you* **listen to reason?** (=be persuaded by advice) **4** **anything within reason** anything that is not too much to expect: *He'll do anything within reason for me, but he won't break the law.* **5** **it stands to reason** it is clear to all sensible people: *It stands to reason that he won't go if we don't pay him.*

USAGE **1** Some people think a sentence such as *The reason for my absence was* **because** *I was ill* is bad English. It may be better to say: *The reason for my absence was* **that** *I was ill.* **2** Compare **cause** and **reason**. A **cause** is something that produces a result; a **reason** is something that explains or excuses an action: *The* **cause** *of the accident was the fact that he was driving too fast.*|*The* **reason** *why he was driving so fast was that he was late for an important meeting* –see EXCUSE (USAGE)

reason² *v* **1** [I] to use one's REASON¹ (2): *She can reason very clearly.* **2** [T +*that*] to have or give an opinion based on REASON¹(2) (that): *I reasoned that since she had not answered my letter she must be angry with me.*

reason with sbdy. *v prep* [T] to try to persuade by fair argument: *You should reason with the child instead of just telling him to obey.*

rea·son·a·ble /'riʸzənəbəl/ *adj* **1** sensible: *a perfectly reasonable thing to do* –opposite **unreasonable**; compare LOGICAL **2** (esp. of prices) fair; not too much: *to charge a very reasonable price* –**reasonableness** *n* [U]

rea·son·a·bly /'riʸzənəbliʸ/ *adv* **1** sensibly; fairly; rather: *The car is in reasonably good condition.*

rea·soned /'riʸzənd/ *adj* [A] (of a statement, argument, etc.,) clearly thought out: *a (well-)reasoned statement*

rea·son·ing /'riʸzənɪŋ/ *n* [U] the use of one's ●REASON¹ (2): *Your reasoning ●was quite correct.*

re·as·sure /‚riʸə'ʃʊər/ *v* **-sured, -suring** [T *about*] to make free from fear: *The doctor reassured the sick man (about his health).* –**reassurance** /‚riʸə'ʃʊərəns/ *n* [C;U]: *She won't believe it in spite of all our reassurances.* –**reassuringly** *adv*

re·bate /'riʸbeʸt/ *n* a return of part of a payment: *The company is offering a $500 rebate if you buy a new car.* –compare DISCOUNT

reb·el¹ /'rɛbəl/ *n* a person who REBELS: *She became a rebel when her father was put in prison.*

SPELLING NOTE

Words with the sound /r/ may be spelled **wr-**, like **wrong**.

re·bel[2] /rɪ'bɛl/ v -ll- [I *against*] to fight with violence (against anyone in power, esp. the government): *The slaves rebelled against their masters.*

re·bel·lion /rɪ'bɛlyən/ n [C;U] an act or the state of REBELling –compare REVOLUTION (1)

re·bel·lious /rɪ'bɛlyəs/ adj (seeming) disobedient and hard to control: *rebellious behavior* –**rebelliously** adv –**rebelliousness** n [U]

re·birth /riᵞ'bɜrθ, 'riᵞbɜrθ/ n [S] *fml* a renewal of life; change of spirit: *the rebirth of learning in the Western world*

re·born /riᵞ'bɔrn/ adj [F] *fml or lit* as if born again: *Our hopes of success were reborn.*

re·bound[1] /'rɪ'baʊnd,'riᵞbaʊnd/ v [I] to fly back after hitting something: *The ball rebounded from the wall and I caught it.*|(fig.) *His lies rebounded on* (= had an unexpected effect on) *himself because nobody trusted him any more.*

re·bound[2] /'riᵞbaʊnd/ n **on the rebound: a** while REBOUNDing[1]: *to catch the ball on the rebound* **b** as a quick action in reply to failure in a relationship: *to marry a different person on the rebound*

re·buff /rɪ'bʌf/ n *fml* a rough or cruel answer given to someone who is trying to be friendly or is asking for help: *She met with/suffered a rebuff.* –**rebuff** v [T]: *She rebuffed all my offers of friendship.*

re·build /riᵞ'bɪld/ v -**built** /'bɪlt/, -**building** [T] to build again or build new parts to: *to rebuild a house after a fire*

re·buke /rɪ'byuʷk/ v -**buked**, -**buking** [T] *fml* to give a short (esp. official) scolding to: *to rebuke the child for his disobedience* –**rebuke** n

re·but /rɪ'bʌt/ v -tt- [T] *fml* to prove the falsity of (a statement or charge); REFUTE –**rebuttal** /rɪ'bʌtl/ n

re·cal·ci·trant /rɪ'kælsətrənt/ adj *fml* that refuses to obey or be controlled: *recalcitrant behavior* –**recalcitrance** n [U]: *The teacher was surprised by the recalcitrance of the children.*

re·call[1] /rɪ'kɔl/ v **1** [T +v-ing/that; not be +v-ing] to remember: *I can't recall seeing him/where he lives/how to do it.* **2** [T from, to] to call or take back: *The government recalled the general after he lost the battle.|The makers have recalled a lot of cars that were unsafe.*

re·call[2] /rɪ'kɔl, 'riᵞkɔl/ n **1** [S;U] (a) call to return: *the recall of the general from abroad* **2** [U] the power to remember something learned or experienced: *Mary has total recall and never forgets anything.*

re·cant /rɪ'kænt/ v [I;T] *fml* to say publicly that one no longer holds (a former political or religious belief): *She recanted (her faith) and became a Muslim/Christian.* –**recantation** /,riᵞkæn'teᵞʃən/ n [C;U]

re·ca·pit·u·late /,riᵞkə'pɪtʃə,leᵞt/ also **recap** /'riᵞkæp/ *infml*– v -**lated**, -**lating** [I;T] to repeat (the chief points of something that has been said): *He recapitulated the main arguments for accepting the employers' offer.* –**recapitulation** /,riᵞkə,pɪtʃə'leᵞʃən/ n [C;U]

re·cap·ture /riᵞ'kæptʃər/ v -**tured**, -**turing** [T] **1** to CAPTURE again: *The police recaptured the escaped criminal.* **2** *lit* to bring back into the mind: *a book that recaptures the happiness of youth*

re·cede /rɪ'siᵞd/ v -**ceded**, -**ceding** [I *from*] **1** (of things) to move back or away: *His hair is beginning to recede (from his forehead).* **2** to slope backwards: *a receding chin*

re·ceipt /rɪ'siᵞt/ n **1** [C] a written statement that one has received money: *Ask her to give you a receipt when you pay the bill.* **2** [U *of*] the event of receiving: **On receipt of** (=when he receives) *your payment, he will send the package.*

re·ceipts /rɪ'siᵞts/ n [P] the money received from a business: *The receipts have increased since last year.*

re·ceive /rɪ'siᵞv/ v -**ceived**, -**ceiving 1** more *fml than* get– [T] to get: *to receive a letter/a lot of attention/a blow on the head* **2** [I;T] *fml* to accept as a visitor or member; welcome: *She was received into the club.* **3 on the receiving end (of)** *infml* suffering (unpleasant actions done to one): *We were on the receiving end of several complaints.*

re·ceiv·er /rɪ'siᵞvər/ n **1** [C] the part of a telephone that is held to one's ear –see TELEPHONE (USAGE) **2** [C] a radio or television set **3** [*the* S] the person officially appointed to take charge of the affairs of a company or person that a LAWSUIT has been brought against or that has become BANKRUPT: *His business has failed and is in the hands of the receiver.*

re·cent /'riᵞsənt/ adj having happened or come into existence only a short time ago: *recent history/a recent copy of the newspaper* –see NEW (USAGE) –**recentness** n [U]

re·cent·ly /'riᵞsəntliᵞ/ adv not long ago; lately: *I've only recently begun to learn French.*

re·cep·ta·cle /rɪ'sɛptəkəl/ n *tech or fml* a container

re·cep·tion /rɪ'sɛpʃən/ n **1** [C] an act of receiving; welcome: *to get a very friendly reception* **2** [C] a large formal party: *give/hold a reception|a wedding reception* **3** [U] *BrE* for RECEPTION DESK **4** [U] the receiving of radio or television signals: *Radio reception isn't very good here.*

reception desk /·'·· ,·/ n the desk just inside a hotel where guests are received: *Leave the keys for me at the reception desk.* –see illustration on page 200

re·cep·tion·ist /rɪ'sɛpʃənɪst/ n a person who receives people arriving in a large office, visiting a doctor, etc. –see illustration on page 200

re·cep·tive /rɪ'sɛptɪv/ adj [*of,to*] (of a person or his/her mind) willing to consider new ideas: *He's not very receptive to my suggestions.* –**receptively** adv –**receptiveness** n [U]

re·cess /'riᵞsɛs, rɪ'sɛs/ n **1** [C;U] a pause for rest during the working day or year: *Congress is in recess now.|The children in this school have recess at 10:15 every morning.* **2** [C] a space in the wall of a room for shelves, cupboards, etc. –compare ALCOVE **3** [C often *pl.*] *lit* a secret inner part of a place

re·ces·sion /rɪ'sɛʃən/ *n* a period of reduced business activity; SLUMP² (1)

rec·i·pe /'rɛsəpiy/ *n* [*for*] a set of instructions for cooking a dish: *a recipe for making bread|to follow a recipe|a recipe book|*(fig.) *a recipe for a happy marriage*

re·cip·i·ent /rɪ'sɪpiyənt/ *n* [*of*] *fml* a person who receives something

re·cip·ro·cal /rɪ'sɪprəkəl/ *adj fml* given and received in return; MUTUAL: *a reciprocal trade agreement between two nations* –**reciprocally** *adv*

re·cip·ro·cate /rɪ'sɪprə,keyt/ *v* **-cated, -cating** *fml* [I;T] to give or do (something) in return: *They invited us to their party, and we reciprocated (their invitation).* –**reciprocation** /rɪ,sɪprə'keyʃən/ *n* [U]

re·cit·al /rɪ'saɪtl/ *n* **1** a performance of poetry or esp. music, given by one performer or written by one writer: *to give a piano recital* **2** *fml* an account; report: *She gave us a long recital of his experiences.*

re·cite /rɪ'saɪt/ *v* **-cited, -citing 1** [I;T] to say (something learned) aloud from memory: *I don't like reciting poetry in public.* **2** [T] to give a list of: *He recited a list of his complaints.* –**recitation** /,rɛsə'teyʃən/ *n* [C;U]

reck·less /'rɛklɪs/ *adj* [*of*] (of a person or behavior) too hasty; not caring about danger: *reckless of danger|reckless driving* –**recklessly** *adv* –**recklessness** *n* [U]

reck·on /'rɛkən/ *v* [T] **1** [+ *to-v*/ among, as] to consider; regard: *She is reckoned (to be) a very good politician.|I reckon him as a friend|among my friends.* **2** [+(*that*)] *infml* to guess; suppose: *I reckon (that) he'll come soon.|How much do you reckon (that) she earns?* **3** to calculate; add up (an amount, cost, etc.): *My pay is reckoned from the 1st of the month.|She reckoned up the cost.*

  reckon on sthg. *v prep* [T +*v-ing*] to expect; depend on; BANK **on**: *We're reckoning on a large profit.|You can't always reckon on seeing him.*

  reckon with sbdy./sthg. *v prep* [T] **1** to have to deal with: *If they try to dismiss you, they'll have the union to reckon with.* **2 to be reckoned with** to be taken into account seriously as a possible opponent, competitor, danger, etc.: *She's a woman to be reckoned with.*

  reckon without sbdy./sthg. *v prep* [T] to fail to consider: *When he decided to change his job, he reckoned without the difficulty of selling his house.*

reck·on·ing /'rɛkənɪŋ/ *n* [U] **1** the act of calculating: *By my reckoning, it must be 60 miles from here to the coast.* **2 day of reckoning** the time when one must suffer for a mistake

re·claim /rɪ'kleym/ *v* [T *from*] **1** to claim the return of: *I want to reclaim some of the tax I paid last year.* **2** to make (land) fit for use: *to*

SPELLING NOTE

Words with the sound /r/ may be spelled **wr-**, like **wrong**.

---

reclaim land from the sea **3** to obtain (useful materials) from a waste product: *to reclaim valuable metal from scrap cars* –**reclamation** /,rɛklə'meyʃən/ *n* [U]

re·cline /rɪ'klaɪn/ *v* **-clined, -clining** [I;T *against,on*] to lie back or down; be or put oneself in a position of rest: *recline on the bed|in a reclining position*

re·cluse /'rɛkluws, rɪ'kluws/ *n* a person who purposely lives alone away from the world –compare HERMIT

rec·og·ni·tion /,rɛkəg'nɪʃən/ *n* [S;U] **1** the act of recognizing: *Please accept this gift **in recognition of|as a recognition of** all your help.* **2** change beyond/out of all recognition to change so as to be impossible to recognize: *Illness and age had changed her out of all recognition.*

rec·og·nize *AmE*‖also **-nise** *BrE* /'rɛkəg,naɪz/ *v* **-nized, -nizing** [T] **1** to know and remember (someone or something one has seen before): *I recognized Mary in the photograph.* **2** [*as*] to accept as being lawful or real, or as having value: *They refused to recognize our new government.|a recognized method of teaching English* **3** [+*that*] to see clearly; be prepared to agree: *I recognize that she is the best worker we have.* **4** to show official gratefulness for: *The government recognized his services by making him a citizen.* –**recognizable** /'rɛkəg,naɪzəbəl, ,rɛkəg'naɪ-/ *adj* –**recognizably** *adv*

re·coil /rɪ'kɔɪl/ *v* [I] **1** [*from*] to draw back suddenly in fear or dislike: *She recoiled from her attacker.* **2** (of a gun) to spring back when fired –**recoil** /'riykɔɪl, rɪ'kɔɪl/ *n* [S;U]

rec·ol·lect /,rɛkə'lɛkt/ *v* [T+*v-ing/that;* not *be* + *v-ing*] *v* to remember (something formerly known): *Do you recollect her name?*

rec·ol·lec·tion /,rɛkə'lɛkʃən/ *n* **1** [U] the power or action of remembering the past **2** [C] something in one's memory of the past: *I have a vague recollection of living in the country when I was very young.*

rec·om·mend /,rɛkə'mɛnd/ *v* **1** [T *as, for*] to make a favorable judgment of; praise: *Can you recommend a good dictionary (to me)?|They recommended her for the job|as a good lawyer.* **2** [T +*v-ing/that*] to advise or suggest: *I recommend that you inquire about the job.* **3** [T *to*] (of a quality) to make (someone or something) attractive: *This hotel has nothing to recommend it (to travelers) except that it's cheap.*

rec·om·men·da·tion /,rɛkəmən'deyʃən, -mɛn-/ *n* **1** [U] advice; the act of RECOMMENDing (1,2): *They bought the car on Paul's recommendation.* **2** [C] a letter or statement that RECOMMENDs (1) (esp. someone for a job)

rec·om·pense¹ /'rɛkəm,pɛns/ *v* **-pensed, -pensing** [T *for*] *fml* to give a RECOMPENSE² to

recompense² *n* [S;U *for*] *fml* (a) reward or payment for trouble or suffering: *They received $5,000 in recompense|as a recompense for the damage to their house.* –compare COMPENSATION

rec·on·cile /'rɛkən,saɪl/ *v* **-ciled, -ciling** [T *with*] **1** to make peace between: *They used to*

quarrel in the past, but now they're completely reconciled. **2** to find agreement between (two seemingly opposing actions or ideas): *How do you reconcile your political principles with your religious beliefs?* –**reconcilable** /ˌrɛkənˈsaɪləbəl, ˈrɛkənˌsaɪ-/ *adj*
reconcile sbdy. **to** sthg. *v prep* [T] to cause to accept: *They never became reconciled to the loss of their children.*

rec·on·cil·i·a·tion /ˌrɛkənˌsɪliˈeʸʃən/ *n* [S;U] (a) peace-making: *There was no hope of a reconciliation between the two families.*

re·con·di·tion /ˌriʸkənˈdɪʃən/ *v* [T] to repair and bring back into working order: *a reconditioned engine*

re·con·nais·sance /rɪˈkɑnəsəns, -zəns/ *n* [C;U] (an) act of reconnoitering (RECONNOITER)

re·con·noi·ter *AmE*‖**-tre** *BrE* /ˌriʸkəˈnɔɪtər, ˌrɛ-/ *v* **-tered, tering** *AmE*‖**-tred, -tring** *BrE* [I;T] to go near (the place where an enemy is) in order to find out the enemy's numbers, position, etc.

re·con·sid·er /ˌriʸkənˈsɪdər/ *v* [I;T] to think again and change one's mind about (a subject): *Won't you reconsider your decision to leave the club?* –**reconsideration** /ˌriʸkənˌsɪdəˈreʸʃən/ *n* [U]

re·con·sti·tute /riʸˈkɑnstəˌtuʷt, -ˌtyuʷt/ *v* [T] **1** to bring back into existence: *We decided to reconstitute the committee under a new chairman.* **2** to bring back (dried food) into its former condition by adding water: *to reconstitute milk powder|reconstituted orange juice*

re·con·struct /ˌriʸkənˈstrʌkt/ *v* [T] **1** to rebuild after destruction or damage **2** to build up a complete description or picture of (something only partly known): *to reconstruct a crime from known facts* –**reconstruction** /ˌriʸkənˈstrʌkʃən/ *n* [C;U]: *a reconstruction of the events leading up to the accident*

re·cord¹ /rɪˈkɔrd/ *v* **1** [T] to write down so that it will be known: *to record the events of the past* **2** [I;T] to preserve (sound or a television broadcast) so that it can be heard and/or seen again: *The broadcast was recorded, not* LIVE² (4).|*She has recorded several songs.* **3** [T] (of an instrument) to show by measuring: *The* THERMOMETER *recorded a temperature of 28 degrees.*

rec·ord² /ˈrɛkərd/ *n* **1** a written statement of facts, amounts, events, etc.: *Keep a record of how much you spend.* **2** the known facts about someone's past behavior: *She has a long criminal record.* **3** the best yet done; the highest/lowest figure ever reached: *to break/make/establish a record for long distance swimming* **4** a circular piece of plastic on which sound is stored: *Have you heard my new record?|Put a record on (the record player); let's listen to some music.* –see illustration on page 399 **5 off the record** *infml* unofficial(ly): *He told us off the record that the company was doing badly this year.* **6 on record** (of facts or events) (ever) recorded: *the coldest winter on record|She is on record as having said that she opposed high taxation.*

rec·ord³ /ˈrɛkərd/ *adj* [A] more, faster, better, etc. than ever before: *a record crop of corn|finished in record time*

record-break·ing /ˈ·· ˌ··/ *adj* (usu. in sport) that goes beyond the former RECORD² (3): *a record-breaking speed*

re·cord·er /rɪˈkɔrdər/ *n* **1** a wooden musical instrument like a whistle **2** → TAPE RECORDER

re·cord·ing /rɪˈkɔrdɪŋ/ *n* (esp. in broadcasting) a performance, speech, etc., that has been RECORDed¹ (2)

record play·er /ˈ·· ˌ··/ ‖also **phonograph** *AmE*– *n* an instrument which can turn the information stored on a RECORD² (4) back into the original sounds, music, etc. –compare STEREO

re·count¹ /rɪˈkaʊnt/ *v* [T] *fml* to tell (a story): *She recounted the story of her travels across Asia.*

re·count² /riʸˈkaʊnt/ *v* [T] to count again: *They had to recount the votes.*

re·count³ /ˈriʸkaʊnt/ *n* a second or new count, esp. of votes

re·coup /rɪˈkuʷp/ *v* [T] to regain (esp. money): *I'll recoup my traveling* EXPENSES *from my employers.*

re·course /ˈriʸkɔrs, -koʷrs, rɪˈkɔrs, rɪˈkoʷrs/ *n* [U] a means of help: *The sick man had recourse to* (=made use of) *drugs to lessen his pain.* –compare RESORT (2)

re·cov·er /rɪˈkʌvər/ *v* **1** [T] to get back (something lost or taken away): *The police recovered the stolen jewelry.|She recovered consciousness soon after the accident.* **2** [I *from*] to return to the proper state of health, strength, ability, etc.: *Has the country recovered yet from the effects of the war?* –**recoverable** *adj*

re·cov·er /riʸˈkʌvər/ *v* [T] to put a new cover on: *These chairs need re-covering.*

re·cov·er·y /rɪˈkʌvəriʸ/ *n* **1** [U *of*] RECOVERing or being RECOVERed (1): *the recovery of the stolen jewels* **2** [S *from*] RECOVERing (2): *She made a quick recovery from her fever.*

re·cre·ate /ˌriʸkriʸˈeʸt/ *v* **-ated, -ating** [T] to make again: *to recreate the scenes of the past in one's imagination*

rec·re·a·tion /ˌrɛkriʸˈeʸʃən/ *n* [C;U] (a form of) amusement: *His only recreations are drinking beer and working in the garden.*

USAGE A **sport** is a form of **recreation** needing physical effort and usually played according to rules. A **game** may be either an example of this, or an activity in which people compete with each other using their brains: *I'm not really interested in* **sports**.|*My favorite* **sports** *are tennis and football.|Let's have a* **game** *of tennis/cards.|Do you have a ticket for the football* **game** *on Saturday?* A **hobby** is a form of **recreation** which people often do on their own, not in order to compete. *Her* **hobbies** *are reading, swimming, and playing the piano.* –**recreational** *adj*

re·crim·i·nate /rɪˈkrɪməˌneʸt/ *v* **-nated, -nating** [I *against*] to blame a person who has treated one badly –**recriminatory** /rɪˈkrɪmənəˌtɔriʸ -ˌtoʷriʸ/ *adj* –**recrimination** /rɪˌkrɪməˈneʸʃən/ *n* [C;U]: *Let's make friends, instead of wasting our time on recrimination(s)*

re·cruit¹ /rɪ'kruʷt/ n [to] a new member of an organization: *recruits to our music club are always welcome.*

recruit² v **1** [I] to find RECRUITS: *a recruiting drive* (=special effort to recruit) *for the army* **2** [T] to get (someone) as a RECRUIT: *to recruit some new members* **–recruitment** n [U]

rec·tan·gle /'rɛk,tæŋgəl/ n tech a shape with four straight sides forming four RIGHT ANGLES **–compare** SQUARE¹ (2), OBLONG

rec·tan·gu·lar /rɛk'tæŋgyələr/ adj tech in the shape of a RECTANGLE

rec·ti·fy /'rɛktə,faɪ/ v **-fied, -fying** [T] fml to put right: *Would you rectify the mistakes in my bill?* **–rectification** /,rɛktəfə'keʸʃən/ n [C;U]

rec·tor /'rɛktər/ n *(the title of)* **1** (in the CHURCH OF ENGLAND) the priest in charge of a PARISH **2** the head of certain schools

rec·to·ry /'rɛktəriʸ/ n **-ries** the house where a RECTOR (1) lives

rec·tum /'rɛktəm/ n **-tums,** or **-ta** /tə/ tech the lowest end of the large bowel, through which solid waste matter passes to the ANUS

re·cum·bent /rɪ'kʌmbənt/ adj fml lying down: *a recumbent figure on the bed*

re·cu·per·ate /rɪ'kuʷpə,reʸt, -'kyuʷ-/ v **-ated, -ating** [I] to get well again after illness: *You'll soon recuperate; all you need is a long vacation.* **–recuperation** /rɪ,kuʷpə'reʸʃən, -,kyuʷ-/ n [U]

re·cur /rɪ'kɜr/ v **-rr-** [I] to happen again, or more than once: *If the pain recurs, take this medicine.* **–recurrence** /rɪ'kɜrəns, -'kʌr-/ n [U]: *the frequent recurrence of the pain* **–recurrent** adj **–recurrently** adv

re·cy·cle /,riʸ'saɪkəl/ v **-cled, -cling** [T] to treat (a used substance) so that it is fit to use again: *One can recycle bottles and use the glass again.|a bag made of recycled paper*

red¹ /rɛd/ adj **-dd- 1** of the color of blood: *Let's paint the door red.* **2** (of hair) of a bright brownish orange or copper color **3** (of the human skin or lips) pink: *to turn red with shame or anger* **–redness** n [U]

red² n **1** [C;U] (a) red color **2** [U] red clothes: *dressed in red* **3 in the red** in debt: *Your account is in the red.* **–opposite in the black 4 see red** to become angry suddenly and lose control of oneself

Red adj,n often derog for COMMUNIST

red-blood·ed /,· '··◄/ adj apprec (of a person, behavior, etc.) bold and strong: *a red-blooded young man*

red car·pet /,· '··/ n [A;S] a special ceremonial welcome to a guest: *They gave her the red-carpet treatment.*

Red Cross /,· '·/ n [the U] an international Christian organization that looks after sick and wounded people: *The Red Cross is active in a lot of different countries.*

red·den /'rɛdn/ v [I;T] to (cause to) turn red: *She reddened (with embarrassment) when they praised her so much.|The sunset red-

dened the clouds.

red·dish /'rɛdɪʃ/ adj slightly red

re·dec·o·rate /riʸ'dɛkə,reʸt/ ‖also **do** sthg.↔ **over** AmE– v **-rated, -rating** [I;T] to put new paint or paper on, buy new furniture for, etc. (a room or the inside of a building): *to redecorate the living room/house/office*

re·deem /rɪ'diʸm/ v [T] **1** fml to buy or gain the freedom of: *to redeem someone from sin* **2** [from] to regain with money (what was PAWNED or MORTGAGEd) **3** to carry out; fulfill: *to redeem one's promise* **4 redeeming feature** a single good point in a person or thing that is bad in all other ways: *His only redeeming feature is his honesty.* **–redeemable** adj

re·demp·tion /rɪ'dɛmpʃən/ n [U] **1** REDEEMing or being REDEEMed **2 beyond/past redemption** fml too evil to be REDEEMed (1): *a criminal past all redemption*

re·de·ploy /,riʸdɪ'plɔɪ/ v to rearrange (soldiers, workers, etc.) in a more effective way **–redeployment** n [U]

red-hand·ed /,· '··◄/ adj [F] in the act of doing something wrong: *They caught the thief* **red-handed** *while he was just putting the diamonds in his pocket.*

red·head /'rɛdhɛd/ n infml a person with RED¹ (2) hair: *He married a beautiful redhead.*

red-hot /,· '·◄/ adj (of metal) so hot that it shines red

re·di·rect /,riʸdə'rɛkt, -daɪ-/ v [T] → READDRESS

red-let·ter /,· '··/ n **a red-letter day** a specially happy day that will be remembered: *It was a red-letter day for us when Paul came home from the war.*

re·do /riʸ'duʷ/ v **-did** /'dɪd/, **-done** /'dʌn/, *3rd person sing. present tense* **-does** /'dʌz/, **-doing** [T] to do again: *to redo a piece of work/one's hair*

red·o·lent /'rɛdl-ənt/ adj [F +of, with] fml smelling of; making one think of: *an old house redolent of mystery/redolent with garlic.* **–redolence** n [U]

re·dou·ble /riʸ'dʌbəl/ v **-bled, -bling** [I;T] to (cause to) increase greatly: *The police redoubled their efforts to find the missing child.*

re·doubt·a·ble /rɪ'daʊṭəbəl/ adj lit & humor greatly respected and feared: *a redoubtable opponent*

re·dress¹ /rɪ'drɛs/ v [T] fml **1** to put right (a wrong, injustice, etc.) **2 redress the balance** to make things equal again

re·dress² /'riʸdrɛs, rɪ'drɛs/ n fml satisfaction or payment for a wrong that has been done: *You must SEEK redress in the law courts for the damage to your car.*

red tape /,· '·/ n [U] detailed, often unnecessary rules that delay (esp. government) business

re·duce /rɪ'duʷs, rɪ'dyuʷs/ v **-duced, -ducing** **1** [T from, to] to make smaller, cheaper, etc.: *I bought this shirt because it was reduced (from $10 to $5).|He won't reduce the rent of our house.* **–compare** INCREASE **2** [I] infml (of a person) to lose weight on purpose: *Please don't give me any cake because I'm trying to reduce.* **–reducible** adj reduce sbdy./sthg. **to** sthg. *v prep* [T] **1** to bring (something) to (a smaller number or amount): *The great fire reduced the forest to a few trees.*|*We can reduce his statement to three simple facts.* **2** [*usu. pass.*] to bring (esp. someone) to (a weaker or favorable state): *The class was reduced to silence/to order.*|*She was reduced to begging for her living.* **3 reduce someone to tears** to make someone cry

re·duc·tion /rɪ'dʌkʃən/ *n* [C;U] making or becoming smaller; the amount taken off in making something smaller: *some/a slight reduction in the price of food* | *price reductions* –compare INCREASE

re·dun·dan·cy /rɪ'dʌndənsiʸ/ *n* **-cies** [C;U] (a case of) being REDUNDANT

re·dun·dant /rɪ'dʌndənt/ *adj* **1** not needed; more than is necessary: *In the sentence "She lives alone by herself," the word "alone" is redundant.* **2** *esp. BrE* (of a worker) no longer needed –**redundantly** *adv*

reed /riʸd/ *n* **1** a grasslike plant that grows in wet places **2** (in a musical instrument) a thin piece of wood or metal that produces sound by shaking (VIBRATION) when air is blown over it

reef /riʸf/ *n* a line of sharp rocks or bank of sand on or near the surface of the sea: *The ship was wrecked on a reef.*

reek /riʸk/ *n* [S] a strong unpleasant smell: *a reek of tobacco and beer*

reek of sthg. *v prep* [T *no pass.*] to smell strongly and unpleasantly of: (fig.) *The sale of that house reeks of dishonesty.*

reel¹ /riʸl/ *n* a round object on which a length of sewing thread, wire, film, fishing line, recording TAPE¹ (2), etc., is wound

reel² *v* [T *in, off, out*] to move by winding: *to reel in the fishing line*

reel sthg.↔ **off** *v adv* [T] → RATTLE **off**

reel³ *v* [I] to (seem to) move unsteadily: *He came reeling up the street, drunk.*|*The room reeled before my eyes, and I became unconscious.*|*When I hit him, he reeled (back) and almost fell.*

re·e·lect /ˌriʸə'lɛkt/ *v* [T] to elect again: *The senator was reelected for a third term.* –**reelection** /ˌriʸə'lɛkʃən/ *n* [C;U]: *He's seeking reelection for the third time.*

re·en·try /riʸ'ɛntriʸ/ *n* **-tries** [C;U] (an act of) entering again: *The spacecraft made a successful reentry into the earth's* ATMOSPHERE.

re·fec·to·ry /rɪ'fɛktəriʸ/ *n* **-ries** (in schools, colleges, etc.) a large hall in which meals are served

refer /rɪ'fɜr/ *v* → REFER TO

ref·er·ee¹ /ˌrɛfə'riʸ/ *n* **1** also **ref** /rɛf/ *infml*– a judge in charge of some games –see USAGE **2** a person who is asked to settle a disagreement **3** *BrE* for REFERENCE (3b)

USAGE **Referee** is used in connection with **basketball, billiards, boxing, football, hockey, rugby,** and **wrestling. Umpire** is used in connection with **badminton, baseball, cricket, swimming, tennis,** and **volleyball.**

referee² *v* **-eed, -eeing** [I;T] to act as REFEREE¹ (1) for (a game): *John will referee (the*

football game).

ref·er·ence /'rɛfərəns/ *n* **1** [C;U *to*] (an example of) mentioning: *In the conversation, Janet kept making nasty references to me.* **2** [C;U *to*] (an example of) looking at something for information: *Keep this dictionary on your desk for easy reference.* **3** [C] **a** a piece of written information about someone's character, ability, etc., esp. when he or she is looking for employment: *When you look for a job, good references will help you.* **b** *AmE*‖**referee** *BrE*– a person who provides such information: *Ask Professor Jerome if she will be one of your references.* –see also TESTIMONIAL **4 in/with reference to** *fml* in connection with

reference book /'··· ˌ·/ *n* a book that is looked at for information, e.g. a dictionary

reference li·brar·y /'··· ˌ···/ *n* **1** a collection of REFERENCE BOOKS: *Add this dictionary to your reference library.* **2** → REFERENCE ROOM

reference room /'··· ˌ·/ also **reference library**– *n* the place containing a collection of REFERENCE BOOKS that cannot be taken away but must be used in the place where they are kept

ref·er·en·dum /ˌrɛfə'rɛndəm/ *n* **-dums** *or* **-da** /də/ a direct vote by all the people of a nation or area on some particular political question: *to decide the question by holding a referendum* –compare PLEBISCITE

re·fer to *v prep* **-rr-** [T] **1** (**refer to** sbdy./sthg.) to mention; speak about: *He referred to Rio de Janeiro in his speech about travel.* **2** (**refer to** sthg.) to look at for information: *If you don't know what this means, refer to the dictionary.* **3** (**refer to** sbdy./sthg.) to concern; be directed towards: *The new law does not refer to land used for farming.* **4** (**refer** sbdy./sthg. **to** sbdy.) to send to (someone else) for decision or action: *The store referred the complaint (back) to the makers of the product.*

re·fill¹ /riʸ'fɪl/ *v* [T] to fill again: *The hungry teenagers refilled their plates again and again.*

re·fill² /'riʸfɪl/ *n* (a container holding) a quantity of ink, paper, etc., to REFILL¹ something

re·fi·nance /ˌriʸfə'næns, riʸ'faɪnæns/ *v* **-nanced, -nancing** [T] *AmE* to borrow or lend money to pay off a debt, usu. so that the borrower can obtain lower payments or other advantages: *We'd like to refinance our house and pay for it over 30 years instead of 20.*

refine /rɪ'faɪn/ *v* **-fined, -fining** [T] to make pure: *Oil must be refined before it can be used.*

re·fined /rɪ'faɪnd/ *adj* **1** made pure: *refined oil/sugar* **2** (of a person, behavior, etc.) having or showing education and gentleness of manners: *a refined way of speaking* –opposite **unrefined**

re·fine·ment /rɪ'faɪnmənt/ *n* **1** [C *on*] an addition or improvement: *The addition of a little lemon juice was a perfect refinement to the sauce.* **2** [U] the act of making pure: *the refinement of sugar* **3** [U] the quality of being REFINED (2): *a woman of great refinement*

re·fin·er·y /rɪ'faɪnəriʸ/ *n* **-ies** a building and

apparatus for refining (REFINE) metals, oil, or sugar: *a sugar refinery*

re·flect /rɪˈflɛkt/ *v* **1** [T] to throw back (heat, light, sound, or an image): *The mirror reflected my face.* **2** [T] to express; give an idea of: *Does the letter reflect your real opinions?* **3** [I;T +*that*] to think carefully: *After reflecting for a time he decided not to go.*

reflect on sbdy./sthg. *v prep* [T] **1** to consider carefully: *I have been reflecting on the matter/on what you said.* **2** (of an action or event) to bring blame on: *The lie that you told reflects on your honesty.*

re·flec·tion /rɪˈflɛkʃən/ *n* **1** [C] an image REFLECTed (1) in a mirror or polished surface: *We looked at our reflections in the lake.* **2** [U] the REFLECTING (1) of heat, light, sound, or an image: *The moon looks bright because of the reflection of light.* **3** [C;U] (a) deep and careful thought: *His reflections on Indian politics were very interesting* | *On reflection, he agreed to lend them the money.*

re·flec·tor /rɪˈflɛktər/ *n* a surface that REFLECTs (1) light

re·flex /ˈriːflɛks/ *n* an unintentional movement that is made in reply to some outside influence: *The doctor hit my knee with a hammer to test my reflexes.* | *I can't help closing my eyes when I see a bright light; it's a* **reflex action**.

re·flex·ive /rɪˈflɛksɪv/ *n,adj* (a word) showing that the action in a sentence has its effect on the person or thing that does the action: *In "I enjoyed myself," "myself" is a* **reflexive pronoun**.

re·form¹ /rɪˈfɔrm/ *v* [I;T] to (cause to) improve; make or become right: *Harry has completely reformed/is a completely reformed character now; he's stopped taking drugs.* –**reformer** *n: Susan B. Anthony was a famous social reformer.*

reform² *n* [C;U] (an) action that improves conditions or effectiveness, removes unfairness, etc.: *social reforms* | *a reform of the tax system*

ref·or·ma·tion /ˌrɛfərˈmeɪʃən/ *n* [C;U] (an) improvement; REFORMing¹ or being reformed: *Have you noticed the complete reformation in Harry's character?*

Reformation *n* [*the* S] the religious movement in Europe in the 16th century leading to the establishment of the PROTESTANT churches

re·form·a·to·ry /rɪˈfɔrməˌtɔriː/ also **reform school** /ˈ·ˌ·ˌ/– *n* -**ries** *AmE* a special school for boys or girls who have done things against the law, where they live and receive training

re·fract /rɪˈfrækt/ *v* [T] (of water, glass, etc.) to cause (light) to change direction when passing through at an angle –**refraction** /rɪˈfrækʃən/ *n* [U]: *Refraction makes a straight stick look bent if it is partly in water.*

re·frain¹ /rɪˈfreɪn/ *v* [I *from*] to hold oneself back from doing something: *Please refrain from smoking.*

refrain² *n* a part of a song that is repeated, esp. at the end of each VERSE (2): *They all sang the refrain.*

re·fresh /rɪˈfrɛʃ/ *v* [T] to make fresh again: *A hot bath will refresh you.* | *He refreshed himself with a glass of beer.* | *I looked at the map to* **refresh my memory** *of* (=make me remember again) *the road.*

re·fresh·er course /rɪˈfrɛʃər ˌkɔrs, -ˌkoʷrs/ *n* a training course given to a group of members of the same profession to bring their knowledge up to date: *to hold/attend a refresher course on modern teaching methods*

re·fresh·ing /rɪˈfrɛʃɪŋ/ *adj* **1** producing a feeling of comfort and new strength: *a refreshing sleep* **2** pleasantly new and interesting: *It's refreshing to talk to such a truthful person.* –**refreshingly** *adv*

re·fresh·ment /rɪˈfrɛʃmənt/ *n* **1** [U] being REFRESHED **2** [C *often pl.*] *fml* food and drink: *Refreshments will be served after the meeting.*

re·frig·er·ate /rɪˈfrɪdʒəˌreɪt/ *v* -**ated**, -**ating** [T] to make (food, liquid, etc.) cold, as a way of preserving; freeze: *refrigerated meat/beer* –**refrigeration** /rɪˌfrɪdʒəˈreɪʃən/ *n* [U]

re·frig·er·a·tor /rɪˈfrɪdʒəˌreɪtər/ *n* also **fridge** *infml* | also **ice box** *AmE infml*– a large box in which food or drink can be kept for a time at a low temperature –see illustration on page 379

re·fu·el /ˌriːˈfyuʷəl/ *v* -**l**- *AmE* | -**ll**- *BrE* [I;T] to (cause to) fill up again with FUEL: *The plane refueled at Cairo.*

ref·uge /ˈrɛfyuːdʒ/ *n* [C;U] (a place that provides) protection or shelter from danger: *a mountain refuge for climbers* | *They* **took refuge** (=found shelter) *under a tree.*

ref·u·gee /ˌrɛfyʊˈdʒiː, ˈrɛfyʊˌdʒiː/ *n* a person who has been driven from his/her country for political reasons or during a war

re·fund¹ /rɪˈfʌnd/ *v* [T] to give (money) as a REFUND²: *They refunded (us) our money.*

re·fund² /ˈriːfʌnd/ *n* [C;U] (a) repayment: *to demand a refund on unsatisfactory goods*

re·fus·al /rɪˈfyuːzəl/ *n* [C;U +*to-v*] (a case of) refusing: *My offer to buy the house met with* (=was answered with) *a cold refusal.*

re·fuse¹ /rɪˈfyuːz/ *v* -**fused**, -**fusing** [I;T +*to-v*] not to accept or do or give: *He asked her to marry him, but she refused (to marry him).* | *She refused his offer.* –opposite **accept**

USAGE **Refuse**, **reject**, **decline**, and **turn down** are all used to show failure to agree to an offer or request, but they are not exactly the same. **Decline** suggests a polite refusal (esp. of an offer or invitation) but **refuse** is less polite and suggests more firmness: *I'm afraid I must* **decline** *your invitation/***decline** *to answer that question.* | *The prisoner* **refused** *to give his name.* | *They've* **refused** *(us) permission to build on this land.* **Turn down** is similar to **refuse:** *I wrote to them about the job, but they* **turned** *me* **down.** **Reject** suggests a complete refusal to consider (an offer or suggestion) or to accept (a person): *The workers have* **rejected** *the company's pay offer.* | *He feels* **rejected** *by society.*

SPELLING NOTE

Words with the sound /r/ may be spelled **wr-**, like **wrong**.

ref·use² /ˈrɛfjuʷs/ n [U] *fml* waste material: *kitchen refuse*

re·fute /rɪˈfjuʷt/ v **-futed, -futing** [T] to prove to be wrong: *I refuted him/his argument easily.|to refute the claim that the world is flat* –see also IRREFUTABLE **–refutation** /ˌrɛfjuˈteʸʃən/ n [C;U]

re·gain /rɪˈgeʸn/ v [T] to get or win (something) back: *to regain one's health|I regained my balance.* (=got back on my feet after slipping) **2** *lit* to reach (a place) again: *to regain the shore*

re·gal /ˈriʸgəl/ adj very splendid; of or like a king or queen: *regal manners|a regal old lady* **–regally** adv

re·gale sbdy. **with** sthg. /rɪˈgeʸl/ v prep **-galed, -galing** [T] to give enjoyment to (oneself or another) with: *He regaled us with some stories about his youth.*

re·ga·lia /rɪˈgeʸlyə/ n [U] ceremonial clothes and ornaments, esp. those used at royal ceremonies: *a king's regalia*

re·gard¹ /rɪˈgɑrd/ n [U] **1** respect: *I hold her in high/low/the greatest regard.* **2** [*for, to*] respectful attention: *You have no regard for my feelings!* **3** **in/with regard to** → REGARDING

regard² v [T] **1** [*as,with*] to consider: *I have always regarded him highly/with the greatest admiration.|I regard him as my friend.* **2** *fml* to look at: *She regarded him thoughtfully.*

re·gard·ing /rɪˈgɑrdɪŋ/ also **as regards, in re, re–** prep *fml* (esp. in business letters) on the subject of; in connection with: *Regarding your recent enquiry . . .*

re·gard·less /rɪˈgɑrdlɪs/ adv *infml* whatever may happen: *Get the money, regardless!*

    regardless of prep without worrying about: *They decorated the house regardless of the cost.*

re·gards /rɪˈgɑrdz/ n [P] good wishes: *Give him my (best) regards.*

re·gat·ta /rɪˈgɑtə, -ˈgæ-/ n a meeting for races between rowing or sailing boats

re·gen·cy /ˈriʸdʒənsiʸ/ n [U] (the period of) government by a REGENT

re·gent /ˈriʸdʒənt/ n (*often cap.*) a person who governs in place of a king or ruling queen who is ill, absent, or still a child **–regent** adj [after n]: *the Prince Regent*

reg·gae /ˈrɛgeʸ/ n [U] (*often cap.*) a type of popular music from the West Indies with a strong, continually repeated BEAT² (3)

re·gime /reʸˈʒiʸm, rɪ-/ n a particular (type of) government: *The country is under a military regime.*

reg·i·ment¹ /ˈrɛdʒəmənt/ n [C] a large military group, commanded by a COLONEL: *His regiment is going abroad.* **–regimental** /ˌrɛdʒəˈmɛntəl/ adj [A]: *the regimental band*

reg·i·ment² /ˈrɛdʒəˌmɛnt/ v [T] *derog* to control (people) firmly: *Children today don't like being regimented.* **–regimentation** /ˌrɛdʒəmɛnˈteʸʃən, -mən-/ n [U]

re·gion /ˈriʸdʒən/ n **1** a fairly large area or part: *the southern region of Brazil|a pain in the region of the heart* **2** **in the region of** about: *It will cost in the region of $200.* **–regional** adj: *strange regional customs*

–regionally adv

reg·is·ter¹ /ˈrɛdʒəstər/ n **1** (a book containing) a record or list: *to keep a register of births and deaths|The teacher can't find his school attendance register.* –see also CASH REGISTER **2** *tech* the range of a human voice or musical instrument

register² v **1** [T] to put into an official list or record: *to register the birth of a baby* **2** [I] to enter one's name on a list: *to register at a hotel/as an elector* **3** [T] to show; record: *The* THERMOMETER *registered 35°C.|She/Her face registered anxiety.* **4** [T] to send by REGISTERED MAIL: *a registered letter*

registered mail /ˌ··· ˈ·/ *AmE*‖**registered post** *BrE*– n [U] a postal service which, for an additional charge, protects the sender of a valuable letter or package against loss

registered nurse /ˌ··· ˈ·/ *also* **RN–** (in the US) a trained person who is officially allowed to practice as a nurse

reg·is·trar /ˈrɛdʒəˌstrɑr/ n a keeper of official records, esp. in a university or college

reg·is·tra·tion /ˌrɛdʒəˈstreʸʃən/ n [U] the act of REGISTERing² (1,2)

reg·is·try /ˈrɛdʒəstriʸ/ n **-tries** a place where records are kept

re·gress /rɪˈgrɛs/ v [I] to return to an earlier, less developed state –compare PROGRESS **–regression** /rɪˈgrɛʃən/ n [U]

re·gret¹ /rɪˈgrɛt/ v **-tt-** [T +v-ing/that] to be sorry about (a sad fact or event): *to regret someone's death|We've always regretted selling the farm.|She regrets that she can't come.|(fml) We* **regret to inform you** (=we are sorry to say) *that you owe the bank $1000.*

regret² n [U] unhappiness (at the loss of something, at a sad event, etc.): *They said goodbye with great regret.|He said he* **had no regrets** (=he did not feel sorry) *about leaving the university.* **–regretful** /rɪˈgrɛtfəl/ adj **–regretfully** adv

re·gret·ta·ble /rɪˈgrɛtəbəl/ adj that one should feel sorry about: *Your choice of friends is most regrettable.* **–regrettably** adv: *regrettably unable to attend*

re·group /ˌriʸˈgruʷp/ v [I,T] to (cause to) form into new groups or into groups again

reg·u·lar¹ /ˈrɛgyələr/ adj **1** happening, coming, doing something, again and again with the same length of time between each occasion: *They could hear the regular* TICK *of the clock.|a regular customer|regular working hours|regular attendance at church* **2** *AmE* ordinary; average: *regular size* –opposite **irregular** **3** not varying: *You must drive at a regular speed.* **4** [A no comp.] professional; not just employed for a time: *the regular army* **5** *apprec* evenly shaped: *He has regular* FEATURES. (=of the face) **6** [A no comp.] *infml* complete; thorough: *That child is a regular actor; when he cries, he's only pretending.*

regular² n **1** *infml* a REGULAR¹ (1) visitor, customer, etc. **2** a soldier who is a member of an army kept by a country all the time

reg·u·lar·i·ty /ˌrɛgyəˈlærətiʸ/ n [U] the quality of being REGULAR¹

reg·u·lar·ly /ˈrɛgyələrliʸ/ adv at REGULAR¹ (1)

times: *Take the medicine regularly three times a day.*

reg·u·late /'regyə‚leʸt/ *v* **-lated, -lating** [T] **1** to fix or control: *to regulate one's habits| Your watch is always slow; it needs to be regulated.* (=made to work correctly) **2** to control by rules; to keep (something) within limits: *This government office regulates large business companies.*

reg·u·la·tion /‚regyə'leʸʃən/ *n* **1** [C] an official rule or order: *regulations governing the sale of guns* **2** [U] control; bringing of order: *the regulation of public spending*

re·gur·gi·tate /ri'gɜrdʒə‚teʸt/ *v* **-tated, -tating** [T] *fml* to bring (food already swallowed) up again to the mouth: (fig.) *He can regurgitate facts,* (=say them from memory) *but he can't think for himself.* **—regurgitation** /ri‚gɜrdʒə'teʸʃən/ *n* [U]

re·ha·bil·i·tate /‚riʸhə'bilə‚teʸt, ‚riʸə-/ *v* **-tated, -tating** [T] **1** to make able to live an ordinary life again, as by training: *to rehabilitate criminals* **2** to put back into good condition: *to rehabilitate old houses* **—rehabilitation** /‚riʸhə‚bilə'teʸʃən, ‚riʸə-/ *n* [U]

re·hash /riʸ'hæʃ/ *v* [T] *infml* to use (the same ideas) again in a new form which is not really different or better: *a politician who keeps rehashing the same old speech* **—rehash** /'riʸhæʃ/ *n*

re·hears·al /ri'hɜrsəl/ *n* [C;U] the act or an occasion of rehearsing (REHEARSE): *This play will need a lot of rehearsal(s).|At a* **dress rehearsal** *all the actors wear the clothes they will wear in the performance.*

re·hearse /ri'hɜrs/ *v* **-hearsed, -hearsing** [I;T] to practise (something) for later performance: *The actors were rehearsing (a play) in the theater.*

re·house /‚riʸ'hɑʊz/ *v* **-housed, -housing** [T] to put (someone) into a new or better house: *a plan to rehouse poor people in better homes*

reign¹ /reʸn/ *n* a period of REIGNing: *during the reign of King George*

reign² *v* [I *over*] **1** to be the king or queen **2** *lit* to exist: *The thunder died away and silence reigned once more.*

re·im·burse /‚riʸɪm'bɜrs/ *v* **-bursed, -bursing** *fml* to pay (money) back to (a spender): *We will reimburse you (for) the cost.|You/The cost will be reimbursed.* **—reimbursement** *n* [U]

rein /reʸn/ *n* **1** [*usu. pl.*] a long narrow band usu. of leather, by which a horse is controlled and guided **2** **give (free) rein to** to give freedom to (feelings or desires): *to give free rein to one's imagination* **3** **keep a tight rein on** to control firmly

re·in·car·nate /‚riʸɪn'kɑrneʸt/ *v* **-nated, -nating** [T *as; usu. pass.*] to cause to return to life in a new body, after death: *I believe I will be reincarnated as a snake.*

re·in·car·na·tion /‚riʸɪnkɑr'neʸʃən/ *n* **1** [U]

SPELLING NOTE
Words with the sound /r/ may be spelled **wr-**, like **wrong**.

---

the act of being REINCARNATEd: *Buddhists believe in reincarnation.* **2** [C] the creature that results: *He claims to be a reincarnation of Napoleon.*

rein·deer /'reʸndɪər/ *n* **reindeer** a type of large deer with long branching horns

re·in·force /‚riʸɪn'fɔrs, -'foʷrs/ *v* **-forced, -forcing** [T] to strengthen by adding esp. materials or people: *to reinforce a coat by sewing pieces of leather on the elbows|to reinforce an army|to reinforce an argument* **—reinforcement** *n* [U]: *This roof needs some reinforcement.*

re·in·force·ments /‚riʸɪn'fɔrsmənts, -'foʷrs-/ *n* [P] more people, supplies, etc. sent to REINFORCE an army: (fig.) *When we worked until two a.m., they brought us coffee and other reinforcements.*

re·in·state /‚riʸɪn'steʸt/ *v* **-stated, -stating** [T *as, in*] to put back into a position formerly held: *He was dismissed, but was later reinstated (as a toolmaker/in his former job).* **—reinstatement** *n* [C;U]

re·it·er·ate /riʸ'ɪtə‚reʸt/ *v* **-ated, -ating** [T] to repeat several times: *The miners have reiterated their demands for more money.* **—reiteration** /riʸ‚tə'reʸʃən/ *n* [C;U]

re·ject¹ /ri'dʒɛkt/ *v* [T] **1** to refuse to accept: *She rejected my suggestion.* **2** to throw away as useless or imperfect: *to choose the good apples and reject the bad ones* **—see** REFUSE (USAGE)

re·ject² /'riʸdʒɛkt/ *n* something REJECTed¹ (2)

re·jec·tion /ri'dʒɛkʃən/ *n* [C;U] (an example of) REJECTing or being rejected: *I'm trying to get a job, but have so far only received rejections.|I was annoyed at her rejection of my offer.*

re·joice /ri'dʒɔɪs/ *v* **-joiced, -joicing** [I;T +*to-v/that*] *fml & lit* to feel or show great joy: *to rejoice at/over good news*

re·joic·ing /ri'dʒɔɪsɪŋ/ *n* [U] *fml* great joy, esp. shown by a number of people

re·join·der /ri'dʒɔɪndər/ *n* an answer, esp. a rude one

re·ju·ve·nate /ri'dʒuʷvə‚neʸt/ *v* **-nated, -nating** [I;T *often pass.*] to make or become young again: *The mountain air will rejuvenate you.* **—rejuvenation** /ri‚dʒuʷvə'neʸʃən/ *n* [U]

re·lapse /ri'læps/ *v* **-lapsed, -lapsing** [I *into*] to fall back (into a bad state) after an improvement; return: *He relapsed into his old bad habits.* **—relapse** /'riʸlæps, ri'læps/ *n*: *He was getting over his illness, but then he had a relapse.*

re·late /ri'leʸt/ *v* **-lated, -lating** [T] *fml* **1** to tell (a story): *He related (to us) the story of his escape.* **2** to see or show a connection between: *I can't relate those two ideas.*

relate to *v prep* [T] **1** [*often neg.*] to have a friendly relationship with: *She doesn't relate very well to her mother.|(fig.) She can relate to almost any kind of music.* **2** (**relate** sthg. **to** sthg.) also **relate with**— to connect (one thing) with (another): *I can't relate what he does to what he says.* **3** (**relate to** sbdy./sthg.) →REFER TO (3)

re·lat·ed /ri'leʸṭɪd/ *adj* [*by, to*] connected; of

the same family or kind: *She is related to me by marriage.* –opposite **unrelated**

re·la·tion /rɪˈleɪʃən/ n 1 [C] → RELATIVE[1] 2 [U] also **relationship**– connection: *the relation between wages and prices*

re·la·tions /rɪˈleɪʃənz/ n [P *between, with*] way of treating and thinking of each other: *to have/establish friendly relations with someone*

re·la·tion·ship /rɪˈleɪʃənˌʃɪp/ n [C;U] 1 family or personal connection: *I'm not going to give my boyfriend the job just because of our relationship.|There's a good relationship between the police and the local people here.* 2 → RELATION (2)

rel·a·tive[1] /ˈrɛlətɪv/ also **relation**– n *fml* a member of one's family: *My uncle is my nearest relative.*

relative[2] *adj* compared to each other or to something else: *the relative costs of building in stone and brick|After his money troubles, he's now living in relative comfort.* –compare ABSOLUTE

rel·a·tive·ly /ˈrɛlətɪvliʲ/ *adv* quite; when compared to others: *She walks relatively fast for a small child.*

relative pro·noun /ˌ··· ˈ··/ n *tech* a word like *who, which,* or *that. In the sentence "the man who lives next door is a doctor," "who" is a relative pronoun.*

rel·a·tiv·i·ty /ˌrɛləˈtɪvətiʲ/ n [U] (*often cap.*) the relationship between time, size, and mass, which is said to change with increased speed: *Einstein's* THEORY *of relativity*

re·lax /rɪˈlæks/ v 1 [I;T] to make or become less active or worried: *Sit down and relax!|The music will help to relax you.* –compare UNWIND 2 [I;T] to make or become less stiff or tight: *His muscles relaxed.* –compare TENSE[3] 3 [T] to make (effort or control) less severe: *You must not relax your control for a moment.*

re·lax·a·tion /ˌriʲlækˈseɪʃən/ n 1 [C;U] (something done for) rest and amusement: *Playing the piano is one of his favorite relaxations.* 2 [U] the act of RELAXing or condition of being RELAXed: *the relaxation of controls on government spending*

re·lay[1] /ˈriʲleɪ/ n [C;U] 1 one part of a team or organization, that takes its turn in keeping an activity going continuously, a new group replacing the first one: *groups of men working in/by relay(s) to clear the blocked railway line|A relay (race) is a race in which each member of each team runs part of the distance.* 2 a system or apparatus that receives and passes on messages by telephone, radio, etc.: *This broadcast is coming from England by relay.*

re·lay[2] /ˈriʲleɪ, rɪˈleɪ/ v **-layed, -laying** [T] 1 to lay out by RELAY[1] (2): *to relay a broadcast* 2 to pass or send from one group or person to another: *He relayed the message too late.*

re·lease[1] /rɪˈliʲs/ v **-leased, -leasing** [T] 1 [*from*] *more formal than* **set free**– to set free; allow to come out: *to release a prisoner from prison/a man from a promise* 2 to allow **a** (a new movie or record) to be shown or bought

publicly **b** (a news story) to be known and printed

release[2] n 1 [S;U *from*] a setting free: *After his release from prison he came home.* 2 [C] a letter or message that sets free: *The governor signed a release for the prisoner.* 3 a new movie or record that has been RELEASED[1] (2): *I'd like to see some of the latest releases.*

rel·e·gate /ˈrɛləˌɡeɪt/ v **-gated, -gating** [T *to*] to put into a lower or worse position: *to relegate the old furniture to the children's room|Everyone was surprised when the football team was relegated (to a lower division).*

re·lent /rɪˈlɛnt/ v [I] to have or show pity; become less cruel: (fig.) *In the morning the storm relented a little.*

re·lent·less /rɪˈlɛntlɪs/ *adj* without pity: *a relentless enemy* –**relentlessly** *adv* : *He beat the dog relentlessly.*

rel·e·vant /ˈrɛləvənt/ *adj* [F *to*] connected with the subject: *His nationality isn't relevant to whether he's a good lawyer/isn't a relevant point.* –opposite **irrelevant** –**relevance** n [U *to*]: *What you say has no relevance to what we're talking about.* –**relevantly** *adv*

re·li·a·ble /rɪˈlaɪəbəl/ *adj* able to be trusted; dependable: *She may forget; she's not very reliable.|a reliable pair of boots* –opposite **unreliable** –**reliability** /rɪˌlaɪəˈbɪlətiʲ/ n [U] –**reliably** /rɪˈlaɪəbliʲ/ *adv: I am reliably informed that he takes drugs.*

re·li·ant /rɪˈlaɪənt/ *adj* [F *on*] depending on: *We should not be reliant on military power alone.* –compare SELF-RELIANT –**reliance** n [U *on*]

rel·ic /ˈrɛlɪk/ n 1 a part of the body or clothing of a holy person which is kept and respected after his/her death 2 something old that reminds us of the past: *This stone ax is a relic of ancient times.*

re·lief /rɪˈliʲf/ n 1 [S;U] (a) feeling of comfort at the ending of anxiety, fear, or pain: *a drug for the relief of pain|You're safe! What a relief!* 2 [U] help for people in trouble: *The government sent relief* (=money, food, clothes) *to the people who lost their homes in the flood.* 3 [C] a person or group taking from another the responsibility for a duty: *The relief for the military guard is expected soon.|a relief driver* 4 [C;U] (a shape or) decoration which stands out above the rest of the surface it is on

re·lieve /rɪˈliʲv/ v **-lieved, -lieving** [T] 1 to lessen (pain or trouble): *a drug that relieves headaches* 2 to take a duty from (someone) as a RELIEF (3): *The guard will be relieved at midnight.* 3 to give variety to; make more interesting: *to relieve a dull evening with a little dancing*

relieve sbdy. **of** sthg. *v prep* [T] to take from (someone) (something heavy to carry or hard to do): *Let me relieve you of that heavy package.*

re·lieved /rɪˈliʲvd/ *adj* [F + *to-v/(that)*] given RELIEF (1): *Your mother will be very relieved (to hear that you are safe).*

re·li·gion /rɪˈlɪdʒən/ n [C;U] (a particular system of) belief in one or more gods, esp. the belief that he/she/they made the world and can control it

re·li·gious /rɪˈlɪdʒəs/ *adj* [A] **1** of or concerning religion: *a religious service* **2** (of a person or behavior) obeying the rules of a religion very carefully: *a very religious man* **3** performing duties very carefully, as a matter of conscience

re·li·gious·ly /rɪˈlɪdʒəsliʸ/ *adv* faithfully and regularly: *He washes the floor religiously every morning.*

re·lin·quish /rɪˈlɪŋkwɪʃ/ *v* [T] *fml* to give up; yield: *He relinquished his claim to the land.*

rel·ish¹ /ˈrelɪʃ/ *n* **1** [U] (a great deal of) enjoyment, esp. of food; pleasure: *He drank the wine with relish.* **2** [C;U] (a) substance eaten with a meal, such as PICKLES (2) or SAUCE, to add taste and interest: *a spoonful of relish*

relish² *v* [T + *v-ing*] to enjoy; be pleased with: *John won't relish having to wash all those dishes.*

re·live /ˌriʸˈlɪv/ *v* **-lived, -living** [T] to experience again in the imagination: *to relive one's school days in conversation with an old friend*

re·lo·cate /riʸˈloʷkeʸt/ *v* **-cated, -cating** [I;T] to move to or set up in a new place: *to relocate the factory outside Atlanta|We're relocating outside Atlanta.* **–relocation** /ˌriʸloʷˈkeʸʃən/ *n* [U]

re·luc·tant /rɪˈlʌktənt/ *adj* [F + *to-v*] unwilling, and therefore perhaps slow to act: *to give a reluctant promise|He was very reluctant to help.* **–reluctance** *n* [U] **–reluctantly** *adv*

re·ly on/upon sthg. /rɪˈlaɪ/ *v prep* **-lied, -lying** [T + *v-ing*] to trust (esp. that something will happen or someone will do something): *You can't rely on the weather.|Don't rely on me/my going to India.* (=perhaps I won't go)*|You can rely on me (to help you).*

re·main /rɪˈmeʸn/ *v* **1** [I] to stay or be left behind after others have gone: *Of the seven brothers only four now remain; the rest are dead.* **2** to continue to be (in an unchanged state): *Peter became a judge, but John remained a fisherman/remained poor.* **–see** STAY (USAGE)

re·main·der /rɪˈmeʸndər/ *n* [*the* U +*sing./pl.v*] what is left over; the rest: *The remainder of the books are in the box.|The remainder is in the box.*

re·mains /rɪˈmeʸnz/ *n* [P] **1** [*of*] parts which are left: *the remains of dinner/of an old castle* **2** *fml* a dead body: *His remains lie in the churchyard.*

re·make /ˌriʸˈmeʸk/ *v* **-made** /ˈmeʸd/, **-making** [T] to make (esp. a movie) again: *They're remaking "Gone with the Wind."* **–remake** /ˈriʸmeʸk/ *n*

re·mand /rɪˈmænd/ *v* [T *usu. pass.*] to send back to prison from a court of law, to be tried later (often in the phrase **remanded in custody**) **–remand** *n* [C;U]: *He's on remand.* (=in prison waiting for a trial)

SPELLING NOTE

Words with the sound /r/ may be spelled **wr-**, like **wrong**.

---

re·mark¹ /rɪˈmɑrk/ *v* [T +*that*] to say, esp. something which one has just noticed; give as an opinion: *He remarked that it was getting late.*

remark on/upon sthg. *v prep* [T] to say or write something about: *Everyone remarked loudly on his absence.*

remark² *n* [*about, on*] a spoken or written opinion; COMMENT¹: *to make/pass rude remarks about her appearance*

re·ma·rk·able /rɪˈmɑrkəbəl/ *adj* worth speaking of; unusual or noticeable: *a most remarkable sunset* **–remarkably** *adv*: *a remarkably fine day|It's remarkably easy.* –see Study Notes on page 363

re·me·di·al /rɪˈmiʸdiʸəl/ *adj* [*no comp.*] curing or helping; providing a REMEDY: *to do remedial exercises for a weak back* **–remedially** *adv*

rem·e·dy¹ /ˈremədiʸ/ *n* **-dies** [C;U *for*] a cure: *Alcohol is the best remedy for colds.|Take a vacation; it's a good remedy for unhappiness.*

remedy² *v* **-died, -dying** [T] to put or make right (anything bad): *to remedy an injustice/a fault/a loss*

re·mem·ber /rɪˈmembər/ *v* **1** [I;T +*v-ing* (*that*)] to keep in the memory; call back into the mind: *Certainly I mailed your letter; I remember mailing it.|I can't remember how to get there/where she lives/what happened then.* **–opposite forget 2** [I;T +*to-* *v*] to take care not to forget: *Remember to mail my letter!* **3** [T] *often euph* to give money or a present to: *She always remembers me at Christmas.*

USAGE Note the difference between **remember** +*v-ing* and **remember** +*to-v*: *I remember locking the door as I left the house.* (=I locked it and can call this event to mind)*|I remembered to lock the door as I left the house.* (=I took care not to forget to do this).

remember sbdy. **to** sbdy. *v prep* [T] *infml* to send (someone's) greetings to: *Please remember me to your mother.*

re·mem·brance /rɪˈmembrəns/ *n* **1** [C;U *of*] the state or act of remembering: *a church service in remembrance of those killed in the war* –see MEMORY **2** [C *of*] something kept or given to remind one: *He gave me his photograph as a remembrance (of him).*

re·mind /rɪˈmaɪnd/ *v* [T +*that/of*] to tell or cause (someone) to remember (a fact, or to do something): *Remind me to write to Mother.|She reminded me that I hadn't written to Mother.|I've forgotten how to do this; will you remind me?|The sight of the clock reminded me that I was late/reminded me to leave at once.*

remind sbdy. **of** sbdy./sthg. *v prep* [T] cause (someone) to remember (someone or something) by seeming the same: *This hotel reminds me of the one we stayed in last year.*

re·mind·er /rɪˈmaɪndər/ *n* something, esp. a letter, to make one remember: *He hadn't paid the bill, so the store sent him a reminder.*

rem·i·nisce /ˌreməˈnɪs/ *v* **-nisced, -niscing** [I] to talk pleasantly about the past: *The old friends sat reminiscing (about their youth).*

–**reminiscence** n [C;U]

rem·i·nis·cent /ˌrɛməˈnɪsənt/ adj [F of] that
reminds one of; like: *This hotel is reminiscent
of the one we stayed in last year.|The taste is
reminiscent of chicken.*

re·miss /rɪˈmɪs/ adj [F] fml careless, esp.
about a duty: *It was remiss of me not to
answer your letter.*

re·mis·sion /rɪˈmɪʃən/ n **1** [U] the act of
REMITting (1) **2** [C;U] a period when a
disease that sometimes gets better and sometimes worse (**remittant disease**) is less
severe: *He went into remission last month.* **3**
[C;U] (a) lessening of the time a person has
to stay in prison: *The prisoner was given six
months' remission for good behavior.*

re·mit /rɪˈmɪt/ v **-tt-** fml **1** [T] to free someone
from (a debt or punishment) **2** [I;T] to send
(money) by mail: *to remit a check*

re·mit·tance /rɪˈmɪtns/ n an amount of
money REMITted (2)

rem·nant /ˈrɛmnənt/ n **1** a part that remains:
the remnants of a feast **2** a small piece of cloth
left over from a larger piece and sold cheap:
to go to a remnant sale

re·mod·el /ˌriˈmɑdl/ v **-l-** AmE‖**-ll-** BrE [T]
to change the shape of: *to remodel a kitchen*

rem·on·strate /rɪˈmɑnstreʸt/ v **-strated,
-strating** [I against,with] fml to complain;
express disapproval: *to remonstrate with him*
(=complain to him) *about his behavior*
–**remonstrance** /rɪˈmɑnstrəns/ n [C;U]

re·morse /rɪˈmɔrs/ n sorrow for having done
wrong: *He felt/He was filled with remorse
after hitting the child.* –**remorseful** /rɪ
ˈmɔrsfəl/ adj –**remorsefully** adv –**remorseless**
adj –**remorselessly** adv

re·mote /rɪˈmoʷt/ adj [from] **1** distant in
space, time, or manner: *remote stars|the
remote future|a remote village|Her manner
was polite but remote.* (=not friendly) **2**
widely separated; not close: *The connection
between these two ideas is very remote.* **3**
(esp. of a chance or possibility) slight: *I
haven't the remotest idea what you mean.*
–**remoteness** n [U]

remote con·trol /·ˌ· ·ˈ·/ n [U] a system for
controlling machinery from a distance by
radio signals

re·mote·ly /rɪˈmoʷtliʸ/ adv to a very small
degree: *She isn't remotely interested in what
you're saying.*

re·mov·al /rɪˈmuʷvəl/ n [C;U] (an) act of
removing

removal van /·ˈ·· ˌ·/ n BrE for MOVING VAN

re·move /rɪˈmuʷv/ v **-moved, -moving 1** [T
from] to take away (from a place); get rid of:
*Remove your hat.|to remove a child from a
class|to remove mud from your shoes* **2** [T
from] fml to dismiss: *That officer must be
removed (from his position).* **3 removed from**
distant from: *What you say is far removed
from what you said before.* **4 -remover** a
chemical for cleaning off the stated (unwanted) substance: *paint-remover*

re·mu·ner·ate /rɪˈmyuʷnəˌreʸt/ v **-ated, -ating**
[T for] fml to reward; pay (someone) for
work or trouble –**remuneration** /rɪˌmyuʷ
nəˈreʸʃən/ n [S;U]: *to receive (a small*

remuneration –*see* PAY (USAGE)

re·mu·ner·a·tive /rɪˈmyuʷnəˌreʸtɪv, -rətɪv/
adj fml (of work) well-paid; profitable

Ren·ais·sance /ˈrɛnəˌsɑns, -ˌzɑns, ˌrɛnə
ˈsɑns, -ˈzɑns/ n the period in Europe between the 14th and 17th centuries, when the
art, literature, and ideas of ancient Greece
were discovered again and widely studied:
the poetry of the early Renaissance –compare
MIDDLE AGES

rend /rɛnd/ v **rent** /rɛnt/, **rending** [T apart] lit
to divide by force; split: (fig.) *A terrible cry
rent the air.*

ren·der /ˈrɛndər/ v [T] fml **1** to give (esp.
help): *You have rendered me a service.* **2** to
cause to be: *His fatness renders him unable to
touch his toes.* **3** to perform: *to render the
song beautifully*

ren·der·ing /ˈrɛndərɪŋ/ n [of] → RENDITION

ren·dez·vous /ˈrɑndəˌvuʷ, -deʸ-/ n **-vous** /
ˌvuʷz/ French **1** an arrangement to meet at a
certain time and place **2** the place (and time)
chosen for meeting: *John arrived late for his
rendezvous with Joan under the station clock.*
3 a popular place for people to meet: *This
club is a rendezvous for writers.* –**rendezvous**
v **-voused,** /ˌvuʷd/, **-vousing** /ˌvuʷɪŋ/ [I] tech:
*The two spacecraft rendezvoused success-
fully.*

ren·di·tion /rɛnˈdɪʃən/ n a performance (of a
play or piece of music): *a splendid rendition
of the song*

ren·e·gade /ˈrɛnəˌgeʸd/ n derog a person who
deserts one country or belief to join another;
TRAITOR

re·new /rɪˈnuʷ, rɪˈnyuʷ/ v [T] **1** to give new
life and freshness to: *I came back from my
vacation with renewed strength.* **2** to replace
(something old) with something new of the
same kind: *to renew one's library card* **3** to
repeat (an action): *In the morning the enemy
renewed their attack.* –**renewal** n [C;U]

re·new·a·ble /rɪˈnuʷəbəl, rɪˈnyuʷ-/ adj that
can or must be RENEWed (esp. 2): *This ticket
is renewable after twelve months.*

re·nounce /rɪˈnaʊns/ v **-nounced, -nouncing**
[T] more fml than **give up- 1** to give up (esp.
a claim): *She renounced her claim to the
property.* **2** to say formally that one has no
more connection with: *He renounced his
religion and became a Muslim.*

ren·o·vate /ˈrɛnəˌveʸt/ v **-vated, -vating** [T] to
repair; put back into good condition: *to
renovate an old house* –**renovation** /ˌrɛnə
ˈveʸʃən/ n [C;U]

re·nown /rɪˈnaʊn/ n [U] fame: *a painter
of some renown/of great/high renown* –**renowned** adj: *renowned as an inventor
|renowned for his inventions*

rent¹ /rɛnt/ n [C;U] (a sum of) money paid
regularly for the use of a room, building,
television set, piece of land, etc.: *The young
man paid a rent of $50 a week.|to pay a
high/low rent|to pay more/less rent*

rent² v [T] **1** [from] to pay rent for the use of: *I
rent a room from Mrs. Alberto.* **2** to allow to
be used in return for rent: *to rent (out) a
room to Mrs. Sanders.* **3** esp. AmE to pay
money for the use of (a car, boat, etc.) for a

short time: *to rent a suit*

USAGE In *AmE* you **rent** things for a short time, and the owner **rents** them (**out**), but in *BrE* you **hire** them and the owner **hires** them **out**: *Let's rent (AmE)||hire (BrE) a car for the weekend.* In both *AmE* and *BrE* you **rent** things for a longer period: *Is that your* TYPEWRITER, *or do you rent it?* In *AmE* and *BrE*, you **rent** a house or an apartment, but in *AmE* the owner **rents** it (**out**) and in *BrE* the own

rent³ *n* a large tear, (as if) in cloth

rent⁴ *v past tense & participle of* REND

rent·al /'rɛntəl/ *n fml* a sum of money fixed to be paid as rent: *to pay the television rental*

rent-free /ˌ· '·◄/ *adv,adj* (used) without payment of rent: *to live rent-free|a rent-free apartment*

re·nun·ci·a·tion /rɪˌnʌnsiˈeɪʃən/ *n* [C;U] a case or the act of renouncing (RENOUNCE (1))

re·or·ga·nize ||also **-nise** *BrE* /riˈɔrgəˌnaɪz/ *v* **-nized, -nizing** [I;T] to ORGANIZE (something) again, esp. in a better way **–reorganization** /riˌɔrgənəˈzeɪʃən, ˌriɔr-/ *n* [U]

rep¹ /rɛp/ *n infml* a salesman; sales representative: *Our rep will call on Monday.*

rep² *n infml* a REPERTORY (1) theater or company: *the local rep*

re·paid /riˈpeɪd/ *v past tense & participle of* REPAY

re·pair¹ /rɪˈpɛər/ *v* [T] **1** to mend (something worn or broken): *to repair a broken watch/ a road/old shoes* **2** *fml* to put right (a wrong, mistake, etc): *How can I repair the wrong I have done her?* –see also IRREPARABLE **–repairable** *adj*

repair² *n* **1** [*usu. pl.*] an act or result of mending: *to carry out the repairs to my damaged car* **2** in (a) good/bad (state of) **repair** in good/bad condition

rep·a·ra·tion /ˌrɛpəˈreɪʃən/ *n* [U] *fml* repayment for loss or wrong: *to ask/make reparation for the sorrow one has caused*

rep·ar·tee /ˌrɛpərˈtiʸ, -ˈteʸ, ˌrɛpar-/ *n* [U] (the power to make) quick amusing answers in conversation: *I enjoy listening to their* WITTY *repartee.*

re·past /rɪˈpæst||rɪˈpɑst/ *n fml* a meal

re·pa·tri·ate /riʸˈpeʸtriʸˌeʸt/ *v* **-ated, -ating** [T] to bring or send (someone) back to his/her own country **–repatriation** /riʸˌpeʸtriʸˈeʸʃən/ *n* [U]

re·pay /rɪˈpeʸ/ *v* **-paid** /'peʸd/, **-paying** [T] **1** to return what is owed; pay back: *When will you repay me the $5 I lent you?* –see Study Notes on page 481 **2** [*by, for, with*] to reward: *How can I ever repay you for your kindness?*

re·pay·a·ble /rɪˈpeʸəbəl/ *adj* (of money) that can or must be paid back: *The debt is repayable at the end of the month.*

re·pay·ment /rɪˈpeʸmənt/ *n* [C;U] the action of paying back; something paid back:

SPELLING NOTE

Words with the sound /r/ may be spelled **wr-**, like **wrong**.

---

a/some small repayment for all you have done

re·peal /rɪˈpiʸl/ *v* [T] to put an official end to (a law): *to repeal a property law* **–repeal** *n* [U]

re·peat¹ /rɪˈpiʸt/ *v* [T] **1** [*that*] to say or do again: *to repeat a word/a mistake* **2** to say (something heard or learned): *Don't repeat what I told you.* **3 not bear repeating** (of words) to be too bad to say again **4 repeat oneself** to say or to be the same thing again and again: *History seems to be repeating itself.*

repeat² *n* a REPEATED¹ (1) performance: *I wish we could see more new programs on television, not repeats all the time.*

re·peat·ed /rɪˈpiʸtɪd/ *adj* [A] done again and again: *His repeated failure is very sad.* **–repeatedly** *adv*

re·pel /rɪˈpɛl/ *v* **-ll-** [T] **1** to drive back (as if) by force: *to repel an attack* **2** to cause feelings of dislike in

re·pel·lent¹ /rɪˈpɛlənt/ *adj* causing great dislike; nasty: *repellent behavior*

repellent² *n* [C;U] (a) substance that drives something, esp. insects, away: *a mosquito repellent*

re·pent /rɪˈpɛnt/ *v* [I;T *+v-ing/of*] *fml* to be sorry for (wrongdoing): *He repented (of) his wickedness.* **–repentance** *n* [U] **–repentant** *adj*: *her repentant face*

re·per·cus·sion /ˌriʸpərˈkʌʃən/ *n* a far-reaching effect (of some action or event): *The President's death had unexpected repercussions.*

rep·er·toire /'rɛpərˌtwar, -ˌtwɔr/ *n* the collection of plays, pieces of music, etc., that a performer or theater company can perform: (*fig.*) *He has a large repertoire of funny stories.*

rep·er·to·ry /'rɛpərˌtɔriʸ, -ˌtoʷriʸ/ *n* **-ries 1** [U] also **rep** *infml*– the practice of performing several plays, with the same actors and in the same theater, one after the other on different days: *a repertory theater/company* **2** [C] →REPERTOIRE

rep·e·ti·tion /ˌrɛpəˈtɪʃən/ *n* [C;U] the act of REPEATING¹ (1) or something repeated: *This accident is a repetition of one that happened here three weeks ago.*

rep·e·ti·tious /ˌrɛpəˈtɪʃəs/ also **repetitive** /rɪˈpɛtətɪv/– *adj derog* containing parts that are said or done too many times: *a repetitious speech*

re·place /rɪˈpleʸs/ *v* **-placed, -placing** [T] **1** to put (something) back in the right place: *He replaced the book on the shelf.* **2** to take the place of: *George has replaced Ed as captain of the team.* **3** [*with, by*] to change (one person or thing) for another, often better, newer, etc.: *We've replaced the old adding machine with a computer.|You'll have to replace those tires; they're badly worn.* **–replaceable** *adj*

USAGE Compare **replace** and **displace**: Like the second sense of **replace**, **displace** can mean "to fill and take place of," but when it is used of people it usually suggests sadness, anger, or lack of justice: *The old adding machine has been* **replaced** *by a modern computer.|It's very unfair that I should be* displaced *by a younger person.*

re·place·ment /rɪˈpleʸsmənt/ *n* **1** [U] the act of replacing (REPLACE (3)) **2** [C] someone or something that REPLACEs (2): *We need a replacement for the secretary who left.*

re·play /ˌriʸˈpleʸ/ *v* **-played, -playing** [I;T] to play (esp. a game) again: *The teams tied, so they'll replay (the game) on Wednesday.* –**replay** /ˈriʸpleʸ/ *n*

re·plen·ish /rɪˈplɛnɪʃ/ *v* [T] to fill up again; put new supplies into: *to replenish the refrigerator* –**replenishment** *n* [U]

re·plete /rɪˈpliʸt/ *adj* [F *with*] *fml* quite full, esp. of food: *She felt replete with food and drink.*

rep·li·ca /ˈrɛplɪkə/ *n* a close copy, e.g. of a painting or other work of art

re·ply¹ /rɪˈplaɪ/ *v* **-plied, -plying** [I;T +*that*/ *to*] *more fml than* **answer**– to answer; say or do as an answer: *"Did you forget to do it?" I asked. "Of course not," she replied.|Have you replied to his letter?* –see ANSWER (USAGE)

reply² *n* **-plies** [C;U] an act of replying: *What did you say* **in reply to** *his suggestion?*

re·port¹ /rɪˈpɔrt, rɪˈpoʷrt/ *n* **1** [C] an account or description of events, experiences, etc.: *to read some newspaper reports of the accident|a company's report for the year* **2** [C] the noise of an explosion or shot: *a loud report* **3** [C;U] (a piece of) talk that spreads without official support; RUMOR

report² *v* **1** [T +*v-ing/that*] to tell of; make known; give or write an account of: *They reported the appearance of a new star/that they had seen a new star.|to report the President's speech for a newspaper* **2** [I *for, to*] to go somewhere and say that one is there (and ready for work or duty): *They report for work at 8.00 a.m.* **3** [T *for, to*] to make a complaint about: *He reported the boy (to the teacher) (for making a noise).* –**reportedly** *adv*: *He reportedly left before I did, although he is not here yet.*

 report on sthg. *v prep* [T *to*] to provide information about: *He reported on the whole event (to the senator).*

report card /ˈ·ˌ·ˌ·/ *AmE*‖**school report** *BrE*– *n* (in education) a written statement by teachers about a child's work at school which contains GRADEs (=marks for the standard of schoolwork)

re·port·er /rɪˈpɔrtər, -ˈpoʷr-/ *n* a person who writes about news for a newspaper, or for radio or television –compare JOURNALIST

re·pose /rɪˈpoʷz/ *n* [U] *fml* rest; quiet sleep; calm: *She lay on the bed, in repose.* –**repose** *v* **-posed, -posing** [I;T]

rep·re·hen·si·ble /ˌrɛprɪˈhɛnsəbəl/ *adj* (of a person or behavior) deserving to be blamed –**reprehensibly** *adv*

rep·re·sent /ˌrɛprɪˈzɛnt/ *v* [T] **1** to show; be a sign or picture of; stand for: *This painting represents a storm at sea.|a tall stone figure representing Victory|The red lines on the map represent railroads.* **2** to act officially for (another person or people): *to represent one's fellow-members at the club meeting* **3** [+ *to-v/as*] to describe (perhaps falsely) as:

She represents herself as a supporter of the union.

rep·re·sen·ta·tion /ˌrɛprɪzɛnˈteʸʃən, -zən-/ *n* **1** [U] the act of REPRESENTing (2) or the condition of being REPRESENTed (2): *They demanded political representation.* **2** [C *of*] something that REPRESENTs (1): *This painting is a representation of a storm at sea.*

rep·re·sent·a·tive¹ /ˌrɛprɪˈzɛntətɪv/ *adj* **1** [*of*] typical; being an example (of what others are like): *Are your opinions representative of those of the other students?* –opposite **unrepresentative** **2** (of a system of government) in which the people and their opinions are REPRESENTed (2)

representative² *n* [*of*] a person acting in place of one or more others: *They sent a representative to the meeting.* –see also SALESPERSON

re·press /rɪˈprɛs/ *v* [T] to control or hold back (natural feelings, actions, etc.): *I could hardly repress my laughter.* –**repressed** *adj*: *a repressed desire to steal* –**repression** /rɪˈprɛʃən/ *n* [U]: *the repression of my feelings/ of political opposition.*

re·pres·sive /rɪˈprɛsɪv/ *adj derog* (of a law or other kind of control) hard and cruel: *a repressive political system that allows no freedom*

re·prieve¹ /rɪˈpriʸv/ *v* **-prieved, -prieving** [T] to give a REPRIEVE² to: *to reprieve the prisoner*

reprieve² *n* an official order delaying the punishment of a prisoner who was to die: *to* GRANT³ (1) *him a reprieve|(fig.) It was time for the children to go to bed, but they begged for a reprieve.*

rep·ri·mand /ˈrɛprəˌmænd, ˌrɛprəˈmænd/ *v* [T] to scold officially and severely –**reprimand** /ˈrɛprəˌmænd/ *n* [C;U]

re·print¹ /ˌriʸˈprɪnt/ *v* [T] to print (a book) again when supplies have run out

re·print² /ˈriʸˌprɪnt/ *n* a REPRINTed book

re·pris·al /rɪˈpraɪzəl/ *n* [C;U] (an act of) punishing others for harm done to oneself: *to drop bombs on an enemy village in reprisal/as a reprisal*

re·proach¹ /rɪˈproʷtʃ/ *n* **1** [U] blame: *She gave me a look of reproach.|His manners are* **above/beyond reproach.** (=perfect) **2** [C] a word or words of blame: *When he came home drunk, he was greeted with loud reproaches.* –**reproachful** /rɪˈproʷtʃfəl/ *adj* –**reproachfully** *adv*

reproach² *v* [T *for, with*] to blame (someone), not angrily but sadly: *He reproached her for being lazy.*

rep·ro·bate /ˈrɛprəˌbeʸt/ *adj,n usu. humor* (a person) of bad character: *an old reprobate who spends all his money on beer*

re·pro·duce /ˌriʸprəˈduʷz, -ˈdyuʷs/ *v* **-duced, -ducing** [I;T] **1** to produce the young of (oneself or one's own kind): *Some tropical fish reproduce (themselves) by laying eggs.* **2** to produce a copy (of): *a painting that reproduces every detail of the scene*

re·pro·duc·tion /ˌriʸprəˈdʌkʃən/ *n* **1** [U] the act or method of producing young **2** [U] copying: *The quality of reproduction isn't very good on this recording.* **3** [C] a copy, esp. of a work of art: *a cheap reproduction of a great painting* **–reproductive** *adj* [A] : *the female reproductive system|to print a book by modern reproductive methods*

re·prove /rɪ'pruʷv/ *v* **-proved, -proving** [T *for*] *fml* to scold for bad behavior: *to reprove a child (for staying out late)* **–reproof** /rɪ'pruʷf/ *n* [C;U] **–reproving** *adj* : *a reproving voice* **–reprovingly** *adv*

rep·tile /'rɛptəl, -taɪl/ *n* a rough-skinned creature whose blood changes temperature according to the temperature around it: *Snakes and* LIZARDS *are reptiles.* **–reptilian** /rɛp'tɪliʸən, -'tɪlyən/ *adj*

re·pub·lic /rɪ'pʌblɪk/ *n* a nation, usu. governed by elected representatives, whose head of state is a president

re·pub·li·can¹ /rɪ'pʌblɪkən/ *adj* [no comp.] belonging to or favoring a REPUBLIC: *a republican system of government |republican ideas*

republican² *n* a person who believes in a REPUBLICAN government

Republican *n,adj* (a member or supporter) of the **Republican Party**, one of the two largest political parties of the US **–see also** DEMOCRAT

re·pu·di·ate /rɪ'pyuʷdiʸ,eʸt/ *v* **-ated, -ating** [T] to refuse to accept or recognize: *to repudiate offers of friendship|He repudiated the charge of having shot his sister.* **–repudiation** /rɪ,pyuʷdiʸ'eʸʃən/ *n* [U]

re·pug·nance /rɪ'pʌgnəns/ *n* [S;U *to*] a feeling of strong dislike: *She turned away from him in repugnance.* **–repugnant** *adj*

re·pulse /rɪ'pʌls/ *v* **-pulsed, -pulsing** [T] **1** to drive back (an enemy attack), REPEL **2** to refuse coldly (an offer of friendship) **–repulse** *n*

re·pul·sion /rɪ'pʌlʃən/ *n* [S;U] strong dislike and fear: *He looked with repulsion at the dead body.* **–repulsive** /rɪ'pʌlsɪv/ *adj*: *a repulsive smell* **–repulsively** *adv* **–repulsiveness** *n* [U]

rep·u·ta·ble /'rɛpyətəbəl/ *adj* respectable; well spoken of: *a reputable firm of builders* **–opposite disreputable** **–reputably** *adv*

rep·u·ta·tion /,rɛpyə'teʸʃən/ *n* [S;U] **1** also **repute–** (an) opinion held by others (about someone or something); the degree to which one is well thought of: *The restaurant has a good reputation.|He has the reputation of being a coward.|If this matter becomes known, it will ruin your reputation.* **–compare** CHARACTER, CHARACTERISTIC **2 live up to one's reputation** to behave in the way people have come to expect

re·pute /rɪ'pyuʷt/ *n* [U] *fml* **1** →REPUTATION: *a man of low* (=bad) *repute* **2** good REPUTATION: *a hotel of (some) repute*

re·put·ed /rɪ'pyuʷtɪd/ *adj* [A;F +to-v] generally supposed (to be); considered (as): *the reputed father of her baby|She is reputed*

to be the best singer in America. **–reputedly** *adv*

re·quest¹ /rɪ'kwɛst/ *n* **1** a polite demand: *He made a request for help/that I should help him.* **2** [C] something that has been asked for: *Do they play requests on this radio show?* (=records that have been asked for by listeners) **3 at someone's request** because someone asked: *I bought it at your request/ at the request of my father.* **4 on request** when asked for: *The band will play on request.*

request² *v* [T +*that/of*] more *fml* than **ask–** to demand politely: *The judge requested silence.*

req·ui·em /'rɛkwiʸəm/ *n* (a piece of music for) a Christian ceremony (MASS) for the soul of a dead person

re·quire /rɪ'kwaɪər/ *v* **-quired, -quiring 1** [T +*v-ing/that*] more *fml* than **need–** to need: *This suggestion requires careful thought.|His health requires that he should go to bed early.* **2** [T +*that*] *fml* to demand; order, expecting obedience: *All passengers are required to show their tickets.|to pass the required examinations to become a doctor*

re·quire·ment /rɪ'kwaɪərmənt/ *n* more *fml* than **need–** **1** something needed or demanded: *This store can supply all your requirements.* **2 meet someone's requirements** to do or be what someone REQUIRES

req·ui·site /'rɛkwəzɪt/ *n,adj* [*for*] (something) needed for a purpose: *sports requisites|Do you have the requisite stamp on your passport?*

req·ui·si·tion /,rɛkwə'zɪʃən/ *n* [C;U *for,on*] (a) formal demand, esp. by the army: *The soldiers made a requisition on the village for horses.* **–requisition** *v* [T]: *The army requisitioned the stores of gasoline.*

res·cue¹ /'rɛskyuʷ/ *v* **-cued, -cuing** [T *from*] to save from harm or danger; set free: *to rescue a man from drowning/a cat from a high tree* **–rescuer** *n*

rescue² *n* an act of rescuing (RESCUE¹): *A rescue team is trying to reach the trapped miners.|Jean couldn't do her school work, but her mother came to her rescue.* (=helped her)

re·search¹ /rɪ'sɜrtʃ, 'riʸsɜrtʃ/ *n* [U] advanced study of a subject, so as to learn new facts: *research students/workers|to do some research/carry out some research on diseases of the blood*

research² *v* [I;T] to do RESEARCH¹ (on or for): *to research a subject|We've been researching for three years with no result.* **–researcher** *n*

re·sem·ble /rɪ'zɛmbəl/ *v* **-bled, -bling** [T *in*] to look or be like: *She resembles her sister in appearance but not in character.* **–resemblance** /rɪ'zɛmbləns/ *n* [C;U *between*]: *There's a strong resemblance between the two sisters.*

re·sent /rɪ'zɛnt/ *v* [T +*v-ing*] to feel angry or bitter at: *He resents being called a fool.* **–resentful** /rɪ'zɛntfəl/ *adj*: *to give him a resentful look* **–resentfully** *adv*

re·sent·ment /rɪ'zɛntmənt/ *n* [U] the feeling of RESENTING bad treatment: *I don't bear you*

SPELLING NOTE

Words with the sound /r/ may be spelled **wr-**, like **wrong**.

any resentment. (=I don't feel angry with you)

res·er·va·tion /ˌrɛzər'veⁱʃən/ n **1** [C;U +*that*] a doubt in one's mind: *I have some reservations about the truth of his story.*|*I accept your offer* **without reservation(s)**. (=with no uncertainty) **2** [C] (in the US) a piece of land set apart for North American Indians to live on **3** [C] *AmE*‖**booking** *BrE*– a case or the act of reserving (RESERVE¹ (2)), esp. a seat or a room: *All reservations must be made two weeks in advance.*|*She ordered tickets from the reservations desk at the theater.*

re·serve¹ /rɪ'zɜrv/ v **-served, -serving** [T] **1** to keep for a special purpose: *These seats are reserved for old people.* **2** *AmE*‖also **book**– to arrange in advance to have (something): *to reserve a seat on the plane*

reserve² n **1** [C *of*] a store (of something) kept for future use: *to keep a reserve/some reserves of food* **2** [C] the military force that a country keeps for use if needed: *to call out the reserve(s)* **3** [C] a piece of land RESERVED for a (stated) purpose: *to go and see the lions in the nature reserve* **4** [U] (of a person or character) the quality of being RESERVED (1): *the well-known reserve of the Scots* **5 in reserve** ready for use if needed

re·served /rɪ'zɜrvd/ adj **1** (of a person) not liking to talk about himself or his feelings –compare DEMONSTRATIVE **2** having been RESERVED¹ (2): *reserved seats*

res·er·voir /'rɛzərv,wɑr, -,wɔr/ n a place where liquid is stored, esp. a man-made lake to provide water for a city

re·shuf·fle /riⁱ'ʃʌfəl/ n a changing around of the positions of people employed in an organization: *a reshuffle in the company* –**reshuffle** v **-fled, -fling** [I;T]

re·side /rɪ'zaɪd/ v **-sided, -siding** [I] *fml* to have one's home; live: *to reside abroad*

res·i·dence /'rɛzədəns/ n **1** [C] *fml* the place where one lives; a house –see HOUSE (USAGE) **2** [U] the state of residing (RESIDE): *They took up residence in Jamaica.* **3 in residence** actually living in a place

res·i·den·cy /'rɛzədənsiⁱ/ n **-cies** *AmE* the period after hospital training during which a medical doctor receives training in a special field of medicine

res·i·dent¹ /'rɛzədənt/ adj [in] living in a place: *a resident doctor* (=living in the hospital) –opposite **non-resident**

resident² n **1** a person who lives in a place, not a visitor: *This hotel serves meals to residents only.* –opposite **non-resident 2** *AmE* a doctor of medicine serving a period of RESIDENCY –compare INTERN

res·i·den·tial /ˌrɛzə'denʃəl, -tʃəl/ adj (of part of a town) consisting of private houses, without offices or factories

re·sid·u·al /rɪ'zɪdʒuⁿəl/ adj remaining; left over

res·i·due /'rɛzə,duⁿ, -,dyuⁿ/ n [*usu. sing.*] *tech* what is left, esp. after chemical treatment

re·sign /rɪ'zaɪn/ v [I;T *from*] **1** to leave (a job or position): *to resign from a committee*|*to resign one's post* **2 resign oneself to** to accept (something unpleasant) without complaint: *You must resign yourselves to waiting a little longer.* –see RESIGNED

res·ig·na·tion /ˌrɛzɪg'neⁱʃən/ n **1** [C;U] (an act of) RESIGNING (1): *You have the choice between resignation and dismissal.* **2** [U] the state of being RESIGNED: *to accept one's fate with resignation* **3** [C] a written statement to inform that one intends to RESIGN (1): *to hand in/send in my resignation*

re·signed /rɪ'zaɪnd/ adj [to] accepting something unpleasant without complaint: *He seems quite resigned (to his mother's death).* –see also RESIGN (2) –**resignedly** /rɪ'zaɪnɪdliⁱ/ adv

re·sil·ient /rɪ'zɪlyənt/ adj **1** (of a substance) able to spring back to the former shape when pressure is removed: *Rubber is more resilient than wood.* **2** (of living things) strong enough to recover from difficulty, disease, etc.: *He has a resilient character and will soon be cheerful again.* –**resilience, -cy** n [S;U]: *Rubber has more resilience than wood.* –**resiliently** adv

res·in /'rɛzən/ n **1** [U] a thick sticky liquid from certain trees such as the FIR **2** [C] any of various man-made plastic substances, used in industry –**resinous** /'rɛzənəs/ adj

re·sist /rɪ'zɪst/ v [I;T +*v-ing*] **1** to oppose; stand or fight against (force): *to resist an enemy attack*|*to resist being carried off*|*If you are attacked, don't resist.* **2** to remain unchanged or unharmed by: *the power to resist disease* **3** [*usu. neg.*] to force oneself not to yield to or accept: *She could hardly resist laughing.* –**resistible** adj –opposite **irresistible**

re·sist·ance /rɪ'zɪstəns/ n **1** [S;U] (an act of) RESISTING (1): opposition: *The committee put up a lot of resistance to the chairman's plan.* **2** [U] the (stated) force opposed to anything moving: *wind resistance to a plane* **3** [U] the ability (of a living body) to RESIST (2) disease: *Mary has great powers of resistance and will get well quickly.* **4** [U] the power of a substance to RESIST (2) the passing through it of an electric current

re·sis·tant /rɪ'zɪstənt/ adj having or showing RESISTANCE (3) (to): *rats that are resistant to poison*

res·o·lute /'rɛzə,luⁿt/ adj (of a person or his character) firm; determined in purpose –**resolutely** adv –**resoluteness** n [U]

res·o·lu·tion /ˌrɛzə'luⁿʃən/ n **1** [U] also **resolve**– the quality of being RESOLUTE: *You should show more resolution.* **2** [U *of*] the action of resolving (RESOLVE¹ (1)): *The lawyer's advice led to the resolution of all our difficulties.* **3** [C +*to-v*] a formal decision made by a group vote: *At the meeting, there was a resolution for/against building a new library* **4** [C +*to-v*] a decision: *my New Year's resolution* (=one made on January 1st for the year ahead) *to stop smoking* –compare RESOLVE²

re·solve¹ /rɪ'zɑlv/ v **-solved, -solving 1** [T] to settle or clear up (a difficulty): *There weren't enough beds, but the matter was resolved by* making George sleep on the floor. **2** [I;T +*to-v*/*that*] to decide: *To resolve to work harder*/*that one will work harder* **3** [I;T +*to-v*/*that*] (of a committee or public body) to make a RESOLUTION (3) (that): *Congress has resolved that . . .*

resolve² *n fml* **1** [C +*to-v*] → RESOLUTION (4): *a firm resolve to avoid doing anything dishonest* **2** [U]→RESOLUTION (1)

res·o·nant /'rɛzənənt/ *adj* (of a sound) deep, full, clear, and continuing: *the resonant note of a bell*–**resonance** *n* [U]: *The bell-like resonance of his voice filled the great church.* –**resonantly** *adv* –**resonate** /'rɛzə,neʸt/ *v* -**nated, -nating** [I]

re·sort /rɪ'zɔrt/ *n* **1** [C] a vacation place, or place considered good for the health: *a health*/*mountain resort* **2** [U *to*] the action of RESORTING TO: *to pass the examination without resort to cheating* –compare RE-COURSE **3 as a**/**in the last resort** if everything else fails: *In the last resort we can always sleep in the car for a night.*

resort to *v prep* [T +*v-ing*] to turn to (often something bad) for help: *She resorted to stealing when she had no more money.*

re·sound /rɪ'zaʊnd/ *v* **1** [I *through, throughout*] (of a sound) to be loudly and clearly heard: *Their laughter resounded through the hall.* **2** [I *with*] (of a place) to be filled (with sound): *The hall resounded with laughter.*

re·sound·ing /rɪ'zaʊndɪŋ/ *adj* [A] **1** (of a sound) loud and clear; ECHOing² (1): *a resounding crash* **2** very great: *a resounding success* –**resoundingly** *adv*

re·source /'riʸsɔrs, -soʷrs, rɪsɔrs, -'soʷrs/ *n* **1** [*usu. pl.*] a possession (esp. of a country) in the form of wealth or goods: *a country rich in* **natural resources** (=minerals, oil, etc.) **2 a** means of comfort or help: *Religion is her only resource now.* **3 leave someone to his**/**her own resources** to let someone pass the time as he/she wishes

re·source·ful /rɪ'sɔrsfəl, -'soʷrs-/, *adj apprec* (of a person) good at finding a way around difficulties –**resourcefully** *adv* –**resourcefulness** *n* [U]

re·spect¹ /rɪ'spɛkt/ *n* **1** [S;U *for*] admiration; feeling of honor: *He is held in the greatest respect by the whole village.* –opposite **disrespect 2** [U *for, to*] attention (to); care (for); *to have no respect for the speed limit* –compare SELF-RESPECT **3** [C] a detail; point: *The new job is better paid, but in some respects less interesting.* **4 with respect to** *fml* concerning: *With respect to the recent flood, please report the number of sheep that were drowned.*

respect² *v* [T] **1** to feel RESPECT¹ (1) for: *The teacher feels that her students don't respect her.* **2** to show RESPECT¹ (2) for: *I promise to respect your wishes.*

re·spect·a·ble /rɪ'spɛktəbəl/ *adj* **1** showing or having standards acceptable to society: *It's*

---

not respectable to be drunk in the street./*to put on a clean shirt and look respectable* **2** quite good; enough in amount or quality: *a respectable income* –**respectability** /rɪ,spɛktə'bɪləṭiʸ/ *n* [U] –**respectably** /rɪ'spɛktəbliʸ/ *adv*

re·spect·ful /rɪ'spɛktfəl/ *adj* [*to*] feeling or showing RESPECT¹ (1) (to): *The crowd waited in respectful silence for the President to speak.* –opposite **disrespectful** –**respectfully** *adv*

re·spec·tive /rɪ'spɛktɪv/ *adj* [A] of or for each one; particular and separate: *They went home to their respective houses.*

re·spec·tive·ly /rɪ'spɛktɪvliʸ/ *adv* each separately in the order mentioned: *The nurses and the miners received pay increases of 8% and 12% respectively.* (=the nurses got 8% and the miners got 12%).

re·spects /rɪ'spɛkts/ *n* [P] polite formal greetings: *Give my respects to your wife.*

res·pi·ra·tion /,rɛspə'reʸʃən/ *n* [U] *fml & tech* the action of breathing: *Respiration is difficult at great heights.* –see also ARTIFICIAL RESPIRATION

res·pi·ra·tor /'rɛspə,reʸṭər/ *n* an apparatus that is worn over the nose and mouth, to help people to breathe

res·pi·ra·to·ry /'rɛspərə,tɔriʸ, -,toʷriʸ, rɪ'spaɪrə-/ *adj* [A] connected with breathing: *respiratory diseases*

res·pite /'rɛspɪt/ *n* [C;U *from*; *usu. sing.*] (a short period of) pause or rest, during a time of effort, pain, or trouble: *The noise went on all night without (a moment's) respite.*

re·splend·ent /rɪ'splɛndənt/ *adj* bright and shining; splendid; (fig.) *George arrived, resplendent in a new white suit.* –**resplendence** *n* [U] –**resplendently** *adv*

re·spond /rɪ'spand/ *v* **1** [I;T *to*] *more fml than* **answer**– to answer: *They still haven't responded to my letter.* –see ANSWER (USAGE) **2** [I *by, to, with*] to act in answer: *He responded (to my suggestion) with a laugh*/*by laughing.*

respond to sthg. *v prep* [T *no pass.*] (esp. of a disease) to get better or do the right thing as a result of: *The disease failed to respond to drugs.*

re·sponse /rɪ'spans/ *n more fml than* **answer**– [C;U *to*] (an action as) an answer: *He made*/*gave no response (to my question).*/*There has been very little response to our call for help.*/*to open the door* **in response to** *a knock*

re·spon·si·bil·i·ty /rɪ,spansə'bɪləṭiʸ/ *n* -**ties 1** [U *for,to*] the condition of being RESPONSIBLE (1): *I take full responsibility for breaking the window.* **2** [U] the quality of being RESPONSIBLE (2,3): *He holds a position of great responsibility in the company.* **3** [C] something for which one is RESPONSIBLE (1): *The mother of a family has many responsibilities.*

re·spon·si·ble /rɪ'spansəbəl/ *adj* **1** [F *for, to*] having the duty of looking after someone or something, so that one can be blamed (by the stated person) if things go wrong: *I am responsible to the director for making sure that the company is profitable.* **2** trustworthy:

You can leave the children with him; he's very responsible. –opposite **irresponsible 3** (of a job) needing a trustworthy person to do it **4 be responsible for** to be the cause of: Who is responsible for breaking the mirror?

re·spon·si·bly /rɪ'spɒnsəbli^y/ adv in a RE-SPONSIBLE (2) way: I'll trust you to behave responsibly while I'm out. –opposite **irresponsibly**

re·spon·sive /rɪ'spɒnsɪv/ adj [to] answering readily with words or feelings: The child is very responsive to kindness. |a responsive smile –opposite **unresponsive** –**responsively** adv –**responsiveness** n [U]

rest¹ /rɛst/ n **1** [C;U from] (a period of) freedom from action or anything tiring: I'm tired: let's take/stop for a rest. |to get a good night's rest (sleep) |Sunday is my day of rest. |The machine is **at rest**. (=not moving) |The car rolled down the hill and **came to rest** at the bottom. **2** [C] a support (for the stated thing): an armrest |a headrest |Use this shelf as a rest for your camera. **3 set someone's mind/fears at rest** to free someone from anxiety

rest² v **1** [I;T] to (allow to) take a REST¹ (1): I always rest for an hour after dinner. |Sit down and rest your feet. **2** [T against, on] to lean or support: Rest your bike against the wall. **3** [I] to lie buried: Let him rest in peace. **4** [I] to stop being active: Let the argument rest there, because we'll never agree. |I will not rest (have peace of mind) until this matter is settled. **5 rest assured** to be certain: Rest assured/You can rest assured that we will do all we can.

rest on/upon sbdy./sthg. v prep [I] **1** to lean on; be supported by: The bridge rests on stone arches. |(fig.) Your argument rests on evidence that can't be proved. **2** (of sight or the eyes) to be directed towards: His eyes rested on the peaceful valley below.

rest with sbdy. v prep [T no pass.] to be the responsibility of: The decision rests with you.

rest³ n [U +sing. pl. v] what is left; the ones that still remain: We'll eat some of the butter and keep the rest (of it) for breakfast. |He's only got one shirt, because all the rest (of them) are being washed. |John is American and the rest of us are Canadian.

res·tau·rant /'rɛstərənt, -ˌrɑnt/ n a place where meals are sold and eaten –compare CAFÉ –SEE ILLUSTRATION ON PAGE 581

res·tau·ra·teur /ˌrɛstərə'tɜr/ n the owner of a restaurant, esp. one who runs it himself/herself

rest·ful /'rɛstfəl/ adj peaceful; giving one a feeling of REST¹ (1): We spent a restful evening watching television. –**restfully** adv –**restfulness** n [U]

rest home /'· ·/ n an establishment where old or sick people are looked after

res·ti·tu·tion /ˌrɛstə'tu^wʃən, -'tyu^w-/ n [U of] fml the act of returning something lost or stolen to its owner, or of paying for damage: to make restitution (of something, to someone)

res·tive /'rɛstɪv/ adj unwilling or unable to keep still: a restive horse –**restively** adv

rest·less /'rɛstlɪs/ adj never quiet; always

moving around: We spent a very restless night. –**restlessly** adv –**restlessness** n [U]

re·stor·a·tive /rɪ'stɔrətɪv, -'sto^wr-/ n,adj fml (a food, medicine, etc) that brings back health and strength

re·store /rɪ'stɔr, rɪ'sto^wr/ v **-stored, -storing** [T] **1** [to] to give or bring back: to restore stolen property |to call in the army to restore law and order/ I feel quite restored (to health) after my vacation. |The Republican Party was restored to power at the election. **2** to put (old buildings, furniture, or works of art) back into the original state –**restoration** /ˌrɛstə'rey^yʃən/ n [C;U]: the restoration of public order after a time of violence |the restoration of a painting/house

re·strain /rɪ'streyn/ v [T from] to control; prevent (from doing something): If you can't restrain your dog (from biting people), you'll have to lock him up

re·strained /rɪ'streynd/ adj calm and controlled; not showing strong feelings –see also UNRESTRAINED

re·straint /rɪ'streynt/ n **1** [U] apprec the quality of being RESTRAINED or RESTRAINING oneself: I think you showed great restraint in not hitting him after what he said. **2** [C] often derog something that RESTRAINs: He hates the restraints of life in a small town.

re·strict /rɪ'strɪkt/ v [T to] to keep within limits: I restrict myself to (smoking) two cigarettes a day. |laws to restrict the sale of alcohol –**restriction** /rɪ'strɪkʃən/ n [C;U]: to be allowed to drink without restriction |the many restrictions of army life

re·strict·ed /rɪ'strɪktɪd/ adj **1** [no comp.] controlled, esp. by law: The sale of alcohol is restricted in some states. **2** [to] for a particular purpose, or for the use of a particular group only: a restricted area, where only the army is allowed to go **3** limited: restricted space in a small house

re·stric·tive /rɪ'strɪktɪv/ adj often derog that RESTRICTs: He finds the job too restrictive. –**restrictively** adv

rest room /'· ·/ n AmE a public TOILET, in a hotel, restaurant, etc.

re·sult¹ /rɪ'zʌlt/ v [I from] to happen as an effect or RESULT² (1): His illness resulted from eating bad food. |He added a chemical to the beer, and the resulting mixture was poisonous.

result in sthg. v prep [T +v-ing; no pass.] to have as a RESULT² (1); cause: The accident resulted in the death of two passengers/in two passengers dying.

re·sult² n **1** [C;U] what happens because of an action or event: His illness is/the result of (eating) bad food. | Your hard work is beginning to show results. (=have a noticeable effect). |He was late **as a result of** (=because of) the snow. **2** [C usu. pl.] (the news of) a person's or team's success or failure in an examination, sports match, etc.: I heard the football results on the radio. |When will you know your examination results? **3** [C] the answer to a sum

re·sult·ant /rɪ'zʌltənt/ adj [A] happening as an effect: The drivers all sounded their horns *and the resultant noise was unbearable.*

re·sume /rɪ'zuʷm/ *v* **-sumed, -suming** *fml* **1** [I;T +*v-ing*] to begin (something, or doing something) again after a pause: *We'll stop now and resume (working) at two o'clock.* **2** [T] to take again: *to resume one's seat* **-resumption** /rɪ'zʌmpʃən/ *n* [U]: *the resumption of business after a holiday*

ré·su·mé, resume /'rɛzə‚meʸ, 'reʸ-, ‚rɛzə 'meʸ, ‚reʸ-/ *n* **1** →SUMMARY **2** *esp. AmE*‖also **curriculum vitae**– a short written account of one's education and past employment, used esp. when looking for a new job

re·sur·gence /rɪ'sɜrdʒəns/ *n* [S;U] a return to power, life, and activity: *(a) resurgence of nationalist feeling* **-resurgent** *adj* [A]

res·ur·rect /‚rɛzə'rɛkt/ *v* [T] to bring back into use, fashion, or attention: *to resurrect an old custom*

res·ur·rec·tion /‚rɛzə'rɛkʃən/ *n* **1** [U] renewal (of life, hope, etc.) **2** [*the S*] (*often cap.*) (in Christian belief) the rising of Christ from his grave

re·sus·ci·tate /rɪ'sʌsə‚teʸt/ *v* **-tated, -tating** [T] to bring back to life: *to try to resuscitate a drowned man* **-resuscitation** /rɪ‚sʌsə'teʸʃən/ *n* [U]

re·tail¹ /'riʸteʸl/ *n* [U] the sale of goods in stores to CUSTOMERs, for their own use, not for resale: *the retail of goods*|*retail prices* –compare WHOLESALE

retail² *adv* by RETAIL¹; from a RETAILER: *to buy it* retail –compare WHOLESALE

re·tail·er /'riʸteʸlər/ *n* someone who sells things by RETAIL¹; shopkeeper

re·tain /rɪ'teʸn/ *v* [T] to keep possession of; avoid losing: *to retain one's balance* |*to retain a lot of facts in one's memory* –see also RETENTION

re·take /‚riʸ'teʸk/ *v* **-took** /'tʊk/, **-taken** /'teʸ kən/, **-taking** [T] to photograph again (esp. a scene in film or television) **-retake** /'riʸteʸk/ *n* : *The third retake was successful.*

re·tal·i·ate /rɪ'tæliʸ‚eʸt/ *v* **-ated, -ating** [I *against, by*] to pay back evil with evil: *Mary kicked Susan, and Susan retaliated (by biting her).* **-retaliation** /rɪ‚tæliʸ'eʸʃən/ *n* [U]

re·tard /rɪ'tɑrd/ *v* [T] *esp. fml or tech* to make slow; cause to happen later: *Cold weather retards the growth of the crops.*

re·tard·ed /rɪ'tɑrdɪd/ *adj* (of a person) less developed in MENTAL ability than others: *Retarded children learn more slowly than others.*|*a home for retarded adults*

retch /rɛtʃ/ *v* [I] to try to be sick (VOMIT) but without success

re·ten·tion /rɪ'tɛnʃən, -tʃən/ *n* [U] the state or action of RETAINING: *the retention of facts in the mind* **-retentive** /rɪ'tɛntɪv/ *adj* : *He has a very retentive memory.* **-retentively** *adv* **-retentiveness** *n* [U]

re·think /‚riʸ'θɪŋk/ *v* **-thought** /'θɔt/, **-thinking** [I;T] to think again; reconsider (a subject): *We'd better rethink the whole plan* **-rethink**

SPELLING NOTE

Words with the sound /r/ may be spelled **wr-**, like **wrong**.

/'riʸθɪŋk/ *n* [S]

ret·i·cent /'rɛtəsənt/ *adj* (of a person or behavior) silent; not saying as much as is known or felt: *She was reticent about her reasons for leaving the job.* **-reticence** *n* [U] **-reticently** *adv*

ret·i·na /'rɛtn-ə/ *n* **-nas** or **-nae** /'rɛtn‚iʸ/ the light-sensitive area of nerve-endings at the back of the eye

ret·i·nue /'rɛtn‚uʷ, -‚yuʷ/ *n* a group of servants and followers traveling with an important person: *The President's retinue is arriving.*

re·tire /rɪ'taɪər/ *v* **-tired, -tiring** **1** [I;T] to (cause to) stop working at one's job, profession, etc., usu. because of age: *My father retired at the age of 60.* **2** [I *from, to*] to go away or back: *The senators retired to the committee-room to make their decision.* **3** [I] *fml* to go to bed

re·tired /rɪ'taɪərd/ *adj* (of a person) having stopped working, usu. because of age: *My father is retired*|*is a retired doctor.*

re·tire·ment /rɪ'taɪərmənt/ *n* **1** [C;U] a case or the act of retiring (RETIRE (1)): *He was given a gold watch on his retirement.* **2** [U] the period after one has RETIRED (1): *He wants to write a book during his retirement.*

re·tir·ing /rɪ'taɪərɪŋ/ *adj* **1** avoiding the company of others: *He has a retiring nature and hates parties.* **2** [A] at which one RETIRES (1): *What's the retiring age for miners?*

re·tort /rɪ'tɔrt/ *v,n* [T +*that*] (to make) a quick, usu. angry or amusing answer: *He retorted that it was all my fault.* –see ANSWER (USAGE)

re·trace /rɪ'treʸs, riʸ-/ *v* **-traced, -tracing** [T] to go over again; go back over: *She retraced her steps* (=went back) *along the path to try to find her lost ring.*

re·tract /rɪ'trækt/ *v* [I;T] **1** to admit that (something one said earlier) should not have been said: *The political prisoner refused to retract (his speeches against the government).* **2** to (cause to) draw back or in: *A cat can retract its CLAWs, but a dog can't.* **-retractable** *adj* **-retraction** /rɪ'trækʃən/ *n* [C;U]

re·treat¹ /rɪ'triʸt/ *v* [I *from, to*] (esp. of an army) to move away; go back, esp. when forced to do so: *The defeated army had to retreat hastily (from the field of battle).* –compare ADVANCE¹ (1)

retreat² *n* **1** [C;U *from, to*] (an act of) RETREATING: *Napoleon's retreat from Moscow* **2** [S] a military signal for RETREATing: *to sound the retreat by beating a drum* **3** [C] a place into which one can go for peace and safety

re·tri·al /'riʸ‚traɪəl/ *n* an act of trying a law case again: *to demand a retrial*

ret·ri·bu·tion /‚rɛtrə'byuʷʃən/ *n* [S;U *for*] *fml* (a) deserved punishment: *Do evil actions bring retribution after death?*

re·trieve /rɪ'triʸv/ *v* **-trieved, -trieving** [T *from*] to regain; find and bring back: *I ran back to retrieve the bag I had left in the train*|*to retrieve information from a computer system.* **-retrieval** *n* [U]

ret·ro·grade /'rɛtrə‚greʸd/ *adj* moving back

James and Maria decided to **eat out** tonight. Maria called a nearby restaurant to **make a reservation.**

When they got to the restaurant, they were **seated** at a table and their **waiter** brought them **drinks** and gave them **menus.** Later the waiter came back to **take their orders.**

WAITER: Are you ready **to order** now?
MARIA: Yes. **I'd like** the roast chicken.
JAMES: And **I'll have** the broiled fish. Could we see the **wine list,** please?
MARIA: Oh, and could you bring us some water?
WAITER: Of course.

After they had eaten, the waiter brought the **check.**

JAMES: Do you take **credit cards?**
WAITER: No, sir, we don't. But you can **pay by check.**
JAMES: That's all right. We'll **pay cash.**

James and Maria **paid the check** and decided to leave the waiter a good **tip** because the **service** had been excellent.

JAMES: I like this place a lot.
MARIA: Me too. Let's come back soon.

towards an earlier and worse state

ret·ro·gress /ˌrɛtrəˈgrɛs/ v [I *to*] *esp. fml or tech* to go back (to an earlier and worse state) –**retrogression** /ˌrɛtrəˈgrɛʃən/ n [U]

ret·ro·spect /ˈrɛtrəˌspɛkt/ n [U] the act of looking back towards the past: *One's school life seems happier* **in retrospect** *than it really was.*

re·tro·spec·tive /ˌrɛtrəˈspɛktɪv/ adj concerned with the past: *retrospective thoughts*

re·turn¹ /rɪˈtɜrn/ v **1** [I *from, to*] to come or go back: *to return home* | *to return to Washington* | *What time does your husband return (from work)?* | *The temperature soon returned to the seasonal average.* | *Let's return to the subject of my vacation.* **2** [I] to give, put, or send back: *Don't forget to return my keys (to me).* | *We returned the empty bottles (to the store).* | *He returned the gun to his pocket.* **3** [I] to happen again: *Spring will soon return.* **4** [T] to state officially, esp. in answer to a demand: *The* JURY *returned a* VERDICT (=gave a judgment) *of "Not Guilty."* **5 return a favor** to do a kind action in return for another

return² n **1** [C *from, to*] an act of RETURNing¹ (1): *We look forward to your return (from China).* | *On his return he found her asleep.* **2** [U] the act of RETURNing¹ (2) something: *The library is demanding the return of the books.* **3** [C *of*] a case of happening again: *the return of spring* **4** [C *often pl.*] a profit: *These shares bring in a good return/good returns.* **5** [C] an official statement or set of figures given in answer to a demand: *a tax return* **6 by return (of mail)** by the next mail **7 in return (for)** in exchange (for); in payment (for): *He gave her some roses in return for her kindness.*

return³ adj BrE for ROUND TRIP: *a return ticket*

re·turn·a·ble /rɪˈtɜrnəbəl/ adj that must or can be given or sent back: *returnable bottles*

re·un·ion /riˈyuʷnyən/ n **1** [U] the state of being together again **2** [C] a meeting of friends after a separation: *to hold a reunion of former students of the college*

re·u·nite /ˌriʸyuʷˈnaɪt/ v -**nited, -niting** [I;T *with*] to (cause to) come or join together again: *After the war, the soldiers were reunited with their families.*

rev¹ /rɛv/ n *infml* for REVOLUTION (4)

rev² v -**vv-** [T *up*] *infml* to increase the speed of (an engine): *Don't rev (up) your engine so loudly.*

Rev. *written abbrev. said as:* REVEREND: *the Rev. J. Jeffrey*

re·val·ue /riʸˈvælyuʷ/ v -**ued, -uing** to increase the exchange value of a country's money: *to revalue the dollar* –see also DEVALUE (1) –**revaluation** /riʸˌvælyuʷˈeʸʃən/ n [C;U]

re·veal /rɪˈviʸl/ v [T] **1** to allow to be seen: *The curtains opened, to reveal a darkened stage.* **2** [+ *that*] to make known: *She suddenly revealed (the fact) that she was not married.*

re·veal·ing /rɪˈviʸlɪŋ/ adj allowing something to be seen or known: *a very revealing dress* | *revealing remarks*

rev·eil·le /ˈrɛvəliʸ/ n [S] music played as a signal to waken soldiers in the morning

rev·el /ˈrɛvəl/ v **-l-** AmE‖**-ll-** BrE [I] *old use or humor* to pass the time in dancing, feasting, etc.: *They were drinking and reveling all night.* –**reveler** AmE‖**reveller** BrE n

revel in sthg. v prep [T +v-*ing*] to enjoy greatly: *She revels in hearing about my difficulties.*

rev·e·la·tion /ˌrɛvəˈleʸʃən/ n **1** [U *of*] the making known (of something secret) **2** [C] a (surprising) fact that is made known: *We listened to her strange revelations about her past.*

rev·el·ry /ˈrɛvəlriʸ/ n [U] wild noisy dancing and feasting; REVELing

re·venge¹ /rɪˈvɛndʒ/ v -**venged, -venging** [T] **1** to do something in REVENGE² for (some harm done to oneself): *to revenge an injustice* **2** to do something in REVENGE² for harm done to: *Hamlet revenged his dead father.* (=killed the man who killed him)

USAGE **Revenge** and **avenge** are very similar in meaning, but to **avenge** or **take vengeance** suggests the idea of correcting an injustice, while to **revenge** or **take revenge** suggests satisfying the desire to harm someone who has harmed you.

revenge² n [S;U *for, on*] (a) punishment given to someone in return for harm done to oneself: *The village was bombed* **in revenge for** *protecting enemy soldiers.*

rev·e·nue /ˈrɛvəˌnuʷ, -ˌnyuʷ/ n [U] income, esp. that which the government receives as tax

re·ver·ber·ate /rɪˈvɜrbəˌreʸt/ v -**ated, -ating** [I] (of sound) to be thrown back again and again: ECHO² repeatedly: *The thunder reverberated across the valley.* –**reverberation** /rɪˌvɜrbəˈreʸʃən/ n [C;U]

re·vere /rɪˈvɪər/ v -**vered, -vering** [T] *fml* to give great respect and admiration to: *She revered her father all her life.*

Rev·er·end /ˈrɛvərənd/ n [A;S] (a title of respect for) a CLERGYMAN (=a Christian religious leader): *(The) Reverend Donald Jones*

rev·er·ent /ˈrɛvərənt/ adj having or showing a feeling of great respect or admiration: *He spoke in a quiet, reverent voice* –opposite **irreverent** –**reverence** n [S;U *for*] –**reverently** adv

rev·er·ie /ˈrɛvəriʸ/ n [C;U *about*] (a state of) pleasant thoughts and dreams while awake: *She fell into a reverie about the past.*

re·ver·sal /rɪˈvɜrsəl/ n [C;U *of*] (a case of) being REVERSEd² (2,3): *He suffered a reversal of fortune and lost all his money.*

re·verse¹ /rɪˈvɜrs/ adj [A] opposite in position; back; being the REVERSE³ (1): *the reverse side of the cloth* | *Please read the names on the list* **in reverse order**. (=from the end to the beginning)

reverse² v -**versed, -versing 1** [I;T] to (cause to) go backwards: *He reversed the car through the gate.* | *The car reversed through* the gate. **2** [T] to change (a direction or judgment) to the opposite: *He reversed the court's judgment and set the prisoner free.* **3** [T] to change around (proper order or positions): *Today we'll reverse the usual order of the lesson and start with a written exercise.* **4** **reverse the charges**‖also **call collect** *AmE*– to make a telephone call to be paid for by the person receiving it –**reversible** *adj: This coat is reversible; you can wear it inside out.*

reverse³ *n* **1** [*the* U *of*] the opposite: *He did the reverse of what we expected; instead of being angry, he bought us a drink.* **2** [U] also **reverse gear**– the position of the controls that causes backward movement, esp. in a car: *Put the car in reverse.*

re·vert to sbdy./sthg. /rɪˈvɜrt/ *v prep* [T] **1** [+*v-ing*] to go back to (a former condition, habit, subject of conversation): *He's stopped taking drugs now, but he may revert to taking them again.* **2** *law* (of property) to go back to (an owner) –**reversion** /rɪˈvɜrʒən/ *n* [U *to*]: *reversion to bad habits*

re·view¹ /rɪˈvyuʷ/ *n* **1** an act of REVIEWing² (1): *After a careful review of political events, he decided not to vote at all.* **2** a magazine or newspaper article giving judgments on a new book, play, television show, etc. **3** a show of the armed forces, in the presence of a king or an important general: *a naval review* **4** **be/come under review** to be/start to be considered with a view to possible changes: *The company's wage system is coming under review.*

review² *v* **1** [T] to consider and judge (an event or state of affairs); go over again in the mind: *The government is reviewing its education policy.* **2** [I;T] to write a REVIEW¹ (2) of (a play, book, etc.): *The play was well-reviewed* (=was praised) *in all the newspapers.* **3** [I;T] *AmE*‖**revise** *BrE*– to study again (lessons already learned): *I should review for tomorrow's exam.*

re·view·er /rɪˈvyuʷər/ *n* a person who REVIEWs² (2) plays, books, etc.

re·vile /rɪˈvaɪl/ *v* **-viled, -viling** [T] *fml* to curse; speak very strongly and angrily to or of

re·vise /rɪˈvaɪz/ *v* **-vised, -vising 1** [T] to read through (a piece of writing) carefully, making improvements and correcting mistakes **2** [T] to change (opinions, intentions, etc.) because of new information or more thought **3** [I;T] *BrE* for REVIEW² (3)

re·vi·sion /rɪˈvɪʒən/ *n* **1** [C;U] (an act of) revising (REVISE¹ (1)) **2** [C] a piece of writing that has been REVISEd¹ (1)

re·vi·tal·ize ‖also **-ise** *BrE* /riʸˈvaɪtl̩ˌaɪz/ *v* **-ized, -izing** [T] to put new strength or power into –**revitalization** /riʸˌvaɪtl-əˈzeʸʃən/ *n* [U]

re·viv·al /rɪˈvaɪvəl/ *n* **1** [C;U *of*] (a) rebirth or renewal; reviving or being REVIVEd: *There has been a/some revival of interest in the fashions of the 1930's.* **2** [C] a new performance of an old play after many years **3** [C] **a** a renewal of religious spirit **b** in some churches, a set of special services intended to bring this about: *We had a revival at our church last week.*

re·vive /rɪˈvaɪv/ *v* **-vived, -viving** [I;T] **1** to make or become conscious or healthy again: *That rose will revive if you water it.* **2** to bring or come back into use or existence: *to revive an old custom*

re·voke /rɪˈvoʷk/ *v* **-voked, -voking** [T] to put an end to (a law, decision, permission, etc.); CANCEL (1)

re·volt¹ /rɪˈvoʷlt/ *v* **1** [I *against*] to act violently against those in power: *The people revolted against the military government.* **2** [T] to shock; cause (someone) to feel violent dislike and sickness: *Such cruelty revolted him.* –see also REVULSION; compare DISGUST

revolt² *n* [C;U *against*] (an example of) the act of REVOLTing¹ (1): *The whole nation is in (a state of) revolt.*

re·volt·ing /rɪˈvoʷltɪŋ/ *adj* very nasty and unpleasant: *a revolting smell of bad eggs* –**revoltingly** *adv*

rev·o·lu·tion /ˌrɛvəˈluʷʃən/ *n* **1** [C;U] (a time of) great social change, esp. the changing of a ruler and/or political system by force: *the Russian revolution.* –compare REBELLION **2** [C *in*] a complete change (in ways of thinking or acting): *The invention of air travel caused a revolution in our way of living*‖*the computer revolution* **3** [C;U] (one complete) circular movement around a fixed point: *The earth makes one complete revolution around the sun each year.* **4** [C] also **rev** *infml*– (in a machine) one complete circular movement on a central point, as of a wheel: *a speed of 100 revolutions per minute* –see also REVOLVE

rev·o·lu·tion·ar·y¹ /ˌrɛvəˈluʷʃəˌnɛriʸ/ *adj* **1** [A *no comp.*] connected with (a) REVOLUTION (1): *a revolutionary leader* **2** completely new and different; being a REVOLUTION (2): *a revolutionary new way of growing rice*

revolutionary² *n* **-ies** a person who favors or joins in a REVOLUTION (1)

rev·o·lu·tion·ize ‖also **-ise** *BrE* /ˌrɛvəˈluʷʃəˌnaɪz/ *v* **-ized, -izing** [T] to cause a complete change in; cause a REVOLUTION (2) in: *The discovery of the new drug has revolutionized the treatment of many diseases.*

re·volve /rɪˈvalv/ *v* **-volved, -volving** [I;T *on, around*] to (cause to) spin around (on a central point); make REVOLUTIONs (4): *The wheels began to revolve slowly.*‖*The earth revolves around the sun once a year.*‖*revolving doors*

revolve around sbdy./sthg. *v prep* [T not *be* +*v-ing; no pass.*] to have as a center or main subject: *A baby's life revolves mainly around its mother and father.*

re·volv·er /rɪˈvalvər/ *n* a type of small gun (PISTOL)

re·vue /rɪˈvyuʷ/ *n* a light theatrical show with songs, dances, and jokes, esp. about the events and fashions of the present time

re·vul·sion /rɪˈvʌlʃən/ *n* [S;U *against*] (a) feeling of being shocked and REVOLTed¹ (2): *We looked away in revulsion from the scene of the accident.*

re·ward¹ /rɪˈwɔrd/ *v* [T *for, with*] to give a REWARD to (someone): *He rewarded the boy (for bringing back the lost dog).*‖*How can I reward you for all your help?*

reward² *n* [C;U *for*] (something given or gained as) return for work or service: *She got nothing* **in reward** *(for her kindness).|The police are offering a reward for information about the robbery.*

re·ward·ing /rɪˈwɔrdɪŋ/ *adj* (of an experience or action) worth doing or having; WORTH- WHILE: *Nursing can be a very rewarding job.* –opposite **unrewarding**

re·wire /ˌriʸˈwaɪər/ *v* **-wired, -wiring** [T] to put new electric wires into (a building)

re·write /ˌriʸˈraɪt/ *v* **-wrote** /ˈroʷt/, **-written** /ˈrɪtn/, **-writing** [T] to write again in a different, esp. more suitable, way

rhap·so·dy /ˈræpsədiʸ/ *n* **-dies** [*about, over*] an expression of (too) great praise and wild excitement: *Mother* **went into a rhapsody** *over the beauty of the scene.*

rhet·o·ric /ˈretərɪk/ *n* [U] **1** the art of speaking or writing so as to persuade people effectively **2** *derog* speech or writing that sounds fine and important, but is really insincere or without meaning **–rhetorical** /rɪˈtɔrɪkəl, -ˈtɑr-/ *adj* [A] **–rhetorically** *adv*

rhe·tor·i·cal ques·tion /ˌ·,··· ˈ·· ·/ *n* a question asked only for effect, and not expecting any answer

rheu·mat·ic /ruʷˈmætɪk/ *adj* connected with or having RHEUMATISM: *a rheumatic condition of the joints |a rheumatic old woman*

rheu·ma·tism /ˈruʷmə,tɪzəm/ *n* [U] a disease causing pain and stiffness in the joints or muscles

rhi·noc·er·os /raɪˈnɑsərəs/ also **rhino** /ˈraɪnoʷ/ *infml– n* **-oses** *or* **-os** a large, heavy, thick-skinned animal of Africa or Asia, with either one or two horns on its nose

rho·do·den·dron /ˌroʷdəˈdendrən/ *n* a bush that is grown for its large bright flowers, and keeps its leaves in winter (is EVERGREEN)

rhu·barb /ˈruʷbɑrb/ *n* [U] a broad-leaved garden plant whose thick juicy stems are boiled with sugar and eaten

rhyme¹ /raɪm/ *n* **1** a word that RHYMES² with another: *"Bold" and "cold" are rhymes.* **2** [U] the use of words that RHYME² in poetry: *Shakespeare sometimes wrote in rhyme.* **3** [C] a short and not serious piece of writing, using words that RHYME² **4** **rhyme or reason** (only used in NEGATIVES², questions, etc.) any sense or meaning: *There doesn't seem to be (any) rhyme or reason in his actions. Is he crazy?*

rhyme² *v* **rhymed, rhyming** [I *with*; not *be* + *v-ing*] (of words or lines of poetry) to end with the same sound (as another word, or as each other): *"House" rhymes with "mouse."|The last two lines of this poem don't rhyme very well.*

rhythm /ˈrɪðəm/ *n* [C;U] (a) regular, repeated pattern of sounds or movements in speech, dancing, music, etc.: *the exciting rhythms of African drum music|*(fig.) *the rhythm of the seasons*

SPELLING NOTE

Words with the sound /r/ may be spelled **wr-**, like **wrong**.

rhyth·mic /ˈrɪðmɪk/ *adj* having RHYTHM: *the rhythmic beating of one's heart* **–rhyth- mically** *adv*

RI , R.I. *written abbrev. said as:* Rhode Island /ˌroʷd ˈaɪlənd/ (a state in the US)

rib¹ /rɪb/ *n* one of the 12 pairs of bones running around the chest of a person or animal, from the SPINE to where they join at the front

rib² *v* **-bb-** [T] *infml* to make fun of (someone) in a friendly way: *All the boys ribbed him for keeping a pet pig.*

rib·ald /ˈrɪbəld/ *adj* humorously rude and disrespectful: *ribald jokes|a crowd of ribald soldiers* **–ribaldry** /ˈrɪbəldriʸ/ *n* [U]

rib·bon /ˈrɪbən/ *n* [C;U] (a piece of) silk or other cloth woven in a long narrow band and used for tying the hair, for decoration, etc.: *a black* TYPEWRITER *ribbon*

rib cage /ˈ· ·/ *n* the wall of RIBs that encloses and protects the lungs

rice /raɪs/ *n* [U] (the seeds of) a food grain grown in wet tropical places, esp. in India and China: *Would you like rice with your meat?|Rice pudding is a sweet dish made by baking rice with milk and sugar.*

rich /rɪtʃ/ *adj* **1** (of a person) wealthy; possessing a lot of money or property –compare POOR (1) **2** [F *in*] containing a lot of a certain thing: *This fish is rich in oil.* **3** (of possessions) costly, valuable, and beautiful: *rich silk|furniture* **4** (of food) containing a lot of cream, sugar, eggs, etc.: *a very rich Christmas cake* **5** (of land) good for growing plants in: *rich soil* –opposite **poor** **6** (of a sound or color) deep and strong: *the rich notes of the church* ORGAN (3)*|a rich dark red* **–richness** *n* [U]

rich·es /ˈrɪtʃɪz/ *n* [P] *lit* wealth: *All his riches are no good to him if he is so ill.*

rich·ly /ˈrɪtʃliʸ/ *adv* splendidly; in a large quantity: *a dress richly ornamented with jewels|You* **richly** (=fully) **deserve** *to be punished.*

rick /rɪk/ *n* a large pile of wheat stems (STRAW), dried grass (HAY), or wood for burning

rick·et·y /ˈrɪkətiʸ/ *adj* weakly joined and likely to break: *a rickety old cart*

rick·shaw, -sha /ˈrɪkʃɔ/ *n* a small vehicle used in East Asia for carrying one or two passengers and powered by a man either pulling or cycling

ric·o·chet /ˈrɪkə,ʃeʸ/ *v* **-cheted** /,ʃeʸd/, **-cheting** /,ʃeʸɪŋ/ [I *off*] (of a stone, bullet, etc.) to change direction when it hits a surface at an angle: *The bullet ricocheted off the bridge.*

rid /rɪd/ *v* → RID OF

rid·dance /ˈrɪdns/ *n* **Good riddance!** (said when one is glad that someone or something has gone) –see also RID OF

rid·dle /ˈrɪdl/ *n* a difficult and amusing question to which one must guess the answer: (fig.) *Robert's character is a complete riddle* (=mystery) *to me.*

riddle sbdy./sthg. **with** sthg. *v, prep* **-dled, -dling** [T *often pass.*] to make full of (holes): *The tent's riddled with holes.|Don't move or I'll riddle you with bullets!*

ride¹ /raɪd/ *v* **rode** /roʷd/, **ridden** /ˈrɪdn/, **rid-**

ing 1 [I;T] to travel along, sitting on and controlling (a horse, or other animal, a bicycle, or a motorcycle): *Can you ride a bicycle?|We rode across the fields.|He got on his bicycle and rode off down the road.|The king rode on an elephant.|Alison is learning to ride.* (=ride a horse) –compare DRIVE 2 [I *in*] to be carried along sitting in a vehicle not controlled by oneself: *She gets sick when she rides in a bus.* **3** *infml esp. AmE* to cause intentional and continual difficulty to; annoy: *Leave him alone and stop riding him; he's doing his best.* **4** *infml* **let something ride** to let something continue; take no action about something

ride out sthg. *v adv* [T] to come safely through (bad weather, trouble, difficult times, etc.): *to ride out the storm/the* RECESSION

ride up *v adv* [I] (of clothing) to move upwards or out of place: *Her tight skirt rides up when she sits down.*

ride² *n* **1** a journey on an animal, in a vehicle, etc., esp. for pleasure: *Shall we go for a ride in the car?|Could you give me a ride to the post office?* –compare DRIVE **2 take someone for a ride** *infml* to deceive someone

rid·er /ˈraɪdər/ *n* a person who rides esp. a horse

ridge /rɪdʒ/ *n* a long narrow raised part of any surface, such as the top of a range of mountains or of a sloping roof where the two sloping surfaces meet: *He walked along the mountain ridge/sat on the ridge of the roof.*

rid·i·cule¹ /ˈrɪdə,kjuʷl/ *n* [U] unkind laughter; being made fun of: *His behavior deserves ridicule rather than blame.*

ridicule² *v* **-culed, -culing** [T] to laugh unkindly at; make unkind fun of: *They all ridiculed the idea.*

ri·dic·u·lous /rɪˈdɪkyələs/ *adj derog* silly; deserving RIDICULE¹: *She looks ridiculous in those tight pants.* **–ridiculously** *adv* : *The examination was ridiculously easy.* **–ridiculousness** *n* [U]

rid·ing /ˈraɪdɪŋ/ *n* [U] the skill or exercise of traveling on a horse: *a riding lesson*

rid sbdy./sthg. **of** sbdy./sthg. *v prep* **rid of** *or* **ridded of, ridding of** [T] **1** to make free of: *You must rid yourself of these old-fashioned ideas.|He's gone, and I'm glad to be rid of him.* (=to be free of him again) **2 get rid of: a** to free oneself from (something unwanted): *Try to get rid of your bad cold.* **b** to drive, throw, or give away or destroy: *How can I get rid of the flies in the kitchen?*

rife /raɪf/ *adj* [F] *esp. lit* **1** (of bad things) widespread; common: *Disease and violence were rife in the city.* **2** [*with*] full (of bad things): *The city was rife with disease and violence.*

ri·fle¹ /ˈraɪfəl/ *n* a long-barreled gun fired from the shoulder

rifle² *v* **-fled, -fling** [T] to search through and steal everything valuable out of (a place): *Somebody has been rifling my drawers.*

rift /rɪft/ *n* [*between, in*] *fml & lit* a crack; narrow opening made by breaking: *The sun appeared through a rift in the clouds.|*(fig.)

The argument caused a rift between the two friends.

rig¹ /rɪg/ *v* **-gg-** [T] to provide (a ship) with the necessary ropes, sails, etc.: *a fully-rigged vessel*

rig sthg. ↔ **up** *v adv* [T] *infml* to put together for a short time out of materials easily found: *Let's try to rig up some sort of shelter.*

rig² *n* **1** the way a ship's sails are arranged: *Judging by its rig, I'd say it was a fishing boat.* **2** a piece of apparatus (for the stated purpose): *They built an* OIL RIG *to get the oil out of the ground.*

rig³ *v* **-gg-** [T] to arrange (an event) dishonestly for one's own advantage: *They complained that the election was rigged.*

rig·ging /ˈrɪgɪŋ/ *n* [*the* U] all the ropes, sails on a ship: *The ship lost most of her rigging in the storm.*

right¹ /raɪt/ *adj* **1** [A] on or belonging to the side of the body that does not contain the heart: *Most people write with their right hand.* **2** [A] on, by, or in the direction of this side: *a right turn, not a left turn* –opposite **left**

right² *n* **1** [U] the RIGHT¹ (1) side or direction: *Keep to the right!| Take the second turn on the right.* **2** [C] the right hand: *Hit him with your right.* **3** [U] (*often cap.*) political parties or groups (such as the REPUBLICAN party) that favor fewer political changes and less state control, and generally support business or those in official positions rather than the workers: *The right opposes the new taxes.|a new party of the far Right* –compare LEFT²

right³ *adj* **1** [F +*to-v*] just; morally good: *I'll try to do whatever is right.|It's not right, in fact it's wrong, to tell lies.|I was right in selling/right to sell the farm.* **2** correct; true: *Is that the right time?|"Is this Times Square?" "Yes, that's right."* –opposite **wrong 3 in one's right mind** altogether sensible; not mad or crazy: *She's not in her right mind if she thinks she's going to win this game.* **–rightness** *n* [U]

right⁴ *n* **1** [U] what is RIGHT³ (1): *She's old enough to know the difference between right and wrong.* **2** [S;U *of, to*] (a) morally just or lawful claim: *She has a right/has no right to say that.|You have the right to remain silent.|She has the/the right to half your money.|She is American by right of marriage.* **3 in one's own right** because of a personal claim that does not depend on anyone else: *The First Lady is respected in her own right.* (=not because she is married to the President) **4 in the right** having justice on one's side –opposite **in the wrong** –see also RIGHTS

right⁵ *adv* **1** towards the RIGHT² (1): *He turned right.* –opposite **left 2** [*adv + adv/prep*] *infml* exactly: *right now|right in the middle|He's right here.* **3** [*adv +adv/prep*] directly; completely: *right after breakfast|right in front of you|Go right back to the beginning.|I'll be right over.* **4** properly; correctly: *to guess right|Did I do it right?* –opposite **wrong 5** Yes; I agree: *"You're coming tomorrow aren't you?" "Right. What time are you expecting me?"* **6 right away** at once; without delay **7 right on** *infml* an expression used as an encouragement to a speaker

right⁶ *v* [T] to put (something) right or upright again: *The cat righted itself during the fall, and landed on its feet.*

right an·gle /ˌ· '··/ *n* an angle of 90 degrees, as at any of the four corners of a square –**right-angled** /ˌ· '··◄/ *adj*

right·eous /'raɪtʃəs/ *adj* [no comp.] *lit & bibl* **1** (doing what is) lawful and morally good: *a righteous man*|*"I never drink or smoke," he said in a righteous voice.* **2** (of feelings) having good or just cause: *righteous anger* –**righteously** *adv* –**righteousness** *n* [U]

right·ful /'raɪtfəl/ *adj* [A] lawful; according to a just claim: *Who is the rightful owner of this car?* –**rightfully** *adv* –**rightfulness** *n* [U]

right-hand /'· ·/ *adj* [A] **1** on or to the right side: *Make a right-hand turn.* **2** of, for, with, or done by the right hand –opposite **left-hand 3 someone's right-hand man** a person's most useful and valuable helper

right-hand·ed /ˌ· '··◄/ *adj* using the right hand for most actions rather than the left: *Most people are right-handed.* –opposite **left-handed**

right·ly /'raɪtliʸ/ *adv* correctly; truly; justly: *He believed,* **rightly or wrongly,** *that she was guilty.*

right of way /ˌ· ·· '·/ *n* **rights of way 1** [C] *law* a right to follow a path across someone else's land: *We have a right of way across his field to our house.* **2** [the U] the right of traffic to drive, cross, pass, etc., before other vehicles

rights /raɪts/ *n* [P] **1** the political, social, etc., advantages to which someone has a just claim, morally or in law: *to fight for women's rights* **2 by rights** in justice; if things were done properly: *I shouldn't by rights be at this party at all; I should be studying tonight.* **3 within one's rights** not going beyond one's just claims: *You'd be within your rights to refuse to work on Sunday.*

right wing /ˌ· '·◄/ *adj,n* [U] (the members) of a political party (esp. a REPUBLICAN party) or group, favoring fewer political changes, CAPITALISM, etc.: *a right wing politician*|*The right wing of the party is opposed to this plan.* –opposite **left wing**; compare FASCIST, RIGHT² (3)

rig·id /'rɪdʒɪd/ *adj* stiff; not easy to bend: *a tent supported on a rigid framework*|*She was rigid with fear.*|(fig.) *He's very rigid in his ideas on marriage.* –**rigidly** *adv* –**rigidity** /rɪ'dʒɪdətiʸ/ *n* [U]

rig·ma·role /'rɪgmə,roʷl/ also **rigamarole** /'rɪgəmə,roʷl/– *n* [S;U] *infml derog* a long meaningless story or set of actions: *He had to go through all the rigmarole of swearing in front of the judge and kissing the Bible.*

rig·or *AmE*||**-our** *BrE* /'rɪgər/ *n* [U] **1** hardness; lack of mercy: *He deserves to be punished with the full rigor of the law.* **2**

---

severe conditions: *the rigor(s) of a Canadian winter*

rig·or mor·tis /ˌrɪgər 'mɔrtɪs/ *n* [U] *Latin* the stiffening of the muscles after death

rig·or·ous /'rɪgərəs/ *adj* **1** careful and thorough: *The new cars are given rigorous safety checks.* **2** severe; painful: *the rigorous hardships of the journey* –**rigorously** *adv*

rile /raɪl/ *v* **riled, riling** [T] *infml* up to annoy; make angry: *It riles me when he makes stupid remarks.*|*Talk to him gently or he'll get riled up.*

rim /rɪm/ *n* **1** the outside edge or border of esp. a round or circular object: *the rim of a cup*|*of a wheel* **2 -rimmed** having a rim or rims of: *horn-rimmed glasses* –**rimless** *adj* : *She wore rimless glasses.*

rind /raɪnd/ *n* [C;U] the thick, sometimes hard, outer covering of certain foods or fruits, esp. of BACON and MELONS *a piece of* BACON *rind*|*cheese rind*|*This cheese has a very thick rind.*

USAGE The skin of the orange, grapefruit and lemon can be called either **rind** or **peel**. When used in cooking, they are usu. called **peel**.

ring¹ /rɪŋ/ *n* **1** [C] a circular band, esp. one worn on the finger: *She wears a gold wedding ring to show that she's married.*|*rings of oil around a wrecked ship*|*the rings of the* PLANET *Saturn* | *A key ring is for carrying keys on.* **2** [C] a circular line, mark, or arrangement: *children dancing in a ring*|*count the rings of a tree when it is cut across* **3** [the S] any closed-in central space where performances take place, as in a CIRCUS (1,2) or for BOXING **4** [C] a group of people who work together, esp. dishonestly, to control business affairs for their own advantage: *a drug ring* **5 run rings around someone** to do things much better and faster than someone

ring² *v* **ringed, ringing** [T *with*] to make, put, or be a ring round: *Police ringed the building.*

ring³ *v* **rang** /ræŋ/, **rung** /rʌŋ/, **ringing 1** [T] to cause (a bell) to sound: *The cyclist rang his bell loudly.*|*Ring the bell for* (=to call) *your secretary.* **2** [I] (of a bell, telephone, etc.) to sound: *The telephone's ringing.*|*The bell rang loudly.* **3** [I *for*] to ring a bell as a sign that one wants something: *She rang for a drink.* **4** [I *with*] (of the ears) to be filled with a continuous sound: *The crash really made my ears ring.*| **5 ring a bell** *infml* to remind one of something **6 ring false/true** to sound untrue/true; *It was a clear excuse, but it didn't really ring true.* **7** [I;T *up*] *BrE* for CALL¹ (5)

ring off *v adv* [I] *BrE* for HANG up: *I'd better ring off now; the baby's crying.*

ring out *v adv* [I] (of a voice, bell, etc.) to sound loudly and clearly: *A loud shot rang out.*

ring sthg.↔ **up** *v adv* [T] to calculate and record the amount of a sale on a CASH REGISTER: *Could you ring up the milk and eggs and tell me how much they cost?*

ring⁴ *n* **1** [C;S] (an act of making) the sound of a bell: *He gave several loud rings at the door.*

2 [S] a quality: *Her story had a ring of truth about it.* **3 give someone a ring** to telephone someone: *I'll give you a ring tonight.* –see TELEPHONE (USAGE)

ring·lead·er /'rɪŋ,liʸdər/ n a person who leads others to do wrong or make trouble

ring·let /'rɪŋlɪt/ n a long hanging curl of hair

ring·mas·ter /'rɪŋ,mæstər/ n a person, esp. a man, whose job is directing performances in the CIRCUS (1,2) ring

ring road /'· ·/ n BrE for BELTWAY

ring·side /'rɪŋsaɪd/ adj,n [A] (at) the edge of a RING¹ (3) where things are happening: *We had ringside seats for the big fight and saw it all.*

rink /rɪŋk/ n a specially prepared surface, either of ice, or of any hard material, for skating (SKATE) on

rinse¹ /rɪns/ v **rinsed, rinsing** [T *out*] **1** to wash (esp. clothes) in clean water so as to take away soap, dirt, etc.: *I'll just rinse (out) these shirts.|Rinse your mouth (out).* **2** to wash (soap, dirt, etc.) out (of something) with clean water: *Rinse the soap out of these shirts/your hair.*

rinse² n **1** [C] an act of rinsing (RINSE¹): *Give the shirts at least three rinses.* **2** [C;U] (a) liquid for coloring the hair: *a (bottle of) blue rinse for gray hair*

ri·ot¹ /'raɪət/ n **1** [C] a lot of violent actions, noisy behavior, etc., by a number of people together: *The army was called in to* PUT **down** (1) *a riot.|The football players* **ran riot** (=became violent and uncontrollable) *after the defeat of their team.* **2** [S] *infml* a very funny and successful occasion or person: *I hear the new show is a riot; let's go and see it!*

riot² v [I] to take part in a RIOT¹ (1): *The crowds are rioting for more pay/rioting against the government.* –**rioter** n: *The government called in troops against the rioters.*

ri·ot·ous /'raɪətəs/ adj **1** (of people or behavior) wild and disorderly: *a riotous crowd* **2** *apprec* (of an occasion) noisy and exciting: *They spent a riotous night drinking and singing.* –**riotously** adv

rip¹ /rɪp/ v **-pp-** [I;T] to tear or be torn quickly and violently: *The sail ripped under the force of the wind.|He ripped the cloth with his knife.|I ripped the letter open.*

rip into sbdy. v prep [T] to scold severely: *The employer ripped into his secretary when she forgot to give him a message.*

rip sbdy./sthg.↔ **off** v adv [T] *infml* **1** to charge (someone) too much: *They really ripped us off at that hotel.* **2** to steal: *Someone's ripped off my car!* –see also RIP-OFF

rip sthg.↔ **up** v adv [T] to tear violently into pieces: *She ripped the letter up angrily.*

rip² n a long tear or cut: *a rip in the shirt*

RIP /,ɑr aɪ 'piʸ/ abbrev. for: rest in peace (written on gravestones)

rip·cord /'rɪpkɔrd/ n the cord that one pulls to open a PARACHUTE after jumping from an aircraft

ripe /raɪp/ adj **1** (of fruit and crops) fully grown and ready to be eaten: *a field of ripe corn* –opposite **unripe 2** (esp. of cheese) old

enough to be eaten **3** [F *for; no comp.*] ready for; fit for: *land ripe for industrial development|I won't tell her the news until* **the time is ripe.** (=it is a suitable time) –**ripeness** n

rip·en /'raɪpən/ v [I;T] to make or become ripe: *The sun ripens the corn.|The corn ripens in the sun.*

rip-off /'· ·/ n *infml* an act of charging too much –see also RIP **off**

rip·ple¹ /'rɪpəl/ v **-pled, -pling 1** [I;T] to (cause to) move in RIPPLES² (1): *The wind rippled the surface of the cornfield.* **2** [I] to make a sound like gently running water: *a rippling stream*

ripple² n **1** [C] a very small wave; gentle waving movement: *ripples on a pool when the wind blows* **2** [S] a sound of or like gently running water: *I heard the ripple of the stream.*

rise¹ /raɪz/ v **rose** /roʷz/, **risen** /'rɪzən/, **rising** [I] **1** to go up; get higher: *The river is rising after the rains.|Smoke rose from the factory chimneys.|Her voice rose higher and higher with excitement.|The price of bread has risen by 15%.|The road rises steeply from the village.|He rose to an important position in the firm.|My spirits rose* (=I became happier) *when I heard the news.* –opposite **fall 2** (of the sun, moon, or stars) to come up; appear above the horizon: *The sun rises in the east.* –opposite **set 3** *fml* to get out of bed; get up: *She rises before it is light.* **4** also **arise** *fml*– to stand up from lying, kneeling, or sitting: *She rose to greet her guests.* **5** to show above the surroundings: *trees rising over the roof-tops* **6** (of wind or storms) to get stronger **7** (esp. of a river) to begin: *The Rhine River rises in Switzerland.|The argument rose from/out of a misunderstanding.* **8** to come up to the surface of a liquid: *The bubbles rose to the top of the lake.* **9** (of unbaked bread) to swell as the YEAST works: *The bread won't rise quickly if the room is too cold.* **10 rise again** also **rise from the dead**– to come back to life after being dead **11 rise to the occasion** to show that one can deal with a difficult matter: *When the unexpected guests came, we rose to the occasion by making a meal.*

USAGE Do not confuse **rise**, which is always [I] and means "to go up to a higher position," and **raise**, which is always [T] and means "to move someone or something to a higher position": *They* **raised** *the curtain and the play began.|The curtain* **rose** *and the play began.* **Arise** can mean the same as **rise**, but this is very formal; its usual meaning is "to come into being": *A problem has* **arisen** *with the new computer.*

rise against sbdy./sthg. v prep [T] to REBEL against (rule or rulers); begin to oppose: *The people rose (up) against their leaders.*

rise² n **1** [C *in*] an increase (in price, amount, temperature, etc.): *a rise in the cost of living* **2** [U] the act of growing greater or more powerful: *the rise and fall of the Roman Empire* **3** [C] an upward slope; small hill: *a house on top of a small rise* **4** [C] BrE for RAISE² **5 give rise to** to be the cause of; lead to (esp. bad things): *These bad conditions have* given rise to *a lot of crime.*

risk[1] /rɪsk/ *n* **1** [C;S;U] a danger: *There's some/a great/no/not much risk (of fire).| Miners face a lot of risks in their daily lives.|The disease is spreading, and all young children are* **at risk**. (in danger)| *You have to* take/**run** *a lot of* **risks** (=do dangerous things) *in my job.* **2** [C] (in insurance) (a person or thing that is) a danger: *I'm afraid I'm a poor risk for life insurance, because my health is so bad.|to* INSURE *it for all risks* **3 at one's own risk** agreeing to bear any loss or danger: *"Anyone swimming in this lake does so* **at his own risk**.*" (notice)* **4 at the risk of** with danger of: *She saved my life* **at the risk of** *losing her own.*

risk[2] *v* [T] **1** to place in danger: *to risk one's health* **2** [+*v-ing*] to take the chance of: *He risked his parents' anger by marrying me.* **3 risk one's neck** to endanger one's life

risk·y /'rɪskiʸ/ *adj* **-ier, -iest** (esp. of an action) dangerous: *You drove too fast around that corner. It was a risky thing to do.* –**riskily** *adv* –**riskiness** *n* [U]

ris·qué /rɪ'skeʸ/ *adj* (of a joke, story, etc.) slightly rude; concerned with sex: *a very risqué conversation*

rite /raɪt/ *n* a form of behavior with a fixed pattern, usu. for a religious purpose: *funeral rites*

rit·u·al /'rɪtʃuʷəl/ *n* [C;U] one or more ceremonies or customary acts which are often repeated in the same form: *the ritual of morning prayers in school|Christian ritual* (=the form of church service) –**ritual** *adj : ritual dancing* –**ritually** *adv*

ri·val[1] /'raɪvəl/ *n* [*for, in*] a person with whom one competes: *Bob and I were rivals for the job.*

rival[2] *adj* [A] competing: *Michael left and joined a rival company.*

rival[3] *v* **-l-** *AmE*‖**-ll-** *BrE* [T] to equal; be as good as: *Ships can't rival aircraft for speed.* –see also UNRIVALED

ri·val·ry /'raɪvəlriʸ/ *n* **-ries** [C;U *in, with*] competition; (a case of) being RIVALS[1]: *the many rivalries of office life|Should we encourage international rivalry in sports?*

riv·er /'rɪvər/ *n* a wide natural stream of water flowing between banks into a lake, into another wider stream, or into the sea: *to go swimming in the river/sailing on the river|the Amazon River* –compare STREAM[1]

riv·er·bed /'rɪvər,bɛd/ *n* the ground over which a river flows between its banks

riv·er·side /'rɪvər,saɪd/ *n* [A;S] the land on or near the banks of a river: *to tie up the boat by the riverside|an old riverside inn*

riv·et[1] /'rɪvɪt/ *n* a metal pin for fastening metal plates (as when building a ship)

rivet[2] *v* [T] **1** to fasten with RIVETS[1] **2** to attract and hold (someone's attention) strongly: *The strange sound riveted the attention of a passing policeman.|His attention was riveted*

SPELLING NOTE

Words with the sound /r/ may be spelled **wr-**, like **wrong**.

---

on the tennis match.

riv·et·ing /'rɪvətɪŋ/ *adj* very interesting; holding one's attention: *a riveting book about World War II.*

R.N, RN *abbrev. for:* REGISTERED NURSE: *Maria Pires, R.N.*

roach /roʷtʃ/ *n AmE for* COCKROACH

road /roʷd/ *n* a smooth prepared track along which wheeled vehicles can travel: *a road map of the US|Drive on the right side of the road.|I have to stop and rest; I've been* **on the road** (=traveling) *for twelve hours.|My address is 21 Forest Road.* –see STREET (USAGE)

road·block /'roʷdblak/ *n* a bar or other object(s) used for closing a road, esp. to stop traffic

road·side /'roʷdsaɪd/ *n* (at or near) the edge of the road: *We ate our meal by the roadside/at a roadside inn.*

road·way /'roʷdweʸ/ *n* [S] the middle part of a road where vehicles drive: *Don't stop on the roadway; go to the side.* –compare FOOTPATH, SIDEWALK

roam /roʷm/ *v* [I;T] to wander with no very clear aim (through, around, etc.): *to roam the hills |roaming from place to place*

roar[1] /rɔr, roʷr/ *v* **1** [I] to give a deep loud continuing sound: *The lion/The crowd/ The engine roared.|The traffic roars past along/down the hill.* **2** [I;T +*that/out*] to say or express with a deep loud continuing sound: *The crowd roared their approval.|He* **roared with laughter/pain/anger.**

roar[2] *n* a deep loud continuing sound: *the roar of an angry lion/of a crowd|roars of laughter*

roar·ing /'rɔrɪŋ, 'roʷrɪŋ/ *adv* very (great): *He came home* **roaring drunk**.*|The party was a* **roaring success**.*|The new restaurant is* **doing a roaring trade**. (=operating very successfully)

roast[1] /roʷst/ *v* [I;T] to cook or be cooked by dry heat, either in front of an open fire or in a hot box (OVEN): *to roast a chicken|roasted coffee beans|The meat is roasting nicely.* –see COOK (USAGE)

roast[2] *n* **1** [C] a large piece of ROASTED[1] meat: *Let's have a roast for Sunday dinner.* **2** [A] ROASTED[1]: *a roast chicken|roast potatoes| roast beef*

roast·ing /'roʷstɪŋ/ *adj,adv* [*no comp.*] very (hot): *a roasting (hot) summer day*

rob /rab/ *v* **-bb-** [I;T *of*] to take the property of (a person or organization) unlawfully: *to rob a bank|(fig.) You have robbed me of my happiness!* –see THIEF (USAGE)

rob·ber /'rabər/ *n* a person who robs: *a band/a* GANG (1) *of robbers* –see THIEF (USAGE)

rob·ber·y /'rabəriʸ/ *n* **-ies** [C;U] **1** (an example of) the crime of taking someone else's property; robbing: *He was charged with robbery.* **2 highway robbery** *infml* charging too much money: *$3 for a beer? It's highway robbery!*

robe[1] /roʷb/ *n* a long flowing garment **a** for informal occasions: *a bath robe* –see illustration on page 55 **b** for official or ceremonial occasions: *a judge's black robes*

robe² *v* **robed, robing** [I;T *in*] to dress in ROBEs; put on a ROBE

rob·in /'rɑbɪn/ *n* a small brown bird with a red breast

ro·bot /'rowbɑt, -bət/ *n* a machine that can move and do some of the work of a person: *Some of the work in the car factory is now done by robots.*

ro·bust /row'bʌst, 'rowbʌst/ *adj* having or showing very good health: *a robust baby* |*a robust company* –**robustly** *adv* –**robustness** *n* [U]

rock¹ /rɑk/ *v* **1**[I;T] to (cause to) move regularly backwards and forwards or from side to side: *She rocked the child in her arms.*|*The boat rocked (to and fro) on the water.* **2** [T] to cause great shock and surprise to: *The news of the President's murder rocked the nation.*

rock² *n* **1** [U] stone forming part of the earth's surface: *a passage cut through (the) solid rock* **2** [C] a large piece or mass of stone: *danger from falling rocks*|*ships driven onto the rocks by a storm* **3 on the rocks: a** (of alcoholic drinks) with ice: WHISKEY *on the rocks* **b** (esp. of a marriage or business) in difficulties

rock³ *n* [U] → ROCK 'N' ROLL

rock and roll /ˌ· · '·/ *n* [U] → ROCK 'N' ROLL

rock bot·tom /ˌ· '···◄/ *n* [U] (esp. of prices) the lowest point; the bottom; *Prices have reached rock bottom.*

rock·er /'rɑkər/ *n* **1** one of the curved pieces of wood underneath a ROCKING CHAIR, ROCK-ING HORSE, or CRADLE¹ (1) **2** *AmE* for ROCK-ING CHAIR **3 off one's rocker** *infml* mad; crazy

rock·er·y /'rɑkəriy/ *n* **-ies** → ROCK GARDEN

rock·et¹ /'rɑkɪt/ *n* **1** a tube-shaped machine driven by burning gases, used for space travel, and to power bombs or MISSILES (1) **2** a model of this, packed with gunpowder and used as FIREWORKs

rocket² *v* [I *up*] (esp. of levels, amounts, etc.) to rise quickly and suddenly: *The price of sugar has rocketed.* –compare PLUMMET

rock gar·den /'· ˌ··/ also **rockery**– *n* a (part of a) garden laid out as a heap of rocks with low-growing plants growing between them

rock·ing chair /'·· ˌ·/ ‖also **rocker** *AmE*– *n* a chair fitted with ROCKERs (1)

rocking horse /'·· ˌ·/ *n* a wooden horse fitted with ROCKERs (1), for a child to ride on

rock 'n' roll /ˌrɑk ən 'rowl/ also **rock, rock and roll**– *n* [U] popular modern dance music with a strong, loud beat, which usu. repeats the same few phrases and is played on electric instruments

rock·y /'rɑkiy/ *adj* **-ier, -iest** full of, made of, or like rock: *a rocky path up the mountain* –**rockiness** *n* [U]

rod /rɑd/ *n* a long thin stiff pole or bar of wood, metal, or plastic: *a fishing rod*

rode /rowd/ *v past tense of* RIDE

ro·dent /'rowdnt/ *n* a member of the family of small plant-eating animals with strong sharp teeth, that includes rats, mice, and rabbits

ro·de·o /'rowdiyˌow, row'deyow/ *n* **-os** in Canada and the western US, a public performance at which COWBOYs ride wild horses,

catch cattle with ropes, etc.

roe /row/ *n* [C;U] (a) mass of eggs or male seed (SPERM) in a fish, often eaten as food

rogue /rowg/ *n becoming rare* **1** a very dishonest person, esp. a man: *Don't buy a used car from that rogue.* **2** *humor* a person who likes playing tricks: *You little rogue –where are my shoes?*

ro·guish /'rowgɪʃ/ *adj becoming rare* (typical of a person) who is playful and fond of playing tricks: *a roguish smile* –**roguishly** *adv*– **roguishness** *n* [U]

role /rowl/ *n* the part taken by someone in life or in any activity, esp. the part of some particular actor in a play: *Olivier played the role of Hamlet.*|*to fulfill her role as a mother* –see TITLE ROLE

roll¹ /rowl/ *n* **1** [*of*] a piece of the stated material that has been rolled into a tube –see illustration on page 683 **2** a small long or round loaf for one person: *breakfast rolls* **3** (often cap.) an official list of names: *The teacher* **called the roll.** (=read the list aloud to see if everyone was there)

roll² *v* **1** [I;T] to move by turning over and over, or from side to side: *The ball rolled into the hole.*|*The dog rolled over onto its back.*|*We rolled the barrels of oil onto the ship.* **2** [I] to move steadily and smoothly along (as if) on wheels: *The train rolled slowly into the station.*|*The clouds are rolling away.* **3** [T *up*] to form into a tube or other stated shape by curling around and around: *He rolled up the map.*|*She rolled the clay into a ball.*|*Please roll me a cigarette.* –opposite **unroll**|*She's a doctor and mother* **rolled into one.** (=combined in one person) **4** [I] (of a ship) to swing from side to side with the movement of the waves –compare PITCH¹ (6) **5** [T] to make (flat) by pressing with a ROLLER (1) or ROLLING PIN: *Roll the pastry as flat as you can.* **6** [I] to make a long deep sound like that of a lot of quick strokes: *The thunder/drums rolled.* **7** [I;T] (of the eyes) to move around and around: *His eyes rolled (with fear) when he heard the news.* **8** [I] *infml* to be helpless with laughter: *His jokes kept us rolling all evening.* **9** [I;T] to throw (DICE): *She rolled a seven and won the game.*|*It's your turn to roll.*

roll sthg.↔ **back** *v adv* [T] *AmE* to reduce (esp. prices): *The government has rolled back the price of oil.*

roll by *v adv* [I] to go steadily past: *The years rolled by.*

roll in¹ *v adv* [I] to come or arrive in large quantities: *Invitations kept rolling in.*

roll in² sthg. *v prep* [T *no pass.*] to have plenty of (money): *She's rolling in money.*

roll sthg.↔ **out** *v adv* [T] to spread (a piece of material) out flat and thin by pressing with a ROLLER (1) or a ROLLING PIN: *roll out the pastry* –compare ROLL² (5)

roll up *v adv* **1** [T] (**roll** sthg.↔ **up**) to roll (SLEEVEs (1)) up one's arms; roll (pants) up one's legs **2** [I] *infml* to arrive in a vehicle: *The movie actors rolled up in a Cadillac.*

roll³ *n* **1** [S] a long deep sound as of a lot of quick strokes: *a roll of thunder/of drums* **2**

[C] a rolling movement, over and over or to and fro sideways: *the slow roll of a ship on the rough sea*

roll call /ˈ· ·/ *n* [U] the time or act of reading out a list of names to see who is there: *I arrived just before roll call.*

roll·er /ˈroʷlər/ *n* **1** a tube-shaped piece of wood, metal, hard rubber, etc., that rolls over and over, as used **a** in a machine, for crushing, pressing, printing, etc. **b** for smoothing the surface of grass or roads **c** for moving heavy things that have no wheels: *They pushed the boat down to the water on rollers.* **d** for shaping: *She puts her hair into rollers to curl it.* **2** a rod around which something is rolled up: *a big map on a roller*

roller coast·er /ˈ·· ˌ··/ *n* a kind of small railroad with sharp slopes and curves, popular in amusement parks

roller skate /ˈ·· ˌ·/ *n* [often *pl.*] a wheeled frame for fitting under a shoe, or a shoe with wheels fixed on, allowing the wearer to move quickly on any smooth surface, such as a road —**roller-skate** *v* **-skated, -skating** [I]

roll·ing /ˈroʷlɪŋ/ *adj* [A] (of land) rising and falling in long gentle slopes: *a rolling plain*

rolling pin /ˈ·· ˌ·/ *n* a tube-shaped piece of wood or other material, for spreading pastry out flat and thin before cooking

rolling stock /ˌ·· ˈ·/ *n* [U] everything on wheels that belongs to a railroad, such as engines and cars

Ro·man /ˈroʷmən/ *n,adj* (a citizen) of the ancient empire or the city of Rome

Roman Cath·o·lic /ˌ·· ˈ···/ *n,adj* (a member) of the branch of the Christian religion whose leader (**POPE**) rules from Rome: *Her family is Roman Catholic.*| *All the members of her family are Roman Catholics.*

ro·mance /roʷˈmæns, ˈroʷmæns/ *n* **1** [C] a story of love, adventure, strange happenings, etc., often set in a distant time or place: *a romance about a king who married a poor girl* **2** [U] the quality that such stories have; the quality in the human mind that hopes for such experiences in real life: *the romance of life in the Wild West* **3** [C] a love affair: *I think he is having a little romance with Julia.*

Roman nu·mer·al /ˌ·· ˈ···/ *n* any of a set of signs, originally used in ancient Rome and sometimes now, for numbers, as in I, II, III, IV, V, etc. —compare ARABIC NUMERAL

ro·man·tic¹ /roʷˈmæntɪk/ *adj* **1** belonging to or suggesting ROMANCE: *a very romantic love story* **2** sometimes *derog* fanciful; not practical: *She has romantic ideas about becoming a famous actress.* —**romantically** *adv*

romantic² *n* a ROMANTIC¹ (2) person: *She was a romantic who went off to the South Seas to paint pictures.*

ro·man·ti·cize ‖also **-cise** *BrE* /roʷˈmæntə ˌsaɪz/ *v* **-cized, -cizing** [I;T] *derog* to tell improbable and ROMANTIC¹ (2) stories

---

SPELLING NOTE

Words with the sound /r/ may be spelled **wr-**, like **wrong**.

(about): *Just keep to the facts and stop romanticizing!*

romp /rɑmp/ *v* [I *around*] to play noisily and roughly with a lot of running and jumping: *children romping in the garden* —**romp** *n*

romp·ers /ˈrɑmpərz/ *n* [P] a one-piece garment for babies combining a top and short trouser-like bottom: *a pair of rompers* —see PAIR (USAGE)

roof¹ /ruʷf, rʊf/ *n* **1** the outside covering on top of a building, closed vehicle, tent, etc.: *The rain's coming in. We have to fix the roof.* —compare CEILING —see illustration on page 337 **2** a house; home: *She and I can't live under the same roof.* **3 a/no roof over one's head** somewhere/nowhere to live **4 hit/raise the roof** to make a loud noise, esp. of angry or excited complaint: *Your father will raise the roof when he hears what you've done.* **5 roof of the/one's mouth** the bony upper part of the inside of the mouth; PALATE

roof² *v* [T *with*] to put a roof on: *a house roofed with lead*

roof·ing /ˈruʷfɪŋ, ˈrʊ-/ *n* [U] material for making or covering roofs

rook /rʊk/ *v* [T (*of*)] *infml* to cheat (someone), as by charging a very high price or by winning money at a card game: *$20! You've been rooked!*

rook·ie /ˈrʊkiʸ/ *n AmE infml* a new soldier or member of the police force; RECRUIT

room¹ /ruʷm, rʊm/ *n* **1** [C] a division of a building, with its own walls, floor, and CEILING: *I want a double room* (=for two people) *with a view.* **2** [U +*to-v*] space that could be filled, or that is enough for any purpose: *There's no room to move.*|*Move along and make room for me!*|*A piano takes up a lot of room.* **3** [U *for*] **a** a need for: *There's plenty of room for improvement in his work.* **b** reason for: *There's no room for doubt.* —see PLACE (USAGE) **4 -room** having a certain number or size of rooms: *a six-room house* —**roomful** /ˈruʷmfʊl, ˈrʊm-/ *n* [*of*]: *a roomful of noisy children* [*of*]:

room² *v* [I *at, with*] *AmE* to lodge; have a room or rooms (at, with): *He's rooming at our house/with us.*

rooming house /ˈ·· ˌ·/ *n AmE* a building divided into separate rooms that can be rented

room·mate /ˈruʷm-meʸt, ˈrʊm-/ *n* a person with whom one shares a lodging: *Bill and I are roommates.*

room serv·ice /ˈ· ˌ··/ *n* [U] a service provided by a hotel, by which food, drink, etc., are sent up to a person's room

room·y /ˈruʷmiʸ, ˈrʊmiʸ/ *adj* **-ier, -iest** with plenty of space: *a roomy house/car* —**roominess** *n* [U]

roost /ruʷst/ *v* [I] (of a bird) to sit and sleep for the night

roost·er /ˈruʷstər/ *esp. AmE*‖also **cock-** *n* a fully-grown male bird, esp. a chicken

root¹ /ruʷt, rʊt/ *n* **1** [often *pl.*] the part of a plant that grows down into the soil in search of food and water: *Pull the plant up by the/by its roots.* **2** the part of a tooth, hair, or organ that holds it to the rest of the body **3** the origin; cause; central part or base: *Let's get to/get at the root of this matter.* **4** *tech* (in MATHEMATICS) a number that when multiplied by itself a stated number of times gives another stated number: *3 is the* **square root** *of 9* ($3 \times 3 = 9$).|*3 is the* **cube root** *of 27* ($3 \times 3 \times 3 = 27$). **5 take root** (of plants or ideas) to become established and begin to grow –see also ROOTS

root² /v/ [I;T] to (cause to) form roots: *Try to root this plant in the garden.*|*Do roses root easily?*

root sbdy./sthg.↔ **out** *v adv* [T] to get rid of completely (someone or something bad); destroy: *This disease could easily be rooted out.*

root³ *v* [I *around, for*] to search (for something) by turning things over: *Who's been rooting around among my papers?*

root⁴ *v* →ROOT FOR

root beer /'· ·/ *n* [C;U] (esp. in the US) a sweet gassy non-alcoholic drink made from various roots

root crop /'· ·/ *n* a crop that is grown for its roots, such as CARROTS

root·ed /'ruʷtɪd, 'rʊtɪd/ *adj* [F *to*] fixed (as if by roots): *He stood rooted (to the spot).*| *a deeply rooted dislike of cats*

root for sbdy./sthg. *v prep* [T] *AmE infml* to support or cheer for someone or something: *Let's root for our team.*

root·less /'ruʷtlɪs, 'rʊt-/ *adj* homeless and without ROOTS –**rootlessness** *n* [U]

roots /ruʷts, rʊts/ *n* [P] the feeling of belonging by origin to one particular place: *Her roots are in Texas where she was born.*

rope¹ /roʷp/ *n* **1** [C;U] (a piece of) strong thick cord made by twisting –compare STRING¹ **2 know the ropes** to know from experience the rules and customs in a place or activity: *I've done this before so I know the ropes. Would you like me to show you how to do it?*

rope² *v* **roped, roping** [T] **1** [*up*] to tie up with a rope: *roped chests of tea* **2** *esp.* *AmE* to catch (an animal) with a rope; LASSO²: *rope the cow*

rope sbdy.↔ **in** *v adv* [T] *infml* to persuade someone to help in one's plans or join an activity: *I've been roped in to help sell the tickets.*

rope sthg.↔ **off** *v adv* [T] to separate (an area) from the rest with ropes: *They've roped off one end of the room.*

rope lad·der /'· ·'··/ *n* a ladder made of two long ropes connected by cross pieces of wood, rope, or metal

ro·sa·ry /'roʷzəriʸ/ *n* -**ries** (esp. in the ROMAN CATHOLIC religion) a set of prayers or the string of BEADS (=small decorative balls) used to count them

rose¹ /roʷz/ **1** (the brightly-colored, sweet-smelling flower of) a bush with strong prickly stems and divided leaves **2** [A] (of) a color from pink to a deep purplish red **3 a bed of roses** a very pleasant state to be in

rose² *v past tense of* RISE

ro·sé /roʷ'zeʸ/ *n* [U] also **pink**– a type of light pink wine: *a glass of rosé*

rose·mar·y /'roʷz,mɛəriʸ/ *n* [U] a low bush whose sweet-smelling leaves are used in cooking

ro·sette /roʷ'zɛt/ *n* a bunch of narrow silk bands (RIBBONS) made up in the form of a rose and usu. worn as a sign of something: *The winner of the competition was given a red rosette.*

ros·ter /'rɑstər/ *n* a list of people's names (that shows when it is each person's turn to do a certain job)

ros·trum /'rɑstrəm/ *n* -**trums** *or* -**tra**/trə/ a raised place (PLATFORM) for a public speaker, CONDUCTOR (1), etc.: *the teacher on his rostrum*

ros·y /'roʷziʸ/ *adj* -**ier**, -**iest 1** (esp. of the human skin) pink: *rosy cheeks* **2** (esp. of the future) giving hope: *Things don't look very rosy at my company, so I'm looking for another job.* –**rosiness** *n* [U]

rot¹ /rɑt/ *v* -**tt**- [I;T] to (cause to) decay: *The rain has rotted the roof beams.*|(fig.) *They left him to rot in prison for 20 years.* –see also ROTTEN

rot² *n* [U] **1** (the action of) decay: *an old hollow tree full of rot*|(fig.) *How can we* **stop the rot** *in our society?* **2** *BrE infml* foolish remarks or ideas: *Don't talk rot!*

ro·ta·ry /'roʷtəriʸ/ *adj* (of movement) turning around a fixed point, like a wheel: *the rotary movement of the blades*

ro·tate /'roʷteʸt/ *v* -**tated**, -**tating** [I;T] **1** to (cause to) turn around a fixed point: *The earth rotates once every 24 hours.*|*You can rotate the wheel with your hand.* **2** to (cause to) take turns or come around in regular order: *to rotate the crops*

ro·ta·tion /roʷ'teʸʃən/ *n* **1** [U] the action of rotating (ROTATE): *the rotation of the earth*|*The seasons follow each other* **in rotation.** (=coming around one after the other) **2** [C] one complete turn around a fixed point: *to make ten rotations a second*

ro·tis·ser·ie /roʷ'tɪsəriʸ/ *n* an apparatus for cooking meat by turning it over and over on a bar (SPIT³ (1)), over direct heat

ro·tor /'roʷtər/ *n* a part of a machine that ROTATEs (1), esp. the system of blades that raise a HELICOPTER into the air

rot·ten /'rɑtn/ *adj* **1** decayed; gone bad: *rotten eggs*|*a rotten branch* **2** bad; unkind; *What a rotten thing to do to her!* –**rottenness** *n* [U]

ro·tund /roʷ'tʌnd/ *adj* *fml or humor* (of a person) fat and round –**rotundity** *n* [S;U]

rou·ble /'ruʷbəl/ *n* → RUBLE

rouge /ruʷʒ/ *n* [U] a red substance used for coloring the cheeks

rough¹ /rʌf/ *adj* **1** having an uneven surface; not smooth: *The rough road made the car shake.*|*A cat's tongue is rough.* **2** not gentle, tender, or polite; using force: *a rough voice*|*Play nicely and don't be rough!* **3** not delicate or comfortable; simple: *Life was rough in the American West in the last century.* **4** (of weather, the sea, or a sea journey) stormy and violent; not calm **5** [*no comp.*] (of plans, calculations, etc.) not (yet) in detail or the finished form; not exact: *a rough drawing*|*I have a rough idea where it* is. **6** *infml* unfortunate and perhaps unfair: *She's been having a rough time recently.*|*It's* **rough on** (=unfortunate for) *him, having to do two people's work.* **7 rough and ready** simple and without comfort –**roughness** *n* [U]

rough² *n* [U] **1** the uneven ground with long grass on a GOLF course: *He lost his ball in the rough.* **2 in the rough** in an incomplete or undetailed form: *Draw it in the rough first.* **3 take the rough with the smooth** to accept bad things as well as good things without complaining

rough³ *v* **rough it** *infml* to live in a simple and not very comfortable way

  rough sbdy.↔ **up** *v adv* [T] *infml* to attack (someone) roughly

rough⁴ *adv* in a ROUGH¹ (2) way: *Those boys certainly* **play (it) rough!**

rough·age /'rʌfɪdʒ/ *n* [U] coarse matter contained in food, that helps the bowels to work: *Brown bread provides valuable roughage.*

rough·en /'rʌfən/ *v* [I;T] to make or become rough

rough·ly /'rʌfliʸ/ *adv* **1** in a rough manner: *He pushed her away roughly.* **2** about; more or less: *There were roughly 200 people there.*

rough·neck /'rʌfnɛk/ *n AmE infml* **1** a rough bad-tempered man **2** a member, not the leader, of a team who are making (DRILLing¹ (1)) an oil well

rou·lette /ruʷˈlɛt/ *n* [U] a game of chance in which a small ball is spun around a moving wheel and falls into a hole marked with a number

round¹ /raʊnd/ *adj* **1** circular: *a round plate* **2** shaped like a ball; SPHERICAL **3** (of parts of the body) fat and curved: *the child's round red cheeks* **4** [A] (of numbers) complete; and not less: *a round dozen* **5** in round figures (of numbers) not exactly, but to the nearest 10, 100, 1,000, etc., without small amounts: *The car cost $9,878; that's $10,000 in round figures.*

round² *adv* **1**‖also **around** *AmE*– moving in a circle; measured in a circle: *The wheels went round and round.*|*He works* **all year round.**(=during the whole year) **2** on all sides; in a circular position: *The children gathered round to hear the story.* **3** *BrE* for AROUND

round³ *prep esp. BrE* for AROUND

round⁴ *n* **1** [*of*] a number or set (of events): *a continual round of parties*|*a second round of wage claims* (=by trade unions for their members)|*We won the first round* (=set of games) *of the Football Cup.* **2** a regular set of visits to a number of houses, offices, etc.: *The doctor made her daily rounds at the hospital.* **3** a share given out to everyone present: *I'll buy you all a* **round of drinks! 4 a** (in GOLF) a complete game including all the holes **b** (in BOXING) one of the periods of

fighting in a match, separated by short rests: *He was knocked out in the second round.* **5** one single shot: *He fired round after round.*| *I've only got two rounds left.* (=bullets for two shots) **6** a type of song for three or four voices, in which each sings the same tune, one starting a line after another has just finished it

round⁵ *v* **1** [T] to travel around: *She rounded the corner at 95 miles per hour.* **2** [I;T] to make or become round: *round one's lips to whistle*

  round sthg.↔ **off** *v adv* **1** [T *by, with*] to end suitably and satisfactorily: *We rounded off the evening with a hot drink/by singing a song.* **2** [*to*] to change (an exact figure) to the closest whole number: *round off $1.95 to $2.00/$1.20 to $1.00*

  round sbdy./sthg.↔ **up** *v adv* [T] to gather together (scattered things, people, or animals, esp. cattle): *Round up a few friends to help you!*

round·a·bout¹ /'raʊndəˌbaʊt/ *n* **1** *BrE* for TRAFFIC CIRCLE **2** *BrE* for MERRY-GO-ROUND

roundabout² *adj* (of the way to somewhere) indirect; not the shortest: (fig.) *I heard the news in a roundabout way.*

round-shoul·dered /'· ˌ··/ *adj* with bent shoulders; with a back that is not upright

round trip /ˌ· '·/ *n* a journey to a place and back again

round-trip /ˌ· '·◂/ *AmE*‖**return** *BrE*– *adj* (of a ticket or its cost) for a trip from one place to another and back again: *a round-trip ticket*

rouse /raʊz/ *v* **roused, rousing** [T *from, out of*] to waken: *He's very hard to rouse in the morning.*|(fig.) *The speaker tried to rouse the people (from their lack of interest).*|*roused to anger*

rous·ing /'raʊzɪŋ/ *adj* that makes people excited: *a very rousing speech about freedom*

rout /raʊt/ *v* [T] to defeat completely and drive away: *They routed the enemy.* –**rout** *n*: *the total rout of the enemy forces*

route¹ /ruʷt, raʊt/ *n* a way planned or followed from one place to another: *the shortest route from Boston to Washington*

route² *v* **routed, routing** [T *by, through*] to send by a particular ROUTE¹: *They routed the goods through Italy by way of Germany.*

rou·tine¹ /ruʷˈtiʸn/ *n* [C;U] the regular fixed ordinary way of working or doing things: *Please do it according to routine.*|*These two babies have different daily routines.*

routine² *adj* [A] regular; not unusual: *a routine medical examination*|*a dull routine job* –**routinely** *adv*

rove /roʷv/ *v* **roved, roving** [I;T] to wander; move continually (around): *to rove the seas in search of adventure*

rov·er /'roʷvər/ *n lit* a wanderer

row¹ /roʷ/ *v* [I;T] **1** to move (a boat) through the water with OARS (=long poles with flat ends): *You should learn to row (a boat).* **2** to travel or carry in this way: *He rowed (the boat) across the lake.*

row² /roʷ/ *n* [*of*] **1** a neat line (of people or things) side by side: *a row of houses/of cups on a shelf*|*Children standing hand in hand in* a row. (=side by side) **2** a line of seats in a theater: *We have front row seats for this play.*

row³ /raʊ/ *n infml* **1** [C] a noisy quarrel, sometimes with violent actions: *He's always having rows with his wife.* **2** [S] a noise: *Stop making such a row; I can't sleep!*

row⁴ /raʊ/ [I *with*] *infml* to quarrel, often noisily or violently: *They always row about money.*

row·boat /'roʷboʷt/ *AmE*‖**rowing boat** /'·· ‚·/ *BrE– n* a small boat that is moved through the water with OARs (=long poles with flat ends)

row·dy /'raʊdiʸ/ *adj* **-dier, -diest** noisy and rough: *a rowdy evening in the park*‖*rowdy behavior/children* **–rowdily** *adv* **–rowdiness** *n* [U]

roy·al /'rɔɪəl/ *adj* [A] for, belonging to, or connected with a king or queen: *the royal palaces*‖*the Royal Navy* **–royally** *adv*

Royal High·ness /‚·· '··/ *n* (the words used when speaking to or of) a prince or princess: *Thank you very much, Your Royal Highness.*‖*His Royal Highness, Prince Charles*

roy·al·ist /'rɔɪəlɪst/ *adj,n* (typical of) someone who supports a king or queen or believes that a country should be ruled by one

roy·al·ty /'rɔɪəltiʸ/ *n* **-ties 1** [U] royal power and rank **2** [U] people of the royal family: *The flag is only raised when royalty is present.* **3** [C] a payment made to a writer of a book, piece of music, etc. as part of the profit from selling that work: *The writer gets a 5% royalty on every copy of his new book.*

RPM *abbrev. for:* REVOLUTIONs (4) per minute, a measure of engine speed

RSVP *abbrev. for: French* répondez s'il vous plaît; please reply (written on invitations)

rub¹ /rʌb/ *v* **-bb- 1** [T *with, together*] to slide (one surface) with pressure, to and fro or around and around against (another): *She rubbed the window (with a cloth).*‖*He rubbed his hands (together) to warm them/with pleasure.*‖*He rubbed polish on the table.* **2** [I *against, on*] (of a surface) to slide in this way (against/on another): *This tire seems badly worn; it must be rubbing against/on something.* **3 rub someone the wrong way** *infml* to annoy someone: *I don't like him; he rubs me the wrong way.*

rub sbdy./sthg.↔ **down** *v adv* [T] to dry or make smooth by rubbing: *rubbing herself down after a swim*‖*Rub the door down before you paint it.*

rub sthg. **in** *v adv* [T] **1** to make (liquid) go into a surface by rubbing: *Rub the polish in well.* **2 rub it in** *infml* to keep talking about something that another person wants to forget: *"You've put on some weight." "I know; don't rub it in!"*

rub off *v adv* [I *on, onto*] to come off a surface (onto another) by rubbing: (fig.) *I hope that some of her good qualities will rub off onto you.*

rub sthg.↔ **out** *v adv* [T] to remove (esp. pencil writing) with an ERASER (=a piece of rubber): *to rub out a word/a dirty mark on the paper*

rub² *n* [S] an act of rubbing: *Give me a back rub.*

rub·ber /'rʌbər/ *n* **1** [U] a substance, made either from the juice of a tropical tree or chemically, which keeps out water and springs back into position when stretched **2** [C *usu. pl.*] *AmE* a shoe of this substance worn over another shoe to keep it dry **3** [C] *esp. BrE* for ERASER

rubber band /‚·· '·, '·· ‚·/ *n* a thin circular piece of rubber used for fastening things together: *Put a rubber band around your hair/around this bunch of flowers.*

rub·ber·y /'rʌbəriʸ/ *adj often derog* strong and springy like rubber: *The meat's a little rubbery. You didn't cook it long enough!*

rub·bish /'rʌbɪʃ/ *n* [U] **1** →TRASH **2** *esp. BrE* silly remarks; nonsense: *He's talking rubbish.* **–rubbishy** *adj*

rub·ble /'rʌbəl/ *n* [U] (a mass of) broken stones or bricks: *After the bombing, her house was just a heap of rubble.*

ru·bel·la /ruʷ'bɛlə/ *n* [U] *tech* → GERMAN MEASLES

ru·ble, rouble /'ruʷbəl/ *n* (a coin or note worth) the standard amount in the money system of the USSR

ru·by /'ruʷbiʸ/ *n* **-bies** [A;C] (the color of) a deep red precious stone: *a ruby ring*‖*ruby wine*

ruck·sack /'rʌksæk, 'rʊk-/ *n* → KNAPSACK

rud·der /'rʌdər/ *n* a wooden or metal blade at the back of a ship or aircraft that swings to and fro to control the direction

rud·dy /'rʌdiʸ/ *adj* **-dier, -diest** (of the face) pink and healthy-looking: *the ruddy cheeks of the children* **–ruddiness** *n* [U]

rude /ruʷd/ *adj* **1** (of a person or behavior) not at all polite: *It's rude to say you don't like the food, when we spent so long preparing it.*‖*Don't be so rude to your father.* **2** [A] simple and roughly made: *a rude hut* **3** [A] sudden and violent: *a rude shock* **–rudeness** *n* [U] **–rudely** *adv*

ru·di·men·ta·ry /‚ruʷdə'mɛntəriʸ/ *adj* (of facts, knowledge, etc.) simple; coming or learned first: *I have only the most rudimentary knowledge of chemistry.*

ru·di·ments /'ruʷdəmənts/ *n* [P] the RUDIMENTARY parts (of a subject): *to learn the rudiments of grammar/of Italian*

rue /ruʷ/ *v* **rued, ruing** [T +*v-ing*] *old use & humor* to be sorry about (something one has done or not done): *I never went to college, and I've rued it bitterly all my life.*‖*She'll* **rue the day** (=always be sorry that) *she married him.*

rue·ful /'ruʷfəl/ *adj* feeling or showing that one RUEs something: *a rueful smile* **–ruefully** *adv*

ruff /rʌf/ *n* **1** a kind of stiff white collar worn in Europe in the 16th century **2** a ring of hair or feathers around the neck of an animal or bird

ruf·fi·an /'rʌfiʸən/ *n becoming rare* a bad, perhaps violent, man: *He was attacked by a band of ruffians.*

ruf·fle¹ /'rʌfəl/ *v* **-fled, -fling 1** [T *up*] to move the smooth surface of; make uneven: *The* *bird ruffled (up) its feathers.* **2** [I;T] to make or become rather angry: *Don't get so ruffled.*

ruffle² *n* a band of cloth sewn in folds as a decoration around the neck or wrists of a garment; FRILL

rug /rʌg/ *n* **1** a thick usu. woolen floor mat, smaller than a CARPET¹ (2) –see illustration on page 399 **2** a large warm woolen covering to wrap around oneself when traveling **3** *infml humor* a small HAIRPIECE or TOUPEE for a man **4 sweep (something) under the rug** to keep (something) secret

rug·by /'rʌgbiʸ/ also **rugby football** /,·· '··/ *fml*, **rugger** /'rʌgər/ *infml*– *n* [U] (*sometimes cap.*) a type of football played with an oval ball, by two teams

rug·ged /'rʌgɪd/ *adj* (of a thing) large, rough, and strong-looking: *rugged hills*|(fig.) *a rug-ged good-looking man* **–ruggedly** *adv* **–rug-gedness** *n* [U]

ru·in¹ /'ruʷɪn/ *n* **1** [U] (the cause, of) destruc-tion and decay: *an ancient temple which has fallen into ruin*|*Drink was his father's ruin and it will be the ruin of him too!* **2** [C] a RUINED² (1) building: *an interesting old ruin on top of the hill*

ruin² *v* [T] **1** to destroy and spoil (com-pletely): *an ancient ruined city*|*She poured water all over my painting and ruined it.* **2** to cause total loss of money to: *I was ruined by that law case.*

ru·in·ous /'ruʷənəs/ *adj* causing destruction or total loss of money: *The cost will be ruinous.*|*a ruinous war* **–ruinously** *adv*

ru·ins /'ruʷɪnz/ *n* [P] the remains of a building or buildings: *the ruins of an ancient castle*| *The castle is now* **in ruins.**

rule¹ /ruʷl/ *n* **1** [C +*that*] **a** a principle or order which guides behavior, says how things hap-pen, are to be done, etc.: *It's against the rules to pick up the ball.*|*We have a rule that the loser of the game buys*|*that the loser should buy everyone a drink.* **b** the usual way that something happens: *the rules of grammar* **2** [U] power to RULE² (1); time or manner of ruling: *Their country is under foreign rule.* (=governed by foreigners)|*Her rule lasted 20 years.*|*the rule of law* **3** [C] →RULER (2): *a two-foot rule* **4 as a rule** usually; generally **5 rules and regulations** small annoying RULES¹ (1) usu. in large numbers: *You must obey all the rules and regulations about car insurance.* USAGE When speaking of scientific facts it is usual to call them **laws** rather than **rules:** *the law that oil floats on water.*

rule² *v* **ruled, ruling 1** [I;T *over*] to have and use the highest form of power over (a coun-try, people, etc.) esp. as a king/queen or government: *The king ruled (the country*|*the people) for 30 years.* **2** [I;T +*that*/*on, against*] (esp. in law) to decide officially: *The judge ruled that he has to pay $500.* –compare RULING¹ **3** [T] to draw (a line) with the help of a RULER² or some kind of straight edge **4 be**

ruled by to be influenced or controlled by: *Don't let yourself be ruled by your feelings in this matter.*

rule sbdy./sthg↔ **out** *v adv* [T] not to con-sider; EXCLUDE (2): *We can't* **rule out the possibility** *that he'll come.*

rul·er /'ruʷlər/ *n* **1** a person who RULES² (1) **2** a long narrow flat piece of hard material with straight edges, marked with inches or CEN-TIMETERs, and used for measuring things or for drawing straight lines: *a 12-inch ruler*

rul·ing¹ /'ruʷlɪŋ/ *n* [C +*that*/*on*] an official decision: *The judge has made*/*given several rulings on these matters.* –compare RULE²(2)

ruling² *adj* [A] most powerful: *Painting is her ruling* PASSION. (=interest)

rum /rʌm/ *n* [U] a strong alcoholic drink made from the juice of the sugar CANE (=plant)

rum·ble /'rʌmbəl/ *v* **-bled, -bling** [I] to make or move with a deep continuous rolling sound: *The thunder rumbled in the dis-tance.*|*The heavy cart rumbled down the rough street.* **–rumble** *n* [S]

ru·mi·nant /'ruʷmənənt/ *adj,n* (an animal) that RUMINATEs (2): *The cow is a ruminant.*

ru·mi·nate /'ruʷmə,neʸt/ *v* **-nated, -nating** [I] **1** [*about, over*] (of a person) to think deeply: *Let me ruminate over this plan of yours.* **2** (of cattle, deer, etc.) to bring back food from the stomach and CHEW it (=bite it over and over again) **–rumination** /,ruʷmə'neʸʃən/ *n* [U]

rum·mage /'rʌmɪdʒ/ *v* **-maged, -maging** [I *around, through, among*] to turn things over while trying to find something: *Who's been rummaging around among my papers?* **–rummage** *n* [S *around*]

rummage sale /'·· ,·/ *n AmE* a sale of used clothes and other things to get money for some good work such as helping the poor –compare GARAGE SALE

rum·my /'rʌmiʸ/ *n* [U] any of several simple card games for two or more players, played with two sets (PACKs) of cards

ru·mor /'ruʷmər/ *n AmE*‖also **rumour** *BrE* **1** [U] unofficial news; common talk, perhaps untrue: **Rumor has it** *that he's found a new job.* **2** [C +*that*/*about, of*] a story that reaches one through this: *All kinds of strange rumors about Jean are going around.*

ru·mored /'ruʷmərd/ *adj AmE*‖also **ru-moured** *BrE* [F +*to-v*/*that*] reported un-officially: *It's rumored that Jean's getting married.*|*The company is rumored to be in serious difficulties.*

rump /rʌmp/ *n* the part of an animal at the back just above the legs

rum·ple /'rʌmpəl/ *v* **-pled, -pling** [T] to disar-range (hair, clothes, etc.); make untidy: *her rumpled curls*

rum·pus /'rʌmpəs/ *n* [S] *infml* a noisy argu-ment, quarrel, or disagreement: *to* **kick up** (=make) **a rumpus**

run¹ /rʌn/ *v* **ran** /ræn/, **run** /rʌn/, **running 1** [I] to move on one's legs at a speed faster than walking: *I had to run to catch the bus.*|*The children came running when she called them.*|*He ran a mile in four minutes.* **2**

[T] to cause to take part in a race: *He's running his horse in the next race.* **3** [I;T] to (cause to) move quickly: *A thought ran through my mind.*|*Could you* **run your eyes over** *the list of figures?* (=look at it quickly)|*The car ran down the hill out of control.* **4** [I;T] to (cause to) work or be in operation: *Don't touch the engine while it's running.*|*This machine runs on/by electricity.*|*Run the engine for a moment.*|(fig.) *Is everything running smoothly at the office?* **5** [I not be +*v-ing*] to pass; stretch; continue: *The road runs along the river bank.* **6** [I;T] to (cause to) travel as arranged: *This bus doesn't run on Sundays.* **7** [I] (of a liquid) to flow: *to wash in running water* **8** [I] (of a container) to pour out liquid: *Your nose is running.*|*The well has run dry.* **9** [T] to cause (liquid) to flow (into): *Run the water until it gets hot.*|*I'm going to run a bath.* **10** [I] (melt and) spread by the action of heat or water: *I'm afraid the colors of your shirt ran when I washed it.* **11** [I against,for,in] *esp. AmE* to be or become a CANDIDATE (=a person trying to get elected) (in an election); compete (for an office, against someone else) in this way: *He's decided to run for President/to run in the next election.* **12** [I] to continue in operation, performance, etc.: *Her play ran in New York for 18 months.* **13** [T] *infml* to take (somebody or something) to somewhere in a vehicle: *Can I run you home?* **14** [T] to control; be in charge of and cause to work: *His parents run a small hotel.*|*Who runs this company?* **15** **run into the ground** to tire (oneself or someone else) out with hard work **16 run short: a** to use almost all one has and not have enough left: *We're running short of oil.* **b** also **run low–** to become less than enough: *The supply of oil is running low.*

run after sbdy./sthg. *v prep* [T] **1** to chase: *a dog running after rabbits* **2** *infml* to try to gain the attention and company of: *He's always running after her.*

run along *v adv* [I *often in commands*] *infml* (used esp. to children) to leave; go away: *Run along now, all of you! I'm busy.*

run around *v adv* [I] to go about in company (with, together): *Her husband found out that she'd been running around with another man.*

run away *v adv* [I *from*] to escape by running: *She hit the child, and he ran away.* –see also RUNAWAY

run away/off with sbdy./sthg. *v adv prep* [T] **1** to carry off; gain control of: *Don't let your temper run away with you.* **2** to take (someone of the opposite sex) away: *He ran away with his teacher's wife.* **3** to steal: *He's run away with all my jewels.*

run down *v adv* **1** [T] (**run** sbdy./sthg.↔ **down**) to knock down and hurt (a person or animal) with one's vehicle –compare RUN **into**, RUN **over 2** [T] (**run** sbdy./sthg.↔ **down**) to chase and catch (a person or animal): *to run down a criminal* **3** [T] (**run** sbdy./sthg. ↔ **down**) to speak of without respect; DISPARAGE: *She's jealous of your success; that's*

why she's always running you down. **4** [I] (esp. of a clock, or of an electric BATTERY) to lose power and stop working, e.g. because it needs winding up: (fig.) *an industry that is running down* –see also RUN-DOWN

run sbdy./sthg. **in** *v adv* [T] *infml* (of the police) to catch (a criminal); ARREST¹ (1): *He was run in for being in possession of drugs.*

run into sbdy./sthg. *v prep* [T] **1 a** to cause (a vehicle) to meet (something) with force: *to run one's car into a tree* **b** (of a vehicle) to meet (something) with force: *to run into a lamppost* –compare RUN **down**, RUN **over 2** also **run to–** to add up to; reach (a length or amount): *a debt running into thousands of dollars* **3** *infml* to meet (someone) by chance

run off with sbdy./sthg. *v adv prep* [T] → RUN **away with**

run out *v adv* [I] to come to an end or have no more: *Our supply of sugar has run out-*|*Time is running out.*|*Can you give me a cigarette? I've run out.*

run out of sthg. *v adv prep* [T] to use all one's supply of; have no more of: *We're running out of time.*|*to run out of gasoline*

run over *v adv* **1** [I] (of liquids or their containers) to overflow: *The water/The cup ran over.* **2** [T] (**run** sbdy./sthg.↔ **over**) (of a vehicle or its driver) to knock down and pass over the top of: *He was run over by a bus.*|*The bus ran him over/ran over him.* –compare RUN **into**, RUN **down**

run through *v prep* [T] **1** (**run through/over** sthg.) to repeat for practice: *Let's run through the first scene again.* **2** (**run through** sthg.) to read or examine quickly: *I'll just run through this list of figures.* **3** (**run** sthg. **through** sthg.) to pass or draw right through (something): *She ran her fingers through her hair/a line through the word on the page.*

run to sthg. *v prep* [T] → RUN **into** (2)

run sthg.↔ **up** *v adv* [T] **1** to raise (a flag): *They ran up the flag in honor of the victory.* **2** to cause (one's bills or debts) to grow: *She ran up a large bill for all her new clothes.*

run² *n* **1** [C] an act of RUNNING¹ (1): *He went for a run before breakfast.*|*a five-mile run* **2** [C] a journey esp. by train: *It's a 55-minute run from New York to Philadelphia.* **3** [S] a continuous set of performances of a play, movie, etc.: *The play had a run of three months.* **4** [S *of*] continuous set of similar events: *I've had a run of bad luck recently.* **5** [S *on*] eager buying or selling: *There's been a great run on beer in this hot weather.*|*a run on the dollar* (=selling dollars in the money market) **6** [C] a usu. enclosed area where the stated animals are kept: *a chicken run* **7** [C] a sloping course for the stated downhill sport: *a SKI-run* **8** [C] in BASEBALL a point won by a player reaching the home base safely **9** *AmE*||**ladder** *BrE–* a fault in a stocking caused by stiches coming undone **10 a (good) run for one's money** *infml* a plenty of opposition in a competition **b** good results for money spent or effort made: *He died at 92: I think he had a good run for his money.* **11 in the long run** after enough time; in the end: *It'll be cheaper in the long run to build it in* *stone.* **12 on the run** trying to escape or to hide, esp. from the police **13 the run of (a place)** the freedom to visit or use (a place): *While we're away, you can have the run of the house.*

run·a·way /ˈrʌnə͵weɪ/ *adj* [A] **1** out of control: *a runaway horse* **2** having escaped by running: *a runaway child* see also RUN **away** –**run-away** *n*

run-down[1] /ˈ· ·/ *n* a detailed report of a set of events: *He gave me a run-down on everything that had happened while I was away.*

run-down[2] /͵· ˈ· ◄/ *adj* in poor health or condition: *You need a vacation; you look run-down.|an old run-down hotel* –see also RUN **down**

rung[1] /rʌŋ/ *n* one of the cross-bars that form the steps of a ladder

rung[2] *v past participle of* RING[3]

run-in /ˈ· ·/ *n AmE infml* a quarrel or disagreement, esp. with the police or an official body: *I've had a run-in with the law.*

run·ner /ˈrʌnər/ *n* **1** a person who runs, esp. in a race or as a sport: *only six runners in the race|a long-distance runner* **2** one of the two thin blades on which a SLEDGE (=wheelless carriage) slides over the snow

runner bean /ˈ·· ͵·/ *n BrE* for STRING BEAN

runner-up /͵·· ˈ·/ *n* **runners-up** the person or team that comes second in a race or competition

run·ning[1] /ˈrʌnɪŋ/ *n* **1** [U] the act or sport of running **2 in/out of the running** with some/no hope of winning: *Charles is still* **in the running** *for the job of director.*

running[2] *adj* [A] **1** (of water) flowing (from TAPS[1] (1)): *This hotel has hot and cold running water in every room.* **2** done while one is running along: *a running jump/ fight/ kick* **3** continuous: *He has a* **running battle** *with his wife over which of them is to use the car.|A* **running commentary** *is an account of a (sports) event given by a broadcaster while it is actually happening.* **4** for or concerned with running as a sport: *Where are my running shoes?* **5** giving out liquid: *a running nose/sore* **6 in running order** (of a machine) working properly

running[3] *adv (after a plural noun with a number)* one after the other without a break: *She won the prize three times running.*

running mate /ˈ·· ͵·/ *n* (in US politics) a person with whom another is RUNNING[1](11) for a pair of political positions of greater and lesser importance, esp. those of President and Vice-President: *Reagan and Bush were running mates in 1980.*

run·ny /ˈrʌniʲ/ *adj* **-nier, -niest** *infml* **1** more liquid than is usual or expected: *runny eggs* **2** (of the nose or eyes) producing liquid, as when one has a cold

run-of-the-mill /͵· · · ˈ· ◄/ *adj often derog* ordinary; not special or exciting: *a run-of-*

the-mill job in an office

run·way /ˈrʌnweɪ/ *n* a specially prepared hard surface, on which aircraft land and TAKE **off** (=leave the ground)

ru·pee /ruːˈpiʲ, ˈruːpiʲ/ *n* (a note or coin worth) a standard measure of money in India, Pakistan, Sri Lanka, etc.

rup·ture[1] /ˈrʌptʃər/ *n* **1** [C;U] (a) sudden breaking apart or bursting: *the rupture of a blood vessel* **2** [C] → HERNIA

rupture[2] *v* **-tured, -turing** **1** [I;T] to break or burst: *He'll rupture a muscle if he goes on dancing like that!* **2** [T] to give (oneself) a HERNIA: *He ruptured himself lifting a heavy weight.*

ru·ral /ˈrʊərəl/ *adj* of or like the COUNTRYSIDE; concerning country or village life: *people living in rural areas* –compare URBAN, RUSTIC –**rurally** *adv*

ruse /ruːz, ruːs/ *n* a trick to deceive an opponent: *The fox pretended to be dead as a ruse to confuse the hunters.*

rush[1] /rʌʃ/ *v* **1** [I;T] to (make someone or something) hurry or act quickly: *There's plenty of time; we don't have to rush.|They rushed up the stairs.|Let me think about it and don't rush me.* **2** [T] to attack suddenly and all together: *Maybe if we all rush him at once, he'll drop his gun.*

rush[2] *n* **1** [C] a sudden rapid hasty movement **2** [S;U +to-v] (too much) haste: *We don't have to leave yet; what's all the rush?|the rush* (=hurried demand) *for tickets for the football game* **3** [U] great activity and excitement: *I hate shopping during the Christmas rush when everyone's buying presents.*

rush[3] *n* a grasslike water plant whose long thin hollow stems are often dried and made into mats, baskets, etc.

rush hour /ˈ· ·/ *n* either of the two periods in the day when people are traveling to and from work in a city, and the streets, buses, and trains are crowded: *I try to get to work before the rush hour/before the rush-hour traffic starts.*

rusk /rʌsk/ *n* a kind of hard dry bread

rus·set /ˈrʌsɪt/ *n,adj* [S;U] *esp. lit* (of) a reddish brown or golden brown color

Rus·sian /ˈrʌʃən/ *adj n* (of or related to) **a** the language and people of Russia **b** the chief language, people, and state of the USSR: *the Russian language|Do you speak Russian?*

rust[1] /rʌst/ *n* [U] **1** the reddish brown surface that forms on iron and some other metals when attacked by water and air –see also RUSTY **2** the color of this: *a rust-colored dress*

rust[2] *v* [I;T] to (cause to) become covered with RUST (1): *The rain will rust the iron roof.|The lock has rusted and needs oil.*

rus·tic[1] /ˈrʌstɪk/ *adj often apprec* **1** connected with or suitable for the country; RURAL: *The village has a certain rustic charm.* **2** simple and rough, esp. as compared to (that of) the town: *their rustic way of speaking* –compare URBAN, RURAL

rustic[2] *n often derog* a person from the country, esp. a farm worker

rus·tle[1] /ˈrʌsəl/ *v* **-tled, -tling** **1** [I;T] **a** (of paper, dry leaves, silk, etc.) to make slight sounds when moved or rubbed together: *Her long silk skirt rustled as she walked.* **b** to cause to make these sounds: *Stop rustling that newspaper!* **c** to move along making the sounds: *The tiger rustled through the bushes.* **2** [T] *AmE* to steal (cattle or horses that are left loose in open country)

rustle sthg.↔**up** *v adv* [T *for*] to find a supply of; collect or prepare quickly: *I'll try and rustle up something to eat.*

rustle² *n* [S] a sound of rustling (RUSTLE¹ (1)): *We heard a rustle of leaves.*

rus·tler /'rʌslər/ *n AmE* a cattle thief; person who RUSTLES¹ (2)

rus·tling /'rʌslɪŋ/ *n* [U] **1** the sound of something that RUSTLES¹ (1): *He heard the rustling of a mouse in the box.* **2** *esp. AmE* the crime of stealing cattle or horses

rust·y /'rʌstiʸ/ *adj* **-ier, -iest 1** covered with

RUST¹ (1): *a rusty nail* **2** [F] (of one's knowledge of a subject) mostly forgotten: *My Greek history is a little rusty.* **–rustiness** *n* [U]

rut /rʌt/ *n* **1** a deep narrow track left in soft ground by a wheel: *The farm trucks have worn ruts in this field.* **2 be in/get into a rut** to be in/get into a fixed and dull way of life: *Don't let yourself get into a rut; find some new friends or change your job.*

ruth·less /'ruʷθlɪs/ *adj* (of a person or behavior) very cruel; without pity: *a ruthless enemy|his ruthless treatment of the conquered nation* **–ruthlessly** *adv* **–ruthlessness** *n* [U]

rye /raɪ/ *n* [U] a grass plant grown in cold countries for its grain, used for making flour: *rye bread|I'd like my sandwich on rye.* (=on rye bread)

S, s

> **SPELLING NOTE**
> Words with the sound /s/, may be spelled **c-**, like **city**, or **ps-**, like **psychology**.

S, s /ɛs/ **S's, s's** *or* **Ss, ss** the 19th letter of the English alphabet

S *written abbrev. said as:* south(ern)

-'s /z, s, ɪz/ *v short for:* **1** is: *What's that?* **2** has: *He's gone.* **3** us (only in the phrase **let's**) USAGE The short forms of **am, are, had, has, is, will,** and **would** are not used at the end of the sentence: *I'm not coming but they* **are.**|*They're not coming but I* **am.**|*She's wondering where he is.*

Sab·bath /'sæbəθ/ *n* [S] **1** the 7th day of the week; Saturday, kept as a day of rest and worship by Jews and some Christians **2** Sunday, kept as such a day by most Christian churches

sab·bat·i·cal /sə'bætɪkəl/ *n* a period, allowed with pay, in which one may leave one's place of work to travel and study: *Mary is away on Sabbatical this term.*

sa·ber *AmE*‖**sabre** *BrE* /'seʸbər/ *n* a heavy military sword, or a sword like this used in FENCING **–compare** FOIL²

sa·ble /'seʸbəl/ *n* [C;U] (the dark fur of) a small animal of northern Europe and Asia

sab·o·tage¹ /'sæbə͵taʒ/ *n* [U] intentional damage, usu. carried out secretly, to machines, buildings, etc., to weaken a business or a country

sabotage² *n* **-taged, -taging** [T] to practice SABOTAGE¹ on

sab·o·teur /͵sæbə'tɜr/ *n* a person who practices SABOTAGE¹

sac /sæk/ *n tech* a part shaped like a bag inside a plant or animal, usu. containing a particular liquid

sac·cha·rin /'sækərɪn/ *n* [U] a very sweet-tasting chemical used in place of sugar

esp. by people who want to reduce their weight or who must not eat sugar

sac·cha·rine /'sækərɪn, 'sækə͵raɪn, -͵riʸn/ *adj* very, esp. unpleasantly sweet

sa·chet /sæ'ʃeʸ/ *n* a small packet of a sweet smelling substance for putting among clothes in a drawer to give them a pleasant smell

sack¹ /sæk/ *n* [C] **1** *esp. AmE* a bag of strong usu. brown paper often with a flat bottom, such as large food stores give to people for carrying away the food they have bought: *a* GROCERY sack|*a paper sack* **2 a** a large bag, usu. of strong cloth or leather, used for storing or moving flour, coal, vegetables, grain, etc. **b** also **sackful** /'sækful/– the amount in one of these **3 hit the sack** *infml* to go to bed

sack² *v* [T] *BrE infml* for FIRE

sack out *v adv* [I] *AmE infml* to go to sleep; esp. for the night: *I'm ready to sack out.*

sack³ *v* [T] (of an army in former times) to destroy buildings, etc. in (a conquered city); PLUNDER: *The army sacked the city.*

sac·ra·ment /'sækrəmənt/ *n* (used esp. in the CATHOLIC church) any of several Christian ceremonies (including BAPTISM, the EUCHARIST, and marriage) considered as started by Jesus Christ or as signs of blessing or truth **–sacramental** /͵sækrə'mentəl/ *adj*

sa·cred /'seʸkrɪd/ *adj* religious in nature or use; holy by connection with God: *sacred music|sacred writings* **–see also** PROFANE

sacred cow /͵· '·/ *n derog* a thing or idea so much accepted that not even honest doubts about it are allowed

sac·ri·fice¹ /'sækrə͵faɪs/ *n* [C;U] **1** (an) offering to God or a god; esp. of an animal by killing it in a ceremony **2 a**/the loss or giving up of something of value, esp. for a particular purpose: *She made a lot of sacrifices to get an education.*

sacrifice² *v* **-ficed, -ficing 1** [I;T] to make an offering of (something) as a SACRIFICE¹ (1) **2**

[T] to give up or lose, esp. for some purpose or belief: *She sacrificed her life to save the child.*

sac·ri·fi·cial /ˌsækrəˈfɪʃəl/ *adj* of or being (a) SACRIFICE¹ (1): *a sacrificial lamb* –**sacrificially** *adv*

sac·ri·lege /ˈsækrəlɪdʒ/ *n* [C;U] (an act of) treating a holy thing without respect: (fig.) *I think it would be a sacrilege to destroy this beautiful old building.* –**sacrilegious** /ˌsækrəˈlɪdʒəs, -ˈliʸ-/ *adj* –**sacrilegiously** *adv*

sac·ro·sanct /ˈsækrowˌsæŋkt/ *adj often derog or humor* too holy or important to be allowed to suffer any harm or disrespect: *My weekends are sacrosanct; I never work then.*

sad /sæd/ *adj* -dd- **1** unhappy; feeling or causing grief or sorrow: *The news of his death made me very sad.|a sad day for our team* **2** [A] deserving blame; bad: *It's a sad state of affairs when children aren't taught to read properly.* –**sadly** *adv: He walked sadly away.* –**sadness** *n* [U]

sad·den /ˈsædn/ *v* [I;T] to make or become sad: *We were saddened by the death of our friend.*

sad·dle¹ /ˈsædl/ *n* **1** a usu. leather seat made to fit over the back of a horse, camel, etc. **2** a piece of meat from the back of a sheep or deer: *a saddle of lamb* **3** a seat on a bicycle, motorcycle, etc. **4 in the saddle** *infml* in a position to direct a job; in control

saddle² *v* -dled, -dling [T *with, upon*] to give (someone) an unpleasant duty, responsibility, etc.: *He's saddled with a large house which he can't sell.*

saddle up *v adv* [I;T(=**saddle** sthg. ↔ **up**)] to put a SADDLE on a horse: *They saddled up and rode away.*

sad·dle·bag /ˈsædlˌbæg/ *n* a bag on a horse, bicycle, motorcycle, etc., fixed behind, across, or below the SADDLE

sa·dism /ˈseʸdɪzəm, ˈsæ-/ *n* [U] unnatural fondness for cruelty to other people, sometimes as a way of getting sexual pleasure –compare MASOCHISM –**sadist** *n* –**sadistic** /səˈdɪstɪk/ *adj* –**sadistically** *adv*

sa·fa·ri /səˈfɑriʸ, səˈfæriʸ/ *n* a trip through wild country, esp. in Africa, hunting or photographing big animals: *to go* **on safari**

safe¹ /seʸf/ *adj* **1** [F *from*] out of danger; not threatened by harm; protected: *You will be safe from attack inside the building.| As soon as the animals were in their cages, we were safe.* **2** [F] not hurt; unharmed: *She came through the storm safe and sound.* (=completely unharmed) **3** [*for*] not allowing danger or harm: *Is this a safe place to swim?|Keep these papers in a safe place.* –opposite **unsafe 4** not likely to cause risk or disagreement: *It's safe to say that crime will continue at a high rate this year.* **5 on the safe side** *infml* taking no risks; being more careful than may be necessary: *Let's be on the safe*

side and take more money than we think we'll need. **6 play it safe** to take no risks –**safely** *adv* –**safeness** *n* [U]

safe² *n* a box or cupboard with thick metal sides and a lock used for protecting valuable things from thieves

safe-de·pos·it /ˌ· ·ˈ··/ *n* [U] safe storing of small valuable objects, usu. in small boxes (**safe-deposit boxes**) in a special room in a bank

safe·guard /ˈseʸfgɑrd/ *v,n* [C;T *against*] (to be) a means of protection: *The new law contains safeguards against the misuse of government power.*

safe·keep·ing /ˌseʸfˈkiʸpɪŋ/ *n* [U] the action or state of protection from harm for things of value: *Put your important papers in the bank for safekeeping.*

safe·ty /ˈseʸftiʸ/ *n* [U] the condition of being safe; freedom from danger, harm, or risk: *My main concern is for the safety of my family.|She led the children to a place of safety.|The safety of the ship is the captain's responsibility.*

safety belt /ˈ·· ˌ·/ *n* → SEAT BELT

safety match /ˈ·· ˌ·/ *n* a match which can be lighted only when rubbed along a special surface on its box

safety pin /ˈ·· ˌ·/ *n* a wire pin which is bent so that its point is covered when the pin is being used

safety ra·zor /ˈ·· ˌ··/ *n* a RAZOR with a cover over its blade, to protect the skin from being cut

safety valve /ˈ·· ˌ·/ *n* a part of a machine which allows gas, steam, etc., to escape when the pressure becomes too great: (fig.) *I think that sports are a safety valve for people's violent feelings.*

saf·fron /ˈsæfrən/ *n* [U] **1** powder of a deep orange color used for coloring and for giving a special taste to food **2** an orange-yellow color

sag¹ /sæg/ *v* -gg- [I *down*] to sink or bend downwards, esp. from the usual or correct position: *The branch sagged (down) under the weight of the apples.|(fig.) My spirits sagged* (=I became less happy) *when I saw all the work I had to do.*

sag² *n* [S *in*] (a) downward bending or sinking: *a sag in the floor*

sa·ga /ˈsɑgə/ *n* a long story about a time in history, group of people, etc.

sa·ga·cious /səˈgeʸʃəs/ *adj lit* wise –**sagaciously** *adv* –**sagacity** /səˈgæsətiʸ/ *n* [U]

sage¹ /seʸdʒ/ *n,adj* (a person, esp. an old man, who is) wise as a result of long thinking and experience –**sagely** *adv*

sage² *n* [U] a type of MINT¹ used in cooking

sage·brush /ˈseʸdʒbrʌʃ/ *n* [U] a type of short bushy plant very common on the dry plains of the western US

Sag·it·tar·i·us /ˌsædʒəˈtɛəriʸəs/ *n* see ZODIAC

said¹ /sɛd/ *v* past tense and past participle of SAY

said² *adj* [the A] *fml* the particular (person, thing, etc.) spoken of before: *John James Smith is charged with stealing. The said John*

Smith was seen leaving the store at the times stated.

sail[1] /seɪl/ n **1** [C;U] a piece of strong cloth fixed in position on a ship to move it through the water by the force of the wind: *a ship* **in full sail** (=with all its sails spread) **2** [S] a short trip, usu. for pleasure, in a boat with these: *Let's go for a sail this afternoon.* **3** [C] any of the broad wind-catching blades of a WINDMILL **4 set sail** to begin a trip at sea

sail[2] v **1** [I;T] **a** (of a ship) to travel on the water: *to watch the ships sail by* **b** to command or direct (a ship) on the water: *The captain sailed the ship through the passage.* **2** [I] to travel by ship: *We sailed across the Atlantic in five days.* **3** [I] to begin a voyage: *We sail/Our ship sails tomorrow (for New York).* **4** to move smoothly or easily: *birds sailing across the sky|She sailed through the examination.* (=she passed easily)

sail·boat /'seɪlˌboʷt/ *AmE* ‖**sailing boat** /'·· ˌ·/ *BrE*– *n* a boat driven by one or more sails, esp. a small boat used for racing and pleasure trips

sail·ing /'seɪlɪŋ/ *n* [U] **1** the skill of directing the course of a ship **2** the sport of riding in or directing a small boat with sails

sail·or /'seɪlər/ *n* **1** a person with a job on a ship, esp. one who is not a ship's officer **2** a member of a navy

saint /seɪnt/ *n* **1** a person officially recognized after death as especially holy and worthy of formal honor in the Christian church **2** *infml* a person with a holy or completely unselfish way of life: *My mother was a real saint.* –**sainthood** *n* [U]

Saint *n* [A] (a title before a SAINT's (1) name): *Saint Joan of Arc*

saint·ly /'seɪntliʸ/ *adj* **-lier, -liest** of or like a SAINT: *a saintly man/life* –**saintliness** *n* [U]

sake /seɪk/ *n* **1 for the sake of: a** for the good of: *Do it for my sake.* (=to please me) **b** for the purpose of: *He's just talking for the sake of hearing his own voice.* **2 for God's/ goodness/pity('s) sake** *infml* **a** (used when asking strongly for something): *For goodness sake, don't tell him!* **b** (shows annoyance): *What's the matter now, for God's sake?*

sa·la·cious /sə'leɪʃəs/ *adj fml* sexually improper or shocking; OBSCENE: *a salacious movie* –**salaciously** *adv*

sal·ad /'sæləd/ *n* [C;U] a mixture of vegetables served cold, sometimes with other foods added: *a green salad* (=mostly LETTUCE)| *chicken salad*

sa·la·mi /sə'lɑmiʸ/ *n* [U] a large SAUSAGE with a strong salty taste

sal·a·ried /'sæləriʸd/ *adj* having a SALARY, as opposed to wages: *salaried workers |a salaried job*

sal·a·ry /'sæləriʸ/ *n* **-ries** [C;U] fixed regular pay each month for a job: *a high/low salary* –*see* PAY (USAGE)

sale /seɪl/ *n* **1** an act of selling; contract or agreement exchanging something for money: *The sale of my house hasn't been easy.|I hope I'll make a sale tody.* **2** a special offering of goods at lower prices than usual: *I got this hat cheap at a/in the sale.|regular*

price *$5 sale price $2.50* –see also RUMMAGE SALE **3** →AUCTION: *There's a furniture sale every Tuesday.* **4** the total amount sold of something offered to be sold: *We're hoping for a large sale of our new product.|We have very good sales figures this month.* (=we sold a lot) **5 for sale** offered to be sold, esp. by a private owner: *The sign on the house says "For Sale".* **6 on sale a** offered to be sold, esp. in a store: *Will the new product be on sale next month?* **b** *AmE* at or in a SALE (2): *I bought this dress on sale for $35, it used to be $85.*

sales /seɪlz/ *adj* [A] of, for, or related to selling: *the sales department of a company|the sales director*

sales·clerk /'seɪlzklɜrk/ *AmE*‖**shop assistant** *BrE*– *n* a person who serves buyers in a store

sales·person /'seɪlzˌpɜrsən/ **salesman** /-mən/ *masc.*, **saleswoman** /-ˌwʊmən/ *fem.*– *n* **-people** /-ˌpiʸpəl/ a person whose job is to sell goods either in a store or directly to businesses, homes, etc.

sales slip /'· ·/ *n AmE* a receipt given at a store

sales tax /'· ·/ *n* [C;U] (in most places in the US) (an amount or rate of) money charged as tax in addition to the ordinary sale price of an article

sa·li·ent /'seɪliʸənt/ *adj fml* most noticeable or important: *the salient points of the speech*

sa·line /'seɪliʸn, -laɪn/ *adj* of, related to, or containing salt: *a saline lake*

sa·li·va /sə'laɪvə/ *n* [U] the natural watery liquid produced in the mouth –**salivary** /'sæləˌvɛriʸ/ *adj* :*the salivary* GLANDS

sal·i·vate /'sæləˌveɪt/ *v* **-vated, -vating** [I] to produce SALIVA in the mouth, esp. at the sight or thought of food –**salivation** /ˌsæləˈveɪʃən/ [U]

sal·low /'sæloʷ/ *adj* (of the skin) yellow and unhealthy-looking –**sallowness** *n* [U]

salm·on /'sæmən/ *n* **salmon** or **salmons** **1** [C;U] a large fish with silvery skin and yellowish-pink flesh eaten as food: *I like salmon, but it's expensive.* **2** [U] a yellowish-pink color like the flesh of a salmon

sa·lon /sə'lɑn/ *n* a stylish or fashionable business: *a beauty salon*

sa·loon /sə'luʷn/ *n* **1** (esp. formerly in the American west) a public drinking place **2** a room for the social use of a ship's passengers **3** *BrE* for SEDAN

salt[1] /sɔlt/ *n* **1** [U] a very common white solid with many uses, esp. in cooking to improve the taste of food: *The vegetables need more salt.|Please pass the salt.* **2** [C] *tech* a chemical substance which may be formed by the combining of an acid and a BASE[1] (4) or metal **3** [C] **old salt** an old, experienced sailor **4 rub salt in someone's wound(s)** to make someone's sorrow, pain, etc., even worse **5 the salt of the earth** a person or people regarded as admirable **6 take something with a grain/ pinch of salt** to accept that something is probably completely untrue **7 worth one's salt** *infml* worthy of respect, or of one's pay

salt[2] *v* [T] to add salt to; put salt on: *Have you*

salted the vegetables?

salt sthg.↔ **away** *v adv* [T] *infml* **1** to save (esp. money) for the future

salt³ *adj* **1** containing, full of, or tasting of salt; salty: *salt water* **2** [A] formed by salty water: *a salt lake*

salt·cel·lar /'sɔlt,sɛlər/ *n* **1** a small, open dish for salt, used at meals **2** → SALTSHAKER

salt·shak·er /'sɔlt,ʃeʸkər/ *AmE*‖also **saltcellar**– *n* a container with one or more holes in the top for shaking salt out usu. kept on the table

salt·wa·ter /'sɔlt,wɔtər, -,wɑ-/ *adj* [A] being or belonging to salty water or sea water: *saltwater fish* –opposite **freshwater**

salt·y /'sɔlti/ *adj* **-ier, -iest** of, containing, or tasting of salt –**saltiness** *n* [U]

sa·lu·bri·ous /sə'luʷbriʸəs/ *adj fml or lit* favorable to good health; WHOLESOME: *They live in a very salubrious area.* –**salubriousness** *n* [U]

sal·u·tar·y /'sælyə,tɛriʸ/ *adj* causing improvement or a good effect: *The accident was a salutary experience; I'll never drink and drive again.*

sal·u·ta·tion /,sælyə'teʸʃən/ *n* [C;U] *fml* (an) expression of greeting by words or action

sa·lute¹ /sə'luʷt/ *v* **-luted, -luting 1** [I;T] to make a SALUTE² (1a) (to): *to salute an officer* **2** [T] *lit* to greet, esp. with words or a sign: *He saluted his friend with a wave.*

salute² *n* **1** [C] a military sign of recognition, such as **a** a raising of the right hand to the forehead **b** a ceremonial firing of guns or lowering of flags **2** [C;U] *lit* a greeting; SALUTATION

sal·vage¹ /'sælvɪdʒ/ *n* [U] **1** the act of saving things from destruction, esp. of saving a wrecked ship or its goods from the sea **2** property saved from being destroyed: *a sale of salvage from the wreck*

salvage² *v* **-vaged, -vaging** [T] to save (goods or property) from loss or damage: *We were unable to salvage anything when the factory burned down.*

sal·va·tion /sæl'veʸʃən/ *n* [U] **1** (esp. in the Christian religion) the saving or state of being saved from SIN **2** *fml* saving or preservation from loss, ruin, or failure: *The people have no food; their salvation depends on quick action.*

Salvation Ar·my /·,·· ·'··/ *n* [S] a Christian organization that has military uniforms and ranks, and is best known for its help to poor people

salve¹ /sæv/ *n* [C;U] (an) oily paste (OINTMENT) for putting on a cut, wound, etc.

salve² *v* **salved, salving** [T] *lit* to make (esp. feelings) less painful; SOOTHE: *He tried to salve his conscience with excuses, but he knew he was wrong.*

sal·ver /'sælvər/ *n* a fine metal plate, esp. of silver, for serving food, drink, etc., formally

---

SPELLING NOTE

Words with the sound /s/, may be spelled **c-**, like **city**, or **ps-**, like **psychology**.

---

sal·vo /'sælvoʷ/ *n* **-vos** *or* **-voes** [*of*] a firing of several guns at once, in a ceremony or battle

Sa·mar·i·tan /sə'mærətn/ *n* **good Samaritan** a person who gives help to someone in need

sam·ba /'sæmbə, 'sɑmbə/ *n* a fast dance of Brazilian origin

same¹ /seʸm/ *adj* [*the, this, that, these, those* +*adj*] **1** not changed or different; not another: *Father sits in the same chair every evening.*|*She wears the same red dress to every party.*|*You've made the same mistakes as last time/that you made last time.* **2** alike in every way: *We eat (much) the same thing for breakfast every day.*|*Men and women should get the same pay for doing the same jobs.* **3** **one and the same** exactly the same **4** **same here** *infml* the same with me; me too: *"I think I ate too much." "Same here. I did too."*

same² *pron* **1** the same thing, person, etc.: *All the newspapers say the same.*|*Thanks for helping me; I'll do the same for you sometime.* **2** **same to you!** *infml* (in answer to a greeting or sometimes an angry wish) I wish you the same thing: *"Merry Christmas." "Same to you!"*

same·ness /'seʸmnɪs/ *n* [U] the state of being (almost) the same; very close likeness: *I don't like his books because they all have a certain sameness about them.*

sam·ple¹ /'sæmpəl/ *n,adj* (being) a small part representing the whole; typical small quantity, thing, etc.: *The nurse took a sample of my blood/a blood sample for tests.*|*Here are some sample questions from last year's exam.*

sample² *v* **-pled, -pling** [T] **1** to take and examine a SAMPLE¹ of; test: *She sampled the wine before giving it to the others.* **2** to get to know about by experience; TRY **out:** *to sample the pleasures of country life*

sam·u·rai /'sæmə,raɪ/ *n* **-rai** *or* **-rais** a military nobleman in Japan in former times

san·a·to·ri·um /,sænə'tɔriʸəm, -'toʷriʸəm/ ‖also **sanitarium, sanatarium** /,sænə'tɛəriʸ əm/ *AmE*– *n* **-riums** *or* **-ria** /riʸə/ a kind of hospital for sick people who are getting better and need treatment, rest, etc.

sanc·ti·fy /'sæŋktə,faɪ/ *v* **-fied, -fying** [T] *fml* to make holy: *The priest sanctified the church with a special ceremony.* –**sanctification** /,sæŋktəfə'keʸʃən/ *n* [U]

sanc·ti·mo·ni·ous /,sæŋktə'moʷniʸəs/ *adj derog* making a show of being religious; pretending to be holy: *sanctimonious behavior* –**sanctimoniously** *adv* –**sanctimoniousness** *n* [U]

sanc·tion¹ /'sæŋkʃən/ *n* **1** [U] *fml* permission or approval: *The army acts only with the sanction of the government.* **2** [C] an action taken against a person or esp. a country that has broken a law or rule: *We will establish sanctions against any country that trades with our enemies.* **3** [C] something that forces people to keep a rule or standard: *a moral sanction*

sanction² *v* [T] *fml* to accept, approve, or permit: *The church would not sanction his second marriage.*

sanc·ti·ty /'sæŋktətiʸ/ *n* [U] holiness;

satchel

SACREDness: *the sanctity of a formal promise*
sanc·tu·ar·y /'sæŋktʃuᵂɛriʸ/ n -ies 1 [C] the part of a Christian religious building considered most holy 2 [C;U] (a place of) protection or safety from harm, esp. for a person escaping from officers of the law 3 [C] an area for birds or animals where they may not be hunted

sanc·tum /'sæŋktəm/ n -tums or -ta /tə/ 1 a holy place 2 a private place or room where one can be alone

sand¹ /sænd/ n [U] the small loose grains of material found on beaches and in deserts, used for making cement, glass, etc.

sand² v [T] 1 [*down*] to make smoother by rubbing, usu. with SANDPAPER 2 to put sand on: *The roads were sanded after the snowstorm.*

san·dal /'sændl/ n a light open-sided shoe worn in warm weather

san·dal·wood /'sændl̩wʊd/ n [U] 1 a hard yellowish sweet-smelling Asian wood 2 a brown color

sand·bank /'sændbæŋk/ n a bank of sand in a river, harbor, etc.

sand·box /'sændbɑks/ AmE‖**sandpit** BrE– n a box, or place in the ground, containing sand for children to play in

sand·cas·tle /'sænd₁kæsəl/ n a small model, esp. of a castle, built in sand by children

sand dune /'· ·/ n → DUNE

sand·pa·per /'sænd₁peʸpər/ v,n [T;U] (to rub with) paper covered on one side with sand or fine grainy material, used for making rough surfaces smoother

sand·pit /'sænd₁pɪt/ n BrE for SANDBOX

sand·stone /'sændstoʷn/ n [U] soft rock formed by sand fixed in a natural cement

sand·storm /'sændstɔrm/ n a windstorm in which sand is blown around in a desert

sand·wich¹ /'sændwɪtʃ, 'sænwɪtʃ/ n two pieces of bread with some other food between them, eaten with the hands: *a cheese sandwich*

sandwich² v [T *in, between*] to put tightly in between two other things: *a piece of plastic sandwiched between two pieces of glass*

sandwich board /'··· ₁·· / n a pair of advertising signs for hanging at the front and back of a person (**sandwich man**) who walks around in public

sand·y /'sændiʸ/ adj -ier, -iest 1 containing or full of sand 2 (esp. of hair) yellowish-brown in color, like sand –**sandiness** n [U]

sane /seʸn/ adj 1 healthy in mind; not mad or CRAZY (1) –opposite **insane** 2 produced by good reasonable thinking; sensible: *a sane eductional policy* –**sanely** adv

sang /sæŋ/ v past tense of SING

sang·froid /₁sɑŋ'frwɑ, ₁sɑ̃-/ n [U] French calm courage; self-control

san·guine /'sæŋgwɪn/ adj fml expecting the best; showing OPTIMISM: *a person of sanguine temper*

san·i·tar·i·um /₁sænə'tɛəriʸəm/ n -iums or -ia /iʸə/ AmE for SANATORIUM

san·i·tar·y /'sænə₁tɛriʸ/ adj 1 of or concerning health, esp. the treatment or removal of waste, dirt, or infection: *the local council's*

sanitary department 2 clean; free from danger to health: *It's not very sanitary to let flies come near food.*

sanitary nap·kin /₁···· '··/ AmE‖**sanitary towel** BrE– n soft paper worn between a woman's legs during her PERIOD (5) to take up the flow from the WOMB

san·i·ta·tion /₁sænə'teʸʃən/ n [U] means for protecting public health, esp. by the removing and treatment of waste

san·i·ty /'sænətiʸ/ n [U] the quality of being SANE –opposite **insanity**

sank /sæŋk/ v past tense of SINK

San·ta Claus /'sæntə ₁klɔz, 'sæntiʸ-/ ‖also **Father Christmas** BrE– n an imaginary old man in red clothes with a long white beard believed by children to bring presents at Christmas

sap¹ /sæp/ n 1 [U] the watery juice carrying food through a plant 2 [C] infml a stupid person likely to be tricked or treated unfairly: *Didn't you know I was joking, you sap?*

sap² v -pp- [T] to weaken or destroy, esp. over a long time: *Her long illness gradually sapped her strength.*

sap·ling /'sæplɪŋ/ n a young tree

sap·phire /'sæfaɪər/ n [C;U] a precious stone of a transparent bright blue color

sar·casm /'sɑr₁kæzəm/ n [U] speaking or writing using expressions which clearly mean the opposite to what is felt: *"It was a good idea to put the dog in the same room as my cat," she said with sarcasm.*

sar·cas·tic /sɑr'kæstɪk/ adj using or marked by SARCASM: *a sarcastic remark/person* –**sarcastically** adv

sar·dine /sɑr'diʸn/ n 1 a young small fish, e.g. the HERRING, esp. as food preserved in oil 2 like sardines infml packed, crowded, etc., very tightly together

sar·don·ic /sɑr'dɑnɪk/ adj SCORNFUL; CYNICAL –**sardonically** adv

sa·ri /'sɑriʸ/ n a length of light cloth wrapped around the body, worn esp. by Hindu women

sash¹ /sæʃ/ n a length of cloth worn around the waist, or (usu. as a mark of honor) over one shoulder

sash² n a frame into which sheets of glass are fixed to form part of a window, door, etc.

sash win·dow /'· ₁··/ n a window of two SASHes² which opens by sliding one up or down –compare CASEMENT WINDOW

sass /sæs/ n [U] AmE infml for SAUCE (2): *Don't give me any of your sass!*

sas·sa·fras /'sæsə₁fræs/ n [U] (the dried outer covering of the root of) a type of small tree of Asia and North America, used to make a kind of tea

sass·y /'sæsiʸ/ adj -ier, -iest AmE infml for SAUCY: *a sassy child*

sat /sæt/ v past tense and participle of SIT

Sa·tan /'seʸtn/ n the devil

sa·tan·ic /sə'tænɪk, seʸ-/ adj very cruel, evil, or wicked; FIENDISH –**satanically** adv

satch·el /'sætʃəl/ n a small bag, usu. with a band for carrying over the shoulder: *He carries his books in his school satchel.*

sate /seɪt/ v **sated, sating** [T usu. pass.] fml to satisfy with more than enough of something: I've been eating all morning and I'm completely sated.

sat·el·lite /'sætḷ‚aɪt/ n **1** a heavenly body or man-made object which moves around a larger one (a PLANET): The moon is a satellite of the earth.|The broadcast came from Europe by satellite. **2** something, esp. a country, that depends on the power of another

sa·ti·ate /'seɪʃiʸ‚eʸt/ v **-ated, -ating** [T usu. pass] to satisfy fully, esp. too fully

sat·in /'sætn/ adj,n [U] (made of) a kind of very fine shiny smooth silk cloth

sat·in·y /'sætn-iʸ/ also **satin**– adj very pleasantly smooth, shiny, and soft, like satin: satiny skin

sat·ire /'sætaɪər/ n [C;U on] (a work of) literature, etc., intended to show the foolishness of something in an amusing way: The play is a satire on the government's defense policy. –compare SATYR

sa·tir·i·cal /sə'tɪrɪkəl/ also **satiric** /sə'tɪrɪk/– adj being or using SATIRE –**satirically** adv

sat·i·rize also **-rise** BrE /'sætə‚raɪz/ v **-rized, -rizing** [T] to use SATIRE against: a book satirizing the military government

sat·is·fac·tion /‚sætɪs'fækʃən/ n **1** [C;U] (something that causes) contentment or pleasure: I always get a feeling of satisfaction from doing a job properly. –opposite **dissatisfaction 2** [U] fml fulfilment of a need, desire, etc.: satisfaction of public demand **3** [U] fml condition of being certain: It's been proved **to my satisfaction** (= I am fully persuaded) that you're telling the truth.

sat·is·fac·to·ry /‚sætɪs'fæktəriʸ/ adj good enough; pleasing: Of all the radios he tried, only one was satisfactory.|Sales are up 20% from last year; that's very satisfactory. –opposite **unsatisfactory** –**satisfactorily** adv

sat·is·fy /'sætɪs‚faɪ/ v **-fied, -fying** [T] **1** to make (someone) happy; please: She told me that she was not satisfied with my examination results.|Some people are very hard to satisfy. –opposite **dissatisfy 2** to be or give enough for; fulfill (a need, desire, etc.): You can't vote until you have satisfied certain conditions. **3** [that/of] to cause to believe fully: Are you satisfied that he is telling the truth?

sat·is·fy·ing /'sætɪs‚faɪ-ɪŋ/ adj giving satisfaction: a satisfying meal/job –**satisfyingly** adv

sat·u·rate /'sætʃə‚reʸt/ v **-rated, -rating** [T with] **1** to make completely wet; SOAK[1] (2): The blood saturated his shirt. **2** to fill completely: It's hard to get a teaching job now; the MARKET[1] (4) is saturated. (= there are too many teachers and not enough jobs) –**saturation** /‚sætʃə'reʸʃən/ n [U]

Sat·ur·day /'sætərdiʸ, -‚deʸ/ n the 7th and last day of the week; day before Sunday: He'll

---

SPELLING NOTE

Words with the sound /s/, may be spelled **c-**, like **city**, or **ps-**, like **psychology**.

---

arrive (on) Saturday.|She arrived (on) Saturday morning.|We do our shopping (on) Saturdays.

Sat·urn /'sætərn/ n the PLANET which is 6th in order from the sun and is surrounded by large rings

sat·yr /'sætər, 'seʸ-/ n (in ancient literature) a god usu. represented as half human and half goat –compare SATIRE

sauce /sɔs/ n **1** [C;U] a thick, usu. cooked liquid put on or eaten with food: TOMATO sauce|a white sauce for fish|apple sauce **2** also **sass** AmE– [U] infml disrespectful (but often harmless) talk, as to a parent, teacher, etc.: That's enough of your sauce, young man! **3** [U] infml alcoholic drink; WHISKEY

sauce·pan /'sɔs-pæn/ n a deep usu. round metal cooking pot with a handle and usu. a lid –see illustration on page 379

sau·cer /'sɔsər/ n a small plate with edges curving up, made for putting a cup on –see illustration on page 379

sau·cy /'sɔsiʸ/ also **sassy** AmE– adj **-cier, -ciest** infml disrespectful, or producing sexual interest, in an amusing way –**saucily** adv –**sauciness** n [U]

sau·er·kraut /'sauər‚kraut/ n [U] a dish made from small pieces of a leafy vegetable (CABBAGE) allowed to become sour by keeping them in salt

sau·na /'sɔnə, 'saunə/ also **sauna bath** /'·· ‚·/– n (a room or building for) a Finnish type of bath in steam

saun·ter /'sɔntər, 'sɑn-/ v [I] to walk in an unhurried way –**saunter** n [S]: Let's take a saunter down to the lake.

sau·sage /'sɔsɪdʒ/ n [C;U] a thin edible tube of animal skin filled with meat, bread, SPICES, etc.: Would you prefer sausage or BACON with your eggs?

sau·té[1] /sɔ'teʸ, soʷ-/ n a SAUTÉed[2] dish: a sauté of potatoes and onions

sauté[2] v **-téed** or **-téd, -téeing** or **-téing** [T] to cook quickly in a little hot oil or fat: Sauté the onions for five minutes.

sav·age[1] /'sævɪdʒ/ adj **1** forcefully cruel or violent; fierce; FEROCIOUS: a savage dog| savage anger|a savage attack in the newspapers **2** [A] uncivilized: savage people/customs –**savagely** adv –**savageness** n [U]

savage[2] n an uncivilized person

savage[3] v **-aged, -aging** [T] (esp. of an animal) to attack and bite fiercely: savaged by a mad dog

sav·age·ry /'sævɪdʒriʸ/ n **-ries** [C;U] (an act of) SAVAGE[1] (1) behavior: He beat the dog with great savagery.|the savageries of war

sa·van·na, -nah /sə'vænə/ n [C;U] (an open flat area of) grassy land in a warm country

save[1] /seʸv/ v **saved, saving 1** [T from] to make safe from danger: Help! Save me!|He saved his friend from falling. **2** [I;T up, for] to keep (esp. money) for later use: Children should learn to save.|We're saving (up) for a new car.|She saved her strength for the last minutes of the race. **3** [T +v-ing/from] to make unnecessary (for): Will you go to the store for me? It'll save (me) a trip.|It'll save (me) going into town.|a labor-saving

machine 4 [T] (of a soccer player, esp. a GOALKEEPER) to stop one's opponents from getting (a goal): *He saved three goals.* **5 save one's breath** to keep silent because talking would be useless: *Save your breath; you'll never change her mind.*

save on sthg. *v prep* [T] to avoid the waste of: *If we all go in one car, we'll save on gasoline.*

save² *n* (in soccer) a quick action by the GOALKEEPER which prevents the opponents scoring (SCORE²) a goal

save³ also **saving** *–prep lit & old use* leaving out; except: *He answered all the questions save one.*|*Save for one old lady, the bus was empty.*

sav·er /ˈseʸvər/ *n* **1** something that prevents loss or waste: *a time-saver* **2** a person who saves money

saving grace /ˌ·· ˈ·/ *n* a saving quality or fact that makes something acceptable in spite of weakness, faults, etc.; REDEEMing feature: *The movie's saving grace is its beautiful photography.*

sav·ings /ˈseʸvɪŋz/ *n* [P] money saved, esp. in a bank

savings ac·count /ˈ·· ·ˌ/ *n* a bank account which earns interest from money DEPOSITed into it

savings bank /ˈ·· ·ˌ·/ *n* a bank which has only interest-earning kinds of accounts

sav·ior *AmE*‖**saviour** *BrE* /ˈseʸvyər/ *n* **1** [C] a person or thing that saves from danger or loss: *She was her country's savior during the war.* **2** [S] (*usu. cap.*) (in the Christian religion) Jesus Christ

sa·vor¹ *AmE*‖**savour** *BrE* /ˈseʸvər/ *n* [S;U] a taste or smell: *The meat had cooked too long and lost its savor.*

savor² *AmE*‖**savour** *BrE v* [T] to enjoy, as by tasting, slowly and purposefully: *She drank the wine slowly, savoring every drop.*

sa·vor·y *AmE*‖**savoury** *BrE* /ˈseʸvəriʸ/ *adj* **1** pleasant or attractive in taste **2** (of food) not sweet

sav·vy /ˈsæviʸ/ *adj infml* having practical knowledge and ability: *He's a savvy New Yorker; he knows how to get things cheap.* *–savvy n* [U]: *It takes a lot of savvy to succeed in this business.*

saw¹ /sɔ/ *n* a hand- or power-driven tool for cutting hard materials

saw² *v* **sawed, sawed** *AmE*‖also **sawn** /sɔn/, **sawing 1** [I;T *up, off, etc.*] to cut with a SAW: *He sawed the logs up into little pieces.*|*The tree was nearly sawn through.*|*She sawed off a dead branch.* **2** [I *at*] to move one's hand, a knife, etc., backwards and forwards, (as if) cutting with a SAW: *He sawed at the loaf of bread with his knife.*

saw³ *v* past tense of SEE

saw·dust /ˈsɔdʌst/ *n* [U] dust or very small pieces of wood made by a SAW in cutting

Sax·on /ˈsæksən/ *adj* of or concerning a people of north Germany who conquered and settled in England in the Fifth century *–see* also ANGLO-SAXON

sax·o·phone /ˈsæksəˌfoʷn/ also **sax** /sæks/ *infml – n* a metal musical wind instrument

usu. used in JAZZ and dance music *–***saxophonist** *n* /ˈsæksˈəfɔnɪst/ *n*

say¹ /seʸ/ *v* **said** /sɛd/ **saying,** *3rd person sing. present tense* **says** /sɛz/ **1** [T] to pronounce (a sound, word, etc.): *"I'd like another drink," he said.*|*Have you said your prayers?*|*"I think I'll go home now," I said to myself.* (=thought) **2** [I;T +(*that*)] to express (a thought, intention, etc.) in words: *He said he would like another drink.*|*Don't believe anything he says.*|*Who can say how it happened?*|*"Will we win?" "I can't say."* (=I don't know)|*My watch says* (=shows) *5:30.* *–see Study Notes on page 481* **3** [T +(*that*) (*usu. in commands*)] to suppose; ASSUME(1): *Say your plan fails: then what do we do?* **4 it goes without saying** of course; clearly: *It goes without saying that our plans depend on the weather.* **5 that is to say** also **i.e.** *abbrev. –* in other words; expressed another (more exact) way **6 they say** people say; it's usually thought **7 to say nothing of** as well as; including: *three people hurt, to say nothing of the damage to the building* **8 you don't say (so)!** *infml* (an expression of surprise) **9 you said it** *infml esp. AmE* you're right; I agree: *"Let's go home." "You said it! I'm tired."*

USAGE Compare **say, tell, inform, speak,** and **talk; 1 Say** is nearly always [T] and can only have words (not a person) as its object: *He said "I'm tired."*|*He said (that) he was tired.*|*He said a few words then sat down.* **Tell** is nearly always [T] and can have one object or two: words, or a person, or both: *He told us (that) he was tired.*| *He told (us) a funny story.* **Inform** (*fml*) is always [T] and its object is always a person: *He informed us that he was tired.* Of all these words, only **say** can be used with the actual words spoken, and only **tell** can be used for commands: *He said "Open the door".*|*He told me to open the door.* **2 Speak** and **talk** are usually [I]. They are very close in meaning, but **talk** sometimes gives the idea of a conversation, rather than of a single person making statements: *We talked for hours (about politics).*|*The director spoke to us about the company's plans.* **Speak** and **talk** are sometimes [T], but can never have a person as their object: *Do you speak French?*|*You're talking nonsense!*

say² *n* [S;U] **1 (a)** power or right of (sharing in) decision: *The unions had no say*|*very little say in the new pay agreement.* **2 have one's say** to have the chance to say something, esp. to express one's opinion

say³ *interj AmE infml* (used for expressing surprise or a sudden idea): *Say, haven't I seen you somewhere before?*

say·ing /ˈseʸɪŋ/ *n* a well-known wise statement; PROVERB: *As the saying goes, "There's no smoke without fire."*

SC, S.C. *written abbrev.* said as: South Carolina /ˌsaʊθ ˌkærəˈlaɪnə/ (a state in the US)

scab /skæb/ *n* **1** a hard mass of dried blood which forms over a cut or wound **2** *derog infml* a worker who does the work of one who is on STRIKE² (1)

scab·bard /ˈskæbərd/ *n* a leather or metal

tube enclosing the blade of a sword, knife, etc.

scab·by /'skæbiʸ/ *adj* **-bier, -biest** covered with SCABS (1)

scads /skædz/ *n* [P] *AmE infml* large numbers or amounts: *There were scads of people at the concert.*

scaf·fold /'skæfəld, -foʷld/ *n* **1** a framework around a building being built, for workmen to stand on **2** a raised stage for the killing of criminals (esp. in former times) by hanging: *His life of murder led him to the scaffold.* (=death by hanging)

scaf·fold·ing /'skæfəldɪŋ, -,foʷl-/ *n* [U] poles and boards used in a system of SCAFFOLDs (1)

scal·a·wag /'skælə,wæg/ *AmE*‖**scallywag** *BrE*– *n usu.* humor a trouble-making or dishonest person; RASCAL

scald¹ /skɔld/ *v* [T] **1** to burn with hot liquid: *He scalded his tongue on/with the hot coffee.|They were scalded to death by steam from the burst pipe.* **2** to clean (e.g. dishes) with boiling water or steam

scald² *n* a skin burn from hot liquid or steam

scald·ing /'skɔldɪŋ/ *adj* boiling or nearly boiling: *scalding hot water*

scale¹ /skeʸl/ *n* **1** a pair of pans for weighing an object by comparing it with a known weight: *a laboratory scale used for weighing gold* –see PAIR (USAGE) **2** any weighing machine: *He weighed himself on the bathroom scales.* –see illustration on page 683

scale² *n* **1** [C] a set of numbers or standards for measuring or comparing: *a pay scale for all the workers in the company|wind forces measured on a standard scale* **2** [C] a set of marks, esp. numbers, on an instrument at exactly fixed distances apart, used for measuring: *a ruler with a metric scale* **3** [C] a set of numbers comparing measurements on a map or model with actual measurements: *a scale of 1 inch to the mile|a scale model/ drawing* (=made according to a scale)|*a large/small-scale map* **4** [C;U] size, esp. in relation to other things or to what is usual: *a large-scale business operation|business on a large/grand scale* **5** [C] a set of musical notes in upward or downward order: *the scale of A* (=with the note A for its base) **6 to scale** according to a fixed rule for reducing the size of something in a drawing, model, etc.: *The plan of the building was carefully drawn to scale, except one part which was out of scale.*

scale³ *n* **1** [C] one of the small stiff pieces forming the outer body covering of fish, snakes, etc. **2** [U] grayish material forming inside hot water pipes, pots in which water is boiled, etc. –see also FUR (3)

scale⁴ *v* scaled, scaling [T] **1** to climb up: *scale a wall/ladder* **2** to increase or reduce, esp. by a fixed rate: *Income tax is scaled according to how much you earn.*

scal·lion /'skælyən/ also **green onion** *AmE*

SPELLING NOTE
Words with the sound /s/, may be spelled **c-**, like **city**, or **ps-**, like **psychology**.

‖also **spring onion** – *n* an onion whose round white part is small

scal·lop /'skɑləp, 'skæləp/ also **scollop**– *n* **1** an edible sea animal (a MOLLUSC) which has a pair of rounded shells **2** one of a row of small curves forming an edge or pattern: *a dress with scallops around the neck*

scal·ly·wag /'skæliʸ,wæg/ *n BrE* for SCAL-AWAG

scalp¹ /skælp/ *n* the skin on the top of the human head, where hair grows

scalp² *v* [T] **1** (esp. of American Indians in former times) to cut off the SCALP¹ of (a dead enemy) as a mark of victory **2** *AmE infml* to buy and then resell (as theater tickets) at very high prices for profit

scal·pel /'skælpəl/ *n* a small sharp knife used by doctors in operations

scal·y /'skeʸliʸ/ *adj* **-ier, -iest** covered with SCALES³ (1) or SCALE³ (2) **–scaliness** *n* [U]

scamp /skæmp/ *n* a trouble-making but usu. playful child

scam·per /'skæmpər/ *v* [I] to run quickly and usu. playfully: *The mouse scampered into its hole.*

scan¹ /skæn/ *v* **-nn-** [T] **1** to examine closely, esp. in search: *He was scanning the sky for planes.* **2** to look at quickly without careful reading: *to scan the list of names*

scan² *n* [S] an act of SCANNING, esp. a searching look

scan·dal /'skændl/ *n* **1** [C;U] (something which causes) a public feeling that something is not proper: *The news about the Senator's private life caused a scandal.* **2** [U] true or false talk which brings shame to another: *I wish you'd stop repeating scandal about the neighbors!*

scan·dal·ize‖also **-ise** *BrE* /'skændl,aɪz/ *v* **-ized, -izing** [T] to offend (someone's) feelings of what is right or proper

scan·dal·ous /'skændl-əs/ *adj* offensive to feelings of what is right or proper: *scandalous behavior* **–scandalously** *adv*

Scan·di·na·vi·an /,skændə'neʸviʸən/ *adj* of or concerning the people or languages of Denmark, Norway, Sweden, and Iceland

scant /skænt/ *adj* hardly enough: *He paid scant attention to what was said.*

scant·y /'skæntiʸ/ *adj* **-ier, -iest** hardly big enough; almost too small, few, etc.: *a scanty breakfast* **–scantily** *adv* **–scantiness** *n* [U]

scape·goat /'skeʸpgoʷt/ *n* a person or thing taking the blame for the fault of others

scar¹ /skɑr/ *n* a mark remaining on the skin from a wound, cut, etc.: (fig.) *a country showing the scars of recent war*

scar² *v* **-rr-** [T] to mark with a SCAR: *scarred for life by the accident*

scarce /skeərs/ *adj* not much or many; hard to find; not PLENTIFUL: *Good fruit is scarce in winter, and costs a lot.* –compare COMMON; see RARE (USAGE)

scarce·ly /'skeərsliʸ/ *adv* hardly; almost not; BARELY: *She scarcely spoke a word of English.* –compare RARELY

scar·ci·ty /'skeərsəṭiʸ/ *n* **-ties** [C;U *of*] a state of being SCARCE; lack: *scarcities of all kinds of goods*

scare[1] /skɛər/ v **scared, scaring 1** [I;T] **a** to cause sudden fear to; FRIGHTEN: *Don't let the noise scare you; it's only the wind.* **b** to become afraid: *a woman who doesn't scare (easily)* **2** [T *off, away*] to cause to go by making afraid: *He made a noise and scared off the animals.|The high price is scaring away possible buyers.*

scare[2] n [S] a sudden feeling of fear: *What a scare you gave me, appearing suddenly in the dark!*

scare[3] adj [A] intended to cause fear: *scare stories about war, printed in the newspapers*

scare·crow /'skɛərkrowˌ/ n an object in the shape of a person, set up in a field to keep birds away from crops

scared /skɛərd/ adj [+*to-v/that*] afraid or made anxious: *Why won't you come on the trip? Are you scared?|I'm scared to fly in a plane. I'm scared that it might crash.|I was scared stiff/out of my wits/to death by the dog.*

scarf /skɑrf/ n **scarfs** or **scarves** /skɑrvz/ a piece of cloth for wearing around the neck, head, or shoulders for protection against the cold or for decoration

scar·let /'skɑrlɪt/ adj,n [U] (of) a very bright red color

scarlet fe·ver /ˌ·· '··/ n [U] a serious disease marked by a painful throat and red spots on the skin

scar·y /'skɛəriy/ adj **-ier, -iest** infml causing fear: *a dark scary street|a scary story*

scath·ing /'skeyðɪŋ/ adj bitterly cruel in judgment: *scathing remarks|She was very scathing about my work.* **–scathingly** adv

scat·ter /'skæṭər/ v **1** [I;T] **a** to cause (a group) to separate widely: *The gunshot scattered the birds.* **b** (of a group) to do this: *The birds scattered.* **2** [T *with, on, over*] to spread widely by throwing: *to scatter seed on the field/ scatter the field with seed|*(fig.) *He scatters money around as if he were rich.*

scat·ter·brain /'skæṭərˌbreyn/ n infml a likeable but careless or forgetful person **–scatterbrained** adj

scav·enge /'skævɪndʒ/ v **-enged, -enging** [I;T] to search for (usable objects) among waste: *homeless dogs scavenging for food* **–compare** SCROUNGE

scav·eng·er /'skævɪndʒər/ n **1** a creature (such as the VULTURE or JACKAL) which feeds on waste or decaying flesh **2** a person who SCAVENGES

sce·nar·i·o /sɪ'nɛəriyˌow, -'nær-, -'nɑr-/ n **-os** a description of a possible course of action or events or of the story of a movie, play, etc.

scene /siyn/ n **1** [C] **a** (in a play) any of the divisions, often within an ACT[2] (3), during which there is no change of place **b** (in a movie, broadcast, etc.) a single piece of action in one place **2** [C] a view of a place: *a beautiful scene from our hotel window|a painter of street scenes* **3** [C] a place where something happens: *objects found at the scene of the crime* **4** [C] an event regarded as like something in a play or film: *angry scenes in the classroom* **5** [C] a show of anger or feelings, esp. between two people in public:

Why did you **make a scene** *in the restaurant?* **6** [S] infml an area of activity: *the music scene|the film scene* **7 behind the scenes** out of sight; secretly: *decisions made behind the scenes, without public knowledge* **8 set the scene** to prepare; make ready: *The unjust peace agreement set the scene for another war.* –see VIEW (USAGE)

sce·ner·y /'siynəriy/ n [U] **1** the set of painted backgrounds used on a theater stage **2** natural surroundings, esp. in beautiful and open country –see VIEW (USAGE)

sce·nic /'siynɪk/ adj of, concerning, or showing natural SCENERY: *a scenic road/route along the coast* **–scenically** adv

scent[1] /sɛnt/ n **1** [C] a smell, esp. **a** as left by a hunted animal **b** a particular usu. pleasant smell: *the scent of roses* **2** [U] BrE for PERFUME **3** [S] a way to a discovery; TRACK[1] (1): *a scientist who thinks she's* **on the scent** *of a cure for heart disease*

scent[2] v [T] **1** (esp. of animals) to smell, esp. to tell the presence of by smelling: (fig.) *She scented danger.* **2** [usu. pass.] to fill with a SCENT[1] (1b): *the air, scented with spring flowers*

scep·ter AmE‖**sceptre** BrE /'sɛptər/ n a short rod carried by a ruler as a sign of power

scep·tic /'skɛptɪk/ n BrE for SKEPTIC

scep·ti·cal /'skɛptɪkəl/ adj [*of, about*] BrE for SKEPTICAL

sched·ule[1] /'skɛdʒuwˌəl, -dʒəl/ n **1** a timetable of things to be done, dealt with, etc.; PROGRAM[1] (3): *a factory production schedule* –compare CURRICULUM **2** a formal list, such as **a** a list of prices: *a schedule of mailing rates* **b** AmE a timetable of trains, buses, etc. **3 ahead of/on/behind schedule** before/at/after the planned time

schedule[2] v **-uled, -uling** [T] **1** [*for*] to plan for a certain future time: *The meeting is scheduled to take place next week.* **2** to put (a flight, train, etc.) into a regular timetable: *Are you going by a scheduled flight or by* CHARTER[1] (2)?

scheme[1] /skiym/ n **1** a plan in a simple form; a general arrangement; system: *a scheme to improve education* **2** a clever dishonest plan: *a scheme to escape taxes*

scheme[2] v **schemed, scheming** [I +*to-v*] to make secret dishonest plans; PLOT[2] (4) **–schemer** n

schism /'sɪzəm, 'skɪzəm/ n [C;U] (a) separation between parts originally of the same group, esp. the Christian church

schiz·oid /'skɪtsɔɪd/ adj tech of or like SCHIZOPHRENIA

schiz·o·phre·ni·a /ˌskɪtsə'friyniyə/ n [U] tech a disorder of the mind causing a person to draw away from other people into a life in the imagination

schiz·o·phren·ic /ˌskɪtsə'frɛnɪk/ adj,n tech (typical of) a person with SCHIZOPHRENIA

schlepp, schlep /ʃlɛp/ v AmE infml **1** [T] to carry around usu. something heavy which makes one tired: *I schlepped all these books home with me.* **2** [I *around*] to spend a lot of time and effort in getting from one place to another: *I had to schlepp on a train and a bus* *in order to get here.*

schol·ar /'skɑlər/ *n* **1** a person with great knowledge of a subject; LEARNED person **2** the holder of a SCHOLARSHIP (1)

schol·ar·ly /'skɑlərli⁄/ *adj* concerned with serious detailed study; of or like a SCHOLAR (1)

schol·ar·ship /'skɑlər,ʃɪp/ *n* **1** [C] a sum of money given to a student by an official body, to pay (partly) for a course of study **2** [U] the knowledge, work, or method of SCHOLARs (1); exact and serious study: *Her book is a fine piece of scholarship.*

scho·las·tic /skə'læstɪk/ *adj* [A] of or concerning schools and teaching

school[1] /skuʷl/ *n* **1** [C;U] (study at) a place of education for children: *an* ELEMENTARY/*a* SECONDARY *school*|*new schools built by the government*|*She walked home after school.* **2** [C] the students (and teachers) at such a place: *The whole school was sorry when she left.* **3** [C;U] an establishment for teaching a particular subject, skill, etc.: *She goes to (an) art school.*|NIGHT SCHOOL **4** [C] (in certain universities) a department concerned with a particular subject: *the School of Law* **5** [C] a group of people with the same methods, opinions, style of painting, etc.: *Rembrandt and his school*|*There are different* **schools of thought** *on the best way of doing this.* **6** [C;U] *AmE* for UNIVERSITY

school[2] *v* [T *in*] to teach, train, or bring under control: *well schooled in obedience*

school[3] *n* [*of*] a large group of one kind of fish or certain sea animals swimming together

school·boy /'skuʷlbɔɪ/ **schoolgirl** /-gɜrl/ *fem.– n* a boy attending school

school·ing /'skuʷlɪŋ/ *n* [U] education or attendance at school: *He had only five years of schooling.*

school·mas·ter /'skuʷl,mæstər/ **schoolmistress** /-,mɪstrɪs/ *fem– n esp. BrE* a male teacher at a school

school re·port /ˌ· ·'·/ *n BrE* for REPORT CARD

schoo·ner /'skuʷnər/ *n* **1** a fast sailing ship **2** a large tall drinking glass, esp. for beer

sci·ence /'saɪəns/ *n* **1** [U] (the study of) knowledge which depends on testing facts and stating general natural laws **2** [C;U] **a** any of the branches usu. studied at universities, such as PHYSICS, BIOLOGY, chemistry, and ENGINEERING (**the sciences**): *I'm studying science.* –compare ARTS, HUMANITIES; see also NATURAL SCIENCE **b** anything which may be studied exactly: *the science of cooking*|*military science* –see also SOCIAL SCIENCE

science fic·tion /ˌ·· '··/ also **sci-fi** /ˌsaɪ 'faɪ/ *infml– n* [U] stories about imaginary developments in science and their effect on life

sci·en·tif·ic /ˌsaɪən'tɪfɪk/ *adj* **1** [A *no compt.*] of, being, or concerning science: *The microscope is a scientific instrument.*|*She has a*

scientific mind. **2** needing or showing exact knowledge, skill, or use of a system: *She has a very scientific approach to political problems.* –opposite **unscientific** (for 2) –**scientifically** *adv*

sci·en·tist /'saɪəntɪst/ *n* a person who works in a science, esp. PHYSICS, chemistry, or BIOLOGY

scim·i·tar /'sɪmətər/ *n* a curved sword that is sharp on the outer edge, formerly used in the Middle East

scin·til·lat·ing /'sɪntəl,eʸtɪŋ/ *adj* (esp. of speech) full of interest; quick and clever: *scintillating conversation*

scis·sors /'sɪzərz/ *n* [P] two sharp blades with handles at one end, fastened at the center so that they cut when they close: *I cut his hair with scissors.*|*Do you have any scissors?* –compare SHEARS; see PAIR (USAGE); see illustration on page 467

scoff /skɔf, skɑf/ *v* [I *at*] to speak or act disrespectfully; laugh unkindly (at); RIDICULE[2]: *I told them my ideas but they scoffed at them.* –**scoffer** *n*

scold /skoʷld/ *v* [I;T] to speak in an angry and complaining way (to), esp. to blame: *I hate to scold (you), but you shouldn't stay out so late at night!* –**scolding** *n* [C;U]

scol·lop /'skɑləp/ *n* → SCALLOP

scone /skoʷn, skɑn/ *n BrE* for BISCUIT

scoop[1] /skuʷp/ *n* **1** a container for moving liquids or loose soft materials: *a kitchen scoop*|*a measuring scoop*|*two scoops of ice-cream* **2** a report made by a newspaper before any other newspapers –compare EXCLUSIVE[2]

scoop[2] *v* [T] **1** [*up, out, out of*] to take up or out, (as if) with a scoop[1] (1): *to scoop up a handful of sand*|*to scoop some sugar out of the bag* **2** (of a newspaper) to make a news report before (another newspaper): *The "News" scooped the other newspapers with an early report on the election.*

scoot /skuʷt/ *v* [I] *infml* to run quickly

scoot·er /'skuʷtər/ *n* **1** also **motor scooter**–a small motorcycle, with a covering over the engine at the back **2** a child's vehicle with two small wheels, an upright handle fixed to the front wheel, and a narrow board for one foot, pushed by the other foot touching the ground

scope /skoʷp/ *n* [U] **1** the limits of a question, subject, etc.; RANGE[1] (6): *The committee was not interested in people's private lives. This subject was outside the scope of their inquiry.* **2** [*for*] chance for action or thought: *There's not much scope for* INITIATIVE *in this job.*

scorch[1] /skɔrtʃ/ *v* **1** [I;T] to burn so as to change a thing's color, taste, or feeling but not completely destroy it: *to scorch a shirt with an iron that's too hot*|(fig.) *fields scorched by the sun* **2** [I] *infml* to travel very fast: *The car scorched down the road at 100 miles an hour.*

scorch·er /'skɔrtʃər/ *n* [S] *infml* a very hot day

scorch·ing /'skɔrtʃɪŋ/ *adj,adv* (in a way) that SCORCHes: *scorching heat*|*a scorching hot day*

SPELLING NOTE

Words with the sound /s/, may be spelled **c-**, like **city**, or **ps-**, like **psychology**.

score[1] /skɔr, skoᵂr/ n **1** the number of points, GOALs (3), etc., gained in a game, sport, competition, examination, etc.: *The score stood at/was 2 to 1 at half time.|He got a low score on the test.* **2 a** a written copy of a piece of music, esp. for a large group of performers: *a full score* (=showing all the parts in separate lines on the page) **b** the music for a movie or play: *There were some good songs in that movie. Who wrote the score?* **3** [*usu. sing.*] a reason; account: *We have enough money; don't worry* **on that score. 4** an old disagreement or hurt kept in mind; GRUDGE[2] (1): *I have* **a score/an old score to settle** *with him.* (=I want to make sure he is punished) **5 know the score** *infml* to understand the true and usu. unfavorable facts of a matter

score[2] v **scored, scoring 1** [I;T] to gain (points, GOALs (3), etc.) in a sport, game, competition, examination, etc.: *He scored three points/times in the last half of the game.|She scored the highest marks on the exam.* **2** [I] to record the SCORE[1] (1) of a sports event as it is played: *Who will score for us?* **3** [T] to mark or cut one or more lines (as) with a sharp instrument: *Score the paper to make it easy to fold.* **4** [I;T *off, against, over*] to make (a clever and successful point), esp. in an argument against someone: *I hate conversations where people try to score (points) off each other.* **5** [I;T] to gain or win (a success, victory, prize, etc.): *This writer has scored again with another popular book.* **6** [T] to write or arrange a piece of music esp. for a large group of performers
score sthg.↔ **out** v adv [T] *fml* to draw a line through (written words) to show that they should not be read; CROSS **out**

score[3] *determiner, n* **score** or **scores 1** (a group of) 20: *threescore or three score* (=60) **2 scores (of)** large numbers (of): *scores of people, perhaps 80 or more*

score·board /'skɔrbɔrd, 'skoᵂrbɔrᵂd/ n a board on which the SCORE[1] (1) of a game is recorded as it is played

scor·er /'skɔrər, 'skoᵂrər/ n **1** a person who keeps the SCORE[1] (1) of a sports event as it is played **2** a player who scores points, GOALs (3), etc.

scorn[1] /skɔrn/ n [U] strong, usu. angry disrespect; CONTEMPT : *He* **poured scorn on** *my suggestion.|I told him my suggestion, but he* **laughed it to scorn.** −**scornful** /'skɔrnfəl/ adj −**scornfully** adv

scorn[2] v [T] *usu. lit* **1** [+ *to-v/v-ing*] to refuse because of pride: *She scorned our offers of help.* **2** to feel scorn[1] (1) for

Scor·pi·o /'skɔrpiᵞoᵂ/ n see ZODIAC

scor·pi·on /'skɔrpiᵞən/ n a tropical insect with a curving tail which stings poisonously

scotch /skɑtʃ/ v [T] *fml* to put an end to: *to scotch a false rumor by explaining the true facts*

Scotch n [C;U] also *fml* **Scotch whiskey** /₁· '··/− (a glass of) a strong alcoholic drink (WHISKEY) made in Scotland

scotch tape /₁· '·/ AmE‖**sellotape** BrE− n *tdmk* (*often cap.*) sticky thin clear material (CELLULOID) in long narrow pieces sold in

rolls, for fastening paper, repairing light objects, etc.

scot-free /₁skɑt 'friᵞ/ adj [F] *infml* without harm or punishment: *The man escaped scot-free from the accident.*

Scot·land Yard /₁skɑtlənd 'yɑrd/ n [U] (the main office of) the London police

Scot·tish /'skɑtɪʃ/ also **Scots** /skɑts/− adj of, being, concerning, or typical of Scotland

USAGE **Scots** is less common than **Scottish**, and is normally only used of people: *a well-known* **Scots/Scottish** *actor/the* **Scottish** *islands.* **Scotch** is normally only used of the products of Scotland: **Scotch** wool/ BEEF/WHISKY. **Scottish** and **Scots** are polite.

scoun·drel /'skaʊndrəl/ n a wicked selfish person; VILLAIN

scour[1] /skaʊər/ v [T *for*] to go through (an area) thoroughly in search of someone or something: *the police scoured the area looking for the lost child.*

scour[2] v [T] **1** [*down, out, off*] to clean (a surface) by hard rubbing with a rough material: *scour out a dirty pan|scour off the dirt from the floor* **2** [*out*] (of water) to form by wearing away: *The river had scoured out a passage in the sand.*

scour·er /'skaʊərər/ n → SCOURING PAD

scourge /skɜrdʒ/ n a cause of great harm or suffering: *the scourge of war*

scouring pad /'·· ₁·/ also **scourer**− n a small ball of metal or plastic wire for cleaning pots and pans

scout[1] /skaʊt/ v [I *around, for*] to go looking for something: *He scouted around for a store that was open late.*

scout[2] n **1** a soldier, ship or aircraft sent out to search for information about the land, the enemy, etc. **2 a** → BOY SCOUT **b** AmE for GIRL SCOUT

scowl[1] /skaʊl/ v to make a SCOWL[2]; FROWN angrily

scowl[2] n an angry threatening expression of the face; angry FROWN

scrab·ble /'skræbəl/ v **-bled, -bling** [I *around*] to move wildly and quickly (as if) looking for something: *She scrabbled around on the floor picking up the coins she'd dropped.*

scrag·gly /'skrægliᵞ/ adj **-glier, -gliest** AmE *infml* (esp. of things that grow) poor and uneven-looking; badly grown: *a scraggly beard*

scrag·gy /'skrægiᵞ/ adj **-gier, -giest** thin and bony: *a scraggy-looking dog*

scram /skræm/ v **-mm-** [I *usu. in commands*] *infml* to go away fast; run away: *You're not wanted here, so scram!*

scram·ble[1] /'skræmbəl/ v **-bled, -bling 1** [I] to move or climb quickly, esp. over a rough or steep surface: *I scrambled up the rock.* **2** [I +*to-v/for*] to struggle with others eagerly or in a disorderly way: *people scrambling for shelter/scrambling to get out of the way* **3** [T] to mix the white and yellow parts of (eggs) together while cooking them: *scrambled eggs* **4** [T] to mix together without order; JUMBLE: *scrambled words*

scramble[2] n [S] **1** an act of moving or climbing over a rough surface: *It's quite a scramble* *to get to the top of the hill.* **2** an eager and disorderly struggle: *a scramble for the best seats*

scrap[1] /skræp/ *n* **1** [C] a small piece: *a scrap of paper|scraps of news/food* **2** [A;U] material which cannot be used for its original purpose but which may still have some value: *scrap metal/scrap paper* –see also SCRAPS

scrap[2] *v* **-pp-** [T] to get rid of as no longer useful or wanted; DISCARD[1] (1)

scrap[3] *n infml* a usu. sudden, not serious, fight or quarrel: *It wasn't a real fight; it was just a scrap.*

scrap[4] *v* **-pp-** [I *with*] *infml* to quarrel or fight

scrap·book /'skræpbʊk/ *n* a book of empty pages in which a collection of photographs, newspaper articles, etc., is fastened

scrape[1] /skreʸp/ *v* **scraped, scraping 1** [T] to remove (material) from a surface by repeated rubbing or by pulling an edge firmly across it: *I scraped the skin off the vegetables with a knife.* **2** [T *down*] to clean or make (a surface) smooth in this way: *She scraped the door (down) before painting it again.* **3** [I;T *on, against*] to (cause to) rub roughly: *He scraped his chair against the wall.|He scraped (=hurt) his knee when he fell.* **4** [I *along, by, through*] **a** to live with only just enough money: *scraping by on very small wages* **b** to succeed by doing work of the lowest acceptable quality: *She just scraped through (=passed) the examination by one point.*

scrape sthg.↔ **up/together**– *v adv* [T] to gather (a total, esp. of money) with difficulty by putting small amounts together: *She scraped up enough money to buy the car.*

scrape[2] *n* **1** an act or sound of scraping (SCRAPE) **2** a wound made by scraping (SCRAPE): *He suffered a few cuts and scrapes.* **3** a difficult or unpleasant state of affairs

scrap heap /'· ·/ *n* **1** [C] a pile of waste material, esp. metal **2** [*the* S] an imaginary place where unwanted things, people, or ideas go: *Put that plan on the scrap heap; it'll never work.*

scrap·py[1] /'skræpiʸ/ *adj* **-pier, -piest 1** made of disconnected bits; not well arranged or planned: *a scrappy, badly-written report*

scrappy[2] *adj* **-pier, -piest** *AmE infml* liking to fight

scraps /skræps/ *n* [P] pieces of food not eaten at a meal, and thrown away: *Feed the scraps to the dog.*

scratch[1] /skrætʃ/ *v* **1** [I;T] to rub and tear or mark (a surface) with something pointed or rough, e.g. CLAWS or FINGERNAILS: *Be careful of the cat; it'll scratch (you)!|an accident in which the table top was scratched|a dog scratching at the door to be let in|She scratched her elbow on a nail.* **2** [T] to remove or mark in this way: *He scratched the paint off the gate as he drove through.|He*

SPELLING NOTE

Words with the sound /s/, may be spelled **c-**, like **city**, or **ps-**, like **psychology**.

scratched his name on the wall with a knife. **3** [I;T] to rub (a part of the body) lightly to stop ITCHING[1] (1): *The cat likes to be scratched behind its ears.|He scratched his arm where he had been bitten by an insect.* **4** [I;T] to remove (oneself, a horse, etc.) from a race or competition before it starts: *The horse (was) scratched on the day of the race.|(fig.): That's not a good idea. Let's scratch it.* **5 scratch the surface** to deal with only the beginning of a matter or only a few of many cases: *I've only scratched the surface in my studying. I still have hours of reading to do.*

scratch[2] *n* **1** [C] a mark or sore place made by SCRATCHING[1] (1): *a scratch on the table top made by her ring|He got a few cuts and scratches in the accident.* **2** [C] a sound made by SCRATCHING[1] (1): *The record was spoiled by scratches.* **3** [S] an act of SCRATCHING[1] (3): *My back needs a good scratch.* **4** [A] made or put together in a hurry using whatever could be found: *a scratch football team* **5 from scratch** *infml* starting from the beginning or with nothing: *She cooks everything from scratch.* **6 up to scratch** *infml* at or to a good enough standard: *The piano player was not feeling well, and her performance wasn't up to scratch.* **7 without a scratch** *infml* without even the smallest amount of hurt or damage

scratch pad /'· ·/ *n esp. AmE* a small pile of loosely joined pieces of paper (PAD) for writing informal notes

scratch pa·per /'· ,··/ *AmE‖*also **scrap paper**– *n* [U] paper, esp. in sheets already used on one side, which may be used for informal notes

scratch·y /'skrætʃiʸ/ *adj* **-ier, -iest 1** (of a recording) spoiled by SCRATCHes[2] (2) **2** (of clothes) hot, rough, and pricking: *These wool pants are scratchy.* –**scratchiness** *n* [U]

scrawl[1] /skrɔl/ *v* [T] to write in a careless, awkward, or unskillful way

scrawl[2] *n* [usu. sing.] something written awkwardly, or fast and carelessly: *just a scrawl on a card to say she was having a good time*

scraw·ny /'skrɔniʸ/ *adj* **-nier, -niest** *derog* (of people or animals) without much flesh on the bones; thin: *a scrawny little man/dog*

scream[1] /skriʸm/ *v* **1** [I] to cry out loudly on a high note, in fear, pain, excitement, or sometimes laughter: *The man was screaming with pain.|to scream for help|I screamed with laughter at the joke.* **2** [T +*that/out*] to express in this way: *He screamed (out) a warning to us.|(fig.) The newspaper screamed the news on the front page.*

scream[2] *n* **1** [C] a sudden loud cry expressing pain, fear, excitement, or sometimes laughter: *We heard a terrible scream.|(fig.) the scream of the electric saw as it cut the log* **2** [S] *infml* a very funny person, or thing: *She thought it was a scream when I fell off my chair.*

scream·ing·ly /'skriʸmɪŋliʸ/ *adv* **screamingly funny** *infml* very funny

screech /skriʸtʃ/ *v* [I;T] (of people, animals, or machinery) to give out an unpleasant high sharp sound, as in terror or pain: *birds screeching in the trees|(fig.) The car* *screeched to a stop.* –**screech** *n: a screech of brakes*

screen[1] /skriᵞn/ *n* **1** [C] an upright frame used as a small movable wall for dividing a room, protecting people from view, from cold air, etc: *They put a screen around his bed so that the doctor could examine him.* **2** [C] also **window screen**– a frame holding a fine wire net, put into a window to keep insects out **3** [C] something that protects, shelters, or hides: *a screen of trees to keep out the wind*|(fig.) *His job at the bank was just a screen for his life as a spy.* **4** [C] a surface on which a movie is shown: *She first appeared on the screen* (=acted in her first movie) *ten years ago.* **5** [S] the movie industry: *a play written for the screen* (=to be shown as a movie)|*a* **screen test** (=test of one's ability to act in movies) **6** [C] the front surface of an electrical instrument, esp. a television, on which pictures or information appear

screen[2] *v* [T] **1** [*from*] to shelter or protect from light, wind, etc.: *He screened his eyes with his hand.* **2** [*off, from*] to hide from view, (as) with a SCREEN (1): *Her movements were screened by a large rock, which stopped us from seeing her.*|*Part of the room was screened off for the new baby.* **3** to test (people) to see whether they are loyal, suitable for a job, etc.: *100 carefully screened people were invited to have dinner with the President.* **4** to show (a movie) for a group of people to see: *a new movie, first screened only last month*

screen door /ˌ· '·/ *n* a door made of a wood or metal frame holding a wire net, used to keep insects out

screen·play /'skriᵞnpleᵞ/ *n* a story written for a movie

screw[1] /skruʷ/ *n* **1** a type of usu. metal fastener similar to a nail but having a raised circular edge (THREAD (3)), so that it holds firmly when fastened into a material by turning (usu. with a SCREWDRIVER) –compare BOLT[1] (1), NAIL[1] (1) **2** an act of turning one of these: *Give it another screw to tighten it.* **3** → PROPELLER **4 have a screw loose** *humor* be slightly crazy

screw[2] *v* **1** [T] to fasten with one or more screws: *The table legs are screwed to the top.*|*It won't move; it's screwed to the floor.* **2** [I;T] **a** to turn or tighten (a screw or something that moves in the same way): *Screw the two pipes together end to end.*|*Screw the lid on tightly.* **b** (of such a thing) to turn or tighten: *The two pieces screw together easily.* –see also UNSCREW **3** [T *out of*] *infml* to get by forcing, or by dishonest means: *He screwed the others out of their share of the money.* **4** [I;T] *taboo* to have sex (with someone) **5 have one's head screwed on (right)** to be sensible; do nothing foolish

screw sthg.↔ **up** *v adv* [T] **1** *infml* to ruin: *The bad weather screwed up our plans for a picnic.* **2** to twist a part of the face, esp. to express disapproval or uncertainty: *She screwed up her eyes in the bright light.* **3 screw up one's courage** to stop oneself from being afraid: *He screwed up his courage and*

asked her to go out with him.

screw·ball /'skruʷbɔl/ *n infml esp. AmE* a person whose ideas or actions seem wild or crazy, usu. in a harmless way

screw·driv·er /'skruʷˌdraɪvər/ *n* a tool with a narrow blade at one end, which turns SCREWs into and out of their places

screw·y /'skruʷiᵞ/ *adj* **-ier, -iest** *infml* seeming strange, and often funny or annoying; crazy (1,2): *Something has gone screwy in my calculation.*|*He's a little screwy.*

scrib·ble[1] /'skrɪbəl/ *v* **-bled, -bling 1** [I;T] to write (meaningless marks): *The little girl can't write yet, but she loves to scribble with a pencil.* **2** [T] to write carelessly or in a hurry: *He scribbled me a note.*

scribble[2] *n* **1** [C] a meaningless written mark: *scribbles on the wall* **2** [S;U] (a way of) writing which is careless and hard to read: *His writing is nothing but (a) scribble.*

scribe /skraɪb/ *n* a person employed to copy things in writing, esp. in times before the invention of printing

scrimp /skrɪmp/ *v* **scrimp and save** to save (money) slowly and with difficulty, esp. by living poorly: *She had to scrimp and save to pay for her trip.*

script /skrɪpt/ *n* **1** [C;U] the set of letters used in writing a language; ALPHABET: *words printed in Arabic script* **2** [U] writing done by hand, esp. with the letters or words joined **3** [C] the written form of a speech, play, or broadcast

scrip·tur·al /'skrɪptʃərəl/ *adj* according to a holy writing, esp. the Bible

scrip·ture /'skrɪptʃər/ *n* [C;U] *(often cap.)* holy writings, esp. the Bible

script·writ·er /'skrɪptˌraɪtər/ *n* a writer of SCRIPTs (3)

scroll /skroʷl/ *n* a long straight piece of skin or paper with writing on it, that can be rolled up, esp. as used formerly

scrooge /skruʷdʒ/ *n infml & derog (sometimes cap.)* for MISER

scro·tum /'skroʷtəm/ *n* **-ta** /tə/ *or* **-tums** *tech* the bag of flesh holding the TESTICLEs of male animals

scrounge /skraundʒ/ *v* **scrounged, scrounging 1** [T *off*] *often derog* to get (money or whatever else one needs), without work or payment, or by persuading others: *He's always scrounging off his friends.* **2** [I *around*] to go looking for things: *He scrounged around in people's desks looking for a pen.* –**scrounger** *n*

scrub[1] /skrʌb/ *v* **-bb- 1** [I;T] to clean by hard rubbing, e.g. with a stiff brush: *He scrubbed the floor clean*/*the dirt off the floor.* **2** [T] to cause not to happen; CANCEL (1): *We've had to scrub our vacation plans this year; we don't have any money.*

scrub[2] *n* [S] an act of SCRUBbing[1] (1): *Give that floor a good hard scrub.*

scrub[3] *n* [A;U] low-growing bushes and short trees growing in poor soil

scruff /skrʌf/ *n* **the scruff of the neck** the flesh at the back of the neck: *caught*/*grabbed by the scruff of the neck*

scruff·y /'skrʌfiᵞ/ *adj* **-ier, -iest** dirty and

untidy; SHABBY: *a scruffy hotel/boy*

scrump·tious /'skrʌmpʃəs/ *adj infml* (esp. of food) very good; DELICIOUS

scru·ple /'skruʷpəl/ *n* **1** [C] a moral principle which keeps one from doing something wrong: *a man with no scruples, who will do anything to get what he wants* **2** [U] the desire to do what is right; conscience: *He acted wrongly and without scruple.*

scru·pu·lous /'skruʷpyələs/ *adj* **1** correct even in the smallest detail; exact; PAINSTAK-ING (1): *The nurse treated him with the most scrupulous care.* **2** carefully doing only what is right; exactly honest; CONSCIENTIOUS: *She is very scrupulous in her business activities; everybody trusts her.* –opposite **unscrupulous** (for 2) **–scrupulously** *adv* **–scrupulousness** *n* [U]

scru·ti·nize ‖also **-nise** *BrE* /'skruʷtn,aɪz/ *v* **-nized, -nizing** [T] to give SCRUTINY to; examine closely: *She scrutinized his work carefully before allowing him to send it out.*

scru·ti·ny /'skruʷtn-iʸ/ *n* [U] careful and thorough examination: *She SUBJECTed³ his work to close scrutiny.*

scu·ba /'skuʷbə/ *n* [A;C] an instrument used for breathing while swimming under water, made of one or more containers of air under pressure fastened to the back, and connected by a rubber pipe to the mouth: *While I was in Florida, I went* **scuba diving.**

scud /skʌd/ *v* **-dd-** [I] *lit* (esp. of clouds and ships) to move along quickly as if driven: *Clouds scudded across the sky.*

scuff /skʌf/ *v* [T *up*] to make a rough mark on the smooth surface of (shoes, a floor, etc.); SCRAPE¹ (3): *The floor was badly scuffed where they had been dancing.*

scuf·fle /'skʌfəl/ *v,n* **-fled, -fling** [I] (to be in) a disorderly fight, usu. not serious or long

scull¹ /skʌl/ *n* a small light racing boat for one person rowing with a pair of light OARs

scull² *v* [I;T] to row (a SCULL¹)

sculp·tor /'skʌlptər/ *n* an artist who does SCULPTURE

sculp·ture¹ /'skʌlptʃər/ *n* **1** [U] the art of shaping solid figures (e.g. people or things) out of stone, wood, metal, etc.: *to study sculpture in art school* **2** [C;U] (a piece of) work produced by this art: *There are some interesting sculptures in this church.*

sculp·ture² also **sculpt** /skʌlpt/– *v* **-tured, -turing** [I;T] to make (esp. works of SCULPTURE) by shaping: *sculptured pillars*|(fig.) *The water had sculptured the rocks into strange shapes.*

scum /skʌm/ *n* **1** [S;U] a filmy covering of impure material on the surface of a liquid **2** [U +*sing./pl. v*] *derog* worthless evil people: *He says people who* TORTURE *other people are* **the scum of the earth.** (=the worst people in the world) **–scummy** *adj* **-mier, -miest**

scur·ri·lous /'skɜrələs, 'skʌr-/ *adj* making or

---

containing very rude, improper, or evil statements: *a scurrilous attack in the newspapers* **–scurrilously** *adv* **–scurrilousness** *n* [U]

scur·ry¹ /'skɜriʸ, 'skʌriʸ/ *v* **-ried, -rying** [I] to move quickly with short steps; hurry: *The mouse scurried into its hole.*

scurry² *n* [S] a movement or esp. sound of SCURRYing: *I heard the scurry of feet in the hall.*

scut·tle¹ /'skʌtl/ *v* **-tled, -tling** [T] to sink (a ship, esp. one's own) by making holes in the bottom of it

scuttle² *v* [I] to run with short quick steps, esp. to escape; SCURRY: *The children scuttled off/away when they saw the policeman.*

scythe¹ /saɪð/ *n* a long-handled tool with a curving blade for cutting long grass

scythe² *v* **scythed, scything** [I;T *down, off*] to cut (grass) with a SCYTHE

SE *written abbrev. said as:* southeast(ern)

sea /siʸ/ *n* **1** [C; U] the great body of salty water that covers most of the earth's surface; ocean: *boats sailing on the sea*|*Most of the earth is covered by sea.*|*sea water*|*sea travel*|*(a) seacoast*|*We went* **by sea,** *not by air.* **2** [C] a large body of salty water smaller than an ocean, or enclosed by land: *the Red Sea*|*the Mediterranean Sea* **3** [S *of*] a large mass or quantity: *The actor looked out from the stage onto a sea of faces.* **4** [C] movement of waves on water: *The ship ran into strong winds and heavy seas.* **5 at sea** *infml* as if lost; not understanding; BEWILDERed: *He felt completely at sea in his new school.*

sea·bed /'siʸbɛd/ *n* [S] the land at the bottom of the sea

sea·far·ing /'siʸ,fɛərɪŋ/ *adj* [A] *esp. lit* having strong connections with the sea and sailing: *a seafaring nation*

sea·food /'siʸfuʷd/ *n* [U] fish and fishlike animals (esp. SHELLFISH) from the sea which can be eaten

sea·front /'siʸfrʌnt/ *n* [C;U] the part of a coastal town that is on the edge of the sea, often with a broad path along it for vacation visitors

sea·gull /'siʸgʌl/ *n* → GULL

sea horse /'· ·/ *n* a very small fish with a neck and head that look like those of a horse

seal¹ /siʸl/ *v* [T] **1** to fix a SEAL² (1) onto: *an official statement signed and sealed* **2** [*up, down*] to fasten or close with a SEAL³ (1,2) or a tight cover or band of something: *She sealed the package with sticky TAPE.*|*a sealed envelope/bottle*|(fig.) **My lips are sealed**; *I won't tell you.* **3** to make certain, formal, or solemn: *They sealed their agreement by shaking hands.*

seal sbdy./sthg.↔ **in** *v adv* [T] to keep inside without a chance to escape: *Cook the meat quickly at first to seal in the juices.*|*The door closed behind us and sealed us in the dark room.*

seal sthg.↔ **off** *v adv* [T] to close tightly so as not to allow entrance or escape: *The police sealed off the building. No one could go in or out.*

seal² *n* **1** the official mark of a government,

company, etc., fixed to some formal and official writings: *This letter carries the Presidential seal.*|(fig.) *The new car has my* **seal of approval.** (=I think it is very good) **2** a small piece of paper, wax, or wire, fastened across an opening to protect it: *The seal on this wine bottle is broken.* **3** a tight connection in a machine, for keeping a gas or liquid in or out: *The seal is worn out, and the machine is losing oil.*

seal³ *n* **seals** *or* **seal** a large fish-eating sea animal with broad flat limbs (FLIPPERs) suitable for swimming

sealing wax /'·· ,·/ *n* [U] a usu. red solid substance, which melts and then hardens quickly and is used for fixing SEALs² (1)

sea li·on /'·· ,··/ *n* **sea lions** *or* **sea lion** a SEAL³ of the Pacific Ocean

seam /siʸm/ *n* **1** a line of stitches joining two pieces of cloth, leather, etc. **2** the line where two edges meet: *seamless stockings* (=with no join) **3** a narrow band of mineral between masses of other rocks: *a coal seam*

sea·man /'siʸmən/ *n* **-men** /mən/ a member of a navy, or a sailor on a ship, who is not an officer

sea·man·ship /'siʸmən,ʃɪp/ *n* [U] the skill of handling a ship and directing its course

seam·stress /'siʸmstrɪs/ *n* a woman whose job is sewing

seam·y /'siʸmiʸ/ *adj* **-ier, -iest** bad; unpleasant: **the seamy side** *of city life* **–seaminess** *n* [U]

sé·ance /'seʸɑns/ *n* a meeting where people try to talk to or receive messages from dead people

sea·plane /'siʸpleʸn/ *n* an aircraft which takes off from and lands on water

sea·port /'siʸpɔrt, -poʷrt/ *n* a town with a harbor used by large ships

sear /sɪər/ *v* [T] **1** to burn with a sudden powerful heat *searing pain* **2** to cook the outside of (a piece of meat) quickly

search¹ /sɜrtʃ/ *v* [I;T *for*] to look through, or examine (a place or person) thoroughly or carefully to try to find something: *The police searched the woods for the lost child.*|*She searched (through) her pockets for a cigarette.*|*The police searched the thief but found nothing.*|*Scientists are still searching for a cure to the common cold.* **–searcher** *n*

search² *n* [C *for*] an act of searching: *a long search for the lost child*|*birds flying south* **in search of** *winter sun*

search·ing /'sɜrtʃɪŋ/ *adj* sharp and thorough; anxious to discover the truth: *She gave me a searching look.* **–searchingly** *adv*

search·light /'sɜrtʃlaɪt/ *n* a large usu. movable light with a powerful beam, used when searching for aircraft in the sky, missing or escaped people, etc. **–compare** FLOODLIGHT

search par·ty /'·· ,··/ *n* **-ties** a group of people searching, esp. for a lost person: *The search party has found the child.*

search war·rant /'·· ,··/ *n* a written order sometimes given by a court to police to allow them to search a place, as to look for stolen goods

sea·shell /'siʸʃɛl/ *n* a shell of a small sea animal

sea·shore /'siʸʃɔr, -ʃoʷr/ *n* [U] land along the edge of the sea, usu. sand or rocks –see SHORE (USAGE)

sea·sick /'siʸˌsɪk/ *adj* feeling sick because of the movement of a ship on water **–seasickness** *n* [U]

sea·side /'siʸsaɪd/ *n* [*the* S] the edge of the sea, esp. as a vacation place: *a seaside town*|*a vacation at*|*by the seaside* –see SHORE (USAGE)

sea·son¹ /'siʸzən/ *n* **1** a period of time each year, e.g. **a** spring, summer, fall, or winter **b** marked by weather or particular activities: *the rainy season*|*the football season*|*My* **season ticket** *means that I can go to the ball games any number of times during the stated period.* **2 in season: a** (of fresh foods) at the time when they are usually ready for eating: *Fruit is cheapest in season.* **b** (of certain female animals) in HEAT¹ (3) **c** (of animals) permitted to be hunted at the time –opposite **out of season**

season² *v* [T] **1** [*with*] to give special taste to (a food) by adding salt, pepper, a SPICE, etc. **2** to make (wood) hard and fit for use by gradual drying: *You should use only seasoned wood when you build a house.*

sea·son·a·ble /'siʸzənəbəl/ *adj* suitable or typical for the time of year: *seasonable weather* **–seasonably** *adv*

sea·son·al /'siʸzənəl/ *adj* happening or active at a particular season: *seasonal employment at a summer camp*

sea·soned /'siʸzənd/ *adj* with a great deal of experience in the stated activity: *a seasoned traveler*|*news reporter*

sea·son·ing /'siʸzənɪŋ/ *n* [C;U] something that SEASONs food

seat¹ /siʸt/ *n* **1** a place for sitting: *Using all our chairs, we'll have seats for ten people.*|*the front*|*back seat of a car*|*tickets for good seats at the theater* –see illustration on page 95 **2** the part on which one sits: *The seat of the chair is broken.*|(euph) *My seat is sore from riding a horse.* **3** a place as a member of an official body: *to win*|*lose a seat in Congress in an election* **4** [*of*] a place where a particular activity happens: *a famous university and* **seat of learning 5 take/have a seat** please sit down **6 to take a back seat (to someone)** *infml* to allow someone else to take control or have a more important job

seat² *v* [T] **1** to cause or help to sit: *He seated himself near the window.*|(fml) *Please be seated.* (=sit down) –see also UNSEAT **2** (of a room, table, etc.) to have room for seats for: *a large hall which seats 1,000* –see SIT (USAGE)

seat belt /'· ·/ also **safety belt**– *n* a fixed belt fastened around a person in a car or plane to protect him/her from sudden movement, esp. in an accident –see illustration on page 95

seat·ing /'siʸtɪŋ/ *n* [U] provision of seats: *Do we have enough seating for the guests?*

sea ur·chin /'· ,··/ *n* a small ball-shaped sea

sea·weed /'siʸwiʸd/ n [U] a usu. dark green plant growing in the sea

sea·wor·thy /'siʸ,wɜrðiʸ/ adj (of a ship) in good condition and fit for a sea voyage –**seaworthiness** n [U]

se·cede /sɪ'siʸd/ v -**ceded, -ceding** [I from] fml to officially leave a group or organization, esp. because of disagreement –**secession** /sɪ'sɛʃən/ n [U]

se·clud·ed /sɪ'kluʷdɪd/ adj very quiet and private: a secluded country house

se·clu·sion /sɪ'kluʷʒən/ n [U] the state of being SECLUDED: The famous actor now lives in seclusion.

sec·ond¹ /'sɛkənd/ determiner,adv,n,pron **1** 2nd **2** [C] an imperfect article that is sold at a lower price: If you want to buy dishes cheaply, you can get factory seconds. **3** [C] a person who helps another, esp. in a BOXING match or DUEL¹ **4 second to none** infml the best: As a tennis player Ann is second to none.

second² n **1** a length of time equal to 1/60 of a minute **2** a measure of an angle equal to 1/3600 of a degree (or 1/60 of a MINUTE¹ (1))

second³ v [T] to support (a formal suggestion (MOTION¹ (3)) at a meeting so that argument or voting may follow: "Will anyone second this motion?" "I second it, Madam Chairwoman." –**seconder** n

sec·ond·ar·y /'sɛkən,dɛriʸ/ adj **1** (of education or a school) for children over 11 years old: secondary schools/teachers –compare PRIMARY (2) **2** developing from something earlier or original: a secondary infection caused by a cold **3** [to] of second rank, value, importance, etc.: a matter of secondary importance

second-class /,·· '·◄/ adj **1** regarded as below a standard; INFERIOR: He regards women as second-class citizens. **2** being SECOND CLASS: a second-class letter –compare FIRST-CLASS –**second-class** adv: traveling second-class

second class n [U] **1** (in the US and Canada) a class of mail for newspapers and magazines **2** the ordinary type of seating or living arrangements on a train or boat: a second-class seat|We're traveling second class. –see also FIRST CLASS

second-de·gree /,·· ·'·◄/ adj of the next to the most serious kind: second-degree murder|second-degree burns

second-guess /,·· '·/ v [I;T] AmE infml to find fault with (someone, something), esp. after an event has taken place

sec·ond·hand¹ /,sɛkənd'hænd◄/ adj,adv **1** used by an earlier owner; not new: a secondhand car|I got this book secondhand. **2** passed on from someone else: It was a secondhand report, based on what others had

told him. –see also HAND¹ (8), FIRSTHAND

secondhand² adj [A] dealing in SECONDHAND¹ goods: a secondhand shop

second na·ture /,·· '··/ n [U] a very firmly fixed habit: It's second nature for me to lock the doors at night.

second-rate /,·· '·◄/ adj of less than the best quality; INFERIOR¹: a second-rate movie/actor

se·cre·cy /'siʸkrəsiʸ/ n [U] **1** the practice of keeping secrets: Secrecy is important to our plans. **2** the state of being kept secret: The secrecy of the plan was closely guarded.

se·cret¹ /'siʸkrɪt/ adj [from] kept from the view or knowledge of others: secret plans| These plans must be kept secret (from the enemy).|a secret meeting place in the forest|Adrian is a secret admirer of Helen, though he has never spoken to her. –**secretly** adv

secret² n **1** something kept hidden or known only to a few: Our relationship must remain a secret.|Can you **keep** (=not tell) **a secret?**| The meeting was held **in secret. 2** something unexplained; mystery: the secret of how life on earth began|What is the secret of your success? (=how do you do it?)

secret a·gent /,·· '··/ n a person gathering information secretly, esp. for a foreign government; SPY

sec·re·tar·i·al /,sɛkrə'tɛəriʸəl/ adj of or concerning the work of a secretary: secretarial school

sec·re·tar·i·at /,sɛkrə'tɛəriʸət/ n an official department with a high-ranking government officer as its head: the United Nations Secretariat in New York

sec·re·tar·y /'sɛkrə,tɛriʸ/ n -ies **1** a person with the job of preparing letters, arranging meetings, etc., for another: a job as **private secretary** to the company chairman **2** a high-ranking government officer, as **a** (in the US) a nonelected director of a large department: Secretary of the TREASURY|Secretary of State Jones flew to London yesterday. **b** (in Britain) a minister: The Home/Foreign Secretary **3** an officer of an organization who keeps records, writes official letters, etc.: a union secretary

se·crete¹ /sɪ'kriʸt/ v -**creted, -creting** [T] (esp. of an animal or plant organ) to produce (a usu. liquid substance): Many animals secrete oil.

secrete² v [T] to put into a hidden place; hide

se·cre·tion /sɪ'kriʸʃən/ n **1** [C;U] (the production of) usu. liquid material by part of a plant or animal **2** [U] the act of hiding something

se·cre·tive /'siʸkrətɪv, sɪ'kriʸtɪv/ adj fond of keeping secrets –**secretively** adv –**secretiveness** n [U]

secret serv·ice /,·· '··/ n [the S] a government department dealing with special kinds of police work: The Secret Service is responsible for protecting the President.

sect /sɛkt/ n a group of people, sometimes within a larger group, having a special set of (esp. religious) beliefs

sec·tar·i·an /sɛk'tɛəriʸən/ adj resulting from division into SECTS: sectarian differences|sec-

tarian violence –opposite **non-sectarian** –**sectarianism** *n* [U]

sec·tion[1] /'sɛkʃən/ *n* **1** [C] a separate part of a larger object, place, group, etc.: *the business section of a city|the brass section* (=those who play brass instruments) *of a band|a bookcase which comes apart into sections|signals controlling each section of railroad track* **2** [C] a representation of something as if it were cut from top to bottom and looked at from the side –compare ELEVATION (3), PLAN[1] (3)

section[2] *v* [T] **1** to divide into SECTIONs **2** to cut or show a SECTION[1] from –**sectional** *adj*: *sectional furniture|a sectional drawing*

sec·tor /'sɛktər/ *n* **1** a part of an area of activity, esp. of business: *employment in the public and private sectors* (=those controlled by the government, and by private business)|*the banking sector* **2** an area of military operation: *the French sector in Berlin*

sec·u·lar /'sɛkyələr/ *adj* not connected with a church; not religious: *secular music*

se·cure[1] /sɪ'kyuər/ *adj* **1** [*from, against*] safe; protected against danger or risk: *a castle secure from attack|a secure job* (=not likely to be lost) **2** closed, firm, or tight enough for safety: *Make the windows secure before leaving the house.* **3** having no doubt or anxiety; CONFIDENT: *a secure belief|The boy felt secure near his parents.*–opposite **insecure** (for **1,3**) –**securely** *adv*

secure[2] *v* -**cured, -curing** [T] **1** [*for*] *fml* to get, esp. as the result of effort: *He's secured himself a good job.* **2** to fasten tightly: *They secured the windows as the storm began.* **3** [*from, against*] to make safe: *The soldiers secured the camp against attack.*

se·cu·ri·ty /sɪ'kyuərəṭiy/ *n* **1** [U] **1** the state of being SECURE: *He lost his feeling of security when he left home.* **2** something which protects: *The money is my security against hardship.* **3** valuable property promised to a lender of money in case repayment is not made: *He used his house as security to borrow the money.* –compare GUARANTEE[1] (3) **4** protection against lawbreaking, violence, etc.: *For security reasons the passengers have to be searched.|Tight security was in force during the President's visit.*

se·dan /sɪ'dæn/ *AmE*‖**saloon** *BrE*– *n* a car for four to seven passengers with a roof, closed sides and windows –see illustration on page 95

se·date[1] /sɪ'deyt/ *adj* not easily troubled; calm; quiet: *a sedate old lady* –**sedately** *adv* –**sedateness** *n* [U]

sedate[2] *v* -**dated, -dating** [T] to make sleepy or calm, esp. with a SEDATIVE –**sedation** /sɪ'deyʃən/ *n* [U]: *He's under sedation and resting quietly in bed.*

sed·a·tive /'sɛdəṭɪv/ *adj,n* (a drug) causing sleep: *The doctor gave him a sedative to help him sleep.*

sed·en·tar·y /'sɛdnteriy/ *adj fml* used to or needing to be performed while sitting: *sedentary jobs/workers*

sed·i·ment /'sɛdəmənt/ *n* [S;U] solid material that settles to the bottom of a liquid: *(a) brown sediment in the bottom of the coffee cup*

se·di·tion /sɪ'dɪʃən/ *n* [U] *fml* speaking, writing, or action intended to make people disobey a government –**seditious** /sɪ'dɪʃəs/ *adj*: *a seditious speech/speaker*

se·duce /sɪ'duws, sɪ'dyuws/ *v* -**duced, -ducing** [T] **1** to persuade (usu. someone young and without sexual experience) to have sex with one **2** to cause or persuade (someone) to do something wrong by making it seem attractive; ENTICE: *The warm weather seduced me away from my studies.* –**seducer** *n* –**seduction** /sɪ'dʌkʃən/ *n* [C;U]

se·duc·tive /sɪ'dʌktɪv/ *adj* having qualities likely to SEDUCE; very desirable or attractive: *her seductive voice|a seductive offer of higher pay* –**seductively** *adv* –**seductiveness** *n* [U]

see[1] /siy/ *v* **saw** /sɔ/, **seen** /siyn/, **seeing 1** [I not *be +v-ing*] to use the eyes; have or use the power of sight: *It was so dark he could hardly see (to do his work).|He doesn't see very well with his right eye.* **2** [T +(*that*); not *be +v-ing*] to get sight of; notice, examine, or recognize by looking: *I looked for her but I couldn't see her in the crowd.|I saw the train come/coming into the station.|Can you see where I put my glasses?|He saw his dog killed by the car.|(fig.) You and I have seen* (=experienced) *some good times together.| (fig.) This old house has* **seen better days**. (=is in bad condition) **3** [I;T +(*that*); not *be + v-ing*] to understand: *"Do you see what I mean?" "Yes, now I see." "I can't see why you don't like it.* **4** [I;T] to find out or decide: *Will you see if Mary wants her coffee yet?|"Can I go and stay with my friends?" "We'll see."* (=we'll decide later) **5** [T +(*that*); not *be +v-ing*] to make sure; take care: *See that you're there at eight o'clock.* **6** [T +*v-ing*; not *be +v-ing*] to form a picture in the mind of; imagine: *I can't see her lending me any money.* (=I'm sure she won't) **7** [T] to visit, call upon, or meet: *Come and see me when you're in New York.|The doctor can't see you yet. He's seeing someone else at the moment.|We haven't* **seen much of** *you lately.* (=we haven't been together) **8** [T] to go with; ACCOMPANY (1): *I'll see you home.* **9 let me see** (used for expressing a pause for thought): *"Do you recognize this music?" "Let me see . . . Yes, now I do."* **10 see fit to** to decide to **11 see the last of** *infml* to be finished with; have no further association with: *He's an annoying man and I'll be glad to see the last of him.* **12 see the light: a** to understand or accept an idea or the truth of something **b** to have a religious experience which changes one's belief **c** to be born or come to exist **13 see one's way to** to feel able to **14 see red** to be very angry **15 see stars** to see flashes of light, esp. as the result of being hit on the head **16 see things** to think that one sees something that is not there: *I must be seeing things; I can't believe they've got another new car!* **17 So I see** What you say is already clear or easy to see: *"I'm afraid I'm a* *little late." "So I see."*

USAGE Compare **see**, **look**, and **watch**: To **see** is to experience with the eyes; to **look** is to use the eyes on purpose and with attention; and to **watch** is to look at something in which there is movement: *The ball was going so fast that I didn't see it.|If you look carefully at the photograph, you can see John among the crowd.|The children are watching television/the football game.*

see sbdy./sthg. **off** *v adv* [T] to go to the airport, station, etc., with (someone who is beginning a trip): *He saw his friend off at the bus station.*

see about sthg. *v prep* [T +*v-ing*] to make arrangements for; take action about: *It's time for me to see about dinner/to see about cooking dinner.*

see sbdy./sthg.↔ **out** *v adv* [T] **1** to go to the door with (someone who is leaving): *"I'll see you out."* **2** to last until the end of: *Will our supplies see the winter out?*

see through¹ sbdy./sthg. *v prep* [T] to recognize the truth about (an excuse, false statement, etc.)

see sbdy. **through**² (sthg.) *v adv; prep* [T] to provide for until the end of (a time or difficulty): *enough money to see him through (a year abroad)*

see to sbdy./sthg. *v prep* [T +*v-ing*] to attend to; take care of: *If I cook lunch, will you see to the children?*

see² *n* the office of, or area governed by, a BISHOP –compare DIOCESE

seed¹ /siʸd/ *n* **1** [C;U] the part of some plants that may grow into a new plant: *a bag of grass seed* **2** [C] something from which growth begins; GERM² (2): *seeds of future trouble* **3** a SEEDed² (4) player in a competition –**seedless** *adj*: *a seedless orange*

seed² *v* **1** [I] (of a plant) to grow and produce seed **2** [T *with*] to plant seeds in (a piece of ground) **3** [T] to remove seeds from (fruit) **4** [T] to place (esp. a tennis player at the start of a competition) in order of likelihood to win: *He was an unknown player who wasn't seeded.*

seed·ling /'siʸdlɪŋ/ *n* a young plant grown from a seed

seed·y /'siʸdiʸ/ *adj* **-ier, -iest** **1** having a poor, worn-out appearance: *a seedy and unpleasant part of the town* **2** full of seeds: *a seedy orange* –**seedily** *adv* –**seediness** *n* [U]

see·ing /'siʸɪŋ/ also **seeing that** /'·· ·/, **seeing as** *infml*– *conj* as it is true that: *Seeing (that) she's old enough to get married, I don't think you can stop her.*

seek /siʸk/ *v* **sought** /sɔt/, **seeking 1** [I;T *after, for, out*] *fml* to make a search (for); try to find or get (something): *He sought out his friend in the crowd.|to seek (after) the truth| seek public office* **2** [T] *fml* to ask for; go to request: *You should seek advice from*

your lawyer. **3** [T +*to-v*] *lit* to try; make an attempt: *They sought to punish him for his crime but he escaped.* –**seeker** *n*

seem /siʸm/ *v* **1** [+*to-v*; not *be*+*v-ing*] to give the idea or effect of being; appear: *She always seems (to be) sad.|I seem to have caught a cold.|There seems (to be) every hope that business will get better.* **2** [*it* +I +(*that*)] to appear to be true: *It seems (as if) there will be a storm soon.*

seem·ing /'siʸmɪŋ/ *adj* [A] that seems to be, but perhaps is not real: *a seeming piece of good luck which led to a lot of trouble*

seem·ing·ly /'siʸmɪŋliʸ/ *adv* as far as one can tell; EVIDENTly: *Seemingly we can do nothing.*

seem·ly /'siʸmliʸ/ *adj* **-lier, -liest** (esp. of behavior) pleasing by being suitable to an occasion or to social standards –opposite **unseemly** –**seemliness** *n* [U]

seen /siʸn/ *v* past participle of SEE¹

seep /siʸp/ *v* [I] (of a liquid) to flow slowly through small openings in a material; OOZE²: *Water had seeped into the house through the walls.* –**seepage** /'siʸpɪdʒ/ *n* [S;U]

see·saw¹ /'siʸsɔ/ *n* a board balanced in the middle for children to sit on at opposite ends so that when one end goes up the other goes down, used for fun

seesaw² *v* [I] to move up and down: *seesawing prices*

seethe /siʸð/ *v* **seethed, seething** [I] **1** (of a liquid) to move about as if boiling **2** to be very excited or angry: *a country seething with political unrest*

seg·ment¹ /'sɛgmənt/ *n* any of the parts into which something may be divided; SECTION¹ (1): *a dish of orange segments*

seg·ment² /sɛg'mɛnt, 'sɛgmɛnt/ *v* [I;T] to (cause to) divide into SEGMENTs¹ –**segmentation** /ˌsɛgmən'teʸʃən/ *n* [S;U]

seg·re·gate /'sɛgrəˌgeʸt/ *v* **-gated, -gating** [T] to separate from the rest of a social group: *He went to a school where boys and girls were segregated.* –compare INTEGRATE

seg·re·ga·tion /ˌsɛgrə'geʸʃən/ *n* [U] the separation of esp. a social or racial group from others, e.g. by laws against using the same schools, hotels, buses, etc. –opposite **integration**; compare APARTHEID

seis·mic /'saɪzmɪk/ *adj tech* of or caused by EARTHQUAKEs

seize /siʸz/ *v* **seized, seizing** [T] **1** to take hold of eagerly and forcefully; GRAB: *He seized my hand.|She seized (hold of) the child and pulled it away from the road.|*(fig.) *She seized (on) the chance of a trip abroad.* **2** to take control of by official order or by force: *The weapons were seized by the police.|The enemy army seized the fort.|*(fig.) *She was seized by a desire to be a singer.*

sei·zure /'siʸʒər/ *n* **1** [U] the act of seizing (SEIZE): *The courts ordered the seizure of all her property.* **2** [C] a sudden attack of an illness: *a heart seizure*

sel·dom /'sɛldəm/ *adv* not often; rarely: *He very seldom eats breakfast.|He seldom, if ever, reads a book.* –see NEVER (USAGE)

se·lect¹ /sɪ'lɛkt/ *v* [T] to choose: *He selected a*

SPELLING NOTE

Words with the sound /s/, may be spelled **c-**, like **city**, or **ps-**, like **psychology**.

shirt to match his suit.

select² /,· ·'· ◄/ *adj* **1** [A] carefully chosen: *A select group of people were invited to the first performance.* **2** limited to certain members; EX-CLUSIVE¹ (1): *a select club*

se·lec·tion /sɪ'lɛkʃən/ *n* **1** [C;U] the act of SELECTing, or a thing selected: *the selection of a wine to go with dinner* **2** [C] a collection, e.g. of goods for sale: *The store has a fine selection of cheeses.*

se·lec·tive /sɪ'lɛktɪv/ *adj* **1** careful in choosing: *He is always very selective when he chooses his suits.* **2** concerning only certain articles; not general: *selective controls on goods brought into the country for sale* **–selectively** *adv* **–selectivity** /sɪˌlɛk'tɪvəṭiʸ/ *n* [U] **–selectiveness** /sɪ'lɛktɪvnɪs/ *n* [U]

se·lec·tor /sɪ'lɛktər/ *n* a person or instrument that SELECTs

self /sɛlf/ *n* selves /sɛlvz/ **1** [C;U] a person with his/her own nature, character, abilities, etc.: *Knowledge of self increases as one gets older.* **2** [C] a typical part of one's mental or physical nature: *back to her old self after a long illness*

self-ad·dressed /,· ·'· ◄/ *adj* addressed for return to the sender: *Please enclose a self-addressed envelope with your order.*

self-as·sur·ance /,· ·'··/ *n* [U] sure belief in one's own abilities; SELF-CONFIDENCE **–self-assured** /,· ·'· ◄/ *adj*

self-cen·tered /,· ·'·· ◄/ *adj* interested only in oneself; selfish

self-con·fessed /,· ·'· ◄/ *adj* [A] admitted by oneself to be the stated kind of person; AVOWED: *a self-confessed criminal* –see also CONFESSED

self-con·fi·dence /,· ·'··/ *n* [U] belief in one's own power to do things successfully **–self-confident** *adj*

self-con·scious /,· ·'··/ *adj* nervous and uncomfortable about oneself as seen by others **–self-consciously** *adv* **–self-consciousness** *n* [U]

self-con·tained /,· ·'· ◄/ *adj* **1** complete in itself; having no part shared with anything else: *a self-contained factory* **2** (of a person) habitually not showing feelings or depending on the friendship of others

self-con·trol /,· ·'·/ *n* [U] control over one's feelings: *She never loses her self-control, even when things don't go well.* **–self-controlled** /,· ·'· ◄/ *adj*

self-de·feat·ing /,· ·'··/ *adj* having the effect of preventing its own success: *a self-defeating plan*

self-de·fense /,· ·'·/ *n* [U] the act or skill of defending oneself: *He shot the man in self-defense.* (=only to protect himself)

self-de·ni·al /,· ·'··/ *n* [U] the habit of not allowing oneself pleasures

self-de·ter·mi·na·tion /,· ···'··/ *n* [U] the right of the people of a place to make a free decision about the form of their government, esp. whether or not to be independent of another country

self-dis·ci·pline /,· ·'··/ *n* [U] the training of oneself to control one's emotions, desires, and actions

self-ef·fac·ing /,· ·'·· ◄/ *adj* keeping oneself from attracting attention; modest –see also EFFACE

self-em·ployed /,· ·'· ◄/ *adj* earning money from one's own business and not as pay from an employer

self-ev·i·dent /,· '··· ◄/ *adj* plainly true without need of proof: *It's self-evident that our football team isn't very good; they've lost every game this season.*

self-ex·plan·a·to·ry /,· ·'···/ *adj* (esp. of speaking or writing) explaining itself; needing no further explanation

self-gov·ern·ment /,· ·'···/ *n* [U] government without outside control; independence

self-im·por·tance /,· ·'··/ *n* [U] too high an opinion of one's own importance **–self-important** /,· ·'·· ◄/ *adj*: *He's just a self-important clerk.*

self-im·posed /,· ·'· ◄/ *adj* (of a duty, etc.) that one has forced oneself to accept: *a self-imposed limit of three cigarettes a day*

self-in·dul·gence /,· ·'··/ *n* [U] the too easy allowance of pleasure or comfort to oneself **–self-indulgent** /,· ·'· ◄/ *adj*

self-in·ter·est /,· '··, ,· '··/ *n* [U] concern for what is best for oneself: *I don't really like my rich uncle, but I'm always friendly to him out of self-interest.*

self·ish /'sɛlfɪʃ/ *adj* concerned with one's own advantage without care for others: *a selfish boy|to act for purely selfish reasons* –opposite **unselfish** **–selfishly** *adv* **–selfishness** *n* [U]

self·less /'sɛlflɪs/ *adj* completely unselfish **–selflessly** *adv* **–selflessness** *n* [U]

self-made /,· '· ◄/ *adj* raised to success and wealth by one's own efforts alone: *a self-made man*

self-pit·y /,· '··/ *n* [U] too great pity for one's own sorrows or troubles

self-pos·sessed /,· ·'· ◄/ *adj* having firm control over one's own feelings and actions, esp. in difficult or unexpected conditions; calm **–self-possession** /,· ·'··/ *n* [U]

self-pres·er·va·tion /,· ···'··/ *n* [U] the natural tendency to keep oneself from death or harm

self-re·li·ant /,· ·'··/ *adj* able to act without depending on the help of others **–self-reliance** *n* [U]

self-re·spect /,· ·'·/ *n* [U] proper pride in oneself; the feeling that one need not be ashamed of oneself –see also RESPECT (2)

self-right·eous /,· ·'··/ *adj derog* too proud of one's own rightness or goodness **–self-righteously** *adv* **–self-righteousness** *n* [U]

self-sac·ri·fice /,· ·'··/ *n* [U] the giving up of one's pleasure or interests in favor of others or of a worthier purpose **–self-sacrificing** *adj*

self-sat·is·fied /,· ·'··/ *adj* too pleased with oneself; SMUG; COMPLACENT **–self-satisfaction** /,· ·'··/ *n* [U]

self-seek·ing /,· '·· ◄/ *n,adj* [U] (action) that works only for one's own advantage: *a dishonorable self-seeking politician*

self-serv·ice /,· '·· ◄/ *adj,n* [U] (working by) the system in which buyers take what they want and then pay at a special desk: *a self-*

service gas station/restaurant

self-styled /ˌ· ˈ·◄/ *adj* [A] *usu. derog* given the stated title by oneself, usu. without any right to it: *a self-styled "doctor" who has no qualifications*

self-suf·fi·cient /ˌ· ·ˈ·◄/ *adj* [in] able to provide for one's needs without outside help: *The US is not self-sufficient in oil.* –**self-sufficiency** /ˌ· ·ˈ··/ *n* [U]

sell /sɛl/ *v* sold /soʷld/, selling **1** [I;T *to*] to give (property or goods) in exchange for money: *I sold my car to my friend for $500.*|*I sold my friend my car for $500.*|*Before they moved to Boston, they sold their house.*|*I went to the market to buy, not to sell.*|*Do you sell cigarettes in this store?* –compare BUY **2** [I *at, for*] to be bought; get buyers; gain a sale: *This newspaper is selling for/at 25 cents.*|*The tickets cost too much and sold badly/wouldn't sell.* **3** [T] to help or cause to be bought: *Bad news sells newspapers.* **4** [T *on, to*] *infml* to persuade (someone) to accept a product, idea, etc.: *I'm completely sold on this new machine; it saves so much time!*|*What a stupid excuse! You'll never sell that to anyone!* **5 sell oneself**: **a** to make oneself or one's ideas seem attractive to others **b** to give up one's principles for money or other gain

sell sthg.↔**off** *v adv* [T] to get rid of (goods) by selling, usu. cheaply: *They're selling off their furniture because they're moving to Canada.*

sell (sbdy./sthg.)↔ **out** *v adv* [I;T] **1** [*of*] to sell all of (what was for sale): *Sorry, the tickets are sold out; there are no more left.*|*We're sold out of milk.* **2** to be disloyal to (one's principles or friends), esp. for money: *He sold out (his artistic standards) and now just writes for money.* –see also SELLOUT

sell·er /ˈsɛlər/ *n* **1** a person who sells –compare BUYER **2** a product with the stated amount of sales: *Her new book is already a best-seller.* (=very many copies have been sold)

sell·out /ˈsɛlaʊt/ *n* **1** a performance, sports event, etc., for which all tickets are sold **2** an act of disloyalty to one's principles or friends; BETRAYAL –see also SELL **out**

selves /sɛlvz/ *n pl. of* SELF

se·man·tics /səˈmæntɪks/ *n* [U] the study of the meanings of words –**semantic** *adj*

sem·a·phore /ˈsɛməˌfɔr, -ˌfoʷr/ *n* [U] a system of sending messages, using two flags held one in each hand

sem·blance /ˈsɛmbləns/ *n* [S] an appearance; outward form: *a semblance of peace*

se·men /ˈsiʸmən/ *n* [U] the liquid produced by the male sex organs, carrying SPERM

se·mes·ter /səˈmɛstər/ *n* either of the two periods into which a year at schools and universities, usu. in the US, is divided: *I'm taking Spanish this semester.* –compare TERM

SPELLING NOTE

Words with the sound /s/, may be spelled **c-**, like **city**, or **ps-**, like **psychology**.

---

sem·i·cir·cle /ˈsɛmiʸˌsɜrkəl/ *n* half a circle –**semicircular** /ˌsɛmiʸˈsɜrkyələr/ *adj*

sem·i·co·lon /ˈsɛmiʸˌkoʷlən/ *n* the mark (;) used to separate different parts of a list and independent parts of a sentence

sem·i·de·tached /ˌsɛmiʸdɪˈtætʃt◄, ˌsɛmaɪ-/ *adj,n* (being) one of a pair of joined houses

sem·i·fi·nal /ˈsɛmiʸˌfaɪnl, ˈsɛmaɪ-, ˌsɛmiʸ ˈfaɪnl◄, ˌsɛmaɪ-/ *n* (in sports) one of a pair or set of matches whose winners then compete against one another to decide the winner of the whole competition

sem·i·nar /ˈsɛməˌnɑr/ *n* a small class of students working on usu. advanced subjects of their own choosing with the help of a teacher

sem·i·nar·y /ˈsɛməˌnɛriʸ/ *n* **-ies** a college for training the CLERGY (=religious leaders)

sem·i·pre·cious /ˌsɛmiʸˈprɛʃəs◄, ˌsɛmaɪ-/ *adj* (of a jewel, stone, etc.) of lower value than a PRECIOUS STONE

Se·mit·ic /səˈmɪṭɪk/ *adj* **1** of the Jews, Arabs, and various other peoples in ancient times: *a Semitic language* –compare ANTI-SEMITISM **2** Jewish

sem·o·li·na /ˌsɛməˈliʸnə/ *n* [U] hard grains of crushed wheat used in making certain food: *semolina* SPAGHETTI

sen·ate /ˈsɛnɪt/ *n* (*usu. cap.*) **1** the smaller (UPPER) of the two law-making groups (HOUSES[1] (2)) in some countries such as the US: *The Senate has voted to support the President's defense plans.* –compare CONGRESS **2** the governing council at some universities

sen·a·tor /ˈsɛnəṭər/ *n* [A;C] (*often cap.*) a member of a SENATE (1): *Senator Davis will see you now.*

send /sɛnd/ *v* sent /sɛnt/, sending **1** [T *to*] to cause or order (a person or thing) to go somewhere without going there oneself: *If you need money I'll send it to you/I'll send you some.*|*He was sent (by his mother) to buy some milk.*|*They sent their children to school in Boston.* **2** [I *for*] to cause a message, request, or order to go out: *Send for a doctor!* **3** [T] to cause to be in a particular state: *The news sent the family into great excitement.* **4** to cause to move quickly and uncontrollably: *The explosion sent glass flying everywhere.* **5** [I;T] (of a radio or the person using it) to TRANSMIT: *The ship's radio sent out signals for help.*

send sthg.↔ **off** *v adv* [T] to mail (a letter, package, etc) –see also SEND-OFF

send away/off *v adv* **1** [T] (**send** sbdy.↔ **away**) to send to another place: *He sent his son away/off to school in Pennsylvania.* **2** [I *for*] to order goods to be sent by mail: *I couldn't get this lamp in town, so I sent away for it.* –see also SEND-OFF

send sbdy./sthg.↔**down** *v adv* [T] to cause to go down: *Bad news sent market prices down.*

send sthg.↔ **out** *v adv* [T] to send from a central point: *to send out invitations/orders*|*the sun sending out light*

send sbdy./sthg. **up** *v adv* [T] **1** to cause to go up: *a fire sending up smoke into the air* **2** *infml AmE* to send (someone) to prison

send-off /'· ·/ *n* a usu. planned show of good wishes at the start of a trip, new business, etc.: *The team was given a great send-off at the airport.* –see also SEND **off**

se·nile /'siʸnaɪl, 'sɛnaɪl/ *adj* weak in body or in mind because of old age –**senility** /sɪ'nɪləṭiʸ/ *n* [U]

sen·ior[1] /'siʸnyər/ *n* **1** a person who is older or higher in rank than another **2** *AmE* a student in the last year of a high school or university course –compare FRESHMAN, SOPHOMORE

senior[2] *adj* **1** [F *to; no comp.*] older or of higher rank: *He is senior to me.* **2** of high rank: *a meeting of the most senior army officers* –compare JUNIOR

Senior *n* [after *n*] *esp. AmE* the older: *John Smith Senior* –compare JUNIOR; see MAJOR (USAGE)

senior cit·i·zen /,·· '···/ *n* an old person, esp. one over the age of 60 or 65

se·nior·i·ty /siʸn'yɔrəṭiʸ, -'yɑr-/ *n* [U] the quality of being SENIOR[2] (1) in rank or age

sen·sa·tion /sɛn'seʸʃən/ *n* **1** [C;U] (a) direct feeling coming from the senses: *He could feel no sensation in his arm.* **2** [C] a general feeling in the mind or body: *The train had stopped, but I had the sensation that it was still moving.* **3** [C] (a cause of) a state of excited interest: *The discovery was/caused a great sensation.*

sen·sa·tion·al /sɛn'seʸʃənəl/ *adj* **1** causing or intended to cause excited interest: *a sensational murder/news report* **2** *infml* wonderful; very good or exciting: *You won? That's sensational!* –**sensationally** *adv*

sen·sa·tion·al·ism /sɛn'seʸʃənəl,ɪzəm/ *n* [U] usu. *derog* the intentional producing of excitement or shock, e.g. by books, magazines, etc., of low quality

sense[1] /sɛns/ *n* **1** [S;U] (a) power to understand and make judgments about something: *a sense of values/direction|a successful man with good business sense* –see SENSIBLE (USAGE) **2** [S] a feeling, esp. one that is hard to describe exactly: *a sense of fear|a sense that someone was standing behind him* **3** [U] good and esp. practical understanding and judgment: *Haven't you got enough sense to know you can't spend more than you earn.* –see also COMMON SENSE, NONSENSE; see SENSIBLE (USAGE) **4** [C *of*] any of the five SENSES (1): *to lose one's sense of smell/taste* **5** [C] a meaning: *"man" in its broadest sense, meaning both men and women* **6 in a sense** in one way of speaking; partly: *You are right in a sense, but you don't know all the facts.* **7 make sense: a** to have a clear meaning: *No matter how you read it, this sentence doesn't make (any) sense.|I can't* **make sense of** (=understand) *it.* **b** to be a wise course of action: *It makes sense to take care of your health.* **8 talk sense** *infml* to speak reasonably **9 there's no sense in** *infml* there's no good reason for: *There's no sense in going by boat when the plane is just as cheap and much quicker.*

sense[2] *v* **sensed, sensing** [T *that*] to have a feeling, without being told directly, of: *The horse sensed danger and stopped.|She sensed*

that her husband was worried.

sense·less /'sɛnslɪs/ *adj* **1** in a sleeplike state, as after a blow on the head; unconscious **2** foolish; purposeless: *senseless violence* –**senselessly** *adv* –**senselessness** *n* [U]

sens·es /'sɛnsɪz/ *n* [P] **1** the five natural powers of sight, hearing, feeling, tasting, and smelling, which give a person or animal feelings and information about the outside world **2** one's powers of (reasonable) thinking: *Are you crazy? Have you* **taken leave of your senses?**

sen·si·bil·i·ty /,sɛnsə'bɪləṭiʸ/ *n* -ties [C;U] *fml* (a) tender or delicate feeling: *She plays the piano with great sensibility.* –see SENSIBLE (USAGE)

sen·si·ble /'sɛnsəbəl/ *adj* **1** reasonable and practical; having or showing good sense: *a sensible child/plan/idea* **2** [F *of*] *fml* knowing; recognizing: *He was sensible of the trouble he caused.* **3** (of clothing, etc.) practical rather than fashionable: *a sensible summer suit|sensible shoes* –**sensibly** *adv*

USAGE **Sensible**, in its usual meaning of "reasonable and practical", concerns your ability to understand and make judgments (your **sense**[1] (3)). But **sensibility**, which is not related to this meaning of **sensible**, concerns your ability to experience delicate feelings, and it is closer to **sensitive**: a **sensitive** person has great **sensibility** and is quick to enjoy or suffer.

sen·si·tive /'sɛnsəṭɪv/ *adj* **1** [*to*] quick to show or feel the effect of something: *sensitive to cold/pain|light-sensitive photographic paper |a sensitive scale* **2** showing delicate feelings or judgment: *a sensitive performance/actor* –opposite **insensitive 3** sometimes *derog* easily offended **4** dealing with secret government work: *sensitive official papers* –see SENSIBLE (USAGE) –**sensitively** *adv* –**sensitivity** /,sɛnsə'tɪvəṭiʸ/ also **sensitiveness** /'sɛnsəṭɪvnɪs/ *n* [U]

sen·so·ry /'sɛnsəriʸ/ *adj* of the bodily senses: *sensory* PERCEPTION

sen·su·al /'sɛnʃuwəl, -tʃuw-/ *adj* **1** sometimes *derog* interested in giving pleasure to one's own body, e.g. by sex, food, and drink –compare SENSUOUS **2** of, or seen, felt, etc. by the senses: *sensual experiences*

sen·su·ous /'sɛnʃuwəs, -tʃuw-/ *adj* of or causing pleasant feelings of the senses: *The cat stretched itself with sensuous pleasure in the sun.* –compare SENSUAL –**sensuously** *adv* –**sensuousness** *n* [U]

sent /sɛnt/ *v past tense and participle of* SEND

sen·tence[1] /'sɛntəns/ *n* **1** a group of words that forms a statement, command, EXCLAMATION, or question, usu. contains a subject and a verb, and (in writing) begins with a capital letter and ends with one of the marks . ! ? The following are all sentences: *"Sing the song again." "How well he sings!" "Who sang at the concert last night?"* –compare CLAUSE, PHRASE **2** a punishment for a criminal found guilty in court: *The sentence was ten years (in prison).|the death sentence|The judge* **gave/passed/pronounced sentence on** *him.*

sentence² *v* **-tenced, -tencing** [T *to*] (of a judge or court) to give a punishment to: *He was sentenced to three years in prison.*

sen·ti·ment /'sɛntəmənt/ *n* [C;U] **1** (a) tender or fine feeling of pity, love, sadness, etc.: *There's no place for sentiment in business!* **2** (a) thought or judgment arising from feeling: *strong public sentiment on the question of unemployment*

sen·ti·men·tal /ˌsɛntə'mɛntəl◄/ *adj* **1** having or coming from tender feelings rather than reasonable or practical ones: *The clock doesn't work very well, but we keep it for sentimental reasons. It belonged to my grandfather.* **2** showing too much of such feelings, esp. of a weak or silly kind: *sentimental love stories* **–sentimentally** *adv* **–sentimentality** /ˌsɛntəmɛn'tælətiʸ/ *n* [U] *often derog*

sen·ti·nel /'sɛntən-əl/ *n* *lit & old use* a guard; SENTRY

sen·try /'sɛntriʸ/ *n* **-tries** a soldier standing as a guard

sep·a·ra·ble /'sɛpərəbəl/ *adj* that can be separated **–**opposite **inseparable**

sep·a·rate¹ /'sɛpəˌreʸt/ *v* **-rated, -rating 1** [I;T *from, into*] to set or move apart: *Separate the two pipes by unscrewing them.*|*The teacher separated the children into two groups*/*separated the boys from the girls.* **2** [T] to keep apart; mark a division between: *two towns separated by a river* **3** [I;T *up, into*] to break or divide up into parts: *An orange separates (up) into 10 or 12 pieces.* **4** [I] (of a husband and wife) to live apart, esp. by a formal agreement

sep·a·rate² /'sɛpərɪt/ *adj* **1** not the same; different: *This word has three separate meanings.* **2** [A] not shared with another; INDIVIDUAL: *We have separate rooms.* **3** [F *from*] apart: *Keep the boys separate from the girls.* **–separateness** *n* [U] **–separately** *adv*

sep·a·ra·tion /ˌsɛpə'reʸʃən/ *n* **1** [C;U] (a) breaking or coming apart **2** [C;U *from*] (a time of) being or living apart: *He was unhappy because of his separation from his mother.* **3** [C] *law* a formal agreement by a husband and wife to live apart **–**compare DIVORCE

sep·a·rat·ist /'sɛpərətɪst/ *n* a member of a group that wants to become separate from a larger political or religious body

se·pi·a /'siʸpiʸə/ *n* [U] (the color of) a brown paint or ink: *an old sepia photograph*

Sep·tem·ber /sɛp'tɛmbər/ also **Sept.** *written abbrev–* *n* the ninth month of the year

sep·tic /'sɛptɪk/ *adj* infected by disease bacteria

sep·ul·cher *AmE*‖**sepulchre** *BrE* /'sɛpəlkər/ *n* *old use & bibl* a burial place; TOMB **–sepulchral** /sə'pʌlkrəl/ *adj*

se·quel /'siʸkwəl/ *n* **1** [*to*] something that follows something else, esp. as a result **2** a story, movie, etc., which continues the

action of an earlier one

se·quence /'siʸkwəns/ *n* **1** [C] a group of things arranged in an order, esp. following one another in time: *a sequence of historical plays by Shakespeare* **2** [U] the order in which things or events follow one another; SUCCESSION: *Please keep the cards in sequence. Don't mix them up.*|*The* **sequence of events** *on the night of the murder still isn't known.*

se·quin /'siʸkwɪn/ *n* a very small round shiny piece of metal or plastic sewn onto a piece of clothing for decoration

ser·e·nade¹ /ˌsɛrə'neʸd/ *n* a song or other music sung or played in the open air at night, esp. to a woman by a lover

serenade² *v* **-naded, -nading** [T] to sing or play a SERENADE¹ to

se·rene /sə'riʸn/ *adj* completely calm and peaceful: *a serene summer night*|*a serene trust in God* **–serenely** *adv* **–serenity** /sə'rɛnətiʸ/ *n* [U]

serf /sɜrf/ *n* a person, not quite a slave, forced to stay and work on his/her master's land, esp. in a FEUDAL system

serf·dom /'sɜrfdəm/ *n* [U] the state or fact of being a SERF

serge /sɜrdʒ/ *n* [U] a type of strong cloth used esp. for suits, coats, and dresses

ser·geant /'sɑrdʒənt/ *n* [A;C] **1** a NONCOMMISSIONED OFFICER of upper rank in the army, air force, or MARINE CORPS **2** a police officer with next to the lowest rank

sergeant ma·jor /ˌ·· '·· ◄/ *n* [A;C] a NONCOMMISSIONED OFFICER of the highest rank in the US army or MARINE CORPS

se·ri·al¹ /'sɪəriʸəl/ *adj* of, happening, or arranged in a SERIES or row of things in order: *placed in serial order*|*The police know the serial numbers of the stolen traveler's checks.* **–serially** *adv*

serial² *n* a written or broadcast story appearing in parts at fixed times

se·ri·al·ize ‖also **-ise** *BrE* /'sɪəriʸəˌlaɪz/ *v* **-ized, -izing** [T] to print or broadcast (a book already written) as a SERIAL² **–serialization** /ˌsɪəriʸələ'zeʸʃən/ *n* [C;U]

se·ries /'sɪəriʸz/ *n* **series** a group of things of the same kind, coming one after another in order: *a television series* (=a series of shows on television) *about modern art*|*After a series of unsuccessful attempts, he has at last passed his driving test.*|*The Mexican team will be playing a series of games in Brazil this year.*

se·ri·ous /'sɪəriʸəs/ *adj* **1** thoughtful; solemn; not cheerful; GRAVE² (1): *a serious expression on her face*|*Do you think he is serious about leaving his wife?* (=does he really intend to do it?) **2** not slight: *serious damage*|*serious crime* **3** of an important kind; needing great skill or thought: *a serious artist*|*piece of art* **–seriousness** *n* [U]

se·ri·ous·ly /'sɪəriʸəsliʸ/ *adv* **1** in a serious way: *to study music seriously*|*seriously wounded* **2** **take (someone/something) seriously** to treat (someone or something) as important or true and needing thought and attention

ser·mon /'sɜrmən/ *n* **1** a talk given

(PREACHed) as part of a church service **2** *infml* a (too) long and solemn warning or piece of advice

ser·pent /'sɜrpənt/ *n lit* a snake

ser·rat·ed /sə'reʸtɪd, 'sɛreʸtɪd/ *adj* having a row of connected V-shapes like teeth (as on a saw): *a serrated edge|a serrated knife*

se·rum /'sɪərəm/ *n* **-rums** *or* **-ra** /rə/ [C;U] (a) liquid containing disease-fighting substances and prepared for putting into a person's or animal's blood —compare VACCINE

serv·ant /'sɜrvənt/ *n* **1** a person who is paid to work for another in the other's house: *They have two servants: a cook and a gardener.* **2** [*of*] *fml* a person used for the service or purposes of another: *A politician should be a servant of the people.* —see also CIVIL SERVANT

serve¹ /sɜrv/ *v* **served, serving 1** [I;T *as, in, on, under*] to work or do a useful job (for): *Serve your country.|Our gardener has served the family for 20 years.|He served in the army/on the committee.|They served under the king.* **2** [T *with*] to provide with something necessary or useful: *a single pipeline serving all the houses with water* **3** [I;T *as, for*] to be suitable for (a purpose): *One room had to serve as/for both bedroom and living room.|I don't have a hammer, but this stone should serve (my purpose).* **4** [I;T *with*] to offer (food) for eating: *Please serve the coffee now.|What time is breakfast served in this hotel?|The waitress was serving at the next table.* **5** [T] (of a person in a store) to attend to (a customer): *Are you being served?* (=Is someone else attending to you?) **6** [T] to spend (a period of time) in prison: *He served ten years/a long sentence for his crime.|He served time* (=was in prison) *for murder.* **7** [I;T] (in tennis, VOLLEYBALL, etc.) to begin play by striking (the ball) to the opponent **8** [T] *law* to deliver (an official order to appear in court) to (someone): *serve a SUMMONS on him/him (with) a summons* **9 serve someone right** *infml* to be a suitable punishment for someone: *After all you've eaten, it'll serve you right if you get a pain in your stomach.*

serve² *also* **service-** *n* an act or manner of serving (SERVE¹ (7)) in tennis: *He has a good fast serve.|It's your serve.* (=your turn to serve)

serv·er /'sɜrvər/ *n* something used in serving food, esp. a specially shaped tool for putting a particular kind of food onto a plate

serv·ice¹ /'sɜrvɪs/ *n* **1** [U] attention to buyers in a store or to guests in a hotel, restaurant, etc.: *The service in this place is slow/bad. Sometimes you have to wait ten minutes for service.* **2** [C *usu. pl.*] *fml* an act or job done for someone: *You may need the services of a lawyer in this affair.* **3** [U] work or duty done for someone: *He died in the service of his country.* **4** [U] the repair of a machine: *Take your car for service/for regular service.* **5** [C;U] a business or organization doing useful work or supplying a need: *Is there any train service here on Sundays?|good telephone service* **6** [C] a fixed form of public worship; a religious ceremony: *Our church*

has three services each Sunday. **7** [C] a government department: *the* CIVIL SERVICE **8** [C;U] (duty in) any of the armed forces: *He saw active service in the last war.* **9** [C] → SERVE² **10** [C] the dishes, tools, etc., needed to serve a stated food, number of people, or meal: *a silver tea service/service for eight* **11** [A] something for the use of people working in a place, esp. servants in a house: *a service entrance|a service* ELEVATOR **12** [C *usu. pl.*; A] a business or job that does not produce goods: *Tourism is a service industry.* **13 at your service** *polite or pomp* willing to do what you command: *If you need any help, I am at your service.* **14 of service** useful; helpful: *(polite) Can I be of service to you?* —compare DISSERVICE

service² *v* **-iced, -icing** [T] to repair or put in good condition: *to service the car*

serv·ice·a·ble /'sɜrvɪsəbəl/ *adj* that can be used; fit for (long or hard) use: *a serviceable pair of shoes*

serv·ice·man /'sɜrvɪs,mæn, -mən/ *n* **-men** /,mɛn, -mən/ a male member of the army, navy, etc.

service sta·tion /'·· ,··/ *n esp. AmE* for GAS STATION

ser·vile /'sɜrvəl, -vaɪl/ *adj derog* behaving like a slave; allowing complete control by another: *servile obedience to his employer* —**servility** /sər'vɪlətiʸ *n* [U]

ser·vi·tude /'sɜrvə,tuʷd, -,tyuʷd/ *n* [U *to*] *lit* the condition of a slave or of one who is forced to obey another: *a life of servitude to the enemy conquerors*

ses·sion /'sɛʃən/ *n* **1** a formal meeting of an organization, esp. a law-making body or court: *The next session of Congress will begin in November.|This court is now in session.* **2** *esp. AmE* one of the parts of the year when teaching is given at a university: *the summer session* —see also SEMESTER **3** a meeting or period of time used esp. by a group for a particular purpose: *a dance session*

set¹ /sɛt/ *v* **set, setting 1** [T] to put so as to stay in a place: *Set that heavy load down here.|(fig.) His great ability sets him apart* (=makes him clearly different) *from the others.* **2** [T] to put into order for use: *Set the table for dinner.* (=put the plates, glasses, etc. on it) **3** [T] to fix or determine (a rule, time, standard, number, etc.): *The price has been set at $1000.|He set a land speed record.* **4** [T] to fix firmly (a part of the body, esp. to show one's feelings): *He set his jaw and refused to agree.|The child has set his heart on it.* (=wants it very much)|*I've set my mind to it.* (=firmly decided on it) **5** [I] (esp. of the sun) to pass downwards out of sight: *In the winter the sun sets early.* —opposite **rise 6** [T] to cause to be: *I opened the cage and set the bird free.* **7** [T] to cause to start: *Your remarks have set me thinking.* **8** [T] to give (a piece of work) for (someone) to do, esp. in the phrase **set a task** [T *usu. pass.*] to give a particular SETTING (3) to: *The book is set in 17th-century Spain.* **10** [T] to write music for (words): *Has the poem ever been set (to music)?* **11** [T *in/with*] to fix (a precious stone) into (a piece of jewelry): *set a diamond in a ring|a ring set with three diamonds* **12** [I;T] **a** to put (a broken bone or limb) into a fixed position so that it will mend **b** (of a broken bone or limb) to become joined in a fixed position **13** [I] (of a liquid, paste, jelly, etc.) to become solid **14** [T] to arrange (hair) when wet to give the desired style when dry **15 all set: a** not needing anything further: *Would you like more coffee or are you all set?* **b** ready: *Are you all set for your trip tomorrow?* **16 set foot in/on** to enter; visit: *Nobody has ever set foot on that island.* **17 set fire/a match to** to cause (something) to burn in the stated way **18 set someone's teeth on edge** to give someone the unpleasant sensation caused by certain acid tastes or high sounds **19 set store by** to feel to be of the stated amount of importance: *I set great store by your support.* **20 set the pace** to fix the speed for others to follow **21 set right** to make just, healthy, correct, etc.: *This medicine will set you right.* **22 set to work** to start working –see SIT (USAGE)

set about sthg. *v prep* [T +*v-ing*] to begin to do; start: *She set about answering letters as soon as she arrived at the office.*

set sbdy./sthg. **against** sbdy./sthg. *v prep* [T] to cause to oppose: *a war which set family against family*

set sthg.↔ **aside** *v adv* [T] **1** also **set** sthg.↔ **by**– to save for a special purpose: *Set aside a little money each week.* **2** to pay no attention to: *Setting aside what I think, what would you like to do?*

set back *v adv* [T] **1** (**set** sthg.↔ **back**) to place at a distance behind something: *a house set 50 feet back from the road* **2** (**set** sthg.↔**back**) to make late: *The bad weather will set back our building plans (by three weeks).* **3** (**set** sbdy. **back** sthg.) *infml* to cost (someone) (a large amount of money): *That's a nice suit; it must have set you back a lot.* –see also SETBACK

set sbdy./sthg.↔**down** *v adv* [T] to write; make a record of: *I have set down everything that happened, as I remember it.*

set in *v adv* [I] (of a disease, unfavorable weather, etc.) to begin and (probably) continue: *Winter sets in early in the north.|The wound was treated before infection could set in.*

set off *v adv* **1** [I] also **set out**– to begin a trip: *She set off on a trip across Europe.* **2** [T] (**set** sthg.↔ **off**) to cause to explode: *The bomb could be set off at any time.* **3** [T] (**set off** sthg.) to cause (sudden activity): *The discovery of gold in California set off a rush to get there.* **4** [T] (**set** sthg.↔ **off**) to make (one thing) look better by putting it near something different: *a white belt to set off her blue dress*

set on *v prep* [T] **1** (**set on** sbdy.) also **set**

upon sbdy.– (esp. of a group) to attack: *He was set on by robbers.* **2** (**set** sbdy./sthg. **on** sbdy.) to cause to attack or chase: *If you come to my house again, I'll set the dog on you!*

set out *v adv* **1** [I *from, for*] → SET off (1) **2** [I +*to-v*] to begin a course of action: *He set out to paint the whole house but finished only the front.* **3** [T] (**set** sthg.↔ **out**) also **set** sthg. **forth** *fml or pomp*– to explain in order, esp. in writing: *The reasons for my decision are set out in my report.* **4** [T] (**set** sthg.↔ **out**) to arrange or spread out in order: *The meal was set out on a long table.*

set sthg.↔ **up** *v adv* [T] **1** to raise into position: *Roadblocks were set up by the police to catch the escaped prisoner.* **2** to establish (an organization, business, etc.): *The mayor set up a committee to inquire into local unemployment.*

set (sbdy.) **up as** sthg. *v adv prep* [T] to establish (oneself or someone else) in business as: *He set (himself) up as a house painter and soon became successful.* –see also **set up** SHOP¹

set² *adj* **1** fixed; arranged: *I have to study at set hours each day.* **2** (of part of the body, manner, state of mind, etc.) fixed in position; unmoving: *a set smile|set opinions that will never change* **3** [F *on,upon*] determined; of a fixed intention: *I can't stop you if you're set on going.* **4** [F +*to-v/for*] ready; prepared: *I was (all) set to leave the house when the telephone rang.*

set³ *n* **1** [C] a group of naturally connected things that belong together: *a set of tools* **2** [C] an apparatus for receiving television or radio signals: *a color television set|Is your set* (=television) *working?* **3** [C] scenery for a play, movie, etc.: *a stage set|Everyone must be on the set* (=the place where the movie is made) *by eight o'clock.* **4** [C] a group of games in a tennis match **5** [*the* S] a position of part of the body: *From the set of her shoulders I could see that she was tired.*

set·back /ˈsetbæk/ *n* a return to a less good position: *She seemed better after her illness, but then she had a sudden setback.* –see also SET **back**

set·tee /seˈtiʸ/ *n* a long seat for more than one person, with a back and usu. arms; SOFA

set·ter /ˈsetər/ *n* **1** a long-haired dog often trained to point out the positions of animals for shooting **2** a person or thing that sets: *a trendsetter|a typesetter*

set·ting /ˈsetɪŋ/ *n* **1** [U] the action of a person or thing that sets: *the setting of the sun* **2** [C] the way or position in which something, esp. an instrument, is set: *This machine has two settings, fast and slow.* **3** [C] a set of surroundings; background: *high mountains forming a beautiful setting for a movie|Our story has its setting in ancient Rome.|a diamond in a gold setting*

set·tle /ˈsetl/ *-tled, -tling* **1** [I;T] to go and live (in): *They got married and settled in San Francisco.* **2** [I;T] to (place so as to) stay and be comfortable: *He settled himself in his chair.* **3** [I;T] to (cause to) go downwards: *A* *bird settled* (=came down and landed) *on the branch.|Shake the bag to settle the sugar in it.* **4** [I;T] to make or become quiet, calm, still, etc.: *This medicine should settle your nerves.|Settle down, children. Stop running around!* **5** [I;T +*that/on,upon*] to make the last arrangements (about); decide: *That's settled; we'll do it tomorrow!|We've settled on Canada* (=decided to go there) *for our vacation, but we haven't settled on when to go.* **6** [I;T] to end (an argument, esp. in law); bring (a matter) to an agreement: *They settled their quarrel in a friendly way.|The two companies* **settled out of court**. (=ended their argument without going to a court of law) **7** [T] to pay (a bill or money claimed)

settle down *v adv* **1** [I;T (=**settle** sbdy. **down**)] to (cause to) sit comfortably: *She settled (herself) down in a chair with a book.* **2** [I] to establish a home and live a quiet life: *I want to get married and settle down.* **3** [I] to become used to a way of life, job, etc.: *I'm sure he'll soon settle down in his new school.* –see also SETTLE (4)

settle for sthg. *v prep* [T] to accept (something less than hoped for): *I want $500 for my car, and I won't settle for less.*

settle in *v adv* [I;T (=**settle** sbdy. **in**)] to (help to) get used to a new home, job, etc.: *It was the first time she had left home, so it took her a while to settle in.*

settle up *v adv* [I *with*] to pay what is owed: *He settled up with the hospital after he got out.*

set·tled /ˈsɛtld/ *adj* unlikely to change; fixed: *settled weather/habits* –opposite **unsettled**

set·tle·ment /ˈsɛtlmənt/ *n* **1** [C] a small village in an area with few people: *a settlement on the edge of the desert* **2** [U] the movement of a new population into a place to live there: *the settlement of the American West* **3** [C] an agreement or decision ending an argument, question, etc.: *the settlement of the law case* **4** [C] a payment of money claimed: *a settlement of a bill*

set·tler /ˈsɛtlər/ *n* one of a new population, usu. in an area with few people: *early settlers ,in Australia*

set·up /ˈsɛtʌp/ *n* [S] an arrangement or organization: *He's new to the office and doesn't know the setup yet.* –see also SET **up** (2)

sev·en /ˈsɛvən/ *determiner,n,pron* (the number) 7 –**seventh** *determiner,n,pron,adv*

sev·en·teen /ˌsɛvənˈtiᵛn◄/ *determiner,n, pron* (the number) 17 –**seventeenth** *determiner,n,pron,adv*

sev·en·ty /ˈsɛvəntiʸ/ *determiner,n,pron* -**ties** (the number) 70 –**seventieth** /ˈsɛvəntiʸiθ/ *determiner,n,pron,adv*

sev·er /ˈsɛvər/ *v more fml than* cut *or* break– **1** [T *from*] to cut; divide, esp. into two parts: *His arm was severed from his body in the accident.|a severed* ARTERY **2** [I] to break: *The rope severed under the heavy weight.*

sev·er·al¹ /ˈsɛvərəl/ *determiner,pron* a few but not many; some: *several visits to New York|several hundred people|Several of the apples are bad.* –see Study Notes on page 550

several² *adj* [A] *fml & lit* separate; different;

RESPECTIVE: *They shook hands and went their several ways.*

sev·er·ance /ˈsɛvərəns/ *n* [C;U] the/an act or result of SEVERING: *(a) severance of relations between the two countries*

severance pay /ˈ··· ˌ·/ *n* [U] money paid by a company to a worker losing his job through no fault of his own

se·vere /səˈvɪər/ *adj* **1** not kind or gentle in treatment; STERN; STRICT (1): *a severe look on her face|severe military rules* **2** very harmful or painful: *severe pain|the severest winter in ten years* –compare MILD (2) **3** plain; without decoration; AUSTERE: *the severe beauty of a simple church* –compare STRICT (1) –**severely** *adv* –**severity** /səˈvɛrətiʸ/ *n* -**ties** [C;U]

sew /soʷ/ *v* **sewed**, **sewn** /soʷn/, **sewing** [I;T] to join or fasten (cloth, leather, etc.) by stitches made with thread; make or mend with needle and thread: *Would you sew on this button/sew this button onto my shirt?| Who taught you how to sew?* –**sewing** *n* [U]: I used to hate sewing before we got a **sewing machine**

sew sthg.↔**up** *v adv* [T] **1** to close or repair by sewing **2** *infml* to put into one's control; determine or settle: *They've got the election sewn up; they're sure to win.*

sew·age /ˈsuʷɪdʒ/ *n* [U] the waste material and water carried in SEWERS

sew·er /ˈsuʷər/ *n* a man-made passage or large pipe under the ground for carrying away water and waste material

sex /sɛks/ *n* **1** [U] the condition of being either male or female: *In the space marked "sex," put an "M" for male or an "F" for female.* **2** [C] the set of all male or all female creatures: *a member of the opposite sex* **3** [A] connected with the bodily system of producing children: *sex organs* **4** [U] SEXUAL INTERCOURSE or activity connected with this act: *Do you think sex without marriage is wrong?|There's a lot of sex and violence in this film.*

sex·ism /ˈsɛksɪzəm/ *n* [U] the opinion that one sex, esp. women, is less able in most ways than the other, esp. men

sex·ist /ˈsɛksɪst/ *adj,n* (a person) showing SEXISM: *I'm tired of his sexist jokes about women drivers!*

sex·less /ˈsɛkslɪs/ *adj* **1** sexually uninteresting; not SEXY **2** not male or female; NEUTER¹ (2)

sex·tant /ˈsɛkstənt/ *n* an instrument used on a ship or aircraft to calculate its position

sex·u·al /ˈsɛkʃuʷəl/ *adj* of sex or the sexes: *sexual* REPRODUCTION*|sexual excitement* –see EROTIC (USAGE) –**sexually** *adv*

sexual in·ter·course /ˌ··· ˈ···/ *also* **intercourse**– *n* [U] the bodily act between two animals or people in which the male sex organ enters the female

sex·u·al·i·ty /ˌsɛkʃuʷˈælətiʸ/ *n* [U] fondness for, or interest in, sexual activity

sex·y /ˈsɛksiʸ/ *adj* -**ier**, -**iest** exciting in a sexual way: *sexy girls/pictures/clothes* –see EROTIC (USAGE) –**sexily** *adv*

SF *abbrev. for:* SCIENCE FICTION

Sgt. *written abbrev. said as:* SERGEANT

sh, shh, ssh /ʃ/ *interj* (used for demanding silence or less noise): *Sh! You'll wake the baby!*

shab·by /'ʃæbiʸ/ *adj* **-bier, -biest 1** (esp. of clothes) appearing poor because of long wear; (of people) poorly dressed: *a shabby old coat* **2** ungenerous or not worthy; unfair; MEAN¹ (1,2): *What a shabby trick, making me walk home!* –**shabbily** *adv* –**shabbiness** *n* [U]

shack /ʃæk/ *n* a small roughly built house; hut

shack·le¹ /'ʃækəl/ *n* **1** a band for fastening around the wrist or ankle of an animal, prisoner, etc. to prevent movement **2** [*usu. pl.*] *lit* something that prevents freedom of action or expression: *bound by the shackles of out-of-date beliefs*

shackle² *v* **-led, -ling** [T] to bind (as if) with SHACKLES: *hands shackled together|shackled by old customs*

shade¹ /ʃeʸd/ *n* **1** [U] shelter from direct light, esp. from sunlight outdoors, made by something blocking it: *sitting in the shade of a tree* **2** [C] something that keeps out light or its full brightness: *a lampshade|a green eyeshade* **3** [C] a degree of color: *a lighter/deeper shade of blue* **4** [C] a slight difference in degree; NUANCE: *a word with several shades of meaning* **5** [C] a little bit: *That music is just a shade too loud.*

USAGE **Shade** is any area sheltered from the sun; a **shadow** is a clear shape made by the **shade** of a particular person or thing. Compare: *The trees in the garden provide plenty of shade.|The child saw its shadow on the ground.*

shade² *v* **shaded, shading** [T] **1** to shelter from direct light or heat: *She shaded her eyes from the sun with her hand.* **2** [*in*] to represent the effect of shade or shadow on (an object in a picture): *to shade in the background of a drawing*

shad·ow¹ /'ʃædoʷ/ *n* **1** [C;U] (an area of) greater darkness where direct light, esp. sunlight, is blocked by something: *As the sun set, the shadows became large.|The tree* CAST (=produced) *its shadow on the wall.|His shadow followed him along the road.* (=because the sun was in front of him) **2** [C] a form from which the real substance has gone: *After his illness, he was only a shadow of his former self.* **3** [S] (used only in NEGATIVES², questions, etc.) a slightest bit; TRACE² (2): *not a shadow of doubt* –see SHADE¹ (USAGE)

shadow² *v* [T] **1** to make a shadow on; darken (as) with a shadow **2** to follow and watch closely; shadow secretly: *She was shadowed everywhere by the secret police.*

shad·ow·y /'ʃædoʷiʸ/ *adj* **-ier, -iest 1** hard to see or know about clearly; not DISTINCT (2): *a shadowy and little-known historical figure* **2** full of shade; in shadow: *the shadowy depths of the forest*

SPELLING NOTE
Words with the sound /ʃ/ may be spelled **ch-**, like **chauffeur**.

shad·y /'ʃeʸdiʸ/ *adj* **-ier, -iest 1** in or producing shade: *shady trees* **2** *infml* not very honest: *a shady politician*

shaft /ʃæft/ *n* **1** the long handle of a spear, hammer, axe, etc. **2** one of the pair of poles that an animal is fastened between to pull a vehicle **3** a bar which turns, or around which a belt or wheel turns, to pass power through a machine: *a* PROPELLER *shaft* **4** a beam of light: *a shaft of sunlight* **5** a long passage, usu. up and down or sloping: *a mine shaft|an* ELEVATOR *shaft*

shag·gy /'ʃægiʸ/ *adj* **-gier, -giest** consisting of or covered with long, rough hair: *a shaggy beard/dog/coat* –**shagginess** *n* [U]

shake¹ /ʃeʸk/ *v* **shook** /ʃʊk/, **shaken** /'ʃeʸkən/, **shaking 1** [I;T] to (cause to) move quickly up and down and to and fro: *The explosion shook the house.|The house shook.|She was shaking with laughter/anger/fear.|Shake the bottle before use.|She shook the sand from her shoes.* (=removed it by shaking) **2** [I;T] to take and hold (someone's right hand) in one's own, as a sign of greeting, goodbye, or agreement: *They shook hands (with each other).* **3** [T *up*] to trouble the mind or feelings of; upset: *She was badly shaken (up) by the sad news.* **4 shake one's head** to move one's head from side to side to say "no"

shake sbdy./sthg.↔**off** *v adv* [T] to get rid of; escape from: *I've had a bad cold for a week. I just can't shake it off.*

shake sthg.↔**out** *v adv* [T] to open or spread with a shaking movement: *He shook out the dirty mat.*

shake sthg.↔**up** *v adv* [T] **1** to rearrange; make changes in (an organization): *The new chairman will shake up the company.* –see SHAKE-UP **2** to mix by shaking

shake² *n* an action of shaking: *She answered "no" with a shake of the head.*

shake-up /'· ·/ *n* a rearrangement of an organization: *a company shake-up with twelve people losing their jobs* –see also SHAKE up

shak·y /'ʃeʸkiʸ/ *adj* **-ier, -iest 1** shaking or unsteady, e.g. from nervousness or weakness **2** not solid or firm; undependable: *an unsafe shaky ladder|shaky in her beliefs* –**shakily** *adv* –**shakiness** *n* [U]

shale /ʃeʸl/ *n* [U] soft rock which naturally divides into thin sheets

shall /ʃəl; *strong* ʃæl/ *v negative contraction* **shan't** /ʃænt/ *BrE*) [I + *to-v*] **1** *fml esp. BrE* (used with *I* and *we* to show the future): *We shall be away next week.|I shall have finished the book by Friday.* **2** *fml* or *esp. BrE* (used with *you, he, she, it, they* to show a promise, command, or law): *It shall be done as you wish.|This law shall have effect in all the land.* **3** (used, esp. with *I* and *we*, in questions or offers that ask the hearer to decide): *Shall I (=Do you want me to) open the window?* –see also SHOULD, WILL; see Study Notes on page 434

USAGE In modern speech **will,** or the short form **'ll,** is used much more often than **shall** in the first and second meanings; but in the third meaning, **shall** is always used.

shal·lot /ʃəˈlɑt, ˈʃælət/ *n* a small onion-like vegetable

shal·low /ˈʃæloʷ/ *adj* **1** not deep; not far from top to bottom: *the shallow end of the swimming pool* **2** lacking deep or serious thinking; SUPERFICIAL: *a shallow thinker whose opinions aren't worth much* –**shallowly** *adv* –**shallowness** *n* [U]

sham¹ /ʃæm/ *n* **1** [S] something false pretending to be the real thing: *The agreement was a sham. Nobody intended to keep to it.* **2** [A] not real; copying the real thing: *sham jewelry*

sham² *v* **-mm-** [I;T] to put on the false appearance of (some disease, condition, etc.): *He isn't really ill; he's shamming.*

sham·ble /ˈʃæmbəlz/ *v* **-bled, -bling** [I] to walk awkwardly, dragging the feet: *shambling along the street*

sham·bles /ˈʃæmbəlz/ *n* [S] *infml* a scene of great disorder; MESS¹ (1): *After the party the house was a shambles.*

shame¹ /ʃeʸm/ *n* **1** [U] the painful feeling of one's own guilt, wrongness, or failure or that of a close friend, relative, etc.: *I feel no shame for my action. I did what was right. I was filled with shame when I remembered how badly I'd behaved at the party.* **2** [U] loss of honor; DISGRACE: *Your bad behavior brings shame on the whole school.* **3** [S] an unfortunate state of affairs; something that ought not to be: **What a shame** *that it rained so much during your vacation.* **4 put someone/something to shame** to show someone/something to be less good by comparison: *Your beautiful roses put my few little flowers to shame.*

shame² *v* **shamed, shaming** [T] to bring dishonor to; DISGRACE: *He shamed his family by being sent to prison.*

shame·faced /ˈʃeʸmfeʸst/ *adj* showing suitable shame: *He made his excuses in a shame-faced way.* –**shamefacedly** /ˌʃeʸmˈfeʸsɪdliʸ, ˈʃeʸm͵feʸstliʸ/ *adv*

shame·ful /ˈʃeʸmfəl/ *adj* deserving blame; which one ought to be ashamed of –**shamefully** *adv*

shame·less /ˈʃeʸmlɪs/ *adj* **1** (of a person) unable to feel shame: *an immodest and shameless person* **2** done without shame; INDECENT: *shameless disloyalty* –**shamelessly** *adv*

sham·poo¹ /ʃæmˈpuʷ/ *n* **-poos 1** [C;U] a usu. liquid soaplike product used for washing the hair, CARPETS, etc.: *creamy shampoo for dry hair* **2** [C] an act of SHAMPOOing²

shampoo² *v* **-pooed, -pooing,** [I;T] to wash with SHAMPOO¹: *I want to shampoo before we go out.*

sham·rock /ˈʃæmrɑk/ *n* [C;U] a type of CLOVER with three leaves on each stem, used as the national sign of Ireland

shan't /ʃænt/ *v BrE short for:* shall not: *Shall I go, or shan't I?*

shan·ty /ˈʃæntiʸ/ *n* **-ties** a small roughly built usu. wooden house; SHACK

shape¹ /ʃeʸp/ *n* **1** [C;U] the appearance or form of something: *a cake in the shape of a heart We saw a shape through the mist, but we couldn't see what it was. What shape will future society have?* **2** [U] *infml* state or condition: *He's exercising a lot to* **get into shape.** (=develop a good physical condition) *Our garden is in good shape after the rain.* **3 take shape** to begin to be like the finished form: *ideas taking shape in his mind* –**shapeless** *adj*

shape² *v* **shaped, shaping 1** [T] to make or influence the form of: *The bird shaped its nest from mud and sticks/shaped mud and sticks into a nest. My time at school shaped my future.* **2** [I] to develop well or in the stated way: *Our vacation plans are shaping (up) well.*

shaped /ʃeʸpt/ *adj* having a certain shape: *a cloud shaped like a camel a heart-shaped cake*

shape·ly /ˈʃeʸpliʸ/ *adj* **-lier, -liest** (esp. of a woman's body) having a good-looking shape –**shapeliness** *n* [U]

share¹ /ʃɛər/ *n* **1** [S] the part belonging or owed to, or done by, a person: *If you want a share in/of the pay, you'll have to do your share of the work.* **2** *esp. BrE* for STOCK¹ (3)

share² *v* **shared, sharing 1** [I;T *with,among, between*] to use, pay, have, etc., with others: *We don't have enough books for everyone. Some of you will have to share. Everyone in the house shares the bathroom. He's sure we'll win the game, but I don't share his faith in the team. Children should be taught to share (their toys).* **2** [T *among,between*] to divide and give out in shares: *His property was shared between his children.* **3 share and share alike** *infml* to have an equal share in everything –**sharer** *n*

share·hold·er /ˈʃɛər͵hoʷldər/ *n esp. BrE* for STOCKHOLDER

shark /ʃɑrk/ *n* **1** a large dangerous fish with sharp teeth **2** *infml* a person clever at getting money from others in dishonest ways

sharp¹ /ʃɑrp/ *adj* **1** having a thin cutting edge or a fine point: *a sharp knife/needle/nail* –opposite **blunt 2** quick and sensitive: *a sharp mind/sharp eyes* **3** causing a sensation like that of cutting, biting, or stinging: *a sharp wind/a sharp taste/a sharp pain* **4** not rounded: *a sharp nose* **5** having a quick change in direction; sudden: *a sharp turn/a sharp rise/fall in prices* **6** clear in shape or detail; DISTINCT (2): *a sharp photographic image* **7** quick and strong: *a sharp blow on the head* **8** (of words) intended to hurt; angry: *a sharp scolding* **9** [after *n*] (of a note in music) raised by ¹/₂ TONE (5) (in the phrases **F sharp, C sharp,** etc.) –compare FLAT¹ (6) –**sharply** *adv* –**sharpness** *n* [U]

sharp² *adv* [after *n*] exactly at the stated time: *The meeting starts at three o'clock sharp.*

sharp·en /ˈʃɑrpən/ *v* [I;T] to make or become sharp: *to sharpen a pencil/knife*

sharp·en·er /ˈʃɑrpənər/ *n* a machine or tool for SHARPENing –see illustration on page 467

shat·ter /ˈʃætər/ *v* [I;T] to (cause to) break suddenly into small pieces; SMASH: *A stone shattered the window. The glass shattered.* (fig.) *Hopes of reaching an agreement were shattered away.*

shave¹ /ʃeʸv/ *v* **shaved, shaving 1** [I;T *off*] to cut off (hair or beard) from (one's face, etc.)

with a RAZOR: *I've shaved off my beard.*|*I cut myself while I was shaving.*|*Do you shave your legs?* **2** [T *off*] to cut off (very thin pieces) from (a surface): *She shaved the bottom of the door to make it close properly.* **3** **-shaven** /'ʃeʸvən/ having been SHAVED: *a clean shaven face* (=with no beard)

shave² *n* **1** an act or result of shaving (SHAVE) **2 a close shave** *infml* a narrow escape

shav·er /'ʃeʸvər/ *n* a tool for shaving (SHAVE), esp. an electric RAZOR

shav·ing /'ʃeʸvɪŋ/ *n* **1** [U] the act of closely cutting off hair **2** [*C usu. pl.*] a very thin piece cut from a surface with a sharp blade: *wood shavings made with a PLANE¹*

shawl /ʃɔl/ *n* a piece of cloth for wearing over a woman's head and shoulders

she¹ /ʃiʸ/ *pron* (used as the subject of a sentence) **1** that female person or animal already mentioned, seen, heard, etc.: *That's an intelligent woman. Who is she?* **2** (used of things, esp. countries and certain vehicles, that are thought of as female): *The ship has come in, but she will leave in ten minutes.*

she² /ʃiʸ/ *n* a female person or animal: *Is your dog a he or a she?*|*a she-goat*

sheaf /ʃiʸf/ *n* **sheaves** /ʃiʸvz/ **1** a bunch of grain plants tied together **2** [*of*] a handful of long or thin things laid or tied together; BUNDLE¹ (1): *She had a sheaf of notes in front of her.*

shear /ʃɪər/ *v* **sheared, sheared** *or* **shorn** /ʃɔrn, ʃoʷrn/, **shearing** [T] to cut wool from (sheep)

shears /ʃɪərz/ *n* **1** [P] large scissors: *kitchen shears* **2** any of various heavier cutting tools which work like scissors

sheath /ʃiʸθ/ *n* **sheaths** /ʃiʸðz, ʃiʸθs/ a closefitting case for a knife or sword blade

sheathe /ʃiʸð/ *v* **sheathed, sheathing** [T] to put into a SHEATH (1)

shed¹ /ʃɛd/ *n* a lightly built building, usu. for storing things: *a toolshed*|*cattle shed*|*woodshed*|*garden shed* –compare HUT

shed² *v* **shed, shedding** [T] **1** to cause to flow out: *He shed tears of sorrow.*|*arguments which shed new light on the question* (=make it clearer)|*They wanted to bring down the government, but without shedding blood.* (=without causing death) –see also BLOODSHED **2** (of a plant or animal) to throw off naturally: *trees shedding their leaves in autumn*|*Some snakes shed their skin each year.*

she'd /ʃiʸd/ *short for:* **1** she would **2** she had

sheen /ʃiʸn/ *n* [S;U] (a) brightness on a surface: *hair with a beautiful sheen*

sheep /ʃiʸp/ *n* **sheep 1** a grass-eating animal that is kept for its wool and its meat –compare RAM, EWE; see MEAT (USAGE) **2 black sheep** an unsatisfactory member of a group: *After he had been in prison, Peter was regarded as the black sheep of the family.* **3 the sheep and the goats** those who are good,

able, successful, etc., and those who are not: *a hard examination, intended to separate the sheep from the goats*

sheep·dog /'ʃiʸpdɔg/ *n* a dog trained to drive sheep and keep them together

sheep·ish /'ʃiʸpɪʃ/ *adj* slightly ashamed and afraid of others: *a sheepish smile* **–sheepishly** *adv* **–sheepishness** *n* [U]

sheer¹ /ʃɪər/ *adj* **1** [A] pure; unmixed with anything else; nothing but: *He won by sheer luck/determination.* **2** very steep; straight up and down: *a sheer cliff* **3** very thin and almost transparent: *ladies' sheer stockings*

sheer² *adv* straight up or down: *The mountain rises sheer from the plain.*

sheer³ *v* [I *off,away*] to turn (as if) to avoid hitting something; change direction quickly: *The boat came close to the rocks and then sheered away.*

sheet /ʃiʸt/ *n* **1** a large piece of cloth used in a pair on a bed: *We change the sheets* (=put clean ones on the bed) *every week.* –see illustration on page 55 **2** a piece of paper: *wrapped in a sheet of newspaper* **3** a broad stretch or piece of something thin: *a sheet of ice over the lake*|*sheet metal* (=metal in sheets) **4** a moving or powerful wide mass: *rain coming down in sheets*

sheik, sheikh /ʃiʸk, ʃeʸk/ *n* [A;C] **1** an Arab chief or prince **2** a Muslim religious leader or teacher

shelf /ʃɛlf/ *n* **shelves** /ʃɛlvz/ **1** a flat long and narrow board fixed against a wall or in a frame, for placing things on: *Please put the book back on the shelf when you've finished with it.* –see illustration on page 55 **2** something with a shape like one of these, esp. a narrow surface (LEDGE) of rock

shell¹ /ʃɛl/ *n* **1** [C;U] a hard covering of an animal, egg, fruit, nut, or seed: *The sea shore was covered with shells.*|*a SNAIL shell*|*a nutshell*|*some pieces of eggshell* –see also SEASHELL **2** [C] the outside frame of a building **3** [C] an explosive for firing from a large gun: *shells bursting all around*

shell² *v* **1** [T] to remove from a natural shell or POD: *to shell PEAs* **2** [I;T] to fire SHELLs¹ (3) (at): *The enemy lines were weakened by shelling before the attack.*

shell out (sthg.) *v adv* [I;T] *infml* to pay (money): *He wouldn't shell out for his share of the meal.*

she'll /ʃɪl; *strong* ʃiʸl/ *short for:* **1** she will: *She'll come if she can.* **2** she shall

shell·fish /'ʃɛl,fɪʃ/ *n* **shellfish** [C;U] any animal without a SPINE that lives in water and has a shell: *The LOBSTER is a shellfish.*

shel·ter¹ /'ʃɛltər/ *n* **1** [U] protection, esp. from the weather: *In the storm I took shelter under a tree.* **2** [C] a building or enclosure offering protection: *a bus shelter* (=roofed enclosure at a bus stop)

shel·ter² *v* **1** [T *from*] to give shelter to: *to shelter a plant from the sun*|*sheltering the homeless* **2** [I *from*] to find shelter: *In the rain people were sheltering in the doorways of stores.*

shel·tered /'ʃɛltərd/ *adj* protected from harm, risk, or unpleasant realities: *a shel-*

SPELLING NOTE

Words with the sound /ʃ/ may be spelled **ch-**, like **chauffeur**.

tered life with no worries about money

shelve /ʃɛlv/ v **shelved, shelving 1** [T] to put on a shelf; arrange on shelves **2** [T] to put aside (usu. a plan) until a later time: *We've shelved our vacation plans because the baby is ill.* **3** [I *down,up*] (of land) to slope gradually

shelv·ing /'ʃɛlvɪŋ/ n [U] (material for) shelves

shep·herd¹ /'ʃɛpərd/ n a man or boy who takes care of sheep in the fields

shepherd² v [T] to lead or take care of like sheep: *We shepherded the children into the bus.*

shep·herd·ess /'ʃɛpərdɪs/ n (esp. in poetry and art) a woman or girl who takes care of sheep in the fields

sher·bet /'ʃɜrbɪt/ n [U] *AmE* a frozen dessert, usu. with the taste of fruit

sher·iff /'ʃɛrɪf/ n [A;C] (in the US) an elected officer responsible for public order

sher·ry /'ʃɛriʸ/ n **-ries** [C;U] strong wine from Spain, often drunk before a meal

she's /ʃiʸz/ *short for:* **1** she is: *She's working in an office.* **2** she has: *She's got a new job.*

shield¹ /ʃiʸld/ n **1** a broad piece of metal, wood, etc. carried by soldiers in former time as a protection from arrows or blows **2** a representation of this used for a BADGE, (in the US) road sign, etc. **3** a protective cover, esp. on a machine: *The spacecraft was fitted with a heat shield.*

shield² v [T *from*] to protect or hide from harm or danger: *She lied to the police to shield her friend.*

shift¹ /ʃɪft/ v [I;T] **1** to change in position or direction; move from one place to another: *Fasten the load down to stop it from shifting at high speed.|The wind shifted from the south to the west.|*(fig.) *Don't try to shift the blame onto me!* **2 shift for oneself** to take care of oneself; live as one can **3 shift (gear(s)** *AmE‖*also **change gear(s)**– to cause the engine of a vehicle to be in a different GEAR¹ (2): *Shift gears when you go up that hill.*

shift² n [C] **1** a change in position, direction, or character: *a shift in the wind/in political opinion* **2** [C +*sing. v*] (a group of workers for) a period of work in a factory, etc.: *I work (on) the day/night shift|The night shift is arriving now.|shift work*

shift·less /'ʃɪftlɪs/ adj lazy; lacking in purpose or ability **–shiftlessly** adv **–shiftlessness** n [U]

shift·y /'ʃɪftiʸ/ adj **-ier, -iest** looking dishonest; not to be trusted **–shiftily** adv

shil·ling /'ʃɪlɪŋ/ n **1** an amount of money used in Britain until 1971: *One shilling = 12 (old) pence = ¹/₂₀ of £1.* **2** an amount of money in some African countries, equal to 100 cents

shim·mer /'ʃɪmər/ v [I] to shine with a soft trembling light: *water shimmering in the moonlight*

shin¹ /ʃɪn/ n the bony front part of the leg between the knee and ankle

shin² ‖also **shinny** *AmE*– v **-nn-** [I *up, down*] to climb (a tree, pole, etc.) quickly and easily, using the hands and legs: *She shinned up a tree to get a better view.*

shine¹ /ʃaɪn/ v **shone** /ʃoʷn/, **shining 1** [I] to give off light; look bright: *a fine morning with the sun shining (down)|The polished surface shone in the sun.|*(fig.) *She's a good student generally, but sports are where she really shines.* (=shows special ability) **2** [T] to direct (a lamp, etc.): *Shine your light over here.*

shine² v **shined, shining** [T] to polish; make bright by rubbing: *Shine your shoes before going out.*

shine³ n [S] **1** brightness; shining quality: *The wooden surface had a beautiful shine.* **2** an act of polishing: *These shoes need a shine.* **3 (come) rain or shine** in good or bad weather; whatever happens: *I promise we'll be there, rain or shine.*

shin·gle /'ʃɪŋgəl/ n **1** a small thin piece of building material (such as wood or ASBESTOS) laid in rows to cover a roof or wall –see illustration on page 337 **2 hang up/out one's shingle** *infml AmE* to establish an office as a doctor, lawyer, etc.

shin·ny /'ʃɪniʸ/ v **-nied, -nying** *AmE* for SHIN²

shin·y /'ʃaɪniʸ/ adj **-ier, -iest** (esp. of a smooth surface) looking as if polished; bright: *a shiny new coin* **–shininess** n [U]

ship¹ /ʃɪp/ n **1** a large boat for carrying people or goods on the sea: *life on board ship|We went by plane, but sent all our furniture on a ship/by ship.* **2** *infml* a large aircraft or spacecraft

ship² v **-pp-** [T] **1** to carry or send by ship: *I'm flying to Florida, but my car is being shipped.* **2 ship water** (of a boat) to take in water over the side

ship·ment /'ʃɪpmənt/ n **1** [C] a load of goods sent together: *A large shipment of grain has just arrived.* **2** [U] the action of sending, carrying, and delivering goods: *articles lost in shipment*

ship·per /'ʃɪpər/ n a dealer who sends and delivers goods: *wine shippers*

ship·ping /'ʃɪpɪŋ/ n [U] **1** ship traffic; ships as a group **2** the sending and delivery of something: *a shipping charge* (=charge for shipping) *of $5*

ship·shape /'ʃɪpʃeʸp/ adj clean and neat; in good order

ship·wreck¹ /'ʃɪp-rɛk/ n [C;U] a/the destruction of a ship, by hitting rocks or sinking

shipwreck² v [T] to cause to suffer SHIPWRECK: *sailors shipwrecked on an island*

ship·yard /'ʃɪp-yɑrd/ n a place where ships are built or repaired

shirk /ʃɜrk/ v [I;T +*v-ing*] to avoid (something unpleasant) because of laziness, etc.: *We shouldn't shirk our cleaning job.|to shirk one's responsibilities* **–shirker** n

shirt /ʃɜrt/ n a piece of clothing for the upper part of the body, usu. of light cloth with a collar and SLEEVES –compare SWEATSHIRT

shirt·sleeves /'ʃɜrtsliʸvz/ n [P] **in one's shirtsleeves** wearing nothing over one's shirt: *On hot days the men in the office work in their shirtsleeves.*

shiv·er¹ /'ʃɪvər/ v [I] (esp. of people) to shake, as from cold or fear; tremble: *It was* *so cold that we were all shivering.* **–shivery** *adj*

shiver[2] *n* a feeling of SHIVERING[1]: *That strange noise sends shivers (up and) down my spine.* (=my back)

shoal[1] /ʃoʷl/ *n* a bank of sand not far below the surface of the water, making it dangerous to boats

shoal[2] *n* a large group of fish swimming together: (fig.) *People arrived in shoals.*

shock[1] /ʃak/ *n* **1** [C;U] (the state caused by) something unexpected and usu. very unpleasant: *The bad news left us all speechless from shock.|His death came as a great shock to us all.* **2** [C;U] (a) violent force, as from a hard blow, crash, explosion, etc.: *The shock of the explosion was felt far away.* **3** [C;U] the sudden violent effect of electricity passing through the body **4** [U] *tech* weakness after physical damage to the body: *She is still in shock after her accident.*

shock[2] *v* [T] to cause unpleasant or angry surprise: *I was shocked by his sudden death/his rudeness.*

shock·ing /ˈʃakɪŋ/ *adj* **1** very improper, wrong, or sad: *a shocking accident* **2** very bad though not evil: *What a shocking waste of time!* **–shockingly** *adv*

shock·proof /ˈʃakpruʷf/ *adj* (esp. of a watch) not easily damaged by being dropped, hit, etc.

shod /ʃad/ *adj lit* wearing shoes: *poor, badly-shod children*

shod·dy /ˈʃadiʸ/ *adj* **-dier, -diest 1** made or done cheaply and badly: *shoddy workmanship* **2** ungenerous or not worthy; dishonorable: *a shoddy trick* **–shoddily** *adv* **–shoddiness** *n* [U]

shoe /ʃuʷ/ *n* **1** an outer covering for the human foot, usu. of leather and having a hard base (**sole**) and a support (**heel**) under the heel of the foot: *to put on/take off one's shoes* –compare BOOT[1] (1), SANDAL, SLIPPER –see illustration on page 123 **2** → HORSESHOE **3** **in someone's shoes** in someone's position; experiencing what another has to experience: *I'm glad I'm not in his shoes!* **4** **the shoe is on the other foot** *infml* the state of affairs has changed to the opposite of what it was: *the shoe is on the other foot now that you've lost all your money.*

shoe·horn /ˈʃuʷhɔrn/ *n* a curved piece of metal or plastic for putting inside the back of a shoe when putting it on, to help the foot go in easily

shoe·lace /ˈʃuʷleʸs/ ‖also **shoestring** *AmE*– *n* a thin cord or piece of leather used to tie the front parts of a shoe together

shoe·string /ˈʃuʷˌstrɪŋ/ *n* **1** *AmE* for SHOE-LACE **2** **on a shoestring** on a very small amount of money: *He started his business on a shoestring and built it up.*

shone /ʃoʷn/ *v* past tense and participle of SHINE[1]

shoo[1] /ʃuʷ/ *interj* (said, usu. not angrily, to animals or small children) go away!

shoo[2] *v* [T] **shooed, shooing** to drive away (as if) by saying "SHOO": *He shooed the children out of the kitchen.*

shook /ʃʊk/ *v* past tense of SHAKE

shoot[1] /ʃuʷt/ *v* **shot** /ʃat/, **shooting 1** [I;T] to fire (a weapon): *I'm coming out with my hands up. Don't shoot!|He shot at a bird, but missed it.* (Compare *He shot a bird and killed it.*) **2** [T] to send or fire (a bullet, arrow, etc.) from a weapon: *They shot their way out of prison.|I shot an arrow at the wall.* **3** [T] to hit, wound, or kill with a gun: *He shot a bird.|He was shot three times in the arm.|She shot him dead.|He goes to the country every year to shoot wild duck.* (=for sport) **4** [I;T] to send or come out quickly or suddenly: *She shot him an angry look.|Blood shot out of the wound.* **5** [I] to go fast or suddenly: *He shot past me in his fast car.|Pain shot through his arm.* **6** [I;T] to throw or kick a ball to try to make a point in a game: *in a good position to shoot* **7** [I;T] to make a photograph or movie (of): *This movie was shot in California.* **8** [T] to pass quickly by or along: *a boat shooting the* RAPIDS[2] **9 shoot one's mouth off** *infml* to talk too freely **10 shoot the bull** *AmE infml* to have an informal, not very serious conversation: *They sat around shooting the bull until late at night.* **11 shoot the works** *infml, esp. AmE* **a** to use all one's effort **b** to risk all one's money in a game –see FIRE (USAGE)

shoot sbdy./sthg.↔ **down** *v adv* [T] **1** to bring down and destroy (an aircraft) by shooting **2** *infml* to say "no" firmly to (a person or idea): *another idea shot down by the chairman*

shoot out *v adv* **1** [I;T (=shoot sthg.↔ out)] to (cause to) come out suddenly: *Water shot out of the broken pipe.* **2** [T *with*] (**shoot** sthg. **out**) *infml* to decide (a quarrel) by shooting: *The boys are going to shoot it out (with each other).*

shoot up *v adv* [I] **1** to go upwards, increase, or grow quickly: *Flames shot up into the air.|Prices have shot up lately.* **2** *infml* to take (a drug) directly into the BLOODSTREAM by using a needle

shoot[2] *n* **1** a new growth from a plant, esp. a young stem and leaves **2** an occasion for shooting (esp. animals): *a weekend shoot*

shooting star /ˌ·· ˈ·/ also **falling star**– *n* a METEOR from space which burns brightly as it passes through the earth's air

shop[1] /ʃap/ *n* **1** *esp. BrE* for STORE[2] (1): *a card shop* **2** a place where things are made or repaired; WORKSHOP: *the paint shop in a car factory|a repair shop* **3 set up shop** to start in business: *He's set up shop as a lawyer in town.* **4 talk shop** to talk about one's work, esp. on a social occasion

shop[2] *v* **-pp-** [I *for*] to visit stores in order to buy; buy goods: *Did you go shopping today? |I was shopping for some new clothes, but I couldn't find anything.* –compare WINDOW-SHOPPING; see CUSTOMER (USAGE) **–shopper** *n*

shop around *v adv* [I] to compare prices in

different stores: (fig.) *We shopped around
before deciding which church to join.*

shop as·sist·ant /'·· ·,··/ *n esp. BrE* for SALES-
CLERK

shop·keep·er /'ʃɑp,kiʸpər/ *n esp. BrE* for
STOREKEEPER

shop·lift /'ʃɑp,lɪft/ *v* [I;T] to take (goods)
from a store without paying –see also LIFT¹
(4) –see THIEF (USAGE) –**shoplifter** *n*

shopping bag /'·· ,·/ *AmE*‖**carrier bag** *BrE–*
n a cheap strong paper or plastic bag esp.
with handles for carrying goods away from a
store –see illustration on page 683

shopping cen·ter /'·· ,··/ ‖also **shopping
mall, mall** *AmE– n* a group of stores of different kinds, usu. in an area outside a city,
planned and built as a whole

shop stew·ard /'· ,··/ *n* a labor union officer
elected by union members in a particular
place of work

shop·worn /'ʃɑpwɔrn, -woʷrn/ *adj* **1** (of
ideas) no longer fresh, interesting, or valuable **2** *AmE*‖**shopsoiled** /'ʃɑpsɔɪld/ *BrE–*
slightly soiled or dirty from being in a store a
long time

shore¹ /ʃɔr, ʃoʷr/ *n* [C;U] the land along the
edge of a large stretch of water: *to walk along
the shore|to see a boat about a mile from|off
the shore|The sailors got into trouble while
they were on shore.* (=on land) –see also
ASHORE

USAGE The land along the edge of a river is
the **bank**, and the land along the edge of the
sea or a lake is the **shore**. **Coast** is used for the
whole area bordering the sea. Compare *We
walked along the* **shore**.*|My parents live on
the south* **coast** (=near the sea, but not
necessarily right on the edge). When considered as a place of enjoyment, the **coast** is
called the **seaside** or the **seashore**, and the
part of the shore that is covered by sand or
smooth stones is called the **beach**: *We're taking the children to the* **seaside/seashore** *on
Saturday.|We spent the whole day lying on
the* **beach**.

shore² *v* **shored, shoring** [T *up*] to strengthen
or give support to (something weak or in
danger of failing): *government action to
shore up farm prices*

shorn /ʃɔrn, ʃoʷrn/ *v past participle of* SHEAR

short¹ /ʃɔrt/ *adj* **1** not far from one end to the
other; little in distance or length (opposite
long) or in height (opposite **tall**): *It's only
a short way/distance from here.|A straight
line is the shortest distance between two
points.|He's a short man, shorter than his
wife.* **2** lasting only a little time: *a short visit
of only half an hour|only a short time ago|I've
got such a short memory that I can't remember what you told me yesterday.* **3** not having
or being enough: *"I'm short of money this
week; can you lend me some?" "Sorry; I'm
pretty short myself."|These goods are in short
supply; the price will be high.|I need $10 but
I'm $1 short; I've only got $9.|Our car broke
down only two miles short of where we
wanted to go.* **4** rudely impatient: *I'm sorry I
was short with you; I ought to have answered
your question more politely.|He's very*

short-tempered. (=becomes angry easily) **5**
[A] (of a drink) of a kind (such as SPIRITS¹ (7))
usu. served in a small glass **6 for short** as a
shorter way of saying the same name: *My
name is Alexander, "Al " for short.* **7 in short**
to put it into a few words; all I mean is: *You
can't make me! I won't do it! In short–no!*
8 short and sweet *infml* not wasting words
or time; short and direct in expression **9
short for** a shorter form of, or way of
saying: *The usual word "TV" is short for
"television."* **10 short of: a** up to but not
including: *threats of every action short of war*
b except for; without: *There's no way to cross
the river, short of swimming.* –**shortness** *n*
[U]

short² *adv* suddenly; ABRUPTly (1): *The driver
stopped short when the child ran into the
street.*

short³ *n* → SHORT CIRCUIT

short·age /'ʃɔrtɪdʒ/ *n* [C;U *of*] a condition of
having less than needed; an amount lacking:
food shortages during the war

short·bread /'ʃɔrtbrɛd/ *n* [U] a thin hard
sweet COOKIE made with a lot of butter

short·cake /'ʃɔrtkeʸk/ *n* [U] *AmE* a cake
over which sweetened fruit is poured: *straw-
berry shortcake*

short-change /,· '·/ *v* -**changed, -changing**
[T] to give back less than enough money
(CHANGE² (4)) to (a buyer)

short-cir·cuit /,· '··/ *v* [I;T] to (cause to) have
a SHORT CIRCUIT

short circuit also **short–** *n* a faulty electrical
connection that usu. puts the power supply
out of operation

short·com·ing /'ʃɔrt,kʌmɪŋ/ *n* [usu. pl.] a
fault; DEFECT: *In spite of all my friend's
shortcomings, I still like him.*

short cut /'· ·/ *n* a quicker more direct way

short·en /'ʃɔrtn/ *v* [I;T] to make or become
shorter: *Shorten this report to 2000 words.*
–compare LENGTHEN

short·fall /'ʃɔrtfɔl/ *n* an amount lacking
to reach the amount needed or expected:
*Owing to bad weather, there will be a
shortfall in wheat supplies this year.*

short·hand /'ʃɔrthænd/ *n* [U] rapid writing in
a system using signs or shorter forms for
letters, words, etc.: *The secretary made notes
in shorthand.* –compare LONGHAND

short-lived /,ʃɔrt'laɪvd, -'lɪvd◄/ *adj* lasting
only a short time

short·ly /'ʃɔrtliʸ/ *adv* **1** soon; in a little time:
Mr. Perez will be back shortly. **2** impatiently;
not politely: *He answered very shortly.*

shorts /ʃɔrts/ *n* [P] **1** pants ending at or above
the knees, worn in playing games, by child-
ren, etc. **2** *AmE* men's short UNDERPANTS
–see illustration on page 123 –see PAIR
(USAGE)

short·sight·ed /,ʃɔrt'saɪtɪd◄/ *adj* **1** *BrE* for
NEARSIGHTED **2** not considering what is likely
to happen in the future: *It's very shortsighted
not to spend money on repairing your house.*
–opposite **farsighted** –**shortsightedly** *adv*
–**shortsightedness** *n* [U]

short-term /,· '·◄/ *adj* concerning a short
period of time; in or for the near future:

short-term planning/borrowing –see also
LONG-TERM

short wave /ˌ· '·◄/ n [U] radio broadcasting
or receiving on waves of less than 60 meters
in length: *a short-wave radio*

shot¹ /ʃɑt/ n **1** [C] an action of shooting a
weapon: *He fired three shots.|He was
wounded by a shot in the leg.* **2** [C] a kick,
throw, etc., of a ball intended to win a point:
His shot went to the right of the goal. **3** [C] a
person who shoots with the stated degree of
skill: *She's a good/poor shot.* **4** [C] a chance
or attempt to do something; TRY² (1); GO² (3):
*It's not easy, but I'd like to have a shot at
it.|Looking for her in the library was a **long
shot*** (=an attempt unlikely to succeed); *I
had no idea where she was.* **5** [C] a sending up
of a spacecraft or ROCKET: *a moon shot* (=for
a voyage to the moon) **6** [U] nonexplosive
metal balls for shooting from some kinds of
guns, esp. CANNONs in former times and
SHOTGUNs **7** [C] a photograph or a short con-
tinuous action in a movie: *fashion shots|an
action shot* **8** [C] *infml* a taking of a drug into
the bloodstream through a needle; INJEC-
TION: *a shot of* PENICILLIN **9** [C] *infml* a small
drink (esp. of WHISKEY) all swallowed at
once **10 big shot** *derog* an important person
11 like a shot *infml* quickly and eagerly: *He
accepted the offer like a shot.* **12 shot in the
arm** *infml* something which acts to bring
back a better, more active condition: *The big
sale was a shot in the arm to the failing company.* **13 shot in the dark** *infml* a wild guess
unsupported by arguments

shot² *adj* [F] *AmE infml* ruined or completely
worn by hard use: *My nerves are shot. I need
a vacation.|This car is shot.*

shot³ *v past tense and participle of* SHOOT

shot·gun /ˈʃɑtgʌn/ n a gun which fires a
quantity of small metal balls (SHOT (6)) and is
used esp. for shooting birds

should /ʃəd; *strong* ʃʊd/ v *negative contraction* **shouldn't** /ˈʃʊdnt/ [I +*to*-v] **1 a** ought to:
*you should be ashamed of yourself.|He
shouldn't have/oughtn't to have said that.*
(=he said it but it was bad to do so)|*I should
write a letter this evening, but I want to watch
television.* **b** (to show that something can be
naturally expected): *They should be/ought
to be here soon.* **2 a** *BrE* (in reported speech
with a past verb) shall: *I thought I should
succeed.* (=I thought "I shall succeed.") **b**
BrE (used instead of *shall* in "if" sentences
with a past tense verb): *I should (but She
would) be surprised if he came.|I should stay
out of trouble if I were you.* (=You ought
to . . .) **c** (used after *that* in certain expressions of feeling): *It's odd that you should mention that.* **d** *BrE* (used after *that* with certain
verbs like *demand, insist,* and *recommend* to
refer to a later action): *They demanded that
John should go.‖AmE that John go.* **e** *fml*
(used in "if" sentences about what is

SPELLING NOTE
Words with the sound /ʃ/ may be
spelled ch-, like **chauffeur**.

---

possible in the future): *If I should die, you
would get the money.|Should any visitors call*
(=if they call) *tell them I'm busy.* **3 I should
have thought** *esp. BrE* (shows surprise): *20
degrees? I should have thought it was colder
than that.* **4** *BrE* **I should like** I want: *I should
like a bath.|I should like to ask a question.*
–see LIKE (USAGE) **5** *esp. BrE* **I should
think** I believe: *"Can you come?" "Yes, I
should think so."*

USAGE In ordinary speech **would,** or the
short form **'d,** is used more often than **should**
in meanings 2a, 2b, 3, and 4. In the other
meanings, **should** is always used.

shoul·der¹ /ˈʃoʷldər/ n **1** the part of the body
at each side of the neck where the arms are
connected: *If you stand on my shoulders,
you will be able to see over the wall.* **2** the part
of a garment that covers this part of the body
3 something like this part of the body in
shape, such as a slope on a mountain near
the top, or the outward curve on a bottle
below the neck **4 head and shoulders above**
very much better than: *This book stands/is
head and shoulders above all others.* **5
shoulder to shoulder** side by side; close
together

shoulder² v [T] **1** to place (a load) on the
shoulder(s): (fig.) *to shoulder the responsibility of high political office* **2** to push with
the shoulders: *He shouldered his way to the
front of the crowd.*

shoulder blade /ˈ·· ˌ·/ n either of the two flat
bones on each side of the upper back

should·n't /ˈʃʊdnt/ v *short for:* should not:
You shouldn't laugh at him.

USAGE **Shouldn't** and **oughtn't** (*esp. BrE*)
mean that something is wrong; **don't have to**
and **needn't** (*esp. BrE*) mean that something
is unnecessary: *You don't have to talk so
loud. I can hear you.|You shouldn't talk so
loud. You'll wake the baby.*

shout¹ /ʃaʊt/ v [I;T +*(that)*/out] to give a
loud cry (of); speak or say very loudly: *I can
hear you. There's no need to shout.|"Help!"
he shouted.|He shouted for help.*

shout sbdy.↔ **down** v adv [T] to prevent (a
speaker) from being heard, by shouting: *The
crowd shouted down the unpopular speaker.*

shout² n a loud cry or call: *a warning
shout|shouts of delight from the crowd*

shove /ʃʌv/ v **shoved, shoving** [I;T] to push,
esp. in a rough careless way: *There was a
lot of **pushing and shoving** to get on the
bus.|Shove the chair into the corner, would
you?*

shove sbdy. **around** v adv [T] *infml* → PUSH
around; ORDER **around**

shove off v adv [I] **1** (of a boat or a person in
it) to leave the shore **2** [*esp. in commands*]
infml Go away: *Shove off! I'm busy.*

shove² n a strong push: *We gave the car a
good shove and moved it out of the mud.*

shov·el¹ /ˈʃʌvəl/ n **1** a usu. long-handled tool
with a broad blade for lifting and moving
loose material –compare SPADE **2** a part like
this on a digging or earth-moving machine

shovel² v **-l-** *AmE‖*-ll-** *BrE* [I;T] to move,
make, or work (as if) with a SHOVEL: *He*

shoveled a path through the snow.|She shoveled the papers into her desk.

show¹ /ʃoʷ/ v **showed, shown** /ʃoʷn/, **showing**
1 [T] to allow or cause to be seen: Let me show you the photographs from my vacation.|The painting shows a girl holding a baby. **2** [I] to appear; be able to be seen: Don't worry about that dirt on your pants. It won't show.|(fig.) She did very little work on this report, and it shows! (=it is very clear to see) **3** [T] to go with and guide: May I show you to your seat? |The visitors were **shown around** the castle. **4** [T +(that)] to prove or make clear (to): His remarks showed he didn't understand.|Will you show me how to use this machine?|This report shows the accident to have been the driver's fault. **5** [I;T] (esp. of a movie) to be offered at present: "What's showing at the theater?" "They're showing a Russian movie." **6** [T] to cause to be felt in one's actions: They showed their enemies no mercy. **7 it (all) goes to show** infml it proves the point: It all goes to show that crime doesn't pay. **8 show one's face** to appear before people: I'm surprised he dared to show his face here after his behavior last week. **9 show one's hand** to make one's power or intentions clear **10 to show for** as a profit or reward from: She's got nothing to show for her life's work except a lot of memories.

show sbdy. **around** (sthg.) v prep; adv [T] to be a guide to (someone) on a first visit to (a place): Before you start work, I'll show you around the office.

show off v adv [I] to behave so as to try to get people to admire one, one's abilities, etc.: Don't look at him! He's just showing off! –see also SHOW-OFF

show up v adv **1** [I;T (=**show** sthg.↔**up**)] to (cause to) be easily seen: This bright sunlight really shows up the cracks in the wall. **2** [T] (**show** sbdy./sthg.↔ **up**) make known the esp. unpleasant truth about **3** [I] infml to arrive; be present: Did everybody show up for the party?

show² n **1** [C] a performance, esp. in a theater or on radio or television: What television shows do you usually watch? **2** [C] a collection of things for the public to look at; EXHIBIT² (2): a cat/flower/car show **3** [S] a showing: The army put on a show of strength. (=showed their strength openly)|The vote was taken by **a show of hands**. (=decided by counting the raised hands of voters) **4** [S] an outward appearance, as opposed to what is really true, happening, etc.: I made a show of interest, but I really didn't care about what he was saying. **5** [U] grandness; splendid appearance or ceremony **6** [S] infml an organization or activity: He's in charge of the whole show. **7 on show** being shown to the public

show busi·ness /'· ˌ··/ also **show biz** /'ʃoʷ ˌbɪz/ infml– n [U] the business of performing; the job of people who work in movies, the theater, etc.

show·down /'ʃoʷdaʊn/ n infml a settlement of a disagreement in an open direct way

show·er¹ /'ʃaʊər/ n **1** a short-lasting fall of rain or snow: Some showers are expected this afternoon. –see WEATHER (USAGE) **2** a fall of many small things or drops of liquid: The bucket fell over, sending a shower of water into the street. **3 a** a washing of the body by standing under running water: to take a shower **b** an apparatus for this –see illustration on page 51 **4** AmE a party given on some occasion by (usu. a woman's) friends at which they give suitable gifts: a baby/wedding shower

shower² v **1** [I;T] to pour down in SHOWERs (on): It's started to shower.|Nuts showered down from the tree.|(fig.) They showered gifts on her/showered her with gifts. **2** [I] to take a SHOWER¹ (3a)

show·er·y /'ʃaʊəriʸ/ adj (e.g. of weather) bringing rain from time to time but not for long

show·ing /'ʃoʷɪŋ/ n **1** [C] an act of putting on view: a showing of new fashions **2** [S] a record of success or quality; performance: a good/poor showing by the local team

show·man /'ʃoʷmən/ n **-men** /mən/ **1** a person whose business is producing plays, musical shows, etc. **2** a person who always behaves as if performing for others –**showmanship** /'ʃoʷmənˌʃɪp/ n [U]

shown /ʃoʷn/ v past participle of SHOW¹

show-off /'· ·/ n infml a person who SHOWs¹ off

show·room /'ʃoʷruʷm, -rʊm/ n a large room where examples of goods for sale may be looked at

show·y /'ʃoʷiʸ/ adj **-ier, -iest** too colorful, bright, attention-getting, etc. –**showily** adv

shrank /ʃræŋk/ v past tense of SHRINK

shrap·nel /'ʃrapnəl/ n [U] metal scattered in small pieces from an exploding bomb or SHELL¹ (3)

shred¹ /ʃrɛd/ n **1** [C] a small narrow piece torn or roughly cut off: His coat was torn to shreds/was in shreds. **2** [S] (used in NEGATIVES², questions, etc.) a smallest piece; bit: There isn't a shred of truth in that statement.

shred² v **-dd-** [T] to cut or tear into SHREDs: shredded CABBAGE

shrew /ʃruʷ/ n **1** a bad-tempered scolding woman **2** a small mouselike animal

shrewd /ʃruʷd/ adj **1** clever in judgment: a shrewd lawyer who knows all the tricks **2** well-reasoned and likely to be right: a shrewd guess –**shrewdly** adv –**shrewdness** n [U]

shrew·ish /'ʃruʷɪʃ/ adj typical of a bad-tempered woman (SHREW (1)) –**shrewishly** adv

shriek¹ /ʃriʸk/ v [I;T] to cry out with a high sound; SCREECH: "Help!" the boy shrieked.|They were all shrieking with laughter.

shriek² n a wild high cry (e.g. of pain or terror)

shrill /ʃrɪl/ adj (of a sound) high and sounding sharp; PIERCING: a shrill whistle –**shrilly** /'ʃrɪl-liʸ, 'ʃrɪliʸ/ adv –**shrillness** n [U]

shrimp /ʃrɪmp/ n **shrimp** or **shrimps 1** a small sea creature with long legs and a fanlike tail –compare PRAWN **2** derog a small person

shrine /ʃraɪn/ n a place for worship; place held in respect for its religious or other connections: *Stratford, Shakespeare's shrine*

shrink¹ /ʃrɪŋk/ v **shrank** /ʃræŋk/, **shrunk** /ʃrʌŋk/ or **shrunken** /'ʃrʌŋkən/, **shrinking 1** [I;T] to (cause to) become smaller, as from the effect of heat or water: *Washing wool in hot water will shrink it/make it shrink.*|(fig.) *The number of students has shrunk in recent years.* **2** [I] to move back and away: *The nervous dog shrank into a corner.*

shrink from sthg. v prep [T +v-ing] to be afraid of; avoid because of fear; RECOIL from: *He shrank from (the thought of) having to kill anyone*|*The young woman shrank from all responsibilities.*

shrink² n AmE humor infml for PSYCHIATRIST

shrink·age /'ʃrɪŋkɪdʒ/ n [U] the act or amount of SHRINKING (1); loss in size: *As a result of shrinkage, the shirt is now too small to wear.*

shriv·el /'ʃrɪvəl/ v **-l-** AmE|**-ll-** BrE [I;T up] to (cause to) dry out and become smaller by twisting into small folds: *plants shriveling (up) in the dry heat*

shroud¹ /ʃraʊd/ n **1** the cloth for covering a dead body at burial **2** something that covers and hides: *A shroud of secrecy hangs over/surrounds the plan.*

shroud² v [T usu. pass.] to cover and hide: *hills shrouded in mist*| *a mystery shrouded in uncertainty*

shrub /ʃrʌb/ n a low bush

shrub·ber·y /'ʃrʌbəri/ n **-ies** [C;U] (part of a garden planted with) SHRUBs forming a mass or group –see illustration on page 337

shrug /ʃrʌg/ v **-gg-** [I;T] to raise (one's shoulders), esp. as an expression of doubt, lack of interest, etc.: *He shrugged (his shoulders), saying he didn't know and didn't care.* –**shrug** n: *She answered with a shrug.*

shrug sthg. **off** v adv [T] to treat as unimportant or easily dealt with: *She can shrug off her troubles and keep smiling.*

shuck /ʃʌk/ n, v [C;T] esp. AmE (to remove) an outer covering on a plant or animal; shell, POD, or HUSK

shucks /ʃʌks/ interj AmE infml an inoffensive expression of annoyance or disappointment: *"You can't go to the party." "Shucks! I was looking forward to it."*

shud·der¹ /'ʃʌdər/ v [I +to-v/at] to shake uncontrollably for a moment, as from fear or strong dislike; tremble: *He shuddered at the sight of the dead body.*|(fig.) *I shudder to think what your father will say when he sees this broken window.*

shudder² n an act of SHUDDERing: *She gave a shudder in the cold.*

shuf·fle¹ /'ʃʌfəl/ v **-fled, -fling 1** [I;T] to mix up the order of (playing cards): *It's your turn to shuffle.*|(fig.) *shuffling papers around on her desk* **2** [I] to walk slowly or without lifting

one's feet: *The old woman shuffled across the room.*

shuffle² n **1** [S] a slow dragging walk **2** [C] an act of shuffling (SHUFFLE¹ (1)) cards **3** [C] → SHAKE-UP: *a shuffle of government officials*

shun /ʃʌn/ v **-nn-** [T + v-ing] to avoid; keep away from: *He was shunned by society.*|*We shunned seeing other people.*

shunt /ʃʌnt/ v **1** [T] to move (a train or railroad car) from one track to another, esp. to a SIDING **2** [I] (of a train or railroad car) to move in this way: (fig.) *Smith has been shunted to a smaller office.*

shush /ʃʌʃ, ʃʊʃ/ v **1** [I in commands] to become quiet; HUSH: *Shush! Don't cry!* **2** [T] to tell to be quiet, e.g. by saying "SH"

shut /ʃʌt/ v **shut, shutting 1** [I;T] to put or go into a covered, blocked, or folded-together position; close: *Shut the gate so that the dog can't get out.*|*He shut his eyes and tried to sleep.*|*She shut the book.*|*The doors shut, and the train moved off.* **2** [T] to keep or hold by closing: *He shut himself in his room to think.*|*She shut her skirt in the door and tore it.* **3** [I;T] to stop in operation; SHUT **down**: *The stores shut at 5:30.*|*He lost his job when they shut the factory.* –see OPEN (USAGE)

shut sbdy. ↔ **away** v adv [T] to keep guarded away from others; ISOLATE: *She shut herself away in her country house.*

shut (sthg.↔) **down** v adv [I;T] (of a business or factory) to stop operation, esp. for a long time: *The company shuts down for one week at Christmas.* –see also SHUTDOWN

shut sthg.↔ **off** v adv [T] **1** to cause to stop in flow or operation, usu. by turning a handle or pressing a button: *They shut off the water before going on vacation.* **2** to keep separate or away: *a valley shut off by mountains from the rest of the world*

shut up v adv **1** [I in commands] infml to stop talking; be quiet: *Shut up! I'm trying to think.* **2** [T] (**shut** sbdy. **up**) infml to make (someone) stop talking: *Can't you shut your friend up?* **3** [T] (**shut** sbdy. **up**) to keep enclosed: *He shut himself up in his room.*

shut·down /'ʃʌtdaʊn/ n a stopping of work, e.g. in a factory because of a labor quarrel, vacation, lack of demand, etc. –see also SHUT **down**

shut·ter¹ /'ʃʌtər/ n **1** one of a pair of wooden or metal covers that can be closed in front of a window –see illustration on page 337 **2** a part of a camera which opens for a very short time to let light fall on the film

shutter² v [T] to close with SHUTTERs¹ (1): *an empty town, with all the stores shuttered and the people gone*

shut·tle /'ʃʌtl/ n a regular service to and fro by air, bus, etc.: *There is a shuttle (bus service) between the town center and the train station.*|*a space shuttle* (=a spacecraft that can make regular trips to space)

shuttle² v **-tled, -tling** [I;T] to move to and fro often or regularly: *The airplane shuttles passengers from Boston to New York.*

shut·tle·cock /'ʃʌtl,kɒk/ n a small light object which is hit across a net in the game of BADMINTON

SPELLING NOTE

Words with the sound /ʃ/ may be spelled **ch-**, like **chauffeur**.

shy[1] /ʃaɪ/ adj **shyer** or **shier, shyest** or **shiest 1** not bold; nervous in the company of others; BASHFUL: *When the children met the President, they were too shy to speak.*|*a shy smile* **2** (of animals) unwilling to come near people **3 once bitten, twice shy** *infml* a person who has been tricked will be more careful in the future **4 -shy** afraid of; not liking: *She's camera-shy and hates being photographed.* –**shyly** adv –**shyness** n [U]

shy[2] v **shied, shying** [I] **1** [at] (of a horse) to make a sudden movement, e.g. from fear: *The horse shied at the loud noise, and its rider fell off.* **2** [off, away] to avoid something unpleasant, as by moving aside: *They shied away from buying the house when they learned the price.*

shy·ster /'ʃaɪstər/ n AmE infml a dishonest person, esp. a lawyer

sib·ling /'sɪblɪŋ/ n fml a brother or sister

sic /sɪk/ adv Latin (usu. in BRACKETs after a word in writing) written in this wrong way intentionally; not my mistake: *The writer tells us that the war lasted from 939* (sic) *to 1945!*

sick /sɪk/ adj **1** not well; ill; having a disease: *visiting my sick uncle in the hospital*|*a sick cow*|*The sick and wounded were allowed to go free.* –see DISEASE (USAGE) **2** [F] upset in the stomach so as to want to throw up what is in it; feeling NAUSEA: *He began to feel sick when the ship started to move.* **3** [F of] tired of; having too much of: *I'm sick of listening to your complaints; be quiet!* **4** unnaturally cruel; MORBID: *a sick joke*/*mind* **5** [A] for illness: *sick pay*|*sick leave* **6 be sick** to throw up what is in the stomach; VOMIT: *I thought I was going to be sick when I saw the car accident.* **7 make someone sick** *infml* to be strongly displeasing to someone: *Your complaining makes me sick!* **8 -sick** feeling sick from the stated kind of travel: *carsick*| *seasick*

sick·en /'sɪkən/ v **1** [T] to cause strong feelings of dislike in; NAUSEATE: *a sickening sight* **2** [I for] to become ill; show signs of a disease: *The animal began to sicken and soon died.*

sick leave /'· ·/ n [on U] (permitted amount of) time spent away from a job during illness

sick·ly /'sɪkliy/ adj **-lier, -liest 1** often ill; weak and unhealthy: *a sickly child* |*a sickly-looking plant* **2** unpleasantly weak or pale: *His face was a sickly yellow.* **3** causing a sick feeling: *a sickly smell*

sick·ness /'sɪknɪs/ n **1** [C;U] the condition of being ill; an illness or disease: *absence due to sickness* –compare HEALTH **2** [U] the condition of feeling sick; NAUSEA: *He suffers from carsickness.*

sick pay /'· ·/ n [U] pay for time spent away from a job during illness

sick·room /'sɪk-ruʷm, -rʊm/ n a room where someone lies ill in bed

side[1] /saɪd/ n **1** an upright surface of something, not the top, bottom, front, or back: *The front door is locked; we'll have to go around to the side of the house.*|*The sides of the bowl were beautifully painted.*|*The house*

was halfway up the side of the hill/up the hillside. **2** any of the flat surfaces of something: *A cube has six sides.*|*Which side of the box is up?* (=which is the top?) **3** an edge or border: *A square has four equal sides.*|*I sat on the side of the road/on the roadside.* **4** either of the two surfaces of a thin flat object: *Write on only one side of the paper.* **5** a part, place, or division according to a real or imaginary central line: *She lives on the other side of town*|*the left/right side of his face*|*Cars drive on the left side of the road in the United States.* **6** the right or left part of the body, esp. from the shoulder to the top of the leg: *I've got a pain in my left side.* **7** the place next to something or someone: *On one side of the window was a mirror, and on the other a painting.*|*His daughter walked by his side.*|*During her illness he never left her side.* **8** a part to be considered, usu. in opposition to another: *Try to look at all sides of the question before deciding.*|*Her kindness was a side of her character that I had never seen before.* **9** (a group which holds) a position in a quarrel, war, etc.: *In most wars neither side wins.*|*Whose side are you on; mine or hers?*|*I never take sides.* (=support one side against the other) **10** [C] a sports team: *Our side is winning.* **11** the part of a line of a family that is related to a particular person: *He's Scottish on his mother's side.* **12 on the short/easy/low** etc. **side** a little too short/ easy/low etc.: *I like the house but I think the price is on the high side.* **13 on the side** as a (sometimes dishonest) additional activity: *He's a teacher, but he makes a little money on the side by repairing cars in his free time.* –see also SIDELINE **14 put on/to one side** to take out of consideration for the present; keep for possible use later **15 side by side** next to one another: *They lined up side by side for the photograph.* **16 -sided** having a certain number or kind of sides: *an eight-sided coin*|*a steep-sided mountain*

side[2] adj [A] **1** at, from, towards, etc., the side: *a side door* **2** besides the main or regular thing: *Certain drugs have harmful side effects.*|*We must keep to the main point and not talk about side issues.*|*The main dish was meat, with various vegetables as side dishes.*

side[3] v **sided, siding** [I with, against] to support one party in a quarrel, fight, etc., against another: *Mother sided with David (against Father) in the argument.*

side·board /'saɪdbɔrd, -boʷrd/ n a piece of DINING ROOM furniture like a low cupboard, used to hold dishes, spoons, etc.

side·burns /'saɪdbɜrnz/ AmE|**sideboards** /'saɪdbɔrdz, -boʷrdz/ BrE– n [P] growths of hair on the sides of a man's face, esp. when worn long

side·car /'saɪdkɑr/ n a usu. enclosed seat fastened to the side of a motorcycle to hold a passenger

side ef·fect /'· ·,·/ n an effect in addition to the intended one: *Medicines sometimes have unpleasant side effects.*

side·kick /'saɪd,kɪk/ n AmE infml a usu. less important companion or helper

side·light /ˈsaɪdlaɪt/ n **1** either of a pair of small lamps fixed on either side of the front of a vehicle –see also HEADLIGHT –see illustration on page 95 **2** a piece of interesting though not very important information: *The general's private letters can give some interesting sidelights on the history of the war.*

side·line /ˈsaɪdlaɪn/ n an activity in addition to one's regular job: *Jane's a doctor, but she does some writing as a sideline.* –compare **on the** SIDE¹ (13)

side·long /ˈsaɪdlɒŋ/ adv,adj directed sideways: *a sidelong blow/smile*

side or·der /ˈ· ˌ··/ n AmE a restaurant order for a separate dish in addition to the main dish

side·show /ˈsaɪdʃoʊ/ n **1** a separate small show at a fair or CIRCUS (1), usu. with some amusement or game **2** a usu. amusing activity beside a more serious main one

side·step /ˈsaɪdstɛp/ v **-pp-** [I;T] **1** to take a step to the side to avoid (e.g. a blow) **2** to avoid (an unwelcome question, duty, etc.): *to sidestep a problem*

side street /ˈ· ·/ n a narrow less important street, esp. one that meets a main street –compare BACK STREET

side·swipe /ˈsaɪdswaɪp/ n, v **-swiped, swiping** [C;T] AmE (to strike with) a blow directed along the side: *He sideswiped the parked car.*

side·track /ˈsaɪdtræk/ v [T] to cause (someone) to leave one subject or activity and follow another usu. less important one: *The children were going to do their homework, but they got sidetracked by a movie on television.*

side·walk /ˈsaɪdwɔk/ AmE‖**pavement** BrE– n a PAVED surface or path at the side of a street for people to walk on –see illustration on page 337

side·ways /ˈsaɪdweɪz/ adv,adj to or towards one side: *to step sideways/a sideways jump*

sid·ing /ˈsaɪdɪŋ/ n **1** [C] a short railway track connected to a main track, used for railroad cars not in use, etc. **2** [U] AmE wood or metal in lengths for nailing up to the side of a building

si·dle /ˈsaɪdl/ v **-dled, -dling** [I up] to walk secretively or nervously, as if one is ready to turn and go the other way: *He sidled up to the stranger and tried to sell him the stolen ring.*

siege /siːdʒ/ n an operation by an armed force surrounding a defended place to force it to yield, usu. by blocking its supplies.

si·er·ra /siˈɛrə/ n a row, range, or area of sharply-pointed mountains

si·es·ta /siˈɛstə/ n a short sleep after the midday meal, as is the custom in hot countries

sieve¹ /sɪv/ n **1** a tool of wire or plastic net on a frame, used for separating large from small solid pieces, or solid things from liquid **2**

SPELLING NOTE
Words with the sound /s/ may be spelled **c-**, like **city**, or **ps-** like **psychology**.

head/memory like a sieve infml a mind that forgets quickly

sieve² v **sieved, sieving** [T] to put through a SIEVE; separate using a sieve: *Sieve the flour first.|Sieve out the stones from the soil.*

sift /sɪft/ v [I;T] **1** to put (something) through a SIEVE or net: (fig.) *The snow sifted through the crack in the roof.* **2** [through] to make a close examination of (things in a mass or group): *He sifted through his papers to find the lost letter.*

sigh¹ /saɪ/ v [I] **1** to let out a deep breath slowly and with a sound expressing tiredness, sadness, pleasure, etc. **2** lit (of the wind) to make a sound like this

sigh² n an act or sound of SIGHing (1): *We all heaved* (=made) *a sigh of* RELIEF.

sight¹ /saɪt/ n **1** [U] the power of seeing; EYESIGHT: *The woman lost her sight in a car accident.* **2** [U] presence in one's view; the range of what can be seen: *He never lets his children out of his sight.|The house is hidden from sight by a row of trees.|The boat was within sight of land.|Keep out of sight! You can't be seen here.|*(fig.) *I believe that peace is now in sight.* (=near) **3** [C] something that is seen: *the familiar sight of the mailman going along the street* **4** [C usu. pl.] something worth seeing: *We'll take you to see the sights when you're in New York.* –see also SIGHTSEEING **5** [S] something which looks very bad or laughable: *What a sight you are, with paint all over your clothes!* **6** [C often pl.] a part of an instrument or weapon which guides the eye in aiming **7** [S] infml a lot: *That meal was a sight better than the last one I ate here.|She earns a sight more than I do.* **8 at first sight** at the first time of seeing or meeting: *love at first sight* **9 catch sight of** to see for a moment: *I caught sight of her hurrying away.* **10 lose sight of** to stop seeing or being conscious of: *We shouldn't lose sight of* (=forget) *the main purpose of the meeting.*

sight² v [T] to get a view of, esp. after a time of looking; see for the first time: *The sailors gave a shout when they sighted land.|Several rare birds have been sighted in this area.* –**sighting** n

sight·ed /ˈsaɪtɪd/ adj (of a person) able to see; not blind

sight·see·ing /ˈsaɪtˌsiːɪŋ/ n [U] visiting places of interest usu. while on a vacation: *We often go sightseeing.* –see also SIGHT¹ (4) –**sightseer** /ˈsaɪtˌsiːər/ n

sign¹ /saɪn/ n **1** a standard mark; something which is seen and represents a known meaning; SYMBOL: *Written music uses lots of signs* **2** a board or notice giving information, warning, etc.: *Pay attention to the traffic/road signs.* **3** [+ to- v] a movement of the body intended to express a meaning; signal: *She put her finger to her lips as a sign to be quiet.* **4** something that shows the presence or coming of something else: *All the signs are that business will get better.|Swollen ankles can be a sign of heart disease.* **5** also **sign of the zodiac**– any of the 12 divisions of the year represented by groups of stars

sign² v **1** [I;T] to write (one's name) on a

paper, etc., esp. for official purposes: *The papers are ready to be signed.|She signed her name on the check/signed the check.* **2** [I;T *to*] to make a movement as a sign to (someone); signal: *The policeman signed (to) me to stop.|People who are unable to speak* (MUTES) *sign what they want to say with their hands.* (=use SIGN LANGUAGE). **3** [I;T +*to-v*] to SIGN **up/on**: *The football team has signed two new players.*

sign sthg.↔ **away** *v adv* [T] to give up formally (ownership, a claim, a right, etc.), by signing a paper: *He signed away his share in the property.*

sign for sthg. *v prep* [T] to sign one's name to show that one has received; formally accept: *The mailman asked me to sign for the letter.*

sign in *v adv* [I] to record one's name when arriving –opposite **sign out**

sign on *v adv* [I;T (=**sign** sbdy.↔ **on**)] to (cause to) join a working force, by signing a paper; ENLIST (1): *She signed on as a newspaper reporter.*

sign out *v adv* [I] to record one's name when leaving –opposite **sign in**

sign up *v adv* [I;T (=**sign** sbdy.↔ **up**) +*to -v*] to (cause to) sign an agreement to take part in something, or to take a job; ENLIST (1): *I've signed up (to take a course) at the local college.*

sig·nal¹ /ˈsɪgnəl/ *n* **1** a sound or action understood to give a message: *A red light is often used as a danger signal. |American Indians sometimes used to send smoke signals.|When I look at my watch, it's a signal for us to leave.* **2** a railroad apparatus, usu. with colored lights, near the track to direct train drivers **3** → TRAFFIC LIGHT **4** the waves sent by radio or television: *We live too far from the city to get a strong television signal.*

signal² *v* **-l-** *AmE*||**-ll-** *BrE* **1** [I *to, for*] to give a signal: *She was signaling wildly, waving her arms.* **2** [I;T +*to-v/that*] to express, warn, or tell by a signal or signals: *The policeman signaled (to) the traffic to move forward.|The thief signaled (his friend) that the police were coming.* **3** [T] to be a sign of; MARK²: *The defeat signaled the end of the war.*

signal³ *adj* [A] *lit* noticeable; important; OUTSTANDING (1): *a signal example of courage* –**signally** *adv*

sig·na·to·ry /ˈsɪgnəˌtɔriʸ, -ˌtoʷriʸ/ *n* **-ries** *fml* any of the people or countries that sign an agreement, esp. one between nations

sig·na·ture /ˈsɪgnətʃər/ *n* **1** [C] a person's name written by his/her own hand, at the end of a letter, check, etc. **2** [U] the act of signing one's name: *to witness someone's signature*

sig·nif·i·cance /sɪgˈnɪfəkəns/ *n* [S;U] importance; meaning; value: *an industry of great significance to the country* –opposite **insignificance**

sig·nif·i·cant /sɪgˈnɪfəkənt/ *adj* **1** of noticeable importance: *a significant increase in crime* –opposite **insignificant 2** having a special meaning: *a significant smile* –**significantly** *adv*

sig·ni·fy /ˈsɪgnəˌfaɪ/ *v* **-fied, -fying** *fml* **1** [T +*that*] to be a sign of; mean: *A fever usually signifies a disorder of the body/that there is something wrong with the body.* **2** [I;T] to express (esp. an opinion) by an action: *They signified their agreement by raising their hands.*

sign lan·guage /ˈ·· ˌ··/ *n* [U] a system of hand movements for expressing meanings, as used by the DEAF (1) and MUTE¹, by some American Indians, etc.

sign of the zo·di·ac /ˌ··· ˈ···/ *n* see ZODIAC

sign·post /ˈsaɪnpoʷst/ *n* a sign showing directions and distances, e.g. by a road

si·lage /ˈsaɪlɪdʒ/ *n* [U] grass or other plants cut and stored in a SILO for cattle food

si·lence¹ /ˈsaɪləns/ *n* [U] **1** absence of sound; stillness: *nothing but silence in the empty house|The silence was broken by a loud cry.* **2** the state of not speaking or making a noise: *She received the bad news in silence.* **3** failure to mention a particular thing: *I can't understand the government's silence on such an important matter.*

silence² *v* **-lenced, -lencing** [T] **1** to cause to stop making a noise: *The enemy's guns were silenced by repeated bombings.* **2** to force to stop expressing opinions, etc.: *The judge silenced them by putting them in prison.*

si·lenc·er /ˈsaɪlənsər/ *n* an apparatus for reducing noise, esp. of a gun

si·lent /ˈsaɪlənt/ *adj* **1** not speaking; not using spoken expression: *a silent prayer|silent reading|a silent movie* (=one with no sound) **2** free from noise; quiet: *the silent hours of the night* **3** (of a letter in a word) not having a sound; not pronounced: *silent "k" in "know"* –**silently** *adv*

sil·hou·ette¹ /ˌsɪluʷˈɛt/ *n* **1** a picture of something in solid black against a background; the shadow-like shape of something esp. of a person seen from the side: *His silhouette appeared on the curtain.* **2 in silhouette** as a dark shape against a light background

silhouette² *v* **-etted, -etting** [T *usu. pass.*] to cause to appear as a SILHOUETTE: *birds silhouetted against the sky*

sil·i·con /ˈsɪlɪˌkɑn, -kən/ *n* [U] a simple substance (ELEMENT) that is nonmetallic and found in nature in great quantities

silicon chip /ˌ··· ˈ·/ *n* → MICROPROCESSOR

silk /sɪlk/ *n* [U] fine thread which is produced by a kind of insect (SILKWORM) and made into cloth: *a dress of the finest silk*

silk·en /ˈsɪlkən/ *adj lit* **1** soft, smooth, or shiny like silk; SILKY: *silken hair* **2** made of silk: *silken garments*

silk·worm /ˈsɪlk-wɜrm/ *n* an insect (CATERPILLAR) which produces a COCOON of silk

silk·y /ˈsɪlkiʸ/ *adj* **-ier, -iest** like silk; soft, smooth, or shiny: *the cat's fine silky fur* –**silkiness** *n* [U]

sill /sɪl/ *n* the flat piece at the base of an opening or frame, esp. a WINDOWSILL

sil·ly /ˈsɪliʸ/ *adj* **-lier, -liest** foolish; not serious or sensible: *It's silly to go out in the rain if you don't have to.*

si·lo /ˈsaɪloʷ/ *n* **-los 1** a usu. round tower on a farm for storing SILAGE **2** an underground base from which a MISSILE may be fired

silt /sɪlt/ *n* [U] loose sand, mud, etc., carried in running water and then dropped at the entrance to a harbor, etc.

silt up *v adv* [I;T (=**silt** sthg.↔ **up**)] to fill or become filled with SILT

sil·ver¹ /ˈsɪlvər/ *n* [U] **1** a soft whitish precious metal that is a simple substance (ELEMENT), can be brightly polished, and is used esp. in jewelry and coins **2** coins made of silver or of some metal like it: *Could you give me $1 in silver, please?* **3** spoons, forks, dishes, etc., for the table, made of silver or a metal like it: *to polish the silver*

silver² *adj* **1** made of silver: *Is your ring silver?* **2** like silver in color: *a silver-haired old man*

silver an·ni·ver·sa·ry /ˌ·· ··'····/ *n* the 25th ANNIVERSARY of some important event, usu. a wedding

silver birch /ˌ·· '·/ *n* the common white BIRCH tree

sil·ver·fish /ˈsɪlvərˌfɪʃ/ *n* **-fish** or **-fishes** a type of small silver colored wingless insect found in houses and sometimes harmful to paper and cloth

silver plate /ˌ·· '·◄/ *n* [U] metal with a thin outer surface of silver

sil·ver·smith /ˈsɪlvərˌsmɪθ/ *n* a maker of jewelry, etc., in silver

sil·ver·ware /ˈsɪlvərˌwɛər/ *n* [U] *AmE* knives, forks, spoons and other utensils made of silver, SILVER PLATE or STAINLESS steel used when eating

sil·ver·y /ˈsɪlvəriy/ *adj* **1** like silver in shine and color **2** having a pleasant musical sound

sim·i·lar /ˈsɪmələr/ *adj* [to] like or alike; of the same kind: *bread, cake, and other similar foods|We have similar opinions; my opinions are similar to his.* –**similarly** *adv*

sim·i·lar·i·ty /ˌsɪmə'lærətiy/ *n* **-ties 1** [U] the quality of being alike: *How much similarity is there between the two religions?* **2** [C] a point of likeness

sim·i·le /ˈsɪməliy/ *n* an expression comparing two things, using the words *like* or *as*: "*As white as snow*" is a simile. –compare METAPHOR

sim·mer /ˈsɪmər/ *v* [I;T] to (cause to) cook gently in liquid at just below boiling point: *Let the soup simmer.|*(fig.) *simmering with anger/excitement* –see COOK (USAGE)

simmer down *v adv* [I] to become calmer; control one's excitement: *Simmer down; don't lose your temper.*

simmer² *n* [S] a heat just below boiling: *Bring the vegetables to a simmer.*

sim·per /ˈsɪmpər/ *v* [I] to smile in a silly unnatural way –**simperingly** *adv* –**simper** *n*

sim·ple /ˈsɪmpəl/ *adj* **1** not decorated; plain: *simple but well-prepared food|buildings in a simple style* **2** easy to understand or do; not difficult: *a simple explanation* **3** of the ordi-

nary kind, without special qualities, etc.: *A knife is one of the simplest of tools.|a simple case of stealing* **4** not mixed with anything else; pure: *the simple truth* **5** easily tricked; foolish: *You may be joking, but he's simple enough to believe you.* –compare COMPLICATED

sim·ple·ton /ˈsɪmpəltən/ *n* a weak-minded trusting person

sim·plic·i·ty /sɪm'plɪsətiy/ *n* [U] the state of being simple: *a beautiful simplicity of style|He believes everything with childlike simplicity.*

sim·pli·fy /ˈsɪmpləˌfaɪ/ *v* **-fied, -fying** [T] to make plainer, easier, or less full of detail: *Try to simplify your explanation for the children.* –see also OVERSIMPLIFY; compare COMPLICATE –**simplification** /ˌsɪmpləfə'keyʃən/ *n* [C;U]

sim·ply /ˈsɪmpliy/ *adv* **1** in a simple way; easily, clearly, or naturally: *On her small income, they live very simply.* **2** just; only: *I don't like driving; I do it simply to get to work.* **3** really; very (much): *simply wonderful*

sim·u·late /ˈsɪmyəˌleyt/ *v* **-lated, -lating** [T] *fml* to give the effect or appearance of; IMITATE: *He shook a sheet of metal to simulate the noise of thunder.* –**simulation** /ˌsɪmyə'leyʃən/ *n* [C;U]

sim·u·lat·ed /ˈsɪmyəˌleytɪd/ *adj* made to look, feel, etc., like the real thing: *a simulated fur coat*

si·mul·ta·ne·ous /ˌsaɪməl'teyniyəs/ *adj* happening at the same moment: *a flash of lightning and a simultaneous crash of thunder* –**simultaneously** *adv*

sin¹ /sɪn/ *n* **1** [C;U] (an example of) disobedience to God; the breaking of holy law: *the sin of pride|to commit a sin* –compare CRIME **2** [C] *esp. humor* something that should not be done: *He thinks it's a sin to stay in bed after eight o'clock.*

sin² *v* **-nn-** [I *against*] to break God's laws; do wrong

since¹ /sɪns/ *adv,prep,conj* (with the present tense, or with *have* or *had*) between a point in the past and now: *It's a long time since our last vacation.|Her husband died ten years ago, but she's since remarried.|We've been friends (ever) since we left school.|Since leaving Paris, we've visited Brussels and Amsterdam.* –see AGO (USAGE)

since² *conj* as it is true that: *Since you can't answer the question, I'll ask someone else.* –see Study Notes on page 144

sin·cere /sɪn'sɪər/ *adj* without deceit or falseness; real, true, or honest: *a sincere admiration of his qualities* –opposite **insincere** –**sincerely** *adv*

sin·cer·i·ty /sɪn'sɛrətiy/ *n* [U] the quality of being sincere; honesty –opposite **insincerity**

si·ne·cure /ˈsaɪnəˌkyʊər, ˈsɪ-/ *n* an easy, well-paid job

sin·ew /ˈsɪnyuw/ *n* [C;U] a strong cord in the body connecting a muscle to a bone; TENDON

sin·ew·y /ˈsɪnyuwiy/ *adj* **1** (of meat) containing SINEW; not easy to cut or eat **2** having strong muscles

sin·ful /'sɪnfəl/ adj 1 wicked 2 infml shameful; seriously wrong or bad: a sinful waste of time and money –**sinfully** adv –**sinfulness** n [U]

sing /sɪŋ/ v sang /sæŋ/, sung /sʌŋ/, singing 1 [I;T to, for] to produce (music, songs, etc.) with the voice: Birds sing loudest in the early morning.|The children were singing Christmas songs.|I'll try and sing the baby to sleep. (=make him sleep by singing) 2 [I] to make or be filled with a ringing sound: A bullet sang past my ear. 3 [I;T of] lit to tell about, or praise in poetry: Poets sang the king's praises; they sang of his brave deeds. 4 [I] AmE infml (of a criminal) to give information to the police –**singer** n

sing out v adv [I;T (=sing sthg. out)] to sing or call loudly

sing. written abbrev. said as: singular

singe /sɪndʒ/ v singed, singeing [T] 1 to burn off the ends from (hair, threads, etc.): He got too near the fire and singed his beard. 2 to burn lightly on the surface; SCORCH[1] (1): He singed the shirt with a hot iron.

sing·ing /'sɪŋɪŋ/ n [U] the art or sound of singing: to study singing|a poor singing voice

sin·gle[1] /'sɪŋgəl/ adj 1 [A] only one: A single tree gave shade from the sun.|Her single aim was to make money 2 having only one part; not double or MULTIPLE[1]: For strong sewing use double, not single thread. 3 [A] separate; considered by itself: There's no need to write down every single word I say. 4 unmarried: He's still single. 5 [A] for only one person: a single bed –compare DOUBLE[1]

single[2] n 1 a record with only one short song on each side –compare LP 2 infml a $1 note 3 a room for one person in a hotel 4 an unmarried person: a singles bar

single[3] v → SINGLE OUT

single file /ˌ·· '·/ n,adv (moving in) a line of people, vehicles, etc., one behind another: to go (in) single file along the narrow passage

single-hand·ed /ˌ·· '··◄/ adj,adv done by one person; without help from others: a single-handed sailing trip|He rebuilt his house single-handed. –**single-handedly** adv

single-mind·ed /ˌ·· '··◄/ adj with one clear purpose –**single-mindedly** adv [U] –**single-mindedness** n [U]

single sbdy./sthg. **out** v adv -gled, -gling [T for] to choose from a group, esp. for special treatment: They all did wrong. Why single him out for punishment?

sin·gles /'sɪŋgəlz/ n singles a match, esp. of tennis, with one player against one –compare DOUBLES

sin·gly /'sɪŋgliy/ adv separately; one by one: Some guests came singly, others in groups.

sing·song /'sɪŋsɔŋ/ n 1 [A;S] a repeated rising and falling of the voice in speaking: to talk in (a) singsong (voice)

sin·gu·lar[1] /'sɪŋgyələr/ adj 1 (in grammar) of a word or form representing only one thing: The noun "mouse" is singular; it is the singular form of "mice." –compare PLURAL 2 fml unusual: a woman of singular intelligence –**singularity** /ˌsɪŋgyə'lærətiy/ n -ties [C;U]

singular[2] n (a word in) a form representing

only one: "Trousers" has no singular.

sin·gu·lar·ly /'sɪŋgyələrliy/ adv fml particularly; very: a singularly intelligent woman

sin·is·ter /'sɪnɪstər/ adj threatening evil: a sinister look on his face|a sinister-looking crack in the wall

sink[1] /sɪŋk/ v sank /sæŋk/, sunk /sʌŋk/, sinking 1 [I;T] to (cause to) go down below a surface, or to the bottom of water: This rubber ball won't sink; it floats.|They sank the ship with bombs.|The moon sank below the hills.|This lack of money will sink our plans. (=make them fail) 2 [I] to go down in number, strength, value, etc.: The population of the village is slowly sinking.|He's sinking (=losing strength) fast and won't live much longer. 3 [I] to fall, e.g. from lack of strength: He fainted and sank to the ground. 4 [T] to dig out or force into the earth: to sink a well|a mine SHAFT[1] (5) 5 [T in, into] to put (money, labor, etc.) into; INVEST: I've sunk all my money into buying a new house. –**sinkable** adj

sink in v adv [I] 1 to become fully understood: The lesson has sunk in; she won't make the same mistake again. 2 to enter a solid through the surface: If the ink sinks in, it'll be hard to remove it.

sink (sthg.) **into** sthg. v prep [T] to put, force, or go below or into: The hungry dog sank its teeth into the meat.

sink[2] n 1 a large basin in a kitchen, for washing pots, vegetables, etc. –see illustration on page 379 2 also **lavatory** AmE||also **washbasin** esp. BrE– a basin for washing hands and face –see illustration on page 51

sin·ner /'sɪnər/ n a person who SINS; one who has disobeyed God

sin·u·ous /'sɪnyuwəs/ adj fml twisting like a snake; full of curves: a sinuous road through the mountains

si·nus /'saɪnəs/ n any of the air-filled spaces in the bones of the face that have an opening into the nose

sip[1] /sɪp/ v -pp- [I;T at] to drink, taking only a little at a time: She politely sipped her drink.

sip[2] n a very small amount of a drink; slight taste: Have a sip of this to see if you like it.

si·phon[1], syphon /'saɪfən/ n 1 a tube bent so that a liquid is drawn upwards and then downwards through it to a lower level 2 a kind of bottle for holding SODA WATER

siphon[2], syphon v [T off, out] to take away by a SIPHON[1] (1): to siphon (out) gasoline from a TANK (1)

sir /sər; strong sɜr/ n (a respectful or formal way to address a man): Thank you, sir.|"Can we go home now, sir?" asked the schoolchildren.

Sir n 1 [A] (a title used before the name of a KNIGHT[1] (1,2) or BARONET): Sir Harold Wilson|Sir Harold 2 (used at the beginning of a formal letter): Dear Sir, ... –compare MADAM

sire /saɪər/ v sired, siring [T] (esp. of a horse) to be the father of: This horse has sired several race winners. –**sire** n

si·ren /'saɪrən/ n 1 an apparatus for making a loud warning sound, used on ships, police cars, etc. **2** a dangerous beautiful woman

sir·loin /'sɜːlɔɪn/ also **sirloin steak–** /,·· '·/ *n* [C;U] (a piece of) meat from cattle (BEEF) cut from the best part of the lower back

sis·sy /'sɪsiʸ/ *n, adj* **-sies** *infml* **1** (a boy who looks or acts) like a girl **2** a cowardly person

sis·ter /'sɪstər/ *n* [C] a female relative with the same parents: *Joan and Mary are sisters.|Joan is Mary's sister.* –see illustration on page 247 **2** [A] (of women or things considered female) in the same group; fellow: *a sister ship|sister societies in various cities* **3** [A;C] (a title for) a woman member of a religious group, esp. a NUN: *Sister Mary Grace|a Christian sister* –compare BROTHER –**sisterly** *adj*

sis·ter·hood /'sɪstər,hʊd/ *n* **1** [U] a sisterly relationship between women **2** [C] a society of women leading a religious life –compare BROTHERHOOD

sister-in-law /'·· · ,·/ *n* **sisters-in-law 1** the sister of one's husband or wife **2** the wife of one's brother **3** the wife of the brother of one's husband or wife –see illustration on page 247 –compare BROTHER-IN-LAW

sit /sɪt/ *v* **sat** /sæt/, **sitting 1** [I] to rest in a position with the upper body upright and supported at the bottom of the back, e.g. on a chair or other seat: *He sat at his desk working.|sitting by the fire* –compare STAND¹ (1) **2** [I;T *down*] to (cause to) go into this position; (cause to) take a seat: *Sit down please, children, and we'll start our lesson.|She sat the baby (down) on the grass.* **3** [I] (of an animal or bird) to be in or go into a position with the tail end of the body resting on a surface **4** [I] to lie; rest; have a place: *books sitting unread on the shelf |a village sitting on the side of a hill* **5** [I] to have a position in an official body: *He sits on several committees.* **6** [I] (of an official body) to have a meeting: *The court sat until all the arguments had been heard.* **7 sit tight** *infml* to keep in the same position; not move: *If your car breaks down, sit tight and wait for the police.*

USAGE One **sits** *at* a table or desk; *on* a chair, a BENCH, a SOFA, a bicycle, or the ground; *in* a car, a garden, or an armchair.

sit around *v adv* [I] *infml* to do nothing, esp. while waiting or while others act

sit back *v adv* [I] to take no more active part; rest: *to sit back and enjoy the results of hard work*

sit in *v adv* [I] **1** [*for,as*] to take another's regular place, e.g. in a meeting or office job: *The president is ill, so the secretary is sitting in for her at the meeting.* **2** to take part in a SIT-IN

sit out *v adv* [T] **1** to remain seated during (a dance); not take part in **2** also **sit through–** to stay until the end of (a performance), esp. without enjoyment

sit up *v adv* **1** [I;T (=**sit** sbdy. **up**)] to (help

to) rise to a sitting position: *The loud noise made her sit up in bed.|She sat the old man up in bed.* **2** [I *for*] to stay up late; not go to bed: *Don't sit up (for me) if I'm late.*

si·tar /sɪ'tɑr/ *n* a Indian stringed musical instrument

site¹ /saɪt/ *n* **1** a place where something of special interest was or happened: *the site of the Battle of Waterloo* **2** a piece of ground for building on: *the site of a planned new town*

site² *v* **sited, siting** [T *usu. pass.*] to place on a SITE¹ (2); LOCATE (2): *a house beautifully sited to catch the sunshine*

sit-in /'· ·/ *n* an act of dissatisfaction and anger by a group of people who enter a public place, stop its usual business, and refuse to leave: *There's a sit-in at the local hospital because the government is trying to close it.* –see also SIT in

sit·ting¹ /'sɪtɪŋ/ *n* **1** a period of time spent seated in a chair: *I read the book in/at a single sitting.* **2** a serving of a meal for a number of people at one time: *two sittings for dinner, one at seven and one at eight* **3** a meeting of an official body; SESSION

sitting² *adj* [A] that now has a seat on an official body, such as Congress: *The sitting member will be hard to defeat in the election.*

sitting room /'·· ,·/ *n* esp. BrE for LIVING ROOM

sit·u·at·ed /'sɪtʃuʷ,eʸtɪd/ *adj* [F] in a particular place; LOCATED (2)

sit·u·a·tion /,sɪtʃuʷ'eʸʃən/ *n* **1** a position or condition at the moment; state of affairs: *I'm in a difficult situation.* **2** esp. BrE fml a job: *the "Situations Wanted" advertisements in the newspaper*

situation com·e·dy /,··,·· '··/ also **sitcom** /'sɪtkam/– *n* [C;U] a (form of) humorous television show typically having a number of standard characters who appear in different stories each week

six /sɪks/ *determiner,n,pron* (the number) 6 –**sixth** *determiner,n,pron,adv*

six-pack /'· ·/ *n* esp. AmE a set of 6 bottles or cans of a drink, usu. beer, sold in a paper or plastic case for carrying

six·pence /'sɪkspəns/ *n* [C;U] (in Britain until 1971) (a coin worth) the sum of six pennies

six·teen /,sɪk'stiʸn◄/ *determiner,n,pron* (the number) 16 –**sixteenth** *determiner,n,pron, adv*

sixth sense /,· '·/ *n* [S] an ability to see or know that does not come from the five senses; INTUITION

six·ty /'sɪkstiʸ/ *determiner,n,pron* **-ties** (the number) 60 –**sixtieth** /'sɪkstiʸɪθ/ *determiner, n,pron,adv*

siz·a·ble, sizeable /'saɪzəbəl/ *adj* fairly large; CONSIDERABLE: *a sizeable income*

size /saɪz/ *n* **1** [C;U] (a degree of) bigness or smallness: *What's the size of your yard? |rocks of all sizes* **2** [U] bigness: *The company is able to keep its prices down simply because of its size.* **3** [C] any of a set of measures in which objects such as clothes are made: *I take a size 8 shoe.|What size bottle would you like? The small size is 50 cents and* *the large size is 95 cents.* **4 -sized** also **-size–** of a certain size or number: *medium-sized|a good-sized* (=large) *crowd*

size sbdy./sthg.↔ **up** *v adv* **sized, sizing** [T] to form an opinion about; get an idea of: *He sized up his opponent.*

siz·zle /'sɪzəl/ *v* **-zled, -zling** [I] to make a sound as of food cooking in hot fat: *meat sizzling in the pan*

skate¹ /skeʸt/ *n* **1** → ICE SKATE **2** → ROLLER SKATE

skate² *v* **skated, skating** [I] to move on SKATES: *to skate across the lake|to go skating* –**skater** *n*

   skate over/around sthg. *v prep* [T] to avoid treating seriously; GLOSS OVER

skate³ *n* **skate** *or* **skates** [C;U] a large flat sea fish

skate·board /'skeʸtbɔrd, -boʷrd/ *n* a short board with two small wheels at each end for standing on and riding

skein /skeʸn/ *n* [*of*] a loosely wound length of thread or YARN

skel·e·ton /'skɛlətn/ *n* **1** [C] the framework of bones in a human or animal body **2** [C] something forming a framework: *the steel skeleton of a tall building* **3** [A] enough to keep an operation going, and no more: *During the holiday, the Long Island Railroad is providing only a skeleton service with five trains a day.*

skep·tic *AmE*‖**sceptic** *BrE* /'skɛptɪk/ *n* a SKEPTICAL person, esp. about the claims of a religion

skep·ti·cal *AmE*‖**sceptical** *BrE* /'skɛptɪkəl/ *adj* [(of, about)] unwilling (habitually) to believe a claim or promise; doubting; distrustful: *I'm skeptical of/about our getting there on time.* –**skeptically** *adv* –**skepticism** /'skɛptə,sɪzəm/ *n* [U]

sketch¹ /skɛtʃ/ *n* **1** a rough drawing: *Rembrandt's sketches for his paintings* **2** a short description in words: *The speaker gave us a sketch of life in the 1890s.* **3** a short informal piece of acting

sketch² *v* **1** [I;T] to draw SKETCHES¹ (1) or make a sketch of **2** [T *in, out*] to describe roughly with few details: *to sketch in/out the main points of our plan*

sketch·y /'skɛtʃiʸ/ *adj* **-ier, -iest** not thorough or complete; without details; rough: *a sketchy knowledge of history* –**sketchily** *adv* –**sketchiness** *n* [U]

skew·er¹ /'skyuʷər/ *n* a long wooden or metal pin for holding pieces of meat together while cooking

skewer² *v* [T] to fasten or make a hole through, esp. with a SKEWER¹: *Skewer the chicken before cooking.*

ski¹ /skiʸ/ *n* **skis** either of a pair of long thin narrow pieces of wood, plastic, or metal, fastened to a boot and used for traveling on snow

ski² *v* **skied, skiing** [I] to go on SKIS: *to go skiing|to ski down a hill|learning to ski* –see also WATER SKIING –**skier** *n*

skid¹ /skɪd/ *v* **-dd-** [I] (of a vehicle or a wheel) to slip sideways out of control

skid² *n* an act or path of SKIDDing: *The car*

went into a skid|skid marks on the road

skiff /skɪf/ *n* a small light boat for rowing or sailing by one person

skill /skɪl/ *n* [C;U] practical knowledge and power; (an) ability to do something (well): *a pilot of great skill* |*Reading and writing are different skills.* –see GENIUS (USAGE)

skilled /skɪld/ *adj* [*in*] having or needing skill: *a skilled job/electrician* –opposite **unskilled**

skil·let /'skɪlɪt/ *n AmE* for FRYING PAN –see illustration on page 379

skim /skɪm/ *v* **-mm-** **1** [T *off*] to remove (floating fat or solids) from the surface of a liquid: *to skim (off) the cream from the milk*|(fig.) *The politicians were skimming off money from several unlawful businesses.* **2** [I;T *through*] to read quickly to get the main ideas; SCAN¹ (2) **3** [I; T] to (cause to) move swiftly over (a surface): *to skim stones over a lake|birds skimming the waves*

skimp /skɪmp/ *v* [I;T *on*] to spend, or use less (of) than is really needed: *to skimp on food*

skimp·y /'skɪmpiʸ/ *adj* **-ier, -iest** not being enough; almost too small: *a skimpy meal/dress* –**skimpily** *adv* –**skimpiness** *n* [U]

skin¹ /skɪn/ *n* **1** [U] the natural outer covering of an animal or human body, from which hair may grow: *a skin disease|Babies have soft skin.* **2** [C;U] this part of an animal body used as leather, fur, etc.: *a sheepskin coat* **3** [C] a natural outer covering of some fruits and vegetables; PEEL: *banana skins* **4** [C;U] the solid surface that forms over a liquid, when it gets cool: *Paint in a can forms a skin when the lid is left off.* **5** **by the skin of one's teeth** *infml* narrowly; only just: *We caught the train by the skin of our teeth.* **6** **get under someone's skin** *infml* to annoy or excite someone deeply **7** **-skinned** having a certain type or color of skin: *pale-skinned| smooth-skinned* –see also THICK-SKINNED

skin² *v* **-nn-** [T] to remove the skin from: *to skin a deer/an onion*

skin-deep /ˌ· '·◄/ *adj* not deep or lasting: *Their differences of opinion are only skin-deep.*

skin-dive /'· ·/ *v* **-dived, -diving** [I] to swim under water without heavy breathing apparatus or a protective suit: *to go skin-diving* –**skin diver** *n* –compare FROGMAN –**skin diving** *n* [U]

skin flick /'· ·/ *n AmE* a movie showing a lot of sex

skin·flint /'skɪn,flɪnt/ *n derog* a person who is not generous; MISER

skin·ny /'skɪniʸ/ *adj* **-nier, -niest** *derog* thin; without much flesh –see THIN (USAGE)

skin-tight /ˌ· '·◄/ *adj* (of clothes) fitting tightly against the body

skip¹ /skɪp/ *v* **-pp-** **1** [I] to move in a light dancing way, with quick steps and jumps: *The little boy skipped along at his mother's side.* **2** [I] to move in no fixed order: *The speaker kept skipping from one subject to another.* **3** [I;T] to pass over or leave out: *to skip (over) the uninteresting parts of a book|to skip a meeting/a meal* **4** [I] to jump over a rope passed repeatedly beneath one's feet, as a game

skip² *n* a light quick stepping and jumping movement

skip·per /'skɪpər/ *n infml* a captain of a ship, sports team, etc. **–skipper** *v* [T]: *Who's going to skipper the boat this year?*

skir·mish¹ /'skɜrmɪʃ/ *n* **1** a fight between small groups of soldiers, ships, etc. **2** a slight exchange of arguments between opponents

skirmish² *v* [I *with*] to fight in a SKIRMISH¹

skirt¹ /skɜrt/ *n* **1** a woman's outer garment that fits around the waist and hangs down –see illustration on page 123 **2** a part of a coat or dress that hangs below the waist

skirt² *v* [T] to be or go around the outside of: *a road skirting the town*|(fig.) *Her speech skirted* (=avoided) *all the questions; it was very disappointing.*

skit /skɪt/ *n* [*on*] a short humorous acted-out scene, often copying and making fun of something

skulk /skʌlk/ *v* [I] to move about secretly, through fear or for some evil purpose: *robbers skulking in the corners, ready to jump out*

skull /skʌl/ *n* **1** the bone of the head **2** **skull and crossbones** a sign for death or danger, used esp. on PIRATES'¹ (1) flags in former times

skull·cap /'skʌlkæp/ *n* a simple closefitting cap for the top of the head

skunk /skʌŋk/ *n* a small black and white North American animal which gives out an unpleasant smelling liquid when attacked

sky /skaɪ/ *n* **skies 1** [C;U] the upper air; the space above the earth: *The sky turned dark as the storm came near.*|*We expect sunny skies for the next week.* –compare HEAVEN **2** **The sky's the limit** *infml* There is no upper limit: *How much do you want to spend? The sky's the limit!*

sky blue /ˌ· '·◂/ *n* [U] the pleasant bright blue color of a clear sunny sky **–sky-blue** *adj*

sky-high /ˌ· '·◂/ *adv, adj infml* very high; to a very high level: *Prices have gone sky-high.*

sky·lark /'skaɪlɑrk/ *n* small bird (LARK) that sings as it flies up

sky·light /'skaɪlaɪt/ *n* a window in a roof

sky·line /'skaɪlaɪn/ *n* a shape or picture made by scenery (esp. tall city buildings) against the background of the sky

sky·rock·et /'skaɪˌrɑkɪt/ *v* [I] to go up suddenly and steeply: *The price of gasoline has skyrocketed.*

sky·scrap·er /'skaɪˌskreɪpər/ *n* a very tall city building –see illustration on page 673

slab /slæb/ *n* a thick flat piece of metal, stone, food, etc.: *a house built on a cement slab*|*a slab of cake*/*cheese*

slack¹ /slæk/ *adj* **1** (of a rope, wire, etc.) not pulled tight **2** not firm; weak; loose: *slack laws*/*control* **3** not busy or active: *Business is slack right now.* **4** not properly careful or

---

SPELLING NOTE

Words with the sound /s/, may be spelled **c-**, like **city**, or **ps-**, like **psychology**.

---

attentive: *You've been slack in your work recently.* **–slackly** *adv* **–slackness** *n* [U]

slack² *v* [I] **1** to be lazy; not work well or quickly enough: *You're always slacking!* **2** [*off, up*] to reduce (in) speed, effort, or tightness; SLACKEN: *He always slacks off towards the end of the day.* **–slacker** *n*

slack³ *n* [U] the part of a rope, wire, etc., that hangs loose: *Pull the rope tight to* **take up**/**in the slack.** (=make the rope tighter)

slack·en /'slækən/ *v* [I;T *off, up*] to make or become SLACK¹; reduce in activity, force, or tightness: *The train slackened speed.*|*Slacken (up) the tent ropes before it rains.* –compare TIGHTEN, LOOSEN

slacks /slæks/ *n* [P] pants, esp. of an informal kind –see PAIR (USAGE)

slag /slæg/ *n* [U] waste material left when metal is separated from its natural rock

slain /sleɪn/ *v past participle of* SLAY

slake /sleɪk/ *v* **slaked, slaking** [T] *fml* to satisfy (thirst) with a drink; QUENCH

slam¹ /slæm/ *v* **-mm-** **1** [I;T] to shut loudly and violently: *Please don't slam the door.*|*The door slammed (shut).* **2** [T] to push, move, etc., quickly and violently: *He slammed the papers down on the desk and angrily walked out.* **3** [T] (often used in newspapers) to attack with words: *"The Mayor slams Local Government Spending."*

slam² *n* [S] the act or loud noise of a door closing violently: *He shut the door with a slam.*

slan·der¹ /'slændər/ *n* [C;U] (the offense of making) an intentionally false spoken report, story, etc., which unfairly damages the good opinion held about a person by others –compare LIBEL

slander² *v* [T] to speak SLANDER against; harm by making a false statement **–slanderous** /'slændərəs/ *adj*

slang /slæŋ/ *n* [U] language that is not usu. acceptable in serious speech or writing; very informal words and expressions: *Slang often goes in and out of fashion quickly.*|*army slang*| "BROKE" *is a slang word for "having no money."*

slant¹ /slænt/ *v* **1** [I;T] to put or be at an angle; (cause to) SLOPE: *The roof slants upwards from left to right.* **2** [T] to express (facts, a report, etc.) in a way favorable to a particular opinion: *The report of the meeting was slanted to make it seem that an agreement was reached.*

slant² *n* **1** [S] a SLANTING direction or position: *a steep upward slant*|*a line drawn at*/*on a slant* **2** [C] a particular way of looking at or expressing (news or facts): *an interesting new slant on the presidential elections*

slap¹ /slæp/ *n* a quick blow with the flat part of the hand: *She gave him a slap on the cheek.*

slap² *v* **-pp-** [T] **1** to strike quickly with the flat part of the hand: *to slap someone on the face*/*on the cheek*/*on the back* **2** to place thickly, roughly, or carelessly: *to slap paint on a wall*

slap³ *adv* [*adv + prep*] *infml* directly; right; SMACK³: *The car ran slap into the store window.*

slap·dash /'slæpdæʃ/ adj careless and hurried: a slapdash piece of work

slap·stick /'slæp,stɪk/ n [U] humorous acting (COMEDY) that depends on fast action and simple jokes

slash¹ /slæʃ/ v 1 [I;T at] to cut with long sweeping violent strokes: to slash at the bushes with a stick|The car tires had been slashed. 2 [T] to reduce (an amount, price, etc.) steeply: "This week only; prices slashed!" (store advertisement)

slash² n 1 a long sweeping cut or blow 2 a straight cut making an opening in a garment

slat /slæt/ n a thin flat piece of wood, plastic, etc., esp. in furniture or BLINDS³ (2) −**slatted** adj

slate¹ /sleɪt/ n 1 [U] heavy rock easily split into flat thin pieces 2 [C] a small piece of this used for covering a roof 3 [C] an imaginary record of past mistakes, disagreements, etc.: Let's forget our quarrel and start again with a clean slate. 4 [C] AmE a list of people, esp. those of the same party, entered in an election

slate² v slated, slating 1 [T] to cover (a roof) with SLATES¹ (2) 2 [T (for); usu. pass.] AmE a to choose for a purpose or office: She's slated to be the next president of the company. b to expect or plan to happen: a meeting slated to take place/slated for next week

slaugh·ter¹ /'slɔtər/ n [U] 1 the killing of many people or animals, esp. cruelly or wrongly; MASSACRE 2 the killing of animals for meat

slaughter² v [T] 1 to kill (esp. many people) cruelly or wrongly; MASSACRE: people needlessly slaughtered 2 to kill (animals) for food; BUTCHER −see KILL (USAGE) 3 infml to defeat severely in a game

slaugh·ter·house /'slɔtər,haʊs/ n -houses /,haʊzɪz/ a building where animals are killed for meat

slave¹ /sleɪv/ n 1 a person owned in law by another; servant without personal freedom 2 [of, to] a person completely in the control of another person or thing: a slave to fashion/drink

slave² v slaved, slaving [I away] to work like a slave; work hard: I've been slaving away all weekend in the kitchen.

slave driv·er /'· ,··/ n infml a person who makes other people work very hard

slave la·bor AmE‖**slave labour** BrE /,· '··/ n [U] 1 work done by slaves 2 humor work done for little or no pay, or forced to be done

slav·er /'slævər, 'slɑ-, 'sleɪ-/ v [I] to let liquid (SALIVA) come out of the mouth; DROOL

slav·er·y /'sleɪvəriɪ/ n [U] 1 the system of having slaves 2 the condition of being a slave

Slav·ic /'slɑvɪk, 'slæ-/ also **Slavonic** /slə'vɑnɪk/− adj of or concerning the Eastern European people (**Slavs**), including Russians, Czechs, Poles, Yugoslavs, etc.

slav·ish /'sleɪvɪʃ/ adj 1 slavelike; showing complete dependence on others 2 copying or copied very closely from something else; not fresh or changed: a slavish translation −**slavishly** adv

slay /sleɪ/ v slew /sluw/, slain /sleɪn/, slaying

esp. AmE or lit to kill violently; murder −**slayer** n

slea·zy /'sliɪziɪ/ adj -zier, -ziest cheap, dirty, and poor-looking: a sleazy hotel in a poor part of town −**sleaziness** n [U]

sled¹ /slɛd/ n a small vehicle for sliding along snow used esp. in play and sport

sled² v -dd- 1 [I] to go down slopes on a SLED¹: to go sledding 2 [I;T] to travel or carry on a SLED¹

sledge /slɛdʒ/ n a vehicle for carrying heavy loads on snow or ice −compare SLED¹, SLEIGH

sledge·ham·mer /'slɛdʒ,hæmər/ n a large heavy hammer used to drive in posts, break stones, etc.

sleek /sliɪk/ adj 1 (esp. of hair or fur) smooth and shining, as from good health and care 2 (too) neat, fashionable, or stylish in appearance −**sleekness** n [U]

sleep¹ /sliɪp/ n [S;U] 1 (a period of) the natural resting state of unconsciousness of the body: I haven't had enough sleep lately.|You'll feel better after a good (night's) sleep. 2 **get to sleep** to succeed in sleeping: The children were so excited that they couldn't get to sleep. 3 **go to sleep** to begin to sleep; fall asleep 4 **put to sleep: a** euph to kill (a suffering animal) mercifully **b** infml to make (a person) unconscious, e.g. for an operation

sleep² v slept /slɛpt/, sleeping 1 [I] to rest in sleep: He likes to sleep for an hour in the afternoon.|I didn't sleep well last night 2 [T] to provide beds or sleeping-places for (a number of people): The back seat of the car folds down to sleep two.

sleep in v adv [I] 1 → SLEEP late 2 to sleep at one's place of work: a big house with two servants who slept in

sleep late v adv [I] to sleep longer than usual in the morning

sleep sthg. ↔ off v adv [T] v to get rid of the effect of something by sleeping: to sleep off a big dinner

sleep on sthg. v prep [T] to delay deciding on (a question) until the next day; spend a night considering: I'll sleep on it tonight and give you my answer tomorrow.

sleep through sthg. v prep [T] not to wake up during; be asleep and miss hearing, seeing, etc.: I slept through the movie.

sleep together v adv [I] euph (of two people) to have sex

sleep with sbdy. v prep [T] euph to have sex with

sleep·er /'sliɪpər/ n 1 a person sleeping: a heavy sleeper (=difficult to wake up) 2 a train with beds 3 AmE infml something (e.g. a book, play, movie, etc.) that has a delayed or unexpected success

sleeping bag /'·· ,·/ n a large warm bag for sleeping in, e.g. when camping

sleeping pill /'·· ,·/ also **sleeping tablet** /'·· ,··/− n a pill which helps a person to sleep

sleep·less /'sliɪplɪs/ adj 1 not providing sleep: a sleepless night 2 esp. lit not able to sleep: He lay sleepless on his bed. −**sleeplessness** n [U]

sleep·walk·er /'sliɪp,wɔkər/ n a person who

walks around while asleep –**sleepwalking** *n* [U] –**sleepwalk** *v* [I]

sleep·y /'sliʸpiʸ/ *adj* -**ier**, -**iest** **1** tired and ready for sleep **2** quiet; inactive or slow-moving: *a sleepy country town* –**sleepily** *adv* –**sleepiness** *n* [U]

sleet[1] /sliʸt/ *n* [U] partly frozen rain –see WEATHER (USAGE) –**sleety** *adj* -**ier**, -**iest**

sleet[2] *v* [*it* + I] (of SLEET) to fall

sleeve /sliʸv/ *n* **1** a part of a garment for covering an arm: *a dress with short/long sleeves* **2** a stiff envelope for keeping a RECORD[2] (4) in **3 have/keep something up one's sleeve** to keep something secret for use at the right time in the future **4 wear one's heart on one's sleeve** to be in the habit of showing one's feelings to others **5** -**sleeved** having sleeves of a certain length or shape: *a short-sleeved shirt* –**sleeveless** /'sliʸvlɪs/ *adj*

sleigh /sleyʸ/ *n* a vehicle which slides along snow and is pulled by a horse – compare SLED[1], SLEDGE

sleight of hand /ˌslaɪt əv 'hænd/ *n* [U] skill and quickness of the hands in doing tricks: *to make a coin disappear by sleight of hand*

slen·der /'slɛndər/ *n* **1** delicately or gracefully thin; SLIM: *a slender woman/tree* –see THIN (USAGE) **2** slight; hardly enough: *only the slenderest chance of success* –**slenderness** *n* [U]

slen·der·ize ‖also -**ise** *BrE* /'slɛndəˌraɪz/ -**ized**, -**izing** *v* [I;T] *AmE* to make (oneself) thinner by eating less, playing sports, etc.

slept /slɛpt/ *v* past tense & participle of SLEEP

sleuth /sluʷθ/ *n infml* for DETECTIVE

slew[1] /sluʷ/ *v* past tense of SLAY

slew[2] *n* [(*of*) *usu. sing.*] *infml esp. AmE* a large number; a lot: *a whole slew of people*

slice[1] /slaɪs/ *n* **1** [*of*] a thin flat piece cut from something: *a slice of bread|Cut the cake into slices.*|(fig.) *The workers are hoping for a slice* (=a share) *of the company's profits.* **2** a kitchen tool for lifting and serving pieces of food **3** (in sports like GOLF and tennis) a shot which makes the ball move away from a straight course **4 a slice of life** a representation or experience of life as it really is: *a book to amuse you, not to give you a slice of life*

slice[2] *v* **sliced**, **slicing** **1** [T *up*] to cut into SLICES[1] (1): *to slice up a cake|A loaf of sliced bread, please.* **2** [I;T *into*] to cut with a knife: *He sliced (into) his fingers by accident when cutting vegetables.* **3** [I;T] to hit (a ball) with a SLICE[1] (3) **4 any way you slice it** *AmE infml* however you consider it

slick[1] /slɪk/ *adj* **1** clever or effective, but often not honest: *a slick job of selling* **2** spoken too easily to be really true: *slick excuses* –**slickly** *adv* –**slickness** *n* [U]

slick[2] *n* → OIL SLICK

slick sthg.↔ **back/down** *v adv* [T] to make (esp. hair) flat and shiny with water, oil, etc.

slide[1] /slaɪd/ *v* **slid** /slɪd/, **sliding** **1** [I;T] to

SPELLING NOTE

Words with the sound /s/, may be spelled **c-**, like **city**, or **ps-**, like **psychology**.

(cause to) go smoothly over a surface: *He slid along the ice.*|*He slid his glass across the table.* **2** [I] to go silently and unnoticed; slip: *She slid out of the room when no one was looking.* **3 let something slide** *infml* to pay no attention to something, esp. though laziness

slide[2] *n* **1** a slipping movement over a surface: *The car went into a slide on the ice.* **2** a track or apparatus for sliding down: *a children's playground slide* **3** a fall; downward turn: *a rockslide* (=a sudden fall of rocks down a hill)|*to stop the slide in living standards* **4** a piece of film in a frame for passing light through to show a picture: *They showed slides of their vacation.*|*a slide show* **5** a small glass plate to put an object on for seeing under a microscope

sliding scale /ˌ·· '·/ *n* a system of pay, taxes, etc., calculated by rates which may vary according to changing conditions

slight[1] /slaɪt/ *adj* **1** not great; not considerable: *a slight pain/improvement* **2** not strong-looking; thin and delicate: *a slight old lady* **3 in the slightest** (only used in NEGATIVES[2], questions, etc.) at all: *"Do you mind if I open the window?" "Not in the slightest, please do."* –**slightness** *n* [U]

slight[2] *v* [T] to treat without respect, or as if unimportant –**slightingly** *adv*

slight[3] *n* a SLIGHTing act; INSULT: *She took it as a slight when nobody noticed her..*

slight·ly /'slaɪtliʸ/ *adv* **1** to a small degree; a little: *slightly drunk* **2** in a SLIGHT[1] (2) way: *a slightly-built framework*

slim /slɪm/ *adj* -**mm**- **1** (esp. of people) attractively thin; not fat –see THIN (USAGE) **2** (of hope, probability, etc.) poor; slight: *Our chances of winning are slim.* –**slimness** *n* [U]

slim down *v* -**mm**- [I] to make oneself SLIM[1] (1); get thinner: *I don't want any cake: I'm trying to slim down.*

slime /slaɪm/ *n* [U] nasty, bad-smelling mud or sticky liquid

slim·y /'slaɪmiʸ/ *adj* -**ier**, -**iest** **1** like, being, or covered with SLIME; unpleasantly slippery **2** insincerely humble: *a slimy manner* –**sliminess** *n* [U]

sling[1] /slɪŋ/ *v* **slung** /slʌŋ/, **slinging** [T] **1** to throw, esp. roughly or with effort: *He slung his coat over his shoulder.* **2** to move or hang with a rope, etc.: *The line of flags was slung up between two trees.*

sling[2] *n* **1** a piece of cloth for hanging from the neck to support a damaged arm or hand –see illustration on page 201 **2** an apparatus of ropes, etc., for lifting heavy objects **3** a length of cord with a piece of leather in the middle, for throwing stones

sling·shot /'slɪŋʃɑt/ *n AmE* a small Y-shaped stick with a rubber band fastened between the forks, used by children to shoot small stones at objects

slink /slɪŋk/ *v* **slunk** /slʌŋk/, **slinking** [I] to move quietly and secretly, as if ashamed: *to slink away into the night*

slip[1] /slɪp/ *v* -**pp**- **1** [I] to slide out of place or fall by sliding: *The old lady slipped and fell on the ice.*|*The hammer slipped and hit my* *fingers instead of the nail.* **2** [I;T] to move smoothly, secretly, or unnoticed: *She slipped into/out of the room when no one was looking.|As the years slipped by/past, I thought less about her.* **3** [I;T] to put on or take off (a garment): *Slip into/Slip on some old clothes, and come and help me in the garden.* **4** [I] to get worse or lower: *He has slipped in my opinion since I found out more about him.|Standards are slipping in this hotel.* **5** [T] to give secretly: *She slipped the waiter $5 to get a good table.* **6** let slip: **a** to fail to take (a chance, offer, etc.) **b** to say without intending **7** slip a disc to get a SLIP-PED DISC **8** slip one's mind to be forgotten or unnoticed: *I'm sorry I forgot your birthday; it completely slipped my mind.* **9** slip something over on someone *AmE infml* to trick someone

slip up *v adv* [I] to make a slight mistake: *The secretary slipped up and the letter was never sent.* –see also SLIP-UP

slip² *n* **1** an act of slipping or sliding **2** a usu. slight mistake: *"Too" was a slip of the pen: I meant to write "to".* –see ERROR (USAGE) **3** a woman's undergarment like a short dress not covering the arms or neck **4** → SLIPWAY **5** give someone the slip *infml* to escape from someone

slip³ *n* **1** a small piece of paper: *a slip marking his place in the book* **2** slip of a boy/girl *becoming rare* a small thin boy or girl

slip·knot /ˈslɪpnɒt/ *n* a knot that can be tightened around something by pulling one of its ends

slipped disc /ˌ· ˈ·/ *n* [S] a painful displacement of one of the connecting parts in the human back

slip·per /ˈslɪpər/ *n* a light shoe with the top made of soft material, usu. worn indoors: *a pair of slippers|dancing slippers* –see illustration on page 55

slip·per·y /ˈslɪpəriʸ/ *adj* **-ier, -iest** **1** difficult to hold or to stand on, drive on, etc., without slipping: *Drive carefully; the roads are wet and slippery.* **2** *infml* not to be trusted; SHIFTY –**slipperiness** *n* [U]

slip·shod /ˈslɪpʃɒd/ *adj* careless; not exact or thorough: *a slipshod piece of work*

slip-up /ˈ· ·/ *n* a slight mistake –see also SLIP¹ up

slip·way /ˈslɪpweʸ/ *n* also **slip**– a sloping track for moving ships into or out of water

slit¹ /slɪt/ *v* **slit, slitting** [T] to make a SLIT² in; make a cut along: *to slit an envelope (open) with a knife*

slit² *n* a narrow cut or opening

slith·er /ˈslɪðər/ *v* [I] **1** to move in a slipping or twisting way like a snake **2** to slide unsteadily: *She slithered across the ice.*

sliv·er /ˈslɪvər/ *n* [*of*] a small thin sharp piece cut or torn off: *a sliver of glass from the broken window*

slob /slɒb/ *n* *infml* a rude, lazy, or carelessly-dressed person

slob·ber /ˈslɒbər/ *v* **1** [I;T] to let (liquid) fall from the lips: *a dog slobbering at the sight of food* **2** [I (*over*)] to express fond feelings too openly and indelicately: *bad poetry, slobber-*

ing over the beauties of nature

slog /slɒg/ *v* **-gg-** [I] to do hard dull work: *to slog away at a job* –**slogger** *n*

slo·gan /ˈsloʷgən/ *n* a short phrase expressing a usu. political or advertising message –compare MOTTO

sloop /sluʷp/ *n* **1** a kind of small sailing ship **2** a small armed ship such as a CUTTER (1)

slop¹ /slɒp/ *v* **-pp-** **1** [T] to cause some of (a liquid) to go over the side of a container; SPILL¹ (1) **2** [I] (of a liquid) to do this: *Some of the soup slopped over the edge of the bowl.*

slop² *n* [U] *derog* tasteless liquid food

slope¹ /sloʷp/ *v* **sloped, sloping** [I] to lie in a sloping direction; be at an angle: *a sloping roof|The road slopes up/down slightly at this point.*

slope² *n* **1** a surface that slopes: *to climb a steep slope|a SKI slope* **2** a degree of sloping; a measure of an angle from a level direction: *a slope of 30 degrees*

slop·py /ˈslɒpiʸ/ *adj* **-pier, -piest** **1** (e.g. of clothes) loose, informal, and careless or dirty-looking **2** not careful or thorough enough: *a sloppy piece of writing* **3** silly in showing feelings –**sloppily** *adv* –**sloppiness** *n* [U]

slops /slɒps/ *n* [P] food waste, esp. for feeding to animals

slosh /slɒʃ/ *v* [I] **1** to go through water or mud: *sloshing along in our rubber boots* **2** (of liquid) to move around against the sides of a container

slot¹ /slɒt/ *n* **1** a long straight narrow opening, esp. in a machine or tool: *to put a coin in the slot* **2** *infml* a position in a list, system, etc.: *The 7 o'clock slot on the radio is usually filled with a news broadcast.*

slot² *v* **-tt-** [T] **1** to cut a SLOT¹ (1) in **2** [*in, into*] to put into a SLOT¹ (2); find a place for: *I'm going to try to slot in some time for reading on my vacation.*

sloth /sloʊθ, sloʷθ/ *n* **1** [U] *esp. lit* unwillingness to work; laziness **2** [C] a slow-moving animal of Central and South America

sloth·ful /ˈsloʊθfəl, ˈsloʷθ-/ *adj* *lit* unwilling to work or be active; lazy –**slothfully** *adv* –**slothfulness** *n* [U]

slot ma·chine /ˈ· ·ˌ·/ *n* *AmE* a machine with one long handle, into which people put money to try to win more money

slouch¹ /slaʊtʃ/ *n* **1** [S] a tired-looking round-shouldered way of standing or walking **2** [C] a lazy, useless person

slouch² *v* [I] to stand or walk with a SLOUCH¹: *a slouching figure*

slough sthg.↔**off** /slʌf/ *v adv* [T] (esp. of a snake) to throw off (dead outer skin): *(fig.) She sloughed off all her responsibilities.*

slov·en·ly /ˈslʌvənliʸ/ *adj* untidy; not clean or orderly: *slovenly people/work* –**slovenliness** *n* [U]

slow¹ /sloʷ/ *adj* [+*to-v*] not moving or acting quickly; having less than a usual or average speed: *slow music/poison|a slow train/walk|The government was slow to act on the committee's report.* (=took a long time) –compare FAST **2** not quick in understanding; dull in mind **3** [F or after *n*] (of a clock) showing a time that is earlier than the true time: *The clock is two minutes slow.* –opposite **fast** –**slowly** *adv* –**slowness** *n* [U]

slow² *adv* slowly

slow³ *v* [I;T *up, down*] to make or become slower: *The train slowed as it went around the curve.|Business slows up/down in summer.*

slow mo·tion /ˌ· '··/ *n* [U] action which takes place at a much slower speed than in real life, esp. as shown in movies

sludge /slʌdʒ/ *n* [U] **1** thick mud **2** dirty waste oil in an engine

slue /sluʷ/ *v* **slued, sluing** [I;T *around*] *AmE* to cause to turn or swing violently

slug¹ /slʌg/ *n* a small limbless creature, related to the SNAIL but with no shell

slug² *n* **1** a lump or piece of metal **2** *AmE* **a** a coin-shaped object unlawfully put into a machine in place of a coin **b** *infml* a bullet

slug³ *v* -**gg**- [T] *AmE infml* to strike with a heavy blow

slug·gish /'slʌgɪʃ/ *adj* slow-moving; not very active or quick: *a sluggish stream/feeling rather sluggish in the heat of the day* –**sluggishly** *adv* –**sluggishness** *n* [U]

sluice¹ /sluʷs/ *n* a passage for water with an opening (**sluice gate**) through which the flow can be controlled

sluice² *v* **sluiced, sluicing** [T *out, down*] to wash with floods of water: *to sluice out the cowshed*

slum¹ /slʌm/ *n* **1** [*often pl.*] an area of the city with poor living conditions and dirty unrepaired buildings **2** *infml* a very untidy place –**slummy** *adj* -**ier**, -**iest**

slum² *v* -**mm**- [I] *infml* to amuse oneself by visiting a place on a much lower social level

slum·ber /'slʌmbər/ *n,v* [C;U;I] *lit* (to be in) a state of sleep: *waking from her slumber(s)/slumbering peacefully*

slump¹ /slʌmp/ *v* [I] **1** to sink down; fall heavily or in a heap: *He slumped into his chair.* **2** to go down in number or strength: *Sales have slumped in the last month.*

slump² *n* **1** a time of seriously bad business conditions and high unemployment; DEPRESSION (4) –compare RECESSION **2** *esp. AmE* a lowering of activity, number, force, etc.: *Nothing interesting is happening, I'm in a slump.*

slung /slʌŋ/ *v past tense & participle of* SLING

slunk /slʌŋk/ *v past tense & participle of* SLINK

slur¹ /slɜr/ *v* -**rr**- [T] to pronounce (a sound in a word) unclearly

slur² *n* **1** [S] a SLURRING¹ way of speaking **2** [C] an unfair damaging remark: *a slur on the company's good name*

slurp /slɜrp/ *v* [I;T] *infml* to eat (soft food) or drink noisily: *children slurping their milk*

slush /slʌʃ/ *n* [U] **1** partly melted snow; **2** literature, movies, etc., concerned with silly love stories –**slushy** *adj* -**ier**, -**iest**

slut /slʌt/ *n derog* a woman who acts in a

SPELLING NOTE

Words with the sound /s/, may be spelled **c**-, like **city**, or **ps**-, like **psychology**.

sexually immodest or immoral way –**sluttish** *adj*

sly /slaɪ/ *adj* **slier** *or* **slyer**, **sliest** *or* **slyest 1** clever in deceiving; CRAFTY: *a sly old fox* **2 on the sly** secretly –**slyly** *adv* –**slyness** *n* [U]

smack¹ /smæk/ *v* [T] **1** to strike loudly, with the flat part of the hand: *The child was crying because his mother had smacked his legs.* **2** to open and close (one's lips) noisily **3** to put so as to make short loud sound: *She smacked the book angrily on the table.*

smack of sthg. *v prep* [T] to have a taste or suggestion of: *a plan that smacks of disloyalty*

smack² *n* (the sound of) a quick loud forceful blow: *If you don't stop making that noise, you'll get a smack!|The book hit the floor with a loud smack.*

smack³ *adv* [*adv + prep*] *infml* **1** with force: *to run smack into a wall* **2** *esp. AmE* **smack-dab** /ˌ· '·/ squarely; directly; right: *There it was, smack-dab in the middle of the room.*

smack⁴ *n* a small sailing boat used for fishing

small¹ /smɔl/ *adj* **1** not large; of less than average size, weight, importance, etc.: *a book written for small children|The girl is small for her age.|The Indian elephant is smaller than the African elephant.|You made one or two small mistakes, but otherwise your work was good.* –see Study Notes on page 550 **2** [A] doing only a limited amount of a business or activity: *to be a small businessman* (=own a small business) **3** [A] very little; slight: *She had small hope of success.|You've been eating far too much;* **small wonder** *you're getting fat.* (=it's not surprising) –compare BIG –**smallness** *n* [U]

small² *adv* in a small manner: *He writes so small I can't read it.*

small change /ˌ· '·/ *n* [U] **1** money in coins of small value **2** (of a person or thing) not important

small-mind·ed /ˌ· '··◁/ *adj* having narrow selfish interests; unwilling to listen to others –compare OPEN-MINDED, BROADMINDED –**small-mindedness** *n* [U]

small·pox /'smɔlpɑks/ *n* [U] a serious infectious disease until recent times, causing spots which left marks on the skin

small talk /'· ·/ *n* [U] light conversation on unimportant subjects

small-time /ˌ· '·◁/ *adj* limited in activity, ability, etc.; unimportant: *a small-time criminal*

smart¹ /smɑrt/ *adj* **1** *esp. AmE* good or quick in thinking; intelligent **2** quick and forceful: *a smart blow on the head* **3** used by, concerning, etc., very fashionable people: *a smart restaurant* **4 play it smart** *esp. AmE* to act wisely –**smartly** *adv* –**smartness** *n* [U]

smart² *v* [I] **1** to cause or feel a painful stinging sensation, usu. not lasting long: *His knee was smarting.* **2** [*over, under*] to be hurt in one's feelings: *She was still smarting over his unkind words.*

smart al·eck /'smɑrt ˌælɪk/ *n infml* a person who annoys others by claiming to know everything and trying to sound clever

smart·en up /'smɑrtn/ *v adv* [I;T (=**smarten** sbdy./sthg.↔ **up**)] **1** to make or become good-looking, neat, or stylish: *Some new paint will smarten up the house.* **2** *infml* to become smart: *He better smarten up or he'll loose his job.*

smash¹ /smæʃ/ *v* [I;T] **1** [*up*] to (cause to) break into pieces violently: *to smash a window*|*The dish smashed on the floor.*|*to smash (up) one's car* **2** to go, drive, or hit forcefully against something solid; crash: *He smashed his foot through the door.*|*They smashed their way out of the building.*

smash² *n* **1** a powerful blow: *a smash that sent his opponent to the floor* **2** (the noise of) a violent breaking: *the smash of glasses breaking* **3** also **smash hit** /ˌ· '·/– a very successful new play, movie, etc.; HIT² (3): *a new musical smash* **4** a hard downward attacking shot, esp. in tennis **5** → SMASH-UP

smash-up /'· ·/ also **smash–** *n* a road or railroad accident: *a five-car smash-up*

smat·ter·ing /'smætərɪŋ/ *n* [S *of*] a small amount of knowledge: *I know a smattering of Italian.*

smear¹ /smɪər/ *n* **1** a mark made by SMEARing² **2** a charge made intentionally to try to turn public feelings against someone: *a* **smear campaign** *against the leader of the opposition party*

smear² *v* **1** [T] to cause (a sticky or oily material) to spread across: *Prepare the dish by smearing butter on it*|*by smearing it with butter.* **2** [I] (of such material) to do this: *Be careful; the paint may smear.*

smell¹ /smɛl/ *v* **smelled** *or* **smelt** /smɛlt/, **smelling** **1** [I] to have or use the sense of the nose: *an old dog who can hardly smell any longer* **2** [T +*v-ing* (*that*)] to notice, examine, or recognize by this sense: *to smell cooking*|*I could smell that the milk wasn't fresh.*|*He can always smell when rain is coming.*|(fig.) *I could smell trouble.* **3** [I *of*, *like*] to have a particular smell: *a sweet-smelling flower*|*This book smells old.* **4** [I *of*] to have an unpleasant smell; STINK: *The meat had started to smell.*

    smell sbdy./sthg.↔**out** *v adv* [T] to find (as if by smelling): *to smell out a news story*

smell² *n* **1** [U] the power of using the nose: *dogs that track by smell alone* **2** [C] a quality that has an effect on the nose: *Some flowers have strong smells.*|*There's a nice smell of coffee in the restaurant.* **3** [S] an act of SMELLing¹ (2) something: *Have a smell of this wine: is it all right?*

smell·y /'smɛliʸ/ *adj* **-ier**, **-iest** unpleasant-smelling –**smelliness** *n* [U]

smelt /smɛlt/ *v* [T] to melt (metal-containing earth (ORE)) so as to separate and remove the metal

smile¹ /smaɪl/ *n* an expression of the face with the mouth turned up at the ends and the eyes bright, that usu. expresses amusement, happiness, approval, etc.

smile² *v* **smiled**, **smiling** **1** [I] to have or make a smile: *The children were smiling happily as they ran out of the school.*|*He smiled at me.* **2** [T] to express with a smile: *She smiled a*

greeting. **3** [I *on*] to act or look favorably: *The weather smiled on us: it was a fine day.* –**smilingly** *adv*

smirk /smɜrk/ *v,n* [C;I] (to make) a silly satisfied smile

smite /smaɪt/ *v* **smote** /smoʷt/, **smitten** /'smɪtn/, **smiting** [T] **1** *old use & lit* to strike hard: *He smote his enemy with his sword.* **2** [*usu. pass.*] to have a powerful sudden effect on: *smitten by*/*with a feeling of sadness*

smith /smɪθ/ *n* **1** a worker in metal: *a blacksmith*|*a goldsmith* **2** a maker: *a gunsmith*

smith·er·eens /ˌsmɪðəˈriʸnz/ *n* (**in**)**to smithereens** *infml* into very small pieces: *The glass was smashed to smithereens.*

smock /smɑk/ *n* a loose shirtlike garment usu. worn over one's other clothes while working

smog /smɑg, smɔg/ *n* [U] the unhealthy mixture of FOG¹, smoke, and vehicle waste gases in the air in some large cities

smoke¹ /smoʷk/ *n* **1** [U] gas that can be seen in the air and is usu. given off by burning: *smoke from a chimney*|*the smell of tobacco smoke* **2** [C] **a** an act of smoking: *a short smoke on his pipe* **b** *infml* something (esp. a cigarette) for smoking **3 go up in smoke** to end without results, esp. suddenly –**smokeless** *adj*

smoke² *v* **smoked**, **smoking** **1** [I;T] to breathe in smoke from (esp. tobacco, as in cigarettes): *Do you mind if I smoke?*|*She smokes 20 cigarettes a day.* **2** [I] to send out smoke: *smoking chimneys* **3** [T] to preserve and give a special taste to (meat, fish, etc.) by hanging it in smoke **4** [T] to darken with smoke, esp. by allowing smoke to settle on a surface: *smoked glass*

    smoke sbdy./sthg.↔**out** *v adv* [T] to fill a place with smoke to force (a person, animal, etc.) to come out from hiding

smok·er /'smoʷkər/ *n* **1** a person who smokes **2** a railroad car where smoking is allowed –opposite **non-smoker**

smoke screen /'· ·/ *n* **1** a cloud of smoke made to hide an activity from enemy sight **2** something which hides one's real intentions

smok·y /'smoʷkiʸ/ *adj* **-ier**, **-iest** **1** filled with or producing smoke: *a smoky fire*/*room* **2** with the taste or appearance of smoke: *a smoky mist*|*smoky-tasting fish* –**smokiness** *n* [U]

smol·der *AmE*‖**smoulder** *BrE* /'smoʷldər/ *v* [I] **1** to burn slowly without a flame **2** to have violent feelings that are kept from being expressed: *smoldering anger*

smooth¹ /smuʷð/ *adj* **1** having an even surface; not rough: *The sea looks calm and smooth.*|*a baby's smooth skin*|*a smooth road* **2** even in movement without sudden changes: *to bring a car to a smooth stop* **3** (of a liquid mixture) without lumps; evenly thick: *Beat the mixture until it's smooth.* **4** (of a taste) not bitter or sour; pleasant in the mouth: *a smooth pipe tobacco* **5** too pleasant or polite in manner: *I don't trust that salesman; he's too smooth.* –**smoothly** *adv* –**smoothness** *n* [U]

smooth² v [T] **1** [*out, down*] to make smooth: *to smooth out a tablecloth*|(fig.) *This agreement will smooth the way for peace.* **2** [*away*] to remove (roughness) from a surface: *a face cream that claims to smooth away lines*
smooth sthg.↔**over** v adv [T] to make (difficulties) seem unimportant: *to smooth over the bad feelings*

smote /smoᵂt/ v *past tense of* SMITE

smoth·er /'smʌðər/ v **1** [I;T] to die or kill from lack of air; SUFFOCATE: *a baby smothered in bed accidentally*|*to smother a fire*|(fig.) *They smothered all opposition.* **2** [T] to cover thickly: *cake smothered with*/*in cream*|(fig.) *She smothered Bruce with kisses.*

smudge¹ /smʌdʒ/ v **smudged, smudging** [I;T] to make or become dirty with a mark of rubbing: *He smudged the ink with his hand.*

smudge² n a dirty mark –**smudgy** adj **-ier, -iest**

smug /smʌg/ adj **-gg-** too pleased with oneself –**smugly** adv –**smugness** n [U]

smug·gle /'smʌgəl/ v **-gled, -gling** [T] to take (esp. goods) from one country to another illegally: *It's a serious crime to smuggle drugs into the U.S.* –**smuggler** /'smʌglər/ n –**smuggling** n [U]

smut /smʌt/ n **1** [C;U] (a small piece of) dirt or SOOT that makes dark marks **2** [U] morally offensive books, stories, etc.

smut·ty /'smʌtiʸ/ adj **-tier, -tiest** morally improper: *a smutty joke*/*book* –**smuttily** adv –**smuttiness** n [U]

snack /snæk/ n an amount of food smaller than a meal; something eaten informally between meals
snack bar /'· ·/ n an informal public eating place that serves SNACKs

snag¹ /snæg/ n **1** a hidden or unexpected difficulty **2** a pulled thread in cloth, esp. in a stocking

snag² v **-gg-** [T] **1** to catch on and cause a SNAG¹ (2): *I snagged my stockings on the chair.* **2** AmE infml to catch or get, esp. by a quick action: *She got snagged by the police while stealing the purse.*

snail /sneʸl/ n **1** a small animal (MOLLUSK) with a soft body, no limbs, and a hard shell on its back **2** snail's pace a very slow speed

snake¹ /sneʸk/ n a cold-blooded animal (REPTILE) with a long limbless body, a fork-shaped tongue, and often a poisonous bite

snake² v **snaked, snaking** [I;T] to move in a twisting way: *a train snaking (its way) through the mountains*

snake charm·er /'· ˌ··/ n a person who controls snakes, usu. by playing music, as a public performance

snap¹ /snæp/ v **-pp- 1** [I *at*] to (try to) close the jaws quickly: *The dog snapped at my ankles.* **2** [I;T] to (cause to) break suddenly off or in

---

SPELLING NOTE
Words with the sound /s/, may be spelled **c-**, like **city**, or **ps-**, like **psychology**.

---

two: *The branch snapped under all the snow.*|(fig.) *After waiting an hour, my patience snapped and I went home.* **3** [I;T] to move so as to cause a sound of SNAPping¹ (1,2): *The lid snapped shut.* **4** [I;T *at*] to say or speak quickly, usu. in an annoyed way: *"You're late!," she snapped.*|*I asked him the time and he just snapped at me.* **5** [T] infml to photograph; take a SNAPSHOT of **6 snap one's fingers** to make a noise by moving the second finger quickly along the thumb **7 snap out of it** infml to free oneself quickly from a bad state of mind
snap sthg.↔ **up** v adv [T] to take or buy quickly and eagerly: *to snap up a bargain* (=to buy goods at a cheap price)

snap² n **1** [C] an act or sound of SNAPping¹: *He called the waiter with a snap of his fingers.* **2** a small metal fastener for a garment, in which one part is pressed into the hollow space of another **3** [C] infml for SNAPSHOT **4 It's a snap.** (=something easy)

snap³ adj [A] done in haste and without warning: *a snap decision*

snap·py /'snæpiʸ/ adj **-pier, -piest 1** → LIVELY (1): *snappy conversation* **2 Make it snappy!** infml Hurry up!

snap·shot /'snæpʃɑt/ also **snap** infml– n an informal picture taken with a hand-held camera

snare¹ /snɛər/ n a trap for catching an animal, esp. by means of a rope

snare² v **snared, snaring** [T] to catch (as if) in a SNARE¹: *to snare a rabbit*

snarl¹ /snɑrl/ v [I] (of an animal) to make a low angry sound while showing the teeth: *a snarling dog*|(fig.) *The old man snarled angrily at the children.*

snarl² n an act or sound of SNARLing¹; angry GROWL

snarl³ v [T *up; usu. pass.*] to make confused or difficult; TANGLE: *Traffic was badly snarled (up) near the accident.*

snarl-up /'· ·/ n a confused state, esp of traffic

snatch¹ /snætʃ/ v [T] to get hold of hastily and forcefully: *The thief snatched her handbag and ran.* –**snatcher** n
snatch at sthg. v prep [T] to try to SNATCH; make every effort to get: *to snatch at a chance*

snatch² n **1** an act of SNATCHing¹ (at) something: *He made a brave snatch at victory but failed.* **2** a short and incomplete period of something: *to sleep in snatches*|*As I walked past the house, I heard a snatch of music.*

sneak¹ /sniʸk/ v [I;T] to go or take quietly and secretly: *to sneak past a guard*|*to sneak around to the back door*|*I sneaked a look at the plans that were lying on her desk.*
sneak up v adv [I *on*] to come quietly and secretly near: *Don't sneak up on*/*behind me like that!*

sneak² n a person who acts secretly and should not be trusted

sneak·er /'sniʸkər/ n AmE a cloth shoe with a rubber bottom, worn informally or for sports: *a pair of sneakers*

sneak·ing /'sniʸkɪŋ/ adj [A] **1** secret; not expressed, as if shameful: *a sneaking desire to* *eat a cake* **2** (of a feeling or belief) not proved but probably right: *a sneaking suspicion that the plan won't work*

sneak·y /'sniˠkiˠ/ *adj* **-ier, -iest** acting or done secretly and deceitfully –**sneakiness** *n* [U]

sneer¹ /sniər/ *v* [I] **1** to express proud dislike and disrespect by a kind of unpleasant one-sided smile **2** [*at*] to behave as if something is not worthy of serious notice: *Don't sneer at their religion.* –**sneeringly** *adv*

sneer² *n* a SNEERing look or remark

sneeze /sniˠz/ *v,n* **sneezed, sneezing** [C;I] (to produce) a sudden uncontrolled burst of air out of the nose and mouth: *The dust made him sneeze.|a loud sneeze*

snick·er /'snɪkər/ ‖also **snigger** *esp. BrE*– *v,n* [C;I *at*] (to make) a laugh in a low disrespectful way

snide /snaɪd/ *adj* amusing, but in a way that is intended to hurt the feelings; MEAN¹ (2): *a snide remark* –**snidely** *adv* –**snideness** *n* [U]

sniff¹ /snɪf/ *v* **1** [I *at*] to draw air into the nose with a sound, esp. in short repeated actions **2** [I;T *at*] to do this to discover a smell (in or on): *dogs sniffing (at) the ground*

  sniff at sthg. *v prep* [T] to refuse proudly: *You shouldn't sniff at such a good offer.*

sniff² *n* an act or sound of SNIFFing

snif·fle /'snɪfəl/ also **snuffle**– *v* **-fled, -fling** [I] to SNIFF repeatedly, as when one is crying or has a cold

snig·ger /'snɪgər/ *v,n* [C;I *at*] *esp. BrE* for SNICKER

snip¹ /snɪp/ *n* **1** [C] a short quick cut with scissors: *make a snip in the cloth* **2** *derog infml* a small or unimportant person

snip² *v* **-pp-** [T] to cut with scissors, esp. in short quick strokes: *to snip off the corner of a page|snip a hole in the paper*

snipe /snaɪp/ *v* **sniped, sniping** [I *at*] **1** to shoot from a hidden position at unprotected people **2** to attack in a nasty indirect way –**sniper** *n*

snip·pet /'snɪpɪt/ *n* [*of*] a small piece of something: *a snippet of poetry*

snip·py /'snɪpiˠ/ *adj* **-pier, -piest** *infml* quick and impolite: *a snippy answer*

snitch¹ /snɪtʃ/ *v infml* **1** [I] to steal usu. a small thing **2** [T *to, on*] *derog* to give information to the police, etc. against someone; INFORM

snitch² *n derog infml* one who SNITCHes¹ (2)

sniv·el /'snɪvəl/ *v* **-l-** *AmE‖***-ll-** *BrE* [I] to act or speak in a weak complaining way: *If you fail, don't come sniveling back to me.* –**sniveler** *n*

snob /snɒb/ *n* **1** a person who dislikes those he/she feels to be of lower social class, and admires people of a higher social class **2** a person who is too proud of having special knowledge in a subject: *a musical snob who likes only Mozart* –**snobbish** *adj* –**snobbishly** *adv* –**snobbishness** *n* [U]

snob·ber·y /'snɒbəriˠ/ *n* [U] the behavior of a SNOB

snook·er¹ /'snʊkər/ *n* [U] a game like BILLIARDS played on a table with 15 red balls and seven balls of other colors

snooker² *v* [T] *infml* to put into a difficult

position; trap or trick

snoop /snuˠp/ *v* [I] to look into, or concern oneself with other people's property or activities without permission: *I caught him snooping (around) in my office.* –**snoopy** *adj* **-ier, -iest** –**snoop** *n* –**snooper** *n*

snoot·y /'snuˠtiˠ/ *adj* **-ier, -iest** *infml* proudly rude; SUPERCILIOUS: *He's too snooty to be interested in his old friends now that he's rich.* –**snootily** *adv* –**snootiness** *n* [U]

snooze /snuˠz/ *v,n* **snoozed, snoozing** [I;S] *infml* (to have) a short sleep; DOZE

snore¹ /snɔr, snoˠr/ *v* **snored, snoring** [I] to breathe noisily through the nose and mouth while asleep –**snorer** *n*

snore² *n* a noisy way of breathing when asleep: *His snores woke her up.*

snor·kel /'snɔrkəl/ *n* an air tube that can rise above the surface of water, allowing a swimmer under water to breathe

snort /snɔrt/ *v* [I] to make a rough noise by blowing air down the nose, sometimes to express anger or impatience –**snort** *n*

snout /snaʊt/ *n* the long nose of any of various animals (such as pigs)

snow¹ /snoˠ/ *n* **1** [U] water frozen into small flat white bits (FLAKEs) that fall like rain in cold weather and cover the ground thickly **2** [C] a fall of this: *one of the heaviest snows this winter* –see WEATHER (USAGE)

snow² *v* **1** [*it* + I] (of snow) to fall: *Look! It's snowing.* **2** [T] *AmE infml* to persuade or win the respect of (someone) as by making oneself sound important: *I was really snowed by her smooth manners and polite talk.*

snow·ball¹ /'snoˠbɔl/ *n* a ball pressed together from snow, as thrown at each other by children

snowball² *v* [I] to grow bigger at a faster and faster rate: *The effect of rising prices has snowballed.*

snow·bound /'snoˠbaʊnd/ *adj* blocked or kept indoors by heavy snow

snow·drift /'snoˠ,drɪft/ *n* a deep bank of snow formed by the wind

snow·drop /'snoˠdrɒp/ *n* a small white European flower which appears in the early spring

snowed in /, ˈ ·/ *adj* **1** unable to travel because of snow: *We were snowed in* (=could not leave home) *for three days last winter.* **2** also **snowed up**– impossible for people to travel in or out because of snow: *The town was snowed in twice last year.*

snowed un·der /, · ˈ··/ *adj* having more work than one can easily deal with, esp. in a short time: *Don't even talk to me at the moment; I'm completely snowed under.*

snow·fall /'snoˠfɔl/ *n* **1** [C] a fall of snow **2** [S;U] the amount of snow that falls: *an average snowfall of five inches per year*

snow·flake /'snoˠfleˠk/ *n* a small flat bit of frozen water which falls as snow

snow·man /'snoˠmæn/ *n* **-men** /mɛn/ a figure of a man made out of snow, esp. by children

snow·plow *AmE‖***-plough** *BrE* /'snoˠplaʊ/ *n* an apparatus or vehicle for pushing snow off roads

snow·storm /'snoˠstɔrm/ *n* a very heavy fall

of snow, esp. blown by strong winds

snow-white /ˌ· ˈ·◄/ *adj* as white as snow; pure white

snow·y /ˈsnoʷiʸ/ *adj* **-ier, -iest 1** full of snow or snowing: *snowy weather* **2** pure white: *snowy (white) hair* **–snowiness** *n* [U]

snub¹ /snʌb/ *v* **-bb-** [T] to treat rudely, by paying no attention: *I greeted her as we passed in the street, but she just snubbed me.*

snub² *n* an act of snubbing

snub³ *adj* [A] (of a nose) short and flat at the end

snuff¹ /snʌf/ *n* [U] tobacco made into powder for breathing into the nose

snuff² *v* → SNUFF OUT

snuf·fle /ˈsnʌfəl/ *v,n* **-fled, -fling** [C;I] → SNIFFLE

snuff sthg.↔**out** *v adv* [T] to put out (a candle flame) by pressing

snug /snʌg/ *adj* **-gg- 1** warm and comfortable; cosy: *a snug little room with a warm fire|lying snug in bed* **2** (of clothes) fitting closely **–snugly** *adv* **–snugness** *n* [U]

snug·gle /ˈsnʌgəl/ *v* **-gled, -gling** [I *up, down*] to settle into a warm comfortable position; NESTLE: *Snuggle up to me and I'll keep you warm.*

so¹ /soʷ/ *adv* **1** to such a degree: *He was so fat that he couldn't get through the hole.|He held his hands a little way apart, and said "The fish was so long."|I'm so glad* (=very glad) *you could come!|You shouldn't worry so.|*(used like *as*, in NEGATIVE comparisons) *She doesn't run so fast as she used to.* –see AS (USAGE) **2** in this way; in that way: *First you turn on the engine, so.|She was washing her hair, and while she was so employed, she heard a noise.|It so happens that we have the same birthday.|He keeps all his papers just/exactly so.* (=neatly arranged) **3** (used in place of something stated already): *He hopes he'll win and I hope so too.|Are you married?* **If so,** (=if that is true) *give your wife's name.|"Is it true she's got a new job?" "So she says."|He's very young, but* **even so** (=even though that is true) *he ought to know better.|"Is it interesting?" "Yes,* **more so** (=more interesting) *than I expected."* **4** (followed by *be, have, do,* or a verb like *will, can,* or *should,* and then its subject) also: *I enjoyed the book and so did my wife.|I'd like another drink, and so would John.|"Ann can play the piano." "So can I!"* (compare *"Ann can't play the piano." "Nor can I."* (=I, also, can't play the piano)) **5** (followed by *there* or a pronoun subject and then *be, have, do,* or a verb like *will, can,* or *should*) indeed: *"There's a fly in your coffee." "So there is!"|"Look, your wife has just come in." "So she has!"* **6 and so on/forth** and other things of that kind: *pots, pans, dishes, and so on* **7 so as to** in order to: *The test questions are kept secret, so as to prevent cheating.|He did it so*

as not to be caught. **8 So long!** *infml* Goodbye!

so² *conj* **1** with the result that; therefore: *I had broken my glasses, so I couldn't see what was happening.|I had a headache, so I went to bed.* **2** [*that*] with the purpose that: *I packed him a little food so/so that he wouldn't be hungry.* –see Study Notes on page 144 **3 So what?** *infml* Why should I care?

so³ *adj* [F] true: *You know very well that it just isn't so.|Is that really so?*

soak¹ /soʷk/ *v* [I;T] **1** [*in*] to (cause to) remain in a liquid: *Leave the dirty clothes to soak.* **2** [*in, into, through*] (of a liquid) to enter (a solid) through its surface: *The ink had soaked through the thin paper.*

soak sthg.↔**up** *v adv* [T] to draw in (a liquid) through a surface: *His handkerchief soaked up the blood.*

soak² *n* an act or state of SOAKING (1): *Give the clothes a good soak before you wash them.*

soaked /soʷkt/ *adj* [F] thoroughly wet, e.g. from rain: *You're soaked! Take off those wet clothes!*

soak·ing /ˈsoʷkɪŋ/ *adv,adj* very (wet): *My coat's soaking/soaking wet.*

so-and-so /ˈ· · ˌ·/ *n* **so-and-sos 1** [U] someone or something; a certain one not named: *a list of people, with so-and-so saying he'll give $5, so-and-so $2, etc.* **2** [C] *euph* (used instead of a stronger word) a rude, wicked, etc., person: *That so-and-so who repaired my watch charged me $20.*

soap¹ /soʷp/ *n* [U] a product made from fat and used with water for washing: *a bar/cake of soap|soap powder* –compare DETERGENT **–soapy** *adj* **-ier, -iest**: *soapy water|a cheese with a soapy taste*

soap² *v* [T] to rub soap on or over: *I was just soaping myself when the telephone rang.*

soap op·er·a /ˈ· ˌ·· ·/ *n* a continuing television or radio story (SERIAL) about the lives and problems of its imaginary characters

soar /sɔr,soʷr/ *v* [I] **1** (*lit*) to fly; go fast or high on wings: *birds soaring over the hills* **2** to rise far or fast: *The temperature soared to 35°C.|soaring prices|The cliffs soar 500 feet into the air.*

sob /sɑb/ *v* **-bb-** [I] to breathe while weeping, in sudden short bursts: *a little boy sobbing in the corner|She sobbed herself to sleep.* (=wept until she fell asleep) **–sob** *n*: *"Don't be so cruel to me!" she said with a sob.*

so·ber¹ /ˈsoʷbər/ *adj* **1** in control of oneself; not drunk **2** thoughtful, serious, or solemn **–soberly** *adv* **–sobriety** /səˈbraɪəṭiʸ, soʷ-/ *n* [U]

sober² *v* [I;T] to make or become serious or thoughtful: *Her illness had a sobering effect on her.*

sober up *v adv* [I;T (=**sober** sbdy. **up**)] to make or become SOBER¹ (1); get or be no longer drunk: *I hope this coffee sobers him up.*

so-called /ˌ· ˈ·◄/ *adj* [A] improperly or falsely named: *so-called Christians who show no love to anyone*

soc·cer /ˈsɑkər/ also **football, Association**

Football *BrE– n* [U] a football game between two teams of eleven players using a round ball which is kicked but not handled

so·cia·ble /ˈsoʷʃəbəl/ *adj* fond of being with other people; friendly –opposite **unsociable** –**sociability** /ˌsoʷʃəˈbɪlətiʸ/ *n* [U] –**sociably** /ˈsoʷʃəbliʸ/ *adv*

so·cial /ˈsoʷʃəl/ *adj* **1** of or concerning human society or its organization: *opinions on various social questions* **2** based on rank in society: *people of different social classes* **3** shared with friends: *We have an active social life.* (=We spend a lot of time meeting friends, etc.) **4** forming groups or living together by nature: *social insects such as ants* –see also ANTISOCIAL –**socially** *adv*

so·cial·ism /ˈsoʷʃəˌlɪzəm/ *n* [U] a belief or system (sometimes considered to include COMMUNISM) aiming at the establishment of a society in which every person is equal

so·cial·ist[1] /ˈsoʷʃəlɪst/ *n* **1** a believer in SOCIALISM **2** (*usu. cap.*) a member of a SOCIALIST political party

socialist[2] *adj* of, concerning, or following SOCIALISM: *socialist principles*

so·cial·ize ‖also **-ise** *BrE* /ˈsoʷʃəˌlaɪz/ *v* **-ized, -izing** [I *with*] to spend time with other people in a friendly way: *There will be no socializing during business hours!*

socialized med·i·cine /ˌ··· ˈ···/ *n* [U] *AmE* medical care provided by a government and paid for by taxes

social sci·ence /ˌ··· ˈ···/ also **social studies**– *n* [C;U] (a branch of) the study of people in society, usu. including history, politics, ECONOMICS, SOCIOLOGY, and ANTHROPOLOGY –see also NATURAL SCIENCE

social se·cu·ri·ty /ˌ··· ·ˈ···/ *n* [U] **1** *AmE* (often cap.) the system of government payment to people too old to work or to a worker's family after his or her death **2** *BrE* for WELFARE

social work /ˈ··· ˌ·/ *n* [U] work done by government or private organizations to improve bad social conditions –**social worker** *n*

so·ci·e·ty /səˈsaɪətiʸ/ *n* **-ties 1** [C;U] a large group of people with shared customs, laws, etc.: *a history of ancient society* **2** [U] people living together, considered as a whole: *Society has a right to expect obedience to the law.* **3** [C] an organization of people with similar aims, interests, etc.; club: *a film society* **4** [U] *fml* the companionship of others: *to spend time in the society of one's friends* **5** [U] the fashionable people in an area: *a society occasion|Her marriage to a truck driver shocked Boston society.*

so·ci·ol·o·gy /ˌsoʷsiʸˈaləʤiʸ, ˌsoʷʃiʸ-/ *n* [U] the scientific study of societies and human behavior in groups –compare ANTHROPOLOGY –**sociological** /ˌsoʷsiʸəˈlaʤɪkəl, ˌsoʷʃiʸ-/ *adj* –**sociologist** /ˌsoʷsiʸˈaləʤɪst, ˌsoʷʃiʸ-/ *n*

sock /sak/ *n* a soft covering for the foot and lower part of the leg, usu. worn inside a shoe –see illustration on page 123

sock·et /ˈsakɪt/ *n* an opening, hollow place, or machine part into which something fits: *eye sockets|to put an electric light bulb into a socket*

sod /sad/ *n* [C;U] (a piece of) earth with grass and roots growing in it

so·da /ˈsoʷdə/ *n* [C;U] **1** → SODA WATER: *whiskey and soda* **2** *AmE*‖also **pop**– (a drink or a container of) a sweet (flavored) drink containing gas (CARBON DIOXIDE): *I like orange soda.|two orange sodas*

soda wa·ter /ˈ·· ˌ··/ *n* [C;U] (a drink or a container of) water filled with gas (CARBON DIOXIDE)

sod·den /ˈsadn/ *adj* heavy with wetness: *sodden clothes*

so·di·um /ˈsoʷdiʸəm/ *n* [U] a silver-white metal that is a simple substance (ELEMENT), found only in combination with other substances

so·fa /ˈsoʷfə/ *n* a comfortable seat wide enough for two or three people to sit on

soft /sɔft/ *adj* **1** not firm against pressure; not hard or stiff: *a soft chair/bed|His foot sank into the soft snow.|a book with a soft cover* **2** smooth and delicate to the touch: *soft skin* **3** restful and pleasant to the senses, esp. the eyes: *soft lights|soft colors* –opposite **harsh 4** quiet; not loud: *soft music* **5** *infml* easily persuaded; weak: *Don't let him do that; you're too soft with him.* **6** (of a drink) containing no alcohol: *We're serving soft drinks at our party, but no* **hard drinks** (=drinks containing alcohol) **7** (of water) without certain minerals; allowing soap to act easily: *We're lucky that the local water is soft.* **8** not of the worst or most harmful kind: *soft PORNOGRAPHY|soft drugs like* CANNABIS –opposite **hard** (for 1, 2, 5, 7, 8) **9** *infml* foolish or mad: *soft in the head* **10 have a soft spot for** to be fond of –**softly** *adv* –**softness** *n* [U]

soft-boiled /ˌ· ˈ· ◂/ *adj* (of an egg) boiled not long enough for the inside to become solid –see also HARD-BOILED

soft·en /ˈsɔfən/ *v* [I;T *up*] to make or become soft, gentle, less stiff, or less severe: *a cream for softening dry skin|In the heat the frozen ground began to soften (up).* –compare HARDEN

soft·heart·ed /ˌsɔftˈhɑrtɪd◂/ *adj* having tender feelings; easily moved to pity –opposite **hard-hearted** –**softheartedness** *n* [U]

soft lens /ˌ· ˈ·/ *n* lenses a CONTACT LENS made of soft plastic material

soft-spo·ken /ˌ· ˈ··◂/ *adj* having a gentle voice

soft·ware /ˈsɔftwɛər/ *n* [U] the set of PROGRAMS[1] (4) for use with a computer system –see also HARDWARE (2)

soft·wood /ˈsɔftwʊd/ *n* [U] wood from trees that is easy to cut –opposite **hardwood**

sog·gy /ˈsagiʸ/ *adj* **-gier, -giest** heavy or lacking firmness as a result of wetness: *soggy ground after the heavy rain|If you boil the vegetables too long, they'll get soggy.* –**soggily** *adv* –**sogginess** *n* [U]

soil[1] /sɔɪl/ *n* [U] the top covering of the earth in which plants grow; ground: *rich/sandy soil* –see LAND (USAGE)

soil[2] *v* [T] to make dirty: *The shirt collar was badly soiled, and I couldn't get it clean.*

sol·ace /ˈsalɪs/ *n* [C;U] (something that provides) comfort in grief or anxiety

so·lar /'so^wlər/ *adj* of, from, or concerning the sun or the sun's light: *solar time|a solar heating system* –compare LUNAR

solar sys·tem /'·· ,·'/ *n* **1** [*the* S] the sun together with the bodies (PLANETs) going around it **2** [C] such a system around another star

sold /so^wld/ *v past tense & participle of* SELL

sol·der¹ /'sadər/ *n* [U] soft metal used when melted for joining other metal surfaces

solder² *v* [T] to join or repair with SOLDER: *to solder two wires together*

sol·dier /'so^wldʒər/ *n* a member of an army, esp. one who is not an officer

sole¹ /so^wl/ *n* **1** the bottom surface of the foot **2** the part of a sock, shoe, etc., covering this, esp. not including the heel

sole² *v* **soled, soling** [T] to put a SOLE¹ on (a shoe): *to have one's shoes soled* –compare HEEL²

sole³ *n* **sole** *or* **soles** [C;U] a flat fish often eaten as food

sole⁴ *adj* [A] **1** only: *The sole survivor of the crash was a baby.* **2** belonging to one person and no other; unshared: *The sole responsibility for this job is yours.*

sole·ly /'so^wl-li^y, 'so^wli^y/ *adv* not including others; only

sol·emn /'saləm/ *adj* **1** serious: *a solemn moment in our country's history* **2** of the most formal kind: *a solemn wedding service in church* –**solemnly** *adv*

so·lem·ni·ty /sə'lɛmnəti^y/ *n* **-ties 1** [U] the quality of being solemn **2** [C *usu. pl.*] a formal act proper for a solemn event: *all the solemnities of the occasion*

sol·em·nize ‖also **-nise** *BrE* /'saləm,naɪz/ *v* **-nized, -nizing** [T] *lit or fml* to perform a formal religious ceremony of (esp. marriage) –**solemnization** /,saləmnə'ze^yʃən/ *n* [U]

so·lic·it /sə'lɪsɪt/ *v* **1** [I;T *for*] to ask for (money, help, a favor, etc.): *Beggars are not allowed to solicit in public places.|to solicit votes* **2** [I] to offer oneself for sex for pay, esp. in public: *The police charged her with soliciting.*

so·lic·i·tor /sə'lɪsətər/ *n* **1** *AmE* a person who comes to people's doors to sell or SOLICIT (1) **2** a law officer of a city or STATE¹ (4) **3** (esp. in England) a kind of lawyer who gives advice, appears in lower courts, and prepares cases for a BARRISTER to argue in a high court

so·lic·it·ous /sə'lɪsətəs/ *adj* [*about, of, for*] *fml* anxious to help; carefully interested –**solicitously** *adv* –**solicitousness** *n* [U]

sol·id¹ /'salɪd/ *adj* **1** not needing a container to hold its shape; not liquid or gas: *The milk is frozen solid.* **2** having an inside filled up; not hollow: *solid rubber tires* **3** made of material tight together: *solid rock* **4** without spaces or breaks; CONTINUOUS; *I waited for three solid hours.* **5** of good quality; firm and

well made: *solid furniture|a solid old house built 100 years ago* **6** [A] completely of one material without mixture of others: *a solid gold watch* **7** [A] *AmE* completely of one color without a mixture of others: *a solid blue dress* **8** *tech* having length, depth, and height; three-DIMENSIONAL: *A* SPHERE *is a solid figure.* –**solidly** *adv* –**solidity** /sə'lɪdəti^y/ *n* [U]

solid² *n* **1** a SOLID¹ (1) object; something that does not flow: *Water becomes a solid when it freezes.* **2** an object with length, width, and height **3** [*usu. pl.*] an article of non-liquid food: *He's still too ill to take solids.*

sol·i·dar·i·ty /,salə'dærəti^y/ *n* [U] agreement of interests, aims, or standards among a group

so·lid·i·fy /sə'lɪdə,faɪ/ *v* **-fied, -fying** [I;T] to make or become solid, hard, or firm: *the mixture will solidify as it cools.* –**solidification** /sə,lɪdəfə'ke^yʃən/ *n* [U]

so·lil·o·quy /sə'lɪləkwi^y/ *n* **-quies** a speech made to oneself alone, esp. in a play

sol·i·taire /'salə,tɛər/ *n* [U] *AmE* a card game for one player: *to play solitaire*

sol·i·tar·y /'salə,tɛri^y/ *adj* **1** (fond of being) alone: *He's a rather solitary young man.* **2** in a lonely place **3** [A] used in NEGATIVEs², questions, etc. single; SOLE⁴: *Can you give me one solitary piece of proof for what you say?* –see ALONE (USAGE) –**solitarily** /,salə'tɛərəli^y/ *adv*

sol·i·tude /'salə,tu^wd, -,tyu^wd/ *n* [U] the quality or state of being alone and away from other people

so·lo¹ /'so^wlo^w/ *n* **-los** a piece of music played or sung by one person –compare DUET

solo² *adj,adv* without a companion: *my first solo flight* (=flying a plane by myself)|*Have you ever flown solo?|She has a good solo voice.* (=suitable for singing alone)

so·lo·ist /'so^wlo^wɪst/ *n* a performer of a musical SOLO¹

sol·stice /'salstɪs, 'so^wl-/ *n* either the shortest day in the year (the **winter solstice,** December 22 in the northern half of the world) or the longest day in the year (the **summer solstice,** June 22 in the northern half of the world) –compare EQUINOX

sol·u·ble /'salyəbəl/ *adj* [*in*] that can be DISSOLVEd (1): *Salt is soluble in water.* –opposite **insoluble** –**solubility** /,salyə'bɪləti^y/ *n* [U]

so·lu·tion /sə'lu^wʃən/ *n* **1** [C] an answer to a difficulty or problem: *It's difficult to find a solution to this question.* **2** [C;U] (a) liquid containing a solid or gas mixed into it: *a sugar solution* (=sugar in water)

solve /salv/ *v* **solved, solving** [T] to find an answer to or way of dealing with: *to solve a problem/puzzle/mystery* –see also INSOLUBLE –**solvable** *adj*

sol·vent¹ /'salvənt/ *adj* having enough money to pay all that is owed; not in debt –opposite **insolvent** –**solvency** *n* [U]

solvent² *n* [C;U] (a) liquid able to DISSOLVE (1) a solid substance: *Alcohol and gasoline are useful solvents.*

som·ber *AmE*‖**sombre** *BrE* /'sambər/ *adj* **1**

sadly serious; GLOOMY **2** (esp. of colors) dark: *a somber business suit* –**somberly** *adv* –**somberness** *n* [U]

some¹ /sʌm/ *determiner,pron* **1** a certain amount or number (of): *Some parts of the country are very mountainous.|He asked for money and I gave him some.* (compare *but I didn't give him any).|Some of those stories* (=not all) *are very good.|The fire went on for some time* (=quite a long time) *before it was brought under control.* –see Study Notes on page 550 **2** an unknown (one): *There must be some reason for what he did.* **3** some ... or (an)other not a particular one; a person or thing that is not stated exactly: *I read it in some book or other.|I met him somewhere or other.|Somebody or other will have to go.*

USAGE In NEGATIVE statements, **any** or **no** are used instead of **some**: *I don't have any socks.|I have no socks.* If **some**, **somebody**, etc., are used in questions, it means that we think the answer will be "yes," but if **any**, **anybody**, etc. are used, we do not know what the answer will be: *Is there something to eat?* (=I can smell food)|*Is there anything to eat?* (=I'm hungry!)

some² /səm; *strong* sʌm/ *determiner* (used like *a, an*) a little; a few: *I saw some boys* (or *a boy) I knew.|Would you like some tea* (or *a cup of tea)?* –see Study Notes on page 550

some·bod·y /ˈsʌm,bɑdiʸ, -,bʌdiʸ, -bədiʸ/ also **someone** /ˈsʌmwʌn, -wən/ – *pron* a person; some person but not a particular or known one:|*There's somebody on the telephone for you.|You'd better ask someone to help you.* –see EVERYBODY, SOME (USAGE)

some·day /ˈsʌmdeʸ/ *adv* at some future time: *Maybe someday I'll be rich.*

some·how /ˈsʌmhaʊ/ ‖also **someway** *AmE infml*– *adv* in some way not yet known: *We'll get the money somehow.|The book has disappeared somehow.*

some·place /ˈsʌmpleʸs/ *adv* *AmE* for SOMEWHERE

som·er·sault /ˈsʌmər,sɔlt/ *v,n* [C; I] (to do) a rolling backward or forward movement in which the feet go over the head before the body returns upright –compare CARTWHEEL

some·thing /ˈsʌmθiŋ/ *pron* **1** some unknown thing; a certain thing: *I think I dropped something.|I was looking for something cheaper.* –see SOME (USAGE) **2** a thing of some value; a thing better than nothing: *At least we didn't lose any money. That's something!|You can't get something for nothing.* (=a profit without any risk or effort) –compare NOTHING **3** or something (used when the speaker is not sure): *He said he was tired or something.* **4** something like: **a** rather like: *shaped something like a potato* **b** infml about: *something like 1,000 people* **5** something to do with (having) a connection with: *His job has something to do with oil.* –see also SOME¹ (3)

some·time¹ /ˈsʌmtaɪm/ *adv* at some uncertain time: *We'll go there sometime next summer.|Our house was built sometime around 1905.*

sometime² *adj* [A] *fml* having been once;

former: *the sometime chairman of General Motors*

some·times /ˈsʌmtaɪmz/ *adv* [no comp.] now and then, but not very often: *Sometimes I wonder why I ever listen to him.|Sometimes he comes by train and sometimes by car.* (=he comes either by train or by car) –see NEVER (USAGE)

some·way /ˈsʌmweʸ/ *adv* *AmE infml* for SOMEHOW

some·what /ˈsʌmhwʌt, -hwɑt, -wʌt, -wɑt/ *adv* **1** a little; rather: *somewhat cold weather|It somewhat surprised me.*

some·where /ˈsʌmhwɛr, -wɛər/ also **someplace** *AmE*– *adv* in or to some place: *He's somewhere in the building.|I don't like this restaurant. Let's go somewhere else.* –see also NOWHERE –see SOME¹ (USAGE)

son /sʌn/ *n* **1** someone's male child –compare DAUGHTER –see illustration on page 247 **2** (used by an older man to a much younger man or boy): *What's your name, son?*

so·na·ta /səˈnɑtə/ *n* a piece of music for one or two instruments, one of which is a piano

song /sɔŋ/ *n* **1** [C] a usu. short piece of music with words for singing: *a lovesong/*FOLKsong|*That's my favorite song.* **2** [U] the act or art of singing: *She suddenly* **burst into song.** (=started singing) **3** [C;U] the music-like sound of a bird: *the song of the blackbird*

song·bird /ˈsɔŋbɜrd/ *n* a bird that can sing well

son·ic /ˈsɑnɪk/ *adj* of or concerning sound waves

son-in-law /ˈ·· ·,·/ *n* **sons-in-law** the husband of someone's daughter –compare DAUGHTER-IN-LAW –see illustration on page 247

son·net /ˈsɑnɪt/ *n* a 14-line poem with a formal pattern of line endings (RHYMEs)

so·no·rous /səˈnɔrəs, -ˈnoʷr-, ˈsɑnərəs/ *adj fml* having a pleasantly full loud sound: *a sonorous bell/voice* –**sonorously** *adv*

soon /suʷn/ *adv* **1** [adv + adv/adj/prep] before long; within a short time: *soon after the party|Please do it as soon as possible–* **the sooner the better.**|*He got married as soon as* (=not later than when) *he left the university.|***No sooner had we sat down** *than* (=the moment we sat down) *we had to get up again.* –see HARDLY (USAGE) **2** (with *as, than*) willingly: *I'd sooner/rather die than marry you!|"Let's go to a movie." "I'd just as soon stay home, if you don't mind."* **3 sooner or later** at some time certainly; if not soon then later: *Don't worry; she'll get here sooner or later.*

soot /sʊt/ *n* [U] black powder produced by burning, sometimes carried into the air by smoke –**sooty** *adj* **-ier, -iest**

soothe /suʷð/ *v* **soothed, soothing** [T] **1** to make less angry or anxious; comfort or calm: *Have a drink to soothe your nerves.|soothing words* **2** to make less painful: *to soothe a sore throat|soothing medicine* –**soothingly** *adv*

so·phis·ti·cat·ed /səˈfɪstəkeʸtɪd/ *adj* **1** having or showing signs of experience in social life and behavior; no longer natural or simple:

The child is quite sophisticated for his age|sophisticated tastes. –opposite **unsophisticated** **2** not easily understood; COMPLICATED: *sophisticated machinery/arguments* –**sophistication** /səˌfɪstɪˈkeʸʃən/ *n* [U]

soph·o·more /ˈsɑfəˌmɔr, -ˌmoʷr, ˈsɑfmɔr, moʷr/ *n* (in the US) a student in the second year of a high school or university —compare FRESHMAN; SENIOR

sop·o·rif·ic /ˌsɑpəˈrɪfɪk/ *adj* causing one to fall asleep: *a soporific drug/speech* –**soporifically** *adv*

sop·ping /ˈsɑpɪŋ/ *adv,adj infml* very (wet): *Our clothes are sopping/sopping wet.*

sop·py /ˈsɑpiʸ/ *adj* **-pier, -piest** *infml* (of a person, story, etc.) too full of tender feelings like sorrow and love; SENTIMENTAL (2)

so·pra·no /səˈprænoʷ, -ˈprɑ-/ *n* **-nos** (a person with) a singing voice in the highest usual range, above ALTO –**soprano** *adj*

sor·cer·er /ˈsɔrsərər/ **sorceress** /-rɪs/ *fem.– n* a person believed to do magic by using the power of evil spirits –**sorcery** *n* [U]

sor·did /ˈsɔrdɪd/ *adj* **1** unpleasant and shameful: *a sordid attempt to cheat his brother* **2** very dirty and poor: *a sordid little house.* –**sordidly** *adv* –**sordidness** *n* [U]

sore¹ /sɔr, soʷr/ *adj* **1** painful or aching from a wound, infection, or hard use: *a sore throat from a cold|My feet are sore from all that running yesterday.* **2** [A] likely to cause offense: *Don't joke about his weight; it's really a sore point with him.* **3** [F] *infml esp. AmE* angry, esp. from feeling unjustly treated: *Don't get sore. I didn't mean any harm.* –**soreness** *n* [U]

sore² *n* a painful usu. infected place on the body

sore·head /ˈsɔrhɛd, ˈsoʷr-/ *n AmE infml* a bad-tempered person

sore·ly /ˈsɔriʸ, ˈsoʷr-/ *adv* severely or painfully; greatly: *John's in the hospital and he's sorely missed by the family.*

so·ror·i·ty /səˈrɔrətiʸ, -ˈrɑr-/ *n* **-ties** (at some universities in the US) a club of women students usu. living in the same house –compare FRATERNITY (3)

sor·row¹ /ˈsɑroʷ, ˈsɔr-/ *n* [C;U *over, at, for*] (a cause of) unhappiness; sadness; grief: *sorrow at the death of a friend|the joys and sorrows of life|He expressed his sorrow for what he had done.* –**sorrowful** /ˈsɑrəwfəl, ˈsɔr-/ *adj* –**sorrowfully** *adv*

sorrow² *v* [I *over, at, for*] *lit* to feel or express sorrow; grieve: *sorrowing over his lost youth*

sor·ry¹ /ˈsɑriʸ, ˈsɔriʸ/ *adj* **-rier, -riest 1** [F +*to-v/(that)*] grieved; sad: *I'm sorry to say that we have failed.|I was sorry to hear your bad news.* **2** [+(*that*)/*for, about*] unhappy at one's past actions: *If you're really sorry, I'll forgive you.|I'm sorry I broke your pen.* **3** [F] (used for expressing polite refusal, disagreement, etc.): *(I'm) sorry, but you can't bring*

SPELLING NOTE
Words with the sound /s/, may be spelled **c-**, like **city**, or **ps-**, like **psychology**.

---

your dog in here. **4** [A] causing pity mixed with disapproval: *He was a sorry sight in his dirty old clothes.* **5 be/feel sorry for** to feel pity towards: *I feel sorry for whoever marries him!*

USAGE One says *I'm very sorry (to hear that)* when told of a death. To feel pity for someone is to feel **sorry for** him/her. When one steps on someone's foot, one says *I'm sorry* or **Excuse me** (*AmE*).

sorry² *interj* **1** (used for expressing polite refusal, disagreement, etc.): *Sorry; you can't come in.* **2** *esp. BrE* (used for asking someone to repeat something): *"I'm cold." "Sorry?" "I said, I'm cold."*

sort¹ /sɔrt/ *n* **1** [*of*] a group of people, things, etc., all sharing certain qualities; type; kind: *What sort of food do you like best?|people of all sorts|all sorts of people* –see KIND (USAGE) **2** [*usu. sing.*] *infml* a person: *She's not such a bad sort* (=quite a nice person) *when you get to know her.* **3 sort of** *infml* rather; in a way: *I sort of thought you might say that.* **4 of sorts** of a poor or doubtful kind: *It's a painting of sorts, but not a very good one.* **5 out of sorts** feeling unwell or annoyed

sort² *v* [I;T *through, over, out*] to put (things) in order; place according to kind, rank, etc.: *a job sorting letters in the Post Office|Can you sort these clothes into two piles, please?* –**sorter** *n*

sort sthg.↔**out** *v adv* [T] [*from*] to separate from a mass: *Will you sort out the papers to be thrown away, and put the rest back?*

sor·tie /ˈsɔrtiʸ, sɔrˈtiʸ/ *n* **1** a short attack made by an army from a position of defense **2** a short trip into an unfamiliar or unfriendly place: (fig.) *His first sortie into the world of movie-making wasn't very successful.*

SOS /ˌɛs oʷ ˈɛs/ *n* an international signal calling for help, used esp. by ships in trouble

so-so /ˈ· ·, ˌ· ˈ·◄/ *adj,adv infml* not very bad(ly) and not very good/well: *a so-so tennis player|Business is only so-so.*

sot·to vo·ce /ˌsɑtoʷ ˈvoʷtʃiʸ/ *adv* in a soft voice so that other people cannot hear

souf·flé /suʷˈfleʸ/ *n* [C;U] a light airy dish made from eggs, flour, milk, and often cheese

sought /sɔt/ *n past tense & participle of* SEEK

soul¹ /soʷl/ *n* **1** [C] the part of a person that is not the body and is thought not to die: *She's dead, but her soul's in heaven.* **2** [U] an attractive quality of sincerity and deep feeling: *a stylish performance but lacking in soul* **3** [C] a person: *You mustn't tell this to a soul.|She's a dear old soul.* **4** [U] → SOUL MUSIC: *a soul group* **5 keep body and soul together** to have just enough money, food, etc., to live **6** a central or most important part of: *The football team is the soul of this town.* **7 the soul of** a fine example of: *Your son is the soul of charm.*

soul² *adj* [A] *AmE infml* of or concerning black people in the US: *soul food*

soul-de·stroy·ing /ˈ· ·ˌ·/ *adj* very uninteresting: *a soul-destroying job making screws*

soul·ful /ˈsoʷlfəl/ *adj* full of feeling; expressing deep feeling: *a soulful look/song* –**soulfully** *adv* –**soulfulness** *n* [U]

soul·less /'so^wl-lɪs/ *adj* having no warm or friendly human qualities: *a big soulless office building*

soul mu·sic /'· ˌ··/ also **soul–** *n* [U] a type of popular music usu. performed by black singers supposed to show feelings strongly and directly

sound¹ /saʊnd/ *n* **1** [C;U] what can be heard; (something that causes) a sensation in the ear: *to hear the sound of voices/strange sounds from the next room/Sound travels* (in **sound waves**) *at 1,100 feet per second* –see NOISE (USAGE.) **2** [S] an idea produced by something read or heard: *From the sound of it, I'd say the matter was serious.* –**soundless** *adj* –**soundlessly** *adv*

sound² *v* **1** [I not *be* +*v-ing*] to seem when heard: *Your idea sounds (like) a good one./Does this sentence sound right?/I heard about your accident; it sounds as if you'll need a new car.* **2** [I;T] to (cause to) make a sound: *The school bell sounded at eight o'clock./ Sound your horn to warn the other driver.*

sound off *v adv* [I *on, about*] usu. *derog* to express an opinion freely and forcefully: *He's always sounding off about the behavior of young people.*

sound sbdy.↔**out** *v adv* [T *on, about*] to try to find out the opinion or intentions of

sound³ *adj* **1** in good condition; without disease or damage: *in sound health* –opposite **unsound 2** solid; firm; strong: *We're pleased with the company's sound performance this year.* **3** based on truth or good judgment; not likely to be wrong: *sound advice/judgment* **4** (of sleep) deep and untroubled –**soundly** *adv* –**soundness** *n* [U]

sound⁴ *adv* SOUNDLY (4) (esp. in the phrase **sound asleep**)

sound⁵ *n* a water passage connecting two larger bodies of water and wider than a STRAIT

sound ef·fects /'· ·ˌ·/ *n* [P] sounds produced to give the effect of natural sounds needed in a broadcast or movie

sound·proof¹ /'saʊndpru^wf/ *adj* keeping sound from getting in or out: *a soundproof room*

soundproof² *v* [T] to make SOUNDPROOF: *He soundproofed the bedroom so that he can practice playing his drums.*

sound·track /'saʊndtræk/ *n* the recorded music from a movie

soup /su^wp/ *n* [U] liquid cooked food containing small pieces of meat, fish, or vegetables

soup sthg.↔**up** *v adv* [T] *infml* to increase the power of (a car or engine)

sour¹ /saʊər/ *adj* **1** having the taste that is not bitter, salty, or sweet, and is produced esp. by acids: *sour green apples* **2** having the taste of chemical action by bacteria (FERMENTATION): *This milk has gone sour; it has a sour taste.* **3** bad-tempered; unsmiling: *He gave me a sour look.* –**sourly** *adv* –**sourness** *n* [U]

sour² *v* [I;T] to make or become sour: *The*

milk has soured overnight./(fig.) *an argument that has soured relations between us*

source /sɔrs, so^wrs/ *n* **1** [*of*] a place from which something comes: *to find the source of the engine trouble/Do you have any other source of income apart from your job?* **2** the place where a stream of water starts: *Where is the source of the Amazon River?* –compare SPRING² (1)

south¹ /saʊθ/ *adv* (*often cap.*) towards the south: *to travel south/Mexico is south of the US.*

south² *n* [*the* S] (*often cap.*) **1** one of the four main points of the compass, on the right of a person facing the rising sun **2** the part of a country which is further south than the rest: *The South of this country is warmer than the North.* **3** the states in the southern part of the US that were once part of the CONFEDERACY (2)

south·bound /'saʊθbaʊnd/ *adj* traveling towards the south: *To get to Washington, take the southbound train.*

south·east¹ /ˌsaʊθ'i^yst◂/ *adv* (*often cap.*) towards the southeast: *windows facing southeast*

southeast² *n* [*the* S] (*often cap.*) (the direction of) the point of the compass that is halfway between south and east

south·east·er·ly /ˌsaʊθ'i^ystərli^y/ *adj* **1** towards or in the southeast: *in a southeasterly direction* **2** (of a wind) coming from the southeast

south·east·ern /ˌsaʊθ'i^ystərn/ *adj* (*often cap.*) of or belonging to the southeast part, esp. of a country

south·east·ward /ˌsaʊθ'i^ystwərd/ *adj fml* going towards the southeast –**southeastwards**‖also **southeastward** *AmE*– *adv*

south·er·ly /'sʌðərli^y/ *adj* **1** towards the south: *the southerly shore of the lake* **2** (of a wind) coming from the south: *warm southerly winds*

south·ern /'sʌðərn/ *adj* (*often cap.*) of or belonging to the south part, esp. of the world or a country: *the southern US/the warm southern sun*

South·ern·er /'sʌðərnər/ *n* a person who lives in or comes from the southern part of a country

south·ern·most /'sʌðərnˌmo^wst/ *adj fml* furthest south: *the southernmost station on the railroad line*

south·paw /'saʊθpɔ/ *n* *AmE infml* a LEFT-HANDED (1) person: *a southpaw* BASE-BALL PITCHER²

South Pole /ˌ· '·/ *n* [*the* S] (the lands around) the most southern point on the surface of the earth –see also NORTH POLE

south·ward /'saʊθwərd/ *adj* going towards the south: *a southward journey* –**southwards**‖also **southward** *AmE*– *adv*: *to sail southwards*

south·west¹ /ˌsaʊθ'wɛst◂/ *adv* (*often cap.*) towards the southwest: *to sail southwest*

southwest² *n* [*the* S] (*often cap.*) (the direction of) the point of the compass which is halfway between south and west

south·west·er /ˌsaʊθ'wɛstər/ also **sou'wester**

/ˌsaʊˈwɛstər/– **1** a strong wind or storm from the southwest **2** a hat of shiny material (OILSKIN) worn esp. by sailors in storms

south·west·er·ly /ˌsaʊθˈwɛstərliʸ/ adj **1** towards or in the southwest **2** (of a wind) coming from the southwest

south·west·ern /ˌsaʊθˈwɛstərn/ adj (often cap.) of or belonging to the southwest part, esp. of a country

south·west·ward /ˌsaʊθˈwɛstwərd/ adj going towards the southwest –**southwestwards**‖ also **southwestward** AmE– adv

sou·ve·nir /ˌsuʷvəˈnɪər, ˈsuʷvəˌnɪər/ n an object kept as a reminder of an event, trip, place, etc.: I bought this bag as a souvenir of my visit to Tokyo.

sov·er·eign¹ /ˈsɑvərən/ n **1** a ruler such as a king or queen **2** a former British gold coin worth £1

sovereign² adj **1** in control of a country; ruling: Sovereign power must lie with the people. **2** (of a country) independent and self-governing –**sovereignty** n [U]

So·vi·et /ˈsoʷviʸɪt, -ˌɛt/ adj of or concerning the USSR (the **Soviet Union**) or its people

sow¹ /saʊ/ n a fully grown female pig –compare BOAR, HOG¹ (1)

sow² /soʷ/ v sowed, sown /soʷn/ or sowed, sowing [I;T with/on] to plant or scatter (seeds) on (a piece of ground): to sow grass/ to sow a field with grass –compare REAP

soy·bean /ˈsɔɪbiʸn/ also **soya bean** /ˈsɔɪə ˌbiʸn/– n (the bean of) a plant native to Asia which produces oil

spa /spɑ/ n a place with a spring of mineral water where people come for cures of various diseases

space¹ /speʸs/ n **1** [C;U] something measurable in length, width, or depth; room: Is there enough space at the table for 10 people?|Keep some space between you and the car ahead.|a parking space|a town with some open space (=land not built on) near the center|Six people have been killed on this road in the space of a year. (=during this length of time) **2** [U] that which surrounds all objects and continues outwards in all directions: He didn't see me; he was just looking out into space. **3** [U] what is outside the earth's air; where other heavenly bodies move: to travel through space to the moon|a space station|in outer space

space² v spaced, spacing [T out] to place apart; arrange with spaces between: Space the desks three feet apart.

space·craft /ˈspeʸs-kræft/ n spacecraft a vehicle able to travel in SPACE¹ (3)

space·ship /ˈspeʸsˌʃɪp, ˈspeʸʃˌʃɪp/ n (esp. in stories) a spacecraft for carrying people

spa·cious /ˈspeʸʃəs/ adj having a lot of room; ROOMY –**spaciousness** n [U]

spade¹ /speʸd/ n **1** a tool like a SHOVEL (1) but with a blade to push into the ground, for

digging earth **2 call a spade a spade** infml to speak the plain truth

spade² n a playing card with one or more figures shaped like a black pointed leaf printed on it: the six of spades –see CARDS (USAGE)

spa·ghet·ti /spəˈgɛtiʸ/ n [U] an Italian food of flour paste (PASTA) in long strings –compare MACARONI

span¹ /spæn/ n **1** a stretch between two limits, esp. in time: over a span of three years **2** a length of time over which something continues or works well: a short memory span **3** the length of a bridge, arch, etc., between supports –see also WINGSPAN

span² v -nn- [T] to form a bridge over; stretch over: A bridge spanned the stream.|(fig.) He was born in 1880 and died in 1930, so his life spanned two centuries.

span·gle /ˈspæŋgəl/ n a small piece of shiny metal sewn in large numbers esp. on dresses; SEQUIN

span·iel /ˈspænyəl/ n a small short-legged dog with long ears and long wavy hair

spank /spæŋk/ v [T] to strike (esp. a child) with the open hand, esp. on the BUTTOCKS –**spank** n –**spanking** n: If you don't stop that noise, you'll get a spanking!

span·ner /ˈspænər/ n BrE for WRENCH² (3)

spar¹ /spɑr/ n a thick pole, esp. one used on a ship to support sails or ropes –compare MAST

spar² v -rr- [I with] **1** to BOX³ without hitting hard, as in practice (between **sparring partners**) **2** to fight with words: a government official sparring with newspaper reporters

spare¹ /spɛər/ v spared, sparing [T] **1** to afford to give: Can you spare me five minutes?|We're so busy that no one can be spared for any other work. **2** esp. old use to treat with mercy; not harm: Take my money but spare my life! **3** to keep from giving (someone) (something unnecessary): Spare me all the details of the meeting; just tell me about what they decided. **4** (only used in NEGATIVEs², questions, etc.) to keep from using, spending, etc.: No trouble/expense (=money) was spared to make sure they enjoyed themselves.

spare² adj **1** not in use but kept for use: a spare tire/bedroom **2** not needed for use; free: something to do in her spare time|Do you have a spare minute to look at this report? **3** rather thin; LEAN² (1): her spare figure

spare³ n a second object of the same kind that is kept for possible use: This tire is damaged. Do you have a spare?

spar·ing /ˈspɛərɪŋ/ adj [in, of] using or giving little; FRUGAL (1): Be sparing in the amount of oil you use, or you will spoil the meal. –opposite unsparing –**sparingly** adv

spark¹ /spɑrk/ n **1** a small piece of burning material thrown out by a fire or by the striking together of two hard objects **2** a flash of light produced by electricity passing across a space **3** [of] a very small but important amount, esp. of a quality: a spark of cleverness/politeness

spark² v **1** [I] to produce SPARKs¹ (1) or a

SPARK[1] (2) **2** [T] *AmE*‖ also **spark off**– to lead to; to be the direct cause of: *to spark an argument*

spar·kle /'spɑrkəl/ *v* **-kled, -kling** [I] **1** to shine in small flashes: *a diamond that sparkled in the sunlight*|(fig) *a sparkling* (=a bright and lively) *conversation* **2** (of a drink) to give off gas in small bubbles: *sparkling wine* –compare STILL[1] (3) –**sparkle** *n* [C;U]: (fig.) *a conversation full of sparkle*

spark plug /'· ·/ also **sparking plug** /'·· ,·/ *BrE*– *n* the part which makes an electric SPARK in a gasoline engine

spar·row /'spærowʷ/ *n* a small brownish bird very common in many parts of the world

sparse /spɑrs/ *adj* scattered; thin or few: *lots of bare floor and only sparse furniture* –**sparsely** *adv* –**sparseness** *n* [U]

spar·tan /'spɑrtn/ *adj* simple and without attention to comfort; severe: *a rather spartan meal of meat and boiled potatoes*

spasm /'spæzəm/ *n* **1** a sudden uncontrolled tightening of muscles **2** [*of*] a sudden violent effort, feeling, or act; FIT[3] (2): *spasms of grief/laughter/coughing*

spas·mod·ic /spæz'mɑdɪk/ *adj* **1** of or like a SPASM: *spasmodic pain* **2** not continuous; irregular; with pauses between: *spasmodic increases in the population* –**spasmodically** *adv*

spas·tic /'spæstɪk/ *n,adj* (a person) suffering from a disease in which some parts of the body will not move because the muscles stay tightened

spat[1] /spæt/ *n AmE* a short unimportant quarrel

spat[2] *v past tense & participle of* SPIT

spate /speʸt/ *n* [S *of*] a large number or amount, esp. coming together in time: *a spate of accidents on a dangerous stretch of road*

spa·tial /'speʸʃəl/ *adj fml* of, concerning, or being in space –**spatially** *adv*

spat·ter /'spætər/ *v* [I;T *with, on*] to cause (drops of liquid) to scatter on: *The car spattered my clothes with mud/spattered mud on my clothes.*|*A little oil spattered on the wall.*

spat·u·la /'spætʃələ/ *n* a tool with a wide flat blade, for spreading, mixing, or lifting soft substances –see illustration on page 379

spawn[1] /spɔn/ *v* **1** [I;T] (of fish and FROGs, etc.) to lay (eggs) in large quantities together **2** [T] to produce in large numbers: *The computer industry has spawned hundreds of new companies.*

spawn[2] *n* [U] the eggs of water animals like fishes and FROGs

speak /spiʸk/ *v* **spoke** /spoʷk/, **spoken** /'spoʷkən/, **speaking 1** [I] to say things; talk: *I'd like to speak to/with you about my idea.*|*I was so shocked I could hardly speak.*|*After their argument, they're still not speaking (to each other)/not* **on speaking terms**. (=willing to talk and be polite to each other) –see SAY (USAGE) **2** [T] to express or say: *Are you speaking the truth?* **3** [T] to be able to talk in (a language): *Do you speak English?*|*We need a French-speaking secretary.* **4** [I] to make a speech: *I've invited her to speak to our club on Chinese politics.* **5** [I] to express

thoughts, ideas, etc., in some other way than by talk: *Actions speak louder than words.*|*Everything at the party spoke of careful planning.* **6 so to speak** as one might say; rather **7 speak one's mind** to express one's thoughts directly: *He always speaks his mind, so many people think he's rude.* **8 to speak of** (only used in NEGATIVEs[2], questions, etc.) worth mentioning; of much value or amount: *There's been no rain to speak of, only a few drops.*

speak for sbdy./ sthg. *v prep* [T] **1** to express the thoughts, opinions, etc., of: *a powerless group with no one to speak for them* **2** to get the right to (something) in advance; RESERVE[1]: *You can't buy this car; It's already been spoken for.*

speak out *v adv* [I] to speak boldly, freely, and plainly: *The newspapers are afraid to speak out against the government.*

speak up *v adv* [I] **1** to speak more loudly: *Speak up, please. I can't hear you.* **2** → SPEAK **out**: *She spoke up in defense of her beliefs.*

speak·er /'spiʸkər/ *n* **1** a person making a speech: *an interesting speaker* **2** a person who speaks a language: *a speaker of English* **3** →LOUDSPEAKER –see illustration on page 399

spear[1] /spɪər/ *n* a pole with a sharp point at one end used formerly for throwing as a weapon

spear[2] *v* [T] to make a hole in or catch (as) with the point of a spear; IMPALE: *He speared a piece of meat with his fork.*

spear·head /'spɪərhɛd/ *v,n* [C;T] (to be) the leader (of an attack); (be) a leading force: *The attack on the President was spearheaded by several senators.*

spear·mint /'spɪər,mɪnt/ *n* [U] a common MINT plant used for its fresh taste, e.g. in CHEWING GUM

spe·cial[1] /'spɛʃəl/ *adj* of a particular kind; not ordinary or usual: *A special train was provided for the football supporters.*|*a special friend of mine*|*Since it's a special occasion, let's have a bottle of wine with dinner.*

special[2] *n* something that is not of the regular or ordinary kind: *a two-hour television special*

spe·cial·ist /'spɛʃəlɪst/ *n* [*in*] a person who has special knowledge or training in a field of work or study: *a heart specialist*|*He's a specialist in Roman coins.*

spe·cial·ize ‖also **-ise** *BrE* /'spɛʃə,laɪz/ *v* **-ized, -izing** [I *in*] to limit one's study, business, etc., to particular things or subjects: *a doctor who specializes in tropical diseases* –**specialization** /,spɛʃələ'zeʸʃən/ *n* [C;U]

spe·cial·ized ‖also **-ised** *BrE* /'spɛʃə,laɪzd/ *adj* developed for one particular use: *specialized tools/knowledge.*

spe·cial·ly /'spɛʃəliʸ/ *adv* **1** for one particular purpose: *I made a cake specially for you.* **2** → ESPECIALLY: *It's not specially hot today.*

spe·cial·ty /'spɛʃəltiʸ/ *n* **-ties 1** a special field of work or study: *Her specialty is ancient Greek poetry.* **2** [*of*] a particularly fine product: *Fish baked in pastry is the specialty of this restaurant.*

spe·cies /'spiʸʃiʸz, -siʸz/ *n* **-cies** [*of*] a group of plants or animals of the same kind, which are alike in all important ways and can breed together –compare GENUS

spe·cif·ic /spɪ'sɪfɪk/ *adj* **1** detailed and exact: *You say that your factory is in Quebec. Can you be a little more specific?* **2** [A] particular; certain; fixed: *a specific tool for each job* –**specificity** /ˌspɛsə'fɪsətiʸ/ *n* [U] –**specifically** /spɪ'sɪfɪkliʸ/ *adv: They told us specifically to avoid the main road.|a book written specifically for school children in Nigeria*

spec·i·fi·ca·tion /ˌspɛsəfə'keʸʃən/ *n* **1** [C *usu. pl.*] any of the parts of a detailed plan or set of descriptions or directions: *According to the radio's specifications, this wire should go into that hole.* **2** [U *of*] the action of SPECIFYing

spe·ci·fy /'spɛsəˌfaɪ/ *v* **-fied, -fying** [T] to mention exactly; choose or name: *Please specify when you will be away/the dates of your absence.*

spec·i·men /'spɛsəmən/ *n* **1** a single typical thing or example: *a fine specimen of a mountain lion* **2** a piece or amount of something to be shown, tested, etc.: *The doctor will need a specimen of your blood.*

spe·cious /'spiʸʃəs/ *adj fml* seeming right or correct but not so in fact: *a specious argument* –**speciously** *adv* –**speciousness** *n* [U]

speck /spɛk/ *n* [*of*] a small spot or mark: *a speck of dirt in my eye*

speck·le /'spɛkəl/ *n* a small colored mark, esp. one of a large number –**speckled** *adj: speckled bird's eggs*

spec·ta·cle /'spɛktəkəl/ *n* **1** a grand public show or scene **2** a silly sight; something to laugh at: *to make a spectacle of oneself*

spec·ta·cles /'spɛktəkəlz/ also **specs** /spɛks/ *infml– n more fml than* **glasses** *n* [P] glasses to help a person to see: *I can't read the newspaper without my spectacles.* –see PAIR (USAGE)

spec·tac·u·lar¹ /spɛk'tækyələr/ *adj* grandly unusual; attracting excited notice –**spectacularly** *adv*

spectacular² *n* a SPECTACULAR¹ entertainment: *a television spectacular with lots of famous stars*

spec·ta·tor /'spɛkteʸtər/ *n* a person who watches (esp. an event or sport) without taking part –compare PERFORMER

spec·ter *AmE‖-***tre** *BrE* /'spɛktər/ *n* a spirit without a body; GHOST (1)

spec·trum /'spɛktrəm/ *n* **-tra** /trə/ *or* **-trums** **1** the set of bands of colored light in the order of their WAVELENGTHs, into which a beam of light may be separated **2** a range of any of various kinds of waves: *a radio/sound spectrum|(fig.) the wide spectrum of opinion on this question*

spec·u·late /'spɛkyəˌleʸt/ *v* **-lated, -lating** **1** [I;T +(*that*)] to think (about a matter)

SPELLING NOTE

Words with the sound /s/, may be spelled **c-**, like **city**, or **ps-**, like **psychology**.

---

without facts that would lead to a firm result: *We can only speculate about what will happen next.* **2** [I *in*] to buy or deal in goods, SHARES¹ (2), etc., in the hope of a large profit: *speculating in gold mines* –**speculator** *n* –**speculation** /ˌspɛkyə'leʸʃən/ *n* [C;U]: *His belief that business will improve is pure speculation.* (=only a guess)

spec·u·la·tive /'spɛkyələtɪv, -ˌleʸtɪv/ *adj* based on speculation (SPECULATE): *a speculative guess/sale* –**speculatively** *adv*

speech /spiʸtʃ/ *n* **1** [U] the act or power of speaking; spoken language: *Only humans have the power of speech.* **2** [U] a way of speaking: *By your speech I can tell you're from Texas.* **3** [C] an act of speaking formally to a group of listeners: *to give/make a speech|The President's speech was reported in the newspapers.*

speech·less /'spiʸtʃlɪs/ *adj* [*with*] unable for the moment to speak because of strong feeling, shock, etc.: *speechless with anger* –**speechlessly** *adv* –**speechlessness** *n* [U]

speed¹ /spiʸd/ *n* **1** [C] rate of movement: *a speed of 55 miles per hour|to move along at a slow speed|to keep within/exceed the* **speed limit** (=the fastest speed allowed by law on a road) **2** [U] swift movement: *They won because of their speed with the ball.* **3** a part of a highway for cars traveling at high speeds

speed up *v adv* [I;T (=**speed** sthg.↔**up**)] to (cause to) go faster: *The company president wants us to speed up production of the new car.*

speed² *v* **sped** /spɛd/ *or* **speeded, speeding** **1** [I;T] to (cause to) go quickly: *We saw a car speeding away.|The time sped quickly by.* **2** [I] to break the speed limit: *Was I really speeding, officer?*

speed·boat /'spiʸdboʷt/ *n* a small power-driven boat built for high speed

speed·om·e·ter /spɪ'dɑmətər/ *n* an instrument in a vehicle for telling its speed –see illustration on page 95

speed·way /'spiʸdweʸ/ *n* **-ways** **1** a track for a type of motorcycle or car racing **2** a part of a highway for cars traveling at high speeds

speed·y /'spiʸdiʸ/ *adj* **-ier, -iest** going, working, or passing fast; quick; swift: *a speedy journey* –**speedily** *adv* –**speediness** *n* [U]

spell¹ /spɛl/ *v* **spelled** *or* AmE‖**spelt** /spɛlt/ *BrE*, **spelling** **1** [T *with*] to name in order the letters of (a word): *My name is spelled S-M-I-T-H.* **2** [I] to form words from letters: *to learn to spell* **3** [T *no pass.*] (of letters in order) to form (a word): *B-O-O-K spells "book."* **4** [T] to mean: *This vote spells defeat for the administration.* –**speller** *n*

spell sthg.↔ **out** *v adv* [T] **1** to explain in a very detailed way: *to spell out the government's plans in a newspaper article* **2** to write or say (a word) letter by letter

spell² *n* (magic words used to produce) a condition caused by magical power

spell³ *n* an unbroken period of time: *a spell of bad weather|a hot spell*

spell·bound /'spɛlbaʊnd/ *adj* [F] with the attention held as if by magic: *The children sat spellbound as the old man told his story.*

spell·ing /'spɛlɪŋ/ n [C;U] the way of forming words from letters: *Her spelling has improved.|British and American spellings of some words are different.*

spend /spɛnd/ v **spent** /spɛnt/, **spending 1** [I;T *on, for*] to give out (esp. money) in payment: *to spend $5,000 for/on a new car |cuts in government spending* **2** [T *in*] to pass or use (time): *Come and spend the weekend with us.|to spend three years in prison* **3** [T] *lit* to wear out or use completely: *The storm soon spent itself.*

spend·thrift /'spɛnd,θrɪft/ n a person who spends money wastefully

spent /spɛnt/ adj **1** already used; no longer for use: *spent bullets/matches* **2** worn out; EXHAUSTED: *tired and spent*

sperm /spɜrm/ n **sperm** or **sperms 1** [C] a cell produced by the sex organs of a male animal, which is able to unite with the female egg to produce new life **2** [U] the liquid from the male sex organs in which these swim; SEMEN

spew /spyuʷ/ v [I;T] **1** to send or come out in a flood: *The burst pipe was spewing out water.* **2** [*up*] *infml for* VOMIT[1]

sphere /sfɪər/ n **1** a round figure in space; ball-shaped mass **2** an area of existence, action, etc.: *His main sphere of influence is the world of banking.*

spher·i·cal /'sfɛrɪkəl, 'sfɪər-/ adj having the form of a SPHERE (1)

sphinx /sfɪŋks/ n an ancient Egyptian image of a lion with a human head

spice[1] /spaɪs/ n **1** [C;U] a vegetable product used esp. in the form of powder for giving a taste to other foods **2** [S;U] interest or excitement: *a few good stories to add spice to the speech*

spice[2] v **spiced, spicing** [T *up, with*] to add SPICE[1] to

spick-and-span /,spɪk ən 'spæn/ adj clean and bright; like new

spic·y /'spaɪsiʸ/ adj **-ier, -iest 1** containing or tasting like SPICE[1] (1): *I don't like spicy food.* **2** exciting and perhaps slightly improper: *spicy stories*

spi·der /'spaɪdər/ n a small eight-legged creature which makes silk threads, usu. into nets for catching insects

spi·der·y /'spaɪdəriʸ/ adj long and thin like a SPIDER'S legs: *the old lady's spidery writing*

spike[1] /spaɪk/ n a usu. long piece of metal with a point at one end: *spikes along the top of a fence|spikes on the bottom of running shoes* **–spiky** adj **-ier, -iest** *infml*

spike[2] v **spiked, spiking** [T] **1** to fix with SPIKES[1]; drive SPIKES into **2** esp. AmE to add an alcoholic drink to a nonalcoholic one

spill /spɪl/ v **spilled** or **spilt** /spɪlt/, **spilling 1** [I;T] to (cause to) pour out accidentally, e.g. over the edge of a container: *My hand slipped and I spilled my drink on my leg.|*(fig.) *The crowd spilled over* (=spread) *from the church into the streets.* **2 spill the beans** *infml* to tell a secret too soon or to the wrong person

spin[1] /spɪn/ v **spun** /spʌn/, **spinning** [I;T] **1** to make (thread) by twisting (cotton, wool, etc.): *to spin thread|to spin wool into*

thread|(fig.) *to spin a* YARN (=to tell a story which is not true) **2** to (cause to) turn around and around fast; WHIRL[1]: *to spin a* TOP[4]*|I spun around to see who had spoken.*

spin sthg.⇔**out** v adv [T] to make longer, esp. unnecessarily; stretch: *to spin out a story to make a book*

spin[2] n **1** [C] an act of spinning **2** [S] a short trip for pleasure: *Come for a spin in my car.*

spin·ach /'spɪnɪtʃ/ n [U] a vegetable with broad green leaves

spi·nal /'spaɪnl/ adj of, for, or concerning the SPINE (1): *spinal disease*

spin·dle /'spɪndl/ n **1** a round pointed rod used for twisting the thread in spinning **2** a machine part around which something turns

spin·dly /'spɪndliʸ/ adj long, thin, and weak-looking: *a young horse with spindly legs*

spin-dry /,· '·/ v **-dried, -drying** [T] to remove water from (wet clothes) in a machine (**spin dryer**), that spins around and around fast

spine /spaɪn/ n **1** also **spinal column** /'·· ,··/, **backbone**– the row of bones down the center of the back of humans and some animals **2** the end of a book where the pages are fastened together **3** a stiff sharp-pointed plant or animal part; prickle

spine·less /'spaɪnlɪs/ adj **1** lacking moral courage esp. in dealing with others: *He's too spineless to ask for more money.* **2** (of an animal) having no SPINE (1) **–spinelessly** adv **–spinelessness** n [U]

spinning wheel /'·· ,·/ n a small machine used esp. formerly for spinning thread

spin-off /'· ·/ n a useful product or result besides the main one

spin·ster /'spɪnstər/ n *sometimes derog* an unmarried woman, esp. an older one –compare BACHELOR

spi·ral[1] /'spaɪrəl/ n a curve winding around a center and moving continuously either towards the center or upwards: *a spiral spring|a spiral staircase*

spiral[2] v **-l-** *AmE*||**-ll-** *BrE* [I] to move in a SPIRAL[1]; rise or fall in a winding way: *The damaged plane spiraled towards the earth.|The President is worried about spiraling prices.*

spire /spaɪər/ n a tower rising steeply to a point, as on a church

spir·it[1] /'spɪrɪt/ n **1** [C *in* + U] a person's soul or mind: *His spirit was troubled.|I can't come to your wedding, but I'll be there in spirit.* (=I'll think about you on the day)*|The religious leader has been dead for a long time but his spirit lives on in the work of others.* **2** [C] a being without a body, such as a GHOST (1): *There are evil spirits in this old house.* **3** [*the* S *of*] the central quality or force of something that makes it special: *the 17th-century spirit of inquiry* **4** [U] force, effort, or excitement shown: *a horse with a lot of spirit|They always lose because they have no* **team spirit**. (=no feeling of loyalty to the team) **5** [S] an intention or feeling in the mind; ATTITUDE (1): *You should take my remarks in the right spirit, without feeling offended.|He came to the party, but didn't really* **enter into the spirit**

of it. (=didn't try to enjoy it) **6** [*the S of*] the real intended meaning of a law, rule, etc., rather than what it actually says: *Judges often try to apply the spirit of the law.* –opposite **letter 7** [C *usu. pl.*] a strong alcoholic drink, such as WHISKEY or BRANDY, produced by DISTILLing: *I prefer spirits to beer.*

spirit² *v* [T *away, off*] to take in a secret mysterious way:*The crowd waited outside the theater to see her, but she was spirited away through the back door.*

spir·it·ed /'spɪrɪtɪd/ *adj* **1** active and excited; ANIMATED: *a spirited argument/defense* **2** **-spirited** having a certain kind of character or feeling: HIGH-SPIRITED|PUBLIC SPIRITED

spirit lev·el /'·· ,··/ also **level** *AmE*– *n* a tool for testing whether a surface is level

spir·its /'spɪrɪts/ *n* [P] the cheerful or sad state of one's mind: *in high spirits* (=cheerful)

spir·it·u·al¹ /'spɪrɪtʃuʷəl/ *adj* **1** nonmaterial; of the nature of spirit: *one's spiritual nature* –compare INTELLECTUAL **2** religious; holy: *spiritual songs|an adviser in spiritual matters* –**spiritually** *adv*

spiritual² *n* a religious song sung originally by the black people of the US

spir·it·u·al·ism /'spɪrɪtʃuʷə,lɪzəm, -tʃə,lɪz əm/ *n* [U] the belief that dead people may send messages to living people usu. through a person (MEDIUM²) with special powers –**spiritualist** *n*

spit¹ /spɪt/ *v* **spit** *AmE*|also **spat** /spæt/, **spit·ting** [I;T *out, up*] to force (liquid) from the mouth: *to spit on the ground|He's very ill and spitting (up) blood.|The baby spit up* (=VOMITED) *on the rug.|* (fig.) *She angrily spat out her answer.*

spit² *n* [U] the liquid in the mouth; SALIVA

spit³ *n* **1** a thin pointed rod for sticking meat onto, for cooking over a fire **2** a small usu. sandy point of land running out into a stretch of water

spite¹ /spaɪt/ *n* [U] **1** unreasonable dislike for and desire to annoy another person: *I'm sure she took my parking space just* **out of/from spite. 2 in spite of** taking no notice of; although something is true: *I went out in spite of the rain.* –see Study Notes on page 144 –**spiteful** /'spaɪtfəl/ *adj* –**spitefully** *adv* –**spitefulness** *n* [U]

spite² *v* **spited, spiting** [T] to treat with SPITE¹; annoy intentionally: *He took her to the movies just to spite me.*

spit·tle /'spɪtl/ *n* [U] → SPIT²; SALIVA

splash¹ /splæʃ/ *v* [I;T] **a** (of a liquid) to fall or strike noisily, in drops, waves, etc.: *The rain splashed on the window.* **b** to cause (a liquid) to do this; throw a liquid (at): *children splashing water in the bath|He splashed his face with cold water.*

splash² *n* **1** a SPLASHing¹ act, movement, or noise: *I fell into the water with a splash.* **2** a

---

SPELLING NOTE

Words with the sound /s/, may be spelled **c-**, like **city**, or **ps-**, like **psychology**.

---

mark made by SPLASHing¹: *a splash of paint on the floor*

splat /splæt/ *n,adv* [S; *adv + prep*] (with) a noise of something wet hitting a surface

splay /spleʸ/ *v* **splayed, splaying** [I;T *out*] to (cause to) spread out or become larger at one end

splen·did /'splɛndɪd/ *adj* **1** grand in appearance; glorious: *a splendid golden crown* **2** very fine; excellent: *a splendid day* –**splen·didly** *adv* –**splendor** *AmE*||**-dour** *BrE* /'splɛndər/ *n* [U] grand beauty: *the splendor of the high distant mountains*

splice /splaɪs/ *v* **spliced, splicing** [T *to, together*] to fasten end to end, by weaving (ropes), sticking (pieces of film), etc.: *The recording tape's broken; can you splice these two pieces together?*

splint /splɪnt/ *n* a flat piece of wood, metal, etc., used for keeping a broken bone in position

splin·ter¹ /'splɪntər/ *n* **1** [C] a small needle-like piece broken off something: *to get a splinter in one's finger* **2** [A] a group that has separated from a larger body: *They disagreed with the party's decision, so they formed* **a splinter** group.

splinter² *v* [I;T] to (cause to) break into small needle-like pieces

split¹ /splɪt/ *v* **split, splitting 1** [I;T] to (cause to) divide along the length, esp. by a blow or tear: *This soft wood splits easily.|His coat split down the back.* **2** [I;T *up, into*] to divide into separate often opposing parts or groups: *We split (up) into two groups, and searched the forest.|The book is split up into 12 CHAP-TERS.|an argument which split the political party|Who was the first person to split the atom?* **3** [T] to divide among people; share: *I'll come with you, and we'll split the cost of the gas.* **4** [I *up, with*] to end a friendship, marriage, etc.: *Did you know that John and Mary split up?* (=that their marriage ended) **5** [I] *AmE* (of shares in the ownership of a company) to be multiplied so that each holder gets a certain, often stated, number for each one held: *The stock has lately split 2 for 1.*

split² *n* **1** a cut or break made by splitting: *to fix a split in my pants* **2** a division or separation within a group: *a split in the party*

split-lev·el /,· '··◄/ *adj* (of a building) having floors at different heights in different parts

split sec·ond /,· '··◄/ *n* a small part of a second; moment –**split-second** *adj*

split·ting /'splɪtɪŋ/ *adj* (esp. of a headache) very painful

splut·ter¹ /'splʌtər/ *n* a wet SPITTING¹ noise: *The fire went out with a few splutters as the rain fell.*

splutter² *v* **1** [I;T] to say or talk quickly and as if confused: *"But, but . . .," he spluttered.* –see also SPUTTER **2** [I] to make a wet SPIT-ting¹ noise

spoil¹ /spɔɪl/ *v* **spoiled** or **spoilt** /spɔɪlt/, **spoil·ing** [T] to make useless; ruin: *The visit was spoiled by an argument.|He spoiled the soup by putting too much salt in it.* **2** [I] to decay or lose goodness: *The fruit has spoiled in the hot* *sun.* **3** [T] to treat very or too well: *This hotel advertises that it spoils its guests.|a spoiled and selfish child who gets too much attention*

spoil² *n* [C;U] things taken without payment, as by an army or by thieves: *to divide up the spoil(s)*

spoil·sport /ˈspɔɪlspɔrt, -spoʷrt/ *n* a person who puts an end to someone else's fun

spoke¹ /spoʷk/ *n* any of the bars which connect the outer ring of a wheel to the center, as on a bicycle

spoke² *v past tense of* SPEAK

spo·ken /ˈspoʷkən/ *v* **1** *past participle of* SPEAK **2** -**spoken** speaking in a certain way: *well-spoken|soft-spoken*

spokes·man /ˈspoʷksmən/ **spokeswoman** /-ˌwʊmən/ *fem.*, also **spokesperson** /-ˌpɜrsən/– *n* -**men** /mən/ a person chosen to speak for a group officially

sponge¹ /spʌndʒ/ *n* **1** [C] a simple sea creature which grows a spreading rubber-like frame full of small holes **2** [C;U] a piece of this animal's frame or of rubber or plastic like it, used for washing the body, dishes, etc.

sponge² *v* **sponged, sponging 1** [T *off, down*] to clean with a wet cloth or SPONGE¹ (2): *to sponge down the car* **2** [T] to remove (liquid) in this way: *to sponge blood from a wound* **3** [I *on, from*] *derog* to get money, meals, etc., free by taking advantage of another's good nature; FREELOAD –**sponger** *n*: *He's a real sponger; he always comes by at dinnertime for a free meal.*

sponge cake /ˈ· ·/ *n* [C;U] (a) light cake made from eggs, sugar, and flour

spon·gy /ˈspʌndʒiʸ/ *adj* -**gier, -giest** like a SPONGE¹ (1); soft and wet: *The grass is spongy after the rain.* –**sponginess** *n* [U]

spon·sor¹ /ˈspɑnsər/ *n* **1** a person who takes responsibility for a person or thing: *the sponsor of a* BILL¹ (2) *in Congress* **2** a business which pays for a show, sports event, etc., usu. in return for advertising –**sponsorship** *n* [U]

sponsor² *v* [T] to act as SPONSOR for: *The baseball game is being sponsored by a cigarette company.*

spon·ta·ne·ous /spɑnˈteʸniʸəs/ *adj* produced from natural feelings or causes; unplanned: *a spontaneous cheer from the crowd* –**spontaneously** *adv* –**spontaneity** /ˌspɑntəˈniʸəṭiʸ, -ˈneʸ-/ *n* [U]

spoof /spuʷf/ *n* a funny untrue copy or description; PARODY¹ (2): *a magazine spoof of college life*

spook¹ /spuʷk/ *n infml* a spirit; GHOST (1)

spook² *v* [T] *infml esp. AmE* to cause to be suddenly afraid: *That movie spooked me!*

spook·y /ˈspuʷkiʸ/ *adj* -**ier, -iest** *infml* causing fear in a strange way; EERIE: *a spooky old house*

spool /spuʷl/ *n* **1** a wheel for winding wire, thread, camera film, etc., around **2** *AmE* for REEL¹

spoon¹ /spuʷn/ *n* **1** a tool for mixing, serving, and eating food: *a silver/wooden spoon|a* TEASPOON –see illustration on page 379 **2** → SPOONFUL: *two spoons of sugar*

spoon² *v* [T *up, out*] to take up or move with a spoon: *Spoon (out) the mixture into glasses.*

spoon-feed /ˈ· ·, ˌ· ˈ·/ *v* -**fed, -feeding** [T] **1** to feed (esp. a baby) with a spoon **2** to teach (people or a subject) in very easy lessons

spoon·ful /ˈspuʷnfʊl/ also **spoon–** *n* **spoonfuls** the amount that a spoon will hold: *two teaspoonfuls of sugar*

spo·rad·ic /spəˈrædɪk/ *adj* happening irregularly: *sporadic fighting* –**sporadically** *adv*

spore /spɔr, spoʷr/ *n* a very small seedlike cell produced by some plants, which is able to develop into a new plant

sport¹ /spɔrt, spoʷrt/ *n* **1** [C;U] a game or activity done for physical exercise and pleasure: *Do you think football is an exciting sport?* –see RECREATION (USAGE) **2** [C] a person who accepts defeat or a joke without becoming angry or upset: *You're a sport/a good sport to laugh at the trick we played on you.*

sport² *v* [T] to wear publicly: *She came in today sporting a fur coat.*

sport·ing /ˈspɔrṭɪŋ, ˈspoʷr-/ *adj* **1** [A] of or concerning outdoor sports: *a painter of sporting scenes* **2** fair-minded and generous, esp. in sports: *It was very sporting of them to let our team bat first.* –opposite **unsporting 3** offering a fair risk: *a sporting chance of winning* –**sportingly** *adv*

sports /spɔrts, spoʷrts/ *n* **1** [A] also **sport** *AmE*– (esp. of clothes) *informal: a sport(s)* JACKET **2** for, or connected with sports: *the sports page of the paper*

sports car /ˈ· ·/ *n* a low usu. open fast car

sports·cast /ˈspɔrts-kæst, ˈspoʷrts-/ *n* a broadcast of sporting news or a sporting event

sports·man /ˈspɔrtsmən, ˈspoʷr-/ **sportswoman** /-ˌwʊmən/ *fem.– n* -**men** /mən/ **1** a person who plays sports **2** a good SPORT¹ (2)

sports·man·like /ˈspɔrtsmən,laɪk, ˈspoʷrts-/ *adj* showing good SPORTSMANSHIP –opposite **unsportsmanlike**

sports·man·ship /ˈspɔrtsmən,ʃɪp, ˈspoʷrts-/ *n* [U] a spirit of fair play and graceful winning and losing

spot¹ /spɑt/ *n* **1** [C] a usu. round part or area different from the main surface, e.g. in color: *a white dress with blue spots* **2** [C] a particular place: *Spain is our favorite vacation spot.|Wherever she's needed she's quickly* **on the spot.** (=at the place of action) **3** [C] a dirty mark: *to clean off ink spots with soap and water* **4** [S] a difficult position; FIX² (1): *Now that we've lost the key we're really in a spot!* **5** [A] limited to a few times or places: *We don't have to test everyone; we'll just make spot* CHECKS¹ (3). **6 hit the spot** *infml* to satisfy a need, such as thirst or hunger

spot² *v* -**tt-** [T] **1** to pick out with the eye; recognize: *to spot a friend in a crowd* **2** to mark with spots: *white cloth spotted with green|a spotted dog*

spot·less /ˈspɑtlɪs/ *adj* completely clean: *a spotless house|(fig.) a spotless* REPUTATION –**spotlessly** *adv* –**spotlessness** *n* [U]

spot·light¹ /ˈspɑtlaɪt/ *n* **1** [C] a lamp with a

narrow beam that can be directed, used esp. in theaters **2** [*the* S] public attention: *in the political spotlight this week*

spotlight² *v* [T] to direct attention to, (as if) with a SPOTLIGHT: *an article spotlighting crime in the cities*

spot·ter /'spɒtər/ *n* a person who keeps watch for a particular thing, esp. during a war: *an airplane spotter.*

spot·ty /'spɒtiʸ/ *adj* **-tier, -tiest 1** having spots **2** *AmE* with some parts different from others; irregular; PATCHY: *The book was spotty; it had some good parts and some bad.*

spouse /spaʊs, spaʊz/ *n usu. fml or law* a husband or wife

spout¹ /spaʊt/ *v* **1** [I;T *out*] to throw or come out in a forceful stream: *a well spouting oil* **2** [T] to pour out in a stream of words: *She's always spouting Shakespeare.*

spout² *n* an opening from which liquid comes out, such as a tube or pipe: *the spout of a teapot*

sprain /spreyⁿ/ *v* [T] to damage (a joint in the body) by sudden twisting: *to sprain one's ankle* **–sprain** *n* : *a bad sprain of the ankle*

sprang /spræŋ/ *v past tense of* SPRING¹

sprawl /sprɔl/ *v* **1** [I;T *out*] to stretch out (oneself or one's limbs) awkwardly in lying or sitting: *She sprawled (herself) out in a comfortable chair* **2** [I *out*] to spread ungracefully: *The city sprawls for miles in each direction.* **–sprawl** *n*

spray¹ /spreyʸ/ *n* **1** [U] water in very small drops blown from the sea, a waterfall, etc.: *We parked the car by the sea and it got covered with spray.* **2** [C;U] (a can or other container holding) liquid to be SPRAYED² out under pressure: *spray paint/insect spray* (=to kill insects)

spray² *v* [I;T *with/on*] to scatter or be scattered in small drops under pressure: *to spray paint on a wall/spray a wall with paint* (fig.) *They sprayed the President's car with bullets.*

spray³ *n* (an arrangement of flowers, jewels, etc. in the shape of) a small branch with its leaves and flowers

spray·er /'spreyʸər/ *n* a person or apparatus that SPRAYS² out a liquid

spread¹ /sprɛd/ *v* **spread, spreading 1** [I;T *out*] to (cause to) open, reach, or stretch out; make or become longer, broader, wider, etc.: *a ship with sails spread/The fire/The news soon spread through the whole of the town.* **2** [I *over, for*] to cover a large area or period of time: *His interests now spread over several subjects.* **3** [T *with, on*] to put (a covering) on: *to spread butter on bread/spread a piece of bread with butter* **4** [T *over*] to scatter, share, or divide over an area, period of time, etc.; DISTRIBUTE: *to spread the cost over three years* **5** [I;T] to make or become widely known: *If I tell you this secret, don't spread it around.*

spread² *n* **1** [S] the act or action of spreading: *the spread of a disease/one's interests/the city* **2** [C *usu. sing.*] a distance, area, or time of spreading: *a tree with a spread of 100 feet/The students' ages show a wide spread./a 1,000-ACRE spread in Texas* **3** [C] a newspaper or magazine article or advertisement usu. running across one or more pages: *a two-page spread* **4** [C] a large or grand meal: *Our host had a fine spread waiting for us.* **5** [C;U] a soft food for spreading on bread: *a dish of cheese spread*

spread-ea·gle /'· ˌ··/ *v* **-gled, -gling** [I;T *usu.pass.*] to put or go into a position with arms and legs spread out: *to lie spread-eagled on the bed*

spree /spriʸ/ *n* a time of free and wild fun, spending, drinking, etc.

sprig /sprɪg/ *n* a small end of a stem or branch with leaves: *soup with a sprig of* PARSLEY

spright·ly /'spraɪtliʸ/ *adj* **-lier, -liest** cheerful and active; LIVELY (1): *a sprightly dance/old man* –compare SPRY **–sprightliness** *n* [U]

spring¹ /sprɪŋ/ *v* **sprang** /spræŋ/, **sprung** /sprʌŋ/, **springing 1** [I] to jump; BOUND⁵ (1): *She sprang to her feet/sprang over the wall.* **2** [I *up*] to happen or appear quickly from nothing; arise: *A wind suddenly sprang up./Towns sprang up in the desert when gold was found there.* **3** [I;T] to open or close with a SPRING² (3): *The box sprang open when I touched the button.* **4** [T *on*] to produce as a surprise: *to spring a surprise party on someone* **5 spring a leak** (of a ship, container, etc.) to begin to let liquid through a crack, hole, etc.

spring² *n* **1** [C] a place where water comes up naturally from the ground –compare SOURCE (2) **2** [C] (*often cap.*) the season between winter and summer in which leaves and flowers appear **3** [C] an object, usu. a length of metal wound around, which returns to its original shape after being pushed, pulled, etc.: *a watch-spring/What an uncomfortable chair! It needs new springs.* **4** [U] the quality of this object; elasticity: *not much spring in this old bed* **5** [C] an act of springing: *The cat made a spring at the mouse.*

spring·board /'sprɪŋbɔrd -boʷrd/ *n* a board for jumping off to give height to a DIVE² (1) or jump: (fig.) *a springboard to success*

spring-clean·ing /ˌ· '··/ *AmE*‖**spring clean** /'· ·/ *BrE*– *n* [S] a thorough cleaning of one's house, esp. in the spring

spring fe·ver /ˌ· '··/ *n* [U] a lazy or restless feeling thought to come at the beginning of spring

spring·y /'sprɪŋiʸ/ *adj* **-ier, -iest** having SPRING² (4)

sprin·kle /'sprɪŋkəl/ *v* **-kled, -kling** [T *with/on*] to scatter in drops or small grains: *to sprinkle water on the grass/the grass with water* (fig.) *a book sprinkled with humor*

sprin·kler /'sprɪŋklər/ *n* an apparatus for scattering drops of water: *a garden sprinkler/a sprinkler system in a building for protection against fire*

sprin·kling /'sprɪŋklɪŋ/ *n* [*of*] a small scattered group or amount: *a sprinkling of* *snow/of new faces in the crowd*

sprint¹ /sprɪnt/ v [I] to run at one's fastest speed for a short distance –see WALK (USAGE) –**sprinter** n

sprint² n **1** an act of SPRINTing **2** a short race: *the 100 meters sprint*

sprite /spraɪt/ n a fairy, esp. a playful one

sprout¹ /spraʊt/ v [I;T *from, up*] to (cause to) grow or send up new growth: *leaves beginning to sprout from trees*

sprout² n **1** a new growth on a plant; SHOOT² (1) **2** → BRUSSELS SPROUT

spruce¹ /spruːˢ/ n [C;U] (the wood of) a tree with short needle-shaped leaves found in northern parts of the world

spruce² adj tidy and clean –**sprucely** adv: *sprucely dressed*

spruce³ v **spruced, sprucing** [T *up*] to make SPRUCE²: *to spruce oneself (up) for a party*

sprung /sprʌŋ/ v past participle of SPRING¹

spry /spraɪ/ adj (esp. of old people) active; quick in movement: *a spry old lady* –compare SPRIGHTLY

spud /spʌd/ n infml a potato

spun /spʌn/ v past tense & participle of SPIN¹

spur¹ /spɜr/ n **1** a pointed object worn on the heel of a rider's boot to urge on a horse **2** a force leading to action; INCENTIVE: *news which will be a spur to continued effort* **3 on the spur of the moment** without preparation or planning: *We hadn't planned to go to Europe; we just bought tickets on the spur of the moment.*

spur² v **-rr-** [T] **1** to prick (a horse) with SPURS¹ (1) **2** [+*to-v/on*] to urge to faster action or greater effort: *She spurred on her team to try harder.*

spu·ri·ous /ˈspjʊəriʸəs/ adj **1** like something else but false: *a spurious signature* **2** bad in reasoning; WRONG: *a spurious argument* –**spuriously** adv –**spuriousness** n [U]

spurn /spɜrn/ v [T] to refuse with angry pride; SCORN² (1): *She spurned all offers of help.*

spurt¹ /spɜrt/ n **1** a short sudden increase of effort; BURST²: *She had a spurt of energy and finished her work in two hours.* **2** a sudden coming out of liquid or gas: *a spurt of blood*

spurt² v [I *out, from*] to flow out suddenly: *Water spurted from the broken pipe.*

sput·ter /ˈspʌtər/ v **1** [I;T] to say or speak in confusion; SPLUTTER² (1) **2** [I] to make repeated soft explosive sounds: *The car's engine sputtered for a moment and then died.* –**sputter** n

spy¹ /spaɪ/ n **spies** a person employed to find out secret information, as from an enemy or company

spy² v **spied, spying 1** [I *into, on, upon*] to watch secretly: *He's always spying on neighbors.|to spy into the affairs of others.* **2** [I *on, upon*] to act as a SPY¹ **3** [T] esp. lit to catch sight of: *She spied her friend in the crowd.*

sq. written abbrev. said as: square: *6 sq. meters*

squab·ble /ˈskwɒbəl/ v,n **-bled, -bling** [C; I] (to have) a quarrel over something unimpor-

tant: *What are you children squabbling about now?*

squad /skwɒd/ n a group of people working as a team: *The bomb squad has arrived.*

squad car /'· ·/ AmE‖also **patrol car** esp. BrE– n a car used by the police for PATROLing² (1) the streets

squad·ron /ˈskwɒdrən/ n a large group of, soldiers with TANKs (2), of warships, or of aircraft in an airforce: *The squadron is ready for duty.*

squal·id /ˈskwɒlɪd/ adj very dirty and uncared-for: *squalid living conditions* –**squalidly** adv –**squalor** /ˈskwɒlər/ n [U]: *a part of the city now sunk into squalor*

squall /skwɔl/ n a sudden strong wind often bringing rain or snow –**squally** adj

squan·der /ˈskwɒndər/ v [T] to spend foolishly; use up wastefully: *The government is squandering our money on atomic weapons.*

square¹ /skwɛər/ n **1** a shape with four straight equal sides forming four RIGHT ANGLES: *Draw a square with sides of 10 centimeters.|a square of cloth* –compare RECTANGLE, OBLONG **2** (the buildings surrounding) a broad open place at the meeting of streets: *The market is held in the town square.|He lives near Washington Square.* –see STREET (USAGE) **3** a number equal to another number multiplied by itself: *16 is the square of 4.* –see also SQUARE ROOT **4** a straight-edged often L-shaped tool for drawing and measuring right angles **5** infml now rare a person who does not follow the latest ideas, styles, etc.: *Don't ask her advice about clothes; she's a real square!* **6 square one**, the very beginning; starting point: *All my papers were lost in the fire, so now I'm back to square one.*

square² adj **1** [no comp.] having four equal sides and four right angles: *A handkerchief is usually square.|a square tower* **2** (nearly) forming a right angle: *a square jaw|square shoulders* **3** level: *That shelf isn't square on the wall; can you straighten it?* **4** [A no comp.] being a measurement of area equal to that of a square with sides of a particular length: *144 square inches equals 1 square foot.* **5** [after n; no comp.] being the stated length on all four sides: *The room is 6 meters square.* **6** [F no comp.] paid and settled: *Our account is all square.* **7** [F no comp.] equal in points; TIED² (3): *The teams are all square at one game each.* **8** infml now rare of or like a SQUARE¹ (5); old-fashioned **9 square deal** fair and honest treatment: *I don't think I'm getting a square deal at that garage.* –see also FAIR² (2) and **square 10 a square meal** a good satisfying meal: *three square meals a day* –**squarely** adv –**squareness** n [U]

square³ v **squared, squaring 1** [T] to make square: *He squared off the end of the piece of wood.|"I won't be threatened," she said, squaring her shoulders.* **2** [T] to mark squares on: *squared paper* **3** [T usu. pass.] to multiply (a number) by itself once: *2 squared equals 4.* (written $2^2=4$) **4** [I;T *with*] to (cause to) fit a particular explanation or standard: *His statement doesn't square with the facts.* **5** [T] to pay or pay for; settle: *I squared my account at the store.*

square sthg. **away** *v adv* [T *often pass.*] *AmE infml* to put in order; settle correctly: *to help a new man to get himself/his things squared away*

  square up *v adv* [I] *infml* to settle a bill: *Let's square up: how much is the bill?*

square⁴ also **squarely**– *adv* [*adv* + *prep*] *infml* directly; with nothing in the way: *He looked her square in the eye.*

square knot /'· ·/ *n AmE* a kind of double knot that will not come undone easily: *Tie the rope in a square knot.*

square root /,· '··/ *n* the number not less than 0 which when multiplied by itself equals a particular number: *3 is the square root of 9.* (because 3x3=9) –see also SQUARE¹ (3)

squash¹ /skwɑʃ, skwɔʃ/ *v* **1** [I;T] to force or be forced into a flat shape or a small space: *I sat on my hat and squashed it.|Can I squash in next to you?* **2** [T] to force into silence or inactivity: *squashed by an unkind remark*

squash² *n* **1** [C] an act or sound of SQUASH-ing: *I heard a squash when I dropped the bag.* **2** [U] a game played in a walled court with RACKETS¹ and a rubber ball

squash³ *n* **squash** *or* **squashes** [C; U] any of a group of large fairly solid vegetables including GOURDS and PUMPKINS

squat¹ /skwɑt/ *v* **-tt-** [I] **1** to sit on a surface with one's legs drawn fully up or under the body **2** to live in a place without permission; be a SQUATTER

squat² *adj* ungracefully short or low and thick: *an ugly squat building*

squat·ter /'skwɑtər/ *n* a person who lives on a piece of land or in an empty building without permission

squaw /skwɔ/ *n* an American Indian woman

squawk /skwɔk/ *n,v* [C;I] (to make) a loud rough-sounding cry, esp. as made by birds: *hens squawking at the sight of a cat*(fig.) *Don't squawk about the work! You're being well-paid.*

squeak /skwiʸk/ *n,v* [C;I] (to make) a very high but not loud sound: *a squeaking door/the squeak of a mouse* –**squeaky** *adj* **-ier, -iest**: *a squeaky voice*

squeal /skwiʸl/ *n,v* [C;I] (to make) a long very high sound or cry: *squealing tires/pigs/squeals of delight from the children*

squeam·ish /'skwiʸmɪʃ/ *adj* easily shocked; unable to stand unpleasantness: *It's a violent movie, so don't go if you're squeamish.* –**squeamishly** *adv* –**squeamishness** *n* [U]

squeeze¹ /skwiʸz/ *v* **squeezed, squeezing** **1** [T] to press together; COMPRESS¹ (1): *to squeeze an orange/squeeze out a wet cloth* **2** [I;T] to fit by forcing, CROWDING, or pressing: *The car was full, but I squeezed in anyway.|We squeezed seven people into the car.*

SPELLING NOTE

Words with the sound /s/, may be spelled **c-**, like **city**, or **ps-**, like **psychology**.

---

3 [T *from, out of*] to force out by pressure: *to squeeze toothpaste out of a tube*

squeeze² *n* **1** [C] an act of pressing in from opposite sides or around: *She gave his hand a gentle squeeze.* **2** [C] a small amount SQUEEZEd¹ (3) out: *a squeeze of lemon* **3** [S] a condition of CROWDING or pressing: *There's room for one more, but it'll be a squeeze.* **4** [C] a difficult state of affairs caused by short supplies, tight controls, etc.: *a HOUS-ING/CREDIT squeeze*

squelch¹ /skwɛltʃ/ *v* [T] to force into silence or inactivity; crush: *a desire for freedom which nothing could squelch*

squelch² *n,v* (to make) a sound of partly liquid material being pressed down, e.g. when stepping through mud

squid /skwɪd/ *n* **squid** *or* **squids** a sea creature with 10 arms at one end of a long body

squig·gle /'skwɪɡəl/ *n infml* a short wavy or twisting line: *What do these squiggles on the map mean?* –**squiggly** *adj*

squint¹ /skwɪnt/ *v* [I] **1** to look with almost closed eyes, as at a bright light **2** [not *be* +*v-ing*] to have a SQUINT²

squint² *n* a disorder of the eye muscles caus-ing the eyes to look in two different directions

squire /skwaɪər/ *n* (esp. formerly) the main landowner in an English country area

squirm /skwɜrm/ *v* [I] to twist the body around, as from discomfort or nervousness: *questions that made him squirm*

squir·rel /'skwɜrəl, 'skwʌrəl/ *n* a small four-legged animal with a long furry tail that climbs trees and eats nuts

squirt¹ /skwɜrt/ *v* **1** [I;T] to force or be forced out in a thin stream: *to squirt oil into a lock| water squirting from a hole in the pipe* **2** [T *with*] to hit with a stream of liquid: *I was squirted with water.*

squirt² *n* **1** a quick thin stream; JET¹ (1) **2** *infml derog* a young unimportant person

Sr. [after *n*] written abbrev. said as: SENIOR

Ssh /ʃ/ *interj* → SH

St. *n* written abbrev. said as: **1** [after *n*] Street: *Maple St.* **2** [A] SAINT: *St. Andrew*

stab¹ /stæb/ *n* **1** a wound made with a pointed weapon: *a stab in the chest* **2** a sudden painful feeling; PANG: *a stab of guilt* **3 take a stab at** to try to: *Take a stab at (answering) question 3.*

stab² *v* **-bb-** [I;T *at*] to strike forcefully with a pointed weapon: *Julius Caesar was stabbed in the chest/stabbed to death.*

stab·bing /'stæbɪŋ/ *adj* (esp. of pain) sharp and sudden

sta·bil·i·ty /stə'bɪlətiʸ/ *n* [U] the state of being STABLE³; steadiness: *the stability of their mar-riage* –opposite **instability**

sta·bi·lize ‖also **-lise** *BrE* /'steʸbə,laɪz/ *v* **-lized, -lizing** [I;T] to make or become firm or steady: *The price of coffee has been rising and falling, but has now stabilized.* –**stabil-ization** /,steʸbələ'zeʸʃən/ *n* [U]

sta·bi·liz·er ‖also **-liser** *BrE* /'steʸbə,laɪzər/ *n* an apparatus or chemical that STABILIZEs something: *The ship's stabilizers make it comfortable even in bad weather.*

sta·ble¹ /'steʸbəl/ *n* [*often pl.*] **1** a building for keeping and feeding horses in **2** a group of racing horses with one owner

stable² v **-bled, -bling** [T] to put in a STABLE¹ (1)

stable³ adj not easily moved, upset, or changed; firm: *a stable chair/government/character* –opposite **unstable** –**stably** adv

stack¹ /stæk/ n [of] **1** an orderly pile: *a stack of papers/dishes* **2** infml a large amount or number: *stacks of work to do*

stack² v [I;T] **1** [up] to make into a neat pile; arrange in a STACK: *The chairs were neatly stacked at the back of the hall.* **2** [against] infml esp. AmE to arrange unfairly and dishonestly: *He said his opponent had cheated by stacking the cards.*

stack up v adv, infml AmE **1** [I against] to compare; measure; match: *How does this product stack up against the competition's?* **2** [I] to be as a result or condition: *That's how things stack up today.*

sta·di·um /ˈsteʸdiʸəm/ n **-diums** or **-dia** /diʸə/ a large sports ground with rows of seats built around a sports field

staff¹ /stæf/ n the group of workers who do the work of an organization: *The school's teaching staff is excellent.|a staff of 15|She's* **on the staff of** *the new university.*

staff² v [T with] to supply with STAFF; provide the workers for: *a hospital staffed with 20 doctors*

staff³ n a thick stick used as a support or as a mark of office

stag /stæg/ n **stags** or **stag 1** a fully grown male deer **2 stag party** a party for men only, esp. just before a man gets married

stage¹ /steʸdʒ/ n **1** [C] a period in a course of events: *The plan is still in its early stages/at an early stage.* **2** [C] a part of a journey: *We traveled by (easy) stages, stopping often along the way.* **3** [C] the raised floor on which plays are performed in a theater: *The actor was* **on stage** *for hours.* **4** [the S] work in the theater: *When she was five years old, she decided that she wanted to go on the stage.* (=become an actress)

stage² v **staged, staging** [T] **1** to perform or arrange for public show; put on: *to stage an art show/a football game* **2** to cause to happen, esp. for public effect: *to stage a one-day* STRIKE² (1)

stage·coach /ˈsteʸdʒkoʷtʃ/ n (in former times) a horse-drawn closed vehicle carrying passengers: *to travel* **by stagecoach**

stage fright /ˈ· ·/ n [U] nervousness felt when performing in public

stage man·ag·er /ˈ· ˌ···/ n a person in charge of a theater stage during a performance

stag·ger¹ /ˈstægər/ v **1** [I] to move unsteadily on one's feet: *a drunk man staggering across the street* **2** [T] to arrange not to come at the same time: *Our vacations are staggered; John's off for a week, then I'm off for a week.*

stagger² n an unsteady movement of a person having difficulty walking: *She walked with a stagger after her accident.*

stag·ger·ing /ˈstægərɪŋ/ adj almost unbelievable; very surprising: *a staggering*

rise in the cost of gas –**staggeringly** adv

stag·ing /ˈsteʸdʒɪŋ/ n **1** [C;U] the action or art of producing a play: *a new staging of "Hamlet"* **2** [U] movable boards and frames for standing on

stag·nant /ˈstægnənt/ adj (of water) not flowing or moving, and often bad-smelling: (fig.) *Business is stagnant at the moment.* (=inactive) –**stagnantly** adv

stag·nate /ˈstægneʸt/ v **-nated, -nating** [I] to become STAGNANT; stop moving or developing –**stagnation** /stægˈneʸʃən/ n [U]

staid /steʸd/ adj serious and dull by habit; unadventurous –**staidly** adv –**staidness** n [U]

stain¹ /steʸn/ v [I;T] **1** to change the color of, in a way that is lasting: *teeth stained by years of smoking|stained* (=colored) *glass windows in a church* **2** to darken using chemicals: *to stain the chairs to match the dark table*

stain² n [C;U] **1** a STAINed place or spot: *bloodstains on my shirt|*(lit.) *the stain upon his honor* **2** a chemical for darkening esp. wood

stain·less /ˈsteʸnlɪs/ adj not easily broken down chemically (esp. RUSTed) by air and water: *a set of stainless steel knives*

stair /steɑr/ n **1** → STAIRS **2** a step in a set of stairs

stair·case /ˈsteɑrkeʸs/ also **stairway** /-weʸ/– n a set of stairs with its supports and side parts

stairs /steɑrz/ n [P] a fixed length of steps built for going from one level to another, esp. inside a building: *to go up and down the stairs|a* **flight of stairs** –see also DOWNSTAIRS, UPSTAIRS

stake¹ /steʸk/ n **1** [C] a pointed piece of wood for driving into the ground as a mark, for holding a rope, etc. **2** [the S] (in former times) a post to which a person was tied in order to be killed by burning **3** [C] also **stakes**– something that may be gained or lost; INTEREST¹ (4): *Profit-sharing gives workers a stake in their company's business.|He lost his stake* (=money he had STAKEd²) *when the horse finished last.* **4 at stake** at risk

stake² v **staked, staking** [T +(that)/on] **1** to risk (esp. money) on a result; BET: *Even though the stakes* (=amount risked) *were high, he decided to join the card game.|Don't fail. I've staked all my hopes on you.* **2** [T out, off] to mark (an area of ground) with STAKEs (1): *Stake off part of the field.* **3 stake (out) one's/a claim** to make a claim; state that something is one's by right: *He staked a claim to the land where he found the oil.*

stake out v adv [T] infml to cause (a place) to be watched secretly all the time by police: *The police staked out the drug dealer's house.* –**stakeout** n

sta·lac·tite /stəˈlæktaɪt/ n a sharp downward-pointing part of a cave roof like an ICICLE, formed over a long time by water dropping from the roof –compare STALAGMITE

sta·lag·mite /stəˈlægmaɪt/ n an upward-pointing part of a cave floor formed by drops from a STALACTITE and often joining it to form a solid pillar

stale /steˠl/ *adj* no longer fresh: *pieces of stale bread for the birds*|(fig.) *the same stale jokes I've heard 50 times before* –**staleness** *n* [C;U]

stale·mate /'steˠlmeˠt/ *n* [C;U] **1** (in the game of CHESS) a position from which neither player can win **2** a condition in which neither side in a quarrel, argument, etc., can get an advantage

stalk¹ /stɔk/ *v* **1** [T] to hunt (esp. an animal) by following it quietly and staying hidden: *to stalk a criminal* **2** [I] to walk stiffly and proudly: *She was so angry with him that she stalked out of the house.*

stalk² *n* the main part of a plant supporting its leaves, fruits, or flowers; stem: *a stalk of corn.*

stall¹ /stɔl/ *n* **1** an indoor enclosure (in a BARN or STABLE) for one animal: *cattle in their stalls* **2** a small enclosed space: *a* SHOWER¹ (3b) *stall* **3** a table or small open-fronted shop in a public place: *a market stall*|*a bookstall*

stall² *v* **1** [I] *infml* to delay: *Stop stalling and answer my question!* **2** [I;T] **a** (of an engine) to stop through lack of power or speed: *The car stalled on the hill.* **b** to cause or force (an engine) to do this

stal·lion /'stælyən/ *n* a fully-grown male horse –compare MARE

stalls /stɔlz/ *n* [P] *BrE* for ORCHESTRA (2)

stal·wart¹ /'stɔlwərt/ *adj* strong and unmoving in body, mind, purpose, etc.: *a stalwart supporter/fighter* –**stalwartly** *adv* –**stalwartness** *n* [U]

stalwart² *n* a firm follower, esp. of a political party

sta·men /'steˠmən/ *n tech* the male POLLEN-producing part of a flower

stam·i·na /'stæmənə/ *n* [U] the strength of body or mind to fight tiredness, illness, etc.; power to keep going: *You need great stamina to run in the 10,000 meter race.*

stam·mer¹ /'stæmər/ *v* [I;T] to speak or say with pauses and repeated sounds, either habitually or because of excitement, fear, etc.: *She stammers when she feels nervous.*|*He stammered his thanks.* –compare STUTTER –**stammerer** *n*

stammer² *n* [usu. sing.] the fault of STAMMERing in speech

stamp¹ /stæmp/ *v* **1** [I;T *on*] to put (the feet) down hard: *She was stamping around in the cold trying to keep her feet warm.*|*He stamped his foot angrily.* **2** [T *with/on*] to mark (a pattern, sign, letters, etc.) by pressing: *This machine stamps the date on all letters/stamps all letters with the date.*|*The title was stamped in gold on the book.* **3** [T] to stick a stamp onto: *Has this letter been stamped?*

stamp sthg.↔ **out** *v adv* [T] to put an end to completely; ERADICATE: *to stamp out a disease*

SPELLING NOTE

Words with the sound /s/, may be spelled **c-**, like **city**, or **ps-**, like **psychology**.

---

stamp² *n* **1** also **postage stamp** *fml*– a small piece of paper for sticking on a piece of mail, on certain official papers, etc. **2** (a mark made by) an instrument or tool for printing onto a surface: *The stamp in the library book shows it must be returned tomorrow.*|(fig.) *Her words have the stamp of truth.* –see illustration on page 467 **3** an act of stamping, e.g. with the foot

stam·pede¹ /stæm'piˠd/ *n* a sudden rush of fearful animals: (fig.) *a stampede to buy gold before the price goes up*

stampede² *v* **-peded, -peding** [I;T *into*] to drive or go in a disorderly or unreasonable rush: *We shouldn't be stampeded into doing anything foolish.*

stance /stæns/ *n* **1** a way of standing, esp. in various sports **2** a way of thinking; ATTITUDE (1)

stanch /stɔntʃ, stɑntʃ/ *AmE*‖also **staunch** *esp. BrE v* to stop the flow of (esp. blood)

stand¹ /stænd/ *v* **stood** /stʊd/, **standing 1** [I] to support oneself upright on one's feet: *I couldn't get a seat on the bus, so I had to stand.* –compare SIT **2** [I;T *up*] to (cause to) rise to a position of doing this: *He stood (up) when the lady entered the room.*|*He stood the child on the chair so that she could see.* **3** [I] to be in or take a particular position like this: *Stand back and let the man through.*|(fig.) *Stand firm; don't let them change your opinion.* **4** [I] to be in height: *The building stands over 200 feet high.* **5** [I;T] to be, put, or rest upright or on a base: *Few houses were left standing after the bomb hit.*|*The table stood in the corner.*|*Stand the ladder against the wall.* **6** [I +*to-v*] to be in a particular condition: *How do things stand at the moment?*|*My bank account stands at $500.*|*If this new law is passed, we stand to lose* (=will be in a position to lose) *a lot of money.* **7** [I] to remain unmoving or unchanged: *The machinery has been standing idle* (=unused) *for months.*|*Let the mixture of liquids stand overnight.*|*My offer of help still stands.* **8** [T +*v-ing*/not *be+v-ing*] (usu. used in NEGATIVES², questions, etc.) to accept successfully; bear: *I can't stand getting up early.*|*This work will not stand close examination.*|*He seems to like me, but I can't stand the sight of him.* –see BEAR (USAGE) **9** [T] to pay the cost of (something) for: *Let me stand you a drink.* **10** [I *for*] *BrE* for RUN¹ (11) **11** [I] *AmE* (of a vehicle) to park for a short time, as for waiting or loading (used esp. on signs in the phrase **no standing**) **12 know how/where one stands (with someone)** to know how someone feels about one: *He always says what he thinks, so you always know where you stand with him.* **13 stand a chance** to have a chance: *You don't stand a chance of getting the job!* **14 standing on one's head** *infml* with great ease: *I could do that job standing on my head.* **15 stand on one's hands/head** to support oneself on the hands/head and hands, with the feet in the air **16 stand on one's own (two) feet/legs** to be able to do something without help from others **17 stand something on its head** to change or upset something violently: *It was a discovery which stood the scientific world on its head.* **18 it stands to reason** it is clear to all sensible people; it is OBVIOUS **19 stand trial** to be tried in court

stand by[1] sbdy./sthg. *v prep* [T] to support; be loyal to: *Please stand by me in my hour of need.*|*I'll stand by my promise.*

stand by[2] *v adv* [I] **1** to remain inactive: *How can you stand by and watch your child ruin his life?* **2** (esp. in radio and military use) to stay ready: *Stand by to receive a message/ to fire.* –see also STANDBY

stand for sthg. *v prep* [T] **1** to be a sign or short form of; represent; mean: *What does "ESL" stand for? "English-as-a-Second-Language."* **2** to have as a principle; support: *Before we elect her to Congress, we want to know what she stands for.* **3**[+ *v-ing*] (used in NEGATIVE[2] sentences) to accept; PUT **up with:** *I won't stand for being treated like a child.*

stand in *v adv* [I *for*] to act as a STAND-IN: *She's standing in for him while he's on vacation.*

stand out *v adv* [I] **1** to have an easily-seen shape, color, etc.: *The road sign is easy to read; the words stand out well.* **2** to be much better or the best; *Among mystery writers, Agatha Christie stood out as the best.*

stand up *v adv* **1** [I *to, under*] to stay in good condition after hard use: *a good floor wax that will stand up to continual traffic* **2** [I] to be accepted as true or proven: *The charges you've made would never stand up in court.*

stand up for sbdy./ sthg. *v adv prep* [T] to defend against attack: *You have to stand up for your rights!*

stand[2] *n* **1** a strong effort of defense: *In February 1916 the French Army made a stand at Verdun.* **2** a clear, publicly-stated position: *If he wants my vote, he'll have to* **take a stand** *on the question of East-West relations.* **3** a piece of furniture for putting something on: *a hat stand*|*music stand* (for holding sheets of music) **4** also **stall**– a small often outdoor store or place for showing things: *a newsstand* (=selling newspapers) **5** a place where taxis wait for passengers **6** [*usu. pl.*] an open-fronted building at a sports ground with rows of seats or standing space rising behind each other: *He kicked the ball into the stands.* **7** *AmE* for WITNESS STAND: *Will the next witness take the stand?*

stand·ard[1] /'stændərd/ *n* **1** an acceptable degree of quality: *a teacher who sets high standards for his pupils/the standard of one's work.* **2** something fixed as a rule for measuring weight, value, etc.: *The government has an official standard for the purity of silver.* **3** a ceremonial flag: *the royal standard*

standard[2] *adj* **1** ordinary; not rare or special: *These nails come in three standard sizes.* **2** [A] generally recognized as correct or acceptable: *It's one of the standard books on the subject.*|*standard spelling/pronunciation* –compare NONSTANDARD, SUBSTANDARD

stand·ard·ize ‖also **-ise** *BrE* /'stændər‚daɪz/ *v* **-ized, -izing** [T] to make alike in every case: *a system of standardized road signs/a standar-*

dized test. –**standardization** /‚stændərdə'zeyʃən/ *n* [U]

standard of liv·ing /‚· · · '··/ *n* the degree of wealth and comfort in everyday life enjoyed by a person, country, etc.: *to have a high/low standard of living*

stand·by /'stændbaɪ/ *n* **-bys** a person or thing that is kept ready to be used: *If the electricity fails, the hospital has a standby power apparatus.*|*Keep the police* **on standby** *in case there's trouble.* –see also STAND **by**

stand-in /'· ·/ *n* a person who takes the place or job of another for a time –see also STAND **in**

stand·ing[1] /'stændɪŋ/ *adj* [A] remaining; kept in use or force: *We have a standing invitation; we can visit them whenever we like.*|*a standing army*|*a standing order for the newspaper to be delivered daily.*

standing[2] *n* [U] **1** rank; position in a system, organization, or list: *a lawyer of high standing* **2** continuance; time during which something has kept on; DURATION: *friends of* **long standing**

stand·off·ish /‚stænd'ɔfɪʃ/ *adj* rather unfriendly; coldly formal –**standoffishly** *adv* –**standoffishness** *n* [U]

stand·point /'stændpɔɪnt/ *n* a position from which things are seen and opinions formed; POINT[1] (20) **of view**

stand·still /'stænd‚stɪl/ *n* [S] a condition of no movement or activity; stop: *to bring the car to a standstill*

stank /stæŋk/ *v past tense of* STINK

stan·za /'stænzə/ *n* a group of lines forming a division of a poem

sta·ple[1] /'steypəl/ *n* **1** a small piece of thin wire which is driven through sheets of paper to hold them together **2** a small U-shaped piece of metal for holding e.g. electrical wire in place

staple[2] *v* **-pled, -pling** [T] to fasten with STAPLES

staple[3] *n* **1** something, esp. a food, that forms the most important part: *a staple diet of rice and vegetables* **2** a main product: *the staples among American farm products*

sta·pler /'steyplər/ *n* a hand instrument for driving STAPLES[1] into paper –see illustration on page 467

star[1] /star/ *n* **1** a brightly-burning heavenly body of great size esp. one very far away **2** *infml* any heavenly body, such as a PLANET, that appears as a bright point in the sky –see SHOOTING STAR **3** a five or more pointed figure, e.g. for wearing as a mark of office, rank, etc., or as a sign to show quality: *He only stays at five star* (=the best) *hotels.* **4** [*usu. pl.*] a heavenly body regarding as determining one's fate: *She was born under an unlucky star.*|*Thank your lucky stars.* **5** a famous or very skillful performer: *a movie/football star* **6** → ASTERISK **7 see stars** to see flashes of light, esp. as a result of being hit on the head –**starless** *adj*

star[2] *v* **-rr-** **1** [T] to mark with one or more stars **2** [I;T *in*] to have or appear as a main performer: *an old movie starring Charlie Chaplin*|*Humphrey Bogart starred in this* *movie.*

star·board /'starbərd/ *n* [S] the right side of a ship or aircraft as one faces forward –compare PORT²

starch¹ /startʃ/ *v* [T] to stiffen with STARCH² (2): *to starch a shirt*

starch² *n* **1** [C;U] (a white tasteless substance forming an important part of) a food such as grain, rice, beans, and potatoes **2** [U] a product made from this for stiffening cloth

starch·y /'startʃiʸ/ *adj* **-ier, -iest 1** full of, or like, STARCH² (1): *starchy foods* **2** *infml* stiffly correct and formal

star·dom /'stardəm/ *n* [U] the position of a famous performer

stare /stɛər/ *v* **stared, staring** [I;T *at*] to look fixedly (at) with wide-open eyes, as in wonder, fear, or deep thought: *It's rude to stare (at other people).* | *He sat staring into space, thinking.* | *The teacher stared the class into silence.* –**stare** *n*: *She gave him a long cool stare.*

stare sbdy. down *v adv* [T] to make (a person or animal) look away under the power of a long steady look

star·fish /'star,fɪʃ/ *n* **starfish** *or* **starfishes** a flat sea animal with five arms forming a star shape

stark¹ /stark/ *adj* **1** hard, bare, or severe in appearance: *the stark shape of rocks against the sky* **2** [A] pure; complete; UTTER: *stark terror/madness* –**starkly** *adv*

stark² *adv* **stark naked** *infml* completely NAKED

star·let /'starlɪt/ *n* a young actress who has had some success, but who isn't yet very famous

star·light /'starlaɪt/ *n* [U] the light given by the stars

star·ling /'starlɪŋ/ *n* a common greenish-black European bird

star·ry /'stariʸ/ *adj* **-rier, -riest** filled with stars: *a starry winter sky*

starry-eyed /'·· ,·/ *adj* full of unreasonable hopes; dreamy

Stars and Stripes /,· · '·/ *n AmE pomp* the flag of the US

Star-Span·gled Ban·ner /,· ·· '·/ *n [the + S]* **1** the NATIONAL ANTHEM (=song) of the US **2** *AmE pomp* the flag of the US

star-stud·ded /'· ,··/ *adj infml* filled with famous performers: *a star-studded cast*

start¹ /start/ *v* **1** [I;T *up*] to bring or come into being; begin: *How did the trouble start up?* | *I'm trying to start a swimming club in our town.* **2** [I;T *+to-v/v-ing*] to put into or go into activity, operation, etc.: *It started to rain/started raining.* | *If everyone is ready we can start.* | *The clock keeps starting and stopping; what's wrong with it?* | *I can't start the car.* (=the car's engine) | *I can't get the fire started.* (=can't light the fire) | *The movie starts in ten minutes; hurry up!* –compare

---

SPELLING NOTE

Words with the sound /s/, may be spelled **c-**, like **city**, or **ps-**, like **psychology**.

---

stop¹ **3** [I *off, out, for*] to begin something, usu. a journey: *It's a long trip; we'll have to* **start out/off** *early and* **start back** *for home in the afternoon.* | *She started out studying medicine, but now she's a lawyer.* **4** [I *at,from*] to go from a particular point; have a beginning or lower limit: *The train starts from Moscow and goes all the way to Siberia.* | *Prices start at $5.* **5** [T] to begin using: *Start each page on the second line.* **6** [I *at*] to make a quick uncontrolled movement, as from sudden surprise; be STARTLEd: *The touch on his shoulder made him start.* **7 to start with** also **for a start, for starters** (*infml*)– (used before the first in a list of facts, reasons, etc.). *It won't work; to start with, it's a bad idea, and secondly, it'll cost too much.* **8 start (all) over again** *AmE* also **start (all) over**– to begin again as before

USAGE **1** Both **start** and **begin** are used in the patterns [T + *to-v*] and [T + *v-ing*] with the same meaning; but the [T + *to-v*] pattern is better a if **begin** or **start** are themselves in the *-ing* form: *I think it's* **beginning/starting** *to rain*; or b if the verb that follows concerns one's feelings, ideas, etc.: *I began to realize that she was right.* | *I started to wonder if...* **2 Begin** cannot be used instead of **start** in the following meanings: *We* **started** (*out*) *for Boston* (=began our journey). | *They've* **started** (brought into existence) *a new political party.* | *I can't start the car.* | *The car won't start.* **Commence** is used like **begin** but is very formal.

start² *n* **1** [C] an act or place of starting: *The runner lined up at the start.* | *It was love from the start.* **2** [C] the beginning of something: *The movie was dull at the start, but it became exciting later on.* –compare FINISH **3** [C *usu. sing.*] a sudden uncontrolled movement, e.g. of surprise: *I woke up with a start.* **4** [C;U] the amount by which someone is ahead of someone else: *The thieves have (a) three day start on/over the police; I doubt if they will be caught.*

start·er /'startər/ *n* **1** a person, horse, car, etc., in a race or match at the start –compare BEGINNER **2** a person who gives the signal for a race to begin **3** an apparatus for starting an engine

star·tle /'startl/ *v* **-tled, -tling** [T] to cause to jump with sudden surprise: *You startled me! I didn't hear you come in.*

star·va·tion /star'veʸʃən/ *n* [U] suffering or death from lack of food

starve /starv/ *v* **starved, starving** [I;T] **1** to (cause to) die or suffer from lack of food: *They got lost in the desert and starved to death.* | (fig.) *He's starving himself trying to lose weight.* **2** [I] *infml* very hungry: *Let's get something to eat; I'm starving!*

state¹ /steʸt/ *n* **1** [C] a condition in which a person or thing is: *the state of one's health* | *a happy state of mind* **2** [C;U] (*often cap.*) a country or its government: *Should industry be controlled by the state?* | *state-owned railroads* | *state secrets* –see RACE (USAGE) **3** [A;U] the formality and ceremony connected with high-level government: *the*

President's state visit to Britain|a state occa-sion **4** [C] (*often cap.*) any of the smaller partly self-governing parts making up certain nations: *the 50 states of the US|the state of Texas* **5** [C] *infml* a very nervous or excited condition: *He* **got into a state** *before the examination began.* **6 lie in state** (of a dead body) to be placed in a public place so that people may honor it

state² *v* **stated, stating** [T] *fml* **1** [+(*that*)] to say, express, or put into words: *This book states the case for women's rights very clearly.* **2** to set in advance; name: *Theater tickets must be used on the stated date.*

state·ly /'steˠtliˠ/ *adj* **-lier, -liest 1** formal and grand: *a stately old lady* **2** grand in style or size: *A* **stately home** *is a large country house, usu. of historical interest.* **–stateliness** *n* [U]

state·ment /'steˠtmənt/ *n* **1** something that is stated; a formal declaration: *Do you believe the witness's statement?* **2** a list showing amounts of money paid, received, owing, etc., and their total: *I get a statement from my bank every month.*

States /steˠts/ *n infml* the US: *How long have you lived in the States?*

state's ev·i·dence /ˌ· '···/ *n AmE* **turn state's evidence** (of a criminal) to give information in a court of law against other criminals, esp. in order to receive less punishment oneself: *The bank robber turned state's evidence against his partners and received a lighter prison sentence in return.*

state·side /'steˠtsaɪd/ *adj,adv infml* of, in, or towards the United States of America

states·man /'steˠtsmən/ **stateswoman** /-ˌwʊmən/ *fem–* *n* **-men** /mən/ a political leader, esp. one who is wise and fair-minded **–statesmanship** *n* [U]

stat·ic /'stætɪk/ *adj* **1** not moving or changing: *static prices* **2** (of electricity) not flowing in a current: *static electricity in some people's hair*

sta·tion¹ /'steˠʃən/ *n* **1** also **depot** *AmE–* a building on a railroad or bus line where passengers or goods are picked up: *a station hotel/waiting-room|a subway station* **2** a building that is a center for a particular service: *a police/fire/gas station* **3** a company or apparatus that broadcasts on television or radio: *I can't get* (=hear) *many foreign stations on this little radio.* **4** a usu. small military establishment: *a naval station*

station² *v* [T] to put into a place; POST⁶: *Guards were stationed around the prison.*

sta·tion·ar·y /'steˠʃəˌnɛriˠ/ *adj* standing still; not moving: *The car was stationary when the accident happened.*

station break /'·· ˌ·/ *n AmE* a pause during a radio or television broadcast for local stations to give their names

sta·tion·er /'steˠʃənər/ *n* a person who sells STATIONERY

sta·tion·er·y /'steˠʃəˌnɛriˠ/ *n* [U] materials for writing; paper, ink, pencils, etc.

station wag·on /'·· ˌ··/ *AmE‖***estate car** *BrE– n* a private motor vehicle with a lot of room in the back for putting bags, cases, etc. inside **–see illustration on page 95**

stat·is·ti·cian /ˌstætəˈstɪʃən/ *n* a person who works with STATISTICS

sta·tis·tics /stəˈtɪstɪks/ *n* [P;U] (the science which deals with) collected numbers representing facts or measurements: *These statistics show deaths per 1,000 of the population.* **–statistical** *adj* **–statistically** *adv*

stat·ue /'stætʃuˠ/ *n* a likeness esp. of a person or animal, made in stone, metal, etc.

stat·u·esque /ˌstætʃuˈwˠɛsk/ *adj* (esp. of a tall woman) having a grand or noble appearance

stat·u·ette /ˌstætʃuˈwˠɛt/ *n* a very small STATUE

stat·ure /'stætʃər/ *n* [U] *fml* **1** a person's natural height **2** quality or position gained by proved worth: *a woman of (high) stature, respected by many*

sta·tus /'steˠtəs, 'stæ-/ *n* **-tuses 1** [C;U] position in law or in relation to others: *What's your status in this country? Are you a citizen?* **2** [U] recognition and respect by others: *Her family name gave her status in the group.|They bought a new car because it was a* **status symbol**. (=sign of PRESTIGE).

status quo /ˌsteˠtəs ˈkwoˠ, ˌstæ-/ *n* [*the* S] *Latin* the existing state of affairs

stat·ute /'stætʃuˠt/ *n fml* a written law

stat·u·to·ry /'stætʃəˌtoriˠ, -ˌtoˠriˠ/ *adj fml* fixed by STATUTE: *statutory control of wages*

staunch¹ /stɔntʃ, stɑntʃ/ *adj* dependably loyal; firm: *a staunch friend* **–staunchly** *adv* **–staunchness** *n* [U]

staunch² *v* → STANCH

stave sthg.↔**off** /steˠv/ *v adv* **staved, staving** [T] to keep away; keep back for a time: *enough food to stave off hunger*

stay¹ /steˠ/ *v* **1** [I] to remain; continue to be: *I stayed late at the party last night.|Can you stay for dinner, or do you have to go?|Don't turn here; stay on the same road.|Please stay seated.|The workers* **stayed out on strike** (=did not go to work because of a disagreement with their employer) *for a week.|You'll have to keep working hard to stay ahead of the others.* **2** [I] to live in a place for a while; be a visitor or guest: *My wife's mother is staying with us this week.|I'm going to stay at a hotel tonight.* **3** [T] to last or; continue for the whole length of: *to stay the course in a mile race* **4 stay put** to remain in one place; not move: *I like to stay put by the fire on a cold day.*

stay on *v adv* [I] to remain after the usual or expected time for leaving: *He will be 65 next month, but he is staying on as chairman.*

stay² *n* **1** [C] a usu. limited time of living in a place: *a short stay in the hospital* **2** [C;U] a delay ordered by a judge: *The prisoner was given a stay of EXECUTION.* (=the judgment was not carried out)

stead·fast /'stɛdfæst/ *adj* faithful; steadily loyal: *They were steadfast in their support of their friend.* **–steadfastly** *adv*

stead·y¹ /'stɛdiˠ/ *adj* **-ier, -iest 1** firm; sure in position or movement: *a steady hand/steady nerves* **2** moving or developing evenly; regular: *a steady growth in industry|a steady east wind* **–opposite** **unsteady** (for **1, 2**) **3** not changing; STABLE³: *a steady income/job* **–steadily** *adv* **–steadiness** *n*

steady² *v* **-ied, -ying** [I;T] to make or become

steady, regular, or less changing: *She started to fall, then steadied herself.|A drink will steady your nerves.*

steak /steɪk/ *n* [C;U] a flat piece of esp. BEEF or fish: *Two steaks, please.* –compare CHOP² (2)

steal¹ /stiːl/ *v* **stole** /stoʷl/, **stolen** /'stoʷlən/, **stealing 1** [I;T] to take (what belongs to another) without any right: *She used to steal money from her father's drawer|*(fig.) *to steal a kiss* (=to kiss someone quickly, without permission) **2** [I] to move secretly and quietly: *He stole out of the house without anyone seeing him.* **3 steal the show** to get all the attention expected by someone else at a public event –see THIEF (USAGE)

steal² *n* [S] *infml, esp. AmE* something for sale that is very cheap; BARGAIN¹ (2): *At $10 this camera was a steal!*

stealth /stɛlθ/ *n* [U] the action of acting secretly or unseen: *She took the money* **by stealth** –**stealthy** *adj* **-ier -iest** –**stealthily** *adv*

steam¹ /stiːm/ *n* **1** [U] water in the state of a gas, produced by boiling **2** [A] using this under pressure to produce power or heat: *a steam engine|a steam bath* **3** [U] *infml* feelings considered as trapped by self- control: *I was so angry I let/worked off steam by taking a long walk.* **4 under one's own steam** by one's own power or effort

steam² *v* **1** [I] to send out steam: *steaming hot coffee* **2** [I] to travel by steam power: *The ship steamed into the harbor.* **3** [T] to cook in steam: *steamed vegetables* **4** [T] to use steam on, esp. for unsticking or softening: *to steam open a letter*

steam up *v adv* **1** [I;T (=steam sthg.↔ up)] to cover or be covered with steam: *Her glasses (became) steamed up when she came into the warm room.* **2** [T *usu. pass.*] *infml* to make angry or excited: *Don't get all steamed up about it; it's not important.*

steam·er /'stiːmər/ *n* → STEAMSHIP

steam·roll·er¹ /'stiːm,roʷlər/ *n* a heavy machine with very wide wheels for flattening road surfaces

steamroller² *v* [T] *infml* to crush or force using very great power or pressure: *He was steamrollered into signing the agreement.*

steam shov·el /'· ,··/ *AmE*‖also **excavator**– *n* a large machine that digs and moves earth in a bucket at the end of a two-part arm

steam·ship /'stiːm,ʃɪp/ *n* a large non-naval ship driven by steam power

steed /stiːd/ *n lit* a horse for riding

steel¹ /stiːl/ *n* [U] iron in a hard strong form containing some CARBON and sometimes other metals, and used for making knives, machines, etc.: (fig.:) **nerves of steel** (=strong nerves)

steel² *v* [T] to harden (oneself) enough to do something: *He steeled himself to go in and say he was sorry.*

SPELLING NOTE

Words with the sound /s/, may be spelled **c-**, like *city*, or **ps-**, like **psychology**.

---

steel·works /'stiːlwɜrks/ *n* **steelworks** a factory where steel is made

steel·y /'stiːliː/ *adj* **-ier, -iest** like steel, esp. in color or hardness: *steely blue eyes|steely determination*

steep¹ /stiːp/ *adj* **1** rising or falling quickly or at a large angle: *a steep hill|a steep rise in prices* **2** *infml* (of a demand) unreasonable; too much: *She's asking $2,000 for her old car, which I think is a little steep.* –**steeply** *adv* –**steepness** *n* [U]

steep² *v* [I;T] to leave or be left in a liquid, for softening, cleaning, etc.; SOAK: *Leave that dirty shirt to steep (in hot water) for a while.*

stee·ple /'stiːpəl/ *n* a church tower with the top rising to a point (SPIRE)

stee·ple·chase /'stiːpəl,tʃeɪs/ *n* a race for people or horses, with many jumps to be made during the run

stee·ple·jack /'stiːpəl,dʒæk/ *n* a person whose work is building or repairing tall chimneys, STEEPLEs, etc.

steer¹ /stɪər/ *v* [I;T] **1** to direct the course of (e.g. a ship or vehicle): *to steer a car around a corner|to steer a conversation* –see LEAD (USAGE) **2 steer clear** of to keep away from; avoid

steer² *n* a male animal of the cattle family with its sexual organs removed (ox), esp. a young one raised for its meat –compare BULLOCK

steer³ *n* **bum steer** *infml, esp. AmE* a piece of bad advice or misleading information: *give someone a bum steer*

steering wheel /'·· ,·/ *n* the wheel which one turns to control a car's or ship's direction of movement –see illustration on page 95

stel·lar /'stɛlər/ *adj tech* of or concerning the stars

stem¹ /stɛm/ *n* **1** the central part of a plant above the ground, from which the leaves grow, or the smaller part which supports a leaf or flower **2** any narrow upright part which supports another: *the stem of a wine glass* **3 -stemmed** having a certain kind of stem: *a smooth-stemmed plant|a long-stemmed glass*

stem² *v* **-mm-** [T] to stop (the flow of): *to stem the flow of blood from the wound*

stem from sthg. *v prep* [T +*v-ing*] to have as origin: *Her interest in flowers stems from her childhood in the country.*

stench /stɛntʃ/ *n fml* a strong bad smell

sten·cil¹ /'stɛnsəl/ *n* a piece of paper, metal, etc., in which patterns or letters have been cut out

stencil² *v* **-l-** *AmE*‖**-ll-** *BrE* [T] to copy by using a STENCIL¹

ste·nog·ra·pher /stə'nɑgrəfər/ *n esp. AmE* a person who is employed to record speech in SHORTHAND and make copies on a TYPEWRITER

ste·nog·ra·phy /stə'nɑgrəfiː/ also **steno** /'stenoʷ/ *esp. AmE, infml*– *n* [U] SHORTHAND writing

step¹ /stɛp/ *n* **1** the act of putting one foot in front of the other in order to move along: *Take two steps forward and two steps back.* **2** the sound this makes –compare FOOTSTEP **3**

the distance between the feet when stepping: *The door is three steps away.|It's just a step* (=a short distance) *from my house to his.* –compare PACE¹ (2) **4** a flat edge, esp. in a set of surfaces each higher than the other, on which the foot is placed for climbing up and down; stair, RUNG of a ladder, etc.: *Be careful of the step outside the door.|She was standing on the church steps.|A* **flight of steps** led up to the house. **5** an act, esp. in a set of actions: *Our first step must be a change in working hours; then we will decide how to improve conditions.|We should* **take steps** (=take action) *to help them.* **6** a movement of the feet in dancing: *a fast step|Do you know this step?* **7 in step/out of step** (esp. of soldiers) stepping with the left and right leg at the same time/a different time than the others **8 step by step** gradually **9 watch one's step** *infml* to behave or act carefully

step² *v* **-pp-** [I] **1** [*on*] to put one foot down usu. in front of the other, in order to move along: *to step forward/aside|She stepped on a loose stone and twisted her ankle.* **2** to walk: *Step into the house while you're waiting.* **3** **step out of line** to act differently from others or from what is expected

step down/aside *v adv* [I] **1** to give one's place to another person, esp. in elections **2** to give up a job; RESIGN: *She stepped down from her position as president of the company.*

step in *v adv* [I] to enter an argument, plan, etc., between other people by saying or doing something: *Mother stepped in and stopped the children from fighting.*

step up sthg. *v adv* [T] *infml* to increase (an amount of something) in size or speed: *to step up the work*

step·lad·der /'stɛp,lædər/ *n* a short ladder with a folding support behind it

steppe /stɛp/ *n* a large area of land without trees, esp. in the Soviet Union

stepping-stone /'·· ,·/ *n* **1** one of a row of large stones, which one walks on to cross a river **2** a way of getting ahead: *This job is a stepping-stone to a better one.*

ster·e·o¹ /'stɛriy,ow, 'stɪər-/ *also* **stereo set** /'··· ,·/– *n* **-os** a record player which gives out sound from two places by means of two LOUDSPEAKERs –see also HI-FI

stereo² *also* **stereophonic** /,stɛriyə'fɑnɪk, ,stɪər-/ *fml* – *adj* which gives out, or is given out as, sound coming from two different places: *a stereo recording|record player* –compare MONO

ster·e·o·type¹ /'stɛriyə,taɪp, 'stɪər-/ *n* a fixed pattern which represents a type of person or event: *He's the stereotype of an army officer.*

stereotype² *v* **-typed, -typing** [T] to think of (a thing or person) as an example of a general type: *She has a stereotyped view of teachers, believing that they are all as bad as hers were.*

ster·ile /'stɛrəl/ *adj* **1** (of living things) unable to produce young –compare FERTILE **2** made free from all GERMs and bacteria: *a sterile room in a hospital* –sterility /stə'rɪlətiy/ *n* [U]

ster·i·lize ‖*also* **-lise** *BrE* /'stɛrə,laɪz/ *v* **-lized,**

-lizing [T] to make STERILE (1,2) –**sterilization** /,stɛrələ'zeyʃən/ *n* [U]

ster·ling¹ /'stɜrlɪŋ/ *n* **1** [U after *n*] *tech* the type of money used in Britain, based on the pound (£): *The value of sterling has risen.|the pound sterling* **2** [U] forks, spoons, knives, etc. made of sterling silver

sterling² *adj* [A] **1** *tech* (of gold and esp. silver) of standard value **2** of good true qualities: *a sterling helper*

stern¹ /stɜrn/ *adj* **1** showing firmness towards the behavior of others: *a stern teacher|a stern look* **2** difficult to bear: *a stern punishment* –**sternly** *adv* –**sternness** *n* [U]

stern² *n* the back end of a ship –compare BOW⁵

steth·o·scope /'stɛθə,skowp/ *n* a medical instrument which fits into a doctor's ears, used for listening to the heart, the breathing, etc. –see illustration on page 201

ste·ve·dore /'stiyvə,dɔr, -,dowr/ *also* **longshoreman** *AmE* – *n* a person whose job is loading and unloading ships; DOCKER

stew¹ /stuw, styuw/ *n* [C;U] a meal of meat, vegetables, etc., cooked together in liquid –see COOK(USAGE)

stew² *v* [I;T] **1** to cook (something) slowly and gently in liquid **2 stew in one's own juice** *infml* to be left to suffer as a result of one's own actions

stew·ard /'stuwərd, 'styuw-/ *n* **1** a man who controls supplies of food in a club, college, etc. **2** a man who serves passengers on a ship or plane; a male FLIGHT ATTENDANT **3** one of the people who arranges a public event such as a horse race

stew·ard·ess /'stuwərdɪs, 'styuw-/ *n* a woman who serves passengers on a plane or ship; a female FLIGHT ATTENDANT

stick¹ /stɪk/ *n* **1** a usu. small thin piece of wood **2** a thin rod of wood used for a special purpose: *He uses a walking stick to support him when he goes out.* **3** [*of*] a thin rod of any material: *a stick of CHEWING GUM* **4 get the wrong end of the stick** *infml* to misunderstand

stick² *v* **stuck** /stʌk/, **sticking 1** [T] to push (a pointed object) into or through something: *Don't stick pins into the chair!* **2** [I;T] to (cause to) be fixed with a sticky substance: *Stick a stamp on the letter.* **3** [I] to become or remain fixed: *The paper's sticking to my hand/is stuck on my hand.|The door's stuck, and I can't get out.|I got stuck in traffic for an hour.* **4** [T] *infml* to put: *He stuck a flower in his buttonhole.* **5** [T *with*] to give (someone) a difficult or unpleasant responsibility: *We were stuck with paying the bill.* **6 stick one's neck out** *infml* to take a risk: *A politician supporting an unpopular law is sticking his neck out: he may lose the next election.*

stick around *v adv* [I] *infml* to stay or wait in a place

stick by sbdy./sthg. *v prep* [T] *infml* to continue to support: *to stick by a friend*

stick out *v adv* **1** [I;T (=**stick** sthg.↔**out**)] to (cause to) be positioned beyond the rest: *Her ears stick out.|Don't stick your tongue out at me!* **2** [I] *infml* to be clearly seen: *It really sticks out that we aren't welcome here.*

stick to sthg. *v prep* [T] **1** to refuse to leave or change: *to stick to one's plans* **2** also **stick with** to continue to work hard at: *to stick to the job*

stick together *v adv* [I] *infml* (of two or more people) to stay loyal to each other: *Although they have many other friends, the two brothers have always stuck together.*

stick up for sbdy./ sthg. *v adv prep* [T] *infml* to defend by words or actions: *When they hit you, stick up for yourself instead of crying.*

stick·er /'stɪkər/ *n* a small piece of sticky paper with a picture or message on it: *political stickers on cars*

stick-in-the-mud /'· · · ,·/ *n* **-muds** *infml* a person who will not change or accept new things

stick·ler /'stɪklər/ *n* [*for*] a person who thinks a particular quality is very important: *She's a stickler for the truth.*

stick shift /'· ·/ *n AmE* for GEAR SHIFT

stick-to-it·ive·ness /ˌstɪk'tuʷətəvnɪs/ *n* [U] *apprec infml* (of a person) the quality of being firm and steady, esp. in spite of difficulties

stick·y /'stɪkiʸ/ *adj* **-ier, -iest 1** made of or containing material which can stick to anything else: *His fingers are sticky with jam.* **2** (of weather) hot and HUMID –**stickily** *adv* –**stickiness** *n* [U]

stiff¹ /stɪf/ *adj* **1** not easily bent: *stiff paper|Shoes are stiff when they're new.* **2** painful when moving or moved: *stiff aching muscles* **3** in an almost solid state; firm: *Beat the mixture until it is stiff.* **4** formal; not friendly: *a stiff smile* **5** [A] *infml* (of a drink of strong alcohol) large and without water or other liquid added: *a stiff whisky* **6** difficult to do: *a stiff examination* –**stiffly** *adv* –**stiffness** *n* [U]

stiff² *adv infml* **1 bore someone stiff** to make someone very tired with dull talk **2 scare someone stiff** to make someone very afraid

stiff·en /'stɪfən/ *v* [I;T] to make or become STIFF¹ (1,2,4) *a shirt with a stiffened collar|He stiffened at her rude remarks.*

sti·fle /'staɪfəl/ *v* **-fled, -fling** [T] to cause difficulty in breathing properly: *a stifling hot day|*(fig.) *It was a dull conversation and I had to stifle* (=keep back) *a* YAWN

stig·ma /'stɪgmə/ *n* **-mas,** *or* **-mata** /stɪg'matə,'stɪgmətə/ a sign of shame; feeling of being ashamed: *There is a stigma about having to ask for money.*

stile /staɪl/ *n* an arrangement of steps which must be climbed to cross a fence or wall outdoors

still¹ /stɪl/ *adj* **1** not moving: *Keep still while I tie your shoe.* **2** quiet or silent: *The room was still at the end of the speech.* –**stillness** *n* [U]

still² *v* [T] *lit* to make quiet or calm: *The food stilled the baby's cries.*

still³ *n* [S] *lit* quietness or calm: *the still of the evening*

still⁴ *adv* [*no comp.*] **1** at a particular time; even later than expected: *Are you still here? You should have gone home hours ago.|"Have you finished your dinner yet?" "No I still haven't finished it".* **2** even so; in spite of that: *We knew he probably wouldn't win, but it's still unfair that he didn't get a higher mark.|It's raining. Still, we have to go out.* –see Study Notes on page 144 **3** (used for making comparisons stronger): *It's cold now, but it'll be still/even colder at night.|The first question is difficult, the second is more difficult, and the third is still/even more difficult.*

still·born /'stɪlbɔrn, ˌstɪl'bɔrn◄/ *adj* born dead

stilt /stɪlt/ *n* one of a pair of poles, with supporting pieces for the foot, which can allow the user to walk raised above the ground

stilt·ed /'stɪltɪd/ *adj* (of a style of writing or speaking) very formal and unnatural

stim·u·lant /'stɪmyələnt/ *n* **1** anything taken into the body, usu. a drug, which increases activity for a time **2** anything (e.g. praise) which encourages more activity

stim·u·late /'stɪmyəˌleʸt/ *v* **-lated, -lating** [T] **1** to excite (the body or mind): *Exercise stimulates the body.* **2** to encourage: *She was stimulated into new efforts.* –**stimulation** /stɪmyə'leʸʃən/ *n* [U]

stim·u·lus /'stɪmyələs/ *n* **-li** /ˌlaɪ/ something which is the cause of activity: *Light is a stimulus to growth in plants.*

sting¹ /stɪŋ/ *v* **stung** /stʌŋ/, **stinging 1** [I;T] to (cause to) feel a sharp pain: *My eyes are stinging from the smoke.|The smoke is stinging my eyes.* **2** [I;T] to prick with or have a STING² (1): *An insect stung me.|a stinging* NETTLE

sting² *n* **1** a sharp organ used as a weapon by some animals, often poisonous **2** a pain-producing substance on a plant's surface: NETTLES *have a sting.* **3** a sharp pain, esp. caused by a plant or insect

stin·gy /'stɪndʒiʸ/ *adj* **-gier, -giest** *infml* unwilling to give, esp. money: *a stingy person* –**stinginess** *n* [U]

stink /stɪŋk/ *v,n* **stank** /stæŋk/, **stunk** /stʌŋk/, **stinking** [I *of*] (to give) a strong bad smell: *The place stank of bad fish.*

stint¹ /stɪnt/ *v* [T *of*] to give too small an amount (of): *Don't stint yourself; take all you want.*

stint² *n* a fixed amount, esp. of work: *doing a stint in the army*

stip·ple /'stɪpəl/ *v* **-pled, -pling** [I;T] to draw or paint by using dots

stip·u·late /'stɪpyəˌleʸt/ *v* **-lated, -lating** [T +(*that*)] to demand as a condition: *She stipulates three things before she will agree to go.*

stip·u·la·tion /ˌstɪpyə'leʸʃən/ *n* a condition of agreement: *She agreed, but with several stipulations.*

stir¹ /stɜr/ *v* **-rr- 1** [T] to move around and mix (esp. liquid) e.g. with a spoon: *He stirred his coffee.* **2** [I;T] to (cause to) move from a position: *She stirred in her sleep.|The wind*

stirred her hair. **3** [T] to excite (people's feelings): *The story stirred her sympathy.|stirring music*
stir up sthg. *v adv* [T] to cause (trouble): *Don't stir up trouble unnecessarily.*

stir² *n* **1** [C] an act of STIRRING¹: *Give the mixture a few stirs.* **2** [S] public excitement: *The news caused quite a stir.*

stir·rup /'stɪrəp, 'stɪrəp/ *n* a metal piece for the rider's foot to go in, hanging from the sides of a horse's SADDLE

stitch¹ /stɪtʃ/ *n* **1** [C] a movement of a needle and thread through cloth in sewing: *to put a stitch in a shirt* **2** [C] a turn of the wool around the needle when KNITting: *to drop* (=lose) *a stitch* **3** [C] the piece of thread or wool seen in place after the completion of such a movement: *a short/ loose stitch* **4** [U] a particular style used when sewing or KNITting: *feather stitch in sewing* **5** [S] a sharp pain in the side, esp. caused by running **6 in stitches** *infml* laughing helplessly

stitch² *v* [I;T] to sew: *Will you stitch a button on this shirt?*

stoat /stəʊt/ *n* a small brown furry animal of the WEASEL family that eats other animals

stock¹ /stɒk/ *n* **1** [C *of*] a supply of something for use: *The country's stocks of coal are getting low.|I like to keep a good stock* (=a lot) *of food in the house.* **2** [U] (supply of) goods for sale: *We've been losing a lot of stock through* (=because of) *stealing.|"Do you have any blue shirts* **in stock?"** *"No, they're/we're* **out of stock."** (=we have none for sale) **3** [C;U] the money (CAPITAL) owned by a company, divided into SHARES¹ (2): *He bought several* SHARES *of stock in the company.* **4** [U] farm animals, esp. cattle; LIVESTOCK **5** [U] a liquid made from the juices of meat, vegetables, etc., used in cooking **6** [U] a family line, esp. of the stated sort: *a man of farming stock* **7** [C] a piece of wood used as a support or handle, e.g. for a gun or tool **8 take stock (of)** to consider the state of things so as to take a decision: *He took stock of his situation and decided he needed a long vacation.* –compare STOCK-TAKING

stock² *v* [T] **1** to keep supplies of: *They stock all types of shoes.* **2** to supply: *a store well stocked with goods*
stock up *v* [I *with*] to collect a full store of goods: *We should stock up with food for the holidays.*

stock·ade /stɒ'keɪd/ *n* a fence of upright pieces of wood (STAKEs) built for defense

stock·bro·ker /'stɒk,brəʊkər/ *n* a person whose job is buying and selling STOCKs¹ (3) and SHAREs¹ (2)

stock com·pa·ny /'· ,··/ *n* **1** a group of actors who perform a certain set of plays **2** a business company owned by all the people who have bought shares in it

stock ex·change /'· ·,·/ also **stock market** /'· ,··/ –*n* [*the* S] (*usu. caps.*) the place where STOCKs¹ (3) and SHAREs¹ (2) are bought and sold

stock·hold·er /'stɒk,həʊldər/ *AmE*||also

shareholder– *n* an owner of shares in a business

stock·ing /'stɒkɪŋ/ *n* a close-fitting, usu. nylon, covering for a woman's foot and leg –compare SOCK –see PAIR (USAGE)

stock·pile /'stɒkpaɪl/ *v,n* **-piled, -piling** [T] (to keep) a large store of materials for future use

stock-still /,· '·/ *adj* without the slightest movement: *She stood stock-still and listened.*

stock·tak·ing /'stɒk,teɪkɪŋ/ *n* [U] the making of a list of goods held in a business

stock·y /'stɒkiy/ *adj* **-ier, -iest** thick, short, and strong in body –**stockily** *adv* –**stockiness** *n*

stodg·y /'stɒdʒiy/ *adj* **-ier, -iest 1** (of food) thick; heavy **2** dull and difficult: *a stodgy book* **3** (of a person) dull; old-fashioned

sto·i·cal /'stəʊɪkəl/ also **stoic** /'stəʊɪk/,–*adj* patient when suffering –**stoic** *n* –**stoically** *adv* –**stoicism** /'stəʊɪ,sɪzəm/ *n* [U]: *to bear all one's misfortunes with stoicism*

stoke /stəʊk/ *v* **stoked, stoking** [T *up*] to fill (an enclosed fire) with material (FUEL) which is burned to give heat, power, etc.: *to stoke up the fire with coal*

stole¹ /stəʊl/ *n* a long straight piece of material worn on the shoulders by women, esp. for a social occasion

stole² *v past tense of* STEAL

sto·len /'stəʊlən/ *v past participle of* STEAL

stol·id /'stɒlɪd/ *adj* showing no excitement –**stolidly** *adv*

stom·ach¹ /'stʌmək/ *n* **1** a baglike organ in the body where food is DIGESTed (=broken down for use by the body) after being eaten **2** the front part of the body below the chest; ABDOMEN

stomach² *v* [T] (used only in NEGATIVEs², questions, etc.) to accept without displeasure: *I can't stomach his jokes.*

stom·ach·ache /'stʌmək,eɪk/ *n* [C;U] (a) continuing pain in the ABDOMEN: *I've got a terrible stomachache!*

stomp /stɒmp, stɔmp/ *v* [I] *infml* to walk or dance with a heavy step: *stomping up the stairs*

stone¹ /stəʊn/ *n* **1** [C] a piece of rock, esp. not very large, either of natural shape or cut out specially for building **2** [U] solid mineral material; a type of rock: *sandstone| limestone|a stone surface* **3** [C] a single hard seed inside some fruits, such as the CHERRY, PLUM, and PEACH **4** [C] →PRECIOUS STONE **5** [C] →GRAVESTONE –see also HAILSTONE, MILLSTONE, STEPPING-STONE **6 leave no stone unturned** to try every way possible (of doing) **7 stone's throw** a short distance: *only a stone's throw from his house to the station*

stone² *v* **stoned, stoning** [T] **1** to throw stones at (someone), esp. as a punishment: *The criminal was stoned to death.* **2** to take the seeds or STONEs¹ (3) out of (fruit): *stoned peaches*

stone³ *n* **stone** *or* **stones** (in Britain) (a measure of weight equal to) 14 pounds (lbs): *He weighs 13 stone(s).|a 20-stone man*

stoned /stəʊnd/ *adj* [F] *infml* **1** under the influence of drugs **2** very drunk

stone·ma·son /'sto^{w}n,me^{y}sən/ also **mason** n a person whose job is cutting stone into shape for building

stone·ware /'sto^{w}nwɛər/ n [U] pots and other vessels made from a special hard clay that contains a hard stone (FLINT)

stone·work /'sto^{w}nwɜrk/ n [U] the parts of a building made of stone

ston·y /'sto^{w}ni^y/ adj **-ier, -iest 1** containing or covered with stones: *stony ground* **2** cruel; showing no pity or feeling: *a stony heart* –**stonily** adv

stood /stʊd/ v past tense & participle of STAND

stool /stu^{w}l/ n **1** a seat without a supporting part for the back or arms: *a piano stool|a bar stool* –see illustration on page 581 **2** fml & tech a piece of solid waste matter passed from the body

stoop /stu^{w}p/ v [I;T] to bend (the head and shoulders) forwards and down –**stoop** n [S]: *an old woman with a stoop*

stoop to sthg. v prep [T +v-ing] to fall to a low standard of behavior by (doing): *I wouldn't stoop to stealing money.*

stop¹ /stɑp/ v **-pp- 1** [I;T +v-ing] to (cause to) cease moving or continuing an activity: *We stopped working at 12:00.|Do the buses stop (=so that people can get on/off) at the train station?|He held out his hand to stop the bus.* (=as a signal)|*Stop making so much noise.* **2** [I;T] to (cause to) end: *I wish the rain would stop.|The railroad line stops at Los Angeles.* (=goes no further) –compare START¹ **3** [T from] to prevent: *I'm going and you can't stop me.|You have to stop her from telling such lies.* **4** [I] stay; stop one's journey: *Let's stop for a bite to eat.* **5** [T up] to block: *There's something inside stopping (up) the pipe.* **6** [T] to prevent from being given or paid: *The bank stopped (payment of) his check because he had no money in his account.* **7 stop short of** to decide against (a strong action): *She wouldn't stop short of stealing if she thought it would help her children.* –**stoppable** adj [no comp.]

stop by v adv, v prep [I; T (=**stop by** sthg.)] esp. AmE to make a short visit (esp. to someone's house): *I was in the neighborhood, so I thought I'd stop by (his house).*

stop off v adv [I at] infml to make a short visit to a place while making a journey somewhere else: *We'll stop off at a restaurant for dinner.*

stop over v adv [I] esp. AmE to make a short stay before continuing a journey: *We stopped over in Rome before continuing to Athens.* –see STOPOVER

stop² n **1** an act of stopping or the state of being stopped: *We had to make a few stops on the way.* **2** a place on a road where buses or other public vehicles stop for passengers: *a bus stop* **3** esp. BrE a dot used as a mark of PUNCTUATION, esp. a PERIOD (4) **4** an object

which prevents movement: *a doorstop* **5** a set of pipes on an ORGAN (3) with a movable part to provide a certain type of note **6 pull all the stops out** to do everything possible to complete an effect or action: *she pulled all the stops out to finish the work in time.*

stop·cock /'stɑpkɑk/ n a VALVE or TAP which controls the flow of water in a pipe

stop·gap /'stɑpgæp/ n something or someone that fills a need for a time: *to act as a stopgap while the secretary's away*

stop·light /'stɑp-laɪt/ n AmE a red light in a traffic signal that signals cars to stop

stop·o·ver /'stɑp,o^{w}vər/ n a short stay between parts of a journey, e.g. a long plane trip: *We made a stopover in Rome on the way to Athens.* –see STOP **over**

stop·page /'stɑpɪdʒ/ n **1** a blocked state which stops movement, as in a waste pipe or a pipe in the body **2** the act of stopping something, esp. work or pay

stop·per /'stɑpər/ n an object which fits in and closes the opening to a bottle or JAR

stop·watch /'stɑpwɑtʃ/ n a watch which can be stopped and started at any time, so that the time taken by an action can be measured exactly

stor·age /'stɔrɪdʒ, 'sto^{w}rɪdʒ/ n [U] **1** the act of storing: *storage space* **2** a place for storing goods: *Her furniture is in storage while she finds a new house.*

store¹ /stɔr, sto^{w}r/ v **stored, storing** [T in, up] to keep somewhere for future use: *to store food in the cupboard|to store one's furniture in a* WAREHOUSE

store² n **1** a room or building where goods are regularly kept and sold: *a clothing store|a department store|most of the large stores are in the center of town.* –see also CHAIN¹ (2) **store 2** AmE‖also **shop** esp. BrE– such a place, esp. small or selling special kinds of goods: *a candy store* –see illustration on page 673 **3** a large building in which articles are stored; WAREHOUSE **4** [of] a supply for future use: *This animal makes a store of nuts for the winter.* **5 in store** about to happen: *There's a shock in store for him.* **6 set... store by** to feel to be of (the stated amount of) importance: *He sets great store by his sister's ability.*

store·house /'stɔrhaʊs, 'sto^{w}r-/ n **-houses** /,haʊzɪz/ → STORE² (2): (fig.) *She is a storehouse of good ideas.*

store·keep·er /'stɔr,ki^{y}pər, 'sto^{w}r-/ esp. AmE‖also **shopkeeper** esp. BrE – n a person, usu. the owner, in charge of a small store

store·room /'stɔr-ru^{w}m, -rʊm, 'sto^{w}r-/ n a room where goods are kept until needed

stork /stɔrk/ n a large usu. white bird, with a long beak, neck, and legs, which walks in water looking for food

storm¹ /stɔrm/ n a rough weather condition with wind, rain, etc.: *a thunderstorm|a snowstorm|a sandstorm* –see WEATHER (USAGE)

storm² v **1** [T] to attack with sudden violence: *to storm the city* **2** [I at] to show violent anger: *He stormed around the house, breaking things.*

storm·y /'stɔrmiʸ/ *adj* **-ier, -iest 1** having storms: *stormy weather|a stormy day* **2** noisy and angry: *a stormy argument*

sto·ry¹ *AmE*||**storey** *BrE*– /'stɔriʸ, 'stoʷriʸ/ *n* **-ries** a floor or level in a building: *There are three stories including the ground floor.*

story² *n* **-ries 1** an account of events, real or imagined: *to tell a story* **2** *infml* (used by and to children) a lie (esp. in the phrase **to tell stories**) –see also TALL STORY **3** (material for) an article in a newspaper, magazine, etc.: *This event will be a good story for the paper.* –see HISTORY (USAGE)

stout¹ /staʊt/ *adj* **1** rather fat and heavy: *He became stout as he grew older.* **2** strong; thick: *He cut a stout stick to help him walk.* **3** [A] brave; determined: *a stout supporter of the team* –**stoutly** *adv* –**stoutness** *n* [U]

stout² *n* [U] a strong dark beer

stout·heart·ed /ˌstaʊt'hɑrtɪd◄/ *adj lit* brave; of a firm character

stove /stoʷv/ also **range** *AmE*||**cooker** *BrE* – *n* an enclosed apparatus for cooking or heating which works by burning coal, oil, etc., or by electricity –see FIRE¹ (3), HEATER –see illustration on page 379

stow /stoʷ/ *v* [T *away*] to put away or pack, esp. for some time: *to stow goods (away)* in boxes

stow·a·way /'stoʷəˌweʸ/ *n* a person who hides on a ship or plane to get a free journey

strad·dle /'strædl/ *v* **-dled, -dling** [T] **1** to sit or stand with the legs on either side of: *to straddle a horse|to sit straddling the fence* **2** (to appear to) favor both sides, esp. regarding a decision.

strag·gle /'strægəl/ *v* **-gled, -gling 1** to move or spread untidily, without ordered shape: *straggling branches* **2** to fall away from the main group while walking or marching: *Stop straggling behind! Hurry up!* –**straggler** *n*

strag·gly /'strægliʸ/ *adj* **-glier, -gliest** growing or spreading out in an untidy shape: *straggly hair*

straight¹ /streʸt/ *adj* **1** not bent or curved: *a straight line|She has straight, not curly hair.* **2** level or upright: *Put the mirror straight.|Put the pole up straight.* **3** honest; truthful: *a straight answer* –see on the LEVEL¹ (4) **4** [F] correct: *Just to* **put the record straight,** *this is what really happened.* **5** (of alcohol) without added water: *a straight whiskey|to drink whiskey straight* –compare NEAT (3) **6** serious: *a straight play|It was difficult to keep a straight face when he fell over the dog.* **7** *infml* for HETEROSEXUAL **8** *AmE* following one after the other: *four straight wins* **9 set someone straight** to give correct information (to someone who has a wrong opinion) often sharply: *He thought I would pay for the drinks, but I set him straight.* –**straightness** *n* [U]

straight² *adv* [*adv* +*adv/prep*] **1** in a straight line: *Sit up straight.|straight down the road|straight|right in front of you.* **2** directly: *Go straight home|I went straight|right to bed after dinner.* **3 straight off** /ˌ· '·/ also **straightaway** /ˌstreʸtə'weʸ/– at once: *I told her straight off that it was a foolish idea.*

straight³ *n* a straight part, esp. on a race track: *The cars crashed on the straight.*

straight·en /'streʸtn/ *v* [I;T *up, out*] to make or become straight, level, or neat: *Straighten your tie.*

straighten sthg.↔ **out** *v adv* [T] to remove the confusions or difficulties in: *to straighten out one's business affairs*

straighten up *v adv* [I] to get up from a bent-over position

straight·for·ward /ˌstreʸt'fɔrwərd/ *adj* simple and honest; without hidden meanings –**straightforwardly** *adv*

straight·laced /ˌstreʸt'leʸst◄/ *adj derog* having severe ideas about morals

strain¹ /streʸn/ *n* **1** [C] a breed or type of plant or animal: *This strain of wheat can grow during a cold spring.* **2** [S] *lit* a way of using words: *Her letters were written in a happy strain.* **3** [C] *lit* a tune; notes of music: *the strains of a well-known song*

strain² *v* **1** [I;T *at*] to stretch or pull tightly: *He strained at the rope and the boat moved.* **2** [I;T] to make great efforts (with): *to strain to hear|straining to understand|She strained her ears to hear what was happening.* **3** [T] to damage or weaken (a part of the body): *to strain a muscle* **4** [I *against*] to press oneself closely: *She strained against the ropes which tied her.* **5** [T] *fml* to force beyond acceptable or truthful limits: *to strain the truth* **6** [T] to separate (a liquid from a solid) by pouring through a narrow space, esp. the fine holes in a STRAINER: *to strain the vegetables*

strain³ *n* **1** [C;U] (the force causing) the condition of being STRAINED² (1): *The rope broke under the strain.* **2** [C *on*] a fact or state which tests the powers, esp. of mind and body: *The additional work put a great strain on him.* **3** [C; U] a state of TENSION (2): *She's under a great strain at the moment; her child's very ill.* **4** [C;U] damage to a part of the body caused by too great effort: *heart strain* –compare SPRAIN

strained /streʸnd/ *adj* **1** not natural in behavior; unfriendly: *His manner was strained.* **2** nervous or tired: *a strained face at the end of the day*

strain·er /'streʸnər/ *n* an instrument for separating solids from liquids, such as a SIEVE, a COLANDER, or a FILTER¹ (1)

strait /streʸt/ *n* [*usu. pl.*] (*often cap. as part of a name*) a narrow passage of water connecting two seas: *the Straits of Gibraltar*

strait·jack·et /'streʸtˌdʒækɪt/ *n* a garment which holds the arms down, preventing a person from violent movement

straits /streʸts/ *n* [P] a difficult position in life: *Now that I've lost my job, I'm* **in serious straits.**

strand /strænd/ *n* [*of*] a single piece or thread: *Many strands are twisted together to form a rope.*

strand·ed /'strændɪd/ *adj* in a helpless position, unable to get away: *a whale stranded on the shore|stranded in the middle of the traffic*

strange /streʸndʒ/ *adj* **1** hard to accept or understand; surprising: *It's strange you've never met him.* **2** not known before;

unfamiliar: *in a strange land.* –**strangely** *adv:* *He's been acting very strangely lately.* –**strangeness** *n* [U]

strang·er /ˈstreʸndʒər/ *n* **1** a person who is unfamiliar: *They never talk to strangers.* **2** a person in an unfamiliar place: *I'm a stranger in this town. Can you tell me the way to the station?* –compare FOREIGNER

stran·gle /ˈstræŋgəl/ *v* **-gled, -gling** [T] to kill by pressing on the throat –**strangulation** /ˌstræŋgyəˈleʸʃən/ *n* [U]: *Death was caused by strangulation.*

stran·gle·hold /ˈstræŋgəlˌhoʷld/ *n* a strong hold around the neck: (fig.) *the stranglehold of large companies on industry*

strap[1] /stræp/ *n* a strong narrow band of material, such as leather, used as a fastening: *a watch strap*

strap[2] *v* **-pp-** [T] **1** to fasten in place with STRAPS[1]: *to strap a bag onto one's back* **2** to beat with a STRAP[1]

strapped /stræpt/ *adj AmE* lacking something, esp. money: *strapped for cash*

strap·ping /ˈstræpɪŋ/ *adj* [A] big and strong: *a fine, strapping man*

stra·ta /ˈstreʸṭə, ˈstræṭə, ˈstrɑṭə/ *n pl. of* STRATUM

strat·a·gem /ˈstræṭədʒəm/ *n* a trick to deceive an enemy

stra·te·gic /strəˈtiʸdʒɪk/ also **strategical** /kəl/– *adj* done for reasons of STRATEGY: *a strategic decision*/*strategic weapons* –**strategically** *adv*

strat·e·gy /ˈstræṭədʒiʸ/ *n* **-gies 1** [U] the art of planning a war: *a general who was a master of strategy* –compare TACTICS **2** [C;U] (a piece of) skillful planning: *He uses strategy to get what he wants.*|*economic strategy* –**strategist** *n*

strat·i·fy /ˈstræṭəˌfaɪ/ *v* **-fied, -fying** [I;T] to arrange or become arranged in separate levels or strata (STRATUM): *a stratified society*|*stratified rock* –**stratification** /ˌstræṭəfəˈkeʸʃən/ *n* [U]

strat·o·sphere /ˈstræṭəˌsfɪər/ *n* [*the* S] the outer part of the air which surrounds the earth, starting at about six miles above the earth –compare ATMOSPHERE

stra·tum /ˈstreʸṭəm, ˈstræ-, ˈstrɑ-/ *n* **-ta** /ṭə/ **1** a band of rock of a certain kind **2** a level of people in society; social class: *The meeting was attended by people from several social strata.*

straw /strɔ/ *n* **1** [U] dried stems of grain plants, such as wheat, used for animals to sleep on, for making baskets, mats, etc. **2** [C] **a** one stem of wheat, rice, etc. **b** a thin paper or plastic tube for sucking up liquid **3** *AmE* **straw vote** an unofficial vote to discover general feeling **4 the last straw** an addition to a set of troubles which makes them too much to bear

straw·ber·ry /ˈstrɔˌberiʸ, -bəriʸ/ *n* **-ries** a

SPELLING NOTE

Words with the sound /s/, may be spelled **c-**, like **city**, or **ps-**, like **psychology**.

---

plant which grows near the ground, or its red juicy fruit

stray[1] /streʸ/ *v* **strayed, straying** [I] to wander away: *Our dog strayed from home.*|(fig.) *Her thoughts strayed from the subject.*

stray[2] *n* **strays** an animal lost from its home

stray[3] *adj* [A] **1** lost from home: *stray cats* **2** met or happening by chance: *hit by a stray shot*

streak[1] /striʸk/ *n* [*of*] **1** a thin line or band: *streaks of gray in her black hair*|(fig.) *a streak of cruelty in his character* **2 be on a winning/losing streak** to have repeated success/failure for a period

streak[2] *v* **1** [I] to move very fast: *The cat streaked across the road with the dog behind it.* **2** to cover with STREAKS[1] (1): *a face streaked with dirt*

streak·y /ˈstriʸkiʸ/ *adj* **-ier, -iest** marked with STREAKS[1] (1): *streaky bacon* (=with lines of fat among the meat)

stream[1] /striʸm/ *n* **1** a natural flow of water, usu. smaller than a river: *to cross a stream*|(fig.) *a stream of people going into the house* **2** [*usu. sing.*] (the direction of) a current of water: (fig.) *He doesn't have the courage to go against the stream (of public opinion).* –see also DOWNSTREAM, UPSTREAM

stream[2] *v* **1** [I] to flow fast and strong; pour out: *The pipe broke, and water streamed onto the floor.*|(fig.) *They streamed out of the movie theater.* **2** [I *out*] to float in the air: *The wind caught her hair, and it streamed out behind her.*

stream·er /ˈstriʸmər/ *n* a long narrow flag, piece of paper, or BANNER, used for decorating buildings at a time of public enjoyment

stream·line /ˈstriʸmlaɪn/ *v* **-lined, -lining** [T] to form into a smooth shape which moves easily through water or air: *a streamlined racing car*|(fig.) *to streamline a business* (=to make it more effective)

street /striʸt/ *n* a road in a town or city with houses or other buildings on one or both sides: *101 Main Street* –see illustration opposite

USAGE A **street** is in the middle of a town, and a **road** is usually in the country. The **way** to a place is either **a** the direction, and the instructions needed for getting there: *Can you tell me the* **way** *to City Hall?* or **b** one's journey from one place to another: *A funny thing happened on my* **way** *to the theater!*

street·car /ˈstriʸtkɑr/ *AmE*‖**tram** *BrE*– *n* a public vehicle for many passengers, usu. driven by electricity, that runs along metal lines set in the road

strength /streŋkθ, streŋθ/ *n* [U] **1** the quality or degree of being strong: *He hasn't got enough strength to get out of bed.*|*strength of character*|*I bought it* **on the strength of** (=because of) *her advice.* **2** something providing strength or power: *Her knowledge of the subject is the strength of her argument.* –compare WEAKNESS **3** force, measured in numbers: *They came* **in strength** (=a lot of them came) *to see the fight.*

strength·en /ˈstreŋkθən, ˈstreŋθən/ *v* [I;T] to make or become stronger: *to strengthen a*

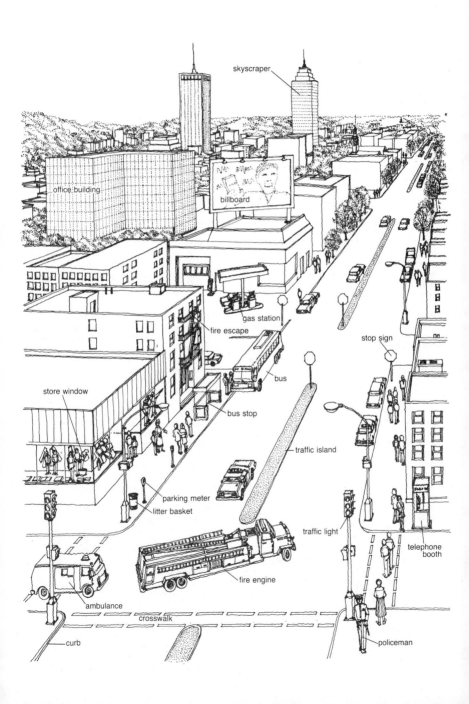

skyscraper

office building

billboard

gas station

fire escape

bus

store window

bus stop

stop sign

traffic island

parking meter

litter basket

traffic light

telephone booth

fire engine

ambulance

crosswalk

curb

policeman

fence|*The wind strengthened during the night.* –compare WEAKEN

stren·u·ous /'strɛnyuʷəs/ *adj* **1** needing great effort: *a strenuous day* **2** showing great activity: *a strenuous supporter of women's rights* –**strenuously** *adv* –**strenuousness** *n* [U]

stress¹ /strɛs/ *n* [C;U] **1** force or pressure caused by difficulties in life: *He's under stress because he has too much work to do.* **2** force of weight caused by something heavy: *The heavy trucks put stress on the bridge.* **3** the degree of force put on a part of a word: *In "under," the main stress is on "un."*

stress² *v* [T] to give importance to (a matter): *She stressed the need for careful spending.*

stress mark /'· ·/ *n* a mark (' *or* ˌ *or* ◀) to show that STRESS¹ (3) falls on a certain part of a word

stretch¹ /strɛtʃ/ *v* **1** [I;T] to make or become wider or longer: *My wool coat stretched when I washed it.*|*Rubber bands stretch.* (=are elastic)|(fig.) *You are stretching my patience to the limit.* **2** [I] to spread out: *The sea stretched (out) as far as I could see.* **3** [I;T *out*] to straighten (the limbs or body) to full length: *He stretched (himself) out in front of the fire.* **4** **stretch one's legs** to take a walk, esp. after sitting for a long time

stretch² *n* **1** [C] an act of stretching, esp. the body **2** [U] the (degree of) ability to increase in length or width: *stretch socks* **3** [C] a level area of land or water: *a wide stretch of road*|*the finishing stretch (in a race)* **4** [C *of*] a continuous period of time: *a stretch of ten years abroad*|*They had to stand for hours* **at a stretch**. (=without stopping)

stretch·er /'strɛtʃər/ *n* a framework on which a sick person can be carried

strew /struʷ/ *v* **strewed, strewn** /struʷn/ *or* **strewed, strewing** [T *on, over, with*] to scatter: *There were papers strewn all over the floor.*|*They strewed the earth with seeds.*

strick·en /'strɪkən/ *adj* experiencing the effects of trouble, illness, etc.: *stricken by debts*|*grief-stricken*

strict /strɪkt/ *adj* **1** severe, esp. in rules of behavior: *They are very strict with their children.* –compare LENIENT **2 a** exact: *a strict interpretation of the rules* **b** complete: *He told me about it in strict secrecy.* –**strictly** *adv* –**strictness** *n* [U]

stric·ture /'strɪktʃər/ *n fml* an expression of blame: *the strictures of the public on the private lives of the famous*

stride¹ /straɪd/ *v* **strode** /stroʷd/, **stridden** /'strɪdn/, **striding** [I] to walk with long steps or cross with one long step: *He strode over the stream.*

stride² *n* **1** a long step in walking **2 make great strides** to improve or do well **3 take (something) in one's stride** to accept and deal with easily: *Some people would have been shocked, but she takes it all in her stride.* –see

SPELLING NOTE

Words with the sound /s/, may be spelled **c-**, like **c**ity, or **ps-**, like **ps**ychology.

WALK (USAGE)

stri·dent /'straɪdnt/ *adj* with a hard sharp sound or voice: *a strident speaker*|*voice* –**stridently** *adv*

strife /straɪf/ *n* [U] trouble between people; quarreling: *family*|*political strife*

strike¹ /straɪk/ *v* **struck** /strʌk/, **striking 1** [I;T] *more fml than* **hit**– to hit: *She struck him in the face.*|*He struck out at his attackers.*|*The army struck* (=attacked) *at dawn.*|(fig.)*We must strike a blow for freedom.* **2** [T] to make or put into action by hitting: *He struck a light.* (=by lighting a match)|*She struck a match and lit a cigarette.*|*She struck a note on the piano*|*The clock struck 12.* (=12 o'clock)|(fig.) *We should be able to* **strike a bargain**. (=reach an agreement)|*It's difficult to* **strike a balance** (=be fair to everybody) *between the two courses of action.* **3** [T] to have an effect on; AFFECT with: *How does the room strike you?* (=what do you think of it?)|*That strikes me as a good idea.* (=I think it is good) | *They were* **struck dumb** *with fear.*|*The noise struck terror into their hearts*|*The whole village was* **struck down** *by a strange illness.* **4** [T] to come suddenly to the mind of: *If a better idea strikes you, let me know.*|*It strikes me* (=I think) *that we should stay here for the night.* **5** [I] to stop working because of disagreement: *The union struck for better working conditions.* **6** [T] to discover (a material or place): *They struck oil under the sea.* **7** [I *off, out*] to start going: *They struck off on a new course.*|*He struck out* (=began to swim) *towards the shore.*|*After he'd worked for his father for years, he decided to* **strike out on his own**. (=to start to work for himself) **8** [T] to lower (sails, a flag, or a tent): *The army* **struck camp** (=took down their tents) *and moved on.* –compare PITCH **9 strike it rich** to find sudden wealth **10 strike while the iron's hot** to use a favorable occasion as soon as it comes, without losing time **11 within striking distance** very near –see also STRICKEN

strike sbdy.↔ **off** *v adv* [T] to dismiss (someone) from a professional body by removing his/her name from an official list

strike up *v adv* **1** [I;T (=**strike up** sthg.) to begin playing: *to strike up a song* **2** [T *with*] (**strike up** sthg.) to start to make (a friendship): *They struck up a friendship on the plane.*

strike² *n* **1** a time when no work is done because of disagreement, e.g. over pay or working conditions: *We decided to* **go on strike** *because the company wasn't paying us enough money.* **2** success in finding esp. a mineral in the the the earth: *an oil strike*

strik·er /'straɪkər/ *n* a person on STRIKE² (1)

strik·ing /'straɪkɪŋ/ *adj* which draws the attention: *a very striking woman*|*a striking idea* –**strikingly** *adv*

string¹ /strɪŋ/ *n* **1** [C;U] (a) thin cord: *pictures hung on string* | *nylon string* –compare ROPE **2** [C] a thin piece of material stretched across a musical instrument (a **stringed instrument**), to give sound –see STRINGS **3** [C *of*] a set (of things) connected together on a thread: *a* *string of onions*/BEADS | (fig.) *a string of complaints*/*curses* **4 no strings attached** (esp. of an agreement) with no limiting conditions **5 pull strings** to use influence, esp. secretly: *He had to pull a few strings to get that job.*

string² *v* **strung** /strʌŋ/, **stringing** [T] **1** to put one or more STRINGS¹ (2) on (a musical instrument) **2** to thread (BEADS) on a string: (fig.) *to string phrases*/*words together* **3 highly strung** also **high strung** *infml*– (of a person) very sensitive, easily excited, etc.

string sbdy. **along** *v adv infml* [T] to encourage (someone's) hopes deceitfully: *He will never be paid the money they promised him; they're just stringing him along.*

string sthg.↔ **out** *v adv* [T] to spread (something) out in a line: *He strung out 12 pairs of socks on the clothes line.*

string up *v adv* [T] **1** (**string** sthg. ↔**up**) to hang (something) high: *They strung up colored lights around the room.* **2** (**string** sbdy. ↔**up**) *infml* to put to death by hanging, as a punishment

string bean /'· ·/ *AmE*‖**runner bean** *BrE*– *n* a green bean with long green PODS (=seed containers) which are eaten as food

strin·gent /'strɪndʒənt/ *adj* (of rules) severe; which must be obeyed –**stringently** *adv* –**stringency** *n* [U]: *the stringency of wartime rules*

strings /strɪŋz/ *n* [P] the set of (players with) instruments with STRINGS¹ (2) in an ORCHESTRA

string·y /'strɪŋiʸ/ *adj* **-ier, -iest** like string; having very thin flesh or muscle: *a stringy body*/*arm*|*stringy hair* –**stringiness** *n* [U]

strip¹ /strɪp/ *v* **-pp- 1** [T *off*] to remove (the covering or parts of): *Elephants strip the leaves off*/*from trees: They stripped the shirt from his back.* **2** [I;T *off*] to undress: *He stripped off his clothes and jumped into the water.*|*He stripped to the waist.*

strip² *n* [*of*] a narrow piece: *a strip of land*/*paper*

stripe /straɪp/ *n* a band of color, among one or more other colors: *Tigers have orange fur with black stripes.*|*A sergeant has three stripes on his sleeve.* –**striped** *adj*

strip·per /'strɪpər/ *n infml* a STRIPTEASE performer

strip·tease /'strɪptiʸz, ˌstrɪp'tiʸz/ also **strip show** /'· ·/– *n* [C;U] (a) removal of clothes by a person, esp. a woman, performed as a show

strive /straɪv/ *v* **strove** /stroʷv/, *or* **strived, striven** /'strɪvən/ *or* **strived, striving** [I +*to-v*/*for, against*] to struggle hard (to get or conquer): *She strove for recognition as an artist*/*to be recognized as an artist.*

strode /stroʷd/ *v past tense of* STRIDE

stroke¹ /stroʷk/ *v* **stroked, stroking** [T] to pass the hand over gently, esp. for pleasure: *The cat likes being stroked.*

stroke² *n* **1** [C] a blow, esp. with (the edge of) a weapon: *a stroke of the whip* **2** [S *of*] an unexpected piece (of luck) **3** [C] a sudden illness in part of the brain which can cause loss of movement in parts of the body

stroll /stroʷl/ *v* [I] to walk, esp. slowly, for pleasure

stroll·er /'stroʷlər/ *n* **1** a person who STROLLs or is strolling **2** *AmE* a folding chair on wheels for pushing a small child along

strong /strɔŋ/ *adj* **stronger** /'strɔŋɡər/, **strongest** /'strɔŋɡɪst/ **1** having (a degree of) power, esp. of the body: *his strong arm*|*She was not very strong after her illness.* **2** not easily broken, spoiled, or changed: *strong shoes*|*strong beliefs*|*a strong argument*|*Languages are her strong point.* (=something she does well) **3** [after *n*] of a certain number: *Our club is 50 strong.* **4** (esp. of drinks) having a lot of the material which gives taste: *The coffee is too strong; I can't drink it.* –compare WEAK (3) **5** (**still**) **going strong** active, esp. when old: *Grandfather's old clock is still going strong.* –**strongly** *adv*

strong·box /'strɔŋbɑks/ *n* a usu. metal box or SAFE² for keeping valuable things

strong·hold /'strɔŋhoʷld/ *n* **1** a fort **2** a place where an activity is common: *The village is a stronghold of old customs.*

strong lan·guage /ˌ· '··/ *n* [U] *euph* swearing; curses

strong-mind·ed /ˌ· '···◄/ *adj* firm in beliefs, wishes, etc. –**strong-mindedness** *n* [U]

strove /stroʷv/ *v past tense of* STRIVE

struck /strʌk/ *v past tense & participle of* STRIKE

struc·tur·al /'strʌktʃərəl/ *adj* of or concerning STRUCTURE, esp. of a building: *a structural fault* –**structurally** *adv*

struc·ture¹ /'strʌktʃər/ *n* **1** [U *of*] the way in which parts are formed into a whole: *the structure of the brain*/*a sentence* **2** [C] anything formed of many parts, esp. a building: *a tall structure*

structure² *v* **-tured, -turing** [T] to arrange (esp. ideas) into a whole form: *to structure one's argument*

strug·gle¹ /'strʌɡəl/ *v* **-gled, -gling** [I *against, with*] to make violent movements, esp. when fighting against a person or thing: *She struggled with the attacker.*|(fig.) *They struggled against poverty.* (=lack of money)

struggle² *n* a hard fight or bodily effort: *the struggle between the two teams*|*The struggle for human rights.*

strum /strʌm/ *v* **-mm-** [I;T *on*] to play a stringed instrument (STRING¹ (2)) informally, esp. without skill: *strumming (on) a GUITAR*

strung /strʌŋ/ *v past tense & participle of* STRING

strut¹ /strʌt/ *v* **-tt-** [I] to walk in a proud strong way, trying to look important: *The male bird strutted in front of the female.*

strut² *n* a piece of wood or metal holding the weight of a part of a building, an aircraft, etc.

stub¹ /stʌb/ *n* **1** a short end, esp. of a cigarette or pencil **2** the piece of a check or ticket left as a record after use

stub² *v* **-bb-** [T] to hurt (one's toe) by hitting it against something hard

stub out ↔sthg. *v adv* [T] to stop (a cigarette) from burning by pressing the end against something

stub·ble /'stʌbəl/ n [U] short stiff pieces of something which grows, esp. a short beard or the remains of wheat after being cut –**stubbly** adj -**blier, -bliest**

stub·born /'stʌbərn/ adj determined; with a strong will; a stubborn child who won't listen to his parents –**stubbornly** adv –**stubbornness** n [U]

stub·by /'stʌbiʸ/ adj -**bier, -biest** short and thick: his stubby fingers

stuck¹ /stʌk/ adj [F] 1 unable to move or be moved; fixed in place: The door's stuck.|His head is stuck in the window.|(fig.) Can you help me with this math problem? I'm stuck. 2 fixed by sticky material: The paper is stuck to my finger.|A piece of candy is stuck on that chair.

stuck² v past tense & participle of STICK

stuck-up /ˌ·'◄/ adj infml proud in manner: too stuck-up to speak to his old friends

stud¹ /stʌd/ n a male animal, esp. a horse kept for breeding

stud² n 1 a fastener used instead of a button and buttonhole, esp. one with two separate parts which are pressed together 2 a nail or flat-topped object used for decoration

stud³ v -**dd-** [T] to cover with (something like) STUDS²: a star-studded sky

stu·dent /'stuʷdnt, 'styuʷ-/ n 1 a person who is studying at a place of education or training 2 [of] a person with a stated interest: a student of human nature

stud·ied /'stʌdiʸd/ adj fml carefully considered before being expressed: a studied remark

stu·di·o /'stuʷdiʸˌoʷ, 'styuʷ-/ n -**os 1** a workroom for a painter, photographer, etc. 2 a room from which broadcasts are made: a television studio 3 a place where movies are made: Universal studios

studio a·part·ment /ˌ··· ·'··/ also **studio–** n AmE a single room used for both living and sleeping in

stu·di·ous /'stuʷdiʸəs, 'styuʷ-/ adj 1 eager to study; studying hard 2 fml careful: to pay studious attention to detail –**studiously** adv –**studiousness** n [U]

stud·y¹ /'stʌdiʸ/ n -**ies 1** [U] the act of studying: weeks of study to prepare for the examination 2 [C;U] a subject studied: to give time to one's studies 3 [C] a thorough inquiry into, esp. including a piece of writing on, a particular subject: to make a study of Shakespeare's plays 4 [C] a room used for studying

study² v **studied, studying 1** [I;T] to spend time in learning (a subject): She studies French. 2 [T] to examine carefully: She studied the shape of the wound.

stuff¹ /stʌf/ n [U] 1 material of any sort, of which something is made: What's this strange stuff on the floor? 2 infml things in a mass; matter: I can't carry all my stuff in this bag. 3

do one's stuff infml to show one's ability as expected

stuff² v 1 [T] to push (a substance) into; fill with a substance: to stuff a shoe with newspaper/stuff the newspaper into the shoe|(infml) He stuffed himself with food. 2 to fill the skin of (a dead animal), to make it look real: a stuffed elephant 3 to put STUFFING (2) inside: to stuff a chicken

stuff·ing /'stʌfɪŋ/ n [U] 1 material used as a filling for something: to use feathers as stuffing 2 special food placed inside a bird or piece of meat before cooking

stuff·y /'stʌfiʸ/ adj -**ier, -iest 1** having air which is not fresh: a stuffy room 2 (of ideas) dull, old-fashioned, etc. –**stuffily** adv –**stuffiness** n [U]

stum·ble /'stʌmbəl/ v -**bled, -bling** [I] 1 to catch the foot on the ground while moving along and start to fall: She stumbled and fell. 2 to stop or make mistakes in speaking or reading aloud: She stumbled over the long word. –**stumble** n

stumble across/on sbdy./sthg. v prep [T] to meet or discover by chance

stumbling block /'·· ˌ·/ n something which prevents action or causes worry: The stumbling block is that I don't drive; how can I get there?

stump¹ /stʌmp/ n the part of something left after the rest has been cut down, cut off, or worn down: a tree stump|the stump of a tooth/pencil

stump² v 1 [I] to move heavily: He stumped angrily up the stairs. 2 [T] infml to cause (someone) to be unable to reply; BAFFLE: Her question stumped him; he couldn't answer.

stump·y /'stʌmpiʸ/ adj -**ier, -iest** short and thick

stun /stʌn/ v -**nn-** [T] 1 to make unconscious by hitting the head 2 to shock or surprise: I was completely stunned by his refusal to help.

stung /stʌŋ/ v past tense & participle of STING

stunk /stʌŋk/ v past participle of STINK

stun·ning /'stʌnɪŋ/ adj infml very attractive; beautiful –**stunningly** adv

stunt¹ /stʌnt/ v [T] to prevent (full growth) (of): Lack of food may stunt the growth.

stunt² n 1 an act of bodily skill, often dangerous: In the movie he had to do such dangerous stunts as driving a car into the sea. 2 also **publicity stunt–** an action which gains attention: These newspaper articles are a stunt to raise interest in new products.

stunt man /'· ·/ **stunt woman** /'· ˌ··/ fem.– n a person who does dangerous acts in a movie so that the actor does not have to take risks

stu·pe·fy /'stuʷpəˌfaɪ, 'styuʷ-/ v -**fied, -fying** [T] fml to make unable to think; surprise very much: I was stupefied at the sight of so much gold. –**stupefaction** /ˌstuʷpə'fækʃən, ˌstyuʷ-/ n [U]

stu·pen·dous /stuʷ'pɛndəs, styuʷ-/ adj surprisingly great: a stupendous success –**stupendously** adv

stu·pid /'stuʷpɪd, 'styuʷ-/ adj silly or foolish: a stupid person|a stupid thing to do –**stupidly**

SPELLING NOTE

Words with the sound /s/, may be spelled **c-**, like **city**, or **ps-**, like **psychology**.

adv **–stupidity** /stuʷˈpɪdətiʸ, styuʷ-/ *n* **-ties** [C;U]

stu·por /ˈstuʷpər, ˈstyuʷ-/ *n* a state in which one cannot think or use the senses: *I was in a* DRUNKEN *stupor when I left the party.*

stur·dy /ˈstɜrdiʸ/ *adj* **-dier, -diest** strong and firm, esp. in body: *a sturdy horse* **–sturdily** *adv* **–sturdiness** *n* [U]

stut·ter /ˈstʌtər/ *v* [I] to speak with difficulty in producing sounds, esp. habitually holding back the first consonant –compare STAMMER **–stutter** *n: to speak with a stutter* **–stutterer** *n*

sty[1] /staɪ/ *n* **sties** → PIGSTY (1)

sty[2], **stye** *n* an infected swollen place on the eyelid

style[1] /staɪl/ *n* **1** [C;U] a general way of doing something: *the modern style of building|a formal style of writing* **2** [C] fashion, esp. in clothes: *the style of the 30's* **3** [C] a type or sort, esp. of goods: *They sell every style of mirror.|a hair style* **4** [U] high quality of social behavior, appearance, or manners: *She gives dinner parties* **in style**, (=in a grand way) *with the best food and wine.* **5 -style** in the manner of a certain person, place, etc.: *He wears his hair short, military-style.*

style[2] *v* **styled, styling** [T] to form in a certain pattern, shape, etc.: *The dress is carefully styled.*

styl·ish /ˈstaɪlɪʃ/ *adj* fashionable **–stylishly** *adv* **–stylishness** *n* [U]

styl·ist /ˈstaɪlɪst/ *n* a person who is concerned with styles of appearance: *a hair stylist*

sty·lis·tic /staɪˈlɪstɪk/ *adj fml* of or concerning style, esp. in writing or art: *stylistic differences between the two books* **–stylistically** *adv*

styl·ize ‖also **-ise** *BrE* /ˈstaɪlaɪz/ *v* **-ized, -izing** [T] *fml* (in art or description) to present in a fixed, often unnatural style

sty·lus /ˈstaɪləs/ *n* **-luses** *or* **-li** /laɪ/ the needle-like instrument in a RECORD PLAYER that picks up the sound signals from a record

suave /swɑv/ *adj* having very good smooth manners which sometimes hide bad character **–suavely** *adv*

sub /sʌb/ *n infml* **1** → SUBSTITUTE[1] **2** → SUBMARINE[1] (1)

sub·com·mit·tee /ˈsʌbkə,mɪtiʸ/ *n* a smaller group formed from a larger committee to deal with a certain matter in more detail: *The subcommittee has decided…*

sub·con·scious[1] /,sʌbˈkɑnʃəs, -tʃəs/ *adj* (of thoughts, feelings, etc.) present at a hidden level of the mind –see CONSCIOUS (USAGE) **–subconsciously** *adv*

subconscious[2] also **unconscious** *–n* [*the* S] the hidden level of the mind and the thoughts that happen there

sub·con·ti·nent /,sʌbˈkɑntənənt, ˈsʌb,kɑn-/ *n* a large mass of land that forms part of a CONTINENT

sub·di·vide /,sʌbdəˈvaɪd, ˈsʌbdə,vaɪd/ *v* **-vided, -viding** [I;T] to divide (something that is already divided) into smaller parts: *to subdivide a house into apartments* **–subdivision** /ˈsʌbdə,vɪʒən/ *n* [U]

sub·due /səbˈduʷ, -ˈdyuʷ/ *v* **-dued, -duing** [T] to conquer or gain control of: *Napoleon sub-*

dued most of Europe.|She tried to subdue her anger.

sub·dued /səbˈduʷd, -ˈdyuʷd/ *adj* **1** gentle; reduced in strength of light, sound, etc.: *subdued lighting|a subdued voice* **2** unnaturally quiet in behavior

sub·hu·man /,sʌbˈhyuʷmən/ *adj* of less than human qualities: *subhuman behavior*

sub·ject[1] /ˈsʌbdʒɪkt/ *n* **1** something being considered: *Don't change the subject; answer the question.|a book on the subject of insects* **2** a branch of knowledge studied, as part of an education: *She's taking six subjects in her first year of college.* **3** something represented in art: *The subject of the painting is the Battle of Waterloo.* **4** a person owing loyalty to a certain state or royal ruler: *a subject of the King* –compare CITIZEN **5** a person or animal used in an EXPERIMENT: *an experiment to discover the effects of smoking, with mice as the subjects* **6** (in grammar) the noun, PRONOUN, etc., which is most closely related to the verb in forming a sentence: *In the sentence "Mary hit John," "Mary" is the subject of the sentence.* –compare OBJECT[1] (4)

subject[2] *adj* **1** [*to*] governed by someone or something else; not independent: *a subject race|subject to the law* **2** [F *to*] likely or tending (to have): *The arrangements are subject to change.*

sub·ject[3] /səbˈdʒɛkt/ *v* [T] **1** to cause to experience: *They were subjected to great suffering.* **2** to cause to be controlled or ruled: *These people have been subjected by another tribe.* **–subjection** /səbˈdʒɛkʃən/ *n* [U] **subject** sbdy. **to** sthg. *v prep* [T]

sub·jec·tive /səbˈdʒɛktɪv/ *adj* **1** influenced by personal feelings: *This is a very subjective judgment of her abilities.* –see also OBJECTIVE **2** existing only in the mind; imaginary: *a subjective image of water in the desert* **–subjectively** *adv* **–subjectivity** /,sʌbdʒɛkˈtɪvətiʸ/ *n* [U]

subject to /ˈsʌbdʒɪkt tə, tu, ,tuʷ (*as for* to)/ *prep* depending on: *Our plans are subject to change, depending on the weather.*

sub·ju·gate /ˈsʌbdʒə,geʸt/ *v* **-gated, -gating** [T] to conquer and take power over: *a subjugated people* **–subjugation** /,sʌbdʒəˈgeʸʃən/ *n* [U]

sub·let /sʌbˈlɛt/ also **sublease** /sʌbˈliʸs/ *–v* **-tt-** [I;T] to rent to someone else (part of) a property that one has rented for oneself: *He rents the house and sublets a room to a friend.|She sublets her apartment during the summer when she's away on vacation.*

sub·lime /səˈblaɪm/ *adj* very noble or wonderful; causing pride, joy, etc.: *sublime music* **–sublimely** *adv*

sub·ma·rine[1] /ˈsʌbmə,riʸn, ,sʌbməˈriʸn/ *n* **1** also **sub** *infml*– a ship, esp. a warship, which can stay under water **2** → HERO SANDWICH

sub·ma·rine[2] /,sʌbməˈriʸn◂/ *adj tech* growing or used under or in the sea: *submarine plant life|a submarine pipeline*

sub·merge /səbˈmɜrdʒ/ *v* **-merged, -merging** [I;T] to (cause to) go under the surface of water: *The submarine submerged and then* *rose to the surface.|dangerous submerged rocks*

sub·mis·sion /səbˈmɪʃən/ n **1** [U *to*] the acceptance of someone else's power; obedience: *his submission to his father's wishes* **2** [C] *fml* a suggestion

sub·mis·sive /səbˈmɪsɪv/ adj gentle and willing to obey orders –**submissively** adv –**submissiveness** n [U]

sub·mit /səbˈmɪt/ v **-tt- 1** [I;T *to*] to yield (oneself); agree to obey: *to submit (oneself) to another's wishes* **2** [T] to offer for consideration: *to submit new plans*

sub·nor·mal /ˌsʌbˈnɔrməl/ adj less than is usual, esp. in power of the mind: *He was born subnormal and will never learn to speak.*

sub·or·di·nate¹ /səˈbɔrdn-ɪt/ n,adj [*to*] *fml* (a person) of a lower rank or position

sub·or·di·nate² /səˈbɔrdn,eʸt/ v **-nated, -nating** *fml* to put in a position of less importance: *He subordinated his own wishes to those of the group.* –**subordination** /səˌbɔrdnˈeʸʃən/ n [U]

sub·poe·na /səˈpiʸnə/ v,n **-naed, -naing** [C;T] *law* (to give) a written order to attend a court of law

sub·scribe /səbˈskraɪb/ v **-scribed, -scribing 1** [I *to*] to pay regularly in order to receive a magazine, newspaper, etc.: *I subscribe to "Language and Speech."* **2** [I;T *to*] to give (money) with other people in support of some good aim: *She subscribes to an animal protection society.* –**subscriber** n

sub·scrip·tion /səbˈskrɪpʃən/ n **1** [C] an amount of money given, esp. regularly, in order to receive a magazine, newspaper, etc. **2** [U] the act of subscribing (SUBSCRIBE): *The library was paid for by public subscription.*

sub·se·quent /ˈsʌbsəkwənt/ adj [A;F *to*] *fml* coming after something else, sometimes as a result of it: *We made plans for a visit, but subsequent difficulties with the car prevented it.* –**subsequently** adv

sub·ser·vi·ent /səbˈsɜrviʸənt/ adj [*to*] habitually willing to do what others want –**subserviently** adv –**subservience** n [U]

sub·side /səbˈsaɪd/ v **-sided, -siding** [I] **1** (of bad weather conditions) to go back to the usual level: *The floods subsided* (=went down).|(fig.) *His anger quickly subsided.* **2** (of a building, land, etc.) to sink gradually further into the ground

sub·sid·ence /səbˈsaɪdns, ˈsʌbsədəns/ n [C;U] (an example of) the fact of subsiding (SUBSIDE); the sinking of land or buildings

sub·sid·i·ar·y /səbˈsɪdiʸˌɛriʸ/ n,adj **-ies** [*to, of*] (something which is) connected but of second importance to the main company, plan, work, etc.: *This company is a subsidiary of the main company.*

sub·si·dize ‖also **-dise** *BrE* /ˈsʌbsəˌdaɪz/ v **-dized, -dizing** [T] (of governments, large

---

organizations, etc.) to pay part of the costs of (something) for (someone): *subsidized housing* –**subsidization** /ˌsʌbsədəˈzeʸʃən/ n [U]

sub·si·dy /ˈsʌbsədiʸ/ n **-dies** money paid, esp. by the government to an organization, to make prices lower, goods cheaper, etc.: *government subsidies to farmers*

sub·sist /səbˈsɪst/ v [I *on*] to stay alive when having small amounts of money or food: *They subsisted on bread and water.* –**subsistence** n [U]: *to live* **at subsistence level** (=with just enough food to stay alive)

sub·son·ic /ˌsʌbˈsɑnɪk◄/ adj (flying at a speed) below the speed of sound: *subsonic aircraft* –see also SUPERSONIC

sub·stance /ˈsʌbstəns/ n **1** [C] a material; type of matter: *Salt is a useful substance.* **2** [*the* S;U] the important part; the real meaning: *The substance of the argument was that too many people have too little money.*

sub·stand·ard /ˌsʌbˈstændərd/ adj not good enough; an unacceptable kind: *substandard work/clothing*

sub·stan·tial /səbˈstænʃəl, -tʃəl/ adj **1** solid; strongly made: *a substantial desk* **2** noticeable; important; of some size or value: *to make substantial changes|a substantial amount of money* –see also INSUBSTANTIAL

sub·stan·tial·ly /səbˈstænʃəliʸ, -tʃəliʸ/ adv quite a lot: *to help substantially*

sub·stan·ti·ate /səbˈstænʃiʸˌeʸt, -tʃiʸ-/ v **-ated, -ating** [T] *fml* to prove the truth of: *Can you substantiate your claim?* –**substantiation** /səbˌstænʃiʸˈeʸʃən, -tʃiʸ-/ n [U]

sub·sti·tute¹ /ˈsʌbstəˌtuʷt, -ˌtyuʷt/ also **sub** *infml*– n [C; *the* S *for*] a person or thing acting in place of another: *The teacher was sick today, so we had a substitute.|Money is no substitute for happiness.*

substitute² v **-tuted, -tuting 1** [T *for*] to put (something or someone) in place of another: *They don't like potatoes, so we substituted rice.* **2** [I *for*] to act as a SUBSTITUTE¹; be used instead of: *She substituted for the worker who was ill.* –**substitution** /ˌsʌbstəˈtuʷʃən, -ˈtyuʷ-/ n [C;U]

sub·ter·fuge /ˈsʌbtərˌfyuʷdʒ/ n [C;U] (deceit by) a trick or dishonest way of doing something

sub·ter·ra·ne·an /ˌsʌbtəˈreʸniʸən/ adj underground: *subterranean rivers*

sub·ti·tles /ˈsʌbˌtaɪtlz/ n [P] words printed over a movie in a foreign language to translate what is being said: *a French movie with English subtitles*

sub·tle /ˈsʌtl/ adj **1** delicate, hardly noticeable, and usu. pleasant: *a subtle taste|subtle differences in meaning* **2** clever, esp. in deceiving: *a subtle way of making us spend more money* –**subtly** /ˈsʌtliʸ, ˈsʌtl-iʸ/ adv: *subtly different*

sub·tle·ty /ˈsʌtltiʸ/ n **-ties 1** [U] the quality of being SUBTLE: *the subtlety of her argument* **2** [C] a SUBTLE idea or detail

sub·tract /səbˈtrækt/ v [T *from*] to take (a part or amount) from something larger: *If you subtract 1 from 30, you'll be left with 29.*

SPELLING NOTE

Words with the sound /s/, may be spelled **c-**, like **city**, or **ps-**, like **psychology**.

–compare ADD –**subtraction** /səb'trækʃən/ n [C;U]

sub·urb /'sʌbɜrb/ n [often pl.] an outer area of a town or city, usu. where people live rather than work: a suburb of Boston|I live in the suburbs. –**suburban** /sə'bɜrbən/ adj: suburban life

sub·ur·bi·a /sə'bɜrbiʸə/ n [U] often derog the SUBURBS

sub·ver·sive /səb'vɜrsɪv, -zɪv/ adj which tries to destroy those in power: Many people in government dislike this magazine because it prints subversive ideas. –**subversively** adv –**subversiveness** n [U]

sub·vert /səb'vɜrt/ v [T] fml to try to destroy the power and influence of (esp. a governing body) –**subversion** /səb'vɜrʒən, -ʃən/ n [U]

sub·way /'sʌbweʸ/ AmE‖**underground** BrE– n [C; the S] a railroad system in which the trains run in passages under the surface of the ground: We're late because we took the wrong subway.|It's quicker to go **by subway**. –compare METRO

suc·ceed /sək'siʸd/ v 1 [I in] to gain a purpose or reach an aim; do well: She succeeded the second time she took the examination. –compare FAIL¹ (1,3) 2 [T] to follow after: A silence succeeded his words. –compare PRECEDE 3 [T] to be the next to take a position or rank after: Mr. McCarthy succeeded Mr. Lawrence as our teacher.

suc·cess /sək'sɛs/ n 1 [U] the act of SUCCEEDing (1) in something: Success at last! 2 [C] a person or thing that SUCCEEDs (1)

suc·cess·ful /sək'sɛsfəl/ adj having succeeded; having gained an aim: a successful businesswoman –opposite unsuccessful –**successfully** adv

suc·ces·sion /sək'sɛʃən/ n 1 [U] the fact of following one after the other: His words came out in quick succession. 2 [C of] a set of people or things following on one after the other: a succession of rainy days 3 [U] the act or right of SUCCEEDing (2) someone in a position

suc·ces·sive /sək'sɛsɪv/ adj following one after the other: two visits on successive days –**successively** adv

suc·ces·sor /sək'sɛsər/ n a person or thing that comes after another: Our last director wasn't very good; I hope his successor will be better.

suc·cinct /sək'sɪŋkt/ adj fml clearly expressed in few words –**succinctly** adv –**succinctness** n [U]

suc·cor AmE‖**-cour** BrE /'sʌkər/ n,v [T;U] fml & lit (to provide with) help given in difficulty

suc·cu·lent /'sʌkyələnt/ adj apprec juicy: a succulent fruit/piece of meat –**succulence** n [U]

suc·cumb /sə'kʌm/ v [I to] fml to yield: He succumbed to persuasion.

such /sʌtʃ/ predeterminer,determiner,pron 1 so great; so good, bad, or unusual: Don't be such a fool!|He told us such funny stories that we all laughed.|He wrote to her every day, such was his love for her. 2 of the same kind; of that kind: chairs, tables, and all such furniture|He said, "Get out!" or some such rude remark.|They're dirty and untidy; I can't understand such people.|You can borrow my old car, such as it is. (=it's not a very good car)|They enjoy plays, movies, and such|and suchlike.|He's a good man and is known as such (=known as a good man) to everyone. 3 **such as** (used before an example): people such as my sister|animals such as horses, cattle, and deer

USAGE Compare **such** and **so** in these examples: It was **such** an interesting meeting. (=the meeting was **so** interesting)|There were **such** a lot of people. (=there were **so** many people)|It was **such** a shock. (=it was **so** shocking)

such·like /'sʌtʃlaɪk/ pron,adj [A] infml (things) of that kind: tennis, swimming, and suchlike (summer sports)

suck /sʌk/ v 1 [I;T] to draw (liquid) into the mouth by using the lips and muscles at the side of the mouth: to suck milk through a straw 2 [I;T at] to eat (something) by holding it in the mouth and melting it: sucking (away at) a piece of candy|(fig.) The baby was sucking its thumb. 3 [T] current sucked them under the water.

suck·er /'sʌkər/ n 1 a person or thing that sucks 2 something which sticks to a surface by SUCTION: You stick this hook to the wall with a sucker.|Flies have suckers on their feet. 3 infml a foolish person who is easily cheated 4 a new growth from the root or lower stem of a plant

suck·le /'sʌkəl/ v -led, -ling [I;T] (esp. of animals) to feed (the young) with milk from the mother's breast –see also NURSE² (2)

suc·tion /'sʌkʃən/ n [U] the act of drawing air or liquid away so that **a** another gas or liquid enters or **b** a solid sticks to another surface, because of the pressure of the air outside: We'll get the water out with a **suction pump**.

sud·den /'sʌdn/ adj 1 happening quickly and unexpectedly: a sudden illness 2 **all of a sudden** unexpectedly –**suddenly** adv –**suddenness** n [U]

suds /sʌdz/ also **soapsuds**– n [P] the bubbles formed by soap when mixed with water

sue /suʷ/ v sued, suing [I;T for] to bring a claim in law against (someone): The senator says that the newspaper story about him is completely untrue, and that he intends to sue (the person who wrote it).

suede, suède /sweʸd/ n [U] soft leather with a rough surface: suede shoes

su·et /'suʷɪt/ n [U] hard fat used in cooking, made from the KIDNEYs of an animal

suf·fer /'sʌfər/ v 1 [I] to experience pain or difficulty: He suffered terribly all through his illness.|Many companies are suffering because of loss of business. 2 [T] to experience (something painful): The army suffered heavy losses (=many soldiers were killed) in the battle. 3 [I] to grow worse; lessen in quality: He drank a lot and his work suffered.

suffer from sthg. v prep [T] to experience (something unpleasant, e.g. an illness), esp.

over a period of time: *My mother suffers from headaches.*

suf·fer·ance /ˈsʌfərəns/ *n* **on sufferance** with permission, though not welcomed

suf·fer·er /ˈsʌfərər/ *n* a person who suffers, esp. from a stated illness: *a new drug to help headache sufferers*

suf·fer·ing /ˈsʌfərɪŋ/ *n* [C;U] (an experience of) pain or difficulty: *There was a great deal of suffering during the war.*

suf·fice /səˈfaɪs/ *v* **-ficed, -ficing** [I *for*; not be +*v-ing*] *fml* to be enough: *Her income suffices for her needs.*

suf·fi·cien·cy /səˈfɪʃənsiʸ/ *n* [S *of*] *fml* a supply which is enough –opposite **insufficiency**

suf·fi·cient /səˈfɪʃənt/ *adj* enough: *$30 should be sufficient for a new pair of shoes.* –opposite **insufficient**

suf·fix /ˈsʌfɪks/ *n* (in grammar) an AFFIX that is placed at the end of a word –compare PREFIX

suf·fo·cate /ˈsʌfəˌkeʸt/ *v* **-cated, -cating** [I;T] to (cause to) die because of lack of air –**suffocation** /ˌsʌfəˈkeʸʃən/ *n* [U]

suf·fra·gette /ˌsʌfrəˈdʒɛt/ *n* (in the early 20th century) a woman who was a member of a group which tried to gain **suffrage** (=the right to vote) for women

sug·ar¹ /ˈʃʊgər/ *n* [U] a sweet usu. white substance obtained from plants (esp. **sugar cane** and **sugar beet**) and used in food: *I take sugar in tea, but not in coffee.*

sugar² *v* [T] to put sugar in: *to sugar one's tea*

sug·ar·y /ˈʃʊgəriʸ/ *adj* **1** containing sugar **2** too sweet, nice, kind, etc.

sug·gest /səgˈdʒɛst, səˈdʒɛst/ *v* [T] **1** [+*v-ing (that)*] to say or write (an idea to be considered): *I suggest finishing now/(that) we finish now.* **2** [(*that*)] to give signs (of): *Her expression suggested anger/(that) she was angry.*

sug·gest·i·ble /səgˈdʒɛstəbəl, səˈdʒɛs-/ *adj* easily influenced: *a suggestible child/She's at a suggestible age.*

sug·ges·tion /səgˈdʒɛstʃən, səˈdʒɛs-/ *n* **1** [C +(*that*)] something suggested: *The teacher made some useful suggestions to help us prepare for the examination.* **2** [U] the act of suggesting: *I went there on your suggestion.* **3** [C *of*] a slight sign: *a suggestion of a smile on her face*

sug·ges·tive /səgˈdʒɛstɪv, səˈdʒɛs-/ *adj* which suggests thoughts of sex: *a suggestive remark* –**suggestively** *adv*

su·i·ci·dal /ˌsuʷəˈsaɪdl/ *adj* **1** with a tendency to SUICIDE: *feeling suicidal* **2** likely to lead to death or destruction: *a suicidal attempt to climb a dangerous mountain* –**suicidally** *adv*

su·i·cide /ˈsuʷəˌsaɪd/ *n* **1** [U] the act of killing oneself: *to* **commit suicide** **2** [C] an example of this: *the prisoner's suicide attempt*

suit¹ /suʷt/ *n* **1** a a set of outer clothes of the same material, usu. including a short

coat (JACKET) with pants or skirt: *a three piece suit* (=pants, JACKET, VEST) –see illustration on page 123 **b** a set of clothes for a special purpose: *a bathing suit* **2** one of the four sets of cards used in games –see CARDS (USAGE) **3** → LAWSUIT **4** **follow suit** to do the same as someone else has

suit² *v* **1** [I;T] to satisfy or please; be convenient for: *It's a small house but it suits us/our needs.* **2** [T] to match or look right with: *That color doesn't suit him.* **3** **be suited (to/for)** to be fit, suitable, or of the right kind (for): *He found he wasn't suited to/for the job and left after three months.*/*I'm surprised they're getting married: they don't seem very well suited (for each other).* **4** **suit oneself** *infml* to do what one likes: *"The others are going out, but I think I'll stay at home." "Suit yourself."*

sui·ta·ble /ˈsuʷtəbəl/ *adj* [*for*] fit (for a purpose); right; convenient: *Is she suitable for the job?* –opposite **unsuitable** –**suitably** *adv*

suit·case /ˈsuʷtkeʸs/ *n* a flat box for carrying clothes and possessions when traveling –see illustration on page 17

suite /swiʸt/ *n* **1** [*of*] a set of rooms, esp. in a hotel **2** [*of*] a set of furniture, esp. a SETTEE and two chairs: *a living-room suite* **3** a piece of music with several loosely connected parts

suit·or /ˈsuʷtər/ *n old use* a man wishing to marry a woman

sul·fur *AmE*‖**sulphur** *BrE* /ˈsʌlfər/ *n* [U] a simple substance (ELEMENT) that is found as a light yellow powder

sulk /sʌlk/ *v* [I] to show lasting annoyance, esp. silently and for slight cause –**sulky** *adj* **-ier, -iest** –**sulkily** *adv* –**sulkiness** *n* [U]

sul·len /ˈsʌlən/ *adj* **1** silently showing dislike and lack of cheerfulness: *a rather sullen-looking woman* **2** dark and unpleasant: *a sullen sky* –**sullenly** *adv* –**sullenness** *n* [U]

sul·tan /ˈsʌltən/ *n* a Muslim ruler, as formerly in Turkey

sul·try /ˈsʌltriʸ/ *adj* **-trier, -triest** **1** (of weather) hot, airless, and uncomfortable **2** causing strong sexual attraction: *a sultry smile* –**sultriness** *n* [U]

sum¹ /sʌm/ *n* **1** [C] a usu. simple calculation, such as adding or dividing: *learning to do sums at school* **2** [C *of*] an amount: *I've spent a large sum/large sums of money on repairing the car.* **3** [the S *of*] the total produced when numbers, amounts, etc., are added together: *The sum of 6 and 4 is 10.*

sum² *v* → SUM UP

sum·ma·rize ‖also **-rise** *BrE* /ˈsʌməˌraɪz/ *v* **-rized, -rizing** [T] to make or give a SUMMARY (1) of (something longer) –see also SUM UP

sum·ma·ry¹ /ˈsʌməriʸ/ *n* **-ries** [*of*] a short account giving the main points

summary² *adj fml* done at once, esp. (of punishments) without considering mercy: *summary dismissal/EXECUTION (1)*

sum·mer /ˈsʌmər/ *n* [C;U] the season between spring and fall when the sun is hot: *warm summer weather* | *the hottest summer in 20 years* –**summery** *adj*: *warm and summery*/*a summery dress*

sum·mer·house /ˈsʌmərˌhaʊs/ *n* **-houses**

SPELLING NOTE

Words with the sound /s/, may be spelled **c-**, like **city**, or **ps-**, like **psychology**.

/ˌhauzɪz/ a small building in a garden, with seats in the shade

sum·mer·time /'sʌmər,taɪm/ n [the U] the season of summer; the time of hot weather

summing-up /ˌ·· '·/ also **summation** /sə'meʸʃən/– n **summings-up** a SUMMARY[1], esp. spoken by a judge at the end of a court case –see also SUM UP

sum·mit /'sʌmɪt/ n **1** [C of] the top, esp. the highest part of a mountain: *When we reached the summit, we placed a flag there.*|(fig.) *She has now reached the summit of her* AMBITIONS. **2** [A;C] (a meeting) between heads of state: *The President is attending the summit (meeting) in Moscow.*

sum·mon /'sʌmən/ v [T to] fml to give an official order (to come, do, etc.): *to be summoned (in) to the presence of the General* **summon** sthg. ↔ **up** v adv [T] to draw (a quality) out of oneself, esp. with an effort: *She summoned up all her strength and pushed open the door.*

sum·mons[1] /'sʌmənz/ n **-monses** an order to appear in a court of law: *They* **served** *her with* **a summons.**

summons[2] v [T] to give a SUMMONS[1] to; order to appear in court

sump·tu·ous /'sʌmptʃuʷəs/ adj expensive and grand: *a sumptuous feast* –**sumptuously** adv –**sumptuousness** n [U]

sum up v, adv **-mm- 1** [I;T (=**sum** sthg.↔ **up**)] to give the main points of (a report, a meeting, etc.); SUMMARIZE –see also SUMMING-UP **2** [T] (**sum** sbdy./sthg.↔ **up**) to consider and judge quickly: *to sum up the problem*

sun[1] /sʌn/ n **1** [the S] the burning star in the sky, from which the earth receives light and heat **2** [the S;U] light and heat from the sun: *to sit in the sun*|*I've got a headache; I think I've had too much sun.* **3** [C] a star around which PLANETS may turn

sun[2] v **-nn-** [T] to place (oneself) in sunlight: *She was sunning herself in the garden.*

sun·bathe /'sʌnbeʸð/ v **-bathed, -bathing** [I] to sit or lie in strong sunlight in order to make the body brown –**sunbather** n

sun·beam /'sʌnbiʸm/ n a beam of sunlight

Sun·belt /'sʌnbɛlt/ n [the S;U] AmE infml the southern and southwestern states of the US: *Many are attracted to the warm weather in the Sunbelt.*

sun·burn /'sʌnbɜrn/ n [U] (the condition of having) sore skin after experiencing too much strong sunlight –**sunburned** /'sʌnbɜrnd/ also **sunburnt** /'sʌnbɜrnt/ adj

sun·choke /'sʌnʃoʷk/ n →JERUSALEM ARTICHOKE

sun·dae /'sʌndiʸ, -deʸ/ n a dish of ice cream with fruit, sweet-tasting juice, nuts, etc.

Sun·day /'sʌndiʸ, -deʸ/ also **Sun.** written abbrev.– n the first day of the week; the day between Saturday and Monday: *She'll arrive (on) Sunday.*

Sunday school /'·· ˌ·/ n [C;U] religious teaching for children on a Sunday

sun·di·al /'sʌn,daɪəl/ n an apparatus, used esp. in former times, which shows the time according to where the shadow of a pointer falls

sun·down /'sʌndaʊn/ n [S] →SUNSET

sun·dry /'sʌndriʸ/ adj [A] various: *books, pens, and sundry other articles*

sun·flow·er /'sʌn,flaʊər/ n a plant with a large yellow flower, and seeds used to make cooking oil

sung /sʌŋ/ v past participle of SING

sun·glass·es /'sʌn,glæsɪz/ n [P] glasses with dark glass in them to protect the eyes from the sun –see PAIR (USAGE)

sunk /sʌŋk/ v past participle of SINK

sunk·en /'sʌŋkən/ adj **1** which has (been) sunk: *a sunken ship* **2** hollow; having fallen lower than the surrounding surface: *sunken eyes*

sun·lamp /'sʌnlæmp/ n a lamp which gives out ULTRAVIOLET light like that which comes from the sun

sun·light /'sʌnlaɪt/ n [U] natural light from the sun

sun·lit /'sʌn,lɪt/ adj brightly lit by the sun

sun·ny /'sʌniʸ/ adj **-nier, -niest 1** having bright sunlight: *a sunny room/day* **2** cheerful: *a sunny smile* **3** AmE **sunny-side up** /ˌ··· '·/ (of an egg) fried (FRY=cook in hot fat) on one side only, not turned over in the pan –**sunnily** adv –**sunniness** n [U]

sun·rise /'sʌnraɪz/ n [C;U] the time when the sun appears after the night

sun·set /'sʌnsɛt/ n [C;U] the time when the sun disappears as night begins: *They stopped work at sunset.*|*a beautiful sunset*

sun·shade /'sʌnʃeʸd/ n **1** →PARASOL **2** →AWNING

sun·shine /'sʌnʃaɪn/ n [U] strong sunlight: *I was sitting in the garden, enjoying the sunshine.*

sun·stroke /'sʌnstroʷk/ also **heatstroke**– n [U] an illness caused by the effects of too much strong sunlight

sun·tan /'sʌntæn/ also **tan**– n the brownness of the skin after the effects of sunshine –**suntanned** adj

su·per[1] /'suʷpər/ adj infml wonderful

super[2] n infml for SUPERINTENDENT

su·per·an·nu·ate /ˌsuʷpər'ænyuʷ,eʸt/ v **-ated, -ating** to dismiss (someone) from work because of old age, usu. with a PENSION

su·per·an·nu·at·ed /ˌsuʷpər'ænyuʷ,eʸtɪd/ adj fml **1** too old for work **2** old-fashioned: *superannuated ideas*

su·perb /su'pɜrb/ adj excellent; wonderful: *The food was superb.* –**superbly** adv

su·per·cil·i·ous /ˌsuʷpər'sɪliʸəs/ adj derog (as if) thinking others of little importance; HAUGHTY –**superciliously** adv –**superciliousness** n [U]

su·per·fi·cial /ˌsuʷpər'fɪʃəl/ adj **1** on the surface; not deep: *Don't worry about that crack in the wall; it's only superficial.*|*a superficial wound* **2** often derog not serious or searching in thought, ideas, etc.: *a rather superficial person* –**superficiality** /ˌsuʷpər,fɪʃiʸ'æləti/ n [U] –**superficially** /ˌsuʷpər'fɪʃəli/ adv

su·per·flu·ous /su'pɜrfluʷəs/ adj more than is necessary; not needed or wanted –**superfluously** adv –**superfluousness** n [U]

su·per·high·way /ˌsuʷpər'haɪweʸ/ n AmE

wide, usu. long HIGHWAY for fast-moving traffic

su·per·hu·man /ˌsuʷpərˈhyuʷmən◄/ adj seeming beyond human powers: *superhuman strength/patience*

su·per·im·pose /ˌsuʷpərɪmˈpoʷz/ v -posed, -posing [T *on*] to put (one thing) over something else or over each other, esp. so as to show the form of both: *to superimpose one film image on another*

su·per·in·tend /ˌsuʷpərɪnˈtɛnd/ v [T] to be in charge of and direct; SUPERVISE

su·per·in·tend·ent /ˌsuʷpərɪnˈtɛndənt/ n a person in charge of some work, building, etc.

su·pe·ri·or¹ /səˈpɪəriʸər, su-/ adj 1 [A] of higher rank or class: *I'll report you to your superior officer.* –see MAJOR (USAGE) 2 of high quality: *superior wool* –opposite **inferior** (for **1,2**) 3 *derog* (as if) thinking oneself better than others: *a superior smile* –**superiority** /səˌpɪəriʸˈɔrəṭiʸ, -ˈɑr-, su-/ n [U]

superior² n 1 a person of higher rank, esp. in a job: *I'll have to ask my superiors about that.* –compare INFERIOR² 2 [*after n*] (*usu. cap.*) (a title for) the head of a religious group: *Mother Superior*

su·per·la·tive¹ /səˈpɜrləṭɪv, su-/ n 1 [*the* S] the highest degree of comparison of an adjective or adverb: *"Good" becomes "best" in the superlative.* 2 [C] a word in this form –compare COMPARATIVE² –see Study Notes on page 135 –**superlatively** adv

superlative² adj *fml* best; greatest: *of superlative quality*

su·per·man /ˈsuʷpərˌmæn/ n -men /ˌmɛn/ (in stories) a man with powers of mind and body much greater than others'

su·per·mar·ket /ˈsuʷpərˌmɑrkɪt/ n a large store where one serves oneself with food and other goods –see illustration opposite

su·per·nat·u·ral /ˌsuʷpərˈnætʃərəl◄/ adj not explained by natural laws but by the powers of gods, magic, etc.: *supernatural powers/an interest in the supernatural* –compare UNNATURAL –**supernaturally** adv

su·per·pow·er /ˈsuʷpərˌpaʊər/ n one of the most (militarily) powerful nations in the world, as the US and Russia

su·per·sede /ˌsuʷpərˈsiʸd/ v -seded, -seding [T] to take the place of as an improvement: *This big old computer has now been superseded by a smaller modern one.*

su·per·son·ic /ˌsuʷpərˈsɑnɪk◄/ adj faster than the speed of sound: *a supersonic aircraft* –see SUBSONIC

su·per·star /ˈsuʷpərˌstɑr/ n an unusually famous performer, esp. a popular musician or a movie actor

su·per·sti·tion /ˌsuʷpərˈstɪʃən/ n [C;U *that*] (a) belief which is not based on reason but on magic or old ideas: *It's a common superstition that black cats are unlucky.*

SPELLING NOTE

Words with the sound /s/, may be spelled **c-**, like **city**, or **ps-**, like **psychology**.

---

su·per·sti·tious /ˌsuʷpərˈstɪʃəs/ adj strongly influenced by SUPERSTITION –**superstitiously** adv

su·per·struc·ture /ˈsuʷpərˌstrʌktʃər/ n an arrangement of parts (e.g. the upper parts of a ship) built up on top of the rest

su·per·vise /ˈsuʷpərˌvaɪz/ v -vised, -vising [I;T] to keep watch over (work and workers) as the person in charge –**supervision** /ˌsuʷpərˈvɪʒən/ n [U]: *The work was done under my supervision.* –**supervisor** /ˈsuʷpərˌvaɪzər/ n –**supervisory** /ˌsuʷpərˈvaɪzəriʸ◄/ adj

su·pine /ˈsuʷˈpaɪn/ adj *fml* lying on one's back looking upward: *lying supine on the floor* –compare PRONE (2)

sup·per /ˈsʌpər/ n [C;U] the last meal of the day, taken in the evening

sup·plant /səˈplænt/ v [T] *fml* to take the place of, esp. unfairly or improperly: *The President was supplanted by a political rival.*

sup·ple /ˈsʌpəl/ adj bending or moving easily, esp. in the joints of the body –**suppleness** n [U]

sup·ple·ment¹ /ˈsʌpləmənt/ n an additional amount of something, e.g. a separate part of a newspaper

sup·ple·ment² /ˈsʌpləˌmɛnt/ n [T *by*, *with*] to make additions to: *He supplements his wages from the factory by working as a gardener on weekends.*

sup·ple·men·ta·ry /ˌsʌpləˈmɛntəriʸ/ adj [*to*] additional: *The hospital has a supplementary water supply for use if the main supply fails.*

sup·pli·cate /ˈsʌpliˌkeʸt/ v -cated, -cating [I;T *for*] *fml or lit* to beg (someone), esp. for help –**supplication** /ˌsʌpliˈkeʸʃən/ n [C;U]

sup·pli·er /səˈplaɪər/ n a person or company that supplies something, esp. goods

sup·plies /səˈplaɪz/ n [P] necessary materials for daily life, esp. for a group of people over a period of time –see also SUPPLY²

sup·ply¹ /səˈplaɪ/ v -plied, -plying [T] 1 [*to*] to give (something that is needed): *The government supplies free books to all public schools.* 2 [*with*] to give things to (a person) for use: *Everyone who works for the railroad is supplied with a uniform.*

supply² n -plies 1 [C;U] (a) system of supplying: *difficulties with the food/water supply* 2 [C] an amount: *a large supply of food* –see also SUPPLIES 3 [U] the rate at which an amount is provided: *The supply of heat is limited in the mornings.* 4 **in short supply** scarce

supply and de·mand /ˌ·, · ·ˈ·/ n [U] the balance between the amount of goods for sale and how much is needed, esp. as shown in price changes

sup·port¹ /səˈpɔrt, səˈpoʷrt/ v [T] 1 to bear the weight of: *Do you think those shelves can support so many books?* 2 to provide money for (a person) to live on: *She has a large family to support.* 3 to approve of and encourage: *to support the workers' demand for higher wages* 4 to be loyal to, esp. by attending games or performances: *Which football team do you support?* 5 to strengthen (an idea, opinion, etc.); be in favor of: *The*

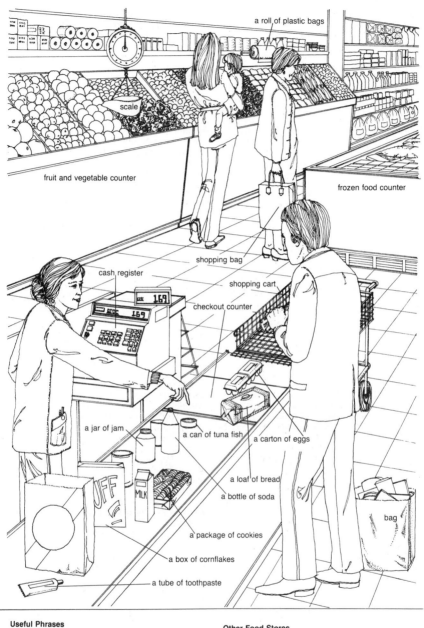

a roll of plastic bags

scale

fruit and vegetable counter

frozen food counter

shopping bag

cash register

shopping cart

checkout counter

a jar of jam

a can of tuna fish

a carton of eggs

a loaf of bread

a bottle of soda

a package of cookies

a box of cornflakes

a tube of toothpaste

bag

Useful Phrases

to make a shopping list   to compare prices
to go shopping   to get in line
to weigh (vegetables)   to check out

I need ─
a pound of potatoes/tomatoes/apples/cheese
a half (a) pound of butter/ground beef/onions
a bunch of carrots/radishes
a head of lettuce/cabbage/broccoli/cauliflower
a dozen eggs
a half (a) dozen eggs

Other Food Stores

There's a ─
butcher
bakery
fruit and vegetable stand/
    greengrocer
fish market
─ on the corner.

popularity of the new party supports the idea that people want a change.

support² *n* **1** [U] the act of SUPPORTing¹: *We are staying away from work* **in support of** *our demands.* **2** [C] something which bears the weight of something else: *the supports of the bridge* **3** [U] money to live: *a means of support* (such as a job) **4** [U] encouragement and help: *Thank you for all your support.* –**supportive** *adj* [A]

sup·port·er /sə'pɔrtər, -'powr-/ *n* a person who loyally supports (an activity), defends (a principle), etc.: *a supporter of women's rights/of the Los Angeles football team*

sup·pose¹ /sə'powz/ *v* **-posed, -posing** [T +(*that*)/not *be* +v-ing] **1** to consider as probable: *I suppose he's gone home.|I suppose she won't agree/I don't suppose she'll agree.* **2** to believe: *I suppose you're right.|He was commonly supposed (to be) dead.* **3** **be supposed to** /sə'powstə, -tʊ, -,tuʷ/: **a** to be expected, because of duty, law, etc., to: *Everyone is supposed to wear a seat belt in the car.|You're not supposed to smoke in here.* (=you are not allowed to) **b** *infml* to be generally considered to be: *I haven't seen it myself, but it is supposed to be a really good movie.*

suppose² also **supposing**– *conj* **1** if; what will happen if: *Suppose it rains, what will we do?|Suppose a bear should come out of the forest.* **2** (used in making a suggestion): *Suppose we wait a while.*

sup·pos·ed·ly /sə'powzɪdliʸ/ *adv* as believed; as it appears: *Supposedly, she's a rich woman.*

sup·po·si·tion /,sʌpə'zɪʃən/ *n* **1** [U +(*that*)] the act of supposing (SUPPOSE¹) or guessing: *His belief that things will improve is pure supposition.* (=is based only on guessing) **2** [C] a guess: *My supposition is that he stole the money.*

sup·press /sə'prɛs/ *v* [T] **1** to crush (esp. an action or state) by force: *Opposition to the government was quickly suppressed.|to suppress one's feelings of anger* **2** to prevent from appearing: *to suppress the truth/a smile* –**suppression** /sə'prɛʃən/ *n* [U]

su·prem·a·cy /sə'prɛməsiʸ, sʊ-/ *n* [U] the state of being SUPREME: *Britain's naval supremacy in the 19th century*

su·preme /sə'priʸm, sʊ-/ *adj* **1** highest in position, of power: *the supreme command|The matter will have to be decided by the* **Supreme Court.** (=the highest law court in many countries) **2** highest in degree: *supreme happiness/courage* –**supremely** *adv*

sur·charge /'sɜrtʃɑrdʒ/ *n* an amount charged in addition to the usual amount

sure¹ /ʃʊər/ *adj* **1** [F +(*that*)] having no doubt: *I think so, but I'm not sure.|Are you sure this is the right bus?|I'm not sure whether he's telling the truth.* –opposite **unsure 2** [F

+*to-v*] certain (to happen): *It's a really good movie; you're sure to enjoy it.* **3** to be trusted: *One thing is sure; he couldn't have gone far.|Those black clouds are a sure sign it's going to rain.* **4** **make sure of something/that**: **a** to find out for certain: *I'll just make sure (that) the car's locked.* **b** to arrange so: *Make sure you get here before midnight.* **5** **sure of oneself** believing in one's own abilities, actions, etc. –**sureness** *n* [U]

USAGE **Sure** cannot be used of events: *It is* **certain** (not ***sure**) *that he will come.* In *AmE*, both **certainly** and **sure** or **surely** can be used when giving a firm "yes" or "no." In *BrE*, only **certainly** is used: *"May I borrow your knife?" "***Certainly***"/(esp. AmE)* **"Sure!"***|"Did you enjoy the movie?" "I* **certainly** *did!"/(esp. AmE infml) "I* **sure** *did!"*

sure² *adv* **1** *esp. AmE infml* certainly: *Sure I will.|She sure is tall.* **2** **for sure** certainly so: *She won't lend you any money, and that's for sure.*

sure·ly /'ʃʊərliʸ/ *adv* **1** safely: *slowly but surely* **2** I believe or hope: *Surely you remember him?|You know him, surely?* **3** *esp. AmE* of course

sur·e·ty /'ʃʊərətiʸ/ *n* **-ties** [C;U] **1** money given to make sure that a person will appear in court –see also BAIL **2** a person who takes responsibility for another's behavior

surf¹ /sɜrf/ *n* [U] the white water (FOAM) formed by waves when they break on rocks, etc.

surf² *v* [I] to ride as a sport over breaking waves near the shore, on a special narrow board (a **surfboard**) –**surfer** *n*

sur·face¹ /'sɜrfəs/ *n* **1** [C] the outer part: *the earth's surface|marks on the surface of the table* **2** [C] the top of a body of liquid: *A wave broke across the surface of the pool.* **3** [*the* S] what is easily seen, not the main (hidden) part: *He seems quiet* **on the surface,** *but he's very different when you get to know him.*

surface² *v* **-faced, -facing 1** [I] to come to the surface of water: *fish surfacing to catch insects|(fig.) old arguments surfacing again* **2** [T] to cover (e.g. a road) with hard material

surface³ *adj* (of mail) traveling by land and sea: *Surface mail takes longer than* AIRMAIL.

sur·feit /'sɜrfɪt/ *n* [*of; usu. sing.*] *old use or humor* too large an amount, esp. of food

surge¹ /sɜrdʒ/ *n* [*usu. sing.*] a powerful forward movement, of or like a wave: *a surge of people/electric current|(fig.) a surge of anger*

surge² *v* **surged, surging** [I] **1** to move in or like powerful waves: *The crowd surged past him.* **2** [*up*] (of a feeling) to arise powerfully: *Anger surged (up) within her.*

sur·geon /'sɜrdʒən/ *n* a doctor whose job is to practice SURGERY

sur·ger·y /'sɜrdʒəriʸ/ *n* **-ies** [U] the performing of medical operations: *Many lives have been saved by surgery.|Your condition is serious; you will need surgery.* (=you must have an operation)

sur·gi·cal /'sɜrdʒɪkəl/ *adj* [A] of, by, or for SURGERY: *a surgical knife*

sur·ly /'sɜrliʸ/ *adj* **-lier, -liest** angry, bad-mannered, etc.: *a surly fellow/look*

sur·mise /sər'maɪz/ v -mised, -mising [I;T+*that*] *fml* to suppose as a reasonable guess: *From the look on his face, I surmised that he opposed the idea.* –**surmise** /sər'maɪz, 'sɜrmaɪz/ n

sur·mount /sər'maʊnt/ v [T] *fml* to conquer (esp. difficulties) –**surmountable** *adj*

sur·name /'sɜrneʸm/ n one's family name: *Alan Smith's surname is Smith.* –see also FIRST NAME

sur·pass /sər'pæs/ v [T] *fml* to go beyond, in amount or degree: *to surpass all expectation*

sur·plus /'sɜrplʌs, -pləs/ n,adj (an amount) more than what is needed or used: *Mexico has a large surplus of oil/has plenty of surplus oil.* –opposite **deficit**

sur·prise¹ /sər'praɪz, sə'praɪz/ n 1 [U] the feeling caused by an unexpected event 2 [A;C] an unexpected event: *It was a pleasant surprise to see him again.|a surprise meeting* 3 **take by surprise** to happen when unexpected: *When he offered me the job, it took me by surprise/I was completely taken by surprise.*

surprise² v -prised, -prising [T] 1 to cause surprise to: *The taste surprised him; it was not as he had imagined it.|I was surprised to hear that his wife had left him.* 2 to come on or attack when unprepared: *They surprised us with a visit.*

sur·pris·ing /sər'praɪzɪŋ, sə'praɪ-/ adj causing surprise: *It's not surprising that they lost the game.* –**surprisingly** adv –see Study Notes on page 363

sur·re·al·ism /sə'riʸə‚lɪzəm/ n [U] a modern dreamlike type of art and literature in which the artist connects unrelated images and objects –**surrealist** adj,n

sur·re·al·is·tic /sə‚riʸə'lɪstɪk/ adj 1 of a strange dreamlike quality 2 (as if) concerning SURREALISM

sur·ren·der¹ /sə'rɛndər/ v 1 [I;T *to*] to yield as a sign of defeat: *to surrender (oneself/one's army) to the enemy* 2 [T] *fml* to give up possession of: *I surrender my claim to the money.* –compare GIVE **up**

surrender² n [U] the act of SURRENDERing

sur·rep·ti·tious /‚sɜrəp'tɪʃəs, ‚sʌr-/ adj done, gained, etc., secretly: *a surreptitious kiss* –**surreptitiously** adv –**surreptitiousness** n [U]

sur·round /sə'raʊnd/ v [T *by*] to be or go around on every side: *The prison is surrounded by a high wall.|The police surrounded the house.|(fig.) surrounded by comforts*

sur·round·ing /sə'raʊndɪŋ/ adj [A] around and nearby: *in the surrounding area*

sur·round·ings /sə'raʊndɪŋz/ n [P] everything that surrounds a place or person, esp. as it affects the quality of life: *She grew up in comfortable surroundings.* –see ENVIRONMENT (USAGE)

sur·veil·lance /sɜr'veʸləns/ n [U] a close watch kept on someone, esp. someone believed to have criminal intentions: *The police have been keeping him under surveillance.*

sur·vey¹ /sər'veʸ, 'sɜrveʸ/ v -veyed, -veying [T] 1 to look at (a person, place, etc.) as a whole: *to survey the view* 2 to examine the condition of (a building): *Has the house been properly surveyed?* 3 to make a map of (an area of land): *to survey the east coast*

sur·vey² /'sɜrveʸ/ n 1 a general view or examination (of a place or condition): *The latest survey of public opinion shows that the current Administration is unpopular.* 2 (an) examination of a house, esp. for someone who may buy it: *Make sure you get a thorough survey.* 3 the making of a map

sur·vey·or /sər'veʸər/ n a person whose job is to SURVEY¹ (2,3) buildings or land

sur·viv·al /sər'vaɪvəl/ n 1 [U] the fact or likelihood of surviving (SURVIVE): *hopes of survival* 2 [C] something which has continued to exist from an earlier time: *That fashion is a survival from the 1970's.*

sur·vive /sər'vaɪv/ v -vived, -viving [I;T] to continue to live (after): *Both parents were killed by the explosion, but the children survived.|She survived the accident.*

sur·vi·vor /sər'vaɪvər/ n a person who has continued to live after coming close to death, or after other people have died

sus·cep·ti·ble /sə'sɛptəbəl/ adj [*to*] 1 easily influenced: *susceptible to suggestion* 2 [F] likely to suffer (from): *susceptible to the cold* –**susceptibility** /sə‚sɛptə'bɪləti̯ʸ/ n [U *to*]

sus·pect¹ /sə'spɛkt/ v [T not be +*v-ing*] 1 [+(*that*)] to believe to exist or be true; think likely: *We suspected that he was lost, even before we were told.* 2 [*of*] to believe to be guilty: *They suspect him of murder.* 3 to be doubtful about the value of: *I suspect his judgment.*

sus·pect² /'sʌspɛkt/ n a person who is SUSPECTed¹ (2) of guilt, esp. in a crime

sus·pect³ /'sʌspɛkt/ adj of uncertain truth, quality, etc.: *That is a rather suspect answer; I don't believe it.*

sus·pend /sə'spɛnd/ v [T] 1 [*from*] to hang from above: *to suspend a rope from a tree* 2 [*usu. pass.*] to hold still in liquid or air: *dust suspended in the sunlight* 3 to delay or stop for a period of time: *to suspend punishment* 4 to prevent from belonging to a group, etc., for a time, usu. because of misbehavior: *She was suspended from school.*

sus·pend·ers /sə'spɛndərz/ *AmE*‖**braces** *BrE*– n [P] elastic cloth bands worn over the shoulders to hold up men's pants: *a pair of suspenders* –see PAIR (USAGE)

sus·pense /sə'spɛns/ n [U] a state of uncertain expectation: *We've been kept in suspense waiting for the examination results.*

sus·pen·sion /sə'spɛnʃən, -tʃən/ n 1 [U] the act of SUSPENDing or state of being suspended 2 [C;U] the apparatus fixed to the wheels of a car, etc., to lessen the effects of rough road surfaces

sus·pi·cion /sə'spɪʃən/ n 1 [U] **a** the act of SUSPECTing¹ or state of being suspected: *She is under suspicion of murder.* **b** lack of trust: *She always treated us with suspicion.* 2 [C +(*that*)] **a** a feeling of SUSPECTing¹: *I have a suspicion that he's right.* **b** a belief about someone's guilt: *The police have their suspicions about who killed him.* 3 [S *of*] a slight amount (of something seen, heard, tasted, etc.): *a suspicion of onion in the soup*

sus·pi·cious /sə'spɪʃəs/ *adj* **1** [*of*] SUSPECTing[1] guilt; not trusting: *She was suspicious of us/our intentions.|The man's strange behavior made the police suspicious.* **2** making people think one is guilty: *He is a suspicious character.* (=person) **–suspiciously** *adv*

sus·tain /sə'steɪn/ *v* [T] **1** to keep strong; strengthen: *A light meal will not sustain us through the day.* **2** to keep (in existence) over a long period: *She owes her success to sustained hard work.|He couldn't sustain his interest in the job.* **3** to suffer (pain, etc.): *They sustained severe injuries in the accident.*

sus·te·nance /'sʌstənəns/ *n* [U] *fml* **1** the ability of food to keep people strong **2** food which does this

svelte /svɛlt/ *adj* (esp. of a woman) thin and graceful

SW *written abbrev. said as:* southwest(ern)

swab[1] /swɑb/ *n* **1** an object for taking in liquids, drying or cleaning, as a MOP or PAD **2** (a piece of material which will hold) liquid to be tested for infection

swab[2] *v* **-bb-** [T *down*] to clean (esp. the floors (DECKs) of a ship)

swag·ger[1] /'swægər/ *v* [I] to walk with a proud swinging movement: *He swaggered down the street after winning the fight.* **–swaggerer** *n* **–swaggeringly** *adv*

swagger[2] *n* [S] a proud manner of walking

swal·low[1] /'swɑlow/ *v* **1** [T] to move (food or drink) down the throat from the mouth: *to swallow a mouthful of bread/soup* **2** [I] to make the same movement of the throat, esp. as a sign of nervousness: *He swallowed and walked into the examination room.* **3** [T] *infml* to accept: *to swallow a story* (=to believe it without doubting)

   swallow sbdy./sthg.↔ **up** *v adv* [T] to take in, causing to disappear: *Higher living costs have swallowed up our pay raise.*

swallow[2] *n* an act of swallowing

swallow[3] *n* a small bird with pointed wings and a double-pointed tail

swam /swæm/ *v past tense of* SWIM

swamp[1] /swɑmp, swɔmp/ *n* [C;U] (an area of) soft wet land; (a) BOG: *The land is dangerous; it's mainly swamp.* **–swampy** *adj* **-ier, -iest**

swamp[2] *v* [T] to fill with water, esp. causing to sink: (fig.) *We were swamped with work after the holidays.*

swan /swɑn/ *n* a large white bird with a long neck, which lives on rivers and lakes

swank /swæŋk/ *n* [U] **1** a quality of grace, beauty, and fashion; stylishness **2** *infml* unpleasantly proud behavior

swank·y /'swæŋkiy/ *adj* **-ier, -iest** *infml* very fashionable or expensive: *a really swanky hotel*

swap[1], **swop** /swɑp/ *v* **-pp-** [I;T] *infml* to ex-

change (goods or positions): *I'll swap six old stamps for three of the new ones.|I liked her coat and she liked mine, so we swapped.*

swap[2], **swop** *n* [*usu. sing.*] *infml* an exchange: *to do a swap*

swarm[1] /swɔrm/ *n* a large group (of insects, esp. bees) moving in a mass: (fig.) *A swarm of tourists was passing through the gates of the castle.*

swarm[2] *v* [I] to move in a crowd: *As the fire spread, people came swarming out of the building.*

   swarm with sbdy./sthg. *v prep* [T] to be full of (moving crowds of people, insects, etc.): *The place was swarming with tourists.*

swarth·y /'swɔrðiy, -θiy/ *adj* **-ier, -iest** (of a person) having a dark skin

swat[1] /swɑt/ *v* **-tt-** [T] to hit (an insect) with a flat object, esp. so as to kill it

swat[2] *n* an act of SWATting

swathe /swɑð, swɔð, sweyð/ *v* **swathed, swathing** [T *in*] *lit or fml* to wrap around in cloth: (fig.) *hills swathed in mist*

sway[1] /swey/ *v* **swayed, swaying 1** [I;T] to (cause to) swing from side to side: *The trees swayed in the wind.* **2** [T] to influence: *When choosing a job, don't be swayed just by promises of high earnings.*

sway[2] *n* [U] **1** SWAYing movement: *The sway of the ship made him fall over.* **2** *old use & lit* power to rule: *under Caesar's sway*

swear /swɛər/ *v* **swore** /swɔr, swowr/, **sworn** /sworn, swowrn/, **swearing 1** [I *at*] to curse; use bad language: *Stop swearing in front of the children.* **2** [T *+to-v/(that)*] to state or promise formally or by an OATH (1): *He swore to obey/he would obey the king.|* (*infml*) *Peter says he was there, but I swear I never saw him.* **3** [T *to*] to cause to take an OATH (1): *I can't tell you anything about it: I've been sworn to secrecy.*

   swear by sthg. *v prep* [T +*v-ing*] *infml* to trust in: *He swears by taking a cold bath every morning, and says he has never been ill.*

   swear sbdy.↔ **in** *v adv* [T] to cause to take an OATH (1) of loyalty: *The new President was sworn in.*

swear·word /'swɛərwɜrd/ *n* a word used in SWEARing (1)

sweat[1] /swɛt/ *n* **1** [U] also **perspiration**– liquid which comes out from the body through the skin to cool it: *I was covered in sweat after running to catch the bus.* **2** [S] an anxious state: *in a cold sweat* **3** [S] *infml* hard work: *Digging that hole was quite a sweat.*

sweat[2] *v* **sweated** *or* **sweat, sweating** [I] **1** to have SWEAT[1] (1) coming out through the skin: *sweating in the heat/with fear* **2** *infml* to work very hard, esp. for little money

sweat·er /'swɛtər/ *n* a KNITted garment, often made of wool, with long SLEEVEs, worn over the top of the body –compare PULLOVER –see illustration on page 123

sweat·shirt /'swɛt-ʃɜrt/ *n* a loose cotton garment with long SLEEVEs for the upper part of the body: *When he goes running, he wears shorts and a sweatshirt.*

sweat·shop /'swɛt-ʃɑp/ *n* a factory or work-

SPELLING NOTE

Words with the sound /s/, may be spelled **c-**, like **city**, or **ps-**, like **psychology**.

room where workers produce goods by heavy labor for very little money

sweat·y /'swɛtiʸ/ *adj* **-ier, -iest 1** covered in or smelly with SWEAT¹: *sweaty feet* **2** unpleasantly hot; causing one to SWEAT²: *sweaty weather/work*

sweep¹ /swiʸp/ *v* **swept** /swɛpt/, **sweeping 1** [T] to clean or remove by brushing: *He swept the floor.|She swept the dirt away.* –compare BRUSH² **2** [I;T] to move quickly and powerfully (all over): *The crowd swept through the gates.|A storm swept (over) the country.|*(fig.) *The new dance swept the country.* (=was soon popular everywhere) **3** [I;T] to be or move in a curve across (an area): *The hills sweep around the hidden valley.|The security camera swept the store.* **4** [I] (of a person) to move (away) in a proud firm manner: *She swept angrily from the room.* **5 sweep someone off his/her feet: a** to cause someone to fall suddenly in love with one **b** to persuade someone completely and suddenly

sweep up *v adv* [I;T (=**sweep** sthg.↔ **up**)] to collect and remove (dirt, dust, etc.) by sweeping the floor

sweep² *n* **1** an act of sweeping: *This room needs a good sweep.* **2** a swinging movement, as of the arm: *with a sweep of his sword* **3** [*usu. sing.*] a long curved line or area of country: *the long sweep of the distant hills|*(fig.) *the broad sweep of her argument* (=covering all parts of the subject) **4** →SWEEPSTAKES **5** *infml* for CHIMNEYSWEEP **6 clean sweep: a** a complete removal or change: *to make a clean sweep of all the old ideas* **b** a complete victory: *It's a clean sweep for Germany; they finished first, second, and third in the race.*

sweep·er /'swiʸpər/ *n* a person or thing that sweeps: *a street-sweeper*

sweep·ing /'swiʸpɪŋ/ *adj* **1** including many things: *sweeping changes* **2** too general: *a sweeping statement*

sweep·stakes /'swiʸpsteʸks/ also **sweep-stake–** *n* **sweepstakes** a form of betting (BET²), usu. on a horserace

sweet¹ /swiʸt/ *adj* **1** having a taste like that of sugar: *a sweet apple|sweet wine|This tea is too sweet for me.* (=contains too much sugar) –compare BITTER¹ (1) **2** pleasant to the senses: *sweet music|the sweet smell of freshly-picked flowers* **3** (esp. of small or young things) charming; lovable: *Your little boy looks very sweet in his new coat.* **4** gentle or attractive in manner: *a sweet temper/smile* –**sweetly** *adv* –**sweetness** *n* [U]

sweet² *n esp. BrE* a small piece of sweet substance, e.g. chocolate, eaten for pleasure –compare CANDY

sweet corn /'· ·/ *n* [U] *BrE* for CORN¹ (1)

sweet·en /'swiʸtn/ *v* **1** [I;T] to make or become sweeter: *Shall I sweeten* (=add sugar to) *your coffee?|Apples sweeten as they become ripe.* **2** [T] *infml* to make an offer, a business deal, etc., more attractive by adding extra money, advantages, etc.: *The company sweetened the job with an extra week's vacation.*

sweet·en·er /'swiʸtn-ər, 'swiʸtnər/ *n* a substance used instead of sugar to make food and drink taste sweet

sweet·heart /'swiʸthɑrt/ *n becoming rare* (a word used to address) a person whom one loves

sweet pea /'· ·/ *n* a climbing plant with sweet-smelling flowers

sweet po·ta·to /'· ·,··/ also **yam–** *n* a type of plant whose yellowish fleshy root is eaten as a vegetable

swell¹ /swɛl/ *v* **swelled, swollen** /'swoʷlən/ *or* **swelled, swelling 1** [I *up*] to increase in fullness and roundness: *Her ankle swelled (up) after the fall.|*(fig.) *His heart swelled with pride as he watched his daughter win the race.* –see also SWOLLEN **2** [I;T *out*] to fill, giving a round shape: *The wind swelled (out) the sails.|The sails swelled out in the wind.*

swell² *n* [S] **1** the movement of large stretches of the sea up and down, without separate waves **2** an increase of sound: *the great swell of the ORGAN* (3)

swell³ *adj AmE infml* (*becoming rare*) very good; of good quality: *a swell teacher*

swell·ing /'swɛlɪŋ/ *n* a swollen place on the body: *a nasty swelling on my foot*

swel·ter·ing /'swɛltərɪŋ/ *adj infml* very hot: *Open the window; it's sweltering in here!*

swept /swɛpt/ *v past tense & participle of* SWEEP

swerve¹ /swɜrv/ *v* **swerved, swerving 1** [I] to turn suddenly to one side: *The car swerved to avoid the dog.* **2** [I;T *from*] to (cause to) change from a course or purpose: *Nothing will swerve him from his aims.*

swerve² *n* a swerving movement (SWERVE¹ (1)): *a sudden swerve to the left*

swift¹ /swɪft/ *adj* [+to-v] *more fml than* **quick–** rapid; quick in action: *a swift runner|He was swift to take offense.* –**swiftly** *adv* –**swiftness** *n* [U]

swift² *n* a small bird with long wings, similar to a SWALLOW³

swig /swɪg/ *v* **-gg-** [T] *infml* to drink, esp. in large mouthfuls –**swig** *n: a swig of beer*

swill¹ /swɪl/ *v* [T *down*] **1** [*out*] to wash by pouring large amounts of water: *to swill the yard* **2** *infml* to drink, esp. in large amounts

swill² *n* **1** [U] pig food, mostly uneaten human food in partly liquid form **2** [S] an act of SWILLING¹ (2)

swim¹ /swɪm/ *v* **swam** /swæm/, **swum** /swʌm/, **swimming 1** [I] to move through water by moving the limbs and/or tail: *We're all going swimming.|Some snakes can swim.* **2** [T] to cross or complete (a distance) by doing this: *to swim a river/a mile* **3** [I *with, in*] to be full of or covered with liquid: *soup swimming with fat* **4** [I] to cause one to feel DIZZY; seem to spin around: *I was tired, and my head was swimming.* –**swimmer** *n*

swim² *n* an act or occasion of swimming: *Let's go for a swim!*

swim·ming /'swɪmɪŋ/ *n* [U] the act or sport of those who swim

swimming pool /'·· ,·/ *n* a special pool for swimming in: *They have a swimming pool in their yard.*

swimming trunks /'·· ˌ·/ n [P] a man's garment worn for swimming –see PAIR (USAGE)

swim·suit /'swɪmsuʷt/ n → BATHING SUIT

swin·dle¹ /'swɪndl/ v **-dled, -dling** [T out of] to cheat (someone), esp. getting money illegally: *He's swindled me out of $100!* **–swindler** n

swindle² n an act of swindling (SWINDLE): *a tax swindle*

swine /swaɪn/ n swine **1** old use or tech a pig: *swine fever* **2** infml a nasty unpleasant person

swing¹ /swɪŋ/ v swung /swʌŋ/, **swinging 1** [I;T] to (cause to) move backwards and forwards or around and around, from a fixed point; (cause to) move in a curve: *They were swinging their arms as they walked.*|*The sign was swinging in the wind.*|*The children were swinging on the gate/on a rope.*|*The door swung open/shut.*|*He swung his arm and hit me in the face.* **2** [I] to turn quickly: *He swung around and said, "Why are you following me?"*|*The car swung into the parking lot and nearly hit me.*|(fig.) *Public opinion has swung against the President since the last tax increase.* **3** [I] to walk rapidly and actively with light steps: *swinging gaily down the street* **4** [I] infml to have or play with a pleasing exciting beat: *That music/That band really swings.*

swing² n **1** [C;U] an act or the manner of swinging: *with a swing of his arms*|*Would you like a swing on my rope?* **2** [C] (a ride on) a seat hanging on ropes or chains, on which one moves backwards and forwards: *The children are playing on the swings in the park.* **3** [C] a large change: *There's been a big swing in public opinion since the election.* **4 in full swing** (of a party, event, work, etc.) at the most active part

swing·ing /'swɪŋɪŋ/ adj **1** active and full of life: *a swinging party* **2** fashionably free and modern, esp. in sex life **–swingingly** adv **–swinger** n

swipe¹ /swaɪp/ n a sweeping stroke or blow: *He took a swipe at me.*

swipe² v swiped, swiping **1** [I;T at] to (try to) hit violently, esp. with a swing of the arm: *He swiped at the ball, but missed it.* **2** [T] infml to steal

swirl¹ /swɜrl/ v [I] to move with twisting turns: *The water swirled around his feet.*

swirl² n **1** a SWIRLING¹ movement: *She danced with a swirl of her skirt.* **2** a twisting mass (of water, dust, etc.): *swirls of smoke*

swish /swɪʃ/ v **1** [I;T] to (cause to) cut through the air making a sharp whistling noise: *to swish a whip*|*the cow's swishing tail* **2** [I] (esp. of clothes) to make a soft sound in movement: *swishing silk* **–swish** n

switch¹ /swɪtʃ/ n **1** an apparatus for stopping an electric current from flowing **2** a complete change, esp. unexpected: *a sudden switch in*

our plans **3** a small thin stick **4** AmE an apparatus for causing a train to turn onto another railroad line

switch² v [I;T] **1** to change or exchange: *They switched positions.*|*He got tired of teaching and switched to painting.* **2** [to] to move or change by a SWITCH¹ (1): *She switched the lights from green to red.*

switch off v adv **1** [I;T (=**switch** sthg.↔**off**)] to turn off (an electric light or apparatus) by means of a SWITCH¹ (1) –see OPEN (USAGE) **2** [I] infml → TUNE **out:** *He just switches off when you try to talk to him.*

switch on v adv [I;T (=**switch** sthg.↔**on**)] to turn on (an electric light or apparatus) by means of a SWITCH¹ (1) –see OPEN (USAGE)

switch over v adv [I] **1** [to, from] to change completely: *to switch over to the opposite political party* **2** to change from one radio or television CHANNEL (4) to another

switch·blade /'swɪtʃbleʸd/ AmE||**flick knife** BrE– n a knife with a blade inside the handle that springs into position when a button is pressed

switch·board /'swɪtʃbɔrd, -boʷrd/ n a central board which connects different telephone lines, e.g. within a company

swiv·el /'swɪvəl/ v **-l-** AmE||**-ll-** BrE [I;T around] to (cause to) turn around; PIVOT²: *a swiveling chair*|*She swiveled around as I came into the room.*

swol·len¹ /'swoʷlən/ adj **1** having got bigger, often because of water or air inside: *Her foot was very swollen after her accident.* **2** [A] too great or proud: *a swollen opinion of oneself* **–swollenness** n [U]

swollen² v past participle of SWELL¹

swoon /swuʷn/ v [I] esp. old use to lose consciousness; FAINT² **–swoon** n

swoop¹ /swuʷp/ v [I down] to descend sharply, esp. in attack: *The bird swooped to catch the mouse.*|(fig.) *As the thieves ran out of the bank, the waiting policemen swooped down (on them).*

swoop² n **1** a SWOOPING action **2 at one fell swoop** all at the same time

swop /swɑp/ v,n **-pp-** → SWAP

sword /sɔrd, soʷrd/ n **1** a weapon with a long sharp steel blade, used esp. in former times **2 cross swords (with)** to be opposed (to), esp. in argument

sword·fish /'sɔrdˌfɪʃ, 'soʷrd-/ n **-fish** or **-fishes** a large fish with a long sword-like upper jaw

swords·man /'sɔrdzmən, 'soʷrdz-/ n **-men** /mən/ a skilled fighter with a sword

swore /swɔr, swoʷr/ v past tense of SWEAR

sworn¹ /swɔrn, swoʷrn/ adj [A] complete, and with no possibility of changing: *sworn enemies*

sworn² v past participle of SWEAR

swum /swʌm/ v past participle of SWIM¹

swung /swʌŋ/ v past tense & participle of SWING¹

syc·a·more /'sɪkəˌmɔr, -ˌmoʷr/ n [C;U] (the hard wood of) any of several types of tree

syc·o·phant /'sɪkəfənt/ n derog a person who tries too much to please (FLATTERs) those in positions of power, so as to gain advantage

---

SPELLING NOTE

Words with the sound /s/, may be spelled **c-**, like **city**, or **ps-**, like **psychology**.

for himself –**sycophantic** /ˌsɪkə'fæntɪk/ *adj*

syl·la·ble /'sɪləbəl/ *n* part of a (word) which contains a vowel sound: *There are two syllables in "window:" "win" and "dow."*

syl·la·bus /'sɪləbəs/ *n* -**buses** *or* -**bi** /ˌbaɪ/ an arrangement of subjects for study, esp. a course of studies leading to an examination

sym·bol /'sɪmbəl/ *n* **1** [*of*] a sign or object which represents a person, idea, etc.: *A horseshoe is a symbol of good luck.* –compare EMBLEM **2** a letter or figure which expresses a sound, number, or chemical substance: *"H_2O" is the symbol for water.*

sym·bol·ic /sɪm'bɑlɪk/ also **symbolical** /-kəl/ *adj* [*of*] of, as, or using a SYMBOL (1): *The Christian ceremony of* BAPTISM *is a symbolic act.* –**symbolically** *adv*

sym·bol·ism /'sɪmbəˌlɪzəm/ *n* [U] the use of SYMBOLS (1), esp. in literature, painting, film, etc.

sym·bol·ize‖also **-ise** *BrE* /'sɪmbəˌlaɪz/ *v* -**ized**, -**izing** [T] to represent by SYMBOLS (1); be a symbol of: *In the wedding ceremony, the rings symbolize the union of the two partners.* –**symbolization** /ˌsɪmbələ'zeⁱʃən/ *n* [U]

sym·met·ri·cal /sə'mɛtrɪkəl/ also **symmetric** /sə'mɛtrɪk/– *adj* having both sides exactly alike –opposite **asymmetric** –**symmetrically** *adv*

sym·me·try /'sɪmətriⁱ/ *n* [U] (the pleasing effect resulting from) the exact likeness between the opposite sides of something

sym·pa·thet·ic /ˌsɪmpə'θɛtɪk/ *adj* [*to*] feeling or showing sympathy: *She was sympathetic to my ideas.*|*I told the teacher I was feeling ill, but he wasn't very sympathetic.* –opposite **unsympathetic** –**sympathetically** *adv*

sym·pa·thies /'sɪmpəθiⁱz/ *n* [P] feelings of support: *Although I pity him, my sympathies are with his family.*

sym·pa·thize‖also **-thise** *BrE* /'sɪmpəˌθaɪz/ *v* -**thized**, -**thizing** [I *with*] to feel or show sympathy or approval: *It's hard to sympathize with her political opinions.* –**sympathizer** *n*

sym·pa·thy /'sɪmpəθiⁱ/ *n* [U] **1** (the expression of) pity for the sufferings of other people: *She pressed his hand in sympathy.*|*I didn't get much sympathy from the doctor when I told her about my illness.* **2** agreement in or understanding of the feelings of others: *I have a lot of sympathy for his opinions.*

sym·pho·ny /'sɪmfəniⁱ/ *n* -**nies** a piece of music for a large group of instruments (ORCHESTRA), usu. having four parts (MOVEMENTS) –**symphonic** /sɪm'fɑnɪk/ *adj*

symp·tom /'sɪmptəm/ *n* [*of*] an outward sign of an inward, often bad, condition: *Yellowness of the eyes is one of the symptoms of* JAUNDICE.|*His attempt to kill himself is a symptom of his unhappiness.* –**symptomatic** /ˌsɪmptə'mætɪk/ *adj* [*of*]

syn·a·gogue /'sɪnəˌgɑg, -ˌgɔg/ *n* a place where Jews meet for religious worship

syn·chro·nize‖also **-nise** *BrE* /'sɪŋkrəˌnaɪz/ *v* -**nized**, -**nizing** **1** [T] to set (clocks and watches) to show the same time **2** [I;T] to (cause to) happen at the same speed: *They synchronized their steps.* –**synchronization** /ˌsɪŋkrənə'zeⁱʃən/ *n* [U]

syn·di·cate¹ /'sɪndəkɪt/ *n* a group of businesses or people combined together for a particular purpose, e.g. making money: *A syndicate of businessmen is building a new hotel here.*

syn·di·cate² /'sɪndəˌkeⁱt/ *v* -**cated**, -**cating** [I;T] to form into a SYNDICATE¹ –**syndication** /ˌsɪndə'keⁱʃən/ *n* [U]

syn·drome /'sɪndroʷm/ *n* a set of qualities, happenings, SYMPTOMS, etc., typical of a general condition

syn·od /'sɪnəd/ *n* an important meeting of church members to make decisions on church matters

syn·o·nym /'sɪnəˌnɪm/ *n tech* a word with the same meaning as another word: *"Sad" and "unhappy" are synonyms.* –compare ANTONYM

syn·on·y·mous /sɪ'nɑnəməs/ *adj* [*with*] having the same or nearly the same meaning (as): *Being a woman is synonymous with being a second-class citizen, in her opinion.* –**synonymously** *adv*

syn·op·sis /sɪ'nɑpsɪs/ *n* -**ses** /ˌsiⁱz/ a short account of something longer, e.g. the story of a movie, play, or book

syn·tax /'sɪntæks/ *n* [U] the rules of grammar which are used for ordering and connecting words in a sentence –**syntactic** /sɪn'tæktɪk/ *adj* –**syntactically** *adv*

syn·the·sis /'sɪnθəsɪs/ *n* -**ses** /ˌsiⁱz/ [C;U] (something made by) the combining of separate things, ideas, etc., into a complete whole: *The beliefs of that group are a synthesis of Eastern and Western religions.* –compare ANALYSIS

syn·the·size‖also **-sise** *BrE* /'sɪnθəˌsaɪz/ *v* -**sized**, -**sizing** [T] to make up or produce by combining parts; (esp.) to make something similar to a natural product by combining chemicals: *to synthesize a drug*

syn·thet·ic /sɪn'θɛtɪk/ *adj* not naturally produced; ARTIFICIAL (1); produced by synthesizing (SYNTHESIZE): *a new kind of cigarette made of synthetic tobacco* –**synthetically** *adv*

syph·i·lis /'sɪfəlɪs/ *n* [U] a serious VENEREAL DISEASE

sy·phon /'saɪfən/ *n,v* →SIPHON

sy·ringe¹ /sə'rɪndʒ, 'sɪrɪndʒ/ *n* a pipe used in science and medicine, into which liquid can be sucked and from which it can be pushed out, esp. through a needle, to put drugs into the body

syringe² *v* -**ringed**, -**ringing** [T] to treat or clean (a diseased part, wound, etc.) using a SYRINGE¹

syr·up /'sɪrəp, 'sɜrəp/ *n* [U] **1** thick sweet liquid, esp. sugar and water: *Canned fruit usually has a lot of syrup with it.* **2** medicine in the form of a thick sweet liquid

syr·up·y /'sɪrəpiⁱ, 'sɜr-/ *adj* **1** like or containing SYRUP **2** too sweet; SENTIMENTAL (2) –compare SUGARY

sys·tem /'sɪstəm/ *n* **1** [C] a group of related parts working together: *the postal system*|*This drug has an effect on your whole system.* (=the way your body works) **2** [C *of*] an ordered set of ideas, methods, or ways of working: *What are the differences between the American and British systems of government?|She has a special system for winning money on horse races.* **3** [U] orderly methods: *You need some system in your life if you want to succeed.*

sys·tem·at·ic /ˌsɪstə'mætɪk/ *adj apprec* based on a regular plan or fixed method; thorough:

The police made a systematic search of the room. –**systematically** *adv*

sys·tem·a·tize‖also **-tise** *BrE* /'sɪstəmə,taɪz/ *v* **-tized, -tizing** to arrange in a system or by a set method –**systematization** /ˌsɪstəmətə'zeʸʃən/ *n* [U]

systems an·a·lyst /'·· ,···/ *n* a COMPUTER worker who plans how such a machine may be used to carry out various operations

T, t

T, t /tiʸ/ **T's, t's** *or* **Ts, ts 1** the 20th letter of the English alphabet **2 to a T** *infml* exactly; perfectly: *The dress fits her to a T.* –see also T-SHIRT

't /t/ *pron old use & lit* it: *'tis* (=it is): *'Twas* (=it was) *a cold night.*

tab /tæb/ *n* **1** a small piece of cloth, paper, etc., fixed to something, e.g. to help in handling, or as a sign of what it is: *Hang your coat up by the tab on the collar.|I sewed tabs with my name on in all my school clothes.* **2** *esp. AmE infml* a bill **3 keep tabs/a tab on** *infml* to watch closely: *Keep tabs on your spending.*

tab·by /'tæbiʸ/ *n* **-bies** a cat with dark bands on its fur, esp. a female cat

tab·er·na·cle /'tæbər,nækəl/ *n* a movable framework of wood, used in worship by the Jews in former times

ta·ble¹ /'teʸbəl/ *n* **1** [C] a piece of furniture with a flat top supported by one or more upright legs: *a kitchen table|At the restaurant, we asked for a table for two.* **2** [A] made to be placed and used on such a piece of furniture: *a table lamp* **3** [S] the food served at a meal **4** [C] the people sitting at a table: *The whole table was amused by John's funny stories.* **5** [C] a printed or written collection of figures, facts, or information, arranged in orderly rows across and down the page: *a bus timetable|There is a table of contents at the front of this dictionary.* **6 at the table** during a meal: *It is bad manners to blow your nose at the table.* **7 turn the tables (on someone)** to seize a position of strength from someone, after having been in a position of weakness

table² *v* **-bled, -bling** [T] **1** to set aside (a matter, report, etc.) for consideration by a committee, etc. for a time without a specified end **2** to put (facts, figures, information, etc.) into the form of a TABLE¹ (5)

tab·leau /'tæbloʷ, tæ'bloʷ/ *n* **-leaux** /'tæbloʷz, tæ'bloʷz/ *or* **-leaus** a representation of a scene, esp. on a stage, by a group of people who do not move or speak

ta·ble·cloth /'teʸbəl,klɔθ/ *n* **-cloths** /ˌklɔðz, ˌklɔθs/ a cloth for covering a table, esp. during a meal –see illustration on page 379

ta·ble d'hôte /ˌtabəl 'doʷt, ˌtæ-/ *adj,adv* [A] French (of a complete meal in a hotel or restaurant) served at a fixed price –compare A LA CARTE

ta·ble·spoon /'teʸbəl,spuʷn/ *n* **1** a large spoon used for serving food **2** also **table-spoonful** /'teʸbəl,spuʷn,fʊl/– the amount held by this; a measurement used in cooking

tab·let /'tæblɪt/ *n* **1** a small round solid piece of medicine; a PILL: *The doctor told me to take two tablets before every meal.* **2** a flat block esp. of stone or metal with words cut into it

table ten·nis /'·· ,···/ also **ping-pong** *infml*– *n* [U] an indoor game played on a table by two or four players who use PADDLES to hit a small ball to each other across a net

tab·loid /'tæblɔɪd/ *n* a newspaper with rather small pages, many pictures, and little serious news

ta·boo /tə'buʷ, tæ-/ *n* **-boos** [C;U] (an act, subject, etc. forbidden by) a religious or social feeling of strong disapproval: *a taboo against sex before marriage* –**taboo** *adj*: *Certain words are taboo in general conversation.*

tab·u·late /'tæbyə,leʸt/ *v* **-lated, -lating** [T] to arrange (facts, figures, etc.) in the form of a table or list –**tabular** /'tæbyələr/ *adj*: *This information will be clear when it's in tabular form.* –**tabulation** /ˌtæbyə'leʸʃən/ *n* [U]

tac·it /'tæsɪt/ *adj* [A] expressed or understood without being put into words: *a tacit agreement* –**tacitly** *adv*

tac·i·turn /'tæsə,tɜrn/ *adj fml* usually silent; not liking to say a lot –**taciturnity** /ˌtæsə'tɜrnətiʸ/ *n* [U] –**taciturnly** *adv* /'tæsə,tɜrnliʸ/

tack¹ /tæk/ *n* **1** [C] a small nail with a sharp point and flat head: *He hammered a tack into the wall to hang a picture.* **2** [C;U] (a change in) the direction of a sailing ship as shown by the position of its sails: *The captain ordered a change of tack.|(fig.) If you can't persuade him, try a new tack and offer him money.* **3** [C] a long loose stitch used for fastening pieces of cloth together before sewing them properly

tack² *v* **1** [T] to fasten to a solid surface with a TACK¹ (1): *She tacked a notice to the board.* **2** [I] to change the course of a sailing ship **3** [T] to sew (cloth) with long loose stitches: *He tacked the pieces of cloth together before sewing them properly.*

tack sthg.↔ **on** *v adv* [T *to*] *infml* to add to the end of a speech, book, etc.: *She tacked a few words on to the letter her sister had written.*

tack·le¹ /'tækəl/ *n* **1** [C] (in football or RUGBY)

an act of stopping, or trying to stop, an opponent who has the ball **2** [U] the equipment used in a sport: *Don't forget to bring your fishing tackle.* **3** [C;U] a system of ropes and wheels (PULLEYs) for working a ship's sails, raising heavy weights, etc.

tackle² *v* **-led, -ling 1** [T] to take action about: *How can we tackle this problem?* **2** [I;T] (in football or RUGBY) to seize and stop (an opponent) by forcing to the ground **3** [T] *infml* to seize and attack: *The robber tried to run away, but a man tackled him.*

tack·y¹ /'tækiʸ/ *adj* **-ier, -iest** sticky: *The paint is still tacky so don't touch it.*

tacky² *adj AmE infml* lacking style; SHABBY: *The dress she wore to the party looked really tacky.*

tact /tækt/ *n* [U] the ability to do or say the right thing at the right time; skill in dealing with people: *A school teacher has to have tact.* **–tactful** /'tæktfəl/ *adj* **–tactfully** *adv* **–tactless** *adj* **–tactlessly** *adv* **–tactlessness** *n* [U]

tac·tic /'tæktɪk/ *n* a means of getting a desired result: *She used a clever tactic to get the job.*

tac·ti·cal /'tæktɪkəl/ *adj* of or related to a TACTIC or TACTICS: *a tactical decision|tactical skill in battle* **–tactically** *adv*

tac·tics /'tæktɪks/ *n* [U + *pl. v*] the art of arranging military forces so as to gain success in battle: (fig.) *clever tactics for winning a game/an election* **–**compare STRATEGY (1)

tac·tile /'tæktəl, -tail/ *adj tech* of the sense of touch; felt by touch: *a tactile sensation*

tad·pole /'tædpoʷl/ *n* a small black water creature that grows into a FROG or TOAD

taf·fy /'tæfiʸ/ **-fies** *n* [C;U] (a piece of) CHEWable candy made by boiling sugar or MOLASSES and pulling it until it reaches the correct color and firmness

tag¹ /tæg/ *n* **1** a small piece of paper, material, etc., fixed to something to give information about it: *a name/price tag* **2** a metal or plastic point at the end of a cord, SHOELACE, etc. **3** a phrase or sentence spoken (too) often

tag² *v* **-gg- 1** [T] to fasten a TAG¹ (1) to (something) **2** [T *on, onto, to*] to fix (something) onto something else: *He tagged a request for money to the end of his letter.* **3** [I *along, on*] *infml* to follow closely: *a child tagging along behind its mother|Why are you tagging along? You weren't invited!*

tag³ *n* [U] a children's game in which one player chases and tries to touch the others

tail¹ /teʸl/ *n* **1** the movable long growth at the back of a creature's body: *a dog's tail* **2** anything like this in appearance or position: *the tails of a coat|a* COMET's *tail|the* **tail end** (=back end) *of a plane/a procession|the* **tail end** (=last part) *of the movie* **3** the side of a coin which does not have the head of a ruler on it (esp. in the phrase **heads or tails**) **–**compare HEAD (6) **4** [C] *infml* a person employed to watch and follow someone: *The police put a tail on the criminal.* **5 turn tail** to run away **6 -tailed** having a certain kind of tail: *long-tailed|bushy-tailed* **–tailless** *adj*

tail² *v* [T] *infml* to follow closely behind (someone): *The police have been tailing me,*

so they know I'm here.

tail off/away *v adv* [I] to lessen in quantity, strength, or quality: *His voice tailed off as his courage failed.*

tail·coat /'teʸlkoʷt/ *n* a man's formal evening coat with the lower back part divided into two

tail·light /'teʸl-lait/ *n* a red light at the back of a vehicle so that it can be seen in the dark **–**see illustration on page 95

tai·lor¹ /'teʸlər/ *n* a person who makes outer garments, esp. for men

tailor² *v* [I;T] to make (an outer garment) by cutting and sewing cloth, esp. to fit a particular person: (fig.) *We can tailor our insurance to meet your needs.*

tailor-made /,·· '·◂/ *adj* [*for*] (of clothes) made specially to fit the wearer: *a tailor-made suit|*(fig.) *This job is tailor-made for John.* **–**see also READY-MADE

tails /teʸlz/ *n* [P] a TAILCOAT: *The men wore tails at the wedding.*

taint¹ /teʸnt/ *v* [T] to infect or make morally impure; spoil: *The warm weather's tainted this meat.|tainted money*

taint² *n* [S;U *of*] *fml* (a) slight touch of decay, infection, or evil influence: *the taint of disloyalty|a taint of madness*

take¹ /teʸk/ *v* **took** /tʊk/, **taken** /'teʸkən/, **taking** [T] **1** to get; have; use: *We're going to take* (=buy or rent) *an apartment in Manhattan.|Do you take the bus or the train when you go home?|Let's take a walk.|Take a seat.|Did you take your medicine?|*(esp. *AmE*) *I think I'll take a bath.* **2** to obtain; receive; accept: *I won't take less than $1,500 for my car.|Why should I take the blame?|You never take my advice.|I don't think it will work, but I'll* **take a chance** *and try it.|This machine only takes ten-cent coins* (DIMEs). (=it will work only if you put ten-cent coins into it)*|This bottle takes* (=has room for) *a quart.* **3** to get possession of; gain; seize; win: *The city was taken by the enemy.|Jane took second place in the race.* **4** to hold with the hands: *She took his arm and led him across the street.* **5** to remove from someone's possession, by stealing or by mistake: *Who has taken my pen?* **6** to remove; subtract: *If you take 5 from 12 you get 7.* **7** to copy from an original, with changes: *This play was taken from a book by Mark Twain.* **8** to carry from one place to another: *We usually take the children to school in the car.|*(fig.) *Her ability took her to the top of her profession.* **–**see Study Notes on page 481 **9** to need: *That takes some believing!* (=is hard to believe)*|It takes a lot of money to buy a house like that.|It took me four hours to drive there.|The trip from Baltimore to Washington takes 55 minutes.* **10** to record: *The policeman took my name and address.|I had my picture taken.* (=I was photographed)*|The nurse took my temperature.* (=with a THERMOMETER) **11** to understand; think; suppose: *I took his smile to mean yes/as meaning yes.|I take it you agree.* (=I ASSUME you agree)*|Do you take me for a fool?* (=Do you think I am a fool?) **12** to act towards in a stated way: *I always take your suggestions seriously*. **13** to do; perform; put into effect: *The government took these measures to deal with unemployment.|Are you willing to take* (=swear) *the oath?* **14** to cause to become: *She was taken ill and had to go to the hospital*. **15 take for granted: a** to accept (a fact, an action, etc.) without questioning if it is true or will happen: *I just took it for granted that you knew*. **b** to treat (a person) without consideration or kindness: *He never thanks you for your help; he just takes you for granted*. **16 take it from me** also **take my word for it**– believe me when I say: *You can take it from me that he won't do his work in time*. **17 take one's time (over): a** to use as much time as is necessary; not hurry **b** to take more time than is reasonable **18 take place** to happen **19 take the law into one's own hands** to take no notice of society's rules and act alone, usu. by force **20 take the rough with the smooth** to accept bad things as well as good things, without complaining

take sbdy. **aback** *v adv* [T] to surprise and confuse: *I was very taken aback by his rudeness*.

take after sbdy. *v prep* [T] **1** to look or behave like (an older relative): *Mary takes after her mother; she's always cheerful*. **2** *AmE* to chase

take sthg.↔ **apart** *v adv* [T] to separate (a small machine) into pieces: *She took the watch apart to fix it*. –compare TAKE[1] **down**

take sbdy./sthg. ↔ **back** *v adv* [T] **1** to admit that one was wrong in (what one said): *I'm sorry I was rude; I take back what I said*. –compare WITHDRAW (2) **2** to agree to receive back (something or someone): *The store promised to take the toy back if it broke.|If my husband leaves me, I won't take him back*.

take sthg. ↔ **down** *v adv* [T] **1** to separate (a large machine or article) into pieces: *to take down a dangerous bridge* –compare TAKE[1] **apart**, PUT **up 2** to make a record of: *Let me just take down your phone number*. **3** to take from a public place: *They took down the notices*. –opposite **put up**

take sbdy./sthg. ↔ **in** *v adv* [T] **1** to provide a home for (a person): *He had nowhere to live, so we took him in*. **2** to include: *This is the total cost of the trip, taking in everything*. **3** to make (clothes) narrower: *The dress was too big, so I took it in*. –opposite **let out 4** to understand: *I didn't take in what you were saying*. **5** to deceive: *Don't be taken in by her promises*.

take off *v adv* **1** [T] (**take** sthg.↔ **off**) to remove (esp. clothes): *Take your coat off*. –opposite **put on 2** [I] (esp. of a plane) to rise into the air –compare LAND[1] (2) **3** [T] (**take** sbdy.↔ **off**) *infml* to copy (someone's speech or manners): *to take off members of the President's family* –compare IMPERSONATE, MIMIC; see also TAKEOFF

take on *v adv* [T] **1** (**take** sbdy.↔ **on**) to start to employ: *The company took on a new clerk*. –opposite **lay off 2** (**take on** sthg.) to begin to have (a quality or appearance): *Her*

face took on a new expression. **3** (**take** sbdy. ↔ **on**) to start a fight with: *Why don't you take on someone your own size?* **4** (**take** sthg. ↔ **on**) to accept (responsibility): *Don't take on too much work*.

take sbdy./sthg. ↔ **out** *v adv* [T] **1** to remove from inside: *to have a tooth taken out* **2** to go somewhere with (a person): *I'm taking the children out to the movies tonight*. **3** to obtain officially; get: *Have you taken out insurance yet?* **4 take someone out of himself/herself** to amuse or interest someone who is feeling unhappy **5 take it/a lot out of someone** *infml* to use all someone's strength: *The long journey really took it/a lot out of everyone*.

take sthg. **out on** sbdy. *v adv prep* [T] *infml* to express (one's feelings) by making (someone else) suffer: *It's not my fault that you've had a bad day; don't take it out on me*.

take over *v adv* [I;T (=**take** sthg.↔ **over**)] to gain control over or responsibility for: *Our chairman has left, so Paula will take over (his job)*. –see also TAKEOVER

take to sbdy./sthg. *v prep* [T] **1** to like: *Jean took to Paul as soon as they met*. **2** [+*v-ing*] to begin as a practice, habit, etc.: *John's taken to drinking a lot*. **3** to go to for rest, escape, etc.: *Father's ill, so he has taken to his bed.|The criminal took to the woods to hide*.

take sbdy./sthg.↔ **up** *v adv* [T] **1** [+*v-ing*] to begin to do; interest oneself in: *John took up writing poetry while at school*. **2** to fill: *The work took up all of Sunday.|books taking up space* **3** to continue: *I'll take up the story where I finished yesterday*. **4** [*with*] to complain or ask about: *I will take this matter up with a lawyer*. **5** [*on*] to accept the offer of (a person): *Can I take you up on your offer of a meal?* **6** to make (clothes) shorter –opposite **let down 7 taken up (with)** very busy (with): *He can't help; he's too taken up with his own problems*.

take up with sbdy. *v adv prep* [T] *infml* to become friendly with

take[2] *n* **1** [*usu. sing.*] *infml* the amount of money taken by a business, thief, etc. **2** a scene that is photographed for a movie

take·off /'teɪk-ɔf/ *n* **1** [C;U] the beginning of a flight, e.g. when a plane rises from the ground: *a smooth takeoff|Takeoff is at 12 o'clock*. –compare LANDING (1) **2** [C] *infml* an amusing copy of someone's behavior: *a funny takeoff on leading politicians* –see also TAKE[1] **off**

take-out //'· ·/ also **carry-out**– *adj,n* [A] *AmE* **1** (of food) bought at a restaurant from which meals are taken out to be eaten: *a take-out dinner* **2** of a restaurant that sells this food: *a take-out restaurant*

take·o·ver /'teɪk,oʷvər/ *n* an act of gaining control, esp. of a business company or government –see also TAKE **over**

tak·ings /'teɪkɪŋz/ *n* [P] receipts of money, esp. by a store: *to count the takings*

tal·cum pow·der /'tælkəm ˌpaʊdər/ also **talc** /tælk/– *n* [U] very fine powder which is put on the body to dry it, or make it smell nice

tale /teɪl/ *n* **1** a story: *a tale of adventure* **2** a false or unkind account: *Children shouldn't tell tales.*

tal·ent /'tælənt/ *n* [C;U *for*] (a) special natural ability or skill: *a talent for drawing|musical/artistic talent* –see GENIUS (USAGE) –**talented** *adj: a very talented actor*

tal·is·man /'tælɪsmən, -lɪz-/ *n* **-mans** an object which is believed to have magic powers of protection

talk¹ /tɔk/ *v* **1** [I] to speak; produce human words: *Human beings can talk; animals can't.|I want to talk to you about something.|She's talking to her father.* **2** [I] to express thoughts as if by speech: *People who cannot speak can talk by using signs.* **3** [T] to express in words: *Talk sense!* **4** [T] to be able to speak (a language): *to talk French* –see SAY (USAGE)

talk back to sbdy. *v adv prep* [T] to reply without respect or fear

talk down to sbdy. *v adv prep* [T] to speak to (someone) in a way that makes one seem of higher rank or greater importance

talk sbdy. **into** sthg. *v prep* [T] to persuade (someone) to do (something): *She talked me into buying her car.* –compare TALK¹ **out of**

talk sbdy. **out of** sthg. *v adv prep* [T] **1** to persuade (someone) not to do (something): *She talked him out of killing himself.* –compare TALK¹ **into 2 talk one's way out of** to escape from (trouble) by talking

talk sthg.↔ **over** *v adv* [T *with*] to speak about thoroughly: *I have an important matter to talk over with you.*

talk² *n* **1** [C *with*] a conversation: *I met Mrs Young at the meeting and had a long talk with her.* **2** [C *on, about*] an informal speech: *The teacher gave a talk on modern poetry.* **3** [U] a particular way of speech or conversation: *baby talk* **4** [U] empty or meaningless speech: *His threats were just talk. Don't worry!* –see also TALKS

talk·a·tive /'tɔkətɪv/ *adj* liking to talk a lot –**talkativeness** *n* [U]

talk·er /'tɔkər/ *n* a person who talks: *a good/bad talker*

talking-to /'·· ,·/ *n* **-tos** *infml* a scolding

talks /tɔks/ *n* [P] a formal exchange of opinions and views: *The two presidents met for talks.| peace talks*

tall /tɔl/ *adj* **1** having a greater than average height: *a tall man/building/tree* **2** [after *n*] having the stated height: *four feet tall* –see HIGH (USAGE) –**tallness** *n* [U]

tall·boy /'tɔlbɔɪ/ *BrE* for HIGHBOY

tall or·der /,· '··/ *n* a request that is unreasonably difficult to perform

tal·low /'tæloʷ/ *n* [U] hard animal fat used for making candles

tall sto·ry /,· '··/ *n* a story that is difficult to believe

tal·ly¹ /'tæliʸ/ *n* **-lies** an account; record of points; SCORE¹ (1)

tally² *v* **-lied, -lying** [I;T *with*] to (cause to) agree or equal exactly: *Your figures don't tally with mine.*

Tal·mud /'talmʊd, -məd, 'tæl-/ *n* [*the* + R] the body of Jewish law concerned with religious and nonreligious life

tal·on /'tælən/ *n* a sharp curved nail on the feet of some hunting birds

tam·bou·rine /,tæmbə'riʸn/ *n* a circular frame with a skin stretched over it, with small metal plates round the edge, which is shaken or beaten to make a musical sound

tame¹ /teʸm/ *adj* **1** not fierce or wild; trained to live with people: *a tame animal* **2** *infml* dull; unexciting: *a tame football game/party* –**tamely** *adv* –**tameness** *n* [U]

tame² *v* **tamed, taming** [T] to train (something wild or dangerous, esp. an animal) to be gentle –**tamable, tameable** *adj* –**tamer** *n: a lion-tamer*

tam·per with sthg. /'tæmpər/ *v prep* [T] to make changes in (something) without permission: *My car wouldn't start after he tampered with it.*

tam·pon /'tæmpɑn/ *n* a mass of cotton fitted into a woman's sex organ to take in (ABSORB) the monthly bleeding

tan¹ /tæn/ *v* **-nn- 1** [T] to change (animal skin) into leather by a special treatment **2** [I;T] to make or become brown, esp. by sunlight: *Janet tanned quickly in the sun.*

tan² *n* **1** [U] a yellowish brown color: *These shoes are tan, not dark brown.* **2** [C] → SUNTAN

tan·dem¹ /'tændəm/ *n* a bicycle built for two riders sitting one behind the other

tandem² *adv* (usu. of two people riding a bicycle) one behind the other: *to ride tandem*

tang /tæŋ/ *n* [usu. *sing.*] a strong taste or smell: *the tang of the sea air* –**tangy** *adj* **-ier, -iest**

tan·gent /'tændʒənt/ *n* **1** a straight line touching a curve but not cutting across it **2 go off at/on a tangent** *infml* to change suddenly from one course of action, thought, etc., to another –**tangential** /tæn'dʒɛnʃəl, -tʃəl/ *adj* –**tangentially** *adv*

tan·ger·ine /,tændʒə'riʸn, 'tændʒə,riʸn/ *n* [C;U] (the color of) a small sweet orange with a loose skin

tan·gi·ble /'tændʒəbəl/ *adj* **1** that can be felt by touch –opposite **intangible 2** clear and certain; real: *tangible proof* –**tangibility** /,tændʒə'bɪlətiʸ/ *n* [U] –**tangibly** /'tæn dʒəbliʸ/ *adv*

tan·gle¹ /'tæŋgəl/ *v* **-gled, -gling** [I;T] to make or become a mass of disordered and twisted threads: *Your hair's so tangled that I can't comb it.|(fig.) tangled thoughts* –opposite **untangle**

tangle with sbdy. *v prep* [T] *infml* to quarrel or argue with

tangle² *n* a confused mass or disordered state of hair, thread, etc.: *wool in a tangle*

tan·go /'tæŋgoʷ/ *n* **-gos** [C;U] (music for) a spirited dance of Spanish-American origin –**tango** *v* [I]

tank /tæŋk/ *n* **1** a large container for storing liquid or gas: *the gas tank of a car|a fish tank* **2** a large, heavy, armored vehicle with a gun, which moves on metal belts

tan·kard /'tæŋkərd/ *n* a large drinking cup, usu. with a handle and lid

tank·er /'tæŋkər/ *n* a ship or road vehicle built for carrying large quantities of gas or liquid:

oil coming by tanker

tan·ner /'tænər/ n a person whose job is making animal skin into leather by TANNING[1] (1)

tan·ta·lize‖also **-lise** *BrE* /'tæntəl‚aız/ v **-lized, -lizing** [T] to raise the hopes of (a person or animal) by keeping something strongly desired just out of reach: *A tantalizing smell of food reached the hungry prisoners.*

tan·ta·mount /'tæntə‚maunt/ adj [F *to*] equal in value, force, or effect: *Your answer is tantamount to a refusal.*

tan·trum /'tæntrəm/ n a sudden uncontrolled attack of anger

tap[1] /tæp/ ‖also **faucet** *AmE*– n **1** an apparatus for letting out liquid or gas from a pipe, barrel, etc. **2** an apparatus put on a telephone to listen secretly to phone conversations **3 on tap: a** (of beer) from a barrel **b** ready for use when needed: *plenty of information on tap*

tap[2] v **-pp-** [T] **1** to open (a barrel) so as to draw off liquid **2** to use or draw from: *to tap the nation's natural mineral wealth* **3** to listen to (telephone conversations) through a secret telephone connection

tap[3] v **-pp-** [I;T *on*] to strike (the hand, foot, etc.) lightly against something: *The teacher tapped her fingers on the desk impatiently.|I tapped on the window to let them know I'd arrived.* –**tap** n: *a tap on the shoulder*

tap danc·ing /'· ‚·'/ n [U] stage dancing in which the dancer beats time to music with his/her feet, wearing special shoes

tape[1] /teyp/ n **1** [C;U] (a length of) narrow material, used e.g. for tying up packages **2** a [C;U] (a) MAGNETIC band on which sound can be recorded **b** [C] also **tape recording** /'· ·‚·/– a length of this on which sound has been recorded: *some tapes of her songs*

tape[2] v **taped, taping 1** [I;T] also **tape-record** /'· ·‚·/– to record (sound) on TAPE[1] (2) by using a TAPE RECORDER **2** [T *up*] to fasten or tie (a package, packet, etc.) with TAPE[1] (1): *Have you finished taping all the presents up yet?*

tape deck /'· ·/ n the apparatus in a TAPE RECORDER that records and plays back sound

tape meas·ure /'· ‚·/ n a narrow band of cloth or steel, marked with divisions of length, used for measuring

ta·per[1] /'teypər/ v [I;T *off*] to (cause to) become gradually narrower towards one end: *The stick tapered off to a point.*

taper[2] n a very long thin candle

tape re·cord·er /'· ·‚··/ n an apparatus which can record and play back sound on TAPE[1] (2)

tap·es·try /'tæpıstriy/ n **-tries** [C;U] (a piece of) heavy cloth on which a picture, pattern, etc., is woven: *a beautiful tapestry on the wall|tapestry chair covers*

tape·worm /'teypwɜrm/ n a long flat worm that lives in the bowels of people and animals

tap·i·o·ca /‚tæpiy'oʷkə/ n [U] small hard white grains of food made from the roots of a tropical plant

tap·pet /'tæpıt/ n a part of the VALVE (1) system of an engine

tar[1] /tɑr/ n [U] a black substance, thick and sticky when hot and hard when cold, used for making roads, preserving wood, etc.

tar[2] v **-rr-** [I;T] to cover with TAR[1]: *to tar a road*

ta·ran·tu·la /tə'ræntʃələ/ n a large hairy poisonous SPIDER

tar·dy /'tɑrdiy/ adj **-dier, -diest 1** slow in acting or happening **2** *AmE* late –**tardily** adv [U] –**tardiness** n [U]

tar·get /'tɑrgıt/ n **1** anything fired at, esp. a round board with circles on it, used in shooting practice **2** [*of*] a person or thing that people blame or laugh at: *He is the target of many jokes.* **3** a total or object which one desires to reach: *My target is to save $25 a week.*

tar·iff /'tærıf/ n **1** a tax collected by a government, usu. on goods coming into a country **2** a list of fixed prices charged by a hotel, restaurant, etc.

tar·nish /'tɑrnıʃ/ v [I;T] to make or become dull, discolored, or less bright: *tarnished brass*|(fig.) *tarnished honor* –**tarnish** n [U]

tar·ot /'tæroʷ, tæ'roʷ/ n (a set of) 22 cards used for telling the future

tar·pau·lin /tɑr'pɔlın, 'tɑrpələn/ also **tarp** /tɑrp/– n [C;U] (a sheet or cover of) heavy cloth that water will not pass through

tar·ra·gon /'tærə‚gɑn, -gən/ n [U] (the strong-smelling leaves of) a plant used for giving a special taste to food

tar·ry /'tæriy/ v **-ried, -rying** [I] *old use & lit* to stay in a place; delay

tart[1] /tɑrt/ n [C;U] (an) open fruit PIE; circle of pastry cooked with fruit or JAM on it

tart[2] adj **1** sharp to the taste; not sweet **2** bitter; SARCASTIC –**tartly** adv –**tartness** n [U]

tar·tan /'tɑrtn/ n **1** [U] Scottish woolen cloth woven with bands of different colors crossing each other **2** [C] a special pattern on this cloth, used as the sign of a particular Scottish CLAN

tar·tar[1] /'tɑrtər/ n [U] **1** a hard chalky substance that forms on the teeth –compare PLAQUE **2** also **cream of tartar** /‚· · '··/– a white powder used in making medicine

tartar[2] n a fierce person with a violent temper

tartar sauce, tartare sauce /'tɑrtər ‚sɔs/ n [U] a thick SAUCE eaten with fish

task /tæsk/ n **1** a piece of esp. hard work to be done; duty: *the task of sweeping the floors|She finds looking after her old father a difficult task.* **2 take someone to task** to scold someone severely

task force /'· ·/ n a military force or a group of police, sent to a place for a special purpose

task·mas·ter /'tæsk‚mæstər/ n a person who gives jobs, esp. hard and unpleasant ones, to other people: *Our teacher's a hard taskmaster.*

tas·sel /'tæsəl/ n a bunch of threads tied into a round ball at one end and hung on clothes, curtains, etc. for decoration –**tasseled** *AmE*‖ **tasselled** *BrE* adj

taste[1] /teyst/ v **tasted, tasting 1** [T] to test the TASTE[2] (1) of (food or drink) by taking a little into the mouth: *I always taste the wine before allowing the waiter to fill my glass.* **2** [T] to experience the TASTE[2] (1) of: *I've got a cold, so I can't taste what I'm eating.* **3** [I] to have a particular TASTE² (1): *These oranges taste good.│This soup tastes salty.*

taste² *n* **1** [C;U] the sensation of saltiness, sweetness, bitterness, etc., that is produced when food or drink is put in the mouth: *Sugar has a sweet taste.│This cake has no/very little taste.│I've got a cold, so I've lost my sense of taste.* **2** [C] a small quantity of food or drink: *I had a taste of soup to see if it was good.│*(fig.) *a taste* (=short experience) *of freedom* **3** [C;U] the ability to enjoy and judge beauty, art, music, etc.: *a taste for music│She has good taste in clothes.*

taste·ful /'teʸstfəl/ *adj* having or showing good TASTE² (3) **–tastefully** *adv* **–tastefulness** *n* [U]

taste·less /'teʸstlɪs/ *adj* **1** having no TASTE² (1): *tasteless medicine* **2** having or showing poor TASTE² (3): *tasteless furniture* **–tastelessly** *adv* **–tastelessness** *n* [U]

tast·er /'teʸstər/ *n* a person whose job is testing the quality of food and drink by tasting them

tast·y /'teʸstiʸ/ *adj* **-ier, -iest** having a pleasant taste: *a tasty meal* **–tastily** *adv*

tat·tered /'tætərd/ *adj* old and torn

tat·ters /'tætərz/ *n* [P] old, torn clothing or bits of cloth: *His shirt was in tatters.*

tat·too¹ /tæ'tuʷ/ *n,v* **-toos** [C;T] (to make) a picture, message, etc., on the skin by pricking it with a pin and then pouring colored DYES in: *A heart was tattooed on his chest.│He wants his hand tattooed.│The tattoo read "I love Sally."*

tattoo² *n* **-toos** **1** a rapid beating of drums played as a signal **2** an outdoor military show with music, usu. at night: *the Edinburgh tattoo*

taught /tɔt/ *v past tense & participle of* TEACH

taunt /tɔnt, tɑnt/ *v* [T] to try to make (someone) angry or unhappy by making unkind remarks: *They taunted him for being afraid of water.* **–tauntingly** *adv* **–taunt** *n* [often pl.]: *cruel taunts about his dead father*

Tau·rus /'tɔrəs/ *n* see ZODIAC

taut /tɔt/ *adj* **1** tightly drawn; stretched tight: *Pull the string taut!│taut muscles* **–opposite** **slack 2** showing signs of anxiety: *a taut expression on her face* **–tautly** *adv* **–tautness** *n* [U]

tau·tol·o·gy /tɔ'tɑlədʒiʸ/ *n* **-gies** [C;U] (an) unnecessary repeating of the same idea in different words (as in *He sat alone by himself.*) **–tautological** /ˌtɔtḷ'ɑdʒɪkəl/ *adj*

tav·ern /'tævərn/ *n old use* a bar (10a)

taw·dry /'tɔdriʸ/ *adj* **-drier, -driest** cheaply showy; lacking good TASTE² (3): *tawdry jewelry* **–tawdriness** *n* [U]

taw·ny /'tɔniʸ/ *adj* **-nier, -niest** brownish yellow

tax¹ /tæks/ *v* **1** [T] to charge a tax on: *Cigarettes are heavily taxed in New York.│Why don't we tax the rich more heavily?* **2** [I;T] to make heavy demands (on); tire: *a long taxing journey│to tax one's patience* **–taxable** *adj*

tax² *n* [C;U] (a sum of) money paid to the government according to income, property, goods bought, etc.: *The government in-*

creased income tax to pay for defense.│Half of my wages go to taxes.*

tax·a·tion /tæk'seʸʃən/ *n* [U] the act of taxing; money raised from taxes: *We must increase taxation if we are to spend more on education.*

tax-free /ˌ· '·◄/ *adj,adv* free from taxation: *tax-free income│You can live on this little island tax-free.*

tax·i¹ /'tæksiʸ/ also **taxicab** /'tæksiʸˌkæb/ *fml│*also **cab** *esp. AmE– n* **-is** *or* **-ies** a car and driver which may be hired by the public: *I came by taxi.*

taxi² *v* **-ied, -iing** *or* **-ying** [I] (of a plane) to move along the ground before taking off

tax·i·der·my /'tæksəˌdɜrmiʸ/ *n* [U] the art of preserving and filling the skins of dead animals, so that they look like the living creature **–taxidermist** *n*

taxi stand /'·· ˌ·/ also **cabstand** *AmE*, **taxi rank** *BrE– n* a place where taxis wait to be hired

TB *abbrev. for:* TUBERCULOSIS

tea /tiʸ/ *n* **1** [U] the dried leaves of a bush grown in Asia: *a packet of tea* **2** [C;U] a hot brown drink made by pouring boiling water onto these leaves: *a cup of tea with milk and sugar│Give me two teas* (=cups of tea) *and a coffee, please.* **3** [C;U] a small meal, usu. served in the afternoon with a cup of TEA (2): *We had a tea for the author of that new book.* **4** [U] a medicinal drink made like tea: HERB *tea* **5 one's cup of tea** *infml* the sort of thing one likes: *Tennis isn't my cup of tea; let's watch television instead.*

tea·bag /'tiʸbæg/ *n* a small bag with tea leaves inside, put into boiling water to make tea

teach /tiʸtʃ/ *v* **taught** /tɔt/, **teaching** [I;T +that/v-ing/to] to give (someone) training or lessons in (a particular subject, skill, etc.): *She teaches my son history.│Mary teaches politics to college students.│I teach young children.│My religion teaches that war is wrong.│He taught the boys (to play) baseball.│I taught them what to do.│Teach me how to swim.│She taught me to sing/taught singing.│My husband teaches at a local school.* **–compare** LEARN

teach·er /'tiʸtʃər/ *n* a person who teaches, esp. as a profession: *a history/music teacher*

teach-in /'· ˌ·/ *n infml* an exchange of opinions about a subject of interest, as held in a college by students, teachers, guest speakers, etc.

teach·ing /'tiʸtʃɪŋ/ *n* **1** [U] the work of a teacher **2** [C;U] something that is taught: *to follow Christ's teaching/ teachings│the teachings of Freud*

tea·cup /'tiʸkʌp/ *n* a cup in which tea is served

teak /tiʸk/ *n* [C;U] a large tree or its very hard wood used for making furniture, ships, etc.

tea·leaf /'tiʸliʸf/ *n* **-leaves** /liʸvz/ one of the small pieces of leaf used for making tea

team¹ /tiʸm/ *n* **1** a group of people who work, play, or act together: *The school baseball team was winning.│Both teams of politicians are very skilled.│Football is a team sport.* **2** two or more animals pulling the same vehicle: *a team of oxen/horses*

team² *v* → TEAM UP

team spir·it /ˌ·ˈ···/ *n* [U] the feeling of loyalty among members of a team working happily together

team·ster /ˈtiʸmstər/ *n* **1** *AmE* a person who drives a truck, esp. as a job **2** a person who drives a team of animals

team up *v adv* [I *with*] to work together; combine: *I teamed up with Jane to do the job.*

team·work /ˈtiʸmwɜrk/ *n* [U] the ability of a group to work well together

tea·pot /ˈtiʸpɑt/ *n* a vessel with a handle and a SPOUT (=bent pouring pipe), from which tea is served –see illustration on page 379

tear¹ /tɪər/ *n* a drop of salty liquid that flows from the eye during pain or sadness: *to burst into tears*|*He was in tears.* (=crying)

tear² /tɛər/ *v* **tore** /tɔr, toʷr/ **torn** /tɔrn, toʷrn/, **tearing** **1** [T] to pull apart or into pieces by force, esp. so as to leave irregular edges: *Why did you tear the cloth instead of cutting it with scissors?*|*an old torn dress*|*He tore a hole in his pants climbing over the wall.* **2** [T *away, off, out, up*] to remove by force: *Our roof was torn off in the storm.*|(fig.) *The T.V. show was so interesting that I couldn't tear myself away.* **3** [I] to become torn (TEAR² (1)): *This material tears easily, so be careful when you wear it.* **4** [I] to move excitedly with great speed: *The excited children tore noisily down the street.*

tear sthg.↔ **down** *v adv* [T] to pull down (esp. a building); destroy

tear into sbdy. *v prep* [T *no passive*] to attack violently, esp. with words

tear sthg.↔ **up** *v adv* [T] to destroy completely by tearing: *He tore up her letter angrily.*

tear³ /tɛər/ *n* a torn (TEAR² (1)) place in cloth, paper, etc.

tear·drop /ˈtɪərdrɑp/ *n* a single TEAR¹

tear·ful /ˈtɪərfəl/ *adj* crying; weeping, or likely to weep –**tearfully** *adv* –**tearfulness** *n* [U]

tea·room /ˈtiʸruʷm, -rʊm/ *n* a restaurant where tea and light meals are served

tease /tiʸz/ *v* **teased, teasing** [I;T] **1** to make unkind jokes about or laugh unkindly at (a person): *At school, they teased me because I was fat.* **2** to annoy (an animal) on purpose: *Stop teasing the cat!*

teas·er /ˈtiʸzər/ *n infml* **1** a difficult question **2** also **tease–** a person who likes to TEASE

tea·spoon /ˈtiʸspuʷn/ *n* **1** a small spoon used for mixing sugar into tea, coffee, etc. **2** also **teaspoonful** /ˈtiʸspuʷn,fʊl/– the amount held by this

teat /tiʸt, tɪt/ *n* a NIPPLE (1), usu. of an animal

tech·ni·cal /ˈtɛknɪkəl/ *adj* **1** having special knowledge, esp. of an industrial or scientific subject: *technical experts*|*This law book is too technical; I can't understand it.* **2** of or related to a particular subject, esp. a practical or scientific one: *a technical college*|*technical training* –**technically** *adv*

tech·ni·cal·i·ty /ˌtɛknəˈkælətiʸ/ *n* -**ties** a small detail or rule: *a technicality in the law*

tech·ni·cian /tɛkˈnɪʃən/ *n* a skilled worker in esp. a scientific or industrial subject

tech·nique /tɛkˈniʸk/ *n* [C;U] (a) way of doing some specialist activity or artistic work: *perfect piano technique*|*different techniques of photography*

tech·nol·o·gy /tɛkˈnɑlədʒiʸ/ *n* -**gies** [C;U] the branch of knowledge dealing with scientific and industrial methods and their practical use in industry –**technologist** *n* –**technological** /ˌtɛknəˈlɑdʒɪkəl/ *adj*: *The development of the steam engine was a great technological advance.* –**technologically** *adv*

ted·dy bear /ˈtɛdiʸ ˌbɛər/ also **teddy–** *n* a toy bear filled with soft material

te·di·ous /ˈtiʸdiʸəs/ *adj* long and tiring; dull: *a tedious book/speaker* –**tediously** *adv* –**tediousness** *n* [U]

te·di·um /ˈtiʸdiʸəm/ *n* [U] TEDIOUSNESS

tee /tiʸ/ *n* (in GOLF) (the area surrounding) the small heap of sand or small nail-shaped object, from which the player first hits the ball

teem¹ /tiʸm/ *v* [I *with*] *esp. lit* to be or have present in large numbers: *a river teeming with fish*

teem² *v* [I] *infml* to rain very heavily: *The rain teemed down for hours.*|*It's really teeming outside.*

teen·age /ˈtiʸneʸdʒ/ also **teenaged** /ˈtiʸneʸdʒd/– *adj* [A] of, for, or being a TEENAGER: *teenage fashions*|*a teenage boy*

teen·ag·er /ˈtiʸneʸdʒər/ *n* a young person of between 13 and 19 years old –see CHILD (USAGE)

teens /tiʸnz/ *n* [P] the period of one's life from the age of 13 to 19: *She's in her teens.*

tee shirt /ˈtiʸ ʃɜrt/ *n* → T-SHIRT

tee·ter /ˈtiʸtər/ *v* [I *on*] to stand or move in an unsteady way: *to teeter along in high shoes*

teeth /tiʸθ/ *n* [P] **1** *plural of* TOOTH **2** armed to the teeth very heavily armed

teethe /tiʸð/ *v* **teethed, teething** [I] (of babies) to grow teeth

tee·to·tal·er *AmE*‖-**taller** *BrE* /ˌtiʸˈtoʷtl-ər/ *n* a person who never drinks alcohol

tel·e·com·mu·ni·ca·tions /ˌtɛləkəˌmyuʷnəˈkeʸʃənz/ *n* [P] the receiving or sending of messages by telephone, television, telegraph, or radio: *a telecommunications SATELLITE*

tel·e·gram /ˈtɛləˌgræm/ *n* [C;U] a message sent by telegraph

tel·e·graph¹ /ˈtɛləˌgræf/ *n* [U] a method of sending messages along wire by electric signals: *The news was sent by telegraph.*

telegraph² *v* [I;T +(*that*)/*to*] to send by TELEGRAPH¹: *We telegraphed her the news.*|*They telegraphed us to come.* –**telegraphic** /ˌtɛləˈgræfɪk/ *adj* –**telegraphically** *adv*

te·lep·a·thy /təˈlɛpəθiʸ/ *n* [U] the sending of thoughts from one person's mind to another's without the ordinary use of the senses –**telepathic** /ˌtɛləˈpæθɪk/ *adj* –**telepathically** *adv*

tel·e·phone¹ /ˈtɛləˌfoʷn/ also **phone** *infml*– *n* an apparatus which sends sounds, esp. speech, over long distances by electrical means: *He told me the news by telephone.*|*She's on the telephone* (=talking to someone by means of the telephone) *at the moment.* –see illustration on page 467

USAGE **Telephone** can be used as a noun or a verb, and so can the short form **phone.** If you want to **telephone** your mother (or **call** her, **ring** her, **give** her a **ring**), you **dial** her **(phone) number,** which can be found in the **directory/telephone book.** If it is a long-distance call, you may have to ask the **operator** to connect you. The phone will **ring,** and if your mother is at home she will **answer** it by picking up the **receiver.** If she is too busy to speak to you, she may ask you to **call back** later; if she doesn't want to speak to you, she may **hang up** (=replace the **receiver**); or if she is already **on the phone** when you call her, her number is **busy** *AmE*/**engaged** *BrE.* A telephone in a public place is a **telephone booth** *AmE*/**call box** *BrE.*

telephone² also **phone** *infml– v* **-phoned, -phoning** [I;T] **1** [*to*]to speak (a message) to (someone) by telephone: *I telephoned your aunt with the news.*|*Did you telephone Bob?*|*I telephoned my mother to come.*|*You can telephone your order (through) to the store.* **2** to (try to) reach (a place or person) by telephone: *I've been telephoning him all morning, but he's not there.*|*You can't telephone the city direct from here.*

telephone booth /'··· ,·/ also **phone booth**‖also **call box** *BrE–* a small enclosure containing a telephone for use by the public –see illustration on page 673

telephone ex·change /'··· ·,·/ *n* a place where telephone connections are made

tel·e·pho·to lens /,tɛlə,fowtow 'lɛnz/ *n* a LENS that allows a camera to take clear enlarged pictures of distant objects

tel·e·scope¹ /'tɛlə,skowp/ *n* a tubelike scientific instrument which makes distant objects appear nearer and larger –compare MICROSCOPE

telescope² *v* **-scoped, -scoping** [I;T] to make or become shorter by one part sliding over another: *This instrument will telescope small enough to fit into this box.*

tel·e·scop·ic /,tɛlə'skɑpɪk/ *adj* **1** of, like, or seen through a TELESCOPE¹: *a telescopic LENS/picture of the moon* **2** made of parts that slide over one another to make the whole shorter

tel·e·vise /'tɛlə,vaɪz/ *v* **-vised, -vising** [T] to broadcast by television: *The tennis match will be televised.*

tel·e·vi·sion /'tɛlə,vɪʒən/ also **TV** *AmE*‖also **telly** *BrE infml– n* **1** [C] also **television set–** /'···· ,·/ a boxlike apparatus for receiving pictures and sound –see illustration on page 399 **2** [U] the method of broadcasting pictures and sound by means of electrical waves; the news, plays, advertisements, etc., shown in this way: *watching television*|*What's on television tonight?*|*Emily works in television.* (=the industry of television broadcasting)

tel·ex¹ /'tɛlɛks/ *n* **1** [U] an international service providing a telegraphic method of sending printed messages **2** [C] a message sent in this way: *A telex arrived from Hong Kong.*

telex² *v* [I;T +(*that*)/*to*] to send (a message) to (a person, place, etc.) by TELEX¹ (1): *Telex*

Paris that prices have increased.|*Telex him to come.*

tell /tɛl/ *v* **told** /towld/, **telling 1** [T +(*that*)/*to*] to make (something) known in words to (someone); express in words; speak: *Did you tell Aunt Joan the news about Paul?*|*John told us he'd seen you in town.*|*Can you tell me what time the party starts?*|*I always tell my daughter a story before she goes to sleep.*|*Are you telling me the truth?* –see Study Notes on page 481 **2** [T +(*that*)] to warn; advise: *I told you David wouldn't want a drink.*|*I told you not to buy that car, and now look what's happened!*|*I told you so!* **3** [T] to order; direct: *Do you think children should do as they're told?*|*I told you to get here early, so why are you late?* **4** [T] to show; make known: *This light tells you if the machine is on or off.* **5** [I;T +(*that*)/*whether, if, from*] to recognize; know: *It was so dark I couldn't tell it was you.*|*I can't tell if it's him or not.*|*"Which team will win?" "Who can tell?"* **6** [I] to be noticeable; have an effect: *In the last stage of the race, her tiredness began to tell (on her).* **7** [I] to speak someone's secret to someone else: *If I whisper my secret to you, will you promise not to tell?* **8 all told** altogether; when all have been counted **9 tell the time** to read the time from a clock or watch **10 there is/was/will be no telling** it is/was/will be impossible to know **11 you can never tell** also **you never can tell–** one can never be sure about something because one can easily be deceived without knowing it –see ORDER (USAGE)

tell sbdy.↔ **off** *v adv* [T] *infml* to scold

tell on sbdy./sthg. *v prep* [T] **1** also **tell upon** sbdy./sthg. *fml–* to have a bad effect on: *All those late nights are telling on your work.* **2** *infml* (used esp. by children) to inform against: *I missed the lesson and John told on me.*

tell·er /'tɛlər/ *n* **1** a person employed to receive and pay out money in a bank **2** a person who counts votes at an election

tell·ing /'tɛlɪŋ/ *adj* **1** very effective: *a telling argument* **2** that shows one's feelings or opinions: *a telling remark*

tell·tale /'tɛlteʸl/ *n infml* a person who informs about other people's secrets, wrong actions, etc.

telltale² *adj* [A] that makes a fact known: *the telltale look of jealousy in his eyes*

tel·ly /'tɛliʸ/ *n* **-lies** [C;U] *BrE infml* for TELEVISION

te·mer·i·ty /tə'mɛrətiʸ/ *n* [U] *fml* foolish boldness; RASHNESS: *He had the temerity to ask for higher wages after only a day's work.*

tem·per¹ /'tɛmpər/ *n* **1** [C] a particular state or condition of the mind: *Carol's in a bad temper.* (=angry)|*She has a sweet temper.* (=is calm by nature) **2** [C;U] an angry state of mind: *John's in a temper today.* **3** [U] *tech* the degree to which a substance, esp. a metal, has been hardened or strengthened **4 fly/get into a temper** to become angry suddenly **5 keep one's temper** to stay calm **6 lose one's temper** to become angry **7 -tempered** having a certain kind of temper or nature:

bad-tempered|even-tempered (=calm)

temper² v [T] **1** tech to harden and strengthen (esp. metal): *Steel is tempered by heating and then cooling it.* **2** fml to soften; make less severe: *justice tempered with mercy*

tem·per·a·ment /'tɛmpərəmənt/ n [C;U] a person's nature; one's usual way of thinking or acting: *an excitable temperament*

tem·per·a·men·tal /ˌtɛmpərə'mɛntəl/ adj **1** having frequent changes of temper: *The actor was so temperamental that people refused to work with him.* **2** caused by one's nature: *a temperamental dislike of sports* **–temperamentally** adv

tem·per·ance /'tɛmpərəns/ n [U] **1** self-control; being TEMPERATE (1) **2** total avoidance of alcoholic drinks

tem·per·ate /'tɛmpərɪt/ adj **1** practicing or showing self-control: *temperate behavior* **2** (of parts of the world) free from very high or very low temperatures: *a temperate* CLIMATE

tem·per·a·ture /'tɛmpərətʃər/ n [C;U in, of] **1** the degree of heat or coldness: *the average temperature in Detroit|a change of temperature* **2** have/run a temperature to have a higher bodily temperature than usual **3** take someone's temperature to measure the temperature of someone's body with a THERMOMETER

tem·pest /'tɛmpɪst/ n lit a violent storm **–tempestuous** /tɛm'pɛstʃuʷəs/ adj: *the tempestuous sea/wind*|(fig.) *a tempestuous meeting* **–tempestuously** adv **–tempestuousness** n [U]

tem·ple¹ /'tɛmpəl/ n a building for public worship in certain religions: *a Buddhist temple*

temple² n one of the flat places on each side of the forehead

tem·po /'tɛmpoʷ/ n **-pos** or **-pi** /piʸ/ the speed at which music is played: (fig.) *the fast tempo of city life*

tem·po·ral /'tɛmpərəl/ adj fml **1** of or related to material affairs, as opposed to SPIRITUAL religious affairs: *the temporal power of the state* **2** tech of or limited by time: *"When" is a temporal* CONJUNCTION (1).

tem·po·rar·y /'tɛmpəˌrɛriʸ/ adj lasting only for a limited time: *a temporary job* **–compare** PERMANENT **–temporarily** /ˌtɛmpə'rɛɔrəliʸ/ adv: *I was temporarily delayed.* **–temporariness** /'tɛmpəˌrɛriʸnɪs/ n [U]

tempt /tɛmpt/ v [T] **1** to (try to) persuade (someone) to do something bad: *He tried to tempt me to cheat on the examination.|to tempt him with money* **2** to attract: *a tempting meal|The warm sun tempted us to go out.* **–tempter** (**temptress** /'tɛmptrɪs/ fem.) n **–temptingly** adv

temp·ta·tion /tɛmp'teʸʃən/ n [+to-v] **1** [U] the act of TEMPTing or the state of being tempted: *the temptation to smoke a cigarette* **2** [C] something that attracts or tempts: *the temptations of a big city*

ten /tɛn/ determiner,n,pron (the number) 10 **–tenth** determiner,n,pron,adv

ten·a·ble /'tɛnəbəl/ adj fml **1** that can be defended: *not a tenable argument* **–opposite untenable** (of an office, position, etc.) that can be held by somebody: *How long is the post tenable (for)?*

te·na·cious /tə'neʸʃəs/ adj firm and unyielding: *a tenacious defense of the city* **–tenaciously** adv **–tenaciousness** n [U] **–tenacity** /tə'næsəṭiʸ/ n [U]

ten·an·cy /'tɛnənsiʸ/ n **-cies** [C;U] (the length of time during which a person can have) the use of a room, land, building, etc., for which rent has been paid: *a tenancy agreement which will last for six months*

ten·ant /'tɛnənt/ n a person who pays rent for the use of a room, building, land, etc.: *Do you own your house or are you a tenant?*

tend¹ /tɛnd/ v [I] **1** [+to-v] to be likely (to do something); have a tendency: *Janet tends to get angry if you ask her stupid questions.|It tends to be cold at this time of year.* **2** to move or develop in a certain direction: *Prices are tending upwards.*

tend² v [T] more fml than **look after** to take care of; look after: *She tended her husband lovingly during his illness.|a farmer tending his sheep*

tend·en·cy /'tɛndənsiʸ/ n **-cies** [C +to-v/towards] a natural likelihood: *She's always had a tendency to be thin.*

ten·der¹ /'tɛndər/ adj **1** soft; easy to bite through: *tender meat* **–opposite tough 2** sore; easily hurt: *His wound is still tender.* **3** gentle and loving: *a tender heart* **4** [A] lit young; inexperienced: *a child of tender years* **–tenderly** adv **–tenderness** n [U]

tend·er² n **1** a person who takes care of something **2** a vehicle carrying coal, pulled behind a railroad engine

ten·der³ n **1** a statement of the price one would charge for doing a job **2** also **legal tender–** money which by law must be accepted when offered in payment

tender⁴ v [T] fml to offer; present: *"Passengers must tender the exact amount of money."* (notice on a bus)|*The Senator tendered his* RESIGNATION (3).

tender for sthg. v prep [T] to make a formal offer to do (a piece of work) at a certain price

ten·der·heart·ed /ˌtɛndər'hɑrtɪd◄/ adj easily moved to love, pity, or sorrow **–tenderheartedly** adv

ten·don /'tɛndən/ n a thick strong cord that connects a muscle to a bone; SINEW

ten·dril /'tɛndrəl/ n a thin curling stem of a climbing plant

ten·e·ment /'tɛnəmənt/ also **tenement house** /'··· ˌ·/– n a large building divided into apartments, esp. in the poorer areas of a city

ten·et /'tɛnɪt/ n fml a principle or belief: *the tenets of our Church*

Tenn. written abbrev. said as: Tennessee /ˌtɛnə'siʸ/ (a state in the US)

ten·nis /'tɛnɪs/ n [U] a game played between two people (**singles**) or two pairs of people (**doubles**) who use RACKETS to hit a small ball from one side of a low net to the other, on a specially marked area (a **tennis court**): *Would you like to play a game of tennis?|a tennis ball*

ten·or /'tɛnər/ n **1** [C;U] (a man with) the highest natural male singing voice **–compare** BASS **2** [C] an instrument with the same range of notes as this **3** [C *usu. sing.*] *fml* the general meaning: *I understood the tenor of his speech but not the details.*

tense¹ /tɛns/ *n* [C;U] any of the forms of a verb that show the time of the action or state expressed: *"I am" is present tense, "I was" is past tense, and "I will be" is future tense.*

tense² *adj* **1** stretched tight; stiff: *tense muscles/nerves* **2** nervous; anxious: *a tense moment before we heard the news* –**tensely** *adv* –**tenseness** *n* [U]

tense³ *v* **tensed, tensing** [I;T *up*] to make or become TENSE² (1) –compare RELAX (2)

ten·sion /'tɛnʃən, -tʃən/ *n* **1** [U] the degree of tightness of a wire, rope, etc.: *If the tension of this string is increased, it will break.* **2** [C;U] (a feeling of) nervous anxiety, worry, or pressure: *I am suffering from nervous tension.|the tensions of life in a big city* **3** [U] electric power: *Danger! High tension wires.*

tent /tɛnt/ *n* a movable shelter made of cloth supported by poles and ropes: *Before it got dark the campers* PITCHed (=put up) *their tent in a field.*

ten·ta·cle /'tɛntəkəl/ *n* a long snakelike boneless limb on certain creatures, used for moving, seizing, touching, etc.: *the tentacles of an octopus*

ten·ta·tive /'tɛntətɪv/ *adj* made or done only as a suggestion; not certain: *We've made tentative plans for a vacation but haven't really decided yet.* –**tentatively** *adv* –**tentativeness** *n* [U]

ten·ter·hooks /'tɛntər,hʊks/ *n* **on tenterhooks** in a state of anxious expectation

ten·u·ous /'tɛnyuʷəs/ *adj* very thin; not strong: *a tenuous connection between the movie and the book on which it is based* –**tenuously** *adv* –**tenuousness** *n* [U]

ten·ure /'tɛnyər/ *n* [U] *fml* **1** the right of holding land or a job: *the tenure of an office|conditions of tenure* **2** the length of time one holds office **3** *AmE* the right to stay in an office without needing to have a new contract of employment, usu. given after a particular number of years: *She finally received tenure at the university.*

te·pee /'tiʸpiʸ/ *n* a round tent of the type used by North American Indians

tep·id /'tɛpɪd/ *adj* (esp. of liquid) only slightly warm: (fig.) *a rather tepid welcome* –**tepidity** /tɛ'pɪdətiʸ, tə-/ *n* –**tepidly** /'tɛpɪdliʸ/ *adv*

te·qui·la /tə'kiʸlə/ *n* [U] a strong alcoholic drink made in Mexico

term¹ /tɜrm/ *n* **1** [C;U *in, of, during*] one of the three periods of time into which the school or university year is divided: *the summer term|During the term, we have examinations.* –compare SEMESTER **2** [C] a fixed period of time: *The President is elected for a four-year term.|a term of office* **3** [C] a word or expression, esp. one used in a particular activity, profession, etc.: *a medical term* **4 in the long/short term** over a long/short period of time: *In the short term we will lose money, but in the long term we will make a profit.* –see also TERMS

term² *v* [T] to name; call: *The chairman of this meeting is termed the "Speaker."*

ter·mi·nal¹ /'tɜrmənəl/ *adj* **1** of, having, or being an illness that will cause death: *terminal patients* (=people who are dying) **2** of or at the end of something –**terminally** *adv*

terminal² *n* **1** a bus or railroad station usu. in the center of town, esp. for passengers going to or arriving from an airport **2** a point at which connections can be made to an electric system (CIRCUIT) or messages passed to or from a computer

ter·mi·nate /'tɜrmə,neʸt/ *v* **-nated, -nating** [I;T] *more fml than* **end**– to bring or come to an end: *to terminate a contract* –**termination** /,tɜrmə'neʸʃən/ *n* [C;U]

ter·mi·nol·o·gy /,tɜrmə'nɑlədʒiʸ/ *n* **-gies** [C;U] (a system of) specialized words and expressions used in a particular science, profession, or activity: *I don't understand scientific terminology.* –**terminological** /,tɜrmənl'ɑdʒɪkəl/ *adj* –**terminologically** *adv*

ter·mi·nus /'tɜrmənəs/ *n* **-ni** /,naɪ/ *or* **-nuses** the end of a railroad or bus line

ter·mite /'tɜrmaɪt/ *n* an antlike tropical insect that destroys wood, and builds hills of earth

term pa·per /,· '··/ *also* **paper**– *n* a usu. long piece of writing on a particular subject for school

terms /tɜrmz/ *n* [P] **1** the conditions of an agreement, contract, etc.: *The terms of the agreement are quite clear.* **2** conditions of payment, prices, etc.: *We sell furniture at very reasonable terms.* **3 come to terms with** to accept (something unpleasant): *He seems to have come to terms with losing his sight.* **4 in no uncertain terms** clearly and usu. angrily: *He told me in no uncertain terms to go away.* **5 in terms of/in... terms** with regard to: *In terms of property, we're quite rich.* **6 on good/bad/friendly/equal terms** having a good, bad, etc., relationship: *Now that I'm no longer working for him, we can meet on equal terms.* **7 on speaking terms** friendly enough to speak: *After their argument, they weren't on speaking terms.* **8 think in terms of** to consider: *We're thinking in terms of moving.*

ter·race /'tɛrəs/ *n* **1** a flat area next to a house, used as an outdoor living area **2** a flat area cut from a slope: *The trees grew in terraces on the side of the mountain.* –**terrace** *v* **-raced, -racing** [T]: *The garden was terraced.*

ter·ra cot·ta /,tɛrə 'kɑtə/ *n* [U] (articles made from) hard reddish-brown baked clay

ter·ra fir·ma /,tɛrə 'fɜrmə/ *n* [U] *Latin, pomp* dry land: *After the rough sea voyage, we were glad to reach terra firma.*

ter·rain /tə'reʸn/ *n* [C;U] a stretch of land considered esp. with regard to its physical character: *rocky terrain*

ter·ra·pin /'tɛrəpɪn/ *n* **terrapin** *or* **terrapins** a small TURTLE that lives in fresh water

ter·res·tri·al /tə'rɛstriʸəl/ *adj* **1** of or related to the earth, rather than the moon, space, etc. **2** of or living on land, rather than in water: *a terrestrial animal* –**terrestrially** *adv*

ter·ri·ble /'tɛrəbəl/ *adj* **1** very severe indeed: *a terrible war/accident* **2** *infml* very bad: *a terrible play*

ter·ri·bly /'tɛrəbliʸ/ *adv* **1** very badly, severely, etc.: *He played that game terribly.* **2** *infml* very: *I've been terribly worried about you.* –see Study Notes on page 363

ter·ri·er /ˈtɛriⁱər/ *n* a small dog originally used for hunting

ter·rif·ic /təˈrɪfɪk/ *adj infml* **1** very good; enjoyable; excellent: *a terrific party* **2** very great: *She drove at a terrific speed.* **–terrifically** /təˈrɪfɪkliⁱ/ *adv*

ter·ri·fy /ˈtɛrə,faɪ/ *v* **-fied, -fying** [T] to fill with terror or fear: *Heights terrify me!|I am terrified of heights.*

ter·ri·to·ry /ˈtɛrə,tɔriⁱ, -,toʷriⁱ/ *n* **-ries** [C;U] **1** (an area of) land, esp. ruled by one government: *Canadian territory|We traveled through unknown territory.* **2** (an) area regarded by a person, animal, group, etc., as belonging to it alone: *animals fighting for their territory* **–territorial** /,tɛrəˈtɔriⁱəl, -ˈtoʷr-/ *adj: a country's territorial possessions*

ter·ror /ˈtɛrər/ *n* **1** [C;U] (a cause of) great fear: *They ran from the enemy in terror.|the terrors of war* **2** [C] *infml* an annoying person: *That child's a real terror!*

ter·ror·ism /ˈtɛrə,rɪzəm/ *n* [U] the illegal use of (threats of) violence to obtain political demands **–terrorist** *adj,n: Terrorists were responsible for the bomb explosion.*

ter·ror·ize ‖also **-ise** *BrE* /ˈtɛrə,raɪz/ *v* **-ized, -izing** [T] to fill (someone) with terror

terror-strick·en /ˈ·· ,··/ also **terror-struck** /ˈ·· ,·/– *adj* filled with great terror

ter·ry·cloth /ˈtɛriⁱ,klɔθ/ also **terry** /ˈtɛriⁱ/– *n* [U] a thick usu. cotton material with uncut threads on both sides used for making TOWELS, bathmats, etc.

terse /tɜrs/ *adj* (of a speaker or speech) short; using few words **–tersely** *adv* **–terseness** *n* [U]

ter·ti·ar·y /ˈtɜrʃiⁱ,ɛriⁱ, -ʃəriⁱ/ *adj fml* third in place, degree, or rank

test¹ /tɛst/ *n* **1** a number of questions, jobs, etc., set to measure someone's ability or knowledge; short examination: *a history test| I've passed my driving test.* **2** a practical examination or trial: *Before buying the car, I went for a test drive.|atom bomb tests* **3** something used as a standard when judging: *Colleges will use this as a test for progress.* **4** **put something to the test** to find out the qualities of something by using it in certain conditions **–tester** *n*

test² *v* **1** [T] to examine by means of a test: *I have to have my eyes tested.* **2** [T] to be a difficult test for: *These wet roads really test a car's tires.* **3** [I;T] to search by means of tests: *testing (the ground) for oil*

tes·ta·ment /ˈtɛstəmənt/ *n fml* for WILL² (4) (esp. in the phrase **last will and testament**) –see also OLD TESTAMENT, NEW TESTAMENT

test ban /ˈ· ·/ *n* an agreement between nations to stop testing bombs: *a test ban TREATY*

test case /ˈ· ·/ *n* a case in a court of law which establishes a particular principle, which is then used as a standard for other cases

tes·ti·cle /ˈtɛstɪkəl/ *n* one of the two round SPERM-producing organs in the male, below the PENIS

tes·ti·fy /ˈtɛstə,faɪ/ *v* **-fied, -fying** [I;T +(*that*)/*against, for, to*] to make a solemn statement; bear witness: *The teacher testified to the pupil's ability.|One witness testified that he'd seen the robbery.*

tes·ti·mo·ni·al /,tɛstəˈmoʷniⁱəl/ *n* **1** a formal written statement of a person's character, ability, etc. –compare REFERENCE (3) **2** something given or done to show thanks

tes·ti·mo·ny /ˈtɛstə,moʷniⁱ/ *n* **-nies** [C;U] a formal statement, as made by a witness in a court of law

test pi·lot /ˈ· ,··/ *n* a pilot who flies new aircraft in order to test them

test tube /ˈ· ·/ *n* a small tube of thin glass, closed at one end, used in scientific tests

tes·ty /ˈtɛstiⁱ/ *adj* **-tier, -tiest** impatient; easily annoyed **–testily** *adv* **–testiness** *n* [U]

tet·a·nus /ˈtɛtn-əs/ also **lockjaw** *infml*– *n* [U] a serious disease caused by infection in a cut or wound which stiffens the muscles, esp. of the jaw

tête-à-tête /,teʸt ə ˈteʸt, ,tɛt ə ˈtɛt/ *adv* (of two people) together in private: *They had dinner tête-à-tête.* **–tête-à-tête** *n: The two women had a tête-à-tête* (=private conversation) *in the corner.*

teth·er /ˈtɛðər/ *n* **1** a rope or chain to which an animal is tied **2** **at the end of one's tether** unable to suffer any more **–tether** *v* [T]: *a dog tethered to a post*

Tex. *written abbrev. said as:* Texas /ˈtɛksəs/ (a state in the US)

text /tɛkst/ *n* **1** [C;U] the words in a book as opposed to notes, pictures, etc.: *Children's books often have more pictures than text.* **2** [C] the original words or printed form of a speech, article, book, etc.: *The original text of "Hamlet"* **3** [C] a sentence from the Bible to be talked about, esp. by a priest in a SERMON **–textual** /ˈtɛkstʃuʷəl/ *adj: textual differences between the two copies of this book*

text·book /ˈtɛkstbʊk/ *n* a standard book for the study of a subject, esp. used in schools

tex·tile /ˈtɛkstaɪl, ˈtɛkstəl/ *n* any material made by weaving: *a textile factory|silk and cotton textiles*

tex·ture /ˈtɛkstʃər/ *n* [C;U] **1** the degree of roughness or smoothness, coarseness or fineness, of a surface, as felt by touch: *the smooth texture of silk|the delicate texture of her skin* **2** **-textured** having a certain kind of TEXTURE: *coarse-textured cloth|fine-textured skin*

tha·lid·o·mide /θəˈlɪdə,maɪd/ *n* [U] a drug formerly used for making people calm or sleepy, until it was discovered that it caused unborn babies to develop wrongly, esp. without limbs

than /ðən, ðɛn; *strong* ðæn/ *conj,prep* (used in comparisons, to show a difference): *She's older than me/than I am.|They arrived earlier than usual.|more than a week.|less than $100* –see ME, HARDLY (USAGE), DIFFERENT (USAGE)

thank /θæŋk/ *v* [T *for*] **1** to express gratefulness to (someone); give thanks to: *The old lady thanked me for helping her.* –see also THANK YOU **2** **have (oneself) to thank** to be responsible for something bad: *You've only* *got yourself to thank for the accident.* (=it's your own fault) **3 thank God/good-ness/heaven** (an expression of pleasure at the end of anxiety: *Thank God my son's alive!*

thank·ful /ˈθæŋkfəl/ *adj* [+*to-v/that*] glad that something good has happened: *I was thank-ful to be/that I was free.|a thankful smile* –**thankfully** *adv* –**thankfulness** *n* [U]

thank·less /ˈθæŋklɪs/ *adj* **1** not feeling or showing thanks **2** not rewarded with thanks: *a thankless job* –**thanklessly** *adv* –**thankless-ness** *n* [U]

thanks /θæŋks/ *n* [P] **1** words expressing gratefulness: *Give thanks to God.|to return a borrowed book with thanks* **2 thanks to** because of: *Thanks to your stupidity, we lost the game.*

thanks·giv·ing /ˌθæŋksˈgɪvɪŋ/ *n* [C;U] (an) expression of gratefulness, esp. to God

Thanksgiving also **Thanksgiving Day** /·ˈ·· ˌ·/– *n* a holiday in the US and Canada, on which God is thanked for a year of success and good fortune, usu. marked with a feast

thank-you /ˈθæŋk yuʷ/ *n* an expression of thanks: *a special thank-you for all your help*

thank you /ˈ· ·/ also **thanks** *infml– interj* (used politely to mean) I am grateful to you: *Thank you for the present.|"Would you like a cup of coffee?" "No, thank you."*

USAGE If one is offered something that one does not want, one replies *"No, thank you."* A reply of **"Thank you"** means that one wants it: *"Have a drink!" "Thank you. I'll have a beer, please."*

that¹ /ðæt/ *determiner,pron* those /ðoʷz/ **1** the one or amount stated; the one that is further in place, time, or thought: *You look in this box here, and I'll look in that box over there.|That's my sister up there on the stage.|Who told you that?|that story?|Look at that!|We saw a movie, and after that* (=then) *we went home.|Do they always dance like that* (=in the way just shown) *in New York?* **2 that is (to say)** in other words **3 that's that** that settles the matter: *You can't go, and that's that.* –compare THIS¹

that² /ðæt/ *adv infml* so; as much as that: *I don't like him all that much.*

that³ /ðət; *strong* ðæt/ *conj* **1** (introduces various kinds of CLAUSEs. It is often left out.): *It's true (that) she's French.|I believe (that) you want to go home.|He was so rude (that) she refused to speak to him.|I saw him on the day (that)* (=when) *he ar-rived.|There's no proof (that) she was there.* **2** [U] **a** (*used as a subject*) who or which: *Did you see the letter that/which came today?* –see USAGE 1b (*Used as object. It is often left out*) whom or which: *Did you get the books (that/which) I sent you?|Here's the man (that/whom) I was telling you about.*

USAGE 1 **That³** (2) can be used instead of **who** or **which,** and is particularly useful when you are talking about both people and things: *the people and machines that produce the nation's wealth.* **2 That** cannot be used instead of **who** or **which** when they add more information to the sentence: *He broke his leg, which* (not **that) was very sad.|This is

my father, who (not **that) lives in Chicago.* But compare: *Which of my brothers did you meet–the one who/that lives in Atlanta or the one who/that lives in San Francisco?*

thatch /θætʃ/ *n* [U] roof covering made of STRAW, REEDS, etc. –**thatched** *adj: Our house has a thatched roof.|a thatched house*

thaw /θɔ/ *v* [I;T *out*] to (cause to) increase in temperature and so become liquid or soft: *The snow is thawing.|In the mountains, it doesn't thaw in summer.* (=the snow and ice do not melt) –compare FREEZE **2** [I] (of a person) to become friendlier, less formal, etc. –**thaw** *n: There was a thaw in the spring.* (=a warmer period when snow and ice melted)

the¹ /ðə *before a consonant,* ðiʸ *before a vowel; strong* ðiʸ/ *definite article,determiner* **1** (used before singular and plural nouns, when it is clearly understood who or what is meant): *We have a cat and two dogs. The cat* (=our cat) *is black, and the dogs* (=our dogs) *are white.|The sun* (=there is only one sun) *is shining.|The sky is blue.|Take these letters to the post office.* (=there is only one post office near here, and you know where it is)|*the Queen of Denmark* (=Denmark has only one queen)|*I spoke to her on the telephone.|We went to the South of France last year.* **2** (used as part of some names): *the Rhine|the Atlantic|the Alps* **3** (used before an adjective to make it into a noun): *the poor* (=poor people)|*the old* (=old people)|*The English* (=English people) *drink a lot of beer.|I can't do the impossible.* (=things that are impossible) **4** (used before a singular noun to make it general): *The lion is a wild animal.* (=lions are wild animals) **5** (used before names of musical instruments): *She plays the piano.* **6** (used before names of measures) each: *This cloth is sold by the yard.|paid by the hour|How many miles does your car do to the gallon?* **7** (used before the plural of 20, 30, 40, etc., to show a period of 10 years): *In the 30's* (=from 1930 to 1939) *there was a lot of unemployment.*

USAGE 1 With certain words, **the** is not used except when there is something else before or after the noun that tells us which one or what kind is meant. This is true of **a** nouns such as *music, history, time, beauty, work* (=ABSTRACT nouns). We say *Life is difficult* but *The life of a writer is difficult.* **b** nouns such as *wine, silk, coal, gold, sugar* (=[U] nouns). Compare: *She gave us wine and cheese; I drank* **the** *wine, but I didn't eat the cheese.* **c** names of times, after *at, by, on: at sunset|by night|on Monday* (but *on* **the** *Mon-day after Christmas,* because *after Christmas* tells us which Monday is meant). 2 *The* is not used **a** with most names of diseases: *He's got* SMALLPOX. **b** in many expressions about organizations and means of traveling: *by car|at school|in bed|in prison* **c** in expres-sions like: *She became President.|They crowned him king.|They appointed her cap-tain.* **d** when someone is directly addressed: *Come here, doctor!* **e** with **man** or **woman** in meaning 4: *Man is related to the monkey.*

the² *adv* **1** (used in comparisons, to show that two things happen together): *The more he eats, the fatter he gets.* **2** (used in comparisons, to show that something or someone is better, worse, etc., than before): *She's had a vacation, and looks (all) the better for it.* **3** (showing that something or someone is more than any other): *Of all her children, Mary is the tallest/the most intelligent.*

the·a·ter *AmE*‖also **theatre** *esp. BrE* /'θiʸəţər/ *n* **1** [C] a place for the performance of plays: *New York's theaters* **2** [U] the work of people who write or act in plays: *I'm interested in the theater.* **3** [C] a scene of important military events: *He fought in the Pacific theater of World War II.*

the·at·ri·cal /θiʸ'ætrɪkəl/ *adj* **1** of or for the theater: *a theatrical company* **2** (of behavior) showy; not natural **–theatrically** *adv*

thee /ðiʸ/ *pron old use* (*object form of* THOU) you

theft /θɛft/ *n* [C;U] (an example of) the act of stealing

their /ðər; *strong* ðɛər/ *determiner* (*possessive form of* THEY) of those people, animals, or things already mentioned: *They washed their faces.|Everyone waved their flags.*

theirs /ðɛərz/ *pron* (*possessive form of* THEY) of those people, animals, or things already mentioned: *The money is theirs.|I do my work, and the others do theirs.*

them /ðəm, əm; *strong* ðɛm/ *pron* (*object form of* THEY): *Where are my shoes? I can't find them.|What have you done with them?|He bought them drinks.*

theme /θiʸm/ *n* **1** the subject of a talk or piece of writing **2** a tune on which a piece of music is based

theme song /'· ·/ *n* a song or tune played often during a musical play or movie

them·selves /ðəm'sɛlvz, ðɛm-/ *pron* **1** (used as the object of a verb, or after a PREPOSITION, when the same people, animals, or things do the action and are the objects of the action): *The children are enjoying themselves.|They're feeling pleased with themselves.* **2** (used to make *they*, or the name of a group of people or things, stronger): *They built the house themselves.|The team themselves were delighted.*

then¹ /ðɛn/ *adv* **1** at that time: *We lived in the country then.|Will we still be alive then?|I'll be married by then.|From then on, (=starting then) he worked harder.* **2** next; afterwards: *Let's have a drink and then go home.* **3** in that case; therefore: *If you want to go home, then go.* **4** besides; and also: *You must ask Carol to the party, and then there's Paul too.* **5** but then however: *He lost the race, but then he never expected to win.*

then² *adj* [A] at that time in the past: *the then president of the country*

thence /ðɛns/ *adv fml* from there: *We can fly to London and thence to Paris.* –see also HENCE

the·o·lo·gian /ˌθiʸə'loʷdʒən/ *n* a person who has studied THEOLOGY

the·ol·o·gy /θiʸ'alədʒiʸ/ *n* [U] the study of religion and of God **–theological** /ˌθiʸə'ladʒɪkəl/ *adj* **–theologically** *adv*

the·o·rem /'θiʸərəm, 'θɪərəm/ *n tech* (esp. in MATHEMATICS) a STATEMENT that can be shown to be true by reasoning

the·o·rize ‖also **-rise** *BrE* /'θiʸə͵raɪz/ *v* **-rized, -rizing** [I *about, on*] *fml* to form a THEORY (1) or theories

the·o·ry /'θiʸəriʸ, 'θɪəriʸ/ *n* **-ries 1** [C +(*that*)] a reasoned argument, intended to explain a fact or event; an idea that has not yet been proved to be true: *the theory that man is descended from monkeys|She has a theory about the murder.* –compare HYPOTHESIS **2** [U] the general principles of a science or art as opposed to its practice: *The plans are good in theory, but they won't work in practice.| musical theory* **–theoretical** /ˌθiʸə'rɛţɪkəl/ also **theoretic–** *adj: theoretical science|a theoretical possibility* **–theoretically** *adv: Theoretically it's my job, but in fact I don't do it.* **–theorist** /'θiʸərɪst/ *n*

ther·a·peu·tic /ˌθɛrə'pyuʷţɪk/ *adj* of or related to the treating or curing of a disease: *a therapeutic exercise*

ther·a·py /'θɛrəpiʸ/ *n* [U] the treatment of illnesses of the mind or body, esp. without operations: OCCUPATIONAL *therapy* (=with lots of activity)|PHYSIOTHERAPY **–therapist** *n: a speech therapist*

there¹ /ðɛər/ *adv* **1** to, at, or in that place: *I live there.|Go over there.|It's cold out there.* **2** at that point: *I read to the bottom of the page and decided to stop there.* **3** (used for drawing attention to someone or something): *There goes John.* (=I can see John going past) –compare HERE **4** (used for comforting someone or for expressing satisfaction, encouragement, victory, etc.): *There, it's finished.|There, there, stop crying.|There, I told you I was right.* **5 then and there** also **there and then–** at that time and place: *Then and there she quit her job.* **6 There you are: a** There is what you wanted **b** I told you so: *There you are. I said he would fail.*

there² /ðɛər, ðər/ *pron* (used to show that someone or something exists or happens): *There's a cat on the roof.|There are some letters for you.|There was a knock on the door.|Is there a telephone near here?*

there·a·bouts /ˌðɛərə'bauts, 'ðɛərə͵bauts/ ‖ also **thereabout** /ˌðɛərə'baut, 'ðɛərə͵baut/ *AmE– adv* near that place, time, number, etc.: *a boy of six or thereabouts*

there·af·ter /ðɛər'æftər/ *adv fml* after that; afterwards: *Thereafter we heard no more about it.*

there·by /ðɛər'baɪ, 'ðɛərbaɪ/ *adv fml or law* by that means; by doing or saying that: *He became a citizen, thereby gaining the right to vote.*

there·fore /'ðɛərfɔr, -foʷr/ *adv* for that reason; so: *I don't know much about China; therefore I can't advise͵ you about it.|She's nice, and therefore popular.* –see Study Notes on page 144

there·in /ðɛər'ɪn/ *adv fml or law* in that: *She would never marry him, and therein lay the cause of his unhappiness.*

there-of /ðɛər'ʌv, -'ɒv/ *adv fml or law* of that; of it

there-to /ðɛər'tuʷ/ *adv fml or law* to that; to it: *The judge wrote a letter and signed his name thereto.*

there-up-on /ˈðɛərəˌpɒn, -ˌpɔn, ˌðɛərəˈpɒn, -'pɔn/ *adv fml* because of that; at that moment: *He thereupon asked her to marry him.*

ther-mal /ˈθɜrməl/ *adj* of, producing, or caused by heat: *thermal springs* (=hot-water springs)

ther-mom-e-ter /θər'mɑmətər/ *n* an instrument for measuring and showing temperature –see illustration on page 201

ther-mos bot-tle /ˈθɜrməs ˌbɑtl̩/ also **thermos** *AmE*‖**thermos flask** *BrE*– *n tdmk* a bottle having thin glass walls between which a VACUUM is kept, used for keeping the contents either hot or cold

ther-mo-stat /ˈθɜrməˌstæt/ *n* an apparatus that can be set to keep a particular level of temperature in a room, apparatus, etc.

the-sau-rus /θɪ'sɔrəs/ *n* **-ruses** *or* **-ri** /raɪ/ a book of words put in lists according to their meaning

these /ðiʸz/ *determiner,pron, plural of* THIS[1]

the-sis /ˈθiʸsɪs/ *n* **-ses** /siʸz/ **1** an opinion or statement put forward and supported by reasoned argument **2** a long piece of writing done for a university degree

they /ðeʸ/ *pron* (used as the subject of a sentence) **1** those people, animals, or things already mentioned: *John and Mary are here; they come every week.|Take these books; they might be useful.* **2** people; everyone: *They say prices will increase.|They* (=the people in power) *still haven't fixed that hole in the road.*

they'd /ðeʸd/ *short for:* **1** they had: *If only they'd been here.* **2** they would: *They'd never believe you.*

they'll /ðeʸl, ðɛl/ *short for:* **1** they will **2** they shall

they're /ðər; *strong* ðɛər, ðeʸər/ *short for:* they are

they've /ðeʸv/ *short for:* they have

thick[1] /θɪk/ *adj* **1** having a large distance between opposite surfaces; not thin: *a thick board|book|thick wire* **2** [after *n*] measuring in depth or width: *ice five inches thick* **3** (of liquid) not flowing easily: *thick soup* **4** [F *with*] full of; covered with: *The air was thick with smoke.* **5** (of a voice) not clear in sound: *His voice sounded thick because of his cold.|a thick* ACCENT[1] (1) **6** closely packed together; DENSE (1,2): *a thick forest|thick mist* **7** *infml* (of a person) stupid **8 as thick as thieves** *infml* very friendly –**thick** *adv*: *The flowers grew thickest near the wall.* –**thickly** *adv*

thick[2] *n* [S] **1** the part, place, time, etc., of greatest activity: *in the thick of the fight|the traffic* **2 through thick and thin** through both good and bad times

thick-en /ˈθɪkən/ *v* [I;T] to make or become thick: *Thicken the soup by adding flour.|(fig.) The* PLOT[1] (3) *thickened.* (=the story became more confusing)

thick-et /ˈθɪkɪt/ *n* a thick growth of bushes and small trees

thick-ness /ˈθɪknɪs/ *n* [C;U] the state or degree of being thick: *The beam has a thickness of four inches|is four inches in thickness.*

thick-set /ˌθɪk'sɛt◀/ *adj* having a short broad body

thick-skinned /ˌ· '·◀/ *adj sometimes derog* insensitive; not worried by disapproval –see also THIN-SKINNED

thief /θiʸf/ *n* **thieves** /θiʸvz/ a person who steals

USAGE **Thief** is a general word for a person who **steals**. A **thief** who takes things from stores without paying is a **shoplifter.** Someone who **steals** things from people's pockets in the street, on a bus, etc., is a **pickpocket.** A **mugger** is a person who **robs** with violence, usually in a public place. **Burglars** and **housebreakers** both steal from houses, but a **burglar** usually steals at night. A **robber** is more violent and steals from banks, people, etc. One **steals** things but one **burglarizes/breaks into** places: *My wedding ring was stolen when the house was burglarized/broken into.* One **robs** people or places (of things), but one **mugs** only people: *They robbed the bank and stole $50,000.|He knocked me down and robbed me of my watch.|My brother got mugged on his way from work and is now in the hospital.*

thieve /θiʸv/ *v* **thieved, thieving** [I] to steal things; act as a thief

thigh /θaɪ/ *n* the top part of the human leg between the knee and the HIP

thim-ble /ˈθɪmbəl/ *n* a small hard cap put over the finger that pushes the needle when sewing

thin[1] /θɪn/ *adj* **-nn- 1** having a small distance between opposite surfaces; not thick: *a thin board|thin ice|a thin shirt* **2** having little fat on the body; not fat: *She looked thin after her illness.* –see USAGE **3** (of a liquid) watery; flowing easily: *thin soup* **4** widely separated; not DENSE (1): *Your hair's getting very thin.* **5** lacking in strength; weak: *thin high musical notes|a thin excuse* –**thin** *adv*: *Don't cut the bread so thin.* –**thinly** *adv*: *Spread the butter thinly.* –**thinness** *n* [U]: *Despite its thinness this glass is very strong.*

USAGE **1 Thin** is a general word to describe people who have little or no fat on their bodies. If someone is **thin** in a pleasant way, we say they are **slim** or (less common) **slender,** but if they are too **thin** they are **skinny** (*infml*), **underweight,** or (worst of all) **emaciated:** *I wish I were as slim as you!|She looks very thin/skinny/underweight after her illness.|After weeks with little or no food, the prisoners were emaciated.* The opposite of **thin** in this sense is **fat,** but this is not very polite. **Plump, overweight, heavy, chubby** (esp. of babies), and **matronly** (only of older women) are all more polite ways of saying the same things. A person who is very fat is **obese. 2** Things that are long and **thin,** in the sense of having a short distance from one side to another, are **narrow** (opposite **wide**): *a narrow country road|a long narrow room.* **3 Fine** is used to describe things that are **thin,** when one is giving the idea of careful sensitive work: *She used a fine pen to draw the* *map.*|**fine** *silk thread* –opposite **thick.**

thin² *v* **-nn-** [I;T *out*] to make or become thin or less DENSE (1,2): *The mist thinned.*|*to thin out* (=separate) *the plants*

thine¹ /ðaɪn/ *pron old use, bibl, or lit (possessive form of* THOU) that/those belonging to THEE; yours

thine² *determiner old use, bibl, or lit (before a vowel or* h) THY

thing /θɪŋ/ *n* **1** [C] any material object; an object that is not named: *What do you use this thing for?*|*My daughter enjoys making things out of clay.*|*I haven't got a thing* (=any suitable garment) *to wear.*|*It's so dark I can't see a thing.* (=anything) **2** [C] a remark, subject, or idea: *What a nasty thing to say to your sister!*|*There's one more thing I want to say.*|*He says the first thing that comes into his head.* **3** [C] an act; deed: *What's the next thing we have to do?*|*I expect great things from you!*|*The first thing is for you to talk to your teacher.* (=that is what you should do first) **4** [C] a creature; person, animal, etc.: *There wasn't a living thing in the woods.* **5** [S] *infml* something necessary or desirable: *A glass of cold beer is just the thing on a hot day.* **6** [S] *infml* an activity very satisfying to one personally: *Everyone should be free to do their own thing.* **7 first thing** early; before anything else: *First thing in the morning I have a cup of coffee.* **8 for one thing** (used for introducing a reason): *For one thing it costs too much, and for another it's the wrong color.* **9 have a thing about** *infml* to have a strong like or dislike for **10 it's a good thing** it's lucky: *It's a good thing George can't hear us!* **11 make a thing about/of** to give too much importance to: *I disagree with you, but let's not make a thing about/of it.*

thing·a·ma·jig, thingumajig /'θɪŋəmədʒɪg/ also **thingamabob** /'θɪŋəməbɑb/– *n infml* a person or thing whose name one has forgotten: *a new thingamajig for opening bottles*

things /θɪŋz/ *n* [P] **1** one's personal possessions; belongings: *Pack your things. We're going.* **2** the general state of affairs: *Things are getting worse and worse.* **3 be seeing things** to see things which do not exist; have HALLUCINATIONS

think /θɪŋk/ *v* **thought** /θɔt/, **thinking 1** [I;T *about*] to use the power of reason; use the mind to form opinions; have (a thought): *Do you still think in English when you're speaking French?*|*Can animals think?*|*Think hard before you answer the question.*|*Think* (=consider the matter carefully) *before you accept his offer!*|*thinking great thoughts*|*What are you thinking about?*|*thinking people* (=those who use reason) **2** [T +(*that*)] to believe; consider: *I think (that) he's wrong, don't you?*|*Who do you think murdered the old lady?*|*She thinks of herself as a great poet.*|*"Do you think it will rain?" "Yes, I think so.*|*No, I don't think so.*" **3** [T] (used *after* cannot and could not and in the infinitive after try, want, *etc.*) to remember: *I can't think what his name is.*|*I'm trying to think how to get there.* **4** [I;T +(*that*)] to expect: *We didn't think we'd be this late.*|*I thought as*

much. (used when one has heard some news, to mean "that's just what I expected") **5** [I] to direct the mind in a particular way: *to think big* **6 think aloud/out loud** to speak one's thoughts as they come **7 think twice** to think very carefully about something –**thinker** *n*: *Bertrand Russell, one of the great thinkers of our age* –**think** *n* [S *about*] *infml*

think of sbdy./sthg. *v prep* [T +*v-ing*] **1** also **think about** sbdy./sthg.– to consider; have in one's mind: *We're thinking of going to France for our vacation.*|*You must learn to think of other people.* **2** also **think about** sbdy./sthg.– to have as an opinion about: *What do you think of this plan?* **3** (used *after* cannot *and* could not *and in the infinitive after* try, want, *etc.*) to remember: *I can't think of his name.* **4** to suggest: *I thought of the idea first.* **5 not think much of** to have a low opinion of **6 think better of** to decide against: *I was going to go, but I thought better of it.* **7 think highly/well/little/poorly/**etc. **of someone** or **something** to have a good/bad/ etc. opinion of someone or something **8 think nothing of** to regard as usual or easy: *She thinks nothing of walking ten miles.* **9 think nothing of it** do not thank me for it

think sthg.↔**out**‖also **think** sthg.↔ **through** *AmE*– *v adv* [T] to consider carefully and in detail (a plan, problem, etc.)

think sthg.↔ **over** *v adv* [T] to consider carefully: *It's a good offer, but I have to think it over.*

think sthg.↔ **up** *v adv* [T] to invent (esp. an idea): *to think up a plan/an excuse*

think·ing /'θɪŋkɪŋ/ *n* [U] **1** the act of using one's mind to produce thoughts **2** opinion; judgment; thought: *What's the Administration's thinking on this matter?*

thin·ner /'θɪnər/ *n* [U] a liquid added esp. to paint to make it spread more easily

thin-skinned /ˌ· '·◄/ *adj sometimes derog* sensitive; easily offended –see also THICK-SKINNED

third /θɜrd/ *determiner,adv,n,pron* 3rd

third de·gree /ˌ· ·'·◄/ *n* [*the* S] *infml* rough treatment of a prisoner by the police in order to obtain information or a statement of guilt: (fig.) *When I got to work two hours late, my boss gave me the third degree.*

third di·men·sion /ˌ· ·'··/ *n* [*the* S] depth; the quality that makes an object appear solid

third par·ty /ˌ· '·◄/ *n tech* **1** a person in a law case who is not one of the two main people concerned **2** a person not named in an insurance agreement but protected by the insurance in the event of an accident –see also PARTY (5)

third-rate /ˌ· '·◄/ *adj* of very poor quality

Third World /ˌ· '·◄/ *n* the industrially less developed countries of the world, esp. in Asia and Africa

thirst /θɜrst/ *n* **1** [C;S;U] the need to drink; desire for drink: *Running five miles gave him a thirst.*|*suffering from thirst* **2** [S *for*] a strong desire: *the thirst for excitement*

thirst for/after sthg. *v prep* [T] *lit* to have a strong desire for: *Our people thirst for independence.*

thirst·y /ˈθɜrstiʸ/ *adj* **-ier, -iest 1** feeling or causing thirst: *Salty food makes one thirsty.* **2** [F *for*] having a strong desire for: *She was thirsty for power.* **–thirstily** *adv*

thir·teen /ˌθɜrˈtiʸn◂/ *determiner,n,pron* (the number) 13 **–thirteenth** *determiner,n,pron, adv*

thir·ty /ˈθɜrtiʸ/ *determiner,n,pron* **-ties** (the number) 30 **–thirtieth** /ˈθɜrtiʸɪθ/ *determiner, n,pron,adv*

this¹ /ðɪs/ *determiner,pron* **these** /ðiʸz/ **1** the one or amount (going to be) stated; the one that is near in place, time, or thought: *Who told you this story/this?|You look in this box here, and I'll look in that box over there.|Would you carry this box for me?|I saw Mrs. Jones this morning.* (=earlier today)*|Do it like this.* (=in the way I'm showing you) **–compare** THAT **2** *infml* (used in stories) a certain: *Then this man came up to me in the street...*

this² *adv infml* so; as much as this: *I've never been out this late before.|Cut off about this much thread...*

this·tle /ˈθɪsəl/ *n* a wild plant with prickly leaves and usu. purple flowers

thith·er /ˈθɪðər, ˈðɪðər/ *adv old use* to that place; in that direction

thong /θɔŋ, θɑŋ/ *n* a narrow length of leather used as a fastening, whip, etc.

tho·rax /ˈθɔræks, ˈθoʷr-/ *n* **-races** /rəˌsiʸz/ or **-raxes** *tech* the part of the body between the neck and ABDOMEN; chest

thorn /θɔrn/ *n* **1** [C] a sharp pointed prickle growing on a plant: *the thorns on a rose bush* **2** [C;U] (*usu. in comb.*) a bush, plant, or tree having such prickles: *a* HAWTHORN **3 thorn in one's flesh/side** a continual cause of annoyance **–thorny** *adj* **-ier, -iest**: (fig.) *a thorny* (=difficult) *question* **–thorniness** *n* [U]

thor·ough /ˈθɜroʷ, ˈθʌroʷ/ *adj* [A] complete and careful: *a thorough search|a thorough worker* **–thoroughly** *adv*: *After a hard day's work, I feel thoroughly tired.* **–thoroughness** *n* [U]

thor·ough·bred /ˈθɜrəˌbrɛd, ˈθʌrə-, ˈθoʷroʷ-, ˈθʌroʷ-/ *adj,n* (an animal, esp. a horse) of pure breed

thor·ough·fare /ˈθɜrəˌfɛər, ˈθʌrə-, ˈθoʷroʷ-, ˈθʌroʷ-/ *n* a road for public traffic: *a busy thoroughfare*

those /ðoʷz/ *determiner,pron plural of* THAT: *Will those* (=the people) *who want to join the club please sign here?*

thou /ðaʊ/ *pron old use or bibl* (used as the subject of a sentence with special old forms of verbs) the person to whom one is speaking; you: *"Thou shalt* (=you shall) *not kill."*

though¹ /ðoʷ/ *conj* **1** in spite of the fact that; even if: *Though/Even though it's hard work, I enjoy it.|He spoke firmly though pleasantly.* **2 as though** as if: *He behaves as though he were rich.* **–see also** ALTHOUGH

though² *adv* in spite of everything; however: *It's hard work. I enjoy it, though.*

thought¹ /θɔt/ *n* **1** [U] the act or way of thinking; consideration: *She sat, deep in thought.|ancient Greek thought* (=way of thinking)*|Give the matter plenty of*

thought.*|Without thought for her own safety, she jumped into the river to save him.* **2** [C;U] something that is thought; (an) idea, opinion, etc.: *What are your thoughts on the subject?* **3** [U] *of* intention: *I had no thought of annoying you.* **4 second thought** a thought that a past decision may not be correct: *I said I wouldn't go; but on second thoughts I think I will.*

thought² *v past tense & participle of* THINK

thought·ful /ˈθɔtfəl/ *adj* **1** thinking deeply: *The girl looked thoughtful and sad.* **2** paying attention to the feelings of other people: *It was very thoughtful of you to visit me.* **–thoughtfully** *adv* **–thoughtfulness** *n* [U]

thought·less /ˈθɔtlɪs/ *adj* careless; selfish: *How thoughtless of you to forget my birthday.* **–thoughtlessly** *adv* **–thoughtlessness** *n* [U]

thought-out /ˌ· ˈ·◂/ *adj* produced after the stated consideration: *a well thought-out plan*

thou·sand /ˈθaʊzənd/ *determiner,n,pron* **-sand** or **-sands** (the number) 1,000 **–see** Study Notes on page 550 **–thousandth** *determiner,n,pron,adv*

thrash /θræʃ/ *v* **1** [T] to beat with a whip or stick **2** [T] to defeat thoroughly **3** [I *around*] to move wildly about: *The fish thrashed around in the net.|The children were thrashing around in bed.*

thrash sthg.↔ out *v adv* [T] to reach agreement about (a problem) or produce (a decision) by much talk and consideration: *After a long argument, we thrashed out a plan.*

thread¹ /θrɛd/ *n* **1** [C;U] (a length of) very fine cord, used in sewing or weaving: *cotton/nylon thread|*(fig.) *His life* **hangs by a thread.** (=is in very great danger) **2** [C] a line of reasoning in an argument or story: *to lose the thread of one's argument* **3** [C] a raised line around the outside of a screw

thread² *v* [T] to pass a thread through: *to thread a needle|to thread buttons on a string|*(fig.) *I threaded my way through the crowd.*

thread·bare /ˈθrɛdbɛər/ *adj* (of cloth, clothes, etc.) worn thin; very worn and old

threat /θrɛt/ *n* **1** [C;U] a warning that one is going to hurt, punish, etc.: *I obeyed, but only under threat of death.|a threat to kill me* **2** [C *to, of; usu. sing.*] a (sign of) possible danger: *The killer is a threat to everyone.|The clouds brought a threat of rain.*

threat·en /ˈθrɛtn/ *v* **1** [I;T +*to-v/with*] to express or be a threat to: *I was threatened with punishment if I didn't obey.|a threatening letter|She threatened to murder me.|Noisy traffic threatens our peaceful way of life.|While danger threatens we must all take care.* **2** [T] to give warning of (something bad): *The black clouds threatened rain.* **–threateningly** *adv*

three /θriʸ/ *determiner,n,pron* (the number) 3

three-di·men·sion·al /ˌ· ·ˈ···◂/ *adj* having length, depth, and height

three-quar·ter /ˌ· ˈ··◂/ *adj* consisting of three FOURTHS ($^3/_4$) of the whole: *a three-quarter length coat*

thresh /θrɛʃ/ *v* [I;T] to separate the grain

from (corn, wheat, etc.) by beating
–**thresher** *n*

thresh·old /'θrɛʃhoʷld, -ʃoʷld/ *n* **1** a piece of wood or stone fixed beneath the door into a house **2** [*usu. sing.*] the place or point of beginning: *Scientists are now* **on the threshold of** *a new discovery.*

threw /θruʷ/ *v past tense of* THROW

thrice /θraɪs/ *predeterminer,adv old use* three times

thrift /θrɪft/ *n* [U] wise careful use of money and goods –**thrifty** *adj* **-ier, -iest**: *a thrifty housewife/meal* –**thriftily** *adv*

thrill¹ /θrɪl/ *v* [I;T *at, to*] to (cause to) feel a THRILL² or thrills: *a thrilling story* –**thrillingly** *adv*

thrill² *n* (something producing) a sudden very strong feeling of excitement, pleasure, or fear

thrill·er /'θrɪlər/ *n* a book, play, or movie that tells a very exciting story, esp. of crime and violence

thrive /θraɪv/ *v* **throve** /θroʷv/ *or* **thrived, thrived** *or* **thriven** /'θrɪvən/, **thriving** [I *on*] to develop well and be healthy; be successful: *a thriving business*|(fig.) *He thrives on hard work.*

throat /θroʷt/ *n* **1** the passage from the back of the mouth down inside the neck: *a sore throat* **2** the front of the neck **3 force/thrust/ram something down somebody's throat** to force someone to accept something, esp. one's ideas, opinions, etc., unwillingly **4 jump down someone's throat** to attack somebody in words strongly and unexpectedly

throat·y /'θroʷtiʸ/ *adj* **-ier, -iest** having a low rough voice: *a throaty laugh*

throb /θrɑb/ *v* **-bb-** [I] to beat strongly and rapidly: *My heart was throbbing with excitement.*|*throbbing with pain* –**throb** *n: the throb of machinery*

throes /θroʷz/ *n* [P] **1** *esp. lit* severe pains (esp. in the phrase **death throes**) **2 in the throes of** struggling with: *a country in the throes of war*

throm·bo·sis /θrɑm'boʷsɪs/ *n* **-ses** /siʸz/ [C;U] the condition of having a blood CLOT in a blood vessel

throne /θroʷn/ *n* **1** [C] the ceremonial chair of a king, queen, etc. **2** [S] the rank or office of a king or queen: *She was only fifteen when she came to the throne.*

throng¹ /θrɔŋ, θrɑŋ/ *n* a large crowd of people: *A throng of people is here.*|*Throngs of people are gathering.*

throng² *v* [I;T] to go (as if) in a crowd: *People thronged to see the play.*

throt·tle¹ /'θrɑtl/ *v* **-tled, -tling** [T] to seize (someone) tightly by the throat and so stop his/her breathing; STRANGLE: *She was throttled to death.*

throttle² *n* a part of a pipe (VALVE) that opens and closes to control the flow of liquid into an engine

through¹ /θruʷ/ *prep* **1** into at one side, and out at the other: *Water flows through this pipe.*|*She pushed her way through the crowd.*|*We couldn't see through the mist.*|*She drove straight through the town.* **2** by way of;

by means of: *She climbed in through the window.*|*I got this book through the library.* **3** because of: *The war was lost through bad organization.* –see Study Notes on page 144 **4** past: *I drove through a red light.* (=a TRAFFIC LIGHT showing "Stop")|*Did you get through* (=did you pass) *your examination?* **5** to or at the end of: *I don't think the old man will live through the night.*|*I read right through the book.* **6** all over; among the parts of: *We traveled through France and Belgium.*|*I searched through all my papers.* **7** *AmE* (*esp. in expressions of time*) up to and including: *Wednesday through Sunday*

through² *adv* **1** in at one side and out at the other: *I opened the gate and let them through.* **2** all the way from beginning to end: *She read the letter through.*|*Does this train go right through to New Haven?* **3** to a successful end: *I failed the examination, but she got through.* (=passed) **4** connected by telephone: *"Can you put me through to Mr. Jones?"* **5** [*with*] to or at the end; finished: *Are you through with your work yet?*|*I'm through with alcohol.* (=I won't drink any more) **6 through and through** completely; in every way

through³ *adj* [A] going all the way from one end to the other: *a through train*|*a through road*

through·out /θruʷ'aʊt/ *adv* **1** in every part: *The house is painted throughout.* **2** from beginning to end: *The prince remained loyal throughout.* –**throughout** *prep: throughout the country/night*

throw¹ /θroʷ/ *v* **threw** /θruʷ/, **thrown** /θroʷn/, **throwing 1** [I;T] to send through the air by a sudden movement or straightening of the arm: *She threw the ball 50 feet.*|*Throw me the ball.* **2** [T] to move or put suddenly, or with force: *She threw off her clothes and jumped into the water.*|*The two fighters threw themselves at each other.*|*The new system has thrown us all into confusion.* **3** [T] to cause to fall off: *The horse threw him.* **4** [T] to move (a SWITCH, handle, etc.) in order to connect or disconnect parts of a machine **5** [T] to make (one's voice) appear to come from somewhere other than one's mouth **6** [T] to shape (an object) out of clay when making POTTERY **7** [T] *infml* to arrange or give (a party, dinner, etc.) **8** [T] *infml* to confuse; shock: *His behavior really threw me.* **9 throw a fit** to have a sudden attack of uncontrolled temper **10 throw oneself at someone: a** to rush violently towards someone **b** to attempt forcefully to win the love of someone **11 throw oneself into** to work very busily at –**thrower** *n*

throw *sthg.*↔ **away** *v adv* [T] **1** also **throw** *sthg.*↔ **out**– to get rid of (something); DISCARD: *I must have thrown away the theater tickets by accident.* **2** to lose by foolishness: *He threw away the chance of a good job.*

throw *sthg.*↔ **in** *v adv* [T] *infml* to supply in addition, without increasing the price: *The room costs fifteen dollars a night, with the meals thrown in.*

throw *sbdy./sthg.*↔ **off** *v adv* [T] to free oneself from: *to throw off a cold*

throw sthg.↔ **open** *v adv* [T *to*] to allow people to enter: *to throw the gardens open to the public*

throw sbdy./sthg.↔ **out** *v adv* [T] **1** to refuse to accept: *The committee threw out my suggestions.* **2** to dismiss; force to leave: *The teacher threw me out for making too much noise.* **3** → THROW sthg.↔ **away** (1)

throw sbdy.↔ **over** *v adv* [T] to end a relationship with

throw sbdy./sthg.↔ **together** *v adv* [T] **1** to make hastily: *I just threw the meal together.* **2** to bring together: *Chance threw us together at a party.*

throw up *v adv* **1** [I;T (=**throw up** sthg.)] for VOMIT **2** [T] (**throw** sthg.↔ **up**)to stop doing: *to throw up a job* **3** (**throw up** sthg.) to build hastily: *They threw up those buildings in a few months.*

throw² *n* **1** an act of throwing **2** the distance to which something is thrown: *a throw of 100 feet|a record throw*

thru /θruʷ/ *adv,adj,prep AmE infml* through

thrush /θrʌʃ/ *n* a small bird with a brownish back and spotted breast

thrust /θrʌst/ *v* **thrust, thrusting 1** [T] to push forcefully and suddenly: *We thrust our way through the crowd.* **2** [I *at*] to make a sudden forward stroke with a sword, knife, etc. –**thrust** *n* [C;U]: *the thrust (=force) of an engine|a sword thrust*

thud /θʌd/ *n* a dull sound caused by a heavy object striking something soft: *He fell to the floor with a thud.* –**thud** *v* **-dd-** [I]

thug /θʌg/ *n* a violent criminal

thumb¹ /θʌm/ *n* **1** the short thick finger which is set apart from the other four **2 stick out like a sore thumb** *infml* to seem out of place **3 thumbs up** (an expression of satisfaction, victory, or approval) **4 under somebody's thumb** *infml* under the control or influence of someone

thumb² *v* [I;T] **1** [*through*] to look through (a book) quickly **2** *infml* to ask for (a free ride) from passing motorists by holding out one's thumb; HITCHHIKE: *to thumb a ride to Boston*

thumb·nail /ˈθʌmneʸl/ *n* **1** [C] the hard flat piece at the end of the thumb **2** [A] small; short: *a thumbnail sketch*

thumb·tack /ˈθʌmtæk/ *n AmE* a short nail with a broad flat head for pressing with one's thumb into a board or wall, to hold a picture or notice in place

thump¹ /θʌmp/ *v* [I;T] to strike with a heavy blow: *I'll thump you on the head!|He thumped (=walked with a heavy step) down the stairs.*

thump² *n* (the dull sound of) a heavy blow

thun·der¹ /ˈθʌndər/ *n* [U] the loud explosive noise that follows a flash of lightning: *After the lightning came the thunder.|*(fig.) *the thunder of distant guns* –**thunderous** /ˈθʌndərəs/ *adj:* (fig.) *thunderous (=very loud)* APPLAUSE –**thunderously** *adv*

USAGE Note the word order in this fixed phrase: **thunder and lightning.**

thunder² *v* **1** [I] to produce thunder: *I'm always afraid when it thunders. (=when there is thunder)|*(fig.)*The guns thundered in the*

distance. 2 to shout loudly: *"Get out!" he thundered.*

thun·der·bolt /ˈθʌndər,boʷlt/ *n* a flash of lightning, with thunder

thun·der·clap /ˈθʌndər,klæp/ *n* a single loud crash of thunder

thun·der·cloud /ˈθʌndər,klaʊd/ *n* a large dark cloud producing thunder and lightning: (fig.) *The thunderclouds of war are coming.*

thun·der·storm /ˈθʌndər,stɔrm/ *n* a storm of heavy rain with thunder and lightning

thun·der·struck /ˈθʌndər,strʌk/ *adj* [F] very surprised indeed

thun·der·y /ˈθʌndəriʸ/ *adj* (of the weather) giving signs that thunder is likely

Thurs·day /ˈθɜrzdiʸ, -deʸ/ also **Thurs.** *written abbrev.*– the 5th day of the week: *He'll arrive (on) Thursday.|I'm always home on Thursday evenings.|(esp. AmE) She works Thursdays.*

thus /ðʌs/ *adv fml* **1** in this way: *We hope the new machine will work faster, thus reducing our costs.* **2** as a result –see Study Notes on page 144 **3 thus far** up until now

thwart /θwɔrt/ *v* [T] to oppose successfully: *My plans were thwarted by the weather.*

thy /ðaɪ/ *determiner old use* (*possessive form of* THOU) belonging to THEE; your

thyme /taɪm/ *n* [U] (the dried leaves of) a plant, used for giving a special taste to food

thy·roid /ˈθaɪrɔɪd/ also **thyroid gland** /ˈ·· ,ˈ/– *n* an organ in the neck that controls growth and activity

ti·ar·a /tiʸˈærə, tiʸˈɛərə, tiʸˈɑrə/ *n* a piece of jewelry like a small crown, esp. as worn on the head by women on formal occasions

tic /tɪk/ *n* a sudden movement of the muscles, esp. in the face, usu. caused by a nervous illness

tick¹ /tɪk/ *n* **1** the short regularly repeated sound of a clock or watch **2** *BrE* for CHECK¹ (3)

tick² *v* **1** [I] (of a clock, watch, etc.) to make a regularly repeated short sound **2** [T *off*] *BrE* for CHECK² (15) **3 make someone or something tick** *infml* to provide a person or thing with reasons for acting, behaving, working in a particular way: *We're trying to find out what makes her tick.*

tick sbdy.↔ **off** *v adv* [T] *infml* to anger

tick³ *n* a very small insect-like creature that fixes itself to animals and sucks their blood

tick·er·tape /ˈtɪkər,teʸp/ *n* [U] very long narrow lengths of paper often thrown during public rejoicings

tick·et /ˈtɪkɪt/ *n* **1** a printed piece of paper or card which shows that a person has paid for a journey on a bus, entrance into a theater, etc.: *a bus/train/movie ticket* –see illustration on page 17 **2** a piece of card or paper that shows the price, size, etc., of an object for sale **3** a printed notice of an offence against the driving laws: *a parking ticket*

tick·ing /ˈtɪkɪŋ/ *n* [U] the thick strong coarse cloth used for making MATTRESS and PILLOW covers

tick·le¹ /ˈtɪkəl/ *v* **-led, -ling 1** [T] to touch (someone's body) lightly to produce laughter or nervous excitement **2** [I;T] to give or feel a sensation of nervous excitement: *These rough sheets tickle.* **3** [T] to delight or amuse

tickle² *n* [C;U] (an) act or feeling of tickling (TICKLE¹ (1,2))

tick·lish /'tɪklɪʃ/ *adj* **1** (of a (part of a) person) sensitive to tickling **2** (of a problem, etc.) difficult: *a ticklish question*

tick-tack-toe, tic-tac-toe /ˌtɪk tæk 'towˈ/ *n* [U] *AmE* a game played by two people writing the marks O and X in turn on a pattern of nine squares, with the purpose of writing three such marks in a row

tid·al /'taɪdl/ *adj* of, having, or related to the TIDE (1): *tidal currents|a tidal wave* (=very large dangerous ocean wave)

tid·bit /'tɪd,bɪt/ *n AmE* **1** a small good-tasting piece of food **2** *infml* an interesting piece of news

tide¹ /taɪd/ *n* **1** [C] (a current caused by) the regular rise and fall of the seas: *The sea comes right up to the cliffs when the tide is in.| Strong tides make swimming dangerous.| (fig.) the tide of public opinion* **2** [U] *old use* time; season: *Christmastide*

tide² *v* **tided, tiding** → TIDE sbdy. OVER (sthg.)

tide·mark /'taɪdmɑrk/ *n* the highest point reached by a TIDE (1) on the shore

tide sbdy. **over** (sthg.) *v adv; prep* **tided, tiding** [T] to help (someone) through (a difficult period): *Can you lend me ten dollars, to tide me over ((for) the next few days)?*

tide·wa·ter /'taɪd,wɔt̬ər, -wɑ-/ *n* [U] **1** water that flows onto the land when the TIDE is very high **2** the water in the TIDAL parts of rivers and streams **3** *AmE* low coastal land

ti·dings /'taɪdɪŋz/ *n* [P] *old use* news

ti·dy¹ /'taɪdiʸ/ *adj* **-dier, -diest 1** (liking things to be) neatly arranged: *a tidy room/person* **2** *infml* quite large: *a tidy income* **-tidily** *adv* **-tidiness** *n* [U]

tidy² *v* **-died, -dying** [I;T *up*] to make neat

tie¹ /taɪ/ *n* **1** also **necktie** *AmE*– a band of cloth worn around the neck and tied in a knot at the front –see also BOW TIE **2** a cord, string, etc., used for fastening something **3** something that unites; BOND¹ (1): *family ties/ties of friendship* **4** something that limits one's freedom: *Young children can be a tie.* **5** an equality of results, votes, etc.: *The result of the election was a tie.* –compare DRAW¹ (6) **6** *AmE* any of the row of heavy pieces of wood, metal, etc., supporting a railroad track

tie² *v* **tied, tying 1** [I;T *up*] to fasten or be fastened with a cord, string, band, etc.: *to tie up a package|Tie your shoelaces.|My dress ties (up) in the back.|to tie a dog to a fence* **2** [T] to make (a knot or BOW³ (3)): *to tie a knot* **3** [I *with, for*] to be equal in a competition: *to tie for second place*

tie sbdy. **down** *v adv* [T] **1** to limit the freedom of: *She feels her job is tying her down.* **2** to force to take a particular position, make a decision, etc.: *She tied him down to a date for the meeting.*

tie in *v adv* [I *with*] to be in agreement with: *This story doesn't tie in with the facts.*

tie sthg.↔ **up** *v adv* [T] **1** [*in*] to limit the free use of (money, property, etc.) by certain conditions **2** [*with*] to connect: *The police are trying to tie up his escape from prison with the murder.* –compare TIE IN **in 3 tied up** very busy

tier /tɪər/ *n* any of a number of levels, esp. of seats, rising one behind or above another: *Their wedding cake had three tiers.*

tiff /tɪf/ *n* a slight quarrel: *a lovers' tiff*

ti·ger /'taɪgər/ **tigress** *fem.*– *n* a fierce Asian large wild cat that has yellow fur with black bands

tight¹ /taɪt/ *adj* **1** fitting (too) closely; leaving no free room or time: *tight shoes|a tight* SCHEDULE **2** closely fastened; firmly fixed in place: *This drawer is so tight I can't open it.|Are you sure this joint/roof is completely tight/watertight?* (=made so that water cannot pass through) **3** fully stretched: *Pull the thread tight.* **4** (of money) difficult to obtain **5** *infml* (of a person) **a** drunk **b** not generous with money **6 in a tight corner/spot** in a difficult position **-tightly** *adv* **-tightness** *n* [U]

tight² *adv* **1** closely; firmly; tightly: *She held him tight and kissed him.* **2 sit tight** to stay where one is

tight·en /'taɪtn/ *v* [I;T *up*] to make or become tighter: *The government is tightening up (on)* (=becoming firmer about) *the driving laws.* –compare LOOSEN, SLACKEN

tight·fist·ed /ˌtaɪt'fɪstɪd◂/ also **tight–** *adj infml* very ungenerous with money

tight·rope /'taɪt-rowp/ *n* a tightly stretched rope or wire, high above the ground, on which performers walk and do tricks

tights /taɪts/ *n* [P] a very close-fitting garment worn esp. by women, and made of thin material covering the legs and lower part of the body –see PAIR (USAGE)

ti·gress /'taɪgrɪs/ *n* a female tiger

tile /taɪl/ *n* a thin piece of baked clay or plastic, metal, etc. used for covering roofs, walls, floors, etc. **-tile** *v* **tiled, tiling** [T]: *to tile a roof|a tiled floor*

till¹ /tɪl, tl/ *prep, conj* → UNTIL

till² /tɪl/ *n* a drawer where money is kept in a store

till³ /tɪl/ *v* [T] *old use* to cultivate (the ground): *to till the soil*

till·er /'tɪlər/ *n* a long handle fastened to the RUDDER of a boat, to turn it

tilt¹ /tɪlt/ *v* [I;T] to (cause to) slope by raising one end

tilt² *n* **1** a slope: *She wore her hat at a tilt.* **2 (at) full tilt** *infml* at full speed

tim·ber /'tɪmbər/ *n* **1** [U] wood or growing trees to be used for building **2** [C] a wooden beam

time¹ /taɪm/ *n* **1** [U] a continuous measurable quantity from the past, through the present, and into the future; the passing of minutes, days, months, and years: *The universe exists in space and time.|In time* (=after a certain period) *you'll forget him.|Only time will tell if you're right.|The men are working against time to finish the bridge.* (=it must be finished soon and there is still much to do) **2** [S;U] a limited period e.g. between two events or for the completion of an action:

Learning English takes quite a long time.|Take more time and care over your work.|I don't have much time, (=I am in a hurry) so tell me quickly.|She stays in **all the time**. (=she never goes out)|I'll be back in no time. (=very soon) **3** [U] a system of measuring time: Daylight Saving Time **4** the period in which an action is completed, esp. a performance in a race: Her time was just under four minutes. **5** [S;U] a particular point in the day stated in hours, minutes, and sometimes seconds: "What's the time?" "It's one o'clock."|"What time's Tony coming to dinner?" "Four o'clock."|This clock **keeps good time**. (=works correctly) **6** [S;U] a particular moment or occasion: It's time to go to bed.|**Closing time** at this bar is two o'clock.|He's in a good mood, so **now's the time** to tell him you've crashed his car.|They arrived **ahead of time**. (=early)|I told you **at the time** (=when the thing we are talking about happened) that I thought you were being foolish.|He comes here **from time to time**. (=occasionally)|Do the trains ever run **on time** (=at the right time) here?|The people came in **two at a time**. (=in groups of two)|I've told you **time after time/time and again** (=repeatedly) not to do that. **7** [C] a period: in ancient times|We had a good time (=enjoyed ourselves) at the party.|a writer who is **ahead of her time** (=has ideas too modern or original for the period in which she lives)|**At one time** (=formerly) I used to like her, but not anymore.|He lived **for a time** (=for a short period) in Spain. **8** [U] the rate of speed of a piece of music: You **beat time** and I'll play.|The players at the back aren't **keeping time**. **9 at the same time** in spite of this; yet: He can be very rude, but at the same time, I can't help liking him. **10 for the time being** for a limited period: I'll let you keep the book for the time being. but I'll want it back next week. **11 have no time for** infml to dislike **12 in good time: a** at the right time **b** early enough **13 in one's own good time** infml when one is ready and not before **14 in time** early enough: We must make sure we arrive in time to get a good seat. **15 have the time of one's life** to have a very enjoyable experience
USAGE To **spend** time suggests using it in a sensible or useful way, but to **pass** time gives the idea of too much time that must be filled: We **spent** the day painting the outside of the house.|How do you **pass** the time now that you're no longer working? To **waste** time suggests that it has been badly used: We **wasted** an hour trying to find a parking space!

time² v timed, timing [T] **1** [usu. pass.] to set the time at which (something) happens or is to happen: The bell is timed to ring at six o'clock.|She timed her visit well, and arrived at the right moment. **2** to record the speed of or time taken by: We timed our journey. It took us two hours.

time bomb /'· ·/ n a bomb that can be set to explode at a particular time

time card /'· ·/ also **time sheet** /'· ·/– n a card or sheet on which the hours worked by a

worker are recorded

time-hon·ored /'· ¸··/ adj respected because of age or long use: a time-honored custom

time·keep·er /'taɪmˌkiʸpər/ n a person who records the time of competitors in a race, work done by others, etc.

time lag /'· ·/ also **lag**– n the period of time in between two connected events

time·less /'taɪmlɪs/ adj lasting forever; not changed by time: the timeless beauty of the stars –timelessly adv –timelessness n [U]

time lim·it /'· ¸··/ n a period of time within which something must be done

time·ly /'taɪmliʸ/ adj -lier, -liest happening at just the right time: a timely warning

tim·er /'taɪmər/ n a person or machine that records time

times¹ /taɪmz/ prep multiplied by: 3 times 3 = 9 is usually written 3 x 3 = 9.

times² n [P] **1** the present time: a sign of the times **2** occasions on which something was done: I played tennis five times last week. **3 at times** sometimes **4 behind the times** old-fashioned **5 for old times' sake** because of happy times in the past **6 move with the times** to develop at the same rate as changing fashions and social customs

time·ta·ble /'taɪmˌteʸbəl/ n esp. BrE for SCHEDULE (2b)

time·worn /'taɪmwɔrn, -woʷrn/ adj lit showing signs of decay through age

tim·id /'tɪmɪd/ adj fearful; lacking courage –timidity /tɪˈmɪdəţiʸ/ n [U] –timidly /'tɪmɪdliʸ/ adv

tim·ing /'taɪmɪŋ/ n [U] (judgment in) the arrangement and control of events, actions, etc.: a dancer with perfect timing

tim·o·rous /'tɪmərəs/ adj fml afraid; nervous –timorously adv

tim·pa·ni /'tɪmpəniʸ/ n timpani [C;U] a set of KETTLEDRUMS: The timpani is too loud. –timpanist /'tɪmpənɪst/ n

tin¹ /tɪn/ n **1** [U] a soft whitish metal that is a simple substance (ELEMENT), used to cover (PLATE) metal objects with a protective shiny surface **2** [C] esp. BrE for CAN²

tin² v -nn- [T] BrE for CAN³ (1)

tin³ adj made of tin

tinc·ture /'tɪŋktʃər/ n [C;U] a medical substance mixed with alcohol

tin·der /'tɪndər/ n [U] fml any material that catches fire easily: The plants are as dry as tinder.

tin·foil /'tɪnfɔɪl/ n [U] a very thin bendable sheet of shiny metal, used as a protective wrapping, esp. for food

tinge /tɪndʒ/ v tinged, tingeing or tinging [T] to give a small amount of a color to: black hair tinged with gray|(fig.) Her admiration for him was tinged with jealousy. –tinge n [S of]: a tinge of sadness in her voice

tin·gle /'tɪŋgəl/ v -gled, -gling [I] to feel a slight prickly sensation: My fingers tingled with the cold. –tingle n [S]: (fig.) a tingle of fear/excitement

tin·ker¹ /'tɪŋkər/ n a person who travels from place to place mending metal pots, pans, etc.

tinker² v [I with] to try to repair something

without useful results: *Don't tinker with my television.*

tin·kle /'tɪŋkəl/ *v* **-kled, -kling** [I;T] to (cause to) make light ringing sounds: *The bell tinkled as he opened the shop door.* **–tinkle** *n* [*usu. sing.*]: *the tinkle of glasses*

tin·ny /'tɪniʸ/ *adj* **-nier, -niest** **1** of, like, or containing tin **2** having a thin metallic sound: *a tinny bell*

tin·sel /'tɪnsəl/ *n* [U] thin sheets or threads of shiny material used for decoration, esp. at Christmas

tint /tɪnt/ *n* a pale or delicate shade of a color **–tint** *v* [T]: *She tinted her hair red.* (=gave her hair a slight red color)

ti·ny /'taɪniʸ/ *adj* **-nier, -niest** very small –see Study Notes on page 550

tip¹ /tɪp/ *n* **1** the usu. pointed end of something: *the tip of one's nose/fingers* **2** a small end, cap, or point **3** **have (something) on the tip of one's tongue** to be about to remember (a name, word, etc.) **–tip** *v* **-pp-** [T]

tip² *v* **-pp-** **1** [I;T] to (cause to) lean at an angle: *The child tipped the plate, and the cake fell off it.* **2** [I;T *over, up*] to (cause to) fall over: *I'm sorry I tipped the bottle over.* **3** [T] to raise or touch the BRIM of (one's hat) as a greeting

tip³ *v* **-pp-** [I;T] to give a small amount of money to (a waiter, etc.) as thanks for a service performed **–tip** *n*: *I gave the taxi driver a large tip for being so helpful.* **–tipper** *n*: *He's a good tipper; he always leaves at least 20%.*

tip⁴ *v* **-pp-** [T] to strike lightly: *to tip the ball*

tip⁵ *n* [C *on*] a helpful piece of advice: *tips on cooking*

tip sbdy.↔ off *v adv* [T +*that/about*] to give secret information or a warning to: *The police were tipped off that the criminals were planning to rob the bank.*

tip-off /'· ·/ *n* a piece of secret information; warning: *a tip-off about the robbery*

tip·ster /'tɪpstər/ *n* a person who gives advice about the likely winners of horse and dog races

tip·sy /'tɪpsiʸ/ *adj* **-sier, -siest** slightly drunk **–tipsily** *adv* **–tipsiness** *n* [U]

tip·toe¹ /'tɪptoʷ/ *n* **on tiptoe** on one's toes with the rest of the feet raised above the ground

tiptoe² *v* **-toed, -toeing** [I] to walk on TIPTOE¹

ti·rade /'taɪreʸd, taɪ'reʸd/ *n* a long scolding speech

tire¹ /taɪər/ *v* **tired, tiring** [I;T *of*] to make tired: *a tiring day/She never tires of talking.*

tire sbdy.↔ out *v adv* [T] to make or become completely tired: *I'm tired out, so I'll go to bed.*

tire² *AmE*‖**tyre** *BrE* *n* a thick rubber band, solid or filled with air, that fits around the outside edge of a wheel, esp. on a motor vehicle or bicycle, as a running surface to aid to soften shocks –see illustration on page 95

tired /taɪərd/ *adj* **1** needing to rest or sleep **2** [F *of*] no longer interested in; annoyed with: *I'm tired of your stupid remarks.* **–tiredly** *adv* **–tiredness** *n* [U]

tire·less /'taɪərlɪs/ *adj* never getting tired: *a tireless worker* **–tirelessly** *adv*

tire·some /'taɪərsəm/ *adj* annoying: *a tiresome child* **–tiresomely** *adv*

tis·sue /'tɪʃuʷ/ *n* **1** [U] animal or plant cells, esp. those that make up a particular organ: *lung tissue/leaf tissue* **2** [C;U] (a piece of) soft thin paper –see illustration on page 51

tit¹ /tɪt/ *n infml* **1** for BREAST (1) **2** for NIPPLE

tit² *n* a small European bird: *a blue tit*

tit for tat /,tɪt fər 'tæt/ *n infml* something unpleasant done in return for something unpleasant one has suffered

tit·il·late /'tɪtl,eʸt/ *v* **-lated, -lating** [T] to excite pleasantly: *a titillating piece of news* **–titillation** /,tɪtl'eʸʃən/ *n* [U]

ti·tle /'taɪtl/ *n* **1** [C] a name given to a book, painting, play, etc.: *The title of the play is "Hamlet."* **2** [C] a word or name, such as "Mr.," "Senator," "Doctor," "General," etc., used before a person's name as a sign of rank, profession, etc. **3** [S;U *to*] *tech* the lawful right to ownership or possession: *Do they have any title to this land?* **4** a noble title such as "Lord"

title² *v* **-tled, -tling** [T] *AmE* to give a title to a book, movie, etc.

ti·tled /'taɪtld/ *adj* having a noble title, such as "Lord"

title deed /'·· ,·/ *n* a paper showing a person's right of ownership of property

title role /,·· '·/ *n* the chief part (ROLE) in a play, after which the play is named

tit·ter /'tɪtər/ *v* [I] to laugh quietly in a nervous or silly way **–titter** *n*

tit·tle-tat·tle /'tɪtl ,tætl/ *n* [U] *infml* for GOSSIP¹ (1)

tit·u·lar /'tɪtʃələr/ *adj* holding a title but not having the duties or power of office: *He's the titular head of the party, but he has no real power.*

tiz·zy /'tɪziʸ/ *n infml* [*usu. sing.*] a state of excited confusion

TN *written abbrev. said as:* Tennessee /,tɛnə'siʸ/ (a state in the US)

to¹ /tə, tʊ; *strong* tuʷ/ *prep* **1** going in the direction of; towards: *the road to town/He pointed to the moon./She threw the ball to me.* (=for me to catch it) **2** as far as; so as to reach: *We went to San Francisco./They sent him to prison./The traffic lights changed to green./Count from 1 to 20./They stayed here from Monday to/till Friday./ten to twelve feet of water* (=between ten and twelve) **3** (used with words about sending, giving, or belonging): *I'm writing a letter/writing to John./She wants a room to herself.* **4** touching or facing: *The paper stuck to the wall./sitting with my back to/towards the engine* **5** in connection with: *kind to animals/the key to the door/They live* **next door to** *me.* **6** (used with words about addition): *Add 2 to 4.* **7** (of the clock) before: *It's five (minutes) to four.* (= 3:55. **Till** is not used here.) **8** per; in each: *There are 100 cents to the dollar.*

to² *adv* **1** into consciousness: *After he hit his head, he didn't* **come to** *for half an hour.* **2** so as to be shut: *The wind blew the door to.* **3** **close/near to** really close: *When we got close to the birds, they flew away.*

to³ (**to** can be used before a verb to show it is

in the INFINITIVE) **1** (after certain verbs): *He wants to go.|You ought to understand.* **2** (describing what someone asked, advised, warned, etc.) **a**: *He told them to shoot.* (=He said "Shoot!") **b** (after *how, what, when, where, whether, which, who, whom, whose*): *Tell me where to go!|He wondered what to do.* **3** (after some nouns): *They made an attempt to land.* **4** (after some adjectives): *I'm sorry to hear it.* **5** (when using a verb like a noun): *To wear boots would be safest.|It would be safest to wear boots.* **6** (when speaking of purpose): *He said it to annoy her/so as to annoy her.|I want some scissors to cut my nails with/in order to cut my nails.|There were plenty of things to eat.* –see Study Notes on page 144 **7** (with *too* and *enough*, when speaking of result): *He's too fat to dance.|It's cold enough to snow.*

USAGE In general, it is a good idea to avoid putting any other word between **to** and the verb that follows it, as in *He tried to quietly leave the room.* This is called a **split infinitive.** But sometimes there is no other way to arrange the sentence, as in *Your job is to really understand these children.*

toad /tow̥d/ *n* an animal like a large FROG (1)

toad·stool /'tow̥dstuʷl/ *n* a fleshy, usu. poisonous plant (FUNGUS) that looks like the MUSHROOM

to-and-fro /ˌ· · '·/ *adj* backwards and forwards or from side to side: *a to-and-fro movement* –**to and fro** *adv*: *The teacher walked to and fro in front of the class.*

toast¹ /tow̥st/ *n* **1** [U] bread made brown by being heated **2** [C] a call on other people to drink and wish for someone's success and happiness: *to drink a toast to the newly married pair* **3** [*the* S] the person or thing in whose honor this is done

toast² *v* [T] to make (bread, cheese, etc.) brown by holding it close to heat: (fig.) *to toast* (=warm) *one's feet by the fire* –see COOK (USAGE)

toast³ *v* [T] to drink and wish for the success and happiness of (someone or something): *He was toasted by all his friends.*

toast·er /'tow̥stər/ *n* an electric apparatus for TOASTING bread –see illustration on page 379

to·bac·co /tə'bækow̥/ *n* [U] a plant or its large leaves, prepared for smoking in cigarettes, pipes, etc.

to·bac·co·nist /tə'bækənɪst/ *n* a person who sells tobacco, cigarettes, etc.

to·bog·gan /tə'bɑgən/ *n* a board curved up at the front, for carrying people over snow, esp. down slopes –**toboggan** *v* [I]: *children tobogganing in the snow*

to·day /tə'deɪ/ *adv,n* **1** (on) this present day: *Today's my birthday!|Are we going shopping today?* **2** (at) this present time; now: *the young people of today|People travel more today than they used to.*

tod·dle /'tɑdl/ *v* -dled, -dling [I *about*] to walk with short unsteady steps, as a small child does

tod·dler /'tɑdlər/ *n* a child who has just learned to walk –see CHILD (USAGE)

to-do /tə 'duʷ/ *n* [*usu. sing.*] *infml* a state of

excited confusion: *What a to-do about nothing!*

toe¹ /tow̥/ *n* **1** one of the five parts at the end of each foot –compare FINGER¹ **2 on one's toes** ready for action

toe² *v* **toed, toeing** [T] **toe the line** to obey orders

toe·nail /'tow̥neɪl/ *n* one of the hard flat pieces that cover the ends of the fronts of the toes

tof·fee, toffy /'tɔfiʸ, 'tɑfiʸ/ *n* -fees, -fies [C;U] (a piece of) a hard brown candy made by boiling sugar and butter

to·ga /'tow̥gə/ *n* a loose outer garment worn by the ancient Romans

to·geth·er /tə'gɛðər/ *adv* **1** into one group; so as to be joined: *The people gathered together.|Tie the ends together.|Add these numbers together.* **2** with one another: *Her eyes are too close together.|We went to school together.* **3** at the same time: *Why do all the bills seem to come together?* **4 together with** as well as; in addition to: *He sent her some roses, together with a nice letter.* **6 get it/one's act together** *infml* to arrange (oneself or things) in an orderly way; to work in a way that has good results

to·geth·er·ness /tə'gɛðərnɪs/ *n* [U] a feeling of being united with other people; friendliness

tog·gle /'tɑgəl/ *n* an instrument used to hold something or keep it tight, esp. a kind of pin used in boating

togs /tɑgz, tɔgz/ *n* [P] *infml* for clothes

toil /tɔɪl/ *v* [I] *fml or lit* **1** to work hard and untiringly **2** to move with tiredness, difficulty, or pain: *The slaves toiled up the hill pulling the heavy blocks.* –**toil** *n* [U]

toi·let /'tɔɪlɪt/ *n* **1** [C] (a room with) a large seatlike bowl connected to a pipe (DRAIN), used for getting rid of the body's waste matter –see illustration on page 51 **2** [U] *fml* the act of washing, dressing oneself, and taking care of one's appearance

toilet pa·per /'·· ˌ·'·/ *n* [U] thin paper for cleaning the body when waste matter has been passed from it –see illustration on page 51

toi·let·ries /'tɔɪlətriʸz/ *n* [P] articles or substances used in dressing, washing, etc.

toilet wa·ter /'·· ˌ·'·/ *n* [U] a pleasant-smelling but not very strong PERFUME¹ (2)

to·ken /'tow̥kən/ *n* **1** [A;C] a sign or reminder; small part meant to represent something greater: *The whole family wore black as a token of their grief.|a token payment|a token* STRIKE² **2** [C] a piece of metal in the shape of a coin used instead of money, for a particular purpose: *a bus/subway token*

told /tow̥ld/ *v past tense & participle of* TELL

tol·er·a·ble /'tɑlərəbəl/ *adj* fairly good; that can be TOLERATED –see also INTOLERABLE –**tolerably** *adv*: *I feel tolerably well today.*

tol·er·ance /'tɑlərəns/ *n* **1** [C;U *for, of, to*] the ability to suffer pain, hardship, etc., without being damaged: *He has no tolerance of cold weather.* **2** [U *for*] the quality of allowing people to behave in a way that may not please one, without becoming annoyed: *He has no tolerance for people who disagree* *with him.* **3** [U] → TOLERATION

tol·er·ant /ˈtɑlərənt/ *adj* showing or practising TOLERANCE (2) **–tolerantly** *adv*

tol·er·ate /ˈtɑləˌreʸt/ *v* **-ated, -ating** [T] to allow (something one does not like) to be practiced or done: *I can't tolerate bad manners.* –see BEAR (USAGE)

tol·er·a·tion /ˌtɑləˈreʸʃən/ *n* [U] **1** the quality or practice of allowing opinions, beliefs, behavior, etc., different from one's own, to be held and practiced freely: *religious toleration* **2** → TOLERANCE (2)

toll¹ /toʷl/ *n* **1** a tax paid to use a road, bridge, etc. **2** [*usu. sing.*] the cost in health, life, etc., from something: *the death toll from road accidents*|*Years of worry have* **taken their toll** *on him.*

toll² *v* [I;T] to ring (a bell) slowly and repeatedly **–toll** *n* [S]: *the toll of the bell*

toll call /ˈ· ·/ *n* a telephone call for which the charge is higher than for local calls: *My phone bill was very high because I made so many toll calls to Houston.*|*For more information, call this number* **toll free.** (=without extra charge)

toll·gate /ˈtoʷlgeʸt/ *n* a gate at which a TOLL¹ (1) must be paid

tom·a·hawk /ˈtɑməˌhɔk/ *n* a small light ax used by North American Indians

to·ma·to /təˈmeʸtoʷ/ *n* **-toes** **1** [C;U] (a) soft red fruit eaten as a vegetable **2** [C] the plant on which this fruit grows

tomb /tuʷm/ *n* a grave, esp. a large decorated one

tom·boy /ˈtɑmbɔɪ/ *n* **-boys** a spirited young girl who likes to be rough and noisy **–tomboyish** *adj*

tomb·stone /ˈtuʷmstoʷn/ *n* → GRAVESTONE

tom·cat /ˈtɑmkæt/ also **tom** /tɑm/ *infml*– *n* a male cat

tome /toʷm/ *n lit or humor* a large book

tom·fool·er·y /ˌtɑmˈfuʷləriʸ/ *n* [U] foolish behavior

to·mor·row /təˈmɔroʷ, -ˈmɑr-/ *adv,n* **1** (on) the day after today: *Tomorrow's my birthday!*|*We're going to a party tomorrow.*| *tomorrow night* –compare YESTERDAY **2** (in) the future: *tomorrow's world*

tom-tom /ˈtɑm tɑm/ *n* a long narrow drum, beaten with the hands

ton /tʌn/ *n* **tons** *or* **ton** **1** a measurement of weight equal in the US to 2,000 pounds and in Britain to 2,240 pounds **2** also **metric ton**– a measurement of weight equal to one thousand kilos **3** a measurement of **a** the size of a ship equal to one hundred CUBIC feet **b** the amount of goods a ship can carry equal to forty CUBIC feet **4** [*of*] *infml* a very large quantity or weight: *I bought tons of food.*|*This book weighs a ton!*

tone¹ /toʷn/ *n* **1** [C] a sound, esp. of a musical instrument or singing voice, considered with regard to its quality **2** [C] a particular quality of the voice; manner of expression: *to speak in low tones*|*I don't like your tone (of voice).* **3** [C] a variety of a color: *a picture painted in tones of blue* **4** [U] the general quality: *Her funny opening speech set the tone for the evening.* **5** [C] also **step** *AmE*– *tech* a fixed

distance between musical notes in a SCALE² (5): *There is a tone between B and C sharp; B and C are half a tone apart.* **–tonal** /ˈtoʷnl/ *adj*

tone² *v* **toned, toning**→TONE DOWN, TONE IN, TONE UP

tone-deaf /ˈ· ·/ *adj* unable to tell the difference between musical notes

tone sthg.↔ **down** *v adv* **toned, toning** [T] to reduce the violence or force of: *You must tone down your language; stop swearing.*

tone in *v adv* **toned, toning** [I *with*] to match: *Your hat and shoes tone in well with your dress.*

tone·less /ˈtoʷnlɪs/ *adj* lacking color and spirit; lifeless: *a toneless voice* **–tonelessly** *adv*

tone sbdy./sthg.↔ **up** *v adv* **toned, toning** [T] to make stronger, more healthy, etc.: *Swimming is the best way to tone up your body.*

tongs /tɑŋz, tɔŋz/ *n* [P] an instrument with two movable arms, used for holding or lifting: *She used the tongs to put the coal onto the fire.* –see PAIR (USAGE)

tongue /tʌŋ/ *n* **1** [C] the movable fleshy organ in the mouth, used for tasting, producing speech, etc. **2** [C;U] this organ taken from an animal such as the ox, used as food **3** [C] an object like a TONGUE (1) in shape or purpose, such as the piece of material under the LACES in a shoe: (fig.) *tongues of flame* **4** [C] a spoken language: *My native tongue is English.* **5** **hold one's tongue** *usu. in commands* to remain silent **6** **(with) (one's) tongue in (one's) cheek** *infml* saying or doing something one does not seriously mean **7** **-tongued:** **a** having a certain kind of tongue: *a fork-tongued snake* **b** having a certain way of speaking: *sharp-tongued*

tongue-tied /ˈ· ·/ *adj* unable to speak freely, e.g. through nervousness

tongue twist·er /ˈ· ˌ··/ *n* a word or phrase difficult to speak quickly

ton·ic /ˈtɑnɪk/ *n* anything which increases health or strength: *Country air is a good tonic.*|*The doctor gave me a special tonic.* (=medicine) **–tonic** *adj*

tonic wa·ter /ˈ·· ˌ··/ also **tonic**– [U] gassy water made bitter with QUININE, often added to alcoholic drinks: *a gin and tonic*

to·night /təˈnaɪt/ *adv,n* (on) this present night, or the one after today: *tonight's TV news*|*Let's go to bed early tonight; we were out late last night.*

ton·nage /ˈtʌnɪdʒ/ *n* [U] **1** the amount of goods a ship can carry, or its size, expressed in TONS (3) **2** the total shipping of a navy, port, or country, expressed in TONS (3)

ton·sil /ˈtɑnsəl/ *n* one of two small organs at the sides of the throat near the back of the tongue

ton·sil·li·tis, tonsilitis /ˌtɑnsəˈlaɪṭɪs/ *n* [U] a disease of the TONSILS

too /tuʷ/ *adv* **1** [+*to-v*] more than enough; more than is good: *You're going too fast, slow down!*|*This dress is too small* (=not big enough) *for me.*|*It's too cold to go swimming.*|*He wasn't too pleased.* (=he was rather annoyed) **2** also; as well: *I can dance; I can sing, too.* (Compare *I can't dance; I can't*

sing, either.) –see Study Notes on page 144
USAGE One can say *The day is* **too** *hot or It's*
too *hot a day* (notice the word order); but **too**
cannot be used in the pattern **too** + adjective
+ noun, so one cannot say **a* **too** *hot day.*

took /tʊk/ *v past tense of* TAKE[1]

tool /tuʷl/ *n* **1** any instrument such as an ax,
hammer, spade, etc., for doing a special job
–see MACHINE (USAGE) **2** a person unfairly
used by another for the other person's own
purposes

toot /tuʷt/ *v* [I;T] to (cause to) make a short
warning sound as with a horn, whistle, etc.:
The cyclist tooted his horn. –**toot** *n: to give a
short toot on the horn*

tooth /tuʷθ/ *n* **teeth** /tiʸθ/ **1** one of the small
hard bony objects in the mouth, used for
biting and tearing food **2** any of the pointed
parts that stand out from a comb, SAW, etc. **3**
long in the tooth *infml* old **4 sweet tooth** a
liking for food which is sweet and sugary **5**
tooth and nail very violently: *to fight tooth
and nail* –see also TEETH

tooth·ache /'tuʷθeʸk/ *n* [C;U] (a) pain in a
tooth

tooth·brush /'tuʷθbrʌʃ/ *n* a small brush used
for cleaning the teeth –see illustration on
page 51

tooth·paste /'tuʷθpeʸst/ *n* [U] a substance
used for cleaning the teeth –see illustration
on page 51

tooth·pick /'tuʷθ,pɪk/ *n* a small pointed piece
of wood used for removing food stuck between the teeth

top[1] /tɑp/ *n* **1** [A;C] the highest or upper part:
*the top of the page/hill | The mountain tops
were hidden in mist. | They live on the top
floor. | the top* (=upper surface) *of my
desk | the table top* **2** [*the* S *of*] the best or most
important position: *He started life at the bottom and worked his way to the top.* –compare
BOTTOM **3** [C] a cover: *I can't unscrew the top
of this bottle.* **4** [C] a garment worn on the
upper part of the body **5 at the top of (one's)
voice** as loudly as possible **6 at top speed** very
fast **7 off the top of one's head** without time to
consider; without careful thought: *I can't
give you an answer off the top of my head.* **8
on top of** *infml* having gained mastery of or
control over: *I don't feel on top of this problem yet.* **9 on top (of)** in addition (to): *He lost
his job, and on top of that his wife left him.* **10
on top of the world** very happy **11 to top it all
(off)** to complete good or bad fortune: *His
house burned down, his car was stolen, and
to top it all off he lost his job.*

top[2] *adj* at the top; first or best: *Fred is our top
man.*

top[3] *v* **-pp-** [T] **1** to form or be a top for: *a cake
topped with cream* **2** to be higher, better, or
more than: *Their profits have topped ours
this year.* **3** to remove the top from (a vegetable, fruit, etc.) **4 top billing** the position of
chief actor or actress in a play

top *sthg.↔* **off** *v adv* [T *with*] *AmE* to complete successfully: *Let's top off the evening
with a drink.*

top[4] *n* a child's toy that spins and balances on
its point

to·paz /'toʷpæz/ *n* [C;U] (a precious stone
cut from) a transparent yellowish mineral

top·coat /'tɑpkoʷt/ *n* → OVERCOAT

top dog /ˌ· '·/ *n infml* the person in the most
important position

top hat /ˌ· '·/ *n* a man's formal tall silk hat

top-heav·y /ˌ· '··/ *adj* [F] not properly
balanced because of too much weight at the
top

top·ic /'tɑpɪk/ *n* a subject for conversation,
talk, writing, etc.

top·i·cal /'tɑpɪkəl/ *adj* of, related to, or being
a subject of present interest: *Recent events
have made this movie very topical.* –**topically**
adv

USAGE **Topical** has the same connection
with time as **local** has with place: *a book of
great* **topical** *interest* (=interesting now but
not always) | *a book of great* **local** *interest*
(=interesting here but not everywhere)

top·less /'tɑplɪs/ *adj* (of a woman or a garment) leaving the upper part of the body,
including the breasts, bare

top·most /'tɑpmoʷst/ *adj* highest

to·pog·ra·phy /tə'pɑgrəfiʸ/ *n* [U] (the science
of describing or mapping) the character of a
place, esp. as regards the shape and height of
the land –**topographer** *n* –**topographical**
/ˌtɑpə'græfɪkəl/ *adj* –**topographically** *adv*

top·ping /'tɑpɪŋ/ *n* [C;U] something put on
top of food: *cream topping*

top·ple /'tɑpəl/ *v* **-pled, -pling** [I;T *over*] to
make or become unsteady and fall down:
(fig.) *The government was toppled by the
army.*

top-se·cret /ˌ· '··◄/ *adj* to be kept very
secret: *top-secret military information*

top-sy-tur·vy /ˌtɑpsiʸ 'tɜrviʸ◄/ *adv,adj* in a
state of confusion

torch /tɔrtʃ/ *n* **1** a mass of burning material
tied to a stick and used to give light **2** *AmE*
for BLOWTORCH **3 carry a torch for** to be in
love with (someone, esp. a person who does
not return the love)

torch·light /'tɔrtʃlaɪt/ *n* [U] light produced by
TORCHes (1): *a torchlight procession*

tore /tɔr, toʷr/ *v past tense of* TEAR[2]

to·re·a·dor /'tɔriʸə,dɔr/ *n* one of the men who
takes part in a Spanish BULLFIGHT riding on a
horse –compare MATADOR

tor·ment[1] /'tɔrment/ *n* [C;U] (a cause of) very
great pain or suffering: *He was in torment
after the operation. | to suffer torments | That
child is a torment to his parents.*

tor·ment[2] /tɔr'ment, 'tɔrment/ *v* [T] to cause
to suffer pain –**tormentor** *n*

torn[1] /tɔrn, toʷrn/ *adj* [*apart, between*]
divided by opposing forces: *He was torn between the desire to leave his wife and go away,
and his love for his children.*

torn[2] *v past participle of* TEAR[2]

tor·na·do /tɔr'neʸdoʷ/ *n* **-does** *or* **-dos** a very
violent wind that spins at great speeds

tor·pe·do /tɔr'piʸdoʷ/ *n* **-does** a long explosive
shell, driven along under the sea by its own
motors, used to destroy ships –**torpedo** *v*
-doed, -doing [T]: *We torpedoed the enemy
ships.*

tor·pid /'tɔrpɪd/ *adj fml* inactive; slow: *a tor-*

pid mind **–torpidly** *adv* **–torpor** /'tɔrpər/ *n* [U]

tor·rent /'tɔrənt, 'tɑr-/ *n* a violently rushing stream: *The rain fell* **in torrents.**|*A torrent of water swept down the valley.*|(fig.) *a torrent of bad language* **–torrential** /tɔ'rɛnʃəl, -tʃəl, tə-/ *adj: torrential rain*

tor·rid /'tɔrɪd, 'tɑr-/ *adj* **1** very hot: *torrid weather* **2** concerning strong uncontrolled feelings: *a torrid story of sex and violence* **–torridly** *adv*

tor·sion /'tɔrʃən/ *n* [U] *tech* twisting or turning; being twisted or turned

tor·so /'tɔrsoʷ/ *n* **-sos** the human body without the head and limbs; TRUNK (2)

tor·toise /'tɔrtəs/ *n* a slow-moving land animal with a soft body covered by a hard shell **–compare** TURTLE

tor·toise·shell /'tɔrtə,ʃɛl, 'tɔrtəs,ʃɛl/ *n* [U] (the color of) the hard brown and yellow shell of the TORTOISE or TURTLE, used for making combs, boxes, etc.

tor·tu·ous /'tɔrtʃuʷəs/ *adj* **1** twisted; winding **2** not direct; DEVIOUS or deceiving: *a tortuous argument* **–tortuously** *adv* **–tortuousness** *n* [U]

tor·ture¹ /'tɔrtʃər/ *n* **1** [U] the causing of severe pain, done out of cruelty, to find out information, etc. **2** [C;U] (a) severe pain or suffering: *the tortures of jealousy*

torture² *v* **-tured, -turing** [T] to cause great pain to (a person or animal) out of cruelty, as a punishment, etc.: *The prisoner was tortured to make him admit to the crime.* **–torturer** *n*

toss /tɔs/ *v* **1** [T *to, around*] to throw: *We tossed around a ball.*|*He tossed the keys to Ann.* **2** [I;T *around*] to (cause to) move about rapidly: *The boat was tossed around in the stormy sea.*|*Unable to sleep, he tossed and turned all night.*|*The horse tossed its head back.* **3** [T] to mix lightly: *to toss a* SALAD **4** [I;T *up, for*] to throw (a coin) to decide something according to which side lands face upwards: *There's only one cake and two of us, so let's toss for it.* **–toss** *n* [C;S]: *a quick toss of the head*|*Our team won the toss so we play first.*

toss sthg.↔ **off** *v adv* [T] to produce quickly with little effort: *She tossed off a few ideas for advertising the new product.*

toss-up /'··/ *n* [S] *infml* an even chance: *It's a toss-up between the two of them as to who will get the job.*

tot /tɑt/ *n* **1** a very small child: *a tiny tot* **2** *esp. BrE* a small amount of a strong alcoholic drink: *a tot of rum*/*whiskey*

to·tal¹ /'toʷtl/ *adj* complete; whole: *the total population of Mexico*|*total silence* **–totally** *adv: I totally agree with you.* **–see** Study Notes on page 363

total² *n* a number or quantity obtained by adding; complete amount: *Add these numbers together and tell me the total.*|*A total of two hundred people visited the castle.*|**In total,** *there were two hundred visitors.*

total³ *v* **-l-** *AmE*||**-ll-** *BrE* [T] to equal a total of; add up to: *Your debts total one thousand dollars.*

to·tal·i·tar·i·an /toʷ,tælə'tɛəriʸən/ *adj* of or being a political system in which one political group controls everything and does not allow opposition parties to exist

to·tal·i·ty /toʷ'tælətiʸ/ *n* [U] *fml* completeness

tote /toʷt/ *v* **toted, toting** [T] *infml* to carry

tote bag /'··/ *n* a large bag for carrying books, small goods, etc.

to·tem /'toʷtəm/ *n* (a representation of) an animal, plant, or object thought to have a close relationship with the family group: *The North American Indians used to make* **totem poles.** (=tall poles with totems painted onto them)

tot·ter /'tɑtər/ *v* [I] to move or walk in an unsteady way: *The old lady tottered down the stairs.*

tot·ter·y /'tɑtəriʸ/ *adj* unsteady; shaky

tou·can /'tuʷkæn, -kən/ *n* a brightly colored tropical bird with a large beak

touch¹ /tʌtʃ/ *v* **1** [I;T] to be not separated from (something) by any space: *Stand close together so that your shoulders are touching.*|*The branches hung down and touched the water.* **2** [I;T] to feel or press with a part of the body, esp. the hands or fingers: *Visitors are asked not to touch the paintings.*|*You can look, but you can't touch.*|*He touched the bell, and a servant appeared.*|(fig.) *In his talk he* **touched on** (=mentioned shortly) *the state of affairs in Africa.* **3** [T *usu. negative*] to take action concerning; handle; use: *He swore he'd never touch a drink* (=whisky, alcohol) *again.*|*He put away the book he was writing and didn't touch it again for years.*|*You haven't touched* (=eaten) *your food; I hope you're not ill.* **4** [T *usu. negative*] to compare with; be equal to: *No one can touch the Swiss at making watches.* **5** [T] to cause to feel pity: *His sad story so touched me*/*my heart that I nearly cried.*|*a touching story* **6** **touch wood** to touch something made of wood in order to turn away bad luck **–touchable** *adj*

touch down *v adv* [I] (of a plane) to land

touch off sthg. *v adv* [T] to cause to explode: (fig.) *His stupid remarks touched off a fight.*

touch sthg.↔ **up** *v adv* [T] to improve by making small changes or additions

touch² *n* **1** [U] the sense by which a material object is known to be hard, smooth, rough, cold, hot, etc.: *A cat's fur is soft to the touch.* (=feels soft) **2** [C] an act of touching: *He felt the touch of her hand on his shoulder.* **3** [U] connection so as to receive information: *I'm trying to* **get in touch with** *my brother.*|*Please write; it would be nice to* **keep in touch**/*I don't want us to* **lose touch.**|*I'd like to go back to teaching, but I'm* **out of touch** *with my subject now.*|(fig.) *I think you've* **lost touch with** *reality.* **4** [S *of*] a slight amount: *This soup needs a touch of salt.*|*She's got a touch of fever.* **5** [C] a slight added detail that improves or completes something: *I'm just putting* **the finishing touches** *on the cake.* **6** [S;U] skill, esp. in artistic performance: *The piano player had a delicate touch.*|*He's lost another game; do you think he's* **losing his touch**?

touch-and-go /,···'·◄/ *adj* risky; of uncertain result: *It was touch-and-go whether he would* *get there in time.*

touch·down /'tʌtʃdaʊn/ *n* **1** (in American football) an action giving a team six points, made by carrying or catching the ball beyond the opposing team's GOAL (2) line **2** the landing of a plane

touched /tʌtʃt/ *adj* [F] **1** feeling grateful: *I was very touched by their present.* **2** *infml* slightly mad

touch·stone /'tʌtʃstoʷn/ *n* anything used as a test or standard; CRITERION

touch·y /'tʌtʃiʸ/ *adj* **-ier, -iest** easily offended; too sensitive **–touchily** *adv* **–touchiness** *n* [U]

tough¹ /tʌf/ *adj* **1** strong; not easily weakened: *Only tough breeds of sheep can live in the mountains.* | **as tough as nails** (=very tough) **2** difficult to cut or eat: *tough meat* –opposite **tender 3** difficult to do; demanding effort: *a tough lesson/job* **4** rough; hard: *The government will get tough with people who avoid paying taxes.* | *a tough criminal* **5** *infml* too bad; unfortunate: *Tough luck!* **–toughly** *adv* **–toughness** *n* [U]

tough² *n infml* a rough violent person, esp. a criminal

tough·en /'tʌfən/ *v* [I;T *up*] to make or become TOUGH¹ (1,2)

tou·pee /tuʷ'peʸ/ *n* a piece of false hair that fits over a place on a man's head where the hair no longer grows

tour¹ /tʊər/ *n* **1** [*around*] a journey during which several places are visited: *a tour around Europe* | *The singer is currently* **on tour** *in South America.* **2** [*around*] a short trip to or through a place: *We went on a guided tour around the castle.* **3** [*in*] a period of duty at a single place or job, esp. abroad: *a two-year tour in Germany*

tour² *v* [I;T] to visit as a tourist: *We're touring Italy on our vacation.*

tour de force /ˌtʊər də 'fɔrs, -'foʷrs/ *n* [S] *French* a show of strength or skill

tour·ism /'tʊərɪzəm/ *n* [U] **1** the business of providing lodging, food, and services for tourists **2** the practice of traveling for pleasure

tour·ist /'tʊərɪst/ *n* a person traveling for pleasure: *a cheap tourist hotel*

tour·na·ment /'tʊərnəmənt, 'tɜr-/ *n* **1** a number of competitions between players, played until the most skillful wins: *a tennis tournament* **2** (in former times) a competition of courage and skill between noble soldiers (KNIGHTs) fighting with weapons

tour·ni·quet /'tʊərnɪkɪt, 'tɜr-/ *n* anything, esp. a band of cloth, twisted tightly around a limb to stop bleeding

tou·sle /'taʊzəl/ *v* **-sled, -sling** [T] to disarrange (esp. the hair); make untidy

tout¹ /taʊt/ *v* [I *for*] to try to persuade people to buy one's goods, use one's services, etc.: *touting for business*

tout² *n* a person who TOUTs¹

tow¹ /toʷ/ *v* [T] to pull (a vehicle) along by a rope or chain

tow² *n* [C;U] **1** an act of TOWing or the state of being TOWed **2 in tow** *infml* following closely behind: *She arrived with her children in tow.*

to·ward /tɔrd, toʷrd, tə'wɔrd/ also **towards**
/tɔrdz, toʷrdz, tə'wɔrdz/– *prep* **1** in the direction of: *She was walking toward town when I met her.* | *He stood with his back toward me.* **2** not long before: *Toward the end of the afternoon, it began to rain.* **3** in relation to: *What are his feelings toward us?* **4** for part payment of: *We save $15 a week toward our trip to Mexico.*

tow·el¹ /'taʊəl/ *n* a piece of cloth or paper used for drying wet things –see illustration on page 51

towel² *v* **-l-** *AmE*‖**-ll-** *BrE* [T] to rub or dry with a TOWEL¹

to·wel·ing *AmE*‖**towelling** *BrE* /'taʊəlɪŋ/ *n* [U] thickish cloth, used for making esp. TOWELs¹

tow·er¹ /'taʊər/ *n* a tall building standing alone or forming part of a castle, church, etc.: *the Tower of London* | *the Eiffel Tower* | *a radio/television tower*

tower² *v* [I *above, over*] to be very tall, esp. in relation to the surroundings: *The mountains towered over the town in the valley.* | *towering trees*

town /taʊn/ *n* **1** [C] a large group of houses and other buildings where people live and work –compare CITY, VILLAGE **2** [S] the business or shopping center of such a place: *We went into (the) town to do some shopping today.* | *I was* **in town** *on business last week.* **3** [C] the people who live in a TOWN (1): *The whole town is in agreement about the plan.* **4 go to town** *infml* to act freely, esp. by spending a lot of money **5 (out) on the town** *infml* enjoying oneself, esp. at night

town hall /ˌ· '·/ *n* a building used for a town's local government offices and public meetings

town·ship /'taʊnʃɪp/ *n* **1** (in the US and Canada) a town, or town and the area around it, that has certain powers of local government **2** (in South Africa) a place where nonwhite citizens live

towns·peo·ple /'taʊnzˌpiʸpəl/ also **townsfolk** /'taʊnzfoʷk/– *n* [*the* P] the people who live in a town

tox·ic /'taksɪk/ *adj* poisonous: *a toxic drug* | *toxic waste from a factory* **–toxicity** /tak'sɪsəṭiʸ/ *n* [U]

tox·i·col·o·gy /ˌtaksɪ'kalədʒiʸ/ *n* [U] the scientific and medical study of poisons **–toxicologist** *n*

tox·in /'taksɪn/ *n* a poison produced by bacteria in a plant or animal body

toy /tɔɪ/ *n* [A;C] **1** an object for children to play with: *a toy soldier* **2** (being) a small breed of dog: *a toy* POODLE

toy with sthg. *v prep* [T] to play with purposelessly: *a child toying with food* | (fig.) *He toyed with* (=considered, but not seriously) *the idea of changing his job.*

trace¹ /treʸs/ *v* **traced, tracing** [T] **1** to follow the course, line, history, development, etc., of: *The criminal was traced to Chicago.* | *His family can trace its history back to the tenth century.* | *to trace the beginnings of the women's rights movement* | *I can't trace* (=find) *the letter you sent me.* **2** to copy the lines or shape of (a drawing, map, etc.) using transparent paper (**tracing paper**) **–traceable** *adj*

trace² *n* **1** [C;U] a mark or sign showing the former presence or passing of something or someone: *The police found no trace of the man.|lost without trace* **2** [C] a very small amount of something: *traces of poison in the dead man's blood*

trac·ing /'treʸsɪŋ/ *n* a copy of a map, drawing, etc., made by tracing (TRACE¹ (2))

track¹ /træk/ *n* **1** a line or number of marks left by a person, animal, vehicle, etc., that has passed before: *We followed the fox's tracks.|The police are* **on his track** (=following him) *and hope to catch him soon.* **2** a rough path or road: *a bicycle track* **3** the metal lines on which a train runs **4** a course specially prepared for racing: *a racetrack* **5** one of the pieces of music on a long-playing record or TAPE¹ (2) **6 a one-track mind** *infml* a tendency to give all one's attention to one subject **7 in one's tracks** *infml* where one is; suddenly: *He stopped in his tracks when he saw her.* **8 keep/lose track (of)** to keep/not keep oneself informed about a person, state of affairs, etc. **9 off the beaten track** not well-known or often visited **10 on the right/wrong track** thinking or working correctly/incorrectly **11 the wrong side of the tracks** the less outwardly pleasant part of a town where poorer people live: *He never let her forget that she was from the wrong side of the tracks.*

track² *v* [T] to follow the track of something or someone **–tracker** *n: Because it had snowed, the trackers had no problem finding the criminals.*

track sbdy./sthg.↔ **down** *v adv* [T] to find by hunting or searching

track meet /'· ·/ *n* a sports competition with a variety of running and jumping events

track·suit /'træksuʷt/ *n* a warm loose-fitting suit worn by people when training for sports

tract¹ /trækt/ *n* a short article, esp. about a religious or moral subject

tract² *n* **1** a wide stretch of land **2** *tech* a system of related organs, with one purpose: *the* DIGESTIVE *tract*

trac·ta·ble /'træktəbəl/ *adj fml* easily controlled **–tractability** /ˌtræktə'bɪləṭiʸ/ *n* [U]

trac·tion /'trækʃən/ *n* [U] (the power used for) pulling a heavy load over a surface: *steam traction*

trac·tor /'træktər/ *n* a motor vehicle with large wheels and thick tires used for pulling farm machinery or other heavy objects

trade¹ /treʸd/ *n* **1** [U] the business of buying and selling goods: *a trade agreement between the US and Mexico* **2** [C] a particular business or industry: *He works in the cotton/tourist trade.* **3** [C] a job, esp. one needing special skills: *the trade of a printer|He's a printer* **by trade**. **4** [*the*] the people who work in a particular business or industry: *This talk is only likely to be of interest to the trade.* –see JOB (USAGE)

trade² *v* **traded, trading 1** [I *in, with*] to carry on trade: *He trades in meat.|to trade with another country* **2** [T *for*] to buy, sell, or

exchange: *They traded their clothes for food.*

trade sthg.↔ **in** *v adv* [T *for*] to give in part payment for something new: *to trade an old car in for a new one* **–trade-in** /'· ·/ *n*

trade·mark /'treʸdmɑrk/ *n* a special mark or a name for a product to show that it is made by a particular producer

trade name /'· ·/ also **brand name**– *n* a name given to a particular product, by which it may be recognized among those made by other producers

trad·er /'treʸdər/ *n* a person who buys and sells goods

trade school /'· ·/ *n* a high school where students are taught a TRADE (3)

trades·man /'treʸdzmən/ *n* **-men** /mən/ **1** a person who buys and sells goods, esp. a storekeeper **2** a skilled worker

trade un·ion /'· ˌ··/ *n esp. BrE* for LABOR UNION

trade wind /'· ·/ *n* a tropical wind that blows towards the EQUATOR (=the imaginary line running around the middle of the earth)

tra·di·tion /trə'dɪʃən/ *n* **1** [U] the passing down of opinions, beliefs, practices, customs, etc., from the past to the present **2** [C] an opinion, belief, custom, etc., passed down in this way: *It is a tradition that women get married in long white dresses.* **–traditional** *adj: the traditional Christmas dinner* **–traditionally** *adv*

traffic¹ /'træfɪk/ *n* [U] **1** moving vehicles in roads or streets, ships in the seas, planes in the sky, etc. –compare CIRCULATION (2) **2** trade; buying and selling: *the illegal traffic in drugs*

traffic² *v* **-ck-** → TRAFFIC IN

traffic cir·cle /'·· ˌ··/ also **rotary** *AmE*‖**roundabout** *BrE*– *n* a central space at a road crossing which makes cars go in a circle around it

traffic in sthg. *v prep* **-ck-** [T *with*] to carry on trade, esp. of an illegal kind, in (the stated goods): *trafficking in stolen goods* **–trafficker** *n* [*in*]

traffic light /'·· ˌ·/ also **traffic signal** /'·· ˌ··/ *n* a set of electrically powered colored lights used for controlling and directing traffic on roads –see illustration on page 673

trag·e·dy /'trædʒədiʸ/ *n* **-dies 1** [C] a serious play that ends sadly: *Shakespeare's "Hamlet" is a very famous tragedy.* **2** [U] these plays considered as a group –compare COMEDY **3** [C;U] a terrible, unhappy, or unfortunate event: *It was a tragedy that she died so young.* **–tragic** /'trædʒɪk/ *adj: a tragic actress|a tragic accident* **–tragically** *adv*

trail¹ /treʸl/ *v* **1** [I;T *along, behind*] to drag or be dragged behind: *The child was trailing a toy car on a string.|Her long skirt was trailing (along) behind her.* **2** [T] to follow the tracks of: *The hunters trailed the elephant for hours.* **3** [I *along, behind*] to walk tiredly: *The defeated army trailed back to camp.* **4** [I] (of a plant) to grow over or along the ground

trail² *n* **1** the track or smell of a person or animal **2** a path across rough country **3** a stream of dust, smoke, etc., behind something moving

trail·er /'treʸlər/ *n* **1** a vehicle pulled by

another vehicle: *a car pulling a boat on a trailer* –see illustration on page 95 **2** *AmE*‖**caravan** *BrE*– a vehicle which can be pulled by car, which contains apparatus for cooking and sleeping, and in which people live or travel, usu. for vacations **3** an advertisement for a new movie, showing small parts of it

train¹ /treᵞn/ *n* **1** a line of connected railroad cars drawn by an engine: *to travel* **by train 2** a long line of moving people, vehicles, or animals **3** a part of the back of a long dress that spreads over the ground **4** a chain of related events, thoughts, etc.: *The telephone rang and interrupted my* **train of thought.**

train² *v* **1** [I;T *+to-v/for*] to give or be given teaching and practice in a profession or skill: *to train soldiers to fight*|*She is training to be a doctor.*|*He spends two hours a day training for the race.* **2** [T *on, upon*] to aim (a gun) at something or someone **3** [T] to direct the growth of (a plant) –**trainable** *adj* –**trainer** *n*

train·ee /treᵞ'niᵞ/ *n* a person who is being trained: *a trainee reporter*

train·ing /'treᵞnɪŋ/ *n* [S;U] **1** the act of TRAINing² (1) or being trained; instruction: *to* **go into training** *for a match* **2 in/out of training** in/not in a good healthy condition for a sport, test of skill, etc. **3 in training** in preparation (for action)

trait /treᵞt/ *n* a particular quality of someone or something; CHARACTERISTIC: *Generosity is her best trait.*

trai·tor /'treᵞt̬ər/ *n* a person who is disloyal, esp. to his/her country –**traitorous** *adj esp. lit* –**traitorously** *adv*

tra·jec·to·ry /trə'dʒɛktəriᵞ/ *n* -**ries** *tech* the curved path of an object fired through the air: *the trajectory of a bullet*

tram /træm/ *n BrE* for STREETCAR

tramp¹ /træmp/ *v* **1** [I] to walk with firm heavy steps **2** [I;T] to walk steadily through or over: *They tramped (through) the woods all day.*

tramp² *n* **1** [C] a person with no home or job, who wanders from place to place **2** [S] the sound of heavy walking: *the tramp of the soldiers' feet on the road* **3** [C] a long walk **4** [C] *esp. AmE* a woman considered to be sexually immoral

tram·ple /'træmpəl/ *v* -**pled, -pling** [I;T *down, on, over, upon*] to step heavily with the feet (on); crush: (fig.) *to trample on someone's feelings*

tram·po·line /ˌtræmpə'liᵞn, 'træmpəˌliᵞn/ *n* an apparatus consisting of a sheet of material held to a metal frame by springs, on which ACROBATs and GYMNASTs jump up and down

trance /træns/ *n* a sleeplike condition of the mind (esp. in the phrase **in a trance**)

tran·quil /'træŋkwəl/ *adj* calm; quiet; peaceful: *a tranquil lake/smile* –**tranquility** /træŋ'kwɪlət̬iᵞ/ *n* [U] –**tranquilly** /'træŋ kwəliᵞ/ *adv*

tran·quil·ize also **-quillize** *AmE*‖also **-ise** *BrE* /'træŋkwəˌlaɪz/ *v* -**ized, -izing** [T] to make calm: *a tranquilizing drug*

tran·quil·iz·er also **-quillizer** *AmE*‖ also **-liser** *BrE* /'træŋkwəˌlaɪzər/ *n* a drug used for

reducing nervous anxiety and making a person calm

trans·act /træn'sækt, -'zækt/ *v* [T] to carry (a piece of business, etc.) through to an agreement

trans·ac·tion /træn'sækʃən, -'zæk-/ *n* **1** [U] the act of TRANSACTing **2** [C] something transacted; a piece of business

trans·at·lan·tic /ˌtrænsət'læntɪk, ˌtrænz-/ *adj* connecting or concerning countries on both sides of the Atlantic Ocean: *a translantic agreement*|*a transatlantic flight*

tran·scend /træn'sɛnd/ *v* [T] *lit* to go or be above or beyond: *The size of the universe transcends our imagination.* –**transcendence** also **transcendency**– *n* [U]

tran·scen·den·tal /ˌtrænsɛn'dɛntəl/ *adj* going beyond human knowledge, thought, belief, and experience: *transcendental* MEDITATION

trans·con·ti·nen·tal /ˌtrænskɑntən'ɛntəl, ˌtrænz-/ *adj* crossing a CONTINENT: *a transcontinental railroad*

tran·scribe /træn'skraɪb/ *v* -**scribed, -scribing** [T] **1** to make a full copy of (esp. notes or recorded matter) **2** [*for*] to arrange (a piece of music) for an instrument or voice other than the original –**transcription** /træn 'skrɪpʃən/ *n* [C;U]

tran·script /'trænˌskrɪpt/ *n* a written or printed copy; something TRANSCRIBEd

trans·fer¹ /'trænsfər, træns'fɜr/ *v* -**rr- 1** [I;T] to (cause to) move from one place, job, vehicle, etc., to another: *The office was transferred from Chicago to Los Angeles.*|*He is hoping to transfer/be transferred to another team.*|*At Boston, we transferred from a train to a bus.* **2** [T] to give the ownership of (property) to another person –**transferable** *adj* –**transference** /træns'fɜrəns, 'træns fərəns/ *n* [U]

trans·fer² /'trænsfər/ *n* **1** [C;U] (an example of) the act of TRANSFERring: *He wants a transfer to another team.* **2** [C] a drawing, pattern, etc., for sticking or printing onto a surface: *a transfer of Mickey Mouse on a shirt* **3** [C] someone or something that has TRANSFERred¹ (1) or been transferred

trans·fig·ure /træns'fɪgyər/ *v* -**ured, -uring** [T] to change in appearance, and make glorious: *a face transfigured with joy* –**transfiguration** /trænsˌfɪgyə'reᵞʃən/ *n* [C;U]

trans·fix /træns'fɪks/ *v* [T *with; usu. pass.*] to make unable to move or think because of terror, shock, etc.

trans·form /træns'fɔrm/ *v* [T] to change completely in form, appearance, or nature: *The magician transformed the piece of cloth into a rabbit.*|*to transform heat into power* –**transformation** /ˌtrænsfər'meᵞʃən/ *n* [C;U]

trans·form·er /træns'fɔrmər/ *n* an apparatus for changing electrical force (VOLTAGE)

trans·fu·sion /træns'fyuʷʒən/ *n* [C;U] (a case of) putting the blood of one person into the body of another: *The driver had to have a blood transfusion after the accident.* –**transfuse** /træns'fyuʷz/ *v* -**fused, -fusing** [T]

trans·gress /træns'grɛs, trænz-/ *v* [T] *fml* **1** to go beyond (a proper limit) **2** to break (a law, agreement, etc.) –**transgression** /træns'grɛʃ*ə*n, trænz-/ *n* [C;U] –**transgressor** /træns'grɛs*ə*r, trænz-/ *n*

tran·sient[1] /'trænʃ*ə*nt, -tʃ*ə*nt, -ʒ*ə*nt/ *adj* **1** also **transitory** /'trænsə,tɔri*y*, -,to*w*ri*y*, 'trænz-/– lasting for only a short time: *transient happiness* **2** (of a person) passing through a place or staying for only a short period of time: *New York City has a large transient population.* –**transience** *n* [U]

transient[2] *n esp. AmE* A guest who stays in a hotel for only a short time

tran·sis·tor /træn'zɪstər, -'sɪs-/ *n* **1** a small electrical apparatus, esp. used in radios, televisions, etc. –compare VALVE (2) **2** also **transistor radio** /·,·· '··-/– a radio that has these instead of VALVE*s*

tran·sit /'trænsɪt, -zɪt/ *n* [U] the act of moving people or goods from one place to another: *His letter must have gotten lost* **in transit.**

tran·si·tion /træn'zɪʃ*ə*n, -'sɪ-/ *n* [C;U] (an act of) changing or passing from one state, subject, or place to another: *We hope there will be a peaceful transition to the new system.* –**transitional** *adj: a transitional period* –**transitionally** *adv*

tran·si·tive /'trænsətɪv, -zə-/ *adj,n* (a verb) that takes a direct OBJECT[1] (4) –see also INTRANSITIVE –see Study Notes on page 745

trans·late /træns'le*y*t, trænz-, 'trænsle*y*t, 'trænz-/ *v* **-lated, -lating** [I;T] to change (speech or writing) from one language into another: *The book was translated from French into English.* –compare INTERPRET –**translation** /træns'le*y*ʃ*ə*n, trænz-/ *n* [C;U]: *I've only read Tolstoy's books* **in translation.** –**translator** /træns'le*y*tər, trænz-, 'træns,le*y*tər, 'trænz-/ *n*

trans·lu·cent /træns'lu*w*s*ə*nt, trænz-/ *adj* not transparent but clear enough to allow light to pass through –**translucence** also **translucency**– *n* [U]

trans·mis·sion /træns'mɪʃ*ə*n, trænz-/ *n* **1** [U] the act of TRANSMITting or of being transmitted **2** [C] something broadcast by television or radio **3** [C] the parts of a vehicle that carry power from the engine to its wheels

trans·mit /træns'mɪt, trænz-/ *v* **-tt-** [I;T] **1** to send out (electric signals, messages, news, etc.); broadcast **2** [T] to send or carry from one person, place, or thing to another: *to transmit a disease*

trans·mit·ter /træns'mɪtər, trænz-/ *n* **1** an apparatus that sends out radio or television signals **2** someone or something that TRANSMIT*s*

trans·par·en·cy /træns'pærənsi*y*, -'pɛər-/ *n* **-cies 1** [C] a piece of photographic film, on which a picture can be seen when light is passed through **2** [U] the state of being transparent

trans·par·ent /træns'pærənt, -'pɛər-/ *adj* that can be seen through: *Glass is transparent.| Her silk dress was almost transparent.*|(fig.) *a transparent* (=clear) *meaning*|(fig.) *a transparent lie* –compare OPAQUE –**transparently** *adv*

tran·spire /træn'spaɪər/ *v* **-spired, -spiring** [I] **1** [+*that*] (of an event, secret, etc.) to become gradually known: *It later transpired that the senator had lied about the money he had received from a private company.* **2** *infml* to happen: *Let's wait and see what transpires.* USAGE This second sense of **transpire**, meaning "to happen," is thought by some teachers to be incorrect.

trans·plant[1] /træns'plænt/ *v* [T] **1** to move (a plant) from one place and plant it in another **2** to move (an organ, piece of skin, hair, etc.) from one part of the body to another or from one person to another: *to transplant a heart* –**transplantation** /,trænsplæn'te*y*ʃ*ə*n/ *n* [U]

trans·plant[2] /'trænsplænt/ *n* **1** something TRANSPLANTed **2** an act or operation of TRANSPLANTing[1] (2): *to do a heart transplant*

trans·port /træns'pɔrt, -'po*w*rt/ *v* [T] **1** to carry (goods, people, etc.) from one place to another **2** (in former times) to send (a criminal) to a distant land as a punishment –**transportable** *adj*

trans·por·ta·tion /,trænspɔr'te*y*ʃ*ə*n/ *n* **1** [U] *AmE*‖also **transport** /'trænspɔrt, -po*w*rt/– the act of TRANSPORTing (1) or of being TRANSPORTed[1]: *The transportation of goods by air is very expensive.* **2** [U] *AmE*‖also **transport**– a means or system of carrying passengers or goods from one place to another: *a public transportation system*|*I'd like to go to the concert, but I have no transportation.* (=method of getting there) **3** [C] a ship or plane for carrying soldiers or supplies USAGE 1 You **ride** a horse, bicycle, or anything else that sit on with your legs hanging down. You **drive** (=control and guide) a car or any other wheeled vehicle that you sit inside, and your passengers are **riding** in it or being **driven.** The person in control of a train or bus **drives** it; the person in control of a plane **flies** (FLY) or **pilots** it, and on a boat the person in control **sails** or **pilots** it. –see also LEAD (USAGE) 2 You **get on(to)** anything you **ride**, and later **get off it** or (*fml*) **dismount** from it; you **get on(to)** a bus or train and later **get off** it or (*fml*) **alight** from it; you **get on/off** a boat or (*fml*) **embark/disembark**; you **get on** or **board** a plane, and later **get off it**; and you **get into** and **out of** a car or taxi. 3 Notice the pattern [**by + U**], which can be used with all forms of transportation: *You can go from the airport to the center of town* **by car, by taxi, by** *bus, or even* **by** HELICOPTER.

trans·port·er /træns'pɔrtər, -'po*w*r-/ *n* a long vehicle on which a number of cars can be carried

trans·pose /træns'po*w*z/ *v* **-posed, -posing** [T] **1** to change the order or position of (two or more things): *to transpose the letters of a word* **2** to change the KEY[1] (4) of (a piece of music) –**transposition** /,trænspə'zɪʃ*ə*n/ *n*

trans·verse /,træns'vɜrs◂, 'trænz-/ *adj* lying or placed across: *a transverse beam* –**transversely** *adv*

trans·ves·tite /træns'vɛstaɪt, trænz-/ *adj,n* (of or being) a person who likes to wear the clothes of the opposite sex –**transvestism** /træns'vɛstɪzəm, trænz-/ *n* [U]

trap[1] /træp/ *n* **1** an apparatus for catching and holding animals: *a mouse caught in a trap* **2** a plan for deceiving and tricking a person: *The police set a trap for the criminals.* **3** a light two-wheeled vehicle pulled by a horse **4** *infml* a mouth: *Keep your trap shut!* (=be quiet)

trap² *v* **-pp-** [T *for, into*] to catch in a trap or by a trick: *to trap animals for fur*|*He trapped me into admitting I had done it.*

trap·door /ˌtræp'dɔr, -'doʷr/ *n* a small door covering an opening in a floor or roof

tra·peze /træ'piʸz/ *n* a short bar hung high above the ground from two ropes, used by ACROBATS and GYMNASTS

trap·per /'træpər/ *n* a person who traps wild animals, esp. for their fur

trap·pings /'træpɪŋz/ *n* [P] articles of dress or decoration, esp. as a sign of rank: *He wore all the trappings of high office.*

trash /træʃ/ *n* [U] **1** something worthless or of low quality **2** *AmE* for RUBBISH (1)

trash·can /'træʃkæn/ *n* *AmE* for GARBAGE CAN

trash·y /'træʃiʸ/ *adj* **-ier, -iest** worthless: *trashy ideas/books* –**trashiness** *n* [U]

trau·ma /'trɔmə, 'traumə/ *n* **-mas** *or* **-mata** /mətə/ damage to the mind caused by a sudden shock

trau·mat·ic /trɔ'mætɪk, trɔ-, trau-/ *adj* (of an experience) deeply shocking –**traumatically** *adv*

trav·el¹ /'trævəl/ *v* **-l-** *AmE*||**-ll-** *BrE* **1** [I] to go from place to place; make a journey: *to travel around the world for a year*|(fig.) *His mind traveled back to* (=he remembered) *his childhood.* **2** [I;T] to pass, go, or move through (a place or distance): *At what speed does light travel?*|*The news traveled fast.*|*We traveled thousands of miles.* **3** **travel light** to travel without much LUGGAGE

travel² *n* [U] the act of traveling

USAGE Although **travel** (verb) is a general word for going from one place to another, the nouns **travel** [U] and **travels** [P] usually suggest traveling for long distances and long periods of time: *He came home after years of foreign travel.*|*She wrote a book about her travels in South America.* A **trip/journey** is the time spent and the distance covered in going from one place to another: *I go to work by train, and the trip takes 40 minutes.*|*an uncomfortable journey in a crowded train.* **Voyage** is similar, but is mainly used of sea journeys (or sometimes journeys in space), and a **journey** by plane is a **flight**: *Take some books to read on the trip/journey/voyage/flight.* A journey made for religious reasons is a **pilgrimage**, and a difficult and dangerous journey made by a group of people for a special purpose is an **expedition**: *a pilgrimage to Mecca*|*Scott's famous expedition to the South Pole.*

travel a·gen·cy /'·· ˌ···/ also **travel bureau** /'·· ˌ···/ – *n* **-cies** a business that arranges people's journeys

travel a·gent /'·· ˌ··/ *n* a person who owns or works in a TRAVEL AGENCY

trav·el·er *AmE*||**traveller** *BrE* /'trævələr/ *n* a person on a journey

traveler's check /'··· ˌ·/ *n* a check sold by a

bank to a person intending to travel abroad, exchangeable at most banks for the money of the particular country

travels /'trævəlz/ *n* [P] traveling; journeys –see TRAVEL² (USAGE)

tra·verse /trə'vɜrs, 'trævərs/ *v* **-versed, -versing** [T] *fml* to pass across, over, or through: *The lights traversed the sky searching for enemy planes.*

trav·es·ty /'trævɪstiʸ/ *n* **-ties** a copy, account, or example of something that completely misrepresents it: *His trial was a travesty of justice.*

trawl¹ /trɔl/ *v* [I;T] to fish with a TRAWL²: *boats out trawling (the lake) for fish*

trawl² *n* a large wide-mouthed fishing net that is drawn along the sea bottom

trawl·er /'trɔlər/ *n* a fishing vessel that uses a TRAWL²

tray /treʸ/ *n* a flat piece of wood or metal with raised edges, used for carrying small articles: *a tray/ trayful of glasses* –see illustration on page 581

treach·er·ous /'trɛtʃərəs/ *adj* **1** disloyal; deceitful **2** dangerous: *treacherous currents* –**treacherously** *adv*

treach·er·y /'trɛtʃəriʸ/ *n* **-ies 1** [U] disloyalty; deceit; unfaithfulness; falseness –compare TREASON **2** [C *usu. pl.*] a TREACHEROUS (1) action

trea·cle /'triʸkəl/ *n* [U] *BrE* for MOLASSES

tread¹ /trɛd/ *v* **trod** /trɑd/, **trodden** /'trɑdn/ *or* **trod, treading 1** [I *on*] to walk or step: *Don't tread on the flowers!* **2** [T] to walk on, over, or along: *Every day he trod the same path to school.* **3** [T] to press firmly with the feet: *They crush the juice out of the fruit by treading it.* **4** **tread on somebody's toes** to offend somebody **5** **tread water** to stay upright in deep water with the head above the surface, by moving the legs

tread² *n* **1** [S] the act, manner, or sound of walking: *a noisy tread* **2** [C;U] the raised pattern on a tire **3** [C] the part of a stair on which the foot is placed

trea·dle /'trɛdl/ *n* an apparatus worked by the feet to drive a machine: *the treadle of a sewing machine*

trea·son /'triʸzən/ *n* [U] (the crime of) disloyalty to one's country –compare TREACHERY –**treasonable** also **treasonous**– *adj*: *a treasonable crime against the state* –**treasonably** *adv*

treas·ure¹ /'trɛʒər/ *n* **1** [U] wealth in the form of gold, silver, jewels, etc. **2** [C] a very valuable object: *the nation's art treasures*

treasure² *v* **-ured, -uring** [T] to keep or regard as precious: *a treasured memory*

treas·ur·er /'trɛʒərər/ *n* a person in charge of the money belonging to a club, organization, etc.

treasure trove /'trɛʒər ˌtroʷv/ *n* [U] valuable objects found hidden in the ground and claimed by no one

treas·ur·y /'trɛʒəriʸ/ *n* **-ies** [*of*] **1** a collection of valuable things: *This book is a treasury of useful information.* **2** [*the* S] (*usu. cap.*) the government department that controls and spends public money: *The Treasury is spend-*

ing less this year.

treat¹ /triˠt/ v [T] **1** to act or behave towards: *She treats us as/like children.* **2** to deal with; handle; consider: *This glass must be treated with care.|He treated the idea as a joke.* **3** to try to cure by medical means: *to treat a disease* **4** to buy or give (someone) something special: *I'm going to treat myself to a vacation in the mountains.* **5** to put (a substance) through a chemical or industrial action in order to change it: *treated pigskin* –**treatable** *adj*

treat² *n* something that gives pleasure, esp. when unexpected: *It's a great treat for her to go to the theater.|This is my treat.* (=I will pay for everything)

trea·tise /ˈtriˠtɪs/ *n* [on] a serious book or article that examines a particular subject

treat·ment /ˈtriˠtmənt/ *n* [C;U] the act, manner, or method of treating someone or something: *He's gone to the hospital for special treatment.*

trea·ty /ˈtriˠtiˠ/ *n* **-ties** a formal agreement, esp. between countries

tre·ble¹ /ˈtrɛbəl/ *n* **1** [C] (a person with or a musical part for) a high singing voice **2** [U] the upper half of the whole range of musical notes –compare BASS³

treble² *adv,adj* **1** in three parts; three together: *They have the treble advantage of power, money, and influence.* –see also TRIPLE² **2** (of a voice or musical instrument) high in sound: *to sing treble* –compare BASS²

treble³ *predeterminer* three times: *He earns treble my wages.|The house is worth treble what they paid for it.*

treble⁴ *v* **-bled, -bling** [I;T] to make or become three times as great –see also TRIPLE¹

tree /triˠ/ *n* a tall plant with a wooden trunk and branches: *an apple tree|the trees in the wood* –**treeless** /ˈtriˠlɪs/ *adj*

trek /trɛk/ *v* **-kk-** [I] to make a long hard journey, esp. on foot –**trek** *n: a long trek through the mountains*

trel·lis /ˈtrɛlɪs/ *n* [C;U] (a) light upright wooden framework, esp. used as a support for climbing plants

trem·ble /ˈtrɛmbəl/ *v* **-bled, -bling** [I] **1** to shake uncontrollably: *to tremble with fear/cold/excitement|The whole house trembled as the train went by.* **2** [+to-v/for] to feel fear or anxiety: *I tremble to think what will happen.* –**tremble** *n* [S] *infml: He was all a-tremble.* (=trembling) –**tremblingly** *adv*

tre·men·dous /trɪˈmɛndəs/ *adj* **1** very great in size, amount, or degree: *to travel at a tremendous speed|a tremendous explosion* **2** wonderful: *We went to a tremendous party last night.* –**tremendously** *adv*

trem·or /ˈtrɛmər/ *n* a shaking movement: *an earth tremor* (=small EARTHQUAKE)*|a tremor of fear*

trem·u·lous /ˈtrɛmyələs/ *adj* slightly shaking; nervous: *a tremulous voice* –**tremulously** *adv* –**tremulousness** *n* [U]

trench /trɛntʃ/ *n* a long narrow hole cut in the ground; ditch –compare DUGOUT (2)

trend /trɛnd/ *n* **1** a general direction; tendency: *the trend of rising unemployment|the latest trends* (=fashions) *in women's clothes* **2 set the trend** to start or popularize a fashion

trend·set·ter /ˈtrɛnd₁sɛtər/ *n infml* a person who starts or popularizes a particular style or fashion

trend·y /ˈtrɛndiˠ/ *adj* **-ier, -iest** *infml, sometimes derog* very fashionable: *a trendy dress/girl* –**trendiness** *n* [U]

trep·i·da·tion /₁trɛpəˈdeˠʃən/ *n* [U] *fml* a state of anxiety: *in fear and trepidation*

tres·pass¹ /ˈtrɛspəs, -pæs/ *v* [I] to go onto privately-owned land without permission –**trespasser** *n*

trespass upon/on sthg. *v prep* [T] *fml* to make too much use of: *It would be trespassing upon their generosity to accept any more.*

trespass² *n* [C;U] (an example of) the act of TRESPASSING¹

tress·es /ˈtrɛsɪz/ *n* [P] *lit* a woman's long hair

tres·tle /ˈtrɛsəl/ *n* a wooden beam fixed to a pair of legs, used esp. as a support for a table (**trestle table**)

tri·al /ˈtraɪəl/ *n* **1** [C;U] (an act of) hearing and judging a person or case in a court: *The murder trial lasted six weeks.|He is on trial.* (=being tried in a court of law) **2** [C;U] (an act of) testing to find quality, value, usefulness, etc.: *a trial period|She took the car on trial.* (=for a short time, to test it) **3** [C] a cause of worry or trouble: *That child is a trial to his parents.* **4 stand trial** to be tried in court: *to stand trial for murder* **5 trial and error** a way of getting satisfactory results by trying several methods and learning from one's mistakes: *learning to cook by trial and error*

tri·an·gle /ˈtraɪ₁æŋgəl/ *n* **1** a flat figure with three straight sides and three angles **2** a small three-sided musical instrument made of steel, played by being struck with a steel rod **3** *AmE|*setsquare *BrE*– a flat three-sided object used for drawing straight lines and angles exactly –**triangular** /traɪˈæŋgyələr/ *adj: a triangular piece of land*

tribe /traɪb/ *n* a group of people of the same race, beliefs, language, etc., under the leadership of a chief or chiefs: *American Indian tribes|The whole tribe is angry.* –see RACE (USAGE) –**tribal** /ˈtraɪbəl/ *adj: tribal music* –**tribalism** *n* [U]: *the tribalism* (=the importance of tribal feeling) *of black Africa*

tribes·man /ˈtraɪbzmən/ *n* **-men** /mən/ a (male) member of a tribe

trib·u·la·tion /₁trɪbyəˈleˠʃən/ *n* [C;U] *fml* (a cause of) trouble, grief, and suffering: *the trials and tribulations of modern life*

tri·bu·nal /traɪˈbyuˠnl, trɪ-/ *n* **1** a court of justice **2** a court of people officially appointed to deal with special matters: *He had to stand before a military tribunal.*

trib·une /ˈtrɪbyuˠn/ *n* **1** an official of Ancient Rome elected by the ordinary people to protect their interests **2** a popular leader; person who defends popular interests and rights

trib·u·tar·y /ˈtrɪbyə₁tɛriˠ/ *n* **-ies** a stream or river that flows into a larger stream or river: *the tributaries of the Rhine*

trib·ute /ˈtrɪbyuˠt/ *n* [C;U] **1** something done, said, or given to show respect or admiration for someone: *We pay* **tribute** *to his courage.* **2** (a) payment made by one ruler or country to another as the price of peace, protection, etc.

trice /traɪs/ *n* **in a trice** *infml* in the shortest possible time

trick¹ /trɪk/ *n* **1** an act needing special skill, esp. done to confuse or amuse: *magic tricks|No one understood how I did the card trick.* **2** a special skill: *John taught me the trick of opening a bottle of wine properly.* **3** something done to deceive or make someone look stupid: *He got the money by a trick.|The children loved to* **play tricks on** *their teacher.* **4** the cards played or won in one game of cards –see CARDS (USAGE) **5 do the trick** *infml* to fulfill one's purpose: *This medicine ought to do the trick.* (=cure the disease)

trick² *adj* [A] *infml* **1** made for playing tricks: *a trick spoon that melts in hot liquid* **2** full of hidden difficulties: *a trick question*

trick³ *v* [T *into*] to cheat (someone): *She tricked me into paying for her meal at the restaurant.*

trick·er·y /ˈtrɪkəriʸ/ *n* [U] the use of tricks to deceive or cheat

trick·le /ˈtrɪkəl/ *v* **-led, -ling** [I] to flow in drops or in a thin stream: *Blood trickled down his face.* –**trickle** *n* [S]: (fig.) *We only had a trickle of customers at the store today.*

trick·ster /ˈtrɪkstər/ *n* a person who deceives or cheats people

trick·y /ˈtrɪkiʸ/ *adj* **-ier, -iest 1** (of work, a state of affairs, etc.) difficult to handle or deal with; delicate **2** (of a person or actions) clever and deceitful; SLY: *a tricky politician* –**trickiness** *n* [U]

tri·cy·cle /ˈtraɪsɪkəl/ *n* a bicycle with three wheels, two at the back and one at the front: *We bought our son a tricycle.*

tri·dent /ˈtraɪdnt/ *n* a forklike instrument or weapon with three points

tried¹ /traɪd/ *adj* found to be good by testing: *a tried method*

tried² *v* past tense & participle of TRY¹

tri·fle /ˈtraɪfəl/ *n* **1** a thing of little value or slight importance: *wasting one's money on trifles* **2** a very small amount of money **3 a trifle** to some degree; rather: *He's a trifle angry.*

trifle with sbdy./sthg. *v prep* **-fled, -fling** [T] to treat without seriousness or respect: *The general is not a man to be trifled with.*

tri·fling /ˈtraɪflɪŋ/ *adj* of little importance or value

trig·ger¹ /ˈtrɪɡər/ *n* the small tongue of metal pressed by the finger to fire a gun

trigger² *v* [T *off*] to start (esp. a chain of events): *Price increases trigger off demands for wage increases.*

trig·o·nom·e·try /ˌtrɪɡəˈnɑmətriʸ/ *n* the branch of MATHEMATICS (=the science of numbers) that deals with the relationship between the sides and angles of TRIANGLES (=three-sided figures)

trill /trɪl/ *n* (a sound like) the rapid repeating of two musical notes, for special effect –**trill** *v* [I;T]: *birds trilling their songs*

tril·o·gy /ˈtrɪlədʒiʸ/ *n* **-gies** a group of three related books, plays, etc., connected by common subject matter

trim¹ /trɪm/ *v* **-mm-** [T] **1** [*off*] to make neat, even, or tidy by cutting: *to have one's hair trimmed|to trim off loose threads* **2** [*with*] to decorate: *a coat trimmed with fur* **3** to reduce: *to trim one's costs* **4** to move (a sail) into the desired position

trim² *adj* **-mm-** tidy; neat in appearance: *a trim figure/garden* –**trimly** *adv*

trim³ *n* **1** [S] an act of cutting: *to give one's hair a trim* **2** [U] proper condition; fitness

tri·mes·ter /traɪˈmɛstər/ *n AmE* a TERM¹ (1) of three months at a school or college

trim·ming /ˈtrɪmɪŋ/ *n* [*usu. pl.*] something used for TRIMMING¹ (2); a pleasant addition: *duck served with all the trimmings* (=vegetables, potatoes, etc.)

trin·ket /ˈtrɪŋkɪt/ *n* a small piece of jewelry of low value

tri·o /ˈtriʸoʷ/ *n* **-os 1** a group of three people, esp. musicians: *A trio is playing tonight.* **2** [C] a piece of music written for three singers or musicians

trip¹ /trɪp/ *v* **-pp- 1** [I;T *over, up*] to (cause to) catch one's foot and lose one's balance: *He tripped over a root and fell.|The boy put his leg out to trip the teacher.* **2** [I,T *up*] to (cause to) make a mistake: *The lawyer always tries to trip witnesses up by asking confusing questions.* **3** [I] to move or dance with quick light steps: *The little girl tripped lightly down the path.*

trip² *n* **1** a journey from one place to another: *a trip to Europe|a business trip|a day trip* (=journey for pleasure lasting just one day) *to the country* **2** a fall; act of tripping

tri·par·tite /traɪˈpɑrtaɪt/ *adj* **1** having three parts **2** (of an agreement) agreed on by three parties

tripe /traɪp/ *n* [U] **1** the wall of the stomach of the cow or ox, eaten as food **2** *infml* worthless or stupid talk, writing, etc.: *Why do you read such tripe?*

tri·ple /ˈtrɪpəl/ *v* **-pled, -pling** [I;T] to (cause to) grow to three times the amount –see also TREBLE⁴

triple² *adj* **1** having three parts **2** three times repeated: *a triple dose* (=amount) *of medicine* –see also TREBLE²

tri·plet /ˈtrɪplɪt/ *n* any of three children born of the same mother at the same time

tri·plex /ˈtrɪplɛks, ˈtraɪ-/ also **triplex apart·ment** /ˌ·· ·ˈ··/– *n AmE* an apartment having rooms on three floors –compare DUPLEX

trip·li·cate /ˈtrɪpləkɪt/ *adj* consisting of three parts that are exactly alike: *triplicate copies of the contract* –**triplicate** *n*: *The contract has been written in triplicate.*

tri·pod /ˈtraɪpɑd/ *n* a three-legged support, e.g. for a camera

trite /traɪt/ *adj* (of remarks, ideas, etc.) too often used to be meaningful or effective –**tritely** *adv* –**triteness** *n* [U]

tri·umph /ˈtraɪəmf/ *n* [C;U] (the joy caused by) a complete victory or success: *a triumph over the enemy|his examination triumph| shouts of triumph* –**triumphant** /traɪˈʌmfənt/

adj: a triumphant army –**triumphantly** *adv*
triumph² *v* [I] [*over*] to be victorious (over): *to triumph over all one's difficulties*
tri·um·phal /traɪˈʌmfəl/ *adj* of, related to, or marking a TRIUMPH¹: *a triumphal arch*
triv·i·a /ˈtrɪviʸə/ *n* [P] unimportant or useless things; TRIFLEs (1)
triv·i·al /ˈtrɪviʸəl/ *adj* of little importance: *Why do you get angry over such trivial matters?* –**trivially** *adv* –**triviality** /ˌtrɪviʸˈæləţiʸ/ *n* -**ties** [C;U]
trod /trad/ *v past tense & participle of* TREAD¹
trod·den /ˈtradn/ *v past participle of* TREAD¹
troll /trowl/ *n* (in ancient Scandinavian stories) one of a race of friendly or evil beings, living in caves or hills
trol·ley /ˈtraliʸ/ *n* -**leys 1** any of various small low carts or vehicles, esp. one pushed by hand **2** also **trolley car** /ˈ·· ˌ·/ *AmE*– an electric STREETCAR: *When we were in San Francisco, we took the trolley.*
trol·ley·bus /ˈtraliʸˌbʌs/ *n* a bus that draws power from electric wires running above it
trom·bone /tramˈbown/ *n* a large brass musical instrument with a long sliding tube –**trombonist** *n*
troop¹ /truwp/ *n* **1** a band of people or animals: *a troop of monkeys/children* **2** a body of soldiers, esp. on horses or in armored vehicles: *The troop is advancing.*
troop² *v* [I] to move together in a group: *Everyone trooped into the meeting.*
troop·er /ˈtruwpər/ *n* **1** a soldier in the CAVALRY **2** *AmE* a member of a STATE police force
troops /truwps/ *n* [P] soldiers
tro·phy /ˈtrowfiʸ/ *n* -**phies 1** a prize given for winning a race, competition, etc. **2** something taken after much effort, esp. in war or hunting: *to hang the lion's head on the wall as a trophy*
trop·ic /ˈtrapɪk/ *n* one of the two imaginary lines (lines of LATITUDE) drawn around the world at about 23½° north (**the tropic of Cancer**) and south (**the tropic of Capricorn**) of the imaginary line around the middle of the world (EQUATOR)
trop·i·cal /ˈtrapɪkəl/ *adj* of, related to, or living in the tropics: *tropical flowers/the tropical sun* **2** very hot: *tropical weather* –**tropically** *adv*
trop·ics /ˈtrapɪks/ *n* [*the* P] the hot area between the tropics: *living in the tropics*
trot¹ /trat/ *n* [S] **1** (of a horse) a fairly quick movement between a walk and a GALLOP **2** a fairly fast human speed between a walk and a run
trot² *v* -**tt**- [I;T] to (cause to) move at a TROT¹
trou·ba·dour /ˈtruwbəˌdɔr, -ˌdowr/ *n* a traveling singer and poet in former times
trou·ble¹ /ˈtrʌbəl/ *v* -**bled, -bling 1** [T] to make anxious, nervous, worried, etc.: *You look troubled; what's worrying you?* **2** [I;T +*to-v/for*] (esp. in polite expressions) to cause inconvenience to (someone else or oneself): *I'm sorry to trouble you, but can you tell me the time?/May I trouble you for the salt?* (=please pass it to me) **3** [T] to cause (someone) pain as a disease does: *He's been troubled with a bad back for years.*

trouble² *n* **1** [C;U] (a) difficulty, worry, anxiety, annoyance, etc.: *to have trouble getting the car started/Paying rent is the least of my troubles at present.* **2** [U *with*] danger; risk; a difficulty or dangerous state of affairs: *The little boy looked as though he was in trouble, so I swam out to save him.* / *He told a lie rather than get into trouble.* (=be blamed for doing wrong) **3** [S;U] (an) inconvenience; effort: *I hope we haven't put you to any trouble.* / *We must thank him for taking the trouble* (=causing himself work) *to cook us a meal.* **4** [C;U] (an example of) political or social disorder: *There's been a lot of trouble in this country in the past year.* **5** [S *with*] a bad point; fault: *The trouble with you is that you're stupid. That's your trouble!* **6** [U] (a) medical condition; illness: *heart/back trouble* **7 ask/look for trouble** to behave so as to cause difficulty or danger for oneself
trou·ble·mak·er /ˈtrʌbəlˌmeʸkər/ *n* a person who habitually causes trouble
trou·ble·shoot·er /ˈtrʌbəlˌʃuʷţər/ *n* a person employed to find and remove causes of trouble, usu. in an organization
trou·ble·some /ˈtrʌbəlsəm/ *adj* causing trouble or anxiety: *a troublesome child*
trough /trɔf/ *n* **1** a long narrow boxlike container, esp. for holding water or food for animals **2** a long narrow hollow area, e.g. between two waves; DEPRESSION (3) **3** *tech* (in METEOROLOGY) an area of lower pressure between two areas of high pressure
troupe /truwp/ *n* a group of singers, actors, dancers, etc.: *The whole troupe was swinging from ropes.*
troup·er /ˈtruwpər/ *n* a member of a TROUPE
trou·sers /ˈtrauzərz/ *n* [P] →PANTS (1): *a new pair of trousers*
trous·seau /ˈtruwsow, truwˈsow/ *n* -**seaux** /sowz, ˈsowz/ *or* -**seaus** the personal possessions, esp. clothes, that a woman brings with her when she marries
trout /traut/ *n* **trout** [C;U] (the flesh of) a fish with darkish spots on its brown skin, used for food
trow·el /ˈtrauəl/ *n* **1** a tool with a flat blade for spreading cement, PLASTER, etc. **2** a small spade-like garden tool with a curved blade
tru·ant /ˈtruwənt/ *n* a student who purposely stays away from school without permission –see also **play** HOOKY –**truancy** /ˈtruwənsiʸ/ *n* [U]: *Truancy is common at this school.*
truce /truws/ *n* (an agreement between two enemies for) the stopping of fighting for a period
truck¹ /trʌk/ *n* **1** also **lorry** *BrE*– a large motor vehicle for carrying big goods: *Heavy trucks aren't allowed to cross this bridge./The goods were taken to the harbor by truck.* –see illustration on page 95 **2** an open container with wheels for carrying goods: *coal trucks* –**trucker** /ˈtrʌkər/ *n: A trucker's life can be lonely.*
truck² *v* →TRUCK sthg.↔ IN
truck farm /ˈ· ·/ *AmE*‖**market garden** *BrE*– *n* an area for growing vegetables and fruit for sale –**truck farmer** /ˈ· ˌ··/ *n*
truck·load /ˈtrʌk-lowd/ *n* *AmE* an amount

being carried or to be carried by a truck
truck sthg.↔**in** v adv [T] *AmE* to deliver (esp.
food) by truck from one area to another: *The
grapes were trucked in to New York from
California.*

truc·u·lent /'trʌkyələnt/ adj fierce; always
willing to quarrel or attack –**truculence** n [U]
–**truculently** adv

trudge¹ /trʌdʒ/ v **trudged, trudging** [I] to
walk with heavy steps, slowly and with
effort: *to trudge through deep snow*

trudge² n a long tiring walk

true /truʷ/ adj **truer, truest 1** in accordance
with fact or reality; actual: *a true story*|*Is the
news true?*|*Is it true you're going away?*|*The
book is very true to life.* (=like actual life) **2**
real; sincere: *true love*|*I have a true interest in
your future.* **3** [*to*] faithful; loyal: *a true
friend*|*to stay true to one's principles* **4** exact:
a true copy **5** correctly fitted or placed: *If the
door's not exactly true, it won't close right.* **6**
come true to happen just as one wished,
expected, dreamed, etc. **7 true to type**
behaving or acting just as one would expect

true-life /ˌ· ˈ·◄/ adj [A] based on fact: *a
true-life adventure story*

truf·fle /'trʌfəl, 'truʷ-/ n **1** a fleshy FUNGUS
that grows underground and is highly
regarded as a food **2** a soft candy

tru·ism /'truʷɪzəm/ n a statement that is so
clearly true that there is no need to mention
it –compare CLICHÉ, PLATITUDE

tru·ly /'truʷliⁱ/ adv **1** exactly: *He cannot truly
be described as stupid, but he is lazy.* **2** really:
I am truly grateful to you.|*a truly beautiful
view* **3 yours truly** (used at the end of a
formal letter before the signature) –compare
FAITHFULLY, SINCERELY

trump¹ /trʌmp/ n (in card games) any card of
a SUIT chosen to be of higher rank than the
other SUITs (fig.) *Then, he* **played his trump
card** (=used an important advantage at the
last minute) *and brought in a witness.*

trump² v [T] to beat (a card) by playing a
TRUMP¹

trump up sthg. v adv [T] to invent (a false
reason, story, etc.): *The President wanted to
get rid of him, so he was sent to prison on a
trumped-up charge.*

trum·pet¹ /'trʌmpɪt/ n **1** a brass wind instrument, played by pressing three buttons in
various combinations **2** a loud cry, esp. of an
elephant

trumpet² v [I] **1** to play a TRUMPET¹ (1) **2** (esp.
of an elephant) to make a loud sound –**trum-
peter** n

trun·cate /'trʌŋkeⁱt/ v **-cated, -cating** [T] *fml*
to shorten (something) by cutting a part or
end off it: (fig.) *a truncated report*

trun·cheon /'trʌntʃən/ n *BrE* for NIGHTSTICK

trun·dle /'trʌndl/ v **-dled, -dling** [I;T] to
(cause to) move heavily on wheels: *to trundle
a cart along the street*

trunk /trʌŋk/ n **1** the thick main stem of a tree
2 the human body apart from the head and
limbs **3** a large box in which clothes or
belongings are stored or packed for travel **4**
the very long nose of an elephant **5**
AmE‖**boot** *BrE*– an enclosed space at the

back of a car for bags, boxes, etc. –see illustration on page 95

trunks /trʌŋks/ n [P] a short trouser-like garment worn by men, esp. for swimming –see
PAIR (USAGE)

truss¹ /trʌs/ v [T *up*] to tie up firmly with
cord, rope, etc.: *to truss (up) a chicken
before cooking it*

truss² n **1** a framework of beams built to
support a roof, bridge, etc. **2** a special belt
worn to support muscles in a case of HERNIA

trust¹ /trʌst/ n **1** [U *in*] firm belief in the
honesty or worth of someone or something;
faith: *I don't place any trust in his promise.*|*It
took the teacher a long time to gain the children's trust.* (=it was a long time before they
trusted him) **2** [U] responsibility: *a position
of trust* **3** [U] care; keeping: *After their
parents' death, the children were put in my
trust.* **4** [C;U] (an arrangement for) the holding and controlling of property for someone
else: *money* **held in trust** *for a child*|*to set up a
trust* **5** a group of companies that have combined together **6 take on trust** to accept
without proof

trust² v **1** [T] to believe in the honesty and
worth of; have faith in: *Don't trust him, he's
dishonest.*|*Trust my judgment!* **2** [I;T
+(*that*)] *fml* to hope: *I trust you enjoyed
yourself.*

trust in sbdy./sthg. v prep [T] to have faith
in

trust·ee /trʌˈstiⁱ/ n a person or company that
holds and controls property for someone
else

trust·ful /'trʌstfəl/ also **trusting** /'trʌstɪŋ/–
adj (too) ready to trust others: *the trustful
nature of a small child* –**trustfully** adv
–**trustfulness** n [U]

trust·wor·thy /'trʌstˌwɜrðiⁱ/ adj worthy of
trust; dependable –**trustworthiness** n [U]

trust·y /'trʌstiⁱ/ adj **-ier, -iest** old use or
humor faithful: *My trusty old car will get us
home safely.*

truth /truʷθ/ n **truths** /truʷðz, truʷθs/ **1** [U]
that which is true; the true facts: *You must
always tell the truth.* **2** [U] the quality of
being true: *I don't doubt the truth of his
information.* **3** [C] a fact or principle
accepted as true: *the truths of science* **4 in
truth** in fact; really

truth·ful /'truʷθfəl/ adj **1** (of a statement,
account, etc.) true: *a truthful account of what
happened* **2** (of a person) who habitually tells
the truth: *a truthful boy* –**truthfully** adv
–**truthfulness** n [U]

try¹ /traɪ/ v **tried, trying 1** [T +v-ing/*out*] to
test by use and experience: *Have you tried
this new soap?*|*It seems like a good idea; I'll
try it out.* **2** [I;T +to-v] to attempt: *I don't
think I can do it, but I'll try.*|*Please try to
come.* **3** [T] to attempt to open (a door,
window, etc.): *I think the door's locked, but
I'll try it just in case.* **4** [T] to examine (a
person thought guilty or a case) in a court of
law: *They're going to try him for murder.* **5**
[T] to test (someone's patience); annoy: *I've
had a very trying time at work today.* **6** *AmE*
to try one's luck to attempt something to see

if one can be successful
USAGE Note the difference between *He* **tried** *to climb the mountain.* (=but he couldn't)|*He* **tried** *climbing the mountain.* (=he climbed it, to see what it was like).

try sthg.↔ **on** *v adv* [T] to put on (a garment, hat, shoe, etc.) to see if it fits

try out sthg./sbdy. *v adv* [T] to test (something or someone) by use and experience: *The idea seems fine but we need to try it out for practice.*

try out for sthg. *AmE v adv prep* [T] to make an attempt to get or win; compete for: *He tried out for the play, but he didn't make it.*

try² *n* **tries** an attempt: *Let me have a try.|It was a good try, but it didn't succeed.*

tsar, czar, tzar /zɑr, tsɑr/ **tsarina, czarina, tzarina** /zɑˈriʸnə, tsɑ-/ *fem.– n →* CZAR

T-shirt, tee shirt /ˈtiʸ ʃɜrt/ *n* a close-fitting collarless garment for the upper body, with short arms

tsp. *written abbrev. said as:* TEASPOON: *one tsp. of salt*

tub /tʌb/ *n* **1** a large round usu. wooden vessel, for packing, storing, washing, etc. **2** *AmE* for BATHTUB

tu·ba /ˈtuʷbə, ˈtyuʷbə/ *n* a large brass wind instrument that produces low notes

tub·by /ˈtʌbi/ *adj* **-bier, -biest** *infml* short and fat

tube /tuʷb, tyuʷb/ *n* **1** a hollow round pipe of metal, glass, rubber, etc., used esp. for holding liquids **2** a small soft metal container, fitted with a cap, for holding TOOTHPASTE, paint, etc. –see illustration on page 55 **3** any hollow pipe or organ in the body **4** [*the* S] *AmE infml* television **5** → CATHODE RAY TUBE

tu·ber /ˈtuʷbər, ˈtyuʷ-/ *n* a fleshy swollen underground stem, such as the potato

tu·ber·cu·lo·sis /tuˌbɜrkyəˈloʷsɪs, tyʊ-/ also **TB–** *n* [U] a serious infectious disease that usu. attacks the lungs –**tubercular** /tʊˈbɜr kyələr, tyʊ-/ *adj*

tub·ing /ˈtuʷbɪŋ, ˈtyuʷ-/ *n* [U] metal, plastic, etc., in the form of a tube

tu·bu·lar /ˈtuʷbyələr, ˈtyuʷ-/ *adj* of, being, or made of a tube or tubes: *tubular metal furniture*

tuck¹ /tʌk/ *v* [T] to put into a desired or convenient position: *Tuck your shirt into your trousers.|He had a book tucked under his arm.*

tuck sthg.↔ **away** *v adv* [T] to put in a safe or hidden place: *She's got a lot of money tucked away.*

tuck sbdy. **in** *v adv* [T] to make (someone) comfortable in bed by pulling the bedclothes tight

tuck² *n* [C] a flat fold of material sewn into a garment

Tues. *written abbrev. said as:* Tuesday

Tues·day /ˈtuʷzdiʸ, -deʸ, ˈtyuʷz-/ *n* the third day of the week: *He'll arrive (on) Tuesday.|I have a music lesson on Tuesday.|(esp. AmE) She works Tuesdays.|He arrived on a Tuesday.*

tuft /tʌft/ *n v* [*of*] a bunch (of hair, feathers, grass, etc.) –**tufted** *adj*

tug¹ /tʌg/ *v* **-gg-** [I;T *at*] to pull hard with force or much effort: *The little child tugged at my arm to attract my attention.*

tug² *n* a sudden strong pull

tug·boat /ˈtʌgboʷt/ also **tug–** *n* a small powerful boat used for guiding large vessels into or out of harbors, etc.

tug-of-war /ˌ·· ·ˈ·/ *n* [C;U] a test of strength in which two teams pull against each other on a rope

tu·i·tion /tuʷˈɪʃən, tyuʷ-/ *n* [U] **1** the charge to students for instruction, esp. at a university or private school **2** instruction; teaching: *Tuition fees have gone up again.*

tu·lip /ˈtuʷlɪp, ˈtyuʷ-/ *n* a garden plant that grows from a BULB (1), or its large colorful cup-shaped flowers

tum·ble¹ /ˈtʌmbəl/ *v* **-bled, -bling** [I] to fall or roll over suddenly, helplessly, or in disorder: *to tumble down the stairs|The children tumbled off the bus at the park.*

tumble² *n* a fall

tum·bler /ˈtʌmblər/ *n* a drinking glass with no handle or stem

tum·my /ˈtʌmiʸ/ *n* **-mies** *infml* stomach: *a tummy ache*

tu·mor *AmE*‖**tumour** *BrE* /ˈtuʷmər, ˈtyuʷ-/ *n* a mass of diseased cells in the body –compare GROWTH

tu·mult /ˈtuʷmʌlt, ˈtyuʷ-/ *n* [C;U] *fml* (a state of) confused noise and excitement –**tumultuous** /tʊˈmʌltʃuʷəs, tyʊ-/ *adj: a tumultuous welcome* –**tumultuously** *adv*

tu·na /ˈtuʷnə, ˈtyuʷnə/ *n* **tuna** or **tunas** [C;U] (the flesh of) a large sea fish, used for food: *a can of tuna fish*

tun·dra /ˈtʌndrə/ *n* [*the* S;U] a cold treeless plain in the far north of Europe, Asia, and North America

tune¹ /tuʷn, tyuʷn/ *n* **1** an arrangement of musical sounds: *Do you know the tune to this song?* **2** **change one's tune** to change one's opinion, behavior, etc. **3** **in/out of tune: a** at/not at the correct musical level (PITCH²): *The piano is out of tune.* **b** in/not in agreement or sympathy: *His ideas were in tune with mine.* **4** **to the tune of** to the amount of: *We were robbed to the tune of fifty dollars.*

tune² *v* **tuned, tuning** [T *up*] **1** to set (a musical instrument) at the proper musical level (PITCH²) **2** to put (an engine) in good working order

tune in *v adv* [I;T (=**tune in** sthg.)] **1** to set (a radio) to receive broadcasts from a particular radio station: *We always tune in at 10 o'clock to hear the news.* **2** **tuned in (to)** in touch with what people are thinking, saying, feeling, etc.: *A politician must be tuned in to popular feelings if he is to be successful.*

tune out *v adv* **1** [T] to cut radio broadcasts by changing the signals **2** [I;T (=**tune** sbdy.↔ **out**)] *infml* to stop listening: *When he started to complain, I tuned (him) out.*

tune up *v adv* [I] to set an instrument at the proper musical level

tune·ful /ˈtuʷnfəl, ˈtyuʷn-/ *adj* having a pleasing tune; pleasant to listen to –**tunefully** *adv*

tune·less /ˈtuʷnlɪs, ˈtyuʷn-/ *adj* unmusical; unpleasant to listen to –**tunelessly** *adv*

tun·er /'tu^wnər, 'tyu^w-/ n **1** the part of a radio or television that changes the signals into sound and/or pictures –see illustration on page 399 **2** a person who TUNES² (1) musical instruments: *a piano tuner*

tune-up /'· ·/ n an act of tuning (TUNE² (2)) an engine

tu·nic /'tu^wnɪk, 'tyu^w-/ n **1** a loose armless outer garment **2** a short coat worn by policemen, soldiers, etc., as part of a uniform

tuning fork /'·· ˌ·/ n a small steel instrument that produces a fixed musical note when struck, used in tuning (TUNE² (1)) musical instruments

tun·nel¹ /'tʌnl/ n an underground or underwater passage (for a road, railroad, etc.) through or under a hill, town, etc.

tunnel² v **-l-** *AmE*‖**-ll-** *BrE* [I] to make a TUNNEL¹ under or through (a hill, river, etc.)

tur·ban /'tɜrbən/ n **1** a man's head-covering of Muslim origin, consisting of a long length of cloth wound around the head **2** a woman's small tight-fitting hat

tur·bine /'tɜrbət, -baɪn/ n an engine or motor driven by the pressure of a liquid or gas

tur·bot /'tɜrbət/ n [C;U] (the flesh of) a large fish with a flat diamond-shaped body, used for food

tur·bu·lence /'tɜrbyələns/ n [U] **1** the state of being TURBULENT **2** irregular and violent movement of the air: *The flight was very uncomfortable because of turbulence.*

tur·bu·lent /'tɜrbyələnt/ adj violent; disorderly; uncontrolled; stormy: *turbulent weather/winds*‖*a turbulent period of history*

tu·reen /tə'ri^yn/ n a large deep dish with a lid, from which soup is served

turf¹ /tɜrf/ n **turfs 1** [C;U] (a piece of) the surface of the soil with grass growing in it **2** [*the* S] horseracing **3** *infml* one's own neighborhood

turf² v [T] to cover (a piece of land) with TURF¹ (1)

tur·gid /'tɜrdʒɪd/ adj **1** swollen, as by a liquid or inner pressure **2** (of language or style) too solemn and self-important –**turgidly** adv –**turgidity** /tɜr'dʒɪdəti^y/ n [U]

tur·key /'tɜrki^y/ n **-keys 1** [C;U] (the flesh of) a large bird bred for its meat which is used as food, esp. at Christmas and Thanksgiving **2 cold turkey** *infml* a method of curing drug dependence by stopping the drug completely and at once (esp. in the phrase **go cold turkey**) **3** *infml esp. AmE* **talk turkey** to speak seriously and plainly, esp. about business matters

Turk·ish bath /ˌtɜrkɪʃ 'bæθ/ n a steam bath and MASSAGE

tur·moil /'tɜrmɔɪl/ n [S;U] a state of confusion, excitement, and trouble: *The whole town was* **in turmoil.**

turn¹ /tɜrn/ v **1** [I;T] to (cause to) go around: *The wheel turned slowly.*|*Turn the hands of the clock until they point to nine o'clock.*|*She turned the key in the lock.*|*to turn the pages of a book* **2** [I *around*] to bend around; look around: *He turned and waved.* **3** [T] to go around: *The car turned the corner.* **4** [I;T] to (cause to) change direction: *She turned the*

car *into the narrow street.*|*The car turned into the hotel entrance.*|*Turn right here and then left at the end of the street.*|*The police turned* (=pointed) *their guns at the robbers.*|(fig.) *Her condition has turned for the worse.*|(fig.) *He has turned to crime.* (=become a criminal)|(fig.) *We must now turn our attention to the coming elections.* **5** [T *in, down, back*] to fold: *He turned the corner of the page down so that he could find his place.* **6** [I;T] to (cause to) become (different): *He claimed to have invented a substance to turn iron into gold.*|*In 50 years this place has turned from a little village into a large town.*|*The heat has turned the grass brown.*|*He turns nasty if you laugh at him.*|*The heat has turned the milk.* (=made it sour)|*Don't let all this praise* **turn your head.** (=make you proud) **7** [T not *be* +*v-ing*] to become; reach; pass (a certain age, time, amount, etc.): *He has turned 40.*|*It's just turned three o'clock.* (=is just after three o'clock) **8** [T *away, out*] to cause to go; send; drive: *My father would turn me out if he knew I took drugs.* **9 turn loose** to let (a person or thing) go: *They turned the woman loose when the real criminal was found.* **10 turn one's hand to** to begin to practice (a skill) **11 turn one's stomach** to make one feel sick **12 turn over a new leaf** to abandon one's previous bad behavior **13 turn the tables** to change a situation in one's favor

turn (sbdy.) **against** sbdy./sthg. v prep [T] (to cause (someone)) to become opposed to or an enemy of (someone or something): *She turned the child against his own father.*

turn away v adv **1** [I] to refuse to look at something or someone **2** [T] (**turn** sbdy.↔ **away**) to refuse to admit: *We were turned away from the restaurant because we weren't properly dressed.*

turn back v adv [I;T (=**turn** sbdy.↔ **back**)] v to (cause to) return in the direction from which one has come: *We had to turn back because the road was blocked by snow.*

turn sbdy./sthg.↔ **down** v adv [T] **1** to lessen the force, strength, loudness, etc., of (a radio, heating system, etc.): *Turn that radio down at once!* **2** to refuse (a request, person, etc.): *to turn down an offer*

turn in v adv **1** [I] *infml* to go to bed **2** [T] (**turn** sbdy./sthg.↔ **in/over**) to deliver to the police

turn off v adv **1** [T] (**turn** sthg.↔ **off**) to stop a flow of (water, gas, electricity, etc.): *Turn off the television!* **2** [I;T (=**turn off** sthg.)] to leave (one road) for another: *We turned off the main road a few miles back.* **3** [T] (**turn** sbdy. **off**) *infml* to (cause to) dislike: *He really turns me off.*

turn on v adv [T] **1** (**turn** sthg.↔ **on**) to cause (water, gas, electricity, etc.) to flow: *He turned on the light.*|(fig.) *She turns on her charm whenever she wants anything.* –see OPEN (USAGE) **2** (**turn on** sbdy.) to attack (someone) suddenly **3** (**turn** sbdy. **on**) *infml* to excite or interest (a person), esp. sexually

turn out v adv **1** [T] (**turn** sthg.↔ **out**) to stop (a light, etc.) **2** [I] to come out or gather as for a meeting, public event, etc.: *Crowds turned out for the procession.* –compare TURNOUT **3** [T] (**turn** sthg. **out**) to produce: *This factory can turn out a hundred cars a day.* **4** [I +*to-v*] to happen to be in the end: *His statement turned out to be false.|The party turned out a success.* **5** [*usu. pass.*] to dress: *She was well turned out for the party.*

turn over *v adv* **1** [T] (**turn** sthg.↔ **over**) to think about; consider: *to turn an idea over in one's mind* **2** [I] (of an engine) to run at the lowest speed **3** [T *to*] → TURN **in** (2) –compare TURNOVER

turn to sbdy./sthg. *v prep* [T] **1** to go to for help **2** to look at (the stated page) in a book

turn up *v adv* **1** [T] (**turn** sthg.↔ **up**) to find: *to turn up new information* **2** [I] to be found: *The missing bag turned up, completely empty, in an old car.* **3** [T] (**turn** sthg.↔ **up**) to shorten (a garment) **4** [I] to arrive: *She turns up late for everything.|Don't worry, something will turn up.* (=happen) **5** [T] (**turn** sthg.↔ **up**) to increase the force, strength, loudness, etc., of (a radio, heating system, etc.) by using controls

turn² *n* **1** [C] an act of turning; single movement completely around a fixed point: *To open the safe, give the wheel three turns to the left and then two turns to the right.* **2** [C] a change of direction: *a turn in the road|river|Take* (=follow) *the second turn on the right.* **3** [S] a movement or development in direction: *I'm afraid there's been a* **turn for the worse.** (=things have become worse)*|How do you explain this strange* **turn of events**? (=this strange happening)*|Will there be a turn* (=change) *in government thinking this year?* **4** [*the* S *of*] a point of change in time: *at the turn of the century|the turn of the hour* **5** [C +*to-v*] a rightful chance or duty to do something: *It's my turn to drive next.|You've missed your turn so you'll have to wait.|We* **took turns** *at driving the car.* (=first she did it, then I did it, then she, etc.)*|Would you like a turn* (to play)*?|We visited each old lady* **in turn.** (=one after the other)*|I hope I haven't spoken* **out of turn?** (=spoken when I should have remained silent) **6** [C] *infml* an attack of illness: *He had one of his funny turns again last night.* **7** [S] *infml* a shock: *You gave me quite a turn when you shouted out like that.* **8** (a person who gives) a usu. short performance esp. in a theater, circus, show, etc.: *a* COMEDY (=amusing) *turn|the star turn* **9** a **good turn** a useful or helpful action: *He did me a good turn when he sold me his car; it's in really good condition.* **10** to **a turn** (esp. of food) perfectly cooked: *This meat's* **done to a turn.**

turn·coat /'tɜrnkoʷt/ *n derog* a person who changes his party, principles, or loyalty

turning point /'·· ,·/ *n* a point in time of important change: *The arrival of the Romans was a turning point in our history.*

tur·nip /'tɜrnɪp/ *n* [C;U] (a plant with) a large yellowish root used for food

turn·out /'tɜrnaʊt/ *n* [*usu. sing.*] the number of people who attend a meeting, vote, etc.: *They usually get a turnout of a hundred or*

more at their meetings.|a big turnout at the election –compare TURN **out**

turn·o·ver /'tɜrn,oʷvər/ *n* [S] the amount of business done, workers hired, articles sold, etc., in a particular period: *a turnover of $5,000 a week* –compare TURN **over**

turn·pike /'tɜrnpaɪk/ also **pike**– *n AmE* a special road for the use of fast-traveling vehicles, esp. such a road where one has to pay

turn·stile /'tɜrnstaɪl/ *n* a small gate with arms, which allows people to pass one at a time, usu. after payment

turn·ta·ble /'tɜrn,teʸbəl/ *n* the round spinning surface on which a record is played –see illustration on page 399

tur·pen·tine /'tɜrpən,taɪn/ *infml*– *n* [U] a thin oil, used for thinning or removing paint

tur·quoise /'tɜrkwɔɪz, -kɔɪz/ *adj,n* [U] (the color of) a bluish-green, precious mineral

tur·ret /'tɜrɪt, 'tʌr-/ *n* **1** a small tower, usu. at a corner of a larger building **2** (on a TANK (2) plane, warship, etc.) a low heavily-armored steel DOME, with guns on it –**turreted** *adj*

tur·tle /'tɜrtl/ *n* **turtles** *or* **turtle** an animal that lives esp. in water, with a soft body covered by a hard horny shell –compare TORTOISE

tur·tle·neck /'tɜrtl,nɛk/ ‖also **polo neck** *BrE*– *n* a round rolled collar, usu. woolen: *a turtleneck sweater*

tusk /tʌsk/ *n* a very long pointed tooth, usu. one of a pair, that comes out near the mouth in certain animals such as the elephant

tus·sle /'tʌsəl/ *v* **-sled, -sling** [T *with*] *infml* to fight roughly without weapons; struggle roughly –**tussle** *n*

tu·tor /'tuʷtər, 'tyuʷ-/ *n* a teacher who gives private instruction to a single pupil or a very small class –**tutor** *v* [I;T *in*]

tu·to·ri·al /tuʷ'tɔriʸəl, -'toʷr-, tyuʷ-/ *adj* of or related to a TUTOR or his duties

tux·e·do /tʌk'siʸdoʷ/ also **tux** /tʌks/ *infml*, **dinner jacket**– *n* **-dos** *AmE* **1** a suit of formal evening clothes, usu. for men and often black in color, including coat, trousers, white shirt, black BOW TIE, etc. **2** just this coat, usu. black in color –see illustration on page 123

TV /,tiʸ 'viʸ/ *abbrev. for:* television

twad·dle /'twɑdl/ *n* [U] *infml* foolish talk or writing; nonsense

twang /twæŋ/ *n* **1** a quick ringing sound such as that made by pulling, then freeing a very tight string **2** a quality of speech, in which the voice sounds as though it is coming through the nose

'twas /twʌz, twɑz; *weak* twəz/ *short for* (*old use or lit*) it was

tweak /twiʸk/ *v* [T] to seize, pull, and twist (the ear or nose) with a sudden movement –**tweak** *n*

tweed /twiʸd/ *n* [U] a coarse woolen cloth: *a tweed suit*

tweet /twiʸt/ *v,n* [C;I] (to make) the short weak high noise of a small bird; CHIRP

tweez·ers /'twiʸzərz/ *n* [P] a small metal tool with two joined arms or parts, esp. used for picking up or pulling out small objects –see PAIR (USAGE)

twelve /twɛlv/ *determiner,n,pron* (the number) 12 –**twelfth** /twɛlfθ/ *determiner,adv,n, pron*

twen·ty /'twɛntiʸ, 'twɛniʸ/ *determiner,n,pron* **-ties** (the number) 20 –**twentieth** *determiner, n,pron,adv*

twenty-one¹ /ˌ··'·◄/ *determiner,n,pron* (the number) 21

twenty-one² /ˌ··'·/ *n* → BLACKJACK (1)

twice /twaɪs/ *predeterminer,adv* two times: *I've read the book twice.*|*I work twice as hard as you.*|*He eats twice what you eat/twice the amount that you eat.*

twid·dle /'twɪdl/ *v* **-dled, -dling** [T] to move (the fingers) or play with (something) aimlessly: *He just sat there, twiddling his thumbs.*

twig /twɪg/ *n* a small thin woody stem growing from a branch –**twiggy** *adj*

twi·light /'twaɪlaɪt/ *n* [U] the time when day is about to become night, and there is little light, or (less common) when night is about to become day –compare DUSK

twill /twɪl/ *n* [U] strong woven cotton cloth

twin /twɪn/ *n* **1** either of two children born of the same mother at the same time: *Jean and John are twins.*|*my twin sister* **2** either of two people or things closely connected or very like each other: *twin towns*|*twin beds* (=two single beds in a room)

twine¹ /twaɪn/ *n* [U] strong cord or string made by twisting threads together

twine² *v* **twined, twining** [I;T] to twist; wind: *The stems twined around the tree trunk.*

twinge /twɪndʒ/ *n* a sudden sharp pain: (fig.) *a twinge of conscience*

twin·kle /'twɪŋkəl/ *v* **-kled, -kling** [I *with*] to shine with an unsteady light: *stars twinkling in the sky*|*Her eyes twinkled* (=were bright) *with amusement.* –**twinkle** *n* [S]: *a twinkle of delight in his eyes*

twin·kling /'twɪŋklɪŋ/ *n* [S] a moment: **in the twinkling of an eye** (=a very short time)

twirl /twɜrl/ *v* [I;T] to (cause to) turn around and around quickly; (cause to) spin –**twirl** *n*

twist¹ /twɪst/ *v* **1** [T *around, together*] to twist: *to make a rope by twisting threads*|*She twisted her hair around her fingers to make it curl.* **2** [T] to turn: *Twist the handle and the box will open.*|*I twisted my foot.* (=hurt it by turning it sharply) **3** [I;T] to (cause to) change shape; bend: *The child twisted the wire into the shape of a star.*|*to twist* (=bend and break) *an apple off a tree*|(fig.)*He twisted my words* (=changed the meaning of what I said) *to make me look guilty.*|(fig.) *I gave her the $5 after she twisted my arm.* (=persuaded me)

twist² *n* **1** [C] an act of twisting **2** [C;U] something, such as thread, rope, etc., made by twisting two or more lengths together **3** [C] a bend: *a road with a lot of twists in it* **4** [C] an unexpected change or development: *a strange twist of fate/events* –**twisty** *adj* **-ier, -iest**: *a twisty road*

twist·er /'twɪstər/ *n* **1** a person or thing that twists **2** *AmE infml* a TORNADO or WHIRLWIND

twit /twɪt/ *n infml esp. BrE* a stupid fool

twitch¹ /twɪtʃ/ *v* [I;T] **1** to (cause to) move suddenly and quickly: *The horse twitched its ears.* **2** to give a sudden quick pull to (some-

thing): *I felt someone twitch my coat.*

twitch² *n* **1** a repeated short sudden movement of a muscle, done without conscious control –compare TIC **2** a sudden quick pull

twit·ter /'twɪtər/ *v* [I] **1** (of a bird) to make a number of short rapid sounds **2** [*on, about*] (of a person) to talk quickly and nervously: *always twittering on about something unimportant* –**twitter** *n* [S;U]: *the twitter of birds in the trees*

two /tuʷ/ *determiner,n,pron* **twos 1** (the number) 2 –compare SECOND **2 in two** into two parts: *cut it in two*

two-bit /'· ·/ *adj AmE infml* of small importance

two·faced /ˌtuʷ'feʸst◄/ *adj* deceitful; insincere

two·fold /'tuʷfoʷld, ˌtuʷ'foʷld◄/ *adj AmE* having two parts: *a twofold idea*

two-piece /ˌ· '·◄/ *adj* [A] consisting of two matching parts: *a two-piece suit*

two·some /'tuʷsəm/ *n* [*usu. sing.*] *infml* a group of two people or things

two-time /'· ·/ *v* **-timed, -timing** [I;T] *infml* to be deceitfully disloyal to (one's husband, wife, or lover): *I was two-timing (him), and he never knew it.*

two-way /ˌ· '·◄/ *adj* moving or allowing movement in both directions: *a two-way street*|*two-way traffic*

TX *written abbrev. said as:* Texas /'tɛksəs/ (a state in the US)

ty·coon /taɪ'kuʷn/ *n* a businessman or industrialist with great wealth and power

ty·ing /taɪ-ɪŋ/ *v pres. participle of* TIE²

tyke /taɪk/ *n esp. AmE* a small child

type¹ /taɪp/ *n* **1** [C] a particular kind, class, or group; group or class of people or things very like each other: *What type of plant is this?*|*She's the type of person that I admire.* **2** [C;U] (one of the) small blocks of metal or wood with the shapes of letters on them, used in printing **3** [U] printed words

type² *v* **typed, typing** [I;T] to write (something) with a TYPEWRITER

type·cast /'taɪpkæst/ *v* **-cast, -casting** [T] to repeatedly give (an actor) the same kind of part: *They always typecast me as a murderer because my face looks evil.*

type·face /'taɪpfeʸs/ *n* the size and style of the letters used in printing

type·writ·er /'taɪpˌraɪtər/ *n* a machine that prints letters by means of keys which are struck by the fingers –see illustration on page 467

ty·phoid /'taɪfɔɪd/ also **typhoid fever** /ˌ·· '··/– *n* an infectious disease causing fever and often death, caused by bacteria in food or drink

ty·phoon /taɪ'fuʷn/ *n* a very violent tropical storm

ty·phus /'taɪfəs/ *n* [U] an infectious disease, carried by lice (LOUSE) and FLEAS, that causes severe fever

typ·i·cal /'tɪpɪkəl/ *adj* [*of*] combining and showing the main signs of a particular kind, group, or class: *a typical eighteenth-century church*|*It was typical of him to arrive so late.* –**typically** *adv*: *typically American*

typ·i·fy /'tɪpə,faɪ/ v **-fied, -fying** [T] to serve as a typical example of: *the high quality that typifies all her work*

typ·ist /'taɪpɪst/ n a person employed mainly for typing (TYPE²) letters

ty·po /'taɪpoʷ/ n **-pos** *AmE infml* a mistake made in typing (TYPE²)

tyr·an·nize ‖ also **-nise** *BrE* /'tɪrə,naɪz/ v **-nized, -nizing** [I;T] to use power over (a person, country, people, etc.) with unjust cruelty

tyr·an·ny /'tɪrəniʸ/ n [U] **1** the use of cruel or unjust power to rule a person or country **2** government by a cruel ruler with complete power **–tyrannical** /tɪ'rænɪkəl, taɪ-/ adj **–tyrannically** adv

ty·rant /'taɪrənt/ n a person with complete power, who rules cruelly and unjustly

tyre /taɪər/ n *BrE* for TIRE

tzar /zɑr, tsɑr/ n [A;C] → CZAR

U, u

U, u /yuʷ/ **U's, u's** or **Us, us** the 21st letter of the English alphabet

u·biq·ui·tous /yuʷ'bɪkwətəs/ adj *fml* appearing, happening, done, etc., everywhere

ud·der /'ʌdər/ n the bag-like organ of a cow, female goat, etc., from which milk is produced

UFO /,yuʷ ɛf 'oʷ/ n UFO's *abbrev. for:* unidentified (IDENTIFY) flying object; a spacecraft thought to come from another world in space

ugh /ʊx, ʌg/ interj (an expression of dislike): *Ugh! This medicine tastes terrible.*

ug·ly /'ʌgliʸ/ adj **-lier, -liest 1** unpleasant to see: *an ugly face|Some parts of the city are rather ugly.* **2** very unpleasant: *An ugly scene developed in the crowd when a group of boys started fighting.* –see BEAUTIFUL (USAGE) **–ugliness** n [U]

UHF /,yuʷ eʸtʃ 'ɛf/ also **ultrahigh frequency** /,ʌltrahaɪ 'friʸkwənsiʸ/ *fml–* n [U] (the sending out of radio waves at) the rate of 300,000,000 to 3,000,000,000 per second, producing excellent sound quality –compare VHF

UK /,yuʷ 'keʸ/ n *abbrev. for:* United Kingdom (of Great Britain and Northern Ireland)

u·ku·le·le /,yuʷkə'leʸliʸ/ n a musical instrument like a small GUITAR

ul·cer /'ʌlsər/ n a rough place on the skin or inside the body which may bleed or produce poisonous matter: *a stomach ulcer|mouth ulcers*

ul·te·ri·or /ʌl'tɪəriʸər/ adj hidden or kept secret, esp. because bad: *He has an ulterior motive for seeing her: he's going to ask for some money.*

ul·ti·mate /'ʌltəmɪt/ adj [A] **1** (the) last; being at the end or happening in the end: *The ultimate responsibility lies with the President.* **2** *infml* greatest or best: *This is the ultimate in bicycles; you'll never find a better one.*

ul·ti·mate·ly /'ʌltəmɪtliʸ/ adv in the end: *Many gave their opinions, but ultimately the decision was the President's.*

ul·ti·ma·tum /,ʌltə'meʸtəm/ n **-tums** or **-ta** /tə/ a statement of something that must be done under a threat of force: *They gave us this ultimatum: if we didn't move out of the house before the end of the week, they would throw us out.*

ul·tra·ma·rine /,ʌltrəmə'riʸn◀/ adj,n [U] (of) a very bright blue color

ul·tra·son·ic /,ʌltrə'sɑnɪk◀/ adj (of sound waves) beyond the range of human hearing

ul·tra·vi·o·let /,ʌltrə'vaɪəlɪt◀/ adj (of light) beyond the purple end of the SPECTRUM and unable to be seen by human beings: *ultraviolet RAYS* –compare INFRARED

um·bil·i·cal cord /ʌm'bɪlɪkəl ,kɔrd/ n the tube of flesh which joins the young to the mother before birth, and through which the young is fed

um·brage /'ʌmbrɪdʒ/ n **take umbrage** to show that one's feelings have been hurt

um·brel·la /ʌm'brelə/ n **1** an arrangement of cloth over a folding frame with a handle, used for keeping rain off the head –see illustration on page 123 **2** a protecting power: *a country under the umbrella of the United Nations*

um·pire¹ /'ʌmpaɪər/ n a judge in charge of a game, esp. baseball

USAGE This word is used in connection with **baseball, football, tennis,** and **basketball.** –see REFEREE (USAGE)

umpire² v **-pired, -piring** [I;T] to act as UMPIRE¹ for (a game)

ump·teen /,ʌmp'tiʸn◀/ determiner,pron *infml* a large number (of): *I've seen that movie umpteen times.* **–umpteenth** n,determiner: *That's the umpteenth time I've told you not to do that!*

UN /,yuʷ 'ɛn/ n *abbrev. for:* United Nations

un·a·bat·ed /,ʌnə'beʸtɪd/ adj (of a wind, a person's strength, etc.) without losing force: *The storm continued unabated.* –see also ABATE

un·a·ble /ʌn'eʸbəl/ adj [F +to-v] not able; without the power, knowledge, time, etc., to do something: *He seems unable to understand you.|I'd like to go, but I'm unable to.* –compare INABILITY

un·a·bridged /,ʌnə'brɪdʒd◀/ adj (esp. of something written) not shortened; not ABRIDGED

un·ac·com·pa·nied /,ʌnə'kʌmpəniʸd◀/ adj **1** not accompanied (ACCOMPANY); without someone or something else going with one: *Children unaccompanied by an ADULT will not be admitted.* **2** without music as ACCOMPANIMENT: *an unaccompanied song*

un·ac·count·a·ble /,ʌnə'kauntəbəl/ adj surprising; not easily explained: *unaccount-*

able behavior –see also ACCOUNT FOR –**unaccountably** *adv*

un·a·dul·ter·at·ed /ˌʌnəˈdʌltəˌreɪtɪd/ *adj* **1** (esp. of food) not mixed with impure substances **2** [A] complete; UTTER: *unadulterated nonsense*

un·af·fect·ed /ˌʌnəˈfɛktɪd/ *adj* **1** not AFFECTED¹ (1): *People in the south of the country were unaffected by the storms in the north.* **2** not AFFECTED; natural in behavior or character: *the unaffected delight of a child*

un·A·mer·i·can /ˌʌn əˈmɛrɪkən◁/ *adj* (esp. of political activity and loyalty) unfavorable to the US; against American customs and ways: *People used to be imprisoned for un-American activities.*

u·nan·i·mous /yuʷˈnænəməs/ *adj* (of people) all agreeing; (of decisions) made with everyone agreeing: *The vote was unanimous/The voters were unanimous.* –**unanimously** *adv* –**unanimity** /ˌyuʷnəˈnɪmətiʸ/ *n* [U]

un·ap·proach·a·ble /ˌʌnəˈproʷtʃəbəl◁/ *adj* (of a person) not APPROACHABLE, difficult to talk to; not seeming to encourage friendliness

un·armed /ˌʌnˈɑrmd◁/ *adj* not carrying ARMS (1); without weapons

un·as·sum·ing /ˌʌnəˈsuʷmɪŋ◁/ *adj* not showing a wish to be noticed; quiet in manner

un·at·tached /ˌʌnəˈtætʃt◁/ *adj* **1** not connected **2** not married or ENGAGED (3) –see also ATTACH

un·at·tend·ed /ˌʌnəˈtɛndɪd◁/ *adj* alone; without people present or in charge: *Your car will be damaged if you leave it unattended here.*

un·a·wares /ˌʌnəˈwɛərz/ *adv* **1** unintentionally or without noticing **2 take someone unawares** to surprise someone

un·bal·anced /ˌʌnˈbælənst◁/ *adj* (of a person, his/her character, etc.) slightly crazy: *He became a little unbalanced after his wife died.*

un·bear·a·ble /ʌnˈbɛərəbəl/ *adj* not bearable; too bad to be borne: *unbearable heat* |*The pain was unbearable.* –**unbearably** *adv*

un·be·liev·a·ble /ˌʌnbɪˈliʸvəbəl/ *adj* very surprising: *It's unbelievable how many children she has!* –see also BELIEVABLE –**unbelievably** *adv*

un·bend /ʌnˈbɛnd/ *v* -**bent** /ˈbɛnt/, -**bending** [I] to behave in an informal manner, esp. when usu. formal; RELAX: *She was very formal at first, but then she unbent a little and told a funny story.*

un·bend·ing /ˌʌnˈbɛndɪŋ◁/ *adj* refusing to change opinions, decisions, etc.

un·born /ˌʌnˈbɔrn◁/ *adj* not yet born

un·bound·ed /ˌʌnˈbaʊndɪd◁/ *adj* limitless; far-reaching: *unbounded joy* –see also BOUND²

un·bri·dled /ˌʌnˌbraɪdld◁/ *adj esp. lit* not controlled: *unbridled anger*

un·bur·den /ʌnˈbɜrdn/ *v* [T *of*] to free (oneself, one's mind, etc.) by talking about a secret trouble: *She unburdened herself (of her secret) to me.* –see also BURDEN²

un·but·ton /ʌnˈbʌtn/ *v* [T] to unfasten the buttons of

un·called-for /ʌnˈkɔld ˌfɔr/ *adj* not deserved or right: *Such rudeness is completely uncalled-for.*

un·can·ny /ʌnˈkæniʸ/ *adj* -**nier**, -**niest** mysterious; not natural or usual: *It seemed uncanny to hear her voice from the other side of the world.* –**uncannily** *adv*

un·cared-for /ʌnˈkɛərd ˌfɔr/ *adj* not well looked after: *His face is dirty and his clothes uncared-for.*

un·cer·e·mo·ni·ous /ˌʌnsɛrəˈmoʷniʸəs/ *adj* **1** informal: *an unceremonious but sincere welcome* **2** not done politely; rudely quick: *She finished the meal with unceremonious haste.* –see also CEREMONIOUS –**unceremoniously** *adv* –**unceremoniousness** *n* [U]

un·cer·tain /ʌnˈsɜrtn/ *adj* **1** [F] not certain; doubtful: *I'm uncertain about how to get there.* **2** undecided or unable to decide: *Our vacation plans are still uncertain.* **3** changeable: *uncertain weather* –**uncertainly** *adv* –**uncertainty** /ʌnˈsɜrtn-tiʸ/ *n* -**ties** [C;U]

un·char·i·ta·ble /ʌnˈtʃærətəbəl/ *adj* not kind or fair in judging others: *an uncharitable remark* –see also CHARITY

un·chart·ed /ˌʌnˈtʃɑrtɪd◁/ *adj lit* (of a place) not known well enough for records, esp. maps, to be made: *the uncharted forests of Brazil*

un·checked /ˌʌnˈtʃɛkt◁/ *adj* not prevented from moving, developing, etc.; not CHECKED² (3): *The disease spread unchecked.*

un·cle /ˈʌŋkəl/ *n* [A;C] **1** (*often cap.*) the brother of one's father or mother, or the husband of one's aunt: *He's my uncle.*|*Take me swimming, Uncle (Jack)!* –see illustration on page 247 **2 say uncle** *AmE infml* to admit defeat; give up

un·clean /ˌʌnˈkliʸn◁/ *adj* not clean; not considered pure, esp. in a religious way: *In ancient times LEPERS were thought unclean.*

Uncle Sam /ˌʌŋkəl ˈsæm/ *n infml* the US

Uncle Tom /ˌʌŋkəl ˈtɑm/ *n derog* (a name for) a black person who is very friendly to whites and who is habitually willing to do what whites want

un·com·fort·a·ble /ʌnˈkʌmftəbəl, ʌnˈkʌmfərtəbəl/ *adj* not comfortable: *an uncomfortable chair* |(fig.) *I felt uncomfortable* (=EMBARRASSED) *when Carl and Jane started arguing with each other.* –**uncomfortably** *adv*

un·com·mit·ted /ˌʌnkəˈmɪtɪd◁/ *adj* [*to*] not COMMITTED; not having given loyalty to any one thing, group, belief, etc.: *She will join the club later, but at the moment wants to remain uncommitted.*

un·com·mon·ly /ʌnˈkɑmənliʸ/ *adv fml & old use* very; unusually: *That's uncommonly kind of you.* –see also COMMONLY

un·com·pro·mis·ing /ʌnˈkɑmprəˌmaɪzɪŋ/ *adj* refusing to change ideas or decisions; HARDLINE: *He is uncompromising in his ideas about education.* –**uncompromisingly** *adv*

un·con·cerned /ˌʌnkənˈsɜrnd◁/ *adj* [*about*] not CONCERNED (1); not worried or anxious: *She must have hurt herself, but she seemed* *quite unconcerned.* **–unconcernedly** /ˌʌnkən'sɜrnɪdliʲ/ *adv*

un·con·di·tion·al /ˌʌnkən'dɪʃənəl◂/ *adj* not limited by any conditions: *unconditional freedom/unconditional surrender* **–unconditionally** *adv*

un·con·scious¹ /ˌʌn'kɑnʃəs◂, -tʃəs/ *adj* **1** having lost consciousness: *She hit her head and was unconscious for several minutes.* **2** not intentional: *an unconscious action* –see CONSCIOUS (USAGE) **–unconsciously** *adv* **–unconsciousness** *n* [U]

unconscious² *n* → SUBCONSCIOUS

un·cork /ʌn'kɔrk/ *v* [T] to open (esp. a bottle) by removing the CORK¹ (2)

un·count·able /ˌʌn'kaʊntəbəl/ *adj* that cannot be counted: *An* **uncountable noun** *is marked* [U] *in this dictionary.* –opposite **countable** –see Study Notes on page 550

un·couth /ʌn'kuʷθ/ *adj* not having good manners; rough in speech and ways: *an uncouth young man*

un·cov·er /ʌn'kʌvər/ *v* [T] to remove a covering from: (fig.)*The police have uncovered a plan to shoot the President.*

un·crit·i·cal /ˌʌn'krɪtɪkəl◂/ *adj* [*of*] not CRITICAL (1); not making any judgments; (unwisely) accepting, without deciding if good or bad **–uncritically** *adv*

unc·tu·ous /'ʌŋktʃuʷəs/ *adj fml* too smooth in speech; showing insincere kindness, interest, etc. **–unctuously** *adv* **–unctuousness** *n* [U]

un·cut /ˌʌn'kʌt◂/ *adj* **1** (of a movie or story) not cut; not made shorter **2** (of a diamond or precious stone) not shaped for use in jewelry, etc.

un·daunt·ed /ˌʌn'dɔntɪd◂, -'dɑn-/ *adj* not at all discouraged by danger or difficulty; bold

un·de·cid·ed /ˌʌndɪ'saɪdɪd◂/ *adj* **1** in doubt: *I'm undecided about where to go for my vacation.* **2** without any decision or result being reached: *The match was left undecided.*

un·de·ni·a·ble /ˌʌndɪ'naɪəbəl◂/ *adj* clearly and certainly so, in existence, etc.: *His skill is undeniable, but he works too slowly.* **–undeniably** *adv*

un·der¹ /'ʌndər/ *adv* in or to a lower place; below: *She pushed him into the water and held him under.* (=below the surface)*|children of seven and under* (=younger)

under² *prep* **1** directly below; covered by: *to breathe under water|The insect crept under the door.|What are you wearing under your coat?* **2** less than; below: *under $5|children under seven* (=younger than seven) –opposite **over 3** working for; controlled by: *She has three secretaries under her.* **4** during the rule of: *Spain under Franco* **5** in the class of (a heading): *Rabbits come under "Animals" in the list.* **6** (used to express various states or conditions): *Under present conditions no change is possible.|under the influence of alcohol|The matter is still under discussion.* (=being talked about)*|I am under contract, so I must finish the job.|I was* **under the impression** (=I thought) *that he was honest, but in fact he was a thief.|to work under great*

difficulties **7 under age** too young in law, esp. for drinking alcohol, entering certain public places alone, driving a car, etc. **8 under cover (of)** hidden or sheltered (by): *They escaped under cover of darkness.* –compare BELOW, BENEATH

un·der·arm /'ʌndərˌɑrm/ *adj,adv* **1** of the ARMPIT **2** (esp. in sports) (done) with the hand not moving above the shoulder –see also OVERHAND

un·der·car·riage /'ʌndərˌkærɪdʒ/ *n* the wheels of an aircraft

und·er·charge /ˌʌndər'tʃɑrdʒ/ *v* **-charged, -charging** [I;T] to take too small an amount of money from (someone); charge too little: *I think he undercharged me by mistake.* –opposite **overcharge**

un·der·clothes /'ʌndərˌkloʷz, -ˌkloʷðz/ also **underclothing** /'ʌndərˌkloʷðɪŋ/ [U]– *n* [P] → UNDERWEAR

un·der·coat /'ʌndərˌkoʷt/ *n* a covering of paint put onto a surface as a base for a top covering of paint

un·der·cov·er /ˌʌndər'kʌvər◂/ *adj* acting or done secretly, esp. as a SPY¹: *an undercover agent*

un·der·cur·rent /'ʌndərˌkɜrənt, -ˌkʌr-/ *n* a hidden current of water beneath the surface: (fig.) *An undercurrent of violence could be felt as you walked around the town.*

un·der·cut /ˌʌndər'kʌt, 'ʌndərˌkʌt/ *v* **-cut, -cutting** [T] to sell goods or services more cheaply than (a competitor)

un·der·dog /'ʌndərˌdɔg/ *n* **1** a person, country, etc., which is expected to lose in a competition with another **2** a small, poor, weak person, country, etc., that is always treated badly by others –compare DOG¹ (6)

un·der·done /ˌʌndər'dʌn◂/ *adj* not completely cooked –see also OVERDONE

un·der·es·ti·mate /ˌʌndər'ɛstəˌmeʲt/ *v* **-mated, -mating** [I;T] to have too low an opinion of the degree or number of: *I underestimated the cost of the journey, and now have no money left.* –see also OVERESTIMATE

un·der·foot /ˌʌndər'fʊt/ *adv* below one's feet; for walking on: *The ground was stony underfoot.*

un·der·go /ˌʌndər'goʷ/ *v* **-went** /'wɛnt/, **-gone** /'gɔn, 'gɑn/, **-going** [T] to experience (esp. suffering or difficulty): *She is undergoing treatment at the hospital.*

un·der·grad·u·ate /ˌʌndər'grædʒuʷɪt/ also **undergrad** /'ʌndərˌgræd/ *infml– n* a university student who has not yet taken his/her first degree –see also GRADUATE

un·der·ground¹ /'ʌndərˌgraʊnd/ *adj* **1** below the surface of the earth: *an underground passage* **2** secret; representing a political view which is not acceptable to the government: *an underground newspaper* **–underground** /ˌʌndər'graʊnd/ *adv*

un·der·ground² /'ʌndərˌgraʊnd/ *n BrE* for SUBWAY

un·der·growth /'ʌndərˌgroʷθ/ *n* [U] bushes, tall plants, etc., growing around and under trees: *to hide in the undergrowth*

un·der·hand /'ʌndərˌhænd/ also **underhanded** /ˌʌndər'hændɪd◂/– *adj* dishonest, esp. secretly: *He won the election in a very underhand manner.*

un·der·lie /ˌʌndər'laɪ/ *v* **-lay** /'leʸ/, **-lain** /'leʸn/, **-lying** [T] (of feelings and qualities) to form a (hidden) explanation of: *Does some personal difficulty underlie his lack of interest in work?*

un·der·line /'ʌndərˌlaɪn, ˌʌndər'laɪn/ also **underscore–** *v* **-lined, -lining** [T] to mark (one or more words) by drawing a line underneath, esp. to show importance or to give force: (fig.) *The accident at the factory underlines* (=shows the importance of) *the need for better safety standards.*

un·der·manned /ˌʌndər'mænd◄/ *adj* →UNDERSTAFFED –see also MAN²

un·der·mine /ˌʌndər'maɪn, 'ʌndərˌmaɪn/ *v* **-mined, -mining** [T] to wear away (something) from beneath, removing support: *The house is unsafe since the* FOUNDATIONS *were undermined by floods.|Illness undermined his strength.*

un·der·neath¹ /ˌʌndər'niʸθ/ *prep,adv* under; below: *The insect crept underneath the door.*

underneath² *n* [S] the lower part of something; bottom surface: *a mark on the underneath of the table*

un·der·nour·ish /ˌʌndər'nɜrɪʃ, -'nʌr-/ *v* [T] to feed with too little and/or bad quality food, causing lack of growth –see also NOURISH –**undernourishment** *n* [U]

un·der·pants /'ʌndərˌpænts/ *n* [P] short, close-fitting underclothes, covering the lower part of the body –see PAIR¹ (USAGE) –see illustration on page 123

un·der·pass /'ʌndərˌpæs/ *n* a road or (esp.) a path for walkers that goes under another road

un·der·pay /ˌʌndər'peʸ/ *v* **-paid** /'peʸd/, **-paying** [I;T] to pay less than the sufficient amount or the amount deserved –**underpaid** /ˌʌndər'peʸd◄/ *adj: Doctors are seldom underpaid.*

un·der·priv·i·leged /ˌʌndər'prɪvəlɪdʒd◄/ *adj* (of people) not having the advantages of other people

un·der·rate /ˌʌndər'reʸt/ *v* **-rated, -rating** [T] to have too low an opinion of (ability, strength, etc.): *We underrated his powers as a speaker.* –see also OVERRATE

un·der·score /ˌʌndər'skɔr, -'skoʷr/ *v* **-scored, -scoring** [T] → UNDERLINE

un·der·shirt /'ʌndərˌʃɜrt/ *AmE*‖**vest** *BrE–* *n* a short undergarment, usu. without coverings for the arms, worn on the upper part of the body next to the skin –compare T-SHIRT

un·der·side /'ʌndərˌsaɪd/ *n* the part underneath; lower side or surface: *the underside of a car*

un·der·signed /'ʌndərˌsaɪnd/ *adj* **the undersigned** the person(s) whose signature(s) is/are lower on the paper: *The undersigned (persons) wish to be considered for election: John Smith, Joe Brown, Mary Jones.*

un·der·sized /ˌʌndər'saɪzd◄/ also **undersize** /ˌʌndər'saɪz◄/– *adj* too small or smaller than usual

un·der·staffed /ˌʌndər'stæft◄/ also **undermanned–** *adj* having too few workers: *The*

office *has been understaffed since the secretary left.*

un·der·stand /ˌʌndər'stænd/ *v* **-stood** /'stʊd/, **-standing** [not *be* +*v-ing*] **1** [I;T] to know or get the meaning of (something): *Do you understand (this idea)?|I can't understand modern art.* **2** [T] to know or feel closely the nature of (a person, feelings, etc.): *I can't understand him when he behaves so badly.|I understand how you feel.* **3** [T +(*that*)] *fml* or *polite* to have been informed; have found out (a fact): *I understand you're coming to work for us.* **4** [T +(*that*)] to take or judge (as the meaning): *By "children" it's understood (that) they mean people under 14.|We understood them to mean that they would wait for us.* **5 make oneself understood** to make one's meaning clear to others, esp. in speech –**understandable** *adj* –**understandably** *adv: He was understandably upset when he lost the game.*

un·der·stand·ing /ˌʌndər'stændɪŋ/ *n* **1** [C;U] the act of understanding; power to judge: *According to my understanding of the letter, he owes you money.* **2** [S;U] sympathy: *There is (a) deep understanding between them.* **3** [C] a private, not formal, agreement: *We have come to an understanding.* (=reached an agreement)

un·der·state /ˌʌndər'steʸt, 'ʌndərˌsteʸt/ *v* **-stated, -stating** [T] to cause (something) to seem less important than it is: *They understated the seriousness of the crime.* –see also OVERSTATE

un·der·state·ment /'ʌndərˌsteʸtmənt/ *n* (a) statement which is not strong enough: *To say the book was "not bad" is an understatement; it was excellent!*

un·der·stud·y /'ʌndərˌstʌdiʸ/ *n* **-ies** an actor who learns an important part in a play so as to take the place of the person who plays that part, if necessary

un·der·take /ˌʌndər'teʸk/ *v* **-took** /'tʊk/, **-taken** /'teʸkən/, **-taking** [T] **1** to take up (a position); start on (work): *She undertook responsibility for the cost of the changes.* **2** [+*to-v/*(*that*)] to promise or agree: *She undertook to pay back the money within six months.*

un·der·tak·er /'ʌndərˌteʸkər/ *n* a person whose job it is to arrange funerals

un·der·tak·ing /'ʌndərˌteʸkɪŋ, ˌʌndər'teʸ-/ *n* **1** a piece of work, or something needing effort: *To start a new farm is a large undertaking.* **2** [+*to-v/*(*that*)] a promise: *I want a firm undertaking that you won't be late again.*

under-the-ta·ble /ˌ··· '··◄/ also **under-the-counter** /ˌ··· '··◄/– *adj infml* (bought or sold) secretly, esp. against the law: *an under-the-table business arrangement* –see also COUNTER¹ (2)

un·der·tone /'ʌndərˌtoʷn/ *n* a quiet voice: *He spoke in an undertone so that the others wouldn't hear.*

un·der·wa·ter /ˌʌndər'wɔtər◄, -'wɑ-/ *adj, adv* (used, done, etc.) below the surface of the water: *underwater swimming|underwater movies|an underwater camera|They swam underwater.*

un·der·wear /'ʌndər‚wɛər/ also **underclothes** [P], **underclothing**– n [U] the clothes worn next to the body under other clothes, such as UNDERSHIRTS, UNDERPANTS, BRAS, etc. –see illustration on page 123

un·der·weight /'ʌndər‚weʸt, ‚ʌndər'weʸt◄/ adj [after n] weighing too little: *He is several pounds underweight.* –see also OVERWEIGHT; see THIN (USAGE)

un·der·went /‚ʌndər'wɛnt/ v past tense of UNDERGO

un·der·world /'ʌndər‚wɜrld/ n 1 (usu. cap.) (in ancient stories) the place where the spirits of the dead live 2 the criminal world

un·de·sir·a·ble¹ /‚ʌndɪ'zaɪərəbəl◄/ adj fml not DESIRABLE; unpleasant; not wanted: *Long delays are undesirable, but sometimes unavoidable.* –**undesirability** /‚ʌndɪ‚zaɪərə'bɪlətiʸ/ n [U]

undesirable² n a person not wanted or liked by other people

un·de·vel·oped /‚ʌndɪ'vɛləpt◄/ adj (usu. of a place) not DEVELOPed; in its natural state, esp. not having industry, mining, modern farming, etc.

un·dis·tin·guished /‚ʌndɪ'stɪŋgwɪʃt◄/ adj not DISTINGUISHED; ordinary; not excellent: *an undistinguished performance/writer*

un·di·vid·ed /‚ʌndɪ'vaɪdɪd◄/ adj complete: *to give one's undivided attention*

un·do /ʌn'duʷ/ v -did /'dɪd/, -done /'dʌn/, -doing, 3rd pers. sing. present tense does /'dʌz/ [T] 1 to unfasten (what is tied or wrapped): *to undo the string around a package|He undid the package.* –see also UNDONE (1), DO up (1,2) 2 to remove the effects of: *The sudden fire undid months of hard work.*

un·do·ing /ʌn'duʷɪŋ/ n [S] the cause of ruin, failure, etc.: *Our attempt to climb higher was our undoing; we fell off the rock.*

un·done /‚ʌn'dʌn◄/ adj 1 [F] unfastened or loose: *Your button has come undone.* 2 not done: *a pile of work still undone*

un·doubt·ed /ʌn'daʊtɪd◄/ adj known for certain to be (so): *his undoubted wealth* –**undoubtedly** adv: *That is undoubtedly true.*

un·dreamed-of /ʌn'driʸmd əv, -‚ʌv, -‚av/ also **undreamt-of** /ʌn'drɛmt əv, -‚ʌv, -‚av/– adj [A] better than could have been imagined: *undreamed-of happiness/wealth*

un·dress /ʌn'drɛs/ v 1 [I] to take one's clothes off: *The doctor asked me to undress.|I (got) undressed and went to bed.* 2 [T] to take the clothes off (someone): *He undressed the baby and put her in the bath.*

un·due /‚ʌn'duʷ◄, -'dyuʷ◄/ adj [A] too much; not suitable: *with undue haste*

un·du·late /'ʌndʒə‚leʸt, -dyə-/ v -lated, -lating [I] to move or lie like waves rising and falling: *undulating hills* –**undulation** /‚ʌndʒə'leʸʃən, -dyə-/ n [C;U]

un·du·ly /ʌn'duʷliʸ, -'dyuʷ-/ adv too much (so); very: *not unduly worried|not worried unduly*

un·earth /ʌn'ɜrθ/ v [T] to dig up: *to unearth a box buried under a tree|(fig.) to unearth a secret*

un·earth·ly /ʌn'ɜrθliʸ/ adj 1 not natural; GHOSTLY: *to feel an unearthly presence in the room* 2 infml (of time) very inconvenient, esp. because too early or late: *What an unearthly time of night to call!*

un·eas·y /‚ʌn'iʸziʸ◄/ adj -ier, -iest not comfortable, esp. because worried or anxious: *uneasy about the future* –**uneasily** adv –**uneasiness** also **unease** /ʌn'iʸz/- n [U] lit

un·ec·o·nom·ic /‚ʌnɛkə'namɪk, -iʸkə-/ also **uneconomical** /‚ʌnɛkə'namɪkəl, -iʸkə-/– adj not producing profit; wasteful: *an uneconomic use of time* –compare ECONOMICAL –**uneconomically** adv

un·ed·u·cat·ed /ʌn'ɛdʒə‚keʸtɪd/ adj not EDUCATEd; showing a lack of (good) education: *uneducated speech*

un·em·ployed /‚ʌnɪm'plɔɪd◄/ adj not having a job: *The unemployed are hoping for work at the new factory.*

un·em·ploy·ment /‚ʌnɪm'plɔɪmənt/ n [U] 1 a lack of jobs for a large number of people in a society: *Unemployment became worse as factories closed.* 2 the condition of lacking a job: *He was thrown into unemployment when the hospital closed.* –compare EMPLOYMENT

un·en·light·ened /‚ʌnɪn'laɪtnd/ adj not ENLIGHTENed; not having knowledge, sometimes because uneducated; IGNORANT

un·en·vi·a·ble /ʌn'ɛnviʸəbəl/ adj unpleasant; not to be wished for: *The policeman had the unenviable job of telling the woman that her husband was missing.* –compare ENVIABLE

un·e·qual /ʌn'iʸkwəl/ adj 1 [in, to] not of equal size, value, etc.: *unequal amounts| amounts unequal in size* 2 [F to] (of a person) not having enough strength, ability, etc.: *He was unequal to the job.* –**unequally** adv

un·e·qualed AmE∥**unequalled** BrE /ʌn'iʸkwəld/ adj the greatest possible: *unequaled courage*

un·e·quiv·o·cal /‚ʌnɪ'kwɪvəkəl/ adj not EQUIVOCAL; totally clear in meaning –**unequivocally** adv

un·er·ring /ʌn'ɜrɪŋ, -'ɛr-/ adj without making a mistake: *With unerring judgment/aim she threw the ball through the hole.* –**unerringly** adv

un·e·ven /ʌn'iʸvən/ adj 1 not smooth or even: *Her hair has been badly cut and the ends are uneven.* 2 of varying quality: *a rather uneven* (=sometimes bad) *piece of writing* –**unevenly** adv –**unevenness** n [U]

un·fail·ing /ʌn'feʸlɪŋ/ adj (esp. of something good) never ceasing to be (so): *with unfailing interest/courage* –**unfailingly** adv

un·faith·ful /ʌn'feʸθfəl/ adj [to] not FAITHFUL; disloyal to one's marriage partner or lover by having a sexual relationship with another person

un·fath·om·a·ble /ʌn'fæðəməbəl/ adj which cannot be understood: *an unfathomable mystery* –**unfathomably** adv

un·fa·vor·a·ble AmE∥**unfavourable** BrE /ʌn'feʸvərəbəl/ adj not favorable; not good: *unfavorable weather|I've been hearing unfavorable reports about your work.* –**unfavorably** adv

un·feel·ing /ʌn'fiʸlɪŋ/ adj cruel; not sympathetic towards others: *an unfeeling ATTITUDE towards other people* –**unfeelingly** adv

un·flag·ging /ʌnˈflægɪŋ/ *adj* without tiring or stopping: *an unflagging interest in the job*

un·flinch·ing /ʌnˈflɪntʃɪŋ/ *adj* fearless; firm: *unflinching courage* –**unflinchingly** *adv*

un·fold /ʌnˈfoʷld/ *v* **1** [T] to open from a folded position: *She opened the envelope, took out the letter, and unfolded it carefully.* **2** [I;T] to make or become clear, more fully known, etc.: *The story unfolds slowly as the movie goes on.*

un·fore·seen /ˌʌnfɔrˈsiʸn◂, -foʷr-/ *adj* not FORESEEN; unexpected: *unforeseen delays*

un·for·get·ta·ble /ˌʌnfərˈgɛtəbəl/ *adj* (of an experience) too good or bad to be forgotten: *We went to a beautiful lake and spent an unforgettable day.* –**unforgettably** *adv*

un·for·tu·nate¹ /ʌnˈfɔrtʃənɪt/ *adj* **1** not FORTUNATE; unlucky: *an unfortunate accident/ man* **2** unsuitable: *an unfortunate remark*

unfortunate² *n* sometimes pomp an unlucky person, esp. one who has no social advantages, no home, etc.

un·for·tu·nate·ly /ʌnˈfɔrtʃənɪtliʸ/ *adv* I am afraid that...: *Unfortunately, we arrived too late to catch the plane.* –compare FORTUNATELY

un·found·ed /ˌʌnˈfaʊndɪd◂/ *adj* not supported by facts; without base: *The suggestion that I wanted to leave is completely unfounded.*

un·furl /ʌnˈfɜrl/ *v* [T] to unroll and open (a flag, sail, etc.)

un·gain·ly /ʌnˈgeʸnliʸ/ *adj* not graceful; awkward in movement; CLUMSY (1) –**ungainliness** *n* [U]

un·gov·ern·a·ble /ʌnˈgʌvərnəbəl/ *adj fml* uncontrollable: *an ungovernable temper* –see also GOVERN (2)

un·gra·cious /ʌnˈgreʸʃəs/ *adj* not GRACIOUS; not polite: *an ungracious refusal* –**ungraciously** *adv*

un·grate·ful /ʌnˈgreʸtfəl/ *adj* not grateful –**ungratefully** *adv*

un·guard·ed /ʌnˈgɑrdɪd◂/ *adj* careless over what is made known: *An unguarded remark let everyone know his secret.*

un·hap·pi·ly /ʌnˈhæpəliʸ/ *adv* **1** in an unhappy way **2** *fml* for UNFORTUNATELY: *Unhappily, we never saw her again.*

un·hap·py /ʌnˈhæpiʸ/ *adj* **-pier, -piest 1** not happy **2** *fml* unsuitable: *an unhappy choice of words, which was certain to hurt someone's feelings* –**unhappiness** *n* [U]

un·health·y /ʌnˈhɛlθiʸ/ *adj* **-ier, -iest 1** not generally in good health: *They're unhealthy because they don't get good food and fresh air.* **2** not likely to give good health: *unhealthy weather* **3** unnatural: *an unhealthy interest in cruelty* –opposite **healthy** –**unhealthily** *adv* –**unhealthiness** *n* [U]

un·heard /ˌʌnˈhɜrd◂/ *adj* not listened to: *Her complaints went unheard.*

unheard-of /·ˈ· ˌ·/ *adj* very strange and unusual: *It's unheard-of to pass the examination so young.*

un·hinge /ʌnˈhɪndʒ/ *v* **-hinged, -hinging** [T] to drive (a person) crazy; to cause (the mind) to become UNBALANCED: *The terrible experience unhinged him/his mind.*

un·hook /ʌnˈhʊk/ [T] **1** to remove from a hook: *to unhook the meat* **2** to unfasten the hooks of: *to unhook a dress*

u·ni·corn /ˈyuʷnəˌkɔrn/ *n* an imaginary horselike animal with one horn growing forwards from its forehead

un·i·den·ti·fied /ˌʌnaɪˈdɛntəˌfaɪd◂, ˌʌnə-/ *adj* whose name, nature, or origin has not been found: *An unidentified man was seen near the scene of the murder.* –see also UFO

u·ni·form¹ /ˈyuʷnəˌfɔrm/ *adj* with every part the same; regular: *a uniform color* –**uniformity** /ˌyuʷnəˈfɔrmətiʸ/ *n* [U] –**uniformly** /ˈyuʷnəˌfɔrmliʸ/ *adv*

uniform² *n* [C;U] a certain type of clothing which all members of a group wear, esp. in the army, a school, or the police: *New York City policemen wear dark blue uniforms.|school uniform* –**uniformed** *adj*: *Two policemen came to the door: one was a uniformed officer, and the other was in plain clothes.* (=not *wearing a uniform*)

u·ni·fy /ˈyuʷnəˌfaɪ/ *v* **-fied, -fying** [T] **1** to make (parts) into one (whole): *Spain was unified in the 16th century.* **2** to make all the same: *to unify the systems* –**unification** /ˌyuʷnəfəˈkeʸʃən/ *n* [U]

u·ni·lat·er·al /ˌyuʷnəˈlætərəl/ *adj* done by or having an effect on only one of the groups in an agreement –compare BILATERAL, MULTILATERAL

un·im·peach·a·ble /ˌʌnɪmˈpiʸtʃəbəl◂/ *adj fml* blameless; that cannot be doubted: *an unimpeachable character/witness*

un·in·formed /ˌʌnɪnˈfɔrmd◂/ *adj* not informed; (done) without enough knowledge: *an uninformed opinion*

un·in·hab·it·a·ble /ˌʌnɪnˈhæbɪtəbəl◂/ *adj* not HABITABLE; unfit to be lived in

un·in·hib·it·ed /ˌʌnɪnˈhɪbɪtɪd◂/ *adj* not INHIBITED; free in action and behavior, esp. doing and saying what one likes –**uninhibitedly** *adv*

un·in·ter·est·ed /ʌnˈɪntrəstɪd, -ˈɪntəˌrɛstɪd/ *adj* [*in*] not interested –see DISINTERESTED (USAGE)

un·in·ter·rupt·ed /ˌʌnɪntəˈrʌptɪd◂/ *adj* continuous –**uninterruptedly** *adv*

un·ion /ˈyuʷnyən/ *n* **1** [U] the act of joining or state of being joined into one: *the union of two people in marriage* **2** [C] (*often cap.*) a group of countries or states joined together: *the Soviet Union* **3** [C] a club or society, esp. a LABOR UNION: *Do you belong to a union?|The Teachers Union is holding elections today.* **4** [C;U] *fml* (a) marriage: *a union blessed by the Church*

un·ion·ize ||also **-ise** *BrE* /ˈyuʷnyəˌnaɪz/ *v* **-ized, -izing** [I;T] to (cause to) form a LABOR UNION –**unionization** /ˌyuʷnyənəˈzeʸʃən/ *n* [U]

Union Jack /ˈ·· ˌ·/ *n* the national flag of Great Britain

u·nique /yuʷˈniʸk/ *adj* **1** [*no comp.*] being the only one of its type: *This stamp is unique; there are no others like it.* **2** *infml* unusual: *That's a rather unique dress.* –**uniquely** *adv* –**uniqueness** *n* [U]

USAGE Although **unique** is often used to

mean "unusual," this is thought by many teachers to be incorrect.

u·ni·sex /'yuʷnə,sɛks/ adj infml (usu. of clothes and HAIRDRESSERs) which can be used by both male and female: a unisex hairdresser (=for both men and women)

u·ni·son /'yuʷnəsən, -zən/ n in unison: a in perfect agreement b together

u·nit /'yuʷnɪt/ n 1 a thing or group regarded as being a complete whole: an army unit|The family is a small social unit.|a unit of housing (=a house, apartment, etc.) 2 a piece of furniture, storage apparatus, etc., which can be fitted with others of the same type: a kitchen unit 3 an amount or quantity taken as a standard of measurement: The YEN is the standard unit of money in Japan. 4 a the smallest whole number; the number 1 b any whole number less than 10

U·ni·tar·i·an /,yuʷnə'tɛəriʸən/ adj,n (a member) of a branch of the Christian church

u·nite /yuʷ'naɪt/ v -nited, -niting 1 [I;T] to join together into one: The threat of a foreign attack united the government and its opponents. 2 to act together for a purpose: They united (in their attempts) to form a club.

u·nit·ed /yuʷ'naɪtɪd/ adj 1 joined in a state of love, agreement, etc.: a very united family 2 [A] with everyone concerned having the same aim: to make a united effort 3 [A] (cap. in names) joined in a political organization: the United States (of America)|the United Nations –unitedly adv

u·ni·ty /'yuʷnəti̯/ n [S;U] (a) state of being united: a new unity between different branches of the church|The argument spoiled their former unity.

u·ni·ver·sal /,yuʷnə'vɜrsəl◄/ adj 1 concerning all members of a group: There was universal agreement that you should become chairman. 2 for all people or every purpose; widespread: a subject of universal interest –universality /,yuʷnəvər'sæləti̯/ n [U] –universally /,yuʷnə'vɜrsəli̯/ adv

u·ni·verse /'yuʷnə,vɜrs/ n (often cap.) all space and the matter which exists in it: Did God make the universe?

u·ni·ver·si·ty /,yuʷnə'vɜrsəti̯/ n -ties [C;U] a place of education at the highest level, where degrees are given: Several new universities have recently been built in Nigeria.|I spent three years at a university.|a university LECTURER (=teacher)

un·kempt /,ʌn'kɛmpt◄/ adj (esp. of hair) not neat or tidy

un·kind /,ʌn'kaɪnd◄/ adj not kind; cruel or thoughtless –unkindly adv –unkindness n [C;U]

un·known /,ʌn'noʷn◄/ n,adj (a person or thing) whose name, value, or origin is not known: an unknown quantity

un·law·ful /ʌn'lɔfəl/ adj against the law: an unlawful action –unlawfully adv

un·leash /ʌn'liʸʃ/ v [T] to set free (a dog) from a LEASH. (fig.) All her anger was unleashed upon us.

un·leav·ened /,ʌn'lɛvənd◄/ adj (of bread) made without YEAST, and therefore flat

un·less /ʌn'lɛs, ən-/ conj if not; except if: I'll

go unless he telephones.|Don't leave the building unless I tell you to.

un·like /,ʌn'laɪk◄/ adj,prep [F] not like; different: She's very unlike her mother.|It's unlike him to be late; he's usually on time.

un·like·ly /,ʌn'laɪkliʸ◄/ adj [+to-v] not likely; improbable: He may come, but it's very unlikely.|They're unlikely to marry.|It seems unlikely that they'll come. –unlikeliness also unlikelihood– n [U]

un·load /ʌn'loʷd/ v 1 [T] to remove (a load) from (something): to unload the books/the car 2 [I;T] to have (a load) removed: The train is unloading at the moment. 3 [I;T] to remove the CHARGE² (7) from (a gun) or film from (a camera)

un·lock /ʌn'lɑk/ v [T] to unfasten the lock of: She unlocked the door and then opened it.

un·looked-for /ʌn'lʊkt ,fɔr/ adj lit unexpected

un·loose /ʌn'luʷs/ v -loosed, -loosing [T] lit to set free

un·loos·en /ʌn'luʷsən/ v [T] to loosen: He sat down and unloosened his belt.

un·luck·y /,ʌn'lʌkiʸ◄/ adj -ier, -iest not lucky: He's very unlucky; he never wins anything.|She was unlucky enough to fall and break her leg on her first day at school.

un·made /,ʌn'meʸd◄/ adj (of a bed) not made ready for sleeping

un·mask /ʌn'mæsk/ v [T] to show the hidden truth about: to unmask the thief

un·men·tion·a·ble /ʌn'mɛnʃənəbəl, -tʃənə-/ adj too unpleasant to be spoken of –see also MENTION

un·mis·tak·a·ble /,ʌnmɪ'steʸkəbəl◄/ adj clearly recognizable; that cannot be thought to be otherwise: the unmistakable sound of a baby crying –see also MISTAKE –unmistakably adv

un·mit·i·gat·ed /,ʌn'mɪtə,geʸtɪd◄/ adj [A] in every way bad; not lessened or excused in any way: He is an unmitigated liar! –see also MITIGATE

un·moved /,ʌn'muʷvd◄/ adj 1 not feeling pity 2 not worried; calm –see also MOVE¹ (6)

un·nat·u·ral /ʌn'nætʃərəl/ adj 1 not natural; unusual: Her hair is an unnatural color. 2 against ordinary ways of behaving: unnatural sexual practices –compare SUPERNATURAL –unnaturally adv: an unnaturally large nose

un·nec·es·sar·y /ʌn'nɛsə,sɛriʸ/ adj not necessary or wanted; additional to what is needed or expected: That was an unnecessary remark; it would have been better to keep silent. –unnecessarily /,ʌn-nɛsə'sɛərəliʸ/ adv: unnecessarily rude

un·nerve /ʌn'nɜrv/ v -nerved, -nerving [T] to take away the courage of: The accident unnerved him, and he hasn't driven since. –see also NERVE²

un·ob·tru·sive /,ʌnəb'truʷsɪv/ adj not easily seen or noticed: She's a quiet unobtrusive student, but always does well on examinations. –see also OBTRUSIVE –unobtrusively adv –unobtrusiveness n [U]

un·of·fi·cial /,ʌnə'fɪʃəl◄/ adj not official; informal: an unofficial meeting|an unofficial

STRIKE² (1) –**unofficially** *adv*

un·or·tho·dox /ʌn'ɔːθəˌdɒks/ *adj* not ORTHO-DOX; not according to usual beliefs, methods, etc.: *She has an unorthodox style of playing tennis, but she usually wins.*

un·pack /ʌn'pæk/ *v* [I;T] to remove (possessions) from (a container): *I'm just going to unpack (my clothes/my case).* –see also PACK

un·par·al·leled /ʌn'pærəˌleld/ *adj* too great to be equaled: *an unparalleled success* –see also PARALLEL³

un·pleas·ant /ʌn'plɛzənt/ *adj* not pleasant; causing dislike; not enjoyable; unkind: *unpleasant smells/weather/She was very unpleasant to me.* –**unpleasantly** *adv* –**unpleasantness** *n* [U]

un·prec·e·dent·ed /ʌn'prɛsəˌdɛntɪd/ *adj* never having happened before: *unprecedented rainfall/price increases*

un·pre·ten·tious /ˌʌnprɪ'tɛnʃəs, -tʃəs/ *adj* not PRETENTIOUS; not showing signs of wealth, importance, etc.: *an unpretentious little house/They are rich but have an unpretentious style of living.* –**unpretentiously** *adv* –**unpretentiousness** *n* [U]

un·prin·ci·pled /ʌn'prɪnsəpəld/ *adj* (done) without regard to usual standards of honorable behavior: *He is totally unprincipled in money matters; you can't trust him.*

un·print·a·ble /ʌn'prɪntəbəl/ *adj* (of words) unacceptable for printing, usu. because offensive

un·pro·fes·sion·al /ˌʌnprə'fɛʃənəl/ *adj* (esp. of behavior) not suitable in a certain profession or activity, esp. because bad in some way –see also PROFESSIONAL¹ (2) –**unprofessionally** *adv*

un·pro·voked /ˌʌnprə'voʷkt◄/ *adj* (esp. of a bad action) not caused by another action: *The judge said that their attack on the old woman had been unprovoked.*

un·qual·i·fied /ʌn'kwɒləˌfaɪd/ *adj* **1** [+*to-v*] not having suitable knowledge or QUALIFICATIONS: *I am unqualified to talk on this subject.* **2** not limited: *We are in unqualified agreement./an unqualified success* (=very successful)

un·ques·tion·a·ble /ʌn'kwɛstʃənəbəl/ *adj* which cannot be QUESTIONED² (2); certain –**unquestionably** *adv*: *She is unquestionably our best player.*

un·rav·el /ʌn'rævəl/ *n* -**l**- *AmE*‖-**ll**- *BrE* **1** [I;T] **a** to cause (threads, cloth, etc.) to become separated or unwoven **b** (of threads, cloth, etc.) to become separated or unwoven **2** [T] to make clear (a mystery)

un·re·al /ˌʌn'riʸəl◄/ *adj* (of an experience) seeming imaginary or unlike reality

un·rea·son·a·ble /ʌn'riʸzənəbəl/ *adj* **1** unfair in demands; not sensible or showing reason **2** (of prices, costs, etc.) too great –**unreasonably** *adv* –**unreasonableness** *n* [U]

un·rea·son·ing /ʌn'riʸzənɪŋ/ *adj* not using the power of reason: *unreasoning anger*

un·re·lent·ing /ˌʌnrɪ'lɛntɪŋ◄/ *adj* continuous; without decreasing in power: *a week of unrelenting activity* –compare RELENTLESS –**unrelentingly** *adv*

un·re·lieved /ˌʌnrɪ'liʸvd◄/ *adj* continuous or complete: *unrelieved anxiety/sadness*

un·re·mit·ting /ˌʌnrɪ'mɪtɪŋ◄/ *adj* never stopping: *unremitting activity*

un·re·quit·ed /ˌʌnrɪ'kwaɪtɪd◄/ *adj* *fml* not given in return (esp. in the phrase **unrequited love**)

un·re·served /ˌʌnrɪ'zɜːvd◄/ *adj* without limits or RESERVATIONS: *You have my unreserved admiration.* –**unreservedly** /ˌʌnrɪ'zɜːv ɪdliʸ/ *adv*

un·rest /ʌn'rɛst/ *n* [U] dissatisfaction, esp. socially: *Unemployment causes social unrest.*

un·re·strained /ˌʌnrɪ'streɪnd◄/ *adj* not RESTRAINED; not held back or reduced: *unrestrained anger/violence*

un·ri·valed *AmE*‖**unrivalled** *BrE* /ʌn'raɪ vəld/ *adj* unequaled; very good: *an unrivaled knowledge of art*

un·roll /ʌn'roʷl/ *v* [I;T] to open from a rolled position: *They unrolled the cloth onto the table.*

un·ru·ly /ʌn'ruʷliʸ/ *adj* -**lier**, -**liest** wild in behavior; uncontrollable: *unruly children* –**unruliness** *n* [U]

un·said /ʌn'sɛd/ *adj* (thought of but) not spoken: *She left her fears unsaid.*

un·san·i·tar·y /ʌn'sænəˌtɛriʸ/ also **insanitary**– *adj* which is likely to harm the health by causing disease: *unsanitary conditions* –opposite **sanitary**

un·sa·vor·y *AmE*‖**unsavoury** *BrE* /ʌn'seʸ vəriʸ/ *adj* unpleasant or unacceptable in moral values: *an unsavory character* (=person)

un·scathed /ʌn'skeʸðd/ *adj* not harmed: *He walked away from the accident completely unscathed.*

un·screw /ʌn'skruʷ/ *v* [T] **1** to remove the screw(s) from (something) **2** to undo by twisting: *I can't unscrew (the top of) this bottle.*

un·scru·pu·lous /ʌn'skruʷpyələs/ *adj* not caring about honesty and fairness: *unscrupulous business methods* –opposite **scrupulous** –**unscrupulously** *adv* –**unscrupulousness** *n* [U]

un·seat /ʌn'siʸt/ *v* [T] to remove from a position of power, e.g. a seat in the Senate

un·seem·ly /ʌn'siʸmliʸ/ *adj esp. old use* not suitable (in behavior) –opposite **seemly** –**unseemliness** *n* [U]

un·set·tle /ʌn'sɛtl/ *v* -**tled**, -**tling** [T] **1** to make less calm, more dissatisfied, etc.: *The sudden changes unsettled her.* **2** to cause illness to (esp. the stomach): *Foreign food always unsettles me/my stomach.*

un·set·tled /ˌʌn'sɛtld◄/ *adj* not settled; changeable

un·shake·a·ble /ʌn'ʃeʸkəbəl/ *adj* firm (in belief): *an unshakable belief in God*

un·sight·ly /ʌn'saɪtliʸ/ *adj* not pleasant to look at; ugly –**unsightliness** *n* [U]

un·skilled /ˌʌn'skɪld◄/ *adj* **1** not trained for a particular type of job: *unskilled workers* **2** not needing special skill: *an unskilled job* –opposite **skilled**

un·so·phis·ti·cat·ed /ˌʌnsə'fɪstəˌkeʸtɪd◄/ *adj* not SOPHISTICATED (1); simple in likes, dislikes, etc.; inexperienced in the world and social life

un·sound /ˌʌn'saʊnd◄/ *adj* **1** not healthy, strong, or SOUND³: *Most of the building is in good condition, but the roof is unsound.* **2** (of ideas) not having a firm base in fact

un·spar·ing /ʌn'speərɪŋ/ *adj* holding nothing back, esp. money or help –opposite **sparing** –**unsparingly** *adv*

un·speak·a·ble /ʌn'spiʸkəbəl/ *adj* terrible: *unspeakable pain* –**unspeakably** *adv*: *unspeakably cruel*

un·stud·ied /ʌn'stʌdiʸd/ *adj fml* natural; without effort: *unstudied grace*

un·swerv·ing /ʌn'swɜrvɪŋ/ *adj* firm in purpose, esp. loyal

un·tan·gle /ʌn'tæŋgəl/ *v* **-gled, -gling** [T] to remove TANGLEs from; make free from twisted parts: *Can you untangle these wires?*

un·tapped /ˌʌn'tæpt◄/ *adj* not used or drawn from: *The sea is an untapped supply of* ENERGY (2).

un·ten·a·ble /ʌn'tɛnəbəl/ *adj* (esp. of a belief or argument) which cannot be defended: *an untenable position*

un·think·a·ble /ʌn'θɪŋkəbəl/ *adj* which one cannot believe has happened, or cannot wish to happen: *Failure at this late stage is unthinkable.*

un·think·ing /ʌn'θɪŋkɪŋ/ *adj* careless; done or said without considering the effect; THOUGHTLESS –**unthinkingly** *adv*

un·ti·dy /ʌn'taɪdiʸ/ *adj* **-dier, -diest** not tidy; not neatly arranged: *an untidy room*

un·tie /ʌn'taɪ/ *v* **-tied, -tying** [T] to undo (a knot or something tied): *Untie the string/the dog.*

un·til /ʌn'tɪl, ən-/ also **till**– *prep,conj* up to the time when; up to as late as: *Wait until tomorrow.|We won't start until (=before) Jane comes.|Keep driving straight until you get to the hospital, and then turn left.*

un·time·ly /ʌn'taɪmliʸ/ *adj fml* **1** happening too soon: *The accident put an untimely end to the party.* **2** not suitable for the occasion: *an untimely show of temper* –**untimeliness** *n* [U]

un·tir·ing /ʌn'taɪərɪŋ/ *adj* not showing tiredness, esp. in spite of hard work –**untiringly** *adv*

un·to /'ʌntuʷ/ *prep old use & bibl* to: *She spoke unto him.*

un·told /ˌʌn'toʷld◄/ *adj* **1** too great to be counted; limitless: *untold wealth* **2** not told or expressed: *an untold story*

un·to·ward /ˌʌn'tɔrd, -'toʷrd/ *adj fml* unfortunate; not wanted: *an untoward event*

un·truth /ʌn'truʷθ/ *n* **-truths** /'truʷðz, 'truʷθs/ *fml euph* a lie

un·truth·ful /ʌn'truʷθfəl/ *adj* not truthful; lying, esp. habitually: *an untruthful boy* –**untruthfully** *adv*

un·used¹ /ˌʌn'yuʷzd◄/ *adj* not having been used: *Put away the unused plates and cups.*

un·used² /ˌʌn'yuʷst/ *adj* [F+*to*] not accustomed: *He's unused to flying, so he gets nervous in planes.*

un·u·su·al /ʌn'yuʷʒuʷəl, -ʒəl/ *adj* not usual; rare; not common; interesting because different from others: *There's been an unusual*

amount of rain this month.|She has a most unusual face.

un·u·su·al·ly /ʌn'yuʷʒuʷəliʸ, -ʒəliʸ/ *adv* **1** in an unusual way **2** very; more than is common: *He's unusually fond of chocolate.*

un·veil /ʌn'veʸl/ *v* [I;T] to remove a VEIL or covering (from): *They unveiled the plaque to open the new school.*

un·war·rant·ed /ʌn'wɔrəntɪd, -'wɑr-/ *adj* (done) without good reason; not with just cause: *an unwarranted interruption*

un·well /ʌn'wɛl/ *adj* [F] not well; ill, esp. for a short time

un·wield·y /ʌn'wiʸldiʸ/ *adj* awkward to move, esp. because it is large, heavy, etc.: *a large, unwieldy box*

un·wind /ʌn'waɪnd/ *v* **-wound** /'waʊnd/, **-winding 1** [I;T] **a** to undo (something wound around): *He unwound the wool from the ball.* **b** (of something wound around) to become undone **2** [I] *infml* for RELAX

un·wit·ting /ˌʌn'wɪtɪŋ◄/ *adj* [A] not knowing or intended: *unwitting rudeness* –**unwittingly** *adv*

un·zip /ʌn'zɪp/ *v* **-pp-** [T] to open by undoing a ZIPPER (fastener)

up¹ /ʌp/ *adv* **1** from below towards a higher place; away from the floor, the ground, or the bottom: *Can you lift that box up onto the shelf for me?|We swam a long way under water and then came up for air.|The sleeping dog jumped up when it saw its master.|It gets hot after the sun has come up. (=appeared above the horizon. The sun comes out from behind a cloud.)* **2** in a high place: *flying 10,000 miles up in the air* **3** into an upright or raised position: *Stand up when the teacher comes in!|He turned his collar up to keep his neck dry.|They're putting up (=building) a new house.* **4** out of bed: *to get up early|to stay up late* **5** towards or in the north: *traveling up to Cape Cod from New York* **6** (showing a higher level or better condition): *Production has gone up this year. (=we have produced more)|The temperature's gone up ten degrees.* **7** along; towards the person speaking: *He came up to me and asked my name.* **8** (showing more noise, strength, activity, etc.): *Please turn the radio up.|Speak up! I can't hear you.* **9** (so as to be) completely finished: *The money's all used up.|Eat up your vegetables.|Time's up! (=it is time to finish now)* **10** into parts or pieces: *to tear up a newspaper|They divided up the money.* **11** firmly; tightly; safely: *to tie up a parcel|He nailed up the door, so they couldn't open it.* **12** so as to be together: *Please add up these numbers.|to collect up the fallen apples* **13** on top (in phrases like **right side up, wrong end up**) **14 up against** having to face: *to come up against a problem|a difficulty|We're really **up against it** (=in difficulties) now.* **15 up and down: a** higher and lower: *to jump up and down* **b** backwards and forwards: *to walk up and down* –compare DOWN

up² *adj* [*no comp.*] **1** [A] directed or going up: *the up stairs* **2** (of a road) being repaired: *"Road Up"* (on a sign) **3 up and about** out of bed: *She's not very ill; she'll soon be up and about again.* **4** *infml* **What's up?** What's the matter? **5 up to: a** busy with; doing something bad: *The children are very quiet; I wonder what they're up to.* **b** good enough for; intelligent enough for: *Michael's not really up to that job.|My German isn't up to translating that letter.|Do you feel up to going out?* (=well enough to go out) **c** the duty or responsibility of: *It's up to the cleaners to lock the doors at night.|It's up to you (to decide) whether to go or not.*

up³ *prep* **1** to or in a higher place; upwards by way of: *He ran up the hill.|The water got up my nose.|His office is up those stairs.* **2** along; to or at the far end of: *They live just up the road.* **3** against the direction of (the current of a river) –opposite **down 4 up and down: a** higher and lower on: *climbing up and down a ladder* **b** backwards and forwards along: *His eyes moved up and down the rows of people, looking for his son.*

up⁴ *v* **-pp-** *infml* **1** [T] to raise; increase: *to up the price of gasoline* **2** [I not be + *v*-*ing*] to get or jump up (and): *He upped and left.*

up-and-com-ing /ˌ· · '·-◄/ *adj* [A] showing signs of being about to succeed, usu. in a profession, work, etc.: *an up-and-coming actress* –compare UPCOMING

up·braid /ʌpˈbreɪd/ *v* [T] *fml or old use* to scold

up·bring·ing /ˈʌpˌbrɪŋɪŋ/ *n* [S] (a way of) training and caring for a child: *He has had a good upbringing.* –see also BRING up

up·com·ing /ˈʌpˌkʌmɪŋ/ *adj AmE* about to happen –compare UP-AND-COMING

up·date /ˌʌpˈdeɪt, ˈʌpdeɪt/ *v* **-dated, -dating** [T] to make more modern or UP-TO-DATE

up·end /ʌpˈɛnd/ *v* [T] to cause to stand on end: *We'll have to upend the cupboard to get it through the door.*

up·grade /ˌʌpˈgreɪd, ˈʌpgreɪd/ *v* **-graded, -grading** [T] to give a higher position to (esp. an employed person) –opposite **downgrade**

up·heav·al /ʌpˈhiːvəl/ *n* [C;U] (a) great change and movement: *all the upheaval of moving house*

up·hill /ˌʌpˈhɪl◄/ *adj,adv* on an upward slope: *walking uphill|*(fig.) *an uphill* (=difficult) *job* –opposite **downhill**

up·hold /ʌpˈhoʊld/ *v* **-held** /ˈhɛld/, **-holding** [T] **1** to support; prevent from being weakened or taken away: *to uphold the right to free speech* **2** to declare to be right; CON-FIRM: *The judge upheld the lower court's decision.* –**upholder** *n*

up·hol·ster /ʌpˈhoʊlstər, əˈpoʊl-/ *v* [T] to fit (a chair) with soft coverings over filling material (PADDING) –**upholsterer** *n*

up·hol·ster·y /ʌpˈhoʊlstəriː, əˈpoʊl-/ *n* [U] the material used in making CARPETs, curtains, soft chairs, etc.

up·keep /ˈʌpkiːp/ *n* [U *of*] the act or cost of keeping something repaired and in order: *We can no longer afford the upkeep of a large house.*

up·land /ˈʌplənd, -lænd/ *n* the higher land in an area: *the upland areas of the country*

up·lift /ˌʌpˈlɪft/ *v* [T] to encourage cheerful or

holy feelings in: *uplifting words*

up·on /əˈpɑn, əˈpɔn/ *prep fml* for ON¹ (1)

up·per¹ /ˈʌpər/ *adj* [A] **1** in a higher position or rank (than something lower): *the upper part of the body* **2 have/get the upper hand** to have or get control

upper² *n* the top part of a shoe or boot above the HEEL and SOLE

upper class /ˌ·· '·-◄/ *n* [*the* U] **1** (in the US) a social class whose members are very rich: *This part of town is where the upper class live.* **2** (esp. in Europe) a small class whose members belong to a few old, sometimes noble, and usu. very rich families –see also MIDDLE CLASS, WORKING CLASS; see UPPER CLASS (USAGE) –**upper-class** *adj: Tennis used to be only an upper-class sport.*

up·per·cut /ˈʌpərˌkʌt/ *n* (in BOXING) a blow with the hand moving upwards to the opponent's chin

upper hand /ˌ·· '·/ *n* [*the* S] control (esp. in the phrase **have/get the upper hand**)

up·per·most /ˈʌpərˌmoʊst/ *adv,adj* in the highest or strongest position: *uppermost in my mind ...* (=what I think about most)

up·right¹ /ˈʌp-raɪt/ *adj* **1** (standing) straight up, esp. habitually: *a tall upright young man* **2** honest, fair, responsible, etc.: *an upright citizen*

upright² *adv* straight up; not bent

up·ris·ing /ˈʌpˌraɪzɪŋ/ *n* an act of REBELling against the rulers, esp. the government

up·roar /ˈʌp-rɔr, -roʷr/ *n* [S;U] confused noisy activity, esp. shouts

up·roar·i·ous /ʌpˈrɔriʸəs, -ˈroʷr-/ *adj* **1** noisy, esp. with laughter **2** very amusing; causing loud laughter: *an uproarious movie* –**uproariously** *adv*

up·root /ˌʌpˈruʷt, -ˈrʊt/ *v* [T] to tear up by the roots: (fig.) *to uproot oneself and move across the country*

ups and downs /ˌ· · '·/ *n* [P] good and bad periods: *Life is full of ups and downs.*

up·set¹ /ʌpˈsɛt/ *v* **-set, -setting** [T] **1** to knock over, causing confusion: *to upset a cup of coffee|*(fig.) *Her plans were upset by the change in the weather.* **2** to cause to worry, not be calm, etc.: *His violent temper upset the children.* **3** to make ill in the stomach: *The foreign food upset me/my stomach.*

up·set² /ʌpˈsɛt◄/ *adj* **1** [F] worried; feeling unhappy about something **2** slightly ill: *an upset stomach*

up·set³ /ˈʌpsɛt/ *n* **1** [C;U] the act of upsetting, or state of being in confusion: *a complete upset of our plans* **2** [C] a slight illness, usu. of the stomach: *a stomach upset*

up·shot /ˈʌpʃɑt/ *n* [S] the result in the end; OUTCOME: *The two leaders talked for several hours, and the upshot was a new peace agreement.*

up·side down /ˌʌpsaɪd ˈdaʊn/ *adv* **1** in a position with the top turned to the bottom **2** in disorder: *Everything's upside down in this house.*

up·stage¹ /ˌʌpˈsteɪdʒ/ *adv* towards the back of the stage in the theater

up·stage² /ʌpˈsteɪdʒ/ *v* **-staged, -staging** [T]

to take attention away from (someone else) for oneself

up·stairs /ˌʌp'stɛɑrz◄/ adv,adj [A;F] at, to, or on the upper floor(s) of a building: *He ran upstairs.|an upstairs bedroom* –see also DOWNSTAIRS –**upstairs** n

up·start /'ʌpstɑrt/ n derog a person who has risen too suddenly or unexpectedly to a high position

up·stream /ˌʌp'striʸm◄/ adv,adj (moving) against the current, stream, etc. –opposite **downstream**

up·surge /'ʌpsɜrdʒ/ n [of] a sudden appearance of anger, feeling, etc.: *an upsurge of joy*

up·take /'ʌpteʸk/ n ability to understand esp. something new (in the phrase **quick/slow on the uptake**)

up·tight /ˌʌp'taɪt◄/ adj infml very worried, nervous, etc.

up-to-date /ˌ· ·'·◄/ adj **1** modern **2 bring someone/something up-to-date** to tell someone/include in something the latest information

up·town /ˌʌp'taʊn◄/ adj,adv AmE at or in the living areas in the upper, often northern, part of a town or city, not the business center –compare DOWNTOWN

up·ward /'ʌpwərd/ adj [A] going up: *the upward path to the hilltop|an upward movement of prices* –opposite **downward**

up·wards /'ʌpwərdz/ also **upward** AmE– adv going up: *The sun rose upwards in the sky.* **2** with a particular side facing up: *He lay on the floor face upwards.* –see also DOWNWARDS

u·ra·ni·um /yʊ'reʸniʸəm/ n [U] a heavy RADIOACTIVE white metal that is a simple substance (ELEMENT (1))

U·ra·nus /yʊ'reʸnəs, 'yʊərənəs/ n the PLANET seventh in order from the sun

ur·ban /'ɜrbən/ adj [A] of a town or city: *urban life* –compare RURAL –**urbanize** /'ɜrbəˌnaɪz/ v -ized, -izing [T]: *One large company succeeded in urbanizing the little town.* –**urbanization** /ˌɜrbənə'zeʸʃən/ n [U]

ur·bane /ɜr'beʸn/ adj (of a person or his/her behavior) smoothly polite –**urbanely** adv –**urbanity** /ɜr'bænəti/ n [U]

urban re·new·al /ˌ·· ·'··/ n the repairing or tearing down of buildings, esp. in a poor area of a city

urban sprawl /ˌ·· '·/ n the uncontrolled spread of the URBAN area: *All the new housing developments 25 miles outside of the city were part of the urban sprawl.*

ur·chin /'ɜrtʃɪn/ n a small dirty untidy child: *a street urchin*

urge¹ /ɜrdʒ/ v urged, urging [T] **1** [on] to drive or force (forward); encourage: *to urge the team on* **2** to beg or strongly persuade: *They urged us to go with them.* **3** [on] to tell of with force; STRESS (2): *She urged on us the need for speed.*

urge² n [+to-v] a strong wish or need: *powerful sexual urges|She felt the/an urge to hit him.*

ur·gent /'ɜrdʒənt/ adj very important and needing to be dealt with quickly or first: *It's not urgent; it can wait until tomorrow.* –**urgently** adv –**urgency** n [U]

u·ri·nal /'yʊərənl/ n a men's LAVATORY for urinating (URINATE)

u·ri·nate /'yʊərəˌneʸt/ v -nated, -nating [I] to pass URINE from the body

u·rine /'yʊərɪn/ n [U] liquid waste material, passed from the body

urn /ɜrn/ n **1** a large container (VASE), esp. one in which the ashes of a dead person are kept **2** a large container in which tea or coffee may be heated and kept

us /əs; strong ʌs/ pron (object form of WE): *Did he see us?|That house is too small for us.*

U.S., US /ˌyuʷ 'es◄/ n abbrev. for: **1** also **U.S.A.** /ˌyuʷ ɛs 'eʸ/– the United States (of America) **2** of the United States: *the U.S. Navy*

us·age /'yuʷsɪdʒ, -zɪdʒ/ n **1** [U] the way of using something; the type or degree of use **2** [C;U] the generally accepted way of using a language: *modern English usage*

use¹ /yuʷs/ n **1** [U] the act of using or state of being used: *Do you approve of the use of guns by the police?* **2** [U] the ability or right to use something: *He was wounded in the war and lost the use of both legs.|to be given the use of the library* **3** [C;U] the purpose or reason for using something: *a new machine for the kitchen with several different uses* **4** [U] the usefulness or advantage given by something: *Is this book of any use?|What's the use of worrying?* **5** in use being used

use² /yuʷz/ v used, using [T] **1** to employ for a purpose; put to use: *a pan used for cooking eggs|The company now uses a computer to do all its accounts.* **2** to finish; CONSUME (2): *All the paper has been used.|The car's using too much oil.* **3** derog to treat (someone) with consideration only for one's own advantage –**usable** adj –**user** n

use sthg.↔ up v adv [T] to finish completely

use³ /yuʷs/ v used /yuʷst/ [I +to-v] (used in the past tense only, to show that something happened always or regularly): *I used to go swimming on Saturdays, but now I don't.|He didn't use to/used not to like fish, but now he does.|It used to be thought that the earth was flat.|She doesn't work here now, but she used to.|Didn't she use to live in Detroit?|I'm surprised to see you smoking; you never used to.* –see Study Notes on page 000

USAGE **1 Used to** and **would** are both used of things that happened always or regularly in the past, but **would** is not used at the beginning of a story: *We used to swim every day when we were children. We would run down to the lake and jump in...* **2** The usual question form of **used to** is *Did(n't) she* **use/used to?** In the NEGATIVE², *She didn't* **used/use to** are possible, but *She never* **used to,** which expresses the same idea, is probably more common.

used¹ /yuʷzd/ adj (usu. of goods) which has already had an owner; SECOND-HAND: *used cars*

used² /yuʷst/ adj [F to] accustomed: *to get used to Mexican food |I'm not used to getting up so early.* –opposite **unused**

use·ful /'yuʷsfəl/ adj **1** effective in use: *a useful idea* **2** helpful: *She's a useful person to* *have around.* –**usefulness** [U]

use·less /'yuʷslɪs/ *adj* not of any use –**uselessly** *adv* –**uselessness** *n* [U]

ush·er¹ /'ʌʃər/ **usherette** /ˌʌʃə'rɛt/ *fem.*– *n* a person who shows people to their seats on an important occasion, e.g. in church at weddings, etc., or in a movie theater

usher² *v* [T *in, out*] *fml* to bring (in): *She ushered him into the room.*

U.S.S.R., USSR /ˌyuʷ ɛs ɛs 'ɑr/ *abbrev. for:* Union of Soviet Socialist Republics (Soviet Union)

usu. *adv written abbrev. said as:* usually

u·su·al /'yuʷʒuʷəl, -ʒəl/ *adj* **1** happening most often; customary: *We will meet at the usual time.* –see also UNUSUAL **2 as usual** generally has happened before: *As usual, he arrived last.*

u·su·al·ly /'yuʷʒuʷəliʸ, -ʒəliʸ/ *adv* often; generally: *I'm not usually so late.|I'm not late, usually.* –see NEVER (USAGE)

u·surp /yuʷ'sɜrp, yuʷ'zɜrp/ *v* [T] *fml* to seize for oneself (power or position), esp. illegally –**usurper** *n*

u·su·ry /'yuʷʒəriʸ/ *n* [U] *derog* the practice of lending money to be paid back at a high rate of interest

UT *written abbrev. said as:* Utah /'yuʷtɔ, -tɑ/ (a state in the US)

u·ten·sil /yuʷ'tɛnsəl/ *n fml or tech* an object for use in a particular way, esp. a tool: *kitchen utensils*

u·ter·us /'yuʷtərəs/ *n* **-i** /ˌaɪ/ *or* **-uses** *tech* for WOMB

u·til·i·ty /yuʷ'tɪlətiʸ/ *n* **-ties 1** [U] the degree of usefulness **2** [C] any useful service for the public, such as gas, water, and electricity

u·til·ize ‖also **-ise** *BrE* /'yuʷtl̩ˌaɪz/ *v* **-ized, -izing** [T] *fml* to make (good) use of; use: *to utilize one's abilities in a suitable job* –**utiliz-able** *adj* –**utilization** /ˌyuʷtl̩ə'zeʸʃən/ *n* [U]

ut·most /'ʌtmoʷst/ also **uttermost** /'ʌtər ˌmoʷst/ *lit– adj,n* [A] (effort) of the greatest degree: *with her utmost strength|to do one's utmost* (=make the greatest possible effort)

u·to·pi·a /yuʷ'toʷpiʸə/ *n* (*often cap.*) an imaginary perfect society –**utopian** *adj*

ut·ter¹ /'ʌtər/ *adj* [A] complete: *It's an utter mystery.|He's an utter fool.* –**utterly** *adv* –see Study Notes on page 363

utter² *v* [T] to speak (sound) esp. for a short time: *to utter a cry|He uttered a few words, and then fell to the ground.*

ut·ter·ance /'ʌtərəns/ *n fml or tech* **1** [U] the act of speaking **2** [C] something spoken

U-turn /'yuʷ tɜrn/ *n* a turning movement in a car, taking one back in the direction one came from

V, v

V, v /viʸ/ **V's, v's** *or* **Vs, vs 1** the 22nd letter of the English alphabet **2** the ROMAN NUMERAL (number) for 5

v *written abbrev. said as:* verb

V¹ *n* a thing or part shaped like the letter V: *She cut the material out in a V.*

V² *written abbrev. said as:* VOLT

v. also **vs.** /'vɜrsəs/ *abbrev for:* VERSUS

VA, Va. *written abbrev. said as:* Virginia /vərdʒɪnyə/ (a state in the US)

va·can·cy /'veʸkənsiʸ/ *n* **-cies 1** [C] an unfilled place, such as a hotel room that is not being used **2** [C] an unfilled job in a factory, office, etc.: *We've only got vacancies for metal workers at present.* **3** [U] the state of being VACANT

va·cant /'veʸkənt/ *adj* **1** (of a house, room, seat, space, etc.) not being used or lived in **2** (of a job) not at present filled: *Are there any vacant positions in your company?* **3** showing lack of active or serious thought: *a vacant expression on his face* –**vacantly** *adv: He stared vacantly into space.*

va·cate /'veʸkeʸt/ *v* **-cated, -cating** [T] to move out of; stop using or living in: *You must vacate the hotel room by Friday.*

va·ca·tion /veʸ'keʸʃən, və-/ also **holiday** *esp. BrE*– *n* a time of rest, amusement, and RECREATION away from one's job or school: *Where did you go for your vacation?* –**vacation** *v* [I] *AmE: vacationing in Europe*

USAGE **Vacation** is the general *AmE* word for an official period of rest from work, which one may spend at home or visiting another place; the general *BrE* word is **holiday**: *In this job you get two weeks' vacation (AmE)/holiday (BrE) a year.|Tom is on vacation this week.* A period of any other absence from work is called a **leave of absence** and the person is said to be **on leave**. If the absence is due to illness, it is called **sick leave**. Soldiers go **on leave**, not **on vacation**.

vac·ci·nate /'væksəˌneʸt/ *v* **-nated, -nating** [T *against*] to introduce VACCINE into the body of (someone), as a protection against a disease –**vaccination** /ˌvæksə'neʸʃən/ *n* [C;U *against*]

vac·cine /væk'siʸn/ *n* [C;U] a poisonous substance (containing a VIRUS) used for protecting people against diseases –compare SERUM

vac·il·late /'væsəˌleʸt/ *v* **-lated, -lating** [I *between*] to be continually changing from one opinion or feeling to another; be uncertain of what action to take –**vacillation** /ˌvæsə'leʸʃən/ *n* [C;U]

vac·u·ous /'vækyuʷəs/ *adj fml* foolish, esp. in showing no sign of ideas, thought, or feeling: *a vacuous expression* –**vacuously** *adv*

vac·u·um¹ /'vækyuʷm, -yuʷəm/ *n* a space that is completely empty of all gas, esp. from which all air has been taken away: (fig.) *Her death left a vacuum* (=emptiness) *in his life.*

vacuum² *v* [I;T] *infml* to clean (a house, room, floor, etc.) using a VACUUM CLEANER: *I've been vacuuming all morning.*

vacuum clean·er /'·· ˌ··/ *n* an apparatus

which cleans floor coverings by drawing up the dirt from them in air

vacuum flask /'·· ,·/ $n \rightarrow$ FLASK (3)

vag·a·bond /'væɡəˌbɒnd/ n *old use* a usu. lazy or worthless person who lives an irregular or wandering life –compare VAGRANT

va·ga·ry /'veɪɡəriʸ, vəˈɡɛəriʸ/ n **-ries** [*often pl.*] an unusual or purposeless idea, act, or thought: *the vagaries of love*

va·gi·na /vəˈdʒaɪnə/ n the passage which leads from the outer sex organs of women or female animals, to the organ (WOMB) in which young are formed –**vaginal** /'vædʒənl/ *adj*

va·grant[1] /'veɪʸɡrənt/ n a person who lives a wandering life with no steady home or work –compare VAGABOND –**vagrancy** n [U]

vagrant[2] *adj* [A] going from place to place with no fixed purpose: *a vagrant life*

vague /veɪʸɡ/ *adj* **1** not clearly seen, described, expressed, felt, or understood: *the vague shapes of animals in the mist*|*I couldn't recognize the woman from the vague description of her that you gave me.* **2** not expressing oneself clearly: *The policeman was rather vague when I asked him how to get to the station.* –**vaguely** *adv* –**vagueness** n [U]

vain /veɪʸn/ *adj* **1** full of self-admiration; thinking too highly of one's appearance, abilities, etc. **2** without result; useless: *After a number of vain attempts to climb the mountain, we were forced to return to camp.* **3 in vain** uselessly; without success: *We tried in vain to make him change his mind.* –**vainly** *adv*

val·ance /'væləns/ n *AmE* a narrow piece of wood or cloth above a window that hides the rod on which curtains hang

vale /veɪʸl/ n (as part of a place name or in poetry) a broad low valley: *the Vale of Tears*

val·en·tine /'vælənˌtaɪn/ n (*often cap.*) a greeting card sent to a lover on **Saint Valentine's Day** (February 14th)

val·et /'vælɪt, 'væleʸ, væ'leʸ/ n **1** a man's personal male servant, who looks after his clothes, etc. **2** a male worker in a hotel who cleans and presses the clothes of people staying there

val·iant /'vælyənt/ *adj fml or lit* (of a person or act) very brave, esp. in war; HEROIC –**valiantly** *adv*

val·id /'vælɪd/ *adj* **1** (of a reason, argument, etc.) having a strong firm base; that can be defended: *The fact that you went to bed late isn't a valid excuse for arriving late at work.* **2** that can be used legally: *a train ticket valid for three months* –opposite **invalid 3** *law* written or done in a proper manner so that a court of law would agree with it –**validity** /vəˈlɪdət̬iʸ/ n: *The judge did not question the validity of my statement.* –**validly** /'vælɪdliʸ/ *adv*

val·i·date /'vælɪˌdeɪt/ v **-dated, -dating** [T] *fml* to make VALID: *In order to validate the agreement between yourself and your employer, you must both sign it.* –opposite **invalidate** –**validation** /ˌvælɪˈdeɪʃən/ n [C;U]

va·lise /vəˈliʸs/ n *becoming rare* a small bag used while traveling, esp. for carrying clothes

val·ley /'væliʸ/ n **-leys** the land lying between two lines of hills or mountains, often with a river running through it

USAGE A deep narrow mountain **valley** with steep sides is a **ravine** or **gorge**, or (if it is very large) a **canyon**.

val·or *AmE*‖**valour** *BrE* /'vælər/ n [U] *fml or lit* great bravery, esp. in war

val·u·a·ble /'vælyəbəl, 'vælyuʷə-/ *adj* **1** worth a lot of money: *a valuable diamond* **2** very useful: *Your help has been very valuable.* –see WORTHLESS (USAGE)

val·u·a·bles /'vælyəbəlz, 'vælyuʷə-/ n [P] things (such as pieces of jewelry) that are worth a lot of money: *You should put your valuables in the bank.*

val·u·a·tion /ˌvælyuʷ'eɪʸʃən/ n **1** [U;C *of*] the action of calculating how much money something is worth: *The company's business is the valuation of property*|*making valuations of property.* **2** [C *of*] a value or price (esp. of land or property) decided upon in this way: *a valuation of \$7,000*

val·ue[1] /'vælyuʷ/ n **1** [U] the degree of usefulness of something: *You'll find this map of great value*|*of little value in helping you to get around the city.*|*The government sets a higher value on defense* (=considers it more important) *than on education.* **2** [C;U] the worth of something in money or as compared with other goods for which it might be changed: *Because of continual price increases, the value of the dollar has fallen in recent years.*|*I bought this old painting for \$50, but its real value must be about \$500.*|*The thieves took some clothes and a few books, but nothing of great value.* **3** [U] worth compared with the amount paid: *We offer the best value in the city: only three dollars for lunch with coffee and dessert.*|*You always get value for your money at that store.* (=the goods are always worth the price charged) –see also VALUES; WORTHLESS (USAGE) –**valueless** *adj*

value[2] v **-ued, -uing** [T] **1** to calculate the value, price, or worth of (something): *He valued the house and its contents at \$75,000.* **2** to consider to be of great worth: *I've always valued your friendship very highly.*

val·u·er /'vælyuʷər/ n a person whose work is to decide how much money things are worth

val·ues /'vælyuʷz/ n [P] standards; people's ideas about the worth of certain qualities: *Moral values have changed a lot in the last 50 years.*

valve /vælv/ n **1** a doorlike part of a pipe, which controls the flow of liquid, air, gas, etc., through the pipe: *You put air into a bicycle tire through the valve.*|*The valves of the heart allow the blood to pass in one direction only.* **2** also **tube** *AmE*– a closed glass tube with no air in it, used for controlling a flow of electricity, as (esp. formerly) in radio or television –compare TRANSISTOR

vam·pire /'væmpaɪər/ n an evil spirit which is believed to live in a dead body and suck the blood of sleeping people

van /væn/ n a covered road vehicle for carrying goods and sometimes people: *a newspaper van*|*a police van*|*Packages are delivered* **by van**. –compare TRUCK –see illustration on page 95

van·dal /'vændl/ *n* a person who intentionally damages or destroys beautiful or useful things: *All the seat-covers on the train had been torn by vandals.*

van·dal·ism /'vændl,ɪzəm/ *n* [U] intentional, needless, and usu. widespread damage and destruction, esp. of public property

van·dal·ize‖also **-ise** *BrE* /'vændl,aɪz/ *v* **-ized, -izing** [T] to damage or destroy (esp. a piece of public property) intentionally: *We can't use any of the public telephones around here; they've all been vandalized.*

vane /veʸn/ *n* a bladelike part of certain machines, which has a flat surface that makes it possible to use the force of wind or water as the driving power: *the vanes of a* PROPELLER

van·guard /'vængɑrd/ *n* **1** [C] the soldiers marching at the front of an army, or sent on ahead to protect it against surprise attack: *The vanguard is under attack.* **2** [*the* U] the leading part of any kind of advancement in human affairs: *In the modern world, the scientists are* **in the vanguard of** *all industrial development.*

va·nil·la /və'nɪlə/ *n* [U] a substance obtained from a tropical plant, used for giving a special taste to certain sweet foods: *vanilla ice cream*

van·ish /'vænɪʃ/ *v* [I] **1** to disappear: *With a wave of his hand, the magician made the rabbit vanish.* **2** to cease to exist: *Many types of animal have now vanished from the earth.*

van·i·ty /'vænəṭiʸ/ *n* [U] the quality of being too proud of oneself or one's appearance, abilities, etc.

van·quish /'væŋkwɪʃ, 'væn-/ *v* [T] *lit* to conquer; defeat completely

va·por *AmE*‖**vapour** *BrE* /'veʸpər/ *n* **1** [C;U] a gaslike form of a liquid (such as mist or steam): *A cloud is a mass of vapor in the sky.* **2** [U] *tech* the gas to which the stated liquid or solid can be changed by the action of heat: *water vapor*

va·por·ize‖also **-ise** *BrE* /'veʸpə,raɪz/ *n* **-ized, -izing** [I;T] to (cause to) change into VAPOR: *Water vaporizes when boiled.*

var·i·a·ble¹ /'veəriʸəbəl/ *adj* **1** likely to change; not staying the same; not steady: *The winds today will be light and variable.* –opposite **invariable 2** that can be intentionally varied: *The speed of the toy boat is variable.* –**variability** /,veəriʸə'bɪləṭiʸ/ *n* [U] –**variably** /'veəriʸəbliʸ/ *adv*

variable² *n usu. tech* something (such as temperature) which can vary in quantity or size: *The time of the journey depends on a number of variables, such as the amount of traffic on the road.*

var·i·ance /'veəriʸəns/ *n* **at variance (with)** in opposition (to); not in agreement (with): *What he did was at variance with what he promised to do.*

var·i·ant¹ /'veəriʸənt/ *adj* [A *no comp.*] different; varying: *variant spellings*

variant² *n* a different form, esp. of a word or phrase

var·i·a·tion /,veəriʸ'eʸʃən/ *n* [C;U] (an example or degree of) the action of varying: *price variations in different stores*

var·i·cose veins /,værəkoʷs 'veʸnz/ *n* a medical condition in which the blood vessels (esp. of the leg) have become greatly swollen

var·ied /'veəriʸd/ *adj* **1** of different kinds: *Opinions on the play were varied.* **2** not staying the same; changing: *to lead a varied life*

var·i·e·gat·ed /'veəriʸə,geʸṭid/ *adj* (esp. of a flower or leaf) marked irregularly in spots, lines, masses, etc., of different colors –**variegation** /,veəriʸə'geʸʃən/ *n* [U]

va·ri·e·ty /və'raɪəṭiʸ/ *n* **-ties 1** [U] the state of varying; difference of condition or quality: *My last job lacked variety; I was doing the same things all the time.* **2** [S *of*] a group or collection containing different sorts of the same thing or people: *The box contains a variety of toys.* **3** [C] a type which is different from others in a group: *That farmer is always looking for new varieties of wheat.* **4** [U] a theater or television show including singing, dancing, acts of skill, etc.: *a variety show*

var·i·ous /'veəriʸəs/ *adj* [A] **1** different: *There are various ways of cooking an egg.* **2** several; a number of: *Various people said they had seen the accident.* –see DIFFERENT (USAGE) –**variously** *adv*: *The depth of this cave has been variously calculated at from 200 yards to 500 yards.*

var·nish¹ /'vɑrnɪʃ/ *n* **1** [C;U] (a) liquid which, when brushed onto articles made esp. of wood, gives a clear hard shiny surface **2** [*the* S] the shiny appearance produced by using this substance: *Hot plates may spoil the varnish on a table.* –compare LACQUER

varnish² *v* [T] to cover with VARNISH¹: *to varnish a table* –compare LACQUER

var·y /'veəriʸ/ *v* **-ied, -ying** [I;T] to be, make, or become different: *Opinions on this matter vary.*|*She varies her eating habits a lot.*

vase /veʸs, veʸz, vɑz/ *n* a glass or clay container, used as a decoration or to put flowers in –see illustration on page 399

vas·ec·to·my /væ'sektəmiʸ/ *n* **-mies** [C;U] (an operation for) removing a man's ability to become a father by cutting the small tube that carries the male seeds (SPERM)

vast /væst/ *adj* very large and wide; great in size or amount: *The vast plains stretch for 600 miles.* –see Study Notes on page 550 –**vastness** *n* [U]

vast·ly /'væstliʸ/ *adv* very greatly: *His piano playing has improved vastly since last year.*

vat /væt/ *n* a very large barrel or container for holding liquids (such as WHISKEY, beer, etc.), esp. when they are being made

vault¹ /vɔlt/ *n* **1** a roof or CEILING formed, as in most churches, by a number of arches **2** an underground room in which the bodies of the dead are placed, or in which valuable things are stored

vault² *v* [I;T] to jump over (something) in one movement using the hands or a pole to gain more height: *to vault over a gate*|*to pole-vault*

vault³ *n* a jump made by VAULTing² –see also POLE VAULT

VD *n* [U] → VENEREAL DISEASE

-'ve /v, əv/ *v short for* have: *We've finished.*

veal /viʸl/ *n* [U] meat from the young of a cow (CALF) –see MEAT (USAGE)

veer /vɪər/ *v* [I] to turn or change direction: *The car was out of control and suddenly veered across the road.*|*We were talking about food, and then suddenly the conversation veered around to stomach diseases.*

veg·e·ta·ble /'vɛdʒtəbəl, 'vɛdʒətə-/ *n* a (part of a) plant that is grown for food: *meat and vegetables*|*We grow many different vegetables: potatoes, onions, beans, etc.*

veg·e·tar·i·an /ˌvɛdʒə'tɛəriʸən/ *n* a person who does not eat meat or fish, but only vegetables, grains, fruit, etc. **–vegetarian** *adj: a vegetarian restaurant/meal* **–vegetarianism** *n* [U]

veg·e·tate /'vɛdʒə,teʸt/ *v* **-tated, -tating** [I] to live a dull life without interests or social activity

veg·e·ta·tion /ˌvɛdʒə'teʸʃən/ *n* [U] plants in general: *the strange and colorful vegetation of the tropical forest*

ve·he·ment /'viʸəmənt/ *adj* fiercely strong; violent: *She made a vehement attack on the government's plan to close the school.* **–vehemently** *adv* **–vehemence** *n* [U]

ve·hi·cle /'viʸəkəl/ *n* **1** something in or on which people or goods can be carried, esp. along roads (such as a bicycle, car, truck, or bus) **2** *fml* something by means of which something else can be passed on or spread: *Television has become an important vehicle for spreading political ideas.*

ve·hic·u·lar /viʸ'hɪkyələr/ *adj fml* concerning vehicles on roads: *vehicular traffic*

veil¹ /veʸl/ *n* **1** [C] a covering of fine cloth or net for the head or face, worn esp. by women, sometimes for religious reasons **2** [S of] something which covers or hides something else: *a veil of mist*|(fig.) *No one knew what the army was doing; there was a veil of secrecy over their activities.*

veil² *v* [T] to cover with a VEIL

veiled /veʸld/ *adj* **1** wearing a VEIL¹ (1) **2** hidden; expressed indirectly: *veiled threats*

vein /veʸn/ *n* **1** [C] a tube that carries blood from any part of the body to the heart –compare ARTERY (1) **2** [C] one of a system of thin lines which runs in a pattern through leaves and the wings of certain insects **3** [C] a crack in rock, filled with useful metal: *a vein of silver* –compare SEAM (3) **4** [S] a style or MOOD: *speaking in a serious vein*|*a number of jokes all in the same vein* **5** [S] a small, but noticeable amount: *There is a vein of truth in all her stories.*

ve·loc·i·ty /və'lɑsəṭiʸ/ *n* **-ties** [C;U] *tech* (a) speed in a certain direction; rate of movement

ve·lour, velours /və'luər/ *n* [U] a heavy cloth made from silk, cotton, etc., with a soft slightly furry surface

vel·vet /'vɛlvɪt/ *n* [U] a fine closely-woven cloth made esp. of silk but also of nylon,

cotton, etc., with a short soft furry surface on one side only

vel·vet·y /'vɛlvɪṭiʸ/ *adj* like VELVET; very soft

ve·nal /'viʸnl/ *adj fml* **1** (of a person) acting unfairly or wrongly, in return for money or other reward: *venal judges* **2** (of an action) done, not for the proper or honest reasons, but for money **–venality** /viʸ'næləṭiʸ/ *n* [U] **–venally** /'viʸnl-iʸ/ *adv*

ven·det·ta /vɛn'dɛṭə/ *n* a long-lasting and violent quarrel between families

vend·ing ma·chine /'vɛndɪŋ məˌʃiʸn/ *n* a machine from which cigarettes, drinks, stamps, etc., can be obtained by putting a coin into it

ven·dor, vender /'vɛndər/ *n* **1** a seller of small articles that can be carried around or pushed on a cart: *a fruit vendor* **2** *law* the seller of a house, land, etc.

ve·neer /və'nɪər/ *n* **1** [C;U] a thin covering of good quality wood forming the outer surface of an article made of a cheaper material **2** [S of] an outer appearance which hides the unpleasant reality: *a veneer of good manners*

ven·er·a·ble /'vɛnərəbəl/ *adj* (of an old person or thing) considered to deserve great respect or honor, because of character, religious or historical importance, etc. –see OLD (USAGE)

ven·er·ate /'vɛnə,reʸt/ *v* **-ated, -ating** [T] *fml* to treat with great respect and honor, and sometimes worship **–veneration** /ˌvɛnə'reʸʃən/ *n* [U]

ve·ne·re·al dis·ease /vəˌnɪəriʸəl dɪ'ziʸz/ *also* **VD**– *n* [C;U] (a type of) disease passed from one person to another during sexual activity

venge·ance /'vɛndʒəns/ *n* [U] **1** severe harm or damage done to another person as a punishment for harm he/she has done to oneself, one's family, etc.: *He took vengeance on those who had tried to murder him.* –see also REVENGE **2 with a vengeance** *infml* to a high degree; with greater force than is usual: *The wind's blowing with a vengeance today.*

venge·ful /'vɛndʒfəl/ *adj lit* showing a fierce desire to punish a person for the harm he/she has done to oneself **–vengefully** *adv*

ven·i·son /'vɛnəsən/ *n* [U] the flesh of a deer as food –see MEAT (USAGE)

ven·om /'vɛnəm/ *n* [U] **1** liquid poison which certain snakes, insects, and other creatures use in biting or stinging **2** great hatred: *Her speech against the government was full of venom.* **–venomous** *adj: a venomous snake/look* **–venomously** *adv*

vent¹ /vɛnt/ *v* [T *on*] to give expression to (one's feelings): *It's wrong to vent your anger on the children.*

vent² *n* **1** a hole, opening, or pipe by which gases, smoke, air, or liquid can enter or escape from an enclosed space –see illustration on page 337 **2** a long narrow straight opening at the bottom of a coat, at the sides, or back **3 give vent to** to express freely (a strong feeling): *He gave vent to his anger by shouting at the children.*

ven·ti·late /'vɛntəl,eʸt/ *v* **-lated, -lating** [T] to allow fresh air to enter (a room, building, etc.): *a smoky, badly-ventilated bar*

ven·ti·la·tion /ˌventəl'eɪʃən/ *n* [U] (the system that is used for) the passing into and around a room, building, etc., of fresh air: *The workers complained that the factory's lack of ventilation made them feel ill.*

ven·ti·la·tor /'ventəlˌeɪtər/ *n* any arrangement or apparatus for the ventilating (VEN-TILATE) of a room, building, etc.

ven·tril·o·quism /ven'trɪləˌkwɪzəm/ *n* [U] the art of speaking or singing without moving the lips or jaws, so that the sound seems to come from somewhere else –**ventriloquist** /ven'trɪləkwɪst/ *n*

ven·ture¹ /'ventʃər/ *v* **-tured, -turing 1** [I;T +*to-v*] to risk going somewhere or doing something dangerous: *Don't venture too near the edge of the well; you might fall in.* **2** [T +*to-v*] to take the risk of saying (something that may be opposed or considered foolish): *I venture to say that by the year 2500 there'll be men living on the moon.|to venture a suggestion*

venture² *n* an attempt; course of action (esp. in business) of which the result is uncertain
USAGE **Venture** (noun or verb) suggests some risk to one's life or money: *a business venture|Nobody ventured (=dared) to speak to the angry king.* An **adventure** is an exciting experience, which may or may not be dangerous as well. The plural **adventures** is often used in the title of a story about the exciting activities of a particular character: *"The* **Adventures** *of Sinbad the Sailor."*

Ve·nus /'viːnəs/ *n* the PLANET second in order from the sun, and next to the earth

ve·ran·da, -dah /və'rændə/ *n* → PORCH

verb /vɜrb/ *n* a word or phrase that tells what someone or something is, does, or experiences: *In "She is tired" and "He wrote a letter," "is" and "wrote" are verbs.* –see Study Notes on page 745

ver·bal /'vɜrbəl/ *adj* **1** spoken, not written: *a verbal agreement* **2** connected with words and their use: *verbal skill* –compare VERBOSE

ver·bal·ize ‖ also **-ise** *BrE* /'vɜrbəˌlaɪz/ *v* **-ized, -izing** [I;T] *fml* to express (something) in words

ver·bal·ly /'vɜrbəliy/ *adv* in spoken words and not in writing

verbal noun /ˌ·· '·/ also **gerund**– *n* a noun which describes an action or experience and ends in *-ing* like a PRESENT PARTICIPLE: *"Building" is a verbal noun in "The building of the bridge was slow work," but not in "The bank was a tall building."*

ver·ba·tim /vər'beɪtɪm/ *adj,adv* repeating the actual words exactly: *His memory was so good that he could repeat many plays of Shakespeare verbatim.*

ver·bi·age /'vɜrbiyɪdʒ/ *n* [U] too many unnecessary words in speech or writing

ver·bose /vər'boʷs/ *adj fml* using too many words: *Your report is twice as long as it needs to be; it's too verbose.* –compare VERBAL –**verbosely** *adv* –**verbosity** /vər'bɑs·əṭiy/ *n* [U]

ver·dant /'vɜrdnt/ *adj lit* green with freshly growing plants or grass: *verdant fields*

ver·dict /'vɜrdɪkt/ *n* **1** the official decision made by a JURY in a court of law, at the end of a trial: *Members of the* JURY, *what is your verdict? Guilty, or not guilty?* **2** *infml* a statement of (carefully considered) opinion: *The general verdict on the party was that it had been very enjoyable.*

verge /vɜrdʒ/ *n* the edge or border of a road, path, etc.: *the verge of the desert*|(fig.) *She tried to hide her grief, but she was* **on the verge of** (=very near to) *tears.*

verge on/upon sthg. *v prep* **verged, verging** [T] to be near to (the stated quality or condition): *His strange behavior sometimes verges on madness.*

ver·i·fy /'verəˌfaɪ/ *v* **-fied, -fying** [T +*that*] to make sure that (a fact, statement, etc.) is true: *The police are verifying the prisoner's statement by questioning several witnesses.* –**verifiable** *adj* –**verification** /ˌverəfə'keɪʃən/ *n* [U]

ver·i·si·mil·i·tude /ˌverəsə'mɪləˌtuʷd, -ˌtyuʷd/ *n* [U] *fml* the quality of seeming to be true; likeness to reality

ver·i·ta·ble /'verəṭəbəl/ *adj* [A] (used to give force to an expression) that may be described as; real: *The meal was a veritable feast.* –**veritably** *adv*

ver·mil·ion /vər'mɪlyən/ *adj,n* [U] bright reddish-orange (color)

ver·min /'vɜrmɪn/ *n* [U] **1** any usu. small animal or bird that causes damage and is difficult to control: *To a farmer a fox is vermin because it steals and kills chickens.* **2** any kind of unpleasant biting insect (such as a FLEA, LOUSE, etc.) that lives on the body of man or animals: *Vermin is found in large numbers on many wild, farmyard, and* DOMESTIC¹ (2) *animals.* –**verminous** *adj*

ver·mouth /vər'muʷθ/ *n* [U] a drink made from wine with the addition of bitter or strong-tasting substances from roots and HERBS

ver·nac·u·lar /vər'nækyələr/ *adj,n* (using) the native spoken language of a country or area: *In some churches they speak* LATIN, *but in others they use the vernacular.*

ver·ru·ca /və'ruʷkə/ *n* a small hard often infectious growth on the skin, usu. on the bottom of the feet

ver·sa·tile /'vɜrsəṭl, -ˌtaɪl/ *adj* **1** having many different kinds of skill or ability: *She's a very versatile performer; she can act, sing, dance, and play the piano.* **2** having many different uses: *Nylon is a versatile material.* –**versatility** /ˌvɜrsə'tɪləṭiy/ *n* [U]

verse /vɜrs/ *n* **1** [U] written language in the form of poetry: *Not all verse is great poetry.*|*comic verse* –see also BLANK VERSE **2** [C] a set of lines which form one part of a poem or song: *Today I learned three verses of a poem at school.* **3** [C] one of the (groups of) sentences that together form one numbered division (CHAPTER) of one of the books of the Bible

versed /vɜrst/ *adj* [F *in*] possessing a thorough knowledge (of a subject, an art, etc.); experienced (esp. in the phrase **well versed in**)

ver·sion /'vɜrʒən, -ʃən/ *n* [*of*] **1** one person's account of an event: *The two newspapers gave different versions of what happened.* **2** a slightly different form, copy, or style of an article: *This dress is a cheaper version of the one we saw in the store.* **3** a translation: *The King James Version of the Bible first appeared in 1611.*

ver·sus /'vɜrsəs/ *vs. AmE*‖also **v.** *esp. BrE*–*prep abbrev. for:* (against): *The boxing match today is Ali versus Frazier.*

ver·te·bra /'vɜrtəbrə/ *n* -**brae** /ˌbriʸ, ˌbreʸ/ one of the small hollow bones down the center of the back which form the SPINE

ver·te·brate /'vɜrtəbrɪt, -ˌbreʸt/ *adj,n tech* (an animal, bird, fish, etc.) which has a SPINE –see also INVERTEBRATE

ver·ti·cal /'vɜrtɪkəl/ *adj* (of an object, line, or surface) forming an angle of 90 degrees with the level ground, or with a straight line in a figure; upright: *The northern side of the mountain is almost vertical.* –compare HORIZONTAL –**vertically** *adv*

ver·ti·go /'vɜrtɪˌgoʷ/ *n* [U] a feeling of great unsteadiness, sickness, or faintness, caused usu. by looking down from a great height

verve /vɜrv/ *n* [U] life, force, and eager enjoyment: *playing the piano with great verve*

ver·y¹ /'veriʸ/ *adv* **1** especially; to a great degree: *It's very warm today.|a very good cake|a very exciting book|The traffic in the city moves very slowly.|Thank you very much.* –see Study Notes on page 363 **2** (used with SUPERLATIVE¹ (2) adjectives, or words like *same, own, first, last,* to make them stronger): *the very best movie I've seen this year|This is the very last time I offer to help you.|There have been three accidents in this very same place.|my very own boat* **3 very well** (in answer to a suggestion, request, or plan) all right (but I don't particularly want to): *"Please come home early." "Very well, if I must."*

USAGE One says **very** *big* or *the* **very** *biggest,* but **much** *bigger* –see MUCH (USAGE)

ver·y² *adj* [A] *(used for giving force to an expression)* actual: *This is the very pen he used when he was writing the book.|I'll go this very minute.* (=at once)*|I found it at the very bottom of the box.|The very walls* (=Even the walls) *of the old city are full of history.*

very high fre·quen·cy /ˌ·· · '···/ *n* [U] → VHF

ves·pers /'vespərz/ *n* [U] (in some divisions of the Christian church) the evening service

ves·sel /'vesəl/ *n fml* **1** a usu. round container, such as a glass, pot, bucket, or barrel, used esp. for holding liquids: *a drinking vessel* **2** a ship or large boat: *a fishing vessel* –see also BLOOD VESSEL

vest¹ /vest/ *n AmE* a close-fitting garment without arms that reaches to the waist and is often worn under a jacket as part of a 3-piece suit

vest² *v* → VEST sthg. IN sbdy.

vested in·ter·est /ˌ·· '··/ *n often derog* a personal reason for doing or continuing something, because one gains advantage from it:

The tobacco companies have a vested interest in claiming that cigarette smoking isn't harmful.

ves·ti·bule /'vestəˌbyuʷl/ *n fml* a wide passage or small room just inside the outer door of a (public) building; entrance hall

ves·tige /'vestɪdʒ/ *n* [*of*] the very small slight remains (of something): *the last vestiges of Inca civilization|There's not a vestige* (=not the slightest bit) *of truth in his statement.*

vest sthg. **in** sbdy. *v prep* [T *usu. pass.*] *fml* to give legally (a right or power) to (a person or group): *In the US, the right to make new laws is vested in the representatives of the people.*

vest·ment /'vestmənt/ *n* [*often pl.*] *fml* a ceremonial garment, esp. as worn by priests for church services

ves·try /'vestriʸ/ *n* -**tries** a room in a church **a** where the priest and church singers put on their ceremonial garments or **b** which is used for prayer meetings, church business, etc.

vet /vet/ **1** also **veterinarian** /ˌvetərə'neəriʸən, ˌvetrə-/ *AmE fml*‖**veterinary surgeon** /ˌ·····' ···/ *BrE fml*– a trained animal doctor **2** *AmE* for VETERAN (2)

vet·er·an /'vetərən, 'vetrən/ *n,adj* **1** [A *of*] (a person) who in the past has had long experience, esp. in war: *Grandfather is a veteran (soldier) of the First World War.|At the age of 12 the boy was already a veteran traveler, having been all over the world with his father.* **2** also **vet** *AmE*– any person, young or old, who has served any length of time in the armed forces, esp. during a war: *My brother is a Vietnam veteran.*

vet·er·i·nar·y /'vetərəˌneəriʸ, 'vetrə-/ *adj* [A] connected with the medical care and treatment of sick animals: *veterinary science* –see also VET

ve·to¹ /'viʸtoʷ/ *n* -**toes** **1** [C;U] (esp. in politics) the official right or power to refuse permission for an action, or to forbid something to be done: *to exercise one's veto* **2** [C on] a refusal to give permission for something; act of forbidding something completely

veto² *v* -**toed, -toing** [T] to prevent or forbid (some action); refuse to allow (something): *The senator's plan to reduce defense spending was vetoed by the President.*

vex /veks/ *v* [T] *esp. old use* to displease (someone); cause (someone) to feel angry or bad-tempered –**vexation** /vek'seʸʃən/ *n* [C;U]

VHF *n* [U] very high FREQUENCY (2); (the sending out of radio waves at) the rate of 30,000,000 to 300,000,000 per second: *This radio station broadcasts only on VHF.|a VHF radio* –see also UHF

vi·a /'vaɪə, 'viʸə/ *prep* traveling or sent through (a place) on the way: *We flew to Athens via Paris and Rome.|(infml) I sent a message to Mary via her sister.*

vi·a·ble /'vaɪəbəl/ *adj* able to succeed in operation: *This plan looks all right in principle, but in practice it wouldn't be viable.* –**viability** /ˌvaɪə'bɪlətiʸ/ *n* [U] –**viably** /'vaɪəbliʸ/ *adv*

vi·a·duct /'vaɪəˌdʌkt/ *n* a long high bridge

STUDY NOTES verbs ▮

transitive verbs

like and **thank** are both TRANSITIVE verbs. This means that they must be followed by a noun or noun phrase as a direct OBJECT. If you take away the direct object the sentence no longer makes sense. So we can say:

*Anne **likes** apples.*
*They **thanked** Mrs. Jones.*

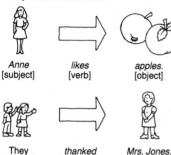

Anne	likes	apples.
[subject]	[verb]	[object]

They	thanked	Mrs. Jones.
[subject]	[verb]	[object]

In the dictionary, transitive verbs are shown like this [T]:

thank *v* [T] to express gratefulness to (someone); give thanks to: *The old lady thanked me for helping her.*

intransitive verbs

rise and **arrive** are both INTRANSITIVE verbs. This means that their meaning is complete without a direct object. So we can say:

*The family **arrived**.*
*The sun **rose**.*

The family	arrived.
[subject]	[verb]

The sun	rose.
[subject]	[verb]

In the dictionary, intransitive verbs are shown like this [I]:

rise *v* [I] (of the sun, moon, or stars), to come up; appear above the horizon: *The sun rises in the east.*

We can add other nouns to both [T] (transitive) and [I] (intransitive) verbs, but these are not direct objects:

They thanked Mrs. Jones for the presents.   *The sun rises every morning.*

Many verbs, like **speak** and **stop**, can be both [T] (transitive) and [I] (intransitive). These verbs look like this in the dictionary:

speak *v* **1** [I] to say things; talk: *I'd like to speak to you about my idea.* **3** [T] to be able to talk in (a language): *Do you speak English?*

stop *v* [I;T] to (cause to) cease moving or continuing an activity: *Do the buses stop at the train station?* | *He held out his hand to stop the bus.*

Some verbs, like **become**, do not have an [I] or a [T] after them for some or all of their meanings. These verbs must be followed by another word for their meaning to be complete, but the word can be a noun or an adjective or an adverb. These nouns, adjectives, and adverbs always tell us something about the subject of a sentence. For example:

become *v* to come to be: *She became a lawyer.* | *The weather became warmer.*

Other verbs like **become** are **appear, be, feel, look, remain,** and **seem.**

For more information on verbs turn to page 501.

which carries a road or railroad line across a valley

vi·al /'vaɪəl/ n a small bottle, esp. one of liquid medicines

vi·brant /'vaɪbrənt/ adj **1** alive; forceful; powerful and exciting: *a city vibrant with life* **2** (of color or light) pleasantly bright and strong **–vibrantly** adv

vi·brate /'vaɪbreʸt/ v -brated, -brating [I;T] to (cause to) shake continuously and very rapidly with a fine slight movement: *Tom's heavy footsteps upstairs make the old house vibrate.*

vi·bra·tion /vaɪ'breʸʃən/ n [C;U] (a) slight continuous shaky movement: *Our house is near the airport, and you can feel the vibrations when a plane flies over.*

vic·ar /'vɪkər/ n (in the CHURCH OF ENGLAND) a priest in charge of a church and the area (PARISH) belonging to it

vic·ar·age /'vɪkərɪdʒ/ n a VICAR's house

vi·car·i·ous /vaɪ'keəriʸəs, vɪ-/ adj experienced by the imagination through watching or reading about other people; indirect: *He gets vicarious pleasure by going to watch sex films.* **–vicariously** adv

vice¹ /vaɪs/ n **1** [C;U] (any particular kind of) evil living, esp. in sexual practices, taking of harmful drugs, etc.: *In spite of the police, there's usually a certain amount of vice in all big cities.* **2** [C;U] (an example of) wickedness of character **–opposite virtue 3** [C] *infml, often humor* a bad habit: *Smoking is my only vice.*

vice² n BrE for VISE

vice·roy /'vaɪsrɔɪ/ n a king's or queen's representative ruling for him/her in another country: *When Britain ruled India, the British king was represented there by a viceroy.*

vi·ce ver·sa /ˌvaɪsə 'vɜrsə, ˌvaɪs, ˌvaɪsiʸ/ adv in the opposite way from that just stated: *When she wants to go out, he wants to stay in, and vice versa.* (=when he wants to go out, she wants to stay in)

vi·cin·i·ty /və'sɪnəṭiʸ/ n [U] the surroundings; neighborhood: *Are there any stores in this vicinity/in the vicinity of your house?*

vi·cious /'vɪʃəs/ adj **1** cruel; having or showing hate and the desire to hurt: *He gave the dog a vicious blow with his stick.* **2** dangerous; able or likely to cause severe hurt: *a vicious-looking knife* **3 vicious circle** a set of events in which cause and effect follow each other in a circular pattern: *"Crime leads to prison, which leads to unemployment, which leads to crime. It's a vicious circle."* **–viciously** adv **–viciousness** n [U]

vic·tim /'vɪktɪm/ n [of] a person, animal, or thing that suffers pain, harm, etc., as a result of other people's actions, or of illness, bad luck, etc.: *Four people were killed in the explosion, but the police have not yet named the victims.*

vic·tim·ize‖also **-ise** BrE /'vɪktə,maɪz/ v -ized, -izing [T] to cause (someone) to suffer unfairly: *When she lost her job, she felt she'd been victimized because of her political views.* **–victimization** /ˌvɪktəmə'zeʸʃən/ n [U]

vic·tor /'vɪktər/ n fml or lit a winner in a battle, race, game, or other kind of struggle

Vic·to·ri·an /vɪk'tɔriʸən, -'toʷr-/ adj,n **1** (any person) of or living in the time when Queen Victoria ruled (1837–1901): *Victorian furniture/Florence Nightingale was a famous Victorian.* **2** like the middle-class society in the time of Queen Victoria; very respectable and religious in a formal way: *His opinions about sex are very Victorian.*

vic·to·ry /'vɪktəriʸ/ n -ries [C;U in, over] (an) act of winning or state of having won (in war or in any kind of struggle): *The officers led their men to victory in battle.|The hockey team had a string of victories* (=a number of wins) *last season.* **–compare** DEFEAT **–victorious** /vɪk'tɔriʸəs, -'toʷr-/ adj: *the victorious team* **–victoriously** adv

vict·uals /'vɪtlz/ n [P] old use food and drink

vid·e·o¹ /'vɪdiʸoʷ/ adj[A] **1** connected with or used in the showing of pictures by television: *a video* DISPLAY *system* **–compare** AUDIO **2** using VIDEOTAPE¹: *a video recording*

video² also **videocassette recorder** /ˌ····ˈ· ·,··/ fml– n an instrument which records pictures and sound using VIDEOTAPE¹: *I'm going to record that television play on my video.*

vid·e·o·disk /'vɪdiʸoʷ,dɪsk/ n a disk like a RECORD² (4) on which television pictures (and sound) can be recorded

vid·e·o·tape¹ /'vɪdiʸoʷ,teʸp/ n **1** [U] a long narrow band of MAGNETIC material on which television pictures (and sound) are recorded **2** [C] also **videocassette**– a CASSETTE (1) containing a length of this

videotape² v -taped, -taping [T] to record (a television show) on VIDEOTAPE¹

vie /vaɪ/ v vied, vying [I with, for] to compete (against someone) (for something): *They are vying (with each other) for the lead in the play.*

view¹ /vyuʷ/ n **1** [U] ability to see or be seen from a particular place; sight: *My view of the harbor was blocked by the new building.| The valley was hidden from view in the mist.|When we reached the top of the mountain, we came in view of* (=were able to see) *a wide plain below|a wide plain came into view.* (=was able to be seen)|*He fell off his bicycle in full view of his friends.* (=seen by all of them) **2** [C of] (a picture or photograph of) something seen from a particular place, esp. a stretch of pleasant country: *There's no view from my bedroom window except of some factory chimneys.* **3** [S of] a special chance to see someone or something: *If you stand here, you'll get a better view of the procession.* **4** [C] a personal opinion, belief, idea, etc., about something: *In my view, he's a fool.|What are your views on free education?* **5 in view of** considering; taking into consideration: *In view of his youth, the police have decided not to* PROSECUTE. **6 keep something in view** to remember something as a possibility or for future consideration if a favorable chance comes **7 on view** being shown to the public: *Our new range of cars will be on view from next week.* **8 take a dim/poor view of** infml to think unfavorably about **9 with a view to doing something** with the aim of; in order to do something: *He put a new roof on his house with a view to increasing its value.*

USAGE 1 Compare **scenery, scene,** and **view:** The general appearance of the country, considered for its beauty, is **scenery:** *the beautiful* **scenery** *of the Great Lakes.* A **view** is the part of the **scenery** that can be seen from one place: *There's a fine* **view** *of the mountains from our hotel window.* **Scene** can mean the same as **view,** but a **scene** is more likely to include people and movement: *a happy* **scene** *of children playing in the garden.* 2 Like **view, prospect** and **outlook** also describe what you see when you look from a particular place. But all three words have common fig. meanings. **View** in this sense is like **opinion,** and what is expected to happen in the future is the **outlook** or **prospect:** *What are your* **views** *on the government's plan for education?*|*Business is bad, and the* **outlook** *for next year is even worse.*|*The* **prospect** *of the coming examinations made us all nervous.*

view² *v* [T] **1** *esp. tech* to examine; look at thoroughly: *Several possible buyers have come to view the house.* **2** to consider; regard; think about: *He viewed his son's absence from school very badly.* (=did not approve of it)|*How do you view this matter?* (=what is your opinion about it?)

view·er /ˈvyuʷər/ *n* a person watching television

view·point /ˈvyuʷpɔint/ *n* → POINT¹ (20)

vig·il /ˈvɪdʒəl/ *n* [C;U] (an act of) remaining watchful for some purpose (e.g. on guard, in prayer, or looking after sick people), esp. during the night (esp. in the phrases **keep vigil, all-night vigil**)

vig·i·lant /ˈvɪdʒələnt/ *adj fml* continually watchful or on guard: *A vigilant police force helps to control crime.* –**vigilance** [U] –**vigilantly** *adv*

vig·i·lan·te /ˌvɪdʒəˈlæntiʸ/ *n esp. derog* a member of an unofficial organization which keeps order and punishes crime in an area where an official body either does not exist or does not work properly

vig·or *AmE*‖**vigour** *BrE* /ˈvɪgər/ *n* [U] forcefulness; strength shown in power of action –**vigorous** *adj:* *a vigorous speech in defense of the government* –**vigorously** *adv*

vile /vaɪl/ *adj* hateful; shameful; evil; low and worthless: *Would you be so vile as to steal a coat from a blind man?* **2** *infml* very bad or unpleasant: *This food is vile!* –**vilely** *adv* –**vileness** *n* [U]

vil·i·fy /ˈvɪləˌfaɪ/ *v* **-fied, -fying** [T] *fml* to say bad things about; abuse –**vilification** /ˌvɪləfəˈkeʸʃən/ *n* [U]

vil·la /ˈvɪlə/ *n* a pleasant house with a garden, esp. one in the country or used for vacations: *We're renting a villa in the south of France for the summer.*

vil·lage /ˈvɪlɪdʒ/ *n* a collection of houses and other buildings (such as a church, school, and one or more stores) in a country area, smaller than a town: *The whole village* (=all

the people in the village) *is going to the baker's funeral today.*

vil·lag·er /ˈvɪlɪdʒər/ *n* a person who lives in a village

vil·lain /ˈvɪlən/ *n* (esp. in old plays, movies, and stories) a wicked person, esp. the main bad character: *The villain carried off the young girl and tied her to the railroad line.* –opposite **hero** –**villainous** *adj*

vil·lain·y /ˈvɪləniʸ/ *n* [U] *esp. lit* wicked behavior

vin·ai·grette /ˌvɪnəˈgrɛt/ *n* [U] a sharp-tasting mixture of oil, VINEGAR, salt, pepper, etc., served with some cold dishes of meat, fish, and vegetables

vin·di·cate /ˈvɪndəˌkeʸt/ *v* **-cated, -cating** [T] to prove to be true or right; free from blame: *The government's actions have been vindicated by the improvement in living standards.* –**vindication** /ˌvɪndəˈkeʸʃən/ *n* [S;U *of*]

vin·dic·tive /vɪnˈdɪktɪv/ *adj* showing the desire to harm someone who has harmed oneself –**vindictively** *adv* –**vindictiveness** *n* [U]

vine /vaɪn/ *n* **1** any creeping or climbing plant (such as the IVY, the CUCUMBER, etc.) **2** a climbing plant that produces bunches of juicy green or purple fruit (GRAPES)

vin·e·gar /ˈvɪnɪgər/ *n* [U] an acid-tasting liquid made usu. from MALT or sour wine, used in preserving or adding taste to food

vine·yard /ˈvɪnyərd/ *n* a piece of land planted with VINES (2) for wine production

vin·tage¹ /ˈvɪntɪdʒ/ *adj* [A] **1** (of wines) made in a year when the VINTAGE² produced wines of high quality **2** produced in or being a time famous for high quality and lasting value: *a vintage silent movie*|*a vintage performance by Heifetz* **3** (of a car) made between 1916 and 1930

vintage² *n* (a fine wine produced from) the gathering of GRAPES in a particular year: *The vintage was earlier than usual this year.*|*He has some rare old vintages in his collection of wines.*

vi·nyl /ˈvaɪnl/ *n* [U] firm bendable plastic used instead of leather, rubber, wood, etc.: *vinyl floor covering*

vi·o·la /viʸˈoʷlə/ *n* a stringed musical instrument, like the VIOLIN but a little larger

vi·o·late /ˈvaɪəˌleʸt/ *v* **-lated, -lating** [T] **1** to disregard or act against (a promise, law, etc.): *A country isn't respected if it violates an international agreement.* **2** *esp. lit* to break, spoil, or destroy (something that ought to be respected): *to violate a grave* **3** *lit or euph* to have sex with (a woman) by force; RAPE –compare DEFILE –**violation** /ˌvaɪəˈleʸʃən/ *n* [C;U]: *They have been fishing in our waters, in violation of the recent agreement.*

vi·o·lence /ˈvaɪələns/ *n* [U] **1** very great force in action or feeling: *The wind blew with great violence.* **2** use of bodily force to hurt or harm: *The police used unnecessary violence on the crowd.*|*robbery with violence*

vi·o·lent /ˈvaɪələnt/ *adj* using, showing, or produced by great damaging force: *The madman was violent and had to be locked up.*|*a violent storm*|*She was in a violent* *mood.* | *He died a violent death.* –**violently** *adv*

vi·o·let /'vaɪəlɪt/ *n,adj* **1** [C] a small plant with sweet-smelling dark purplish-blue flowers **2** [U] (having) a purplish-blue color

vi·o·lin /ˌvaɪə'lɪn/ *n* a four-stringed musical instrument, supported between the left shoulder and the chin and played by drawing a BOW³ (2) across the strings –**violinist** *n*

vi·o·lon·cel·lo /ˌvaɪələn'tʃɛloʷ/ *n* -**los** *fml* for CELLO

VIP /ˌviʸ aɪ 'piʸ/ *n infml* a very important person; person of great influence or fame: *Only the VIP's were permitted to ride in the cars.*

vi·per /'vaɪpər/ *n* a small poisonous snake

vir·gin¹ /'vɜrdʒɪn/ *n* a person who has never had sexual relations with a member of the opposite sex –**virginal** *adj*

virgin² *adj* **1** [A] without sexual experience **2** fresh; unspoiled: *no footmarks on the virgin snow*

vir·gin·i·ty /vər'dʒɪnətiʸ/ *n* [U] the state of being a VIRGIN¹: *She was 19 when she lost her virginity.* (=had sex with a man for the first time)

Virgin Mar·y /ˌvɜrdʒɪn 'mɛəriʸ/ *n* (in the Christian religion) Mary, the mother of Christ

Vir·go /'vɜrgoʷ/ *n* see ZODIAC

vir·ile /'vɪrəl/ *adj usu. apprec* (of a man) having strong and manly qualities, esp. in matters of sex: *a virile young sportsman*

vi·ril·i·ty /və'rɪlətiʸ/ *n* [U] *usu. apprec* male sexual power; manly qualities

vir·tu·al /'vɜrtʃuʷəl/ *adj* [A] almost what is stated; in fact though not in name: *The king was so much under the influence of his wife that she was the virtual ruler of the country.*

vir·tu·al·ly /'vɜrtʃuʷəliʸ/ *adv* almost; very nearly: *The dinner's virtually ready; I only have to finish the vegetables.*

vir·tue /'vɜrtʃuʷ/ *n* **1** [U] goodness, nobleness, and worth of character: *a man of the highest virtue* –opposite **vice 2** [C] any good quality of character or behavior: *Among her many virtues are loyalty, courage, and truthfulness.* –opposite **vice 3** [C;U] (an) advantage: *One of the virtues of this curtain material is that it's easily washable.* **4 by virtue of** as a result of; by means of: *Though she isn't American by birth, she's an American citizen by virtue of her marriage to an American.*

vir·tu·o·so /ˌvɜrtʃuʷ'oʷsoʷ/ *n* -**sos** a very skillful performer in one of the arts, esp. music –**virtuosity** /ˌvɜrtʃuʷ'asətiʸ/ *n* [U]

vir·tu·ous /'vɜrtʃuʷəs/ *adj* possessing, showing, or practicing VIRTUE(*s*) (1,2) –**virtuously** *adv*

vir·u·lent /'vɪryələnt, 'vɪrə-/ *adj* **1** (of a poison, a disease caused by bacteria, etc.) very powerful, quick-acting, and dangerous to life or health **2** (of a feeling or its expression) very bitter; full of hatred –**virulence** *n* [U] –**virulently** *adv*

vi·rus /'vaɪrəs/ *n* a living thing even smaller than bacteria which causes infectious disease in the body, in plants, etc.: *the common cold virus* | *virus infections* –compare GERM

vi·sa /'viʸzə/ *n* an official mark put onto a PASSPORT giving a foreigner permission to enter, pass through, or leave a particular country: *Do Americans need a visa to visit Canada?*

Visa *n* [U] *tdmk* a name of an American CREDIT CARD

vis·age /'vɪzɪdʒ/ *n lit* the human face, esp. with regard to its expression or appearance

vis-à-vis /ˌviʸz ə 'viʸ/ *prep fml or pomp* with regard to; when compared to: *This year's profits show an improvement vis-à-vis last year's.*

vis·count /'vaɪkaʊnt/ **viscountess** /-ɪs/ *fem.–n* [A;C] *(often cap.)* (the title of) a British nobleman next in rank below an EARL

vis·cous /'vɪskəs/ *adj* (of a liquid) thick and sticky; that does not flow easily –**viscosity** /vɪs'kasətiʸ/ *n* [U]

vise /vaɪs/ *AmE* ‖**vice** *BrE n* a tool with metal jaws, used for holding a piece of wood or metal firmly in place so that it can be worked on

vis·i·bil·i·ty /ˌvɪzə'bɪlətiʸ/ *n* [U] (esp. in official weather reports) the degree of clearness with which objects can be seen according to the weather: *We had a splendid view of the mountains because of the very good visibility.* | *The mist was so thick that visibility was only ten feet.* (=you could see only ten feet)

vis·i·ble /'vɪzəbəl/ *adj* that can be seen; noticeable to the eye –opposite **invisible** –**visibly** *adv: She was visibly anxious about the examination.*

vi·sion /'vɪʒən/ *n* **1** [U] the ability to see: *I've had my eyes tested and the report says that my vision is perfect.* **2** [U] power of imagination and expression; wisdom in understanding the true meaning of facts, esp. with regard to the future: *a man of vision* | *We need someone with real vision to lead the party.* **3** [C *of*] something that is without bodily reality, seen (as) in a dream, in the imagination, or as a religious experience: *She saw/had a vision in which God seemed to appear before her.* | *She has a clear vision of the future she wants.* | (fig.) *There was so much traffic on the way to the airport that I had visions of missing the plane.* (=I thought I would miss it)

vi·sion·ar·y¹ /'vɪʒəˌneriʸ/ *adj* **1** *apprec* having or showing VISION (2) **2** fanciful; existing in the mind only and unlikely to happen

visionary² *n* -**ies** a person whose aims show VISION (2) and are noble or excellent but often impractical

vis·it /'vɪzɪt/ *v* **1** [I;T] to go and spend time in (a place) or with (a person): *While we're in Europe, we ought to visit Holland.* | *Aunt Jane usually visits us for two or three weeks in the spring.* | *When we were in New York, we visited the World Trade Center and the Statue of Liberty.* | *Visiting hours in the hospital* (=the times when sick people may be visited) *are from 4:30 to 6:00.* **2** [T] to go to (a place) in order to make an official examination: *Prisons should to be visited from time to time by government officials.* **3** [I] to talk casually: *We didn't go out last night; we just sat around and visited.*

visit sthg. **on** sbdy. *v prep* [T] *fml or bibl* to direct (one's anger, a punishment, etc.) against: *God has visited his anger on us.*

visit² *n* an act or time of visiting: *He visits his father once a week.*|*We've just had a visit from the police.* (=the police have visited us)|*I think you should* **pay a visit** *to the doctor*/**pay the doctor** **a visit** *about your arm.*

vis·it·a·tion /ˌvɪzəˈteɪʃ*ə*n/ *n* [*by, of*] a formal visit by someone in charge (esp. by a high official person to discover whether things are in good order)

vis·i·tor /ˈvɪzəṭər/ *n* [*to*] a person who visits: *Visitors to the castle are asked not to take photographs.*

vi·sor /ˈvaɪzər/ *n* **1** the part of the HELMET which protects the face **2** the front part of a cap which protects the eyes from sunshine; PEAK

vis·ta /ˈvɪstə/ *n* a distant view, to which the eye is directed between narrow limits, e.g. by rows of trees

vis·u·al /ˈvɪʒuʷəl/ *adj* gained by or connected with seeing: *Visual knowledge of a place of battle helps a general plan his attack.*|*The* **visual arts** *are painting,* SCULPTURE, ETC., *as opposed to music and literature.* –**visually** *adv: Visually the chair is very pleasing, but it's uncomfortable.*

visual aid /ˌ··· ˈ·/ *n* an object that can be looked at (such as a picture, map, or movie) which is used for helping people to learn

vis·u·al·ize‖also **-ise** *BrE* /ˈvɪʒuʷəˌlaɪz/ *v* **-ized, -izing** [T +*v-ing*/*as*] to form a picture of (something or someone) in the mind; imagine: *She described the place carefully, and I tried to visualize it.*|*Can you visualize living on the moon?* –**visualization** /ˌvɪʒuʷələˈzeɪʃ*ə*n/ *n* [U]

vi·tal /ˈvaɪṭl/ *adj* **1** [*to, for*] very necessary; of the greatest importance: *This point is vital to my argument.*|*Your support is vital for the success of my plan.*|*He was lucky that the bullet hadn't entered a* **vital organ**. (=one which is necessary for life) **2** full of life and force: *Their leader's vital and cheerful manner filled the group with courage.* **3** **vital statistics** certain official facts about people's lives, esp. their births, marriages, and deaths

vi·tal·i·ty /vaɪˈtæləṭiʸ/ *n* [U] lively forcefulness of character or manner: *He has a pleasant voice, but his singing lacks vitality.*

vi·tal·ly /ˈvaɪṭl-iʸ/ *adv* in the highest possible degree: *It is vitally important to switch off the electricity before attempting to repair the television.*

vi·ta·min /ˈvaɪṭəmɪn/ *n* any one of several chemical substances which are present in certain foods, and are important for growth and good health: *This type of bread has added vitamins.*|*Oranges contain vitamin C.*

vi·ti·ate /ˈvɪʃiʸˌeʸt/ *v* **-ated, -ating** [T] *fml* to spoil; harm the quality of: *The report is vitiated by continual spelling mistakes.*

vit·re·ous /ˈvɪtriʸəs/ *adj tech* of or like glass: *Vitreous rocks are hard and shiny.*|*vitreous* CHINA

vit·ri·ol·ic /ˌvɪtriʸˈɑlɪk/ *adj* (of a feeling or its expression) bitter and violent: *vitriolic remarks*

vi·va·cious /vɪˈveʸʃəs, vaɪ-/ *adj* full of life and high spirits –**vivaciously** *adv* –**vivacity** /vɪˈvæsəṭiʸ, vaɪ-/ *n* [U] –**vivaciousness** /vɪˈveʸʃəsnɪs, vaɪ-/ *n* [U]

viv·id /ˈvɪvɪd/ *adj* **1** (of light or color) bright and strong: *a vivid flash of lightning*|*vivid red hair* **2** that produces sharp clear pictures in the mind; lifelike: *a child with a vivid imagination*|*a vivid description* –**vividly** *adv* –**vividness** *n* [U]

viv·i·sec·tion /ˌvɪvəˈsɛkʃən/ *n* [U] the practice of performing operations on living animals, esp. in order to increase medical knowledge

vix·en /ˈvɪksən/ *n* a female fox

viz. /vɪz/ *adv* that is to say: *On most midwestern farms, you'll find four kinds of animal, viz. horses, chickens, cattle, and pigs.* USAGE Usually read aloud as "NAMELY."

vo·cab·u·lar·y /voʷˈkæbyəˌlɛriʸ, və-/ *n* **-ies 1** all the words known to a particular person, or used in a particular kind of work, etc.: *Our baby's just starting to talk; he's got a vocabulary of about ten words.*|*I find it difficult to understand the vocabulary of the law courts.* **2** a list of words, usu. in alphabetical order and with explanations of their meanings, less complete than a dictionary

vo·cal /ˈvoʷkəl/ *adj* **1** [A] connected with or produced by or for the voice: *The tongue is one of the vocal organs.*|*I like instrumental better than vocal music.* **2** *infml* expressing oneself freely and noisily in words: *She was very vocal at the meeting.* –**vocally** *adv*

vocal cords /ˈ·· ˌ·/ *n* [P] thin bands of muscle at the upper end of a person's air passage (WINDPIPE) that produce sound

vo·cal·ist /ˈvoʷkəlɪst/ *n* a singer of popular songs, esp. one who sings with a band

vo·ca·tion /voʷˈkeʸʃən/ *n* **1** [S;U *for*] a particular fitness or ability (for a certain kind of work, esp. of a worthy kind): *She's a good doctor because she has a real vocation for looking after the sick.* **2** [C] a job, esp. a worthy one for which one has a VOCATION (1): *Teaching children is more than just a way of making money: it's a vocation.* **3** [S] a special call from God to be a priest, MONK, etc. –see JOB (USAGE)

vo·ca·tion·al /voʷˈkeʸʃənəl/ *adj* preparing for a particular type of job: *vocational training for pilots*

vo·cif·er·ous /voʷˈsɪfərəs/ *adj fml* noisy in the expression of one's feelings: *vociferous demands for higher wages* –**vociferously** *adv* [U] –**vociferousness** *n* [U]

vod·ka /ˈvɑdkə/ *n* [U] a strong, colorless, and almost tasteless alcoholic drink, first made in Russia and Poland

vogue /voʷg/ *n* the fashion or custom at a certain time: *High boots were the vogue for women last year.*|*Long hair for men is no longer* **in vogue**/*has* **gone out of vogue**. (=is no longer fashionable)

voice¹ /vɔɪs/ *n* **1** [C;U] the sound(s) produced by people when speaking and singing:

He had such a bad cold he lost his voice.|She lowered her voice (=spoke quietly) *as she told me the secret.|We could hear the children's voices in the garden.|She has a good voice for singing|a good singing voice.|He* **gave voice to** (=expressed) *his fears that the government's policies weren't working.* **2** [U] (the expressing of) an opinion: *The crowd was large, but they were all* **of one voice.** (=they all said the same thing)|*He was very angry at first but in the end the* **voice of reason** *won.* **3** [C *usu. sing.*] *tech* the form of the verb which shows whether the subject of a sentence acts (**active voice**) or is acted on (**passive voice**) **4 at the top of one's voice** very loudly **5 raise one's voice: a** to speak louder **b** to speak loudly and angrily (to someone): *Don't raise your voice to me.* **6 -voiced** having a voice of the stated kind: *loud-voiced|soft-voiced|sweet-voiced*

voice² *v* **voiced, voicing** [T] to express in words, esp. forcefully: *The chairman voiced the feeling of the meeting when he demanded more pay.*

void¹ /vɔɪd/ *adj* **1** [F *of*] *fml* empty (of); without; lacking: *That part of the town is completely void of interest for visitors.* –see also DEVOID **2** *esp. law* (of any kind of official agreement) having no value or effect from the beginning: *An agreement signed by a child is void.* –see also NULL AND VOID

void² *n* [S] an empty space, esp. the space around our world and beyond the stars: *A ball of fire seemed to fall out of the void, disappearing before it reached the earth.*|(fig.)*The child's death left a painful void in her parents' lives.*

vol. *n abbrev. said as:* VOLUME (1)

vol·a·tile /ˈvɑlətl, -ˌtaɪl/ *adj* **1** (of a person or his/her character) quickly-changing and undependable **2** (of a liquid or oil) easily changing into a gas: *Gasoline is volatile.* –**volatility** /ˌvɑləˈtɪlətiʸ/ *n* [U]

vol·ca·no /vɑlˈkeʸnoʷ/ *n* **-noes** *or* **-nos** a mountain with a large opening (CRATER) at the top through which melting rock (LAVA), steam, gases, etc., escape from time to time with explosive force from inside the earth (ERUPT): *An active volcano may erupt at any time.*|*An extinct volcano has ceased to be able to erupt.* –**volcanic** /vɑlˈkænɪk/ *adj: volcanic rocks|activity*

vole /voʷl/ *n* a small short-tailed animal of the rat and mouse family, which lives in fields, woods, banks of rivers, etc.: *a water vole*

vo·li·tion /voʊˈlɪʃən, vɑʷ-/ *n* [U] *fml* the act of using one's will in choosing a course of action: *I didn't ask him to go; he went of his own volition.*

vol·ley /ˈvɑliʸ/ *n* **-leys 1** a number of shots, arrows, stones, etc., fired or thrown at the same time: *A volley of shots was heard.*|(fig.) *a volley of curses* **2** (esp. in tennis) a hitting of a ball which has not touched the ground first

vol·ley·ball /ˈvɑliʸˌbɔl/ *n* [U] a game in which a large ball is struck by hand across a net without being allowed to touch the ground

volt /voʷlt/ *n* a standard measure of electrical force used in causing a flow of electrical

current along wires –compare AMP

volt·age /ˈvoʷltɪdʒ/ *n* [C;U] electrical force measured in VOLTS

vol·u·ble /ˈvɑlyəbəl/ *adj often derog* talking with a great flow of words: *Ted's a voluble speaker at meetings; he doesn't give much chance to others to say anything.* –**volubility** /ˌvɑlyəˈbɪlətiʸ/ *n* [U] –**volubly** /ˈvɑlyəbliʸ/ *adv*

vol·ume /ˈvɑlyəm, -yuʷm/ *n* **1** [U] (degree of) loudness of sound: *The television is too loud; turn the volume down.* **2** [U *of*] size or quantity thought of as measurement of the space filled by something: *The volume of this container is 100,000 cubic feet.* –compare AREA **3** [C] a book, esp. one of a set of the same kind: *We have a set of Dickens' works in 24 volumes.* **4** [C;U] *esp. tech* amount produced by some kind of (industrial) activity: *The volume of passenger travel on the railroads is increasing again.*

vo·lu·mi·nous /vəˈluʷmənəs/ *adj* **1** (of a garment) very loose and full; using much cloth: *a voluminous skirt* **2** containing or able to hold a lot: *a voluminous shopping bag|a voluminous report* –**voluminously** *adv*

vol·un·tar·y /ˈvɑlənˌteriʸ/ *adj* **1** (of a person or an action) acting or done willingly, without payment and without being forced: *He made a voluntary statement to the police.*|*At election time the party needs a lot of voluntary helpers.* –compare COMPULSORY **2** [A] controlled or supported by people who give their money, services, etc., free: *Many social services are still provided by voluntary organizations.* –**voluntarily** /ˌvɑlənˈterəliʸ, ˈvɑlənˌterər-/ *adv: She made the promise quite voluntarily; I didn't force her to.*

vol·un·teer¹ /ˌvɑlənˈtɪər/ *n* a person who VOLUNTEERS² (1,2): *This work costs us nothing; it's all done by volunteers.*

volunteer² *v* **1** [I +*to-v*] to offer one's services or help without payment; offer (to do something), esp. when others are unwilling: *He volunteered to help me move.* **2** [I +*to-v/for*] to offer to join the armed forces of one's own free will **3** [T] to tell (something) without being asked: *My friend volunteered an interesting piece of news.*

vo·lup·tu·ous /vəˈlʌptʃuʷəs/ *adj* (esp. connected with women) that suggests or expresses sexual pleasure: *The dancer's movements were slow and voluptuous.*|*She had a large voluptuous mouth.* –**voluptuously** *adv* –**voluptuousness** *n* [U]

vom·it¹ /ˈvɑmɪt/ *v* [I;T] to throw up (the contents of the stomach) through the mouth; be sick: *The unpleasant smell made her feel so sick that she began to vomit.*

vomit² *n* [U] food or other matter that has been VOMITED¹

voo·doo /ˈvuʷduʷ/ *n* [U] (*often cap.*) (esp. in the West Indies) a set of magical beliefs and practices, used as a form of religion

vo·ra·cious /vəˈreʸʃəs, vɔ-, voʷ-/ *adj fml* eating or desiring large quantities of food: *Pigs are voracious eaters.*|(fig.) *She's a voracious reader.* –**voracity** /vəˈræsətiʸ, vɔ-, voʷ-/ *n* [U] –**voraciously** /vəˈreʸʃəsliʸ, vɔ-, voʷ-/ *adv*

vor·tex /'vɔrtɛks/ n -texes or -tices /-tə,siʸz/ esp. lit a circular moving mass of anything, esp. water or wind, which causes objects to be drawn into its hollow center, as in a WHIRLPOOL or WHIRLWIND

vote¹ /voʷt/ n 1 [C] an act of making a choice or decision on a matter by means of voting: Since there is some disagreement on this matter, let's take a vote on it/let's put it to the vote. 2 [C] a choice or decision as expressed by voting: There were 15 votes in favor of my suggestion, and 23 against.|She will certainly not get my vote (=I will not vote for her) at the next election.|You must cast (=record) your vote before eight o'clock tonight. 3 [S] the whole number of such choices made by a particular set of people: In elections in New York, the Irish vote is very important. 4 [the S] the right to vote in political elections: In the U.S., people get the vote at the age of 18. 5 vote of thanks a public expression of thanks: Mrs. Jones proposed (=called for) a vote of thanks to Dr. Brown for his interesting talk.

vote² v voted, voting 1 [I +to-v/(that)/for, against, on] to express one's choice officially from among the possibilities offered (by marking a piece of paper, raising one's hand at a meeting, etc.): You're only 16; you're too young to vote.|Did you vote for Reagan in the last election?|The railroad workers have voted to go back to work on Monday.|The sign said "Vote Democratic." (=vote for this party)|(fig. infml) I vote we go home. 2 [T] to agree, by a vote, to provide (something): Congress has voted the city a large sum of money for low-income housing. 3 [T] infml to agree as the general opinion: The party was voted a great success.

vot·er /'voʷtər/ n a person who is voting

voting booth AmE‖also **polling booth** esp. BrE– n a partly enclosed place inside a building used for voting where people record their votes secretly

vouch /vautʃ/→VOUCH FOR

vouch·er /'vautʃər/ n 1 law a receipt or official declaration, written or printed, given to prove that accounts are correct or that money has already been paid 2 esp. BrE a kind of ticket that may be used instead of money for a particular purpose: a travel voucher|Some companies give their workers luncheon vouchers, which they can use to buy a meal.

vouch for sbdy./sthg. v prep [T] 1 to declare one's belief in (someone or something),

from one's own personal experience or knowledge: I've read this report carefully and I can vouch for its accuracy. 2 to take responsibility for (someone's future behavior)

vow¹ /vau/ n a solemn promise: All the men took/made a vow of loyalty to their leader.

vow² v [T +to-v/(that)] to declare or swear solemnly (that one will do something): When young Ernie was caught stealing, he vowed he'd never do it again.

vow·el /'vauəl/ n 1 a human speech sound in which the breath is let out without any stop or any closing of the air passage in the mouth: The vowel sounds of American English are represented in this dictionary by /iʸ, ɪ, eʸ, ɛ, æ, ɑ, ɔ, oʷ, ʊ, uʷ, ʌ, ɜ, ə/. 2 a letter used for representing any of these: The vowels in the English alphabet are a, e, i, o, u, and sometimes y. –compare CONSONANT, DIPHTHONG

voy·age¹ /'vɔɪ-ɪdʒ/ n a long journey made by boat or ship (or in space): The voyage from America to France used to take two months.|a voyage to the moon

voyage² v -aged, -aging [I] lit or fml to make a long journey by sea –see TRAVEL (USAGE)

vs. AmE‖also **v.** /'vɜrsəs/ written abbrev. said as: VERSUS

VT, Vt. written abbrev. said as: Vermont /vər'mant/ (a state in the US)

vul·gar /'vʌlgər/ adj 1 very rude, low, or bad-mannered; going against the accepted standards of polite society: The old lady was shocked by the children's vulgar language.| Putting food into one's mouth with a knife is considered vulgar in the US. 2 showing a lack of fine feeling or good judgment in the choice of what is beautiful: The house was full of expensive but very vulgar furniture. –**vulgarly** adv

vul·gar·i·ty /vʌl'gærəṭiʸ/ n -ties 1 [U] the quality of being VULGAR 2 [C often pl.] VULGAR speech or action

vul·ner·a·ble /'vʌlnərəbəl/ adj [to] easily harmed, hurt, or attacked; sensitive: We're in a vulnerable position here, with the enemy on the hill above us.|She looked so young and vulnerable that I felt a great desire to protect her. –**vulnerability** /,vʌlnərə'bɪləṭiʸ/ n [U to] –**vulnerably** /'vʌlnərəbliʸ/ adv

vul·ture /'vʌltʃər/ n a large ugly tropical bird with almost featherless head and neck, which feeds on dead animals

vy·ing /'vaɪ-ɪŋ/ v pres. participle of VIE

W, w

W, w /'dʌbəl,yuʷ/ **W's, w's** or **Ws, ws** the 23rd letter of the English alphabet

W written abbrev. said as: **a** west(ern) **b** WATT

WA written abbrev. said as: Washington /'waʃɪŋtən, 'wɔ-/ (a state in the US)

Wac /wæk/ n a member of the women's army CORPS

wack·y /'wækiʸ/ adj **-ier, -iest** AmE infml (of people, ideas, behavior, etc.) silly or strange **–wackiness** n [U]

wad /wad/ n [of] **1** a thick collection of things, such as pieces of paper, folded, pressed, or fastened together: a wad of dollar bills **2** a thick soft mass of material used for filling an empty space, hole, etc.: wads of cotton in one's ears to keep out noise

wad·dle /'wadl/ v **-dled, -dling** [I along] to walk with short steps, moving one's body from one side to the other, like a duck **–waddle** n

wade /weʸd/ v **waded, wading** [I across, into, through] to walk through water: We had to wade across the river, and the water came up to our knees.

wade through sthg. v prep [T] infml to finish (something long or unpleasant) with effort: I waded through that long report at last.

wa·fer /'weʸfər/ n **1** a very thin COOKIE eaten esp. with ice cream **2** a thin round piece of bread used in the Christian religious ceremony of Holy COMMUNION

waf·fle /'wafəl/ n a large light sweet cake, usu. marked with raised squares, often covered with a sweet liquid, and common in America

waft /waft, wæft/ v [I;T] esp. lit to (cause to) move lightly on, or as if on, wind or waves: Cooking smells wafted along the hall.

wag /wæg/ v **-gg-** [I;T] (esp. of a dog) to shake (its tail) quickly and repeatedly from side to side: The dog wagged its tail.|Look at the dog's tail wagging; he must be happy to see us. –compare WAGGLE **–wag** n

wage¹ /weʸdʒ/ n [A;S] wages: a weekly wage of $350

wage² v **waged, waging** [T] fml to begin and continue (a struggle of some kind): to wage war|The police are waging a war on/against crime in the city.

wa·ger /'weʸdʒər/ v [T +(that)] fml to BET²: I'll wager ($5) he's there by now. **–wager** n

wag·es /'weʸdʒɪz/ n [P] a payment for labor or services, usu. received daily or weekly –see PAY (USAGE)

wag·gle /'wægəl/ v **-gled, -gling** [I;T] to (cause to) move frequently from side to side: Can you waggle your ears? –compare WAG **–waggle** n [S]

wag·on AmE‖**waggon** BrE /'wægən/ n **1** a strong four-wheeled road vehicle, mainly for heavy loads, drawn by horses or oxen: He takes his fruit to market **by wagon/on a** **wagon. 2** a small copy of this as a child's toy

waif /weʸf/ n esp. lit an uncared-for or homeless child: a pitiful little waif

wail /weʸl/ v [I;T +that/with] to cry out (something) with a long sound suggesting grief or pain: The wind wailed in the chimney all night.|"You've taken my money," she wailed. **–wail** n: the wails of a lost child

waist /weʸst/ n (the part of a garment that goes around) the narrow part of the human body just above the legs and HIPs: What do you measure around the waist?|It's a nice skirt, but too big around the waist.

waist·line /'weʸstlaɪn/ n a line measured around the waist at its narrowest part: Your waistline is getting bigger.

wait¹ /weʸt/ v [I +to-v/for, about, around] **1** to stay somewhere without doing anything until somebody or something comes or something happens: We waited and waited.|We waited 20 minutes (for a bus).|We're waiting anxiously to hear the examination results.|Try not to keep her waiting.|"What's for dinner?" "Wait and see." (=Wait, and you'll soon know the answer)|(fig.) The business can wait until after dinner. **2** wait on tables to serve meals, esp. as a regular job

USAGE Compare **wait** and **expect**. To **wait** suggests staying in the same place and/or taking no action until something happens: I spent an hour **waiting** for a bus.|We can't start the meeting yet; we're **waiting** for John (to arrive). If you **expect** something, you think it will probably happen, arrive, etc., whether you want it to or not: I'm **expecting** a big telephone bill this month.|We were **expecting** 12 guests (=we thought 12 would come), but only seven came. –see also HOPE (USAGE)

wait on/upon sbdy. v prep [T] **1** esp. old use to attend as a servant **2** wait on someone hand and foot to serve someone very humbly: Don't expect me to wait on you hand and foot; make your own breakfast!

wait up v adv [I for] infml to delay going to bed: Don't wait up (for me); I'll be home very late.

wait² n **1** an act or period of waiting: We had a long wait for a bus. **2** lie in wait (for someone) to hide, waiting to attack (someone): The robbers were lying in wait for me as I came out of the bank.

wait·er /'weʸtər/ **waitress** /'weʸtrɪs/ fem.– n a person who serves food at the tables in a restaurant –see illustration on page 581

waiting list /'·· ,·/ n a list of people who want something (such as theater tickets or a job): There's a long waiting list of people who want an apartment in that building.

waiting room /'·· ,·/ n a room for people who are waiting, e.g. to see a doctor –see illustration on page 200

waive /weyv/ v **waived, waiving** [T] fml to give up willingly (a right, a rule, etc.): *We cannot waive this rule except in case of illness.*

wake¹ /weyk/ v **woke** /wowk/ or **waked, waked** or **woken** /'wowkən/, **waking** [I;T up] **1** to (cause to) cease to sleep: *I usually wake (up) at eight o'clock.|The children's shouts woke us up.*|(fig.) *The company has only just woken up to* (=become conscious of the possibility of) *using computers.* **2 Wake up** infml Listen!; Pay attention!

USAGE **Waken, awake,** and **awaken** can all be used in the patterns [I] and [T], though **awake** is usually [I] and **waken/awaken** are usually [T]. But **wake** (up) is the most common and least formal word in both patterns.

wake² n a gathering to watch and grieve over a dead person on the night before the burial

wake³ n a track or path, esp. one left by a ship in water: *the broad white wake of the great ship*|(fig.) *hunger and disease* **in the wake of** (=as a result of) *the war*

wake·ful /'weykfəl/ adj not able to sleep; sleepless: *a wakeful night/baby* –**wakefully** adv –**wakefulness** n [U]

wak·en /'weykən/ v [I;T up] fml to (cause to) wake: *We were wakened by a loud noise.*

wak·ing /'weykɪŋ/ adj [A] of the time when one is awake: *She spends all her waking hours working.*

walk¹ /wɔk/ v **1** [I;T] to (cause to) move at a walk: *Do you walk to work, or do you come by bus?|to walk (for) ten miles|She likes walking.* **2** [T] to pass over, through, or along on foot: *tired out after walking the streets of Boston all day|to walk a* TIGHTROPE **3** [T] to take (an animal) for a walk; exercise: *He's walking the dog.* **4** [T] to go on foot with (someone), usu. to a stated place: *I'll walk you to the bus stop.*

USAGE **Walk** is the usual word for moving on foot at a normal speed: *Do you* **walk** *to work, or do you go by bus?* To **amble** or **stroll** is to walk in an easy, unhurried way, esp. for pleasure. To **stride** is to walk purposefully with long steps, and to **march** is to walk with forceful regular steps as soldiers do. **Run** is the general word for moving quickly on one's legs. **Race, dash,** and **sprint** all suggest running very fast for a short distance: *I* **raced/dashed/sprinted** *down the road to catch the bus.* To **jog** is to run in a steady unhurried way as a form of exercise: *She goes* **jogging** *every morning.*

walk into sthg. v prep [T] to meet through carelessness: *He walked right into the trap.*

walk off/away with sthg. v adv prep [T] infml **1** to steal: *Someone's walked off with my bicycle.* **2** to win easily: *She walked off with first prize.*

walk out v adv [I of] to go on STRIKE² (1) –**walkout** /'wɔk-aut/ n: *There's been an unofficial walkout at the car factory.*

walk out on sbdy. v adv prep [T] infml to leave suddenly, esp. in a time of trouble; desert: *She walked out on her friends in the middle of the party.*

walk over sbdy. v prep [T] infml to treat

badly: *Don't let them walk (all) over you like that.*

walk² n **1** (of people and creatures) a natural and unhurried way of moving on foot from one place to another **2** a (usu. short) journey on foot: *Let's go for/have/take a short walk.|The station's just a ten-minute walk from here.* **3** a place, path, or course for walking: *There is a beautiful walk along the river.* (=beside the river)

walk·ie-talk·ie /,wɔkiy 'tɔkiy/ n infml a two-way radio that can be carried, allowing one to talk as well as listen

walk-in /'·· ·/ adj infml esp. AmE large enough to be walked into: *a walk-in closet*

walking pa·pers /'·· ,··/ n AmE infml official notice that one's services are no longer needed: *I got my walking papers at work today.* (=I was fired)

walking stick /'·· ,·/ n a stick used by someone to support himself/herself while walking

walk-on /'·· ·/ n a small, usu. non-speaking, part in a play

walk-up /'·· ·/ n, adj AmE infml (an apartment in) a building with no elevator

walk·way /'wɔk-wey/ n AmE a passage used for walking, esp. one connecting different sections of a building or garden

wall¹ /wɔl/ n **1** an upright dividing surface (esp. of stone or brick) intended for defense or safety, or for enclosing something: *a garden surrounded by stone walls|the city wall of London*|(fig.) *a wall of fire/wall of silence* **2** the side of a building or a room: *Hang that picture on the wall.* **3 bang/run one's head against a (brick) wall** infml to try to do something difficult with very little hope of success **4 with one's back to the wall** fighting with no way of escape

wall² v [T in, up] to provide, close with, or surround with a wall: *an old walled town in Portugal*

wall sthg.↔ **off** v adv [T from] to separate with one or more walls: *This part of the house is walled off because it has a dangerous floor.*

wal·la·by /'wɒləbiy/ n **-bies** or **-by** a KANGAROO of small to middle size

wal·let /'wɒlɪt, 'wɔ-/ n a small flat leather case which can usu. be folded, for holding papers and paper money –compare PURSE

wal·lop /'wɒləp/ v [T] infml to hit with force: *to wallop someone|He hit the floor with a wallop.* –**wallop** n

wal·low /'wɒlow/ v [I in] to move or roll around happily in deep mud, dirt, water, etc.: *Pigs enjoy wallowing in mud.*|(fig.) *wallowing in self-pity/her success* –**wallow** n [in]: *animals having a wallow in the mud*

wall·pa·per /'wɔl,peypər/ n [U] decorative paper to cover the walls of a room –**wallpaper** v [I;T]: *We've decided to wallpaper the bedroom.*

wal·nut /'wɔlnʌt, -nət/ n **1** [C] an edible nut with a round rough shell **2** [C;U] the tree that produces these nuts, or its wood

wal·rus /'wɔlrəs, 'wɒl-/ n **walruses** or **walrus** a large SEAL³-like sea-animal with two long teeth (TUSKs) standing out from the face

waltz¹ /wɔlts/ n (music for) a slow social dance for a man and a woman: *I like dancing the waltz.|a waltz by Strauss*

waltz² v [I;T] to (cause to) dance a WALTZ: *Can you waltz?|He waltzed her across the room.*

wan /wɑn/ adj esp. lit appearing ill, weak, and tired: *a wan smile* –**wanly** adv –**wanness** n [U]

wand /wɑnd/ n a thin stick used by a person who does magic tricks: *He waved his magic wand and pulled a rabbit out of the hat.*

wan·der /'wɑndər/ v 1 [I;T about] to move around (an area) without a fixed course, aim, or purpose: *The lost child was wandering (around) the streets.*|(fig.) *He's getting old, and his mind's beginning to wander a little.* (=to become confused) 2 [I off] to move away (from the main idea): *Don't wander off the point.* –**wanderer** n

wan·der·lust /'wɑndər,lʌst/ n [S;U] a strong desire not to stay in one place

wane¹ /weɪn/ v **waned, waning** [I] to become gradually smaller or less after being full or complete: *The moon waxes and wanes every month.*

wane² n **on the wane** becoming smaller, weaker, or less: *The government's popularity is on the wane.*

wan·gle /'wæŋgəl/ v **-gled, -gling** [T] infml to get (something) from someone, esp. by cleverness or a trick: *I wangled an invitation (out of George).*

wan·na /'wɑnə, 'wɔnə/ want to

USAGE **Want to** is sometimes pronounced in this way. It may be written **wanna** in stories to show an informal way of speaking: *I don't wanna go.* (=I don't want to go.) Many teachers don't like this form.

want¹ /wɑnt, wɔnt/ v [not *be+v-ing*] 1 [T +*to-v*] to have a strong desire to or for; feel a strong desire to have: *I want a rest|I want to rest.|I want this letter (to be) opened now!|What do you want for your birthday?* (=What present would you like?)|*Do you want anything else to eat?* 2 [T +*v-ing*] to need: *The house wants painting.* 3 [T +*to-v*] ought to: *You want to see a doctor about your cough.* 4 [T] to wish or demand the presence of: *I wasn't wanted at the office, so I left.* 5 [T usu. pass.] (esp. of the police) to hunt or look for in order to catch: *He is wanted for murder.|He is a wanted man.* 6 [I] to lack enough food, clothing, shelter, etc.: *You shall never want while I have any money left.*

    want for sthg. v prep [T usu. in NEGATIVES²] fml (of a person) to lack (esp. food, clothing, shelter, money, love, attention, etc.): *They have never wanted for anything.* (=have always had everything they need)

want² n 1 [S;U] lack, absence, or need: *The plants died for/from want of water.|I'll take this one for want of a better.* 2 [U] severe lack of things necessary to life: *How terrible to live in want!*

want ad /'· ·/ n esp. AmE a small newspaper advertisement stating that something or someone is wanted (such as a job, a person for a job, or a particular thing)

want·ing /'wɑntɪŋ, 'wɔn-/ adj **be found (to be)**

wanting (in) to be considered not good enough, strong enough, or full enough of

wan·ton /'wɑntən, 'wɔn-/ adj 1 lit wild and full of fun: *wanton behavior at the party* 2 having no just cause or no good reason: *wanton cruelty* –**wantonly** adv

wants /wɑnts, wɔnts/ n [P] needs: *My wants are few and are soon satisfied.*

war¹ /wɔr/ n [C;U] 1 (an example or period of) armed fighting between nations: *He fought in both World Wars.|Is war necessary?|a prisoner of war|Those two countries have been at war (with each other) for a long time.* –compare BATTLE 2 a struggle between opposing forces or for a particular purpose: *class war|to wage war on/against disease* 3 **(having) been through the wars** infml (having) been hurt or damaged: *Your car looks as if it's been through the wars!*

war² v **-rr-** [I with, against, for] lit to take part in or direct a war: *a meeting between the generals of the warring forces*

war·ble /'wɔrbəl/ v **-bled, -bling** [I;T] (esp. of birds) to sing with a clear, continuous, yet varied note –compare TRILL –**warble** [*the S of*] n

ward¹ /wɔrd/ n 1 a division of a hospital: *the children's ward* 2 a division of a city, esp. for political purposes: *Which ward does she represent on the council?* 3 a person, esp. a child, who is under the protection of another person or of a law court (=is a **ward of court**) –compare GUARDIAN (2)

ward² v → WARD OFF

war dance /'· ·/ n a dance performed esp. by tribes in preparation for battle or after a victory

war·den /'wɔrdn/ n 1 a person who looks after a place (and people): *the warden of an old people's home* 2 an official who helps to see that certain laws are obeyed: *A traffic warden sees that all cars are properly parked.* 3 AmE the head of a prison

ward off sthg. v adv [T] protect oneself against (a blow, a danger, a cold, etc.): *Brushing your teeth regularly helps to ward off tooth decay.*

ward·robe /'wɔrdroʷb/ n 1 a cupboard or large upright box, with a door, in which one hangs up clothes 2 a collection of clothes (esp. of one person or for one activity): *a new summer wardrobe*

ware·house /'weərhaʊs/ n **-houses** /,haʊzɪz/ a building for storing things, esp. to be sold or before being moved

wares /weərz/ n [P] lit articles for sale, usu. not in a store: *The baker traveled around the town selling his wares.*

war·fare /'wɔrfeər/ n [U] (type of) war: *chemical warfare*

war·head /'wɔrhɛd/ n the explosive front end of a bomb or esp. MISSILE

war·i·ly /'weərəli/ adv see WARY –**wariness** n [U]

war·like /'wɔrlaɪk/ adj ready for war or liking war: *a warlike appearance/nation*

warm¹ /wɔrm/ adj 1 having or giving a pleasant feeling of heat: *warm milk|a warm fire|a warm sunny day* 2 able to keep in heat or keep out cold: *warm clothes* **3** showing or marked by strong feeling, esp. good feeling: *warm support for the local team|warm friendship|a warm welcome* **4** giving a pleasant feeling of cheerfulness or friendliness: *warm colors|a warm voice* –compare COOL **5** [F] (esp. in children's games) near a hidden object, the right answer to a question, etc.: *You're getting warm; you've nearly found the answer!* –opposite **cool** or **cold** –**warmly** *adv: They greeted each other warmly.* –**warmness** *n* [U]

warm² *v* [I;T] to make or become warm: *They warmed their hands/themselves by the fire.|a warming fire/drink|The soup is warming in the pot on the stove.* –compare COOL²

warm over *v adv* [T] *usu. derog, esp. AmE infml* **1** to make or become warm **2** to use (the same arguments) again: *He never has any new ideas but just keeps giving us the same ones warmed over.*

warm to/towards sbdy./sthg. *v prep* [T] *infml* to begin to like or be interested in: *The more he spoke, the more he warmed to his subject.*

warm up *v adv* [I;T (=**warm** sbdy./sthg.↔ **up**)] **1** to make or become warm: *Come and warm yourself up by the fire.|The room soon warmed up.* **2** to make or become ready for action or performance: *The singers are warming up before the concert.|Let's warm up the car engine a little before we start.* –**warm-up** */'· ·/ n: After a warm-up of 15 minutes, the game began.*

warm-blood·ed /ˌ· '··◄/ *adj tech* (of birds, MAMMALS, etc.) able to keep the temperature of the body high whether the outside temperature is high or low –see also COLD-BLOODED

warm-heart·ed /ˌ· '··◄/ *adj* having or showing warm friendly feelings –see also COLD-HEARTED –**warm-heartedness** *n* [U]

war·mon·ger /'wɔrˌmʌŋgər, -ˌmɑŋ-/ *n derog* a person who encourages war

warmth /wɔrmθ/ *n* [U] the state or quality of being warm: *the warmth of the fire/of her feelings*

warn /wɔrn/ *v* [I;T +*that/of,against*] to tell of something bad that may happen; tell of how to prevent something bad: *The morning paper warned (us) of serious delays at the airport.|Drivers have been warned to avoid the roads through the center of town.|She warned the company that profits would be low that year.|a red warning light on a car*

warn·ing /'wɔrnɪŋ/ *n* **1** [C;U +*to-v/of*] the act of warning or the state of being warned: *They attacked without warning.|a warning not to go there* **2** [C +*to-v/of*] something that warns: *Let that be a warning to you.|The accident served as a warning of what may happen.*

warp¹ /wɔrp/ *n* [S] **1** a twist out of a true level or straight line: *There's a warp in this table top.* **2** [*the*] *tech* threads running along the length of cloth –compare WEFT

warp² *v* [I;T] to (cause to) turn or twist out of shape: *A record warps if it gets too hot.|*(fig.) *the warped mind of a violent killer*

war·path /'wɔrpæθ/ *n* **on the warpath** starting to fight or struggle: *Those politicians are on the warpath for higher taxes again.*

war·rant¹ /'wɔrənt, 'wɑr-/ *n* an official written order, esp. allowing the police to take certain action: *You can't search my house without a* **search warrant**.

warrant² *v* [T] **1** [+*v-ing*] to cause (an action) to appear right or reasonable: *The old car doesn't warrant a new engine.|His illness doesn't warrant (his) staying home for a week.* –see also UNWARRANTED **2** [+(*that*)] *infml old use* to declare as if certain: *I'll warrant (you) (that) he's back there drinking again!*

war·ran·ty /'wɔrəntiʸ, 'wɑr-/ *n* -**ties** [C;U] *tech* a written GUARANTEE¹ (1): *We'll repair your car without charging because it's still* **under warranty**.

war·ren /'wɔrən, 'wɑr-/ *n* **1** a system of underground passages in which a number of rabbits live –compare BURROW **2** *usu. derog* a place in which too many people live, or in which one gets lost easily: *a warren of narrow old streets*

war·ri·or /'wɔriʸər, 'wɑr-/ *n lit* a soldier or experienced fighter

war·ship /'wɔrʃɪp/ *n* a naval ship used for war, esp. one armed with guns

wart /wɔrt/ *n* a small hard ugly swelling on the skin, esp. of the face or hands

war·time /'wɔrtaɪm/ *n* [U] a period during which a war is going on –opposite **peacetime**

war·y /'wɛəriʸ/ *adj* -**ier**, -**iest** [*of*] careful; looking out for danger: *Our dog is a little wary of strangers.* –**warily** *adv* –**wariness** *n* [U]

was /wəz; *strong* wʌz, wɑz/ *v past tense of* BE, 1st and 3rd person singular: *I/He was*

Wash. *written abbrev. said as:* Washington /'wɑʃɪŋtən, 'wɔ-/ (a state in the US)

wash¹ /wɑʃ, wɔʃ/ *v* **1** [T *down, off, out, with*] to clean with liquid: *to wash clothes/one's car/a dog/one's hands/oneself (with soap and water)* **2** [I *with*] to clean oneself or a part of one's body with liquid: *I always wash before dinner.* **3** [I] to bear cleaning with liquid without damage: *These clothes only wash in cold water.* **4** [I;T *against, over*] to flow over or against (something) continually: *The waves washed (against/over) the shore.* **5** [T *away, off*] to cause to be carried by liquid: *The waves washed him off the rocks into the sea.* **6** [I *used in* NEGATIVE² (1) *sentences*] *infml* to be believed: *His story just won't wash (with me).* **7 wash one's hands of** *infml* to refuse to be responsible for: *I wash my hands of you and all your wild ideas!*

wash sthg.↔ **down** *v adv* [T] **1** to clean with a lot of water: *to wash down the car/the walls* **2** [*with*] to swallow (food or medicine) with the help of liquid: *Wash the dry cake down with coffee.*

wash out *v adv* **1** [I;T (=**wash** sthg.↔ **out**) *of*] to remove or be removed by washing: *Was she able to wash the dirty mark out of her coat?|Do you think these ink spots will wash out?* **2** [T] (**wash** sthg.↔ **out**) to prevent or destroy by water, esp. rain: *The baseball*

game was washed out (by rain). –see also
WASHOUT

wash up *v adv infml* **1** [I] *AmE* to wash
one's face and hands **2** [T] (**wash** sbdy./sthg.
⟵ **up**) (of waves) to bring in to the shore:
*The sea washed up the body of the drowned
sailor.*

wash² *n* **1** [S] the act or an action of washing
or being washed: *Go upstairs and have a
wash.|Give the car a good wash.* **2** [*the* S]
things to be washed, or being washed; LAUN-
DRY: *I've got no clean shirts; they're all in the
wash.* –see also WASHING **3** [S;U] a movement of water (usu. caused by the passing of
a boat) –compare WAKE³ **4** [C;U] the liquid
with which something is washed or colored:
She rinses her mouth out with mouthwash.

wash·a·ble /'wɑʃəbəl, 'wɔ-/ *adj* that can be
washed without damage: *washable cotton*

wash·ba·sin /'wɑʃ,beʸsən, 'wɔʃ-/|also **wash-
bowl** /'wɑʃboʷl, 'wɔʃ-/ *AmE– n* a large fixed
basin for water for washing the hands and
face, esp. in a bathroom –compare SINK²

wash·cloth /'wɑʃklɔθ, 'wɔʃ-/ *n AmE*‖**face-
cloth** *esp. BrE n* **-cloths** /klɔðz, klɔθs/ a small
cloth used to wash face and body

washed-out /ˌ· '·◄/ *adj* very tired: *She felt
washed-out after working all night.|Go and
get some rest; you look washed-out!*

washed up /ˌ· '·◄/ *adj infml* (esp. of people)
finished; with no further possibilities of success: *He's (all) washed-up in this town.*

wash·er /'wɑʃər, 'wɔ-/ *n* **1** a person or
machine that washes **2** a ring of metal, rubber, etc., between a NUT (2) and BOLT¹ (1), or
between two pipes, to make a better, tighter
joint **3** → WASHING MACHINE

wash·ing /'wɑʃɪŋ, wɔ-/ *n* [U] things (esp.
clothes) washed or to be washed: *Hang the
washing out to dry.* –see also WASH² (2),
LAUNDRY (2)

washing ma·chine /'·· ·ˌ·/ *n* a machine for
washing clothes

wash·out /'wɑʃaʊt, 'wɔʃ-/ *n infml* a failure:
*The plan was a washout after all, and cost us a
lot of money.* –see also WASH **out** (2)

wash·room /'wɑʃruʷm, -rʊm, 'wɔʃ-/ *n AmE*
for LAVATORY

was·n't /'wʌzənt, 'wɑz-/ *short for* was not: *I
wasn't at school yesterday because I was ill.*

wasp /wɑsp, wɔsp/ *n* a flying stinging insect
related to the bee, which is usu. colored
yellow and black

WASP, Wasp *n infml* **1** a white American of
British or Northern European ancestry who
belongs to the PROTESTANT religion **2** *abbrev*
White ANGLO-SAXON PROTESTANT

wast·age /'weʸstɪdʒ/ *n* [S;U] wasting; something wasted: *A quarter of the goods were
damaged; that's a wastage of 25%.*

waste¹ /weʸst/ *n* **1** [S;U] loss, wrong use, or
lack of full use: *These new weapons are a
waste of money.|The meeting was a complete
waste of time.* (=nothing was done or
decided)|*Don't let all this good food go to
waste!* **2** [U] used, damaged, or unwanted
matter: *A lot of poisonous waste from the
chemical works goes into the river.|Waste
from the body passes out from the bowels.*

–compare LAY WASTE, REFUSE² **3** [C] *often lit*
an unused or useless stretch of land or water:
*No crops will grow on these stony wastes.|the
Arctic wastes*

waste² *v* **wasted, wasting 1** [I;T] to use
wrongly, not use, or use too much of: *I've
wasted a lot of money on that useless
car.|Don't waste electricity; turn off the lights
when you go out.* –see TIME (USAGE) **2** [I;T
away] to (cause to) lose flesh, strength, etc.,
slowly: *Since he became ill, he has been wasting away.* **3** [T] *AmE infml* to kill

waste³ *adj* [A] **1** (esp. of areas of land)
empty; not productive; ruined or destroyed:
waste land **2** got rid of as worthless or
damaged: *waste material/paper* **3** used for
holding or carrying away what is worthless or
no longer wanted: *waste pipes*

waste·ful /'weʸstfəl/ *adj* tending to waste or
marked by waste: *wasteful habits* –**wastefully**
adv –**wastefulness** *n* [U]

waste·pa·per bas·ket /'weʸstˌpeʸpər
ˌbæskɪt/|also **wastebasket** /'weʸstˌbæskɪt/
AmE– n a container for used or unnecessary
material (esp. paper) in a house or office
–see illustration on page 467

watch¹ /wɑtʃ, wɔtʃ/ *v* **1** [I;T] to look at (some
activity or event): *Do you often watch televi-
sion?|They watched the sun set/setting until it
disappeared behind the trees.* –see SEE
(USAGE) **2** [T +*to-v/for*] to look for; expect and wait (for): *She watched (for) a
chance to cross the road.|She watched to see
what I would do.* **3** [T +(*that*)] to take care
of, be careful with, or pay attention to: *I'll
watch the baby while you are away.|Watch
that the milk doesn't boil over.|You have to
watch what you say when you talk to the
general.* **4** [T] to attend carefully to (some-
one or someone's action): *Watch Jim.|Watch
Jim do/doing it.|Watch how to do this.* **5
Watch it!** *infml* Be careful! : *Watch it when
you handle the glasses!* –**watcher** *n*

watch out *v adv* [I] *infml* (esp. in giving
orders) to take care: *Watch out! There's a car
coming.*

watch over sbdy./sthg. *v adv* [T] to guard
and protect; take care of

watch² *n* **1** [C] a small clock to be worn or
carried: *a wristwatch|My watch has stopped.*
–see CLOCK (USAGE) **2** [S] one or more
people ordered to watch a place or a person:
*In spite of the watch on the house, the thief
escaped.* **3** [C;U] (sailors who have to be on
duty during) a period of two or four hours at
sea: *You'll be on the first watch
tonight.|Who's on watch now?* **4 keep (a)
close/careful watch on** to fix one's attention
on, carefully: *The government is keeping (a)
close watch on rising prices.*

watch·dog /'wɑtʃdɔg, 'wɔtʃ-/ *n* **1** a fierce dog
kept to guard property **2** a person or group
that tries to guard against bad or dishonest
behavior: *a government watchdog on television advertisements*

watch·ful /'wɑtʃfəl, 'wɔtʃ-/ *adj* [*for*] careful
to notice things: *She was watchful for any
sign of activity in the empty house.*
–**watchfully** *adv* –**watchfulness** *n* [U]

watch·mak·er /'watʃ,meʸkər, 'wɔtʃ-/ n a person who makes or repairs watches or clocks

watch·man /'watʃmən, 'wɔtʃ-/ n **-men** /mən/ a guard, esp. of a building: *Call the* **night watchman** *if there is any trouble tonight.*

watch·word /'watʃwɜrd, 'wɔtʃ-/ n a word or phrase used as a sign of recognition among members of a group; PASSWORD

wa·ter¹ /'wɔtər, 'wɑ-/ n [U] **1** the most common liquid, which falls from the sky as rain, forms rivers, lakes, and seas, and is drunk by people and animals: *The prisoner was given only bread and water.|The hotel has hot and cold water in all the bedrooms.|After all the rain, most of the town was* **under water**.|*The goods came* **by water**, (=by boat) *not by air.* **2 above water** *infml* out of difficulty: *We don't make much money, but we are able to* **keep our heads above water**. (=we have enough money for our needs) **3 in/into hot water** *infml* in/into trouble: *We'll get into hot water if the teacher hears about this.* **4 throw cold water on** *infml* to speak against; point out difficulties in (a plan, idea, etc.) esp. in an unhelpful way –see also WATERS

water² v **1** [T] to pour water on (plants or land): *It's very dry: we must water the garden.* **2** [I] (esp. of the eyes or mouth) to form or let out something like water: *My eyes watered when I cut the onions.|The sight of the food made my mouth water.*

water sthg.↔ down v adv [T often pass.] to weaken (a liquid) by adding water: *This beer has been watered down!|(fig.) a watered-down political statement that won't offend anyone*

wa·ter·borne /'wɔtər,bɔrn, ,boʷrn, 'wɑ-/ adj supported or carried by water: *waterborne trade/diseases*

water clos·et /'·· ,·/ n fml for WC

wa·ter·col·or /'wɔtər,kʌlər, 'wɑ-/ n [C;U] (a picture painted with) paint mixed with water: *She mostly paints in watercolors.|Have you sold any more watercolors?* –compare OILS

wa·ter·cress /'wɔtər,krɛs, 'wɑ-/ also **cress**– n [U] a hot-tasting plant grown in water and used as food, esp. in SALADS

wa·ter·fall /'wɔtər,fɔl, 'wɑ-/ n water falling straight down over rocks, sometimes from a great height

wa·ter·front /'wɔtər,frʌnt, 'wɑ-/ n [usu. sing.] land near a stretch of water, esp. when used as a port: *to walk along the waterfront*

wa·ter·hole /'wɔtər,hoʷl, 'wɑ-/ n a small area of water in dry country, where wild animals go to drink

watering can /'··· ,·/ n a container with a long SPOUT² for watering garden plants

wa·ter·logged /'wɔtər,lɔgd, ,lɑgd, 'wɑ-/ adj (of land or a floating object) full of water: *The boat became so waterlogged that it sank.|The game couldn't be played because the ground was waterlogged.*

water main /'··· ,·/ n a large underground pipe carrying a supply of water

wa·ter·mark /'wɔtər,mɑrk, 'wɑ-/ n **1** a mark showing the height to which water has risen **2** a mark made on paper by the maker, seen only when it is held up to the light

wa·ter·mel·on /'wɔtər,mɛlən, 'wɑ-/ n [C;U] a large round fruit with juicy red flesh and black seeds

water po·lo /'·· ,·/ n [U] a game played by two teams of swimmers with a ball in a pool

wa·ter·proof /'wɔtər,pruʷf, 'wɑ-/ adj,n (something, such as an outer garment) which does not allow water to go through: *Put on your waterproof (coat) before you go out in the rain.|Is the tent waterproof?*

wa·ters /'wɔtərz, 'wɑ-/ n [P] **1** sea near (or belonging to) the stated country: *fishing in Icelandic waters* **2** the water of the stated river, lake, etc.: *This is where the waters of the Amazon flow out into the sea.*

wa·ter·shed /'wɔtər,ʃɛd, 'wɑ-/ n **1** the high land separating two river systems **2** the point of an important change from one state of affairs to another: *Leaving her first job was a watershed in her life.*

wa·ter·side /'wɔtər,saɪd, 'wɑ-/ n [the S] the edge of a natural body of water

water ski·ing /'·· ,··/ n [U] the sport in which one travels over water on SKIS¹, pulled by a boat: *to go water skiing*

wa·ter·tight /'wɔtər,taɪt, 'wɑ-/ adj **1** through which no water can go: *a watertight box* **2** allowing or having no mistakes : *a watertight argument/plan/excuse*

wa·ter·way /'wɔtər,weʸ, 'wɑ-/ n a stretch of water up which a ship can go, such as part of a river: *Canals and rivers form the* **inland waterways** *of a country.*

wa·ter·works /'wɔtər,wɜrks, 'wɑ-/ n [P] buildings, pipes, and supplies of water forming a public water system: *He has a job at the waterworks.*

wa·ter·y /'wɔtəriʸ, 'wɑ-/ adj **1** containing (too much) water: *watery soup* **2** very pale in color: *walls painted a watery yellow color*

watt /wɑt/ n a measure of electrical power: *A* KILOWATT *is 1000 watts.*

wave¹ /weʸv/ v **waved, waving 1** [I;T *at*] to move (one's hand, or something held in the hand) as a signal, esp. in greeting: *The children waved their flags as the President passed.|They're waving (at us).|They waved goodbye.|The policeman waved the traffic on.* (=signaled to the drivers to move) **2** [I] to move in the air, backwards and forwards or up and down: *The trees waved in the wind.* **3** [I;T] to (cause to) lie in regular curves: *I'm going to have my hair waved.*

wave sthg.↔aside v adv to push aside without giving attention to (esp. ideas, suggestions, etc.): *He waved aside my offer of help.*

wave² n **1** the movement of the hand in waving: *The President gave the crowd a wave.* **2** one of a number of raised lines of water on the surface, esp. of the sea: *In bad weather, we get very large waves on the shore.* **3** an evenly curved part of the hair: *natural waves in her hair* **4** a suddenly rising and increasing feeling, way of behavior, etc.: *The police are worried about the recent wave of violence.* –see also HEAT WAVE **5** a form in which some forms of ENERGY (2), such as light and sound, move: *radio waves*

wave band /'· ·/ *n* a set of sound waves of similar lengths: *WXYZ can be heard on the long wave band.*

wave·length /'weᵛvlɛŋkθ, -lɛŋθ/ *n* a radio signal sent out on radio WAVES² (5) that are a particular distance apart: (fig.) *You and I are* **on different wavelengths.** (=have completely different beliefs, ways of thinking, etc.)

wa·ver /'weᵛvər/ *v* [I *between*] to be unsteady or uncertain: *He wavered between accepting and refusing.*

wav·y /'weᵛviᵛ/ *adj* **-ier, -iest** having regular curves: *wavy hair* **–waviness** *n* [U]

wax¹ /wæks/ *n* [U] a solid material made of fats or oils, which changes to a thick liquid when melted by heat: *a wax candle*|*wax paper*|*wax in the ears* (=a natural substance) –see also BEESWAX

wax² *v* [T] to put wax on, esp. as a polish: *to wax the floor*

wax³ *v* [I] (esp. of the moon) to grow –compare WANE

wax·works /'wækswɜrks/ *n* **waxworks** a place where one can see models of human beings made in wax: *Madame Tussaud's is a famous waxworks in London.*

way¹ /weᵛ/ *n* **1** [C] the (right) road(s), path(s), etc., to follow in order to reach a place: *Is this the way out?*|*Please show me the way to the shopping center.*|*If you* **lose your way**, *ask a policeman.*|*Move* **out of my way** *so I can pass.*|(fig.) *Nothing must* **stand in the way of** (=prevent) *our plans.*|*I met him on* **the way** *home.* (=as I was going home)|*There is a* **right of way** *across this field* (=we are allowed to walk across it) –see USAGE **2** [C] a direction: *Which way is the house from here?*|*Come this way.* **3** [S] the distance to be traveled in order to reach a place or point: *We're a long way from home.*|*Christmas is still a long way off.* **4** [C +to-v/(that)] a manner or method: *He has a funny way of laughing.*|*What is the best way to do it?*|*Those two girls do their hair the same way.*|*She hasn't got a job, but she has* **ways and means** *of getting money.* **5** [U] forward movement: *The car broke down, and I had to* **make my way** *on foot.*|(fig.) *The party got* **under way** (=started) *at nine o'clock.* **6** [C] a degree or point: *In many ways yours is a better plan.*|*In a way I can see what you mean, though I disagree with you.* **7** [C] (part of the name of) a road or path: *Westpath Way* –see STREET (USAGE) **8 by the way** (used to introduce a new subject in speech) in addition **9 by way of: a** going through: *You can get to San Francisco by way of the Golden Gate Bridge.* **b** with the intention of: *By way of introducing himself, he showed me his card.* **10 get one's own way** to do or get what one wants, in spite of others **11 give way** to yield: *We refused to give way to their demands for more money.* **12 have it both ways** to gain advantage from opposing opinions or actions: *You'll have to decide whether you want to pass your examinations or just have a good time; you can't have it*

both ways! **13 under way** moving forward: *Work on the new bridge is now under way.*

USAGE Compare **in the way** and **on the way:** *I couldn't get through the gate because your car was* **in the way.** (=blocking the entrance)|*I saw the accident* **on the way** *to work* (=while I was traveling to work).

way² *adv* [*adv+adv*] *esp. AmE* far: *The movie was made way back in 1929.*|*We're way behind with our work.*

way·far·er /'weᵛˌfɛərər/ *n old use & lit* a traveler on foot –compare PEDESTRIAN¹

way·lay /'weᵛleᵛ, weᵛ'leᵛ/ *v* **-laid** /leᵛd, 'leᵛd/, **-laying** [T] to stop (a person going somewhere) for a special purpose: *She waylaid me after the lesson and asked where I had been the week before.*

way-out /ˌ· '· ◄/ *adj infml* unusual or strange, far

way·side /'weᵛsaɪd/ *n* [*the* S] the side of the road: *They stopped by the wayside to rest.*

way·ward /'weᵛwərd/ *adj* changeable and not easy to guide (in character): *wayward behavior*|*a wayward son*

WC also **water closet** *BrE fml*– *n* a TOILET which is emptied by a flow of water

we /wiᵛ/ *pron* (used as the subject of a sentence) the people who are speaking; I and one or more others: *Shall we* (=you and I) *sit together, Mary?*|*May we* (=I and the others) *go now, sir?*

weak /wiᵛk/ *adj* **1** not strong; not strong enough to work or last properly: *I still feel a bit weak after my illness.*|*The shelf's too weak to hold all those books.*|*a weak heart*|*weak eyes*|(fig.) *She's good at history, but rather weak at French.* **2** not strong in character: *The teacher's so weak that the students do what they want.* –see also WEAK-KNEED **3** containing too much water: *weak soup/tea* **–weakly** *adv*

weak·en /'wiᵛkən/ *v* [I;T] to (cause to) become weak, esp. in health or character: *The illness weakened her heart.*|*a country weakened by war and disease*|*She asked so many times that in the end we weakened and let her go.* –compare STRENGTHEN

weak-kneed /ˌ· '· ◄/ *adj* habitually afraid and nervous; cowardly

weak·ling /'wiᵛk-lɪŋ/ *n* a person lacking strength in body or character

weak·ness /'wiᵛknɪs/ *n* **1** [U] the state of being weak, esp. in mind, body, or character **2** [C] a fault; weak part: *The cost of your plan is its main weakness.*|*Drinking is his weakness.* –compare STRENGTH **3** [C *for*] a strong liking, esp. for something which is bad for one: *a weakness for chocolate*

weal /wiᵛl/ *n* a mark on the skin; WELT: *The dog was covered in weals where it had been beaten*

wealth /wɛlθ/ *n* **1** [U] (a large amount of) money and possessions: *her great wealth*|*a man of wealth* **2** [S *of*] a large number: *a wealth of examples*

wealth·y /'wɛlθiᵛ/ *adj* **-ier, -iest** (of a person) rich **–wealthiness** *n* [U]

wean /wiᵛn/ *v* [T] to accustom (a young child or animal) to food instead of mother's milk: *Most babies are weaned by the time they are* *one.*|(fig.) *How can we wean him from his habit of getting drunk every night?*

weap·on /'wɛpən/ n a tool for harming or killing in attack or defense: *guns, bombs, gas, and other weapons*

wear[1] /wɛər/ v **wore** /wɔr, wowʳr/, **worn** /wɔrn, wowʳrn/, **wearing 1** [T] to have (esp. clothes) on the body: *He's wearing a new coat.*|*Does your brother wear glasses?*|*She's wearing her diamonds.* (=jewelry) –compare HAVE **on** (1) –see DRESS[1] (USAGE) **2** [T] to bear or keep in a particular way: *He wears his hair very short.* **3** [T] to have (a particular expression on the face): *She wore an angry expression.* **4** [I;T] to reduce or be reduced by continued use: *I liked this shirt, but the collar is worn.*|*The water has worn down the rocks.*|*The noise wore her nerves (to nothing).* **5** [T] to produce by wear, use, rubbing, etc.: *You've worn a hole in your sock.*|*The villagers had worn a path through the fields.* **6** [T] to last in the stated condition: *Good wool wears well.* **7 wear the pants in one's family** to have the controlling influence or power in the family –**wearable** *adj*

  wear away v adv [I;T (=**wear** sthg.↔**away**)] to (cause to) disappear by use, rubbing, etc.: *In the last hundred years, the wind has worn the rocks away.*

  wear sbdy./sthg. **down** v adv [T] to reduce the strength or size of: *We wore down the opposition after several hours of argument.*

  wear off v adv [I] to be reduced until it disappears: *The pain is wearing off.*

  wear on v adv [I] **1** to pass slowly (in time): *The meeting wore on all afternoon.* **2 (wear on** sbdy.**)** to have a negative effect on (somebody)

  wear out v adv **1** [I;T (=**wear** sthg.↔**out**)] also **wear through**– to (cause to) be reduced to nothing or a useless state by use: *Her shoes wear out quickly when she goes walking.*|*worn-out old shoes* **2** [T] (**wear** sbdy.↔**out**) to tire greatly: *If you don't stop working, you'll wear yourself out.* –see also WORN-OUT

wear[2] n [U] **1** use which reduces the material: *This mat has had a lot of wear.*|*I spent the whole night at the party, but the next morning I was* **none the worse for wear.** (=still fresh and active) **2** damage from use: *These shoes I bought last week are already showing signs of wear*/**wear and tear.** **3** the quality of lasting in use: *There's still plenty of wear in these tires.*

wear[3] n [U] (used esp. in business) clothes of the stated type, or for the stated purpose: *men's wear*|*sports wear*

wear·ing /'wɛərɪŋ/ adj tiring: *She's very wearing when she talks on and on.*|*It's a very wearing job.*

wea·ri·some /'wɪəriʸsəm/ adj which makes one feel tired and BORED[4]: *a wearisome day*

wea·ry[1] /'wɪəriʸ/ adj **-rier, -riest** [of] tired: *You look weary after your long journey.*|*a weary smile* –**wearily** adv –**weariness** n [U]

weary[2] v **-ried, -rying** [I;T *with, of*] to (cause to) become WEARY: *He soon wearied of (=grew tired of) his job on the farm.*

wea·sel /'wiʸzəl/ n a small thin furry animal which can kill other small animals

weasel out v adv **-l-** AmE||**-ll-** BrE [I *of*] AmE infml to escape (from a duty): *He's trying to weasel out of his responsibilities.*

weath·er[1] /'wɛðər/ n [U] **1** the condition of wind, rain, sunshine, snow, etc., at a certain time or over a period of time: *good weather*|*The people here are nice, but the weather is terrible.*|*What will the weather be like tomorrow?* **2 under the weather** not very well or happy

USAGE 1 **Wind** is a general word for a moving current of air. A **breeze** is a pleasant gentle wind; a **gust** is a sudden strong rush of **air;** and a **gale** is a very strong wind: *There's a nice* **breeze** *down by the sea.*|*A* **gust** *of wind blew the door shut.*|*Our chimney was blown down in a* **gale.** 2 **Rain** is water falling from the clouds; icy, partly frozen rain is called **sleet;** hard frozen drops of rain are called **hail;** and frozen rain falling in soft white pieces is **snow.** 3 If it is raining heavily, we say it is **pouring** (down), if only very lightly, it is **drizzling** (DRIZZLE). 4 A **shower** is a fall of rain that does not last long. A heavy fall of rain (or snow), together with strong winds and (sometimes) thunder and lightning, is a **storm.** A **blizzard** is a severe snowstorm, and a **hurricane** is a storm with very high winds. The yearly season of rainy weather in some tropical countries is called the **monsoon.**

weather[2] v **1** [T] to pass safely through (a storm or difficulty): *The ship weathered the storm, and arrived safely.*|*The examination was difficult, but I think I weathered it pretty well.* **2** [I;T] to change or be changed by being open to the air and weather: *Rocks weather until they are worn away.*

weather-beat·en /'·· ,···/ adj marked or damaged by the wind, sun, etc.: *a weather-beaten* (=brown and lined) *face*

weath·er·cock /'wɛðər,kɑk/ also **weather vane** /'·· ,·/– n a small metal apparatus, often shaped like a cock and fixed to the top of a building, which is blown around by the wind and so shows its direction

weather fore·cast /'·· ,··/ n a description of weather conditions as they are expected to be by people who study them –**weather forecaster** n

weath·er·man /'wɛðər,mæn/ n **-men** /,mɛn/ a person who makes WEATHER FORECASTS, as on television and the radio

weave[1] /wiʸv/ v **wove** /wowʳv/, **woven** /'wowʳvən/, **weaving 1** [I] to form threads into material by crossing one thread under and over a set of longer threads stretched out on a LOOM: *Do you know how to weave?* **2** [T] to make by doing this: *to weave a mat*|(fig. lit) *He wove an interesting story from a few facts in a history book.*

weave[2] n the way in which a material is woven and the pattern formed by this: *a loose/fine weave*

weave[3] v **weaved, weaving** [I;T] to move along, turning and changing direction frequently: *weaving in and out between the cars*|*He weaved his way through the crowd.*

weav·er /'wiʸvər/ n a person whose job is to weave cloth

web /wɛb/ n **1** a net of thin threads spun (SPIN) by some insects, esp. SPIDERS, to trap other insects **2** a detailed arrangement or network: *a web of deceit* (=a set of lies)

webbed /wɛbd/ adj having skin between the toes, as on a duck's foot: *webbed feet*

web-foot·ed /,· '··◄/ also **web-toed** /,· '·◄/– adj having WEBBED feet: *Ducks are web-footed.*

wed /wɛd/ v **wedded** or **wed, wedding** [I;T not be +v-ing] *lit* to marry: *They were wed in the spring.*

we'd /wiʸd/ *short for* **1** we had **2** we would

wed·ding /'wɛdɪŋ/ n a marriage ceremony, esp. with a party or meal after a church service: *Have you been invited to their wedding?* –compare MARRIAGE

wedding ring /'·· ,·/ n a usu. gold ring, used in the marriage ceremony and worn to show that one is married

wedge¹ /wɛdʒ/ n **1** a V-shaped piece of wood, one end being thin and the other quite wide, used e.g. for holding a door open: *Put a wedge under the door, so that it will stay open.* **2** something shaped like this: *shoes with wedge heels*

wedge² v **wedged, wedging** [T] to fix firmly with a WEDGE¹: *Wedge the door (open/shut).*|(fig.) *The people sitting close to me wedged me in/into the corner.*

wed·lock /'wɛdlɑk/ n [U] *old use* **1** the state of being married **2 born out of wedlock** born of unmarried parents; ILLEGITIMATE (1)

Wednes·day /'wɛnzdiʸ, -deʸ/ also **Wed.** *written abbrev.* –n the fourth day of the week; day between Tuesday and Thursday: *He'll arrive (on) Wednesday.*|*He'll arrive on Wednesday afternoon.*|*I always go to the bank on Wednesdays.*|(esp. AmE) *She works Wednesdays.*|*He arrived on a Wednesday.*

wee /wiʸ/ adj **1** very small: *a wee child* **2** very early: *the wee hours of the morning*

weed¹ /wiʸd/ n an unwanted wild plant: *The garden's full of weeds.*

weed² v [I;T] to remove WEEDS¹ (from): *to weed the garden*|*to weed the grass out of/from the rose garden*

weed sbdy./sthg.↔ **out** v adv [T] to get rid of (things or people that are not wanted): *He weeded out the books he no longer needed.*

weed·y /'wiʸdiʸ/ adj **-ier, -iest** *infml* **1** full of WEEDS **2** weak in body: *Who was that weedy young man I saw you with?*

week /wiʸk/ n **1** a period of seven days (and nights), esp. from Sunday to Saturday: *The flight to Accra goes twice a week.*|*I'll see you next week.* **2** also **work week** – the period of time during which one works, as in a factory or office: *She works a 60-hour week.*|*The five-day week is usual in most companies.* **3 week in, week out** also **day in, day out**– without change or rest

week·day /'wiʸkdeʸ/ n a day of the week **a** not Saturday or Sunday: *I only work on week-days, not on Saturday or Sunday.* **b** not Sunday: *There is one train timetable for weekdays and another for Sundays.*

week·end /'wiʸkɛnd/ n Saturday and Sunday

week·ly¹ /'wiʸkliʸ/ adj,adv (happening or appearing) once a week or every week: *a weekly visit/magazine*

weekly² n **-lies** a magazine or newspaper which appears once a week

weep /wiʸp/ v **wept** /wɛpt/, **weeping** [I;T over] *fml or lit* to let fall (tears) from the eyes: *They wept over their failure.*|*I could weep when I think of all the money we've lost.* –compare CRY

weep·y /'wiʸpiʸ/ adj **-ier, -iest** *infml* tending to cry: *not very well, and feeling weepy*

weft /wɛft/ n the threads of a material woven across the downward set of threads –compare WARP¹ (2)

weigh /weʸ/ v **1** to find the weight of, esp. by a machine: *to weigh oneself* **2** to have a certain weight: *It weighs six pounds.*|*I weigh less than I used to.* **3** to consider or compare carefully: *He weighed the ideas in his mind.* **4 weigh anchor** to raise an ANCHOR

weigh sbdy./sthg. **down** v adv [T with] to make heavy (with a load): *I was weighed down with shopping bags.*|(fig.) *weighed down with responsibilities*

weigh on sbdy./sthg. v prep [T] to cause worry to: *His lack of money weighed on his mind.*

weigh sthg.↔ **out** v adv [T] to measure in amounts by weight: *I weighed out half a pound of flour and added it to the mixture.*

weight¹ /weʸt/ n **1** [U] the heaviness of anything, esp. as measured by a certain system; amount which something weighs: *two pounds in weight*|*What's the weight of your suitcase?*|*to* **put on/lose weight** (=to become heavier/lighter)|*She is* **under/over weight.** (=too light/too heavy) **2** [C] a piece of metal of a standard heaviness, which can be balanced against a substance to measure equal heaviness of that substance: *a one-pound weight* **3** [C] a usu. heavy object, esp. one used for holding something down: *a paperweight*|*You shouldn't lift heavy weights after an operation.*|(fig.) *The loss of the money is a weight on my mind.* (=a worry) **4** [U] value or importance: *Don't worry what he thinks; his opinion doesn't* **carry much weight. 5 pull one's weight** to join in work or activity equally with others **6 throw one's weight around** to give orders to others, because one thinks oneself important

weight² v [T with] to put a weight on or add a heavy material to: *Fishing nets are weighted so that they sink in the water.*

weight sbdy./sthg.↔ **down** v adv [T with; usu. pass.] to load heavily; WEIGH **down**: *weighted down with shopping bags*

weight·ed /'weʸtɪd/ adj [F towards, against] giving advantage: *The system of elections is weighted in favor of the main political parties.*

weight·less /'weʸtlɪs/ adj having no weight, as when in space –**weightlessness** n [U]

weight lift·ing /'· ,··/ n [U] the sport of lifting specially shaped weights above the head –**weight lifter** n

weight·y /'weʸtiʸ/ adj **-ier, -iest** important and serious: *a weighty problem/argument*

–weightily *adv* **–weightiness** *n* [U]

weir /wɪər/ *n* a wall across a river, stopping or controlling the flow of the water above it

weird /wɪərd/ *adj* **1** strange; unnatural **2** *infml* unusual and not sensible or acceptable: *He has some weird ideas.* **–weirdly** *adv* **–weirdness** *n* [U]

wel·come¹ /'wɛlkəm/ *interj* [*to*] (an expression of pleasure at someone's arrival or return): *Welcome home/ back!/Welcome to America.*

welcome² *v* **-comed, -coming** [T] to meet or greet, esp. with pleasure: *The President welcomed the Prince when he arrived./They welcomed him with flowers./a welcoming smile/*(fig.) *They welcomed the idea/my suggestion.* (=they were pleased with it)

welcome³ *adj* **1** acceptable and wanted: *a welcome suggestion/You are always welcome at my house./a welcome change* **2** [F +*to-v/to*] allowed freely (to have), sometimes because not wanted: *He's coming to visit you? You're welcome to him!/You're welcome to try, but you won't succeed.* **3 You're welcome** (a polite expression when thanked for something): *"Thank you!" "You're welcome."* **4 make (someone) welcome** to receive (a guest) with friendliness

welcome⁴ *n* a greeting to or a receiving of an arriving person: *The First Lady gave the foreign minister a* **warm welcome.***/an official welcome for the hero.*

weld /wɛld/ *v* [I;T *to, together*] **a** to join (usu. metals) by pressing or melting them together when hot **b** (of metals) to become joined in this way **–weld** *n: a weld in the pipe*

weld·er /'wɛldər/ *n* a person whose job is to make WELDed joints

wel·fare /'wɛlfɛər/ *n* [U] **1** well-being; comfort and good health: *We're thinking only of his welfare: we want him to be happy in his new school* **2** *AmE*‖**social security** *BrE* – (the system of) government money paid to people who are without jobs, ill, or poor: *on welfare*

welfare state /'·· ,·/ *n* (a country with) a system of government-provided health care, unemployment pay, etc.

well¹ /wɛl/ *n* **1** a place where water comes from underground: *to find a well in the desert/well water* **2** a hole like this through which oil is drawn from underground **3** an enclosed space in a building running straight up and down, e.g. for an ELEVATOR or stairs: *the stair well*

well² *v* [I *out, up*] (of liquid) to rise and flow (from): *Blood welled (out) from the cut./Tears welled (up) in her eyes.*

well³ *adv* **better** /'bɛtər/, **best** /bɛst/ **1** in a good way; kindly, satisfactorily, etc.: *She paints very well./a well-dressed young man/ They speak well of him at school./She business is doing well.* (=succeeding) | *She did well* (=gained a good profit) *out of the sale of her house.* **–opposite badly 2** thoroughly: *Wash it well before you dry it.* **3** [*adv + prep/ adv*] very much: *I can't reach it; it's well above my head.*| *He arrived well*

within the time. **4** justly; suitably: *I couldn't very well say no./You did well to tell him./You may well ask!* (=we are all wondering) **5 as well: a** in addition; also; too: *I'm going to Mexico, and John's going as well.* –see Study Notes on page 144 **b** with as good a result: *We might (just) as well have stayed at home. It's no fun here!* **6 as well as** in addition to: *I'm learning French as well as English./He was kind as well as sensible.* –see Study Notes on page 144 **7 (It's) just as well** (as a reply) There's no harm done; There's no loss: *"I was too late to see the movie." "(It's) just as well; it wasn't very good."* **8 pretty well** almost: *The work is pretty well finished.* **9 Well done!** (said when someone has been successful): *You've passed your examination. Well done!* **10 well out of** lucky to be free from (an affair): *It's lucky you left before the trouble started; you were well out of it.* **11 well up on** knowing a great deal about: *well up on the latest fashions*

well⁴ *interj* **1** (used for showing surprise, doubt, acceptance, etc.): *She's got a new job. Well, well!/Well, what a surprise./Well, all right, I agree.* **2** (used when continuing a story): *Well, then she said…* **3 Oh well!** (used for showing cheerfulness when something bad has happened): *"Oh well, I shouldn't complain; it could have been worse."*

well⁵ *adj* **better, best** [F] **1** healthy: *I'm not feeling very well./She was ill for a month, but she's nearly well now.*|(esp. *AmE*) *He's not a well man.* **2** right; in an acceptable state: *to make sure that all is well* **3 It's all very well** (shows dissatisfaction): *It's all very well (for you) to say you're sorry, but I've been waiting here for two hours!*

we'll /wɪl; *strong* wiʸl/ *v* short for **1** we will **2** we shall

well-ad·vised /,· ·'·◄/ *adj* sensible: *You would be well-advised to see the doctor about that pain.*

well-bal·anced /,· '··◄/ *adj* **1** (of people and their characters) sensible and not controlled by unreasonable feelings **2** (of food) containing the right amounts of what is good for the body: *a well-balanced diet*

well-be·ing /,· '··◄/ *n* [U] personal and bodily comfort, esp. good health: *The warm summer weather always gives me a sense of well-being.*

well-bred /,· '·◄/ *adj* well-behaved and polite: *a well-bred voice*

well-done /,· '·◄/ *adj* (of food, esp. meat) cooked for a longer rather than shorter period of time **–compare** RARE²

well-earned /,· '·◄/ *adj* much deserved: *a well-earned rest after so much hard work*

well-found·ed /,· '··◄/ *adj* based on facts: *My fears that the game would be spoiled by rain were well-founded.*

well-groomed /,· '·◄/ *adj* having a very, neat clean appearance: *"Well-groomed young person wanted as secretary to the president."* (job advertisement)

well-heeled /,· '·◄/ *adj infml* rich

well-in·formed /,· ·'·◄/ *adj* knowing a lot

about several subjects or a particular subject

well-in·ten·tioned /ˌ· ·ˈ··◄/ also **well-meaning–** adj acting in the hope of good results, though often failing: *It was a well-intentioned effort to help.*

well-known /ˌ· ˈ·◄/ adj known by many people: *a well-known fact* –see FAMOUS (USAGE)

well-mean·ing /ˌ· ˈ··◄/ adj →WELL-INTENTIONED: *a well-meaning person/effort*

well-nigh /ˌwɛl ˈnaɪ◄/ adv fml almost: *well-nigh impossible*

well-off /ˌ· ˈ·◄/ adj 1 [F for] rich: *They're very well-off.* –opposite **badly-off** 2 **you don't know when you're well off** you're more fortunate than you know

well-read /ˌwɛl ˈrɛd◄/ adj having read many books and gained much useful information: *a well-read student*

well-spo·ken /ˌ· ˈ··◄/ adj speaking in a way which is correct and polite

well-thought-of /ˌ· ˈ· ·◄/ adj (of a person) liked and admired generally

well-timed /ˌ· ˈ·◄/ adj said or done at the most suitable time: *well-timed advice*

well-to-do /ˌ· · ˈ·◄/ adj infml rich

well-wish·er /ˈ· ·ˌ··, ˌ· ˈ··/ n a person giving good wishes to another, esp. on a special occasion

well-worn /ˌ· ˈ·◄/ adj (of phrases) with little meaning, because over-used

Welsh /wɛlʃ/ adj of Wales, its people, or their language

welt /wɛlt/ a raised mark on the skin e.g. from a stroke of a whip

wel·ter /ˈwɛltər/ n [S] a disordered mixture: *a welter of confused ideas*

wench /wɛntʃ/ n old use a girl, esp. in the country

wend /wɛnd/ v lit **wend one's way** to move or travel over a distance, esp. slowly

went /wɛnt/ v past tense of GO

wept /wɛpt/ v past tense and past participle of WEEP

were /wər; strong wɜr/ v negative short form **weren't** /wɜrnt, ˈwɜrənt/ past tense of BE

we're /wɪr; strong wɪər/ short for: we are

were·wolf /ˈwɛərwʊlf, ˈwɪər-/ n -wolves /wʊlvz/ (in stories) a man who sometimes turns into a WOLF

west¹ /wɛst/ adv (often cap.) towards the west: *to travel west*|*She sat facing West, watching the sun go down.*

west² n (often cap.) [the S] one of the four main points of the compass, which is on the left of a person facing north: *the west door of the church*|*The sun sets in the west.*|*The road goes from east to west through the center of town.*

West n [the S] 1 the western part of the world, esp. western Europe and the United States: *Leaders from the West have been invited to peace talks in Moscow.* 2 the part of a country which is further west than the rest 3 (in the US) the part of the country west of the Mississippi settled later than the eastern US

west·bound /ˈwɛstbaʊnd/ adj traveling towards the west: *To get to Houston, take the westbound train.*

west·er·ly /ˈwɛstərliʸ/ adj 1 [A] towards or in the west: *the westerly shore of the lake*|*in a westerly direction* 2 (of a wind) coming from the west: *a soft westerly wind*

west·ern¹ /ˈwɛstərn/ adj (often cap.) of or belonging to the west part of the world or of a country: *the Western nations*

western² n (often cap.) a movie or story about life in the West of the US in the past

West·ern·er /ˈwɛstərnər/ n AmE someone who lives in or comes from the WEST

West In·di·an /ˌ· ˈ····/ adj of or from the West Indies: *West Indian cooking*

west·ward /ˈwɛstwərd/ adj going towards the west: *a westward journey* –compare WESTERLY **westward** AmE‖**westwards** BrE adv: *They traveled westward.*

wet¹ /wɛt/ adj 1 covered with liquid; not dry: *I can't go out till my hair's dry; it's still wet from being washed.*|*wet ground*|*wet paint* (=still sticky)|*Don't go out, you'll get wet.* 2 rainy: *wet weather*|*We can't go out; it's too wet.* 3 **wet blanket** derog a person who discourages others, prevents them enjoying themselves, etc. –**wetness** n [U]

wet² v wet or **wetted**, **wetting** [T] 1 to cause to be wet: *Wet the cloth and clean the table with it.* 2 **all wet** infml wrong: *You're all wet. Minnesota did not win that game.* 3 **wet behind the ears** young and without experience 4 **wet one's whistle** infml take a drink 5 **wet the bed** to pass water from the body in bed, because of a loss of control while asleep

we've /wiʸv/ short for: we have

whack¹ /hwæk, wæk/ v [T] to hit with a noisy blow

whack² n 1 (the noise made by) a hard blow 2 [usu. sing.] infml a try; attempt: *If you can't open it, let me have a whack at it.* 3 **out of whack** AmE not working properly: *The washer is out of whack; you'll have to do your clothes by hand.*

whale /hweʸl, weʸl/ n 1 a very large animal which lives in the sea, and looks like a fish but is a MAMMAL: *The Blue Whale is the world's biggest living animal.* 2 **whale of a time** infml a very enjoyable social occasion, party, etc.

whal·ing /ˈhweʸlɪŋ, ˈweʸ-/ n [U] the hunting of WHALES to produce oil and other materials

wharf /hwɔrf, wɔrf/ n **wharves** /hwɔrvz, wɔrvz/ or **wharfs** a place, usu. made of stone, where ships can be tied up to unload goods –compare DOCK¹ (1)

what /hwʌt, hwɑt, wʌt, wɑt; weak hwət, wət/ predeterminer, determiner, pron 1 (used in questions about an unknown thing, person, or kind of thing/person): *What are you doing?*|*What color is it?*|*What time will you come?*|*"I got up at four o'clock." "What did you say?" "You did what?" "What?"* (Some people think *"What?"* is not very polite here. Compare PARDON.) *"What do you do?" "I'm a teacher."* 2 the thing or things that: *She told me what to do.*|*I know what you mean.*|*Show me what you bought.*|*I gave her what books* (=the books that) *I had.* 3 (shows surprise): *What a strange thing to say!*|*What a pity!*

(compare *How sad!*)|*What beautiful weather!* **4 what for?** *infml* why?: *"I'm going to Paris." "What for?"* –see also FOR¹ (2) **5 what have you** *infml* anything (else) like that: *In his pocket I found a handkerchief, string, old candy, and what have you.* **6 what if?** what will happen if?: *What if we move the picture over here?*|*What if she doesn't come?* **7 what is/was something like?** (used when asking for a description): *"What's the new teacher like?" "He's got a red beard."*|*"What's it like, being an actor?"* **8 what's his/her/its name** also **what d'you call him/her/it**– *infml* (used when speaking of a person or thing whose name one cannot remember): *Mary's gone out with what's his name: you know, the boy with the red car.* **9 what the...?** *infml* (used with various words to show anger or surprise) what: *What the devil are you doing?*|*What the* HELL *does he want?* **10 what with** because of (esp. something bad): *What with all this work and so little sleep, I don't think I can do this job much longer.* –see WHICH (USAGE)

what·ev·er¹ /hwɒtˈevər, wɒt-/ also **whatsoever** /ˌhwɒtsoʊˈevər, hwɒt-, wʌt-, wɒt-/– *lit determiner,pron* **1** any(thing) at all that: *Goats eat whatever (food) they can find.* **2** no matter what: *Whatever you do, don't keep him waiting!*

whatever² *pron* **1** also **whatnot**– anything (else) like that: *Anyone seen carrying bags, boxes, or whatever, was stopped by the police.* **2** (*showing surprise*) what?: *Look at that strange animal! Whatever is it?* –see EVER (USAGE)

whatever³ also **whatsoever**– *adj* [after *n*]a (*used in* NEGATIVES² (1), *questions, etc.*) at all: *I have no money whatsoever.*

wheat /hwiʸt, wiʸt/ *n* [A;U] a plant or its grain, from which flour is made: *a field of wheat*|*wheat bread/products.*

wheat·en /ˈhwiʸtn, ˈwiʸtn/ *adj* made from wheat (flour)

whee·dle /ˈhwiʸdl, ˈwiʸ-/ *v* **-dled, -dling** [I;T] to persuade (someone) to do what one wants by pleasant but insincere behavior or words
　　wheedle sthg. out *v adv* [T *of*] to obtain from someone by insincerely pleasant persuading: *He wheedled ten dollars out of his father so he could go out.*

wheel¹ /hwiʸl, wiʸl/ *n* **1** [C] a circular object with an outer frame which turns around an inner part (HUB), used for making vehicles move, driving machinery, etc. **2** [*the* S] the STEERING WHEEL of a car or guiding wheel of a ship: *I'm getting tired; will you* **take the wheel?** (=drive instead of me)|*John's* **at the wheel** (=driving) *now.* **3 -wheeler** a vehicle with the stated number of wheels: *a three-wheeler*

wheel² *v* **1** [T] to move ((something on) a wheeled object): *The nurse wheeled the table up to the bed.* **2** [I *around*] to turn suddenly: *I called him as he was running away, and he wheeled around and looked at me.* **3** [I] (of birds) to fly around and around in circles: *GULLs wheeling over the sea*

wheel·bar·row /ˈhwiʸlˌbæroʷ, ˈwiʸl-/ *n* a small cart with one wheel at the front, two legs, and two handles at the back for pushing: *Put those stones in the wheelbarrow; don't carry them.*

wheel·base /ˈhwiʸlbeʸs, ˈwiʸl-/ *n* the distance between the front and back AXLES on a vehicle

wheel·chair /ˈhwiʸltʃɛər, ˈwiʸl-/ *n* a chair with large wheels used by a person who cannot walk –see illustration on page 201

wheeze /hwiʸz, wiʸz/ *v* **wheezed, wheezing** [I] to make a noisy whistling sound e.g. when breathing with difficulty: *The old man was wheezing after running for the bus.* –**wheeze** *n*

wheez·y /ˈhwiʸziʸ, ˈwiʸ-/ *adj* **-ier, -iest** that WHEEZEs, esp. habitually: *a wheezy old bicycle pump* –**wheezily** *adv*

whelk /hwɛlk, wɛlk/ *n* a sea animal which lives in a shell, and is sometimes used as food, esp. in Europe

when¹ /hwɛn, wɛn/ *adv,conj* **1** at what time? at the time that: *When will they come?*|*She'll tell us when to open it.*|*I jumped up when she called.* **2** considering that; although; as: *I can't tell you anything when you won't listen.*|*Why do you want a new job when you've got such a good one already?* –see HARDLY (USAGE)

when² *pron* (*in questions*) what time: **Since when** has he had a beard?

whence /hwɛns, wɛns/ *adv* old use (from) where; (from) which: *They returned to the land (from) whence they came.*|*the river Cam, whence comes the name of the town, Cambridge*

when·ev·er /hwɛˈnevər, wɛ-, hwə-, wə-/ *adv,conj* **1** at whatever time: *Whenever we see him, we speak to him.*|*Come whenever you like.* **2** (*showing surprise*) at what time?: *Whenever did you have time to do it?* –see EVER (USAGE)

where¹ /hwɛər, wɛər/ *adv,conj* at or to what place? at or to the place that: *Where do you live?*|*the office where I work*|*I asked her where to put it.*|*Sit where you like.*

where² *pron* what place: *Where do you come from?*

where·a·bouts¹ /ˈhwɛərəˌbauts, ˈwɛər-, ˌhwɛərəˈbauts, ˌwɛər-/ *adv,conj* where?; near what place?: *Whereabouts did I leave my bag?*

where·a·bouts² /ˈhwɛərəˌbauts, ˈwɛər-/ *n* [U +*sing./pl. v*] the place where someone or something is: *The escaped prisoner's whereabouts is/are still unknown.*

where·as /hwɛərˈæz, wɛər-/ *conj* (shows an opposite) but; although: *They want a house, whereas we would rather live in an apartment.*

where·by /hwɛərˈbaɪ, wɛər-/ *adv fml* by which: *a law whereby all children receive free education*

where·in /hwɛərˈɪn, wɛər-/ *adv,conj fml* in what; in which

where·of /hwɛərˈʌv, -ˈɒv, wɛər-/ *adv,conj fml* of what; of which

where·so·ev·er /ˌhwɛərsoʷˈevər, ˌwɛər-/ *conj,adv lit* for WHEREVER (1)

where·up·on /ˌhwɛərə'pɑn, -'pɔn, ˌwɛər-, 'hwɛərəˌpɑn, -ˌpɔn, 'wɛər-/ *conj fml* after which: *He saw me coming, whereupon he ran off in the other direction.*

wher·ev·er /hwɛər'ɛvər, wɛər-, hwər-, wər-/ *adv,conj* **1** to or at whatever place: *Wherever you go, I go too.|Sleep wherever you like.* **2** (showing surprise) to or at what place?: *Wherever have you been?* –see also EVER (USAGE)

where·with·al /'hwɛərwɪˌðɔl, -ˌθɔl, 'wɛər-/ *n* [*the* S +*to-v*] the necessary means, esp. money (to do something): *I'd like a new car, but I lack the wherewithal (to pay for it).*

whet /hwɛt, wɛt/ *v* **-tt-** [T] **1** *fml* to sharpen: *She whetted her knife on the stone.* **2 whet someone's appetite** to make someone wish for more: *That short climb whetted her appetite; now she wants to climb a bigger mountain.*

wheth·er /'hwɛðər, 'wɛ-/ *conj* **1** (shows a choice between possibilities): *He asked me whether/if she was coming.* (=He asked, "Is she coming?")|*I'll find out whether/if she's ready.|He wondered whether to go or not.|Please tell me whether or not you like it.* **2** (shows that it does not matter which is chosen): *I'll go, whether you come with me or stay at home.* (=I'll go whatever happens)| *Whether you like it or not, I'm going to bed.*

whew /hwyuʷ, hwuʷ, hyuʷ/ *interj* → PHEW

which /hwɪtʃ, wɪtʃ/ *determiner,pron* **1** (used in questions, when a choice is to be made): *Which shoes should I wear, the red ones or the brown ones?|Which of these books is yours?* **2** (shows what thing or things is/are meant): *Did you see the letter which/that came today?|This is the book which/that I told you about.* **3** (used esp. in written language, after a COMMA, to add more information to a sentence) **a** (about a thing or things): *The train, which takes only two hours to get there, is more convenient than the bus, which takes three.* **b** (about the first part of the sentence): *She said she'd been waiting for half an hour, which was true.* (=she had in fact been waiting for half an hour)

USAGE Compare **which** and **what**: 1 **Which** is used when a choice must be made. **What** is used in questions about something unknown: **What** *color do you want?*|**Which** *color do you want, red or blue?* 2 **Which** can be followed by *of*, but **what** cannot: **Which** *of the movies did you like best?* –see WHO, THAT (USAGE)

which·ev·er /hwɪ'tʃɛvər, wɪ-/ *determiner,pron* **1** any (one) of the set that: *Take whichever seat you like.|I'll give it to whichever of you wants it.* **2** no matter which: *You get the same result, whichever way you do it.* **3** (showing surprise) which?: *Whichever did you choose?*

whiff /hwɪf, wɪf/ *n* [S *of*] a short-lasting smell or movement of air: *Something good must be cooking; I got a whiff of it through the window.*

while¹ /hwaɪl, waɪl/ *n* **1** [S] a length of time, esp. a short one: *Just wait for a while and then I'll help you.* **2 worth one's/someone's**

time and trouble: *Do you think it's worth our while waiting for a bus, or should we just walk?|If you join our company, we'll* **make it worth your while**. (=we'll pay you well) –see also WORTHWHILE

while² *conj* **1** during the time that: *They arrived while we were having dinner.|While she read, I cooked the dinner.* **2** although; WHEREAS: *Their country has plenty of oil, while ours has none.*

while sthg. ↔ **a·way, wile away** *v adv* **whiled, whiling** to pass (time) lazily: *to while away the hours thinking about his next trip*

whim /hwɪm, wɪm/ *n* a sudden idea or wish, often not reasonable: *a sudden whim to buy a cream cake*

whim·per /'hwɪmpər, 'wɪm-/ *v* **1** [I] (esp. of a creature that is afraid) to make small weak cries **2** [I;T] to speak or say in a small trembling voice: *"Don't hurt me!" he whimpered.* –**whimper** *n*: *The dog gave a whimper of pain/fear.*

whim·si·cal /'hwɪmzɪkəl, 'wɪm-/ *adj* fanciful; with strange ideas –**whimsically** *adv*

whine¹ /hwaɪn, waɪn/ *v* **whined, whining** [I] **1** to make a high sad cry: *The dog whined at the door because it wanted to go out.* **2** to complain in an unnecessarily sad voice: *Stop whining, Peter!* –**whine** *n*: *the whines of the child| dog|*(fig.) *the whine of a car*

whin·ny /'hwɪniʸ, 'wɪniʸ/ *v* **-nied, -nying** [I] to make a gentle sound which horses make –**whinny** *n* **-nies**

whip¹ /hwɪp, wɪp/ *n* **1** a long piece of rope or leather fastened to a handle, used for hitting animals or people **2** a sweet food made of beaten eggs and other foods whipped together **3** a member of Congress or Parliament who is responsible for making other members of his/her party attend at voting time

whip² *v* **-pp-** **1** [T] to beat with a WHIP¹ (1) **2** [I;T] to move (something) quickly: *He whipped out his gun.|The wind whipped* (=moved quickly and fiercely) *across the plain.* **3** [T] to beat until stiff (esp. cream or the white part of eggs): *whipped cream* –compare WHISK² (2), BEAT¹ (3)

whip sthg. ↔ **up** *v adv* [T] **1** to cause (feelings) to rise, become stronger, etc.: *They're trying to whip up support for the new political party.* **2** to make quickly: *to whip up a meal*

whip·ping /'hwɪpɪŋ, 'wɪ-/ *n* a beating, esp. as a punishment

whir *AmE*‖**whirr** *BrE* /hwɜr, wɜr/ *v* **-rr-** [I] to make a regular sound like something turning, or moving up and down, very quickly: *the whirring sound of an insect's wings* –**whir** *n*: *the whir of the sewing machine*

whirl¹ /hwɜrl, wɜrl/ *v* [I;T] to (cause to) move around and around very fast: *the whirling dancers|The leaves were picked up by the wind and whirled into the air.*

whirl² *n* **1** [S] the act or sensation of WHIRLing¹: *My head's* **in a whirl** (=confused); *I must sit down and think.* **2** [C] very fast confused movement or activity: *a whirl of social activity*

whirl·pool /'hwɜrlpuʷl, 'wɜrl-/ n a place with circular currents of water in a sea or river, which can draw objects into it: *The floating sticks were sucked into the whirlpool.*

whirl·wind /'hwɜrl,wɪnd, 'wɜrl-/ n a tall pipe-shaped body of air moving rapidly in a circle: *A whirlwind destroyed the town.*

whisk¹ /hwɪsk, wɪsk/ n 1 [*usu. sing.*] a quick movement, esp. to brush something off: *with a whisk of his hand* 2 a small hand-held tool for beating eggs, whipping cream, etc.: *an egg whisk* –see illustration on page 379

whisk² v [T] 1 to move or remove quickly: *The horse was whisking its tail to brush the flies off its back.|She whisked the cups away.|She whisked him (off) home.* 2 to beat (esp. eggs), esp. with a WHISK¹ (2)

whisk·er /'hwɪskər, 'wɪ-/ n [*usu. pl.*] one of the long stiff hairs that grows near the mouth of a cat, rat, etc.

whisk·ers /'hwɪskərz, 'wɪ-/ n [P] hair growing on the sides of a man's face –compare BEARD

whis·key /'hwɪskiʸ, 'wɪ-/ -keys [C;U] a strong alcoholic drink (SPIRIT¹ (7)) made from MALT, esp. that produced in the US and Ireland: *a bottle of whiskey|Two whiskeys, please.*

whis·ky /'hwɪskiʸ, 'wɪ-/ -kies [C;U] WHISKEY produced esp. in Scotland and Canada

whis·per¹ /'hwɪspər, 'wɪ-/ v [I;T] to speak (words) very quietly, using the breath but not the voice: *The children were whispering together in the corner.|"Listen!" she whispered, "and don't make a noise!"|*(fig.) *the wind whispering in the trees*

whisper² n whispered words: *She said it* **in a whisper,** *so I couldn't hear.|*(fig.) *the whisper of the wind in the trees*

whist /hwɪst, wɪst/ n [U] a card game for two pairs of players

whis·tle¹ /'hwɪsəl, 'wɪ-/ n 1 a simple musical instrument for making a high sound by passing air or steam through: *The* REFEREE *blew his whistle, and the game stopped.* 2 the high sound made by passing air or steam through a small tube-shaped instrument, a mouth, or a beak: *He gave a loud whistle of surprise.*

whistle² v -tled, -tling 1 [I] to make a WHISTLE¹ (2), esp. with the mouth, so as to make music or to attract attention: *He whistled to me from the other side of the street.|*(fig.) *The wind whistled around them.* 2 [T] to produce (music) by doing this: *He whistled a popular tune.*

white¹ /hwaɪt, waɪt/ adj 1 a of the color of snow and milk: *white paint|white hair* (=when one is very old) b pale in color: *white wine|white-faced with fear* 2 (of a person) of a pale-skinned race –compare BLACK¹ (3), FAIR¹ (4) 3 (of coffee) with milk or cream –opposite black **–whiteness** n [U]

white² n 1 [U] the color which is white 2 [C] a person of a pale-skinned race: *There were both whites and blacks at the meeting.* 3 [C] the white part of the eye 4 [C;U] the part of an egg which is colorless, but white after cooking: *Beat three egg whites until stiff.*

white-col·lar /,· '··/ adj [A] not of the people who work with their hands; of office workers, etc.: *a white-collar job* –see also BLUE-COLLAR

White House /'· ·/ n the official home in Washington D.C. of the President of the United States

whit·en /'hwaɪtn, 'waɪtn/ v [I;T] to (cause to) become (more) white: *This soap will whiten your wash.* **–whitener** n

white pa·per /'· ,··/ n an official government report on a certain subject: *a new white paper on education*

white·wash¹ /'hwaɪtwɑʃ, -wɔʃ, 'waɪt-/ n [U] 1 a white liquid mixture made from lime, used esp. for painting walls 2 an attempt to hide something wrong: *What he said was just whitewash to hide his mistake.*

whitewash² v [T] 1 to cover with WHITEWASH¹ (1): *whitewashing the farm buildings* 2 to try to hide (something wrong)

whith·er /'hwɪðər, 'wɪ-/ adv,conj old use 1 to which (place): *the place whither* (=to which) *he went* –compare WHENCE 2 to what place?: *Whither goes he?* (=Where is he going?)

whit·ing /'hwaɪtɪŋ, 'waɪ-/ n **whiting** or **whitings** a sea fish used for food

whit·tle /'hwɪtl, 'wɪtl/ v -tled, -tling [T *down, away*] to cut (wood) to a smaller size by taking off small thin pieces: *whittling down a piece of wood|*(fig.) *Lack of sleep whittled his strength away.*

whiz , whizz /hwɪz, wɪz/ v -zz- [I] *infml* to move very fast, often with a noisy sound: *Cars were whizzing past.*

whiz kid /'· ·/ n *infml* an unusually intelligent or successful young person

who /huʷ/ pron (*used esp. as the subject of a verb*) 1 (*used in questions*) what person or people?: *Who's at the door?|Who are they?|Who won the race?* 2 (shows what person or people is/are meant): *The woman who/that wrote this letter works in a hospital.|Do you know the people who/that live here?|A mailman is a man who/that delivers letters.* 3 (used esp. in written language, after a COMMA, to add more information about a person or people): *This is my father, who lives in Chicago.* (=and he lives in Chicago)

USAGE Except in very formal language, **who** can be used instead of **whom** as an object in questions: **Who** *did you see?|***Who** *was she dancing with?* –see THAT (USAGE)

WHO /,dʌbəlyuʷeʸtʃ 'oʷ, huʷ/ n abbrev. for: the World Health Organization; an international organization which aims to improve the health of people throughout the world

whoa /woʷ, hwoʷ, hoʷ/ interj (a call to a horse) stop

who'd /huʷd/ short for 1 who had 2 who would

who·ev·er /huʷ'ɛvər/ pron 1 anybody at all that: *I'll take whoever wants to go.* 2 no matter who: *Whoever it is, I don't want to see them/him.* 3 (showing surprise) who?: *Whoever can that be knocking at the door?*

whole¹ /hoʷl/ adj 1 not spoiled or divided: *a can of whole* PEACHES (=not cut in half)|*to swallow it whole* (=without breaking it up in the mouth) 2 [A] not less than (a); all (the): *I* spent the whole day in bed.|the whole truth|He drank a whole bottle of wine.

whole² n [usu. sing.] **1** [of] the complete amount, thing, etc.: *The whole of the morning was wasted.|We can't treat the group* **as a whole,** *but must pay attention to each member.* **2** the sum of the parts: *Two halves make a whole.* **3 on the whole** generally; mostly: *On the whole, I like it.*

whole-heart·ed /ˌ· '··◄/ adj with all one's ability, sincerity, etc.: *to give one's whole-hearted attention/sympathy* –see also HALF-HEARTED –**wholeheartedly** adv

whole wheat /ˌ· '·◄/ AmE‖**wholemeal** /'howlmiʸl/ BrE– adj [A] made without removing the covering of the grain: *whole wheat flour|whole wheat bread* (=a type of brown bread)

whole·sale¹ /'howlseʸl/ n [U] the business of selling goods in large quantities, esp. to storekeepers –compare RETAIL

wholesale² adj,adv **1** of or concerned in selling in large quantities esp. for selling again: *a wholesale wine dealer* –compare RETAIL **2** in too large, unlimited numbers: *a wholesale rush from the burning building.*

whole·sal·er /'howl,seʸlər/ n a businessman who sells WHOLESALE² (1) goods

whole·some /'howlsəm/ adj **1** good for the body: *wholesome food* **2** good in effect, esp. morally: *Such movies are not wholesome for young children.* –**wholesomeness** n [U]

who'll /huʷl/ short for: who will

whol·ly /'howliʸ, 'howl-liʸ/ adv completely: *not wholly to blame for the accident*

whom /huʷm/ pron (the object form of WHO, used esp. in formal speech or writing): *Whom did you see?|I met a woman whom I know.|This is the man with whom I talked.|The government official, to whom I spoke recently, agrees.* –see WHO, THAT (USAGE)

whoop /huʷp, hwuʷp, wuʷp/ v,n [C;I] (to make) a loud cry, as of joy

whop·per /'hwɑpər, 'wɑ–/ n infml **1** a big thing: *Did you catch that fish? What a whopper!* **2** a big lie: *He told a real whopper to excuse his lateness.*

whore /hɔr, howr/ n derog infml for PROSTITUTE

whorl /hwɔrl, hwɜrl, wɔrl, wɜrl/ n the shape which a line makes when going around in a SPIRAL, e.g. in some seashells

who's /huʷz/ short for **1** who is: *Who's he talking about?* **2** who has: *Who's he brought to dinner?* **3** infml who does: *Who's he mean?*

whose /huʷz/ determiner,pron **1** (used in questions) of whom?: *Whose house is this?|Whose is that car?* **2** of whom: *That's the man whose house burned down.* **3** of which: *a picture whose artist is not known*

who·so·ev·er /ˌhuʷsoʷ'ɛvər/ pron old use for WHOEVER(1,2)

why /hwaɪ, waɪ/ adv,conj **1** for what reason: *Why did you do it?|They asked him why he was so dirty.|Is there a reason why you can't come?|I see why it won't work.* **2 Why not** (making a suggestion): *Why not go by bus?*

WI written abbrev. said as: Wisconsin

/wɪs'kɑnsən/ (a state in the US)

wick /wɪk/ n **1** a piece of twisted thread in a candle, which burns as the wax melts **2** a piece of material in an oil lamp which draws up oil while burning

wick·ed /'wɪkɪd/ adj very bad; evil: *a wicked man|*(fig.) *a wicked waste of money* –**wickedly** adv –**wickedness** n [U]

USAGE **Wicked** and **evil** are very strong words for people or acts that are seriously morally wrong: *a wicked/evil murderer.* Disobedient children are usually called **naughty** or, if one finds their bad behavior amusing, **mischievous.**

wick·er /'wɪkər/ also **wickerwork** /'wɪkər,wɜrk/– n [A;U] example(s) of objects produced by weaving TWIGs, REEDs, etc.: *wicker furniture.*

wick·et /'wɪkɪt/ n (in cricket) **1** AmE also **hoop**– a metal arch through which the ball is driven in croquet **2 a** either of two sets of three sticks (STUMPs), at which the ball is thrown (BOWLed) **b** also **pitch**– the stretch of grass between these two sets

wide¹ /waɪd/ adj **1** [after n] large from side to side or edge to edge: *The skirt's too wide.|The garden is eight yards long and six yards wide.|The gate isn't wide enough for me to drive the car through.* **2** covering a large space or range of things: *over the wide seas|wide interests* –compare NARROW¹ **3** also **wide open**– fully open: *wide eyes*

wide² adv **1** completely (open), esp. the mouth: *open wide/wide open|She was wide-eyed with surprise.|wide-awake* (=fully awake) **2** [of] (in sport) far away from the right point: *The ball went wide (of the* PITCHER).

wide·ly /'waɪdliʸ/ adv **1** over a wide space or range of things: *widely known|She is widely read/has read widely.* (=many types of book)|*It's widely believed* (=by many people) *that the senator will lose the election.* **2** to a large degree: *widely different*

wid·en /'waɪdn/ v [I;T] to make or become (wide or) wider: *to widen a road* –compare NARROW²

wide·spread /ˌwaɪd'sprɛd◄/ adj found, placed, etc., in many places: *a widespread disease/belief*

wid·ow /'wɪdoʷ/ n a woman whose husband has died, and who has not married again

wid·owed /'wɪdoʷd/ adj left alone after the death of one's husband/wife

wid·ow·er /'wɪdoʷər/ n a man whose wife has died, and who has not married again

width /wɪdθ, wɪtθ/ n size from side to side: *The width of the garden is six yards.* **2** [C] a piece of material of the full width, as it was woven: *We need four widths of curtain material to cover the window.*

wield /wiʸld/ v [T] to control the action of: *She wields a lot of power in the government.|*(old use & lit) *to wield a weapon*

wife /waɪf/ n wives /waɪvz/ the woman to whom a man is married: *My wife is a company director.|the President and his wife* –compare HUSBAND

wife·ly /'waɪfliʸ/ adj esp. old use having or

showing the good qualities of a wife

wig /wɪg/ n an arrangement of false hair to make a covering for the head: *The actress wore a black wig over her* BLOND *hair.|In England judges wear wigs in court.*

wig·gle /ˈwɪgəl/ v **-gled, -gling** [I;T] to (cause to) move in small esp. side to side movements: *to wiggle one's toes* **–wiggle** n [I;T]: *She walks with a wiggle.*

wig·wam /ˈwɪgwɑm, -wɔm/ n a tent of the type used by some North American Indians

wild¹ /waɪld/ adj **1** usu. living in natural conditions or having natural qualities; not TAME or CULTIVATED: *a wild animal/flower/the wild hills* **2** not CIVILIZED; SAVAGE: *wild tribes* **3** having or showing strong feelings, esp. of anger: *He looked wild with anger.* **4** (of natural forces) violent; strong: *a wild wind* **5** having or showing lack of thought or control: *I'll make a wild guess.* (=because I don't know any facts)|*a wild throw* **6** [F *about*] having a great (sometimes unreasonable) liking (for): *She's wild about racing cars.* **–wildness** n [U]

wild² n [*the* C;S] natural areas full of animals and plants, with few people: *The lion escaped and returned to the wild.|lost in the wilds (of an unknown country)*

wild³ adv **run wild** to behave as one likes, without control

wild·cat /ˈwaɪldkæt/ adj [A] (in industry) happening unofficially and unexpectedly: *wildcat* STRIKES

wil·der·ness /ˈwɪldərnɪs/ n **1** [*the* S] old use & bibl an area of land with little life, esp. a desert **2** [C *of*] an unchanging empty stretch of land, water, etc.: *in a wilderness of houses|That garden's a wilderness.* (=not controlled in growth)

wild·fire /ˈwaɪldfaɪər/ n **like wildfire** very fast: *The news spread/went around like wildfire.*

wild·fowl /ˈwaɪldfaʊl/ n [P] birds that are shot for sport, esp. waterbirds

wile /waɪl/ v **-wiled, wiling** →WHILE **away**

wild-goose chase /ˌ· ˈ· ·/ n (**lead someone on**) **a wild-goose chase** (to cause someone) a useless search

wild·life /ˈwaɪldlaɪf/ n [U] animals (and plants) which live in a wild state: *The island is full of interesting wildlife.*

wild·ly /ˈwaɪldliy/ adv in a wild way: *He ran wildly down the street.|His answer was wildly wrong.* (=very greatly wrong)

wiles /waɪlz/ n [P] tricks; deceitful PERSUASION: *She was tricked by the salesman's wiles into buying worthless goods.*

will·ful AmE‖**wilful** BrE /ˈwɪlfəl/ adj **1** having the intention of doing what one likes, in spite of other people: *a willful child|willful behavior* **2** [A] done on purpose: *willful behavior|willful damage to the farmer's crops* **–willfully** adv **–willfulness** n [U]

will¹ /l, əl, wəl/ *strong* wɪl/ v *negative short form* **won't** /woʷnt/ [I + *to*-v] **1** (used to show the future): *They say that it will rain tomorrow.* –see Study Notes on page 434 **2** to be willing to; be ready to: *I won't go!|We can't find anyone who will take the job.|The door*

won't shut.|Will you have some coffee? (used when offering something politely) **3** (used when asking someone to do something): *Will you telephone me later please?|Shut the door, will you?|You won't tell him, will you?* (=I hope not) **4** (shows what always happens): *Accidents will happen.|Oil will float on water.* **5** (used like **can**, to show what is possible): *This car will hold six people.* **6** (used like **must**, to show what is likely): *That will be the mailman at the door now.* –see also WOULD; see SHALL (USAGE)

will² /wɪl/ n **1** [C;U] the power in the mind to choose one's actions: *Free will makes us able to choose our way of life.* **2** [C;U] intention or power to make things happen: *the will to live|He didn't have the will to change.* **3** [U] what is wished or intended (by the stated person): *Her death is God's will.* **4** [C] the written wishes of a person in regard to sharing his property among other people after his death: *Have you made your will yet?|I was left $1,000 in my grandfather's will.* **5 at will** as one wishes **6 -willed** having a certain kind of WILL² (1): *a strong-willed man*

will³ v [T] **1** [+ (*that*)] to make or intend (to happen) esp. by power of the mind: *We willed him to stop, but he just drove past.* **2** [*to*] law to leave (possessions or money) in a WILL² (4) to be given after one's death: *My grandfather willed me his watch.*

will·ing /ˈwɪlɪŋ/ adj [+ *to*-v] ready (to do something): *Are you willing to help?|a willing helper* **–willingly** adv **–willingness** n [U + *to*-v]

wil·low /ˈwɪloʷ/ n [C;U] (the wood from) a tree which grows near water, with long thin branches

wil·low·y /ˈwɪloʷiy/ adj pleasantly thin and graceful: *a girl with a willowy figure*

will·pow·er /ˈwɪlˌpaʊər/ n [U] strength of WILL² (2): *He doesn't have the willpower to stop eating so much.*

wil·ly-nil·ly /ˌwɪliy ˈnɪliy/ adv regardless of whether (generally) wanted or not: *They introduced the new laws willy-nilly.*

wilt /wɪlt/ v [I] (of a plant) to become less fresh and start to die: *The flowers are wilting for lack of water.* |(fig.) *I'm wilting* (=becoming tired and weak) *in this heat.*

wi·ly /ˈwaɪliy/ adj **-ier, -iest** clever in tricks, esp. for getting what one wants: *a wily fox* –see also WILES **–wiliness** n [U]

wimp /wɪmp/ n AmE infml derog a person, esp. a man, lacking firmness of mind or strength of character

win¹ /wɪn/ v **won** /wʌn/, **winning 1** [I;T] to be the best or first in (a struggle, competition, or race): *She won the race.|Who won? |Who won the election?|to win at cards|the winning team* **2** [T] to be given (something) as the result of success in a competition, race, or game of chance: *She won a prize cup/$100.|I won $20 at cards.* **3** [T] to gain (for oneself) by effort or ability: *By her hard work she won a place for herself/won herself a place on the school team.*

USAGE Compare **win**, **earn**, and **gain**. To **win** is to be successful in (a contest, a war, a game, etc.) and perhaps to receive (a prize) as a result: *Who is going to win the election?*|*She won $1000 in a competition.* If you work for money (or any other reward), you **earn** it, and this also suggests that you deserve what you have worked for: *You've been working very hard and I think you've earned* (=you deserve) *a rest.*|*She earns $1000 a month working for a newspaper.* To **gain** is to obtain (something useful and desirable) and, unlike **win** and **earn**, it is not used in connection with money: *By reducing our prices, we gained an advantage over our opponents.*|*She gained useful experience while working for the newspaper.*

win sbdy.↔ **over** *v adv* [T *to*] to gain the support of (someone), often by persuading: *He disagrees, but we can win him over to our point of view.*

win² *n* (esp. in sport) a victory or success: *three wins and two losses*

wince /wɪns/ *v* **winced, wincing** [I *at*] to close one's eyes, move suddenly, etc., (as if) drawing away from something unpleasant: *I could see him wince when I told him how much the repairs would cost.* –compare JUMP¹ (3), START¹ (6)

winch /wɪntʃ/ *v,n* [C;T] (to move by) a machine for pulling up heavy objects by means of a turning part: *They winched the car out of the ditch.*|*They used a winch to lift the car.*

wind¹ /wɪnd/ *n* **1** [C;U] strongly moving air: *high/strong/heavy winds*|*We couldn't play tennis because there was too much wind.* –compare BREEZE, AIR; see WEATHER (USAGE) **2** [U] breath or breathing: *He couldn't get his wind* (=could not breathe properly) *after his run.* –compare WINDPIPE **3** [U] (the condition of having) air or gas in the stomach: *You get wind when you eat too quickly.* **4 get wind of** *infml* to hear about, esp. accidentally or unofficially: *If anyone gets wind of our plans, we'll be in trouble.* **5 (something) in the wind** (something secret) about to happen/being done **6 second wind: a** a steady breathing regained during exercise which has at first made one breathless **b** ability to try hard again (esp. in the phrase **get one's second wind**)

wind² /wɪnd/ *v* [T] to cause to be breathless: *He hit him in the stomach and winded him.*

wind³ /waɪnd/ *v* **wound** /waʊnd/, **winding 1** [T *around*] to place around several times: *to wind a cloth around the wounded arm*|*I wound my arm around the back of the chair.* **2** [T *up*] to tighten the working parts by turning: *to wind a clock* **3** [T] to turn; move by turning (a handle): *to wind down the car window* **4** [I] to follow a direction in a twisting shape: *The path winds through the woods.*

wind down *v adv* [I] **1** (of a clock or watch) to work more slowly before at last stopping **2** (of a person) to rest until calmer, after work or excitement

wind up *v adv* **1** [I;T (=**wind** sthg.↔ **up**) *with*] to come to, or bring to, an end: *to wind up the evening with a drink*|*to wind up a*

company **2** [I] *infml* to put oneself (in a certain state or place), accidentally: *He wound up feeling ashamed of himself.*|*You'll wind up in the hospital, if you drive so fast.* –compare END **up**

wind·bag /'wɪndbæg/ *n infml* a person who talks too much, esp. about dull things

wind·break /'wɪndbreɪk/ *n* a fence, wall, etc., intended to prevent the wind coming through with its full force

wind·break·er /'wɪnd,breɪkər/ *n AmE* a short coat usually fastened closely at wrists and neck, which is intended to keep out the wind –see also PARKA

wind·fall /'wɪndfɔl/ *n* **1** a piece of fruit blown down off a tree: *These apples are windfalls, but they're good.* **2** an unexpected lucky gift, esp. money: *a windfall of $1,000 from a distant relative*

wind·ing /'waɪndɪŋ/ *adj* of a twisting turning shape: *a winding road through the old town*|*winding stairs* –see WIND³ (4)

wind in·stru·ment /'wɪnd ,ɪnstrəmənt/ *n* any musical instrument played when air is blown through it

wind·mill /'wɪnd,mɪl/ *n* a building containing a machine that crushes corn, provides electricity, pumps water, etc., and is driven by large sails which are turned around by the wind

win·dow /'wɪndoʊ/ *n* a (usu.) glass opening, esp. in the wall of a house, to let in light and air –see illustration on page 337

window dress·ing /'·· ,··/ *n* [U] the art or practice of arranging goods in a store window to attract people

win·dow·pane /'wɪndoʊ,peɪn/ *n* one whole piece of glass in a window

window screen /'·· ,·/ *n* →SCREEN¹ (2)

window shade /'·· ,·/ *n AmE for* BLIND³ (1)

window-shop·ping /'·· ,··/ *n* [U] looking at the goods shown in store windows without necessarily intending to buy: *to go window-shopping*

win·dow·sill /'wɪndoʊ,sɪl/ *n* the flat shelf formed by the wood or stone below a window

wind·pipe /'wɪndpaɪp/ *n* the tube which forms an air passage from the throat to the top of the lungs

wind·shield /'wɪndʃiɪld/ *AmE*‖**windscreen** *BrE*– *n* the piece of glass or transparent material across the front of a car which the driver looks through –see illustration on page 95

windshield wip·er /'·· ,··/ *also* **wiper**– *n* a movable arm which clears rain from the WINDSHIELD of a car –see illustration on page 95

wind·sock /'wɪndsɑk/ *n* a tube-like piece of material, fastened to a pole at airports, which shows the direction of the wind

wind·swept /'wɪndswɛpt/ *adj* **1** (of country) open to the wind: *a bare windswept plain* **2** (as if) blown into an untidy state: *a windswept appearance*

wind·y /'wɪndiɪ/ *adj* **-ier, -iest** with a lot of wind: *windy weather*|*a windy hillside* –**windily** *adv* –**windiness** *n* [U]

wine /waɪn/ n [C;U] (an) alcoholic drink made from GRAPEs or other fruit: *a glass of wine*|*the wines of Alsace*|*apple wine*

wing¹ /wɪŋ/ n **1** one of the limbs by which a bird or insect flies **2** one of the parts standing out from the side of a plane which supports it in flight **3** any part of an object or group which stands out from the side: *the west wing of the house* **4** (in sport) the position or player on the far right or left of the field **5** a group representing certain views within a political party: *Which wing of the party is she on?* –see also LEFT WING, RIGHT WING **6 under someone's wing** being protected, helped, etc., by someone: *to take the new students under one's wing*

wing² v [I;T] **1** *lit* to fly (as if) on wings: *birds winging their way across the sky* **2** *AmE infml* **wing it** to do or say something without preparation: IMPROVISE: *The teacher hadn't prepared for the class, so he had to wing it.*

wings /wɪŋz/ n [P] (either of) the sides of a stage, where an actor is hidden from view: *She stood watching* **in the wings.**

wing·span /'wɪŋspæn/ n the distance from the end of one wing to the end of the other, when both are stretched out –see also SPAN

wink¹ /wɪŋk/ v [I] **1** [*at*] to close and open one eye rapidly, usu. as a signal between people, esp. of amusement: *He winked at her, and she knew he was only pretending to be angry.* **2** (of a light) to flash on and off: *The car's right hand side light winks when it turns right.* –compare BLINK

wink² n **1** [C] a WINKing¹ movement: *with a wink of the eye*|*He gave me a wink.* **2** [S *only in* NEGATIVE² *sentences*] (used of sleep) a short time: *I didn't sleep a wink*/*get a wink of sleep.* –compare BLINK

win·ner /'wɪnər/ n a person or animal that has won or is thought likely to win –compare LOSER

win·ning /'wɪnɪŋ/ adj which attract(s): *winning ways*|*a winning smile*

win·nings /'wɪnɪŋz/ n [P] money which has been won in a game, by BETting on a (horse) race, etc.

win·o /'waɪnoʷ/ n -os *AmE infml* a person who is an alcoholic, esp. one who drinks cheap wine

win·some /'wɪnsəm/ adj old use nice-looking; attractive: *a winsome appearance*

win·ter¹ /'wɪntər/ n [C;U] the coldest season, between autumn and spring: *I go on vacation in the winter.*|*a very cold winter*|*last winter*|*winter sports* (=on snow or ice)

winter² v [I *in*] to spend the winter: *to winter in a warm country*

win·ter·time /'wɪntər,taɪm/ n [*the* U] the winter season: *Heating bills are highest in (the) wintertime.*

win·try /'wɪntriʸ/ also **wintery** /'wɪntəriʸ/– adj like winter, esp. cold or snowy: *wintry clouds*|*a wintry scene*

wipe¹ /waɪp/ v **wiped, wiping** [T] **1** to pass a cloth or other material against (something) to remove dirt, liquid, etc.: *Wipe your feet/shoes (on the mat).*|*Wipe the table.* **2**

[*away, off*] to remove by doing this: *to wipe the tears away*

wipe sbdy./sthg.↔ **out** v adv [T] to destroy all of: *The enemy wiped out the whole nation.*

wipe up v adv [T] (**wipe** sthg.↔ **up**] to remove (liquid/dirt SPILLed or dropped) with a cloth: *Wipe up that mess!*

wipe² n a wiping (WIPE¹) movement: *Give your nose a good wipe.*

wip·er /'waɪpər/ n → WINDSHIELD WIPER

wire¹ /waɪər/ n **1** [C;U] (a piece of) thin metal like a thread: *a wire fence*|*They tied his hands with wire.*|BARBED WIRE|*The string wasn't strong enough, so we used wire.* –compare CABLE **2** [C] metal like this used for carrying electricity from one place to another **3** *infml*, *esp. AmE* a telegram

wire² v **wired, wiring** [T] **1** [*up*] to connect up wires in (something), esp. in an electrical system: *to wire (up) a house*/*to re-wire it* **2** [+*that*] to send a telegram to: *He wired me (about) the results of the examination.*

wire net·ting /,· '··/ n a material made of wires woven together into a network, used esp. as a fence

wire serv·ice /'· ,··/ n *AmE* an organization that gathers news and sends it to SUBSCRIBERs, esp. newspapers

wire·tap /'waɪərtæp/ v -pp- [I;T] *esp. AmE* to TAP² (3) telephone lines

wir·ing /'waɪərɪŋ/ n [*the* U] the arrangement of the wired electrical system in a building: *good wiring*|*This old wiring needs replacing.*

wir·y /'waɪəriʸ/ adj -ier, -iest rather thin, with strong muscles: *a wiry body* –**wiriness** n [U]

Wisc. *written abbrev. said as:* Wisconsin /'wɪs'kɑnsən/ (a state in the US)

wis·dom /'wɪzdəm/ n [U] the quality of being wise: *to have*/*show great wisdom*

wisdom tooth /'·· ,·/ n (in humans) one of the four large back teeth, which do not usu. appear until the rest of the body has stopped growing

wise¹ /waɪz/ adj usu. *fml & polite* **1** having or showing good sense, judgment, the ability to understand what happens and decide on the right action: *a wise man*/*decision*|*It was wise of you to leave when you did.* **2 none the wiser** knowing no more than before: *I was still none the wiser, even after he'd told me how to use the machine.* –**wisely** adv

wise² v **wised, wising** →WISE UP

wise·crack /'waɪzkræk/ v,n [C;T] *infml* (to make) a joking remark or reply

wise guy /'· ·/ n *infml* a person who thinks he knows more than others

wise up v adv [I;T] *AmE infml* to (cause to) learn the right information

wish¹ /wɪʃ/ v [*not* be+v-ing] **1** [T +*that*] to want (what is at present impossible): *I wish the weather weren't so cold.*|*I wish I could fly.* **2** [I *for*] to want and try to cause a particular thing: *You have everything you could wish for.* **3** [T] to hope that (someone) has (something): *We wish you a merry Christmas*/*good luck*/*a safe journey.* **4** [I;T] *fml* to want: *Do you wish to eat alone?*|*Do you wish me to come back later?* –see HOPE (USAGE)

wish sbdy./sthg. **on** sbdy. v prep [T] [*usu. in*

questions or in NEGATIVE² *sentences*] to hope that someone else should have: *She's a difficult person; I wouldn't wish her on my worst enemy.*

wish² *n* **1** [+*to-v*] a feeling of wanting, esp. what at present is impossible: *a wish to see the world|a wish for peace* **2** a desire for and attempt to make a particular thing happen, esp. by magic (esp. in the phrase **make a wish**) **3** what is wished for: *his last wish* (=before death)

wish·bone /'wɪʃbown/ *n* a V-shaped bone in a cooked chicken or other farm bird

wish·ful think·ing /,wɪʃfəl 'θɪŋkɪŋ/ *n* [U] acting as though something is true or will happen because one would like it to be: *He says he's sure to get a job when he leaves the university, but it may be just wishful thinking.*

wish·y-wash·y /'wɪʃiy,waʃiy, -,wɔʃiy/ *adj derog* without strength; weak: *wishy-washy ideas*

wisp /wɪsp/ *n* [*of*] **1** a small separate piece: *a wisp of hair|wisps of grass* **2** a small thin twisting bit (of smoke or steam)

wist·ful /'wɪstfəl/ *adj* having or showing a wish which may not be satisfied, or thoughts of past happiness which may not return: *to look wistful* –**wistfully** *adv*: *He thought wistfully of days gone by.* –**wistfulness** *n* [U]

wit /wɪt/ *n* **1** [C;U] (a person who has) the ability to say things which are both intelligent and amusing: *conversation full of wit|Oscar Wilde was a famous wit.* –see also WITTY **2** [U] power of thought; INTELLIGENCE (1): *He didn't have the wit to say no.* **3 at one's wits' end** made too worried by difficulties to know what to do next **4 have/keep one's wits about one** to be ready to act sensibly: *You need to keep your wits about you when you're driving in New York.* **5 -witted** having the stated type of ability or understanding: *quick-witted|dim-witted* (=stupid)

witch /wɪtʃ/ *n* a woman who has, or is believed to have, magic powers –compare WIZARD

witch·craft /'wɪtʃkræft/ *n* [U] the practice of magic to make things (esp. bad things) happen

witch·doc·tor /'wɪtʃ,daktər/ *n* a man in an undeveloped society who is believed to have magical powers

witch-hunt /'·· ·/ *n* a search for people whose political views are disliked, so that they may be made to suffer, removed from power, etc.

with /wɪð, wɪθ/ *prep* **1** among or including; in the presence of: *staying with* (=at the house of) *a friend|Mix the flour with some milk.|Leave your dog with me.|Connect this wire with that one.* (=so that they are joined) **2** having; showing: *a book with a green cover|They fought with courage.* –opposite **without 3** by means of; using: *to eat with a spoon|Cut it with the scissors.|What will you buy with the money?|This photograph was taken with a cheap camera.* **4** (shows the idea of covering, filling, or containing): *covered with dirt|I filled it with sugar.|made with eggs* **5** in support of; in favor of: *I agree with every*

word.|*You're either with me or against me.* **6** in the same direction as: *to sail with the wind|carried along with the crowd* **7** at the same time and rate as: *The wine improves with age.* **8** (used in comparisons): *to compare apples and pears|level with the street* **9** against: *Stop fighting with your brother.* **10** (shows separation from): *to break with the past* **11** in spite of: *With all his faults, I still like him.* **12** because of: *singing with joy|grass wet with rain|eyes bright with excitement|With John away,* (=John is away) *we've got more room.* **13** concerning; in the case of: *angry with him|in love with him|Be patient with them.|What's the matter with your foot?* **14** (used in exclamations expressing a wish or command): *On with the dance!* (=let the dancing continue)|*Down with school!|Off to bed with you!* (=Go to bed!)

with·draw /wɪð'drɔ, wɪθ-/ *v* **-drew** /'druw/, **-drawn** /'drɔn/, **-drawing 1** [I;T *from*] to (cause to) move away or back: *to withdraw the army|The army withdrew.* **2** [T *from*] to take away or back: *to withdraw $50 from a bank account|*(fig.) *to withdraw a remark* –compare DEPOSIT **3** [I;T *from*] to (cause to) not take part in: *He withdrew (his horse) from the race.*

with·draw·al /wɪð'drɔəl, wɪθ-/ *n* [C;U] (an example of) the act of WITHDRAWING or state of being WITHDRAWN

with·drawn /wɪð'drɔn, wɪθ-/ *adj* quiet and concerned with one's own thoughts

with·er /'wɪðər/ *v* [I;T *away*] (of a plant) to make or become reduced in size, color, etc.: *The cold withered the leaves.|*(fig.) *withered hopes|The flowers withered in the cold.* –compare WILT

with·er·ing /'wɪðərɪŋ/ *adj* (of an expression or remark) which causes one to be silent and/or uncertain: *The teacher gave me a withering look.* –**witheringly** *adv*

with·hold /wɪθ'howld, wɪð-/ *v* **-held** /'held/, **-holding** [T *from*] to keep (back) on purpose: *to withhold information*

with·in /wɪ'ðɪn, wɪ'θɪn/ *adv,prep* **1** *fml* inside: *within the building|"Apartments for Rent. Inquire Within."* (= an advertisement) **2** not beyond; not more than: *They'll arrive within an/the hour.|to keep within the law* (=not break it) –see INSIDE (USAGE)

withholding tax /·'·· ,·/ *n* [C;U] *AmE* a part of a worker's wages withheld (WITHHOLD) by an employer to pay part of the worker's income tax

with·out /wɪ'ðaut, wɪ'θaut/ *adv,prep* **1** not having: *to go out without a coat|a night without sleep|We couldn't have done it without Mary.* **2** (before *-ing* verbs) not: *He left without telling me|Can you wash it without breaking it?* –see also DO **without**, GO **without**

with·stand /wɪθ'stænd, wɪð-/ *v* **-stood** /'stud/, **-standing** [T] to oppose without yielding; RESIST: *to withstand an attack|Children's furniture must be able to withstand kicks and blows.*

wit·ness¹ /'wɪtnɪs/ *n* **1** [*to*] also **eyewitness** –a person who is present when something happens: *There were no witnesses when the accident happened.* **2** a person who tells in a court of law what he saw happen, what he knows about someone, etc. **3** [*to*] a person who signs an official paper to show that he has seen the maker sign it: *a witness to the* WILL² (4) **4** [*to*] a sign or proof (of): *The success of the show* **bears witness to** *our good planning.*

witness² *v* [T] **1** to be present at the time of and see: *Did anybody witness the accident?* **2** to be present as a WITNESS¹ (3) at the making of: *to witness the* WILL² (4)/*the signature*

witness stand /'·· ¸·/ *AmE*||also **witness box** *esp.BrE* – *n* the raised area where witnesses stand in court when being questioned

wit·ti·cism /'wɪtə‚sɪzəm/ *n* a WITTY remark

wit·ty /'wɪtiʸ/ *adj* **-tier, -tiest** having or showing an intelligent mind and amusing way of expressing thoughts: *a witty speaker*|*a witty remark* –**wittily** *adv* –**wittiness** *n* [U]

wives /waɪvz/ *n pl. of* WIFE

wiz·ard /'wɪzərd/ *n* **1** (esp. in stories) a man who has magic powers –compare WITCH **2** also **wiz** *infml*– a person with unusual abilities of a certain kind: *He's a wizard at playing the piano.*

wiz·ened /'wɪzənd/ *adj* (as if) dried up, with lines in the skin: *wizened apples*|*a wizened old lady*

wk *written abbrev. for:* week

wob·ble /'wɑbəl/ *v* **-bled, -bling** [I;T] to move unsteadily from one direction to another: *The table's wobbling.*|*You're making the table wobble*/*wobbling the table with your foot.* –**wobble** *n: a wobble in her voice*

wob·bly /'wɑbliʸ/ *adj* **-blier, -bliest** tending to WOBBLE: *wobbly handwriting*

woe /woʷ/ *n* [C;U] *esp. old use* (something causing) great sorrow: *a tale of woe* (=a story of misfortune)|*He told her all his woes.*

woe·be·gone /'woʷbɪ‚gɔn, -‚gɑn/ *adj* very sad in appearance

woe·ful /'woʷfəl/ *adj* **1** very sad: *woeful eyes* **2** which makes one sorry: *a woeful lack of understanding* –**woefully** *adv*

woke /woʷk/ *v past tense of* WAKE

wo·ken /'woʷkən/ *v past participle of* WAKE

wolf¹ /wʊlf/ *n* **wolves** /wʊlvz/ **1** a wild animal of the dog family which hunts other animals in a group (PACK¹ (2)) **2** *derog* a man who always seeks women for sex only –**wolfish** *adj*

wolf² *v* [T *down*] to eat quickly, in large amounts: *He wolfed his meal.*

wom·an /'wʊmən/ *n* **women** /'wɪmɪn/ **1** a fully grown human female: *Is your doctor a man or a woman?* **2** women in general **3** [A] female: *women workers* –see GENTLEMAN (USAGE)

wom·an·hood /'wʊmən‚hʊd/ *n* [U] the condition or period of being a woman

wom·an·ish /'wʊmənɪʃ/ *adj usu. derog* (of a man) like a woman in character, behavior, appearance, etc.: *a womanish walk* –compare EFFEMINATE

wom·an·ize ||also **-ise** *BrE* /'wʊmə‚naɪz/ *v* **-ized, -izing** [I] (of men) to habitually spend time with many women, esp. in order to have sexual relationships –**womanizer** *n*

wom·an·kind /'wʊmən‚kaɪnd/ *n* [U] women considered together as one body

wom·an·ly /'wʊmənliʸ/ *adj* having or showing the qualities suitable to a woman –**womanliness** *n* [U]

womb /wuʷm/ *n* also **uterus**– *n* the female sex organ of a MAMMAL where her young develop before they are born

wom·en·folk /'wɪmɪn‚foʷk/ *n* [P] *old use or humor infml* women

women's lib·er·a·tion /‚·· ··'·‚·/ also **women's lib** /‚·· '·/ *infml*– *n* [U] a movement to obtain social and political rights for women equal to those of men –compare FEMINISM

won /wʌn/ *v past tense and past participle of* WIN

won·der¹ /'wʌndər/ *v* **1** [I *about*] to express a wish to know: *I wonder if she knows we're here.*|*I wonder why they didn't arrive.*|*I wonder what really happened.* **2** [I;T +*that/at*] to be surprised and want to know (why): *I wonder at his rudeness.*|*I wonder (that) he can come here after what happened.*

USAGE Compare **wonder** (in the second meaning) and **admire:** You can **wonder** *at* (=be very much surprised by) both good and bad things, but you **admire** only good things (=look at them with pleasure and respect), without any feelings of surprise: *Arriving in New York, she* **wondered** *at the tall buildings and crowded streets.*|*She* **admired** *the fine stores and beautiful buildings.*

wonder² *n* **1** (something which causes) a feeling of strangeness, surprise, and admiration: *They were filled with wonder at the sight of the great new waterfall.*|*The temple of Diana was one of the seven* **Wonders of the World** *in ancient times.* **2** [C] a wonderful act or producer of such acts: (*infml*) *She's a wonder, the way she arranges everything.* **3 It's a/no wonder (that)** It's (not) surprising: *It's a wonder you recognized me after all these years.* **4 work wonders** to bring unexpectedly good results: *She looked so tired before, but her two week vacation has worked wonders.*

wonder³ *adj* [A] which is unusually good of its kind: *wonder drugs*

won·der·ful /'wʌndərfəl/ *adj* unusually good: *wonderful news* –**wonderfully** *adv*

wont /woʷnt, wɔnt, wɑnt, wʌnt/ *n* [S] *fml* a habit or custom: *He spoke for too long, as is his wont.*

won't /woʷnt/ *short for* will not: *I won't go!*

woo /wuʷ/ *v* **wooed, wooing** [T] **1** *old use* (of a man) to pay attention to (a woman one hopes to marry) –compare COURT² (3) **2** to make efforts to gain (the support of): *to woo the voters before an election*

wood /wʊd/ *n* **1** [U] the material of which trees are made, which is cut and dried in various forms for burning, making paper or furniture, etc.: *Put some more wood on the fire.*|*Most doors are made of wood.* **2** [C] →WOODS

wood·cut·ter /'wʊd‚kʌtər/ *n* (esp. in fairy stories) a man whose job is to cut down trees

wood·ed /'wʊdɪd/ *adj* having woods; covered with growing trees: *wooded hills*

wood·en /'wʊdn/ *adj* **1** made of wood: *a*

wooden bed **2** stiff; unbending: *wooden movements* **–woodenly** *adv*

wood·land /ˈwʊdlənd, -lænd/ *n* [U] wooded country: *large areas of woodland*|*woodland birds*

wood·peck·er /ˈwʊdˌpɛkər/ *n* a bird with a long beak, which can make holes in the wood of trees and pull out insects

woods /wʊdz/ *n* [P] a place where trees grow, smaller than a forest: *a walk in the woods*

wood·wind /ˈwʊdˌwɪnd/ *n* (the players of) the set of (wooden) instruments in an ORCHESTRA which are played by blowing: *The woodwinds are too loud.*

wood·work /ˈwʊdwɜrk/ *n* [U] **1** wooden objects, esp. furniture; **2** the parts of a house that are made of wood: *a mouse behind/in the woodwork*

woodworking /ˈwʊdˌwɜrkɪŋ/ *n* [U] *AmE* the skill of making wooden objects, esp. furniture; CARPENTRY: *He does woodworking.*

wood·worm /ˈwʊdwɜrm/ *n* **-worms** *or* **-worm** [C;U] the small soft wormlike young (LARVA) of certain BEETLEs, which makes holes in wood: *The stairs are unsafe because of woodworm.*

wood·y /ˈwʊdiʸ/ *adj* **-ier, -iest 1** of or with woods: *a woody valley* **2** of or like wood: *plants with woody stems*

woof /wʊf/ *n,interj infml* (a word used for describing the sound (BARK) made by a dog)

wool /wʊl/ *n* [U] **1** the soft thick hair which sheep and some goats have **2** thick thread or cloth made from this: KNITting *wool*|*a wool suit* –compare WORSTED **3** soft material from plants, such as cotton before it is spun: *cotton wool* **4 pull the wool over someone's eyes** to trick someone or hide the facts from him/her

wool·en *AmE*‖**woollen** *BrE* /ˈwʊlən/ *adj* made of wool: *a woolen coat*

wool·ens *AmE*‖**woollens** *BrE* /ˈwʊlənz/ *n* [P] garments made of wool, esp. KNITted –see also WOOLLY[2]

wool·ly /ˈwʊliʸ/ *adj* **-lier, -liest 1** of or like wool: *woolly socks* **2** (of thoughts) not clear in the mind: *His ideas are a little woolly.*

woolly[2] *n* **-lies** [*usu. pl.*] *infml* a garment made of wool, esp. KNITted: *winter woollies*

woolly-head·ed /ˌ·· ˈ···◄/ *adj* tending not to think clearly or have sensible ideas

woo·zy /ˈwuʷziʸ, ˈwʊziʸ/ *adj* **-zier, -ziest** *infml* unsteady; DIZZY

word[1] /wɜrd/ *n* **1** [C] (a written representation of) one or more sounds which can be spoken to represent an idea, object, action, etc.: *What is the French word for "bread?"*|*I know the tune but not the words.*|*Tell me what happened in your own words.* (=not repeating what somebody else said)|**Words fail me!** (=I'm too surprised/shocked to say anything)|*He told me what happened,* **word for word.** (=repeating everything that was said) **2** [S] the shortest (type of) statement: *Don't say a word to anybody.*|*I don't believe a word of it.*|*He never has a good word to say about me.* (=is always expressing disapproval of me) **3** [C] a short speech or conversation: *Can I have a few words with you?*|*a*

word with you?|*Let me give you a word or two of advice.* **4** [U +*that*] a message or news: *My friend* **sent word** *that he was still alive and well.* **5** [S +(*that*)] a promise: *I give* **you my word** *(of honor) I won't tell your secret.*|*He always* **keeps his word**; *he's* **a man of his word.**|*She said she wouldn't do it, and she was* **as good as her word.** (=she didn't do it) **6** [C *usu. sing.*] an order: *When I give the* **word**, *start writing.* **7 from the word go** from the beginning **8** (**get**) **a word in edgewise** (*used in* NEGATIVEs[2], *questions, etc.*) (to make) a remark made in spite of others who are speaking all the time: *He talks so much that no one else can get a word in edgewise.* **9 have words (with)** *euph* to argue angrily (with) **10 in other words** expressing the same thing in different words; which is the same as saying **11** (**not**) **in so many words** (not) expressed with that meaning but only suggested: *"Did she say she liked him?" "Not in so many words, (but...)"*

word[2] *v* [T] to express in words: *He worded the explanation well.*|*a carefully-worded letter*

word·ing /ˈwɜrdɪŋ/ *n* [S] the words chosen to express something: *The wording of a business agreement should be exact.*

word pro·ces·sor /ˈ·· ˌ···/ *n* a machine like a TYPEWRITER with a very small computer and a VDU. Writing can be seen on the SCREEN[1] (6) and can be changed before the machine produces a piece of paper with printed words on it –see illustration on page 467 –**word processing** *n* [U]

word·y /ˈwɜrdiʸ/ *adj* **-ier, -iest** using or containing too many words: *a wordy explanation* –compare VERBOSE

wore /wɔr, woʷr/ *v past tense of* WEAR

work[1] /wɜrk/ *n* **1** [U] activity which uses effort, esp. with a special purpose, not for amusement: *Digging in the garden all afternoon is hard work.*|*The road is closed; there are men* **at work** *repairing it.*|*The repairman arrived and* **went to work on** *the television.* (=began to repair it) **2** [U] what one is working on: *I'm taking some work home from the office this evening.* **3** [U] (the nature or place of) a job or business: *What kind of work do you do?*|*She got home very late from work.*|*Are you allowed to smoke at work?*|*My husband is* **out of work.** (=has no job) **4** [U] what is produced by work, esp. of the hands: *This mat is my own work.* (=I made it)|(fig.) *The broken window must be the work of that boy.* **5** [C *usu. pl.*] a work of art; object produced by painting, writing, etc.: *the works of Shakespeare* (=plays and poems) –see also WORKS **6 have one's work cut out for one** to have something difficult to do, esp. in the time allowed: *You'll have your work cut out for you to finish that job by tomorrow!* **7 make short work of** to finish quickly and easily

USAGE This is a general word that can be used of activities of the mind and of the body. **Labor** can be used instead, but it expresses the idea of tiring and unpleasant effort. –see JOB (USAGE)

work² *v* **1** [I;T] to (cause to) be active or use effort or power: *She's been working in the garage all afternoon.|I'm working on a new book.* (=writing one)|*She worked hard at her studies.|This machine works by/on electricity.|I think the teacher works us too hard.* (=we have to work too hard)|*Press the button that works the machine.* **2** [I;T] to be employed: *My mother works in an office.|He worked his way through college.* (=did jobs to earn the money to pay for school) **3** [I] to be active in the proper way, without failing: *Does this light work?|I don't think your plan will work.* (=succeed) **4** [I;T] to (cause to) reach a state or position by small movements: *The screw worked itself loose and the door fell off the cupboard.|He gradually worked his way to the front of the crowd.|*(fig.) *He worked himself into a temper.* **5** [T] to produce (an effect): *I think a long vacation would work wonders for your health.* **6** [T] to work in (a large area) usu. moving around: *The salesman worked both sides of the street.*
USAGE Although almost everyone **works,** expressions like **worker, workman,** and **out of work** are used particularly of people who work with their hands. –see also WORKING CLASS

work sthg.↔ **off** *v adv* [T] to remove, by work or activity: *to work off one's anger/to work off some extra weight*

work out *v adv* **1** [T] (**work** sthg.↔ **out**) to calculate the answer to: *to work out a math problem* **2** [I] to have an answer which can be calculated: *The cost works out to $20a day.* **3** [I;T (=**work** sthg. **out**)] to (cause to) have a good result: *Things will work themselves out.|I hope the new job works out for you.* **4** [I] *infml* to exercise: *to work out in the* GYM-NASIUM –see also WORKOUT

work over *v adv* [T] *infml esp. AmE* to attack violently: *After the robbers had taken the old man's money, they worked him over.*

work up *v adv* **1** [T] (**work** sbdy. ↔ **up**) to excite the feelings, esp. anger, tears, etc., of (esp. oneself): *The politician worked the crowd up until they were really angry.* –see also WORKED UP **2** [I;T (=**work** sthg.↔ **up**) to] to develop (towards): *She's working up to what she wants to say.|I've been playing tennis and have really worked up a thirst.*

work·bench /ˈwɜrkbentʃ/ *n* (a table with) a hard surface for working on with tools: *a* CARPENTER *at his workbench*

work·day /ˈwɜrkdeɪ/ *also* **working day** /ˈ··ˌ·/– *n* **1** a day which is not a holiday **2** the amount of time during which one works each day

worked up /ˌ· ˈ·/ *adj* [F] very excited; showing strong feelings, esp. when worried: *That child gets worked up about going to school and leaves the house crying every day.* –see WORK² up (1)

work·er /ˈwɜrkər/ *n* **1** a person or animal that works **2** a hard worker: *She's a real worker; she gets twice as much done as anybody else.* **3** *also* **workingman** /ˈwɜrkɪŋˌmæn/ a person who works with his hands, WORKING CLASS

person: *a factory worker*

work force /ˈ·· ·/ *n* [S] the people who work in industry generally, considered as a group: *the work force of this country|The factory has a work force of 250.*

work·ing /ˈwɜrkɪŋ/ *adj* [A] **1** concerning or including work: *The visiting head of state had a working breakfast with the President.* **2** who works with the hands: *a working man/woman* –see also WORKMAN **3** (of time) spent in work: *the working day/week* **4** used in work, business, etc.: *a working tool|in* **working order** (=in a state of working well)

working class /ˈ·· ˌ·/ *n,adj* [C +*sing./ pl.v;often pl. with sing. meaning*] (of) the social class to which people belong who work with their hands: *a working-class home|"The working class is/The working classes are getting angry about unemployment"*, *she said.* –compare MIDDLE CLASS, UPPER CLASS
USAGE **Working class** can be used in any of the following patterns: 1 Sing. with sing. v.: *The* **working class** *doesn't support this political party.* 2 Pl. with sing. meaning: *The* **working classes** *are getting angry about unemployment.* 3 As an adj: *This is a* **work-ing-class** *area.|Most of the people in this area are* **working-class. Lower class, middle class,** and **upper class** can all be used in the same ways.

working knowl·edge /ˌ·· ˈ··/ *n* [S] enough practical knowledge to do something: *She has a working knowledge of car engines and can do most repairs.*

work·ings /ˈwɜrkɪŋz/ *n* [P] the way in which something works or acts: *I will never under-stand the workings of an engine.*

work·man /ˈwɜrkmən/ *n* **-men** /mən/ a man who works with his hands, esp. in a particular skill or trade: *The workmen fixed the water system.|a good workman*

work·man·like /ˈwɜrkmənˌlaɪk/ *adj* having or showing the qualities of a good workman: *workmanlike methods*

work·man·ship /ˈwɜrkmənˌʃɪp/ *n* [U] (signs of) skill in making things: *good workmanship|Look at the workmanship in this old table.*

work·out /ˈwɜrk-aʊt/ *n infml* a period of bodily exercise and training, esp. for a sport –see also WORK² out (4)

works¹ /wɜrks/ *n* [*the* P] the moving parts (of a machine)

works² *n* **works** an industrial place of work; factory: *a gas works*

work·shop /ˈwɜrkʃɑp/ *n* **1** a room or place, as in a factory or business, where things are produced, repairs are done, etc. **2** a class of students or professionals meeting to study some subjects: *I'm taking a writing/dance workshop on Wednesdays.*

work week /ˈ· ·/ *n* →WEEK (2)

world /wɜrld/ *n* **1** [*the* S] the body in space on which we live; the earth: *He's the richest man in the world.|the Second World War* (=be-tween many countries of the world) **2** [C] a PLANET or star system, esp. one which may contain life: *a strange creature from another world* **3** [*the* S] a particular part of the earth or of life on earth: *the Third World* (=the poorer countries)|*the animal world* (=animals and their lives) **4** [*the* S] a particular area of human activity: *the world of football* **5** [*the* S] people in general; everyone: *The whole world knows about it.* **6** [*the* S] human life (and its affairs): *He's very young and inexperienced, and doesn't know about* **the ways of the world.**|*She has* **brought** *four children* **into the world.** (=given birth to four children) **7** [S *of*] a large number or amount: *The medicine did me a world of good.*|*The new fire makes a world of difference: I'm much warmer now.* **8 for all the world as if/like** exactly as if/like **9 in the world** (in a question expressing surprise): *What in the world* (=whatever) *are you doing?* **10 not for the world** certainly not: *I wouldn't hurt her for the world.* **11 out of this world** *infml* unusually good; wonderful **12 worlds apart** completely different: *Their ways of life are worlds apart.* **13 (have) the best of both worlds** (to have) the advantages which each choice offers, without having to choose between them

world-class /ˌ· '·◄/ *adj* among the best in the world: *a world-class football player*

world·ly /'wɜrldliʸ/ *adj* **-lier, -liest 1** [A; *no comp.*] of the material world: *all my worldly goods* **2** concerned with the ways of society, esp. social advantage; not SPIRITUAL **–worldliness** *n* [U]

worldly-wise /ˌ·· '·◄/ *adj* experienced in the ways of people: *too worldly-wise to expect too much of human nature*

world pow·er /ˌ· '··/ *n* an important nation whose trade, politics, etc., have an international effect

World Se·ries /ˌ· '···/ *n* [*the* S] a group of BASEBALL games played in the fall in the US to determine which of the teams is the best: *Do you think the Yankees will win the World Series this year?*

world war /ˌ· '·◄/ *n* a war in which many nations of the world join: *World War I (WWI)* (=that of 1914-1918)|*World War II* (=that of 1939-45)

world·wide /ˌwɜrld'waɪd◄/ *adj,adv* in or over all the world: *French cheeses are famous worldwide.*

worm¹ /wɜrm/ *n* **1** a small thin tube-like creature with no backbone or limbs, esp. the one which lives in and moves through earth (**earthworm**): *The dog has worms.* (=which live inside the body) **2** a person who is thought worthless, cowardly, etc.

worm² *v* [T] **1** [*in, into*] to move by twisting or effort: *He wormed himself through the opening.*|(fig.) *He* **wormed his way** *into her heart.* **2** to remove living worms from the body of, esp. by chemical means: *to worm a dog*

worm sthg. **out** *v adv* [T *of*] to obtain (information) by questioning, esp. over a period of time: *I wormed the secret out (of them).*

worn /wɔrn, woʷrn/ *v past participle of* WEAR¹

worn-out /ˌ· '·◄/ *adj* **1** completely finished by continued use: *worn-out shoes* **2** [F] very tired: *She was worn-out after three sleepless nights.* –see also WEAR out (2), OUTWORN

wor·ried /'wɜriʸd, 'wʌriʸd/ *adj* [*about*] anxious: *a worried look* **–worriedly** *adv*

wor·ry¹ /'wɜriʸ, 'wʌriʸ/ *v* **-ried, -rying 1** [I;T *about, over*] to be or make anxious: *It worries me that he's working so hard.*|*Worrying about your health can make you ill.*|*Don't worry!* **2** [T] (esp. of a dog) to chase and bite (an animal): *The dog was found worrying sheep, and had to be shot.*

worry² *n* **-ries** [C;U] (a cause of) a feeling of anxiety: *Money is just one of our worries.* (=there are others)|*lines of worry* (=caused by worrying) *on her face*

worse¹ /wɜrs/ *adj* **1** (COMPARATIVE² *of* BAD) lower in quality; more bad; less good: *worse weather than last week*|*I'm better at history than Laurie, but worse at French.*|*He may be late. Worse still, he may not come at all.* **2** [F] (COMPARATIVE² *of* ILL) more ill: *At least, he's no worse.* –compare BETTER¹ **3 none the worse (for)** not harmed (by): *He's none the worse for his fall from the window.*

worse² *adv* (COMPARATIVE² *of* BADLY) **1** in a worse way: *You're behaving worse than an animal.* **2** to a worse degree; more: *It's hurting worse than before.* –compare BETTER²

worse³ *n* [U] **1** something worse: *I thought that what happened was bad enough, but what followed was even worse.* –compare BETTER³ **2 a change for the worse** a bad change

wors·en /'wɜrsən/ *v* [I;T] to (cause to) become worse: *The rain has worsened our difficulties.* –compare BETTER⁴

wor·ship¹ /'wɜrʃɪp/ *n* [U] **1** (the act of showing) great respect, admiration, etc., esp. to God or a god: *They joined in worship together.* **2** a religious service: *They attended worship.*

worship² *v* **-p-** *AmE*||**-pp-** *BrE* **1** [I;T *at*] to show great respect, admiration, etc.:(fig.)*He worships the very ground she walks on.*|*His admirers worshiped at his feet.* **2** [I] to attend a church service: *to worship regularly* **–worshiper** *n*

worst¹ /wɜrst/ *adj* (SUPERLATIVE² *of* BAD) [A] the lowest in quality; the most bad: *This is the worst accident in years.*|*the worst driver I know* –compare BEST¹

worst² *adv* (SUPERLATIVE² *of* BADLY) in the worst way; most badly: *Who suffered worst?*|*the worst-dressed man* –compare BEST²

worst³ *n* [*the* S] **1** the most bad thing or part; the greatest degree of badness: *I've seen bad work, but this is the worst.*|*The worst of it is that I could have prevented the accident.*|*Tell me the worst!* (=the worst part of the news) –compare BEST³ **2 at worst** if the worst happens; if one thinks of it in the worst way: *He's a fool at best, and at worst he's a criminal.* **3 do one's worst** to do as much harm as one can (esp. when not much harm can be done): *Let the enemy do his worst; we are ready for him.* **4 get the worst of (it)** to be defeated in: *John got the worst of the argument.* **5 if (the) worst comes to (the) worst** if the worst difficulties happen; if there is no better way: *If worst comes to worst and the car won't start, we can* *always go by bus.*

wor·sted /ˈwʊstɪd, ˈwɜrstɪd/ *n* [U] wool cloth: *a worsted suit* –compare WOOL (2)

worth¹ /wɜrθ/ *prep* **1** of the value of: *This house is worth a lot of money.* **2** having possessions amounting to: *She's worth $1,000,000.* **3** good enough for; deserving: *The food's not worth eating.|Don't lock the door; it isn't worth the trouble/worth it.*

worth² *n* [U] value: *property of little or no worth*

worth·less /ˈwɜrθlɪs/ *adj* **1** of no value: *a worthless action* **2** (of a person) of bad character: *a worthless member of society*

USAGE Things of great value are **valuable**, and very **valuable** things are **priceless**: *a priceless 16th century Chinese plate.* **Invaluable** is similar in meaning, but is used of qualities rather than things: *Your help has been invaluable; we couldn't have done the job without you.* Things of little or no value are **valueless** or **worthless**.

worth·while /ˌwɜrθˈhwaɪl◂, -ˈwaɪl◂/ *adj* worth doing; worth the trouble taken: *We had a long wait, but it was worthwhile because we got the tickets.*

wor·thy /ˈwɜrðiʸ/ *adj* **-thier, -thiest 1** [A;F +to-v/of] deserving: *worthy of help/dislike|a worthy winner|not worthy to be chosen* **2** *esp. old use* to be admired, respected, etc.: *a worthy man* **3 -worthy: a** fit or safe to travel in or on: *This boat isn't seaworthy; it may sink.* **b** deserving: *a praiseworthy action|a newsworthy event* –**worthily** *adv* –**worthiness** *n* [U]

would /d, əd, wəd; *strong* wʊd/ *v negative short form* **wouldn't** /ˈwʊdnt/ [I +*to*-v] **1 a** (describing WILL in the past): *They said it would be fine.* (=They said, "It will be fine") **b** (used instead of WILL with a past tense verb): *They couldn't find anyone who would* (=who was willing to) *take the job.|She would be surprised if he came.* **2 a** (shows what always happened) used to: *We used to work in the same office. We would often have coffee together.* –see USE³ (USAGE) –see Study Notes on page 434 **b** (shows that one is annoyed at something usual or typical): *That's exactly like him: he would lose the key!* **3 would you** (used when politely asking someone to do something): *Would you please lend me your pencil?*

wound¹ /wuʷnd/ *n* a damaged place in the body, usu. a hole or tear through the skin, esp. done on purpose by a weapon: *only a flesh wound* (=not deep)|(fig.) *a wound to her pride*

wound² /wuʷnd/ *v* [T] to cause a wound to: *The shot wounded his arm.|She wounded him in the arm.*

USAGE People get **wounded** in war or fighting, and **injured** in accidents. Both words are more serious than **hurt**: *He was seriously wounded by an enemy bullet.|They were badly injured when their car hit a tree.|I hurt my foot when I dropped the hammer on it.*

wound³ /waʊnd/ *v past tense and past participle of* WIND³

wove /woʷv/ *v past tense of* WEAVE

wo·ven /ˈwoʷvən/ *v past participle of* WEAVE

wow¹ /waʊ/ *interj infml* (an expression of surprise and admiration): *Wow! Look at her new car!*

wow² *v* [T] *AmE infml* to excite greatly: *The singer really wowed the crowd.*

wran·gle /ˈræŋgəl/ *v,n* **-gled, -gling** [I *with*] (to have) an angry or noisy argument

wran·gler /ˈræŋglər/ *n AmE* a COWBOY, esp. one who takes care of horses in the western US

wrap¹ /ræp/ *v* [T] **-pp- 1** [*up, in*] to cover (in a material folded around): *I wrapped the book in brown paper before I mailed it.|They wrapped up my new shoes in the store.* **2** [*around*] to fold (a material) over: *I wrapped the RUG around the sick man's legs to keep him warm.*

wrap up *v adv* **1** [I] to wear warm clothes: *In cold weather you should wrap up well.* **2** [I;T] (=**wrap** sthg.↔**up**)] *infml* to complete or finish (a business arrangement, a meeting, etc.): *Let's wrap up (this meeting).* **3 wrapped up in** giving complete love or attention to: *He's so wrapped up in her, he can't see her faults.*

wrap² *n becoming rare* a garment or piece of material which is used as a covering, esp. a SCARF *or* SHAWL

wrap·per /ˈræpər/ *n* a piece of paper used as a cover for something: *a candy wrapper.*

wrap·ping /ˈræpɪŋ/ *n* [C;U] material used for folding around and covering something: *wrapping paper around a present*

wrath /ræθ/ *n* [U] *lit* great anger: *the wrath of God* –**wrathful** /ˈræθfəl/ *adj* –**wrathfully** *adv*

wreak /riʸk/ *v* [T *on*] *esp. lit* to do (violence) or express (strong feelings) in violence: *to wreak VENGEANCE (on someone)*

wreath /riʸθ/ *n* **wreaths** /riʸðz, riʸθs/ **1** an arrangement of flowers or leaves, esp. in a circle, esp. one given at a funeral –compare GARLAND **2** a curl of smoke, mist, gas, etc.

wreathe /riʸð/ *v* **wreathed, wreathing** [T *in*] *lit* to circle around and cover completely: *Mist wreathed the hilltops.|(fig.) She/her face was wreathed in smiles.*

wreck¹ /rɛk/ *n* **1** [C] a ship lost at sea or (partly) destroyed on rocks: *the wreck of the Titanic* –see also SHIPWRECK **2** [C;U] (a person or thing) in the state of being ruined or destroyed: *He's a complete wreck after his illness.|My plan's a complete wreck; we can't go on with it.*

wreck² *v* [T] to destroy: *The ship was wrecked on the rocks.|The weather has completely wrecked our plans.*

wreck·age /ˈrɛkɪdʒ/ *n* [U *of*] the broken parts of a destroyed thing: *the wreckage of the cars which were in the accident*

wren /rɛn/ *n* a very small bird which sings

wrench¹ /rɛntʃ/ *v* [T] **1** to pull hard with a twisting or turning movement: *He closed the door so hard that he wrenched the handle off.* **2** to twist and damage (a joint of the body): *to wrench one's ankle*

wrench² *n* **1** an act of twisting and pulling **2** painful grief at a separation: *the wrench of leaving one's family* **3** *AmE*‖a metal hand tool with jaws for fitting over and twisting screwed parts (NUTS¹ (2))

wrest /rɛst/ v [T *from, out of*] *fml* to pull (away) violently: *She wrested it from his hands.*|(fig.) *to wrest the truth out of someone*

wres·tle /ˈrɛsəl/ v **-tled, -tling 1** [I *with*] to fight by holding and throwing the body: *She wrestled with her attacker, and forced him to the ground.*|(fig.) *wrestling with a difficult examination paper* **2** [I;T] to fight (someone) like this as a sport (**wrestling**) –compare BOX³ –**wrestler** n

wretch /rɛtʃ/ n **1** a poor or unhappy person: *unlucky wretches with no homes* **2** a person or animal disliked and thought bad and useless –**wretched** /ˈrɛtʃɪd/ adj: *feeling wretched after an illness*|*Wretched child, why can't she behave?* –**wretchedly** adv –**wretchedness** n [U]

wrig·gle /ˈrɪgəl/ v **-gled, -gling** [I;T] to twist (a part of the body) from side to side: *He wriggled uncomfortably on the hard chair.*|(fig.) *You know it's your fault, so don't try to* **wriggle out of** *it.* (=escape from it)

wriggle² n a wriggling (WRIGGLE¹) movement

wring¹ /rɪŋ/ v **wrung** /rʌŋ/, **wringing** [T] **1** a to twist (esp. the neck, causing death) b to press hard on; SQUEEZE: *He wrung his hands in sorrow.* **2** [*out, from*] a to twist and/or press (wet clothes) to remove water: *Wring those wet things out.* b to press (water) from clothes: *Wring the water out (of the cloth).*|(fig.) *They wrung the truth out of me in the end.* **3 wringing wet** very wet

wring² n an act of WRINGING

wring·er /ˈrɪŋər/ n a machine with rollers between which water is pressed from clothes, sheets, etc.

wrin·kle¹ /ˈrɪŋkəl/ n **1** a line in something which is folded or crushed, esp. on the skin when a person is old **2** a small problem: *The plan is good, but there are still some wrinkles to be worked out.* –**wrinkly** adj **-klier, -kliest**

wrinkle² v **-kled, -kling** [I;T *up*] to (cause to) form into lines, folds, etc.: *He wrinkled (up) his nose at the bad smell.*|*the wrinkled face of the old man*

wrist /rɪst/ n the joint between the hand and the lower part of the arm

wrist·watch /ˈrɪst-wɑtʃ/ n a watch made to be fastened on the wrist with a band (STRAP)

writ /rɪt/ n an official paper given in law to tell someone (not) to do a particular thing

write /raɪt/ v **wrote** /rowt/, **written** /ˈrɪtn/, **writing 1** [I;T] to make (marks that represent letters or words) by using esp. a pen or pencil on paper: *The children are learning to write.*|*Write the address on the envelope.* **2** [T] to express and record in this way: *to write a report/a book* **3** [I;T] to be a writer of (books, plays, etc.): *She writes for the stage.* **4** [I;T *+to-v/v-ing/that/to*] to produce and send (a letter): *He writes me a letter every day, but I don't* **write back** (=reply) *very often.*| *I wish he would write more often.*|*He wrote to ask me to come.*

write sthg.↔**down** v adv [T] to record in writing (esp. what has been said): *Write your idea down while it's clear in your mind.*

write in v adv **1** [I *for*] also **write away** *AmE*– to send a letter to a company asking for something or giving an opinion: *We wrote in for a free book, but the company never replied.* **2** [T] *AmE* (**write** sbdy.↔**in**) to vote for (someone) by writing the name on a voting paper –see also WRITE-IN

write sbdy./sthg.↔**off** v adv [T *as*] to regard as being lost, having failed, etc.: *We'll just have to write off our plans if we can't find the money.*|*The newspapers wrote him off as a failure, but he proved them wrong.* –see also WRITE-OFF

write sthg.↔**out** v adv [T] **1** to write in full: *to write out a report* **2** to write (something official): *to write out a check/receipt*

write sthg.↔**up** v adv [T] to write (again) in a complete and useful form: *to write up one's notes* –see also WRITE-UP

write-in /ˈ· ·/ n *AmE* a vote given by writing the name of the person voted for –see also WRITE **in** (2)

write-off /ˈ· ·/ n anything which is completely ruined: *The car was a write-off after the accident.* –see also WRITE **off** (1)

writ·er /ˈraɪtər/ n a person who writes, esp. as a job

write-up /ˈ· ·/ n *infml* a written report, esp. one giving a judgment, as of goods or a play: *The concert got a good write-up in the local newspaper.* –see also WRITE **up**

writhe /raɪð/ v **writhed, writhing** [I] to twist the body, as when in great pain: *writhing with/in pain*

writ·ing /ˈraɪtɪŋ/ n **1** [U] the activity of writing, esp. books: *Writing is a difficult way of earning a living.* **2** [U] handwriting: *I can't read the doctor's writing.* **3** [C;U] written work or form: *Put that down in writing.*|*Darwin's scientific writings*

writing pa·per /ˈ·· ,·/ also **notepaper**– n [U] smooth, good quality paper for writing letters on

writ·ten /ˈrɪtn/ v past participle of WRITE

wrong¹ /rɒŋ/ adj **1** not correct: *the wrong answer*|*The clock's wrong; it's later than the time it shows.*|*This is the wrong time* (=not a suitable time) *to ask for a pay raise.* **2** [F] evil; against moral standards: *Telling lies is wrong.*|*It's wrong to tell lies.* –opposite **right** –**wrongly** adv

wrong² adv **1** wrongly: *You've spelled the word wrong.* –opposite **right 2 get it wrong** to misunderstand **3 go wrong: a** to make a mistake: *The plan didn't succeed, but I can't see where I went wrong.* **b** to stop working properly: *Something's gone wrong with the car.*

wrong³ n **1** [U] standards according to which some things are bad: *to know right from wrong* –opposite **right 2** [C] *fml* any seriously bad or unjust action: *He did you a terrible wrong.*

wrong⁴ v [T] to be unfair to or cause difficulty, pain, etc., to: *I wronged him by saying he could never improve his work.*

wrong·do·ing /ˌrɒŋˈduwɪŋ, ˈrɒŋˌduwɪŋ/ n [U] (an example of) bad, evil, or illegal be-

havior –**wrongdoer** *n*
wrong·ful /'rɔŋfəl/ *adj* unjust; unlawful: *wrongful imprisonment* –**wrongfully** *adv*
wrote /roʷt/ *v past tense of* WRITE
wrought /rɔt/ *adj old use & lit* made or done: *carefully wrought works of literature| wrought by hand*
wrought i·ron /,· '·· ◂/ *n* [U] iron shaped into

a useful form or pleasing pattern: *a wrought-iron gate*
wrung /rʌŋ/ *v past tense and past participle of* WRING
wry /raɪ/ *adj* **wrier, wriest 1** showing dislike, lack of pleasure, etc.: *a wry face* (=expression)/*smile* **2** (of humor) bitterly IRONIC –**wryly** *adv*

X, x

X, x /ɛks/ **X's, x's** *or* **Xs, xs 1** the 24th letter of the English alphabet **2** the ROMAN NUMERAL (number) for 10
x *n* (in MATHEMATICS) a quantity that is unknown until a calculation has been made: *If 3x=6, x=2.*
xen·o·pho·bi·a /,zɛnə'foʷbiʸə/ *n* [U] unreasonable fear and dislike of foreigners or strangers –**xenophobic** *adj*
xe·rox /'zɪəraks, 'ziʸraks/ *v,n* [IT] *tdmk* (*often cap.*) (to make) a photographic copy of (something printed or written) on a special electric copying machine; PHOTOCOPY
X·mas /'krɪsməs, 'ɛksməs/ *n infml* Christmas
x-rat·ed /'ɛks ,reʸṭɪd/ *adj* (in the US) a movie

that children under 17 are not allowed to see: *"Night Terror" is an x-rated movie.*
x-ray /'ɛks reʸ/ *v* [T] (*often cap.*) to photograph, examine, or treat by means of x-RAYS: *They x-rayed her leg to find out if the bone was broken.*
X-ray *n* **1** [*usu. pl.*] a powerful unseen beam of light which can pass through substances that are not transparent, and which is used esp. for photographing medical conditions inside the body **2** a photograph taken using this
xy·lo·phone /'zaɪlə,foʷn/ *n* a musical instrument made up of a set of flat wooden bars which produce musical notes when struck with small wooden hammers

Y, y

SPELLING NOTE
Words with the sound /y/ may be spelled **u-**, like **use**, or **eu**, like **Europe**.

Y, y /waɪ/ **Y's, y's** *or* **Ys, ys** the 25th letter of the English alphabet
yacht /yat/ *n* **1** a sailing boat, esp. one used for pleasure –compare DINGHY **2** a large, often motor-driven boat used for pleasure
yacht·ing /'yaṭɪŋ/ *n* [U] (the act of) sailing, traveling, or racing in a YACHT: *She went yachting.*
yak /yæk/ *n* a long-haired ox of central Asia
yam /yæm/ *n* **1** a tropical climbing plant whose root is eaten as a vegetable **2** *AmE* for SWEET POTATO
yam·mer /'yæmər/ *v* [I] *AmE infml* **1** to complain in a sad voice **2** to talk noisily and continuously
yank /yæŋk/ *v* [I;T] *infml* to pull suddenly and sharply: *He yanked (on) the rope.* –**yank** *n*
Yan·kee /'yæŋkiʸ/ also **Yank** /yæŋk/– *n infml sometimes derog* **1** a citizen of the United States of America **2** *AmE* a person born or living in the northern or northeastern states in the US
yap /yæp/ *v* **-pp-** [I] (esp. of dogs) to make short sharp excited noises (sharp BARKs) –**yap** *n: The dog gave a loud yap.*
yard¹ /yard/ *n* a measure of length that is a

little less than a meter; three feet; 36 inches
yard² *n* **1** an enclosed or partly enclosed area next to or around a house or other building **2** an enclosed area used for a particular business: *shipyard|coalyard*
yard goods /'·· ·/ *n* [P] *AmE* materials, such as cloth, sold in measures of a yard
yard·stick /'yard,stɪk/ *n* a standard of measurement or comparison: *Is money the only yardstick of success?*
yarn /yarn/ *n* **1** [U] thread, e.g. of wool or cotton **2** [C] *infml* a long and sometimes untrue story: *He would often **spin (us) a yarn** about his adventures in the navy.*
yawn /yɔn/ *v* [I] **1** to open the mouth wide and breathe in deeply, as when tired or uninterested **2** to be or become wide open: *A yawning hole* –**yawn** *n: I gave a loud yawn, but he just kept on talking.*
yd., yd *written abbrev. said as:* YARD(s)¹
ye /yiʸ/ *pron old use* you
yeah /yɛə/ *adv infml* yes
year /yɪər/ *n* **1** also **calendar year**– a period of 365 or 366 days divided into 12 months beginning on January 1st and ending on December 31st –see also LEAP YEAR **2** a period of 365 days measured from any point: *I arrived here two years ago today.* **3** a period of (about) a year in the life of an organization: *We take our exams in June, at the end of the school year.* **4 all year round** during the whole year

year·ling /'yıərlıŋ/ *n* an animal, esp. a young horse, between one and two years old

year·ly /'yıərliʸ/ *adj,adv* [A] (happening, appearing, etc.) every year or once a year

yearn /yɜrn/ *v* [I +*to-v/for*] *esp. lit* to have a strong, loving, or sad desire: *They yearned to return home.|He yearned for her presence/for her to come home.* –**yearning** *n* [C;U]

yeast /yiʸst/ *n* [U] a form of very small plant life that is used in making bread, and for producing alcohol in beer and wine –**yeasty** *adj*: *This beer tastes very yeasty.*

yell /yɛl/ *v* [I;T *at, out*] to say, shout, or cry loudly: *He yelled (out) orders at everyone.|Don't yell at me like that!* –**yell** *n*: *yells of excitement*

yel·low /'yɛloʷ/ *adj,n* [U] (of) a color like that of butter, gold, or the middle part (YOLK) of an egg –**yellow** *v* [I;T]: *That paper has yellowed with age.*

yellow pag·es /'·· ,··/ *n* [P] (the part of) a telephone DIRECTORY that lists businesses according to the goods and services they offer

yelp /yɛlp/ *v,n* [I] (to make) a short sharp high cry, as of pain or excitement: *The dog yelped/gave a yelp when I hit him.*

yen¹ /yɛn/ *n* **yen** the standard amount (UNIT (3)) of money in Japan

yen² *n infml* [S +*to-v/for*] a strong desire: *He has a yen to travel.*

yes /yɛs/ *adv* (used as an answer expressing agreement or willingness): *"Are you ready?" "Yes, I am."|"Go and close the door." "Yes, sir."* –opposite **no**

yes-man /'yɛs mæn/ *n derog* a person who always agrees with his/her employer, leader, etc.

yes·ter·day /'yɛstərdiʸ, -,deʸ/ *adv,n* 1 (on) the day before today: *I saw her at yesterday's meeting.|She came to dinner yesterday/yesterday afternoon.* –compare TOMORROW 2 (of) a short time ago: *the fashions of yesterday*

yet¹ /yɛt/ *adv* 1 (*used only in questions and* NEGATIVE*s²*) by a particular time; even sooner than expected; already: *Has John arrived yet?|She hasn't answered yet.|John hasn't done much work yet, but Anne has already finished.|He hasn't called as yet.* (=up till now)–see ALREADY (USAGE) 2 in the future; in spite of the way things seem now: *We may win yet.|The plan may even yet succeed.* 3 even; still: *yet another reason|a yet worse mistake*

yet² *conj* even so; but: *strange yet true|She's a funny girl; yet you can't help liking her.* –see Study Notes on page 144

yew /yuʷ/ *n* [C;U] (the wood of) a tree with small dark green leaves and small red berries

yield /yiʸld/ *v* 1 [I;T] to give; produce: *His business yields big profits.* 2 [I;T *to*] to give up control (of); SURRENDER: *We were forced to yield (our position to the enemy).* 3 [I] to

---

bend, break, etc., because of a strong force: (fig.) *The government will yield under pressure from the army.*

yip·pee /'yıpiʸ, yıp'iʸ/ *interj infml* (a cry of delight, happiness, success, etc.)

yo·del /'yoʷdl/ *v* **-l-** *AmE‖***-ll-** *BrE* [I;T] to sing (a song) with many rapid changes between the natural voice and a very high voice –**yodel** *n*

yo·ga /'yoʷgə/ *n* [U] a Hindu system of exercises to free the self from the body, will, and mind

yo·gi /'yoʷgiʸ/ *n* **-gis** a person who teaches YOGA

yogurt, yoghurt /'yoʷgərt/ *n* [U] milk that has turned thick and slightly acid through the action of certain bacteria and is eaten, not drunk

yoke¹ /yoʷk/ *n* 1 a wooden bar used for joining together two animals, esp. oxen, in order to pull heavy farm vehicles, etc. 2 a frame fitted across a person's shoulders for carrying two equal loads

yoke² *v* **yoked, yoking** [T *together*] to join (as if) with a YOKE¹: *Yoke the oxen together.*

yo·kel /'yoʷkəl/ *n humor or derog* a simple or foolish country person

yolk /yoʷk/ *n* [C;U] the yellow central part of an egg –compare WHITE² (4)

yon·der /'yɑndər/ *also* **yon** /yɑn/– *adj,adv* [A; after *n*] *lit or old use* over there: *He has walked to yonder hill.*

you /yə, yʊ; *strong* yuʷ/ *pron* (used as subject or object) 1 the person or people being spoken to: *You are my only friend.|You should all listen carefully.|You fool!* 2 a person; anyone: *You can't trust him.* (=it's impossible to trust him) –compare ONE² (2)

you-all /yuʷ 'ɔl, 'yuʷ ɔl, yɔl/ *pron AmE* (*esp. Southern*) *infml* (to more than one person) you: *You-all are going to fill up this plane.*

you'd /yəd, yʊd; *strong* yuʷd/ *short for* 1 you had 2 you would

you'll /yəl, yʊl; *strong* yuʷl/ *short for* 1 you will 2 you shall

young¹ /yʌŋ/ *adj* **younger** /'yʌŋgər/, **youngest** /'yʌŋgıst/ 1 in an early stage of life or development; recently born or begun: *a young girl/plant/country* 2 of, for, concerning, or having the qualities of a young person: *a young manner* –compare OLD –**youngish** /'yʌŋıʃ/ *adj*

young² *n* [P] 1 [*the*] young people considered as a group 2 young animals: *The lion fought to protect her young.*

young·ster /'yʌŋstər/ *n* a young person

your /yər; *strong* yʊər, yɔr, yoʷr/ *determiner* (POSSESSIVE² *form of* YOU) of the person or people being spoken to: *Your hands are dirty.|You are all invited, and bring your friends.*

you're /yər; *strong* yʊər, yɔr, yoʷr/ *short for:* you are

yours /yʊərz, yɔrz, yoʷrz/ *pron* 1 (POSSESSIVE² *form of* YOU) of the person or people being spoken to: *This is our room, and yours* (=your room) *is down the passage.* 2 (*usu. cap.*) (written at the end of a letter): **Sincerely yours|Yours truly,** *John Brown*

SPELLING NOTE

Words with the sound /y/ may be spelled **u-**, like **use**, or **eu**, like **Europe**.

your·self /yər'sɛlf/ *pron* **-selves** /'sɛlvz/ **1** (used as the object of a verb, or after a preposition, when the person being spoken to does the action and is the object of the action): *You'll hurt yourself.|Are you all enjoying yourselves?|Why not buy yourself* (=for yourself) *some shoes?* **2** (used to make YOU stronger): *You yourself know that it's true.|You and Mary will have to carry it (by) yourselves.*

youth /yuʷθ/ *n* **youths** /yuʷðz, yuʷθs/ **1** [U] the period of being young; early life **2** [C] a young person, esp. a young male: *a gang of youths* –see CHILD (USAGE) **3** [*the* U *of*] young men and women considered as a group: *The youth of that country is not ready to fight.*

youth·ful /'yuʷθfəl/ *adj* **1** of or having the qualities of youth: *youthful* ENTHUSIASM **2** young –**youthfully** *adv* –**youthfulness** *n* [U]

you've /yəv, yuv; *strong* yuʷv/ *short for* you have

yule /yuʷl/ *n rare* (*sometimes cap.*) Christmas

yule·tide /'yuʷltaɪd/ *n esp. lit or pomp* (*sometimes cap.*) Christmas: *Yuletide greetings*

Z, z

Z, z /ziʸ/ **Z's, z's** *or* **Zs, zs** the 26th and last letter of the English alphabet

za·ny /'zeʸniʸ/ *adj* **-nier, -niest** foolish in an amusing way: *She made us all laugh with her zany tricks.*

zeal /ziʸl/ *n* [U] eagerness; keenness: *She shows great zeal for knowledge.*

zeal·ous /'zɛləs/ *adj* [+*to-v/for, in*] eager; enthusiastic: *zealous for fame/in doing his duty/to succeed* –**zealously** *adv* –**zealousness** *n* [U]

ze·bra /'ziʸbrə/ *n* **zebras** *or* **zebra** a horse-like African wild animal with broad dark brown and white lines all over the body

ze·nith /'ziʸnɪθ/ *n* [*usu. sing*] the highest point, e.g. of hope or fortune: *Rome's power reached its zenith under the emperor Trajan.*

zep·pe·lin /'zɛpəlɪn/ *n* a large AIRSHIP used by the Germans in World War I

ze·ro /'zɪəroʷ, 'ziʸroʷ/ *n* **-ros** *or* **-roes 1** the name of the sign 0 and of the number it stands for **2** the point between + and – on a scale; on the CENTIGRADE scale, the temperature at which water freezes: *It was five below zero last night.*

USAGE In saying a number, **zero** is generally used for **0** in scientific matters. When giving a telephone number, ADDRESS or ZIP CODE, American speakers usually use **O** /oʷ/.

zest /zɛst/ *n* [S;U] (a feeling of) eager excitement: *She entered into the work with zest/with a zest which surprised us all.*

zig·zag[1] /'zɪgzæg/ *n* a line shaped like a row of z's: *to go in a zigzag|a zigzag path*

zigzag[2] *v* **-gg-** [I] to go in a ZIGZAG[1]: *The path zigzags up the hill.*

zinc /zɪŋk/ [U] a bluish-white metal that is a simple substance (ELEMENT) used in the production of other metals

zip /zɪp/ *v* **-pp- 1** [T] to open or close with a ZIPPER: *He zipped the bag open/shut.* **2** [I] to make the sound of something moving quickly through the air: *The bullet zipped past my head.*

zip sbdy./sthg.↔**up** *v adv* [T] to fasten (a person into something) with a ZIPPER *Will you zip me up/zip up my dress?* –opposite **unzip**

zip·per /'zɪpər/ *AmE*‖**zip** *BrE– n* a fastener made of two sets of metal or plastic teeth and a sliding piece that draws them together, used esp. on clothes

zip code /'· ·/ *n AmE*‖**postcode** *BrE–* a group of numbers that can be added to the address on letters so that they may be delivered more quickly

zo·di·ac /'zoʷdiʸˌæk/ *n* **1** [*the* S] an imaginary belt through space along which the sun, the moon, and the nearest heavenly bodies (PLANETs) appear to travel and which is divided into 12 equal parts (SIGNs[1] (5)) **2** [C] a circular representation of this with pictures and names for each part (SIGN[1] (5)), esp. as used in ASTROLOGY by people who believe in the influence of the stars on one's character and fate

zone /zoʷn/ *n* a division or area marked off from others by particular qualities: *a war/danger zone|a US postal zone*

zoo /zuʷ/ *also* **zoological garden** /ˌ····· '··, ··ˌ··· '·–/ *n fml–* **zoos** a park where many kinds of living animals are kept for show

zo·ol·o·gy /zoʷɑlədʒiʸ/ *n* [U] the scientific study of animals, and of where and how they live –**zoological** /ˌzoʷə'lɑdʒɪkəl/ *adj* –**zoologist** /zoʷ'ɑlədʒɪst/ *n*

zoom[1] /zuʷm/ *v* [I] **1** (of an aircraft) to go quickly upwards **2** *infml* (of a driver or vehicle) to go quickly: *Jack went zooming past in his new car.* **3** [*in, out*] (of a movie camera) to move quickly between a distant and a close-up view: *The camera zoomed in on the child's face.*

zoom[2] *n* [S] (the deep low sound of) the upward flight of an aircraft

zuc·chi·ni /zuʷ'kiʸniʸ/ *n* **-ni** *or* **-nis** *AmE* a type of long round vegetable with a thin dark-green skin and soft light-green flesh eaten cooked as a vegetable

Word Building
and
List of Irregular Verbs

Word building

In English there are many word endings (SUFFIXES) and beginnings (PREFIXES) that can be added to a word to change its meaning or to make it into a different part of speech. The most common ones are shown in the tables here. Many more are listed on pages 784–789.

making verbs

The endings **-ize** and **-ify** can be added to many nouns and adjectives to make them into verbs, like this:

American		Americanize
modern	**-ize**	modernize
popular		popularize
legal		legalize

*We must make the factory more **modern**. We must **modernize** the factory.*

simple		simplify
pure	**-ify**	purify
liquid		liquefy
beauty		beautify

*The story is very **simple**. It has been **simplified**.*

making adverbs

The ending **-ly** can be added to very many adjectives in English to make them into adverbs, like this:

stupid		stupidly
quick	**-ly**	quickly
easy		easily
main		mainly

*His behavior was **stupid**. He behaved **stupidly**.*

making nouns

The endings **-er**, **-ment**, and **-ation** can be added to many verbs to make them into nouns, like this:

drive		driver
teach	**-er**	teacher
open		opener
fasten		fastener

*John **drives** a bus. He is a bus **driver**.*
*A can **opener** is a tool for **opening** cans.*

develop		development
amaze	**-ment**	amazement
pay		payment
retire		retirement

*Children **develop** very quickly. Their **development** is very quick.*

examine		examination
organize	**-ation**	organization
admire		admiration
associate		association

*The doctor **examined** me carefully. He gave me a careful **examination**.*

The endings **-ity** and **-ness** can be added to many adjectives to make them into nouns, like this:

stupid		stupidity
pure	**-ity**	purity
cruel	**-ty**	cruelty
odd		oddity

*Don't be so **cruel**. I hate **cruelty**.*

dark		darkness
deaf	**-ness**	deafness
kind		kindness
happy		happiness

*It's very **dark** in here; the **darkness** makes it impossible to see.*

making adjectives from nouns

The endings **-y**, **-ic**, **-ical**, **-ful**, and **-less** can be added to many nouns to make them into adjectives, like this:

dirt		dirty
hair	**-y**	hairy
smell		smelly
bush		bushy

There is a lot of **dirt** *in this room. The room is very* **dirty**.

atom		atomic
history	**-ic**	historical
poetry	**-ical**	poetic
economy		economic

The book was about the **economic** *situation in England. It was about England's* **economy**. (– see -ICAL (USAGE), page 787)

pain		painful (= causing pain)
hope	**-ful**	hopeful (= full of hope)
care		careful (= taking care)

His broken leg caused him a lot of **pain**. *It was very* **painful**.

pain		painless
hope	**-less**	hopeless
care		careless

The operation didn't cause him any **pain**. *It was* **painless**.

making adjectives from verbs

The ending **-able** can be added to many verbs to make them into adjectives, like this:

wash		washable
love	**-able**	lovable
debate		debatable
break		breakable

You can **wash** *this coat. It's* **washable**.

opposites

These PREFIXes can be added to the beginning of some words to change them to their opposites. Note that in some cases the meaning of the NEGATIVE form is not the exact opposite, it may have a slightly different meaning. Look up the words in the dictionary for all their different meanings.

	happy	unhappy
un-	fortunate	unfortunate
	wind	unwind
	block	unblock

I'm not very **happy**. *In fact I'm very* **unhappy**.

in-	efficient	inefficient
im-	possible	impossible
il-	literate	illiterate
ir-	regular	irregular

It's just not **possible** *to do that. It's* **impossible**.

	agree	disagree
dis-	approve	disapprove
	honest	dishonest

I don't **agree** *with everything you said; I* **disagree** *with the last part.*

	centralize	decentralize
de-	increase	decrease
	ascend	descend
	inflate	deflate

increase *means to make or become larger in amount or number.* **decrease** *means to make or become smaller in amount or number.*

	sense	nonsense
non-	payment	nonpayment
	resident	nonresident
	conformist	nonconformist

The hotel serves meals to **residents** (= people who are staying in the hotel) *only.* **Non-residents** *are not allowed in.*

Word building

Word beginnings

a-[1] /ə/ (*makes adjectives and adverbs*) **asleep** sleeping | **alive** living

a-[2] /e^y, æ, ə/ not: **atypical** not typical

aero- /'ɛərow, 'ɛərə/ relating to air: **aerodynamics** the study of forces on a body moving through air

Afro- /'æfrow/ relating to Africa: **Afro-Asian** relating to both Africa and Asia

ambi- /'æmbi^y, 'æmbɪ, æm'bɪ/ both; double: **ambivalent** having both POSITIVE and NEGATIVE feelings towards someone or something | **ambidextrous** able to use both hands equally well

Anglo- /'æŋglow, 'æŋglə/ relating to England: **Anglo-American** relating to both England and America

ante- /'æntɪ/ before: **antedate** to write a date on a letter, paper, etc. which comes before the real date –compare **post-**

anti- /'ænti^y, 'æntɪ, 'æntaɪ/ **1** having a feeling or opinion against: **antinuclear** opposing the use of nuclear weapons and power –compare **pro- 2** opposite to or of: **anticlimax** a much less satisfying end (CLIMAX) than expected | **antihero** the main character in a book or play who lacks the qualities of a typical hero **3** preventing or acting against: **antifreeze** a liquid put into water in a car to stop it from freezing

arch- /ɑrtʃ, ɑrk/ chief; first: **archbishop** a chief bishop

astro- /'æstrow, 'æstrə, ə'strɑ/ relating to the stars, planets, and space: **astronomy** the study of the planets and stars

audi-, audio-, /'ɔdi^y, 'ɔdə/ 'ɔdi^{y}ow/ relating to sound and hearing: **audiovisual** using or relating to both sound and sight

auto- /'ɔtow, 'ɔtə, ɔ'tɑ/ **1** self: **autobiography** a book about one's own life written by oneself **2** without help: **automatic** working by itself without human operation

be- /bɪ/ (*makes verbs*) to make; become; treat as: **belittle** to say that a person or thing is small or unimportant

bi- /baɪ/ two; twice: **biplane** a plane with two wings | **bilingual** able to speak two languages equally well | **biweekly** happening once every two weeks, or twice a week

bio- /'baɪow, baɪ'ɑ/ relating to life and living things: **biochemistry** the scientific study of the chemistry of living things | **biodegradable** able to be broken down into harmless products by the action of living things

by- /baɪ/ **1** less important: **by-product** something formed in addition to the main product **2** near: **bypass** a road near a city or town so

that drivers can go around it rather than through it

cent-, centi- /'sɛnt/ /'sɛntə/ 100; 100th: **Centigrade** a scale of temperature in which water boils at 100° | **centimeter** a measurement of length = 0.01 meters

co- /kow/ together; with: **co-worker** a person with whom one works

contra- /'kɑntrə/ opposite; against: **contradict** to say the opposite of (a statement, opinion, etc)

counter- /'kauntər/ opposite; against: **counter-revolution** a movement opposing a revolution | **counterattack** an attack opposing another attack

de- /di^y, dɪ/ the reverse or opposite of: **deemphasize** to make less important | **devalue** to make (the value of something such as a currency) less

deca-, dec- /'dɛkə/ /dɛk/ ten: **decade** a period of ten years

deci- /'dɛsə/ a tenth part: **deciliter** 0.1 liters

dis- /dɪs/ **1** the opposite of: **discontented** not happy; not contented | **disagree** to have a different opinion; not agree **2** to reverse; remove: **disconnect** to remove a connection of (something, esp. something electrical)

en-, em- /ɪn, ɛn/ /ɪm, ɛm/ (*makes verbs*) **1** to put in, on, or around: **encase** to cover completely (as) with a case | **enclose** to put a wall or fence around **2** to make; cause to be: **enlarge** to make larger | **empower** to give (someone) the right or power to do something

equi- /'i^{y}kwi^y, 'i^{y}kwə, ɪ'kwɪ/ equal: **equidistant** equally distant | **equivalent** (of amount, number, etc.) same; equal

Euro- /'yuərow, 'yuərə/ European: **Eurodollar** a US dollar held in Europe, esp. by a European bank, and used in international trade

ex- /ɛks/ no longer being; former: **ex-husband** a man who was a woman's husband, but who is now DIVORCED from her

extra- /'ɛkstrə/ beyond; outside: **extrasensory** beyond the five sense of sight, smell, sound, taste and touch

fore- /fɔr, fow^r/ **1** earlier; before: **foresee** to guess what is going to happen in the future **2** placed in front of; before; front part of: **forearm** the front part of the arm, below the elbow | **forefront** the most forward place

geo- /'dʒi^{y}ow, dʒi^y'ɑ/ relating to the earth: **geology** the study of the materials (soil, rocks, etc.) which make up the earth | **geography** the study of the seas, rivers, towns, etc., on the surface of the earth

hecto- /'hɛktoʷ, -tə/ 100: **hectoliter** 100 liters

hetero- /'hɛtəro, 'hɛtərə/ other; different: **heterogeneous** of (many) different kinds | **heterosexual** attracted to people of the opposite sex —compare **homo-**

homo- /'hoʷmoʷ, 'hoʷmə, 'hɑ-/ same; like: **homogeneous** formed of parts of the same kind | **homosexual** attracted to people of the same sex —compare **hetero-**

hyper- /'haɪpər/ above or too (much): **hypercritical** too critical

in- /ɪn/ **1** also **il-** /ɪl/, **im-** /ɪm/, **ir-** /ɪr/ not: **inexact** not exact **2** in; into; on: **inset** something put in as an addition into something else

USAGE **in-** meaning "not" usually changes to **il-** before *l*: **illegal** not legal; **im-** before *b*, *m*, or *p*: **imbalance** lack of balance | **immobile** not mobile | **impatient** not patient; **ir-** before *r*: **irregular** not regular or even; not usual

inter- /'ɪntər/ between; among: **international** having to do with more than one nation | **intermarriage** marriage between members of different groups, families, etc.

intra-, intro- /'ɪntrə/ /'ɪntroʷ, -trə/ inside: **introspection** looking into one's own thoughts and feelings | **intravenous** inside a VEIN

kilo- /'kɪloʷ, 'kɪlə/ 1,000: **kilogram** 1,000 grams; **kilometer** 1,000 meters

macro- /'mækroʷ, -rə/ large; great: **macroeconomics** the study of the economics of a country or countries

mal- /mæl/ bad; wrong: **malformation** the condition of being shaped wrongly **malfunction** a fault in the operation of a machine

mega- /'mɛgə/ million: **megawatt** 1,000,000 WATTS (units of electric power)

micro- /'maɪkroʷ, -rə/ **1** very small: **microcomputer** a very small computer **2** a millionth: **microsecond** a millionth (0.000 000 1) of a second

mid- /mɪd/ middle: **midpoint** a point at or near the center or middle | **midway** halfway or in a middle position

milli- /'mɪlə/ a thousandth: **milligram** 1,000th (=0.001) of a gram (a measurement of weight) | **millimeter** 1,000th (=0.001) of a meter (a measurement of length)

mis- /mɪs/ **1** bad; wrong: **misspelling** a wrong spelling | **misjudge** to have a wrong opinion of **2** the opposite of: **mistrust** not to trust

mono- /'mɑnoʷ, 'mɑnə, mə'nɑ/ one; single: **monorail** a railway with only one rail | **monopoly** a situation where only one person or group sells a particular thing, produces something, etc. | **monosyllabic** (of a word) having one syllable

multi- /'mʌltiʸ, -tɪ, -tə/ many; more than one: **multi-colored** having many colors | **multistory** (of a building) having many levels or floors

neo- /'niʸoʷ, 'nɪʸə/ new; a later kind of: **neoclassical** a new or later kind of classical style: *the neoclassical architecture of America*

non- /nɑn/ not: **nonstop** without stopping before the end | **nonpayment** not having

paid: *He is in trouble for nonpayment of his taxes.*

out- /aʊt/ **1** outside: **outdoors** in the open air **2** more than; beyond: **outgrow** to grow too big for: *The girl has outgrown her clothes.*

over- /'oʷvər/ **1** too much: **overexcited** too excited | **overpopulation** the condition of having too many people (in a country) **2** across; above: **overland** across or by land

photo- /'foʷtoʷ, 'foʷtə/ **1** light: **photoelectric cell** an instrument which starts an electrical apparatus working by means of light **2** photography: **photocopy** (to make) an exact copy of (a letter, drawing, etc.) using a special machine

post- /poʷst/ after; later than: **postwar** belonging to the time after a war | **postdoctoral** relating to university study done after receiving a DOCTORAL degree

pre- /priʸ/ before: **prewar** before a war | **preschool** relating to children who are too young to go to school

pro- /proʷ/ in favor of: **pro-education** in favor of education —compare **anti-**

pseudo- /'suʷdoʷ, -də/ not real; false: **pseudonym** a false name, used esp. by a writer of books | **pseudomodern** seeming to be (but not) modern

psych-, psycho- /saɪk/ /'saɪkoʷ, -kə/ relating to the mind: **psychotherapy** the treatment of disorders of the mind | **psychology** the study of the mind and of behavior

quadr-, quadri- /kwɑdr/ /'kwɑdrə/ four: **quadrilateral** (a figure) with four sides

quasi- /'kweʸzaɪ, 'kwɑziʸ/ seeming or like: **quasiscientific** seeming to be scientific

quin- /kwɪn/ five: **quintet** (music for) five players or singers together

re- /riʸ, rɪ/ again: **remake** to make (esp. a film) again | **rethink** to think about again

USAGE When **re-** means "again", it is pronounced /riʸ/. In other words beginning with **re-**, it is usually pronounced /rɪ/ (or /riʸ/ before a vowel). Compare **recover** (–to get better) /rɪ'kʌvər/ and **re-cover** (–to cover again) /ˌriʸ'kʌvər/

self- /sɛlf/ of or by oneself, independent: **self-explanatory** that explains itself | **self-control** control of oneself | **self-employed** working for oneself

semi- /'sɛmiʸ, 'sɛmaɪ/ **1** half: **semicircle** half a circle **2** partly: **semisolid** partly solid and partly liquid | a **semi-detached** *house* a house partly joined to another house by one shared wall

sub- /sʌb/ **1** under: **submarine** a ship which can travel under water **2** a smaller part of: **subregion** a small part of a region **3** less than: **subhuman** having less than human qualities

super- /'suʷpər/ greater or more than: **supersonic** faster than the speed of sound | **superstar** a very famous and popular performer

tele- /'tɛlə/ at or over a long distance: **telescope** an instrument for looking at objects that are far away | **telephone** an electrical apparatus for talking to other people a long distance away

thermo- /'θɜrmoʷ, θər'ma/ heat: **thermometer** an instrument for measuring temperature | **thermodynamics** the study of the relationship between heat and mechanical energy

trans- /træns, trænz/ **1** across; on the other side of: **transatlantic** crossing, on the other side of, or concerning countries on both sides of the Atlantic **2** change: **transform** to change completely in form, appearance, or nature

tri- /traɪ/ three: **triangle** a flat figure with three straight sides

ultra- /'ʌltrə/ **1** beyond: **ultrasonic** (of sound waves) beyond the range of human hearing **2**

very; excessively: **ultramodern** very modern | **ultramarine** a very bright blue color

un- /ʌn/ **1** (*makes adjectives and adverbs*) not: **uncomfortable** not comfortable | **unhappy** not happy | **unwashed** not washed **2** (*makes verbs*) to make the opposite of; reverse: **undress** to take one's clothes off | **unlock** to unfasten the lock of | **untie** to undo (a knot or something tied)

vice- /vaɪs/ next in rank or importance: **vice-president** the person next in official rank below a president: *the Vice-President of the United States*

Word endings

-ability, **-ibility** /ə'bɪlətiʸ/ (*makes nouns from adjectives ending in* **-able**, **-ible**) **flexibility** the quality of being flexible (= easy to bend or change) | **reliability** the quality of being reliable; able to be trusted

-able, **-ible** /əbəl/ (*makes adjectives*) **1** able to be …ed: **washable** able to be washed | **drinkable** that can be drunk **2** showing or having: **knowledgeable** having a good deal of knowledge | **reasonable** showing or having reason or good sense

-age /ɪdʒ/ (*makes nouns*) **baggage** all the bags and containers with which a person travels | **storage** a place for storing goods | **passage** the action of going across, by, over, etc.

-al, **-ial** /əl/ /iʸəl, yəl, əl/ **1** (*makes adjectives*) **political** of or concerning politics | **manorial** of or belonging to a manor **2** (*makes nouns*) **arrival** the act of arriving | **refusal** the act of refusing

-an, **-ian**, **-ean** /ən/ /iʸən, yən, ən/ **1** (*makes adjectives and nouns from names of places or people*) **American** a person belonging to or connected with America | **Christian** a person who believes in the teachings of Jesus Christ **2** (*makes adjectives*) **Dickensian** of or like Dickens or his books **3** (*makes nouns from words ending in* **-ic**, **-ics**, *and* **-y**) **historian** a person who studies and/or writes about history

-ance, **-ence** /əns/ (*makes nouns*) **1** importance the quality or state of being important | **patience** the quality of being patient **2** an example of: **performance** an act of PERFORMing in a play, film, etc.

-ant, **-ent** /ənt/ **1** (*makes adjectives*) **pleasant** pleasing to the senses, feelings, or mind | **different** unlike; not of the same kind **2** (*makes nouns*) **servant** a person who works for another in the other's house | **student** a

person who is studying at a school, college, etc. | **disinfectant** a chemical used to DISINFECT | **deodorant** a substance that removes unpleasant smells (ODORs)

-ar /ər/ **1** (*makes nouns*) see **-ER²** **2** (*makes adjectives*) **muscular** having big muscles; strong-looking

-arian /'ɛəriʸən/ (*makes nouns and adjectives*) **vegetarian** someone who does not eat meat or fish | **librarian** a person who is in charge of or helps to run a library

-ary /ɛriʸ, əriʸ/ **1** (*makes nouns*) a person or thing connected with or a place for: **library** a building or room which contains books that can be read and usually borrowed **2** (*makes adjectives*) **customary** established by custom; usual

-ate /ɪt, eʸt *for adj and n*; eʸt *for v*/ **1** (*makes adjectives*) showing; full of: **considerate** showing consideration for **2** (*makes verbs*) to act as; cause to become: **activate** to cause to be active | **regulate** to bring order or method to; make REGULAR **3** (*makes nouns*) a group of people: **electorate** all the people in a place or country who can vote

-ation /'eʸʃən/ (*makes nouns*) **declaration** an act of declaring | **hesitation** an act of hesitating (= pausing in or before an action) | **exploration** the act or an action of exploring (EXPLORE) (= to travel to a place for the purpose of discovery)

-ative /ətɪv, eʸtɪv/ (*makes adjectives*) **imaginative** using or having imagination | **talkative** liking to talk a lot

-ator /eʸtər/ (*makes nouns*) a person or thing that does something: **narrator** a person who NARRATES | **generator** a machine which makes energy, usu. electricity

-cide /saɪd/ (*makes nouns*) kill: **suicide** the act of killing oneself | **insecticide** a chemical substance made to kill insects

-cracy /krəsiʸ/ (*makes nouns*) a government or class characterized by …: **democracy** a government that is DEMOCRATIC; government

787

by elected representatives of the people

-cy /siʸ/ (*makes nouns*) **accuracy** the quality of being ACCURATE (= exact and correct)

-d /d, ɪd, t / see -ED

-dom /dəm/ (*makes nouns*) **1** the state of being (something): **boredom** the state of being BORED (= uninterested because of something dull) **2 kingdom** the country rules by a king or queen: *the United Kingdom*

-ean /iʸən, yən, ən/ see -AN

-ed, -d /d /d, ɪd, t/ **1** (*makes regular past tenses and past participles*) *we* **laughed** | *I have* **waited** | *a man* **wanted** *by the police* **2** (*makes adjectives*) *a* **bearded** *man* (= a man with a beard) | *a long-***tailed** *cat*

-ee /iʸ/ (*makes nouns*) **1** somebody to whom something is done: **employee** a person who is employed | **trainee** a person who is being trained | **refugee** a person who has been driven from his/her country **2** somebody who is or does something: **absentee** a person who is absent from work, etc.

-eer /ɪər/ (*makes nouns*) a person who does an activity: **mountaineer** a person who climbs mountains | **profiteer** someone who makes large profits in times of war or difficulty

-en /ən/ **1** (*makes adjectives*) made of: **golden** of or like gold | **wooden** made of wood **2** (*makes verbs*) to cause to be or to have: **darken** to make or become dark: *The sky darkened after sunset.* | **soften** to make or become soft

-ent /ənt/ see -ANT

-er¹, -r /ər/ (*makes the comparative of short adjectives and adverbs*) **hotter** more hot | **safer** more safe –see Study Notes on page 135

-er², -ar, -or, -r /ər/ (*makes nouns*) **1** a person who does an activity: **baseball player** a person who plays baseball | **teacher** a person who teaches | **liar** a person who tells lies | **actor** a person who acts | **writer** a person who writes **2** a person who lives in (a place): **New Yorker** a person who lives in New York | **villager** a person who lives in a village **3** a thing that: **broiler** an apparatus on which food is cooked under direct heat | **heater** a machine for heating air, water, etc.

-ery, -ry /əriʸ/ (*makes nouns*) **1** the art of or quality of: **cookery** the art of cooking | **bravery** the quality of being brave **2** a place where something is done: **bakery** a place where bread is baked and/or sold

-es /z, s, ɪz/ see -S

-ese /iʸz, iʸs/ (*makes adjectives and nouns*) relating to a country, its language or people, or a style: **Japanese** of or relating to the people, language, or country of Japan | **journalese** in the style of the language used in newspapers

-esque /ɛsk/ having a manner or style like: **picturesque** looking like a picture: *a picturesque old village*

-ess /ɪs/ female: **actress** a woman who acts in plays and films | **lioness** a female lion

-est, -st /ɪst/ (*makes the superlative of many short adjectives and adverbs*) **highest** the most high: *Mount Everest is the highest*

mountain in the world. | **hottest** the most hot: *the hottest day of the year* –see Study Notes on page 135

-ette /ɛt/ (*makes nouns*) small: **kitchenette** a small kitchen

-fold /fowld/ (*makes adjectives*) times; multiplied by: **fourfold** four times (an amount)

-ful¹ /fəl/ (*makes adjectives*) **delightful** causing delight; highly pleasing | **painful** causing pain

-ful² /fʊl/ (*makes nouns*) the amount that a container holds: **cupful** the amount held by a cup | **spoonful** the amount held by a spoon

-fy /faɪ/ see -IFY

-hood /hʊd/ (*makes nouns*) the state or period of being: **childhood** the time or condition of being a child | **womanhood** the state or period of being a woman

-ial /iʸəl, yəl, əl/ see -AL

-ian /iʸən, yən, ən/ see -AN

-ibility /əˈbɪləṭiʸ/ see -ABILITY

-ible /əbəl/ see -ABLE

-ic /ɪk/ (*makes adjectives*) **poetic** of, like, or connected with poets or poetry –see -ICAL (USAGE)

-ical /ɪkəl/ (*makes adjectives*) connected with: **historical** connected with history

USAGE Some pairs of words ending in -ic and -ical have different meanings. For example, **historic** means 'having a long history' or 'being remembered in history,' but **historical** means 'something that happened in the past' or 'relating to the study of history.'

-ics /ɪks/ (*makes nouns*) a science or particular activity: **economics** the scientific study of the way industry and trade produce and use wealth | **athletics** the sport of exercising the body by running, jumping, etc.

-ie /iʸ/ see Y (2)

-ify, -fy /əˌfaɪ/ /faɪ/ (*makes verbs*) to make or become: **purify** to make pure | **simplify** to make simple | **clarify** to make clearer or easier to understand

-ing /ɪŋ/ **1** (*makes the present participle of verbs*) *she's* **sleeping** | *I'm* **waiting** *for you.* **2** (*makes nouns from verbs*) **Running** *keeps you healthy.* | *a* **sleeping** *pill* (= a pill to make a person sleep) | *a beautiful* **painting** | **Painting** *is fun.*

-ise /aɪz/ see -IZE

-ish /ɪʃ/ (*makes adjectives*) **1** relating to a country, its language, or people: **British** of Britain | **Swedish** of Sweden **2** like; typical of: **childish** (*often derog*) of or typical of a child | **foolish** like a fool; without good sense; stupid | **3** rather: **reddish** slightly red | **smallish** rather small **4** approximately: **fortyish** about forty | **sixish** at about 6 o'clock

-ism /ɪzəm/ (*makes nouns*) **1** the ideas, principles, or teaching of: **socialism** a belief in equality and in public ownership | **Buddhism** a religion of east and central Asia, based on the teachings of the Buddha **2** a practice or activity: **terrorism** the practice of using violence to obtain political demands **3** a quality or characteristic: **heroism** the quality of being a HERO (= someone who acts with great courage)

-ist /ɪst/ **1** (*makes nouns and adjectives*) a follower of a movement: **socialist** a person who believes in SOCIALISM **2** (*makes nouns*) someone who studies, produces, plays, or operates: **guitarist** someone who plays the guitar | **pianist** someone who plays the piano | **machinist** a person who operates a machine | **linguist** someone who studies language | **novelist** someone who writes NOVELS

-ite /aɪt/ (*makes nouns and adjectives*) **1** a follower of a movement: **Trotskyite** a supporter of Trotsky's ideas **2** someone who lives in (the stated place) **Brooklynite** a person who lives in Brooklyn

-ity, -ty /ətiʸ/ /tiʸ/ (*makes nouns*) the quality or an example of: *It was an act of* **stupidity** *to drive so fast.* | **cruelty** *to animals*

-ive /ɪv/ (*makes adjectives*) having a tendency, character, or quality: **creative** creating new ideas and things | **descriptive** that describes | **explosive** that can explode

-ize, -ise /aɪz/ (*makes verbs*) **popularize** to make popular | **legalize** to make legal | **criticize** to find fault with; judge severely

USAGE Both **-ize** and **-ise** are used in British English, but only **-ize** is generally used in American English.

-less /lɪs/ (*makes adjectives*) **1** without: **hopeless** without hope | **painless** causing no pain | **careless** without taking care | **powerless** without power or strength **2** that never . . .s; that cannot be . . .ed: **tireless** never getting tired | **countless** that cannot be counted

-let /lɪt/ (*makes nouns*) small: **booklet** a small book, usually with paper covers | **piglet** a young pig

-like /laɪk/ (*makes adjectives*) like or similar to: **childlike** of or typical of a child

-logy, -ology /lədʒiʸ/ 'alədʒiʸ/ (*makes nouns*) the science or study of: **geology** the study of the materials which make up the earth | **sociology** the scientific study of societies and human groups

-ly /liʸ/ **1** (*makes adverbs from adjectives*) *Please drive* **carefully.** | *The man was walking very* **slowly. 2** (*makes adjectives and adverbs*) happening regularly: **hourly** happening every hour | **daily** happening each day **3** (*makes adjectives*) having the manner of: **motherly** having or showing the love, kindness, etc., of a mother **4** (*makes adverbs*) from a particular point of view: *Some people didn't like the film, but* **personally** *I thought it was very good.*

-ment /mənt/ (*makes nouns from verbs*) **1** the act or result of: **government** the act or method of ruling a country | **encirclement** the action or result of making a circle around something | **development** the action or result of developing **2** the condition of: **confinement** the state of being CONFINED (enclosed within limits); the time during which a woman about to give birth has to stay in bed

-most /moʷst/ (*makes the superlative of some adjectives and adverbs*) most: **topmost** nearest the top | **northernmost** nearest the north

-ness /nɪs/ (*makes nouns*) **goodness** the quality of being good | **loudness** the quality of being loud

-ology /'alədʒiʸ/ see -LOGY

-or /ər/ see -ER

-ory /ˌɔriʸ, oʷriʸ, əriʸ/ **1** (*makes adjectives*) **satisfactory** causing SATISFACTION; good enough **2** (*makes nouns*) place or thing used for: **observatory** a place where scientists look at stars, etc.

-ous /əs/ (*makes adjectives*) **dangerous** able to or likely to cause danger | **spacious** having a lot of space

-phile /faɪl/ (*makes nouns*) a person who is attracted to: **Anglophile** a person who likes England

-philia /'fɪliʸə, 'fiʸlyə/ (*makes nouns*) love of: **Anglophilia** a love of England –compare **-phobia**

-phobia /'foʷbiʸə/ (*makes nouns*) very strong fear or dislike: **Anglophobia** a dislike of England | **claustrophobia** a fear of being in a closed space –compare **-philia**

-ry /riʸ/ see -ERY

-s, -es /z, s, ɪz/ **1** (*makes the plural of nouns*) *one* **cat**, *three* **cats** | *one* **glass**, *two* **glasses 2** (*makes the third person singular of the present tense of verbs*) *she* **sings** | *He* **likes** *reading.* | *He* **watches** *television.*

-ship /ʃɪp/ (*makes nouns*) **1** the state or condition of having or being: **friendship**: *the condition of having a friendly relationship* | **partnership**: *the state of being a partner, esp. in business.* **2** skill; craft: **scholarship** the knowledge, work or method of SCHOLARS | **workmanship** skill in making things | **musicianship** skill in performing or judging music

-some /səm/ **1** (*makes nouns*) **twosome** a group of two people or things **2** (*makes adjectives*) causing; producing: **fearsome** causing fear | **troublesome** causing trouble

-ster /stər/ (*makes nouns*) a person who does an activity or who is of a certain group: **youngster** a young person

-th /θ/ (*makes adjectives from numbers, except for those ending in 1, 2, or 3*) **sixth** | **hundredth** | **fortieth**

-ty /tiʸ/ see -ITY

-ule /yuʷl/ a small kind of: **globule** a drop of liquid

-ure /yər, ər/ (*makes nouns from verbs*) **closure** the act of closing | **failure** lack of success; failing

-ward, -wards /wərd/ /wərdz/ (*makes adjectives and adverbs*) in the direction of: **backward** directed toward the back, the beginning, or the past | **homeward** going toward home

-ware /wɛər/ (*makes nouns*): **hardware** metal goods for the home and garden, such as pans, tools, etc. | **ironware** goods made from iron

-ways /weʸz/ see -WISE

-wise, -ways /waɪz, weʸz/ **1** (*makes adjectives and adverbs*) in the manner or direction

of: **lengthways** in the direction of the length |
clockwise in the direction in which the hands
of a clock move **2** (*often infml*) (*makes adverbs*) with regard to: **moneywise** with regard
to money: *I'm having a lot of problems
moneywise.*

-y /iʸ/ **1** (*makes nouns*) **jealousy** a JEALOUS

feeling | **sympathy** pity for the suffering of
another **2** also **-ie** – (*infml*) (*makes nouns*)
names for people: **granny** grandmother |
Jamie James **3** (*makes nouns*) names for animals, used esp. by small children: **doggy** dog
4 (*makes adjectives*) **noisy** making a lot of
noise | **sunny** having bright sunlight

List of irregular verbs

The list below shows those verbs that have irregular past tense, PAST PARTICIPLE, or PRESENT PARTICIPLE forms. (–see Dictionary Skills Workbook page 000)

The INFINITIVE form is shown first, e.g. **begin**
2 = past tense, e.g. *As I was walking home it* **began** *to rain.*
3 = past participle, e.g. *It* **had** *already* **begun** *to rain before I left home.*
4 = present participle, e.g. *It is* *just* **beginning** *to rain now.*
The number 2/3 means that the past tense and past participle are the same form. The pronunciation of each form is shown at its own place in the dictionary.

abide 2/3 abode *or* abided 4 abiding
arise 2 arose 3 arisen 4 arising
awake 2 awoke *or* awaked 3 awaked *or* awoken
  4 awaking
be –see BE
bear 2 bore 3 borne 4 bearing
beat 2 beat 3 beaten *or* beat 4 beating
become 2 became 3 become 4 becoming
befall 2 befell 3 befallen 4 befalling
begin 2 began 3 begun 4 beginning
behold 2/3 beheld 4 beholding
bend 2/3 bent 4 bending
bereave 2/3 bereaved *or* bereft 4 bereaving
beseech 2/3 besought *or* beseeched 4 beseeching
beset 2/3 beset 4 besetting
bet 2/3 bet *or* betted 4 betting
bid[1] 2/3 bid 4 bidding
bid[3] 2 bade *or* bid 3 bidden *or* bid 4 bidding
bide 2/3 bided *or* bode 4 biding
bind 2/3 bound 4 binding
bite 2 bit 3 bitten 4 biting
bleed 2/3 bled 4 bleeding
bless 2/3 blessed *or* blest 4 blessing
blow 2 blew 3 blown 4 blowing
break 2 broke 3 broken 4 breaking
breed 2/3 bred 4 breeding
bring 2/3 brought 4 bringing
broadcast 2/3 broadcast ‖ *also* broadcasted *AmE*
  4 broadcasting
build 2/3 built 4 building
burn 2/3 burned *or* burnt 4 burning
burst 2/3 burst 4 bursting
buy 2/3 bought 4 buying
cast 2/3 cast 4 casting
catch 2/3 caught 4 catching
chide 2 chided *or* chid
  3 chided *or* chid *or* chidden 4 chiding
choose 2 chose 3 chosen 4 choosing
cleave 2 cleaved *or* cleft *or* clove
  3 cleaved *or* cleft *or* cloven 4 cleaving
cling 2/3 clung 4 clinging
clothe 2/3 clothed *or* clad 4 clothing
come 2 came 3 come 4 coming
cost 2/3 cost 4 costing
creep 2/3 crept 4 creeping
cut 2/3 cut 4 cutting
dare 2/3 dared 4 daring
deal 2/3 dealt 4 dealing
dig 2/3 dug 4 digging
dive 2 dived ‖ *also* dove *AmE* 3 dived 4 diving
do –see DO
draw 2 drew 3 drawn 4 drawing
dream 2/3 dreamed *or* dreamt 4 dreaming
drink 2 drank 3 drunk 4 drinking
drive 2 drove 3 driven 4 driving
dwell 2/3 dwelt *or* dwelled 4 dwelling
eat 2 ate 3 eaten 4 eating
fall 2 fell 3 fallen 4 falling
feed 2/3 fed 4 feeding
feel 2/3 felt 4 feeling

fight 2/3 fought 4 fighting
find 2/3 found 4 finding
flee 2/3 fled 4 fleeing
fling 2/3 flung 4 flinging
fly 2 flew 3 flown 4 flying
forbear 2 forbore 3 forborne 4 forbearing
forbid 2 forbade *or* forbad 3 forbidden *or* forbid
  4 forbidding
forecast 2/3 forecast *or* forecasted 4 forecasting
foresee 2/3 foresaw 4 foreseeing
foretell 2/3 foretold 4 foretelling
forget 2 forgot 3 forgotten 4 forgetting
forgive 2 forgave 3 forgiven 4 forgiving
forsake 2 forsook 3 forsaken 4 forsaking
forswear 2 forswore 3 forsworn 4 forswearing
freeze 2 froze 3 frozen 4 freezing
get 2 got 3 got *esp. BrE* ‖ gotten *AmE*
  4 getting –see GET (USAGE)
gild 2/3 gilden *or* gilt 4 gilding
give 2 gave 3 given 4 giving
go 2 went 3 gone 4 going
grind 2/3 ground 4 grinding
hang[1] 2/3 hung 4 hanging
hang[2] 2/3 hanged 4 hanging
have –see HAVE
hear 2/3 heard 4 hearing
heave 2/3 heaved 4 heaving
heave 2 hove 4 heaving
hew 2 hewed 3 hewn *or* hewed 4 hewing
hide 2 hid 3 hidden *or* hid 4 hiding
hit 2/3 hit 4 hitting
hold 2/3 held 4 holding
hurt 2/3 hurt 4 hurting
keep 2/3 kept 4 keeping
kneel 2/3 knelt *or* kneeled 4 kneeling
knit 2/3 knit *or* knitted 4 knitting
know 2 knew 3 known 4 knowing
lay 2/3 laid 4 laying
lead 2/3 led 4 leading
lean 2/3 leaned *esp. AmE* ‖ leant *esp. BrE*
  4 leaning
leap 2/3 leaped *esp. AmE* ‖ leapt *esp. BrE*
  4 leaping
learn 2/3 learned *or* learnt 4 learning
leave 2/3 left 4 leaving
lend 2/3 lent 4 lending
let 2/3 let 4 letting
lie 2 lay 3 lain 4 lying
light 2/3 lighted *or* lit 4 lighting
lose 2/3 lost 4 losing
make 2/3 made 4 making
mean 2/3 meant 4 meaning
meet 2/3 met 4 meeting
mislay 2/3 mislaid 4 mislaying
mislead 2/3 misled 4 misleading
misspell 2/3 misspelled *or* misspelt 4 misspelling
misspend 2/3 misspent 4 misspending
mistake 2 mistook 3 mistaken 4 mistaking
misunderstand 2/3 misunderstood
  4 misunderstanding

outbid 2 outbid 3 outbid ‖ *also* outbidden *AmE*
   4 outbidding
outdo 2 outdid 3 outdone 4 outdoing
outshine 2/3 outshone 4 outshining
overcome 2 overcame 3 overcome
   4 overcoming
overdo 2 overdid 3 overdone 4 overdoing
overhang 2/3 overhung 4 overhanging
overhear 2/3 overheard 4 overhearing
override 2 overrode 3 overridden 4 overriding
overrun 2 overran 3 overrun 4 overrunning
oversee 2 oversaw 3 overseen 4 overseeing
overshoot 2/3 overshot 4 overshooting
oversleep 2/3 overslept 4 oversleeping
overtake 2 overtook 3 overtaken
   4 overtaking
overthrow 2 overthrew 3 overthrown
   4 overthrowing
partake 2 partook 3 partaken 4 partaking
pay 2/3 paid 4 paying
prove 2/3 proved ‖ *also* proven *esp. AmE*
   4 proving
read 2/3 read 4 reading
rebuild 2/3 rebuilt 4 rebuilding
redo 2 redid 3 redone 4 redoing
relay 2/3 relayed 4 relaying
remake 2/3 remade 4 remaking
rend 2/3 rent ‖ *also* rended *AmE* 4 rending
repay 2/3 repaid 4 repaying
rewrite 2 rewrote 3 rewritten 4 rewriting
rid 2 rid *or* ridded 3 rid 4 ridding
ride 2 rode 3 ridden 4 riding
ring² 2/3 ringed 4 ringing
ring³ 2 rang 3 rung 4 ringing
rise 2 rose 3 risen 4 rising
run 2 ran 3 run 4 running
saw 2 sawed 3 sawn ‖ *also* sawed *AmE*
   4 sawing
say 2/3 said 4 saying
see 2 saw 3 seen 4 seeing
seek 2/3 sought 4 seeking
sell 2/3 sold 4 selling
send 2/3 sent 4 sending
set 2/3 set 4 setting
sew 2 sewed 3 sewn ‖ *also* sewed *AmE*
   4 sewing
shake 2 shook 3 shaken 4 shaking
shave 2 shaved 3 shaved *or* shaven 4 shaving
shear 2 sheared 3 sheared *or* shorn 4 shearing
shed 2/3 shed 4 shedding
shine¹ 2/3 shone 4 shining
shine² 2/3 shined 4 shining
shoot 2/3 shot 4 shooting
show 2 showed 3 shown ‖ *also* showed *AmE*
   4 showing
shrink 2 shrank *or* shrunk 3 shrunk *or* shrunken
   4 shrinking
shut 2/3 shut 4 shutting
sing 2 sang 3 sung 4 singing
sink 2 sank ‖ *also* sunk *AmE*
   3 sunk ‖ *also* sunken *AmE* 4 sinking
sit 2/3 sat 4 sitting
slay 2 slew 3 slain 4 slaying
sleep 2/3 slept 4 sleeping
slide 2/3 slid 4 sliding
sling 2/3 slung 4 slinging
slink 2/3 slunk 4 slinking
slit 2/3 slit 4 slitting
smell 2/3 smelled *esp. AmE* ‖ smelt *esp. BrE*
   4 smelling
smite 2 smote 3 smitten *or* smote 4 smiting
sow 2 sowed 3 sown *or* sowed 4 sowing
speak 2 spoke 3 spoken 4 speaking
speed 2/3 sped ‖ *also* speeded *AmE* 4 speeding
spell 2/3 spelled *esp. AmE* ‖ spelt *esp. BrE*
   4 spelling
spend 2/3 spent 4 spending

spill 2/3 spilled *or* spilt 4 spilling
spin 2/3 spun 4 spinning
spit 2/3 spit *AmE* ‖ *also* spat 4 spitting
split 2/3 split 4 splitting
spoil 2/3 spoiled *or* spoilt 4 spoiling
spread 2/3 spread 4 spreading
spring 2 sprang ‖ *also* sprung *AmE* 3 sprung
   4 springing
stand 2/3 stood 4 standing
steal 2 stole 3 stolen 4 stealing
stick 2/3 stuck 4 sticking
sting 2/3 stung 4 stinging
stink 2 stank *or* stunk 3 stunk 4 stinking
strew 2 strewed 3 strewn *or* strewed
   4 strewing
stride 2 strode 3 stridden 4 striding
strike 2 struck 3 struck ‖ *also* stricken *AmE*
   4 striking
string 2/3 strung 4 stringing
strive 2 strove 3 striven ‖ *also* strived *AmE*
   4 striving
swear 2/3 swore 4 swearing
sweep 2/3 swept 4 sweeping
swell 2/3 swelled *or* swollen 4 swelling
swim 2 swam 3 swum 4 swimming
swing 2/3 swung 4 swinging
take 2 took 3 taken 4 taking
teach 2/3 taught 4 teaching
tear 2 tore 3 torn 4 tearing
tell 2/3 told 4 telling
think 2/3 thought 4 thinking
thrive 2 throve *or* thrived 3 thrived *or* thriven
   4 thriving
throw 2 threw 3 thrown 4 throwing
thrust 2/3 thrust 4 thrusting
tread 2 trod 3 trodden *or* trod 4 treading
unbend 2/3 unbent 4 unbending
undergo 2 underwent 3 undergone
   4 undergoing
understand 2/3 understood 4 understanding
undertake 2 undertook 3 undertaken
   4 undertaking
undo 2 undid 3 undone 4 undoing
unwind 2/3 unwound 4 unwinding
uphold 2/3 upheld 4 upholding
upset 2/3 upset 4 upsetting
wake 2 woke *or* waked 3 waked *or* woken
   4 waking
waylay 2/3 waylaid 4 waylaying
wear 2 wore 3 worn 4 wearing
weave 2 wove 3 woven 4 weaving
weave 2/3 weaved 4 weaving
wed 2/3 wedded *or* wed 4 wedding
weep 2/3 wept 4 weeping
wet 2/3 wetted *or* wet 4 wetting
win 2/3 won 4 winning
wind² 2/3 winded 4 winding
wind³ 2/3 wound 4 winding
withdraw 2 withdrew 3 withdrawn
   4 withdrawing
withhold 2/3 withheld 4 withholding
withstand 2/3 withstood 4 withstanding
wring 2/3 wrung 4 wringing
write 2 wrote 3 written 4 writing

Pronunciation

American English This Dictionary shows pronunciations used by speakers of the most common American English dialects. Sometimes more than one pronunciation is shown. For example, many Americans say *wh* in *which* as /hw/, while many others say this *wh* as /w/, pronouncing *which* and *witch* the same way: /wɪtʃ/. We show *which* as /hwɪtʃ, wɪtʃ/. This indicates that both pronunciations are possible. We have not, however, shown all American dialects. For example, some Americans do not use the sound /ɔ/ in many of the places we have shown it. These speakers say /ɑ/ in those places instead of /ɔ/, so that *caught* and *cot* are both said as /kɑt/.

Use of the hyphen When more than one pronunciation is given for a word, we usually show only the part of the pronunciation that differs from the first pronunciation, replacing the parts that are the same with a hyphen: **economics** /ˌɛkə'nɑmɪks, ˌiʸ-/.

Symbols The symbols used in this Dictionary are based on the symbols of the International Phonetic Alphabet (IPA) with a few modifications: /iʸ/, /eʸ/, /oʷ/, /uʷ/, and /y/.

The symbols /iʸ/, /eʸ/, /oʷ/, and /uʷ/ are used to help show how the sounds are said. In English these vowels tend to be longer than in many languages. They begin with the "pure" vowel sound /i/, /e/, /o/, or /u/ and end in a short "glide" sound, in which the tongue moves in the direction of /y/ or /w/. We show this glide as /ʸ/ or /ʷ/. These glides are usually stronger if the vowel is stressed, as in **see** /siʸ/, than if it is not, as in **many** /'mɛniʸ/.

The symbol /y/, which is closer to English spelling than the /j/ used in IPA, is used for the first sound in *you*: /yuʷ/.

Foreign words English pronunciations have been shown for foreign words, even though some speakers may use a pronunciation closer to that of the original language. The English pronunciations, however, sometimes include sounds that do not normally occur in English, such as /x/ and nasalized vowels: **chutzpah** /'hʊtspə, 'xʊt-/ **croissant** /kwa'sant, krwa'sɑ̃/.

Abbreviations No pronunciations are shown for most abbreviations, either because they are not spoken (these are labeled *written abbrev.*) or because they are pronounced by saying the names of the letters, with main stress on the last letter and secondary stress on the first: **CPA** /ˌsiʸ piʸ 'eʸ/. Pronunciations have been shown where an abbreviation is spoken like an ordinary word: **NATO** /'neʸt̬oʷ/, or where an abbreviation looks as if it might be pronounced like an ordinary word, but is not: **AD** /ˌeʸ 'diʸ/ (not like **ad** /æd/).

Words derived from main words A form of a main word may come at the end of the entry for that word. If the derived word is pronounced by saying the main word and adding an ending (see list on page 786), no separate pronunciation is given. If the addition of the ending causes a change in the pronunciation of the main word, the pronunciation for the related word is given. For example: **anticlimax** /ˌænti'klaɪmæks/ **anticlimactic** /ˌæntɪklɪ'mæktɪk/.

There are a few pronunciation changes that we do not show at these entries: (1) When an *-ly* or *-er* ending is added to a main word ending in /-bəl/ /-kəl/, /-pəl/, /-gəl/, or /-dəl/, the /ə/ is usually omitted. For example, *reliable* is shown as /rɪ'laɪəbəl/.

When *-ly* is added to it, it becomes /rɪ'laɪəbliʸ/. This difference is not shown. (2) When *-ly* or *-ity* is added to words ending in *-y* /iʸ/, the /iʸ/ becomes /ə/: **angry** /'æŋgriʸ/ becomes **angrily** /'æŋgrəliʸ/. This is not shown.

Stress In English words of two or more syllables, at least one syllable is said with more force than the others. The sign /'/ is placed before the syllable with the most force. We say it has *main stress*: **paper** /'peʸpər/ **article** /'ɑrtɪkəl/. Some words also have *secondary stress* (less strong than main stress) on another syllable. The sign /ˌ/ is placed before such a syllable: **information** /ˌɪnfər'meʸʃən/ **motorcycle** /'moʷt̬ər,saɪkəl/.

Compound words with a space or hyphen Many compounds are written with either a space or a hyphen between the parts. When all parts of the compound appear in the Dictionary as separate main words, the full pronunciation of the compound is not shown. Only its stress pattern is given. Each syllable is represented by a dot /·/, and the stress marks are placed before the dots that represent the syllables with stress. For example: **bus stop** /'· ·/ **town hall** /ˌ· '·/.

Sometimes a compound contains a main word with an ending. If the main word is in the Dictionary and the ending is a common one, only a stress pattern is shown. For example: **washing machine** /'·· ·,·/. *Washing* is not a main word in the Dictionary, but *wash* is; so only a stress pattern is shown because *-ing* is a common ending. But if any part is not a main word, the full pronunciation is given: **helter-skelter** /ˌhɛltər 'skɛltər/.

Stress shift A number of compounds may have a shift in stress when they are used before some nouns. For example, the compound *plate glass* would have the pattern /ˌ· '·/ when spoken by itself or in a sentence like *The window was made of plate glass*. But the phrase *plate glass window* would usually have the pattern /ˌ· · '··/. The mark /◄/ shows this. For example: **plate glass** /ˌ· '· ◄/. Stress shift can also happen with some single words: **artificial** /ˌɑrt̬ə'fɪʃəl ◄/ **independent** /ˌɪndɪ'pɛndənt ◄/.

Syllabic consonants The sounds /n/, /l/, and /m/ can be syllabic. That is, they can themselves form a syllable, especially when they are at the end of a word (following certain consonants). In **sudden** /'sʌdn/ for example, the /n/ is syllabic; there is no vowel between the /d/ and the /n/.

/ə/ This symbol means that /ə/ may either be pronounced or left out. For example, some people say *travel* with /ə/ in the second syllable– /'trævəl/ –and some people say *travel* with a syllabic /l/ (without /ə/). We show this by giving the pronunciation as /'trævəl/. The /ə/ is also used in certain other situations, most often after a vowel and before /r/. For example, some people pronounce the first syllable of *cereal* with the same vowel as in *here*– /'sɪəriʸəl/. Other people use a vowel more like the one in *sit*– /'sɪriʸəl/. We therefore show *cereal* as /'sɪəriʸəl/.

/t̬/ /t̬/ as in *tip* or *sit*, is a voiceless sound. Many Americans, however, use a voiced sound like a quick English /d/ for the *t* in words like *latter*, *party*, and *little*. The *t* in these words, shown in this Dictionary as /t̬/, sounds like the *d* in *ladder*, *hardy*, and *ladle*. This sound usually occurs between vowels (esp. before an unstressed vowel), between *r* and a vowel, or before a syllabic *l*.

Pronunciation table

VOWELS	
Symbol	Key Word
i^y	beat
ɪ	bit
e^y	bay
ɛ	bet
æ	bat
ɑ	box, car
ɔ	bought, horse
o^w	bone
ʊ	book
u^w	boot
ʌ	but
ə	banana, sister
aɪ	by
aʊ	bound
ɔɪ	boy
ɜr	burn
ɪər	beer
ɛər	bare
ʊər	tour

CONSONANTS	
Symbol	Key Word
p	pan
b	ban
t	tip
d	dip
k	cap
g	gap
tʃ	church
dʒ	judge
f	fan
v	van
θ	thing
ð	then
s	sip
z	zip
ʃ	ship
ʒ	measure
h	hot
m	sum
n	sun
ŋ	sung
w	wet
hw	what
l	lot
r	rot
y	yet

/t̬/ means that the /t/ sound is said as a voiced sound (like a quick English /d/).

/ə/ means that /ə/ may or may not be used.

/ˈ/ shows main stress.

/ˌ/ shows secondary stress.

/◄/ shows stress shift.